Webster's New Spanish Dictionary

Webster's New Spanish Dictionary

Copyright © 2004 by Chambers Harrap Publishers Ltd. All rights reserved.

Published by Wiley Publishing, Inc., Hoboken, New Jersey

For general information on our other products and services or to obtain technical support please contact our Customer Care Department within the U.S. at 800-762-2974, outside the U.S. at 317-572-3993 or fax 317-572-4002.

Wiley also publishes its books in a variety of electronic formats. Some content that appears in print may not be available in electronic books. For more information about Wiley products, visit our web site at www.wiley.com.

Library of Congress Cataloging-in-Publication Data is available from the publisher.

ISBN-13: 978-0-7645-9854-8
ISBN-10: 0-7645-9854-6

Manufactured in the United States of America

10 9 8 7 6 5 4 3 2 1

Contents/Índice

Preface

This new pocket-sized dictionary is aimed at students at beginner and intermediate level. It covers all the essential words and phrases needed and packs a wealth of vocabulary into its pages.

Content is fully up to date with the latest changes in language and in the world. In particular, there is excellent coverage of computing terms (including e-mail and the Internet), as well as Latin American Spanish.

A number of extra features add to the effectiveness of the dictionary as a learning tool. We have included false friend boxes to help the user avoid common translation pitfalls, and grammar notes to indicate correct usage. In the pronunciation guides, special attention has been given to the problems Spanish speakers encounter in pronouncing English.

As regards presentation, adverbs and phrasal verbs have separate entries, and each part of speech within an entry starts on a new line. This makes for a clear layout of the text, so the book is easy to consult.

Prefacio

Este nuevo diccionario de bolsillo, dirigido a estudiantes de nivel elemental e intermedio, recoge todas las palabras y expresiones básicas, incluyéndose en sus páginas una gran cantidad de vocabulario.

El contenido refleja los cambios en el lenguaje y en el mundo. En particular, contiene una excelente selección de términos de informática (además del correo electrónico e Internet) y del español de América.

La utilidad del diccionario como herramienta de aprendizaje ha sido potenciada con varios elementos adicionales. Hemos incluido cuadros sobre falsos amigos para evitar trampas en las traducciones y notas gramaticales que indican el uso correcto de las palabras. Las guías sobre la pronunciación prestan especial atención a los problemas que tienen los hablantes nativos de español al pronunciar el inglés.

En lo que respecta a la presentación, los adverbios y los "phrasal verbs" tienen entradas individuales, y cada categoría gramatical comienza en una nueva línea. Esto hace que la presentación del texto sea más clara y que el libro sea fácil de consultar.

Structure of Entries

> **ceviche** *nm* ≋ raw fish marinated in lemon and garlic

- The equals sign = introduces an explanation when there is no direct translation.

> **inocentada** *nf Fam* ≈ April Fool's joke; **hacer una i. a algn** to play an April Fool's joke on sb

- The sign ≈ introduces a word that has a roughly equivalent status but is not identical.

> **aflojar 1** *vt* to loosen
> **2** *vi (viento etc)* to weaken, to grow weak
> **3 aflojarse** *upr* to come *o* work loose; *(rueda)* to go down

- The different grammatical categories are cleary indicated, introduced by a bold Arabic numeral.

> **abrir²** (*pp* **abierto**) **1** *vi* to open
> **2** *vt* (**a**) to open; *(cremallera)* to undo (**b**) *(gas, grifo)* to turn on (**c**) *Jur* **a.** (**un**) **expediente** to start proceedings
> **3 abrirse** *upr* (**a**) to open; *Fig* **a. paso** to make one's way (**b**) *Fam* **¡me abro!** I'm off!

- Usage and field labels are clearly shown.

> **reconocer** [34] *vt* (**a**) to recognize (**b**) *(admitir)* to recognize, to admit (**c**) *Med (paciente)* to examine

- A number before an irregular Spanish verb refers the user to the verb tables in the middle of the book for information on how to conjugate it.

> **bland** [blænd] *adj (food)* soso(a)
>
> 🖉 Note that the Spanish word **blando** is a false friend and is never a translation for the English word **bland**. In Spanish, **blando** means "soft".

- Usage notes warn the user when a word is a false friend.

> **acodarse** *upr* to lean (**en on**)

- The most common prepositions used are given after the translation.

> **acústica** *nf* acoustics *sing*

- The number of a translation is indicated where this is ambiguous.

Estructura de las entradas

> **ceviche** *nm* = raw fish marinated in lemon and garlic

- Cuando no es posible dar una traducción se ofrece una explicación precedida por el signo igual (=).

> **inocentada** *nf Fam* ≃ April Fool's joke; **hacer una i. a algn** to play an April Fool's joke on sb

- El signo ≃ precede a una traducción que tiene un significado aproximado pero no idéntico.

> **aflojar 1** *vt* to loosen
> **2** *vi (viento etc)* to weaken, to grow weak
> **3 aflojarse** *vpr* to come *o* work loose; *(rueda)* to go down

- Las diferentes categorías gramaticales están separadas por un número en negrita.

> **abrir²** *(pp* **abierto)** **1** *vi* to open
> **2** *vt* **(a)** to open; *(cremallera)* to undo **(b)** *(gas, grifo)* to turn on **(c)** *Jur* **a. (un) expediente** to start proceedings
> **3 abrirse** *vpr* **(a)** to open; *Fig* **a. paso** to make one's way **(b)** *Fam* **¡me abro!** I'm off!

- Las marcas de uso y de campo semántico están claramente indicadas.

> **reconocer** [34] *vt o* **(a)** to recognize **(b)** *(admitir)* to recognize, to admit **(c)** *Med (paciente)* to examine

- Los números que aparecen detrás de los verbos irregulares remiten a las tablas verbales que se encuentran en el medio del diccionario.

> **blando,-a** *adj* soft
>
> > 🖉 Observa que la palabra inglesa **bland** es un falso amigo y no es la traducción de la palabra española **blando**. En inglés, **bland** significa "soso".

- Las notas de uso informan sobre los falsos amigos.

> **acodarse** *vpr* to lean **(en on)**

- Las preposiciones más comunes aparecen después de las traducciones.

> **acústica** *nf* acoustics *sing*

- El número de la traducción aparece en los casos en los que éste es ambiguo.

Abbreviations used in this dictionary
Abreviaturas usadas en este diccionario

abbreviation	*abbr, abr*	abreviatura
adjective	*adj*	adjetivo
adverb	*adv*	adverbio
agriculture	*Agr*	agricultura
somebody, someone	*algn*	alguien
Latin American Spanish	*Am*	español de América
anatomy	*Anat*	anatomía
Andean Spanish (Bolivia, Chile Colombia, Ecuador, Peru)	*Andes*	español andino (Bolivia, Chile, Colombia, Ecuador, Perú)
approximately	*aprox*	aproximadamente
architecture	*Archit*	arquitectura
Argentinian Spanish	*Arg*	español de Argentina
architecture	*Arquit*	arquitectura
article	*art*	artículo
astronomy	*Astron*	astronomía
Australian	*Austral*	australiano
motoring	*Aut*	automóviles
auxiliary	*aux*	auxiliar
aviation	*Av*	aviación
biology	*Biol*	biología
Bolivian Spanish	*Bol*	español de Bolivia
botany	*Bot*	botánica
British English	*Br*	inglés británico
Central American Spanish	*CAm*	español centroamericano
Canary Islands Spanish	*Can*	español de Canarias
Caribbean Spanish (Cuba, Puerto Rico, Dominican Republic, Venezuela)	*Carib*	español caribeño (Cuba, Puerto Rico, República Dominicana, Venezuela)
chemistry	*Chem*	química
Chilean Spanish	*Chile*	español de Chile
cinema	*Cin*	cine
Colombian Spanish	*Col*	español de Colombia
commerce	*Com*	comercio
comparative	*comp*	comparativo
computers	*Comput*	informática
conditional	*cond*	condicional
conjunction	*conj*	conjunción
building industry	*Constr*	construcción
sewing	*Cost*	costura
Costa Rican Spanish	*CRica*	español de Costa Rica
Spanish from the Southern Cone region (Argentina, Uruguay, Paraguay, Chile)	*CSur*	español del Cono Sur (Argentina, Uruguay, Paraguay, Chile)
Cuban Spanish	*Cuba*	español de Cuba
cookery	*Culin*	cocina
definite	*def*	definido
defective	*defect*	defectivo
demonstrative	*dem*	demostrativo
sport	*Dep*	deporte
economics	*Econ*	economía
Ecuadorian Spanish	*Ecuad*	español de Ecuador
education	*Educ*	educación
electricity	*Elec*	electricidad
especially	*esp*	especialmente
Peninsular Spanish	*Esp*	español de España
etcetera	*etc*	etcétera
euphemism	*Euph, Euf*	eufemismo
feminine	*f*	femenino

familiar	*Fam*	familiar
pharmacy	*Farm*	farmacia
railways	*Ferroc*	ferrocarriles
figurative use	*Fig*	uso figurado
finance	*Fin*	finanzas
physics	*Fís*	física
formal use	*Fml*	uso formal
photography	*Fot*	fotografía
feminine plural	*fpl*	plural femenino
football	*Ftb*	fútbol
future	*fut*	futuro
geography	*Geog*	geografía
geology	*Geol*	geología
geometry	*Geom*	geometría
present participle	*ger*	gerundio
Guatemalan Spanish	*Guat*	español de Guatemala
history	*Hist*	historia
humorous	*Hum*	humorístico
imperative	*imperat*	imperativo
imperfect	*imperf*	imperfecto
impersonal	*impers*	impersonal
printing	*Impr*	imprenta
industry	*Ind*	industria
indefinite	*indef*	indefinido
indeterminate	*indet*	indeterminado
indicative	*indic*	indicativo
infinitive	*infin*	infinitivo
computers	*Informát*	informática
insurance	*Ins*	seguros
interjection	*interj*	interjección
interrogative	*interr*	interrogativo
invariable	*inv*	invariable
ironic	*Irón*	irónico
law	*Jur*	derecho
linguistics	*Ling*	lingüística
literature	*Lit*	literatura
phrase	*loc*	locución
masculine	*m*	masculino
mathematics	*Math, Mat*	matemáticas
medicine	*Med*	medicina
meteorology	*Met*	meteorología
Mexican Spanish	*Méx*	español de México
military	*Mil*	militar
mining	*Min*	minas
masculine plural	*mpl*	plural masculino
music	*Mus, Mús*	música
noun	*n*	nombre
nautical	*Naut, Náut*	náutica
neuter	*neut*	neutro
feminine noun	*nf*	nombre femenino
plural feminine noun	*nfpl*	nombre femenino plural
masculine noun	*nm*	nombre masculino
masculine and feminine noun	*nmf/nm,f*	nombre masculino y femenino
plural masculine noun	*nmpl*	nombre masculino plural
plural noun	*npl*	nombre plural
optics	*Opt*	óptica
ornithology	*Orn*	ornitología
Panamanian Spanish	*Pan*	español de Panamá
Paraguayan Spanish	*Par*	español de Paraguay
pejorative	*Pej*	peyorativo
personal	*pers*	personal
Peruvian Spanish	*Perú*	español de Perú
pejorative	*Pey*	peyorativo
pharmacy	*Pharm*	farmacia

photography	*Phot*	fotografía
physics	*Phys*	física
plural	*pl*	plural
politics	*Pol*	política
possessive	*pos, poss*	posesivo
past participle	*pp*	participio pasado
prefix	*pref*	prefijo
preposition	*prep*	preposición
present	*pres*	presente
present participle	*pres p*	gerundio
Puerto Rican Spanish	*PRico*	español de Puerto Rico
pronoun	*pron*	pronombre
psychology	*Psi, Psy*	psicología
past tense	*pt*	pretérito
chemistry	*Quím*	química
radio	*Rad*	radio
railways	*Rail*	ferrocarriles
relative	*rel*	relativo
religion	*Rel*	religión
Spanish from the River Plate region (Argentina, Uruguay, Paraguay)	*RP*	español de los países ribereños del Río de la Plata
somebody, someone	*sb*	alguien
Scottish	*Scot*	escocés
insurance	*Seg*	seguros
singular	*sing*	singular
something	*sth*	algo
subjunctive	*subj*	subjuntivo
superlative	*superl*	superlativo
bullfighting	*Taurom*	tauromaquia
technical	*Tech, Téc*	técnica
telephones	*Tel*	teléfonos
textiles	*Tex*	textiles
theatre	*Th*	teatro
television	*TV*	televisión
typography	*Typ*	tipografía
university	*Univ*	universidad
Uruguayan Spanish	*Urug*	español de Uruguay
American English	*US*	inglés norteamericano
usually	*usu*	usualmente
verb	*v*	verbo
auxiliary verb	*v aux*	verbo auxiliar
Venezuelan Spanish	*Ven*	español de Venezuela
intransitive verb	*vi*	verbo intransitivo
impersonal verb	*v impers*	verbo impersonal
reflexive verb	*vpr*	verbo pronominal
transitive verb	*vt*	verbo transitivo
vulgar	*Vulg*	vulgar
zoology	*Zool*	zoología
cultural equivalent	≃	equivalente cultural
registered trademark	®	marca registrada

Spanish Pronunciation Guide

The pronunciation of most Spanish words is predictable as there is a close match between spelling and pronunciation. The table below gives an explanation of that pronunciation. In the dictionary text therefore, pronunciation is only given when the word does not follow these rules, usually because it is a word of foreign origin. In these cases, the IPA (International Phonetic Alphabet) is used (see column 2 of the table below).

Letter in Spanish	IPA Symbol	Example in Spanish	Pronunciation (example in English)
Vowels			
Note that all vowel sounds in Spanish are shorter than in English			
a	a	ala	Similar to the sound in "father" but more central
e	e	ecó	Similar to the sound in "met"
i	i	iris	Like the vowel sound in "meat" but much shorter
o	o	oso	off, on
u	u	uva	Like the vowel sound in "soon" but much shorter
Semiconsonants			
"i" in the diphthongs: ia, ie, io, iu	j	hiato, hielo, avión, viuda	yes
"u" in the diphthongs: ua, ue, ui, uo	w	suave, fuego, huida	win
Consonants			
b	b	bomba (at beginning of word or after m)	boom
	β	abajo (all other contexts)	A "b" pronounced without quite closing the lips completely

Letter in Spanish	IPA Symbol	Example in Spanish	Pronunciation (example in English)
c	θ (in Spain)	ceño (before e) cinco (before i)	thanks (in Spain)
	s (in Latin America and southern Spain)		sun (in Latin America and southern Spain)
	k	casa (all other contexts)	cat
ch	tʃ	caucho	arch
d	d	donde (at beginning of word or after n) aldea (after l)	day
	ð	adorno (all other contexts)	Similar to the sound in "mother" but less strong
f	f	furia	fire
g	χ	gema (before e) girasol (before i)	Like an "h" but pronounced at the back of the throat (similar to Scottish "loch")
	g	gato (at beginning of word) lengua (after n)	goose
	ɣ	agua (all other contexts)	Like a "w" pronounced while trying to say "g"
j	χ	jabalí	Like an "h" but pronounced at the back of the throat (similar to Scottish "loch")
l	l	lado	lake
ll	j	lluvia	million
	ʒ		In some regions (eg the Rio de la Plata area of South America) it is pronounced like the "s" in "pleasure"
m	m	mano	man
n	n	nulo	no
	ŋ	manco, fango (before c and g)	parking
ñ	ɲ	año	onion
p	p	papa	pool

Letter in Spanish	IPA Symbol	Example in Spanish	Pronunciation (example in English)
r	r	dorado (in between vowels) hablar (at end of syllable or word)	A rolled "r" sound (similar to Scottish "r")
	rr	rosa (at beginning of word) alrededor (after l) enredo (after n)	A much longer rolled "r" sound (similar to Scottish "r")
rr	rr	arroyo	A much longer rolled "r" sound (similar to Scottish "r")
s	s	saco	sound
sh	ʃ	show	show
t	t	tela	tea
v	b	invierno (after "n")	boom
	β	ave (all other contexts)	A "b" pronounced without quite closing the lips completely
x	ks	examen	extra
y	j	ayer	yellow
	ʒ		In some regions (eg the Rio de la Plata area of South America) it is pronounced like the "s" in "pleasure"
z	θ (in Spain)	zapato	thanks (in Spain)
	s (in Latin America and southern Spain)		sun (in Latin America and southern Spain)

Pronunciación del inglés

Para ilustrar la pronunciación inglesa, en este diccionario utilizamos los símbolos del AFI (Alfabeto Fonético Internacional). En el siguiente cuadro, para cada sonido del inglés hay ejemplos de palabras en inglés y palabras en español donde aparece un sonido similar. En los casos en los que no hay sonido similar en español, ofrecemos una explicación de cómo pronunciarlos.

Carácter AFI	Ejemplo en inglés	Ejemplo en español
Consonantes		
[b]	**b**a**bb**le	**b**e**b**é
[d]	**d**ig	**d**e**d**o
[dʒ]	**g**iant, **j**ig	se pronuncia como [ʒ] en "plea**s**ure" pero con una "**d**" adelante, o como "**gi**" en italiano: **Gi**ovanna
[f]	**f**it, **ph**ysics	**f**aro
[g]	**g**rey, bi**g**	**g**ris
[h]	**h**appy	"**h**" aspirada
[j]	**y**ellow	se pronuncia como "**y**" o "**ll**" en España: **y**o, **ll**uvia
[k]	**c**lay, ki**ck**	**c**asa
[l]	**l**ip	**l**abio
	pi**ll**	pape**l**
[m]	**m**u**mm**y	**m**a**m**á
[n]	**n**ip, pi**n**	**n**ada
[ŋ]	si**ng**	se pronuncia como "**n**" antes de "**c**": ba**n**co
[p]	**p**i**p**	**p**a**p**á
[r]	**r**ig, **wr**ite	sonido entre "**r**" y "**rr**"
[s]	**s**ick, **sc**ience	**s**apo
[ʃ]	**sh**ip, na**ti**on	**sh**ow
[t]	**t**ip, bu**tt**	**t**ela
[tʃ]	**ch**ip, bat**ch**	cau**ch**o
[θ]	**th**ick	**z**apato (como se pronuncia en España)

Carácter AFI	Ejemplo en inglés	Ejemplo en español
[ð]	this	se pronuncia como la "d" de "hada" pero más fuerte
[v]	vague, give	se pronuncia como "v" de vida, con los dientes apoyados sobre el labio inferior
[w]	wit, why	whisky
[z]	zip, physics	"s" con sonido zumbante
[ʒ]	pleasure	se pronuncia como "y" o "ll" en el Río de la Plata: yo, lluvia
[χ]	loch	jota

Vocales

En inglés, las vocales marcadas con dos puntos son mucho más alargadas

[æ]	rag	se pronuncia "a" con posición bucal para "e"
[ɑ:]	large, bath	"a" muy alargada
[ʌ]	cup	"a" breve y cerrada
[e]	set	se pronuncia como "e" de elefante pero más corta
[3:]	curtain, were	se pronuncia como una "e" larga con posición bucal entre "o" y "e"
[ə]	utter	se pronuncia como "e" con posición bucal para "o"
[ɪ]	big, women	"i" breve, a medio camino entre "e" e "i"
[i:]	leak, wee	"i" muy alargada
[ɒ]	lock	"o" abierta
[ɔ:]	wall, cork	"o" cerrada y alargada
[ʊ]	put, look	"u" breve
[u:]	moon	"u" muy alargada

Pronunciación del inglés

Carácter AFI	Ejemplo en inglés	Ejemplo en español
Diptongos		
[aɪ]	why, high, lie	aire
[aʊ]	how	aura
[eə]	bear	"ea" pronunciado muy brevemente y con sonido de "e" más marcado que el de "a"
[eɪ]	day, make, main	reina
[əʊ]	show, go	"ou" como en COU
[ɪə]	here, gear	hielo pronunciado con el sonido de "i" más marcado y alargado que el de "e"
[ɔɪ]	boy, soil	voy
[ʊə]	poor	cuerno pronunciado con el sonido de "u" más marcado y alargado que el "e"

Spanish – English
Español – Inglés

A, a [a] *nf (la letra)* A, a
a *(abr* **área**) area
a *prep*

> combines with the article **el** to form the contraction **al** (e.g. **al centro** to the centre).

(**a**) *(dirección)* to; **ir a Colombia** to go to Colombia; **llegar a Valencia** to arrive in Valencia; **subir al tren** to get on the train; **ir al cine** to go to the cinema; **vete a casa** go home

(**b**) *(lugar)* at, on; **a la derecha** on the right; **a la entrada** at the entrance; **a lo lejos** in the distance; **a mi lado** at *o* by my side, next to me; **al sol** in the sun; **a la mesa** at (the) table

(**c**) *(tiempo)* at; **a las doce** at twelve o'clock; **a los sesenta años** at the age of sixty; **a los tres meses/la media hora** three months/half an hour later; **al final** in the end; **al principio** at first

(**d**) *(distancia)* away; **a 100 km de aquí** 100 km from here

(**e**) *(manera)* **a la inglesa** (in the) English fashion *o* manner *o* style; **escrito a máquina** typed, typewritten; **a mano** by hand

(**f**) *(proporción)* **a 90 km por hora** at 90 km an hour; **a 300 pesetas el kilo** 300 pesetas a kilo; **tres veces a la semana** three times a week

(**g**) *Dep* **ganar cuatro a dos** to win four (to) two

(**h**) *(complemento indirecto)* to; *(procedencia)* from; **díselo a Javier** tell Javier; **te lo di a ti** I gave it to you; **comprarle algo a algn** to buy sth from sb; *(para algn)* to buy sth for sb; *(complemento directo de persona)* **saludé a tu tía** I said hello to your aunt

(**i**) *Fam* **ir a por algn/algo** to go and fetch sb/sth

(**j**) *(verbo + a + infin)* to; **aprender a nadar** to learn (how) to swim; **fueron a ayudarle** they went to help him

(**k**) *(nombre + a + infin)* **distancia a recorrer** distance to be covered

(**l**) **a decir verdad** to tell (you) the truth; **a no ser por ...** if it were not for ...; **a no ser**

que unless; **a ver** let's see; **¡a comer!** lunch/dinner/*etc* is ready!; **¡a dormir!** bedtime!; **¿a que no lo haces?** *(desafío)* I bet you don't do it!

abad *nm* abbot

abadía *nf* abbey

abajeño,-a *nm,f Am* lowlander

abajo 1 *adv* (**a**) *(en una casa)* downstairs; **el piso de a.** the downstairs flat (**b**) *(dirección)* down, downwards; **ahí/aquí a.** down there/here; **la parte de a.** the bottom (part); **más a.** further down; **hacia a.** down, downwards; **calle a.** down the street; **echar algo a.** to knock sth down; **venirse a.** *(edificio)* to fall down; *Fig (proyecto)* to fall through

2 *interj* **¡a. la censura!** down with censorship!

abalanzarse [40] *upr* **a. sobre/contra** to rush towards

abalear *vt Andes, CAm, Ven* to shoot at

abalorio *nm* (**a**) *(cuenta)* glass bead (**b**) *(baratija)* trinket

abanderado,-a *nm,f* standard bearer

abandonado,-a *adj* (**a**) abandoned; **tiene a su familia muy abandonada** he takes absolutely no interest in his family (**b**) *(desaseado)* untidy, unkempt

abandonar 1 *vt* (**a**) *(lugar)* to leave, to quit; *(persona, cosa)* to abandon; *(proyecto, plan)* to give up (**b**) *Dep (carrera)* to drop out of

2 abandonarse *upr* to let oneself go

abandono *nm* (**a**) *(acción)* abandoning, desertion (**b**) *(de proyecto, idea)* giving up (**c**) *(descuido)* neglect

abanicarse *upr* to fan oneself

abanico *nm* (**a**) fan (**b**) *(gama)* range; **un amplio a. de posibilidades** a wide range of possibilities

abaratar 1 *vt* to cut *o* reduce the price of

2 abaratarse *upr (artículos)* to become cheaper, to come down in price; *(precios)* to come down

abarcar [44] *vt (incluir)* to cover

abarrotado,-a *adj* packed, crammed (**de** with)

abarrotar *vt* to pack, to cram (**de** with); **el público abarrotaba la sala** the room was packed (with people)

abarrote *nm Andes, CAm, Méx* grocer's (shop), grocery store; **abarrotes** groceries; **tienda de abarrotes** grocer's (shop), grocery store

abarrotería *nf Andes, CAm, Méx* grocer's (shop), grocery store

abarrotero,-a *nm,f Andes, CAm, Méx* grocer

abastecedor,-a *nm,f* supplier

abastecer [33] **1** *vt* to supply

2 abastecerse *vpr* **a. de** to be supplied with

abastecimiento *nm* supplying; **a. de agua** water supply

abasto *nm* (a) *Fam* **no doy a.** I can't cope, I can't keep up (b) **mercado de abastos** wholesale food market

abatible *adj* folding, collapsible; **asiento a.** reclining seat

abatido,-a *adj* downcast

abatir 1 *vt* (a) *(derribar)* to knock down, to pull down (b) *(matar)* to kill; **a. a tiros** to shoot down (c) *(desanimar)* to depress, to dishearten

2 abatirse *vpr* *(desanimarse)* to lose heart, to become depressed

abdicación *nf* abdication

abdicar [44] *vt & vi* to abdicate

abdomen *nm* abdomen

abdominales *nmpl* sit-ups

abecedario *nm* alphabet

abedul *nm* birch

abeja *nf* bee; **a. reina** queen bee

abejorro *nm* bumblebee

aberración *nf* aberration

aberrante *adj* deviant

abertura *nf* (hueco) opening, gap; *(grieta)* crack, slit

abertzale *adj & nmf* Basque nationalist

abeto *nm Bot* fir (tree); **a. rojo** spruce

abierto,-a *adj* (a) open; *(grifo)* (turned) on; **a. de par en par** wide open (b) *(persona)* open-minded

abigarrado,-a *adj* (mezclado) jumbled, mixed up

abismal *adj* abysmal; *Fig* **una diferencia a.** a world of a difference

abismo *nm* abyss; *Fig* **al borde del a.** on the brink of ruin; *Fig* **entre ellos media un a.** they are worlds apart

ablandar 1 *vt* to soften

2 ablandarse *vpr* (a) to soften, to go soft (b) *(persona)* to mellow

abnegación *nf* abnegation, self-denial

abnegado,-a *adj* selfless, self-sacrificing

abocado,-a *adj* (a) **está a. al fracaso** it is doomed to failure (b) *(vino)* medium dry

abochornar *vt* to shame, to embarrass

abofetear *vt* to slap

abogacía *nf* legal profession

abogado,-a *nm,f* lawyer, solicitor; *(en tribunal supremo)* lawyer, *Br* barrister; **a. de oficio** legal aid lawyer; **a. defensor** counsel for the defense; **a. del diablo** devil's advocate; **a. laboralista** union lawyer

abogar [42] *vt* to plead; **a. a favor de** to plead for, to defend; **a. por algo** to advocate *o* champion sth

abolengo *nm* ancestry, lineage

abolición *nf* abolition

abolir *vt defect* to abolish

abolladura *nf* dent

abollar *vt* to dent

abominable *adj* abominable

abominar *vt & vi* **a. (de)** to abominate, to loathe

abonado,-a 1 *nm,f* subscriber

2 *adj Fin (pagado)* paid; **a. en cuenta** credited

abonar 1 *vt* (a) *Agr* to fertilize (b) *(pagar)* to pay (for) (c) *(subscribir)* to subscribe

2 abonarse *vpr* to subscribe (**a** to)

abonero,-a *nm,f Méx* hawker, street trader

abono *nm* (a) *Agr (producto)* fertilizer; *(estiércol)* manure (b) *(pago)* payment (c) *(a revista etc)* subscription; *(billete)* season ticket (d) *Méx (plazo)* instalment; **pagar en abonos** to pay by instalments

abordar *vt* (persona) to approach; *(barco)* to board; **a. un asunto** to tackle a subject

aborigen (pl aborígenes) **1** *adj* native, indigenous; *esp Austral* aboriginal

2 *nmf* native; *esp Austral* aborigine

aborrecer [33] *vt* to detest, to loathe

abortar 1 *vi* (involuntariamente) to miscarry, to have a miscarriage; *(intencionadamente)* to abort, to have an abortion

2 *vt* to abort

abortista *nmf* abortionist

aborto *nm* miscarriage; *(provocado)* abortion

abotargado,-a *adj* swollen

abotonar *vt (ropa)* to button (up)

abovedado,-a *adj* vaulted, arched

abracadabra *nm* abracadabra

abrasador,-a *adj* scorching

abrasar 1 *vt & vi* to scorch

2 abrasarse *vpr* to burn

abrazadera *nf* clamp

abrazar [40] **1** *vt* to embrace, to hug; *Fig (doctrina)* to embrace

2 abrazarse *vpr* **a. a algn** to embrace sb; **se abrazaron** they embraced each other
abrazo *nm* embrace, hug; **un a., abrazos** *(en carta)* best wishes
abrecartas *·nm inv* letter-opener, paperknife
abrefácil *nm* Com **caja con a.** easy-open carton
abrelatas *nm inv* tin-opener, *US* can opener
abreviar [43] **1** (a) *vt* to shorten; *(texto)* to abridge; *(palabra)* to abbreviate
2 *vi* to be quick o brief; **para a.** to cut a long story short
abreviatura *nf* abbreviation
abridor *nm (de latas, botellas)* opener
abrigado,-a *adj* wrapped-up; **ir muy a.** to be well wrapped-up
abrigar [42] *vt* (a) to keep warm; **esta chaqueta abriga mucho** this cardigan is very warm (b) *(proteger)* to protect, to shelter (c) *(esperanza)* to cherish; *(duda)* to have, to harbour
abrigo *nm* (a) *(prenda)* coat, overcoat; **ropa de a.** warm clothes (b) **al a. de** protected o sheltered from
abril *nm* April
abrillantador *nm* polish
abrillantar *vt* to polish
abrir ¹ *nm* **en un a. y cerrar de ojos** in the twinkling of an eye
abrir ² *(pp abierto)* **1** *vi* to open
2 *vt* (a) to open; *(cremallera)* to undo (b) *(gas, grifo)* to turn on (c) *Jur* **a. (un) expediente** to start proceedings
3 abrirse *vpr* (a) to open; *Fig* **a. paso** to make one's way (b) *Fam* **¡me abro!** I'm off!
abrochar *vt,* **abrocharse** *vpr (botones)* to do up; *(camisa)* to button (up); *(cinturón)* to fasten; *(zapatos)* to tie up; *(cremallera)* to do up
abrumado,-a *adj* overwhelmed
abrumador,-a *adj* overwhelming
abrumar *vt* to overwhelm, to crush; **tantos problemas me abruman** all these problems are getting on top of me
abrupto,-a *adj* (a) *(terreno)* steep, abrupt (b) *Fig* abrupt, sudden
absceso *nm* abscess
absentismo *nm* absenteeism; **a. laboral** absenteeism from work
absolución *nf* (a) *Rel* absolution (b) *Jur* acquittal
absolutamente *adv* absolutely, completely; **a. nada** nothing at all
absoluto,-a *adj* absolute; **en a.** not at all, by no means

absolutorio,-a *adj Jur* **sentencia absolutoria** verdict of not guilty
absolver [4] *(pp absuelto)* *vt* (a) *Rel* to absolve (b) *Jur* to acquit
absorbente *adj* (a) *(papel)* absorbent (b) *Fig* absorbing, engrossing
absorber *vt* to absorb
absorción *nf* absorption
absorto,-a *adj* absorbed, engrossed (**en** in)
abstemio,-a **1** *adj* teetotal, abstemious
2 *nm,f* teetotaller
abstención *nf* abstention
abstenerse [24] *vpr* to abstain (**de** from); *(privarse)* to refrain (**de** from)
abstinencia *nf* abstinence; **síndrome de a.** withdrawal symptoms
abstracción *nf* abstraction
abstracto,-a *adj* abstract
abstraer [25] **1** *vt* to abstract
2 abstraerse *vpr* to become lost in thought
abstraído,-a *adj (ensimismado)* absorbed, engrossed (**en** in); *(distraído)* absent-minded
absuelto,-a *pp* **de absolver**
absurdo,-a **1** *adj* absurd
2 *nm* absurdity, absurd thing
abuchear *vt* to boo, to jeer at
abucheo *nm* booing, jeering
abuela *nf* grandmother; *Fam* grandma, granny; *Fig* old woman
abuelo *nm* (a) grandfather; *Fam* grandad, grandpa; *Fig* old man (b) **abuelos** grandparents
abulense **1** *adj* of/from Avila
2 *nmf* person from Avila
abulia *nf* apathy, lack of willpower
abultado,-a *adj* bulky, big
abultar **1** *vi* to be bulky; **abulta mucho** it takes up a lot of space
2 *vt* to exaggerate
abundancia *nf* abundance, plenty; *Fig* **nadar en la a.** to be rolling in money
abundante *adj* abundant, plentiful
abundar *vi* to abound, to be plentiful
abur *interj Fam* cheerio!, see you!
aburrido,-a *adj* (a) **ser a.** to be boring (b) **estar a.** to be bored; **estar a. de** *(harto)* to be tired of
aburrimiento *nm* boredom; **¡qué a.!** how boring!, what a bore!
aburrir **1** *vt* to bore
2 aburrirse *vpr* to get bored; **a. como una ostra** to be bored stiff
abusado,-a *adj Méx* astute, shrewd
abusar *vi* (a) *(propasarse)* to go too far (b) **a. de** *(situación, persona)* to take

(unfair) advantage of; *(poder, amabilidad)* to abuse; **a. de la bebida/del tabaco** to drink/smoke too much o to excess; *Jur* **a. de un niño/una mujer** to abuse a child/woman

abusivo,-a *adj (precio)* exorbitant

abuso *nm* abuse

abyecto,-a *adj* abject

a. C. *(abr antes de Cristo)* BC

a/c *Com (abr* **a cuenta)** on account

acá *adv* (a) *(lugar)* here, over here; **más a.** nearer; **¡ven a.!** come here! (b) **de entonces a.** since then

acabado,-a 1 *adj* (a) *(terminado)* finished (b) *Fig (persona)* worn-out, spent
2 *nm* finish

acabar 1 *vt* to finish (off); *(completar)* to complete
2 *vi* (a) to finish, to end; **a. bien** to have a happy ending; **a. con algo** *(terminarlo)* to finish sth; *(romperlo)* to break sth (b) **a. de ...** to have just ...; **acaba de entrar** he has just come in; **no acaba de convencerme** I'm not quite convinced (c) **acabaron casándose** o **por casarse** they ended up getting married; **acabó en la cárcel** he ended up in jail
3 acabarse *vpr* to finish, to come to an end; **se nos acabó la gasolina** we ran out of *Br* petrol o *US* gas; *Fam* **¡se acabó!** that's that!

acabóse *nm Fam* **esto es el a.** this is the end

acacia *nf* acacia

academia *nf* academy; **a. de idiomas** language school

académico,-a *adj & nm,f* academic

acaecer [33] *v impers* to happen, to occur

acallar *vt* to silence

acalorado,-a *adj* (a) hot (b) *Fig (excitado)* worked up, excited; *(debate etc)* heated, angry

acalorarse *vpr* (a) to get warm o hot (b) *Fig* to get excited o worked up

acampada *nf* camping; **ir de a.** to go camping; **zona de a.** camp site, *US* campground

acampanado,-a *adj* bell-shaped; *(prendas)* flared

acampar *vi* to camp

acantilado *nm* cliff

acantonar *vt (tropas)* to billet, to quarter *(en* in)

acaparar *vt* (a) *(productos)* to hoard; *(el mercado)* to corner (b) *Fig* to monopolize

acápite *nm Am (párrafo)* paragraph

acaramelado,-a *adj* (a) *(color)* caramel-coloured (b) *(pareja)* lovey-dovey, starry-eyed

acariciar [43] *vt* to caress; *(pelo, animal)* to stroke; *(esperanza)* to cherish

acarrear *vt* (a) *(transportar)* to carry, to transport (b) *Fig (conllevar)* to entail

acaso *adv* perhaps, maybe; **¿a. no te lo dije?** did I not tell you, by any chance?; **por si a.** just in case; **si a. viene ...** if he should come ...

acatamiento *nm* respect; *(de la ley)* observance

acatar *vt* to observe, to comply with

acatarrado,-a *adj* **estar a.** to have a cold

acatarrarse *vpr* to catch a cold

acaudalado,-a *adj* rich, wealthy

acaudalar *vt* to accumulate, to amass

acaudillar *vt* to lead

acceder *vi* **a.** *(consentir)* to accede to, to consent to; *(tener acceso)* to gain admittance to; *Informát* to access

accesible *adj* accessible; *(persona)* approachable

acceso *nm* (a) *(entrada)* access, entry; *Informát* **a. al azar** random access; *Univ* **prueba de a.** entrance examination; **a. a Internet** Internet access (b) *(carretera)* approach, access (c) *Med & Fig* fit

accesorio,-a *adj & nm* accessory

accidentado,-a 1 *adj (terreno)* uneven, hilly; *(viaje, vida)* eventful
2 *nm,f* casualty, accident victim

accidental *adj* accidental; **un encuentro a.** a chance meeting

accidente *nm* (a) accident; **por a.** by chance; **a. laboral** industrial accident (b) *Geog* **accidentes geográficos** geographical features

acción *nf* (a) action; *(acto)* act; **poner en a.** to put into action; **ponerse en a.** to go into action; **campo de a.** field of action; **película de a.** adventure film (b) *Fin* share

accionar *vt* to drive

accionista *nmf* shareholder

acebo *nm (hoja)* holly; *(árbol)* holly tree

acechar *vt* to lie in wait for; **un grave peligro nos acecha** great danger awaits us

acecho *nm* **estar al a. de** *(esperar)* to lie in wait for

acedía *nf (pez)* dab

aceite *nm* oil; **a. de girasol/maíz/oliva** sunflower/corn/olive oil

aceitera *nf* (a) *Culin* oil bottle; **aceiteras** oil and vinegar set (b) *Aut* oil can

aceitero,-a 1 *adj* oil
　2 *nm,f* oil merchant
aceitoso,-a *adj* oily
aceituna *nf* olive; **a. rellena** stuffed olive
aceitunado,-a *adj* olive, olive-coloured
aceitunero,-a *nm,f* **(a)** *(recolector)* olive picker *o* harvester **(b)** *(vendedor)* olive seller
acelerado,-a *adj* accelerated, fast
acelerador *nm* Aut accelerator
acelerar *vt* to accelerate
acento *nm* **(a)** accent; *(de palabra)* stress **(b)** *(énfasis)* stress, emphasis
acentuar [30] **1** *vt* **(a)** to stress **(b)** *Fig* to emphasize, to stress
　2 acentuarse *vpr* Fig to become more pronounced *o* noticeable
aceña *nf* watermill
acepción *nf* meaning, sense
aceptable *adj* acceptable
aceptación *nf* **(a)** acceptance **(b)** **tener poca a.** to have little success, not to be popular
aceptar *vt* to accept
acequia *nf* irrigation ditch *o* channel
acera *nf* Br pavement, US sidewalk; *Fam Pey* **ser de la a. de enfrente** to be gay *o* queer
acerado *nm* pavement
acerbo,-a *adj* harsh, bitter
acerca *adv* **a. de** about
acercamiento *nm* bringing together, coming together; *Pol* rapprochement
acercar [44] **1** *vt* to bring near *o* nearer, to bring (over); *Fig* to bring together; **¿te acerco a casa?** can I give you a lift home?
　2 acercarse *vpr* **(a)** **acercarse (a)** to approach **(b)** *(ir)* to go; *(venir)* to come
acerico *nm* pincushion
acero *nm* steel; **a. inoxidable** stainless steel
acérrimo,-a *adj* *(partidario)* staunch; *(enemigo)* bitter
acertado,-a *adj* **(a)** *(solución)* right, correct; *(decisión)* wise **(b)** **no estuviste muy a. al decir eso** it wasn't very wise of you to say that
acertante 1 *nmf* winner
　2 *adj* winning
acertar [1] **1** *vt* *(pregunta)* to get right; *(adivinar)* to guess correctly; **a. las quinielas** to win the pools
　2 *vi* to be right; **acertó con la calle que buscaba** she found the street she was looking for
acertijo *nm* riddle
acervo *nm* **a. cultural** cultural tradition *o* heritage

achacar [44] *vt* *(atribuir)* to attribute
achacoso,-a *adj* ailing, unwell
achaque *nm* ailment, complaint
achicar [44] **1** *vt* **(a)** *(amilanar)* to intimidate **(b)** *(encoger)* to reduce, to make smaller **(c)** *(barco)* to bale out
　2 achicarse *vpr* **(a)** *(amilanarse)* to lose heart **(b)** *(encogerse)* to get smaller
achicharrar *vt* to burn to a crisp
achicoria *nf* chicory
achinado,-a *adj* **(a)** *(ojos)* slanting **(b)** Am Indian-looking
acholado,-a *adj* Andes Pey half-caste
achuchar *vt* *(empujar)* to shove
achuchón *nm* *(empujón)* push, shove
aciago,-a *adj* ill-fated, fateful
acicalado,-a *adj* well-dressed, smart
acicalarse *vpr* to dress up, to smarten up
acicate *nm* Fig *(aliciente)* spur, incentive
acidez *nf* *(de sabor)* sharpness, sourness; *Quím* acidity; *Med* **a. de estómago** heartburn
ácido,-a 1 *adj* *(sabor)* sharp, tart; *Quím* acidic; *Fig* *(tono)* harsh
　2 *nm* Quím acid
acierto *nm* *(buena decisión)* good choice *o* idea; **con gran a.** very wisely
aclamación *nf* acclamation, acclaim
aclamar *vt* to acclaim
aclaración *nf* explanation
aclarado *nm* rinsing, rinse
aclarar 1 *vt* **(a)** *(explicar)* to clarify, to explain; *(color)* to lighten, to make lighter **(b)** *(enjuagar)* to rinse
　2 *v impers* Met to clear (up)
　3 aclararse *vpr* **(a)** *(decidirse)* to make up one's mind; *(entender)* to understand **(b)** Met to clear (up)
aclaratorio,-a *adj* explanatory
aclimatación *nf* Br acclimatization, US acclimation
aclimatar 1 *vt* Br to acclimatize, US to acclimate **(a** to)
　2 aclimatarse *vpr* Fig **a. a algo** to get used to sth
acné *nf* acne
acobardar 1 *vt* to frighten
　2 acobardarse *vpr* to get frightened, to lose one's nerve
acodarse *vpr* to lean **(en** on)
acogedor,-a *adj* cosy, warm
acoger [53] **1** *vt* **(a)** *(recibir)* to receive; *(a invitado)* to welcome **(b)** *(persona desvalida)* to take in
　2 acogerse *vpr* Fig **a. a** to take refuge in; *(amnistía)* to avail oneself of; **a. a la ley** to have recourse to the law
acogida *nf* reception, welcome

acojonado,-a adj muy Fam shit-scared

acojonante adj muy Fam damn o Br bloody great o terrific

acojonarse vpr muy Fam (acobardarse) to shit oneself, to be shit-scared

acolchar vt (rellenar) to pad; (prenda) to quilt

acometer vt (a) (emprender) to undertake (b) (atacar) to attack

acometida nf (ataque) attack; (de gas etc) connection

acomodado,-a adj well-off, well-to-do

acomodador,-a nm,f (hombre) usher; (mujer) usherette

acomodar 1 vt (a) (alojar) to lodge, to accommodate (b) (en cine etc) to find a place for
   2 acomodarse vpr (a) to make oneself comfortable (b) (adaptarse) to adapt

acomodaticio,-a adj (a) accommodating, easy-going (b) Pey pliable

acompañante 1 nmf companion
   2 adj accompanying

acompañar vt (a) to accompany; le acompañó hasta la puerta she saw him to the door; me acompañó al médico he came with me to see the doctor; ¿te acompaño a casa? can I walk you home?; Fml le acompaño en el sentimiento my condolences (b) (adjuntar) to enclose

acompasado,-a adj (rítmico) rhythmic

acomplejado,-a adj estar a. to have a complex (por about)

acomplejar 1 vt a. alguien to give sb a complex
   2 acomplejarse vpr a. por to develop a complex about

acondicionado,-a adj aire a. air conditioning

acondicionador nm conditioner

acondicionar vt to prepare, to set up; (mejorar) to improve; (cabello) to condition

acongojar vt to distress

aconsejable adj advisable

aconsejar vt to advise

acontecer [33] v impers to happen, to take place

acontecimiento nm event

acopio nm store, stock; **hacer a. de** to store

acoplar 1 vt (a) to fit (together), to join (b) Téc to couple, to connect
   2 acoplarse vpr (nave espacial) to dock

acorazado,-a 1 adj (a) armoured, armour-plated
   2 nm battleship

acordado,-a adj agreed; **según lo a.** as agreed

acordar [2] **1** vt to agree; (decidir) to decide
   2 acordarse vpr to remember; **no me acuerdo (de Silvia)** I can't remember (Silvia)

acorde 1 adj in agreement
   2 nm Mús chord

acordeón nm (a) (instrument) accordion (b) Col, Méx Fam (en examen) crib

acordonado,-a adj cordoned off, sealed off

acordonar vt (a) (zona) to cordon off, to seal off (b) (atar) to lace up

acorralar vt to corner

acortar vt to shorten; **a. distancias** to cut down the distance

acosar vt to harass; Fig **a. a algn a preguntas** to bombard sb with questions

acoso nm harassment; **a. sexual** sexual harassment

acostar [2] **1** vt to put to bed
   2 acostarse vpr (a) to go to bed (b) Fam **a. con algn** to sleep with sb, to go to bed with sb

acostumbrado,-a adj (a) usual, customary; **es lo a.** it is the custom (b) **a. al frío/calor** used to the cold/heat

acostumbrar 1 vi **a. a** (soler) to be in the habit of
   2 vt **a. a algn a algo** (habituar) to get sb used to sth
   3 acostumbrarse vpr (habituarse) **a. a algo** to get used to sth

acotación nf (a) (en escrito) (marginal) note; Teatro stage direction (b) (en mapa) elevation mark

acotamiento nm Méx (arcén) verge; (de autopista) Br hard shoulder, US shoulder

acotar vt (a) (área) to enclose; Fig (tema) to delimit (b) (texto) to annotate (c) (mapa) to mark with elevations

ácrata adj & nmf anarchist

acre¹ adj (a) (sabor) sour, bitter; (olor) acrid (b) Fig (palabras) bitter, harsh; (crítica) biting

acre² nm (medida) acre

acrecentar [1] vt to increase

acreditación nf badge

acreditar vt (a) to be a credit to (b) (probar) to prove (c) (embajador) to accredit (d) Fin to credit

acreditativo,-a adj which proves, which gives proof

acreedor,-a nm,f Com creditor

acribillar vt to riddle, to pepper; **a. a algn a balazos** to riddle sb with bullets

acrílico,-a adj acrylic

acriollarse vpr Am to adopt native ways

acritud *nf (mordacidad)* acrimony
acrobacia *nf* acrobatics *sing*
acróbata *nmf* acrobat
acta *nf* (a) *(de reunión)* minutes, record (b) *(certificado)* certificate, official document; **a. notarial** affidavit; **A. Única (Europea)** Single European Act

> Takes the masculine articles **el** and **un**.

actitud *nf* attitude
activar *vt* (a) to activate (b) *(avivar)* to liven up
actividad *nf* activity
activista *nmf* activist
activo,-a **1** *adj* active; **en a.** on active service
  2 *nm Fin* assets
acto *nm* (a) act, action; **a. sexual** sexual intercourse; **en el a.** at once; **a. seguido** immediately afterwards; *Mil* **en a. de servicio** in action; **hacer a. de presencia** to put in an appearance (b) *(ceremonia)* ceremony (c) *Teatro* act
actor *nm* actor
actriz *nf* actress
actuación *nf* (a) performance (b) *(intervención)* intervention, action
actual *adj* current, present; *(al día)* up-to-date; **un tema muy a.** a very topical subject
actualidad *nf* (a) present time; **en la a.** at present; **estar de a.** to be fashionable; **temas de a.** topical subjects (b) *(hechos)* current affairs
actualizar [40] *vt* to update, to bring up to date; *Informát (software, hardware)* to upgrade
actualmente *adv (hoy en día)* nowadays, these days; *(ahora)* at the moment, at present

> 🖉 Observa que las palabras inglesas **actual** y **actually** son falsos amigos y no son la traducción de las palabras españolas **actual** y **actualmente**. En inglés, **actual** significa "real, verdadero", y **actually** significa "en realidad".

actuar [30] *vi* (a) to act; **a. como** *o* **de** to act as (b) *Cin & Teatro* to perform, to act
acuarela *nf* watercolour
Acuario *nm* Aquarius
acuario *nm* aquarium
acuartelar *vt* to confine to barracks
acuático,-a *adj* aquatic; **esquí a.** water-skiing
acuchillar *vt* to knife, to stab
acuciante *adj* urgent, pressing
acuciar [43] *vt* to urge on

acudir *vi* *(ir)* to go; *(venir)* to come, to arrive; **nadie acudió en su ayuda** nobody came to help him; **no sé dónde a.** I don't know where to turn
acueducto *nm* aqueduct
acuerdo *nm* agreement; **¡de a.!** all right!, O.K.!; **de a. con** in accordance with; **de común a.** by common consent; **estar de a. en algo** to agree on sth; **ponerse de a.** to agree; **a. marco** framework agreement
acumular **1** *vt* to accumulate
  2 acumularse *vpr* (a) to accumulate, to build up (b) *(gente)* to crowd
acunar *vt* to rock
acuñar *vt* *(moneda)* to mint; *(frase)* to coin
acuoso,-a *adj* watery; *(jugoso)* juicy
acupuntura *nf* acupuncture
acurrucarse [44] *vpr* to curl up, to snuggle up
acusación *nf* (a) accusation (b) *Jur* charge
acusado,-a **1** *nm,f* accused, defendant
  2 *adj (marcado)* marked, noticeable
acusar **1** *vt* (a) to accuse (**de** of); *Jur* to charge (**de** with) (b) *(golpe etc)* to feel; *Fig* **su cara acusaba el cansancio** his face showed his exhaustion (c) *Com* **a. recibo** to acknowledge receipt
  2 acusarse *vpr* (a) *(acentuarse)* to become more pronounced (b) *Fig (notarse)* to show
acuse *nm* **a. de recibo** acknowledgment of receipt
acusica *adj & nmf Fam* telltale
acústica *nf* acoustics *sing*
acústico,-a *adj* acoustic
adán *nm Fam* untidy *o* slovenly person
adaptable *adj* adaptable
adaptación *nf* adaptation
adaptador *nm* adapter
adaptar **1** *vt* (a) to adapt (b) *(ajustar)* to adjust
  2 adaptarse *vpr* to adapt oneself (**a** to)
adecentar *vt* to tidy (up), to clean (up)
adecuado,-a *adj* appropriate, suitable
adecuar [47] *vt* to adapt
adefesio *nm (persona)* freak; *(cosa)* monstrosity
a. de J.C. (*abr* **antes de Jesucristo**) BC
adelantado,-a *adj* (a) advanced; *(desarrollado)* developed; *(precoz)* precocious (b) *(reloj)* fast (c) **pagar por a.** to pay in advance
adelantamiento *nm* overtaking; **hacer un a.** to overtake
adelantar **1** *vt* (a) to move *o* bring forward; *(reloj)* to put forward; *Fig* to

advance (**b**) *Aut* to overtake (**c**) *(fecha)* to bring forward; *Fig* **a. (los) acontecimientos** to get ahead of oneself

2 *vi* (**a**) to advance (**b**) *(progresar)* to make progress (**c**) *(reloj)* to be fast

3 adelantarse *upr* (**a**) *(ir delante)* to go ahead (**b**) *(reloj)* to gain, to be fast (**c**) **el verano se ha adelantado** we are having an early summer

adelante 1 *adv* forward; **más a.** *(lugar)* further on; *(tiempo)* later; **seguir a.** to keep going, to carry on; **llevar a. un plan** to carry out a plan

2 *interj* **¡a!** come in!

adelanto *nm* (**a**) advance; *(progreso)* progress (**b**) **el reloj lleva diez minutos de a.** the watch is ten minutes fast (**c**) *(de dinero)* advance payment

adelfa *nf* oleander, rosebay

adelgazamiento *nm* slimming

adelgazar [40] *vi* to slim, to lose weight

ademán *nm* (**a**) gesture (**b**) **ademanes** manners

además *adv* moreover, furthermore; **a., no lo he visto nunca** what's more, I've never seen him; **a. de él** besides him

adentrarse *upr* **a. en** *(bosque)* to go deep into; *(asunto)* to study thoroughly

adentro 1 *adv (dentro)* inside; **mar a.** out to sea; **tierra a.** inland

2 *nmpl* **decir algo para sus adentros** to say sth to oneself

adepto,-a *nm,f* follower, supporter

> 🖉 Observa que la palabra inglesa **adept** es un falso amigo y no es la traducción de la palabra española **adepto**. En inglés, **adept** significa "experto".

aderezar [40] *vt (comida)* to season; *(ensalada)* to dress

aderezo *nm (de comida)* seasoning; *(de ensalada)* dressing

adeudar 1 *vt* to owe

2 adeudarse *upr* to get into debt

adherencia *nf* adherence; *Aut* roadholding

adherir [5] 1 *vt* to stick on

2 adherirse *upr* **a. a** to adhere to; *(partido)* to join

adhesión *nf* adhesion; *(a partido)* joining; *(a teoría)* adherence

adhesivo,-a *adj & nm* adhesive

adicción *nf* addiction; **crear a.** to be addictive

adición *nf* addition

adicional *adj* additional

adicto,-a 1 *nm,f* addict

2 *adj* addicted (**a** to)

adiestrar *vt* to train

adinerado,-a 1 *adj* wealthy, rich

2 *nm,f* rich person

adiós *(pl* **adioses)** **1** *interj* goodbye; *Fam* bye-bye; *(al cruzarse)* hello

2 *nm* goodbye

aditivo,-a *adj & nm* additive

adivinanza *nf* riddle, puzzle

adivinar *vt* to guess; **a. el pensamiento de algn** to read sb's mind

adivino,-a *nm,f* fortune-teller

adjetivo,-a 1 *nm* adjective

2 *adj* adjectival

adjudicación *nf* award; *(en subasta)* sale

adjudicar [44] 1 *vt* (**a**) *(premio, contrato)* to award (**b**) *(en subasta)* to sell

2 adjudicarse *upr* to appropriate, to take over

adjuntar *vt* to enclose

adjunto,-a 1 *adj* (**a**) enclosed, attached (**b**) *Educ* assistant

2 *nm,f Educ* assistant teacher

adm., admón. *(abr* **administración**) admin.

administración *nf* (**a**) *(gobierno)* administration, authorities; *Pol* **a. central** central government; **a. pública** civil service (**b**) *(de empresa)* administration, management (**c**) *(oficina)* (branch) office

administrador,-a 1 *nm,f* administrator

2 *adj* administrating

administrar 1 *vt* (**a**) to administer (**b**) *(dirigir)* to run, to manage

2 administrarse *upr* to manage one's own money

administrativo,-a 1 *adj* administrative

2 *nm,f (funcionario)* official

admirable *adj* admirable

admiración *nf* (**a**) admiration; **causar a.** to impress (**b**) *Ling* exclamation mark

admirador,-a *nm,f* admirer

admirar 1 *vt* (**a**) to admire (**b**) *(sorprender)* to amaze, to astonish

2 admirarse *upr* to be amazed, to be astonished

admisible *adj* admissible, acceptable

admisión *nf* admission; **reservado el derecho de a.** *(en letrero)* the management reserves the right to refuse admission

admitir *vt* (**a**) to admit, to let in (**b**) *(aceptar)* to accept; **no se admiten cheques** *(en letrero)* no cheques accepted (**c**) *(tolerar)* to allow (**d**) *(reconocer)* to admit, to acknowledge; **admito que mentí** I admit that I lied

admonición *nf* warning

ADN *nm* *(abr* **ácido desoxirribonucleico**) DNA

adobar *vt Culin* to marinate

adobe *nm* adobe

adobo *nm* marinade

adoctrinar *vt* to indoctrinate

adolecer [33] *vi* a. de *(carecer de)* to lack; *Fig Fml* to suffer from

adolescencia *nf* adolescence

adolescente *adj & nmf* adolescent

adonde *adv* where

adónde *adv interr* where (to)?

adondequiera *adv* wherever

adopción *nf* adoption

adoptar *vt* to adopt

adoptivo,-a *adj (hijo)* adopted; *(padres)* adoptive; *Fig* país a. country of adoption

adoquín *nm* cobble, paving stone

adorable *adj* adorable

adorar *vt* (a) *Rel* to worship (b) *Fig* to adore

adormecer [33] 1 *vt* to send to sleep, to make sleepy

  2 adormecerse *vpr* (a) *(dormirse)* to doze off (b) *(brazo etc)* to go to sleep, to go numb

adormecido,-a *adj* sleepy, drowsy

adormilarse *vpr* to doze, to drowse

adornar *vt* to adorn, to decorate

adorno *nm* decoration, adornment; de a. decorative

adosado,-a *adj* adjacent; *(casa)* semidetached

adquirir [31] *vt* to acquire; *(comprar)* to purchase

adquisición *nf* acquisition; *(compra)* buy, purchase

adquisitivo,-a *adj* poder a. purchasing power

adrede *adv* deliberately, on purpose

adrenalina *nf* adrenalin

adriático,-a *nm* el (Mar) A. the Adriatic (Sea)

adscribir *(pp adscrito)* **1** *vt* (a) *(atribuir)* to ascribe to (b) *(a un trabajo)* to appoint to

  2 adscribirse *vpr* to affiliate (a to)

adscrito,-a *pp de* adscribir

aduana *nf* customs

aduanero,-a 1 *adj* customs

  2 *nm,f* customs officer

aducir [10] *vt (motivo, pretexto)* to give

adueñarse *vpr* a. de to take over; *(pánico etc)* to take hold of

aduje *pt indef de* aducir

adulación *nf* adulation

adular *vt* to adulate

adulterar *vt* to adulterate

adulterio *nm* adultery

adúltero,-a 1 *adj* adulterous

2 *nm,f (hombre)* adulterer; *(mujer)* adulteress

adulto,-a *adj & nm,f* adult

adusto,-a *adj* harsh, severe

aduzco *indic pres de* aducir

advenedizo,-a *adj & nm,f* upstart

advenimiento *nm* advent, coming

adverbio *nm* adverb

adversario,-a 1 *nm,f* adversary, opponent

  2 *adj* opposing

adversidad *nf* adversity; *(revés)* setback

adverso,-a *adj* adverse

advertencia *nf* warning

advertido,-a *adj* warned; *(informado)* informed; estás o quedas a. you've been warned

advertir [5] *vt* (a) to warn; *(informar)* to inform, to advise; *Fam* te advierto que yo tampoco lo vi mind you, I didn't see it either (b) *(notar)* to realize, to notice

adviento *nm* Advent

adyacente *adj* adjacent

aéreo,-a *adj* (a) aerial (b) *Av* air; tráfico a. air traffic; *Com* por vía aerea by air

aero- *pref* aero-

aeróbic *nm* aerobics *sing*

aerodinámico,-a *adj* aerodynamic; de línea aerodinámica streamlined

aeródromo *nm* aerodrome

aeromodelismo *nm* aeroplane modelling

aeromoza *nf Am* air hostess

aeronáutica *nf* aeronautics *sing*

aeronáutico,-a *adj* la industria aeronáutica the aeronautics industry

aeronave *nf* airship

aeroplano *nm* light aeroplane

aeropuerto *nm* airport

aerosol *nm* aerosol

aerostático,-a *adj* globo a. hot-air balloon

a/f *(abr a* favor*)* in favour

afable *adj* affable

afamado,-a *adj* famous, well-known

afán *nm (pl* afanes*)* (a) *(esfuerzo)* effort (b) *(celo)* zeal

afanador,-a *nm,f Méx* cleaner

afanar 1 *vt Fam (robar)* to pinch

  2 afanarse *vpr* a. por conseguir algo to do one's best to achieve sth

afanoso,-a *adj* (a) *(persona)* keen, eager (b) *(tarea)* hard, tough

afección *nf* disease

afectación *nf* affectation

afectado,-a *adj* affected

afectar *vt* a. a to affect; le afectó mucho she was deeply affected; nos afecta a

todos it concerns all of us

afecto *nm* affection; **tomarle a. a algn** to become fond of sb

afectuoso,-a *adj* affectionate

afeitado *nm* shave

afeitar *vt*, **afeitarse** *vpr* to shave

afeminado,-a *adj* effeminate

aferrado,-a *adj* **a. a** clinging to

aferrar 1 *vt Náut* to anchor, to moor

 2 aferrarse *vpr* to clutch, to cling; *Fig* **a. a una creencia** to cling to a belief

Afganistán *n* Afghanistan

afgano,-a *adj & nm,f* Afghan

afianzamiento *nm* strengthening, reinforcement

afianzar [40] 1 *vt* to strengthen, to reinforce

 2 afianzarse *vpr* (persona) to become established

afiche *nm Am* poster

afición *nf* (a) liking; **tiene a. por la música** he is fond of music (b) *Dep* **la a.** the fans

aficionado,-a 1 *nm,f* (a) enthusiast; **un a. a la música** a music lover (b) *(no profesional)* amateur

 2 adj (a) keen, fond; **ser a. a algo** to be fond of sth (b) *(no profesional)* amateur

aficionarse *vpr* to become fond (**a** of), to take a liking (**a** to)

afilado,-a *adj* sharp

afilar *vt* to sharpen

afiliación *nf* affiliation

afiliado,-a *nm,f* member

afiliarse [43] *vpr* to become a member

afín *adj* (semejante) kindred, similar; *(relacionado)* related

afinar *vt* (a) *(puntería)* to sharpen (b) *(instrumento)* to tune

afincarse [44] *vpr* to settle down

afinidad *nf* affinity

afirmación *nf* affirmation; **afirmaciones** *(declaración)* statement

afirmar (a) *vt (aseverar)* to state, to declare (b) *(afianzar)* to strengthen, to reinforce

afirmativo,-a *adj* affirmative; **en caso a. ...** if the answer is yes ...

aflicción *nf* affliction

afligir [57] 1 *vt* to afflict

 2 afligirse *vpr* to grieve, to be distressed

aflojar 1 *vt* to loosen

 2 vi *(viento etc)* to weaken, to grow weak

 3 aflojarse *vpr* to come o work loose; *(rueda)* to go down

aflorar *vi* (río) to come to the surface; *(sentimiento)* to surface, to show

afluencia *nf* inflow, influx; **gran a. de**

público great numbers of people

afluente *nm* tributary

afluir [37] *vi* to flow (**a** into)

afónico,-a *adj* **estar a.** to have lost one's voice

aforismo *nm* aphorism

aforo *nm (capacidad)* seating capacity

afortunado,-a *adj* fortunate; **las Islas Afortunadas** the Canaries

afrenta *nf Fml* affront

África *n* Africa

africano,-a *adj & nm,f* African

afrodisíaco,-a *adj & nm* aphrodisiac

afrontar *vt* to confront, to face; **a. las consecuencias** to face the consequences

afuera 1 *adv* outside; **la parte de a.** the outside; **más a.** further out; **salir a.** to come o go out

 2 nfpl afueras outskirts

agachar 1 *vt* to lower

 2 agacharse *vpr* to duck

agalla *nf* (a) *(de pez)* gill (b) **tiene agallas** she's got guts

agarraderas *nfpl Fam* **tener buenas a.** to be well-connected

agarrado,-a *adj* (a) *Fam* stingy, tight (b) **baile a.** cheek-to-cheek dancing

agarrar 1 *vt* (a) to grasp, to seize; **agárralo fuerte** hold it tight (b) *Am (tomar)* to take; **a. un taxi** to take a taxi (c) *Fam (pillar)* to catch; **a. una borrachera** to get drunk o pissed

 2 agarrarse *vpr* to hold on; **agarraos bien** hold tight

agarrotarse *vpr* (a) *(músculo)* to stiffen (b) *(máquina)* to seize up

agasajar *vt* to smother with attentions

ágata *nf* agate

> Takes the masculine articles **el** and **un**.

agazaparse *vpr* to crouch (down)

agencia *nf* agency; *(sucursal)* branch; **a. de viajes** travel agency; **a. de seguros** insurance agency; **a. inmobiliaria** estate agency

agenciarse [43] *vpr* (a) to get oneself; **se agenció una moto** he got himself a motorbike (b) **agenciárselas** to manage

agenda *nf* diary

agente *nmf* agent; **a. de policía** *(hombre)* policeman; *(mujer)* policewoman; **a. de bolsa** stockbroker; **a. de seguros** insurance broker

agigantado,-a *adj* **a pasos agigantados** by leaps and bounds

ágil *adj* agile

agilidad *nf* agility

agilización *nf* speeding up

agilizar [40] *vt (trámites)* to speed up

agitación *nf (intranquilidad)* restlessness; *(social, político)* unrest

agitado,-a *adj* agitated; *(persona)* anxious; *(mar)* rough; **una vida muy agitada** a very hectic life

agitar 1 *vt (botella)* to shake; *(multitud)* to agitate

  2 agitarse *vpr (persona)* to become agitated; *(mar)* to become rough

aglomeración *nf* agglomeration; *(de gente)* crowd

aglomerar 1 *vt* to bring together

  2 aglomerarse *vpr* to mass o gather together

agnóstico,-a *adj & nm,f* agnostic

agobiado,-a *adj Fig* **a. de problemas** snowed under with problems; *Fig* **a. de trabajo** up to one's eyes in work

agobiante *adj (trabajo)* overwhelming; *(lugar)* claustrophobic; *(calor)* oppressive; *(persona)* tiresome, tiring

agobiar [43] 1 *vt* to overwhelm

  2 agobiarse *vpr (con problemas)* to be over-anxious; *(por el calor)* to suffocate

agobio *nm* (a) *(angustia)* anxiety (b) *(sofoco)* suffocation

agolpamiento *nm* crowd, crush

agolparse *vpr* to crowd, to throng

agonía *nf* dying breath, last gasp

agonizante *adj* dying

agonizar [40] *vi* to be dying

agosto *nm* August; *Fam* **hacer su a.** to make a packet

agotado,-a *adj* (a) *(cansado)* exhausted, worn out (b) *Com* sold out; *(existencias)* exhausted; *(libro)* out of print

agotador,-a *adj* exhausting

agotamiento *nm* exhaustion

agotar 1 *vt* (a) *(cansar)* to exhaust, to wear out (b) *(acabar)* to exhaust, to use up *(completely)*

  2 agotarse *vpr* (a) *(acabarse)* to run out, to be used up; *Com* to be sold out (b) *(persona)* to become exhausted o tired out

agraciado,-a *adj* (a) *(hermoso)* pretty (b) *(ganador)* winning; **ser a. con** to win

agradable *adj* pleasant

agradar *vi* to please; **no me agrada** I don't like it

agradecer [33] *vt* (a) *(dar las gracias)* to thank for; **les agradezco su atención** (I) thank you for your attention; **te lo agradezco mucho** thank you very much (b) *(estar agradecido)* to be grateful to; **te agradecería que vinieras** I'd be grateful if you'd come (c) *(uso impers)* **siempre se agradece un descanso** a rest is always welcome

agradecido,-a *adj* grateful; **le estoy muy a.** I am very grateful to you

agradecimiento *nm* gratitude

agrado *nm* pleasure; **no es de su a.** it isn't to his liking

agrandar 1 *vt* to enlarge, to make larger

  2 agrandarse *vpr* to enlarge, to become larger

agrario,-a *adj* agrarian; **política agraria** agricultural policy

agravamiento *nm* aggravation

agravante 1 *adj Jur* aggravating

  2 *nm Jur* aggravating circumstance

agravar 1 *vt* to aggravate

  2 agravarse *vpr* to worsen, to get worse

agraviar [43] *vt* to offend, to insult

agravio *nm* offense, insult

agredir *vt defect* to assault

agregación *nf* aggregation

agregado,-a 1 *adj Educ* **profesor a.** *(escuela)* secondary school teacher; *Univ* assistant teacher

  2 *nm,f Pol* attaché

agregar [42] 1 *vt* (a) *(añadir)* to add (b) *(destinar)* to appoint

  2 agregarse *vpr* **a. a** to join

agresión *nf* aggression

agresividad *nf* aggressiveness

agresivo,-a *adj* aggressive

agresor,-a 1 *nm,f* aggressor, attacker

  2 *adj* attacking

agriarse *vpr* to turn sour

agrícola *adj* agricultural

agricultor,-a *nm,f* farmer

agricultura *nf* agriculture; **a. biológica** o **ecológica** organic farming

agridulce *adj* bittersweet

agrietar 1 *vt* to crack; *(piel, labios)* to chap

  2 agrietarse *vpr* to crack; *(piel)* to get chapped

agringarse [42] *vpr Am Pey* to behave like a gringo

agrio,-a 1 *adj* sour

  2 *nmpl* **agrios** citrus fruits

agrónomo,-a *nm,f* **(ingeniero) a.** agronomist

agropecuario,-a *adj* farming, agricultural

agrupación *nf* association

agrupar 1 *vt* to group

  2 agruparse *vpr* (a) *(congregarse)* to group together, to form a group (b) *(asociarse)* to associate

agua *nf* water; **a. potable** drinking water; **a. corriente/del grifo** running/tap water;

a. dulce/salada fresh/salt water; **a. mineral sin/con gas** still/fizzy o sparkling mineral water; **a. de colonia** (eau de) cologne; *Fig* **estar con el a. al cuello** to be up to one's neck in it; **aguas jurisdiccionales** territorial waters; **aguas residuales** sewage

Takes the masculine articles **el** and **un**.

aguacate nm (*árbol*) avocado; (*fruto*) avocado (pear)

aguacero nm shower, downpour

aguado,-a adj watered down

aguafiestas nmf inv spoilsport, wet blanket

aguafuerte nm (a) *Arte* etching (b) *Quím* nitric acid

aguamala nf *Carib, Col, Ecuad, Méx* jellyfish

aguamarina nf aquamarine

aguamiel nm o nf (a) *Am* (*bebida*) = water mixed with honey or cane syrup (b) *Carib, Méx* (*jugo*) maguey juice

aguanieve nf sleet

aguantar 1 vt (a) (*soportar*) to tolerate; **no lo aguanto más** I can't stand it any longer (b) (*sostener*) to support, to hold; **aguanta esto** hold this (c) **aguanta la respiración** hold your breath
  2 aguantarse vpr (a) (*contenerse*) to keep back; (*lágrimas*) to hold back; **no pude aguantarme la risa** I couldn't help laughing (b) (*resignarse*) to resign oneself

aguante nm endurance; **tener mucho a.** (*ser paciente*) to be very patient; (*tener resistencia*) to be strong, to have a lot of stamina

aguar [45] vt to water down; *Fig* **a. la fiesta a algn** to spoil sb's fun

aguardar 1 vt to await
  2 vi to wait

aguardiente nm liquor, brandy

aguarrás nm turpentine

aguatero,-a nm,f *Am* water seller

aguaviva nf *RP* jellyfish

agudeza nf (a) sharpness; (*del dolor*) acuteness (b) *Fig* (*ingenio*) witticism, witty saying

agudización nf (a) sharpening (b) (*empeoramiento*) worsening

agudizar [40] 1 vt to intensify, to make more acute
  2 agudizarse vpr to intensify, to become more acute

agudo,-a adj (*dolor*) acute; (*voz*) high-pitched; (*sonido*) treble, high; *Fig* (*ingenioso*) witty; *Fig* (*sentido*) sharp, keen

agüero nm omen

aguijón nm sting; *Fig* (*estímulo*) spur

águila nf eagle; **á. real** golden eagle; *Méx* **¿á. o sol?** heads or tails?

Takes the masculine articles **el** and **un**.

aguileño,-a adj aquiline; **nariz aguileña** aquiline nose

aguinaldo nm Christmas box; **pedir el a.** to go carol singing

agüita nf *Chile* (herbal) tea

aguja nf (a) needle; (*de reloj*) hand; (*de tocadiscos*) stylus (b) *Arquit* spire (c) *Ferroc* point, *US* switch

agujerear vt to make holes in

agujero nm (a) hole; **a. negro** black hole (b) *Econ* deficit, shortfall

agujetas nfpl stiffness; **tener a.** to be stiff

agur interj *Fam* bye!, see you!

aguzar [40] vt (a) (*afilar*) to sharpen (b) *Fig* **a. el oído** to prick up one's ears; **a. la vista** to look attentively; **aguzar el ingenio** to sharpen one's wits

ahí adv there; **a. está** there he/she/it is; **ve por a.** go that way; **está por a.** it's over there; **setenta o por a.** seventy or thereabouts; **de a.** hence

ahijado,-a nm,f godchild; (*niño*) godson; (*niña*) goddaughter; **ahijados** godchildren

ahínco nm eagerness; **con a.** eagerly

ahíto,-a adj (*de comida*) full, stuffed; (*harto*) fed up

ahogado,-a 1 adj (a) (*en líquido*) drowned; **morir a.** to drown (b) (*asfixiado*) suffocated
  2 nm,f drowned person

ahogar [42] 1 vt (a) (*en líquido*) to drown (b) (*asfixiar*) to suffocate
  2 ahogarse vpr (a) (*en líquido*) to drown, to be drowned; *Fig* **a. en un vaso de agua** to make a mountain out of a molehill (b) (*asfixiarse*) to suffocate (c) (*motor*) to be flooded

ahondar 1 vt to deepen
  2 vi to go deep; *Fig* **a. en un problema** to go into a problem in depth

ahora 1 adv (a) (*en este momento*) now; **a. mismo** right now; **de a. en adelante** from now on; **por a.** for the time being (b) **a. voy** I'm coming; **a. vuelvo** I'll be back in a minute (c) **hasta a.** (*hasta el momento*) until now, so far; (*hasta luego*) see you later
  2 conj **a. bien** (*sin embargo*) however; (*y bueno*) well then

ahorcado,-a 1 nm,f hanged person
  2 adj hanged

ahorcar [44] 1 *vt* to hang
  2 ahorcarse *vpr* to hang oneself

ahorita, ahorita *adv* Andes, CAm, Carib, Méx Fam (**a**) (*en el presente*) (right) now; **a. voy** I'm just coming (**b**) (*pronto*) in a second (**c**) (*hace poco*) just now, a few minutes ago

ahorrador,-a *adj* thrifty

ahorrar 1 *vt* to save
  2 ahorrarse *vpr* **ahórrate los comentarios** keep your comments to yourself

ahorrativo,-a *adj* thrifty

ahorro *nm* (**a**) saving; **a. energético** energy saving (**b**) **ahorros** savings; *Fin* **caja de ahorros** savings bank

ahuecar [44] *vt* (**a**) to hollow out; *Fam* **a. el ala** to clear off, to beat it (**b**) (*voz*) to deepen

ahuevado,-a *adj* Andes, CAm Fam (*tonto*) **estar a. con algo** to be bowled over by sth

ahumado,-a *adj* (*cristal, jamón*) smoked; (*bacon*) smoky; **salmón a.** smoked salmon

ahumar 1 *vt* to smoke
  2 *vi* (*echar humo*) to smoke, to give off smoke

ahuyentar *vt* to scare away

aindiado,-a *adj* Am Indian-like

airado,-a *adj* angry

airar 1 *vt* to anger
  2 airarse *vpr* to get angry

airbag ['era, air'a] *nm* (*pl* **airbags**) airbag

aire *nm* (**a**) air; **a. acondicionado** air conditioning; **al a.** (*hacia arriba*) into the air; (*al descubierto*) uncovered; **al a. libre** in the open air; **en el a.** (*pendiente*) in the air; *Rad* on the air; **hacerse a.** to fan oneself; **saltar por los aires** to blow up; **tomar el a.** to get some fresh air; **necesito un cambio de aires** I need a change of scene (**b**) *Aut* choke (**c**) (*viento*) wind; **hace a.** it's windy (**d**) (*aspecto*) air, appearance (**e**) **él va a su a.** he goes his own sweet way (**f**) **darse aires** to put on airs

airear *vt* (*ropa, lugar*) to air; *Fig* (*asunto*) to publicize

airoso,-a *adj* graceful, elegant; *Fig* **salir a. de una situación** to come out of a situation with flying colours

aislacionismo *nm* isolationism

aislado,-a *adj* (**a**) isolated (**b**) *Téc* insulated

aislamiento *nm* (**a**) isolation (**b**) *Téc* insulation

aislante 1 *adj* **cinta a.** insulating tape
  2 *nm* insulator

aislar *vt* (**a**) to isolate (**b**) *Téc* to insulate

ajar *vt* to wear out

ajedrez *nm* (**a**) (*juego*) chess (**b**) (*piezas y tablero*) chess set

ajeno,-a *adj* belonging to other people; **los bienes ajenos** other peoples' goods; **por causas ajenas a nuestra voluntad** for reasons beyond our control

ajetreado,-a *adj* (very) busy, hectic

ajetreo *nm* activity, hard work, bustle

ají *nm* (**a**) Andes, RP (*pimiento*) chilli (pepper) (**b**) Andes, RP (*salsa*) = sauce made from oil, vinegar, garlic and chilli

ajiaco *nm* (**a**) Andes, Carib (*estofado*) = chilli-based stew (**b**) Méx (*estofado con ajo*) = tripe stew flavoured with garlic

ajillo *nm* Culin **al a.** fried with garlic

ajo *nm* garlic; **cabeza/diente de a.** head/clove of garlic; *Fam* **estar en el a.** to be in on it

ajonjolí *nm* sesame

ajorca *nf* bracelet; (*en el tobillo*) anklet

ajuar *nm* (*de novia*) trousseau

ajustado,-a *adj* tight

ajustador,-a *nm,f* fitter

ajustar *vt* (**a**) to adjust (**b**) (*apretar*) to tighten (**c**) *Fin* (*cuenta*) to settle; *Fig* **ajustarle las cuentas a algn** to settle a score with sb

ajuste *nm* (**a**) adjustment; *Téc* assembly; *TV* **carta de a.** test card (**b**) (*de precio*) fixing; (*de cuenta*) settlement; *Fig* **a. de cuentas** settling of scores

ajusticiar [43] *vt* to execute

al (*contracción de a* + *el*) (**a**) *ver* **a** (**b**) (*al* + *infin*) **al salir** on leaving; **está al caer** it's about to happen; **al parecer** apparently

ala 1 *nf* (**a**) wing; *Fig* **cortarle las alas a algn** to clip sb's wings (**b**) (*de sombrero*) brim
  2 *nmf Dep* winger

> Takes the masculine articles **el** and **un**.

alabanza *nf* praise

alabar *vt* to praise

alabastro *nm* alabaster

alacena *nf* (food) cupboard

alacrán *nm* scorpion

alambicado,-a *adj* intricate

alambique *nm* still

alambrada *nf*, **alambrado** *nm* wire fence

alambrar *vt* to fence with wire

alambre *nm* wire; **a. de púas** barbed wire

alambrista *nmf* tightrope walker

alameda *nf* (**a**) poplar grove (**b**) (*paseo*) avenue, boulevard

álamo *nm* poplar

alano,-a *nm,f* (**perro**) **a.** mastiff

alarde *nm* (*ostentación*) bragging,

boasting; **hacer a. de** to show off

alardear *vi* to brag, to boast; **a. de rico** *o* **de riqueza** to flaunt one's wealth

alargadera *nf Elec* extension

alargado,-a *adj* elongated

alargar [42] **1** *vt* (a) to lengthen; *(estirar)* to stretch; **ella alargó la mano para cogerlo** she stretched out her hand to get it (b) *(prolongar)* to prolong, to extend (c) *(dar)* to pass, to hand over; **alárgame ese jersey** can you pass me that sweater?

2 alargarse *vpr* (a) to get longer (b) *(prolongarse)* to go on (c) **¿puedes a. a casa?** can you give me a lift home?

alarido *nm* screech, shriek; **dar un a.** to howl

alarma *nf* alarm; **la a. saltó** the alarm went off; **falsa a.** false alarm; **señal de a.** alarm (signal)

alarmado,-a *adj* alarmed

alarmante *adj* alarming

alarmar 1 *vt* to alarm

2 alarmarse *vpr* to be alarmed

alazán,-ana *adj & nm,f* **(caballo) a.** chestnut

alba *nf* dawn, daybreak

Takes the masculine articles **el** and **un**.

albacea *nmf (hombre)* executor; *(mujer)* executrix

albahaca *nf* basil

albanés,-esa *adj & nm,f* Albanian

Albania *n* Albania

albañal *nm* sewer, drain

albañil *nm* bricklayer

albañilería *nf* bricklaying; **pared de a.** *(obra)* brick wall

albarán *nm Com* delivery note, despatch note

albaricoque *nm* apricot

albaricoquero *nm* apricot tree

albatros *nm inv* albatross

albedrío *nm* will; **libre a.** free will

alberca *nf* (a) *(depósito)* water tank (b) *Méx (piscina)* swimming pool

albergar [42] **1** *vt (alojar)* to house, to accommodate; *Fig (sentimientos)* to cherish, to harbour

2 albergarse *vpr* to stay

albergue *nm* hostel; **a. juvenil** youth hostel

albino,-a *adj & nm,f* albino

albóndiga *nf* meatball

albores *nmpl* beginning; **en los a. de ...** at the beginning of ...

albornoz *nm* bathrobe

alborotado,-a *adj* (a) worked up, agitated (b) *(desordenado)* untidy, messy (c)

(mar) rough; *(tiempo)* stormy

alborotar 1 *vt* (a) *(agitar)* to agitate, to work up (b) *(desordenar)* to make untidy, to turn upside down

2 *vi* to kick up a racket

3 alborotarse *vpr* (a) to get excited *o* worked up (b) *(mar)* to get rough; *(tiempo)* to get stormy

alboroto *nm* (a) *(jaleo)* din, racket (b) *(desorden)* disturbance, uproar

alborozo *nm* merriment, gaiety

albufera *nf* lagoon

álbum *nm* album

alcachofa *nf* (a) *Bot* artichoke (b) *(de tubo, regadera)* rose, sprinkler

alcalde *nm* mayor

alcaldesa *nf* mayoress

alcaldía *nf* (a) *(cargo)* mayorship (b) *(oficina)* mayor's office

alcalino,-a *adj* alkaline

alcance *nm* (a) reach; **al a. de cualquiera** within everybody's reach; **dar a. a** to catch up with; **fuera del a. de los niños** out of the reach of children (b) *Fig* scope; *(de noticia)* importance

alcancía *nf* money box; *(cerdito)* piggy bank

alcanfor *nm* camphor

alcantarilla *nf* sewer; *(boca)* drain

alcantarillado *nm* sewer system

alcanzar [40] **1** *vt* (a) to reach; *(persona)* to catch up with; **la producción alcanza dos mil unidades** production is up to two thousand units (b) **alcánzame la sal** *(pasar)* pass me the salt (c) *(conseguir)* to attain, to achieve

2 *vi (ser suficiente)* to be sufficient; **con un kilo no alcanza para todos** one kilo won't be enough for all of us

alcaparra *nf (fruto)* caper; *(planta)* caper bush

alcatraz *nm Orn* gannet

alcaucil *nm RP* artichoke

alcayata *nf* hook

alcazaba *nf* fortress, citadel

alcázar *nm* (a) *(fortaleza)* fortress, citadel (b) *(castillo)* castle, palace

alcista 1 *adj (bolsa)* rising, bullish; **tendencia a.** upward tendency

2 *nmf (bolsa)* bull

alcoba *nf* bedroom

🖋 Observa que la palabra inglesa **alcove** es un falso amigo y no es la traducción de la palabra española **alcoba**. En inglés, **alcove** significa "hueco".

alcohol *nm* alcohol

alcoholemia *nf* blood alcohol level;

prueba de a. Breathalyser® test

alcohólico,-a adj & nm,f alcoholic

alcoholímetro nm Breathalyser®

alcoholismo nm alcoholism

alcoholizado,-a adj & nm,f alcoholic

alcornoque nm cork oak

alcurnia nf lineage, ancestry; **de alta a.** of noble lineage

alcuzcuz nm couscous

aldaba nf (llamador) door knocker

aldabonazo nm (a) loud knock (b) (advertencia) warning

aldea nf village

aldeano,-a 1 adj village
  2 nm,f villager

aleación nf alloy

aleatorio,-a adj random

alebrestarse vpr Col (ponerse nervioso) to get nervous o excited

aleccionador,-a adj (instructivo) instructive; (ejemplar) exemplary

aleccionar vt (instruir) to teach, to instruct; (adiestrar) to train

aledaño,-a 1 adj adjoining, adjacent
  2 nmpl aledaños outskirts

alegar [42] vt (a) (aducir) to claim; Jur to allege (b) (presentar) to put forward

alegato nm argument

alegoría nf allegory

alegrar 1 vt (a) (complacer) to make happy o glad; **me alegra que se lo hayas dicho** I am glad you told her (b) Fig (avivar) to enliven, to brighten up
  2 alegrarse vpr to be glad, to be happy; **me alegro de verte** I am pleased to see you; **me alegro por ti** I am happy for you

alegre adj (a) (contento) happy, glad (b) (color) bright; (música) lively; (lugar) pleasant, cheerful (c) Fig (borracho) tipsy, merry

alegría nf joy, happiness

alejado,-a adj far away, remote

alejar 1 vt to move further away
  2 alejarse vpr to go away, to move away; **no te alejes de mí** keep close to me

aleluya nm o nf hallelujah, alleluia

alemán,-ana 1 adj & nm,f German
  2 nm (idioma) German

Alemania n Germany; **A. del Este/Oeste** East/West Germany; **A. Occidental/Oriental** West/East Germany

alentador,-a adj encouraging; **un panorama poco a.** a rather bleak outlook

alentar [1] vt Fig to encourage

alergia nf allergy

alérgico,-a adj allergic

alero nm eaves

alerón nm Av aileron

alerta nf & adj alert; **estar en estado de a.** to be (on the) alert

alertar vt to alert (de to); **nos alertó del peligro** he alerted us to the danger

aleta nf (de pez) fin; (de foca, de nadador) flipper

aletargado,-a adj lethargic

aletargar [42] **1** vt to make lethargic
  2 aletargarse vpr to become lethargic

aletear vi to flutter o flap its wings

alevín nm (pescado) young fish; Fig (principiante) beginner

alevosía nf (traición) treachery; (premeditación) premeditation

alevoso,-a adj (persona) treacherous; (acto) premeditated

alfabético,-a adj alphabetic

alfabetización nf teaching to read and write; **campaña de a.** literacy campaign

alfabeto nm alphabet

alfajor nm CSur = large biscuit filled with toffee and coated with coconut

alfalfa nf lucerne, alfalfa

alfarería nf (a) (arte) pottery (b) (taller) potter's workshop; (tienda) pottery shop

alfarero,-a nm,f potter

alféizar nm sill, windowsill

alférez nm second lieutenant

alfil nm bishop

alfiler nm pin; (broche) pin, brooch; (de corbata) tiepin; (para tender) peg; Andes, RP, Ven **a. de gancho** (imperdible) safety pin

alfiletero nm pin box, pin case

alfombra nf rug; (moqueta) carpet

alfombrar vt to carpet

alfombrilla nf rug, mat

alforja nf (para caballos) saddlebag; (para hombro) knapsack

alga nf alga; (marina) seaweed

> Takes the masculine articles **el** and **un**.

algarabía nf hubbub; hullabaloo

algarrobo nm carob tree

algazara nf din, row

álgebra nf algebra

> Takes the masculine articles **el** and **un**.

álgido,-a adj culminating, critical; **el punto a.** the climax

algo 1 pron indef (a) (afirmativo) something; (interrogativo) anything; **a. así** something like that; **¿a. más?** anything else?; **por a. será** there must be a reason for it; Fam **a. es a.** it's better than nothing (b) (cantidad indeterminada) some; **¿queda a. de pastel?** is there any cake left?

2 *adv (un poco)* quite, somewhat; **se siente a. mejor** she's feeling a bit better

algodón *nm* cotton; **a. (hidrófilo)** *Br* cotton wool, *US* absorbent cotton; **a. de azúcar** *Br* candy floss, *US* cotton candy

algodonero,-a 1 *nm,f* cotton grower

2 *adj* cotton

alguacil *nm* bailiff

alguien *pron indef (afirmativo)* somebody, someone; *(interrogativo)* anybody, anyone

alguno,-a 1 *adj* **(a)** *(delante de nombre)* *(afirmativo)* some; *(interrogativo)* any; **algunos días** some days; **algunas veces** some times; **alguna que otra vez** now and then; **¿has tomado alguna medicina?** have you taken any medicine?; **¿le has visto alguna vez?** have you ever seen him? **(b)** *(después de nombre)* not at all; **no vino persona alguna** nobody came

> **algún** is used instead of **alguno** before masculine singular nouns (e.g. **algún día** some day).

2 *pron indef* **(a)** someone, somebody; **a. dirá que ...** someone might say that ...; **a. que otro** some **(b)** **algunos,-as** some (people)

alhaja *nf* jewel

alhelí *nm (pl alhelíes)* wallflower, stock

aliado,-a 1 *adj* allied

2 *nm,f* **los Aliados** the Allies

alianza *nf* **(a)** *(pacto)* alliance **(b)** *(anillo)* wedding ring

aliarse *[29]* *vpr* to become allies, to form an alliance

alias *adv & nm inv* alias

alicaído,-a *adj* **(a)** *Fig (débil)* weak, feeble **(b)** *Fig (deprimido)* down, depressed

alicatar *vt* to tile

alicates *nmpl* pliers

aliciente *nm* **(a)** *(atractivo)* lure, charm **(b)** *(incentivo)* incentive

alienación *nf* alienation

alienado,-a *adj* insane, deranged

alienar *vt* to alienate

alienígena *adj & nmf* alien

aliento *nm* **(a)** breath; **sin a.** breathless **(b)** *(ánimo)* encouragement

aligerar 1 *vt (acelerar)* to speed up; **a. el paso** to quicken one's pace

2 *vi Fam* **¡aligera!** hurry up!

alijo *nm* haul; **un a. de drogas** a consignment of drugs

alimaña *nf* vermin

alimentación *nf (comida)* food; *(acción)* feeding; *Téc* supply

alimentar 1 *vt* **(a)** *(dar alimento)* to feed; *(ser nutritivo)* to be nutritious **(b)** *Fig*

(sentimientos) to nourish **(c)** *Informát* to feed; *Téc* to supply

2 alimentarse *vpr* **a. con** *o* **de** to live on

alimentario,-a *adj* food

alimenticio,-a *adj* nutritious; **productos alimenticios** food products, foodstuffs; **valor a.** nutritional value

alimento *nm* **(a)** *(comida)* food **(b)** *Fig* **tiene poco a.** it is not very nourishing

alimón *adv* **al a.** together

alineación *nf* **(a)** alignment **(b)** *Dep (equipo)* line-up

alineado,-a *adj* aligned, lined-up; **países no alineados** non-aligned countries

alineamiento *nm* alignment

alinear 1 *vt* to align, to line up

2 alinearse *vpr* to line up

aliñar *vt* to season, to flavour; *(ensalada)* to dress

aliño *nm* seasoning, dressing

alioli *nm* garlic mayonnaise

alisar *vt,* **alisarse** *vpr* to smooth

aliscafo, alíscafo *nm RP* hydrofoil

alistar 1 *vt Mil* to recruit, to enlist

2 alistarse *vpr* **(a)** *Mil* to enlist, to enrol **(b)** *Am (prepararse)* to get ready

aliviar *[43]* **1** *vt (dolor)* to soothe, to relieve; *(carga)* to lighten, to make lighter

2 aliviarse *vpr (dolor)* to diminish, to get better

alivio *nm* relief

aljibe *nm* cistern, tank

allá *adv* **(a)** *(lugar alejado)* there, over there; **a. abajo/arriba** down/up there; **¡a. voy!** here I go!; **más a.** further on; **más a. de** beyond; **el más a.** the beyond **(b)** *(tiempo)* **a. por los años veinte** back in the twenties **(c)** **a. tú** that's your problem

allanamiento *nm Jur* **a. de morada** breaking and entering

allanar *vt* **(a)** *(terreno)* to level, to flatten; *Fig (camino)* to smooth **(b)** *Jur* to break into

allegado,-a 1 *adj* close

2 *nm,f* close friend

allende *adv Fml* beyond; **a. los mares** overseas

allí *adv* there, over there; **a. abajo/arriba** down/up there; **de a. para acá** back and forth; **por a.** *(movimiento)* that way; *(posición)* over there

alma *nf* soul; **no había ni un a.** there was no soul

> Takes the masculine articles **el** and **un**.

almacén *nm* **(a)** *(local)* warehouse; *(habitación)* storeroom **(b)** *Com* **(grandes) almacenes** department store **(c)** *Andes,*

RP (de alimentos) grocer's (shop), grocery store

almacenaje *nm* storage, warehousing

almacenamiento *nm* storage, warehousing; *Informát* storage

almacenar *vt* to store

almacenista *nmf (vendedor)* wholesaler; *(propietario)* warehouse owner

almanaque *nm* calendar

almeja *nf* clam; *muy Fam* pussy

almena *nf* merlon

almendra *nf* almond; **a. garapiñada** sugared almond

almendro *nm* almond tree

almiar *nm* haystack

almíbar *nm* syrup

almidón *nm* starch

almidonar *vt* to starch

alminar *nm* minaret

almirante *nm* admiral

almizcle *nm* musk

almohada *nf* pillow; *Fam* **consultarlo con la a.** to sleep on it

almohadilla *nf* (small) cushion

almohadón *nm* large pillow, cushion

almorrana *nf Fam* pile

almorzar [2] 1 *vi* to have lunch

  2 *vt* to have for lunch

almuerzo *nm* lunch

aló *interj Andes, Carib (al teléfono)* hello!

alocado,-a *adj* thoughtless, rash

alocución *nf* speech, address

alojamiento *nm* accommodation; **dar a.** to accommodate

alojar 1 *vt* to accommodate

  2 alojarse *vpr* to stay

alondra *nf* lark; **a. común** skylark

alpaca *nf* alpaca

alpargata *nf* canvas sandal, espadrille

Alpes *npl* **los A.** the Alps

alpinismo *nm* mountaineering, climbing

alpinista *nmf* mountaineer, climber

alpino,-a *adj* Alpine; **esquí a.** downhill skiing

alquilar *vt* to hire; *(pisos, casas)* to rent; **se alquila** *(en letrero)* to let

alquiler *nm* **(a)** *(de pisos, casas)* renting, letting; **a. de coches** car hire; **de a.** *(pisos, casas)* to let, rented; *(coche)* for hire; *(televisión)* for rent **(b)** *(precio)* hire, rental; *(de pisos, casas)* rent

alquimia *nf* alchemy

alquitrán *nm* tar

alrededor 1 *adv (lugar)* round, around; **mira a.** look around; **a. de la mesa** round the table; **a. de las dos** around two o'clock; **a. de quince** about fifteen;

  2 *nmpl* **alrededores** surrounding area;

en los alrededores de Murcia in the area round Murcia

alta *nf* **dar de** *o* **el a.** *(a un enfermo)* to discharge from hospital

> Takes the masculine articles **el** and **un**.

altamente *adv* highly, extremely

altanería *nf* arrogance

altanero,-a *adj* arrogant

altar *nm* altar

altavoz *nm* loudspeaker

alterable *adj* changeable

alteración *nf* **(a)** *(cambio)* alteration **(b)** *(alboroto)* quarrel, row; **a. del orden público** disturbance of the peace **(c)** *(excitación)* agitation

alterar 1 *vt* to alter, to change; **a. el orden público** to disturb the peace

  2 alterarse *vpr* **(a)** *(cambiar)* to change **(b)** *(inquietarse)* to be upset **(c)** *(alimentos)* to go off

altercado *nm* quarrel, argument

alternar 1 *vt* to alternate

  2 *vi (relacionarse)* to meet people, to socialize

  3 alternarse *vpr* to alternate

alternativa *nf* alternative

alternativo,-a *adj* alternative

alterno,-a *adj* alternate; **días alternos** alternate days

alteza *nf* Highness; **Su A. Real** His/Her Royal Highness

altibajos *nmpl Fig* ups and downs

altiplano *nm* high plateau

altísimo *nm* **el A.** the Almighty

altisonante *adj* grandiloquent

altitud *nf* altitude

altivez *nf* arrogance, haughtiness

altivo,-a *adj* arrogant, haughty

alto¹ *nm* **(a)** *(interrupción)* stop, break **(b)** *Mil* halt; **dar el a.** to order to halt; **un a. el fuego** a cease-fire

alto²,-a 1 *adj (persona, árbol, edificio)* tall; *(montaña, techo, presión)* high; *(sonido)* loud; *Fig (precio, tecnología)* high; *(tono)* high-pitched; **los pisos altos** the top floors; **en lo a.** at the top; **alta sociedad** high society; **clase alta** upper class; **en voz alta** aloud, in a loud voice; **a altas horas de la noche** late at night

  2 *adv* **(a)** high, high up **(b)** *(sonar, hablar etc)* loud, loudly; **pon la radio más alta** turn the radio up; **¡habla más a.!** speak up!

  3 *nm* **(a)** *(altura)* height; **¿cuánto tiene de a.?** how tall/high is it?; *Fig* **por todo lo a.** in a grand way **(b)** *(elevación)* hill

altoparlante *nm Am* loudspeaker

altozano *nm* hillock, hill

altramuz *nm* lupin

altruista 1 *adj* altruistic

  2 *nmf* altruist

altura *nf* (**a**) height; **de 10 m de a.** 10 m high (**b**) (*nivel*) level; **a la misma a.** on the same level; *Geog* on the same latitude; **a la a. del cine** by the cinema; *Fig* **estar a la a. de las circunstancias** to meet the challenge; *Fig* **no está a su a.** he does not measure up to him; *Fig* **a estas alturas** at this stage (**c**) *Rel* **alturas** heaven

alubia *nf* bean

alucinación *nf* hallucination

alucinado,-a *adj Fam* amazed

alucinante *adj Fam* brilliant, mind-blowing

alucinar 1 *vt* to hallucinate; *Fig* (*encantar*) to fascinate

  2 *vi Fam* to be amazed, to be spaced out

alucinógeno,-a 1 *adj* hallucinogenic

  2 *nm* hallucinogen

alud *nm* avalanche

aludido,-a *adj Fig* **darse por a.** to take it personally

aludir *vi* to allude to, to mention

alumbrado,-a 1 *adj* lit

  2 *nm Elec* lighting; **a. público** street lighting

alumbrar 1 *vt* (*iluminar*) to light, to illuminate

  2 *vi* (*parir*) to give birth

aluminio *nm* aluminium

alumnado *nm* (*de colegio*) pupils; *Univ* student body

alumno,-a *nm,f* (**a**) (*de colegio*) pupil; **a. externo** day pupil; **a. interno** boarder (**b**) *Univ* student

alusión *nf* allusion, mention

aluvión *nm* downpour; *Fig* **un a. de preguntas** a barrage of questions

alverja, alverjana *nf Am* pea

alza *nf* (**a**) rise; **en a.** rising; **jugar al a.** (*bolsa*) to bull the market (**b**) *Mil* sight

> Takes the masculine articles **el** and **un**.

alzado,-a 1 *adj* raised, lifted; **votación a mano alzada** vote by a show of hands

  2 *nm Arquit* elevation

alzamiento *nm* (*rebelión*) uprising

alzar [**40**] **1** *vt* to raise, to lift; **a. el vuelo** to take off; **a. los ojos/la vista** to look up; **álzate el cuello** turn your collar up

  2 alzarse *vpr* (**a**) (*levantarse*) to get up, to rise (**b**) (*rebelarse*) to rise, to rebel (**c**) **a. con la victoria** to win, to be victorious

AM *nf* (*abr* **amplitude modulation**) AM

a.m. *adv* a.m.

ama *nf* (*señora*) lady of the house; (*dueña*) owner; **a. de casa** housewife; **a. de llaves** housekeeper

> Takes the masculine articles **el** and **un**.

amabilidad *nf* kindness; *Fml* **tenga la a. de esperar** would you be so kind as to wait?

amable *adj* kind, nice; *Fml* **¿sería usted tan a. de ayudarme?** would you be so kind as to help me?

amado,-a 1 *adj* loved, beloved

  2 *nm,f* sweetheart

amaestrar *vt* to train; (*domar*) to tame

amagar [**42**] *vt* (*amenazar*) to threaten; **amaga tormenta** a storm is threatening

amago *nm* (**a**) (*indicio*) first sign; **a. de infarto** onset of a heart attack (**b**) (*intento*) attempt (**c**) *Fig* (*amenaza*) threat

amainar *vi* (*viento etc*) to drop, to die down

amalgama *nf* amalgam

amalgamar *vt* to amalgamate

amamantar *vt* to breast-feed; *Zool* to suckle

amancay *nm Andes* amaryllis

amancebarse *vpr* to cohabit

amanecer [**33**] **1** *v impers* to dawn; **¿a qué hora amanece?** when does it get light?; **amaneció lluvioso** it was rainy at daybreak

  2 *vi* **amanecimos en Finlandia** we were in Finland at daybreak; **amaneció muy enfermo** he woke up feeling very ill

  3 *nm* dawn, daybreak; **al a.** at dawn

amanerado,-a *adj* mannered, affected

amansar *vt* (**a**) to tame (**b**) *Fig* (*apaciguar*) to tame, to calm

amante *nmf* lover; **a. del arte** art lover

amañar *vt* to fix, to fiddle; (*elecciones*) to rig

amapola *nf* poppy

amar 1 *vt* to love

  2 amarse *vpr* to love each other

amaraje *nm Av* landing at sea

amargado,-a 1 *adj* (*rencoroso*) embittered, bitter; *Fam* (*agobiado*) pissed off; **estoy a. con los exámenes** I'm pissed off with the exams

  2 *nm,f* bitter person

amargar [**42**] **1** *vt* to make bitter; *Fig* to embitter, to sour

  2 amargarse *vpr Fig* to become embittered *o* bitter; **no te amargues por eso** don't let that make you bitter

amargo,-a *adj* bitter

amargor *nm*, **amargura** *nf* bitterness

amarillento,-a *adj* yellowish

amarillo,-a *adj & nm* yellow; **prensa amarilla** gutter press

amarilloso,-a *adj Ven* yellowish

amarra *nf* mooring rope; **soltar amarras** to cast off, to let go

amarradero *nm* mooring

amarrar *vt Náut* to moor, to tie up; *(atar)* to tie (up), to bind

amarrete,-a *adj Andes, RP Fam* mean, tight

amasar *vt* (a) *Culin* to knead (b) *Fig (fortuna)* to amass

amasiato *nm CAm, Méx* cohabitation, common-law marriage

amasijo *nm Fam* hotchpotch, jumble

amasio,-a *nm,f CAm, Méx* live-in lover, common-law partner

amateur *adj & nmf* amateur

amatista *nf* amethyst

amazona *nf* (a) *(jinete)* horsewoman (b) *(en mitología)* Amazon

Amazonas *n* el A. the Amazon

amazónico,-a *adj* Amazonian

ambages *nmpl* hablar sin a. to go straight to the point

ámbar *nm* amber

Amberes *n* Antwerp

ambición *nf* ambition

ambicionar *vt* to have as an ambition; **ambiciona ser presidente** his ambition is to become president

ambicioso,-a 1 *adj* ambitious

  2 *nm,f* ambitious person

ambidextro,-a *nm,f* ambidextrous person

ambientación *nf Cin & Teatro* setting

ambientado,-a *adj (bar etc)* lively

ambientador *nm* air freshener

ambiental *adj* environmental

ambientar 1 *vt* (a) *(bar etc)* to liven up (b) *Cin & Teatro* to set

  2 ambientarse *vpr (adaptarse)* to get used to

ambiente 1 *nm* (a) *(gen)* environment; *Fig (medio)* environment, milieu (b) *Andes, RP (habitación)* room

  2 *adj* environmental; **temperatura a.** room temperature

ambigüedad *nf* ambiguity

ambiguo,-a *adj* ambiguous

ámbito *nm* field, sphere; **empresa de á. nacional** nationwide company

ambos,-as *adj pl Fml* both; **por a. lados** on both sides

ambulancia *nf* ambulance

ambulante *adj* travelling, mobile; **biblioteca a.** mobile library

ambulatorio *nm* surgery, clinic

amedrentar *vt* to frighten, to scare

amén¹ *nm* amen

amén² *adv* a. de in addition to

amenaza *nf* threat

amenazador,-a, amenazante *adj* threatening, menacing

amenazar [40] *vt* to threaten; **a. de muerte a algn** to threaten to kill sb

amenizar [40] *vt* to liven up

ameno,-a *adj* entertaining

América *n* America; **A. Central/del Norte/del Sur** Central/North/South America

americana *nf (prenda)* jacket

americano,-a *adj & nm,f* American

amerindio,-a *adj & nm,f* Amerindian, American Indian

ameritar *vt Am* to deserve

amerizar [40] *vi* to land at sea

ametralladora *nf* machine gun

ametrallar *vt* to machine-gun

amianto *nm* asbestos

amigable *adj* friendly

amígdala *nf* tonsil

amigdalitis *nf* tonsillitis

amigo,-a 1 *nm,f* friend; **hacerse a. de** to make friends with; **hacerse amigos** to become friends; **son muy amigos** they are very good friends

  2 *adj (aficionado)* fond (**de** of)

amilanar 1 *vt* to frighten, to scare

  2 amilanarse *vpr* to be frightened o daunted

aminorar *vt* to reduce; **a. el paso** to slow down

amistad *nf* (a) friendship (b) **amistades** friends

amistoso,-a *adj* friendly

amnesia *nf* amnesia

amnistía *nf* amnesty

amo *nm* (a) *(dueño)* owner (b) *(señor)* master

amodorrarse *vpr* to become sleepy o drowsy

amoldar 1 *vt* to adapt, to adjust

  2 amoldarse *vpr* to adapt oneself

amonestación *nf* (a) rebuke, reprimand; *Dep* warning (b) *Rel* **amonestaciones** banns

amonestar *vt* (a) *(advertir)* to rebuke, to reprimand; *Dep* to warn (b) *Rel* to publish the banns of

amoniaco, amoníaco *nm* ammonia

amontonar 1 *vt* to pile up, to heap up

  2 amontonarse *vpr* to pile up, to heap up; *(gente)* to crowd together

amor *nm* love; **hacer el a.** to make love; **a. propio** self-esteem; **¡por el a. de Dios!** for God's sake!

amoral adj amoral

amoratado,-a adj (de frío) blue with cold; (de un golpe) black and blue

amordazar [40] vt (perro) to muzzle; (persona) to gag

amorfo,-a adj amorphous

amorío nm love affair, flirtation

amoroso,-a adj loving, affectionate

amortajar vt to shroud, to wrap in a shroud

amortiguador nm Aut shock absorber

amortiguar [45] vt (golpe) to cushion; (ruido) to muffle; (luz) to subdue

amortización nf repayment

amortizar [40] vt to pay off

amotinado,-a nm,f rioter; Mil mutineer

amotinamiento nm riot, rioting; Mil mutiny

amotinar 1 vt to incite to riot; Mil to incite to mutiny

2 amotinarse vpr to rise up; Mil to mutiny

amparar 1 vt to protect

2 ampararse vpr to seek refuge

amparo nm protection, shelter; **al a. de la ley** under the protection of the law

amperio nm ampère, amp

ampliación nf enlargement; (de plazo, casa) extension

ampliar [29] vt to enlarge; (casa, plazo) to extend

amplificador nm amplifier

amplificar [44] vt to amplify

amplio,-a adj large, roomy; (ancho) wide, broad; **en el sentido más a. de la palabra** in the broadest sense of the word

amplitud nf (a) spaciousness; a. de miras broad-mindedness (b) (de espacio) room, space (c) Fís amplitude

ampolla nf (a) Med blister; Fig **levantar ampollas** to raise people's hackles (b) (de medicina) ampoule

ampuloso,-a adj pompous, bombastic

amputar vt Med to amputate; Fig to cut out

amueblar vt to furnish

amuermar vt Fam (a) (atontar) to make feel dopey o groggy (b) (aburrir) to bore

amuleto nm amulet; a. de la suerte lucky charm

amurallar vt to wall, to fortify

anacronismo nm anachronism

ánade nm duck; á. real mallard

anales nmpl annals

analfabetismo nm illiteracy

analfabeto,-a nm,f illiterate

analgésico,-a adj & nm analgesic

análisis nm inv analysis; a. de sangre blood test

analista nmf analyst

analizar [40] vt to analyse

analogía nf analogy

analógico,-a adj analogue

análogo,-a adj analogous, similar

ananá nm (pl ananaes), **ananás** nm (pl ananases) pineapple

anaquel nm shelf

anaranjado,-a adj & nm orange

anarquía nf anarchy

anarquismo nm anarchism

anarquista adj & nmf anarchist

anatomía nf anatomy

anatómico,-a adj anatomical

anca nf haunch; ancas de rana frogs' legs

> Takes the masculine articles el and un.

ancestral adj ancestral

ancho,-a 1 adj wide, broad; **a lo a.** breadthwise; **te está muy a.** it's too big for you

2 nm (a) (anchura) width, breadth; **2 m de a.** 2 m wide; **¿qué a. tiene?** how wide is it? (b) Cost width

3 nfpl Fam **a mis** o **tus anchas** at ease, comfortable

anchoa nf anchovy

anchura nf width, breadth

anciano,-a 1 adj very old

2 nm,f old person; **los ancianos** old people

ancla nf anchor

> Takes the masculine articles el and un.

anclar vt & vi to anchor

andadas nfpl **volver a las a.** to go back to one's old tricks

andaderas nfpl baby-walker

andadura nf walking

ándale interj CAm, Méx Fam come on!

Andalucía n Andalusia

andaluz,-a adj & nm,f Andalusian

andamiaje, andamio nm scaffolding

andanza nf adventure, happening

andar¹ nm a. o andares nmpl walk, gait

andar² [8] **1** vi (a) to walk (b) (coche etc) to move; **este coche anda despacio** this car goes very slowly (c) (funcionar) to work; **esto no anda** this doesn't work (d) Fam **anda por los cuarenta** he's about forty; **anda siempre diciendo que ...** he's always saying that ...; **¿cómo andamos de tiempo?** how are we off for time?; **tu bolso debe a. por ahí** your bag must be over there somewhere

2 vt (recorrer) to walk

andariego,-a adj fond of walking

andén nm (a) (en estación) platform (b)

Andes, CAm (acera) Br pavement, *US* sidewalk (**c**) *Andes (bancal de tierra)* terrace

Andes *nmpl* Andes

andinismo *nm Am* mountaineering

andinista *nmf Am* mountaineer

andino,-a *adj & nm,f* Andean

andrajo *nm* rag, tatter

andrajoso,-a *adj* ragged, tattered

androide *nm* android

andurriales *nmpl Fam* out-of-the-way place

anécdota *nf* anecdote

anecdótico,-a *adj* anecdotal

anegar [42] *vt*, **anegarse** *upr* to flood

anejo,-a 1 *adj* attached, joined (**a** to)
2 *nm* appendix

anemia *nf* anaemia

anestesia *nf* anaesthesia

anestésico,-a *adj & nm* anaesthetic

anexar *vt* to annex

anexión *nf* annexation

anexionar *vt* to annex

anexo,-a 1 *adj* attached, joined (**a** to)
2 *nm* appendix

anfetamina *nf* amphetamine

anfibio,-a 1 *adj* amphibious
2 *nm* amphibian

anfiteatro *nm* (**a**) amphitheatre (**b**) *Cin & Teatro* gallery

anfitrión,-ona *nm,f* host, *f* hostess

ángel *nm* (**a**) angel; **á. de la guarda** guardian angel (**b**) *Am (micrófono)* hand-held microphone

angelical, angélico,-a *adj* angelic

angina *nf* angina; **tener anginas** to have tonsillitis; *Med* **a. de pecho** angina pectoris

anglófono,-a 1 *adj* English-speaking
2 *nm,f* English speaker

anglosajón,-ona *adj & nm,f* Anglo-Saxon

Angola *n* Angola

angosto,-a *adj Fml* narrow

anguila *nf* eel; **a. de mar** conger eel

angula *nf* elver

angular *adj* angular; *Fot* (**objetivo**) **gran a.** wide-angle lens; **piedra a.** cornerstone

ángulo *nm* angle; *(rincón)* corner

angustia *nf* anguish

angustiar [43] *vt* to distress

angustioso,-a *adj* distressing

anhelar *vt* to long for, to yearn for

anhelo *nm* longing, yearning

anhídrido *nm* **a. carbónico** carbon dioxide

anidar *vi* to nest

anilla *nf* ring; **carpeta de anillas** ringbinder

anillo *nm* ring; **a. de boda** wedding ring

ánima *nf* soul

> Takes the masculine articles **el** and **un**.

animación *nf (diversión)* entertainment

animado,-a *adj (fiesta etc)* lively

animador,-a *nm,f* (**a**) entertainer; *TV* presenter; **a. cultural** cultural organizer (**b**) *Dep* cheerleader

animadversión *nf* ill feeling, animosity

animal 1 *nm* animal; *Fig (basto)* brute; *(necio)* dunce
2 *adj* animal

animar 1 *vt* (**a**) *(alentar)* to encourage (**b**) *(alegrar) (persona)* to cheer up; *(fiesta, bar)* to liven up, to brighten up
2 animarse *upr* (**a**) *(persona)* to cheer up; *(fiesta, reunión)* to brighten up (**b**) **¿te animas a venir?** do you fancy coming along?

anímico,-a *adj* **estado a.** frame *o* state of mind

ánimo *nm* (**a**) *(espíritu)* spirit; **estado de á.** frame *o* state of mind (**b**) **con á. de** *(intención)* with the intention of (**c**) *(valor, coraje)* courage; **dar ánimos a** to encourage; **¡á.!** cheer up!

animosidad *nf* animosity

animoso,-a *adj* cheerful

aniñado,-a *adj* childlike; *Pey* childish

aniquilación *nf* annihilation

aniquilar *vt* to annihilate

anís *nm* (**a**) *(bebida)* anisette (**b**) *(grano)* aniseed

anisete *nm* anisette

aniversario *nm* anniversary

ano *nm* anus

anoche *adv* last night; *(por la tarde)* yesterday evening; **antes de a.** the night before last

anochecer [33] **1** *v impers* to get dark; **cuando anochece** at nightfall, at dusk
2 *vi* to be somewhere at dusk; **anochecimos en Cuenca** we were in Cuenca at dusk
3 *nm* nightfall, dusk

anodino,-a *adj (insustancial)* insubstantial; *(soso)* insipid, dull

anomalía *nf* anomaly

anómalo,-a *adj* anomalous

anonadado,-a *adj* **me quedé/dejó a.** I was astonished

anonimato *nm* anonymity; **permanecer en el a.** to remain anonymous *o* nameless

anónimo,-a 1 *adj* (**a**) *(desconocido)*

anonymous (**b**) *Com* **sociedad anónima** public liability company, *US* incorporated company

2 *nm (carta)* anonymous letter

anorak *nm (pl* **anoraks)** anorak

anorexia *nf* anorexia

anormal 1 *adj* (**a**) abnormal (**b**) *(inhabitual)* unusual; **una situación a.** an irregular situation (**c**) *Med* subnormal

2 *nmf Med* subnormal person

anotación *nf* (**a**) annotation (**b**) *(apunte)* note

anotar 1 *vt* (**a**) to annotate (**b**) *(apuntar)* to take down, to make a note of

2 anotarse *vpr RP (en curso)* to enrol

anquilosado,-a *adj Fig* fossilized; **a. en el pasado** locked in the past

anquilosarse *vpr Fig* to stagnate

ansia *nf* (**a**) *(deseo)* longing, yearning (**b**) *(ansiedad)* anxiety (**c**) *Med* sick feeling

> Takes the masculine articles **el** and **un**.

ansiar [**29**] *vt* to long for, to yearn for

ansiedad *nf* anxiety; **con a.** anxiously

ansioso,-a *adj* (**a**) *(deseoso)* eager (**por** for) (**b**) *(avaricioso)* greedy

antagónico,-a *adj* antagonistic

antagonismo *nm* antagonism

antagonista 1 *adj* antagonistic

2 *nmf* antagonist

antaño *adv* in the past, formerly

antártico,-a 1 *adj* Antarctic

2 *nm* **el A.** the Antarctic

Antártida *nf* Antarctica

ante¹ *nm* (**a**) *Zool* elk, moose (**b**) *(piel)* suede

ante² *prep* (**a**) before, in the presence of; *Jur* **a. notario** in the presence of a notary; **a. todo** most of all (**b**) *(en vista de)* faced with, in view of; **a. la crisis energética** faced with the energy crisis

anteanoche *adv* the night before last

anteayer *adv* the day before yesterday

antecedente 1 *adj* previous

2 *nm* antecedent

3 *nmpl* (**a**) **antecedentes** *(historial)* record; *Jur* **antecedentes penales** criminal record (**b**) *Fig* **poner en antecedentes** to put in the picture

anteceder *vt* to precede, to go before

antecesor,-a *nm,f* (**a**) *(en un cargo)* predecessor (**b**) *(antepasado)* ancestor

antedicho,-a *adj* above-mentioned

antelación *nf* notice; **con poca a.** at short notice; **con un mes de a.** a month beforehand, with a month's notice

antemano *adv* **de a.** beforehand, in advance

antena *nf* (**a**) *Rad & TV* aerial; **a. parabólica** satellite dish; **en a.** on the air (**b**) *Zool* antenna, feeler

anteojo *nm* (**a**) telescope (**b**) **anteojos** *(binoculares)* binoculars; *Am (gafas)* glasses, spectacles

antepasado,-a *nm,f* ancestor

antepecho *nm (de ventana)* sill; *(pretil)* parapet, guardrail

antepenúltimo,-a *adj* antepenultimate; **el capítulo a.** the last chapter but two

anteponer [**19**] *(pp* **antepuesto)** *vt Fig* to give preference to

anteproyecto *nm* preliminary plan, draft; *Pol* **a. de ley** draft bill

antepuesto,-a *pp* de anteponer

antepuse *pt indef* de anteponer

anterior *adj* (**a**) previous; **el día a.** the day before (**b**) *(delantero)* front; **parte a.** front part

anterioridad *nf* **con a.** before; **con a. a** prior to, before

anteriormente *adv* previously, before

antes *adv* (**a**) *(tiempo)* before; **a. de las tres** before three o'clock; **mucho a.** long before; **la noche a.** the night before; **cuanto a.** as soon as possible (**b**) *(antaño)* in the past; **a. llovía más** it used to rain more in the past (**c**) *(lugar)* before; **a. del semáforo** before the traffic lights (**d**) **a. prefiero hacerlo yo** I'd rather do it myself; **a. (bien)** on the contrary

antesala *nf* antechamber, anteroom; *Fig* **en la a. de** on the eve of

anti- *pref* anti-

antiadherente *adj* nonstick

antiaéreo,-a *adj* anti-aircraft

antibiótico,-a *adj* & *nm* antibiotic

anticaspa *adj* anti-dandruff

anticiclón *nm* anticyclone, high pressure area

anticipación *nf* bringing forward; **con a.** in advance

anticipadamente *adv* in advance

anticipado,-a *adj* brought forward; **elecciones anticipadas** early elections; **gracias anticipadas** thanks in advance; *Com* **por a.** in advance

anticipar 1 *vt (acontecimiento)* to bring forward; *(dinero)* to pay in advance; **no anticipemos acontecimientos** we'll cross that bridge when we come to it

2 anticiparse *vpr* (**a**) *(adelantarse)* to beat to it; **iba a decírtelo, pero él se me anticipó** I was going to tell you, but he beat me to it (**b**) *(llegar pronto)* to arrive early; *Fig* **a. a su tiempo** to be ahead of one's time

anticipo *nm (adelanto)* advance; **pedir un a.** to ask for an advance (on one's wages)

anticonceptivo,-a *adj & nm* contraceptive

anticongelante *adj & nm (de radiador)* antifreeze; *(de parabrisas)* de-icer

anticonstitucional *adj* unconstitutional

anticuado,-a *adj* antiquated

anticuario,-a *nm,f* antique dealer

anticucho *nm Andes (brocheta)* kebab

anticuerpo *nm* antibody

antídoto *nm* antidote

antier *adv Am Fam* the day before yesterday

antiestético,-a *adj* ugly, unsightly

antifaz *nm* mask

antigás *adj* **careta/mascarilla a.** gas mask

antigualla *nf Pey* museum piece

antigüedad *nf* (a) *(período histórico)* antiquity; **en la a.** in olden days, in former times (b) *(en cargo)* seniority (c) **tienda de antigüedades** antique shop

antiguo,-a *adj* (a) old, ancient (b) *(pasado de moda)* old-fashioned (c) *(en cargo)* senior (d) *(anterior)* former

antihigiénico,-a *adj* unhygienic, unhealthy

antihistamínico,-a *adj & nm* antihistamine

Antillas *nfpl* **las A.** the West Indies, the Antilles

antinatural *adj* unnatural, contrary to nature

antiniebla *adj inv* **luces a.** foglights

antipatía *nf* antipathy, dislike; **tener a.** to dislike

antipático,-a *adj* unpleasant; **Pedro me es a.** I don't like Pedro

antípodas *nfpl* **las A.** the Antipodes

antiquísimo,-a *(superl de* **antiguo)** *adj* very old, ancient

antirrobo 1 *adj inv* antitheft; **alarma a.** burglar alarm; *(para coche)* car alarm

  2 *nm (para coche)* car alarm; *(para casa)* burglar alarm

antisemita 1 *adj* anti-Semitic

  2 *nmf* anti-Semite

antiséptico,-a *adj & nm* antiseptic

antítesis *nf inv* antithesis

antivirus *nm inv Informát* antivirus system

antojadizo,-a *adj* capricious, unpredictable

antojarse *vpr* (a) **cuando se me antoja** when I feel like it; **se le antojó un helado** he fancied an ice-cream (b) *(suponer)* **se me antoja que no lo sabe** I have the feeling that he doesn't know

antojitos *nmpl Méx* snacks, appetizers

antojo *nm* (a) *(capricho)* whim, caprice; *(de embarazada)* craving; **a su a.** in one's own way, as one pleases (b) *(en la piel)* birthmark

antología *nf* anthology

antonomasia *nf* **por a.** par excellence

antorcha *nf* torch

antro *nm* dump, hole; *Fig* **a. de perdición** den of vice

antropología *nf* anthropology

antropólogo,-a *nm,f* anthropologist

anual *adj* annual; **ingresos anuales** yearly income

anualidad *nf* annual payment, annuity

anuario *nm* yearbook

anudar *vt* (a) *(atar)* to knot, to tie (b) *Fig (unir)* to join, to bring together

anulación *nf* cancellation; *(de matrimonio)* annulment; *(de ley)* repeal

anular[1] *nm* ring finger ·

anular[2] *vt* (a) *Com (pedido)* to cancel; *Dep (gol)* to disallow; *(matrimonio)* to annul; *Jur (ley)* to repeal (b) *Informát* to delete

anunciador,-a *adj* **empresa anunciadora** advertising company

anunciante *nm* advertiser

anunciar [43] 1 *vt* (a) *(producto etc)* to advertise (b) *(avisar)* to announce

  2 anunciarse *vpr* to advertise oneself; **a. en un periódico** to put an advert in a newspaper

anuncio *nm* (a) *(comercial)* advertisement, advert, ad (b) *(aviso)* announcement (c) *(cartel)* notice, poster

anzuelo *nm* (fish) hook

añadidura *nf* addition; **por a.** besides, on top of everything else

añadir *vt* to add (a to)

añejo,-a *adj* (a) *(vino, queso)* mature (b) *(estropeado)* stale

añicos *nmpl* smithereens; **hacer a.** to smash to smithereens

añil 1 *adj* indigo, blue

  2 *nm* (a) *Bot* indigo plant (b) *(color)* indigo

año *nm* (a) year; **el a. pasado** last year; **el a. que viene** next year; **hace años** a long time ago, years ago; **los años noventa** the nineties; **todo el a.** all the year (round); **a. luz** light year (b) **¿cuántos años tienes?** how old are you?; **tiene seis años** he's six years old; **entrado en años** getting on

añoranza *nf* longing, yearning

añorar *vt (pasado)* to long for, to yearn for; *(país)* to feel homesick for, to miss

APA *nf (abr* **Asociación de Padres de Alumnos**) = Spanish association for parents of schoolchildren, ≃ PTA

> Takes the masculine articles **el** and **un**.

apabullar *vt* to bewilder

apacentar [1] *vt* to put out to pasture, to graze

apacible *adj* mild, calm

apaciguar [45] 1 *vt (calmar)* to pacify, to appease
  2 apaciguarse *vpr (persona)* to calm down; *(tormenta)* to abate

apadrinar *vt* (a) *(en bautizo)* to act as godfather to; *(en boda)* to be best man for (b) *(artista)* to sponsor

apagado,-a *adj* (a) *(luz, cigarro)* out (b) *(color)* dull; *(voz)* sad; *(mirada)* expressionless, lifeless; *(carácter, persona)* spiritless

apagar [42] *vt (fuego)* to put out; *(luz, tele etc)* to turn off, to switch off; *(color)* to soften; *(sed)* to quench

apagón *nm* power cut, blackout

apaisado,-a *adj* (a) oblong (b) *(papel)* landscape

apalabrar *vt (concertar)* to make a verbal agreement on

apalancar [44] 1 *vt* to lever up
  2 apalancarse *vpr Fam* to ensconce oneself, to settle down

apalear¹ *vt* to beat, to thrash

apalear² *vt Agr (grano)* to winnow

apañar 1 *vt* to mend, to fix
  2 apañarse *vpr Fam* **apañárselas** to manage

apaño *nm* mend, repair

apapachar *vt Méx Fam (mimar)* to cuddle; *(consentir)* to spoil

apapacho *nm Méx Fam (mimo)* cuddle

aparador *nm (mueble)* sideboard; *(de tienda)* shop window

aparato *nm* (a) *(piece of)* apparatus, *(dispositivo)* device; *(instrumento)* instrument; **a. de radio/televisión** radio/television set; **a. digestivo** digestive system; **a. eléctrico** thunder and lightning (b) *Tel* **¿quién está al a.?** who's speaking? (c) *(ostentación)* display

aparatoso,-a *adj* (a) *(pomposo)* ostentatious, showy (b) *(espectacular)* spectacular (c) *(grande)* bulky

aparcamiento *nm (en la calle)* parking place; *(parking) Br* car park, *US* parking lot

aparcar [44] *vt* to park

aparcería *nf Agr* sharecropping

apareamiento *nm* (a) *(de cosas)* pairing off (b) *(de animales)* mating

aparear *vt*, **aparearse** *vpr* to mate

aparecer [33] 1 *vi* (a) to appear; **no aparece en mi lista** he is not on my list (b) to turn up, to show up; **¿apareció el dinero?** did the money turn up?; **no apareció nadie** nobody turned up
  2 aparecerse *vpr* to appear

aparejado,-a *adj* **llevar** *o* **traer a.** to entail

aparejador,-a *nm,f* quantity surveyor

aparejar *vt* (a) *(caballo)* to harness (b) *(emparejar)* to pair off

aparejo *nm* (a) *(equipo)* equipment (b) *(de caballo)* harness

aparentar 1 *vt* (a) *(fingir)* to affect (b) *(tener aspecto)* to look; **no aparenta esa edad** she doesn't look that age
  2 *vi* to show off

aparente *adj* (a) apparent; **sin motivo a.** for no apparent reason (b) *Fam (conveniente)* suitable

aparición *nf* (a) appearance (b) *(visión)* apparition

apariencia *nf* appearance; **en a.** apparently; *Fig* **guardar las apariencias** to keep up appearances

apartado,-a 1 *adj (lugar)* remote, isolated; **mantente a. de él** keep away from him
  2 *nm* (a) *(párrafo)* section, paragraph (b) **a. de correos** Post Office Box

apartamento *nm* (small) flat, apartment

apartar 1 *vt* (a) *(alejar)* to move away, to remove; **a. la mirada** to look away (b) *(guardar)* to put aside
  2 *vi* **¡aparta!** move out of the way!
  3 apartarse *vpr (alejarse)* to move over, to move away; **apártate de en medio** move out of the way

aparte 1 *adv* (a) aside; **ponlo a.** put it aside; **modestia/bromas a.** modesty/joking apart (b) **eso hay que pagarlo a.** *(separadamente)* you have to pay for that separately (c) **a. de eso** *(además)* besides that; *(excepto)* apart from that (d) **eso es caso a.** that's completely different
  2 *nm* (a) *Teatro* aside (b) *Ling* **punto y a.** full stop, new paragraph

apasionado,-a 1 *adj* passionate; **a. de la música** very fond of music
  2 *nm,f* enthusiast

apasionante *adj* exciting

apasionar *vt* to excite, to thrill; **le apasiona el jazz** he is mad about jazz

apatía *nf* apathy

apático,-a 1 *adj* apathetic
  2 *nm,f* apathetic person
apátrida 1 *adj* stateless
  2 *nmf* stateless person
apdo. (*abr* **apartado**) P.O. Box
apeadero *nm* halt
apearse *vpr* (*de un autobús, tren*) to get off, to alight; (*de un coche*) to get out; **se apeó en Jerez** he got off in Jerez
apechugar [42] *vi* **a. con** to shoulder
apedrear *vt* to throw stones at
apegado,-a *adj* devoted, attached (**a** to)
apegarse [42] *vpr* to become devoted *o* attached (**a** to)
apego *nm* love, affection; **tener a. a** to be attached to
apelación *nf* appeal; **interponer a.** to lodge an appeal
apelar *vi* (**a**) *Jur* to appeal (**b**) (*recurrir*) to resort (**a** to)
apellidarse *vpr* to have as a surname, to be called
apellido *nm* surname; **a. de soltera** maiden name
apelmazado,-a *adj* stodgy
apelotonar 1 *vt* to pile up, to put into a pile
  2 apelotonarse *vpr* (*gente*) to crowd together
apenado,-a *adj* (**a**) (*entristecido*) sad (**b**) *Andes, CAm, Carib, Méx* (*avergonzado*) ashamed, embarrassed
apenar 1 *vt* to sadden
  2 apenarse *vpr* (**a**) (*entristecerse*) to be saddened (**b**) *Andes, CAm, Carib, Méx* (*avergonzarse*) to be ashamed, to be embarrassed
apenas *adv* (**a**) (*casi no*) hardly, scarcely; **a. come** he hardly eats anything; **a. (si) hay nieve** there is hardly any snow (**b**) (*tan pronto como*) scarcely; **a. llegó, sonó el teléfono** no sooner had he arrived than the phone rang
apéndice *nm* appendix
apendicitis *nf* appendicitis
apercibir 1 *vt* to warn
  2 apercibirse *vpr* **apercibirse (de)** to notice
aperitivo *nm* (*bebida*) apéritif; (*comida*) appetizer
apero *nm* (*usu pl*) equipment, tools; **aperos de labranza** farming implements
apertura *nf* (**a**) (*comienzo*) opening (**b**) *Pol* liberalization
apestar 1 *vi* to stink (**a** of)
  2 *vt* to infect with the plague
apetecer [33] *vi* **¿qué te apetece para cenar?** what would you like for supper?;

¿te apetece ir al cine? do you fancy going to the cinema?
apetecible *adj* tempting, inviting
apetito *nm* appetite; **tengo mucho a.** I'm really hungry
apetitoso,-a *adj* appetizing, tempting; (*comida*) delicious, tasty
apiadarse *vpr* to take pity (**de** on)
ápice *nm* (**a**) (*punta*) apex (**b**) *Fig* **ni un á.** not a bit
apicultura *nf* beekeeping, apiculture
apilar *vt*, **apilarse** *vpr* to pile up, to heap up
apiñarse *vpr* to crowd together
apio *nm* celery
apisonadora *nf* roadroller, steamroller
apisonar *vt* to roll
aplacar [44] **1** *vt* to placate, to calm
  2 aplacarse *vpr* to calm down
aplanar *vt* to level
aplastante *adj* crushing; *Pol* **victoria a.** landslide victory
aplastar *vt* (**a**) to flatten, to squash (**b**) *Fig* (*vencer*) to crush
aplatanarse *vpr* *Fam* to become lethargic
aplaudir *vt* (**a**) to clap, to applaud (**b**) *Fig* to applaud
aplauso *nm* applause
aplazamiento *nm* postponement, adjournment; (*de un pago*) deferment
aplazar [40] *vt* to postpone, to adjourn; *Fin* (*pago*) to defer
aplicación *nf* application
aplicado,-a *adj* hard-working
aplicar [44] **1** *vt* to apply
  2 aplicarse *vpr* (**a**) (*esforzarse*) to apply oneself, to work hard (**b**) (*norma, ley*) to apply, to be applicable
aplique *nm* wall light, wall lamp
aplomo *nm* aplomb
apocado,-a *adj* shy, timid
apocamiento *nm* timidity, lack of self-confidence
apocarse [44] *vpr* to become frightened
apodar *vt* to nickname
apoderado,-a *nm,f* (**a**) agent, representative (**b**) (*de torero, deportista*) manager
apoderarse *vpr* to take possession (**de** of), to seize; *Fig* **el miedo se apoderó de ella** she was seized by fear
apodo *nm* nickname
apogeo *nm* height; **estar en pleno a.** (*fama etc*) to be at its height
apolillarse *vpr* to get moth-eaten
apolítico,-a *adj* apolitical
apología *nf* apology, defence
apoltronarse *vpr* *Fam* to vegetate

apoplejía *nf* apoplexy

apoquinar *vt Fam* to cough up, to fork out

aporrear *vt* to beat, to hit, to thrash; *(puerta)* to bang; *Fam* **a. el piano** to bang (away) on the piano

aportación *nf* contribution

aportar 1 *vt* to contribute
2 *vi Náut* to reach port

aposentarse *vpr* to stay, to lodge

aposento *nm* room

aposta *adv* on purpose, intentionally

apostar¹ [2] 1 *vt* to bet; **te apuesto una cena a que no viene** I bet you a dinner that he won't come
2 *vi* to bet (**por** on); **a. a los caballos** to bet on horses; **apuesto a que sí viene** I bet she will come
3 apostarse *vpr* to bet; **me apuesto lo que quieras** I bet you anything

apostar² *vt (situar)* to post, to station

apostilla *nf* note

apóstol *nm* apostle

apóstrofo *nm* apostrophe

apostura *nf* good bearing

apoteósico,-a *adj* enormous, tremendous

apoyacabezas *nm Aut* headrest

apoyar 1 *vt* (a) to lean (b) *(causa)* to support
2 apoyarse *vpr* (a) **a. en** to lean on; **apóyate en mi brazo** take my arm (b) **a. en** *(opinión)* to be based on, to rest on

apoyo *nm* support

apreciable *adj* appreciable, noticeable

apreciación *nf* appreciation

apreciar [43] 1 *vt* (a) to appreciate (b) *(percibir)* to notice, to see
2 apreciarse *vpr* to be noticeable

aprecio *nm* regard, esteem; **tener a. a algn** to be fond of sb

aprehender *vt (alijo, botín)* to apprehend, to seize

aprehensión *nf* seizure

apremiante *adj* urgent, pressing

apremiar [43] *vi* to be urgent; **el tiempo apremia** time is at a premium

aprender *vt* to learn; **así aprenderás** that'll teach you

aprendiz,-a *nm,f* apprentice, trainee

aprendizaje *nm* (a) learning (b) *(instrucción)* apprenticeship, traineeship

aprensión *nf* apprehension

aprensivo,-a *adj* apprehensive

apresar *vt* to seize, to capture

aprestar 1 *vt* to prepare, to get ready
2 aprestarse *vpr* to get ready

apresurado,-a *adj (persona)* in a hurry; *(cosa)* hurried

apresuramiento *nm* haste, hurry

apresurar 1 *vt (paso etc)* to speed up
2 apresurarse *vpr* to hurry up

apretado,-a *adj* (a) *(ropa, cordón)* tight; **íbamos todos apretados en el coche** we were all squashed together in the car (b) *(día, agenda)* busy

apretar [1] 1 *vt (botón)* to press; *(nudo, tornillo)* to tighten; **a. el gatillo** to pull the trigger; **me aprietan las botas** these boots are too tight for me
2 *vi* **apretaba el calor** it was really hot
3 apretarse *vpr* to squeeze together, to cram together; *Fig* **a. el cinturón** to tighten one's belt

apretón *nm* squeeze; **a. de manos** handshake

apretujar 1 *vt* to squeeze, to crush
2 apretujarse *vpr* to squeeze together, to cram together

aprieto *nm* tight spot, fix, jam; **poner a algn en un a.** to put sb in an awkward position

aprisa *adv* quickly

aprisionar *vt (atrapar)* to trap

aprobación *nf* approval

aprobado *nm Educ* pass

aprobar [2] *vt* (a) *(autorizar)* to approve (b) *(estar de acuerdo con)* to approve of (c) *Educ* to pass (d) *Pol (ley)* to pass

aprontar 1 *vt (preparar)* to quickly prepare *o* get ready
2 aprontarse *vpr RP (prepararse)* to get ready; **aprontate para cuando llegue tu papá!** just wait till your father gets back!

apropiado,-a *adj* suitable, appropriate

apropiarse [43] *vpr* to appropriate

aprovechado,-a *adj* (a) mal **a.** *(recurso, tiempo)* wasted; **bien a.** *(espacio)* well-planned (c) *(egoísta)* self-seeking

aprovechamiento *nm* use

aprovechar 1 *vt* (a) to make good use of, to make the most of; **aprovechamos bien la tarde** we've done lots of things this afternoon (b) *(recursos etc)* to take advantage of; **a. la ocasión** to seize the opportunity
2 *vi* **¡que aproveche!** enjoy your meal!, bon appétit!
3 aprovecharse *vpr* to use to one's advantage, to take advantage; **a. de algn** to take advantage of sb; **a. de algo** to make the most of sth

aprovisionar *vt* to supply, to provide; **a. las tropas** to give supplies to the troops

aproximación *nf* (a) approximation (b) *(en lotería)* consolation prize

aproximadamente *adv* approximately, roughly

aproximado,-a *adj* approximate; **un cálculo a.** a rough estimate

aproximar 1 *vt* to bring *o* put nearer

2 aproximarse *vpr* **aproximarse (a)** to approach

aproximativo,-a *adj* approximate, rough

aptitud *nf* aptitude; **prueba de a.** aptitude test

apto,-a *adj* (a) *(apropiado)* suitable, appropriate; *Cin* **a. para todos los públicos** *Br* U, *US* G (b) *(capacitado)* capable, able (c) *Educ* passed

apuesta *nf* bet, wager

apuesto,-a *adj* good-looking; *(hombre)* handsome

apunado,-a *adj Andes* **estar a.** to have altitude sickness

apunarse *vpr Andes* to get altitude sickness

apuntador,-a *nm,f Teatro* prompter

apuntalar *vt* to prop up, to shore up, to underpin

apuntar 1 *vt* (a) *(con arma)* to aim (b) *(señalar)* to point out (c) *(anotar)* to note down, to make a note of (d) *(indicar)* to indicate, to suggest; **todo parece a. a ...** everything seems to point to ...

2 *vi* **cuando apunta el día** when day breaks

3 apuntarse *vpr* (a) *(en una lista)* to put one's name down (b) *Fam* **¿te apuntas?** are you game?; **me apunto** count me in

apunte *nm (usu pl)* note; **tomar apuntes** to take notes

apuñalar *vt* to stab

apurado,-a 1 *adj* (a) *(necesitado)* in need; **a. de dinero** hard up for money; **a. de tiempo** in a hurry (b) *(preocupado)* worried; *(avergonzado)* embarrassed (c) *(situación)* awkward, difficult (d) *(afeitado)* close

2 *nm (afeitado)* close shave

apurar 1 *vt* (a) *(terminar)* to finish off, to end (b) *(preocupar)* to worry

2 apurarse *vpr* (a) *(preocuparse)* to worry, to get worried; **no te apures** don't worry (b) *(darse prisa)* to rush, to hurry, to pester; **apúrate** get a move on

apuro *nm* (a) *(situación difícil)* tight spot, fix, jam; **estar en un a.** to be in a tight spot (b) *(escasez de dinero)* hardship; **pasar apuros** to be hard up (c) *(vergüenza)* embarrassment; **¡qué a.!** how embarrassing!

aquejado,-a *adj* suffering *(de* from*)*

aquel,-ella *adj dem* (a) that; **a. niño** that boy (b) **aquellos,-as** those; **aquellas niñas** those girls

aquél,-élla *pron dem m,f* (a) that one; *(el anterior)* **aquél/aquélla ... éste/ésta** the former ... the latter (b) **todo a. que** anyone who, whoever (c) **aquéllos,-as** those; *(los anteriores)* the former

> Note that **aquél** and its various forms can be written without an accent when there is no risk of confusion with the adjective.

aquella *adj dem f ver* **aquel**

aquélla *pron dem f ver* **aquél**

aquello *pron neut f* that, it

aquellos,-as *adj dem pl ver* **aquel,-ella**

aquéllos,-as *pron dem m,fpl ver* **aquél,-élla**

aquí *adv* (a) *(lugar)* here; **a. arriba/fuera** up/out here; **a. está** here it is; **a. mismo** right here; **de a. para allá** up and down, to and fro; **hasta a.** this far; **por a., por favor** this way please; **está por a.** it's around here somewhere (b) *(tiempo)* **de a. en adelante** from now on; **de aquí a junio** between now and June; **hasta a.** up till now

aquietar *vt* to pacify, to calm down

ara *nf Fml* **en aras de** for the sake of

> Takes the masculine articles **el** and **un**.

árabe 1 *adj (de Arabia)* Arab

2 *nmf (persona)* Arab

3 *nm (idioma)* Arabic

Arabia *n* Arabia; **A. Saudita** Saudi Arabia

arado *nm* plough

Aragón *n* Aragon

aragonés,-esa *adj & nm,f* Aragonese

arancel *nm* tariff, customs duty

arancelario,-a *adj* tariff, duty; **derechos arancelarios** duties; **barreras arancelarias** customs barriers

arandela *nf Téc* washer; *(anilla)* ring

araña *nf* (a) spider (b) *(lámpara)* chandelier

arañar *vt* to scratch

arañazo *nm* scratch

arar *vt* to plough

araucaria *nf* araucaria, monkey puzzle tree

arbitraje *nm* (a) arbitration (b) *Dep* refereeing; *Ten* umpiring

arbitrar *vt* (a) to arbitrate (b) *Dep* to referee; *Ten* to umpire

arbitrariedad *nf* (a) arbitrariness (b) *(acto)* arbitrary action

arbitrario,-a *adj* arbitrary

arbitrio *nm (voluntad)* will; *(juicio)* judgement

árbitro,-a *nm,f* (a) *Dep* referee; *(de tenis)* umpire (b) *(mediador)* arbitrator

árbol *nm* (a) *Bot* tree (b) *Téc* shaft (c) *Náut* mast (d) *(gráfico)* tree (diagram); **á. genealógico** family *o* genealogical tree

arbolado,-a 1 *adj* wooded
2 *nm* woodland

arboleda *nf* grove

arbusto *nm* bush, shrub

arca *nf* (a) chest (b) *(para caudales)* strongbox, safe; **arcas públicas** Treasury

> Takes the masculine articles **el** and **un**.

arcada *nf* (a) arcade; *(de puente)* arch (b) *(náusea)* retching

arcaico,-a *adj* archaic

arcén *nm* verge; *(de autopista) Br* hard shoulder, *US* shoulder

archi- *pref* super-

archiconocido,-a *adj* extremely well-known

archipiélago *nm* archipelago

archivador *nm* filing cabinet

archivar *vt* (a) *(documento etc)* to file (away) (b) *(caso, asunto)* to shelve (c) *Informát* to save

archivo *nm* (a) file (b) *(archivador)* filing cabinet (c) **archivos** archives (d) *Informát* file; **a. adjunto** attachment

arcilla *nf* clay

arco *nm* (a) *Arquit* arch (b) *Mat & Elec* arc (c) *(de violín)* bow (d) *(para flechas)* bow; **tiro con a.** archery (e) **a. iris** rainbow (f) *Am Dep (portería)* goal, goalmouth

arder *vi* to burn; *Fam* **la conversación está que arde** the conversation is really heating up; **Juan está que arde** Juan is really fuming

ardid *nm* scheme, plot

ardiente *adj* (a) *(encendido)* burning; **capilla a.** chapel of rest (b) *Fig (fervoroso)* eager

ardilla *nf* squirrel

ardor *nm* (a) heat; *Med* **a. de estómago** heartburn (b) *Fig* ardour, fervour

ardoroso,-a *adj Fig* ardent, passionate

arduo,-a *adj* arduous

área *nf* (a) area; *Dep* penalty area (b) *(medida)* are *(100 square metres)*

> Takes the masculine articles **el** and **un**.

arena *nf* (a) sand; **playa de a.** sandy beach (b) *Taurom* bullring

arengar [42] *vt* to harangue

arenisca *nf* sandstone

arenoso,-a *adj* sandy

arenque *nm* herring; *Culin* **a. ahumado** kipper

arepa *nf Carib, Col* = pancake made of maize flour

arete *nm Andes, Méx* earring

argamasa *nf* mortar

Argel *n* Algiers

Argelia *n* Algeria

argelino,-a *adj & nm,f* Algerian

Argentina *n* Argentina

argentino,-a *adj & nm,f* Argentinian, Argentine

argolla *nf* (a) *(aro)* (large) ring (b) *Col, Méx (alianza)* wedding ring

argot *nm (popular)* slang; *(técnico)* jargon

argucia *nf* ruse

argüende *nm Méx Fam* (a) *(alboroto)* rumpus, shindy; **armar (un) a.** to kick up a rumpus (b) *(enredo, confusión)* mess, trouble; **meterse en un a.** to get into a mess

argüir [62] *vt* (a) *(deducir)* to deduce, to conclude (b) *(argumentar)* to argue

argumentación *nf* argument

argumentar *vt* = argüir

argumento *nm* (a) *Lit & Teatro (trama)* plot (b) *(razonamiento)* argument

arguyo *indic pres de* argüir

aridez *nf* aridity; *Fig* dryness

árido,-a *adj* arid; *Fig* dry

Aries *nm* Aries

ariete *nm Mil* battering ram

ario,-a *adj & nm,f* Aryan

arisco,-a *adj (persona)* unfriendly, stand-offish; *(animal)* unfriendly

arista *nf* edge

aristocracia *nf* aristocracy

aristócrata *nmf* aristocrat

aristocrático,-a *adj* aristocratic

aritmética *nf* arithmetic

arma *nf* weapon; **a. blanca** knife; **a. de fuego** firearm; **a. homicida** murder weapon; **a. nuclear** nuclear weapon; *Fig* **a. de doble filo** double-edged sword

> Takes the masculine articles **el** and **un**.

armada *nf* navy

armado,-a *adj* armed; **ir a.** to be armed; **lucha armada** armed struggle

armador,-a *nm,f* shipowner

armadura *nf* (a) *(armazón)* frame (b) *Hist* suit of armour

armamentista *adj* arms; **la carrera a.** the arms race

armamento *nm* armaments; **a. nuclear** nuclear weapons

armar 1 *vt* (a) *(tropa, soldado)* to arm (b) *(piezas)* to fit *o* put together, to assemble (c) *Fam* **armaron un escándalo** they created a scandal

2 armarse *vpr* to arm oneself; *Fig* **a. de paciencia** to summon up one's patience; *Fig* **a. de valor** to pluck up courage; *Fam* **se armó la gorda** all hell broke loose

armario *nm* (*para ropa*) wardrobe; (*de cocina*) cupboard; **a. empotrado** built-in wardrobe *o* cupboard

armatoste *nm* (*cosa*) monstrosity

armazón *nm* frame; (*de madera*) timberwork; *Arquit* shell

Armenia *n* Armenia

armería *nf* gunsmith's (shop)

armiño *nm* ermine

armisticio *nm* armistice

armonía *nf* harmony

armonioso,-a *adj* harmonious

armonizar [40] *vt & vi* to harmonize

aro *nm* (a) (*gen*) hoop; *Fam* **pasar por el a.** to knuckle under (b) *Am* (*pendiente*) earring

aroma *nm* aroma; (*de vino*) bouquet

aromático,-a *adj* aromatic

arpa *nf* harp

Takes the masculine articles **el** and **un**.

arpía *nf* (*en mitología*) harpy; *Fig* harpy, old witch

arpón *nm* harpoon

arquear *vt*, **arquearse** *vpr* to bend, to curve

arqueología *nf* archaeology

arqueólogo,-a *nm,f* archaeologist

arquero,-a *nm,f* (a) (*tirador*) archer (b) *Am* (*portero de fútbol*) goalkeeper

arquetipo *nm* archetype

arquitecto,-a *nm,f* architect

arquitectónico,-a *adj* architectural

arquitectura *nf* architecture

arrabalero,-a *adj Pey* coarse

arrabales *nmpl* slums

arraigado,-a *adj* deeply rooted

arraigar [42] *vi* to take root

arraigo *nm Fig* roots; **una tradición con mucho a.** a deeply-rooted tradition

arrancar [44] **1** *vt* (a) (*planta*) to uproot, to pull up; **a. de raíz** to uproot (b) (*extraer*) to pull *o* tear off *o* out; (*diente, pelo*) to pull out; *Fig* (*confesión etc*) to extract; **arranca una hoja del cuaderno** tear a page out of the notebook (c) (*coche, motor*) to start; *Informát* to boot

2 *vi* (a) *Aut & Téc* to start; *Informát* to boot (up) (b) (*empezar*) to begin; **a. a llorar** to burst out crying

arranque *nm* (a) *Aut & Téc* starting (b) (*comienzo*) start (c) *Fam* (*arrebato*) outburst, fit

arrasar 1 *vt* to devastate, to destroy

2 *vi* (*en elecciones etc*) to win by a landslide

arrastrado,-a *Fam* **1** *adj* wretched

2 *nm,f* bad egg

arrastrar 1 *vt* to pull (along), to drag (along); **vas arrastrando el vestido** your dress is trailing on the ground; **lo arrastró la corriente** he was swept away by the current

2 arrastrarse *vpr* to drag oneself; *Fig* (*humillarse*) to crawl

arrastre *nm* (a) pulling, dragging; *Fam* **para el a.** (*persona*) on one's last legs; (*cosa*) done for (b) (**pesca de**) **a.** trawling (c) *Am Fam* **tener a.** to have a lot of influence

arrayán *nm* myrtle

arre *interj* gee up!, giddy up!

arrear *vt* (a) to spur on; (*caballos*) to urge on (b) *Fam* (*bofetada*) to give

arrebatador,-a *adj Fig* captivating, fascinating

arrebatar 1 *vt* (*coger*) to snatch, to seize; *Fig* (*cautivar*) to captivate, to fascinate

2 arrebatarse *vpr* (*enfurecerse*) to become furious; (*exaltarse*) to get carried away

arrebato *nm* outburst, fit

arreciar [43] *vi* (*viento, tormenta*) to get worse

arrecife *nm* reef

arreglado,-a *adj* (a) (*reparado*) repaired, fixed (b) (*solucionado*) settled (c) (*habitación*) tidy, neat (d) (*persona*) well-dressed, smart

arreglar 1 *vt* (a) to arrange; (*problema*) to sort out; (*habitación*) to tidy; (*papeles*) to put in order (b) (*reparar*) to repair, to fix (c) (*vestir*) to get ready

2 arreglarse *vpr* (a) (*vestirse*) to get ready (b) *Fam* **arreglárselas** to manage (c) (*reconciliarse*) to make up

arreglo *nm* (a) arrangement; (*acuerdo*) compromise (b) (*reparación*) repair; **no tiene a.** it is beyond repair; *Fam* **¡no tienes a.!** you're hopeless! (c) *Fml* **con a. a** in accordance with

arrellanarse *vpr* to sit back

arremangarse [42] *vpr* to roll one's sleeves *o* trousers up

arremeter *vi* to attack

arremolinarse *vpr* to whirl about; *Fig* (*gente*) to crowd together, to cram together

arrendamiento *nm* (a) (*alquiler*) renting (b) (*precio*) rent

arrendar [1] *vt* (*piso*) to rent; (*dar en arriendo*) to let on lease; (*tomar en* *arriendo)* to take on lease

arrendatario,-a *nm,f* leaseholder, lessee; *(inquilino)* tenant

arreos *nmpl* (a) *(de caballería)* harness, trappings (b) *(adornos)* adornments

arrepentido,-a *adj* regretful

arrepentimiento *nm* regret

arrepentirse [5] *upr* a. de to regret; *Rel* to repent

arrestar *vt* to arrest, to detain; *(encarcelar)* to put in prison

arresto *nm* arrest; *Jur* a. domiciliario house arrest

arriar [29] *vt (bandera)* to strike; *(velas)* to lower

arriba 1 *adv* up; *(encima)* on the top; ahí a. up there; de a. abajo from top to bottom; *Fam* mirar a algn de a. abajo to look sb up and down; desde a. from above; hacia a. upwards; de un millón para a. from one million upwards; más a. higher up, further up; a. del todo right on o at the top; la parte de a. the top (part); vive a. he lives upstairs; véase más a. see above

2 *interj* get up!, up you get!; ¡a. la República! long live the Republic!; ¡a. las manos! hands up!

3 *prep Am* a. (de) on top of

arribar *vi* to reach port, to arrive

arribeño,-a *Am* 1 *adj* highland

2 *nm,f* highlander

arribista *nmf* parvenu, social climber

arriendo *nm* lease; *(de un piso)* renting; dar en a. to let out on lease; tomar en a. to take on lease

arriesgado,-a *adj* (a) *(peligroso)* risky (b) *(temerario)* fearless, daring

arriesgar [42] 1 *vt* to risk

2 arriesgarse *upr* to risk; se arriesga demasiado he's taking too many risks

arrimar 1 *vt* to move closer, to bring near o nearer; *Fam* a. el hombro to lend a hand

2 arrimarse *upr* to move o get close, to come near o nearer

arrinconar *vt* (a) *(poner en un rincón)* to put in a corner (b) *(abandonar)* to put away, to lay aside (c) *(acorralar)* to corner

arrobo *nm* rapture, enthralment

arrocero,-a *adj* la industria arrocera the rice industry

arrodillarse *upr* to kneel down

arrogancia *nf* arrogance

arrogante *adj* arrogant

arrojadizo,-a *adj* arma arrojadiza missile

arrojado,-a *adj (osado)* bold, daring

arrojar 1 *vt* (a) *(tirar)* to throw, to fling (b) *Com (saldo)* to show

2 arrojarse *upr* to throw oneself, to fling oneself

arrojo *nm* daring, courage

arrollador,-a *adj Fig* overwhelming; *(éxito)* resounding; *(personalidad)* captivating

arrollar *vt* 1 *(atropellar)* to run over, to knock down

2 *vi Dep & Pol* to win easily

arropar 1 *vt* to wrap up; *(en la cama)* to tuck in

2 arroparse *upr* to wrap oneself up

arrostrar *vt* to face

arroyo *nm* brook, stream

arroz *nm* rice; a. con leche rice pudding

arruga *nf (en la piel)* wrinkle; *(en la ropa)* crease

arrugar [42] 1 *vt (piel)* to wrinkle; *(ropa)* to crease; *(papel)* to crumple (up)

2 arrugarse *upr (piel)* to wrinkle; *(ropa)* to crease

arruinado,-a *adj* bankrupt, ruined

arruinar 1 *vt* to ruin

2 arruinarse *upr* to be ruined

arrullar 1 *vt (bebé)* to lull

2 *vi (paloma)* to coo

arrullo *nm* (a) *(de paloma)* cooing (b) *(nana)* lullaby

arrumaco *nm Fam* kissing and hugging; *(halago)* flattery

arsenal *nm* arsenal

arsénico *nm* arsenic

arte *nm o nf* (a) art; bellas artes fine arts; *Fam* por amor al a. for the love of it (b) *(habilidad)* skill

> Takes the masculine articles el and un.

artefacto *nm* device; a. explosivo explosive device

arteria *nf* artery; *(carretera)* highway

artesanal *adj* handmade

artesanía *nf* (a) *(cualidad)* craftsmanship (b) *(objetos)* crafts, handicrafts

artesano,-a 1 *nm,f* craftsman, *f* craftswoman

2 *adj* handmade

ártico,-a 1 *adj* arctic; el océano Á. the Arctic Ocean

2 *nm* el Á. the Arctic

articulación *nf* (a) *Anat* joint, articulation (b) *Téc* joint

articulado,-a *adj (tren etc)* articulated

articular *vt* to articulate

artículo *nm* article; a. de fondo leader (article)

artífice *nmf* author; *Fig* el a. del acuerdo the architect of the agreement

artificial *adj* artificial; *Tex* man-made *o* synthetic
artificio *nm* (**a**) artifice; **fuego de a.** firework (**b**) *(artimaña)* ruse
artillería *nf* artillery; **a. antiaérea** anti-aircraft guns
artillero *nm* artilleryman
artilugio *nm* gadget, device
artimaña *nf* trick, ruse
artista *nmf* artist; **a. de cine** film star
artístico,-a *adj* artistic
artritis *nf* arthritis
arveja *nf Andes, Carib, RP* pea
arzobispo *nm* archbishop
as *nm* ace
asa *nf* handle

Takes the masculine articles **el** and **un**.

asado,-a **1** *adj Culin* roast; **pollo a.** roast chicken; *Fig* **a. de calor** roasting, boiling hot
   2 *nm Culin* roast; *Col, CSur (barbacoa)* barbecue
asaduras *nfpl* offal; *(de ave)* giblets
asalariado,-a **1** *adj* salaried
   2 *nm,f* wage earner, salaried worker
asaltador,-a *nm,f,* **asaltante** *nmf* attacker; *(en un robo)* robber
asaltar *vt* to assault, to attack; *(banco)* to rob; *Fig* to assail
asalto *nm* (**a**) assault, attack; **a. a un banco** bank robbery (**b**) *(en boxeo)* round
asamblea *nf* meeting; **a. general** general meeting
asar **1** *vt* to roast
   2 asarse *vpr Fig* to be roasting, to be boiling hot
ascendencia *nf* ancestry, ancestors; **de a. escocesa** of Scottish descent
ascender [3] **1** *vt (en un cargo)* to promote
   2 *vi* (**a**) to move upward; *(temperatura)* to rise; **la factura asciende a ...** the bill adds up to ... (**b**) *(al trono)* to ascend (**c**) *(de categoría)* to be promoted
ascendiente *nmf* ancestor
ascensión *nf* (**a**) climb (**b**) *(al trono)* accession
ascenso *nm* promotion; *(subida)* rise
ascensor *nm Br* lift, *US* elevator
asco *nm* disgust, repugnance; **me da a.** it makes me (feel) sick; **¡qué a.!** how disgusting *o* revolting!
ascua *nf* ember; *Fig* **en ascuas** on tenterhooks

Takes the masculine articles **el** and **un**.

aseado,-a *adj* tidy, neat

asear **1** *vt* to clean, to tidy up
   2 asearse *vpr* to wash, to get washed
asediar [43] *vt* to besiege
asedio *nm* siege
asegurado,-a *adj* (**a**) insured (**b**) *(indudable)* secure
asegurador,-a **1** *adj* insurance
   2 *nm,f* insurer
asegurar **1** *vt* (**a**) to insure (**b**) *(garantizar)* **me aseguró que ...** he assured me that ...; **a. el éxito de un proyecto** to ensure the success of a project (**c**) *(cuerda)* to fasten
   2 asegurarse *vpr* (**a**) to make sure; **a. de que ...** to make sure that ... (**b**) *Seg* to insure oneself
asemejarse *vpr* **a. a** to look like
asentado,-a *adj (establecido)* established, settled
asentamiento *nm* settlement
asentar [1] **1** *vt* **a. la cabeza** to settle down
   2 asentarse *vpr* (**a**) *(establecerse)* to settle down, to establish oneself (**b**) *(té, polvo)* to settle
asentimiento *nm* assent, consent
asentir [5] *vi* to assent, to agree; **a. con la cabeza** to nod
aseo *nm* (**a**) cleanliness, tidiness (**b**) **aseos** *o* **(cuarto de) a.** bathroom; *(retrete)* toilet
asequible *adj* affordable; *(comprensible)* easy to understand; *(alcanzable)* attainable
aserrín *nm* sawdust
asesinar *vt* to murder; *(rey, ministro)* to assassinate
asesinato *nm* murder; *(de rey, ministro)* assassination
asesino,-a **1** *adj* murderous
   2 *nm,f* killer; *(hombre)* murderer; *(mujer)* murderess; *Pol* assassin
asesor,-a **1** *nm,f* adviser; **a. fiscal** tax adviser
   2 *adj* advisory
asesoramiento *nm* (**a**) *(acción)* advising (**b**) *(consejo)* advice
asesorar **1** *vt* (**a**) to advise, to give (professional) advice to (**b**) *Com* to act as consultant to
   2 asesorarse *vpr* to consult
asesoría *nf* consultant's office
asestar *vt* to deal; **a. un golpe a algn** to deal sb a blow
aseverar *vt* to assert
asfalto *nm* asphalt
asfixia *nf* asphyxiation, suffocation
asfixiante *adj* asphyxiating, suffocating; *Fam* **hace un calor a.** it's stifling

asfixiar [43] *vt*, **asfixiarse** *vpr* to asphyxiate, to suffocate

así *adv* (a) *(de esta manera)* like this *o* that, this way, thus; **ponlo a.** put it this way; **a. de grande/alto** this big/tall; **algo a.** something like this *o* that; **¿no es a.?** isn't that so *o* right?; **a. es la vida** such is life; **a. a.** so-so; **a. sin más,** *Am* **a. no más** *o* **nomás** just like that (b) **a las seis o a.** around six o'clock; **diez años o a.** ten years more or less (c) **a. como** as well as (d) **a. tenga que …** *(aunque)* even if I have to … (e) **aun a.** and despite that (f) **a. pues** so; **a. que … so …** (g) **a. que llegues** as soon as

Asia *n* Asia; **A. Menor** Asia Minor

asiático,-a *adj & nm,f* Asian

asidero *nm (asa)* handle; *Fig* pretext, excuse

asiduidad *nf* assiduity; **con a.** frequently, regularly

asiduo,-a 1 *adj* assiduous

2 *nm,f* regular customer

asiento *nm* (a) seat; **a. trasero/delantero** front/back seat; **tome a.** take a seat (b) *(poso)* sediment (c) *Fin* entry

asignación *nf* (a) *(de dinero)* assignment, allocation (b) *(de puesto)* appointment (c) *(paga)* allowance

asignar *vt* (a) to assign, to allocate (b) *(nombrar)* to appoint

asignatura *nf* subject; **a. pendiente** failed subject

asilado,-a *nm,f* refugee

asilar *vt* to grant *o* give political asylum to

asilo *nm* asylum; **a. de ancianos** old people's home; *Pol* **a. político** political asylum

asimilación *nf* assimilation

asimilar *vt* to assimilate

asimismo *adv* also, as well

asir [46] *vt* to grasp, to seize

asistencia *nf* (a) *(presencia)* attendance; **falta de a.** absence (b) **a. médica/técnica** medical/technical assistance (c) *(público)* audience, public

asistenta *nf* charlady, cleaning lady

asistente 1 *adj* attending; **el público a.** the audience

2 *nmf* (a) *(ayudante)* assistant; **a. social** social worker (b) **los asistentes** the public

asistido,-a *adj* assisted; **a. por ordenador** computer-assisted; *Aut* **dirección asistida** power steering

asistir 1 *vt* to assist, to help

2 *vi* **a. (a)** to attend, to be present (at)

asma *nf* asthma

Takes the masculine articles **el** and **un**.

asno *nm* donkey, ass

asociación *nf* association

asociado,-a 1 *adj* associated

2 *nm,f* associate, partner

asociar [43] **1** *vt* to associate

2 asociarse *vpr* (a) to be associated (b) *Com* to become partners

asolar [2] *vt* to devastate, to destroy

asomar 1 *vt* to put out, to stick out; **asomó la cabeza por la ventana** he put his head out of the window

2 *vi* to appear

3 asomarse *vpr* (a) to lean out; **a. a la ventana** to lean out of the window (b) *(entrar)* to pop in; *(salir)* to pop out

asombrar 1 *vt* to amaze, to astonish

2 asombrarse *vpr* to be astonished; **a. de algo** to be amazed at sth

asombro *nm* amazement, astonishment

asombroso,-a *adj* amazing, astonishing

asomo *nm* trace, hint

asonada *nf* putsch, uprising

asorocharse *vpr Andes* to get altitude sickness

aspa *nf* (a) *(de molino)* arm; *(de ventilador)* blade (b) *(cruz)* cross

Takes the masculine articles **el** and **un**.

aspaviento *nm* **hacer aspavientos** to wave one's arms about

aspecto *nm* (a) look, appearance (b) *(de un asunto)* aspect

aspereza *nf* roughness; *Fig* **limar asperezas** to smooth things over

áspero,-a *adj* rough; *Fig (carácter)* surly

aspersión *nf* sprinkling

aspersor *nm* sprinkler

aspiración *nf* (a) inhalation, breathing in (b) *(pretensión)* aspiration

aspiradora *nf* vacuum cleaner

aspirante *nmf* candidate, applicant

aspirar 1 *vt* (a) *(respirar)* to inhale, to breathe in (b) *Téc (absorber)* to suck in, to draw in

2 *vi Fig* **a. a algo** to aspire after sth

aspirina *nf* aspirin

asquear *vt* to disgust

asquerosidad *nf* filthy *o* revolting thing; **¡que a.!** how revolting!

asqueroso,-a 1 *adj (sucio)* filthy; *(desagradable)* revolting, disgusting

2 *nm,f* filthy *o* revolting person

asta *nf* (a) *(de bandera)* staff, pole; **a media a.** at half-mast (b) *Zool (cuerno)* horn

Takes the masculine articles **el** and **un**.

asterisco *nm* asterisk

astilla *nf* splinter
astillero *nm* shipyard
astral *adj* astral; **carta a.** birth chart
astringente *adj & nm* astringent
astro *nm* star
astrología *nf* astrology
astrólogo,-a *nm,f* astrologer
astronauta *nmf* astronaut
astronave *nf* spaceship
astronomía *nf* astronomy
astronómico,-a *adj* astronomical
astrónomo,-a *nm,f* astronomer
astucia *nf* shrewdness; *(artimaña)* ruse
asturiano,-a *adj & nm,f* Asturian
Asturias *n* Asturias
astuto,-a *adj* astute, shrewd
asumir *vt* to assume
asunción *nf* assumption
asunto *nm* (a) subject; **no es a. tuyo** it's none of your business (b) **Asuntos Exteriores** Foreign Affairs
asustar 1 *vt* to frighten, to scare
    2 asustarse *vpr* to be frightened, to be scared
atacante *nmf* attacker, assailant
atacar [44] *vt* to attack, to assault; *Fig* **me ataca los nervios** he gets on my nerves
atado,-a *adj* tied; *(ocupado)* tied up
atadura *nf Fig* hindrance
atajar *vi* to take a shortcut (**por** across *o* through)
atajo *nm* (a) shortcut (b) *(grupo)* bunch
atalaya *nf* watchtower
atañer *v impers* to concern, to have to do with; **eso no te atañe** that has nothing to do with you
ataque *nm* (a) attack, assault; **a. aéreo** air raid (b) *Med* fit; **a. cardíaco** *o* **al corazón** heart attack; **a. de nervios/tos** fit of hysterics/coughing
atar 1 *vt* (a) to tie; (b) **a. cabos** to put two and two together; *Fam* **loco de a.** as mad as a hatter (b) *Fig* to tie down
    2 atarse *vpr Fig* to get tied up; **átate los zapatos** do your shoes up
atardecer [33] 1 *v impers* to get *o* grow dark
    2 *nm* evening, dusk
atareado,-a *adj* busy
atascado,-a *adj* stuck
atascar [44] 1 *vt (bloquear)* to block, to obstruct
    2 atascarse *vpr* (a) *(bloquearse)* to become obstructed, to become blocked (b) *Fig (estancarse)* to get bogged down
atasco *nm* traffic jam
ataúd *nm* coffin

ataviarse [29] *vpr* to dress oneself up
atavío *nm* dress, attire
ate *nm Méx* quince jelly
atemorizar [40] *vt* to frighten, to scare
atemperar *vt* to moderate, to temper
Atenas *n* Athens
atención 1 *nf* attention; **llamar la a.** to attract attention; **prestar/poner a.** to pay attention (**a** to)
    2 *interj* attention!
atender [3] 1 *vt* to attend to; *(petición)* to agree to
    2 *vi (alumno)* to pay attention (**a** to)
atenerse [24] *vpr* (**a**) *(a reglas etc)* to abide (**a** by); **a. a las consecuencias** to bear the consequences (**b**) *(remitirse)* to go by; **me atengo a sus palabras** I'm going by what he said; **no saber a qué a.** not to know what to expect
atentado *nm* attack; **a. terrorista** terrorist attack
atentamente *adv* **le saluda a.** *(en carta)* yours sincerely *o* faithfully
atentar *vi* **a. a** *o* **contra** to commit a crime against; **a. contra la vida de algn** to make an attempt on sb's life
atento,-a *adj* (**a**) attentive; **estar a. a** to be mindful *o* aware of (**b**) *(amable)* thoughtful, considerate; **atentos saludos de** *(en carta)* yours faithfully
atenuante 1 *adj* attenuating
    2 *nm Jur* extenuating circumstance
atenuar [30] *vt* (**a**) to attenuate; *Jur* to extenuate (**b**) *(importancia)* to lessen, to diminish
ateo,-a 1 *adj* atheistic
    2 *nm,f* atheist
aterciopelado,-a *adj* velvety; *(vino)* smooth
aterido,-a *adj* **a. de frío** stiff with cold, numb
aterrador,-a *adj* terrifying
aterrar 1 *vt* to terrify
    2 aterrarse *vpr* to be terrified
aterrizaje *nm Av* landing; **a. forzoso** forced landing
aterrizar [40] *vi* to land
aterrorizar [40] 1 *vt* to terrify; *Mil & Pol* to terrorize
    2 aterrorizarse *vpr* to be terrified
atesorar *vt* to accumulate; *(dinero)* to hoard
atestado¹ *nm Jur* affidavit, statement; **atestados** testimonials
atestado²,-a *adj* packed, crammed; **estaba a. de gente** it was full of people
atestar ¹ *vt Jur* to testify

atestar² *vt (abarrotar)* to pack, to cram (**de** with)

atestiguar [45] *vt* (**a**) *Jur* to testify to (**b**) *Fig* to vouch for

atiborrar 1 *vt* to pack, to stuff (**de** with)

2 atiborrarse *vpr Fam* to stuff oneself (**de** with)

ático *nm* attic

atinado,-a *adj (juicioso)* sensible; *(pertinente)* pertinent

atinar *vi* to get it right; **a. a hacer algo** to succeed in doing sth; **a. al blanco** to hit the target; **atinó con la solución** he found the solution

atingencia *nf Am* connection; *(observación)* comment

atípico,-a *adj* atypical

atisbar *vt* to make out

atisbo *nm Fig* slight sign, inkling

atizar [40] **1** *vt* (**a**) *(fuego)* to poke, to stoke (**b**) *Fig (rebelión)* to stir up; *(pasión)* to rouse, to excite

atlántico,-a 1 *adj* Atlantic

2 *nm* **el (océano) A.** the Atlantic (Ocean)

atlas *nm inv* atlas

atleta *nmf* athlete

atlético,-a *adj* athletic

atletismo *nm* athletics *sing*

atmósfera *nf* atmosphere

atmosférico,-a *adj* atmospheric

atole, atol *nm CAm, Méx* = drink made of corn meal

atolladero *nm* fix, jam; **estar en un a.** to be in a jam

atolondrado,-a *adj* stunned, bewildered; *(atontado)* stupid

atolondrar 1 *vt* to confuse, to bewilder

2 atolondrarse *vpr* to be confused, to be bewildered

atómico,-a *adj* atomic

átomo *nm* atom

atónito,-a *adj* amazed, astonished

atontado,-a *adj* (**a**) *(tonto)* silly, foolish (**b**) *(aturdido)* bewildered, amazed

atontar 1 *vt* to confuse, to bewilder

2 atontarse *vpr* to be o get confused, to be bewildered

atorarse *vpr* (**a**) *(atragantarse)* to choke (**con** on) (**b**) *Am (atascarse)* to get stuck

atormentar 1 *vt* to torment

2 atormentarse *vpr* to torment oneself, to suffer agonies

atornillar *vt* to screw on

atorón *nm Méx* traffic jam

atorrante *adj CSur (holgazán)* lazy

atosigar [42] *vt* to harass

atracador,-a *nm,f (de banco)* (bank) robber; *(en la calle)* attacker, mugger

atracar [44] **1** *vt* to hold up; *(persona)* to rob

2 *vi Náut* to come alongside, to tie up

3 atracarse *vpr (de comida)* to stuff oneself (**de** with), to gorge oneself (**de** on)

atracción *nf* attraction; **parque de atracciones** funfair

atraco *nm* hold-up, robbery; **a. a mano armada** armed robbery

atracón *nm Fam* binge, blowout; **darse un a. de comer** to make a pig of oneself

atractivo,-a 1 *adj* attractive, appealing

2 *nm* attraction, appeal

atraer [25] *vt* to attract

atragantarse *vpr* to choke (**con** on), to swallow the wrong way; *Fig* **esa chica se me ha atragantado** I can't stand that girl

atraigo *indic pres de* **atraer**

atraje *pt indef de* **atraer**

atrancar [44] **1** *vt (puerta)* to bolt

2 atrancarse *vpr* to get stuck; *(al hablar, leer)* to get bogged down

atrapar *vt* to catch

atrás *adv* (**a**) *(lugar)* at the back, behind; **hacia/para a.** backwards; **puerta de a.** back o rear door; *Fig* **echarse a.** to back out (**b**) *(tiempo)* previously, in the past, ago; **un año a.** a year ago; **venir de muy a.** to go o date back a long time

atrasado,-a *adj* late, slow; *(pago)* overdue; *(reloj)* slow; *(país)* backward; *Prensa* **número a.** back number

atrasar 1 *vt* to put back

2 *vi (reloj)* to be slow

3 atrasarse *vpr* (**a**) to remain o stay behind, to lag behind (**b**) *(tren)* to be late

atraso *nm* (**a**) delay (**b**) *(de país)* backwardness (**c**) *Fin* **atrasos** arrears

atravesado,-a *adj (cruzado)* lying crosswise; *(persona)* difficult; **lo tengo a.** I can't stand him

atravesar [1] **1** *vt* (**a**) *(calle)* to cross (**b**) *(muro)* to pierce, to go through (**c**) *(poner a través)* to lay across, to put across, to put crosswise

2 atravesarse *vpr* to get in the way; *Fig* **se me ha atravesado Luis** I can't stand Luis

atrayente *adj* attractive

atreverse *vpr* to dare; **a. a hacer algo** to dare to do sth

atrevido,-a *adj* (**a**) *(osado)* daring, bold (**b**) *(insolente)* insolent, impudent (**c**) *(ropa etc)* daring, risqué

atrevimiento *nm* (**a**) *(osadía)* daring, audacity (**b**) *(insolencia)* insolence, impudence

atribuir [37] **1** *vt* to attribute, to ascribe

2 atribuirse *vpr* to assume

atribular *vt* to afflict
atributo *nm* attribute
atril *nm* music stand
atrochar *vi* to take a short cut
atrocidad *nf* atrocity
atrofiar [43] *vt*, **atrofiarse** *vpr* to atrophy
atropellado,-a *adj* hasty, impetuous
atropellar *vt* to knock down, to run over
atropello *nm* (**a**) *Aut* knocking down, running over (**b**) *(abuso)* abuse
atroz *adj* (**a**) *(bárbaro)* atrocious (**b**) *Fam (hambre, frío)* enormous, tremendous
ATS *nmf (abr* **ayudante técnico sanitario)** = qualified Spanish nurse
atuendo *nm* dress, attire
atún *nm* tuna, tunny
aturdido,-a *adj* stunned, dazed
aturdimiento *nm* confusion, bewilderment
aturdir *vt* (**a**) *(con un golpe)* to stun, to daze (**b**) *(confundir)* to bewilder, to confuse
aturrullar *vt* to confuse, to bewilder
atuve *pt indef de* **atenerse**
audacia *nf* audacity
audaz *adj* audacious, bold
audible *adj* audible
audición *nf* (**a**) hearing (**b**) *Teatro* audition
audiencia *nf* (**a**) *(público)* audience; *TV &Rad* **horas de máxima a.** prime time; **índice de a.** viewing figures, ratings (**b**) *(entrevista)* audience (**c**) *Jur* court hearing
audiovisual *adj* audio-visual
auditivo,-a 1 *adj* auditory; **comprensión auditiva** listening comprehension
2 *nm* receiver
auditor *nm Fin* auditor
auditorio *nm* (**a**) *(público)* audience (**b**) *(sala)* auditorium, hall
auge *nm* peak; *Econ* boom; *Fig* **estar en a.** to be thriving o booming
augurar *vt* to augur
augurio *nm* omen
aula *nf (en colegio)* classroom; *Univ* lecture room; **a. magna** amphitheatre

Takes the masculine articles **el** and **un**.

aulaga *nf* gorse
aullar *vt* to howl, to yell
aullido *nm* howl, yell
aumentar 1 *vt* to increase; *(precios)* to put up; *(producción)* to step up; *Fot* to enlarge; *Opt* to magnify
2 *vi (precios)* to go up, to rise; *(valor)* to appreciate

3 aumentarse *vpr* to increase, to be on the increase
aumento *nm* increase; *Opt* magnification; **a. de precios** rise in prices; **ir en a.** to be on the increase
aun *adv* even; **a. así** even so, even then; **a. más** even more
aún *adv* still; *(en negativas)* yet; **a. está aquí** he's still here; **ella no ha venido a.** she hasn't come yet
aunar *vt* to unite, to join
aunque *conj* although, though; *(enfático)* even if, even though; **a. no vengas** even if you don't come
aúpa *interj* up!, get up!
aura *nf* aura

Takes the masculine articles **el** and **un**.

aureola *nf* halo
auricular *nm* (**a**) *Tel* receiver (**b**) **auriculares** earphones, headphones
aurora *nf* daybreak, dawn
auscultar *vt* to sound (with a stethoscope)
ausencia *nf* absence
ausentarse *vpr* to leave
ausente 1 *adj* absent
2 *nmf* absentee
ausentismo *nm Am* absenteeism
austeridad *nf* austerity
austero,-a *adj* austere
austral 1 *adj* southern
2 *nm Fin* = former standard monetary unit of Argentina
Australia *n* Australia
australiano,-a *adj & nm,f* Australian
Austria *n* Austria
austríaco,-a *adj & nm,f* Austrian
autenticidad *nf* authenticity
auténtico,-a *adj* authentic
autentificar [44] *vt* to authenticate
autismo *nm* autism
autista *adj* autistic
auto¹ *nm RP (coche)* car
auto² *nm Jur* decree, writ; **autos** *(pleito)* papers, documents
autoadhesivo,-a *adj* self-adhesive
autobiografía *nf* autobiography
autobiográfico,-a *adj* autobiographical
autobombo *nm Fam* self-praise, blowing one's own trumpet
autobús *nm* bus
autocar *nm* coach
autocrítica *nf* self-criticism
autóctono,-a *adj* indigenous
autodefensa *nf* self-defence
autodisciplina *nf* self-discipline
autoedición *nf Informát* desktop publishing

autoescuela *nf* driving school, school of motoring

autogobierno *nm* self-government

autógrafo *nm* autograph

autómata *nm* automaton

automático,-a *adj* automatic

automatización *nf* automation

automatizar [40] *vt* to automate

automotor,-a 1 *adj* self-propelled
  2 *nm Ferroc* diesel train

automóvil *nm* car

automovilismo *nm* motoring

automovilista *nmf* motorist

automovilístico,-a *adj* car; **accidente a.** car accident

autonomía *nf* (**a**) autonomy (**b**) *(región)* autonomous region

autonómico,-a *adj* autonomous, self-governing; **elecciones autonómicas** elections for the autonomous parliament; **televisión autónomica** regional television

autónomo,-a *adj* autonomous

autopista *nf* motorway; *Informát* **autopista de la información** information superhighway

autopsia *nf* autopsy, postmortem

autor,-a *nm,f (hombre)* author; *(mujer)* authoress; *(de crimen)* perpetrator

autoridad *nf* authority

autoritario,-a *adj* authoritarian

autorizado,-a *adj* authoritative, official

autorizar [40] *vt* to authorize

autorretrato *nm* self-portrait

autoservicio *nm* self-service; *(supermercado)* supermarket

autostop *nm* hitch-hiking; **hacer a.** to hitch-hike

autostopista *nmf* hitch-hiker

autosuficiencia *nf* self-sufficiency

autosuficiente *adj* self-sufficient

auxiliar [43] 1 *adj & nmf* auxiliary, assistant
  2 *vt* to help, to assist

auxilio *nm* help, assistance; **primeros auxilios** first aid

auyama *nf Carib, Col* pumpkin

Av. *(abr* **Avenida)** Ave

aval *nm Com & Fin* endorsement

avalancha *nf* avalanche

avalar *vt* to guarantee, to endorse

avance *nm* (**a**) advance (**b**) *Fin* advance payment (**c**) *TV* **a. informativo** news summary, *US* news in brief

avanzado,-a *adj* advanced; **de avanzada edad** advanced in years

avanzar [40] *vt* to advance

avaricia *nf* avarice

avaricioso,-a *adj* greedy

avaro,-a 1 *adj* avaricious, miserly
  2 *nm,f* miser

avasallar *vt* to subdue

avatares *nmpl* quirks

Avda. = **Av.**

AVE *nf (abr* **Alta Velocidad Española)** High Speed Train

ave *nf* bird; **aves de corral** poultry; **a. de rapiña** bird of prey

> Takes the masculine articles **el** and **un**.

avecinarse *vpr* to approach, to come near

avellana *nf* hazelnut

avellano *nm* hazelnut tree

avena *nf* oats

avendré *indic fut de* **avenir**

avenencia *nf* compromise

avengo *indic pres de* **avenir**

avenida *nf* avenue

avenido,-a *adj* **bien/mal avenidos** on good/bad terms

avenir [27] 1 *vt* to reconcile
  2 **avenirse** *vpr* to be on good terms; *(consentir)* to agree (**en** to)

aventajado,-a *adj (destacado)* outstanding, exceptional; *(en cabeza)* in the lead

aventajar *vt* (**a**) to be ahead o in front of (**a** of) (**b**) *(superar)* to surpass, to outdo

aventar [1] 1 *vt* (**a**) *Agr* to winnow (**b**) *(el fuego)* to fan (**c**) *Andes, CAm, Méx (tirar)* to throw (**d**) *CAm, Méx, Perú (empujar)* to push, to shove
  2 **aventarse** *vpr Méx* (**a**) *(tirarse)* to throw oneself (**b**) *(atreverse)* **a. a hacer algo** to dare to do sth

aventón *nm Méx* **dar a. a algn** to give sb a ride; **pedir a.** to hitch a ride

aventura *nf* (**a**) adventure (**b**) *(amorosa)* (love) affair

aventurado,-a *adj* risky

aventurarse *vpr* to venture

aventurero,-a *adj* adventurous

avergonzado,-a *adj* ashamed

avergonzar [63] 1 *vt* to shame
  2 **avergonzarse** *vpr* to be ashamed (**de** of)

avería *nf* breakdown

averiado,-a *adj* out of order; *(coche)* broken down

averiar [29] 1 *vt* to break
  2 **averiarse** *vpr (estropearse)* to malfunction, to go wrong; *(coche)* to break down

averiguación *nf* enquiry

averiguar [45] *vt* to ascertain

aversión *nf* aversion

avestruz *nm* ostrich

aviación *nf* (a) aviation; **accidente de a.** plane crash; **a. civil** civil aviation (b) *Mil* air force

aviador,-a *nm,f.*aviator, flier; *Mil (piloto)* air force pilot

aviar [29] *vt (preparar)* to prepare, to get ready

avícola *adj* poultry

avicultura *nf* aviculture; *(de aves de corral)* poultry keeping

avidez *nf* avidity, eagerness

ávido,-a *adj* avid; **a. de** eager for

avinagrado,-a *adj* vinegary, sour; *Fig* sour

avinagrarse *vpr* to turn sour; *Fig* to become sour o bitter

avión¹ *nm* aircraft, *Br* aeroplane, *US* airplane; **viajar en a.** to fly, to go by plane; **por a.** *(en carta)* airmail

avión² *nm Orn* martin

avioneta *nf* light aircraft o plane

avíos *nmpl Culin* ingredients

avisar *vt* (a) *(informar)* to inform; **avísame cuando hayas acabado** let me know when you finish (b) *(advertir)* to warn; **ya te avisé** I warned you (c) *(llamar)* to call for; **a. a la policía** to notify the police; **a. al médico** to send for the doctor

aviso *nm* (a) notice; *(advertencia)* warning; *(nota)* note; **hasta nuevo a.** until further notice; **sin previo a.** without notice (b) **estar sobre a.** to know what's going on, to be in on it (c) *Am (anuncio)* advertisement; **a. clasificado** classified advertisement

avispa *nf* wasp

avispado,-a *adj Fam* quick-witted

avispero *nm (nido)* wasps' nest

avistar *vt* to see, to sight

avituallamiento *nm* provisioning

avivar *vt (fuego)* to stoke (up); *(pasión)* to intensify; *(paso)* to quicken

avizor,-a *adj* **estar ojo a.** to be on the alert o on the lookout

axila *nf* armpit, axilla

axioma *nm* axiom

ay *interj (dolor)* ouch!

aya *nf (niñera)* nanny

| Takes the masculine articles **el** and **un**. |

ayer 1 *adv* yesterday; **a. por la mañana/ por la tarde** yesterday morning/afternoon; **a. por la noche** last night; **antes de a.** the day before yesterday

2 *nm* **el a.** yesteryear

ayuda *nf* help, assistance; **ir en a. de algn** to come to sb's assistance; **a. al desarrollo** development aid

ayudante *nmf* assistant; *Med* **a. técnico-sanitario** nurse

ayudar 1 *vt* to help; **¿en qué puedo ayudarle?** (how) can I help you?

2 ayudarse *vpr* (a) *(unos a otros)* to help (b) **a. de** to use, to make use of

ayunar *vi* to fast

ayunas *nfpl* **en a.** without having eaten breakfast

ayuno *nm* fasting; **guardar/hacer a.** to fast

ayuntamiento *nm (institución)* town council; *(edificio)* town hall

azabache *nm* jet; **negro a.** jet black

azada *nf* hoe

azafata *nf* (a) *Av* air hostess (b) *(de congresos)* stewardess; *(de concurso)* hostess

azafate *nm Andes (bandeja)* tray

azafrán *nm* saffron

azahar *nm (del naranjo)* orange blossom; *(del limonero)* lemon blossom

azar *nm* chance; **por a.** by chance; **al a.** at random; **juegos de a.** games of chance; **los azares de la vida** the ups and downs of life

azaroso,-a *adj* hazardous, dangerous

azogue *nm* mercury, quicksilver

azorado,-a *adj* embarrassed

azorar 1 *vt* to embarrass

2 azorarse *vpr* to be embarrassed

Azores *nfpl* **las (Islas) A.** the Azores

azotar *vt* to beat; *(con látigo)* to whip, to flog; *Fig* to scourge

azote *nm* (a) *(golpe)* smacking; *(latigazo)* lash, stroke (of the whip) (b) *Fig* scourge

azotea *nf* flat roof

azteca *adj & nmf* Aztec

azúcar *nm o nf* sugar; **a. blanco** refined sugar; **a. moreno** brown sugar

azucarado,-a *adj* sweetened

azucarero,-a 1 *nm o nf* sugar bowl

2 *adj* sugar

azucena *nf* white lily

azufre *nm* sulphur

azul *adj & nm* blue; **a. celeste** sky blue; **a. marino** navy blue; **a. turquesa** turquoise; **sangre a.** blue blood

azulado,-a *adj* bluish

azulejo *nm (glazed)* tile

azuzar [40] *vt* **a. los perros a algn** to set the dogs on sb

B

B, b [be] *nf (la letra)* B, b
baba *nf* dribble; *Fig* **se le caía la b.** he was delighted
babear *vi (niño)* to dribble; *(adulto, animal)* to slobber
babel *nm o nf* bedlam
babero *nm* bib
Babia *n Fig* **estar en B.** to be daydreaming
babor *nm Náut* port, port side
babosa *nf* slug
babosada *nf CAm, Méx Fam (disparate)* daft thing
baboso,-a 1 *adj* (a) *Fam (despreciable)* slimy (b) *Am Fam (tonto)* daft, stupid
2 *nm,f Fam* (a) *(persona despreciable)* creep (b) *Am (tonto)* twit, idiot
babucha *nf* slipper
baca *nf Aut* roof rack
bacalao *nm (pez)* cod
bache *nm* (a) *(en carretera)* pot hole (b) *Av* air pocket (c) *Fig* bad patch; **pasar un b.** to go through a bad patch
bachillerato *nm* = academically orientated Spanish secondary school course for pupils aged 14-17
bacilo *nm* bacillus
bacon *nm* bacon
bacteria *nf* bacterium; **bacterias** bacteria
bacteriológico,-a *adj* bacteriological; **guerra bacteriológica** germ warfare
báculo *nm* walking stick; *(de obispo)* crosier
badén *nm Aut* bump
bádminton *nm* badminton
bafle *nm* loudspeaker
bagaje *nm* baggage
bagatela *nf (baratija)* knick-knack; *Fig* trifle
Bagdad *n* Baghdad
Bahamas *npl* **las (Islas) B.** the Bahamas
bahía *nf* bay
baila(d)or,-a *nm,f* flamenco dancer
bailar *vt & vi* to dance; *Fig* **b. al son que le tocan** to toe the line; *Fam* **¡que me quiten lo baila(d)o!** but at least I had a good time!
bailarín,-ina *nm,f* dancer; *(clásico)* ballet dancer
baile *nm* (a) *(danza)* dance (b) *(fiesta popular)* dance; *(formal)* ball; **b. de disfraces** fancy dress ball
baja *nf* (a) *(descenso)* drop, fall; *Fin* **jugar a la b.** to bear (b) *Mil* loss, casualty (c) **dar de b. a algn** *(despedir)* to lay sb off; **darse de b.** *(por enfermedad)* to take sick leave; *(de un club)* to resign (**de** from), to drop out (**de** of)
bajada *nf* (a) *(descenso)* descent (b) *(cuesta)* slope (c) **b. de bandera** *(de taxi)* minimum fare
bajamar *nf* low tide
bajar 1 *vt* (a) to come/go down; **b. la escalera** to come/go downstairs (b) *(descender)* to bring/get/take down; *(volumen)* to turn down; *(voz, telón)* to lower; *(precios etc)* to reduce, to cut; *(persiana)* to let down; *(cabeza)* to bow o lower
2 *vi* (a) to go/come down (b) *(apearse)* to get off; *(de un coche)* to get out (**de** of) (c) *(disminuir)* to fall, to drop
3 bajarse *vpr* (a) to come/go down (b) *(apearse)* to get off; *(de un coche)* to get out (**de** of)
bajativo *nm Andes, RP (licor)* digestive liqueur; *(tisana)* herbal tea
bajeza *nf* despicable action
bajial *nm Perú* lowland
bajinis: • **por lo bajinis** *loc adv Fam* on the sly
bajío *nm* (a) sandbank (b) *(terreno bajo)* lowland
bajista 1 *adj Fin* bearish; **tendencia b.** downward trend
2 *nmf* (a) *Fin* bear (b) *Mús* bass guitarist
bajo,-a 1 *adj* (a) *(persona)* short; *(sonido)* faint, soft; **en voz baja** in a low voice; **planta baja** ground floor; **de baja calidad** of poor quality; **la clase baja** the lower class (b) *Fig (vil)* base, contemptible
2 *nm* (a) *Mús* bass (b) *(planta baja)* ground floor
3 *adv* low; **hablar b.** to speak quietly; *Fig* **por lo b.** on the sly
4 *prep* (a) *(lugar)* under, underneath; **b. tierra** underground; **b. la lluvia** in the rain (b) *Pol & Hist* under; **b. la República** under the Republic (c) **b. cero** *(temperatura)*

below zero (**d**) *Jur* under; **b. juramento** under oath; **b. pena de muerte** on pain of death; **b. fianza** on bail

bajón *nm* (**a**) *(bajada)* sharp fall, decline (**b**) *Com* slump (**c**) *(de salud)* relapse, deterioration

bajorrelieve *nm* bas-relief

bajura *nf* **pesca de b.** coastal fishing

bala *nf* bullet; *Fig* **como una b.** like a shot

balacear *vt Am (tirotear)* to shoot

balacera *nf Am* shootout

balada *nf* ballad

baladí *adj* (*pl* **baladíes**) trivial

balance *nm* (**a**) *Fin* balance; *(declaración)* balance sheet; *Fig* **hacer b. de una situación** to take stock of a situation (**b**) *(resultado)* outcome

balancear 1 *vt* to rock

2 balancearse *upr (en mecedora)* to rock; *(en columpio)* to swing

balanceo *nm* rocking, swinging; *(de barco, avión)* rolling; *Am Aut* wheel balance

balanza *nf* scales; *Fig* **estar en la b.** to be in the balance *o* in danger; **b. comercial** balance of trade; **b. de pagos** balance of payments

balar *vi* to bleat

balaustrada *nf* balustrade, railing

balazo *nm* *(disparo)* shot; **matar a algn de un b.** to shoot sb dead (**b**) *(herida)* bullet wound

balboa *nm Fin* = standard monetary unit of Panama

balbucear *vi (adulto)* to stutter, stammer; *(niño)* to babble

balbuceo *nm* *(de adulto)* stuttering, stammering; *(de niño)* babbling

balbucir *vi defect* = **balbucear**

Balcanes *nmpl* **los B.** the Balkans

balcón *nm* balcony

baldado,-a *adj Fam* shattered

baldar *vt* to cripple, to maim

balde¹ *nm* pail, bucket

balde² *loc adv* (**a**) **de b.** *(gratis)* free (**b**) **en b.** *(en vano)* in vain

baldío,-a *adj (terreno)* uncultivated, waste; *(esfuerzo)* vain, useless

baldosa *nf* (ceramic) floor tile; *(para pavimentar)* flagstone, paving stone

balear¹ 1 *adj* Balearic

2 *nmf* person from the Balearic Islands

balear² *vt Am (disparar)* to shoot

Baleares *npl* **las (Islas) B.** the Balearic Islands

baleo *nm Am* shootout

balido *nm* bleating, bleat

balística *nf* ballistics *sing*

balístico,-a *adj* ballistic

baliza *nf* (**a**) *Náut* buoy (**b**) *Av* beacon

ballena *nf* whale

ballet *nm* ballet

balneario *nm* spa, health resort

balompié *nm* football

balón *nm* (**a**) ball, football; *Fig* **b. de oxígeno** boost (**b**) *(bombona)* gas cylinder

baloncesto *nm* basketball

balonmano *nm* handball

balonvolea *nm* volleyball

balsa *nf* (**a**) *Náut* raft (**b**) *Fig* **como una b. de aceite** very quiet

bálsamo *nm* balsam, balm

balsero,-a *nm,f (de Cuba)* = refugee fleeing Cuba on a raft

Báltico *nm* **el (Mar) B.** the Baltic (Sea)

baluarte *nm Fig* stronghold

bambas® *nfpl* trainers

bambolear *vi,* **bambolearse** *upr* to swing; *(persona, árbol)* to sway; *(mesa, silla)* to wobble

bambú *nm* (*pl* **bambúes**) bamboo

banal *adj* banal, trivial

banalidad *nf* triviality, banality

banana *nf* banana

banano *nm (árbol)* banana tree; *Col (fruto)* banana

banca *nf* (**a**) *(asiento)* bench (**b**) *Com & Fin* (the) banks; *(actividad)* banking; **b. electrónica** electronic banking (**c**) *(en juegos)* bank

bancario,-a *adj* banking

bancarrota *nf Fin* bankruptcy; **estar en b.** to be bankrupt

banco *nm* (**a**) bench (**b**) *Com & Fin* bank (**c**) **b. de arena** sandbank (**d**) *(de peces)* shoal, school (**e**) *Geol* layer

banda *nf* (**a**) *Mús* band (**b**) *Cin* **b. sonora** sound track (**c**) *(de pájaros)* flock (**d**) *(cinta)* sash (**e**) *(lado)* side; *Ftb* **línea de b.** touchline; **saque de b.** throw-in

bandada *nf* flock

bandazo *nm* **dar bandazos** to lurch

bandeja *nf* tray; *Fig* **servir algo a algn en b.** to hand sth to sb on a plate

bandera *nf* flag; **b. azul** *(en playa)* blue flag

banderín *nf* pennant, small flag

bandido *nm* bandit, outlaw

bando¹ *nm* (**a**) *Jur (edicto)* edict, proclamation (**b**) *bandos* banns

bando² *nm* faction, side; **pasarse al otro b.** to go over to the other side, to change allegiances

bandolero *nm* bandit, outlaw

banquero,-a *nm,f* banker

banqueta *nf* (**a**) *(asiento)* stool (**b**) *(para*

los pies) footstool (**c**) *CAm, Méx (acera) Br* pavement, *US* sidewalk

banquete *nm* banquet, feast; **b. de bodas** wedding reception

banquillo *nm* (**a**) *Jur* dock (**b**) *Dep* bench

banquina *nf RP (arcén)* verge; *(de autopista) Br* hard shoulder, *US* shoulder

bañadera *nf* (**a**) *Arg (bañera)* bath (**b**) *RP (vehículo)* minibus

bañado *nm Bol, RP (terreno)* marshy area

bañador *nm (de mujer)* bathing o swimming costume; *(de hombre)* swimming trunks

bañar 1 *vt* (**a**) to bath (**b**) *(cubrir)* to coat, to cover; **b. en oro** to goldplate

2 bañarse *vpr (en baño)* to have o take a bath; *(en mar, piscina)* to go for a swim; *Am (ducharse)* to have a shower

bañera *nf* bath, bathtub

bañista *nmf* bather, swimmer

baño *nm* (**a**) bath; **tomar un b.** to have o take a bath; *Fig* **darse un b. de sol** to sunbathe; **b. de sangre** bloodbath (**b**) *(de oro etc)* coat; *(de chocolate etc)* coating, covering (**c**) *(cuarto de baño)* bathroom; *(lavabo)* toilet

bar *nm* bar, pub

barahúnda *nf* din, uproar

baraja *nf* pack, deck

barajar *vt (cartas)* to shuffle; *Fig (nombres, cifras)* to juggle with

baranda, barandilla *nf (de escalera)* handrail, banister; *(de balcón)* handrail

baratija *nf* trinket, knick-knack

baratillo *nm* flea market

barato,-a 1 *adj* cheap

2 *adv* cheaply

baraúnda *nf* din, uproar

barba *nf* (**a**) *Anat* chin (**b**) *(pelo)* beard; *Fig* **100 pesetas por b.** 100 pesetas a head

barbacoa *nf* barbecue

barbaridad *nf* (**a**) atrocity (**b**) *(disparate)* piece of nonsense; **no digas barbaridades** don't talk nonsense (**c**) **una b.** a lot; **costar una b.** to cost a fortune

barbarie *nf* savagery, cruelty

bárbaro,-a 1 *adj* (**a**) *Hist* barbarian (**b**) *(cruel)* barbaric, barbarous (**c**) *Fam (enorme)* massive (**d**) *RP Fam (estupendo)* tremendous, terrific

2 *nm,f Hist* barbarian

barbecho *nm* fallow land; **dejar en b.** to leave fallow

barbería *nf* barber's (shop)

barbero *nm* barber

barbilla *nf* chin

barbitúrico ▸ *nm* barbiturate

barbudo,-a *adj* with a heavy beard

barca *nf* small boat

barcaza *nf* lighter

barcelonés,-esa 1 *adj* of/from Barcelona

2 *nm,f* person from Barcelona

barco *nm* boat, ship; **b. de pasajeros** liner; **b. de vapor** steamer

baremo *nm* scale

barítono *nm* baritone

barlovento *nm* windward

barman *nm* barman

barniz *nm* (**a**) *(en madera)* varnish; *(en cerámica)* glaze (**b**) *Fig* veneer

barnizar [40] *vt (madera)* to varnish; *(cerámica)* to glaze

barómetro *nm* barometer

barón *nm* baron

baronesa *nf* baroness

barquero,-a *nm,f (hombre)* boatman; *(mujer)* boatwoman

barquillo *nm* wafer

barra *nf* (**a**) bar; **b. de pan** French loaf, baguette; **b. de labios** lipstick (**b**) *(mostrador)* bar; **b. americana** = bar where hostesses chat with clients (**c**) *Dep* **b. fija** horizontal bar; **barras paralelas** parallel bars (**d**) *Andes, RP Fam (grupo de amigos)* gang, group of friends; **b. brava** = group of violent soccer supporters

barraca *nf* (**a**) *(caseta)* shack, hut (**b**) *(en Valencia y Murcia)* thatched farmhouse

barracón *nm Mil* prefabricated hut

barranco *nm (despeñadero)* cliff, precipice; *(torrentera)* gully, ravine

barranquismo *nm Dep* canyoning

barrena *nf* twist drill

barrenar *vt Téc* to drill

barrendero,-a *nm,f* sweeper, street sweeper

barreno *nm* (**a**) *(taladro)* large drill (**b**) *Min* charge

barreño *nm* tub

barrer 1 *vt* to sweep

2 *vi (en elecciones)* to win by a landslide

barrera *nf* barrier

barriada *nf* (**a**) *(barrio popular)* neighbourhood, area (**b**) *Am (barrio de chabolas)* shanty town

barricada *nf* barricade

barrida *nf* landslide victory

barriga *nf* belly; *Fam* tummy

barrigón,-ona, barrigudo,-a *adj* potbellied

barril *nm* barrel; **cerveza de b.** draught beer

barrillo *nm* pimple, spot

barrio *nm* area, district; **del b.** local; **el B. Gótico** the Gothic Quarter; **b. chino**

red-light district; **barrios bajos** slums

barrizal *nm* mire, quagmire

barro *nm* (a) *(lodo)* mud (b) *(arcilla)* clay; **objetos de b.** earthenware

barroco,-a *adj* baroque

barruntar *vt (sospechar)* to suspect; *(presentir)* to have a feeling

barrunto *nm (presentimiento)* feeling, presentiment; *(sospecha)* suspicion

bartola: • **a la bartola** *loc adv Fam* **tenderse** *o* **tumbarse a la b.** to laze around, to idle away one's time

bártulos *nmpl Fam* things, bits and pieces

barullo *nm (alboroto)* row, din; *(confusión)* confusion

basar 1 *vt* to base (**en** on)

2 basarse *upr (teoría, película)* **b. en** to be based on; **¿en qué te basas para decir eso?** what grounds do you have for saying that?

basca *nf Fam* people, crowd

báscula *nf* scales; *(para camiones)* weighbridge

bascular *vi* to tilt

base *nf* (a) base; **sueldo b.** minimum wage; *Informát* **b. de datos** database (b) *(de argumento, teoría)* basis; **en b.** a on the basis of; **a b. de estudiar** by studying; **a b. de productos naturales** using natural products (c) *(de partido)* grass roots; **miembro de b.** rank and file member (d) *(nociones)* grounding

básico,-a *adj* basic

basílica *nf* basilica

básquet *nm* basketball

bastante 1 *adj* (a) *(suficiente)* enough; **b. tiempo/comida** enough time/food; **bastantes platos** enough plates (b) *(abundante)* quite a lot of; **hace b. calor/frío** it's quite hot/cold; **bastantes amigos** quite a lot of friends

2 *adv* (a) *(suficiente)* enough; **con esto hay b.** that is enough; **no soy lo b. rico (como) para ...** I am not rich enough to ... (b) *(considerablemente)* fairly, quite; **me gusta b.** I quite like it; **vamos b. al cine** we go to the cinema quite *o* fairly often

bastar 1 *vi* to be sufficient *o* enough, to suffice; **basta con tres** three will be enough; **¡basta de tonterías!** enough of this nonsense!; **basta con tocarlo para que se abra** you only have to touch it and it opens; **¡basta (ya)!** that's enough!, that will do!

2 bastarse *upr* **b. a sí mismo** to be self-sufficient, to rely only on oneself

bastardilla *nf Impr* italics

bastardo,-a *adj & nm,f* bastard

bastidor *nm* (a) frame (b) *Teatro* **bastidores** wings; *Fig* **entre bastidores** behind the scenes

bastión *nm* bastion

basto,-a *adj (cosa)* rough, coarse; *(persona)* coarse, uncouth

bastón *nm* stick, walking stick

bastos *nmpl Naipes* ≃ clubs

basura *nf Br* rubbish, *US* garbage, *US* trash

basurero *nm* (a) *(persona) Br* dustman, *US* garbage man (b) *(lugar) Br* rubbish tip *o* dump, *US* garbage dump

bata *nf (para casa)* dressing gown; *(de médico etc)* white coat; *(de científico)* lab coat

batacazo *nm* (a) crash, bang (b) *CSur Fam (triunfo inesperado)* surprise victory;

batalla *nf* battle; **librar b.** to do *o* join battle; **b. campal** pitched battle

batallar *vi* to fight, quarrel

batallón *nm* battalion

batata *nf* sweet potato

batatazo *nm Am* = **batacazo**

bate *nm Dep* bat; **b. de béisbol** baseball bat

batear 1 *vi* to bat

2 *vt* to hit

batería 1 *nf* (a) battery (b) *Mús* drums (c) **b. de cocina** pots and pans, set of pans

2 *nmf* drummer

batiburrillo *nm* jumble, mess

batida *nf* (a) *(de la policía)* raid (b) *(en caza)* beat

batido,-a 1 *adj* (a) *Culin* whipped (b) *Dep* **tierra batida** clay

2 *nm* milk shake

batidora *nf (eléctrica)* mixer

batiente *adj* **reírse a mandíbula b.** to laugh one's head off

batín *nm* short dressing gown

batir 1 *vt* (a) to beat (b) *(huevo)* to beat; *(nata)* to whip, to whisk (c) *(récord)* to break (d) *(en caza)* to beat

2 batirse *upr* to fight

batuta *nf Mús* baton; *Fig* **llevar la b.** to be in charge

baúl *nm* (a) *(cofre)* trunk (b) *RP (maletero) Br* boot, *US* trunk

bautismo *nm* baptism, christening

bautizar [40] *vt* to baptize, to christen; *(vino)* to water down

bautizo *nm* baptism, christening

Baviera *n* Bavaria

baya *nf* berry

bayeta *nf* floorcloth

bayo,-a *adj* whitish yellow

bayoneta *nf* bayonet

baza *nf* trick; *Fig* **meter b.** to butt in

bazar *nm* bazaar

bazo *nm* spleen

bazofia *nf* rubbish

be *nf (letra)* b; *Am* **be baja** *o* **corta** v *(to distinguish from "b")*; *Am* **be alta** *o* **grande** *o* **larga** b *(to distinguish from "v")*

beatería *nf* sanctimoniousness

beato,-a *adj (piadoso)* devout; *Pey* prudish, sanctimonious

bebe,-a *nm,f Andes, RP* baby

bebé *nm* baby; **b. probeta** test-tube baby

bebedero *nm* drinking trough, water trough

bebedor,-a *nm,f* (hard *o* heavy) drinker

beber *vt & vi* to drink

bebible *adj* drinkable

bebida *nf* drink; **darse a la b.** to take to drink

bebido,-a *adj* drunk

beca *nf* grant

becar [44] *vt* to award a grant to

becario,-a *nm,f* grant holder

becerro *nm* calf

bechamel *nf* bechamel; **salsa b.** bechamel sauce, white sauce

becuadro *nm Mús* natural sign

bedel *nm* beadle

begonia *nf* begonia

beige *adj & nm inv* beige

béisbol *nm* baseball

bejuco *nm (en América)* liana; *(en Asia)* rattan

Belén *n* Bethlehem

belén *nm* nativity scene, crib

belga *adj & nmf* Belgian

Bélgica *n* Belgium

Belgrado *n* Belgrade

Belice *n* Belize

bélico,-a *adj* warlike, bellicose; *(preparativos etc)* war; **material b.** armaments

belicoso,-a *adj* warlike, bellicose; *(agresivo)* aggressive

beligerancia *nf* belligerence

beligerante *adj* belligerent; **los países beligerantes** the countries at war

bellaco,-a 1 *adj* wicked, roguish

   2 *nm,f* scoundrel, rogue

belleza *nf* beauty

bello,-a *adj* beautiful

bellota *nf Bot* acorn; *Fig* **animal de b.** blockhead

bemol 1 *adj Mús* flat

   2 *nm* **esto tiene bemoles** this is a tough one

bencina *nf Chile (gasolina) Br* petrol, *US* gas

bencinera *nf Chile Br* petrol station, *US* gas station

bendecir [12] *vt* to bless; **b. la mesa** to say grace; **¡Dios te bendiga!** God bless you!

bendición *nf* blessing

bendito,-a 1 *adj* blessed; *(maldito)* damned

   2 *nm,f (bonachón)* good sort, kind soul; *(tontorrón)* simple soul

beneficencia *nf* beneficence, charity

beneficiado,-a *adj* favoured; **salir b. de algo** to do well out of sth

beneficiar [43] **1** *vt* to benefit

   2 beneficiarse *vpr* **b. de** *o* **con algo** to profit from *o* by sth

beneficiario,-a *nm,f* beneficiary; **margen b.** profit margin

beneficio *nm* (a) *Com & Fin* profit (**b**) *(bien)* benefit; **en b. propio** in one's own interest; **un concierto a b. de ...** a concert in aid of ...

beneficioso,-a *adj* beneficial

benéfico,-a *adj* charitable

benemérita *nf* **la B.** the Spanish Civil Guard

beneplácito *nm Fml* approval, consent

benevolencia *nf* benevolence

benevolente, benévolo,-a *adj* benevolent

bengala *nf* flare

benigno,-a *adj (persona)* gentle, benign; *(clima)* mild; *(tumor)* benign

benjamín,-ina *nm,f* youngest child

beodo,-a *adj* drunk

berberecho *nm* (common) cockle

berbiquí *nm Téc* drill

berenjena *nf Br* aubergine, *US* eggplant

Berlín *n* Berlin

berlina *nf (coche)* saloon; *(carruaje)* sedan

berlinés,-esa 1 *adj* of/from Berlin

   2 *nm,f* Berliner

berma *nf Andes (arcén)* verge; *(de autopista) Br* hard shoulder, *US* shoulder

bermejo,-a *adj* reddish

bermellón *nm* vermilion

Bermudas 1 *nfpl* **las (Islas) B.** Bermuda

   2 *nmpl* **bermudas** *(prenda)* Bermuda shorts

Berna *n* Bern

berrear *vi* to bellow, low

berrido *nm* bellowing, lowing

berrinche *nm Fam* rage, tantrum

berro *nm* cress, watercress

berza *nf* cabbage

besar 1 *vt* to kiss

   2 besarse *vpr* to kiss

beso *nm* kiss

bestia 1 *nf* beast, animal; **b. de carga** beast of burden

2 *nmf Fam Fig* brute, beast

3 *adj Fig* brutish, boorish; **a lo b.** rudely

bestial *adj* bestial; *Fam (enorme)* huge, tremendous; *(extraordinario)* fantastic, terrific

bestialidad *nf* (a) *Fam (estupidez)* stupidity (b) *(crueldad)* act of cruelty (c) *Fam* **una b. de** tons of, stacks of

best-seller *nm* best-seller

besugo *nm* (a) *(pez)* sea bream (b) *(persona)* idiot, half-wit

besuquear *Fam* **1** *vt* to kiss, to cover with kisses

2 besuquearse *upr* to smooch

betabel *nf Méx Br* beetroot, *US* beet

betarraga *nf Andes Br* beetroot, *US* beet

betún *nm (para el calzado)* shoe polish; *Quím* bitumen

biberón *nm* baby's bottle, feeding bottle

Biblia *nf* Bible

bíblico,-a *adj* biblical

bibliografía *nf* bibliography

bibliorato *nm RP* file

biblioteca *nf* (a) *(institución)* library; **b. ambulante** mobile library (b) *RP (mueble)* bookcase

bibliotecario,-a *nm,f* librarian

bicameral *adj Pol* bicameral, two-chamber

bicarbonato *nm* bicarbonate; **b. sódico** bicarbonate of soda

bicentenario *nm Br* bicentenary, *US* bicentennial

bíceps *nm inv* biceps

bicha *nf* snake

bicho *nm* (a) *(bug, insect; ¿qué b. te ha picado?* what's bugging you? (b) *Taurom* bull (c) *Fam* **todo b. viviente** every living soul; **un b. raro** a weirdo, an oddball

bici *nf Fam* bike

bicicleta *nf* bicycle; **montar en b.** to ride a bicycle

bicolor *adj* two-coloured; *Pol* **gobierno b.** two-party government

bidé *nm* bidet

bidón *nm* drum

biela *nf Aut* connecting rod

Bielorrusia *n* Belarus

bien¹ 1 *adv* (a) *(correctamente)* well; **habla b. (el) inglés** she speaks English well; **responder b.** to answer correctly; **hiciste b. en decírmelo** you were right to tell me; **las cosas le van b.** things are going well for him; **¡b.!** good!, great!; **¡muy b.!** excellent, first class!; **¡qué b.!** great!, fantastic!

(b) *(de salud)* well; **sentirse/encontrarse/estar b.** to feel well

(c) **vivir b.** to be comfortably off; **¡está b.!** *(¡de acuerdo!)* fine!, all right!; **¡ya está b.!** that's (quite) enough!; **aquí se está muy b.** it's really nice here; **esta falda te sienta b.** this skirt suits you; *Fam* **ese libro está muy b.** that book is very good; *Fam* **su novia está muy b.** his girlfriend is very nice

(d) *(intensificador)* very, quite; **b. temprano** very early, nice and early; **b. caliente** pretty hot; **b. es verdad que ...** it's quite clear that ...

(e) **más b.** rather, a little

(f) **b. podía haberme avisado** she might have let me know

(g) *(de buena gana)* willingly, gladly; **b. me tomaría una cerveza** I'd really love a beer

2 *conj* **ahora b.** now, now then; **o b.** or, or else; **b. ... o b. ... either ... or ...;** **no b.** as soon as; **no b. llegó ...** no sooner had she arrived than ...; **si b.** although, even if

3 *adj* **la gente b.** the wealthy, the upper classes

bien² *nm* (a) *(bondad)* good; **el b. y el mal** good and evil; **un hombre/familia de b.** a good man/family (b) *(bienestar)* **por el b. de** for the good of; **lo hace por tu b.** he does it for your sake (c) **bienes** goods; **bienes de equipo** capital goods; **bienes gananciales** communal property; **bienes inmuebles** real estate; **bienes de consumo** consumer goods

bienal *nf* biennial exhibition

bienestar *nm* *(personal)* well-being, contentment; *(comodidad)* ease, comfort; **la sociedad del b.** the affluent society

bienhechor,-a *nm,f (hombre)* benefactor; *(mujer)* benefactress

bienintencionado,-a *adj* well-meaning, well-intentioned

bienio *nm* biennium, two-year period

bienvenida *nf* welcome; **dar la b. a algn** to welcome sb

bienvenido,-a *adj* welcome

bife *nm Andes, RP (bistec)* steak

bifocal *adj* bifocal; **gafas bifocales** bifocals

bifurcación *nf* bifurcation; *(de la carretera)* fork

bifurcarse **[44]** *upr* to fork, to branch off

bigamia *nf* bigamy

bígamo,-a 1 *adj* bigamous

2 *nm,f* bigamist

bigote *nm (de persona)* moustache; *(de animal) (usu pl)* whiskers

📝 Observa que la palabra inglesa **bigot** es un falso amigo y no es la traducción de la palabra española **bigote**. En inglés, **bigot** significa "intolerante".

bilateral *adj* bilateral; **acuerdo b.** bilateral agreement

bilbaíno,-a 1 *adj* of/from Bilbao
2 *nm,f* person from Bilbao

bilingüe *adj* bilingual

bilis *nf* bile

billar *nm* (a) *(juego)* billiards *sing*; **b. americano** pool; **b. ruso** snooker (b) *(mesa)* billiard table

billete *nm* (a) ticket; **b. de ida** *Br* single (ticket), *US* one-way ticket; **b. de ida y vuelta** *Br* return (ticket), *US* round-trip (ticket); (b) *(de banco) Br* note, *US* bill; **un b. de mil pesetas** a thousand peseta note

billetera *nf*, **billetero** *nm* wallet, *US* billfold

billón *nm* trillion

bimensual *adj* twice-monthly, bimonthly

bimotor 1 *adj* twin-engined
2 *nm* twin-engined plane

binario,-a *adj* binary

bingo *nm* (a) *(juego)* bingo (b) *(sala)* bingo hall

binomio *nm* binomial

biodegradable *adj* biodegradable

biofísica *nf* biophysics *sing*

biografía *nf* biography

biográfico,-a *adj* biographical

biógrafo,-a *nm,f* biographer

biología *nf* biology

biológico,-a *adj* biological; *(agricultura, productos)* organic

biólogo,-a *nm,f* biologist

biomasa *nf* bio-mass

biombo *nm* (folding) screen

biopsia *nf* biopsy

bioquímica *nf* biochemistry

bioquímico,-a 1 *adj* biochemical
2 *nm,f* biochemist

bióxido *nm* dioxide; **b. de carbono** carbon dioxide

bipartidismo *nm* two-party system

biquini *nm* bikini

birlar *vt Fam* to pinch, to nick

Birmania *n* Burma

birmano,-a *adj & nm,f* Burmese

birome *nf RP* ballpoint pen, *Br* Biro®

birrete *nm* cap, beret; *Rel* biretta; *Univ* mortar-board

birria *nf Fam* rubbish

bis 1 *nm* encore
2 *adv* twice

bisabuela *nf* great-grandmother

bisabuelo *nm* great-grandfather; **bisabuelos** great-grandparents

bisagra *nf* hinge; **partido b.** party holding the balance of power

bisbisar, bisbisear *vt* to whisper

bisexual *adj & nmf* bisexual

bisiesto *adj* **año b.** leap year

bisnieto,-a *nm,f (niño)* great-grandson; *(niña)* great-granddaughter; **mis bisnietos** my great-grandchildren

bisonte *nm* bison, American buffalo

bisoño,-a *adj* inexperienced

bisté, bistec *nm* steak

bisturí *nm* scalpel

bisutería *nf* imitation jewellery

bit *nm Informát* bit

bíter *nm* bitters

bizantino,-a *adj Fig* **discusiones bizantinas** hair-splitting arguments

bizco,-a 1 *adj* cross-eyed
2 *nm,f* cross-eyed person

bizcocho *nm* sponge cake

biznieto,-a *nm,f* = bisnieto,-a

blanca *nf Fam* **estar sin b.** to be flat broke

blanco¹,-a 1 *adj* white; *(tez)* fair
2 *nm,f (hombre)* white man; *(mujer)* white woman; **los blancos** whites

blanco² *nm* (a) *(color)* white (b) *(hueco)* blank; **dejó la hoja en b.** he left the page blank; **votos en b.** blank votes; *Fig* **pasar la noche en b.** to have a sleepless night; **me quedé en b.** my mind went blank (c) *(diana)* target; **dar en el b.** to hit the target; *Fig* **ser el b. de todas las miradas** to be the centre of attention

blancura *nf* whiteness

blandengue *adj Pey* weak, soft

blandir *vt* to brandish

blando,-a *adj* soft

📝 Observa que la palabra inglesa **bland** es un falso amigo y no es la traducción de la palabra española **blando**. En inglés, **bland** significa "soso".

blanquear *vt* (a) to whiten (b) *(encalar)* to whitewash (c) *(dinero)* to launder

blanquecino,-a *adj* whitish

blanqueo *nm* (a) whitening (b) *(encalado)* whitewashing (c) *(de dinero)* laundering

blanquillo *nm CAm, Méx (huevo)* egg

blasfemar *vi* to blaspheme (**contra** against)

blasfemia *nf* blasphemy

blasón *nm* coat of arms

bledo *nm Fam* **me importa un b.** I couldn't give a damn

blindado,-a *adj Mil* armoured, armour-plated; *(antibalas)* bullet-proof; **coche b.** bullet-proof car; **puerta blindada** reinforced door, security door

blindaje *nm* armour; *(vehículo)* armour plating

bloc *nm* pad; **b. de notas** notepad

bloomer ['blumer], **blúmer** *nm CAm, Carib* panties, *Br* knickers

bloque *nm* (a) block; en b. en bloc; **b. de pisos** *BR* (block of) flats, *US* apartment block (b) *Pol* bloc; **el b. comunista** the Communist Bloc

bloquear *vt* (a) to block (b) *Mil* to blockade

bloqueo *nm* blockade; *Dep* block

blues *nm* blues

blusa *nf* blouse

blusón *nm* loose blouse, smock

bluyín *nm*, **bluyines** *nmpl Andes, Ven* jeans

boato *nm* show, ostentation

bobada *nf* nonsense; **decir bobadas** to talk nonsense

bobalicón,-ona *Fam* **1** *adj* simple, stupid **2** *nm,f* simpleton, idiot

bobería *nf* = bobada

bobina *nf* (a) reel (b) *Elec* coil

bobo,-a 1 *adj (tonto)* stupid, silly; *(ingenuo)* naïve **2** *nm,f* fool

boca *nf* (a) mouth; **b. abajo** face downward; **b. arriba** face upward; *Fig* **a pedir de b.** in accordance with one's wishes; *Fig* **andar de b. en b.** to be the talk of the town; *Fam* **¡cierra la b!** shut up!; *Fam* **con la b. abierta** open-mouthed; *Fam* **se le hizo la b. agua** his mouth watered; **el b. a b.** kiss of life, mouth-to-mouth resuscitation (b) **la b. del metro** the entrance to the *Br* underground *o US* subway station; **b. de riego** hydrant

bocacalle *nf* entrance to a street

bocadillo *nm* (a) *(con pan)* sandwich; **un b. de jamón/tortilla** a ham/an omelette sandwich (b) *(de cómic)* balloon

bocado *nm* (a) *(mordedura)* bite (b) *(de caballo)* bit

bocajarro: •a bocajarro *loc adv* point-blank

bocanada *nf* (a) *(de vino)* mouthful (b) *(de humo)* puff; **una b. de viento** a gust of wind

bocata *nm* sandwich

bocazas *nmf inv Fam* bigmouth, blabbermouth

boceto *nm Arte* sketch, outline; *(esquema)* outline, plan

bochinche *nm Fam* uproar; **armar un b.** to kick up a row

bochorno *nm* (a) *(tiempo)* sultry *o* close weather; *(calor sofocante)* stifling heat (b) *Fig (vergüenza)* shame, embarrassment

bochornoso,-a *adj* (a) *(tiempo)* sultry, close, muggy; *(calor)* stifling (b) *Fig (vergonzoso)* shameful, embarrassing

bocina *nf* horn; **tocar la b.** to blow *o* sound one's horn

bocinazo *nm* hoot, toot

bocón,-ona *nm,f Am Fam* bigmouth

boda *nf* wedding, marriage; **bodas de plata** silver wedding

bodega *nf* (a) wine cellar; *(tienda)* wine shop (b) *Náut* hold (c) *(almacén)* warehouse (d) *Am* grocery store, grocer's (shop)

bodegón *nm* still-life

bodrio *nm Fam* rubbish, trash

body *nm* bodystocking, leotard

BOE *nm* (*abr* **Boletín Oficial del Estado**) Official Gazette

bofetada *nf*, **bofetón** *nm* slap on the face; **dar una b./un b. a algn** to slap sb's face

boga *nf Fig* **estar en b.** to be in vogue

bogar [42] *vi* (a) *(remar)* to row (b) *(navegar)* to sail

bogavante *nm* lobster

bogotano,-a 1 *adj* of/from Bogotá **2** *nm,f* person from Bogotá

bohío *nm Am* hut, cabin

boicot *nm (pl* **boicots)** boycott

boicotear *vt* to boycott

boicoteo *nm* boycott

bóiler *nm Méx* boiler

boina *nf* beret

bol *nm* bowl

bola *nf* (a) ball; *(canica)* marble; **b. de nieve** snowball; **no dar pie con b.** to be unable to do anything right (b) *Fam (mentira)* fib, lie; **meter bolas** to tell fibs (c) *(rumor)* rumour; **corre la b. por ahí de que te has echado novio** they say you've got yourself a boyfriend

bolchevique *adj & nmf* Bolshevik

bolear *vt Méx (sacar brillo)* to shine, to polish

bolera *nf* bowling alley

bolería *nf Méx* shoeshine store

boleta *nf* (a) *Méx, RP (para votar)* ballot, voting slip (b) *CSur (comprobante)* receipt (c) *CAm, CSur (multa)* parking ticket (d) *Méx (boletín)* (school) report card

boletería *nf Am (de cine, teatro)* box office; *(de estación)* ticket office

boletero,-a nm,f Am box office attendant

boletín nm bulletin; **B. Oficial del Estado** Official Gazette

boleto nm (a) (de rifa) ticket (b) Am (de tren, metro) ticket (c) Méx (para espectáculo) ticket

boli nm Fam pen, Br Biro®

boliche nm (a) (juego) bowling (b) (bola) jack (c) (lugar) bowling alley (d) CSur Fam (bar) small bar

bólido nm Aut racing car

bolígrafo nm ballpoint (pen), Br Biro®

bolita nf CSur (bola) marble; **jugar a las bolitas** to play marbles

bolívar nm Fin = standard monetary unit of Venezuela

Bolivia n Bolivia

boliviano,-a adj & nm,f Bolivian

bollar vt to dent

bollo nm (a) Culin bun, bread roll (b) (abolladura) dent

bolo¹ nm (pieza) skittle, pin; **bolos** (juego) (ten-pin) bowling

bolo²,-a nm,f CAm Fam (borracho) drunk

bolsa¹ nf bag; Méx (de mano) Br handbag, US purse; Av **b. de aire** air pocket; **b. de deportes** sports bag; **b. de la compra** shopping bag; **b. de viaje** travel bag

bolsa² nf Fin Stock Exchange; **jugar a la b.** to play the market

bolsillo nm (en prenda) pocket; **de b.** pocket, pocket-size; **libro de b.** paperback; **lo pagó de su b.** he paid for it out of his own pocket

bolso nm Br handbag, US purse

boludear vi RP Fam (a) (hacer tonterías) to mess about (b) (decir tonterías) to talk rubbish (c) (perder el tiempo) to waste one's time

boludo,-a nm,f RP Fam (estúpido) idiot, twit

bomba¹ nf pump; Andes, Ven (gasolinera) Br petrol station, US gas station; **b. de aire** air pump; **b. de incendios** fire engine; Andes, Ven **b. (de gasolina)** (surtidor) Br petrol pump, US gas pump

bomba² nf bomb; **b. atómica/de hidrógeno/de neutrones** atomic/hydrogen/neutron bomb; **b. de relojería** time bomb; **b. fétida** stink bomb; Fam **noticia b.** shattering piece of news; Fam **pasarlo b.** to have a whale of a time

bombacha nf RP (braga) panties, Br knickers; **bombachas** (pantalones) = loose-fitting trousers worn by cowboys

bombardear vt to bomb, to shell; **b. a algn a preguntas** to bombard sb with questions

bombardeo nm bombing, bombardment

bombardero nm Av bomber

bombazo nm bomb blast

bombear vt (a) (agua etc) to pump (b) (pelota) to blow up

bombeo nm (de líquido) pumping; **estación de b.** pumping station

bombero,-a nm,f (a) (de incendios) firefighter; (hombre) fireman; (mujer) firewoman; **cuerpo de bomberos** Br fire brigade, US fire department; **parque de bomberos** fire station (b) Ven (de gasolinera) Br petrol-pump o US gas-pump attendant

bombilla nf (light) bulb

bombillo nm CAm, Carib, Col, Méx light bulb

bombín nm bowler hat

bombita nf RP light bulb

bombo nm (a) Mús bass drum; Fig **a b. y platillo(s)** with a great song and dance; Fam **darse b.** to blow one's own trumpet (b) (de sorteo) lottery drum

bombón nm chocolate

bombona nf cylinder; **b. de butano** butane gas cylinder

bombonera nf chocolate box

bonachón,-ona adj good-natured, easy-going

bonaerense 1 adj of/from Buenos Aires **2** nmf person from Buenos Aires

bonanza nf (a) Náut (tiempo) fair weather; (mar) calm at sea (b) Fig (prosperidad) prosperity

bondad nf goodness; Fml **tenga la b. de esperar** please be so kind as to wait

bondadoso,-a adj kind, good-natured

bonete nm Rel cap, biretta; Univ mortar-board

boniato nm sweet potato

bonificación nf bonus

bonificar [44] vt Com to give a bonus to

bonito¹,-a adj pretty, nice

bonito² nm tuna

bono nm (a) (vale) voucher (b) Fin bond, debenture; **bonos del tesoro** o **del Estado** Treasury bonds

bono-bus nm bus pass

boom nm boom

boomerang nm boomerang

boquerón nm anchovy

boquete nm hole

boquiabierto,-a adj open-mouthed; **se quedó b.** he was flabbergasted

boquilla nf (a) (de cigarro) tip; (de pipa) mouthpiece; **decir algo de b.** to pay lip service to sth (b) Mús mouthpiece (c) (orificio) opening

borbotar, borbotear *vi* to bubble

borbotón *nm* bubbling; *Fig* **salir a borbotones** to gush forth

borda *nf Náut* gunwale; **arrojar** *o* **echar por la b.** to throw overboard; **fuera b.** *(motor)* outboard motor

bordado,-a 1 *adj* embroidered; **el examen me salió b.** I made a good job of that exam
  2 *nm* embroidery

bordar *vt* **(a)** to embroider **(b)** *Fig* to do excellently

borde¹ *nm (de mesa, camino)* edge; *Cost* hem, edge; *(de vasija)* rim, brim; **al b. de** on the brink of, on the verge of; **al b. del mar** at the seaside

borde² *Fam* **1** *adj* stroppy
  2 *nmf* stroppy person

bordear *vt* to go round the edge of, to skirt

bordillo *nm Br* kerb, *US* curb

bordo *nm* **a b.** on board; **subir a b.** to go on board

bordó *adj inv RP* maroon, burgundy

borla *nf* tassel

borne *nm Elec* terminal

borra *nf* **(a)** *(pelusa)* fluff **(b)** *(poso)* sediment, dregs

borrachera *nf (embriaguez)* drunkenness; **agarrarse** *o* **cogerse una b.** to get drunk;

borracho,-a 1 *adj* **(a)** *(bebido)* drunk; **estar b.** to be drunk **(b)** *(bizcocho)* with rum
  2 *nm,f* drunkard, drunk

borrador *nm* **(a)** *(escrito)* rough copy, first draft **(b)** *(croquis)* rough *o* preliminary sketch **(c)** *(de pizarra)* duster

borraja *nf* **quedar en agua de borrajas** to come to nothing, to fizzle *o* peter out

borrar 1 *vt* **(a)** *(con goma)* to erase, to rub out; *(pizarra)* to clean **(b)** *Informát* to delete
  2 borrarse *vpr (de un club etc)* to drop out, to withdraw

borrasca *nf* area of low pressure

borrascoso,-a *adj* stormy

borrego,-a *nm,f* **(a)** *yearling* lamb **(b)** *Fam (persona)* sheep

borrico *nm* ass, donkey; *Fam Fig* ass, dimwit

borrón *nm* blot, smudge

borroso,-a *adj* blurred; **veo b.** I can't see clearly, everything's blurred

Bosnia *n* Bosnia; **B. y Herzegóvina** Bosnia-Herzegovina

bosnio,-a *adj & nm,f* Bosnian

bosque *nm* wood

bosquejar *vt (dibujo)* to sketch, outline; *(plan)* to draft, to outline

bosquejo *nm (de dibujo)* sketch, study; *(de plan)* draft, outline

bostezar [40] *vi* to yawn

bostezo *nm* yawn

bota *nf* **(a)** boot; *Fig* **ponerse las botas** to make a killing **(b)** *(de vino)* wineskin

botana *nf Méx* snack, appetizer

botánica *nf* botany

botánico,-a 1 *adj* botanic; **jardín b.** botanic gardens
  2 *nm,f* botanist

botar 1 *vi* **(a)** *(saltar)* to jump **(b)** *(pelota)* to bounce
  2 *vt* **(a)** *(barco)* to launch **(b)** *(pelota)* to bounce **(c)** *Am (arrojar)* to throw out

botarate *nmf* madcap, fool

bote¹ *nm* **(a)** jump, bound; **dar botes** to jump up and down; **de un b.** with one leap **(b)** *(de pelota)* bounce, rebound

bote² *nm (lata)* can, tin; *(para propinas)* jar *o* box for tips; *(en lotería)* jackpot; *Fam* **chupar del b.** to scrounge

bote³ *nm (lancha)* boat; **b. salvavidas** lifeboat

bote⁴ *nm* **de b. en b.** packed, full to bursting

botella *nf* **(a)** bottle **(b)** *Cuba (autostop)* **dar b. a algn** to give sb a lift; **hacer b.** to hitchhike

botellín *nm* small bottle

botepronto *nm Fam* **a b.** all of a sudden

botica *nf* pharmacy, *Br* chemist's (shop), *US* drugstore; *Fam* **hay de todo como en b.** there's everything under the sun

boticario,-a *nm,f* pharmacist, *Br* chemist, *US* druggist

botijo *nm* earthenware pitcher *(with spout and handle)*

botín¹ *nm (de un robo)* loot, booty

botín² *nm (calzado)* ankle boot

botiquín *nm* **(a)** medicine chest *o* cabinet; *(portátil)* first-aid kit **(b)** *(enfermería)* first-aid post

botón *nm* button; **pulsar el b.** to press the button; **b. de muestra** sample

botones *nm inv (en hotel)* bellboy, *US* bellhop; *(recadero)* messenger, errand boy

boutique *nf* boutique

bóveda *nf* vault

bovino,-a *adj* bovine; **ganado b.** cattle

box *nm (pl boxes)* **(a)** *(de caballo)* stall **(b)** *(de coches)* pit **(c)** *Am (boxeo)* boxing

boxeador *nm* boxer

boxear *vi* to box

boxeo *nm* boxing

boya nf (a) Náut buoy (b) (corcho) float
boyante adj buoyant
boy-scout nm boy scout
bozal nm (a) (para perro) muzzle (b) Am (cabestro) halter
bracero nm (day) labourer
bragas nfpl panties, Br knickers
bragueta nf (de pantalón etc) fly, flies
braguetazo nm Fam dar el b. to marry for money
braille nm braille
bramar vi to low, to bellow
bramido nm lowing, bellowing
brandy nm brandy
branquia nf gill
brasa nf ember, red-hot coal; **chuletas a la b.** barbecued chops
brasero nm brazier
brasier nm Carib, Col, Méx bra
Brasil n Brazil
brasileño,-a, RP **brasilero,-a** adj & nm,f Brazilian
bravata nf piece o act of bravado
bravo,-a 1 adj (a) (valiente) brave, courageous (b) (feroz) fierce, ferocious; **un toro b.** a fighting bull (c) (mar) rough, stormy
  2 interj **¡b.!** well done!, bravo!
bravucón,-ona nm,f boaster, braggart
bravura nf (a) (de animal) ferocity, fierceness (b) (de persona) courage, bravery (c) (de toro) fighting spirit
braza nf (a) Náut fathom (b) (en natación) breaststroke; **nadar a b.** to do the breaststroke
brazada nf (en natación) stroke
brazalete nm (a) (insignia) armband (b) (pulsera) bracelet
brazo nm arm; (de animal) foreleg; (de sillón, tocadiscos) arm; **en brazos** in one's arms; **ir del b.** to walk arm in arm; Fig **no dar su b. a torcer** not to give in, stand firm; **b. de gitano** = type of Swiss roll containing cream
brea nf tar, pitch
brebaje nm concoction, brew
brecha nf (en muro) opening, gap; Mil & Fig breach; Fig **estar siempre en la b.** to be always in the thick of things
brécol nm broccoli
bregar [42] vi to fight
Bretaña nf (a) Brittany (b) **Gran B.** Great Britain
brete nm Fig **poner a algn en un b.** to put sb in a tight spot
bretel nm CSur strap; **un vestido sin breteles** a strapless dress

breva nf early fig; Fam **de higos a brevas** once in a blue moon; Fam **¡no caerá esa b.!** no such luck!
breve adj brief; **en b., en breves momentos** shortly, soon; **en breves palabras** in short
brevedad nf briefness; (concisión) brevity; **con la mayor b. posible** as soon as possible
brevet nm Chile (de avión) pilot's licence; Ecuad, Perú (de automóvil) Br driving licence, US driver's license; RP (de velero) sailor's licence
brezo nm heather
bribón,-ona 1 adj roguish, dishonest
  2 nm,f rogue, rascal
bricolaje nm do-it-yourself, DIY
brida nf (a) (rienda) rein, bridle (b) Téc flange
bridge nm Naipes bridge
brigada 1 nf (a) Mil brigade (b) (de policías) squad; **b. antiterrorista** anti-terrorist squad
  2 nm Mil sergeant major
brigadier nm brigadier
brillante 1 adj brilliant
  2 nm diamond
brillantez nf brilliance
brillantina nf brilliantine
brillar vi (resplandecer) to shine; (ojos, joyas) to sparkle; (lentejuelas etc) to glitter; **b. por su ausencia** to be conspicuous by one's absence
brillo nm (resplandor) shine; (del sol, de la luna) brightness; (de lentejuelas etc) glittering; (del cabello, tela) sheen; (de color) brilliance; (de pantalla) brightness; (de zapatos) shine; **sacar b. a** to shine, to polish
brilloso,-a adj Am shining
brincar [44] vi to skip
brinco nm skip
brindar 1 vi to drink a toast; **b. por algn/algo** to drink to sb/sth
  2 vt (a) (oportunidad) to offer, to provide (b) Taurom to dedicate (a to)
  3 brindarse vpr to offer (a to), to volunteer (a to)
brindis nm (a) toast (b) Taurom dedication (of the bull)
brío nm energy
brioso,-a adj energetic, vigorous
brisa nf breeze; **b. marina** sea breeze
británico,-a 1 adj British; **las Islas Británicas** the British Isles
  2 nm,f Briton; **los británicos** the British
brizna nf (de hierba) blade; (de carne) string

broca *nf Téc* bit

brocha *nf (para pintar)* paintbrush; **b. de afeitar** shaving brush

broche *nm* (a) *(joya)* brooch; *Fig* **poner el b. de oro** to finish with a flourish (b) *(de vestido)* fastener

bróculi *nm* broccoli

broma *nf (chiste)* joke; **bromas aparte** joking apart; **en b.** as a joke; **¡ni en b.!** not on your life!; **b. pesada** practical joke; **gastar una b.** to play a joke

bromear *vi* to joke

bromista 1 *adj* fond of joking o playing jokes

    2 *nmf* joker, prankster

bronca *nf* (a) *(riña)* quarrel, row (b) **echar una b. a algn** to bawl sb out (c) *RP Fam (rabia)* **me da b.** it hacks me off; **el jefe le tiene b.** the boss can't stand him

bronce *nm* bronze

bronceado,-a 1 *adj* suntanned, tanned

    2 *nm* suntan, tan

bronceador,-a 1 *adj* **leche bronceadora** suntan cream

    2 *nm* suntan cream o lotion

broncearse *vpr* to get a tan o a suntan

bronco,-a *adj* rough, coarse

bronquitis *nf inv* bronchitis

brotar *vi (planta)* to sprout; *(agua)* to spring, to gush; *(lágrimas)* to well up; *(epidemia)* to break out

brote *nm* (a) *Bot (renuevo)* bud, shoot; *(de agua)* gushing (b) *(de epidemia, violencia)* outbreak

bruces: • **de bruces** *loc adv* face downwards; **se cayó de b.** he fell flat on his face

bruja *nf* witch, sorceress

brujería *nf* witchcraft, sorcery

brujo,-a 1 *nm* wizard, sorcerer

    2 *adj Méx Fam* **estar b.** to be broke

brújula *nf* compass

bruma *nf* mist

brumoso,-a *adj* misty

bruñir *vt* to polish

brusco,-a *adj* (a) *(persona)* brusque, abrupt (b) *(repentino)* sudden, sharp

Bruselas *n* Brussels; **coles de B.** Brussels sprouts

brusquedad *nf* brusqueness, abruptness

brutal *adj* brutal

brutalidad *nf* brutality

bruto,-a 1 *adj* (a) *(necio)* stupid, thick; *(grosero)* coarse, uncouth (b) *Fin* gross; **peso b.** gross weight (c) **un diamante en b.** an uncut diamond

    2 *nm,f* blockhead, brute

búcaro *nm* earthenware jug

bucear *vi* to swim under water

buche *nm* maw; *(de ave)* craw; *Fam (estómago)* belly, stomach

bucle *nm* curl, ringlet

budín *nm* pudding

budismo *nm* Buddhism

budista *adj & nmf* Buddhist

buen *adj (delante de un nombre masculino singular)* good; **¡b. viaje!** have a good trip!; *ver* **bueno,-a**

buenamente *adv* **haz lo que b. puedas** just do what you can; **si b. puedes** if you possibly can

buenaventura *nf* good fortune, good luck; **echar la b. a algn** to tell sb's fortune

bueno,-a 1 *adj* (a) *good;* **un alumno muy b.** a very good pupil; **una buena película** a good film; **lo b.** the good thing

    (b) *(amable) (con* **ser)** *good, kind;* **el b. de Carlos** good old Carlos; **es muy buena persona** he's a very kind soul

    (c) *(sano) (con* **estar)** *well, in good health*

    (d) *(tiempo) good;* **hoy hace buen tiempo** it's fine today; **mañana hará b.** it will be fine o a nice day tomorrow

    (e) *(conveniente) good;* **no es b. comer tanto** it's not good for you to eat so much; **sería b. que vinieras** it would be a good idea if you came

    (f) *(considerable)* considerable; **un buen número de** a good number of; **una buena cantidad** a considerable amount

    (g) *(grande) good, big;* **un buen trozo de pastel** a nice o good big piece of cake

    (h) *Fam (atractivo)* gorgeous, sexy; **¡Rosa está muy buena!** Rosa's a bit of all right!; **una tía buena** a good-looking girl

    (i) *Irón* fine, real, proper; **¡en buen lío te has metido!** that's a fine mess you've got yourself into!

    (j) **¡buenas!** *(saludos)* hello!; **buenas tardes** *(desde mediodía hasta las cinco)* good afternoon; *(desde las cinco)* good evening; **buenas noches** *(al llegar)* good evening; *(al irse)* good night; **buenos días** good morning

    (k) *(locuciones)* **de buenas a primeras** suddenly, all at once; **estar de buenas** to be in a good mood; **los buenos tiempos** the good old days; **por las buenas** willingly; **por las buenas o por las malas** willy-nilly; **un susto de los buenos** a real fright; *Irón* **¡estaría b.!** I should jolly well hope not!; *Irón* **librarse de una buena** to get off scot free

buen is used instead of **bueno** before masculine singular nouns (e.g. **buen hombre** good man). The comparative form of **bueno** is **mejor** (better), and the superlative form is **el mejor** (masculine) or **la mejor** (feminine) (the best).

2 *interj* (a) *(vale)* all right, OK (b) *(expresa sorpresa)* hey! (c) *Col, Méx (al teléfono)* hello

buey *nm* ox, bullock

búfalo,-a *nm,f* buffalo

bufanda *nf* scarf

bufar *vi* (a) *(toro)* to snort; *(caballo)* to neigh (b) *(persona)* to be fuming

bufé *nm* buffet; **b. libre** self-service buffet meal

bufete *nm (despacho de abogado)* lawyer's office

buffet *nm (pl buffets)* = **bufé**

bufido *nm (de toro)* snort; *(de caballo)* neigh

bufón,-ona *nm,f* clown, buffoon

buhardilla *nf* attic, garret

búho *nm* owl; **b. real** eagle owl

buhonero,-a *nm,f* pedlar, hawker

buitre *nm* vulture

bujía *nf* (a) *Aut* spark plug (b) *Fís* candle-power

bulbo *nm* bulb

buldog *nm* bulldog

bulevar *nm* boulevard

Bulgaria *n* Bulgaria

búlgaro,-a *adj & nm,f* Bulgarian

bulín *nm RP Fam* bachelor pad

bulla *nf* (a) *(muchedumbre)* crowd, mob (b) *(ruido)* din; **armar b.** to kick up a din

bullicio *nm* din, hubbub

bullir *vi* (a) *(hervir)* to boil, to bubble (up) (b) **b. de gente** to be teeming with people

bulto *nm* (a) *(cosa indistinta)* shape, form (b) *(maleta, caja)* piece of luggage (c) *Med* lump (d) **hacer mucho b.** to be very bulky; *Fam* **escurrir el b.** to pass the buck

bumerán, bumerang *nm* boomerang

bungalow *nm* bungalow

búnker *nm* bunker

buñuelo *nm* doughnut

BUP *nm (abr Bachillerato Unificado Polivalente)* = academically orientated Spanish secondary school course for pupils aged 14-17

buque *nm* ship; **b. de guerra** warship; **b. de pasajeros** liner, passenger ship; **b. insignia** flagship

burbuja *nf* bubble; **hacer burbujas** to bubble, make bubbles

burbujear *vi* to bubble

burdel *nm* brothel

Burdeos *n* Bordeaux

burdo,-a *adj* coarse, rough

burgalés,-esa 1 *adj* of/from Burgos
2 *nm,f* person from Burgos

burgués,-esa *adj & nm,f* bourgeois

burguesía *nf* bourgeoisie

burla *nf* gibe, jeer; **hacer b. de algo/algn** to make fun of sth/sb; **hacer b. a algn** to stick one's tongue out at sb

burladero *nm Taurom* refuge in bullring

burlar 1 *vt* (a) *(engañar)* to deceive (b) *(eludir)* to dodge, to evade
2 burlarse *vpr* to make fun (**de** of), to laugh (**de** at)

burlón,-ona *adj* mocking

buró *nm* (a) *Pol* executive committee (b) *(escritorio)* bureau, desk (c) *Méx (mesa de noche)* bedside table

burocracia *nf* bureaucracy

burócrata *nmf* bureaucrat

burocrático,-a *adj* bureaucratic

buromática *nf* office automation

burrada *nf (comentario)* stupid o foolish remark; *(hecho)* stupid o foolish act

burro,-a 1 *nm,f* (a) *(animal)* donkey, ass; *Fam Fig* **bajarse del b.** to climb o back down (b) *Fam (estúpido)* dimwit, blockhead (c) **b. de carga** dogsbody, drudge
2 *adj Fam* (a) *(necio)* stupid, dumb (b) *(obstinado)* stubborn

bursátil *adj* stock-market

bus *nm* bus

busca *nf* search; **ir en b. de** to go in search of

buscapersonas *nm* pager

buscapleitos *nmf inv* troublemaker

buscar [44] 1 *vt* (a) to look o search for; **b. una palabra en el diccionario** to look up a word in the dictionary (b) **ir a b. algo** to go and get sth, to fetch sth; **fue a buscarme a la estación** she picked me up at the station
2 buscarse *vpr Fam* **b. la vida** to try and earn one's living; *Fam* **te la estás buscando** you're asking for it; **se busca** *(en anuncios)* wanted

buseta *nf Col, CRica, Ecuad, Ven* minibus

búsqueda *nf* search, quest; *Informát* search

busto *nm* bust

butaca *nf* (a) *(sillón)* armchair, easy chair (b) *Cin & Teatro* seat; **b. de platea** o **patio** seat in the stalls

butano *nm* butane; **(gas) b.** butane gas

butifarra *nf* sausage

buzo *nm* (a) *(persona)* diver (b) *Arg, Col (sudadera)* sweatshirt (c) *Col, Urug (jersey)* sweater, *Br* jumper

buzón *nm Br* letter box, *US* mailbox; *Informát (de correo electrónico)* (electronic) mailbox; **echar una carta al b.** to *Br* post *o US* mail a letter; **b. de voz** voice mail

byte *nm Informát* byte

C, c [θe] *nf (la letra)* C, c

C (a) *(abr* **Celsius)** C (b) *(abr* **centígrado)** C

c/ (a) *(abr* **calle)** St; Rd (b) *(abr* **cargo)** cargo, freight (c) *(abr* **cuenta)** a/c

C., Ca *(abr* **compañía)** Co

cabal 1 *adj* (a) *(exacto)* exact, precise (b) *(honesto)* honest, upright

2 *nmpl Fam* **no está en sus cabales** he's not in his right mind

cábala *nf Fig* **hacer cábalas sobre algo** to speculate about sth

cabalgadura *nf* mount

cabalgar [42] *vt & vi* to ride

cabalgata *nf* cavalcade; **la c. de los Reyes Magos** the procession of the Three Wise Men

caballa *nf* mackerel

caballar *adj* **ganado c.** horses

caballería *nf* (a) *(cabalgadura)* mount, steed (b) *Mil* cavalry

caballeriza *nf* stable

caballero *nm* (a) gentleman; **¿qué desea, c.?** can I help you, sir?; **ropa de c.** menswear (b) *Hist* knight (c) **caballeros** *(en letrero)* gents

caballeroso,-a *adj* gentlemanly, chivalrous

caballete *nm* (a) *(de pintor)* easel (b) *Téc* trestle (c) *(de nariz)* bridge

caballito *nm* (a) **c. de mar** seahorse (b) **caballitos** merry-go-round, *US* carousel

caballo *nm* (a) horse; **a c.** on horseback; **montar a c.** to ride; *Fig* **a c. entre ...** halfway between ... (b) *Téc* **c. de vapor** horse power (c) *(pieza de ajedrez)* knight (d) *Naipes* queen (e) *Fam (heroína)* horse, smack

cabaña *nf* cabin

cabaret *nm (pl* **cabarets)** cabaret

cabecear 1 *vi* to nod

2 *vt Dep* to head

cabecera *nf* (a) top, head (b) *Impr* headline

cabecilla *nmf* leader

cabellera *nf* head of hair

cabello *nm* (a) hair (b) *Culin* **c. de ángel** = sweet made of gourd and syrup

cabelludo,-a *adj* **cuero c.** scalp

caber [9] *vi* (a) to fit, to be (able to be) contained; **cabe en el maletero** it fits in the boot; **¿cabemos todos?** is there room for all of us?; **en este coche/jarro caben ...** this car/jug holds ...; **no cabe por la puerta** it won't go through the door; **no c. en sí de gozo** to be beside oneself with joy; **no me cabe en la cabeza** I can't understand it; **no cabe duda** there is no doubt; **cabe la posibilidad de que ...** there is a possibility *o* chance that ...; **no está mal dentro de lo que cabe** it isn't bad, under the circumstances

(b) **cabe señalar que ...** we should point out that ...

(c) *Mat* **doce entre cuatro caben a tres** four into twelve goes three (times)

cabestrillo *nm* sling

cabeza 1 *nf* head; **en c.** in the lead; **por c.** a head, per person; *Fig* **a la c. de** at the front *o* top of; *Fig* **estar mal de la c.** to be a mental case; **c. de turco** scapegoat; **el** *o* **la c. de familia** the head of the family

2 *nm* **c. rapada** skinhead

cabezada *nf* (a) *(golpe)* butt, blow on the head (b) *Fam* **echar una c.** to have a snooze; **dar cabezadas** to nod

cabezal *nm Téc* head; *(de tocadiscos)* pick-up

cabezota *Fam* **1** *adj* pigheaded

2 *nmf* pigheaded person

cabezudo *nm* = carnival figure with a huge head

cabida *nf* capacity; **dar c. a** to leave room for

cabildo *nm Rel* chapter

cabina *nf* cabin; **c. telefónica** telephone box, telephone booth

cabinera *nf Col* air hostess

cabizbajo,-a *adj* crestfallen

cable *nm* cable; *Fam* **echarle un c. a algn** to give sb a hand

cableoperador *nm* cable company, cable operator

cabo *nm* (a) *(extremo)* end; **al c. de** after; **de c. a rabo** from start to finish (b) *Mil* corporal; *(policía)* sergeant (c) *Náut* rope, cable; *Fig* **atar cabos** to put two and two together; *Fig* **no dejar ningún c.**

suelto to leave no loose ends (**d**) *Geog* cape; **Ciudad del C.** Cape Town; **C. Verde** Cape Verde

cabra *nf* goat; *Fam* **estar como una c.** to be off one's head

cabré *indic fut de* **caber**

cabreado,-a *adj muy Fam* pissed off

cabrear *muy Fam* **1** *vt* to make angry, *Br* to piss off

  2 cabrearse *vpr* to get *Br* pissed off *o US* pissed

cabreo *nm muy Fam* anger

cabrío,-a *adj* **macho c.** billy goat; **ganado c.** goats

cabriola *nf* skip

cabrito *nm Zool* kid

cabro,-a *nm,f Chile Fam* kid

cabrón,-ona *nm,f Vulg (hombre) Br* bastard, *US* asshole; *(woman)* bitch

cabronada *nf muy Fam* dirty trick

cabuya *nf* (**a**) *(planta)* agave (**b**) *(fibra)* fibre hemp (**c**) *CAm, Col, Ven (cuerda)* rope

caca *nf Fam* poopoo

cacahuete, *CAm, Méx* **cacahuate** *nm* peanut

cacao *nm* (**a**) *Bot* cacao (**b**) *(polvo, bebida)* cocoa (**c**) *Fam (lío)* mess

cacarear 1 *vi (gallina)* to cluck

  2 *vt Fig* to boast about

cacareo *nm* (**a**) *(de gallina)* clucking (**b**) *Fig* boasting, bragging

cacatúa *nf* cockatoo

cacereño,-a 1 *adj* of/from Cáceres

  2 *nm,f* person from Cáceres

cacería *nf* (**a**) *(actividad)* hunting, shooting (**b**) *(partida)* hunt, shoot

cacerola *nf* saucepan

cacha *nf Fam (muslo)* thigh; **estar cachas** to be really muscular

cachalote *nm* sperm whale

cacharro *nm* (**a**) *(earthenware)* pot *o* jar (**b**) *Fam (cosa)* thing, piece of junk (**c**) **cacharros** *(de cocina)* pots and pans

caché *nm Informát* **(memoria) c.** cache memory

cachear *vt* to frisk, to search

cachemir *nm*, **cachemira** *nf* cashmere

cacheo *nm* frisk, frisking

cachetada *nf Am* slap

cachete *nm* (**a**) *(bofetada)* slap (**b**) *Am (mejilla)* cheek

cachila *nf RP (automóvil)* vintage car

cachimba *nf* (**a**) *(pipa)* pipe (**b**) *RP (pozo)* well

cachiporra *nf* club, truncheon

cachivache *nm Fam* thing, knick-knack

cacho¹ *nm Fam (pedazo)* bit; piece; *Fig*

¡qué c. de animal! what a nasty piece of work!

cacho² *nm Andes, Ven (cuerno)* horn

cachondearse *vpr Fam* **c. de** to take the mickey out of

cachondeo *nm Fam* laugh; **tomar algo a c.** to take sth as a joke

cachondo,-a *adj Fam* (**a**) *(sexualmente)* randy (**b**) *(divertido)* funny

cachorro,-a *nm,f (de perro)* pup, puppy; *(de gato)* kitten; *(de otros animales)* cub, baby

cacique *nm (jefe)* local boss

caco *nm Fam* thief

cacofonía *nf* cacophony

cacto *nm*, **cactus** *nm inv Bot* cactus

cada *adj (de dos)* each; *(de varios)* each, every; **c. día** every day; **c. dos días** every second day; **c. vez más** more and more; **¿c. cuánto?** how often?; **c. dos por tres** every other minute; **cuatro de c. diez** four out of (every) ten; **¡tienes c. cosa!** you come up with some fine ideas!

cadalso *nm* scaffold

cadáver *nm (de persona)* corpse, (dead) body; *(de animal)* body, carcass; **ingresar c.** to be dead on arrival

cadena *nf* (**a**) chain; *(correa de perro)* lead, leash (**b**) *TV* channel (**c**) *Ind* line; **c. de montaje** assembly line; **trabajo en c.** assembly line work (**d**) *Geog* **c. montañosa** mountain range (**e**) *Jur* **c. perpetua** life imprisonment (**f**) *Aut* **cadenas** tyre chains

cadencia *nf* rhythm; *Mús* cadenza

cadera *nf* hip

cadete *nm* cadet; *RP (chico de los recados)* errand boy, office junior

caducar [**44**] *vi* to expire

caducidad *nf* expiry; **fecha de c.** *(en alimentos)* ≃ sell-by date; *(en medicinas)* to be used before

caduco,-a *adj* (**a**) *Bot* deciduous (**b**) *(anticuado)* out-of-date

caer [**39**] **1** *vi* to fall; **dejar c.** to drop; *Fig* **está al c.** *(llegar)* he'll arrive any minute now; *(ocurrir)* it's on the way

  (**b**) *(fecha)* to fall; **su cumpleaños cae en sábado** his birthday falls on a Saturday

  (**c**) *(entender)* to understand, to see; **ya caigo** I get it; **no caí** I didn't twig

  (**d**) *(hallarse)* to be; **cae por Granada** it is somewhere near Granada

  (**e**) **me cae bien/mal** I like/don't like her

  (**f**) **al c. el día** in the evening; **al c. la noche** at nightfall

  2 caerse *vpr* to fall (down); **me caí de la moto** I fell off the motorbike; **se le ha cayó**

el pañuelo she dropped her handkerchief

café *nm* (a) coffee; **c. solo/con leche** black/white coffee (b) *(cafetería)* café

cafeína *nf* caffeine

cafetal *nm* coffee plantation

cafetera *nf* coffee-maker

cafetería *nf* snack bar, coffee bar; *Ferroc* buffet car

cafetero,-a *adj* (a) coffee (b) *Fam* **es muy c.** *(persona)* he loves coffee

cafiche *nm Andes Fam (proxeneta)* pimp

cafre *nmf* savage, beast

cagado,-a *adj muy Fam (cobarde)* coward; **estar c. de miedo** to be shit-scared

cagar [42] *muy Fam* **1** *vi* (a) to (have a) shit (b) *(estropear)* to ruin, to spoil; **cagarla** to cock it up

2 cagarse *vpr* to shit oneself; **c. de miedo** to be shit-scared; **¡me cago en diez!** *Br* bloody hell!, *US* goddamn it!

caída *nf* (a) fall; *(de pelo, diente)* loss (b) *(de precios)* drop (c) *Pol* downfall, collapse

caído,-a 1 *adj* fallen

2 *nmpl* **los caídos** the fallen

caigo *indic pres de* **caer**

caimán *nm* alligator

Cairo *n* **El C.** Cairo

caja *nf* (a) box; **c. fuerte** safe; *Fam TV* **la c. tonta** the idiot box (b) *(de leche etc)* carton (c) *(de embalaje)* crate, case; **una c. de cerveza** a crate of beer (d) *Fin (en tienda)* cash desk; *(en banco)* cashier's desk (e) *Aut* **c. de cambios** gearbox (f) *Com* **c. de ahorros o de pensiones** savings bank (g) *(féretro)* coffin

cajero,-a *nm,f* cashier; **c. automático** cash point, cash dispenser

cajetilla *nf* packet, pack

cajón *nm* (a) *(en un mueble)* drawer; *Fig* **c. de sastre** jumble; *Fam* **de c.** obvious, self-evident (b) *(caja grande)* crate, chest

cajuela *nf CAm, Méx (maletero) Br* boot, *US* trunk

cal¹ *nf* lime; *Fig* **a c. y canto** hermetically; *Fam* **una de c. y otra de arena** six of one and half a dozen of the other

cal² *(abr* **caloría(s))** cal

cala *nf* (a) *Geog* creek, cove (b) *Náut* hold

calabacín *nm Bot* (a) *(pequeño) Br* courgette, *US* zucchini (b) *(grande) Br* marrow, *US* squash

calabaza *nf* pumpkin, gourd

calabobos *nm inv Fam* drizzle

calabozo *nm* (a) *(prisión)* jail, prison (b) *(celda)* cell

calada *nf Fam (de cigarrillo)* drag, puff

calado,-a 1 *adj* soaked

2 *nm Náut* draught

calamar *nm* squid *inv*; *Culin* **calamares a la romana** squid fried in batter

calambre *nm* (a) *Elec (descarga)* electric shock; **ese cable da c.** that wire is live (b) *(en músculo)* cramp

calamidad *nf* calamity

calaña *nf* kind, sort; **una persona de mala c.** a bad sort

calar 1 *vt* (a) *(mojar)* to soak, to drench (b) *(agujerear)* to pierce, to penetrate (c) *Fam (a alguien)* to rumble; **¡te hemos calado!** we've got your number!

2 *vi* (a) *(prenda)* to let in water (b) *Náut* to draw

3 calarse *vpr* (a) *(prenda, techo)* to let in water; *(mojarse)* to get soaked (b) *(el sombrero)* to pull down (c) *Aut* to stall

calavera 1 *nf* (a) *(cráneo)* skull (b) *Méx Aut* **calaveras** tail lights

2 *nm* tearaway

calcar [44] *vt* (a) *(un dibujo)* to trace (b) *Fig (imitar)* to copy, to imitate

calceta *nf* (a) *(prenda)* stocking (b) **hacer c.** to knit

calcetín *nm* sock

calcinar *vt* to burn

calcio *nm* calcium

calco *nm* tracing; **papel de c.** carbon paper

calcomanía *nf* transfer

calculadora *nf* calculator

calcular *vt* (a) *Mat* to calculate (b) *(evaluar)* to (make an) estimate (c) *(suponer)* to figure, to guess

cálculo *nm* (a) calculation; **según mis cálculos** by my reckoning (b) *Med* gallstone (c) *Mat* calculus

caldear *vt* to heat up

caldera *nf* (a) *(industrial)* boiler; *(olla)* cauldron (b) *Urug (hervidor)* kettle

caldereta *nf* stew

calderilla *nf* small change

caldo *nm* stock, broth; **c. de cultivo** culture medium; *Fig* breeding ground

calé *adj & nm* gypsy

calefacción *nf* heating; **c. central** central heating

calefaccionar *vt CSur (calentar)* to heat (up), to warm (up)

calefactor *nm* heater

calefón *nm CSur (calentador)* water heater

caleidoscopio *nm* kaleidoscope

calendario *nm* calendar

calentador *nm* heater

calentamiento *nm Dep* warm-up

calentar [1] *vt* (a) *(agua, horno)* to heat; *(comida, habitación)* to warm up; *Fig* **no me calientes la cabeza** don't bug me (b) *Fam (pegar)* to smack (c) *Fam (excitar)* to arouse (sexually), to turn on

2 calentarse *vpr* (a) to get hot *o* warm, to heat up (b) *Fig* **se calentaron los ánimos** people became very excited

calentón,-ona, calentorro,-a *adj Fam* randy

calentura *nf* fever, temperature

calesita *nf RP* merry-go-round, carousel

calibrar *vt* to gauge, to bore

calibre *nm* (a) *(de arma)* calibre (b) *Fig (importancia)* importance

calidad *nf* (a) quality; **de primera c.** first-class; **un vino de c.** good-quality wine (b) **en c. de as**

cálido,-a *adj* warm; **una cálida acogida** a warm welcome

calidoscopio *nm* = **caleidoscopio**

caliente *adj* (a) hot (b) *Fig (debate)* heated; **en c.** in the heat of the moment (c) *Fam (cachondo)* hot, randy

calificación *nf* (a) qualification (b) *Educ* mark

calificar [44] *vt* (a) to describe (**de** as); **le calificó de inmoral** he called him immoral (b) *(examen)* to mark, to grade

calificativo *nm* epithet

caligrafía *nf* calligraphy; *(modo de escribir)* handwriting

calima *nf* haze, mist

calimocho *nm* = drink made with wine and Coca-Cola®

calina *nf* = **calima**

cáliz *nm* chalice

caliza *nf* limestone

calizo,-a *adj* lime

callado,-a *adj* quiet; **te lo tenías muy c.** you were keeping that quiet

callar 1 *vi* (a) *(dejar de hablar)* to stop talking; **¡calla!** be quiet!, *Fam* shut up! (b) *(no hablar)* to keep quiet, to say nothing

2 *vt (noticia)* not to mention, to keep to oneself

3 •callarse *vpr* to stop talking, to be quiet; **¡cállate!** shut up!

calle *nf* (a) street, road; **c. de dirección única** one-way street; **c. mayor** *Br* high street, *US* main street; **el hombre de la c.** the man in the street (b) *Dep* lane

calleja *nf* narrow street

callejero,-a 1 *nm (mapa)* street directory

2 *adj* street; **gato c.** alley cat

callejón *nm* back alley *o* street; **c. sin salida** cul-de-sac, dead end

callejuela *nf* narrow street, lane

callista *nmf* chiropodist

callo *nm* (a) *Med* callus, corn; *Fam* **dar el c.** to slog (b) *Culin* **callos** tripe

calma *nf* (a) calm; **¡c.!** calm down!; **en c.** calm; **tómatelo con c.** take it easy (b) *Met* calm weather; **c. chicha** dead calm

calmante *nm* painkiller

calmar 1 *vt (persona)* to calm (down); *(dolor)* to soothe, to relieve

2 calmarse *vpr* (a) *(persona)* to calm down (b) *(dolor, viento)* to ease off

caló *nm* gypsy dialect

calor *nm* (a) heat; **hace c.** it's hot; **tengo c.** I'm hot; **entrar en c.** to warm up (b) *Fig (afecto)* warmth

caloría *nf* calorie

calote *nm RP Fam* swindle

calumnia *nf* (a) calumny (b) *Jur* slander

calumniar [43] *vt* (a) to calumniate (b) *Jur* to slander

caluroso,-a *adj* hot; *(acogida etc)* warm

calva *nf* bald patch

calvicie *nf* baldness

calvinismo *nm* Calvinism

calvo,-a 1 *adj* bald; **ni tanto ni tan c.** neither one extreme nor the other

2 *nm* bald man

calza *nf* wedge

calzada *nf* road, carriageway

calzado *nm* shoes, footwear

calzador *nm* shoehorn

calzar [40] 1 *vt* (a) *(poner calzado)* to put shoes on; **¿qué número calzas?** what size do you take? (b) *(mueble)* to wedge

2 calzarse *vpr* **c. los zapatos** to put on one's shoes

calzón *nm* (a) *Dep* shorts (b) *Andes, RP* **calzones** *(bragas)* panties, *Br* knickers (c) *Méx* **calzones** *(calzoncillos)* underpants

calzonazos *nm inv Fam* henpecked husband

calzoncillos *nmpl* underpants, pants

calzoneta *nm CAm* swimming trunks

cama *nf* bed; **estar en** *o* **guardar c.** to be confined to bed; **hacer la c.** to make the bed; **irse a la c.** to go to bed; **c. doble/sencilla** double/single bed; **c. turca** couch

camada *nf* litter; *(de pájaros)* brood

camafeo *nm* cameo

camaleón *nm* chameleon

cámara 1 *nf* (a) *(aparato)* camera; **a c. lenta** in slow motion (b) *Pol* Chamber, House; **C. Alta/Baja** Upper/Lower House (c) *Aut* inner tube (d) *(habitación)* room, chamber; **c. de gas** gas chamber; **c. frigorífica** cold-storage room; **música de c.** chamber music

2 *nmf* *(hombre)* cameraman; *(mujer)* camerawoman

camarada *nmf* comrade

camaradería *nf* camaraderie

camarera *nf* *(de hotel)* chambermaid

camarero,-a *nm,f* **(a)** *(de restaurante)* *(hombre)* waiter; *(mujer)* waitress; *(trás la barra)* *(hombre)* barman; *(mujer)* barmaid **(b)** *(de avión)* *(hombre)* steward; *(mujer)* stewardess

camarilla *nf* clique

camarón *nm* (common) prawn

camarote *nm* cabin

camba *Bol Fam* **1** *adj* of/from the forested lowland region of Bolivia

2 *nmf* person from the forested lowland region of Bolivia

cambalache *nm RP (tienda)* junk shop

cambiante *adj* changing; *(carácter)* changeable

cambiar **[43]** **1** *vt* **(a)** to change; **c. algo de sitio** to move sth **(b)** *(intercambiar)* to swap, to exchange **(c)** *(dinero)* to change

2 *vi* to change; **c. de casa** to move (house); **c. de idea** to change one's mind; **c. de trabajo** to get another job; **c. de velocidad** to change gear

3 **cambiarse** *vpr* **(a)** *(de ropa)* to change (clothes) **(b)** *(de casa)* to move (house)

cambiazo *nm Fam* switch

cambio *nm* **(a)** *(cambio)*; *(de impresiones)* exchange; **c. de planes** change of plans; **un c. en la opinión pública** a shift in public opinion; *Fig* **a c. de** in exchange for; **en c.** on the other hand **(b)** *(dinero)* change; **¿tienes c. de mil pesetas?** have you got change for a thousand pesetas? **(c)** *Fin (de divisas)* exchange; *(de acciones)* price **(d)** *Aut* gear change; **c. automático** automatic transmission

cambista *nmf* moneychanger

Camboya *n* Cambodia

cambur *nm Ven (plátano)* banana

camelar *vt*, **camelarse** *vpr Fam* **(a)** to cajole **(b)** *(galantear)* to win over

camelia *nf* camellia

camello,-a 1 *nm,f* camel

2 *nm Fam (traficante de drogas)* (drug) pusher

camellón *nm Col, Méx (en avenida)* Br central reservation, *US* median (strip)

camelo *nm Fam* **(a)** *(engaño)* hoax **(b)** *(trola)* cock-and-bull story

camerino *nm* dressing room

Camerún *n* Cameroon

camilla *nf* **(a)** stretcher **(b)** **mesa c.** = small round table under which a heater is placed

caminante *nmf* walker

caminar 1 *vi* to walk

2 *vt* to cover, to travel; **caminaron 10 km** they walked for 10 km

caminata *nf* long walk

camino *nm* **(a)** *(ruta)* route, way; **ir c. de** to be going to; **ponerse en c.** to set off; *Fig* **ir por buen/mal c.** to be on the right/wrong track; **abrirse c.** to break through; **a medio c.** half-way; **en el c.** o **de c.** a on the way to; **estar en c.** to be on the way; **nos coge** o **pilla de c.** it is on the way **(b)** *(vía)* path, track **(c)** *(modo)* way

camión *nm* **(a)** truck, *Br* lorry; **c. cisterna** tanker; **c. de la basura** *Br* dustcart, *US* garbage truck; **c. frigorífico** refrigerated truck **(b)** *CAm, Méx (autobús)* bus

camionero,-a *nm,f* truck o *Br* lorry driver

camioneta *nf* van

camisa *nf* shirt; **en mangas de c.** in one's shirtsleeves; *Fig* **cambiar de c.** to change sides; **c. de fuerza** straightjacket

camiseta *nf* **(a)** *(de uso interior)* *Br* vest, *US* undershirt **(b)** *(de uso exterior)* T-shirt **(c)** *Dep* shirt; **sudar la c.** to run oneself into the ground

camisón *nm* nightdress, *Fam* nightie

camomila *nf* camomile

camorra *nf Fam* trouble

camorrista 1 *adj* quarrelsome, rowdy

2 *nmf* troublemaker

camote *nm Andes, CAm, Méx (batata)* sweet potato

campal *adj* **batalla c.** pitched battle

campamento *nm* camp

campana *nf* bell; **pantalones de campana** bell-bottom trousers

campanada *nf* peal o ring of a bell

campanario *nm* belfry, bell tower

campanilla *nf* **(a)** small bell **(b)** *Anat* uvula **(c)** *Bot* bell flower

campante *adj Fam* **se quedó tan c.** he didn't bat an eyelid

campaña *nf* **(a)** campaign; **c. electoral** election campaign; **c. publicitaria** advertising campaign **(b)** *Mil* campaign; **hospital/ambulancia de c.** field hospital/ambulance **(c)** *RP (campo)* countryside

campar *vi Fam* **c. por sus respetos** to do as one pleases

campechano,-a *adj* unpretentious

campeón,-ona *nm,f* champion; **c. mundial** world champion

campeonato *nm* championship; **un tonto de c.** an utter idiot

campera *nf* **(a)** **camperas** *(botas)* cowboy boots **(b)** *RP (chaqueta)* jacket

campero,-a adj country, rural; **(botas) camperas** leather boots

campesino,-a nm,f (hombre) country-man; (mujer) countrywoman

campestre adj rural

camping nm campsite; **hacer** o **ir de c.** to go camping

campiña nf open country

campista nmf camper

campo nm (a) country, countryside; **a c. traviesa** o **través** cross-country; **trabaja (en) el c.** he works (on) the land; **trabajo de c.** fieldwork (b) (parcela) field (c) Fís & Fot field (d) (ámbito) field; **c. de acción** field of action; Mil **c. de batalla** battle-field; **c. de concentración** concentration camp; **c. de trabajo** work camp (e) Dep field; (de fútbol) pitch; (de golf) course (f) RP (hacienda) farm (g) Andes (sitio) room, space

camposanto nm cemetery

camuflaje nm camouflage

camuflar vt to camouflage

cana nf (gris) grey hair; (blanco) white hair; **tener canas** to have grey hair; Fam **echar una c. al aire** to let one's hair down

Canadá n Canada

canadiense adj & nmf Canadian

canal nf (a) (artificial) canal; (natural) channel; **C. de la Mancha** English Chan-nel (b) TV, Elec & Informát channel

canalizar [40] vt to channel

canalla 1 nm swine, rotter
2 nf riffraff, mob

canallesco,-a adj rotten, despicable

canalón nm gutter

canapé nm (a) Culin canapé (b) (sofá) couch, sofa

canario,-a 1 adj & nm,f Canarian; **Islas Canarias** Canary Islands, Canaries
2 nm Orn canary

canasta nf basket

canastilla nf small basket; (de un bebé) layette

canasto nm big basket, hamper

cancán nm frilly petticoat; RP **cancanes** (leotardos) Br tights, US pantyhose

cancela nf wrought-iron gate

cancelación nf cancellation

cancelar vt (a) (acto etc) to cancel (b) (deuda) to pay off (c) Chile, Ven (compra) to pay for

cáncer nm cancer; **c. de pulmón/mama** lung/breast cancer

cancerbero,-a nm,f Ftb goalkeeper

cancerígeno,-a adj carcinogenic

canceroso,-a adj cancerous

cancha nf ground; Ten court

canchero,-a adj RP Fam (desenvuelto) streetwise, savvy

canciller nm chancellor

cancillería nf Am foreign ministry

canción nf song

candado nm padlock

candela nf fire

candelabro nm candelabrum

candelero nm candlestick; Fig **en el c.** at the top

candente adj red-hot; Fig **tema c.** topical issue

candidato,-a nm,f candidate; (a un pues-to) applicant

candidatura nf (a) (lista) list of candid-ates (b) **presentar su c.** to submit one's application

candidez nf candour

cándido,-a adj ingenuous, naive

> 🖉 Observa que la palabra inglesa **candid** es un falso amigo y no es la traducción de la palabra española **cándido**. En inglés, **candid** significa "franco, sincero".

candil nm oil lamp; Méx (candelabro) chandelier

candilejas nfpl Teatro footlights

candor nm innocence, naivety

> 🖉 Observa que la palabra inglesa **candour** es un falso amigo y no es la traducción de la palabra española **candor**. En inglés, **candour** significa "sinceridad, franqueza".

candoroso,-a adj innocent, pure

canela nf cinnamon

canelones nmpl cannelloni

cangrejo nm (de mar) crab; (de río) fresh-water crayfish

canguro 1 nm kangaroo
2 nmf Fam baby-sitter

caníbal adj & nmf cannibal

canica nf marble

caniche nm poodle

canícula nf dog days, midsummer heat

canijo,-a adj Fam puny, weak

canilla nf (a) Fam (espinilla) shinbone (b) RP (grifo) Br tap, US faucet

canillera nf Am (cobardía) cowardice; (miedo) fear

canillita nm Andes, RP newspaper ven-dor

canino,-a 1 adj canine; Fam **tener un hambre canina** to be starving
2 nm (colmillo) canine

canjear vt to exchange

cano,-a adj (blanco) white; (gris) grey

canoa nf canoe

canódromo nm dog o greyhound track

canon nm (a) canon, norm (b) Mús & Rel canon (c) Com royalty

canónigo nm canon

canonizar [40] vt to canonize

canoso,-a adj (de pelo blanco) white-haired; (de pelo gris) grey-haired; (pelo) white, grey

cansado,-a adj (a) (agotado) tired, weary; **estar c.** to be tired (b) **ser c.** (pesado) to be boring o tiresome

cansador,-a adj Andes, RP (que cansa) tiring; (que aburre) boring

cansancio nm tiredness, weariness; Fam **estoy muerto de c.** I'm on my last legs

cansar 1 vt to tire

2 vi to be tiring

3 cansarse vpr to get tired; **se cansó de esperar** he got fed up (with) waiting

Cantabria n Cantabria

cantábrico,-a adj Cantabrian; **Mar C.** Bay of Biscay

cántabro,-a adj & nm,f Cantabrian

cantaleta nf Am **la misma c.** the same old story

cantante 1 nmf singer

2 adj singing; **llevar la voz c.** to rule the roost

cantaor,-a nm,f flamenco singer

cantar[1] vt & vi (a) Mús to sing; Fig **en menos que canta un gallo** in a flash (b) Fam (confesar) to sing, to spill the beans (c) Fam (oler mal) to hum

cantar[2] nm Literario song; Fam **¡eso es otro c.!** that's a totally different thing!

cantarín,-ina adj (voz) singsong

cántaro nm pitcher; Fig **llover a cántaros** to rain cats and dogs

cante nm (a) (canto) singing; **c. hondo, c. jondo** flamenco (b) Fam **dar el c.** to attract attention

cantegril nm Urug shanty town

cantera nf (a) (de piedra) quarry (b) Fig Ftb young players

cantero nm (a) (masón) stonemason (b) Cuba, RP (parterre) flowerbed

cantidad 1 nf quantity; (de dinero) amount, sum; **en c.** a lot; Fam **c. de gente** thousands of people

2 adv Fam a lot; **me gusta c.** I love it

cantimplora nf water bottle

cantina nf canteen

cantinero,-a nm,f bar attendant

canto[1] nm (a) (arte) singing (b) (canción) song

canto[2] nm (borde) edge; **de c.** on its side

canto[3] nm (guijarro) pebble, stone; **c. rodado** (grande) boulder; (pequeño) pebble

cantor,-a 1 adj singing; **pájaro c.** songbird

2 nm,f singer

canturrear vi to hum, to croon

canutas nfpl Fam **pasarlas c.** to have a hard time

canuto nm (a) (tubo) tube (b) Fam (porro) joint

caña nf (a) (vaso) glass; (de cerveza) glass of beer (b) Bot reed; (tallo) cane, stem; **c. de azúcar** sugar cane (c) (de pescar) rod (d) Fam **darle c. al coche** to go at full speed (e) Andes, Cuba, RP (aguardiente) cane spirit, cheap rum

cañada nf gully, ravine

cáñamo nm hemp

cañería nf (piece of) piping; **cañerías** plumbing

cañero,-a nm,f Am (trabajador) = worker on sugar plantation

cañí adj & nmf (pl **cañís**) Fam gypsy

caño nm (tubo) tube; (tubería) pipe

cañón nm (a) Mil cannon; Fig **estar siempre al pie del c.** to be always ready for a fight (b) (de fusil) barrel (c) Geog canyon

cañonazo nm gunshot

caoba nf mahogany

caos nm chaos

caótico,-a adj chaotic

cap. (abr **capítulo**) ch

capa nf (a) (prenda) cloak, cape; **de c. caída** low-spirited (b) (de pintura) layer, coat; Culin coating (c) Geol stratum, layer

capacidad nf (a) (cabida) capacity (b) (aptitud) capacity, ability

capacitación nf qualification

capacitar vt (autorizar) to authorize

capar vt to castrate

caparazón nm shell

capataz,-a nm,f (hombre) foreman; (mujer) forewoman

capaz adj (a) capable, able; **ser c. de hacer algo** (tener la habilidad de) to be able to do sth; (atreverse a) to dare to do sth; **si se entera es c. de despedirle** if he finds out, he could quite easily sack him (b) Am **es c. que** it is likely that

capcioso,-a adj captious; **pregunta capciosa** catch question

capea nf amateur bullfight

capear vt (dificultad etc) to dodge, to shirk; Fig **c. el temporal** to weather the storm

capellán nm chaplain

caperuza nf hood

capicúa adj **número c.** reversible number; **palabra c.** palindrome

capilar *adj* hair; **loción c.** hair lotion

capilla *nf* chapel; **c. ardiente** chapel of rest

capirote *nm Fam* **tonto de c.** silly idiot

capital 1 *nf* capital

  2 *nm Fin* capital; **c. activo** *o* **social** working *o* share capital

  3 *adj* capital, main; **de importancia c.** of capital importance; **pena c.** capital punishment

capitalismo *nm* capitalism

capitalista *adj & nmf* capitalist

capitalizar [40] *vt* to capitalize

capitán,-ana *nm,f* captain; **c. general** *Br* field marshal, *US* general of the army

capitanear *vt* (a) *Mil & Náut* to captain, to command (b) *(dirigir)* to lead; *Dep* to captain

capitulación *nf* agreement; *Mil* capitulation; **capitulaciones matrimoniales** marriage settlement

capitular *vi* (a) *Mil* to capitulate, to surrender (b) *(convenir)* to reach an agreement

capítulo *nm* (a) *(de libro)* chapter (b) *Fig* **dentro del c. de ...** *(tema)* under the heading of ...

capó *nm Aut Br* bonnet, *US* hood

capón *nm* rap on the head with the knuckles

capota *nf Aut* folding hood *o* top

capote *nm* (a) *Taurom* cape (b) *Mil* greatcoat

capricho *nm* (a) *(antojo)* whim, caprice (b) *Mús* caprice, capriccio

caprichoso,-a *adj* whimsical

Capricornio *nm* Capricorn

cápsula *nf* capsule

captar *vt* (a) *(ondas)* to receive, to pick up (b) *(comprender)* to understand, to grasp (c) *(interés etc)* to attract

captura *nf* capture

capturar *vt (criminal)* to capture; *(cazar, pescar)* to catch; *Mil* to seize

capucha *nf* hood

capuchino *nm (café)* cappuccino

capullo *nm* (a) *(de insecto)* cocoon (b) *Bot* bud (c) *Vulg (prepucio)* foreskin (d) *muy Fam (persona despreciable) Br* dickhead, *US* jerk

caqui 1 *adj (color)* khaki

  2 *nm (fruto)* persimmon

cara 1 *nf* (a) face; **c. a c.** face to face; **c. a la pared** facing the wall; **poner mala c.** to pull a long face; **tener buena/mala c.** to look good/bad; *Fig* **c. de circunstancias** serious look; *Fig* **dar la c.** to face the consequences (of one's acts); *Fig* **dar la**
c. por algn to stand up for sb; *Fig* **(de) c. a** with a view to; *Fig* **echarle a algn algo en c.** to reproach sb for sth; *Fig* **plantar c. a algn** to face up to sb

  (b) *(lado)* side; *(de moneda)* right side; **¿c. o cruz?** heads or tails?; **echar algo a c. o cruz** to toss (a coin) for sth

  (c) *Fam (desfachatez)* cheek, nerve; **¡qué c. (más dura) tienes!** what a cheek you've got!

  2 *nm Fam (desvergonzado)* cheeky person

carabela *nf* caravel

carabina *nf* (a) *(arma)* carbine, rifle (b) *(persona)* chaperon

carabinero *nm* (a) *(marisco)* scarlet shrimp, = type of large red prawn (b) *Chile (policía)* military policeman

caracense 1 *adj* of/from Guadalajara

  2 *nmf* person from Guadalajara

caracol 1 *nm* (a) *(de tierra)* snail; *Am* shell (b) *(rizo)* kiss-curl

  2 *interj* **¡caracoles!** good heavens!

caracola *nf* conch

carácter *nm (pl* **caracteres)** (a) *(temperamento)* character; **de mucho c.** with a strong character; **tener buen/mal c.** to be good-natured/bad-tempered (b) *Fig (índole)* nature; **con c. de invitado** as a guest (c) *Impr* character

característica *nf* characteristic

característico,-a *adj* characteristic

caracterizar [40] *vt* to characterize

caradura *nmf Fam* cheeky devil; **¡qué c. eres!** you're so cheeky!

carajillo *nm Fam* = coffee with a dash of brandy

carajo *interj Vulg* shit!; **¡vete al c.!** go to hell!

caramba *interj Fam (sorpresa)* good grief!; *(enfado)* damn it!

carámbano *nm* icicle

carambola *nf Br* cannon, *US* carom

caramelo *nm* (a) *(dulce) Br* (boiled) sweet, *US* candy (b) *(azúcar quemado)* caramel; *Culin* **a punto de c.** syrupy

carantoña *nf* caress

caraota *nf Ven* bean

caraqueño,-a 1 *adj* of/from Caracas

  2 *nm,f* person from Caracas

carátula *nf* (a) *(cubierta)* cover (b) *(máscara)* mask

caravana *nf* (a) *(vehículo)* caravan (b) *(de tráfico) Br* tailback, *US* backup (c) *Urug (aro, pendiente)* earring

caray *interj* God!, good heavens!

carbón *nm* coal; **c. vegetal** charcoal; **c. mineral** coal

carboncillo *nm* charcoal

carbonero *nm* coal merchant

carbónico,-a *adj* carbonic; **agua carbónica** mineral water

carbonilla *nf* coal dust

carbonizar [40] 1 *vt* to carbonize, to char; **morir carbonizado** to be burnt to death

2 carbonizarse *upr* to carbonize, to char

carbono *nm* carbon

carburador *nm* carburettor

carburante *nm* fuel

carburar *vi Fam (funcionar)* to work properly

carca *adj & nmf Fam* old fogey; *Pol* reactionary

carcaj *nm* quiver

carcajada *nf* guffaw

carcamal *nm Fam* old fogey

cárcel *nf* prison, jail

carcelario,-a *adj* prison, jail

carcelero,-a *nm,f* jailer, warder

carcoma *nf* woodworm

carcomer 1 *vt* to eat away

2 carcomerse *upr* to be consumed (**de** with)

cardar *vt* (a) *(lana, algodón)* to card (b) *(pelo)* to backcomb

cardenal *nm* (a) *Rel* cardinal (b) *Med* bruise

cárdeno,-a *adj* purple

cardíaco,-a, cardiaco,-a 1 *adj* cardiac, heart; **ataque c.** heart attack

2 *nm,f* person with a heart condition

cardinal *adj* cardinal; **punto/número c.** cardinal point/number

cardiólogo,-a *nm,f* cardiologist

cardo *nm (con espinas)* thistle

carear *vt* (a) *Jur* to bring two people face to face (b) *(cotejar)* to compare

carecer [33] *vi* **c. de** to lack

carencia *nf* lack (**de** of)

carente *adj* lacking; **c. de interés** lacking interest

careo *nm Jur* confrontation

carestía *nf* (a) *(falta)* lack, shortage (b) *Fin* high price *o* cost

careta *nf* mask; **c. antigás** gas mask

carey *nm* tortoiseshell

carezco *indic pres de* **carecer**

carga *nf* (a) *(acción)* loading (b) *(cosa cargada)* load; *(de avión, barco)* cargo, freight; *Fig* **c. afectiva** emotional content (c) *Fin (gasto)* debit; **c. fiscal** tax charge (d) *Fig (obligación)* burden (e) *Mil & Elec* charge

cargado,-a *adj* (a) loaded (b) *(bebida)* strong; **un café c.** a strong coffee (c)

(ambiente) heavy; **atmósfera cargada** stuffy atmosphere (d) *Fig* burdened; **c. de deudas** up to one's eyes in debt (e) *Elec* charged

cargamento *nm* (a) *(carga)* load (b) *(mercancías)* cargo, freight

cargante *adj Fam* annoying

cargar [42] 1 *vt* (a) to load; *(mechero, pluma)* to fill; *(batería)* to charge; *Fig* **c. las culpas a algn** to put the blame on sb (b) *Com* to charge; **cárguelo a mi cuenta** charge it to my account; *Fam Educ* **me han cargado las matemáticas** I failed maths

2 *vi* (a) **c. con** *(llevar)* to carry; *Fig* **c. con la responsabilidad** to take the responsibility; *Fig* **c. con las consecuencias** to suffer the consequences (b) *Mil* **c. contra** to charge

3 cargarse *upr* (a) *Fam* **te la vas a c.** you're asking for trouble and you're going to get it (b) *Fam (estropear)* to smash, to ruin (c) *Fam (matar)* to kill, to bump off

cargo *nm* (a) *(puesto)* post, position; **alto c.** *(puesto)* top job, high ranking position; *(persona)* top person (b) **estar al c. de** to be in charge of; **correr a c. de** *(gastos)* to be met by; **hacerse c. de** to take charge of; **hazte c. de mi situación** please try to understand my situation; **c. de conciencia** weight on one's conscience (c) *Fin* charge, debit; **con c. a mi cuenta** charged to my account (d) *Jur* charge, accusation

cargosear *vt CSur* to annoy, to pester

cargoso,-a *adj CSur* annoying

carguero *nm* (a) *(avión)* transport plane (b) *(barco)* freighter

cariarse *upr* to decay

caribe *nm (idioma)* Carib; **el (mar) C.** the Caribbean Sea

caricatura *nf* caricature

caricaturizar [40] *vt* to caricature

caricia *nf* caress, stroke

caridad *nf* charity

caries *nf inv* decay, caries

carilla *nf* page, side of a piece of paper

cariño *nm* (a) *(amor)* affection; **coger/ tener c. a algo/algn** to grow/to be fond of sth/sb; **con c.** *(en carta)* love (b) *(querido)* darling (c) *(abrazo)* cuddle

cariñoso,-a *adj* loving, affectionate

carisma *nm* charisma

carismático,-a *adj* charismatic

caritativo,-a *adj* charitable

cariz *nm* look

carmesí *adj & nm* crimson

carmín *nm (de color)* **c.** carmine; **c. (de labios)** lipstick

carnal *adj* (**a**) *(de carne)* carnal (**b**) *(pariente)* first; **primo c.** first cousin

carnaval *nm* carnival

carne *nf* (**a**) flesh; *Fam* **ser de c. y hueso** to be only human; *Fig* **c. de cañón** cannon fodder; **c. de gallina** goosepimples; **c. viva** raw flesh (**b**) *(alimento)* meat; **c. de cerdo/cordero/ternera/vaca** pork/lamb/veal/beef (**c**) *(de fruta)* pulp

carné *nm* card; **c. de conducir** *Br* driving licence, *US* driver's license; **c. de identidad** identity card

carnear *vt Andes, RP (sacrificar)* to slaughter, to butcher

carnero *nm* ram; *Culin* mutton

carnet *nm* = **carné**

carnicería *nf* (**a**) butcher's (shop) (**b**) *Fig (masacre)* slaughter

carnicero,-a *nm,f* butcher

cárnico,-a *adj* **productos cárnicos** meat products

carnitas *nfpl Méx* = small pieces of fried or grilled pork

carnívoro,-a 1 *adj* carnivorous
2 *nm,f* carnivore

carnoso,-a *adj* fleshy

caro,-a 1 *adj* expensive, dear
2 *adv* **salir c.** to cost a lot; **te costará c.** *(amenaza)* you'll pay dearly for this

carozo *nm RP (de fruta, aceituna)* stone, *US* pit

carpa *nf* (**a**) *(pez)* carp (**b**) *(de circo)* big top; *(en parque, la calle)* marquee (**c**) *Am (de camping)* tent

Cárpatos *nmpl* Carpathians

carpeta *nf* file, folder

> *Observa que la palabra inglesa **carpet** es un falso amigo y no es la traducción de la palabra española **carpeta**. En inglés, **carpet** significa "alfombra".*

carpetazo *nm* **dar c. a un asunto** to shelve a matter

carpintería *nf* (**a**) *(oficio)* carpentry; **c. metálica** metalwork (**b**) *(taller)* carpenter's (shop)

carpintero,-a *nm,f* carpenter

carraca *nf* rattle

carraspear *vi* to clear one's throat

carraspeo *nm* clearing of the throat

carraspera *nf* hoarseness

carrera *nf* (**a**) run; *(de media)* run, ladder; **a la c.** in a hurry (**b**) *(competición)* race; **c. contra reloj** race against the clock; **c. de coches** rally, meeting; **echar una c. a algn** to race sb; **c. de armamentos** arms race (**c**) *(estudios)* university course; **hacer la c. de derecho/físicas** to study law/

physics (at university) (**d**) *(profesión)* career, profession

carrerilla *nf* run; **tomar c.** to take a run; **de c.** parrot fashion

carreta *nf* cart

carrete *nm* *(de hilo)* reel; *(de película)* spool; *(de cable)* coil

carretera *nf* road; **c. de acceso** access road; *(en autopista)* slip road; **c. de circunvalación** *Br* ring road, *US* beltway; **c. comarcal** minor road; *Méx* **c. de cuota** toll road; **c. nacional** *Br* ≃ A road, *US* ≃ state highway

carretero,-a *adj Am* road; **un accidente c.** a road accident

carretilla *nf* wheelbarrow

carricoche *nm* caravan

carril *nm* (**a**) *Ferroc* rail (**b**) *Aut* lane

carrillo *nm* cheek; *Fam* **comer a dos carrillos** to devour, to gobble up

carriola *nf* (**a**) *(cama)* truckle bed (**b**) *Méx (coche de bebé)* Br pram, *US* baby carriage

carro *nm* (**a**) *(carreta)* cart; *RP Fam* **¡pará el c.!** hold your horses! (**b**) *Mil* **c. de combate** tank (**c**) *(de máquina de escribir)* carriage (**d**) *Andes, CAm, Carib, Méx* car (**e**) *Méx (vagón)* car; **c. comedor** dining car

carrocería *nf Aut* bodywork

carroña *nf* carrion

carroza 1 *nf* (**a**) *(coche de caballos)* coach, carriage (**b**) *(de carnaval)* float
2 *nmf Fam* old fogey

carruaje *nm* carriage, coach

carrusel *nm Andes* roundabout, merry-go-round

carta *nf* (**a**) letter; **c. certificada/urgente** registered/express letter (**b**) *(menú)* menu; **a la c.** à la carte; **c. de vinos** wine list (**c**) *Naipes* card; **echar las cartas a algn** to tell sb's fortune; *Fig* **poner las cartas sobre la mesa** to put *o* lay one's cards on the table, to come clean (**d**) *Geog (mapa)* chart (**e**) *Fig* **adquirir c. de naturaleza** to become widely accepted; **tomar cartas en un asunto** to take part in an affair

cartabón *nm* set square

cartearse *vpr* to correspond (**con** with), to exchange letters (**con** with)

cartel *nm* poster; **pegar/fijar carteles** to put *o* stick up bills

cartél *nm Com* cartel

cartelera *nf* billboard, *Br* hoarding; *Prensa* **c. de espectáculos** entertainments section *o* page

cartera *nf* (**a**) *(de bolsillo)* wallet, *US*

billfold (**b**) *(de mano)* handbag; *(para documentos etc)* briefcase; *(de colegial)* satchel, schoolbag (**c**) *Pol (ministerio)* portfolio (**d**) *Com* portfolio; **c. de pedidos** order book

carterista *nm* pickpocket

cartero,-a *nm,f (hombre) Br* postman, *US* mailman; *(mujer) Br* postwoman, *US* mailwoman

cartilla *nf* (**a**) *(libreta)* book; **c. de ahorros** savings book (**b**) *(libro)* first reader; *Fam* **leerle la c. a algn** to tell sb off

cartografía *nf* cartography

cartón *nm* (**a**) *(material)* card, cardboard; **c. piedra** papier mâché (**b**) *(de cigarrillos)* carton

cartucho *nm* (**a**) *(de balas)* cartridge (**b**) *(de papel)* cone

cartulina *nf* card

casa *nf* (**a**) *(edificio)* house; **c. de huéspedes** boarding house; **c. de socorro** first-aid post (**b**) *(hogar)* home; **vete a c.** go home; **en c. de Daniel** at Daniel's; **de andar por c.** everyday (**c**) *(empresa)* company, firm; **c. matriz/principal** head/central office

casación *nf Jur* annulment

casadero,-a *adj* of marrying age

casado,-a 1 *adj* married
2 *nm,f* married person; **los recién casados** the newlyweds

casamiento *nm* marriage; *(boda)* wedding

casar[1] **1** *vt* to marry
2 *vi* to match, to go o fit together
3 casarse *upr* to marry, to get married; **c. por la iglesia/por lo civil** to get married in church/in a registry office

casar[2] *vt Jur* to annul, to quash

cascabel *nm* bell

cascada *nf* waterfall, cascade

cascanueces *nm inv* nutcracker

cascar **[44] 1** *vt* (**a**) to crack (**b**) *Fam* **cascarla** to kick the bucket, to snuff it
2 *vi Fam (charlar)* to chat away
3 cascarse *upr* to crack

cáscara *nf* shell; *(de fruta)* skin, peel; *(de grano)* husk

cascarón *nm* eggshell

cascarrabias *nmf inv Fam* short-tempered person

casco *nm* (**a**) *(para la cabeza)* helmet (**b**) *(de caballo)* hoof (**c**) *(envase)* empty bottle (**d**) **c. urbano** city centre (**e**) *(de barco)* hull (**f**) **cascos** *(auriculares)* headphones

cascote *nm* piece of rubble o debris

caserío *nm* country house

casero,-a 1 *adj* (**a**) *(hecho en casa)* homemade (**b**) *(persona)* home-loving
2 *nm,f (dueño) (hombre)* landlord; *(mujer)* landlady

caseta *nf* hut, booth; *(de feria, exposición)* stand, stall; *Méx* **c. de cobro** tollbooth; *Méx* **c. telefónica** phone box, phone booth

casete 1 *nm (magnetófono)* cassette player o recorder
2 *nf (cinta)* cassette (tape)

casi *adv* almost, nearly; **c. mil personas** almost one thousand people; **c. ni me acuerdo** I can hardly remember it; **c. nunca** hardly ever; **c. nadie** hardly anyone; **c. me caigo** I almost fell

casilla *nf* (**a**) *(de casillero)* pigeonhole; *Andes, RP* **c. de correos** PO Box; *CAm, Carib, Méx* **c. postal** PO Box (**b**) *(recuadro)* box (**c**) *Fig* **sacar a algn de sus casillas** to drive sb mad

casillero *nm* pigeonholes

casino *nm* casino

caso *nm* case; **el c. es que ...** the fact o thing is that ...; **el c. Mattei** the Mattei affair; **(en) c. contrario** otherwise; **en c. de necesidad** if need be; **en cualquier c.** in any case; **en el mejor/peor de los casos** at best/worst; **en ese c.** in such a case; **en todo c.** in any case; **en un c. extremo, en último c.** as a last resort; **hacer c. a o de algn** to pay attention to sb; **hacer c. omiso de** to take no notice of; **no venir al c.** to be beside the point; **pongamos por c.** let's say

caspa *nf* dandruff

casquete *nm* (**a**) *(de bala)* case, shell (**b**) *Geog* **c. polar** polar cap

> 📖 Observa que la palabra inglesa **casket** es un falso amigo y no es la traducción de la palabra española **casquete**. En inglés, **casket** significa "cofre, ataúd".

casquillo *nm (de bala)* case

cassette *nm & nf* = **casete**

casta *nf* (**a**) *(linaje)* lineage, descent (**b**) *(animales)* breed; **de c.** thoroughbred, purebred (**c**) *(división social)* caste

castaña *nf* chestnut; *Fig* **sacarle a algn las castañas del fuego** to save sb's bacon

castañetear *vi (dientes)* to chatter

castaño,-a 1 *adj* chestnut-brown; *(pelo, ojos)* brown, dark
2 *nm Bot* chestnut

castañuela *nf* castanet

castellano,-a 1 *adj* Castilian
2 *nm,f (persona)* Castilian
3 *nm (idioma)* Spanish, Castilian

castidad *nf* chastity
castigar [42] *vt* (**a**) to punish (**b**) *(dañar)* to harm, to ruin (**c**) *Jur & Dep* to penalize
castigo *nm* punishment; *Jur* penalty; *Dep* **área de c.** penalty area
Castilla *n* Castile
castillo *nm* castle
castizo,-a *adj* pure, authentic
casto,-a *adj* chaste
castor *nm* beaver
castrar *vt* to castrate
castrense *adj* military
casual 1 *adj* accidental, chance
2 *nm Fam* chance
casualidad *nf* chance, coincidence; **de** *o* **por c.** by chance; **dio la c. que ...** it so happened that ...; **¿tienes un lápiz, por c.?** do you happen to have a pencil?; **¡que c.!** what a coincidence!

> 🖉 Observa que la palabra inglesa **casualty** es un falso amigo y no es la traducción de la palabra española **casualidad**. En inglés, **casualty** significa "víctima".

casualmente *adv* by chance
cata *nf* tasting
cataclismo *nm* cataclysm
catador,-a *nm,f* taster
catalán,-ana 1 *adj & nm,f* Catalan
2 *nm (idioma)* Catalan
catalejo *nm* telescope
catalepsia *nf* catalepsy
catalizador *nm* catalyst; *Aut* catalytic converter
catalizar [40] *vt Fig* to act as a catalyst for
catalogar [42] *vt* (**a**) to catalogue (**b**) *(clasificar)* to classify
catálogo *nm* catalogue
Cataluña *n* Catalonia
cataplasma *nf* (**a**) *Farm* cataplasm, poultice (**b**) *Fam (pelmazo)* bore
catapulta *nf* catapult; *Fig* springboard
catapultar *vt* to catapult
catar *vt* to taste
catarata *nf* (**a**) waterfall (**b**) *Med* cataract
catarro *nm* (common) cold
catastral *adj* **valor c.** rateable value
catastro *nm* land registry
catástrofe *nf* catastrophe
catastrófico,-a *adj* catastrophic
catear *vt* (**a**) *Fam (suspender)* to fail, *US* to flunk (**b**) *Am (casa)* to search
catecismo *nm* catechism
cátedra *nf* (professorial) chair; **le han dado la c.** they have appointed him professor
catedral *nf* cathedral

catedrático,-a *nm,f Educ* (**a**) *Univ* professor (**b**) *(de instituto)* head of department
categoría *nf* category; *Fig* class; **de c.** *(persona)* important; *(vino etc)* quality
categórico,-a *adj* categoric; **un no c.** a flat refusal
cateto,-a *nm,f Pey* yokel, bumpkin
catire,-a *adj Carib (rubio)* blond, blonde
catolicismo *nm* Catholicism
católico,-a *adj & nm,f* Catholic
catorce *adj & nm inv* fourteen
catre *nm Fam* bed
Cáucaso *n* Caucasus
cauce *nm* (**a**) *(de un río)* bed (**b**) *Fig (canal)* channel; **cauces oficiales** official channels
caucho *nm* (**a**) rubber (**b**) *Am (cubierta)* tyre
caudal *nm* (**a**) *(de un río)* flow (**b**) *(riqueza)* wealth, riches
caudaloso,-a *adj (río)* plentiful
caudillo *nm* leader, head
causa *nf* (**a**) cause; **a** *o* **por c. de** because of (**b**) *(ideal)* cause (**c**) *Jur (caso)* case; *(juicio)* trial
causante 1 *adj* causal, causing
2 *nmf* **el c. del incendio** the person who caused the fire
causar *vt* to cause, to bring about; **me causa un gran placer** it gives me great pleasure; **c. buena/mala impresión** to make a good/bad impression
cáustico,-a *adj* caustic
cautela *nf* caution
cautivar *vt* (**a**) to capture, to take prisoner (**b**) *Fig (fascinar)* to captivate
cautiverio *nm*, **cautividad** *nf* captivity
cautivo,-a *adj & nm,f* captive
cauto,-a *adj* cautious, wary
cava 1 *nf (bodega)* wine cellar
2 *nm (vino espumoso)* cava, champagne
cavar *vt* to dig
caverna *nf* cave; **hombre de las cavernas** caveman
cavernícola *nmf* cave dweller
caviar *nm* caviar
cavidad *nf* cavity
cavilar *vt* to ponder
cayado *nm* (**a**) *(de pastor)* crook (**b**) *(de obispo)* crosier, crozier
cayuco *nm Am* small flat-bottomed canoe
caza 1 *nf* (**a**) hunting; **ir de c.** to go hunting; **c. furtiva** poaching (**b**) *(animales)* game; **c. mayor/menor** big/small game (**c**) *Fig (persecución)* hunt; **c. de brujas** witch hunt

2 *nm Av* fighter, fighter plane

cazabe *nm Am* cassava bread

cazabombardero *nm Av* fighter bomber

cazador,-a *nm,f* hunter; **c. furtivo** poacher

cazadora *nf* (waist-length) jacket

cazar [40] *vt* to hunt; *Fam* **cazarlas al vuelo** to be quick on the uptake

cazatalentos *nmf inv* head-hunter

cazo *nm* (**a**) *(cacerola)* saucepan (**b**) *(cucharón)* ladle

cazuela *nf* saucepan; *(guiso)* casserole, stew; **a la c.** stewed

c/c *(abr* cuenta corriente) c/a

CC. OO. *nfpl (abr* Comisiones Obreras) = Spanish left-wing trade union

CD-ROM *nm* CD-ROM

cebada *nf* barley

cebar 1 *vt* (**a**) *(animal)* to fatten; *(persona)* to feed up (**b**) *(anzuelo)* to bait (**c**) *(fuego, caldera)* to stoke, to fuel; *(máquina, arma)* to prime (**d**) *RP (mate)* to prepare, to brew

2 cebarse *vpr* **c. con** *(ensañarse)* to delight in tormenting

cebo *nm* bait

cebolla *nf* onion

cebolleta *nf* (**a**) *(especie)* chives (**b**) *(cebolla tierna)* spring onion

cebra *nf* zebra; **paso de c.** *Br* zebra crossing, *US* crosswalk

cecear *vi* to lisp

ceceo *nm* lisp

cedazo *nm* sieve

ceder 1 *vt* to give, to hand over; *Aut* **c. el paso** to give way

2 *vi* (**a**) *(cuerda, cable)* to give way (**b**) *(lluvia, calor)* to diminish, to slacken (**c**) *(consentir)* to give in

cederrón *nm* CD-ROM

cedro *nm* cedar

cédula *nf* (**a**) document, certificate; *Am* **c. de identidad** identity card (**b**) *Com & Fin* bond, certificate, warrant

C(E)E *nf (abr* Comunidad (Económica) Europea) E(E)C

cegador,-a *adj* blinding

cegar [1] *vt* (**a**) to blind (**b**) *(puerta, ventana)* to wall up

ceguera *nf* blindness

CEI *(abr* Comunidad de Estados Independientes) CIS

Ceilán *n* Ceylon

ceja *nf* eyebrow

cejar *vi* **c. en el empeño** to give up

celada *nf* trap, ambush

celador,-a *nm,f* attendant; *(de una cárcel)* warder

celda *nf* cell; **c. de castigo** punishment cell

celebración *nf* (**a**) *(festejo)* celebration (**b**) *(de juicio etc)* holding

celebrar 1 *vt* (**a**) to celebrate; **celebro que todo saliera bien** I'm glad everything went well (**b**) *(reunión, juicio, elecciones)* to hold (**c**) *(triunfo)* to laud

2 celebrarse *vpr* to take place, to be held

célebre *adj* famous, well-known

celebridad *nf* (**a**) celebrity, fame (**b**) *(persona)* celebrity

celeste 1 *adj* (**a**) *(de cielo)* celestial (**b**) *(color)* sky-blue

2 *nm* sky blue

celestial *adj* celestial, heavenly

celibato *nm* celibacy

célibe *adj & nmf* celibate

celo *nm* (**a**) zeal (**b**) **en c.** *(macho)* in rut; *(hembra)* on *o* in heat (**c**) **celos** jealousy; **tener celos (de algn)** to be jealous (of sb)

celo® *nm Fam Br* Sellotape®, *US* Scotch tape®

celofán *nm* cellophane®

celosía *nf* lattice

celoso,-a *adj* (**a**) jealous (**b**) *(cumplidor)* conscientious

celta 1 *adj* Celtic

2 *nmf* Celt

3 *nm (idioma)* Celtic

célula *nf* cell

celular 1 *adj* (**a**) cellular (**b**) **coche c.** police van (**c**) *Am* **teléfono c.** mobile phone, cellphone

2 *nm Am* mobile, cellphone

celulitis *nf inv* cellulitis

celuloide *nm* celluloid

celulosa *nf* cellulose

cementerio *nm* cemetery, graveyard; **c. de coches** scrapyard

cemento *nm* cement; **c. armado** reinforced cement

cena *nf* evening meal; *(antes de acostarse)* supper; **la Última C.** the Last Supper

cenagal *nm* marsh, swamp

cenar 1 *vi* to have supper *o* dinner

2 *vt* to have for supper *o* dinner

cencerro *nm* cowbell

cenefa *nf* *(de ropa)* edging, trimming; *(de suelo, techo)* ornamental border, frieze

cenetista 1 *adj* = of or related to the CNT (Confederación Nacional del Trabajo)

2 *nmf* member of the CNT

cenicero *nm* ashtray

cenit *nm* zenith

ceniza *nf* ash

cenizo *nm Fam (gafe)* jinx

censo *nm* census; **c. electoral** electoral roll

censor *nm* censor

censura *nf* (a) censorship (b) *Pol* **moción de c.** vote of no confidence

censurar *vt* (a) *(libro, película)* to censor (b) *(criticar)* to censure, to criticize

centavo *nm Am Fin* cent, centavo

centella *nf* spark

centellear *vi* to flash, to sparkle

centelleo *nm* flashing, sparkling

centena *nf,* **centenar** *nm* hundred; **a centenares** in hundreds

centenario *nm* centenary, hundredth anniversary

centeno *nm* rye

centésimo,-a *adj & nm,f* hundredth

centígrado,-a *adj* centigrade

centilitro *nm* centilitre

centímetro *nm* centimetre

céntimo *nm* cent

centinela *nm* sentry

centollo *nm* spider crab

centrado,-a *adj* (a) centred (b) *(equilibrado)* balanced

central 1 *adj* central
2 *nf* (a) *Elec* **c. nuclear/térmica** nuclear/coal-fired power station (b) *(oficina principal)* head office

centralismo *nm* centralism

centralita *nf Tel* switchboard

centralizar [40] *vt* to centralize

centrar 1 *vt* (a) to centre (b) *(esfuerzos, atención)* to concentrate, to centre (**en** on)
2 centrarse *vpr* (a) to be centred o based (b) **c. en** *(concentrarse)* to concentrate on

céntrico,-a *adj* centrally situated; **zona céntrica** centrally situated area

centrifugar [42] *vt* to centrifuge; *(ropa)* to spin-dry

centrista *Pol* **1** *adj* centre; **partido c.** centre party
2 *nmf* centrist

centro *nm* (a) middle, centre; **c. de la ciudad** town o city centre (b) *(establecimiento)* institution, centre; **c. comercial** shopping centre

Centroamérica *n* Central America

centroamericano,-a *adj & nm,f* Central American

centrocampista *nmf Ftb* midfielder

centuria *nf* century

ceñido,-a *adj* tight-fitting, clinging

ceñirse [6] *vpr* (a) *(atenerse, limitarse)* to limit oneself, to stick (**a** to); **c. al tema** to keep to the subject; **ciñéndonos a este caso en concreto** coming down to this particular case (b) **c. a** *(prenda)* to cling to

ceño *nm* scowl, frown; **con el c. fruncido** frowning

CEOE *nf (abr* **Confederación Española de Organizaciones Empresariales)** = Spanish employers' organization, ≃ CBI

cepa *nf* (a) *(de vid)* vine (b) *Fig* **vasco de pura c.** *(origen)* Basque through and through

cepillar 1 *vt* (a) to brush (b) *(en carpintería)* to plane (down) (c) *Fam (robar)* to pinch
2 cepillarse *vpr* (a) *(con cepillo)* to brush (b) *Fam (matar)* to do in (c) *muy Fam* to lay

cepillo *nm* brush; *(en carpintería)* plane; **c. de dientes** toothbrush; **c. del pelo** hairbrush

cepo *nm* (a) *(para cazar)* trap (b) *Aut* clamp

CEPYME *nf (abr* **Confederación Española de la Pequeña y Mediana Empresa)** = Spanish confederation of small and medium-sized businesses

cera *nf* wax; *(de abeja)* beeswax

cerámica *nf* ceramics *sing*

cerca¹ *adv* (a) near, close; **ven más c.** come closer; **ya estamos c.** we are almost there (b) **c. de** *(al lado de)* near, close to; **el colegio está c. de mi casa** the school is near my house (c) **c. de** *(casi)* nearly, around; **c. de cien personas** about one hundred people (d) **de c.** closely; **lo vi muy de c.** I saw it close up

cerca² *nf* fence, wall

cercado *nm* (a) *(lugar cerrado)* enclosure (b) *(valla)* fence, wall

cercanía *nf* (a) proximity, nearness (b) **cercanías** outskirts, suburbs; **(tren de) cercanías** suburban train

cercano,-a *adj* nearby; **el C. Oriente** the Near East

cercar [44] *vt* (a) *(tapiar)* to fence, to enclose (b) *(rodear)* to surround

cercenar *vt* to cut off, to amputate

cerciorar 1 *vt* to assure
2 cerciorarse *vpr* to make sure

cerco *nm* (a) circle, ring (b) *Mil (sitio)* siege; **poner c. (a una ciudad)** to besiege (a town)

cerda *nf* (a) *Zool* sow (b) *(pelo)* bristle; **cepillo de c.** bristle brush

Cerdeña *n* Sardinia

cerdo *nm* (a) *(animal)* pig (b) *(carne)* pork (c) *Fam* pig, arsehole

cereal *nm* cereal

cerebral *adj* (a) cerebral (b) *(frío)* calculating

cerebro *nm* brain; *Fig (inteligencia)* brains

ceremonia *nf* ceremony

ceremonioso,-a *adj* ceremonious, formal; *Pey* pompous, stiff

cereza *nf* cherry

cerezo *nm* cherry tree

cerilla *nf* match

cerillo *nm CAm, Méx* match

cernerse [3] *vpr Fig* to loom (**sobre** above)

cernícalo *nm* kestrel

cernirse [54] *vpr* = **cernerse**

cero *nm* zero; *Dep* nil; *Fig* **partir de c.** to start from scratch; *Fig* **ser un c. a la izquierda** to be useless *o* a good-for-nothing

cerquillo *nm Am Br* fringe, *US* bangs

cerrado,-a *adj* (**a**) closed, shut; **a puerta cerrada** behind closed doors (**b**) *(reservado)* reserved; *(intransigente)* uncompromising, unyielding; *Fam (torpe)* thick; *(acento)* broad; *(curva)* tight, sharp (**c**) *(barba)* bushy

cerradura *nf* lock

cerrajero,-a *nm,f* locksmith

cerrar [1] **1** *vt* to shut, to close; *(grifo, gas)* to turn off; *(luz)* to turn off, to switch off; *(cremallera)* to do up; *(negocio)* to close down; *(cuenta)* to close; *(carta)* to seal; *(puños)* to clench; **c. con llave** to lock; **c. el paso a algn** to block sb's way; *Fam* **c. el pico** to shut one's trap

2 *vi* to close, to shut

3 cerrarse *vpr* to close, to shut; *Fam* **c. en banda** to stick to one's guns

cerro *nm* hill; *Fig* **irse por los cerros de Ubeda** to beat around the bush

cerrojo *nm* bolt; **echar el c. (de una puerta)** to bolt (a door)

certamen *nm* competition, contest

certero,-a *adj* accurate

certeza, certidumbre *nf* certainty; **saber (algo) con c.** to be certain (of sth); **tener la c. de que ...** to be sure *o* certain that ...

certificado,-a 1 *adj* (**a**) certified (**b**) *(correo)* registered

2 *nm* certificate

certificar [44] *vt* (**a**) to certify (**b**) *(carta)* to register

cervatillo *nm* fawn

cervecería *nf* (**a**) *(bar)* pub, bar (**b**) *(fábrica)* brewery

cerveza *nf* beer; **c. de barril** draught beer; **c. dorada** *o* **ligera** lager; **c. negra** stout

cervical *adj* cervical

cesante *adj (destituido)* dismissed, *Br* sacked; *CSur, Méx (parado)* unemployed

cesantear *vt CSur* to make redundant

cesar 1 *vi* **c. (de)** to stop, to cease; **sin c.** incessantly

2 *vt (empleado)* to dismiss, *Br* to sack

cesárea *nf* Caesarean (section)

cese *nm* (**a**) cessation, suspension (**b**) *(despido)* dismissal

Cesid *nm (abr* **Centro Superior de Investigación de la Defensa)** = Spanish military intelligence and espionage service

césped *nm* lawn, grass

cesta *nf* basket; **c. de Navidad** Christmas hamper

cesto *nm* basket

cetáceo *nm* cetacean, whale

cetrino,-a *adj* sallow

cetro *nm* sceptre

Ceuta *n* Ceuta

ceutí 1 *adj* of/from Ceuta

2 *nmf* person from Ceuta

ceviche *nm* = raw fish marinated in lemon and garlic

chabacano,-a 1 *adj* cheap

2 *nm Méx (fruto)* apricot; *(árbol)* apricot tree

chabola *nf* shack; **barrio de chabolas** shanty town

chacal *nm* jackal

chacarero,-a *nm,f Andes, RP* farmer

chacha *nf* maid

cháchara *nf Fam* small talk, chinwag; **estar de c.** to have a yap

chachi *adj* smashing

chacinados *nmpl RP* pork products

chacinería *nf* pork butcher's (shop)

chacra *nf Andes, RP* farm

chafar *vt* (**a**) *Fam (plan etc)* to ruin, to spoil (**b**) *(aplastar)* to squash, to flatten

chal *nm* shawl

chalado,-a *adj Fam* crazy, nuts (**por** about)

chalé *nm (pl* **chalés**) = **chalet**

chaleco *nm Br* waistcoat, *US* vest; *(de punto)* sleeveless pullover; **c. antibalas** bullet-proof vest; **c. salvavidas** life jacket

chalet *nm* villa

chalupa *nf* (**a**) *(embarcación)* boat, launch (**b**) *Méx (torta)* = small tortilla with a raised rim to contain a filling

chamaco,-a *nm,f Méx Fam* kid

chamarra *nf* sheepskin jacket

chamba *nf CAm, Méx, Perú, Ven Fam (trabajo)* job

chambelán *nm* chamberlain

chambergo *nm* heavy coat

chambón,-ona *nm,f Am Fam* sloppy *o* shoddy worker

chamizo *nm* thatched hut

champa *nf CAm (tienda de campaña)* tent

champán, champaña *nm o nf* champagne

champiñón *nm* mushroom

champú *nm* shampoo

chamuscar [44] *vt* to singe, to scorch

chamusquina *nf* singeing, scorching; *Fam* **esto me huele a c.** there's something fishy going on here

chancaca *nf CAm (torta)* syrup cake

chance 1 *nm Am* opportunity
2 *adv Méx* maybe

chancear *vi Am* to joke, to horse around

chanchada *nf Am* (a) *(porquería)* **no hagas chanchadas** stop that, don't be disgusting! (b) *Fam (jugarreta)* dirty trick

chancho,-a *nm,f Am* pig, hog, *f* sow

chanchullo *nm Fam* fiddle, wangle

chancla *nf Br* flip-flop, *US* thong

chanclo *nm (zueco)* clog; *(de goma)* overshoe, galosh

chándal *nm* track *o* jogging suit

changa *nf Bol, RP (trabajo temporal)* odd job

changador *nm RP (cargador)* porter

changarro *nm Méx* small shop

chantaje *nm* blackmail; **hacer c. a algn** to blackmail sb

chantajear *vt* to blackmail

chantajista *nmf* blackmailer

chanza *nf* joke

chapa *nf* (a) *(de metal)* sheet (b) *(de madera)* panel-board (c) *(tapón)* bottle top, cap (d) *(de adorno)* badge (e) *RP Br* number plate, *US* license plate (f) *Col (cerradura)* lock

chapado,-a *adj (metal)* plated; **c. en oro** gold-plated; *Fig* **c. a la antigua** old-fashioned

chaparro *nm Bot* holm oak

chaparrón *nm* downpour, heavy shower

chapopote *nm Carib, Méx* bitumen, pitch

chapotear *vi* to splash about, to paddle

chapucero,-a *adj (trabajo)* slapdash, shoddy; *(persona)* bungling

chapulín *nm CAm, Méx (saltamontes)* grasshopper

chapurrear *vt* to speak badly *o* with difficulty; **sólo chapurreaba el francés** he spoke only a few words of French

chapuza *nf* (a) *(trabajo mal hecho)* shoddy piece of work (b) *(trabajo ocasional)* odd job

chapuzón *nm (baño corto)* dip; **darse un c.** to have a dip

chaqué *nm* morning coat

chaqueta *nf* jacket; *Pol* **cambiar de c.** to change sides

chaquetero,-a *nm,f Fam Pol* turncoat

chaquetilla *nf* short jacket

charanga *nf Mús* brass band

charca *nf* pond, pool

charco *nm* puddle

charcutería *nf* delicatessen

charla *nf* *(conversación)* talk, chat; *(conferencia)* informal lecture *o* address; *Informát* chat

charlar *vi* to talk, to chat; *Informát* to chat

charlatán,-ana 1 *adj (parlanchín)* talkative; *(chismoso)* gossipy
2 *nm,f* (a) *(parlanchín)* chatterbox; *(chismoso)* gossip; *(bocazas)* bigmouth (b) *(embaucador)* trickster, charmer

charol *nm* (a) *(piel)* patent leather; **zapatos de c.** patent leather shoes (b) *Andes (bandeja)* tray

charola *nf CAm, Méx* tray

charqui *nm Andes, RP (carne)* jerked *o* salted beef

chárter *adj inv (vuelo)* **c.** charter (flight)

chasca *nf Andes (greña)* mop of hair

chascar [44] *vt (lengua)* to click; *(dedos)* to snap; *(látigo)* to crack

chascarrillo *nm* shaggy dog story

chasco *nm Fam* disappointment; **llevarse un c.** to be disappointed

chasis *nm inv* chassis

chasquear *vt (lengua)* to click; *(dedos)* to snap; *(látigo)* to crack

chasqui *nm* = Inca messenger *o* courier

chasquido *nm (de la lengua)* click; *(de los dedos)* snap; *(de látigo, madera)* crack

chatarra *nf* scrap (metal), scrap iron; *Fam* junk

chato,-a 1 *adj* (a) *(nariz)* snub; *(persona)* snub-nosed (b) *(objeto)* flat, flattened (c) *PRico, RP Fam (sin ambiciones)* commonplace; **una vida chata** a humdrum existence
2 *nm (small)* glass of wine

chau *interj Andes, RP Fam* bye!, see you!

chaucha 1 *adj RP Fam* dull, boring
2 *nf Bol, RP* green bean

chauvinista *adj & nmf* chauvinist

chaval,-a *nm,f Fam (chico)* boy, lad; *(chica)* girl

chaveta *nf* (a) *(clavija)* cotter pin (b) *Fam (cabeza)* nut, head; **perder la c.** *(volverse loco)* to go off one's rocker (c) *Andes (navaja)* penknife

chavo,-a *Fam* **1** *nm,f Méx (chico)* guy; *(chica)* girl
2 *nm (dinero)* **no tener un c.** to be broke

che *interj RP Fam* **¿qué hacés, c.?, ¿cómo andás, c.?** how are things *o* how's it going, then?; **c., ¡vení para acá!** over here, you!

checo,-a *adj* Czech

checoslovaco,-a 1 *adj* Czechoslovakian, Czech

   2 *nm,f (persona)* Czechoslovakian, Czechoslovak, Czech

Checoslovaquia *n* Czechoslovakia

chele,-a *CAm* **1** *adj (rubio)* blond, blonde; *(de piel blanca)* fair-skinned

   2 *nm,f (rubio)* blond(e) person; *(de piel blanca)* fair-skinned person

chelín *nm* shilling

chepa *nf Fam* hump

cheque *nm* cheque; **c. al portador** cheque payable to bearer; **c. de viaje** *o* **(de) viajero** traveller's cheque

chequeo *nm Med* checkup; *Aut* service

chévere *adj Andes, CAm, Carib, Méx Fam* great, fantastic

chic *adj inv* chic, elegant

chicano,-a *adj & nm,f* chicano

chicha¹ *nf Andes* = alcoholic drink made from fermented maize

chicha² *nf* **calma c.** dead calm

chícharo *nm CAm, Méx* pea

chicharra *nf* (a) *(insecto)* cicada (b) *Méx, RP (timbre)* electric buzzer

chiche *nm* (a) *Andes, RP Fam (juguete)* toy (b) *Andes, RP (adorno)* delicate ornament (c) *CAm, Méx muy Fam (pecho)* tit

chichón *nm* bump, lump

chichonera *nf* helmet

chicle *nm* chewing gum

chico,-a 1 *nm,f (muchacho)* boy, lad; *(muchacha)* girl

   2 *adj* small, little

chicoria *nf* chicory

chicote *nm Am (látigo)* whip

chiflado,-a *adj Fam* mad, crazy (**por** about)

chiflar *vt* (a) *(silbar)* to hiss (at), to boo (at) (b) *Fam* **le chiflan las motos** he's really into motorbikes

chiflido *nm Am* whistle, whistling

chigüín,-ina *nm,f CAm Fam* kid

chiíta *adj & nmf* Shiite

chilango,-a *Méx Fam* **1** *adj* of/from Mexico City

   2 *nm,f* person from Mexico City

Chile *n* Chile

chile *nm* chilli (pepper)

chileno,-a *adj & nm,f* Chilean

chillar *vi (persona)* to scream, to shriek; *(ratón)* to squeak; *(frenos)* to screech, to squeal; *(puerta)* to creak, to squeak

chillido *nm (de persona)* scream, shriek; *(de ratón)* squeak; *(de frenos)* screech, squeal; *(de puerta)* creaking, squeaking

chillón,-ona *adj* (a) *(voz)* shrill, high-pitched; *(sonido)* harsh, strident (b) *(color)* loud, gaudy

chilpotle *nm Méx* = smoked or pickled jalapeño chilli

chimbo,-a *adj Col, Ven Fam* (a) *(de mala calidad)* crap, useless (b) *(complicado)* screwed-up

chimenea *nf* (a) *(hogar abierto)* fireplace, hearth (b) *(conducto)* chimney; *(de barco)* funnel, stack

chimichurri *nm RP* = barbecue sauce made from garlic, parsley, herbs and vinegar

China *n* China

china *nf* (a) *(piedra)* pebble, small stone; *Fam* **tocarle a uno la c.** to get the short straw (b) *Fam (droga)* deal

> *♪* Observa que la palabra inglesa **china** es un falso amigo y no es la traducción de la palabra española **china**. En inglés, **china** significa "loza, porcelana".

chinampa *nf Méx* = man-made island for growing flowers, fruit and vegetables, found in Xochimilco near Mexico City

chinche 1 *nf* bug, bedbug; *Fam* **caer como chinches** to fall like flies

   2 *nmf Fam* nuisance, pest

chincheta *nf Br* drawing pin, *US* thumbtack

chinchín *interj* **¡c.!** cheers!, (to) your (good) health!

chinchulín *nm,* **chinchulines** *nmpl Andes, RP (plato)* = piece of sheep or cow intestine, plaited and then roasted

chinesco,-a *adj* **sombras chinescas** shadow theatre

chingado,-a *adj muy Fam (estropeado)* bust, *Br* knackered

chingana *nf Perú Fam* bar

chingar [42] *vt* (a) *(fastidiar)* to annoy (b) *muy Fam (estropear)* to bust, *Br* to knacker (c) *Vulg (joder)* to fuck, to screw

chino¹ *nm (piedrecita)* pebble, stone

chino²,-a *adj* (a) *(de la China)* Chinese; *Fam* **eso me suena a c.** it's all Greek to me (b) *Am (mestizo)* of mixed ancestry

chip *nm (pl* **chips)** *Informát* chip

chipirón *nm* baby squid

Chipre *n* Cyprus

chipriota *adj & nmf* Cypriot

chiqueo *nm Méx* cuddle

chiquilín,-ina *nm,f RP* small boy, *f* small girl

chiquillo,-a *nm,f* kid

chiquito,-a *adj* tiny

chirimiri *nm* drizzle, fine misty rain

chirimoya *nf* custard apple

chiringuito *nm (en playa etc)* refreshment stall; *(en carretera)* roadside snack bar

chiripa *nf* fluke, lucky stroke; *Fam Fig* **de o por c.** by a fluke, by chance; **cogió el tren por c.** it was sheer luck that he caught the train

chiripá *nm (pl* **chiripaes)** *Bol, CSur =* garment worn by gauchos as trousers

chirla *nf* small clam

chirona *nf Fam* clink, nick

chirriar **[29]** *vi (puerta etc)* to creak; *(frenos)* to screech, to squeal

chirrido *nm (de puerta etc)* crack, cracking; *(de frenos)* screech, squeal

chisme *nm* (a) *(habladuría)* piece of gossip (b) *Fam (trasto)* knick-knack; *(cosa)* thing

chismorrear *vi Fam* to gossip

chismorreo *nm Fam* gossip, gossiping

chismoso,-a **1** *adj* gossipy
  2 *nm,f* gossip

chispa *nf* (a) spark; **echar chispas** to fume (b) *Fam (un poco)* bit, tiny amount (c) *Fam (agudeza)* wit, sparkle; *(viveza)* liveliness

chispear *vi* (a) to spark, to throw out sparks (b) *(lloviznar)* to spit

chiste *nm* joke; **contar un c.** to tell a joke; **c. verde** blue joke, dirty joke

chistera *nf* top hat

chistoso,-a *adj (persona)* funny, witty; *(anécdota)* funny, amusing

chivarse *vpr Fam* to tell tales

chivatazo *nm Fam* tip-off; **dar el c.** to squeal

chivato,-a **1** *nm,f Fam (delator) Br* grass, *US* rat; *(acusica)* telltale
  2 *nm* (a) *(luz)* warning light (b) *(alarma)* alarm bell (c) *Ven Fam (pez gordo)* big cheese

chivito *nm Urug =* steak sandwich *(containing cheese and salad)*

chivo,-a *nm,f Zool* kid, young goat; *Fig* **c. expiatorio** scapegoat

chocante *adj* (a) *(persona)* off-putting (b) *(sorprendente)* surprising, startling; *(raro)* strange

chocar **[44]** **1** *vi* (a) *(topar)* to crash, to collide; **c. con o contra** to run into, to collide with (b) *(en discusión)* to clash
  2 *vt* (a) to knock; *(la mano)* to shake; *Fam* **¡chócala!, ¡choca esos cinco!** shake (on it)!, put it there! (b) *(sorprender)* to surprise

chochear *vi* (a) to be senile *o* in one's dotage (b) **c. con algn** to dote on sb

chocho,-a **1** *adj (senil)* senile; **viejo c.** old dodderer
  2 *nm* (a) *(altramuz)* lupin (b) *muy Fam Br* fanny, *US* beaver

choclo *nm Andes, RP (mazorca)* corncob, ear of maize *o US* corn; *(granos)* sweetcorn; *(cultivo)* maize, *US* corn

chocolate *nm* (a) chocolate; **c. con leche** milk chocolate (b) *Fam (droga)* dope

chocolatina *nf* bar of chocolate, chocolate bar

chófer *nm (pl* **chóferes)** *Am* **chofer** *nm (pl* **choferes)** driver; *(particular)* chauffeur

chollo *nm Fam (ganga)* bargain, snip

chomba *nf Arg* polo shirt

chompa *nf Andes* sweater, *Br* jumper

chompipe *nm CAm, Méx* turkey

chongo *nm Méx* (a) *(moño)* bun (b) **chongos zamoranos** *(dulce) =* Mexican dessert made from milk curds, served in syrup

chonta *nf Am* palm tree

chop *nm CSur* (a) *(jarra)* beer mug/glass (b) *(cerveza)* (glass of) beer

chopo *nm* poplar

chopp *nm CSur =* chop

choque *nm* (a) impact; *(de coches etc)* crash, collision; **c. frontal** head-on collision; **c. múltiple** pile-up (b) *Fig (contienda)* clash

choricear, chorizar *vt Fam* to pinch

chorizo *nm* (a) chorizo, highly-seasoned pork sausage (b) *Fam (ratero)* thief, pickpocket

chorlito *nm Orn* plover; *Fam Fig* **cabeza de c.** scatterbrain

choro *nm Andes* mussel

chorra *Fam* **1** *nmf (tonto)* idiot, fool
  2 *nf (suerte)* luck

chorrada *nf Fam* piece of nonsense

chorrear *vi* to drip, to trickle; *Fam* **c. de sudor** to pour with sweat; *Fam* **tengo el abrigo chorreando** my coat is dripping wet

chorro *nm* (a) *(de agua etc)* spurt; *(muy fino)* trickle; **salir a chorros** to gush forth (b) *Téc* jet (c) *Fig* stream, flood

chovinismo *nm* chauvinism

chovinista **1** *adj* chauvinistic
  2 *nmf* chauvinist

choza *nf* hut, shack

christmas *nm* Christmas card

chubasco *nm* heavy shower, downpour

chubasquero *nm* raincoat

chúcaro,-a *adj Andes, CAm, RP* (a) *(animal)* wild (b) *(persona)* unsociable

chuchería *nf Fam Br* sweet, *US* candy

chueco,-a **1** *adj Am (torcido)* twisted;

(patizambo) bowlegged; *Méx, Ven Fam (cojo)* lame

2 *nm,f Am (patizambo)* bowlegged person; *Méx, Ven Fam (cojo)* lame person

chufa *nf* groundnut

chulear *vi Fam* to strut around; **c. de** to go on about

chuleta *nf* (a) chop, cutlet; **c. de cerdo** pork chop (b) *Educ Fam* crib

chullo *nm Andes* woollen cap

chulo,-a *Fam* **1** *nm,f* show-off

2 *nm (proxeneta)* pimp

3 *adj (bonito)* smashing

chungo,-a *adj Fam* dodgy

chuño *nm Andes, RP* potato starch

chupa *nf Arg* short jacket

chupachups® *nm* lollipop

chupacirios *nmf inv Fam Pey* holy Joe

chupado,-a *adj* (a) *(flaco)* skinny, thin (b) *Fam* **está c.** it's dead easy

chupamedias *nmf Andes, RP, Ven Fam* toady, sycophant

chupar 1 *vt* (a) to suck (b) *(lamer)* to lick (c) *(absorber)* to soak up, to absorb

2 *vi* to suck

3 chuparse *vpr* (a) **está para c. los dedos** it's really mouthwatering (b) *Fam* to put up with; **nos chupamos toda la película** we sat through the whole film

chupatintas *nm inv Pey* penpusher

chupe *nm Andes, Arg* stew

chupete *nm Br* dummy, *US* pacifier

chupi *adj Fam* great, terrific, fantastic

chupón *nm* (a) lollipop (b) *(desatrancador)* plunger

churrasco *nm* barbecued meat

churrería *nf* fritter shop

churrete *nm* dirty mark, grease spot

churro *nm* (a) = dough formed into sticks or rings, fried in oil and covered in sugar (b) *Fam (chapuza)* mess

chusco *nm* chunk of stale bread; *Mil Fam* ration bread

chusma *nf* rabble, mob

chutar 1 *vi Dep (a gol)* to shoot (b) *Fam* **¡y vas que chutas!** and then you're well away!

2 chutarse *vpr Fam (drogas)* to shoot up

chute *nm* (a) *Dep* shot (b) *Fam (drogas)* fix

CI *nm (abr coeficiente intelectual)* IQ

Cía., cía *(abr compañía)* Co

cianuro *nm* cyanide

cibercafé *nm Informát* Internet cafe, cybercafe

ciberespacio *nm Informát* cyberspace

cibernética *nf* cybernetics *sing*

cicatero,-a 1 *adj* stingy, mean

2 *nm,f* miser

cicatriz *nf* scar

cicatrizar [40] *vt & vi Med* to heal

cíclico,-a *adj* cyclical

ciclismo *nm* cycling

ciclista 1 *adj* cycling

2 *nmf* cyclist

ciclo *nm* cycle; *(de conferencias etc)* course, series

ciclocróss *nm* cyclo-cross

ciclomotor *nm* moped

ciclón *nm* cyclone

ciego,-a 1 *adj (persona)* blind; *Fam (borracho)* blind drunk; *(de droga)* stoned; **a ciegas** blindly

2 *nm,f* blind person; **los ciegos** the blind

cielo *nm* (a) sky (b) *Rel* heaven; *Fig* **caído del c.** *(oportuno)* heaven-sent; *(inesperado)* out of the blue; **¡c. santo!** good heavens! (c) *Arquit* **c. raso** ceiling (d) **c. de la boca** roof of the mouth

ciempiés *nm* centipede

cien *adj & nm inv* hundred; **c. libras** a o one hundred pounds; **c. por c.** one hundred percent

ciénaga *nf* marsh, bog

ciencia *nf* (a) science; *Fig* **saber algo a c. cierta** to know sth for certain; **c. ficción** science fiction; **c. infusa** intuition; **ciencias ocultas** the occult (b) *(conocimiento)* knowledge

cieno *nm* mud, mire

científico,-a 1 *adj* scientific

2 *nm,f* scientist

cientista *nmf CSur* **c. social** social scientist

ciento *adj* hundred; **c. tres** one hundred and three; **por c.** percent

cierne *nm Fig* **en ciernes** budding

cierre *nm* (a) *(acción)* closing, shutting; *(de fábrica)* shutdown; *TV* close-down; **c. patronal** lockout (b) *(de bolso)* clasp; *(de puerta)* catch; *(prenda)* fastener; **c. de seguridad** safety lock; **c. centralizado** central locking; *Am* **c. relámpago** *Br* zip, *US* zipper

cierto,-a 1 *adj* (a) *(verdadero)* true; *(seguro)* certain; **estar en lo c.** to be right; **lo c. es que ...** the fact is that ...; **por c.** by the way (b) *(algún)* certain; **ciertas personas** certain o some people

2 *adv* certainly

ciervo,-a *nm,f* deer; *(macho)* stag; *(hembra)* doe, hind

cifra *nf* (a) *(número)* figure, number (b) *(código)* cipher, code

cifrar *vt* to express in figures

cigala *nf* Norway lobster, scampi

cigarra *nf* cicada

cigarrillo *nm* cigarette

cigarro *nm* (a) *(puro)* cigar (b) *(cigarrillo)* cigarette

cigüeña *nf* (a) *Orn* stork (b) *Téc* crank

cigüeñal *nm* crankshaft

cilindrada *nf Aut* cylinder capacity

cilíndrico,-a *adj* cylindrical

cilindro *nm* cylinder

cima *nf* summit

cimbrearse *upr* to sway

cimentar *vt* to lay the foundations of; *Fig (amistad)* to strengthen

cimientos *nmpl* foundations; **echar** *o* **poner los c.** to lay the foundations

cinc *nm* zinc

cincel *nm* chisel

cincelar *vt* to chisel

cinco *adj & nm* five

cincuenta *adj & nm inv* fifty

cine *nm* (a) *(local)* cinema, *US* movie theater (b) *(arte)* cinema; **c. mudo/sonoro** silent/talking films

cineasta *nmf* movie director, movie maker

cinéfilo,-a *nm,f (que va al cine)* (keen) moviegoer *o Br* filmgoer; *(que entiende de cine)* movie *o Br* film buff

cinematográfico,-a *adj* cinematographic; **la industria cinematográfica** the movie *o Br* film industry

cíngaro,-a *adj & nm,f* gypsy

cínico,-a 1 *adj* shameless

2 *nm,f* shameless person; **es un c.** he's shameless, he has no shame

> 🔎 Observa que la palabra inglesa **cynic** es un falso amigo y no es la traducción de la palabra española **cínico**. En inglés, **cynic** significa tanto "descreído, suspicaz" como "desaprensivo".

cinismo *nm* shamelessness

> 🔎 Observa que la palabra inglesa **cynicism** es un falso amigo y no es la traducción de la palabra española **cinismo**. En inglés, **cynicism** significa "descreimiento, suspicacia"

cinta *nf* (a) *(tira)* band, strip; *(para adornar)* ribbon; *Cost* braid, edging (b) *Téc & Mús* tape; **c. adhesiva/aislante** adhesive/insulating tape; **c. de vídeo** video tape; **c. transportadora** conveyor belt (c) *Cin* film

cinto *nm* belt

cintura *nf* waist

cinturón *nm* belt; *Fig* **apretarse el c.** to tighten one's belt; **c. de seguridad** safety belt; *Am* **c. de miseria** = slum or shanty

town area round a large city

ciprés *nm* cypress

circense *adj* circus

circo *nm* circus

circuito *nm* circuit

circulación *nf* (a) circulation (b) *Aut (tráfico)* traffic

circular 1 *adj & nf* circular

2 *vi (moverse)* to circulate; *(líquido)* to flow; *(tren, autobús)* to run; *Fig (rumor)* to go round; **circule por la izquierda** *(en letrero)* keep to the left

circulatorio,-a *adj* circulatory; *Aut* **un caos c.** traffic chaos

círculo *nm* circle; *Fig* **c. vicioso** vicious circle

circuncisión *nf* circumcision

circundante *adj* surrounding

circundar *vt* to surround, to encircle

circunferencia *nf* circumference

circunloquio *nm* circumlocution

circunscribirse *(pp circunscrito)* *upr* **c. a** to confine *o* limit oneself to

circunscripción *nf* district; **c. electoral** constituency

circunscrito,-a *adj* circumscribed

circunspecto,-a *adj* circumspect

circunstancia *nf* circumstance; **en estas circunstancias ...** under the circumstances ...

circunstancial *adj* circumstantial

cirio *nm* wax candle

cirrosis *nf* cirrhosis

ciruela *nf* plum; **c. claudia** greengage; **c. pasa** prune

ciruelo *nm* plum tree

cirugía *nf* surgery; **c. estética** *o* **plástica** plastic surgery

cirujano,-a *nm,f* surgeon

cisma *nm* (a) *Rel* schism (b) *Pol* split

cisne *nm* swan

cisterna *nf* cistern, tank

cistitis *nf inv* cystitis

cita *nf* (a) appointment; **darse c.** to come together (b) *(amorosa)* date (c) *(mención)* quotation

citación *nf Jur* citation, summons *sing*

citado,-a *adj* aforementioned

citar 1 *vt* (a) *(dar cita)* to arrange to meet, to make an appointment with (b) *(mencionar)* to quote (c) *Jur* to summons

2 citarse *upr* to arrange to meet, to make a date (**con** with)

cítrico,-a 1 *adj* citric, citrus

2 *nmpl* **cítricos** citrus fruits

ciudad *nf* town; *(capital)* city; *Méx* **c. perdida** shanty town

ciudadanía *nf* citizenship

ciudadano,-a 1 *nm,f* citizen; **el c. de a pie** the man in the street

2 *adj* civic

cívico,-a *adj* civic

civil 1 *adj* (a) civil; **matrimonio c.** civil marriage (b) *Mil* civilian

2 *nm* member of the Guardia Civil

civilización *nf* civilization

civilizado,-a *adj* civilized

civilizar [40] *vt* to civilize

civismo *nm* (a) *(urbanidad)* public-spiritedness (b) *(cortesía)* civility

cizaña *nf Bot* bearded darnel; *Fig* **sembrar c.** to sow discord

cl *(abr* **centilitro(s))** cl

clamar *vt* to cry out for, to clamour for

clamor *nm* clamour

clamoroso,-a *adj* resounding

clan *nm* clan

clandestinidad *nf* **en la c.** underground

clandestino,-a *adj* clandestine, underground; **aborto c.** backstreet abortion

clara *nf (de huevo)* white

claraboya *nf* skylight

clarear *vi* (a) *(amanecer)* to dawn (b) *(despejar)* to clear up (c) *(transparentar)* to wear thin, to become transparent

clarete *adj & nm* claret

claridad *nf* (a) *(luz)* light, brightness (b) *(inteligibilidad)* clarity; **con c.** clearly

clarificador,-a *adj* clarifying

clarificar [44] *vt* to clarify

clarín *nm* bugle

clarinete *nm* clarinet

clarividente 1 *adj* (a) far-sighted (b) *(lúcido)* lucid

2 *nmf (persona)* clairvoyant

claro,-a 1 *adj* (a) clear; **dejar algo c.** to make sth clear (b) *(líquido, salsa)* thin (c) *(color)* light

2 *interj* of course!; **¡c. que no!** of course not!; **¡c. que sí!** certainly!

3 *nm* (a) *(espacio)* gap, space; *(en un bosque)* clearing (b) *Met* bright spell

4 *adv* clearly

clase *nf* (a) *(grupo)* class; **c. alta/media** upper/middle class; **clases pasivas** pensioners; **primera/segunda c.** first/second class (b) *(tipo)* kind, sort; **toda c. de ...** all kinds of ... (c) *Educ (curso)* class; *(aula)* classroom; **c. particular** private class o lesson (d) *(estilo)* class; **tener c.** to have class

clásico,-a 1 *adj* classical; *(típico)* classic; *(en el vestir)* classic

2 *nm* classic

clasificación *nf* (a) classification; *Dep* league table (b) *(para campeonato,* *concurso)* qualification

clasificar [44] 1 *vt* to classify, to class

2 clasificarse *vpr Dep* to qualify

claudicar [44] *vi* to give in

claustro *nm* (a) *Arquit* cloister (b) *(reunión)* staff meeting

claustrofobia *nf* claustrophobia

cláusula *nf* clause

clausura *nf* (a) *(cierre)* closure; **ceremonia de c.** closing ceremony (b) *Rel* enclosure

clausurar *vt* to close

clavadista *nmf CAm, Méx* diver

clavar 1 *vt* (a) to nail; *(clavo)* to bang o hammer in; *(estaca)* to drive in (b) *Fam (timar)* to sting o fleece

2 clavarse *vpr* **c. una astilla** to get a splinter

clave 1 *nf* key; **la palabra c.** the key word

2 *nm* harpsichord

clavel *nm* carnation

clavícula *nf* collarbone

clavija *nf Téc* jack

clavo *nm* (a) nail; *Fig* **dar en el c.** to hit the nail on the head (b) *Bot* clove

claxon *nm (pl* **cláxones)** horn; **tocar el c.** to sound the horn

clemencia *nf* mercy, clemency

clementina *nf* clementine

cleptómano,-a *adj & nm,f* kleptomaniac

clerical *adj* clerical

clericó *nm RP* = drink made of white wine and fruit

clérigo *nm* priest

clero *nm* clergy

cliché *nm* (a) *Fig (tópico)* cliché (b) *Fot* negative (c) *Impr* plate

cliente *nmf* customer, client

clientela *nf* clientele

clima *nm* climate

climatizado,-a *adj* air-conditioned

climatizar [40] *vt* to air-condition

clímax *nm inv* climax

clínica *nf* clinic

clínico,-a *adj* clinical

clip *nm* clip

clítoris *nm inv* clitoris

cloaca *nf* sewer, drain

clorhídrico,-a *adj* hydrochloric

cloro *nm* chlorine

cloroformo *nm* chloroform

cloruro *nm* chloride; **c. sódico** sodium chloride

clóset *nm (pl* **clósets)** *Am* fitted cupboard

club *nm (pl* **clubs** o **clubes)** club; **c. náutico** yacht club

cm *(abr* **centímetro(s))** cm

CNT *nf (abr* **Confederación Nacional del**

Trabajo) = Spanish anarchist trade union federation

coacción *nf* coercion

coaccionar *vt* to coerce

coactivo,-a *adj* coercive

coadyuvar *vt* to assist

coagular *vt & vi,* **coagularse** *vpr* to coagulate; *(sangre)* to clot; *(leche)* to curdle

coágulo *nm* coagulum, clot

coalición *nf* coalition

coartada *nf* alibi

coartar *vt* to restrict

coba *nf-Fam* **dar c. a algn** to soft-soap sb

cobalto *nm* cobalt

cobarde 1 *adj* cowardly
2 *nmf* coward

cobardía *nf* cowardice

cobaya *nf* guinea pig

cobertizo *nm* shed, shack

cobertor *nm* bedspread

cobertura *nf* cover; *(de noticia)* coverage

cobija *nf Am* blanket

cobijar 1 *vt* to shelter
2 cobijarse *vpr* to take shelter

cobijo *nm* shelter; *Fig (protección)* protection

cobra *nf* cobra

cobrador,-a *nm,f* (a) *(de autobús)* *(hombre)* conductor; *(mujer)* conductress (b) *(de luz, agua etc)* collector

cobrar 1 *vt* (a) *(dinero)* to charge; *(cheque)* to cash; *(salario)* to earn (b) *Fig (fuerza)* to gain, to get; **c. ánimos** to take courage *o* heart; **c. importancia** to become important
2 *vi Fam* to catch it
3 cobrarse *vpr* **¿se cobra?** *(al pagar)* take it out of this, please

cobre *nm* (a) copper (b) *Am (moneda)* copper cent

cobrizo,-a *adj* copper, copper-coloured

cobro *nm (pago)* collecting; *(de cheque)* cashing; *Tel* **llamada a c. revertido** *Br* reverse-charge call, *US* collect call

coca *nf* (a) *Bot* coca (b) *Fam (droga)* cocaine, coke

cocaína *nf* cocaine

cocainómano,-a *nm,f* cocaine addict

cocalero,-a *Bol, Perú* **1** *adj* **región cocalera** coca-producing area; **productor c.** coca farmer *o* producer
2 *nm,f* coca farmer *o* producer

cocción *nf* cooking; *(en agua)* boiling; *(en horno)* baking

cocer [41] 1 *vt* to cook; *(hervir)* to boil; *(hornear)* to bake
2 *vi (hervir)* to boil

3 cocerse *vpr* (a) *(comida)* to cook; *(hervir)* to boil; *(hornear)* to bake (b) *(tramarse)* to be going on

cochambroso,-a *adj* squalid

coche *nm* (a) car; **en c.** by car; **c. de carreras** racing car; **c. de bomberos** fire engine; **c. fúnebre** hearse (b) *Ferroc* carriage, coach; **c. cama** sleeping car, sleeper (c) *(de caballos)* carriage, coach

cochecito *nm (de niño) Br* pram, *US* baby carriage

cochera *nf* (a) garage (b) *(de autobuses)* depot

cochinillo *nm* suckling pig

cochino,-a 1 *nm,f* (a) *(macho)* pig; *(hembra)* sow (b) *Fam (persona)* filthy person, pig
2 *adj (sucio)* filthy, disgusting

cocido *nm* stew

cociente *nm* quotient

cocina *nf* (a) kitchen (b) *(aparato)* cooker, stove; **c. eléctrica/de gas** electric/gas cooker (c) *(arte)* cooking; **c. casera** home cooking; **c. española** Spanish cooking *o* cuisine

cocinar *vt & vi* to cook

cocinero,-a *nm,f* cook

cocktail *nm* = **cóctel**

coco¹ *nm* coconut; *Fam (cabeza)* nut; **comerle el c. a algn** to brainwash sb; **comerse el c.** to get obsessed

coco² *nm Fam (fantasma)* bogeyman

cocodrilo *nm* crocodile

cocoliche *nm RP Fam* = pidgin Spanish spoken by Italian immigrants

cocotero *nm* coconut palm

cóctel *nm* cocktail; **c. Molotov** Molotov cocktail

coctelera *nf* cocktail shaker

codazo *nm* (a) *(señal)* nudge with one's elbow (b) *(golpe)* blow with one's elbow

codearse *vpr* to rub shoulders (**con** with), to hobnob (**con** with)

codeína *nf* codeine

codicia *nf* greed

codiciar [43] *vt* to covet

codicioso,-a *adj* covetous, greedy

codificar [44] *vt (ley)* to codify; *(mensajes)* to encode

código *nm* code; **c. de circulación** highway code; **c. postal** *Br* postcode, postal code, *US* zip code

codo *nm* elbow; *Fig* **c. con c.** side by side; *Fam* **hablar por los codos** to talk nonstop

codorniz *nf* quail

coeficiente *nm* (a) coefficient (b) *(grado)* rate; **c. intelectual** intelligence quotient

coercitivo,-a *adj* coercive

coetáneo,-a *adj & nm,f* contemporary

coexistencia *nf* coexistence

coexistir *vi* to coexist

cofia *nf* bonnet

cofradía *nf (hermandad)* brotherhood; *(asociación)* association

cofre *nm (arca)* trunk, chest; *(para joyas)* box, casket

coger [53] **1** *vt* **(a)** *(del suelo)* to take; *(del suelo)* to pick (up); *(fruta, flores)* to pick; *(asir)* to seize, to take hold of; *(bus, tren)* to take, to catch; *(pelota, ladrón, resfriado)* to catch; *(entender)* to grasp; *(costumbre)* to pick up; *(velocidad, fuerza)* to gather; *(atropellar)* to run over, to knock down **(b)** *Am Vulg* to fuck

2 *vi Fam* **cogió y se fue** he upped and left

3 cogerse *vpr (agarrarse)* to hold on

cogida *nf* goring

cogollo *nm (de lechuga)* heart

cogotazo *nm Fam* blow on the back of the neck

cogote *nm* nape *o* back of the neck

cohabitación *nf* cohabitation

cohabitar *vi* to live together, to cohabit

cohecho *nm Jur* bribery

coherencia *nf* coherence

coherente *adj* coherent

cohesión *nf* cohesion

cohete *nm* rocket; **c. espacial** space rocket

cohibido,-a *adj* inhibited

cohibir 1 *vt* to inhibit

2 cohibirse *vpr* to feel inhibited

COI *nm Dep (abr* **Comité Olímpico Internacional**) IOC

coima *nf Andes, RP Fam* bribe, *Br* backhander

coincidencia *nf* coincidence

coincidir *vi* **(a)** to coincide **(b)** *(concordar)* to agree; **todos coincidieron en señalar que** everyone agreed that **(c)** *(encontrarse)* to meet by chance

coito *nm* coitus, intercourse

cojear *vi (persona)* to limp, to hobble; *(mueble)* to wobble

cojera *nf* limp

cojín *nm* cushion

cojinete *nm Téc* bearing; **c. de agujas/bolas** needle/ball bearing

cojo,-a 1 *adj (persona)* lame; *(mueble)* rickety

2 *nm,f* lame person

cojón *nm Vulg* ball; **de cojones** *(estupendo)* fucking brilliant *o* good; *(pésimo)* fucking awful *o* bad

cojonudo,-a *adj muy Fam Br* bloody *o US* goddamn brilliant

cojudez *nf Andes muy Fam* **¡qué c.!** *(acto)* what a *Br* bloody *o US* goddamn stupid thing to do!; *(dicho)* what a *Br* bloody *o US* goddamn stupid thing to say!

cojudo,-a *adj Andes muy Fam Br* bloody *o US* goddamn stupid

col *nf* cabbage; **c. de Bruselas** Brussels sprout

cola¹ *nf* **(a)** *(de animal)* tail; *(de vestido)* train; *(de pelo)* ponytail; *Am (de persona) Br* bum, *US* fanny; **a la c.** at the back *o* rear; *Fam* **traer c.** to have consequences **(b)** *(fila) Br* queue, *US* line; **hacer c.** *Br* to queue (up), *US* to stand in line

cola² *nf (pegamento)* glue

colaboración *nf* **(a)** collaboration **(b)** *Prensa* contribution

colaboracionismo *nm Pol* collaboration

colaborador,-a 1 *nm,f* **(a)** collaborator **(b)** *Prensa* contributor

2 *adj* collaborating

colaborar *vi* to collaborate, to cooperate

colación *nf* **sacar** *o* **traer (algo) a c.** to bring (sth) up

colada *nf* wash, laundry; **hacer la c.** to do the washing *o* laundry

colador *nm* colander, sieve; *(de té, café)* strainer

colapsar 1 *vt* to bring to a standstill

2 colapsarse *vpr* to come to a standstill

colapso *nm* **(a)** *Med* collapse **(b)** *Aut* **c. circulatorio** traffic jam, hold-up

colar [2] **1** *vt* **(a)** *(líquido)* to strain, to filter **(b)** *(por agujero)* to slip

2 *vi Fam* **esa mentira no cuela** that lie won't wash

3 colarse *vpr* **(a)** to slip in; *(a fiesta)* to gatecrash; *(en una cola)* to jump the queue **(b)** *Fam (pasarse)* to go too far

colateral *adj* collateral

colcha *nf* bedspread

colchón *nm* mattress

colchoneta *nf* air bed

colear *vi* **(a)** to wag its tail; *Fam* **vivito y coleando** alive and kicking **(b)** *Fam* **el asunto aún colea** we haven't heard the last of it yet

colección *nf* collection

coleccionable *adj & nm* collectable

coleccionar *vt* to collect

coleccionista *nmf* collector

colecta *nf* collection

colectividad *nf* community

colectivo,-a 1 *adj* collective

2 *nm* **(a)** *(asociación)* association **(b)** *Andes (taxi)* (collective) taxi **(c)** *Arg (autobús)* bus

colega *nmf* (a) colleague (b) *Fam (amigo)* pal, *Br* mate, *US* buddy

colegiado,-a *nm,f Dep* referee

colegial,-ala 1 *adj (escolar)* school

  2 *nm,f (alumno)* schoolboy; *(alumna)* schoolgirl; **los colegiales** the schoolchildren

colegio *nm* (a) *(escuela)* school; **c. privado** private school, *Br* public *o* independent school (b) *(profesional)* association, college; **c. de abogados** the Bar; *Pol* **c. electoral** electoral college (c) *Univ* **c. mayor** *o* **universitario** hall of residence

colegir [58] *vt* to infer, to deduce

cólera¹ *nf* anger, rage

cólera² *nm Med* cholera

colérico,-a *adj* furious

colesterol *nm* cholesterol

coleta *nf* pigtail, ponytail; *Fig* **cortarse la c.** to retire

coletazo *nm* **dar los últimos coletazos** to be on one's last legs

coletilla *nf* postcript

colgado,-a *adj* (a) *Fam* **dejar (a algn) c.** to leave (sb) in the lurch (b) *Fam* weird; *(drogado)* high

colgante 1 *nm (joya)* pendant

  2 *adj* hanging

colgar [2] **1** *vt* (a) to hang (up); *(colada)* to hang (out) (b) *(ahorcar)* to hang

  2 *vi* (a) to hang (**de** from); *Fig* **c. de un hilo** to hang by a thread (b) *Tel* to hang up

  3 colgarse *vpr (ahorcarse)* to hang oneself

colibrí *nm* hummingbird

cólico *nm* colic

coliflor *nf* cauliflower

colijo *indic pres de* **colegir**

colilla *nf* (cigarette) end *o* butt

colimba *nf Arg Fam* military service

colina *nf* hill

colindante *adj* adjoining, adjacent

colindar *vi* to be adjacent (**con** to)

colirio *nm* eye-drops

colisión *nf* collision, crash; *(de ideas)* clash

colisionar *vi* to collide, to crash

colitis *nf* colitis

colla *Bol* **1** *adj* of/from the altiplano

  2 *nmf* = indigenous person from the altiplano

collage *nm* collage

collar *nm* (a) *(adorno)* necklace (b) *(de perro)* collar

colmado,-a *adj* full, filled; *(cucharada)* heaped

colmar *vt* (a) to fill (right up); *(vaso, copa)* to fill to the brim; *Fig* to shower (**de** with) (b) *(ambiciones)* to fulfil, to satisfy

colmena *nf* beehive

colmillo *nm* eye *o* canine tooth; *Zool (de carnívoro)* fang; *(de jabalí, elefante)* tusk

colmo *nm* height; **el c. de** the height of; **¡eso es el c.!** that's the last straw!; **para c.** to top it all

colocación *nf* (a) *(acto)* positioning (b) *(disposición)* lay-out (c) *(empleo)* job, employment

colocado,-a *adj* (a) *(empleado)* employed (b) *Fam (drogado)* high

colocar [44] **1** *vt* (a) to place, to put (b) *Fin (invertir)* to invest (c) *(emplear)* to give work to (d) *Fam (drogar)* to stone

  2 colocarse *vpr* (a) *(situarse)* to put oneself (b) *(emplearse)* to take a job (**de** as) (c) *Fam (drogarse)* to get high

colofón *nm* (a) *(apéndice)* colophon (b) *Fig* climax

Colombia *n* Colombia

colombiano,-a *adj & nm,f* Colombian

Colón *n* Columbus

colón *nm Fin* = standard monetary unit of Costa Rica and El Salvador

colonia¹ *nf* colony; *(campamento)* summer camp; *Méx (barrio)* district

colonia² *nf (perfume)* cologne

colonial *adj* colonial

colonialismo *nm* colonialism

colonización *nf* colonization

colonizar [40] *vt* to colonize

coloquial *adj* colloquial

coloquio *nm* discussion, colloquium

color *nm* colour; *Cin & Fot* **en c.** in colour; **de colores** multicoloured; **persona de c.** coloured person

colorado,-a 1 *adj* red; **ponerse c.** to blush

  2 *nm* red

🖉 Observa que la palabra inglesa **coloured** es un falso amigo y no es la traducción de la palabra española **colorado**. En inglés, **coloured** significa "coloreado".

---

colorante *nm* colouring

colorear *vt* to colour

colorete *nm* rouge

colorido *nm* colour

colorín *nm* goldfinch

colosal *adj* colossal

columna *nf* column; *Anat* **c. vertebral** vertebral column, spinal column

columpiar [43] **1** *vt* to swing

  2 columpiarse *vpr* to swing

columpio *nm* swing

coma¹ *nf* (a) *Ling & Mús* comma (b) *Mat*

point; **tres c. cinco** three point five

coma² *nm Med* coma

comadre *nf* (**a**) *(madrina)* = godmother of one's child, or mother of one's godchild (**b**) *Am Fam (amiga)* friend

comadreja *nf* weasel

comadreo *nm* gossip, gossiping

comadrona *nf* midwife

comal *nm CAm, Méx* = flat clay or metal dish used for baking "tortillas"

comandancia *nf* command

comandante *nm* (**a**) *Mil* commander, commanding officer (**b**) *Av* captain

comandar *vt* to command

comando *nm* (**a**) *Mil* commando (**b**) *Informát* command

comarca *nf* region

comarcal *adj* regional

comba *nf* (**a**) *(curvatura)* curve, bend (**b**) *(cuerda)* skipping rope; **saltar a la c.** to skip, *US* to jump rope

combar *vt* to bend

combate *nm* combat; *(en boxeo)* fight; *Mil* battle; **fuera de c.** out for the count; *(eliminado)* out of action

combatiente 1 *adj* fighting
  2 *nmf* combatant

combatir 1 *vt* to combat
  2 *vi* **c. contra** to fight against

combativo,-a *adj* spirited, aggressive

combinación *nf* (**a**) combination (**b**) *(prenda)* slip

combinado,-a 1 *adj* combined
  2 *nm* (**a**) *(cóctel)* cocktail (**b**) *Dep* line-up

combinar *vt*, **combinarse** *vpr* to combine

combustible 1 *nm* fuel
  2 *adj* combustible

combustión *nf* combustion

comedia *nf* comedy

comediante,-a *nm,f* *(hombre)* actor; *(mujer)* actress

comedido,-a *adj* self-restrained, reserved

comedor *nm* dining room

comensal *nmf* companion at table

comentar *vt* **c. algo con algn** to talk sth over with sb; **me han comentado que** I've been told that

comentario *nm* (**a**) comment, remark; *(crítica)* commentary; **sin c.** no comment (**b**) **comentarios** *(cotilleos)* gossip

comentarista *nmf* commentator

comenzar [51] *vt & vi* to begin, to start; **comenzó a llover** it started raining *o* to rain; **comenzó diciendo que ...** he started by saying that ...

comer 1 *vt* (**a**) to eat (**b**) *(en juegos)* to take, to capture
  2 *vi* to eat; **dar de c. a algn** to feed sb
  3 comerse *vpr* (**a**) to eat (**b**) *Fig (saltarse)* to skip

comercial *adj* commercial

comercialización *nf* marketing

comercializar [40] *vt* to market

comerciante *nmf* merchant

comerciar [43] *vi* to trade; **comercia con oro** he trades in gold

comercio *nm* (**a**) commerce, trade; **c. exterior** foreign trade; *Informát* **c. electrónico** e-commerce; **c. justo** fair trade (**b**) *(tienda)* shop

comestible 1 *adj* edible
  2 *nmpl* **comestibles** food, foodstuff(s); **tienda de comestibles** grocer's shop, *US* grocery store

cometa 1 *nm Astron* comet
  2 *nf* *(juguete)* kite

cometer *vt* *(error, falta)* to make; *(delito, crimen)* to commit

cometido *nm* (**a**) *(tarea)* task, assignment (**b**) *(deber)* duty; **cumplir su c.** to do one's duty

comezón *nm* itch

cómic *nm* comic

comicios *nmpl* elections

cómico,-a 1 *adj* (**a**) comical, funny (**b**) *Teatro* **actor c.** comedian
  2 *nm,f* comic; *(hombre)* comedian; *(mujer)* comedienne

comida *nf* (**a**) *(alimento)* food (**b**) *(almuerzo, cena)* meal

comidilla *nf Fam* **la c. del pueblo** the talk of the town

comienzo *nm* beginning, start; **a comienzos de** at the beginning of; **dar c. (a algo)** to begin *o* start (sth)

comillas *nfpl* inverted commas; **entre c.** in inverted commas

comilón,-ona 1 *adj* greedy, gluttonous
  2 *nm,f* big eater, glutton

comilona *nf Fam* big meal, feast

comino *nm* cumin, cummin; *Fam* **me importa un c.** I don't give a damn (about it)

comisaría *nf* police station

comisario *nm* (**a**) *(de policía)* police inspector (**b**) *(delegado)* commissioner; **c. europeo** European Commissioner

comisión *nf* (**a**) *Com (retribución)* commission; **a** *o* **con c.** on a commission basis (**b**) *(comité)* committee; **la C. Europea** the European Commission

comité *nm* committee

comitiva *nf* suite, retinue

como 1 *adv* (**a**) *(manera)* how; **me gusta c. cantas** I like the way you sing; **dilo c. quieras** say it however you like

(**b**) *(comparación)* as; **blanco c. la nieve** as white as snow; **habla c. su padre** he talks like his father

(**c**) *(según)* as; **c. decíamos ayer** as we were saying yesterday

(**d**) *(en calidad de)* as; **c. presidente** as president; **lo compré c. recuerdo** I bought it as a souvenir

(**e**) *(aproximadamente)* about; **c. a la mitad de camino** halfway; **c. unos diez** about ten

2 *conj* (**a**) (+ *subjunctive*) *(si)* if; **c. no estudies vas a suspender** if you don't study hard, you'll fail

(**b**) *(porque)* as, since; **c. no venías me marché** as you didn't come, I left

(**c**) **c. si** as if; **c. si nada** *o* **tal cosa** as if nothing had happened; *Fam* **c. si lo viera** I can imagine perfectly well

cómo 1 *adv* (**a**) **¿c.?** *(¿perdón?)* what?

(**b**) *(interrogativo)* how; **¿c. estás?** how are you?; **¿c. lo sabes?** how do you know?; **¿c. es de grande/ancho?** how big/wide is it?; **¿a c. están los tomates?** how much are the tomatoes?; **¿c. es que no viniste a la fiesta?** *(por qué)* how come you didn't come to the party?; *Fam* **¿c. es eso?** how come?

(**c**) *(exclamativo)* how; **¡c. has crecido!** you've really grown a lot!; **¡c. no!** but of course!

2 *nm* **el c. y el porqué** the whys and wherefores

cómoda *nf* chest of drawers

comodidad *nf* (**a**) comfort (**b**) *(conveniencia)* convenience

> 🖉 Observa que la palabra inglesa **commodity** es un falso amigo y no es la traducción de la palabra española **comodidad**. En inglés, **commodity** significa "producto básico".

comodín *nm Naipes* joker

cómodo,-a *adj* (**a**) comfortable; **ponerse c.** to make oneself comfortable (**b**) *(útil)* handy, convenient

comoquiera *adv* (**a**) however, whatever way; **c. que sea** one way or another (**b**) **c. que no estaba enterado** *(puesto que)* as he didn't know

compa *nmf Fam* pal, *Br* mate, *US* buddy

compacto,-a *adj* compact; **disco c.** compact disc

compadecer [33] 1 *vt* to feel sorry for, to pity

2 compadecerse *vpr* to have *o* take pity (**de** on)

compadre *nm* (**a**) *(padrino)* = godfather of one's child, or father of one's godchild (**b**) *Am Fam (amigo)* friend, mate

compadrear *vi RP* to brag, to boast

compaginar *vt* to combine

compañerismo *nm* companionship, comradeship

compañero,-a *nm,f* companion; **c. de colegio** school friend; **c. de piso** flat-mate

compañía *nf* company; **hacer c. (a algn)** to keep (sb) company; **c. de seguros/de teatro** insurance/theatre company

comparable *adj* comparable

comparación *nf* comparison; **en c.** comparatively; **en c. con** compared to; **sin c.** beyond compare

comparar *vt* to compare (**con** with)

comparativo,-a *adj & nm* comparative

comparecencia *nf* appearance

comparecer [33] *vi Jur* to appear (**ante** before)

comparsa *nf* band of revellers

compartimento, compartimiento *nm* compartment; **c. de primera/segunda clase** first-/second-class compartment

compartir *vt* to share

compás *nm* (**a**) *Téc* (pair of) compasses (**b**) *Náut* compass (**c**) *Mús (división)* time; *(intervalo)* beat; *(ritmo)* rhythm; **c. de espera** *Mús* bar rest; *Fig (pausa)* delay; **al c. de** in time to

compasión *nf* compassion, pity; **tener c. (de algn)** to feel sorry (for sb)

compasivo,-a *adj* compassionate

compatible *adj* compatible

compatriota *nmf* compatriot; *(hombre)* fellow countryman; *(mujer)* fellow countrywoman

compendiar [43] *vt* to abridge, to summarize

compendio *nm* compendium

compenetrarse *vpr* to understand each other *o* one another

compensación *nf* compensation

compensar 1 *vt (pérdida, error)* to make up for; *(indemnizar)* to compensate (for)

2 *vi* to be worthwhile; **este trabajo no compensa** this job's not worth my time

competencia *nf* (**a**) *(rivalidad, empresas rivales)* competition (**b**) *(capacidad)* competence (**c**) *(incumbencia)* field, province; **no es de mi c.** it's not up to me

competente *adj* competent

competición *nf* competition, contest

competido,-a *adj* hard-fought

competidor,-a 1 *nm,f* (**a**) *Com & Dep*

competitor (**b**) (*participante*) contestant
2 *adj* competing
competir [6] *vi* to compete (**con** with *o* against; **en** in; **por** for)
competitividad *nf* competitivity
competitivo,-a *adj* competitive
compilar *vt* to compile
compinche *nmf* (**a**) (*compañero*) chum, pal (**b**) (*cómplice*) accomplice
complacencia *nf* (**a**) (*satisfacción*) satisfaction (**b**) (*indulgencia*) indulgence

> *ℓ* Observa que la palabra inglesa **complacency** es un falso amigo y no es la traducción de la palabra española **complacencia**. En inglés, **complacency** significa "autocomplacencia".

complacer [60] **1** *vt* to please; *Fml* **me complace presentarles a ...** it gives me great pleasure to introduce to you ...
2 complacerse *vpr* to delight (**en** in), to take pleasure (**en** in)
complaciente *adj* obliging
complejidad *nf* complexity
complejo,-a *adj & nm* complex
complementar 1 *vt* to complement
2 complementarse *vpr* to complement (each other), to be complementary to (each other)
complementario,-a *adj* complementary
complemento *nm* complement; *Ling* object
completamente *adv* completely
completar *vt* to complete
completo,-a *adj* (**a**) (*terminado*) complete; **por c.** completely (**b**) (*lleno*) full; **al c.** full up to capacity
complexión *nf* build; **de c. fuerte** well-built

> *ℓ* Observa que la palabra inglesa **complexion** es un falso amigo y no es la traducción de la palabra española **complexión**. En inglés, **complexion** significa "tez".

complicación *nf* complication
complicado,-a *adj* (**a**) (*complejo*) complicated (**b**) (*implicado*) involved
complicar [44] **1** *vt* (**a**) to complicate (**b**) **c. en** (*involucrar*) to involve in
2 complicarse *vpr* to get complicated; **c. la vida** to make life difficult for oneself
cómplice *nmf* accomplice
complot *nm* (*pl* **complots**) conspiracy, plot
componente 1 *adj* component
2 *nm* (**a**) (*pieza*) component; (*ingrediente*) ingredient (**b**) (*persona*) member

componer [19] (*pp* **compuesto**) **1** *vt* (**a**) (*formar*) to compose, to make up (**b**) *Mús & Lit* to compose (**c**) (*reparar*) to mend, to repair
2 componerse *vpr* (**a**) **c. de** (*consistir*) to be made up of, to consist of (**b**) (*arreglarse*) to dress up (**c**) *Fam* **componérselas** to manage
comportamiento *nm* behaviour
comportar 1 *vt* to entail, to involve
2 comportarse *vpr* to behave; **c. mal** to misbehave
composición *nf* composition
compositor,-a *nm,f* composer
compostelano,-a *adj* from Santiago de Compostela
compostura *nf* composure
compota *nf* compote
compra *nf* (*acción*) buying; (*cosa comprada*) purchase, buy; **ir de c.** to go shopping
comprador,-a *nm,f* purchaser, buyer
comprar *vt* (**a**) to buy (**b**) *Fig* (*sobornar*) to bribe, to buy off
compraventa *nf* buying and selling; **contrato de c.** contract of sale
comprender *vt* (**a**) (*entender*) to understand; **se comprende** it's understandable (**b**) (*contener*) to comprise, to include
comprensible *adj* understandable
comprensión *nf* understanding
comprensivo,-a *adj* understanding

> *ℓ* Observa que la palabra inglesa **comprehensive** es un falso amigo y no es la traducción de la palabra española **comprensivo**. En inglés, **comprehensive** significa "amplio, detallado".

compresa *nf* (**a**) (*para mujer*) sanitary towel (**b**) *Med* compress
comprimido,-a 1 *nm Farm* tablet
2 *adj* compressed; **escopeta de aire c.** air rifle
comprimir *vt* to compress
comprobante *nm* (*de compra etc*) voucher, receipt
comprobar [2] *vt* to check
comprometer 1 *vt* (**a**) (*arriesgar*) to compromise, to jeopardize (**b**) (*obligar*) to compel, to force
2 comprometerse *vpr* (**a**) **c. a hacer algo** to undertake to do sth (**b**) (*novios*) to become engaged
comprometido,-a *adj* (**a**) (*situación*) difficult (**b**) (*para casarse*) engaged
compromiso *nm* (**a**) (*obligación*) obligation, commitment; **sin c.** without obligation; **por c.** out of a sense of duty (**b**) **poner (a algn) en un c.** to put (sb) in a

difficult o embarrassing situation (**c**) *(acuerdo)* agreement; *Fml* **c. matrimonial** engagement; **soltero y sin c.** single and unattached

> *♪* Observa que la palabra inglesa **compromise** es un falso amigo y no es la traducción de la palabra española **compromiso**. En inglés, **compromise** significa "solución negociada".

compuesto,-a 1 *adj* (**a**) compound (**b**) **c. de** composed of
     2 *nm* compound

compulsar *vt* to make a certified true copy of

compungido,-a *adj (arrepentido)* remorseful; *(triste)* sorrowful, sad

compuse *pt indef de* **componer**

computadora *nf* computer

cómputo *nm* calculation

comulgar [42] *vi* (**a**) to receive Holy Communion (**b**) *Fig* **no comulgo con sus ideas** I don't share his ideas

común 1 *adj* (**a**) common; **de c. acuerdo** by common consent; **hacer algo en c.** to do sth jointly; **poco c.** unusual; **por lo c.** generally (**b**) *(compartido)* shared, communal; **amigos comunes** mutual friends
     2 *nm Br Pol* **los Comunes** the Commons

comuna *nf Am (municipalidad)* municipality

comunal *adj* communal

comunero,-a *nm,f Perú, Méx (indígena)* = member of an indigenous village community

comunicación *nf* (**a**) communication; **ponerse en c. (con algn)** to get in touch (with sb) (**b**) *(comunicado)* communication; **c. oficial** communiqué (**c**) *Tel* connection; **se nos cortó la c.** we were cut off (**d**) *(unión)* link, connection

comunicado,-a 1 *adj* **una zona bien comunicada** a well-served zone; **dos ciudades bien comunicadas** two towns with good connections (between them)
     2 *nm* communiqué; **c. de prensa** press release

comunicar [44] **1** *vt* to communicate; **comuníquenoslo lo antes posible** let us know as soon as possible
     2 *vi* (**a**) to communicate (**b**) *Tel* to be engaged; **está comunicando** it's engaged
     3 comunicarse *upr* to communicate

comunicativo,-a *adj* communicative

comunidad *nf* community; **C. Europea** European Community; **C. de Estados**

Independientes Commonwealth of Independent States

comunión *nf* communion

comunismo *nm* communism

comunista *adj & nmf* communist

comunitario,-a *adj* (**a**) of o relating to the community (**b**) *(de UE)* of o relating to the EU; **la política agraria comunitaria** the common agricultural policy

con *prep* (**a**) with; **córtalo c. las tijeras** cut it with the scissors; **voy cómodo c. este jersey** I'm comfortable in this sweater
     (**b**) *(compañía)* with; **vine c. mi hermana** I came with my sister
     (**c**) **c. ese frío/niebla** in that cold/fog; **estar c. (la) gripe** to have the flu
     (**d**) *(contenido)* with; **una bolsa c. dinero** a bag (full) of money
     (**e**) *(a)* to; **habló c. todos** he spoke to everybody; **sé amable c. ella** be nice to her
     (**f**) *(con infinitivo)* **c. llamar será suficiente** it will be enough just to phone
     (**g**) *(+ que + subjuntivo)* **bastará c. que lo esboces** a general idea will do
     (**h**) **c. tal (de) que ...** provided that ...; **c. todo (y eso)** even so

conato *nm* attempt; **c. de asesinato** attempted murder

concebible *adj* conceivable, imaginable

concebir [6] **1** *vt* (**a**) *(plan, hijo)* to conceive (**b**) *(entender)* to understand
     2 *vi (mujer)* to become pregnant, to conceive

conceder *vt* to grant; *(premio)* to award

concejal,-a *nm,f* town councillor

concejo *nm* council

concentración *nf* concentration; *(de manifestantes)* gathering; *(de coches, motos)* rally; *(de equipo)* base

concentrado *nm* concentrate

concentrar 1 *vt* to concentrate
     2 concentrarse *upr* (**a**) to concentrate (en on) (**b**) *(reunirse)* to gather

concepción *nf* conception

concepto *nm* (**a**) *(idea)* concept; **tener buen/mal c. de** to have a good/a bad opinion of; **bajo/por ningún c.** under no circumstances (**b**) **en c. de** under the heading of (**c**) *(en factura)* item

concerniente *adj* **c.** (**a**) concerning, regarding; *Fml* **en lo c. a** with regard to

concernir [54] *v impers* (**a**) *(afectar)* to concern; **en lo que a mí concierne** as far as I am concerned; **en lo que concierne a** with regard/respect to (**b**) *(corresponder)* to be up to

concertación *nf* compromise, agreement

concertar [1] **1** *vt* (a) *(cita)* to arrange; *(precio)* to agree on; *(acuerdo)* to reach (b) *(una acción etc)* to plan, to co-ordinate
  2 *vi* to agree, to tally

concesión *nf* (a) concession (b) *(de un premio, contrato)* awarding

concesionario,-a *nm,f* dealer

concha *nf* (a) *Zool (caparazón)* shell; *(carey)* tortoiseshell (b) *Andes, RP Vulg Br* fanny, *US* beaver (c) *Ven (de árbol)* bark; *(de fruta)* peel, rind; *(del pan)* crust; *(de huevo)* shell

conchabarse *vpr* to gang up

concheto,-a *RP Fam* **1** *adj* posh
  2 *nm,f* rich kid

conchudo,-a *nm,f Perú, RP Vulg* prick, *Br* dickhead

conciencia *nf* (a) conscience; **tener la c. tranquila** with a clear conscience (b) *(conocimiento)* consciousness, awareness; **a c.** conscientiously; **tener/tomar c. (de algo)** to be/to become aware (of sth)

concienciar [43], *Am* **concientizar** [40] **1** *vt* **c. de** to make aware of
  2 **concienciarse** *vpr* to become aware (de of)

concienzudo,-a *adj* conscientious

concierto *nm* (a) *Mús* concert; *(composición)* concerto (b) *(acuerdo)* agreement

conciliar [43] *vt* to reconcile; **c. el sueño** to get to sleep

concilio *nm* council

conciso,-a *adj* concise

conciudadano,-a *nm,f* fellow citizen

concluir [37] *vt* to conclude

conclusión *nf* conclusion; **sacar una c.** to draw a conclusion

concluyente *adj* conclusive

concomerse *vpr* to be consumed; **c. de envidia** to be green with envy

concordar [2] **1** *vi* to agree; **esto no concuerda con lo que dijo ayer** this doesn't fit in with what he said yesterday
  2 *vt* to bring into agreement

concordia *nf* concord

concretamente *adv* specifically

concretar *vt (precisar)* to specify, to state explicitly; *(fecha, hora)* to fix

concreto,-a 1 *adj* (a) *(preciso, real)* concrete (b) *(particular)* specific; **en c.** specifically; **en el caso c. de ...** in the specific case of ...
  2 *nm Am* concrete

concurrencia *nf* (a) *(de dos cosas)* concurrence (b) *(público)* audience

concurrido,-a *adj* crowded, busy

concurrir *vi* (a) *(gente)* to converge (**en** on), to meet (**en** in) (b) *(coincidir)* to concur, to coincide (c) *(participar)* to compete; *(en elecciones)* to be a candidate

concursante *nmf* (a) contestant, competitor (b) *(para un empleo)* candidate

concursar *vi* to compete, to take part

concurso *nm* (a) *(competición)* competition; *(de belleza etc)* contest; *TV* quiz show; **presentar (una obra) a c.** to invite tenders (for a piece of work) (b) *Fml (ayuda)* help

> 📝 Observa que la palabra inglesa **concourse** es un falso amigo y no es la traducción de la palabra española **concurso**. En inglés, **concourse** significa "vestíbulo".

condal *adj* of o relating to a count; **la Ciudad C.** Barcelona

conde *nm* count

condecoración *nf* decoration

condecorar *vt* to decorate

condena *nf* (a) *Jur* sentence (b) *(desaprobación)* condemnation, disapproval

condenado,-a 1 *adj* (a) *Jur* convicted; **c. a muerte** condemned to death (b) *Rel & Fam* damned; **c. al fracaso** doomed to failure
  2 *nm,f* (a) *Jur* convicted person; *(a muerte)* condemned person (b) *Rel* damned person

condenar 1 *vt* (a) *Jur* to convict, to find guilty; **c. a algn a muerte** to condemn sb to death (b) *(desaprobar)* to condemn
  2 **condenarse** *vpr Rel* to be damned

condensado,-a *adj* condensed; **leche condensada** condensed milk

condensador *nm* condenser

condensar *vt*, **condensarse** *vpr* to condense

condesa *nf* countess

condescender [3] *vi* (a) to condescend (b) *(ceder)* to comply (with), to consent (to)

condescendiente *adj* (a) *(displicente)* condescending (b) *(complaciente)* complacent

condición *nf* (a) condition; **en buenas/ malas condiciones** in good/bad condition; **condiciones de trabajo** working conditions; **con la c. de que ... on** the condition that ... (b) *(manera de ser)* nature, character (c) **en su c. de director** *(calidad)* in his capacity as director

condicional *adj* conditional

condicionar *vt* (a) to condition (b) **una**

cosa condiciona la otra one thing determines the other

condimentar *vt* to season, to flavour

condimento *nm* seasoning, flavouring

condolerse [4] *vpr* **c. de** to sympathize with

condominio *nm Am (edificio) Br* block of flats, *US* condominium

condón *nm* condom

condonar *vt (ofensa)* to condone; *(deuda)* to cancel

cóndor *nm* condor

conducir [10] 1 *vt (coche)* to drive; *(electricidad)* to conduct

2 *vi* (a) *Aut* to drive; **permiso de c.** *Br* driving licence, *US* driver's license (b) *(camino, actitud)* to lead; **eso no conduce a nada** this leads nowhere

conducta *nf* behaviour, conduct; **mala c.** misbehaviour, misconduct

conducto *nm* (a) *(tubería)* pipe; *Fig* **por conductos oficiales** through official channels (b) *Anat* duct, canal

conductor,-a 1 *nm,f Aut* driver

2 *nm Elec* conductor

conectar *vt* (a) to connect up (b) *Elec* to plug in, to switch on

coneja *nf* doe rabbit

conejillo *nm* **c. de Indias** guinea pig

conejo *nm* rabbit

conexión *nf* connection

confabularse *vpr* to conspire, to plot

confección *nf* (a) *Cost* dressmaking, tailoring; **la industria de la c.** the rag trade (b) *(de un plan etc)* making, making up

confeccionar *vt* to make (up)

confederación *nf* confederation

conferencia *nf* (a) lecture; **dar una c. (sobre algo)** to give a lecture (on sth) (b) **c. de prensa** press conference (c) *Tel* long-distance call

conferenciante *nmf* lecturer

conferir [5] *vt Fml (honor, privilegio)* to confer

confesar [1] 1 *vt* to confess, to admit; *(crimen)* to own up to; *Rel (pecados)* to confess

2 *vi Jur* to own up

3 • **confesarse** *vpr* to confess; **c. culpable** to admit one's guilt; *Rel* to go to confession

confesión *nf* confession, admission; *Rel* confession

confesionario *nm Rel* confessional

confeti *nm (pl* **confetis)** confetti

confiado,-a *adj* (a) *(seguro)* self-confident (b) *(crédulo)* gullible, unsuspecting

confianza *nf* (a) *(seguridad)* confidence;

tener c. en uno mismo to be self-confident (b) **de c.** reliable (c) **tener c. con algn** to be on intimate terms with sb; **con toda c.** in all confidence; **tomarse (demasiadas) confianzas** to take liberties

confiar [29] 1 *vt (entregar)* to entrust; *(información, secreto)* to confide

2 *vi* **c. en** to trust; **confío en ella** I trust her; **no confíes en su ayuda** don't count on his help

3 **confiarse** *vpr* to confide (**en** *o* **a** in); **c. demasiado** to be over-confident

confidencia *nf* confidence

confidencial *adj* confidential

confidente,-a *nm,f* (a) *(hombre)* confidant; *(mujer)* confidante (b) *(de la policía)* informer

configuración *nf* configuration; *Informát* configuration

configurar *vt* to shape, to form

confín *nm* limit, boundary

confinar *vt Jur* to confine

confirmación *nf* confirmation

confirmar *vt* to confirm; *Prov* **la excepción confirma la regla** the exception proves the rule

confiscar [44] *vt* to confiscate

confite *nm Br* sweet, *US* candy

confitería *nf* (a) confectioner's (shop), *US* candy store (b) *CSur* café

confitura *nf* preserve, jam

conflagración *nf Fig* **c. mundial** world war

conflictividad *nf* **c. laboral** industrial unrest

conflictivo,-a *adj (asunto)* controversial; *(época)* unsettled; **niño c.** problem child

conflicto *nm* conflict; **c. laboral** industrial dispute

confluencia *nf* confluence

confluir [37] *vi* to converge; *(caminos, ríos)* to meet, to come together

conformar 1 *vt* to shape

2 **conformarse** *vpr* to resign oneself, to be content

conforme 1 *adj* (a) *(satisfecho)* satisfied; **c.** agreed, all right; **no estoy c.** I don't agree (b) **c. a** in accordance *o* keeping with

2 *conj* (a) *(según, como)* as; **c. lo vi/lo oí** as I saw/heard it (b) *(a medida que)* as; **la policía los detenía c. iban saliendo** the police were arresting them as they came out

conformidad *nf* (a) approval, consent (b) **en c. con** in conformity with

conformismo *nm* conformity

conformista *adj & nmf* conformist

confort nm (pl **conforts**) comfort; **todo c.** (en anuncio) all mod cons

confortable adj comfortable

confortar vt to comfort

confraternizar [40] vi to fraternize

confrontación nf (a) (enfrentamiento) confrontation (b) (comparación) contrast

confrontar vt (a) to confront (b) (cotejar) to compare, to collate

confundir 1 vt (a) to confuse (con with); **c. a una persona con otra** to mistake somebody for somebody else (b) (persona) to mislead (c) (turbar) to confound

2 confundirse vpr (a) (equivocarse) to be mistaken; Tel **se ha confundido** you've got the wrong number (b) (mezclarse) to mingle; **se confundió entre el gentío** he disappeared into the crowd

confusión nf confusion

confuso,-a adj (a) confused; (formas, recuerdo) blurred, vague (b) (mezclado) mixed up

congelación nf (a) freezing (b) Fin freeze; **c. salarial** wage freeze (c) Med frostbite

congelado,-a 1 adj frozen; Med frostbitten

2 nmpl **congelados** frozen food

congelador nm freezer

congelar 1 vt to freeze

2 congelarse vpr (a) to freeze; Fam **me estoy congelando** I'm freezing (b) Med to get o become frostbitten

congeniar [43] vi to get on (con with)

congénito,-a adj congenital

congestión nf congestion; Med **c. cerebral** stroke

congestionar vt to congest

conglomerado nm conglomerate

conglomerar vt, **conglomerarse** vpr to conglomerate

congoja nf sorrow, grief

congraciarse [43] vpr to ingratiate oneself (con with)

congratular vt Fml to congratulate (por on)

congregación nf congregation

congregar [42] vt, **congregarse** vpr to congregate, to assemble

congresista nmf member of a congress

congreso nm congress, conference; Pol **c. de los Diputados** Br ≃ Parliament, US ≃ Congress

congrio nm conger (eel)

congruente adj coherent, suitable

conjetura nf conjecture; **por c.** by guesswork

conjeturar vt to conjecture

conjugación nf conjugation

conjugar [42] vt to conjugate; Fig (planes, opiniones) to combine

conjunción nf conjunction

conjuntar vt to co-ordinate

conjuntivitis nf conjunctivitis

conjunto,-a 1 nm (a) (grupo) collection, group (b) (todo) whole; **de c.** overall; **en c.** on the whole (c) Mús (pop) group, band (d) (prenda) outfit, ensemble (e) Mat set (f) Dep team

2 adj joint

conjurar 1 vt to exorcise; (peligro) to ward off

2 conjurarse vpr to conspire, to plot

conjuro nm (a) (exorcismo) exorcism (b) (encantamiento) spell, incantation

conllevar vt to entail

conmemoración nf commemoration

conmemorar vt to commemorate

conmigo pron pers with me; **vino c.** he came with me; **él habló c.** he talked to me

conminar vt to threaten, to menace

conmoción nf commotion, shock; **c. cerebral** concussion

conmocionar vt to shock; Med to concuss

conmovedor,-a adj touching; **una película conmovedora** a moving film

conmover [4] vt to touch, to move

conmutador nm (a) Elec switch (b) Am Tel switchboard

conmutar vt to exchange; Jur to commute; Elec to commutate

connivencia nf connivance, collusion

connotación nf connotation

cono nm cone; **C. Sur** South America

conocedor,-a adj & nm,f expert; (de vino, arte etc) connoisseur

conocer [34] **1** vt (a) to know; **dar (algo/algn) a c.** to make (sth/sb) known (b) (a una persona) to meet (c) (reconocer) to recognize; **te conocí por la voz** I recognized you by your voice

2 conocerse vpr (dos personas) to know each other; (por primera vez) to meet

conocido,-a 1 adj known; (famoso) well-known

2 nm,f acquaintance

conocimiento nm (a) knowledge; **con c. de causa** with full knowledge of the facts (b) (conciencia) consciousness; **perder/recobrar el c.** to lose/regain consciousness (c) **conocimientos** knowledge

conque conj so

conquense 1 adj of/from Cuenca

2 nmf person from Cuenca

conquista *nf* conquest

conquistador,-a *nm,f* conqueror

conquistar *vt (país, ciudad)* to conquer; *Fig (puesto, título)* to win; *(a una persona)* to win over

consabido,-a *adj* (a) *(bien conocido)* well-known (b) *(usual)* familiar, usual

consagración *nf* (a) *Rel* consecration (b) *(de un artista)* recognition

consagrar 1 *vt* (a) *Rel* to consecrate (b) *(artista)* to confirm (c) *(tiempo, vida)* to devote

  2 **consagrarse** *vpr* (a) **c. a** *(dedicarse)* to devote oneself to, to dedicate oneself to (b) *(lograr fama)* to establish oneself

consciente *adj* (a) conscious, aware; **ser c. de algo** to be aware of sth (b) *Med* conscious

conscripto *nm Andes, Arg* conscript

consecución *nf* (a) *(de un objetivo)* achievement (b) *(obtención)* obtaining

consecuencia *nf* (a) consequence; **a o como c. de** as a consequence o result of; **en c.** therefore; **tener o traer (malas) consecuencias** to have (ill) effects; **sacar como o en c.** to come to a conclusion (b) *(coherencia)* consistency; **actuar en c.** to be consistent

consecuente *adj* consistent

consecutivo,-a *adj* consecutive; **tres días consecutivos** three days in a row

conseguir [6] *vt* (a) to get, to obtain; *(objetivo)* to achieve (b) **conseguí terminar** I managed to finish

consejero,-a *nm,f* (a) *(asesor)* adviser (b) *Pol* councillor (c) *Com* **c. delegado** managing director

consejo *nm* (a) *(recomendación)* advice; **un c.** a piece of advice (b) *(junta)* council; **c. de ministros** cabinet; *(reunión)* cabinet meeting; **c. de administración** board of directors; **c. de guerra** court martial

consenso *nm* consenso

consensuar *vt* to approve by consensus

consentido,-a *adj* spoiled

consentimiento *nm* consent

consentir [5] 1 *vt* (a) *(tolerar)* to allow, to permit; **no consientas que haga eso** don't allow him to do that (b) *(mimar)* to spoil

  2 *vi* to consent; **c. en** to agree to

conserje *nm* commissionaire; *(en escuela etc)* janitor

conserva *nf* tinned o canned food

conservación *nf* (a) preservation (b) *(mantenimiento)* maintenance, upkeep

conservador,-a 1 *adj & nm,f* conservative; *Pol* Conservative

  2 *nm (de museo)* curator

conservadurismo *nm* conservatism

conservante *nm* preservative

conservar 1 *vt* to conserve, to preserve; *(mantener)* to keep up, to maintain; *(alimentos)* to preserve

  2 **conservarse** *vpr* (a) *(tradición etc)* to survive (b) **c. bien** *(persona)* to age well

conservatorio *nm* conservatory

considerable *adj* considerable

consideración *nf* (a) consideration; **tomar algo en c.** to take sth into account (b) *(respeto)* regard (c) **de c.** important, considerable; **herido de c.** seriously injured

considerado,-a *adj* (a) *(atento)* considerate, thoughtful (b) **estar bien/mal c.** to be well/badly thought of

considerar *vt* to consider; **lo considero imposible** I think it's impossible

consigna *nf* (a) *(para maletas) Br* left-luggage office, *US* checkroom (b) *Mil* orders, instructions

consignar *vt* (a) *(puesto)* to allocate; *(cantidad)* to assign (b) *(mercancía)* to ship, to dispatch

consigo¹ *pron pers* (a) *(tercera persona) (hombre)* with him; *(mujer)* with her; *(cosa, animal)* with it; *(plural)* with them; *(usted)* with you (b) **hablar c. mismo** to speak to oneself

consigo² *indic pres de* **conseguir**

consiguiente *adj* resulting, consequent; **por c.** therefore, consequently

consistencia *nf* (a) consistency (b) *(de argumento)* soundness

consistente *adj* (a) *(firme)* firm, solid (b) *(teoría)* sound (c) **c. en** consisting of

> *Observa que la palabra inglesa* **consistent** *es un falso amigo y no es la traducción de la palabra española* **consistente**. *En inglés,* **consistent** *significa "consecuente".*

consistir *vi* to consist (**en** of); **el secreto consiste en tener paciencia** the secret lies in being patient

consistorial *adj* **casa c.** town hall

consola *nf* console table; *Informát* console

consolación *nf* consolation; **premio de c.** consolation prize

consolador,-a 1 *adj* consoling, comforting

  2 *nm* dildo

consolar [2] 1 *vt* to console, to comfort

  2 **consolarse** *vpr* to console oneself, to take comfort (**con** from)

consolidar *vt,* **consolidarse** *vpr* to consolidate

consomé nm clear soup, consommé

consonancia nf **en c. con** in keeping with

consonante adj & nf consonant

consorcio nm consortium

consorte 1 adj **príncipe c.** prince consort

  2 nmf (cónyuge) partner, spouse

conspicuo,-a adj prominent, outstanding

conspiración nf conspiracy, plot

conspirar vi to conspire, to plot

constancia nf (a) constancy, perseverance (b) (testimonio) proof, evidence; **dejar c. de algo** to put sth on record

constante 1 adj constant; (persona) steadfast

  2 nf constant feature; Mat constant

constantemente adv constantly

constar vi (a) (figurar) to figure, to be included (**en** in); **c. en acta** to be on record (b) **me consta que ...** I am absolutely certain that ... (c) **c. de** to be made up of, to consist of

constatar vt to state; (comprobar) to check

constelación nf constellation

consternación nf consternation

consternar vt to dismay

constipado,-a 1 adj **estar c.** to have a cold o a chill

  2 nm cold, chill

> ♪ Observa que la palabra inglesa **constipated** es un falso amigo y no es la traducción de la palabra española **constipado**. En inglés, **constipated** significa "estreñido".

constiparse vpr to catch a cold o a chill

constitución nf constitution

constitucional adj constitutional

constituir [37] 1 vt (a) (formar) to constitute; **estar constituido por** to consist of (b) (suponer) to represent (c) (fundar) to constitute, to set up

  2 **constituirse** vpr **c. en** to set oneself up as

constituyente adj & nmf constituent

constreñir [6] vt (a) (forzar) to compel, to force (b) (oprimir) to restrict (c) Med to constrict

construcción nf (a) construction; (sector) the building industry; **en c.** under construction (b) (edificio) building

constructivo,-a adj constructive

constructor,-a 1 nm,f builder

  2 adj **empresa constructora** builders, construction company

construir [37] vt to build, to manufacture

> ♪ Observa que el verbo inglés **to construe** es un falso amigo y no es la traducción del verbo español **construir**. En inglés, **to construe** significa "interpretar".

consuelo nm consolation

cónsul nmf consul

consulado nm consulate

consulta nf (a) consultation; **obra de c.** reference book (b) Med surgery; (despacho) consulting room; **horas de c.** surgery hours

consultar vt to consult, to seek advice (**con** from); (libro) to look up

consultivo,-a adj consultative, advisory

consultorio nm (a) Med medical centre (b) Prensa problem page, advice column

consumado,-a adj (a) consummated; **hecho c.** fait accompli, accomplished fact (b) Fig (artista) consummate

consumar vt to complete, to carry out; (crimen) to commit

consumición nf (a) consumption (b) (bebida) drink

consumidor,-a 1 nm,f consumer

  2 adj consuming

consumir 1 vt to consume

  2 **consumirse** vpr (al hervir) to boil away; Fig (persona) to waste away

consumismo nm consumerism

consumo nm consumption; **bienes de c.** consumer goods; **sociedad de c.** consumer society

contabilidad nf Com (a) (profesión) accountancy (b) (de empresa, sociedad) accounting, book-keeping

contabilizar [40] vt Com to enter in the books; Dep to score

contable nmf accountant

contactar vi **c. con** to contact, to get in touch with

contacto nm contact; Aut ignition; **perder el c.** to lose touch; **ponerse en c.** to get in touch

contado,-a 1 adj few and far between; **contadas veces** very seldom; **tiene los días contados** his days are numbered

  2 nm **pagar al c.** to pay cash

contador,-ora 1 nm,f Am (persona) accountant; **c. público** Br chartered accountant, US certified public accountant

  2 nm (aparato) meter; **c. de agua** water meter

contagiar [43] 1 vt Med to pass on

  2 **contagiarse** vpr (a) (persona) to get infected (b) (enfermedad) to be contagious

contagio nm contagion

contagioso,-a *adj* contagious; *Fam (risa)* infectious

contaminación *nf* contamination; *(del aire)* pollution

contaminar *vt* to contaminate; *(aire, agua)* to pollute

contante *adj* dinero c. **(y sonante)** hard o ready cash

contar [2] 1 *vt* (**a**) *(sumar)* to count (**b**) *(narrar)* to tell
  2 *vi* (**a**) to count (**b**) c. con *(confiar en)* to count on; *(tener)* to have
  3 contarse *vpr Fam* ¿qué te cuentas? how's it going?

contemplación *nf* contemplation; *Fam* no andarse con contemplaciones to make no bones about it

contemplar *vt* to contemplate; *(considerar)* to consider; *(estipular)* to stipulate

contemporáneo,-a *adj & nm,f* contemporary

contención *nf* muro de c. retaining wall; c. salarial wage restraint

contencioso,-a 1 *adj* contentious; *Jur* litigious
  2 *nm Jur* legal dispute

contendiente *nmf* contender, contestant

contenedor *nm* container

contener [24] 1 *vt* (**a**) to contain (**b**) *(pasiones etc)* to restrain, to hold back
  2 contenerse *vpr* to control oneself, to hold (oneself) back

contenido *nm* content, contents

contentar 1 *vt* (**a**) *(satisfacer)* to please (**b**) *(alegrar)* to cheer up
  2 contentarse *vpr* (**a**) *(conformarse)* to make do (con with), to be satisfied (con with) (**b**) *(alegrarse)* to cheer up

contento,-a *adj* happy, pleased (con with)

contestación *nf* answer; dar c. to answer

contestador *nm* c. automático answering machine

contestar *vt* (**a**) to answer (**b**) *Fam (replicar)* to answer back

contestatario,-a *adj* anti-establishment

contexto *nm* context

contienda *nf* struggle

contigo *pron pers* with you

contiguo,-a *adj* contiguous (**a** to), adjoining

continente *nm* (**a**) *Geog* continent (**b**) *(compostura)* countenance

contingencia *nf* contingency

contingente *nm* contingent

continuación *nf* continuation; a c. next

continuamente *adv* continuously

continuar [30] *vt & vi* to continue, to carry on (with); **continúa en Francia** he's still in France; **continuará** to be continued

continuidad *nf* continuity

continuo,-a 1 *adj* (**a**) continuous; *Aut* línea continua solid white line (**b**) *(reiterado)* continual, constant
  2 *nm* continuum

contonearse *vpr* to swing one's hips

contorno *nm* (**a**) outline (**b**) contornos surroundings, environment

contorsión *nf* contortion

contorsionarse *vpr* to contort o twist oneself

contra 1 *prep* against; **en c. de** against
  2 *nm* los pros y los contras the pros and cons

contraataque *nm* counterattack

contrabajo *nm* double bass

contrabandista *nmf* smuggler; c. de armas gunrunner

contrabando *nm* smuggling; c. de armas gunrunning; pasar algo de c. to smuggle sth in

contracción *nf* contraction

contracepción *nf* contraception

contrachapado *nm* plywood

contracorriente 1 *nf* crosscurrent
  2 *adv* ir (**a**) c. to go against the tide

contradecir [12] *(pp* contradicho*)* *vt* to contradict

contradicción *nf* contradiction

contradictorio,-a *adj* contradictory

contraer [25] 1 *vt* to contract; c. matrimonio con algn to marry sb
  2 contraerse *vpr* to contract

contraigo *indic pres de* contraer

contraindicación *nf* contraindication

contraje *pt indef de* contraer

contralor *nm Am* = inspector of public spending

contraloría *nf Am* = office controlling public spending

contraluz *nm* view against the light; a c. against the light

contramaestre *nm* (**a**) *(en buque)* boatswain (**b**) *(capataz)* foreman

contramano: • a contramano *loc adv* the wrong way o direction

contrapartida *nf* en c. in return

contrapelo: • a contrapelo *loc adv* the wrong way; *Fig* against the grain

contrapesar *vt* (**a**) to counterbalance, to counterpoise (**b**) *Fig (compensar)* to offset, to balance

contrapeso *nm* counterweight

contraportada *nf* back page

contraposición nf contrast

contraproducente adj counterproductive

contraprogramación nf TV competitive scheduling

contrapunto nm counterpoint

contrariamente adv **c. a ...** contrary to...

contrariar [29] vt (a) (oponerse a) to oppose, to go against (b) (disgustar) to upset

contrariedad nf (a) (contratiempo) obstacle, setback (b) (disgusto) annoyance

contrario,-a 1 adj (a) opposite; **lo c. de** the opposite of; **en el lado/sentido c.** on the other side/in the other direction; **al c., por el c.** on the contrary; **de lo c.** otherwise; **todo lo c.** quite the opposite (b) (perjudicial) contrary (**a** to)

2 nm,f opponent, rival

3 nf **llevar la contraria** to be contrary

contrarrestar vt to offset, to counteract

contrasentido nm contradiction

contraseña nf password

contrastar vt to contrast (**con** with)

contraste nm (a) contrast (b) (en oro, plata) hallmark

contrata nf contract

contratar vt to hire, to engage

contratiempo nm setback, hitch

contratista nmf contractor

contrato nm contract; **c. de trabajo** work contract; **c. de alquiler** lease, leasing agreement; **c. basura** short-term contract with poor conditions

contravenir [27] vt to contravene, to infringe

contraventana nf shutter

contribución nf (a) contribution (b) (impuesto) tax

contribuir [37] **1** vt to contribute (**a** to)

2 vi (a) to contribute (b) (pagar impuestos) to pay taxes

contribuyente nmf taxpayer

contrincante nmf rival, opponent

control nm (a) control; **c. a distancia** remote control (b) (inspección) check; (de policía etc) checkpoint

controlador,-a nm,f **c. (aéreo)** air traffic controller

controlar 1 vt (a) to control (b) (comprobar) to check

2 controlarse vpr to control oneself

controversia nf controversy

controvertido,-a adj controversial

contumaz adj obstinate

contundente adj (a) (arma) blunt (b) (argumento) forceful, convincing

contusión nf contusion, bruise

conuco nm Carib, Col small farm, Br smallholding

convalecencia nf convalescence

convaleciente adj & nmf convalescent

convalidar vt to validate; (documento) to ratify

convencer [49] vt to convince; **c. a algn de algo** to convince sb about sth

convencimiento nm conviction; **tener el c. de que ...** to be convinced that ...

convención nf convention

convencional adj conventional

convenido,-a adj agreed; **según lo c.** as agreed

conveniencia nf (a) (provecho) convenience (b) **conveniencias sociales** social proprieties

conveniente adj (a) (oportuno) convenient; (aconsejable) advisable (b) (precio) good, fair

convenio nm agreement; **c. laboral** agreement on salary and conditions

convenir [27] vt & vi (a) (acordar) to agree; **c. una fecha** to agree on a date; **sueldo a c.** salary negotiable; **c. en** to agree on (b) (ser oportuno) to suit, to be good for; **conviene recordar que ...** it's as well to remember that ...

convento nm (de monjas) convent; (de monjes) monastery

convergente adj convergent

converger [53] vi to converge

conversación nf conversation

conversada nf Am Fam chat

conversar vi to converse, to talk

conversión nf conversion

converso,-a nm,f convert

convertible adj convertible

convertir [54] **1** vt to change, to convert

2 convertirse vpr (a) **c. en** to turn into, to become (b) Rel to be converted (**a** to)

convexo,-a adj convex

convicción nf conviction; **tengo la c. de que ...** I am convinced that ..

convicto,-a adj convicted

convidado,-a adj & nm,f guest

convidar vt to invite

convincente adj convincing

convite nm reception

convivencia nf life together; Fig coexistence

convivir vi to live together; Fig to coexist (**con** with)

convocar [44] vt to summon; (reunión, elecciones) to call

convocatoria nf (a) (a huelga etc) call (b) Educ diet

convulsión *nf* Med convulsion; *(agitación social)* upheaval

convulsivo,-a *adj* convulsive

conyugal *adj* conjugal; **vida c.** married life

cónyuge *nmf* spouse; **cónyuges** married couple, husband and wife

coña *nf muy Fam* **estar de c.** to be joking

coñac *nm* brandy, cognac

coñazo *nm muy Fam* pain, drag; **dar el c.** to be a real pain

coño 1 *nm Vulg* cunt
2 *interj Vulg* for fuck's sake!

cooperación *nf* co-operation

cooperador,-a *nm,f* collaborator, co-operator

cooperante *nmf* aid worker

cooperar *vi* to co-operate (**con** with)

cooperativa *nf* co-operative

coordenada *nf* co-ordinate

coordinación *nf* co-ordination

coordinador,-a *nm,f* co-ordinator

coordinadora *nf* co-ordinating committee; **c. general** joint committee

coordinar *vt* to co-ordinate

copa *nf* (a) glass; **tomar una c.** to have a drink (b) *(de árbol)* top (c) *Dep* cup (d) *Naipes* **copas** hearts

copar *vt* to take up

copartícipe *adj & nmf (socio)* partner; *(colaborador)* collaborator; *(copropietario)* joint owner, co-owner

Copenhague *n* Copenhagen

copetín *nm RP* pre-lunch/pre-dinner drinks

copia *nf* copy; *Informát* **c. de seguridad** backup; *Informát* **hacer una c. de seguridad de algo** to back up sth

copiar **[43]** *vt* to copy

copiloto *nm Av* copilot; *Aut* co-driver

copioso,-a *adj* abundant, copious

copistería *nf* photocopying service

copla *nf* verse, couplet

copo *nm* flake; *(de nieve)* snowflake; **copos de maíz** cornflakes

coproducción *nf* co-production, joint production

cópula *nf* (a) *(coito)* copulation, intercourse (b) *Ling* conjunction

copular *vi* to copulate (**con** with)

coqueta *nf* dressing table

coquetear *vi* to flirt (**con** with)

coqueto,-a 1 *adj* coquettish
2 *nm,f* flirt

coraje *nm* (a) *(valor)* courage (b) *(ira)* anger, annoyance; *Fig* **dar c. a algn** to infuriate sb; **¡qué c.!** how maddening!

coral¹ *nm Zool* coral

coral² *nf Mús* choral, chorale

Corán *nm* Koran

coraza *nf* armour; *Fig* protection

corazón *nm* (a) heart; *Fig* **de (todo) c.** in all sincerity; *Fig* **tener buen c.** to be kind-hearted (b) *(parte central)* heart; *(de fruta)* core (c) *Naipes* **corazones** hearts

corazonada *nf* hunch, feeling

corbata *nf* tie, *US* necktie; **con c.** wearing a tie

Córcega *n* Corsica

corchete *nm* (a) *Impr* square bracket (b) *Cost* hook and eye, snap fastener

corcho *nm* cork; *(de pesca)* float

cordel *nm* rope, cord

cordero,-a *nm,f* lamb

cordial *adj* cordial, warm

cordialidad *nf* cordiality, warmth

cordillera *nf* mountain chain *o* range

córdoba *nm Fin* = monetary unit of Nicaragua

cordón *nm* string; *(de zapatos)* shoelace; *Anat* **c. umbilical** umbilical cord; **c. policial** police cordon; *CSur, Cuba (de la vereda)* Br kerb, *US* curb

cordura *nf* common sense

Corea *n* Korea; **C. del Norte/Sur** North/South Korea

coreano,-a *adj & nm,f* Korean

corear *vt* (a) *(cantar a coro)* to sing in chorus (b) *(aclamar)* to applaud

coreografía *nf* choreography

cornada *nf Taurom* goring

corneja *nf* crow

córner *nm Ftb* corner (kick); **sacar un c.** to take a corner

corneta *nf* bugle; **c. de llaves** cornet

cornisa *nf* cornice

cornudo *nm Fam (marido)* cuckold

coro *nm Mús* choir; *Teatro* chorus; *Fig* **a c.** all together

corona *nf* (a) crown (b) *(de flores etc)* wreath, garland; **c. funeraria** funeral wreath

coronación *nf* (a) coronation (b) *Fig (culminación)* crowning point

coronar *vt* to crown

coronel *nm* colonel

coronilla *nf* crown of the head; *Fam* **estar hasta la c. (de)** to be fed up (with)

corpiño *nm (vestido)* bodice; *Arg (sostén)* bra

corporación *nf* corporation

corporal *adj* corporal; **castigo c.** corporal punishment; **olor c.** body odour, BO

corporativo,-a *adj* corporative

corpulento,-a *adj* corpulent, stout

corpus *nm* corpus

corral *nm* farmyard, *US* corral; *(de casa)* courtyard

correa *nf* (a) *(tira)* strap; *(de reloj)* watchstrap; *(de pantalón)* belt; *(de perro)* lead, leash (b) *Téc* belt

corrección *nf* (a) *(rectificación)* correction (b) *(urbanidad)* courtesy, politeness

correcto,-a *adj* (a) *(sin errores)* correct (b) *(educado)* polite, courteous (**con** to); *(conducta)* proper

corredera *nf* puerta/ventana de c. sliding door/window

corredizo,-a *adj* sliding; **nudo c.** slipknot; **techo c.** sunroof

corredor,-a *nm,f* (a) *Dep* runner (b) *Fin* **c. de bolsa** stockbroker

corregir [58] 1 *vt* to correct

2 **corregirse** *vpr* to mend one's ways

correo *nm* (a) *(sistema)* post, mail; **echar al c.** to post; **por c.** by post; **c. aéreo** airmail; **c. certificado** registered post; *Informát* **c. electrónico** electronic mail, e-mail; *Informát* **me envió un c.** (**electrónico**) *(un mensaje)* she e-mailed me, she sent me an e-mail; **(tren) c.** mail train (b) **correos** *(edificio)* post office

correr 1 *vi* (a) to run; *(coche)* to go fast; *(conductor)* to drive fast; *(viento)* to blow; *Fig* **no corras, habla más despacio** don't rush, speak slower; **c. prisa** to be urgent (b) **c. con los gastos** to foot the bill; **corre a mi cargo** I'll take care of it

2 *vt* (a) *(cortina)* to draw; *(cerrojo)* to close; *(aventura etc)* to have; **c. el riesgo** o **peligro** to run the risk (b) *(mover)* to pull up, to draw up

3 **correrse** *vpr* (a) *(moverse)* to move over (b) *Fam* **c. una juerga** to go on a spree (c) *muy Fam (tener orgasmo)* to come

correspondencia *nf* (a) correspondence (b) *Ferroc* connection

corresponder 1 *vi* (a) to correspond (a to; **con** with) (b) *(incumbir)* to concern, to be incumbent upon; **esta tarea te corresponde a ti** it's your job to do this (c) *(pertenecer)* to belong; **me dieron lo que me correspondía** they gave me my share

2 **corresponderse** *vpr* (a) *(ajustarse)* to correspond (b) *(dos cosas)* to tally; **no se corresponde con la descripción** it does not match the description (c) *(dos personas)* to love each other

correspondiente *adj* corresponding (a to)

corresponsal *nmf* correspondent

corrida *nf* **c.** (**de toros**) bullfight

corrido,-a *adj* (a) *(avergonzado)* abashed (b) **de c.** without stopping; **se lo sabe de c.** she knows it by heart

corriente 1 *adj* (a) *(común)* common (b) *(agua)* running (c) *(mes, año)* current, present; **el diez del c.** the tenth of this month (d) *Fin (cuenta)* current (e) **estar al c.** to be up to date

2 *nf* (a) current, stream; *Fig* **ir** o **navegar contra c.** to go against the tide; *Fam* **seguirle** o **llevarle la c. a algn** to humour sb; *Elec* **c. eléctrica** (electric) current (b) *(de aire)* draught (c) *(tendencia)* trend, current

corrijo *indic pres de* **corregir**

corrillo *nm* small group of people talking; *Fig* clique

corro *nm* (a) circle, ring (b) *(juego)* ring-a-ring-a-roses

corroborar *vt* to corroborate

corroer [38] *vt* to corrode; *Fig* **la envidia le corroe** envy eats away at him

corromper *vt* (a) *(pudrir)* to turn bad, to rot (b) *(pervertir)* to corrupt, to pervert

2 **corromperse** *vpr* (a) *(pudrirse)* to go bad, to rot (b) *(pervertirse)* to become corrupted

corrosivo,-a *adj* corrosive; *Fig (mordaz)* caustic

corrupción *nf* (a) *(putrefacción)* rot, decay (b) *Fig* corruption; *Jur* **c. de menores** corruption of minors

corrupto,-a *adj* corrupt

corsé *nm* corset

cortacésped *nm* o *nf* lawnmower

cortado,-a 1 *adj* (a) cut (up) (b) *(leche)* sour (c) *(labios)* chapped (d) *Fam (tímido)* shy

2 *nm* small coffee with a dash of milk

cortafuego *nm* firebreak

cortapisa *nf* *Fig* restriction, limitation

cortar 1 *vt* (a) to cut; *(carne)* to carve; *(árbol)* to cut down; *Fam* **c. por lo sano** to take drastic measures; *Fam* **cortó con su novio** she split up with her boyfriend (b) *(piel)* to chap, to crack (c) *(luz, teléfono)* to cut off (d) *(paso, carretera)* to block

2 **cortarse** *vpr* (a) *(herirse)* to cut oneself (b) **c. el pelo** to have one's hair cut (c) *(leche etc)* to curdle (d) *Tel* **se cortó la comunicación** we were cut off (e) *Fam (aturdirse)* to become all shy

cortaúñas *nm inv* nail clippers

corte¹ *nm* (a) cut; **c. de pelo** haircut; *TV* **c. publicitario** commercial break; **c. de mangas** ≃ V-sign (b) *(sección)* section; **c. transversal** cross section (c) *Fam* rebuff; **dar un c. a algn** to cut sb dead

corte² nf (a) (real) court (b) **Las Cortes** (Spanish) Parliament

cortejar vt to court

cortejo nm (a) (galanteo) courting (b) (comitiva) entourage, retinue; **c. fúnebre** funeral cortège

cortés adj courteous, polite

cortesía nf courtesy, politeness

corteza nf (de árbol) bark; (de queso) rind; (de pan) crust

cortijo nm Andalusian farm o farmhouse

cortina nf curtain; **c. de humo** smoke screen

corto,-a 1 adj (a) (distancia, tiempo) short; Fam **c. de luces** dim-witted; **c. de vista** short-sighted; Aut **luz corta** dipped headlights (b) Fam **quedarse c.** (calcular mal) to underestimate (c) (apocado) timid, shy
  2 nm Cin short (film)

cortocircuito nm short circuit

cortometraje nm short (film)

corvo,-a adj curved, bent

cosa nf (a) thing; **no he visto c. igual** I've never seen anything like it; **no ser gran c.** not to be up to much (b) (asunto) matter, business; **eso es c. tuya** that's your business o affair; **eso es otra c.** that's different (c) **hace c. de una hora** about an hour ago

coscorrón nm knock o blow on the head

cosecha nf (a) Agr harvest, crop (b) (año del vino) vintage

cosechadora nf combine harvester

cosechar vt to harvest, to gather (in)

coser vt (a) to sew; Fam **es c. y cantar** it's a piece of cake (b) Med to stitch up

cosmético,-a adj & nm cosmetic

cósmico,-a adj cosmic

cosmonauta nmf cosmonaut

cosmopolita adj & nmf cosmopolitan

cosmos nm inv cosmos

coso nm (a) Taurom bullring (b) CSur Fam (objeto) whatnot, thing

cosquillas nfpl tickling; **hacer c. a algn** to tickle sb; **tener c.** to be ticklish

cosquilleo nm tickling

costa¹ nf coast; (litoral) coastline; (playa) beach, seaside

costa² nf **a c. de** at the expense of; **a toda c.** at all costs, at any price; **vive a c. mía** he lives off me

costado nm side; **de c.** sideways; **es catalana por los cuatro costados** she's Catalan through and through

costal nm sack

costanera nf CSur seaside promenade

costar [2] vi (a) to cost; **¿cuánto cuesta?** how much is it?; **c. barato/caro.** to be

cheap/expensive (b) Fig **te va a c. caro** you'll pay dearly for this; **c. trabajo o mucho** to be hard; **me cuesta hablar francés** I find it difficult to speak French; **cueste lo que cueste** at any cost

costarricense adj & nmf, **costarriqueño,-a** adj & nm,f Costa Rican

coste nm cost; **a precio de c.** (at) cost price; **c. de la vida** cost of living

costear 1 vt to afford, to pay for; **c. los gastos** to foot the bill
  2 costearse upr to pay for

costero,-a 1 adj coastal; **ciudad costera** seaside town
  2 nf Méx **costera** seaside promenade

costilla nf (a) Anat rib (b) Culin cutlet

costo¹ nm cost

costo² nm Fam (hachís) dope, shit, stuff

costoso,-a adj costly, expensive

costra nf crust; Med scab

costumbre nf (a) (hábito) habit; **como de c.** as usual; **tengo la c. de levantarme temprano** I usually get up early; **tenía la c. de …** he used to … (b) (tradición) custom

costura nf (a) sewing (b) (confección) dressmaking; **alta c.** haute couture (c) (línea de puntadas) seam

costurera nf seamstress

costurero nm sewing basket

cota nf Geog height above sea level; Fig rating

cotejar vt to compare

cotidiano,-a adj daily; **vida cotidiana** everyday life

cotilla nmf Fam busybody, gossip

cotillear vi Fam to gossip (**de** about)

cotilleo nm Fam gossip

cotización nf (a) Fin (market) price, quotation (b) (cuota) membership fees, subscription

cotizar [40] **1** vt Fin to quote
  2 vi to pay national insurance
  3 cotizarse upr Fin **c. a** to sell at

coto nm (a) enclosure, reserve; **c. de caza** game reserve (b) **poner c. a** to put a stop to

cotorra nf parrot; Fig (persona) chatterbox

COU nm Educ (abr **Curso de Orientación Universitaria**) = one-year course which prepares students aged 17-18 for Spanish university entrance examinations

country ['kauntri] nm Arg = luxury suburban housing development

coyote nm coyote, prairie wolf

coyuntura nf (a) Anat articulation, joint (b) Fig (circunstancia) juncture; **la c.**

económica the economic situation
coz *nf* kick; **dar una c.** to kick
C.P. (*abr* **código postal**) *Br* postcode, *US* zip code
crac(k) *nm* (a) *Fin* crash (b) (*droga*) crack
cráneo *nm* cranium, skull
cráter *nm* crater
creación *nf* creation
creador,-a *nm,f* creator
crear *vt* to create
creatividad *nf* creativity
creativo,-a *adj* creative
crecer [33] *vi* (a) to grow; **c. en importancia** to become more important (b) (*al tricotar*) to increase
creces *nfpl* **con c.** fully, in full; **devolver con c.** to return with interest
crecido,-a *adj* (*persona*) grown-up
creciente *adj* growing, increasing; **cuarto c.** crescent
crecimiento *nm* growth
credencial *nf* credential; (**cartas**) **credenciales** credentials
credibilidad *nf* credibility
crédito *nm* (a) *Com & Fin* credit (b) (*confianza*) belief; **dar c.** to believe
credo *nm* creed
crédulo,-a *adj* credulous, gullible
creencia *nf* belief
creer [36] 1 *vt* (a) to believe (b) (*pensar*) to think; **creo que no** I don't think so; **creo que sí** I think so; **ya lo creo** I should think so
 2 *vi* to believe; **c. en** to believe in
 3 **creerse** *vpr* (a) to consider oneself to be; **¿qué te has creído?** what *o* who do you think you are? (b) **no me lo creo** I can't believe it
creíble *adj* credible, believable
creído,-a 1 *adj* arrogant, vain
 2 *nm,f* big head
crema *nf* cream
cremallera *nf Br* zip (fastener), *US* zipper
crematorio **(horno) c.** crematorium
cremoso,-a *adj* creamy
crepe *nm* crêpe, pancake
crepería *nf* creperie
crepitar *vi* to crackle
crepúsculo *nm* twilight
crespo,-a *adj* frizzy
crespón *nm* crepe
cresta *nf* (a) crest; (*de gallo*) comb (b) (*de punk*) mohican
Creta *n* Crete
cretino,-a 1 *adj* stupid, cretinous
 2 *nm,f* cretin
creyente *nmf* believer
crezco *indic pres de* **crecer**

cría *nf* (a) (*cachorro*) young (b) (*crianza*) breeding, raising
criada *nf* maid
criadero *nm* nursery
criadilla *nf Culin* bull's testicle
criado,-a 1 *adj* **mal c.** spoilt
 2 *nm,f* servant
crianza *nf* (*de animales*) breeding; *Fig* **vinos de c.** vintage wines
criar [29] *vt* (a) (*animales*) to breed, to raise; (*niños*) to bring up, to rear (b) (*producir*) to have, to grow
criatura *nf* (a) (living) creature (b) (*crío*) baby, child
criba *nf* sieve
cribar *vt* to sieve, to sift
crimen *nm* (*pl* **crímenes**) murder; **c. de guerra** war crime
criminal *nmf & adj* criminal
crin *nf*, **crines** *nfpl* mane
crío,-a 1 *nm Fam* kid
 2 *adj* babyish
criollo,-a *adj & nm,f* Creole
críquet *nm* cricket
crisantemo *nm* chrysanthemum
crisis *nf inv* crisis (b) (*ataque*) fit, attack; **c. nerviosa** nervous breakdown
crispación *nf* tension
crispar *vt* to make tense; *Fig* **eso me crispa los nervios** that sets my nerves on edge
cristal *nm* (a) crystal; **c. de roca** rock crystal (b) (*vidrio*) glass; (*de gafas*) lense; (*de ventana*) (window) pane
cristalera *nf* window
cristalería *nf* (*conjunto*) glassware; (*vasos*) glasses
cristalino,-a *adj* crystal clear
cristalizar [40] *vi* to crystallize
cristiandad *nf* Christendom
cristianismo *nm* Christianity
cristiano,-a *adj & nm,f* Christian
Cristo *nm* Christ
criterio *nm* (a) (*pauta*) criterion (b) (*opinión*) opinion (c) (*discernimiento*) discretion; **lo dejo a tu c.** I'll leave it up to you
crítica *nf* (a) criticism (b) *Prensa* review; **tener buena c.** to get good reviews (c) (*conjunto de críticos*) critics
criticar [44] 1 *vt* to criticize
 2 *vi* (*murmurar*) to gossip
crítico,-a 1 *adj* critical
 2 *nm,f* critic
criticón,-ona *nm,f Fam* fault-finder
Croacia *n* Croatia
croar *vi* to croak
croata 1 *adj* Croatian
 2 *nmf* Croat, Croatian

croché *nm* crochet
croissant *nm* croissant
crol *nm* crawl
cromo *nm* (a) *(metal)* chromium, chrome (b) *(estampa)* picture card
cromosoma *nm* chromosome
crónica *nf* (a) account, chronicle (b) *Prensa* feature, article
crónico,-a *adj* chronic
cronista *nmf Prensa* feature writer
cronología *nf* chronology
cronológico,-a *adj* chronological
cronometrar *vt* to time
cronómetro *nm* stopwatch
croqueta *nf* croquette
croquis *nm inv* sketch
cruce *nm* (a) *(acción)* crossing; *(de carreteras)* crossroads; *(de razas)* crossbreeding (b) *Tel* crossed line
crucero *nm Náut* cruise; *(barco)* cruiser
crucial *adj* crucial
crucificar [44] *vt* to crucify
crucifijo *nm* crucifix
crucigrama *nm* crossword (puzzle)
crudeza *nf* crudeness, coarseness
crudo,-a 1 *adj* (a) raw; *(comida)* under-done; *Fam Fig* **lo veo muy c.** it doesn't look too good (b) *(clima)* harsh (c) *(color)* cream
   2 *nm (petróleo)* crude
cruel *adj* cruel
crueldad *nf* cruelty; *Fig (del clima)* severity
cruento,-a *adj* bloody
crujido *nm (de puerta)* creak, creaking; *(de dientes)* grinding
crujiente *adj* crunchy
crujir *vi (madera)* to creak; *(comida)* to crunch; *(dientes)* to grind
cruz *nf* (a) cross; **C. Roja** Red Cross; **c. gamada** swastika (b) **¿cara o c.?** ≃ heads or tails?
cruza *nf Am* cross, crossbreed
cruzada *nf* crusade
cruzado,-a 1 *adj* (a) crossed; **con los brazos cruzados** arms folded (b) *Cost* double-breasted (c) *(atravesado)* lying across (d) *(animal)* crossbred
   2 *nm Hist* crusader
cruzar [40] **1** *vt* (a) to cross (b) *(palabras, miradas)* to exchange (c) *(animal, planta)* to cross, to crossbreed
   2 *vi (atravesar)* to cross
   3 cruzarse *vpr* to cross; **c. con algn** to pass sb
cta. *Com (abr* **cuenta**) a/c
cta. cte. *Com (abr* **cuenta corriente**) c/a
c/u *(abr* **cada uno**) ea

cuaderno *nm* notebook
cuadra *nf* (a) *(establo)* stable (b) *Am* block (of houses)
cuadrado,-a 1 *adj* (a) *Geom* square (b) *(complexión física)* broad, stocky (c) *Fig (mente)* rigid
   2 *nm* (a) *Geom* square (b) *Mat* square; **elevar (un número) al c.** to square (a number)
cuadrar 1 *vt* (a) *Mat* to square (b) *Andes (aparcar)* to park
   2 *vi (coincidir)* to square, to agree (**con** with); *(sumas, cifras)* to tally
   3 cuadrarse *vpr (soldado)* to stand to attention
cuadriculado,-a *adj* **papel c.** square paper
cuadrilátero,-a 1 *adj* quadrilateral
   2 *nm (en boxeo)* ring
cuadrilla *nf (equipo)* gang, team; *Mil* squad; *Taurom* bullfighter's team
cuadro *nm* (a) *Geom* square; **tela a cuadros** checked cloth (b) *Arte* painting, picture (c) *Teatro* scene (d) *Elec & Téc* panel; **c. de mandos** control panel (e) *(gráfico)* chart, graph
cuádruple *adj* quadruple, fourfold
cuajada *nf* curd
cuajar 1 *vt (leche)* to curdle; *(sangre)* to clot
   2 *vi* (a) *(nieve)* to lie (b) *(moda)* to catch on; *(plan, esfuerzo)* to get off the ground
cual 1 *pron rel (precedido de artículo)* (a) *(persona) (sujeto)* who; *(objeto)* whom (b) *(cosa)* which
   2 *pron* (a) **tal c.** exactly as (b) *Literario (comparativo)* such as, like
cuál 1 *pron interr* which (one)?, what?; **¿c. quieres?** which one do you want?
   2 *adj interr* which
   3 *loc adv* **a c. más tonto** each more stupid than the other
cualidad *nf* quality
cualificado,-a *adj* qualified
cualquier *adj indef* any; **c. cosa** anything; **en c. momento** at any moment o time
cualquiera *(pl* **cualesquiera**) **1** *adj indef* (a) *(indefinido)* any; **un profesor c.** any teacher (b) *(corriente)* ordinary

> Note that **cualquier** is used before singular nouns (e.g. **cualquier hombre** any man).

   2 *pron indef* (a) *(persona)* anybody; **c. te lo puede decir** anybody can tell you (b) *(cosa, animal)* anyone (c) **c. que sea** whatever it is
   3 *nmf Fig* **ser un c.** to be a nobody; **es una c.** she's a tart

cuando 1 *adv (de tiempo)* when; **c. más** at the most; **c. menos** at least; **de c. en c., de vez en c.** from time to time

2 *conj* (a) *(temporal)* when; **c. quieras** whenever you want; **c. vengas** when you come (b) *(condicional) (si)* if (c) *(concesiva) (aunque)* **(aun) c.** even if

3 *prep* during, at the time of; **c. la guerra** during the war; **c. niño** as a child

cuándo *adv interr* when?; **¿desde c.?** since when?; **¿para c. lo quieres?** when do you want it for?

cuantía *nf* quantity, amount

cuantioso,-a *adj* substantial, considerable

cuanto,-a 1 *adj* all; **gasta c. dinero gana** he spends all the money *o* as much as he earns; **unas cuantas niñas** a few girls

2 *pron rel* as much as; **coma c. quiera** eat as much as you want; **regala todo c. tiene** he gives away everything he's got

3 *pron indef pl* **unos cuantos** a few

4 *adv* (a) *(tiempo)* **c. antes** as soon as possible; **en c.** as soon as

(b) *(cantidad)* **c. más ... más** the more ... the more; **c. más lo miro, más me gusta** the more I look at it, the more I like it; **cuantas más personas (haya) mejor** the more the merrier

(c) **en c. a** with respect to, regarding; **en c. a Juan** as for Juan, as far as Juan is concerned

cuánto,-a 1 *adj & pron interr (sing)* how much?; *(pl)* how many?; **¿cuántas veces?** how many times?; **¿c. es?** how much is it?

2 *adv* how, how much; **¡cuánta gente hay!** what a lot of people there are!

cuarenta *adj & nm inv* forty; *Fam* **cantarle a algn las c.** to give sb a piece of one's mind

cuarentena *nf Med* quarantine

cuarentón,-ona *nm,f* forty-year-old

cuaresma *nf* Lent

cuartear *vt* to quarter

cuartel *nm Mil* barracks; **c. general** headquarters; *Fig* **no dar c.** to give no quarter

cuartelada *nf,* **cuartelazo** *nm* putsch, military uprising

cuartelillo *nm Mil* post, station

cuarteto *nm* quartet

cuartilla *nf* sheet of paper

cuarto,-a 1 *nm* (a) *(habitación)* room; **c. de baño** bathroom; **c. de estar** living room (b) *(cuarta parte)* quarter; **c. de hora** quarter of an hour; *Dep* **cuartos de final** quarter finals (c) *Fam* **cuartos** *(dinero)* dough, money

2 *adj & nm,f* fourth

cuarzo *nm* quartz

cuate *nmf Méx Fam* pal, *Br* mate, *US* buddy

cuatro 1 *adj & nm inv* four

2 *nm Fam* a few; **cayeron c. gotas** it rained a little bit

cuatrocientos,-as *adj & nm* four hundred

Cuba *n* Cuba

cuba *nf* cask, barrel; *Fam* **como una c.** (as) drunk as a lord

cubalibre *nm* rum/gin and coke

cubano,-a *adj & nm,f* Cuban

cubata *nm Fam* = cubalibre

cubertería *nf* cutlery

cúbico,-a *adj* cubic; *Mat* **raíz cúbica** cube root

cubierta *nf* (a) cover (b) *(de rueda)* tyre (c) *Náut* deck (d) *(techo)* roof

cubierto,-a 1 *adj* (a) covered; *(piscina)* indoors; *(cielo)* overcast (b) *(trabajo, plaza)* filled

2 *nm* (a) *(en la mesa)* place setting (b) **cubiertos** cutlery

cubil *nm* lair

cubismo *nm* cubism

cubito *nm* little cube; **c. de hielo** ice cube

cubo *nm* (a) bucket; **c. de la basura** rubbish bin (b) *Mat* cube (c) *(de rueda)* hub

cubrecama *nm* bedspread

cubrir *(pp* cubierto*)* **1** *vt* to cover

2 cubrirse *vpr (cielo)* to become overcast

cucaracha *nf* cockroach

cuchara *nf* spoon

cucharada *nf* spoonful; **c. rasa/colmada** level/heaped spoonful

cucharilla *nf* teaspoon; **c. de café** coffee spoon

cucharón *nm* ladle

cuchichear *vi* to whisper

cuchicheo *nm* whispering

cuchilla *nf* blade; **c. de afeitar** razor blade

cuchillada *nf,* **cuchillazo** *nm* stab

cuchillo *nm* knife

cuchitril *nm Fam* hovel, hole

cuclillas: •**en cuclillas** *loc adv* **en c.** crouching; **ponerse en c.** to crouch down

cuco,-a 1 *nm* cuckoo

2 *adj Fam (astuto)* shrewd, crafty

cucurucho *nm* (a) *(para helado)* cornet (b) *(de papel)* paper cone

cuello *nm* (a) neck (b) *(de camisa etc)* collar

cuenca *nf* (a) *Geog* basin (b) *(de los ojos)* socket

cuenco *nm* earthenware bowl

cuenta *nf* (a) *(factura)* bill (b) *Fin (de*

banco) account; **c. corriente** current account (**c**) *(cálculo)* count; **hacer cuentas** to do sums; **c. atrás** countdown (**d**) *(de collar)* bead (**e**) *(locuciones)* **caer en la c., darse c.** to realize; **dar c.** to report; **tener en c.** to take into account; **traer c.** to be worthwhile; **más sillas de la c.** too many chairs; **en resumidas cuentas** in short; **pedir cuentas** to ask for an explanation; **trabajar por c. propia** to be self-employed

cuentagotas *nm inv* dropper

cuentakilómetros *nm inv (distancia)* mileometer; *(velocidad)* speedometer

cuento *nm* story; *Lit* short story; **contar un c.** to tell a story; *Fig* **eso no viene a c.** that's beside the point; **c. chino** tall story; **c. de hadas** fairy story

cuerda *nf* (**a**) *(cordel)* rope; *Fig* **bajo c.** dishonestly; **c. floja** tightrope; **cuerdas vocales** vocal chords (**b**) *(de instrumento)* string (**c**) *(del reloj)* spring; **dar c. al reloj** to wind up a watch

cuerdo,-a *adj* sane

cueriza *nf Andes Fam* beating, leathering

cuerno *nm* horn; *(de ciervo)* antler; *Fam* **¡vete al c.!** get lost!; *Fam* **ponerle cuernos a algn** to be unfaithful to sb

cuero *nm* (**a**) leather; **chaqueta de c.** leather jacket (**b**) **c. cabelludo** scalp; *Fam* **en cueros (vivos)** (stark) naked

cuerpo *nm* (**a**) body; **de c. entero** full-length; *Fig* **tomar c.** to take shape (**b**) *(cadáver)* corpse; **de c. presente** lying in state (**c**) *(parte)* section, part (**d**) *(grupo)* corps, force; **c. de bomberos** fire brigade; **c. diplomático** diplomatic corps

cuervo *nm* raven

cuesta 1 *nf* slope; **c. abajo** downhill; **c. arriba** uphill

　2 *loc adv* **a cuestas** on one's back *o* shoulders

cuestión *nf* (**a**) *(asunto)* matter, question; **es c. de vida o muerte** it's a matter of life or death; **en c. de unas horas** in just a few hours (**b**) *(pregunta)* question

cuestionario *nm* questionnaire

cueva *nf* cave

cuezo *indic pres de* **cocer**

cuico,-a *nm,f Méx Fam* cop

cuidado 1 *nm* (**a**) care; **con c.** carefully; **tener c.** to be careful; **estar al c. de** *(cosa)* to be in charge of; *(persona)* to look after; **me trae sin c.** I couldn't care less (**b**) *Med* **cuidados intensivos** intensive care

　2 *interj* **¡c.!** look out!, watch out!; **¡c. con lo que dices!** watch what you say!; **¡c. con el escalón!** mind the step!

cuidadoso,-a *adj* careful

cuidar 1 *vt* to care for, to look after; **c. de que todo salga bien** to make sure that everything goes all right; **c. los detalles** to pay attention to details

　2 cuidarse *vpr* **cuídate** look after yourself

cuitlacoche *nm CAm, Méx* corn smut, = edible fungus which grows on maize

culata *nf* (**a**) *(de arma)* butt (**b**) *Aut* cylinder head

culebra *nf* snake

culebrilla *nf Med* ringworm

culebrón *nm* soap opera

culinario,-a *adj* culinary

culminación *nf* culmination

culminante *adj (punto)* highest; *(momento)* culminating

culminar *vi* to culminate

culo *nm* (**a**) *Fam (trasero)* backside; *Vulg* **¡vete a tomar por c.!** fuck off! (**b**) *(de recipiente)* bottom

culpa *nf* (**a**) blame; **echar la c. a algn** to put the blame on sb; **fue c. mía** it was my fault; **por tu c.** because of you (**b**) *(culpabilidad)* guilt

culpabilidad *nf* guilt, culpability

culpable 1 *nmf* offender, culprit

　2 *adj* guilty; *Jur* **declararse c.** to plead guilty

culpar *vt* to blame; **c. a algn de un delito** to accuse sb of an offence

cultivado,-a *adj* (**a**) *Agr* cultivated (**b**) *(con cultura)* cultured, refined

cultivar *vt* (**a**) to cultivate (**b**) *Biol* to culture

cultivo *nm* (**a**) cultivation; *(planta)* crop (**b**) *Biol* culture

culto,-a 1 *adj* educated; *(palabra)* learned

　2 *nm* cult; *Rel* worship

cultura *nf* culture

cultural *adj* cultural

culturismo *nm* body building

culturista *nmf* body builder

cumbre *nf* (**a**) *(de montaña)* summit, top; *(conferencia)* **c.** summit conference (**b**) *Fig (culminación)* pinnacle

cumple *nm Fam* birthday

cumpleaños *nm inv* birthday; **¡feliz c.!** happy birthday!

cumplido,-a 1 *adj* (**a**) completed; *(plazo)* expired; **misión cumplida** mission accomplished (**b**) *(cortés)* polite

　2 *nm* compliment

cumplidor,-a *adj* reliable, dependable

cumplimiento *nm* fulfilment; **c. de la ley** observance of the law

cumplir 1 *vt* (**a**) to carry out, to fulfil; *(deseo)* to fulfil; *(promesa)* to keep;

(sentencia) to serve (**b**) **ayer cumplí veinte años** I was twenty (years old) yesterday

2 *vi* (**a**) *(plazo)* to expire, to end (**b**) **c. con el deber** to do one's duty

3 cumplirse *vpr* (**a**) *(deseo, sueño)* to be fulfilled, to come true (**b**) *(plazo)* to expire

cúmulo *nm* pile, load

cuna *nf* (**a**) *(plazo)* cot (**b**) *Fig (origen)* cradle

cundir *vi* (**a**) **me cunde mucho el trabajo o el tiempo** I seem to get a lot done (**b**) *(extenderse)* to spread; **cundió el pánico** panic spread; **cundió la voz de que ...** rumour had it that ...

cuneta *nf (de la carretera)* gutter; **quedarse en la c.** to be left behind

cuña *nf* (**a**) *(pieza)* wedge; **c. publicitaria** commercial break (**b**) *Andes, RP Fam (enchufe)* **tener c.** to have friends in high places

cuñado,-a *nm,f (hombre)* brother-in-law; *(mujer)* sister-in-law

cuño *nm* **de nuevo c.** newly-coined

cuota *nf* (**a**) *(de club etc)* membership fees, dues (**b**) *(porción)* quota, share (**c**) *Méx* **carretera de c.** toll road

cupe *pt indef de* **caber**

cupiera *subj imperf de* **caber**

cupo *nm* ceiling; *Mil* **excedente de c.** exempt from military service

cupón *nm* coupon, voucher

cúpula *nf* dome, cupola; *(líderes)* leadership

cura 1 *nm Rel* priest

2 *nf Med* cure; *Fig* **no tiene c.** there's no remedy

curación *nf* cure, treatment

curandero,-a *nm,f* quack

curar 1 *vt* (**a**) *(sanar)* to cure; *(herida)* to dress; *(enfermedad)* to treat (**b**) *(carne, pescado)* to cure

2 *vi (sanar)* to recover, to get well; *(herida)* to heal up

3 •**curarse** *vpr* to recover, to get well; *(herida)* to heal up; **c. en salud** to make sure

curcuncho,-a *adj Andes Fam* hunchbacked

curiosear *vi* to pry

curiosidad *nf* curiosity; **tener c. de** to be curious about

curioso,-a 1 *adj* (**a**) *(indiscreto)* curious, inquisitive (**b**) *(extraño)* strange, odd; **lo c. es que ...** the strange thing is that ... (**c**) *(limpio)* neat, tidy

2 *nm,f (mirón)* onlooker (**b**) *(chismoso)* nosey-parker, busybody

curita *nf Am Br* sticking-plaster, *US* Band-aid®

currante *nmf Fam* worker

currar, currelar *vi Fam* to graft, to grind

currículum *nm (pl* **curricula)** **c. vitae** curriculum vitae

curro *nm Fam* job

cursar *vt (estudiar)* to study; *(enviar)* to send

cursi *adj* vulgar

cursillo *nm* short course; **c. de reciclaje** refresher course

cursivo,-a *adj* **letra cursiva** italics

curso *nm* (**a**) *(año académico)* year; *(clase)* class (**b**) *Fig* **año/mes en c.** current year/month; **en el c. de** during (**c**) *(de acontecimientos, río)* course (**d**) *Fin* **moneda de c. legal** legal tender

cursor *nm* cursor

curtido,-a *adj* (**a**) *(piel)* weatherbeaten; *(cuero)* tanned (**b**) *Fig (persona)* hardened

curtiembre *nf Andes, RP* tannery

curtir *vt* (**a**) *(cuero)* to tan (**b**) *Fig (avezar)* to harden, to toughen

curva *nf* (**a**) curve (**b**) *(en carretera)* bend; **c. cerrada** sharp bend

curvilíneo,-a *adj* curvaceous

curvo,-a *adj* curved

cuscús *nm* couscous

cúspide *nf* summit, peak; *Fig* peak

custodia *nf* custody

custodiar [43] *vt* to watch over

cutáneo,-a *adj* cutaneous, skin; *Med* **erupción cutánea** rash

cutícula *nf* cuticle

cutis *nm* complexion

cuyo,-a *pron rel & pos (de persona)* whose; *(de cosa)* of which; **en c. caso** in which case

cv *(abr* **caballos de vapor)** hp

D

D, d [de] *nf (la letra)* D, d

D. *(abr* **don)** Mr

Da. *(abr* **doña)** Mrs/Miss

dactilar *adj* **huellas dactilares** finger-prints

dádiva *nf (regalo)* gift, present; *(donativo)* donation

dadivoso,-a *adj* generous

dado¹,-a *adj* **(a)** given; **en un momento d.** at a certain point **(b) ser d. a** to be given to **(c) d. que** since, given that

dado² *nm* die, dice

daga *nf* dagger

dalia *nf* dahlia

dálmata *nm* Dalmatian (dog)

daltónico,-a *adj* colour-blind

dama *nf* **(a)** *(señora)* lady **(b)** *(en damas)* king **(c) damas** *(juego) Br* draughts, *US* checkers

damasco *nm* **(a)** *(tela)* damask **(b)** *Andes, CAm, Carib, RP (albaricoque)* apricot

damnificado,-a *nm,f* victim, injured person

danés,-esa 1 *adj* Danish
2 *nm,f (persona)* Dane
3 *nm* **(a)** *(idioma)* Danish **(b) gran d.** *(perro)* Great Dane

Danubio *nm* **el D.** the Danube

danza *nf* dancing; *(baile)* dance

danzar [40] *vt & vi* to dance

dañar *vt (cosa)* to damage; *(persona)* to hurt, to harm

dañino,-a *adj* harmful, damaging (**para** to)

daño *nm (a cosa)* damage; *(a persona) (físico)* hurt; *(perjuicio)* harm; **se hizo d. en la pierna** he hurt his leg; *Jur* **daños y perjuicios** (legal) damages

dar [11] 1 *vt* **(a)** *(recado, recuerdos)* to pass on, to give; *(noticia)* to tell
(b) *(mano de pintura, cera)* to apply, to put on
(c) *(película)* to show, to screen; *(fiesta)* to throw, to give
(d) *(cosecha)* to produce, to yield; *(fruto, flores)* to bear; *(beneficio, interés)* to give, to yield
(e) *(bofetada etc)* to deal; **d. a algn en la cabeza** to hit sb on the head

(f) dale a la luz switch the light on; **d. la mano a algn** to shake hands with sb; **d. los buenos días/las buenas noches a algn** to say good morning/good evening to sb; **me da lo mismo, me da igual** it's all the same to me; **¿qué más da?** what difference does it make?

(g) *(hora)* to strike; **ya han dado las nueve** it's gone nine (o'clock)

(h) d. de comer a to feed

(i) d. a conocer *(noticia)* to release; **d. a entender a algn que ...** to give sb to understand that ...

(j) d. por *(considerar)* to assume, to consider; **lo dieron por muerto** he was assumed dead, he was given up for dead; **d. por descontado/sabido** to take for granted, to assume

2 *vi* **(a) me dio un ataque de tos/risa** I had a coughing fit/an attack of the giggles

(b) d. a *(ventana, habitación)* to look out onto, to overlook; *(puerta)* to open onto, to lead to

(c) d. con *(persona)* to come across; **d. con la solución** to hit upon the solution

(d) d. de sí *(ropa)* to stretch, to give

(e) d. en to hit; **el sol me daba en los ojos** the sun was (shining) in my eyes

(f) d. para to be enough *o* sufficient for; **el presupuesto no da para más** the budget will not stretch any further

(g) le dio por nadar he took it into his head to go swimming

(h) d. que hablar to set people talking; **el suceso dio que pensar** the incident gave people food for thought

3 darse *vpr* **(a) se dio un caso extraño** something strange happened

(b) *(hallarse)* to be found, to exist

(c) d. a to take to; **se dio a la bebida** he took to drink

(d) d. con *o* **contra** to bump *o* crash into

(e) dárselas de to consider oneself

(f) d. por satisfecho to feel satisfied; **d. por vencido** to give in

(g) se le da bien/mal el francés she's good/bad at French

dardo *nm* dart

dársena *nf* dock

datar 1 *vt* to date

2 *vi* **d. de** to date back to *o* from

dátil *nm* date

dato *nm* (**a**) piece of information; **datos personales** personal details (**b**) *Informát* **datos** data

d.C. (*abr* **después de Cristo**) AD

dcha. (*abr* **derecha**) rt.

de *prep*

> **de** combines with the article **el** to form the contraction **del** (e.g. **del hombre** of the man).

(**a**) (*pertenencia*) of; **el título de la novela** the title of the novel; **el coche/hermano de Sofía** Sofía's car/brother; **las bicicletas de los niños** the boys' bicycles

(**b**) (*procedencia*) from; **de Madrid a Valencia** from Madrid to Valencia; **soy de Palencia** I'm from *o* I come from Palencia

(**c**) (*descripción*) **el niño de ojos azules** the boy with blue eyes; **el señor de la chaqueta** the man in the jacket; **el bobo del niño** the silly boy; **un reloj de oro** a gold watch; **un joven de veinte años** a young man of twenty

(**d**) (*contenido*) of; **un saco de patatas** a sack of potatoes

(**e**) **gafas de sol** sunglasses; **goma de borrar** eraser, *Br* rubber

(**f**) (*oficio*) by, as; **es arquitecto de profesión** he's an architect by profession; **trabaja de secretaria** she's working as a secretary

(**g**) (*acerca de*) about; **curso de informática** computer course

(**h**) (*tiempo*) **a las tres de la tarde** at three in the afternoon; **de día** by day; **de noche** at night; **de lunes a jueves** from Monday to Thursday; **de pequeño** as a child; **de año en año** year in year out

(**i**) (*precio*) at; **patatas de 30 pesetas el kilo** potatoes at 30 pesetas a kilo

(**j**) **una avenida de 15 km** an avenue 15 km long; **una botella de litro** a litre bottle

(**k**) (*con superlativo*) in; **el más largo de España** the longest in Spain

(**l**) (*causa*) with, because of; **llorar de alegría** to cry with joy; **morir de hambre** to die of hunger

(**m**) (*condicional*) **de haber llegado antes** if he had arrived before; **de no ser así** if that wasn't the case; **de ser cierto** if it was *o* were true

(**n**) **lo mismo de siempre** the usual thing

(**o**) **de cuatro en cuatro** in fours, four at a time

deambular *vi* to saunter, to stroll

debajo *adv* underneath, below; **el mío es el de b.** mine is the one below; **está d. de la mesa** it's under the table; **por d. de lo normal** below normal; **salió por d. del coche** he came out from under the car

debate *nm* debate

debatir 1 *vt* to debate

2 debatirse *upr* to struggle; **d. entre la vida y la muerte** to fight for one's life

debe *nm* Com debit, debit side

deber¹ *nm* (**a**) duty; **cumplir con su d.** to do one's duty (**b**) *Educ* **deberes** homework

deber² **1** *vt* (*dinero, explicación*) to owe

2 *vi* (**a**) must, to have to; **debe (de) comer** he must eat; **debe (de) irse ahora** she has to leave now; **la factura debe pagarse mañana** the bill must be paid tomorrow; **el tren debe llegar a las dos** the train is expected to arrive at two

(**b**) (*consejo*) **deberías visitar a tus padres** you ought to visit your parents; **debería haber ido ayer** I should have gone yesterday; **no debiste hacerlo** you shouldn't have done it

(**c**) (*suposición*) **deben de estar fuera** they must be out

3 deberse *upr* **d. a** to be due to; **esto se debe a la falta de agua** this is due to lack of water

debidamente *adv* duly, properly

debido,-a *adj* (**a**) due; **a su d. tiempo** in due course; **con el d. respeto** with due respect (**b**) (*adecuado*) proper; **más de lo d.** too much; **tomaron las debidas precauciones** they took the proper precautions; **como es d.** properly (**c**) **d. a** because of, due to; **d. a que** because of the fact that

débil *adj* weak; (*luz*) dim; **punto d.** weak spot

debilidad *nf* weakness; *Fig* **tener d. por** (*persona*) to have a soft spot for; (*cosa*) to have a weakness for

debilitamiento *nm* weakening

debilitar 1 *vt* to weaken, to debilitate

2 debilitarse *upr* to weaken, to grow weak

débito *nm* (**a**) (*deuda*) debt (**b**) (*debe*) debit

debut *nm* début, debut

debutar *vi* to make one's début *o* debut

década *nf* decade; **en la d. de los noventa** during the nineties

decadencia *nf* decadence

decadente *adj & nmf* decadent

decaer [39] *vi* to deteriorate

decaído,-a adj down
decaimiento nm (**a**) (*debilidad*) weakness (**b**) (*desaliento*) low spirits
decano,-a nm,f Univ dean
decantarse vpr to lean towards; **d. por** to come down on the side of
decapitar vt to behead, to decapitate
decena nf (about) ten; **una d. de veces** (about) ten times; **por decenas** in tens
decencia nf (**a**) (*decoro*) decency (**b**) (*honradez*) honesty
decenio nm decade
decente adj decent; (*decoroso*) modest
decepción nf disappointment

> 🖉 Observa que la palabra inglesa **deception** es un falso amigo y no es la traducción de la palabra española **decepción**. En inglés, **deception** significa "engaño".

decepcionante adj disappointing
decepcionar vt to disappoint
decididamente adv (**a**) (*resueltamente*) resolutely (**b**) (*definitivamente*) definitely
decidido,-a adj determined, resolute
decidir 1 vt & vi to decide
  2 **decidirse** vpr to make up one's mind; **d. a hacer algo** to make up one's mind to do sth; **d. por algo** to decide on sth
décima nf tenth
decimal adj & nm decimal; **el sistema métrico d.** the decimal system
décimo,-a 1 adj & nm,f tenth
  2 nm (**a**) (*parte*) tenth (**b**) (*billete de lotería*) tenth part of a lottery ticket
decir¹ nm saying
decir² [12] (*pp* **dicho**) 1 vt (**a**) to say; **dice que no quiere venir** he says he doesn't want to come
  (**b**) **d. una mentira/la verdad** to tell a lie/the truth
  (**c**) Tel **dígame** hello
  (**d**) **¿qué me dices del nuevo jefe?** what do you think of the new boss?
  (**e**) (*mostrar*) to tell, to show; **su cara dice que está mintiendo** you can tell from his face that he's lying
  (**f**) (*sugerir*) to mean; **esta película no me dice nada** this film doesn't appeal to me; **¿qué te dice el cuadro?** what does the picture mean to you?
  (**g**) **querer d.** to mean
  (**h**) (*locuciones*) **es d.** that is (to say); **por así decirlo** as it were, so to speak; **digamos** let's say; **digo yo** in my opinion; **el qué dirán** what people say; **ni que d. tiene** needless to say; **¡no me digas!** really!; **¡y que lo digas!** you bet!
  2 **decirse** vpr **¿cómo se dice "mesa" en inglés?** how do you say "mesa" in English?; **se dice que ...** they say that ...; **sé lo que me digo** I know what I am saying
decisión nf (**a**) (*resolución*) decision; **tomar una d.** to take o make a decision (**b**) (*resolución*) determination; **con d.** decisively
decisivo,-a adj decisive
decisorio,-a adj decision-making
declamar vt & vi to declaim, to recite
declaración nf (**a**) declaration; **d. de (la) renta** tax declaration o return (**b**) (*afirmación*) statement; **hacer declaraciones** to comment (**c**) Jur **prestar d.** to give evidence
declarante nmf Jur witness
declarar 1 vt (**a**) to declare; **d. la guerra a** to declare war on (**b**) (*afirmar*) to state (**c**) Jur **d. culpable/inocente a algn** to find sb guilty/not guilty
  2 vi (**a**) to declare (**b**) Jur to testify
  3 **declararse** vpr (**a**) **d. a favor/en contra de** to declare oneself in favour of/against; **d. en huelga** to go on strike; **d. a algn** to declare one's love for sb (**b**) (*guerra, incendio*) to start, to break out (**c**) Jur **d. culpable** to plead guilty
declinar vt & vi to decline
declive nm (**a**) (*del terreno*) incline, slope (**b**) (*de imperio etc*) decline
decolaje nm Am take-off
decolar vi Am to take off
decolorante nm bleaching agent
decolorar 1 vt to fade; (*pelo*) to bleach
  2 **decolorarse** vpr to fade
decomisar vt to confiscate, to seize
decoración nf decoration
decorado nm scenery, set
decorador,-a nm,f (**a**) decorator (**b**) Teatro set designer
decorar vt to decorate
decorativo,-a adj decorative
decoro nm (**a**) (*respeto*) dignity, decorum (**b**) (*pudor*) modesty, decency
decoroso,-a adj (**a**) (*correcto*) seemly, decorous (**b**) (*decente*) decent, modest
decrecer [33] vi to decrease, to diminish
decrépito,-a adj decrepit
decretar vt to decree
decreto nm decree; **d.-ley** decree
dedal nm thimble
dedicación nf dedication
dedicar [44] 1 vt to dedicate; (*tiempo, esfuerzos*) to devote (**a** to)
  2 **dedicarse** vpr **¿a qué se dedica Vd.?** what do you do for a living?; **los fines de semana ella se dedica a pescar** at weekends she spends her time fishing
dedicatoria nf dedication

dedillo *nm* **saber algo al d.** to have sth at one's fingertips, to know sth very well

dedo *nm* (*de la mano*) finger; (*del pie*) toe; **d. anular/corazón/índice/meñique** ring/middle/index/little finger; **d. pulgar, d. gordo** thumb; *RP* **hacer d.** to hitchhike; *Fig* **elegir a algn a d.** to hand-pick sb

deducción *nf* deduction

deducible *adj Com* deductible

deducir [10] **1** *vt* (a) to deduce, to infer (b) *Com* to deduct
2 deducirse *vpr* **de aquí se deduce que ...** from this it follows that ...

deductivo,-a *adj* deductive

defecar [44] *vi* to defecate

defecto *nm* defect, fault; **d. físico** physical defect

defectuoso,-a *adj* defective, faulty

defender [3] **1** *vt* to defend (**de** from); **d. del frío/viento** to shelter from the cold/wind
2 defenderse *vpr* (a) to defend oneself (b) *Fam* **se defiende en francés** he can get by in French

defendido,-a *adj Jur* defendant

defensa 1 *nf* defence; **en d. propia, en legítima d.** in self-defence; **salir en d. de algn** to come out in defence of sb
2 *nm Dep* defender, back

defensiva *nf* defensive; **estar/ponerse a la d.** to be/go on the defensive

defensivo,-a *adj* defensive

defensor,-a *nm,f* defender; **abogado d.** counsel for the defence; **el defensor del pueblo** the ombudsman

deferencia *nf* deference; **en** *o* **por d. a** out of deference for

deficiencia *nf* deficiency, shortcoming; **d. mental** mental deficiency; **d. renal** kidney failure

deficiente 1 *adj* deficient
2 *nmf* **d. mental** mentally retarded person
3 *nm Educ* fail

déficit *nm* (*pl* **déficits**) deficit; (*carencia*) shortage

deficitario,-a *adj* showing a deficit

definición *nf* definition; **por d.** by definition

definido,-a *adj* clear; *Ling* definite

definir *vt* to define

definitivamente *adv* (a) (*para siempre*) for good, once and for all (b) (*con toda seguridad*) definitely

definitivo,-a *adj* definitive; **en definitiva** in short

deflación *nf Econ* deflation

deflacionista *adj Econ* deflationary

deformación *nf* deformation

deformar 1 *vt* to deform, to put out of shape; (*cara*) to disfigure; *Fig* (*la verdad, una imagen*) to distort
2 deformarse *vpr* to go out of shape, to become distorted

deforme *adj* deformed; (*objeto*) misshapen

defraudación *nf* fraud; **d. fiscal** tax evasion

defraudar *vt* (a) (*decepcionar*) to disappoint (b) (*al fisco*) to defraud, to cheat; **d. a Hacienda** to evade taxes

defunción *nf Fml* decease, demise

degeneración *nf* degeneration

degenerado,-a *adj* & *nm,f* degenerate

degenerar *vi* to degenerate

degollar [2] *vt* to behead

degradación *nf* degradation

degradante *adj* degrading

degradar *vt* to degrade

degustación *nf* tasting

degustar *vt* to taste, to sample

dehesa *nf* pasture, meadow

deificar [44] *vt* to deify

dejadez *nf* slovenliness

dejado,-a *adj* (a) (*descuidado*) untidy, slovenly (b) (*negligente*) negligent, careless (c) *Fam* **d. de la mano de Dios** godforsaken

dejar 1 *vt* (a) to leave; **déjame en paz** leave me alone; **d. dicho** to leave word *o* a message
(b) (*prestar*) to lend
(c) (*abandonar*) to give up; **d. algo por imposible** to give sth up; **dejé el tabaco y la bebida** I gave up smoking and drinking
(d) (*permitir*) to let, to allow; **d. caer** to drop; **d. entrar/salir** to let in/out
(e) (*omitir*) to leave out, to omit
(f) (*ganancias*) to produce
(g) (+ *adj*) to make; **d. triste** to make sad; **d. preocupado/sorprendido** to worry/surprise
(h) (*posponer*) **dejaron el viaje para el verano** they put the trip off until the summer
2 *v aux* **d. de** + *inf* to stop, to give up; **dejó de fumar el año pasado** he gave up smoking last year; **no deja de llamarme** she's always phoning me up
3 dejarse *vpr* (a) **me he dejado las llaves dentro** I've left the keys inside (b) (*locuciones*) **d. barba** to grow a beard; **d. caer** to flop down; **d. llevar por** to be influenced by

del (*contracción de* **de** + **el**) *ver* **de**

delantal *nm* apron

delante *adv* (a) in front; **la entrada de d.** the front entrance (b) **d. de** in front of; *(en serie)* ahead of (c) **por d.** in front; **se lo lleva todo por d.** he destroys everything in his path; **tiene toda la vida por d.** he has his whole life ahead of him

delantera *nf* (a) *(ventaja)* lead; **tomar la d.** take the lead (b) *Ftb* forward line, forwards

delantero,-a 1 *adj* front

2 *nm Ftb* forward; **d. centro** centre forward

delatar *vt* (a) to inform against (b) *Fig* to give away

delator,-a *nm,f* informer

delegación *nf* (a) *(acto, delegados)* delegation (b) *(oficina)* local office, branch; **D. de Hacienda** Tax Office (c) *Méx (distrito municipal)* district; *(comisaría)* police station

delegado,-a *nm,f* (a) delegate; **d. de Hacienda** chief tax inspector (b) *Com* representative

delegar [42] *vt* to delegate (**en** to)

deleitar 1 *vt* to delight

2 deleitarse *vpr* to delight in, to take delight in

deleite *nm* delight

deletrear *vt* to spell (out)

deleznable *adj* brittle

delfín *nm* dolphin

delgadez *nf* slimness

delgado,-a *adj* slim; *(capa)* fine

deliberación *nf* deliberation

deliberado,-a *adj* deliberate

deliberar *vi* to deliberate (on), to consider

delicadeza *nf* (a) *(finura)* delicacy, daintiness (b) *(tacto)* tactfulness; **falta de d.** tactlessness

delicado,-a *adj* (a) delicate (b) *(exigente)* fussy, hard to please (c) *(sensible)* hypersensitive

delicia *nf* delight; **hacer las delicias de algn** to delight sb

delicioso,-a *adj* *(comida)* delicious; *(agradable)* delightful

delictivo,-a *adj* criminal, punishable

delimitar *vt* to delimit

delincuencia *nf* delinquency

delincuente *adj & nmf* delinquent; **d. juvenil** juvenile delinquent

delineante *nmf (hombre)* draughtsman; *(mujer)* draughtswoman

delinear *vt* to delineate, to outline

delinquir [48] *vi* to break the law, to commit an offence

delirante *adj* delirious

delirar *vi* to be delirious

delirio *nm* delirium; **delirios de grandeza** delusions of grandeur

delito *nm* crime, offence

delta *nm* delta; **ala d.** hang-glider

demacrado,-a *adj* emaciated

demagogia *nf* demagogy

demagogo,-a *nm,f* demagogue

demanda *nf* (a) *Jur* lawsuit (b) *Com* demand

demandado,-a 1 *nm,f* defendant

2 *adj* in demand

demandante *nmf* claimant

demandar *vt* to sue

demarcar [44] *vt* to demarcate

demás 1 *adj* **los/las d.** the rest of; **la d. gente** the rest of the people

2 *pron* **lo/los/las d.** the rest; **por lo d.** otherwise, apart from that; **y d.** etcetera

demasía *nf* **en d.** excessively

demasiado,-a 1 *adj (singular)* too much; *(plural)* too many; **hay demasiada comida** there is too much food; **quieres demasiadas cosas** you want too many things

2 *adv* too (much); **es d. grande/caro** it is too big/dear; **fumas/trabajas d.** you smoke/work too much

demencia *nf* dementia, insanity

demente 1 *adj* insane, mad

2 *nmf* mental patient

democracia *nf* democracy

demócrata 1 *adj* democratic

2 *nmf* democrat

democrático,-a *adj* democratic

democratizar [40] *vt* to democratize

demografía *nf* demography

demográfico,-a *adj* demographic; **crecimiento d.** population growth

demoledor,-a *adj Fig* devastating

demoler [4] *vt* to demolish

demonio *nm* devil, demon; *Fam* **¿cómo/dónde demonios ...?** how/where the hell ...?; *Fam* **¡demonio(s)!** hell!, damn!; *Fam* **¡d. de niño!** you little devil!

demora *nf* delay

demorar 1 *vt* (a) *(retrasar)* to delay, to hold up (b) *(tardar)* **demoraron tres días en pintar la casa** it took them three days to paint the house

2 *vi Am (tardar)* **¡no demores!** don't be late!; **demorar en hacer algo** *(llevar tiempo)* to take one's time doing sth; *(retrasarse)* to take too long doing sth; **no demoraron en venir** they came immediately

3 demorarse *vpr* (a) *(retrasarse)* to be delayed, to be held up (b) *(detenerse)* to dally

demostrable *adj* demonstrable

demostración *nf* demonstration; **una d. de fuerza/afecto** a show of strength

demostrar [2] *vt* (**a**) *(mostrar)* to show, to demonstrate (**b**) *(evidenciar)* to prove

demudado,-a *adj* pale

denegar [1] *vt* to refuse; *Jur* **d. una demanda** to dismiss a claim

denigrante *adj* humiliating

denigrar *vt* to humiliate

denominación *nf* denomination; **d. de origen** *(vinos)* = guarantee of region of origin

denominado,-a *adj* so-called

denominador *nm* denominator

denominar *vt* to name, to designate

denotar *vt* to denote

densidad *nf* density; **d. de población** population density

denso,-a *adj* dense

dentadura *nf* teeth, set of teeth; **d. postiza** false teeth, dentures

dental *adj* dental

dentera *nf* **me da d.** it sets my teeth on edge

dentífrico,-a **1** *adj* **pasta/crema dentífrica** toothpaste

2 *nm* toothpaste

dentista *nmf* dentist

dentro *adv* (**a**) *(en el interior)* inside; **aquí d.** in here; **por d.** (on the) inside; **por d. está triste** deep down (inside) he feels sad (**b**) **d. de** *(lugar)* inside (**c**) **d. de poco** shortly, soon; **d. de un mes** in a month's time; **d. de lo que cabe** all things considered

denuncia *nf* (**a**) *Jur* report (**b**) *(crítica)* denunciation

denunciar [43] *vt* (**a**) *(delito)* to report (**a** to) (**b**) *(criticar)* to denounce

deparar *vt* to give; **no sabemos qué nos depara el destino** we don't know what fate has in store for us

departamento *nm* (**a**) department (**b**) *Ferroc* compartment (**c**) *(territorial)* province, district (**d**) *Arg (piso) Br* flat, *US* apartment

dependencia *nf* (**a**) dependence (**de** on) (**b**) **dependencias** premises

depender *vi* to depend (**de** on); *(económicamente)* to be dependent (**de** on)

dependienta *nf* shop assistant

dependiente **1** *adj* dependent (**de** on)

2 *nm* shop assistant

depilación *nf* depilation; **d. a la cera** waxing

depilar *vt* to remove the hair from; *(cejas)* to pluck

depilatorio,-a *adj & nm* depilatory; **crema depilatoria** hair-remover, hair-removing cream

deplorable *adj* deplorable

deplorar *vt* to deplore

deponer [19] *(pp* **depuesto)** *vt* (**a**) *(destituir)* to remove from office; *(líder)* to depose (**b**) *(actitud)* to abandon

deportado,-a *nm,f* deportee, deported person

deportar *vt* to deport

deporte *nm* sport; **hacer d.** to practise sports; **d. de aventura** adventure sport

deportista **1** *nmf (hombre)* sportsman; *(mujer)* sportswoman

2 *adj* sporty

deportividad *nf* sportsmanship

deportivo,-a **1** *adj* sports; **club/chaqueta d.** sports club/jacket

2 *nm* *Aut* sports car

deposición *nf* removal from office; *(de un líder)* deposition

depositar **1** *vt* (**a**) *Fin* to deposit (**b**) *(colocar)* to place, to put

2 depositarse *vpr* to settle

depósito *nm* (**a**) *Fin* deposit; **en d.** on deposit (**b**) *(de agua, gasolina)* tank (**c**) **d. de basuras** rubbish tip **o** dump; **d. de cadáveres** mortuary, morgue

depravación *nf* depravity

depravar *vt* to deprave

depre *nf Fam* downer, depression

depreciación *nf* depreciation

depreciar [43] **1** *vt* to reduce the value of

2 depreciarse *vpr* to depreciate, to lose value

depredador,-a **1** *adj* predatory

2 *nm,f* predator

depresión *nf* depression; **d. nerviosa** nervous breakdown

depresivo,-a *adj* depressive

deprimente *adj* depressing

deprimido,-a *adj* depressed

deprimir **1** *vt* to depress

2 deprimirse *vpr* to get depressed

deprisa *adv* quickly

depuesto,-a *pp de* deponer

depuración *nf* (**a**) *(del agua)* purification (**b**) *(purga)* purge

depurador,-a *adj* **planta depuradora** purification plant

depuradora *nf* purifier

depurar *vt* (**a**) *(agua)* to purify (**b**) *(partido)* to purge (**c**) *(estilo)* to refine

derecha *nf* (**a**) *(mano)* right hand (**b**) *(lugar)* right, right-hand side; **a la d.** to **o** on the right, on the right-hand side (**c**) *Pol* **la d.** the right; **de derechas** right-wing

101   **derechista ▸ desahogarse**

derechista *nmf* right-winger
derecho,-a 1 *adj* (**a**) *(de la derecha)* right
(**b**) *(recto)* upright, straight
2 *nm* (**a**) *(privilegio)* right; **derechos
civiles/humanos** civil/human rights; **tener d. a** to be entitled to, to have the right
to; **estar en su d.** to be within one's rights;
no hay d. it's not fair; **d. de admisión** right
to refuse admission (**b**)*Jur* law; **d. penal/
político** criminal/constitutional law (**c**)
Com **derechos** duties; **derechos de autor**
royalties; **derechos de matrícula** enrolment fees
3 *adv* **siga todo d.** go straight ahead
deriva *nf* drift; **ir a la d.** to drift
derivado *nm* *(producto)* derivative, by-
product
derivar 1 *vt* to divert; *(conversación)* to
steer
2 *vi* (**a**) to drift (**b**) **d. de** to derive from
3 derivarse *upr* (**a**) **d. de** *(proceder)* to
result o stem from (**b**) **d. de** *Ling* to be
derived from
dermatitis *nf inv* dermatitis
dermatólogo,-a *nm,f* dermatologist
derogar [42] *vt* to repeal
derramamiento *nm* spilling; **d. de sangre** bloodshed
derramar 1 *vt* to spill; *(lágrimas)* to shed
2 derramarse *upr* to spill
derrame *nm* *Med* discharge; **d. cerebral**
brain haemorrhage
derrapar *vi* to skid
derredor *nm* **en d. de** round, around
derretir [6] *vt*, **derretirse** *upr* to melt;
(hielo, nieve) to thaw
derribar *vt* (**a**) *(edificio)* to pull down, to
knock down (**b**) *(avión)* to shoot down
(**c**) *(gobierno)* to bring down
derrocar [44] *vt* to bring down; *(violentamente)* to overthrow
derrochador,-a 1 *adj* wasteful
2 *nm,f* wasteful person, squanderer
derrochar *vt* to waste, to squander
derroche *nm* (**a**) *(de dinero, energía)*
waste, squandering (**b**) *(abundancia)*
profusion, abundance
derrota *nf* (**a**) defeat (**b**) *Náut* (ship's)
course
derrotar *vt* to defeat, to beat
derrotero *nm* (**a**) *Fig* path, course o plan
of actiòn (**b**) *Náut* sailing directions
derrotista *adj & nmf* defeatist
derruido,-a *adj* in ruins
derruir [37] *vt* to demolish
derrumbar 1 *vt* *(edificio)* to knock down,
to pull down
2 derrumbarse *upr* to collapse, to fall

down; *(techo)* to fall in, to cave in
desabastecido,-a *adj* **d. de** out of
desaborido,-a 1 *adj* (**a**) *(comida)* tasteless (**b**) *Fig (persona)* dull
2 *nm,f Fig* dull person
desabrido,-a *adj* (**a**) *(comida)* tasteless
(**b**) *(tiempo)* unpleasant (**c**) *Fig (tono)*
harsh; *(persona)* moody, irritable
desabrigado,-a *adj* **ir/estar d.** to be
lightly dressed
desabrochar 1 *vt* to undo
2 desabrocharse *upr* (**a**) **desabróchate la
camisa** undo your shirt (**b**) *(prenda)* to
come undone
desacatar *vt* to disobey
desacato *nm* lack of respect, disrespect
(**a** for); *Jur* **d. al tribunal** contempt of
court
desacertado,-a *adj* unwise
desacierto *nm* mistake, error
desaconsejar *vt* to advise against
desacorde *adj* **estar d. con** to be in
disagreement with
desacreditar *vt* (**a**) *(desprestigiar)* to discredit, to bring into discredit (**b**) *(criticar)*
to disparage
desactivador,-a *nm,f* bomb disposal expert
desactivar *vt* *(bomba)* to defuse
desacuerdo *nm* disagreement
desafiante *adj* defiant
desafiar [29] *vt* to challenge
desafinado,-a *adj* out of tune
desafinar 1 *vi* to sing out of tune; *(instrumento)* to play out of tune
2 *vt* to put out of tune
3 desafinarse *upr* to go out of tune
desafío *nm* challenge
desaforado,-a *adj* wild
desafortunado,-a *adj* unlucky, unfortunate
desagradable *adj* unpleasant, disagreeable
desagradar *vi* to displease
desagradecido,-a 1 *adj* ungrateful
2 *nm,f* ungrateful person
desagrado *nm* displeasure
desagraviar [43] *vt* to make amends for
desaguar [45] *vt* to drain
desagüe *nm* *(vaciado)* drain; *(cañería)*
waste pipe, drainpipe
desaguisado *nm* mess
desahogado,-a *adj* (**a**) *(acomodado)*
well-off, well-to-do (**b**) *(espacioso)* spacious, roomy
desahogarse [42] *upr* to let off steam; **se
desahogó de su depresión** he got his
depression out of his system

desahogo nm (a) (alivio) relief (b) **vivir con d.** to live comfortably

desahuciado,-a adj (a) (enfermo) hopeless (b) (inquilino) evicted

desahuciar [43] vt (a) (desalojar) to evict (b) (enfermo) to deprive of all hope

desahucio nm eviction

desairado,-a adj (a) (humillado) spurned (b) (sin gracia) awkward

desairar vt to slight, to snub

desaire nm slight, rebuff

desajustar 1 vt to upset

2 desajustarse vpr (piezas) to come apart

desajuste nm upset; **d. económico** economic imbalance; **un d. de horarios** clashing timetables

desalentador,-a adj discouraging, disheartening

desalentar [1] 1 vt to discourage, to dishearten

2 desalentarse vpr to get discouraged, to lose heart

desaliento nm discouragement

desaliñado,-a adj scruffy, untidy

desaliño nm scruffiness, untidiness

desalmado,-a adj cruel, heartless

desalojamiento nm (de inquilino) eviction; (de público) removal; (de lugar) evacuation

desalojar vt (a) (inquilino) to evict; (público) to move on; (lugar) to evacuate (b) (abandonar) to move out of, to abandon

desalojo nm = desalojamiento

desamor nm lack of affection

desamortizar [40] vt to alienate, to disentail

desamparado,-a 1 adj (persona) helpless, unprotected; (lugar) abandoned, forsaken

2 nm,f helpless o abandoned person

desamparar vt (a) to abandon, to desert (b) Jur to renounce, to relinquish

desamparo nm helplessness

desamueblado,-a adj unfurnished

desandar [8] vt **d. lo andado** to retrace one's steps

desangrarse vpr to lose (a lot of) blood

desanimado,-a adj (a) (persona) downhearted, dejected (b) (fiesta etc) dull, lifeless

desanimar 1 vt to discourage, to dishearten

2 desanimarse vpr to lose heart, to get discouraged

desánimo nm discouragement, dejection

desapacible adj unpleasant

desaparecer [33] vi to disappear

desaparecido,-a 1 adj missing

2 nm,f missing person

desaparición nf disappearance

desapego nm indifference, lack of affection

desapercibido,-a adj (a) (inadvertido) unnoticed; **pasar d.** to go unnoticed (b) (desprevenido) unprepared

desaprensivo,-a 1 adj unscrupulous

2 nm,f unscrupulous person

desaprobar [2] vt (a) (no aprobar) to disapprove of (b) (rechazar) to reject

desaprovechar vt (a) (dinero, tiempo) to waste; **d. una ocasión** to fail to make the most of an opportunity

desarmable adj that can be taken to pieces

desarmador nm Méx screwdriver

desarmar vt (a) (desmontar) to dismantle, to take to pieces (b) Mil to disarm

desarme nm disarmament; **d. nuclear** nuclear disarmament

desarraigado,-a adj rootless, without roots

desarraigar [42] vt to uproot

desarraigo nm rootlessness

desarreglado,-a adj (a) (lugar) untidy (b) (persona) untidy, slovenly

desarreglar vt (a) (desordenar) to make untidy, to mess up (b) (planes etc) to spoil, to upset

desarreglo nm difference of opinion

desarrollado,-a adj developed; **país d.** developed country

desarrollar 1 vt to develop

2 desarrollarse vpr (a) (persona, enfermedad) to develop (b) (tener lugar) to take place

desarrollo nm development; **países en vías de d.** developing countries

desarticular vt to dismantle; **d. un complot** to foil a plot

desaseado,-a adj unkempt

desasir [46] 1 vt to release

2 desasirse vpr to get loose; **d. de** to free o rid oneself of

desasosegar [1] vt to make restless o uneasy

desasosiego nm restlessness, uneasiness

desastrado,-a 1 adj untidy, scruffy

2 nm,f scruffy person

desastre nm disaster; **eres un d.** you're just hopeless

desastroso,-a adj disastrous

desatar 1 vt to untie, to undo; (provocar) to unleash

2 desatarse *vpr* (**a**) *(zapato, cordón)* to come undone (**b**) *(tormenta)* to break; *(pasión)* to run wild

desatascar [44] *vt* to unblock, to clear

desatender [3] *vt* to neglect, not to pay attention to

desatento,-a *adj* inattentive; *(descortés)* impolite, discourteous

desatinado,-a *adj* unwise

desatino *nm* blunder

desatornillar *vt* to unscrew

desatrancar [44] *vt* to unblock; *(puerta)* to unbolt

desautorizar [40] *vt* (**a**) to disallow (**b**) *(huelga etc)* to ban, to forbid (**c**) *(desmentir)* to deny

desavenencia *nf* disagreement

desaventajado,-a *adj* at a disadvantage

desayunar 1 *vi* to have breakfast; *Fml* to breakfast

2 *vt* to have for breakfast

desayuno *nm* breakfast

desazón *nf* unease

desazonar *vt* to cause unease to, to worry

desbancar [44] *vt* to oust

desbandada *nf* scattering; **hubo una d. general** everyone scattered

desbandarse *vpr* to scatter, to disperse

desbarajuste *nm* confusion, disorder

desbaratar *vt* to ruin, to wreck; *(jersey)* to unravel

desbloquear *vt* (**a**) *(negociaciones)* to get going again (**b**) *(créditos, precios)* to unfreeze

desbocado,-a *adj (caballo)* runaway

desbocarse *vpr (caballo)* to bolt, to run away

desbolado,-a *RP Fam* **1** *adj* messy, untidy

2 *nm,f* untidy person

desbolarse *vpr RP Fam* to undress, to strip

desbole *nm RP Fam* mess, chaos

desbordante *adj* overflowing, bursting

desbordar 1 *vt* to overflow; *Fig* to overwhelm

2 *vi* to overflow (**de** with)

2 desbordarse *vpr* to overflow, to flood

descabalgar [42] *vi* to dismount

descabellado,-a *adj* crazy, wild

descafeinado,-a *adj* (**a**) *(café)* decaffeinated (**b**) *Fig* watered-down, diluted

descalabrar *vt* (**a**) to wound in the head (**b**) *Fig* to damage, to harm

descalabro *nm* setback, misfortune

descalificar [44] *vt* to disqualify

descalzarse [40] *vpr* to take one's shoes off

descalzo,-a *adj* barefoot

descambiar [43] *vt* to exchange

descaminado,-a *adj* **ir d.** to be on the wrong track

descampado *nm* waste ground

descansado,-a *adj* (**a**) *(persona)* rested (**b**) *(vida, trabajo)* restful

descansar *vi* (**a**) to rest, to have a rest; *(corto tiempo)* to take a break (**b**) *Euf* **que en paz descanse** may he/she rest in peace

descansillo *nm* landing

descanso *nm* (**a**) rest, break; **un día de d.** a day off (**b**) *Cin & Teatro* interval; *Dep* half-time, interval (**c**) *(alivio)* relief (**d**) *(rellano)* landing

descapotable *adj & nm* convertible

descarado,-a 1 *adj* (**a**) *(insolente)* cheeky, insolent; *(desvergonzado)* shameless (**b**) *Fam* **d. que sí/no** *(por supuesto)* of course/course not

2 *nm,f* cheeky person

descarga *nf* (**a**) unloading (**b**) *Elec & Mil* discharge

descargar [42] 1 *vt* (**a**) to unload (**b**) *Elec* to discharge (**c**) *(disparar)* to fire; *(golpe)* to deal

2 *vi (tormenta)* to burst

3 descargarse *vpr (batería)* to go flat

descargo *nm Jur* discharge; **testigo de d.** witness for the defence

descarnado,-a *adj* crude

descaro *nm* cheek, nerve; **¡qué d.!** what a cheek!

descarriar [29] 1 *vt* to lead astray, to put on the wrong road

2 descarriarse *vpr* to go astray, to lose one's way

descarrilar *vi* to go off the rails, to be derailed

descartar 1 *vt* to rule out

2 descartarse *vpr Naipes* to discard cards; **me descarté de un cinco** I got rid of a five

descascarillarse *vpr* to chip, to peel

descendencia *nf* descendants; **morir sin d.** to die without issue

descendente *adj* descending, downward

descender [3] 1 *vi* (**a**) *(temperatura, nivel)* to fall, to drop (**b**) **d. de** to descend from

2 *vt* to lower

descendiente *nmf* descendant

descenso *nm* (**a**) descent; *(de temperatura)* fall, drop (**b**) *Dep* relegation

descentrado,-a *adj* off-centre

descentralizar [40] *vt* to decentralize

descifrar *vt* to decipher; *(mensaje)* to decode; *(misterio)* to solve; *(motivos, causas)* to figure out

descojonarse *vpr muy Fam (reírse)* to piss oneself laughing

descolgar [2] 1 *vt (el teléfono)* to pick up; *(cuadro, cortinas)* to take down
2 descolgarse *vpr* to let oneself down, to slide down

descolorido,-a *adj* faded

descombros *nmpl* rubble, debris

descompasado,-a *adj* inconsistent

descomponer [19] *(pp* descompuesto*)*
1 *vt* **(a)** to break down **(b)** *(corromper)* to rot, to decompose
2 descomponerse *vpr* **(a)** *(corromperse)* to rot, to decompose **(b)** *(ponerse nervioso)* to lose one's cool **(c)** *Am (el tiempo)* to turn nasty

descomposición *nf* **(a)** *(de carne)* decomposition, rotting; *(de país)* disintegration **(b)** *Quím* breakdown

descompostura *nf* **(a)** *Am (malestar)* unpleasant turn **(b)** *Méx, RP (avería)* breakdown

descompuesto,-a *adj* **(a)** *(podrido)* rotten, decomposed **(b)** *(furioso)* furious

descomponer *pt indef de* descomponer

descomunal *adj* huge, massive

desconcertante *adj* disconcerting

desconcertar [1] 1 *vt* to disconcert
2 desconcertarse *vpr* to be bewildered, to be puzzled

desconchón *nm* bare patch

desconcierto *nm* chaos, confusion

desconectar *vt* to disconnect

desconexión *nf* disconnection

desconfiado,-a *adj* distrustful, wary

desconfianza *nf* distrust, mistrust

desconfiar [29] *vi* **d. (de)** to distrust, to mistrust

descongelar *vt (nevera)* to defrost; *(créditos)* to unfreeze

descongestionar *vt* to clear

desconocer [34] *vt* not to know, to be unaware of

desconocido,-a 1 *adj* unknown; *(irreconocible)* unrecognizable
2 *nm* **lo d.** the unknown
3 *nm,f* stranger

desconsiderado,-a 1 *adj* inconsiderate, thoughtless
2 *nm,f* inconsiderate o thoughtless person

desconsolado,-a *adj* disconsolate, grief-stricken

desconsuelo *nm* grief, sorrow

descontado,-a *adj Fam* **dar por d.** to take

for granted; **por d.** needless to say, of course

descontar [2] *vt* **(a)** to deduct **(b)** *Dep (tiempo)* to add on

descontento,-a 1 *adj* unhappy
2 *nm* dissatisfaction

descontrol *nm Fam* lack of control; **había un d. total** it was absolute chaos

descontrolarse *vpr* to lose control

desconvocar *vt* to call off

descorchar *vt* to uncork

descornarse [2] *vpr Fam (trabajar)* to slave (away)

descorrer *vt* to draw back

descortés *adj* impolite, discourteous

descortesía *nf* discourtesy, impoliteness

descoser *vt* to unstitch, to unpick

descosido *nm (en camisa etc)* open seam; *Fam* **como un d.** like mad, wildly

descoyuntar *vt* to dislocate

descrédito *nm* disrepute, discredit

descremado,-a *adj* skimmed

describir *(pp* descrito*) vt* to describe

descripción *nf* description

descriptivo,-a *adj* descriptive

descrito,-a *pp de* describir

descuajaringar [42] *vt Fam* to pull o take to pieces

descuartizar [40] *vt* to cut up, to cut into pieces

descubierto,-a 1 *adj* open, uncovered; **a cielo d.** in the open
2 *nm* **(a)** *Fin* overdraft **(b)** **al d.** in the open; **poner al d.** to uncover, to bring out into the open

descubridor,-a *nm,f* discoverer

descubrimiento *nm* discovery

descubrir *(pp* descubierto*) vt* to discover; *(conspiración)* to uncover; *(placa)* to unveil

descuento *nm* discount

descuidado,-a *adj* **(a)** *(desaseado)* untidy, neglected **(b)** *(negligente)* careless, negligent **(c)** *(desprevenido)* off one's guard

descuidar 1 *vt* to neglect, to overlook
2 *vi* **descuida, voy yo** don't worry, I'll go
3 descuidarse *vpr (despistarse)* to be careless; **como te descuides, llegarás tarde** if you don't watch out, you'll be late

descuido *nm* **(a)** oversight, mistake; **por d.** inadvertently, by mistake **(b)** *(negligencia)* negligence, carelessness

desde *adv* **(a)** *(tiempo)* since; **d. ahora** from now on; **d. el lunes/entonces** since Monday/then; **espero d. hace media hora** I've been waiting for half an hour; **no lo he visto d. hace un año** I haven't seen him for a year; **¿d. cuándo?** since when?; **d. siempre** always

(**b**) *(lugar)* from; **d. aquí** from here; **d. arriba/abajo** from above/below

(**c**) **d. luego** of course

(**d**) **d. que** ever since; **d. que lo conozco** ever since I've known him

desdecir [12] *(pp desdicho)* **1** *vi* **d. de** not to live up to

2 desdecirse *vpr* to go back on one's word

desdén *nm* disdain

desdentado,-a *adj* toothless

desdeñar *vt* to disdain

desdeñoso,-a *adj* disdainful

desdibujarse *vpr* to become blurred *o* faint

desdicha *nf* misfortune; **por d.** unfortunately

desdichado,-a 1 *adj* unfortunate

2 *nm,f* poor devil, wretch

desdigo *indic pres de* **desdecir**

desdiré *indic fut de* **desdecir**

desdoblar *vt* to unfold

deseable *adj* desirable

desear *vt* (**a**) to desire; **deja mucho que d.** it leaves a lot to be desired (**b**) *(querer)* to want; **¿qué desea?** can I help you?; **estoy deseando que vengas** I'm looking forward to your coming (**c**) **te deseo buena suerte/feliz Navidad** I wish you good luck/a merry Christmas

desecar [44] *vt* to dry up

desechable *adj* disposable, throw-away

desechar *vt* (**a**) *(tirar)* to discard, to throw out *o* away (**b**) *(oferta)* to turn down, to refuse; *(idea, proyecto)* to drop, to discard

desechos *nmpl* waste

desembalar *vt* to unpack

desembarcar [44] 1 *vt (mercancías)* to unload; *(personas)* to disembark

2 *vi* to disembark

desembarco, desembarque *nm (de mercancías)* unloading; *(de personas)* disembarkation

desembocadura *nf* mouth

desembocar [44] *vi* **d. en** *(río)* to flow into; *(calle, situación)* to lead to

desembolsar *vt* to pay out

desembolso *nm* expenditure

desembragar [42] *vt Aut* to declutch

desembrollar *vt Fam* (**a**) *(aclarar)* to clarify, to clear up (**b**) *(desenredar)* to disentangle

desembuchar *vt Fig* to blurt out; *Fam* **¡desembucha!** out with it!

desempañar *vt* to wipe the condensation from; *Aut* to demist

desempaquetar *vt* to unpack, to unwrap

desempatar *vi Dep* to break the deadlock

desempate *nm* play-off; **partido de d.** play-off, deciding match

desempeñar *vt* (**a**) *(cargo)* to hold, to occupy; *(función)* to fulfil; *(papel)* to play (**b**) *(recuperar)* to redeem

desempleado,-a 1 *adj* unemployed, out of work

2 *nm,f* unemployed person; **los desempleados** the unemployed

desempleo *nm* unemployment; **cobrar el d.** to be on the dole

desempolvar *vt* (**a**) to dust (**b**) *Fig (pasado)* to revive

desencadenar 1 *vt* (**a**) to unchain (**b**) *(provocar)* to unleash

2 desencadenarse *vpr* (**a**) *(prisionero)* to break loose; *(viento, pasión)* to rage (**b**) *(conflicto)* to start, to break out

desencajar 1 *vt (pieza)* to knock out; *(hueso)* to dislocate

2 desencajarse *vpr* (**a**) *(pieza)* to come out; *(hueso)* to become dislocated (**b**) *(cara)* to become distorted

desencaminado,-a *adj* = **descaminado, -a**

desencanto *nm* disenchantment

desenchufar *vt* to unplug

desenfadado,-a *adj* carefree, free and easy

desenfado *nm* ease

desenfocado,-a *adj* out of focus

desenfoque *nm* incorrect focusing; *Fig (de asunto)* wrong approach

desenfrenado,-a *adj* frantic, uncontrolled; *(vicio, pasión)* unbridled

desenfreno *nm* debauchery

desenganchar *vt* to unhook; *(vagón)* to uncouple

desengañar 1 *vt* **d. a algn** to open sb's eyes

2 desengañarse *vpr* (**a**) to be disappointed (**b**) *Fam* **¡desengáñate!** get real!

desengaño *nm* disappointment; **llevarse** *o* **sufrir un d. con algo** to be disappointed in sth

desengrasar *vt* to degrease, to remove the grease from

desenlace *nm* (**a**) result, outcome; **un feliz d.** a happy end (**b**) *Cin & Teatro* ending, dénouement

desenmarañar *vt (pelo)* to untangle; *(problema)* to unravel; *(asunto)* to sort out

desenmascarar *vt* to unmask

desenredar vt to untangle, to disentangle

desenrollar vt to unroll; (cable) to unwind

desenroscar [44] vt to unscrew

desentenderse [3] vpr se desentendió de mi problema he didn't want to have anything to do with my problem

desenterrar [1] vt (a) (cadáver) to exhume, to disinter; (tesoro etc) to dig up (b) (recuerdo) to revive

desentonar vi (a) Mús to sing out of tune, to be out of tune (b) (colores etc) not to match (c) (persona, comentario) to be out of place

desentrañar vt (misterio) to unravel, to get to the bottom of

desentrenado,-a adj out of training o shape

desentumecer [33] vt to put the feeling back into

desenvoltura nf ease

desenvolver [4] (pp desenvuelto) 1 vt to unwrap
   2 desenvolverse vpr (a) (persona) to manage, to cope (b) (hecho) to develop

desenvuelto,-a adj relaxed

deseo nm wish; (sexual) desire; **formular un d.** to make a wish

deseoso,-a adj eager; **estar d. de** be eager to

desequilibrado,-a 1 adj unbalanced
   2 nm,f unbalanced person

desequilibrar 1 vt to unbalance, to throw off balance
   2 desequilibrarse vpr to become mentally disturbed

desequilibrio nm imbalance; **d. mental** mental disorder

deserción nf desertion

desertar vi to desert

desértico,-a adj desert

desertización nf desertification

desertor,-a nm,f deserter

desesperación nf (desesperanza) despair; (exasperación) desperation

desesperado,-a adj (a) (sin esperanza) desperate, hopeless (b) (exasperado) exasperated, infuriated

desesperante adj exasperating

desesperar 1 vt to drive to despair; (exasperar) to exasperate
   2 desesperarse vpr to despair

desestabilizar [40] vt to destabilize

desestatización nf Am privatization

desestatizar vt Am to privatize

desestimar vt to reject

desfachatez nf cheek, nerve

desfalco nm embezzlement, misappropriation

desfallecer [33] vi (a) (debilitarse) to feel faint; (desmayarse) to faint (b) (desanimarse) to lose heart

desfasado,-a adj (a) outdated (b) (persona) old-fashioned, behind the times (c) Téc out of phase

desfase nm gap; **d. horario** time lag

desfavorable adj unfavourable

desfigurar vt (cara) to disfigure; (verdad) to distort

desfiladero nm narrow pass

desfilar vi (a) to march in single file (b) Mil to march past, to parade

desfile nm Mil parade, march past; **d. de modas** fashion show

desfogar [42] 1 vt to give vent to
   2 desfogarse vpr to let off steam

desgajar 1 vt (arrancar) to rip o tear out; (rama) to tear off
   2 desgajarse vpr to come off

desgana nf (a) (inapetencia) lack of appetite (b) (apatía) apathy, indifference; **con d.** reluctantly, unwillingly

desganado,-a adj (a) estar d. (inapetente) to have no appetite (b) (apático) apathetic

desgañitarse vpr Fam to shout oneself hoarse

desgarbado,-a adj ungraceful, ungainly

desgarrador,-a adj harrowing

desgarrar vt to tear

desgarrón nm big tear, rip

desgastar 1 vt to wear out
   2 desgastarse vpr (consumirse) to wear out; (persona) to wear oneself out

desgaste nm wear; **d. del poder** wear and tear of power

desgracia nf (a) misfortune; **por d.** unfortunately (b) (deshonor) disgrace (c) **desgracias personales** loss of life

desgraciadamente adv unfortunately

desgraciado,-a 1 adj unfortunate; (infeliz) unhappy
   2 nm,f unfortunate person; **un pobre d.** a poor devil

desgravable adj tax-deductible

desgravación nf deduction; **d. fiscal** tax deduction

desgravar vt to deduct

desguazar [40] vt (un barco) to break up; Aut to scrap

deshabitado,-a adj uninhabited, unoccupied

deshabitar vt to abandon, to vacate

deshacer [15] (pp deshecho) **1** vt (a) (paquete) to undo; (maleta) to unpack (**b**) *(plan)* to destroy, to ruin (**c**) *(acuerdo)* to break off (**d**) *(disolver)* to dissolve; *(derretir)* to melt

2 deshacerse *vpr* (**a**) to come undone o untied (**b**) **d. de algn/algo** to get rid of sb/ sth (**c**) *(afligirse)* to go to pieces; **d. en lágrimas** to cry one's eyes out (**d**) *(disolverse)* to dissolve; *(derretirse)* to melt (**e**) *(niebla)* to fade away, to disappear

deshecho,-a *adj* (**a**) *(cama)* unmade; *(maleta)* unpacked; *(paquete)* unwrapped (**b**) *(roto)* broken, smashed (**c**) *(disuelto)* dissolved; *(derretido)* melted (**d**) *(abatido)* devastated, shattered (**e**) *(cansado)* exhausted, tired out

desheredar *vt* to disinherit

deshidratar *vt* to dehydrate

deshielo *nm* thaw

deshilachar *vt* to fray

deshilvanado,-a *adj Fig (inconexo)* disjointed

deshonesto,-a *adj* (**a**) dishonest (**b**) *(indecente)* indecent, improper

deshonor *nm*, **deshonra** *nf* dishonour

deshonrar *vt* (**a**) to dishonour (**b**) *(a la familia etc)* to bring disgrace on

deshora: • a deshora *loc adv* at an inconvenient time; **comer a d.** to eat at odd times

deshuesar *vt (carne)* to bone; *(fruta)* to stone

deshumanizar [40] *vt* to dehumanize

desidia *nf* apathy

desierto,-a 1 *nm* desert

2 *adj* (**a**) *(deshabitado)* uninhabited (**b**) *(vacío)* empty, deserted (**c**) *(premio)* void

designación *nf* designation

designar *vt* (**a**) to designate (**b**) *(fecha, lugar)* to fix

designio *nm* intention, plan

desigual *adj* (**a**) uneven (**b**) *(lucha)* unequal (**c**) *(carácter)* changeable

desigualdad *nf* (**a**) inequality (**b**) *(del terreno)* unevenness

desilusión *nf* disappointment, disillusionment

desilusionar *vt* to disappoint, to disillusion

desinfectante *adj & nm* disinfectant

desinfectar *vt* to disinfect

desinflar 1 *vt* to deflate; *(rueda)* to let down

2 desinflarse *vpr* to go flat

desintegración *nf* disintegration

desintegrar *vt*, **desintegrarse** *vpr* to disintegrate

desinterés *nm* (**a**) *(indiferencia)* lack of interest, apathy (**b**) *(generosidad)* unselfishness

desinteresado,-a *adj* selfless, unselfish

desintoxicar [44] 1 *vt* to detoxicate; *(de alcohol)* to dry out

2 desintoxicarse *vpr Med* to detoxicate oneself; *(de alcohol)* to dry out

desistir *vi* to desist

deslavazado,-a *adj* disjointed

deslave *nm Am* landslide *(caused by flooding or rain)*

desleal *adj* disloyal; *(competencia)* unfair

deslealtad *nf* disloyalty

deslenguado,-a *adj (insolente)* insolent, cheeky; *(grosero)* coarse, foul-mouthed

desliar [29] *vt* to unwrap

desligar [42] 1 *vt* (**a**) *(separar)* to separate (**b**) *(desatar)* to untie, to unfasten

2 desligarse *vpr* **d. de** to disassociate oneself from

desliz *nm* mistake, slip; **cometer** o **tener un d.** to slip up

deslizar [40] 1 *vi* to slide

2 deslizarse *vpr* (**a**) *(patinar)* to slide (**b**) *(fluir)* to flow

deslucir [35] *vt* (**a**) *(espectáculo)* to spoil (**b**) *(metal)* to make dull

deslumbrador,-a, deslumbrante *adj* dazzling; *Fig* stunning

deslumbrar *vt* to dazzle

desmadrarse *vpr Fam* to go wild

desmadre *nm Fam* hullabaloo

desmandarse *vpr* to get out of hand, to run wild; *(caballo)* to bolt

desmano: • a desmano *loc adv* out of the way; **me coge a d.** it is out of my way

desmantelar *vt* (**a**) to dismantle (**b**) *Náut* to dismast, to unrig

desmaquillador,-a 1 *nm* make-up remover

2 *adj* **leche desmaquilladora** cleansing cream

desmaquillarse *vpr* to remove one's make-up

desmarcarse [44] *vpr Dep* to lose one's marker

desmayado,-a *adj* unconscious; **caer d.** to faint

desmayarse *vpr* to faint

desmayo *nm* faint, fainting fit; **tener un d.** to faint

desmedido,-a *adj* disproportionate, out of all proportion; *(ambición)* unbounded

desmejorar *vi*, **desmejorarse** *vpr* to deteriorate, to go downhill

desmelenarse *vpr Fam* to let one's hair down

desmembración *nf*, **desmembramiento** *nm* dismemberment

desmemoriado,-a adj forgetful, absent-minded

desmentir [5] vt to deny

desmenuzar [40] vt (a) (deshacer) to break into little pieces, to crumble; (carne) to cut into little pieces (b) (asunto) to examine in detail

desmerecer [33] vi to lose value

desmesura nf excess

desmesurado,-a adj excessive

desmilitarizar [40] vt to demilitarize

desmontable adj that can be taken to pieces

desmontar 1 vt (a) (desarmar) to take to pieces, to dismantle (b) (allanar) to level
2 vi **d. (de)** to dismount, to get off

desmoralizar [40] vt to demoralize

desmoronarse upr to crumble, to fall to pieces

desnatado,-a adj (leche) skimmed

desnivel nm (en el terreno) drop, difference in height

desnivelar vt to throw out of balance

desnucarse [44] upr to break one's neck

desnuclearizar vt to denuclearize

desnudar 1 vt to undress
2 desnudarse upr to get undressed

desnudismo nm nudism

desnudista adj & nmf nudist

desnudo,-a 1 adj naked, nude
2 nm Arte nude

desnutrición nf malnutrition

desnutrido,-a adj undernourished

desobedecer [33] vt to disobey

desobediencia nf disobedience

desobediente 1 adj disobedient
2 nmf disobedient person

desocupado,-a adj (a) (vacío) empty, vacant (b) (ocioso) free, not busy (c) (sin empleo) unemployed

desocupar vt to empty, to vacate

desodorante adj & nm deodorant

desolación nf desolation

desolar vt to devastate

desollar [2] 1 vt to skin
2 • desollarse upr to scrape; **me desollé el brazo** I scraped my arm

desorbitado,-a adj (precio) exorbitant

desorden nm untidiness, mess; **¡qué d.!** what a mess!; **d. público** civil disorder

desordenado,-a adj messy, untidy

desordenar vt to make untidy, to mess up

desorganizar [40] vt to disorganize, to disrupt

desorientación nf disorientation

desorientar 1 vt to disorientate
2 desorientarse upr to lose one's sense

of direction, to lose one's bearings; Fig to become disorientated

despabilado,-a adj (a) (sin sueño) wide awake (b) (listo) quick, smart

despachar vt (a) (asunto) to get through (b) (correo) to send, to dispatch (c) (en tienda) to serve (d) Fam (despedir) to send packing, to sack (e) Am (facturar) to check in

despacho nm (a) (oficina) office; (en casa) study (b) (venta) sale (c) (comunicación) dispatch

despachurrar vt Fam to squash, to flatten

despacio adv (a) (lentamente) slowly (b) (en voz baja) quietly

despampanante adj Fam stunning

desparpajo nm self-assurance; **con d.** in a carefree manner

desparramar vt, **desparramarse** upr to spread, to scatter; (líquido) to spill

despavorido,-a adj terrified

despecho nm spite; **por d.** out of spite

despectivo,-a adj derogatory, disparaging

despedazar [40] vt to cut o tear to pieces

despedida nf farewell, goodbye; **d. de soltera/soltero** hen/stag party

despedido,-a adj **salir d.** to be off like a shot

despedir [6] 1 vt (a) (empleado) to fire, Br to sack (b) (decir adiós) to see off, to say goodbye to (c) (olor, humo etc) to give off
2 despedirse upr (a) (decir adiós) to say goodbye (**de** to) (b) Fig to forget, to give up; **ya puedes despedirte del coche** you can say goodbye to the car

despegado,-a adj (a) unstuck (b) (persona) couldn't-care-less

despegar [42] 1 vt to take off, to detach
2 vi Av to take off
3 despegarse upr to come unstuck

despego nm detachment

despegue nm take-off

despeinado,-a adj dishevelled, with untidy hair

despejado,-a adj clear; (cielo) cloudless

despejar 1 vt to clear; (misterio, dudas) to clear up
2 despejarse upr (a) (cielo) to clear (b) (persona) to clear one's head

despeje nm Dep clearance

despellejar vt to skin

despelotarse upr Fam (a) (desnudarse) to strip (b) **d. de risa** to laugh one's head off

despensa *nf* pantry, larder

despeñadero *nm* cliff, precipice

despeñarse *upr* to go over a cliff

desperdiciar [43] *vt* to waste; *(oportunidad)* to throw away

desperdicio *nm* (a) *(acto)* waste (b) **desperdicios** *(basura)* rubbish; *(desechos)* scraps, leftovers

desperdigar [42] *vt*, **desperdigarse** *upr* to scatter, to separate

desperezarse [40] *upr* to stretch (oneself)

desperfecto *nm* (a) *(defecto)* flaw, imperfection (b) *(daño)* damage

despertador *nm* alarm clock

despertar [1] 1 *vt* to wake (up), to awaken; *Fig (sentimiento etc)* to arouse
  2 **despertarse** *upr* to wake (up)

despiadado,-a *adj* merciless

despido *nm* dismissal, sacking

despierto,-a *adj* (a) *(desvelado)* awake (b) *(vivo)* quick, sharp

despilfarrar *vt* to waste, to squander

despilfarro *nm* wasting, squandering

despintar *vi*, **despintarse** *upr (ropa)* to fade

despiole *nm RP Fam* rumpus, shindy

despistado,-a 1 *adj* (a) *(olvidadizo)* scatterbrained (b) *(confuso)* confused
  2 *nm,f* scatterbrain

despistar 1 *vt* (a) *(hacer perder la pista a)* to lose, to throw off one's scent (b) *Fig* to mislead
  2 **despistarse** *upr* (a) *(perderse)* to get lost (b) *(distraerse)* to switch off

despiste *nm* (a) *(cualidad)* absentmindedness (b) *(error)* slip-up

desplazamiento *nm (viaje)* trip, journey; **dietas de d.** travelling expenses

desplazar [40] 1 *vt* to displace
  2 **desplazarse** *upr* to travel

desplegar [1] 1 *vt* (a) to open (out), to spread (out) (b) *(energías etc)* to use, to deploy
  2 **desplegarse** *upr* (a) *(abrirse)* to open (out), to spread (out) (b) *Mil* to deploy

despliegue *nm* (a) *Mil* deployment (b) *(de medios etc)* display

desplomarse *upr* to collapse; *(precios)* to slump, to fall sharply

desplumar *vt* to pluck

despoblar [2] *vt* to depopulate

despojar *vt* (a) to strip (**de** of) (b) *Fig* to divest, to deprive (**de** of)

despojo *nm* (a) stripping (b) **despojos** leftovers, scraps

desposado,-a *adj Fml* newly-wed

desposar *vt Fml* to marry

desposeer [36] *vt* **d. de** to dispossess of; *(autoridad)* to strip of

desposeído *nm* **los desposeídos** the have-nots

déspota *nmf* despot

despótico,-a *adj* despotic

despotismo *nm* despotism

despotricar [44] *vi* to rant and rave (**contra** about)

despreciable *adj* despicable, contemptible; *(cantidad)* negligible

despreciar [43] *vt* (a) *(desdeñar)* to scorn, to despise (b) *(rechazar)* to reject, to spurn

desprecio *nm* (a) *(desdén)* scorn, disdain (b) *(desaire)* slight, snub

desprender 1 *vt* (a) *(separar)* to remove, to detach (b) *(olor, humo etc)* to give off
  2 **desprenderse** *upr* (a) *(soltarse)* to come off *o* away (b) **d. de** to rid oneself of, to free oneself from (c) **de aquí se desprende que ...** it can be deduced from this that ...

desprendido,-a *adj Fig* generous, unselfish

desprendimiento *nm* (a) loosening, detachment; **d. de tierras** landslide (b) *Fig (generosidad)* generosity, unselfishness

despreocupado,-a *adj* (a) *(tranquilo)* unconcerned (b) *(descuidado)* careless; *(estilo)* casual

despreocuparse *upr* (a) *(tranquilizarse)* to stop worrying (b) *(desentenderse)* to be unconcerned, to be indifferent (**de** to)

desprestigiar [43] *vt* to discredit, to run down

desprestigio *nm* discredit, loss of reputation; **campaña de d.** smear campaign

desprevenido,-a *adj* unprepared; **coger** *o* **pillar a algn d.** to catch sb unawares

desprolijo,-a *adj Am (casa)* messy, untidy; *(cuaderno)* untidy; *(persona)* unkempt, dishevelled

desproporción *nf* disproportion, lack of proportion

desproporcionado,-a *adj* disproportionate

desprovisto,-a *adj* **d. (de)** lacking, without, devoid (of)

después *adv* (a) afterwards, later; *(entonces)* then; *(seguidamente)* next; **una semana d.** a week later; **poco d.** soon after (b) *(lugar)* next (c) **d. de** after; **d. de la guerra** after the war; **mi calle está d. de la tuya** my street is the one after yours; **d. de cenar** after eating; **d. de todo** after all (**d**) **d. de que** after; **d. de que vi-niera** after he came

despuntar 1 *vt* to blunt, to make blunt

2 *vi* (**a**) *(día)* to dawn (**b**) *(destacar)* to excel, to stand out

desquiciar [43] 1 *vt (persona)* to unhinge

2 desquiciarse *vpr (persona)* to go crazy

desquitarse *vpr* to take revenge (**de** for)

desquite *nm* revenge

destacado,-a *adj* outstanding

destacamento *nm* detachment

destacar [44] 1 *vt Fig* to emphasize, to stress

2 *vi* to stand out

3 destacarse *vpr* to stand out

destajo *nm* piecework; **trabajar a d.** to do piecework

destapador *nm Am* bottle opener

destapar 1 *vt* to take the lid off; *(botella)* to open; *Fig (asunto)* to uncover; *RP (caño)* to unblock

2 destaparse *vpr* to get uncovered

destartalado,-a *adj* rambling; *(desvencijado)* ramshackle

destello *nm* flash, sparkle

destemplado,-a *adj* (**a**) *(voz, gesto)* sharp, snappy; **con cajas destempladas** rudely, brusquely (**b**) *(tiempo)* unpleasant (**c**) *(enfermo)* indisposed, out of sorts (**d**) *Mús* out of tune, discordant

desteñir [6] 1 *vt & vi* to discolour

2 desteñirse *vpr* to lose colour, to fade

desternillarse *vpr* **d. (de risa)** to split one's sides laughing

desterrar [1] *vt* to exile

destiempo: • **a destiempo** *loc adv* at the wrong time *o* moment

destierro *nm* exile

destilado,-a *adj* distilled; **agua destilada** distilled water

destilar *vt* to distil

destilería *nf* distillery

destinado,-a *adj* destined, bound; *Fig* **d. al fracaso** doomed to failure

destinar *vt (dinero etc)* to set aside, to assign (**b**) *(empleado)* to appoint

destinatario,-a *nm,f* (**a**) *(de carta)* addressee (**b**) *(de mercancías)* consignee

destino *nm* (**a**) *(rumbo)* destination; **el avión con d. a Bilbao** the plane to Bilbao (**b**) *(sino)* fate, fortune (**c**) *(de empleo)* post

destitución *nf* dismissal from office

destituir [37] *vt* to dismiss *o* remove from office

destornillador *nm* screwdriver

destornillar *vt* to unscrew

destreza *nf* skill

destrozado,-a *adj* (**a**) *(roto)* torn-up, smashed (**b**) *(cansado)* worn-out, exhausted (**c**) *(abatido)* shattered

destrozar [40] *vt* (**a**) *(destruir)* to destroy; *(rasgar)* to tear to shreds *o* pieces (**b**) *(afligir)* to shatter; *(vida, reputación)* to ruin

destrozo *nm* (**a**) destruction (**b**) **destrozos** damage

destrucción *nf* destruction

destructivo,-a *adj* destructive

destructor,-a 1 *adj* destructive

2 *nm Náut* destroyer

destruir [37] *vt* to destroy

desubicado,-a *nm,f Andes, RP* **ser un d.** to have no idea how to behave, to be clueless

desusado,-a *adj* old-fashioned, outdated

desuso *nm* disuse; **caer en d.** to fall into disuse; **en d.** obsolete, outdated

desvalido,-a *adj* defenceless

desvalijar *vt (robar)* to clean out, to rob; *(casa, tienda)* to burgle

desvalorizar [40] *vt* to devalue

desván *nm* attic, loft

desvanecerse [33] *vpr* (**a**) *(disiparse)* to vanish, to fade away (**b**) *(desmayarse)* to faint

desvariar [29] *vi* to talk nonsense

desvarío *nm* (**a**) *(delirio)* raving, delirium (**b**) *(disparate)* nonsense

desvelado,-a *adj* awake, wide awake

desvelar 1 *vt* to keep awake

2 desvelarse *vpr* (**a**) *(despabilarse)* to stay awake (**b**) *(desvivirse)* to devote oneself (**por** to) (**c**) *CAm, Méx (quedarse despierto)* to stay up *o* awake

desvencijar 1 *vt* to take apart

2 desvencijarse *vpr* to fall apart

desventaja *nf* (**a**) disadvantage; **estar en d.** to be at a disadvantage (**b**) *(inconveniente)* drawback

desventura *nf* misfortune, bad luck

desvergonzado,-a 1 *adj* (**a**) *(indecente)* shameless (**b**) *(descarado)* insolent

2 *nm,f* (**a**) *(sinvergüenza)* shameless person (**b**) *(fresco)* insolent *o* cheeky person

desvergüenza *nf* (**a**) *(indecencia)* shamelessness (**b**) *(atrevimiento)* insolence; **tuvo la d. de negarlo** he had the cheek to deny it (**c**) *(impertinencia)* insolent *o* rude remark

desvestir [6] 1 *vt* to undress

2 desvestirse *vpr* to undress, to get undressed

desviación *nf* deviation; *(de carretera)*

diversion, detour; *Med* **d. de columna** slipped disc

desviar [29] 1 *vt* (río, carretera) to divert; (golpe, conversación) to deflect; **d. la mirada** to look away

2 desviarse *upr* to go off course; (coche) to turn off; *Fig* **d. del tema** to digress

desvincular 1 *vt* to separate

2 desvincularse *upr* to separate, to cut oneself off

desvío *nm* diversion, detour

desvirgar [42] *vt* to deflower

desvirtuar [30] *vt* to distort

desvivirse *upr* to bend over backwards

detalladamente *adv* in (great) detail

detallado,-a *adj* detailed, thorough

detallar *vt* to give the details of

detalle *nm* (a) detail; **entrar en detalles** to go into details (b) (delicadeza) nice thought, nicety; ¡**qué d.!** how nice!, how sweet! (c) (toque decorativo) touch, ornament

detallista 1 *adj* perfectionist

2 *nmf Com* retailer

detectar *vt* to detect

detective *nmf* detective; **d. privado** private detective o eye

detector,-a *nm,f* detector; **d. de incendios** fire detector

detención *nf* (a) *Jur* detention, arrest (b) **con d.** carefully, thoroughly

detener [24] 1 *vt* (a) to stop, to halt (b) *Jur* (arrestar) to arrest, to detain

2 detenerse *upr* to stop

detenidamente *adv* carefully, thoroughly

detenido,-a 1 *adj* (a) (parado) standing still, stopped (b) (arrestado) detained (c) (minucioso) detailed, thorough

2 *nm,f* detainee, person under arrest

detenimiento *nm* **con d.** carefully, thoroughly

detentar *vt* to hold

detergente *adj & nm* detergent

deteriorar 1 *vt* to spoil, to damage

2 deteriorarse *upr* (a) (estropearse) to get damaged (b) (empeorar) to get worse

deterioro *nm* (a) (empeoramiento) deterioration, worsening (b) (daño) damage; **ir en d. de** to be to the detriment of

determinación *nf* (a) determination; **con d.** determinedly (b) (decisión) decision

determinado,-a *adj* (a) (preciso) definite, precise (b) (resuelto) decisive, resolute (c) *Ling* definite

determinante *adj* decisive

determinar 1 *vt* (a) (fecha etc) to fix, to

set (b) (decidir) to decide on (c) (condicionar) to determine (d) (ocasionar) to bring about

2 determinarse *upr* to make up one's mind to

detestable *adj* detestable, repulsive

detestar *vt* to detest, to hate

detonante *nm* detonator; *Fig* trigger

detonar *vt* to detonate

detractor,-a *nm,f* detractor

detrás *adv* (a) behind, on o at the back (**de** of) (b) **d. de** behind

detrimento *nm* detriment; **en d. de** to the detriment of

detuve *pt indef de* **detener**

deuda *nf* debt; **estoy en d. contigo** (monetaria) I am in debt to you; (moral) I am indebted to you; **d. del Estado** public debt; **d. pública** national debt

deudor,-a 1 *adj* indebted

2 *nm,f* debtor

devaluación *nf* devaluation

devaluar [30] *vt* to devalue

devanar 1 *vt* (hilo) to wind; (alambre) to coil

2 devanarse *upr Fam* **d. los sesos** to rack one's brains

devaneo *nm* dabbling

devastador,-a *adj* devastating

devastar *vt* to devastate, to ravage

devengar [42] *vt Com* to earn, to accrue

devenir [27] *vi* to become

devoción *nf* (a) *Rel* devoutness (b) (al trabajo etc) devotion; *Fam* **Juan no es santo de mi d.** Juan isn't really my cup of tea

devolución *nf* (a) giving back, return; *Com* refund, repayment (b) *Jur* devolution

devolver [4] (pp **devuelto**) **1** *vt* to give back, to return; (dinero) to refund

2 *vi* (vomitar) to vomit, to throw o bring up

3 devolverse *upr Am* to go o come back, to return

devorar *vt* to devour

devoto,-a 1 *adj* pious, devout

2 *nm,f* (a) *Rel* pious person (b) (seguidor) devotee

devuelto,-a *pp de* **devolver**

DF *nm* (abr **Distrito Federal**) (en México) Mexico City

DGI *nf RP* (abr **Dirección General Impositiva**) *Br* ≃ Inland Revenue, *US* ≃ IRS

DGT *nf* (abr **Dirección General de Tráfico**) = government department responsible for road transport

di (a) *pt indef de* **dar** (b) *imperat de* **decir**

día nm day; **¿qué d. es hoy?** what's the date today?; **d. a d.** day by day; **de d.** by day; **durante el d.** during the daytime; **de un d. para otro** overnight; **un d. sí y otro no** every other day; **pan del d.** fresh bread; **hoy (en) d.** nowadays; **el d. de mañana** in the future; **Fig estar al d.** to be up to date; **Fig poner al d.** to bring up to date; **d. festivo** holiday; **d. laborable** working day; **d. libre** free day, day off; **es de d.** it is daylight; **hace buen/mal d.** it's a nice/bad day, the weather is nice/bad today

diabetes nf diabetes

diabético,-a adj & nm,f diabetic

diablo nm devil; Fam **¡al d. con ...!** to hell with ...!; Fam **vete al d.** get lost; Fam **¿qué/cómo diablos ...?** what/how the hell ...?

diablura nf mischief

diácono nm deacon

diadema nf tiara

diáfano,-a adj clear

diafragma nm diaphragm; Fot aperture; Med cap

diagnosis nf inv diagnosis

diagnosticar [44] vt to diagnose

diagnóstico nm diagnosis

diagonal adj & nf diagonal; **en d.** diagonally

diagrama nm diagram; Informát **d. de flujo** flowchart

dial nm dial

dialecto nm dialect

dialogar [42] vi to have a conversation; (para negociar) to talk

diálogo nm dialogue

diamante nm diamond

diámetro nm diameter

diana nf (a) Mil reveille (b) (blanco) bull's eye.

diapositiva nf slide

diariamente adv daily, every day

diariero,-a nm,f Andes, RP newspaper seller

diario,-a 1 nm (a) Prensa (daily) newspaper (b) (memorias) diary; Náut **d. de a bordo, d. de navegación** logbook
2 adj daily; **a d.** daily, every day

diarrea nf diarrhoea

diatriba nf diatribe

dibujante nmf (a) drawer (b) (de cómic) cartoonist (c) Téc (hombre) draughtsman; (mujer) draughtswoman

dibujar vt to draw

dibujo nm (a) drawing; **dibujos animados** cartoons (b) (arte) drawing; **d. artístico** artistic drawing; **d. lineal** draughtsmanship

diccionario nm dictionary; **buscar/mirar una palabra en el d.** to look up a word in the dictionary

dicha nf happiness

dicharachero,-a adj talkative and witty

dicho,-a adj (a) said; **mejor d.** or rather; **d. de otro modo** to put it another way; **d. sea de paso** let it be said in passing; **d. y hecho** no sooner said than done (b) **dicha persona** (mencionado) the above-mentioned person

dichoso,-a adj (a) (feliz) happy (b) Fam damned; **¡este d. trabajo!** this damned job!

diciembre nm December

dictado nm dictation; Fig **dictados** dictates

dictador,-a nm,f dictator

dictadura nf dictatorship

dictáfono® nm Dictaphone®

dictamen nm (juicio) ruling; (informe) report

dictaminar vi to rule (**sobre** on)

dictar vt (a) to dictate (b) (ley) to enact; (sentencia) to pass

dictatorial adj dictatorial

didáctico,-a adj didactic

diecinueve adj & nm inv nineteen

dieciocho adj & nm inv eighteen

dieciséis adj & nm inv sixteen

diecisiete adj & nm inv seventeen

diente nm tooth; Téc cog; (de ajo) clove; **d. de leche** milk tooth; **dientes postizos** false teeth; Fig **hablar entre dientes** to mumble; Fig **poner los dientes largos a algn** to make sb green with envy

diera subj imperf de **dar**

diéresis nf inv diaeresis

diesel adj & nm diesel

diestra nf right hand

diestro,-a 1 adj (a) (hábil) skilful, clever (b) **a d. y siniestro** right, left and centre **2** nm Taurom bullfighter, matador

dieta nf (a) diet; **estar a d.** to be on a diet (b) **dietas** expenses o subsistence allowance

dietética nf dietetics sing

dietista nmf dietician

diez adj & nm inv ten

difamación nf defamation, slander; (escrita) libel

difamar vt to defame, to slander; (por escrito) to libel

diferencia nf difference; **a d. de** unlike

diferencial 1 adj distinguishing
2 nm differential

diferenciar [43] 1 vt to differentiate, to distinguish (**entre** between)

2 diferenciarse *vpr* to differ (**de** from), to be different (**de** from)

diferente 1 *adj* different (**de** from *o US* than)

2 *adv* differently

diferido,-a *adj TV* **en d.** recorded

difícil *adj* difficult, hard; **d. de creer/hacer** difficult to believe/do; **es d. que venga** it is unlikely that she'll come

dificultad *nf* difficulty; *(aprieto)* trouble, problem

dificultar *vt* to make difficult

dificultoso,-a *adj* difficult, hard

difuminar *vt* to blur

difundir *vt*, **difundirse** *vpr* to spread

difunto,-a 1 *adj* late, deceased

2 *nm,f* deceased

difusión *nf* (**a**) *(de noticia)* spreading; **tener gran d.** to be widely broadcast (**b**) *Rad & TV* broadcasting

difuso,-a *adj* diffuse

digerir [5] *vt* to digest; *Fig* to assimilate

digestión *nf* digestion; **corte de d.** sudden indigestion

digestivo,-a *adj* easy to digest

digitador,-a *nm,f Am* keyboarder

digital *adj* digital; **huellas digitales** fingerprints; **tocadiscos d.** CD player

digitalizar *vt* digitize

digitar *vt Am* to key

dígito *nm* digit

dignarse *vpr* **d. (a)** to deign to, to condescend to

dignidad *nf* dignity

digno,-a *adj* (**a**) *(merecedor)* worthy; **d. de admiración** worthy of admiration; **d. de mención/verse** worth mentioning/seeing (**b**) *(decoroso)* decent, good

digo *indic pres de* **decir**

dije *pt indef de* **decir**

dilación *nf* delay, hold-up; **sin d.** without delay

dilatado,-a *adj* (**a**) *(agrandado)* dilated (**b**) *(vasto)* vast, extensive

dilatar 1 *vt* (**a**) *(agrandar)* to expand (**b**) *(pupila)* to dilate

2 dilatarse *vpr* (**a**) *(agrandarse)* to expand (**b**) *(pupila)* to dilate

dilema *nm* dilemma

diligencia *nf* (**a**) *diligence;* **con d.** diligently (**b**) **diligencias** formalities

diligente *adj* diligent

dilucidar *vt* to elucidate, to clarify

diluir [37] 1 *vt* to dilute

2 diluirse *vpr* to dilute

diluviar [43] *v impers* to pour with rain

diluvio *nm* flood; **el D. (Universal)** the Flood

diluyo *indic pres de* **diluir**

dimensión *nf* (**a**) dimension, size; **de gran d.** very large (**b**) *Fig (importancia)* importance

diminutivo,-a *adj & nm* diminutive

diminuto,-a *adj* minute, tiny

dimisión *nf* resignation; **presentar la d.** to hand in one's resignation

dimitir *vi* to resign (**de** from); **d. de un cargo** to give in *o* tender one's resignation

Dinamarca *n* Denmark

dinámica *nf* dynamics *sing*

dinámico,-a *adj* dynamic

dinamita *nf* dynamite

dinamitar *vt* to dynamite

dinamo, dínamo *nf* dynamo

dinar *nm Fin* dinar

dinastía *nf* dynasty

dineral *nm Fam* fortune

dinero *nm* money; **d. contante (y sonante)** cash; **d. efectivo** *o* **en metálico** cash; **gente de d.** wealthy people

dinosaurio *nm* dinosaur

diócesis *nf inv* diocese

dios *nm* god; **¡D. mío!** my God!; **¡por D.!** for goodness sake!; **a la buena de D.** any old how; **hacer algo como D. manda** to do sth properly; *Fam* **ni d.** nobody; *Fam* **todo d.** everybody

diosa *nf* goddess

diploma *nm* diploma

diplomacia *nf* diplomacy

diplomarse *vpr* to graduate

diplomático,-a 1 *adj* diplomatic; **cuerpo d.** diplomatic corps

2 *nm,f* diplomat

diptongo *nm* diphthong

diputación *nf* **d. provincial** ≃ county council

diputado,-a *nm,f Br* ≃ Member of Parliament, MP; *US (hombre)* Congressman; *(mujer)* Congresswoman; **Congreso de Diputados** *Br* ≃ House of Commons, *US* ≃ Congress; **d. provincial** ≃ county councillor

dique *nm* dike

diré *fut de* **decir**

dirección *nf* (**a**) direction; *Aut (en letrero)* **d. prohibida** no entry; **calle de d. única** one-way street (**b**) *(señas)* address; *Informát* **d. de correo electrónico** e-mail address (**c**) *Cin & Teatro* direction (**d**) *(destino)* destination (**e**) *Aut & Téc* steering (**f**) *(dirigentes)* management; *(cargo)* directorship; *(de un partido)* leadership; *(de un colegio)* headship

direccional *nm Col, Méx Aut Br* indicator, *US* turn signal

directa *nf Aut* top gear

directamente *adv* directly, straight away

directiva *nf* board of directors, management

directivo,-a *adj* directive; **junta directiva** board of directors

directo,-a *adj* direct; *TV & Rad* **en d.** live

director,-a *nm,f* director; *(de colegio)* *(hombre)* headmaster; *(mujer)* headmistress; *(de periódico)* editor; **d. de cine** (film) director; **d. de orquesta** conductor; **d. gerente** managing director

directorio *nm Informát* directory; *Andes, Méx* **d. telefónico** telephone directory

directriz *nf* directive; *Mat* directrix

dirigente 1 *adj* leading; **clase d.** ruling class

2 *nmf* leader

dirigir [57] **1** *vt* to direct; *(empresa)* to manage; *(negocio, colegio)* to run; *(orquesta)* to conduct; *(partido)* to lead; *(periódico)* to edit; *(coche, barco)* to steer; **d. la palabra a algn** to speak to sb

2 dirigirse *vpr* (a) **d. a** o **hacia** to go to, to make one's way towards (b) *(escribir)* to write; **diríjase al apartado de correos 42** write to PO Box 42 (c) *(hablar)* to speak

discapacidad *nf* disability

discar *vt Andes, RP* to dial

discernir [54] *vt* to discern

disciplina *nf* discipline

disciplinado,-a *adj* disciplined

discípulo,-a *nm,f* disciple

disco *nm* (a) disc; **d. de freno** brake disc (b) *Mús* record; **d. compacto** compact disc (c) *Informát* disk; **d. duro** o **fijo/ flexible** hard/floppy disk (d) *Dep* discus (e) *Tel* dial

discográfico,-a *adj* **casa/compañía discográfica** record company

disconforme *adj* **estar d. con** to disagree with

discontinuo,-a *adj* discontinuous; *Aut* **línea discontinua** broken line

discordante *adj* discordant; **ser la nota d.** to be the odd man out

discordia *nf* discord; **la manzana de la d.** the bone of contention; **sembrar d.** to sow discord

discoteca *nf* (a) *(lugar)* discotheque (b) *(colección)* record collection

discreción *nf* (a) discretion (b) **a d.** at will

discrecional *adj* optional; **servicio d.** special service

discrepancia *nf (desacuerdo)* disagreement; *(diferencia)* discrepancy

discrepar *vi (disentir)* to disagree (de with; en on); *(diferenciarse)* to be different (de from)

discreto,-a *adj* (a) discreet (b) *(mediocre)* average

discriminación *nf* discrimination

discriminar *vt* (a) to discriminate against (b) *Fml (diferenciar)* to discriminate between, to distinguish

disculpa *nf* excuse; **dar disculpas** to make excuses; **pedir disculpas a algn** to apologize to sb

disculpar 1 *vt* to excuse

2 disculparse *vpr* to apologize (**por** for)

discurrir *vi* (a) *(reflexionar)* to think (b) *Fig (transcurrir)* to pass, to go by (c) *Fml (río)* to wander

discurso *nm* speech; **dar** o **pronunciar un d.** to make a speech

discusión *nf* argument

discutir 1 *vi* to argue (**de** about)

2 *vt* to discuss, to talk about

disecar [44] *vt* (a) *(animal)* to stuff (b) *(planta)* to dry

diseminar *vt* to disseminate, to spread

disentir [54] *vi* to dissent, to disagree (**de** with)

diseñar *vt* to design

diseño *nm* design; **d. de interiores** interior design

disertar *vi* to expound (**sobre** on o upon)

disfraz *nm* disguise; *(para fiesta)* fancy dress; **fiesta de disfraces** fancy dress party

disfrazar [40] **1** *vt* to disguise

2 disfrazarse *vpr* to disguise oneself; **d. de pirata** to dress up as a pirate

disfrutar 1 *vi* (a) *(gozar)* to enjoy oneself (b) *(poseer)* **d. (de)** to enjoy

2 *vt* to enjoy

disgregar [42] *vt* (a) to disintegrate, to break up (b) *(dispersar)* to disperse

disgustado,-a *adj* upset, displeased

disgustar 1 *vt* to upset

2 disgustarse *vpr* (a) *(molestarse)* to get upset, to be annoyed (b) *(dos amigos)* to quarrel

> ℓ Observa que el verbo inglés **to disgust** es un falso amigo y no es la traducción del verbo español **disgustar**. En inglés, **to disgust** significa "repugnar, indignar".

disgusto *nm* (a) *(preocupación)* annoyance; **llevarse un d.** to get upset; **dar un d. a algn** to upset sb (b) *(desgracia)* trouble; **a d.** unwillingly; **sentirse** o **estar a d.** to feel ill at ease (c) *(desavenencia)* fall-out, disagreement

🖉 Observa que la palabra inglesa **disgust** es un falso amigo y no es la traducción de la palabra española **disgusto**. En inglés, **disgust** significa "repugnancia, asco".

disidente adj & nmf dissident

disimuladamente adv surreptitiously

disimulado,-a adj (a) (persona) sly, crafty (b) (oculto) hidden, concealed

disimular vt to conceal, to hide

disimulo nm pretence

disipar 1 vt (niebla) to drive away; (temor, duda) to dispel

  2 disiparse vpr (gaseosa) to go flat; (niebla, temor etc) to disappear

disketera nf Informát disk drive

dislexia nf dyslexia

dislocar [44] vt to dislocate

disminución nf decrease

disminuir [37] **1** vt to reduce

  2 vi to diminish

disolución nf dissolution

disolvente adj & nm solvent

disolver [4] (pp disuelto) vt to dissolve

disparar 1 vt (pistola etc) to fire; (flecha, balón) to shoot; **d. a algn** to shoot at sb

  2 dispararse vpr (a) (arma) to go off, to fire (b) (precios) to rocket

disparatado,-a adj absurd

disparate nm (a) (dicho) nonsense; **decir disparates** to talk nonsense (b) (acto) foolish act

disparidad nf disparity

disparo nm shot; Dep **d. a puerta** shot

dispensar vt (a) (disculpar) to pardon, to forgive (b) (eximir) to exempt

dispersar 1 vt to disperse; (esparcir) to scatter

  2 dispersarse vpr to disperse

disperso,-a adj (separado) dispersed; (esparcido) scattered

displicencia nf condescension, disdain

displicente adj condescending, disdainful

disponer [19] (pp dispuesto) **1** vt (a) (arreglar) to arrange, to set out (b) (ordenar) to order

  2 vi **d. de** to have at one's disposal

  3 disponerse vpr to prepare, to get ready

disponible adj available

disposición nf (a) (uso) disposal; **a su d.** at your disposal o service (b) (colocación) arrangement, layout (c) **no estar en d. de** not to be prepared to (d) (orden) order, law

dispositivo nm device

dispuesto,-a adj (a) (ordenado) arranged (b) (a punto) ready (c) (decidido)

determined; **no estar d. a** not to be prepared to (**d**) **según lo d. por la ley** in accordance with what the law stipulates

disputa nf (discusión) argument; (contienda) contest

disputar 1 vt (a) (premio) to compete for (b) Dep (partido) to play

  2 disputarse vpr (premio) to compete for

disquete nm Informát diskette, floppy disk

disquetera nf Informát disk drive

distancia nf distance; **a d.** from a distance

distanciamiento nm distancing

distanciar [43] **1** vt to separate

  2 distanciarse vpr to become separated; (de otra persona) to distance oneself

distante adj distant, far-off

distar vi to be distant o away; Fig to be far from; **dista mucho de ser perfecto** it's far from (being) perfect

distender [3] vt Fig to ease, to relax

distensión nf Pol détente

distinción nf distinction; **a d. de** unlike; **sin d. de** irrespective of

distinguido,-a adj distinguished

distinguir [59] **1** vt (a) (diferenciar) to distinguish (b) (reconocer) to recognize (c) (honrar) to honour

  2 vi (diferenciar) to discriminate

  3 distinguirse vpr to distinguish oneself

distintivo,-a 1 adj distinctive, distinguishing

  2 nm distinctive sign o mark

distinto,-a adj different

distorsión nf (a) distortion (b) Med sprain

distracción nf (a) entertainment; (pasatiempo) pastime, hobby (b) (descuido) distraction, absent-mindedness

distraer [25] **1** vt (a) (atención) to distract (b) (divertir) to entertain, to amuse

  2 distraerse vpr (a) (divertirse) to amuse oneself (b) (abstraerse) to let one's mind wander

distraído,-a adj (a) (divertido) entertaining (b) (abstraído) absent-minded

distribución nf (a) distribution (b) (disposición) layout

distribuidor,-a 1 adj distributing

  2 nm,f (a) distributor (b) Com wholesaler

distribuir [37] vt to distribute; (trabajo) to share out

distrito nm district; **d. postal** postal district

disturbio nm riot, disturbance

disuadir vt to dissuade

disuasión nf dissuasion

disuelto,-a pp de **disolver**

DIU nm (abr **dispositivo intrauterino**) IUD

diurético,-a adj & nm diuretic

diurno,-a adj daytime

divagar [42] vi to digress, to wander

diván nm divan, couch

divergencia nf divergence

divergente adj diverging

diversidad nf diversity

diversificar [44] 1 vt to diversify
2 diversificarse vpr to be diversified o varied; (empresa) to diversify

diversión nf fun

diverso,-a adj different; **diversos** several, various

divertido,-a adj amusing, funny

divertir [5] 1 vt to amuse, to entertain
2 divertirse vpr to enjoy oneself, to have a good time; **¡que te diviertas!** enjoy yourself!, have fun!

dividendo nm dividend

dividir 1 vt to divide (**en** into); Mat **15 dividido entre 3** 15 divided by 3
2 dividirse vpr to divide, to split up

divinidad nf divinity

divino,-a adj divine

divisa nf (a) (emblema) symbol, emblem (b) Com **divisas** foreign currency

divisar vt to make out, to discern

división nf division

divisorio,-a adj dividing

divorciado,-a 1 adj divorced
2 nm,f (hombre) divorcé; (mujer) divorcée

divorciar [43] 1 vt to divorce
2 divorciarse vpr to get divorced; **se divorció de él** she divorced him, she got a divorce from him

divorcio nm divorce

divulgación nf disclosure

divulgar [42] vt to disclose; Rad & TV to broadcast

dizque adv Andes, Carib, Méx apparently

DNI nm (abr **Documento Nacional de Identidad**) Identity Card, ID card

do nm Mús (de solfa) doh, do; (de escala diatónica) C; **do de pecho** high C

doberman nm Doberman (pinscher)

dobladillo nm hem

doblaje nm Cin dubbing

doblar 1 vt (a) to double; **me dobla la edad** he is twice as old as I am (b) (plegar) to fold o turn up (c) (torcer) to bend (d) (la esquina) to go round (e) (película) to dub
2 vi (a) (girar) to turn; **d. a la derecha/**

izquierda to turn right/left (b) (campanas) to toll
3 doblarse vpr (a) (plegarse) to fold (b) (torcerse) to bend

doble 1 adj double; **arma de d. filo** double-edged weapon
2 nm (a) double; **gana el d. que tú** she earns twice as much as you do (b) Dep **dobles** doubles

doblegar [42] 1 vt to bend
2 doblegarse vpr to give in

doblez 1 nm (pliegue) fold
2 nm o nf Fig two-facedness, hypocrisy

doce adj & nm inv twelve

docena nf dozen

docencia nf teaching

docente adj teaching; **centro d.** educational centre

dócil adj docile

doctor,-a nm,f doctor

doctorado nm Univ doctorate, PhD

doctrina nf doctrine

documentación nf documentation; (DNI, de conducir etc) papers

documental adj & nm documentary

documentar 1 vt to document
2 documentarse vpr **d. (sobre)** to research, to get information (about o on)

documento nm document; **d. nacional de identidad** identity card

dogma nm dogma

dogmático,-a adj & nm,f dogmatic

dogo nm bulldog

dólar nm dollar

dolarización nf dollarization

dolencia nf ailment

doler [4] 1 vi to hurt, to ache; **me duele la cabeza** I've got a headache; **me duele la mano** my hand is sore
2 dolerse vpr to be sorry o sad

dolido,-a adj estar **d.** to be hurt

dolor nm (a) Med pain; **d. de cabeza** headache; **d. de muelas** toothache (b) (pena) grief, sorrow

dolorido,-a adj (a) (dañado) sore, aching (b) (apenado) hurt

doloroso,-a adj painful

domar vt to tame; (caballo) to break in

domesticar [44] vt to domesticate; (animal) to tame

doméstico,-a adj domestic; **animal d.** pet

domiciliación nf payment by standing order

domiciliar [43] vt (a) to house (b) Fin to pay by standing order

domiciliario,-a adj arresto **d.** house arrest

domicilio *nm* home, residence; *(señas)* address; **sin d. fijo** of no fixed abode; **d. fiscal** registered office

dominación *nf* domination

dominante *adj* (**a**) dominant (**b**) *(déspota)* domineering

dominar 1 *vt* (**a**) to dominate, to rule (**b**) *(situación)* to control; *(idioma)* to speak very well; *(asunto)* to master; *(paisaje etc)* to overlook

2 *vi* (**a**) to dominate (**b**) *(resaltar)* to stand out

3 dominarse *vpr* to control oneself

domingo *nm inv* Sunday; **D. de Resurrección** *o* **Pascua** Easter Sunday

dominguero,-a *nm,f Fam (excursionista)* weekend tripper; *(conductor)* weekend driver

dominical 1 *adj* Sunday

2 *nm (suplemento)* Sunday supplement

dominicano,-a *adj & nm,f* Dominican; **República Dominicana** Dominican Republic

dominio *nm* (**a**) *(poder)* control; *(de un idioma)* command; **d. de sí mismo** self-control (**b**) *(ámbito)* scope, sphere; **ser del d. público** to be public knowledge (**c**) *(territorio)* dominion (**d**) *Informát* domain

dominó, dómino *nm* dominoes

don¹ *nm* (**a**) *(habilidad)* gift, talent; **tener el d. de** to have a knack for; **tener d. de gentes** to get on well with people (**b**) *(regalo)* present, gift

don² *nm* **Señor D. José García** Mr José Garcia; **D. Fulano de Tal** Mr So-and-So; **un d. nadie** a nobody

donaire *nm* grace, elegance

donante *nmf* donor; *Med* **d. de sangre** blood donor

donar *vt Fml* to donate; *(sangre)* to give

donativo *nm* donation

doncella *nf Literario* (**a**) *(joven)* maid, maiden (**b**) *(criada)* maid, housemaid

donde *adv rel* where; **a o en d.** where; **de o desde d.** from where; **está d. lo dejaste** it is where you left it; *Fam* **está d. su tía** he's at his aunt's

> **donde** combines with the preposition **a** to form **adonde** when following a noun, a pronoun or an adverb expressing location (e.g. **el sitio adonde vamos** the place where we're going; **es allí adonde iban** that's where they were going).

dónde *adv interr* where?; **¿de d. eres?** where are you from?; **¿por d. se va a la playa?** which way is it to the beach?

> **dónde** can combine with the preposition **a** to form **adónde** (e.g. **¿adónde vamos?** where are we going?).

dondequiera *adv* everywhere; **d. que vaya** wherever I go

donostiarra 1 *adj* of/from San Sebastián

2 *nmf* person from San Sebastián

doña *nf (Señora)* **D. Leonor Benítez** Mrs Leonor Benítez

dopaje *nm Dep* drug-taking

dopar 1 *vt (caballo etc)* to dope

2 doparse *vpr* to take drugs

doping *nm Dep* drug-taking

doquier, doquiera *adv Literario* **por d.** everywhere

dorada *nf (pez)* gilthead bream

dorado,-a 1 *adj* golden

2 *nm Téc* gilding

dorar *vt* (**a**) to gild (**b**) *Culin* to brown

dormido,-a *adj* (**a**) asleep; **quedarse d.** to fall asleep; *(no despertarse)* to oversleep, to sleep in (**b**) *(pierna, brazo)* numb

dormilón,-ona 1 *adj Fam* sleepyheaded

2 *nm,f* sleepyhead

3 *nf Ven* **dormilona** nightdress

dormir [7] *vi* to sleep; **tener ganas de d.** to feel sleepy;

2 *vt* **d. la siesta** to have an afternoon nap

3 dormirse *vpr* to fall asleep; **se me ha dormido el brazo** my arm has gone to sleep

dormitar *vi* to doze, to snooze

dormitorio *nm* (**a**) *(de una casa)* bedroom (**b**) *(de colegio, residencia)* dormitory; **ciudad d.** dormitory town

dorsal 1 *adj* **espina d.** spine

2 *nm Dep* number

dorso *nm* back; **instrucciones al d.** instructions over; **véase al d.** see overleaf

dos *adj & nm inv* two; **los d.** both; **nosotros/vosotros d.** both of us/you; *Fam* **cada d. por tres** every other minute; *Fam* **en un d. por tres** in a flash

doscientos,-as *adj & nm* two hundred

dosel *nm* canopy

dosificación *nf* dosage

dosificar [44] *vt* (**a**) to dose (**b**) *(esfuerzos, energías)* to measure

dosis *nf inv* dose

dossier *nm* dossier

dotación *nf (dinero)* grant; *(personal)* personnel, staff; *(de barco)* crew

dotado,-a *adj* (**a**) *(persona)* gifted (**b**) *(equipado)* equipped; **d. de** provided with

dotar *vt* **d. de** to provide with

dote *nf* (**a**) *(de novia)* dowry (**b**) **dotes** *(talento)* gift, talent

doy *indic pres de* **dar**

dpto. (*abr* **departamento**) Dept

Dr. (*abr* **doctor**) Dr

Dra. (*abr* **doctora**) Dr

dragar [42] *vt* to dredge

dragón *nm* dragon

drama *nm* drama

dramático,-a *adj* dramatic

dramatismo *nm* drama, dramatic quality

dramaturgo,-a *nm,f* playwright, dramatist

drástico,-a *adj* drastic

drenar *vt* to drain

driblar *vi* to dribble

droga *nf* drug; **d. blanda/dura** soft/hard drug

drogadicto,-a *nm,f* drug addict

drogar [42] 1 *vt* to drug
  2 **drogarse** *vpr* to drug oneself, to take drugs

droguería *nf* hardware and household goods shop

dto. (*abr* **descuento**) discount

dual *adj* dual

dualidad *nf* duality

dubitativo,-a *adj* doubtful

Dublín *n* Dublin

dublinés,-esa 1 *adj* of/from Dublin
  2 *nm,f* Dubliner

ducha *nf* shower; **darse/tomar una d.** to take/have a shower

ducharse *vpr* to shower, to have o take a shower

ducho,-a *adj* expert; **ser d. en** to be well versed in

duda *nf* doubt; **sin d.** without a doubt; **no cabe d.** (there is) no doubt; **poner algo en d.** to question sth; **sacar a algn de dudas** to dispel sb's doubts

dudar 1 *vi* (**a**) to doubt (**b**) (*vacilar*) to hesitate (**en** to); **dudaba entre ir o quedarme** I hesitated whether to go o to stay (**c**) **d. de algn** (*desconfiar*) to suspect sb
  2 *vt* to doubt

dudoso,-a *adj* (**a**) **ser d.** (*incierto*) to be uncertain o doubtful (**b**) **estar d.** (*indeciso*) to be undecided (**c**) (*poco honrado*) dubious

duelo¹ *nm* (*combate*) duel

duelo² *nm* (*luto*) mourning

duende *nm* (**a**) (*espíritu*) goblin, elf (**b**) (*encanto*) magic, charm

dueña *nf* owner; (*de pensión*) landlady

dueño *nm* owner; (*de casa etc*) landlord; *Fig* **ser d. de sí mismo** to be self-possessed

Duero *n* **el D.** the Douro

dulce 1 *adj* (**a**) (*sabor*) sweet (**b**) (*carácter, voz*) gentle (**c**) (*metal*) soft (**d**) **agua d.** fresh water
  2 *nm* (**a**) *Culin* (*pastel*) cake (**b**) (*caramelo*) *Br* sweet, *US* candy

dulzura *nf* (**a**) sweetness (**b**) *Fig* gentleness, softness

duna *nf* dune

dúo *nm* duet

duodécimo,-a *adj & nm,f* twelfth

dúplex *nm* (**a**) (*piso*) duplex, duplex apartment (**b**) *Tel* link-up

duplicado,-a 1 *adj* **por d.** in duplicate
  2 *nm* duplicate, copy

duplicar [44] 1 *vt* to duplicate; (*cifras*) to double
  2 **duplicarse** *vpr* to double

duplo,-a *adj & nm,f* double

duque *nm* duke

duquesa *nf* duchess

duración *nf* duration, length; **disco de larga d.** long-playing record

duradero,-a *adj* durable, lasting

durante *prep* during; **d. el día** during the day; **d. todo el día** all day long; **viví en La Coruña d. un año** I lived in La Coruña for a year

durar *vi* (**a**) to last (**b**) (*ropa, calzado*) to wear well, to last

durazno *nm* (*fruto*) peach; (*árbol*) peach tree

dúrex *nm Méx Br* Sellotape®, *US* Scotch tape®

dureza *nf* (**a**) hardness; (*severidad*) harshness, severity (**b**) (*callosidad*) corn

---

🔲 Observa que la palabra inglesa **duress** es un falso amigo y no es la traducción de la palabra española **dureza**. En inglés, **duress** significa "coacción".

---

duro,-a 1 *adj* (**a**) hard; *Dep* **juego d.** rough play (**b**) (*resistente*) tough; (*severo*) hard (**c**) (*clima*) harsh
  2 *nm* (*moneda*) 5-peseta coin
  3 *adv* hard; **trabajar d.** to work hard

DVD *nm Informát* (*abr* **Disco Versátil Digital**) DVD

E, e [e] *nf (la letra)* E, e
E (*abr* **Este**) E
e *conj* and

> **e** is used instead of **y** in front of words beginning with "i" or "hi" (e.g. **apoyo e interés** support and interest; **corazón e hígado** heart and liver).

ebanista *nm* cabinet-maker
ébano *nm* ebony
ebrio,-a *adj* inebriated; **e. de dicha** drunk with joy
ebullición *nf* boiling; **punto de e.** boiling point
eccema *nm* eczema
echar 1 *vt* (a) *(lanzar)* to throw; *Fig* **e. una mano** to give a hand; *Fig* **e. una mirada/una ojeada** to have a look/a quick look o glance
(b) *(carta)* to post; *(vino, agua)* to pour; **e. sal al estofado** to put salt in the stew; **e. gasolina al coche** to put *Br* petrol o *US* gas in the car
(c) *(expulsar)* to throw out; *(despedir)* to fire, *Br* to sack
(d) *(humo, olor etc)* to give off
(e) *Fam (película)* to show
(f) **le echó 37 años** he reckoned she was about 37
(g) **e. de menos** o **en falta** to miss
(h) **e. abajo** *(edificio)* to demolish
2 *vi* (+ **a** + *infin)* *(empezar)* to begin to; **echó a correr** he ran off
3 echarse *vpr* (a) *(tumbarse)* to lie down; *(lanzarse)* to throw oneself; *Fig* **la noche se nos echó encima** it was night before we knew it
(b) **échate a un lado** stand aside; *Fig* **e. atrás** to get cold feet
(c) *Fam* **e. novio/novia** to get a boyfriend/girlfriend
(d) (+ **a** + *infin)* *(empezar)* to begin to; **e. a llorar** to burst into tears; **e. a reír** to burst out laughing; **e. a perder** *(comida)* to go bad
ecléctico,-a *adj & nm,f* eclectic
eclesiástico,-a 1 *adj* ecclesiastical
2 *nm* clergyman
eclipsar *vt* to eclipse

eclipse *nm* eclipse
eco *nm* echo; *Fig* **hacerse e. de una noticia** to publish an item of news; **tener e.** to arouse interest
ecografía *nf* scan
ecología *nf* ecology
ecológico,-a *adj* ecological; *(alimentos)* organic; *(detergente)* environmentally-friendly
ecologista 1 *adj* ecological; *Pol* **partido e.** ecology party
2 *nmf* ecologist
economía *nf* (a) economy; **con e.** economically (b) *(ciencia)* economics *sing*
económico,-a *adj* (a) economic (b) *(barato)* economical, inexpensive (c) *(persona)* thrifty
economista *nmf* economist
economizar [40] *vt & vi* to economize
ecosistema *nm* ecosystem
ecotasa *nf* ecotax
ecoturismo *nm* ecotourism
ecuación *nf* equation
Ecuador *n* Ecuador
ecuador *nm Geog* equator
ecualizador *nm* **e. (gráfico)** graphic equalizer
ecuánime *adj* (a) *(temperamento)* equable, even-tempered (b) *(juicio)* impartial
ecuatorial *adj* equatorial; **Guinea E.** Equatorial Guinea
ecuatoriano,-a *adj & nm,f* Ecuadorian
ecuestre *adj* equestrian
ecuménico,-a *adj* ecumenical
eczema *nm* eczema
edad *nf* age; **¿qué e. tienes?** how old are you?; **la tercera e.** senior citizens; **E. Media** Middle Ages
edición *nf* (a) *(publicación)* publication; *(de sellos)* issue (b) *(conjunto de ejemplares)* edition
edicto *nm* edict, proclamation
edificante *adj* edifying
edificar [44] *vt* to build
edificio *nm* building
edil,-a *nm,f* town councillor
Edimburgo *n* Edinburgh
editar *vt* (a) *(libro, periódico)* to publish;

(disco) to release (**b**) *Informát* to edit
editor,-a 1 *adj* publishing
  2 *nm,f* publisher
editorial 1 *adj* publishing
  2 *nf* publishers, publishing house
  3 *nm Prensa* editorial, leader article
edredón *nm Br* duvet, *US* comforter
educación *nf* (**a**) education; **e. física** physical education (**b**) *(formación)* upbringing (**c**) **buena/mala e.** *(modales)* good/bad manners; **falta de e.** bad manners
educado,-a *adj* polite
educador,-a 1 *adj* educating
  2 *nm,f* educationalist
educar [44] *vt (hijos)* to raise; *(alumnos)* to educate; *(la voz)* to train
educativo,-a *adj* educational; **sistema e.** education system
edulcorante *nm* sweetener
EE.UU. *(abr* **Estados Unidos**) USA
efectista *adj* spectacular
efectivamente *adv* quite!, yes indeed!
efectividad *nf* effectiveness
efectivo,-a 1 *adj* effective; **hacer algo e.** to carry sth out; *Fin* **hacer e. un cheque** to cash a cheque
  2 *nm* (**a**) *Fin* **en e.** in cash (**b**) *Mil* **efectivos** forces
efecto *nm* (**a**) *(resultado)* effect; **efectos especiales/sonoros** special/sound effects; **efectos personales** personal belongings *o* effects; **a efectos de ...** for the purposes of ...; **en e.** quite!, yes indeed! (**b**) *(impresión)* impression; **causar** *o* **hacer e.** to make an impression (**c**) *Dep* spin
efectuar [30] *vt* to carry out; *(viaje)* to make; *Com (pedido)* to place
efeméride *nf* event
efervescente *adj* effervescent; **aspirina e.** soluble aspirin
eficacia *nf (de persona)* efficiency; *(de remedio etc)* effectiveness
eficaz *adj (persona)* efficient; *(remedio, medida etc)* effective
eficiencia *nf* efficiency
eficiente *adj* efficient
efigie *nf* effigy
efímero,-a *adj* ephemeral
efusivo,-a *adj* effusive
EGB *nf Educ (abr* **Enseñanza General Básica**) = formerly, stage of Spanish education system for pupils aged 6-14
Egeo *n* **el (Mar) E.** the Aegean Sea
egipcio,-a *adj & nm,f* Egyptian
Egipto *n* Egypt
egocéntrico,-a *adj* egocentric, self-centred

egoísmo *nm* egoism, selfishness
egoísta 1 *adj* ego(t)istic, selfish
  2 *nmf* ego(t)ist, selfish person
egregio,-a *adj* eminent, illustrious
egresar *vi Am* to leave school, *US* to graduate
Eire *n* Eire, Republic of Ireland
ej. *(abr* **ejemplo**) example
eje *nm* (**a**) *Téc (de rueda)* axle; *(de máquina)* shaft (**b**) *Mat* axis (**c**) *Hist* **El E.** the Axis
ejecución *nf* (**a**) *(de orden)* carrying out (**b**) *(ajusticiamiento)* execution (**c**) *Mús* performance
ejecutar *vt* (**a**) *(orden)* to carry out (**b**) *(ajusticiar)* to execute (**c**) *Mús* to perform, to play (**d**) *Informát* to run
ejecutiva *nf Pol* executive
ejecutivo,-a 1 *adj* executive; *Pol* **el poder e.** the government
  2 *nm* executive
ejecutor,-a *nm,f* (**a**) *Jur* executor (**b**) *(verdugo)* executioner
ejemplar 1 *nm* (**a**) *(de libro)* copy; *(de revista, periódico)* number, issue (**b**) *(espécimen)* specimen
  2 *adj* exemplary, model
ejemplificar [44] *vt* to exemplify
ejemplo *nm* example; **por e.** for example; **dar e.** to set an example
ejercer [49] 1 *vt* (**a**) *(profesión etc)* to practise (**b**) *(influencia)* to exert (**c**) **e. el derecho de/a ...** to exercise one's right to ...
  2 *vi* to practise (**de** as)
ejercicio *nm* (**a**) *(ejercitación; de profesión)* practice; **hacer e.** to take *o* do exercise (**b**) *Fin* tax year; **e. económico** financial *o* fiscal year
ejercitar *vt* to practise
ejército *nm* army
ejote *nm CAm, Méx* green bean
el 1 *art def m* (**a**) (**b**) *(no se traduce)* **el Sr. García** Mr. García; **el hambre/destino** hunger/fate (**c**) *(con partes del cuerpo, prendas de vestir)* **me he cortado el dedo** I've cut my finger; **métetelo en el bolsillo** put it in your pocket (**d**) *(con días de la semana)* **el lunes** on Monday

> **el** is used instead of **la** before feminine nouns which are stressed on the first syllable and begin with "a" or "ha" (e.g. **el agua, el hacha**). Note that **el** combines with the prepositions **a** and **de** to produce the contracted forms **al** and **del**.

  2 *pron* (**a**) the one; **el de las once** the eleven o'clock one; **el que tienes en la mano** the one you've got in your hand; **el**

que quieras whichever one you want (**b**) (*no se traduce*) **el de tu amigo** your friend's

él *pron pers* (**a**) (*sujeto*) (*persona*) he; (*animal, cosa*) it (**b**) (*complemento*) (*persona*) him; (*animal, cosa*) it

> Usually omitted in Spanish as a subject except for emphasis or contrast.

elaboración *nf* (**a**) (*de un producto*) manufacture, production (**b**) (*de una idea*) working out, development

elaborar *vt* (**a**) (*producto*) to manufacture, to produce (**b**) (*teoría*) to develop

elasticidad *nf* elasticity; *Fig* flexibility

elástico,-a *adj & nm* elastic

elección *nf* choice; *Pol* election

elector,-a *nm,f* elector

electorado *nm* electorate

electoral *adj* electoral; **campaña e.** election campaign; **colegio e.** polling station

electoralismo *nm* electioneering

electricidad *nf* electricity

electricista *nmf* electrician

eléctrico,-a *adj* electric

electrificar [44] *vt* to electrify

electrizar [40] *vt* to electrify

electrochoque *nm* electric shock therapy

electrocutar *vt* to electrocute

electrodo *nm* electrode

electrodoméstico *nm* (domestic) electrical appliance

electroimán *nm* electromagnet

electromagnético,-a *adj* electromagnetic

electrón *nm* electron

electrónica *nf* electronics *sing*

electrónico,-a *adj* electronic

elefante *nm* elephant

elegancia *nf* elegance

elegante *adj* elegant

elegía *nf* elegy

elegir [58] *vt* (**a**) to choose (**b**) *Pol* to elect

elemental *adj* (**a**) (*fundamental*) basic, fundamental (**b**) (*simple*) elementary

elemento *nm* (**a**) element (**b**) (*componente*) component, part (**c**) (*individuo*) type, individual (**d**) **elementos** elements; (*fundamentos*) rudiments

elepé *nm* LP (record)

elevación *nf* elevation; **e. de precios** rise in prices; **e. del terreno** rise in the ground

elevado,-a *adj* (**a**) high; (*edificio*) tall (**b**) (*pensamiento etc*) lofty, noble

elevalunas *nm inv* *Aut* **e. eléctrico** electric windows

elevar 1 *vt* to raise

2 elevarse *vpr* (**a**) (*subir*) to rise; (*edificio*) to stand (**b**) **e. a** (*cantidad*) to amount o come to

elijo *indic pres de* **elegir**

eliminación *nf* elimination

eliminar *vt* to eliminate

eliminatoria *nf* *Dep* heat, qualifying round

eliminatorio,-a *adj* qualifying, eliminatory

élite *nf* elite, élite

elitista *adj* elitist

elixir *nm* (*enjuage bucal*) mouthwash; *Literario* elixir

ella *pron pers f* (**a**) (*sujeto*) she; (*animal, cosa*) it, she (**b**) (*complemento*) her; (*animal, cosa*) it, her

> Usually omitted in Spanish as a subject except for emphasis or contrast.

ellas *pron pers fpl ver* **ellos**

ello *pron pers neut* it; **por e.** for that reason

ellos *pron pers mpl* (**a**) (*sujeto*) they (**b**) (*complemento*) them

> Usually omitted in Spanish as a subject except for emphasis or contrast.

elocuencia *nf* eloquence

elocuente *adj* eloquent; **los hechos son elocuentes** the facts speak for themselves

elogiar [43] *vt* to praise

elogio *nm* praise

elote *nm CAm, Méx* corncob, ear of maize

El Salvador *n* El Salvador

elucidar *vt* to elucidate

eludir *vt* to avoid

emanar *vi* to emanate; *Fig* **e. de** (*derivar*) to derive o come from

emancipar 1 *vt* to emancipate

2 emanciparse *vpr* to become emancipated

embadurnar *vt* to daub, to smear (**de** with)

embajada *nf* embassy

embajador,-a *nm,f* ambassador

embalaje *nm* packing, packaging

embalar *vt* to pack

embalarse *vpr* to speed up; *Fig* **no te embales** hold your horses

embalsamar *vt* to embalm

embalsar 1 *vt* to dam; (*problema*) to contain

2 embalsarse *vpr* to form a pool

embalse *nm* dam, reservoir

embarazada 1 *adj* pregnant; **dejar e.** to get pregnant

2 *nf* pregnant woman, expectant mother

> 🖉 Observa que la palabra inglesa **embar-rassed** es un falso amigo y no es la traduc-ción de la palabra española **embarazada**. En inglés **embarrassed** significa "avergon-zado".

embarazar [40] *vt Fig* to hinder

embarazo *nm* (**a**) *(preñez)* pregnancy (**b**) *(obstáculo)* obstacle (**c**) *(turbación)* embarrassment

embarazoso,-a *adj* awkward, embar-rassing

embarcación *nf* (**a**) *(nave)* boat, craft (**b**) *(embarco)* embarkation

embarcadero *nm* quay

embarcar [44] 1 *vt* to ship
  2 *vi* to embark, to go on board
  3 embarcarse *vpr* (**a**) *Náut* e. (**en**) to go on board (**b**) *Av* to board (**b**) **e. en un proyecto** to embark on a project

embarco *nm* embarkation

embargar [42] *vt* (**a**) *Jur* to seize, to impound (**b**) *Fig* **le embarga la emoción** he's overwhelmed with joy

embargo *nm* (**a**) *Jur* seizure of property (**b**) *Com & Pol* embargo (**c**) **sin e.** how-ever, nevertheless

embarque *nm* *(de persona)* boarding; *(de mercancías)* loading; **tarjeta de e.** board-ing card

embarrancar [44] *vi*, **embarrancarse** *vpr Náut* to run aground

embaucador,-a 1 *adj* deceitful
  2 *nm,f* swindler, cheat

embaucar [44] *vt* to swindle, to cheat

embeber 1 *vt* to soak up
  2 embeberse *vpr* to become absorbed *o* engrossed

embelesar *vt* to fascinate

embellecer [33] *vt* to embellish

embestida *nf* (**a**) onslaught (**b**) *Taurom* charge

embestir [6] *vt* (**a**) *Taurom* to charge (**b**) *(atacar)* to attack

emblandecer [33] 1 *vt* to soften
  2 emblandecerse *vpr Fig* to relent

emblema *nm* emblem

embobado,-a *adj* fascinated

embobarse *vpr* to be fascinated *o* besot-ted (**con** by)

embolia *nf* embolism

émbolo *nm* piston

embolsar *vt*, **embolsarse** *vpr* to pocket

emborrachar *vt*, **emborracharse** *vpr* to get drunk

emboscada *nf* ambush; **tender una e.** to lay an ambush

embotar *vt* to blunt; *Fig (sentidos)* to dull; *(mente)* to befuddle

embotellado *nm* bottling

embotellamiento *nm Aut* traffic jam

embotellar *vt* (**a**) to bottle (**b**) *(tráfico)* to block

embragar [42] *vi Aut* to engage the clutch

embrague *nm* clutch

embravecerse [33] *vpr* (**a**) *(enfadarse)* to become enraged (**b**) *(mar)* to become rough

embriagador,-a *adj* intoxicating

embriagar [42] 1 *vt* to intoxicate; *Fig* to enrapture
  2 embriagarse *vpr* to get drunk; *Fig* to be enraptured

embriaguez *nf* intoxication

embridar *vt* to bridle

embrión *nm* embryo

embrollar 1 *vt* to confuse, to muddle
  2 embrollarse *vpr* to get muddled *o* confused

embrollo *nm* (**a**) *(lío)* muddle, confusion (**b**) *(aprieto)* fix, jam

embrujado,-a *adj (persona)* bewitched; *(sitio)* haunted

embrujo *nm* spell, charm; *Fig* attraction, fascination

embrutecer [33] *vt* to stultify

embuchar *vt* to stuff

embudo *nm* funnel

embuste *nm* lie, trick

embustero,-a *nm,f* cheater, liar

embutido *nm* sausage

embutir *vt* (**a**) *(carne)* to stuff (**b**) *(meter)* to stuff *o* cram *o* squeeze (**en** into) (**c**) *(incrustar)* to inlay

emergencia *nf* emergency; **salida de e.** emergency exit; **en caso de e.** in an emergency

emerger [53] *vi* to emerge

emigración *nf* emigration; *(de pájaros)* migration

emigrado,-a *nm,f* emigrant; *Pol* émigré

emigrante *adj & nmf* emigrant

emigrar *vi* to emigrate; *(pájaros)* to mi-grate

emilio *nm Fam Informát* e-mail (mes-sage)

eminencia *nf* eminence; *(genio)* genius

eminente *adj* eminent

emirato *nm* emirate

emisario,-a *nm,f* emissary

emisión *nf* (**a**) emission (**b**) *(de bonos, sellos)* issue (**c**) *Rad & TV* broadcasting

emisora *nf* radio *o* television station

emitir *vt* (**a**) to emit; *(luz, calor)* to give off

(**b**) *(opinión, juicio)* to express (**c**) *Rad & TV* to transmit (**d**) *(bonos, sellos)* to issue

emoción *nf* (**a**) emotion (**b**) *(excitación)* excitement; **¡qué e.!** how exciting!

emocionado,-a *adj* deeply moved o touched

emocionante *adj* (**a**) *(conmovedor)* moving, touching (**b**) *(excitante)* exciting, thrilling

emocionar 1 *vt* (**a**) *(conmover)* to move, to touch (**b**) *(excitar)* to thrill

2 emocionarse *vpr* (**a**) *(conmoverse)* to be moved (**b**) *(excitarse)* to get excited

emotivo,-a *adj* emotional

empacar [44] *vt* (**a**) *(mercancías)* to pack (**b**) *Am* to annoy

empachar *vt* to give indigestion to

empacho *nm* *(de comida)* indigestion, upset stomach; *Fig* surfeit

empadronar *vt*, **empadronarse** *vpr* to register

empalagar [42] *vi* to pall

empalagoso,-a *adj* (**a**) *(dulce)* sickly sweet (**b**) *Fig (persona)* smarmy

empalizada *nf* fence

empalmar 1 *vt* (**a**) *(unir)* to join; *(cuerdas, cables)* to splice (**b**) *Ftb* to volley

2 *vi* to converge; *Ferroc* to connect

3 empalmarse *vpr Vulg* to get a hard-on

empalme *nm* (**a**) connection (**b**) *Ferroc* junction; *(en carretera)* intersection, T-junction

empanada *nf* pie

empanadilla *nf* pasty

empanado,-a *adj (filete etc)* breaded, in breadcrumbs

empantanarse *vpr* (**a**) *(inundarse)* to become flooded (**b**) *Fig* to be bogged down

empañar *vt*, **empañarse** *vpr (cristales)* to steam up

empapado,-a *adj* soaked

empapar 1 *vt* (**a**) *(mojar)* to soak (**b**) *(absorber)* to soak up

2 empaparse *vpr* (**a**) *(persona)* to get soaked (**b**) *Fam Fig* **empaparse (de)** to take in

empapelar *vt* to wallpaper

empaque *nm* bearing, presence

empaquetar *vt* to pack

emparedado *nm* sandwich

emparejar *vt (cosas)* to match; *(personas)* to pair off

empastar *vt (diente)* to fill

empaste *nm (de diente)* filling

empatado,-a *adj* drawn; **estar/ir empatados** to be drawing

empatar 1 *vi Dep* to tie, to draw

2 *vt* (**a**) *Dep* **e. el partido** to equalize (**b**) *Am (unir)* to join

empate *nm Dep* draw, tie

empecinarse *vpr* to dig one's heels in

empedernido,-a *adj (fumador, bebedor)* hardened

empedrado,-a 1 *adj* cobbled

2 *nm* (**a**) *(adoquines)* cobblestones (**b**) *(acción)* paving

empeine *nm* instep

empellón *nm* push, shove

empeñar 1 *vt* to pawn

2 empeñarse *vpr* (**a**) *(insistir)* to insist (**en** on), to be determined (**en** to) (**b**) *(endeudarse)* to get into debt

empeño *nm* (**a**) *(insistencia)* insistence; **poner e. en algo** to put a lot of effort into sth (**b**) *(deuda)* pledge; **casa de empeños** pawnshop

empeoramiento *nm* deterioration, worsening

empeorar 1 *vi* to deteriorate, to worsen

2 *vt* to make worse

3 empeorarse *vpr* to deteriorate, to worsen

empequeñecer [33] *vt Fig* to belittle

emperador *nm* emperor

emperatriz *nf* empress

emperifollarse *vpr Fam* to get dolled up

emperrarse *vpr* to dig one's heels in, to become stubborn

empezar [51] *vt & vi (a hacer algo)* to begin; *(algo)* to start, to commence

empinado,-a *adj (cuesta)* steep

empinar 1 *vt* to raise; *Fam* **e. el codo** to drink

2 empinarse *vpr (persona)* to stand on tiptoe

empírico,-a *adj* empirical

emplasto *nm* poultice

emplazamiento *nm* (**a**) *(colocación)* site, location (**b**) *Jur* summons sing

emplazar¹ [40] *vt* to locate, to situate

emplazar² [40] *vt* (**a**) *Jur* to summons (**b**) *(a una reunión etc)* to call

empleado,-a *nm,f* employee; *(de oficina, banco)* clerk; **empleada del hogar** servant, maid

emplear *vt* (**a**) *(usar)* to use; *(contratar)* to employ (**b**) *(dinero, tiempo)* to spend

empleo *nm* (**a**) *(oficio)* job; *Pol* employment (**b**) *(uso)* use; **modo de e.** instructions for use

emplomar *vt Am (diente)* to fill

empobrecer [33] **1** *vt* to impoverish

2 empobrecerse *vpr* to become impoverished o poor

empobrecimiento *nm* impoverishment

empollar *vt* (**a**) *(huevos)* to sit on (**b**) *Fam (estudiar)* to bone up on, *Br* to swot up

empollón,-ona *nm,f Br Fam* swot, *US* grind

empolvar 1 *vt* to cover in dust

2 empolvarse *vpr (la cara)* to powder

emponzoñar *vt* to poison

emporcar [44] *vt* to foul, to dirty

emporio *nm* (**a**) *Com* emporium, trading o commercial centre (**b**) *Am* department store

emporrarse *vpr Fam* to get high

empotrado,-a *adj* fitted

emprendedor,-a *adj* enterprising

emprender *vt* to undertake; *Fam* **emprenderla con algn** to pick on sb

empresa *nf* (**a**) *Com & Ind* firm, company; **e. punto com** dot com (company); **e. de trabajo temporal** temping agency (**b**) *Pol* **la libre e.** free enterprise (**c**) *(tarea)* undertaking

empresariado *nm* employers

empresarial *adj* (**a**) *(de empresa)* business; **(ciencias) empresariales** business studies (**b**) *(espíritu)* entrepreneurial; **organización e.** employers' organization

empresario,-a *nm,f* (**a**) *(hombre)* businessman; *(mujer)* businesswoman (**b**) *(patrón)* employer

empréstito *nm Fin* debenture loan

empujar *vt* to push, to shove

empuje *nm* push; *Fig (brío)* verve, get-up-and-go

empujón *nm* push, shove; **dar empujones** to push and shove

empuñadura *nf (de espada)* hilt

empuñar *vt* to grasp, to seize

emular *vt* to emulate

emulsión *nf* emulsion

en *prep* (**a**) *(posición)* in, on, at; **en Madrid/Bolivia** in Madrid/Bolivia; **en la mesa** on the table; **en el bolso** in the bag; **en casa/el trabajo** at home/work

(**b**) *(movimiento)* into; **entró en el cuarto** he went into the room

(**c**) *(tiempo)* in, on, at; **en 1940** in 1940; **en verano** in summer; *Am* **en la mañana** in the morning; **cae en martes** it falls on a Tuesday; **en ese momento** at that moment

(**d**) *(transporte)* by, in; **en coche/tren** by car/train; **en avión** by air

(**e**) *(modo)* **en español** in Spanish; **en broma** jokingly; **en serio** seriously

(**f**) *(reducción, aumento)* by; **los precios aumentaron en un diez por ciento** the prices went up by ten percent

(**g**) *(tema, materia)* at, in; **bueno en deportes** good at sports; **experto en política** expert in politics

(**h**) *(división, separación)* in; **lo dividió en tres partes** he divided it in three

(**i**) *(con infinitivo)* **fue rápido en responder** he was quick to answer; **la conocí en el andar** I recognized her by her walk; **ser sobrio en el vestir** to dress simply

enaguas *nfpl* underskirt, petticoat

enajenación *nf*, **enajenamiento** *nm* alienation; **e. mental** mental derangement, insanity

enajenar 1 *vt* (**a**) *Jur* to alienate (**b**) *(turbar)* to drive insane

2 enajenarse *vpr (enloquecer)* to go insane

enaltecer [33] *vt* (**a**) *(alabar)* to praise, to extol (**b**) *(ennoblecer)* to do credit to

enamorado,-a 1 *adj* in love

2 *nm,f* person in love

enamorar 1 *vt* to win the heart of

2 enamorarse *vpr* to fall in love (**de** with)

enano,-a *adj & nm,f* dwarf

enardecer [33] 1 *vt (sentimientos)* to rouse, to stir up; *(persona)* to fill with enthusiasm

2 enardecerse *vpr Fig* to become excited

encabezamiento *nm (de carta)* heading; *(de periódico)* headline; *(preámbulo)* foreword, preamble

encabezar [40] *vt* (**a**) *(carta, lista)* to head; *(periódico)* to lead (**b**) *(rebelión, carrera, movimiento)* to lead

encabritarse *vpr* (**a**) *(caballo)* to rear (up) (**b**) *Fig (persona)* to get cross

encadenar *vt* to chain

encajar 1 *vt* (**a**) *(ajustar)* to insert; **e. la puerta** to push the door to (**b**) *Fam (asimilar)* to take (**c**) *(comentario)* to get in; **e. un golpe a algn** to land sb a blow

2 *vi* (**a**) *(ajustarse)* to fit (**b**) *Fig* **e. con** to fit (in) with, to square with

encaje *nm* lace

encalar *vt* to whitewash

encallar *vi* (**a**) *Náut* to run aground (**b**) *Fig* to flounder, to fail

encaminado,-a *adj* **estar bien/mal e.** to be on the right/wrong track

encaminar 1 *vt* to direct

2 encaminarse *vpr* to head (**a** for; **hacia** towards)

encandilar *vt* to dazzle

encantado,-a *adj* (**a**) *(contento)* delighted; **e. de conocerle** pleased to meet you (**b**) *(embrujado)* enchanted

encantador,-a 1 *adj* charming, delightful

2 *nm,f* magician

encantamiento *nm* spell

encantar *vt (hechizar)* to bewitch, to cast a spell on; *Fig* **me encanta nadar** I love swimming

encanto *nm* (**a**) *(atractivo)* charm; **ser un e.** to be charming (**b**) *(hechizo)* spell

encapricharse *vpr* **e. con** to set one's mind on; *(encariñarse)* to take a fancy to; *(enamorarse)* to get a crush on

encapuchado,-a *adj* hooded

encaramarse *vpr* to climb up

encarar 1 *vt* to face, to confront
  2 encararse *vpr* **e. con** to face up to

encarcelar *vt* to imprison, to jail

encarecer [33] **1** *vt* to put up the price of
  2 encarecerse *vpr* to go up (in price)

encarecidamente *adv* earnestly, insistently; **le rogamos e. que ...** we would earnestly request you to ...

encarecimiento *nm* increase *o* rise in price

encargado,-a 1 *nm,f Com (hombre)* manager; *(mujer)* manager, manageress; *(responsable)* person in charge
  2 *adj* in charge

encargar [42] **1** *vt* (**a**) to put in charge of, to entrust with (**b**) *Com (mercancías)* to order, to place an order for; *(encuesta)* to commission
  2 encargarse *vpr* **e. de** to see to, to deal with

encargo *nm* (**a**) *Com* order; **hecho de e.** *(a petición)* made to order (**b**) *(recado)* errand (**c**) *(tarea)* job, assignment

encariñarse *vpr* **e. con** to become fond of, to get attached to

encarnación *nf* incarnation, embodiment

encarnado,-a *adj (rojo)* red

encarnar *vt* to personify, to embody

encarnizado,-a *adj* fierce

encarrilar *vt (coche, tren)* to put on the road *o* rails; *Fig* to put on the right track

encasillar *vt* to pigeonhole

encausar *vt* to prosecute

encauzar [40] *vt* to channel

encenagarse [42] *vpr* to get covered in mud

encendedor *nm* lighter

encender [3] **1** *vt* (**a**) *(luz, radio, tele)* to switch on, to put on; *(cigarro, vela, fuego)* to light; *(cerilla)* to strike, to light (**b**) *Fig* to inflame, to stir up
  2 encenderse *vpr* (**a**) *(fuego)* to catch; *(luz)* to go *o* come on (**b**) *(cara)* to blush, to go red

encendido *nm* ignition

encerado *nm (pizarra)* blackboard

encerar *vt* to wax, polish

encerrar [1] **1** *vt* (**a**) to shut in; *(con llave)* to lock in (**b**) *Fig (contener)* to contain, to include
  2 encerrarse *vpr* to shut oneself up *o* in; *(con llave)* to lock oneself in

encestar *vi Dep* to score (a basket)

enchaquetado,-a *adj* smartly dressed

encharcar [44] **1** *vt* to flood, to swamp
  2 encharcarse *vpr* to get flooded

enchilada *nf Culin* = stuffed corn tortilla seasoned with chilli

enchironar *vt Fam* to put away

enchufado,-a 1 *adj Fam* **estar e.** to have good connections *o* contacts
  2 *nm,f Fam (favorito)* pet

enchufar *vt* (**a**) *Elec* to plug in (**b**) *(unir)* to join, to connect (**c**) *Fam (para un trabajo)* to pull strings for

enchufe *nm* (**a**) *Elec (hembra)* socket; *(macho)* plug (**b**) *Fam* contact

enchufismo *nm Fam* string-pulling

encía *nf* gum

enciclopedia *nf* encyclopedia

encierro *nm Pol (protesta)* sit-in

encima *adv* (**a**) on top; *(arriba)* above; *(en el aire)* overhead; **déjalo e.** put it on top; **¿llevas cambio e.?** do you have any change on you?; *Fig* **quitarse algo de e.** to get rid of sth; **ahí e.** up there (**b**) *(además)* besides (**c**) **e. de** *(sobre)* on; *(en el aire)* above; *Fig (además)* besides; **e. de la mesa** on the table (**d**) **por e.** above; *Fig* **por e. de sus posibilidades** beyond his abilities; **leer un libro por e.** to skip through a book

encimera *nf (de cocina)* worktop

encina *nf* holm oak

encinta *adj* pregnant

enclaustrarse *vpr* to shut oneself up

enclave *nm* enclave

enclenque *adj (débil)* puny; *(enfermizo)* sickly

encoger [53] **1** *vi (contraerse)* to contract; *(prenda)* to shrink
  2 *vt* to contract; *(prenda)* to shrink
  3 encogerse *vpr (contraerse)* to contract; *(prenda)* to shrink; **e. de hombros** to shrug (one's shoulders)

encolar *vt (papel)* to paste; *(madera)* to glue

encolerizar [40] **1** *vt* to infuriate, to anger
  2 encolerizarse *vpr* to become furious

encomendar [1] **1** *vt* to entrust with, to put in charge of
  2 encomendarse *vpr* **e. a** to entrust oneself to

encomienda *nf* (a) assignment, mission (b) *(paquete postal)* parcel

encomio *nm* praise

enconado,-a *adj* (a) *(discusión)* bitter, fierce (b) *Med* inflamed, sore

enconarse *vpr* (a) *(exasperarse)* to get angry o irritated (b) *Med (herida)* to become inflamed o sore

encono *nm* spitefulness, ill feeling

encontrado,-a *adj (contrario)* conflicting

encontrar [2] **1** *vt* (a) *(hallar)* to find; **no lo encuentro** I can't find it; **lo encuentro muy agradable** I find it very pleasant (b) *(dar con)* to meet; *(problema)* to run into, to come up against

2 encontrarse *vpr* (a) *(persona)* to meet (b) *(sentirse)* to feel, to be; **e. a gusto** to feel comfortable (c) *(estar)* to be

encontronazo *nm* (a) *(choque)* collision, crash (b) *Fig (de ideas etc)* clash

encorvar 1 *vt* to bend

2 encorvarse *vpr* to stoop o bend (over)

encrespar 1 *vt* (a) *(pelo)* to curl (b) *(mar)* to make choppy o rough (c) *Fig (enfurecer)* to infuriate

2 encresparse *vpr* (a) *(mar)* to get rough (b) *Fig (enfurecerse)* to get cross o irritated

encrucijada *nf* crossroads

encrudecer [33] *vi*, **encrudecerse** *vpr* to get worse

encuadernación *nf* (a) *(oficio)* bookbinding (b) *(cubierta)* binding

encuadernador,-a *nm,f* bookbinder

encuadernar *vt* to bind

encuadrar *vt* (a) *(imagen etc)* to frame (b) *(fig (encajar)* to fit, to insert

encuadre *nm Cin & TV* framing

encubierto,-a *adj (secreto)* hidden; *(operación)* covert

encubridor,-a *nm,f Jur* accessory (after the fact), abettor

encubrir *vt* to conceal

encuentro *nm* (a) encounter, meeting (b) *Dep* meeting, match; **e. amistoso** friendly (match)

encuesta *nf* (a) *(sondeo)* (opinion) poll, survey (b) *(investigación)* investigation, inquiry

encuestador,-a *nm,f* pollster

encuestar *vt* to poll

encumbrar 1 *vt* to exalt

2 encumbrarse *vpr* to rise to a high (social) position

ende: • **por ende** *loc adv* therefore

endeble *adj* weak, feeble

endeblez *nf* weakness, feebleness

endémico,-a *adj Med* endemic; *Fig* chronic

endemoniado,-a *adj* (a) *(poseso)* possessed (b) *Fig (travieso)* mischievous

enderezar [40] **1** *vt (poner derecho)* to straighten out; *(poner vertical)* to set upright

2 enderezarse *vpr* to straighten up

endeudarse *vpr* to get o fall into debt

endiablado,-a *adj* (a) *(poseso)* possessed (b) *(travieso)* mischievous, devilish

endibia *nf* endive

endiosar *vt* to deify

endomingarse [42] *vpr Fam* to put on one's Sunday best

endosar *vt* (a) *(cheque)* to endorse (b) *Fam* **e. algo a algn** *(tarea)* to lumber sb with sthg

endrina *nf Bot* sloe

endrogarse [42] *vpr Am* to take drugs, to use drugs

endulzar [40] *vt* to sweeten

endurecer [33] **1** *vt* to harden

2 endurecerse *vpr* to harden, to become hard

enebro *nm* juniper

enema *nm* enema

enemigo,-a 1 *adj* enemy; **soy e. de la bebida** I'm against drink

2 *nm,f* enemy

enemistad *nf* hostility, enmity

enemistar 1 *vt* to set at odds, to cause a rift between

2 enemistarse *vpr* to become enemies; **e. con algn** to fall out with sb

energético,-a *adj* energy

energía *nf* energy; **e. hidráulica/nuclear** hydro-electric/nuclear power; *Fig* **e. vital** vitality

enérgico,-a *adj* energetic; *(decisión)* firm; *(tono)* emphatic

energúmeno,-a *nm,f Fam (hombre)* madman; *(mujer)* mad woman; **ponerse como un e.** to go up the wall

enero *nm* January

enervante *adj* enervating

enervar *vt* to enervate

enésimo,-a *adj* (a) *Mat* nth (b) *Fam* umpteenth; **por enésima vez** for the umpteenth time

enfadado,-a *adj (enojado)* angry; *(molesto)* annoyed; **estamos enfadados** we've fallen out with each other

enfadar 1 *vt* to make angry o annoyed

2 enfadarse *vpr* (a) to get angry (con with) (b) *(dos personas)* to fall out

enfado *nm* anger; *(desavenencia)* fall-out

enfangarse [42] *vpr* to get muddy; *Fig* to

get involved (in dirty business)

énfasis *nm inv* emphasis, stress; **poner e. en algo** to lay stress on sth

enfático,-a *adj* emphatic

enfatizar [40] *vt* to emphasize, to stress

enfermar *vi*, **enfermarse** *vpr* to become *o* fall ill, to be taken ill

enfermedad *nf* illness; *(contagiosa)* disease

enfermería *nf* infirmary

enfermero,-a *nm,f (mujer)* nurse; *(hombre)* male nurse

enfermizo,-a *adj* unhealthy, sickly

enfermo,-a 1 *adj* ill; **caer e.** to be taken ill; *Fam* **esa gente me pone e.** those people make me sick
  2 *nm,f* ill person; *(paciente)* patient

enfervorizar [40] *vt* to enthuse

enfilar *vi* **e. hacia** to make for

enflaquecer [33] *vt (adelgazar)* to make thin; *(debilitar)* to weaken

enfocado,-a *adj Fot* **bien/mal enfocado** in/out of focus

enfocar [44] *vt* (a) *(imagen)* to focus; *(persona)* to focus on (b) *(tema)* to approach (c) *(con linterna)* to shine a light on

enfoque *nm* (a) focus; *(acción)* focusing (b) *(de un tema)* approach

enfrentamiento *nm* clash

enfrentar 1 *vt* (a) *(situación, peligro)* to confront (b) *(enemistar)* to set at odds
  2 enfrentarse *vpr* (a) **e. con** *o* **a** to face up to, to confront (b) *Dep* **enfrentarse (a)** *(rival)* to meet

enfrente *adv* (a) opposite, facing; **la casa de e.** the house opposite *o* across the road (b) **e. de.** opposite (to), facing; **e. del colegio** opposite the school

enfriamiento *nm* (a) *(proceso)* cooling (b) *Med (catarro)* cold, chill

enfriar [29] 1 *vt* to cool (down), to chill
  2 *vi* to cool down
  3 enfriarse *vpr* (a) to get *o* go cold (b) *(resfriarse)* to get *o* catch a cold (c) *Fig (pasión)* to cool down

enfurecer [33] 1 *vt* to enrage, to infuriate
  2 enfurecerse *vpr* to get furious, to lose one's temper

enfurruñarse *vpr Fam* to sulk

engalanar 1 *vt* to deck out, to adorn
  2 engalanarse *vpr* to dress up, to get dressed up

enganchado,-a *adj Fam* **estar e. (a la droga)** to be hooked (on drugs)

enganchar 1 *vt* (a) to hook; *Ferroc* to couple (b) *Fam (pillar)* to nab
  2 engancharse *vpr* to get caught *o*

hooked; *Fam (a la droga)* to get hooked

enganche *nm (gancho)* hook; *Ferroc* coupling

engañabobos *nm inv (persona)* con man, confidence trickster; *(truco)* con trick

engañar 1 *vt* to deceive, to mislead; *(estafar)* to cheat, to trick; *(mentir a)* to lie to; *(al marido, mujer)* to be unfaithful to
  2 engañarse *vpr* to deceive oneself

engañifa *nf Fam* swindle

engaño *nm* (a) deceit; *(estafa)* fraud, swindle; *(mentira)* lie (b) *(error)* mistake, misunderstanding

engañoso,-a *adj (palabras)* deceitful; *(apariencias)* deceptive; *(consejo)* misleading

engarzar [40] *vt* (a) *(unir)* to link (b) *(engastar)* to mount, to set

engastar *vt* to set, to mount

engatusar *vt Fam* to coax; **e. a algn para que haga algo** to coax sb into doing sth

engendrar *vt* (a) *Biol* to engender (b) *Fig* to give rise to, to cause

engendro *nm* freak

englobar *vt* to include

engomar *vt* to gum, to glue

engordar 1 *vt* to fatten (up), to make fat
  2 *vi* (a) to put on weight, to get fat; **he engordado 3 kilos** I've put on 3 kilos (b) *(comida, bebida)* to be fattening

engorro *nm Fam* bother, nuisance

engorroso,-a *adj Fam* bothersome, tiresome

engranaje *nm* (a) *Téc* gearing (b) *Fig* machinery

engranar *vt Téc* to engage

engrandecer [33] *vt* to exalt

engrasar *vt* (a) *(lubricar)* to lubricate, to oil (b) *(manchar)* to make greasy, to stain with grease

engrase *nm* lubrication

engreído,-a *adj* vain, conceited

engreírse [56] *vpr* to become vain *o* conceited

engrosar [2] *vt (incrementar)* to enlarge; *(cantidad)* to increase, to swell

engrudo *nm* paste

enguatar *vt* to pad

engullir *vt* to gobble up

enharinar *vt* to cover with flour

enhebrar *vt* to thread

enhorabuena *nf* congratulations; **dar la e. a algn** to congratulate sb

enigma *nm* enigma

enigmático,-a *adj* enigmatic

enjabonar *vt* to soap

enjalbegar [42] *vt* to whitewash

enjambre *nm* swarm

enjaular *vt* (**a**) *(animal)* to cage (**b**) *Fam* to put inside, to put in jail

enjuagar [42] *vt* to rinse

enjuague *nm* rinse; **e. bucal** mouthwash

enjugar [42] *vt*, **enjugarse** *vpr* (**a**) *(secar)* to mop up; *(lágrimas)* to wipe away (**b**) *(deuda, déficit)* to clear, to wipe out

enjuiciamiento *nm* (**a**) *(opinión)* judgement (**b**) *Jur (civil)* lawsuit; *(criminal)* trial, prosecution

enjuiciar [43] *vt* (**a**) *(juzgar)* to judge, to examine (**b**) *Jur (criminal)* to indict, to prosecute

enjundia *nf Fig (sustancia)* substance; *(importancia)* importance

enjuto,-a *adj* lean, skinny

enlace *nm* (**a**) *(unión)* link, connection; **e. químico** chemical bond (**b**) *Ferroc* connection (**c**) *(casamiento)* marriage (**d**) *(persona)* liaison officer; **e. sindical** shop steward

enlatado,-a *adj* canned, tinned

enlatar *vt* to can, to tin

enlazar [40] *vt & vi* to link, to connect (**con** with)

enlodar *vt* (**a**) *(enfangar)* to muddy, to cover with mud (**b**) *Fig (reputación)* to stain, to besmirch

enloquecedor,-a *adj* maddening

enloquecer [33] **1** *vi* to go mad

2 *vt* (**a**) *(volver loco)* to drive mad (**b**) *Fam* **me enloquecen las motos** I'm mad about motorbikes

3 **enloquecerse** *vpr* to go mad, to go out of one's mind

enlosar *vt* to tile

enlucir [35] *vt (pared)* to plaster; *(plata, oro)* to polish

enlutado,-a *adj* in mourning

enmadrado,-a *adj* **estar e.** to be tied to one's mother's apron strings

enmarañar **1** *vt* (**a**) *(pelo)* to tangle (**b**) *Fig (complicar)* to complicate, confuse

2 **enmarañarse** *vpr* (**a**) *(pelo)* to get tangled (**b**) *Fig (situación)* to get confused, to get into a mess *o* a muddle

enmarcar [44] *vt* to frame

enmascarar **1** *vt* (**a**) to mask (**b**) *(problema, la verdad)* to mask, to disguise

2 **enmascararse** *vpr* to put on a mask

enmendar [1] **1** *vt (corregir)* to correct, to put right; *Jur* to amend

2 **enmendarse** *vpr (persona)* to reform, to mend one's ways

enmienda *nf* correction; *Jur & Pol* amendment

enmohecerse [33] *vpr (metal)* to rust, to

get rusty; *Bot* to go mouldy

enmoquetar *vt* to carpet

enmudecer [33] *vi (callar)* to fall silent; *Fig* to be dumbstruck

ennegrecer [33] *vt*, **ennegrecerse** *vpr* to blacken, to turn black

ennoblecer *vt* to ennoble

enojadizo,-a *adj* irritable, touchy

enojado,-a *adj (enojado)* angry; *(molesto)* annoyed;

enojar 1 *vt* to anger, to annoy

2 **enojarse** *vpr* to get angry, to lose one's temper

enojo *nm* anger, annoyance

enorgullecer [33] **1** *vt* to fill with pride

2 **enorgullecerse** *vpr* to be *o* feel proud (**de** of)

enorme *adj* enormous

enormidad *nf* enormity; *Fam* **una e.** loads

enraizado,-a *adj* rooted

enraizar [40] *vi*, **enraizarse** *vpr (persona)* to put down roots; *(planta, costumbre)* to take root

enrarecerse [33] *vpr (aire)* to become rarefied

enredadera *nf* climbing plant, creeper

enredar 1 *vt* (**a**) *(pelo)* to entangle, to tangle up (**b**) *Fig (asunto)* to confuse, to complicate (**c**) *Fig (implicar)* to involve (**en** in) (**d**) *(confundir)* to mix up

2 **enredarse** *vpr* (**a**) *(pelo)* to get entangled, to get tangled (up) *o* in a tangle (**b**) *Fig (asunto)* to get complicated *o* confused (**c**) *Fig* **e. con** *(involucrarse)* to get involved with (**d**) *(confundirse)* to get mixed up

enredo *nm* (**a**) *(maraña)* tangle (**b**) *Fig (lío)* muddle, mess

enrejado *nm (de ventana)* lattice

enrevesado,-a *adj* complicated, difficult

enriquecer [33] **1** *vt* to make rich; *Fig* to enrich

2 **enriquecerse** *vpr* to get *o* become rich, to prosper; *Fig* to become enriched

enrocar [44] *vi (en ajedrez)* to castle

enrojecer [33] **1** *vt* to redden, to turn red

2 *vi (ruborizarse)* to blush

3 **enrojecerse** *vpr* to blush

enrolarse *vpr* to enrol, to sign on; *Mil* to enlist, to join up

enrollado,-a *adj* (**a**) rolled up (**b**) *(persona)* great (**c**) *Fam* **estar e. con algn** *(estar saliendo con)* to go out with sb

enrollar 1 *vt* to roll up; *(cable)* to coil; *(hilo)* to wind up

2 **enrollarse** *vpr* (**a**) *Fam (hablar)* to chatter, to go on and on (**b**) *Fam* **e. con**

algn *(tener relaciones)* to have an affair with sb

> 🖉 Observa que el verbo inglés **to enrol** es un falso amigo y no es la traducción del verbo español **enrollar**. En inglés, **to enrol** significa "matricular, inscribir".

enroque *nm (en ajedrez)* castling

enroscar [44] 1 *vt* (**a**) (to coil (round), to wind (**b**) *(tornillo, tapón)* to screw in o on

  2 enroscarse *vpr* to coil, to wind

ensaimada *nf* = kind of spiral pastry from Majorca

ensalada *nf* salad

ensaladera *nf* salad bowl

ensaladilla *nf* e. rusa Russian salad

ensalzar [40] *vt (enaltecer)* to exalt; *(elogiar)* to praise, to extol

ensamblador *nm Informát* assembler

ensamblaje *nm Téc* assembly

ensamblar *vt* to assemble

ensanchar 1 *vt* to enlarge, to widen; *Cost* to let out

  2 ensancharse *vpr* to get wider

ensanche *nm* enlargement, widening; *(de ciudad)* urban development

ensangrentado,-a *adj* bloodstained, covered in blood

ensangrentar [1] *vt* to stain with blood, to cover in blood

ensañarse *vpr* e. con to be brutal with; *(cebarse)* to delight in tormenting

ensartar *vt* (**a**) *(perlas etc)* to string together (**b**) *(mentiras etc)* to reel off, to rattle off

ensayar *vt* to test, to try out; *Teatro* to rehearse; *Mús* to practise

ensayista *nmf* essayist

ensayo *nm* (**a**) *(prueba)* test, trial (**b**) *Teatro* rehearsal; **e. general** dress rehearsal (**c**) *(escrito)* essay

enseguida, en seguida *adv (inmediatamente)* at once, straight away; *(poco después)* in a minute, soon; **e. voy** I'll be right there

ensenada *nf* inlet, cove

enseña *nf* ensign, standard

enseñanza *nf* (**a**) *(educación)* education (**b**) *(de idioma etc)* teaching (**c**) **enseñanzas** teachings

enseñar *vt* (**a**) to teach; **e. a algn a hacer algo** to teach sb how to do sth (**b**) *(mostrar)* to show; *(señalar)* to point out

enseres *nmpl (bártulos)* belongings, goods; *(de trabajo)* tools

ensillar *vt* to saddle (up)

ensimismado,-a *adj (en la lectura etc)* engrossed; *(abstraído)* lost in thought

ensimismarse *vpr (en la lectura etc)* to become engrossed; *(abstraerse)* to be lost in thought

ensombrecer [33] 1 *vt* to cast a shadow over

  2 ensombrecerse *vpr* to darken

ensopar *vt Am* to soak

ensordecedor,-a *adj* deafening

ensordecer [33] 1 *vt* to deafen

  2 *vi* to go deaf

ensortijado,-a *adj* curly

ensuciar [43] 1 *vt* (**a**) to get dirty (**b**) *Fig (reputación)* to harm, to damage

  2 ensuciarse *vpr* to get dirty

ensueño *nm* dream; **una casa de e.** a dream house

entablado *nm* (**a**) *(entarimado)* planking, planks (**b**) *(suelo)* wooden floor

entablar *vt* (**a**) *(conversación)* to open, to begin; *(amistad)* to strike up; *(negocios)* to start (**b**) *(en juegos de tablero)* to set up (**c**) *(pleito)* to initiate

entablillar *vt Med* to splint

entallado,-a *adj (vestido)* close-fitting; *(camisa)* fitted

entallar 1 *vt* to take in at the waist

  2 *vi* to fit at the waist

entarimado *nm* parquet floor

entarimar *vt* to cover with parquet

ente *nm* (**a**) *(institución)* organization, body; **e. público** public service organization (**b**) *(ser)* being

entendederas *nfpl Fam* brains; **ser duro de e.** to be slow on the uptake

entender [3] 1 *vt (comprender)* to understand; **a mi e.** to my way of thinking; **dar a algn a e. que ...** to give sb to understand that ...

  2 *vi* (**a**) *(comprender)* to understand (**b**) **e. de** *(saber)* to know about

  3 entenderse *vpr* (**a**) *(comprenderse)* to be understood, to be meant (**b**) *Fam* **e. (bien) con** to get on (well) with

entendido,-a 1 *nm,f* expert

  2 *adj* **tengo e. que ...** I understand that ...

entendimiento *nm* understanding

enterado,-a 1 *adj* knowledgeable, well-informed; **estar e.** to be in the know; **estar e. de ...** to be aware of ...

  2 *nm,f (listillo)* know-all

enteramente *adv* entirely, completely

enterar 1 *vt* to inform (**de** about o of)

  2 enterarse *vpr* to find out; **me he enterado de que ...** I understand ...; **ni me enteré** I didn't even realize it

entereza *nf* strength of character

enternecedor,-a *adj* moving, touching

enternecer [33] 1 *vt* to move, to touch

2 enternecerse *vpr* to be moved *o* touched

entero,-a 1 *adj* (**a**) *(completo)* entire, whole; **por e.** completely (**b**) *Fig (íntegro)* honest, upright (**c**) *Fig (firme)* strong

2 *nm* (**a**) *Mat* whole number (**b**) *Fin* point

enterrador *nm* gravedigger

enterramiento *nm* burial

enterrar [1] *vt* to bury

entidad *nf* organization; **e. comercial** company, firm

entierro *nm* (**a**) burial (**b**) *(ceremonia)* funeral

entomología *nf* entomology

entonación *nf* intonation

entonar 1 *vt* (**a**) *(canto)* to sing (**b**) *Med* to tone up

2 *vi* to be in harmony, to be in tune (**con** with)

entonces *adv* then; **por aquel e.** at that time; **el e. ministro** the then minister

entornar *vt (ojos etc)* to half-close; *(puerta)* to leave ajar

entorno *nm* environment

entorpecer [33] *vt (obstaculizar)* to hinder, to impede

entrada *nf* (**a**) entrance (**b**) *(billete)* ticket; *(recaudación)* takings (**c**) **de e.** for a start (**d**) *Culin* entrée (**e**) *Com* entry; *(pago inicial)* down payment, deposit; **e. de capital** capital inflow (**f**) *Com* **entradas** *(ingresos)* receipts, takings (**g**) *(en la frente)* receding hairline

entrado,-a *adj* **e. en años** advanced in years; **hasta bien entrada la noche** well into the night

entramado *nm* framework; *(de sistema etc)* network

entramparse *vpr Fam* to get into debt

entrante 1 *adj* coming; **el mes e.** next month; **el ministro e.** the incoming minister

2 *Culin* starter

entrañable *adj* (**a**) *(lugar)* intimate, close (**b**) *(persona)* affectionate, warmhearted

entrañar *vt* to entail

entrañas *nfpl* bowels

entrar 1 *vi* (**a**) to come in, to go in, to enter; **Fig no me entran las matemáticas** I can't get the hang of maths (**b**) *(encajar)* to fit (**c**) **el año que entra** next year, the coming year (**d**) *(venir)* to come over; **me entró dolor de cabeza** I got a headache; **me entraron ganas de reír** I felt like laughing

2 *vt* (**a**) to introduce (**b**) *Informát* to enter

entre *prep* (**a**) *(dos)* between (**b**) *(más de dos)* among(st)

entreabierto,-a *adj (ojos etc)* half-open; *(puerta)* ajar

entreacto *nm* interval, intermission

entrecejo *nm* space between the eyebrows; **fruncir el e.** to frown, to knit one's brow

entrecortado,-a *adj (voz)* faltering, hesitant

entrecot *nm* fillet steak

entrecruzar [40] *vt*, **entrecruzarse** *vpr* to entwine

entredicho *nm* (**a**) *Jur* injunction (**b**) **estar en e.** to be suspect; **poner algo en e.** to bring sth into question

entrega *nf* (**a**) *(de productos)* delivery; *(de premios)* presentation (**b**) *(fascículo)* part, instalment (**c**) *(devoción)* selflessness

entregar [42] **1** *vt* to hand over; *(deberes etc)* to give in, to hand in; *Com* to deliver

2 entregarse *vpr* (**a**) *(rendirse)* to give in, to surrender (**b**) **e. a** to devote oneself to; *Pey* to indulge in

entreguismo *nm Pol* appeasement

entrelazar [40] *vt*, **entrelazarse** *vpr* to entwine

entremedias *adv* in between; *(mientras tanto)* meanwhile, in the meantime

entremés *nm Culin* hors d'oeuvres

entremeterse *vpr* = entremeterse

entremezclarse *vpr* to mix, to mingle

entrenador,-a *nm,f* trainer, coach

entrenamiento *nm* training

entrenar *vi*, **entrenarse** *vpr* to train

entrepierna *nf* crotch, crutch

entresacar [44] *vt* to pick out, to select

entresijos *nmpl* nooks and crannies

entresuelo *nm* mezzanine

entretanto 1 *adv* meanwhile

2 *nm* **en el e.** in the meantime

entretejer *vt* to interweave

entretención *nf Am* amusement, entertainment

entretener [24] **1** *vt* (**a**) *(divertir)* to entertain, to amuse (**b**) *(retrasar)* to delay; *(detener)* to hold up, to detain

2 entretenerse *vpr* (**a**) *(distraerse)* to amuse oneself, to while away the time (**b**) *(retrasarse)* to be delayed, to be held up

entretenido,-a *adj* enjoyable, entertaining

entretenimiento *nm* entertainment, amusement

entretiempo: •de entretiempo *loc adj* **ropa de e.** lightweight clothing

entrever [28] *vt* to glimpse, to catch sight of; *Fig* dejó e. que ... she hinted that ...

entrevista *nf* interview

entrevistador,-a *nm,f* interviewer

entrevistar 1 *vt* to interview

2 entrevistarse *upr* **e. con algn** to have an interview with sb

entristecer [33] **1** *vt* to sadden, to make sad

2 entristecerse *upr* to be sad (**por** about)

entrometerse *upr* to meddle, to interfere (**en** in)

entrometido,-a 1 *nm,f* meddler, busybody

2 *adj* interfering

entroncar *vi* to connect

entumecer [33] **1** *vt* to numb

2 entumecerse *upr* to go numb

entumecido,-a *adj* numb

enturbiar [43] **1** *vt* (**a**) *(agua)* to make cloudy (**b**) *Fig (asunto)* to cloud, to obscure

2 enturbiarse *upr* to become cloudy

entusiasmar 1 *vt* to fill with enthusiasm

2 entusiasmarse *upr* to get excited *o* enthusiastic (**con** about)

entusiasmo *nm* enthusiasm; **con e.** enthusiastically

entusiasta 1 *adj* enthusiastic, keen (**de** on)

2 *nmf* enthusiast

enumerar *vt* to enumerate

enunciado *nm (de teoría, problema)* wording

envainar *vt* to sheathe

envanecer [33] **1** *vt* to make proud *o* vain

2 envanecerse *upr* to become conceited *o* proud, to give oneself airs

envasado,-a 1 *nm (en botella)* bottling; *(en paquete)* packing; *(en lata)* canning

2 *adj* **e. al vacío** vacuum-packed

envasar *vt (embotellar)* to bottle; *(empaquetar)* to pack; *(enlatar)* to can, to tin

envase *nm* (**a**) *(acto)* packing; *(de botella)* bottling; *(de lata)* canning (**b**) *(recipiente)* container (**c**) *(botella vacía)* empty

envejecer [33] **1** *vi* to grow old

2 *vt* to age

envejecimiento *nm* ageing

envenenar *vt* to poison

envergadura *nf* (**a**) *(importancia)* importance, scope; **de gran e.** large-scale (**b**) *(de pájaro, avión)* span, wingspan; *Náut* breadth (of sail)

envés *nm* other side

envestidura *nf* investiture

enviado,-a *nm,f* envoy; *Prensa* **e.**

especial special correspondent

enviar [29] *vt* to send

enviciarse [43] *upr* to become addicted (**con** to)

envidia *nf* envy; **tener e. de algn** to envy sb

envidiable *adj* enviable

envidiar [43] *vt* to envy; **no tener nada que e.** to be in no way inferior (**a** to)

envidioso,-a *adj* envious

> 🖉 Observa que la palabra inglesa **invidious** es un falso amigo y no es la traducción de la palabra española **envidioso**. En inglés, **invidious** significa "ingrato" o "injusto".

envilecer [33] *vt* to degrade, to debase

envío *nm* sending; *(remesa)* consignment; *(paquete)* parcel; **gastos de e.** postage and packing; **e. contra reembolso** cash on delivery

enviudar *vi (hombre)* to become a widower, to lose one's wife; *(mujer)* to become a widow, to lose one's husband

envoltorio *nm*, **envoltura** *nf* wrapper, wrapping

envolver [4] *(pp* envuelto) **1** *vt* (**a**) *(con papel)* to wrap (**b**) *(cubrir)* to envelop (**c**) *(en complot etc)* to involve (**en** in)

2 envolverse *upr* (**a**) to wrap oneself up (**en** in) (**b**) *(implicarse)* to become involved (**en** in)

enyesar *vt* to plaster; *Med* to put in plaster

enzima *nf* enzyme

épica *nf* epic poetry

epicentro *nm* epicentre

épico,-a *adj* epic

epidemia *nf* epidemic

epilepsia *nf* epilepsy

epílogo *nm* epilogue

episcopal *adj* episcopal

episodio *nm* episode

epístola *nf* epistle

epitafio *nm* epitaph

epíteto *nm* epithet

época *nf* time; *Hist* period, epoch; *Agr* season; **en esta é. del año** at this time of the year; **hacer é.** to be a landmark; **mueble de é.** period furniture

equidad *nf* equity

equilátero *adj* equilateral

equilibrar *vt* to balance

equilibrio *nm* balance

equilibrismo *nm* balancing act

equilibrista *nmf* (**a**) tightrope walker (**b**) *Am Pol* opportunist

equipaje *nm* luggage; **hacer el e.** to pack, do the packing

equipar *vt* to equip, to furnish (**con** *o* **de** with)

equiparable *adj* comparable (**a** to; **con** with)

equiparar *vt* to compare (**con** with), to liken (**con** to)

equipo *nm* (**a**) *(de expertos, jugadores)* team (**b**) *(aparatos)* equipment; **e. de alta fidelidad** hi-fi stereo system (**c**) *(ropas)* outfit

equis *nf* = name of the letter X in Spanish

equitación *nf* horse *o* US horseback riding

equitativo,-a *adj* equitable, fair

equivalente *adj* equivalent

equivaler [26] *vi* to be equivalent (**a** to)

equivocación *nf* error, mistake

equivocado,-a *adj* mistaken, wrong

equivocar [44] **1** *vt* to mix up

2 equivocarse *vpr* to make a mistake; *Tel* **se equivocó de número** he dialled the wrong number; **se equivocó de fecha** he got the wrong date

equívoco,-a 1 *adj* equivocal, misleading

2 *nm* misunderstanding

era¹ *nf (época)* era, age

era² *nf Agr* threshing floor

era³ *pt indef de* **ser**

erario *nm* exchequer, treasury

eras *pt indef de* **ser**

erección *nf* erection

erecto,-a *adj* upright; *(pene)* erect

eres *indic pres de* **ser**

erguir [55] **1** *vt* to erect

2 erguirse *vpr* to straighten up, to stand/sit up straight

erial *nm* uncultivated land

erigir [57] **1** *vt* to erect

2 erigirse *vpr* **e. en algo** to set oneself up in sth

erizado,-a *adj* bristly, prickly

erizarse [40] *vpr* to bristle, to stand on end

erizo *nm* hedgehog; **e. de mar** *o* **marino** sea urchin

ermita *nf* hermitage

> *𝄃* Observa que la palabra inglesa **hermit** es un falso amigo y no es la traducción de la palabra española **ermita**. En inglés, **hermit** significa "ermitaño".

ermitaño,-a *nm,f* hermit

erosión *nf* erosion

erosionar *vt* to erode

erótico,-a *adj* erotic

erotismo *nm* eroticism

erradicar [44] *vt* to eradicate

errante *adj* wandering

errar [50] **1** *vt* to miss, to get wrong

2 *vi* (**a**) *(vagar)* to wander, to roam (**b**) *(fallar)* to err

errata *nf* erratum, misprint

erre *nf* **e. que e.** stubbornly, pigheadedly

erróneo,-a *adj* erroneous, wrong

error *nm* error, mistake; *Informát* bug; **por e.** by mistake, in error; *Impr* **e. de imprenta** misprint; **caer en un e.** to make a mistake

Ertzaintza *nf* = Basque police force

eructar *vi* to belch, to burp

eructo *nm* belch, burp

erudición *nf* erudition

erudito,-a 1 *adj* erudite, learned

2 *nm,f* scholar

erupción *nf* (**a**) *(de volcán)* eruption (**b**) *(en la piel)* rash

es *indic pres de* **ser**

esa *adj dem ver* **ese**

ésa *pron dem ver* **ése**

esbelto,-a *adj* slender

esbirro *nm* henchman

esbozar [40] *vt* to sketch, to outline

esbozo *nm* sketch, outline, rough draft

escabeche *nm* brine

escabechina *nf* massacre

escabroso,-a *adj* (**a**) *(espinoso)* tricky (**b**) *(indecente)* crude

escabullirse *vpr* to slip away, to scuttle *o* scurry off

escacharrar *vt Fam* to break

escafandra *nf* diving suit; **e. espacial** spacesuit

escala *nf* (**a**) scale; *(de colores)* range; **e. musical** scale; **en gran e.** on a large scale (**b**) *(parada)* *Náut* port of call; *Av* stopover; **hacer e. en** to call in at, to stop over in (**c**) *(escalera)* ladder, stepladder

escalada *nf* (**a**) climb (**b**) *Fig (de violencia)* escalation; *(de precios)* rise

escalador,-a *nm,f* climber, mountaineer

> *𝄃* Observa que la palabra inglesa **escalator** es un falso amigo y no es la traducción de la palabra española **escalador**. En inglés, **escalator** significa "escalera mecánica".

escalafón *nm (graduación)* rank; *(de salarios)* salary *o* wage scale

escalar *vt* to climb, to scale

escaldar *vt* to scald

escalera *nf* (**a**) stair; **e. de incendios** fire escape; **e. mecánica** escalator; **e. de caracol** spiral staircase (**b**) *(escala)* ladder (**c**) *Naipes* run

escalerilla *nf (de piscina)* steps; *Náut* gangway; *Av* (boarding) ramp

escalfar *vt* to poach

escalinata *nf* stoop

escalofriante *adj* hair-raising, blood-curdling

escalofrío *nm* shiver; **me dio un e.** it gave me the shivers

escalón *nm* step; **e. lateral** *(en letrero)* ramp

escalonar *vt* to place at intervals, to space out

escalope *nm* escalope

escalpelo *nm* scalpel

escama *nf Zool* scale; *(de jabón)* flake

escamarse *vpr* to smell a rat, to become suspicious

escamotear *vt Fam* to diddle out of, to do out of

escampar *vi* to stop raining, to clear up

escanciar [43] *vt (vino)* to pour out, to serve

escandalizar [40] **1** *vt* to scandalize, to shock

   2 escandalizarse *vpr* to be shocked (**de** at o by)

escándalo *nm* (a) *(alboroto)* racket, din; **armar un e.** to kick up a fuss (b) *(desvergüenza)* scandal

escandaloso,-a *adj* (a) *(ruidoso)* noisy, rowdy (b) *(ofensivo)* scandalous

Escandinavia *n* Scandinavia

escandinavo,-a *adj & nm,f* Scandinavian

escáner *nm Med & Informát* scanner

escaño *nm Parl* seat

escapada *nf* (a) *(de prisión)* escape; *(en ciclismo)* breakaway (b) *(viaje rápido)* flying visit, quick trip

> 🖉 Observa que la palabra inglesa **escapade** es un falso amigo y no es la traducción de la palabra española **escapada**. En inglés, **escapade** significa "aventura".

escapar 1 *vi* to escape, to run away

   2 escaparse *vpr* (a) to escape, to run away; **se me escapó de las manos** it slipped out of my hands; **se me escapó el tren** I missed the train (b) *(gas etc)* to leak, to escape

escaparate *nm* shop window

escapatoria *nf* escape; **no tener e.** to have no way out

escape *nm* (a) *(de gas etc)* leak, escape (b) *Téc* exhaust; **tubo de e.** exhaust (pipe) (c) *(huida)* escape; *(escapatoria)* way out

escaquearse *vpr Fam* to duck out; **e. de hacer algo** to worm one's way out of doing sth

escarabajo *nm* beetle

escaramuza *nf Mil* skirmish; *Fig (riña)* squabble, brush

escarbar *vt* (a) *(suelo)* to scratch; *(fuego)* to poke (b) *Fig* to inquire into, to investigate

escarceo *nm* attempt

escarcha *nf* hoarfrost, frost

escarchado,-a *adj (fruta)* crystallized, candied

escardar *vt* to hoe

escardillo *nm* weeding hoe

escarlata *adj* scarlet

escarlatina *nf* scarlet fever

escarmentar [1] *vi* to learn one's lesson

escarmiento *nm* punishment, lesson

escarnio *nm* derision, mockery

escarola *nf* curly endive

escarpado,-a *adj (paisaje)* craggy; *(pendiente)* steep

escasear *vi* to be scarce

escasez *nf* scarcity

escaso,-a *adj* scarce; *(dinero)* tight; *(conocimientos)* scant; **e. de dinero** short of money

escatimar *vt* to skimp on; **no escatimó esfuerzos para ...** he spared no efforts to ...

escayola *nf* (a) plaster of Paris, stucco (b) *Med* plaster

escayolar *vt Med* to put in plaster

escena *nf* (a) scene (b) *(escenario)* stage; **poner en e.** to stage

escenario *nm* (a) *Teatro* stage (b) *(entorno)* scenario; *(de crimen)* scene; *(de película)* setting

escénico,-a *adj* scenic

escenografía *nf Cin* set design; *Teatro* stage design

escepticismo *nm* scepticism

escéptico,-a *adj & nm,f* sceptic

escindirse *vpr* to split (off) (**en** into)

escisión *nf* split

esclarecer [33] *vt* to shed light on

esclava *nf* bangle

esclavitud *nf* slavery

esclavizar [40] *vt* to enslave

esclavo,-a *adj & nm,f* slave

esclusa *nf* lock, sluicegate

escoba *nf* brush, broom

escocer [41] **1** *vi* to sting, to smart

   2 escocerse *vpr (piel)* to chafe

escocés,-esa 1 *adj* Scottish, Scots; **falda escocesa** kilt

   2 *nm,f (hombre)* Scotsman; *(mujer)* Scotswoman

Escocia *n* Scotland

escoger [53] *vt* to choose

escogido,-a *adj* chosen, selected;

(producto) choice, select; *Lit* **obras escogidas** selected works

escolar 1 *adj (curso, año)* school
  2 *nmf (niño)* schoolboy; *(niña)* schoolgirl

escolaridad *nf* schooling

escollo *nm* reef; *Fig* pitfall

escolta *nf* escort

escoltar *vt* to escort

escombros *nmpl* rubbish, debris

esconder 1 *vt* to hide (**de** from), to conceal (**de** from)
  2 esconderse *vpr* to hide (**de** from)

escondidas *adv* **a e.** secretly

escondite *nm* (**a**) *(lugar)* hiding place, hide-out (**b**) *(juego)* hide-and-seek

escondrijo *nm* hiding place, hide-out

escopeta *nf* shotgun; **e. de aire comprimido** air gun; **e. de cañones recortados** sawn-off shotgun

escopetazo *nm* gunshot

escorbuto *nm* scurvy

escoria *nf* (**a**) *(de metal)* slag (**b**) *Fig* scum, dregs

Escorpio *nm* Scorpio

escorpión *nm* scorpion

escotado,-a *adj* low-cut

escote *nm* low neckline

escotilla *nf* hatch, hatchway

escozor *nm* stinging, smarting

escribiente *nmf* clerk

escribir (*pp* **escrito**) **1** *vt* to write; **e. a mano** to write in longhand; **e. a máquina** to type
  2 escribirse *vpr* (**a**) *(dos personas)* to write to each other, to correspond (**b**) **se escribe con h** it is spelt with an h

escrito,-a 1 *adj* written; **e. a mano** handwritten, in longhand; **por e.** in writing
  2 *nm* writing

escritor,-a *nm,f* writer

escritorio *nm* (**a**) *(mueble)* writing desk, bureau; *(oficina)* office (**b**) *Informát* desktop

escritura *nf* (**a**) *Jur* deed, document; **e. de propiedad** title deed (**b**) *Rel* **Sagradas Escrituras** Holy Scriptures

escrúpulo *nm* (**a**) scruple; **una persona sin escrúpulos** an unscrupulous person (**b**) *(esmero)* care (**c**) **me da e.** *(asco)* it makes me feel squeamish

escrupuloso,-a *adj* (**a**) *(honesto)* scrupulous (**b**) *(meticuloso)* painstaking (**c**) *(delicado)* squeamish

escrutar *vt* (**a**) to scrutinize (**b**) *(votos)* to count

escrutinio *nm* (**a**) scrutiny (**b**) *(de votos)* count

escuadra *nf* (**a**) *(instrumento)* square (**b**) *Mil* squad; *Náut* squadron; *Dep* team; *(de coches)* fleet

escuadrilla *nf* *Náut* squadron

escuadrón *nm* *Av* squadron

escuálido,-a *adj* emaciated

escucha *nf* listening; **escuchas telefónicas** phone tapping; **estar a la e. de** to be listening out for

escuchar 1 *vt* to listen to; *(oír)* to hear
  2 *vi* to listen; *(oír)* to hear

escudarse *vpr* *Fig* **e. en algo** to hide behind sth

escudería *nf* motor racing team

escudilla *nf* bowl

escudo *nm* (**a**) *(arma defensiva)* shield (**b**) *(blasón)* coat of arms

escudriñar *vt* to scrutinize

escuela *nf* school; **e. de Bellas Artes** Art School; **e. de conducir/de idiomas** driving/language school

escueto,-a *adj* plain, unadorned

escuezo *indic pres de* **escocer**

esculcar [44] *vt Am* to search

esculpir *vt* to sculpt; *(madera)* to carve; *(metal)* to engrave

escultor,-a *nm,f (hombre)* sculptor; *(mujer)* sculptress; *(de madera)* woodcarver; *(de metales)* engraver

escultura *nf* sculpture

escultural *adj* sculptural; *(persona)* statuesque

escupidera *nf* (**a**) *(recipiente)* spittoon (**b**) *(orinal)* chamberpot

escupir 1 *vi* to spit
  2 *vt* to spit out

escupitajo *nm* *Fam* spit

escurreplatos *nm inv* dish rack

escurridizo,-a *adj* (**a**) *(resbaladizo)* slippery (**b**) *Fig (huidizo)* elusive, slippery

escurridor *nm* colander; *(escurreplatos)* dish rack

escurrir 1 *vt (plato, vaso)* to drain; *(ropa)* to wring out; **e. el bulto** to wriggle out
  2 escurrirse *vpr* (**a**) *(platos etc)* to drip (**b**) *(escaparse)* to run *o* slip away (**c**) *(resbalarse)* to slip

escúter *nm* *(motor)* scooter

ese,-a *adj dem* (**a**) that (**b**) **esos,-as** those

ése,-a *pron dem m,f* (**a**) that one (**b**) **ésos,-as** those *(ones)*; *Fam* **¡ni por ésas!** no way!; *Fam* **¡no me vengas con ésas!** come off it!

> Note that **ése** and its various forms can be written without an accent when there is no risk of confusion with the adjective.

esencia *nf* essence

esencial *adj* essential; **lo e.** the main thing

esencialmente *adv* essentially

esfera *nf* (a) sphere; *Fig* sphere, field (b) *(de reloj de pulsera)* dial; *(de reloj de pared)* face

esférico,-a 1 *adj* spherical

　2 *nm (balón)* ball

esfinge *nf* sphinx

esforzarse [2] *upr* to make an effort (**por** to)

esfuerzo *nm* effort

esfumarse *upr Fam* to beat it

esgrima *nf Dep* fencing

esgrimir *vt* to wield

esguince *nm* sprain

eslabón *nm* link

eslavo,-a 1 *adj* Slav, Slavonic

　2 *nm,f (persona)* Slav

　3 *nm (idioma)* Slavonic

eslip *nm (pl* **eslips)** men's briefs, underpants

eslogan *nm (pl* **eslóganes)** slogan; **e. publicitario** advertising slogan

eslora *nf Náut* length

eslovaco,-a 1 *adj & nm,f* Slovak, Slovakian

　2 *nm (idioma)* Slovak

Eslovaquia *n* Slovakia

Eslovenia *n* Slovenia

esloveno,-a 1 *adj & nm,f* Slovene

　2 *nm (idioma)* Slovene

esmaltar *vt* to enamel

esmalte *nm* enamel; *(de uñas)* nail polish *o* varnish

esmerado,-a *adj* painstaking, careful

esmeralda *nf* emerald

esmerarse *upr* to be careful; *(esforzarse)* to go to great lengths

esmero *nm* great care

esmoquin *nm (pl* **esmóquines)** dinner jacket, *US* tuxedo

esnifar *vt Fam (drogas)* to sniff

esnob *(pl* **esnobs)** 1 *adj (persona)* snobbish; *(restaurante etc)* posh

　2 *nmf* snob

esnobismo *nm* snobbery, snobbishness

ESO *nf (abr* **Enseñanza Secundaria Obligatoria)** = mainstream secondary education in Spain for pupils aged 12-16

eso *pron neut* that; **¡e. es!** that's it!; **por e.** that's why; *Fam* **a e. de las diez** around ten; *Fam* **e. de las Navidades sale muy caro** this whole Christmas thing costs a fortune

esófago *nm* oesophagus

esos,-as *adj dem pl ver* **ese,-a**

ésos,-as *pron dem m,fpl ver* **ése,-a**

esotérico,-a *adj* esoteric

espabilado,-a *adj* (a) *(despierto)* wide awake (b) *(niño)* bright

espabilar 1 *vt* to wake up

　2 **espabilarse** *upr* to wake up, to waken up

espachurrar *vt* to squash

espacial *adj* spatial, spacial; **nave e.** space ship

espaciar [43] *vt* to space out

espacio *nm* (a) space; *(de tiempo)* length; **a doble e.** double-spaced (b) *Rad & TV* programme

espacioso,-a *adj* spacious, roomy

espada 1 *nf* (a) sword; **estar entre la e. y la pared** to be between the devil and the deep blue sea; **pez e.** swordfish (b) *Naipes* spade

　2 *nm Taurom* matador

> 🖉 Observa que la palabra inglesa **spade** es un falso amigo y no es la traducción de la palabra española **espada**. En inglés, **spade** significa "pala".

espadaña *nf* belfry

espaguetis *nmpl* spaghetti

espalda *nf* (a) *Anat* back; **espaldas** back; **a espaldas de algn** behind sb's back; **por la e.** from behind; **volver la e. a algn** to turn one's back on sb; *Fam* **e. mojada** wetback (b) *(en natación)* backstroke

espaldar *nm (de silla)* back

espaldilla *nf* shoulder blade

espantapájaros *nm inv* scarecrow

espantar 1 *vt* (a) *(asustar)* to frighten, to scare (b) *(ahuyentar)* to frighten away

　2 **espantarse** *upr* to get *o* feel frightened (**de** of), to get *o* feel scared (**de** of)

espanto *nm* fright; *Fam* **de e.** dreadful, shocking

espantoso,-a *adj* dreadful

España *n* Spain

español,-a 1 *adj* Spanish

　2 *nm,f* Spaniard; **los españoles** the Spanish

　3 *nm (idioma)* Spanish

esparadrapo *nm* sticking plaster

esparcimiento *nm (relajación)* relaxation

esparcir [52] 1 *vt (papeles, semillas)* to scatter; *Fig (rumor)* to spread

　2 **esparcirse** *upr* (a) to be scattered (b) *(relajarse)* to relax

espárrago *nm* asparagus

espartano,-a *adj Fig* spartan

espasmo *nm* spasm

espástico,-a *adj* spastic

espátula *nf Culin* spatula; *Arte* palette

knife; *Téc* stripping knife; *(de albañil)* trowel

especia *nf* spice

especial *adj* special; **en e.** especially; **e. para ...** suitable for ...

especialidad *nf* speciality, *US* specialty; *Educ* main subject

especialista *nmf* specialist

especializarse [40] *vpr* to specialize (**en** in)

especialmente *adv (exclusivamente)* specially; *(muy)* especially

especie *nf* (a) *Biol* species *inv* (b) *(clase)* kind; **una e. de salsa** a kind of sauce (c) *Com* **en e.** in kind

específicamente *adv* specifically

especificar [44] *vt* to specify

específico,-a *adj* specific; **peso e.** specific gravity

espécimen *nm (pl* **especímenes)** specimen

espectacular *adj* spectacular

espectacularidad *nf* **de gran e.** really spectacular

espectáculo *nm* (a) *(escena)* spectacle, sight; *Fam* **dar un e.** to make a spectacle of oneself (b) *Teatro, Cin & TV* show; **montar un e.** to put on a show

espectador,-a *nm,f Dep* spectator; *(de accidente)* onlooker; *Teatro & Cin* member of the audience; **los espectadores** the audience; *TV* the viewers

espectro *nm* (a) *Fís* spectrum (b) *(fantasma)* spectre (c) *(gama)* range

especulación *nf* speculation; **e. del suelo** land speculation

especulador,-a *nm,f Fin* speculator

especular *vi* to speculate

especulativo,-a *adj* speculative

espejismo *nm* mirage

espejo *nm* mirror; *Aut* **e. retrovisor** rearview mirror

espeleología *nf* potholing, speleology

espeluznante *adj* hair-raising, horrifying

espera *nf* wait; **en e. de ...** waiting for ...; **a la e. de** expecting; **sala de e.** waiting room

esperanza *nf* hope; **tener la e. puesta en algo** to have one's hopes pinned on sth; **e. de vida** life expectancy; **en estado de buena e.** expecting, pregnant

esperanzador,-a *adj* encouraging

esperanzar *vt* to give hope to

esperar **1** *vi* (a) *(aguardar)* to wait (b) *(tener esperanza de)* to hope

2 *vt* (a) *(aguardar)* to wait for; **espero a mi hermano** I'm waiting for my brother

(b) *(tener esperanza de)* to hope for; **espero que sí** I hope so; **espero que vengas** I hope you'll come (c) *(estar a la espera de)* to expect; **te esperábamos ayer** we were expecting you yesterday (d) *Fig (bebé)* to expect

esperma (a) *nm Biol* sperm (b) *Am (vela)* candle

espermaticida *nm* spermicide

espermatozoide *nm* spermatozoid

esperpéntico,-a *adj Fam* grotesque

espesar **1** *vt* to thicken

2 espesarse *vpr* to thicken, to get thicker

espeso,-a *adj (bosque, niebla)* dense; *(líquido)* thick; *(masa)* stiff

espesor *nm* thickness; **3 m de e.** 3 m thick

espesura *nf* denseness

espetar *vt Fig* to spit out

espía *nmf* spy

espiar [29] **1** *vi* to spy

2 *vt* to spy on

espichar *vi Fam* **espichar(la)** *(morir)* to kick the bucket

espiga *nf* (a) *(de trigo)* ear (b) *Téc* pin

espigado,-a *adj* slender

espina *nf* (a) *Bot* thorn (b) *(de pescado)* bone (c) *Anat* **e. dorsal** spinal column, spine (d) *Fig* **ése me da mala e.** there's something fishy about that one

espinaca *nf* spinach

espinal *adj* spinal; **médula e.** spinal marrow

espinazo *nm* spine, backbone

espinilla *nf* (a) *Anat* shin (b) *(en la piel)* spot

espinillera *nf Dep* shin pad

espino *nm* hawthorn; **alambre de e.** barbed wire

espionaje *nm* spying, espionage; **novela de e.** spy story

espiral *adj & nf* spiral

espirar *vi* to breathe out, to exhale

espiritismo *nm* spiritualism

espíritu *nm* (a) *(espíritu)* spirit; **e. deportivo** sportsmanship (b) *Rel (alma)* soul; **el E. Santo** the Holy Ghost

espiritual *adj* spiritual

espléndido,-a *adj* (a) *(magnífico)* splendid (b) *(generoso)* lavish, generous

esplendor *nm* splendour

esplendoroso,-a *adj* magnificent

espliego *nm* lavender

espolear *vt* to spur on

espolio *nm* = expolio

espolvorear *vt* to sprinkle (**de** with)

esponja *nf* sponge

esponjoso,-a *adj* spongy; *(bizcocho)* light

esponsales *nmpl* betrothal, engagement

espontaneidad *nf* spontaneity; **con e.** naturally

espontáneo,-a 1 *adj* spontaneous

2 *nm Taurom* = spectator who spontaneously joins in the bullfight

esporádico,-a *adj* sporadic

esposado,-a *adj* (**a**) *(recién casado)* newly married (**b**) *(con esposas)* handcuffed

esposar *vt* to handcuff

esposas *nfpl* handcuffs

esposo,-a *nm,f* spouse; *(hombre)* husband; *(mujer)* wife

esprint *nm* sprint

esprintar *vi* to sprint

espuela *nf* spur

espuerta *nf* hod

espuma *nf* foam; *(de olas)* surf; *(de cerveza)* froth, head; *(de jabón)* lather; **e. de afeitar** shaving foam

espumoso,-a *adj* frothy; *(vino)* sparkling

esputo *nm* spit

esquela *nf* notice, announcement; **e. mortuoria** announcement of a death

esquelético,-a *adj* (**a**) *Anat* skeletal (**b**) *(flaco)* skinny

esqueleto *nm.* (**a**) skeleton (**b**) *Constr* framework

esquema *nm* diagram

esquemático,-a *adj* *(escueto)* schematic; *(con diagramas)* diagrammatic

esquí *nm* (**a**) *(objeto)* ski (**b**) *(deporte)* skiing; **e. acuático** waterskiing

esquiador,-a *nm,f* skier

esquiar [29] *vi* to ski

esquilar *vt* to shear

esquimal *adj & nmf* Eskimo

esquina *nf* corner; *Dep* **saque de e.** corner (kick)

esquinazo *nm* **dar e. a algn** to give sb the slip

esquirla *nf* splinter

esquirol *nm* *Ind* blackleg, scab

esquivar *vt* *(a una persona)* to avoid; *(un golpe)* to dodge

esquivo,-a *adj* cold, aloof

esquizofrenia *nf* schizophrenia

esquizofrénico,-a *adj & nm,f* schizophrenic

esta *adj dem ver* **este,-a**

ésta *pron dem f ver* **éste,-a**

está *indic pres de* **estar**

estabilidad *nf* stability

estabilizar [40] *vt* to stabilize

estable *adj* stable

establecer [33] **1** *vt* to establish; *(fundar)* to set up, to found; *(récord)* to set

2 establecerse *vpr* to settle

establecimiento *nm* establishment

establo *nm* cow shed

estaca *nf* stake, post; *(de tienda de campaña)* peg

estacada *nf* fence; *Fig* **dejar a algn en la e.** to leave sb in the lurch

estacazo *nm* blow with a stick

estación *nf* (**a**) station; **e. de servicio** service station; **e. de esquí** ski resort (**b**) *(del año)* season

estacional *adj* seasonal

estacionamiento *nm* *Aut (acción)* parking; *(lugar) Br* car park, *US* parking lot

estacionar *vt*, **estacionarse** *vpr Aut* to park

estacionario,-a *adj* stationary

estada *nf*, **estadía** *nf Am* stay

estadio *nm* (**a**) *Dep* stadium (**b**) *(fase)* stage, phase

estadista *nmf* *Pol (hombre)* statesman; *(mujer)* stateswoman

estadística *nf* statistics *sing*; **una e.** a statistic

estado *nm* (**a**) *Pol* state (**b**) *(situación)* state, condition; **en buen e.** in good condition; **e. de salud** condition, state of health; **e. de excepción** state of emergency; **estar en e.** to be pregnant; **e. civil** marital status; *Com* **e. de cuentas** statement of accounts (**c**) *Mil* **e. mayor** general staff

Estados Unidos *npl* the United States

estadounidense 1 *adj* United States, American

2 *nmf* American

estafa *nf* swindle

estafador,-a *nm,f* swindler

estafar *vt* to swindle

estafeta *nf* **e. de Correos** sub-post office

estalactita *nf* stalactite

estalagmita *nf* stalagmite

estallar *vi* (**a**) to burst; *(bomba)* to explode, to go off; *(guerra)* to break out (**b**) *Fig (de cólera etc)* to explode; **e. en sollozos** to burst into tears

estallido *nm* explosion; *(de guerra)* outbreak

estambre *nm* *Bot* stamen

Estambul *n* Istanbul

estamento *nm* *Hist* estate; *Fig (grupo)* group

estampa *nf* print, image

> 🖉 Observa que la palabra inglesa **stamp** es un falso amigo y no es la traducción de la palabra española **estampa**. En inglés, **stamp** significa "sello, tampón".

estampado,-a 1 *adj (tela)* ▸ printed

2 *nm* (**a**) *(tela)* print (**b**) *(proceso)* printing

estampar *vt* (**a**) *(tela)* to print (**b**) *(dejar impreso)* to imprint (**c**) *Fig (bofetada, beso)* to plant, to place

estampida *nf* (**a**) *(estampido)* bang (**b**) *(carrera rápida)* stampede; **de e.** suddenly

estampido *nm* bang

estampilla *nf Am* (postage) stamp

estancado,-a *adj (agua)* stagnant; *Fig* static, at a standstill; **quedarse e.** to get stuck *o* bogged down

estancar [44] **1** *vt* (**a**) *(agua)* to hold back (**b**) *Fig (asunto)* to block; *(negociaciones)* to bring to a standstill

2 estancarse *vpr* to stagnate; *Fig* to get bogged down

estancia *nf* (**a**) *(permanencia)* stay (**b**) *(habitación)* room (**c**) *Am (hacienda)* ranch, farm

estanco,-a 1 *nm* tobacconist's

2 *adj* watertight

estándar *(pl* **estándares)** *adj & nm* standard

estandarizar [40] *vt* to standardize

estandarte *nm* standard, banner

estanque *nm* pool, pond

estanquero,-a *nm,f* tobacconist

estante *nm* shelf; *(para libros)* bookcase

estantería *nf* shelves, shelving

estaño *nm* tin

estar [13] **1** *vi* (**a**) to be; **está en la playa** he is at the beach; **e. en casa** to be in, to be at home; **estamos en Caracas** we are in Caracas; **¿está tu madre?** is your mother in?; **¿cómo estás?** how are you?; **los precios están bajos** prices are low; **el problema está en el dinero** the problem is money; **e. en lo cierto** to be right; **e. en todo** not to miss a trick

(**b**) *(+ adj)* to be; **está cansado/enfermo** he's tired/ill; **está vacío** it's empty

(**c**) *(+ adv)* to be; **está bien/mal** it's all right/wrong; **e. mal de dinero** he's short of money; **estará enseguida** it'll be ready in a minute

(**d**) *(+ ger)* to be; **está escribiendo** she is writing; **estaba comiendo** he was eating

(**e**) *(+ a + fecha)* to be; **¿a cuántos estamos?** what's the date (today)?; **estamos a 2 de Noviembre** it is the 2nd of November

(**f**) *(+ precio)* to be at; **están a 100 pesetas el kilo** they're at 100 pesetas a kilo

(**g**) *(locuciones)* **e. al caer** to be just round the corner; **¿estamos?** OK?

(**h**) *(+ de)* **e. de más** not to be needed; **e. de paseo** to be out for a walk; **e. de vacaciones/viaje** to be (away) on holiday/a trip; **estoy de jefe hoy** I'm the boss today

(**i**) *(+ para)* **estará para las seis** it will be finished by six; **hoy no estoy para bromas** I'm in no mood for jokes today; **el tren está para salir** the train is just about to leave

(**j**) *(+ por)* **está por hacer** it has still to be done; **eso está por ver** it remains to be seen; **estoy por esperar** *(a favor de)* I'm for waiting

(**k**) *(+ con)* to have; **e. con la gripe** to have the flu, to be down with flu; **estoy con Jaime** *(de acuerdo con)* I agree with Jaime

(**l**) *(+ sin)* to have no; **e. sin luz/agua** to have no light/water

(**m**) *(+ que)* **está que se duerme** he is nearly asleep; *Fam* **está que rabia** he's hopping mad

2 estarse *vpr* **¡estáte quieto!** keep still!, stop fidgeting!

estatal *adj* state; **enseñanza e.** state education

estático,-a *adj* static

estatua *nf* statue

estatura *nf* (**a**) height; **¿cuál es tu e.?** how tall are you? (**b**) *(renombre)* stature

estatus *nm* status; **e. quo** status quo

estatutario,-a *adj* statutory

estatuto *nm Jur* statute; *(de ciudad)* by-law; *(de empresa etc)* rules

este¹ **1** *adj* eastern; *(dirección)* easterly

2 *nm* east; **al e. de** to the east of

este²,-a *adj dem* (**a**) this (**b**) **estos,-as** these

éste,-a *pron dem m,f* (**a**) this one; **aquél ... é.** the former ... the latter (**b**) **éstos,-as** these (ones); **aquéllos ... é.** the former ... the latter

> Note that **éste** and its various forms can be written without an accent when there is no risk of confusion with the adjective.

esté *subj pres de* **estar**

estela *nf (de barco)* wake; *(de avión)* vapour trail; *(de cometa)* tail

estelar *adj* (**a**) *Astron* stellar (**b**) *Fig Cin & Teatro* star

estentóreo,-a *adj* stentorian, thundering

estepa *nf* steppe

estera *nf* rush mat

estercolero *nm* dunghill; *Fig* pigsty

estéreo *nm & adj* stereo

estereofónico,-a *adj* stereophonic, stereo

estereotipar *vt* to stereotype

estereotipo *nm* stereotype

estéril *adj* (a) sterile (b) *Fig (esfuerzo)* futile

esterilidad *nf* (a) sterility (b) *Fig* futility, uselessness

esterilizar [40] *vt* to sterilize

esterilla *nf* small mat

esterlina *adj & nf* sterling; **libra e.** pound (sterling)

esternón *nm* sternum, breastbone

estero *nm Am* marsh, swamp

estertor *nm* death rattle

estética *nf* aesthetics *sing*

esteticienne, esteticista *nf* beautician

estético,-a *adj* aesthetic; **cirugía estética** plastic surgery

estibador *nm* docker, stevedore

estiércol *nm* manure, dung

estigma *nm* stigma; *Rel* stigmata

estilarse *vpr* to be in vogue, to be fashionable

estilete *nm (punzón)* stylus; *(puñal)* stiletto

estilístico,-a *adj* stylistic

estilizar [40] *vt* to stylize

estilo *nm* (a) style; *(modo)* manner, fashion; **algo por el e.** something like that; **e. de vida** way of life (b) *(en natación)* stroke (c) *Ling* **e. directo/indirecto** direct/indirect speech

estilográfica *nf* **(pluma) e.** fountain pen

estima *nf* esteem, respect

estimación *nf* (a) *(estima)* esteem, respect (b) *(valoración)* evaluation; *(cálculo aproximado)* estimate

estimado,-a *adj* esteemed, respected; **E. Señor** *(en carta)* Dear Sir

estimar *vt* (a) *(apreciar)* to esteem (b) *(considerar)* to consider, to think; **lo estimo conveniente** I think it appropriate (c) *(valorar)* to value

estimativo,-a *adj* approximate, estimated

estimulante 1 *adj* stimulating
2 *nm* stimulant

estimular *vt* (a) to stimulate (b) *Fig* to encourage

estímulo *nm Biol & Fís* stimulus; *Fig* encouragement

estío *nm* summer

estipendio *nm* stipend, fee

estipular *vt* to stipulate

estirado,-a *adj Fig* stiff

estirar 1 *vt* to stretch; *Fig (dinero)* to spin out; *Fig* **e. la pata** to kick the bucket

2 estirarse *vpr* to stretch

estirón *nm* pull, jerk, tug; *Fam* **dar o pegar un e.** to shoot up *o* grow quickly

estirpe *nf* stock, pedigree

estival *adj* summer; **época e.** summertime

esto *pron neut* this, this thing, this matter; *Fam* **e. de la fiesta** this business about the party

estocada *nf Taurom* stab

Estocolmo *n* Stockholm

estofado *nm* stew

estoico,-a 1 *adj* stoical
2 *nm,f* stoic

estómago *nm* stomach; **dolor de e.** stomach ache

Estonia *n* Estonia

estonio,-a 1 *adj & nm,f* Estonian
2 *nm (lengua)* Estonian

estoque *nm Taurom* sword

estorbar 1 *vt* (a) *(dificultar)* to hinder, to get in the way of (b) *(molestar)* to disturb
2 *vi* to be in the way

estorbo *nm* (a) *(obstáculo)* obstruction, obstacle (b) *(molestia)* nuisance

estornino *nm* starling

estornudar *vi* to sneeze

estornudo *nm* sneeze

estos,-as *adj dem pl ver* **este,-a**

éstos,-as *pron dem m,fpl ver* **éste,-a**

estoy *indic pres de* **estar**

estrabismo *nm* squint

estrado *nm* platform; *Mús* bandstand; *Jur* stand

estrafalario,-a *adj Fam* outlandish

estragos *nmpl* **hacer e. en** to wreak havoc with *o* on

estrambótico,-a *adj Fam* outlandish, eccentric

estrangulador,-a *nm,f* strangler

estrangular *vt* to strangle; *Med* to strangulate

estraperlo *nm* black market; **tabaco de e.** black market cigarettes

Estrasburgo *n* Strasbourg

estratagema *nf Mil* stratagem; *Fam* trick, ruse

estratega *nmf* strategist

estrategia *nf* strategy

estratégico,-a *adj* strategic

estratificar [44] *vt* to stratify

estrato *nm* stratum

estraza *nf* **papel de e.** brown paper

estrechamente *adv (íntimamente)* closely, intimately; **e. relacionados** closely related

estrechamiento *nm* (a) narrowing; **e. de calzada** *(en letrero)* road narrows (b) *(de amistad etc)* tightening

estrechar 1 *vt* (**a**) to make narrow·(**b**) *(mano)* to shake; *(lazos de amistad)* to tighten; **me estrechó entre sus brazos** he hugged me

2 estrecharse *vpr* to narrow, to become narrower

> 🖉 Observa que el verbo inglés **to stretch** es un falso amigo y no es la traducción del verbo español **estrechar**. En inglés, **to stretch** significa "estirar, desplegar".

estrechez *nf* (**a**) narrowness; *Fig* **e. de miras** narrow-mindedness (**b**) *Fig (dificultad económica)* want, need; **pasar estrecheces** to be hard up

estrecho,-a 1 *adj* (**a**) narrow; *(ropa, zapato)* tight; *(amistad, relación)* close, intimate (**b**) *Fig* **e. de miras** narrow-minded

2 *nm Geog* strait, straits

estregar *vt* to scrub

estrella *nf* star; **e. de cine** film star; *Zool* **e. de mar** starfish; **e. fugaz** shooting star

estrellado,-a *adj* (**a**) *(en forma de estrella)* star-shaped (**b**) *(cielo)* starry (**c**) *(huevos)* scrambled

estrellar 1 *vt Fam* to smash

2 estrellarse *vpr (morir)* to die in a car crash; *Aut & Av* **e. contra** *(chocar)* to crash into

estrellato *nm* stardom

estremecedor,-a *adj* bloodcurdling

estremecer [33] *vt*, **estremecerse** *vpr* to shake

estrenar *vt* (**a**) to use for the first time; *(ropa)* to wear for the first time (**b**) *Teatro & Cin* to premiere

estreno *nm Teatro* first performance; *Cin* premiere

estreñido,-a *adj* constipated

estreñimiento *nm* constipation

estrépito *nm* din, racket

estrepitoso,-a *adj* deafening; *Fig (fracaso)* spectacular

estrés *nm* stress

estresante *adj* stressful

estría *nf* (**a**) *(en la piel)* stretch mark (**b**) *Arquit* flute, fluting

estribar *vi* **e. en** to lie in, to be based on

estribillo *nm (en canción)* chorus; *(en poema)* refrain

estribo *nm* (**a**) stirrup; *Fig* **perder los estribos** to lose one's temper, to lose one's head (**b**) *Arquit* buttress; *(de puente)* pier, support

estribor *nm* starboard

estricto,-a *adj* strict

estridente *adj* strident

estrofa *nf* verse

estropajo *nm* scourer

estropear 1 *vt (máquina, cosecha)* to damage; *(fiesta, plan)* to spoil, to ruin; *(pelo, manos)* to ruin

2 estropearse *vpr* to be ruined; *(máquina)* to break down

estropicio *nm Fam (destrozo)* damage; *(ruido)* crash, clatter

estructura *nf* structure; *(armazón)* frame, framework

estructurar *vt* to structure

estruendo *nm* roar

estrujar 1 *vt (limón etc)* to squeeze; *(ropa)* to wring; *(apretar)* to crush

2 estrujarse *vpr Fam* **e. los sesos** *o* **el cerebro** to rack one's brains

estrujón *nm* tight squeeze, big hug

estuche *nm* case; *(para lápices)* pencil case

estuco *nm* stucco

estudiante *nmf* student

estudiantil *adj* student

estudiar [43] *vt & vi* to study

estudio *nm* (**a**) study; *(encuesta)* survey; *Com* **e. de mercado** market research (**b**) *(sala)* studio; **e. cinematográfico/de grabación** film/recording studio (**c**) *(apartamento)* studio (flat) (**d**) **estudios** studies

estudioso,-a 1 *adj* studious

2 *nm,f* specialist

estufa *nf (calentador)* heater; *(de leña)* stove

estupefaciente *nm* drug, narcotic

estupefacto,-a *adj* astounded, flabbergasted

estupendamente *adv* marvellously, wonderfully

estupendo,-a *adj* super, marvellous; **¡e.!** great!

estupidez *nf* stupidity

estúpido,-a 1 *adj* stupid

2 *nm,f* idiot

estupor *nm* amazement, astonishment

estuve *pt indef de* **estar**

esvástica *nf* swastika

ETA *nf (abr* **Euzkadi Ta Askatasuna** *(Patria Vasca y Libertad))* ETA

etapa *nf* stage; **por etapas** in stages

etarra *nmf* = member of ETA

etc. *(abr* **etcétera***)* etc

etcétera *nf* etcetera

éter *nm* ether

etéreo,-a *adj* ethereal

eternidad *nf* eternity; *Fam* **una e.** ages

eterno,-a *adj* eternal

ética *nf* ethic; *(ciencia)* ethics *sing*

ético,-a *adj* ethical

etílico,-a *adj* ethylic; **alcohol e.** ethyl alcohol; **en estado e.** intoxicated; **intoxicación etílica** alcohol poisoning

etimología *nf* etymology

etimológico,-a *adj* etymological

etiope, etíope *adj & nmf* Ethiopian

Etiopía *nf* Ethiopia

etiqueta *nf* (a) *(de producto)* label (b) *(ceremonia)* etiquette; **de e.** formal

etiquetar *vt* to label

etnia *nf* ethnic group

étnico,-a *adj* ethnic

ETT *nf (abr* **Empresa de Trabajo Temporal)** temping agency

eucalipto *nm* eucalyptus

eucaristía *nf* eucharist

eufemismo *nm* euphemism

euforia *nf* euphoria

eufórico,-a *adj* euphoric

eureka *interj* eureka!

euro *nm (moneda)* euro

eurocomunismo *nm* Eurocommunism

eurodiputado,-a *nm,f* Euro MP

euromisil *nm* Euromissile

Europa *nf* Europe

europeísmo *nm* Europeanism

europeizar [40] *vt* to europeanize

europeo,-a *adj & nm,f* European

euscalduna 1 *adj* Basque; *(que habla vasco)* Basque-speaking
   2 *nmf* Basque speaker

euskera *adj & nm* Basque

eutanasia *nf* euthanasia

evacuación *nf* evacuation

evacuar [47] *vt* to evacuate

evadir 1 *vt (respuesta, peligro, impuestos)* to avoid; *(responsabilidad)* to shirk
   2 evadirse *vpr* to escape

evaluación *nf* evaluation; *Educ* assessment; **e. continua** continuous assessment

evaluar [30] *vt* to evaluate, to assess

evangélico,-a *adj* evangelical

evangelio *nm* gospel

evangelista *nm* evangelist

evaporación *nf* evaporation

evaporar 1 *vt* to evaporate
   2 evaporarse *vpr* to evaporate; *Fig* to vanish

evasión *nf (fuga)* escape; *Fig* evasion; **e. fiscal** o **de impuestos** tax evasion

evasiva *nf* evasive answer

evasivo,-a *adj* evasive

evento *nm* (a) *(acontecimiento)* event (b) *(incidente)* contingency, unforeseen event

eventual *adj* (a) *(posible)* possible; *(gastos)* incidental (b) *(trabajo, obrero)* casual, temporary

eventualidad *nf* contingency

eventualmente *adv* by chance; **los problemas que e. surjan** such problems as may arise

---

📖 Observa que las palabras inglesas **eventual** y **eventually** son falsos amigos y no son la traducción de las palabras españolas **eventual** y **eventualmente**. En inglés, **eventual** significa "final" o "consiguiente" y **eventually** "finalmente".

---

evidencia *nf* obviousness; **poner a algn en e.** to show sb up

evidenciar [43] *vt* to show, to demonstrate

evidente *adj* obvious

evidentemente *adv* obviously

evitar *vt* to avoid; *(prevenir)* to prevent; *(desastre)* to avert

evocador,-a *adj* evocative

evocar [44] *vt (traer a la memoria)* to evoke; *(acordarse de)* to recall

evolución *nf* evolution; *(desarrollo)* development

evolucionar *vi* to develop; *Biol* to evolve; **el enfermo evoluciona favorablemente** the patient is improving

ex 1 *pref* former, ex-; **ex alumno** former pupil, ex-student; **ex combatiente** *Br* ex-serviceman, *f* ex-servicewoman, *US* (war) veteran; **ex marido** ex-husband
   2 *nmf Fam* **mi ex** my ex

exabrupto *nm* sharp comment

exacerbar [47] *vt* (a) *(agravar)* to exacerbate, to aggravate (b) *(irritar)* to exasperate, to irritate
   2 exacerbarse *vpr* (a) *(agravarse)* to get worse (b) *(irritarse)* to feel exasperated

exactamente *adv* exactly, precisely

exactitud *nf* accuracy; **con e.** precisely

exacto,-a *adj* exact; **¡e.!** precisely!; **para ser e.** to be precise

exageración *nf* exaggeration

exagerado,-a *adj* exaggerated; *(excesivo)* excessive

exagerar 1 *vt* to exaggerate
   2 *vi* to overdo it

exaltado,-a 1 *adj (persona)* excitable, hot-headed
   2 *nm,f Fam* fanatic

exaltar 1 *vt (ensalzar)* to praise, to extol
   2 exaltarse *vpr (acalorarse)* to get over-excited, to get carried away

examen *nm* examination, exam; **e. de conducir** driving test; *Med* **e. médico** checkup

examinador,-a *nm,f* examiner

examinar 1 *vt* to examine

  2 examinarse *vpr* to take o sit an examination

exasperante *adj* exasperating

exasperar 1 *vt* to exasperate

  2 exasperarse *vpr* to become exasperated

Exc., Exca., Exc.a (*abr* **Excelencia**) Excellency

excavación *nf* excavation; *(en arqueología)* dig

excavadora *nf* digger

excavar *vt* to excavate, to dig

excedencia *nf* leave (of absence)

excedente *adj & nm* excess, surplus

exceder 1 *vt* to exceed, to surpass

  2 excederse *vpr* to go too far

excelencia *nf* (a) excellence; **por e.** par excellence (b) *(título)* **Su E.** His/Her Excellency

excelente *adj* excellent

excelso,-a *adj* sublime, lofty

excentricidad *nf* eccentricity

excéntrico,-a *adj* eccentric

excepción *nf* exception; **a e.** with the exception of, except for; **de e.** exceptional; *Pol* **estado de e.** state of emergency

excepcional *adj* exceptional

excepto *adv* except (for), apart from

exceptuar [30] *vt* to except, to exclude

excesivo,-a *adj* excessive

exceso *nm* excess; **en e.** in excess, excessively; **e. de equipaje** excess baggage; **e. de velocidad** speeding

excitable *adj* excitable

excitación *nf (sentimiento)* excitement

excitante 1 *adj* exciting; *Med* stimulating

  2 *nm* stimulant

excitar 1 *vt* to excite

  2 excitarse *vpr* to get excited

exclamación *nf* exclamation

exclamar *vt & vi* to exclaim, to cry out

excluir [37] *vt* to exclude; *(rechazar)* to reject

exclusión *nf* exclusion

exclusiva *nf Prensa* exclusive; *Com* sole right

exclusive *adv (en fechas)* exclusive

exclusivo,-a *adj* exclusive

Excma. (*abr* **Excelentísima**) Most Excellent

Excmo. (*abr* **Excelentísimo**) Most Excellent

excomulgar [42] *vt Rel* to excommunicate

excomunión *nf* excommunication

excremento *nm* excrement

exculpar *vt* to exonerate

excursión *nf* excursion

excursionista *nmf* tripper; *(a pie)* hiker

excusa *nf (pretexto)* excuse; *(disculpa)* apology

excusado *nm (retrete)* toilet

excusar 1 *vt* (a) *(justificar)* to excuse (b) *(eximir)* (**de** from)

  2 excusarse *vpr (disculparse)* to apologize

execrar *vt* to execrate, to abhor

exención *nf* exemption; **e. de impuestos** tax exemption

exento,-a *adj* exempt, free (**de** from)

exequias *nfpl* funeral rites

exhalar *vt* to exhale, to breathe out; *(gas)* to give off, to emit; *(suspiro)* to heave

exhaustivo,-a *adj* exhaustive

exhausto,-a *adj* exhausted

exhibición *nf* exhibition

exhibicionista *nmf* exhibitionist

exhibir 1 *vt* (a) *(mostrar)* to exhibit, to display (b) *(lucir)* to show off

  2 exhibirse *vpr* to show off, to make an exhibition of oneself

exhortar *vt* to exhort

exhumar *vt* to exhume

exigencia *nf* (a) demand (b) *(requisito)* requirement

exigente *adj* demanding, exacting

exigir [57] *vt* to demand

exiguo,-a *adj* minute

exilado,-a 1 *adj* exiled, in exile

  2 *nm,f* exile

exilar 1 *vt* to exile, to send into exile

  2 exilarse *vpr* to go into exile

exiliado,-a *adj & nm,f* = **exilado,-a**

exiliar [43] *vt*, **exiliarse** *vpr* = **exilar**

exilio *nm* exile

eximio,-a *adj* distinguished, eminent

eximir *vt* to exempt (**de** from)

existencia *nf* (a) *(vida)* existence (b) *Com* **existencias** stock, stocks

existente *adj* existing; *Com* in stock

existir *vi* to exist, to be (in existence)

éxito *nm* success; **con é.** successfully; **tener é.** to be successful

> 🖉 Observa que la palabra inglesa **exit** es un falso amigo y no es la traducción de la palabra española **éxito**. En inglés, **exit** significa "salida".

exitoso,-a *adj* successful

éxodo *nm* exodus

exonerar *vt* to exonerate

exorbitante *adj* exorbitant, excessive

exorcista *nmf* exorcist

exorcizar [40] *vt* to exorcize

exótico,-a *adj* exotic

expandir 1 *vt* to expand

　2 expandirse *vpr (gas etc)* to expand; *(noticia)* to spread

expansión *nf* (a) expansion; *(de noticia)* spreading (b) *(diversión)* relaxation, recreation

expansionarse *vpr Fig (divertirse)* to relax, to let one's hair down

expatriado,-a *adj & nm,f* expatriate

expatriar [29] 1 *vt* to exile, to banish

　2 expatriarse *vpr* to leave one's country

expectación *nf* excitement

expectativa *nf* expectancy; **estar a la e. de** to be on the lookout for

expectorante *nm* expectorant

expedición *nf* expedition

expedientar *vt* to place under enquiry

expediente *nm* (a) *(informe)* dossier, record; *(ficha)* file; *Educ* **e. académico** student's record; **abrirle e. a algn** to place sb under enquiry (b) *Jur* proceedings, action

expedir [6] *vt* (a) *(carta)* to send, to dispatch (b) *(pasaporte etc)* to issue

expedito,-a *adj* free, clear

expendedor,-a 1 *nm,f* seller

　2 *nm* **e. automático** vending machine

expendeduría *nf* tobacconist's

expensas *nfpl* **a e. de** at the expense of

experiencia *nf* (a) experience; **por e.** from experience (b) *(experimento)* experiment

experimentado,-a *adj* experienced

experimental *adj* experimental

experimentar 1 *vi* to experiment

　2 *vt* to undergo; *(aumento)* to show; *(pérdida)* to suffer; *(sensación)* to experience, to feel; *Med* **e. una mejoría** to improve, to make progress

experimento *nm* experiment

experto,-a *nm,f* expert

expiar [29] *vt* to expiate, to atone for

expirar *vi* to expire

explanada *nf* esplanade

explayarse *vpr* to talk at length (about)

explicación *nf* explanation

explicar [44] 1 *vt* to explain

　2 explicarse *vpr (persona)* to explain (oneself); **no me lo explico** I can't understand it

explicativo,-a *adj* explanatory

explícito,-a *adj* explicit

exploración *nf* exploration; *Téc* scanning; *Med (interna)* exploration; *(externa)* examination; *Mil* reconnaissance

explorador,-a *nm,f* (a) *(persona)* explorer (b) *Med* probe; *Téc* scanner

explorar *vt* to explore; *Med (internamente)* to explore; *(externamente)* to examine; *Téc* to scan; *Mil* to reconnoitre

explosión *nf* explosion, blast; **hacer e.** to explode; **motor de e.** internal combustion engine; **e. demográfica** population explosion

explosionar *vt & vi* to explode, to blow up

explosivo,-a *adj & nm* explosive

explotación *nf* (a) *(abuso)* exploitation (b) *(uso)* exploitation, working; *Agr* cultivation (of land); *(granja)* farm

explotador,-a *nm,f* exploiter

explotar 1 *vi (bomba)* to explode, to go off

　2 *vt* (a) *(aprovechar)* to exploit; *(recursos)* to tap; *(tierra)* to cultivate (b) *(abusar de)* to exploit

expoliar [43] *vt* to plunder, to pillage

exponente *nmf* exponent

exponer [19] *(pp* **expuesto)** 1 *vt* (a) *(mostrar)* to exhibit, to display (b) *(explicar)* to expound, to put forward (c) *(arriesgar)* to expose

　2 exponerse *vpr* to expose oneself (**a** to); **te expones a perder el trabajo** you run the risk of losing your job

exportación *nf* export

exportador,-a 1 *adj* exporting

　2 *nm,f* exporter

exportar *vt* to export

exposición *nf* (a) *Arte* exhibition; **e. universal** world fair; **sala de exposiciones** gallery (b) *(de hechos, ideas)* exposé (c) *Fot* exposure

exprés *adj* express; **(olla) e.** pressure cooker; **(café) e.** espresso (coffee)

expresamente *adv* specifically, expressly

expresar 1 *vt* to express; *(manifestar)* to state

　2 expresarse *vpr* to express oneself

expresión *nf* expression; **la mínima e.** the bare minimum

expresivo,-a *adj* expressive

expreso,-a 1 *adj* express; **con el fin e. de** with the express purpose of

　2 *nm Ferroc* express (train)

　3 *adv* on purpose, deliberately

exprimidor *nm* squeezer, juicer

exprimir *vt (limón)* to squeeze; *(zumo)* to squeeze out; *Fig (persona)* to exploit, to bleed dry

expropiar [43] *vt* to expropriate

expuesto,-a *adj* (a) *(sin protección)* exposed; **estar e. a** to be exposed to (b) *(peligroso)* risky, dangerous (c) *(exhibido)* on display, on show

expulsar *vt* (a) to expel, to throw out; *Dep (jugador)* to send off (b) *(gas etc)* to belch out

expulsión *nf* expulsion; *Dep* sending off

expurgar [42] *vt* to expurgate; *Fig* to purge

expuse *pt indef de* **exponer**

exquisito,-a *adj* exquisite; *(comida)* delicious; *(gusto)* refined

extasiado,-a *adj* ecstatic; **quedarse e.** to go into ecstasies *o* raptures

extasiarse [29] *vpr* to go into ecstasies *o* raptures

éxtasis *nm inv* ecstasy

extender [3] 1 *vt* (a) to extend; *(agrandar)* to enlarge (b) *(mantel, mapa)* to spread (out), to open (out); *(mano, brazo)* to stretch (out) (c) *(crema, mantequilla)* to spread (d) *(cheque)* to make out; *(documento)* to draw up; *(certificado)* to issue

2 **extenderse** *vpr* (a) *(en el tiempo)* to extend, to last (b) *(en el espacio)* to spread out, to stretch (c) *(rumor, noticia)* to spread, to extend (d) *Fig (hablar demasiado)* to go on

extendido,-a *adj* (a) extended; *(mapa, plano)* spread out, open; *(mano, brazo)* outstretched (b) *(costumbre, rumor)* widespread

extensible *adj* extending

extensión *nf (de libro etc)* length; *(de cuerpo)* size; *(de terreno)* area, expanse; *(edificio anexo)* extension; **en toda la e. de la palabra** in every sense of the word; **por e.** by extension

extensivo,-a *adj* **hacer e.** to extend; **ser e. a** to cover

extenso,-a *adj (terreno)* extensive; *(libro, película)* long

extenuar [30] 1 *vt* to exhaust

2 **extenuarse** *vpr* to exhaust oneself

exterior 1 *adj* (a) *(de fuera)* outer; *(puerta)* outside (b) *(política, deuda)* foreign; *Pol* **Ministerio de Asuntos Exteriores** Ministry of Foreign Affairs, *Br* ≃ Foreign Office, *US* ≃ State Department

2 *nm* (a) *(parte de fuera)* exterior, outside (b) *(extranjero)* abroad (c) **exteriores** *Cin* location

exteriorizar [40] *vt* to show

exteriormente *adv* outwardly

exterminar *vt* to exterminate

exterminio *nm* extermination

externalización *nf Com* outsourcing

externo,-a 1 *adj* external; *Farm* **de uso e.** for external use only

2 *nm,f Educ* day pupil

extinción *nf* extinction

extinguir [59] 1 *vt (fuego)* to extinguish, to put out; *(raza)* to wipe out

2 **extinguirse** *vpr (fuego)* to go out; *(especie)* to become extinct, to die out

extinto,-a *adj* extinct

extintor *nm* fire extinguisher

extirpar *vt* (a) *Med* to remove (b) *Fig* to eradicate, to stamp out

extorsión *nf* extortion

extorsionar *vt* to extort

extra 1 *adj* (a) *(suplementario)* extra; **horas e.** overtime; **paga e.** bonus (b) *(superior)* top-quality

2 *nm* extra

3 *nmf Cin & Teatro* extra

extra- *pref* extra-; **extramatrimonial** extramarital

extracción *nf* (a) extraction (b) *(en lotería)* draw

extracto *nm* (a) extract; **e. de fresa** strawberry extract; **e. de regaliz** liquorice; *Fin* **e. de cuenta** statement of account (b) *(resumen)* summary

extractor *nm* extractor

extradición *nf* extradition

extraer [25] *vt* to extract, to take out

extraescolar *adj (actividad etc)* extracurricular

extrafino,-a *adj* superfine

extralimitarse *vpr* to overstep the mark

extranjería *nf* **ley de e.** law on aliens

extranjero,-a 1 *adj* foreign

2 *nm,f* foreigner

3 *nm* abroad; **en el e.** abroad

extrañar 1 *vt* (a) *(sorprender)* to surprise; **no es de e.** it's hardly surprising (b) *Am (echar de menos)* to miss

2 **extrañarse** *vpr* **e. de** to be surprised at

extrañeza *nf* (a) *(sorpresa)* surprise, astonishment (b) *(singularidad)* strangeness

extraño,-a 1 *adj* strange; *Med* **cuerpo e.** foreign body

2 *nm,f* stranger

extraoficial *adj* unofficial

extraordinaria *nf (paga)* bonus

extraordinario,-a *adj* extraordinary; *Prensa* **edición extraordinaria** special edition

extrarradio *nm* outskirts, suburbs

extraterrestre *nmf* alien

extravagancia *nf* extravagance

extravagante *adj* odd, outlandish

extravertido,-a *adj* = extrovertido,-a

extraviado,-a *adj* lost, missing

extraviar [29] 1 *vt* to mislay, to lose

2 **extraviarse** *vpr* to be missing, to get mislaid

extremadamente *adv* extremely

extremado,-a *adj* extreme

Extremadura *n* Estremadura

extremar 1 *vt* **e. la prudencia** to be extremely careful

2 extremarse *upr* to take great pains, to do one's utmost

extremaunción *nf* extreme unction

extremeño,-a 1 *adj* of/from Estremadura

2 *nm,f* person from Estremadura

extremidad *nf* (**a**) *(extremo)* end, tip (**b**) *Anat (miembro)* limb, extremity

extremista *adj & nmf* extremist

extremo,-a 1 *nm (de calle, cable)* end; *(máximo)* extreme; **en e.** very much; **en último e.** as a last resort

2 *nm,f (en fútbol)* winger; **e. derecha/izquierda** outside right/left

3 *adj* extreme; **E. Oriente** Far East

extrovertido,-a *adj & nm,f* extrovert

exuberante *adj* exuberant; *(vegetación)* lush, abundant

eyaculación *nf* ejaculation; **e. precoz** premature ejaculation

eyacular *vi* to ejaculate

eyectable *adj* **asiento e.** ejector seat

F, f ['efe] *nf (la letra)* F, f

fa *nm Mús* F

fabada *nf* stew of beans, pork sausage and bacon

fábrica *nf* factory; **marca de f.** trademark; **precio de f.** factory *o* ex-works price

> 🖉 Observa que la palabra inglesa **fabric** es un falso amigo y no es la traducción de la palabra española **fábrica**. En inglés, **fabric** significa "tejido".

fabricación *nf* manufacture; **de f. casera** home-made; **de f. propia** our own make; **f. en cadena** mass production

fabricante *nmf* manufacturer

fabricar [44] *vt* (**a**) *Ind* to manufacture (**b**) *Fig (mentiras etc)* to fabricate

fabril *adj* manufacturing

fábula *nf* fable

fabuloso,-a *adj* fabulous

faca *nf* large curved knife

facción *nf* (**a**) *Pol* faction (**b**) **facciones** *(rasgos)* features

faccioso,-a 1 *adj* seditious
 2 *nm,f* rebel

faceta *nf* facet

facha¹ *nf Fam* appearance, look

facha² *nmf Pey* fascist

fachada *nf* façade

facial *adj* facial

fácil *adj* (**a**) easy; **f. de comprender** easy to understand (**b**) *(probable)* likely, probable; **es f. que ...** it's (quite) likely that ...

facilidad *nf* (**a**) *(sencillez)* easiness (**b**) *(soltura)* ease (**c**) *(servicio)* facility; **dar facilidades** to make things easy; *Com* **facilidades de pago** easy terms (**d**) **f. para los idiomas** gift for languages

facilitar *vt (proporcionar)* to provide, to supply (**a** with)

fácilmente *adv* easily

facineroso,-a *adj* criminal

facsímil, facsímile *nm* facsimile

factible *adj* feasible

fáctico,-a *adj* **poderes fácticos** vested interests

factor *nm* (**a**) factor (**b**) *Ferroc* luggage clerk

factoría *nf (fábrica)* factory

factura *nf* (**a**) *Com* invoice (**b**) *Arg (bollo)* = rolls and pastries

facturación *nf* (**a**) *Com* invoicing (**b**) *(de equipajes) (en aeropuerto)* check-in; *(en estación)* registration

facturar *vt* (**a**) *Com* to invoice (**b**) *(en aeropuerto)* to check in; *(en estación)* to register

facultad *nf* faculty; **facultades mentales** faculties

facultativo,-a 1 *adj* optional
 2 *nm,f* doctor

faena *nf* (**a**) *(tarea)* task (**b**) *Fam (mala pasada)* dirty trick (**c**) *Taurom* performance

faenar *vi* to fish

fagot *nm Mús* bassoon

fainá *nf Urug (plato)* = baked dough made with chickpea flour and olive oil, served with pizza

faisán *nm* pheasant

faja *nf* (**a**) *(corsé)* girdle, corset (**b**) *(banda)* sash (**c**) *(de terreno)* strip

fajo *nm (de ropa etc)* bundle; *(de billetes)* wad

falacia *nf* fallacy

falaz *adj* (**a**) *(erróneo)* fallacious (**b**) *(engañoso)* deceitful

falda *nf* (**a**) *(prenda)* skirt; **f. pantalón** culottes (**b**) *(de montaña)* slope, hillside (**c**) *(de mesa)* cover (**d**) *(regazo)* lap

faldero,-a *adj* **perro f.** lapdog

falencia *nf* (**a**) *Am Com (bancarrota)* bankruptcy (**b**) *CSur (error)* fault

falla¹ *nf Am (defecto)* defect, fault

falla² *nf Geol* fault

fallar¹ 1 *vi Jur* to rule
 2 *vt (premio)* to award

fallar² 1 *vi* to fail; **le falló la puntería** he missed his aim; *Fig* **no me falles** don't let me down
 2 *vt* to miss

fallecer [33] *vi Fml* to pass away, to die

fallecido,-a *adj* deceased

fallecimiento *nm* demise

fallido,-a *adj* unsuccessful, vain

fallo¹ *nm* (**a**) *(error)* mistake; **f. humano** human error (**b**) *(del corazón, de los frenos)* failure

fallo² nm (**a**) Jur judgement, sentence (**b**) (en concurso) awarding

falluto,-a RP Fam **1** adj phoney, hypocritical

  2 nm,f hypocrite

falo nm phallus

falsear vt (**a**) (informe etc) to falsify; (hechos, la verdad) to distort (**b**) (moneda) to forge

falsedad nf (**a**) falseness, (doblez) hypocrisy (**b**) (mentira) falsehood

falsificar [44] vt to falsify; (cuadro, firma, moneda) to forge

falso,-a adj (**a**) false; **dar un paso en f.** (tropezar) to trip, to stumble; Fig to make a blunder; **jurar en f.** to commit perjury (**b**) (persona) insincere

falta nf (**a**) (carencia) lack; **por f. de** for want o lack of; **sin f.** without fail; **f. de educación** bad manners

  (**b**) (escasez) shortage

  (**c**) (ausencia) absence; **echar algo/a algn en f.** to miss sth/sb

  (**d**) (error) mistake; (defecto) fault, defect; **f. de ortografía** spelling mistake; **sacar faltas a algo/a algn** to find fault with sth/sb

  (**e**) Jur misdemeanour

  (**f**) (en fútbol) foul; (en tenis) fault

  (**g**) **hacer f.** to be necessary; **(nos) hace f. una escalera** we need a ladder; **harán f. dos personas para mover el piano** it'll take two people to move the piano; **no hace f. que ...** there is no need for ...

faltante nm Am deficit

faltar vi (**a**) (no estar) to be missing; **¿quién falta?** who is missing?

  (**b**) (escasear) to be lacking o needed; **le falta confianza en sí mismo** he lacks confidence in himself; **¡lo que me faltaba!** that's all I needed!; **¡no faltaría o faltaba más!** (por supuesto) (but) of course!

  (**c**) (quedar) to be left; **¿cuántos kilómetros faltan para Managua?** how many kilometres is it to Managua?; **ya falta poco para las vacaciones** it won't be long now till the holidays; **faltó poco para que me cayera** I very nearly fell

  (**d**) **f. a la verdad** not to tell the truth; **f. al deber** to fail in one's duty; **f. a su palabra/promesa** to break one's word/promise; **f. al respeto a algn** to treat sb with disrespect

falto,-a adj **f. de** lacking in

fama nf (**a**) fame, renown; **de f. mundial** world-famous (**b**) (reputación) reputation

famélico,-a adj starving, famished

familia nf family; **estar en f.** to be among friends; **f. numerosa** large family

familiar 1 adj (**a**) (de la familia) family; **empresa f.** family business (**b**) (conocido) familiar

  2 nmf relation, relative

familiaridad nf familiarity

familiarizarse [40] vpr **f. con** to familiarize oneself with

famoso,-a 1 adj famous

  2 nm famous person

fan nmf fan

fanático,-a 1 adj fanatical

  2 nm,f fanatic

fanatismo nm fanaticism

fanfarrón,-ona Fam **1** adj boastful

  2 nm,f show-off

fanfarronear vi Fam (chulear) to show off; (bravear) to brag, to boast

fango nm (**a**) (barro) mud (**b**) Fig degradation

fantasear vi to daydream, to dream

fantasía nf fantasy; **joya de f.** imitation jewellery

fantasioso,-a adj imaginative

fantasma nm (**a**) (espectro) ghost (**b**) Fam (fanfarrón) braggart, show-off

fantasmal adj ghostly

fantástico,-a adj fantastic

fantoche nm Pey nincompoop, ninny

faraón nm Pharaoh

fardar vi Fam to show off

fardo nm bundle

farfullar vt to jabber

faringe nf pharynx

faringitis nf pharyngitis

fariseo,-a nm,f (falso) hypocrite

farmacéutico,-a 1 adj pharmaceutical

  2 nm,f pharmacist, Br chemist, US druggist

farmacia nf (**a**) (tienda) Br chemist's (shop), US drugstore (**b**) (ciencia) pharmacology

fármaco nm medicine, medication

faro nm (**a**) (torre) lighthouse (**b**) (de coche) headlight, headlamp

farol nm (**a**) lantern; (en la calle) streetlight, streetlamp (**b**) Fam (fanfarronada) bragging; **tirarse un f.** to brag (**c**) (en naipes) bluff

farola nf streetlight, streetlamp

farolear vi Fam to brag

farolillo nm Fig **ser el f. rojo** to bring up the rear

farragoso,-a adj confused, rambling

farruco,-a adj Fam cocky

farsa nf farce

farsante *nmf* fake, impostor

fascículo *nm Impr* instalment

fascinador,-a, fascinante *adj* fascinating

fascinar *vt* to fascinate

fascismo *nm* fascism

fascista *adj & nmf* fascist

fase *nf* (**a**) *(etapa)* phase, stage (**b**) *Elec & Fís* phase

fastidiado,-a *adj Fam* (**a**) *(roto)* broken (**b**) *(enfermo)* sick; **tiene el estómago f.** he's got a bad stomach

fastidiar [43] 1 *vt* (**a**) *(molestar)* to annoy, to bother; *(dañar)* to hurt; *Fam* **¡no fastidies!** you're kidding! (**b**) *Fam (estropear)* to damage, to ruin; *(planes)* to spoil

2 **fastidiarse** *vpr* (**a**) *(aguantarse)* to put up with it, to resign oneself; **que se fastidie** that's his tough luck (**b**) *Fam (estropearse)* to get damaged, to break down (**c**) **me he fastidiado el tobillo** I've hurt my ankle

fastidio *nm* nuisance

fastuoso,-a *adj* (**a**) *(acto)* splendid, lavish (**b**) *(persona)* lavish, ostentatious

fatal 1 *adj* (**a**) *Fam (muy malo)* awful, dreadful (**b**) *(mortal)* deadly, fatal (**c**) *(inexorable)* fateful, inevitable

2 *adv Fam* awfully, terribly; **lo pasó f.** he had a rotten time

fatalidad *nf* (**a**) *(destino)* fate (**b**) *(desgracia)* misfortune

> ♪ Observa que la palabra inglesa **fatality** es un falso amigo y no es la traducción de la palabra española **fatalidad**. En inglés, **fatality** significa "víctima mortal".

fatalista 1 *adj* fatalistic

2 *nmf* fatalist

fatiga *nf* (**a**) *(cansancio)* fatigue (**b**) **fatigas** *(dificultades)* troubles, difficulties

fatigar [42] 1 *vt* to tire, to weary

2 **fatigarse** *upr* to tire, to become tired

fatigoso,-a *adj* tiring, exhausting

fatuo,-a *adj* (**a**) *(envanecido)* vain, conceited (**b**) *(necio)* fatuous, foolish

fauces *nfpl Fig* jaws

fauna *nf* fauna

favor *nm* favour; **por f.** please; **¿puedes hacerme un f.?** can you do me a favour?; **estar a f. de** to be in favour of; **haga el f. de sentarse** please sit down

favorable *adj* favourable; **f. a** in favour of

favorecedor,-a *adj* flattering

favorecer [33] *vt* (**a**) to favour (**b**) *(sentar bien)* to flatter

favoritismo *nm* favouritism

favorito,-a *adj & nm,f* favourite

faz *nf* (*pl* **faces**) *Literario (cara)* face

fe *nf* (**a**) faith; **de buena/mala fe** with good/dishonest intentions (**b**) *(certificado)* certificate; **fe de bautismo/matrimonio** baptism/marriage certificate (**c**) *Impr* **fe de erratas** errata

fealdad *nf* ugliness

febrero *nm* February

febril *adj* (**a**) *Med* feverish (**b**) *(actividad)* hectic

fecha *nf* (**a**) date; **f. límite** *o* **tope** deadline; **f. de caducidad** sell-by date; **hasta la f.** so far; **en f. próxima** at an early date (**b**) **fechas** *(época)* time; **el año pasado por estas fechas** this time last year

fechar *vt* to date

fechoría *nf* *(de niños)* mischief; *Literario* misdeed

fécula *nf* starch

fecundación *nf* fertilization; **f. in vitro** in vitro fertilization

fecundar *vt* to fertilize

fecundo,-a *adj* fertile

federación *nf* federation

federal *adj & nmf* federal

fehaciente *adj* (**a**) *Fml* authentic, reliable (**b**) *Jur* irrefutable; **documento** *o* **prueba f.** irrefutable proof

felicidad *nf* happiness; **(muchas) felicidades** *(en cumpleaños)* many happy returns

felicitación *nf* **tarjeta de f.** greetings card

felicitar *vt* to congratulate (**por** on); **¡te felicito!** congratulations!

feligrés,-esa *nm,f* parishioner

felino,-a *adj & nm* feline

feliz *adj* (**a**) *(contento)* happy; **¡felices Navidades!** Happy *o* Merry Christmas! (**b**) *(decisión etc)* fortunate

felonía *nf* treachery

felpa *nf* (**a**) *Tex* plush; **oso** *o* **osito de f.** teddy bear (**b**) *(para el pelo)* hairband

felpudo *nm* mat, doormat

femenino,-a *adj* feminine; *(equipo, ropa)* women's; **el sexo f.** the female sex, women

feminismo *nm* feminism

feminista *adj & nmf* feminist

fémur *nm* femur

fenecer [33] *vi Euf* to pass away, to die

fenomenal 1 *adj* (**a**) phenomenal (**b**) *Fam (fantástico)* great, terrific

2 *adv Fam* wonderfully, marvellously; **lo pasamos f.** we had a fantastic time

fenómeno,-a 1 *nm* (**a**) phenomenon (**b**) *(prodigio)* genius (**c**) *(monstruo)* freak

2 *adj Fam* fantastic, terrific

3 *interj* fantastic!, terrific!

feo,-a 1 *adj* ugly; *(asunto etc)* nasty

2 *nm Fam* **hacerle un f. a algn** to offend sb

féretro *nm* coffin

feria *nf* fair; **f. de muestras/del libro** trade/book fair

feriado,-a *Am* **1** *adj* **día f.** (public) holiday

2 *nm* (public) holiday

ferial *adj* **recinto f.** *(de exposiciones)* exhibition centre; *(de fiestas)* fairground

ferina *adj* **tos f.** whooping cough

fermentar *vi* to ferment

fermento *nm* ferment

ferocidad *nf* ferocity, fierceness

feroz *adj* fierce, ferocious; **el lobo f.** the big bad wolf

férreo,-a *adj* ferreous; *Fig* iron

ferretería *nf* ironmonger's (shop), hardware store

ferrocarril *nm Br* railway, *US* railroad

ferroviario,-a *adj* rail, *Br* railway

ferry *nm* ferry

fértil *adj* fertile

fertilidad *nf* fertility

fertilizante 1 *adj* fertilizing

2 *nm* fertilizer

fertilizar [40] *vt* to fertilize

ferviente *adj* fervent

fervor *nm* fervour

fervoroso,-a *adj* fervent

festejar *vt* to celebrate

festejos *nmpl* festivities

festín *nm* feast, banquet

festival *nm* festival

festividad *nf* festivity

festivo,-a 1 *adj* (a) *(ambiente etc)* festive (b) **día f.** holiday

2 *nm* holiday

feta *nf RP* slice

fetal *adj* foetal

fetiche *nm* fetish

fétido,-a *adj* stinking, fetid

feto *nm* foetus

feudalismo *nm* feudalism

feudo *nm* fief; *Pol* stronghold

FEVE *nm* (*abr* **Ferrocarriles de Vía Estrecha**) = Spanish narrow-gauge railways

FF.AA. *nfpl* (*abr* **Fuerzas Armadas**) Armed Forces

FF.CC. *nmpl* (*abr* **ferrocarriles**) railways

fiabilidad *nf* reliability, trustworthiness

fiable *adj* reliable, trustworthy

fiaca *nf Méx, CSur Fam (pereza)* laziness

fiador,-a *nm,f* guarantor; **salir** *o* **ser f. de algn** *(pagar fianza)* to stand bail for sb; *(avalar)* to vouch for sb

fiambre *nm* (a) *Culin* cold meat (b) *Fam (cadáver)* stiff, corpse

fiambrera *nf* lunch box

fianza *nf (depósito)* deposit; *Jur* bail; **en libertad bajo f.** on bail

fiar [29] 1 *vt* (a) *(avalar)* to guarantee (b) *(vender sin cobrar)* to sell on credit

2 *vpr* **fiarse (de)** to trust

fiasco *nm* fiasco

fibra *nf* fibre; *(de madera)* grain; **f. de vidrio** fibreglass

ficción *nf* fiction

ficha *nf* (a) *(tarjeta)* filing card; **f. técnica** specifications, technical data; *Cin* credits (b) *(en juegos)* counter; *(de ajedrez)* piece, man; *(de dominó)* domino

fichado,-a *adj* **está f. por la policía** he has a police record

fichaje *nm Dep* signing

fichar 1 *vt* (a) to put on file (b) *Dep* to sign up

2 *vi* (a) *(en el trabajo) (al entrar)* to clock in; *(al salir)* to clock out (b) *Dep* to sign

fichero *nm* card index

ficticio,-a *adj* fictitious

fidedigno,-a *adj* reliable, trustworthy; **fuentes fidedignas** reliable sources

fidelidad *nf* faithfulness; **alta f.** high fidelity, hi-fi

fideo *nm* noodle

fiebre *nf* fever; **tener f.** to have a temperature

fiel 1 *adj* (a) *(leal)* faithful, loyal (b) *(exacto)* accurate, exact

2 *nm* (a) *(de balanza)* needle, pointer (b) *Rel* **los fieles** the congregation

fieltro *nm* felt

fiera *nf* (a) wild animal; *Fam* **estaba hecho una f.** he was hopping mad (b) *Taurom* bull

fiero,-a *adj (salvaje)* wild; *(feroz)* fierce, ferocious

fierro *nm Am (hierro)* iron

fiesta *nf* (a) *(entre amigos)* party (b) **día de f.** holiday (c) *Rel* feast; **f. de guardar** holy day of obligation (d) *(festividad)* celebration, festivity

figura *nf* figure

figurado,-a *adj* figurative; **en sentido f.** figuratively

figurar 1 *vi (en lista)* to figure

2 **figurarse** *vpr* (a) to imagine, to suppose; **ya me lo figuraba** I thought as much (b) **¡figúrate!, ¡figúrese!** just imagine!

figurinista *nmf Teatro & Cin* costume designer

fijador *nm* (a) *(gomina)* gel (b) *Fot* fixative

fijamente *adv* mirar f. to stare

fijar 1 *vt* to fix; **prohibido f. carteles** *(en letrero)* post no bills

2 fijarse *vpr* (a) *(darse cuenta)* to notice (b) *(poner atención)* to pay attention, to watch

fijo,-a *adj* (a) fixed; **sin domicilio f.** of no fixed abode (b) *(trabajo)* steady

fila *nf* (a) file; **en f. india** in single file; **poner en f.** to line up (b) *(de cine, teatro)* row (c) *Mil* **filas** ranks; **llamar a algn a filas** to call sb up; **¡rompan filas!** fall out!, dismiss!

filamento *nm* filament

filantropía *nf* philanthropy

filántropo,-a *nm,f* philanthropist

filarmónico,-a *adj* philharmonic

filatelia *nf* philately, stamp collecting

filete *nm* *(de carne, pescado)* fillet

filiación *nf* *Pol* affiliation

filial 1 *adj* (a) *(de hijos)* filial (b) *Com* subsidiary

2 *nf Com* subsidiary

filigrana *nf* (a) filigree (b) *Fig* **filigranas** intricacy, intricate work

Filipinas *npl* **(las) F.** (the) Philippines

filipino,-a *adj & nm,f* Philippine, Filipino

film *nm* film

filmar *vt* to film, to shoot

filme *nm* film

fílmico,-a *adj* film

filmoteca *nf (archivo)* film library

filo *nm* (cutting) edge; **al f. de la medianoche** on the stroke of midnight; *Fig* **de doble f.** double-edged

filón *nm* (a) *Min* seam, vein (b) *Fig (buen negocio)* gold mine

filoso,-a *adj Am* sharp

filosofal *adj* **piedra f.** philosopher's stone

filosofía *nf* philosophy; *Fig* **con f.** philosophically

filosófico,-a *adj* philosophical

filósofo,-a *nm,f* philosopher

filtración *nf* filtration; *(de información)* leak

filtrar 1 *vt* (a) to filter (b) *(información)* to leak

2 • filtrarse *vpr* (a) *(líquido)* to seep (b) *(información)* to leak out

filtro *nm* filter

fin *nm* (a) *(final)* end; **dar o poner f. a** to put an end to; **llegar o tocar a su f.** to come to an end; **en f.** anyway; **¡por o al f.!** at last!; **f. de semana** weekend; **al f. y al cabo** when all's said and done; **noche de F. de Año** New Year's Eve (b) *(objetivo)* purpose, aim; **a f. de** in order to, so as to;

a f. de que in order that, so that; **con el f. de** with the intention of

final 1 *adj* final

2 *nm* end; **al f.** in the end; **f. de línea** terminal; **f. feliz** happy ending; **a finales de octubre** at the end of October

3 *nf Dep* final

finalidad *nf* purpose, aim

finalista 1 *nmf* finalist

2 *adj* in the final

finalizar [40] *vt & vi* to end, to finish

finalmente *adv* finally

financiación *nf* financing

financiar [43] *vt* to finance

financiero,-a 1 *adj* financial

2 *nm,f* financier

financista *nmf Am* financier, financial expert

finanzas *nfpl* finances

finca *nf (inmueble)* property; *(de campo)* country house

finés,-esa *adj & nm,f* = **finlandés,-esa**

fingido,-a *adj* feigned, false; **nombre f.** assumed name

fingir [57] 1 *vt* to feign

2 fingirse *vpr* to pretend to be

finlandés,-esa 1 *adj* Finnish

2 *nm,f (persona)* Finn

3 *nm (idioma)* Finnish

Finlandia *n* Finland

fino,-a 1 *adj* (a) *(hilo, capa)* fine (b) *(flaco)* thin (c) *(educado)* refined, polite (d) *(oído)* sharp, acute; *(olfato)* keen (e) *(humor, ironía)* subtle

2 *nm (vino)* = type of dry sherry -

finta *nf (en boxeo)* feint; *(en fútbol)* dummy

finura *nf* (a) *(refinamiento)* refinement, politeness (b) *(sutileza)* subtlety

firma *nf* (a) signature (b) *(empresa)* firm, company

firmamento *nm* firmament

firmante *adj & nmf* signatory; **el o la abajo f.** the undersigned

firmar *vt* to sign

firme 1 *adj* (a) firm; *Fig* **mantenerse f.** to hold one's ground; **tierra f.** terra firma (b) *Mil* **¡firmes!** attention!

2 *nm (de carretera)* road surface

3 *adv* hard

firmemente *adv* firmly

firmeza *nf* firmness

fiscal 1 *adj* fiscal, tax

2 *nmf Jur* public prosecutor, *US* district attorney

fisco *nm* treasury, exchequer

fisgar [42] *vi Fam* to snoop, to pry

fisgón,-ona *nm,f* snooper

fisgonear *vi* to snoop, to pry

física *nf* physics *sing*

físico,-a 1 *adj* physical
 2 *nm,f (profesión)* physicist
 3 *nm* physique

fisión *nf* fission

fisioterapeuta *nmf* physiotherapist

fisioterapia *nf Med* physiotherapy

fisonomía *nf* physiognomy

fisonomista *nmf Fam* **ser buen/mal f.** to be good/no good at remembering faces

fisura *nf* fissure

flácido,-a *adj* flaccid, flabby

flaco,-a 1 *adj* (a) *(delgado)* skinny (b) *Fig* **punto f.** weak spot
 2 *nm,f Am Fam (como apelativo)* **¿cómo estás, flaca?** hey, how are you doing?

flagelar *vt* to flagellate

flagelo *nm (látigo)* whip; *Fig* scourge

flagrante *adj* flagrant; **en f. delito** red-handed

flamante *adj* (a) **nuevecito f.** *(nuevo)* brand-new (b) *(vistoso)* splendid, brilliant

flamenco,-a 1 *adj* (a) *Mús* flamenco (b) *(de Flandes)* Flemish
 2 *nm* (a) *Mús* flamenco (b) *Orn* flamingo (c) *(idioma)* Flemish

flan *nm* crème caramel

🖉 Observa que la palabra inglesa **flan** es un falso amigo y no es la traducción de la palabra española **flan**. En inglés, **flan** significa "tarta".

---

flanco *nm* flank, side

flanquear *vt* to flank

flaquear *vi (fuerzas, piernas)* to weaken, to give way

flaqueza *nf* weakness

flash *nm Fot* flash

flato *nm* wind, flatulence

flatulencia *nf* flatulence

flauta *nf* flute; **f. dulce** recorder

flautín *nm (instrumento)* piccolo

flautista *nmf Mús* flute player, flautist, *US* flutist

flecha *nf* arrow

flechazo *nm Fig (enamoramiento)* love at first sight

fleco *nm* fringe

flema *nf* phlegm

flemático,-a *adj* phlegmatic

flemón *nm* gumboil, abscess

flequillo *nm Br* fringe, *US* bangs

fletar *vt* to charter

flete *nm* (a) *(alquiler)* charter (b) *(carga)* freight

flexibilidad *nf* flexibility

flexible *adj* flexible

flexión *nf* (a) *Gram* inflection (b) **flexiones** push-ups, *Br* press-ups

flexionar *vt* to bend; *(músculo)* to flex

flexo *nm* reading lamp

flipante *adj Fam* great, cool

flipar *vt Fam* **le flipan las motos** he's crazy about motorbikes

flirtear *vi* to flirt

flirteo *nm* flirting

flojear *vi (ventas etc)* to fall off, to go down; *(piernas)* to weaken, to grow weak; *(memoria)* to fail; *Andes Fam (holgazanear)* to laze around o about

flojedad *nf* weakness

flojera *nf Fam* weakness, faintness

flojo,-a *adj* (a) *(tornillo, cuerda etc)* loose, slack (b) *(perezoso)* lazy, idle; *(exámen, trabajo, resultado)* poor

flor *nf* (a) flower; **en f.** in blossom; *Fig* **en la f. de la vida** in the prime of life; *Fig* **la f. y nata** the cream (of society) (b) **a f. de piel** skin-deep

flora *nf* flora

floreado,-a *adj* flowery

florecer [33] *vi* (a) *(plantas)* to flower (b) *Fig (negocio)* to flourish, to thrive

floreciente *adj Fig* flourishing, prosperous

Florencia *n* Florence

florero *nm* vase

floricultura *nf* flower growing, floriculture

florido,-a *adj* (a) *(con flores)* flowery (b) *(estilo)* florid

floripondio *nm Pey (adorno)* heavy ornamentation

florista *nmf* florist

floristería *nf* florist's (shop)

flota *nf* fleet

flotador *nm* (a) *(de pesca)* float (b) *(para nadar)* rubber ring

flotar *vi* to float

flote *nm* floating; **a f.** afloat; **sacar a f. un negocio** to put a business on a sound footing

flotilla *nf* flotilla

fluctuación *nf* fluctuation

fluctuar [30] *vi* to fluctuate

fluidez *nf* fluency

fluido,-a 1 *adj* fluid; *(estilo etc)* fluent
 2 *nm* fluid; **f. eléctrico** current

fluir [37] *vi* to flow

flujo *nm* (a) flow (b) rising tide; **f. y reflujo** ebb and flow (c) *Fís* flux (d) *Med* discharge (e) *Informát* stream

flúor *nm* fluorine

fluorescente *adj* fluorescent

fluvial *adj* river

FM *nf* (*abr* **Frecuencia Modulada**) FM

FMI *nm* (*abr* **Fondo Monetario Internacional**) IMF

fobia *nf* phobia (**a** about)

foca *nf* seal

foco *nm* (**a**) *Elec* spotlight, floodlight (**b**) (*de ideas, revolución etc*) centre, focal point (**c**) *Am* (*de coche*) (car) headlight; (*farola*) street light (**d**) *Col, Méx* (*bombilla*) light bulb

fofo,-a *adj* soft; (*persona*) flabby

fogata *nf* bonfire

fogón *nm* (*de cocina*) ring

fogonazo *nm* flash

fogosidad *nf* ardour, fire

fogoso,-a *adj* fiery, spirited

fogueo *nm* **cartucho de f.** blank cartridge

fólder *nm* *Andes, CAm, Méx* (*carpeta*) folder

folio *nm* sheet of paper

folklore *nm* folklore

folklórico,-a *adj* **música folklórica** folk music

follaje *nm* foliage

follar *muy Fam* **1** *vi* to screw, to shag
2 *vt* (*suspender*) to fail
3 follarse *vpr* **f. a algn** to screw sb, to shag sb

folletín *nm* (**a**) (*relato*) newspaper serial (**b**) *Fig* melodrama

folleto *nm* leaflet; (*turístico*) brochure

follón *nm* *Fam* (**a**) (*alboroto*) rumpus, shindy; **armar (un) f.** to kick up a rumpus (**b**) (*enredo, confusión*) mess, trouble; **meterse en un f.** to get into a mess (**c**) **un f. de** (*montón*) a load of

follonero,-a *nm,f* troublemaker

fomentar *vt* to promote

fomento *nm* promotion

fonda *nf* inn

fondear *vi* to anchor

fondista *nmf* *Dep* long-distance runner

fondo¹ *nm* (**a**) (*parte más baja*) bottom; **a f.** thoroughly; **al f. de la calle** at the bottom of the street; **tocar f.** *Náut* to touch bottom; *Fig* to reach rock bottom; *Fig* **en el f. es bueno** deep down he's kind; **bajos fondos** dregs of society; **doble f.** false bottom
(**b**) (*de habitación*) back; (*de pasillo*) end
(**c**) (*segundo término*) background; **música de f.** background music
(**d**) *Prensa* **artículo de f.** leading article
(**e**) *Dep* **corredor de f.** long-distance runner; **esquí de f.** cross-country skiing
(**f**) *RP* (*patio*) back patio
(**g**) *Carib, Méx* (*prenda*) petticoat

fondo² *nm* *Fin* fund; **cheque sin fondos** bad cheque; *Fam* **f. común** kitty

fonendoscopio *nm* stethoscope

fonética *nf* phonetics *sing*

fonético,-a *adj* phonetic

fono *nm* *Am Fam* phone

fontanería *nf* plumbing

fontanero,-a *nm,f* plumber

footing *nm* jogging; **hacer f.** to go jogging

forajido,-a *nm,f* outlaw

foráneo,-a *adj* foreign

forastero,-a *nm,f* outsider, stranger

forcejear *vi* to wrestle, to struggle

forcejeo *nm* struggle

fórceps *nm inv* forceps

forense 1 *adj* forensic
2 -*nmf* **(médico)** **f.** forensic surgeon

forestal *adj* forest; **repoblación f.** reafforestation

forjado,-a *adj* wrought

forjar *vt* (*metal*) to forge; *Fig* to create, to make

forma *nf* (**a**) form, shape; **en f. de L** L-shaped; **¿qué f. tiene?** what shape is it? (**b**) (*manera*) way; **de esta f.** in this way; **de f. que** so that; **de todas formas** anyway, in any case; **no hubo f. de convencerla** there was no way we could convince her; **f. de pago** method of payment (**c**) *Dep* form; **estar en f.** to be on form; **estar en baja f.** to be off form (**d**) *Rel* **Sagrada F.** Host (**e**) **formas** (*modales*) manners

formación *nf* (**a**) formation (**b**) (*educación*) upbringing (**c**) (*enseñanza*) training; **f. profesional** vocational training

formal *adj* (**a**) formal (**b**) (*serio*) serious, serious-minded (**c**) (*fiable*) reliable, dependable

formalidad *nf* (**a**) formality (**b**) (*seriedad*) seriousness (**c**) (*fiabilidad*) reliability (**d**) **formalidades** (*trámites*) formalities

formalizar [40] 1 *vt* to formalize
2 formalizarse *vpr* to settle down

formar 1 *vt* (**a**) to form; **f. parte de algo** to be a part of sth (**b**) (*educar*) to bring up; (*enseñar*) to educate, to train
2 formarse *vpr* (**a**) to be formed, to form; **se formó un charco** a puddle formed; **f. una impresión de algo** to get an impression of sth (**b**) (*educarse*) to be educated o trained

formatear *vt* *Informát* to format

formato *nm* format; (*del papel*) size

formica® *nf* Formica®

formidable *adj* (**a**) (*estupendo*) wonderful, terrific (**b**) (*espantoso*) formidable

fórmula *nf* formula; *Aut* **f. uno** formula one

formular *vt (quejas, peticiones)* to make; *(deseo)* to express; *(pregunta)* to ask; *(una teoría)* to formulate

formulario *nm* form

fornicación *nf* fornication

fornicar [44] *vi* to fornicate

fornido,-a *adj* strapping, hefty

foro *nm* **(a)** forum **(b)** *(mesa redonda)* round table **(c)** *Teatro* back (of the stage) **(d)** *Jur* law court, court of justice

forofo,-a *nm,f Fam* fan, supporter

forrado,-a *adj* lined; *Fam* **estar f.** to be well-heeled, to be well-off

forraje *nm* fodder

forrar 1 *vt (por dentro)* to line; *(por fuera)* to cover

2 forrarse *vpr Fam (de dinero)* to make a packet

forro *nm* **(a)** *(por dentro)* lining; *(por fuera)* cover, case **(b)** *RP Fam (preservativo)* rubber, condom

fortalecer [33] *vt* to fortify, to strengthen

fortaleza *nf* **(a)** strength; *(de espíritu)* fortitude **(b)** *Mil* fortress, stronghold

fortificante 1 *adj* fortifying

2 *nm* tonic

fortificar [44] *vt* to fortify

fortísimo,-a *adj* very strong

fortuito,-a *adj* fortuitous

fortuna *nf* **(a)** *(destino)* fortune, fate **(b)** *(suerte)* luck; **por f.** fortunately **(c)** *(capital)* fortune

forzado,-a *adj* forced; **a marchas forzadas** at a brisk pace; **trabajos forzados** hard labour

forzar [2] *vt* **(a)** *(obligar)* to force; **f. a algn a hacer algo** to force sb to do sth **(b)** *(puerta, candado)* to force, to break open

forzosamente *adv* necessarily

forzoso,-a *adj* obligatory, compulsory; *Av* **aterrizaje f.** forced landing

fosa *nf* **(a)** *(sepultura)* grave **(b)** *(hoyo)* pit **(c)** *Anat* **fosas nasales** nostrils

fosforescente *adj* phosphorescent

fósforo *nm (cerilla)* match

fósil *adj & nm* fossil

fosilizarse [40] *vpr* to fossilize, to become fossilized

foso *nm* **(a)** *(hoyo)* pit **(b)** *(de fortificación)* moat **(c)** *(en garaje)* inspection pit

foto *nf Fam* photo; **sacar/echar una f.** to take a photo

fotocopia *nf* photocopy

fotocopiadora *nf* photocopier

fotocopiar [43] *vt* to photocopy

fotogénico,-a *adj* photogenic

fotografía *nf* **(a)** photograph; **echar** *o* **hacer** *o* **sacar fotografías** to take photographs **(b)** *(arte)* photography

fotografiar [29] *vt* to photograph, to take a photograph of

fotográfico,-a *adj* photographic

fotógrafo,-a *nm,f* photographer

fotograma *nm* still, shot

fotomatón *nm* passport photo machine

fotómetro *nm* light meter, exposure meter

FP *nf Educ (abr* **Formación Profesional***)* vocational training

frac *nm (pl* **fracs** *o* **fraques***)* dress coat, tails

fracasado,-a 1 *adj* unsuccessful

2 *nm,f (persona)* failure

fracasar *vi* to fail

fracaso *nm* failure

> 🖉 Observa que la palabra inglesa **fracas** es un falso amigo y no es la traducción de la palabra española **fracaso**. En inglés, **fracas** significa "gresca, refriega".

fracción *nf* **(a)** fraction **(b)** *Pol* faction

fraccionamiento *nm Méx (urbanización)* housing estate

fraccionar *vt,* **fraccionarse** *vpr* to break up, to split up

fraccionario,-a *adj* fractional; **moneda fraccionaria** small change

fractura *nf* fracture

fracturar *vt,* **fracturarse** *vpr* to fracture, to break

fragancia *nf* fragrance

fragata *nf* frigate

frágil *adj* **(a)** *(quebradizo)* fragile **(b)** *(débil)* frail

fragmentar 1 *vt* to fragment

2 fragmentarse *vpr* to break up

fragmento *nm* fragment; *(de novela etc)* passage

fragor *nm* din

fragua *nf* forge

fraguar [45] *vt* **(a)** *(metal)* to forge **(b)** *(plan)* to think up, to fabricate; *(conspiración)* to hatch

fraile *nm* friar, monk

frailecillo *nm* puffin

frambuesa *nf* raspberry

francamente *adv* frankly

francés,-esa 1 *adj* French; *Culin* **tortilla francesa** plain omelette

2 *nm,f (hombre)* Frenchman; *(mujer)* Frenchwoman

3 *nm (idioma)* French

Francfort, Francfurt *n* Frankfurt; *Culin* **salchicha estilo f.** frankfurter

Francia *n* France

francmasón,-ona *nm,f* freemason

franco¹,-a *adj* (**a**) *(persona)* frank (**b**) *Com* **f. a bordo** free on board; **f. fábrica** ex-works; **puerto f.** free port (**c**) *CSur (día)* **me dieron el día f.** they gave me the day off

franco² *nm Fin (moneda)* franc

francotirador,-a *nm,f* sniper

franela *nf* (**a**) *(paño)* flannel (**b**) *Bol, Col, Ven (camiseta)* T-shirt

franja *nf* (**a**) *(de terreno)* strip; *(de bandera)* stripe; *Cost* fringe, border

franquear *vt* (**a**) *(atravesar)* to cross; *Fig (dificultad, obstáculo)* to overcome (**b**) *(carta)* to frank (**c**) *(camino, paso)* to free, to clear

franqueo *nm* postage

franqueza *nf* frankness

franquicia *nf* exemption; *Com* franchise

franquismo *nm Hist* (**a**) *(ideología)* Francoism (**b**) **el f.** *(régimen)* the Franco regime

franquista *adj & nmf* Francoist

frasco *nm* small bottle, flask

frase *nf (oración)* sentence; *(expresión)* phrase; **f. hecha** set phrase o expression

fraternidad *nf* brotherhood, fraternity

fraternizar [40] *vi* to fraternize

fraterno,-a *adj* fraternal, brotherly

fraude *nm* fraud; **f. fiscal** tax evasion

fraudulento,-a *adj* fraudulent

fray *nm Rel* brother

frazada *nf Am* blanket

frecuencia *nf* frequency; **con f.** frequently, often

frecuentar *vt* to frequent

frecuente *adj* frequent

frecuentemente *adv* frequently, often

fregadero *nm* (kitchen) sink

fregado¹ *nm* (**a**) *(lavado)* washing (**b**) *Fam (follón)* racket

fregado²,-a *adj Am Fam* (**a**) *(persona) (difícil)* tiresome, annoying (**b**) *(objeto) (roto)* broken

fregar [1] *vt* (**a**) *(lavar)* to wash; *(suelo)* to mop (**b**) *Am Fam (molestar)* to annoy, to irritate (**c**) *Am Fam (romper)* to bust, to break

fregón,-ona *adj Am* annoying

fregona *nf* mop

freidora *nf* (deep fat) fryer

freír [56] *(pp frito)* **1** *vt* to fry

2 freírse *vpr* to fry; *Fig* **f. de calor** to be roasting

frenar *vt* to brake; *Fig (inflación etc)* to slow down; *(impulsos)* to restrain

frenazo *nm* sudden braking; **dar un f.** to jam on the brakes

frenesí *nm* frenzy

frenético,-a *adj* frantic

freno *nm* (**a**) brake; **pisar/soltar el f.** to press/release the brake; **f. de disco/tambor** disc/drum brake; **f. de mano** handbrake (**b**) *(de caballería)* bit (**c**) *Fig* curb, check; **poner f. a algo** to curb sth

frente 1 *nm* front; **al f. de** at the head of; **chocar de f.** to crash head on; **hacer f. a algo** to face sth, to stand up to sth

2 *nf Anat* forehead; **f. a f.** face to face

3 *adv* **f. a** in front of, opposite

fresa *nf* (**a**) strawberry (**b**) *Téc* milling cutter

fresca *nf Fam* cheeky remark

fresco,-a 1 *adj* (**a**) *(frío)* cool (**b**) *(comida, fruta)* fresh (**c**) *(reciente)* fresh, new (**d**) *(descarado)* cheeky, shameless; **se quedó tan f.** he didn't bat an eyelid; **¡qué f.!** what a nerve!

2 *nm* (**a**) *(frescor)* fresh air, cool air; **al f.** in the cool (**b**) *Arte* fresco

frescor *nm* freshness

frescura *nf* (**a**) freshness (**b**) *(desvergüenza)* cheek, nerve

fresno *nm* ash tree

fresón *nm* (large) strawberry

frialdad *nf* coldness

fríamente *adv* coolly

fricción *nf* (**a**) friction (**b**) *(masaje)* massage

friega *nf* rub

friegaplatos *nmf inv (persona)* dishwasher

frigider *nm Andes* refrigerator, fridge

frígido,-a *adj* frigid

frigorífico,-a 1 *nm* refrigerator, fridge

2 *adj* **cámara frigorífica** cold store

frijol, fríjol *nm Andes, CAm, Carib, Méx* bean

frío,-a 1 *adj* (**a**) cold (**b**) *(indiferente)* cold, cool, indifferent; **su comentario me dejó f.** her remark left me cold

2 *nm* cold; **hace f.** it's cold

friolento,-a *adj Am* sensitive to the cold

friolera *nf Fam* **la f. de diez mil pesetas/ dos horas** a mere ten thousand pesetas/ two hours

friolero,-a *adj* sensitive to the cold

fritanga *nf* fried food; *Am* greasy food

frito,-a 1 *adj* (**a**) *Culin* fried (**b**) *Fam* exasperated, fed up; **me tienes f.** I'm sick to death of you

2 *nm* **fritos** fried food

frívolo,-a *adj* frivolous

frondoso,-a *adj* leafy, luxuriant

frontera *nf* frontier

fronterizo,-a *adj* frontier, border; **países fronterizos** neighbouring countries

frontón *nm Dep* pelota

frotar 1 *vt* to rub

2 frotarse *vpr* to rub; **f. las manos** to rub one's hands together

fructífero,-a *adj (árbol)* fruit-bearing; *(esfuerzo)* fruitful

frugal *adj* frugal

fruncir [52] *vt* (**a**) *Cost* to gather (**b**) *(labios)* to purse, to pucker; **f. el ceño** to frown, to knit one's brow

frustración *nf* frustration

frustrado,-a *adj* frustrated; **intento f.** unsuccessful attempt

frustrante *adj* frustrating

frustrar 1 *vt* to frustrate; *(defraudar)* to disappoint

2 frustrarse *vpr* (**a**) *(esperanza)* to fail, to go awry (**b**) *(persona)* to be frustrated *o* disappointed

fruta *nf* fruit; **f. del tiempo** fresh fruit

frutería *nf* fruit shop

frutero,-a 1 *nm,f* fruiterer

2 *nm* fruit dish *o* bowl

frutilla *nf Bol, CSur, Ecuad* strawberry

fruto *nm* fruit; **frutos secos** nuts; **dar f.** to bear fruit; *Fig (dar buen resultado)* to be fruitful; **sacar f. de algo** to profit from sth

fu *interj* **ni fu ni fa** so-so

fucsia *nf* fuchsia

fuego *nm* (**a**) fire; **fuegos artificiales** fireworks (**b**) *(lumbre)* light; **¿me da f., por favor?** have you got a light, please? (**c**) *Culin* **a f. lento** on a low flame; *(al horno)* in a slow oven

fuel, fuel-oil *nm* diesel

fuente *nf* (**a**) fountain; *Chile, Col, Méx, Ven* **f. de soda** *(cafetería)* cafe *(serving soft drinks and alcohol)* (**b**) *(recipiente)* dish, serving dish (**c**) *(de información)* source

fuera¹ *adv* (**a**) outside, out; **quédate f.** stay outside; **sal f.** go out; **desde f.** from (the) outside; **por f.** on the outside; **la puerta de f.** the outer door; **f. de** out of; **f. de serie** extraordinary; *Fig* **estar f. de sí** to be beside oneself (**c**) *Dep* **el equipo de f.** the away team; **jugar f.** to play away; **f. de juego** offside

fuera² **1** *subj imperf de* **ir**

2 *subj imperf de* **ser**

fuero *nm* (**a**) *Hist* code of laws (**b**) *Fig* **en tu f. interno** deep down, in your heart of hearts

fuerte 1 *adj* strong; *(dolor)* severe; *(sonido)* loud; *(comida)* heavy; **el plato f.** the main course; *Fig* the most important event

2 *nm* (**a**) *(fortaleza)* fort (**b**) *(punto fuerte)* forte, strong point

3 *adv* **¡abrázame f.!** hold me tight!; **comer f.** to eat a lot; **¡habla más f.!** speak up!; **¡pégale f.!** hit him hard!

fuerza *nf* (**a**) *(fortaleza)* strength; *Fig* **a f. de** by dint of (**b**) *(violencia)* force; **a la f.** *(por obligación)* of necessity; *(con violencia)* by force; **por f.** of necessity; **f. mayor** force majeure (**c**) *Fís* force (**d**) *(cuerpo)* force; **las fuerzas del orden** the forces of law and order; **f. aérea** air force; **fuerzas armadas** armed forces

fuese 1 *subj imperf de* **ir**

2 *subj imperf de* **ser**

fuete *nm Am* whip

fuga *nf* (**a**) *(huida)* escape; **darse a la f.** to take flight (**b**) *(de gas etc)* leak

fugarse [42] *vpr* to escape; **f. de casa** to run away from home

fugaz *adj* fleeting, brief

fugitivo,-a *nm,f* fugitive

fui 1 *pt indef de* **ir**

2 *pt indef de* **ser**

fulana *nf* whore, tart

fulano,-a *nm,f* so-and-so; *(hombre)* what's-his-name; *(mujer)* what's-her-name; **Doña Fulana de tal** Mrs So-and-so

fular *nm* headscarf

fulgor *nm Literario* brilliance, glow

fullería *nf* cheating; **hacer fullerías** to cheat

fullero,-a 1 *adj* cheating

2 *nm,f* cheat

fulminante *adj (cese)* summary; *(muerte, enfermedad)* sudden; *(mirada)* withering

fulminar *vt Fig* to strike dead; **f. a algn con la mirada** to look daggers at sb

fumada *nf Am (calada)* pull, drag

fumado,-a *adj Fam (colocado)* stoned

fumador,-a *nm,f* smoker; **los no fumadores** nonsmokers

fumar 1 *vt & vi* to smoke; **no f.** *(en letrero)* no smoking

2 fumarse *vpr* to smoke; **f. un cigarro** to smoke a cigarette

> Observa que el verbo inglés **to fume** es un falso amigo y no es la traducción del verbo español **fumar**. En inglés, **to fume** significa "despedir humo".

fumigar [42] *vt* to fumigate

funambulista *nmf*, **funámbulo,-a** *nm,f* tightrope walker

función *nf* (**a**) function; **en f. de** according to (**b**) *(cargo)* duties; **entrar en funciones** to take up one's duties; **presidente**

en funciones acting president (**c**) *Cin &
Teatro* performance

funcionamiento *nm* operation; **poner/
entrar en f.** to put/come into operation

funcionar *vi* to work; **no funciona** (*en
letrero*) out of order

funcionario,-a *nm,f* civil servant; **f. público** public official

funda *nf* cover; (*de gafas etc*) case; (*de
espada*) sheath; **f. de almohada** pillowcase

fundación *nf* foundation

fundador,-a *nm,f* founder

fundamental *adj* fundamental

fundamentar *vt* to base (**en** on)

fundamento *nm* basis, grounds; **sin f.**
unfounded

fundar 1 *vt* (**a**) (*empresa*) to found (**b**)
(*teoría*) to base, to found
2 fundarse *vpr* (**a**) (*empresa*) to be founded (**b**) (*teoría*) to be based (**en** on)

> *ℓ* Observa que el verbo inglés **to fund** es
> un falso amigo y no es la traducción del ver-
> bo español **fundar**. En inglés, **to fund** sig-
> nifica "financiar".

fundición *nf* (**a**) (*de metales*) smelting
(**b**) (*fábrica*) foundry

fundir 1 *vt* (**a**) to melt; (*bombilla, plomos*)
to blow (**b**) (*unir*) to unite, to join
2 fundirse *vpr* (**a**) (*derretirse*) to melt (**b**)
(*bombilla, plomos*) to blow (**c**) (*unirse*) to
merge (**d**) *RP Fam* (*arruinarse*) to go bust,
to be ruined

fúnebre *adj* (**a**) (*mortuorio*) funeral; **coche f.** hearse (**b**) (*lúgubre*) mournful,
lugubrious

funeral *nm* funeral

funeraria *nf* undertaker's, *US* funeral
home

funesto,-a *adj* ill-fated, fatal; (*consecuencias*) disastrous

fungir [57] *vi Méx* to act (**de** *o* **como** as)

funicular *nm* funicular (railway)

furcia *nf Pey* whore, tart

furgón *nm Aut* van

furgoneta *nf* van

furia *nf* fury; **ponerse hecho una f.** to
become furious, to fly into a rage

furibundo,-a *adj* furious, enraged

furioso,-a *adj* furious; **ponerse f.** to get
furious

furor *nm* fury, rage; *Fig* **hacer f.** to be all
the rage

furtivo,-a *adj* furtive, stealthy; **caza/pes-
ca furtiva** poaching; **cazador/pescador f.**
poacher

furúnculo *nm Med* boil

fuselaje *nm* fuselage

fusible *nm* fuse

fusil *nm* gun, rifle

fusilamiento *nm* shooting, execution

fusilar *vt* to shoot, to execute

fusión *nf* (**a**) (*de metales*) fusion; (*del
hielo*) thawing, melting; **punto de f.** melting point (**b**) *Com* merger

fusionar *vt*, **fusionarse** *vpr* (**a**) *Fís* to
fuse (**b**) *Com* to merge

fustán *nm Am* petticoat

fútbol *nm* soccer, *Br* football

futbolín *nm Br* table football, *US* foosball

futbolista *nmf* soccer player, *Br* footballer

fútil *adj* futile, trivial

futilidad *nf* futility, triviality

futurista *adj* futuristic

futuro,-a 1 *adj* future
2 *nm* future; **en un f. próximo** in the near
future; *CSur, Méx* **a f.** in the future

G, g [xe] *nf (la letra)* G, g
gabán *nm* overcoat
gabardina *nf (prenda)* raincoat
gabinete *nm* (a) *(despacho)* study; **g. de abogados** lawyers' office (b) *Pol* cabinet
gaceta *nf* gazette
gachas *nfpl* porridge
gacho,-a *adj* **con la cabeza gacha** hanging one's head
gaditano,-a 1 *adj* of/from Cadiz
2 *nm,f* person from Cadiz
gafar *vt Fam* to put a jinx on, to bring bad luck to
gafas *nfpl* glasses, spectacles; **g. de sol** sunglasses
gafe *adj & nm Fam* **ser g.** to be a jinx

> ✎ Observa que la palabra inglesa **gaffe** es un falso amigo y no es la traducción de la palabra española **gafe**. En inglés, **gaffe** significa "metedura de pata, desliz".

gafete *nm Méx* badge
gaita *nf* bagpipes
gajes *nmpl Fam Irón* **g. del oficio** occupational hazards
gajo *nm* (a) *(de naranja, pomelo etc)* segment (b) *(rama desprendida)* torn-off branch
gala *nf* (a) *(vestido)* full dress; **de g.** dressed up; *(ciudad)* decked out (b) *(espectáculo)* gala; **hacer g. de** to glory in (c) **galas** finery
galán *nm* (a) handsome young man; *Hum* ladies' man (b) *Teatro* leading man
galante *adj* gallant
galantear *vt* to court
galanteo *nm* courtship
galantería *nf* gallantry
galápago *nm* turtle
galardón *nm* prize
galardonado,-a *nm,f* prizewinner
galardonar *vt* to award a prize to
galaxia *nf* galaxy
galeón *nm* galleon
galeote *nm* galley slave
galera *nf* (a) *Náut* galley (b) *(carro)* covered wagon (c) *Impr* galley proof
galería *nf* (a) *Arquit* covered balcony (b) *(museo)* art gallery (c) *Teatro* gallery, gods
Gales *n* **(el país de) G.** Wales
galés,-esa 1 *adj* Welsh
2 *nm,f (hombre)* Welshman; *(mujer)* Welshwoman; **los galeses** the Welsh
3 *nm (idioma)* Welsh
galgo *nm* greyhound
Galicia *n* Galicia
galimatías *nm inv Fam* gibberish
gallardo *adj* (a) *(apuesto)* smart (b) *(valeroso)* brave
gallego,-a 1 *adj* (a) Galician (b) *CSur, Cuba Pey* Spanish
2 *nm,f* (a) Galician, person from Galicia (b) *CSur, Cuba Pey* Spaniard
3 *nm (idioma)* Galician
galleta *nf* (a) *Culin Br* biscuit, *US* cookie (b) *Fam (cachete)* slap
gallina 1 *nf* hen
2 *nmf Fam* coward, chicken
gallinero *nm* (a) hen run (b) *Teatro* **el g.** the gods
gallito *nm Fam (peleón)* bully
gallo *nm* (a) cock, rooster; *Fam Fig* **en menos que un canto de g.** before you could say Jack Robinson (b) *Fam Mús* off-key note
galón¹ *nm Mil* stripe
galón² *nm (medida)* gallon, *Br* = 4.55 l, *US* = 3.79 l
galopante *adj Fig (inflación etc)* galloping
galopar *vi* to gallop
galope *nm* gallop; **a g. tendido** flat out
galpón *nm Am* shed
gama *nf* range; *Mús* scale
gamba *nf* prawn
gamberrismo *nm* hooliganism
gamberro,-a 1 *nm,f* hooligan
2 *adj* uncouth
gamo *nm* fallow deer
gamonal *nm Andes, CAm, Ven* local boss
gamuza *nf* (a) *Zool* chamois (b) *(trapo)* chamois *o* shammy leather
gana *nf* (a) *(deseo)* wish (**de** for); **de buena g.** willingly; **de mala g.** reluctantly; *Fam* **no me da la g.** I don't feel like it (b) **tener ganas de (hacer) algo** to feel like

(doing) sth; **quedarse con las ganas** not to manage (**c**) (*apetito*) appetite; **comer con ganas** to eat heartily

ganadería *nf* (**a**) (*crianza*) livestock farming (**b**) (*conjunto de ganado*) livestock

ganadero,-a *nm,f* livestock farmer

ganado *nm* (**a**) livestock (**b**) *Fam Fig* (*gente*) crowd

ganador,-a 1 *adj* winning
2 *nm,f* winner

ganancia *nf* profit

ganar 1 *vt* (**a**) (*sueldo*) to earn (**b**) (*victoria*) to win (**c**) (*aventajar*) to beat (**d**) (*alcanzar*) to reach
2 ganarse *vpr* (**a**) to earn; **g. el pan** to earn one's daily bread (**b**) (*merecer*) to deserve; **se lo ha ganado** he deserves it

ganchillo *nm* crochet work

gancho *nm* (**a**) hook (**b**) *Fam Fig* (*gracia, atractivo*) charm (**c**) *Andes, CAm, Méx* (*horquilla*) hairpin (**d**) *Andes, CAm, Méx, Ven* (*percha*) hanger

gandul,-a *nm,f* loafer

ganga *nf* bargain

gangoso,-a *adj* nasal

gangrena *nf* gangrene

gansada *nf Fam* silly thing to say/do

ganso,-a 1 *nm,f* (**a**) goose; (*macho*) gander (**b**) *Fam* dolt
2 *adj Fam* ginormous; **pasta gansa** bread, dough

ganzúa *nf* picklock

gañán *nm* (*obrero*) farmhand; *Fam* (*bribón*) cheat

garabatear *vt & vi* to scribble

garabato *nm* scrawl

garaje *nm* garage

garante *nmf Fin* guarantor

garantía *nf* (**a**) guarantee (**b**) *Jur* (*fianza*) bond, security

garantizar [40] *vt* to guarantee

garbanzo *nm* chickpea

garbeo *nm Fam* (*paseo*) stroll; **darse un g.** to go for a stroll

garbo *nm* grace

garfio *nm* hook, grappling iron

gargajo *nm* spit

garganta *nf* (**a**) throat (**b**) (*desfiladero*) narrow pass

gargantilla *nf* short necklace

gárgaras *nfpl* (**a**) gargling; *Fam* **¡vete a hacer g.!** get lost! (**b**) *Am* (*licor*) gargling solution

gárgola *nf* gargoyle

garita *nf* (*caseta*) hut; *Mil* sentry box

garito *nm Fam* joint

garra *nf* (**a**) *Zool* claw; (*de ave*) talon (**b**)

Fig (*fuerza*) force; **tener g.** to be compelling

garrafa *nf* carafe

garrafal *adj* monumental

garrapata *nf* tick

garrote *nm* (**a**) (*porra*) club (**b**) *Jur* garrotte

garrucha *nf* pulley

gárrulo,-a *adj Fig* garrulous

garúa *nf Andes, RP, Ven* drizzle

garza *nf* heron

gas *nm* (**a**) gas; **g. ciudad** town gas; **gases (nocivos)** fumes; **g. de escape** exhaust fumes (**b**) (*en bebida*) fizz; **agua con g.** fizzy water (**c**) *Med* **gases** flatulence

gasa *nf* gauze

gaseosa *nf* lemonade

gasfitería *nf Chile, Ecuad, Perú* plumber's (shop)

gasfitero,-a *nm,f Chile, Ecuad, Perú* plumber

gasoducto *nm* gas pipeline

gasoil, gasóleo *nm* diesel oil

gasolina *nf Br* petrol, *US* gasoline

gasolinera, *Méx* **gasolinería** *nf Br* petrol *o US* gas station

gastado,-a *adj* (*zapatos etc*) worn-out; *Fig* (*frase*) hackneyed

gastar 1 *vt* (**a**) (*consumir*) (*dinero, tiempo*) to spend; (*gasolina, electricidad*) to consume (**b**) *Fig* (*malgastar*) to waste (**c**) (*ropa*) to wear; **¿qué número gastas?** what size do you take? (**d**) **g. una broma a algn** to play a practical joke on sb
2 gastarse *vpr* (**a**) (*zapatos etc*) to wear out (**b**) (*gasolina etc*) to run out

gasto *nm* expenditure; **gastos** expenses; **gastos de viaje** travelling expenses

gatas: • a gatas *loc adv* on all fours

gatear *vi* (**a**) to crawl (**b**) (*trepar*) to climb

gatillo *nm* (*de armas*) trigger; **apretar el g.** to pull the trigger

gato *nm* (**a**) cat (**b**) *Aut & Téc* jack

gauchada *nf CSur* favour

gaucho,-a 1 *adj RP Fam* (*servicial*) helpful, obliging
2 *nm,f* gaucho

gaveta *nf* (**a**) (*cajón*) drawer (**b**) *Am Aut* (*guantera*) glove compartment

gavilán *nm Orn* sparrowhawk

gavilla *nf* (*de ramillas etc*) sheaf

gaviota *nf* seagull

gay *adj inv & nm* (*pl* **gays**) homosexual, gay

gazapo *nm* (**a**) (*error*) misprint (**b**) *Zool* young rabbit

gaznate *nm* gullet

gazpacho *nm Culin* gazpacho

gel *nm* gel; **g. (de ducha)** shower gel

gelatina *nf (ingrediente)* gelatin; *Culin* jelly

gema *nf* gem

gemelo,-a 1 *adj & nm,f* (identical) twin
2 *nmpl* **gemelos** (a) *(de camisa)* cufflinks (b) *(anteojos)* binoculars

gemido *nm* groan

Géminis *nm* Gemini

gemir **[6]** *vi* to groan

generación *nf* generation

general 1 *adj* general; **por lo** *o* **en g.** in general, generally;
2 *nm Mil & Rel* general

Generalitat *nf* Catalan/Valencian/Balearic parliament

generalización *nf* (a) generalization (b) *(extensión)* spread

generalizar **[40] 1** *vt* (a) to generalize (b) *(extender)* to spread
2 generalizarse *vpr* to become widespread *o* common

generalmente *adv* generally

generar *vt* to generate

género *nm* (a) *(clase)* kind, sort (b) *Arte & Lit* genre (c) *(mercancía)* article (d) *Ling* gender (e) *Biol* genus; **el g. humano** mankind

generosidad *nf* generosity

generoso,-a *adj* (a) generous (**con** to) (b) *(vino)* full-bodied

Génesis *nm Rel* Genesis

genética *nf* genetics *sing*

genético,-a *adj* genetic

genial *adj* brilliant; *Fam* terrific

> ℘ Observa que la palabra inglesa **genial** es un falso amigo y no es la traducción de la palabra española **genial**. En inglés, **genial** significa "cordial, amable".

genio *nm* (a) *(carácter)* temperament; *(mal carácter)* temper; **estar de mal g.** to be in a bad mood (b) *(facultad)* genius

genocidio *nm* genocide

Génova *n* Genoa

gente *nf* (a) people (b) *(familia)* folks (c) *Am* respectable people

gentil *adj* (a) *(amable)* kind (b) *(pagano)* pagan

> ℘ Observa que la palabra inglesa **genteel** es un falso amigo y no es la traducción de la palabra española **gentil**. En inglés, **genteel** significa "fino, distinguido".

gentileza *nf* kindness; *Fml* **por g. de** by courtesy of

gentío *nm* crowd

gentuza *nf Pey* riffraff

genuino,-a *adj* *(puro)* genuine; *(verdadero)* authentic

geografía *nf* geography

geología *nf* geology

geometría *nf* geometry

geranio *nm* geranium

gerencia *nf* management

gerente *nmf* manager

germano,-a 1 *adj* German, Germanic
2 *nm,f* German

germen *nm* (a) *Biol* germ (b) *Fig (inicio)* germ; *(fuente)* origin

germinar *vi* to germinate

gerundio *nm* gerund

gesta *nf* heroic exploit

gestación *nf* gestation

gestar *vt* to gestate

gesticular *vi* to gesticulate

gestión *nf* (a) *(administración)* management (b) **gestiones** *(negociaciones)* negotiations; *(trámites)* formalities

gestionar *vt* to take steps to acquire *o* obtain; *(negociar)* to negotiate

gesto *nm* (a) *(mueca)* face (b) *(con las manos)* gesture

gestor,-a *nm,f* ≃ solicitor

giba *nf* hump

gibar *vt Fam* to annoy

Gibraltar *n* Gibraltar; **el peñón de G.** the Rock of Gibraltar

gibraltareño,-a 1 *adj* of/from Gibraltar
2 *nm,f* Gibraltarian

gigante,-a 1 *nm,f* giant
2 *adj* giant, enormous

gigantesco,-a *adj* gigantic

gigoló *nm* gigolo

gil, gila *nm,f CSur Fam* twit, idiot

gili, gilí *nm muy Fam* = **gilipollas**

gilipollas *nmf muy Fam Br* prat, *US* dork

gimnasia *nf* gymnastics

gimnasio *nm* gymnasium

gimotear *vi* to whine

Ginebra *n* Geneva

ginebra *nf (bebida)* gin

ginecología *nf* gynaecology

ginecólogo,-a *nm,f* gynaecologist

gira *nf Teatro & Mús* tour

girar 1 *vi* (a) *(dar vueltas)* to spin (b) **g. a la derecha/izquierda** to turn right/left
2 *vt Fin* (a) *(expedir)* to draw (b) *(dinero)* to transfer

girasol *nm* sunflower

giratorio,-a *adj* revolving

giro *nm* (a) *(vuelta)* turn (b) *(de acontecimientos)* direction (c) *(frase)* turn of phrase (d) *Fin* draft; **g. telegráfico** money order; **g. postal** postal *o* money order

gis nm Andes, Méx chalk

gitano,-a adj & nm,f gypsy, gipsy

glacial adj icy

glaciar nm glacier

glándula nf gland

glasear vt Culin to glaze

global adj comprehensive; **precio g.** all-inclusive price

globalmente adv as a whole

globo nm (a) balloon (b) (esfera) globe (c) (lámpara) globe, glass lampshade

glóbulo nm globule

gloria nf (a) (fama) glory (b) Rel heaven; Fam Fig **estar en la g.** to be in seventh heaven (c) Fam (delicia) delight

glorieta nf (a) (plazoleta) small square (b) (encrucijada de calles) Br roundabout, US traffic circle (c) (en un jardín) arbour

glorificar [44] vt to glorify

glorioso,-a adj glorious

glosa nf (a) gloss (b) Lit (comentario) notes, commentary

glosar vt (a) (explicar) to gloss; (texto) to interpret (b) (comentar) to comment on

glosario nm glossary

glotón,-ona 1 adj greedy
2 nm,f glutton

glotonería nf gluttony

glucosa nf Quím glucose

gobernación nf government; Pol & Hist Ministerio de la G. Br ≃ Home Office, US ≃ Department of the Interior

gobernador,-a nm,f governor

gobernante adj ruling

gobernar [1] 1 vt to govern; (un país) to rule
2 vi Náut to steer

gobiernista Am **1** adj government
2 nmf government supporter

gobierno nm (a) Pol government (b) (mando) running (c) Náut steering (d) Náut (timón) rudder

goce nm enjoyment

gofio nm Am Can roasted maize meal

gol nm goal

goleada nf lots of goals; **ganar por g.** to win by a barrowload

golear vt to hammer

golf nm golf; **palo de g.** golf club

golfista nmf golfer

golfo¹,-a 1 nm,f good-for-nothing
2 nf **golfa** Fam Pey tart

golfo² nm Geog gulf; **el g. Pérsico** the Persian Gulf

golondrina nf swallow

golosina nf Br sweet, US candy

goloso,-a adj sweet-toothed

golpe nm (a) blow; (llamada) knock; (puñetazo) punch; **de g.** all of a sudden; **g. de estado** coup d'état; **g. de suerte** stroke of luck; **no dar ni g.** not to lift a finger (b) Aut bump (c) (desgracia) blow; **un duro g.** a great blow (d) (de humor) witticism

golpear vt to hit; (con el puño) to punch; (puerta, cabeza) to bang

golpiza nf Am beating

goma nf (a) rubber; **g. de pegar** glue; **g. de borrar** eraser, Br rubber (b) (elástica) rubber band (c) Cuba, CSur (neumático) tyre (d) Fam (preservativo) rubber

gomaespuma nf foam rubber

gomal nm Am Agr rubber plantation

gomería nf CSur tyre centre

gomero nm Am (a) Bot gum tree (b) (recolector) rubber collector

gomina nf hair cream

góndola nf (a) (embarcación) gondola (b) Bol, Chile (autobús) (long distance) bus

gordo,-a 1 adj (a) (carnoso) fat (b) (grueso) thick (c) (importante) big; **me cae g.** I can't stand him; **de g.** in a big way
2 nm,f (a) fat person; Fam fatty (b) Am Fam (como apelativo) ¿cómo estás, gorda? hey, how are you doing?
3 nm **el g.** (de lotería) the jackpot

gordura nf fatness

gorgorito nm trill

gorila nm (a) gorilla (b) Fig (en discoteca etc) bouncer

gorjear 1 vi to chirp
2 •gorjearse vpr Am **g. de algn** to laugh at sb's expense

gorjeo nm chirping

gorra nf cap; (con visera) peaked cap; Fam **de g.** free

gorrión nm sparrow

gorro nm (a) cap (b) Fam **estar hasta el g. (de)** to be up to here (with)

gorrón,-ona nm,f sponger

gota nf (a) drop; (de sudor) bead; **g. a g.** drop by drop; **ni g.** not a bit (b) Med gout

gotear v impers to drip; **el techo gotea** there's a leak in the ceiling

gotera nf leak

gótico,-a adj Gothic

gozar [40] 1 vt to enjoy
2 vi (disfrutar) **g. (de)** to enjoy

gozne nm hinge

gozo nm pleasure

grabación nf recording

grabado nm (a) (arte) engraving (b) (dibujo) drawing

grabadora nf tape recorder

grabar *vt* (**a**) *(sonidos, imágenes)* to record (**b**) *Informát* to save (**c**) *Arte* to engrave

gracia *nf* (**a**) *(atractivo)* grace (**b**) *(chiste)* joke; **hacer** *o* **tener g.** to be funny (**c**) *(indulto)* pardon

gracias *nfpl (agradecimiento)* thanks; **g. a Dios** thank God, thank goodness; **g. a** thanks to; **muchas** *o* **muchísimas g.** thank you very much

gracioso,-a 1 *adj* (**a**) *(divertido)* funny (**b**) *(garboso)* graceful
   2 *nm,f Teatro* comic character

grada *nf* (**a**) *(peldaño)* step (**b**) **gradas** *(en estadio)* terraces

gradación *nf* (**a**) gradation (**b**) *Mús* scale

graderío *nm* tiers of seats; *Dep* terraces, *US* bleachers

gradiente 1 *nm* gradient
   2 *nf Am* slope

grado *nm* (**a**) degree (**b**) *Mil* rank (**c**) **de buen g.** willingly, gladly

graduable *adj* adjustable

graduación *nf* (**a**) gradation (**b**) *Mil* rank

graduado,-a *nm,f* graduate

gradual *adj* gradual

gradualmente *adv* gradually

graduar [30] **1** *vt* (**a**) *Educ & Mil* to confer degree *o* a rank on (**b**) *(regular)* to regulate
   2 graduarse *vpr* (**a**) *Educ & Mil* to graduate (**b**) **g. la vista** to have one's eyes tested

gráfico,-a 1 *adj* graphic; **diseño g.** graphic design
   2 *nm* graph

grafista *nmf* graphic designer

gragea *nf Med* pill

grajo,-a 1 *nm,f Orn* rook
   2 *nm Am* body odour

gral. *(abr* **General***)* gen

gramática *nf* grammar

gramo *nm* gram, gramme

gran *adj* = **grande**

grana *nf* scarlet

granada *nf* (**a**) *(fruto)* pomegranate (**b**) *Mil* grenade

granate 1 *adj inv (color)* maroon
   2 *nm (color)* maroon

Gran Bretaña *n* Great Britain

grande *adj* (**a**) *(tamaño)* big, large; *Fig (persona)* great (**b**) *(cantidad)* large; **vivir a lo g.** to live in style; *Fig* **pasarlo en g.** to have a great time

> **gran** is used instead of **grande** before masculine singular nouns (e.g. **gran hombre** great man).

grandeza *nf* (**a**) *(importancia)* greatness (**b**) *(grandiosidad)* grandeur; **delirios de g.** delusions of grandeur

grandioso,-a *adj* grandiose

granel: •a granel *loc adv (sin medir exactamente)* loose

granero *nm Agr* granary

granito *nm* granite

granizada *nf*, **granizado** *nm* iced drink

granizar [40] *v impers* to hail

granizo *nm* hail

granja *nf* farm

granjear *vt*, **granjearse** *vpr* to gain

granjero,-a *nm,f* farmer

grano *nm* (**a**) grain; *(de café)* bean; **ir al g.** to get to the point (**b**) *(espinilla)* spot

granuja *nm* (**a**) *(pilluelo)* ragamuffin (**b**) *(estafador)* con-man

grapa *nf* (**a**) staple (**b**) *Constr* cramp (**c**) *CSur (bebida)* grappa

grapadora *nf* stapler

grapar *vt* to staple

grasa *nf* grease

grasiento,-a *adj* greasy

graso,-a *adj (pelo)* greasy; *(materia)* fatty

gratificar [44] *vt* (**a**) *(satisfacer)* to gratify (**b**) *(recompensar)* to reward

gratinar *vt Culin* to cook in a sauce until golden brown

gratis *adj inv & adv* free

gratitud *nf* gratitude

grato,-a *adj* pleasant

gratuito,-a *adj* (**a**) *(de balde)* free (of charge) (**b**) *(arbitrario)* gratuitous

grava *nf* *(guijas)* gravel; *(en carretera)* chippings

gravamen *nm Jur* (**a**) *(carga)* burden (**b**) *(impuesto)* tax

gravar *vt Jur* (**a**) *(cargar)* to burden (**b**) *(impuestos)* to tax

grave *adj* (**a**) *(importante)* serious (**b**) *(muy enfermo)* seriously ill (**c**) *(voz, nota)* low

gravedad *nf* (**a**) *(seriedad, importancia)* seriousness (**b**) *Fís* gravity

gravilla *nf* chippings

gravitar *vi* (**a**) *Fís* to gravitate (**b**) **g. sobre** to rest on

gravoso,-a *adj* (**a**) *(costoso)* costly (**b**) *(molesto)* burdensome

graznar *vi (de pájaro)* to squawk; *(de pato)* to quack; *(de cuervo)* to caw

graznido *nm* *(un sonido)* squawk; *(varios)* squawking; *(de pato)* quack; *(de cuervo)* caw

Grecia *n* Greece

gregario,-a *adj* gregarious; **instinto g.** herd instinct

gremio *nm* (a) *Hist* guild (b) *(profesión)* profession

greña *nf* lock of entangled hair; *Fam* andar a la g. to squabble

gres *nm* artículos de g. stoneware

gresca *nf* (a) *(bulla)* racket (b) *(riña)* row

griego,-a *adj & nm,f* Greek

grieta *nf* crack; *(en la piel)* chap

grifo *nm* (a) *(llave)* Br tap, US faucet (b) *Perú (gasolinera)* Br petrol station, US gas station

grillete *nm* shackle

grillo *nm* cricket

gringo,-a *Fam* 1 *adj* (a) *(estadounidense)* gringo, American (b) *Am (extranjero)* foreign
  2 *nm,f* (a) *(estadounidense)* gringo, American (b) *Am (extranjero)* = non-Spanish-speaking foreigner

gripa *nf Col, Méx* flu

gripe *nf* flu

gris *adj & nm* grey

grisáceo,-a *adj* greyish

gritar *vt & vi* to shout

grito *nm* shout; **a voz en g.** at the top of one's voice

Groenlandia *n* Greenland

grosella *nf (fruto)* redcurrant; **g. negra** blackcurrant; **g. silvestre** gooseberry

grosería *nf* (a) *(ordinariez)* rude word o expression (b) *(rusticidad)* rudeness

grosero,-a *adj (tosco)* coarse; *(maleducado)* rude

grosor *nm* thickness

grotesco,-a *adj* grotesque

grúa *nf* (a) *Constr* crane (b) *Aut Br* breakdown van o truck, *US* tow truck

grueso,-a 1 *adj* thick; *(persona)* stout
  2 *nm (parte principal)* bulk

grulla *nf Orn* crane

grumo *nm* lump; *(de leche)* curd

gruñido *nm* grunt

gruñir *vi* to grunt

gruñón,-ona *adj* grumpy

grupa *nf* hindquarters

grupo *nm* (a) group; *Informát* g. de noticias newsgroup (b) *Téc* unit, set

gruta *nf* cave

guaca *nf Am (sepultura)* = pre-Columbian Indian tomb

guacal *nm* (a) *CAm, Méx (calabaza)* calabash (b) *Carib, Col, Méx (jaula)* cage

guacamayo,-a *nm,f Orn* macaw

guacamol, guacamole *nm Culin* guacamole

guachafita *nf Am* uproar

guachimán *nm Am* night watchman

guacho,-a *adj & nm,f Andes, RP* (a) *muy Fam (persona huérfana)* orphan (b) *Fam (sinvergüenza)* bastard, swine

guaco *nm Am (cerámica)* = pottery object found in pre-Columbian Indian tomb

guadaña *nf* scythe

guagua¹ *nf Can, Cuba* bus

guagua² *nf Andes* baby

guajiro,-a *nm,f Cuba Fam (campesino)* peasant

guajolote *nm CAm, Méx* (a) *(pavo)* turkey (b) *(tonto)* fool, idiot

guampa *nf Bol, CSur* horn

guanajo *nm Carib* turkey

guantazo *nm* slap

guante *nm* glove

guantera *nf Aut* glove compartment

guapo,-a *adj* (a) *(hombre)* handsome, good-looking; *(mujer)* pretty, good-looking (b) *Am (matón)* bully

guaraca *nf Am* sling

guarache *nm Méx (sandalia)* sandal

guarangada *nf Bol, CSur* rude remark

guarango,-a *adj Bol, CSur* rude

guarda *nmf* guard; **g. jurado** security guard

guardabarros *nm inv Aut Br* mudguard, *US* fender

guardabosque *nmf* gamekeeper

guardacoches *nmf inv* parking attendant

guardacostas *nm inv (persona)* coastguard; *(embarcación)* coastguard vessel

guardaespaldas *nm inv* bodyguard

guardafangos *nm inv Andes, CAm, Carib Aut Br* mudguard, *US* fender

guardameta *nmf Dep* goalkeeper

guardapolvo *nm* overalls

guardar 1 *vt* (a) *(conservar)* to keep (b) *(un secreto)* to keep; **g. silencio** to remain silent; **g. cama** to stay in bed (c) *(poner en un sitio)* to put away (d) *(reservar)* to keep (e) *Informát* to save
  2 **guardarse** *vpr* **g. de hacer algo** *(abstenerse)* to be careful not to do sth; **guardársela a algn** to have it in for sb

guardarropa *nm* (a) *(cuarto)* cloakroom (b) *(armario)* wardrobe

guardería *nf* g. infantil nursery (school)

guardia 1 *nf* (a) *(vigilancia)* watch (b) **la G. Civil** the civil guard (c) *(turno de servicio)* duty; *Mil* guard duty; **de g.** on duty; **farmacia de g.** duty chemist
  2 *nmf* policeman; *(mujer)* policewoman

guardián,-ana *nm,f* watchman

guarecer [33] 1 *vt* to shelter
  2 **guarecerse** *vpr* to take shelter o refuge (de from)

guarida *nf (de animal)* lair; *(refugio)* hideout

guarismo *nm* digit

guarnecer [33] *vt* (a) *Culin* to garnish (b) *(dotar)* to provide (de with) (c) *Mil* to garrison

guarnición *nf* (a) *Culin* garnish (b) *Mil* garrison

guarro,-a 1 *adj* filthy
2 *nm,f* pig

guarura *nm Méx Fam* bodyguard

guasa *nf* mockery

guasearse *upr Fam* **g. de** to make fun of

guaso,-a *adj Am* peasant

guasón,-ona 1 *adj* humorous
2 *nm,f* joker

guata *nf* (a) *(relleno)* padding (b) *Am (barriga)* paunch

Guatemala *n* (a) *(país)* Guatemala (b) *(ciudad)* Guatemala City

guatemalteco,-a *adj & nm,f* Guatemalan

guay *adj inv Fam* brilliant, terrific

guayabera *nf* short jacket

guayabo,-a *nm,f Am Fig (chica bonita)* pretty young girl; *(chico guapo)* good-looking boy

guepardo *nm* cheetah

güero,-a *adj Méx Fam* blond, blonde

guerra *nf* war; **en g.** at war; **g. bacteriológica** germ warfare; **g. civil/fría/mundial/ nuclear** civil/cold/world/nuclear war; *Fam* **dar g.** to be a real nuisance

guerrero,-a 1 *nm,f* warrior
2 *adj* warlike

guerrilla *nf* (a) *(partida armada)* guerrilla force *o* band (b) *(lucha)* guerrilla warfare

güevón,-ona *nm,f Andes, Arg, Ven muy Fam (estúpido)* Br prat, *US* dork

guía 1 *nmf (persona)* guide
2 *nf* (a) *(norma)* guideline (b) *(libro)* guide; *(lista)* directory; **g. de teléfonos** telephone directory

guiar [29] **1** *vt* (a) *(indicar el camino)* to guide (b) *Aut* to drive; *Náut* to steer; *(caballo, bici)* to ride
2 guiarse *upr* **g. por** to be guided by, to go by

guija *nf* pebble

guijarro *nm* pebble

guinda *nf (fruto)* morello (cherry)

guindilla *nf* chilli

guineo *nm Andes, CAm* banana

guiñapo *nm* (a) *(andrajo)* rag (b) *Fig (persona)* wreck; **poner a algn como un g.** to tear sb to pieces

guiñar *vt* to wink

guiño *nm* wink

guión *nm* (a) *Cin & TV* script (b) *Ling* hyphen, dash (c) *(esquema)* sketch

guionista *nmf* scriptwriter

guiri *nmf Fam* foreigner

guirigay *nm* hubbub

guirnalda *nf* garland

guisa *nf* way, manner; **a g. de** as, by way of

guisado *nm Culin* stew

guisante *nm* pea

guisar *vt* to cook

guiso *nm* dish; *(guisado)* stew

guita *nf* (a) *(cuerda)* rope (b) *Fam* dough

guitarra 1 *nf* guitar
2 *nmf* guitarist

guitarreada *nf CSur* singalong *(to guitars)*

guitarrista *nmf* guitarist

gula *nf* gluttony

gurí,-isa *nm,f RP Fam (niño)* kid, child; *(joven) (hombre)* lad; *(mujer)* lass

gusano *nm* worm; *(oruga)* caterpillar; *Fam Pey (exiliado cubano)* = anti-Castro Cuban living in exile; **g. de seda** silkworm

gustar 1 *vt* (a) **me gusta el vino** I like wine; **me gustaban los caramelos** I used to like sweets; **me gusta nadar** I like swimming; **me gustaría ir** I would like to go (b) *Fml* **¿gustas?** would you like some?; **cuando gustes** whenever you like
2 *vi* **g. de** to enjoy

gusto *nm* (a) *(sentido)* taste (b) *(en fórmulas de cortesía)* pleasure; **con (mucho) g.** with (great) pleasure; **tanto g.** pleased to meet you (c) **estar a g.** to feel comfortable *o* at ease; **por g.** for the sake of it; **ser de buen/mal g.** to be in good/bad taste; **tener buen/mal g.** to have good/bad taste; **tenemos el gusto de comunicarle que ...** we are pleased to inform you that ...

gutural *adj* guttural

H

H, h [atʃe] *nf (la letra)* H,h; **bomba H** H-bomb

ha *indic pres de* **haber**

haba *nf* broad bean

> Takes the masculine articles **el** and **un**.

Habana *nf* **La H.** Havana

habano *nm* Havana cigar

haber [14] **1** *v aux* (a) *(en tiempos compuestos)* to have; **lo he visto** I have seen it; **ya lo había hecho** he had already done it

(b) **h. de** + *infin (obligación)* to have to; **has de ser bueno** you must be good

2 *v impers (special form of present tense:* **hay**) (a) *(existir, estar) (singular used also with plural nouns)* **hay** there is/are; **había** there was/were; **había un gato en el tejado** there was a cat on the roof; **había muchos libros** there were a lot of books; **hay 500 km entre Madrid y Granada** it's 500 km from Madrid to Granada

(b) **h. que** + *infin* it is necessary to; **hay que trabajar** you've got to *o* you must work; **habrá que comprobarlo** I/you/we/*etc* will have to check it

(c) *(tener lugar)* **habrá una fiesta** there will be a party; **hoy hay partido** there's a match today; **los accidentes habidos en esta carretera** the accidents which have happened on this road

(d) **había una vez** ... once upon a time ...; **no hay de qué** you're welcome, don't mention it; **¿qué hay?** how are things?

3 *nm* (a) *Fin* credit; **haberes** assets

(b) **en su h.** in his possession

habichuela *nf (judía)* kidney bean; *Carib, Col (judía verde)* green bean

hábil *adj* (a) *(diestro)* skilful (b) *(astuto)* smart (c) **días hábiles** working days

habilidad *nf* (a) *(destreza)* skill (b) *(astucia)* cleverness

habilitar *vt* (a) *(espacio)* to fit out (b) *(persona)* to entitle (c) *Fin (financiar)* to finance

habiloso,-a *adj Chile* shrewd, astute

habitación *nf (cuarto)* room; *(dormitorio)* bedroom; **h. individual/doble** single/double room

habitante *nmf* inhabitant

habitar **1** *vt* to live in, to inhabit

2 *vi* to live

hábitat *nm (pl* **hábitats**) habitat

hábito *nm* (a) *(costumbre)* habit (b) *Rel* habit

habitual *adj* usual, habitual; *(cliente, lector)* regular

habituar [30] **1** *vt* to accustom (a to)

2 habituarse *vpr* **habituarse a** to get used to, to become accustomed to

habla *nf* (a) *(idioma)* language; **países de h. española** Spanish-speaking countries (b) *(facultad de hablar)* speech; **quedarse sin h.** to be left speechless (c) *Tel* **¡al h.!** speaking!

> Takes the masculine articles **el** and **un**.

hablado,-a *adj* spoken; **el inglés h.** spoken English; **mal h.** coarse, foul-mouthed

hablador,-a *adj (parlanchín)* talkative; *(chismoso)* gossipy

habladuría *nf (rumor)* rumour; *(chisme)* piece of gossip

hablante *nmf* speaker

hablar **1** *vi* (a) to speak, to talk; **h. con algn** to speak to sb (b) **¡ni h.!** certainly not!; *Fam* **¡quién fue a h.!** look who's talking!

2 *vt* (a) *(idioma)* to speak; **habla alemán** he speaks German (b) *(tratar un asunto)* to talk over, to discuss

3 hablarse *vpr* (a) to speak *o* talk to one another (b) **se habla español** *(en letrero)* Spanish spoken

habré *indic fut de* **haber**

hacendado,-a *nm,f Am* farmer

hacendoso,-a *adj* hardworking

hacer [15] **1** *vt* (a) *(crear, producir, fabricar)* to make; **h. una casa** to build a house

(b) *(obrar, ejecutar)* to do; **eso no se hace** it isn't done; **hazme un favor** do me a favour; **¿qué haces?** *(en este momento)* what are you doing?; *(para vivir)* what do you do (for a living)?; **tengo mucho que h.** I have a lot to do; **h. deporte** to do sports; **h. una carrera/medicina** to do a degree/medicine

(c) *(conseguir)* *(amigos, dinero)* to make

(d) *(obligar)* to make; **hazle callar/**

trabajar make him shut up/work
(**e**) (*arreglar*) to make; **h. la cama** to make the bed
(**f**) *Mat (sumar)* to make; **y con éste hacen cien** and that makes a hundred
(**g**) (*dar aspecto*) to make look; **el negro le hace más delgado** black makes him look slimmer
(**h**) (*sustituyendo a otro verbo*) to do; **ya no puedo leer como solía hacerlo** I can't read as well as I used to
(**i**) (*representar*) to play; **h. el bueno** to play the (part of the) goody
(**j**) **¡bien hecho!** well done!

2 *vi* (**a**) (*actuar*) to play; **hizo de Desdémona** she played Desdemona
(**b**) **h. por** *o* **para** + *infin* to try to; **hice por venir** I tried to come
(**c**) (*fingir*) to pretend; **h. como si** to act as if
(**d**) (*convenir*) to be suitable; **a las ocho si te hace** will eight o'clock be all right for you?

3 *v impers* (**a**) **hace calor/frío** it's hot/cold
(**b**) (*tiempo transcurrido*) ago; **hace mucho (tiempo)** a long time ago; **hace dos días que no le veo** I haven't seen him for two days; **hace dos años que vivo en Glasgow** I've been living in Glasgow for two years

4 hacerse *upr* (**a**) (*volverse*) to become, to grow; **h. viejo** to grow old
(**b**) (*simular*) to pretend; **h. el dormido** to pretend to be sleeping
(**c**) **h. con** (*apropiarse*) to get hold of
(**d**) **h. a** (*habituarse*) to get used to; **enseguida me hago a todo** I soon get used to anything

hacha *nf* (**a**) (*herramienta*) axe (**b**) *Fam* **ser un h. en algo** to be an ace *o* a wizard at sth

> Takes the masculine articles **el** and **un**.

hachís *nm* hashish

hacia *prep* (**a**) (*dirección*) towards, to; **h. abajo** down, downwards; **h. adelante** forwards; **h. arriba** up, upwards; **h. atrás** back, backwards (**b**) (*tiempo*) at about, at around; **h. las tres** at about three o'clock

hacienda *nf* (**a**) *Am* (*finca agrícola*) estate, *US* ranch (**b**) *Fin* Treasury; **h. pública** public funds *o* finances; **Ministerio de H.** ≈ Exchequer, Treasury

hacinamiento *nm* (**a**) *Agr* stacking; *Fig* (*montón*) piling (**b**) (*de gente*) overcrowding

hacinar 1 *vt Agr* to stack; *Fig (amontonar)* to pile up, to heap up
2 hacinarse *upr* **h. en** (*gente*) to be packed into

hada *nf* fairy; **cuento de hadas** fairy tale; **h. madrina** fairy godmother

> Takes the masculine articles **el** and **un**.

hado *nm* destiny
hago *indic pres de* **hacer**
halagar [42] *vt* to flatter
halago *nm* flattery
halagüeño,-a *adj* (*noticia, impresión*) promising
halcón *nm* falcon; **h. peregrino** peregrine (falcon)
hálito *nm* (**a**) (*aliento*) breath (**b**) (*vapor*) vapour
hallar 1 *vt* (*encontrar*) to find; (*averiguar*) to find out; (*descubrir*) to discover
2 hallarse *upr* (*estar*) to be, to find oneself; (*estar situado*) to be situated
hallazgo *nm* (**a**) (*descubrimiento*) discovery (**b**) (*cosa encontrada*) find
hamaca *nf* hammock; (*mecedora*) rocking chair
hambre *nf* (*apetito*) hunger; (*inanición*) starvation; (*catástrofe*) famine; **tener h.** to be hungry

> Takes the masculine articles **el** and **un**.

hambriento,-a *adj* starving
hamburguesa *nf* hamburger
hampa *nf* underworld

> Takes the masculine articles **el** and **un**.

han *indic pres de* **haber**
harapo *nm* rag; **hecho un h.** in tatters
haré *indic fut de* **hacer**
harén *nm* (*pl* **harenes**) harem
harina *nf* flour
hartar 1 *vt* (**a**) (*cansar, fastidiar*) to annoy (**b**) (*atiborrar*) to satiate; **el dulce harta enseguida** sweet things soon fill you up
2 hartarse *upr* (**a**) (*saciar el apetito*) to eat one's fill (**b**) (*cansarse*) to get fed up (**de** with), to grow tired (**de** of)
harto,-a 1 *adj* (**a**) (*de comida*) full (**b**) (*cansado*) fed up; **¡me tienes h.!** I'm fed up with you!; **estoy h. de trabajar** I'm fed up working (**c**) *Andes, CAm, Carib, Méx (mucho)* lots of; **tiene h. dinero** he's got lots of money
2 *adv* (**a**) *Fml (muy)* very (**b**) *Andes, CAm, Carib, Méx (muy, mucho)* really
hartura *nf* bellyful; **¡qué h.!** what a drag!
has *indic pres de* **haber**
hasta 1 *prep* (**a**) (*lugar*) up to, as far as,

down to (**b**) *(tiempo)* until, till, up to; **h. el domingo** until Sunday; **h. el final** right to the end; **h. la fecha** up to now; **h. luego** see you later (**c**) *(con cantidad)* up to, as many as (**d**) *(incluso)* even (**e**) *CAm, Col, Méx (no antes de)* **pintaremos la casa h. fin de mes** we won't paint the house till the end of the month

2 *conj* **h. que** until

hastiado,-a *adj* sick, tired (**de** of)

hastiar [29] *vt* to sicken

hastío *nm* weariness

hato *nm* bundle

hay *indic pres de* **haber**

Haya *nf* **La H.** The Hague

haya¹ *nf* (**a**) *Bot (árbol)* beech (**b**) *(madera)* beech (wood)

> Takes the masculine articles **el** and **un**.

haya² *subj pres de* **haber**

haz¹ *nm* (**a**) *Agr* sheaf (**b**) *(de luz)* shaft

haz² *nf (de hoja)* top side

haz³ *imperat de* **hacer**

hazaña *nf* deed, exploit

hazmerreír *nm* laughing stock

he¹ *adv* **he ahí/aquí ...** there/here you have ...

he² *indic pres de* **haber**

hebilla *nf* buckle

hebra *nf* thread; *(de carne)* sinew; *(de madera)* grain; **pegar la h.** to chat

hebreo,-a 1 *adj* Hebrew

2 *nm,f* Hebrew

hecatombe *nf* disaster

hechicería *nf* witchcraft

hechicero,-a 1 *adj* bewitching

2 *nm,f (hombre)* wizard, sorcerer; *(mujer)* witch, sorceress

hechizar [40] *vt* (**a**) *(embrujar)* to cast a spell on (**b**) *Fig (fascinar)* to bewitch, to charm

hechizo *nm* (**a**) *(embrujo)* spell (**b**) *Fig (fascinación)* fascination, charm

hecho,-a 1 *adj* (**a**) made, done; **¡bien h.!** well done! (**b**) *(carne)* done (**c**) *(persona)* mature, (**d**) *(frase)* set; *(ropa)* ready-made

2 *nm* (**a**) *(realidad)* fact; **de h.** in fact; **el h. es que ...** the fact is that ... (**b**) *(acto)* act, deed (**c**) *(suceso)* event, incident

hechura *nf (forma)* shape; *Cost* cut

hectárea *nf* hectare

hectolitro *nm* hectolitre

heder [3] *vi* to stink, to smell foul

hediondo,-a *adj* foul-smelling

hedor *nm* stink, stench

hegemonía *nf* hegemony

helada *nf* frost

heladera *nf RP (nevera)* refrigerator, fridge

heladería *nf* ice-cream parlour

helado,-a 1 *nm* ice cream

2 *adj* (**a**) *(muy frío)* frozen, freezing cold; **estoy h. (de frío)** I'm frozen (**b**) *Fig* **quedarse h.** *(atónito)* to be flabbergasted

helar [1] 1 *vt (congelar)* to freeze

2 *v impers* to freeze; **anoche heló** there was a frost last night

3 helarse *vpr (congelarse)* to freeze

helecho *nm Bot* fern

hélice *nf* (**a**) *Av & Náut* propeller (**b**) *Anat, Arquit & Mat* helix

helicóptero *nm Av* helicopter

helipuerto *nm Av* heliport

hematoma *nm Med* haematoma

hembra *nf* (**a**) *Bot & Zool* female (**b**) *(mujer)* woman (**c**) *Téc* female; *(de tornillo)* nut; *(de enchufe)* socket

hemiciclo *nm Fam* (Spanish) parliament

hemisferio *nm* hemisphere

hemorragia *nf Med* haemorrhage

hemos *indic pres de* **haber**

henchir [6] *vt* to stuff

hender [3] *vt (resquebrajar)* to crack, to split; *Fig (olas)* to cut

hendidura *nf* crack

hendir [5] *vt* = **hender**

heno *nm* hay

heráldica *nf* heraldry

herbicida *nm* weedkiller, herbicide

herbívoro,-a 1 *adj* herbivorous, grass-eating

2 *nm,f Zool* herbivore

herbolario *nm* herbalist's (shop)

herboso,-a *adj* grassy

hercio *nm* Herz

heredad *nf* (**a**) *(finca)* country estate (**b**) *(conjunto de bienes)* private estate

heredar *vt* (**a**) *Jur* to inherit (**b**) **ha heredado la sonrisa de su madre** she's got her mother's smile

heredero,-a *nm,f (hombre)* heir; *(mujer)* heiress; **príncipe h.** crown prince

hereditario,-a *adj* hereditary

hereje *nmf Rel* heretic

herejía *nf Rel* heresy

herencia *nf* (**a**) *Jur* inheritance, legacy (**b**) *Biol* heredity

herida *nf (lesión)* injury; *(corte)* wound

herido,-a *nm,f* injured person; **no hubo heridos** there were no casualties

herir [5] 1 *vt* (**a**) *(físicamente) (lesionar)* to injure; *(cortar)* to wound (**b**) *(emocionalmente)* to hurt, to wound (**c**) *(vista)* to offend

2 herirse *vpr* to injure *o* hurt oneself

hermana nf (a) sister (b) Rel (monja) sister

hermanado,-a adj twinned; **ciudad hermanada** twin town

hermanar 1 vt (a) (personas) to unite spiritually (b) (ciudades) to twin (c) (unir) to unite, to combine
  2 hermanarse vpr (a) (ciudades) to twin (b) (combinar) to combine

hermanastro,-a nm,f (hombre) stepbrother; (mujer) stepsister

hermandad nf (a) (grupo) fraternity, brotherhood, sisterhood (b) (relación) brotherhood, sisterhood

hermano nm (a) brother; **h. político** brother-in-law; **primo h.** first cousin (b) Rel (fraile) brother (c) **hermanos** brothers and sisters

herméticamente adv **h. cerrado** hermetically sealed

hermético,-a adj (a) (cierre) hermetic, airtight (b) Fig (abstruso) secretive

hermetismo nm airtightness; Fig impenetrability

hermoso,-a adj beautiful, lovely; (grande) fine

hermosura nf beauty

héroe nm hero

heroico,-a adj heroic

heroína nf (a) (mujer) heroine (b) (droga) heroin

heroinómano,-a nm,f heroin addict

heroísmo nm heroism

herrador nm blacksmith

herradura nf horseshoe

herramienta nf Téc tool; **caja de herramientas** toolbox

herrar [1] vt (a) (caballo) to shoe (b) (ganado) to brand

herrería nf forge, smithy

herrero nm blacksmith, smith

herrumbre nf rust

hervidero nm Fig (lugar) hotbed

hervir [5] 1 vt (hacer bullir) to boil
  2 vi (a) Culin to boil; **romper a h.** to come to the boil (b) (abundar) to swarm, to seethe (**de** with)

heterodoxo,-a adj unorthodox

heterogéneo,-a adj heterogeneous

hez nf (a) (usu pl) (poso) sediment, dregs (b) **heces** faeces

hiato nm Ling hiatus

híbrido,-a adj & nm,f hybrid

hice pt indef de **hacer**

hiciste pt indef de **hacer**

hidalgo nm Hist nobleman, gentleman

hidalguía nf nobility; Fig chivalry, gentlemanliness

hidratación nf (a) Quím hydration (b) (de la piel) moisturizing

hidratante adj moisturizing; **crema/leche h.** moisturizing cream/lotion

hidráulico,-a adj hydraulic; **energía hidráulica** hydro-electric energy

hidroavión nm seaplane, US hydroplane

hidrocarburo nm hydrocarbon

hidrófilo,-a adj absorbent; **algodón h.** Br cotton wool, Am absorbent cotton

hidrógeno nm Quím hydrogen

hidroterapia nf Med hydrotherapy

hiedra nf ivy

hiel nf (a) Anat bile (b) Fig bitterness, gall

hielo nm ice; Fig **romper el h.** to break the ice

hiena nf hyena

hierba nf (a) grass; **mala h.** Bot weed; Fig (persona) bad lot; Fam Hum **y otras hierbas** among others (b) Culin herb; **h. luisa** lemon verbena (c) Fam (marihuana) grass

hierbabuena nf mint

hierro nm (a) (metal) iron; **h. forjado** wrought iron (b) (punta de arma) head, point (c) (marca en el ganado) brand

hígado nm (a) Anat liver (b) Euf guts

higiene nf hygiene

higiénico,-a adj hygienic; **papel h.** toilet paper

higo nm Fam Fig **hecho un h.** wizened, crumpled

higuera nf Bot fig tree

hija nf daughter

hijastro,-a nm,f (hombre) stepson; (mujer) stepdaughter

hijo nm (a) son, child; Pey **h. de papá** rich kid; Vulg **h. de puta** o Méx **de la chingada** bastard, US asshole (b) **hijos** children

hijoputa nm Vulg bastard, US asshole

hilacha nf, **hilacho** nm loose o hanging thread

hilandería nf mill; (de algodón) cotton mill

hilandero,-a nm,f spinner

hilar vt & vi (a) to spin (b) Fig (idea, plan) to work out; **h. muy fino** to split hairs

hilaridad nf hilarity, mirth

hilera nf line, row

hilo nm (a) Cost thread; (grueso) yarn (b) Fig (de historia, discurso) thread; (de pensamiento) train; **perder el h.** to lose the thread; **h. musical** background music (c) Tex linen

hilvanar vt (a) Cost to tack, to baste (b) Fig (ideas etc) to outline

himno nm hymn; **h. nacional** national anthem

hincapié *nm* **hacer h. en** *(insistir)* to insist on; *(subrayar)* to emphasize, to stress

hincar [44] 1 *vt (clavar)* to drive (in); **h. el diente a** to sink one's teeth into

2 hincarse *vpr* **h. de rodillas** to kneel (down)

hincha *Fam* **1** *nmf Ftb* fan, supporter

2 *nf (antipatía)* grudge, dislike; **me tiene h.** he's got it in for me

hinchada *nf Ftb Fam* fans, supporters

hinchado,-a *adj* (a) inflated, blown up (b) *Med (cara etc)* swollen, puffed up; *(estómago)* bloated (c) *Fig (estilo)* bombastic, pompous

hinchar 1 *vt* (a) *(inflar)* to inflate, to blow up (b) *Fig (exagerar)* to inflate, to exaggerate

2 hincharse *vpr* (a) *Med* to swell (up) (b) *Fam* **me hinché de comida** I stuffed myself; **me hinché de llorar** I cried for all I was worth

hinchazón *nf Med* swelling

hindú *adj & nmf* Hindu

hipermercado *nm* hypermarket

hipertensión *nf* high blood pressure

hípica *nf* (horse) riding

hípico,-a *adj* horse; **club h.** riding club

hipnotizar [40] *vt* to hypnotize

hipo *nm* hiccups, hiccough; **me ha dado h.** it's given me the hiccups

hipocondríaco,-a *adj & nm,f* hypochondriac

hipocresía *nf* hypocrisy

hipócrita 1 *adj* hypocritical

2 *nmf* hypocrite

hipódromo *nm* racetrack, racecourse

hipopótamo *nm* hippopotamus

hipoteca *nf Fin* mortgage

hipotecar [44] *vt* (a) *Fin* to mortgage (b) *Fig* to jeopardize

hipótesis *nf inv* hypothesis

hipotético,-a *adj* hypothetical

hiriente *adj* offensive, wounding; *(palabras)* cutting

hirsuto,-a *adj* hirsute, hairy; *(cerdoso)* bristly

hispánico,-a *adj* Hispanic, Spanish

hispanidad *nf* **el Día de la H.** Columbus Day *(12 October)*

hispano,-a 1 *adj (español)* Spanish; *(español y sudamericano)* Hispanic; *(sudamericano)* Spanish American

2 *nm,f (hispanoamericano)* Spanish American; *(estadounidense)* Hispanic

Hispanoamérica *nf* Latin America

hispanoamericano,-a *adj & nm,f* Latin American

hispanohablante 1 *adj* Spanish-speaking

2 *nmf* Spanish speaker

histeria *nf* hysteria; **un ataque de h.** hysterics

histérico,-a *adj* hysterical; *Fam Fig* **me pones h.** you're driving me mad

historia *nf* (a) history; **esto pasará a la h.** this will go down in history (b) *(narración)* story, tale; *Fam* **¡déjate de historias!** don't give me that!

historiador,-a *nm,f* historian

historial *nm* (a) *Med* medical record, case history (b) *(antecedentes)* background

historiar [29] *vt* to recount

histórico,-a *adj* (a) historical (b) *(auténtico)* factual, true; **hechos históricos** true facts (c) *(de gran importancia)* historic, memorable

historieta *nf* (a) *(cuento)* short story, tale (b) *(tira cómica)* comic strip

hito *nm* milestone; **mirar de h. en h.** to stare at

hizo *pt indef de* hacer

hnos. *(abr* Hermanos) Bros

hocico *nm* (a) *(de animal)* snout (b) *(de persona)* mug, snout; *Fam* **meter los hocicos en algo** to stick *o* poke one's nose into sth

hogar *nm* (a) *(casa)* home (b) *(de la chimenea)* hearth, fireplace (c) *Fig* **formar** *o* **crear un h.** *(familia)* to start a family

hogareño,-a *adj (vida)* home, family; *(persona)* home-loving, stay-at-home

hoguera *nf* bonfire

hoja *nf* (a) *Bot* leaf (b) *(pétalo)* petal (c) *(de papel)* sheet, leaf; **h. de cálculo** spreadsheet (d) *(de libro)* leaf, page (e) *(de metal)* sheet (f) *(de cuchillo, espada)* blade (g) *(impreso)* hand-out, printed sheet (h) *(de puerta o ventana)* leaf

hojalata *nf* tin, tin plate

hojaldre *nm Culin* puff pastry

hojarasca *nf* fallen *o* dead leaves

hojear *vt* to leaf through, to flick through

hola *interj* hello!, hullo!, hi!

Holanda *n* Holland

holandés,-esa 1 *adj* Dutch

2 *nm,f (hombre)* Dutchman; *(mujer)* Dutchwoman

3 *nm (idioma)* Dutch

holding *nm Fin* holding company

holgado,-a *adj* (a) *(ropa)* loose, baggy (b) *(económicamente)* comfortable (c) *(espacio)* roomy; **andar h. de tiempo** to have plenty of time

holgar [2] *vi* (a) *(no trabajar)* to be idle

(**b**) (*sobrar*) **huelga decir que ...** it goes without saying that ...

holgazán,-ana 1 *adj* lazy, idle

2 *nm,f* lazybones, layabout

holgura *nf* (**a**) (*ropa*) looseness (**b**) (*espacio*) space, roominess; *Téc* play, give (**c**) (*bienestar económico*) affluence, comfort; **vivir con h.** to be comfortably off, to be well-off

hollar [2] *vt Fig* to walk on; **terrenos jamás hollados** uncharted territory

hollín *nm* soot

hombre 1 *nm* (**a**) man; **de h. a h.** man-to-man; **¡pobre h.!** poor chap!; **ser muy h.** to be every inch a man; **h. de estado** statesman; **h. de negocios** businessman (**b**) (*especie*) mankind, man

2 *interj* (**a**) (*saludo*) hey!, hey there!; **¡h., Juan!** hey, Juan! (**b**) **¡sí h.!, ¡h. claro!** (*enfático*) sure!, you bet!; **¡anda, h.!** (*incredulidad*) oh come on!

hombría *nf* manliness, virility

hombrera *nf* shoulder pad

hombrillo *nm Ven* (*arcén*) verge; (*de autopista*) *Br* hard shoulder, *US* shoulder

hombro *nm* shoulder; **a hombros** on one's shoulders; **encogerse de hombros** to shrug one's shoulders; **mirar a algn por encima del h.** to look down one's nose at sb

hombruno,-a *adj* mannish, butch

homenaje *nm* homage, tribute; **rendir h. a algn** to pay homage *o* tribute to sb

homenajear *vt* to pay tribute to

homicida 1 *nmf* (*hombre*) murderer; (*mujer*) murderess

2 *adj* homicidal; **el arma h.** the murder weapon

homicidio *nm* homicide

homogéneo,-a *adj* homogeneous, uniform

homologable *adj* comparable (**con** with)

homologar [42] *vt* to give official approval *o* recognition to

homólogo,-a 1 *adj* (*equiparable*) comparable

2 *nm,f* (*persona con mismas condiciones*) counterpart

homosexual *adj & nmf* homosexual

homosexualidad *nf* homosexuality

honda *nf* (*arma*) sling

hondo,-a *adj* (**a**) (*profundo*) deep; **plato h.** soup dish (**b**) *Fig* (*pesar*) profound, deep

hondonada *nf Geog* hollow, depression

hondura *nf* depth; *Fig* **meterse en honduras** (*profundizar*) to go into too much detail

Honduras *n* Honduras

hondureño,-a *adj & nm,f* Honduran

honestidad *nf* (**a**) (*honradez*) honesty, uprightness (**b**) (*decencia*) modesty

honesto,-a *adj* (**a**) (*honrado*) honest, upright (**b**) (*decente*) modest

hongo *nm* (**a**) *Bot* fungus; **h. venenoso** toadstool (**b**) (*sombrero*) *Br* bowler (hat), *US* derby

honor *nm* (**a**) (*virtud*) honour; **palabra de h.** word of honour (**b**) **en h. a la verdad ...** to be fair ...; **es un h. para mí** it's an honour for me (**c**) **hacer h. a** to live up to

honorable *adj* honourable; *Pol* **el H. =** head of the Catalan government

honorario,-a 1 *adj* honorary

2 *nmpl* **honorarios** fees, fee

honorífico,-a *adj* honorary

honra *nf* (**a**) (*dignidad*) dignity, self-esteem (**b**) (*fama*) reputation, good name (**c**) (*honor*) honour; **me cabe la h. de ...** I have the honour of ...; **¡a mucha h.!** and proud of it!

honradez *nf* honesty, integrity

honrado,-a *adj* (**a**) (*de fiar*) honest (**b**) (*decente*) upright, respectable

honrar *vt* (**a**) (*respetar*) to honour (**b**) (*enaltecer*) to be a credit to

honrilla *nf* self-respect, pride

honroso,-a *adj* (*loable*) honourable

hora *nf* (**a**) hour; **media h.** half an hour; **a altas horas de la madrugada** in the small hours; **dar la h.** to strike the hour; **(trabajo) por horas** (work) paid by the hour; **h. punta,** *Am* **h. pico** (*de mucho tráfico*) rush hour; (*de agua, electricidad*) peak times; **horas extra** overtime (hours) (**b**) *Fig* time; **¿qué h. es?** what time is it?; **a su h.** at the proper time; **a última h.** at the last moment; **la h. de la verdad** the moment of truth (**c**) (*cita*) appointment; **pedir h.** (*al médico etc*) to ask for an appointment

horadar *vt* (*perforar*) to drill *o* bore a hole in

horario,-a 1 *nm* timetable, *US* schedule

2 *adj* time; *Rad* **señal horaria** pips

horca *nf* gallows *sing*

horcajada: • **a horcajadas** *loc adv* astride

horchata *nf Culin* = sweet, milky drink made from chufa nuts or almonds

horda *nf* horde, mob

horizonte *nm* horizon

horma *nf* (*de zapato*) last

hormiga *nf* ant

hormigón *nm Constr* concrete; **h. armado** reinforced concrete

hormiguear *vi* to itch, to tingle; **me hormigueaba la pierna** I had pins and needles in my leg

hormigueo *nm* (a) pins and needles, tingling o itching sensation (b) *Fig* anxiety

hormiguero *nm* (a) anthill (b) *Fig* **ser un h.** *(lugar)* to be swarming (with people)

hormona *nf* hormone

hornada *nf* (a) *(pan)* batch (b) *Fig* set, batch

hornillo *nm* *(de cocinar)* stove; *(placa)* hotplate

horno *nm* *(cocina)* oven; *Téc* furnace; *(para cerámica, ladrillos)* kiln; *Culin* **pescado al h.** baked fish; *Fam Fig* **esta habitación es un h.** this room is boiling hot

Hornos *nm* **Cabo de H.** Cape Horn

horóscopo *nm* horoscope

horquilla *nf* (a) *(del pelo)* hairpin, *Br* hair-grip, *US* bobby-pin (b) *(estadística)* chart (c) **h. de precios** price range

horrendo,-a *adj* horrifying, horrible

hórreo *nm Agr* granary

horrible *adj* horrible, dreadful, awful

horripilante *adj* hair-raising, scary

horror *nm* (a) horror, terror; **¡qué h.!** how awful!; *Fam* **tengo h. a las motos** I hate motorbikes (b) *Fam Fig* **me gusta horrores** *(muchísimo)* I like it an awful lot

horrorizar [40] *vt* to horrify, to terrify

horroroso,-a *adj* (a) *(que da miedo)* horrifying, terrifying (b) *Fam (muy feo)* hideous, ghastly (c) *Fam (malísimo)* awful, dreadful

hortaliza *nf* vegetable

hortelano,-a *nm,f Br* market gardener, *US* truck farmer

hortensia *nf Bot* hydrangea

hortera *adj Fam (persona)* flashy; *(cosa)* tacky, kitsch

horterada *nf Fam* tacky thing o act

hosco,-a *adj* (a) *(poco sociable)* surly, sullen (b) *(tenebroso)* dark, gloomy (c) *(difícil)* tough

hospedaje *nm* lodgings, *Br* accommodation, *US* accommodations

hospedar 1 *vt* to put up, to lodge

2 hospedarse *vpr* to stay (**en** at)

hospicio *nm* orphanage

hospital *nm* hospital

hospitalario,-a *adj* (a) *(acogedor)* hospitable (b) *Med* hospital; **instalaciones hospitalarias** hospital facilities

hospitalidad *nf* hospitality

hospitalizar [40] *vt* to take o send into hospital, to hospitalize

hostal *nm* guest house

hostelería *nf (negocio)* catering business; *(estudios)* hotel management

hostelero,-a *nm,f (hombre)* landlord; *(mujer)* landlady

hostería *nf CSur* inn, lodging house

hostia 1 *nf* (a) *Rel* host (b) *Vulg (tortazo)* bash (c) *Vulg* **estar de mala h.** to be in a foul mood; **ser la h.** *(fantástico)* to be *Br* bloody o *US* goddamn amazing; *(penoso)* to be *Br* bloody o *US* goddamn awful

2 *interj Vulg* damn! *Br* bloody hell!

hostiar [29] *vt Vulg* to bash, to sock

hostigar [42] *vt* (a) to harass (b) *(caballerías)* to whip

hostil *adj* hostile

hostilidad *nf* hostility

hotel *nm* hotel

hotelero,-a 1 *adj* hotel; **el sector h.** the hotel sector

2 *nm,f* hotel-keeper, hotelier

hoy *adv* (a) *(día)* today (b) *Fig (presente)* now; **h. (en) día** nowadays; **h. por h.** at the present time

hoya *nf Geog* dale, valley

hoyo *nm* (a) *(agujero)* hole, pit (b) *(sepultura)* grave (c) *(de golf)* hole

hoyuelo *nm* dimple

hoz *nf Agr* sickle; **la h. y el martillo** the hammer and sickle

HR *nm (abr* **Hostal Residencia)** boarding house

huachafo,-a *adj Perú Fam* tacky

huasipungo *nm Andes* = plot of land given to Indian for his own use in exchange for work on the landowner's farm

huaso,-a *nm,f Chile Fam* farmer, peasant

hube *pt indef de* **haber**

hubiera *subj imperf de* **haber**

hucha *nf* piggy bank

hueco,-a 1 *adj* (a) *(vacío)* empty, hollow (b) *(sonido)* resonant

2 *nm* (a) *(cavidad)* hollow, hole (b) *(sitio no ocupado)* empty space (c) *(rato libre)* free time

huele *indic pres de* **oler**

huelga *nf* strike; **estar en** o **de h.** to be on strike; **h. de brazos caídos** go-slow; **h. de celo** work-to-rule

huelguista *nmf* striker

huella *nf* (a) *(del pie)* footprint; *(coche)* track; **h. dactilar** fingerprint (b) *Fig (vestigio)* trace, sign; **dejar h.** to leave one's mark

huérfano,-a *nm,f* orphan

huero,-a *adj Fig* empty

huerta *nf Agr* (a) *(parcela) Br* market garden, *US* truck farm (b) *(región)* = irrigated area used for cultivation

huerto *nm (de verduras)* vegetable garden, kitchen garden; *(de frutales)* orchard

hueso *nm* (a) *Anat* bone; **estar en los**

huesos to be all skin and bone (**b**) *(de fruto)* stone, *US* pit (**c**) *Fig (difícil)* hard work; *(profesor)* hard nut (**d**) *Méx (enchufe)* contact

huésped,-a *nm,f (invitado)* guest; *(en hotel etc)* lodger, boarder; **casa de huéspedes** guesthouse

hueste *nf Mil* army, host

huesudo,-a *adj* bony

huevada *nf Andes, RP muy Fam (dicho)* garbage, bullshit, *Br* bollocks

huevera *nf (caja)* egg box

huevo *nm* (**a**) *egg*; **h. duro** hard-boiled egg; **h. escalfado** poached egg; **h. frito** fried egg; **h. pasado por agua**, *Am* **h. tibio** *o* **a la copa** soft-boiled egg; **huevos revueltos** scrambled eggs (**b**) *muy Fam (usu pl)* balls; **hacer algo por huevos** to do sth even if it kills you; **tener huevos** to have guts

huida *nf* flight, escape

huidizo,-a *adj* elusive

huipil *nm CAm, Méx* = traditional Indian woman's dress or blouse

huir [37] *vi* to run away (**de** from), to flee; **h. de la cárcel** to escape from prison; **h. de algn** to avoid sb

hule *nm* (**a**) *(tela impermeable)* oilcloth, oilskin (**b**) *(de mesa)* tablecloth (**c**) *Am* rubber

hulla *nf* soft coal

humanidad *nf* (**a**) *(género humano)* humanity, mankind (**b**) *(cualidad)* humanity, humaneness (**c**) *(bondad)* compassion, kindness

humanitario,-a *adj* humanitarian

humano,-a 1 *adj* (**a**) *(relativo al hombre)* human (**b**) *(compasivo)* humane
2 *nm* human (being); **ser h.** human being

humear *vi (echar humo)* to smoke; *(arrojar vapor)* to steam, to be steaming hot

humedad *nf (atmosférica)* humidity; *(de lugar)* dampness; **a prueba de h.** dampproof

humedecer [33] **1** *vt* to moisten, to dampen
2 humedecerse *vpr* to become damp *o* wet *o* moist

húmedo,-a *adj (casa, ropa)* damp; *(clima)* humid, damp, moist

humildad *nf* humility; *(pobreza)* humbleness

humilde *adj* humble, modest; *(pobre)* poor

humillación *nf* humiliation

humillante *adj* humiliating, humbling

humillar 1 *vt (rebajar)* to humiliate, to humble
2 humillarse *vpr* **humillarse ante algn** to humble oneself before sb

humita *nf Andes, Arg (pasta de maíz)* = paste made of mashed maize *o US* corn, used to make steamed dumplings

humo *nm* (**a**) smoke; *(gas)* fumes; *(vapor)* vapour, steam (**b**) **¡qué humos tiene!** she thinks a lot of herself!

humor *nm* (**a**) *(genio)* mood; **estar de buen/mal h.** to be in a good/bad mood (**b**) *(carácter)* temper; **es persona de mal h.** he's bad-tempered (**c**) *(gracia)* humour; **sentido del h.** sense of humour

humorismo *nm* humour

humorista *nmf* humorist; **h. gráfico** cartoonist

humorístico,-a *adj* humorous, funny

hundido,-a *adj* (**a**) *(barco)* sunken; *(ojos)* deep-set (**b**) *Fig (abatido)* down, demoralized

hundimiento *nm* (**a**) *(de edificio)* collapse (**b**) *(de barco)* sinking (**c**) *(de tierra)* subsidence (**d**) *Fig Fin* crash, slump; *(ruina)* downfall

hundir 1 *vt* (**a**) *(barco)* to sink (**b**) *(edificio)* to bring o knock down (**c**) *Fig (desmoralizar)* to demoralize
2 hundirse *vpr* (**a**) *(barco)* to sink (**b**) *(edificio)* to collapse (**c**) *Fig (empresa)* to collapse, to crash

húngaro,-a 1 *adj* Hungarian
2 *nm,f (persona)* Hungarian
3 *nm (idioma)* Hungarian

Hungría *n* Hungary

huracán *nm* hurricane

huraño,-a *adj Pey* unsociable

hurgar [42] **1** *vi (fisgar)* to poke one's nose in
2 *vt (fuego etc)* to poke, to rake
3 hurgarse *vpr* **h. las narices** to pick one's nose

hurón,-ona 1 *nm Zool* ferret
2 *nm,f Fam Fig (fisgón)* busybody, nosey-parker

hurraca *nf Orn* = **urraca**

hurtadillas *adv* **a h.** stealthily, on the sly

hurtar *vt* to steal, to pilfer

hurto *nm* petty theft, pilfering

husmear 1 *vt (olfatear)* to sniff out, to scent
2 *vi Fig (curiosear)* to snoop, to pry

huyo *indic pres de* **huir**

— I —

I, i [i] *nf (la letra)* I, i; **i griega** Y, y
IB *nm Educ (abr* **Instituto de Bachillerato**) ≃ state secondary school
ib. *(abr* **ibídem**) ibid.
ibérico,-a *adj* Iberian
Iberoamérica *n* Latin America
iberoamericano,-a *adj & nm,f* Latin American
iceberg *nm (pl* **icebergs**) iceberg
ICONA *nm Antes (abr* **Instituto Nacional para la Conservación de la Naturaleza**) = Spanish national institute for conservation
icono *nm* icon; *Informát* icon
iconoclasta 1 *adj* iconoclastic
   2 *nmf* iconoclast
iconografía *nf* iconography
ictericia *nf Med* jaundice
íd. *(abr* **ídem**) id
I+D *(abr* **Investigación más Desarrollo**) R&D
ida *nf* **billete de i. y vuelta** *Br* return ticket, *US* round-trip ticket; **idas y venidas** comings and goings
idea *nf* (a) idea; **i. fija** fixed idea (b) *(noción)* idea; **hacerse a la i. de** to get used to the idea of; *Fam* **ni i.** no idea, not a clue (c) *(opinión)* opinion; **cambiar de i.** to change one's mind (d) *(intención)* intention; **a mala i.** on purpose
ideal *adj & nm* ideal
idealismo *nm* idealism
idealista 1 *adj* idealistic
   2 *nmf* idealist
idealizar [40] *vt* to idealize, to glorify
idear *vt* (a) *(inventar)* to devise, to invent (b) *(concebir)* to think up, to conceive
ídem *adv* idem, ditto; *Fam* **í. de í.** exactly the same
idéntico,-a *adj* identical
identidad *nf* (a) identity; **carnet de i.** identity card (b) *(semejanza)* identity, sameness
identificación *nf* identification
identificar [44] **1** *vt* to identify
   2 identificarse *vpr* to identify oneself; *Fig* **i. con** to identify with
ideología *nf* ideology
ideológico,-a *adj* ideological

idílico,-a *adj* idyllic
idilio *nm* (a) *Lit* idyll (b) *Fig (romance)* romance, love affair
idioma *nm* language
idiomático,-a *adj* idiomatic
idiosincrasia *nf* idiosyncrasy
idiota 1 *adj* idiotic, stupid
   2 *nmf* idiot, fool
idiotez *nf* idiocy, stupidity
ido,-a *adj* (a) *(distraído)* absent-minded (b) *Fam (chiflado)* crazy, nuts
idólatra 1 *adj* idolatrous
   2 *nmf (hombre)* idolater; *(mujer)* idolatress
idolatrar *vt* to worship; *Fig* to idolize
idolatría *nf* idolatry
ídolo *nm* idol
idóneo,-a *adj* suitable, fit
iglesia *nf* (a) *(edificio)* church (b) **la I.** *(institución)* the Church
ignominia *nf* ignominy
ignominioso,-a *adj* ignominious, shameful
ignorancia *nf* ignorance
ignorante 1 *adj* (a) *(sin instrucción)* ignorant (b) *(no informado)* ignorant, unaware *(de* of)
   2 *nmf* ignoramus
ignorar 1 *vt* (a) *(algo)* not to know (b) *(a algn)* to ignore
   2 ignorarse *vpr* to be unknown
ignoto,-a *adj* unknown
igual 1 *adj* (a) *(idéntico)* the same, alike; **son todos iguales** they're all the same; **es i.** it doesn't matter; **i. que** the same as (b) *(equivalente)* equal; **a partes iguales** fifty-fifty (c) *Dep (empatados)* even; **treinta iguales** thirty all (d) *Mat* equal; **tres más tres i. a seis** three plus three equals six (e) **al i. que** just like (f) **por i.** equally
   2 *nm* equal; **de i. a i.** on an equal footing; **sin i.** unique, unrivalled
   3 *adv* (a) **lo haces i. que yo** you do it the same way I do (b) *(probablemente)* probably; **i. vengo** I'll probably come (c) *Andes, RP (aún así)* anyway, still; **estaba nublado pero i. fuimos a la playa** it was cloudy but we still went to the beach *o* we went to the beach anyway

igualar 1 vt (**a**) to make equal (**b**) (nivelar) to level (**c**) Dep **i. el partido** to equalize, to square the match

2 igualarse vpr (**a**) to be equal (**b**) **igualarse con algn** to place oneself on an equal footing with sb

igualdad nf (**a**) equality; **i. ante la ley** equality before the law (**b**) (identidad) sameness; **en i. de condiciones** on equal terms

igualitario,-a adj egalitarian

igualmente adv equally; (también) also, likewise; Fam **encantado de conocerlo – ¡i.!** pleased to meet you – likewise!

ijada nf, **ijar** nm Anat flank

ikastola nf = primary school in the Basque Country where classes are given entirely in Basque

ikurriña nf = Basque national flag

ilegal adj illegal

ilegalidad nf illegality

ilegalmente adv illegally

ilegible adj illegible, unreadable

ilegítimo,-a adj illegitimate

ileso,-a adj unhurt, unharmed

ilícito,-a adj illicit, unlawful

ilimitado,-a adj unlimited, limitless

Ilmo. (abr **Ilustrísimo**) His Excellence o Excellency

ilógico,-a adj illogical

iluminación nf (alumbrado) illumination, lighting

iluminar vt (**a**) to illuminate, to light (up) (**b**) Fig (a persona) to enlighten; (tema) to throw light upon

ilusión nf (**a**) (esperanza) hope; (esperanza vana) illusion, delusion; **hacerse ilusiones** to build up one's hopes (**b**) (sueño) dream (**c**) (emoción) excitement, thrill; **me hace i. verla** I'm looking forward to seeing her; **¡qué i.!** how exciting!

ilusionar 1 vt (**a**) (esperanzar) to build up sb's hopes (**b**) (entusiasmar) to excite, to thrill

2 ilusionarse vpr (**a**) (esperanzarse) to build up one's hopes (**b**) (entusiasmarse) to be excited (**con** about)

iluso,-a adj easily deceived, gullible

ilusorio,-a adj illusory, unreal

ilustración nf (**a**) (grabado) illustration, picture; (ejemplo) illustration (**b**) (erudición) learning, erudition; Hist **la I.** the Enlightenment

ilustrado,-a adj (**a**) (con dibujos, ejemplos) illustrated (**b**) (erudito) learned, erudite

ilustrar 1 vt (**a**) to illustrate (**b**) (aclarar) to explain, to make clear

2 ilustrarse vpr to acquire knowledge (**sobre** of), to learn (**sobre** about)

ilustrativo,-a adj illustrative

ilustre adj illustrious, distinguished

imagen nf (**a**) image; **ser la viva i. de algn** to be the spitting image of sb; **tener buena i.** to have a good image (**b**) Rel image, statue (**c**) TV picture

imaginación nf imagination; **eso son imaginaciones tuyas** you're imagining things

imaginar 1 vt to imagine

2 imaginarse vpr to imagine; **me imagino que sí** I suppose so

imaginario,-a adj imaginary

imaginativo,-a adj imaginative

imán nm magnet

imbatible adj unbeatable

imbatido,-a adj unbeaten, undefeated

imbécil 1 adj stupid, silly

2 nmf idiot, imbecile

imbecilidad nf stupidity, imbecility

imborrable adj indelible

imbuir [37] vt Fml to imbue

imitación nf imitation

imitar vt to imitate; (gestos) to mimic; **este collar imita al oro** this necklace is imitation gold

impaciencia nf impatience

impacientar 1 vt **i. a algn** to make sb lose patience, to exasperate sb

2 impacientarse vpr to get o grow impatient (**por** at)

impaciente adj (deseoso) impatient; (intranquilo) anxious

impactante adj **una noticia i.** a sensational piece of news

impactar vt to shock, to stun

impacto nm impact; Mil hit

impar adj Mat odd; **número i.** odd number

imparable adj Dep unstoppable

imparcial adj impartial, unbiased

imparcialidad nf impartiality

impartir vt (clases) to give

impasible adj impassive

impávido,-a adj fearless

impecable adj impeccable

impedido,-a 1 adj disabled, handicapped

2 nm,f disabled o handicapped person

impedimento nm impediment; (obstáculo) hindrance, obstacle

impedir [6] vt (obstaculizar) to impede, to hinder; (imposibilitar) to prevent, to stop; **i. el paso** to block the way

impeler vt Téc to drive, to propel; Fig to drive, to impel

impenetrable *adj* impenetrable
impenitente *adj Rel* impenitent, unrepentant
impensable *adj* unthinkable
impepinable *adj Fam* dead sure, certain
imperante *adj (gobernante)* ruling; *(predominante)* prevailing
imperar *vi (gobernar)* to rule; *(predominar)* to prevail
imperativo,-a 1 *adj* imperative
2 *nm Ling* imperative
imperceptible *adj* imperceptible
imperdible *nm* safety pin
imperdonable *adj* unforgivable, inexcusable
imperecedero,-a *adj* imperishable; *Fig* enduring
imperfección *nf* (a) imperfection (b) *(defecto)* defect, fault
imperfecto,-a *adj* (a) imperfect, fallible (b) *(defectuoso)* defective, faulty (c) *Ling* imperfect
imperial *adj* imperial
imperialismo *nm* imperialism
impericia *nf* incompetence
imperio *nm* empire; **el i. de la ley** the rule of law
imperioso,-a *adj* (a) *(autoritario)* imperious (b) *(ineludible)* urgent, imperative; **una necesidad imperiosa** a pressing need
impermeable 1 *adj* impermeable, impervious; *(ropa)* waterproof
2 *nm* raincoat, mac
impersonal *adj* impersonal
impertérrito,-a *adj* undaunted, fearless
impertinencia *nf* impertinence
impertinente 1 *adj (insolente)* impertinent; *(inoportuno)* irrelevant
2 *nmpl* **impertinentes** lorgnette
imperturbable *adj* imperturbable, unruffled
ímpetu *nm* (a) *(impulso)* impetus, momentum (b) *(violencia)* violence (c) *(energía)* energy
impetuosidad *nf* (a) *(violencia)* violence (b) *(fogosidad)* impetuosity, impulsiveness
impetuoso,-a *adj* (a) *(violento)* violent (b) *(fogoso)* impetuous, impulsive
impío,-a *adj* ungodly, irreligious
implacable *adj* relentless, implacable
implantar *vt (costumbres)* to implant, to instil; *(reformas)* to introduce; *Med* to implant
implicación *nf (participación)* involvement; *(significado)* implication
implicancia *nf CSur* implication
implicar [44] *vt* (a) *(involucrar)* to involve, to implicate (**en** in) (b) *(conllevar)* to imply
implícito,-a *adj* implicit, implied
implorar *vt* to implore, to beg
impoluto,-a *adj* pure, spotless
imponente *adj* (a) *(impresionante)* imposing, impressive (b) *(sobrecogedor)* stunning (c) *Fam (atractivo)* terrific, tremendous, smashing
imponer [19] *(pp* **impuesto)** **1** *vt* (a) to impose (b) *(respeto)* to inspire (c) *Fin* to deposit
2 *vi (impresionar)* to be impressive;
3 *imponerse* *vpr* (a) *(infundir respeto)* to command respect (b) *(prevalecer)* to prevail (c) *(ser necesario)* to be necessary
imponible *adj Fin* taxable
impopular *adj* unpopular, disliked
importación *nf (mercancía)* import; *(acción)* importing; **artículos de i.** imported goods
importancia *nf* importance, significance; **dar i. a** to attach importance to; **sin i.** unimportant
importante *adj* important, significant; **una suma i.** a considerable sum
importar¹ 1 *vi* (a) *(atañer)* **eso no te importa a tí** that doesn't concern you, that's none of your business (b) *(tener importancia)* to be important; **no importa** it doesn't matter; *Fam* **me importa un bledo** *o* **un pito** I couldn't care less (c) *(molestar)* **¿te importaría repetirlo?** would you mind repeating it?; **¿te importa si fumo?** do you mind if I smoke?
2 *vt (valer)* to amount to; **los libros importan 2.000 pesetas** the books come to 2,000 pesetas
importar² *vt* to import
importe *nm Com & Fin* amount, total
importunar *vt* to bother, to pester
imposibilidad *nf* impossibility
imposibilitar *vt* (a) *(impedir)* to make impossible, to prevent (b) *(incapacitar)* to disable, to cripple
imposible *adj* impossible; **me es i. hacerlo** I can't (possibly) do it
imposición *nf* (a) *(disciplina, condiciones)* imposing (b) *Fin* deposit; *(impuesto)* taxation
impostor,-a *nm,f (farsante)* impostor
impotencia *nf* powerlessness, helplessness; *Med* impotence
impotente *adj* powerless, helpless; *Med* impotent
impracticable *adj* (a) *(inviable)* impracticable, unviable (b) *(camino)* impassable

imprecar [44] *vt* to imprecate, to curse
imprecisión *nf* imprecision, vagueness
impreciso,-a *adj* imprecise, vague
impregnar 1 *vt* to impregnate (**de** with)
  2 impregnarse *vpr* to become impregnated
imprenta *nf* (**a**) *(taller)* printer's, print works (**b**) *(aparato)* printing press (**c**) **libertad de i.** freedom of the press
imprescindible *adj* essential, indispensable
impresentable *adj* unpresentable
impresión *nf* (**a**) *Fig (efecto)* impression; **causar i.** to make an impression (**b**) *Fig (opinión)* impression; **cambiar impresiones** to exchange impressions (**c**) *Impr (acto)* printing; *(edición)* edition (**d**) *(huella)* impression, imprint
impresionable *adj* impressionable
impresionante *adj* impressive, striking; *Fam* **un error i.** *(tremendo)* a terrible mistake
impresionar *vt* (**a**) *(causar admiración)* to impress; *(sorprender)* to stun, to shock (**b**) *Fot* to expose
impresionismo *nm Arte* impressionism
impresionista *adj & nmf* impressionist
impreso,-a 1 *adj* printed
  2 *nm* (**a**) *(papel, folleto)* printed matter (**b**) *(formulario)* form; **i. de solicitud** application form (**c**) **impresos** *(de correos)* printed matter
impresora *nf Informát* printer; **i. láser** laser printer; **i. de chorro de tinta** inkjet printer
imprevisible *adj* unforeseeable, unpredictable
imprevisión *nf* lack of foresight
imprevisto,-a 1 *adj* unforeseen, unexpected
  2 *nm (incidente)* unforeseen event
imprimir *(pp* **impreso)** *vt* (**a**) *Impr & Informát* to print (**b**) *(marcar)* to stamp
improbable *adj* improbable, unlikely
ímprobo,-a *adj (inmoral)* dishonest, corrupt
improcedente *adj* (**a**) inappropriate, unsuitable (**b**) *Jur* inadmissible
improductivo,-a *adj* unproductive
improperio *nm* insult, offensive remark
impropio,-a *adj (inadecuado)* inappropriate, unsuitable; **i. de** uncharacteristic of
improvisación *nf* improvisation; *Mús* extemporization
improvisado,-a *adj (espontáneo)* improvised, impromptu, ad lib; *(provisional)* makeshift; **discurso i.** impromptu speech

improvisar *vt* to improvise; *Mús* to extemporize
improviso *adj* **de i.** unexpectedly, suddenly; *Fam* **coger** *o* **pillar a algn de i.** to catch sb unawares
imprudencia *nf* imprudence, rashness; *(indiscreción)* indiscretion
imprudente *adj* imprudent, unwise; *(indiscreto)* indiscreet
impudicia *nf (falta de pudor)* immodesty; *(desvergüenza)* shamelessness
impudor *nm* immodesty; *(desvergüenza)* shamelessness
impuesto,-a 1 *nm Fin* tax; **i. sobre la renta** income tax; **libre de impuestos** tax-free; **i. sobre el valor añadido** value-added tax
  2 *adj* imposed
impugnar *vt (teoría)* to refute, to disprove; *(decisión)* to challenge, to contest
impulsar *vt* to impel, to drive
impulsivo,-a *adj* impulsive
impulso *nm* impulse, thrust; *Dep* **tomar i.** to take a run-up
impune *adj* unpunished
impunemente *adv* with impunity
impunidad *nf* impunity
impureza *nf* impurity
impuro,-a *adj* impure
impuse *pt indef de* **imponer**
imputar *vt* to impute, to attribute
inabarcable *adj* unfathomable
inabordable *adj* unapproachable, inaccessible
inacabable *adj* interminable, endless
inaccesible *adj* inaccessible
inaceptable *adj* unacceptable
inactividad *nf* inactivity; *Fin* lull, stagnation
inactivo,-a *adj* inactive
inadaptación *nf* maladjustment
inadaptado,-a 1 *adj* maladjusted
  2 *nm,f* misfit
inadecuado,-a *adj* unsuitable, inappropriate
inadmisible *adj* inadmissible
inadvertido,-a *adj (desapercibido)* unnoticed, unseen; **pasar i.** to escape notice, to pass unnoticed
inagotable *adj* (**a**) *(recursos etc)* inexhaustible (**b**) *(persona)* tireless, indefatigable
inaguantable *adj* unbearable, intolerable
inalámbrico,-a 1 *adj* cordless
  2 *nm* cordless telephone
inalcanzable *adj* unattainable, unachievable

inalterable *adj* (**a**) unalterable (**b**) *(persona)* impassive, imperturbable

inamovible *adj* immovable, fixed

inanición *nf* starvation; *Med* inanition

inanimado,-a *adj* inanimate

inapreciable *adj* (**a**) *(valioso)* invaluable, inestimable (**b**) *(insignificante)* insignificant, trivial

inasequible *adj* (**a**) *(producto)* unaffordable (**b**) *(meta)* unattainable, unachievable (**c**) *(persona)* unapproachable, inaccessible (**d**) *(cuestión)* incomprehensible

inaudito,-a *adj* (**a**) *(sin precedente)* unprecedented (**b**) *Fig (escandaloso)* outrageous

inauguración *nf* inauguration, opening

inaugural *adj* inaugural, opening; **ceremonia i.** inaugural ceremony

inaugurar *vt* to inaugurate, to open

inca *adj & nmf* Inca

incalculable *adj* incalculable, indeterminate

incandescente *adj* white-hot, incandescent

incansable *adj* tireless, indefatigable

incapacidad *nf* (**a**) incapacity, inability; **i. física** physical disability (**b**) *(incompetencia)* incompetence, inefficiency

incapacitado,-a *adj (imposibilitado)* incapacitated, disabled; *(desautorizado)* incapacitated

incapacitar *vt* (**a**) to incapacitate, to disable (**b**) *(inhabilitar)* to disqualify, to make unfit (**para** for)

incapaz *adj* (**a**) unable (**de** to), incapable (**de** of); **soy i. de continuar** I can't go on (**b**) *Jur* unfit

incario *nm* = period of the Inca empire

incautación *nf Jur* seizure, confiscation

incautarse *vpr Jur* **i. de** to seize, to confiscate

incauto,-a *adj* (**a**) *(imprudente)* incautious, unwary (**b**) *(crédulo)* gullible

incendiar [43] **1** *vt* to set fire to, to set alight

2 incendiarse *vpr* to catch fire

incendiario,-a 1 *adj* incendiary; *Fig (discurso etc)* inflammatory

2 *nm,f (persona)* arsonist, fire-raiser

incendio *nm* fire; **i. forestal** forest fire

incentivar *vt* to give an incentive to

incentivo *nm* incentive

incertidumbre *nf* uncertainty, doubt

incesante *adj* incessant, never-ending

incesto *nm* incest

incestuoso,-a *adj* incestuous

incidencia *nf* (**a**) *(repercusión)* impact, effect; **la huelga tuvo escasa i.** the strike had little effect (**b**) *(hecho)* incident (**c**) *Fís* incidence

incidente *nm* incident

incidir *vi* (**a**) *(incurrir)* to fall (**en** into) (**b**) **i. en** *(afectar)* to affect, to influence

incienso *nm* incense

incierto,-a *adj (inseguro)* uncertain

incineración *nf (de basuras)* incineration; *(de cadáveres)* cremation

incinerar *vt (basura)* to incinerate; *(cadáveres)* to cremate

incipiente *adj* incipient, budding

incisión *nf* incision, cut

incisivo,-a 1 *adj (mordaz)* incisive, cutting; *(cortante)* sharp

2 *nm Anat* incisor

inciso *nm (paréntesis)* digression; **a modo de i.** in passing, incidentally

incitación *nf* incitement

incitante *adj* (**a**) *(instigador)* inciting (**b**) *(provocativo)* provocative

incitar *vt* to incite, to urge

incivil *adj* uncivil, rude

inclemencia *nf* inclemency, harshness

inclemente *adj* inclement, harsh

inclinación *nf* (**a**) *(de terreno)* slope, incline; *(del cuerpo)* stoop (**b**) *(reverencia)* bow (**c**) *Fig (tendencia)* tendency, inclination, penchant

inclinado,-a *adj* inclined, slanting; *Fig* **me siento i. a creerle** I feel inclined to believe him

inclinar 1 *vt* (**a**) to incline, to bend; *(cabeza)* to nod (**b**) *Fig (persuadir)* to persuade, to induce

2 inclinarse *vpr* (**a**) to lean, to slope, to incline (**b**) *(al saludar)* to bow; **i. ante** to bow down to (**c**) *Fig (optar)* **i. a** to be o feel inclined to; **me inclino por éste** I'd rather have this one, I prefer this one

incluido,-a *adj* (**a**) *(después del sustantivo)* included; *(antes del sustantivo)* including; **servicio no i.** service not included; **i. I.V.A.** including VAT; **todos pagan, incluidos los niños** everyone has to pay, including children (**b**) *(adjunto)* enclosed

incluir [37] *vt* (**a**) to include (**b**) *(contener)* to contain, to comprise (**c**) *(adjuntar)* to enclose

inclusión *nf* inclusion

inclusive *adv* (**a**) *(incluido)* inclusive; **de martes a viernes i.** from Tuesday to Friday inclusive; **hasta la lección ocho i.** up to and including lesson eight (**b**) *(incluso)* even

incluso *adv* even; **i. mi madre** even my mother

incoar *vt defect Jur* to initiate

incógnita *nf* (**a**) *Mat* unknown quantity, unknown (**b**) *(misterio)* mystery

incógnito *nm* **de i.** incognito

incoherencia *nf* incoherence

incoherente *adj* incoherent

incoloro,-a *adj* colourless

incólume *adj Fml* unharmed; **salir i.** to escape unharmed

incombustible *adj* incombustible, fire-proof

incomodar 1 *vt* (**a**) *(causar molestia)* to inconvenience, to put out (**b**) *(fastidiar)* to bother, to annoy

2 incomodarse *vpr* (**a**) *(tomarse molestias)* to put oneself out, to go out of one's way (**b**) *(disgustarse)* to get annoyed *o* angry

incomodidad *nf* *(falta de comodidad)* discomfort; *(molestia)* inconvenience

incómodo,-a *adj* uncomfortable; **sentirse i.** to feel uncomfortable *o* awkward

incompatibilidad *nf* incompatibility; *Jur* **i. de caracteres** mutual incompatibility

incompatible *adj* incompatible

incompetencia *nf* incompetence

incompetente *adj & nmf* incompetent

incompleto,-a *adj* incomplete; *(inacabado)* unfinished

incomprensible *adj* incomprehensible

incomprensión *nf* lack of understanding, failure to understand; *(indiferencia)* lack of sympathy

incomunicado,-a *adj* (**a**) *(aislado)* isolated; **el pueblo se quedó i.** the town was cut off (**b**) *(en la cárcel)* in solitary confinement

incomunicar [44] *vt* (**a**) *(ciudad)* to isolate, to cut off (**b**) *(recluso)* to place in solitary confinement

inconcebible *adj* inconceivable, unthinkable

inconcluso,-a *adj* unfinished

incondicional 1 *adj* unconditional; *(apoyo)* wholehearted; *(amigo)* faithful; *(partidario)* staunch

2 *nm* die-hard

inconexo,-a *adj* *(incoherente)* incoherent, confused

inconformismo *nm* nonconformity

inconformista *adj & nmf* nonconformist

inconfundible *adj* unmistakable, obvious

incongruencia *nf* incongruity

incongruente *adj* incongruous

inconmensurable *adj* immeasurable, vast

inconsciencia *nf Med* unconsciousness; *Fig (irreflexión)* thoughtlessness; *(irresponsabilidad)* irresponsibility

inconsciente *adj* (**a**) *(con estar)* *(desmayado)* unconscious (**b**) *(con ser)* *(despreocupado)* unaware (**de** of); *Fig (irreflexivo)* thoughtless, irresponsible

inconsecuente *adj* inconsistent

inconsistente *adj* flimsy; *(argumento)* weak

inconstancia *nf* inconstancy, fickleness

inconstante *adj* inconstant, fickle

incontable *adj* countless, innumerable

incontenible *adj* uncontrollable, irrepressible

incontestable *adj* indisputable, unquestionable

incontinencia *nf* incontinence

incontrolable *adj* uncontrollable

incontrolado,-a 1 *adj* uncontrolled

2 *nm,f* troublemaker

inconveniencia *nf* (**a**) inconvenience (**b**) *(impropiedad)* unsuitability

inconveniente 1 *adj* (**a**) inconvenient (**b**) *(inapropiado)* unsuitable

2 *nm* *(objeción)* objection; **poner inconvenientes** to raise objections (**b**) *(desventaja)* disadvantage, drawback; *(problema)* difficulty; **¿tienes i. en acompañarme?** would you mind coming with me?

incordiar [43] *vt Fam* to bother, to pester

incordio *nm Fam* nuisance, pain

incorporación *nf* incorporation

incorporar 1 *vt* (**a**) to incorporate (**en** into) (**b**) *(levantar)* to help to sit up

2 incorporarse *vpr* (**a**) **i. a** *(sociedad)* to join; *(trabajo)* to start; **Mil i. a filas** to join up (**b**) *(en la cama)* to sit up

incorrección *nf* (**a**) *(falta)* incorrectness, inaccuracy; *(gramatical)* mistake (**b**) *(descortesía)* discourtesy, impropriety

incorrecto,-a *adj* (**a**) *(equivocado)* incorrect, inaccurate (**b**) *(grosero)* impolite, discourteous

incorregible *adj* incorrigible

incrédulo,-a 1 *adj* (**a**) incredulous, disbelieving (**b**) *Rel* unbelieving

2 *nm,f* (**a**) disbeliever (**b**) *Rel* unbeliever

increíble *adj* incredible, unbelievable

incrementar 1 *vt* to increase

2 incrementarse *vpr* to increase

incremento *nm* *(aumento)* increase; *(crecimiento)* growth; **i. de la temperatura** rise in temperature

increpar *vt Fml* to rebuke, to reprimand

incruento,-a *adj* bloodless

incrustar *vt* (**a**) *(insertar)* to encrust *o*

incrust (**b**) *(embutir)* to inlay; **incrustado con perlas** inlaid with pearls

incubadora *nf* incubator

incubar *vt* to incubate

incuestionable *adj* unquestionable, indisputable

inculcar [**44**] *vt (principios, ideas)* to instil (**en** into)

inculpado,-a *nm,f* **el i.** the accused

inculpar *vt* to accuse (**de** of), to blame (**de** for); *Jur* to charge (**de** with)

inculto,-a 1 *adj (ignorante)* uneducated, uncouth
  2 *nm,f* ignoramus

incultura *nf (ignorancia)* ignorance, lack of culture

incumbencia *nf* **no es de mi i.** it doesn't come within my province, it isn't my concern

incumbir *vi* to be incumbent (**a** upon); **esto no te incumbe** this is none of your business

incumplimiento *nm (de un deber)* nonfulfilment; *(de una orden)* failure to execute; **i. de contrato** breach of contract

incumplir *vt* not to fulfil; *(deber)* to fail to fulfil; *(promesa, contrato)* to break; *(orden)* to fail to carry out

incurrir *vi (cometer)* to fall (**en** into); **i. en delito** to commit a crime; **i. en (un) error** to fall into error

incursión *nf* raid, incursion

incursionar *vi Am* (**a**) *(en ciudad, territorio)* to make an incursion (**b**) **i. en algo** *(tema, asunto)* to dabble in sth

indagar [**42**] *vt* to investigate, to inquire into

indebido,-a *adj* (**a**) *(desconsiderado)* improper, undue (**b**) *(ilegal)* unlawful, illegal

indecencia *nf* indecency, obscenity

indecente *adj* (**a**) *(impúdico)* indecent (**b**) *(impresentable)* dreadful

indecible *adj* unspeakable; *(inefable)* indescribable; **sufrir lo i.** to suffer agonies

indecisión *nf* indecision, hesitation

indeciso,-a *adj* (**a**) *(vacilante)* hesitant, irresolute (**b**) *(resultados etc)* inconclusive

indefenso,-a *adj* defenceless, helpless

indefinidamente *adv* indefinitely

indefinido,-a *adj* (**a**) *(indeterminado)* indefinite; *(impreciso)* undefined, vague (**b**) *Ling* indefinite

indeleble *adj* indelible

indemne *adj (persona)* unharmed, unhurt; *(cosa)* undamaged

indemnización *nf* (**a**) *(acto)* indemnification (**b**) *Fin (compensación)* indemnity,

compensation; **i. por despido** redundancy payment

indemnizar [**40**] *vt* to indemnify, to compensate (**por** for)

independencia *nf* independence

independiente *adj (libre)* independent; *(individualista)* self-reliant

independientemente *adv* (**a**) independently (**de** of) (**b**) *(aparte de)* regardless, irrespective (**de** of)

independizar [**40**] **1** *vt* to make independent, to grant independence to
  2 independizarse *vpr* to become independent

indescifrable *adj* indecipherable

indescriptible *adj* indescribable

indeseable *adj & nmf* undesirable

indeterminación *nf* indecision, irresolution

indeterminado,-a *adj* (**a**) indefinite; *(impreciso)* vague (**b**) *(persona)* irresolute (**c**) *Ling* indefinite

India *nf* (**la**) **I.** India

Indias *nfpl* (**las**) **I.** the Indies; **las I. Orientales/Occidentales** the East/West Indies

indicación *nf* (**a**) *(señal)* indication, sign (**b**) *(instrucción)* instruction, direction; **por i. de algn** at sb's suggestion

indicado,-a *adj* right, suitable; **a la hora indicada** at the specified time; **en el momento menos i.** at the worst possible moment

indicador *nm* (**a**) indicator (**b**) *Téc* gauge, dial, meter; *Aut* **i. del nivel de aceite** (oil) dipstick; *Aut* **i. de velocidad** speedometer

indicar [**44**] *vt (señalar)* to indicate, to show, to point out; **¿me podría i. el camino?** could you show me the way?

indicativo,-a *adj* (**a**) indicative (**de** of) (**b**) *Ling (modo)* **i.** indicative (mood)

índice *nm* (**a**) *(de libro)* index, table of contents (**b**) *(relación)* rate; **í. de natalidad/mortalidad** birth/death rate; *Fin* **í. de precios** price index (**c**) *Anat (dedo)* **í.** index finger, forefinger

indicio *nm* (**a**) *(señal)* indication, sign, token (**de** of) (**b**) *Jur* **indicios** *(prueba)* evidence

índico,-a *adj* Indian; **Océano Í.** Indian Ocean

indiferencia *nf* indifference, apathy

indiferente *adj* (**a**) *(no importante)* unimportant; **me es i.** it makes no difference to me (**b**) *(apático)* indifferent

indígena 1 *adj* indigenous, native (**de** to)
  2 *nmf* native (**de** of)

indigencia *nf Fml* poverty, indigence

indigente *adj Fml* needy, poverty-stricken

indigestarse *vpr* (a) **se le indigestó la comida** the meal gave her indigestion (b) *(sufrir indigestión)* to get indigestion

indigestión *nf* indigestion

indigesto,-a *adj (comida)* indigestible, difficult to digest; **me siento i.** I've got indigestion

indignación *nf* indignation

indignado,-a *adj* indignant (**por** at *o* about)

indignante *adj* outrageous, infuriating

indignar 1 *vt* to infuriate, to make angry
  2 indignarse *vpr* to be *o* feel indignant (**por** at *o* about)

indigno,-a *adj* (a) unworthy (**de** of) (b) *(despreciable)* wretched, dreadful

indio,-a *adj & nm,f* Indian; **en fila india** in single file; *Fam* **hacer el i.** to act the fool

indirecta *nf Fam (insinuación)* hint, insinuation; **tirar** *o* **lanzar una i.** to drop a hint; **coger la i.** to get the message

indirecto,-a *adj* indirect; *Ling* **estilo i.** indirect *o* reported speech

indisciplinado,-a *adj* undisciplined, unruly

indiscreción *nf* indiscretion; *(comentario)* tactless remark

indiscreto,-a *adj* indiscreet, tactless

indiscutible *adj* indisputable, unquestionable

indispensable *adj* indispensable, essential

indisponer [19] *(pp* **indispuesto**) **1** *vt* to upset, to make unwell
  2 indisponerse *vpr* (a) to fall ill, to become unwell (b) *Fig* **i. con algn** to fall out with sb

indispuesto,-a *adj* indisposed, unwell

indispuse *pt indef de* **indisponer**

indistintamente *adv* **pueden escribir en inglés o en español i.** you can write in English or Spanish, it doesn't matter which

indistinto,-a *adj (indiferente)* immaterial, inconsequential

individual 1 *adj* individual; **habitación i.** single room
  2 *nmpl Dep* **individuales** singles

individualismo *nm* individualism

individualista 1 *adj* individualistic
  2 *nmf* individualist

individuo *nm* (a) individual (b) *(tío)* bloke, guy

índole *nf* (a) *(carácter)* character, nature (b) *(clase, tipo)* kind, sort

indolencia *nf* indolence, laziness

indolente 1 *adj* indolent, lazy
  2 *nmf* idler

indomable *adj* (a) *(animal)* untamable (b) *(pueblo)* ungovernable, unruly; *(niño)* uncontrollable; *(pasión)* indomitable

indómito,-a *adj* (a) *(no domado)* untamed; *(indomable)* untamable (b) *(pueblo)* unruly; *(persona)* uncontrollable

Indonesia *n* Indonesia

inducir [10] *vt* (a) *(incitar, mover)* to lead, to induce; **i. a error** to lead into error, to mislead (b) *Elec (corriente)* to induce

inductivo,-a *adj* inductive

indudable *adj* indubitable, unquestionable; **es i. que** there is no doubt that

induje *pt indef de* **inducir**

indulgencia *nf* indulgence, leniency

indulgente *adj* indulgent (**con** towards), lenient (**con** with)

indultar *vt Jur* to pardon

indulto *nm Jur* pardon, amnesty

indumentaria *nf* clothing, clothes

industria *nf* industry

industrial 1 *adj* industrial
  2 *nmf* industrialist

industrialización *nf* industrialization

industrializar [40] *vt* to industrialize

induzco *indic pres de* **inducir**

INE *nm (abr* **Instituto Nacional de Estadística**) = organization that publishes official statistics about Spain

inédito,-a *adj* (a) *(libro, texto)* unpublished (b) *(nuevo)* completely new; *(desconocido)* unknown

inefable *adj* ineffable, indescribable

ineficacia *nf (ineptitud)* inefficiency; *(inutilidad)* ineffectiveness

ineficaz *adj (inepto)* inefficient; *(inefectivo)* ineffective

ineludible *adj* inescapable, unavoidable

INEM *nm (abr* **Instituto Nacional de Empleo**) = Spanish department of employment

ineptitud *nf* ineptitude, incompetence

inepto,-a 1 *adj* inept, incompetent
  2 *nm,f* incompetent person

inequívoco,-a *adj* unmistakable, unequivocal

inercia *nf* (a) *Fís* inertia (b) *Fig (pasividad)* inertia, passivity; **hacer algo por i.** to do sth out of habit

inerte *adj (inanimado)* inert; *(inmóvil)* motionless

inesperado,-a *adj (fortuito)* unexpected, unforeseen; *(imprevisto)* sudden

inestabilidad *nf* instability

inestable *adj* unstable, unsteady

inestimable *adj* inestimable, invaluable
inevitable *adj* inevitable, unavoidable
inexistente *adj* non-existent
inexorable *adj* inexorable
inexperiencia *nf* lack of experience
inexperto,-a *adj* (*inexperto*) inexpert; (*sin experiencia*) inexperienced
inexplicable *adj* inexplicable
inexpugnable *adj* Mil impregnable
infalible *adj* infallible
infamar *vt* to defame, to slander
infame *adj* (*vil*) infamous, vile; (*despreciable*) dreadful, awful
infamia *nf* disgrace, infamy
infancia *nf* childhood, infancy
infanta *nf* infanta, princess
infante *nm* (a) infante, prince (b) Mil infantryman
infantería *nf* Mil infantry; **la i. de marina** the marines
infantil *adj* (a) **literatura i.** (*para niños*) children's literature (b) (*aniñado*) childlike; Pey childish, infantile
infarto *nm* Med infarction, infarct; **i. (de miocardio)** heart attack, coronary thrombosis; Fam **de i.** thrilling, stunning
infatigable *adj* indefatigable, tireless
infección *nf* infection
infeccioso,-a *adj* infectious
infectar **1** *vt* to infect
  2 infectarse *vpr* to become infected (**de** with)
infeliz **1** *adj* unhappy; (*desdichado*) unfortunate
  2 *nmf* Fam simpleton; **es un pobre i.** he is a poor devil
inferior **1** *adj* (a) (*más bajo*) lower (b) (*calidad*) inferior; **de calidad i.** of inferior quality (c) (*cantidad*) lower, less; **i. a la media** below average
  2 *nmf* (*persona*) subordinate, inferior
inferioridad *nf* inferiority; **estar en i. de condiciones** to be at a disadvantage; **complejo de i.** inferiority complex
inferir [5] *vt* Literario (*deducir*) to infer, to deduce (**de** from)
infernal *adj* infernal, hellish; Fig **había un ruido i.** there was a hell of a noise
infestar *vt* (a) **infestado de** (*parásitos*) infested with; (*plantas*) overgrown with (b) (*llenar*) to overrun, to invade; **infestado de turistas** swarming with tourists (c) (*infectar*) to infect
infición *nf* Méx pollution
infidelidad *nf* infidelity, unfaithfulness
infiel **1** *adj* (*desleal*) unfaithful
  2 *nmf* Rel infidel
infierno *nm* (a) Rel hell (b) Fig (*tormento*)

hell; **su vida es un i.** his life is sheer hell (c) (*horno*) inferno; **en verano esto es un i.** in summer it's like an inferno here; Fam **¡vete al i.!** go to hell!, get lost!
infiltración *nf* (*de agua*) infiltration; (*de noticia*) leak
infiltrado,-a *nm,f* infiltrator
infiltrar **1** *vt* to infiltrate; (*noticia*) to leak
  2 infiltrarse *vpr* to infiltrate (**en** into)
ínfimo,-a *adj* Fml (*mínimo*) extremely low; **detalle í.** smallest detail; **ínfima calidad** very poor quality
infinidad *nf* (a) infinity (b) (*sinfín*) great number; **en i. de ocasiones** on countless occasions
infinitivo,-a *adj & nm* Ling infinitive
infinito,-a **1** *adj* infinite, endless
  2 *nm* infinity
  3 *adv* Fam (*muchísimo*) infinitely, immensely
inflación *nf* Econ inflation
inflacionario,-a, inflacionista *adj* Econ inflationary
inflamable *adj* flammable
inflamación *nf* Med inflammation
inflamar **1** *vt* (a) Med to inflame (b) (*encender*) to set on fire, to ignite
  2 inflamarse *vpr* (a) Med to become inflamed (b) (*incendiarse*) to catch fire
inflar **1** *vt* (a) (*hinchar*) to inflate, to blow up; Náut (*vela*) to swell (b) Fig (*exagerar*) to exaggerate
  2 inflarse *vpr* (a) to inflate; Náut (*vela*) to swell (b) Fam **i. de** to overdo; **se inflaron de macarrones** they stuffed themselves with macaroni
inflexible *adj* inflexible
infligir [57] *vt* to inflict
influencia *nf* influence; **ejercer** *o* **tener i. sobre algn** to have an influence on *o* upon sb; **tener influencias** to be influential; **tráfico de influencias** Old-Boy network
influenciar [43] *vt* to influence
influir [37] **1** *vt* to influence
  2 *vi* (a) to have influence (b) **i. en** *o* **sobre** to influence, to have an influence on
influjo *nm* influence
influyente *adj* influential
información *nf* (a) information; **oficina de i.** information bureau (b) **una i.** (*noticia*) a piece of news, news *sing* (c) Tel Br directory enquiries, US information (d) (*referencias*) references
informado,-a *adj* informed; **de fuentes bien informadas** from well-informed sources

informal *adj* (**a**) *(reunión, cena)* informal (**b**) *(comportamiento)* casual (**c**) *(persona)* unreliable, untrustworthy

informalidad *nf* *(incumplimiento)* unreliability; *(desenfado)* informality

informar 1 *vt* to inform (**de** of); *(dar informes)* to report
2 informarse *vpr* *(procurarse noticias)* to find out (**de** about); *(enterarse)* to inquire (**de** about)

informática *nf* computing, information technology

informático,-a 1 *adj* computer, computing
2 *nm,f* (computer) technician

informativo,-a 1 *adj* (**a**) *Rad & TV* news; **boletín i.** news (broadcast) (**b**) *(explicativo)* informative, explanatory
2 *nm Rad & TV* news bulletin

informe *nm* (**a**) report (**b**) **informes** references; **pedir informes sobre algn** to make inquiries about sb

infracción *nf* *(de ley)* infringement, breach (**de** of)

infractor,-a *nm,f* offender

infraestructura *nf* infrastructure

in fraganti *loc adv* in the act; **coger** *o* **pillar a algn i.** to catch sb redhanded

infrahumano,-a *adj* subhuman

infranqueable *adj* impassable; *Fig* insurmountable

infrarrojo,-a *adj* infrared

infrautilizar *vt* to underutilize

infringir [57] *vt* to infringe, to contravene; **i. una ley** to break a law

infructuoso,-a *adj* fruitless, unsuccessful

infundado,-a *adj* unfounded, groundless

infundir *vt* to infuse; *Fig* to instil; **i. dudas** to give rise to doubt; **i. respeto** to command respect

infusión *nf* infusion

infuso,-a *adj* *Fam Irón* **ciencia infusa** sheer genius

ingeniar [43] 1 *vt* to invent, to devise
2 ingeniarse *vpr* **ingeniárselas para hacer algo** to manage to do sth

ingeniería *nf* engineering

ingeniero,-a *nm,f* engineer; **i. agrónomo** agricultural engineer; **i. de caminos** civil engineer; **i. de minas/montes** mining/forestry engineer; **i. de telecomunicaciones** telecommunications engineer; **i. técnico** technician

ingenio *nm* (**a**) *(talento)* talent; *(inventiva)* inventiveness, creativeness; *(agudeza)* wit (**b**) *(aparato)* device

ingenioso,-a *adj* ingenious, clever; *(vivaz)* witty

ingente *adj* huge, enormous

ingenuidad *nf* ingenuousness, naïveté

ingenuo,-a 1 *adj* ingenuous, naïve
2 *nm,f* naïve person

ingerir [5] *vt* *(comida)* to ingest, to consume; *(líquidos, alcohol)* to drink, to consume

Inglaterra *n* England

ingle *nf* *Anat* groin

inglés,-esa 1 *adj* English
2 *nm,f* *(hombre)* Englishman; *(mujer)* Englishwoman; **los ingleses** the English
3 *nm (idioma)* English

ingratitud *nf* ingratitude, ungratefulness

ingrato,-a 1 *adj* (**a**) *(persona)* ungrateful (**b**) *(noticia)* unpleasant (**c**) *(trabajo)* thankless, unrewarding (**d**) *(tierra)* unproductive
2 *nm,f* ungrateful person

ingrediente *nm* ingredient

ingresar 1 *vt* (**a**) *Fin* to deposit, to pay in (**b**) *Med* to admit; **la ingresaron en el hospital** she was admitted to hospital
2 *vi* (**a**) to enter; **i. en el ejército** to enlist in the army, to join the army; **i. en un club** to join a club (**b**) **i. cadáver** to be dead on arrival

ingreso *nm* (**a**) *Fin* deposit; **hacer un i. en una cuenta** to pay money into an account (**b**) *(entrada)* entry (**en** into); *(admisión)* admission (**en** to) (**c**) **ingresos** *(sueldo, renta)* income; *(beneficios)* revenue

inhábil *adj* (**a**) *(incapaz)* unfit; **i. para el trabajo** unfit for work (**b**) **día i.** nonworking day

inhabilitación *nf* (**a**) *Fml (incapacidad)* disablement (**b**) *Jur* disqualification

inhabilitar *vt* (**a**) *Fml (incapacitar)* to disable; **inhabilitado para el trabajo** unfit for work (**b**) *Jur* to disqualify

inhabitable *adj* uninhabitable

> *𝅘* Observa que la palabra inglesa **inhabitable** es un falso amigo y no es la traducción de la palabra española **inhabitable**. En inglés, **inhabitable** significa "habitable".

inhalación *nf* inhalation

inhalador *nm Med* inhaler

inhalar *vt* to inhale

inherente *adj* inherent (**a** in)

inhibición *nf* inhibition

inhibir 1 *vt* to inhibit
2 inhibirse *vpr* (**a**) *(cohibirse)* to be o feel inhibited (**b**) *(abstenerse)* to refrain (**de** from)

inhóspito,-a *adj* inhospitable

inhumación *nf* burial

inhumano,-a *adj* inhumane; *(cruel)* inhuman

inhumar *vt* to bury

INI *nm Antes (abr* **Instituto Nacional de Industria)** = Spanish governmental organization that promotes industry

inicial *adj & nf* initial; **punto i.** starting point

iniciar [43] **1** *vt* (**a**) *(empezar)* to begin, to start; *(discusión)* to initiate; *(una cosa nueva)* to pioneer (**b**) *(introducir)* to initiate

2 iniciarse *vpr* (**a**) **i. en algo** *(aprender)* to start to study sth (**b**) *(empezar)* to begin, to start

iniciativa *nf* initiative; **i. privada** private enterprise; **por i. propia** on one's own initiative

inicio *nm* beginning, start; **a inicios de** at the beginning of

inimitable *adj* inimitable

ininterrumpido,-a *adj* uninterrupted, continuous

iniquidad *nf* iniquity

injerencia *nf* interference, meddling (**en** in)

injerirse *vpr* to interfere, to meddle (**en** in)

injertar *vt Agr & Med* to graft

injerto *nm* graft

injuria *nf (insulto)* insult, affront; *(agravio)* outrage

injuriar [43] *vt (insultar)* to insult; *(ultrajar)* to outrage

injusticia *nf* injustice, unfairness

injustificado,-a *adj* unjustified

injusto,-a *adj* unjust, unfair

inmaculado,-a *adj* immaculate

inmadurez *nf* immaturity

inmaduro,-a *adj* immature

inmediaciones *nfpl* neighbourhood

inmediatamente *adv* immediately, at once

inmediato,-a *adj* (**a**) *(en el tiempo)* immediate; **de i.** at once (**b**) *(en el espacio)* next (**a** to), adjoining

inmejorable *adj (trabajo)* excellent; *(precio)* unbeatable

inmemorial *adj* immemorial; **desde tiempos inmemoriales** since time immemorial

inmensidad *nf* immensity, enormity

inmenso,-a *adj* immense, vast

inmerecido,-a *adj* undeserved, unmerited

inmersión *nf* immersion; *(de submarino)* dive

inmerso,-a *adj* immersed (**en** in)

inmigración *nf* immigration

inmigrante *adj & nmf* immigrant

inmigrar *vi* to immigrate

inminente *adj* imminent, impending

inmiscuirse [37] *vpr* to interfere, to meddle (**en** in)

inmobiliaria *nf Br* estate agent's, *US* real estate company

inmobiliario,-a *adj* property, *US* real-estate; **agente i.** *Br* estate agent, *US* realtor

inmolar *vt Fml* to immolate, to sacrifice

inmoral *adj* immoral

inmoralidad *nf* immorality

inmortal *adj & nmf* immortal

inmortalidad *nf* immortality

inmortalizar [40] *vt* to immortalize

inmóvil *adj* motionless, immobile

inmovilista *adj* ultra-conservative

inmovilizar [40] *vt* (**a**) *(persona, cosa)* to immobilize (**b**) *Fin (capital)* to immobilize, to tie up

inmueble **1** *adj* **bienes inmuebles** real estate

2 *nm* building

inmundicia *nf* (**a**) *(suciedad)* dirt, filth; *Fig* dirtiness (**b**) *(basura)* rubbish, refuse

inmundo,-a *adj* dirty, filthy; *Fig* nasty

inmune *adj* immune (**a** to), exempt (**de** from)

inmunidad *nf* immunity (**contra** against); **i. diplomática/parlamentaria** diplomatic/parliamentary immunity

inmunizar [40] *vt* to immunize (**contra** against)

inmutarse *vpr* to change countenance; **ni se inmutó** he didn't turn a hair

innato,-a *adj* innate, inborn

innecesario,-a *adj* unnecessary

innegable *adj* undeniable

innovación *nf* innovation

innovar *vt & vi* to innovate

innumerable *adj* innumerable, countless

inocencia *nf* (**a**) innocence (**b**) *(ingenuidad)* naïveté

inocentada *nf Fam* ≃ April Fool's joke; **hacer una i. a algn** to play an April Fool's joke on sb

inocente **1** *adj* innocent

2 *nmf* innocent; **día de los Inocentes** Holy Innocents' Day, 28 December, ≃ April Fools' Day

inocuo,-a *adj* innocuous

inodoro,-a **1** *adj* odourless

2 *nm* toilet, lavatory

inofensivo,-a *adj* harmless

inolvidable *adj* unforgettable

inoperante *adj* ineffective

inopia *nf Fig* **estar en la i.** to be in the clouds, to be miles away

inopinado,-a *adj* unexpected

inoportuno,-a *adj* inappropriate; **llegó en un momento muy i.** he turned up at a very awkward moment

inorgánico,-a *adj* inorganic

inoxidable *adj* **acero i.** stainless steel

inquebrantable *adj Fig* unshakable; *(persona)* unyielding

inquietante *adj* worrying

inquietar 1 *vt* to worry

2 inquietarse *vpr* to worry (**por** about)

inquieto,-a *adj* (**a**) *(preocupado)* worried (**por** about) (**b**) *(intranquilo)* restless (**c**) *(emprendedor)* eager

inquietud *nf* (**a**) *(preocupación)* worry (**b**) *(agitación)* restlessness (**c**) *(anhelo)* eagerness

inquilino,-a *nm,f* tenant

inquirir [31] *vt* to investigate

inquisitivo,-a *adj* inquisitive

inri *nm Fam* insult; **para más** *o* **mayor i.** to make matters worse

insaciable *adj* insatiable

insalubre *adj* unhealthy

INSALUD *nm* (*abr* **Instituto Nacional de la Salud**) = Spanish national health service, *Br* ≃ NHS, *US* ≃ Medicaid

insano,-a *adj* (**a**) *(loco)* insane, mad (**b**) *(insalubre)* unhealthy

insatisfecho,-a *adj* dissatisfied

inscribir *(pp* inscrito*)* **1** *vt* (**a**) *(registrar)* to register; **i. a un niño en el registro civil** to register a child's birth (**b**) *(matricular)* to enrol (**c**) *(grabar)* to inscribe

2 inscribirse *vpr* (**a**) *(registrarse)* to register; *(hacerse miembro)* to join (**b**) *(matricularse)* to enrol

inscripción *nf* (**a**) *(matriculación)* enrolment, registration (**b**) *(escrito etc)* inscription

insecticida *nm* insecticide

insecto *nm* insect

inseguridad *nf* (**a**) *(falta de confianza)* insecurity (**b**) *(duda)* uncertainty (**c**) *(peligro)* lack of safety; **la i. ciudadana** the breakdown of law and order

inseguro,-a *adj* (**a**) *(poco confiado)* insecure (**b**) *(dubitativo)* uncertain (**c**) *(peligroso)* unsafe

inseminar *vt* to inseminate

insensatez *nf* foolishness

insensato,-a 1 *adj* foolish

2 *nm,f* fool

insensibilidad *nf* insensitivity

insensible *adj* (**a**) *(indiferente)* insensitive (**a** to), unfeeling (**b**) *(imperceptible)* imperceptible (**c**) *Med* numb

inseparable *adj* inseparable

insertar *vt* to insert

inservible *adj* useless

insidia *nf* (**a**) *(trampa)* malicious ploy (**b**) *(malicia)* maliciousness

insidioso,-a *adj* insidious

insigne *adj* distinguished

insignia *nf* (**a**) *(emblema)* badge (**b**) *(bandera)* flag

insignificancia *nf* (**a**) *(intrascendencia)* insignificance (**b**) *(nadería)* trifle

insignificante *adj* insignificant

insinuación *nf* insinuation

insinuante *adj* insinuating; *(atrevido)* forward

insinuar [30] **1** *vt* to insinuate

2 insinuarse *vpr* **i. a algn** to make advances to sb

insípido,-a *adj* insipid; *Fig* dull, flat

insistencia *nf* insistence; **con i.** insistently

insistente *adj* insistent

insistir *vi* to insist (**en** on); **insistió en ese punto** he stressed that point

insociable *adj* unsociable

insolación *nf Med* sunstroke; **coger una i.** to get sunstroke

insolencia *nf* insolence

insolente *adj* insolent

insolidaridad *nf* unsupportive stance

insólito,-a *adj* *(poco usual)* unusual; *(extraño)* strange, odd

insoluble *adj* insoluble

insolvencia *nf Fin* insolvency

insolvente *adj Fin* insolvent

insomnio *nm* insomnia; **noche de i.** sleepless night

insondable *adj* unfathomable

insonorizado,-a *adj* soundproof

insonorizar [40] *vt* to soundproof

insoportable *adj* unbearable

insospechado,-a *adj* unsuspected

insostenible *adj* untenable

inspección *nf* inspection

inspeccionar *vt* to inspect

inspector,-a *nm,f* inspector; **i. de Hacienda** tax inspector

inspiración *nf* (**a**) inspiration (**b**) *(inhalación)* inhalation

inspirado,-a *adj* inspired

inspirar 1 *vt* (**a**) to inspire (**b**) *(inhalar)* to inhale, to breathe in

2 inspirarse *vpr* **i. en** to be inspired by

instalación *nf* installation; **instalaciones deportivas** sports facilities

instalar 1 *vt* (**a**) to install (**b**) *(puesto, tienda)* to set up

2 instalarse *vpr (persona)* to settle (down)

instancia *nf* (**a**) *(solicitud)* request; **a instancia(s) de** at the request of (**b**) *(escrito)* application form (**c**) *Jur* **tribunal de primera i.** court of first instance (**d**) **en primera i.** first of all; **en última i.** as a last resort

> *Observa que la palabra inglesa* **instance** *es un falso amigo y no es la traducción de la palabra española* **instancia**. *En inglés,* **instance** *significa "caso, ejemplo".*

instantánea *nf* snapshot

instantáneamente *adv* instantly

instantáneo,-a *adj* instantaneous; **café i.** instant coffee

instante *nm* instant, moment; **a cada i.** constantly; **al i.** immediately, right away; **por instantes** with every second; **¡un i.!** just a moment!

instar *vt* to urge

instauración *nf* founding

instaurar *vt* to found

instigador,-a *nm,f* instigator

instigar [42] *vt* to instigate; **i. a la rebelión** to incite a rebellion

instintivo,-a *adj* instinctive

instinto *nm* instinct; **por i.** instinctively; **i. de conservación** survival instinct

institución *nf* institution

instituir [37] *vt* to institute

instituto *nm* (**a**) institute (**b**) *Educ Br* state secondary school, *US* high school

institutriz *nf* governess

instituyo *indic pres de* **instituir**

instrucción *nf* (**a**) *(educación)* education (**b**) *(usu pl) (indicación)* instruction; **instrucciones para el** *o* **de uso** directions for use (**c**) *Jur* preliminary investigation; **la i. del sumario** proceedings; **juez de i.** examining magistrate (**d**) *Mil* drill

instructivo,-a *adj* instructive

instruido,-a *adj* educated, well-educated

instruir [37] *vt* (**a**) to instruct (**b**) *(enseñar)* to educate (**c**) *Mil* to drill (**d**) *Jur* to investigate

instrumental *adj* instrumental

instrumento *nm* instrument

insubordinación *nf* insubordination

insubordinado,-a *adj* insubordinate

insubordinarse *vpr (sublevarse)* to rebel (**contra** against)

insuficiencia *nf* insufficiency

insuficiente 1 *adj* insufficient

2 *nm Educ (nota)* fail

insufrible *adj* insufferable

insular 1 *adj* insular, island

2 *nmf* islander

insulso,-a *adj* insipid

insultante *adj* insulting

insultar *vt* to insult

insulto *nm* insult

insumisión *nf* = refusal to do military service

insumiso,-a 1 *adj* unsubmissive

2 *nm* = person who refuses to do military service

insuperable *adj* (**a**) *(inmejorable)* unsurpassable (**b**) *(problema)* insurmountable

insurgente *adj & nmf* insurgent

insurrección *nf* insurrection

intachable *adj* irreproachable; **conducta i.** impeccable behaviour

intacto,-a *adj* intact

integral 1 *adj* integral; *Culin* **pan i.** wholemeal bread; **arroz i.** brown rice

2 *nf Mat* integral

integrante 1 *adj* integral; **ser parte i. de** to be an integral part of

2 *nmf* member

integrar 1 *vt (formar)* to compose, to make up; **el equipo lo integran once jugadores** there are eleven players in the team

2 integrarse *vpr* to integrate (**en** with)

integridad *nf* integrity

íntegro,-a *adj* (**a**) *(entero)* whole, entire; *Cin & Lit* **versión íntegra** unabridged version (**b**) *(honrado)* upright

intelecto *nm* intellect

intelectual *adj & nmf* intellectual

inteligencia *nf (intelecto)* intelligence; **cociente de i.** intelligence quotient, IQ

inteligente *adj* intelligent

inteligible *adj* intelligible

intemperie *nf* bad weather; **a la i.** in the open (air)

intempestivo,-a *adj* untimely

intención *nf* intention; **con i.** deliberately, on purpose; **con segunda** *o* **doble i.** with an ulterior motive; **tener la i. de hacer algo** to intend to do sth

intencionadamente *adv* on purpose

intencionado,-a *adj* deliberate

intencional *adj* intentional

intendencia *nf* (**a**) *RP (corporación municipal)* town council, *US* city council (**b**) *RP (edificio)* town hall, *US* city hall (**c**) *Chile (gobernación)* administrative region

intendente *nm* (**a**) *RP (alcalde)* mayor (**b**) *Chile (gobernador)* governor

intensidad *nf* intensity; *(del viento)* force

intensificar [44] *vt,* **intensificarse** *vpr* to intensify; *(amistad)* to strengthen

intensivo,-a *adj* intensive; *Agr* **cultivo i.** intensive farming; *Educ* **curso i.** crash course

intenso,-a *adj* intense

intentar *vt* to try, to attempt; *Fam* **¡inténtalo!** give it a go!

intento *nm* attempt; **i. de suicidio** attempted suicide

intentona *nf* putsch

inter- *pref* inter-

intercalar *vt* to insert

intercambiar [43] *vt* to exchange

intercambio *nm* exchange; **i. comercial** trade

interceder *vi* to intercede

interceptar *vt* (a) *(detener)* to intercept (b) *(carretera)* to block; *(tráfico)* to hold up

intercesión *nf* intercession

intercontinental *adj* intercontinental

interdicto *nm* prohibition

interés *nm* (a) *(atención)* interest; **poner i. en** to take an interest in; **tener i. en** *o* **por** to be interested in (b) *(provecho personal)* self-interest; **hacer algo (sólo) por i.** to do sth out of self-interest; **intereses creados** vested interests (c) *Fin* interest; **con un i. del 11 por ciento** at an interest of 11 percent; **tipos de i.** interest rates

interesado,-a **1** *adj* (a) *(atención)* interested (**en** in); **las partes interesadas** the interested parties (b) *(egoísta)* selfish

2 *nm,f* interested person; **los interesados** those interested *o* concerned

interesante *adj* interesting

interesar **1** *vt* (a) *(tener interés)* to interest; **la poesía no me interesa nada** poetry doesn't interest me at all (b) *(concernir)* to concern

2 *vi* *(ser importante)* to be of interest, to be important; **interesaría llegar pronto** it is important to get there early

3 **interesarse** *vpr* **i. por** *o* **en** to be interested in; **se interesó por ti** he asked about *o* after you

interferencia *nf* interference; *Rad & TV* jamming

interferir [5] *vt* (a) to interfere with; *(plan)* to upset (b) *Rad & TV* to jam

interfono *nm Tel* intercom

interinidad *nf* (a) *(temporalidad)* temporariness (b) *(empleo)* temporary employment

interino,-a **1** *adj* *(persona)* acting

2 *nm,f* *(trabajador temporal)* temporary worker

interior **1** *adj* (a) inner, inside, interior; **habitación i.** inner room; **ropa i.** underwear (b) *Pol* domestic, internal (c) *Geog* inland

2 *nm* (a) inside, interior; *Fig* **en su i. no estaba de acuerdo** deep down she disagreed (b) *Geog* interior; *Pol* **Ministerio del I.** *Br* ≃ Home Office, *US* ≃ Department of the Interior

interiorizar [40] *vt* to internalize

interjección *nf Ling* interjection

interlocutor,-a *nm,f* speaker; *(negociador)* negotiator

intermediario *nm Com* middleman

intermedio,-a **1** *adj* intermediate

2 *nm TV* *(intervalo)* break

interminable *adj* endless

intermitente **1** *adj* intermittent

2 *nm Aut Br* indicator, *US* turn signal

internacional *adj* international

internado,-a **1** *nm,f* inmate

2 *nm* *(colegio)* boarding-school

internar *vt (en hospital)* to confine

2 **internarse** *vpr* (a) *(penetrar)* to advance (**en** into) (b) *Dep* to break through

internauta *nmf Informát* Net user

Internet *nf Informát* Internet; **está en I.** it's on the Internet

interno,-a **1** *adj* (a) internal; **por vía interna** internally (b) *Pol* domestic

2 *nm,f (alumno)* boarder; *Med (enfermo)* patient; *(preso)* inmate

3 *nm RP (extensión)* (telephone) extension; **i. 28, por favor** extension 28, please

interponer [19] *(pp* **interpuesto**) **1** *vt* to insert; *Jur* **i. un recurso** to give notice of appeal

2 **interponerse** *vpr* to intervene

interpretación *nf* (a) interpretation (b) *Mús & Teatro* performance

interpretar *vt* (a) to interpret (b) *Teatro (papel)* to play; *(obra)* to perform; *Mús (concierto)* to play, to perform; *(canción)* to sing

intérprete *nmf* (a) *(traductor)* interpreter (b) *Teatro* performer; *Mús (cantante)* singer; *(músico)* performer

interpuse *pt indef de* **interponer**

interrogación *nf* interrogation; *Ling* **(signo de) i.** question *o* interrogation mark

interrogante *nf Fig* question mark

interrogar [42] *vt* to question; *(testigo etc)* to interrogate

interrogatorio *nm* interrogation

interrumpir *vt* to interrupt; *(tráfico)* to block

interrupción *nf* interruption; **i. del embarazo** termination of pregnancy

interruptor *nm Elec* switch

intersección *nf* intersection

interurbano,-a *adj* intercity; *Tel* **conferencia interurbana** long-distance call

intervalo *nm* interval; **habrá intervalos de lluvia** there will be periods of rain

intervención *nf* a (*participación*) intervention, participation (**en** in); (*aportación*) contribution (**en** to) (b) *Med* intervention

intervenir [27] **1** *vi* (*mediar*) to intervene (**en** in); (*participar*) to take part (**en** in); (*contribuir*) to contribute (**en** to)
2 *vt* (a) (*confiscar*) to confiscate, to seize (b) *Tel* (*teléfono*) to tap (c) *Med* to operate on

interventor,-a *nm,f* (*supervisor*) inspector; *Fin* **i. (de cuentas)** auditor

interviú *nf* (*pl* **interviús**) interview

intestino,-a 1 *adj* (*luchas*) internal
2 *nm Anat* intestine

intimar *vi* to become close (**con** to)

intimidad *nf* (*amistad*) intimacy; (*vida privada*) private life; (*privacidad*) privacy; **en la i.** privately, in private

intimidar *vt* to intimidate

íntimo,-a 1 *adj* (a) intimate (b) (*vida*) private; **una boda íntima** a quiet wedding (c) (*amistad*) close
2 *nm,f* close friend, intimate

intolerable *adj* intolerable

intolerancia *nf* intolerance

intolerante 1 *adj* intolerant
2 *nmf* intolerant person

intoxicación *nf* poisoning; **i. alimentaria** food poisoning

---

> 🖉 Observa que la palabra inglesa **intoxication** es un falso amigo y no es la traducción de la palabra española **intoxicación**. En inglés, **intoxication** significa "embriaguez".

---

intoxicar [44] *vt* to poison

> 🖉 Observa que el verbo inglés **to intoxicate** es un falso amigo y no es la traducción del verbo español **intoxicar**. En inglés, **to intoxicate** significa "embriagar, emborrachar".

---

intra- *pref* intra-

intranet *nf Informát* intranet

intranquilidad *nf* worry

intranquilizarse *vpr* to get worried

intranquilo,-a *adj* (*preocupado*) worried; (*agitado*) restless

intransigente *adj* intransigent

intransitable *adj* impassable

intransitivo,-a *adj Ling* intransitive

intratable *adj* (a) (*problema*) intractable

(b) (*persona*) unsociable

intrépido,-a *adj* intrepid

intriga *nf* intrigue; *Cin & Teatro* plot

intrigante 1 *adj* (a) (*interesante*) intriguing, interesting (b) (*maquinador*) scheming
2 *nmf* (*persona*) schemer

intrigar [42] **1** *vt* (*interesar*) to intrigue, to interest
2 *vi* (*maquinar*) to plot

intrincado,-a *adj* (a) (*cuestión, problema*) intricate (b) (*bosque*) dense

intrínseco,-a *adj* intrinsic

introducción *nf* introduction

introducir [10] *vt* (a) to introduce (b) (*meter*) to insert, to put in

intromisión *nf* (*injerencia*) meddling; **perdón por la i.** forgive the intrusion

introspectivo,-a *adj* introspective

introvertido,-a 1 *adj* introverted
2 *nm,f* introvert

intruso,-a 1 *adj* intrusive
2 *nm,f* intruder; *Jur* trespasser

intuición *nf* intuition

intuir [37] *vt* to know by intuition

intuitivo,-a *adj* intuitive

inundación *nf* flood

inundar *vt* to flood; *Fig* (*de trabajo etc*) to swamp

inusitado,-a *adj* unusual

inútil 1 *adj* (a) useless; (*esfuerzo, intento*) vain, pointless (b) *Mil* unfit (for service)
2 *nmf Fam* good-for-nothing

inutilidad *nf* uselessness

inutilizar [40] *vt* to make o render useless; (*máquina etc*) to put out of action

invadir *vt* to invade; *Fig* **los estudiantes invadieron la calle** students poured out onto the street

invalidar *vt* to invalidate

invalidez *nf* (a) *Jur* (*nulidad*) invalidity (b) *Med* (*minusvalía*) disability

inválido,-a 1 *adj* (a) *Jur* (*nulo*) invalid (b) *Med* (*minusválido*) disabled, handicapped
2 *nm,f Med* disabled o handicapped person

invariable *adj* invariable

invasión *nf* invasion

invasor,-a 1 *adj* invading
2 *nm,f* invader

invencible *adj* (a) (*enemigo*) invincible (b) (*obstáculo*) insurmountable

invención *nf* (*invento*) invention; (*mentira*) fabrication

inventar *vt* to invent; (*excusa, mentira*) to make up, to concoct

inventario *nm* inventory

inventiva *nf* inventiveness; *(imaginación)* imagination

invento *nm* invention

inventor,-a *nm,f* inventor

invernadero *nm* greenhouse; **efecto i.** greenhouse effect

invernal *adj* winter, wintry

invernar [1] *vi* to hibernate

inverosímil *adj* unlikely, improbable

inversión *nf* (a) inversion (b) *Fin* investment

inverso,-a *adj* opposite; **en sentido i.** in the opposite direction; **en orden i.** in reverse order

inversor,-a *nm,f Fin* investor

invertebrado,-a *adj & nm Zool* invertebrate

invertido,-a 1 *adj* inverted, reversed
2 *nm,f* homosexual

invertir [5] *vt* (a) *(orden)* to invert, to reverse (b) *(dinero)* to invest (**en** in); *(tiempo)* to spend (**en** on)

investidura *nf* investiture; *Pol* vote of confidence

investigación *nf* (a) *(policial etc)* investigation (b) *(científica)* research

investigador,-a *nm,f* (a) *(detective)* investigator (b) *(científico)* researcher, research worker

investigar [42] *vt* to research; *(indagar)* to investigate

investir [6] *vt* to invest

invidente 1 *adj* unsighted
2 *nmf* unsighted person

invierno *nm* winter

invisible *adj* invisible

invitación *nf* invitation

invitado,-a 1 *adj* invited; **artista i.** guest artist
2 *nm,f* guest

invitar *vt* to invite; **hoy invito yo** it's on me today; **me invitó a una copa** he treated me to a drink

invocar [44] *vt* to invoke

involucrar 1 *vt* to involve (**en** in)
2 involucrarse *vpr* to get involved (**en** in)

involuntario,-a *adj* involuntary; *(impremeditado)* unintentional*

invulnerable *adj* invulnerable

inyección *nf* injection; **poner una i.** to give an injection

inyectar *vt* to inject (**en** into); **i. algo a algn** to inject sb with sth

IPC *nm* (*abr* **Índice de Precios al Consumo**) RPI

ir [16] **1** *vi* (a) to go; **¡vamos!** let's go!; **voy a Lima** I'm going to Lima; **¡ya voy!** (I'm) coming!

(b) *(río, camino)* to lead; **esta carretera va a la frontera** this road leads to the border

(c) *(funcionar)* to work (properly); **el ascensor no va** the lift is out of order

(d) *(desenvolverse)* **¿cómo le va el nuevo trabajo?** how is he getting on in his new job?; **¿cómo te va?** how are things?, how are you doing?

(e) *(sentar bien)* to suit; **el verde te va mucho** green really suits you

(f) *(combinar)* to match; **el rojo no va con el verde** red doesn't go with green

(g) *(vestir)* to wear; **ir con falda** to wear a skirt; **ir de blanco/de uniforme** to be dressed in white/in uniform

(h) *Fam (importar, concernir)* to concern; **eso va por ti también** and the same goes for you; **ni me va ni me viene** I don't care one way or the other

(i) *Fam (comportarse)* to act; **ir de guapo por la vida** to be a flash Harry

(j) **va para abogado** he's studying to be a lawyer

(k) *(ir + por)* **ir por la derecha** to keep (to the) right; *(ir a buscar)* **ve (a)** por **agua** go and fetch some water; *(haber llegado)* **voy por la página 90** I've got as far as page 90

(l) *(locuciones)* **a eso iba** I was coming to that; **¡ahí va!** catch!; **en lo que va de año** so far this year; **ir a parar** to end up; **¡qué va!** of course not!, nothing of the sort!; **va a lo suyo** he looks after his own interests; **¡vamos a ver!** let's see!; **¡vaya!** fancy that!; **¡vaya moto!** what a bike!

2 *v aux* (a) *(ir + gerundio)* **ir andando** to go on foot; **va mejorando** she's improving

(b) *(ir + pp)* **ya van rotos tres** three (of them) have already been broken

(c) *(ir a + inf)* **iba a decir que** I was going to say that; **va a llover** it's going to rain; **vas a caerte** you'll fall

3 irse *vpr* (a) *(marcharse)* to go away, to leave; **me voy** I'm off; **¡vámonos!** let's go!; **¡vete!** go away!; **vete a casa** go home

(b) *(líquido, gas) (escaparse)* to leak

(c) *(direcciones)* **¿por dónde se va a ...?** which is the way to ...? **por aquí se va al río** this is the way to the river

ira *nf* wrath, rage, anger

iracundo,-a *adj* (a) *(irascible)* irascible (b) *(enfadado)* irate, angry

Irak *n* Iraq

Irán *n* Iran

iraní *adj & nmf (pl* **iraníes***)* Iranian

Iraq *n* = **Irak**

iraquí *adj & nmf (pl* **iraquíes***)* Iraqi

irascible *adj* irascible, irritable

iris *nm inv Anat* iris; **arco i.** rainbow

Irlanda *n* Ireland; **I. del Norte** Northern Ireland

irlandés,-esa 1 *adj* Irish
  2 *nm,f (hombre)* Irishman; *(mujer)* Irishwoman; **los irlandeses** the Irish
  3 *nm (idioma)* Irish

ironía *nf* irony

irónico,-a *adj* ironic

IRPF *nm Econ (abr* **impuesto sobre la renta de las personas físicas***)* income tax

irracional *adj* irrational

irradiar [43] *vt* **(a)** *(emitir)* to radiate **(b)** *Am Fig (expulsar)* to expel

irreal *adj* unreal

irrealizable *adj* unattainable, unfeasible; *Fig* unreachable

irreconocible *adj* unrecognizable

irregular *adj* irregular

irregularidad *nf* irregularity

irremediable *adj* irremediable, incurable

irremplazable *adj* irreplaceable

irreparable *adj* irreparable

irreprochable *adj* irreproachable, blameless

irresistible *adj* **(a)** *(impulso, persona)* irresistible **(b)** *(insoportable)* unbearable

irresoluto,-a *adj* irresolute

irresponsable *adj* irresponsible

irrestricto,-a *adj Am* unconditional, complete

irreverente *adj* irreverent

irrigación *nf* irrigation

irrigar [42] *vt* to irrigate, to water

irrisorio,-a *adj* derisory, ridiculous

irritación *nf* irritation

irritante *adj* irritating

irritar 1 *vt* **(a)** *(enfadar)* to irritate, to exasperate **(b)** *Med* to irritate

  2 irritarse *vpr* **(a)** *(enfadarse)* to lose one's temper, to get angry **(b)** *Med* to become irritated

irrompible *adj* unbreakable

irrumpir *vi* to burst **(en** into)

isla *nf* island, isle

islam *nm Rel* Islam

islámico,-a *adj* Islamic

islandés,-esa 1 *adj* Icelandic
  2 *nm,f (persona)* Icelander
  3 *nm (idioma)* Icelandic

Islandia *n* Iceland

isleño,-a 1 *adj* island
  2 *nm,f* islander

islote *nm* small island

ismo *nm Fam* ism

Israel *n* Israel

israelí *adj & nmf (pl* **israelíes***)* Israeli

istmo *nm Geog* isthmus

itacate *nm Méx* packed lunch

Italia *n* Italy

italiano,-a 1 *adj* Italian
  2 *nm,f (persona)* Italian
  3 *nm (idioma)* Italian

itinerante *adj* itinerant, itinerating

itinerario *nm* itinerary, route

IVA *nm Econ (abr* **impuesto sobre el valor añadido***)* VAT

izar [40] *vt* to hoist, to raise

izqda., izqda *(abr* **izquierda***)* left

izqdo., izqdo *(abr* **izquierdo***)* left

izquierda *nf* **(a)** left; **a la i.** on the left; **girar a la i.** to turn left **(b)** *(mano)* left hand **(c)** *Pol* **la i.** the left; **de izquierdas** left-wing

izquierdista *Pol* **1** *adj* leftist, left-wing
  2 *nmf* leftist, left-winger

izquierdo,-a *adj* **(a)** left; **brazo i.** left arm **(b)** *(zurdo)* left-handed

izquierdoso,-a *adj Fam* leftish

J

J, j ['xota] *nf (la letra)* J, j
jabalí *nm (pl jabalíes)* wild boar
jabalina *nf Dep* javelin
jabón *nm* soap; **j. de afeitar/tocador** shaving/toilet soap
jabonera *nf* soap dish
jaca *nf* gelding
jacal *nm Méx* hut
jacinto *nm Bot* hyacinth
jactancia *nf* boastfulness
jactancioso,-a 1 *adj* boastful
   2 *nm,f* braggart
jactarse *vpr* to boast, to brag (**de** about)
jadeante *adj* panting, breathless
jadear *vi* to pant, to gasp
jadeo *nm* panting, gasping
jaez *nm Pey (ralea)* kind, sort
jaiba *nf Andes, CAm, Carib, Méx (cangrejo)* crayfish
jalar 1 *vt* (**a**) *Fam (comer)* to wolf down (**b**) *Andes, CAm, Carib, Méx (tirar)* to pull
   2 jalarse *vpr Fam (comerse)* to wolf down, to scoff
jalbegar [42] *vt* to whitewash
jalea *nf* jelly; **j. real** royal jelly
jalear *vt (animar)* to cheer (on)
jaleo *nm (alboroto)* din, racket; *(riña)* row; *(confusión)* muddle; **armar j.** to make a racket
jalón¹ *nm (estaca)* stake; *Fig (hito)* milestone
jalón² *nm* (**a**) *(tirón)* pull, tug (**b**) *Am Aut* lift
jamaicano,-a *adj & nm,f* Jamaican
jamar *vt Fam* to scoff, to eat
jamás *adv* (**a**) never; **j. he estado allí** I have never been there (**b**) ever; **el mejor libro que j. se ha escrito** the best book ever written (**c**) **nunca j.** never again; **por siempre j.** for ever (and ever)
jamba *nf Arquit* jamb
jamón *nm* ham; **j. de York/serrano** boiled/cured ham
jamona *adj Fam* buxom
Japón *n* (**el**) J. Japan
japonés,-esa 1 *adj* Japanese
   2 *nm,f (persona)* Japanese; **los japoneses** the Japanese
   3 *nm (idioma)* Japanese

japuta *nf (pez)* Ray's bream
jaque *nm (en ajedrez)* check; **dar j. a** to check; **j. mate** checkmate; **j. al rey** check; *Fig* **estar en j.** to be stymied
jaqueca *nf* migraine
jara *nf Bot* rock rose
jarabe *nm* syrup; **j. para la tos** cough mixture
jarana *nf Fam* (**a**) *(juerga)* wild party, spree; **ir de j.** to go on a spree o a binge (**b**) *(jaleo)* racket, din
jaranero,-a 1 *adj* fun-loving, party-loving
   2 *nm,f* pleasure seeker, party-lover
jardín *nm* garden; **j. botánico** botanical garden; **j. de infancia** nursery school, kindergarten
jardinería *nf* gardening
jardinero *nm* gardener
jarra *nf* pitcher; **j. de cerveza** beer mug; *Fig* **de** o **en jarras** (with) arms akimbo, hands on hips
jarro *nm (recipiente)* jug; *(contenido)* jugful; *Fig* **echar un j. de agua fría a** to pour cold water on
jarrón *nm* vase; *(en arqueología)* urn
jaspe *nm* jasper; **como el j.** spotless, like a new pin
Jauja *nf Fig* promised land; **¡esto es J.!** this is the life!
jaula *nf (para animales)* cage
jauría *nf* pack of hounds
jazmín *nm Bot* jasmine
J.C. *(abr* **Jesucristo**) J.C.
jeba = **jeva**
jebo,-a = **jevo,-a**
jeep [jip] *nm Aut* jeep
jefa *nf* female boss, manageress
jefatura *nf* (**a**) *(cargo, dirección)* leadership (**b**) *(sede)* central office; **j. de policía** police headquarters
jefe *nm* (**a**) head, chief, boss; *Com* manager; **j. de estación** stationmaster; **j. de redacción** editor-in-chief; **j. de ventas** sales manager (**b**) *Pol* leader; **J. de Estado** Head of State (**c**) *Mil* officer in command; **comandante en j.** commander-in-chief
Jehová *nm* Jehovah; **testigos de J.** Jehovah's Witnesses

jején *nm Am* gnat

jengibre *nm Bot* ginger

jeque *nm* sheik, sheikh

jerarquía *nf* (a) hierarchy (b) *(categoría)* rank

jerárquico,-a *adj* hierarchical

jeremías *nmf inv* whiner, whinger

jerez *nm* sherry

jerga *nf* *(argot)* *(técnica)* jargon; *(vulgar)* slang; **la j. legal** legal jargon

jerigonza *nf* (a) *(extravagancia)* oddness (b) *(galimatías)* gibberish

jeringa *nf Med* syringe; *Aut* **j. de engrase** grease gun

jeringar [42] *vt Fam* (a) *(molestar)* to pester, to annoy (b) *(romper)* to break

jeringuilla *nf* *(hypodermic)* syringe

jeroglífico,-a 1 *adj* hieroglyphic
2 *nm* (a) *Ling* hieroglyph, hieroglyphic (b) *(juego)* rebus

jersey *nm* *(pl* **jerseis**) sweater, *Br* jumper

Jerusalén *n* Jerusalem

Jesucristo *nm* Jesus Christ

jesuita *adj & nmf* Jesuit

Jesús 1 *nm* Jesus
2 *interj* (a) *(expresa sorpresa)* good heavens! (b) *(al estornudar)* bless you!

jet *nf* jet set

jeta *nf Fam* (a) *(descaro)* cheek; **tener j.** to be cheeky, to have a nerve (b) *(cara)* mug, face (c) *(hocico)* snout

jet-set *nf* jet set

jeva *nf Carib Fam (mujer)* chick, *Br* bird

jevo,-a *nm,f Ven Fam (novio)* guy, boyfriend; *(novia)* girl, girlfriend

jíbaro,-a *nm,f Am* peasant

jícama *nf* yam bean, jicama

jícara *nf CAm, Méx, Ven (bol)* small cup; *(calabaza)* gourd

jilguero *nm Orn* goldfinch

jilipollas *nmf inv muy Fam* = **gilipollas**

jinete *nm* rider, horseman

jinetera *nf Cuba Fam* prostitute

jiñar *vi muy Fam* to shit

jirafa *nf* (a) giraffe (b) *(de micrófono)* boom

jirón *nm* (a) *(trozo desgarrado)* shred, strip; *(pedazo suelto)* bit, scrap; **hecho jirones** in shreds o tatters (b) *Perú (calle)* street

jitomate *nm Méx* tomato

JJOO *nmpl (abr* **Juegos Olímpicos***)* Olympic Games

jocoso,-a *adj* funny, humorous

joda *nf RP muy Fam* (a) *(fastidio)* pain, drag (b) *(broma)* joke; **decir/hacer algo en j.** to say/do sth as a joke (c) *(juerga)* wild party

joder *Vulg* **1** *interj* shit!, *Br* bloody hell!
2 *vt* (a) *(fastidiar)* to piss off; **¡no me jodas!** come on, don't give me that! (b) *(copular)* to fuck (c) *(echar a perder)* to screw up; **¡la jodiste!** you screwed it up! (d) *(romper)* to bugger
3 joderse *vpr* (a) *(aguantarse)* to put up with it; **¡hay que j.!** you'll just have to grin and bear it! (b) *(echarse a perder)* to get screwed up; **¡se jodió el invento!** that's really screwed things up!; **¡que se joda!** to hell with him! (c) *(romperse)* to go bust

jodido,-a *adj Vulg* (a) *(maldito)* damned, *Br* bloody (b) *(molesto)* annoying (c) *(enfermo)* in a bad way; *(cansado)* knackered, exhausted (d) *(estropeado, roto)* bust, kaput, buggered (e) *(difícil)* shitty

jodienda *nf Vulg* (a) *(coito)* fuck (b) *(molestia)* pain in the arse

jofaina *nf* washbasin

jogging ['joging] *nm Urug (ropa)* track o jogging suit

jolgorio *nm Fam (juerga)* binge; *(algazara)* fun

jolín, jolines *interj Fam (sorpresa)* gosh!, good grief!; *(enfado)* blast!, damn!

Jordania *n* Jordan

jornada *nf* (a) **j. (laboral)** *(día de trabajo)* working day; **j. intensiva** continuous working day; **j. partida** working day with a lunch break; **trabajo de media j./j. completa** part-time/full-time work (b) **jornadas** conference

jornal *nm (paga)* day's wage; **trabajar a j.** to be paid by the day

> Observa que la palabra inglesa **journal** es un falso amigo y no es la traducción de la palabra española **jornal**. En inglés, **journal** significa "revista, diario".

jornalero,-a *nm,f* day labourer

joroba 1 *nf (giba)* hump
2 *interj* drat!

jorobado,-a 1 *adj* hunchbacked
2 *nm,f* hunchback

jorobar *Fam* **1** *vt* (a) *(fastidiar)* to annoy, to bother; **me joroba** it really gets up my nose; **¡no jorobes!** *(incredulidad)* pull the other one! (b) *(estropear)* to ruin, to wreck
2 jorobarse *vpr* (a) *(fastidiarse)* to grin and bear it (b) *(estropearse)* to break

jorongo *nm Méx* (a) *(manta)* blanket (b) *(poncho)* poncho

jota¹ *nf* (a) = name of the letter J in Spanish (b) *(cantidad mínima)* jot, scrap; **ni j.** not an iota; **no entiendo ni j.** I don't understand a thing

jota² nf Mús = Spanish dance and music

joven 1 adj young; **de aspecto j.** young-looking

 2 nmf (hombre) youth, young man; (mujer) girl, young woman; **de j.** as a young man/woman; **los jóvenes** young people, youth

jovial adj jovial, good-humoured

joya nf (a) jewel, piece of jewellery; **joyas de imitación** imitation jewellery (b) Fig **ser una j.** (persona) to be a real treasure o gem

joyería nf (tienda) jewellery shop, jeweller's (shop)

joyero,-a 1 nm,f jeweller

 2 nm jewel case o box

juanete nm (en el pie) bunion

jubilación nf (a) (acción) retirement; **j. anticipada** early retirement (b) (pensión) pension

jubilado,-a 1 adj retired

 2 nm,f retired person, pensioner; **los jubilados** retired people

jubilar 1 vt (retirar) to retire, to pension off; Fam Fig to get rid of, to ditch

 2 jubilarse vpr (retirarse) to retire, to go into retirement

júbilo nm jubilation, joy

jubón nm doublet, jerkin

judería nf (barrio) Jewish quarter

judía nf bean; **j. verde** French bean, green bean

judicial adj judicial; **vía j.** legal channels

judío,-a 1 adj Jewish

 2 nm,f Jew

judo nm Dep judo

juego nm (a) game; **j. de azar** game of chance; **j. de cartas** card game; Fig **j. de manos** sleight of hand; Fig **j. de palabras** play on words, pun; **j. de rol** fantasy role-playing game; Fig **j. limpio/sucio** fair/foul play (b) Dep game; **Juegos Olímpicos** Olympic Games; **terreno de j.** Ten court; Ftb field; **fuera de j.** offside (c) (apuestas) gambling; Fig **poner algo en j.** to put sth at stake (d) (conjunto de piezas) set; **j. de café/té** coffee/tea service; Fig **ir a j. con** to match

juerga nf Fam binge, rave-up; **ir de j.** to go on a binge

juerguista 1 adj fun-loving

 2 nmf fun-loving person, raver

jueves nm inv Thursday; **J. Santo** Maundy Thursday

juez nmf judge; **j. de instrucción** examining magistrate; **j. de paz** justice of the peace; Dep **j. de salida** starter; **j. de línea** linesman

jugada nf (a) move; (en billar) shot (b) Fam dirty trick

jugador,-a nm,f player; (apostador) gambler

jugar [32] 1 vi (a) to play; **j. a(l) fútbol/tenis** to play football/tennis; Fig **j. sucio** to play dirty (b) **j. con** (no tomar en serio) to toy with

 2 vt (a) to play (b) (apostar) to bet, to stake

 3 jugarse vpr (a) (arriesgar) to risk; Fam **j. el pellejo** to risk one's neck (b) (apostar) to bet, to stake

jugarreta nf Fam dirty trick

jugo nm juice; Fig **sacar el j. a** (aprovechar) to make the most of; (explotar) to squeeze dry

jugoso,-a adj (a) juicy; **un filete j.** a juicy steak (b) Fig (sustancioso) substantial, meaty; **un tema j.** a meaty topic

juguete nm toy; **pistola de j.** toy gun; Fig **ser el j. de algn** to be sb's plaything

juguetear vi to play

juguetón,-ona adj playful

juicio nm (a) (facultad mental) judgement, discernment; (opinión) opinion, judgement; **a j. de** in the opinion of; **a mi j.** in my opinion (b) (sensatez) reason, common sense; **en su sano j.** in one's right mind; **perder el j.** to go mad o insane (c) Jur trial, lawsuit; **llevar a algn a j.** to take legal action against sb, to sue sb

juicioso,-a adj judicious, wise

julepe nm PRico, RP Fam (susto) scare, fright; **dar un j. a algn** to give sb a scare

julio nm July

junco nm Bot rush

jungla nf jungle

junio nm June

júnior adj Dep junior; **campeonato j. de golf** junior golf championship

junta nf (a) (reunión) meeting, assembly; Pol **j. de gobierno** cabinet meeting (b) (dirección) board, committee; **j. directiva** board of directors (c) Mil junta; **j. militar** military junta (d) (parlamento regional) regional parliament (e) Téc joint

juntar 1 vt (a) (unir) to join, to put together; (piezas) to assemble (b) (reunir) (sellos) to collect; (dinero) to raise

 2 juntarse vpr (a) (unirse) to join; (ríos, caminos) to meet; (personas) to gather (b) (amancebarse) to live together

junto,-a 1 adj together; **dos mesas juntas** two tables side by side; **todos juntos** all together

 2 adv **j. con** together with; **j. a** next to

juntura *nf* (**a**) *Téc* joint, seam (**b**) *Anat* joint

jura *nf* (*acción*) oath; (*ceremonia*) swearing in; **j. de bandera** oath of allegiance to the flag

jurado *nm* (**a**) (*tribunal*) jury; (*en un concurso*) panel of judges, jury (**b**) (*miembro del tribunal*) juror, member of the jury

juramento *nm* (**a**) *Jur* oath; **bajo j.** under oath (**b**) (*blasfemia*) swearword, curse

jurar **1** *vi Jur & Rel* to swear, to take an oath
  2 *vt* to swear; **j. el cargo** to take the oath of office; **j. por Dios** to swear to God
  3 jurarse *vpr Fam* **jurársela(s) a algn** to have it in for sb

jurel *nm* (*pez*) scad, horse mackerel

jurídico,-a *adj* legal

jurisdicción *nf* jurisdiction

jurisdiccional *adj* jurisdictional; **aguas jurisdiccionales** territorial waters

jurista *nmf* jurist, lawyer

justamente *adv* ¡**j.!** precisely!; **j. detrás de** right behind

justicia *nf* justice; **tomarse la j. por su mano** to take the law into one's own hands

justicialismo *nm Pol* = Argentinian nationalistic political movement founded by Juan Domingo Perón

justicialista *adj Pol* = belonging or related to "justicialismo"

justiciero,-a *adj* severe

justificable *adj* justifiable

justificación *nf* justification

justificado,-a *adj* justified, well-grounded

justificante *nm* written proof; **j. de pago** proof of payment

justificar [44] **1** *vt* to justify
  2 justificarse *vpr* to clear oneself, to justify oneself

justo,-a **1** *adj* (**a**) just, fair, right; **un trato j.** a fair deal (**b**) (*apretado*) (*ropa*) tight; **estamos justos de tiempo** we're pressed for time (**c**) (*exacto*) right, accurate; **la palabra justa** the right word (**d**) (*preciso*) **llegamos en el momento j. en que salían** we arrived just as they were leaving (**e**) **lo j.** just enough
  2 *nm,f* just o righteous person; **los justos** the just, the righteous
  3 *adv* (*exactamente*) exactly, precisely; **j. al lado** right beside

juvenil **1** *adj* (*aspecto*) youthful, young; **ropa j.** young people's clothes; **delincuencia j.** juvenile delinquency
  2 *nmf* **los juveniles** the juveniles

juventud *nf* (**a**) (*edad*) youth (**b**) (*jóvenes*) young people

juzgado *nm* court, tribunal; **j. de guardia** police court

juzgar [42] *vt* to judge; **a j. por ...** judging by...

K, k [ka] *nf (la letra)* K, k
ka *nf* = name of the letter K in Spanish
kárate *nm Dep* karate
karateka *nmf Dep* person who does karate
Kenia *n* Kenya
kermés [ker'mes] (*pl* **kermeses**), **kermesse** [ker'mes] (*pl* **kermesses**) *nf* fair,
kermesse
Kg, kg (*abr* **kilogramo(s)**) kg
kilo *nm* (**a**) *(medida)* kilo; *Fam* **pesa un k.**
it weighs a ton (**b**) *Fam (millón)* a million
pesetas
kilogramo *nm* kilogram, kilogramme
kilolitro *nm* kilolitre

kilometraje *nm* ≃ mileage
kilométrico,-a *adj* kilometric, kilometri-
cal; **billete k.** multiple-journey ticket
kilómetro *nm* kilometre
kilovatio *nm* kilowatt; **k. hora** kilowatt-
hour
kínder *nm Andes, Méx* kindergarten, nursery school
kiosco *nm* = quiosco
kiwi *nm* (**a**) *Orn* kiwi (**b**) *(fruto)* kiwi
(fruit), Chinese gooseberry
Kleenex® *nm* Kleenex®, tissue
Km, km (*abr* **kilómetro(s)**) km
Kw, kw (*abr* **kilovatio(s)**) kW

L, l ['ele] *nf (la letra)* L, l

l (*abr* **litro(s)**) l

la¹ 1 *art def f* the; **la mesa** the table

2 *pron dem* the one; **la del vestido azul** the one in the blue dress; **la que vino ayer** the one who came yesterday; *ver* **el**

la² *pron pers f (persona)* her; *(usted)* you; *(cosa)* it; **la invitaré** I'll invite her along; **no la dejes abierta** don't leave it open; **ya la avisaremos, señora** we'll let you know, madam; *ver* **le**

la³ *nm Mús* la, A

laberinto *nm* labyrinth

labia *nf Fam* loquacity; *Pey* glibness; **tener mucha l.** to have the gift of the gab

labio *nm* lip

labor *nf* (**a**) job, task; **l. de equipo** teamwork; **(de profesión) sus labores** housewife (**b**) *Agr* farmwork (**c**) *(de costura)* needlework, sewing

laborable *adj* (**a**) *día l. (no festivo)* working day (**b**) *Agr* arable

laboral *adj* industrial; **accidente l.** industrial accident; **conflictividad l.** industrial unrest; **jornada l.** working day; **Universidad L.** technical training college

laboratorio *nm* laboratory

laborioso,-a *adj* (**a**) *(persona)* hardworking (**b**) *(tarea)* laborious

laborista *Pol* **1** *adj* Labour; **partido l.** Labour Party

2 *nmf* Labour (Party) member/supporter

labrado,-a *adj Arte* carved

labrador,-a *nm,f (granjero)* farmer; *(trabajador)* farm worker

labranza *nf* farming

labrar 1 *vt* (**a**) *Agr* to till (**b**) *(madera)* to carve; *(piedra)* to cut; *(metal)* to work

2 labrarse *vpr Fig* **l. un porvenir** to build a future for oneself

laburar *vi RP Fam* to work

laburo *nm RP Fam* job

laca *nf* (**a**) hair lacquer, hairspray; **l. de uñas** nail polish *o* varnish (**b**) *Arte* lacquer

lacio,-a *adj* (**a**) *(pelo)* lank, limp (**b**) **qué l.!** *(soso)* what a weed!

lacónico,-a *adj* laconic; *(conciso)* terse

lacra *nf* evil, curse; **una l. social** a scourge of society

lacrar *vt* to seal with wax

lacre *nm* sealing wax

lacrimógeno,-a *adj* (**a**) gas **l.** tear gas (**b**) *Fig* **una película lacrimógena** a tearjerker

lactar *vi* to breast-feed

lácteo,-a *adj* **productos lácteos** milk *o* dairy products; *Astron* **Vía Láctea** Milky Way

ladear 1 *vt (inclinar)* to tilt; *(cabeza)* to lean

2 ladearse *vpr* (**a**) *(inclinarse)* to lean, to tilt (**b**) *(desviarse)* to go off to one side

ladera *nf* slope

ladino,-a 1 *adj (astuto)* cunning, crafty

2 *nm,f CAm, Méx, Ven (no blanco)* = Spanish-speaking person of mixed race

lado *nm* (**a**) side; **a un l.** aside; **al l.** close by, nearby; **al l. de** next to, beside; **ponte de l.** stand sideways (**b**) *(en direcciones)* direction; **por todos lados** on/from all sides (**c**) *Fig* **dar de l. a algn** to coldshoulder sb; **por otro l.** *(además)* moreover; **por un l. ..., por otro l. ...** on the one hand ..., on the other hand ...

ladrar *vi* to bark

ladrillo *nm* (**a**) *Constr* brick (**b**) *Fam (pesado)* bore, drag

ladrón,-ona 1 *nm,f* thief, robber; **¡al l.!** stop thief!

2 *nm Elec* multiple socket

lagartija *nf* small lizard

lagarto *nm* lizard

lago *nm* lake

lágrima *nf* (**a**) tear; **llorar a l. viva** to cry one's eyes out (**b**) *(en lámpara)* teardrop

lagrimoso,-a *adj* tearful

laguna *nf* (**a**) small lake (**b**) *Fig (hueco)* gap

La Haya *n* The Hague

laico,-a 1 *adj* lay

2 *nm,f* lay person; *(hombre)* layman; *(mujer)* laywoman

lameculos *nmf inv muy Fam* bootlicker, arselicker

lamentable *adj* regrettable; *(infame)* lamentable

lamentar 1 *vt* to regret; **lo lamento** I'm sorry

2 lamentarse *vpr* to complain

lamento *nm* moan, wail

lamer *vt* to lick

lámina *nf* (**a**) sheet, plate; **l. de acero** steel sheet (**b**) *Impr* plate

laminado,-a 1 *adj* (**a**) laminated (**b**) *(metales)* rolled; **acero l.** rolled steel

2 *nm* lamination

laminar *vt (metal)* to roll

lámpara *nf* (**a**) lamp; **l. de pie** standard lamp (**b**) *Elec (bombilla)* bulb (**c**) *Rad* valve

lamparón *nm Fam* oil *o* grease stain

lana *nf* (**a**) *(de oveja)* wool; **pura l. virgen** pure new wool (**b**) *Andes, Méx Fam (dinero)* dough, cash

lanar *adj* **ganado l.** sheep

lance *nm Literario (episodio)* event, incident

⚠ Observa que la palabra inglesa **lance** es un falso amigo y no es la traducción de la palabra española **lance**. En inglés, **lance** significa "lanza".

lanceta *nf Andes, Méx* sting

lancha *nf* motorboat, launch; **l. motora** speedboat; **l. neumática** rubber dinghy; **l. salvavidas** lifeboat

langosta *nf* (**a**) lobster (**b**) *(insecto)* locust

langostino *nm* king prawn

languidecer [33] *vi* to languish

lánguido,-a *adj* languid; *(sin vigor)* listless

lanudo,-a *adj* woolly, fleecy; *(peludo)* furry

lanza *nf* spear, lance; **punta de l.** spearhead; *Fig* **romper una l. en favor de algn/ de algo** to defend sb/sth

lanzadera *nf* shuttle; **l. espacial** space shuttle

lanzado,-a *adj Fam* reckless; **ir l.** to tear along

lanzagranadas *nm inv Mil* grenade launcher

lanzamiento *nm* (**a**) throwing, hurling (**b**) *Dep (de disco, jabalina)* throw; *(de peso)* put (**c**) *Mil (de cohete etc)* launching (**d**) *Com* launch; **precio de l.** launch price (**e**) *Náut* launch

lanzar [40] 1 *vt* (**a**) *(arrojar)* to throw, to fling (**b**) *Fig (grito)* to let out (**c**) *Náut, Com & Mil* to launch

2 lanzarse *vpr* (**a**) *(arrojarse)* to throw *o* hurl oneself; **l. al suelo** to throw oneself to the ground (**b**) *(emprender)* **l. a** to embark

on; **l. a los negocios** to go into business (**c**) *Fam (irse, largarse)* to scram

lapa *nf* (**a**) *Zool* limpet (**b**) **es una verdadera l.** he/she sticks to you like glue

lapicera *nf CSur* ballpoint (pen), *Br* Biro®; **l. fuente** fountain pen

lapicero *nm* (**a**) *(lápiz)* pencil (**b**) *CAm, Perú (bolígrafo)* ballpoint (pen), *Br* Biro®

lápida *nf* headstone

lapidario,-a *adj* lapidary

lápiz *nm* pencil; **l. labial** *o* **de labios** lipstick; **l. de ojos** eyeliner

lapso *nm* (**a**) *(periodo de tiempo)* period (**b**) *(error)* lapse, slip

lapsus *nm* slip; **l. linguae** slip of the tongue

largar [42] 1 *vt* (**a**) *Fam (golpe, discurso, dinero)* to give (**b**) *Náut* **l. amarras** to cast off

2 largarse *vpr Fam* to clear off, to split; **¡lárgate!** beat it!

largas *nfpl* **dar l. a algo** to put sth off

largavistas *nm inv Bol, CSur* binoculars

largo,-a 1 *adj* (**a**) *(espacio)* long; *(tiempo)* long, lengthy; **pasamos un mes l. allí** we spent a good month there; **a lo l. de** *(espacio)* along; *(tiempo)* through; **a la larga** in the long run (**b**) *(excesivo)* too long; **se hizo l. el día** the day dragged on (**c**) **largos años** many years

2 *nm* (**a**) *(longitud)* length; **¿cuánto tiene de l.?** how long is it? (**b**) *Mús* largo

3 *adv* **l. y tendido** at length; *Fam* **¡l. (de aquí)!** clear off!; **esto va para l.** this is going to last a long time

⚠ Observa que la palabra inglesa **large** es un falso amigo y no es la traducción de la palabra española **largo**. En inglés, **large** significa "grande".

largometraje *nm* feature film, full-length film

laringe *nf* larynx

laringitis *nf* laryngitis

las¹ 1 *art def fpl* the; **l. sillas** the chairs; **lávate l. manos** wash your hands; *(no se traduce)* **me gustan l. flores** I like flowers

2 *pron* **l. que** *(personas)* the ones who, those who; *(objetos)* the ones that, those that; **toma l. que quieras** take whichever ones you want; *ver* **la** *y* **los**

las² *pron pers fpl (ellas)* them; *(ustedes)* you; **l. llamaré mañana (a ustedes)** I'll call you tomorrow; **no l. rompas** don't break them; **Pepa es de l. mías** Pepa thinks the way I do; *ver* **los**

lasaña *nf* lasagna, lasagne

lascivo,-a *adj* lewd, lecherous

láser *nm inv* laser; **impresora l.** laser printer

lástima *nf* pity; **¡qué l.!** what a pity!, what a shame!; **es una l. que ...** it's a pity (that) ...; **estar hecho una l.** to be a sorry sight; **tener l. a algn** to feel sorry for sb

lastimar *vt* to hurt, to injure

lastre *nm* (a) *(peso)* ballast (b) *Fig* dead weight

lata¹ *nf* (a) *(envase)* tin, can; **en l.** tinned, canned (b) *(hojalata)* tin(plate); **hecho de l.** made of tin

lata² *nf Fam* nuisance, drag; **dar la l.** to be a nuisance *o* a pest

latente *adj* latent

lateral 1 *adj* side, lateral; **salió por la puerta l.** he went out by the side door; **escalón l.** *(en letrero)* ramp

2 *nm* side passage; *Aut* **(carril) l.** side lane

latido *nm (del corazón)* beat

latifundio *nm* large landed estate

latigazo *nm* (a) lash (b) *Fam (trago)* drink, swig

látigo *nm* whip

latín *nm* Latin

latino,-a 1 *adj* Latin; **América Latina** Latin America

2 *nm,f* Latin American

Latinoamérica *nf* Latin America

latinomericano,-a *adj & nm,f* Latin American

latir *vi* to beat

latitud *nf* (a) *Geog* latitude (b) **latitudes** region, area

latón *nm* brass

latoso,-a *adj Fam* annoying

laucha *nf Am* mouse

laúd *nm* lute

laurel *nm Bot* laurel, (sweet) bay; *Culin* bay leaf; *Fig* **dormirse en los laureles** to rest on one's laurels

lava *nf* lava

lavable *adj* washable

lavabo *nm* (a) *(pila)* washbasin (b) *(cuarto de aseo)* washroom (c) *(retrete)* lavatory, toilet

lavadero *nm (de coches)* carwash

lavado *nm* wash, washing; *Fig* **l. de cerebro** brainwashing; **l. en seco** dry-cleaning

lavadora *nf* washing machine

lavanda *nf* lavender

lavandería *nf* (a) *(automática) Br* launderette, *US* Laundromat® (b) *(atendida por personal)* laundry

lavaplatos *nm inv* dishwasher

lavar *vt* to wash; **l. en seco** to dry-clean

lavativa *nf* enema

lavatorio *nm Andes, RP (lavabo) Br* washbasin, *US* washbowl

lavavajillas *nm inv* dishwasher

laxante *adj & nm* laxative

laxar *vt (vientre)* to loosen

laxitud *nf* laxity, laxness

lazada *nf (nudo)* bow

lazarillo *nm* **perro l.** guide dog, *US* seeing-eye dog

lazo *nm* (a) *(adorno)* bow (b) *(nudo)* knot; **l. corredizo** slipknot (c) *(para reses)* lasso (d) *Fig (usu pl) (vínculo)* tie, bond

le 1 *pron pers mf (objeto indirecto) (a él)* (to) him; *(a ella)* (to) her; *(a cosa)* (to) it; *(a usted)* (to) you; **lávale la cara** wash his face; **le compraré uno** I'll buy one for her; **¿qué le pasa (a usted)?** what's the matter with you?

2 *pron pers m (objeto directo) (él)* him; *(usted)* you; **no le oigo** I can't hear him; **no quiero molestarle** I don't wish to disturb you

leal 1 *adj* loyal, faithful

2 *nmf* loyalist

lealtad *nf* loyalty, faithfulness

lebrel *nm* greyhound

lección *nf* lesson; *Fig* **dar una l. a algn** to teach sb a lesson; *Fig* **te servirá de l.** let that be a lesson to you

leche *nf* (a) milk; *Anat* **dientes de l.** milk teeth; **l. descremada** *o* **desnatada** skim *o* skimmed milk (b) *Fam* **mala l.** badness (c) **l.!** damn! (d) *muy Fam (golpe)* knock; **dar** *o* **pegar una l. a algn** to clobber sb (e) *Vulg* semen

lechera *nf* (a) *(vasija)* churn (b) *muy Fam* police car

lechería *nf* dairy, creamery

lechero,-a 1 *adj* milk, dairy; **central lechera** dairy co-operative; **vaca lechera** milk cow

2 *nm* milkman

lecho *nm Lit* bed; **l. del río** river-bed; **l. mortuorio** death-bed

lechón *nm* sucking-pig

lechosa *nf Carib* papaya

lechoso,-a *adj* milky

lechuga *nf* lettuce

lechuza *nf* owl

lectivo,-a *adj* school; **horas lectivas** teaching hours

lector,-a 1 *nm,f* (a) *(persona)* reader (b) *Univ* lector, (language) assistant

2 *nm* **l. de microfichas** *(aparato)* microfiche reader

lectura *nf* reading

leer [36] *vt* to read; **léenos el menú** read

out the menu for us; *Fig* **l. entre líneas** to read between the lines

legado *nm (herencia)* legacy

legajo *nm* bundle (of papers)

legal *adj* (a) *Jur* legal, lawful; **requisitos legales** legal formalities (b) *Fam (persona)* honest, trustworthy

legalidad *nf* legality, lawfulness

legalizar [40] *vt* to legalize; *(documento)* to authenticate

legaña *nf* sleep

legar [42] *vt (propiedad etc)* to bequeath; *Fig (tradiciones etc)* to hand down, to pass on

legendario,-a *adj* legendary

legión *nf* legion

legionella *nf* Legionnaire's Disease

legislación *nf* legislation

legislar *vi* to legislate

legislativo,-a *adj* legislative; **el poder l.** parliament

legislatura *nf* legislature

legitimar *vt* to legitimize; *(legalizar)* to legalize

legitimidad *nf Jur* legitimacy; *(licitud)* justice

legítimo,-a *adj* (a) *Jur* legitimate; **en legítima defensa** in self-defence (b) *(auténtico)* authentic, real; **oro l.** pure gold

lego,-a 1 *adj Rel* lay

2 *nm* (a) layman; **ser l. en la materia** to be a layman in the subject (b) *Rel* lay brother

legua *nf (medida)* league; *Fig* **se nota a la l.** it stands out a mile

legumbres *nfpl* pulses

lejanía *nf* distance

lejano,-a *adj* distant, far-off; **parientes lejanos** distant relatives; **el L. Oriente** the Far East

lejía *nf* bleach

lejos *adv* far (away); **a lo l.** in the distance; **de l.** from a distance; *Fig* **ir demasiado l.** to go too far; *Fig* **llegar l.** to go a long way; *Fig* **sin ir más l.** to take an obvious example

lelo,-a *Fam* **1** *adj* stupid, silly

2 *nm,f* ninny

lema *nm* (a) *(divisa)* motto, slogan (b) *(contraseña)* code name

lencería *nf* (a) *(prendas)* lingerie (b) *(ropa blanca)* linen (goods)

lendakari *nm* = head of the Basque government

lengua *nf* (a) tongue; *Fig* **malas lenguas** gossips; *Fam Fig* **irse de la l.** to spill the beans; *Fam Fig* **tirarle a algn de la l.** to draw sb out (b) *Ling* language; **l. materna**

native *o* mother tongue

lenguado *nm (pez)* sole

lenguaje *nm* language; *Informát* language; **l. corporal** body language

lengüeta *nf* (a) *(de zapato)* tongue (b) *Mús* reed

lente 1 *nf* lens; **l. de contacto** contact lens

2 *nm Am* **lentes** *(gafas)* glasses, spectacles; **l. de contacto** contact lens

lenteja *nf* lentil

lentejuela *nf* sequin, spangle

lentilla *nf* contact lens

lentitud *nf* slowness; **con l.** slowly

lento,-a *adj* slow; **a fuego l.** on a low heat

leña *nf* (a) firewood; *Fig* **echar l. al fuego** to add fuel to the fire (b) *Fam (golpes)* knocks

leñazo *nm Fam (golpe)* blow, smash

leñe *interj Fam* damn it!

leño *nm* (a) log (b) *Fam (persona)* blockhead, halfwit

león *nm* lion

leona *nf* lioness

leonera *nf* lion's den; *Fig (habitación)* den

leopardo *nm* leopard

leotardos *nmpl* thick tights

lépero,-a *adj Fam* (a) *CAm, Méx (vulgar)* coarse, vulgar (b) *Cuba (ladino)* smart, crafty

lepra *nf* leprosy

leproso,-a 1 *adj* leprous

2 *nm,f* leper

les 1 *pron pers mfpl (objeto indirecto)* (a *ellos,-as)* them; *(a ustedes)* you; **dales el dinero** give them the money; **l. he comprado un regalo** I've bought you a present

2 *pron pers mpl (objeto directo) (ellos)* them; *(ustedes)* you; **l. esperaré** I shall wait for you; **no quiero molestarles** I don't wish to disturb you

lesbiana *nf* lesbian

leseras *nfpl Chile Fam (tonterías)* nonsense, *Br* rubbish

lesión *nf* (a) *(corporal)* injury (b) *Jur (perjuicio)* damage

lesionar *vt* to injure

leso,-a *adj Jur* **crimen de lesa humanidad** crime against humanity

letal *adj* lethal, deadly

letanía *nf* litany

letargo *nm* lethargy

letón,-ona 1 *adj* Latvian

2 *nm,f* Latvian

3 *nm (idioma)* Latvian, Lettish

Letonia *n* Latvia

letra *nf* (a) letter; **l. de imprenta** block capitals; **l. mayúscula** capital letter; **l.**

minúscula small letter; **l. pequeña** small print (b) *(escritura)* (hand)writing (c) *Mús (texto)* lyrics, words (d) *Fin* **l. (de cambio)** bill of exchange, draft (e) *Univ* **letras** arts

letrado,-a *nm,f* lawyer

letrero *nm (aviso)* notice, sign; *(cartel)* poster; **l. luminoso** neon sign

leucemia *nf* leukaemia

levadizo,-a *adj* **puente l.** drawbridge

levadura *nf* yeast; **l. en polvo** baking powder

levantamiento *nm* (a) raising, lifting; *Dep* **l. de pesos** weightlifting (b) *(insurrección)* uprising, insurrection

levantar 1 *vt* (a) to raise, to lift; *(mano, voz)* to raise; *(edificio)* to erect; *Fig (ánimos)* to raise; **l. los ojos** to look up (b) *(castigo)* to suspend

  2 levantarse *vpr* (a) *(ponerse de pie)* to stand up, to rise (b) *(salir de la cama)* to get up (c) *(concluir)* to finish; **se levanta la sesión** the meeting is closed (d) *Pol* to rise, to revolt; **l. en armas** to rise up in arms (e) *(viento)* to come up; *(tormenta)* to gather

levante *nm* (a) **(el) L.** Levante, = the regions of Valencia and Murcia (b) *(viento)* east wind, Levanter

levar *vt* **l. ancla** to weigh anchor

leve *adj (ligero)* light; *Fig (de poca importancia)* slight

levedad *nf (ligereza)* lightness; *Fig* slightness; *Fig (de ánimo)* levity; **heridas de l.** minor injuries

levemente *adv* slightly

levitar *vi* to levitate

léxico,-a *Ling* **1** *nm (diccionario)* lexicon; *(vocabulario)* vocabulary, word list

  2 *adj* lexical

ley *nf* (a) law; *Parl* bill, act; **aprobar una l.** to pass a bill (b) **oro de l.** pure gold; **plata de l.** sterling silver

leyenda *nf* (a) *(relato)* legend (b) *(en un mapa)* legend; *(en una moneda)* inscription; *(bajo ilustración)* caption

liar [29] 1 *vt* (a) *(envolver)* to wrap up; *(un cigarrillo)* to roll (b) *(enredar)* to muddle up; *(confundir)* to confuse

  2 liarse *vpr* (a) *(embarullarse)* to get muddled up (b) *Fam (salir con)* to get involved; *(besarse)* to neck (c) **l. a bofetadas** to come to blows

libanés,-esa *adj & nm,f* Lebanese

Líbano *n* **el L.** the Lebanon

libelo *nm (difamación)* lampoon, satire

libélula *nf* dragonfly

liberación *nf (de país)* liberation; *(de rehén)* release, freeing

liberal 1 *adj* (a) liberal; *(carácter)* open-minded; *Pol* **Partido L.** Liberal Party; *profesión* **l.** profession (b) *(generoso)* generous, liberal

  2 *nmf* liberal

liberalizar [40] *vt* to liberalize

liberar *vt (país)* to liberate; *(prisionero)* to free, to release

líbero *nm Ftb* sweeper

libertad *nf* freedom, liberty; **en l.** free; *Jur* **(en) l. bajo palabra/fianza** (on) parole/bail; *Jur* **(en) l. condicional** (on) parole; **l. de comercio** free trade; **l. de expresión** freedom of speech

libertador,-a *nm,f* liberator

libertar *vt* to set free, to release

libertinaje *nm* licentiousness

libertino,-a *adj & nm,f* libertine

Libia *n* Libya

libio,-a *adj & nm,f* Libyan

libra *nf (moneda, peso)* pound; **l. esterlina** pound sterling

librador,-a *nm,f Fin* drawer

librar 1 *vt* (a) to free; *Jur* to free, to release (b) *Com (una letra)* to draw (c) **l. batalla** to do *o* join battle

  2 *vi* **libro los martes** *(no ir a trabajar)* I have Tuesdays off

  3 librarse *vpr* to escape; **l. de algn** to get rid of sb

libre *adj* free; **entrada l.** *(gratis)* admission free; *(sin restricción)* open to the public; **l. cambio** free trade; **l. de impuestos** tax-free

librecambio, librecambismo *nm* free trade

librería *nf* (a) *(tienda)* bookshop, *US* bookstore (b) *(estante)* bookcase

> 🖉 Observa que la palabra inglesa **library** es un falso amigo y no es la traducción de la palabra española **librería**. En inglés, **library** significa "biblioteca".

librero,-a 1 *nm,f* bookseller

  2 *nm CAm, Col, Méx (mueble)* bookcase

> 🖉 Observa que la palabra inglesa **librarian** es un falso amigo y no es la traducción de la palabra española **librero**. En inglés, **librarian** significa "bibliotecario".

libreta *nf* notebook; **l. (de ahorro)** savings book

libretista *nmf Am Cin* screenwriter, scriptwriter

libreto *nm Am Cin* script

libro *nm* book; **l. de texto** textbook; *Com* **l. de caja** cashbook; *Fin* **l. mayor** ledger

liceal *nmf Urug Br* secondary school *o US* high school pupil

liceano,-a *nm,f Chile Br* secondary school *o US* high school pupil

liceísta *nmf Ven Br* secondary school *o US* high school pupil

licencia *nf* (a) *(permiso)* permission; *(documentos)* permit, licence; **l. de armas/caza** gun/hunting licence (b) *(libertad abusiva)* licence, licentiousness (c) *Am Aut Br* driving licence, *US* driver's license

licenciado,-a *nm,f* (a) *Univ* graduate; **l. en Ciencias** Bachelor of Science (b) *Am* lawyer

licenciar [43] **1** *vt* (a) *Mil* to discharge (b) *Univ* to confer a degree on
2 licenciarse *vpr Univ* to graduate

licenciatura *nf Univ (título)* (bachelor's) degree (course); *(carrera)* degree (course)

liceo *nm* (a) *(sociedad literaria)* literary society (b) *(escuela) Br* secondary school, *US* high school

licitar *vt Com (pujar)* to bid for

lícito,-a *adj (permisible)* allowed; *Jur* lawful

licor *nm* liquor, spirits

licuadora *nf* liquidizer

licuar [30] *vt* to liquidize

lid *nf (combate)* contest

líder *nmf* leader

liderar *vt* to lead, to head

liderato, liderazgo *nm* leadership; *Dep* top *o* first position

lidia *nf* bullfight, bullfighting

lidiador *nm* bullfighter

lidiar [43] **1** *vt Taurom* to fight
2 *vi* to fight; **l. con** to contend with, to fight against

liebre *nf* (a) hare (b) *Dep* pacemaker

liendre *nf* nit

lienzo *nm* (a) *Tex* linen (b) *Arte* canvas

lifting *nm* face-lift

liga *nf* (a) *Dep & Pol* league; **hacer buena l.** to get on well together (b) *(prenda)* garter

ligamento *nm* ligament

ligar [42] **1** *vt* (a) to join; *Fig (dos personas)* to unite (b) *Fam (coger)* to get
2 *vi Fam* **l. con algn** *(seducir)* to *Br* get off *o US* make out with sb
3 ligarse *vpr (vincularse)* to become attached (**a** to)

ligazón *nf* bond, tie

ligeramente *adv* (a) *(levemente)* lightly (b) *(un poco)* slightly

ligereza *nf* (a) lightness; *(de tela, argumento)* flimsiness (b) *(frivolidad)* flippancy; *(acto)* indiscretion; *(dicho)* indiscreet remark (c) *(rapidez)* speed

ligero,-a 1 *adj* (a) *(peso)* light, lightweight; **l. de ropa** lightly clad (b) *(ágil)* light on one's feet; *(veloz)* swift, quick (c) *(leve)* slight; **brisa/comida ligera** light breeze/meal (d) **a la ligera** lightly
2 *adv (rápido)* fast, swiftly

light *adj inv (tabaco)* mild; *Fig (persona)* lightweight

ligón,-ona *adj & nm,f Fam (hombre)* ladies' man; **es muy ligona** she's hot stuff

ligue *nm* pick-up

liguero,-a 1 *adj Dep* league; **partido l.** league match
2 *nm Br* suspender belt, *US* garter belt

lija *nf* sandpaper; **papel de l.** sandpaper

lijar *vt* to sand *o* sandpaper (down)

lila¹ 1 *nm (color)* lilac
2 *nf (flor)* lilac
3 *adj inv* lilac

lila² Fam 1 *adj (tonto)* dumb, stupid
2 *nmf (tonto)* twit

lima¹ *nf (fruto)* lime

lima² *nf (herramienta)* file; **l. de uñas** nail-file

limar *vt* to file; *Fig* **l. asperezas** to smooth things over

limbo *nm* limbo

limitación *nf* limitation; **l. de velocidad** speed limit

limitar 1 *vt* to limit, to restrict
2 *vi* to border; **l. con** to border on

límite *nm* limit; *Geog & Pol* boundary, border; **caso l.** borderline case; **fecha l.** deadline; **velocidad l.** maximum speed

limítrofe *adj* neighbouring

limo *nm* slime

limón *nm* lemon

limonada *nf* lemon squash

limonero *nm* lemon tree

limosna *nf* alms; **pedir l.** to beg

limpiabotas *nm inv* bootblack, shoeshine

limpiacristales *nm inv* window cleaner

limpiador,-a 1 *adj* cleansing
2 *nm,f (persona)* cleaner
3 *nm (producto)* cleaner

limpiaparabrisas *nm inv Br* windscreen *o US* windshield wiper

limpiar [43] *vt* (a) to clean; *(con un trapo)* to wipe; *(zapatos)* to polish; *Fig* to cleanse (b) *Fam (hurtar)* to pinch, to nick

limpieza *nf (calidad)* cleanliness; *(acción)* cleaning; *Fig (integridad)* integrity; **con l.** cleanly

limpio,-a 1 *adj* (a) *(aseado)* clean (b) *Dep*

juego l. fair play (**c**) *Fin (neto)* net; **beneficios en l.** net profit (**d**) *Fam* **pasar algo a l.** to produce a fair copy of sth
2 *adv* fairly; **jugar l.** to play fair
linaje *nm* lineage
linaza *nf* **aceite de l.** linseed oil
lince *nm* lynx; **tiene ojos de l.** he's eagle-eyed
linchar *vt* to lynch; *Fam (pegar)* to beat up
lindante *adj* bordering
lindar *vi* **l. con** to border on
linde *nm o nf* boundary, limit
lindero,-a 1 *adj* bordering, adjoining
2 *nm* boundary, limit
lindo,-a 1 *adj (bonito)* pretty, lovely; **de lo l.** a great deal
2 *adv Am (bien)* nicely
línea *nf* (**a**) line; **l. aérea** airline; **en líneas generales** roughly speaking; *Informát* **fuera de l.** off-line; **en l.** on-line (**b**) **guardar la l.** to watch one's figure
lineal *adj* linear; **dibujo l.** line drawing
lingote *nm* ingot; *(de oro, plata)* bar
lingüista *nmf* linguist
lino *nm* (**a**) *Bot* flax (**b**) *Tex* linen
linterna *nf* torch
linyera *nmf CSur (vagabundo)* tramp, *US* bum
lío *nm* (**a**) *(paquete)* bundle (**b**) *Fam (embrollo)* mess, muddle; **hacerse un l.** to get mixed up; **meterse en líos** to get into trouble; **armar un l.** to kick up a fuss (**c**) *Fam (relación amorosa)* affair
lioso,-a *adj Fam (asunto)* confusing
lipotimia *nf* fainting fit
liquidación *nf* (**a**) *Com (saldo)* clearance sale (**b**) *Fin* liquidation
liquidar 1 *vt Com (deuda, cuenta)* to settle; *(mercancías)* to sell off
2 liquidarse *vpr Fam* (**a**) *(gastar)* to spend (**b**) **l. a algn** *(matar)* to bump sb off
liquidez *nf Fin* liquidity
líquido,-a 1 *adj* (**a**) liquid (**b**) *Fin* net
2 *nm* (**a**) *(fluido)* liquid (**b**) *Fin* liquid assets; **l. imponible** taxable income
lira *nf (moneda)* lira
lírico,-a *adj* lyrical
lirio *nm* iris
lirismo *nm* lyricism
lirón *nm* dormouse; *Fig* **dormir como un l.** to sleep like a log
Lisboa *n* Lisbon
lisiado,-a 1 *adj* crippled
2 *nm,f* cripple
lisiar [43] *vt* to maim, to cripple
liso,-a 1 *adj* (**a**) *(superficie)* smooth, even; *Dep* **los cien metros lisos** the one hundred metres sprint (**b**) *(pelo, falda)* straight (**c**)

(tela) self-coloured (**d**) *Am (desvergonzado)* rude (**e**) **lisa y llanamente** purely and simply
lisonjero,-a 1 *adj* flattering
2 *nm,f* flatterer
lista *nf* (**a**) *(relación)* list; **l. de espera** waiting list; *(en avión)* standby; **pasar l.** to call the register o the roll; *Informát* **l. de correo** mailing list (**b**) *(franja)* stripe; **a listas** striped
listado,-a 1 *adj* striped
2 *nm* list; *Informát* listing
listar *vt Am* to list
listín *nm* **l. telefónico** telephone directory
listo,-a *adj* (**a**) **ser l.** *(inteligente)* to be clever o smart (**b**) **estar l.** *(a punto)* to be ready
listón *nm Dep* bar; *Fig* **subir el l.** to raise the requirements level
litera *nf (cama)* bunk bed; *(en tren)* couchette
literal *adj* literal
literario,-a *adj* literary
literato,-a *nm,f* writer, author

> *Observa que la palabra inglesa **literate** es un falso amigo y no es la traducción de la palabra española **literato**. En inglés, **literate** significa "alfabetizado".*

literatura *nf* literature
litigar [42] *vi Jur* to litigate
litigio *nm Jur* lawsuit; *Fig* dispute; **en l. in dispute
litografía *nf* (**a**) *(técnica)* lithography (**b**) *(imagen)* lithograph
litoral 1 *nm* coast, seaboard
2 *adj* coastal
litro *nm* litre
Lituania *n* Lithuania
lituano,-a 1 *adj & nm,f* Lithuanian
2 *nm (idioma)* Lithuanian
liturgia *nf* liturgy
liviano,-a *adj (de poco peso)* lightweight
lívido,-a *adj* livid
living ['liin] *(pl* livings*)* *nm* living room
liza *nf* contest
llaga *nf* sore; *(herida)* wound
llama *nf* flame; **en llamas** in flames, ablaze
llamada *nf* call; *Tel* **l. interurbana** long-distance call; **señal de l.** ringing tone
llamado,-a 1 *adj* so-called
2 *nm Am* (**a**) *(en general)* call; *(a la puerta)* knock; *(con timbre)* ring (**b**) *(telefónico)* call; **hacer un l.** to make a phone call (**c**) *(apelación)* appeal, call; **hacer un l. a algn para que haga algo** to call upon sb to do sth; **hacer un l. a la huelga** to call a strike

llamamiento *nm* appeal

llamar 1 *vt* (**a**) *(a)* to call; **l. (por teléfono)** to ring up, to call (**b**) *(atraer)* to draw, to attract; **l. la atención** to attract attention

　2 *vi* *(a la puerta)* to knock

　3 llamarse *vpr* to be called; **¿cómo te llamas?** what's your name?

llamarada *nf* blaze

llamativo,-a *adj* (**a**) *(color, ropa)* loud, flashy (**b**) *(persona)* striking

llanero,-a *nm,f* *(del llano)* plainsman, *f* plainswoman

llaneza *nf* *(sencillez)* simplicity

llano,-a 1 *adj* (**a**) *(superficie)* flat, level (**b**) *(claro)* clear (**c**) *(sencillo)* simple; **el pueblo l.** the common people

　2 *nm* plain

llanta *nf* (**a**) *(de rueda)* wheel rim (**b**) *Am* *(neumático)* tyre

llanto *nm* crying, weeping

llanura *nf* plain

llave *nf* (**a**) *(a)* key; **cerrar con l.** to lock; **llaves en mano** *(en anuncio)* available for immediate occupation; *Aut* **l. de contacto** ignition key (**b**) *Téc* spanner; **l. inglesa** adjustable spanner (**c**) *(interruptor)* switch; **l. de paso** stopcock (**d**) *(en lucha)* lock (**e**) *Impr* brace (**f**) *Chile, Méx* *(grifo)* *Br* tap, *US* faucet

llavero *nm* key-ring

llegada *nf* arrival; *Dep* finish

llegar [42] **1** *vi* (**a**) to arrive; **l. a Madrid** to arrive in Madrid (**b**) *(ser bastante)* to be enough (**c**) *(alcanzar)* **l. a** to reach; **¿llegas al techo?** can you reach the ceiling? (**d**) *Fig* **l. a las manos** to come to blows; **l. a presidente** to become president (**e**) **l. a** + *inf* to go so far as to (**f**) **l. a ser** to become

　2 llegarse *vpr* to stop by

llenar 1 *vt* (**a**) to fill; *(cubrir)* to cover (**b**) *(satisfacer)* to satisfy

　2 *vi* *(comida)* to be filling

　3 llenarse *vpr* to fill (up), to become full

lleno,-a 1 *adj* full (up); *Fig* **de l.** fully

　2 *nm* *Teatro* full house

llevadero,-a *adj* bearable, tolerable

llevar 1 *vt* (**a**) to take; *(hacia el oyente)* to bring; **¿adónde llevas eso?** where are you taking that?; **te llevaré un regalo** I'll bring you a present

　(**b**) *(transportar)* to carry; **dejarse l.** to get carried away

　(**c**) *(prenda)* to wear; **llevaba falda** she was wearing a skirt

　(**d**) *(soportar)* to bear; **¿cómo lleva lo de su enfermedad?** how's he bearing up?

　(**e**) *(tiempo)* **llevo dos años aquí** I've

been here for two years; **esto lleva mucho tiempo** this takes a long time

　(**f**) *(negocio)* to be in charge of

　2 *v aux* (**a**) **l.** + *gerundio* to have been + *present participle*; **llevo dos años estudiando español** I've been studying Spanish for two years

　(**b**) **l.** + *participio pasado* to have + *past participle*; **llevaba escritas seis cartas** I had written six letters

　3 llevarse *vpr* (**a**) to take away; *(premio)* to win; *(recibir)* to get

　(**b**) *(arrastrar)* to carry away

　(**c**) *(estar de moda)* to be fashionable

　(**d**) **l. bien con algn** to get on well with sb

llorar *vi* to cry; *Lit* to weep

llorica *nmf* *Fam* crybaby

lloriquear *vi* to whimper, to snivel

llorón,-ona *adj* **un bebé l.** a baby which cries a lot

lloroso,-a *adj* tearful

llover [4] *v impers* to rain

llovizna *nf* drizzle

lloviznar *v impers* to drizzle

lluvia *nf* rain; **una l. de** lots of; **l. radiactiva** fallout; **l. ácida** acid rain

lluvioso,-a *adj* rainy

lo¹ *art neut* the; **lo mejor** the best (part); **lo mismo** the same thing; **lo mío** mine; **lo tuyo** yours

lo² *pron pers m & neut* (**a**) *(cosa)* it; **debes hacerlo** you must do it; **no lo creo** I don't think so; *(no se traduce)* **no se lo dije** I didn't tell her; *ver* **le** (**b**) **lo que …** what …; **no sé lo que pasa** I don't know what's going on (**c**) **lo cual …** which … (**d**) **lo de …** the business of …; **cuéntame lo del juicio** tell me about the trial

loable *adj* praiseworthy, laudable

loar *vt* to praise

lobo *nm* wolf; **como boca de l.** pitch-dark; *Fam* **¡menos lobos!** pull the other one!

lóbrego,-a *adj* gloomy

lóbulo *nm* lobe

local 1 *adj* local

　2 *nm* *(recinto)* premises, site

localidad *nf* (**a**) *(pueblo)* locality; *(en impreso)* place of residence (**b**) *Cin & Teatro* *(asiento)* seat; *(entrada)* ticket

localizar [40] *vt* (**a**) *(encontrar)* to find (**b**) *(fuego, dolor)* to localize

loción *nf* lotion

loco,-a 1 *adj* mad, crazy; **a lo l.** crazily; **l. por** crazy about; **volverse l.** to go mad; *Fam* **¡ni l.!** I'd sooner die!

　2 *nm,f* madman, *f* madwoman; **hacerse el l.** to act the fool

　3 *nm* *Chile* *(molusco)* = type of abalone

locomotora *nf* locomotive

locomotriz *adj* locomotive

locuaz *adj* loquacious, talkative

locución *nf* phrase

locura *nf* (*enfermedad*) madness, insanity; **con l.** madly; *Fam* **esto es una l.** this is crazy

locutor,-a *nm,f TV & Rad* presenter

locutorio *nm* telephone booth

lodo *nm* mud

logaritmo *nm* logarithm

lógica *nf* logic; **no tiene l.** there's no logic to it

lógico,-a *adj* logical; **era l. que ocurriera** it was bound to happen

logística *nf* logistics *sing o pl*

logotipo *nm* logo

lograr *vt* (a) to get, to obtain; (*premio*) to win; (*ambición*) to achieve (b) **l. hacer algo** to manage to do sth

logro *nm* achievement

loma *nf* hillock, rise

lombriz *nf* worm, earthworm

lomo *nm* (a) back; **a lomo(s)** on the back (b) *Culin* loin (c) (*de libro*) spine

lona *nf* canvas

loncha *nf* slice; **l. de bacon** rasher of bacon

lonche *nm* (a) *Méx, Perú, Ven* (*merienda*) (*en escuela*) mid-morning snack; (*en casa*) (afternoon) tea (b) *Méx, Ven* (*comida rápida*) (mid-morning) snack, *Br* elevenses

lonchería *nf Méx* snack-bar

londinense 1 *adj* of/from London
2 *nmf* Londoner

Londres *n* London

longaniza *nf* spicy (pork) sausage

longevo,-a *adj* long-lived

longitud *nf* (a) length; **2 m de l.** 2 m long; **l. de onda** wavelength; *Dep* **salto de l.** long jump (b) *Geog* longitude

lonja¹ *nf* (*loncha*) slice; **l. de bacon** rasher of bacon

lonja² *nf* **l. de pescado** fish market

loquería *nf Am* mental asylum, mental hospital

lord *nm* (*pl* **lores**) lord; *Br Parl* **Cámara de los Lores** House of Lords

loro *nm* parrot

los¹ 1 *art def mpl* the; **l. libros** the books; **cierra l. ojos** close your eyes; **l. García** the Garcías; *ver* **el, las y lo**
2 *pron* **l. que** (*personas*) those who; (*cosas*) the ones (that); **toma l. que quieras** take whichever ones you want; **esos son l. míos/tuyos** these are mine/yours; *ver* **les**

los² *pron pers mpl* them; **¿l. has visto?** have you seen them?

losa *nf* (stone) slab, flagstone

lote *nm* (a) set (b) *Com* lot (c) *Informát* batch (d) *Fam* **darse el l.** to pet (e) *Am* (*solar*) plot (of land)

loteamiento *nm Bol, Urug* parcelling out, division into plots

loteo *nm Chile, Col* = **loteamiento**

lotería *nf* lottery; **me tocó la l.** I won a prize in the lottery

lotización *nf Ecuad, Perú* = **loteamiento**

loto 1 *nm Bot* lotus
2 *nf* (*lotería*) lottery

loza *nf* (a) (*material*) earthenware (b) (*de cocina*) crockery

lozano,-a *adj* (a) (*persona*) healthy-looking (b) (*plantas*) lush, luxuriant

Ltda. (*abr* **Limitada**) Ltd

lubricante *nm* lubricant

lubricar [44] *vt* to lubricate

lucero *nm* (bright) star

lucha *nf* (a) fight, struggle; **l. de clases** class struggle (b) *Dep* wrestling; **l. libre** freestyle wrestling

luchador,-a *nm,f* (a) fighter (b) *Dep* wrestler

luchar *vi* (a) to fight, to struggle (b) *Dep* to wrestle

lucidez *nf* lucidity

lúcido,-a *adj* lucid, clear

luciérnaga *nf* glow-worm

lucir [35] 1 *vi* (a) (*brillar*) to shine (b) *Am* (*parecer*) to seem (c) *Fam* (*compensar*) **no le luce lo que estudia** his studies don't get him anywhere
2 *vt* (*ropas*) to sport; (*talento*) to display
3 **lucirse** *vpr* (a) (*hacer buen papel*) to do very well (b) (*pavonearse*) to show off

lucrativo,-a *adj* lucrative, profitable

lucro *nm* profit, gain; **afán de l.** greed for money

lúcuma *nf Andes* lucuma, = sweet, pear-shaped fruit

lúdico,-a *adj* relating to games, recreational

luego 1 *adv* (a) (*después*) then, next, afterwards (b) (*más tarde*) later (on); **¡hasta l.!** so long!; **l. de** after (c) **desde l.** of course (d) *Chile, Ven* (*pronto*) soon; *Méx Fam* **l. l. o l. lueguito** right *o* straight away
2 *conj* therefore

lugar *nm* (a) place; **en primer l.** in the first place; **en l. de** instead of; **sin l. a dudas** without a doubt; **tener l.** to take place (b) **dar l. a** to cause, to give rise to

lugareño,-a *adj & nm,f* local

lugarteniente *nmf* lieutenant
lúgubre *adj* gloomy, lugubrious
lujo *nm* luxury; **productos de l.** luxury products; **no puedo permitirme ese l.** I can't afford that
lujoso,-a *adj* luxurious
lujuria *nf* lust

> *Observa que la palabra inglesa* **luxury** *es un falso amigo y no es la traducción de la palabra española* **lujuria***. En inglés,* **luxury** *significa "lujo".*

lujurioso,-a *adj* lecherous, lustful
lumbre *nf* fire
lumbrera *nf* luminary
luminoso,-a *adj* luminous; *Fig* bright
luna *nf* (a) moon; *Fig* **estar en la l.** to have one's head in the clouds; **l. creciente/llena** crescent/full moon; *Fig* **l. de miel** honeymoon (b) *(de escaparate)* pane; *(espejo)* mirror
lunar 1 *adj* lunar
  2 *nm (redondel)* dot; *(en la piel)* mole, beauty spot; **vestido de lunares** spotted dress
lunático,-a *nm,f* lunatic

lunes *nm inv* Monday; **vendré el l.** I'll come on Monday
lupa *nf* magnifying glass
luso,-a *adj & nm,f* Portuguese
lustrabotas *nm inv,* **lustrador,-a** *nm,f Andes, RP* bootblack
lustradora *nf Andes, RP* floor polisher
lustrar *vt* to polish; *(zapatos)* to shine
lustre *nm (brillo)* shine, lustre; *Fig (esplendor)* splendour, glory; **dar** *o* **sacar l. a algo** to polish sth
lustro *nm* five-year period
lustroso,-a *adj* shiny, glossy
luto *nm* mourning
Luxemburgo *n* Luxembourg
luz *nf* (a) light; **apagar la l.** to put out the light; **a la l. de** in the light of; **a todas luces** obviously; *Fig* **dar a l.** *(parir)* to give birth to; *Fig* **dar l. verde a** to give the green light to (b) *Aut* light; **luces de cruce** dipped headlights; **luces de posición** sidelights; **l. larga** headlights (c) **luces** *(inteligencia)* intelligence; **corto de luces** dim-witted (d) **traje de luces** bullfighter's costume
luzco *indic pres de* **lucir**

M

M, m ['eme] *nf (la letra)* M, m
m (**a**) (*abr* **metro(s)**) m (**b**) (*abr* **minu-to(s)**) min
macabro,-a *adj* macabre
macana *nf* (**a**) *Andes, Carib, Méx (palo)* club (**b**) *CSur, Perú, Ven Fam (fastidio)* pain, drag
macanear *vt CSur, Ven (hacer mal)* to botch, to do badly
macanudo,-a *adj Fam* great, terrific
macarra *nm Fam* yob
macarrón *nm* (**a**) macaroon (**b**) *Elec* sheath
macarrones *nmpl* macaroni
macedonia *nf* fruit salad
macerar *vt* to macerate
maceta *nf (tiesto)* plant-pot, flowerpot
machacar [44] **1** *vt* (**a**) to crush; *Dep* to smash (**b**) *Fam (estudiar con ahínco) Br* to swot up on, *US* to bone up on (**c**) *Fam (insistir en)* to harp on about, to go on about
2 *vi* (**a**) *Fam (insistir mucho)* to harp on, to go on (**b**) *Fam (estudiar con ahínco) Br* to swot, *US* to grind (**c**) *(en baloncesto)* to smash
machacón,-ona *Fam* **1** *adj (repetitivo)* repetitious; *(pesado)* boring, tiresome
2 *nm,f (muy estudioso) Br* swot, *US* grind
machamartillo : • a machamartillo *loc adv (con firmeza)* firmly; *(con obstinación)* obstinately
machete *nm* (**a**) *(arma)* machete (**b**) *Arg Fam (chuleta)* crib
machismo *nm* machismo, male chauvinism
machista *adj & nm* male chauvinist
macho 1 *adj* (**a**) *(animal, planta)* male (**b**) *Fam (viril)* manly, virile, macho
2 *nm* (**a**) *(animal, planta)* male (**b**) *Téc (pieza)* male piece o part; *(de enchufe)* plug (**c**) *Fam (hombre viril)* macho, he-man, tough guy
machote *nm Am (borrador)* rough draft
macilento,-a *adj* gaunt
macizo,-a 1 *adj* (**a**) *(sólido)* solid; **de oro m.** of solid gold (**b**) *(robusto)* solid, robust; *Fam (atractivo)* well-built
2 *nm (masa sólida)* mass

macramé *nm* macramé
macro *nf Informát* macro
macro- *pref* macro-
macroeconomía *nf* macroeconomics *sing*
macuto *nm (morral)* knapsack, haversack
madeja *nf (de lana etc)* hank, skein
madera *nf* (**a**) wood; *(de construcción)* timber, *US* lumber; **de m.** wood, wooden (**b**) *Fig* **tiene m. de líder** he has all the makings of a leader
madero *nm* (**a**) *(de construcción)* timber; *(leño)* log (**b**) *muy Fam (policía)* cop; **los maderos** the fuzz *pl*
madrastra *nf* stepmother
madre 1 *nf* (**a**) mother; **es m. de tres hijos** she is a mother of three (children); **m. adoptiva** adoptive mother; **m. alquilada** surrogate mother; **m. de familia** mother, housewife; **m. política** mother-in-law; **m. soltera** unmarried mother; *Fig* **la m. patria** one's motherland; *Méx muy Fam* **me vale m.** I couldn't give a damn o *Br* a toss (**b**) *(de río)* bed
2 *interj* **¡m. de Dios!, ¡m. mía!** good heavens!
madreperla *nf (nácar)* mother-of-pearl
madreselva *nf* honeysuckle
Madrid *n* Madrid
madriguera *nf* burrow, hole
madrileño,-a 1 *adj* of/from Madrid
2 *nm,f* person from Madrid
madrina *nf* (**a**) *(de bautizo)* godmother (**b**) *(de boda)* ≃ bridesmaid (**c**) *Fig (protectora)* protectress
madrugada *nf* (**a**) dawn; **de m.** in the wee small hours (**b**) early morning; **las tres de la m.** three o'clock in the morning
madrugador,-a 1 *adj* early-rising
2 *nm,f* early riser
madrugar [42] *vi* to get up early
madurar 1 *vt Fig (un plan)* to think out
2 *vi* (**a**) *(persona)* to mature (**b**) *(fruta)* to ripen
madurez *nf* (**a**) maturity (**b**) *(de la fruta)* ripeness
maduro,-a *adj* (**a**) mature; **de edad madura** middle-aged (**b**) *(fruta)* ripe

maestría nf mastery; **con m.** masterfully
maestro,-a 1 nm,f (**a**) Educ teacher; **m. de escuela** schoolteacher (**b**) Méx (en universidad) Br lecturer, US professor (**c**) (especialista) master; **m. de obras** foreman (**d**) Mús maestro
2 adj **obra maestra** masterpiece; **llave maestra** master key
mafia nf mafia
mafioso,-a 1 adj of/relating to the mafia
2 nm,f member of the mafia, mafioso
magdalena nf bun, cake
magia nf magic; **por arte de m.** as if by magic
mágico,-a adj (**a**) magic (**b**) Fig (maravilloso) magical, wonderful
magisterio nm teaching
magistrado,-a nm,f judge; Am **primer m.** prime minister
magistral adj (excelente) masterly; **una jugada m.** a master stroke
magistratura nf magistracy
magnánimo,-a adj magnanimous
magnate nm magnate, tycoon
magnesio nm magnesium
magnético,-a adj magnetic
magnetizar [40] vt (**a**) (imantar) to magnetize (**b**) Fig (hipnotizar) to hypnotize
magnetofón, magnetófono nm tape recorder
magnetofónico,-a adj magnetic
magnífico,-a adj magnificent, splendid
magnitud nf magnitude, dimension; **de primera m.** of the first order
magno,-a adj Literario great; **aula magna** main amphitheatre
mago,-a nm,f wizard, magician; **los tres Reyes Magos** the Three Wise Men, the Three Kings
magrear vt muy Fam to grope
magro,-a 1 nm (de cerdo) lean meat
2 adj (sin grasa) lean
magullar 1 vt to bruise, to damage
2 magullarse upr to get bruised, to get damaged
mahometano,-a adj & nm,f Rel Mohammedan, Muslim
mahonesa nf mayonnaise
maillot nm (malla) leotard; Dep shirt
maíz nm maize, US corn
maizal nm field of maize o US corn
majadería nf silly thing, absurdity
majadero,-a nm,f fool, idiot
majara, majareta adj Fam loony, nutty
majestad nf majesty
majestuosidad nf majesty
majestuoso,-a adj majestic, stately
majo,-a adj (bonito) pretty, nice; Fam

(simpático) nice; **tiene un hijo muy m.** she's got a lovely little boy; Fam **ven aquí, m.** come here, dear
mal 1 nm (**a**) evil, wrong (**b**) (daño) harm; **no le deseo ningún m.** I don't wish him any harm (**c**) (enfermedad) illness, disease; Fam **el m. de las vacas locas** mad cow disease
2 adj bad; **un m. año** a bad year; ver **malo,-a**
3 adv badly, wrong; **lo hizo muy m.** he did it very badly; **menos m. que ...** it's a good job (that) ...; **no está (nada) m.** it is not bad (at all); **te oigo/veo (muy) m.** I can hardly hear/see you; **tomar a m.** (enfadarse) to take badly
malabar adj (juegos) **malabares** juggling
malabarista nmf juggler
malapata nf Fam (mala suerte) bad luck
malaria nf malaria
malcriado,-a 1 adj ill-mannered, ill-bred
2 nm,f ill-mannered o uncivil person
malcriar [29] vt to spoil
maldecir [12] 1 vt to curse
2 vi (**a**) (blasfemar) to curse (**b**) (criticar) to speak ill (**de** of)
maldición 1 nf curse
2 interj damnation!
maldito,-a adj (**a**) Fam (molesto) damned, Br bloody (**b**) (endemoniado) damned, cursed; **¡maldita sea!** damn it!
maleante adj & nmf criminal
malear 1 vt Fig to corrupt, to pervert
2 malearse upr to go bad
maleducado,-a 1 adj bad-mannered
2 nm,f bad-mannered person
maleficio nm (hechizo) curse, spell
maléfico,-a adj evil, harmful
malentendido nm misunderstanding
malestar nm (**a**) (molestia) discomfort (**b**) Fig (inquietud) uneasiness; **tengo m.** I feel uneasy
maleta 1 nf suitcase, case; **hacer la m.** to pack one's things o case
2 nm Fam (persona) bungler
maletero nm Aut Br boot, US trunk
maletín nm briefcase
malévolo,-a adj malevolent
maleza nf (**a**) (arbustos) thicket, undergrowth (**b**) (malas hierbas) weeds
malgastar vt & vi to waste, to squander
malhablado,-a 1 adj foul-mouthed
2 nm,f foul-mouthed person
malhechor,-a nm,f wrongdoer, criminal
malhumor nm bad temper o mood; **de m.** in a bad temper o mood

malicia *nf* (a) *(mala intención)* malice, maliciousness (b) *(astucia)* cunning, slyness (c) *(maldad)* badness, evil

malicioso,-a 1 *adj* malicious, spiteful

2 *nm,f* malicious *o* spiteful person

maligno,-a *adj* malignant

malintencionado,-a 1 *adj* ill-intentioned

2 *nm,f* ill-intentioned person

malla *nf* (a) *(prenda)* leotard (b) *(red)* mesh (c) *Perú, RP (bañador)* swimsuit, swimming costume

Mallorca *n* Majorca

mallorquín,-ina *adj & nm,f* Majorcan

malo,-a 1 *adj* (a) bad; **un año m.** a bad year; **estar a malas** to be on bad terms; **por las malas** by force (b) *(persona) (malvado)* wicked, bad; *(travieso)* naughty (c) *(de poca calidad)* bad, poor; **una mala canción/comida** a poor song/meal (d) *(perjudicial)* harmful; **el tabaco es m.** tobacco is harmful (e) **lo m. es que ...** the problem is that ... (f) *(enfermo)* ill, sick

Mal is used instead of **malo** before masculine singular nouns (e.g. **un mal ejemplo** a bad example). The comparative form of **malo** (= worse) is **peor**, the superlative forms (= the worst) are **el peor** (masculine) and **la peor** (feminine).

2 *nm,f Fam* **el m.** the baddy *o* villain

malograr 1 *vt Andes (estropear)* to make a mess of, to ruin

2 **malograrse** *vpr* (a) *(fracasar)* to fail, to fall through (b) *Andes (estropearse) (el tiempo)* to turn nasty; *(máquina)* to break down; *(alimento)* to go off, to spoil

maloliente *adj* foul-smelling

malparado,-a *adj* **salir m.** to end up in a sorry state

malpensado,-a 1 *adj* nasty-minded

2 *nm,f* nasty-minded person

malsonante *adj (grosero)* rude, offensive; **palabras malsonantes** foul language

malta *nf (cebada)* malt

maltratado,-a *adj* battered

maltratar *vt* to ill-treat, to mistreat

maltrecho,-a *adj* in a sorry state, wrecked

malva 1 *adj inv* mauve

2 *nm (color)* mauve

3 *nf Bot* mallow

malvado,-a 1 *adj* evil, wicked

2 *nm,f* villain, evil person

malvender *vt* to sell at a loss

malversar *vt* to misappropriate, to embezzle

Malvinas *npl* **las (Islas) M.** the Falkland Islands

malviviente *nmf CSur* criminal

malvivir *vi* to live very badly

mama *nf* (a) *(de mujer)* breast; *(de animal)* teat (b) *Fam (mamá)* mum, mummy

mamá *nf Fam* mum, mummy; *Col, Méx Fam* **m. grande** grandma

mamada *nf* (a) *(bebé)* feed (b) *Vulg (felatio)* blowjob

mamadera *nf Am* feeding bottle

mamar *vt (leche)* to suck; *Fig (adquirir)* to absorb

mamarracho,-a *nm,f Fam (persona)* ridiculous-looking person, mess, sight; *(cosa)* mess

mameluco *nm Fig* (a) fool, idiot, dimwit (b) *Am* boiler suit

mamey *nm* (a) *(árbol)* mamey, mammee (b) *(fruto)* mamey, mammee (apple)

mamífero,-a *nm,f* mammal

mamón *nm muy Fam Br* prat, *US* jerk

mampara *nf* screen

mamporro *nm Fam* wallop

mampostería *nf* masonry

mamut *nm* mammoth

manada *nf* (a) *Zool (de vacas, elefantes)* herd; *(de ovejas)* flock; *(de lobos, perros)* pack; *(de leones)* pride (b) *Fam (multitud)* crowd, mob; **en manada(s)** in crowds

manager *nmf Dep & Mús* manager

manantial *nm* spring

manar 1 *vi* to flow, to run (**de** from)

2 *vt* to run with, to flow with; **la herida manaba sangre** blood flowed from his wound

manazas *nmf inv Fam* ham-fisted person

mancebo *nm* (a) *(de farmacia)* assistant (b) *Literario (muchacho)* young man

Mancha *n* **el Canal de la M.** the English Channel

mancha *nf* stain, spot; **m. solar** sunspot; **m. de tinta/vino** ink/wine stain

manchado,-a *adj* dirty, stained; **leche manchada** milky coffee

manchar 1 *vt* to stain, to dirty; *Fig* to stain, to blemish

2 **mancharse** *vpr* to get dirty

manchego,-a 1 *adj* of/from La Mancha

2 *nm,f* person from La Mancha

manco,-a 1 *adj* (a) *(de un brazo)* one-armed *(sin brazos)* armless (b) *(de una mano)* one-handed; *(sin manos)* handless

2 *nm,f* (a) *(de brazos)* one-armed/armless person (b) *(de manos)* one-handed/handless person

mancomunidad *nf* community, association

mancornas, mancuernas *nfpl CAm, Chile, Col, Méx, Ven* cufflinks

mandado *nm (recado)* order, errand; **hacer un m.** to run an errand

mandamás *nmf (pl* **mandamases)** *Fam* bigwig, boss

mandamiento *nm* (a) *(orden)* order, command (b) **los Diez Mandamientos** the Ten Commandments

mandar *vt* (a) to order; *Fam* **¿mande?** pardon? (b) *(grupo)* to lead, to be in charge o command of; *Mil* to command (c) *(enviar)* to send; **m. (a) por** to send for; **m. algo por correo** to post sth, to send sth by post; **m. recuerdos** to send regards

mandarina *nf* mandarin (orange), tangerine

mandatario,-a *nm,f Pol* president

mandato *nm* (a) *(orden)* order, command (b) *Jur* writ, warrant (c) *Pol (legislatura)* mandate, term of office

mandíbula *nf* jaw; *Fam* **reír a m. batiente** to laugh one's head off

mandil *nm* apron

Mandinga *nm Am* the Devil

mando *nm* (a) *(autoridad)* command, control (b) **los altos mandos del ejército** high-ranking army officers (c) *Téc (control)* controls; *Aut* **cuadro** o **tablero de mandos** dashboard; **m. a distancia** remote control; **palanca de m.** *Téc* control lever; *(de avión, videojuego)* joystick

mandón,-ona 1 *adj Fam* bossy, domineering

2 *nm,f Fam* bossy o domineering person

3 *nm Am* (mine) foreman

manecilla *nf (de reloj)* hand

manejable *adj* manageable; *(herramienta)* easy-to-use; *(coche)* manoeuvrable

manejar 1 *vt* (a) *(máquina)* to handle, to operate; *Fig (situación)* to handle (b) *(negocio)* to run, to manage (c) *Fig (a otra persona)* to domineer, to boss about (d) *Am (coche)* to drive

2 *vi Am (conducir)* to drive

3 **manejarse** *vpr* to manage

manejo *nm* (a) *(uso)* handling, use; **de fácil m.** easy-to-use (b) *Fig (de un negocio)* management; *(de un coche)* driving (c) *Fig* tricks

manera *nf* (a) way, manner; **a mi/tu m.** (in) my/your way; **de cualquier m.** *(mal)* carelessly, any old how; *(en cualquier caso)* in any case; **de esta m.** in this way; **de ninguna m.** in no way, certainly not; **de todas maneras** anyway, at any rate, in any case; **es mi m. de ser** that's the way I am; **no hay m.** it's impossible (b) **de m. que** so; **de tal m. que** in such a way that (c) **maneras** manners; **de buenas maneras** politely

manga *nf* (a) sleeve; **de m. corta/larga** short-/long-sleeved; **sin mangas** sleeveless; *Fig* **hacer un corte de mangas a algn** ≃ to give sb the fingers; *Fig* **m. por hombro** messy and untidy; *Fig* **sacarse algo de la m.** to pull sth out of one's hat (b) *(de riego)* hose (c) *(del mar)* arm (d) *Dep* leg, round; *Ten* set

mangante *nmf Fam* thief

mangar [42] *vt Fam* to pinch, to nick, to swipe

mango *nm* (a) *(asa)* handle (b) *RP Fam (dinero)* **no tengo un m.** I haven't got a bean, I'm broke

mangonear *vi Fam* (a) *(entrometerse)* to meddle (b) *(dar órdenes)* to throw one's weight around

manguera *nf* hose

mangui *nmf Fam* thief

manguito *nm* (a) *(para las mangas)* oversleeve; *(para flotar)* armband (b) *Téc* sleeve

maní *nm (pl* **maníes)** peanut

manía *nf* (a) *(dislike, ill will;* **me tiene m.** he has it in for me (b) *(costumbre)* habit; **tiene la m. de llegar tarde** he's always arriving late (c) *(afición exagerada)* craze; **la m. de las motos** the motorbike craze (d) *Med* mania

maniaco,-a, maníaco,-a *adj & nm,f Psi* manic; *Fam (obseso)* maniac

maniatar *vt* to tie the hands of

maniático,-a 1 *adj* fussy

2 *nm,f* fusspot

manicomio *nm* mental hospital

manicura *nf* manicure

manido,-a *adj* (a) *(comida)* off (b) *(asunto)* trite, hackneyed

manifestación *nf* (a) demonstration (b) *(expresión)* manifestation, expression

manifestante *nmf* demonstrator

manifestar [1] 1 *vt* (a) *(declarar)* to state, to declare (b) *(mostrar)* to show, to display

2 **manifestarse** *vpr* (a) *(por la calle)* to demonstrate (b) *(declararse)* to declare oneself; **se manifestó contrario a ...** he spoke out against ...

manifiesto,-a 1 *adj* clear, obvious; **poner de m.** *(revelar)* to reveal, to show; *(hacer patente)* to make clear

2 *nm* manifesto

manigua *nf Am Geog* scrubland

manilla *nf* (a) *(de reloj)* hand (b) *Am (palanca)* lever

manillar *nm* handlebar

maniobra *nf* manoeuvre

maniobrar *vi* to manoeuvre

manipulación *nf* manipulation

manipular *vt* to manipulate; *(máquina)* to handle

maniquí *nm (muñeco)* dummy

manitas *nmf inv Fam* (a) **ser un m.** to be handy, to be very good with one's hands (b) **hacer m.** to hold hands

manito *nm Méx Fam* pal, *Br* mate, *US* buddy

manivela *nf Téc* crank

manjar *nm* dish, food

mano 1 *nf* (a) hand; **a m.** *(sin máquina)* by hand; *(asequible)* at hand; **escrito a m.** hand-written; **hecho a m.** hand-made; **m. armada** armed; **estrechar la m. a algn** to shake hands with sb; **de segunda m.** second-hand; **echar una m. a algn** to give sb a hand; **¡manos a la obra!** shoulders to the wheel!; **meter m. a** *(un problema)* to tackle; *Fam* to touch up; **traerse algo entre manos** to be up to sth; **equipaje de m.** hand luggage (b) *(lado)* side; **a m. derecha/izquierda** on the right/left(-hand side) (c) **m. de pintura** coat of paint (d) **m. de obra** labour *(force)* (e) *RP (dirección)* direction *(of traffic)*; **calle de una/doble m.** one-/two-way street

2 *nm Andes, CAm, Carib, Méx Fam* pal, *Br* mate, *US* buddy

manojo *nm* bunch; **ser un m. de nervios** to be a bundle of nerves

manopla *nf* mitten

manoseado,-a *adj (objeto)* worn(-out); *(tema)* hackneyed

manosear *vt* to touch repeatedly, to finger; *Fam* to paw

manotazo *nm* cuff, slap

mansalva: • a mansalva *loc adv (en gran cantidad)* galore

mansedumbre *nf* (a) *(de persona)* meekness, gentleness (b) *(de animal)* tameness, docility

manso,-a *adj* (a) *(persona)* gentle, meek (b) *(animal)* tame, docile (c) *Chile (extraordinario)* great

manta 1 *nf* (a) blanket; **m. eléctrica** electric blanket (b) *(zurra)* beating, hiding (c) *Ven (vestido)* = traditional costume worn by women from Guajira

2 *nmf Fam* lazy person, idler

manteca *nf* (a) *(de animal)* fat; **m. de cacao/cacahuete** cocoa/peanut butter; **m. de cerdo** lard (b) *Am (mantequilla)* butter

mantecado *nm* shortcake

mantel *nm* tablecloth

> 🔎 Observa que la palabra inglesa **mantle** es un falso amigo y no es la traducción de la palabra española **mantel**. En inglés, **mantle** significa "manto, capa".

mantener [24] 1 *vt* (a) *(conservar)* to keep; **mantén el fuego encendido** keep the fire burning; **m. la línea** to keep in trim (b) *(entrevista, reunión)* to have; **m. correspondencia con algn** to correspond with sb (c) *(ideas, opiniones)* to defend, to maintain (d) *(familia)* to support, to feed (e) *(peso)* to support, to hold up

2 **mantenerse** *vpr* (a) *(sostenerse)* to stand (b) **m. firme** *(perseverar)* to hold one's ground (c) *(sustentarse)* to live (**de on**)

mantenimiento *nm* (a) *Téc* maintenance, upkeep; **servicio de m.** maintenance service (b) *(alimento)* sustenance, support (c) **gimnasia y m.** keep fit

mantequilla *nf* butter

manto *nm* cloak

mantón *nm* shawl

mantuve *pt indef de* **mantener**

manual 1 *adj* manual; **trabajo m.** manual labour; *Educ* **trabajos manuales** handicrafts

2 *nm* manual, handbook

manubrio *nm Am (manillar)* handlebars

manufactura *nf* (a) *(fabricación)* manufacture (b) *(fábrica)* factory

manufacturar *vt* to manufacture

manuscrito *nm* manuscript

manutención *nf* maintenance

manzana *nf* (a) apple (b) *(de edificios)* block

manzanilla *nf* (a) *Bot* camomile (b) *(infusión)* camomile tea (c) *(vino)* manzanilla

maña *nf* (a) *(astucia)* cunning (b) *(habilidad)* skill

mañana 1 *nf* morning; **a las dos de la m.** at two in the morning; **de m.** early in the morning; **por la m.** in the morning

2 *nm* tomorrow, the future

3 *adv* tomorrow; **¡hasta m.!** see you tomorrow! **m. por la m.** tomorrow morning; **pasado m.** the day after tomorrow

mañanitas *nfpl Méx* birthday song

mañoco *nm Ven* tapioca

mañoso,-a *adj* skilful

mapa *nm* map; **m. mudo** blank map; *Fam* **borrar del m.** to wipe out

maqueta *nf* (a) *(miniatura)* scale model, maquette (b) *Mús* demo *(tape)*

maquiavélico,-a *adj* Machiavellian

maquila *nf Méx (of machines)* assembly
maquiladora *nf Méx* assembly plant
maquillaje *nm* make-up
maquillar 1 *vt* to make up
  2 maquillarse *vpr* (a) *(ponerse maquillaje)* to put one's make-up on, to make (oneself) up (b) *(usar maquillaje)* to wear make-up
máquina *nf* (a) machine; **escrito a m.** typewritten; **hecho a m.** machine-made; *Fam* **a toda m.** at full speed **m. de afeitar (eléctrica)** (electric) razor *o* shaver; **m. de coser** sewing machine; **m. de escribir** typewriter; **m. fotográfica** *o* **de fotos** camera; **m. tragaperras** *o Am* **tragamonedas** slot machine, one-armed bandit (b) *CAm, Cuba (coche)* car
maquinar *vt* to machinate, to plot
maquinaria *nf* (a) machinery, machines (b) *(de reloj etc) (mecanismo)* mechanism, works
maquinilla *nf* **m. de afeitar** safety razor
maquinista *nmf (de tren)* engine driver
mar 1 *nm o nf* (a) sea; **en alta m.** on the high seas; **m. gruesa** heavy sea; **m. picada** rough sea (b) *Fam* **está la m. de guapa** she's looking really beautiful; **llover a mares** to rain cats and dogs

> Note that the feminine is used in literary language, by people such as fishermen with a close connection with the sea, and in some idiomatic expressions.

2 *nm* sea; **M. del Norte** North Sea; **M. Muerto/Negro** Dead/Black Sea
maracuyá *nf* passion fruit
maraña *nf* tangle
maratón *nm* marathon
maratoniano,-a *adj* marathon
maravilla *nf* marvel, wonder; **de m.** wonderfully; **¡qué m. de película!** what a wonderful film!; *Fam* **a las mil maravillas** marvellously
maravillar 1 *vt* to amaze, to astonish
  2 maravillarse *vpr* to marvel (**con** at), to wonder (**con** at)
maravilloso,-a *adj* wonderful, marvellous
marca *nf* (a) mark, sign (b) *Com* brand, make; **ropa de m.** brand-name clothes; **m. de fábrica** trademark; **m. registrada** registered trademark (c) *Dep (récord)* record; **batir la m. mundial** to break the world record
marcador *nm* (a) marker (b) *Dep (tablero)* scoreboard; *(persona)* scorer (c) *Am (rotulador)* felt-tip pen; *Méx (fluorescente)* highlighter pen

marcaje *nm Dep* marking
marcapasos *nm inv Med* pacemaker
marcar [44] 1 *vt* (a) to mark (b) *Tel* to dial (c) *(indicar)* to indicate, to show; **el contador marca 1.327** the meter reads 1,327 (d) *Dep (gol, puntos)* to score; *(a jugador)* to mark (e) *(cabello)* to set
  2 marcarse *vpr Fam* **m. un farol** to show off, to boast
marcha *nf* (a) march; **hacer algo sobre la m.** to do sth as one goes along; **a marchas forzadas** against the clock (b) **estar en m.** *(vehículo)* to be in motion; *(máquina)* to be working; *(proyecto etc)* to be under way; **poner en m.** to start (c) *Aut* gear; **m. atrás** reverse (gear) (d) *Mús* march (e) *Fam (juerga)* **hay mucha m.** there's lots going on; **ella tiene mucha m.** she likes a good time
marchante,-a *nm,f* (a) *(de arte)* dealer (b) *CAm, Méx, Ven Fam (cliente)* customer, patron
marchar 1 *vi* (a) *(ir)* to go, to walk; *Fam* **¡marchando!** on your way!; **¡una cerveza! – ¡marchando!** a beer, please! – coming right up! (b) *(aparato)* to be on; **m. bien** *(negocio)* to be going well (c) *Mil* to march
  2 marcharse *vpr (irse)* to leave, to go away
marchitar *vt,* **marchitarse** *vpr* to shrivel, to wither
marchito,-a *adj* shrivelled, withered
marchoso,-a *Fam* **1** *adj (persona)* fun-loving, wild
  2 *nm,f* raver, fun-lover
marcial *adj* martial; **artes marciales** martial arts
marcianitos *nmpl (juego)* space invaders
marciano,-a *adj & nm,f* Martian
marco *nm* (a) *(de cuadro etc)* frame (b) *Fig (ámbito)* framework; **acuerdo m.** framework agreement (c) *Fin (moneda)* mark
marea *nf* (a) tide; **m. alta/baja** high/low tide; **m. negra** oil slick (b) *Fig (multitud)* crowd, mob
mareado,-a *adj* (a) sick; *(en un avión)* airsick; *(en un coche)* car-sick, travel-sick; *(en el mar)* seasick (b) *Euf (bebido)* tipsy (c) *(aturdido)* dizzy
marear 1 *vt* (a) to make sick; *(en el mar)* to make seasick; *(en un avión)* to make airsick; *(en un coche)* to make car-sick *o* travel-sick (b) *(aturdir)* to make dizzy (c) *Fam (fastidiar)* to annoy, to pester (d) *Culin* to stir

2 marearse *vpr* (a) to get sick/seasick/airsick/car-sick o travel-sick (b) *(quedar aturdido)* to get dizzy (c) *Euf (emborracharse)* to get tipsy

mareo *nm* (a) *(náusea)* sickness; *(en el mar)* seasickness; *(en un avión)* airsickness; *(en un coche)* car-sickness, travel-sickness (b) *(aturdimiento)* dizziness, light-headedness

marfil *nm* ivory

margarina *nf* margarine

margarita *nf* daisy

margen 1 *nm* (a) *(de papel)* border, edge; *Fig* **dejar algn/algo al m.** to leave sb/sth out; *Fig* **mantenerse al m.** not to get involved; **al m. de** leaving aside (b) *(del papel)* margin (c) *Com* **m. beneficiario** profit margin
2 *nf (de río)* bank

marginación *nf (exclusión)* exclusion

marginado,-a 1 *adj* excluded
2 *nm,f* dropout

marginal *adj* (a) marginal (b) *Pol* fringe

marginar *vt (de un grupo, sociedad)* to leave out, to exclude

maría *nf Fam* (a) *(droga)* marijuana, pot (b) *Educ (asignatura fácil)* easy subject (c) *(ama de casa)* housewife

marica *nm Fam* queer, *Br* poof, *US* fag

maricón *nm muy Fam* queer, *Br* poof, *US* fag

marido *nm* husband

mariguana, marihuana, marijuana *nf* marijuana

marimacho *nm Fam* mannish woman, butch woman

marimandón,-ona *nm,f Fam* domineering person

marimorena *nf Fam* row, fuss; *Fam* **armar(se) la m.** to kick up a racket

marina *nf* (a) *Náut* seamanship (b) *Mil* navy; **m. de guerra** navy; **m. mercante** merchant navy (c) *Geog (zona costera)* seacoast

marinero,-a 1 *nm* sailor, seaman
2 *adj* seafaring

marino,-a 1 *adj* marine; **brisa marina** sea breeze
2 *nm* sailor

marioneta *nf* marionette, puppet

mariposa *nf* (a) *(insecto)* butterfly (b) *(lamparilla)* oil lamp (c) *(en natación)* butterfly

mariposear *vi Fig* (a) *(flirtear)* to flirt (b) *(ser inconstante)* to be fickle

mariposón *nm* (a) *(galanteador)* flirt (b) *Fam (marica)* fairy, pansy

mariquita 1 *nf (insecto) Br* ladybird, *US* ladybug

2 *nm Fam (marica)* queer, *Br* poof, *US* fag

mariscal *nm Mil* marshal; **m. de campo** *Br* field marshal, *US* general of the army

marisco *nm* shellfish; **mariscos** seafood

marisma *nf* marsh

marisquería *nf* seafood restaurant, shellfish bar

marítimo,-a *adj* maritime, sea; **ciudad marítima** coastal town; **paseo m.** promenade

mármol *nm* marble

marmóreo,-a *adj* marble

maroma *nf* (a) *Náut* cable (b) *(cuerda)* thick rope

marqués *nm* marquis

marquesa *nf* marchioness

marquesina *nf* canopy; **m. (del autobús)** bus shelter

marquetería *nf* marquetry, inlaid work

marrano,-a 1 *adj (sucio)* filthy, dirty
2 *nm,f* (a) *Fam (persona)* dirty pig, slob (b) *(animal)* pig

marras: • **de marras** *loc adv* **el individuo de m.** the man in question

marrón 1 *adj (color)* brown
2 *nm* (a) *(color)* brown (b) *Fam (condena)* sentence

marroquí *adj & nmf* Moroccan

marroquinería *nf* leather goods

Marruecos *n* Morocco

marrullero,-a 1 *adj* cajoling, wheedling
2 *nm,f* cajoler, wheedler

Marte *n* Mars

martes *nm inv* Tuesday; **m. y trece** ≃ Friday the thirteenth

martillero *nm CSur* auctioneer

martillo *nm* hammer

mártir *nmf* martyr

martirio *nm* (a) martyrdom (b) *Fig (fastidio)* torment

martirizar [40] *vt* (a) to martyr (b) *Fig (fastidiar)* to torture, to torment

marxista *adj & nmf* Marxist

marzo *nm* March

mas *conj Literario* but

más 1 *adv* (a) *(adicional)* more; **no tengo m.** I haven't got any more
(b) *(comparativo)* more; **es m. alta/inteligente que yo** she's taller/more intelligent than me; **tengo m. dinero que tú** I've more money than you; **m. gente de la que esperas** more people than you're expecting; **m. de** *(con numerales, cantidad)* more than, over
(c) *(superlativo)* most; **es el m. bonito/caro** it's the prettiest/most expensive
(d) *interj* so ..., what a ...; **¡qué casa m. bonita!** what a lovely house! **¡está m.**

guapa! she looks so beautiful!

(**e**) *(después de pron interr e indef)* else; **¿algo m.?** anything else?; **no, nada m.** no, nothing else; **¿quién m.?** who else?; **nadie/alguien m.** nobody/somebody else

(**f**) **cada día** *o* **vez m.** more and more; **estar de m.** to be unnecessary; **traje uno de m.** I brought a spare one; **es m.** what's more, furthermore; **lo m. posible** as much as possible; **m. bien** rather; **m. o menos** more or less; **m. aún** even more; **¿qué más da?** what's the difference?; **todo lo m.** at the most

(**g**) **por m.** (+ *adj/adv*) (+ *que* (+ *subjunctive*)) however (much), no matter how (much); **por m. fuerte que sea** however strong he may be; **por m. que grites no te oirá nadie** no matter how much you shout nobody will hear you

2 *nm* **los m.** the majority, most people; **sus m. y sus menos** its pros and cons

3 *prep Mat* plus; **dos m. dos** two plus *o* and two

masa *nf* (**a**) mass (**b**) *(de cosas)* bulk, volume; **m. salarial** total wage bill (**c**) *(gente)* mass; **en m.** en masse; **medios de comunicación de masas** mass media (**d**) *Culin* dough (**e**) *Constr* mortar (**f**) *RP (pastelito)* shortcake cookie

masacrar *vt* to massacre

masacre *nf* massacre

masaje *nm* massage; **dar masaje(s) (a)** to massage

masajista *nmf (hombre)* masseur; *(mujer)* masseuse

mascar [44] *vt & vi* to chew, to masticate

máscara *nf* mask; **m. de gas** gas mask; **traje de m.** fancy dress

> 🖉 Observa que la palabra inglesa **mascara** es un falso amigo y no es la traducción de la palabra española **máscara**. En inglés, **mascara** significa "rímel".

mascarilla *nf* (**a**) mask; **m. de oxígeno** oxygen mask (**b**) *Med* face mask (**c**) *(cosmética)* face pack

mascota *nf* mascot

masculino,-a *adj* (**a**) *Zool & Bot* male (**b**) *(de hombre)* male, manly; **una voz masculina** a manly voice (**c**) *(para hombre)* men's; **ropa masculina** men's clothes, menswear (**d**) *Ling* masculine

mascullar *vt* to mumble

masificación *nf* overcrowding

masificado,-a *adj* overcrowded

masilla *nf* putty

masivo,-a *adj* massive

masón *nm* freemason, mason

masonería *nf* freemasonry, masonry

masoquista 1 *adj* masochistic

2 *nmf* masochist

máster *nm* master's degree

masticar [44] *vt* to chew

mástil *nm* (**a**) *(asta)* mast, pole (**b**) *Náut* mast (**c**) *(de guitarra)* neck

mastín *nm* mastiff

masturbación *nf* masturbation

masturbar *vt*, **masturbarse** *vpr* to masturbate

mata *nf* (**a**) *(matorral)* bush, shrub; **m. de pelo** head of hair (**b**) *(ramita)* sprig

matadero *nm* slaughterhouse, abattoir

matador *nm* matador, bullfighter

matadura *nf* sore

matambre *nm Andes, RP* = flank steak rolled with boiled egg, olives and red pepper, which is cooked, then sliced and served cold

matamoscas *nm inv (pala)* fly swat

matanza *nf* slaughter

matar *vt* (**a**) to kill; *Fam* **m. el hambre/el tiempo** to kill one's hunger/the time; *Fam* **que me maten si ...** I'll be damned if ... (**b**) *(cigarro, bebida)* to finish off (**c**) *(sello)* to frank

matasellos *nm inv* postmark

matasuegras *nm inv* party blower

mate¹ *adj (sin brillo)* matt

mate² *nm (en ajedrez)* mate; **jaque m.** checkmate

mate³ *nm (infusión)* maté

matemática *nf*, **matemáticas** *nfpl* mathematics *sing*

matemático,-a 1 *adj* mathematical

2 *nm,f* mathematician

materia *nf* (**a**) matter; **m. prima** raw material (**b**) *(tema)* matter, question; **índice de materias** table of contents (**c**) *Educ (asignatura)* subject

material 1 *adj* material, physical; **daños materiales** damage to property

2 *nm* (**a**) material; **m. escolar/de construcción** teaching/building material *o* materials (**b**) *(equipo)* equipment; **m. de oficina** office equipment

materialista *adj & nmf* materialist

materialmente *adv* physically

maternal *adj* maternal, motherly

maternidad *nf* maternity, motherhood

materno,-a *adj* maternal; **abuelo m.** maternal grandfather; **lengua materna** native *o* mother tongue

mates *nfpl Fam Br* maths *sing*, *US* math

matinal *adj* morning; **televisión m.** breakfast television

matiz *nm* (**a**) *(de color)* shade (**b**) *(de*

palabra) shade of meaning, nuance; **un m. irónico** a touch of irony

matización *nf* **hacer una m.** to add a rider

matizar [40] *vt* (a) *Fig (precisar)* to be more precise o explicit about (b) *Arte* to blend, to harmonize (c) *Fig (palabras, discurso)* to tinge; *(voz)* to vary, to modulate

matón,-ona *nm,f Fam* thug, bully

matorral *nm* brushwood, thicket

matraca *nf (ruido)* rattle; *Fam* **dar la m. a algn** to pester o bother sb

matrero,-a *nm,f Am (bandolero)* bandit, brigand

matriarcado *nm* matriarchy

matrícula *nf* (a) registration; **derechos de m.** registration fee; **m. de honor** distinction; **plazo de m.** registration period (b) *Aut (número) Br* registration number, *US* license number; *(placa) Br* number plate, *US* license plate

matriculación *nf* registration

matricular *vt*, **matricularse** *vpr* to register

matrimonial *adj* matrimonial; **agencia m.** marriage bureau; **enlace m.** wedding; **vida m.** married life

matrimonio *nm* (a) marriage; **m. civil/ religioso** registry office/church wedding; **contraer m.** to marry; **cama de m.** double bed (b) *(pareja casada)* married couple; **el m. y los niños** the couple and their children; **el m. Romero** Mr and Mrs Romero, the Romeros

matriz *nf* (a) *Anat* womb, uterus (b) *Mat* matrix (c) *(de documento) (original)* original, master copy (d) *Téc* mould (e) **casa m.** parent company

matrona *nf* midwife

matutino,-a *adj* morning; **prensa matutina** morning papers

maullar *vi* to miaow

maullido *nm* miaowing, miaow

maxilar *nm* jaw, jawbone

máxima *nf* (a) *Met* maximum temperature (b) *(aforismo)* maxim

máxime *adv* especially, all the more so

máximo,-a 1 *adj* maximum, highest; **la máxima puntuación** the highest score

2 *nm* maximum; **al m.** to the utmost; **como m.** *(como mucho)* at the most; *(lo más tarde)* at the latest

mayo *nm* May

mayonesa *nf* mayonnaise

mayor 1 *adj* (a) *(comparativo) (tamaño)* larger, bigger (**que** than); *(edad)* older, elder; **m. que yo** older than me (b) *(superlativo) (tamaño)* largest, biggest;

(edad) oldest, eldest; **la m. parte** the majority; **la m. parte de las veces** most often (c) *(adulto)* grown-up; **ser m. de edad** to be of age (d) *(maduro)* elderly, mature (e) *(principal)* major, main; *Educ* **colegio m.** hall of residence (f) *Mús* major (g) *Com* **al por m.** wholesale; *Fig (en abundancia)* by the score, galore

2 *nm* (a) *Mil* major (b) **mayores** *(adultos)* grown-ups, adults

mayordomo *nm* butler

mayoreo *nm Andes, Méx Com* wholesale

mayoría *nf* majority; **en su m.** in the main; **la m. de los niños** most children; **m. absoluta/relativa** absolute/relative majority; **m. de edad** majority

mayorista 1 *adj* wholesale

2 *nmf* wholesaler; **precios de m.** wholesale prices

mayoritario,-a *adj* majority; **un gobierno m.** a majority government

mayúscula *nf* capital letter

mayúsculo,-a *adj* (a) *Ling (letra)* capital (b) *(error)* very big, enormous

mazacote *nm* (a) *Culin* solid mass, stodge (b) *(mezcla confusa)* hotchpotch

mazapán *nm* marzipan

mazmorra *nf* dungeon

mazo *nm* mallet

mazorca *nf Agr* cob

me *pron pers* (a) *(objeto directo)* me; **no me mires** don't look at me (b) *(objeto indirecto)* me, to me, for me; **¿me das un caramelo?** will you give me a sweet?; **me lo dio** he gave it to me; **me es difícil hacerlo** it is difficult for me to do it (c) *(pron reflexivo)* myself; **me he cortado** I've cut myself; **me voy/muero** *(no se traduce)* I'm off/dying

meada *nf Fam* piss; **echar una m.** to have a piss

meadero *nm Fam Br* bog, *US* john

meandro *nm* meander

mear *Fam* **1** *vi* to (have a) piss

2 mearse *vpr* to wet oneself; *Fig* **m. de risa** to piss oneself (laughing)

MEC *nm (abr* **Ministerio de Educación y Ciencia)** = Spanish ministry of education and science

mecachis *interj Fam* darn it!, damn it!

mecánica *nf* (a) *(ciencia)* mechanics *sing* (b) *(mecanismo)* mechanism, works

mecánico,-a 1 *adj* mechanical

2 *nm,f* mechanic

mecanismo *nm* mechanism

mecanizar [40] *vt* to mechanize

mecanografía *nf* typewriting, typing

mecanografiar [29] *vt* to type

mecanógrafo,-a *nm,f* typist

mecapal *nm CAm, Méx* = porter's leather harness

mecedora *nf* rocking-chair

mecenas *nmf inv* patron

mecer [49] 1 *vt* to rock

    2 mecerse *vpr* to swing, to rock

mecha *nf* (a) *(de vela)* wick (b) *Mil & Min* fuse; *Fam* **aguantar m.** to grin and bear it (c) *(de pelo)* streak; **hacerse mechas** to have one's hair streaked

mechar *vt (carne)* to lard

mechero *nm* (cigarette) lighter

mechón *nm* (a) *(de pelo)* lock (b) *(de lana)* tuft

medalla 1 *nf* medal

    2 *nmf Dep (campeón)* medallist

medallón *nm* medallion

media *nf* (a) stocking; *Am (calcetín)* sock (b) *(promedio)* average; *Mat* mean; **m. aritmética/geométrica** arithmetic/geometric mean (c) **a medias** *(incompleto)* unfinished; *(entre dos)* half and half; **ir a medias** to go halves

> 🖉 Observa que la palabra inglesa **media** es un falso amigo y no es la traducción de la palabra española **media**. En inglés, **media** significa "medios de comunicación".

mediación *nf* mediation, intervention; **por m. de un amigo** through a friend

mediado,-a *adj* half-full, half-empty; **a mediados de mes/semana** about the middle of the month/week

mediador,-a *nm,f* mediator

medialuna *nf* (a) *(símbolo musulmán)* crescent (b) *Am Culin (pasta)* croissant

mediano,-a *adj* (a) middling, average (b) *(tamaño)* medium-sized

medianoche *nf* midnight

mediante *prep* by means of, with the help of, using; **Dios m.** God willing

mediar [43] *vi* (a) *(intervenir)* to mediate, to intervene; **m. en favor de** o **por algn** to intercede on behalf of sb (b) *(tiempo)* to pass; **mediaron tres semanas** three weeks passed

mediático,-a *adj* media

medicación *nf* medication, medical treatment

medicamento *nm* medicine, medicament

medicina *nf* medicine; **estudiante de m.** medical student, medic

médico,-a 1 *nm,f* doctor; **m. de cabecera** family doctor, general practitioner, GP

    2 *adj* medical

medida *nf* (a) measure; **a (la) m.** *(ropa)* made-to-measure; **a m. que avanzaba** as he advanced; **en gran m.** to a great extent (b) *(dimensión)* measurement (c) *(disposición)* measure; **adoptar** o **tomar medidas** to take steps; **m. represiva** deterrent

medidor *nm Am (contador)* meter

medieval *adj* medieval

medievo *nm* Middle Ages

medio,-a 1 *adj* (a) half; **a m. camino** halfway; **m. kilo** half a kilo; **una hora y media** one and a half hours, an hour and a half (b) *(intermedio)* middle; **a media mañana/tarde** in the middle of the morning/afternoon; **clase media** middle class; **punto m.** middle ground (c) *(normal)* average; **salario m.** average wage

    2 *adv* half; **está m. muerta** she is half dead

    3 *nm* (a) *(mitad)* half (b) *(centro)* middle; **en m. (de)** *(en el centro)* in the middle (of); *(entre dos)* in between (c) **medios de transporte** means of transport; **por m. de ...** by means of ...; **medios económicos** means; **medios de comunicación** (mass) media (d) **m. ambiente** environment (e) *Dep (jugador)* half back

medioambiental *adj* environmental

medioambientalista *nmf* environmentalist

mediocre *adj* mediocre

mediocridad *nf* mediocrity

mediodía *nm* (a) *(hora exacta)* midday, noon (b) *(período aproximado)* early afternoon, lunch-time (c) *(sur)* south

medir [6] 1 *vt* (a) *(distancia, superficie, temperatura)* to measure (b) *(moderar)* to weigh; **mide tus palabras** weigh your words

    2 *vi* to measure, to be; **¿cuánto mides?** how tall are you?; **mide 2 m** he is 2 m tall; **mide 2 m de alto/ancho/largo** it is 2 m high/wide/long

meditar *vt & vi* to meditate, to ponder; **m. sobre algo** to ponder over sth

mediterráneo,-a 1 *adj* Mediterranean

    2 *nm* **el M.** the Mediterranean

medrar *vi* to climb the social ladder

medroso,-a *adj* (a) *(temeroso)* fearful, faint-hearted (b) *(que causa miedo)* frightening

médula *nf* (a) marrow; **m. ósea** bone marrow (b) *Fig (lo más profundo)* marrow, pith; **hasta la m.** to the marrow

medusa *nf* jellyfish

megafonía *nf* public-address system, PA system

megáfono *nm* megaphone

megalito *nm* megalith

megalómano,-a adj megalomaniac

mejicano,-a adj & nm,f Mexican

Méjico n Mexico; **ciudad de M.** Mexico City; **Nuevo M.** New Mexico

mejilla nf cheek

mejillón nm mussel

mejor 1 adj (a) (comparativo) better (**que** than); **el m. de los dos** the better of the two; **es m. no decírselo** it's better not to tell her; **es m. que vayas** you'd better go (**b**) (superlativo) best; **el m. de los tres** the best of the three; **tu m. amiga** your best friend; **lo m.** the best thing

2 adv (a) (comparativo) better (**que** than); **cada vez m.** better and better; **ella conduce m.** she drives better; **m. dicho** or rather; **¡mucho** o **tanto m.!** so much the better! (**b**) (superlativo) best; **es el que m. canta** he is the one who sings the best; **a lo m.** (quizás) perhaps; (ojalá) hopefully

mejora nf improvement

mejorar 1 vt to improve; **m. la red vial** to improve the road system; **m. una marca** o **un récord** to break a record

2 vi to improve, to get better

3 mejorarse vpr to get better; **¡que te mejores!** get well soon!

mejoría nf improvement

melancolía nf melancholy

melancólico,-a adj melancholic, melancholy

melé nf Dep scrum

melena nf (head of) hair; (de león) mane

Melilla n Melilla

melindroso,-a 1 adj affected, fussy, finicky

2 nm,f affected o finicky person

mella nf (a) (hendedura) nick, notch; (en plato, taza etc) chip (**b**) (en dentadura) gap (**c**) Fig impression; **hacer m. en algn** to make an impression on sb

mellado,-a adj (sin dientes) gap-toothed

mellizo,-a adj & nm,f twin

melocotón nm peach

melodía nf melody, tune

melodrama nm melodrama

melón nm (a) (fruto) melon (**b**) Fam (tonto) ninny (**c**) muy Fam **melones** (tetas) boobs

melopea nf Fam **coger** o **agarrar/llevar una m.** to get/be drunk o pissed

meloso,-a adj sweet, honeyed

membrana nf membrane

membresía nf Am membership

membrete nm letterhead

membrillo nm (a) Bot quince; (árbol) quince tree; (dulce) quince preserve o jelly (**b**) Fam (tonto) dimwit

memela nf Méx = thick corn tortilla

memo,-a Fam **1** adj silly, stupid

2 nm,f nincompoop, ninny

memorable adj memorable

memorándum nm (pl **memorándums**) memorandum

memoria nf (a) memory; **aprender/saber algo de m.** to learn/know sth by heart; **irse de la m.** to slip one's mind (**b**) (informe) report, statement; **m. anual** annual report (**c**) (recuerdo) memory, recollection (**d**) **memorias** (biografía) memoirs

memorístico,-a adj acquired by memory

memorizar [40] vt to memorize

menaje nm furniture and furnishing; **m. de cocina** kitchen equipment o utensils

mención nf mention; **m. honorífica** honourable mention

mencionar vt to mention

mendicidad nf begging

mendigar [42] vt & vi to beg

mendigo,-a nm,f beggar

mendrugo nm (a) crust o chunk (of stale bread) (**b**) (tonto) dimwit

mene nm Ven = deposit of oil at surface level

menear 1 vt to shake, to move; (cola) to wag, to waggle; Fam (culo) to wiggle

2 menearse vpr to move, to shake; Fam **una tormenta de no te menees** a hell of a storm; Vulg **meneársela** to wank

meneo nm shake; (de cola) wag, waggle; (de culo) wiggle

menester nm (a) **es m.** it is necessary (**b**) **menesteres** (deberes) jobs

menestra nf vegetable stew

mengano,-a nm,f Fam so-and-so, what's-his- o her-name

menguante adj waning, on the wane; **cuarto m.** last quarter

menguar [45] 1 vt (a) to diminish, to reduce (**b**) (en labor de punto) to decrease

2 vi (a) to diminish, to decrease (**b**) (la luna) to wane

menopausia nf Med menopause

menor 1 adj (a) (comparativo) (de tamaño) smaller (**que** than); (de edad) younger (**que** than); **mal m.** the lesser of two evils; **el m. de los dos** the smaller of the two; **ser m. de edad** to be a minor o under age (**b**) (superlativo) (de tamaño) smallest; (de intensidad) least, slightest; (de edad) youngest; **al m. ruido** at the slightest noise; **el m. de los tres** the youngest of the three; **es la m.** she's the youngest child (**c**) *Más* minor (**d**) *Com* **al por m.** retail

2 *nmf* minor; *Jur* **tribunal de menores** juvenile court

menos 1 *adj* (**a**) *(comparativo)* *(con singular)* less; *(con plural)* fewer; **m. dinero/ leche/ tiempo que** less money/milk/time than; **m. libros/pisos que** fewer books/ flats than; *(con cláusula)* **tiene m. años de lo que parece** he's younger than he looks

(**b**) *(superlativo)* **fui el que perdí m. dinero** I lost the least money

2 *adv* (**a**) **m. de** *(con singular)* less than; *(con plural)* fewer than, less than; **m. de media hora** less than half an hour

(**b**) *(superlativo)* *(con singular)* least; *(con plural)* the fewest; *(con cantidad)* the least; **el m. inteligente de la clase** the least intelligent boy in the class; **ayer fue cuando vinieron m. personas** yesterday was when the fewest people came

3 *(locuciones)* **a m. que** (+ subjunctive) unless; **al** o **por lo m.** at least; **echar a algn de m.** to miss sb; **eso es lo de m.** that's the least of it; **¡m. mal!** just as well!; **nada m. que** no less o no fewer than; **ni mucho m.** far from it

4 *prep* (**a**) but, except; **todo m. eso** anything but that

(**b**) *Mat* minus; **tres m. uno** three minus one

menoscabar *vt* (**a**) *(perjudicar)* to damage (**b**) *Fig (desacreditar)* to discredit

menoscabo *nm* harm, damage; **ir en m. de algo** to be to the detriment of sth

menospreciar [43] *vt* to scorn, to disdain

menosprecio *nm* contempt, scorn, disdain

mensáfono *nm* pager

mensaje *nm* message

mensajero,-a *nm,f* messenger, courier

menso,-a *adj Méx Fam* foolish, stupid

menstruación *nf* menstruation

mensual *adj* monthly; **dos visitas mensuales** two visits a month

mensualidad *nf (pago)* monthly payment; *(sueldo)* monthly salary o wage

menta *nf* (**a**) *Bot* mint (**b**) *(licor)* crème de menthe

mental *adj* mental

mentalidad *nf* mentality; **de m. abierta/ cerrada** open-/narrow-minded

mentalizar [40] 1 *vt (concienciar)* to make aware

2 mentalizarse *vpr* (**a**) *(concienciarse)* to become aware (**b**) *(hacerse a la idea)* to come to terms (**a** with)

mentar [1] *vt* to mention, to name

mente *nf* mind; **se me quedó la m. en blanco** my mind went blank; **m. abierta/ tolerante/cerrada** open/broad/closed mind

mentecato,-a *nm,f* fool, idiot

mentir [5] *vi* to lie, to tell lies

mentira *nf* lie; **aunque parezca m.** strange as it may seem; **parece m.** it is unbelievable

mentiroso,-a 1 *adj* lying

2 *nm,f* liar

mentís *nm* denial

mentón *nm Anat* chin

menú *nm* menu

menudeo *nm Andes, Méx Com* retailing

menudillos *nmpl* giblets

menudo,-a 1 *adj* minute, tiny; *(irónico)* tremendous; **la gente menuda** the little ones; **¡m. lío/susto!** what a mess/fright!

2 *adv* **a m.** often

meñique *adj & nm* **(dedo) m.** little finger

meollo *nm* (**a**) *Fig (quid)* essence (**b**) *(miga)* crumb

mercado *nm* market; **M. Común** Common Market; **m. negro** black market; **m. único** single market; **sacar algo al m.** to put sth on the market

mercadotecnia *nf* marketing

mercancía *nf* commodity, goods

mercante *adj* merchant; **barco/marina m.** merchant ship/navy

mercantil *adj* mercantile, commercial

merced *nf Fml* favour, grace; **a m. de** at the mercy of

mercenario,-a *adj & nm,f* mercenary

mercería *nf Br* haberdasher's (shop), *US* notions store

MERCOSUR *nm* (*abr* **Mercado Común del Sur**) = South American economic community consisting of Argentina, Brazil, Paraguay and Uruguay

mercurio *nm* (**a**) *Quím* mercury, quicksilver (**b**) **M.** Mercury

merecer [33] 1 *vt* (**a**) to deserve (**b**) *(uso impers)* **no merece la pena hacerlo** it's not worth while doing it

2 merecerse *vpr* to deserve

merecido,-a 1 *adj* deserved; **ella lo tiene m.** *(recompensa)* she deserves it; *(castigo)* it serves her right

2 *nm* just deserts

merendar [1] *vt* to have as an afternoon snack, to have for tea

2 *vi* to have an afternoon snack, to have tea

merendero *nm (establecimiento)* tea

room, snack-bar; *(en el campo)* picnic spot

merengue *nm Culin* meringue

merezco *indic pres de* **merecer**

meridiano *nm* meridian

meridional 1 *adj* southern

2 *nmf* southerner

merienda *nf* afternoon snack, tea

mérito *nm* merit, worth; **hacer méritos para algo** to strive to deserve sth

merluza *nf (pez)* hake

merma *nf* decrease, reduction

mermar 1 *vt* to cause to decrease *o* diminish

2 *vi* to decrease, to diminish

3 mermarse *vpr* to decrease, to diminish

mermelada *nf* (a) jam; **m. de fresa** strawberry jam (b) *(de agrios)* marmalade; **m. de naranja** orange marmalade

mero,-a *adj* mere, pure; **por el m. hecho de** through the mere fact of

merodear *vi* to prowl

mes *nm* (a) month; **el m. pasado/que viene** last/next month (b) *(cobro)* monthly salary *o* wages; *(pago)* monthly payment (c) *Fam (menstruación)* period

mesa *nf* (a) table; **poner/recoger la m.** to set/clear the table; *(de despacho, etc)* desk; **m. redonda** round table (b) *(junta directiva)* board, executive; **el presidente de la m.** the chairman; **m. electoral** electoral college

mesada *nf* (a) *Am (dinero)* monthly payment (b) *RP (para adolescentes)* (monthly) pocket money, *US* (monthly) allowance (c) *RP (encimera)* worktop

mesero,-a *nm,f CAm, Col, Méx* waiter, *f* waitress

meseta *nf* plateau, tableland, meseta; **la M.** the plateau of Castile

mesilla *nf* **m. de noche** bedside table

mesón *nm* = old-style tavern

mesonero,-a *nm,f* (a) *(en mesón)* innkeeper (b) *Chile, Ven (camarero)* waiter, *f* waitress

mestizo,-a *adj & nm,f* half-breed, half-caste, mestizo

mesura *nf Fml* moderation, restraint

📖 Observa que la palabra inglesa **measure** es un falso amigo y no es la traducción de la palabra española **mesura**. En inglés, **measure** significa "medida".

---

meta *nf* (a) *(objetivo)* goal, aim, objective (b) *(de carrera)* finish, finishing line (c) *Ftb (portería)* goal

metafísica *nf* metaphysics *sing*

metáfora *nf* metaphor

metal *nm* (a) metal; **metales preciosos** precious metals (b) *(timbre de la voz)* timbre (c) *Mús* brass

metálico,-a 1 *adj* metallic

2 *nm* cash; **pagar en m.** to pay (in) cash

metalizado,-a *adj* metallic

metalúrgico,-a 1 *adj* metallurgical

2 *nm,f* metallurgist

metate *nm Guat, Méx* grinding stone

metedura *nf Fam* **m. de pata** blunder

meteorito *nm* meteorite

meteorología *nf* meteorology

meteorológico,-a *adj* meteorological; **parte m.** weather report *o* forecast

meter 1 *vt* (a) *(poner)* to put (**en** in); *Fig* **m. las narices en algo** to poke one's nose into sth (b) *(comprometer)* to involve (**en** in), to get mixed up (**en** in) (c) *Fam Fig (dar)* to give; **m. un rollo** to go on and on; **m. prisa a algn** to hurry sb up (d) *(hacer)* to make; **m. ruido** to make a noise

2 meterse *vpr* (a) *(entrar)* to go *o* come in, to get into (b) *(estar)* to be; **¿dónde te habías metido?** where have you been (all this time)? (c) *(entrometerse)* to meddle (d) **m. con algn** *(en broma)* to get at sb

meterete *nmf RP Fam* meddler

metete *nmf Andes, CAm Fam* meddler, busybody

metiche *nmf Méx, Ven Fam* meddler

meticuloso,-a *adj* meticulous

metido,-a *adj Fam* **estar muy m. en algo** to be deeply involved in sth; **m. en años** getting on (in years)

metódico,-a *adj* methodical

método *nm* (a) method (b) *Educ* course

metodología *nf* methodology

metomentodo *nmf inv Fam* busybody

metralleta *nf* submachine-gun

métrico,-a *adj* metric; **sistema m.** metric system

metro *nm* (a) *(medida)* metre (b) *(tren) Br* underground, *Br* tube, *US* subway

metrópoli *nf* metropolis

metropolitano,-a 1 *adj* metropolitan

2 *nm Fml Br* underground, *Br* tube, *US* subway

mexicano,-a *adj & nm,f* Mexican

México *n* Mexico

mezcla *nf* (a) *(acción)* mixing, blending; *Rad & Cin* mixing (b) *(producto)* mixture, blend

mezclar 1 *vt* (a) *(dos o más cosas)* to mix, to blend (b) *(desordenar)* to mix up (c) *(involucrar)* to involve, to mix up

2 mezclarse *vpr* (a) *(cosas)* to get mixed up; *(gente)* to mingle (b) *(relacionarse)* to get involved (**con** with)

mezcolanza *nf Fml* strange mixture, hotch-potch

mezquino,-a *adj* (**a**) *(persona)* mean, stingy (**b**) *(sueldo)* miserable

mezquita *nf* mosque

m/g *(abr miligramo)* mg

mi¹ *adj* my; **mi casa/trabajo** my house/job; **mis cosas/libros** my things/books

mi² *nm Mús* E; **mi menor** E minor

mí *pron pers* me; **a mí me dio tres** he gave me three; **compra otro para mí** buy one for me too; **por mí mismo** just by myself

mía *adj & pron pos f ver* **mío**

miaja *nf* crumb; *Fig* bit

miche *nm Ven (aguardiente)* = cane spirit flavoured with herbs and spices

michelín *nm Fam* spare tyre

mico *nm* (**a**) *Zool* long-tailed monkey (**b**) *Fam (pequeñajo)* little kid

micra *nf (medida)* micron

micro 1 *nm Fam* mike, microphone
 2 *nm o nf Arg, Chile (microbús)* minibus

microbio *nm* microbe

microbús *nm* (**a**) *(autobús)* minibus (**b**) *Méx (taxi)* (collective) taxi

microchip *nm* (*pl* **microchips**) *Informát* microchip

microficha *nf* microfiche

micrófono *nm* microphone

microonda *nf* **un (horno) microondas** a microwave (oven)

microscopio *nm* microscope

miedica *nmf Fam* scaredy-cat

miedo *nm (pavor)* fear; *(temor)* apprehension; **una película de m.** a horror film; **tener m. de algn/algo** to be afraid of sb/sth; *Fam* **lo pasamos de m.** we had a fantastic time; **un calor de m.** sizzling heat

miedoso,-a *adj* fearful

miel *nf* honey; **luna de m.** honeymoon

miembro *nm* (**a**) *(socio)* member; **estado m.** member state (**b**) *Anat* limb; **m. viril** penis

mientras 1 *conj* (**a**) *(al mismo tiempo que)* while (**b**) *(durante el tiempo que)* when, while; **m. viví en Barcelona** when I lived in Barcelona (**c**) **m. que** *(por el contrario)* whereas (**d**) *Fam (cuanto más)* **m. más/menos ...** the more/less ...
 2 *adv* **m. (tanto)** meanwhile, in the meantime

miércoles *nm inv* Wednesday; **M. de Ceniza** Ash Wednesday

mierda *nf Vulg* (**a**) shit; **ese libro es una m.** that book is crap; **¡vete a la m.!** piss off! (**b**) *Fig (porquería)* dirt, filth (**c**) *(borrachera)* bender

miga *nf (de pan etc)* crumb; *Fig* **hacer buenas migas con algn** to get on well with sb

migaja *nf* (**a**) *(de pan)* crumb (**b**) *Fig* bit, scrap (**c**) **migajas** *(del pan)* crumbs; *Fig* leftovers

migra *nf Méx Fam Pey* = US police border patrol

migraña *nf Med* migraine

mil *adj & nm* thousand; **m. pesetas** a *o* one thousand pesetas

milagro *nm* miracle

milagroso,-a *adj* miraculous

milanesa *nf (de ternera)* Wiener schnitzel, breaded veal escalope

milano *nm Orn* kite; **m. real** red kite

milenario,-a 1 *adj* millenarian, millennial
 2 *nm* millennium

milenio *nm* millennium

milésimo,-a *adj & nm,f* thousandth

mili *nf Fam* military *o* national service; **hacer la m.** to do one's military service

milicia *nf (ejército)* militia; *(servicio militar)* military service

milico *nm Andes, RP Fam Pey (militar)* soldier; **los milicos tomaron el poder** the military took power

milímetro *nm* millimetre

militar 1 *adj* military
 2 *nm* military man, soldier
 3 *vi Pol (en un partido)* to be a member

milla *nf* mile

millar *nm* thousand

millón *nm* million

millonario,-a *adj & nm,f* millionaire

milpa *nf CAm, Méx* cornfield

mimar *vt* to spoil, to pamper

> 🖉 Observa que el verbo inglés **to mime** es un falso amigo y no es la traducción del verbo español **mimar**. En inglés, **to mime** significa "representar con gestos".

mimbre *nm* wicker

mimetismo *nm* mimicry

mímica *nf* mimicry

mimo *nm* (**a**) *(delicadeza)* care (**b**) *Fig (zalamería)* pampering (**c**) *Teatro (actor)* mime

mina *nf* (**a**) mine; **ingeniero de minas** mining engineer (**b**) *(explosivo)* mine; **campo de minas** minefield (**c**) *(de lápiz)* lead; **lápiz de m.** propelling pencil (**d**) *Fig (ganga)* gold mine

minar *vt* (**a**) *Mil & Min* to mine (**b**) *Fig (desgastar)* to undermine

mineral 1 *adj* mineral
 2 *nm* ore

minería *nf* (a) *Min* mining (b) *Ind* mining industry

minero,-a 1 *nm,f* miner
2 *adj* mining

miniatura *nf* miniature

minifalda *nf* miniskirt

minifundio *nm* smallholding

mínima *nf* minimum temperature

minimizar *vt* to minimize

mínimo,-a 1 *adj* (a) (*muy pequeño*) minute, tiny (b) *Mat & Téc* minimum, lowest; **m. común múltiplo** lowest common denominator
2 *nm* minimum; **como m.** at least; **ni lo más m.** not in the least

minipimer® *nm o nf* liquidizer, blender

ministerio *nm* (a) *Pol Br* ministry, *US* department (b) *Rel* ministry

ministro,-a *nm,f* (a) *Pol* minister; **primer m.** Prime Minister (b) *Rel* minister

minoría *nf* minority; *Jur* **m. de edad** minority

minoritario,-a *adj* minority

minucioso,-a *adj* (a) (*persona*) meticulous (b) (*informe, trabajo etc*) minute, detailed

minúsculo,-a *adj* minuscule, minute; **letra minúscula** lower-case *o* small letter

minusválido,-a 1 *adj* handicapped, disabled
2 *nm,f* handicapped person, disabled person

minuta *nf* (a) (*cuenta*) lawyer's bill (b) (*menú*) menu (c) *RP* (*comida*) one-plate meal

minutero *nm* minute hand

minuto *nm* minute

mío,-a 1 *adj pos* of mine; **un amigo m.** a friend of mine; **no es asunto m.** it is none of my business
2 *pron pos* mine; **ese libro es m.** that book is mine; **lo m. es el tenis** tennis is my strong point; *Fam* **los míos** my people *o* folks

miope *nmf* myopic *o* short-sighted person

miopía *nf* myopia, short-sightedness

mira *nf* (a) *Téc* sight (b) *Fig* (*objetivo*) aim, target; **con miras a** with a view to; **amplitud de miras** broad-mindedness

mirada *nf* look; **lanzar** *o* **echar una m. a** to glance at; **levantar la m.** to raise one's eyes; **m. fija** stare

mirador *nm* (a) (*lugar con vista*) viewpoint (b) (*balcón*) bay window, windowed balcony

mirar 1 *vt* (a) to look at (b) (*observar*) to watch (c)·**m. por algn/algo** (*cuidar*) to look after sb/sth (d) (*procurar*) to see;

mira que no le pase nada see that nothing happens to him
2 *vi* (*dar a*) to look, to face; **la casa mira al sur** the house faces south

mirilla *nf* spyhole, peephole

mirlo *nm* blackbird

misa *nf* mass

misántropo,-a 1 *adj* misanthropic
2 *nm,f* misanthrope, misanthropist

miscelánea *nf Méx* (*tienda*) = small general store

miserable 1 *adj* (a) (*mezquino*) (*persona*) despicable; (*sueldo etc*) miserable (b) (*pobre*) wretched, poor; **una vida m.** a wretched life
2 *nmf* (a) (*mezquino*) miser (b) (*canalla*) wretch

miseria *nf* (a) (*pobreza extrema*) extreme poverty (b) (*insignificancia*) pittance; **ganar una m.** to earn next to nothing (c) (*tacañería*) miserliness, meanness

misericordia *nf* mercy, compassion

mísero,-a *adj* miserable, wretched

misil *nm* missile; **m. tierra-aire** surface-to-air missile

misión *nf* mission; **m. cumplida** mission accomplished

misionero,-a *nm,f* missionary

mismísimo,-a *adj superl Fam* (a) (*preciso*) very; **en el m. centro** right in the centre (b) (*en persona*) in person

mismo,-a 1 *adj* (a) same (b) (*uso enfático*) yo m. I myself; **aquí m.** right here
2 *pron* same; **es el m. de ayer** it's the same one as yesterday; **estamos en las mismas** we're back to square one; **lo m.** the same (thing); **dar** *o* **ser lo m.** to make no difference; **por eso m.** that is why; **por uno** *o* **sí m.** by oneself
3 *adv* (a) (*por ejemplo*) for instance; **que venga algn, Juan m.** ask one of them to come, Juan, for instance (b) **así m.** likewise

misógino,-a 1 *adj* misogynous
2 *nm,f* misogynist

miss *nf* beauty queen

míster *nm Ftb* coach, trainer

misterio *nm* mystery

misterioso,-a *adj* mysterious

mitad *nf* (a) half; **a m. de camino** halfway there; **a m. de precio** half-price (b) (*centro*) middle; **en la m. del primer acto** halfway through the first act; *Fam* **eso me parte por la m.** that really screws things up for me

mítico,-a *adj* mythical

mitigar [42] *vt Fml* to mitigate, to palliate; (*luz*) to reduce

mitin *nm Pol* meeting, rally

mito *nm* myth

mitología *nf* mythology

mitote *nm Méx Fam (alboroto)* racket

mixto,-a *adj* mixed

moai *nm* = statue of giant head found on Easter Island

mobiliario *nm* furniture

moca *nm* mocha

mochila *nf* rucksack, backpack

mochuelo *nm Zool* little owl

moción *nf* motion; **m. de censura** vote of censure

moco *nm* snot; **sonarse los mocos** to blow one's nose

mocoso,-a *nm,f Fam* brat

moda *nf* (a) fashion; **a la m., de m.** in fashion; **pasado de m.** old-fashioned (b) *(furor pasajero)* craze

modales *nmpl* manners

modalidad *nf* form, category; *Com* **m. de pago** method of payment; *Dep* **m. deportiva** sport

modelar *vt* to model, to shape

modélico,-a *adj* model

modelo 1 *adj inv & nm* model

   2 *nmf* (fashion) model; **desfile de modelos** fashion show

módem *nm Informát* modem; **m. fax** fax modem

moderación *nf* moderation

moderado,-a *adj* moderate; **un m. aumento de temperatura** a mild increase in temperature

moderador,-a *nm,f* chairperson; *(hombre)* chairman; *(mujer)* chairwoman

moderar 1 *vt* (a) to moderate; *(velocidad)* to reduce (b) *(debate)* to chair

   2 moderarse *vpr* to be moderate

modernizar [40] *vt*, **modernizarse** *vpr* to modernize

moderno,-a *adj* modern

modestia *nf* modesty; **m. aparte** without wishing to be immodest

modesto,-a *adj* modest

módico,-a *adj* moderate; **una módica suma** a modest *o* small sum

modificar [44] *vt* to modify

modismo *nm* idiom

modisto,-a *nm,f* (a) *(diseñador)* fashion designer (b) *(sastre) (hombre)* couturier; *(mujer)* couturière

modo *nm* (a) *(manera)* way, manner; **m. de empleo** instructions for use; = **manera** (b) **modos** manners (c) *Ling* mood

modorra *nf (somnolencia)* drowsiness

modoso,-a *adj* (a) *(educado)* well-behaved (b) *(recatado)* modest

modulación *nf* modulation

modular *vt* to modulate

módulo *nm* module

mofa *nf* mockery; **en tono de m.** in a gibing tone

mofarse *vpr* to laugh (**de** at), to make fun (**de** of)

moflete *nm* chubby cheek

mogollón *nm Fam* (a) **m. de** loads of; **me gusta un m.** I like it loads (b) *(confusión)* commotion; *(ruido)* racket

moho *nm* (a) *Bot* mould (b) *(de metales)* rust

mohoso,-a *adj* (a) mouldy (b) *(oxidado)* rusty

mojado,-a *adj (empapado)* wet; *(húmedo)* damp

mojar 1 *vt* (a) to wet; *(humedecer)* to damp; **m. pan en la leche** to dip *o* dunk bread in one's milk (b) *muy Fam* **mojarla** to have it off

   2 mojarse *vpr* to get wet

mojón *nm* (a) **m. kilométrico** ≃ milestone (b) *muy Fam (mierda)* shit

moka *nm* mocha

molar 1 *vi Fam* **me mola cantidad** I really love it, it's brilliant

   2 *adj & nm Anat* molar

molcajete *nm Méx* mortar

molde *nm* mould; **letras de m.** printed letters; **pan de m.** ≃ sliced bread

moldeador *nm (del pelo)* wave

moldear *vt* to mould

mole 1 *nf* mass, bulk

   2 *nm Méx* (a) *(salsa)* = thick, cooked chilli sauce (b) *(guiso)* = dish served in "mole" sauce

molécula *nf* molecule

moler [4] *vt* (a) *(triturar)* to grind (b) **m. a algn a golpes** to beat sb up

molestar 1 *vt* (a) *(incomodar)* to disturb, to bother (b) *Fml* to bother; **¿le molestaría esperar fuera?** would you mind waiting outside? (c) *(causar malestar a)* to hurt

   2 molestarse *vpr* (a) *(tomarse la molestia)* to bother (b) *(ofenderse)* to take offence, to get upset

molestia *nf* (a) bother; **no es ninguna m.** it is no trouble at all; **perdone las molestias** forgive the inconvenience (b) *Med (dolor)* trouble, slight pain

molesto,-a *adj* (a) *(irritante)* annoying, upsetting (b) **estar m. con algn** *(enfadado)* to be annoyed *o* upset with sb

molinillo *nm* grinder

molino *nm* mill; **m. de agua** watermill; **m. de viento** windmill

mollera *nf Fam* brains; **duro de m.** *(tonto)* dense, thick; *(testarudo)* pigheaded

molón,-ona *adj Fam* flashy, showy

momentáneo,-a *adj* momentary

momento *nm* (a) *(instante)* moment; **al m.** at once; **por momentos** by the minute (b) *(periodo)* time; **de m.** for the time being; **en cualquier m.** at any time

momia *nf* mummy

mona *nf Fam* **coger una m.** to get drunk; **dormir la m.** to sleep it off

Mónaco *n* Monaco

monada *nf Fam* ¡**qué m.!** how cute!

monaguillo *nm Rel* altar boy

monarca *nmf* monarch

monarquía *nf* monarchy

monasterio *nm Rel* monastery

monda *nf* (a) *(piel)* peel, skin (b) *Fam* **ser la m.** *(divertido)* to be a scream

mondadientes *nm inv* toothpick

mondar 1 *vt* to peel

2 mondarse *upr Fam* **m. (de risa)** to laugh one's head off

moneda *nf* (a) *(pieza)* coin; **m. suelta** small change; **acuñar m.** to mint money (b) *Fin* currency; **m. única** single currency

monedero *nm* purse

monería *nf Fam* = **monada**

monetario,-a *adj* monetary

mongol 1 *adj* Mongolian

2 *nmf (persona)* Mongolian

3 *nm (idioma)* Mongolian

mongólico,-a *Med* **1** *adj* Down's syndrome

2 *nm,f* **ser m.** to have Down's syndrome

monigote *nm* (a) *Pey (persona)* wimp (b) *(dibujo)* rough drawing *o* sketch (of a person)

monitor,-a *nm,f* monitor; *(profesor)* instructor

monja *nf* nun

monje *nm* monk

mono,-a 1 *nm* (a) *(animal)* monkey (b) *(prenda) (de trabajo)* boiler suit, overalls; *(de vestir)* catsuit; *Ven (de deporte)* track *o* jogging suit (c) *Fam (droga)* cold turkey

2 *adj Fam (bonito)* pretty, cute

monobloque *nm Arg* tower block

monográfico,-a 1 *adj* monographic

2 *nm* monograph

monólogo *nm* monologue

monopolio *nm* monopoly

monopolizar [40] *vt* to monopolize

monótono,-a *adj* monotonous

monserga *nf Fam* drag

monstruo *nm* (a) *(monster)* (b) *(genio)* genius

monstruoso,-a *adj* (a) *(repugnante)* monstrous (b) *(enorme)* massive, huge

monta *nf Fig* **de poca m.** of little importance

montacargas *nm inv Br* service lift, *US* freight elevator

montado,-a 1 *adj (nata)* whipped

2 *nm* sandwich

montador,-a *nm,f* (a) *(operario)* fitter (b) *Cin & TV* film editor (c) *Teatro* producer

montaje *nm* (a) *Téc (instalación)* fitting; *(ensamblaje)* assembling; **cadena de m.** assembly line (b) *Cin* editing and mounting (c) *Teatro* staging (d) *Fot* montage (e) *Fam (farsa)* farce

montante *nm* (a) *Fin* amount (b) *(de puerta)* post

montaña *nf* mountain; **m. rusa** big dipper

montañismo *nm* mountaineering

montañoso,-a *adj* mountainous

montar 1 *vi* (a) *(subirse)* to get in; *(en bici, a caballo)* to ride (b) *Fin (ascender)* **m. a** to amount to, to come to

2 *vt* (a) *(colocar)* to put on (b) *(máquina etc)* to assemble, *(negocio)* to set up, to start (c) *Culin* to whip (d) *Cin & Fot (película)* to edit, to mount; *(fotografía)* to mount (e) *Teatro (obra)* to stage, to mount (f) *Zool (cubrir)* to mount

3 montarse *upr* (a) *(subirse)* to get on; *(en coche)* to get in (en to) (b) *Fam (armarse)* to break out; *Fam* **montárselo bien** to have things (nicely) worked out *o* set up

monte *nm* (a) *(montaña)* mountain; *(con nombre propio)* mount; **de m.** wild (b) **el m.** *(zona)* the hills

montés *adj (animal)* wild

monto *nm* total

montón *nm* heap, pile; **un m. de** a load of; *Fam* **me gusta un m.** I really love it; *Fam* **del m.** run-of-the-mill, nothing special

montura *nf* (a) *(cabalgadura)* mount (b) *(de gafas)* frame

monumento *nm* monument

monzón *nm* monsoon

moño *nm* (a) *(de pelo)* bun (b) *Am (lazo)* bow

MOPU *nm (abr* **Ministerio de Obras Públicas y Urbanismo)** = Spanish ministry of public works and town planning

moquear *vi* to have a runny nose

moqueta *nf* fitted carpet

mora *nf (zarzamora)* blackberry

morado,-a 1 *adj* purple; *Fam* **pasarlas**

moradas to have a tough time; **ponerse m.** to stuff oneself
2 *nm* purple
moral 1 *adj* moral
2 *nf* (**a**) *(ética)* morals (**b**) *(ánimo)* morale, spirits; **levantar la m. a algn** to raise sb's spirits
moraleja *nf* moral
moralista 1 *adj* moralistic
2 *nmf* moralist
moratoria *nf* moratorium
morbo *nm Fam (interés malsano)* morbid curiosity
morboso,-a *adj (malsano)* morbid
morcilla *nf Br* black pudding, *US* blood sausage; *Fam* **que le den m.** he can drop dead for all I care
mordaz *adj* biting
mordaza *nf* gag
mordedura *nf* bite
morder [4] *vt* to bite; **me ha mordido** it has bitten me; *Fig* **m. el anzuelo** to take the bait
mordida *nf CAm, Méx (soborno)* bribe
mordisco *nm* bite
mordisquear *vt* to nibble (at)
moreno,-a 1 *adj* (**a**) *(pelo)* dark-haired; *(piel)* dark-skinned (**b**) *(bronceado)* tanned; **ponerse m.** to get a suntan; **pan/azúcar m.** brown bread/sugar
2 *nm,f (persona) (de pelo)* dark-haired person; *(de piel)* dark-skinned person
morera *nf Bot* white mulberry
moretón *nm Fam* bruise
morfina *nf* morphine
morfinómano,-a 1 *nm,f* morphine addict
2 *adj* addicted to morphine
morgue *nf Am* morgue
moribundo,-a *adj & nm,f* moribund
morir [7] **1** *vi* to die; **m. de frío/hambre/cáncer** to die of cold/hunger/cancer; **m. de amor** *o* **pena** to die from a broken heart
2 morirse *vpr* to die; **m. de hambre** to starve to death; *Fig* to be starving; **m. de aburrimiento** to be bored to death; **m. de ganas (de hacer algo)** to be dying (to do sth); **m. de risa** to die laughing
mormón,-ona *adj & nm,f* Mormon
moro,-a *nm,f* (**a**) *Hist* Moor; *Fam* **no hay moros en la costa** the coast is clear (**b**) *Pey (musulmán)* Muslim; *(árabe)* Arab
morocho,-a 1 *adj* (**a**) *Andes, RP (moreno)* dark-haired (**b**) *Ven (gemelo)* twin
2 *nm,f* (**a**) *Andes, RP (moreno)* dark-haired person (**b**) *Ven (gemelo)* twin
moronga *nf CAm, Méx Br* black pudding, *US* blood sausage

moroso,-a *nm,f* bad debtor

> 🖉 Observa que la palabra inglesa **morose** es un falso amigo y no es la traducción de la palabra española **moroso**. En inglés, **morose** significa "hosco, huraño".

morral *nm* (**a**) *(para pienso)* nosebag (**b**) *Mil* haversack; *(de cazador)* game bag
morralla *nf* (**a**) *(cosas sin valor)* rubbish, junk (**b**) *(chusma)* scum
morrear *vt,* **morrearse** *vpr Fam* to snog
morreo *nm Fam* snog
morro *nm* (**a**) *(de animal) (hocico)* snout (**b**) *Fam (de persona)* mouth, (thick) lips; **caerse de m.** to fall flat on one's face; **por los morros** without so much as a by-your-leave; *Fam* **¡vaya m.!** what a cheek! (**c**) *(de coche)* nose
morrón *adj* **pimiento m.** (fleshy) red pepper
morsa *nf* walrus
morse *nm* Morse
mortadela *nf* mortadella
mortaja *nf* shroud
mortal 1 *adj* (**a**) mortal (**b**) *(mortífero)* fatal; **un accidente m.** a fatal accident
2 *nmf* mortal
mortalidad *nf* mortality; **índice de m.** death rate
mortandad *nf* death toll
mortecino,-a *adj* colourless
mortero *nm Culin & Mil* mortar
mortífero,-a *adj* deadly, lethal
mortificar [44] *vt* to mortify
mortuorio,-a *adj* death; **lecho m.** death-bed
moruno,-a *adj* Moorish; *Culin* **pincho m.** ≃ kebab
mosaico *nm* mosaic
mosca *nf* fly; **peso m.** flyweight; *Fam* **estar m.** *(suspicaz)* to be suspicious; *(borracho)* to be pissed; *Fam* **por si las moscas** just in case; *Fam* **¿qué m. te ha picado?** what's biting you?
moscada *adj* **nuez m.** nutmeg
moscardón *nm* (**a**) *(insecto)* blowfly (**b**) *Fam (pesado)* pest
moscovita *adj & nmf* Muscovite
Moscú *n* Moscow
mosquearse *vpr Fam* (**a**) *(enfadarse)* to get cross (**b**) *(sospechar)* to smell a rat
mosquetero *nm Hist* musketeer
mosquitero *nm (red)* mosquito net
mosquito *nm* mosquito
mostaza *nf Bot & Culin* mustard
mosto *nm (bebida)* grape juice; *(del vino)* must

mostrador *nm* (**a**) *(de tienda)* counter (**b**) *(de bar)* bar

mostrar 1 *vt* to show; **muéstramelo** show it to me

2 mostrarse *vpr* to be; **se mostró muy comprensiva** she was very understanding

mostrenco,-a 1 *nm,f* (**a**) *(ignorante)* blockhead (**b**) *(gordo)* very fat person

2 *adj* *(sin dueño)* ownerless; **bienes mostrencos** ownerless property

mota *nf* speck

mote[1] *nm* *(apodo)* nickname; **poner m. a algn** to give sb a nickname

mote[2] *nm Andes* stewed maize *o US* corn

moteado,-a *adj* dotted

motín *nm* *(amotinamiento)* mutiny; *(disturbio)* riot

motivación *nf* motivation

motivar *vt* (**a**) *(causar)* to cause; to give rise to (**b**) *(inducir)* to motivate

motivo *nm* (**a**) *(causa)* reason; *(usu pl)* grounds; **con este** *o* **tal m.** for this reason; **con m. de** on the occasion of; **sin m.** for no reason at all; **bajo ningún m.** under no circumstances (**b**) *Arte & Mús* motif, leitmotiv

moto *nf Aut* motorbike; **m. náutica** *o* **acuática** jet ski

motocicleta *nf* motorbike

motociclismo *nm* motorcycling

motociclista *nmf* motorcyclist

motocross *nm* motocross

motoneta *nf Am* (motor) scooter

motonetista *nmf Am* scooter rider

motor,-a 1 *nm* (**a**) *(grande)* engine; *(pequeño)* motor; **m. de reacción** jet engine; **m. de explosión** internal combustion engine; **m. eléctrico** electric motor; *Informát* **m. de busca** search engine

2 *adj Téc* motive

motora *nf* motorboat

motorista *nmf* motorcyclist

motorizar [40] **1** *vt* to motorize

2 motorizarse *vpr Fam* to get oneself a car *o* motorbike

motosierra *nf* power saw

motriz *adj* **fuerza m.** motive power

movedizo,-a *adj* **arenas movedizas** quicksand

mover [4] **1** *vt* (**a**) to move; **m. algo de su sitio** to move sth out of its place (**b**) *(hacer funcionar)* to drive; **el motor mueve el coche** the engine drives the car

2 moverse *vpr* (**a**) to move (**b**) *Fam (gestionar)* to do everything possible (**c**) *(darse prisa)* to hurry up; **¡muévete!** get a move on!

movida *nf Fam* **hay mucha m.** there's a lot going on

movido,-a *adj* (**a**) *Fot* blurred (**b**) *(ocupado)* busy

móvil 1 *adj* mobile; **teléfono m.** mobile phone; *TV & Rad* **unidad m.** outside broadcast unit

2 *nm* (**a**) *(de delito)* motive (**b**) *(teléfono)* mobile

movilización *nf* mobilization

movilizar [40] *vt* to mobilize

movimiento *nm* (**a**) *(gen)* movement; *Fís & Téc* motion; **(poner algo) en m.** (to set sth) in motion; **m. sísmico** earth tremor (**b**) *(actividad)* activity (**c**) *Com & Fin (entradas y salidas)* operations (**d**) *Hist* **el M.** the Falangist Movement

moviola *nf Cin & TV* (**a**) *(cámara)* editing projector (**b**) *(repetición)* action replay

moza *nf* lass, young girl

mozo,-a *nm,f* (**a**) *(niño)* young boy, young lad; *(niña)* young girl (**b**) *(de estación)* porter (**c**) *Mil* conscript (**d**) *Perú, RP (camarero)* waiter, *f* waitress

mucamo,-a *nm,f Andes, RP (en hotel)* chamberperson, *f* chambermaid

muchacha *nf* girl

muchachada *nf Am* group of youngsters

muchacho *nm* boy

muchedumbre *nf (de gente)* crowd

mucho,-a 1 *adj* (**a**) *sing (usu en frases afirmativas)* a lot of, lots of; *(usu en frases negativas)* much; **m. tiempo** a long time; **tengo m. sueño/mucha sed** I am very sleepy/thirsty; **hay m. tonto suelto** there are lots of idiots around; **¿bebes m. café? – no, no m.** do you drink a lot of coffee? – no, not much

(**b**) *(demasiado)* **es m. coche para mí** this car is a bit too much for me

(**c**) **muchos,-as** *(usu en frases afirmativas)* a lot of, lots of; *(usu en frases neg)* many; **tiene muchos años** he is very old

2 *pron* (**a**) a lot, a great deal; **¿cuánta leche queda? – mucha** how much milk is there left? – a lot

(**b**) **muchos,-as** a lot, lots, many; **¿cuántos libros tienes? – muchos** how many books have you got? – lots *o* a lot; **muchos creemos que ...** many of us believe that ...

3 *adv* (**a**) a lot, very much; **lo siento m.** I'm very sorry; **como m.** at the most; **con m.** by far; **m. antes/después** long before/after; **¡ni m. menos!** no way!; **por m. (que)** *(+ subjunctive)* however much

(**b**) *(tiempo)* **hace m. que no viene por aquí** he has not been to see us for a long time (**c**) (a menudo) often; **vamos m. al cine** we go to the cinema quite often

muda nf (de ropa) change of clothes

mudanza nf move; **estar de m.** to be moving; **camión de m.** removal van

mudar 1 vt (**a**) (ropa) to change (**b**) (plumas, pelo) to moult; (piel) to shed, to slough

2 mudarse vpr **m. de casa/ropa** to move house/to change one's clothes

mudo,-a 1 adj (**a**) (que no habla) dumb; **cine m.** silent films (**b**) Fig (callado) speechless

2 nm,f mute

mueble 1 nm piece of furniture; **muebles** furniture; **con/sin muebles** furnished/unfurnished; **m. bar** cocktail cabinet

2 adj movable

mueca nf (**a**) (de burla) mocking face; **hacer muecas** to pull faces (**b**) (de dolor, asco) grimace

muela nf (**a**) Anat molar; **dolor de muelas** toothache; **m. del juicio** wisdom tooth (**b**) Téc (de molino) millstone

muelle¹ nm spring

muelle² nm Náut dock

muermo nm Fam (tedio) boredom; (rollo) drag

muerte nf death; **m. natural** natural death; **dar m. a algn** to kill sb; **odiar a algn a m.** to loathe sb; Fam **de mala m.** lousy, rotten; Fam **un susto de m.** the fright of one's life

muerto,-a 1 adj dead; **caer m.** to drop dead; **m. de hambre** starving; **m. de frío** frozen to death; **m. de miedo** scared stiff; **m. de risa** laughing one's head off; **horas muertas** spare time; Aut **(en) punto m.** (in) neutral

2 nm,f (**a**) (difunto) dead person; **hacerse el m.** to pretend to be dead; Fam **cargar con el m.** to do the dirty work (**b**) (víctima) fatality; **hubo dos muertos** two (people) died

muesca nf notch

muestra nf (**a**) (espécimen) sample, specimen (**b**) (modelo a copiar) model (**c**) (prueba, señal) sign; **dar muestras de** to show signs of; **m. de cariño/respeto** token of affection/respect; **una m. más de ...** yet another example of ...

muestral adj **error m.** margin of error

muestreo nm sampling

mugido nm (de vaca) moo; (de toro) bellow

mugir [57] vi (vaca) to moo, to low; (toro) to bellow

mugre nf filth

mugriento,-a adj filthy

mujer nf (**a**) woman; **dos mujeres** two women; **m. de la limpieza** cleaner; **m. de su casa** houseproud woman (**b**) (esposa) wife; **su futura m.** his bride-to-be

mujeriego 1 adj woman-chasing

2 nm womanizer, woman chaser

muleta nf (**a**) (prótesis) crutch (**b**) Taurom muleta

muletilla nf pet word o phrase

mullido,-a adj soft

mulo nm mule

multa nf fine; Aut ticket

multar vt to fine

multi- pref multi-

multicolor adj multicoloured

multicopista nf duplicator

multilateral adj multilateral

multinacional adj & nf multinational

múltiple adj (**a**) multiple; **accidente m.** pile-up (**b**) **múltiples** (muchos) many

multiplicación nf Mat multiplication

multiplicar [44] **1** vt & vi to multiply (**por** by)

2 multiplicarse vpr (reproducirse, aumentar) to multiply

múltiplo,-a adj & nm multiple

multirriesgo adj inv **póliza m.** multiple risk policy

multitud nf (**a**) (de personas) crowd (**b**) (de cosas) multitude

mundano,-a adj worldly

> 🖋 Observa que la palabra inglesa **mundane** es un falso amigo y no es la traducción de la palabra española **mundano**. En inglés, **mundane** significa "prosaico".

mundial 1 adj worldwide; **campeón m.** world champion; **de fama m.** world-famous

2 nm world championship

mundialmente adv **m. famoso** world-famous, famous worldwide

mundo nm world; **todo el m.** everyone; **correr** o **ver m.** to travel widely; **nada del otro m.** nothing special; **el otro m.** the hereafter

munición nf ammunition

municipal 1 adj municipal

2 nm (municipal) policeman

municipio nm (**a**) (territorio) municipality (**b**) (ayuntamiento) town council

muñeca nf (**a**) wrist (**b**) (juguete, muchacha) doll (**c**) Andes, RP Fam **tener m.** (enchufe) to have friends in high places; (habilidad) to have the knack

muñeco nm (juguete) (little) boy doll; **m. de trapo** rag doll; **m. de nieve** snowman

muñequera nf wristband

muñón *nm Anat* stump

muralla *nf* wall

Murcia *n* Murcia

murciélago *nm Zool* bat

murmullo *nm* murmur

murmuración *nf* gossip

murmurar *vi* (a) *(criticar)* to gossip (b) *(susurrar)* to whisper; *(refunfuñar)* to grumble (c) *Fig (río)* to murmur

muro *nm* wall

murrio,-a *adj Fam* sad, blue

musa *nf* muse

musaraña *nf Fam* **estar mirando a** *o* **pensando en las musarañas** to be day-dreaming *o* in the clouds

musculatura *nf* musculature; **desarrollar la m.** to develop one's muscles

músculo *nm* muscle

musculoso,-a *adj* muscular

museo *nm* museum; **m. de arte** *o* **pintura** art gallery

musgo *nm* moss

música *nf* music; **m. clásica** classical music; **m. de fondo** background music

musical 1 *adj* musical

   2 *nm* musical

músico,-a 1 *adj* musical

   2 *nm,f* musician

muslo *nm* thigh

mustio,-a *adj* (a) *(plantas)* wilted, withered (b) *(persona)* sad, gloomy

musulmán,-ana *adj & nm,f* Muslim, Moslem

mutación *nf Biol* mutation

mutilación *nf* mutilation

mutilado,-a *nm,f* disabled person; **m. de guerra** disabled serviceman

mutilar *vt* to mutilate

mutis *nm Teatro* exit

mutua *nf* mutual benefit society

mutual *nf Arg, Chile, Perú* mutual benefit society

mutualidad *nf* (a) *(reciprocidad)* mutuality (b) *(asociación)* mutual benefit society

mutuo,-a *adj* mutual

muy *adv* very; **m. bueno/malo** very good/bad; **¡m. bien!** very good!; *Fam* **m. mucho** very much; **M. señor mío** Dear Sir; **m. de los andaluces** typically Andalusian; **m. de mañana/noche** very early/late

N, n ['ene] *nf (la letra)* N, n

N (*abr* **Norte**) N

n/ (*abr* **nuestro,-a**) our

nabo *nm* (**a**) *Bot* turnip (**b**) *Vulg (pene)* prick

nácar *nm* mother-of-pearl

nacer [60] *vi* (**a**) to be born; **al n.** at birth; **nací en Montoro** I was born in Montoro; *Fam Fig* **n. de pie** to be born under a lucky star (**b**) *(pájaro)* to hatch (out) (**c**) *(pelo)* to begin to grow (**d**) *(río)* to rise

nacido,-a *adj* born; **n. de padre español** born of a Spanish father; **recién n.** newborn; *Fig* **mal n.** despicable, mean

naciente *adj (nuevo)* new, recent; *(sol)* rising

nacimiento *nm* (**a**) birth; **sordo de n.** deaf from birth; **lugar de n.** birthplace, place of birth (**b**) *Fig (principio)* origin, beginning; *(de río)* source (**c**) *(belén)* Nativity scene, crib

nación *nf* nation; **las Naciones Unidas** the United Nations

nacional 1 *adj* (**a**) national (**b**) *(producto, mercado)* domestic; **vuelos nacionales** domestic flights

2 *nmf* national; *Hist* **los nacionales** the Francoist forces

nacionalidad *nf* nationality

nacionalismo *nm* nationalism

nacionalista *adj & nmf* nationalist

nacionalizar [40] **1** *vt* (**a**) *Econ (banca, industria)* to nationalize (**b**) *(naturalizar)* to naturalize

2 nacionalizarse *vpr* to become naturalized; **n. español** to take up Spanish citizenship

nada 1 *pron* (**a**) *(como respuesta)* nothing; **¿qué quieres? – n.** what do you want? – nothing

(**b**) *(con verbo)* not ... anything; *(enfático)* nothing; **no sé n.** I don't know anything; **yo no digo n.** I'm saying nothing

(**c**) *(con otro negativo)* anything; **no hace nunca n.** he never does anything; **nadie sabía n.** nobody knew anything

(**d**) *(en ciertas construcciones)* anything; **más que n.** more than anything; **sin decir**

n. without saying anything; **casi n.** hardly anything

(**e**) **gracias – de n.** thanks – don't mention it; *Fam* **para n.** not at all; **casi n.** almost nothing; **como si n.** just like that; **un rasguño de n.** an insignificant little scratch; **n. de eso** nothing of the kind; **n. de n.** nothing at all; **n. más verla** as soon as he saw her

2 *adv* not at all; **no me gusta n.** I don't like it at all; **no lo encuentro n. interesante** I don't find it remotely interesting

3 *nf* nothingness; **salir de la n.** to come out of nowhere

nadador,-a *nm,f* swimmer

nadar *vi* (**a**) *Dep* to swim; **n. a braza** to do the breaststroke (**b**) *(flotar)* to float

nadie 1 *pron* (**a**) *(como respuesta)* no one, nobody; **¿quién vino? – n.** who came? – no one (**b**) *(con verbo)* not ... anyone, not ... anybody; *(enfático)* no one, nobody; **no conozco a n.** I don't know anyone *o* anybody; **no vi a n.** I saw no one (**c**) *(con otro negativo)* anyone, anybody; **nunca habla con n.** he never speaks to anybody (**d**) *(en ciertas construcciones)* anybody, anyone; **más que n.** more than anyone; **sin decírselo a n.** without telling anyone; **casi n.** hardly anyone

2 *nm* nobody; **ser un don n.** to be a nobody

nado: • a nado *loc adv* swimming; **cruzar** *o* **pasar a n.** to swim across

NAFTA *nm* (*abr* **North American Free Trade Agreement**) NAFTA

nafta *nf* *RP (gasolina)* *Br* petrol, *US* gas(oline)

nahua, náhuatl 1 *adj* Nahuatl

2 *nmf (individuo)* Nahuatl (Indian)

nailon *nm* nylon

naipe *nm* playing card

nalga *nf* buttock; **nalgas** bottom, buttocks

nana *nf* (**a**) *(canción)* lullaby (**b**) *Col, Méx (niñera)* nanny

napalm *nm* napalm

napias *nfpl Fam* snout

Nápoles *n* Naples

napolitano,-a *adj & nm,f* Neapolitan

naranja 1 *nf* orange; *Fig* **mi media n.** my better half
  2 *adj & nm* (*color*) orange

naranjada *nf* orangeade

naranjo *nm* orange tree

narciso *nm* (**a**) (*blanco*) narcissus; (*amarillo*) daffodil (**b**) *Fig* (*hombre*) narcissist

narcótico *nm* narcotic; (*droga*) drug

narcotizar [40] *vt* (*drogar*) to drug

narcotraficante *nmf* drug trafficker

narcotráfico *nm* drug trafficking

nariz *nf* (**a**) nose; *Fam* **me da en la n. que ...** I've got this feeling that ... (**b**) *Fam* **narices** nose; *Fam* **en mis (propias) narices** right under my very nose; *Fam* **estar hasta las narices de** to be totally fed up with; *Fam* **meter las narices en algo** to poke one's nose into sth; *Fam* **por narices** because I say so; *Fam* **tocarle a algn las narices** to get on sb's wick

narración *nf* narration

narrar *vt* to narrate, to tell

narrativo,-a *adj & nf* narrative

nata *nf* (**a**) cream; **n. batida** *o* **montada** whipped cream (**b**) (*de leche hervida*) skin (**c**) *Fig* cream, best

natación *nf Dep* swimming

natal *adj* **mi país n.** my native country; **su pueblo n.** his home town

natalicio *nm Fml* birthday

natalidad *nf* birth rate; **control de n.** birth control

natillas *nfpl Culin* custard

natividad *nf* Nativity

nativo,-a *adj & nm,f* native

nato,-a *adj* born

natura *nf Literario* nature; **contra n.** against nature

natural 1 *adj* natural; (*fruta, flor*) fresh; **de tamaño n.** life-size; **en estado n.** in its natural state; *Jur* **hijo n.** illegitimate child
  2 *nmf* native

naturaleza *nf* (**a**) nature; **en plena n.** in the wild, in unspoilt countryside; *Arte* **n. muerta** still life (**b**) (*complexión*) physical constitution

naturalidad *nf* (*sencillez*) naturalness; **con n.** naturally, straightforwardly

naturalismo *nm* naturalism

naturalista 1 *adj* naturalistic
  2 *nmf* naturalist

naturalización *nf* naturalization

naturalizar [40] *vt* to naturalize
  2 naturalizarse *vpr* to become naturalized

naturalmente *adv* naturally; **¡n.!** of course!

naturismo *nm* naturism

naturista *nmf* naturist

naufragar [42] *vi* (*barco*) to sink, to be wrecked; (*persona*) to be shipwrecked

naufragio *nm Náut* shipwreck

náufrago,-a *nm,f* shipwrecked person, castaway

náusea *nf* (*usu pl*) nausea, sickness; **me da n.** it makes me sick; **sentir náuseas** to feel sick

nauseabundo,-a *adj* nauseating, sickening

náutico,-a *adj* nautical

navaja *nf* (**a**) (*cuchillo*) penknife, pocketknife; **n. de afeitar** razor (**b**) (*molusco*) razor-shell

navajada *nf*, **navajazo** *nm* stab, gash

navajero *nm Fam* thug

naval *adj* naval

Navarra *n* Navarre

navarro,-a 1 *adj* Navarrese, of/from Navarre
  2 *nm,f* person from Navarre

nave *nf* (**a**) ship; **n. (espacial)** spaceship, spacecraft (**b**) *Ind* plant, building (**c**) (*de iglesia*) nave; **n. lateral** aisle

navegable *adj* navigable

navegación *nf* navigation; **n. costera** coastal shipping

navegador *nm Informát* browser

navegar [42] *vi* (**a**) to navigate, to sail (**b**) *Av* to navigate, to fly (**c**) **n. por Internet** to surf the Net

Navidad(es) *nf(pl)* Christmas; **árbol de Navidad** Christmas tree; **Feliz Navidad, Felices Navidades** Merry Christmas

navideño,-a *adj* Christmas

navío *nm* ship

nazi *adj & nmf* Nazi

nazismo *nm* Nazism

n/c., n/cta. (*abr* **nuestra cuenta**) our account, our acct

neblina *nf* mist, thin fog

nebulosa *nf Astron* nebula

nebuloso,-a *adj* (**a**) *Met* cloudy, hazy (**b**) *Fig* nebulous, vague

necedad *nf* (**a**) (*estupidez*) stupidity, foolishness (**b**) (*tontería*) stupid thing to say *o* to do

necesario,-a *adj* necessary; **es n. hacerlo** it has to be done; **es n. que vayas** you must go; **no es n. que vayas** there is no need for you to go; **si fuera n.** if need be

neceser *nm* (*de aseo*) toilet bag; (*de maquillaje*) make-up bag

necesidad *nf* (**a**) necessity, need; **artículos de primera n.** essentials; **por n.** of necessity; **tener n. de** to need (**b**) (*pobreza*) poverty, hardship (**c**) **hacer**

sus necesidades to relieve oneself

necesitado,-a 1 *adj (pobre)* needy, poor; **n. de** in need of

2 *nmpl* **los necesitados** the needy

necesitar *vt* to need; **se necesita chico** *(en anuncios)* boy wanted

necio,-a 1 *adj* (a) *(tonto)* silly, stupid (b) *Méx (pesado)* boring

2 *nm,f* (a) *(tonto)* fool, idiot (b) *Méx (pesado)* bore

necrología *nf* obituary

néctar *nm* nectar

nectarina *nf* nectarine

neerlandés,-esa 1 *adj* Dutch, of/from the Netherlands

2 *nm,f (persona) (hombre)* Dutchman; *(mujer)* Dutchwoman; **los neerlandeses** the Dutch

3 *nm (idioma)* Dutch

nefasto,-a *adj* (a) *(perjudicial)* harmful (b) *(funesto)* unlucky, ill-fated (c) *(inútil)* hopeless

negación *nf* (a) negation (b) *(negativa)* denial; *(rechazo)* refusal (c) *Ling* negative

negado,-a 1 *adj* **ser n. para algo** to be hopeless *o* useless at sth

2 *nm,f* no-hoper

negar [1] 1 *vt* (a) to deny; **negó haberlo robado** he denied stealing it (b) *(rechazar)* to refuse, to deny; **le negaron la beca** they refused him the grant

2 negarse *vpr* to refuse (**a** to)

negativa *nf* denial

negativo,-a *adj & nm* negative

negligencia *nf* negligence

negociación *nf* negotiation

negociado *nm Andes, RP (chanchullo)* shady deal

negociador,-a *adj* negotiating; **comité n.** negotiating committee

negociante *nmf* dealer; *(hombre)* businessman; *(mujer)* businesswoman

negociar [43] 1 *vt Fin & Pol* to negotiate

2 *vi (comerciar)* to do business, to deal

negocio *nm Com & Fin* business; *(transacción)* deal, transaction; *(asunto)* affair; **hombre de negocios** businessman; **mujer de negocios** businesswoman

negra *nf* (a) *Fig (mala suerte)* bad luck; **tener la n.** to be very unlucky (b) *Mús Br* crotchet, *US* quarter note

negrilla, negrita *adj & nf Impr* bold (face)

negro,-a 1 *adj* (a) black; **estar n.** *(bronceado)* to be suntanned (b) *Fig (suerte)* awful; *(desesperado)* desperate; *(furioso)*

furious; **verlo todo n.** to be very pessimistic; **vérselas negras para hacer algo** to have a tough time doing sth

2 *nm,f (hombre)* black; *(mujer)* black (woman)

3 *nm (color)* black

nene,-a *nm,f (niño)* baby boy; *(niña)* baby girl

nenúfar *nm Bot* waterlily

neocelandés,-esa, neozelandés,-esa 1 *adj* of/from New Zealand

2 *nm,f* New Zealander

neoclásico,-a *adj Arte & Lit* neoclassic, neoclassical

neologismo *nm* neologism

neón *nm* neon

neoyorquino,-a 1 *adj* of/from New York

2 *nm,f* New Yorker

neozelandés,-esa *adj & nm,f* = neocelandés,-esa

nepotismo *nm* nepotism

Neptuno *n* Neptune

nervio *nm* (a) *Anat & Bot* nerve; *(de la carne)* sinew (b) *Fig (fuerza, vigor)* nerve, courage (c) **nervios** nerves; **ataque de nervios** fit of hysterics; **ser un manojo de nervios** to be a bundle of nerves; **tener los nervios de acero** to have nerves of steel

nerviosismo *nm* nerves

nervioso,-a *adj* (a) nervous; **poner n. a algn** to get on sb's nerves (b) *(inquieto)* fidgety

neto,-a *adj* (a) *(peso, cantidad)* net (b) *(nítido)* neat, clear

neumático,-a 1 *adj* pneumatic

2 *nm* tyre; **n. de recambio** spare tyre

neumonía *nf* pneumonia

neurálgico,-a *adj* neuralgic; *Fig* **punto n.** nerve centre

neurólogo,-a *nm,f* neurologist

neurosis *nf* neurosis

neurótico,-a *adj & nm,f* neurotic

neutral *adj* neutral

neutralidad *nf* neutrality

neutralizar [40] *vt* to neutralize

neutro,-a *adj* (a) *(imparcial)* neutral (b) *Ling* neuter

neutrón *nm Fís* neutron; **bomba de neutrones** neutron bomb

nevada *nf* snowfall

nevar [1] *v impers* to snow

nevera *nf* (a) *(frigorífico)* refrigerator, fridge (b) *(portátil)* cool box

nexo *nm* connection, link

ni *conj* (a) **no ... ni, ni ... ni** neither ... nor, not ... or; **no tengo tiempo ni dinero** I have got neither time nor money; **ni ha**

venido ni ha llamado he hasn't come or phoned; **no vengas ni hoy ni mañana** don't come today or tomorrow (**b**) *(ni siquiera)* not even; **ni por dinero** not even for money; **ni se te ocurra** don't even think about it; **¡ni hablar!** no way!

Nicaragua *n* Nicaragua

nicaragüense *adj & nmf* Nicaraguan

nicho *nm* niche

nicotina *nf* nicotine

nido *nm* nest

niebla *nf* fog; **hay mucha n.** it is very foggy

nieto,-a *nm,f (niño)* grandson; *(niña)* granddaughter; **mis nietos** my grandchildren

nieve *nf* (**a**) *Met* snow; *Culin* **a punto de n.** (beaten) stiff (**b**) *Fam (cocaína)* snow (**c**) *Carib, Méx (granizado)* = drink of flavoured crushed ice

nigeriano,-a *adj & nm,f* Nigerian

Nilo *n* **el N.** the Nile

nilón *nm Tex* nylon

nimio,-a *adj (insignificante)* insignificant, petty

ninfómana *nf* nymphomaniac

ninguno,-a 1 *adj* (**a**) *(con verbo)* not ... any; **no leí ninguna revista** I didn't read any magazines; **no tiene ninguna gracia** it is not funny at all (**b**) **en ninguna parte** nowhere; **de ningún modo** no way

> **Ningún** is used instead of **ninguno** before masculine singular nouns (e.g. **ningún hombre** no man).

2 *pron* (**a**) *(persona)* nobody, no one; **n. lo vio** no one saw it; **n. de los dos** neither of the two; **n. de ellos** none of them (**b**) *(cosa)* not ... any of them; *(enfático)* none of them; **me gusta n.** I don't like any of them; **no vi n.** I saw none of them

niña *nf* (**a**) *(girl; ver* **niño,-a** (**b**) *Anat* pupil; *Fig* **es la n. de sus ojos** she's the apple of his eye

niñera *nf* nursemaid, nanny

niñez *nf* infancy; *(a partir de los cuatro años)* childhood

niño,-a *nm,f* (**a**) *(muchacho)* (small) boy; *(muchacha)* (little) girl; **de n.** as a child; **n. prodigio** child prodigy; *Pey* **n. bien o de papá** rich boy, rich kid; *Pey* **n. bonito o mimado** mummy's/daddy's boy (**b**) *(bebé)* baby (**c**) **niños** children; *Fig* **juego de niños** child's play (**d**) *Met* **el N.** el Niño

nipón,-ona *adj & nm,f* Japanese; **los niponés** the Japanese

níquel *nm* nickel

niqui *nm T-shirt*

níspero *nm (fruto)* medlar; *(árbol)* medlar tree

nítido,-a *adj (claro)* clear; *(imagen)* sharp

nitrógeno *nm* nitrogen

nitroglicerina *nf* nitroglycerine

nivel *nm* (**a**) *(altura)* level; **a. del mar** at sea level (**b**) *(categoría)* standard; **n. de vida** standard of living (**c**) *(instrumento)* level; **n. de aire** spirit level (**d**) *Ferroc* **paso a n.** *Br* level crossing, *US* grade crossing

nivelar *vt* (**a**) to level out o off (**b**) *(equilibrar)* to balance out

n *(abr* **número)** no

no 1 *adv* (**a**) *(como respuesta)* no; **¿te gusta? – no** do you like it? – no (**b**) *(en otros contextos)* not; **no vi a nadie** I didn't see anyone; **aún no** not yet; **ya no** no longer, not any more; **no sin antes ...** not without first ...; **¿por qué no?** why not? (**c**) **no fumar/aparcar** *(en letrero)* no smoking/parking (**d**) **no sea que** (+ *subjunctive)* in case (**e**) **es rubia, ¿no?** she's blonde, isn't she?; **llegaron anoche, ¿no?** they arrived yesterday, didn't they? (**f**) *(como prefijo negativo)* non; **la no violencia** non-violence

2 *nm* no; **un no rotundo** a definite no

noble **1** *adj* noble

2 *nmf (hombre)* nobleman; *(mujer)* noblewoman; **los nobles** the nobility

nobleza *nf* nobility

noche *nf* evening; *(después de las diez)* night, night-time; **de n., por la n.** at night; **esta n.** tonight; **mañana por la n.** tomorrow night o evening; **buenas noches** *(saludo)* good evening; *(despedida)* good night; **son las nueve de la n.** it's nine p.m.

nochebuena *nf* Christmas Eve

nochero *nm CSur (vigilante)* nightwatchman

nochevieja *nf* New Year's Eve

noción *nf* (**a**) notion, idea (**b**) **nociones** smattering, basic knowledge; **nociones de español** a smattering of Spanish

nocivo,-a *adj* noxious, harmful

noctámbulo,-a *nm,f* sleepwalker; *Fam* nightbird

nocturno,-a *adj* (**a**) night; **vida nocturna** night life; **clases nocturnas** evening classes (**b**) *Bot & Zool* nocturnal

nodriza *nf* (**a**) *(ama)* wet nurse (**b**) **buque n.** supply ship

nogal *nm Bot* walnut (tree)

nómada 1 *adj* nomadic

2 *nmf* nomad

nombrado,-a *adj (célebre)* famous, well-known

nombramiento *nm* appointment

nombrar *vt* (**a**) *(designar)* to name, to appoint; **n. a algn director** to appoint sb director (**b**) *(mencionar)* to name, to mention

nombre *nm* (**a**) name; **n. de pila** Christian name; **n. y apellidos** full name; *Informát* **n. de dominio** domain name; **a n. de** addressed to; **en n. de** on behalf of (**b**) *Ling* noun; **n. propio** proper noun

nómina *nf* (**a**) *(de sueldo)* pay slip (**b**) *(plantilla)* payroll

nominar *vt* to nominate

nominativo,-a *adj* **cheque n. a** cheque made out to

non *adj* (**a**) *Mat* odd number; **pares y nones** odds and evens (**b**) *Fam* **nones** *(negación)* no; **decir (que) nones** to refuse

nono,-a *adj* = **noveno,-a**

norcoreano,-a *adj & nm,f* North Korean

nordeste *nm* = **noreste**

nórdico,-a 1 *adj* (**a**) *(del norte)* northern (**b**) *(escandinavo)* Nordic
  2 *nm,f* Nordic person

noreste *nm* northeast

noria *nf* (**a**) *(de feria)* big wheel (**b**) *(para agua)* water wheel

norirlandés,-esa 1 *adj* Northern Irish
  2 *nm,f* *(persona)* *(hombre)* Northern Irishman; *(mujer)* Northern Irishwoman; **los norirlandeses** the Northern Irish

norma *nf* norm; **n. de seguridad** safety standard

normal *adj* normal, usual; **lo n.** the normal thing, what usually happens

normalidad *nf* normality; **volver a la n.** to return to normal

normalizar [40] **1** *vt* to normalize, to restore to normal
  2 normalizarse *vpr* to return to normal

normativa *nf* rules

noroeste *nm* northwest

norte *nm* (**a**) north; **al n. de** to the north of (**b**) *Fig* aim, goal

norteafricano,-a *adj & nm,f* North African

Norteamérica *n* North America

norteamericano,-a *adj & nm,f* (North) American

norteño,-a 1 *adj* northern
  2 *nm,f* Northerner

Noruega *n* Norway

noruego,-a 1 *adj* Norwegian
  2 *nm,f* Norwegian
  3 *nm* *(idioma)* Norwegian

nos 1 *pron pers* *(directo)* us; *(indirecto)* (to) us; **n. ha visto** he has seen us; **n. trajo un**

regalo he brought us a present; **n. lo dio** he gave it to us
  2 *pron* *(reflexivo)* ourselves; *(recíproco)* each other; **n. hemos divertido mucho** we enjoyed ourselves a lot; **n. queremos mucho** we love each other very much

nosotros,-as *pron pers pl* (**a**) *(sujeto)* we; **n. lo vimos** we saw it; **somos n.** it is us (**b**) *(complemento)* us; **con n.** with us

> Usually omitted in Spanish except for emphasis or contrast.

nostalgia *nf* nostalgia; *(morriña)* homesickness

nostálgico,-a *adj* nostalgic; *(con morriña)* homesick

nota *nf* (**a**) *(anotación)* note (**b**) *Educ* mark, grade; **sacar buenas notas** to get good marks (**c**) *Fig* *(detalle)* element, quality; **la n. dominante** the prevailing quality (**d**) *Mús* note; *Fam* **dar la n.** to make oneself noticed

notable 1 *adj* *(apreciable)* noticeable; *(destacado)* outstanding, remarkable
  2 *nm* *(nota)* very good

notar 1 *vt* *(percibir)* to notice, to note
  2 notarse *vpr* to be noticeable o evident, to show; **no se nota** it doesn't show; **se nota que …** one can see that …

notaría *nf* *(despacho)* notary's office

notarial *adj* notarial; **acta n.** affidavit

notario,-a *nm,f* notary (public), solicitor

noticia *nf* news *sing*; **una n.** a piece of news; **una buena n.** good news; **no tengo n. de esto** I don't know anything about it

> *Observa que la palabra inglesa* **notice** *es un falso amigo y no es la traducción de la palabra española* **noticia**. *En inglés,* **notice** *significa "aviso, anuncio".*

noticiario, *Am* **noticiero** *nm* (**a**) *Cin* newsreel (**b**) *Rad & TV* television news *sing*

notificación *nf* notification; **sin n. previa** without (previous) notice; *Jur* **n. judicial** summons *sing*

notificar [44] *vt* to notify

notorio,-a *adj* (**a**) *(evidente)* obvious, evident (**b**) *(famoso)* famous, well-known

> *Observa que la palabra inglesa* **notorious** *es un falso amigo y no es la traducción de la palabra española* **notorio**. *En inglés,* **notorious** *significa "tristemente célebre".*

novatada *nf* (**a**) *(broma)* rough joke, rag (**b**) **pagar la n.** to learn the hard way

novato,-a 1 *adj* *(persona)* inexperienced; *Fam* green

2 *nm,f* (**a**) *(principiante)* novice, beginner (**b**) *Univ* fresher

novecientos,-as *adj & nm* nine hundred

novedad *nf* (**a**) *(cosa nueva)* novelty; **últimas novedades** latest arrivals (**b**) *(cambio)* change, development (**c**) *(cualidad)* newness

novedoso,-a *adj* (**a**) *(nuevo)* new, full of novelties (**b**) *(innovador)* innovative

novel 1 *adj* new, inexperienced
2 *nmf* beginner, novice

novela *nf Lit* novel; **n. corta** short story; **n. policíaca** detective story

novelero,-a *adj* (**a**) *(fond of new things* (**b**) *(fantasioso)* highly imaginative

novelesco,-a *adj* (**a**) *(de novela)* novelistic, fictional (**b**) *(extraordinario)* bizarre, fantastic

novelista *nmf* novelist

noveno,-a *adj & nm* ninth; **novena parte** ninth

noventa *adj & nm inv* ninety

novia *nf* (**a**) *(amiga)* girlfriend (**b**) *(prometida)* fiancée (**c**) *(en boda)* bride

noviar *vi CSur, Méx* **n. con algn** to go out with sb; **novian hace tiempo** they've been going out together for a while

noviazgo *nm* engagement

noviembre *nm* November

novillada *nf Taurom* = bullfight with young bulls

novillero,-a *nm,f Taurom* apprentice matador

novillo,-a *nm,f* (**a**) *(toro)* young bull; *(vaca)* young cow (**b**) *Fam Educ* **hacer novillos** to play *Br* truant *o US* hooky

novio *nm* (**a**) *(amigo)* boyfriend (**b**) *(prometido)* fiancé (**c**) *(en boda)* bridegroom; **los novios** the bride and groom

nubarrón *nm Fam* storm cloud

nube *nf* cloud; *Fig* **vivir en las nubes** to have one's head in the clouds; *Fig* **poner a algn por las nubes** to praise sb to the skies

nublado,-a *adj* cloudy, overcast

nublarse *vpr* to become cloudy, to cloud over; *Fig* **se le nubló la vista** his eyes clouded over

nuboso,-a *adj* cloudy

nuca *nf* nape, back of the neck

nuclear *adj* nuclear; **central n.** nuclear power station

núcleo *nm* nucleus; *(parte central)* core; **n. urbano** city centre

nudillo *nm (usu pl)* knuckle

nudista *adj & nmf* nudist

nudo *nm* (**a**) knot; **hacer un n.** to tie a knot; *Fig* **se me hizo un n. en la garganta** I

got a lump in my throat (**b**) *(punto principal)* crux, core (**c**) *(de comunicaciones)* centre

nuera *nf* daughter-in-law

nuestro,-a 1 *adj pos* (**a**) our; **nuestra familia** our family (**b**) *(después del sustantivo)* of ours; **un amigo n.** a friend of ours
2 *pron pos* ours; **este libro es n.** this book is ours

nuevamente *adv* again

Nueva Zelanda *n* New Zealand

nueve *adj & nm inv* nine

nuevo,-a 1 *adj* (**a**) new; *Fam* **¿qué hay de n.?** what's new?; **de n.** again; **Nueva York** New York; **Nueva Zelanda** New Zealand (**b**) *(adicional)* further
2 *nm,f* newcomer; *(principiante)* beginner

nuez *nf* (**a**) walnut; **n. moscada** nutmeg (**b**) *Anat* **n. (de Adán)** Adam's apple

nulidad *nf* (**a**) *(ineptitud)* incompetence (**b**) *Jur* nullity

nulo,-a *adj* (**a**) *(inepto)* useless, totally incapable. (**b**) *(sin valor)* null and void, invalid; **voto n.** invalid vote (**c**) **crecimiento n.** zero growth

núm. *(abr número)* no

numeral *adj & nm* numeral

numerar *vt* to number

numerario,-a 1 *adj* **profesor no n.** teacher on a temporary contract
2 *nm* (**a**) *(miembro)* full member (**b**) *(dinero)* cash

numérico,-a *adj* numerical

número *nm* (**a**) number; **n. de matrícula** *Br* registration number, *US* license number; **n. de serie** serial number; *Fig* **sin n.** countless (**b**) *Prensa* number, issue; **n. atrasado** back number (**c**) *(de zapatos)* size (**d**) *(en espectáculo)* sketch, act; *Fam* **montar un n.** to make a scene

numeroso,-a *adj* numerous

nunca *adv* (**a**) *(como respuesta)* never; **¿cuándo volverás? – n.** when will you come back? – never (**b**) *(con verbo)* never; *(enfático)* not ... ever; **no he estado n. en España** I've never been to Spain; **yo no haría n. eso** I wouldn't ever do that (**c**) *(en ciertas construcciones)* ever; **casi n.** hardly ever; **más que n.** more than ever (**d**) **n. jamás** never ever; *(futuro)* never again

nupcial *adj* wedding, nuptial; **marcha n.** wedding march

nupcias *nfpl Fml* wedding, nuptials; **casarse en segundas n.** to marry again

nutrición *nf* nutrition

nutricionista *nmf* nutritionist

nutrir 1 *vt* to nourish, to feed
  2 nutrirse *vpr* to feed (**de** *o* **con** on)

nutritivo,-a *adj* nutritious, nourishing;
  valor n. nutritional value

ñandutí *nm Par* fine lace
ñapa *nf Ven Fam* bonus, extra

ñato,-a *adj Andes, RP* snub-nosed

O

O, o [o] *nf (la letra)* O, o

o *conj* or; **jueves o viernes** Thursday or Friday; **o ... o** either ... or; **o sea** that is (to say), in other words

> **u** is used instead of **o** in front of words beginning with "o" or "ho" (e.g. **mujer u hombre** woman or man). Note that **ó** (with acute accent) is used between figures.

O. *(abr Oeste)* W

oasis *nm inv* oasis

obcecado,-a *adj Fig* stubborn

obcecar [44] **1** *vt Fig* to blind; **la ira lo obceca** he is blinded by anger

2 obcecarse *vpr Fig* to refuse to budge; *(obsesionarse)* to become obsessed

obedecer [33] **1** *vt* to obey

2 *vi* **o. a** *(provenir)* to be due to; **¿a qué obedece esa actitud?** what's the reason behind this attitude?

obediencia *nf* obedience

obediente *adj* obedient

obertura *nf* overture

obesidad *nf* obesity

obeso,-a *adj* obese

óbice *nm* obstacle; **eso no es ó. para que yo no lo haga** it won't prevent me from doing it

obispo *nm* bishop

objeción *nf* objection; **poner una o.** to raise an objection, to object

objetar **1** *vt* **no tengo nada que o.** I've got no objections

2 *vi Mil* to be a conscientious objector

objetividad *nf* objectivity

objetivo,-a **1** *nm* **(a)** *(fin, meta)* objective, aim **(b)** *Mil* target **(c)** *Cin & Fot* lens; **o. zoom** zoom lens

2 *adj* objective

objeto *nm* **(a)** object; **objetos perdidos** lost property; **mujer o.** sex object **(b)** *(fin)* aim, purpose; **con o. de ...** in order to ...; **tiene por o. ...** it is designed to ... **(c)** *Ling* object

objetor,-a **1** *nm,f* objector; **o. de conciencia** conscientious objector

2 *adj* objecting, dissenting

obligación *nf* **(a)** *(deber)* obligation; **por o.** out of a sense of duty; **tengo o. de ...** I

have to ... **(b)** *Fin* bond, debenture

obligado,-a *adj* obliged; **verse o estar o. a** to be obliged to

obligar [42] *vt* to compel, to force

obligatorio,-a *adj* compulsory, obligatory

obra *nf* **(a)** *(trabajo)* (piece of) work; **por o. de** thanks to **(b)** *Arte* work; **o. maestra** masterpiece **(c)** *(acto)* deed **(d)** *Constr* building site **(e) obras** *(arreglos)* repairs; **carretera en obras** *(en letrero)* roadworks; **cerrado por obras** *(en letrero)* closed for repairs

obrar **1** *vi* **(a)** *(proceder)* to act, to behave; **o. bien/mal** to do the right/wrong thing **(b)** *Fml* **obra en nuestro poder ...** we are in receipt of ...

2 *vt (milagro)* to work

obrero,-a **1** *nm,f* worker, labourer

2 *adj* working; **clase obrera** working class; **movimiento o.** labour movement

obscenidad *nf* obscenity

obsceno,-a *adj* obscene

obscurecer [33] **1** *v impers* to get dark

2 *vt* to darken

3 obscurecerse *vpr (nublarse)* to become cloudy

obscuridad *nf* darkness; *Fig* obscurity

obscuro,-a *adj* **(a)** dark **(b)** *Fig (origen, idea)* obscure; *(futuro)* uncertain, gloomy; *(asunto)* shady; *(nublado)* overcast

obsequiar [43] *vt* to give away

obsequio *nm* gift, present

observación *nf* observation

observador,-a **1** *nm,f* observer

2 *adj* observant

observancia *nf* observance

observar *vt* **(a)** *(mirar)* to observe, to watch **(b)** *(notar)* to notice **(c)** *(cumplir)* to observe

observatorio *nm* observatory

obsesión *nf* obsession

obsesionar **1** *vt* to obsess; **estoy obsesionado con eso** I can't get it out of my mind

2 obsesionarse *vpr* to get obsessed

obsesivo,-a *adj* obsessive

obseso,-a *nm,f* obsessed person; **un o. sexual** a sex maniac

obsoleto,-a adj obsolete
obstaculizar [40] vt to obstruct, to get in the way of
obstáculo nm obstacle
obstante: • no obstante 1 loc adv nevertheless
2 prep notwithstanding
obstetricia nf obstetrics sing
obstinación nf obstinacy
obstinado,-a adj obstinate
obstinarse vpr to persist (en in)
obstrucción nf obstruction; Med blockage
obstruir [37] 1 vt (a) (salida, paso) to block, to obstruct (b) (progreso) to impede, to block
2 obstruirse vpr to get blocked up
obtención nf obtaining
obtener [24] 1 vt (alcanzar) to obtain, to get
2 obtenerse vpr o. de (provenir) to come from
obturador nm Fot shutter
obtuso,-a adj obtuse
obús nm shell
obviar [43] vt (problema) to get round
obvio,-a adj obvious
oca nf goose
ocasión nf (a) (momento) occasion; con o. de ... on the occasion of ...; en cierta o. once (b) (oportunidad) opportunity, chance; aprovechar una o. to make the most of an opportunity (c) Com bargain; de o. cheap; precios de o. bargain prices
ocasional adj (a) (eventual) occasional; trabajo o. casual work; de forma o. occasionally (b) (fortuito) accidental, chance
ocasionar vt to cause, to bring about
ocaso nm (anochecer) sunset; Fig (declive) fall, decline
occidental adj western, occidental
occidente nm west; el O. the West
OCDE nf (abr Organización para la Cooperación y el Desarrollo Económico) OECD
Oceanía n Oceania
oceánico,-a adj oceanic
océano nm ocean
ochenta adj & nm inv eighty
ocho adj & nm inv eight
ochocientos,-as adj & nm eight hundred
ocio nm leisure; en mis ratos de o. in my spare o leisure time
ocioso,-a adj (a) (inactivo) idle (b) (inútil) pointless
ocre nm ochre
octavilla nf (panfleto) handout, leaflet
octavo,-a adj & nm,f eighth

octogenario,-a adj & nm,f octogenarian
octogésimo,-a adj & nm,f eightieth
octubre nm October
ocular adj testigo o. eye witness
oculista nmf ophthalmologist
ocultar 1 vt to conceal, to hide; o. algo a algn to hide sth from sb
2 ocultarse vpr to hide
oculto,-a adj concealed, hidden
ocupación nf occupation
ocupado,-a adj (persona) busy; (asiento) taken; (aseos, teléfono) engaged; (puesto de trabajo) filled
ocupante nmf (de casa) occupant, occupier; (ilegal) squatter; (de vehículo) occupant
ocupar 1 vt (a) to occupy (b) (espacio, tiempo) to take up; (cargo) to hold, to fill (c) CAm, Méx (usar, emplear) to use
2 ocuparse vpr o. de (cuidar) to look after; (encargarse) to see to
ocurrencia nf (agudeza) witty remark, wisecrack; (idea) bright idea

> 🖉 Observa que la palabra inglesa **occurrence** es un falso amigo y no es la traducción de la palabra española **ocurrencia**. En inglés, **occurrence** significa "suceso, incidencia".

ocurrente adj witty
ocurrir 1 v impers to happen, to occur; ¿qué ocurre? what's going on?; ¿qué te ocurre? what's the matter with you?
2 ocurrirse vpr no se me ocurre nada I can't think of anything; se me ocurre que ... it occurs to me that ...
odiar [43] vt to detest, to hate; odio tener que ... I hate having to ...
odio nm hatred, loathing; mirada de o. hateful look
odioso,-a adj hateful
odontología nf dentistry, odontology
odontólogo,-a nm,f dental surgeon, odontologist
odre nm wineskin
OEA nf (abr Organización de Estados Americanos) OAS
oeste nm west
ofender 1 vt to offend
2 ofenderse vpr to get offended (por by), to take offence (por at)
ofensa nf offence
ofensiva nf offensive
ofensivo,-a adj offensive
oferta nf offer; Fin & Ind bid, tender, proposal; Com de o en o. on (special) offer; o. y demanda supply and demand
ofertar vt to offer

off *adj* **voz en o.** *Cin & TV* voice-over; *Teatro* voice offstage

offset *nm Impr* offset

oficial 1 *adj* official
2 *nmf* (**a**) *Mil & Náut* officer (**b**) *(empleado)* clerk (**c**) *(obrero)* skilled worker

oficialismo *nm Am* (**a**) **el o.** *(gobierno)* the Government (**b**) **el o.** *(partidarios del gobierno)* government supporters

oficialista *Am* **1** *adj* pro-government
2 *nmf* government supporter

oficina *nf* office; **o. de empleo** *Br* job centre, *US* job office; **o. de turismo** tourist office; **o. de correos** post office; **horas/horario de o.** business hours

oficinista *nmf* office worker, clerk

oficio *nm* (**a**) *(ocupación)* job, occupation; *(profesión)* trade; **ser del o.** to be in the trade (**b**) *(comunicación oficial)* official letter *o* note; **de o.** ex-officio; **abogado de o.** state-appointed lawyer (**c**) *Rel* service

oficioso,-a *adj (noticia, fuente)* unofficial

> *Observa que la palabra inglesa **officious** es un falso amigo y no es la traducción de la palabra española **oficioso**. En inglés, **officious** significa "excesivamente celoso o diligente".*

ofimática *nf* office automation

ofimático,-a *adj Informát* **paquete o.** business package

ofrecer [33] **1** *vt* (**a**) to offer (**b**) *(aspecto)* to present
2 ofrecerse *vpr* (**a**) *(prestarse)* to offer, to volunteer (**b**) *(situación)* to present itself (**c**) *Fml* **¿qué se le ofrece?** what can I do for you?

ofrecimiento *nm* offering

ofrendar *vt Rel* to offer up

ofrezco *indic pres de* **ofrecer**

oftalmología *nf* ophthalmology

oftalmólogo,-a *nm,f* ophthalmologist

ofuscación *nf*, **ofuscamiento** *nm* blinding, dazzling

ofuscar [44] *vt* (**a**) *Fig (confundir)* to blind (**b**) *(deslumbrar)* to dazzle

oídas: • de oídas *loc adv* by hearsay

oído *nm* (**a**) *(sentido)* hearing (**b**) *(órgano)* ear; **aprender de o.** to learn by ear; *Fig* **hacer oídos sordos** to turn a deaf ear

oír [17] *vt* to hear; **¡oye!** hey!; **¡oiga!** excuse me!; *Fam* **como lo oyes** believe it or not

OIT *nf (abr* **Organización Internacional del Trabajo)** ILO

ojal *nm* buttonhole

ojalá 1 *interj* let's hope so!, I hope so!

2 *conj (+ subjunctive)* **¡o. sea cierto!** I hope it's true!

ojeada *nf* **echar una o.** to have a quick look

ojeras *nfpl* rings *o* bags under the eyes

ojeriza *nf* dislike

ojo 1 *nm* (**a**) eye; **o. morado** black eye; **ojos saltones** bulging eyes; *Fig* **a ojos vista** clearly, openly; *Fig* **calcular a o.** to guess; *Fam* **no pegué o.** I didn't sleep a wink (**b**) *(de aguja)* eye; *(de cerradura)* keyhole (**c**) *(de un puente)* span
2 *interj* careful!, look out!

ojota *nf* (**a**) *Méx (sandalia)* sandal (**b**) *RP (chanclas) Br* flip-flop, *US* thong

okupa *nmf* squatter

ola *nf* wave; **o. de calor** heat wave

ole, olé *interj* bravo!

oleada *nf* wave; *Fig* **o. de turistas** influx of tourists

oleaje *nm* swell

óleo *nm Arte* oil; **pintura** *o* **cuadro al ó.** oil painting

oleoducto *nm* pipeline

oler [65] **1** *vt* (**a**) *(percibir olor)* to smell (**b**) *Fig (adivinar)* to smell, to feel
2 *vi* (**a**) *(exhalar)* to smell; **o. a** to smell of; **o. bien/mal** to smell good/bad (**b**) *Fig (parecer)* to smack (**a** of)
3 olerse *vpr Fig (adivinar)* to feel, to sense; **me lo olía** I thought as much

olfatear *vt* (**a**) *(oler)* to sniff (**b**) *Fig (indagar)* to pry into

olfato *nm* sense of smell; *Fig* good nose, instinct

oligarquía *nf* oligarchy

olimpiada *nf Dep* Olympiad, Olympic Games; **las olimpiadas** the Olympic Games

olímpicamente *adv* **paso o. de estudiar** I couldn't give a damn about studying

olímpico,-a *adj* Olympic; **Juegos Olímpicos** Olympic Games

oliva *nf* olive; **aceite de o.** olive oil

olivar *nm* olive grove

olivo *nm* olive (tree)

olla *nf* saucepan, pot; **o. exprés** *o* **a presión** pressure cooker

olmo *nm* smooth-leaved elm

olor *nm* smell; **o. corporal** body odour

oloroso,-a *adj* fragrant, sweet-smelling

OLP *nf (abr* **Organización para la Liberación de Palestina)** PLO

olvidadizo,-a *adj* forgetful

olvidar 1 *vt* (**a**) to forget; *Fam* **¡olvídame!** leave me alone! (**b**) **olvidé el paraguas allí** I left my umbrella there
2 olvidarse *vpr* to forget; **se me ha olvidado hacerlo** I forgot to do it

olvido *nm* (**a**) *(desmemoria)* oblivion (**b**) *(lapsus)* oversight

ombligo *nm* navel

ominoso,-a *adj* shameful

omisión *nf* omission

omiso,-a *adj* hacer caso o. de to take no notice of

omitir *vt* to omit, to leave out

ómnibus *nm* (*pl* **ómnibus** *o* **omnibuses**) *Cuba, Urug* bus

omnipotente *adj* omnipotent, almighty

omnipresente *adj* omnipresent

omnisciente *adj* omniscient, all-knowing

omnívoro,-a 1 *adj* omnivorous
  2 *nm,f* omnivore

omóplato, omoplato *nm* shoulder blade

OMS *nf* (*abr* **Organización Mundial de la Salud**) WHO

ONCE *nf* (*abr* **Organización Nacional de Ciegos Españoles**) ≃ RNIB

once 1 *adj inv* eleven
  2 *nm inv* eleven; *Ftb* eleven, team

onda *nf* (**a**) *Fís* wave; *Fam Fig* **estar en la o.** to be with it; **o. expansiva** shock wave; *Rad* **o. larga/media/corta** long/medium/short wave (**b**) *(en el agua)* ripple (**c**) *(de pelo)* wave (**d**) *Méx, RP* **¿qué o.?** (*¿qué tal?*) how's it going?, how are things?

ondear *vi* (**a**) *(bandera)* to flutter (**b**) *(de agua)* to ripple

ondulación *nf* undulation; *(de agua)* ripple

ondulado,-a *adj* *(pelo)* wavy; *(paisaje)* rolling

ondulante *adj* undulating

ondular 1 *vt* *(el pelo)* to wave
  2 *vi* *(moverse)* to undulate

oneroso,-a *adj* *(impuesto)* heavy

ONG *nf inv* (*abr* **Organización no Gubernamental**) NGO

onomástica *nf* saint's day

onomatopeya *nf* onomatopoeia

ONU *nf* (*abr* **Organización de las Naciones Unidas**) UN(O)

onubense 1 *adj* of/from Huelva
  2 *nmf* person from Huelva

onza *nf* *(medida)* ounce

OPA *nf* (*abr* **Oferta Pública de Adquisición**) takeover bid

opaco,-a *adj* opaque

ópalo *nm* opal

opción *nf* (**a**) *(elección)* option, choice; *(alternativa)* alternative (**b**) *(posibilidad)* opportunity, chance

opcional *adj* optional

open *nm* *Dep* open

OPEP *nf* (*abr* **Organización de los Países Exportadores de Petróleo**) OPEC

ópera *nf* *Mús* opera

operación *nf* (**a**) *Med* operation; **o. quirúrgica** surgical operation (**b**) *Fin* transaction, deal; **operaciones bursátiles** stock exchange transactions (**c**) *Mat* operation

operador,-a *nm,f* (**a**) *(técnico)* operator (**b**) *Cin (de cámara)* (*hombre*) cameraman; *(mujer)* camerawoman; *(del proyector)* projectionist (**c**) *Tel* operator

operante *adj* operative

operar 1 *vt* (**a**) *Med* **o. a algn (de algo)** to operate on sb (for sth) (**b**) *(cambio etc)* to bring about
  2 *vi Fin* to deal, to do business (**con** with)
  3 operarse *vpr* (**a**) *Med* to have an operation (**de** for) (**b**) *(producirse)* to occur, to come about

operario,-a *nm,f* operator; *(obrero)* worker

operativo,-a 1 *adj* operative
  2 *nm Am* operation

opereta *nf* operetta

opinar *vi* (**a**) *(pensar)* to think (**b**) *(declarar)* to give one's opinion, to be of the opinion

opinión *nf* *(juicio)* opinion; **cambiar de o.** to change one's mind

opio *nm* opium

oponente *nmf* opponent

oponer [19] (*pp* **opuesto**) **1** *vt* *(resistencia)* to offer
  2 oponerse *vpr* *(estar en contra)* to be opposed; **se opone a aceptarlo** he refuses to accept it

oporto *nm* *(vino)* port

oportunidad *nf* opportunity, chance

oportunista *adj & nmf* opportunist

oportuno,-a *adj* (**a**) *(adecuado)* timely; **¡qué o.!** what good timing! (**b**) *(conveniente)* appropriate; **si te parece o.** if you think it appropriate

oposición *nf* (**a**) opposition (**b**) *(examen)* competitive examination

opositar *vi* = to sit a competitive examination

opositor,-a *nm,f* (**a**) *(candidato)* = candidate for a competitive examination (**b**) *Am Pol* opponent

opresión *nf* oppression; **o. en el pecho** tightness of the chest

opresivo,-a *adj* oppressive

opresor,-a 1 *nm,f* oppressor
  2 *adj* oppressive, oppressing

oprimir *vt* (**a**) *(pulsar)* to press (**b**) *(subyugar)* to oppress

oprobio *nm* ignominy, opprobrium

optar *vi* (a) *(elegir)* to choose (**entre** between); **opté por ir yo mismo** I decided to go myself (b) *(aspirar)* to apply (a for); **puede o. a medalla** he's in with a chance of winning a medal

optativo,-a *adj* optional

óptica *nf* (a) *(tienda)* optician's (shop) (b) *(punto de vista)* angle

óptico,-a 1 *adj* optical
2 *nm,f* optician

optimismo *nm* optimism

optimista 1 *adj* optimistic
2 *nmf* optimist

óptimo,-a *adj* optimum, excellent

opuesto,-a *adj* (a) *(contrario)* contrary; **en direcciones opuestas** in opposite directions; **gustos opuestos** conflicting tastes (b) *(de enfrente)* opposite; **el extremo o.** the other end

opulencia *nf* opulence

opulento,-a *adj* opulent

opuse *pt indef de* **oponer**

oración *nf* (a) *Rel* prayer (b) *Ling* clause, sentence

oráculo *nm* oracle

orador,-a *nm,f* speaker, orator

oral *adj* oral; *Med* **por vía o.** to be taken orally

órale *interj Méx Fam* (a) *(venga)* come on! (b) *(de acuerdo)* right!, sure!

orangután *nm* orang-outang, orang-utan

orar *vi Rel* to pray

oratoria *nf* oratory

órbita *nf* (a) orbit (b) *Anat* eye socket

orden 1 *nm* order; **o. público** law and order; **por o. alfabético** in alphabetical order; **de primer o.** first-rate; **o. del día** agenda; **del o. de** approximately
2 *nf* (a) *(mandato)* order; *Mil* **¡a la o.!** sir! (b) *Jur* warrant, order; **o. de registro** search warrant; **o. judicial** court order

ordenado,-a *adj* tidy

ordenador *nm* computer; **o. personal** personal computer

ordenamiento *nm* ordering

ordenanza 1 *nm* *(empleado)* office boy
2 *nf* regulations; **o. municipal** bylaw

ordenar 1 *vt* (a) *(organizar)* to put in order; *(habitación)* to tidy up (b) *(mandar)* to order (c) *Am* *(pedir)* to order
2 **ordenarse** *vpr Rel* to be ordained (**de** as), to take holy orders

ordeñar *vt* to milk

ordinario,-a *adj* (a) *(corriente)* ordinary, common (b) *(grosero)* vulgar, common

orégano *nm* oregano, marjoram

oreja *nf* ear; *(de sillón)* wing

orejero,-a *nm,f Am* *(soplón)* grass

orfanato *nm* orphanage

orfebre *nm* *(del oro)* goldsmith; *(de la plata)* silversmith

orfebrería *nf* gold/silver work

orfelinato *nm* orphanage

orgánico,-a *adj* organic

organigrama *nm* organization chart; *Informát* flow chart

organismo *nm* (a) *(ser vivo)* organism (b) *(institución)* organization, body

organista *nmf* organist

organización *nf* organization

organizado,-a *adj* organized; **viaje o.** package tour

organizador,-a 1 *adj* organizing
2 *nm,f* organizer

organizar [40] 1 *vt* to organize
2 **organizarse** *vpr Fig* *(armarse)* to happen

órgano *nm* organ

orgasmo *nm* orgasm

orgía *nf* orgy

orgullo *nm* (a) *(propia estima)* pride (b) *(arrogancia)* arrogance

orgulloso,-a *adj* (a) **estar o.** *(satisfecho)* to be proud (b) **ser o.** *(arrogante)* to be arrogant o haughty

orientación *nf* (a) *(dirección)* orientation, direction (b) *(guía)* guidance; **curso de o.** induction course

oriental 1 *adj* (a) *(del este)* eastern, oriental; *(del Lejano Oriente)* oriental (b) *Am (uruguayo)* Uruguayan
2 *nmf* (a) *(del Lejano Oriente)* oriental (b) *Am (uruguayo)* Uruguayan

orientar 1 *vt* (a) *(enfocar)* to aim (**a** at), to intend (**a** for); **orientado al consumo** intended for consumption (b) *(indicar camino)* to give directions to; *Fig (aconsejar)* to advise (c) **una casa orientada al sur** a house facing south (d) *(esfuerzo)* to direct
2 **orientarse** *vpr (encontar el camino)* to get one's bearings, to find one's way about

oriente *nm* East, Orient; **el Extremo** o **Lejano/Medio/Próximo O.** the Far/Middle/Near East

orificio *nm* hole, opening; *Anat & Téc* orifice; **o. de entrada** inlet; **o. de salida** outlet

origen *nm* origin; **país de o.** country of origin; **dar o. a** to give rise to

original *adj & nm* original

originalidad *nf* originality

originar 1 *vt* to cause, to give rise to

2 originarse *upr* to originate
originariamente *adv* originally
originario,-a *adj* native
orilla *nf* (*borde*) edge; (*del río*) bank; (*del mar*) shore
orillero,-a *adj Am* (*persona*) suburban
orín¹ *nm* (*herrumbre*) rust
orín² *nm* (*usu pl*) (*orina*) urine
orina *nf* urine
orinal *nm* chamberpot; *Fam* potty
orinar 1 *vi* to urinate
2 orinarse *upr* to wet oneself
oriundo,-a *adj* ser o. de to come from
orla *nf Univ* graduation photograph
ornamentar *vt* to adorn, to embellish
ornamento *nm* ornament
ornar *vt* to adorn, to embellish
ornato *nm* (*atavío*) finery; (*adorno*) decoration
ornitología *nf* ornithology
ornitólogo,-a *nm,f* ornithologist
oro *nm* (**a**) gold; **de o.** gold, golden; **o. de ley** fine gold (**b**) *Naipes* **oros** (*baraja española*) ≃ diamonds
orquesta *nf* orchestra; (*de verbena*) dance band
orquestar *vt* to orchestrate
orquídea *nf* orchid
ortiga *nf* (*stinging*) nettle
ortodoxia *nf* orthodoxy
ortodoxo,-a *adj* orthodox
ortografía *nf* orthography, spelling; **faltas de o.** spelling mistakes
ortográfico,-a *adj* orthographic, orthographical; **signos ortográficos** punctuation
ortopédico,-a *adj* orthopaedic; **pierna ortopédica** artificial leg
oruga *nf* caterpillar
orzuelo *nm Med* sty, stye
os *pron pers pl* (**a**) (*complemento directo*) you; **os veo mañana** I'll see you tomorrow (**b**) (*complemento indirecto*) you, to you; **os daré el dinero** I'll give you the money; **os escribiré** I'll write to you (**c**) (*con verbo reflexivo*) yourselves (**d**) (*con verbo recíproco*) each other; **os queréis mucho** you love each other very much
osa *nf* **O. Mayor** *Br* Great Bear, *US* Big Dipper; **O. Menor** *Br* Little Bear, *US* Little Dipper
osadía *nf* (**a**) (*audacia*) daring (**b**) (*desvergüenza*) impudence
osado,-a *adj* (**a**) (*audaz*) daring (**b**) (*desvergonzado*) shameless
osar *vi* to dare
osario *nm* ossuary

oscilación *nf* (**a**) oscillation (**b**) (*de precios*) fluctuation
oscilante *adj* (**a**) oscillating (**b**) (*precios*) fluctuating
oscilar *vi* (**a**) *Fís* to oscillate (**b**) (*variar*) to vary, to fluctuate
oscuras: • **a oscuras** *loc adv* in the dark; **nos quedamos a o.** we were left in darkness
oscurecer [33] *v impers, vt & vpr* ▶ **obscurecer**
oscuridad *nf* = **obscuridad**
oscuro,-a *adj* = **obscuro,-a**
óseo,-a *adj* osseous, bony; **tejido ó.** bone tissue
osito *nm Fam* **o. (de peluche)** teddy bear
ósmosis, osmosis *nf inv* osmosis
oso *nm* bear; **o. polar** polar bear; **o. hormiguero** anteater; **o. marino** fur seal; *Fam Fig* **hacer el o.** to play the fool
ostensible *adj* ostensible
ostentación *nf* ostentation; **hacer o. de algo** to show sth off
ostentar *vt* (**a**) (*lucir*) to flaunt (**b**) (*cargo*) to hold
ostentoso,-a *adj* ostentatious
osteópata *nmf* osteopath
osteopatía *nf* osteopathy
ostión *nm* (**a**) *Méx* (*ostra*) large oyster (**b**) *Chile* (*vieira*) scallop
ostra *nf* oyster; *Fig* **aburrirse como una o.** to be bored stiff; *Fam* **¡ostras!** *Br* crikey!, *US* gee!
ostracismo *nm* ostracism
OTAN *nf* (*abr* **Organización del Tratado del Atlántico Norte**) NATO
otear *vt* (*horizonte*) to scan, to search
OTI *nf* (*abr* **Organización de Televisiones Iberoamericanas**) = association of all Spanish-speaking television networks
otitis *nf inv* infection and inflammation of the ear, otitis
otoñal *adj* autumn, *US* fall
otoño *nm* autumn, *US* fall
otorgamiento *nm* (*concesión*) granting; (*de un premio*) award
otorgar [42] *vt* (**a**) (*premio*) to award (**a** to); **o. un indulto** to grant pardon (**b**) (*permiso*) to grant (**a** to)
otorrinolaringólogo,-a *nm,f* ear, nose and throat specialist
otro,-a 1 *adj indef* (**a**) (*sin artículo*) (*sing*) another; (*pl*) other; **o. coche** another car; **otras personas** other people (**b**) (*con artículo definido*) other; **el o. coche** the other car (**c**) **otra cosa** something else; **otra vez** again
2 *pron indef* (**a**) (*sin artículo*) (*sing*)

another (one); *(pl) (personas)* others; *(cosas)* other ones; **dame o.** give me another (one); **no es mío, es de o.** it's not mine, it's somebody else's (**b**) *(con artículo definido) (sing)* **el o./la otra** the other (one); *(pl) (personas)* **los otros/las otras** the others; *(cosas)* the other ones (**c**) **hacer o. tanto** to do likewise

ovación *nf* ovation

ovacionar *vt* to give an ovation to, to applaud

oval, ovalado,-a *adj* oval

óvalo *nm* oval

ovario *nm* ovary

oveja *nf* sheep; *(hembra)* ewe; *Fig* **la o. negra** the black sheep

overol *nm Am* overalls

ovillo *nm* ball (of wool); *Fig* **hacerse un o.** to curl up into a ball

ovino,-a *adj* ovine; **ganado o.** sheep *pl*

OVNI *nm (abr* **objeto volador no identificado)** UFO

ovular 1 *adj* ovular

2 *vi* to ovulate

óvulo *nm* ovule

oxidación *nf (metal)* rusting

oxidado,-a *adj (metal)* rusty; *Fig* **su inglés está un poco o.** her English is a bit rusty

oxidar 1 *vt Quím* to oxidize; *(metales)* to rust

2 oxidarse *vpr Quím* to oxidize; *(metales)* to rust, to go rusty

óxido *nm* (**a**) oxide; **ó. de carbono** carbon monoxide (**b**) *(orín)* rust

oxigenado,-a *adj* oxygenated; **agua oxigenada** (hydrogen) peroxide

oxígeno *nm* oxygen; **bomba de o.** oxygen cylinder *o* tank

oye *indic pres & imperat de* **oír**

oyente *nmf* (**a**) *Rad* listener (**b**) *Univ* occasional student

ozono *nm* ozone; **capa de o.** ozone layer

P

P, p [pe] *nf (la letra)* P, p

pabellón *nm* (a) **p. de deportes** sports centre (b) *(en feria)* stand (c) *(bloque)* wing (d) *(bandera)* flag

pábulo *nm Fml Fig* fuel; **dar p. a** to encourage

pacer [60] *vt & vi* to graze, to pasture

pachá *nm Fam Fig* **vivir como un p.** to live like a king

Pachamama *n* Mother Earth

pachanguero,-a *adj Fam Pey (música)* catchy

pachón,-ona *nm,f (perro)* pointer

pachorra *nf Fam* sluggishness; **tener p.** to be phlegmatic

paciencia *nf* patience; **armarse de p.** to grin and bear it

paciente *adj & nmf* patient

pacificación *nf* pacification

pacificador,-a 1 *adj* pacifying

   2 *nm,f* peacemaker

pacificar [44] **1** *vt* to pacify; *Fig (apaciguar)* to appease, to calm

   2 pacificarse *vpr* to calm down

Pacífico *nm* **el (océano) P.** the Pacific (Ocean)

pacífico,-a *adj* peaceful

pacifismo *nm* pacifism

pacifista *adj & nmf* pacifist

paco *nm Andes, Pan Fam (policía)* cop

pacotilla *nf Fam* **de p.** second-rate

pactar *vt* to agree to

pacto *nm* pact; **el P. de Varsovia** the Warsaw Pact; **p. de caballeros** gentlemen's agreement

padecer [33] *vt & vi* to suffer; **padece del corazón** he suffers from heart trouble

padecimiento *nm* suffering

padrastro *nm* (a) stepfather (b) *(pellejo)* hangnail

padrazo *nm* easy-going *o* indulgent father

padre 1 *nm* (a) father; **p. de familia** family man (b) **padres** parents

   2 *adj inv Fam* (a) *(tremendo)* huge; **pegarse la vida p.** to live like a king (b) *Méx (genial)* great

padrenuestro *nm* Lord's Prayer

padrino *nm* (a) *(de bautizo)* godfather;

(de boda) best man; **padrinos** godparents (b) *(espónsor)* sponsor

padrísimo,-a *adj Méx Fam* fantastic, great

padrón *nm* census

padrote *nm Méx Fam (proxeneta)* pimp

paella *nf* paella, = rice dish made with vegetables, meat and/or seafood

paellera *nf* paella pan

pág *(abr* **página)** p

paga *nf (salario)* wage; *(de niños)* pocket money; **p. extra** bonus

pagadero,-a *adj* payable; *Fin* **cheque p. al portador** cheque payable to bearer

pagador,-a *nm,f* payer

pagano,-a *adj & nm,f* pagan, heathen

pagar [42] *vt* (a) to pay; **p. en metálico** *o* **al contado** to pay cash; **p. por** *(producto, mala acción)* to pay for; *Fig* **(ella) lo ha pagado caro** she's paid dearly for it (b) *(recompensar)* to repay

pagaré *nm Fin* promissory note, IOU; **p. del tesoro** treasury note

página *nf* page; **en la p. 3** on page 3; *Fig* **una p. importante de la historia** an important chapter in history; *Informát* **p. personal** home page; *Informát* **p. web** web page

pago *nm* payment; **p. adelantado** *o* **anticipado** advance payment; **p. contra reembolso** cash on delivery; **p. inicial** down payment; **p. por visión** pay-per-view

paila *nf Andes, CAm, Carib* (frying) pan

paipái, paipay *nm (pl* **paipáis)** = large palm fan

país *nm* country, land; **vino del p.** local wine; **P. Vasco** Basque Country; **P. Valenciano** Valencia

paisaje *nm* landscape, scenery

paisano,-a 1 *adj* of the same country

   2 *nm,f (compatriota)* fellow countryman/countrywoman, compatriot; **en traje de p.** in plain clothes

Países Bajos *npl* **(los) P.** the Netherlands, the Low Countries

paja *nf* (a) straw (b) *Fam Fig (bazofia)* padding, waffle (c) *Vulg* **hacerse una p.** to wank

pajar *nm (almacén)* straw loft; *(en el exterior)* straw rick

pajarita *nf* (a) bow tie (b) *(de papel)* paper bird

pájaro *nm* (a) bird; **Madrid a vista de p.** a bird's-eye view of Madrid; **p. carpintero** woodpecker (b) *Fam* **tener pájaros** to have daft ideas

pajita, pajilla *nf* (drinking) straw

Pakistán *n* Pakistan

pakistaní *adj & nmf* Pakistani

pala *nf* (a) shovel; *(de jardinero)* spade; *(de cocina)* slice (b) *Dep (de ping-pong, frontón)* bat, *US* paddle; *(de remo)* blade

palabra *nf* (a) word; **de p.** by word of mouth; **dirigir la p. a algn** to address sb; **juego de palabras** pun *(promesa)* word; **p. de honor** word of honour (c) *(turno para hablar)* right to speak; **tener la p.** to have the floor

palabrería *nf* palaver

palabrota *nf* swearword

palacio *nm (grande)* palace; *(pequeño)* mansion; **P. de Justicia** Law Courts

paladar *nm* (a) palate (b) *(sabor)* taste

paladear *vt* to savour, to relish

palanca *nf* (a) lever (b) *(manecilla)* handle, stick; *Aut* **p. de cambio** *Br* gearstick, *US* gearshift; **p. de mando** control lever (c) *Dep (trampolín)* diving board

palangana *nf* washbasin

palco *nm* box

paleolítico,-a *adj* palaeolithic, paleolithic

paleontología *nf* palaeontology, paleontology

Palestina *n* Palestine

palestino,-a *adj & nm,f* Palestinian

palestra *nf* arena; *Fig* **salir o saltar a la p.** to enter the fray, to take the field

paleta *nf* (a) *(espátula)* slice (b) *(de pintor)* palette; *(de albañil)* trowel (c) *Dep (de pingpong)* bat (d) *CAm, Méx (piruli)* lollipop; *(polo) Br* ice lolly, *US* Popsicle®

paletilla *nf* (a) shoulder blade (b) *Culin* shoulder

paleto,-a *Fam Pey* **1** *adj* unsophisticated, boorish

2 *nm,f* country bumpkin, yokel

paliar [43] *vt* to alleviate, to palliate

paliativo,-a *adj & nm* palliative

palidecer [33] *vi* (a) *(persona)* to turn pale (b) *Fig (disminuir)* to diminish, to be on the wane

palidez *nf* paleness, pallor

pálido,-a *adj* pale

palillero *nm* toothpick case

palillo *nm* (a) *(mondadientes)* toothpick;

palillos chinos chopsticks (b) *Mús* drumstick

palio *nm* (a) canopy (b) *Rel* pallium

palique *nm Fam* chat, small talk

paliza *nf* (a) *(zurra)* thrashing, beating; **darle a algn una p.** to beat sb up (b) *(derrota)* beating (c) *Fam (pesadez)* bore, pain (in the neck)

palma *nf* (a) *Anat* palm (b) *Bot* palm tree (c) **hacer palmas** to applaud

palmada *nf* (a) *(golpe)* slap (b) **palmadas** applause, clapping

palmar *vt Fam* **palmarla** to snuff it, to kick the bucket

palmarés *nm* (a) *(historial)* service record (b) *(vencedores)* list of winners

palmatoria *nf* candlestick

palmera *nf* palm tree

palmo *nm (medida)* span; *Fig* **p. a p.** inch by inch

palo *nm* (a) stick; *(vara)* rod; *(de escoba)* broomstick; *Fig* **a p. seco** on its own (b) *(golpe)* blow; *Fig* **dar un p. a algn** to let sb down (c) **de p.** wooden (d) *Dep (de portería)* woodwork (e) *(de golf)* club (f) *Naipes* suit

paloma *nf* pigeon; *Lit* dove; **p. mensajera** homing o carrier pigeon

palomar *nm* pigeon house, dovecot

palomilla *nf* (a) grain moth (b) *(tuerca)* wing o butterfly nut

palomitas (de maíz) *nfpl* popcorn

palpable *adj* palpable

palpar *vt* to touch, to feel; *Med* to palpate

palpitación *nf* palpitation, throbbing

palpitante *adj* palpitating, throbbing; *(asunto)* burning

palpitar *vi* to palpitate, to throb

palta *nf Andes, RP (fruto)* avocado

palúdico,-a *adj* malarial

paludismo *nm* malaria

palurdo,-a *adj* uncouth, boorish

pamela *nf* broad-brimmed hat

pampa *nf* pampa, pampas

pamplina *nf Fam* nonsense

pan *nm* bread; **p. de molde** loaf of bread; **p. integral** wholemeal o wholewheat bread; **p. rallado** breadcrumbs; **p. dulce** *Méx* cake; *RP* = type of fruitcake eaten at Christmas; *Arg* **p. lactal** sliced bread; *Fam Fig* **más bueno que el p.** as good as gold; *Fam Fig* **es p. comido** it's a piece of cake

pana *nf* corduroy

panacea *nf* panacea

panadería *nf* baker's (shop), bakery

panadero,-a *nm,f* baker

panal *nm* honeycomb

Panamá *n* Panama

panamá *nm (sombrero)* Panama hat
panameño,-a *adj & nm,f* Panamanian
pancarta *nf* placard; *(en manifestación)* banner
pancho *nm RP (perrito caliente)* hot dog
páncreas *nm inv* pancreas
panda[1] *nm* panda
panda[2] *nf* gang
pandereta *nf* tambourine
pandilla *nf Fam* gang
panecillo *nm* bread roll
panel *nm* panel
panera *nf* bread-basket
pánfilo,-a *adj Fam (bobo)* silly, stupid; *(crédulo)* gullible
panfleto *nm* lampoon, political pamphlet
pánico *nm* panic; **sembrar el p.** to cause panic
panocha *nf Bot* corn cob; *(de trigo etc)* ear
panoli *nmf Fam* idiot
panorama *nm (vista)* panorama, view; *Fig* panorama
panorámico,-a *adj* panoramic
panqueque *nm Am* pancake
pantaleta *nf*, **pantaletas** *nfpl Carib, Méx (bragas)* panties, *Br* knickers
pantalla *nf* (a) *Cin, TV & Informát* screen (b) *(de lámpara)* shade (c) *Fig* **servir de p.** to act as a decoy
pantalón *nm (usu pl)* trousers, *US* pants; **p. vaquero** jeans
pantano *nm Geog* (a) *(natural)* marsh, bog (b) *(artificial)* reservoir
panteón *nm* pantheon, mausoleum; **p. familiar** family vault
pantera *nf* panther
pantimedias *nfpl Méx Br* tights, *US* pantyhose
pantomima *nf Teatro* pantomime, mime; *Pey (farsa)* farce
pantorrilla *nf Anat* calf
pantry *nm Ven (comedor diario)* = family dining area off kitchen
pants *nmpl Méx* track *o* jogging suit
pantufla *nf* slipper
panty *nm* (pair of) *Br* tights, *US* pantyhose

🖉 Observa que la palabra inglesa **panties** es un falso amigo y no es la traducción de la palabra española **panty**. En inglés, **panties** significa "bragas".

---

panza *nf Fam* belly, paunch
panzada *nf Fam* bellyful
panzudo,-a, panzón,-ona *adj* pot-bellied, paunchy
pañal *nm Br* nappy, *US* diaper; *Fig* **estar**

en pañales to be in one's infancy
paño *nm* (a) cloth material; *(de lana)* woollen cloth; *(para polvo)* duster, rag; *(de cocina)* dishcloth; *Fig* **paños calientes** half-measures (b) **paños** *(ropa)* clothes; **en paños menores** in one's underclothes
pañoleta *nf* (a) shawl (b) *Taurom* bullfighter's tie
pañuelo *nm* handkerchief; *(pañoleta)* shawl
Papa *nm* **el P.** the Pope
papa *nf* potato; *Fam* **no saber ni p. (de algo)** not to have the faintest idea (about sth); *Am* **papas fritas** *Br* chips, *US* (French) fries; *(de bolsa)* *Br* crisps, *US* (potato) chips
papá *nm Fam* dad, daddy
papada *nf* double chin
papagayo *nm* (a) *(animal)* parrot (b) *Carib, Méx (cometa)* kite
papalote *nm CAm, Méx* kite
papamoscas *nm inv* flycatcher
papanatas *nmf inv* sucker, twit
paparrucha(da) *nf* (piece of) nonsense
papaya *nf* papaya *o* pawpaw fruit
papear *vi Fam* to eat
papel *nm* (a) paper; *(hoja)* piece *o* sheet of paper; **papeles** *(documentos)* documents, identification papers; **p. higiénico** toilet paper; **p. carbón** carbon paper; **p. de carta** writing paper, stationery; *Chile* **p. confort** toilet paper; **p. de aluminio/de estraza** aluminium foil/brown paper; **p. de fumar** cigarette paper; **p. de lija** sandpaper; *Fin* **p. moneda** paper money, banknotes; **p. pintado** wallpaper; *Cuba* **p. sanitario** toilet paper; **p. secante** blotting paper; *Guat, Ven* **p. toilette** *o* **tualé** toilet paper (b) *Cin & Teatro* role, part
papeleo *nm Fam* paperwork
papelera *nf (en despacho)* wastepaper basket; *(en calle)* litter bin
papelería *nf (tienda)* stationer's (shop)
papeleta *nf* (a) *(de rifa)* ticket; *(de votación)* ballot paper; *(de resultados)* report (b) *Fam (dificultad)* tricky problem, difficult job
papeo *nm Fam* grub
paperas *nfpl Med* mumps *sing*
papilla *nf* pap, mush; *(de niños)* baby food
papista *nmf* papist
Papúa Nueva Guinea *n* Papua New Guinea
paquete *nm* (a) *(de cigarrillos etc)* packet; *(postal)* parcel, package (b) *(conjunto)* set, package; *Fin* **p. de acciones** share package (c) *Informát* software

package (**d**) *Fam (castigo)* punishment (**e**) *muy Fam (genitales)* packet, bulge

Paquistán *n* Pakistan

paquistaní *adj & nmf* Pakistani

par 1 *adj Mat* even

2 *nm* (**a**) *(pareja)* pair; *(dos)* couple (**b**) *Mat* even number; **pares y nones** odds and evens (**c**) *(noble)* peer (**d**) *(locuciones)* **a la p.** *(a la vez)* at the same time; **de p. en p.** wide open; *Fig* **sin p.** matchless

para *prep* **a** for; **bueno p. la salud** good for your health; **¿p. qué?** what for?; **p. ser inglés habla muy bien español** for an Englishman he speaks very good Spanish (**b**) *(finalidad)* to, in order to; **p. terminar antes** to o in order to finish earlier; **p. que lo disfrutes** for you to enjoy (**c**) *(tiempo)* by; **p. entonces** by then (**d**) *(a punto de)* **está p. salir** it's about to leave (**e**) *(locuciones)* **decir p. sí** to say to oneself; **ir p. viejo** to be getting old; **no es p. tanto** it's not as bad as all that; **p. mí** in my opinion

parábola *nf* (**a**) *Geom* parabola (**b**) *Rel* parable

parabólico,-a *adj* parabolic; *TV* **antena parabólica** satellite dish

parabrisas *nm inv Aut Br* windscreen, *US* windshield

paraca *nm Fam* para(chutist)

paracaídas *nm inv* parachute

paracaidista *nmf Dep* parachutist; *Mil* paratrooper

parachoques *nm inv Br* bumper, *US* fender

parada *nf* (**a**) stop; **p. de autobús** bus stop; **p. de taxis** taxi stand o rank (**b**) *Ftb* save, stop

paradero *nm* (**a**) *(lugar)* whereabouts *sing* (**b**) *Méx, Perú (apeadero)* stop

parado,-a 1 *adj* (**a**) stopped, stationary; *(quieto)* still; *(fábrica)* at a standstill; *Fig* **salir bien/mal p.** to come off well/badly (**b**) *(desempleado)* unemployed, out of work (**c**) *Fig (lento)* slow (**d**) *Am (de pie)* standing

2 *nm,f* unemployed person

paradoja *nf* paradox

paradójico,-a *adj* paradoxical

parador *nm* roadside inn; **p. nacional** o **de turismo** state-run hotel

parafernalia *nf* paraphernalia *pl*

parafrasear *vt* to paraphrase

paráfrasis *nf inv* paraphrase

paragolpes *nm inv RP (de automóvil) Br* bumper, *US* fender

paraguas *nm inv* umbrella

Paraguay *n* Paraguay

paragüero *nm* umbrella stand

paraíso *nm* (**a**) paradise; **p. terrenal** heaven on earth; *Fin* **p. fiscal** tax haven (**b**) *Teatro* gods, gallery

paraje *nm* spot, place

paralelo,-a *adj & nm* parallel

parálisis *nf inv* paralysis; **p. infantil** poliomyelitis

paralítico,-a *adj & nm,f* paralytic

paralización *nf* (**a**) *Med* paralysis (**b**) *(detención)* halting, stopping

paralizar **[40]** **1** *vt* to paralyse; *(circulación)* to stop

2 **paralizarse** *vpr Fig* to come to a standstill

parámetro *nm* parameter

paramilitar *adj* paramilitary

páramo *nm* bleak plain o plateau, moor

parangón *nm Fml* comparison; **sin p.** incomparable

paranoia *nf* paranoia

paranoico,-a *adj & nm,f* paranoiac, paranoid

parapente *nm (desde montaña)* paragliding, parapenting

parapeto *nm* (**a**) parapet (**b**) *(de defensa)* barricade

parapléjico,-a *adj & nm,f* paraplegic

parar 1 *vt* (**a**) to stop (**b**) *Dep* to save (**c**) *Am (levantar)* to raise

2 *vi* (**a**) to stop; **p. de hacer algo** to stop doing sth; **sin p.** non-stop, without stopping; *Fam* **no p.** to be always on the go (**b**) *(alojarse)* to stay (**c**) *(acabar)* **fue a p. a la cárcel** he ended up in jail

3 **pararse** *vpr* (**a**) to stop; **p. a pensar** to stop to think (**b**) *Am (ponerse en pie)* to stand up

pararrayos *nm inv* lightning rod o conductor

parásito,-a 1 *adj* parasitic

2 *nm* parasite

parasol *nm* sunshade, parasol

parcela *nf* plot

parche *nm* (**a**) patch (**b**) *(emplasto)* plaster (**c**) *Pey (chapuza)* botched-up o slapdash job

parchís *nm Br* ludo, *US* Parcheesi®

parcial 1 *adj* (**a**) *(partidario)* biased (**b**) *(no completo)* partial; **a tiempo p.** part-time

2 *nm (examen)* **p.** class examination

parcialmente *adv* partially, partly

parco,-a *adj (moderado)* sparing; *(frugal)* scant

pardillo,-a 1 *nm,f Pey* yokel, bumpkin

2 *nm Orn* linnet

pardo,-a *adj (marrón)* brown; *(gris)* dark grey

parecer¹ *nm* (a) *(opinión)* opinion (b) *(aspecto)* appearance

parecer² [33] 1 *vi* to seem, to look (like); **parece difícil** it seems o looks difficult; **parecía (de) cera** it looked like wax; *(uso impers)* **parece que no arranca** it looks as if it won't start; **como te parezca** whatever you like; **¿te parece?** is that okay with you?; **parece que sí/no** I think/don't think so; **¿qué te parece?** what do you think of it?

2 **parecerse** (a) *vpr* to be alike; **no se parecen** they're not alike (b) **p. a** to look like, to resemble; **se parecen a su madre** they look like their mother

parecido,-a 1 *adj* (a) alike, similar (b) **bien p.** good-looking

2 *nm* likeness, resemblance; **tener p. con algn** to bear a resemblance to sb

pared *nf* wall

paredón *nm* (a) thick wall (b) *Fam* **le llevaron al p.** he was shot by firing squad

pareja *nf* (a) pair; **por parejas** in pairs (b) *(hombre y mujer)* couple; *(hijo e hija)* boy and girl; **hacen buena p.** they make a nice couple, they're well matched; **p. de hecho** = common-law heterosexual or homosexual relationship (c) *(en naipes)* pair; **doble p.** two pairs (d) *(de baile, juego)* partner

parejo,-a *adj* (a) *(parecido)* similar, alike (b) **ir parejos** to be neck and neck

parentela *nf Fam* relations, relatives

parentesco *nm* relationship, kinship

paréntesis *nm inv* (a) parenthesis, bracket; **entre p.** in parentheses o brackets (b) *(descanso)* break, interruption; *(digresión)* digression

parezco *indic pres de* **parecer**

paria *nmf* pariah

parida *nf Fam* silly thing

pariente *nmf* relative, relation

> Observa que la palabra inglesa **parent** es un falso amigo y no es la traducción de la palabra española **pariente**. En inglés, **parent** significa tanto "padre" como "madre".

parir *vt & vi* to give birth (to)

París *n* Paris

parking *nm Br* car park, *US* parking lot

parlamentario,-a 1 *adj* parliamentary

2 *nm,f Br* Member of Parliament, MP, *US* Congressman, *f* Congresswoman

parlamento *nm* parliament

parlanchín,-ina *adj Fam* talkative, chatty

parné *nm Fam* dough, cash

paro *nm* (a) *(huelga)* strike, stoppage (b) *(desempleo)* unemployment; **estar en p.** to be unemployed; **cobrar el p.** *Br* to be on the dole

parodia *nf* parody

parodiar [43] *vt* to parody

parpadear *vi* *(ojos)* to blink; *Fig (luz)* to flicker

parpadeo *nm* *(de ojos)* blinking; *Fig (de luz)* flickering

párpado *nm* eyelid

parque *nm* (a) park; **p. de atracciones** funfair; **p. zoológico** zoo; **p. nacional/natural** national park/nature reserve; **p. eólico** wind farm; *(de niños)* playpen (c) **p. móvil** total number of cars

parqué *nm* parquet

parqueadero *nm Carib, Col, Pan Br* car park, *US* parking lot

parquear *vt Carib, Col, Pan* to park

parquet *nm* = **parqué**

parquímetro *nm Aut* parking meter

parra *nf* grapevine

párrafo *nm* paragraph

parranda *nf Fam* spree

parricidio *nm* parricide

parrilla *nf* (a) *Culin* grill; **pescado a la p.** grilled fish (b) *Téc* grate (c) *Aut & Dep* starting grid

párroco *nm* parish priest

parronal *nm Chile* vineyard

parroquia *nf* parish; *(iglesia)* parish church

parroquiano,-a *nm,f* (regular) customer

parsimonia *nf* phlegm, calmness

parte 1 *nf* (a) *(sección)* part (b) *(en una repartición)* share (c) *(lugar)* place, spot; **en o por todas partes** everywhere; **se fue por otra p.** he went another way (d) *Jur* party (e) *(bando)* side; **estoy de tu p.** I'm on your side (f) *Euf* **partes** *(genitales)* private parts (g) *(locuciones)* **por mi p.** as far as I am concerned; **de p. de ...** on behalf of ...; *Tel* **¿de p. de quién?** who's calling?; **en gran p.** to a large extent; **en p.** partly; **la mayor p.** the majority; **por otra p.** on the other hand; **tomar p. en** to take part in

2 *nm (informe)* report

partición *nf* *(reparto)* division, sharing out; *(de herencia)* partition; *(de territorio)* partition

participación *nf* (a) participation (b) *Fin (acción)* share; **p. en los beneficios** profit-sharing (c) *(en lotería)* part of a lottery ticket (d) *(notificación)* notice, notification

participante 1 *adj* participating

2 *nmf* participant

participar 1 *vi* (**a**) to take part, to participate (**en** in) (**b**) *Fin* to have a share (**en** in)
(**c**) *Fig* **p. de** to share
 2 *vt* (*notificar*) to notify

partícipe *nmf* (**a**) participant; **hacer p. de
algo** (*notificar*) to inform about sth (**b**)
Com & Fin partner

participio *nm Ling* participle

partícula *nf* particle

particular 1 *adj* (**a**) (*concreto*) particular
(**b**) (*privado*) private, personal (**c**) (*raro*)
peculiar
 2 *nmf* (*individuo*) private individual
 3 *nm* (*asunto*) subject, matter

particularidad *nf* special feature

partida *nf* (**a**) (*salida*) departure (**b**) *Com*
(*remesa*) batch, consignment (**c**) (*juego*)
game (**d**) *Fin* (*entrada*) item (**e**) *Jur* (*certificado*) certificate; **p. de nacimiento** birth
certificate

partidario,-a 1 *adj* **ser/no ser p. de algo**
to be for/against sth
 2 *nm,f* supporter, follower; **es p. del
aborto** he is in favour of abortion

partidista *adj* biased, partisan

partido *nm* (**a**) *Pol* party (**b**) *Dep* match,
game; **p. amistoso** friendly game; **p. de
vuelta** return match (**c**) (*provecho*) advantage; **sacar p. de** to profit from (**d**) *Jur*
(*distrito*) district (**e**) **tomar p. por** to side
with (**f**) **ser un buen p.** to be a good catch

partir 1 *vt* to break; (*dividir*) to split, to
divide; (*cortar*) to cut; **p. a algn por la
mitad** to mess things up for sb
 2 *vi* (**a**) (*marcharse*) to leave, to set out *o*
off (**b**) **a p. de** from
 3 partirse *vpr* to split (up), to break (up);
Fam **p. de risa** to split one's sides laughing

partisano,-a *nm,f* partisan

partitura *nf Mús* score

parto *nm* childbirth, labour; **estar de p.** to
be in labour

parvulario *nm* nursery school, kindergarten

párvulo,-a *nm,f* infant

pasa *nf* raisin; **p. de Corinto** currant

pasable *adj* passable, tolerable

pasaboca *nm Col* snack, appetizer

pasacalle *nm Col, Urug* banner (hung
across street)

pasada *nf* (**a**) **de p.** in passing (**b**) (*jugarreta*) dirty trick (**c**) *Fam* **¡eso es una p.!**
it's too much!

pasadizo *nm* corridor, passage

pasado,-a 1 *adj* (**a**) (*último*) last; **el año/
lunes p.** last year/Monday (**b**) (*anticuado*) dated, old-fashioned; **p. (de moda)**
out of date *o* fashion (**c**) (*alimento*) bad

(**d**) *Culin* cooked; **lo quiero muy p.** I want
it well done (**e**) **p. mañana** the day after
tomorrow
 2 *nm* past

pasador *nm* (**a**) (*prenda*) pin, clasp; (*para el pelo*) (hair) slide (**b**) (*pestillo*) bolt,
fastener

pasaje *nm* (**a**) passage (**b**) (*calle*) alley
(**c**) (*pasajeros*) passengers (**d**) (*billete*)
ticket

pasajero,-a 1 *adj* passing, temporary;
aventura pasajera fling
 2 *nm,f* passenger

pasamanos *nm inv* (*barra*) handrail; (*de
escalera*) banister, bannister

pasamontañas *nm inv* balaclava

pasapalo *nm Ven* snack, appetizer

pasaporte *nm* passport

pasapurés *nm inv Culin* potato masher

pasar 1 *vt* (**a**) to pass; (*objeto*) to pass, to
give; (*mensaje*) to give; (*página*) to turn;
(*trasladar*) to move; **p. algo a limpio** to
make a clean copy of sth
 (**b**) (*tiempo*) to spend, to pass; **p. el rato**
to kill time
 (**c**) (*padecer*) to suffer, to endure; **p.
hambre** to go hungry
 (**d**) (*río, calle*) to cross; (*barrera*) to pass
through *o* over; (*límite*) to go beyond
 (**e**) (*perdonar*) to forgive, to tolerate; **p.
algo (por alto)** to overlook sth
 (**f**) (*introducir*) to insert, to put through
 (**g**) (*examen*) to pass
 (**h**) *Cin* to run, to show
 2 *vi* (**a**) to pass; **¿ha pasado el autobús?**
has the bus gone by?; **ha pasado un
hombre** a man has gone past; **p. de largo**
to go by (without stopping); **el tren pasa
por Burgos** the train goes via Burgos;
pasa por casa mañana come round to
my house tomorrow
 (**b**) **p. a** (*continuar*) to go on to; **p. a ser** to
become
 (**c**) (*entrar*) to come in
 (**d**) (*tiempo*) to pass, to go by
 (**e**) **p. sin** to do without; *Fam* **paso de tí**
couldn't care less about you; *Fam* **yo paso**
count me out
 3 *v impers* (*suceder*) to happen; **¿qué
pasa aquí?** what's going on here?; **¿qué
te pasa?** what's the matter?; *Fam* **¿qué
pasa?** (*saludo*) how are you?; **pase lo
que pase** whatever happens, come what
may
 4 pasarse *vpr* (**a**) **se me pasó la ocasión** I
missed my chance; **se le pasó llamarme**
he forgot to phone me
 (**b**) (*gastar tiempo*) to spend *o* pass time;

pasárselo bien/mal to have a good/bad time
(**c**) *(comida)* to go off
(**d**) *Fam (excederse)* to go too far; **no te pases** don't overdo it
(**e**) **pásate por mi casa** call round at my place

pasarela *nf (puente)* footbridge; *(de barco)* gangway; *(de moda)* catwalk

pasatiempo *nm* pastime, hobby

pascua *nf* (**a**) Easter (**b**) **pascuas** *(Navidad)* Christmas; **¡felices Pascuas!** Merry Christmas!

pascualina *nf RP, Ven* = pie made with spinach and hard-boiled egg

pase *nm* (**a**) pass, permit (**b**) *Cin* showing

pasear 1 *vi* to go for a walk, to take a walk
2 *vt* (**a**) *(persona)* to take for a walk; *(perro)* to walk (**b**) *Fig (exhibir)* to show off
3 pasearse *upr* to go for a walk

paseíllo *nm Taurom* opening parade

paseo *nm* (**a**) walk; *(en bicicleta, caballo)* ride; *(en coche)* drive; **dar un p.** to go for a walk/a ride (**b**) *(avenida)* avenue

pasillo *nm* corridor; *Av* **p. aéreo** air corridor

pasión *nf* passion

pasional *adj* passionate; **crimen p.** crime of passion

pasividad *nf* passivity, passiveness

pasivo,-a 1 *adj* passive; *(inactivo)* inactive
2 *nm Com* liabilities

pasmado,-a *adj (asombrado)* astounded, amazed; *(atontado)* flabbergasted; **dejar p.** to astonish; **quedarse p.** to be amazed

pasmo *nm* astonishment, amazement

paso¹,-a *adj* **ciruela pasa** prune; **uva pasa** raisin

paso² *nm* (**a**) step; *(modo de andar)* gait, walk; *(ruido al andar)* footstep; *Mil* **llevar el p.** to keep in step; *Fig* **a dos pasos** a short distance away; *Fig* **seguir los pasos de algn** to follow in sb's footsteps
(**b**) *(camino)* passage, way; **abrirse p.** to force one's way through; *Aut* **ceda el p.** *(en letrero)* give way; **prohibido el p.** *(en letrero)* no entry; **p. a nivel** *Br* level crossing, *US* grade crossing; **p. de cebra** zebra crossing; **p. de peatones** *Br* pedestrian crossing, *US* crosswalk; **p. elevado** *Br* flyover, *US* overpass; **p. subterráneo** *(para peatones)* subway; *(para coches)* underpass
(**c**) *(acción)* passage, passing; **a su p. por la ciudad** when he was in town; **el p.**

del tiempo the passage of time; **estar de p.** to be just passing through
(**d**) **p. de montaña** mountain pass

pasodoble *nm* paso doble

pasota *nmf Fam* waster

pasta *nf* (**a**) paste; **p. de dientes** o **dentífrica** toothpaste (**b**) *(de pan, pasteles)* dough; *(italiana)* pasta (**c**) *(galleta)* *Br* biscuit, *US* cookie (**d**) *Fam (dinero)* dough, bread

pastar *vt & vi* to graze, to pasture

pastel *nm* (**a**) cake; *(de carne, fruta)* pie (**b**) *Arte* pastel (**c**) *Fam* **descubrir el p.** to spill the beans

pastelería *nf* (**a**) *(tienda)* confectioner's (shop) (**b**) *(dulces)* confectionery

pastelero,-a *nm,f* pastry cook, confectioner

pastiche *nm* (**a**) pastiche (**b**) *Fam (chapuza)* botch(-up)

pastilla *nf* (**a**) tablet, pill; **pastillas para la tos** cough drops (**b**) *(de jabón)* bar (**c**) *Fam* **a toda p.** at full speed

pastizal *nm* grazing land, pasture

pasto *nm* (**a**) *(hierba)* grass (**b**) *(alimento)* fodder; **ser p. de** to fall prey to (**c**) *Am (césped)* lawn, grass

pastor,-a 1 *nm,f* shepherd; *(mujer)* shepherdess; **perro p.** sheepdog
2 *nm* (**a**) *Rel* pastor, minister (**b**) *(perro)* **p. alemán** Alsatian

pastoreo *nm* shepherding

pastoso,-a *adj* pasty; *(lengua)* furry

pata 1 *nf* leg; *Fig* **patas arriba** upside down; **estirar la p.** to kick the bucket; **mala p.** bad luck; **meter la p.** to put one's foot in it; **p. de gallo** crow's foot
2 *nm Perú Fam (amigo)* pal, *Br* mate, *US* buddy

patada *nf (puntapié)* kick, stamp

patalear *vi* to stamp one's feet (with rage)

pataleo *nm* kicking; *(de rabia)* stamping

patán *nm* bumpkin, yokel

patata *nf* potato; **patatas fritas** *Br* chips, *US* (French) fries; *(de bolsa)* *Br* crisps, *US* (potato) chips

patatús *nm inv Fam* dizzy spell, queer turn

paté *nm* pâté

patear 1 *vt (pelota)* to kick; *(pisotear)* to stamp on
2 *vi (patalear)* to stamp (one's foot with rage)

patentar *vt* to patent

patente 1 *nf* (**a**) *(autorización)* licence; *(de invención)* patent (**b**) *CSur (matrícula)* *Br* number plate, *US* license plate
2 *adj (evidente)* patent, obvious

pateo *nm* stamping; *(abucheo)* boo(ing), jeer(ing)

paternal *adj* paternal, fatherly

paternalista *adj* paternalistic

paternidad *nf* paternity, fatherhood

paterno,-a *adj* paternal

patético,-a *adj* moving

patíbulo *nm* scaffold, gallows *sing*

patidifuso,-a *adj Fam* dumbfounded, flabbergasted

patilla *nf* (a) *(de gafas)* leg (b) **patillas** *(pelo)* sideburns

patín *nm* (a) skate; *(patinete)* scooter; **p. de ruedas/de hielo** roller-/ice-skate; **p. en línea** rollerblade (b) *Náut* pedal boat

patinaje *nm* skating; **p. artístico** figure skating; **p. sobre hielo/ruedas** ice-/roller-skating

patinar *vi* (a) to skate; *(sobre ruedas)* to roller-skate; *(sobre hielo)* to ice-skate (b) *(deslizarse)* to slide; *(resbalar)* to slip; *(vehículo)* to skid (c) *Fam (equivocarse)* to put one's foot in it, to slip up

patinazo *nm* (a) skid (b) *Fam (equivocación)* blunder, boob

patinete *nm* scooter

patio *nm* (a) *(de una casa)* yard, patio; *(de recreo)* playground (b) *Teatro & Cin* **p. de butacas** stalls

pato *nm* duck; *Fam* **pagar el p.** to carry the can

patochada *nf* blunder, boob

patógeno,-a *adj* pathogenic

patología *nf* pathology

patológico,-a *adj* pathological

patoso,-a *adj* clumsy, awkward

patota *nf Perú, RP (de gamberros)* street gang

patraña *nf* nonsense

patria *nf* fatherland, native country; **madre p.** motherland; **p. chica** one's home town/region

patriarca *nm* patriarch

patrimonio *nm (bienes)* wealth; *(herencia)* inheritance

patriota *nmf* patriot

patriótico,-a *adj* patriotic

patriotismo *nm* patriotism

patrocinador,-a 1 *adj* sponsoring
  2 *nm,f* sponsor

patrocinar *vt* to sponsor

patrocinio *nm* sponsorship, patronage

patrón,-ona 1 *nm,f* (a) *(jefe)* boss (b) *(de pensión) (hombre)* landlord; *(mujer)* landlady (c) *Rel* patron saint
  2 *nm* (a) pattern (b) *(medida)* standard

patronal 1 *adj* employers'; **cierre p.** lockout; **clase p.** managerial class

2 *nf (dirección)* management

patronato, patronazgo *nm* (a) *(institución benéfica)* foundation (b) *(protección)* patronage

patrono,-a *nm,f* (a) boss; *(empresario)* employer (b) *Rel* patron saint

patrulla *nf* (a) patrol; **estar de p.** to be on patrol; **coche p.** patrol car (b) *(grupo)* group, band; **p. de rescate** rescue party; **p. ciudadana** vigilante group

patrullar 1 *vt* to patrol
  2 *vi* to be on patrol

patrullero *nm CSur (auto)* police (patrol) car

paulatino,-a *adj* gradual

paupérrimo,-a *adj* extremely poor, poverty-stricken

pausa *nf* pause, break; *Mús* rest

pausado,-a *adj* unhurried, calm

pauta *nf* guidelines

pava *nf* (a) *Fam* **pelar la p.** to chat (b) *Arg (tetera)* kettle

pavada *nf RP (tontería)* stupid thing

pavesa *nf* ash

pavimentar *vt* to pave

pavimento *nm (de carretera)* road (surface), *US* pavement; *(de acera)* paving; *(de habitación)* flooring

pavo *nm* (a) turkey; *Fam* **no ser moco de p.** to be nothing to scoff at (b) *Fam (tonto)* twit; *Fam* **estar en la edad del p.** to be growing up

pavonearse *vpr Fam* to show off, to strut

pavoneo *nm Fam* showing off, strutting

pavor *nm* terror, dread

pay *nm Chile, Méx, Ven* pie

payaso *nm* clown; **hacer el p.** to act the clown

payés,-esa *nm,f* = Catalan or Balearic peasant

payo,-a *nm,f* non-gipsy person

paz *nf* peace; *(sosiego)* peacefulness; *Fam* **¡déjame en p.!** leave me alone!, **hacer las paces** to make (it) up

pazguato,-a *adj* (a) *(estúpido)* silly, stupid (b) *(mojigato)* prudish

PC *nm (abr* **personal computer***)* PC

PCE *nm Pol (abr* **Partido Comunista de España***)* = Spanish Communist party

pe *nf Fam* **de pe a pa** from A to Z

peaje *nm* toll; **autopista de p.** *Br* toll motorway, *US* turnpike

peatón *nm* pedestrian

peca *nf* freckle

pecado *nm Rel* sin; **p. capital** *o* **mortal** deadly sin

pecador,-a *nm,f* sinner

pecaminoso,-a *adj* sinful

pecar [44] *vi* to sin; *Fig* **p. por defecto** to fall short of the mark

pecera *nf* fish bowl, fish tank

pecho *nm* (a) chest; *(de mujer)* breast, bust; *(de animal)* breast; **dar el p. (a un bebé)** to breast-feed (a baby); *Fig* **tomar(se) (algo) a p.** to take (sth) to heart (b) *Am (en natación)* breaststroke; **nadar p.** to do the breaststroke

pechuga *nf* (a) *(de ave)* breast (b) *Fam (de mujer)* boob

pectoral *adj* pectoral, chest

peculiar *adj (raro)* peculiar; *(característico)* characteristic

peculiaridad *nf* peculiarity

pedagogía *nf* pedagogy

pedagógico,-a *adj* pedagogical

pedal *nm* pedal

pedalear *vi* to pedal

pedante 1 *adj* pedantic
2 *nmf* pedant

pedantería *nf* pedantry

pedazo *nm* piece, bit; **a pedazos** in pieces; **caerse a pedazos** to fall apart o to pieces; **hacer pedazos** to break o tear to pieces, to smash (up); *Fam* **¡qué p. de coche!** what a terrific car!

pederasta *nm* pederast

pedernal *nm* flint

pedestal *nm* pedestal

pediatra *nmf* paediatrician

pediatría *nf* paediatrics *sing*

pedicuro,-a *nm,f* chiropodist, *US* podiatrist

pedido *nm* (a) *Com* order; **hacer un p.** to place an order with (b) *(petición)* request

pedigrí *nm* pedigree

pedir [6] *vt* (a) to ask (for); **p. algo a algn** to ask sb for sth; **te pido que te quedes** I'm asking you to stay; **p. prestado** to borrow; *Fig* **p. cuentas** to ask for an explanation (b) *Com & (en bar etc)* to order (c) *(mendigar)* to beg

pedo *nm Fam* (a) fart; **tirarse un p.** to fart (b) *(borrachera)* bender

pedrada *nf (golpe)* blow from a stone; *(lanzamiento)* throw of a stone

pedrea *nf (en lotería)* small prizes

pedregoso,-a *adj* stony, rocky

pedrería *nf* precious stones, gems

pedrisco *nm* hailstorm

pega *nf* (a) *Fam (objeción)* objection; **poner pegas** to find fault with (b) **de p.** *(falso)* sham

pegadizo,-a *adj* catchy

pegado,-a *adj* (a) *(adherido)* stuck (b) *(quemado)* burnt

pegajoso,-a *adj (pegadizo)* sticky; *Fig (persona)* tiresome, hard to get rid of

pegamento *nm* glue

pegar [42] **1** *vt* (a) *(adherir)* to stick; *(con pegamento)* to glue; *(coser)* to sew on; *Fam* **no pegó ojo** he didn't sleep a wink; **p. fuego a** to set fire to
(b) *(golpear)* to hit
(c) **p. un grito** to shout; **p. un salto** to jump
(d) *Fam (contagiar)* to give; **me ha pegado sus manías** I've caught his bad habits
(e) *(arrimar)* **p. algo a** o **contra algo** to put o place sth against sth
2 *vi* (a) *(adherirse)* to stick
(b) *(armonizar)* to match, to go; **el azul no pega con el verde** blue and green don't go together o don't match; *Fig* **ella no pegaría aquí** she wouldn't fit in here
(c) *(sol)* to beat down
3 pegarse *vpr* (a) *(adherirse)* to stick; *(pelearse)* to fight
(b) *Fam (darse)* to have, to get; **p. un tiro** to shoot oneself
(c) *(comida)* to get burnt; **se me ha pegado el sol** I've got a touch of the sun
(d) *Fam* **pegársela a algn** to trick o deceive sb
(e) *(arrimarse)* to get close
(f) *Fam Fig* to stick
(g) *Med (enfermedad)* to be catching o contagious; *Fig (melodía)* to be catchy

pegatina *nf* sticker

peinado *nm* hairstyle, *Fam* hairdo

peinar 1 *vt* (a) *(pelo)* to comb (b) *(registrar)* to comb
2 peinarse *vpr* to comb one's hair

peine *nm* comb

peineta *nf* = ornamental comb worn in hair

pela *nf Fam* peseta

pelado,-a 1 *adj* (a) *(cabeza)* shorn; *(piel, fruta)* peeled; *(terreno)* bare (b) *Fam* **saqué un cinco p.** *(en escuela)* I just scraped a pass; **a grito p.** shouting and bawling (c) *Fam (arruinado)* broke, penniless (d) *(desvergonzado)* impudent, insolent
2 *nm Fam* haircut
3 *nm,f* (a) *Andes Fam (niño, adolescente)* kid (b) *CAm, Méx Fam (pobre)* poor person

peladura *nf* peeling

pelagatos *nmf inv Fam* poor devil, nobody

pelaje *nm* (a) fur, hair (b) *Pey (apariencia)* looks, appearance

pelambrera *nf Fam* mop (of hair), long/thick hair

pelapatatas *nm inv* potato peeler

pelar 1 *vt (cortar el pelo a)* to cut the hair of; *(fruta, patata)* to peel; *Fam* **hace un frío que pela** it's brass monkey weather

2 *vi (despellejar)* to peel

3 pelarse *vpr* (a) *(cortarse el pelo)* to get one's hair cut (b) *Fam* **corre que se las pela** he runs like the wind

peldaño *nm* step; *(de escalera de mano)* rung

pelea *nf* fight; *(riña)* row, quarrel; **buscar p.** to look for trouble

peleado,-a *adj* **estar p. (con algn)** not to be on speaking terms (with sb)

pelear 1 *vi* to fight; *(reñir)* to quarrel

2 pelearse *vpr* (a) to fight; *(reñir)* to quarrel (b) *(enemistarse)* to fall out

pelele *nm (muñeco)* straw puppet; *Fig* puppet

pelón,-ona *adj* (a) quarrelsome, aggressive (b) *(vino)* cheap

peletería *nf* furrier's; *(tienda)* fur shop

peletero,-a *nm,f* furrier

peliagudo,-a *adj* difficult, tricky

pelícano *nm* pelican

película *nf* (a) *Cin* movie, *Br* film; **p. de miedo** o **terror** horror film; **p. del Oeste** Western; *Fam* **de p.** fabulous (b) *Fot* film

peligrar *vi* to be in danger, to be threatened; **hacer p.** to endanger, to jeopardize

peligro *nm* danger; *(riesgo)* risk; **con p. de ...** at the risk of ...; **correr (el) p. de ...** to run the risk of ...; **poner en p.** to endanger

peligroso,-a *adj* dangerous, risky

pelirrojo,-a 1 *adj* red-haired; *(anaranjado)* ginger-haired

2 *nm,f* redhead

pellejo *nm* (a) *(piel)* skin (b) *(odre)* wineskin (c) *Fam* **arriesgar** o **jugarse el p.** to risk one's neck

pelliza *nf* fur jacket

pellizcar [44] *vt* to pinch, to nip

pellizco *nm* pinch, nip

pelma *nmf*, **pelmazo,-a** *nm,f (persona)* bore, drag

pelo *nm* (a) *(pelo)* hair; **cortarse el p.** *(uno mismo)* to cut one's hair; *(en la peluquería)* to have one's hair cut; *Fig* **no tiene ni un p. de tonto** he's no fool; *Fig* **no tener pelos en la lengua** to be very outspoken; *Fig* **tomar el p. a algn** to pull sb's leg, to take the mickey out of sb; *Fam* **con pelos y señales** in full detail; *Fam* **por los pelos** by the skin of one's teeth; *Fam* **me puso el p. de punta** it gave me the creeps (b) *(de animal)* fur, coat, hair (c) *Tex (de una tela)* nap, pile (d) *(cerda)* bristle

pelón,-ona *adj (sin pelo)* bald

pelota 1 *nf* (a) ball; *Fam* **devolver la p.** to give tit for tat (b) *Dep* pelota (c) *Fam (cabeza)* nut (d) **hacer la p. a algn** to toady to sb, to butter sb up (e) *muy Fam* **pelotas** *(testículos)* balls; **en pelotas** *Br* starkers, *US* butt-naked

2 *nmf Fam (pelotillero)* crawler

pelotari *nm* pelota player

pelotear *vi Dep* to kick a ball around; *Ten* to knock up

peloteo *nm Ten* knock-up

pelotilla *nf Fam* **hacer la p. (a algn)** to fawn (on sb)

pelotillero,-a *nm,f Fam* crawler

pelotón *nm* (a) *Mil* squad (b) *Fam (grupo)* small crowd, bunch; *(en ciclismo)* pack (c) *(amasijo)* bundle

pelotudo,-a *adj RP Fam* (a) *(estúpido)* stupid (b) *(grande)* great big, massive

peluca *nf* wig

peluche *nm* **osito de p.** teddy bear

peludo,-a *adj* hairy, furry

peluquería *nf* hairdresser's (shop)

peluquero,-a *nm,f* hairdresser

peluquín *nm* toupee

pelusa, pelusilla *nf* (a) *(fluff)* fluff; *(de planta)* down (b) *Fam* jealousy

pelvis *nf inv* pelvis

pena *nf* (a) *(tristeza)* grief, sorrow; *Fig* **me da p. de ella** I feel sorry for her; **¡qué p.!** what a pity! (b) *(dificultad)* hardships, trouble; **no merece** o **vale la p. (ir)** it's not worth while (going); **a duras penas** with great difficulty (c) *(castigo)* punishment, penalty; **p. de muerte** o **capital** death penalty (d) *CAm, Carib, Col, Méx (vergüenza)* shame, embarrassment; **me da p.** I'm ashamed of it

penacho *nm* (a) *(de ave)* crest, tuft (b) *Mil (de plumas)* plume

penal 1 *adj* penal; *Jur* **código p.** penal code

2 *nm* prison, jail

penalidad *nf (usu pl)* hardships, troubles

penalización *nf* penalization; *Dep* penalty

penalizar [40] *vt* to penalize

penalti *nm Dep (pl* **penaltis)** penalty; *Fam* **casarse de p.** to have a shotgun wedding

penar 1 *vt* to punish

2 *vi* to be in torment, to suffer

pendejo,-a *nm,f muy Fam* (a) *Am (tonto)* jerk, idiot (b) *RP Pey (adolescente)* kid

pendenciero,-a *adj* quarrelsome, argumentative

pendiente 1 *adj* (a) *(por resolver)* pending; *Educ* **asignatura p.** failed subject;

Com **p. de pago** unpaid (**b**) **estar p. de** (*esperar*) to be waiting for; (*vigilar*) to be on the lookout for (**c**) (*colgante*) hanging (**de** from)

  2 *nm* (*joya*) earring

  3 *nf* slope; (*de tejado*) pitch

pendón *nm* (**a**) (*bandera*) banner (**b**) *Pey* (*mujer*) slut, whore; (*hombre*) playboy

péndulo *nm* pendulum

pene *nm* penis

penetración *nf* penetration; (*perspicacia*) insight, perception

penetrante *adj* penetrating; (*frío, voz, mirada*) piercing; *Fig* (*inteligencia*) sharp, acute

penetrar 1 *vt* to penetrate; **p. un misterio** to get to the bottom of a mystery

  2 *vi* (*entrar*) to go o get (**en** in)

penicilina *nf* penicillin

península *nf* peninsula

penique *nm* penny, *pl* pence

penitencia *nf* penance

penitenciaría *nf* prison

penitenciario,-a *adj* penitentiary, prison

penoso,-a *adj* (**a**) (*lamentable*) sorry, distressing (**b**) (*laborioso*) laborious, difficult (**c**) *CAm, Carib, Col, Méx* (*vergonzoso*) shy

pensado,-a *adj* (**a**) thought out; **bien p., ... on** reflection, ...; **en el momento menos p.** when least expected; **mal p.** twisted; **tener algo p.** to have sth planned, to have sth in mind; **tengo p. ir** I intend to go (**b**) (*concebido*) designed

pensamiento *nm* (**a**) thought (**b**) (*máxima*) saying, motto (**c**) *Bot* pansy

pensar [1] **1** *vi* to think (**en** o about; **sobre** about o over); *Fig* **sin p.** (*con precipitación*) without thinking; (*involuntariamente*) involuntarily

  2 *vt* (**a**) to think (**de** of); (*considerar*) to think over o about; **piénsalo bien** think it over; *Fam* **¡ni pensarlo!** not on your life! (**b**) (*proponerse*) to intend; **pienso quedarme** I plan to stay (**c**) (*concebir*) to make; **p. un plan** to make a plan; **p. una solución** to find a solution

pensativo,-a *adj* pensive, thoughtful

pensión *nf* (**a**) (*residencia*) boarding house; (*hotel*) guesthouse; **media p.** half board; **p. completa** full board (**b**) (*paga*) pension, allowance; **p. vitalicia** life annuity

pensionista *nmf* pensioner

pentágono *nm* pentagon

pentagrama *nm* staff, stave

penthouse [pent'χaus] *nm* *CSur, Ven* penthouse

penúltimo,-a *adj* & *nm,f* next to the last, penultimate

penumbra *nf* penumbra, half-light

penuria *nf* scarcity, shortage

peña *nf* (**a**) rock, crag (**b**) (*de amigos*) club (**c**) *Fam* (*gente*) people

peñasco *nm* rock, crag

peñón *nm* rock; **el P. de Gibraltar** the Rock of Gibraltar

peón *nm* (**a**) unskilled labourer; **p. agrícola** farmhand (**b**) (*en ajedrez*) pawn

peonada *nf* day's work

peonza *nf* (*spinning*) top

peor 1 *adj* (**a**) (*comparativo*) worse (**b**) (*superlativo*) worst; **en el p. de los casos** if the worst comes to the worst; **lo p. es que** the worst of it is that

  2 *adv* (**a**) (*comparativo*) worse; **¡p. para mí/ti/etc.!** too bad! (**b**) (*superlativo*) worst

pepa *nf* *Col, Ven* (*carozo*) stone, *US* pit (*of fruit*)

pepenador,-a *nm,f* *CAm, Méx* scavenger (*on rubbish tip*)

pepián *nm* *CAm, Méx* = sauce thickened with ground nuts or seeds

pepinillo *nm* gherkin

pepino *nm* cucumber; *Fam* **me importa un p.** I don't give a hoot

pepita *nf* (*de fruta*) pip, seed; (*de metal*) nugget

pepitoria *nf* fricassee; **pollo en p.** fricassee of chicken

peque *nm* *Fam* (*niño*) kid

pequeño,-a 1 *adj* small, little; (*bajo*) short

  2 *nm,f* child; **de p.** as a child

Pequín *n* Peking

pera *nf* (**a**) *Bot* pear; **p. de agua** juicy pear (**b**) *CSur Fam* (*mentón*) chin

peral *nm* pear tree

percance *nm* mishap, setback

percatarse *vpr* **p. de** to realize

percepción *nf* perception

perceptible *adj* (**a**) perceptible (**b**) *Fin* receivable, payable

percha *nf* (*colgador*) (coat) hanger; (*de gallina*) perch

perchero *nm* clothes rack

percibir *vt* (**a**) (*notar*) to perceive, to notice (**b**) (*cobrar*) to receive

percusión *nf* percussion

perdedor,-a 1 *adj* losing

  2 *nm,f* loser

perder [3] **1** *vt* (**a**) to lose (**b**) (*tren, autobús*) to miss; (*tiempo*) to waste; (*oportunidad*) to miss (**c**) (*pervertir*) to be the ruin o downfall of

2 *vi* to lose; **echar (algo) a p.** to spoil (sth); **echarse a p.** to be spoilt; **salir perdiendo** to come off worst

3 perderse *vpr* (**a**) *(extraviarse) (persona)* to get lost; **se me ha perdido la llave** I've lost my key; **no te lo pierdas** don't miss it (**b**) *(pervertirse)* to go to rack and ruin

perdición *nf* undoing, downfall

pérdida *nf* (**a**) loss; **no tiene p.** you can't miss it (**b**) *(de tiempo, esfuerzos)* waste (**c**) *Mil* **pérdidas** losses

perdido,-a *adj* (**a**) *(extraviado)* lost (**b**) *Fam (sucio)* filthy (**c**) *Fam* **loco p.** mad as a hatter (**d**) **estar p. por algn** *(enamorado)* to be crazy about sb (**e**) *(acabado)* finished; **¡estoy p.!** I'm a goner!

perdigón *nm* pellet

perdiguero,-a *adj* partridge-hunting; **perro p.** setter

perdiz *nf* partridge

perdón *nm* pardon, forgiveness; **¡p.!** sorry!; **pedir p.** to apologize

perdonar *vt* (**a**) *(remitir)* to forgive (**b**) **¡perdone!** sorry!; **perdone que le moleste** sorry for bothering you (**c**) *(eximir)* to pardon; **perdonarle la vida a algn** to spare sb's life; **p. una deuda** to write off a debt

perdurable *adj* (**a**) *(eterno)* everlasting (**b**) *(duradero)* durable, long-lasting

perdurar *vi* (**a**) *(durar)* to endure, to last (**b**) *(persistir)* to persist, to continue to exist

perecedero,-a *adj* perishable; **artículos perecederos** perishables

perecer [33] *vi* to perish, to die

peregrinación *nf*, **peregrinaje** *nm* pilgrimage

peregrino,-a 1 *nm,f* pilgrim

2 *adj* **ideas peregrinas** crazy ideas

perejil *nm* parsley

perenne *adj* perennial, everlasting

perentorio,-a *adj* peremptory, urgent

pereza *nf* laziness, idleness

perezoso,-a *adj (vago)* lazy, idle

perfección *nf* perfection; **a la p.** to perfection

perfeccionamiento *nm* (**a**) *(acción)* perfecting (**b**) *(mejora)* improvement

perfeccionar *vt* to perfect; *(mejorar)* to improve, to make better

perfeccionista *adj & nmf* perfectionist

perfectamente *adv* perfectly; **¡p.!** *(de acuerdo)* agreed!, all right!

perfecto,-a *adj* perfect

perfidia *nf* perfidy, treachery

perfil *nm* (**a**) profile; *(contorno)* outline, contour; **de p.** in profile (**b**) *Geom* cross-section

perfilar 1 *vt (dar forma a)* to shape, to outline

2 perfilarse *vpr (tomar forma)* to take shape

perforación *nf*, **perforado** *nm* perforation; *Min* drilling, boring; *Informát (de tarjetas)* punching

perforadora *nf* punch; *Min* drill; *Informát* **p. de teclado** keypunch

perforar *vt* to perforate; *Min* to drill, to bore; *Informát* to punch

perfumar 1 *vt* to perfume

2 perfumarse *vpr* to put on perfume

perfume *nm* perfume, scent

pergamino *nm* parchment

pericia *nf* expertise, skill

periferia *nf* periphery; *(alrededores)* outskirts

periférico,-a 1 *adj* peripheral

2 *nm* (**a**) *Informát* peripheral (**b**) *CAm, Méx (carretera) Br* ring road, *US* beltway

perífrasis *nf inv* periphrasis, long-winded explanation

perilla *nf (barba)* goatee; *Fam* **de perilla(s)** *(oportuno)* at the right moment; *(útil)* very handy

perímetro *nm* perimeter

periódico,-a 1 *nm* newspaper

2 *adj* periodic(al); *Quím* **tabla periódica** periodic table

periodismo *nm* journalism

periodista *nmf* journalist, reporter

periodo, período *nm* period

peripecia *nf* sudden change, vicissitude

periplo *nm* voyage, tour

periquete *nm Fam* **en un p.** in a jiffy

periquito *nm* budgerigar, *Fam* budgie

periscopio *nm* periscope

peritaje *nm (estudios)* technical studies

perito,-a *nm,f* technician, expert; **p. industrial/agrónomo** ≃ industrial/agricultural expert

peritonitis *nf* peritonitis

perjudicar [44] *vt* to harm, to injure; *(intereses)* to prejudice

perjudicial *adj* prejudicial, harmful

perjuicio *nm* harm, damage; **en p. de** to the detriment of; **sin p. de** without prejudice to

perjurar *vi* to commit perjury

perjurio *nm* perjury

perla *nf* pearl; *Fig (persona)* gem, jewel; *Fam* **me viene de perlas** it's just the ticket

permanecer [33] *vi* to remain, to stay

permanencia *nf* (**a**) *(inmutabilidad)* permanence (**b**) *(estancia)* stay

permanente 1 *adj* permanent

2 *nf (de pelo)* permanent wave, perm; **hacerse la p.** to have one's hair permed

permisivo,-a *adj* permissive

permiso *nm* (**a**) *(autorización)* permission (**b**) *(licencia)* licence, permit; **p. de conducir** *Br* driving licence, *US* driver's license; **p. de residencia/trabajo** residence/work permit (**c**) *Mil* leave; **estar de p.** to be on leave

permitir 1 *vt* to permit, to allow; **¿me permite?** may I?

2 permitirse *vpr* (**a**) to permit o allow oneself; **me permito recordarle que** let me remind you that (**b**) **no se permite fumar** *(en letrero)* no smoking

permutar *vt* to exchange

pernicioso,-a *adj* pernicious

pernil *nm (de pantalón)* leg; *(jamón)* leg of pork

pernocta *nf Mil* **(pase de) p.** overnight pass

pero 1 *conj* but; **p., ¿qué pasa aquí?** now, what's going on here?

2 *nm* objection

perogrullada *nf* truism, platitude

perol *nm* large saucepan, pot

perorata *nf* boring speech

perpendicular *adj & nf* perpendicular

perpetrar *vt* to perpetrate, to commit

perpetuar [30] *vt* to perpetuate

perpetuo,-a *adj* perpetual, everlasting; *Jur* **cadena perpetua** life imprisonment

perplejidad *nf* perplexity, bewilderment

perplejo,-a *adj* perplexed, bewildered

perra *nf* (**a**) bitch (**b**) *Fam (moneda)* penny; **estar sin una p.** to be broke

perrera *nf* kennel, kennels

perrería *nf Fam* dirty trick

perro,-a 1 *nm* dog; *Fam* **un día de perros** a lousy day; *Fam* **vida de perros** dog's life; *Culin* **p. caliente** hot dog

2 *adj Fam (vago)* lazy

persecución *nf* (**a**) pursuit (**b**) *Pol (represión)* persecution

perseguir [6] *vt* (**a**) to pursue, to chase; *(correr trás)* to run after, to follow (**b**) *(reprimir)* to persecute

perseverante *adj* persevering

perseverar *vi* (**a**) to persevere, to persist (**b**) *(durar)* to last

persiana *nf* blinds

pérsico,-a *adj* Persian; **golfo P.** Persian Gulf

persignarse *vpr* to cross oneself

persistencia *nf* persistence

persistente *adj* persistent

persistir *vi* to persist

persona *nf* person; **algunas personas** some people; *Fam* **p. mayor** grown-up

personaje *nm* (**a**) *Cin, Lit & Teatro* character (**b**) *(celebridad)* celebrity, important person

personal 1 *adj* personal, private

2 *nm* (**a**) *(plantilla)* staff, personnel (**b**) *Fam (gente)* people

personalidad *nf* personality

personarse *vpr* to present oneself, to appear in person

personero,-a *nm,f Am* representative

personificar [44] *vt* to personify

perspectiva *nf* (**a**) perspective (**b**) *(futuro)* prospect

perspicacia *nf* insight, perspicacity

perspicaz *adj* sharp, perspicacious

persuadir *vt* to persuade; **estar persuadido de que** to be convinced that

persuasión *nf* persuasion

persuasivo,-a *adj* persuasive, convincing

pertenecer [33] *vi* to belong (**a** to)

perteneciente *adj* belonging

pertenencia *nf* (**a**) possessions, property (**b**) *(a un partido etc)* affiliation, membership

pértiga *nf* pole; *Dep* **salto con p.** pole vault

pertinaz *adj* (**a**) persistent (**b**) *(obstinado)* obstinate, stubborn

pertinente *adj* (**a**) pertinent, relevant (**b**) *(apropiado)* appropriate

perturbación *nf* disturbance; **p. del orden público** breach of the peace; *Med* **p. mental** mental disorder

perturbado,-a *adj* (mentally) deranged o unbalanced

perturbador,-a 1 *adj* disturbing

2 *nm,f* unruly person

perturbar *vt (el orden)* to disturb

Perú *n* Peru

peruano,-a *adj & nm,f* Peruvian

perversión *nf* perversion

perverso,-a *adj* perverse, evil

pervertir [5] *vt* to pervert, to corrupt

pervivir *vi* to survive

pesa *nf* weight; **levantamiento de pesas** weightlifting

pesadez *nf* (**a**) heaviness; *(de estómago)* fullness (**b**) *Fam (fastidio)* drag, nuisance

pesadilla *nf* nightmare; **de p.** nightmarish

pesado,-a 1 *adj* (**a**) heavy (**b**) *(aburrido)* tedious, dull; **¡qué p.!** what a drag!

2 *nm,f* bore

pesadumbre *nf* grief, affliction

pésame *nm* condolences, sympathy; **dar**

el p. to offer one's condolences; **mi más sentido p.** my deepest sympathy

pesar 1 *vt* to weigh; *Fig (entristecer)* to grieve

2 *vi* (**a**) to weigh; **¿cuánto pesas?** how much do you weigh? (**b**) *(ser pesado)* to be heavy (**c**) *Fig (tener importancia)* **este factor pesa mucho** this is a very important factor

3 *nm* (**a**) *(pena)* sorrow, grief (**b**) *(arrepentimiento)* regret; **a su p.** to his regret (**c**) **a p. de** in spite of

pesaroso,-a *adj* (**a**) *(triste)* sorrowful, sad (**b**) *(arrepentido)* regretful, sorry

pesca *nf* fishing; *Fam* **y toda la p.** and all that

pescadería *nf* fish shop, fishmonger's (shop)

pescadero,-a *nm,f* fishmonger

pescadilla *nf* young hake

pescado *nm* fish

pescador,-a 1 *adj* fishing

2 *nm,f (hombre)* fisherman; *(mujer)* fisherwoman

pescante *nm* (**a**) *(de carruaje)* coachman's seat (**b**) *Constr* jib, boom (**c**) *Náut* davit

pescar [44] 1 *vi* to fish

2 *vt* (**a**) to fish (**b**) *Fam (coger)* to catch

pescozada *nf*, **pescozón** *nm* slap on the neck/head

pescuezo *nm Fam* neck

pese a (que) *loc adv* in spite of (the fact that)

pesebre *nm* manger, stall

pesero *nm CAm, Méx* fixed-rate taxi service

peseta *nf* peseta

pesetero,-a *nm,f* skinflint

pesimismo *nm* pessimism

pesimista 1 *adj* pessimistic

2 *nmf* pessimist

pésimo,-a *adj* very bad, awful, terrible

peso *nm* (**a**) weight; **al p.** by weight; **p. bruto/neto** gross/net weight; *Fig* **me quité un p. de encima** it took a load off my mind; **p. mosca/pesado** *(en boxeo)* flyweight/heavyweight (**b**) *(importancia)* importance; **de p.** *(persona)* influential; *(razón)* convincing

pespunte *nm* backstitch

pesquero,-a 1 *adj* fishing

2 *nm* fishing boat

pesquisa *nf* inquiry

pestaña *nf* (**a**) eyelash, lash (**b**) *Téc* flange; *(de neumático)* rim

pestañear *vi* to blink; **sin p.** without batting an eyelid

peste *nf* (**a**) *(hedor)* stench, stink (**b**) *Med* plague; *Hist* **la p. negra** the Black Death (**c**) **decir** *o* **echar pestes** to curse

pesticida *nm* pesticide

pestilencia *nf* stench, stink

pestilente *adj* stinking, foul

pestillo *nm* bolt, latch

petaca *nf* (**a**) *(para cigarrillos)* cigarette case; *(para bebidas)* flask (**b**) *Méx (maleta)* suitcase (**c**) *Méx* **petacas** *(nalgas)* buttocks

petaco *nm (de juego)* flipper; **máquina de petacos** pinball machine

pétalo *nm* petal

petardo *nm* (**a**) firecracker, firework; *Mil* petard (**b**) *Fam (persona aburrida)* bore (**c**) *(droga)* joint

petate *nm Mil* luggage

petición *nf* request; *Jur* petition, plea

petiso,-a *adj Andes, RP Fam* short

peto *nm* **pantalón de p.** dungarees

petrificar [44] *vt*, **petrificarse** *upr* to petrify

petróleo *nm* petroleum, oil

📖 Observa que en el inglés británico **petrol** es un falso amigo y no es la traducción de la palabra española **petróleo**. En inglés británico, **petrol** significa "gasolina".

---

petrolero *nm* oil tanker

petulante *adj* arrogant, vain

📖 Observa que la palabra inglesa **petulant** es un falso amigo y no es la traducción de la palabra española **petulante**. En inglés, **petulant** significa "caprichoso".

---

petunia *nf* petunia

peyorativo,-a *adj* pejorative, derogatory

pez¹ *nm* fish; **ella está como p. en el agua** she's in her element; **p. gordo** big shot

pez² *nf* pitch, tar

pezón *nm* nipple

pezuña *nf* hoof

piadoso,-a *adj* (**a**) *(devoto)* pious (**b**) *(compasivo)* compassionate; **mentira piadosa** white lie

pianista *nmf* pianist, piano player

piano *nm* piano

piar [29] *vi* to chirp, to tweet

piara *nf* herd of pigs

PIB *nm Fin* (*abr* **producto interior bruto**) GDP

pibe,-a *nm,f Fam* (**a**) *(hombre)* guy; *(mujer)* girl (**b**) *RP (niño)* kid, boy; *(niña)* kid, girl

picada *nf RP (tapas)* appetizers, snacks

picadero *nm* riding school

picadillo *nm* (**a**) *(de carne)* *Br* minced *o*

US ground meat; *(de verduras)* vegetable salad (**b**) *Chile (tapas)* appetizers, snacks
picado,-a 1 *adj* (**a**) *(carne) Br* minced, *US* ground (**b**) *(fruta)* bad; *(diente)* decayed (**c**) *(mar)* choppy (**d**) *Fam (enfadado)* narked (**e**) **estar p. con** *(en competición)* to be at loggerheads with
2 *nm Av* dive; **caer en p.** to plummet
picador *nm Taurom* mounted bullfighter, picador
picadora *nf Br* mincer, *US* grinder
picadura *nf* (**a**) *(mordedura)* bite; *(de avispa, abeja)* sting (**b**) *(en fruta)* spot; *Med (de viruela)* pockmark; *(en diente)* decay, caries *sing*; *(en metalurgia)* pitting
picajoso,-a 1 *adj* touchy
2 *nm,f* touchy person
picante *adj* (**a**) *Culin* hot, spicy (**b**) *Fig (chiste etc)* risqué, spicy
picantería *nf Andes* cheap restaurant
picapica *nm (polvos de)* **p.** itching powder
picaporte *nm (aldaba)* door knocker; *(pomo)* door handle
picar [44] 1 *vt* (**a**) *(de insecto, serpiente)* to bite; *(de avispas, abejas)* to sting; *(barba)* to prick (**b**) *(comer) (aves)* to peck (at); *(persona)* to nibble, to pick at (**c**) *(de pez)* to bite (**d**) *(perforar)* to prick, to puncture (**e**) *Culin (carne) Br* to mince, *US* to grind (**f**) *(incitar)* to incite, to goad; **p. la curiosidad (de algn)** to arouse (sb's) curiosity
2 *vi* (**a**) *(escocer)* to itch; *(herida)* to smart; *(el sol)* to burn (**b**) *Culin* to be hot (**c**) *(pez)* to bite (**d**) *Fig (dejarse engañar)* to swallow it
3 picarse *upr* (**a**) *(hacerse rivales)* to be at loggerheads (**b**) *(fruta)* to spot, to rot; *(ropa)* to become moth-eaten; *(dientes)* to decay (**c**) *(enfadarse)* to get cross (**d**) *(drogadicto)* to shoot up
picardía *nf* (**a**) *(astucia)* craftiness (**b**) *(palabrota)* swearword (**c**) *(prenda)* baby-doll pyjamas
pícaro,-a 1 *adj* (**a**) *(travieso)* naughty, mischievous; *(astuto)* sly, crafty (**b**) *(procaz)* risqué
2 *nm,f* rascal, rogue
picatoste *nm* crouton
pichi *nm Br* pinafore dress, *US* jumper
pichincha *nf RP Fam* snip, bargain
pichón *nm* young pigeon; **tiro al** *o* **de p.** pigeon shooting
pickles ['pikles] *nmpl RP* pickles
pico *nm* (**a**) *(de ave)* beak, bill; *Fam (boca)* mouth; **tener un p. de oro** to have the gift of the gab (**b**) *(punta)* corner (**c**) *Geog* peak (**d**) *(herramienta)* pick, pickaxe (**e**)

(cantidad) odd amount; **cincuenta y p.** fifty odd; **las dos y p.** just after two (**f**) *(drogas)* fix
picoleto *nm Fam* civil guard
picor *nm* itch, tingling
picoso,-a *adj Méx* spicy, hot
picotazo *nm* peck
picotear *vt & vi* (**a**) *(pájaro)* to peck (**b**) *(comer)* to nibble
pictórico,-a *adj* pictorial
pídola *nf* leapfrog
pie *nm* (**a**) foot; **pies** feet; **a p.** on foot; **de p.** standing up; **de pies a cabeza** from head to foot; **en p.** standing; **el acuerdo sigue en p.** the agreement still stands; **hacer p.** to touch the bottom; **perder p.** to get out of one's depth; *Fig* **a pies juntillas** blindly; *Fig* **al p. de la letra** to the letter, word for word; *Fig* **con buen/mal p.** on the right/wrong footing; *Fig* **con pies de plomo** gingerly, cautiously; *Fig* **dar p. a** to give cause for (**b**) *(de instrumento)* stand; *(de copa)* stem (**c**) *(de página)* foot; *(de una ilustración)* caption; **p. de página** foot of the page (**d**) *(medida)* foot (**e**) *Teatro* cue (**f**) *Lit* foot
piedad *nf* (**a**) *(devoutness)* devoutness, piety (**b**) *(compasión)* compassion, pity
piedra *nf* stone; *(de mechero)* flint; **poner la primera p.** to lay the foundation stone; *Fam Fig* **me dejó** *o* **me quedé de p.** I was flabbergasted
piel *nf* (**a**) skin; **p. de gallina** goose pimples (**b**) *(de fruta, de patata)* skin, peel (**c**) *(cuero)* leather; *(con pelo)* fur
pienso *nm* fodder, feed; **piensos compuestos** mixed feed
pierna *nf* leg
pieza *nf* (**a**) piece, part; **p. de recambio** spare part; *Fig* **me dejó** *o* **me quedé de una p.** I was speechless *o* dumbfounded *o* flabbergasted (**b**) *(habitación)* room (**c**) *Teatro* play
pigmento *nm* pigment
pigmeo,-a 1 *adj* pigmy; *Fig* pygmean
2 *nm,f* Pygmy, Pigmy; *Fig* pygmy, pigmy
pijama *nm* pyjamas
pijo,-a *Fam* **1** *adj* posh; **un barrio p.** a posh area
2 *nm,f (chico)* poor little rich boy; *(chica)* poor little rich girl
3 *nm (pene)* willy
pila *nf* (**a**) *Elec* battery (**b**) *(montón)* pile, heap; *Fig* **una p. de** *(muchos)* piles *o* heaps *o* loads of (**c**) *(lavadero)* basin (**d**) *Fig* **nombre de p.** Christian name
pilar *nm* (**a**) *Arquit* pillar (**b**) *(fuente)* waterhole

píldora *nf* pill; **p. abortiva** morning-after pill; *Fig* **dorar la p. a algn** to butter sb up

pileta *nf* (**a**) *(pila)* sink (**b**) *Am (piscina)* swimming pool

pilila *nf Fam Br* willy, *US* peter

pillaje *nm* looting, pillage

pillar 1 *vt* (**a**) *(robar)* to plunder, to loot (**b**) *(coger)* to catch; *(alcanzar)* to catch up with; **lo pilló un coche** he was run over by a car (**c**) *Fam* to be; **me pilla un poco lejos** it's a bit far for *o* from me
  2 pillarse *vpr* to catch; **p. un dedo/una mano** to catch one's finger/hand

pillo,-a 1 *adj* (**a**) *(travieso)* naughty (**b**) *(astuto)* sly, cunning
  2 *nm,f* rogue

pilotar *vt Av* to pilot, to fly; *Aut* to drive; *Náut* to pilot, to steer

piloto *nm* (**a**) *Av & Náut* pilot; *Aut* driver; **piso p.** show flat; **programa p.** pilot programme (**b**) *(luz)* pilot lamp *o* light

piltrafa *nf* (**a**) *Fam* weakling; **estar hecho una p.** to be on one's last legs (**b**) *(desecho)* scraps

pimentón *nm* paprika, red pepper

pimienta *nf* pepper

pimiento *nm* *(fruto)* pepper; *(planta)* pimiento; **p. morrón** sweet pepper; *Fam* **me importa un p.** I don't give a damn, I couldn't care less

pimpollo *nm* (**a**) *Bot* shoot (**b**) *Fam (hombre)* handsome young man; *(mujer)* elegant young woman

pinacoteca *nf* art gallery

pináculo *nm* pinnacle

pinar *nm* pine grove, pine wood

pincel *nm* brush, paintbrush

pincelada *nf* brushstroke, stroke of a brush

pinchadiscos *nmf inv Fam* disc jockey, DJ

pinchar 1 *vt* (**a**) *(punzar)* to prick; *(balón, globo)* to burst; *(rueda)* to puncture (**b**) *Fam (incitar)* to prod; *(molestar)* to get at, to nag (**c**) *Med* to inject, to give an injection to (**d**) *Tel* to bug
  2 *vi* (**a**) *Aut* to get a puncture (**b**) *Fam* **ni pincha ni corta** he cuts no ice

---

🖉 Observa que el verbo inglés **to pinch** es un falso amigo y no es la traducción del verbo español **pinchar**. En inglés, **to pinch** significa "pellizcar".

---

pinchazo *nm* (**a**) *(punzadura)* prick; *Aut* puncture, blowout (**b**) *(de dolor)* sudden *o* sharp pain

pinche *nm* (**a**) **p. de cocina** kitchen assistant (**b**) *Am (bribón)* rogue

pinchito *nm (de carne)* = type of kebab

pincho *nm* (**a**) *(púa)* barb (**b**) **p. moruno** ≃ shish kebab; **p. de tortilla** = small portion of omelette

ping-pong® *nm* table tennis, ping-pong

pingüe *adj* abundant, plentiful; **pingües beneficios** fat profits

pingüino *nm* penguin

pino *nm* pine; *Fig* **hacer el p.** to do a handstand; *Fam* **en el quinto p.** in the back of beyond

pinole *nm Am* maize *o US* corn drink

pinta 1 *nf* (**a**) *Fam (aspecto)* look; **tiene p. de ser interesante** it looks interesting (**b**) *(mota)* dot; *(lunar)* spot (**c**) *(medida)* pint
  2 *nmf Fam* shameless person

pintada *nf* graffiti

pintado,-a *adj* **recién p.** *(en letrero)* wet paint; *Fam Fig* **nos viene que ni p.** it is just the ticket; *Fam Fig* **te está que ni p.** it suits you to a tee

pintar 1 *vt* (**a**) *(dar color)* to paint (**b**) *(dibujar)* to draw, to sketch
  2 *vi (importar)* to count; *Fig* **yo aquí no pinto nada** I am out of place here
  3 pintarse *vpr* (**a**) *(maquillarse)* to put make-up on (**b**) *Fam* **pintárselas** to manage

pintarraj(e)ar *vt* to daub

pintor,-a *nm,f* painter

pintoresco,-a *adj* (**a**) *(lugar)* picturesque (**b**) *(raro)* eccentric, bizarre

pintura *nf* (**a**) *(arte)* painting; *Fam Fig* **no la puedo ver ni en p.** I can't stand the sight of her (**b**) *(materia)* paint

pinza *nf* *(para depilar)* tweezers; *(para tender)* *Br* clothes peg, *US* clothespin; *(de animal)* pincer, nipper; *Téc* tongs

piña *nf* (**a**) *(de pino)* pine cone; *(ananás)* pineapple (**b**) *Fig (grupo)* clan, clique (**c**) *Fam (golpe)* thump

piñón *nm* (**a**) *(de pino)* pine seed *o* nut (**b**) *Téc* pinion

pío¹ *nm Fam* **no dijo ni p.** there wasn't a cheep out of him

pío²,-a *adj* pious

piojo *nm* louse

piola *adj RP Fam* (**a**) *(simpático)* fun (**b**) *Irón (listo)* smart, clever (**c**) *(lugar)* cosy

piolín *nm Am* cord

pionero,-a *nm,f* pioneer

pipa *nf* (**a**) *(de fumar)* pipe; **fumar en p.** to smoke a pipe (**b**) *(de fruta)* pip; *(de girasol)* sunflower seed

pipí *nm Fam* pee, *Br* wee-wee; **hacer p.** to pee, *Br* to wee-wee

pique *nm* (**a**) resentment (**b**) *(rivalidad)* needle (**c**) **a p. de** on the point of (**d**) **irse**

a p. *Náut* to sink; *(un plan)* to fall through; *(un negocio)* to go bust

piqueta *nf* pickaxe

piquete *nm* (**a**) *(de huelga)* picket (**b**) *Mil* **p. de ejecución** firing squad

pira *nf* pyre

pirado,-a *adj Fam* crazy

piragua *nf* canoe

piragüismo *nm* canoeing

piragüista *nmf* canoeist

pirámide *nf* pyramid

piraña *nf* piranha

pirarse, pirárselas *vpr Fam* to clear off, to hop it

pirata *adj & nmf* pirate

piratear *vt Fig* to pirate

Pirineo(s) *nm(pl)* Pyrenees

pirita *nf* pyrite

pirómano,-a *nm,f Med* pyromaniac; *Jur* arsonist

piropo *nm* **echar un p.** to pay a compliment

pirueta *nf* pirouette; *Fig Pol* **hacer una p.** to do a U-turn

pirulí *nm* lollipop; *TV* television tower

pis *nm Fam* pee, *Br* wee-wee; **hacer p.** to have a pee, *Br* to wee-wee

pisada *nf* step, footstep; *(huella)* footprint

pisapapeles *nm inv* paperweight

pisar *vt* to tread on, to step on

piscifactoría *nf* fish farm

piscina *nf* swimming pool

pisco *nm* pisco, = Andean grape brandy

piscolabis *nm inv Fam* snack

piso *nm* (**a**) *(vivienda)* apartment, *Br* flat; *Pol* **p. franco** safe house (**b**) *(planta)* floor; *(de carretera)* surface

pisotear *vt (aplastar)* to stamp on; *(pisar)* to trample on

pisotón *nm* **me dio un p.** he stood on my foot

pista *nf* (**a**) track; **p. de baile** dance floor; *Dep* **p. de esquí** ski run *o* slope; *Dep* **p. de patinaje** ice rink; *Dep* **p. de tenis** tennis court; **p. de aterrizaje** landing strip; **p. de despegue** runway (**b**) *(rastro)* trail, track (**c**) **dame una p.** give me a clue

pistacho *nm* pistachio nut

pisto *nm Culin* ≃ ratatouille

pistola *nf* (**a**) gun, pistol (**b**) *(para pintar)* spray gun

pistolero *nm* gunman, gangster

pistón *nm* (**a**) *Téc (émbolo)* piston (**b**) *(de arma)* cartridge cap (**c**) *Mús* key

pita *nf* agave

pitada *nf* (**a**) *(silbidos de protesta)* booing, whistling (**b**) *Am Fam (calada)* drag, puff

pitar 1 *vt* (**a**) *(silbato)* to blow (**b**) *Dep* **el árbitro pitó un penalti** the referee awarded a penalty

2 *vi* (**a**) to whistle (**b**) *Aut* to toot one's horn (**c**) *Dep* to referee (**d**) *Fam* **salir pitando** to fly off

pitido *nm* whistle

pitillera *nf* cigarette case

pitillo *nm* (**a**) *(cigarrillo)* cigarette (**b**) *Col (paja)* drinking straw

pito *nm* (**a**) whistle; *Aut* horn; *Fam* **me importa un p.** I don't give a hoot (**b**) *Fam (cigarrillo)* fag (**c**) *Fam (pene)* prick, willie

pitón *nm* (**a**) *(serpiente)* python (**b**) *(de toro)* horn

pitorreo *nm Fam* scoffing, teasing; **hacer algo de p.** to do sth for a laugh

pivot, pivote *nmf* pivot

pizarra *nf* (**a**) *(encerado)* blackboard (**b**) *(roca, material)* slate

pizarrón *nm Am (encerado)* blackboard

pizca *nf* little bit, tiny piece; **ni p.** not a bit; **una p. de sal** a pinch of salt

placa *nf* (**a**) plate (**b**) *(conmemorativa)* plaque

placaje *nm Dep* tackle

placentero,-a *adj* pleasant, agreeable

placer [33] 1 *vt* to please

2 *nm* pleasure; **ha sido un p. (conocerle)** it's been a pleasure (meeting you); *Fml* **tengo el p. de** it gives me great pleasure to; **un viaje de p.** a holiday trip

placidez *nf* placidity

plácido,-a *adj* placid, easy-going

plaga *nf* (**a**) plague (**b**) *Agr* pest, blight

plagar [42] *vt* to cover, to fill

plagiar [43] *vt* (**a**) *(copiar)* to plagiarize (**b**) *Andes, CAm, Méx (secuestrar)* to kidnap

plagiario,-a *nm,f Andes, CAm, Méx (secuestrador)* kidnapper

plagio *nm* plagiarism

plan *nm* (**a**) *(proyecto)* plan (**b**) *(programa)* scheme, programme; *Educ* **p. de estudios** syllabus; **estar a p.** to be on a diet (**c**) *Fam* **en p. de broma** for a laugh; **si te pones en ese p.** if you're going to be like that (about it); **en p. barato** cheaply (**d**) *Fam (cita)* date

plana *nf* (**a**) page; **a toda p.** full page; **primera p.** front page (**b**) *Mil* **p. mayor** staff

plancha *nf* (**a**) iron; *(de metal)* plate (**b**) *Culin* hotplate; **sardinas a la p.** grilled sardines (**c**) *Impr* plate

planchado *nm* ironing

planchar *vt* to iron

planchazo *nm Fam* blunder, boob

planeador *nm* glider

planear 1 *vt* to plan
  2 *vi* to glide

planeta *nm* planet

planetario,-a 1 *adj* planetary
  2 *nm* planetarium

planicie *nf* plain

planificación *nf* planning; **p. familiar** family planning

planificar [44] *vt* to plan

planilla *nf Am* application form

plano,-a 1 *nm* (**a**) (*de ciudad*) map; *Arquit* plan, draft (**b**) *Cin* shot; **un primer p.** a close-up; *Fig* **estar en primer/segundo p.** to be in the limelight/in the background (**c**) *Mat* plane
  2 *adj* flat, even

planta *nf* (**a**) plant (**b**) (*del pie*) sole (**c**) (*piso*) floor, storey; **p. baja** *Br* ground floor, *US* first floor

plantación *nf* (**a**) plantation (**b**) (*acción*) planting

plantado,-a *adj Fam* **dejar a algn p.** to stand sb up

plantar 1 *vt* (**a**) (*árboles, campo*) to plant (**b**) (*poner*) to put, to place; **p. cara a algn** to stand up to sb (**c**) *Fam* **p. a algn en la calle** to throw sb out; **le ha plantado su novia** his girlfriend has ditched him
  2 plantarse *upr* (**a**) to stand (**b**) (*llegar*) to arrive; **en cinco minutos se plantó aquí** he got here in five minutes flat

planteamiento *nm* (*enfoque*) approach

plantear 1 *vt* (**a**) (*problema*) to pose, to raise (**b**) (*planear*) to plan (**c**) (*proponer*) to put forward (**d**) (*exponer*) to present
  2 plantearse *upr* (**a**) (*considerar*) to consider (**b**) (*problema*) to arise

plantel *nm Fig* cadre, clique

plantilla *nf* (**a**) (*personal*) staff, personnel (**b**) (*de zapato*) insole (**c**) (*patrón*) model, pattern

plantón *nm Fam* **dar un p. a algn** to stand sb up

plañir *vi* to mourn

plasmar 1 *vt* (**a**) (*reproducir*) to capture (**b**) (*expresar*) to express
  2 plasmarse *upr* **p. en** to take the shape of

plasta *nmf Fam* bore

plástico,-a 1 *adj* plastic
  2 *nm* (**a**) plastic (**b**) (*disco*) record

plastificar [44] *vt* to coat *o* cover with plastic

plastilina® *nf* Plasticine®

plata *nf* (**a**) silver; (*objetos de plata*) silverware; *Fam* **hablar en p.** to lay (it) on

the line; **p. de ley** sterling silver (**b**) *Am* money

plataforma *nf* platform

plátano *nm* (**a**) (*fruta*) banana (**b**) (*árbol*) plane tree; **falso p.** sycamore

platea *nf Cin & Teatro Br* stalls, *US* orchestra

platear *vt* to silver-plate

platense 1 *adj* of/from the River Plate
  2 *nmf* person from the River Plate

plática *nf CAm, Méx* chat, talk

platicar [44] *vi CAm, Méx* to chat, to talk

platillo *nm* (**a**) saucer; **p. volante** flying saucer (**b**) *Mús* cymbal

platina *nf* (*de tocadiscos*) deck; **doble p.** double deck

platino *nm* (**a**) platinum (**b**) *Aut* **platinos** contact breaker, points

plato *nm* (**a**) plate, dish (**b**) (*parte de una comida*) course; **de primer p.** for starters; **p. fuerte** main course; **p. combinado** one-course meal (**c**) (*guiso*) dish (**d**) (*de balanza*) pan, tray (**e**) (*de tocadiscos*) turntable

plató *nm Cin & TV* (film) set

platudo,-a *adj Am Fam* loaded, rolling in it

plausible *adj* (**a**) (*admisible*) plausible, acceptable (**b**) (*loable*) commendable

playa *nf* (**a**) beach; (*costa*) seaside (**b**) *Am* **p. de estacionamiento** *Br* car park, *US* parking lot

playera *nf* (**a**) (*zapatilla*) *Br* sandshoe, *US* sneaker (**b**) *Méx* (*camiseta*) teeshirt

plaza *nf* (**a**) square (**b**) (*mercado*) market, marketplace (**c**) *Aut* seat (**d**) (*laboral*) post, position (**e**) **p. de toros** bullring

plazo *nm* (**a**) (*periodo*) time, period; (*término*) deadline; **a corto/largo p.** in the short term/in the long run; **el p. termina el viernes** Friday is the deadline (**b**) *Fin* **comprar a plazos** to buy on *Br* hire purchase *o US* an installment plan; **en seis plazos** in six instalments

pleamar *nf* high tide

plebe *nf* masses, plebs

plebeyo,-a 1 *adj* plebeian
  2 *nm,f* plebeian, pleb

plebiscito *nm* plebiscite

plegable *adj* folding, collapsible

plegar [1] 1 *vt* to fold
  2 plegarse *upr* to give way, to bow

plegaria *nf* prayer

pleitear *vi* to conduct a lawsuit, to plead

pleito *nm* (**a**) *Jur* lawsuit, litigation; **poner un p. (a algn)** to sue (sb) (**b**) *Am* (*discusión*) argument

plenilunio *nm* full moon

plenitud *nf* plenitude, fullness; **en la p. de la vida** in the prime of life

pleno,-a 1 *adj* full; **en plena noche** in the middle of the night; **los empleados en p.** the entire staff
  2 *nm* plenary meeting

pletórico,-a *adj* abundant

plexiglás® *nm* (*plástico*) Perspex®, *US* Plexiglass®

pliego *nm* (a) (*hoja*) sheet *o* piece of paper; **p. de condiciones** bidding specifications (b) (*carta*) sealed letter

pliegue *nm* (a) fold (b) (*de vestido*) pleat

plinto *nm Dep* horse

plisar *vt* to pleat

plomería *nf Méx, RP, Ven* plumber's

plomero *nm Méx, RP, Ven* plumber

plomizo,-a *adj* lead, leaden; (*color*) lead-coloured

plomo *nm* (a) (*en metalurgia*) lead (b) *Elec* (*fusible*) fuse (c) (*bala*) slug, pellet

pluma *nf* (a) feather (b) (*estilográfica*) fountain pen (c) *Carib, Méx* (*bolígrafo*) (ballpoint) pen

plumaje *nm* plumage

plumazo *nm* **de un p.** at a stroke

plumero *nm* (a) (*para el polvo*) feather duster (b) *Fam* **se te ve el p.** I can see through you

plumier *nm* pencil box

plural *adj & nm* plural

pluralismo *nm* pluralism

pluriempleo *nm* moonlighting

plus *nm* bonus, bonus payment

plusmarca *nf* record

plusmarquista *nmf* record breaker

plusvalía *nf* capital gain

Plza. (*abr* **Plaza**) Sq

población *nf* (a) (*ciudad*) town; (*pueblo*) village (b) (*habitantes*) population (c) *Chile* (*barrio*) (*callampa*) shanty town

poblado,-a *adj* (a) populated; *Fig* **p. de** full of (b) (*barba*) bushy, thick

poblador,-a *nm,f* settler

poblar [2] *vt* (a) (*con gente*) to settle, to people; (*con plantas*) to plant (b) (*vivir*) to inhabit

pobre 1 *adj* poor; **¡p.!** poor thing!; **un hombre p.** a poor man; **un p. hombre** a poor devil
  2 *nmf* poor person; **los pobres** the poor

pobreza *nf* poverty; *Fig* (*de medios, recursos*) lack

pocho,-a *adj* (a) (*fruta*) bad, overripe (b) *Fig* (*persona*) (*débil*) off-colour; (*triste*) depressed, down (c) *Méx Fam* (*americanizado*) Americanized

pochoclo *nm Arg* popcorn

pocilga *nf* pigsty

pocillo *nm RP* (a) (*pequeño*) small cup (b) *Méx, Ven* (*grande*) enamel mug

pócima, poción *nf* potion; *Pey* concoction, brew

poco,-a 1 *nm* (a) **un p.** (*con adj o adv*) a little; **un p. tarde/frío** a little late/cold (b) **un p.** (*con sustantivo*) a little; **un p. de azúcar** a little sugar
  2 *adj* (a) not much, little; **p. sitio/tiempo** not much *o* little space/time; **poca cosa** not much
  (b) **pocos,-as** not many, few; **pocas personas** not many *o* few people
  (c) **unos,-as pocos,-as** a few
  3 *pron* (a) (*escasa cantidad*) not much; **queda p.** there isn't much left
  (b) (*breve tiempo*) **p. antes/después** shortly *o* a little before/afterwards; **p. de** shortly *o* a little after; **dentro de p.** soon
  (c) **pocos,-as** (*cosas*) few, not many; **tengo muy pocos** I have very few, I don't have very many
  (d) **pocos,-as** (*personas*) few people, not many people; **vinieron pocos** few people came, not many people came
  4 *adv* (a) (*con verbo*) not (very) much, little; **ella come p.** she doesn't eat much, she eats little
  (b) (*con adj*) not very; **es p. probable** it's not very likely
  (c) (*en frases*) **p. a p.** little by little, gradually; **por p.** almost

podadera, *Am* **podadora** *nf* garden shears

podar *vt* to prune

poder¹ *nm* power; *Econ* **p. adquisitivo** purchasing power

poder² **[18] 1** *vi* (a) (*capacidad*) to be able to; **no puede hablar** she can't speak; **no podré llamarte** I won't be able to phone; **no puedo más** I can't take any more; **guapa a más no p.** unbelievably pretty
  (b) (*permiso*) may, might; **¿puedo pasar?** can *o* may I come in?; **¿se puede (entrar)?** may I (come in)?; **aquí no se puede fumar** you can't smoke here
  (c) (*uso impers*) (*posibilidad*) may, might; **puede que no lo sepan** they may *o* might not know; **no puede ser** that's impossible; **puede (ser) (que sí)** maybe, perhaps
  (d) (*deber*) **podrías haberme advertido** you might have warned me
  (e) to cope (**con** with); **no puede con**

tanto trabajo he can't cope with so much work

  2 *vt* (*batir*) to be stronger than; **les puede a todos** he can take on anybody

poderoso,-a *adj* powerful

podio, pódium *nm Dep* podium

podré *indic fut de* **poder**

podrido,-a *adj* (**a**) (*putrefacto*) rotten, putrid (**b**) (*corrupto*) corrupt; *Fam* **p. de dinero** *o Am* **en plata** stinking rich (**c**) *RP Fam* (*harto*) fed up, sick

podrir *vt defect* = **pudrir**

poema *nm* poem

poesía *nf* (**a**) (*género*) poetry (**b**) (*poema*) poem

poeta *nmf* poet

poético,-a *adj* poetic

póker *nm* poker

polaco,-a 1 *adj* Polish

  2 *nm,f* Pole

  3 *nm* (*idioma*) Polish

polaridad *nf* polarity

polarizar [40] *vt* (**a**) *Fís* to polarize (**b**) *Fig* (*ánimo, atención*) to concentrate

polea *nf* pulley

polémica *nf* controversy

polémico,-a *adj* controversial

polemizar [40] *vi* to argue, to debate

polen *nm* pollen

polera *nf RP* polo shirt

poli *Fam* **1** *nmf* cop

  2 *nf* **la p.** the fuzz *pl*

poli- *pref* poly-

policía 1 *nf* police (force)

  2 *nmf* (*hombre*) policeman; (*mujer*) policewoman

policíaco,-a, policiaco,-a, policial *adj* police; **novela/película policíaca** detective story/film

polideportivo *nm* sports centre

poliéster *nm* polyester

polietileno *nm Br* polythene, *US* polyethylene

polifacético,-a *adj* versatile, many-sided; **es un hombre muy p.** he's a man of many talents

poligamia *nf* polygamy

políglota *adj & nmf* polyglot

polígono *nm* polygon; **p. industrial** industrial estate

polilla *nf* moth

poliomielitis *nf* polio, poliomyelitis

politécnico,-a *adj & nm* polytechnic

política *nf* (**a**) politics *sing* (**b**) (*estrategia*) policy

políticamente *adv* **p. correcto** politically correct

político,-a 1 *adj* (**a**) political (**b**)

(*pariente*) in-law; **hermano p.** brother-in-law; **su familia política** her in-laws

  2 *nm,f* politician

póliza *nf* (**a**) (*sello*) stamp (**b**) **p. de seguros** insurance policy

polizón *nm* stowaway

polla *nf* (**a**) *Vulg* (*pene*) prick (**b**) *Orn* **p. de agua** moorhen

pollera *nf* (**a**) *RP* (*occidental*) skirt (**b**) *Andes* (*indígena*) = long skirt worn by Indian women

pollo *nm* (**a**) chicken (**b**) *Fam* (*joven*) lad

polo *nm* (**a**) *Elec & Geog* pole; **P. Norte/Sur** North/South Pole (**b**) (*helado*) *Br* ice lolly, *US* Popsicle® (**c**) (*prenda*) sports shirt, polo neck (sweater) (**d**) *Dep* polo

pololear *vi Chile Fam* to go out (together)

pololo,-a *nm,f Chile Fam* boyfriend, *f* girlfriend

Polonia *n* Poland

poltrona *nf* easy chair

polución *nf* pollution

polvareda *nf* cloud of dust

polvera *nf* powder compact

polvo *nm* (**a**) dust; **limpiar** *o* **quitar el p.** to dust; **en p.** powdered; **polvo(s) de talco** talcum powder (**b**) *Fam* **estar hecho p.** (*cansado*) to be *Br* knackered *o US* bushed; (*deprimido*) to be depressed (**c**) *muy Fam* **echar un p.** to have a screw

pólvora *nf* gunpowder

polvoriento,-a *adj* dusty

polvorín *nm* gunpowder arsenal; *Fig* powder keg

polvorón *nm* sweet pastry

pomada *nf* ointment

pomelo *nm* (*fruto*) grapefruit; (*árbol*) grapefruit tree

pómez *adj inv* **piedra p.** pumice (stone)

pomo *nm* (*de puerta*) knob

pompa *nf* (**a**) bubble (**b**) (*ostentación*) pomp (**c**) *Méx Fam* **pompas** botty

pompis *nm inv Fam* botty

pomposo,-a *adj* pompous

pómulo *nm* cheekbone

ponchar 1 *vt* (**a**) *CAm, Carib, Méx* (*rueda*) to puncture (**b**) *Am* (*en béisbol*) to strike out

  2 poncharse *vpr* (**a**) *CAm, Carib, Méx* (*rueda*) to get a puncture (**b**) *Am* (*en béisbol*) to strike out

ponche *nm* punch

poncho *nm* poncho

ponderar *vt* (**a**) (*asunto*) to weigh up *o* consider (**b**) (*alabar*) to praise

pondré *indic fut de* **poner**

ponencia *nf* paper

poner [19] (*pp* **puesto**) **1** *vt* (a) *to put; (mesa, huevo) to lay; (gesto) to make; (multa) to impose; (telegrama) to send; (negocio) to set up*

(b) *(tele, radio etc) to turn o switch on*

(c) *(+ adj) to make;* **p. triste a algn** *to make sb sad;* **p. colorado a algn** *to make sb blush*

(d) **¿qué llevaba puesto?** *what was he wearing?*

(e) *(decir)* **¿qué pone aquí?** *what does it say here?*

(f) *(suponer) to suppose;* **pongamos que Ana no viene** *supposing Ana doesn't turn up*

(g) *TV & Cin to put on, to show;* **¿qué ponen en la tele?** *what's on the telly?*

(h) *Tel* **ponme con Manuel** *put me through to Manuel*

(i) *(nombrar)* **le pondremos (de nombre) Pilar** *we are going to call her Pilar*

2 *v impers Am Fam (parecer)* **se me pone que ...** *it seems to me that ...*

3 ponerse *vpr* (a) *(ponerse) to put oneself;* **ponte en mi lugar** *put yourself in my place;* **ponte más cerca** *come closer*

(b) *(vestirse) to put on;* **ella se puso el jersey** *she put her sweater on*

(c) *(+ adj) to become;* **p. furioso/malo** *to become furious/ill*

(d) *(sol) to set*

(e) *Tel* **p. al teléfono** *to answer the phone*

(f) **p. a** *to start to;* **p. a trabajar** *to get down to work*

poney *nm* pony

pongo *indic pres de* **poner**

poniente *nm* (a) *(occidente)* West (b) *(viento)* westerly (wind)

ponqué *nm Col, Ven* = large sponge cake, filled with cream and/or fruit, and covered in icing or chocolate

pontífice *nm* Pontiff; **el Sumo P.** His Holiness the Pope

ponzoña *nf* (a) venom, poison (b) **tener p.** *(tristeza)* to be down in the dumps

ponzoñoso,-a *adj* (a) venomous, poisonous (b) *(triste)* down in the dumps

popa *nf* stern; *Fig* **ir viento en p.** to go full speed ahead

popote *nm Méx* drinking straw

populacho *nm Pey* plebs, masses

popular *adj* (a) folk; **arte/música p.** folk art/music (b) *(medida)* popular (c) *(actor)* well-known

popularidad *nf* popularity

popularizar [40] *vt* to popularize

populoso,-a *adj* densely populated

popurrí *nm Mús* medley

póquer *nm* poker

por *prep* (a) *(agente)* by; **pintado p. Picasso** painted by Picasso

(b) **p. qué** why

(c) *(causa)* because of; **p. sus ideas** because of her ideas; **p. necesidad/amor** out of need/love; **suspendió p. no estudiar** he failed because he didn't study

(d) *(tiempo)* **p. la mañana/noche** in the morning/at night; **p. ahora** for the time being; **p. entonces** at that time

(e) *(en favor de)* for; **lo hago p. mi hermano** I'm doing it for my brother('s sake)

(f) *(lugar)* **pasamos p. Córdoba** we went through Córdoba; **p. ahí** over there; **¿p. dónde vamos?** which way are we taking o going?; **p. la calle** in the street; **mirar p. la ventana** to look out the window; **entrar p. la ventana** to get in through the window

(g) *(medio)* by; **p. avión/correo** by plane/post

(h) *(a cambio de)* for; **cambiar algo p. otra cosa** to exchange sth for something else

(i) *(distributivo)* **p. cabeza** a head, per person; **p. hora/mes** per hour/month

(j) *Mat* **dos p. tres, seis** two times three is six; **un 10 p. ciento** 10 percent

(k) *(con infinitivo)* in order to, so as to; **hablar p. hablar** to talk for the sake of it

(l) *(locuciones)* **p. así decirlo** so to speak; **p. más o muy ... que sea** no matter how ... he/she is; **p. mí** as far as I'm concerned

porcelana *nf* porcelain

porcentaje *nm* percentage

porche *nm* porch

porcino,-a *adj* **ganado p.** pigs

porción *nf* portion, part

pordiosero,-a *nm,f* tramp, *US* bum

porfía *nf (obstinación)* obstinacy, stubbornness

porfolio *nm* portfolio

pormenor *nm* detail; **venta al p.** retail

porno *adj inv Fam* porn

pornografía *nf* pornography

pornográfico,-a *adj* pornographic

poro *nm* pore

poroso,-a *adj* porous

poroto *nm RP (judía)* kidney bean

porque *conj* (a) *(causal)* because; **¡p. no!** just because! (b) *(final)* (+ *subjunctive*) so that, in order that

porqué *nm* reason

porquería *nf* (a) *(suciedad)* dirt, filth (b) *(birria) Br* rubbish, *US* garbage (c) *Fam* *(chuchería)* junk food, *Br* rubbish

porra *nf* (a) *(de policía)* truncheon, baton (b) *Fam (locuciones)* ¡una p.! *Br* rubbish!, *US* garbage!; ¡vete a la p.! get lost!

porrazo *nm* thump

porro *nm* (a) *Fam (de droga)* joint (b) *Am (puerro)* leek

porrón *nm* = glass bottle with a spout coming out of its base, used for drinking wine

portaaviones *nm inv* aircraft carrier

portada *nf* (a) *(de libro etc)* cover; *(de periódico)* front page; *(de disco)* sleeve (b) *(fachada)* front, facade

portador,-a *nm,f Com* bearer; *Med* carrier

portaequipajes *nm inv* (a) *Aut (maletero) Br* boot, *US* trunk; *(baca)* roof rack (b) *(carrito)* luggage trolley

portafolios *nm inv* briefcase

portal *nm* (a) *(zaguán)* porch, entrance hall (b) *(puerta de la calle)* main door (c) p. de Belén Nativity scene (d) *Informát* portal

portamaletas *nm inv* = portaequipajes

portaminas *nm inv* propelling pencil

portamonedas *nm inv* purse

portarse *vpr* to behave; p. mal to misbehave

portátil *adj* portable

portaviones *nm inv* = portaaviones

portavoz *nmf* spokesperson; *(hombre)* spokesman; *(mujer)* spokeswoman

portazo *nm* oímos un p. we heard a slam o bang; dar un p. to slam the door

porte *nm* (a) *(aspecto)* bearing (b) *(transporte)* carriage

portento *nm* (a) *(cosa)* wonder, marvel (b) *(persona)* genius

portentoso,-a *adj* extraordinary, prodigious

porteño,-a 1 *adj* of/from Buenos Aires
2 *nm,f* person from Buenos Aires

portería *nf* (a) *(porter's lodge* (b) *Dep* goal

portero,-a *nm,f* (a) *(de vivienda)* porter, caretaker; p. automático Entryphone®
(b) *Dep* goalkeeper

pórtico *nm* (a) *(portal)* portico, porch (b) *(con arcadas)* arcade

portorriqueño,-a *adj & nm,f* Puerto Rican

portuario,-a *adj* harbour, port

Portugal *n* Portugal

portugués,-esa 1 *adj* Portuguese
2 *nm (idioma)* Portuguese

porvenir *nm* future; sin p. with no prospects

pos *adv* en p. de after

pos- *pref* post-

posada *nf* inn

posaderas *nfpl Fam* buttocks

posadero,-a *nm,f* innkeeper

posar 1 *vi (para retrato etc)* to pose
2 *vt* to put o lay down
3 posarse *vpr* to settle, to alight

posdata *nf* postscript

pose *nf* (a) *(postura)* pose (b) *(afectación)* posing

poseedor,-a *nm,f* possessor

poseer [36] *vt* to possess, to own

poseído,-a *adj* possessed

posesión *nf* possession; estar en p. de to have; tomar p. (de un cargo) to take up (a post)

posesivo,-a *adj* possessive

poseso,-a *adj & nm,f* possessed

posguerra *nf* postwar period

posibilidad *nf* possibility; *(oportunidad)* chance

posibilitar *vt* to make possible

posible 1 *adj* possible; de ser p. if possible; en (la medida de) lo p. as far as possible; haré todo lo p. I'll do everything I can; lo antes p. as soon as possible; es p. que venga he might come
2 *nmpl* posibles means

posición *nf* position

positivo,-a *adj* positive

posmoderno,-a *adj* postmodern

poso *nm* dregs, sediment

posponer [19] *vt* (a) *(aplazar)* to postpone, to put off (b) *(relegar)* to put in second place o behind, to relegate

post- *pref* post-

posta *nf* a p. on purpose

postal 1 *adj* postal
2 *nf* postcard

poste *nm* pole; *Dep (de portería)* post

póster *nm* poster

postergar [42] *vt* (a) *(relegar)* to relegate (b) *(retrasar)* to delay; *(aplazar)* to postpone

posteridad *nf* posterity; pasar a la p. to go down in history

posterior *adj* (a) *(lugar)* posterior, rear (b) *(tiempo)* later (a than), subsequent (a to)

posterioridad *nf* posteriority; con p. later

posteriormente *adv* subsequently, later

postgraduado,-a *adj & nm,f* postgraduate

postigo *nm (de puerta)* wicket; *(de ventana)* shutter

postín *nm Fam* boasting, showing off;

darse p. to show off, to swank; **de p.** posh, swanky

postizo,-a 1 *adj* false, artificial; **dentadura postiza** false teeth, dentures

2 *nm* hairpiece

postor *nm* bidder

postrarse *vpr* to prostrate oneself, to kneel down

postre *nm* dessert, sweet

postrero,-a *adj* last

> **Postrer** is used instead of **postrero** before masculine singular nouns (e.g. **el postrer día** the last day).

postrimería *nf (usu pl)* last part *o* period

postular 1 *vt* (a) *(defender)* to call for (b) *Am (candidatar)* to propose, to nominate

2 *vi (en colecta)* to collect

3 postularse *vpr Am* (a) *Pol (para cargo)* to stand, to run (b) *(para trabajo)* to apply (**para** for)

póstumo,-a *adj* posthumous

postura *nf* (a) *(posición)* position, posture (b) *Fig (actitud)* attitude

pos(t)venta *adj* **servicio p.** after-sales service

potable *adj* drinkable; **agua p./no p.** drinking water/not drinking water

potaje *nm* hotpot, stew

pote *nm* pot; *(jarra)* jug

potencia *nf* power; **en p.** potential

potencial 1 *adj* potential

2 *nm* (a) *(potencial)*; **p. eléctrico** voltage; **p. humano** manpower (b) *Ling* conditional (tense)

potenciar [43] *vt* to promote, to strengthen

potente *adj* powerful, strong

potestad *nf* power, authority

potingue *nm Fam Pey* (a) *(bebida)* concoction (b) *(maquillaje)* make-up, face cream/lotion

potra *nf Fam* luck

potrero *nm Am* field, pasture

potro *nm Zool* colt; *(de gimnasia)* horse

poyo *nm* stone bench

pozo *nm* well; *Min* shaft, pit

pozole *nm CAm, Carib, Méx (guiso)* = stew made with maize kernels, pork or chicken and vegetables

PP *nm (abr* **Partido Popular**) = Spanish political party to the right of the political spectrum

práctica *nf* (a) *(práctica)*; **en la p.** in practice (b) *(formación)* placement; **período de prácticas** practical training period

practicante 1 *adj Rel* practising

2 *nmf Med* medical assistant

practicar [44] 1 *vt* to practise; *(operación)* to carry out

2 *vi* to practise

práctico,-a *adj* practical; *(útil)* handy, useful

pradera *nf* meadow

prado *nm* meadow, field

Praga *n* Prague

pragmático,-a 1 *adj* pragmatic

2 *nm,f* pragmatist

pre- *pref* pre-

preámbulo *nm* (a) *(introducción)* preamble (b) *(rodeo)* circumlocution

preaviso *nm* previous warning, notice

precalentamiento *nm* warm-up

precalentar [1] *vt* to preheat

precario,-a *adj* precarious

precaución *nf* (a) *(cautela)* caution; **con p.** cautiously (b) *(medida)* precaution

precaver 1 *vt* to guard against

2 precaverse *vpr* to take precautions (**de** *o* **contra** against)

precavido,-a *adj* cautious, prudent

precedencia *nf* precedence, priority

precedente 1 *adj* preceding

2 *nm* predecessor

3 *nm* precedent; **sin p.** unprecedented

preceder *vt* to precede

precepto *nm* precept

preciarse [43] *vpr* to fancy oneself (**de** as)

precintar *vt* to seal

precinto *nm* seal

> 🖋 Observa que la palabra inglesa **precinct** es un falso amigo y no es la traducción de la palabra española **precinto**. En inglés, **precinct** significa "recinto" o "distrito".

precio *nm* price; **p. de coste** cost price; **a cualquier p.** at any price

preciosidad *nf* (a) *(hermosura) (cosa)* lovely thing; *(persona)* darling (b) *Fml (cualidad)* preciousness

precioso,-a *adj* (a) *(hermoso)* lovely, beautiful (b) *(valioso)* precious, valuable

precipicio *nm* precipice

precipitación *nf* (a) *(prisa)* haste (b) *(lluvia)* rainfall

precipitado,-a *adj (apresurado)* hasty, hurried; *(irreflexivo)* rash

precipitar 1 *vt* (a) *(acelerar)* to hurry, to rush (b) *(arrojar)* to throw, to hurl down

2 precipitarse *vpr* (a) *(persona)* to hurl oneself; *(acontecimientos)* to gather speed (b) *(actuar irreflexivamente)* to hurry, to rush

precisamente *adv (con precisión)* precisely; *(exactamente)* exactly; **p. por**

eso for that very reason

precisar *vt* (a) *(determinar)* to determine, to give full details of; *(especificar)* to specify (b) *(necesitar)* to require, to need

precisión *nf* (a) *(exactitud)* precision, accuracy; **con p.** precisely, accurately (b) *(aclaración)* clarification

preciso,-a *adj* (a) *(necesario)* necessary, essential (b) *(exacto)* accurate, exact; **en este p. momento** at this very moment (c) *(claro)* concise, clear

preconizar [40] *vt* to advocate

precoz *adj* (a) *(persona)* precocious (b) *(fruta)* early

precursor,-a *nm,f* precursor

predecesor,-a *nm,f* predecessor

predecir [12] *(pp* **predicho)** *vt* to foretell, to predict

predestinado,-a *adj* predestined

predeterminar *vt* to predetermine

predicado *nm* predicate

predicador,-a *nm,f* preacher

predicar [44] *vt* to preach

predicción *nf* prediction, forecast

predice *indic pres de* **predecir**

predije *pt indef de* **predecir**

predilección *nf* predilection

predilecto,-a *adj* favourite, preferred

predisponer [19] *(pp* **predispuesto)** *vt* to predispose

predisposición *nf* predisposition

predominante *adj* predominant

predominar *vi* to predominate

predominio *nm* predominance

preescolar *adj* preschool; **en p.** in the nursery school

prefabricado,-a *adj* prefabricated

prefacio *nm* preface

preferencia *nf* preference

preferente *adj* preferable, preferential

preferible *adj* preferable; **es p. que no vengas** you'd better not come

preferido,-a *nm,f* favourite

preferir [5] *vt* to prefer

prefijo *nm* (a) *Tel Br* dialling code, *US* area code (b) *Ling* prefix

pregonar *vt* *(anunciar)* to announce publicly; *Fig (divulgar)* to reveal, to disclose

pregunta *nf* question; **hacer una p.** to ask a question

preguntar **1** *vt* to ask; **p. algo a algn** to ask sb sth; **p. por algn** to ask after o about sb

2 preguntarse *vpr* to wonder; **me pregunto si ...** I wonder whether ...

preguntón,-ona *nm,f Fam.* busybody

prehistoria *nf* prehistory

prehistórico,-a *adj* prehistoric

prejuicio *nm* prejudice; **tener prejuicios** to be prejudiced, to be biased

preliminar *adj & nm* preliminary

preludio *nm* prelude

prematrimonial *adj* premarital

prematuro,-a *adj* premature

premeditación *nf* premeditation; **con p.** deliberately

premeditado,-a *adj* premeditated, deliberate

premiado,-a *adj* prize-winning

premiar [43] *vt* (a) to award a prize to (b) *(recompensar)* to reward

premio *nm* prize, award; *(recompensa)* reward

premisa *nf* premise

premonición *nf* premonition

premura *nf (urgencia)* urgency; **p. de tiempo** haste

prenatal *adj* antenatal, prenatal

prenda *nf* (a) *(prenda)* garment (b) *(garantía)* token, pledge

prendar **1** *vt* to captivate, to delight

2 prendarse *vpr (enamorarse)* to fall in love (**de** with)

prendedor *nm* brooch, pin

prender **1** *vt* (a) *(sujetar)* to fasten, to attach; *(con alfileres)* to pin (b) **p. fuego a** to set fire to (c) *(arrestar)* to arrest

2 *vi (fuego)* to catch; *(madera)* to catch fire; *(planta)* to take root

3 prenderse *vpr* to catch fire

prensa *nf* press; *Fig* **tener buena/mala p.** to have a good/bad press

prensar *vt* to press

preñado,-a *adj* (a) pregnant (b) *Fig (lleno)* pregnant (**de** with), full (**de** of)

preñar *vt (mujer)* to make pregnant; *(animal)* to impregnate

preocupación *nf* worry, concern

preocupado,-a *adj* worried, concerned

preocupar **1** *vt* to worry; **me preocupa que llegue tan tarde** I'm worried about him arriving so late

2 preocuparse *vpr* to worry, to get worried (**por** about); **no te preocupes** don't worry; **p. de algn** to look after sb; **p. de algo** to see to sth

preparación *nf* preparation; *(formación)* training

preparado,-a **1** *adj* (a) *(dispuesto)* ready, prepared; **comidas preparadas** ready-cooked meals (b) *(capacitado)* trained, qualified

2 *nm Farm* preparation

preparador,-a *nm,f* coach, trainer

preparar 1 *vt* (a) to prepare, to get ready;

p. un examen to prepare for an exam (**b**) *Dep (entrenar)* to train, to coach

2 prepararse *vpr* (**a**) to prepare oneself, to get ready (**b**) *Dep (entrenarse)* to train

preparativo *nm* preparation

preparatorio,-a *adj* preparatory

preponderante *adj* preponderant

preposición *nf Ling* preposition

prepotente *adj* domineering; *(arrogante)* overbearing

prerrogativa *nf* prerogative

presa *nf* (**a**) prey; *Fig* **ser p. de** to be a victim of; **p. del pánico** panic-stricken (**b**) *(embalse)* dam

presagiar [43] *vt* to predict, to foretell

presagio *nm* (**a**) *(señal)* omen; **buen/mal p.** good/bad omen (**b**) *(premonición)* premonition

presbiteriano,-a *adj & nm,f* Presbyterian

presbítero *nm* priest

prescindir *vi* **p. de** to do without

prescribir (*pp* **prescrito**) *vt* to prescribe

prescripción *nf* prescription; **p. facultativa** medical prescription

presencia *nf* presence; **hacer acto de p.** to put in an appearance; **p. de ánimo** presence of mind

presencial *adj* **testigo p.** eyewitness

presenciar [43] *vt (ver)* to witness

presentable *adj* presentable; **no estoy p.** I'm not dressed for the occasion

presentación *nf* presentation; *(aspecto)* appearance; *(de personas)* introduction

presentador,-a *nm,f Rad & TV* presenter, host, *f* hostess

presentar 1 *vt* (**a**) to present; *(mostrar)* to show, to display; *(ofrecer)* to offer (**b**) *(una persona a otra)* to introduce; **le presento al doctor Ruiz** may I introduce you to Dr Ruiz

2 presentarse *vpr* (**a**) *(comparecer)* to present oneself; *(inesperadamente)* to turn *o* come up (**b**) *(ocasión, oportunidad)* to present itself, to arise (**c**) *(candidato)* to stand; **p. a unas elecciones** to stand for election, *US* to run for office; **p. a un examen** to sit an examination (**d**) *(darse a conocer)* to introduce oneself (**a** to)

presente 1 *adj* present; **la p. (carta)** this letter; **hacer p.** to declare, to state; **tener p.** *(tener en cuenta)* to bear in mind; *(recordar)* to remember

2 *nm* present

presentimiento *nm* presentiment, premonition; **tengo el p. de que ...** I have the feeling that ...

presentir [5] *vt* to have a presentiment *o* premonition of; **presiento que lloverá** I've got the feeling that it's going to rain

preservación *nf* preservation, protection

preservar *vt* to preserve, to protect (**de** from; **contra** against)

preservativo *nm* sheath, condom

presidencia *nf* (**a**) *Pol* presidency (**b**) *(de una reunión)* *(hombre)* chairmanship; *(mujer)* chairwomanship

presidenciable *nmf Am* potential president

presidencial *adj* presidential

presidente,-a *nm,f* (**a**) *Pol* president; **p. del gobierno** Prime Minister, Premier (**b**) *(de una reunión)* chairperson

presidiario,-a *nm,f* prisoner, convict

presidio *nm* prison, penitentiary

presidir *vt* (**a**) *Pol* to rule, to head (**b**) *(reunión)* to chair, to preside over

presión *nf* pressure; **a** *o* **bajo p.** under pressure; **grupo de p.** pressure group, lobby; **p. arterial** *o* **sanguínea** blood pressure; **p. atmosférica** atmospheric pressure

presionar *vt* to press; *Fig* to pressurize, to put pressure on

preso,-a 1 *adj* imprisoned

2 *nm,f* prisoner

prestación *nf* (**a**) service (**b**) **prestaciones** *(de coche etc)* performance

prestado,-a *adj* **dejar p.** to lend; **pedir p.** to borrow; **vivir de p.** to scrounge

prestamista *nmf* moneylender

préstamo *nm* loan

prestar 1 *vt* (**a**) to lend, to loan; **¿me prestas tu pluma?** can I borrow your pen? (**b**) *(atención)* to pay; *(ayuda)* to give; *(servicio)* to do

2 prestarse *vpr* (**a**) *(ofrecerse)* to offer oneself (**a** to) (**b**) **p. a** *(dar motivo)* to cause; **se presta a (crear) malentendidos** it makes for misunderstandings

presteza *nf* promptness; **con p.** promptly

prestidigitador,-a *nm,f* conjuror, magician

prestigiar [43] *vt* to give prestige to

prestigio *nm* prestige

prestigioso,-a *adj* prestigious

presto,-a *adj Fml* (**a**) *(dispuesto)* ready, prepared (**b**) *(rápido)* swift, prompt

presumible *adj* probable, likely

presumido,-a 1 *adj* vain, conceited

2 *nm,f* vain person

presumir 1 *vt (suponer)* to presume, to suppose

2 *vi* (**a**) *(ser vanidoso)* to show off (**b**)

presume de guapo he thinks he's good-looking

presunción nf (a) (suposición) presumption, supposition (b) (vanidad) vanity, conceit

presunto,-a adj supposed; Jur alleged

presuntuoso,-a adj (a) (vanidoso) vain, conceited (b) (pretencioso) pretentious, showy

> 🖉 Observa que la palabra inglesa **presumptuous** es un falso amigo y no es la traducción de la palabra española **presuntuoso**. En inglés, **presumptuous** significa "impertinente".

presuponer [19] (pp presupuesto) vt to presuppose

presupuestar vt to budget for; (importe) to estimate for

presupuestario,-a adj budgetary

presupuesto nm (a) Fin budget; (cálculo) estimate (b) (supuesto) supposition, assumption

presuroso,-a adj (rápido) quick; (con prisa) in a hurry

pretencioso,-a adj pretentious

pretender vt (a) (intentar) to try; ¿qué pretendes insinuar? what are you getting at? (b) (afirmar) to claim (c) (aspirar a) to try for (d) (cortejar) to court, to woo

pretendiente,-a nm,f (a) (al trono) pretender (b) (a un cargo) applicant, candidate (c) (amante) suitor

pretensión nf (a) (aspiración) aim, aspiration (b) (presunción) pretentiousness

pretérito,-a 1 adj past, former

2 nm Ling preterite, simple past tense

pretextar vt to plead, to allege

pretexto nm pretext, excuse

pretil nm parapet

prevalecer [33] vi to prevail

prevaler [26] vi = prevalecer

prevención nf (a) (precaución) prevention; **en p. de** as a prevention against (b) (medida) precaution

prevenir [27] vt (a) (preparar) to prepare, to get ready (b) (prever) to prevent, to forestall; (evitar) to avoid; **para p. la gripe** to prevent flu; Prov **más vale p. que curar** prevention is better than cure (c) (advertir) to warn

preventivo,-a adj preventive; (medidas) precautionary; Jur **detención** o **prisión preventiva** remand in custody

prever [28] (pp previsto) vt (a) (prevenir) to foresee, to forecast (b) (preparar de antemano) to cater for

previo,-a adj previous, prior; **p. pago de** su importe only on payment; **sin p. aviso** without prior notice

previsible adj predictable

previsión nf (a) (predicción) forecast; **p. del tiempo** weather forecast (b) (precaución) precaution; **en p. de** as a precaution against (c) Andes, RP **p. social** social security

previsor,-a adj careful, far-sighted

previsto,-a adj foreseen, forecast; **según lo p.** as expected

prieto,-a adj (a) (ceñido) tight; **íbamos muy prietos en el coche** we were really squashed together in the car (b) Méx Fam (moreno) dark-skinned

prima nf (a) (gratificación) bonus; **p. de seguro** insurance premium (b) (persona) ver primo,-a

primacía nf primacy

primar 1 vi to have priority, to prevail

2 vt to give a bonus to

primario,-a adj primary

primavera nf spring

primer adj (delante de nm) ver primero,-a

primera nf (a) (en tren) first class (b) Aut (marcha) first gear (c) **a la p.** at the first attempt; Fam **de p.** great, first-class

primero,-a 1 adj first; **a primera hora de la mañana** first thing in the morning; **primera página** o **plana** front page; **de primera necesidad** basic

> **Primer** is used instead of **primero** before masculine singular nouns (e.g. **el primer hombre** the first man).

2 nm,f first; **a primero(s) de mes** at the beginning of the month

3 adv (a) first (b) (más bien) rather, sooner; ver primera

primicia nf novelty; **p. informativa** scoop; **p. mundial** world premiere

primitivo,-a adj (a) primitive (b) (tosco) coarse, rough

primo,-a 1 nm,f (a) cousin; **p. hermano** first cousin (b) Fam (tonto) fool, drip, dunce

2 adj (a) **materia prima** raw material (b) (número) prime

primogénito,-a adj & nm,f first-born

primor nm (a) (delicadeza) delicacy (b) (belleza) beauty

primordial adj essential, fundamental

primoroso,-a adj delicate, exquisite

princesa nf princess

principado nm principality

principal adj main, principal; **lo p. es que ...** the main thing is that ...; **puerta p.** front door

príncipe nm prince

principiante 1 adj novice

2 nmf beginner, novice

principio nm (a) beginning, start; **a principio(s) de** at the beginning of; **al p., en un p.** at first, in the beginning (b) (fundamento) principle; **en p.** in principle (c) **principios** rudiments, basics

pringar [42] **1** vt (ensuciar) to make greasy/dirty

2 vi Fam (trabajar) to work hard

3 pringarse vpr (a) (ensuciarse) to get greasy/dirty (b) Fam (meterse de lleno) to get involved

pringoso,-a adj (grasiento) greasy; (sucio) dirty

pringue nm (grasa) grease

prior,-a nm,f (hombre) prior; (mujer) prioress

priori: • **a priori** loc adv a priori

prioridad nf priority

prioritario,-a adj priority

prisa nf (a) (rapidez) hurry; **date p.** hurry up; **tener p.** to be in a hurry; **de/a p.** in a hurry (b) **correr p.** to be urgent; **me corre mucha p.** I need it right away

prisión nf prison, jail

prisionero,-a nm,f prisoner

prisma nm prism

prismáticos nmpl binoculars, field glasses

priva nf Fam booze

privación nf deprivation

privado,-a adj private

privar 1 vt (despojar) to deprive (**de** of)

2 vi (a) Fam (gustar) to like; (estar de moda) to be fashionable o popular (b) Fam (beber) to booze

3 privarse vpr (abstenerse) to deprive oneself (**de** of), to go without

privativo,-a adj exclusive (**de** of)

privilegiado,-a 1 adj privileged

2 nm,f privileged person

privilegio nm privilege

pro 1 nm advantage; **los pros y los contras** the pros and cons; **en p. de** in favour of

2 prep in favour of; **campaña p. desarme** campaign for disarmament, disarmament campaign

pro- pref pro-

proa nf prow, bows

probabilidad nf probability, likelihood; **tiene pocas probabilidades** he stands little chance

probable adj probable, likely; **es p. que lleva** it'll probably rain

probador nm fitting room

probar [2] **1** vt (a) (comida, bebida) to try

(b) (comprobar) to test, to check (c) (intentar) to try (d) (demostrar) to prove, to show

2 vi to try; **p. a** to attempt o try to

3 probarse vpr (ropa) to try on

probeta nf test tube; **niño p.** test-tube baby

problema nm problem

problemático,-a adj problematic

procedencia nf origin, source

procedente adj (a) (originario) coming (**de** from) (b) (adecuado) appropriate; Jur proper

proceder 1 vi (a) **p. de** (provenir) to come from (b) (actuar) to act (c) (ser oportuno) to be advisable o appropriate; Jur **la protesta no procede** objection overruled (d) **p. a** (continuar) to go on to

2 nm (comportamiento) behaviour

procedimiento nm (a) (método) procedure (b) Jur (trámites) proceedings

procesado,-a 1 nm,f accused

2 nm Informát processing

procesador nm processor; **p. de textos** word processor

procesamiento nm (a) Jur prosecution (b) Informát **p. de datos/textos** data/word processing

procesar vt (a) Jur to prosecute (b) (elaborar, transformar) to process; Informát to process

procesión nf procession

proceso nm (a) process; Informát **p. de datos** data processing (b) Jur trial

proclamación nf proclamation

proclamar vt to proclaim

proclive adj prone, inclined

procreación nf procreation

procrear vt to procreate

procurador,-a nm,f Jur attorney

procuraduría nf Méx **p. general** Ministry of Justice

procurar vt (a) (intentar) to try, to attempt; **procura que no te vean** make sure they don't see you (b) (proporcionar) (to manage) to get

prodigar [42] Fml **1** vt (dar generosamente) to lavish

2 prodigarse vpr **p. en** to be lavish in

prodigio nm prodigy, miracle; **hacer prodigios** to work wonders; **niño p.** child prodigy

prodigioso,-a adj (sobrenatural) prodigious; (maravilloso) wonderful, marvellous

pródigo,-a adj generous, lavish; **ella es pródiga en regalos** she's very generous with presents

producción *nf (acción)* production; *(producto)* product; *Cin* production; **p. en cadena/serie** assembly-line/mass production

producir [10] 1 *vt* (**a**) to produce; *(fruto, cosecha)* to yield, to bear; *(ganancias)* to yield (**b**) *Fig (originar)* to cause, to bring about

2 producirse *vpr* to take place, to happen

productividad *nf* productivity

productivo,-a *adj* productive; *(beneficioso)* profitable

producto *nm* product; *Agr (producción)* produce

productor,-a 1 *adj* producing

2 *nm,f* producer

proeza *nf* heroic deed, exploit

profanación *nf* desecration, profanation

profanar *vt* to desecrate, to profane

profano,-a 1 *adj* profane, secular

2 *nm,f (hombre)* layman; *(mujer)* laywoman

profecía *nf* prophecy

proferir [31] *vt* to utter; **p. insultos** to hurl insults

profesar *vt* to profess

profesión *nf* profession; **de p.** by profession

profesional *adj & nmf* professional

profesionista *adj & nmf Méx* professional

profeso *adv* **ex p.** intentionally

profesor,-a *nm,f* teacher; *Univ* lecturer

profesorado *nm (profesión)* teaching; *(grupo de profesores)* staff

profeta *nm* prophet

profetizar [40] *vt* to prophesy, to foretell

profiláctico,-a 1 *adj* prophylactic

2 *nm* condom

prófugo,-a 1 *adj & nm,f* fugitive

2 *nm Mil* deserter

profundidad *nf* depth; **un metro de p.** one metre deep *o* in depth; *Fig (de ideas etc)* profundity, depth

profundizar [40] *vt & vi (cavar)* to deepen; *Fig (examinar)* to study in depth

profundo,-a *adj* deep; *Fig (idea, sentimiento)* profound

profusión *nf* profusion

progenitor,-a *nm,f (antepasado)* ancestor, progenitor; **progenitores** *(padres)* parents

programa *nm* programme; *Informát* program; *Educ* syllabus

programación *nf Rad & TV* programme planning

programador,-a *nm,f Informát* programmer

programar *vt* to programme; *Informát* to program

progre *adj & nmf Fam* trendy, lefty

progresar *vi* to progress, to make progress

progresista *adj & nmf* progressive

progresivo,-a *adj* progressive

progreso *nm* progress; **hace grandes progresos** he's making great progress

prohibición *nf* prohibition, ban

prohibido,-a *adj* forbidden, prohibited; **prohibida la entrada** *(en letrero)* no admittance; **p. aparcar/fumar** *(en letrero)* no parking/smoking

prohibir *vt* to forbid, to prohibit; **se prohíbe pasar** *(en letrero)* no admittance *o* entry

prohibitivo,-a, prohibitorio,-a *adj* prohibitive

prójimo,-a *nm,f* one's fellow man, one's neighbour

proletariado *nm* proletariat

proletario,-a *adj & nm,f* proletarian

proliferar *vi* to proliferate

prolífico,-a *adj* prolific

prolijo,-a *adj* verbose, long-winded

prólogo *nm* prologue

prolongación *nf* prolonging, extension, prolongation

prolongado,-a *adj* long

prolongar [42] 1 *vt (alargar)* to prolong, to extend

2 prolongarse *vpr (continuar)* to carry on

promedio *nm* average; **como p.** on average

promesa *nf* promise; *Fig* **la joven p. de la música** the promising young musician

prometedor,-a *adj* promising

prometer 1 *vt* to promise; **te lo prometo** I promise

2 *vi* to be promising

3 prometerse *vpr (pareja)* to get engaged

prometido,-a 1 *adj* promised

2 *nm,f (hombre)* fiancé; *(mujer)* fiancée

prominente *adj (elevado)* protruding, projecting; *(importante)* prominent

promiscuo,-a *adj* promiscuous

promoción *nf* promotion; *Educ* **p. universitaria** class, year

promocionar *vt (cosas)* to promote; *(personas)* to give promotion to

promotor,-a 1 *adj* promoting

2 *nm,f* promoter

promover [4] *vt* (**a**) *(cosas, personas)* to promote; *(juicio, querella)* to initiate (**b**) *(causar)* to cause, to give rise to

promulgar [42] *vt* to promulgate

pronombre *nm* pronoun

pronosticar [44] *vt* to predict, to forecast; *Med* to make a prognosis of

pronóstico *nm* (*del tiempo*) forecast; *Med* prognosis

pronto,-a 1 *adj* quick, prompt; *Fml* (*dispuesto*) prepared

2 *nm* (*impulso*) sudden impulse

3 *adv* (**a**) (*deprisa*) quickly, rapidly; **al p.** at first; **de p.** suddenly; **por de** *o* **lo p.** (*para empezar*) to start with (**b**) (*temprano*) soon, early; **¡hasta p.!** see you soon!

pronunciación *nf* pronunciation

pronunciamiento *nm* (**a**) *Mil* uprising, insurrection (**b**) *Jur* pronouncement

pronunciar [43] **1** *vt* to pronounce; (*discurso*) to deliver

2 pronunciarse *vpr* (**a**) (*opinar*) to declare oneself (**b**) (*sublevarse*) to rise up

propagación *nf* propagation, spreading

propagador,-a *nm,f* propagator

propaganda *nf* (*política*) propaganda; (*comercial*) advertising, publicity

propagar [42] **1** *vt* to propagate, to spread

2 propagarse *vpr* to spread

propano *nm* propane

propasarse *vpr* to go too far

propensión *nf* tendency, inclination

propenso,-a *adj* (**a**) (*inclinado*) prone, inclined (**b**) *Med* susceptible

propiamente *adv* **p. dicho** strictly speaking

propiciar [43] *vt* (**a**) (*causar*) to cause (**b**) *Am* (*patrocinar*) to sponsor

propicio,-a *adj* propitious, suitable; **ser p. a** to be inclined to

propiedad *nf* (**a**) (*posesión*) ownership; (*cosa poseída*) property (**b**) (*cualidad*) property, quality; *Fig* **con p.** properly, appropriately

propietario,-a *nm,f* owner

propina *nf* tip; **dar p. (a algn)** to tip (sb)

propinar *vt* to give

propio,-a *adj* (**a**) (*de uno*) own; **en su propia casa** in his own house (**b**) (*correcto*) suitable, appropriate; **juegos propios para su edad** games suitable for their age (**c**) (*característico*) typical, peculiar (**d**) (*mismo*) (*hombre*) himself; (*mujer*) herself; (*animal, cosa*) itself; **el p. autor** the author himself (**e**) **propios,-as** themselves; **los propios inquilinos** the tenants themselves (**f**) *Ling* proper

proponer [19] (*pp* **propuesto**) **1** *vt* to propose, to suggest

2 proponerse *vpr* to intend

proporción *nf* (**a**) proportion; **en p. con** in proportion to (**b**) **proporciones** (*tamaño*) size

proporcionado,-a *adj* (*mesurado*) proportionate, in proportion

proporcional *adj* proportional

proporcionar *vt* (*dar*) to give, to supply, to provide

proposición *nf* (**a**) (*propuesta*) proposal (**b**) (*oración*) clause

propósito *nm* (**a**) (*intención*) intention (**b**) **a p.** (*por cierto*) by the way; (*adrede*) on purpose, intentionally; **a p. de viajes ...** speaking of travelling ...

propuesta *nf* suggestion, proposal

propuesto,-a *pp de* **proponer**

propugnar *vt* to advocate

propulsar *vt* (*vehículo*) to drive; *Fig* (*idea*) to promote

propulsión *nf* propulsion

propulsor,-a *nm,f Fig* (*persona*) promoter

propuse *pt indef de* **proponer**

prórroga *nf* (**a**) (*prolongación*) extension; *Dep Br* extra time, *US* overtime (**b**) (*aplazamiento*) postponement; *Mil* deferment

prorrogar [42] *vt* (**a**) (*prolongar*) to extend (**b**) (*aplazar*) to postpone; *Mil* to defer

prorrumpir *vi* to burst (**en** into)

prosa *nf* prose

proscrito,-a 1 *adj* (*persona*) exiled, banished; (*cosa*) banned

2 *nm,f* exile, outlaw

proseguir [6] *vt & vi* to carry on, to continue

prospección *nf* (**a**) *Min* prospect (**b**) *Com* survey

prospecto *nm* leaflet, prospectus

prosperar *vi* (*negocio, país*) to prosper, to thrive; (*propuesta*) to be accepted

prosperidad *nf* prosperity

próspero,-a *adj* prosperous, thriving; **¡p. año nuevo!** Happy New Year!

prostíbulo *nm* brothel

prostitución *nf* prostitution

prostituir [37] **1** *vt* to prostitute

2 prostituirse *vpr* to prostitute oneself

prostituta *nf* prostitute

protagonista *nmf* (**a**) main character, leading role; **¿quién es el p.?** who plays the lead? (**b**) *Fig* (*centro*) centre of attraction

protagonizar [40] *vt* to play the lead in, to star in

protección *nf* protection

proteccionismo *nm* protectionism

protector,-a 1 *adj* protecting, protective

2 *nm,f* protector

proteger [53] *vt* to protect, to defend
protegido,-a *nm,f (hombre)* protégé; *(mujer)* protégée
proteína *nf* protein
prótesis *nf inv* prosthesis
protesta *nf* protest; *Jur* objection
protestante *adj & nmf Rel* Protestant
protestar *vi* (**a**) to protest; *Jur* to object (**b**) *Fam (quejarse)* to complain
protestón,-ona *nm,f* moaner, grumbler
protocolo *nm* protocol
protón *nm* proton
prototipo *nm* prototype
protuberancia *nf* protuberance
protuberante *adj* protuberant, bulging
prov. *(abr* **provincia***)* prov
provecho *nm* profit, benefit; **¡buen p.!** enjoy your meal!; **sacar p. de algo** to benefit from sth
provechoso,-a *adj* beneficial
proveedor,-a *nm,f* supplier, purveyor; *Informát* **p. de acceso (a Internet)** Internet access provider
proveer [36] *(pp* **provisto***) vt* to supply, to provide
proveniente *adj (procedente)* coming; *(resultante)* arising, resulting
provenir [27] *vi* **p. de** to come from
proverbio *nm* proverb
providencia *nf* providence
provincia *nf* province
provincial *adj* provincial
provinciano,-a *adj & nm,f Pey* provincial
provisión *nf* provision
provisional, *Am* **provisorio,-a** *adj* provisional
provisto,-a *adj* **p. de** equipped with
provocación *nf* provocation
provocado,-a *adj* provoked, caused; **incendio p.** arson
provocador,-a 1 *nm,f* instigator, agent provocateur
  2 *adj* provocative
provocar [44] *vt* (**a**) *(causar)* to cause; **p. un incendio** to start a fire (**b**) *(instigar)* to provoke (**c**) *Carib, Col, Méx Fam (apetecer)* **¿te provoca ir al cine?** would you like to go to the movies?, *Br* do you fancy going to the cinema?; **¿qué te provoca?** what would you like to do?, *Br* what do you fancy doing?
provocativo,-a *adj* provocative
proxeneta *nmf* procurer, pimp
próximamente *adv (pronto)* soon; *Cin & Teatro (en letrero)* coming soon
proximidad *nf* proximity, closeness; **en las proximidades de** close to, in the vicinity of

próximo,-a *adj* (**a**) *(cercano)* near, close (**b**) *(siguiente)* next
proyección *nf* (**a**) projection (**b**) *Cin* showing
proyectar *vt* (**a**) *(luz)* to project (**b**) *(planear)* to plan (**c**) *Cin* to show
proyectil *nm* projectile
proyecto *nm (plan)* project, plan; **tener algo en p.** to be planning sth; **p. de ley** bill
proyector *nm Cin* projector
prudencia *nf* prudence, discretion; *(moderación)* care
prudente *adj* prudent, sensible; *(conductor)* careful; **a una hora p.** at a reasonable time
prueba *nf* (**a**) proof; **en p. de** as a sign of (**b**) *(examen etc)* test; **a p.** on trial; **a p. de agua/balas** waterproof/bullet-proof; **haz la p.** try it (**c**) *Dep* event
pseudo *adj* pseud, pseudo
psicoanálisis *nm inv* psychoanalysis
psicodélico,-a *adj* psychedelic
psicología *nf* psychology
psicológico,-a *adj* psychological
psicólogo,-a *nm,f* psychologist
psicópata *nmf* psychopath
psicosis *nf inv* psychosis
psicotécnico,-a *adj* psychometric
psicoterapeuta 1 *nmf* psychotherapist
  2 *adj* psychotherapeutic
psicoterapia *nf* psychotherapy
psicótico,-a *adj & nm,f* psychotic
psique *nf* psyche
psiquiatra *nmf* psychiatrist
psiquiatría *nf* psychiatry
psiquiátrico,-a 1 *adj* psychiatric; **hospital p.** psychiatric hospital
  2 *nm* psychiatric hospital
psíquico,-a *adj* psychic
PSOE *nm Pol (abr* **Partido Socialista Obrero Español***)* = Spanish political party to the centre-left of the political spectrum
pta(s). *(abr* **peseta(s)***)* peseta(s)
púa *nf* (**a**) *(de planta)* thorn; *(de animal)* quill, spine; *(de peine)* tooth; **alambre de púas** barbed wire (**b**) *Mús* plectrum
pub *nm (pl* **pubs, pubes***)* pub
pubertad *nf* puberty
publicación *nf* publication
publicar [44] *vt* (**a**) *(libro etc)* to publish (**b**) *(secreto)* to publicize
publicidad *nf* (**a**) *Com* advertising (**b**) *(conocimiento público)* publicity
publicitario,-a *adj* advertising
público,-a 1 *adj* public
  2 *nm* public; *Teatro* audience; *Dep* spectators

pucha *interj Andes, RP Fam Euf* (**a**) *(lamento) Br* sugar!, *US* shoot!; **¡p. digo, ya son las doce!** oh, *Br* sugar *o US* shoot! it's twelve o'clock already! (**b**) *(sorpresa)* wow!; **¿cincuenta años? ¡la p.!** fifty years old? get away! *o* never! (**c**) *(enojo) Br* sugar!, *US* shoot!; **¡la p.!, perdí las llaves** *Br* sugar *o US* shoot! I've lost my keys!

pucherazo *nm* rigging of an election

puchero *nm* (**a**) *(olla)* cooking pot; *(cocido)* stew (**b**) **hacer pucheros** to pout

pucho *nm CSur* dog-end

pude *pt indef de* **poder**

pudendo,-a *adj* **partes pudendas** private parts

púdico,-a *adj* modest

pudiente *adj* rich, wealthy

pudor *nm* modesty

pudoroso,-a *adj* modest

pudrir *vt* defect, **pudrirse** *vpr* to rot, to decay

pueblerino,-a *adj Pey (provinciano)* countrified, provincial

pueblo *nm* (**a**) *(población) (pequeña)* village; *(grande)* town (**b**) *(gente)* people; **el p. español** the Spanish people

puente *nm* (**a**) *(bridge; Av* **p. aéreo** *(civil)* air shuttle service; *Mil* airlift; **p. colgante** suspension bridge; **p. levadizo** drawbridge (**b**) *(entre dos fiestas)* ≃ long weekend

puerco,-a 1 *adj* filthy
2 *nm,f* pig
3 *nm* **p. espín** porcupine

puericultura *nf* paediatrics *sing*

pueril *adj* childish, puerile

puerro *nm* leek

puerta *nf* door; *(verja, en aeropuerto)* gate; *Dep* goal; **p. corredera/giratoria** sliding/revolving door; *Fig* **a las puertas, en puertas** imminent; *Fig* **a p. cerrada** behind closed doors

puerto *nm* (**a**) *(de mar)* port, harbour; **p. deportivo** marina (**b**) *(de montaña)* (mountain) pass

Puerto Rico *n* Puerto Rico

puertorriqueño,-a *adj & nm,f* Puerto Rican

pues *conj* (**a**) *(puesto que)* as, since (**b**) *(por lo tanto)* therefore (**c**) *(entonces)* so (**d**) *(para reforzar)* **¡p. claro que sí!** but of course!; **p. como iba diciendo** well, as I was saying; **¡p. mejor!** so much the better!; **¡p. no!** certainly not! (**e**) *(como pregunta)* **¿p.?** why?

puesta *nf* (**a**) **p. de sol** sunset (**b**) *Fig* **p. a punto** tuning, adjusting; *Fig* **p. al día** updating; *Teatro* **p. en escena** staging;

p. en marcha starting-up, start-up; *ver* **puesto,-a**

puestero,-a *nm,f Am* stallholder

puesto,-a 1 *conj* **p. que** since, as
2 *nm* (**a**) *(lugar)* place; *(asiento)* seat (**b**) *(empleo)* position, post, job; **p. de trabajo** job, post (**c**) *(tienda)* stall (**d**) *Mil* post
3 *adj* (**a**) *(colocado)* set, put (**b**) **llevar p.** *(ropa)* to have on; *Fam* **ir muy p.** to be all dressed up (**c**) *Fam (borracho)* drunk (**d**) *Fam* **estar p. en una materia** to be well up in a subject

púgil *nm* boxer

pugilato *nm* boxing

pugna *nf* battle, fight

pugnar *vi* to fight, to struggle (**por** for)

puja *nf* *(acción)* bidding; *(cantidad)* bid

pujante *adj* thriving, prosperous

pujanza *nf* strength, vigour

pujar *vi* (**a**) *(pugnar)* to struggle (**b**) *(en una subasta)* to bid higher

pulcro,-a *adj* (extremely) neat

pulga *nf* flea; *Fam* **tener malas pulgas** to be nasty, to have a nasty streak

pulgada *nf* inch

pulgar *nm* thumb

pulimentar *vt* to polish

pulir *vt* (**a**) *(metal, madera)* to polish (**b**) *(mejorar)* to polish up

pulla *nf* dig

pulmón *nm* lung

pulmonía *nf* pneumonia

pulóver *nm* pullover

pulpa *nf* pulp

pulpería *nf Am* store

púlpito *nm* pulpit

pulpo *nm* octopus

pulque *nm CAm, Méx* pulque, = fermented maguey juice

pulquería *nf CAm, Méx* "pulque" bar

pulsación *nf* pulsation; *(en mecanografía)* stroke, tap; **pulsaciones por minuto** ≃ keystrokes per minute

pulsar *vt (timbre, botón)* to press; *(tecla)* to hit, to strike

pulsera *nf* *(aro)* bracelet; *(de reloj)* watchstrap; **reloj de p.** wristwatch

pulso *nm* (**a**) *pulse; Fig* **tomar el p. a la opinión pública** to sound out opinion (**b**) *(mano firme)* steady hand; **a p.** freehand; **ganarse algo a p.** to deserve sth (**c**) *Fig* trial of strength; **echarse un p.** to arm-wrestle

pulverizador *nm* spray, atomizer

pulverizar [40] *vt (sólidos)* to pulverize; *(líquidos)* to spray; *(un récord)* to smash

puma *nm* puma

puna *nf Andes* (**a**) high moor (**b**) *(mal)*

mountain o altitude sickness

pundonor nf Am self-respect, self-esteem

punta nf (a) (extremo) tip; (extremo afilado) point; (de cabello) end; **sacar p. a un lápiz** to sharpen a pencil; **tecnología p.** state-of-the-art technology; **me pone los nervios de p.** he makes me very nervous (b) (periodo) peak; **hora p.** rush hour (c) (pequeña cantidad) bit; **una p. de sal** a pinch of salt (d) (clavo) nail

puntada nf Am (dolor) stabbing pain

puntaje nm Am (calificación) Br mark, US grade; (en concursos, competiciones) score

puntal nm prop; (travesaño) beam; Fig (soporte) pillar, support

puntapié nm kick

puntear vt (a) (dibujar) to dot (b) Mús (guitarra) to pluck

punteo nm plucking

puntería nf aim; **tener buena/mala p.** to be a good/bad shot

puntero,-a 1 adj leading
   2 nm,f CSur Dep back

puntiagudo,-a adj pointed, sharp

puntilla nf (a) (encaje) lace (b) **dar la p.** Taurom to finish (the bull) off; Fig (liquidar) to finish off (c) **de puntillas** on tiptoe

puntilloso,-a adj touchy

punto nm (a) point; **a p.** ready; Culin **en su p.** just right; **a p. de** on the point of; **hasta cierto p.** to a certain o some extent; **p. muerto** Aut neutral; Fig (impase) deadlock; **p. de vista** point of view (b) (marca) dot; **línea de puntos** dotted line (c) (lugar) place, point (d) **p. y seguido** full stop; **p. y coma** semicolon; **dos puntos** colon; **p. y aparte** full stop, new paragraph (e) (tiempo) **en p.** sharp, on the dot (f) Dep (tanto) point (g) Cost & Med stitch; **hacer p.** to knit

puntuable adj Dep **una prueba p. para** a race counting towards

puntuación nf (a) Ling punctuation (b) Dep score (c) Educ mark

puntual 1 adj (a) punctual (b) (exacto) accurate, precise (c) (caso) specific
   2 adv punctually

puntualidad nf punctuality

puntualizar [40] vt to specify, to clarify

puntuar [30] **1** vt (a) (al escribir) to punctuate (b) Educ (calificar) to mark
   2 vi Dep (a) (marcar) to score (b) (ser puntuable) to count

punzada nf (de dolor) sudden sharp pain

punzante adj (objeto) sharp; (dolor) acute, piercing

punzar [40] vt Téc to punch

puñado nm handful; Fam **a puñados** by the score, galore

puñal nm dagger

puñalada nf stab; Fig **p. trapera** stab in the back

puñeta nf Fam **hacer la p. a algn** to pester sb, to annoy sb; **¡puñetas!** damn!; **¡vete a hacer puñetas!** go to hell!

puñetazo nm punch

puño nm (a) fist (b) (de camisa etc) cuff (c) (de herramienta) handle

pupa nf (a) (herida) cold sore (b) Fam (daño) pain

pupila nf (de ojo) pupil

pupilo,-a nm,f pupil

pupitre nm desk

purasangre adj & nm thoroughbred

puré nm purée; **p. de patata** mashed potatoes; **p. de verduras** thick vegetable soup

pureta nmf old fogey

pureza nf (a) purity (b) (castidad) chastity

purga nf Med purgative; Fig purge

purgante adj & nm purgative

purgar [42] vt Med & Fig to purge

purgatorio nm purgatory

purificación nf purification

purificar [44] vt to purify

purista nmf purist

puritano,-a 1 adj puritanical
   2 nm,f puritan, Puritan

puro,-a 1 adj (a) (sin mezclas) pure; **aire p.** fresh air; **la pura verdad** the plain truth; Pol **p. y duro** hardline (b) (mero) sheer, mere; **no tengo ni p. idea** I haven't (got) a Br bloody o US goddamn clue; **por pura curiosidad** out of sheer curiosity (c) (casto) chaste, pure
   2 nm (cigarro) cigar

púrpura adj inv purple

purpúreo,-a adj purple

pus nm pus

puse pt indef de **poner**

pusilánime adj faint-hearted

pústula nf sore, pustule

puta nf Vulg whore; **de p. madre** great, terrific; **de p. pena** Br bloody o US goddamn awful; **no tengo ni p. idea** I haven't (got) a Br bloody o US goddamn clue; **pasarlas putas** to go through hell, to have a rotten time

putada nf Vulg dirty trick

puteada nf RP muy Fam (insulto) swearword

putear vt (a) Vulg (fastidiar) to fuck o piss around (b) RP muy Fam (insultar) **p. a algn** to call sb for everything, to call sb every name under the sun

puticlub *nm Fam* brothel

puto,-a 1 *adj Vulg* fucking

   2 *nm* male prostitute, stud

putrefacto,-a, pútrido,-a *adj* putre-
fied, rotten

puzzle *nm* jigsaw puzzle

PVC *nm* (*abr* **cloruro de polivinilo**) PVC

PVP *nm* (*abr* **precio de venta al público**)
  RRP

PYME *nf* (*abr* **Pequeña y Mediana Empresa**) SME

Pza. (*abr* **Plaza**) Sq

Q, q [ku] *nf (la letra)* Q, q

que¹ *pron rel* (**a**) *(sujeto) (persona)* who; *(cosa)* that, which; **el hombre q. vino** the man who came; **la bomba q. estalló** the bomb that *o* which went off (**b**) *(complemento) (persona) no se traduce o* that *o* who *o Fml* whom; *(cosa) no se traduce o* that, which; **la chica q. conocí** the girl (that *o* who *o* whom) I met; **el coche q. compré** the car (that *o* which) I bought (**c**) **lo q.** what; **lo q. más me gusta** what I like best (**d**) *(con infinitivo) no se traduce*; **hay mucho q. hacer** there's a lot to do

que² *conj* (**a**) *no se traduce o* that; **dijo q. llamaría** he said (that) he would call; **quiero q. vengas** I want you to come (**b**) *(consecutivo) no se traduce o* that; *(en comparativas)* than; **habla tan bajo q. no se le oye** he speaks so quietly (that) he can't be heard; **más alto q. yo** taller than me (**c**) *(causal) no se traduce* **date deprisa q. no tenemos mucho tiempo** hurry up, we haven't got much time (**d**) *(enfático) no se traduce* **¡q. no!** no!; **¡q. te calles!** I said be quiet! (**e**) *(deseo, mandato) (+ subjunctive) no se traduce*; **¡q. te diviertas!** enjoy yourself! (**f**) *(final)* so that; **ven q. te dé un beso** come and let me give you a kiss (**g**) *(disyuntivo)* whether; **me da igual q. suba o no** it doesn't matter to me whether he comes up or not (**h**) *(locuciones)* **¿a q. no ...?** I bet you can't ...!; **q. yo sepa** as far as I know; **yo q. tú** if I were you

qué 1 *pron interr* (**a**) what; **¿q. quieres?** what do you want?; *Fam* **¿y q.?** so what? (**b**) *(exclamativo) (+ adj)* how; **¡q. bonito!** how pretty! (**c**) *(+ n)* what a; **¡q. lástima!** what a pity! (**d**) *Fam* **¡q. de ...!** what a lot of ...!

2 *adj interr* which; **¿q. libro quieres?** which book do you want?

quebrada *nf Am* stream

quebradero *nm Fig* **q. de cabeza** headache

quebradizo,-a *adj (débil)* fragile; *(cabello, hielo)* brittle

quebrado *nm Mat* fraction

quebradura *nf* (**a**) *(grieta)* crack (**b**) *Med* hernia, rupture

quebrantamiento *nm (de una ley)* violation, infringement

quebrantar 1 *vt (promesa, ley)* to break

2 quebrantarse *vpr* to break down

quebrar [1] 1 *vt (romper)* to break

2 *vi Fin* to go bankrupt

3 quebrarse *vpr* to break; *Med* to rupture oneself

queda *nf* **toque de q.** curfew

quedar 1 *vi* (**a**) *(restar)* to be left, to remain; **quedan dos** there are two left (**b**) *(en un lugar)* to arrange to meet; **quedamos en el bar** I'll meet you in the bar (**c**) **me queda corta** *(ropa)* it is too short for me; **quedaría muy bien allí** *(objeto)* it would look very nice there (**d**) *(acordar)* to agree (**en** to); **¿en qué quedamos?** so what's it to be? (**e**) *(estar situado)* to be; **¿dónde queda la estación?** where's the station? (**f**) *(terminar)* to end; **¿en qué quedó la película?** how did the film end? (**g**) *(locuciones)* **q. en ridículo** to make a fool of oneself; **q. bien/mal** to make a good/bad impression

2 quedarse *vpr* (**a**) *(permanecer)* to stay; **se quedó en casa** she stayed (at) home; **q. sin dinero/pan** to run out of money/bread; **q. con hambre** to still be hungry (**b**) **q. (con)** *(retener)* to keep; **quédese (con) el cambio** keep the change (**c**) *Fam* **q. con algn** to make a fool of sb

quedo *adv* softly, quietly

quehacer *nm* task, chore

queja *nf* complaint; *(de dolor)* groan, moan

quejarse *vpr* to complain (**de** about)

quejica *Fam* **1** *adj* grumpy

2 *nmf* moaner

quejido *nm* groan, cry

quemado,-a *adj* (**a**) burnt, burned; *(del sol)* sunburnt (**b**) *Fig (agotado)* burnt-out

quemador *nm (de cocina etc)* burner

quemadura *nf* burn

quemar 1 *vt* to burn; *Fig (agotar)* to burn out

  2 *vi* to be burning hot; **este café quema** this coffee's boiling hot

  3 quemarse *upr Fig* to burn oneself out

quemarropa: •a quemarropa *loc adv* point-blank

quemazón *nf* smarting

quena *nf* Andean flute

quepo *indic pres de* **caber**

queque *nm Andes, CAm, Méx* sponge (cake)

querella *nf Jur* lawsuit

querer [20] 1 *vt* (**a**) *(amar)* to love (**b**) *(desear)* to want; **¿cuánto quiere por la casa?** how much does he want for the house?; **sin q.** without meaning to; **queriendo** on purpose; **¡por lo que más quieras!** for heaven's sake!; **¿quiere pasarme el pan?** would you pass me the bread? (**c**) **q. decir** to mean (**d**) **no quiso darme permiso** he refused me permission

  2 quererse *upr* to love each other

  3 *nm* love, affection

querido,-a 1 *adj* dear, beloved; **q. amigo** *(en carta)* dear friend

  2 *nm,f (amante)* lover; *(mujer)* mistress

queroseno *nm* kerosene, kerosine

querré *indic fut de* **querer**

quesadilla *nf CAm, Méx* = filled fried tortilla

queso *nm* cheese; **q. rallado** grated cheese; **q. de cerdo** *Br* brawn, *US* head-cheese

quetzal *nm (moneda)* = standard monetary unit of Guatemala

quiché *adj & nm* Quiché

quicio *nm* (**a**) *(de puerta)* doorpost (**b**) *Fig* **fuera de q.** beside oneself; **sacar de q.** *(a algn)* to infuriate; *(algo)* to take too far

quid *nm* crux; **has dado en el q.** you've hit the nail on the head

quiebra *nf Fin (bancarrota)* bankruptcy; *(crack)* crash

quiebro *nm (con el cuerpo)* dodge; *Ftb* dribbling

quien *pron rel* (**a**) *(con prep)* no se traduce o *Fml* whom; **el hombre con q.** vino the man she came with; *Fml* the man with whom she came (**b**) *(indefinido)* whoever, anyone who; **q. quiera venir que venga** whoever wants to can come; **hay q. dice lo contrario** some people say the opposite; *Fig* **q. más q. menos** everybody

quién *pron interr* (**a**) *(sujeto)* who?; **¿q. es?** who is it? (**b**) *(complemento)* who, *Fml* whom; **¿para q. es?** who is it for?; **¿de q. es esa bici?** whose bike is that?

quienquiera *pron indef* (*pl* **quienes-quiera**) whoever

quieto,-a *adj* still; *(mar)* calm; **¡estáte q.!** keep still!, don't move!

quietud *nf* stillness; *(calma)* calm

quijada *nf* jawbone

quilate *nm* carat

quilla *nf* keel

quillango *nm Arg, Chile* hide blanket

quilo *nm* = **kilo**

quilombo *nm RP muy Fam* (**a**) *(burdel)* whorehouse (**b**) *(lío, desorden)* godawful ruckus o rumpus

quimera *nf Fig* fantasy, pipe dream

química *nf* chemistry

químico,-a 1 *adj* chemical

  2 *nm,f* chemist

quimioterapia *nf* chemotherapy

quimono *nm* kimono

quincalla *nf* metal pots and pans, tinware

quince *adj & nm inv* fifteen

quinceañero,-a *adj & nm,f* fifteen-year-old

quincena *nf* fortnight, two weeks

quincenal *adj* fortnightly

quincho *nm CSur* (**a**) *(techo)* thatched roof (**b**) *(refugio)* thatched shelter

quiniela *nf* football pools

quinientos,-as *adj & nm* five hundred

quinina *nf* quinine

quinqué *nm* oil lamp

quinquenal *adj* quinquennial, five-year

quinqui *nm Fam* delinquent, petty criminal

quinta *nf* (**a**) *(casa)* country house (**b**) *Mil* call-up year

quintaesencia *nf* quintessence

quintal *nm (medida)* = 46 kg; **q. métrico** ≃ 100 kg

quinteto *nm* quintet

quinto,-a 1 *adj & nm,f* fifth

  2 *nm Mil* conscript, recruit

quiosco *nm* kiosk; **q. de periódicos** newspaper stand

quirófano *nm* operating theatre

quiromancia *nf* palmistry

quirúrgico,-a *adj* surgical

quise *indic fut de* **querer**

quisque, quisqui *pron Fam* **todo** o **cada q.** everyone, everybody

quisquilloso,-a 1 *adj* fussy, finicky

  2 *nm,f* fusspot

quiste *nm* cyst

quitaesmalte(s) *nm inv* nail varnish o polish remover

quitamanchas *nm inv* stain remover

quitanieves *nm* (máquina) **q.** snow-plough

quitar 1 *vt* (**a**) to remove; *(ropa)* to take off; *(la mesa)* to clear; *(mancha)* to remove; *(dolor)* to relieve; *(hipo)* to stop; *(sed)* to quench; *(hambre)* to take away

(**b**) *(apartar)* to take away, to take off; *Fig* **q. importancia a algo** to play sth down; *Fig* **q. las ganas a algn** to put sb off

(**c**) *(robar)* to steal, to take; *Fig (tiempo)* to take up; *(sitio)* to take

(**d**) *(descontar)* to take off

(**e**) *Fam (apagar)* to turn off

(**f**) **eso no quita para que ...** that's no reason not to be ...

(**g**) **¡quita!** go away!

2 quitarse *vpr* (**a**) *(apartarse)* to move away

(**b**) *(mancha)* to come out; *(dolor)* to go away; **se me han quitado las ganas** I don't feel like it any more

(**c**) *(ropa, gafas)* to take off

(**d**) **q. de beber/fumar** to give up drinking/smoking

(**e**) **q. a algn de encima** to get rid of sb

> 🖉 Observa que el verbo inglés **to quit** es un falso amigo y no es la traducción del verbo español **quitar**. En inglés, **to quit** significa "dejar, abandonar".

---

quizá(s) *adv* perhaps, maybe

R

R, r ['erre] *nf (la letra)* R, r

rábano *nm* radish; *Fam* **me importa un r.** I couldn't care less

rabia *nf* (a) *Fig (ira)* fury, rage; **¡qué r.!** how annoying!; **me da r.** it gets up my nose; **me tiene r.** he's got it in for me (b) *Med* rabies *sing*

rabiar [43] *vi* (a) *Fig (sufrir)* to be in great pain (b) *Fig (enfadar)* to rage; **hacer r. a algn** to make sb see red (c) *Med* to have rabies

rabieta *nf Fam* tantrum; **coger una r.** to throw a tantrum

rabillo *nm (del ojo)* corner

rabino *nm* rabbi

rabioso,-a *adj* (a) *Med* rabid; **perro r.** rabid dog (b) *Fig (enfadado)* furious (c) **de rabiosa actualidad** up-to-the-minute

rabo *nm* tail; *(de fruta etc)* stalk

racanear *vi Fam (ser tacaño)* to be stingy

rácano,-a *adj Fam (tacaño)* stingy, mean

racha *nf (de viento)* gust, squall; *Fam (período)* spell, patch; **a rachas** in fits and starts

racial *adj* **discriminación r.** racial discrimination; **disturbios raciales** race riots

racimo *nm* bunch, cluster

raciocinio *nm* reason

ración *nf* portion

racional *adj* rational

racionalizar [40] *vt* to rationalize

racionamiento *nm* rationing; **cartilla de r.** ration book

racionar *vt (limitar)* to ration; *(repartir)* to ration out

racismo *nm* racism

racista *adj & nmf* racist

radar *nm (pl radares) Téc* radar

radiación *nf* radiation

radiactividad *nf* radioactivity

radiactivo,-a *adj* radioactive

radiador *nm* radiator

radial *adj* (a) *(en forma de estrella)* radial (b) *Am (de la radio)* radio

radiante *adj* radiant *(de* with)

radiar [43] *vt* to broadcast, to transmit

radical *adj* radical

radicalizar [40] *vt*, **radicalizarse** *vpr (conflicto)* to intensify; *(postura)* to harden

radicar [44] *vi (estar)* to be (situated) (**en** in), to be rooted (**en** in)

radio 1 *nf* radio; *(aparato)* radio (set)
  2 *nm* (a) radius; **r. de acción** field of action, scope (b) *(de rueda)* spoke

radioactividad *nf* radioactivity

radioactivo,-a *adj* radioactive

radioaficionado,-a *nm,f* radio ham

radiocasete *nm (pl radiocasetes)* radio cassette

radioescucha *nmf* listener

radiograbador *nm*, **radiograbadora** *nf CSur* radio cassette

radiografía *nf (imagen)* X-ray

radioyente *nmf* listener

ráfaga *nf (de viento)* gust, squall; *(de disparos)* burst

raído,-a *adj* (a) *(gastado)* worn (b) *Fam (desvergonzado)* insolent

raigambre *nf* roots

raíl *nm* rail

raíz *nf (pl raíces)* root; **r. cuadrada** square root; *Fig* **a r. de** as a result of

raja *nf (corte)* cut, slit; *(hendidura)* crack, split

rajar 1 *vt (hender)* to crack, to split; *Fam (acuchillar)* to cut up
  2 *vi Fam* to backbite
  3 rajarse *vpr* (a) *(partirse)* to crack, to split (b) *Fam (echarse atrás)* to back out (c) *Am (acobardarse)* to chicken out

rajatabla: • a rajatabla *loc adv* strictly

ralea *nf Pey* type, sort

ralentí *nm* neutral; **estar al r.** to be ticking over

ralentizar *vt* to slow down

rallado,-a *adj* **queso r.** grated cheese; **pan r.** breadcrumbs

rallador *nm* grater

ralladura *nf* gratings

rallar *vt* to grate

ralo,-a *adj* sparse, thin

rama *nf* branch; *Fam* **andarse o irse por las ramas** to beat about the bush

ramaje *nm* branches

ramalazo *nm Fam (toque)* touch

rambla *nf (avenida)* boulevard, avenue

ramera *nf* prostitute, whore

ramificación *nf* ramification

ramificarse [44] *vpr* to ramify, to branch (out)

ramillete *nm* (*de flores*) posy

ramo *nm* (**a**) (*de flores*) bunch, bouquet (**b**) (*sector*) branch

rampa *nf* ramp; **r. de lanzamiento** launch pad

ramplón,-ona *adj* coarse, vulgar

rana *nf* frog; *Fam* **salir r.** to be a disappointment

ranchero,-a *nm,f* (*granjero*) rancher, farmer

rancho *nm* (**a**) (*granja*) ranch (**b**) *Mil* (*comida*) mess (**c**) *RP* (*en la playa*) = thatched beachside building (**d**) *CSur, Ven* (*en la ciudad*) shack, shanty

rancio,-a *adj* (**a**) (*comida*) stale (**b**) (*antiguo*) ancient

rango *nm* rank; (*jerarquía elevada*) high social standing

ranura *nf* slot

rapar *vt* (*afeitar*) to shave; (*pelo*) to crop

rapaz¹ *adj* predatory; **ave r.** bird of prey

rapaz²,-aza *nm,f* youngster; (*muchacho*) lad; (*muchacha*) lass

rape *nm* (**a**) (*pez*) angler fish (**b**) *Fam* **cortado al r.** close-cropped

rapidez *nf* speed, rapidity

rápido,-a 1 *adj* quick, fast, rapid
2 *adv* quickly
3 *nm* (**a**) (*tren*) fast train (**b**) **rápidos** (*de un río*) rapids

rapiña *nf* robbery, theft; **ave de r.** bird of prey

raptar *vt* to kidnap, to abduct

rapto *nm* (**a**) (*secuestro*) kidnapping, abduction (**b**) *Fig* (*arrebato*) outburst, fit

raqueta *nf* (**a**) (*de tenis*) racket; (*de pingpong*) *Br* bat, *US* paddle (**b**) (*de nieve*) snowshoe

raquítico,-a *adj Fam* (*escaso*) small, meagre; (*delgado*) emaciated

raquitismo *nm* rickets *sing*

rareza *nf* (**a**) rarity, rareness (**b**) (*extravagancia*) eccentricity

raro,-a *adj* (**a**) rare; **rara vez** seldom (**b**) (*extraño*) odd, strange

ras *nm* level; **a r. de** (on a) level with; **a r. de tierra** at ground level

rasante 1 *nf Aut* **cambio de r.** brow of a hill
2 *adj* (*vuelo*) low

rasar *vt* (*nivelar*) to level

rasca *nf Fam* (*frío*) cold

rascacielos *nm inv* skyscraper

rascar [44] **1** *vt* (*con las uñas*) to scratch; (*guitarra*) to strum
2 *vi* to chafe

rasero *nm Fig* **medir con el mismo r.** to treat impartially

rasgado,-a *adj* (*ojos*) slit, almond-shaped

rasgar [42] *vt* to tear, to rip

rasgo *nm* (*característica*) characteristic, feature; (*de la cara*) feature; *Fig* **a grandes rasgos** broadly speaking

rasgón *nm* tear, rip

rasguñar *vt* to scratch, to scrape

rasguño *nm* scratch, scrape

rasilla *nf* (*ladrillo*) tile

raso,-a 1 *adj* (*llano*) flat, level; (*vuelo*) low; (*cielo*) clear, cloudless; **soldado r.** private
2 *nm* satin

raspa *nf* (*de pescado*) bone, backbone

raspador *nm* scraper

raspadura *nf* (*ralladura*) scraping, scrapings

raspar 1 *vt* (*limar*) to scrape (off)
2 *vi* (*ropa etc*) to chafe

rasposo,-a *adj* rough, sharp

rastra *nf Agr* harrow; **a la r., a rastras** dragging; *Fig* (*de mal grado*) grudgingly

rastreador *nm* tracker

rastrear *vt* (*zona*) to comb

rastreo *nm* search

rastrero,-a *adj* creeping; *Fig* (*despreciable*) vile, base

rastrillo *nm* (**a**) rake (**b**) *Fam* (*mercadillo*) flea market

rastro *nm* (**a**) trace, sign; (*en el suelo*) track, trail (**b**) **el R.** = the Madrid flea market

rastrojo *nm* stubble

rasurar *vt*, **rasurarse** *vpr* to shave

rata 1 *nf* rat
2 *nm Fam* (*tacaño*) mean o stingy person

ratero,-a *nm,f* pickpocket

raticida *nm* rat poison

ratificar [44] *vt* to ratify

rato *nm* (**a**) (*momento*) while, time; **a ratos** at times; **al poco r.** shortly after; **hay para r.** it'll take a while; **pasar un buen/mal r.** to have a good/bad time; **ratos libres** free time (**b**) *Fam* **un r.** (*mucho*) very, a lot

ratón *nm* mouse; *Informát* mouse

ratonera *nf* mousetrap

raudal *nm* torrent, flood; *Fig* **a raudales** in abundance

raya *nf* (**a**) (*línea*) line; (*del pantalón*) crease; (*del pelo*) parting; **camisa a rayas** striped shirt; *Fig* **tener a r.** to keep at bay; **pasarse de la r.** to go over the score (**c**) (*de droga*) fix, dose

rayano,-a *adj* bordering (**en** on)

rayar 1 *vt* (*arañar*) to scratch

2 *vi* **r. en** o **con** to border on

rayo *nm* (**a**) ray, beam; **rayos X** X-rays (**b**) (*relámpago*) (flash of) lightning; **¡mal r. la parta!** to hell with her!

rayón *nm* rayon

rayuela *nf* hopscotch

raza *nf* (**a**) (*humana*) race (**b**) (*de animal*) breed (**c**) *Perú* (*descaro*) cheek, nerve

razón *nf* (**a**) (*facultad*) reason; **uso de r.** power of reasoning (**b**) (*motivo*) reason; **r. de más para** all the more reason to (**c**) (*justicia*) rightness, justice; **dar la r. a algn** to say that sb is right; **tienes r.** you're right (**d**) (*proporción*) ratio, rate; **a r. de** at the rate of (**e**) **r. aquí** (*en letrero*) enquire within, apply within

razonable *adj* reasonable

razonado,-a *adj* reasoned, well-reasoned

razonamiento *nm* reasoning

razonar 1 *vt* (*argumentar*) to reason out
    2 *vi* (*discurrir*) to reason

RDA *nf Hist* (*abr* **República Democrática Alemana** o **de Alemania**) GDR

re- *pref* re-

reacción *nf* reaction; **avión de r.** jet (plane); **r. en cadena** chain reaction

reaccionar *vi* to react

reaccionario,-a *adj* & *nm,f* reactionary

reacio,-a *adj* reluctant, unwilling

reactor *nm* reactor; (*avión*) jet (plane)

readaptación *nf* rehabilitation; **r. profesional** industrial retraining

reafirmar *vt* to reaffirm, to reassert

reagrupar *vt,* **reagruparse** *vpr* to regroup

reajuste *nm* readjustment; *Com* **r. de plantillas** downsizing; **r. ministerial** cabinet reshuffle

real¹ *adj* (*efectivo, verdadero*) real; **en la vida r.** in real life

real² *adj* (*regio*) royal

realce *nm* (*relieve*) relief; *Fig* (*esplendor*) splendour

realeza *nf* royalty

realidad *nf* reality; **en r.** in fact, actually; **la r. es que ...** the fact of the matter is that ...

realismo *nm* realism

realista 1 *adj* realistic
    2 *nmf* realist

realizable *adj* feasible

realización *nf* (*ejecución*) carrying out; *Cin* & *TV* production

realizador,-a *nm,f Cin* & *TV* producer

realizar [**40**] **1** *vt* (**a**) (*hacer*) to carry out; (*ambición*) to achieve, to fulfil (**b**) *Cin* & *TV* to produce (**c**) *Fin* to realize

2 realizarse *vpr* (*persona*) to fulfil oneself; (*sueño*) to come true

realmente *adv* really; (*en realidad*) actually, in fact

realzar [**1**] *vt* (*recalcar*) to highlight; *Fig* (*belleza, importancia*) to enhance, to heighten

reanimación *nf* revival

reanimar *vt,* **reanimarse** *vpr* to revive

reanudación *nf* renewal, resumption, re-establishment; **r. de las clases** return to school

reanudar 1 *vt* to renew, to resume; **r. el paso** o **la marcha** to set off again; **r. las clases** to go back to school

2 reanudarse *vpr* to start again, to resume

reaparición *nf* reappearance, recurrence; (*de artista etc*) comeback

reapertura *nf* reopening

rearme *nm* rearmament

reaseguro *nm* reinsurance

reavivar *vt* to revive

rebaja *nf* (*descuento*) reduction, discount; **rebajas** sales; **precio de r.** sale price

rebajar 1 *vt* (**a**) (*precio*) to cut, to reduce; (*cantidad*) to take off (**b**) (*color*) to tone down, to soften; (*intensidad*) to diminish (**c**) (*trabajador*) to excuse, to exempt (**de** from) (**d**) (*humillar*) to humiliate

2 rebajarse *vpr* (*humillarse*) to humble oneself

rebanada *nf* slice

rebanar *vt* to slice, to cut into slices

rebañar *vt* (*plato etc*) to finish off

rebaño *nm* (*de ovejas*) flock; (*de otros animales*) herd

rebasar *vt* (**a**) (*exceder*) to exceed, to go beyond (**b**) *Aut* to overtake

rebatir *vt* to refute

> 🔲 Observa que la palabra inglesa **rebate** es un falso amigo y no es la traducción del verbo español **rebatir**. En inglés, **rebate** significa "devolución".

rebeca *nf* cardigan

rebelarse *vpr* to rebel, to revolt

rebelde 1 *nmf* rebel

2 *adj* rebellious; *Fig* **una tos r.** a persistent cough

rebeldía *nf* (**a**) rebelliousness (**b**) *Jur* default

rebelión *nf* rebellion, revolt

rebenque *nm RP* whip

reblandecer [**33**] *vt* to soften

rebobinar *vt* to rewind

rebosante *adj* overflowing (**de** with), brimming (**de** with)

rebosar 1 *vi* to overflow, to brim over; *Fig*
r. de to be overflowing o brimming with
  2 *vt* (*irradiar*) to radiate
rebotar *vi* (*pelota*) to bounce, to rebound; (*bala*) to ricochet
rebote *nm* (*de pelota*) bounce, rebound;
(*de bala*) ricochet; **de r.** on the rebound
rebozar [40] *vt* to coat in breadcrumbs/
batter
rebozo *nm Am* wrap, shawl
rebullir *vi*, **rebullirse** *vpr* to stir
rebuscado,-a *adj* recherché
rebuznar *vi* to bray
recabar *vt* (*información*) to obtain, to
manage to get
recado *nm* (*mandado*) errand; (*mensaje*)
message; **dejar un r.** to leave a message
recaer [39] *vi* (**a**) *Med* to relapse (**b**)
(*culpa, responsabilidad*) to fall (**sobre** on)
recaída *nf* relapse
recalcar [44] *vt* to stress, to emphasize
recalcitrante *adj* recalcitrant
recalentar [1] *vt* (*comida*) to reheat, to
warm up; (*calentar demasiado*) to overheat
recámara *nf* (**a**) (*de rueda*) tube (**b**) (*habitación*) dressing room (**c**) *CAm, Col,
Méx* (*dormitorio*) bedroom
recamarera *nf CAm, Col, Méx* chambermaid
recambiar [43] *vt* to change (over)
recambio *nm* (*repuesto*) spare (part);
rueda de r. spare wheel (**b**) (*de pluma etc*)
refill
recapacitar *vi* to reflect, to think
recargable *adj* (*pluma*) refillable; (*mechero*) rechargeable
recargado,-a *adj* overloaded; *Fig* (*estilo*)
overelaborate, affected
recargar [42] **1** *vt* (**a**) *Elec* to recharge
(**b**) (*sobrecargar*) to overload; (*adornar
mucho*) to overelaborate (**c**) *Fin* to increase
  2 recargarse *vpr Méx* (*apoyarse*) to lean
(**contra** against)
recargo *nm* extra charge, surcharge
recatado,-a *adj* (*prudente*) prudent, cautious; (*modesto*) modest, decent
recato *nm* (*cautela*) caution, prudence;
(*pudor*) modesty
recaudación *nf* (*cobro*) collection; (*cantidad recaudada*) takings; *Dep* gate
recaudador,-a *nm,f* tax collector
recaudar *vt* to collect
recaudo *nm* **estar a buen r.** to be in safekeeping
recelar *vi* **r. de** to distrust
recelo *nm* suspicion, distrust

receloso,-a *adj* suspicious, distrustful
recepción *nf* reception; (*en hotel*) reception (desk)
recepcionista *nmf* receptionist
receptivo,-a *adj* receptive
receptor,-a 1 *nm,f* (*persona*) recipient
  2 *nm Rad & TV* receiver
recesión *nf* recession
receta *nf* recipe; *Med* prescription
recetar *vt Med* to prescribe
rechace *nm Dep* clearance
rechazar [40] *vt* to reject, to turn down;
Mil to repel, to drive back
rechazo *nm* rejection
rechiflar *vt* (**a**) (*silbar*) to hiss, to boo (**b**)
(*mofarse*) to mock, to jeer at
rechinar *vi* (*madera*) to creak; (*metal*) to
squeak, to screech; (*dientes*) to chatter
rechistar *vi* **sin r.** that's final
rechoncho,-a *adj Fam* chubby, tubby
rechupete: • de rechupete *loc Fam* **me sé
el tema de r.** I know the subject inside
out; **la comida estaba de r.** the food was
mouthwateringly good
recibidor *nm* entrance hall
recibimiento *nm* reception, welcome
recibir 1 *vt* to receive; (*en casa*) to welcome; (*en la estación etc*) to meet
  2 recibirse *vpr Am* (*graduarse*) to graduate, to qualify (**de** as)
recibo *nm* (**a**) (*factura*) invoice, bill; (*resguardo*) receipt; **r. de la luz** electricity bill
(**b**) **acusar r. de** to acknowledge receipt of
reciclado,-a 1 *adj* recycled
  2 *nm* (*reciclaje*) recycling
reciclaje *nm* (*de residuos*) recycling; *Fig*
(*renovación*) retraining; **curso de r.** refresher course
reciclar *vt* (*residuos*) to recycle; *Fig* (*profesores etc*) to retrain
recién *adv* (**a**) (*recientemente*) (*antes de
pp*) recently, newly; **café r. hecho** freshly
made coffee; **r. casados** newlyweds; **r.
nacido** newborn baby (**b**) *Am* (*hace poco*)
recently
reciente *adj* recent
recientemente *adv* recently, lately
recinto *nm* (*cercado*) enclosure; **r. comercial** shopping precinct
recio,-a 1 *adj* (*robusto*) strong, sturdy;
(*grueso*) thick; (*voz*) loud
  2 *adv* hard
recipiente *nm* receptacle, container

📝 Observa que la palabra inglesa **recipient**
es un falso amigo y no es la traducción de la
palabra española **recipiente**. En inglés, **recipient** significa "receptor, destinatario".

recíproco,-a *adj* reciprocal
recital *nm Mús* recital; *Lit* reading
recitar *vt* to recite
reclamación *nf* (**a**) *(demanda)* claim, demand (**b**) *(queja)* complaint
reclamar 1 *vt* to claim, to demand
  2 *vi* (**a**) to protest (**contra** against) (**b**) *Jur* to appeal
reclamo *nm* (**a**) *(publicitario)* appeal (**b**) *(en caza)* decoy bird, lure; *Fig* inducement (**c**) *Am (queja)* complaint (**d**) *Am (reivindicación)* claim
reclinar 1 *vt* to lean (**sobre** on)
  2 reclinarse *vpr* to lean back, to recline
recluir [37] *vt* to shut away, to lock away; *(encarcelar)* to imprison, to intern
reclusión *nf* seclusion; *(encarcelamiento)* imprisonment, internment
recluso,-a *nm,f* prisoner

> 🖉 Observa que la palabra inglesa **recluse** es un falso amigo y no es la traducción de la palabra española **recluso**. En inglés, **recluse** significa "solitario".

recluta *nmf* recruit
reclutamiento *nm (voluntario)* recruitment; *(obligatorio)* conscription
recobrar 1 *vt* to recover, to retrieve; *(conocimiento)* to regain; **r. el aliento** to get one's breath back
  2 recobrarse *vpr* to recover, to recuperate
recochineo *nm Fam* mockery
recodo *nm (de río)* twist, turn; *(de camino)* bend
recogedor *nm* dustpan
recoger [53] **1** *vt* (**a**) *(del suelo etc)* to pick up (**b**) *(datos etc)* to gather, to collect (**c**) *(ordenar, limpiar)* to clean; **r. la mesa** to clear the table (**d**) *(ir a buscar)* to pick up, to fetch (**e**) *(cosecha)* to gather, to pick
  2 recogerse *vpr* (**a**) *(irse a casa)* to go home (**b**) *(pelo)* to lift up
recogida *nf* collection; *Agr (cosecha)* harvest, harvesting
recolección *nf Agr* harvest, harvesting; *(recogida)* collection, gathering

> 🖉 Observa que la palabra inglesa **recollection** es un falso amigo y no es la traducción de la palabra española **recolección**. En inglés, **recollection** significa "recuerdo".

recomendable *adj* recommendable
recomendación *nf* recommendation, reference
recomendado,-a *adj Am (carta, paquete)* registered
recomendar [1] *vt* to recommend

recompensa *nf* reward
recompensar *vt* to reward
recomponer [19] (*pp* **recompuesto**) *vt* to repair, to mend
reconciliación *nf* reconciliation
reconciliar [43] **1** *vt* to reconcile
  2 reconciliarse *vpr* to be reconciled
recóndito,-a *adj* hidden, secret
reconfortante *adj* comforting
reconfortar *vt* to comfort
reconocer [34] *vt* (**a**) to recognize (**b**) *(admitir)* to recognize, to admit (**c**) *Med (paciente)* to examine
reconocimiento *nm* (**a**) recognition (**b**) *Med* examination, checkup
reconquista *nf* reconquest
reconstituyente *nm* tonic
reconstruir [37] *vt* to reconstruct
reconversión *nf* reconversion; **r. industrial** industrial redeployment
reconvertir [5] *vt* to reconvert; *Ind* to modernize
recopilación *nf* (**a**) *(resumen)* summary, résumé (**b**) *(compendio)* compilation, collection
recopilar *vt* to compile, to collect
récord *nm* record
recordar [2] **1** *vt* (**a**) *(rememorar)* to remember (**b**) **r. algo a algn** to remind sb of sth
  2 *vi* to remember
recordatorio *nm (aviso)* reminder; *(de defunción)* notice of death
recordman *nm* record holder
recorrer *vt (distancia)* to cover, to travel; *(país)* to tour, to travel through o round; *(ciudad)* to visit, to walk round
recorrido *nm, Am* **recorrida** *nf (distancia)* distance travelled; *(trayecto)* trip, journey; *(itinerario)* itinerary, route
recortable *adj & nm* cutout
recortar *vt* to cut out
recorte *nm (acción, de periódico)* cutting; *(de pelo)* trim, cut; *Fig (de salarios etc)* cut
recostado,-a *adj* reclining, leaning
recostar [2] **1** *vt* to lean
  2 recostarse *vpr (tumbarse)* to lie down
recoveco *nm (curva)* turn, bend; *(rincón)* nook, corner
recreación *nf* recreation
recrear 1 *vt* (**a**) *(divertir)* to amuse, to entertain (**b**) *(crear de nuevo)* to recreate
  2 recrearse *vpr* to amuse oneself, to enjoy oneself; **r. con** to take pleasure o delight in
recreativo,-a *adj* recreational
recreo *nm* (**a**) *(diversión)* recreation (**b**) *(en el colegio)* break, recreation

recriminar *vt* to recriminate; *(reprochar)* to reproach

recrudecer [33] *vt*, **recrudecerse** *vpr* to worsen

recrudecimiento *nm* worsening

recta *nf* Geom straight line; *(de carretera)* straight stretch; *Dep* **la r. final** the home straight

rectangular *adj* rectangular

rectángulo *nm* rectangle

rectificación *nf* rectification; *(corrección)* correction

rectificar [44] *vt* to rectify; *(corregir)* to correct, to remedy

rectilíneo,-a *adj* straight

rectitud *nf* straightness; *Fig* uprightness, rectitude

recto,-a 1 *adj* (a) *(derecho)* straight (b) *(honesto)* upright, honest (c) Geom right
2 *nm Anat* rectum
3 *adv* straight (on)

rector,-a 1 *adj (principio)* guiding, ruling
2 *nm,f* rector

recua *nf Fig* string, series

recuadro *nm Prensa* box

recubrir *(pp* **recubierto)** *vt* to cover

recuento *nm* count; **hacer (el) r. de** to count

recuerdo *nm* (a) *(memoria)* memory (b) *(regalo etc)* souvenir (c) **recuerdos** regards

recuperación *nf* recovery; *(examen)* resit

recuperar 1 *vt (salud)* to recover; *(conocimiento)* to regain; *(tiempo, clases)* to make up
2 recuperarse *vpr* to recover

recurrir *vi* (a) *Jur* to appeal (b) **r. a** *(a algn)* to turn to; *(a algo)* to make use of, to resort to

> *Observa que el verbo inglés* **to recur** *es un falso amigo y no es la traducción del verbo español* **recurrir**. *En inglés,* **to recur** *significa "repetirse".*

recurso *nm* (a) *resource;* **recursos naturales** natural resources; **como último r.** as a last resort (b) *Jur* appeal

recusar *vt* to challenge, to object to

red *nf* net; *(sistema)* network; *Com (cadena)* chain of supermarkets; *Fig (trampa)* trap; **la R.** *(Internet)* the Net

redacción *nf (escrito)* composition, essay; *(acción)* writing; *Prensa* editing; *(redactores)* editorial staff

redactar *vt* to draft; *Prensa* to edit

redactor,-a *nm,f Prensa* editor

redada *nf* **r. policial** *(en un solo sitio)* raid; *(en varios lugares a la vez)* round-up

redentor,-a *nm,f* redeemer

redicho,-a *adj Fam* affected, pretentious

redil *nm* fold, sheepfold

redimir *vt* to redeem

rédito *nm* yield, interest

redituable *adj* interest-yielding

redoblar 1 *vt* to redouble
2 *vi (tambor)* to roll

redoble *nm* roll; *(de campanas)* peal

redomado,-a *adj* utter, out-and-out

redonda *nf* **a la r.** around

redondear *vt (objeto)* to round, to make round; *(cantidad)* to round up

redondel *nm Fam (círculo)* circle, ring; *Taurom* ring, arena

redondo,-a *adj* (a) *round; Fig* **caer r.** to collapse (b) *(rotundo)* categorical; *(perfecto)* perfect

reducción *nf* reduction

reducido,-a *adj (disminuido)* reduced, decreased; *(pequeño)* limited, small

reducir [10] 1 *vt (disminuir)* to reduce
2 reducirse *vpr* (a) *(disminuirse)* to be reduced, to diminish (b) *(limitarse)* to confine oneself

redundancia *nf* redundancy, superfluousness; **valga la r.** if I might say so again

redundante *adj* redundant

redundar *vi* **r. en** *(resultar)* to result in, to lead to

reduplicar [44] *vt* to redouble

reembolsar *vt* to reimburse; *(deuda)* to repay; *(importe)* to refund

reembolso *nm* reimbursement; *(de deuda)* repayment; *(devolución)* refund; **contra r.** cash on delivery

reemplazar [40] *vt* to replace (**con** with)

reemplazo *nm* replacement; *Mil* call-up

reestructuración *nf* restructuring

reestructurar *vt* to restructure

ref. *(abr* **referencia)** ref

refacción *nf* (a) *Andes, CAm, RP, Ven (reparación)* repair (b) *Méx (recambio)* spare part

refaccionar *vt Am* to repair, to do up

refectorio *nm* refectory, canteen

referencia *nf* reference; **con r. a** with reference to

referéndum *nm (pl* **referéndums)** referendum

referente *adj* **r. a** concerning, regarding

referir [5] 1 *vt* to tell, to relate
2 referirse *vpr (aludir)* to refer (**a** to); **¿a qué te refieres?** what do you mean?

refilón: •**de refilón** *loc adv (de pasada)* briefly

refinado,-a *adj* refined
refinamiento *nm* refinement
refinar *vt* to refine
refinería *nf* refinery
reflector,-a 1 *adj* reflecting
  2 *nm Elec* spotlight, searchlight
reflejar 1 *vt* to reflect
  2 **reflejarse** *vpr* to be reflected (**en** in)
reflejo,-a 1 *nm* (**a**) *(imagen)* reflection (**b**) *(destello)* gleam, glint (**c**) *Anat* reflex (**d**) **reflejos** *(en el cabello)* streaks, highlights
  2 *adj (movimiento)* reflex
reflexión *nf* reflection
reflexionar *vi* to reflect (**sobre** on), to think (**sobre** about)
reflexivo,-a *adj* (**a**) *(persona)* thoughtful (**b**) *Ling* reflexive
reflujo *nm* ebb (tide)
reforma *nf* (**a**) reform; **r. fiscal** tax reform (**b**) *(reparación)* repair
reformador,-a *nm,f* reformer
reformar 1 *vt* to reform; *(edificio)* to renovate
  2 **reformarse** *vpr* to reform
reformatorio *nm* reformatory, reform school
reforzar [2] *vt* to reinforce, to strengthen
refractario,-a *adj* (**a**) *Téc* heat-resistant (**b**) *(persona)* unwilling, reluctant
refrán *nm* proverb, saying
refregar [1] *vt* to rub vigorously; *Fig* **no me lo refriegues** don't rub it in
refrenar 1 *vt (contener)* to restrain, to curb
  2 **refrenarse** *vpr* to restrain oneself
refrendar *vt (firmar)* to endorse, to countersign; *(aprobar)* to approve
refrescante *adj* refreshing
refrescar [44] 1 *vt* to refresh
  2 *vi* (**a**) *(tiempo)* to turn cool (**b**) *(bebida)* to be refreshing
  3 **refrescarse** *vpr* to cool down
refresco *nm* soft drink, refreshments
refriega *nf (lucha)* scuffle, brawl; *(escaramuza)* skirmish
refrigeración *nf (enfriamiento)* refrigeration; *(aire acondicionado)* air conditioning
refrigerado,-a *adj* air-conditioned
refrigerador *nm* refrigerator, fridge
refrigerar *vt* to refrigerate; *(habitación)* to air-condition
refrigerio *nm* snack, refreshments
refuerzo *nm* reinforcement, strengthening
refugiado,-a *adj & nm,f* refugee

refugiarse [43] *vpr* to shelter, to take refuge
refugio *nm* refuge
refulgente *adj* radiant, brilliant
refulgir [57] *vi (brillar)* to shine; *(resplandecer)* to glitter, to sparkle
refunfuñar *vi* to grumble, to moan
refutar *vt* to refute
regadera *nf* (**a**) *(para regar)* watering can; *Fam* **estar como una r.** to be as mad as a hatter (**b**) *Col, Méx, Ven (ducha)* shower
regadío *nm (tierra)* irrigated land
regalado,-a *adj* (**a**) *(gratis)* free; *(muy barato)* dirt-cheap (**b**) **una vida regalada** an easy life
regalar *vt* (**a**) *(dar)* to give (as a present); *(en ofertas etc)* to give away (**b**) **r. el oído a algn** to flatter sb
regaliz *nm* liquorice
regalo *nm* (**a**) gift, present; **de r.** as a present (**b**) *(comodidad)* pleasure, comfort
regalón,-ona *adj CSur Fam (niño)* spoilt
regañadientes: •a regañadientes *loc adv* reluctantly, unwillingly
regañar 1 *vt Fam* to scold, to tell off
  2 *vi* to nag
regañina *nf* scolding, telling-off
regañón,-ona *nm,f Fam* nag
regar [1] *vt* to water
regata *nf* boat race
regatear 1 *vi* (**a**) to haggle, to bargain (**b**) *Dep* to dribble
  2 *vt* **no r. esfuerzos** to spare no effort
regateo *nm* (**a**) *(de precios)* haggling (**b**) *Dep* dribbling
regazo *nm* lap
regeneración *nf* regeneration
regenerar *vt* to regenerate
regentar *vt* to rule, to govern; *(cargo)* to hold
regente *nmf* (**a**) *Pol* regent (**b**) *(director)* manager (**c**) *Méx (alcalde)* mayor, *f* mayoress
régimen *nm (pl* **regímenes**) (**a**) *Pol* regime (**b**) *Med* diet; **estar a r.** to be on a diet
regimiento *nm* regiment
regio,-a *adj* (**a**) *(real)* royal, regal (**b**) *(suntuoso)* sumptuous, luxurious; *Am (magnífico)* splendid, majestic
región *nf* region
regional *adj* regional
regionalista *adj & nmf* regionalist
regir [58] 1 *vt* to govern
  2 *vi* to be in force
  3 **regirse** *vpr* to be guided, to go (**por** by)
registrado,-a *adj* (**a**) *(patentado, inscrito)*

registered; **marca registrada** registered trademark (**b**) *Am (certificado)* registered

registrador,-a *adj* **caja registradora** cash register

registradora *nf Am* cash register

registrar 1 *vt* (**a**) *(examinar)* to inspect; *(cachear)* to frisk (**b**) *(inscribir)* to register (**c**) *(grabar)* to record

2 registrarse *vpr* (**a**) *(inscribirse)* to register, to enrol (**b**) *(detectarse)* to be recorded

registro *nm* (**a**) inspection (**b**) *(inscripción)* registration, recording; *(oficina)* registry office (**c**) *Mús* register

regla *nf* (**a**) *(norma)* rule; **en r.** in order; **por r. general** as a (general) rule; **r. de oro** golden rule (**b**) *(instrumento)* ruler (**c**) *Mat* rule (**d**) *Med (periodo)* period

reglamentación *nf* (**a**) *(acción)* regulation (**b**) *(reglamento)* regulations, rules

reglamentar *vt* to regulate

reglamentario,-a *adj* statutory; *Mil* **arma reglamentaria** regulation gun

reglamento *nm* regulations, rules

reglar *vt* to regulate

regocijar 1 *vt* to delight, to amuse

2 regocijarse *vpr* to be delighted, to rejoice

regocijo *nm (placer)* delight, joy; *(alborozo)* rejoicing, merriment

regodearse *vpr Fam* to delight (**con** in)

regodeo *nm Fam* delight

regordete,-a *adj Fam* plump, chubby

regresar 1 *vi* to return

2 *vt Andes, CAm, Carib, Méx (devolver)* to give back

3 regresarse *vpr Andes, CAm, Carib, Méx (yendo)* to go back, to return; *(viniendo)* to come back, to return

regresión *nf* regression; *(decaimiento)* deterioration, decline

regreso *nm* return

reguero *nm (corriente)* trickle; *(de humo)* trail

regulable *adj* adjustable

regular 1 *vt* (**a**) to regulate, to control (**b**) *(ajustar)* to adjust

2 *adj* (**a**) regular; **por lo r.** as a rule; **vuelo r.** scheduled flight (**b**) *Fam (mediano)* average, so-so

3 *adv* so-so

regularidad *nf* regularity; **con r.** regularly

regularizar [40] *vt* to regularize

regusto *nm* aftertaste

rehabilitar *vt* to rehabilitate; *(edificio)* to convert

rehacer [15] *(pp* **rehecho) 1** *vt* to redo

2 rehacerse *vpr (recuperarse)* to recover, to recuperate

rehén *nm* hostage

rehogar [42] *vt* to brown

rehuir [37] *vt* to shun, to avoid

rehusar *vt* to refuse

reina *nf* queen

reinado *nm* reign

reinante *adj (que reina)* reigning, ruling; *(prevaleciente)* prevailing

reinar *vi* to reign

reincidente *nmf Jur* recidivist

reincidir *vi* to relapse, to fall back (**en** into)

reincorporarse *vpr* **r. al trabajo** to return to work

reino *nm* kingdom; **el R. Unido** the United Kingdom

reinserción *nf* reintegration

reinsertar *vt*, **reinsertarse** *vpr* to reintegrate

reintegrar *vt* (**a**) *(trabajador)* to reinstate (**b**) *(dinero)* to reimburse, to refund

reintegro *nm (en lotería)* winning of one's stake

reír [56] 1 *vi* to laugh

2 reírse *vpr* (**a**) to laugh (**b**) *(mofarse)* to laugh (**de** at), to make fun (**de** of)

reiterar *vt* to reiterate, to repeat

reivindicación *nf* claim, demand

reivindicar [44] *vt* to claim, to demand; **el atentado fue reivindicado por los terroristas** the terrorists claimed responsibility for the attack

reivindicativo,-a *adj* protest

reja *nf* (**a**) *(de ventana)* grill, grating; *Fam* **estar entre rejas** to be behind bars (**b**) *Agr* ploughshare

rejilla *nf (de ventana, ventilador, radiador)* grill; *(de horno)* gridiron; *(para equipaje)* luggage rack

rejoneador,-a *nm,f Taurom* = bullfighter on horseback

rejonear *vt Taurom* to fight on horseback

rejuvenecer [33] *vt* to rejuvenate

relación *nf* (**a**) relationship; *(conexión)* connection, link; **con o en r.** with regard to; **relaciones públicas** public relations (**b**) *(lista)* list (**c**) *(relato)* account (**d**) *Mat & Téc* ratio

relacionado,-a *adj* related (**con** to), connected (**con** with)

relacionar 1 *vt* to relate (**con** to), to connect (**con** with)

2 • relacionarse *vpr* (**a**) to be related, to be connected (**b**) *(alternar)* to mix, to get acquainted

relajación *nf* relaxation

relajante *adj* relaxing

relajar 1 *vt* to relax

2 relajarse *vpr* to relax; *(moral)* to deteriorate

relajo *nm Am Fam (alboroto)* racket, din

relamerse *vpr* to lick one's lips

relamido,-a *adj (afectado)* affected; *(pulcro)* prim and proper

relámpago *nm* flash of lightning; *Fig* **pasó como un r.** he flashed past; *Fig* **visita r.** flying visit

relampaguear *v impers* to flash

relanzar *vt* to relaunch

relatar *vt* to narrate, to relate

relatividad *nf* relativity

relativo,-a *adj* relative (**a** to); **en lo r. a** with regard to, concerning

relato *nm (cuento)* tale, story

relax *nm Fam* relaxation

relegar [42] *vt* to relegate

relente *nm* dew

relevancia *nf* importance

> 🖉 Observa que la palabra inglesa **relevance** es un falso amigo y no es la traducción de la palabra española **relevancia**. En inglés, **relevance** significa "pertinencia".

relevante *adj* important

relevar *vt* to relieve, to take over from; **fue relevado del cargo** he was relieved of his duties

2 relevarse *vpr (turnarse)* to relieve one another

relevo *nm* relief; *Dep* relay

relieve *nm Arte* relief; *Fig* **poner de r.** to emphasize

religión *nf* religion

religioso,-a 1 *adj* religious

2 *nm,f (hombre)* monk; *(mujer)* nun

relinchar *vi* to neigh, to whinny

relincho *nm* neigh, whinny

reliquia *nf* relic

rellamada *nf Tel* redial

rellano *nm* landing

rellenar *vt* (**a**) *(impreso etc)* to fill in (**b**) *(un ave)* to stuff; *(un pastel)* to fill

relleno,-a 1 *nm (de aves)* stuffing; *(de pasteles)* filling

2 *adj* stuffed

reloj *nm* clock; *(de pulsera)* watch; **r. de arena** hourglass; **r. de sol** sundial; **r. despertador** alarm clock

relojería *nf (tienda)* watchmaker's, clockmaker's; **bomba de r.** time bomb

relojero,-a *nm,f* watchmaker, clockmaker

reluciente *adj* shining, gleaming

relucir [35] *vi (brillar)* to shine, to gleam; **sacar a r. un tema** to bring up a subject

relumbrar *vi* to shine, to gleam

reluzco *indic pres de* **relucir**

remachar *vt* to drive home, to hammer home

remache *nm* rivet

remanente *nm (restos)* remainder; *(extra)* surplus

remangar [42] *vt*, **remangarse** *vpr (mangas, pantalones)* to roll up; *(camisa)* to tuck up

remanso *nm* pool; *(lugar tranquilo)* quiet place

remar *vi* to row

remarcar [44] *vt* to stress, to underline

> 🖉 Observa que el verbo inglés **to remark** es un falso amigo y no es la traducción del verbo español **remarcar**. En inglés, **to remark** significa "comentar, observar".

rematadamente *adv* **r. loco** as mad as a hatter

rematar *vt* (**a**) to finish off, to put the finishing touches to (**b**) *Com* to sell off cheaply (**c**) *Dep* to shoot

remate *nm* (**a**) *(final)* end, finish; **para r.** to crown it all (**b**) *Dep* shot at goal (**c**) **de r.** utter, utterly

rembolsar *vt* = **reembolsar**

rembolso *nm* = **reembolso**

remedar *vt* to imitate, to copy

remediar [43] *vt* (**a**) to remedy; *(enmendar)* to repair, to make good (**b**) *(evitar)* to avoid, to prevent; **no pude remediarlo** I couldn't help it

remedio *nm (cura)* remedy, cure; *(solución)* solution; **¡qué r.!** what else can I do?; **no hay más r.** there's no choice; **sin r.** without fail; *Fam* **¡no tienes r.!** you're hopeless!

remedo *nm (imitación)* imitation, copy; *(parodia)* parody

rememorar *vt* to remember, to recall

remendar [1] *vt (ropa)* to patch

remera *nf RP (prenda)* T-shirt

remero,-a *nm,f* rower

remesa *nf (de mercancías)* consignment, shipment; *(de dinero)* remittance

remiendo *nm (parche)* patch

remilgado,-a *adj (afectado)* affected; *(melindroso)* fussy, finicky; *(gazmoño)* prudish

remilgo *nm* affectation; *(gazmoñería)* prudishness

reminiscencia *nf* reminiscence

remise *nm RP* taxi *(in private car without meter)*

remisero,-a *nm,f RP* taxi driver *(of private car without meter)*

remiso,-a adj reluctant

remite nm (en carta) = sender's name and address

remitente nmf sender

remitir 1 vt (a) (enviar) to send (b) (referir) to refer
  2 vi (fiebre, temporal) to subside
  3 remitirse upr **si nos remitimos a los hechos** if we look at the facts; **remítase a la página 10** see page 10

remo nm oar; (deporte) rowing

remoción nf Andes, RP (de objetos) transport, removal; (de heridos) transport

remodelación nf (modificación) reshaping; (reorganización) reorganization; Pol **r. ministerial** o **del gobierno** cabinet reshuffle

remodelar vt to reshape; (reorganizar) to reorganize

remojar vt to soak (**en** in)

remojo nm **dejar** o **poner en r.** to soak, to leave to soak

remojón nm Fam **darse un r.** to go for a dip

remolacha nf Br beetroot, US beet

remolcador nm (a) Náut tug, tugboat (b) Aut Br breakdown van o truck, US tow truck

remolcar [44] vt to tow

remolino nm (de agua) whirlpool, eddy; (de aire) whirlwind

remolón,-ona 1 adj lazy
  2 nm,f **hacerse el r.** to shirk, to slack

remolonear vi to shirk, to slack

remolque nm (acción) towing; (vehículo) trailer; Fig **ir a r. de algn** to trundle along behind sb

remontar 1 vt (a) (subir) to go up (b) (superar) to overcome
  2 remontarse upr (a) (pájaros, aviones) to soar (b) (datar) to go back, to date back (**a** to)

remorder [4] vt to trouble; **me remuerde la conciencia por ...** I've got a bad conscience about ...

remordimiento nm remorse

remoto,-a adj remote, faraway; **no tengo la más remota idea** I haven't got the faintest idea

remover [4] vt (a) (trasladar) to move over (b) (tierra) to turn over; (líquido) to shake up; (comida etc) to stir; (asunto) to stir up

> ♪ Observa que el verbo inglés **to remove** es un falso amigo y no es la traducción del verbo español **remover**. En inglés, **to remove** significa "quitar, despedir".

remozar [40] vt to modernize

remplazar [40] vt = **reemplazar**

remplazo nm = **reemplazo**

remuneración nf remuneration

remunerar vt to remunerate

renacentista adj Renaissance

renacer [60] vi to be reborn; Fig (revivir) to revive, to come back to life

renacimiento nm **el R.** the Renaissance

renacuajo nm tadpole; Fam (niño pequeño) shrimp

renal adj kidney; **insuficiencia r.** kidney failure

rencilla nf quarrel

rencor nm rancour; (resentimiento) resentment; **guardar r. a algn** to have a grudge against sb

rencoroso,-a adj (hostil) rancorous; (resentido) resentful

rendición nf surrender

rendido,-a adj (muy cansado) exhausted, worn out

rendija nf crack, split

rendimiento nm (producción) yield, output; (de máquina, motor) efficiency, performance

rendir [6] 1 vt (a) (fruto, beneficios) to yield, to produce (b) (cansar) to exhaust, to wear out (c) **r. culto** a to worship; **r. homenaje a** to pay homage to
  2 vi (dar beneficios) to pay, to be profitable
  3 rendirse upr (a) to surrender, to give in; **¡me rindo!** I give up! (b) (cansarse) to wear oneself out

renegado,-a adj & nm,f renegade

renegar [1] vt **r. de** to renounce, to disown

renegrido,-a adj blackened

RENFE nf (abr **Red Nacional de los Ferrocarriles Españoles**) = Spanish state railway company

renglón nm line; **a r. seguido** immediately afterwards

rengo,-a adj Andes, RP lame

renguear vi Andes, RP to limp, to hobble

reno nm reindeer

renombrado,-a adj renowned, famous

renombre nm renown, fame

renovable adj renewable

renovación nf (de contrato, pasaporte) renewal; (de una casa) renovation

renovar [2] vt to renew; (edificio) to renovate

renta nf (a) Fin (ingresos) income; (beneficio) interest, return; **r. per cápita** per capita income; **r. fija** fixed-interest security (b) (alquiler) rent

rentable *adj* profitable

rentar 1 *vt (rendir)* to produce, to yield; *Méx (alquilar)* to rent
  2 *vi* to be profitable

renuncia *nf* (a) renunciation (b) *(dimisión)* resignation

renunciar [43] *vi* (a) **r. a** to renounce, to give up; *(no aceptar)* to decline (b) *(dimitir)* to resign

reñido,-a *adj (disputado)* tough, hard-fought

reñir [6] **1** *vt (regañar)* to scold, to tell off
  2 *vi (discutir)* to quarrel, to argue; *(pelear)* to fight; **r. con algn** to fall out with sb

reo *nmf (acusado)* defendant, accused; *(culpable)* culprit

reojo: • **de reojo** *loc adv* **mirar algo de r.** to look at sth out of the corner of one's eye

reparación *nf* repair; *(compensación)* reparation, amends

reparar 1 *vt* to repair; *(ofensa, injuria)* to make amends for; *(daño)* to make good
  2 *vi* **r. en** *(darse cuenta de)* to notice; *(reflexionar sobre)* to think about

reparo *nm* **no tener reparos en** not to hesitate to; **me da r.** I feel embarrassed

repartidor,-a *nm,f* distributor

repartir *vt* (a) *(dividir)* to distribute, to share out (b) *(regalo, premio)* to give out, to hand out; *(correo)* to deliver; *Naipes* to deal

reparto *nm* (a) distribution, sharing out (b) *(distribución)* handing out; *(de mercancías)* delivery (c) *Cin & Teatro* cast

repasador *nm RP (trapo)* tea towel

repasar *vt* (a) to revise, to go over (b) *(ropa)* to mend

repaso *nm* revision

repatear *vt Fam* to annoy, to turn off

repatriar [29] *vt* to repatriate

repecho *nm* short steep slope

repelente *adj* repulsive, repellent; *Fam* **niño r.** little know-all

repeler *vt (rechazar)* to repel, to repulse; *(repugnar)* to disgust

repente *nm Fam (arrebato)* fit, outburst; **de r.** suddenly, all of a sudden

repentino,-a *adj* sudden

repercusión *nf* repercussion

repercutir *vi* (a) *(sonido)* to resound, to reverberate; *(objeto)* to rebound (b) *Fig* **r. en** to have repercussions on, to affect

repertorio *nm* repertoire, repertory

repesca *nf Fam* second chance; *(examen)* resit

repetición *nf* repetition; **r. de la jugada** action replay

repetido,-a *adj* **repetidas veces** repeatedly

repetidor,-a 1 *adj* repeating
  2 *nm,f Fam Educ* = student who is repeating a year

repetir [6] **1** *vt* (a) to repeat (b) *(plato)* to have a second helping
  2 *vi Educ* to repeat a year
  3 repetirse *vpr* (a) *(persona)* to repeat oneself (b) *(hecho)* to recur (c) **el pepino se repite** cucumber repeats (on me/you/him/*etc*)

repicar [44] *vt (las campanas)* to peal, to ring out

repipi *adj Fam* **niño r.** little know-all

repique *nm (de campanas)* peal, ringing

repiquetear *vt & vi (campanas)* to ring; *(tambor)* to beat

repisa *nf* shelf, ledge

replantear *vt,* **replantearse** *vpr* to reconsider, to rethink

replegarse [1] *vpr* to fall back, to retreat

repleto,-a *adj* full (up), jam-packed; **r. de** packed with, crammed with

réplica *nf* (a) answer, reply (b) *(copia)* replica

replicar [44] **1** *vt* to answer back
  2 *vi* (a) to reply, to retort (b) *(objetar)* to argue (c) *Jur* to answer

repliegue *nm Mil* withdrawal, retreat

repoblación *nf* repopulation; **r. forestal** reafforestation

repoblar [2] *vt* to repopulate; *(bosque)* to reafforest

repollo *nm* cabbage

reponer [19] **1** *vt* (a) to put back, to replace (b) *Teatro (obra)* to put on again; *Cin (película)* to rerun; *TV (programa)* to repeat
  2 reponerse *vpr* **r. de** to recover from, to get over

reportaje *nm Prensa & Rad* report; *(noticias)* article, news item

reportar 1 *vt (beneficios etc)* to bring; *Am (informar)* to report
  2 reportarse *vpr Am (presentarse)* to report (**a** to)

reporte *nm Méx (informe)* report; *(noticia)* news item *o* report; **recibí reportes de mi hermano** I was sent news by my brother; **el r. del tiempo** the weather report *o* forecast

reportero,-a *nm,f* reporter

reposar **1** *vt* to rest (**en** on)
  2 *vi (descansar)* to rest, to take a rest; *(té)* to infuse; *(comida)* to stand

reposera *nf RP Br* sun-lounger, *US* beach recliner

reposición *nf TV* repeat; *Cin* rerun, re-showing

reposo *nm* rest; **en r.** at rest

repostar *vt (provisiones)* to stock up with; *Aut (gasolina)* to fill up with

repostería *nf* confectionery; *(tienda)* confectioner's (shop)

repostero,-a *nm,f* confectioner

reprender *vt* to reprimand, to scold

represalia *nf (usu pl)* reprisals, retaliation

representación *nf* (a) representation (b) *Teatro* performance

representante *nmf* representative

representar *vt* (a) to represent (b) *(significar)* to mean, to represent (c) *Teatro (obra)* to perform

representativo,-a *adj* representative

represión *nf* repression

represivo,-a *adj* repressive

reprimenda *nf* reprimand

reprimir *vt* to repress

reprobar [2] *vt (cosa)* to condemn; *(a persona)* to reproach, to reprove; *Am (estudiante, examen)* to fail

réprobo,-a *adj & nm,f* reprobate

reprochable *adj* reproachable

reprochar *vt* to reproach; **r. algo a algn** to reproach sb for sth

reproche *nm* reproach

reproducción *nf* reproduction

reproducir [10] **1** *vt* to reproduce
  2 reproducirse *vpr* (a) to reproduce, to breed (b) *(repetirse)* to recur, to happen again

reproductor,-a *adj* reproductive

reptar *vi* to slither

reptil *nm* reptile

república *nf* republic; **la R. Checa** the Czech Republic

republicano,-a *adj & nm,f* republican

repudiar [43] *vt* to repudiate

repuesto *nm (recambio)* spare part, spare; *Aut* **rueda de r.** spare wheel

repugnancia *nf* loathing, disgust

repugnante *adj* disgusting, revolting

repugnar *vt* to disgust, to revolt

repujar *vt* to emboss

repulsa *nf* rebuff

repulsión *nf* repulsion, repugnance

repulsivo,-a *adj* repulsive, revolting

repuntar *vi Am (mejorar)* to improve

repunte *nm Am (recuperación)* recovery; *(aumento)* rise, increase; **un r. en las ventas** an improvement *o* increase in sales

repuse *pt indef de* **reponer**

reputación *nf* reputation

reputar *vt* to consider, to deem

requemar *vt* to scorch

requerimiento *nm* (a) *(súplica)* request (b) *Jur (aviso)* summons *sing*

> 📖 Observa que la palabra inglesa **requirement** es un falso amigo y no es la traducción de la palabra española **requerimiento**. En inglés, **requirement** significa "requisito".

requerir [5] *vt* (a) to require (b) *(solicitar)* to request (c) *Jur (avisar)* to summon

requesón *nm* cottage cheese

requete- *pref Fam* really, very, incredibly; **requetebueno** brilliant

réquiem *nm (pl réquiems)* requiem

requisa *nf* (a) *(inspección)* inspection (b) *Mil* requisition

requisar *vt* to requisition

requisito *nm* requirement, requisite

res *nf* animal

resabiado,-a *adj Pey* pedantic

resabio *nm* (a) *(mal sabor)* unpleasant *o* bad aftertaste (b) *(vicio)* bad habit

resaca *nf* (a) hangover (b) *Náut* undertow, undercurrent

resaltar *vi* (a) *(sobresalir)* to project, to jut out (b) *Fig* to stand out

resarcir [52] *vt* to compensate

resbalada *nf Am Fam* slip

resbaladizo,-a *adj* slippery

resbalar *vi*, **resbalarse** *vpr* to slip; *Aut* to skid

resbalón *nm* slip

rescatar *vt (persona)* to rescue; *(objeto)* to recover

rescate *nm* (a) *(salvamento)* rescue; *(recuperación)* recovery (b) *(suma)* ransom

rescindir *vt* to rescind, to annul; *(contrato)* to cancel

rescisión *nf* rescission, annulment

rescoldo *nm* (a) embers (b) *Fig (recelo)* lingering doubt

resecarse [44] *vpr* to dry up, to become parched

reseco,-a *adj* very dry, parched

resentido,-a *adj* resentful

resentimiento *nm* resentment

resentirse [5] *vpr* (a) **r. de** to suffer from, to feel the effects of (b) *(ofenderse)* to feel offended; **r. por algo** to take offence at sth, to feel bitter about sth

reseña *nf* review; *Prensa* write-up

reserva 1 *nf* (a) *(de entradas etc)* reservation, booking (b) *(provisión)* reserve, stock; **un vino de r.** a vintage wine (c) *Mil* reserve, reserves (d) *(duda)* reservation
  2 *nmf Dep* reserve, substitute

reservado,-a 1 adj (persona) reserved, quiet

2 nm private room

reservar 1 vt (**a**) (billetes etc) to reserve, to book (**b**) (dinero, tiempo etc) to keep, to save

2 reservarse vpr (**a**) to save oneself (**para** for) (**b**) (sentimientos) to keep to oneself (**c**) **r. el derecho de** to reserve the right to

resfriado,-a 1 nm (catarro) cold; **coger un r.** to catch (a) cold

2 adj **estar r.** to have a cold

resfriarse vpr to catch (a) cold

resfrío nm Andes, RP cold

resguardar vt (proteger) to protect, to shelter (**de** from)

resguardo nm (**a**) (recibo) receipt (**b**) (protección) protection, shelter

residencia nf residence; **r. de ancianos** old people's home

residencial adj residential

residente adj & nmf resident

residir vi (**a**) to reside, to live (**en** in); Fig to lie (**en** in)

residuo nm (**a**) residue (**b**) **residuos** waste

resignación nf resignation

resignado,-a adj resigned

resignarse vpr to resign oneself (**a** to)

resina nf resin

resistencia nf (**a**) resistance (**b**) (aguante) endurance, stamina (**c**) Elec element

resistente adj (**a**) resistant (**a** to) (**b**) (fuerte) tough, hardy

resistir 1 vi (**a**) to resist (**b**) (aguantar) to hold (out)

2 vt (situación, persona) to put up with; (tentación) to resist

3 resistirse vpr to resist; (oponerse) to offer resistance; (negarse) to refuse

resollar [2] vi to breathe heavily; (con silbido) to wheeze

resolución nf (**a**) (solución) solution (**b**) (decisión) resolution

resolver [4] (pp **resuelto**) **1** vt (problema) to solve; (asunto) to settle

2 vi (decidir) to resolve, to decide

3 resolverse vpr (**a**) (solucionarse) to be solved (**b**) (decidirse) to resolve, to make up one's mind (**a** to)

resonancia nf (**a**) (sonora) resonance (**b**) (repercusión) repercussions

resonar [2] vi to resound; (tener eco) to echo

resoplar vi (respirar) to breathe heavily; (de cansancio) to puff and pant; (de enfado) to huff and puff

resoplido nm (silbido) wheezing; (de cansancio) panting; (de enfado) snort

resorte nm (**a**) (muelle) spring (**b**) Fig means

> ⚠️ Observa que la palabra inglesa **resort** es un falso amigo y no es la traducción de la palabra española **resorte**. En inglés, **resort** significa "recurso" o "lugar de vacaciones".

respaldar vt to support, to back (up)

respaldo nm (de silla etc) back; Fig (apoyo) support, backing

respectar vt to concern, to regard; **por lo que a mí respecta** as far as I'm concerned

respectivo,-a adj respective; **en lo r. a** with regard to, regarding

respecto nm

al r., a este r. in this respect; **con r. a, r. a, r. de** with regard to; **r. a mí** as for me, as far as I am concerned

respetable 1 adj respectable

2 nm Fam **el r.** the audience

respetar vt to respect; **hacerse r. de todos** to command everyone's respect

respeto nm (**a**) respect; **por r.** out of consideration (**b**) (recelo) fear

respetuoso,-a adj respectful

respingar [42] vi to shy

respingo nm start, jump

respingón,-ona adj (nariz) snub, up-turned

respiración nf (acción) breathing, respiration; (aliento) breath; **r. artificial** artificial resuscitation

respirar vi to breathe; **¡por fin respiro!** well, that's a relief!

respiratorio,-a adj respiratory

respiro nm (**a**) breathing (**b**) (descanso) breather, break

resplandecer [33] vi to shine

resplandeciente adj (brillante) shining; (esplendoroso) resplendent, radiant

resplandor nm (brillo) brightness; (de fuego) glow, blaze

responder 1 vt to answer

2 vi (**a**) (una carta) to reply (**b**) (reaccionar) to respond (**c**) (protestar) to answer back (**d**) **r. de algn** to be responsible for sb; **r. por algn** to vouch for sb

respondón,-ona adj Fam argumentative, cheeky

responsabilidad nf responsibility

responsabilizar [40] 1 vt to make o hold responsible (**de** for)

2 responsabilizarse vpr to assume o claim responsibility (**de** for)

responsable 1 *adj* responsible

2 *nmf* **el/la r.**; *(encargado)* the person in charge; *(de robo etc)* the perpetrator

respuesta *nf* answer, reply; *(reacción)* response

resquebrajarse *upr* to crack

resquemor *nm* resentment, ill feeling

resquicio *nm* crack, chink

resta *nf* subtraction

restablecer [33] **1** *vt* to re-establish; *(el orden)* to restore

2 restablecerse *upr Med* to recover

restablecimiento *nm* **(a)** re-establishment; *(del orden etc)* restoration **(b)** *Med* recovery

restante *adj* remaining; **lo r.** the rest, the remainder

restar 1 *vt* **(a)** *Mat* to subtract, to take away **(b) r. importancia a algo** to play sth down

2 *vi (quedar)* to be left, to remain

restauración *nf* restoration

restaurador,-a 1 *nm,f* restorer

2 *adj* restoring

restaurante *nm* restaurant

restaurar *vt* to restore

restitución *nf* restitution

restituir [37] *vt (restablecer)* to restore; *(devolver)* to return, to give back

resto *nm* **(a)** rest, remainder; *Mat* remainder **(b) restos** remains; *(de comida)* leftovers

restregar [1] *vt* to rub hard, to scrub

restricción *nf* restriction

restrictivo,-a *adj* restrictive

restringir [57] *vt* to restrict, to limit

resucitar *vt & vi* to resuscitate

resuello *nm* breath, gasp

resuelto,-a *adj (decidido)* resolute, determined

resultado *nm* result; *(consecuencia)* outcome; **dar buen r.** to work, to give results

resultante *adj* resulting

resultar *vi* **(a)** *(ser)* to turn o work out; **así resulta más barato** it works out cheaper this way; **me resultó fácil** it turned out to be easy for me **(b)** *(ocurrir)* **resulta que ...** the thing is ...; **y ahora resulta que no puede venir** and now it turns out that she can't come **(c)** *(tener éxito)* to be successful; **la fiesta no resultó** the party wasn't a success

resultas *nfpl* **a r. de** as a result of

resumen *nm* summary; **en r.** in short, to sum up

resumir 1 *vt* to sum up; *(recapitular)* to summarize

2 resumirse *upr* **(a)** *(abreviarse)* **se resume en pocas palabras** it can be summed up in a few words **(b) r. en** *(saldarse con)* to result in

---

> 🖉 Observa que la palabra inglesa **resume** es un falso amigo y no es la traducción de la palabra española **resumir**. En inglés, **resume** significa "reanudar".

---

resurgir [57] *vi* to reappear

resurrección *nf* resurrection

retablo *nm* altarpiece

retaguardia *nf* rearguard

retahíla *nf* series *sing*, string

retal *nm (pedazo)* scrap

retar *vt* to challenge

retardarse *upr* to be delayed

retardo *nm* delay

retazo *nm (pedazo)* scrap; *(fragmento)* fragment, piece

rete- *pref Méx Fam* very

retén *nm* **(a) r. (de bomberos)** squad (of firefighters) **(b)** *Am (prisión)* reformatory, reform school

retención *nf* retention; *Fin* withholding; **r. de tráfico** (traffic) hold-up, traffic jam

retener [24] *vt* **(a)** *(conservar)* to retain **(b)** *Fin (descontar)* to deduct **(c)** *(detener)* to detain

reticencia *nf* reticence, reserve

reticente *adj* reticent, reserved

retina *nf* retina

retintín *nm (tono irónico)* innuendo, sarcastic tone

retirada *nf* retreat, withdrawal

retirado,-a 1 *adj* **(a)** *(alejado)* remote **(b)** *(jubilado)* retired

2 *nm,f* retired person, *US* retiree

retirar 1 *vt* to take away, to remove; *(dinero)* to withdraw; *(ofensa)* to take back

2 retirarse *upr* **(a)** *(apartarse)* to withdraw, to draw back; *(irse)* to retire **(b)** *(jubilarse)* to retire **(c)** *Mil* to retreat, to withdraw

retiro *nm* **(a)** *(jubilación)* retirement; *(pensión)* pension **(b)** *(lugar tranquilo)* retreat **(c)** *Rel* retreat

reto *nm* challenge

retocar [44] *vt* to touch up

retoño *nm (rebrote)* shoot, sprout; *Fig (niño)* kid

retoque *nm* retouching, touching up; **los últimos retoques** the finishing touches

retorcer [41] **1** *vt (cuerda, hilo)* to twist; *(ropa)* to wring (out)

2 retorcerse *upr* to twist, to become twisted; **r. de dolor** to writhe in pain

retorcido,-a *adj Fig* twisted

retórica *nf* rhetoric

retórico,-a *adj* rhetorical

retornable *adj* returnable; **envase no r.** non-deposit bottle

retornar 1 *vt* to return, to give back

    2 *vi* to return, to come back, to go back

retorno *nm* return

retortijón *nm (dolor)* stomach cramp

retozar [40] *vi* to frolic, to romp

retracción *nf* retraction

retractar 1 *vt* to retract

    2 retractarse *vpr* **r. (de)** to retract, to take back

retraerse *vpr (retirarse)* to withdraw; *(por miedo)* to shy away

retraído,-a *adj* shy, reserved

retraimiento *nm (timidez)* shyness

retransmisión *nf* broadcast, transmission

retransmitir *vt* to broadcast

retrasado,-a 1 *adj* **(a)** *(tren)* late; *(reloj)* slow; **voy r.** I'm behind schedule **(b)** *(país)* backward, underdeveloped **(c)** *(mental)* retarded, backward

    2 *nm,f* **r. (mental)** mentally retarded person

retrasar 1 *vt* **(a)** *(retardar)* to slow down **(b)** *(atrasar)* to delay, to postpone **(c)** *(reloj)* to put back

    2 retrasarse *vpr* to be late, to be delayed; *(reloj)* to be slow

retraso *nm* delay; **con r.** late; **una hora de r.** an hour behind schedule; **r. mental** mental deficiency

retratar 1 *vt (pintar)* to paint a portrait of; *Fot* to take a photograph of; *Fig (describir)* to describe, to depict

    2 retratarse *vpr Fot* to have one's photograph taken

retrato *nm (pintura)* portrait; *Fot* photograph; **r. robot** identikit picture, Photofit® picture; **ser el vivo r. de** to be the spitting image of

retreta *nf* retreat

retrete *nm* lavatory, toilet

retribución *nf (pago)* payment; *(recompensa)* reward

  🖉 Observa que la palabra inglesa **retribution** es un falso amigo y no es la traducción de la palabra española **retribución**. En inglés, **retribution** significa "represalias".

---

retribuir *vt (pagar)* to pay; *(recompensar)* to reward

retro *adj inv Fam (retrógrado)* reactionary; *(antiguo)* old-fashioned

retroactivo,-a *adj* retroactive; **con efecto r.** retrospectively

retroceder *vi* to move back, to back away

retroceso *nm* **(a)** *(movimiento)* backward movement **(b)** *Med* deterioration, worsening **(c)** *Econ* recession

retrógrado,-a *adj & nm,f (reaccionario)* reactionary

retropropulsión *nf Av* jet propulsion

retrospectivo,-a *adj & nf* retrospective

retrovisor *nm Aut* rear-view mirror

retumbar *vi (resonar)* to resound, to echo; *(tronar)* to thunder, to boom

retuve *pt indef de* **retener**

reúma *nm* rheumatism

reumático,-a *adj & nm,f* rheumatic

reumatismo *nm* rheumatism

reunión *nf* meeting; *(reencuentro)* reunion

reunir 1 *vt* to gather together; *(dinero)* to raise; *(cualidades)* to have, to possess; *(requisitos)* to fulfil

    2 reunirse *vpr* to meet, to gather; **r. con algn** to meet sb

revalidar *vt* to ratify, to confirm; *Dep (título)* to retain

revalorizar [40] *vt,* **revalorizarse** *vpr (moneda)* to revalue

revancha *nf* revenge; *Dep* return match

revanchista *adj* vengeful, vindictive

revelación *nf* revelation

revelado *nm Fot* developing

revelar *vt* **(a)** to reveal, to disclose **(b)** *Fot (película)* to develop

revender *vt (entradas)* to tout

reventa *nf (de entradas)* touting

reventado,-a *adj Fam (cansado)* knackered

reventar [1] **1** *vt* **(a)** to burst **(b)** *(romper)* to break, to smash **(c)** *(fastidiar)* to annoy, to bother

    2 *vi (estallar)* to burst; **r. de ganas de hacer algo** to be dying to do sth; **está que revienta** he's bursting at the seams

    3 reventarse *vpr (estallar)* to burst, to explode

reventón *nm (de neumático)* blowout, puncture, flat tyre

reverberación *nf* reverberation

reverberar *vi* to reverberate

reverencia *nf* **(a)** *(respeto)* reverence **(b)** *(inclinación) (de hombre)* bow; *(de mujer)* curtsy

reverenciar [43] *vt* to revere, to venerate

reverendo,-a *adj & nm,f* reverend

reversa *nf Méx* reverse

reversible *adj* reversible

reverso *nm* reverse, back

revertido,-a *adj* **llamada a cobro r.** *Br*

reverse-charge call, US collect call

revertir [5] vi to result (**en** in)

revés nm (**a**) (reverso) reverse; **al** o **del r.** (al·contrario) the other way round; (la parte interior en el exterior) inside out; (boca abajo) upside down; (la parte de detrás delante) back to front; **al r. de lo que dicen** contrary to what they say (**b**) (bofetada) slap; Ten backhand (stroke) (**c**) Fig (contrariedad) setback, reverse; **los reveses de la vida** life's misfortunes; **reveses de fortuna** setbacks, blows of fate

revestimiento nm Téc covering, coating

revestir [6] vt (**a**) (recubrir) to cover (**de** with), to coat (**de** with), to line (**de** with) (**b**) Fig **la herida no reviste importancia** the wound is not serious

revisar vt to check; (coche) to service

revisión nf checking; (de coche) service, overhaul; **r. médica** checkup

revisor,-a nm,f ticket inspector

revista nf (**a**) magazine (**b**) **pasar r. a** to inspect, to review (**c**) Teatro revue

revitalizar [40] vt to revitalize

revivido,-a adj revived

revivir vt & vi to revive

revocar [44] vt to revoke, to repeal

revolcar [2] **1** vt Fam (oponente) to floor, to crush
  2 revolcarse vpr to roll about

revolcón nm fall, tumble; Fam (sexual) romp

revolotear vi to fly about, to flutter about

revoltijo, revoltillo nm mess, jumble

revoltoso,-a adj (travieso) mischievous, naughty

revolución nf revolution

revolucionar vt to revolutionize

revolucionario,-a adj & nm,f revolutionary

revolver [4] (pp **revuelto**) **1** vt (mezclar) to stir, to mix; (desordenar) to mess up; **me revuelve el estómago** it turns my stomach
  2 revolverse vpr (**a**) (agitarse) to roll (**b**) Fig **r. contra algn** to turn against sb (**c**) (el tiempo) to turn stormy; (el mar) to become rough

> 🖉 Observa que el verbo inglés **to revolve** es un falso amigo y no es la traducción del verbo español **revolver**. En inglés, **to revolve** significa "girar".

revólver nm (pl **revólveres**) revolver

revuelo nm Fig stir, commotion

revuelta nf (**a**) (insurrección) revolt (**b**) (curva) bend, turn

revuelto,-a adj (**a**) (desordenado) jumbled, in a mess (**b**) (tiempo) stormy, unsettled; (mar) rough (**c**) (agitado) excited

revulsivo,-a adj & nm revulsive

rey nm king; Rel (**el día de**) **Reyes** (the) Epiphany, 6 January

reyerta nf quarrel, dispute

rezagado,-a nm,f straggler, latecomer

rezagarse vpr to lag o fall behind

rezar [40] **1** vi (**a**) (orar) to pray (**b**) (decir) to say, to read
  2 vt (oración) to say

rezo nm prayer

rezumar vt to ooze; Fig to exude

RFA nf Hist (abr **República Federal de Alemania**) FRG

ría nf estuary

riada nf flood

ribera nf (de río) bank; (zona) riverside, waterfront

ribete nm edging, border

ribetear vt to edge, to border

ricamente adv Fam **tan r.** very well

rico,-a 1 adj (**a**) **ser r.** (adinerado) to be rich o wealthy; (abundante) to be rich; (bonito) to be lovely o adorable; (fértil) to be rich o fertile (**b**) **estar r.** (delicioso) to be delicious
  2 nm,f rich person

rictus nm inv grin

ridiculez nf ridiculous thing; (cualidad) ridiculousness

ridiculizar [40] vt to ridicule

ridículo,-a 1 adj ridiculous
  2 nm ridicule; **hacer el r., quedar en r.** to make a fool of oneself; **poner a algn en r.** to make a fool of sb

riego nm watering, irrigation; **r. sanguíneo** blood circulation

riel nm rail

rienda nf rein; Fig **dar r. suelta a** to give free rein to; Fig **llevar las riendas** to hold the reins, to be in control

riesgo nm risk; **correr el r. de** to run the risk of; **seguro a todo r.** fully comprehensive insurance

riesgoso,-a adj Am risky

rifa nf raffle

rifar vt to raffle (off)

rifle nm rifle

rigidez nf rigidity, stiffness; Fig (severidad) strictness, inflexibility

rígido,-a adj rigid, stiff; Fig (severo) strict, inflexible

rigor nm rigour; (severidad) severity; **con r.** rigorously; **de r.** indispensable

rigurosamente adv rigorously; (meticulosamente) meticulously; (severamente) severely; **r. cierto** absolutely true

riguroso,-a *adj* rigorous; *(severo)* severe, strict

rijo *indic pres de* **regir**

rima *nf* rhyme

rimar *vt & vi* to rhyme (**con** with)

rimbombante *adj (lenguaje)* pompous, pretentious

rímel *nm* mascara

Rin *n* **el R.** the Rhine

rincón *nm* corner; *Fam (lugar remoto)* nook

rinoceronte *nm* rhinoceros

riña *nf (pelea)* fight; *(discusión)* row, quarrel

riñón *nm* kidney; *Fam* **costar un r.** to cost an arm and a leg; *Med* **r. artificial** kidney machine

río *nm* river; **r. abajo** downstream; **r. arriba** upstream

rioja *nm* Rioja (wine)

rioplatense *adj* of/from the River Plate region

ripio *nm (palabras de relleno)* waffle; *Fam* **no perder r.** not to miss a trick

riqueza *nf* (a) wealth (b) *(cualidad)* wealthiness

risa *nf* laugh; *(carcajadas)* laughter; **es (cosa) de r.** it's laughable; **me da r.** it makes me laugh; **tomarse algo a r.** to laugh sth off; *Fig* **morirse** *o* **mondarse de r.** to die *o* fall about laughing; *Fam* **mi hermano es una r.** my brother is a laugh; *Fam Fig* **tener algo muerto de r.** to leave sth lying around

risco *nm* crag, cliff

risible *adj* laughable

risilla, risita *nf* giggle, titter; *(risa falsa)* false laugh

risotada *nf* guffaw

ristra *nf* string

ristre *nm* **en r.** at the ready

risueño,-a *adj* smiling

rítmico,-a *adj* rhythmic; **gimnasia rítmica** eurhythmics *sing*

ritmo *nm* (a) rhythm (b) *(paso)* rate; **llevar un buen r. de trabajo** to work at a good pace

rito *nm* (a) rite (b) *(ritual)* ritual

ritual *adj & nm* ritual

rival *adj & nmf* rival

rivalidad *nf* rivalry

rivalizar [40] *vi* to rival (**en** in)

rizado,-a *adj* (a) *(pelo)* curly (b) *(mar)* choppy

rizar [40] 1 *vt (pelo)* to curl; *(tela, papel)* to crease; *Fig* **r. el rizo** to make things even more complicated

2 rizarse *vpr (pelo)* to curl, to go curly

rizo *nm* (a) *(de pelo)* curl (b) *(en el agua)* ripple

RNE *nf* (*abr* **Radio Nacional de España**) = Spanish state radio station

robalo *nm (pez)* bass

robar *vt* (a) *(objeto)* to steal; *(banco, persona)* to rob; *(casa)* to burgle; *Fig* **en aquel supermercado te roban** they really rip you off in that supermarket (b) *Naipes* to draw

roble *nm* oak (tree)

robledal, robledo *nm* oak grove *o* wood

robo *nm* robbery, theft; *(en casa)* burglary; *Fam (timo)* rip-off

robot *nm* (*pl* **robots**) robot; **r. de cocina** food processor

robótica *nf* robotics *sing*

robustecer [33] *vt* to strengthen

robusto,-a *adj* robust, sturdy

roca *nf* rock

rocalla *nf* pebbles, stone chippings

rocambolesco,-a *adj* incredible, far-fetched

roce *nm* (a) *(fricción)* rubbing; *(en la piel)* chafing (b) *(marca) (en la pared etc)* scuff mark; *(en la piel)* chafing mark, graze (c) *(contacto ligero)* brush, light touch (d) *Fam (trato entre personas)* contact (e) *Fam (discusión)* brush

rociar [29] *vt (salpicar)* to spray, to sprinkle

rocín *nm* nag, hack

rocío *nm* dew

Rocosas *nfpl* **las R.** the Rockies

rocoso,-a *adj* rocky, stony

rodaballo *nm (pez)* turbot

rodado,-a *adj* (a) *(piedra)* smooth, rounded; **canto r.** boulder (b) **tráfico r.** road traffic, vehicular traffic

rodaja *nf* slice; **en rodajas** sliced

rodaje *nm* (a) *(filmación)* filming, shooting (b) *Aut* running in

Ródano *n* **el R.** the Rhone

rodante *adj* rolling

rodar [2] 1 *vt (película etc)* to film, to shoot

2 *vi* to roll, to turn

rodear 1 *vt* to surround, to encircle

2 rodearse *vpr* to surround oneself (**de** with)

rodeo *nm* (a) *(desvío)* detour (b) *(al hablar)* evasiveness; **andarse con rodeos** to beat about the bush; **no andarse con rodeos** to get straight to the point (c) *Am* rodeo

rodilla *nf* knee; **de rodillas** *(arrodillado)* kneeling; **hincarse** *o* **ponerse de rodillas**

to kneel down, to go down on one's knees

rodillera *nf (de pantalón)* knee patch; *Dep* knee pad

rodillo *nm* roller; **r. de cocina** rolling pin

rododendro *nm* rhododendron

roedor *nm* rodent

roer [38] *vt (hueso)* to gnaw; *(galleta)* to nibble at; *Fig (conciencia)* to gnaw at, to nag at; *Fig* **un hueso duro de r.** a hard nut to crack

rogar [2] *vt (pedir)* to request, to ask; *(implorar)* to beg; **hacerse de r.** to play hard to get; **se ruega silencio** *(en letrero)* silence please; **rogamos disculpen la molestia** please forgive the inconvenience

roído,-a *adj* gnawed, eaten away

rojizo,-a *adj* reddish

rojo,-a 1 *adj* (a) red; *Fin* **estar en números rojos** to be in the red (b) *Pol (comunista)* red

  2 *nm (color)* red; **al r. vivo** *(caliente)* red-hot; *Fig (tenso)* very tense

  3 *nm,f Pol (comunista)* red

rol *nm* role; **juego de r.** role play

rollizo,-a *adj* chubby, plump

rollo *nm* (a) *(de papel etc)* roll (b) *Fam (pesadez)* drag, bore; **es el mismo r. de siempre** it's the same old story; **un r. de libro** a boring book (c) *Fam (amorío)* affair

Roma *n* Rome

romana *nf* **calamares a la r.** = squid in batter

romance *nm* (a) *(aventura amorosa)* romance (b) *(idioma)* Romance; *Fig* **hablar en r.** to speak plainly (c) *Lit* narrative poem, ballad

románico,-a *adj & nm* Romanesque

romanticismo *nm* romanticism

romántico,-a *adj & nm,f* romantic

rombo *nm* rhombus

romería *nf Rel* pilgrimage

romero *nm Bot* rosemary

romo,-a *adj* (a) blunt (b) *(nariz)* snub

rompecabezas *nm inv (juego)* (jigsaw) puzzle; *Fig (problema)* riddle, puzzle

rompeolas *nm inv* breakwater, jetty

romper (*pp* **roto**) **1** *vt* (a) to break; *(papel, tela)* to tear; *(vajilla, cristal)* to smash, to shatter (b) *(relaciones)* to break off

  2 *vi* (a) *(olas, día)* to break (b) *(acabar)* to break (**con** with); **rompió con su novio** she broke it off with her boyfriend (c) **r. a llorar** to burst out crying; **r. en llanto** to burst into tears

  3 romperse *vpr* to break; *(papel, tela)* to tear; **se rompió por la mitad** it broke *o*

split in half; *Fig* **r. la cabeza** to rack one's brains

rompevientos *nm RP (jersey)* polo neck jersey; *(anorak)* anorak

rompimiento *nm Am* breaking off

ron *nm* rum

roncar [44] *vi* to snore

roncha *nf (en la piel)* swelling, lump

ronco,-a *adj* hoarse; **quedarse r.** to lose one's voice

ronda *nf* (a) round; *(patrulla)* patrol (b) *(carretera)* ring road; *(paseo)* avenue (c) **pagar una r.** to pay for a round of drinks

rondar 1 *vt* (a) *(vigilar)* to patrol, to do the rounds of (b) *Pey (merodear)* to prowl around, to hang about (c) *(estar cerca de)* to be about *o* approximately; **ronda los cuarenta** she is about forty

  2 *vi* (a) *(vigilar)* to patrol (b) *(merodear)* to prowl around, to roam around

ronquera *nf* hoarseness

ronquido *nm* snore

ronronear *vi* to purr

ronroneo *nm* purring

roña *nf* (a) *(mugre)* filth, dirt (b) *(sarna)* mange

roñica *Fam* **1** *adj* mean, stingy

  2 *nmf* scrooge, miser

roñoso,-a *adj* (a) *(mugriento)* filthy, dirty (b) *(sarnoso)* mangy (c) *Fam (tacaño)* mean, stingy

ropa *nf* clothes, clothing; *Fig* **a quema r.** point-blank; **r. blanca** (household) linen; **r. interior** underwear

---

📖 Observa que la palabra inglesa **rope** es un falso amigo y no es la traducción de la palabra española **ropa**. En inglés, **rope** significa "cuerda, soga".

---

ropaje *nm* clothes

ropero *nm (armario)* r. wardrobe

roque *nm* (a) *(en ajedrez)* rook (b) *Fam* **quedarse r.** to fall fast asleep

rosa 1 *adj inv (color)* pink; **novela r.** romantic novel

  2 *nf Bot* rose; *(en la piel)* birthmark; **r. de los vientos** compass (rose)

  3 *nm (color)* pink

rosáceo,-a *adj* rose-coloured, rosy

rosado,-a 1 *adj (color)* pink, rosy; *(vino)* rosé

  2 *nm (vino)* rosé

rosal *nm* rosebush

rosaleda *nf* rose garden

rosario *nm Rel* rosary; *(sarta)* string, series *sing*

rosbif *nm* roast beef

rosca *nf* (a) *(de tornillo)* thread; **tapón de**

r. screw top; *Fig* **pasarse de r.** to go too far (**b**) *(espiral)* spiral, coil

rosco *nm (pastel)* = ring-shaped roll or pastry; *Fam* **no comerse un r.** not to get one's oats

rosetón *nm* rose window

rosquilla *nf* ring-shaped pastry; *Fam Fig* **venderse como rosquillas** to sell like hot cakes

rosticería *nf Chile, Méx* = shop selling roast chicken

rostro *nm* face; *Fam* **tener mucho r.** to have a lot of nerve; *Fam* **¡vaya r.!** what a cheek!

> 🖉 Observa que la palabra inglesa **rostrum** es un falso amigo y no es la traducción de la palabra española *rostro*. En inglés, **rostrum** significa "estrado".

rotación *nf* rotation

rotativo,-a 1 *adj* rotary, revolving
  2 *nm* newspaper

roto,-a 1 *adj* broken; *(papel)* torn; *(ropa)* in tatters, tattered
  2 *nm (agujero)* hole, tear
  3 *nm,f Chile Fam (trabajador)* worker

rotoso,-a *adj Andes, RP* ragged, in tatters

rótula *nf* (**a**) *Anat* kneecap (**b**) *Téc* ball-and-socket joint

rotulador *nm* felt-tip pen

rotular *vt* to letter, to label

rótulo *nm (letrero)* sign, notice; *(titular)* title, heading

rotundo,-a *adj* categorical; **éxito r.** resounding success; **un no r.** a flat refusal

rotura *nf (ruptura)* breaking; *Med* fracture

roturar *vt* to plough

roulotte *nf Br* caravan, *US* trailer

rozadura *nf* scratch, abrasion

rozamiento *nm* rubbing, friction

rozar [40] 1 *vt* to touch, to rub against, to brush against
  2 *vi* to rub
  3 rozarse *vpr* to rub, to brush (**con** against)

Rte. (*abr* **remite, remitente**) sender

RTVE *nf* (*abr* **Radiotelevisión Española**) = Spanish state broadcasting company

ruana *nf Andes* poncho

rubéola *nf* German measles *sing*, rubella

rubí *nm (pl* rubíes*)* ruby

rubicundo,-a *adj* rosy, reddish

rubio,-a 1 *adj (pelo, persona)* fair, blond, *f* blonde; **r. de bote** peroxide blonde; **tabaco r.** Virginia tobacco
  2 *nm,f* blond, *f* blonde

rublo *nm* rouble

rubor *nm* blush, flush

ruborizarse [40] *vpr* to blush, to go red

ruboroso,-a *adj* blushing, bashful

rúbrica *nf* (**a**) *(de firma)* = flourish added to a signature (**b**) *(título)* title, heading

rubricar [44] *vt* (**a**) *(firmar)* to sign with a flourish (**b**) *(respaldar)* to endorse, to ratify

rudeza *nf* roughness, coarseness

rudimentario,-a *adj* rudimentary

rudimento *nm* rudiment

rudo,-a *adj* rough, coarse

rueda *nf* (**a**) *(wheel)*; *Aut* **r. de recambio** spare wheel; *Aut* **r. delantera/trasera** front/rear wheel; **r. de prensa** press conference; *Fam* **ir sobre ruedas** to go very smoothly (**b**) *(rodaja)* round slice

ruedo *nm* (**a**) *Taurom* bullring, arena (**b**) *(de falda)* hem

ruego *nm* request

rufián *nm* villain, scoundrel

rugby *nm* rugby

rugido *nm (de animal)* roar; *(del viento)* howl; *(de tripas)* rumbling

rugir [57] *vi* to roar; *(viento)* to howl

rugoso,-a *adj* rough

ruibarbo *nm* rhubarb

ruido *nm* noise; *(sonido)* sound; *(jaleo)* din, row; *Fig* stir, commotion; **hacer r.** to make a noise

ruidoso,-a *adj* noisy, loud

ruin *adj* (**a**) *(vil)* vile, despicable (**b**) *(tacaño)* mean, stingy

ruina *nf* ruin; *(derrumbamiento)* collapse; *(de persona)* downfall

ruindad *nf* vileness, meanness; *(acto)* mean act, low trick

ruinoso,-a *adj* dilapidated, tumbledown

ruiseñor *nm* nightingale

ruleta *nf* roulette

ruletear *vi CAm, Méx Fam (en taxi)* to drive a taxi

ruletero *nm CAm, Méx Fam (de taxi)* taxi driver

rulo *nm* (**a**) *(para el pelo)* curler, roller (**b**) *Culin* rolling pin

rulot(a) *nf (pl* rulots*) Br* caravan, *US* trailer

ruma *nf Andes, Ven* heap, pile

Rumanía, Rumania *n* Romania

rumba *nf* rhumba, rumba

rumbo *nm* direction, course; **(con) r. a** bound for, heading for

rumiante *nm* ruminant

rumiar [43] 1 *vt* (**a**) *(mascar)* to chew (**b**) *Fig (pensar)* to ruminate, to reflect on, to chew over
  2 *vi* to ruminate, to chew the cud

rumor *nm* (**a**) rumour (**b**) *(murmullo)* murmur

rumorearse *v impers* to be rumoured

runrún, runruneo *nm* buzz, noise

rupestre *adj* **pintura r.** cave painting

ruptura *nf* breaking; *(de relaciones)* breaking off

rural *adj* rural, country

Rusia *n* Russia

ruso,-a *adj & nm,f* Russian

rústico,-a *adj* rustic, rural

ruta *nf* route, road

rutilar *vi* to sparkle

rutina *nf* routine; **por r.** as a matter of course

rutinario,-a *adj* routine

S, s ['ese] *nf (la letra)* S, s

S (*abr* **Sur**) S

S. (*abr* **San, Santo**) St

s. (*abr* **siglo**) c

S.A. (*abr* **Sociedad Anónima**) *Br* ≃ PLC, *US* ≃ Inc

sábado *nm* Saturday

sabana *nf* savannah

sábana *nf* sheet; *Fam* **se me pegaron las sábanas** I overslept

sabandija *nf (insecto)* creepy-crawly; *(persona)* creep

sabañón *nm* chilblain

sabático,-a *adj* sabbatical

sabelotodo *nmf inv* know-all

saber ¹ *nm* knowledge

saber ² [21] **1** *vt* (a) to know; **hacer s.** to inform; **para que lo sepas** for your information; **que yo sepa** as far as I know; **vete tú a s.** goodness knows; **¡y yo qué sé!** how should I know!; *Fig* **a s.** namely (b) *(tener habilidad)* to be able to; **¿sabes cocinar?** can you cook?; **¿sabes hablar inglés?** can you speak English? (c) *(enterarse)* to learn, to find out; **lo supe ayer** I found this out yesterday

2 *vi* (a) *(tener sabor)* to taste (a of); **sabe a fresa** it tastes of strawberries; *Fig* **me sabe mal** I feel guilty *o* bad about that (b) *Am (soler)* to be accustomed to

sabido,-a *adj* known; **como es s.** as everyone knows

sabiduría *nf* wisdom

sabiendas • **a sabiendas** *loc adv* **lo hizo a s.** he did it in the full knowledge of what he was doing; **a s. de que ...** knowing full well that ...

sabihondo,-a *nm,f Fam (sabelotodo)* know-all; *(pedante)* pedant

sabio,-a 1 *adj (prudente)* wise

2 *nm,f* scholar

sabiondo,-a *nm,f Fam* = sabihondo,-a

sable *nm* sabre

sabor *nm (gusto)* taste, flavour; **con s. a limón** lemon-flavoured; **sin s.** tasteless; **me deja mal s. de boca** it leaves a bad taste in my mouth

saborear *vt (degustar)* to taste; *Fig (apreciar)* to savour

sabotaje *nm* sabotage

saboteador,-a *nm,f* saboteur

sabotear *vt* to sabotage

sabré *indic fut de* saber

sabroso,-a *adj* (a) tasty; *(delicioso)* delicious (b) *(agradable)* delightful

sabueso *nm* bloodhound

sacacorchos *nm inv* corkscrew

sacamuelas *nmf inv Fam* dentist

sacapuntas *nm inv* pencil sharpener

sacar [44] *vt* (a) to take out; *(con más fuerza)* to pull out; **s. dinero del banco** to withdraw money from the bank; **s. la lengua** to stick one's tongue out; *Fig* **s. faltas a algo** to find fault with sth; *Fig* **s. adelante** to help to get on; **s. provecho de algo** to benefit from sth; **s. algo en claro** *o* **en limpio** to make sense of sth (b) *(obtener)* to get; *(dinero)* to get, to make; *(conclusiones)* to draw, to reach; *(entrada)* to get, to buy (c) *(producto, libro, disco)* to bring out; *(nueva moda)* to bring in (d) *(fotografía)* to take; *(fotocopia)* to make (e) *Ten* to serve; *Ftb* to kick off

sacarina *nf* saccharin

sacerdotal *adj* priestly

sacerdote *nm* priest; **sumo s.** high priest

saciar [43] *vt* to satiate; *(sed)* to quench; *(deseos, hambre)* to satisfy; *(ambiciones)* to fulfil

saciedad *nf* satiety; **repetir algo hasta la s.** to repeat sth ad nauseam

saco *nm* (a) sack; **s. de dormir** sleeping bag (b) *Mil* **entrar a s. en una ciudad** to pillage a town (c) *Am (chaqueta)* jacket

sacralizar [40] *vt* to consecrate

sacramento *nm* sacrament

sacrificar [44] **1** *vt* to sacrifice

2 **sacrificarse** *vpr* to make a sacrifice *o* sacrifices

sacrificio *nm* sacrifice

sacrilegio *nm* sacrilege

sacrílego,-a *adj* sacrilegious

sacristán *nm* verger, sexton

sacristía *nf* vestry, sacristy

sacro,-a *adj* sacred

sacudida *nf* (a) shake; *(espasmo)* jolt, jerk; **s. eléctrica** electric shock (b) *(de terremoto)* tremor

sacudir vt (**a**) (agitar) to shake; (alfombra, sábana) to shake out; (arena, polvo) to shake off (**b**) (golpear) to beat (**c**) (conmover) to shock, to stun

sádico,-a 1 adj sadistic
2 nm,f sadist

sadismo nm sadism

sadomasoquista 1 adj sadomasochistic
2 nmf sadomasochist

saeta nf (**a**) (dardo) dart (**b**) (canción) = popular religious song

safari nm (cacería) safari; (parque) safari park

sagacidad nf Fml (listeza) cleverness; (astucia) astuteness, shrewdness

sagaz adj (listo) clever; (astuto) astute, shrewd

Sagitario nm Sagittarius

sagrado,-a adj sacred

sagrario nm tabernacle

Sáhara n Sahara

saharaui adj & nmf Saharan

sahariana nf safari jacket

sainete nm Teatro comic sketch, one-act farce

sajón,-ona adj & nm,f Saxon

sal¹ nf (**a**) salt; **s. fina** table salt; **s. gema** salt crystals; **s. gorda** cooking salt (**b**) Fig (gracia) wit

sal² imperat de **salir**

sala nf room; (en un hospital) ward; Jur courtroom; **s. de estar** lounge, living room; **s. de espera** waiting room; **s. de exposiciones** exhibition hall; **s. de fiestas** nightclub, discotheque; **s. de lectura** reading room

saladito nm RP savoury snack o appetizer

salado,-a adj (**a**) (con sal) salted; (con exceso de sal) salty; **agua salada** salt water (**b**) Fig (encantador) charming (**c**) Am (infortunado) unlucky

salamandra nf salamander

salamanquesa nf gecko

salame, salami nm salami

salar vt to salt, to add salt to

salarial adj salary, wage

salario nm salary, wages; **s. mínimo** minimum wage

salazones nfpl salted meat o fish

salchicha nf sausage

salchichón nm = salami-type sausage

salchichonería nf Méx delicatessen

saldar vt (**a**) Fin (cuenta) to settle; (deuda) to pay off (**b**) Com (vender barato) to sell off (**c**) Fig (diferencias) to settle, to resolve

saldo nm (**a**) saldos sales; **a precio de s.** at bargain prices (**b**) Fin balance (**c**) (de una deuda) liquidation, settlement (**d**) (resto de mercancía) remainder, leftover

saldré indic fut de **salir**

saledizo,-a adj projecting

salero nm (**a**) (recipiente) saltcellar (**b**) Fig (gracia) charm

salgo indic pres de **salir**

salida nf (**a**) (partida) departure; (puerta etc) exit, way out; **callejón sin s.** dead end; **s. de emergencia** emergency exit (**b**) Dep start; **línea de s.** starting line; **s. nula** false start (**c**) **te vi a la s. del cine** I saw you leaving the cinema (**d**) (de un astro) rising; **s. del sol** sunrise (**e**) (profesional) opening; Com outlet (**f**) (recurso) solution, way out; **no tengo otra s.** I have no other option (**g**) Fam (ocurrencia) witty remark, witticism (**h**) Informát output

salido,-a adj (**a**) prominent, projecting (**b**) muy Fam (persona) horny

saliente adj (**a**) projecting, prominent; Fig outstanding (**b**) (cesante) outgoing

salina nf salt mine

salino,-a adj saline

salir [22] **1** vi (**a**) (de un sitio) to go out, to leave; (venir de dentro) to come out; **salió de la habitación** she left the room; **s. de la carretera** to turn off the road
(**b**) (tren etc) to depart
(**c**) (novios) to go out (**con** with)
(**d**) (aparecer) to appear; (revista, disco) to come out; (ley) to come in; (trabajo, vacante) to come up
(**e**) (resultar) to turn out, to turn out to be; **el pequeño les ha salido muy listo** their son has turned out to be very clever; **¿cómo te salió el examen?** how did your exam go?; **s. ganando** to come out ahead o on top; **salió presidente** he was elected president
(**f**) **s. a** (precio) to come to, to work out at; **s. barato/caro** to work out cheap/expensive
(**g**) **ha salido al abuelo** she takes after her grandfather
(**h**) (problema) to work out; **esta cuenta no me sale** I can't work this sum out
(**i**) **¡con qué cosas sales!** the things you come out with!
2 salirse vpr (**a**) (líquido, gas) to leak (out); Fig **s. de lo normal** to be out of the ordinary; **se salió de la carretera** he went off the road
(**b**) Fam **s. con la suya** to get one's own way

saliva nf saliva

salivar vi to salivate

salivazo nm spit

salmantino,-a 1 *adj* of/from Salamanca

  2 *nm,f* person from Salamanca

salmo *nm* psalm

salmón 1 *nm (pescado)* salmon

  2 *adj inv (color)* salmon pink, salmon

salmonete *nm (pescado)* red mullet

salmorejo *nm (salsa)* = sauce made from vinegar, water, pepper and salt

salmuera *nf* brine

salobre *adj (agua)* brackish; *(gusto)* salty, briny

salón *nm* **(a)** *(en una casa)* lounge, sitting room **(b)** **s. de actos** assembly hall; **s. de baile** dance hall **(c)** **s. de belleza** beauty salon; **s. de té** tearoom, teashop **(d)** **s. del automóvil** motor show

salpicadera *nf Méx Br* mudguard, *US* fender

salpicadura *nf* splashing

salpicar [44] *vt* **(a)** *(rociar)* to splash; **me salpicó el abrigo de barro** he splashed mud on my coat **(b)** *Fig (esparcir)* to sprinkle

salpicón *nm* **(a)** splash **(b)** *Culin* cocktail

salpimentar [1] *vt* to season

salpullido *nm* rash

salsa *nf* sauce; *(de carne)* gravy; *Fig* **en su (propia) s.** in one's element

saltador,-a *nm,f Dep* jumper

saltamontes *nm inv* grasshopper

saltar 1 *vt (obstáculo, valla)* to jump (over)

  2 *vi* **(a)** to jump; *Fig* **s. a la vista** to be obvious **(b)** *(cristal etc)* to break, to shatter; *(plomos)* to go, to blow **(c)** *(desprenderse)* to come off **(d)** *(encolerizarse)* to explode, to blow up; **por menos de nada salta** the smallest thing makes him explode

  3 saltarse *vpr* **(a)** *(omitir)* to skip, to miss out; **s. el semáforo/turno** to jump the lights/the queue **(b)** *(botón)* to come off; **se me saltaron las lágrimas** tears came to my eyes

salteado,-a *adj* **(a)** *(espaciado)* spaced out **(b)** *Culin* sauté, sautéed

saltear *vt Culin* to sauté

saltimbanqui *nmf* acrobat, tumbler

salto *nm* **(a)** *(acción)* jump, leap; *Fig (paso adelante)* leap forward; **a saltos** in leaps and bounds; **dar** *o* **pegar un s.** to jump, to leap; **de un s.** in a flash; *Fig* **a s. de mata** every now and then; **s. de agua** waterfall; **s. de cama** negligée **(b)** *Dep* jump; **s. de altura** high jump; **s. de longitud** long jump; **s. mortal** somersault

saltón,-ona *adj* prominent; **ojos saltones** bulging eyes

salubre *adj* salubrious

salubridad *nf* healthiness; **por razones de s.** for health reasons

salud *nf* health; **beber a la s. de algn** to drink to sb's health; *Fam* **¡s.!** cheers!

saludable *adj* **(a)** *(sano)* healthy, wholesome **(b)** *Fig (beneficioso)* good, beneficial

saludar *vt* **(a)** *(decir hola a)* to say hello to, to greet; **saluda de mi parte a** give my regards to; **le saludo atentamente** *(en una carta)* yours faithfully **(b)** *Mil* to salute

saludo *nm* **(a)** greeting; **un s. de** best wishes from **(b)** *Mil* salute

salva *nf Mil* salvo, volley

salvación *nf* salvation

salvado *nm* bran

salvador,-a 1 *nm,f* saviour; *(rescatador)* rescuer

  2 *nm* **El S.** El Salvador

salvadoreño,-a *adj & nm,f* Salvadoran, Salvadorian

salvaguarda *nf (defensa)* protection

salvaguardar *vt* to safeguard (**de** from), to protect (**de** from)

salvaguardia *nf* = salvaguarda

salvajada *nf* brutal act

salvaje *adj* **(a)** *Bot* wild, uncultivated; *Zool* wild; *(pueblo, tribu)* savage, uncivilized **(b)** *Fam (violento)* savage, wild

salvajismo *nm* savagery

salvamento, salvamiento *nm* rescue

salvar 1 *vt* **(a)** to save, to rescue (**de** from) **(b)** *(obstáculo)* to clear; *(dificultad)* to get round, to overcome **(c)** *(exceptuar)* to exclude, to except; **salvando ciertos errores** except for a few mistakes

  2 salvarse *vpr* **(a)** *(sobrevivir)* to survive, to come out alive; *Fam (escaparse)* to escape (**de** from); **¡sálvese quien pueda!** every man for himself!; *Fam* **s. por los pelos** to have a narrow escape **(b)** *Rel* to be saved, to save one's soul

salvavidas *nm inv* life belt

salvedad *nf* **(a)** *(excepción)* exception **(b)** *(reserva)* proviso

salvia *nf Bot* sage

salvo,-a 1 *adj* unharmed, safe; **a s.** safe

  2 *adv (exceptuando)* except (for); **s. que** unless

salvoconducto *nm* safe-conduct

san *adj* saint

sanar 1 *vt (curar)* to cure, to heal

  2 *vi* **(a)** *(persona)* to recover, to get better **(b)** *(herida)* to heal

sanatorio *nm* sanatorium

sanción *nf* **(a)** sanction **(b)** *(aprobación)* sanction, approval **(c)** *Jur* penalty

sancionar *vt* **(a)** *(castigar)* to penalize

(**b**) (*aprobar*) to sanction

sancochar *vt* to parboil; *Am* = to boil in water and salt

sancocho *nm Andes, Ven* (*comida*) = stew of beef, chicken or fish, vegetables and green bananas

sandalia *nf* sandal

sándalo *nm* sandalwood

sandez *nf* piece of nonsense

sandía *nf* watermelon

sándwich *nm* sandwich

sandwichera *nf* toasted sandwich maker

saneamiento *nm* (*de terreno*) drainage, draining; (*de una empresa*) reorganization

sanear *vt* (*terrenos*) to drain; (*empresa*) to reorganize

sangrar 1 *vt* (**a**) to bleed (**b**) *Fam* (*sacar dinero*) to bleed dry
  2 *vi* to bleed

sangre *nf* blood; **donar s.** to give blood; **s. fría** sangfroid; **a s. fría** in cold blood

sangría *nf* (**a**) *Med* bleeding, bloodletting; *Fig* drain (**b**) (*timo*) rip-off (**c**) (*bebida*) sangria

sangriento,-a *adj* (*guerra etc*) bloody

sanguijuela *nf* leech, bloodsucker

sanguinario,-a *adj* bloodthirsty

sanguíneo,-a *adj* blood; **grupo s.** blood group

sanidad *nf* health; **Ministerio de S.** Department of Health

> 🖉 Observa que la palabra inglesa **sanity** es un falso amigo y no es la traducción de la palabra española **sanidad**. En inglés, **sanity** significa "cordura, sensatez".

sanitario,-a 1 *adj* health
  2 *nm* toilet

sano,-a *adj* (**a**) (*bien de salud*) healthy; **s. y salvo** safe and sound (**b**) (*comida*) healthy, wholesome (**c**) **en su s. juicio** in one's right mind

> 🖉 Observa que la palabra inglesa **sane** es un falso amigo y no es la traducción de la palabra española **sano**. En inglés, **sane** significa "cuerdo, sensato".

Santa Claus, *Méx, Ven* **Santa Clos** *n* Santa Claus

santería *nf* (**a**) (*religión*) santería, = form of religion common in the Caribbean, in which people allegedly have contact with the spirit world (**b**) *Am* (*tienda*) = shop selling religious mementos such as statues of saints

santero,-a *nm,f* (*curandero*) = faith healer who calls on the saints to assist with the healing process

santiamén *nm Fam* **en un s.** in a flash, in no time at all

santidad *nf* saintliness, holiness

santificar [44] *vt* to sanctify

santiguarse [45] *vpr* to cross oneself

santo,-a 1 *adj* (**a**) holy, sacred (**b**) (*bueno*) saintly; **un s. varón** a saint
  2 *nm,f* (**a**) saint; *Fam* **¡por todos los santos!** for heaven's sake!; *Fig* **se me fue el s. al cielo** I clean forgot (**b**) (*día onomástico*) saint's day; *Fig* **¿a s. de qué?** why on earth?

santuario *nm* sanctuary, shrine

saña *nf* fury; **con s.** furiously

sapo *nm* toad; *Fam* **echar sapos y culebras** to rant and rave

saque *nm* (**a**) *Ftb* **s. inicial** kick-off; **s. de banda** throw-in; **s. de esquina** corner kick (**b**) *Ten* service

saquear *vt* (*ciudad*) to sack, to plunder; (*casas, tiendas*) to loot

saqueo *nm* (*de ciudades*) sacking, plundering; (*de casa, tienda*) looting

S.A.R. (*abr* **Su Alteza Real**) H.R.H.

sarampión *nm* measles *sing*

sarao *nm* knees-up

sarcasmo *nm* sarcasm

sarcástico,-a *adj* sarcastic

sarcófago *nm* sarcophagus

sardana *nf* sardana, = Catalan dance and music

sardina *nf* sardine

sardónico,-a *adj* sardonic

sargento *nm* sergeant

sarmiento *nm* vine shoot

sarna *nf Med* scabies *sing*; *Zool* mange

sarpullido *nm* rash

sarracina *nf* massacre

sarro *nm* (*sedimento*) deposit; (*en los dientes*) tartar; (*en la lengua*) fur

sarta *nf* string

sartén *nf* frying pan, *US* fry-pan; *Fig* **tener la s. por el mango** to have the upper hand

sastre *nm* tailor

Satanás *n* Satan

satánico,-a *adj* satanic

satélite *nm* satellite; *Fig* **país s.** satellite state; **televisión vía s.** satellite TV

satén *nm* satin

satinar *vt* to gloss, to make glossy

sátira *nf* satire

satírico,-a *adj* satirical

satirizar [40] *vt* to satirize

satisfacción *nf* satisfaction; **s. de un deseo** fulfilment of a desire

satisfacer [15] (*pp* **satisfecho**) *vt* (**a**) (*deseos, necesidades*) to satisfy (**b**) (*requisitos*) to meet, to satisfy (**c**) (*deuda*) to pay

satisfactorio,-a *adj* satisfactory

satisfecho,-a *adj* satisfied; **me doy por s.** that's good enough for me; **s. de sí mismo** self-satisfied, smug

saturar *vt* to saturate

Saturno *n* Saturn

sauce *nm* willow; **s. llorón** weeping willow

saudí, saudita *adj & nmf* Saudi; **Arabia Saudita** Saudi Arabia

sauna *nf* sauna

savia *nf* sap

saxo *nm Fam Mús* sax

saxofón *nm* saxophone

saxofonista *nmf* saxophonist

sayo *nm* cassock, smock

sazonar *vt* to season, to flavour

s/c. (*abr* **su cuenta**) your account

Sdad. (*abr* **sociedad**) Soc.

se¹ *pron* (**a**) (*reflexivo*) (*objeto directo*) (*a él mismo*) himself; (*animal*) itself; (*a ella misma*) herself; (*animal*) itself; (*a usted mismo*) yourself; (*a ellos mismos*) themselves; (*a ustedes mismos*) yourselves (**b**) (*objeto indirecto*) (*a él mismo*) (to/for) himself; (*animal*) (to/for) itself; (*a ella misma*) (to/for) herself; (*animal*) (to/for) itself; (*a usted mismo*) (to/for) yourself; (*a ellos mismos*) (to/for) themselves; (*a ustedes mismos*) (to/for) yourselves; **se compró un nuevo coche** he bought himself a new car; **todos los días se lava el pelo** she washes her hair every day (**c**) (*recíproco*) one another, each other (**d**) (*voz pasiva*) **el vino se guarda en cubas** wine is kept in casks (**e**) (*impersonal*) **nunca se sabe** you never know; **se habla inglés** (*en letrero*) English spoken here; **se dice que ...** it is said that ...

se² *pron pers* (*a él*) (to/for) him; (*a ella*) (to/for) her; (*a usted o ustedes*) (to/for) you; (*a ellos*) (to/for) them; **se lo diré en cuanto les vea** I'll tell them as soon as I see them; **¿se lo explico?** shall I explain it to you?; **¿se lo has dado ya?** have you given it to him yet?

sé¹ *indic pres de* **saber**

sé² *imperat de* **ser**

S.E. (*abr* **Su Excelencia**) HE

sea *subj pres de* **ser**

sebo *nm* (*grasa*) fat

secado *nm* drying

secador *nm* dryer; **s. de pelo** hairdryer

secadora *nf* tumble dryer

secano *nm* dry land

secante *adj* **papel s.** blotting paper

secar [44] **1** *vt* to dry
2 secarse *vpr* (**a**) to dry; **sécate** dry yourself; **s. las manos** to dry one's hands (**b**) (*marchitarse*) to dry up, to wither

sección *nf* section

seco,-a *adj* (**a**) dry; **frutos secos** dried fruit; **limpieza en s.** dry-cleaning; *Fig* **a palo s.** on its own; *Fig* **a secas** just, only (**b**) (*tono*) curt, sharp; (*golpe, ruido*) sharp; *Fig* **frenar en s.** to pull up sharply; *Fig* **parar en s.** to stop dead (**c**) (*delgado*) skinny

secreción *nf* secretion

secretaría *nf* (*oficina*) secretary's office; **S. de Estado** (*en España*) = government department under the control of a *Br* junior minister *o US* under-secretary; (*en Latinoamérica*) department, *Br* ministry; (*en Estados Unidos*) State Department

secretariado *nm* (**a**) (*oficina*) secretariat (**b**) *Educ* secretarial course

secretario,-a *nm,f* secretary; **s. de dirección** secretary to the director; **s. de Estado** (*en España*) *Br* junior minister, *US* under-secretary; (*en Latinoamérica*) minister; (*en Estados Unidos*) Secretary of State

secreto,-a 1 *adj* secret; **en s.** in secret, secretly
2 *nm* secret; **guardar un s.** to keep a secret; **con mucho s.** in great secrecy

secta *nf* sect

sectario,-a *adj* sectarian

sector *nm* (**a**) sector (**b**) (*zona*) area; **un s. de la ciudad** an area of the city

sectorial *adj* sectoral

secuela *nf* consequence

secuencia *nf* sequence

secuestrador,-a *nm,f* (**a**) (*de persona*) kidnapper; (*de un avión*) hijacker (**b**) *Jur* sequestrator

secuestrar *vt* (**a**) (*persona*) to kidnap; (*aviones*) to hijack (**b**) *Jur* to confiscate

secuestro *nm* (**a**) (*de persona*) kidnapping; (*de un avión*) hijacking (**b**) *Jur* confiscation

secular *adj* (**a**) *Rel* secular, lay (**b**) (*antiquísimo*) ancient, age-old

secundar *vt* to back

secundario,-a *adj* secondary

secuoya *nf Bot* redwood, sequoia; **s. gigante** giant sequoia

sed *nf* thirst; **tener s.** to be thirsty

seda *nf* silk

sedal *nm* fishing line

sedante *adj & nm* sedative

sede *nf* (a) headquarters, head office; *(de gobierno)* seat (b) **la Santa S.** the Holy See

sedentario,-a *adj* sedentary

sedición *nf* sedition

sedicioso,-a 1 *adj* rebellious
    2 *nm,f* rebel

sediento,-a *adj* thirsty; *Fig* **s. de poder** hungry for power

sedimentario,-a *adj* sedimentary

sedimentarse *vpr* to settle

sedimento *nm* sediment, deposit

sedoso,-a *adj* silky, silken

seducción *nf* seduction

seducir [10] *vt* to seduce; *(persuadir)* to tempt

seductor,-a 1 *adj* seductive; *(persuasivo)* tempting
    2 *nm,f* seducer

segadora *nf* *(máquina)* reaper, harvester

segar [1] *vt* to reap, to cut

seglar 1 *adj* secular, lay
    2 *nmf* lay person; *(hombre)* layman; *(mujer)* laywoman

segmento *nm* segment

segregación *nf* (a) *(separación)* segregation (b) *(secreción)* secretion

segregar [42] *vt* (a) *(separar)* to segregate (b) *(secretar)* to secrete

seguida *nf* **en s.** immediately, straight away

seguido,-a 1 *adj* (a) *(continuo)* continuous (b) *(consecutivo)* consecutive, successive; **tres veces seguidas** on three consecutive occasions; **tres lunes seguidos** three Mondays in a row
    2 *adv* (a) *(en línea recta)* straight on; **todo s.** straight on *o* ahead (b) *Am (a menudo)* often

seguidor,-a *nm,f* follower

seguimiento *nm* (a) pursuit (b) *Prensa* in- depth coverage (c) **estación de s. (espacial)** tracking station

seguir [6] **1** *vt* (a) to follow (b) *(camino)* to continue (c) *(perseguir)* to chase
    2 *vi* (a) to follow (b) **s.** + *ger (continuar)* to continue, to go on, to keep on; **siguió hablando** he continued *o* went on *o* kept on speaking (c) **s.** + *adj/pp* to continue to be, to be still; **sigo resfriado** I've still got the cold; **sigue con vida** he's still alive
    3 seguirse *vpr* to follow, to ensue

según 1 *prep* (a) according to; **s. la Biblia** according to the Bible (b) *(en función de)* depending on; **varía s. el tiempo (que haga)** it varies depending on the weather
    2 *adv* (a) depending on; **s. estén las cosas** depending on how things stand;

¿vendrás mañana? – s. will you come tomorrow? – it depends (b) *(tal como)* just as; **estaba s. lo dejé** it was just as I had left it (c) *(a medida que)* as; **s. iba leyendo ...** as I read on ...

segundero *nm* second hand

segundo¹,-a 1 *adj* second; *Fig* **decir algo con segundas (intenciones)** to say sth with a double meaning
    2 *nm,f (de una serie)* second (one)

segundo² *nm (tiempo)* second; **sesenta segundos** sixty seconds

seguramente *adv* (a) *(seguro)* surely (b) *(probablemente)* most probably; **s. no lloverá** it isn't likely to rain

seguridad *nf* (a) security; **cerradura de s.** security lock (b) *(física)* safety; **s. en carretera** road safety; **para mayor s.** to be on the safe side (c) *(confianza)* confidence; **s. en sí mismo** self-confidence (d) *(certeza)* sureness; **con toda s.** most probably; **tener la s. de que ...** to be certain that ... (e) **S. Social** ≃ Social Security, *Br* ≃ National Health Service (f) *(fiabilidad)* reliability

seguro,-a 1 *adj* (a) *(cierto)* sure; **estoy s. de que ...** I am sure that ...; **dar algo por s.** to take sth for granted (b) *(libre de peligro)* safe; *Fig* **ir sobre s.** to play safe (c) *(protegido)* secure (d) *(fiable)* reliable (e) **está segura de ella misma** she has self-confidence (f) *(firme)* steady, firm
    2 *nm* (a) *Seg* insurance; **s. a todo riesgo** fully comprehensive insurance; **s. contra terceros** third-party insurance; **s. de vida** life insurance (b) *(dispositivo)* safety catch *o* device (c) *CAm, Méx (imperdible)* safety pin
    3 *adv* for sure, definitely

seis *adj & nm inv* six

seiscientos,-as *adj & nm* six hundred

seísmo *nm (terremoto)* earthquake; *(temblor de tierra)* earth tremor

selección *nf* (a) selection (b) *Dep* team

seleccionador,-a *nm,f* (a) selector (b) *Dep* manager

seleccionar *vt* to select

selectividad *nf* selectivity; *Univ* **(prueba de) s.** entrance examination

selectivo,-a *adj* selective

selecto,-a *adj* select; **ambiente s.** exclusive atmosphere

self-service *nm* self-service cafeteria

sellar *vt (documento)* to seal; *(carta)* to stamp

sello *nm* (a) *(de correos)* stamp; *(para documentos)* seal (b) *(precinto)* seal

selva *nf* jungle

semáforo nm traffic lights

semana nf week; **entre s.** during the week; **S. Santa** Holy Week

semanada nf Am Br (weekly) pocket money, US (weekly) allowance

semanal adj & nm weekly

semanario nm weekly magazine

semblante nm Literario (cara) face; Fig (aspecto) look

sembrado nm sown field

sembrar [1] vt a Agr to sow (b) Fig **s. el pánico** to spread panic

semejante 1 adj (a) (parecido) similar; **nunca he visto nada s.** I've never seen anything like it (b) Pey (comparativo) such; **s. desvergüenza** such insolence

  2 nm (prójimo) fellow being

semejanza nf similarity, likeness

semen nm semen

semental nm stud

semestral adj half-yearly

semestre nm six-month period, semester

semicírculo nm semicircle

semifinal nf semifinal

semifinalista nmf semifinalist

semilla nf seed

semillero nm seedbed

seminario nm (a) Educ seminar (b) Rel seminary

sémola nf semolina

Sena n el S. the Seine

senado nm senate

senador,-a nm,f senator

sencillez nf simplicity

sencillo,-a 1 adj (a) (fácil) simple, easy (b) (natural) natural, unaffected (c) (billete) single (d) (sin adornos) simple, plain

  2 nm Andes, CAm, Méx Fam (cambio) loose change

senda nf, **sendero** nm path

sendos,-as adj pl one each; **con sendas carteras** each carrying a briefcase

senil adj senile

seno nm (a) (pecho) breast (b) Fig bosom, heart; **en el s. de** within (c) Mat sine

sensación nf (a) sensation, feeling; **tengo la s. de que ...** I have a feeling that ... (b) (impresión) sensation; **causar s.** to cause a sensation

sensacional adj sensational

sensacionalista adj sensationalist; **prensa s.** gutter press

sensato,-a adj sensible

sensibilizar [40] vt to make aware; **s. a la opinión pública** to increase public awareness

sensible adj (a) sensitive (b) (perceptible) perceptible

sensiblemente adv noticeably, considerably

ℐ Observa que la palabra inglesa **sensible** es un falso amigo y no es la traducción de la palabra española **sensible**. En inglés, **sensible** significa tanto "sensato" como "práctico".

sensiblero,-a adj over-sentimental, mawkish

sensitivo,-a adj sense; **órgano s.** sense organ

sensorial, sensorio,-a adj sensory

sensual adj sensual

sensualidad nf sensuality

sentada nf (a) sitting (b) Fam (protesta) sit-in (demonstration)

sentado,-a adj (establecido) established, settled; **dar algo por s.** to take sth for granted; **dejar s. que ...** to make it clear that ...

sentar [1] 1 vt (a) to sit (b) (establecer) to establish; **s. las bases** to lay the foundations

  2 vi (a) (color, ropa etc) to suit; **el pelo corto te sienta mal** short hair doesn't suit you (b) **s. bien/mal a** (comida) to agree/disagree with; **la sopa te sentará bien** the soup will do you good (c) **le sentó mal la broma** she didn't like the joke

  3 sentarse vpr to sit, to sit down

sentencia nf (a) sentence; **visto para s.** ready for judgement (b) (aforismo) maxim, saying

sentenciar [43] vt Jur to sentence (a to)

sentido,-a 1 nm (a) sense; **los cinco sentidos** the five senses; **s. común** common sense; **s. del humor** sense of humour (b) (significado) meaning; **doble s.** double meaning; **no tiene s.** it doesn't make sense (c) (dirección) direction; **(de) s. único** one-way (d) (conciencia) consciousness; **perder el s.** to faint

  2 adj deeply felt; Fml **mi más s. pésame** my deepest sympathy

sentimental 1 adj sentimental; **vida s.** love life

  2 nmf sentimental person

sentimiento nm (a) feeling (b) (pesar) sorrow, grief; Fml **le acompaño en el s.** my deepest sympathy

sentir¹ nm (a) (sentimiento) feeling (b) (opinión) opinion, view

sentir² [5] 1 vt (a) to feel; **s. hambre/calor** to feel hungry/hot (b) (lamentar) to regret, to be sorry about; **lo siento**

(mucho) I'm (very) sorry; **siento molestarle** I'm sorry to bother you

2 sentirse *upr* to feel; **me siento mal** I feel ill; **s. con ánimos de hacer algo** to feel like doing sth

senyera *nf* Catalan flag

seña *nf* (a) mark (b) *(gesto)* sign; **hacer señas a algn** to signal to sb (c) *(indicio)* sign (d) **señas** *(dirección)* address

señal *nf* (a) *(indicio)* sign, indication; **en s. de** as a sign of, as a token of (b) *(placa)* sign; **s. de tráfico** road sign (c) *(gesto etc)* signal, sign (d) *(marca)* mark; *(vestigio)* trace (e) *Tel* tone; **s. de llamada** *Br* dialling tone, *US* dial tone (f) *Com* deposit

señalado,-a *adj (importante)* important; **un día s.** a red-letter day

señalar *vt* (a) *(indicar)* to mark, to indicate; **s. con el dedo** to point at (b) *(resaltar)* to point out (c) *(precio, fecha)* to fix, to arrange

señalero *nm Urug Br* indicator, *US* turn signal

señor *nm* (a) *(hombre)* man; *(caballero)* gentleman (b) *Rel* **El S.** the Lord (c) *(con apellido)* Mr; *(tratamiento de respeto)* sir; **el Sr. Gutiérrez** Mr Gutiérrez; **muy s. mío** *(en carta)* Dear Sir (d) *(con título) (no se traduce)* **el s. ministro** the Minister

señora *nf* (a) *(mujer)* woman, *Fml* lady; **¡señoras y señores!** ladies and gentlemen! (b) *Rel* **Nuestra S.** Our Lady (c) *(con apellido)* Mrs; *(tratamiento de respeto)* madam; **la Sra. Salinas** Mrs Salinas; **muy s. mía** *(en carta)* Dear Madam (d) *(con título) (no se traduce)* **la s. ministra** the Minister (e) *(esposa)* wife

señoría *nf* (a) *Jur (hombre)* lordship; *(mujer)* ladyship (b) *Pol* **sus señorías** the honourable gentlemen

señorita *nf* (a) *(joven)* young woman, *Fml* young lady (b) *(tratamiento de respeto)* Miss; **S. Padilla** Miss Padilla (c) *Educ* **la s.** the teacher, Miss

señuelo *nm (en caza)* decoy

sepa *subj pres de* **saber**

separación *nf* (a) separation; *Jur* **s. conyugal** legal separation (b) *(espacio)* space, gap

separado,-a *adj* (a) separate; **por s.** separately, individually (b) *(divorciado)* separated

separar 1 *vt* (a) to separate (b) *(desunir)* to detach, to remove (c) *(dividir)* to divide, to separate (d) *(apartar)* to move away

2 separarse *upr* (a) to separate, to part

company (b) *(matrimonio)* to separate (c) *(apartarse)* to move away **(de** from)

separata *nf* offprint

separatismo *nm* separatism

separatista *adj & nmf* separatist

separo *nm Méx* (prison) cell

sepia 1 *nf (pez)* cuttlefish

2 *adj & nm (color)* sepia

septentrional *adj* northern

septiembre *nm* September; **el 5 de s.** the 5th of September; **en s.** in September

séptimo,-a *adj & nm,f* seventh; **la** *o* **una séptima parte** a seventh

sepulcral *adj (silencio)* deathly

sepulcro *nm* tomb

sepultura *nf* grave

sepulturero,-a *nm,f* gravedigger

sequía *nf* drought

séquito *nm* entourage, retinue

ser¹ *nm* being; **s. humano** human being; **s. vivo** living being

ser² [23] *vi* (a) *(+ adj)* to be; **es alto y rubio** he is tall and fair; **el edificio es gris** the building is grey

(b) *(+ profesión)* to be a(n); **Rafael es músico** Rafael is a musician

(c) **s. de** *(procedencia)* to be *o* come from; **¿de dónde eres?** where are you from?, where do you come from?

(d) **s. de** *(+ material)* to be made of

(e) **s. de** *(+ poseedor)* to belong to; **el perro es de Miguel** the dog belongs to Miguel; **¿de quién es este abrigo?** whose coat is this?

(f) **s. para** *(finalidad)* to be for; **esta agua es para lavar** this water is for washing

(g) *(+ día, hora)* to be; **hoy es 2 de noviembre** today is the 2nd of November; **son las cinco de la tarde** it's five o'clock

(h) *(+ cantidad)* **¿cuántos estaremos en la fiesta?** how many of us will there be at the party?

(i) *(costar)* to be, to cost; **¿cuánto es?** how much is it?

(j) *(tener lugar)* to be; **el estreno será mañana** tomorrow is the opening night

(k) **¿qué es de Gonzalo?** what has become of Gonzalo?

(l) *(auxiliar en pasiva)* to be; **fue asesinado** he was murdered

(m) *(locuciones)* **¿cómo es eso?, ¿cómo puede s.?** how can that be?; **es más** furthermore; **es que ...** it's just that ...; **como sea** anyhow; **lo que sea** whatever; **o sea** that is (to say); **por si fuera poco** to top it all; **sea como sea** in any case, be that as it may; **a no s. que** unless; **de no s.**

por ... had it not been for ...; **eso era de esperar** it was to be expected

> The auxiliary verb **ser** is used with the past participle of a verb to form the passive (e.g. **la película fue criticada** the film was criticized).

serenarse *vpr* to calm down

serenidad *nf* serenity

sereno¹ *nm (vigilante)* nightwatchman

sereno²,-a *adj* (a) calm (b) *Fam* **estar s.** *(sobrio)* to be sober

serial *nm Rad & TV* serial

serie *nf* (a) series *sing*; **fabricación en s.** mass production; **lleva ABS de s.** it has ABS fitted as standard; **fuera de s.** out of the ordinary (b) *Rad & TV* series *sing*

seriedad *nf* (a) seriousness (b) *(formalidad)* reliability, dependability; **falta de s.** irresponsibility

serio,-a *adj* (a) *(severo)* serious; **en s.** seriously (b) *(formal)* reliable, responsible

sermón *nm* sermon

sermonear *vt & vi Fam* to lecture

seropositivo,-a *adj* HIV-positive

serpentear *vi (zigzaguear)* to wind one's way, to meander

serpentina *nf (de papel)* streamer

serpiente *nf* snake; **s. de cascabel** rattlesnake; **s. pitón** python

serranía *nf* mountainous area/country

serrar [1] *vt* to saw

serrín *nm* sawdust

serrucho *nm* handsaw

servicial *adj* helpful, obliging

servicio *nm* (a) service; **s. a domicilio** delivery service (b) *Mil* service; **s. militar** military service; **estar de s.** to be on duty (c) **servicios** *(retrete)* toilet, *US* rest room

servidor,-a *nm,f* servant; *Fam* **un s.** yours truly

servil *adj* servile

servilleta *nf* serviette, napkin

servilletero *nm* serviette ring, napkin ring

servio,-a *adj & nm,f* Serbian

servir [6] **1** *vt* to serve; **¿en qué puedo servirle?** what can I do for you?, may I help you?; **¿te sirvo una copa?** will I pour you a drink?

2 *vi* (a) to serve (b) *(valer)* to be useful, to be suitable; **no sirve de nada llorar** it's no use crying; **ya no sirve** it's no use; **¿para qué sirve esto?** what is this (used) for? (c) **s. de** to serve as, to act as

3 servirse *vpr* (a) *(comida etc)* to help oneself (b) *Fml* **sírvase comunicarnos su**

decisión please inform us of your decision

sésamo *nm* sesame

sesenta *adj & nm inv* sixty

sesgar [42] *vt* (a) *(cortar)* to cut diagonally (b) *(torcer)* to slant

sesgo *nm Fig* slant, turn; **tomar un s. favorable** to take a turn for the better

sesión *nf* (a) *(reunión)* meeting, session; *Jur* session, sitting (b) *Cin* showing

seso *nm* brain

set *nm* Ten set

seta *nf (comestible)* mushroom; **s. venenosa** toadstool

setecientos,-as *adj & nm* seven hundred

setenta *adj & nm inv* seventy

setiembre *nm* September

seto *nm* hedge

seudónimo *nm* pseudonym; *(de escritores)* pen name

severidad *nf* severity

severo,-a *adj* severe

Sevilla *n* Seville

sexismo *nm* sexism

sexista *adj* sexist

sexo *nm* (a) sex (b) *(órgano)* genitals

sexólogo,-a *nm,f* sexologist

sexto,-a *adj & nm,f* sixth

sexual *adj* sexual; **vida s.** sex life

sexualidad *nf* sexuality

sexy *adj* sexy

s/f. *(abr su favor)* your favour

shock *nm* shock

short *nm RP* swimming trunks

show *nm* show

si¹ *conj* (a) *(condicional)* if; **como si** as if; **si no** if not; **si quieres** if you like, if you wish (b) *(pregunta indirecta)* whether, if; **me preguntó si me gustaba** he asked me if I liked it; **no sé si ir o no** *(disyuntivo)* I don't know whether to go or not (c) *(sorpresa)* **¡si está llorando!** but she's crying!

si² *nm (pl sis) Mús* B; *(en solfeo)* ti

sí¹ *pron pers* (a) *(singular) (él)* himself; *(ella)* herself; *(cosa)* itself; *(plural)* themselves; **de por sí, en sí** in itself; **hablaban entre sí** they were talking among themselves *o* to each other; **por sí mismo** by himself *o (uno mismo)* oneself; **decir para sí** to say to oneself

sí² **1** *adv* (a) yes; **dije que sí** I said yes, I accepted, I agreed; **porque sí** just because; **¡que sí!** yes, I tell you!; **un día sí y otro no** every other day (b) *(uso enfático) (no se traduce)* **sí que me gusta** of course I like it; **¡eso sí que no!** certainly not!

2 *nm (pl síes)* yes; **los síes** *(en parlamento)* the ayes

siamés,-esa *nm,f* Siamese twin

sibarita *nmf* sybarite

sicario *nm* hired gunman; *Fam* hitman

Sicilia *n* Sicily

sico- = psico-

sicómoro *nm* sycamore

sida *nm* (*abr* **síndrome de inmunodeficiencia adquirida**) AIDS

sidecar *nm* sidecar

siderurgia *nf* iron and steel industry

siderúrgico,-a *adj* iron and steel; **la industria siderúrgica** the iron and steel industry

sidra *nf Br* cider, *US* hard cider

siempre *adv* (a) always; **s. pasa lo mismo** it's always the same; **como s.** as usual; **a la hora de s.** at the usual time; **eso es así desde s.** it has always been like that; **para s.** for ever; **s. que** (*cada vez que*) whenever; (*a condición de que*) provided, as long as; **s. y cuando** provided, as long as (b) *Am* (*todavía*) still; **s. viven allí** they still live there (c) *Méx Fam* (*enfático*) still; **s. sí quiero ir** I still want to go; **s. no me marcho** I'm still not leaving

sien *nf* temple

sierra *nf* (a) saw; **s. mecánica** power saw (b) *Geog* mountain range, sierra

siervo,-a *nm,f* slave

siesta *nf* siesta, nap; **dormir la s.** to have a siesta *o* an afternoon nap

siete 1 *adj* seven

   2 *nm inv* seven

   3 *nf RP Fam Euf* **¡la gran s.!** *Br* sugar!, *US* shoot!

sietemesino,-a *nm,f* seven-month baby, premature baby

sífilis *nf inv* syphilis

sifón *nm* siphon; **whisky con s.** whisky and soda

sig. (*abr* **siguiente**) following

sigilo *nm* secrecy; **entrar con mucho s.** to tiptoe in

sigilosamente *adv* (*secretamente*) secretly; **entró s. en la habitación** she crept *o* slipped into the room

sigiloso,-a *adj* secretive

sigla *nf* acronym

siglo *nm* century; **el s. veintiuno** the twenty-first century; *Fam* **hace siglos que no le veo** I haven't seen him for ages

signatario,-a *adj & nm,f* signatory

significación *nf* (a) (*sentido*) meaning (b) (*importancia*) significance

significado *nm* meaning

significar [44] *vt* to mean

significativo,-a *adj* significant; (*expresivo*) meaningful

signo *nm* (a) sign; **s. del zodiaco** zodiac sign (b) *Ling* mark; **s. de interrogación** question mark

sigo *indic pres de* **seguir**

siguiente *adj* following, next; **¡el s.!** next, please!; **al día s.** the following day

sílaba *nf* syllable

silbar *vi* to whistle; (*abuchear*) to hiss, to boo

silbato *nm* whistle

silbido *nm* whistle, whistling; (*agudo*) hiss

silenciador *nm* (*de arma*) silencer; (*de coche, moto*) *Br* silencer, *US* muffler

silenciar [43] *vt* (a) (*un sonido*) to muffle (b) (*noticia*) to hush up

silencio *nm* silence; **imponer s. a algn** to make sb be quiet

silencioso,-a *adj* (*persona*) quiet; (*motor etc*) silent

silicio *nm* silicon

silicona *nf* silicone

silla *nf* (a) chair; **s. de ruedas** wheelchair; **s. giratoria** swivel chair (b) (*de montura*) saddle

sillín *nm* saddle

sillón *nm* armchair

silo *nm* silo

silueta *nf* silhouette; (*de cuerpo*) figure

silvestre *adj* wild

simbólico,-a *adj* symbolic; **precio s.** token price

simbolizar [40] *vt* to symbolize

símbolo *nm* symbol

simetría *nf* symmetry

simétrico,-a *adj* symmetrical

simiente *nf* seed

similar *adj* similar

similitud *nf* similarity

simio *nm* monkey

simpatía *nf* liking, affection; **le tengo mucha s.** I am very fond of him

   🖋 Observa que la palabra inglesa **sympathy** es un falso amigo y no es la traducción de la palabra española **simpatía**. En inglés, **sympathy** significa tanto "compasión" como "comprensión".

simpático,-a *adj* (*amable*) nice, likeable; **me cae s.** I like him

   🖋 Observa que la palabra inglesa **sympathetic** es un falso amigo y no es la traducción de la palabra española **simpático**. En inglés, **sympathetic** significa tanto "comprensivo" como "compasivo".

simpatizante *nmf* sympathizer

simpatizar [40] *vi* (a) to sympathize

(**con** with) (**b**) *(llevarse bien)* to hit it off
(**con** with)
simple 1 *adj* (**a**) simple (**b**) *(fácil)* simple,
easy (**c**) *(mero)* mere (**d**) *(persona)* simple, simple-minded
  2 *nm (persona)* simpleton
simpleza *nf* simple-mindedness; *(tontería)* nonsense
simplificar [44] *vt* to simplify
simposio *nm* symposium
simulacro *nm* sham, pretence; **un s. de
ataque** a mock attack
simular *vt* to simulate
simultanear *vt* to combine; **simultanea
el trabajo y los estudios** he's working and
studying at the same time
simultáneo,-a *adj* simultaneous
sin *prep* (**a**) without; **s. dinero/tí** without
money/you; **estamos s. pan** we're out of
bread; **s. hacer nada** without doing
anything; **cerveza s.** alcohol-free beer; **s.
más ni más** without further ado (**b**) *(+
inf)* **está s. secar** it hasn't been dried
sinagoga *nf* synagogue
sincerarse *vpr* to open one's heart (**con**
to)
sinceridad *nf* sincerity; **con toda s.** in all
sincerity
sincero,-a *adj* sincere
sincronizar [40] *vt* to synchronize
sindical *adj (Br* trade *o US* labor) union
sindicalista *nmf* union member, *Br* trade
unionist
sindicar *vt Andes, RP, Ven* to accuse
sindicato *nm* union, trade union
síndrome *nm* syndrome
sinfín *nm* endless number; **un s. de** lots of
sinfonía *nf* symphony
singani *nm Bol* grape brandy
single *nm* (**a**) *(disco)* single, 7-inch (**b**)
CSur (habitación) single room
singular 1 *adj* (**a**) singular (**b**) *(excepcional)* exceptional, unique (**c**) *(raro)* peculiar, odd
  2 *nm Ling* singular; **en s.** in the singular
siniestrado,-a *adj* stricken
siniestro,-a 1 *adj* sinister, ominous
  2 *nm* disaster, catastrophe
sino¹ *nm Fml* fate, destiny
sino² *conj* (**a**) but; **no fui a Madrid, s. a
Barcelona** I didn't go to Madrid but to
Barcelona (**b**) *(excepto)* **nadie s. él** no
one but him; **no quiero s. que me oigan** I
only want them to listen (to me)
sinónimo,-a 1 *adj* synonymous
  2 *nm* synonym
sinóptico,-a *adj* **cuadro s.** diagram, chart
sinsabor *nm (usu pl)* trouble, worry

sintético,-a *adj* synthetic
sintetizador *nm* synthesizer
sintetizar [40] *vt* to synthesize
síntoma *nm* symptom
sintonía *nf* (**a**) *Elec & Rad* tuning (**b**) *Mús
& Rad (de programa)* signature tune (**c**)
Fig harmony
sintonizador *nm Rad* tuning knob
sintonizar [40] *vt* (**a**) *Rad* to tune in to
(**b**) *(simpatizar)* **sintonizaron muy bien**
they clicked straight away
sinuoso,-a *adj (camino)* winding
sinvergüenza 1 *adj (desvergonzado)*
shameless; *(descarado)* cheeky
  2 *nmf (desvergonzado)* rogue; *(caradura)* cheeky devil
sionismo *nm* Zionism
siquiera 1 *adv (por lo menos)* at least; **ni s.**
not even
  2 *conj Fml (aunque)* although, even
though
sirena *nf* (**a**) siren, mermaid (**b**) *(señal
acústica)* siren
Siria *n* Syria
sirimiri *nm* fine drizzle
sirio,-a *adj & nm,f* Syrian
sirviente,-a *nm,f* servant
sisar *vt (hurtar)* to pilfer, to filch
sisear *vi* to hiss
sísmico,-a *adj* seismic
sismógrafo *nm* seismograph
sistema *nm* system; **por s.** as a rule; **s.
nervioso** nervous system; **s. montañoso**
mountain chain
sistemático,-a *adj* systematic
sitiar [43] *vt* to besiege
sitio¹ *nm* (**a**) *(lugar)* place; **en cualquier s.**
anywhere; **en todos los sitios** every-
where; *Fig* **quedarse en el s.** to die (**b**)
(espacio) room; **hacer s.** to make room (**c**)
Méx (parada de taxis) taxi stand *o Br* rank
sitio² *nm* siege; **estado de s.** state of
emergency
sito,-a *adj Fml* situated, located
situación *nf* (**a**) situation; **su s. económica es buena** his financial position is good
(**b**) *(ubicación)* situation, location
situado,-a *adj* situated; *Fig* **estar bien s.**
to have a good position
situar [30] **1** *vt* to locate
  2 situarse *vpr* to be situated *o* located
sketch *nm Cin & Teatro* sketch
S.L. *(abr* **Sociedad Limitada***) Br* ≃ Ltd, *US*
≃ Inc
slip *nm* underpants
slogan *nm* slogan
S.M. *(abr* **Su Majestad***) (rey)* His Majesty;
(reina) Her Majesty

smoking *nm* dinner jacket, *US* tuxedo

s/n. (*abr* **sin número**) = abbreviation used in addresses after the street name, where the building has no number

snob *adj & nmf* = **esnob**

snobismo *nm* = **esnobismo**

so¹ *prep* (*bajo*) under; **so pena de** under penalty of

so² *nm Fam* **¡so imbécil!** you damned idiot!

sobaco *nm* armpit

sobar *Fam* **1** *vt* (*manosear*) to fondle, to paw
2 *vi* (*dormir*) to sleep

soberanía *nf* sovereignty

soberano,-a 1 *adj* (a) sovereign (b) *Fam* huge, great
2 *nm,f* (*monarca*) sovereign

soberbia *nf* pride

soberbio,-a *adj* (a) proud (b) (*magnífico*) splendid, magnificent

sobón,-ona *nm,f Fam* **ser un s.** to be fresh o all hands

sobornar *vt* to bribe

soborno *nm* (*acción*) bribery; (*dinero etc*) bribe

sobra *nf* (a) **de s.** (*no necesario*) superfluous; **tener de s.** to have plenty; **estar de s.** not to be needed; **saber algo de s.** to know sth only too well (b) **sobras** (*restos*) leftovers

sobradamente *adv* only too well

sobrado,-a *adj* (*que sobra*) abundant, more than enough; **sobradas veces** repeatedly; **andar s. de tiempo/dinero** to have plenty of time/money

sobrante 1 *adj* remaining, spare
2 *nm* surplus, excess

sobrar *vi* (a) to be more than enough, (*sing*) to be too much, (*pl*) to be too many; **sobran tres sillas** there are three chairs too many; **sobran comentarios** I've nothing further to add; *Fam* **tú sobras aquí** you are not wanted here (b) (*quedar*) to be left over; **ha sobrado carne** there's still some meat left

sobrasada *nf* sausage spread

sobre¹ *nm* (a) (*para carta*) envelope (b) (*de sopa etc*) packet

sobre² *prep* (a) (*encima de*) on, upon, on top of (b) (*por encima*) over, above (c) (*acerca de*) about, on (d) (*aproximadamente*) about; **vendré s. las ocho** I'll come at about eight o'clock (e) **s. todo** especially, above all

sobre- *pref* super-, over-

sobrealimentado,-a *adj* overfed

sobrecarga *nf* overload

sobrecargar [42] *vt* to overload

sobrecogedor,-a *adj* dramatic, awesome

sobrecoger [53] *vt* (*conmover*) to shock

sobredosis *nf inv* overdose

sobreentenderse *vpr* **se sobreentiende** that goes without saying

sobregiro *nm* overdraft

sobrehumano,-a *adj* superhuman

sobreimpresión *nf Fot & Cin* superimposing

sobrellevar *vt* to endure, to bear

sobremesa¹ *nf* afternoon

sobremesa² *nf* **ordenador de s.** desktop computer

sobrenatural *adj* supernatural

sobrenombre *nm* nickname

sobrepasar 1 *vt* to exceed, to surpass; (*rival*) to beat
2 sobrepasarse *vpr* to go too far

sobrepeso *nm* (*de carga*) overload, excess weight; (*de persona*) excess weight

sobreponerse *vpr* (a) **s. a** (*superar*) to overcome; **s. al dolor** to overcome pain (b) (*animarse*) to pull oneself together

sobreproducción *nf* overproduction

sobresaliente 1 *nm* (*nota*) ≃ A
2 *adj* (*que destaca*) outstanding, excellent

sobresalir [22] *vi* to stick out, to protrude; *Fig* (*destacar*) to stand out, to excel

sobresaltar 1 *vt* to startle
2 sobresaltarse *vpr* to be startled, to start

sobresalto *nm* (*movimiento*) start; (*susto*) fright

sobreseer [36] *vt Jur* to stay; **s. una causa** to stay proceedings

sobretiempo *nm Andes* (a) (*en trabajo*) overtime (b) (*en deporte*) *Br* extra time, *US* overtime

sobretodo *nm* (*abrigo*) overcoat; (*guardapolvo*) overalls

sobrevalorar *vt* to overestimate

sobrevenir [27] *vi* to happen unexpectedly

sobreviviente 1 *adj* surviving
2 *nmf* survivor

sobrevivir *vi* to survive

sobrevolar [2] *vt* to fly over

sobriedad *nf* sobriety; (*en la bebida*) soberness

sobrina *nf* niece

sobrino *nm* nephew

sobrio,-a *adj* sober

socarrón,-ona *adj* (a) (*sarcástico*) sarcastic (b) (*astuto*) sly, cunning

socavar *vt Fig* to undermine

socavón nm (bache) pothole
sociable adj sociable, friendly
social adj social
socialdemócrata 1 adj social democratic
  2 nmf social democrat
socialismo nm socialism
socialista adj & nmf socialist
socializar [40] vt to socialize
sociedad nf (a) society; **s. de consumo** consumer society (b) (asociación) association, society (c) Com company; **s. anónima** Br public (limited) company, US incorporated company; **s. limitada** private limited company
socio,-a nm,f (a) (miembro) member; **hacerse s. de un club** to become a member of a club, to join a club (b) Com (asociado) partner
sociología nf sociology
sociológico,-a adj sociological
sociólogo,-a nm,f sociologist
socorrer vt to help, to assist
socorrido,-a adj handy, useful
socorrista nmf life-saver, lifeguard
socorro nm help, assistance; **¡s.!** help!; **puesto de s.** first-aid post
soda nf soda water
soez adj vulgar, crude
sofá nm (pl **sofás**) sofa, settee; **s. cama** sofa bed, studio couch
Sofía n Sofia
sofisticado,-a adj sophisticated
sofocado,-a adj suffocated
sofocante adj suffocating, stifling; **hacía un calor s.** it was unbearably hot
sofocar [44] 1 vt (a) (ahogar) to suffocate, to smother (b) (incendio) to extinguish, to put out
  2 sofocarse vpr (a) (ahogarse) to suffocate, to stifle (b) Fam (irritarse) to get upset
sofoco nm Fig (vergüenza) embarrassment; **le dio un s.** (disgusto) it gave her quite a turn
sofocón nm Fam shock; **llevarse un s.** to get upset
sofreír [56] vt to fry lightly, to brown
sofrito nm = fried tomato and onion sauce
software nm software
soga nf rope; Fig **estar con la s. al cuello** to be in dire straits
soja nf (a) (planta, fruto) Br soya bean, US soy bean (b) (proteína) soya
sojuzgar [42] vt to subjugate
sol¹ nm (a) sun (b) (luz) sunlight; (luz y calor) sunshine; **hace s.** it's sunny, the sun

is shining; **tomar el s.** to sunbathe; **al o bajo el s.** in the sun; **de s. a s.** from sunrise to sunset (c) Fin = standard monetary unit of Peru
sol² nm Mús G; (solfeo) so
solamente adv only; **no s.** not only; **s. con mirarte lo sé** I know just by looking at you; **s. que ...** except that ...
solapa nf (de chaqueta) lapel; (de sobre, bolsillo, libro) flap
solapadamente adv stealthily, in an underhand way
solapado,-a adj (persona) sly
solapamiento nm overlap
solapar 1 vt Fig to conceal, to cover up
  2 vi to overlap
solar¹ adj solar; **luz s.** sunlight
solar² nm (terreno) plot; (en obras) building site
solario, solárium nm sunbed
solaz nm Fml (descanso) rest, relaxation; (esparcimiento) recreation, entertainment
solazarse [40] vpr (relajar) to relax; (divertir) to entertain oneself, to amuse oneself
soldado nm soldier; **s. raso** private
soldador,-a 1 nm,f welder
  2 nm soldering iron
soldar [2] vt (cable) to solder; (chapa) to weld
soleado,-a adj sunny
soledad nf (estado) solitude; (sentimiento) loneliness
solemne adj (a) (majestuoso) solemn (b) Pey downright
solemnidad nf solemnity
soler [4] vi defect (a) (en presente) to be in the habit of; **solemos ir en coche** we usually go by car; **sueles equivocarte** you are usually wrong (b) (en pasado) **solía pasear por aquí** he used to walk round here
solera nf Fig tradition; **de s.** old-established; **vino de s.** vintage wine
solfa nf (a) Mús solfa; Fam **poner en s.** to ridicule (b) Fam (paliza) thrashing, beating
solicitar vt (información etc) to request, to ask for; (trabajo) to apply for
solícito,-a adj obliging, attentive
solicitud nf (petición) request; (de trabajo) application
solidaridad nf solidarity
solidario,-a adj (a) supportive; **una sociedad solidaria** a caring society (b) Jur jointly responsible
solidarizarse vpr to show one's solidarity (con with)

solidez nf solidity, strength

sólido,-a adj solid, strong

soliloquio nm soliloquy

solista nmf soloist

solitario,-a 1 adj (que está solo) solitary, lone; (que se siente solo) lonely
2 nm (a) (diamante) solitaire (b) Naipes solitaire, patience

soliviantar vt (irritar) to irritate

sollozar [40] vi to sob

sollozo nm sob

solo,-a 1 adj (a) only, single; **ni un s. día** not a single day; **una sola vez** only once, just once (b) (solitario) lonely (c) **hablar s.** to talk to oneself; **se enciende s.** it switches itself on automatically; **a solas** alone, by oneself
2 nm Mús solo

sólo adv only; **tan s.** only; **no s. ... sino (también)** not only ... but (also); **con s., (tan) s. con** just by

> Note that the adverb **sólo** can be written without an accent when there is no risk of confusion with the adjective.

solomillo nm sirloin

soltar [2] 1 vt (a) (desasir) to let go of; **¡suéltame!** let me go! (b) (prisionero) to release (c) (humo, olor) to give off (d) (bofetada) to deal; (carcajada) to let out; **me soltó un rollo** he bored me to tears
2 soltarse vpr (a) (desatarse) to come loose (b) (perro etc) to get loose, to break loose (c) (desprenderse) to come off

soltero,-a 1 adj single, unmarried
2 nm (hombre) bachelor, single man
3 nf **soltera** (mujer) single woman, spinster

solterón, -ona nm,f old bachelor, f old maid

soltura nf (agilidad) agility; (seguridad) confidence, assurance; **habla italiano con s.** he speaks Italian fluently

soluble adj soluble; **café s.** instant coffee

solución nf solution

solucionar vt to solve; (arreglar) to settle

solvencia nf (a) Fin solvency (b) (fiabilidad) reliability; **fuentes de toda s.** completely reliable sources

solventar vt (problema) to solve, to resolve; (deuda, asunto) to settle

solvente adj (a) Fin solvent (b) (fiable) reliable

sombra nf (a) shade (b) (silueta proyectada) shadow; **s. de ojos** eyeshadow; **sin s. de duda** beyond a shadow of doubt (c)

tener buena s. (tener suerte) to be lucky

sombrero nm hat; **s. de copa** top hat; **s. hongo** bowler hat

sombrilla nf parasol, sunshade

sombrío,-a adj (oscuro) dark; (tenebroso) sombre, gloomy; Fig (persona) gloomy, sullen

somero,-a adj superficial, shallow

someter 1 vt (a) to subject; **s. a prueba** to put to the test; **s. algo a votación** to put sth to the vote (b) (rebeldes) to subdue, to put down
2 someterse vpr (a) (subordinarse) to submit (b) (rendirse) to surrender, to yield (c) **s. a un tratamiento** to undergo treatment

somier nm (pl somieres) spring mattress

somnífero nm sleeping pill

somnoliento,-a adj sleepy, drowsy

son nm sound; **al s. del tambor** to the sound of the drum; **venir en s. de paz** to come in peace

sonado,-a adj (a) much talked of (b) (trastocado) mad, crazy

sonajero nm baby's rattle

sonámbulo,-a nm,f somnambulist, sleepwalker

sonar [2] 1 vi (a) to sound; **s. a** to sound like; **suena bien** it sounds good (b) (timbre, teléfono) to ring; **sonaron las cinco** the clock struck five (c) **tu nombre/cara me suena** your name/face rings a bell
2 sonarse vpr **s. (la nariz)** to blow one's nose

sonda nf (a) Med sound, probe (b) **s. espacial** space probe

sondear vt (a) (opinión) to test, to sound out (b) Med to sound, to probe (c) Náut to sound

sondeo nm (a) (encuesta) poll (b) Med sounding, probing (c) Náut sounding

soneto nm Lit sonnet

sonido nm sound

sonoro,-a adj (a) Cin sound; **banda sonora** soundtrack (b) (resonante) loud, resounding (c) Ling voiced

sonreír [56] vi, **sonreírse** vpr to smile; **me sonrió** he smiled at me

sonriente adj smiling

sonrisa nf smile

sonrojarse vpr to blush

sonrojo nm blush

sonsacar [44] vt to wheedle; (secreto) to worm out

sonso,-a adj Am foolish, silly

soñador,-a nm,f dreamer

soñar [2] vt & vi (a) to dream; **s. con** to dream of o about; Fig **¡ni soñarlo!** not on your life! (**b**) (*fantasear*) to daydream, to dream

soñoliento,-a *adj* sleepy, drowsy

sopa *nf* soup; **s. juliana** spring vegetable soup; *Fig* **quedar hecho una s.** to get soaked to the skin

sope *nm Méx* = fried corn tortilla, with beans and cheese or other toppings

sopera *nf* soup tureen

sopero,-a *adj* **cucharada sopera** soup spoon

sopesar *vt* to try the weight of; *Fig* to weigh up

sopetón *nm Fam* slap; **de s.** all of a sudden

soplado *nm* glass-blowing

soplagaitas *nmf inv Fam* (*estúpido, pesado*) jerk; *Br* prat

soplar 1 *vi* (*viento*) to blow

2 *vt* (**a**) (*polvo etc*) to blow away; (*para enfriar*) to blow on (**b**) (*para apagar*) to blow out (**c**) (*para inflar*) to blow up (**d**) (*en examen etc*) **me sopló las respuestas** he whispered the answers to me

soplete *nm* blowlamp, blowtorch

soplido *nm* blow, puff

soplillo *nm* fan; *Fam* **orejas de s.** sticky-out ears

soplo *nm* (**a**) (*acción*) blow, puff; (*de viento*) gust (**b**) *Med* murmur

soplón,-ona *nm,f Fam* (*niño*) telltale, sneak; (*delator*) *Br* grass, *US* rat

soporífero,-a *adj* (**a**) (*que adormece*) soporific, sleep-inducing (**b**) (*aburrido*) boring, dull

soportable *adj* bearable

soportal *nm* porch; **soportales** arcade

soportar *vt* (**a**) (*peso*) to support, to bear (**b**) *Fig* (*calor, ruido*) to bear, to endure; (*situación*) to put up with, to bear; **no te soporto** I can't stand you

soporte *nm* support; **s. publicitario** advertising medium

soprano *nmf* soprano

sorber *vt* (**a**) (*beber*) to sip (**b**) (*absorber*) to soak up, to absorb

sorbete *nm* sorbet, sherbet

sorbo *nm* sip; (*trago*) gulp; **de un s.** in one gulp

sordera *nf* deafness

sórdido,-a *adj* squalid, sordid

sordo,-a 1 *adj* (**a**) (*persona*) deaf; **s. como una tapia** stone-deaf (**b**) (*golpe, ruido, dolor*) dull

2 *nm,f* deaf person; **los sordos** the deaf *pl*; *Fam Fig* **hacerse el s.** to turn a deaf ear

sordomudez *nf* deaf-muteness

sordomudo,-a *adj* deaf and dumb, deaf-mute

2 *nm,f* deaf and dumb person, deaf-mute

soroche *nm Andes, Arg* (*mal de altura*) altitude sickness

sorprendente *adj* surprising

sorprender *vt* (**a**) (*extrañar*) to surprise (**b**) (*coger desprevenido*) to catch unawares, to take by surprise

sorpresa *nf* surprise; **coger de** *o* **por s.** to take by surprise

sorpresivo,-a *adj Am* unexpected, surprising

sortear *vt* (**a**) to draw *o* cast lots for; (*rifar*) to raffle (off) (**b**) (*evitar*) to avoid, to get round

sorteo *nm* draw; (*rifa*) raffle

sortija *nf* ring

sortilegio *nm* spell

S.O.S. *nm* SOS

sosa *nf* soda; **s. cáustica** caustic soda

sosegado,-a *adj* (*tranquilo*) calm, quiet; (*pacífico*) peaceful

sosegar [1] *vt* to calm, to quieten

2 sosegarse *upr* to calm down

sosiego *nm* (*calma*) calmness; (*paz*) peace, tranquillity

soslayo: • **de soslayo** *loc adv* **mirar de s.** to look sideways (at)

soso,-a *adj* lacking in salt; *Fig* (*persona*) insipid, dull

sospecha *nf* suspicion

sospechar 1 *vi* (*desconfiar*) to suspect; **s. de algn** to suspect sb

2 *vt* (*pensar*) to suspect

sospechoso,-a 1 *adj* suspicious; **s. de** suspected of

2 *nm,f* suspect

sostén *nm* (**a**) (*apoyo*) support (**b**) (*sustento*) sustenance (**c**) (*prenda*) bra, brassière

sostener [24] 1 *vt* (**a**) (*sujetar*) to support, to hold up (**b**) (*con la mano*) to hold (**c**) *Fig* (*teoría etc*) to defend, to uphold; **s. que ...** to maintain that ... (**d**) (*conversación*) to hold, to sustain (**e**) (*familia*) to support

2 sostenerse *upr* (*mantenerse*) to support oneself (**b**) (*permanecer*) to stay, to remain

sostenido,-a *adj* (**a**) (*continuado*) sustained (**b**) *Mús* sharp

sostuve *pt indef de* **sostener**

sota *nf Naipes* jack, knave

sotana *nf* cassock, soutane

sótano *nm* basement, cellar

soto *nm* grove

soviético,-a *adj* & *nm,f* Soviet; *Hist* **la Unión Soviética** the Soviet Union

soy *indic pres de* **ser**

soya *nf* = **soja**

SP (*abr servicio público*) = sign indicating public transport vehicle

sport: • **de sport** *loc adj* casual, sports; **chaqueta de s.** sports jacket

spot *nm* (*pl* **spots**) *TV* commercial, advert, ad

spray *nm* (*pl* **sprays**) spray

sprint *nm* sprint

Sr. (*abr Señor*) Mr

Sra. (*abr Señora*) Mrs

S.R.C., s.r.c. (*abr se ruega contestación*) please reply, R.S.V.P.

Srta. (*abr Señorita*) Miss

SS *nf* (*abr Seguridad Social*) Social Security

SS.AA. (*abr Sus Altezas*) Their Royal Highnesses

Sta., sta. (*abr Santa*) St

stand *nm Com* stand

standard *adj & nm* standard

status *nm inv* status

Sto., sto. (*abr Santo*) St

su *adj pos* (*de él*) his; (*de ella*) her; (*de usted, ustedes*) your; (*de animales o cosas*) its; (*impersonal*) one's; (*de ellos*) their; **su coche** his/her/your/their car; **su pata** its leg; **sus libros** his/her/your/their books; **sus patas** its legs

suave *adj* (a) smooth; (*luz, voz etc*) soft (b) *Met* (*templado*) mild

---

♪ Observa que la palabra inglesa **suave** es un falso amigo y no es la traducción de la palabra española **suave**. En inglés, **suave** significa "fino, cortés".

---

suavidad *nf* (a) smoothness; (*dulzura*) softness (b) *Met* mildness

suavizante *nm* (*para el pelo*) (hair) conditioner; (*para la ropa*) fabric softener

suavizar [40] 1 *vt* to smooth (out)

2 **suavizarse** *vpr* (*temperatura*) to get milder; (*persona*) to calm down

subacuático,-a *adj* underwater

subalimentado,-a *adj* undernourished, underfed

subalterno,-a *adj & nm,f* subordinate, subaltern

subarrendar [1] *vt Com* to sublet, to sublease

subasta *nf* auction

subastar *vt* to auction (off), to sell at auction

subcampeón *nm Dep* runner-up

subconsciente *adj & nm* subconscious

subcontratación *nf Com* outsourcing

subdesarrollado,-a *adj* underdeveloped

subdesarrollo *nm* underdevelopment

subdirector,-a *nm,f* assistant director/manager

súbdito,-a *nm,f* subject, citizen; **s. francés** French citizen

subdividir *vt* to subdivide

subestimar *vt* to underestimate

subida *nf* (a) (*de temperatura*) rise; (*de precios, salarios*) rise, increase (b) (*ascenso*) ascent, climb (c) (*pendiente*) slope, hill (d) (*fam* (*drogas*) high

subido,-a *adj* **s. de tono** daring, risqué

subir 1 *vt* (a) to go up (b) (*llevar arriba*) to take up, to bring up (c) (*cabeza, mano*) to lift, to raise (d) (*precio, salario*) to raise, to put up (e) (*volumen*) to turn up; (*voz*) to raise

2 *vi* (a) (*ir arriba*) to go up, to come up (b) **s. a** (*un coche*) to get into; (*un autobús*) to get on; (*un barco, avión, tren*) to board, to get on (c) (*aumentar*) to rise, to go up

3 **subirse** *vpr* (a) to climb up; *Fig* **el vino se le subió a la cabeza** the wine went to his head (b) **s. a** (*un coche*) to get into; (*un autobús, avión, tren*) to get on, to board; (*caballo, bici*) to get on (c) (*cremallera*) to do up; (*mangas*) to roll up

súbitamente *adv* suddenly

súbito,-a *adj* sudden

subjetivo,-a *adj* subjective

sublevación *nf* rising, rebellion

sublevar 1 *vt Fig* (*indignar*) to infuriate, to enrage

2 **sublevarse** *vpr* to rebel, to revolt

sublime *adj* sublime

submarinismo *nm* skin-diving

submarino,-a 1 *adj* submarine, underwater

2 *nm* submarine

subnormal 1 *adj* mentally handicapped

2 *nmf* mentally handicapped person

suboficial *nm* (a) *Mil* noncommissioned officer (b) *Náut* petty officer

subordinado,-a *adj & nm,f* subordinate

subordinar *vt* to subordinate

subproducto *nm* by-product

subrayar *vt* to underline; *Fig* (*recalcar*) to emphasize, to stress

subrepticio,-a *adj* surreptitious

subrutina *nf* subroutine

subsanar *vt* (*error*) to rectify, to put right; (*daño*) to make up for

subscribir (*pp* **subscrito**) *vt* = **suscribir**

subscripción *nf* subscription

subsecretario,-a *nm,f* undersecretary

subsidiario,-a *adj* subsidiary

subsidio *nm* allowance, benefit; **s. de desempleo** unemployment benefit

subsistencia *nf* subsistence

subsistir *vi* to subsist, to remain; *(vivir)* to live on, to survive

subsuelo *nm* subsoil

subte *nm RP Br* underground, *Br* tube, *US* subway

subterráneo,-a 1 *adj* underground
   2 *nm (túnel)* tunnel, underground passage

subtítulo *nm* subtitle

suburbano,-a *adj* suburban

suburbio *nm (barrio pobre)* slums; *(barrio periférico)* suburb

subvención *nf* subsidy

subvencionar *vt* to subsidize

subversión *nf* subversion

subversivo,-a *adj* subversive

subyacente *adj* underlying

subyugar [42] *vt* to subjugate

succionar *vt* to suck (in)

sucedáneo,-a *adj & nm* substitute

suceder 1 *vi* **(a)** *(ocurrir) (uso impers)* to happen, to occur; **¿qué sucede?** what's going on?, what's the matter? **(b)** *(seguir)* to follow, to succeed
   2 sucederse *vpr* to follow one another, to come one after the other

sucesión *nf* **(a)** *(serie)* series *sing*, succession **(b)** *(al trono)* succession **(c)** *(descendencia)* issue, heirs

sucesivamente *adv* **y así s.** and so on

sucesivo,-a *adj* following, successive; **en lo s.** from now on

suceso *nm (hecho)* event, occurrence; *(incidente)* incident; *Prensa* **sección de sucesos** accident and crime reports

> ♪ Observa que la palabra inglesa **success** es un falso amigo y no es la traducción de la palabra española **suceso**. En inglés, **success** significa "éxito".

sucesor,-a *nm,f* successor

suciedad *nf* **(a)** *(dirt)* dirt **(b)** *(calidad)* dirtiness

sucinto,-a *adj* concise, succinct

sucio,-a 1 *adj* dirty; **en s.** in rough; *Fig* **juego s.** foul play; *Fig* **negocio s.** shady business
   2 *adv* **jugar s.** to play dirty

sucre *nm Fin* = standard monetary unit of Ecuador

suculento,-a *adj* succulent, juicy

sucumbir *vi* to succumb, to yield

sucursal *nf Com & Fin* branch, branch office

sudaca *nmf Pey* South American

sudadera *nf* sweatshirt

Sudáfrica *n* South Africa

sudafricano,-a *adj & nm,f* South African

Sudamérica *n* South America

sudamericano,-a *adj & nm,f* South American

sudar *vt & vi* to sweat; *Fam Fig* **s. la gota gorda** to sweat blood

sudeste *nm* southeast

sudoeste *nm* southwest

sudor *nm* sweat; *Fig* **con el s. de mi frente** by the sweat of my brow

sudoroso,-a *adj* sweaty

Suecia *n* Sweden

sueco,-a 1 *adj* Swedish
   2 *nm,f (persona)* Swede
   3 *nm (idioma)* Swedish

suegra *nf* mother-in-law

suegro *nm* father-in-law; **mis suegros** my in-laws

suela *nf (de zapato)* sole

sueldo *nm* salary, wages

suelo *nm* **(a)** *(superficie)* ground; *(de interior)* floor; *Fig* **estar por los suelos** *(precios)* to be rock-bottom **(b)** *(territorio)* soil, land **(c)** *(campo, terreno)* land; **s. cultivable** arable land **(d)** *(de carretera)* surface

suelto,-a 1 *adj* **(a)** *(loose)* loose; *(desatado)* undone **(b)** *Fig* **dinero s.** loose change; **hojas sueltas** loose sheets (of paper); **se venden sueltos** they are sold singly *o* separately *o* loose **(c)** *(en libertad)* free; *(huido)* at large **(d)** *(vestido, camisa)* loose, loose-fitting
   2 *nm (dinero)* (loose) change

sueño *nm* **(a)** *(sleep)* sleep; *(ganas de dormir)* sleepiness; **tener s.** to feel *o* be sleepy **(b)** *(cosa soñada)* dream

suero *nm Med* serum; *(de la leche)* whey

suerte *nf* **(a)** *(fortuna)* luck; **por s.** fortunately; **probar s.** to try one's luck; **tener s.** to be lucky; **¡que tengas s.!** good luck! **(b)** **echar algo a suertes** to draw lots for sth **(c)** *(destino)* fate, destiny **(d)** *Fml (género)* kind, sort, type

suéter *nm* sweater

suficiencia *nf* **(a)** *(engreimiento)* smugness, complacency **(b)** *Educ* **prueba de s.** final exam

suficiente 1 *adj (bastante)* sufficient, enough
   2 *nm Educ* pass

suficientemente *adv* sufficiently; **no es lo s. rico como para ...** he isn't rich enough to ...

sufijo *nm* suffix

sufragar [42] **1** *vt* (*gastos*) to pay, to defray

2 *vi Am* to vote (**por** for)

sufragio *nm Pol* suffrage; (*voto*) vote

sufrido,-a *adj* (*persona*) long-suffering

sufrimiento *nm* suffering

sufrir 1 *vi* to suffer; **s. del corazón** to have a heart condition

2 *vt* (**a**) (*accidente*) to have; (*operación*) to undergo; (*dificultades, cambios*) to experience; **s. dolores de cabeza** to suffer from headaches (**b**) (*aguantar*) to bear, to put up with

sugerencia *nf* suggestion

sugerente *adj* suggestive

sugerir [5] *vt* to suggest

sugestión *nf* suggestion

sugestionar *vt* to influence, to persuade

sugestivo,-a *adj* suggestive; (*atractivo*) alluring

suiche *nm Andes, Ven* switch

suicida 1 *nmf* (*persona*) suicide

2 *adj* suicidal

suicidarse *upr* to commit suicide, to kill oneself

suicidio *nm* suicide

suite *nf* suite

Suiza *n* Switzerland

suizo,-a 1 *adj* Swiss

2 *nm,f* (*persona*) Swiss

3 *nm Culin* éclair

sujetador *nm* (*prenda*) bra, brassière

sujetar 1 *vt* (**a**) (*agarrar*) to hold (**b**) (*fijar*) to hold down, to hold in place (**c**) *Fig* (*someter*) to restrain

2 **sujetarse** *upr* (*agarrarse*) to hold on

sujeto,-a 1 *nm* subject; (*individuo*) fellow, individual

2 *adj* (*atado*) fastened, secure; **s. a** (*sometido*) subject to, liable to

sulfato *nm* sulphate

sulfurar 1 *vt Fam* (*exasperar*) to exasperate, to infuriate

2 **sulfurarse** *upr Fam* to lose one's temper, to blow one's top

sultán *nm* sultan

suma *nf* (**a**) (*cantidad*) sum, amount (**b**) *Mat* sum, addition; **s. total** sum total (**c**) **en s.** in short

sumamente *adv* extremely, highly

sumar 1 *vt Mat* to add, to add up

2 **sumarse** *upr* **s. a** (*huelga*) to join; (*propuesta*) to support

sumario,-a 1 *adj* summary, brief; *Jur* **juicio s.** summary proceedings

2 *nm Jur* summary

sumarísimo,-a *adj Jur* swift, expeditious

sumergible *adj & nm* submersible

sumergir [57] **1** *vt* to submerge, to submerse; (*hundir*) to sink, to plunge

2 **sumergirse** *upr* to submerge, to go underwater; (*hundirse*) to sink

sumidero *nm* drain, sewer

suministrar *vt* to supply, to provide; **s. algo a algn** to supply sb with sth

suministro *nm* supply

sumir *vt* (*hundir*) to sink, to plunge; *Fig* to plunge

sumiso,-a *adj* submissive, obedient

sumo,-a *adj* (*supremo*) supreme; **con s. cuidado** with extreme care; **a lo s.** at (the) most

suntuoso,-a *adj* sumptuous, magnificent

supe *pt indef de* saber

supeditar *vt* to subject (**a** to)

super- *pref* super-

súper *Fam* **1** *adj* super, great

2 *nm* (**a**) (*supermercado*) supermarket (**b**) (*gasolina*) 4-star

superado,-a *adj* outdated, obsolete

superar 1 *vt* (**a**) (*obstáculo etc*) to overcome, to surmount; (*prueba*) to pass (**b**) (*aventajar*) to surpass, to excel

2 **superarse** *upr* to improve o better oneself

superávit *nm* surplus

superdotado,-a 1 *adj* exceptionally gifted

2 *nm,f* genius

superficial *adj* superficial

superficialidad *nf* superficiality

superficie *nf* surface; (*área*) area; *Com* **grandes superficies** hypermarkets

superfluo,-a *adj* superfluous

superhombre *nm* superman

superior 1 *adj* (**a**) (*posición*) top, upper (**b**) (*cantidad*) greater, higher, larger (**a** than) (**c**) (*calidad*) superior; **calidad s.** top quality (**d**) *Educ* higher

2 *nm* (*jefe*) superior

superioridad *nf* superiority

supermán *nm* (*pl* **supermanes**) superman

supermercado *nm* supermarket

superpoblación *nf* overpopulation

superponer [19] *vt* to superimpose

superpotencia *nf* superpower

superproducción *nf* (**a**) *Ind* overproduction (**b**) *Cin* mammoth production

supersónico,-a *adj* supersonic

superstición *nf* superstition

supersticioso,-a *adj* superstitious

supervisar *vt* to supervise

supervisor,-a *nm,f* supervisor

supervivencia *nf* survival

supino,-a *adj* (**a**) *(boca arriba)* supine, face up (**b**) *Fig (absoluto)* total absolute

súpito,-a *adj Am* sudden

suplantar *vt* to supplant, to take the place of

suplementario,-a *adj* supplementary, additional

suplemento *nm* supplement; **sin s.** without extra charge

suplente *adj & nmf (sustituto)* substitute, deputy; *Dep* substitute

supletorio,-a *adj* supplementary, additional; **cama supletoria** extra bed; **teléfono s.** extension

súplica *nf* entreaty, plea

suplicar [44] *vt* to beseech, to beg

suplicio *nm (tortura)* torture; *Fig (tormento)* torment

suplir *vt* (**a**) *(reemplazar)* to replace, to substitute (**b**) *(compensar)* to make up for

suponer [19] *(pp* **supuesto***) vt* (**a**) *(significar)* to mean (**b**) *(implicar)* to entail (**c**) *(representar)* to account for (**d**) *(pensar)* to suppose; **supongo que sí** I suppose so; **supongamos que ...** let's assume that ... (**e**) *(adivinar)* to guess; (**me**) **lo suponía** I guessed as much

suposición *nf* supposition

supositorio *nm* suppository

supremacía *nf* supremacy

supremo,-a *adj* supreme

supresión *nf (de una ley etc)* abolition; *(de restricciones)* lifting; *(de una palabra)* deletion; *(de una rebelión)* suppression; *(omisión)* omission

suprimir *vt (ley, impuesto)* to abolish; *(restricción)* to lift; *(palabra)* to delete, to take/leave out; *(rebelión)* to suppress (**b**) *(omitir)* to omit

supuesto,-a 1 *adj* (**a**) *(asumido)* supposed, assumed; **¡por s.!** of course!; **dar algo por s.** to take sth for granted (**b**) *(presunto)* alleged

2 *nm* assumption; **en el s. de que** on the assumption that

supurar *vi* to suppurate, to fester

supuse *pt indef de* **suponer**

sur *nm* south

Suramérica *n* South America

suramericano,-a *adj & nm,f* South American

surcar [44] *vt Agr* to plough; *Fig (olas)* to cut through

surco *nm Agr* furrow; *(en un disco)* groove

sureño,-a 1 *adj* southern

2 *nm,f* southerner

sureste *nm* = **sudeste**

surf(ing) *nm Dep* surfing

surfista *nmf* surfer

surgir [57] *vi (aparecer)* to arise, to emerge, to appear; *(problema, dificultad)* to crop up

suroeste *nm* = **sudoeste**

surrealista *adj & nmf* surrealist

surtido,-a 1 *adj* (**a**) *(variado)* assorted (**b**) **bien s.** well-stocked

2 *nm* selection, assortment

surtidor *nm* spout; **s. de gasolina** *Br* petrol pump, *US* gas pump

surtir *vt* (**a**) to supply, to provide (**b**) **s. efecto** to have the desired effect

susceptible *adj* susceptible; *(quisquilloso)* oversensitive, touchy

suscitar *vt (provocar)* to cause, to provoke; *(rebelión)* to stir up, to arouse; *(interés etc)* to arouse

suscribir *(pp* **suscrito***)* **1** *vt* (**a**) to subscribe to, to endorse (**b**) *Fml (firmar)* to sign

2 suscribirse *vpr* to subscribe (**a** to)

suscripción *nf* subscription

susodicho,-a *adj* above-mentioned, aforesaid

suspender 1 *vt* (**a**) *(ley)* to suspend; *(reunión)* to adjourn (**b**) *(examen)* to fail; **me han suspendido** I've failed (the exam) (**c**) *(colgar)* to hang, to suspend

2 *vi Educ* **he suspendido** I've failed

suspense *nm* suspense; **novela/película de s.** thriller

suspensión *nf* (**a**) hanging (up), suspension (**b**) *Aut* suspension (**c**) *Fin & Jur* **s. de pagos** suspension of payments

suspensivo,-a *adj* **puntos suspensivos** suspension points

suspenso *nm* (**a**) *Educ* fail (**b**) **en s.** *(asunto, trabajo)* pending; **estar en s.** to be pending

suspicacia *nf* suspiciousness

suspicaz *adj* suspicious; *(desconfiado)* distrustful

suspirar *vi* to sigh

suspiro *nm* sigh

sustancia *nf* substance

sustancial *adj* (**a**) substantial (**b**) *(fundamental)* essential, fundamental

sustantivo,-a 1 *adj* substantive

2 *nm Ling* noun

sustentar *vt* (**a**) *(peso)* to support (**b**) *(familia)* to maintain, to support (**c**) *(teoría)* to support, to defend

sustento *nm* (**a**) *(alimento)* sustenance, food (**b**) *(apoyo)* support

sustitución *nf* substitution, replacement

sustituir [37] *vt* to substitute, to replace

sustituto,-a *nm,f* substitute, stand-in

susto *nm* fright, scare; **llevarse** *o* **darse un s.** to get a fright

sustraer [25] *vt* (**a**) *Mat* to subtract (**b**) *(robar)* to steal, to remove

sustrato *nm* substratum

susurrar *vt* to whisper

susurro *nm* whisper

sutil *adj* (**a**) *(diferencia, pregunta)* subtle (**b**) *(delgado)* thin, fine (**c**) *(aroma)* delicate

sutileza *nf* (**a**) *(dicho)* subtlety (**b**) *(finura)* fineness

suyo,-a *adj & pron pos (de él)* his; *(de ella)* hers; *(de usted, ustedes)* yours; *(de animal o cosa)* its; *(de ellos, ellas)* theirs; **los zapatos no son suyos** the shoes aren't hers; **varios amigos suyos** several friends of his/hers/yours/theirs; *Fam* **es muy s.** he's very aloof; *Fam* **hacer de las suyas** to be up to one's tricks; *Fam* **ir (cada uno) a lo s.** to mind one's own business; *Fam* **salirse con la suya** to get one's (own) way

svástica *nf* swastika

T

T, t [te] *nf (la letra)* T, t

t (*abr* **tonelada(s)**) t

tabacalero,-a 1 *nm,f (vendedor)* tobacco trader
2 *nf* La Tabacalera = Spanish state tobacco monopoly

tabaco *nm* (a) *(planta, hoja)* tobacco; **t. rubio** Virginia tobacco (b) *(cigarrillos)* cigarettes

tábano *nm* horsefly

tabaquismo *nm* nicotine poisoning

tabarra *nf Fam* nuisance, bore; **dar la t.** to go on and on

tabasco® *nm* Tabasco® sauce

taberna *nf* pub, bar; *(antiguamente)* tavern

tabernero,-a *nm,f* publican; *(hombre)* landlord; *(mujer)* landlady

tabique *nm* (a) *(pared)* partition (wall) (b) *Anat* **t. nasal** nasal wall

tabla *nf* (a) board; *Dep* **t. de surf** surfboard; *Dep* **t. de windsurf** sailboard (b) *(de vestido)* pleat (c) *Mat* table (d) **tablas** *(en ajedrez)* stalemate, draw; **quedar en tablas** *(juego)* to end in a draw (e) *Taurom* **tablas** fence (f) *Teatro* **las tablas** the stage; *Fig* **tener (muchas) tablas** to be an old hand

tablado *nm* (a) *(plataforma)* wooden platform (b) *Teatro* stage

tablao *nm Fam* = flamenco bar or show

tablero *nm* (a) *(tablón)* panel, board; **t. de mandos** *(de coche)* dash(board) (b) *(en juegos)* board; **t. de ajedrez** chessboard

tableta *nf (de chocolate)* bar

tablón *nm* plank; *(en construcción)* beam; **t. de anuncios** *Br* noticeboard, *US* bulletin board

tabú *adj & nm (pl* **tabúes**) taboo

tabular *vt* to tabulate

taburete *nm* stool

tacaño,-a 1 *adj* mean, stingy
2 *nm,f* miser

tacatá, tacataca *nm* baby-walker

tacha *nf (defecto)* flaw, defect; **sin t.** flawless, without blemish

tachar *vt* (a) to cross out (b) *Fig* **t. de** to accuse of

tachero *nm RP Fam (de taxi)* taxi driver

tacho *nm Am* bucket

tachón *nm (borrón)* crossing out

tachuela *nf* tack, stud

tácito,-a *adj* tacit

taciturno,-a *adj* (a) *(callado)* taciturn (b) *(triste)* sullen

taco *nm* (a) *(planta, hoja)* plug; *(de billetes)* wad; *(de bota de fútbol)* stud; *(en billar)* cue (b) *(cubo) (de jamón, queso)* cube, piece (c) *Culin (tortilla de maíz)* taco, = rolled-up tortilla pancake (d) *Fam (palabrota)* swearword (e) *Fam (lío)* mess, muddle; **armarse** *o* **hacerse un t.** to get all mixed up (f) **me gusta un t.** I like it a lot (g) *Fam* **tacos** *(años)* years

tacón *nm* heel; **zapatos de t.** high-heeled shoes

taconeo *nm (pisada)* heel-tapping; *(golpe)* stamping with the heels

táctica *nf* tactics

táctico,-a *adj* tactical

táctil *adj* tactile; **pantalla t.** touch screen

tacto *nm* (a) *(sentido)* touch (b) *Fig (delicadeza)* tact; **tener t.** to be tactful

taekwondo *nm* tae kwon do

tafetán *nm* taffeta

tahur *nm* cardsharp

tailandés,-esa 1 *adj* Thai
2 *nm,f (persona)* Thai; **los tailandeses** the Thai *o* Thais
3 *nm (idioma)* Thai

Tailandia *n* Thailand

taimado,-a *adj* sly, crafty

tajada *nf* (a) slice; *Fig* **sacar** *o* **llevarse t.** to take one's share (b) *Fam (borrachera)* drunkenness

tajante *adj* incisive

Tajo *n* **el T.** the Tagus

tal 1 *adj* (a) *(semejante)* such; *(más sustantivo singular contable)* such a; **en tales condiciones** in such conditions; **nunca dije t. cosa** I never said such a thing (b) *(indeterminado)* such and such; **t. día y a t. hora** such and such a day and at such and such a time (c) *(persona)* person called ...; **te llamó una t. Amelia** someone called Amelia phoned you (**d**) *(locuciones)* **t. vez** perhaps, maybe; **como si t. cosa** as if nothing had happened

2 *adv* (**a**) *(así)* just; **t. cual** just as it is; **t. (y) como** just as

(**b**) **¿qué t.?** how are things?; **¿qué t. ese vino?** how do you find this wine?

3 *conj* as; **con t. (de) que** (+ *subjunctive*) so long as, provided

4 *pron (cosa)* something; *(persona)* someone, somebody; **t. para cual** two of a kind; **y t. y cual** and so on

tala *nf* tree felling

taladradora *nf* drill

taladrar *vt* to drill; *(pared)* to bore through; *(papeles)* to punch

taladro *nm* (**a**) *(herramienta)* drill (**b**) *(agujero)* hole

talante *nm* (**a**) *(carácter)* disposition (**b**) *(voluntad)* **de buen t.** willingly; **de mal t.** unwillingly, reluctantly

talar *vt (árboles)* to fell, to cut down

talco *nm* talc; **polvos de t.** talcum powder

talega *nf* bag, sack

talego *nm* (**a**) long bag, long sack (**b**) *Fam (cárcel)* clink, hole (**c**) *Fam (mil pesetas)* = 1,000 peseta note

talento *nm* talent

Talgo *nm* = fast passenger train

talismán *nm* talisman, lucky charm

talla *nf* (**a**) *(de prenda)* size; **¿qué t. usas?** what size are you? (**b**) *(estatura)* height; *Fig* stature; *Fig* **dar la t.** to make the grade (**c**) *(escultura)* carving, sculpture (**d**) *(tallado)* cutting, carving

tallado *nm (de madera)* carving; *(de piedras preciosas)* cutting; *(de metales)* engraving

tallar *vt* (**a**) *(madera, piedra)* to carve, to shape; *(piedras preciosas)* to cut; *(metales)* to engrave (**b**) *(medir)* to measure the height of

tallarines *nmpl* tagliatelle

talle *nm* (**a**) *(cintura)* waist (**b**) *(cuerpo)* (de hombre) build, physique; *(de mujer)* figure, shape

taller *nm* (**a**) *(obrador)* workshop; *Aut* **t. de reparaciones** garage (**b**) *Ind* factory, mill

tallo *nm* stem, stalk

talón *nm* (**a**) *(del pie)* heel (**b**) *(cheque)* cheque

> 🖉 Observa que la palabra inglesa **talon** es un falso amigo y no es la traducción de la palabra española **talón**. En inglés, **talon** significa "garra".

talonario *nm (de cheques)* cheque book;

(de billetes) book of tickets

tamal *nm (comida)* tamale, = steamed maize dumpling with savoury or sweet filling, wrapped in maize husks or a banana leaf

tamaño,-a 1 *adj* such a big, so big a

2 *nm* size; **de gran t.** large; **del t. de** as large as, as big as

tamarindo *nm* tamarind

tambalearse *vpr (persona)* to stagger; *(mesa)* to wobble; *Fig* to teeter

tambero *nm Am (mesonero)* innkeeper, landlord

también *adv (igualmente)* too, also, as well; **tú t. puedes venir** you can come too; **¿lo harás? yo t.** are you going to do it? so am I

tambo *nm RP (granja)* dairy farm

tambor *nm* (**a**) *(Mús, de lavadora, de freno)* drum (**b**) *Anat* eardrum

Támesis *n* **el T.** the Thames

tamiz *nm* sieve

tamizar [40] *vt* to sieve

tampoco *adv* (**a**) *(en afirmativas)* nor, neither; **Juan no vendrá y María t.** Juan won't come and neither will Maria; **yo no sé – yo t.** I don't know – neither do I (**b**) *(en negativas)* either, not ... either; **la Bolsa no sube, pero t. baja** the stock market isn't going up, but it's not going down either

tampón *nm* tampon

tan *adv* (**a**) such; *(más sustantivo singular contable)* such a; **es t. listo** he's such a clever fellow; **no me gusta t. dulce** I don't like it so sweet; **¡qué gente t. agradable!** such nice people!; **¡qué vestido t. bonito!** what a beautiful dress! (**b**) *(comparativo)* **t. ... como** as ... as; **t. alto como tú** as tall as you (are) (**c**) *(consecutivo)* so ... (that); **iba t. deprisa que no lo ví** he was going so fast that I couldn't see him (**d**) **t. siquiera** at least; **t. sólo** only

tanda *nf (conjunto)* batch, lot; *(serie)* series *sing*; **por tandas** in groups

tándem *nm* tandem

tanga *nm* tanga

tangente *nf* tangent; *Fig* **salirse** *o* **escaparse por la t.** to go off at a tangent

Tánger *n* Tangier

tangible *adj* tangible

tango *nm* tango

tanguería *nf* = nightclub for tango dancing

tanguero,-a *nm,f (aficionado)* tango enthusiast

tanque *nm* tank

tantear 1 *vt* (**a**) *Fig* **t. a algn** to sound sb

out; **t. el terreno** to see how the land lies (**b**) *(calcular)* to estimate, to guess

2 *vi Dep* to (keep) score

tanteo *nm* (**a**) *(cálculo)* estimate, guess (**b**) *Dep* score

tanto,-a 1 *nm* (**a**) *(punto)* point (**b**) *(cantidad imprecisa)* so much, a certain amount; **t. por ciento** percentage (**c**) **un t.** a bit; **la casa es un t. pequeña** the house is rather *o* somewhat small (**d**) **estar al t.** *(informado)* to be informed; *(pendiente)* to be on the lookout

2 *adj* (**a**) (+ *singular*) so much; (+ *plural*) so many; **no le des t. dinero** don't give him so much money; **¡ha pasado t. tiempo!** it's been so long!; **no comas tantas manzanas** don't eat so many apples (**b**) **cincuenta y tantas personas** fifty odd people; **en el año sesenta y tantos** in nineteen sixty something (**c**) **t. como** as much as; **tantos,-as como** as many as

3 *pron* (**a**) (+ *singular*) so much; **otro t.** as much again, the same again; **no es** *o* **hay para t.** it's not that bad (**b**) (+ *plural*) so many; **otros tantos** as many again; **uno de tantos** run-of-the-mill; *Fam* **a las tantas** very late, at an unearthly hour

4 *adv* (**a**) *(cantidad)* so much; **t. mejor/ peor** so much the better/worse; **t. más cuanto que** all the more so because (**b**) *(tiempo)* so long (**c**) *(frecuencia)* so often (**d**) **t. ... como** both ... and; **t. tú como yo** both you and I; **t. si vienes como si no** whether you come or not (**e**) *(locuciones)* **por lo t.** therefore; **¡y t.!** oh yes!, and how!

tañer *vt* to play

tapa *nf* (**a**) *(cubierta)* lid; *Andes, RP (de botella)* top; *(de libro)* cover; *(de zapato)* heelplate; *Aut (de cilindro)* head (**b**) *(aperitivo)* appetizer, snack

tapadera *nf* *(tapa)* cover, lid; *Fig* cover, front

tapadillo *nm* **hacer algo de t.** to do sth secretly

tapado *nm* *CSur (abrigo)* overcoat

tapar 1 *vt* (**a**) to cover; *(botella etc)* to put the lid/top on; *(con ropas o mantas)* to wrap up (**b**) *(ocultar)* to hide; *(vista)* to block (**c**) *(encubrir)* to cover up

2 taparse *vpr (cubrirse)* to cover oneself; *(abrigarse)* to wrap up

taparrabos *nm inv* loincloth

tapete *nm* (table) cover; *Fig* **poner algo sobre el t.** to table sth

tapia *nf* garden wall

tapiar **[43]** *vt* (**a**) *(área)* to wall off (**b**) *(puerta, ventana etc)* to wall, to close up

tapicería *nf* (**a**) tapestry; *(de muebles, coche)* upholstery (**b**) *(tienda)* upholsterer's shop/workshop

tapioca *nf* tapioca

tapiz *nm* tapestry

tapizar **[40]** *vt* to upholster

tapón *nm* (**a**) *(de lavabo etc)* stopper, plug; *(de botella)* cap, cork; **t. de rosca** screw-on cap (**b**) *(de oídos)* earplug (**c**) *(en baloncesto)* block (**d**) *Aut* traffic jam (**e**) *Am (plomo)* fuse

taponar 1 *vt (tubería, hueco)* to plug (**b**) *Med (herida)* to tampon

2 taponarse *vpr* **se me han taponado los oídos** my ears are blocked up

taquería *nf* *Méx (quiosco)* taco stall; *(restaurante)* taco restaurant

taquigrafía *nf* shorthand

taquígrafo,-a *nm,f* shorthand writer

taquilla *nf* (**a**) ticket office, booking office; *Cin & Teatro* box-office; **un éxito de t.** a box-office success (**b**) *(recaudación)* takings (**c**) *(armario)* locker

taquillero,-a 1 *adj* popular; **película taquillera** box-office hit

2 *nm,f* booking *o* ticket clerk

tara *nf* (**a**) *(peso)* tare (**b**) *(defecto)* defect, fault

tarántula *nf* tarantula

tararear *vt* to hum

tardanza *nf* delay

tardar 1 *vt (llevar tiempo)* to take; **¿cuánto va a t.?** how long will it take?; **tardé dos horas en venir** it took me two hours to get here

2 *vi (demorar)* to take long; **si tarda mucho, me voy** if it takes much longer, I'm going; **no tardes** don't be long; **a más t.** at the latest

3 tardarse *vpr* **¿cuánto se tarda en llegar?** how long does it take to get there?

tarde 1 *nf* (**a**) *(hasta las cinco)* afternoon (**b**) *(después de las cinco)* evening (**c**) **la t. noche** late evening

2 *adv* (**a**) late; **siento llegar t.** sorry I'm late (**b**) *(locuciones)* **de t. en t.** very rarely, not very often; **(más) t. o (más) temprano** sooner or later

tardío,-a *adj* late, belated

tardo,-a *adj* slow

tarea *nf* job, task; **tareas** *(de ama de casa)* housework; *(de estudiante)* homework

tarifa *nf* (**a**) *(precio)* tariff, rate; *(en transportes)* fare (**b**) *(lista de precios)* price list

tarima *nf* platform, dais

tarjeta *nf* card; **t. postal** postcard; **t. de crédito** credit card; **t. de visita** *Br* visiting card, *US* calling card; *Informát* **t. perforada** punch *o* punched card

tarraconense 1 *adj* of/from Tarragona
　2 *nmf* person from Tarragona

tarro *nm* (a) *(vasija)* jar, pot, tub (b) *Fam (cabeza)* bonce (c) *Am (lata)* tin, can

tarta *nf* tart, pie

tartamudear *vi* to stutter, to stammer

tartamudo,-a 1 *adj* stuttering, stammering
　2 *nm,f* stutterer, stammerer

tartana *nf Fam (coche viejo)* banger, heap

tártaro,-a *adj* **salsa tártara** tartar sauce

tartera *nf* (a) *(fiambrera)* lunch box (b) *(cazuela)* baking tin

tarugo *nm* (a) *(de madera)* lump of wood (b) *Fam (persona)* blockhead

tarumba *adj Fam* crazy, mad; **estar t.** to be bonkers

tasa *nf* (a) *(precio)* fee; **tasas académicas** course fees (b) *(impuesto)* tax; **tasas de aeropuerto** airport tax (c) *(índice)* rate; **t. de natalidad/mortalidad** birth/death rate (d) *(valoración)* valuation, appraisal

tasación *nf* valuation

tasador,-a *nm,f* valuer

tasar *vt* (a) *(valorar)* to value; **t. una casa en 10 millones de pesetas** to value a house at 10 million pesetas (b) *(poner precio)* to set *o* fix the price of

tasca *nf Fam* bar, pub

tata 1 *nf (niñera)* nanny
　2 *nm Am Fam (papá)* dad, daddy, *US* pop

tatarabuelo,-a *nm,f* great-great-grandfather, *f* great-great-grandmother; **tatarabuelos** great-great-grandparents

tataranieto,-a *nm,f* great-great-grandson, *f* great-great-granddaughter; **tataranietos** great-great-grandchildren

tatuaje *nm* tattoo

tatuar [30] *vt* to tattoo

taurino,-a *adj* bullfighting

Tauro *nm* Taurus

tauromaquia *nf* tauromachy, (art of) bullfighting

taxativo,-a *adj* categorical

taxi *nm* taxi

taxímetro *nm* taximeter, clock

taxista *nmf* taxi driver

taza *nf* (a) *(recipiente)* cup; **una t. de café** *(recipiente)* coffee cup; *(contenido)* a cup of coffee (b) *(de retrete)* bowl

tazón *nm* bowl

te *pron pers* (a) *(complemento directo)* you; *(complemento indirecto)* (to/for) you; **no quiero verte** I don't want to see you; **te compraré uno** I'll buy one for you, I'll buy you one; **te lo dije** I told you so (b) *(reflexivo)* yourself; **lávate** wash yourself; *(sin traducción)* **bébetelo todo** drink it up; **no te vayas** don't go

té *nm (pl* **tés)** tea; **té con limón** lemon tea

tea *nf* torch

teatral *adj* (a) **grupo t.** theatre company; **obra t.** play (b) *Fig (teatrero)* theatrical

teatrero,-a *adj* theatrical

teatro *nm* (a) *theatre;* **obra de t.** play; **autor de t.** playwright (b) *Lit* drama

tebeo *nm* children's comic

techar *vt* to roof

techo *nm (de habitación)* ceiling; *(tejado)* roof; *Aut* **t. corredizo** sun roof

tecla *nf* key; *Fig* **dar en la t.** to get it right

teclado *nm* keyboard; *Informát* **t. expandido** expanded keyboard

teclear 1 *vt* to key in
　2 *vi* to drum with one's fingers

técnica *nf* (a) *(tecnología)* technology (b) *(método)* technique (c) *(habilidad)* skill

técnico,-a 1 *adj* technical
　2 *nm,f* technician, technical expert

tecnicolor® *nm* Technicolor®

tecno- *pref* techno-

tecnócrata *nmf* technocrat

tecnología *nf* technology

tecnológico,-a *adj* technological

tecolote *nm CAm, Méx (búho)* owl

tedio *nm* tedium, boredom

tedioso,-a *adj* tedious, boring

teja *nf Constr* tile; *Fam Fig* **a toca t.** on the nail

tejado *nm* roof

tejanos *nmpl* jeans

tejemaneje *nm Fam* (a) *(actividad)* bustle, fuss (b) *(maquinación)* intrigue, scheming

tejer *vt (en el telar)* to weave; *(hacer punto)* to knit; *(telaraña)* to spin; *Fig (plan)* to plot, to scheme

tejido *nm* (a) *fabric;* **t. de punto** knitted fabric (b) *Anat* tissue

tejo *nm Fam* **tirar los tejos a algn** to make a play for sb

tejón *nm* badger

tel. *(abr* **teléfono)** tel.

tela *nf* (a) *Tex* material, fabric, cloth; *(de la leche)* skin; **t. de araña** cobweb; **t. metálica** gauze (b) *Fam (dinero)* dough (c) *Arte* canvas (d) *Fig* **poner en t. de juicio** to question; *Fig* **tiene mucha t.** it's not an easy thing

telar *nm Tex* loom

telaraña *nf* cobweb, spider's web

tele *nf Fam* telly, TV

telearrastre *nm* ski lift

telebanca *nf* telephone banking, home banking

telebasura *nf Fam* junkTV

telecabina *nf* cable car

telecomunicaciones *nfpl* telecommunications

telediario *nm TV* television news bulletin

teledirigido,-a *adj* remote-controlled

telefax *nm* telefax, fax

teleférico *nm* cable car/railway

telefilme, telefilm *nm* TV film

telefonazo *nm* **dar un t. (a algn)** to give (sb) a ring

telefonear *vt & vi* to telephone, to phone

telefonía *nf* **t. móvil** mobile phones

telefónica *nf* **Compañía T.** ≃ British Telecom

telefónico,-a *adj* telephone; **llamada telefónica** telephone call

telefonista *nmf* (telephone) operator

teléfono *nm* telephone, phone; **t. portátil** portable telephone; **t. móvil** car phone; **está hablando por t.** she's on the phone; **te llamó por t.** she phoned you

telegrafiar [29] *vt* to telegraph, to wire

telegráfico,-a *adj* telegraphic; **giro t.** giro, money order

telégrafo *nm* (a) telegraph (b) **telégrafos** post office

telegrama *nm* telegram, cable

teleimpresor *nm,* **teleimpresora** *nf* teleprinter

telele *nm Fam* **darle a uno un t.** to have a fit

telemando *nm* remote control (unit)

telenovela *nf* television serial

teleobjetivo *nm* telephoto lens *sing*

telepático,-a *adj* telepathic

telescopio *nm* telescope

teleserie *nf* television series *sing*

telesilla *nm* chair lift

telespectador,-a *nm,f* TV viewer

telesquí *nm* ski lift

teletexto *nm* teletext

teletienda *nf* home shopping programme

teletipo *nm* teleprinter

teletrabajador,-a *nm,f* teleworker

teletrabajo *nm* teleworking

televidente *nmf* TV viewer

televisar *vt* to televise

televisión *nf* (a) *(sistema)* television (b) *Fam (aparato)* television set; **t. en color/en blanco y negro** colour/black-and-white television; **t. digital** digital television; **t. por cable** cable television; **ver la t.** to watch television

televisivo,-a *adj* television; **espacio t.** television programme

televisor *nm* television set

télex *nm inv* telex

telón *nm Teatro* curtain; *Pol & Hist* **t. de acero** Iron Curtain; **t. de fondo** *Teatro* backdrop; *Fig* background

telonero,-a *adj* **(grupo) t.** support band

tema *nm* (a) *(asunto)* topic, subject; *(de examen)* subject; **temas de actualidad** current affairs (b) *Mús* theme

temario *nm (de examen)* programme

temática *nf* subject matter

temático,-a *adj* thematic

temblar [1] *vi (de frío)* to shiver; *(de miedo)* to tremble (**de** with); *(voz)* to quiver; *(pulso)* to shake

tembleque *nm Fam* shaking fit

temblón,-ona *adj Fam* trembling, shaky

temblor *nm* tremor, shudder; **t. de tierra** earth tremor

tembloroso,-a, tembloso,-a *adj* shaking; *(voz)* quivering; *(de frío)* shivering; *(de miedo)* trembling; **manos temblorosas** shaky hands

temer 1 *vt* to fear, to be afraid of; **temo que esté muerto** I fear he's dead; **temo que no podrá recibirte** I'm afraid (that) he won't be able to see you

2 *vi* to be afraid

3 temerse *vpr* to fear, to be afraid; **¡me lo temía!** I was afraid this would happen!

temerario,-a *adj* reckless, rash

temeridad *nf* (a) *(actitud)* temerity, rashness (b) *(acto temerario)* reckless act

temeroso,-a *adj* (a) fearful, timid (b) *(temible)* frightful

temible *adj* fearful, frightful

temor *nm* (a) fear (b) *(recelo)* worry, apprehension

témpano *nm* ice floe

temperamental *adj* temperamental

temperamento *nm* temperament; **tener t.** to have a strong character

temperatura *nf* temperature

tempestad *nf* storm; *Fig* turmoil, uproar

tempestuoso,-a *adj* stormy, tempestuous

templado,-a *adj* (a) *(agua)* lukewarm; *(clima)* mild, temperate (b) *Mús (afinado)* tuned

templanza *nf* moderation, restraint

templar *vt* (a) to moderate (b) *(algo frío)* to warm up; *(algo caliente)* to cool down (c) *Mús (instrumento)* to tune (d) *Téc (metal)* to temper

temple *nm* (a) *(fortaleza)* boldness, courage (b) *Arte* tempera

templete *nm* bandstand

templo *nm* temple

temporada *nf* (a) season; **t. alta** high o peak season; **t. baja** low o off season (b) *(período)* period, time; **por temporadas** on and off

temporal 1 *adj* temporary, provisional
   2 *nm* storm

temporario,-a *adj Am* temporary

temporero,-a *nm,f* seasonal o temporary worker

tempranero,-a *adj* (a) *(persona)* early-rising (b) *(cosecha)* early

temprano,-a *adj & adv* early

tenacidad *nf* (a) *(perseverancia)* tenacity, perseverance (b) *(de metal)* tensile strength

tenacillas *nfpl (para pelo)* curling tongs

tenaz *adj* tenacious

tenaza *nf*, **tenazas** *nfpl (herramienta)* pliers, pincers; *(para el fuego)* tongs

tendedero *nm* clothes line, drying place

tendencia *nf* tendency

tendencioso,-a *adj* tendentious, biased

tender [3] **1** *vt* (a) *(mantel etc)* to spread out; *(para secar)* to hang out (b) *Am (cama)* to make; *(mesa)* to set, to lay (c) *(red)* to cast; *(puente)* to build; *(vía, cable)* to lay; *(trampa)* to lay, to set (d) *(mano)* to stretch o hold out (e) *(tumbar)* to lay
   2 *vi* to tend (**a** to), to have a tendency (**a** to)
   3 tenderse *vpr* to lie down, to stretch out

tenderete *nm (puesto)* market stall

tendero,-a *nm,f* shopkeeper

tendido *nm* (a) *(de vía, cable)* laying; *(de puente)* construction; **t. eléctrico** electrical installation (b) *Taurom (asientos)* = front tiers of seats

tendón *nm* tendon, sinew

tenebroso,-a *adj (sombrío)* dark, gloomy; *(siniestro)* sinister, shady

tenedor *nm* fork

teneduría *nf* **t. de libros** bookkeeping

tenencia *nf Jur* **t. ilícita de armas** illegal possession of arms

tener [24] **1** *vt* (a) to have, to have got; **tenemos un examen** we've got o we have an exam; **va a t. un niño** she's going to have a baby, she's expecting; **¡ahí (lo) tienes!** here you are!
   (b) *(poseer)* to own, to possess
   (c) *(sostener)* to hold; **tenme el bolso un momento** hold my bag a minute; **ten, es para ti** take this o here you are, it's for you
   (d) **t. calor/frío** to be hot/cold; **t. cariño**

a algn to be fond of sb; **t. miedo** to be frightened
   (e) *(edad)* to be; **tiene dieciocho (años)** he's eighteen (years old)
   (f) *Am (llevar)* **tengo tres años aquí** I've been here for three years
   (g) *(medida)* **la casa tiene 100 metros cuadrados** the house is 100 square metres
   (h) *(contener)* to hold, to contain
   (i) *(mantener)* to keep; **me tuvo despierto toda la noche** he kept me up all night
   (j) **t. por** *(considerar)* to consider, to think; **me tienen por estúpido** they think I'm a fool; **ten por seguro que lloverá** you can be sure it'll rain
   (k) **t. que** to have (got) to; **tengo que irme** I must leave; **tienes/tendrías que verlo** you must/should see it
   2 tenerse *vpr* (a) **t. en pie** to stand (up)
   (b) **t. por** *(considerarse)* to think o consider oneself; **se tiene por muy inteligente** he thinks he's very intelligent

tenga *subj pres de* **tener**

tengo *indic pres de* **tener**

teniente *nm* (a) *Mil* lieutenant (b) **t. (de) alcalde** deputy mayor

tenis *nm* tennis

tenista *nmf* tennis player

tenor[1] *nm Mús* tenor

tenor[2] *nm* **a t. de** according to

tensar *vt (cable etc)* to tighten; *(arco)* to draw

tensión *nf* (a) tension; **en t.** tense (b) *Elec* tension, voltage (c) *Med* **t. arterial** blood pressure; **t. nerviosa** nervous strain (d) *Téc* stress

tenso,-a *adj* (a) *(cuerda, cable)* tense, taut (b) *(persona)* tense; *(relaciones)* strained

tentación *nf* temptation

tentáculo *nm* tentacle

tentador,-a *adj* tempting

tentar [1] *vt* (a) *(palpar)* to feel, to touch (b) *(incitar)* to tempt

tentativa *nf* attempt; *Jur* **t. de asesinato** attempted murder

tentempié *nm Fam (pl* **tentempiés)** (a) *(comida)* snack, bite (b) *(juguete)* tumbler

tenue *adj* (a) *(luz, sonido)* subdued, faint (b) *(delgado)* thin, light

teñir [6] **1** *vt* (a) *(pelo etc)* to dye (b) *Fig* to tinge with
   2 teñirse *vpr* **t. el pelo** to dye one's hair

teocalli *nm Hist* = Mexican pyramid

teología *nf* theology

teorema *nm* theorem

teoría *nf* theory; **en t.** theoretically

teórico,-a adj theoretical
teorizar [40] vi to theorize (**sobre** on)
tepache nm = mildly alcoholic Mexican drink made from fermented pineapple peelings and unrefined sugar
tequila nm tequila
terapeuta nmf therapist
terapia nf therapy
tercer adj third; **el t. mundo** the third world
tercerización nf Am Com outsourcing
tercermundista adj third-world
tercero,-a 1 adj third

> **Tercer** is used instead of **tercero** before masculine singular nouns (e.g. **el tercer piso** the third floor).

 2 nm,f (de una serie) third; **a la tercera va la vencida** third time lucky
 3 nm (mediador) mediator; Jur third party
terceto nm Mús trio
terciar [43] 1 vi **(a)** (mediar) to mediate, to arbitrate **(b)** (participar) to take part, to participate
 2 terciarse vpr **si se tercia** should the occasion arise
terciario,-a adj tertiary
tercio nm **(a)** (parte) (one) third **(b)** (de cerveza) = medium-sized bottle of beer **(c)** Taurom stage, part (of a bullfight)
terciopelo nm velvet
terco,-a adj stubborn, obstinate
tereré nm Arg, Par (mate) = refreshing drink made from maté in cold water with lemon juice
tergiversar vt (verdad) to distort; (palabras) to twist
termal adj thermal
termas nfpl (baños) spa, hot baths o springs
térmico,-a adj thermal; **central térmica** coal- fired power station
terminación nf completion
terminal 1 adj terminal
 2 nf **(a)** (de aeropuerto) terminal; (de autobús) terminus **(b)** Elec & Informát terminal
terminante adj **(a)** (categórico) categorical, final **(b)** (dato, resultado) conclusive
terminantemente adv categorically; **t. prohibido** strictly forbidden
terminar 1 vt **(a)** (acabar) to finish, to complete; (completamente) to finish off
 2 vi **(a)** (acabarse) to finish, to end; **termina en seis** it ends with a six; **no termina de convencerse** he still isn't quite

convinced (**b**) (ir a parar) to end up (**en** in); **terminó por comprarlo** he ended up buying it (**c**) **t. con** (eliminar) to put an end to
 3 terminarse vpr **(a)** to finish, to end, to be over **(b)** (vino, dinero etc) to run out
término nm **(a)** (final) end, finish **(b)** (palabra) term, word; **en otros términos** in other words; **en términos generales** generally speaking **(c)** **t. municipal** district **(d)** **por t. medio** on average **(e)** Fig **en último t.** as a last resort
terminología nf terminology
termo nm Thermos® (flask), flask
termodinámico,-a adj thermodynamic
termómetro nm thermometer
termonuclear adj thermonuclear
termostato nm thermostat
ternera nf calf; (carne) veal
ternero nm calf
terno nm Andes, Méx (traje) three-piece suit
ternura nf tenderness
terquedad nf stubbornness, obstinacy
terracota nf terracotta
terraja adj RP Fam (persona) flashy; (cosa) tacky, kitsch
terrajada nf RP Fam tacky thing/act
terral nm Am (polvareda) dust cloud
Terranova n Newfoundland
terraplén nm embankment
terráqueo,-a adj globo t. (tierra) (the) earth; (esfera) globe
terrateniente nmf landowner
terremoto nm earthquake
terrenal adj un paraíso t. a heaven on earth
terreno nm **(a)** (tierra) (piece of) land, ground; Geol terrain; (campo) field; **ganar/perder t.** to gain/lose ground **(b)** Dep field, ground **(c)** Fig field, sphere
terrestre adj **(a)** (de la tierra) terrestrial, earthly **(b)** (por tierra) by land; **por vía t.** by land
terrible adj terrible, awful
terrícola nmf (en ciencia ficción) earthling
terrier nm terrier
territorio nm territory
terrón nm (de azúcar) lump; (de tierra) clod
terror nm terror; Cin horror
terrorífico,-a adj terrifying, frightening
terrorismo nm terrorism
terrorista adj & nmf terrorist
terroso,-a adj (color) earth-coloured
terruño nm (terreno) piece of land; (patria chica) homeland, native land
terso,-a adj smooth

tersura nf smoothness

tertulia nf get-together; **t. literaria** literary gathering

tesina nf first degree dissertation

tesis nf inv thesis; (opinión) view, theory

tesón nm tenacity, firmness

tesorero,-a nm,f treasurer

tesoro nm (a) treasure (b) (erario) exchequer; **T. Público** Treasury

test nm test

testaferro nm front man

testamentario,-a Jur 1 adj testamentary
2 nm,f executor

testamento nm (a) Jur will; **hacer** o **otorgar t.** to make o draw up one's will (b) Rel Testament

testar vi to make o draw up one's will

testarudo,-a adj stubborn, obstinate

testear vt CSur to test

testículo nm testicle

testificar [44] vt to testify

testigo 1 nmf witness; Jur **t. de cargo/descargo** witness for the prosecution/defence; Jur **t. ocular/presencial** eyewitness; Rel **Testigos de Jehová** Jehovah's Witnesses
2 nm Dep baton

testimoniar [43] vt (a) (dar testimonio) to testify to, to attest to (b) (mostrar) to show

testimonio nm Jur testimony; (prueba) evidence, proof

teta nf Fam (a) tit, boob; **niño de t.** breastfeeding baby (b) (de vaca) udder

tétanos nm tetanus

tetera nf teapot

tetero nm Col, Ven (biberón) baby's bottle

tetilla nf (a) Anat man's nipple (b) (de biberón) (rubber) teat

tetina nf (rubber) teat

tétrico,-a adj gloomy, dull

textil adj & nm textile

texto nm text; **libro de t.** textbook

textual adj textual; (exacto) literal; **en palabras textuales** literally

textura nf Tex texture; (en minerales) structure

tez nf complexion

ti pron pers you; **es para ti** it's for you; **hazlo por ti** do it for your own sake; **piensas demasiado en ti mismo** you think too much about yourself

tía nf (a) (pariente) aunt (b) Fam (mujer) girl, woman

tianguis nm inv CAm, Méx open-air market

tibieza nf tepidity; Fig lack of enthusiasm

tibio,-a adj tepid, lukewarm; Fam **ponerse t. de cerveza** to get pissed

tiburón nm shark

tic nm (pl **tiques**) tic, twitch; **t. nervioso** nervous tic o twitch

ticket nm (pl **tickets**) (billete) ticket; (recibo) receipt

tictac nm tick-tock, ticking

tiempo nm (a) time; **a t. in time; a su (debido) t.** in due course; **a un t., al mismo t.** at the same time; **al poco t.** soon afterwards; **antes de t.** (too) early o soon; **con el t.** in the course of time, with time; **con t.** in advance; **¿cuánto t.?** how long?; **¿cuánto t. hace?** how long ago?; **demasiado t.** too long; **estar a t. de** to still have time to; **hacer t.** to kill time; **¿nos da t. de llegar?** have we got (enough) time to get there?; **t. libre** free time; Fig **dar t. al t.** to let matters take their course

(b) (meteorológico) weather; **¿qué t. hace?** what's the weather like?; **hace buen/mal t.** the weather is good/bad

(c) (edad) age; **¿cuánto** o **qué t. tiene tu niño?** how old is your baby/child?

(d) Mús movement

(e) Dep half

(f) Ling tense

tienda nf (a) shop, store; **ir de tiendas** to go shopping (b) **t. (de campaña)** tent

tienta nf **a tientas** by touch; **andar a tientas** to feel one's way; **buscar (algo) a tientas** to grope (for sth)

tiento nm tact; **con t.** tactfully

tierno,-a adj (a) (blando) tender, soft (b) (reciente) fresh

tierra nf (a) (planeta) earth (b) Agr land, soil (c) (continente) land; **tocar t.** to land (d) (país) country; **t. de nadie** no-man's-land (e) (suelo) ground; Fig **echar** o **tirar por t.** to spoil (f) Elec **(toma de) t.** Br earth, US ground

tierral nm Am cloud of dust

tieso,-a adj (rígido) stiff, rigid; (erguido) upright, erect

tiesto nm flowerpot

tifoidea nf (fiebre) **t.** typhoid (fever)

tifón nm typhoon

tifus nm inv typhus (fever)

tigre nm tiger; Am jaguar

tijeras nfpl (pair of) scissors

tijereta nf (a) (insecto) earwig (b) Dep scissors

tila nf (flor) lime o linden blossom; (infusión) lime o linden blossom tea

tildar vt to call, to brand; **me tildó de ladrón** he called me a thief

tilde nf written accent

tilín *nm* (*sonido*) ting-a-ling; *Fig* **José le hace t.** she fancies José

tilma *nf Méx* woollen blanket

tilo *nm* lime tree

timar *vt* to swindle; **me han timado** they did me

timbal *nm* kettledrum

timbrar *vt* (*carta*) to stamp; (*documento*) to seal

timbre *nm* (**a**) (*de la puerta*) bell (**b**) (*sello*) stamp, seal; *Fin* fiscal *o* revenue stamp (**c**) *Mús* (*sonido*) timbre

timidez *nf* shyness, timidity

tímido,-a *adj* shy, timid; *Fig* (*mejoría*) light; (*intento*) cautious

timo *nm* swindle, fiddle; **es un t.** it's a rip-off

timón *nm* (**a**) *Náut & Av* rudder; **golpe de t.** U-turn (**b**) *Andes Aut* steering wheel

timonel *nm* helmsman

tímpano *nm Anat* eardrum

tina *nf* (**a**) (*tinaja*) pitcher (**b**) (*gran cuba*) vat (**c**) *CAm, Col, Méx* (*bañera*) bathtub

tinaja *nf* large earthenware jar

tinerfeño,-a **1** *adj* of/from Tenerife
  2 *nm,f* person from Tenerife

tinglado *nm* (**a**) (*intriga*) intrigue (**b**) (*cobertizo*) shed

tinieblas *nfpl* darkness

tino *nm* (**a**) (*puntería*) (good) aim; **tener buen t.** to be a good shot (**b**) (*tacto*) (common) sense, good judgement

tinta *nf* (**a**) ink; **t. china** Indian ink; **t. simpática** invisible ink (**b**) *Fig* **medias tintas** ambiguities, half measures

tintar *vt* to dye

tinte *nm* (**a**) dye (**b**) *Fig* (*matiz*) shade, overtone

tintero *nm* inkpot, inkwell; *Fig* **se quedó en el t.** it wasn't said

tintinear *vi* (*vidrio*) to clink; (*campana*) to jingle, to tinkle

tintineo *nm* (*de vidrio*) clinking; (*de campana*) jingling

tinto,-a **1** *adj* (*vino*) red
  2 *nm* (**a**) (*vino*) red wine (**b**) *Col, Ven* (*café*) black coffee

tintorería *nf* dry-cleaner's

tintura *nf* (**a**) (*colorante*) dye (**b**) *Quím* tincture; **t. de yodo** iodine

tío *nm* (**a**) (*pariente*) uncle; **mis tíos** my uncle and aunt (**b**) *Fam* guy, *Br* bloke

tiovivo *nm* roundabout, merry-go-round

tipazo *nm Fam* good figure

tipear *vt & vi Am* to type

típico,-a *adj* (**a**) typical; **eso es t. de Antonio** that's just like Antonio (**b**) (*baile, traje*) traditional

tipificar [**44**] *vt* (**a**) (*normalizar*) to standardize (**b**) (*caracterizar*) to typify

tipismo *nm* local colour

tipo *nm* (**a**) (*clase*) type, kind (**b**) *Fam* (*persona*) guy, *Br* bloke; **t. raro** weirdo (**c**) *Anat* (*de hombre*) build, physique; (*de mujer*) figure; *Fig* **jugarse el t.** to risk one's neck; **aguantar el t.** to keep one's cool *o* head (**d**) *Fin* rate; **t. bancario** *o* **de descuento** bank rate; **t. de cambio/interés** rate of exchange/interest (**e**) **el político t. de la izquierda** the typical left-wing politician

tipografía *nf* typography

tipográfico,-a *adj* typographic; **error t.** printing error

tipógrafo,-a *nm,f* typographer

tiquismiquis *Fam* **1** *nmf inv* fusspot
  2 *nmpl* (**a**) (*escrúpulos*) silly scruples (**b**) (*rencillas*) bickering

tira *nf* (**a**) (*banda, cinta*) strip (**b**) (*de dibujos*) comic strip (**c**) *Fam* **la t. de gente** a lot *o* loads of people (**d**) *Méx Fam* **la t.** (*la policía*) the cops (**e**) **t. y afloja** tug of war

tirabuzón *nm* ringlet

tirachinas *nm inv Br* catapult, *US* slingshot

tirada *nf* (**a**) (*lanzamiento*) throw (**b**) (*impresión*) print run

tirado,-a *adj Fam* (**a**) (*precio*) dirt-cheap (**b**) (*examen*) dead easy (**c**) *Fam* **dejar t.** (**a** algn) to let (sb) down

tirador *nm* (**a**) (*persona*) marksman (**b**) (*pomo*) knob, handle; (*cordón*) bell pull (**c**) (*tirachinas*) *Br* catapult, *US* slingshot

tiraje *nm Am* print run

tiralíneas *nm inv* tracer, drawing *o* ruling pen

tiranía *nf* tyranny

tiránico,-a *adj* tyrannical

tiranizar [**40**] *vt* to tyrannize

tirano,-a *nm,f* tyrant

tirante **1** *adj* (*cable etc*) tight, taut; (*situación, relación*) tense
  2 *nm* (**a**) (*de vestido etc*) strap; **tirantes** *Br* braces, *US* suspenders (**b**) *Téc* brace, stay

tirar **1** *vt* (**a**) (*echar*) to throw
  (**b**) (*dejar caer*) to drop
  (**c**) (*desechar*) to throw away; *Fig* (*dinero*) to squander
  (**d**) (*derribar*) to knock down; **t. la puerta (abajo)** to smash the door in
  (**e**) (*foto*) to take
  (**f**) *Impr* to print
  (**g**) (*beso*) to blow
  2 *vi* (**a**) **t. de** (*cuerda, puerta*) to pull

(**b**) *(chimenea, estufa)* to draw
(**c**) *(funcionar)* to work, to run
(**d**) **ir tirando** to get by
(**e**) **t. a** to tend towards; **tira a rojo** it's reddish
(**f**) **tira a la izquierda** turn left; **¡venga, tira ya!** come on, get going!
(**g**) *(disparar)* to shoot, to fire; *Ftb* **t. a puerta** to shoot at goal
3 tirarse *vpr* (**a**) *(lanzarse)* to throw o hurl oneself; **t. de cabeza al agua** to dive into the water
(**b**) *(tumbarse)* to lie down
(**c**) *Fam (tiempo)* to spend; **me tiré una hora esperando** I waited (for) a good hour
(**d**) *Vulg* **t. a algn** to lay sb

tirita® *nf* Elastoplast®, Band-aid®, plaster

tiritar *vi* to shiver, to shake

tiro *nm* (**a**) *(lanzamiento)* throw (**b**) *(disparo, ruido)* shot; *Ftb* **t. a gol** shot at goal; **t. al blanco** target shooting; **t. al plato** clay pigeon shooting; **t. con arco** archery (**c**) *(de vestido)* shoulder width (**d**) *(de chimenea)* draught; **animal de t.** draught animal

tirón *nm* pull, tug; *(del bolso)* snatch; *Fam* **de un t.** in one go

tirotear *vt* to shoot at, to snipe at

tiroteo *nm* shooting, firing to and fro

tirria *nf Fam* dislike; **le tengo t.** I dislike him, I can't stand him

tísico,-a *adj* tubercular, consumptive

tisis *nf inv* tuberculosis, consumption

tisú *nm* tissue, paper hankie

títere *nm (marioneta)* puppet; **no dejar t. con cabeza** to spare no one

titilar *vi (luz)* to flicker; *(estrella)* to twinkle

titiritero,-a *nm,f* (**a**) puppeteer (**b**) *(acróbata)* travelling acrobat

titubeante *adj (indeciso)* hesitant; *(al hablar)* stammering

titubear *vi* (**a**) *(dudar)* to hesitate, to waver (**b**) *(al hablar)* to stammer

titubeo *nm* (**a**) *(duda)* hesitation (**b**) *(al hablar)* stammering

titulación *nf* qualifications

titulado,-a *adj (licenciado)* graduate; *(diplomado)* qualified

titular¹ 1 *nmf (persona)* holder
2 *nm Prensa* headline
3 *adj* appointed, official

titular² 1 *vt (poner título)* to call
2 titularse *vpr* (**a**) *(película etc)* to be called; **¿cómo se titula?** what is it called?
(**b**) *Educ* to graduate (**en** in)

titularidad *nf Educ* tenure

titulitis 1 *nf* obsession with qualifications
2 *nm Fam* certificate

título *nm* (**a**) title (**b**) *Educ* degree; *(diploma)* diploma (**c**) *Prensa (titular)* headline (**d**) **a t. de ejemplo** by way of example

tiza *nf* chalk; **una t.** a piece of chalk

tiznada *nf Am* **hijo de la t.** son of a bitch

tiznar *vt* to blacken (with soot)

tizne *nm* soot

tizón *nm* half-burnt stick, brand

tlapalería *nf Méx* ironmonger's (shop)

toalla *nf* towel; **tirar la t.** to throw in the towel

toallero *nm* towel *Br* rail o *US* bar

tobera *nf* nozzle

tobillo *nm* ankle

tobogán *nm* slide, chute

toca *nf (sombrero)* headdress; *(de monja)* wimple

tocadiscos *nm inv* record player; **t. digital** o **compacto** CD player

tocado¹ *nm* (**a**) *(peinado)* coiffure, hairdo (**b**) *(prenda)* headdress

tocado²,-a *adj Fam* crazy, touched

tocador *nm* (**a**) *(mueble)* dressing table (**b**) *(habitación)* dressing room; **t. de señoras** powder room

tocante a *loc adv* **en lo t. a ...** with reference to ...

tocar [44] 1 *vt* (**a**) to touch; *Fam Fig* **toca madera** touch wood (**b**) *(instrumento, canción)* to play; *(timbre, campana)* to ring; *(bocina)* to blow (**c**) *(tema, asunto)* to touch on (**d**) *(afectar)* to concern; **por lo que a mí me toca** as far as I am concerned
2 *vi* (**a**) **¿a quién le toca?** *(en juegos)* whose turn is it? (**b**) **me tocó el gordo** *(en rifa)* I won the jackpot (**c**) **t. con** to be next to; *Fig* **t. a su fin** to be coming to an end (**d**) *(llamar)* **t. a la puerta** to knock on the door
3 tocarse *vpr (una cosa con otra)* to touch each other; **¿os tocáis algo?** *(ser parientes)* are you related?

tocarse *vpr (cubrirse)* to cover one's head

tocata 1 *nf Mús* toccata
2 *nm Fam* record player

tocateja: • a tocateja *loc adv* **pagar a t.** to pay on the nail

tocayo,-a *nm,f* namesake

tocho *nm Fam (libro grande)* tome

tocino *nm* lard; **t. ahumado** smoked bacon; **t. de cielo** = sweet made with egg yolk

tocólogo,-a *nm,f* obstetrician

tocuyo *nm Am* coarse cotton cloth

todavía *adv* (a) *(aún)* still; *(en negativas)* yet; **t. la quiere** he still loves her; **t. no** not yet; **no mires t.** don't look yet (b) *(para reforzar)* even, still; **t. más/menos** even more/less

todo,-a 1 *adj* (a) all; **t. el pan** all the bread; **t. el mundo** (absolutely) everybody; **t. el día** all day, the whole *o* entire day; *Fam* **t. quisqui** every Tom, Dick and Harry

(b) *(cada)* every; **t. ciudadano de más de dieciocho años** every citizen over eighteen years of age

(c) *(entero)* complete, thorough; **es toda una mujer** she is every inch a woman

(d) *(todos,-as* all; *(con expresiones de tiempo)* every; **todos los niños** all the children; **todos los martes** every Tuesday

2 *nm (totalidad)* whole

3 *pron* (a) *(sin excluir nada)* all, everything; **ante t.** first of all; **con t.** in spite of everything; **del t.** completely; **después de t.** after all; **eso es t.** that's all, that's it; **estar en t.** to be really with it; **hay de t.** there are all sorts; **lo sé t.** I know all about it; **t. lo contrario** quite the contrary *o* opposite; **t. lo más** at the most

(b) *(cualquiera)* anybody; **t. aquél** *o* **el que quiera** anybody who wants (to)

(c) *(cada uno)* **todos aprobamos** we all passed; **todos fueron** they all went

4 *adv* completely, totally; **volvió t. sucio** he was all dirty when he got back

todopoderoso,-a *adj* all-powerful, almighty

todoterreno *nm* all-terrain vehicle

toga *nf* (a) gown, robe (b) *Hist* toga

Tokio *n* Tokyo

toldo *nm* (a) *(cubierta)* awning (b) *Am (cabaña)* tent, teepee

tolerancia *nf* tolerance

tolerante *adj* tolerant

tolerar *vt* to tolerate; *(situación)* to stand; *(gente)* to put up with

toma *nf* (a) *(acción)* taking; *Elec* **t. de corriente** plug, socket (b) *Med* dose (c) *Mil* capture (d) *Cin* take, shot (e) **t. de posesión** swearing in (f) *Fam Fig* **t. y daca** give and take

tomado,-a *adj* (a) *(voz)* hoarse (b) *Am (borracho)* drunk (c) **tenerla tomada con algn** to have it in for sb

tomadura *nf Fam* **t. de pelo** leg-pull; *(timo)* rip-off

tomar 1 *vt* (a) *(coger)* to take; *(autobús, tren)* to catch; *(decisión)* to make, to take; **toma** here (you are); **t. el sol** to sunbathe; *Av* **t. tierra** to land; *Fam* **tomarla con algn**

to have it in for sb (b) *(comer, beber)* to have (c) **t. algo a mal** to take sth badly; **t. en serio/broma** to take seriously/as a joke (d) *(confundir)* to take (por for) (e) *Mil* to take

2 *vi Am (beber alcohol)* to drink

3 **tomarse** *vpr* (a) *(comer)* to eat; *(beber)* to drink (b) *Fam* **no te lo tomes así** don't take it like that

tomate *nm* tomato; **salsa de t.** *(de lata)* tomato sauce; *(de botella)* ketchup

tomavistas *nm inv cine o* movie camera

tómbola *nf* tombola

tomillo *nm* thyme

tomo *nm* volume; *Fam* **de t. y lomo** utter, out-and-out

ton *nm* **sin t. ni son** without rhyme *o* reason

tonada *nf* (a) *Mús* tune, song (b) *Am (acento)* accent

tonalidad *nf* tonality

tonel *nm* barrel, cask

tonelada *nf* ton; **t. métrica** tonne

tonelaje *nm* tonnage

tonelero,-a *nm,f* cooper

tongo *nm* fix

tónico,-a 1 *nm Med* tonic; *(cosmético)* skin tonic

2 *nf tónica* (a) *(tendencia)* tendency, trend; **tónica general** overall trend (b) *(bebida)* tonic (water) (c) *Mús* tonic

3 *adj* (a) *Ling* tonic, stressed (b) *Mús & Med* tonic

tonificante *adj* invigorating

tonificar [44] *vt* to tone up, to invigorate

tono *nm* tone; **a t. con** in tune *o* harmony with; **subir de t.** *o* **el t.** to speak louder; **un t. alto/bajo** a high/low pitch; *Fig* **darse t.** to put on airs; *Fig* **fuera de t.** inappropriate, out of place; **dar el t.** to set the tone

tontear *vi* (a) to act the clown, to fool about (b) *(galantear)* to flirt

tontería *nf* (a) stupidity, silliness (b) *(dicho, hecho)* silly *o* stupid thing (c) *(insignificancia)* trifle

tonto,-a 1 *adj* silly, dumb

2 *nm,f* fool, idiot; **t. de remate** *o* **de capirote** prize idiot

topacio *nm* topaz

topadora *nf RP* bulldozer

toparse *vpr* **t. con** to bump into; *(dificultades)* to run up against, to encounter; **t. con algo** to come across sth

tope 1 *nm* (a) *(límite)* limit, end; *Fam* **a t.** *(al máximo)* flat out; *Fig* **estar hasta los topes** to be full up; **fecha t.** deadline (b) *Téc* stop, check (c) *Ferroc* buffer

2 *adv Fam* incredibly; **t. difícil** really difficult

tópico,-a 1 *nm* cliché
2 *adj Med & Farm* for external use

> 🖉 Observa que la palabra inglesa **topic** es un falso amigo y no es la traducción de la palabra española **tópico**. En inglés, **topic** significa "tema".

topo *nm* mole
topografía *nf* topography
topónimo *nm* place name
toque *nm* (a) *(de viento)* touch; *Fam* **dar un t. a algn** *(avisar)* to let sb know; *(advertir)* to warn sb (b) *(de campanas)* peal; *Fig* warning; **t. de queda** curfew
toquetear *vt* to fiddle with, to finger
toquilla *nf* (knitted) shawl
tórax *nm* thorax
torbellino *nm* (a) *(de viento)* whirlwind (b) *Fig (confusión)* whirl, turmoil
torcedura *nf (acción)* twist, twisting; *Med* sprain
torcer [41] **1** *vt* (a) *(metal)* to bend; *(cuerda, hilo)* to twist; *Med* to sprain; *Fig (esquina)* to turn (b) *(inclinar)* to slant
2 *vi* to turn (left o right)
3 torcerse *vpr* (a) *(doblarse)* to twist, to bend (b) *Med* **se me torció el tobillo** I sprained my ankle (c) *(plan)* to fall through (d) *(desviarse)* to go off to the side
torcido,-a *adj* twisted; *(ladeado)* slanted, lopsided; *(corbata)* crooked
tordo,-a 1 *adj* dapple-grey
2 *nm Orn* thrush
torear 1 *vt/vi* to fight; *Fam* **t. a algn** to tease o confuse sb; *Fam* **t. un asunto** to tackle a matter skilfully
2 *vi* to fight
toreo *nm* bullfighting
torero,-a *nm,f* bullfighter
tormenta *nf* storm
tormento *nm (tortura)* torture; *(padecimiento)* torment
tormentoso,-a *adj* stormy
tornado *nm* tornado
tornar *Fml* **1** *vt (convertir)* to transform, to turn (**en** into)
2 *vi (regresar)* to return, to go back; **t. en sí** to regain consciousness
3 tornarse *vpr* to become, to turn
tornasolado,-a *adj* iridescent
torneo *nm* (a) *Dep* tournament (b) *Hist* tourney, joust
tornillo *nm* screw
torniquete *nm* (a) turnstile (b) *Med* tourniquet
torno *nm* (a) *Téc* lathe; *(de alfarero)* wheel (b) **en t. a** *(alrededor de)* around; *(acerca de)* about

toro *nm* bull; **¿te gustan los toros?** do you like bullfighting?
toronja *nf* grapefruit
torpe *adj* (a) *(sin habilidad)* clumsy (b) *(tonto)* dim, thick (c) *(movimiento)* slow, awkward
torpedear *vt* to torpedo
torpedo *nm* torpedo
torpeza *nf* (a) *(física)* clumsiness; *(mental)* dimness, stupidity (b) *(lentitud)* slowness, heaviness (c) *(error)* blunder
torre *nf* (a) tower (b) *Mil & Náut* turret (c) *(en ajedrez)* rook, castle
torrefacto,-a *adj* roasted; **café t.** high roast coffee
torrencial *adj* torrential
torrente *nm* (a) *(de agua)* torrent (b) *Fig* **t. de voz** strong o powerful voice
torrezno *nm* = rasher of fried bacon
tórrido,-a *adj* torrid
torrija *nf* French toast
torsión *nf* (a) *(torcedura)* twist, twisting (b) *Téc* torsion
torso *nm* (a) *Anat* torso (b) *Arte* bust
torta *nf* (a) *Culin* cake (b) *Fam (golpe)* slap, punch
tortazo *nm Fam* (a) *(bofetada)* slap, punch (b) *(golpe)* whack, thump
tortícolis *nf inv* crick in the neck
tortilla *nf* (a) *(egg)* omelette; **t. francesa/española** (plain)/potato omelette (b) *Am* tortilla
tortillera *nf muy Fam* dyke, lesbian
tórtola *nf* dove
tortuga *nf (de tierra)* tortoise, *US* turtle; *(de mar)* turtle
tortuoso,-a *adj* tortuous
tortura *nf* torture
torturar *vt* to torture
tos *nf* cough; **t. ferina** whooping cough
tosco,-a *adj (basto)* rustic, rough; *(persona)* uncouth
toser *vi* to cough
tosquedad *nf* roughness
tostada *nf* (slice of) toast
tostado,-a *adj* (a) *(pan)* toasted (b) *(moreno)* tanned, brown
tostador *nm* toaster
tostar [2] *vt (pan)* to toast; *(café)* to roast; *(carne, pescado)* to brown; *Fig (la piel)* to tan
tostón *nm* (a) *Culin (pan frito)* crouton (b) *Fam (tabarra)* bore, drag
total 1 *adj (completo)* total
2 *nm* (a) *(todo)* whole; **en t.** in all (b) *Mat* total

3 *adv* so, in short; **¿t. para qué?** what's the point anyhow?; *Fam* **t. que ... so ...; t., tampoco te hará caso** he won't listen to you anyway

totalidad *nf* whole, totality; **la t. de** all of; **en su t.** as a whole

totalitario,-a *adj* totalitarian

totalizar [40] **1** *vt* to total

2 *vi* to amount to

tóxico,-a 1 *adj* toxic, poisonous

2 *nm* poison

toxicología *nf* toxicology

toxicólogo,-a *nm,f* toxicologist

toxicomanía *nf* drug addiction

toxicómano,-a *Med* **1** *adj* addicted to drugs

2 *nm,f* drug addict

tozudo,-a *adj* obstinate, stubborn

traba *nf* (**a**) *(de rueda)* chock; *(enlace)* bond, tie (**b**) *Fig (obstáculo)* hindrance, obstacle

trabajador,-a 1 *nm,f* worker, labourer

2 *adj* hard-working

trabajar 1 *vi* to work; **trabaja mucho** he works hard; **t. de camarera** to work as a waitress

2 *vt* (**a**) to work (on); *(la tierra)* to till (**b**) *(asignatura etc)* to work on (**c**) *Fam (convencer)* to (try to) persuade

trabajo *nm* (**a**) *(ocupación)* work; **t. a destajo** piecework; **t. eventual** casual labour; **trabajos manuales** arts and crafts (**b**) *(empleo)* employment, job (**c**) *(tarea)* task, job (**d**) *Educ (redacción)* report, paper (**e**) *(esfuerzo)* effort; **cuesta t. creerlo** it's hard to believe

trabajoadicto,-a *nm,f* workaholic

trabajoso,-a *adj (laborioso)* hard, laborious; *(difícil)* difficult

trabalenguas *nm inv* tongue twister

trabar 1 *vt* (**a**) *(sujetar)* to lock, to fasten; *(un plan)* to obstruct (**b**) *(conversación, amistad)* to start, to strike up (**c**) *Culin* to thicken

2 trabarse *vpr* (**a**) *(cuerdas)* to get tangled up (**b**) *Fig* **se le trabó la lengua** he got tongue-tied

trabazón *nf (de ideas)* link

trabilla *nf (de pantalón)* belt loop

trabuco *nm* blunderbuss

tracción *nf* traction; *Aut* **t. delantera/ trasera** front-/rear-wheel drive; *Aut* **t. en las cuatro ruedas** four-wheel drive

tractor *nm* tractor

tradición *nf* tradition

tradicional *adj* traditional

traducción *nf* translation; **t. directa/inversa** translation from/into a foreign language

traducir [10] **1** *vt* to translate (**a** into)

2 traducirse *vpr Fig* to result (**en** in)

traductor,-a *nm,f* translator

traer [25] **1** *vt* (**a**) to bring; **trae** give it to me (**b**) *(llevar puesto)* to wear (**c**) *(llevar consigo)* to carry (**d**) *(problemas)* to cause; **traerá como consecuencia ...** it will result in ...

2 traerse *vpr (llevar consigo)* to bring along; *Fig* **¿qué se trae entre manos?** what is he up to?

traficante *nmf (de drogas etc)* trafficker, pusher

traficar [44] *vi (ilegalmente)* to traffic (**con** in)

tráfico *nm* (**a**) *Aut* traffic; **t. rodado** road traffic (**b**) *Com* traffic, trade; **t. de drogas** drug traffic

tragaluz *nm* skylight

tragaperras *nf inv* **(máquina) t.** slot machine

tragar [42] **1** *vt* (**a**) *(ingerir)* to swallow (**b**) *Fam (engullir)* to gobble up, to tuck away (**c**) *Fig (a una persona)* to stand, to stomach (**d**) *Fig (creer)* to believe, to swallow

2 tragarse *vpr* (**a**) *(ingerir)* to swallow (**b**) *Fig (creer)* to believe, to swallow

tragedia *nf* tragedy

trágico,-a *adj* tragic

trago *nm* (**a**) *(bebida)* swig; **de un t.** in one go (**b**) *Fig* **pasar un mal t.** to have a bad time of it

tragón,-ona *nm,f* glutton, big eater

traición *nf* treason, betrayal; **a t.** treacherously; **alta t.** high treason

traicionar *vt* to betray; *(delatar)* to give away, to betray

traicionero,-a *adj* treacherous

traidor,-a 1 *adj* treacherous

2 *nm,f* traitor

traigo *indic pres de* **traer**

tráiler *nm (pl tráilers)* (**a**) *Cin* trailer, *US* preview (**b**) *Aut Br* articulated lorry, *US* semitrailer (**c**) *Méx (casa rodante) Br* caravan, *US* trailer

traje¹ *nm* (**a**) *(de hombre)* suit; **t. de baño** bathing suit *o* costume, swimsuit; **t. de paisano** civilian clothes; **t. de luces** bullfighter's costume (**b**) *(de mujer)* dress; **t. de chaqueta** two-piece suit; **t. de novia** wedding dress

traje² *pt indef de* **traer**

trajeado,-a *adj Fam* sharp, dapper

trajearse *vpr* to dress up

trajín *nm Fam* comings and goings, hustle and bustle

trajinar *vi* to run *o* bustle about

trama nf (a) Tex weft, woof (b) Lit plot

tramar vt to plot, to cook up; **¿qué tramas?** what are you up to?

tramitar vt (a) (gestionar) to take the necessary (legal) steps to obtain (b) Fml (despachar) to convey, to transmit (c) Com, Jur & Fin to carry out, to process

trámite nm (paso) step; (formalidad) formality; Com, Jur & Fin procedures, proceedings

tramo nm (de carretera) section, stretch; (de escalera) flight

tramoya nf (maquinaria) stage machinery; (trama) plot, scheme

trampa nf (a) (de caza) trap, snare (b) (puerta) trapdoor (c) (engaño) fiddle; **hacer trampa(s)** to cheat (d) (truco) trick

> 🖉 Observa que la palabra inglesa **tramp** es un falso amigo y no es la traducción de la palabra española **trampa**. En inglés, **tramp** significa "vagabundo".

trampilla nf trapdoor, hatch

trampolín nm (a) (de piscina) diving board (b) (de esquí) ski jump

> 🖉 Observa que la palabra inglesa **trampoline** es un falso amigo y no es la traducción de la palabra española **trampolín**. En inglés, **trampoline** significa "cama elástica".

tramposo,-a 1 adj deceitful

2 nm,f cheat; Naipes cardsharp

tranca nf (a) (garrote) cudgel; Fam **a trancas y barrancas** with great difficulty (b) (en puerta, ventana) bar

trancar 1 vt (asegurar) (con cerrojo) to bolt; (con tranca) to bar

2 trancarse vpr Am (atorarse) to get stuck; **la llave se trancó en la cerradura** the key got stuck in the lock

trance nm (a) (coyuntura) (critical) moment; **estar en t. de ...** to be on the point of ... (b) (éxtasis) trance

tranquilidad nf calmness, tranquillity; **con t.** calmly; **pídemelo con toda t.** don't hesitate to ask me

tranquilizante nm tranquillizer

tranquilizar [40] 1 vt to calm down; **lo dijo para tranquilizarme** he said it to reassure me

2 tranquilizarse vpr (calmarse) to calm down

tranquillo nm Fig knack; **coger el t. a algo** to get the knack of sth

tranquilo,-a adj (a) (persona, lugar) calm; (agua) still; (conciencia) clear; Fam **tú t.** don't you worry (b) (despreocupado) placid, easy-going

transacción nf transaction, deal

transar vi Am Fam (a) (transigir) to compromise, to give in (b) (negociar) to negotiate

transatlántico,-a 1 adj transatlantic

2 nm Náut (ocean) liner

transbordador nm (car) ferry; **t. espacial** space shuttle

transbordar 1 vt to transfer; Náut (mercancías) to tranship

2 vi Ferroc to change trains, US to transfer

transbordo nm (a) Ferroc change, US transfer; **hacer t.** to change, US to transfer (b) Náut transhipment

transcurrir vi (a) (tiempo) to pass, to go by (b) (acontecer) to take place

transcurso nm course o passing (of time); **en el t. de** in the course of, during

transeúnte nmf (a) (peatón) passer-by (b) (residente temporal) temporary resident

transferencia nf transference; Fin transfer; **t. bancaria** banker's order

transferible adj transferable

transferir [5] vt to transfer; Informát to download

transformación nf transformation

transformador nm Elec transformer

transformar 1 vt to transform, to change

2 transformarse vpr to change, to turn (en into); (algo plegable) to convert

tránsfuga nmf (a) Mil deserter (b) Pol turncoat

transfusión nf transfusion

transgénico,-a 1 adj transgenic

2 nmpl transgénicos GM foods

transgredir vt defect to transgress, to break

transgresor,-a nm,f transgressor, lawbreaker

transición nf transition

transido,-a adj Fml **t. de angustia** overcome by anxiety; **t. de dolor** racked with pain

transigente adj tolerant

transigir [57] vi to compromise

transistor nm transistor

transitable adj passable

transitado,-a adj (carretera) busy

transitar vi to pass

transitivo,-a adj transitive

tránsito nm (a) Aut traffic (b) (movimiento) movement, passage; **pasajeros en t.** passengers in transit

transitorio,-a adj transitory

translucirse [35] vpr = traslucirse

transmisión nf (a) transmission (b) Téc

drive; **t. delantera/trasera** front-/rear-wheel drive (**c**) *Rad & TV* transmission, broadcast

transmisor *nm* transmitter

transmitir *vt* (**a**) to transmit, to pass on (**b**) *Rad & TV* to transmit, to broadcast (**c**) *Jur* to transfer, to hand down

transparencia *nf* (**a**) transparency; *Pol* openness (**b**) *Fot* slide

transparentarse *vpr* to be transparent; **esta tela se transparenta** this is see-through material; **se le transparentaban las bragas** you could see her panties

transparente 1 *adj* transparent; *Pol* open **2** *nm* (**a**) *(visillo)* net curtain (**b**) *(pantalla)* shade, blind

transpiración *nf* perspiration

transpirar *vi* to perspire

transplante *nm* transplant; *Med* **t. de corazón/córnea** heart/eye transplant

transponer [**19**] **1** *vt (mudar de sitio)* to transpose, to move about

2 transponerse *vpr (desmayarse)* to faint

transportar *vt* to transport; *(pasajeros)* to carry; *(mercancías)* to ship

transporte *nm* (**a**) transport (**b**) *Com* freight; **t. de mercancías** freight transport; **t. marítimo** shipment

transportista *nmf* carrier

transvase *nm* (**a**) *(de líquidos)* decanting (**b**) *(de ríos)* transfer

transversal *adj* transverse, cross

tranvía *nm Br* tram, tramcar, *US* streetcar

trapecio *nm* trapeze

trapecista *nmf* trapeze artist

trapero,-a 1 *nm Br* rag-and-bone man, *US* junkman

2 *adj* **puñalada trapera** stab in the back

trapichear *vi* to be up to something

trapicheo *nm* jiggery-pokery

trapo *nm* (**a**) *(viejo, roto)* rag (**b**) *(bayeta)* cloth; **t. de cocina** dishcloth; **t. del polvo** duster; *Fam* **poner (a algn) como un t. (sucio)** to tear (sb) apart

tráquea *nf* trachea, windpipe

traqueteo *nm* rattle, clatter

tras *prep* (**a**) *(después de)* after; **uno t. otro** one after the other (**b**) *(detrás)* behind; **sentados uno t. otro** sitting one behind the other (**c**) **andar/ir t.** to be after; **la policía iba t. ella** the police were after her

trasatlántico,-a *adj & nm* = transatlántico,-a

trasbordador *nm* = transbordador

trasbordar *vt & vi* = transbordar

trasbordo *nm* = transbordo

trascendencia *nf* (**a**) *(importancia)* importance, significance (**b**) *(en filosofía)* transcendence

trascendental, trascendente *adj* (**a**) significant, far-reaching (**b**) *(en filosofía)* transcendental

trascender [**3**] *vi* (**a**) *(noticia)* to become known, to leak out (**b**) *(tener consecuencias)* to have far-reaching consequences (**c**) **t. de** to go beyond

trascurrir *vi* = transcurrir

trascurso *nm* = transcurso

trasero,-a 1 *adj* back, rear; **en la parte trasera** at the back

2 *nm Euf* backside

trasferencia *nf* = transferencia

trasferible *adj* = transferible

trasferir [**5**] *vt* = transferir

trasfondo *nm* background

trasformación *nf* = transformación

trasformador *nm* = transformador

trasformar *vt* = transformar

trásfuga *nmf* = tránsfuga

trasfusión *nf* = transfusión

trasgredir *vt* = transgredir

trasgresor,-a *nm,f* = transgresor,-a

trashumancia *nf* = seasonal movement of livestock

trasiego *nm* comings and goings, hustle and bustle

trasladar 1 *vt (cosa)* to move; *(persona)* to move, to transfer

2 trasladarse *vpr* to go, to move

traslado *nm (de casa)* move, removal; *(de personal)* transfer; *Educ* **t. de expediente** transfer of student record

traslucirse [**35**] *vpr* to show (through)

trasluz *nm* **mirar algo al t.** to hold sth against the light

trasmano *nm* **a t.** out of reach; **(me) coge a t.** it's out of my way

trasmisión *nf* = transmisión

trasmisor *nm* = transmisor

trasmitir *vt* = transmitir

trasnochado,-a *adj (desfasado)* old, hackneyed

trasnochador,-a 1 *adj* given to staying up late

2 *nm,f* night bird, nighthawk

trasnochar *vi* to stay up (very) late

traspapelarse *vpr* to get mislaid o misplaced

trasparencia *nf* = transparencia

trasparentarse *vpr* = transparentarse

trasparente *adj & nm* = transparente

traspasar *vt* (**a**) *(atravesar)* to go through; *(río)* to cross (**b**) *(negocio, local)* to transfer; **se traspasa** *(en letrero)* for sale (**c**) *Fig (exceder)* to exceed, to go beyond

> *♪* Observa que el verbo inglés **to trespass** es un falso amigo y no es la traducción del verbo español **traspasar**. En inglés, **to trespass** significa "entrar sin autorización".

traspaso *nm* (**a**) *(de propiedad etc)* transfer (**b**) *Com (venta)* sale

traspié *nm (pl* **traspiés)** stumble, trip; **dar un t.** to trip; *Fig* to slip up

traspiración *nf* = **transpiración**

traspirar *vi* = **transpirar**

trasplante *nm* = **transplante**

trasponer [19] *vt* = **transponer**

trasportar *vt* = **transportar**

trasporte *nm* = **transporte**

traspuesto,-a *adj* **quedarse t.** to faint

trasquilar *vt (oveja)* to shear; *(pelo)* to crop

trastabillar *vi (tambalearse)* to stagger, to totter

trastada *nf Fam* **hacer trastadas** to be up to mischief

trastazo *nm Fam* wallop, thump

traste¹ *nm Mús* fret

traste² *nm* (**a**) *(trasto)* piece of junk (**b**) *Andes, CAm, Carib, Méx* **trastes** dirty dishes; **fregar los trastes** to wash the dishes, *US* to do the washing-up (**c**) *CSur Fam (trasero)* bottom (**d**) *Fig* **dar al t. con un plan** to spoil a plan; **irse al t.** to fall through

trastear *vi (revolver)* to rummage about

trastero *nm (cuarto)* **t.** junk room

trastienda *nf* back shop

trasto *nm (objeto cualquiera)* thing; *(cosa inservible)* piece of junk

trastocar [44] *vt* = **trastornar**

trastornado,-a *adj (loco)* mad, unhinged

trastornar 1 *vt* (**a**) *(planes)* to disrupt (**b**) *Fig (persona)* to unhinge

  2 trastornarse *upr (enloquecer)* to go out of one's mind, to go mad

trastorno *nm (molestia)* trouble, inconvenience; **t. mental** mental disorder *o* disturbance

trasvase *nm* = **transvase**

trasversal *adj* = **transversal**

trata *nf* slave trade *o* traffic; **t. de blancas** white slave trade

tratable *adj* easy to get along with, congenial

tratado *nm* (**a**) *(pacto)* treaty (**b**) *(estudio)* treatise

tratamiento *nm* (**a**) treatment (**b**) *Téc* processing, treatment (**c**) *Informát* processing; **t. de textos** word processing

tratar 1 *vt* (**a**) *(atender)* to treat; **t. bien/mal** to treat well/badly (**b**) *Med* to treat (**c**) *(asunto)* to discuss (**d**) *Informát & Téc* to process (**e**) **me trata de tú** he addresses me as "tu"

  2 *vi* (**a**) *(intentar)* to try (**b**) **t. de** *o* **sobre** *o* **acerca** to be about; **¿de qué trata?** what is it about? (**c**) **t. con** *(tener tratos)* to deal with; *(negociar)* to negotiate with; *(relacionarse)* to move among (**d**) *Com* **t. en** to deal in

  3 tratarse *upr* (**a**) *(relacionarse)* to be on speaking terms (**b**) **se trata de** *(es cuestión de)* it's a question of; **se trata de un caso excepcional** it's an exceptional case

tratativas *nfpl CSur* negotiation

trato *nm* (**a**) *(de personas)* manner; *(contacto)* contact; **malos tratos** ill-treatment (**b**) *(acuerdo)* agreement; **¡t. hecho!** it's a deal! (**c**) *Com* deal

trauma *nm* trauma

traumático,-a *adj* traumatic

traumatizar *vt Med* to traumatize; *Fam* to shock

través 1 *prep* (**a**) **a t. de** *(superficie)* across, over; *(agujero etc)* through; **a t. del río** across the river; **a t. del agujero** through the hole (**b**) *Fig* **a t. de** through; **a t. del periódico** through the newspaper

  2 *adv* **de t.** *(transversalmente)* crosswise; *(de lado)* sideways

  3 *nm (pl* **traveses)** *Fig (desgracia)* misfortune

travesaño *nm Ftb* crossbar

travesía *nf (viaje)* crossing

travesti, travestí *nmf* transvestite

> *♪* Observa que la palabra inglesa **travesty** es un falso amigo y no es la traducción de la palabra española **travesti**. En inglés, **travesty** significa "parodia burda".

travesura *nf* mischief, childish prank

travieso,-a *adj* mischievous

trayecto *nm* (**a**) *(distancia)* distance; *(recorrido)* route; *(trecho)* stretch (**b**) *(viaje)* journey

trayectoria *nf* (**a**) *(de proyectil, geométrica)* trajectory (**b**) *Fig (orientación)* line, course

traza *nf* (**a**) *(apariencia)* looks, appearance; **no lleva trazas de curarse** it doesn't look as if he's going to get better (**b**) *Arquit* plan, design

trazado *nm* (**a**) *(plano)* layout, plan (**b**) *(de carretera, ferrocarril)* route

trazar [40] *vt (línea)* to draw; *(plano)* to design; *Fig (plan)* to sketch out

trazo nm (a) *(línea)* line (b) *(de letra)* stroke

trébol nm (a) trefoil (b) *Naipes* club

trece 1 adj inv thirteen

  2 nm inv thirteen; *Fig* **estar** o **mantenerse** o **seguir en sus t.** to stick to one's guns

trecho nm distance, way; *(tramo)* stretch; **de t. en t.** from time to time

tregua nf *Mil* truce; *Fig* respite

treinta adj & nm inv thirty

treintavo,-a adj & nm thirtieth

treintena nf **una t. de** (about) thirty

tremendista adj over the top

tremendo,-a adj (a) *(terrible)* terrible, dreadful (b) *(muy grande)* enormous; *Fig* tremendous

trementina nf turpentine

trémulo,-a adj *Literario (vacilante)* quivering, tremulous; *(luz)* flickering

tren nm (a) train (b) *Av* **t. de aterrizaje** undercarriage; **t. de lavado** car wash (c) **t. de vida** lifestyle

trenca nf duffle coat

trenza nf *(de pelo)* plait, *esp US* braid

trepador,-a adj climbing

trepar vt & vi to climb

trepidante adj vibrating, shaking; *Fig* **lleva un ritmo de vida t.** he leads a hectic o frantic life

trepidar vi to vibrate, to shake

tres 1 adj inv *(cardinal)* three; *(ordinal)* third; *Fam* **de t. al cuarto** cheap, of little value

  2 nm *(pl* **treses***)* three; **t. en raya** *Br* noughts and crosses, *US* tick-tack-toe

trescientos,-as adj & nm three hundred

tresillo nm (a) *(mueble)* (three-piece) suite (b) *Mús* triplet

treta nf trick, ruse

triángulo nm triangle; *Fig* **t. amoroso** eternal triangle

tribal adj tribal

tribu nf tribe

tribuna nf (a) *(plataforma)* rostrum, dais; **t. de (la) prensa** press box (b) *Dep* stand

tribunal nm (a) *Jur* court; **t. de apelación** court of appeal; **T. Supremo** *Br* High Court, *US* Supreme Court; **t. (tutelar) de menores** juvenile court (b) *(de examen)* board of examiners

tributar vt to pay

tributario,-a adj **sistema t.** tax system

tributo nm (a) *Com* tax (b) **pagar t. a** *(homenaje)* to pay tribute to

triciclo nm tricycle

tricornio nm three-cornered hat

tridimensional adj three-dimensional

trienio nm three-year period

trifásico,-a 1 adj *Elec* three-phase

  2 nm adapter

trigésimo,-a adj & nm,f thirtieth; **t. primero** thirty-first

trigo nm wheat

trigueño,-a adj *Am (pelo)* dark brown; *(persona)* olive-skinned

trilla nf threshing

trillado,-a adj *Fig* well-worn

trilladora nf threshing machine; **t. segadora** combine harvester

trillar vt to thresh

trilogía nf trilogy

trimestral adj quarterly, three-monthly

trimestre nm quarter; *Educ* term

trinar vi (a) to warble (b) *Fam* to rage, to fume; **Santiago está que trina** Santiago is really fuming

trincar¹ [44] vt *Fam (capturar)* to catch

trincar² vt *Fam* to drink

trinchar vt *(carne)* to carve, to slice (up)

trinchera nf trench

trineo nm sledge, sleigh

Trinidad nf **la Santísima T.** the Holy Trinity

trino nm (a) warble, trill (b) *Mús* trill

trío nm trio

tripa nf (a) *(intestino)* gut, intestine; *Fam* tummy; **dolor de t.** stomach ache (b) **tripas** innards

triple adj & nm triple

triplicado,-a adj triplicate; **por t.** in triplicate

triplicar [44] vt to triple, to treble

trípode nm tripod

tríptico nm (a) *(cuadro)* triptych (b) *(folleto)* leaflet

tripulación nf crew

tripulante nmf crew member

tripular vt to man

triquiñuela nf *Fam* trick, dodge

tris nm **estar en un t. de** to be on the verge of

triste adj (a) *(persona, situación)* sad (b) *(lugar)* gloomy

tristeza nf sadness

triturar vt *(machacar)* to grind (up)

triunfador,-a 1 adj winning

  2 nm,f winner

triunfal adj triumphant

triunfar vi to triumph

triunfo nm (a) *(victoria)* triumph, victory; *Dep* win (b) *(éxito)* success

trivial adj trivial

trivialidad nf triviality

trivializar vt to trivialize, to minimize

triza nf bit, fragment; **hacer trizas** to tear to shreds

trocar [64] *vt* to barter

trocear *vt* to cut up (into bits o pieces)

trochemoche: •a trochemoche *loc adv* *Fam* haphazardly

trofeo *nm* trophy

trola *nf Fam* fib

trolebús *nm* trolleybus

tromba *nf* t. **de agua** violent downpour

trombón *nm* trombone

trombosis *nf inv* thrombosis

trompa *nf* (**a**) *Mús* horn (**b**) *(de elefante)* trunk (**c**) *Anat* tube (**d**) *Fam* **estar t.** to be sloshed o plastered

trompazo *nm Fam* bump; **darse** o **pegarse un t.** to have a bump

trompeta *nf* trumpet

trompetista *nmf* trumpet player, trumpeter

trompicón *nm* trip, stumble; **hacer algo a trompicones** to do sth in fits and starts

trompo *nm* spinning top

tronar [2] **1** *vi* to thunder
2 *vt Méx Fam* (**a**) *(destruir, acabar con)* to destroy; **este remedio es para t. anginas** this remedy will clear up tonsillitis (**b**) *(reprobar)* to fail

tronchar 1 *vt (rama, tronco)* to cut down, to fell; *Fig (esperanzas etc)* to destroy
2 troncharse *vpr* **t. de risa** to split one's sides with laughter

troncho *nm* stem, stalk

tronco *nm* (**a**) *Anat* trunk, torso (**b**) *Bot (de árbol)* trunk; *(leño)* log; *Fam Fig* **dormir como un t.** to sleep like a log

tronera *nf* (**a**) *(de billar)* pocket (**b**) *(ventana)* small window; *(de fortificación)* loophole; *Náut* porthole

trono *nm* throne

tropa *nf* (**a**) squad (**b**) **tropas** troops

tropel *nm* throng, mob; **en t.** in a mad rush

tropezar [1] *vi* (**a**) to trip, to stumble (**con** on) (**b**) **t. con algo** to come across sth; **t. con algn/dificultades** to run into sb/difficulties

tropezón *nm* (**a**) *(traspié)* trip, stumble; **dar un t.** to trip (**b**) *(error)* slip-up, faux pas (**c**) *(de comida)* chunk of meat

tropical *adj* tropical

trópico *nm* tropic

tropiezo 1 *nm* (**a**) *(obstáculo)* trip (**b**) *Fig (error)* blunder, faux pas
2 *indic pres de* **tropezar**

trotamundos *nmf inv* globetrotter

trotar *vi* to trot

trote *nm* (**a**) trot; **al t.** at a trot (**b**) *Fam* **ya no está para esos trotes** he cannot keep up the pace any more

trovador *nm* troubadour

trozar *vt Am (carne)* to cut up; *(res, tronco)* to butcher, to cut up

trozo *nm* piece

trucar [44] *vt* to doctor, to alter

trucha *nf* trout

truco *nm* (**a**) *(ardid)* trick; **aquí hay t.** there's something fishy going on here (**b**) **coger el t. (a algo)** to get the knack o hang (of sth)

truculento,-a *adj* horrifying, terrifying

> 🖉 Observa que la palabra inglesa **truculent** es un falso amigo y no es la traducción de la palabra española **truculento**. En inglés, **truculent** significa "agresivo, airado".

trueno *nm* thunder; **un t.** a thunderclap

trueque *nm* barter

trufa *nf* truffle

truhán,-ana *nm,f* rogue, crook

truncar [44] *vt* to truncate; *Fig (vida etc)* to cut short; *Fig (esperanzas)* to shatter

trusa *nf Méx (calzoncillo)* underpants; *(braga)* panties; *Br* knickers

trust *nm (pl* **trusts**) trust, cartel

tu *adj pos* your; **tu libro** your book; **tus libros** your books

tú *pron* you; **de tú a tú** on equal terms

> Usually omitted in Spanish except for emphasis or contrast.

tuba *nf* tuba

tubérculo *nm* (**a**) *Bot* tuber (**b**) *Med* tubercle

tuberculosis *nf inv* tuberculosis

tubería *nf* (**a**) *(de agua)* piping, pipes (**b**) *(de gas)* pipeline

tubo *nm* (**a**) tube; **t. de ensayo** test tube (**b**) *(tubería)* pipe; *Aut* **t. de escape** exhaust (pipe)

tucán *nm* toucan

tuerca *nf* nut

tuerto,-a 1 *adj* one-eyed, blind in one eye
2 *nm,f* one-eyed person

tuerzo *indic pres de* **torcer**

tuétano *nm* marrow; **hasta el t.** to one's fingertips

tufo *nm* foul odour o smell

tugurio *nm* hovel

tul *nm* tulle

tulipa *nf* small tulip

tulipán *nm* tulip

tullido,-a *adj* crippled, disabled

tullir *vt* to cripple

tumba *nf* grave, tomb

tumbar 1 *vt* to knock down o over
2 tumbarse *vpr (acostarse)* to lie down, to stretch out

tumbo *nm* **dar tumbos** to reel

tumbona *nf Br* sun-lounger, *US* beach recliner

tumor *nm* tumour

tumulto *nm* tumult, commotion

tumultuoso,-a *adj* tumultuous, riotous

tuna *nf* (a) *(agrupación musical)* = group of student minstrels (b) *Am (higo chumbo)* prickly pear

> 🖋 Observa que la palabra inglesa **tuna** es un falso amigo y no es la traducción de la palabra española **tuna**. En inglés, **tuna** significa "atún, bonito".

tunante,-a *nm,f* rogue, crook

túnel *nm* tunnel; **el t. del Canal de la Mancha** the Channel Tunnel

Túnez *n* (a) *(país)* Tunisia (b) *(ciudad)* Tunis

túnica *nf* tunic

tuno,-a 1 *nm,f (bribón)* rogue, crook
　2 *nm* = member of a "tuna"

tuntún: • **al tuntún** *loc adv* haphazardly, any old how

tupé *nm (pl* **tupés)** *(flequillo)* quiff

tupido,-a *adj* thick, dense

turba[1] *nf (combustible)* peat

turba[2] *nf (muchedumbre)* mob, crowd

turbado,-a *adj* (a) *(alterado)* disturbed (b) *(preocupado)* worried, anxious (c) *(desconcertado)* confused

turbante *nm* turban

turbar 1 *vt* (a) *(alterar)* to unsettle (b) *(preocupar)* to upset o worry (c) *(desconcertar)* to baffle, to put off
　2 turbarse *vpr* (a) *(preocuparse)* to be o become upset (b) *(desconcertarse)* to be o become confused o baffled

turbina *nf* turbine

turbio,-a *adj (agua)* cloudy; *(negocio etc)* shady, dubious

turborreactor *nm* turbojet (engine)

turbulencia *nf* turbulence

turbulento,-a *adj* turbulent

turco,-a 1 *adj* Turkish
　2 *nm,f (persona)* Turk; *Fig* **cabeza de t.** scapegoat
　3 *nm (idioma)* Turkish

turismo *nm* (a) tourism; **ir de t.** to go touring; **t. rural** rural tourism (b) *Aut* car

turista *nmf* tourist

turístico,-a *adj* tourist; **de interés t.** of interest to tourists

turnarse *vpr* to take turns

turno *nm* (a) *(en juegos etc)* turn, go (b) *(de trabajo)* shift; **estar de t.** to be on duty; **t. de día/noche** day/night shift

turquesa *adj inv & nf* turquoise

Turquía *n* Turkey

turrón *nm* nougat

tute *nm Fam* **darse un t. de algo** to go to town doing sth

tutear 1 *vt* = to address as "tú"
　2 tutearse *vpr* = to address each other as "tú"

tutela *nf* (a) *Jur* guardianship, tutelage (b) *Fig (protección)* protection, guidance

tuteo *nm* = use of the "tú" form of address

tutor *nm* (a) *Jur* guardian (b) *Educ* tutor

tuve *pt indef de* **tener**

tuyo,-a 1 *adj pos (con personas)* of yours; *(con objetos)* one of your; **¿es amigo t.?** is he a friend of yours?; **unas amigas tuyas** some friends of yours; **un libro t.** one of your books
　2 *pron pos* yours; **éste es t.** this one is yours; *Fam* **los tuyos** *(familiares)* your family

TV *nf (abr* **televisión)** TV

TVE *nf (abr* **Televisión Española)** = Spanish state television network

U, u [u] *nf (la letra)* U, u

u *conj (delante de palabras que empiecen por* o o ho*)* or; **siete u ocho** seven or eight; **ayer u hoy** yesterday or today

ubicación *nf* location, position

ubicar [44] **1** *vt Am (situar)* to locate, to situate

2 ubicarse *vpr* to be situated *o* located

ubicuo,-a *adj* ubiquitous

ubre *nf* udder

Ucrania *n* Ukraine

ucraniano,-a *adj & nm,f* Ukrainian

Ud. *(abr* usted*)* you

Uds. *(abr* ustedes*)* you

UE *nf (abr* **Unión Europea***)* EU

UEM *nf (abr* **unión económica y monetaria***)* EMU

ufanarse *vpr* to boast *(de* of*)*

ufano,-a *adj* conceited

ugetista *adj* = relating to the UGT

UGT *nf (abr* **Unión General de los Trabajadores***)* = major socialist trade union in Spain

ujier *nm* usher

úlcera *nf* ulcer

ulcerar *vt,* **ulcerarse** *vpr* to ulcerate

ulterior *adj (siguiente)* subsequent

últimamente *adv* lately, recently

ultimar *vt* (a) *(terminar)* to finalize (b) *Am (matar)* to kill, to finish off

ultimátum *nm (pl* **ultimátums***)* ultimatum

último,-a 1 *adj* (a) *(último)* last; **el ú. día** the last day; **por ú.** finally (b) *(más reciente)* latest; **últimas noticias** latest news (c) *(más alto)* top; **el ú. piso** the top flat (d) *(más bajo)* lowest (e) *(más lejano)* back, last; **la última fila** the back row (f) *(definitivo)* final

2 *nm,f* **llegar el ú.** to arrive last; **a últimos de mes** at the end of the month; **en las últimas** on one's last legs; *Fam* **a la última** up to the minute; **el ú. de la lista** the lowest in the list

ultra *nmf* extreme right-winger; **los ultras** the extreme right

ultra- *pref* ultra-

ultraderecha *nf Pol* extreme right

ultraderechista *Pol* **1** *adj* extreme right-wing

2 *nmf* extreme right-winger

ultraizquierda *nf* extreme left

ultrajar *vt* to outrage, to offend

ultraje *nm* outrage, offence

ultramar *nm* overseas (countries), abroad; **del** *o* **en u.** overseas

ultramarinos *nmpl* groceries; **tienda de u.** greengrocer's (shop)

ultranza: • **a ultranza** *loc adv* (a) *(a todo trance)* at all costs, at any price; **defender algo a u.** to defend sth to the death (b) *(acérrimo)* out-and-out, extreme

ultrasónico,-a *adj* ultrasonic

ultratumba *nf* afterlife

ultravioleta *adj inv* ultraviolet

ulular *vi (viento)* to howl; *(búho)* to hoot

umbral *nm* threshold

umbrío,-a, umbroso,-a *adj* shady

un, una 1 *art indet* (a) a; *(antes de vocal)* an; **un coche** a car; **un huevo** an egg; **una flor** a flower (b) *unos,-as* some; **unas flores** some flowers

2 *adj (delante de nm sing)* one; **un chico y dos chicas** one boy and two girls; *ver también* **uno,-a**

unánime *adj* unanimous

unanimidad *nf* unanimity; **por u.** unanimously

unción *nf* unction

undécimo,-a *adj* eleventh

UNED *nf (abr* **Universidad Nacional de Educación a Distancia***)* = Spanish open university

ungir [57] *vt Rel* to anoint

ungüento *nm* ointment

únicamente *adv* only, solely

único,-a *adj* (a) *(solo)* only; **es el ú. que tengo** it's the only one I've got; **hijo ú.** only child; **lo ú. que quiero** the only thing I want; **el Mercado Ú.** the Single Market; **el Acta Única** the Single European Act (b) *(extraordinario)* unique

unidad *nf* (a) unit (b) *(cohesión)* unity

unido,-a *adj* united; **están muy unidos** they are very attached to one another; **una familia muy unida** a very close family

unifamiliar *adj* **vivienda u.** detached house

unificación *nf* unification

unificar [44] *vt* to unify

uniformar *vt* (**a**) *(igualar)* to make uniform, to standardize (**b**) *(poner un uniforme a)* to put into uniform, to give a uniform to

uniforme 1 *nm (prenda)* uniform
   2 *adj* (**a**) *(igual)* uniform (**b**) *(superficie)* even

uniformidad *nf* (**a**) *(igualdad)* uniformity (**b**) *(de superficie)* evenness

unilateral *adj* unilateral

unión *nf* union

Unión Soviética *n* Soviet Union

unir 1 *vt* (*juntar*) to unite, to join (together); **esta carretera une las dos comarcas** this road links both districts
   2 unirse *vpr* (*juntarse*) to unite, to join

unisex *adj inv* unisex

unísono *nm* unison; **al u.** in unison

unitario,-a *adj* unitary; **precio u.** unit price

universal *adj* universal; **historia u.** world history

universidad *nf* university; **u. a distancia** ≃ Open University; **u. laboral** technical college

universitario,-a 1 *adj* university
   2 *nm,f* university student

universo *nm* universe

uno,-a 1 *num inv* one; **el u.** (number) one; **el u. de mayo** the first of May
   2 *nf* **es la una** *(hora)* it's one o'clock
   3 *adj* **unos,-as** some; **unas cajas** some boxes; **habrá unos** *o* **unas veinte** there must be around twenty
   4 *pron* (**a**) one; **u.** (**de ellos), una (de ellos)** one of them; **unos cuantos** a few; **se miraron el u. al otro** they looked at each other; **de u. en u.** one by one; **un trás otro** one after the other; **una de dos** one of the two
   (**b**) *(persona)* someone, somebody; **u. que pasaba por allí** some passer-by; **vive con u.** she's living with some man; **unos ... otros** some people ... others
   (**c**) *(impers)* you, one; **u. tiene que ...** you have to ...

untar *vt* to grease, to smear; *(mantequilla)* to spread

untura *nf* ointment

uña *nf* (**a**) nail; **morderse** *o* **comerse las uñas** to bite one's fingernails; *Fig* **ser u. y carne** to be hand in glove (**b**) *Zool (garra)* claw; *(pezuña)* hoof

uperizado,-a *adj* **leche uperizada** UHT milk

Urales *nmpl* **los U.** the Urals

uranio *nm* uranium

Urano *nm* Uranus

urbanidad *nf* urbanity, politeness

urbanismo *nm* town planning

urbanístico,-a *adj* town-planning

urbanización *nf* (**a**) *(barrio)* housing development *o* estate (**b**) *(proceso)* urbanization

urbanizar *vt* to build up

urbano,-a *adj* urban, city; **guardia u.** (traffic) policeman

urbe *nf* large city

urdimbre *nf* (**a**) *Tex* warp (**b**) *(trama)* intrigue

urdir *vt* (**a**) *Tex* to warp (**b**) *(tramar)* to plot, to scheme

urgencia *nf* (**a**) urgency (**b**) *(emergencia)* emergency

urgente *adj* urgent; **correo u.** express mail

urgir [57] *vi* to be urgent *o* pressing; **me urge (tenerlo)** I need it urgently

urinario *nm* urinal

urna *nf* (**a**) *Pol* ballot box (**b**) *(vasija)* urn

urólogo,-a *nm,f Med* urologist

urraca *nf* magpie

URSS *nf Hist* (*abr* **Unión de Repúblicas Socialistas Soviéticas**) USSR

urticaria *nf Med* hives

Uruguay *n* Uruguay

uruguayo,-a *adj & nm,f* Uruguayan

usado,-a *adj (ropa)* second-hand, used

usanza *nf Literario* **a la antigua u.** in the old style

usar 1 *vt* (**a**) to use (**b**) *(prenda)* to wear
   2 usarse *vpr* to be used *o* in fashion

usina *nf Am (central eléctrica)* power station; **u. nuclear** nuclear power station

uso *nm* (**a**) use; *Farm* **u. externo/tópico** external/local application (**b**) *(de poder, privilegio)* exercise (**c**) *(de prenda)* wearing; **haga u. del casco** wear a helmet (**d**) *(costumbre)* usage, custom; **al u.** conventional

usted *(pl* **ustedes)** *pron pers Fml* you; **¿quién es u.?, ¿quiénes son ustedes?** who are you?

> Usually omitted in Spanish except for emphasis or contrast. Although formal in peninsular Spanish, it is not necessarily so in Latin American Spanish.

usual *adj* usual, common

usuario,-a *nm,f* user

usura *nf* usury

usurero,-a *nm,f* usurer

usurpar *vt* to usurp

utensilio *nm* utensil; *(herramienta)* tool

útero *nm* uterus, womb

útil 1 *adj* useful; *(día)* working
  2 *nm (herramienta)* tool, instrument
utilidad *nf* usefulness, utility; *(beneficio)*
 profit
utilitario,-a 1 *nm (coche)* utility vehicle
  2 *adj* utilitarian
utilización *nf* use, utilization

utilizar [40] *vt* to use, to utilize
utopía *nf* utopia
utópico,-a *adj & nm,f* utopian
uva *nf* grape; **u. blanca** green grape
UVI *nf (abr* **unidad de vigilancia intensi-**
 va) ICU
úvula *nf* uvula

V, v ['ue] *nf (la letra)* V, v

V *Elec (abr* **voltio(s))** V

vaca *nf* (**a**) cow (**b**) *(carne)* beef

vacaciones *nfpl Br* holidays, *US* vacation; *(viaje)* holiday; **durante las v.** during the holidays; **estar/irse de v.** to be/go on holiday

vacacionista *nmf Am Br* holidaymaker, *US* vacationer

vacante 1 *adj* vacant
2 *nf* vacancy

vaciar [29] **1** *vt* (**a**) *(recipiente)* to empty; *(contenido)* to empty out (**b**) *(terreno)* to hollow out (**c**) *Arte* to cast, to mould
2 vaciarse *vpr* to empty

vacilación *nf* hesitation

vacilante *adj* (**a**) *(persona)* hesitant, irresolute (**b**) *(voz)* hesitant, faltering (**c**) *(luz)* flickering

vacilar *vi* (**a**) *(dudar)* to hesitate; **sin v.** without hesitation (**b**) *(voz)* to falter (**c**) *(luz)* to flicker (**d**) *Fam (jactarse)* to show off

vacilón,-ona *Fam* **1** *adj* (**a**) *(fanfarrón)* swanky (**b**) *(bromista)* jokey, teasing (**c**) *CAm, Méx Fam (juerguista)* fond of partying
2 *nm,f* (**a**) *(fanfarrón)* show-off (**b**) *(bromista)* tease
3 *nm Carib (fiesta)* party

vacío,-a 1 *adj* (**a**) empty; *(hueco)* hollow (**b**) *(sin ocupar)* vacant, unoccupied
2 *nm* (**a**) emptiness, void (**b**) *(hueco)* gap; *(espacio)* (empty) space (**c**) *Fís* vacuum; **envasado al v.** vacuum-packed

vacuna *nf* vaccine

vacunación *nf* vaccination

vacunar 1 *vt* to vaccinate (**contra** against); *Fig* to inure
2 vacunarse *vpr* to get oneself vaccinated

vacuno,-a *adj* bovine; **ganado v.** cattle

vacuo,-a *adj* vacuous, empty

vadear *vt (río)* to ford; *Fig (dificultad)* to overcome

vado *nm* (**a**) *(de un río)* ford (**b**) *Aut* **v. permanente** *(en letrero)* keep clear

vagabundear *vi* to wander, to roam

vagabundo,-a 1 *adj (errante)* wandering; *Pey* vagrant; **perro v.** stray dog
2 *nm,f* wanderer; *(sin casa)* tramp, *US* hobo; *Pey* vagrant, tramp

vagancia *nf* idleness, laziness

vagar [42] *vi* to wander about, to roam about

vagido *nm* cry *(of a newborn baby)*

vagina *nf* vagina

vago,-a 1 *adj* (**a**) *(perezoso)* lazy (**b**) *(indefinido)* vague
2 *nm,f* (**a**) *(holgazán)* layabout (**b**) *Jur* vagrant

vagón *nm (para pasajeros)* carriage, coach, *US* car; *(para mercancías)* truck, wagon, *US* freight car, *US* boxcar

vaguedad *nf* vagueness

vaho *nm (de aliento)* breath; *(vapor)* vapour

vaina 1 *nf* (**a**) *(de espada)* sheath, scabbard (**b**) *Bot* pod (**c**) *Col, Perú, Ven muy Fam (molestia)* bother, pain (in the neck); **¡qué v.!** what a pain!
2 *nmf (persona)* dimwit

vainilla *nf* vanilla

vaivén *nm* (**a**) *(oscilación)* swinging, to-and-fro movement (**b**) *(de gente)* coming and going, bustle; *Fig* **vaivenes** ups and downs

vajilla *nf* crockery, dishes; **una v.** a set of dishes, a dinner service

valdré *indic fut de* **valer**

vale[1] *interj* all right!, O.K.!

vale[2] *nm* (**a**) *(comprobante)* voucher (**b**) *(pagaré)* promissory note, IOU (**c**) *Méx, Ven Fam (amigo)* pal, *Br* mate, *US* buddy

valedero,-a *adj* valid

valenciano,-a *adj* Valencian

valentía *nf* courage, bravery

valentón,-ona *Pey* **1** *adj* bragging, boastful
2 *nm,f* braggart

valer [26] **1** *vt* (**a**) to be worth; **no vale nada** it is worthless; **vale una fortuna** it is worth a fortune; **no vale la pena (ir)** it's not worth while (going) (**b**) *(costar)* to cost; **¿cuánto vale?** how much is it? (**c**) *(proporcionar)* to earn
2 *vi* (**a**) *(servir)* to be useful, to be of use (**b**) *(ser válido)* to be valid, to count; **no**

vale hacer trampa cheating isn't on (**c**) **más vale** it is better; **más vale que te vayas ya** you had better leave now

3 valerse *vpr* **v. de** to use, to make use of; **v. por sí mismo** to be able to manage on one's own

valeroso,-a *adj* brave, courageous

valgo *indic pres de* **valer**

valía *nf* value, worth

validez *nf* validity

válido,-a *adj* valid

valiente *adj* (**a**) (*valeroso*) brave, courageous (**b**) *Irón* **¡v. amigo eres tú!** a fine friend you are!

valija *nf* (**a**) (*maleta*) case, suitcase; **v. diplomática** diplomatic bag (**b**) (*de correos*) mailbag

valioso,-a *adj* valuable

valla *nf* (**a**) (*cerca*) fence; (*muro*) wall; **v. publicitaria** billboard, *Br* hoarding (**b**) *Dep* hurdle; **los 100 metros vallas** the 100 metres hurdle race

vallado *nm* fence

vallar *vt* to fence (in)

valle *nm* valley

vallisoletano,-a 1 *adj* of/from Valladolid

2 *nm,f* person from Valladolid

valor *nm* (**a**) (*valía*) value, worth; (*precio*) price; **objetos de v.** valuables; **sin v.** worthless; **v. alimenticio** food value (**b**) (*valentía*) courage (**c**) *Fin* **valores** securities, bonds

valoración *nf* valuation

valorar *vt* to value, to calculate the value of

valorización *nf* (**a**) (*tasación*) valuation (**b**) (*revalorización*) appreciation

valorizar [40] *vt* (**a**) (*tasar*) to value (**b**) (*revalorizar*) to raise the value of

vals *nm* waltz; **bailar el v.** to waltz

válvula *nf* valve; **v. de seguridad** safety valve

vampiro *nm* vampire

vanagloriarse [43] *vpr* to boast (**de** of)

vandalismo *nm* vandalism

vándalo,-a *nm,f* vandal

vanguardia *nf* (**a**) avant-garde, vanguard; *Fig* **ir a la v. de** to be at the forefront of (**b**) *Mil* vanguard, van

vanguardista 1 *adj* avant-garde

2 *nmf* avant-gardist

vanidad *nf* vanity

vanidoso,-a *adj* vain, conceited

vano,-a *adj* (**a**) (*vanidoso*) vain, conceited (**b**) (*esfuerzo, esperanza*) vain, futile; **en v.** in vain

vapor *nm* (**a**) (*de agua hirviendo*) steam; *Culin* **al v.** steamed (**b**) (*gas*) vapour; **v. de agua** water vapour

vaporizador *nm* vaporizer, spray

vaporizar [40] **1** *vt* to vaporize

2 vaporizarse *vpr* to vaporize, to evaporate

vaporoso,-a *adj* vaporous

vapulear *vt* (*físicamente*) to shake; (*con palabras*) to slate

vaqueriza *nf* cowshed

vaquero,-a 1 *nm* cowherd, cowboy

2 *adj* **pantalón v.** jeans, pair of jeans

3 *nmpl* **vaqueros** (*prenda*) jeans, pair of jeans

vara *nf* pole, rod

varar 1 *vt* to beach, to dock

2 *vi* to run aground

variable *adj & nf* variable

variación *nf* variation

variado,-a *adj* varied; **galletas variadas** assorted *Br* biscuits *o US* cookies

variante *nf* variant; *Aut* detour

variar [29] **1** *vt* to vary, to change

2 *vi* to vary, to change; *Irón* **para v.** as usual, just for a change

varice, várice *nf* = **variz**

varicela *nf* chickenpox

variedad *nf* (**a**) variety (**b**) *Teatro* **variedades** variety show

varilla *nf* (*vara*) rod, stick; (*de abanico, paraguas*) rib

variopinto,-a *adj* diverse, assorted; **un público v.** a varied audience

varios,-as *adj* several

varita *nf* **v. mágica** magic wand

variz *nf* varicose vein

varón *nm* (*hombre*) man; (*chico*) boy; **hijo v.** male child; **sexo v.** male sex

varonil *adj* manly, virile

Varsovia *n* Warsaw

vas *indic pres de* **ir**

vasallo,-a *nm,f Hist* vassal

vasco,-a *adj* Basque; **el País V.** the Basque Country

vascuence *nm* (*idioma*) Basque

vasectomía *nf* vasectomy

vaselina *nf* Vaseline®

vasija *nf* pot

vaso *nm* (**a**) (*para beber*) glass (**b**) *Anat* vessel

🖉 Observa que la palabra inglesa **vase** es un falso amigo y no es la traducción de la palabra española **vaso**. En inglés, **vase** significa "jarrón".

---

vástago *nm* (**a**) *Bot* shoot (**b**) *Fig* (*hilo*) offspring (**c**) *Téc* rod, stem

vasto,-a *adj* vast

Vaticano *nm* el V. the Vatican
vaticinar *vt* to prophesy, to predict
vaticinio *nm* prophecy, prediction
vatio *nm* watt
vaya¹ *interj* ¡v. lío! what a mess!
vaya² *subj pres de* ir
Vd., Vds. (*abr* usted, ustedes) you
ve 1 *imperat de* ir
  2 *indic pres de* ver
vecinal *adj* local
vecindad *nf,* **vecindario** *nm* (a) (*área*) neighbourhood, vicinity (b) (*vecinos*) community, residents (c) *Méx* (*inquilinato*) tenement house
vecino,-a 1 *nm,f* (a) (*persona*) neighbour; el v. de al lado the next-door neighbour (b) (*residente*) resident
  2 *adj* neighbouring, nearby
veda *nf* (*de caza*) closed season; levantar la v. to open the season
vedado,-a *adj* coto v. de caza private hunting ground
vedar *vt* to forbid, to prohibit
vega *nf* fertile plain o lowland
vegetación *nf* (a) *Bot* vegetation (b) *Med* vegetaciones adenoids
vegetal *nm* vegetable
vegetar *vi Fig* to vegetate
vegetariano,-a *adj & nm,f* vegetarian
vehemencia *nf* vehemence
vehemente *adj* vehement
vehículo *nm* vehicle
veinte *adj & nm inv* twenty
veintena *nf* (*veinte*) twenty; una v. de about twenty
vejación *nf* humiliation
vejar *vt* to humiliate
vejatorio,-a *adj* humiliating
vejez *nf* old age
vejiga *nf* bladder
vela¹ *nf* (a) candle (b) *Fam* quedarse a dos velas to be in the dark (c) pasar la noche en v. to have a sleepless night
vela² *nf Náut* sail
velada *nf* evening (party)
velado,-a *adj* (a) (*oculto*) veiled, hidden (b) *Fot* blurred
velador 1 *nm* (a) (*mesa*) table (b) *Andes, Méx* (*mesilla de noche*) bedside table (c) *Méx, RP* (*lámpara*) bedside lamp
  2 *nm Méx* (*sereno*) nightwatchman
velar¹ *vi* (a) v. por to watch over (b) (*hacer guardia*) to keep watch
velar² *Fot* **1** *vt* to blur
  2 velarse *upr* to become blurred
velatorio *nm* vigil, wake
veleidad *nf* fickleness
veleidoso,-a *adj* fickle

velero *nm* sailing boat o ship
veleta 1 *nf* weather vane, weathercock
  2 *nmf Fam* fickle o changeable person
veliz *nf Méx* suitcase, case
vello *nm* hair
vellón *nm* fleece
velloso,-a, velludo,-a *adj* downy
velo *nm* veil
velocidad *nf* (a) (*rapidez*) speed; (*de proyectil etc*) velocity; *Aut* -v. máxima speed limit; *Informát* v. de transmisión bit rate; *Informát* v. operativa operating speed (b) *Aut* (*marcha*) gear
velocímetro *nm* speedometer
velocista *nmf* sprinter
velódromo *nm* cycle track, velodrome
veloz 1 *adj* swift, rapid
  2 *adv* quickly, fast
vena *nf* vein
venado *nm* deer, stag; *Culin* venison
vencedor,-a 1 *nm,f* winner
  2 *adj* winning
vencejo *nm Orn* swift
vencer [49] 1 *vt* (a) (*al enemigo*) to defeat; (*al contrincante*) to beat (b) (*dificultad*) to overcome, to surmount
  2 *vi* (a) (*pago, deuda*) to fall due, to be payable (b) (*plazo*) to expire
  3 vencerse *upr* (*torcerse*) to warp
vencido,-a *adj* (a) *Mil* (*derrotado*) defeated; *Dep* beaten; *Fig* darse por v. to give up, to accept defeat (b) (*pago, deuda*) due, payable (c) (*plazo*) expired (d) *Fam* a la tercera va la vencida third time lucky
vencimiento *nm* (a) *Com* maturity (b) (*de un plazo*) expiry
venda *nf* bandage
vendaje *nm* dressing
vendar *vt* to bandage; *Fig* v. los ojos a algn to blindfold sb
vendaval *nm* gale
vendedor,-a *nm,f* seller; (*hombre*) salesman; (*mujer*) saleswoman
vender 1 *vt* to sell; v. a plazos/al contado to sell on credit/for cash; v. al por mayor/menor to (sell) wholesale/retail
  2 venderse *upr* (a) to sell; este disco se vende bien this record is selling well; se vende (*en letrero*) for sale (b) (*claudicar*) to sell out
vendimia *nf* grape harvest
vendré *indic fut de* venir
Venecia *n* Venice
veneno *nm* poison; (*de serpiente*) venom
venenoso,-a *adj* poisonous
venerable *adj* venerable
veneración *nf* veneration
venerar *vt* to venerate, to revere

venéreo,-a *adj* venereal

venero *nm* spring

venezolano,-a *adj & nm,f* Venezuelan

Venezuela *n* Venezuela

venga *subj pres de* venir

venganza *nf* vengeance, revenge

vengar [42] 1 *vt* to avenge
  2 **vengarse** *vpr* to avenge oneself; **v. de algn** to take revenge on sb

vengativo,-a *adj* vengeful, vindictive

vengo *indic pres de* venir

venia *nf* (a) *Fml (permiso)* permission (b) *(perdón)* pardon

venial *adj* venial

venida *nf* coming, arrival

venidero,-a *adj* future, coming

venir [27] 1 *vi* (a) to come; *Fig* **v. a menos** to come down in the world; *Fig* **v. al mundo** to be born; **el año que viene** next year; *Fig* **me viene a la memoria** I remember; *Fam* **¡venga ya!** *(vamos)* come on!; *(expresa incredulidad)* come off it! (b) **v. grande/pequeño** *(ropa)* to be too big/small; **v. mal/bien** to be inconvenient/convenient; **el metro me viene muy bien** I find the *Br* underground *o US* subway very handy (c) *(en pasivas)* **esto vino provocado por ...** this was brought about by ... (d) **esto viene ocurriendo desde hace mucho tiempo** this has been going on for a long time now
  2 **venirse** *vpr* **v. abajo** to collapse

venta *nf* (a) sale; **en v.** for sale; **a la v.** on sale; **v. a plazos/al contado** credit/cash sale; **v. al por mayor/al por menor** wholesale/retail (b) *(posada)* country inn

ventaja *nf* advantage; **llevar v. a** to have the advantage over; **le sacó 2 m de v.** he beat him by 2 m

ventajoso,-a *adj* advantageous

ventana *nf* (a) window (b) *(de la nariz)* nostril

ventanal *nm* large window

ventanilla *nf* (a) window (b) *(de la nariz)* nostril

ventanuco *nm* small window

ventilación *nf* ventilation; **sin v.** unventilated

ventilar 1 *vt* (a) *(habitación)* to ventilate, to air (b) *Fig (opinión)* to air
  2 **ventilarse** *vpr Fam (terminar)* to finish off

ventisca *nf* blizzard; *(de nieve)* snowstorm

ventosa *nf* sucker; *Med* cupping glass

ventosear *vi* to break wind

ventoso,-a *adj* windy

ventrílocuo,-a *nm,f* ventriloquist

ventura *nf* (a) *(felicidad)* happiness (b) *(suerte)* luck; *(casualidad)* chance

venturoso,-a *adj* lucky, fortunate

Venus *nm* Venus

veo-veo *nm Fam* **el (juego del) v.** I-spy

ver[1] *nm* **de buen v.** good-looking

ver[2] [28] 1 *vt* (a) to see; *(televisión)* to watch; **a v.** let me see, let's see; **a v. si escribes** I hope you'll write; **(ya) veremos** we'll see; *Fam* **había un jaleo que no veas** you should have seen the fuss that was made; **no veo por qué** I can't see why; **a mi modo de v.** as I see it (b) **no tener nada que v. con** to have nothing to do with
  2 **verse** *vpr* (a) *(imagen etc)* to be seen (b) *(encontrarse con algn)* to meet, to see each other; **¡nos vemos!** see you later! (c) **no se pueden ni v.** *(soportarse)* they can't stand (the sight of) each other (d) *Am* **te ves divina** you look divine

vera *nf* edge, border; **a la v. de** beside, next to

veracidad *nf* veracity, truthfulness

veraneante *nmf Br* holidaymaker, *US* (summer) vacationer

veranear *vi* to spend one's summer *Br* holiday *o US* vacation

veraneo *nm* summer *Br* holiday *o US* vacation

veraniego,-a *adj* summer

veranillo *nm* Indian summer; **el v. de San Juan** *(en el hemisferio sur)* = warm spell around 24 June; **el v. de San Martín** *(en el hemisferio norte)* = warm spell around 11 November

verano *nm* summer

veras *nfpl* **de v.** really, seriously

veraz *adj* veracious, truthful

verbal *adj* verbal

verbena *nf* street party

verbo *nm* verb

verborrea *nf Fam* verbosity, verbal diarrhoea

verdad *nf* (a) truth; **es v.** it is true; **a decir v.** to tell the truth; **¡de v!.** really!, truly!; **un amigo de v.** a real friend (b) *(en frase afirmativa)* **está muy bien, ¿(no es) v.?** it is very good, isn't it?; *(en frase negativa)* **no te gusta, ¿v.?** you don't like it, do you?

verdaderamente *adv* truly, really

verdadero,-a *adj* true, real

verde 1 *adj* (a) green (b) *(fruta)* unripe (c) *Fam (chiste, película)* blue; **viejo v.** dirty old man (d) *Fam Fig* **poner v. a algn** to call sb every name under the sun
  2 *nm* (a) *(color)* green (b) *Pol* **los verdes** the Greens

verdear *vi* to turn green
verdor *nm (color)* greenness; *(de plantas)* verdure
verdoso,-a *adj* greenish
verdugo,-a 1 *nm* executioner
  2 *nm,f Fig* tyrant
verdulería *nf* greengrocer's (shop)
verdulero,-a *nm,f* greengrocer
verdura *nf* vegetables, greens
vereda *nf* (a) *(camino)* path, lane (b) *CSur, Perú (acera) Br* pavement, *US* sidewalk
veredicto *nm* verdict
verga *nf* penis
vergonzoso,-a *adj* (a) *(penoso)* shameful, disgraceful (b) *(tímido)* shy, bashful
vergüenza *nf* (a) *(pena)* shame; ¿no te da v.? aren't you ashamed?, have you no shame?; ¡es una v.! it's a disgrace! (b) *(timidez)* shyness, bashfulness; **tener v.** to be shy; **me da v.** I'm too embarrassed
vericueto *nm* winding path; *Fig* los vericuetos the ins and outs
verídico,-a *adj* truthful, true
verificar [44] 1 *vt (comprobar)* to check
  2 verificarse *upr* to take place, to occur
verja *nf (reja)* grating; *(cerca)* railing, railings; *(puerta)* iron gate
vermut, vermú *nm (pl* vermús) (a) *(licor)* vermouth (b) *(aperitivo)* aperitif (c) *Andes, RP (en cine)* early evening showing; *(en teatro)* early evening performance
verosímil *adj* probable, likely; *(creíble)* credible
verruga *nf* wart
versado,-a *adj* well-versed (**en**)
versar *vi* v. **sobre** to be about, to deal with
versátil *adj* (a) versatile (b) *(voluble)* changeable, inconstant
versatilidad *nf* (a) versatility (b) *(volubilidad)* changeableness, inconstancy
versículo *nm* verse
versión *nf* version; **película en v. original** film in the original language
verso *nm* (a) *(poesía)* verse (b) *(línea)* line
vértebra *nf* vertebra
vertebrado,-a *adj & nm* vertebrate
vertedero *nm (de basura) Br* rubbish tip *o* dump, *US* garbage dump
verter [3] 1 *vt* (a) to pour (out) (b) *(basura)* to dump
  2 *vi (río)* to flow, to run (**a** into)
vertical *adj* vertical
vértice *nm* vertex
vertiente *nf* (a) *(de una montaña, un tejado)* slope; *Fig* aspect (b) *Am (manantial)* spring

vertiginoso,-a *adj* dizzy, giddy; *Fig (velocidad)* breakneck
vértigo *nm* vertigo; **me da v.** it makes me dizzy
vesícula *nf* vesicle; **v. biliar** gall bladder
vespa® *nf* (motor) scooter
vespertino,-a 1 *adj* evening
  2 *nm Prensa* evening newspaper
vespino® *nm* moped
vestíbulo *nm (de casa)* hall; *(de edificio público)* foyer
vestido,-a 1 *nm (ropa)* clothes; *(de mujer)* dress
  2 *adj* dressed; **policía v. de paisano** plain-clothes policeman
vestidura *nf* clothing, clothes
vestigio *nm* vestige, trace
vestimenta *nf* clothes, garments
vestir [6] 1 *vt* (a) *(a algn)* to dress (b) *(llevar puesto)* to wear
  2 *vi* (a) to dress; **ropa de (mucho) v.** formal dress (b) *Fam* la seda viste mucho silk always looks very elegant
  3 vestirse *upr* (a) to get dressed, to dress (b) **v. de** to wear, to dress in; *(disfrazarse)* to disguise oneself as, to dress up as
vestuario *nm* (a) *(conjunto de vestidos)* clothes, wardrobe; *Teatro* wardrobe, costumes (b) *(camerino)* dressing room (c) *Dep* changing room
veta *nf Min* vein, seam; *(de carne)* streak
vetar *vt* to veto
veterano,-a *adj & nm,f* veteran
veterinario,-a 1 *nm,f* vet, *Br* veterinary surgeon, *US* veterinarian
  2 *nf veterinaria* veterinary medicine *o* science
veto *nm* veto; **derecho a v.** power *o* right of veto
vetusto,-a *adj Fml* ancient
vez *nf* (a) time; **una v.** once; **dos veces** twice; **cinco veces** five times; **a** *o* **algunas veces** sometimes; **cada v.** each *o* every time; **cada v. más** more and more; **de v. en cuando** now and again, every now and then; **¿le has visto alguna v.?** have you ever seen him?; **otra v.** again; **a la v.** at the same time; **tal v.** perhaps, maybe; **de una v.** in one go; **de una v. para siempre** once and for all; **en v. de** instead of; **érase** *o* **había una v.** *(en cuentos etc)* once upon a time (b) *(turno)* turn (c) **hacer las veces de** to do duty as
v.g(r). *(abr* verbigracia) eg
vía 1 *nf* (a) *Ferroc* track, line (b) *(camino)* road; **v. pública** public thoroughfare; **V. Láctea** Milky Way (c) *Anat* passage, tract; *Farm* **(por) v. oral** to be taken orally (d)

Fig **por v.** oficial through official channels; **por v. aérea/marítima** by air/sea **(e)** **en vías de** in the process of; **países en vías de desarrollo** developing countries

2 *prep (a través de)* via, through; **v. París** via Paris; **transmisión v. satélite** satellite transmission

viable *adj* viable

viaducto *nm* viaduct

viajante *nmf* commercial traveller, travelling salesman, *f* saleswoman

viajar *vi* to travel

viaje *nm (recorrido)* journey, trip; *(largo, en barco)* voyage; **¡buen v.!** bon voyage!, have a good trip!; **estar de v.** to be away (on a trip); **irse o marcharse de v.** to go on a journey *o* trip; **v. de negocios** business trip; **v. de novios** honeymoon

viajero,-a 1 *nm,f* **(a)** traveller **(b)** *(en transporte público)* passenger

2 *adj* **cheque v.** traveller's cheque

vianda *nf RP* **(a)** *(tentempié)* packed lunch **(b)** *(fiambrera)* lunchbox

viandante *nmf* passer-by

viario,-a *adj* road, highway; **red viaria** road network

víbora *nf* viper

vibración *nf* vibration

vibrador *nm* vibrator

vibrar *vt & vi* to vibrate

vicario,-a *nm,f* vicar

vicepresidente,-a *nm,f* **(a)** *Pol* vice-president **(b)** *(de compañía, comité)* vice-chairperson; *(hombre)* vice-chairman; *(mujer)* vice-chairwoman

vicesecretario,-a *nm,f* assistant secretary

viceversa *adv* vice versa

viciado,-a *adj* **(a)** *(corrompido)* corrupt **(b)** *(aire)* foul

viciar **[43] 1** *vt* **(a)** *(corromper)* to corrupt **(b)** *(estropear)* to waste

2 viciarse *vpr* **(a)** *(deformarse)* to go out of shape **(b)** *(corromperse)* to become corrupted

vicio *nm* **(a)** vice **(b)** *(mala costumbre)* bad habit **(c)** *Fam (destreza)* skill

vicioso,-a 1 *adj* **(a)** *(persona)* depraved, perverted **(b)** **círculo v.** vicious circle

2 *nm,f* depraved person; **v. del trabajo** workaholic

vicisitud *nf (usu pl)* vicissitude

víctima *nf* victim

victimar *vt Am* to kill, to murder

victimario,-a *nm,f Am* killer, murderer

victoria *nf* victory

victorioso,-a *adj* victorious

vicuña *nf* vicuña

vid *nf* vine, grapevine

vida *nf* life; *(período)* lifetime; **de toda la v.** lifelong; **en mi v.** never in my life; **de por v.** for life; **ganarse la v.** to earn one's living; **¿qué es de tu v.?** how's life?; **estar con/sin v.** to be alive/dead

vidente *nmf* clairvoyant

vídeo *nm* video; **grabar en v.** to videotape

videocámara *nf* video camera

videoclub *nm* video club

videoconferencia *nf* videoconferencing; *(sesión)* videoconference

videojuego *nm* video game

vidriera *nf* **(a)** stained-glass window **(b)** *Am (escaparate)* shop window

vidrio *nm* glass

viejo,-a 1 *adj* old; **hacerse v.** to grow old; **un v. amigo** an old friend

2 *nm,f* **(a)** *(hombre, padre)* old man; *(mujer, madre)* old woman; **los viejos** old people; *Fam* **mis viejos** my parents **(b)** *RP Fam* **¡mi v.!** *(apelativo cariñoso)* young man *o* fellow!; **¡mi vieja!** *(apelativo cariñoso)* my dear! **(c)** *Chile* **el V. de Pascua** *o* **Pascuero** Father Christmas

3 *nf* **vieja** *Col, Méx, Ven Fam (mujer, chica)* chick, *Br* bird, *US* broad

Viena *n* Vienna

vienés,-esa *adj & nm,f* Viennese

viento *nm* wind; **hace** *o* **sopla mucho v.** it is very windy; *Fam Fig* **¡vete a tomar v.!** get lost!

vientre *nm* **(a)** belly; **hacer de v.** to have a bowel movement **(b)** *(útero)* womb

viernes *nm inv* Friday; **V. Santo** Good Friday

Vietnam *n* Vietnam

vietnamita *adj & nmf* Vietnamese

viga *nf* **(a)** *(de madera)* beam; *(de hierro)* girder

vigencia *nf* validity; **entrar en v.** to come into force *o* effect

vigente *adj* in force

vigésimo,-a *adj & nm,f* twentieth

vigía 1 *nf* watchtower, lookout post

2 *nmf* lookout; *(hombre)* watchman; *(mujer)* watchwoman

vigilancia *nf* vigilance, watchfulness; *Med* **unidad de v. intensiva** intensive care unit

vigilante *nm* watchman; *(de banco)* guard

vigilar 1 *vt* to watch; *(un lugar)* to guard; **vigila que no entren** make sure they don't get in

2 *vi (gen)* to keep watch

vigilia *nf* **(a)** vigil **(b)** *(víspera)* eve **(c)** *Rel (abstinencia)* abstinence

vigor nm (a) vigour; (fuerza) strength (b) en v. in force

vigoroso,-a adj vigorous

VIH nm (abr Virus de la Inmunodeficiencia Humana) HIV

vikingo,-a adj & nm Viking

vil adj Fml vile, base

vileza nf (a) vileness, baseness (b) (acto) vile act, despicable deed

vilipendiar [43] vt Fml to vilify, to revile

villa nf (a) (población) town (b) (casa) villa, country house (c) Arg **v. miseria** shanty town

villancico nm (Christmas) carol

vilo: • **en vilo** loc adv (persona) on tenterhooks; (cosa) up in the air

vinagre nm vinegar

vinagrera nf **vinagreras** oil and vinegar cruets, cruet (stand)

vinagreta nf vinaigrette sauce

vinajeras nfpl cruets

vincha nf Am headband

vinculante adj binding

vincular vt to link, to bind; (relacionar) to relate, to connect

vínculo nm link

vine pt indef de venir

vinícola adj wine-producing

vinicultor,-a nm,f wine producer

vinicultura nf wine production o growing

vinilo nm vinyl

vino nm wine; **tomar un v.** to have a glass of wine; **v. blanco/tinto/dulce/seco** white/red/sweet/dry wine; **v. rosado** rosé

viña nf vineyard

viñedo nm vineyard

viñeta nf illustration

viola nf viola

violación nf (a) (de una persona) rape (b) (de ley, derecho) violation, infringement

violador nm rapist

violar vt (a) (persona) to rape (b) (ley, derecho) to violate, to infringe

violencia nf (a) violence; **la no v.** nonviolence (b) (incomodidad) embarrassment

violentar vt (a) (forzar) to force, to break open; (sitio) to break into, to enter by force (b) (enojar) to infuriate

violento,-a adj (a) violent (b) (situación) embarrassing (c) **sentirse v.** (incómodo) to feel embarrassed o awkward

violeta 1 adj & nm (color) violet
2 nf (flor) violet

violín nm violin; Fam fiddle

violinista nmf violinist

violón nm double bass

violoncelista, violonchelista nmf cellist

violoncelo, violonchelo nm violoncello, cello

viraje nm (a) turn (b) Fig about-face, U-turn

virar vi (a) (girar) to turn round (b) Fig to change

virgen 1 adj (a) (persona, selva) virgin (b) (aceite, lana) pure; (cinta) blank
2 nmf virgin; Fam **ser un viva la v.** to be a devil-may-care person

virginidad nf virginity

Virgo nm Virgo

virgo nm hymen

virguería nf Fam gem, marvel; **hacer virguerías** to work wonders, to be a dab hand

virguero,-a adj Fam smart, great; **esta camisa es muy virguera** that shirt is the business

vírico,-a adj viral

viril adj virile, manly; **miembro v.** penis

virilidad nf virility

virtual adj virtual

virtud nf (a) virtue; Fig **en v. de** by virtue of (b) (propiedad) property, quality

virtuoso,-a 1 adj virtuous
2 nm,f (a) virtuous person (b) (músico) virtuoso

viruela nf smallpox; **viruelas** pockmarks

virulé: • **a la virulé** loc adj Fam (a) (torcido) crooked, twisted (b) **un ojo a la v.** a black eye

virulencia nf virulence

virulento,-a adj virulent

virus nm inv virus

visado nm, Am **visa** nf visa

víscera nf (a) internal organ (b) **vísceras** viscera, entrails

visceral adj (a) Anat visceral (b) Fig profound, deep-rooted

viscoso,-a adj viscous

visera nf (de gorra) peak; (de casco) visor

visibilidad nf visibility; **curva con mala v.** blind corner

visible adj visible; (evidente) evident

visillo nm small lace o net curtain

visión nf (a) vision (b) (vista) sight; Fig **v. de conjunto** overall view; **con v. de futuro** forward-looking (c) (aparición) vision

visionario,-a nm,f visionary; (iluso) person who imagines things

visita nf (a) (acción) visit; **hacer una v.** to pay a visit; **estar de v.** to be visiting (b) (invitado) visitor, guest

visitador,-a *nm,f Farm* pharmaceutical salesman, *f* saleswoman

visitante 1 *nmf* visitor

2 *adj (equipo)* away

visitar *vt* to visit

vislumbrar *vt* to glimpse

viso *nm* (a) *(reflejo)* sheen (b) *Fig* **tener visos de** to seem, to appear

visón *nm* mink

visor *nm Fot* viewfinder

> 📖 Observa que la palabra inglesa **visor** es un falso amigo y no es la traducción de la palabra española **visor**. En inglés, **visor** significa "visera".

víspera *nf (día anterior)* day before; *(de festivo)* eve; **en vísperas de** in the period leading up to

vista *nf* (a) sight; **a la v.** visible; **a primera** *o* **simple v.** at first sight, on the face of it; **con vistas a** with a view to; **en v. de** in view of, considering; **corto de v.** short-sighted; **conocer a algn de v.** to know sb by sight; **perder de v. a** to lose sight of; **quítalo de mi v.** take it away; *Fig* **tener mucha v. para** to have a good eye for; *Fig* **volver la v. atrás** to look back; *Fam* **¡hasta la v.!** goodbye!, see you!; *Fam* **hacer la v. gorda** to turn a blind eye (b) *(panorama)* view; **con vista(s) al mar** overlooking the sea (c) *Jur* trial, hearing

vistazo *nm* glance; **echar un v. a algo** *(ojear)* to have a (quick) look at sth; *(tener cuidado de)* to keep an eye on sth

visto,-a 1 *adj* (a) **está v. que ...** it is obvious that ...; **por lo v.** evidently, apparently; **v. que** in view of the fact that, seeing *o* given that (b) **estar bien v.** to be well looked upon, to be considered acceptable; **estar mal v.** to be frowned upon (c) **estar muy v.** to be old hat

2 *nm* **v. bueno** approval, O.K.

vistoso,-a *adj* eye-catching

visual *adj* visual; **campo v.** field of vision

visualizar [40] *vt* to visualize; *(película)* to view

vital *adj* (a) vital (b) *(persona)* full of vitality

vitalicio,-a *adj* life, for life; **pensión/cargo v.** life pension/permanent post

vitalidad *nf* vitality

vitamina *nf* vitamin

vitamínico,-a *adj* vitamin; **complejo v.** multivitamins

viticultor,-a *nm,f* wine grower

viticultura *nf* wine growing

vitorear *vt* to cheer

vítreo,-a *adj* vitreous

vitrina *nf (aparador)* glass *o* display cabinet; *(de exposición)* glass case, showcase; *Am (escaparate)* shop window

vituallas *nfpl* provisions

vituperar *vt* to condemn

vituperio *nm* condemnation

viudo,-a *nm,f (hombre)* widower; *(mujer)* widow

viva *interj* **¡v.!** hurrah!

vivacidad *nf* vivacity

vivaracho,-a *adj Fam* lively, sprightly

vivaz *adj* (a) lively, vivacious (b) *(perspicaz)* sharp, quick-witted

vivencias *nfpl* personal experience

víveres *nmpl* provisions, supplies

vivero *nm (de plantas)* nursery; *(de peces)* fish farm *o* hatchery; *Fig* breeding ground, hotbed

viveza *nf* (a) liveliness, vivacity; *(en los ojos)* sparkle (b) *(agudeza)* sharpness, quick-wittedness

vividor,-a *nm,f Pey* sponger, scrounger

vivienda *nf* (a) housing (b) *(casa)* house; *(piso)* flat

vivir 1 *vi* to live; **vive de sus ahorros** she lives off her savings; **viven de la pesca** they make their living by fishing

2 *vt* to live through

3 *nm* life

vivito,-a *adj Fam* **v. y coleando** alive and kicking

vivo,-a 1 *adj* (a) alive; **de viva voz** verbally, by word of mouth; **en v.** *(programa)* live; *Fam* **es el v. retrato** *o* **la viva imagen de** she is the spitting image of (b) **al rojo v.** red-hot (c) *(vivaz)* lively, vivacious (d) *(listo)* sharp, clever (e) *(color)* vivid, bright (f) *(descripción)* lively, graphic

2 *nm,f* **los vivos** the living

Vizcaya *n* **el golfo de V.** the Bay of Biscay

V. B. *(abr* **visto bueno)** *(en documento)* approved

vocablo *nm* word, term

vocabulario *nm* vocabulary

vocación *nf* vocation, calling; **con v. europea** with leanings towards Europe

vocacional *adj* vocational

vocal 1 *nf Ling* vowel

2 *nmf* member

vocalista *nmf Mús* vocalist, singer

vocalizar [40] *vt & vi* to vocalize

voceador,-a *nm,f Am* vendor

vocerío *nm* shouting

vocero,-a *nm,f Am* spokesperson; *(hombre)* spokesman; *(mujer)* spokeswoman

vociferante *adj* vociferous

vociferar *vt & vi* to vociferate

vodka *nm* vodka

vol. (*abr* **volumen**) vol

volado,-a *adj Fam* **estar v.** to have a screw loose

volador,-a *adj* flying

volandas: •**en volandas** *loc adv* (*por el aire*) in the air, flying through the air

volante 1 *nm* (**a**) *Aut* steering wheel; **ir al v.** to be driving; **un as del v.** a motor-racing champion (**b**) *Cost* frill, ruffle (**c**) *Med* note

2 *adj* flying; **platillo v.** flying saucer

volantín *nm Am* (*cometa*) small kite

volar [2] 1 *vi* (**a**) to fly; *Fig* **lo hizo volando** he did it in a flash (**b**) *Fam* (*desaparecer*) to disappear, to vanish

2 *vt* (*edificios*) to blow up; (*caja fuerte*) to blow open; *Min* to blast

3 volarse *vpr* (*papel etc*) to be blown away

volátil *adj* volatile

volatinero,-a *nm,f* acrobat

volcán *nm* volcano

volcánico,-a *adj* volcanic

volcar [2] 1 *vt* (**a**) (*cubo etc*) to knock over; (*barco, bote*) to capsize (**b**) (*vaciar*) to empty out (**c**) (*tiempo*) to invest

2 *vi* (*coche*) to turn over; (*barco*) to capsize

3 volcarse *vpr* (**a**) (*vaso, jarra*) to fall over, to tip over; (*coche*) to turn over; (*barco*) to capsize (**b**) *Fig* **v. con** to do one's utmost for

voleibol *nm* volleyball

voleo *nm Fig* **a(l) v.** at random, haphaz-ardly

voltaje *nm* voltage

voltear 1 *vt* (**a**) (*dar la vuelta a*) to turn upside down (**b**) *CSur* (*derribar*) to knock over (**c**) *Andes, CAm, Carib, Méx* (*cabeza*) to turn; **v. la espalda a algn** to turn one's back on sb

2 *vi* (**a**) to turn o roll over (**b**) *Méx* (*doblar la esquina*) to go round

3 voltearse *vpr* (**a**) *Andes, CAm, Carib, Méx* (*volverse*) to turn around (**b**) *Méx* (*vehículo*) to turn over

voltereta *nf* somersault

voltio *nm* volt

voluble *adj* fickle, changeable

⚠ Observa que la palabra inglesa **voluble** es un falso amigo y no es la traducción de la palabra española **voluble**. En inglés, **vol-uble** significa "locuaz".

volumen *nm* volume

voluminoso,-a *adj* voluminous; (*enor-me*) massive, bulky

voluntad *nf* will; **fuerza de v.** willpower;

tiene mucha **v.** he is very strong-willed; **a v.** at will

voluntario,-a 1 *adj* voluntary

2 *nm,f* volunteer; **ofrecerse v.** to volun-teer

voluntarioso,-a *adj* willing

voluptuoso,-a *adj* voluptuous

volver [4] (*pp* **vuelto**) **1** *vi* (**a**) to return; (*venir*) to come back; (*ir*) to go back; **v. en sí** to come round, to recover con-sciousness (**b**) **v. a hacer algo** to do sth again

2 *vt* (**a**) (*convertir*) to turn, to make; **me vas a v. loco** you are driving me mad (**b**) (*dar vuelta a*) to turn; (*boca abajo*) to turn upside down; (*de fuera adentro*) to turn inside out; (*de atrás adelante*) to turn back to front; (*dar la vuelta a*) to turn over; **volverle la espalda a algn** to turn one's back on sb; *Fig* **v. la vista atrás** to look back; **al v. la esquina** on turning the corner

3 volverse *vpr* (**a**) to turn (**b**) (*regresar*) (*venir*) to come back; (*ir*) to go back (**c**) (*convertirse*) to become; **v. loco,-a** to go mad

vomitar 1 *vi* to vomit, to be sick; **tengo ganas de v.** I feel sick, I want to be sick

2 *vt* to vomit, to bring up

vómito *nm* (*lo vomitado*) vomit; (*acción*) vomiting

vomitona *nf Fam* vomit

voracidad *nf* voracity, voraciousness

vorágine *nf* whirlpool; *Fig* maelstrom

voraz *adj* voracious; *Fig* raging, fierce

vórtice *nm* vortex

vos *pron pers Am* (*tú*) you

The **vos** form is used alongside **tú** in many Latin American countries, and in some countries (Argentina, Paraguay and Uru-guay) is the preferred form.

vosotros,-as *pron pers pl* (**a**) (*sujeto*) you (**b**) (*con prep*) you; **entre v.** among your-selves; **sin vosotras** without you

Usually omitted in Spanish except for em-phasis or contrast. In Latin America, **voso-tros** is not used. Instead, **ustedes** is used as the second person plural in all contexts, without necessarily suggesting formality.

votación *nf* (**a**) (*voto*) vote, ballot (**b**) (*acción*) voting

votante *nmf* voter

votar *vi* to vote; **v. a algn** to vote (for) sb

voto *nm* (**a**) vote; **tener v.** to have the right to vote; **v. secreto** secret ballot (**b**) *Rel* vow

vox *nf* esto es v. populi this is common knowledge

voy *indic pres de* ir

voz *nf* (a) voice; **en v. alta** aloud; **en v. baja** in a low voice; **a media v.** in a low voice, softly; **de viva v.** verbally (b) *(grito)* shout; **a voces** shouting; **dar voces** to shout; *Fig* **estar pidiendo algo a voces** to be crying out for sth; *Fig* **secreto a voces** open secret; **a v. en grito** at the top of one's voice (c) **no tener ni v. ni voto** to have no say in the matter; *Fig* **llevar la v. cantante** to rule the roost (d) *Gram* **v. pasiva** passive voice

vudú *nm* voodoo

vuelco *nm* upset, tumble; **dar un v.** *(coche)* to overturn; *Fig* **me dio un v. el corazón** my heart missed a beat

vuelo *nm* (a) flight; **v. chárter/regular** charter/scheduled flight; **v. sin motor** gliding; *Fig* **cazarlas** *o* **cogerlas al v.** to be quick on the uptake (b) *Cost* **una falda de v.** a full skirt

vuelta *nf* (a) *(regreso)* return; *(viaje)* return journey; **a v. de correo** by return of post; **estar de v.** to be back; *Dep* **partido de v.** return match (b) *(giro)* turn; *(en carreras)* lap; *Dep (ciclista)* tour; **dar media v.** to turn round; *Fig* **la cabeza me da**

vueltas my head is spinning; *Fig* **no le des más vueltas** stop worrying about it; **v. de campana** somersault (c) *(dinero)* change (d) **dar una v.** *(a pie)* to go for a walk *o* stroll; *(en coche)* to go for a drive *o* a spin (in the car) (e) *Fig* **no tiene v. de hoja** there's no doubt about it

vuelto,-a 1 *adj* jersey de cuello v. rollneck sweater

2 *nm Am* change

vuestro,-a 1 *adj pos (antes del sustantivo)* your; *(después del sustantivo)* of yours; **v. libro** your book; **un amigo v.** a friend of yours

2 *pron pos* yours; **éstos son los vuestros** these are yours; **lo v.** what is yours, what belongs to you

vulgar *adj* (a) vulgar (b) **el término v.** the everyday term

vulgaridad *nf* vulgarity

vulgarizar [40] *vt (popularizar)* to popularize

vulgarmente *adv* v. llamado commonly known as

vulgo *nm* **el v.** the common people; *Pey* the masses

vulnerable *adj* vulnerable

vulnerar *vt (ley, acuerdo)* to violate

vulva *nf* vulva

WXY

W, w [ue'ðole] *nf (la letra)* W, w
W (*abr* **vatio(s)**) W
walkie-talkie *nm* walkie-talkie
walkman® *nm* Walkman®
wáter *nm (pl* **wáteres**) *Fam* toilet
waterpolo *nm* water polo
Web, web [web] *Informát* **1** *nf (World Wide Web)* **la W.** the Web
  2 *nm o nf (página web)* web site
whisky *nm (escocés)* whisky; *(irlandés, US)* whiskey
windsurf, windsurfing *nm* windsurfing
windsurfista *nmf* windsurfer

xenofobia *nf* xenophobia
xenófobo,-a 1 *adj* xenophobic
  2 *nm,f* xenophobe

Y, y [iri'ea] *nf (la letra)* Y, y
y *conj* **(a)** and; **una chica alta y morena** a tall, dark-haired girl; **son las tres y cuarto** it's a quarter past three **(b)** **¿y qué?** so what?; **¿y si no llega a tiempo?** what if he doesn't arrive in time?; **¿y tú?** what about you?; **¿y eso?** how come?; **y eso que** although, even though; **¡y tanto!** you bet!, and how!; *ver* **e**
ya 1 *adv* **(a)** already; **ya lo sabía** I already knew; **ya en la Edad Media** as far back as the Middle Ages **(b)** *(ahora mismo)* now; **es preciso actuar ya** it is vital that we act now; **¡hazlo ya!** do it at once!; **ya mismo** right away **(c)** *(en el futuro)* **ya hablaremos luego** we'll talk about it later; **ya nos veremos** see you!; **ya verás** you'll see **(d)** **ya no** no longer; **ya no viene por aquí** he doesn't come round here any more **(e)** *(refuerza el verbo)* **ya era hora** about time too; **ya lo creo** of course, I should think so; **¡ya voy!** coming!; **¡ya está!** that's it!
  2 *conj* **ya que** since
yacaré *nm* cayman
yacer [61] *vi* to lie, to be lying
yacimiento *nm* bed, deposit; **yacimientos petrolíferos** oilfields
yaguar *nm* jaguar
yanqui *Pey* **1** *adj* Yankee
  2 *nmf* Yankee, Yank
yarará *nf Am* = large poisonous snake

yaraví *nm Am* = Quechuan song
yarda *nf* yard
yate *nm* yacht
yaya *nf Am Bot* lance-wood; *Fam (abuela)* granny
yedra *nf* = **hiedra**
yegua *nf* mare
yema *nf* **(a)** *(de huevo)* yolk **(b)** *Bot* bud **(c)** **y. del dedo** fingertip **(d)** *Culin* = sweet made from sugar and egg yolk
Yemen *n* Yemen
yen *nm (moneda)* yen
yendo *ger de* **ir**
yerba *nf* **(a)** = **hierba** **(b)** *RP* maté; **y. mate** yerba maté
yerbatero,-a *Am* **1** *nm,f (curandero)* = witch doctor who uses herbs
  2 *adj* maté
yermo,-a *adj* **(a)** *(baldío)* barren, uncultivated **(b)** *(despoblado)* deserted, uninhabited
yerno *nm* son-in-law
yerro *indic pres de* **errar**
yeso *nm* **(a)** *Geol* gypsum **(b)** *Constr* plaster
Yibuti *n* Djibouti
yiu-yitsu *nm* ju-jitsu
yo *pron pers* I; **entre tú y yo** between you and me; **¿quién es?** – **soy yo** who is it? – it's me; **yo no** not me; **yo que tú** if I were you; **yo mismo** I myself

---

Usually omitted as a personal pronoun in Spanish except for emphasis or contrast.

---

yodo *nm* iodine
yoga *nm* yoga
yogur *nm* yogurt, yoghurt
yogurtera *nf* yoghurt maker
yonqui *nmf Fam* junkie, drug addict
yoyo, yoyó *nm* yo-yo
yuca *nf* yucca
Yucatán *n* Yucatan
yudo *nm* judo
yudoka *nmf* judoka
yugo *nm* yoke
Yugoslavia *n* Yugoslavia
yugoslavo,-a, yugoeslavo,-a *adj & nm,f* Yugoslav, Yugoslavian
yugular *nf* jugular

yunque *nm* anvil
yunta *nf* yoke o team of oxen
yuxtaponer [19] (*pp* **yuxtapuesto**) *vt* to
  juxtapose

yuxtaposición *nf* juxtaposition
yuyo *nm* (**a**) *CSur (mala hierba)* weed;
  (hierba medicinal) medicinal herb (**b**)
  Andes (hierba silvestre) wild herb

Z

Z, z ['θeta] *nf (la letra)* Z, z

zacate *nm CAm, Méx* fodder

zafarse *upr (librarse)* to get away (**de** from), to escape (**de** from)

zafio,-a *adj* uncouth

zafiro *nm* sapphire

zaga *nf* **a la z.** behind, at the rear

zaguán *nm* hall, hallway

zaherir *vt* to hurt

zahúrda *nf* pigsty

zaino,-a *adj (caballo)* chestnut; *(toro)* black

Zaire *n* Zaire

zalamería *nf* flattery

zalamero,-a 1 *nm,f* flatterer, fawner
2 *adj* flattering, fawning

zamarra *nf (prenda)* sheepskin jacket

Zambia *n* Zambia

zambo,-a 1 *adj* (a) *(patizambo)* knock-kneed (b) *Am (persona)* half Indian and half Negro
2 *nm,f Am (persona)* = person who is half Indian and half Negro

zambomba *nf* = kind of primitive drum

zambullida *nf* plunge

zambullirse *upr* to plunge

zamparse *upr Fam* to gobble down

zanahoria *nf* carrot

zancada *nf* stride

zancadilla *nf* **ponerle la z. a algn** to trip sb up

zanco *nm* stilt

zancudo,-a 1 *adj* (a) long-legged (b) *Orn* wading; **ave zancuda** wading bird, wader
2 *nm Am* mosquito

zángano,-a 1 *nm (insecto)* drone
2 *nm,f Fam (persona)* idler, lazybones *inv*

zanja *nf* ditch, trench

zanjar *vt (asunto)* to settle

zapallito *nm CSur Br* courgette, *US* zucchini

zapallo *nm Andes, RP* sweet pumpkin

zapata *nf* (a) *(cuña)* wedge (b) *Téc* shoe

zapatear *vi* to tap one's feet

zapatería *nf* shoe shop

zapatero,-a *nm,f (vendedor)* shoe dealer; *(fabricante)* shoemaker, cobbler

zapatilla *nf* slipper; **zapatillas de deporte** trainers

zapato *nm* shoe; **zapatos de tacón** high-heeled shoes

zar *nm* czar, tsar

Zaragoza *n* Saragossa

zaragozano,-a 1 *adj* of/from Saragossa
2 *nm,f* person from Saragossa

zarandear *vt* to shake

zarandeo *nm* shaking

zarcillo *nm* (a) *(pendiente)* earring (b) *Bot* tendril

zarina *nf* czarina, tsarina

zarpa *nf* claw

zarpar *vi* to weigh anchor, to set sail

zarpazo *nm* clawing; **dar** *o* **pegar un z. a** to claw

zarza *nf* bramble, blackberry bush

zarzal *nm* bramble patch

zarzamora *nf (zarza)* blackberry bush; *(fruto)* blackberry

zarzuela *nf* (a) = Spanish operetta (b) **la Z.** = royal residence in Madrid (c) *Culin* = fish stew

zenit *nm* zenith

zigzag *nm (pl zigzags o zigzagues)* zig-zag

zigzaguear *vi* to zigzag

Zimbabwe *n* Zimbabwe

zinc *nm* zinc

zíper *nm CAm, Méx Br* zip, *US* zipper

zócalo *nm* (a) *(de pared)* skirting board (b) *(pedestal)* plinth

zodiaco, zodíaco *nm* zodiac; **signo del z.** sign of the zodiac

zona *nf* zone; *(región)* region; **z. euro** euro zone; **z. verde** park

zoo *nm* zoo

zoología *nf* zoology

zoológico,-a 1 *adj* zoological; **parque z.** zoo
2 *nm* zoo

zoom *nm Cin & Fot* zoom

zopenco,-a *nm,f Fam* dope, halfwit

zopilote *nm Am* buzzard

zoquete 1 *nm f Fam* blockhead
2 *nm CSur (calcetín)* ankle sock

zorra *nf* (a) vixen (b) *Fam* slut

zorro,-a 1 *nm* fox

2 *adj* (**a**) *(astuto)* cunning, sly (**b**) *muy Fam* **no tengo ni zorra (idea)** I haven't got a *Br* bloody *o US* goddamn clue

zorzal *nm Orn* thrush

zozobrar *vi* to be in danger of going under

zueco *nm* clog

zumbado,-a *adj Fam* crazy, mad

zumbar 1 *vi* to buzz, to hum; **me zumban los oídos** my ears are buzzing; *Fam* **salir zumbando** to zoom off

2 *vt Fam* to thrash

zumbido *nm* buzzing, humming

zumo *nm* juice

zurcir [52] *vt Cost* to darn; *Fam* **¡que te zurzan!** go to hell!

zurda *nf (mano)* left hand

zurdo,-a 1 *nm,f (persona)* left-handed person

2 *adj* left-handed

zurrar *vt (pegar)* to beat, to flog

zutano,-a *nm,f Fam* so-and-so; *(hombre)* what's-his-name; *(mujer)* what's-her-name

Spanish Verbs

◆

Regular Spelling Changes

The rules of spelling in Spanish cause a number of verbs to have regular spelling changes. These are listed below.

Spanish verbs fall into three groups depending on whether their infinitive ends in **-ar**, **-er** or **-ir**. The stem of the verb is the part which is left when the **-ar**, **-er** or **-ir** is removed from the infinitive. For example, the stem of **tomar** is **tom**, the stem of **beber** is **beb**, and the stem of **salir** is **sal**.

In the examples given below, the following indicators are used:

> (**1**) = first person singular present indicative
> (**2**) = present subjunctive, all persons
> (**3**) = first person singular preterite

Verbs ending in -ar

Verbs with a stem ending in **c**, for example **buscar**

The **c** changes to **qu** in:

> (**2**) busque, busques, busque, busquemos, busquéis, busquen
> (**3**) busqué

Verbs with a stem ending in **g**, for example **cargar**

The **g** changes to **gu** in:

> (**2**) cargue, cargues, cargue, carguemos, carguéis, carguen
> (**3**) cargué

Verbs with a stem ending in **gu**, for example **averiguar**

The **gu** changes to **gü** in:

> (**2**) averigüe, averigües, averigüe, averigüemos, averigüéis, averigüen
> (**3**) averigüé

Verbs with a stem ending in **z**, for example **realizar**

The **z** changes to **c** in:

> (**2**) realice, realices, realice, realicemos, realicéis, realicen
> (**3**) realicé

Verbs ending in -er *or* -ir

Verbs with a stem ending in **c**, for example **esparcir**

The **c** changes to **z** in:

(**1**) esparzo
(**2**) esparza, esparzas, esparza, esparzamos, esparzáis, esparzan

Verbs with a stem ending in **g**, for example **coger**

The **g** changes to **j** in:

(**1**) cojo
(**2**) coja, cojas, coja, cojamos, cojáis, cojan

Verbs with a stem ending in **qu**, for example **delinquir**

The **qu** changes to **c** in:

(**1**) delinco
(**2**) delinca, delincas, delinca, delincamos, delincáis, delincan

Verbs with a stem ending in **gu**, for example **distinguir**

The **gu** changes to **g** in:

(**1**) distingo
(**2**) distinga, distingas, distinga, distingamos, distingáis, distingan

Models for Regular Conjugation

TOMAR to take

INDICATIVE

PRESENT	**FUTURE**	**CONDITIONAL**
1. tomo	tomaré	tomaría
2. tomas	tomarás	tomarías
3. toma	tomará	tomaría
1. tomamos	tomaremos	tomaríamos
2. tomáis	tomaréis	tomarías
3. toman	tomarán	tomarían

IMPERFECT	**PRETERITE**	**PERFECT**
1. tomaba	tomé	he tomado
2. tomabas	tomaste	has tomado
3. tomaba	tomó	ha tomado
1. tomábamos	tomamos	hemos tomado
2. tomabais	tomasteis	habéis tomado
3. tomaban	tomaron	han tomado

FUTURE PERFECT	**CONDITIONAL PERFECT**	**PLUPERFECT**
1. habré tomado	habría tomado	había tomado
2. habrás tomado	habrías tomado	habías tomado
3. habrá tomado	habría tomado	había tomado
1. habremos tomado	habríamos tomado	habíamos tomado
2. habréis tomado	habríais tomado	habíais tomado
3. habrán tomado	habrían tomado	habían tomado

SUBJUNCTIVE

PRESENT	**IMPERFECT**	**PERFECT/PLUPERFECT**
1. tome	tom-ara/ase	haya/hubiera* tomado
2. tomes	tom-aras/ases	hayas/hubieras tomado
3. tome	tom-ara/ase	haya/hubiera tomado
1. tomemos	tom-áramos/ásemos	hayamos/hubiéramos tomado
2. toméis	tom-arais/aseis	hayáis/hubierais tomado
3. tomen	tom-aran/asen	hayan/hubieran tomado

IMPERATIVE   ### INFINITIVE   ### PARTICIPLE

(tú) toma	**PRESENT**	**PRESENT**
(Vd) tome	tomar	tomando
(nosotros) tomemos		
(vosotros) tomad	**PERFECT**	**PAST**
(Vds) tomen	haber tomado	tomado

* the alternative form 'hubiese' etc is also possible

COMER to eat

INDICATIVE

PRESENT	FUTURE	CONDITIONAL
1. como	comeré	comería
2. comes	comerás	comerías
3. come	comerá	comería
1. comemos	comeremos	comeríamos
2. coméis	comeréis	comeríais
3. comen	comerán	comerían

IMPERFECT	PRETERITE	PERFECT
1. comía	comí	he comido
2. comías	comiste	has comido
3. comía	comió	ha comido
1. comíamos	comimos	hemos comido
2. comíais	comisteis	habéis comido
3. comían	comieron	han comido

FUTURE PERFECT	CONDITIONAL PERFECT	PLUPERFECT
1. habré comido	habría comido	había comido
2. habrás comido	habrías comido	habías comido
3. habrá comido	habría comido	había comido
1. habremos comido	habríamos comido	habíamos comido
2. habréis comido	habríais comido	habíais comido
3. habrán comido	habrían comido	habían comido

SUBJUNCTIVE

PRESENT	IMPERFECT	PERFECT/PLUPERFECT
1. coma	com-iera/iese	haya/hubiera* comido
2. comas	com-ieras/ieses	hayas/hubieras comido
3. coma	com-iera/iese	haya/hubiera comido
1. comamos	com-iéramos/iésemos	hayamos/hubiéramos comido
2. comáis	com-ierais/ieseis	hayáis/hubierais comido
3. coman	com-ieran/iesen	hayan/hubieran comido

IMPERATIVE · INFINITIVE · PARTICIPLE

IMPERATIVE	INFINITIVE	PARTICIPLE
(tú) come	**PRESENT**	**PRESENT**
(Vd) coma	comer	comiendo
(nosotros) comamos		
(vosotros) comed	**PERFECT**	**PAST**
(Vds) coman	haber comido	comido

* the alternative form 'hubiese' etc is also possible

PARTIR to leave

INDICATIVE

PRESENT	FUTURE	CONDITIONAL
1. parto	partiré	partiría
2. partes	partirás	partirías
3. parte	partirá	partiría
1. partimos	partiremos	partiríamos
2. partís	partiréis	partiríais
3. parten	partirán	partirían

IMPERFECT	PRETERITE	PERFECT
1. partía	partí	he partido
2. partías	partiste	has partido
3. partía	partió	ha partido
1. partíamos	partimos	hemos partido
2. partíais	partisteis	habéis partido
3. partían	partieron	han partido

FUTURE PERFECT	CONDITIONAL PERFECT	PLUPERFECT
1. habré partido	habría partido	había partido
2. habrás partido	habrías partido	habías partido
3. habrá partido	habría partido	había partido
1. habremos partido	habríamos partido	habíamos partido
2. habréis partido	habríais partido	habíais partido
3. habrán partido	habrían partido	habían partido

SUBJUNCTIVE

PRESENT	IMPERFECT	PERFECT/PLUPERFECT
parta	parti-era/ese	haya/hubiera* partido
partas	parti-eras/eses	hayas/hubieras partido
parta	parti-era/ese	haya/hubiera partido
partamos	parti-éramos/ésemos	hayamos/hubiéramos partido
partáis	parti-erais/eseis	hayáis/hubierais partido
partan	parti-eran/esen	hayan/hubieran partido

IMPERATIVE	INFINITIVE	PARTICIPLE
(tú) parte	**PRESENT**	**PRESENT**
(Vd) parta	partir	partiendo
(nosotros) partamos		
(vosotros) partid	**PERFECT**	**PAST**
(Vds) partan	haber partido	partido

* the alternative form 'hubiese' etc is also possible

Models for Irregular Conjugation

[1] **pensar PRES** pienso, piensas, piensa, pensamos, pensáis, piensan; **PRES SUBJ** piense, pienses, piense, pensemos, penséis, piensen; **IMPERAT** piensa, piense, pensemos, pensad, piensen

[2] **contar PRES** cuento, cuentas, cuenta, contamos, contáis, cuentan; **PRES SUBJ** cuente, cuentes, cuente, contemos, contéis, cuenten; **IMPERAT** cuenta, cuente, contemos, contad, cuenten

[3] **perder PRES** pierdo, pierdes, pierde, perdemos, perdéis, pierden; **PRES SUBJ** pierda, pierdas, pierda, perdamos, perdáis, pierdan; **IMPERAT** pierde, pierda, perdamos, perded, pierdan

[4] **morder PRES** muerdo, muerdes, muerde, mordemos, mordéis, muerden; **PRES SUBJ** muerda, muerdas, muerda, mordamos, mordáis, muerdan; **IMPERAT** muerde, muerda, mordamos, morded, muerdan

[5] **sentir PRES** siento, sientes, siente, sentimos, sentís, sienten; **PRES SUBJ** sienta, sientas, sienta, sintamos, sintáis, sientan; **PRES P** sintiendo; **IMPERAT** siente, sienta, sintamos, sentid, sientan

[6] **vestir PRES** visto, vistes, viste, vestimos, vestís, visten; **PRES SUBJ** vista, vistas, vista, vistamos, vistáis, vistan; **PRES P** vistiendo; **IMPERAT** viste, vista, vistamos, vestid, vistan

[7] **dormir PRES** duermo, duermes, duerme, dormimos, dormís, duermen; **PRES SUBJ** duerma, duermas, duerma, durmamos, durmáis, duerman; **PRES P** durmiendo; **IMPERAT** duerme, duerma, durmamos, dormid, duerman

[8] **andar PRET** anduve, anduviste, anduvo, anduvimos, anduvisteis, anduvieron; **IMPERF SUBJ** anduviera/anduviese

[9] **caber PRES** quepo, cabes, cabe, cabemos, cabéis, caben; **PRES SUBJ** quepa, quepas, quepa, quepamos, quepáis, quepan; **FUT** cabré; **COND** cabría; **PRET** cupe, cupiste, cupo, cupimos, cupisteis, cupieron; **IMPERF SUBJ** cupiera/cupiese; **IMPERAT** cabe, quepa, quepamos, cabed, quepan

[10] **conducir PRES** conduzco, conduces, conduce, conducimos, conducís, conducen; **PRES SUBJ** conduzca, conduzcas, conduzca, conduzcamos, conduzcáis, conduzcan; **PRET** conduje, condujiste, condujo, condujimos, condujisteis, condujeron; **IMPERF SUBJ** condujera/condujese; **IMPERAT** conduce, conduzca, conduzcamos, conducid, conduzcan

[11] **dar PRES** doy, das, da, damos, dais, dan; **PRES SUBJ** dé, des, dé, demos, deis, den; **PRET** di, diste, dio, dimos, disteis, dieron; **IMPERF SUBJ** diera/diese; **IMPERAT** da, dé, demos, dad, den

[12] **decir PRES** digo, dices, dice, decimos, decís, dicen; **PRES SUBJ** diga, digas, diga, digamos, digáis, digan; **FUT** diré; **COND** diría; **PRET** dije, dijiste, dijo, dijimos, dijisteis, dijeron; **IMPERF SUBJ** dijera/dijese; **PRES P** diciendo; **PP** dicho; **IMPERAT** di, diga, digamos, decid, digan

[13] **ESTAR** to be

INDICATIVE

PRESENT	FUTURE	CONDITIONAL
1. estoy	estaré	estaría
2. estás	estarás	estarías
3. está	estará	estaría
1. estamos	estaremos	estaríamos
2. estáis	estaréis	estaríais
3. están	estarán	estarían

IMPERFECT	PRETERITE	PERFECT
1. estaba	estuve	he estado
2. estabas	estuviste	has estado
3. estaba	estuvo	ha estado
1. estábamos	estuvimos	hemos estado
2. estabais	estuvisteis	habéis estado
3. estaban	estuvieron	han estado

FUTURE PERFECT	CONDITIONAL PERFECT	PLUPERFECT
1. habré estado	habría estado	había estado
2. habrás estado	habrías estado	habías estado
3. habrá estado	habría estado	había estado
1. habremos estado	habríamos estado	habíamos estado
2. habréis estado	habríais estado	habíais estado
3. habrán estado	habrían estado	habían estado

SUBJUNCTIVE

PRESENT	IMPERFECT	PERFECT/PLUPERFECT
1. esté	estuv-iera/iese	haya/hubiera* estado
2. estés	estuv-ieras/ieses	hayas/hubieras estado
3. esté	estuv-iera/iese	haya/hubiera estado
1. estemos	esuv-iéramos/iésemos	hayamos/hubiéramos estado
2. estéis	estuv-ierais/ieseis	hayáis/hubierais estado
3. estén	estuv-ieran/iesen	hayan/hubieran estado

IMPERATIVE

(tú) está		
(Vd) esté		
(nosotros) estemos		
(vosotros) estad		
(Vds) estén		

INFINITIVE

PRESENT
estar

PERFECT
haber estado

PARTICIPLE

PRESENT
estando

PAST
estado

* the alternative form 'hubiese' etc is also possible

[14] **HABER** to have (*auxiliary*)

INDICATIVE

PRESENT	FUTURE	CONDITIONAL
1. he	habré	habría
2. has	habrás	habrías
3. ha/hay*	habrá	habría
1. hemos	habremos	habríamos
2. habéis	habréis	habríais
3. han	habrán	habrían

IMPERFECT	PRETERITE	PERFECT
1. había	hube	
2. habías	hubiste	
3. había	hubo	ha habido*
1. habíamos	hubimos	
2. habíais	hubisteis	
3. habían	hubieron	

FUTURE PERFECT	CONDITIONAL PERFECT	PLUPERFECT
1.		
2.		
3. habrá habido*	habría habido*	había habido*
1.		
2.		
3.		

SUBJUNCTIVE

PRESENT	IMPERFECT	PERFECT/PLUPERFECT
1. haya	hub-iera/iese	
2. hayas	hub-ieras/ieses	
3. haya	hub-iera/iese	haya/hubiera** habido*
1. hayamos	hub-iéramos/iésemos	
2. hayáis	hub-ierais/ieseis	
3. hayan	hub-ieran/iesen	

INFINITIVE	**PARTICIPLE**

PRESENT	PRESENT
haber	habiendo
PERFECT	**PAST**
haber habido*	habido

* 'haber' is an auxiliary verb used with the participle of another verb to form compound tenses (eg he bebido - I have drunk). 'hay' means 'there is/are' and all third person singular forms in their respective tenses have this meaning. The forms highlighted with an asterisk are used only for this latter construction.

** the alternative form 'hubiese' is also possible.

[15] **hacer PRES** hago, haces, hace, hacemos, hacéis, hacen; **PRES SUBJ** haga, hagas, haga hagamos, hagáis, hagan; **FUT** haré; **COND** haría; **PRET** hice, hiciste, hizo, hicimos, hicisteis, hicieron; **IMPERF SUBJ** hiciera/hiciese; **PP** hecho; **IMPERAT** haz, haga, hagamos, haced, hagan

[16] **ir PRES** voy, vas, va, vamos, vais, van; **PRES SUBJ** vaya, vayas, vaya, vayamos, vayáis, vayan; **IMPERF** iba, ibas, iba, íbamos, ibais, iban; **PRET** fui, fuiste, fue, fuimos, fuisteis, fueron; **IMPERF SUBJ** fuera/fuese; **PRES P** yendo; **IMPERAT** ve, vaya, vamos, id, vayan

[17] **oir PRES** oigo, oyes, oye, oímos, oís, oyen; **PRES SUBJ** oiga, oigas, oiga, oigamos, oigáis, oigan; **PRET** oí, oíste, oyó, oímos, oísteis, oyeron; **IMPERF SUBJ** oyera/oyese; **PRES P** oyendo; **PP** oído; **IMPERAT** oye, oiga, oigamos, oíd, oigan

[18] **poder PRES** puedo, puedes, puede, podemos, podéis, pueden; **PRES SUBJ** pueda, puedas, pueda, podamos, podáis, puedan; **FUT** podré; **COND** podría; **PRET** pude, pudiste, pudo, pudimos, pudisteis, pudieron; **IMPERF SUBJ** pudiera/pudiese; **PRES P** pudiendo; **IMPERAT** puede, pueda, podamos, poded, puedan

[19] **poner PRES** pongo, pones, pone, ponemos, ponéis, ponen; **PRES SUBJ** ponga, pongas, ponga, pongamos, pongáis, pongan; **FUT** pondré; **PRET** puse, pusiste, puso, pusimos, pusisteis, pusieron; **IMPERF SUBJ** pusiera/pusiese; **PP** puesto; **IMPERAT** pon, ponga, pongamos, poned, pongan

[20] **querer PRES** quiero, quieres, quiere, queremos, queréis, quieren; **PRES SUBJ** quiera, quieras, quiera, queramos, queráis, quieran; **FUT** querré; **COND** querría; **PRET** quise, quisiste, quiso, quisimos, quisisteis, quisieron; **IMPERF SUBJ** quisiera/quisiese; **IMPERAT** quiere, quiera, queramos, quered, quieran

[21] **saber PRES** sé, sabes, sabe, sabemos, sabéis, saben; **PRES SUBJ** sepa, sepas, sepa, sepamos, sepáis, sepan; **FUT** sabré; **COND** sabría; **PRET** supe, supiste, supo, supimos, supisteis, supieron; **IMPERF SUBJ** supiera/supiese; **IMPERAT** sabe, sepa, sepamos, sabed, sepan

[22] **salir PRES** salgo, sales, sale, salimos, salís, salen; **PRES SUBJ** salga, salgas, salga, salgamos, salgáis, salgan; **FUT** saldré; **COND** saldría; **IMPERAT** sal, salga salgamos, salid, salgan

[23] **ser PRES** soy, eres, es, somos, sois, son; **PRES SUBJ** sea, seas, sea, seamos, seáis, sean; **IMPERF** era, eras, era, éramos, erais, eran; **PRET** fui, fuiste, fue, fuimos, fuisteis, fueron; **IMPERF SUBJ** fuera/fuese; **IMPERAT** sé, sea, seamos, sed, sean

[24] **tener PRES** tengo, tienes, tiene, tenemos, tenéis, tienen; **PRES SUBJ** tenga, tengas, tenga, tengamos, tengáis, tengan; **FUT** tendré; **COND** tendría; **PRET** tuve, tuviste, tuvo, tuvimos, tuvisteis, tuvieron; **IMPERF SUBJ** tuviera/tuviese; **IMPERAT** ten, tenga, tengamos, tened tengan

[25] **traer PRES** traigo, traes, trae, traemos, traéis, traen; **PRES SUBJ** traiga, traigas, traiga, traigamos, traigáis, traigan; **PRET** traje, trajiste, trajo, trajimos, trajisteis, trajeron; **IMPERF SUBJ** trajera/trajese; **IMPERAT** trae, traiga, traigamos, traed, traigan

[26] **valer** PRES valgo, vales, vale, valemos, valéis, valen; **PRES SUBJ** valga, valgas, valga, valgamos, valgáis, valgan; **FUT** valdré; **COND** valdría; **IMPERAT** vale, valga, valemos, valed, valgan

[27] **venir** PRES vengo, vienes, viene, venimos, venís, vienen; **PRES SUBJ** venga, vengas, venga, vengamos, vengáis, vengan; **FUT** vendré; **COND** vendría; **PRET** vine, viniste, vino, vinimos, vinisteis, vinieron; **IMPERF SUBJ** viniera/viniese; **PRES P** viniendo; **IMPERAT** ven, venga, vengamos, venid, vengan

[28] **ver** PRES veo, ves, ve, vemos, veis, ven; **PRES SUBJ** vea, veas, vea, veamos, veáis, vean; **IMPERF** veía, veías, veía, veíamos, veíais, veían; **PRET** vi, viste, vio, vimos, visteis, vieron; **IMPERF SUBJ** viera/viese; **IMPERAT** ve, vea, veamos, ved, vean

[29] **desviar** PRES desvío, desvías, desvía, desviamos, desviáis, desvían; **PRES SUBJ** desvíe, desvíes, desvíe, desviemos, desviéis, desvíen; **IMPERAT** desvía, desvíe, desviemos, desviéis, desvíen

[30] **continuar** PRES continúo, continúas, continúa, continuamos, continuáis, continúan; **PRES SUBJ** continúe, continúes, continúe, continuemos, continuéis, continúen; **IMPERAT** continúa, continúe, continuemos, continuad, continúen

[31] **adquirir** PRES adquiero, adquieres, adquiere, adquirimos, adquirís, adquieren; **PRES SUBJ** adquiera, adquiras, adquiera, adquiramos, adquiráis, adquieran; **IMPERAT** adquiere, adquiera, adquiramos, adquirid, adquieran

[32] **jugar** PRES juego, juegas, juega, jugamos, jugáis, juegan; **PRES SUBJ** juegue, juegues, juegue, juguemos, juguéis, jueguen; **IMPERAT** juega, juegue, juguemos, jugad, jueguen

[33] **agradecer** PRES agradezco, agradeces, agradece, agradecemos, agradecéis, agradecen; **PRES SUBJ** agradezca, agradezcas, agradezca, agradezcamos, agradezcáis, agradezcan; **IMPERAT** agradece, agradezca, agradezcamos, agradeced, agradezcan

[34] **conocer** PRES conozco, conoces, conoce, conocemos, conocéis, conocen; **PRES SUBJ** conozca, conozcas, conozca, conozcamos, conozcáis, conozcan; **IMPERAT** conoce, conozca, conozcamos, conoced, conozcan

[35] **lucir** PRES luzco, luces, luce, lucimos, lucís, lucen; **PRES SUBJ** luzca, luzcas, luzca, luzcamos, luzcáis, luzcan; **IMPERAT** luce, luzca, luzcamos, lucid, luzcan

[36] **leer** PRET leí, leíste, leyó, leímos, leísteis, leyeron; **IMPERF SUBJ** leyera/leyese; **PRES P** leyendo; **PP** leído; **IMPERAT** lee, lea, leamos, leed, lean

[37] **huir** PRES huyo, huyes, huye, huimos, huís, huyen; **PRES SUBJ** huya, huyas, huya, huyamos, huyáis, huyan; **PRET** huí, huiste, huyó, huimos, huisteis, huyeron; **IMPERF SUBJ** huyera/huyese; **PRES P** huyendo; **PP** huido; **IMPERAT** huye, huya, huyamos, huid, huyan

[38] **roer** PRES roo/roigo/royo, roes, roe, roemos, roéis, roen; **PRES SUBJ** roa/roiga/roya, roas, roa, roamos, roáis, roan; **PRET** roí, roíste, royó, roímos, roísteis, royeron; **IMPERF SUBJ** royera/royese; **PRES P** royendo; **PP** roído; **IMPERAT** roe, roa, roamos, roed, roan

[39] **caer PRES** caigo, caes, cae, caemos, caéis, caen; **PRES SUBJ** caiga, caigas, caiga, caigamos, caigáis, caigan; **PRES P** cayendo; **PP** caído; **IMPERAT** cae, caiga caigamos, caed, caigan

[40] **cazar PRET** cacé, cazaste, cazó, cazamos, cazasteis, cazaron; **PRES SUBJ** cace, caces, cacen, cacemos, cacéis, cacen

[41] **cocer PRES** cuezo, cueces, cuece, cocemos, cocéis, cuecen; **PRES SUBJ** cueza, cuezas, cueza, cozamos, cozáis, cuezan; **IMPERAT** cuece, cueza, cozamos, coced, cuezan

[42] **llegar PRET** llegué, llegaste, llegó, llegamos, llegasteis, llegaron; **PRES SUBJ** llegue, llegues, llegue, lleguemos, lleguéis, lleguen

[43] **cambiar PRES** cambio, cambias, cambia, cambiamos, cambiáis, cambian; **PRES SUBJ** cambie, cambies, cambie, cambiemos, cambiéis, cambien; **IMPERAT** cambia, cambie, cambiemos, cambiad, cambien

[44] **sacar PRET** saqué, sacaste, sacó, sacamos, sacasteis, sacaron; **PRES SUBJ** saque, saques, saque, saquemos, saquéis, saquen; **IMPERAT** saca, saque, saquemos, sacad, saquen

[45] **averiguar PRET** averigüé, averiguaste, averiguó, averiguamos, averiguasteis, averiguaron; **PRES SUBJ** averigüe, averigües, averigüe, averigüemos, averigüéis, averigüen; **IMPERAT** averigua, averigüe, averigüemos, averiguad, averigüen

[46] **asir PRES** asgo, ases, ase, asimos, asís, asen; **PRES SUBJ** asga, asgas, asga, asgamos, asgáis, asgan; **IMPERAT** ase, asga, asgamos, asid, asgan

[47] **adecuar PRES** adecuo, adecuas, adecua, adecuamos, adecuáis, adecuan; **PRES SUBJ** adecue, adecues, adecue, adecuemos, adecuéis, adecuen; **IMPERAT** adecua, adecuen, adecuemos, adecuad, adecuen

[48] **delinquir PRES** delinco, delinques, delinque, delinquimos, delinquís, delinquen; **PRES SUBJ** delinca, delincas, delinca, delincamos, delincáis, delincan; **IMPERAT** delinque, delinca, delincamos, delinquid, delincan

[49] **mecer PRES** mezo, meces, mece, mecemos, mecéis, mecen; **PRES SUBJ** meza, mezas, meza, mezamos, mezáis, mezan; **IMPERAT** mece, meza, mezamos, meced, mezan

[50] **errar PRES** yerro, yerras, yerra, erramos, erráis, yerran; **PRES SUBJ** yerre, yerres, yerre, erremos, erréis, yerren; **IMPERAT** yerra, yerre, erremos, errad, yerren

[51] **comenzar PRES** comienzo, comienzas, comienza, comenzamos, comenzáis, comienzan; **PRES SUBJ** comience, comiences, comience, comencemos, comencéis, comiencen; **IMPERAT** comienza, comience, comencemos, comenzad, comiencen

[52] **zurcir PRES** zurzo, zurces, zurce, zurcimos, zurcís, zurcen; **PRES SUBJ** zurza, zurzas, zurza, zurzamos, zurzáis, zurzan; **IMPERAT** zurce, zurza, zurzamos, zurcid, zurzan

[53] **proteger PRES** protejo, proteges, protege, protegemos, protegéis, protegen; **PRES SUBJ** proteja, protejas, proteja, protejamos, protejáis, protejan; **IMPERAT** protege, proteja, protejamos, proteged, protejan

[54] **discernir PRES** discierno, disciernes, discierne, discernimos, discernís, disciernen; **PRES SUBJ** discierna, disciernas, discierna, discernamos, discernáis, disciernan; **IMPERAT** discierne, discierna, discernamos, discernid, disciernan

[55] **erguir PRES** irgo/yergo, irgues/yergues, irgue/yergue, erguimos, erguís, irguen/yerguen; **PRET** erguí, erguiste, irguió, erguimos, erguisteis, irguieron; **PRES SUBJ** irga/yerga, irgas/yergas, irga/yerga, irgamos/yergamos, irgáis/yergáis, irgan/yergan; **IMPERF SUBJ** irguiera/irguiese; **IMPERAT** irgue/yergue, irga/yerga, irgamos/yergamos, erguid, irgan/yergan

[56] **reír PRES** río, ríes, ríe, reímos, reís, ríen; **PRET** reí, reíste, rió, reímos, reísteis, rieron; **PRES SUBJ** ría, rías, ría, riamos, riáis, rían; **IMPERF SUBJ** riera/riese; **IMPERAT** ríe, ría, riamos, reíd, rían

[57] **dirigir PRES** dirijo, diriges, dirige, dirigimos, dirigís, dirigen; **PRES SUBJ** dirija, dirijas, dirija, dirijamos, dirijáis, dirijan; **IMPERAT** dirige, dirija, dirijamos, dirigid, dirijan

[58] **regir PRES** rijo, riges, rige, regimos, regís, rigen; **PRES SUBJ** rija, rijas, rija, rijamos, rijáis, rijan; **IMPERAT** rige, rija, rijamos, regid, rijan

[59] **distinguir PRES** distingo, distingues, distingue, distinguimos, distinguís, distinguen; **PRES SUBJ** distinga, distingas, distinga, distingamos, distingáis, distingan; **IMPERAT** distingue, distinga, distingamos, distinguid, distingan

[60] **nacer PRES** nazco, naces, nace, nacemos, nacéis, nacen; **PRES SUBJ** nazca, nazcas, nazca, nazcamos, nazcáis, nazcan; **IMPERAT** nace, nazca, nazcamos, naced, nazcan

[61] **yacer PRES** yazco/yazgo/yago, yaces, yace, yacemos, yacéis, yacen; **PRES SUBJ** yazca/yazga/yaga; **IMPERAT** yace/yaz, yazca/yazga/yaga, yazcamos/yazgamos/yagamos, yaced, yazcan/yazgan/yagan

[62] **argüir PRES** arguyo, arguyes, arguye, argüimos, argüís, arguyen; **PRET** argüí, argüiste, arguyó, argüimos, argüisteis, arguyeron; **PRES SUBJ** arguya, arguyas, arguya, arguyamos, arguyáis, arguyan; **IMPERF SUBJ** arguyera/arguyese; **IMPERAT** arguye, arguya, arguyamos, argüid, arguyan

[63] **avergonzar PRES** avergüenzo, avergüenzas, avergüenza, avergonzamos, avergonzáis, avergüenzan; **PRET** avergoncé, avergonzaste, avergonzó, avergonzamos, avergonzasteis, avergonzaron; **PRES SUBJ** avergüence, avergüences, avergüence, avergoncemos, avergoncéis, avergüencen; **IMPERAT** avergüenza, avergüence, avergoncemos, avergonzad, avergüencen

[64] **trocar PRES** trueco, truecas, trueca, trocamos, trocáis, truecan; **PRET** troqué, trocaste, trocó, trocamos, trocasteis, trocaron; **PRES SUBJ** trueque, trueques, trueque, troquemos, troquéis, truequen; **IMPERAT** trueca, trueque, troquemos, trocad, truequen

[65] **oler PRES** huelo, hueles, huele, olemos, oléis, huelen; **PRES SUBJ** huela, huelas, huela, olamos, oláis, huelan; **IMPERAT** huele, huela, olamos, oled, huelan

Verbos irregulares ingleses

INFINITIVO	PRETÉRITO	PARTICIPIO
arise	arose	arisen
awake	awoke	awoken
awaken	awoke, awakened	awakened, awoken
be	were/was	been
bear	bore	borne
beat	beat	beaten
become	became	become
begin	began	begun
bend	bent	bent
beseech	besought, beseeched	besought, beseeched
bet	bet, betted	bet, betted
bid	bade, bid	bidden, bid
bind	bound	bound
bite	bit	bitten
bleed	bled	bled
blow	blew	blown
break	broke	broken
breed	bred	bred
bring	brought	brought
build	built	built
burn	burnt, burned	burnt, burned
burst	burst	burst
buy	bought	bought
cast	cast	cast
catch	caught	caught
choose	chose	chosen
cling	clung	clung
clothe	clad, clothed	clad, clothed
come	came	come
cost	cost	cost
creep	crept	crept
cut	cut	cut
deal	dealt	dealt
dig	dug	dug
do	did	done
draw	drew	drawn
dream	dreamt, dreamed	dreamt, dreamed
drink	drank	drunk
drive	drove	driven
dwell	dwelt	dwelt
eat	ate	eaten
fall	fell	fallen
feed	fed	fed
feel	felt	felt

INFINITIVO	PRETÉRITO	PARTICIPIO
fight	fought	fought
find	found	found
flee	fled	fled
fling	flung	flung
fly	flew	flown
forget	forgot	forgotten
forgive	forgave	forgiven
forsake	forsook	forsaken
freeze	froze	frozen
get	got	got, *US* gotten
give	gave	given
go	went	gone
grind	ground	ground
grow	grew	grown
hang	hung/hanged	hung/hanged
have	had	had
hear	heard	heard
hide	hid	hidden
hit	hit	hit
hold	held	held
hurt	hurt	hurt
keep	kept	kept
kneel	knelt	knelt
knit	knitted, knit	knitted, knit
know	knew	known
lay	laid	laid
lead	led	led
lean	leant, leaned	leant, leaned
leap	leapt, leaped	leapt, leaped
learn	learnt, learned	learnt, learned
leave	left	left
lend	lent	lent
let	let	let
lie	lay	lain
light	lit	lit
lose	lost	lost
make	made	made
mean	meant	meant
meet	met	met
mow	mowed	mown, mowed
pay	paid	paid
put	put	put
quit	quit	quit
read	read	read
rend	rent	rent
rid	rid	rid
ride	rode	ridden
ring	rang	rung
rise	rose	risen
run	ran	run
saw	sawed	sawn, sawed

INFINITIVO	PRETÉRITO	PARTICIPIO
say	said	said
see	saw	seen
seek	sought	sought
sell	sold	sold
send	sent	sent
set	set	set
sew	sewed	sewn
shake	shook	shaken
shear	sheared	shorn, sheared
shed	shed	shed
shine	shone	shone
shoe	shod	shod
shoot	shot	shot
show	showed	shown
shrink	shrank	shrunk
shut	shut	shut
sing	sang	sung
sink	sank	sunk
sit	sat	sat
slay	slew	slain
sleep	slept	slept
slide	slid	slid
sling	slung	slung
slink	slunk	slunk
slit	slit	slit
smell	smelled, smelt	smelled, smelt
sow	sowed	sown, sowed
speak	spoke	spoken
speed	sped, speeded	sped, speeded
spell	spelt, spelled	spelt, spelled
spend	spent	spent
spill	spilt, spilled	spilt, spilled
spin	span	spun
spit	spat	spat
split	split	split
spoil	spoilt, spoiled	spoilt, spoiled
spread	spread	spread
spring	sprang	sprung
stand	stood	stood
steal	stole	stolen
stick	stuck	stuck
sting	stung	stung
stink	stank, stunk	stunk
strew	strewed	strewed, strewn
stride	strode	stridden
strike	struck	struck
string	strung	strung
strive	strove	striven
swear	swore	sworn
sweep	swept	swept
swell	swelled	swollen

INFINITIVO	PRETÉRITO	PARTICIPIO
swing	swung	swung
swim	swam	swum
take	took	taken
teach	taught	taught
tear	tore	torn
tell	told	told
think	thought	thought
thrive	thrived, throve	thrived, thriven
throw	threw	thrown
thrust	thrust	thrust
tread	trod	trodden
wake	woke	woken
wear	wore	worn
weave	wove	woven
weep	wept	wept
wet	wet	wet
win	won	won
wind	wound	wound
wring	wrung	wrung
write	wrote	written

English – Spanish
Inglés – Español

A, a [eɪ] n (**a**) (*the letter*) A, a f (**b**) *Mus* **A** la m (**c**) *Br* **A road** ≃ carretera f nacional

a [eɪ, *unstressed* ə] *indef art* (*before vowel or silent h* **an**) (**a**) un, una; **a man/a woman** un hombre/una mujer; **he has a big nose** tiene la nariz grande (**b**) (*omitted in Spanish*) **half a litre/an hour** medio litro/media hora; **a hundred/thousand people** cien/mil personas; **let's have a drink** vamos a beber algo; **he's a teacher** es profesor; **what a pity** qué pena (**c**) (*each*) **60 pence a kilo** 60 peniques el kilo; **to eat grapes two at a time** comer las uvas de dos en dos; **three times a week** tres veces a la semana (**d**) (*a certain*) un/una tal; **a Mr Rees phoned** llamó un tal Sr. Rees

AA [eɪ'eɪ] n (**a**) (*abbr* **Alcoholics Anonymous**) AA, alcohólicos *mpl* anónimos (**b**) (*abbr* **Automobile Association**) ≃ AC

AAA [eɪeɪ'eɪ] n (**a**) *Br* (*abbr* **Amateur Athletic Association**) = federación británica de atletismo aficionado (**b**) *US* (*abbr* **American Automobile Association**) ≃ AC

aback [ə'bæk] *adv* **to be taken a.** quedarse de una pieza (**by** por)

abandon [ə'bændən] **1** n desenfreno m; **with reckless a.** desenfrenadamente

2 vt (*child*) abandonar; (*job*) dejar; (*project*) renunciar a

abase [ə'beɪs] vt **to a. oneself** humillarse

abashed [ə'bæʃt] *adj* desconcertado(a)

abate [ə'beɪt] *vi* (*anger*) apaciguarse; (*storm*) amainar

abattoir ['æbətwɑː(r)] n matadero m

abbey ['æbɪ] n abadía f

abbot ['æbət] n abad m

abbreviate [ə'briːvɪeɪt] vt abreviar

abbreviation [əbriːvɪ'eɪʃən] n abreviatura f

abdicate ['æbdɪkeɪt] vt & vi abdicar

abdication [æbdɪ'keɪʃən] n abdicación f

abdomen ['æbdəmən] n abdomen m

abduct [æb'dʌkt] vt raptar, secuestrar

aberration [æbə'reɪʃən] n aberración f

abet [ə'bet] vt **to aid and a. sb** ser cómplice de algn

abeyance [ə'beɪəns] n **to be in a.** estar en desuso

abhor [əb'hɔː(r)] vt aborrecer

abhorrent [əb'hɒrənt] *adj* aborrecible

abide [ə'baɪd] vt aguantar; **I can't a. it** no lo aguanto

▸ **abide by** vt insep (*promise*) cumplir con; (*rules*) atenerse a

ability [ə'bɪlɪtɪ] n (*capability*) capacidad f, aptitud f; (*talent*) talento m

abject ['æbdʒekt] *adj* (*state*) miserable; (*apology*) rastrero(a)

ablaze [ə'bleɪz] *adj* & *adv* en llamas, ardiendo

able ['eɪbəl] *adj* (*capable*) capaz; **will you be a. to come on Tuesday?** ¿podrás venir el martes?

able-bodied [eɪbəl'bɒdɪd] *adj* sano(a); **a. seaman** marinero m de primera

abnormal ['æb'nɔːməl] *adj* anormal

abnormally [æb'nɔːməlɪ] *adv* anormalmente; (*large*) extraordinariamente

aboard [ə'bɔːd] **1** *adv* a bordo; **to go a.** (*ship*) embarcarse; (*train*) subir

2 prep a bordo de

abode [ə'bəʊd] n *Jur* **of no fixed a.** sin domicilio fijo

abolish [ə'bɒlɪʃ] vt abolir

abolition [æbə'lɪʃən] n abolición f

abominable [ə'bɒmɪnəbəl] *adj* abominable; (*dreadful*) terrible

aborigine [æbə'rɪdʒɪnɪ] n aborigen mf australianó(a)

abort [ə'bɔːt] **1** vt *Med* hacer abortar; *Fig* (*plan etc*) archivar

2 vi *Med* abortar

abortion [ə'bɔːʃən] n *Med* aborto m; **a. law** ley f del aborto; **to have an a.** abortar

abortive [ə'bɔːtɪv] *adj* (*plan*) fracasado(a); (*attempt*) frustrado(a)

abound [ə'baʊnd] vi **to a. in** or **with** abundar en

about [ə'baʊt] *adv* & *prep* (**a**) (*concerning*) acerca de, sobre; **a programme a. Paris** un programa sobre París; **to be worried a. sth** estar preocupado(a) por algo; **to speak a. sth** hablar de algo; **what's it all a.?** (*what's happening?*) ¿qué pasa?; (*story etc*) ¿de qué se trata?; *Fam* **how a. a game of tennis?** ¿qué te parece un partido de tenis?

(**b**) *(around)* por todas partes; **don't leave things lying a.** no dejes las cosas por medio; **there's nobody a.** no hay nadie; **to look a.** mirar alrededor; **to rush a.** correr de un lado para otro; **we went for a walk a. the town** dimos una vuelta por el pueblo

(**c**) *(approximately)* más o menos; **it's a. three o'clock** son más o menos las tres; **it's a. time you got up** ya es hora de que te levantes; **it's just a. finished** está casi terminado; **she's a. forty** tiene unos cuarenta años

(**d**) **it's a. to start** está a punto de empezar; **not to be a. to do sth** no estar dispuesto(a) a hacer algo

about-turn [əbaʊtˈtɜːn], *US* **about-face** [əbaʊtˈfeɪs] *n* media vuelta *f*; **to do an a.** dar media vuelta; *Fig* cambiar de idea por completo

above [əˈbʌv] *adv & prep* (**a**) *(higher than)* encima de, sobre, arriba; **100 m a. sea level** 100 m sobre el nivel del mar; **it's a. the door** está encima de la puerta; **the flat a.** el piso de arriba (**b**) *(greater than)* superior (a); **amounts a. £10** cantidades superiores a las 10 libras; *Fig* **a policy imposed from a.** una política impuesta desde arriba (**c**) **a. all** sobre todo; **he's not a. stealing** es capaz incluso de robar (**d**) *(in book etc)* más arriba

above-board [əˈbʌvˈbɔːd] *adj (scheme)* legítimo(a)

above-mentioned [əˈbʌvmenʃənd] *adj* susodicho(a)

abrasive [əˈbreɪsɪv] **1** *adj (substance)* abrasivo(a); *Fig (voice, wit etc)* cáustico(a)
2 *n* abrasivo *m*

abreast [əˈbrest] *adv* **to walk three a.** ir de tres en fondo; *Fig* **to keep a. of things** mantenerse al día

abridged [əˈbrɪdʒd] *adj (book)* abreviado(a)

abroad [əˈbrɔːd] *adv* **to be a.** estar en el extranjero; **to go a.** irse al extranjero

abrupt [əˈbrʌpt] *adj (manner)* brusco(a); *(tone)* áspero(a); *(change)* súbito(a)

abruptly [əˈbrʌptlɪ] *adv (act)* bruscamente; *(speak)* con aspereza; *(change)* repentinamente

abscess [ˈæbses] *n* absceso *m*; *(on gum)* flemón *m*

abscond [əbˈskɒnd] *vi* huir

absence [ˈæbsəns] *n (of person)* ausencia *f*; *(of thing)* falta *f*

absent [ˈæbsənt] *adj* ausente; *Fig* **an a. look** una mirada distraída

absentee [æbsənˈtiː] *n* ausente *mf*

absenteeism [æbsənˈtiːɪzəm] *n* absentismo *m*

absently [ˈæbsəntlɪ] *adv* distraídamente

absent-minded [æbsəntˈmaɪndɪd] *adj* distraído(a)

absolute [ˈæbsəluːt] *adj* absoluto(a); *(failure)* total; *(truth)* puro(a); **it's an a. disgrace** es una auténtica vergüenza

absolutely [æbsəˈluːtlɪ] **1** *adv (completely)* completamente; **a. wrong** totalmente equivocado(a); **you're a. right** tienes toda la razón
2 *interj* **a.!** ¡desde luego!

absolve [əbˈzɒlv] *vt* absolver (**from** de)

absorb [əbˈzɔːb] *vt (liquid)* absorber; *(sound, blow)* amortiguar; *Fig* **to be absorbed in sth** estar absorto(a) en algo

absorbing [əbˈzɔːbɪŋ] *adj (book, work)* absorbente

abstain [əbˈsteɪn] *vi* abstenerse (**from** de)

abstemious [əbˈstiːmɪəs] *adj* abstemio(a)

abstention [əbˈstenʃən] *n* abstención *f*

abstinence [ˈæbstɪnəns] *n* abstinencia *f*

abstract [ˈæbstrækt] **1** *adj* abstracto(a)
2 *n (of thesis etc)* resumen *m*

abstruse [əbˈstruːs] *adj* abstruso(a)

absurd [əbˈsɜːd] *adj* absurdo(a)

abundance [əˈbʌndəns] *n* abundancia *f*

abundant [əˈbʌndənt] *adj* abundante, rico(a) (**in** en)

abuse **1** *n* [əˈbjuːs] (**a**) *(ill-treatment)* malos tratos; *(misuse)* abuso *m* (**b**) *(insults)* injurias *fpl*
2 *vt* [əˈbjuːz] (**a**) *(ill-treat)* maltratar; *(misuse)* abusar de (**b**) *(insult)* injuriar

abusive [əbˈjuːsɪv] *adj (insulting)* insultante

abysmal [əˈbɪzməl] *adj (conditions)* extremo(a); *Fam (very bad)* fatal, pésimo(a)

abyss [əˈbɪs] *n* abismo *m*; *Fig* extremo *m*

AC [eɪˈsiː] *(abbr* **alternating current**) CA

academic [ækəˈdemɪk] **1** *adj* académico(a); *(career)* universitario(a); *(discussion)* teórico(a); **a. year** año *m* escolar
2 *n* académico(a) *m,f*

academy [əˈkædəmɪ] *n (society)* academia *f*; *Educ* instituto *m* de enseñanza media; **a. of music** conservatorio *m*

accede [ækˈsiːd] *vi* acceder (**to** a)

accelerate [əkˈseləreɪt] **1** *vt (engine)* acelerar; *(step)* aligerar
2 *vi (car, engine)* acelerar

acceleration [əkseləˈreɪʃən] *n* aceleración *f*

accelerator [æk'seləreɪtə(r)] *n* acelerador *m*

accent ['æksənt] *n* acento *m*

accentuate [æk'sentʃʋeɪt] *vt* subrayar

accept [ək'sept] *vt & vi* aceptar; *(theory)* admitir; **do you a. that ...?** ¿estás de acuerdo en que ...?

acceptable [ək'septəbəl] *adj (satisfactory)* aceptable; *(tolerable)* admisible

acceptance [ək'septəns] *n (act of accepting)* aceptación *f*; *(good reception)* aprobación *f*

access ['ækses] *n* acceso *m*; *Comput* **a. provider** proveedor *m* de acceso (a Internet); **a. road** carretera *f* de acceso; **to have a. to sth** tener libre acceso a algo

accessible [ək'sesəbəl] *adj (place, position)* accesible; *(person)* asequible

accession [ək'seʃən] *n* subida *f* (al trono)

accessory [ək'sesərɪ] *n* (**a**) *Jur* cómplice *mf* (**b**) **accessories** accesorios *mpl*; *(for outfit)* complementos *mpl*

accident ['æksɪdənt] *n* accidente *m*; *(coincidence)* casualidad *f*; **it was an a. on my part** lo hice sin querer; **car a.** accidente *m* de carretera; **by a.** por casualidad

accidental [æksɪ'dentəl] *adj* fortuito(a); *(unintended)* imprevisto(a)

accidentally [æksɪ'dentəlɪ] *adv (by chance)* por casualidad; **he did it a.** lo hizo sin querer

accident-prone ['æksɪdəntprəʊn] *adj* propenso(a) a los accidentes

acclaim [ə'kleɪm] **1** *n* aclamación *f*
2 *vt* aclamar

acclimatization [əklaɪmətaɪ'zeɪʃən], *US* **acclimation** [æklɪ'meɪʃən] *n* aclimatación *f*

acclimatize [ə'klaɪmətaɪz], *US* **acclimate** ['æklɪmeɪt] *vt* aclimatar

acclimatized [ə'klaɪmətaɪzd] *adj* aclimatado(a); **to become a.** aclimatarse

accolade ['ækəleɪd] *n* elogio *m*

accommodate [ə'kɒmədeɪt] *vt* (**a**) *(guests)* alojar (**b**) **to a. sb's wishes** complacer a algn

accommodating [ə'kɒmədeɪtɪŋ] *adj (obliging)* complaciente; *(understanding)* comprensivo(a)

accommodation [əkɒmə'deɪʃən] *n (US also accommodations) (lodgings)* alojamiento *m*

accompany [ə'kʌmpənɪ] *vt* acompañar

accomplice [ə'kʌmplɪs] *n* cómplice *mf*

accomplish [ə'kʌmplɪʃ] *vt (aim)* conseguir; *(task, mission)* llevar a cabo

accomplished [ə'kʌmplɪʃt] *adj* dotado(a), experto(a)

accomplishment [ə'kʌmplɪʃmənt] *n* (**a**) *(of task)* realización *f*; *(of duty)* cumplimiento *m* (**b**) **accomplishments** *(talents)* dotes *fpl*

accord [ə'kɔːd] **1** *n (agreement)* acuerdo *m*; **of her/his own a.** espontáneamente
2 *vt (honour etc)* conceder

accordance [ə'kɔːdəns] *n* **in a. with** de acuerdo con

according [ə'kɔːdɪŋ] *prep* **a. to** según; **everything went a. to plan** todo salió conforme a los planes

accordingly [ə'kɔːdɪŋlɪ] *adv* (**a**) **to act a.** *(appropriately)* obrar según y conforme (**b**) *(therefore)* así pues

accordion [ə'kɔːdɪən] *n* acordeón *m*

account [ə'kaʊnt] *n* (**a**) *(report)* informe *m*; **by all accounts** al decir de todos; **I was fearful on her a.** sufría por ella; **it's of no a.** no tiene importancia; **on a. of** a causa de; **on no a.** bajo ningún concepto; **to take a. of, to take into a.** tener en cuenta (**c**) *Com* cuenta *f*; **to keep the accounts** llevar las cuentas; **accounts department** servicio *m* de contabilidad; **to open/close an a.** abrir/cancelar una cuenta; **current a.** cuenta corriente; **a. number** número *m* de cuenta
▸ **account for** *vt insep (explain)* explicar

accountable [ə'kaʊntəbəl] *adj* **to be a. to sb for sth** ser responsable ante algn de algo

accountancy [ə'kaʊntənsɪ] *n* contabilidad *f*

accountant [ə'kaʊntənt] *n* contable *mf*

accredited [ə'kredɪtɪd] *adj* acreditado(a)

accrue [ə'kruː] *vi (interest)* acumularse

accumulate [ə'kjuːmjʋleɪt] **1** *vt* acumular; *(fortune)* amasar
2 *vi* acumularse

accuracy ['ækjʋrəsɪ] *n (of number etc)* exactitud *f*; *(of shot, criticism)* certeza *f*

accurate ['ækjʋrət] *adj (number)* exacto(a); *(shot, criticism)* certero(a); *(answer)* correcto(a); *(observation)* acertado(a); *(instrument)* de precisión; *(translation)* fiel

accusation [ækjʋ'zeɪʃən] *n* acusación *f*

accuse [ə'kjuːz] *vt* acusar

accused [ə'kjuːzd] *n* **the a.** el/la acusado(a)

accustom [ə'kʌstəm] *vt* acostumbrar; **to be accustomed to doing sth** estar acostumbrado(a) a hacer algo

ace [eɪs] *n* (**a**) *Cards & Fig* as *m* (**b**) *(in tennis)* ace *m*

acetate ['æsɪteɪt] *n* acetato *m*

acetone ['æsɪtəʊn] *n* acetona *f*

ache [eɪk] **1** *n* dolor *m*; **aches and pains** achaques *mpl*

2 *vi* doler; **my back aches** me duele la espalda

achieve [ə'tʃiːv] *vt (attain)* conseguir, alcanzar; *(accomplish)* llevar a cabo, realizar

achievement [ə'tʃiːvmənt] *n (attainment)* logro *m*; *(completion)* realización *f*; *(feat)* hazaña *f*

acid ['æsɪd] **1** *adj* ácido(a); *(taste)* agrio(a); *(remark)* mordaz; **a. rain** lluvia ácida; *Fig* **a. test** prueba decisiva

2 *n* ácido *m*

acknowledge [ək'nɒlɪdʒ] *vt* (a) *(recognize)* reconocer; *(claim, defeat)* admitir; *(present)* agradecer; *(letter)* acusar recibo de (b) *(greet)* saludar

acknowledgement [ək'nɒlɪdʒmənt] *n* (a) *(recognition)* reconocimiento *m*; *(of letter)* acuse *m* de recibo (b) **acknowledgements** *(in preface)* menciones *fpl*

acne ['æknɪ] *n* acné *m*

acorn ['eɪkɔːn] *n* bellota *f*

acoustic [ə'kuːstɪk] **1** *adj* acústico(a)

2 *npl* **acoustics** acústica *f*

acquaint [ə'kweɪnt] *vt* **to a. sb with the facts** informar a algn de los detalles; **to be acquainted with the procedure** estar al corriente de como se procede; **to be acquainted with sb** conocer a algn

acquaintance [ə'kweɪntəns] *n* (a) conocimiento *m*; **to make sb's a.** conocer a algn (b) *(person)* conocido(a) *m,f*

acquiesce [ækwɪ'es] *vi* consentir (**in** en)

acquiescent [ækwɪ'esənt] *adj* conforme

acquire [ə'kwaɪə(r)] *vt* adquirir

acquisition [ækwɪ'zɪʃən] *n* adquisición *f*

acquisitive [ə'kwɪzɪtɪv] *adj* codicioso(a)

acquit [ə'kwɪt] *vt* (a) *Jur* **to a. sb of sth** absolver a algn de algo (b) **to a. oneself well** defenderse bien

acquittal [ə'kwɪtəl] *n* absolución *f*

acre ['eɪkə(r)] *n* acre *m* (= *aprox* 40,47 áreas)

acrid ['ækrɪd] *adj (smell, taste)* acre

acrimonious [ækrɪ'məʊnɪəs] *adj (remark)* cáustico(a); *(dispute)* enconado(a)

acrobat ['ækrəbæt] *n* acróbata *mf*

across [ə'krɒs] **1** *adv* a través; **the river is 30 m a.** el río mide 30 m de ancho; **to go a.** atravesar; **to run a.** atravesar corriendo

2 *prep* (a) a través de; **they live a. the road** viven enfrente; **to go a. the street** cruzar la calle (b) *(at the other side of)* al otro lado de

acrylic [ə'krɪlɪk] *adj* acrílico(a)

act [ækt] **1** *n* (a) *(action)* acto *m*, acción *f*; **a. of God** caso *m* de fuerza mayor (b) *(in parliament)* ley *f*, decreto *m* (c) *Th* acto *m*; *(turn in show)* número *m*

2 *vt Th (part)* interpretar; *(character)* representar; *Fig* **to a. the fool** hacer el tonto

3 *vi* (a) *Th* hacer teatro; *Cin* hacer cine; *Fig (pretend)* fingir (b) *(behave)* comportarse (c) *(take action)* actuar, obrar; **to a. on sb's advice** seguir el consejo de algn (d) *(work)* funcionar; *(drug etc)* actuar; **to a. as a deterrent** servir de disuasivo (e) **to a. as director** hacer de director

► **act out** *vt sep* exteriorizar

► **act up** *vi Fam (machine)* funcionar mal; *(child)* dar guerra

acting ['æktɪŋ] **1** *adj* interino(a)

2 *n (profession)* teatro *m*; **he's done some a.** ha hecho algo de teatro

action ['ækʃən] *n* (a) *(deed)* acción *f*; *Mil* acción de combate; **to be out of a.** *(person)* estar fuera de servicio; *(machine)* estar estropeado(a); **to take a.** tomar medidas (b) *Jur* demanda *f* (c) *TV* **a. replay** repetición *f*

activate ['æktɪveɪt] *vt* activar

active ['æktɪv] *adj* activo(a); *(energetic)* vigoroso(a); *(interest)* vivo(a); *Ling* **a. voice** voz activa

activist ['æktɪvɪst] *n* activista *mf*

activity [æk'tɪvɪtɪ] *n (of person)* actividad *f*; *(on street etc)* bullicio *m*

actor ['æktə(r)] *n* actor *m*

actress ['æktrɪs] *n* actriz *f*

actual ['æktʃʊəl] *adj* real, verdadero(a)

> ♪ Note that the Spanish word **actual** is a false friend and is never a translation for the English word **actual**. In Spanish, **actual** means "current, up-to-date, topical".

actually ['æktʃʊəlɪ] *adv (really)* en efecto, realmente; *(even)* incluso, hasta; *(in fact)* de hecho

> ♪ Note that the Spanish word **actualmente** is a false friend and is never a translation for the English word **actually**. In Spanish, **actualmente** means "nowadays, at the moment".

acumen ['ækjʊmən] *n* perspicacia *f*

acupuncture ['ækjʊpʌŋktʃə(r)] *n* acupuntura *f*

acute [ə'kjuːt] *adj* agudo(a); *(pain)* intenso(a); *(hearing)* muy fino(a); *(shortage)* grave; *(mind)* perspicaz

AD [eɪ'diː] *(abbr* **Anno Domini**) d.J.C., d.C.

ad [æd] *n Fam* anuncio *m*

adamant ['ædəmənt] *adj* firme, inflexible

adapt [ə'dæpt] **1** *vt* adaptar (**to** a); **to a. oneself to sth** adaptarse a algo
2 *vi* adaptarse

adaptable [ə'dæptəbəl] *adj (instrument)* ajustable; **he's very a.** se amolda fácilmente a las circunstancias

adaptation [ædəp'teɪʃən] *n* adaptación *f*

adapter, adaptor [ə'dæptə(r)] *n Elec* ladrón *m*

add [æd] **1** *vt (numbers)* sumar; *(one thing to another)* añadir
2 *vi (count)* sumar
▸ **add to** *vt insep* aumentar
▸ **add up** **1** *vt sep* sumar
2 *vi (numbers)* sumar; *Fig* **it doesn't a. up** no tiene sentido; **it doesn't a. up to much** no es gran cosa

added ['ædɪd] *adj* adicional

adder ['ædə(r)] *n* víbora *f*

addict ['ædɪkt] *n* adicto(a) *m,f; Fam* **television a.** teleadicto(a) *m,f*

addicted [ə'dɪktɪd] *adj* adicto(a); **to become a. to sth** enviciarse con algo

addiction [ə'dɪkʃən] *n (to gambling etc)* vicio *m; (to drugs)* adicción *f*

addictive [ə'dɪktɪv] *adj* que crea adicción

addition [ə'dɪʃən] *n Math* adición *f; (increase)* aumento *m*; **an a. to the family** un nuevo miembro de la familia; **in a. to** además de

additional [ə'dɪʃənəl] *adj* adicional

additive ['ædɪtɪv] *n* aditivo *m*

address [ə'dres] **1** *n* (**a**) *(on letter)* dirección *f*, señas *fpl* (**b**) *(speech)* discurso *m*
2 *vt* (**a**) *(letter)* dirigir (**b**) *(speak to)* dirigirse (**to** a); **to a. the floor** tomar la palabra (**c**) *(use form of address to)* tratar de

adenoids ['ædɪnɔɪdz] *npl* vegetaciones *fpl* (adenoideas)

adept [ə'dept] **1** *adj* experto(a) (**at** en)
2 *n* experto(a) *m,f*

📝 Note that the Spanish word **adepto** is a false friend and is never a translation for the English word **adept**. In Spanish, **adepto** means "follower, supporter".

adequate ['ædɪkwɪt] *adj (enough)* suficiente; *(satisfactory)* adecuado(a)

adhere [əd'hɪə(r)] *vi (stick)* pegarse (**to** a)
▸ **adhere to** *vt insep (policy)* adherirse a; *(contract)* cumplir con

adherent [əd'hɪərənt] *n* partidario(a) *m,f*

adhesive [əd'hiːsɪv] **1** *adj* adhesivo(a); *(sticky)* pegajoso(a); **a. tape** cinta adhesiva
2 *n* adhesivo *m*

ad hoc [æd'hɒk] *adj (remark)* improvisado(a); **an a. committee** un comité especial

ad infinitum [ædɪnfɪ'naɪtəm] *adv* hasta el infinito

adjacent [ə'dʒeɪsənt] *adj (building)* contiguo(a); *(land)* colindante; **a. to** contiguo(a) a

adjective ['ædʒɪktɪv] *n* adjetivo *m*

adjoining [ə'dʒɔɪnɪŋ] *adj* contiguo(a); *(land)* colindante; **the a. room** la habitación de al lado

adjourn [ə'dʒɜːn] **1** *vt (postpone)* aplazar; *(court)* levantar
2 *vi* aplazarse (**until** hasta)

adjudicate [ə'dʒuːdɪkeɪt] *vt* juzgar

adjudicator [ə'dʒuːdɪkeɪtə(r)] *n* juez(a) *m,f*

adjust [ə'dʒʌst] **1** *vt (machine etc)* ajustar; *Fig (methods)* variar
2 *vi (person)* adaptarse (**to** a)

adjustable [ə'dʒʌstəbəl] *adj* ajustable

adjustment [ə'dʒʌstmənt] *n* (**a**) *(to machine etc)* ajuste *m; (by person)* adaptación *f* (**b**) *(change)* modificación *f*

ad lib [æd'lɪb] **1** *adv (speak)* sin preparación; *(continue)* a voluntad
2 *adj (speech)* improvisado(a)
3 ad-lib *vi* improvisar

administer [əd'mɪnɪstə(r)] *vt (country)* gobernar; *(justice)* administrar

administration [ədmɪnɪ'streɪʃən] *n (of country)* gobierno *m; (of justice)* administración *f; (governing body)* dirección *f*

administrative [əd'mɪnɪstrətɪv] *adj* administrativo(a)

admirable [æd'mərəbəl] *adj* admirable

admiral ['ædmərəl] *n* almirante *m*

admiration [ædmə'reɪʃən] *n* admiración *f*

admire [əd'maɪə(r)] *vt* admirar

admirer [əd'maɪərə(r)] *n* admirador(a) *m,f*

admissible [əd'mɪsəbəl] *adj* admisible

admission [əd'mɪʃən] *n* (**a**) *(to school etc)* ingreso *m; (price)* entrada *f* (**b**) *(of fact)* reconocimiento *m; (confession)* confesión *f*

admit [əd'mɪt] *vt* (**a**) *(person)* dejar entrar; **to be admitted to hospital** ser ingresado(a) en el hospital (**b**) *(acknowledge)* reconocer; *(crime, guilt)* confesar

admittance [əd'mɪtəns] *n (entry)* entrada *f*

admittedly [əd'mɪtɪdlɪ] *adv* la verdad es que ...

admonish [əd'mɒnɪʃ] *vt* amonestar

ad nauseam [æd'nɔːzɪæm] *adv* hasta la saciedad

ado [ə'duː] *n* **without further a.** sin más

adolescence [ædə'lesəns] *n* adolescencia *f*

adolescent [ædə'lesənt] *n* adolescente *mf*

adopt [ə'dɒpt] *vt* adoptar; *(suggestion)* aceptar

adopted [ə'dɒptɪd] *adj* **a. child** hijo(a) *m,f* adoptivo(a)

adoption [ə'dɒpʃən] *n* adopción *f*; **country of a.** país adoptivo

adore [ə'dɔː(r)] *vt* adorar

adorn [ə'dɔːn] *vt* adornar

adornment [ə'dɔːnmənt] *n* adorno *m*

adrenalin [ə'drenəlɪn] *n* adrenalina *f*

Adriatic [eɪdrɪ'ætɪk] *adj* **the A. (Sea)** el (mar) Adriático

adrift [ə'drɪft] *adv* **to come a.** *(boat)* irse a la deriva; *(rope)* soltarse; *Fig* **to go a.** *(plans)* ir a la deriva

adult [æd'ʌlt] **1** *adj (person)* adulto(a), mayor; *(film, education)* para adultos
2 *n* adulto(a) *m,f*

adulterate [ə'dʌltəreɪt] *vt* adulterar

adulterer [ə'dʌltərə(r)] *n* adúltero *m*

adulteress [ə'dʌltrɪs] *n* adúltera *f*

adultery [ə'dʌltərɪ] *n* adulterio *m*

advance [əd'vɑːns] **1** *n* **(a)** *(movement)* avance *m*; *Fig (progress)* progreso *m*; **to have sth ready in a.** tener algo preparado de antemano; **to make advances (to)** *(person)* insinuarse (a) **(b)** *(loan)* anticipo *m*
2 *adj (before time)* adelantado(a); *Cin & Th* **a. bookings** reservas *fpl* por adelantado
3 *vt* **(a)** *(troops)* avanzar; *(time, date)* adelantar **(b)** *(idea)* proponer; *(opinion)* dar **(c)** *Fin (sum of money)* anticipar
4 *vi (move forward)* avanzar, adelantarse; *(make progress)* hacer progresos; *(gain promotion)* ascender

advanced [əd'vɑːnst] *adj (developed)* avanzado(a); *(student)* adelantado(a); *(course)* superior; *Educ* **A. level** examen *m* superior de segunda enseñanza, ≃ COU *m*

advancement [əd'vɑːnsmənt] *n (progress)* adelanto *m*; *(promotion)* ascenso *m*

advantage [əd'vɑːntɪdʒ] *n* ventaja *f*; *(in tennis)* **a. Velasco** ventaja para Velasco; **to**

take a. of sb/sth abusar de algn/aprovechar algo

advantageous [ædvən'teɪdʒəs] *adj* ventajoso(a)

advent ['ædvent] *n (arrival)* llegada *f*; *(of Christ)* advenimiento *m*; **A.** Adviento *m*

adventure [əd'ventʃə(r)] *n* aventura *f*; **a. sport** deporte *m* de aventura

adventurous [əd'ventʃərəs] *adj* aventurero(a)

adverb ['ædvɜːb] *n* adverbio *m*

adversary ['ædvəsərɪ] *n* adversario(a) *m,f*

adverse ['ædvɜːs] *adj (effect)* desfavorable; *(conditions)* adverso(a); *(winds)* contrario(a)

adversity [əd'vɜːsɪtɪ] *n* adversidad *f*

advert ['ædvɜːt] *n* *Fam* anuncio *m*

advertise ['ædvətaɪz] **1** *vt* anunciar
2 *vi* hacer publicidad; *(in newspaper)* poner un anuncio; **to a. for sth/sb** buscar algo/a algn mediante un anuncio

advertisement [əd'vɜːtɪsmənt] *n* anuncio *m*; **advertisements** publicidad *f*

advertiser ['ædvətaɪzə(r)] *n* anunciante *mf*

advertising ['ædvətaɪzɪŋ] **1** *n* publicidad *f*, propaganda *f*; *(in newspaper)* anuncios *mpl*
2 *adj* publicitario(a); **a. agency** agencia *f* de publicidad

advice [əd'vaɪs] *n* consejos *mpl*; **a piece of a.** un consejo; **to take legal a. on a matter** consultar el caso con un abogado; **to take sb's a.** seguir los consejos de algn

advisable [əd'vaɪzəbəl] *adj* aconsejable

advise [əd'vaɪz] *vt* aconsejar; *(on business etc)* asesorar; **I a. you to do it** te aconsejo que lo hagas

adviser [əd'vaɪzə(r)] *n* consejero(a) *m,f*; *(in business etc)* asesor(a) *m,f*

advisory [əd'vaɪzərɪ] *adj* asesor(a)

advocate 1 *n* [´ædvəkɪt] *Scot Jur* abogado(a) *m,f*; *(supporter)* defensor(a) *m,f*
2 *vt* ['ædvəkeɪt] *(reform)* abogar por; *(plan)* apoyar

aerial ['eərɪəl] **1** *adj* aéreo(a)
2 *n* antena *f*

aerobics [eə'rəʊbɪks] *n sing* aerobic *m*

aerodrome ['eərədrəʊm] *n Br* aeródromo *m*

aerodynamics [eərəʊdaɪ'næmɪks] *n sing* aerodinámica *f*

aeroplane ['eərəpleɪn] *n Br* avión *m*

aerosol ['eərəsɒl] *n* aerosol *m*

aerospace ['eərəʊspeɪs] *adj* aeroespacial

aesthetic [iːsˈθetɪk] *adj* estético(a)

afar [əˈfɑː(r)] *adv* lejos; **from a.** desde lejos

affair [əˈfeə(r)] *n* (*matter*) asunto *m*; (*event*) acontecimiento *m*; **that's my a.** eso es asunto mío; **business affairs** negocios *mpl*; **foreign affairs** asuntos exteriores; **love a.** aventura amorosa

affect [əˈfekt] *vt* (*person, health*) afectar; (*prices, future*) influir en; (*touch emotionally*) conmover

affected [əˈfektɪd] *adj* (**a**) (*unnatural*) afectado(a) (**b**) (*influenced*) influido(a) (**c**) (*touched emotionally*) conmovido(a) (**d**) (*pretended*) fingido(a)

affection [əˈfekʃən] *n* afecto *m*, cariño *m*

affectionate [əˈfekʃənɪt] *adj* cariñoso(a)

affidavit [æfɪˈdeɪvɪt] *n* declaración escrita y jurada

affiliated [əˈfɪlieɪtɪd] *adj* afiliado(a); **to be/become a. (to** *or* **with)** afiliarse (a)

affinity [əˈfɪnɪti] *n* afinidad *f*; (*liking*) simpatía *f*

affirm [əˈfɜːm] *vt* afirmar, sostener

affirmation [æfəˈmeɪʃən] *n* afirmación *f*

affirmative [əˈfɜːmətɪv] **1** *adj* afirmativo(a)
2 *n* he answered in the a. contestó que sí

affix [əˈfɪks] *vt* (*stamp*) pegar

afflict [əˈflɪkt] *vt* afligir

affluence [ˈæfluəns] *n* opulencia *f*

affluent [ˈæfluənt] *adj* (*society*) opulento(a); (*person*) rico(a)

afford [əˈfɔːd] *vt* (**a**) (*be able to buy*) permitirse el lujo de; **I can't a. a new car** no puedo pagar un coche nuevo (**b**) (*be able to do*) permitirse; **you can't a. to miss the opportunity** no puedes perderte la ocasión

affront [əˈfrʌnt] **1** *n* afrenta *f*
2 *vt* afrentar

afield [əˈfiːld] *adv* **far a.** muy lejos

afloat [əˈfləʊt] *adv* **to keep a.** mantenerse a flote

afoot [əˈfʊt] *adv* **there's a plan a.** hay un proyecto en marcha; **there's something strange a.** se está tramando algo

aforementioned [əˈfɔːmenʃənd], **aforesaid** [əˈfɔːsed] *adj* susodicho(a)

afraid [əˈfreɪd] *adj* (**a**) **to be a.** tener miedo (**of sb** de algn; **of sth** de algo); **I'm a. of it** me da miedo (**b**) **I'm a. not** no tema que no; **I'm a. so** me temo que sí; **I'm a. you're wrong** me temo que estás equivocado(a)

afresh [əˈfreʃ] *adv* de nuevo

Africa [ˈæfrɪkə] *n* Africa

African [ˈæfrɪkən] *adj & n* africano(a) (*m,f*)

Afro [ˈæfrəʊ] *adj & n Fam* (*hairstyle*) afro (*m*)

aft [ɑːft] *adv* en popa; **to go a.** ir en popa

after [ˈɑːftə(r)] **1** *adv* después; **soon a.** poco después; **the day a.** el día siguiente
2 *prep* (**a**) (*later*) después de; *US* **it's ten a. five** son las cinco y diez; **soon a. arriving** al poco rato de llegar; **the day a. tomorrow** pasado mañana
(**b**) (*behind*) detrás de, tras; **a. you!** ¡pase usted!; **they went in one a. the other** entraron uno tras otro; **the police are a. them** la policía anda tras ellos
(**c**) (*about*) por; **they asked a. you** preguntaron por ti; **what's he a.?** ¿qué pretende?
(**d**) **he takes a. his uncle** se parece a su tío; **she was named a. her grandmother** le llamaron como su abuela
3 *conj* después que; **a. it happened** después de que ocurriera

after-effect [ˈɑːftərɪfekt] *n* efecto secundario

afterlife [ˈɑːftəlaɪf] *n* vida *f* después de la muerte

aftermath [ˈɑːftəmæθ] *n* secuelas *fpl*

afternoon [ɑːftəˈnuːn] *n* tarde *f*; **good a.!** ¡buenas tardes!; **in the a.** por la tarde

afternoons [ɑːftəˈnuːnz] *adv US* por las tardes

afters [ˈɑːftəz] *npl Fam* postre *m*

after-sales service [ɑːftəseɪlzˈsɜːvɪs] *n Com* servicio *m* posventa

aftershave (lotion) [ˈɑːftəʃeɪv(ˈləʊʃən)] *n* loción *f* para después del afeitado

afterthought [ˈɑːftəθɔːt] *n* ocurrencia *f* tardía

afterwards [ˈɑːftəwədz] *adv* después, más tarde

again [əˈgen] *adv* (**a**) otra vez, de nuevo; **I tried a. and a.** lo intenté una y otra vez; **to do sth a.** volver a hacer algo; **never a.!** ¡nunca más!; **now and a.** de vez en cuando; **once a.** otra vez (**b**) (*besides*) además; **then a.** por otra parte

against [əˈgenst] *prep* (**a**) (*touching*) contra (**b**) (*opposing*) contra, en contra (de); **a. the grain** a contrapelo; **it's a. the law** es ilegal (**c**) **as a.** en contraste con, comparado con

age [eɪdʒ] **1** *n* (**a**) edad *f*; **she's eighteen years of a.** tiene dieciocho años; **to be under a.** ser menor de edad; **to come of a.** llegar a la mayoría de edad; **a. limit** límite *m* de edad; **old a.** vejez *f* (**b**) (*period*) época *f*; **the Iron A.** la Edad de Hierro (**c**) *Fam (long time)* eternidad *f*; **it's ages since I last saw her** hace siglos que no la veo

2 *vt & vi* envejecer

aged¹ [eɪdʒd] *adj* de *or* a la edad de

aged² [eɪdʒɪd] *npl* **the a.** los ancianos

agency ['eɪdʒənsɪ] *n* (**a**) *Com* agencia *f* (**b**) **by the a. of** por medio de

agenda [ə'dʒendə] *n* orden *m* del día

agent ['eɪdʒənt] *n* agente *mf*; *(representative)* representante *mf*

aggravate ['ægrəveɪt] *vt (worsen)* agravar; *(annoy)* molestar

aggregate ['ægrɪgɪt] *n* conjunto *m*; **on a.** en conjunto

aggression [ə'greʃən] *n* agresión *f*

aggressive [ə'gresɪv] *adj (violent)* agresivo(a), violento(a); *(dynamic)* dinámico(a)

aggrieved [ə'griːvd] *adj* apenado(a)

aghast [ə'gɑːst] *adj* espantado(a)

agile ['ædʒaɪl] *adj* ágil

agitate ['ædʒɪteɪt] **1** *vt (shake)* agitar; *Fig (worry)* perturbar

2 *vi Pol* **to a. against sth** hacer campaña en contra de algo

agitator ['ædʒɪteɪtə(r)] *n Pol* agitador(a) *m,f*

AGM [eɪdʒiː'em] *n (abbr* **annual general meeting)** junta *f* general anual

agnostic [æg'nɒstɪk] *n* agnóstico(a) *m,f*

ago [ə'gəʊ] *adv* **a long time a.** hace mucho tiempo; **as long a. as 1910** ya en 1910; **a week a.** hace una semana; **how long a.?** ¿hace cuánto tiempo?

agog [ə'gɒg] *adj* ansioso(a)

agonizing ['ægənaɪzɪŋ] *adj (pain)* atroz; *(decision)* desesperante

agony ['ægənɪ] *n* dolor *m* muy fuerte; *(anguish)* angustia *f*; **he was in a. with his back** tenía un dolor insoportable de espalda

agree [ə'griː] **1** *vi* (**a**) *(be in agreement)* estar de acuerdo; *(reach agreement)* ponerse de acuerdo; *(consent)* consentir; **to a. to do sth** consentir en hacer algo; **to a. with sb** estar de acuerdo con algn (**b**) *(harmonize) (things)* concordar; *(people)* congeniar; **onions don't a. with me** la cebolla no me sienta bien

2 *vt* acordar

agreeable [ə'griːəbəl] *adj (pleasant)* agradable; *(person)* simpático(a); *(in agreement)* de acuerdo

agreement [ə'griːmənt] *n (arrangement)* acuerdo *m*; *Com* contrato *m*; **to reach an a.** llegar a un acuerdo

agricultural [ægrɪ'kʌltʃərəl] *adj* agrícola; *(college)* de agricultura

agriculture ['ægrɪkʌltʃə(r)] *n* agricultura *f*

aground [ə'graʊnd] *adv* **to run a.** encallar, varar

ahead [ə'hed] *adv* delante; *(early)* antes; **go a.!** ¡adelante!; **to be a.** llevar la ventaja; **to go a.** ir adelante; *Fig* **to go a. with sth** llevar algo adelante; *(start)* comenzar algo; **to get a.** triunfar; **to look a.** pensar en el futuro

aid [eɪd] **1** *n* ayuda *f*; *(rescue)* auxilio *m*; **in a. of** a beneficio de; **to come to the a. of sb** acudir en ayuda de algn; **a. worker** cooperante *mf*

2 *vt* ayudar; **to a. and abet sb** ser cómplice de algn

aide [eɪd] *n* ayudante *mf*

AIDS [eɪdz] *n (abbr* **Acquired Immune Deficiency Syndrome)** sida *m*

ailing ['eɪlɪŋ] *adj* achacoso(a)

ailment ['eɪlmənt] *n* enfermedad *f* (leve), achaque *m*

aim [eɪm] **1** *n (with weapon)* puntería *f*; *(target)* propósito *m*

2 *vt (gun)* apuntar (**at** *a or* hacia); *(attack, action)* dirigir (**at** *a or* hacia)

▶ **aim at** *vt insep (target)* tirar para; **to a. at doing sth** tener pensado hacer algo

▶ **aim to** *vt insep* **to a. to do sth** tener la intención de hacer algo

aimless ['eɪmlɪs] *adj* sin objeto, sin propósito

aimlessly ['eɪmlɪslɪ] *adv (wander)* sin rumbo fijo

air [eə(r)] **1** *n* (**a**) aire *m*; **to travel by a.** viajar en avión; **to throw sth up in the a.** lanzar algo al aire; *Fig* **it's still in the a.** todavía queda por resolver; *Aut* **a. bag** airbag *m*; **a. base** base aérea; **a. bed** colchón *m* hinchable; **a. conditioning** aire acondicionado; **A. Force** Fuerzas Aéreas; **a. freshener** ambientador *m*; **a. gun** pistola *f* de aire comprimido; **a. hostess** azafata *f*; **a. letter** carta aérea; **a. pocket** bache *m*; **a. pressure** presión atmosférica; **a. raid** ataque aéreo; **a. terminal** terminal aérea; **a. traffic control** control *m* de tráfico aéreo; **a. traffic controller** controlador(a) *m,f* aéreo(a)

(**b**) *Rad & TV* **to be on the a.** *(programme)* estar emitiendo; *(person)* estar transmitiendo

(**c**) *(appearance)* aspecto *m*

2 *vt (bed, clothes)* airear; *(room)* ventilar; *Fig (grievance)* airear; *(knowledge)* hacer alarde de

airborne ['eəbɔːn] adj (aircraft) en vuelo; (troops) aerotransportado(a)

air-conditioned ['eəkɒndɪʃənd] adj climatizado(a)

aircraft ['eəkrɑːft] n (pl aircraft) avión m; **a. carrier** portaviones m inv

airfield ['eəfiːld] n campo m de aviación

airlift ['eəlɪft] n puente aéreo

airline ['eəlaɪn] n línea aérea

airlock ['eəlɒk] n (in pipe) bolsa f de aire; (in spacecraft) esclusa f de aire

airmail ['eəmeɪl] n correo aéreo; **by a.** por avión

airplane ['eəpleɪn] n US avión m

airport ['eəpɔːt] n aeropuerto m; **a. tax** tasas fpl de aeropuerto

airsick ['eəsɪk] adj **to be a.** marearse en avión

airstrip ['eəstrɪp] n pista f de aterrizaje

airtight ['eətaɪt] adj hermético(a)

airy ['eərɪ] adj (**airier, airiest**) (well-ventilated) bien ventilado(a); (vague, carefree) ligero(a)

aisle [aɪl] n (in church) nave f; (in theatre) pasillo m

ajar [ə'dʒɑː(r)] adj & adv entreabierto(a)

akin [ə'kɪn] adj semejante

alacrity [ə'lækrɪtɪ] n **with a.** con presteza

à la mode [ælə'məʊd] adj US (dessert) con helado

alarm [ə'lɑːm] **1** n (**a**) alarma f; **a. clock** despertador m (**b**) (fear) inquietud f; **to cause a.** provocar temor
2 vt alarmar

alas [ə'læs] interj ¡ay!, ¡ay de mí!

albatross ['ælbətrɒs] n albatros m

albeit [ɔːl'biːɪt] conj aunque, no obstante

album ['ælbəm] n álbum m

alcohol ['ælkəhɒl] n alcohol m

alcoholic [ælkə'hɒlɪk] adj & n alcohólico(a) (m,f)

alcopop ['ælkəʊpɒp] n Br refresco m con alcohol

alcove ['ælkəʊv] n hueco m

> Note that the Spanish word **alcoba** is a false friend and is never a translation for the English word **alcove**. In Spanish, **alcoba** means "bedroom".

ale [eɪl] n cerveza f; **brown/pale a.** cerveza negra/rubia

alert [ə'lɜːt] **1** adj alerta; (lively) despabilado(a)
2 n alerta m; **to be on the a.** estar alerta
3 vt **to a. sb to sth** avisar a algn de algo

A-level ['eɪlevəl] n Br Educ (abbr **Advanced level**) = examen final o diploma

en una asignatura de los estudios pre-universitarios

algae ['ældʒiː] npl algas fpl

algebra ['ældʒɪbrə] n álgebra f

Algeria [æl'dʒɪərɪə] n Argelia

Algerian [æl'dʒɪərɪən] adj & n argelino(a) (m,f)

Algiers [æl'dʒɪəz] n Argel

alias ['eɪlɪəs] **1** n alias m
2 adv alias

alibi ['ælɪbaɪ] n coartada f

alien ['eɪlɪən] **1** adj (foreign) extranjero(a); (from space) extraterrestre; **a. to** ajeno(a) a
2 n (foreigner) extranjero(a) m,f; (from space) extraterrestre mf

alienate ['eɪlɪəneɪt] vt (**a**) **to a. sb** ofender a algn; **to a. oneself from sb** alejarse de algn (**b**) Jur enajenar

alight¹ [ə'laɪt] adj (on fire) ardiendo(a)

alight² [ə'laɪt] vi (get off) apearse (**from** de)

align [ə'laɪn] vt alinear

alike [ə'laɪk] **1** adj (similar) parecidos(as); (the same) iguales
2 adv (in the same way) de la misma manera, igualmente; **dressed a.** vestidos(as) iguales

alimony ['ælɪmənɪ] n Jur pensión alimenticia

alive [ə'laɪv] adj vivo(a); Fig (teeming) lleno(a) (**with** de); **to be a.** estar vivo(a)

alkaline ['ælkəlaɪn] adj alcalino(a)

all [ɔːl] **1** adj todo(a), todos(as); **a. year** (durante) todo el año; **a. kinds of things** todo tipo de cosas; **at a. hours** a todas horas; **at a. times** siempre; **she works a. the time** siempre está trabajando; **a. six of us were there** los seis estábamos allí
2 pron todo(a), todos(as); **after a.** al fin y al cabo; **a. of his work** toda su obra; **a. of us** todos(as) nosotros(as); **a. who saw it** todos los que lo vieron; **a. you can do is wait** lo único que puedes hacer es esperar; **I don't like it at a.** no me gusta en absoluto; **is that a.?** ¿eso es todo?; **most of** or **above a.** sobre todo; **once and for a.** de una vez por todas; **thanks − not at a.** gracias − de nada; **a. in a.** en conjunto; **that's a.** ya está; **the score was one a.** empataron a uno
3 adv **a. by myself** completamente solo(a); **a. at once** (suddenly) de repente; (altogether) de una vez; **a. the better** tanto mejor; **a. the same** de todos modos; **he knew a. along** lo sabía desde el principio; **if it's a. the same to you** si no te importa; **it's a. but impossible** es casi

imposible; **I'm not a. that tired** no estoy tan cansado(a) como eso

4 n **to give one's a.** darse por completo

Allah [ˈælə] n Alá m

allay [əˈleɪ] vt (fears, doubts) apaciguar

allegation [ælɪˈgeɪʃən] n alegato m

allege [əˈledʒ] vt sostener, pretender (that que)

allegedly [əˈledʒɪdlɪ] adv supuestamente

allegiance [əˈliːdʒəns] n lealtad f

allergic [əˈlɜːdʒɪk] adj alérgico(a) (to a)

allergy [ˈælədʒɪ] n alergia f

alleviate [əˈliːvɪeɪt] vt (pain) aliviar

alley [ˈælɪ] n callejón m

alliance [əˈlaɪəns] n alianza f

allied [ˈælaɪd] adj aliado(a)

alligator [ˈælɪgeɪtə(r)] n caimán m

all-in [ˈɔːlɪn] adj (price) todo incluido; Sport a. **wrestling** lucha f libre

alliteration [əlɪtəˈreɪʃən] n aliteración f

all-night [ˈɔːlnaɪt] adj (café etc) abierto(a) toda la noche; (vigil) que dura toda la noche

allocate [ˈæləkeɪt] vt destinar (to para)

allocation [æləˈkeɪʃən] n (a) (distribution) asignación f (b) (amount allocated) cuota f

allot [əˈlɒt] vt asignar

allotment [əˈlɒtmənt] n (a) (distribution) asignación f (b) (land) parcela f

all-out [ˈɔːlaʊt] **1** adj (effort) supremo(a); (attack) concentrado(a)

2 all out adv **to go all out to do sth** emplearse a fondo para hacer algo

allow [əˈlaʊ] vt (a) (permit) permitir; (a request) acceder a; **to a. sb to do sth** permitir que algn haga algo (b) (allot) (time) dejar; (money) destinar

▸ **allow for** vt insep tener en cuenta

allowance [əˈlaʊəns] n (payment) pensión f, subvención f; (discount) descuento m; **to make allowances for sb/sth** disculpar a algn/tener algo en cuenta; **tax a.** desgravación f fiscal; **travel a.** dietas fpl de viaje

alloy [ˈælɔɪ] n aleación f

all right [ɔːlˈraɪt] **1** adj (okay) bien; **thank you very much – that's a.** muchas gracias – de nada

2 adv (a) (well) bien (b) (definitely) sin duda (c) (okay) de acuerdo, vale

all-round [ˈɔːlraʊnd] adj (athlete etc) completo(a)

all-terrain [ɔːltəˈreɪn] adj a. **vehicle** todoterreno m

all-time [ˈɔːltaɪm] adj **an a. low** una baja sin antecedente; **the a. greats** los grandes de siempre

allude [əˈluːd] vi **to a. to** aludir a

alluring [əˈljʊərɪŋ] adj atractivo(a)

allusion [əˈluːʒən] n alusión f

ally [ˈælaɪ] **1** n aliado(a) m,f

2 vt **to a. oneself to/with sb** aliarse a/con algn

almighty [ɔːlˈmaɪtɪ] **1** adj (all-powerful) todopoderoso(a)

2 n **the A.** El Todopoderoso

almond [ˈɑːmənd] n almendra f

almost [ˈɔːlməʊst] adv casi

alms [ɑːmz] npl limosna f

aloft [əˈlɒft] adv arriba

alone [əˈləʊn] **1** adj solo(a); **can I speak to you a.?** ¿puedo hablar contigo a solas?; **let a.** ni mucho menos; **leave it a.!** ¡no lo toques!; **leave me a.** déjame en paz; **to be a.** estar solo(a)

2 adv solamente, sólo

along [əˈlɒŋ] **1** adv **come a.!** ¡anda, ven!; **he'll be a. in ten minutes** llegará dentro de diez minutos; **a. with** junto con

2 prep (the length of) a lo largo de; **to walk a. the street** andar por la calle; **it's just a. the street** está un poco más abajo

alongside [əˈlɒŋsaɪd] **1** adv Naut de costado

2 prep al lado de

aloof [əˈluːf] **1** adj (person) distante

2 adv **to keep oneself a. (from)** mantenerse a distancia (de)

aloud [əˈlaʊd] adv en voz alta

alphabet [ˈælfəbet] n alfabeto m

alphabetical [ælfəˈbetɪkəl] adj alfabético(a)

alphabetically [ælfəˈbetɪkəlɪ] adv por orden alfabético

alpine [ˈælpaɪn] adj alpino(a)

Alps [ælps] npl **the A.** los Alpes

already [ɔːlˈredɪ] adv ya

alright [ɔːlˈraɪt] adj & adv = **all right**

Alsatian [ælˈseɪʃən] n pastor m alemán

also [ˈɔːlsəʊ] adv también, además

also-ran [ˈɔːlsəʊræn] n Fam (person) segundón(ona) m,f

altar [ˈɔːltə(r)] n altar m

alter [ˈɔːltə(r)] **1** vt (plan) cambiar, retocar; (project) modificar; (clothing) arreglar; (timetable) revisar

2 vi cambiar, cambiarse

alteration [ɔːltəˈreɪʃən] n (to plan) cambio m; (to project) modificación f; (to clothing) arreglo m; (to timetable) revisión f, **alterations** (to building) reformas fpl

alternate 1 adj [ɔːlˈtɜːnɪt] alterno(a); **on a. days** cada dos días

2 vt [ˈɔːltəneɪt] alternar

alternately [ɔːl'tɜːnɪtlɪ] *adv* **a. hot and cold** ahora caliente, ahora frío

alternative [ɔːl'tɜːnətɪv] **1** *adj* alternativo(a)

2 *n* alternativa *f*; **I have no a. but to accept** no tengo más remedio que aceptar

alternatively [ɔːl'tɜːnətɪvlɪ] *adv* o bien; **a., you could walk** o bien podrías ir andando

alternator ['ɔːltəneɪtə(r)] *n Aut* alternador *m*

although [ɔːl'ðəʊ] *conj* aunque

altitude ['æltɪtjuːd] *n* altitud *f*

alto ['æltəʊ] *adj & n (male singer, instrument)* alto *(m)*; *(female singer)* contralto *(f)*

altogether [ɔːltə'geðə(r)] *adv (in total)* en conjunto, en total; *(completely)* completamente, del todo

altruism ['æltruːɪzəm] *n* altruismo *m*

aluminium [æljʊ'mɪnɪəm], *US* **aluminum** [ə'luːmɪnəm] *n* aluminio *m*

alumnus [ə'lʌmnəs] *n (pl* **alumni** [ə'lʌmnaɪ]) *US* antiguo alumno

always ['ɔːlweɪz] *adv* siempre

AM [eɪ'em] *Rad (abbr* **amplitude modulation)** AM

am [æm] *1st person sing pres of* be

a.m. [eɪ'em] *(abbr* **ante meridiem)** a.m., de la mañana

amalgamate [ə'mælgəmeɪt] **1** *vt (metals)* amalgamar

2 *vi (metals)* amalgamarse; *(companies)* fusionarse

amalgamation [əmælgə'meɪʃən] *n* fusión *f*

amass [ə'mæs] *vt (money)* amontonar; *(information)* acumular

amateur ['æmətə(r)] **1** *n* amateur *mf*, aficionado(a) *m,f*

2 *adj* aficionado(a); *Pej (work etc)* chapucero(a)

amateurish ['æmətərɪʃ] *adj* chapucero(a)

amaze [ə'meɪz] *vt* asombrar, pasmar; **to be amazed at sth** quedarse pasmado(a) de algo

amazement [ə'meɪzmənt] *n* asombro *m*, sorpresa *f*

amazing [ə'meɪzɪŋ] *adj* asombroso(a), increíble

ambassador [æm'bæsədə(r)] *n* embajador(a) *m,f*

amber ['æmbə(r)] **1** *n* ámbar *m*

2 *adj* ambarino(a); *(traffic light)* amarillo(a)

ambiguity [æmbɪ'gjuːɪtɪ] *n* ambigüedad *f*

ambiguous [æm'bɪgjʊəs] *adj* ambiguo(a)

ambition [æm'bɪʃən] *n* ambición *f*

ambitious [æm'bɪʃəs] *adj* ambicioso(a)

ambivalent [æm'bɪvələnt] *adj* ambivalente

amble ['æmbəl] *vi* deambular

ambulance ['æmbjʊləns] *n* ambulancia *f*; **a. man** ambulanciero *m*

ambush ['æmbʊʃ] **1** *n* emboscada *f*

2 *vt* tender una emboscada a; *Fig* atacar por sorpresa

amen [ɑː'men] *interj* amén

amenable [ə'miːnəbəl] *adj* **I'd be quite a. to doing that** no me importaría nada hacer eso; **a. to reason** razonable

amend [ə'mend] *vt (law)* enmendar; *(error)* subsanar

amendment [ə'mendmənt] *n* enmienda *f*

amends [ə'mendz] *npl* **to make a. to sb for sth** compensar a algn por algo

amenities [ə'miːnɪtɪz] *npl* comodidades *fpl*

America [ə'merɪkə] *n (continent)* América *f*; *(USA)* (los) Estados Unidos; **South A.** América del Sur, Sudamérica *f*

American [ə'merɪkən] *adj & n* americano(a) *(m,f)*; *(of USA)* norteamericano(a) *(m,f)*, estadounidense *(mf)*

amiable ['eɪmɪəbəl] *adj* amable, afable

amicable ['æmɪkəbəl] *adj* amistoso(a)

amid(st) ['æmɪd(st)] *prep* entre, en medio de

amiss [ə'mɪs] *adj & adv* mal; **there's sth a.** algo anda mal; **to take sth a.** tomar algo a mal

ammonia [ə'məʊnɪə] *n* amoníaco *m*

ammunition [æmjʊ'nɪʃən] *n* municiones *fpl*

amnesia [æm'niːzɪə] *n* amnesia *f*

amnesty ['æmnɪstɪ] *n* amnistía *f*

amok [ə'mɒk] *adv Fig* **to run a.** *(child)* desmadrarse; *(inflation etc)* dispararse

among(st) [ə'mʌŋ(st)] *prep* entre

amoral [eɪ'mɒrəl] *adj* amoral

amorous ['æmərəs] *adj* cariñoso(a)

amorphous [ə'mɔːfəs] *adj* amorfo(a)

amount [ə'maʊnt] *n* cantidad *f*; *(of money)* suma *f*; *(of bill)* importe *m*

▸ amount to *vt insep* ascender a; *Fig* equivaler a

amp [æmp], **ampère** ['æmpeə(r)] *n* amperio *m*

amphetamine [æm'fetəmiːn] *n* anfetamina *f*

amphibian [æm'fɪbɪən] *adj & n* anfibio(a) *(m)*

amphibious [æmˈfɪbɪəs] *adj* anfibio(a)

amphitheatre [ˈæmfɪθɪətə(r)] *n* anfiteatro *m*

ample [ˈæmpəl] *adj (enough)* bastante; *(more than enough)* abundante; *(large)* amplio(a)

amplifier [ˈæmplɪfaɪə(r)] *n* amplificador *m*

amputate [ˈæmpjʊteɪt] *vt* amputar

amuck [əˈmʌk] *adv* = **amok**

amuse [əˈmjuːz] *vt* divertir, entretener

amusement [əˈmjuːzmənt] *n (enjoyment)* diversión *f; (laughter)* risa *f; (pastime)* pasatiempo *m;* **a. arcade** salón *m* de juegos; **a. park** parque *m* de atracciones

amusing [əˈmjuːzɪŋ] *adj* divertido(a)

an [æn, *unstressed* ən] *see* **a**

anabolic steroid [ænəbɒlɪkˈstɪərɔɪd] *n* esteroide *m* anabolizante

anaemia [əˈniːmɪə] *n* anemia *f*

anaemic [əˈniːmɪk] *adj* anémico(a); *Fig (weak)* débil

anaesthetic [ænɪsˈθetɪk] *n* anestesia *f*

anaesthetist [əˈniːsθətɪst] *n* anestesista *mf*

analog(ue) [ˈænəlɒg] *n* análogo *m;* **a. computer** ordenador analógico, *Am* computadora analógica; **a. watch** reloj *m* de agujas

analogy [əˈnælədʒɪ] *n* analogía *f*

analyse [ˈænəlaɪz] *vt* analizar

analysis [əˈnælɪsɪs] *n (pl* **analyses** [əˈnælɪsiːz]) análisis *m inv*

analyst [ˈænəlɪst] *n* analista *mf; (psychoanalyst)* psicoanalista *mf*

analytic(al) [ænəˈlɪtɪk(əl)] *adj* analítico(a)

analyze [ˈænəlaɪz] *vt US* = **analyse**

anarchist [ˈænəkɪst] *n* anarquista *mf*

anarchy [ˈænəkɪ] *n* anarquía *f*

anathema [əˈnæθəmə] *n* **the very idea was a. to him** le repugnaba sólo de pensarlo

anatomy [əˈnætəmɪ] *n* anatomía *f*

ancestor [ˈænsestə(r)] *n* antepasado *m*

anchor [ˈæŋkə(r)] **1** *n Naut* ancla *f; Fig* áncora *f;* **to drop a.** echar el ancla; **to weigh a.** zarpar
2 *vt Naut* anclar; *Fig (fix securely)* sujetar
3 *vi* anclar

anchovy [ˈæntʃəvɪ] *n* anchoa *f*

ancient [ˈeɪnʃənt] *adj* antiguo(a)

ancillary [ænˈsɪlərɪ] *adj & n* auxiliar *(mf)*

and [ænd, *unstressed* ənd, ən] *conj* y; *(before i-, hi-)* e; **a hundred a. one** ciento uno; **a. so on** etcétera; **Bill a. Pat** Bill y Pat; **Chinese a. Indian** chino e indio; **come a. see us** ven a vernos; **four a. a half** cuatro y

medio; **she cried a.** **cried** no paró de llorar; **try a. help me** trata de ayudarme; **wait a. see** espera a ver; **worse a. worse** cada vez peor

Andalusia [ændəˈluːzɪə] *n* Andalucía *f*

Andalusian [ændəˈluːzɪən] *adj* andaluz(a)

Andes [ˈændiːz] *npl* **the A.** los Andes

Andorra [ænˈdɔːrə] *n* Andorra

anecdote [ˈænɪkdəʊt] *n* anécdota *f*

anemia [əˈniːmɪə] *n US* = **anaemia**

anesthetic [ænɪsˈθetɪk] *n US* = **anaesthetic**

angel [ˈeɪndʒəl] *n* ángel *m*

anger [ˈæŋgə(r)] **1** *n* cólera *f*
2 *vt* enojar

angina [ænˈdʒaɪnə] *n* angina *f* (de pecho)

angle [ˈæŋgəl] *n* ángulo *m; Fig* punto *m* de vista

angler [ˈæŋglə(r)] *n* pescador(a) *m,f* de caña

Anglican [ˈæŋglɪkən] *adj & n* anglicano(a) *(m,f)*

Anglo-Saxon [æŋgləʊˈsæksən] *adj & n* anglosajón(ona) *(m,f)*

Angola [æŋˈgəʊlə] *n* Angola

angrily [ˈæŋgrɪlɪ] *adv* furiosamente

angry [ˈæŋgrɪ] *adj* (**angrier, angriest**) *(person etc)* enfadado(a); *(voice)* airado(a); **to get a. with sb about sth** enfadarse con algn por algo

anguish [ˈæŋgwɪʃ] *n* angustia *f*

angular [ˈæŋgjʊlə(r)] *adj (shape)* angular; *(face)* anguloso(a)

animal [ˈænɪməl] **1** *adj* animal
2 *n* animal *m; Fig* bestia *f*

animate 1 *adj* [ˈænɪmɪt] vivo(a)
2 *vt* [ˈænɪmeɪt] animar; *Fig* estimular

animated [ˈænɪmeɪtɪd] *adj (lively)* animado(a)

animosity [ænɪˈmɒsɪtɪ] *n* animosidad *f*

aniseed [ˈænɪsiːd] *n* anís *m*

ankle [ˈæŋkəl] *n* tobillo *m;* **a. boots** botines *mpl;* **a. socks** calcetines cortos

annex [əˈneks] *vt (territory)* anexionar

annexe, *US* **annex** [ˈæneks] *n (building)* (edificio *m)* anexo *m*

annihilate [əˈnaɪəleɪt] *vt* aniquilar

anniversary [ænɪˈvɜːsərɪ] *n* aniversario *m;* **wedding a.** aniversario de bodas

announce [əˈnaʊns] *vt* anunciar; *(news)* comunicar; *(fact)* hacer saber

announcement [əˈnaʊnsmənt] *n* anuncio *m; (news)* comunicación *f; (statement)* declaración *f*

announcer [əˈnaʊnsə(r)] *n TV & Rad* locutor(a) *m,f*

annoy [əˈnɔɪ] *vt* molestar, fastidiar; **to**

get annoyed enfadarse, molestarse

annoyance [ə'nɔɪəns] n (feeling) enojo m; (thing) molestia f, fastidio m

annoying [ə'nɔɪɪŋ] adj molesto(a), fastidioso(a)

annual ['ænjʊəl] 1 adj anual
2 n (book) anuario m; (plant) anual m

annually ['ænjʊəlɪ] adv anualmente

annul [ə'nʌl] vt anular

annulment [ə'nʌlmənt] n anulación f

anomaly [ə'nɒməlɪ] n anomalía f

anonymity [ænə'nɪmɪtɪ] n anonimato m

anonymous [ə'nɒnɪməs] adj anónimo(a)

anorak ['ænəræk] n anorak m

anorexia [ænə'reksɪə] n anorexia f

another [ə'nʌðə(r)] 1 adj otro(a); **a. one** otro(a); **without a. word** sin más
2 pron otro(a); **have a.** toma otro(a); **to love one a.** quererse el uno al otro

Ansaphone® ['ɑːnsəfəʊn] n mensáfono m

answer ['ɑːnsə(r)] 1 n (to letter etc) contestación f; (to question) respuesta f; (to problem) solución f; **in a. to your letter** contestando a su carta; **there's no a.** (on telephone) no contestan; (at door) no abren
2 vt contestar a; (problem) resolver; (door) abrir; (phone) contestar
3 vi contestar, responder
► **answer back** vi replicar; **don't a. back!** ¡no seas respondón!
► **answer for** vt insep responder de; **he's got a lot to a. for** es responsable de muchas cosas
► **answer to** vt insep (name) responder a; (description) corresponder a

answerable ['ɑːnsərəbəl] adj **to be a. to sb for sth** ser responsable ante algn de algo

answering machine ['ɑːnsərɪŋməʃiːn] n contestador automático

ant [ænt] n hormiga f; **a. hill** hormiguero m

antagonism [æn'tægənɪzəm] n antagonismo m (**between** entre), hostilidad f (**towards** hacia)

antagonize [æn'tægənaɪz] vt enemistar, malquistar

Antarctic [æn'tɑːktɪk] 1 adj antártico(a); **A. Ocean** océano Antártico
2 n **the A.** la Antártida

Antarctica [æn'tɑːktɪkə] n Antártida

antecedent [æntɪ'siːdənt] n antecedente m

antelope ['æntɪləʊp] n antílope m

antenatal [æntɪ'neɪtəl] adj antenatal; (clinic) prenatal

antenna [æn'tenə] n (a) (pl antennae [æn'teniː]) (of animal, insect) antena f (b) (pl antennas) TV & Rad antena f

anthem ['ænθəm] n motete m; **national a.** himno m nacional

anthology [æn'θɒlədʒɪ] n antología f

anthracite ['ænθrəsaɪt] n antracita f

anthropology [ænθrə'pɒlədʒɪ] n antropología f

anti-aircraft [æntɪ'eəkrɑːft] adj antiaéreo(a)

antibiotic [æntɪbaɪ'ɒtɪk] n antibiótico m

antibody ['æntɪbɒdɪ] n anticuerpo m

anticipate [æn'tɪsɪpeɪt] vt (a) (expect) esperar (b) (predict) prever; (get ahead of) anticiparse a, adelantarse a

anticipation [æntɪsɪ'peɪʃən] n (expectation) esperanza f; (expectancy) ilusión f

anticlimax [æntɪ'klaɪmæks] n (disappointment) decepción f

anticlockwise [æntɪ'klɒkwaɪz] adv Br en sentido opuesto al de las agujas del reloj

antics ['æntɪks] npl payasadas fpl; (naughtiness) travesuras fpl

anticyclone [æntɪ'saɪkləʊn] n anticiclón m

antidote ['æntɪdəʊt] n antídoto m

antifreeze ['æntɪfriːz] n anticongelante m

antihistamine [æntɪ'hɪstəmɪn] n antihistamínico m

antinuclear [æntɪ'njuːklɪə(r)] adj antinuclear

antipathy [æn'tɪpəθɪ] n antipatía f (**to** a)

antiquated ['æntɪkweɪtɪd] adj anticuado(a)

antique [æn'tiːk] 1 adj antiguo(a)
2 n antigüedad f; **a. dealer** anticuario(a) m,f; **a. shop** tienda f de antigüedades

antiquity [æn'tɪkwɪtɪ] n antigüedad f

anti-Semitism [æntɪ'semɪtɪzəm] n antisemitismo m

antiseptic [æntɪ'septɪk] adj & n antiséptico(a) (m)

antisocial [æntɪ'səʊʃəl] adj (delinquent) antisocial; (unsociable) insociable

antithesis [æn'tɪθɪsɪs] n antítesis f

antivirus ['æntɪvaɪrəs] adj Comput (program, software) antivirus

antler ['æntlə(r)] n cuerna f; **antlers** cornamenta f

Antwerp ['æntwɜːp] n Amberes

anus ['eɪnəs] n ano m

anvil ['ænvɪl] n yunque m

anxiety [æŋ'zaɪtɪ] n (concern) inquietud f; (worry) preocupación f; (fear) angustia f; (eagerness) ansia f

anxious ['æŋkʃəs] adj (concerned)

inquieto(a); *(worried)* preocupado(a); *(fearful)* angustiado(a); *(eager)* ansioso(a); **to be a. about sth** estar preocupado(a) por algo

any ['enɪ] **1** *adj (in questions, conditionals)* algún(una); *(in negative clauses)* ningún(una); *(no matter which)* cualquier(a); *(every)* todo(a); **a. doctor will say the same** cualquier médico te dirá lo mismo; **are there a. seats left?** ¿quedan plazas?; **at a. moment** en cualquier momento; **have you a. apples?** ¿tienes manzanas?; **have you a. money?** ¿tienes (algo de) dinero?; **I don't have a. time** no tengo tiempo; **in a. case** de todas formas

2 *pron (in questions)* alguno(a); *(in negative clauses)* ninguno(a); *(no matter which)* cualquiera; **do they have a.?** ¿tienen alguno?; **I don't want a.** no quiero ninguno(a); **I need some paper, have you a.?** necesito papel, ¿tienes?; **you can have a. (one)** coge el/la que quieras

3 *adv* **is there a. more?** ¿hay más?; **I used to like it, but not a. more/longer** antes me gustaba pero ya no; **is he a. better?** ¿está mejor?

anybody ['enɪbɒdɪ] *pron (in questions, conditionals)* alguien, alguno(a); *(in negative clauses)* nadie, ninguno(a); *(no matter who)* cualquiera; **a. but me** cualquiera menos yo; **bring a. you like** trae a quien quieras; **do you see a. over there?** ¿ves a alguien allí?; **I can't find a.** no encuentro a nadie

anyhow ['enɪhaʊ] *adv* **(a)** *(in spite of that)* en todo caso, de todas formas; *(changing the subject)* bueno, pues **(b)** *(carelessly)* desordenadamente, de cualquier modo *or* forma

anyone ['enɪwʌn] *pron* = **anybody**

anyplace ['enɪpleɪs] *adv US* = **anywhere**

anything ['enɪθɪŋ] **1** *pron (in questions, conditionals)* algo, alguna cosa; *(in negative clauses)* nada; *(no matter what)* cualquier cosa; **a. but that** cualquier cosa menos eso; **a. else?** ¿algo más?; **can I do a. for you?** ¿puedo ayudarte en algo?; **hardly a.** casi nada; **if a., I'd buy the big one** de comprar uno compraría el grande; **to run/work like a.** correr/trabajar a más no poder

2 *adv* **is this a. like what you wanted?** ¿viene a ser éste lo que querías?

anyway ['enɪweɪ] *adv* = **anyhow (a)**

anywhere ['enɪweə(r)] *adv* **(a)** *(in questions, conditionals) (situation)* en alguna parte; *(movement)* a alguna parte; **could it be a. else?** ¿podría estar en otro sitio?

(b) *(in negative clauses) (situation)* en ninguna parte; *(movement)* a ninguna parte; *(no matter where)* dondequiera, en cualquier parte; **go a. you like** ve a donde quieras; **we aren't a. near finished** no hemos terminado ni mucho menos

apart [ə'pɑːt] *adv* **(a)** aparte; **to fall a.** deshacerse; **to take sth a.** desmontar algo **(b)** *(distant)* alejado(a); *(separate)* separado(a); **to be poles a.** ser polos opuestos; **you can't tell the twins a.** no se puede distinguir los mellizos el uno del otro **(c)** **a. from** aparte de

apartheid [ə'pɑːtheɪt] *n* apartheid *m*

apartment [ə'pɑːtmənt] *n (large room)* salón *m*; *US (flat)* piso *m*, apartamento *m*; **a. block** bloque *m* de pisos

apathetic [æpə'θetɪk] *adj* apático(a)

apathy ['æpəθɪ] *n* apatía *f*

ape [eɪp] **1** *n* mono *m*
2 *vt* imitar, copiar

apéritif [ə'perɪtiːf] *n* aperitivo *m*

aperture ['æpətʃə(r)] *n (hole, crack)* resquicio *m*, rendija *f*; *Phot* abertura *f*

apex ['eɪpeks] *n (of triangle)* vértice *m*; *Fig* cumbre *f*

aphrodisiac [æfrə'dɪzɪæk] *n* afrodisíaco *m*

apiece [ə'piːs] *adv* cada uno(a)

aplomb [ə'plɒm] *n* aplomo *m*

apocalypse [ə'pɒkəlɪps] *n* apocalipsis *m inv*

apolitical [eɪpə'lɪtɪkəl] *adj* apolítico(a)

apologetic [əpɒlə'dʒetɪk] *adj (remorseful)* de disculpa; **he was very a.** pidió mil perdones

apologetically [əpɒlə'dʒetɪklɪ] *adv* disculpándose, pidiendo perdón

apologize [ə'pɒlədʒaɪz] *vi (say sorry)* disculparse; **they apologized to us for the delay** se disculparon con nosotros por el retraso

apology [ə'pɒlədʒɪ] *n* disculpa *f*, excusa *f*; *Fam* **what an a. for a meal!** ¡vaya birria de comida!

apoplectic [æpə'plektɪk] *adj Med* apopléctico(a); *Fam* **to be a. with rage** estar furioso(a)

apostle [ə'pɒsəl] *n* apóstol *m*

apostrophe [ə'pɒstrəfɪ] *n* apóstrofo *m*

appal, *US* **appall** [ə'pɔːl] *vt* horrorizar; **to be appalled by sth** quedar horrorizado(a) por algo

appalling [ə'pɔːlɪŋ] *adj (horrifying)* horroroso(a); *Fam (very bad)* pésimo(a), fatal

apparatus [æpə'reɪtəs] *n* aparato *m*; *(equipment)* equipo *m*

apparent [əˈpærənt] *adj (obvious)* evidente; *(seeming)* aparente; **to become a.** ponerse de manifiesto

apparently [əˈpærəntlɪ] *adv (seemingly)* por lo visto

apparition [æpəˈrɪʃən] *n* aparición *f*

appeal [əˈpiːl] **1** *n* (**a**) *(request)* solicitud *f*; *(plea)* súplica *f* (**b**) *(attraction)* atractivo *m*; *(interest)* interés *m* (**c**) *Jur* apelación *f*
  2 *vi* (**a**) *(plead)* rogar, suplicar (**to a.**); **to a. for help** solicitar ayuda (**b**) *(attract)* atraer; *(interest)* interesar; **it doesn't a. to me** no me dice nada (**c**) *Jur* apelar

appealing [əˈpiːlɪŋ] *adj (moving)* conmovedor(a); *(attractive)* atractivo(a); *(tempting)* atrayente

appear [əˈpɪə(r)] *vi* (**a**) *(become visible)* aparecer; *(publicly)* presentarse; *(on stage)* actuar; **to a. before a court** comparecer ante un tribunal; **to a. on television** salir en la televisión (**b**) *(seem)* parecer; **he appears relaxed** parece relajado; **so it appears** según parece

appearance [əˈpɪərəns] *n* (**a**) *(becoming visible)* aparición *f*; *(publicly)* presentación *f*; *(on stage)* presentación *f*; *(before court)* comparecencia *f*; *(of book etc)* publicación *f*; **to put in an a.** hacer acto de presencia (**b**) *(look)* apariencia *f*, aspecto *m*; **to all appearances** al parecer

appease [əˈpiːz] *vt* apaciguar; *(curiosity)* satisfacer

appeasement [əˈpiːzmənt] *n Pol* entreguismo *m*

appendices [əˈpendɪsiːz] *pl of* **appendix**

appendicitis [əpendɪˈsaɪtɪs] *n* apendicitis *f*

appendix [əˈpendɪks] *n (pl* **appendices**) apéndice *m*

appetite [ˈæpɪtaɪt] *n* apetito *m*; *Fig* deseo *m*

appetizer [ˈæpɪtaɪzə(r)] *n (drink)* aperitivo *m*; *(snack)* tapa *f*, pincho *m*

applaud [əˈplɔːd] *vt & vi* aplaudir

applause [əˈplɔːz] *n* aplausos *mpl*

apple [ˈæpəl] *n* manzana *f*; **a. tree** manzano *m*

appliance [əˈplaɪəns] *n* dispositivo *m*

applicable [əˈplɪkəbəl] *adj* aplicable

applicant [ˈæplɪkənt] *n (for post)* candidato(a) *m,f*, *(to court, for tickets)* solicitante *mf*

application [æplɪˈkeɪʃən] *n* (**a**) *(of cream)* aplicación *f* (**b**) *(for post etc)* solicitud *f*; **a. form** solicitud *f*; **job a.** solicitud de empleo (**c**) *(effort)* aplicación *f*; **she lacks a.** no se aplica

applied [əˈplaɪd] *adj* aplicado(a)

apply [əˈplaɪ] **1** *vt* aplicar; *(brake)* echar; *(law)* recurrir a; *(force)* usar; **to a. oneself to** dedicarse a
  2 *vi* (**a**) *(refer)* aplicarse (**to a**) (**b**) *(for job)* presentar una solicitud; *(for information, to court)* presentar una petición
  ▸**apply for** *vt insep (post, information)* solicitar; *(tickets)* pedir

appoint [əˈpɔɪnt] *vt (person)* nombrar; *(time, place etc)* fijar, señalar

appointment [əˈpɔɪntmənt] *n* (**a**) *(to post)* nombramiento *m*; *(post)* cargo *m* (**b**) *(meeting)* cita *f*; **to make an a. with** citarse con; *(at doctor's)* pedir hora a

apportion [əˈpɔːʃən] *vt Fig (blame)* echar

appraisal [əˈpreɪzəl] *n* evaluación *f*

appreciable [əˈpriːʃəbəl] *adj (difference)* apreciable; *(sum)* importante

appreciate [əˈpriːʃɪeɪt] **1** *vt* (**a**) *(be thankful for)* agradecer (**b**) *(understand)* entender (**c**) *(value)* apreciar, valorar
  2 *vi (increase in value)* apreciarse

appreciation [əpriːʃɪˈeɪʃən] *n* (**a**) *(of help, advice)* agradecimiento *m*; *(of difficulty)* comprensión *f*; *(of wine etc)* aprecio *m*; *(appraisal)* evaluación *f* (**b**) *(increase in value)* apreciación *f*

appreciative [əˈpriːʃɪətɪv] *adj (thankful)* agradecido(a); *(responsive)* apreciativo(a)

apprehend [æprɪˈhend] *vt (arrest)* detener

apprehension [æprɪˈhenʃən] *n* (**a**) *(arrest)* detención *f* (**b**) *(fear)* aprensión *f*

apprehensive [æprɪˈhensɪv] *adj (fearful)* aprensivo(a)

apprentice [əˈprentɪs] *n* aprendiz(a) *m,f*

apprenticeship [əˈprentɪsʃɪp] *n* aprendizaje *m*

approach [əˈprəʊtʃ] **1** *n* (**a**) *(coming near)* acercamiento *m*; *(to town)* acceso *m*; **a. road** vía *f* de acceso (**b**) *(to problem)* enfoque *m*
  2 *vt (come near to)* acercarse a; *(be similar to)* aproximarse a; *Fig (problem)* abordar; *(person)* dirigirse a; **to a. sb about sth** dirigirse a algn a propósito de algo
  3 *vi* acercarse

approachable [əˈprəʊtʃəbəl] *adj (person)* accesible

appropriate¹ [əˈprəʊprɪət] *adj (suitable)* apropiado(a), adecuado(a); *(convenient)* oportuno(a)

appropriate² [əˈprəʊprɪeɪt] *vt (allocate)* asignar; *(steal)* apropiarse de

approval [əˈpruːvəl] *n* aprobación *f*, visto

bueno; *Com* **to get sth on a.** adquirir algo sin compromiso de compra

approve [ə'pruːv] *vt* aprobar; **approved school** reformatorio *m*
  ► **approve of** *vt insep* aprobar

approving [ə'pruːvɪŋ] *adj (look etc)* aprobatorio(a)

approx [ə'prɒks] *(abbr* **approximately)** aprox.

approximate 1 *adj* [ə'prɒksɪmɪt] aproximado(a)
  2 *vt* [ə'prɒksɪmeɪt] aproximarse a

approximately [ə'prɒksɪmɪtlɪ] *adv* aproximadamente

apricot ['eɪprɪkɒt] *n* albaricoque *m*, *Am* damasco *m*, *Méx* chabacano *m*

April ['eɪprəl] *n* abril *m*; **A. Fools' Day** día *m* uno de abril, ≃ día de los Inocentes (28 de diciembre)

apron ['eɪprən] *n* delantal *m*; *(for workman)* mandil *m*

apt [æpt] *adj* **(a)** *(suitable)* apropiado(a); *(remark)* acertado(a), oportuno(a); *(name)* justo(a); *(description)* exacto(a) **(b)** **to be a. to do sth** ser propenso(a) a hacer algo

aptitude ['æptɪtjuːd] *n* capacidad *f*; **a. test** prueba *f* de aptitud

aptly ['æptlɪ] *adv* acertadamente

aqualung ['ækwəlʌŋ] *n* botella *f* de oxígeno

aquamarine [ækwəmə'riːn] **1** *n (gem)* aguamarina *f*
  2 *adj* de color de aguamarina

aquarium [ə'kweərɪəm] *n* acuario *m*

Aquarius [ə'kweərɪəs] *n* Acuario *m*

aquatic [ə'kwætɪk] *adj* acuático(a)

aqueduct ['ækwɪdʌkt] *n* acueducto *m*

Arab ['ærəb] *adj & n* árabe *(mf)*

Arabian [ə'reɪbɪən] *adj* árabe

Arabic ['ærəbɪk] **1** *adj* árabe, arábigo(a); **A. numerals** numeración arábiga
  2 *n (language)* árabe *m*

arable ['ærəbəl] *adj* cultivable

Aragon ['ærəgɒn] *n* Aragón *m*

arbitrary ['ɑːbɪtrərɪ] *adj* arbitrario(a)

arbitrate ['ɑːbɪtreɪt] *vt & vi* arbitrar

arbitration [ɑːbɪ'treɪʃən] *n* arbitraje *m*

arc [ɑːk] *n* arco *m*; **a. lamp** arco voltaico

arcade [ɑː'keɪd] *n* arcada *f*; *(passageway)* pasaje *m*; **shopping a.** galerías *fpl* (comerciales)

arch [ɑːtʃ] **1** *n* **(a)** *Archit* arco *m*; *(vault)* bóveda *f* **(b)** *Anat* empeine *m*
  2 *vt (back)* arquear

archaeologist [ɑːkɪ'ɒlədʒɪst] *n* arqueólogo(a) *m,f*

archaeology [ɑːkɪ'ɒlədʒɪ] *n* arqueología *f*

archaic [ɑː'keɪɪk] *adj* arcaico(a)

archbishop [ɑːtʃ'bɪʃəp] *n* arzobispo *m*

arched [ɑːtʃt] *adj* arqueado(a)

archeologist [ɑːkɪ'ɒlədʒɪst] *n US* = **archaeologist**

archeology [ɑːkɪ'ɒlədʒɪ] *n US* = **archaeology**

archer ['ɑːtʃə(r)] *n* arquero(a) *m,f*

archery ['ɑːtʃərɪ] *n* tiro *m* con arco

archetypal ['ɑːkɪtaɪpəl] *adj* arquetípico(a)

archipelago [ɑːkɪ'pelɪgəʊ] *n* archipiélago *m*

architect ['ɑːkɪtekt] *n* arquitecto(a) *m,f*

architectural [ɑːkɪ'tektʃərəl] *adj* arquitectónico(a)

architecture ['ɑːkɪtektʃə(r)] *n* arquitectura *f*

archives ['ɑːkaɪvz] *npl* archivos *mpl*

archway ['ɑːtʃweɪ] *n (arch)* arco *m*; *(vault)* bóveda *f*; *(in church)* atrio *m*; *(passage)* pasaje *m*

arctic ['ɑːktɪk] **1** *adj* ártico(a); **A. Circle** círculo *m* polar Ártico
  2 *n* **the A.** el Ártico

ardent ['ɑːdənt] *adj (supporter etc)* apasionado(a); *(desire)* ardiente

ardour, *US* **ardor** ['ɑːdə(r)] *n* pasión *f*, ardor *m*

arduous ['ɑːdjʊəs] *adj* arduo(a), penoso(a)

are [ɑː(r)] *2nd person sing pres, 1st, 2nd, 3rd person pl pres of* **be**

area ['eərɪə] *n (surface)* área *f*, superficie *f*; *(space)* extensión *f*; *(region)* región *f*; *(of town)* zona *f*; *Fig (field)* campo *m*; *US Tel* **a. code** prefijo *m* local

arena [ə'riːnə] *n (stadium)* estadio *m*; *(bullring)* plaza *f*; *(circus)* pista *f*; *Fig (stage)* campo *m* de batalla

Argentina [ɑːdʒən'tiːnə] *n* Argentina *f*

Argentinian [ɑːdʒən'tɪnɪən] *adj & n* argentino(a) *(m,f)*

arguable ['ɑːgjʊəbəl] *adj* discutible

arguably ['ɑːgjʊəblɪ] *adv* **it's a. the best** hay quienes dicen que es el mejor

argue ['ɑːgjuː] **1** *vt (reason)* discutir; *(point of view)* mantener
  2 *vi (quarrel)* discutir; *(reason)* argumentar, razonar; **to a. for** abogar por; **to a. against sth** ponerse en contra de algo

argument ['ɑːgjʊmənt] *n (reason)* argumento *m* **(for** a favor de; **against** en contra de); *(quarrel)* discusión *f*, disputa *f*; **for the sake of a.** por decir algo

argumentative [ɑːgjʊ'mentətɪv] *adj* **she's very a.** le gusta discutir por todo

aria ['ɑːrɪə] *n* aria *f*

arid ['ærɪd] *adj* árido(a)

Aries ['eəriːz] *n* Aries *m*

arise [ə'raɪz] *vi* (*pt* **arose**; *pp* **arisen** [ə'rɪzən]) (*get up*) levantarse; (*happen*) surgir; **should the occasion a.** si se presenta la ocasión

aristocracy [ærɪ'stɒkrəsɪ] *n* aristocracia *f*

aristocrat ['ærɪstəkræt] *n* aristócrata *mf*

arithmetic [ə'rɪθmətɪk] *n* aritmética *f*

ark [ɑːk] *n* arca *f*; **Noah's A.** el arca de Noé

arm [ɑːm] **1** *n* (**a**) brazo *m*; (*of garment*) manga *f*; **to walk a. in a.** ir cogidos(as) del brazo (**b**) *Mil* **arms** armas *fpl*; **arms race** carrera armamentística; **coat of arms** escudo *m*

    2 *vt* armar; **to a. oneself against sth** armarse contra algo

armaments ['ɑːməmənts] *npl* armamentos *mpl*

armchair ['ɑːmtʃeə(r)] *n* sillón *m*

armed ['ɑːmd] *adj* armado(a); **a. forces** fuerzas armadas; **a. robbery** robo *m* a mano armada

Armenia [ɑː'miːnɪə] *n* Armenia

armistice ['ɑːmɪstɪs] *n* armisticio *m*

armour, *US* **armor** ['ɑːmə(r)] *n* (*on vehicle*) blindaje *m*; (*suit of*) **a.** armadura *f*

armoured car, *US* **armored car** [ɑːməd'kɑː(r)] *n* coche *m* blindado

armour-plated ['ɑːmə'pleɪtɪd] *adj* acorazado(a)

armoury, *US* **armory** ['ɑːmərɪ] *n* arsenal *m*

armpit ['ɑːmpɪt] *n* axila *f*, sobaco *m*

army ['ɑːmɪ] *n* ejército *m*

aroma [ə'rəʊmə] *n* aroma *m*

arose [ə'rəʊz] *pt of* **arise**

around [ə'raʊnd] **1** *adv* alrededor; **all a.** por todos los lados; **are the children a.?** ¿están los niños por aquí?; **he looked a.** miró (a su) alrededor

    2 *prep* (**a**) alrededor de; **a. the corner** a la vuelta de la esquina; **a. here** por aquí (**b**) (*approximately*) aproximadamente

arouse [ə'raʊz] *vt* despertar; (*sexually*) excitar

arrange [ə'reɪndʒ] **1** *vt* (**a**) (*order*) ordenar; (*hair, flowers*) arreglar; *Mus* adaptar (**b**) (*plan*) organizar; (*agree on*) quedar en; **to a. a time** fijar una hora; **arranged marriage** boda arreglada

    2 *vi* **I shall a. for him to be there** lo arreglaré para que pueda asistir

arrangement [ə'reɪndʒmənt] *n* (**a**) (*display*) colocación *f*; *Mus* adaptación *f* (**b**) (*agreement*) acuerdo *m* (**c**) **arrangements** (*plans*) planes *mpl*; (*preparations*) preparativos *mpl*

array [ə'reɪ] *n* colección *f*; **a great a. of goods** un gran surtido de productos

arrears [ə'rɪəz] *npl* atrasos *mpl*; **to be in a. with the rent** estar atrasado(a) con el alquiler; **to be paid in a.** cobrar con retraso

arrest [ə'rest] **1** *n* detención *f*; **to be under a.** estar detenido(a)

    2 *vt* (*criminal*) detener; *Fig* (*progress*) frenar

arresting [ə'restɪŋ] *adj* llamativo(a)

arrival [ə'raɪvəl] *n* llegada *f*; **a new a.** un(a) recién llegado(a)

arrive [ə'raɪv] *vi* llegar (**at/in** a)

arrogance ['ærəgəns] *n* arrogancia *f*

arrogant ['ærəgənt] *adj* arrogante

arrow ['ærəʊ] *n* flecha *f*

arse ['ɑːs] *n Vulg* culo *m*

arsenal ['ɑːsənəl] *n* arsenal *m*

arsenic ['ɑːsənɪk] *n* arsénico *m*

arson ['ɑːsən] *n* incendio *m* provocado

art [ɑːt] *n* (**a**) arte *m*; (*drawing*) dibujo *m*; **the arts** las bellas artes; **arts and crafts** artes *fpl* y oficios *mpl*; **a. gallery** galería *f* de arte (**b**) **arts** (*branch of knowledge*) letras *fpl*

artefact ['ɑːtɪfækt] *n* artefacto *m*; (*in archaeology*) objeto *m* de arte

artery ['ɑːtərɪ] *n* arteria *f*

artful ['ɑːtfəl] *adj* (*cunning*) ladino(a)

arthritis [ɑː'θraɪtɪs] *n* artritis *f*

artichoke ['ɑːtɪtʃəʊk] *n* alcachofa *f*, *RP* alcaucil *m*

article ['ɑːtɪkəl] *n* (**a**) artículo *m*; *Press* artículo; **a. of clothing** prenda *f* de vestir (**b**) *Jur* **articles** contrato *m* de aprendizaje

articulate¹ [ɑː'tɪkjʊlɪt] *adj* (*speech*) claro(a); (*person*) que se expresa bien

articulate² [ɑː'tɪkjʊleɪt] *vt & vi* articular; (*words*) pronunciar; *Br* **articulated lorry** camión articulado

artificial [ɑːtɪ'fɪʃəl] *adj* artificial; (*limb*) postizo(a); **a. intelligence** inteligencia *f* artificial

artillery [ɑː'tɪlərɪ] *n* artillería *f*

artisan ['ɑːtɪzæn] *n* artesano(a) *m,f*

artist ['ɑːtɪst] *n* artista *mf*; (*painter*) pintor(a) *m,f*

artistic [ɑː'tɪstɪk] *adj* artístico(a)

artistry ['ɑːtɪstrɪ] *n* arte *m*, talento artístico

as [æz, *unstressed* əz] **1** *adv & conj* (**a**) (*comparison*) **as ... as ...** tan ... como ...; **as far as** hasta; *Fig* **as far as I'm concerned** por lo que a mi respecta; **as many as** tantos(as) como; **as much as** tanto(a) como; **as tall as me** tan alto(a) como yo; **as opposed to** a diferencia de; **as little as**

£5 tan sólos 5 libras ; **as soon as they arrive** en cuanto lleguen; **I'll stay as long as I can** quedaré todo el tiempo que pueda; **just as big** igual de grande; **three times as fast** tres veces más rápido; **the same as** igual que

(**b**) *(manner)* como; **as a rule** por regla general; **as you know** como ya sabéis; **as you like** como quieras; **do as I say** haz lo que yo te digo; **he's working as a doctor** está trabajando de médico; **I thought as much** ya me lo suponía; **it serves as a table** sirve de mesa; **leave it as it is** déjalo tal como está; **he was dressed as a pirate** iba vestido de pirata

(**c**) *(while, when)* mientras (que); **as a child** de niño(a); **as I was eating** mientras comía; **as we were leaving, we saw Pat** al salir vimos a Pat

(**d**) *(though)* aunque; **be that as it may** por mucho que así sea; **young as he is** aunque es joven

(**e**) *(because)* como, ya que

(**f**) *(and so)* igual que; **as do I** igual que yo; **as well** también

(**g**) *(purpose)* para; **so as to do sth** para hacer algo

(**h**) **as for my brother** en cuanto a mi hermano

(**i**) **as from, as of** a partir de

(**j**) **to act as** actuar como si *(+ subj)*; **it looks as if the concert is off** parece ser que no habrá concierto

(**k**) **it's late enough as it is** ya es muy tarde; **as it were** por así decirlo

(**l**) **as long as** *(only if)* siempre que, con tal de que

(**m**) **as regards** en cuanto a, por lo que se refiere a; **as usual** como siempre; **as yet** aún, todavía

2 *rel pron* **such as** tal(es) como

asbestos [æz'bestəs] *n* amianto *m*, asbesto *m*

ascend [ə'send] *vi* subir, ascender

ascendancy [ə'sendənsɪ] *n* dominio *m*, influencia *f*

ascendant [ə'sendənt] *n* **to be in the a.** estar en auge

ascent [ə'sent] *n* subida *f*

ascertain [æsə'teɪn] *vt* averiguar, enterarse de

ascribe [ə'skraɪb] *vt* **to a. sth to sb/sth** imputar algo a alguien/algo

aseptic [ə'septɪk] *adj* aséptico(a)

ash ¹ [æʃ] *n Bot* fresno *m*

ash ² [æʃ] *n* ceniza *f*; **a. bin,** *US* **a. can** cubo *m* de la basura; *Rel* **A. Wednesday** miércoles *m inv* de ceniza

ashamed [ə'ʃeɪmd] *adj* avergonzado(a); **you ought to be a. of yourself!** ¡te debería dar vergüenza!

ashen ['æʃən] *adj (face)* pálido(a)

ashore [ə'ʃɔ:(r)] *adv (position)* en tierra; **to go a.** desembarcar; **to swim a.** nadar hacia tierra

ashtray ['æʃtreɪ] *n* cenicero *m*

Asia ['eɪʒə] *n* Asia; **A. Minor** Asia Menor

Asian ['eɪʒən] *adj & n* asiático(a) *(m,f)*

aside [ə'saɪd] **1** *adv* al lado, aparte; **to cast a.** echar a un lado; **to stand a.** apartarse

2 *prep* **a. from** *(apart from)* aparte de; *(as well as)* además de

3 *n Th* aparte *m*

ask [ɑ:sk] **1** *vt* (**a**) preguntar; **to a. sb a question** hacer una pregunta a algn (**b**) *(request)* pedir, solicitar; **she asked me to post it** me pidió que lo echara al buzón (**c**) *(invite)* invitar

2 *vi (inquire)* preguntar; *(request)* pedir

▶ **ask after** *vt insep* **to a. after sb** preguntar por algn

▶ **ask for** *vt insep (help)* pedir, solicitar; *(person)* preguntar por alguien

▶ **ask out** *vt sep* **to a. sb out** invitar a algn a salir

askance [ə'skæns] *adv* **to look a. at sb** mirar a algn con recelo

askew [ə'skju:] **1** *adj* ladeado(a)

2 *adv* de lado

asleep [ə'sli:p] *adj (person)* dormido(a); *(limb)* adormecido(a); **to fall a.** quedarse dormido(a)

asparagus [ə'spærəgəs] *n inv* espárragos *mpl*

aspect ['æspekt] *n* (**a**) *(of question)* aspecto *m* (**b**) *(of building)* orientación *f*

aspersions [ə'spɜ:ʃənz] *npl* **to cast a. on sb** difamar a algn

asphalt ['æsfælt] *n* asfalto *m*

asphyxiation [æsfɪksɪ'eɪʃən] *n* asfixia *f*

aspiration [æspə'reɪʃən] *n* aspiración *f*

aspire [ə'spaɪə(r)] *vi* **to a. to** aspirar a

aspirin ['æsprɪn] *n* aspirina *f*

ass ¹ [æs] *n Zool* asno(a) *m,f*, burro(a) *m,f*; *Fam Fig* burro(a)

ass ² [æs] *n US Vulg* culo *m*

assailant [ə'seɪlənt] *n* agresor(a) *m,f*, atacante *mf*

assassin [ə'sæsɪn] *n* asesino(a) *m,f*

assassinate [ə'sæsɪneɪt] *vt* asesinar

assassination [əsæsɪ'neɪʃən] *n* asesinato *m*

assault [ə'sɔ:lt] **1** *n Mil* ataque *m* (**on** a); *Jur* agresión *f*

2 *vt Mil* asaltar, atacar; *Jur* agredir; *(sexually)* violar

assemble [ə'sembəl] **1** vt (people) reunir, juntar; (furniture) montar

  2 vi (people) reunirse, juntarse

assembly [ə'semblɪ] n reunión f, asamblea f; Tech montaje m; Ind **a. line** cadena f de montaje; Educ **morning a.** servicio m matinal

assent [ə'sent] **1** n (agreement) asentimiento m; (consent) consentimiento m; (approval) aprobación f

  2 vi asentir, consentir (**to** en)

assert [ə'sɜːt] vt afirmar; **to a. oneself** imponerse; **to a. one's rights** hacer valer sus derechos

assertive [ə'sɜːtɪv] adj enérgico(a)

assess [ə'ses] vt (estimate value) valorar; (damages, price) calcular; (tax) gravar; Fig (effect) evaluar

assessment [ə'sesmənt] n (of value) valoración f; (of damages etc) cálculo m; (of taxes) gravamen m; Fig juicio m

assessor [ə'sesə(r)] n asesor(a) m,f

asset ['æset] n (**a**) ventaja f, **to be an a.** (person) ser de gran valor (**b**) Fin **assets** bienes mpl; **fixed assets** bienes raíces

asshole ['æshəʊl] n US Vulg (unpleasant person) hijo(a) m,f de puta, cabrón(ona) m,f

assiduous [ə'sɪdjʊəs] adj asiduo(a)

assign [ə'saɪn] vt (task) asignar; (property etc) ceder; **to a. sb to a job** designar a algn para un trabajo

assignment [ə'saɪnmənt] n (allocation) asignación f; (task) tarea f; (mission) misión f; (appointment) cita f

assimilate [ə'sɪmɪleɪt] vt asimilar

assist [ə'sɪst] vt & vi ayudar

assistance [ə'sɪstəns] n ayuda f, auxilio m

assistant [ə'sɪstənt] n ayudante mf; **a. manager** subdirector(a) m,f; **shop a.** dependiente(a) m,f; (language) **a.** lector(a) m,f

associate¹ [ə'səʊʃɪeɪt] **1** vt (ideas) relacionar; (companies) asociar; **to be associated with sth** estar relacionado(a) con algo

  2 vi **to a. with** tratar con

associate² [ə'səʊʃɪt] **1** adj asociado(a)

  2 n (colleague) colega mf; (partner) socio(a) m,f; (accomplice) cómplice mf

association [əsəʊsɪ'eɪʃən] n asociación f; (company) sociedad f

assorted [ə'sɔːtɪd] adj surtido(a), variado(a)

assortment [ə'sɔːtmənt] n surtido m, variedad f

assume [ə'sjuːm] **1** vt (power) asumir; (attitude, name) adoptar; **an assumed name** un nombre falso

  2 vi (suppose) suponer

assumption [ə'sʌmpʃən] n (**a**) (of power) toma f; **a. of office** toma de posesión (**b**) (supposition) suposición f

assurance [ə'ʃʊərəns] n (**a**) (guarantee) garantía f (**b**) (confidence) confianza f (**c**) (insurance) seguro m

assure [ə'ʃʊə(r)] vt asegurar

asterisk ['æstərɪsk] n asterisco m

astern [ə'stɜːn] adv a popa

asthma ['æsmə] n asma f

astonish [ə'stɒnɪʃ] vt asombrar, pasmar; **I was astonished** me quedé pasmado(a)

astonishing [ə'stɒnɪʃɪŋ] adj asombroso(a), pasmoso(a)

astonishment [ə'stɒnɪʃmənt] n asombro m; **to my a.** para gran sorpresa mía

astound [ə'staʊnd] vt asombrar, pasmar

astray [ə'streɪ] adv **to go a.** extraviarse; Fig equivocarse; **to lead sb a.** llevar a algn por mal camino

astride [ə'straɪd] prep a horcajadas sobre

astrology [ə'strɒlədʒɪ] n astrología f

astronaut ['æstrənɔːt] n astronauta mf

astronomer [ə'strɒnəmə(r)] n astrónomo(a) m,f

astronomical [æstrə'nɒmɪkəl] adj astronómico(a)

astronomy [ə'strɒnəmɪ] n astronomía f

Asturias [æ'stʊərɪæs] n Asturias

astute [ə'stjuːt] adj astuto(a)

asylum [ə'saɪləm] n (**a**) (protection) asilo m; **to seek political a.** pedir asilo político (**b**) **mental a.** manicomio m

at [æt, unstressed ət] prep (**a**) (position) a, en; **at school/work** en el colegio/trabajo; **at the window** a la ventana; **at the top** en lo alto

  (**b**) (direction) a; **to be angry at sb/sth** enfadarse con algn/por algo; **to laugh at sb** reírse de algn; **to look at sth/sb** mirar algo/a algn; **to shout at sb** gritarle a algn

  (**c**) (time) a; **at Easter/Christmas** en Semana Santa/Navidad; **at six o'clock** a las seis; **at first** al principio; **at last** por fin; **at once** enseguida; **at that time** entonces; **at the moment** ahora

  (**d**) (manner) a, en; **at best/worst** en el mejor/peor de los casos; **at hand** a mano; **at least** por lo menos; **not at all** en absoluto; (don't mention it) de nada

  (**e**) (rate) a; **they retail at 100 pesetas each** se venden a 100 pesetas la unidad; **two at a time** de dos en dos

ate [et, eɪt] pt of **eat**

atheist ['eɪθɪɪst] n ateo(a) m,f

Athens ['æθɪnz] *n* Atenas

athlete ['æθliːt] *n* atleta *mf*

athletic [æθ'letɪk] **1** *adj* atlético(a); *(sporty)* deportista
2 *npl* **athletics** atletismo *m*

Atlantic [ət'læntɪk] *adj* **the A. (Ocean)** el (océano) Atlántico

atlas ['ætləs] *n* atlas *m*

atmosphere ['ætməsfɪə(r)] *n* atmósfera *f*; *Fig (ambience)* ambiente *m*

atmospheric [ætməs'ferɪk] *adj* atmosférico(a)

atom ['ætəm] *n* átomo *m*; **a. bomb** bomba atómica

atomic [ə'tomɪk] *adj* atómico(a)

atone [ə'təʊn] *vi* **to a. for** expiar

atrocious [ə'trəʊʃəs] *adj* atroz

attach [ə'tætʃ] *vt (stick)* pegar; *(fasten)* sujetar; *(document)* adjuntar; **to a. importance to sth** dar importancia a algn; *Fig* **to be attached to** *(be fond of)* tener cariño a

attaché [ə'tæʃeɪ] *n* agregado(a) *m,f*; **a. case** maletín *m*

attachment [ə'tætʃmənt] *n* **(a)** *Tech* accesorio *m*; *(action)* acoplamiento *m* **(b)** *(fondness)* apego *m* **(to** por) **(c)** *Comput (to e-mail)* archivo adjunto, anexo *m*

attack [ə'tæk] **1** *n* **(a)** *(assault)* ataque *m*, asalto *m*; **an a. on sb's life** un atentado contra la vida de algn **(b)** *Med* ataque *m*
2 *vt (assault)* atacar, asaltar; *Fig (problem)* abordar; *(job)* emprender; *Fig (criticize)* atacar

attacker [ə'tækə(r)] *n* asaltante *mf*, agresor(a) *m,f*

attain [ə'teɪn] *vt (aim)* lograr; *(rank, age)* llegar a

attainment [ə'teɪnmənt] *n (achievement)* logro *m*; *(skill)* talento *m*

attempt [ə'tempt] **1** *n* intento *m*, tentativa *f*; **at the second a.** a la segunda; **an a. on sb's life** un atentado contra la vida de algn
2 *vt* intentar; **to a. to do sth** tratar de *or* intentar hacer algo; *Jur* **attempted murder/rape** intento *m* de asesinato/violación

attend [ə'tend] **1** *vt (be present at)* asistir a; *(care for, wait on)* atender
2 *vi (be present)* asistir; *(pay attention)* prestar atención
▸ **attend to** *vt insep (business)* ocuparse de; *(in shop)* atender a

attendance [ə'tendəns] *n* asistencia *f*

attendant [ə'tendənt] *n (in cinema etc)* acomodador(a) *m,f*; *(in museum)* guía *mf*; *(in car park)* vigilante(a) *m,f*

attention [ə'tenʃən] *n* **(a)** atención *f*; **for the a. of Miss Jones** a la atención de la Srta. Jones; **pay a.!** ¡atiende!; **to pay a. to sth/sb** prestar atención a algn/algo **(b)** *Mil* **a.!** ¡firmes!; **to stand to a.** estar firmes

attentive [ə'tentɪv] *adj (listener)* atento(a); *(helpful)* solícito(a)

attest [ə'test] *vi* **to a. to** dar testimonio a

attic ['ætɪk] *n* ático *m*

attire [ə'taɪə(r)] *n Fml* traje *m*

attitude ['ætɪtjuːd] *n* actitud *f*; *(position of body)* postura *f*; **an a. of mind** un estado de ánimo

attorney [ə'tɜːnɪ] *n* **(a)** *US (lawyer)* abogado(a) *m,f*; **A. General** ≃ Ministro(a) *m,f* de Justicia; **district a.** fiscal *mf* **(b)** *Jur* **power of a.** poderes *mpl*

attract [ə'trækt] *vt* atraer; **to a. attention** llamar la atención; **to a. a waiter's attention** llamar a un camarero

attraction [ə'trækʃən] *n* **(a)** *(power)* atracción *f* **(b)** *(attractive thing)* atractivo *m*; *(charm)* encanto *m*; *(incentive)* aliciente *m*; **the main a.** el número fuerte

attractive [ə'træktɪv] *adj* atractivo(a); *(good-looking)* guapo(a); *(idea, proposition)* atrayente

attribute¹ ['ætrɪbjuːt] *n (quality)* atributo *m*

attribute² [ə'trɪbjuːt] *vt* atribuir

attrition [ə'trɪʃən] *n* **war of a.** guerra *f* de desgaste

aubergine ['əʊbəʒiːn] *n Br* berenjena *f*

auburn ['ɔːbən] *adj* castaño rojizo *inv*

auction ['ɔːkʃən] **1** *n* subasta *f*
2 *vt* subastar

auctioneer [ɔːkʃə'nɪə(r)] *n* subastador(a) *m,f*

audacious [ɔː'deɪʃəs] *adj (daring)* audaz; *(bold)* atrevido(a); *(impudent)* descarado(a)

audible ['ɔːdɪbəl] *adj* audible

audience ['ɔːdɪəns] *n* **(a)** *(spectators)* público *m*; *(at concert, conference)* auditorio *m*; *(television)* telespectadores *mpl* **(b)** *(meeting)* audiencia *f*

audio-visual [ɔːdɪəʊ'vɪzjʊəl] *adj* audiovisual; **a. aids** apoyo *m* audiovisual

audit ['ɔːdɪt] **1** *n* revisión *f* de cuentas
2 *vt* revisar, intervenir

audition [ɔː'dɪʃən] **1** *n* prueba *f*
2 *vt* **to a. sb for a part** probar a algn para un papel

auditor ['ɔːdɪtə(r)] *n* revisor(a) *m,f* de cuentas

auditorium [ɔːdɪ'tɔːrɪəm] *n* auditorio *m*

augment [ɔːg'ment] *vt* aumentar

augur ['ɔːgə(r)] *vi* **to a. well** ser de buen agüero

August ['ɔːgəst] *n* agosto *m*

aunt [ɑːnt] *n* (*also Fam* **auntie, aunty** ['ɑːntɪ]) tía *f*

au pair [əʊ'peə(r)] *n* **a. (girl)** au pair *f*

aura ['ɔːrə] *n* aura *f*; *Rel* aureola *f*

aural ['ɔːrəl] *adj* auditivo(a), del oído

auspices ['ɔːspɪsɪz] *npl* **under the a. of** bajo los auspicios de

auspicious [ɔː'spɪʃəs] *adj* de buen augurio

austere [ɒ'stɪə(r)] *adj* austero(a)

austerity [ɒ'sterɪtɪ] *n* austeridad *f*

Australia [ɒ'streɪlɪə] *n* Australia

Australian [ɒ'streɪlɪən] *adj & n* australiano(a) (*m,f*)

Austria ['ɒstrɪə] *n* Austria

Austrian ['ɒstrɪən] *adj & n* austríaco(a) (*m,f*)

authentic [ɔː'θentɪk] *adj* auténtico(a)

author ['ɔːθə(r)] *n* autor(a) *m,f*

authoritarian [ɔːθɒrɪ'teərɪən] *adj* autoritario(a)

authoritative [ɔː'θɒrɪtətɪv] *adj* (*reliable*) autorizado(a); (*authoritarian*) autoritario(a)

authority [ɔː'θɒrɪtɪ] *n* autoridad *f*; **local a.** ayuntamiento *m*

authorize ['ɔːθəraɪz] *vt* autorizar; (*payment etc*) aprobar; **to a. sb to do sth** autorizar a algn a hacer algo

auto ['ɔːtəʊ] *n US* coche *m*, *Andes, CAm, Carib, Méx* carro *m*

autobiography [ɔːtəʊbaɪ'ɒgrəfɪ] *n* autobiografía *f*

autograph ['ɔːtəgrɑːf] 1 *n* autógrafo *m*
2 *vt* (*sign*) firmar; (*book, photo*) dedicar

automata [ɔː'tɒmətə] *pl of* **automaton**

automatic [ɔːtə'mætɪk] 1 *adj* automático(a)
2 *n* (*car*) coche automático; (*gun*) pistola automática

automatically [ɔːtə'mætɪklɪ] *adv* automáticamente

automation [ɔːtə'meɪʃən] *n* automatización *f*; **office a.** ofimática *f*

automaton [ɔː'tɒmətən] *n* (*pl* **automata**) autómata *m*

automobile ['ɔːtəməbiːl] *n US* coche *m*, automóvil *m*, *Andes, CAm, Carib, Méx* carro *m*

autonomous [ɔː'tɒnəməs] *adj* autónomo(a)

autonomy [ɔː'tɒnəmɪ] *n* autonomía *f*

autopsy ['ɔːtɒpsɪ] *n* autopsia *f*

autumn ['ɔːtəm] *n* otoño *m*

auxiliary [ɔːg'zɪljərɪ] *adj* auxiliar

Av., av. (*abbr* **Avenue**) Av., Avda.

avail [ə'veɪl] 1 *n* **to no a.** en vano
2 *vt* **to a. oneself of sth** aprovecharse de algo

available [ə'veɪləbəl] *adj* (*thing*) disponible; (*person*) libre

avalanche ['ævəlɑːnʃ] *n* avalancha *f*

avarice ['ævərɪs] *n* avaricia *f*

Ave (*abbr* **Avenue**) Av., Avda.

avenge [ə'vendʒ] *vt* vengar

avenue ['ævɪnjuː] *n* avenida *f*; *Fig* vía *f*

average ['ævərɪdʒ] 1 *n* promedio *m*, media *f*; **on a.** por término medio
2 *adj* medio(a); (*condition*) regular
3 *vt* sacar la media de; **he averages eight hours' work a day** trabaja una media de ocho horas al día
▶**average out at** *vt insep* salir a una media de

averse [ə'vɜːs] *adj* **to be a. to sth** ser reacio(a) a algo

aversion [ə'vɜːʃən] *n* (*feeling*) aversión *f*; (*thing*) bestia negra

avert [ə'vɜːt] *vt* (*eyes, thoughts*) apartar (**from** de); (*accident*) impedir; (*danger*) evitar

avid ['ævɪd] *adj* (*reader*) voraz

avidly ['ævɪdlɪ] *adv* vorazmente

avocado [ævə'kɑːdəʊ] *n* **a. (pear)** aguacate *m*, *Andes, RP* palta *f*

avoid [ə'vɔɪd] *vt* evitar; (*question*) eludir

avoidable [ə'vɔɪdəbəl] *adj* evitable

await [ə'weɪt] *vt* esperar, aguardar

awake [ə'weɪk] 1 *adj* despierto(a); **to be a.** estar despierto(a)
2 *vt* (*pt* **awoke, awaked**; *pp* **awoken, awaked**) despertar

awaken [ə'weɪkən] *vt & vi* (*pt* **awakened**; *pp* **awoken**) = **awake 2**

awakening [ə'weɪkənɪŋ] *n* despertar *m*

award [ə'wɔːd] 1 *n* (*prize*) premio *m*; (*medal*) condecoración *f*; *Jur* indemnización *f*; (*grant*) beca *f*
2 *vt* (*prize*) conceder, otorgar; (*medal*) dar; (*damages*) adjudicar

aware [ə'weə(r)] *adj* (*informed*) enterado(a); **not that I'm a. of** que yo sepa no; **to be a. of sth** ser consciente de algo; **to become a. of sth** darse cuenta de algo

awareness [ə'weənɪs] *n* conciencia *f* (**of** de)

awash [ə'wɒʃ] *adj* inundado(a) (**with** de)

away [ə'weɪ] *adv* **far a.** lejos; **go a.!** ¡lárgate!; **it's 3 miles a.** está a 3 millas (de distancia); **keep a. from the fire!** ¡no te acerques al fuego!; **right a.** en seguida; **to be a.** (*absent*) estar ausente; (*out*) estar fuera; **to die a.** desvanecerse; **to give sth**

a. regalar algo; *(secret)* revelar algo; **to go a.** irse; *Sport* **to play a.** jugar fuera; **to turn a.** volver la cara; **to work a.** trabajar

awe [ɔː] *n (fear)* temor *m*; *(amazement)* asombro *m*; **he was in a. of his father** le intimidaba su padre

awe-inspiring ['ɔːɪnspaɪərɪŋ] *adj* impresionante, imponente

awesome ['ɔːsəm] *adj* impresionante

awful ['ɔːfʊl] *adj Fam* espantoso(a); **an a. lot of work** muchísimo trabajo

awfully ['ɔːfʊlɪ] *adv Fam* terriblemente

awkward ['ɔːkwəd] *adj (clumsy)* torpe; *(difficult)* pesado(a); *(object)* incómodo(a); *(moment)* inoportuno(a); *(situation)* embarazoso(a); *(problem)* difícil

awning ['ɔːnɪŋ] *n (on ship)* toldo *m*; *(on shop)* marquesina *f*

awoke [ə'wəʊk] *pt of* awake

awoken [ə'wəʊkən] *pp of* **awake, awaken**

axe, *US* **ax** [æks] **1** *n* hacha *f*
2 *vt Fig (jobs)* eliminar; *(costs)* reducir; *(plan)* cancelar; *(person)* despedir·

axis ['æksɪs] *n (pl axes* ['æksiːz]*)* eje *m*

axle ['æksəl] *n* eje *m*; *Tech* árbol *m*

ayatollah [aɪə'tɒlə] *n* ayatolá *m*

Aztec ['æztek] *adj & n* azteca *(mf)*

B

B, b [biː] *n* (**a**) *(the letter)* B, b *f*; *Br Aut* **B road** carretera secundaria (**b**) *Mus* **B** si *m*; **B flat** si bemol

BA [biːˈeɪ] *n (abbr* **Bachelor of Arts**) *(person)* licenciado(a) *m,f* en Filosofía y Letras

babble [ˈbæbəl] *vi (baby)* balbucear; *(brook)* murmurar

babe [beɪb] *n* (**a**) *(baby)* bebé *m* (**b**) *US Fam* **hi, b.!** ¡hola, guapa!

baboon [bəˈbuːn] *n* zambo *m*

baby [ˈbeɪbɪ] *n* (**a**) bebé *m*; niño(a) *m,f*; *Br* **B. Buggy**® sillita *f* de paseo *or* de niño; *US* **b. buggy** *or* **carriage** cochecito *m* de niño; **b. face** cara *f* de niño (**b**) *(animal)* cría *f* (**c**) *Fam (darling)* querido(a) *m,f*

baby-sit [ˈbeɪbɪsɪt] *vi* hacer de canguro

baby-sitter [ˈbeɪbɪsɪtə(r)] *n* canguro *mf*

baby-walker [ˈbeɪbɪwɔːkə(r)] *n* tacataca *m*

bachelor [ˈbætʃələ(r)] *n* (**a**) soltero *m* (**b**) *Univ* licenciado(a) *m,f*; **B. of Arts/Science** licenciado(a) *m,f* en Filosofía y Letras/Ciencias

back [bæk] **1** *n* (**a**) *(of person)* espalda *f*; *(of animal)* lomo *m*; **b. to front** al revés; *Fig* **to get sb's b. up** poner negro a algn; *Fig* **to have one's b. to the wall** estar en un aprieto
(**b**) *(of book)* lomo *m*; *(of chair)* respaldo *m*; *(of coin)* reverso *m*; *(of hand)* dorso *m*; *(of house, car)* parte *f* de atrás; *Fig* **he knows Leeds like the b. of his hand** se conoce Leeds como la palma de la mano
(**c**) *(of stage, cupboard)* fondo *m*; *Fam* **at the b. of beyond** en el quinto pino
(**d**) *Ftb* defensa *mf*
(**e**) *US* **in b. (of)** *(behind)* en la parte de atrás (de), detrás (de); *(to the rear of)* al fondo (de)
2 *adj* (**a**) trasero(a), de atrás; **b. door** puerta *f* de atrás; **b. seat** asiento *m* de detrás; *Fig* **to take a b. seat** pasar al segundo plano; *Aut* **b. wheel** rueda trasera
(**b**) **b. rent** alquiler atrasado; **b. pay** atrasos *mpl*; *Press* **b. number** número *m* atrasado
3 *adv* (**a**) *(to the rear)* atrás; *(towards the rear)* hacia atrás; **b. and forth** de acá para allá
(**b**) **some years b.** hace unos años
4 *vt* (**a**) *(support)* apoyar, respaldar
(**b**) *Fin* financiar
(**c**) *(bet on)* apostar por
(**d**) *(car etc)* dar marcha atrás a
5 *vi* (**a**) *(move backwards)* retroceder
(**b**) *(car etc)* dar marcha atrás
▶ **back away** *vi* retirarse
▶ **back down** *vi* echarse atrás
▶ **back off** *vi* desistir
▶ **back out** *vi (withdraw)* retractarse, volverse atrás
▶ **back up 1** *vt sep* (**a**) *(support)* apoyar (**b**) *Comput (file)* hacer una copia de seguridad de
2 *vi Aut* ir marcha atrás

backache [ˈbækeɪk] *n* dolor *m* de espalda

backbencher [bækˈbentʃə(r)] *n* diputado(a) *m,f* que no es ministro

backbiting [ˈbækbaɪtɪŋ] *n* murmuración *f*

backbone [ˈbækbəʊn] *n Anat* columna *f*

backcloth [ˈbækklɒθ] *n* telón *m* de fondo

backdate [bækˈdeɪt] *vt* antedatar

backdated [bækˈdeɪtɪd] *adj* con efecto retroactivo

backdrop [ˈbækdrɒp] *n* telón *m* de fondo

backer [ˈbækə(r)] *n* (**a**) *Fin* promotor(a) *m,f* (**b**) *Pol* partidario(a) *m,f* (**c**) *(person who bets)* apostante *mf*

backfire [bækˈfaɪə(r)] *vi* (**a**) *Aut* petardear (**b**) *Fig* **our plan backfired** nos salió el tiro por la culata

background [ˈbækɡraʊnd] *n* (**a**) fondo *m*; **to stay in the b.** quedarse en segundo plano; **b. music** música *f* de fondo (**b**) *(origin)* origen *m*; *(past)* pasado *m*; *(education)* formación *f* (**c**) *(circumstances)* antecedentes *mpl* (**d**) *(atmosphere)* ambiente *m*

backhand [ˈbækhænd] *n Sport* revés *m*

backhanded [ˈbækhændɪd] *adj* equívoco(a), ambiguo(a)

backhander [ˈbækhændə(r)] *n Fam (bribe)* soborno *m*

backing [ˈbækɪŋ] *n* (**a**) *(support)* apoyo

m; Com & Fin respaldo financiero (**b**) *Mus* acompañamiento *m*

backlash ['bæklæʃ] *n* reacción violenta y repentina

backlog ['bæklɒg] *n* to have a b. of work tener un montón de trabajo atrasado

backpack ['bækpæk] *n* mochila *f*

backpedal [bæk'pedəl] *vi Fam* dar marcha atrás

backside [bæk'saɪd] *n Fam* trasero *m*, culo *m*

backstage [bæk'steɪdʒ] *adv* entre bastidores

backstroke ['bækstrəʊk] *n* espalda *f*

backtrack ['bæktræk] *vi Fig* volverse atrás

backup ['bækʌp] *n* (**a**) *(support)* apoyo *m*, respaldo *m*; *Comput* **b. (file)** fichero *m* de apoyo (**b**) *US (of traffic)* caravana *f*

backward ['bækwəd] **1** *adj* (**a**) *(movement)* hacia atrás (**b**) *(country)* subdesarrollado(a); *(child)* retrasado(a)
2 *adv esp US* hacia atrás

backwards ['bækwədz] *adv* hacia atrás; **to walk b.** andar de espaldas

backyard [bæk'jɑːd] *n* patio trasero; *US* jardín trasero

bacon ['beɪkən] *n* tocino *m*, beicon *m*

bacteria [bæk'tɪərɪə] *npl* bacterias *fpl*

bad [bæd] **1** *adj* (**a**) *(poor)* malo(a); **to go from b. to worse** ir de mal en peor (**b**) *(decayed)* podrido(a); **to go b.** echarse a perder (**c**) *that's too b.!* ¡qué pena! (**d**) *(wicked)* malo(a); **to use b. language** ser mal hablado(a) (**e**) *(accident)* grave; *(headache)* fuerte (**f**) *(ill)* enfermo(a) (**g**) **b. debt** deuda *f* incobrable
2 *n* lo malo

bade [beɪd] *pt of* bid

badge [bædʒ] *n* insignia *f*; *(metal disc)* chapa *f*

badger ['bædʒə(r)] **1** *n* tejón *m*
2 *vt* acosar

badly ['bædlɪ] *adv* (**a**) mal; **he did b. in the exam** le salió mal el examen; **to be b. off** andar mal de dinero (**b**) *(seriously)* gravemente (**c**) *(very much)* mucho; **to miss sb b.** echar mucho de menos a algn; **we need it b.** nos hace mucha falta

badminton ['bædmɪntən] *n* bádminton *m*

bad-tempered [bæd'tempəd] *adj* **to be b.** *(temperament)* tener mal genio; *(temporarily)* estar de mal humor

baffle ['bæfəl] **1** *vt* desconcertar
2 *n Tech* pantalla acústica

baffling ['bæflɪŋ] *adj* incomprensible, enigmático(a)

bag [bæg] **1** *n* (**a**) *(large)* bolsa *f*; *(handbag)* bolso *m*, cartera *f*, *Méx* bolsa; *Fam* **bags of** montones de; **travel b.** bolsa de viaje (**b**) *(hunting)* caza *f*, *Fam* **it's in the b.** es cosa hecha (**c**) *Pej* **old b.** *(woman)* bruja *f* (**d**) **bags** *(under eyes)* ojeras *fpl*
2 *vt* (**a**) *(put into sacks)* meter en sacos (**b**) *Fam* coger

baggage ['bægɪdʒ] *n* (**a**) equipaje *m* (**b**) *Mil* bagaje *m*

baggy ['bægɪ] *adj* (**baggier, baggiest**) holgado(a); **b. trousers** pantalones anchos

bagpipes ['bægpaɪps] *npl* gaita *f*

Bahamas [bə'hɑːməz] *npl* **the B.** las Bahamas

bail¹ [beɪl] *n Jur* fianza *f*; **on b.** bajo fianza; **to stand b. for sb** salir fiador por algn
► **bail out** *vt sep Fig (person)* sacar de un apuro

bail² [beɪl] *vi Naut* **to b. (out)** achicar

bailiff ['beɪlɪf] *n* (**a**) *Jur* alguacil *m* (**b**) *(steward)* administrador *m*

bait [beɪt] **1** *n* cebo *m*; **to rise to the b.** tragar el anzuelo, picar
2 *vt* (**a**) *(for fishing)* cebar (**b**) *(torment)* hostigar

baize [beɪz] *n* bayeta *f*; **green b.** tapete *m* verde

bake [beɪk] **1** *vt* (**a**) cocer al horno (**b**) *(harden)* endurecer
2 *vi Fam* hacer mucho calor

baked [beɪkt] *adj* al horno; **b. potato** patata *f* or *Am* papa *f* al horno

baker ['beɪkə(r)] *n* panadero(a) *m,f*

bakery ['beɪkərɪ] *n* panadería *f*

baking ['beɪkɪŋ] *n* cocción *f*; **b. dish** fuente *f* para horno; **b. powder** levadura *f* en polvo; **b. tin** molde *m*

balaclava [bælə'klɑːvə] *n* pasamontañas *m inv*

balance ['bæləns] **1** *n* (**a**) *(scales)* balanza *f*, *Fig* **to hang in the b.** estar en juego (**b**) *(equilibrium)* equilibrio *m*; *Pol* **b. of power** equilibrio de fuerzas (**c**) *Fin* saldo *m*; **b. of payments** balanza *f* de pagos; **b. sheet** balance *m*; **credit b.** saldo acreedor (**d**) *(remainder)* resto *m*
2 *vt* (**a**) poner en equilibrio (**on** en) (**b**) *(budget)* equilibrar; **to b. the books** hacer el balance (**c**) *(weigh up)* sopesar
3 *vi* guardar el equilibrio
► **balance out** *vi (figures)* corresponderse

balanced ['bælənst] *adj* equilibrado(a)

balcony ['bælkənɪ] *n* balcón *m*; *Th* anfiteatro *m*

bald [bɔːld] *adj* (**a**) *(person)* calvo(a) (**b**)

(tyre) desgastado(a) (**c**) *(style)* escueto(a)

baldness ['bɔːldnɪs] *n* (**a**) *(of person)* calvicie *f* (**b**) *(of tyre)* desgaste *m* (**c**) *(of style)* sencillez *f*

bale¹ [beɪl] **1** *n (of cloth)* fardo *m*
2 *vt* embalar

bale² [beɪl] *vt* = **bail²**
► **bale out 1** *vi Av* saltar en paracaídas de un avión
2 *vt sep Fig (person)* sacar de apuros a

Balearic [bælɪ'ærɪk] *adj* **the B. Islands** las Islas Baleares

baleful ['beɪlfʊl] *adj* funesto(a), siniestro(a)

Balkan ['bɔːlkən] *adj* **the Balkans** los Balcanes

ball¹ [bɔːl] *n* (**a**) *(in cricket, tennis etc)* pelota *f*; *Ftb* balón *m*; *(in billiards, golf etc)* bola *f*; *Fig* **the b. is in your court** ahora te toca a tí; *Fig* **to play b. with sb** cooperar con algn; *Fam* **to be on the b.** ser un espabilado; *Tech* **b. bearing** rodamiento *m* de bolas (**b**) *(of paper)* bola *f*; *(of wool)* ovillo *m* (**c**) *US* béisbol *m*; *Fig* **it's a whole new b. game** es otra historia (**d**) *very Fam* **balls** cojones *mpl*

ball² [bɔːl] *n (dance)* baile *m*

ballad ['bæləd] *n* balada *f*

ballast ['bæləst] *n Naut* lastre *m*

ballerina [bælə'riːnə] *n* bailarina *f*

ballet ['bæleɪ] *n* ballet *m*; **b. dancer** bailarín(ina) *m,f*

ballistic [bə'lɪstɪk] *adj* balístico(a)

ballistics [bə'lɪstɪks] *n sing* balística *f*

balloon [bə'luːn] **1** *n* (**a**) globo *m* (**b**) *(in cartoon)* bocadillo *m*
2 *vi* hincharse; *Fig* aumentar rápidamente

ballot ['bælət] **1** *n* votación *f*; **b. box** urna *f*; **b. paper** papeleta *f*
2 *vt* someter a votación

ballpoint (pen) ['bɔːlpɔɪnt('pen)] *n* bolígrafo *m*, *CSur* lapicera *f*

ballroom ['bɔːlruːm] *n* salón *m* de baile

ballyhoo [bælɪ'huː] *n Fam (fuss)* jaleo *m*

balm [bɑːm] *n* bálsamo *m*

balmy ['bɑːmɪ] *adj* (**balmier, balmiest**) *(weather)* suave

Baltic ['bɔːltɪk] *adj* báltico(a); **the B. (Sea)** el (mar) Báltico

balustrade ['bæləstreɪd] *n* barandilla *f*

bamboo [bæm'buː] *n* bambú *m*

bamboozle [bæm'buːzəl] *vt Fam* (**a**) *(puzzle)* dejar perplejo (**b**) *(trick)* engañar, embaucar

ban [bæn] **1** *n* prohibición *f*

2 *vt* (**a**) *(prohibit)* prohibir (**b**) *(exclude)* excluir

banal [bə'nɑːl] *adj* banal, trivial

banana [bə'nɑːnə] *n* plátano *m*, banana *f*, *Col* banano *m*, *Ven* cambur *m*; *Fam* **to go bananas** volverse loco(a)

band [bænd] **1** *n* (**a**) *(strip)* tira *f*; *(ribbon)* cinta *f* (**b**) *(stripe)* raya *f* (**c**) *Rad* banda *f* (**d**) *(group)* grupo *m*; *(of youths)* pandilla *f*; *(of thieves)* banda *f* (**e**) *Mus* banda *f*
2 *vi* **to b. together** unirse, juntarse

bandage ['bændɪdʒ] **1** *n* venda *f*
2 *vt* vendar

Band-Aid® ['bændeɪd] *n US* tirita® *f*, *Am* curita *f*

B & B [biːən'biː] *n (abbr* **bed and breakfast**) *(hotel)* = hostal familiar en el que el desayuno está incluido en el precio de la habitación

bandit ['bændɪt] *n* bandido *m*

bandstand ['bændstænd] *n* quiosco *m* de música

bandwagon ['bændwægən] *n Fig* **to jump on the b.** subirse al tren

bandy ['bændɪ] **1** *vt (words, ideas)* intercambiar
2 *adj* (**bandier, bandiest**) torcido(a) hacia fuera
► **bandy about** *vt sep (ideas)* propagar, difundir

bandy-legged ['bændɪ'leg(ɪ)d] *adj* patizambo(a)

bang [bæŋ] **1** *n* (**a**) *(blow)* golpe *m* (**b**) *(noise)* ruido *m*; *(explosion)* estallido *m*; *(of gun)* estampido *m*; **to shut the door with a b.** dar un portazo
2 *npl US* **bangs** flequillo *m*, *Am* cerquillo *m (corto)*
3 *vt* golpear; **to b. sth shut** cerrar algo de golpe
4 *vi* golpear; **to b. shut** cerrarse de golpe
5 *interj (blow)* ¡zas!; **b., b.!** *(of gun)* ¡pum, pum!
6 *adv Fam* justo

banger ['bæŋə(r)] *n* (**a**) *(firework)* petardo *m* (**b**) *Fam (sausage)* salchicha *f* (**c**) *Fam* **old b.** *(car)* tartana *f*

bangle ['bæŋgəl] *n* brazalete *m*

banish ['bænɪʃ] *vt* desterrar

banister ['bænɪstə(r)] *n* pasamanos *m inv*

bank¹ [bæŋk] **1** *n* (**a**) *Com & Fin* banco *m*; **b. account** cuenta bancaria; **b. card** tarjeta bancaria; **b. clerk** empleado(a) *m,f* de banca; **b. draft** letra bancaria; **b. holiday** fiesta *f* nacional; **b. statement** extracto *m* de cuenta (**b**) *(in gambling)* banca *f* (**c**) *(store)* banco *m*

2 vt Com & Fin depositar, ingresar

3 vi Com & Fin **to b. with** tener una cuenta en

▶ **bank on** vt insep contar con

bank² [bæŋk] **1** n (**a**) (mound) loma f; (embankment) terraplén m (**b**) (of river) ribera f; (edge) orilla f

2 vt Av ladear

3 vi Av ladearse

bankbook ['bæŋkbʊk] n libreta f de ahorros

banker ['bæŋkə(r)] n banquero(a) m,f

banking ['bæŋkɪŋ] n banca f

banknote ['bæŋknəʊt] n billete m de banco

bankrupt ['bæŋkrʌpt] **1** adj en quiebra; **to go b.** quebrar

2 vt llevar a la bancarrota

bankruptcy ['bæŋkrʌptsɪ] n quiebra f, bancarrota f

banner ['bænə(r)] n (in demonstration) pancarta f; (flag) bandera f

banns [bænz] npl amonestaciones fpl

banquet ['bæŋkwɪt] n banquete m

banter ['bæntə(r)] **1** n bromas fpl

2 vi bromear

bap [bæp] n bollo m, panecillo m

baptism ['bæptɪzəm] n bautismo m

baptize [bæp'taɪz] vt bautizar

bar [bɑ:(r)] **1** n (**a**) (of gold) barra f; (of chocolate) tableta f; (of soap) pastilla f; Com **b. code** código m de barras (**b**) (of cage) barrote m; Fam **to be behind bars** estar en la cárcel (**c**) (obstacle) obstáculo m (**d**) Jur (dock) banquillo m; (court) tribunal m (**e**) Jur **the B.** (profession) abogacía f; (body of lawyers) colegio m de abogados (**f**) (pub) bar m; (counter) barra f (**g**) Mus compás m

2 vt (**a**) (door) atrancar; (road) cortar (**b**) (exclude) excluir (**from** de) (**c**) (prohibit) prohibir

3 prep salvo; **b. none** sin excepción

barbarian [bɑ:'beərɪən] adj & n bárbaro(a) (m,f)

barbaric [bɑ:'bærɪk] adj bárbaro(a)

barbecue ['bɑ:bɪkju:] **1** n barbacoa f

2 vt asar a la parrilla

barbed [bɑ:bd] adj (**a**) **b. wire** alambre m de púas (**b**) Fig (remark) mordaz

barber ['bɑ:bə(r)] n barbero(a) m,f; **b.'s (shop)** barbería f

barbiturate [bɑ:'bɪtjʊrɪt] n barbitúrico m

bare [beə(r)] **1** adj (**a**) (naked) desnudo(a); (head) descubierto(a); (foot) descalzo(a); (room) sin muebles; **to lay b.** poner al descubierto; **with his b. hands** sólo con las manos (**b**) (basic) mero(a); **the**

b. minimum lo mínimo

2 vt desnudar; (uncover) descubrir

bareback(ed) ['beə'bæk(t)] adv **to ride b.** montar un caballo a pelo

barefaced ['beəfeɪst] adj desvergonzado(a)

barefoot ['beə'fʊt] adj & adv descalzo(a)

barely ['beəlɪ] adv apenas

bargain ['bɑ:gɪn] **1** n (**a**) (agreement) pacto m; (deal) negocio m; **into the b.** por añadidura, además; **to drive a hard b.** imponer condiciones duras; **to strike a b.** cerrar un trato (**b**) (cheap purchase) ganga f; **b. price** precio m de oferta

2 vi (**a**) negociar (**b**) (haggle) regatear

▶ **bargain for** vt insep esperar, contar con

barge [bɑ:dʒ] **1** n gabarra f

2 vt Fam **to b. into** (room) irrumpir en; (person) tropezar con

▶ **barge in** vi Fam (**a**) (go in) entrar sin permiso (**b**) (interfere) entrometerse

baritone ['bærɪtəʊn] adj & n barítono (m)

bark¹ [bɑ:k] **1** n ladrido m

2 vi (dog) ladrar

bark² [bɑ:k] n Bot corteza f

barley ['bɑ:lɪ] n cebada f; **b. sugar** azúcar m cande

barmaid ['bɑ:meɪd] n camarera f

barman ['bɑ:mən] n camarero m, barman m

barn [bɑ:n] n granero m; **b. dance** baile m popular

barnacle ['bɑ:nəkəl] n percebe m

barometer [bə'rɒmɪtə(r)] n barómetro m

baron ['bærən] n barón m

baroness ['bærənɪs] n baronesa f

baroque [bə'rɒk] adj barroco(a)

barrack ['bærək] vt abuchear

barracks ['bærəks] n Mil cuartel m

barrage ['bærɑ:dʒ] n (**a**) (dam) presa f (**b**) Mil barrera f de fuego (**c**) Fig (of questions) lluvia f

barrel ['bærəl] n (**a**) (of wine) tonel m; (of beer, oil) barril m (**b**) (of firearm) cañón m

barren ['bærən] adj estéril; (land) yermo(a)

barricade [bærɪ'keɪd] n barricada f

2 vt levantar barricadas; **to b. oneself in** parapetarse

barrier ['bærɪə(r)] n barrera f

barrister ['bærɪstə(r)] n Br abogado(a) m,f (capacitado(a) para ejercer ante tribunales superiores)

barrow ['bærəʊ] n carretilla f

bartender ['bɑ:tendə(r)] n US camarero m, barman m

barter ['bɑ:tə(r)] vt trocar (**for** por)

base [beɪs] **1** n base f; (foot) pie m; (of

column) basa *f*; *Sport (of team)* concentración *f*; **air/naval b.** base *f* aérea/naval
  2 *vt* **(a)** basar, fundar (**on** en) **(b)** *(troops)* estacionar
  3 *adj* **(a)** *(despicable)* bajo(a), despreciable **(b)** *(metals)* común

baseball ['beɪsbɔːl] *n* béisbol *m*

baseline ['beɪslaɪn] *n (in tennis)* línea *f* de saque

basement ['beɪsmənt] *n* sótano *m*

bases ['beɪsiːz] *pl of* **basis**

bash [bæʃ] **1** *n (heavy blow)* golpetazo *m*; *(dent)* bollo *m*; *Fam (attempt)* intento *m*
  2 *vt* golpear

bashful ['bæʃfʊl] *adj* tímido(a)

basic ['beɪsɪk] **1** *adj* básico(a); **b. pay** sueldo *m* base
  2 *npl* **basics** lo fundamental

basically ['beɪsɪklɪ] *adv* fundamentalmente

basil ['bæzəl] *n* albahaca *f*

basin ['beɪsən] *n* **(a)** *(washbowl)* palangana *f*; *(for washing up)* barreño *m*; *(in bathroom)* lavabo *m*; *(dish)* cuenco *m* **(b)** *(of river)* cuenca *f*

basis ['beɪsɪs] *n (pl* **bases)** base *f*; **on the b. of** en base a

bask [bɑːsk] *vi* tostarse; **to b. in the sun** tomar el sol

basket ['bɑːskɪt] *n* cesta *f*, cesto *m*

basketball ['bɑːskɪtbɔːl] *n* baloncesto *m*

Basque [bæsk, bɑːsk] **1** *adj* vasco(a); **B. Country** País Vasco, Euskadi; **B. flag** ikurriña *f*; **B. nationalist** abertzale *mf*
  2 *n* **(a)** *(person)* vasco(a) *m,f* **(b)** *(language)* vasco *m*, euskera *m*

bass¹ [bæs] *n inv (seawater)* lubina *f*, *(freshwater)* perca *f*

bass² [beɪs] **1** *n* **(a)** *(singer)* bajo *m* **(b)** *(notes)* graves *mpl*; **b. drum** bombo *m*; **b. guitar** bajo *m*
  2 *adj* bajo(a)

bassoon [bə'suːn] *n* fagot *m*

bastard ['bɑːstəd, 'bæstəd] **1** *n* **(a)** *(bastardo(a)* *m,f* **(b)** *Pej* cabrón *m*, hijo *m* de puta; **poor b.!** ¡el pobre!
  2 *adj* bastardo(a)

baste [beɪst] *vt Culin* untar

bastion ['bæstɪən] *n* baluarte *m*, bastión *m*

bat¹ [bæt] **1** *n (in cricket, baseball)* bate *m*; *(in table tennis)* pala *f*; *Fig* **to do sth off one's own b.** hacer algo por cuenta propia
  2 *vi (in cricket, baseball)* batear

bat² [bæt] *n Zool* murciélago *m*

bat³ [bæt] *vt Fam* **without batting an eyelid** sin pestañear

batch [bætʃ] *n (of bread)* hornada *f*, *(of goods)* lote *m*; *Comput* **b. processing** procesamiento *m* por lotes

bated ['beɪtɪd] *adj* **with b. breath** sin respirar

bath [bɑːθ] **1** *n* **(a)** baño *m*; **to have a b.** bañarse; **b. towel** toalla *f* de baño **(b)** *(tub)* bañera *f* **(c)** **baths** piscina *f* municipal
  2 *vt* bañar

bathe [beɪð] **1** *vi* bañarse
  2 *vt* **(a)** *(wound)* lavar **(b)** **he was bathed in sweat** *(covered)* estaba empapado de sudor

bather ['beɪðə(r)] *n* bañista *mf*

bathing ['beɪðɪŋ] *n* baño *m*; **b. cap** gorro *m* de baño; **b. costume** traje *m* de baño; **b. trunks** bañador *m* de hombre

bathrobe ['bɑːθrəʊb] *n* albornoz *m*

bathroom ['bɑːθruːm] *n* cuarto *m* de baño

bathtub ['bɑːθtʌb] *n* bañera *f*

baton ['bætən, 'bætɒn] *n* **(a)** *Mus* batuta *f* **(b)** *(truncheon)* porra *f* **(c)** *Sport* testigo *m*

battalion [bə'tæljən] *n* batallón *m*

batter¹ ['bætə(r)] *vt* aporrear, apalear

batter² ['bætə(r)] *n (in cricket, baseball)* bateador(a) *m,f*

batter³ ['bætə(r)] *Culin* **1** *n* pasta *f* (para rebozar); **fish in b.** pescado rebozado
  2 *vt* rebozar

battered ['bætəd] *adj (car)* abollado(a); *(person)* maltratado(a)

battering ['bætərɪŋ] *n* paliza *f*; **to take a b.** recibir una paliza; *Mil* **b. ram** ariete *m*

battery ['bætərɪ] *n* **(a)** *(for torch, radio)* pila *f*; *Aut* batería *f* **(b)** *Jur* **assault and b.** lesiones *fpl*

battle ['bætəl] **1** *n* batalla *f*; *Fig* lucha *f*; **to do b.** librar batalla; *Fig* **b. cry** lema *m*
  2 *vi* luchar

battlefield ['bætəlfiːld] *n* campo *m* de batalla

battleship ['bætəlʃɪp] *n* acorazado *m*

bauble ['bɔːbəl] *n* chuchería *f*

bawdy ['bɔːdɪ] *adj (joke etc)* verde

bawl [bɔːl] *vi* gritar, chillar

bay¹ [beɪ] *n Geog* bahía *f*, *(large)* golfo *m*; **B. of Biscay** golfo de Vizcaya; **B. of Bengal** golfo de Bengala

bay² [beɪ] *n* **(a)** *(recess)* hueco *m*; **b. window** ventana salediza **(b)** *(in factory)* nave *f*; **cargo b.** bodega *f* de carga

bay³ [beɪ] *n* laurel *m*

bay⁴ [beɪ] **1** *vi (dog)* aullar
  2 *n* ladrido *m*; *Fig* **at b.** acorralado(a); *Fig* **to keep sb at b.** mantener a algn a raya

bayonet [ˈbeɪənɪt] n bayoneta f

bazaar [bəˈzɑː(r)] n (a) (market) bazar m (b) (church) b. (charity sale) rastrillo benéfico

BBC [biːbiːˈsiː] n (abbr **British Broadcasting Corporation**) BBC f

BC [biːˈsiː] (abbr **before Christ**) a.d.C.

be [biː, unstressed bɪ]

En el inglés hablado, y en el escrito en estilo coloquial, el verbo **be** se contrae de forma que **I am** se transforma en **I'm, he/she/it is** se transforman en **he's/she's/it's** y **you/we/they are** se transforman en **you're, we're/they're**. Las formas negativas **is not, are not, was not** y **were not** se transforman en **isn't, aren't, wasn't** y **weren't**.

---

1 vi (pres 1st person sing **am**; 3rd person sing **is**; 2nd person sing & all persons pl **are**; pt 1st & 3rd persons sing **was**; 2nd person sing & all persons pl **were**; pp **been**) (a): ser; **he is very tall** es muy alto; **Madrid is the capital** Madrid es la capital; **sugar is sweet** el azúcar es dulce (b) (nationality, occupation) ser; **he's Italian** es italiano (c) (origin, ownership) ser; **the car is Domingo's** el coche es de Domingo; **this painting is by Goya** este cuadro es de Goya (d) (price) costar; (total) ser; **a return ticket is £24** un billete de ida y vuelta cuesta £24; **how much is a kilo of cod?** ¿a cuánto está el kilo de bacalao?; **how much is it?** ¿cuánto es? (e) (temporary state) estar; **how are you? – I'm very well** ¿cómo estás? – estoy muy bien; **this soup is cold** esta sopa está fría; **to be cold/afraid/hungry** tener frío/miedo/hambre; **to be lucky** tener suerte (f) (location) estar; **Aberdeen is in Scotland** Aberdeen está en Escocia; **Birmingham is 200 miles from London** Birmingham está a 200 millas de Londres (g) (age) tener; **she is thirty (years old)** tiene treinta años

2 v aux (a) (with pres p) estar; **he is writing a letter** está escribiendo una carta; **she was singing** estaba cantando; **they are leaving next week** se van la semana que viene; **we have been waiting for a long time** hace mucho que estamos esperando; **he is coming** (emphatic) es seguro que viene (b) (passive) ser; **he was murdered** fue asesinado; **she is allowed to smoke** se le permite fumar (c) (obligation) **I am to see him this afternoon** debo verle esta tarde; **you are not to smoke here** no se puede fumar aquí

3 v impers (a) (with there) haber; **there is, there are** hay; **there was, there were** había; **there will be** habrá; **there would be** habría; **there have been a lot of complaints** ha habido muchas quejas; **there were ten of us** éramos diez (b) (with it) **it's late** es tarde; **it is said that** se dice que; **who is it? – it's me** ¿quién es? – soy yo; **what is it?** ¿qué pasa? (c) (weather) **it's foggy** hay niebla; **it's cold/hot** hace frío/calor (d) (time) ser; **it's one o'clock** es la una; **it's four o'clock** son las cuatro (e) (date) **it's the 11th/Tuesday today** hoy es 11/martes (f) (in tag questions) **it's lovely, isn't it?** es bonito, ¿no?; **you're happy, aren't you?** estás contento, ¿verdad? **he's not very clever, is he?** no es muy listo, ¿verdad? (g) (unreal conditions) **if I was/were you ...** yo en tu lugar ...; **if you were a millionaire ...** si fueras millonario ... (h) pres & past perfect (visit, go) estar, ir; **I've been to Paris** he estado en París

beach [biːtʃ] **1** n playa f **2** vt varar

beacon [ˈbiːkən] n (a) Av & Naut baliza f (b) (lighthouse) faro m

bead [biːd] n (a) (of necklace etc) cuenta f, **glass b.** abalorio m (b) (of liquid) gota f

beady [ˈbiːdɪ] adj (**beadier, beadiest**) (eyes) pequeños y brillantes

beagle [ˈbiːgəl] n beagle m

beak [biːk] n (a) (of bird) pico m (b) Fam (nose) nariz ganchuda

beaker [ˈbiːkə(r)] n (tumbler) taza alta, jarra f

beam [biːm] **1** n (a) Archit viga f (b) (of light) rayo m; Phys haz m (c) (in gymnastics) barra fija (d) (smile) sonrisa f radiante **2** vi (a) (sun) brillar (b) (smile) sonreír **3** vt (a) (broadcast) difundir, emitir (b) (transmit) transmitir

beaming [ˈbiːmɪŋ] adj (smiling) radiante

bean [biːn] n alubia f, judía f, Andes, CAm, Carib, Méx frijol m, RP poroto m; Fam **to spill the beans** descubrir el pastel; **baked beans** = alubias cocidas en salsa de tomate; **broad b.** haba f; **butter b.** judía blanca, Andes, CAm, Carib, Méx frijol blanco, RP poroto de manteca; **coffee b.**

grano *m* de café; **green/runner b.** judía
verde, *Bol, RP*³ chaucha *f*, *CAm* ejote *m*,
Col, Cuba habichuela *f*, *Chile* poroto
verde, *Ven* vainita *f*; **haricot b.** alubia;
kidney b. frijol

beansprout ['biːnspraʊt] *n* brote *m* de
soja

bear¹ [beə(r)] (*pt* **bore**; *pp* **borne**) **1** *vt* (a)
(*carry*) llevar
   (b) (*support*) sostener
   (c) (*endure*) soportar, aguantar; **I can't
b. him** no lo soporto
   (d) (*fruit*) dar; *Fin* (*interest*) devengar
   (e) **to b. a resemblance to** parecerse a
   (f) **to b. a grudge against sb** guardar
rencor a algn; **to b. in mind** tener presente
   (g) **to b. witness** atestiguar
   (h) (*pt* **born** *passive only, not followed by*
by) (*give birth to*) dar a luz; **he was born in
Wakefield** nació en Wakefield
   2 *vi* (*turn*) girar, torcer; **to b. left** girar a la
izquierda
 ▸ **bear down** *vi* (*approach*) correr (**on**
sobre)
 ▸ **bear out** *vt sep* (*confirm*) confirmar
 ▸ **bear up** *vi* (*endure*) resistir
 ▸ **bear with** *vt insep* tener paciencia
con

bear² [beə(r)] *n* (a) oso *m*; **b. cub** osezno
m; *Astron* **Great B.** Osa *f* Mayor; **Little B.**
Osa Menor (b) *Fin* bajista *mf*

beard [bɪəd] *n* barba *f*

bearer ['beərə(r)] *n* portador(a) *m,f*; (*of
passport, office*) titular *mf*

bearing ['beərɪŋ] *n* (a) (*posture*) porte *m*
(b) (*relevance*) relación *f*; **to have a b. on**
estar relacionado(a) con (c) *Tech* cojinete
m (d) *Naut* bearings posición *f*, orientación *f*; **to get one's bearings** orientarse;
to lose one's bearings desorientarse

beast [biːst] *n* (a) bestia *f*; **b. of burden**
bestia de carga; *Fig* bestia *f*, bruto *m*
(c) **beasts** (*cattle*) reses *fpl*

beastly ['biːstlɪ] *adj* (**beastlier, beast-
liest**) (*beastlike*) asqueroso(a)

beat [biːt] **1** *vt* (*pt* **beat**; *pp* **beaten**
['biːtən]) (a) (*hit*) pegar, golpear;
(*clothes*) sacudir; (*drum*) tocar; **off the
beaten track** en un lugar muy apartado;
Fam **b. it!** ¡lárgate!
   (b) *Culin* batir
   (c) (*defeat*) batir, vencer; **we b. them
5–2** les ganamos 5 a 2
   (d) **to b. a retreat** batirse en retirada
   (e) *Mus* (*time*) marcar
   (f) **to b. the traffic** evitar los embotella-
mientos de tráfico

   (g) *Fam* (*puzzle*) extrañar; **it beats me**
no lo entiendo
   2 *vi* (a) (*heart*) latir
   (b) (*strike*) dar golpes; *Fig* **to b. about
the bush** andarse por las ramas
   3 *n* (a) (*of heart*) latido *m*
   (b) *Mus* ritmo *m*, compás *m*
   (c) (*of policeman*) ronda *f*
   4 *adj Fam* (*exhausted*) agotado(a)
 ▸ **beat down** *vi* (*sun*) apretar
 ▸ **beat off** *vt sep* rechazar
 ▸ **beat up** *vt sep Fam* dar una paliza a

beating ['biːtɪŋ] *n* (a) (*thrashing*) paliza *f*
(b) (*defeat*) derrota *f* (c) (*of drum*) toque
m (d) (*of heart*) latido *m*

beautician [bjuː'tɪʃən] *n* esteticista *mf*

beautiful ['bjuːtɪfʊl] *adj* hermoso(a),
bello(a); (*delicious*) delicioso(a); **b. people** gente guapa

beauty ['bjuːtɪ] *n* belleza *f*, hermosura *f*;
b. contest concurso *m* de belleza; **b.
queen** miss *f*; **b. salon** salón *m* de belleza;
b. spot (*on face*) lunar *m*; (*place*) lugar
pintoresco

beaver ['biːvə(r)] **1** *n* castor *m*
   2 *vi* **to b. away at sth** meterse de lleno en
algo

became [bɪ'keɪm] *pt of* **become**

because [bɪ'kɒz] **1** *conj* porque
   2 *prep* **b. of** a causa de, debido a

beckon ['bekən] *vt & vi* llamar (con la
mano); **to b. to sb** llamar a algn con
señas

become [bɪ'kʌm] **1** *vi* (*pt* **became**; *pp*
become) (*a teacher, doctor*) hacerse;
(*boring, jealous, suspicious*) volverse;
(*old, difficult, stronger*) hacerse; (*happy,
sad, thin*) ponerse; **to b. angry/interes-
ted** enfadarse/interesarse; **what will b.
of him?** ¿qué va a ser de él?
   2 *vt Fml* (*of clothes, colour*) sentar bien a

becoming [bɪ'kʌmɪŋ] *adj* (a) (*dress*) fa-
vorecedor(a) (b) (*behaviour*) conveniente, apropiado(a)

bed [bed] *n* (a) cama *f*; **to get out of b.**
levantarse de la cama; **to go to b.** acostarse; **to make the b.** hacer la cama; *Br* **b.
and breakfast** (*service*) cama y desayuno
m; (*sign*) pensión; **b. linen** ropa *f* de cama
(b) (*of river*) lecho *m*; (*of sea*) fondo *m* (c)
Geol capa *f* (d) (*flower*) **b.** arriate *m*

bedbug ['bedbʌg] *n* chinche *f*

bedclothes ['bedkləʊðz] *npl*, **bedding**
['bedɪŋ] *n* ropa *f* de cama

bedlam ['bedləm] *n* algarabía *f*, alboroto
m

bedraggled [bɪ'drægəld] *adj* (*wet*) mo-
jado(a); (*dirty*) ensuciado(a)

bedridden ['bedrɪdən] *adj* postrado(a) en cama

bedroom ['bedru:m] *n* dormitorio *m*

bedside ['bedsaɪd] *n* at sb's b. junto a la cama de algn; **b. table** mesilla *f* de noche

bedsit ['bedsɪt] *n Fam*, **bedsitter** ['bed'sɪtə(r)] *n* estudio *m*

bedspread ['bedspred] *n* colcha *f*

bedtime ['bedtaɪm] *n* hora *f* de acostarse

bee [bi:] *n* abeja *f*

beech [bi:tʃ] *n* haya *f*

beef [bi:f] *n* carne *f* de vaca, *Méx* carne de res; **roast b.** rosbif *m*
   ▸ **beef up** *vt sep Fam* reforzar

beefburger ['bi:fbɜ:gə(r)] *n* hamburguesa *f*

beefsteak ['bi:fsteɪk] *n* bistec *m*

beehive ['bi:haɪv] *n* colmena *f*

beeline ['bi:laɪn] *n Fam* to make a b. for sth ir directo hacia algo

been [bi:n, bɪn] *pp of* be

beep [bi:p] *n (of apparatus)* pitido *m*; *(of horn)* pito *m*

beer [bɪə(r)] *n* cerveza *f*; **a glass of b.** una caña

beet [bi:t] *n US* remolacha *f*, *Andes* betarraga *f*, *Méx* betabel *f*; *US* **red b.** remolacha

beetle ['bi:təl] *n* escarabajo *m*

beetroot ['bi:tru:t] *n Br* remolacha *f*, *Andes* betarraga *f*, *Méx* betabel *f*

befit [bɪ'fɪt] *vt* convenir a, corresponder a

before [bɪ'fɔ:(r)] **1** *conj* **(a)** *(earlier than)* antes de que (+ *subj*), antes de (+ *infin*); **b. she goes** antes de que se vaya; **b. leaving** antes de salir **(b)** *(rather than)* antes que (+ *infin*)
   2 *prep* **(a)** *(place)* delante de; *(in the presence of)* ante **(b)** *(order, time)* antes de; **b. Christ** antes de Cristo; **b. long** dentro de poco; **b. 1950** antes de 1950; **I saw it b. you** lo vi antes que tú
   3 *adv* **(a)** *(time)* antes; **I have met him b.** ya lo conozco; **not long b.** poco antes; **the night b.** la noche anterior **(b)** *(place)* delante, por delante

beforehand [bɪ'fɔ:hænd] *adv* **(a)** *(earlier)* antes **(b)** *(in advance)* de antemano, con anticipación

befriend [bɪ'frend] *vt* trabar amistad con

beg [beg] **1** *vt* **(a)** *(money etc)* pedir **(b)** *(beseech)* rogar, suplicar; **I b. your pardon!** ¡perdone usted!; **I b. your pardon?** ¿cómo ha dicho usted?
   2 *vi* **(a)** *(solicit)* mendigar; *(dog)* pedir; **to b. for money** pedir limosna **(b)** **to b.**
for help/mercy *(beseech)* implorar ayuda/compasión

began [bɪ'gæn] *pt of* begin

beggar ['begə(r)] *n* **(a)** mendigo(a) *m,f* **(b)** *Fam Euph (chap)* tío *m*

begin [bɪ'gɪn] *vt & vi* *(pt* began; *pp* begun) empezar, comenzar; **to b. again** volver a empezar; **to b. at the beginning** empezar por el principio; **to b. doing** *or* **to do sth** empezar a hacer algo; **to b. with ...** *(initially)* para empezar ...

beginner [bɪ'gɪnə(r)] *n* principiante *mf*

beginning [bɪ'gɪnɪŋ] *n* **(a)** principio *m*, comienzo *m*; **at the b. of May** a principios de mayo; **from the b.** desde el principio; **in the b.** al principio **(b)** *(origin)* origen *m*

begonia [bɪ'gəʊnɪə] *n* begonia *f*

begrudge [bɪ'grʌdʒ] *vt* dar de mala gana; *(envy)* envidiar

beguile [bɪ'gaɪl] *vt (charm)* seducir

begun [bɪ'gʌn] *pp of* begin

behalf [bɪ'hɑ:f] *n* **on b. of**, *US* **in b. of** en nombre de, de parte de; **don't worry on my b.** no te preocupes por mí

behave [bɪ'heɪv] *vi* **(a)** *(person)* portarse, comportarse; **b. yourself!** ¡pórtate bien!; **to b. well/badly** portarse bien/mal **(b)** *(machine)* funcionar

behaviour, *US* **behavior** [bɪ'heɪvjə(r)] *n* **(a)** *(of person)* comportamiento *m*, conducta *f* **(b)** *(of machine)* funcionamiento *m*

behead [bɪ'hed] *vt* decapitar

beheld [bɪ'held] *pt & pp of* behold

behind [bɪ'haɪnd] **1** *prep* **(a)** detrás de; **b. sb's back** a espaldas de algn; **b. the scenes** entre bastidores; **to be b. sb** apoyar a algn; **what motive was there b. the crime?** ¿cuál fue el móvil del crimen? **(b)** **b. the times** *(less advanced than)* anticuado(a)
   2 *adv* **(a)** *(in the rear)* detrás, atrás; **I've left my umbrella b.** se me ha olvidado el paraguas **(b)** *(late)* **to be b. with one's payments** *(late)* estar atrasado(a) en los pagos
   3 *n Fam* trasero *m*

behold [bɪ'həʊld] *vt* *(pt & pp* beheld) *Literary* contemplar

beige [beɪʒ] *adj & n* beige *(m)*

being ['bi:ɪŋ] *n* **(a)** ser *m* **(b)** *(existence)* existencia *f*; **to come into b.** nacer

Belarus [belə'ru:s] *n* Bielorrusia

belated [bɪ'leɪtɪd] *adj* tardío(a)

belch [beltʃ] **1** *vi (person)* eructar
   2 *vt (smoke, flames)* vomitar, arrojar
   3 *n* eructo *m*

beleaguered [bɪ'liːgəd] *adj* asediado(a)

belfry ['belfrɪ] *n* campanario *m*

Belgian ['beldʒən] *adj & n* belga *(mf)*

Belgium ['beldʒəm] *n* Bélgica

Belgrade [bel'greɪd] *n* Belgrado

belie [bɪ'laɪ] *vt* desmentir

belief [bɪ'liːf] *n* (**a**) *(opinion)* creencia *f*; **beyond b.** increíble (**b**) *(opinion)* opinión *f* (**c**) *(faith)* fe *f* (**d**) *(confidence)* confianza *f* (**in** en)

believe [bɪ'liːv] **1** *vi* (**a**) *(have faith)* creer (**b**) **to b. in** *(be in favour of)* ser partidario(a) de (**c**) *(think)* creer; **I b. so** creo que sí

2 *vt* creer

believer [bɪ'liːvə(r)] *n* (**a**) *Rel* creyente *mf* (**b**) partidario(a) *m,f* (**in** de)

belittle [bɪ'lɪtəl] *vt (person)* menospreciar; *(problem)* minimizar

bell [bel] *n (of church)* campana *f*, *(small)* campanilla *f*; *(of school, door, bicycle etc)* timbre *m*; *(on cat)* cascabel *m*; *(on cow)* cencerro *m*; *Fig* **that rings a b.** eso me suena; **b. jar** campana *f*; **b. tower** campanario *m*

bell-bottoms ['belbɒtəmz] *npl* pantalones *mpl* de campana

bellboy ['belbɔɪ], *US* **bellhop** ['belhɒp] *n* botones *m inv*

belligerent [bɪ'lɪdʒərənt] *adj* agresivo(a)

bellow ['beləʊ] *vi (bull)* bramar; *(person)* rugir

bellows ['beləʊz] *npl* **(pair of) b.** fuelle *m*

belly ['belɪ] *n* (**a**) *(of person)* barriga *f*; **b. flop** panzazo *m* (**b**) *(of animal)* panza *f*

bellyache ['belɪeɪk] *n Fam* dolor *m* de vientre

belong [bɪ'lɒŋ] *vi* (**a**) pertenecer (**to** a) (**b**) *(be a member)* ser socio(a) (**to** de); *Pol* **to b. to a party** ser miembro de un partido (**c**) *(have a proper place)* corresponder; **this chair belongs here** esta silla va aquí

belongings [bɪ'lɒŋɪŋz] *npl* efectos *mpl* personales

beloved [bɪ'lʌvɪd, bɪ'lʌvd] **1** *adj* amado(a), querido(a)

2 *n* amado(a) *m,f*

below [bɪ'ləʊ] **1** *prep* debajo de; **b. average** por debajo de la media; **10 degrees b. zero** 10 grados bajo cero

2 *adv* abajo; **above and b.** arriba y abajo; **see b.** véase más abajo

belt [belt] *n* (**a**) cinturón *m*; **blow below the b.** golpe bajo (**b**) *Tech* correa *f*, cinta *f* (**c**) *(area)* zona *f*

2 *vt Fam* pegar una paliza a

▸ **belt along** *vi Fam* ir a todo gas

▸ **belt out** *vt sep Fam (song)* cantar a voz en grito

▸ **belt up** *vi Fam* callarse

beltway ['beltweɪ] *n US* carretera *f* de circunvalación

bemused [bɪ'mjuːzd] *adj* perplejo(a)

bench [bentʃ] *n* (**a**) *(seat)* banco *m* (**b**) *(in parliament)* escaño *m* (**c**) *Jur* **the b.** *(judges)* la magistratura (**d**) *Sport* banquillo *m* (**e**) **b. mark** *Geol* cota *f* de referencia; *Fig* punto *m* de referencia

bend [bend] **1** *vt (pt & pp bent)* doblar; *(back)* encorvar; *(head)* inclinar; *Fam* **to b. the rules** hacer una excepción

2 *vi* (**a**) doblarse; *(road)* torcerse (**b**) **to b. (over)** inclinarse; *Fam* **he bends over backwards to please her** hace lo imposible por complacerla

3 *n (in river, road)* curva *f*, *(in pipe)* recodo *m*; *Br Fam* **round the b.** loco(a) perdido(a)

▸ **bend down** *vi* inclinarse

beneath [bɪ'niːθ] **1** *prep (below)* bajo, debajo de; *Fig* **it's b. him** es indigno de él

2 *adv* debajo

benefactor ['benɪfæktə(r)] *n* bienhechor(a) *m,f*

beneficial [benɪ'fɪʃəl] *adj* (**a**) *(doing good)* benéfico(a) (**b**) *(advantageous)* beneficioso(a)

beneficiary [benɪ'fɪʃərɪ] *n* beneficiario(a) *m,f*

benefit ['benɪfɪt] **1** *vt* beneficiar

2 *vi* sacar provecho (**from** *or* **by** de)

3 *n* (**a**) *(advantage)* beneficio *m*, provecho *m*; **for the b. of** en beneficio de; **I did it for your b.** lo hice por tu bien (**b**) *(allowance)* subsidio *m*; **unemployment b.** subsidio de desempleo (**c**) *(event)* función benéfica

benevolent [bɪ'nevələnt] *adj* benévolo(a)

Bengal [beŋ'gɔːl] *n* Bengala

benign [bɪ'naɪn] *adj* benigno(a)

bent [bent] **1** *adj* (**a**) *(curved)* curvado(a) (**b**) **to be b. on doing sth** *(determined)* estar empeñado(a) en hacer algo (**c**) *Fam (corrupt)* deshonesto(a) (**d**) *very Fam (homosexual)* gay (**e**) *pt & pp of* **bend**

2 *n (inclination)* inclinación *f* (**towards** hacia)

benzine ['benziːn] *n Chem* bencina *f*

bequeath [bɪ'kwiːð] *vt Jur* legar

bequest [bɪ'kwest] *n Jur* legado *m*

bereaved [bɪ'riːvd] *npl* **the b.** los familiares del/de un difunto

bereavement [bɪ'riːvmənt] *n (mourning)* duelo *m*

bereft [bɪ'reft] *adj* **b. of** privado(a) de

beret ['bereɪ] *n* boina *f*

Berlin [bɜː'lɪn] *n* Berlín

Bermuda [bə'mjuːdə] *n* las (Islas) Bermudas; **B. shorts** bermudas *fpl*

Bern [bɜːn] *n* Berna

berry ['berɪ] *n* baya *f*

berserk [bə'sɜːk, bə'zɜːk] *adj* **to go b.** volverse loco(a)

berth [bɜːθ] *Naut* **1** *n* (**a**) *(mooring)* amarradero *m*; *Fig* **to give sb a wide b.** evitar a algn (**b**) *(bed)* litera *f*

2 *vi* atracar

beseech [bɪ'siːtʃ] *vt* (*pt & pp* **besought** *or* **beseeched**) suplicar, implorar

beset [bɪ'set] *vt* (*pt & pp* **beset**) acosar; **it is b. with dangers** está plagado de peligros

beside [bɪ'saɪd] *prep* (**a**) *(next to)* al lado de, junto a (**c**) *(compared with)* comparado con (**c**) **he was b. himself with joy** estaba loco de alegría; **that's b. the point** eso no viene al caso; **to be b. oneself** estar fuera de sí

besides [bɪ'saɪdz] **1** *prep* (**a**) *(in addition to)* además de (**b**) *(except)* excepto, menos; **no one b. me** nadie más que yo

2 *adv* además

besiege [bɪ'siːdʒ] *vt* *(city)* sitiar; *Fig* asediar

besought [bɪ'sɔːt] *pt & pp* of **beseech**

best [best] **1** *adj* (*superl of* **good**) mejor; **b. man** ≃ padrino *m* de boda; **her b. friend** su mejor amiga; **the b. thing would be to phone them** lo mejor sería llamarles; **we had to wait the b. part of a year** tuvimos que esperar casi un año; **with b. wishes from Mary** *(in letter)* con mis mejores deseos, Mary

2 *adv* (*superl of* **well**) mejor; **as b. I can** lo mejor que pueda; **I like this one b.** éste es el que más me gusta; **the world's b. dressed man** el hombre mejor vestido del mundo

3 *n* **the b.** el/la/lo mejor; **all the b.!** ¡que te vaya bien!; **at b.** a lo más; **to be at one's b.** estar en plena forma; **to do one's b.** hacer todo lo posible; **to make the b. of sth** sacar el mejor partido de algo; **to the b. of my knowledge** que yo sepa

bestiality [bestɪ'ælɪtɪ] *n* bestialidad *f*

bestow [bɪ'stəʊ] *vt* *(favour etc)* conceder; *(honours, power)* otorgar (**on** a); *(title etc)* conferir (**on** a)

best-seller [best'selə(r)] *n* best-seller *m*

best-selling ['bestselɪŋ] *adj* **a b. author** un autor de superventas

bet [bet] **1** *n* apuesta *f*

2 *vt* (*pt* **bet** *or* **betted**) apostar

3 *vi* apostar (**on** por); *Fam* **you b.!** ¡ya tanto!

Bethlehem ['beθlɪhem] *n* Belén

betray [bɪ'treɪ] *vt* (**a**) traicionar (**b**) *(be unfaithful to)* engañar (**c**) *(reveal)* revelar

betrayal [bɪ'treɪəl] *n* traición *f*

better ['betə(r)] **1** *adj* (*comp of* **good**) mejor; **that's b.!** ¡así está mejor!; **the weather is b. than last week** hace mejor tiempo que la semana pasada; **to be no b. than ...** no ser más que ...; **to get b.** mejorar

(**b**) *(healthier)* mejor (de salud)

(**c**) **b. off** *(better)* mejor; *(richer)* más rico(a); **you'd be b. off going home** lo mejor es que te vayas a casa

(**d**) **the b. part of the day** la mayor parte del día

2 *adv* (*comp of* **well**) (**a**) mejor; **all the b., so much the b.** tanto mejor; **b. and b.** cada vez mejor; *Prov* **b. late than never** más vale tarde que nunca

(**b**) **we had b. leave** más vale que nos vayamos

(**c**) **to think b. of** *(plan)* cambiar de

3 *n* mejor; **a change for the b.** una mejora; **to get the b. of sb** vencer a algn

4 *vt* (**a**) *(improve)* mejorar

(**b**) *(surpass)* superar

betting ['betɪŋ] *n* apuestas *fpl*; *Br* **b. shop** quiosco *m* de apuestas

between [bɪ'twiːn] **1** *prep* entre; **b. you and me** entre nosotros; **closed b. one and two** cerrado de una a dos

2 *adv* **in b.** *(position)* en medio; *(time)* entretanto, mientras (tanto)

beverage ['bevərɪdʒ] *n* bebida *f*

bevy ['bevɪ] *n* bandada *f*

beware [bɪ'weə(r)] *vi* tener cuidado (**of** con); **b.!** ¡cuidado!; **b. of the dog** *(sign)* cuidado con el perro

bewildered [bɪ'wɪldəd] *adj* desconcertado(a)

bewilderment [bɪ'wɪldəmənt] *n* desconcierto *m*

bewitching [bɪ'wɪtʃɪŋ] *adj* fascinador(a)

beyond [bɪ'jɒnd] **1** *prep* más allá de; **b. belief** increíble; **b. doubt** sin lugar a dudas; **it is b. me why ...** no comprendo por qué ...; **it's b. a joke** eso ya no tiene gracia; **she is b. caring** ya no le importa; **this task is b. me** no puedo con esta tarea

2 *adv* más allá, más lejos

bias ['baɪəs] *n* *(tendency)* tendencia *f* (**towards** hacia); *(prejudice)* prejuicio *m*

bias(s)ed ['baɪəst] *adj* parcial; **to be b.**

against sth/sb tener prejuicio en contra de algo/algn

bib [bɪb] *n* (*for baby*) babero *m*; (*of apron*) peto *m*

Bible ['baɪbəl] *n* Biblia *f*; *Fam* **B. basher, B. thumper** evangelista *mf*

bibliography [bɪblɪ'ɒgrəfɪ] *n* bibliografía *f*

bicarbonate [baɪ'kɑːbənɪt] *n* bicarbonato *m*; **b. of soda** bicarbonato sódico

bicentenary [baɪsen'tiːnərɪ], *US* **bicentennial** [baɪsen'tenɪəl] *n* bicentenario *m*

biceps ['baɪseps] *n* bíceps *m*

bicker ['bɪkə(r)] *vi* reñir

bicycle ['baɪsɪkəl] *n* bicicleta *f*; **b. pump** bomba *f* (de aire); **to go by b.** ir en bicicleta

bid [bɪd] **1** *vt* (*pt* bid *or* bade; *pp* bid *or* bidden ['bɪdən]) (**a**) (*say*) decir; **to b. sb farewell** despedirse de algn (**b**) (*command*) mandar, ordenar; **she bade him be quiet** le mandó que se callase (**c**) (*invite*) invitar; **he bade me sit down me** invitó a sentarme (**d**) (*at auction*) (*pt & pp* bid) pujar

2 *vi* (*pt & pp* bid) (*at auction*) pujar (**for** por)

3 *n* (**a**) (*offer*) oferta *f* (**b**) (*at auction*) puja *f* (**c**) (*attempt*) intento *m*, tentativa *f*

bidder ['bɪdə(r)] *n* **the highest b.** el mejor postor

bidding ['bɪdɪŋ] *n* (**a**) (*at auction*) puja *f* (**b**) (*order*) orden *f*; **to do sb's b.** cumplir la orden de algn

bide [baɪd] *vt* (*pt* bided *or* bode; *pp* bided) esperar; **to b. one's time** esperar el momento oportuno

bidet ['biːdeɪ] *n* bidé *m*

bifocal [baɪ'fəʊkəl] **1** *adj* bifocal

2 *npl* **bifocals** lentes *fpl* bifocales

big [bɪg] **1** *adj* grande (gran *before singular noun*); **a b. clock** un reloj grande; **a b. surprise** una gran sorpresa; **my b. brother** mi hermano mayor; *Fam Ironic* **b. deal!** ¿y qué?; **b. business** los grandes negocios; **b. dipper** montaña rusa; *US Astron* **B. Dipper** Osa *f* Mayor; **b. toe** dedo gordo del pie; *Fam* **b. gun, b. shot** pez gordo; *Fam* **to make the b. time** tener éxito; *Fam* **b. top** carpa *f*

2 *adv* (**a**) (*on a grand scale*) a lo grande (**b**) (*well*) de manera excepcional

bigamy ['bɪgəmɪ] *n* bigamia *f*

bighead ['bɪghed] *n Fam* creído(a) *m,f*, engreído(a) *m,f*

bigheaded [bɪg'hedɪd] *adj* creído(a), engreído(a)

bigot ['bɪgət] *n* intolerante *mf*

⚠ Note that the Spanish word **bigote** is a false friend and is never a translation for the English word **bigot**. In Spanish, **bigote** means "moustache".

bigoted ['bɪgətɪd] *adj* intolerante

bigotry ['bɪgətrɪ] *n* intolerancia *f*

bigwig ['bɪgwɪg] *n Fam* pez gordo

bike [baɪk] *n Fam* (*abbr* **bicycle** *or* **motorbike**) (*bicycle*) bici *f*; (*motorcycle*) moto *f*; **on your b.!** ¡vete de aquí!

bikini [bɪ'kiːnɪ] *n* bikini *m*

bilateral [baɪ'lætərəl] *adj* bilateral

bile [baɪl] *n* bilis *f*

bilingual [baɪ'lɪŋgwəl] *adj* bilingüe

Bill [bɪl] *n Br Fam* **the Old B.** la poli

bill¹ [bɪl] **1** *n* (**a**) (*for gas etc*) factura *f*, recibo *m* (**b**) *esp Br* (*in restaurant*) cuenta *f* (**c**) *Parl* proyecto *m* de ley (**d**) *US* (*banknote*) billete *m* de banco (**e**) (*poster*) cartel *m*; **on the b.** en cartel; **post no bills** (*sign*) prohibido fijar carteles; *Th* **to top the b.** encabezar el reparto; **b. of exchange** letra *f* de cambio; *Pol* **B. of Rights** declaración *f* de derechos

2 *vt* (**a**) (*send bill to*) facturar (**b**) *Th* programar

bill² [bɪl] *n* (*of bird*) pico *m*

billboard ['bɪlbɔːd] *n* (*hoarding*) cartelera *f*

billet ['bɪlɪt] **1** *n* alojamiento *m*

2 *vt* alojar

billfold ['bɪlfəʊld] *n US* cartera *f*, billetero *m*

billiards ['bɪljədz] *n sing* billar *m*

billion ['bɪljən] *n US* mil millones *mpl*; *Br Old-fashioned* billón *m*

billionaire [bɪljə'neə(r)] *n* multimillonario(a) *m,f*

billow ['bɪləʊ] **1** *n* (*of water*) ola *f*; (*of smoke*) nube *f*

2 *vi* (*sea*) ondear; (*sail*) hincharse

billy goat ['bɪlɪgəʊt] *n* macho cabrío

bin [bɪn] *n* (*for storage*) cajón *m*; **bread b.** panera *f*; (*rubbish*) **b.** cubo *m* de la basura

binary ['baɪnərɪ] *adj* **b. number** número binario

bind [baɪnd] *vt* (*pt & pp* bound) (**a**) (*tie up*) atar (**b**) *Med* (*bandage*) vendar (**c**) (*book*) encuadernar (**d**) (*require*) obligar (**e**) (*join etc*) unir

▶ **bind over** *vt sep Jur* obligar legalmente

binder ['baɪndə(r)] *n* (*file*) carpeta *f*

binding ['baɪndɪŋ] *adj* (*promise*) comprometedor(a); (*contract*) vinculante

binge [bɪndʒ] *n Fam* borrachera *f*; **to go on a b.** irse de juerga

bingo ['bɪŋgəʊ] *n* bingo *m*

binoculars [bɪˈnɒkjʊləz] *npl* prismáticos *mpl*, gemelos *mpl*

biochemistry [baɪəʊˈkemɪstrɪ] *n* bioquímica *f*

biodegradable [baɪəʊdɪˈɡreɪdəbəl] *adj* biodegradable

biography [baɪˈɒɡrəfɪ] *n* biografía *f*

biological [baɪəˈlɒdʒɪkəl] *adj* biológico(a); **b. warfare** guerra biológica

biologist [baɪˈɒlədʒɪst] *n* biólogo(a) *m,f*

biology [baɪˈɒlədʒɪ] *n* biología *f*

biorhythm [ˈbaɪəʊrɪðəm] *n* biorritmo *m*

biosphere [ˈbaɪəsfɪə(r)] *n* biosfera *f*

birch [bɜːtʃ] **1** *n* (**a**) *Bot* abedul *m* (**b**) (*rod*) vara *f* (de abedul)
2 *vt* azotar

bird [bɜːd] *n* (**a**) pájaro *m*, ave *f*; *Fig* **to kill two birds with one stone** matar dos pájaros de un tiro; **they're birds of a feather** son tal para cual; **b. of prey** ave de rapiña (**b**) *Br Fam* (*girl*) tía *f*, chica *f*

birdcage [ˈbɜːdkeɪdʒ] *n* jaula *f*

birdie [ˈbɜːdɪ] *n* (*in golf*) birdie *m*

bird's-eye view [bɜːdzaɪˈvjuː] *n* vista *f* de pájaro

bird-watcher [ˈbɜːdwɒtʃə(r)] *n* ornitólogo(a) *m,f*

Biro® [ˈbaɪrəʊ] *n Fam* boli *m*

birth [bɜːθ] *n* (**a**) nacimiento *m*; (*childbirth*) parto *m*; **by b.** de nacimiento▸ **to give b. to a child** dar a luz a un niño; **b. certificate** partida *f* de nacimiento; **b. control** (*family planning*) control *m* de la natalidad; (*contraception*) métodos anticonceptivos; **b. rate** índice *m* de natalidad (**b**) (*parentage*) de noble *b.* (*parentage*) de noble linaje

birthday [ˈbɜːθdeɪ] *n* cumpleaños *m inv*

birthmark [ˈbɜːθmɑːk] *n* antojo *m*

birthplace [ˈbɜːθpleɪs] *n* lugar *m* de nacimiento

Biscay [ˈbɪskeɪ] *n* Vizcaya; **the Bay of B.** el golfo de Vizcaya

biscuit [ˈbɪskɪt] *n* (**a**) *Br* (*sweet, salted*) galleta *f*; *Fam* **that really takes the b.!** ¡eso ya es el colmo! (**b**) *US* (*savoury*) bollo *m*, bizcocho *m*

bisect [baɪˈsekt] *vt* bisegmentar; *Geom* bisecar

bisexual [baɪˈseksjʊəl] *adj* bisexual

bishop [ˈbɪʃəp] *n* (**a**) *Rel* obispo *m* (**b**) (*in chess*) alfil *m*

bison [ˈbaɪsən] *n inv* bisonte *m*

bit¹ [bɪt] *n* (**a**) (*small piece*) trozo *m*, pedazo *m*; **to smash sth to bits** hacer añicos algo; *Fig* **thrilled to bits** muy emocionado(a); *Fig* **to do one's b.** poner de su parte (**b**) (*small quantity*) poco *m*; **a**

b. of sugar un poco de azúcar; **a b. of advice** un consejo; **a b. of news** una noticia; **bits and pieces** trastos *mpl*; *Fig* **b. by b.** poco a poco (**c**) **a b.** (*slightly*) un poco; **a b. longer** un ratito más; **a b. worried** un poco preocupado (**d**) (*coin*) moneda *f*

bit² [bɪt] *n* (*of tool*) broca *f*

bit³ [bɪt] *n Comput* bit *m*

bit⁴ [bɪt] *pt of* **bite**

bitch [bɪtʃ] **1** *n* (**a**) *Zool* (*female*) hembra *f*; (*dog*) perra *f* (**b**) *Fam* (*spiteful woman*) bruja *f*
2 *vi Fam* **to b. (about)** (*criticize*) criticar

bitchy [ˈbɪtʃɪ] *adj Fam* (*spiteful*) maldiciente; (*malicious*) malicioso(a); (*malevolent*) malintencionado(a)

bite [baɪt] **1** *n* (**a**) (*act*) mordisco *m* (**b**) (*wound*) mordedura *f*; (*insect*) **b.** picadura *f* (**c**) (*mouthful*) bocado *m* (**d**) *Fam* (*snack*) bocado *m*
2 *vt* (*pt* **bit**; *pp* **bitten**) morder; (*insect*) picar; **to b. one's nails** morderse las uñas; *Fig* **to b. the dust** (*suffer defeat*) morder el polvo; (*die*) palmarla; *Fam* **to b. sb's head off** echarle una bronca a algn
3 *vi* (**a**) morder; (*insect*) picar (**b**) *Fig* (*take effect*) surtir efecto (**c**) (*fish*) picar

biting [ˈbaɪtɪŋ] *adj* (*wind*) cortante; *Fig* (*criticism*) mordaz

bitten [ˈbɪtən] *pp of* **bite**

bitter [ˈbɪtə(r)] **1** *adj* (**a**) amargo(a) (**b**) (*weather*) glacial; (*wind*) cortante (**c**) (*person*) amargado(a) (**d**) (*struggle*) enconado(a); (*hatred*) implacable
2 *n* (**a**) (*beer*) cerveza amarga (**b**) **bitters** bíter *m*

bitterly [ˈbɪtəlɪ] *adv* **she was b. disappointed** sufrió una terrible decepción

bitterness [ˈbɪtənɪs] *n* (**a**) amargura *f* (**b**) (*of weather*) crudeza *f* (**c**) (*of person*) rencor *m*

bittersweet [bɪtəˈswiːt] *adj* agridulce

bitumen [ˈbɪtjʊmɪn] *n* betún *m*

bizarre [bɪˈzɑː(r)] *adj* (*odd*) extraño(a); (*eccentric*) estrafalario(a)

blab [blæb] *vi Fam* parlotear; (*let out a secret*) chivarse

black [blæk] **1** *adj* (**a**) (*colour*) negro(a); **a b. and white television** un televisor en blanco y negro; *Fig* **b. and white** amaestrado(a); **to put sth down in b. and white** poner algo por escrito; *Av* **b. box** caja negra; **b. coffee** café solo; **b. eye** ojo morado; **b. hole** agujero negro; **b. humour** humor negro; **b. magic** magia negra; **b. market** mercado negro; *Br* **b. pudding** morcilla *f*; **the B. Sea** el Mar

Negro; *Aut* **b. spot** punto negro; *Br* **the B.
Country** = la región de los Midlands; *Fig*
b. sheep oveja negra
(**b**) *(gloomy)* negro(a); *Fig* **a b. day** un
día aciago
2 *n* (**a**) *(colour)* negro *m*
(**b**) *(person)* negro(a) *m,f*
3 *vt* (**a**) *(make black)* ennegrecer
(**b**) *(polish)* lustrar
(**c**) *(boycott)* boicotear
► **black out 1** *vt sep* (**a**) *(extinguish lights in)*
apagar las luces de (**b**) *(censor)* censurar
2 *vi (faint)* desmayarse

blackberry ['blækbərı] *n* zarzamora *f*

blackbird ['blækbɜːd] *n* mirlo *m*

blackboard ['blækbɔːd] *n* pizarra *f*, encerado *m*

blackcurrant [blæk'kʌrənt] *n* grosella
negra

blacken ['blækən] *vt* (**a**) *(make black)*
ennegrecer (**b**) *Fig (defame)* manchar

blackhead ['blækhed] *n* espinilla *f*

blackjack ['blækdʒæk] *n Cards* veintiuna
f

blackleg ['blækleg] *n* esquirol *m*

blacklist ['blæklıst] *n* lista negra

blackmail ['blækmeıl] **1** *n* chantaje *m*
2 *vt* chantajear

blackout ['blækaʊt] *n* (**a**) *(of lights)* apagón *m* (**b**) *Rad & TV* censura *f* (**c**) *(fainting)* pérdida *f* de conocimiento

blacksmith ['blæksmıθ] *n* herrero *m*

bladder ['blædə(r)] *n* vejiga *f*; **gall b.**
vesícula *f* biliar

blade [bleıd] *n* (**a**) *(of grass)* brizna *f* (**b**)
(of knife etc) hoja *f* (**c**) *(of propeller, oar)*
pala *f*

blame [bleım] **1** *n* culpa *f*; **to take the b.
for sth** asumir la responsabilidad de algo
2 *vt* echar la culpa a; **he is to b.** él tiene la
culpa

blameless ['bleımlıs] *adj (person)* inocente; *(conduct)* intachable

blancmange [blə'mɒnʒ] *n* = tipo de
budín dulce

bland [blænd] *adj (food)* soso(a)

♪ Note that the Spanish word **blando** is a
false friend and is never a translation for the
English word **bland**. In Spanish, **blando**
means "soft".

---

blank [blæŋk] **1** *adj* (**a**) *(without writing)*
en blanco; *Fin* **b. cheque** cheque *m* en
blanco (**b**) *(empty)* vacío(a); **a. b. look**
una mirada inexpresiva (**c**) **a b. refusal**
(absolute) una negativa rotunda
2 *n* (**a**) *(space)* espacio *m* en blanco; **to
draw a b.** no tener éxito (**b**) *Mil* cartucho

m de fogueo (**c**) *US (form)* impreso *m*

blanket ['blæŋkıt] **1** *n* manta *f*, *Am* frazada *f*, cobija *f*; *Fig* capa *f*
2 *adj* general

blare [bleə(r)] *vi* resonar
► **blare out** *vt sep* pregonar

blasé ['blɑːzeı] *adj* de vuelta (de todo)

blasphemous ['blæsfəməs] *adj* blasfe-
mo(a)

blasphemy ['blæsfəmı] *n* blasfemia *f*

blast [blɑːst] **1** *n* (**a**) *(of wind)* ráfaga *f* (**b**)
(of horn etc) toque *m*; **at full b.** a toda
marcha (**c**) *(explosion)* explosión *f*; **b.
furnace** alto horno (**d**) *(shock wave)* onda
f de choque
2 *vt* (**a**) *(blow up)* volar; *Fam* **b. (it)!**
¡maldito sea! (**b**) *Fig (destroy)* arruinar
(**c**) *Fig (criticize)* criticar

blasted ['blɑːstıd] *adj* maldito(a)

blast-off ['blɑːstɒf] *n* despegue *m*

blatant ['bleıtənt] *adj (very obvious)* evidente; *(shameless)* descarado(a); **a b. lie**
una mentira patente

blaze¹ [bleız] **1** *n* (**a**) *(burst of flame)*
llamarada *f* (**b**) *(fierce fire)* incendio *m*
(**c**) *(of sun)* resplandor *m* (**d**) *Fig (of
anger)* arranque *m*
2 *vi* (**a**) *(fire)* arder (**b**) *(sun etc)* brillar

blaze² [bleız] *vt* **to b. a trail** abrir un
camino

blazer ['bleızə(r)] *n* chaqueta *f* sport

bleach [bliːtʃ] **1** *n (household)* lejía *f*
2 *vt* (**a**) *(whiten)* blanquear; *(fade)* descolorir (**b**) *(hair)* decolorar

bleachers ['bliːtʃəz] *npl US Sport (seats)*
gradas *fpl*

bleak [bliːk] *adj* (**a**) *(countryside)* desola-
do(a) (**b**) *(weather)* desapacible (**c**) *(future)* poco prometedor(a)

bleary ['blıərı] *adj* (**blearier, bleariest**)
(eyes) (due to tears) lloroso(a); *(due to
tiredness)* cansado(a)

bleary-eyed [blıər'aıd] *adj* con los ojos
llorosos/cansados

bleat [bliːt] **1** *n* balido *m*
2 *vi (animal)* balar

bleed [bliːd] **1** *vi (pt & pp* **bled** [bled])
sangrar
2 *vt Med* sangrar; *Fam* **to b. sb dry**
sacarle a algn hasta el último céntimo

bleeding ['bliːdıŋ] **1** *n (loss of blood)*
pérdida *f* de sangre
2 *adj* (**a**) *Med* sangrante (**b**) *Fam Pej*
puñetero(a)

bleep [bliːp] **1** *n* bip *m*, pitido *m*
2 *vi* pitar

bleeper ['bliːpə(r)] *n Fam* busca *m*, buscapersonas *m inv*

blemish ['blemɪʃ] n (flaw) defecto m; (on fruit) maca f; Fig mancha f; Fig without b. sin tacha

blend [blend] 1 n mezcla f
2 vt (mix) mezclar; (colours) armonizar
3 vi (mix) mezclarse; (colours) armonizar

blender ['blendə(r)] n licuadora f

bless [bles] vt (pt & pp **blessed** or **blest**) (a) bendecir; Fam **b. you!** (after a sneeze) ¡Jesús! (b) **blessed with good eyesight** dotado(a) de buena vista

blessing ['blesɪŋ] n bendición f; (advantage) ventaja f; **a mixed b.** una ventaja relativa

blest [blest] pt & pp of **bless**

blew [bluː] pt of **blow**

blight [blaɪt] 1 n plaga f
2 vt Fig (spoil) arruinar; (frustrate) frustrar

blimey ['blaɪmɪ] interj Fam ¡caramba!, ¡caray!

blind [blaɪnd] 1 adj ciego(a); **a b. man** un ciego; **a b. woman** una ciega; Fig **b. faith** fe ciega; Fig **to turn a b. eye** hacer la vista gorda; **b. alley** callejón m sin salida; Aut **b. corner** curva f sin visibilidad; **b. spot** ángulo muerto; Fam **b. date** cita f a ciegas
2 adv a ciegas; Fam **to get b. drunk** agarrar una curda
3 n (a) (on window) persiana f (b) pl **the b. los ciegos**
4 vt (a) cegar, dejar ciego; Fig **blinded by ambition** cegado por la ambición (b) (dazzle) deslumbrar

blinders ['blaɪndəz] npl US anteojeras fpl

blindfold ['blaɪndfəʊld] 1 n venda f
2 vt vendar los ojos a

blinding ['blaɪndɪŋ] adj cegador(a), deslumbrante

blindly ['blaɪndlɪ] adv a ciegas, ciegamente

blindness ['blaɪndnɪs] n ceguera f

blink [blɪŋk] vi (eyes) pestañear; (lights) parpadear

blinkered ['blɪŋkəd] adj Fig de miras estrechas

blinkers ['blɪŋkəz] npl (on horse) anteojeras fpl

bliss [blɪs] n felicidad f; **it was b.!** ¡fue maravilloso!

blissful ['blɪsfʊl] adj (happy) feliz; (marvellous) maravilloso(a)

blister ['blɪstə(r)] 1 n (on skin) ampolla f, (on paint) burbuja f
2 vi ampollarse

blithe [blaɪð] adj alegre

blithely ['blaɪðlɪ] adv alegremente

blitz [blɪts] 1 n bombardeo aéreo
2 vt bombardear

blizzard ['blɪzəd] n ventisca f

bloated ['bləʊtɪd] adj hinchado(a)

blob [blɒb] n (drop) gota f; (spot) mancha f

bloc [blɒk] n Pol bloque m

block [blɒk] 1 n (a) bloque m; (of wood) taco m; **in b. capitals** en mayúsculas (b) a **b. of flats** un bloque de pisos (c) (group of buildings) manzana f (d) (obstruction) bloqueo m (e) Fin **a b. of shares** un paquete de acciones (f) Fam (head) coco m
2 vt (a) (obstruct) obstruir; Aut **road blocked** (sign) carretera cortada; **to b. the way** cerrar el paso (b) Sport (player) obstaculizar (c) Fin bloquear
► **block up** vt sep bloquear, obstruir; **to get blocked up** (pipe) obstruirse

blockade [blɒ'keɪd] n bloqueo m

blockage ['blɒkɪdʒ] n bloqueo m, obstrucción f (traffic jam) atasco m

blockbuster ['blɒkbʌstə(r)] n Fam exitazo m; Cin & TV gran éxito m de taquilla; (book) éxito de ventas

bloke [bləʊk] n Fam tío m, tipo m

blond [blɒnd] adj & n rubio (m)

blonde [blɒnd] adj & n rubia (f)

blood [blʌd] n (a) sangre f; **b. bank** banco m de sangre; **b. cell** glóbulo m; **b. donor** donante mf de sangre; **b. group** grupo sanguíneo; **b. pressure** tensión f arterial; US **b. sausage** morcilla f, **b. test** análisis m de sangre; **b. transfusion** transfusión f de sangre; **b. vessel** vaso sanguíneo; **blue b.** sangre azul; **high/low b. pressure** hipertensión f/hipotensión f (b) (race) sangre f, raza f

bloodbath ['blʌdbɑːθ] n Fig baño m de sangre

bloodhound ['blʌdhaʊnd] n sabueso m

bloodshed ['blʌdʃed] n derramamiento m de sangre

bloodshot ['blʌdʃɒt] adj inyectado(a) de sangre

bloodstream ['blʌdstriːm] n corriente sanguínea

bloodthirsty ['blʌdθɜːstɪ] adj sanguinario(a)

bloody ['blʌdɪ] 1 adj (**bloodier, bloodiest**) (a) (battle) sangriento(a) (b) (bloodstained) manchado(a) de sangre (c) Br very Fam (damned) condenado(a), puñetero(a), Andes cojudo(a), Méx pinche
2 adv Br very Fam **it's b. difficult!** ¡joder, qué difícil!; **not b. likely!** ¡ni de coña!

bloody-minded [blʌdɪˈmaɪndɪd] *adj Fam* terco(a)
bloom [bluːm] **1** *n* (a) *(flower)* flor *f*; **in full b.** en flor (b) *(on fruit)* vello *m*
2 *vi (blossom)* florecer
blooming [ˈbluːmɪŋ] *adj* (a) *(blossoming)* floreciente (b) *Fam Euph (damned)* maldito(a), condenado(a)
blossom [ˈblɒsəm] **1** *n (flower)* flor *f*
2 *vi* florecer; *Fig* **to b. out** alcanzar la plenitud
blot [blɒt] **1** *n (of ink)* borrón *m*; *Fig* mancha *f*
2 *vt* (a) *(with ink)* emborronar (b) *(dry)* secar
3 *vi (ink)* correrse
▶ **blot out** *vt sep (memories)* borrar; *(view)* ocultar
blotchy [ˈblɒtʃɪ] *adj* (**blotchier, blotchiest**) *(skin etc)* enrojecido(a); *(paint etc)* cubierto(a) de manchas
blotting-paper [ˈblɒtɪŋpeɪpə(r)] *n* papel *m* secante
blouse [blaʊz] *n* blusa *f*
blow¹ [bləʊ] *n* golpe *m*; **to come to blows** llegar a las manos; **it came as a terrible b.** fue un duro golpe
blow² [bləʊ] **1** *vi* (*pt* **blew**; *pp* **blown**) (a) *(wind)* soplar; (b) *(fuse)* fundirse (c) *(tyre)* reventar
2 *vt* (a) *(kiss)* mandar (b) *(trumpet etc)* tocar; *Fig* **to b. one's own trumpet** darse bombo (c) *(one's nose)* sonarse (d) *(fuse)* fundir (e) *Fam (waste)* despilfarrar (f) *Fam (chances)* dar al traste con (g) *(explode)* volar; *Fig* **to b. sb's cover** descubrir la tapadera de algn; *Fam* **to b. one's top** salirse de sus casillas
▶ **blow away** *vt sep & vi* = **blow off**
▶ **blow down** *vt sep* derribar
▶ **blow off 1** *vt sep (by wind)* llevarse
2 *vi (hat)* salir volando
▶ **blow out 1** *vt sep* apagar
2 *vi* apagarse
▶ **blow over** *vi (storm)* calmarse; *(scandal)* olvidarse
▶ **blow up 1** *vt sep* (a) *(building)* volar (b) *(inflate)* inflar (c) *Phot* ampliar
2 *vi (explode)* explotar
blowlamp [ˈbləʊlæmp] *n* soplete *m*
blown [bləʊn] *pp of* **blow**
blowout [ˈbləʊaʊt] *n Aut* reventón *m*; *Fam (meal)* comilona *f*
blowtorch [ˈbləʊtɔːtʃ] *n US* soplete *m*
blow-up [ˈbləʊʌp] *n Phot* ampliación *f*
blubber [ˈblʌbə(r)] **1** *n* grasa *f* de ballena
2 *vi Fam* llorar a moco tendido

bludgeon [ˈblʌdʒən] *vt* aporrear; *Fig* **to b. sb into doing sth** forzar a algn a hacer algo
blue [bluː] **1** *adj* (a) *(colour)* azul; *Fig* **once in a b. moon** de higos a brevas; *Fam* **to scream b. murder** gritar como un loco; **b. jeans** vaqueros *mpl*, tejanos *mpl* (b) *(sad)* triste; **to feel b.** sentirse deprimido (c) *(obscene)* verde; **b. joke** chiste *m* verde
2 *n* (a) *(colour)* azul *m*; *Fam* **the boys in b.** los maderos (b) **out of the b.** *(suddenly)* de repente; *(unexpectedly)* como llovido del cielo
bluebell [ˈbluːbel] *n* campanilla *f*
blueberry [ˈbluːbərɪ] *n* arándano *m*
bluebottle [ˈbluːbɒtəl] *n* moscarda *f*, mosca *f* azul
blue-collar [ˈbluːkɒlə(r)] *adj* **b. worker** obrero(a) *m,f*
blueprint [ˈbluːprɪnt] *n* anteproyecto *m*
blues [bluːz] *n* (a) *Mus* **the b.** el blues (b) *Fam (sadness)* tristeza *f*, melancolía *f*; **to have the b.** sentirse deprimido
bluetit [ˈbluːtɪt] *n* herrerillo *m* común
bluff [blʌf] **1** *n (trick)* farol *m*; **to call sb's b.** hacer que algn ponga sus cartas encima de la mesa
2 *adj (abrupt)* brusco(a); *(forthright)* francote(a)
3 *vi* tirarse un farol; **to b. one's way through sth** hacer colar algo
blunder [ˈblʌndə(r)] **1** *n* metedura *f* de pata; *Fam* patinazo *m*
2 *vi* meter la pata, pegar un patinazo
blunt [blʌnt] **1** *adj* (a) *(knife)* desafilado(a); *(pencil)* despuntado(a); **b. instrument** instrumento *m* contundente (b) *(frank)* directo(a), francote(a); *(statement)* tajante
2 *vt (pencil)* despuntar; *(knife)* desafilar
bluntly [ˈblʌntlɪ] *adv* francamente
blur [blɜː(r)] **1** *n* aspecto borroso
2 *vt (windows)* empañar; *(shape)* desdibujar; *(memory)* enturbiar
blurb [blɜːb] *n (in book)* resumen *m*
blurred [blɜːd] *adj* borroso(a)
blurt [blɜːt] *vt* **to b. out** dejar escapar
blush [blʌʃ] **1** *n* rubor *m*
2 *vi* ruborizarse
blusher [ˈblʌʃə(r)] *n* colorete *m*
blustery [ˈblʌstərɪ] *adj* borrascoso(a)
boar [bɔː(r)] *n* verraco *m*; **wild b.** jabalí *m*
board [bɔːd] **1** *n* (a) *(plank)* tabla *f* (b) *(work surface)* mesa *f*; *(blackboard)* pizarra *f*; *(for games)* tablero *m* (c) *(meals)* pensión *f*; **full b.** pensión completa; **b. and lodging** casa *f* y comida (d) *(committee)* junta *f*, consejo *m*; **b. of directors**

consejo de administración; **b. room** sala f
del consejo (**e**) *Naut* **on b.** a bordo (**f**) *Fig*
above b. en regla; **across-the-b.** general;
to let sth go by the b. abandonar algo
2 *vt* (*ship, plane etc*) embarcarse en,
subir a
3 *vi* (**a**) (*lodge*) alojarse (**b**) (*at school*)
estar interno(a)
▶ **board up** *vt sep* tapar
boarder ['bɔːdə(r)] *n* (**a**) (*in boarding
house*) huésped *mf* (**b**) (*at school*) inter-
no(a) *m,f*
boarding ['bɔːdɪŋ] *n* (**a**) (*embarkation*)
embarque *m*; **b. card, b. pass** tarjeta f de
embarque (**b**) (*lodging*) alojamiento *m*,
pensión f; **b. house** pensión; **b. school**
internado *m*
boardwalk ['bɔːdwɔːk] *n US* paseo marítimo entarimado
boast [bəʊst] **1** *n* jactancia f, alarde *m*
2 *vi* jactarse, alardear (**about** de)
3 *vt* presumir de, alardear de; **the town
boasts an Olympic swimming pool** la
ciudad disfruta de una piscina olímpica
boat [bəʊt] *n* barco *m*; (*small*) barca f,
bote *m*; (*launch*) lancha f; (*large*) buque
m; *Fig* **we're all in the same b.** todos
estamos en el mismo barco; **fishing b.**
barco de pesca
boater ['bəʊtə(r)] *n* canotié *m*, canotier
m
boatswain ['bəʊsən] *n* contramaestre *m*
boatyard ['bəʊtjɑːd] *n* astillero *m*
bob [bɒb] **1** *n* (**a**) (*haircut*) pelo *m* a lo
chico (**b**) *Fam* (*pl* **bob**) (*shilling*) chelín *m*
2 *vi* **to b. up and down** subir y bajar
bobbin ['bɒbɪn] *n* (*of sewing machine*)
canilla f; (*for lace-making*) bolillo *m*
bobby ['bɒbɪ] *n Br Fam* (*policeman*) poli
m
bobby-pin ['bɒbɪpɪn] *n US* (*hairgrip*)
horquilla f
bobsleigh ['bɒbsleɪ] *n* bobsleigh *m*
bode[1] [bəʊd] *pt of* **bide**
bode[2] [bəʊd] *vt & vi* presagiar; **to b. well/
ill** ser de buen/mal agüero
bodice ['bɒdɪs] *n* (**a**) (*sleeveless under-
garment*) corpiño *m* (**b**) (*of dress*) cuerpo *m*
bodily ['bɒdɪlɪ] **1** *adj* físico(a); **b. harm**
daños *mpl* corporales
2 *adv* **to carry sb b.** llevar a algn en
brazos
body ['bɒdɪ] *n* (**a**) cuerpo *m*; **b. language**
expresión f corporal; **b. odour** olor *m*
corporal; **b. piercing** perforaciones *fpl*
en el cuerpo, piercing *m* (**b**) (*corpse*)
cadáver *m* (**c**) (*main part*) parte f principal (**d**) *Aut* carrocería f; *Naut* casco *m* (**e**)

(*organization*) organismo *m*; (*profession*)
cuerpo *m*; **the b. politic** el estado (**f**)
(*group of people*) conjunto *m*, grupo *m*
body-blow ['bɒdɪbləʊ] *n Fig* duro
golpe
body-builder ['bɒdɪbɪldə(r)] *n* culturista *mf*
body-building ['bɒdɪbɪldɪŋ] *n* culturismo *m*
bodyguard ['bɒdɪgɑːd] *n* guardaespaldas *mf inv*
bodywork ['bɒdɪwɜːk] *n Aut* carrocería f
Boer ['bəʊə(r)] *adj* **the B. War** la guerra
del Transvaal
bog [bɒg] *n* (**a**) ciénaga f (**b**) *Br very Fam*
(*lavatory*) meódromo *m*
▶ **bog down** *vt sep* **to get bogged down**
atascarse
bogey ['bəʊgɪ] *n* (**a**) (*spectre*) espectro
m, fantasma *m* (**b**) (*bugbear*) pesadilla f
(**c**) (*in golf*) bogey *m* (**d**) *Fam* (*mucus*)
moco *m*
boggle ['bɒgəl] *vi Fam* **the mind bog-
gles!** ¡es alucinante!
bogus ['bəʊgəs] *adj* falso(a); **b. company**
compañía f fantasma
boil[1] [bɔɪl] **1** *n* **to come to the b.** empezar
a hervir
2 *vt* (*water*) hervir; (*food*) cocer; (*egg*)
cocer, pasar por agua
3 *vi* hervir; *Fig* **to b. with rage** estar
furioso(a)
▶ **boil down** *vi* reducirse (**to** a)
▶ **boil over** *vi* (*milk*) salirse
boil[2] [bɔɪl] *n Med* furúnculo *m*
boiled [bɔɪld] *adj* **b. egg** huevo cocido *or*
pasado por agua
boiler ['bɔɪlə(r)] *n* caldera f; *Br* **b. suit**
mono *m*
boiling ['bɔɪlɪŋ] *adj* **b. water** agua hirviendo; **it's b. hot** (*food*) quema; (*weather*) hace un calor agobiante; **b. point**
punto *m* de ebullición
boisterous ['bɔɪstərəs] *adj* (**a**) (*person,
party*) bullicioso(a) (**b**) (*weather*) borras-
coso(a)
bold [bəʊld] *adj* (**a**) (*brave*) valiente (**b**)
(*daring*) audaz (**c**) (*features*) marcado(a);
Typ **b. type** negrita f (**d**) (*impudent*) des-
carado(a)
Bolivia [bə'lɪvɪə] *n* Bolivia
Bolivian [bə'lɪvɪən] *adj & n* boliviano(a)
(*m,f*)
bollard ['bɒlɑːd] *n Aut* baliza f
bollocks ['bɒləks] *npl Br very Fam* cojones *mpl*; **b.!** (*disagreement*) ¡y un huevo!
Bolshevik ['bɒlʃəvɪk] *adj & n* bolchevique (*mf*)

bolster ['bəʊlstə(r)] **1** n (pillow) cabezal m, travesaño m

2 vt (strengthen) reforzar; (support) apoyar

bolt [bəʊlt] **1** n (**a**) (on door) cerrojo m; (small) pestillo m (**b**) Tech perno m, tornillo m (**c**) (of lightning) rayo m (**d**) (crossbow) flecha f

2 vt (**a**) (lock) cerrar con cerrojo (**b**) Tech sujetar con pernos (**c**) Fam (food) engullir

3 vi (person) largarse; (horse) desbocarse

4 adv **b. upright** derecho

bomb [bɒm] **1** n bomba f; Br Fam **to cost a b.** costar un ojo de la cara; **b. disposal squad** brigada f de artificieros; **b. scare** amenaza f de bomba; **car b.** coche-bomba m; **letter b.** carta-bomba f

2 vt (city etc) bombardear; (by terrorists) volar

3 vi Fam **to b. (along)** (car) ir a toda pastilla

bombard [bɒm'bɑːd] vt bombardear

bombardment [bɒm'bɑːdmənt] n bombardeo m

bombastic [bɒm'bæstɪk] adj rimbombante

bomber ['bɒmə(r)] n (**a**) Av bombardero m; **b. jacket** cazadora f (**b**) terrorista mf que coloca bombas

bombshell ['bɒmʃel] n (**a**) Mil obús m (**b**) Fig (surprise) bomba f (**c**) Fam **a blonde b.** una rubia explosiva

bona fide ['bəʊnə'faɪdɪ] adj (**a**) (genuine) auténtico(a) (**b**) (in good faith) bien-intencionado(a)

bond [bɒnd] **1** n (**a**) (link) lazo m, vínculo m (**b**) Fin bono m (**c**) Jur (bail) fianza f (**d**) (binding agreement) acuerdo m (**e**) (warehouse) depósito m; **in b.** en depósito (**f**) US (guarantee) garantía f (**g**) **bonds** (shackles) cadenas fpl

2 vt (**a**) (join) pegar (**b**) (merchandise) poner en depósito

bondage ['bɒndɪdʒ] n esclavitud f

bone [bəʊn] **1** n (**a**) hueso m; (in fish) espina f, Fig **b. of contention** manzana f de la discordia; Fig **he made no bones about it** no trató de disimularlo; **b. china** porcelana fina (**b**) **bones** (remains) restos mpl; **the bare bones** lo esencial

2 vt (meat) deshuesar; (fish) quitar las espinas a

▸ **bone up on** vt insep Fam empollar

bone-dry ['bəʊn'draɪ] adj completamente seco(a)

bone-idle ['bəʊn'aɪdəl] adj gandul(a)

bonfire ['bɒnfaɪə(r)] n hoguera f, fogata f; Br **B. Night** = fiesta del 5 de noviembre en que de noche se hacen hogueras y hay fuegos artificiales

bonkers ['bɒŋkəz] adj Br Fam chalado(a)

bonnet ['bɒnɪt] n (**a**) (child's) gorra f (**b**) Br Aut capó m

bonus ['bəʊnəs] n (**a**) (on wages) prima f (**b**) Fin (on shares) dividendo m extraordinario (**c**) Br Ins beneficio m

bony ['bəʊnɪ] adj (bonier, boniest) (person) huesudo(a); (fish) lleno(a) de espinas

boo [buː] **1** interj ¡bu!

2 n abucheo m

3 vt abuchear

boob [buːb] n Br Fam (**a**) (silly mistake) patinazo m (**b**) **boobs** (breasts) tetas fpl

booby ['buːbɪ] n **b. prize** premio m de consolación; **b. trap** trampa f; Mil trampa explosiva

boogie ['buːgɪ] vi Fam bailar

book [bʊk] **1** n libro m; Fig **in my b.** según mi punto de vista; Fig **by the b.** según las reglas; **b. end** sujetalibros m inv; Br **b. token** vale m para comprar libros; **savings b.** libreta f de ahorros (**b**) (of stamps) carpeta f, (of matches) cajetilla f (**c**) Com **books** cuentas fpl; **to keep the books** llevar las cuentas

2 vt (**a**) (reserve) reservar; (return flight) cerrar (**b**) (engage) contratar (**c**) (by police) poner una multa a (**d**) Ftb amonestar

▸ **book into** vt insep (hotel) reservar una habitación en

▸ **book out** vi (of hotel) marcharse

▸ **book up** vt sep **booked up** (sign) completo

booking ['bʊkɪŋ] n esp Br (reservation) reserva f; **b. office** taquilla f

bookmaker ['bʊkmeɪkə(r)] n corredor(a) m,f de apuestas

bookseller ['bʊkselə(r)] n librero(a) m,f

bookshelf ['bʊkʃelf] n bookshelves estantería f

bookshop ['bʊkʃɒp] n librería f

bookstall ['bʊkstɔːl] n quiosco m

bookstore ['bʊkstɔː(r)] n US librería f

bookworm ['bʊkwɜːm] n Fam ratón m de biblioteca

boom¹ [buːm] **1** n (**a**) (noise) estampido m, trueno m (**b**) (sudden prosperity) boom m, auge m

2 vi (**a**) (thunder) retumbar; (cannon) tronar (**b**) (prosper) estar en auge

boom² [buːm] n (of microphone) jirafa f

boomerang ['buːməræŋ] *n* bumerang *m*, bumerán *m*

booming ['buːmɪŋ] *adj* (**a**) (*voice, thunder*) que retumba (**b**) (*prosperous*) en auge

boon [buːn] *n* (*blessing*) bendición *f*

boost [buːst] **1** *n* estímulo *m*, empujón *m*
 2 *vt* (**a**) (*increase*) aumentar (**b**) **to b. sb's confidence** subirle la moral a algn (**c**) (*tourism, exports*) fomentar (**d**) (*voltage*) elevar

booster ['buːstə(r)] *n* (**a**) *Elec* elevador *m* de voltaje (**b**) *Rad & TV* (*amplifier*) amplificador *m* (**c**) *Med* **b. (shot)** revacunación *f*

boot¹ [buːt] **1** *n* (**a**) bota *f*; (*short*) botín *m*; *Fig* **he's too big for his boots** es muy creído; *Fam* **to put the b. in** pisotear; *Fam* **she got the b.** la echaron (del trabajo); **b. polish** betún *m* (**b**) *BrAut* maletero *m*, *CAm, Méx* cajuela *f*, *RP* baúl *m*
 2 *vt Fam* (**a**) *Ftb* (*ball*) chutar (**b**) **to b. (out)** echar a patadas (**c**) *Comput* arrancar
 3 *vi Comput* **to b. (up)** arrancar

boot² [buːt] *n* **to b.** además

bootblack ['buːtblæk] *n esp US* limpiabotas *mf inv*

booth [buːð, buːθ] *n* (**a**) (*in language lab etc*) cabina *f*; **telephone b.** cabina telefónica (**b**) (*at fair*) puesto *m*

bootleg ['buːtleg] *adj* de contrabando

bootlegger ['buːtlegə(r)] *n* contrabandista *m*

booty ['buːtɪ] *n* botín *m*

booze [buːz] *Fam* **1** *n* priva *f*
 2 *vi* privar

bop [bɒp] **1** *n* (**a**) *Mus* be-bop *m* (**b**) *Fam* (*dance*) baile *m*
 2 *vi Fam* (*dance*) bailar

Bordeaux [bɔːˈdəʊ] *n* (**a**) (*city*) Burdeos (**b**) (*wine*) burdeos *m*

border ['bɔːdə(r)] **1** *n* (**a**) borde *m*, margen *m* (**b**) *Sewing* ribete *m* (**c**) (*frontier*) frontera *f*; **b. town** pueblo fronterizo (**d**) (*flowerbed*) arriate *m*
 2 *vt Sewing* ribetear
 ▶ **border on** *vt insep* (**a**) *Geog* lindar con (**b**) *Fig* rayar en

borderline ['bɔːdəlaɪn] **1** *n* (**a**) (*border*) frontera *f* (**b**) (*dividing line*) línea divisoria
 2 *adj* (**a**) (*on the border*) fronterizo(a) (**b**) *Fig* (*case etc*) dudoso(a)

bore¹ [bɔː(r)] **1** *vt Tech* taladrar, perforar
 2 *n* (**a**) *Tech* (*hole*) taladro *m* (**b**) (*of gun*) calibre *m*

bore² [bɔː(r)] **1** *vt* aburrir

2 *n* (*person*) pesado(a) *m,f*, pelma *mf*; (*thing*) lata *f*, rollo *m*; **what a b.!** ¡qué rollo!

bore³ [bɔː(r)] *pt of* bear

bored [bɔːd] *adj* aburrido(a); **to be b. stiff** *or* **to tears** estar aburrido(a) como una ostra

boredom ['bɔːdəm] *n* aburrimiento *m*

boring ['bɔːrɪŋ] *adj* (*uninteresting*) aburrido(a); (*tedious*) pesado(a), latoso(a)

born [bɔːn] **1** *pp of* bear; **to be b.** nacer; **I wasn't b. yesterday** no nací ayer
 2 *adj* (*having natural ability*) nato(a); **b. poet** poeta nato

born-again ['bɔːnəgen] *adj Rel* converso(a)

borne [bɔːn] *pp of* bear

borough ['bʌrə] *n* (**a**) (*town*) ciudad *f*; *US* (*municipality*) municipio *m* (**b**) *esp Br* (*constituency*) distrito *m* electoral

borrow ['bɒrəʊ] **1** *vt* (**a**) pedir *or* tomar prestado; **can I b. your pen?** ¿me dejas tu bolígrafo? (**b**) (*ideas etc*) apropiarse
 2 *vi* pedir *or* tomar prestado

borstal ['bɔːstəl] *n Br Fam* reformatorio *m*

Bosnia ['bɒznɪə] *n* Bosnia

Bosnia-Herzegovina
 ['bɒznɪəhɜːtsəgəˈviːnə] *n* Bosnia y Herzegóvina

Bosnian ['bɒznɪən] *adj & n* bosnio(a) (*m,f*)

bosom ['bʊzəm] *n* (**a**) (*breast*) pecho *m*; (*breasts*) pechos *mpl*; **b. friend** amigo(a) *m,f* del alma; *Fig* seno *m*

boss [bɒs] **1** *n* (**a**) (*head*) jefe(a) *m,f*; (*factory owner etc*) patrón(ona) *m,f* (**b**) *esp US Pol* jefe *m*; *Pej* cacique *m*
 2 *vt* **to b. sb about** *or* **around** mandar sobre algn

bossy ['bɒsɪ] *adj* (**bossier, bossiest**) *Fam* mandón(ona)

bosun ['bəʊsən] *n* contramaestre *m*

botanic(al) [bəˈtænɪk(əl)] *adj* botánico(a); **b. garden** jardín botánico

botany ['bɒtənɪ] *n* botánica *f*

botch [bɒtʃ] **1** *vt* chapucear; **a botched job** una chapuza
 2 *n* chapuza *f*

both [bəʊθ] **1** *adj* ambos(as), los dos/las dos; **b. men are teachers** ambos son profesores; **hold it with b. hands** sujétalo con las dos manos
 2 *pron* **b. (of them)** ambos(as), los dos/las dos; **b. of you** vosotros dos
 3 *conj* **b. ... and: b. England and Spain are in Europe** tanto Inglaterra como España están en Europa

bother ['bɒðə(r)] **1** *vt* (**a**) (*disturb*) molestar; (*be a nuisance to*) dar la lata a (**b**) *(worry)* preocupar; *Fam* **I can't be bothered** no tengo ganas

2 *vi* molestarse; **don't b. about me** no te preocupes por mí; **he didn't b. shaving** no se molestó en afeitarse

3 *n* (**a**) *(disturbance)* molestia *f*; *(nuisance)* lata *f* (**b**) *(trouble)* problemas *mpl*

4 *interj Br* ¡maldito sea!

bothersome ['bɒðəsəm] *adj* molesto(a)

bottle ['bɒtəl] **1** *n* (**a**) *(for perfume, ink)* frasco *m*; *Fam* **to hit the b.** darle a la bebida; **baby's b.** biberón *m*; **b. opener** abrebotellas *m inv* (**b**) *Br Fam* **to have a lot of b.** *(nerve)* tener muchas agallas

2 *vt (wine)* embotellar; *(fruit)* enfrascar

▶ **bottle out** *vi Br Fam* encogerse

▶ **bottle up** *vt sep* reprimir

bottle-bank ['bɒtəlbæŋk] *n* contenedor *m* de vidrio

bottled ['bɒtəld] *adj (beer, wine)* en botella, embotellado(a); *(fruit)* envasado(a)

bottle-green ['bɒtəlgriːn] *adj* verde botella

bottleneck ['bɒtəlnek] *n Aut* embotellamiento *m*, atasco *m*

bottom ['bɒtəm] **1** *adj* (**a**) *(lowest)* más bajo(a); *(drawer, shelf)* de abajo; *Aut* **b. gear** primera *f* (**b**) *(last)* último(a); *Fin* saldo *m* final; *Fig* resultado *m* final

2 *n* (**a**) parte *f* inferior; *(of sea, garden, street, box)* fondo *m*; *(of bottle)* culo *m*; *(of page, hill)* pie *m*; *Educ* **to be (at) the b. of the class** ser el último/la última de la clase; **to touch b.** tocar fondo; *Fam* **bottoms up!** ¡salud! (**b**) **to get to the b. of a matter** llegar al meollo de una cuestión; **who is at the b. of all this?** ¿quién está detrás de todo esto? (**c**) *(buttocks)* trasero *m*

▶ **bottom out** *vi Fin* tocar fondo

bottomless ['bɒtəmlɪs] *adj (pit)* sin fondo; *(mystery)* insondable

boudoir ['buːdwɑː(r)] *n* tocador *m*

bough [baʊ] *n* rama *f*

bought [bɔːt] *pt & pp of* **buy**

bouillon ['buːjɒn] *n* caldo *m*

boulder ['bəʊldə(r)] *n* canto rodado *m*

boulevard ['buːləvɑː(r)] *n* bulevar *m*

bounce [baʊns] **1** *vi* (**a**) *(ball)* rebotar (**b**) *(jump)* saltar (**c**) *Fam (cheque)* ser rechazado (por el banco)

2 *vt (ball)* botar

3 *n* (**a**) *(of ball)* bote *m* (**b**) *(jump)* salto *m* (**c**) *(energy)* vitalidad *f*

▶ **bounce back** *vi (recover health)* recuperarse, recobrarse

bouncer ['baʊnsə(r)] *n Fam* gorila *m*

bound¹ [baʊnd] *adj* (**a**) *(tied up)* atado(a) (**b**) *(book)* encuadernado(a) (**c**) *(obliged)* obligado(a) (**d**) **b. (up)** *(linked)* vinculado(a) (**with a**) (**e**) **it's b. to happen** sucederá con toda seguridad; **it was b. to fail** estaba destinado al fracaso

bound² [baʊnd] **1** *vi* saltar

2 *n* salto *m*

bound³ [baʊnd] *pt & pp of* **bind**

bound⁴ [baʊnd] *adj* **b. for** con destino a, rumbo a; **to be b. for** dirigirse a

boundary ['baʊndərɪ] *n* límite *m*

boundless ['baʊndlɪs] *adj* ilimitado(a), sin límites

bounds [baʊndz] *npl* **beyond the b. of reality** más allá de la realidad; **her ambition knows no b.** su ambición no conoce límites; **the river is out of b.** está prohibido bajar al río

bounty ['baʊntɪ] *n* prima *f*, gratificación *f*

bouquet *n* (**a**) [buːˈkeɪ, bəʊˈkeɪ] *(of flowers)* ramillete *m* (**b**) [buːˈkeɪ] *(of wine)* aroma *m*, buqué *m*

bourbon ['bɔːbən] *n US (whiskey)* whisky americano, bourbon *m*

bourgeois [bʊəʒwɑː] *adj & n* burgués(esa) *(m,f)*

bourgeoisie [bʊəʒwɑːˈziː] *n* burguesía *f*

bout [baʊt] *n* (**a**) *(of work)* turno *m*; *(of illness)* ataque *m* (**b**) *(in boxing)* combate *m*

boutique [buːˈtiːk] *n* boutique *f*, tienda *f*

bow¹ [baʊ] **1** *vi* (**a**) hacer una reverencia (**b**) *(give in)* ceder

2 *n (with head, body)* reverencia *f*

▶ **bow out** *vi* retirarse (**of** de)

bow² [bəʊ] *n* (**a**) *Sport & Mus* arco *m*; *Fig* **to have more than one string to one's b.** ser una persona de recursos (**b**) *(knot)* lazo *m*; **b. tie** pajarita *f*

bow³ [baʊ] *n esp Naut* proa *f*

bowel ['baʊəl] *n* (**a**) intestino *m* (**b**) **bowels** entrañas *fpl*

bowl¹ [bəʊl] *n* (**a**) *(dish)* cuenco *m*; *(for soup)* tazón *m*; *(for washing hands)* palangana *f*; *(for washing clothes, dishes)* barreño *m*; *(of toilet)* taza *f* (**b**) *Geol* cuenca *f*

bowl² [bəʊl] **1** *n* bola *f*

2 *vt (in cricket)* lanzar

3 *vi* (**a**) *(play bowls)* jugar a los bolos (**b**) *(in cricket)* lanzar la pelota

▶ **bowl along** *vi Fam (car)* ir volando

▶ **bowl out** *vt sep (in cricket)* eliminar

▶ **bowl over** *vt sep* (**a**) *(knock down)* derribar (**b**) *Fig (astonish)* desconcertar

bow-legged ['bəʊleg(ɪ)d] *adj* patizambo(a)

bowler [ˈbəʊlə(r)] *n (in cricket)* lanzador(a) *m,f*

bowler² [ˈbəʊlə(r)] *n (hat)* bombín *m*

bowling [ˈbəʊlɪŋ] *n (game)* bolos *mpl;* **b. alley** bolera *f;* **b. ball** bola *f* (de jugar a los bolos)

bowls [bəʊlz] *npl Sport* bolos *mpl*

box¹ [bɒks] **1** *n* (a) caja *f;* (*large*) cajón *m;* (*of matches*) cajetilla *f;* **jewellery b.** joyero *m; Th* **b. office** taquilla *f;* **b. office success** éxito taquillero (b) *Press* recuadro *m* (c) *Th* palco *m* (d) *Br Fam (television)* caja tonta

2 *vt (pack)* embalar

box² [bɒks] *Sport* **1** *vi* boxear

2 *vt (hit)* pegar; **to b. sb's ears** dar un cachete a algn

boxcar [ˈbɒkskɑː(r)] *n US* vagón *m* de mercancías, furgón *m* (de mercancías)

boxer [ˈbɒksə(r)] *n* (a) boxeador *m* (b) *(dog)* bóxer *m*

boxing [ˈbɒksɪŋ] *n* boxeo *m;* **b. ring** cuadrilátero *m*

Boxing Day [ˈbɒksɪŋdeɪ] *n Br* = el día de San Esteban *(26 de diciembre)*

boxroom [ˈbɒksruːm] *n* trastero *m*

boy [bɔɪ] *n* (a) *(child)* niño *m,* chico *m;* *(youth)* joven *m;* **b. band** = grupo musical juvenil compuesto por adolescentes varones; *Fam* **oh b.!** ¡vaya! (b) *(son)* hijo *m*

boycott [ˈbɔɪkɒt] **1** *n* boicot *m*

2 *vt* boicotear

boyfriend [ˈbɔɪfrend] *n* novio *m;* *(live-in)* compañero *m*

boyhood [ˈbɔɪhʊd] *n* niñez *f,* juventud *f*

boyish [ˈbɔɪɪʃ] *adj* juvenil, de muchacho

bra [brɑː] *n* sostén *m, Esp* sujetador *m, Carib, Col, Méx* brasier *m, RP* corpiño *m*

brace [breɪs] **1** *n* (a) *(clamp)* abrazadera *f;* *(of drill)* berbiquí *m;* *(for teeth)* aparato *m* (b) *(of wood)* puntal *m* (c) *(pair)* par *m* (d) *Br* **braces** tirantes *mpl*

2 *vt* (a) *(wall)* apuntalar (b) *(strengthen)* reforzar (c) **to b. oneself** prepararse (**for** para)

► **brace up** *vi* cobrar ánimo

bracelet [ˈbreɪslɪt] *n* pulsera *f*

bracing [ˈbreɪsɪŋ] *adj (wind)* fresco(a); *(stimulating)* tonificante

bracken [ˈbrækən] *n* helecho *m*

bracket [ˈbrækɪt] **1** *n* (a) *Typ (round)* paréntesis *m;* *(square)* corchete *m;* *(curly)* llave *f;* **in brackets** entre paréntesis (b) *(support)* soporte *m;* *(for lamp)* brazo *m;* *(shelf)* repisa *f* (c) *(for tax)* sector *m*

2 *vt* (a) *Ling (phrase etc)* poner entre paréntesis (b) *(group together)* agrupar, juntar

brag [bræg] *vi* jactarse (**about** de)

braggart [ˈbrægət] *n* fanfarrón(ona) *m,f*

braid [breɪd] **1** *vt* trenzar

2 *n* (a) *Sewing* galón *m* (b) *esp US (plait)* trenza *f*

Braille [breɪl] *n* braille *m*

brain [breɪn] *n* (a) cerebro *m;* **she's got cars on the b.** está obsesionada por los coches; *Med* **b. death** muerte *f* cerebral; *Fig* **b. drain** fuga *f* de cerebros; **b. wave** idea *f* genial (b) *Fam* **brains** inteligencia *f;* **to have brains** ser inteligente; *Br* **brains** *or US* **b. trust** grupo *m* de expertos (c) *Culin* **brains** sesos *mpl*

brainchild [ˈbreɪntʃaɪld] *n* invento *m,* idea *f* genial

brainpower [ˈbreɪnpaʊə(r)] *n* capacidad *f* intelectual

brainstorm [ˈbreɪnstɔːm] *n* (a) *(outburst)* arranque *m* (b) *(brainwave)* genialidad *f,* lluvia *f* de ideas

brainwash [ˈbreɪnwɒʃ] *vt* lavar el cerebro a

brainy [ˈbreɪnɪ] *adj* (**brainier, brainiest**) *Fam* listo(a)

braise [breɪz] *vt* cocer a fuego lento

brake [breɪk] **1** *n Aut (also pl)* freno *m;* **b. drum** tambor *m* del freno; **b. fluid** líquido *m* de frenos; **b. light** luz *f* de freno

2 *vi* frenar, echar el freno

bramble [ˈbræmbəl] *n* zarza *f,* zarzamora *f*

bran [bræn] *n* salvado *m*

branch [brɑːntʃ] **1** *n* (a) *(of tree)* rama *f;* *(of road)* bifurcación *f;* *(of science etc)* ramo *m; Com* **b. (office)** sucursal *f*

2 *vi (road)* bifurcarse

► **branch off** *vi* desviarse

► **branch out** *vi* diversificarse

brand [brænd] **1** *n* (a) *Com* marca *f;* **b. name** marca de fábrica (b) *(type)* clase *f* (c) *(on cattle)* hierro *m*

2 *vt* (a) *(animal)* marcar con hierro candente (b) *(label)* tildar

brandish [ˈbrændɪʃ] *vt* blandir

brand-new [ˈbrændˈnjuː] *adj* flamante

brandy [ˈbrændɪ] *n* coñac *m,* brandy *m*

brash [bræʃ] *adj* (a) *(impudent)* descarado(a) (b) *(reckless)* temerario(a) (c) *(loud, showy)* chillón(ona)

brass [brɑːs] *n* latón *m; Fam (money)* pasta *f; Mus* instrumentos *mpl* de metal; **b. band** banda *f* de metal

brassiere [ˈbræzɪə(r)] *n* sostén *m,* sujetador *m*

brat [bræt] *n Fam* mocoso(a) *m,f*

bravado [brəˈvɑːdəʊ] *n* bravuconería *f*

brave [breɪv] **1** *adj* valiente, valeroso(a)

2 *n US* (**Indian**) **b.** guerrero *m* indio

3 *vt* (**a**) *(face)* hacer frente a (**b**) *(defy)* desafiar

bravely ['breɪvlɪ] *adv* valientemente

bravery ['breɪvərɪ] *n* valentía *f*, valor *m*

bravo [brɑː'vəʊ] *interj* ¡bravo!

brawl [brɔːl] **1** *n* reyerta *f*

2 *vi* pelearse

brawn [brɔːn] *n* (**a**) *(strength)* fuerza física (**b**) *Br Culin* queso *m* de cerdo

bray [breɪ] **1** *n* *(of donkey)* rebuzno *m*

2 *vi* rebuznar

brazen ['breɪzən] *adj* descarado(a)

Brazil [brə'zɪl] *n* (el) Brasil

brazil [brə'zɪl] *n* **b. nut** nuez *f* del Brasil

Brazilian [brə'zɪlɪən] *adj & n* brasileño(a) *(m,f)*

breach [briːtʃ] **1** *n* (**a**) *(in wall)* brecha *f* (**b**) *(violation)* incumplimiento *m*; **b. of confidence** abuso *m* de confianza; **b. of contract** incumplimiento de contrato; **b. of the law** violación *f* de la ley; **b. of the peace** alteración *f* del orden público (**c**) *(in relations)* ruptura *f*

2 *vt* violar

bread [bred] *n* (**a**) *(food)* pan *m*; **b. and butter** pan con mantequilla, *Am* pan con manteca; *Fig* **our daily b.** el pan nuestro de cada día (**b**) *Fam (money)* pasta *f*, *Am* plata *f*

breadboard ['bredbɔːd] *n* tabla *f* (para cortar el pan)

breadcrumb ['bredkrʌm] *n* miga *f* de pan; **breadcrumbs** pan rallado

breadline ['bredlaɪn] *n* *Fam* miseria *f*; **to be on the b.** vivir en la miseria

breadth [bredθ] *n* (**a**) *(width)* anchura *f*; **it is 2 m in b.** tiene 2 m de ancho (**b**) *(extent)* amplitud *f*

breadwinner ['bredwɪnə(r)] *n* cabeza *mf* de familia

break [breɪk] **1** *vt* (*pt* **broke**; *pp* **broken**) (**a**) *(destroy)* romper; **to b. a leg** romperse la pierna; **to b. a record** batir un récord (b); **to b. even** no tener ni ganancias ni pérdidas; *Fig* **to b. one's back** matarse a trabajar; *Fig* **to b. sb's heart** partirle el corazón a algn; *Fig* **to b. the ice** romper el hielo (**b**) *(fail to keep)* faltar a; **to b. a contract** romper un contrato; **to b. the law** violar la ley

(**c**) *(destroy)* destrozar; *Fin* arruinar

(**d**) *(interrupt)* interrumpir

(**e**) *(code)* descifrar

(**f**) *(fall)* amortiguar

(**g**) **she broke the news to him** le comunicó la noticia

2 *vi* (**a**) romperse; *(clouds)* dispersarse; *(waves)* romper

(**b**) *(storm)* estallar

(**c**) *(voice)* cambiar

(**d**) *(health)* resentirse

(**e**) **when day breaks** al rayar el alba

(**f**) *(story)* divulgarse

3 *n* (**a**) *(fracture)* rotura *f*; *(crack)* grieta *f*; *(opening)* abertura *f*

(**b**) *(in relationship)* ruptura *f*

(**c**) *(pause)* pausa *f*, descanso *m*; *(at school)* recreo *m*; **to take a b.** descansar un rato; *(holiday)* tomar unos días libres; **without a b.** sin parar

(**d**) *Fam (chance)* oportunidad *f*; **a lucky b.** un golpe de suerte

▸ **break away** *vi* (**a**) *(become separate)* desprenderse (**from** de) (**b**) *(escape)* escaparse

▸ **break down 1** *vt sep* (**a**) *(door)* derribar (**b**) *(resistance)* acabar con (**c**) *(costs)* desglosar

2 *vi* (**a**) *Aut* tener una avería (**b**) *(resistance)* ceder (**c**) *(health)* debilitarse (**d**) *(weep)* ponerse a llorar

▸ **break in 1** *vt sep* acostumbrar; **to b. in a pair of shoes** cogerle la forma a los zapatos

2 *vi* *(burglar)* entrar por la fuerza

▸ **break into** *vt insep* (**a**) *(burgle) (house)* allanar; *(safe)* forzar (**b**) **to b. into song** empezar a cantar

▸ **break off** *vt sep* partir

2 *vi* (**a**) *(become detached)* desprenderse (**b**) *(talks)* interrumpirse (**c**) *(stop)* pararse

▸ **break out** *vi* (**a**) *(prisoners)* escaparse (**b**) *(war etc)* estallar; **she broke out in a rash** le salió un sarpullido

▸ **break through 1** *vt insep* (**a**) *(crowd)* abrirse paso por; *(cordon)* romper (**b**) *(clouds)* atravesar

2 *vi* (**a**) *(crowd)* abrirse paso (**b**) *(sun)* salir

▸ **break up 1** *vt sep* *(object)* romper; *(car)* desguazar; *(crowd)* disolver

2 *vi* (**a**) *(object)* romperse (**b**) *(crowd)* disolverse; *(meeting)* levantarse (**c**) *(relationship)* fracasar; *(couple)* separarse (**d**) *Educ* terminar

▸ **break with** *vt insep* *(past)* romper con

breakable ['breɪkəbəl] *adj* frágil

breakage ['breɪkɪdʒ] *n* *(breaking)* rotura *f*

breakaway ['breɪkəweɪ] *adj* disidente

breakdown ['breɪkdaʊn] *n* (**a**) *Aut* avería *f*; *Br* **b. truck** *or* **van** grúa *f* (**b**) (**nervous**) **b.** crisis nerviosa (**c**) *(in communications)* ruptura *f* (**d**) *(analysis)* análisis *m*; *Fin* desglose *m*

breaker ['breɪkə(r)] *n* (**a**) *(wave)* ola *f* grande (**b**) *Tech* trituradora *f* (**c**) *(switch)* interruptor automático

breakfast ['brekfəst] **1** *n* desayuno *m*; **to have b.** desayunar
2 *vi* desayunar

break-in ['breɪkɪn] *n* (**a**) robo *m* *(con allanamiento de morada)*

breaking ['breɪkɪŋ] *n* (**a**) rotura *f*; **b. point** punto *m* de ruptura (**b**) *Jur* **b. and entering** allanamiento *m* de morada

breakthrough ['breɪkθruː] *n* paso *m* adelante, avance *m*

breakwater ['breɪkwɔːtə(r)] *n* rompeolas *m inv*

breast [brest] *n* *(chest)* pecho *m*; *(of woman)* pecho *m*, seno *m*; *(of chicken etc)* pechuga *f*; *Fig* **to make a clean b. of it** dar la cara

breast-feed ['brestfiːd] *vt* dar el pecho a, amamantar a

breaststroke ['breststrəʊk] *n* braza *f*

breath [breθ] *n* (**a**) aliento *m*; *(breathing)* respiración *f*; **in the same b.** al mismo tiempo; **out of b.** sin aliento; **to catch one's b.** recobrar el aliento; **to draw b.** respirar; **under one's b.** en voz baja; *Fig* **to take sb's b. away** dejar pasmado a algn; *Aut* **b. test** alcoholemia *f* (**b**) **to go out for a b. of fresh air** salir a tomar el aire

Breathalyser®, *US* **Breathalyzer**® ['breθəlaɪzə(r)] *n Br* alcoholímetro *m*

breathe [briːð] **1** *vt* respirar; **to b. a sigh of relief** dar un suspiro de alivio
2 *vi* respirar; **to b. in** aspirar; **to b. out** espirar; **to b. heavily** resoplar

breather ['briːðə(r)] *n Fam (rest)* descanso *m*

breathing ['briːðɪŋ] *n* respiración *f*; **b. space** pausa *f*, respiro *m*

breathless ['breθlɪs] *adj* sin aliento, jadeante

breathtaking ['breθteɪkɪŋ] *adj* impresionante

bred [bred] *pt & pp of* **breed**

breeches ['brɪtʃɪz, 'briːtʃɪz] *npl* bombachos *mpl*; **knee b., riding b.** pantalones *mpl* de montar

breed [briːd] **1** *n (of animal)* raza *f*, *Fig (class)* clase *f*
2 *vt (pt & pp* **bred***) (animals)* criar; *Fig (ideas)* engendrar
3 *vi (animals)* reproducirse

breeder ['briːdə(r)] *n* (**a**) *(person)* criador(a) *m,f* (**b**) *(fast)* **b. reactor** reactor *m* generador

breeding ['briːdɪŋ] *n* (**a**) *(of animals)* cría *f*, *Fig* **b. ground** caldo *m* de cultivo (**b**) *(of person)* educación *f*

breeze [briːz] **1** *n* brisa *f*; *Constr* **b. block** bloque *m* de cemento
2 *vi* **to b. in/out** entrar/salir despreocupadamente

breezy ['briːzɪ] *adj* (**breezier, breeziest**) (**a**) *(weather)* ventoso(a) (**b**) *(person)* despreocupado(a)

brevity ['brevɪtɪ] *n* brevedad *f*

brew [bruː] **1** *vt (beer)* elaborar; *(hot drink)* preparar
2 *vi (tea)* reposar; *Fig* **a storm is brewing** se prepara una tormenta; *Fam* **something's brewing** algo se está cociendo
3 *n* (**a**) *(of tea)* infusión *f*; *Fam (of beer)* birra *f* (**b**) *(magic potion)* brebaje *m*

brewer ['bruːə(r)] *n* cervecero(a) *m,f*

brewery ['bruːərɪ] *n* cervecería *f*

brewing ['bruːɪŋ] **1** *adj* cervecero(a)
2 *n (of beer)* elaboración *f* de la cerveza

briar ['braɪə] *n* brezo *m*

bribe [braɪb] **1** *vt* sobornar
2 *n* soborno *m*

bribery ['braɪbərɪ] *n* soborno *m*

bric-a-brac ['brɪkəbræk] *n* baratijas *fpl*

brick [brɪk] *n* ladrillo *m*; *Fam (reliable person)* persona *f* de confianza

bricklayer ['brɪkleɪə(r)] *n* albañil *m*

brickwork ['brɪkwɜːk] *n* ladrillos *mpl*

bridal ['braɪdəl] *adj* nupcial

bride [braɪd] *n* novia *f*; **the b. and groom** los novios

bridegroom ['braɪdgruːm] *n* novio *m*

bridesmaid ['braɪdzmeɪd] *n* dama *f* de honor

bridge¹ [brɪdʒ] **1** *n* puente *m*; *(of nose)* caballete *m*; *(of ship)* puente de mando
2 *vt* (**a**) *(river)* tender un puente sobre (**b**) *(gap)* llenar; *Fin* **bridging loan** crédito *m* a corto plazo

bridge² [brɪdʒ] *n Cards* bridge *m*

bridle ['braɪdəl] **1** *n* brida *f*; *(bit)* freno *m*; **b. path** camino *m* de herradura
2 *vt (horse)* embridar

brief [briːf] **1** *adj* (**a**) *(short)* breve (**b**) *(concise)* conciso(a)
2 *n* (**a**) *(report)* informe *m*; **in b.** en resumen (**b**) *Jur* expediente *m* (**c**) *Mil* instrucciones *fpl* (**d**) **briefs** *(for men)* calzoncillos *mpl*; *(for women)* bragas *fpl*
3 *vt* (**a**) *(inform)* informar (**b**) *(instruct)* dar instrucciones a

briefcase ['briːfkeɪs] *n* cartera *f*, portafolios *m inv*

briefing ['briːfɪŋ] *n (meeting)* reunión informativa

briefly ['briːflɪ] *adv* brevemente; **as b. as possible** con la mayor brevedad (posible)

brigade [brɪ'geɪd] *n* brigada *f*

brigadier [brɪgə'dɪə(r)] *n* general *m* de brigada

bright [braɪt] *adj* (a) *(light, sun, eyes)* brillante; *(colour)* vivo(a); *(day)* claro(a) (b) *(cheerful)* alegre; **to look on the b. side** mirar el lado bueno (c) *(clever)* listo(a), espabilado(a) (d) *(promising)* prometedor(a)

brighten ['braɪtən] *vi (prospects)* mejorarse; *(face)* iluminarse
▸ **brighten up** 1 *vt sep (room etc)* alegrar
2 *vi (weather)* despejarse; *(person)* animarse

brightly ['braɪtlɪ] *adv* brillantemente

brightness ['braɪtnɪs] *n* (a) *(of sun)* resplandor *m*; *(of day)* claridad *f*; *(of colour)* viveza *f* (b) *(cleverness)* inteligencia *f*

brilliance ['brɪljəns] *n* (a) *(of light)* brillo *m*; *(of colour)* viveza *f* (b) *(of person)* brillantez *f*

brilliant ['brɪljənt] 1 *adj* brillante; *(idea)* genial; *Fam (very good)* estupendo(a)
2 *n* brillante *m*

brim [brɪm] 1 *n* borde *m*; *(of hat)* ala *f*; **full to the b.** lleno hasta el borde
2 *vi* rebosar (**with** de)
▸ **brim over** *vi* rebosar

brine [braɪn] *n* salmuera *f*

bring [brɪŋ] *vt (pt & pp* **brought**) (a) *(carry, take)* traer; **could you b. that book?** ¿podrías traerme el libro? (b) *(take to a different position)* llevar; **the war brought hunger to many homes** la guerra llevó el hambre a muchos hogares (c) *(cause)* provocar; **he brought it upon himself** se lo buscó (d) *(persuade)* convencer; **how did they b. themselves to do it?** ¿cómo llegaron a hacerlo? (e) *(lead)* llevar (f) **to b. an action against** acusar
▸ **bring about** *vt sep* provocar
▸ **bring along** *vt sep* traer
▸ **bring back** *vt sep* (a) *(return)* devolver (b) *(reintroduce)* volver a introducir (c) *(make one remember)* traerle a la memoria
▸ **bring down** *vt sep* (a) *(from upstairs)* bajar (b) *(government)* derribar; *Th* **to b. the house down** echar el teatro abajo con los aplausos (c) *(reduce)* rebajar
▸ **bring forward** *vt sep* (a) *(meeting etc)* adelantar (b) *(present)* presentar (c) *Fin* **brought forward** suma y sigue

▸ **bring in** *vt sep* (a) *(yield)* dar (b) *(show in)* hacer entrar (c) *(law etc)* introducir; *(fashion)* lanzar
▸ **bring off** *vt sep* lograr, conseguir
▸ **bring on** *vt sep* provocar
▸ **bring out** *vt sep* (a) *(publish)* publicar (b) *(reveal)* recalcar; **he brings out the worst in me** despierta lo peor que hay en mí
▸ **bring round** *vt sep* (a) *(revive)* hacer volver en sí (b) *(persuade)* convencer
▸ **bring to** *vt sep* reanimar
▸ **bring up** *vt sep* (a) *(educate)* criar, educar (b) *(subject)* plantear (c) *(vomit)* devolver

brink [brɪŋk] *n (edge)* borde *m*; *Fig* **on the b. of ruin** al borde de la ruina; **on the b. of tears** a punto de llorar

brisk [brɪsk] *adj* enérgico(a); *(pace)* rápido(a); *(trade)* activo(a); *(weather)* fresco(a)

bristle ['brɪsəl] 1 *n* cerda *f*
2 *vi* erizarse (b) *(show anger)* enfurecer (**at** con)
▸ **bristle with** *vt insep (be full of)* estar lleno(a) de

Brit [brɪt] *n Fam* británico(a) *m,f*

Britain ['brɪtən] *n* **(Great) B.** Gran Bretaña

British ['brɪtɪʃ] 1 *adj* británico(a); **the B. Isles** las Islas Británicas
2 *npl* **the B.** los británicos

brittle ['brɪtəl] *adj* quebradizo(a), frágil

broach [brəʊtʃ] *vt (subject)* abordar

broad [brɔːd] 1 *adj* (a) *(wide)* ancho(a); *(large)* extenso(a) (b) **a b. hint** *(clear)* una indirecta clara (c) *(daylight)* pleno(a) (d) *(not detailed)* general (e) *(accent)* marcado(a), cerrado(a)
2 *n US Fam (woman)* tía *f*, chica *f*

broadcast ['brɔːdkɑːst] *Rad & TV* 1 *n* emisión *f*
2 *vt (pt & pp* **broadcast**) emitir, transmitir

broadcaster ['brɔːdkɑːstə(r)] *n* locutor(a) *m,f*

broadcasting ['brɔːdkɑːstɪŋ] *n Rad* radiodifusión *f*; *TV* transmisión *f*; *Rad* **b. station** emisora *f*

broaden ['brɔːdən] *vt* ensanchar

broadly ['brɔːdlɪ] *adv* en términos generales

broad-minded [brɔːd'maɪndɪd] *adj* liberal, tolerante

broadsheet ['brɔːdʃiːt] *n* folleto *m*

broccoli ['brɒkəlɪ] *n* brécol *m*

brochure ['brəʊʃə(r), 'brəʊʃjʊə(r)] *n* folleto *m*

broil [brɔɪl] *vt US* asar a la parrilla

broiler ['brɔɪlə(r)] *n* (**a**) *(chicken)* pollo *m* (tomatero) (**b**) *US (grill)* parrilla *f*

broke [brəʊk] **1** *adj Fam* **to be (flat) b.** estar sin blanca
2 *pt of* **break**

broken ['brəʊkən] **1** *adj* (**a**) roto(a); *(machinery)* averiado(a); *(leg)* fracturado(a) (**b**) *(home)* deshecho(a); *(person)* destrozado(a); *(ground)* accidentado(a); **to speak b. English** chapurrear el inglés
2 *pp of* **break**

broken-hearted [brəʊkən'hɑːtɪd] *adj Fig* con el corazón destrozado

broker ['brəʊkə(r)] *n* corredor *m*, agente *mf* de Bolsa

brolly ['brɒlɪ] *n Fam* paraguas *m inv*

bronchitis [brɒŋ'kaɪtɪs] *n* bronquitis *f*

bronze [brɒnz] **1** *n* bronce *m*
2 *adj (material)* de bronce; *(colour)* bronceado(a)

bronzed [brɒnzd] *adj (suntanned)* bronceado(a)

brooch [brəʊtʃ] *n* broche *m*

brood [bruːd] **1** *n (birds)* cría *f; Hum (children)* prole *m*
2 *vi (hen)* empollar; *Fig (ponder)* rumiar; *Fig* **to b. over a problem** darle vueltas a un problema

broody ['bruːdɪ] *adj* (**a**) *Fam (woman)* con ganas de tener hijos (**b**) *(pensive)* pensativo(a) (**c**) *(moody)* melancólico(a)

brook¹ [brʊk] *n* arroyo *m*

brook² [brʊk] *vt (usu in negative)* soportar, aguantar

broom [bruːm] *n* (**a**) escoba *f* (**b**) *Bot* retama *f*

broomstick ['bruːmstɪk] *n* palo *m* de escoba

Bros *Com (abbr* **Brothers)** Hnos

broth [brɒθ] *n* caldo *m*

brothel ['brɒθəl] *n* burdel *m*

brother ['brʌðə(r)] *n* hermano *m*; **brothers and sisters** hermanos

brotherhood ['brʌðəhʊd] *n* hermandad *f*

brother-in-law ['brʌðərɪnlɔː] *n* cuñado *m*

brotherly ['brʌðəlɪ] *adj* fraternal

brought [brɔːt] *pt & pp of* **bring**

brow [braʊ] *n* (**a**) *(forehead)* frente *f* (**b**) *(eyebrow)* ceja *f* (**c**) *(of hill)* cima *f*

brown [braʊn] **1** *adj* (**a**) marrón *m*; *(hair, eyes)* castaño(a); **b. bread** pan *m* integral; **b. paper** papel *m* de estraza; **b. sugar** azúcar moreno (**b**) *(tanned)* moreno(a)
2 *n* marrón *m*
3 *vt Culin* dorar; *(tan)* broncear

Brownie ['braʊnɪ] *n* niña exploradora

brownish ['braʊnɪʃ] *adj* pardusco(a)

browse [braʊz] **1** *vi (in shop)* mirar; *(through book)* hojear
2 *vt Comput* **to b. the Web** navegar por la Web
3 *n* **to have a b. (in)** dar un vistazo (a)

browser ['braʊzə(r)] *n Comput* navegador *m*

bruise [bruːz] **1** *n* morado *m*, cardenal *m*
2 *vt (body)* contusionar; *(fruit)* estropear
3 *vi (body)* magullarse; *(fruit)* estropearse

brunch [brʌntʃ] *n* = combinación de desayuno y almuerzo

brunette [bruː'net] *adj & n* morena *(f)*

brunt [brʌnt] *n* **the b.** lo peor; **to bear the b.** llevar el peso

brush¹ [brʌʃ] **1** *n* (**a**) *(for hair, teeth)* cepillo *m*; *Art* pincel *m*; *(for house-painting)* brocha *f* (**b**) *(with the law)* roce *m*
2 *vt* (**a**) cepillar; **to b. one's hair** cepillarse el pelo; **to b. one's teeth** cepillarse los dientes; *(touch lightly)* rozar
3 *vi* **to b. against** rozar al pasar
► **brush aside** *vt sep* dejar de lado
► **brush off** *vt sep* ignorar
► **brush up** *vt sep* repasar

brush² [brʌʃ] *n (undergrowth)* broza *f*, maleza *f*

brushwood ['brʌʃwʊd] *n* maleza *f*

brusque [bruːsk, brʊsk] *adj* brusco(a); *(words)* áspero(a)

Brussels ['brʌsəlz] *n* Bruselas

brutal ['bruːtəl] *adj* brutal, cruel

brute [bruːt] **1** *adj* bruto(a); **b. force** fuerza bruta
2 *n (animal)* bruto *m*; *(person)* bestia *f*

BSc [biːes'siː] *n (abbr* **Bachelor of Science)** *(person)* licenciado(a) *m,f* en Ciencias

bubble ['bʌbəl] **1** *n* burbuja *f*; **b. bath** espuma *f* de baño; **b. gum** chicle *m*; **soap b.** pompa *f* de jabón
2 *vi* burbujear; *Culin* borbotear

bubbly ['bʌblɪ] **1** *adj* (**bubblier, bubbliest**) efervescente
2 *n Fam* champán *m*, cava *m*

buck¹ [bʌk] **1** *n Zool* macho *m*; *(male deer)* ciervo *m*; *(male goat)* macho cabrío; *Fam* **to pass the b. to sb** echarle el muerto a algn
2 *vi (horse)* corcovear
► **buck up 1** *vt sep Fam* **b. your ideas up!** ¡espabílate!
2 *vi (cheer up)* animarse

buck² [bʌk] *n US Fam* dólar *m*

bucket ['bʌkɪt] **1** n cubo m; Fam **it rained buckets** llovía a cántaros
2 vi Fam (rain) llover a cántaros

buckle ['bʌkəl] **1** n hebilla f
2 vt abrochar con hebilla
3 vi **(a)** (wall, metal) combarse **(b)** (knees) doblarse

bud [bʌd] **1** n (shoot) brote m; (flower) capullo m
2 vi brotar; Fig florecer

Buddhism ['bʊdɪzəm] n budismo m

budding ['bʌdɪŋ] adj en ciernes

buddy ['bʌdɪ] n US Fam amigote m, compinche m

budge [bʌdʒ] vi **(a)** (move) moverse **(b)** (yield) ceder

budgerigar ['bʌdʒərɪgɑː(r)] n periquito m

budget ['bʌdʒɪt] **1** n presupuesto m; Br Pol **the B.** ≃ los Presupuestos Generales del Estado
2 vi hacer un presupuesto (**for** para)

budgie ['bʌdʒɪ] n Fam = **budgerigar**

buff¹ [bʌf] **1** adj & n (colour) color (m) de ante
2 vt dar brillo a

buff² [bʌf] n Fam (enthusiast) aficionado(a) m,f

buffalo ['bʌfələʊ] n (pl buffaloes or buffalo) búfalo m

buffer ['bʌfə(r)] **1** n **(a)** (device) amortiguador m; Rail tope m; **b. zone** zona f de seguridad **(b)** Comput memoria intermedia
2 vt amortiguar

buffet¹ ['bʊfeɪ] n **(a)** (snack bar) bar m; (at railway station) cantina f; Rail **b. car** coche m restaurante **(b)** (self-service meal) bufet m libre **(c)** (item of furniture) aparador m

buffet² ['bʌfɪt] vt golpear

buffoon [bə'fuːn] n bufón m, payaso m

bug [bʌg] **1** n **(a)** (insect) bicho m **(b)** Fam (microbe) microbio m; **the flu b.** el virus de la gripe **(c)** (hidden microphone) micrófono oculto **(d)** Comput error m
2 vt Fam **(a)** **to b. a room** ocultar micrófonos en una habitación; **to b. a phone** pinchar un teléfono **(b)** (annoy) fastidiar, molestar

bugger ['bʌgə(r)] **1** n **(a)** sodomita m **(b)** very Fam Pej (person) gilipollas mf inv; (thing) coñazo m; **poor b.!** ¡el pobre!
2 interj very Fam Pej ¡joder!
3 vt sodomizar
▸ **bugger about** very Fam **1** vi hacer chorradas
2 vt sep **they really buggered him about**

se las hicieron pasar canutas
▸ **bugger off** vi very Fam Pej pirarse; **b. off!** ¡vete a la mierda!
▸ **bugger up** vt sep very Fam jorobar

buggy ['bʌgɪ] n **(a)** Br (baby's pushchair) cochecito m de niño **(b)** US (pram) cochecito m (de niño)

bugle ['bjuːgəl] n bugle m

build [bɪld] **1** vt (pt & pp built) construir
2 n (physique) tipo m, físico m
▸ **build up** vt sep (accumulate) acumular; **to b. up a reputation** labrarse una buena reputación

builder ['bɪldə(r)] n constructor(a) m,f; (contractor) contratista mf

building ['bɪldɪŋ] n edificio m, construcción f; **b. site** obra f; **b. society** sociedad hipotecaria

build-up ['bɪldʌp] n **(a)** (accumulation) aumento m; (of gas) acumulación f **(b)** (publicity) propaganda f

built [bɪlt] pt & pp of **build**

built-in ['bɪlt'ɪn] adj **(a)** (cupboard) empotrado(a) **(b)** (incorporated) incorporado(a)

built-up [bɪlt'ʌp] adj urbanizado(a)

bulb [bʌlb] n **(a)** Bot bulbo m **(b)** (light bulb) bombilla f

Bulgaria [bʌl'geərɪə] n Bulgaria

Bulgarian [bʌl'geərɪən] **1** adj búlgaro(a)
2 n **(a)** (person) búlgaro(a) m,f **(b)** (language) búlgaro m

bulge [bʌldʒ] **1** n protuberancia f; (in pocket) bulto m
2 vi (swell) hincharse; (be full) estar repleto(a)

bulk [bʌlk] n **(a)** (mass) masa f, volumen m; Com **in b.** a granel; **to buy sth in b.** comprar algo al por mayor **(b)** (greater part) mayor parte f

bulky ['bʌlkɪ] adj (bulkier, bulkiest) **(a)** (large) voluminoso(a) **(b)** **this crate is rather b.** esta caja es un armatoste

bull [bʊl] n **(a)** toro m; Fig **to take the b. by the horns** coger al toro por los cuernos **(b)** Fin **b. market** mercado m al alza

bulldog ['bʊldɒg] n bulldog m

bulldoze ['bʊldəʊz] vt (land) nivelar; (building) derribar

bulldozer ['bʊldəʊzə(r)] n bulldozer m

bullet ['bʊlɪt] n bala f; **b. wound** balazo m

bulletin ['bʊlɪtɪn] n boletín m; Rad & TV **news b.** boletín de noticias; US **b. board** tablón m de anuncios

bullet-proof ['bʊlɪtpruːf] adj a prueba de balas; **b. vest** chaleco m antibalas

bullfight ['bʊlfaɪt] n corrida f de toros

bullfighter ['bʊlfaɪtə(r)] n torero(a) m,f

bullfighting ['bʊlfaɪtɪŋ] *n* los toros *mpl*; *(art)* tauromaquia *f*

bullion ['bʊljən] *n (gold, silver)* lingote *m*

bullish ['bʊlɪʃ] *adj Fin (market)* en alza

bullock ['bʊlək] *n* buey *m*

bullring ['bʊlrɪŋ] *n* plaza *f* de toros

bull's-eye ['bʊlzaɪ] *n (of target)* blanco *m*

bully ['bʊlɪ] **1** *n* matón *m*

2 *vt (terrorize)* intimidar; *(bulldoze)* tiranizar

3 *interj Ironic* b. for you! ¡bravo!

bulwark ['bʊlwək] *n* baluarte *m*

bum¹ [bʌm] *n Fam (bottom)* culo *m*

bum² [bʌm] *Fam* **1** *n* **(a)** *US (tramp)* vagabundo *m* **(b)** *(idler)* holgazán(ana) *m,f*

2 *vi* gorronear

▶ **bum around** *vi Fam* vaguear

bumblebee ['bʌmbəlbi:] *n* abejorro *m*

bumbling ['bʌmblɪŋ] *adj* torpe

bump [bʌmp] **1** *n* **(a)** *(swelling)* chichón *m*; *(lump)* abolladura *f*; *(on road)* bache *m* **(b)** *(blow)* choque *m*, golpe *m* **(c)** *(jolt)* sacudida *f*

2 *vt* golpear; **to b. one's head** darse un golpe en la cabeza

3 *vi* chocar (**into** contra)

▶ **bump into** *vt insep (meet)* tropezar con

▶ **bump off** *vt sep Fam* liquidar

bumper ['bʌmpə(r)] **1** *adj* abundante; **b. edition** edición *f* especial

2 *n Aut* parachoques *m inv*

bumptious ['bʌmpʃəs] *adj* presuntuoso(a), engreído(a)

bumpy ['bʌmpɪ] *adj* (**bumpier, bumpiest**) con muchos baches

bun [bʌn] *n* **(a)** *(bread)* panecillo *m*; *(sweet)* bollo *m*; *Fig Euph* **she's got a b. in the oven** está preñada **(b)** *(of hair)* moño *m*

bunch [bʌntʃ] **1** *n (of keys)* manojo *m*; *(of flowers)* ramo *m*; *(of grapes)* racimo *m*; *(of people)* grupo *m*; *(gang)* pandilla *f*

2 *vi* **to b. together** juntarse, agruparse

bundle ['bʌndəl] **1** *n (of clothes)* bulto *m*, fardo *m*; *(of papers)* fajo *m*; *(of wood)* haz *m*

2 *vt* **(a)** *(make a bundle of)* liar, atar **(b)** *(push)* empujar

bung [bʌŋ] **1** *n* tapón *m*

2 *vt Fam* **(a)** *(throw)* arrojar **(b)** *(put)* meter

▶ **bung up** *vt sep Fam* atascar

bungalow ['bʌŋɡələʊ] *n* chalé *m*, bungalow *m*

bungle ['bʌŋɡəl] *vt* chapucear

bunion ['bʌnjən] *n* juanete *m*

bunk [bʌŋk] *n (bed)* litera *f*

bunker ['bʌŋkə(r)] *n* **(a)** *(coal)* carbonera *f* **(b)** *Mil* búnker *m* **(c)** *(in golf)* búnker *m*

bunny ['bʌnɪ] *n Fam (baby talk)* **b. (rabbit)** conejito *m*

bunting ['bʌntɪŋ] *n (material)* lanilla *f*; *(flags)* banderines *mpl*; *Naut* empavesada *f*

buoy [bɔɪ] *n* boya *f*

▶ **buoy up** *vt sep* **(a)** *(keep afloat)* mantener a flote **(b)** *(person, spirits)* alentar, animar

buoyancy ['bɔɪənsɪ] *n* **(a)** *(of object)* flotabilidad *f* **(b)** *Fin* tendencia *f* alcista **(c)** *(optimism)* optimismo *m*

buoyant ['bɔɪənt] *adj* **(a)** *(object)* flotante **(b)** *Fin* con tendencia alcista **(c)** *(optimistic)* optimista

burble ['bɜːbl] *vi* **(a)** *(stream)* murmurar; *(baby)* balbucear **(b)** *(talk quickly)* farfullar

burden ['bɜːdən] **1** *n* carga *f*; *Fig* **to be a b. to sb** ser una carga para algn

2 *vt* cargar (**with** con)

bureau ['bjʊərəʊ] *n (pl* **bureaux)** **(a)** *(desk)* escritorio *m* **(b)** *(office)* agencia *f*, oficina *f* **(c)** *US (chest of drawers)* cómoda *f* **(d)** *US Pol* departamento *m* del Estado

bureaucracy [bjʊə'rɒkrəsɪ] *n* burocracia *f*

bureaucrat ['bjʊərəkræt] *n* burócrata *mf*

bureaucratic [bjʊərə'krætɪk] *adj* burocrático(a)

burgeon ['bɜːdʒən] *vi* florecer

burger ['bɜːɡə(r)] *n Fam (hamburger)* hamburguesa *f*

burglar ['bɜːɡlə(r)] *n* ladrón(ona) *m,f*; **b. alarm** alarma *f* antirrobo

burglarize ['bɜːɡləraɪz] *vt US* robar, desvalijar

burglary ['bɜːɡlərɪ] *n* robo *m* con allanamiento de morada

burgle ['bɜːɡəl] *vt* robar, desvalijar

burial ['berɪəl] *n* entierro *m*

burly ['bɜːlɪ] *adj* (**burlier, burliest**) fornido(a), fuerte

Burma ['bɜːmə] *n* Birmania

Burmese [bɜː'miːz] **1** *adj* birmano(a)

2 *n* **(a)** *(person)* birmano(a) *m,f* **(b)** *(language)* birmano *m*

burn [bɜːn] **1** *n* quemadura *f*

2 *vt (pt & pp* **burnt** *or* **burned)** quemar

3 *vi* **(a)** *(fire)* arder; *(building, food)* quemarse **(b)** *(lamp)* estar encendido(a) **(c)** *(sore)* escocer

▶ **burn down 1** *vt sep* incendiar

2 *vi* incendiarse

▶ **burn out** *vi (people)* quemarse

▸ **burn up** vt sep (energy, calories) quemar

burner ['bɜːnə(r)] n quemador m

burning ['bɜːnɪŋ] adj (a) (on fire) incendiado(a); (hot) abrasador(a) (b) (passionate) ardiente (c) a b. question una cuestión candente

burnt [bɜːnt] **1** adj quemado(a); b. almonds almendras tostadas
2 pt & pp of **burn**

burp [bɜːp] **1** n eructo m
2 vi eructar

burrow ['bʌrəʊ] **1** n madriguera f; (for rabbits) conejera f
2 vi (a) hacer una madriguera (b) (search) hurgar

bursar ['bɜːsə(r)] n tesorero(a) m,f

bursary ['bɜːsərɪ] n beca f

burst [bɜːst] **1** n (a) (explosion) estallido m; (of tyre) reventón m (b) (of applause) arranque m; (rage) arrebato m; b. of gunfire ráfaga f de tiros; b. of laughter carcajadas fpl
2 vt (pt & pp burst) (balloon) reventar; Fig the river b. its banks el río se salió de madre
3 vi (a) reventarse; (shell) estallar (b) (enter suddenly) irrumpir (into en)
▸ **burst into** vt insep to b. into laughter/tears echarse a reír/allorar
▸ **burst open** vi abrirse violentamente
▸ **burst out** vi to b. out laughing echarse a reír

bursting ['bɜːstɪŋ] adj the bar was b. with people el bar estaba atestado de gente; Fam to be b. to do sth reventar por hacer algo

bury ['berɪ] vt (a) enterrar; to be buried in thought estar absorto en pensamientos (b) (hide) ocultar

bus [bʌs] n (pl buses, US busses) autobús m, Andes, CAm, Ven buseta f, Arg colectivo m, CAm, Méx camión m, Chile micro m, Cuba guagua f, Urug ómnibus m; b. conductor revisor m; (driver conductor(a) m,f; b. stop parada f de autobús

bush [bʊʃ] n (a) (shrub) arbusto m (b) Austral the b. el monte; Fam b. telegraph radio f macuto

bushy ['bʊʃɪ] adj espeso(a), tupido(a)

business ['bɪznɪs] n (a) (commerce) negocios mpl; how's b.? ¿cómo andan los negocios?; to be away on b. estar en viaje de negocios; b. deal negocio m; b. hours horas fpl de oficina; b. trip viaje m de negocios (b) (firm) empresa f (c) (matter) asunto m; I mean b. estoy hablando en serio; it's no b. of mine no es asunto mío; to make it one's b. to ...

encargarse de ...; to get down to b. ir al grano; to go about one's b. ocuparse de sus asuntos

businesslike ['bɪznɪslaɪk] adj (practical) eficiente; (methodical) metódico(a); (serious) serio(a)

businessman ['bɪznɪsmən] n hombre m de negocios

businesswoman ['bɪznɪswʊmən] n mujer f de negocios

busker ['bʌskə(r)] n Fam músico(a) m,f callejero(a)

bust[1] [bʌst] n (a) (of woman) pecho m (b) Art busto m

bust[2] [bʌst] Fam **1** vt (a) estropear (b) (person) trincar; (place) hacer una redada en
2 adj (a) (damaged) estropeado(a) (b) to go b. (bankrupt) quebrar

bustle ['bʌsəl] **1** n (activity, noise) bullicio m
2 vi to b. about ir y venir

bustling ['bʌslɪŋ] adj bullicioso(a)

bust-up ['bʌstʌp] n Fam riña f, pelea f

busy ['bɪzɪ] **1** adj (a) ocupado(a), atareado(a); (life) ajetreado(a); (street) concurrido(a) (b) esp US Tel ocupado(a); b. signal señal f de comunicando
2 vt to b. oneself doing sth ocuparse haciendo algo

busybody ['bɪzɪbɒdɪ] n entrometido(a) m,f

but [bʌt] **1** conj (a) pero; b. yet a pesar de todo (b) (after negative) sino; not two b. three no dos sino tres; she's not Spanish b. Portuguese no es española sino portuguesa
2 adv had we b. known de haberlo sabido; we can b. try al menos podemos intentarlo; b. for her we would have drowned si no hubiera sido por ella, nos habríamos ahogado
3 prep salvo, menos; everyone b. her todos menos ella; he's anything b. handsome es todo menos guapo
4 npl ifs and buts pegas fpl

butane ['bjuːteɪn] n butano m; b. gas gas butano

butcher ['bʊtʃə(r)] **1** n carnicero(a) m,f; b.'s (shop) carnicería f
2 vt (animals) matar; (people) masacrar

butler ['bʌtlə(r)] n mayordomo m

butt[1] [bʌt] n (a) (end) extremo m; (of rifle) culata f; (of cigarette) colilla f (b) he was the b. of all the jokes era el blanco de todas las bromas (c) US Fam (bottom) culo m

butt[2] [bʌt] **1** n (with head) cabezazo m

2 *vt (strike with head)* dar un cabezazo a
▶ **butt in** *vi* entrar en la conversación
butt³ [bʌt] *n (barrel)* tonel *m*
butter ['bʌtə(r)] **1** *n* mantequilla *f*, *Am*
manteca *f*; **b. dish** mantequera *f*
2 *vt* untar con mantequilla *or Am* manteca
buttercup ['bʌtəkʌp] *n* ranúnculo *m*,
botón *m* de oro
butterfingers ['bʌtəfɪŋgəz] *n sing Fam*
manazas *mf inv*
butterfly ['bʌtəflaɪ] *n* mariposa *f*
buttock ['bʌtək] *n* nalga *f*; **buttocks** nalgas *fpl*
button ['bʌtən] **1** *n* (a) *(on clothes, machine)* botón *m* (b) *US (badge)* chapa *f*
2 *vt* **to b. (up)** abrochar(se), aboto-
nar(se)
buttonhole ['bʌtənhəʊl] *n* ojal *m*
buttress ['bʌtrɪs] **1** *n* (a) contrafuerte *m*
(b) *(support)* apoyo *m*
2 *vt* apuntalar; *Fig* reforzar, apoyar
buxom ['bʌksəm] *adj (woman)* pechu-
gona
buy [baɪ] **1** *n* compra *f*; **a good b.** una
ganga
2 *vt (pt & pp bought)* (a) comprar; **she
bought that car from a neighbour**
compró ese coche a un vecino (b) *Fam
(believe)* tragar
▶ **buy off** *vt sep* sobornar
▶ **buy out** *vt sep* adquirir la parte de
▶ **buy up** *vt sep* comprar en grandes cantidades
buyer ['baɪə(r)] *n* comprador(a) *m,f*
buzz [bʌz] **1** *n* (a) *(of bee)* zumbido *m*; *(of
conversation)* rumor *m* (b) *Fam (tele-
phone call)* telefonazo *m*
2 *vi* zumbar
buzzer ['bʌzə(r)] *n* timbre *m*
by [baɪ] **1** *prep* (a) *(indicating agent)* por;
composed by Bach compuesto(a) por
Bach; **a film by Almodóvar** una película
de Almodóvar
(b) *(via)* por; **he left by the back door**
salió por la puerta trasera
(c) *(manner)* por; **by car/train** en coche/
tren; **by credit card** con tarjeta de crédito;
by chance por casualidad; **by oneself**
solo(a); **made by hand** hecho(a) a mano;
**you can obtain a ticket by filling in the
coupon** puede conseguir una entrada
llenando el cupón
(d) *(amount)* por; **little by little** poco a
poco; **they are sold by the dozen** se

venden por docenas; **to be paid by the
hour** cobrar por horas
(e) *(by far)* con mucho; **he won by a foot**
ganó por un pie
(f) *(beside)* al lado de, junto a; **side by
side** juntos
(g) **to walk by a building** *(pass)* pasar
por delante de un edificio
(h) *(time)* para; **by now** ya; **by then** para
entonces; **we have to be there by nine**
tenemos que estar allí para las nueve; **by
the time we arrive** (para) cuando lleguemos; **by this time next year** el año que
viene por estas fechas
(i) *(during)* de; **by day/night** de día/
noche
(j) *(in an oath)* por; **by God!** ¡por Dios!
(k) *Math* por
(l) *(according to)* según; **is that O.K. by
you?** ¿te viene bien?
(m) **he had two children by his first
wife** tuvo dos hijos con su primera esposa
(n) *(phrases)* **bit by bit** poco a poco; **day
by day** día a día; **what do you mean by
that?** ¿qué quieres decir con eso?; **by the
way** a propósito
2 *adv* (a) **to go by** *(past)* pasar; **she just
walked by** pasó de largo
(b) **by and by** con el tiempo; **by and
large** en conjunto
bye [baɪ] **1** *n* **by the b.** por cierto
2 *interj Fam* ¡hasta luego!
bye-bye ['baɪbaɪ] *interj Fam* ¡adiós!,
¡hasta luego!
by-election ['baɪɪlekʃən] *n* elección *f*
parcial
bygone ['baɪgɒn] **1** *adj* pasado(a)
2 *npl* **let bygones be bygones** lo pasado
pasado está
by-law ['baɪlɔː] *n* ley *f* municipal
bypass ['baɪpɑːs] **1** *n* (a) *(road)* carretera
f de circunvalación (b) *Med* **b. surgery**
cirugía *f* de by-pass
2 *vt* evitar
by-product ['baɪprɒdʌkt] *n Chem & Ind*
derivado *m*, subproducto *m*; *Fig* consecuencia *f*
byroad ['baɪrəʊd] *n* carretera secundaria
bystander ['baɪstændə(r)] *n* testigo *mf*
byte [baɪt] *n Comput* byte *m*, octeto *m*
byword ['baɪwɜːd] *n* **it became a b. for
modernity** se convirtió en sinónimo de
modernidad

C

C, c [si:] n (a) (the letter) C, c f (b) Mus **C** do m

C (a) (abbr **Celsius**) C (b) (abbr **centigrade**) C

cab [kæb] n US taxi m; **c. driver** taxista mf

cabaret ['kæbəreɪ] n cabaret m

cabbage ['kæbɪdʒ] n col f, berza f; **red c.** (col) lombarda f

cabin ['kæbɪn] n (a) (hut) choza f; **log c.** cabaña f (b) Naut camarote m (c) (of lorry, plane) cabina f

cabinet ['kæbɪnɪt] n (a) (item of furniture) armario m; (glass-fronted) vitrina f; **c. maker** ebanista mf (b) Pol gabinete m, consejo m de ministros

cable ['keɪbəl] **1** n cable m; **c. car** teleférico m; **c. company** cableoperador(a) m,f; **c. TV** televisión f por cable

2 vt & vi cablegrafiar, telegrafiar

caboose [kə'bu:s] n US (on train) furgón m de cola

cache [kæʃ] n (a) (place) alijo m (b) Comput caché f

cackle ['kækəl] vi cacarear

cactus ['kæktəs] n (pl **cacti** ['kæktaɪ]) cactus m

CAD [kæd] n (abbr **computer-aided or -assisted design**) CAD m

cad [kæd] n Br Fam canalla m

caddie ['kædɪ] n (in golf) cadi m

cadet [kə'det] n Mil cadete m

cadge [kædʒ] vt & vi Fam gorronear

Caesarean [siː'zeərɪən] n Med **she had a C.** le hicieron una cesárea; **C. section** operación f cesárea

café ['kæfeɪ], **cafeteria** [kæfɪ'tɪərɪə] n cafetería f

caffeine ['kæfiːn] n cafeína f

cage [keɪdʒ] **1** n jaula f

2 vt enjaular

cagey ['keɪdʒɪ] adj (**cagier, cagiest**) Fam reservado(a)

cagoule [kə'guːl] n (garment) canguro m

Cairo ['kaɪrəʊ] n (el) Cairo

cajole [kə'dʒəʊl] vt engatusar

cake [keɪk] **1** n (a) pastel m, tarta f; Fam Fig **it's a piece of c.** está chupado; **birthday c.** pastel de cumpleaños; **c. shop** pastelería f (b) (of soap) pastilla f

2 vi (mud) endurecerse

3 vt **caked with ...** cubierto(a) de ...

calamity [kə'læmɪtɪ] n calamidad f

calcium ['kælsɪəm] n calcio m

calculate ['kælkjʊleɪt] vt calcular

calculated ['kælkjʊleɪtɪd] adj intencionado(a)

calculating ['kælkjʊleɪtɪŋ] adj (a) **c. machine** calculadora f (b) Pej (person) calculador(a)

calculation [kælkjʊ'leɪʃən] n cálculo m

calculator ['kælkjʊleɪtə(r)] n calculadora f

calendar ['kælɪndə(r)] n calendario m; **c. year** año m civil

calf¹ [kɑːf] n (pl **calves**) (of cattle) becerro(a) m,f, ternero(a) m,f; (of other animals) cría f

calf² [kɑːf] n (pl **calves**) Anat pantorrilla f

calfskin ['kɑːfskɪn] n piel f de becerro

calibre, US caliber ['kælɪbə(r)] n calibre m

call [kɔːl] **1** vt (a) llamar; **to c. sb names** poner verde a algn; **what's he called?** ¿cómo se llama?

(b) (meeting etc) convocar; **to c. sth to mind** traer algo a la memoria

2 vi (a) llamar; Tel **who's calling?** ¿de parte de quién?

(b) **to c. at sb's (house)** pasar por casa de algn; **to c. for sth/sb** pasar a recoger algo/a algn

(c) (trains) parar

(d) **to c. for** (require) exigir; **that wasn't called for** eso no estaba justificado

3 n (a) llamada f, grito m

(b) (visit) visita f; **to pay a c. on sb** visitar a algn

(c) Tel (phone) **c.** llamada f, Am llamado m; **c. box** cabina telefónica; **c. centre** centro m de atención telefónica

(d) Med **to be on c.** estar de guardia

(e) **there's no c. for you to worry** no hay motivo para que te preocupes

▸ **call away** vt sep **to be called away on business** tener que ausentarse por motivos de trabajo

▸ **call back** vi (phone again) llamar otra vez; (visit again) volver

► **call in 1** *vt sep (doctor)* llamar
2 *vi* (**a**) **I'll c. in tomorrow** *(visit)* mañana me paso (**b**) *Naut* hacer escala (**at** en)
► **call off** *vt sep* suspender
► **call on** *vt insep* (**a**) visitar (**b**) **to c. on sb for support** recurrir a algn en busca de apoyo
► **call out 1** *vt sep* (**a**) *(shout)* gritar (**b**) *(doctor)* hacer venir; *(workers)* convocar a la huelga
2 *vi* gritar
► **call up** *vt sep* (**a**) *Tel* llamar (por teléfono) (**b**) *Mil* llamar a filas, reclutar
caller ['kɔːlə(r)] *n* visita *mf*; *Tel* persona *f* que llama
calling ['kɔːlɪŋ] *n esp Rel* llamada *f*, vocación *f*; *US* **c. card** tarjeta *f* de visita;
callous ['kæləs] *adj* insensible, duro(a)
call-up ['kɔːlʌp] *n* llamamiento *m* a filas
calm [kɑːm] **1** *adj* (**a**) *(weather, sea)* en calma (**b**) *(relaxed)* tranquilo(a); **keep c.!** ¡tranquila!
2 *n* (**a**) *(of weather, sea)* calma *f* (**b**) *(tranquillity)* tranquilidad *f*
3 *vt* calmar, tranquilizar
4 *vi* **to c. (down)** calmarse, tranquilizarse
Calor Gas® ['kæləgæs] *n* (gas *m*) butano *m*
calorie, calory ['kælərɪ] *n* caloría *f*
calve [kɑːv] *vi (cow)* parir (un becerro)
calves [kɑːvz] *pl of* **calf¹, calf²**
Cambodia [kæm'bəʊdɪə] *n* Camboya
came [keɪm] *pt of* **come**
camel ['kæməl] *n* camello(a) *m,f*
cameo ['kæmɪəʊ] *n* camafeo *m*
camera ['kæmərə] *n* (**a**) cámara *f or* máquina *f* fotográfica; *Cin & TV* cámara (**b**) *Jur* **in c.** a puerta cerrada
cameraman ['kæmərəmən] *n* cámara *m*
Cameroon [kæmə'ruːn] *n* Camerún
camomile ['kæməmaɪl] *n* camomila *f*; **c. tea** (infusión *f* de) manzanilla *f*
camouflage ['kæməflɑːʒ] **1** *n* camuflaje *m*
2 *vt* camuflar
camp¹ [kæmp] **1** *n* campamento *m*; **c. bed** cama *f* plegable; **c. site** camping *m*
2·vi **to go camping** ir de camping
camp² [kæmp] *adj Fam* afeminado(a); *(affected)* amanerado(a)
campaign [kæm'peɪn] **1** *n* campaña *f*
2 *vi* **to c. for/against** hacer campaña a favor de/en contra de
campaigner [kæm'peɪnə(r)] *n* defensor(a) *m,f* (**for** de)
camper ['kæmpə(r)] *n* (**a**) *(person)* campista *mf* (**b**) *US (vehicle)* caravana *f*

camping ['kæmpɪŋ] *n* **c. ground, c. site** camping *m*
campus ['kæmpəs] *n* campus *m*, ciudad universitaria
can¹ [kæn, *unstressed* kən] *v aux (pt* **could)**

El verbo **can** carece de infinitivo, de gerundio y de participio. En infinitivo o en participio, se empleará la forma correspondiente de **be able to**, por ejemplo: **he wanted to be able to speak English**; **she has always been able to swim**. En el inglés hablado, y en el escrito en estilo coloquial, la forma negativa **cannot** se transforma en **can't** y la forma negativa **could not** no se transforma en **couldn't**.

(**a**) *(be able to)* poder; **he could have come** podría haber venido; **I'll phone you as soon as I c.** te llamaré en cuanto pueda; **she can't do it** no puede hacerlo; **I can't understand why** no entiendo por qué (**b**) *(know how to)* saber; **c. you ski?** ¿sabes esquiar?; **I can't speak English** no sé hablar inglés (**c**) *(be permitted to)* poder; **he can't go out tonight** no le dejan salir esta noche (**d**) *(be possible)* poder; **she could have forgotten** puede (ser) que lo haya olvidado; **they can't be very poor** no deben ser muy pobres; **what c. it be?** ¿qué será?

can² [kæn] **1** *n* (**a**) *(of oil)* bidón *m* (**b**) *US (tin)* lata *f*, bote *m*; **c. opener** abrelatas *m inv*
2 *vt* (**a**) *(fish, fruit)* envasar, enlatar (**b**) *US Fam* desestimar
Canada ['kænədə] *n* Canadá
Canadian [kə'neɪdɪən] *adj & n* canadiense *(mf)*
canal [kə'næl] *n* canal *m*
canary [kə'neərɪ] *n* canario *m*
Canary Islands [kə'neərɪaɪləndz] *npl* (Islas *fpl*) Canarias *fpl*
cancel ['kænsəl] *vt (train, contract)* cancelar; *Com* anular; *(permission)* retirar; *(decree)* revocar
cancellation [kænsɪ'leɪʃən] *n* cancelación *f*; *Com* anulación *f*
cancer ['kænsə(r)] *n* (**a**) *Med* cáncer *m*; **breast c.** cáncer de mama; **c. research** cancerología *f* (**b**) **C.** *(in astrology)* Cáncer *m*
candelabra [kændɪ'lɑːbrə] *n* candelabro *m*
candid ['kændɪd] *adj* franco(a), sincero(a)

Note that the Spanish word **cándido** is a false friend and is never a translation for the English word **candid**. In Spanish, **cándido** means "ingenuous, naïve".

---

candidate ['kændɪdeɪt, 'kændɪdɪt] *n* candidato(a) *m,f*; *(in exam)* opositor(a) *m,f*

candle ['kændəl] *n* vela *f*; *(in church)* cirio *m*

candlelight ['kændəllaɪt] *n* luz *f* de vela; **by c.** a la luz de las velas

candlestick ['kændəlstɪk] *n* candelero *m*, palmatoria *f*; *(in church)* cirial *m*

candour, US **candor** ['kændə(r)] *n* sinceridad *f*, ranqueza *f*

📖 Note that the Spanish word **candor** is a false friend and is never a translation for the English word **candour**. In Spanish, **candor** means "innocence, naïvety".

---

candy ['kændɪ] *n* US caramelo *m*; **c. store** confitería *f*

candyfloss ['kændɪflɒs] *n* Br algodón *m* dulce

cane [keɪn] **1** *n* (a) *Bot* caña *f*; **c. sugar** azúcar *m* de caña (b) *(wicker)* mimbre *m* (c) *(walking stick)* bastón *m*; *(for punishment)* palmeta *f*
2 *vt* castigar con la palmeta

canine ['keɪnaɪn] *adj Zool* canino(a); **c. tooth** colmillo *m*

canister ['kænɪstə(r)] *n* bote *m*

canned [kænd] *adj* enlatado(a); **c. foods** conservas *fpl*

cannelloni [kænə'ləʊnɪ] *n* canelones *mpl*

cannibal ['kænɪbəl] *adj & n* caníbal *(mf)*

cannon ['kænən] **1** *n* (a) *(pl* **cannons** *or* **cannon)** cañón *m*; *Fig* **c. fodder** carne *f* de cañón (b) *Br (in billiards, snooker)* carambola *f*
2 *vi* chocar (**into** contra)

cannonball ['kænənbɔːl] *n* bala *f* de cañón

cannot ['kænɒt, kæ'nɒt] = **can not**

canoe [kə'nuː] *n* canoa *f*; *Sport* piragua *f*

canon ['kænən] *n Rel* canon *m*

canopy ['kænəpɪ] *n* (a) *(on throne)* dosel *m* (b) *(awning)* toldo *m*

can't [kɑːnt] = **can not**

Cantabria [kæn'tæbrɪə] *n* Cantabria *f*

cantankerous [kæn'tæŋkərəs] *adj* intratable

canteen [kæn'tiːn] *n* (a) *(restaurant)* cantina *f* (b) *(set of cutlery)* juego *m* de cubiertos (c) *(flask)* cantimplora *f*

canter ['kæntə(r)] **1** *n* medio galope
2 *vi* ir a medio galope

canvas ['kænvəs] *n* (a) *Tex* lona *f* (b) *(painting)* lienzo *m*

canvass ['kænvəs] *vi* (a) *Pol* hacer propaganda electoral (b) *Com* hacer promoción, buscar clientes

canvasser ['kænvəsə(r)] *n Pol* = persona que hace propaganda electoral de puerta en puerta

canyon ['kænjən] *n* cañón *m*; **the Grand C.** el Gran Cañón

canyoning ['kænjənɪŋ] *n Sport* barranquismo *m*

cap [kæp] **1** *n* (a) gorro *m*; *(soldier's)* gorra *f* (b) *Br Sport* **to win a c. for England** ser seleccionado(a) para el equipo de Inglaterra (c) *(of pen)* capuchón *m*; *(of bottle)* chapa *f*
2 *vt* (a) *(bottle)* poner la chapa a; *Fig* **to c. it all** para colmo (b) *Br Sport* seleccionar

capability [keɪpə'bɪlɪtɪ] *n* habilidad *f*

capable ['keɪpəbəl] *adj* (a) *(skilful)* hábil (b) *(able)* capaz (**of** de)

capacity [kə'pæsɪtɪ] *n* (a) capacidad *f* (b) *(position)* puesto *m*; **in her c. as manageress** en calidad de gerente

cape¹ [keɪp] *n (garment)* capa *f*

cape² [keɪp] *n Geog* cabo *m*, promontorio *m*; **C. Horn** Cabo de Hornos; **C. Town** Ciudad del Cabo; **C. Verde** Cabo Verde

caper ['keɪpə(r)] *n (prank)* travesura *f*

capital ['kæpɪtəl] **1** *n* (a) *(town)* capital *f* (b) *Fin* capital *m*; **c. expenditure** inversión *f* de capital (c) *(letter)* mayúscula *f*
2 *adj* (a) *(city)* capital (b) **c. punishment** pena *f* capital (c) *(primary)* primordial (d) **c. letter** mayúscula *f*

capitalism ['kæpɪtəlɪzəm] *n* capitalismo *m*

capitalist ['kæpɪtəlɪst] *adj & n* capitalista *(mf)*

capitalize ['kæpɪtəlaɪz] *vi Fin* capitalizar; *Fig* **to c. on sth** sacar provecho *or* beneficio de algo

capitulate [kə'pɪtjʊleɪt] *vi* capitular

cappuccino [kæpə'tʃiːnəʊ] *n* (café *m*) capuchino *m*

Capricorn ['kæprɪkɔːn] *n* Capricornio *m*

capsicum ['kæpsɪkəm] *n* pimiento *m*

capsize [kæp'saɪz] **1** *vt* hacer zozobrar
2 *vi* zozobrar

capsule ['kæpsjuːl] *n* cápsula *f*

captain ['kæptɪn] **1** *n* capitán *m*
2 *vt* capitanear

caption ['kæpʃən] *n (under picture)* leyenda *f*; *Cin* subtítulo *m*

captivating ['kæptɪveɪtɪŋ] *adj* seductor(a)

captive ['kæptɪv] **1** *n* cautivo(a) *m,f*
2 *adj* cautivo(a)

captivity [kæp'tɪvɪtɪ] *n* cautiverio *m*

capture ['kæptʃə(r)] **1** *vt* (a) capturar, apresar; *Mil (town)* tomar (b) *(market)* acaparar (**c**) *Fig (mood)* captar

  2 *n (of fugitive)* captura *f; (of town)* toma *f*

car [kɑ:(r)] *n* (**a**) *(vehicle)* coche *m, Andes, CAm, Carib, Méx* carro *m, RP* auto *m;* **c. ferry** transbordador *m* para coches; *Br* **c. park** parking *m,* aparcamiento *m;* **c. wash** túnel *m* de lavado (**b**) *US Rail* coche *m*

carafe [kəˈræf, kəˈrɑ:f] *n* garrafa *f*

caramel [ˈkærəməl] *n* azúcar *m* quemado; *(sweet)* caramelo *m*

carat [ˈkærət] *n* quilate *m*

caravan [ˈkærəvæn] *n* (**a**) *(vehicle)* remolque *m,* caravana *f* (**b**) *(in desert)* caravana *f*

carbohydrate [kɑ:bəˈhaɪdreɪt] *n* hidrato *m* de carbono, carbohidrato *m*

carbon [ˈkɑ:bən] *n* carbono *m;* **c. copy** copia *f* al papel carbón; *Fig* copia exacta; **c. dioxide** dióxido *m* de carbono; **c. paper** papel *m* carbón

carburettor [kɑ:bjʊˈretə(r)], *US* **carburetor** [ˈkɑ:rbəreɪtər] *n* carburador *m*

carcass [ˈkɑ:kəs] *n* res muerta

card [kɑ:d] *n* (**a**) *(card)* tarjeta *f; (of cardboard)* cartulina *f;* **birthday/Christmas c.** tarjeta de cumpleaños/de Navidad (**b**) *(in file)* ficha *f; (identity)* carnet *m;* **c. index** fichero *m* (**c**) **pack of cards** baraja *f,* cartas *fpl;* **(playing) c.** naipe *m,* carta *f; Fig Br* **on** *or US* **in the cards** previsto

cardboard [ˈkɑ:dbɔ:d] *n* cartón *m;* **c. box** caja *f* de cartón; **c. cutout** recortable *m*

cardiac [ˈkɑ:dɪæk] *adj* cardíaco(a); **c. arrest** paro cardíaco

cardigan [ˈkɑ:dɪɡən] *n* rebeca *f*

cardinal [ˈkɑ:dɪnəl] **1** *n Rel* cardenal *m*

  2 *adj* cardinal; **c. numbers** números *mpl* cardinales

care [keə(r)] **1** *vi (be concerned)* preocuparse (**about** por); **I don't c.** no me importa; *Fam* **for all I c.** me trae sin cuidado; *Fam* **he couldn't c. less** le importa un bledo

  2 *n* (**a**) *(attention, protection)* cuidado *m,* atención *f;* **c. of ...** *(on letter)* al cuidado de ...; **medical c.** asistencia *f* médica; **to take c. of** cuidar; *(business)* ocuparse de (**b**) *(carefulness)* cuidado *m;* **take c.** *(be careful)* ten cuidado; *(as farewell)* ¡cuídate! (**c**) *(worry)* preocupación *f*

  ▶ **care for** *vt insep* (**a**) *(look after)* cuidar (**b**) *(like)* gustar, interesar; **would you c. for a coffee?** ¿te apetece un café?

career [kəˈrɪə(r)] **1** *n* carrera *f*

  2 *vi* correr a toda velocidad

carefree [ˈkeəfri:] *adj* despreocupado(a)

careful [ˈkeəfʊl] *adj* cuidadoso(a); *(cautious)* prudente; **be c.!** ¡ojo!; **to be c.** tener cuidado

carefully [ˈkeəfʊlɪ] *adv (painstakingly)* cuidadosamente; *(cautiously)* con cuidado

careless [ˈkeəlɪs] *adj* descuidado(a); *(about clothes)* desaliñado(a); *(driving)* negligente; **a c. mistake** un descuido

carelessly [ˈkeəlɪslɪ] *adv* descuidadamente, a la ligera

carelessness [ˈkeəlɪsnɪs] *n* descuido *m*

caress [kəˈres] **1** *n* caricia *f*

  2 *vt* acariciar

caretaker [ˈkeəteɪkə(r)] *n (in school etc)* bedel *mf; (in block of flats)* portero(a) *m,f*

carfare [ˈkɑ:feər] *n US (precio m del)* billete *m or Am* boleto *m*

cargo [ˈkɑ:ɡəʊ] *n (pl* **cargoes** *or* **cargos)** carga *f,* cargamento *m; Naut* **c. boat** buque *m* de carga, carguero *m*

Caribbean [kærɪˈbɪən, *US* kəˈrɪbɪən] *adj* caribe, caribeño(a); **the C. (Sea)** el (mar) Caribe

caricature [ˈkærɪkətjʊə(r)] *n* caricatura *f*

caring [ˈkeərɪŋ] *adj* solidario(a)

carnage [ˈkɑ:nɪdʒ] *n Fig* carnicería *f*

carnal [ˈkɑ:nəl] *adj* carnal

carnation [kɑ:ˈneɪʃən] *n* clavel *m*

carnival [ˈkɑ:nɪvəl] *n* carnaval *m*

carnivorous [kɑ:ˈnɪvərəs] *adj* carnívoro(a)

carol [ˈkærəl] *n* villancico *m*

carom [ˈkærəm] *n US (in billiards, pool)* carambola *f*

carousel [kærəˈsel] *n US* tiovivo *m*

carp¹ [kɑ:p] *n (fish)* carpa *f*

carp² [kɑ:p] *vi* refunfuñar

carpenter [ˈkɑ:pɪntə(r)] *n* carpintero(a) *m,f*

carpentry [ˈkɑ:pɪntrɪ] *n* carpintería *f*

carpet [ˈkɑ:pɪt] **1** *n* alfombra *f*

  2 *vt Fig* **carpeted with** cubierto(a) de

  𝑄 Note that the Spanish word **carpeta** is a false friend and is never a translation for the English word **carpet**. In Spanish, **carpeta** means "file, folder".

---

carriage [ˈkærɪdʒ] *n* (**a**) *(horse-drawn)* carruaje *m; Rail* vagón *m,* coche *m; (of gun)* cureña *f; (of typewriter)* carro *m* (**b**) *(of goods)* porte *m,* transporte *m*

carriageway [ˈkærɪdʒweɪ] *n Br* carril *m,* autovía *f;* **dual c.** autovía *f*

carrier [ˈkærɪə(r)] *n* (**a**) *(company)* transportista *mf; Br* **c. bag** bolsa *f* de plástico; **c. pigeon** paloma mensajera (**b**) *Med* portador(a) *m,f*

carrot ['kærət] n zanahoria f

carry ['kærɪ] 1 vt (**a**) llevar; (goods) transportar (**b**) (stock) tener; (responsibility, penalty) conllevar, implicar (**c**) **the motion was carried** se aprobó la moción (**d**) (disease) ser portador(a) de
2 vi (sound) oírse
▶**carry away** vt sep llevarse; **to get carried away** entusiasmarse
▶**carry forward** vt sep Fin **carried forward** suma y sigue
▶**carry off** vt sep (prize) llevarse; Fam **to c. it off** salir airoso(a)
▶**carry on** 1 vt sep continuar; (conversation) mantener
2 vi (**a**) continuar, seguir adelante; **c. on!** ¡adelante! (**b**) Fam (make a fuss) hacer una escena; **don't c. on about it!** ¡no te enrolles! (**c**) Fam **to c. on with sb** estar liado(a) con algn
▶**carry out** vt sep (plan) llevar a cabo, realizar; (test) verificar

carryall ['kærɪɔ:l] n US bolsa f (de viaje o de deporte)

carrycot ['kærɪkɒt] n Br cuna f portátil

carsick ['kɑ:sɪk] adj mareado(a) (en el coche)

cart [kɑ:t] 1 n (horse-drawn) carro m; (handcart) carretilla f; US (in supermarket) carrito m
2 vt carretear

cartel [kɑ:'tel] n cártel m

carton ['kɑ:tən] n (of cream etc) caja f

cartoon [kɑ:'tu:n] n (strip) tira cómica, historieta f; Art cartón m; (animated) dibujos mpl animados

cartoonist [kɑ:'tu:nɪst] n caricaturista mf

cartridge ['kɑ:trɪdʒ] n (**a**) cartucho m (**b**) (for pen) recambio m; **c. paper** papel guarro

carve [kɑ:v] vt (**a**) (wood) tallar; (stone, metal) cincelar, esculpir (**b**) (meat) trinchar

cascade [kæ'skeɪd] n cascada f

case[1] [keɪs] n (**a**) caso m; **a c. in point** un buen ejemplo; **in any c.** en cualquier caso, de todas formas; **in c. of doubt** en caso de duda; **just in c.** por si acaso (**b**) Med caso m; **c. history** historial clínico (**c**) Jur causa f

case[2] [keɪs] n (**a**) (suitcase) maleta f, Méx petaca f, RP valija f; (small) estuche m; (soft) funda f (**b**) **a c. of wine** una caja de botellas de vino (**c**) Typ **lower c.** minúscula f; **upper c.** mayúscula f

cash [kæʃ] 1 n dinero efectivo; **to pay c.** pagar al contado or en efectivo; **c. desk** caja f; **c. on delivery** entrega f contra reembolso; **c. dispenser** cajero automático; **c. register** caja registradora
2 vt (cheque) cobrar
▶**cash in** 1 vi Fam Fig **to c. in on sth** sacar provecho de algo
2 vt sep hacer efectivo(a)

cash-and-carry [kæʃən'kærɪ] adj & adv = de venta al por mayor y pago al contado

cashew ['kæʃu:] n c. (**nut**) anacardo m

cashier [kæ'ʃɪə(r)] n cajero(a) m,f

cashmere ['kæʃmɪə(r)] n cachemira f

casino [kə'si:nəʊ] n casino m

cask [kɑ:sk] n tonel m, barril m

casket ['kɑ:skɪt] n (box) cofre m; US (coffin) ataúd m

> 🔊 Note that the Spanish word **casquete** is a false friend and is never a translation for the English word **casket**. In Spanish, **casquete** means "shell case".

casserole ['kæsərəʊl] n (**a**) (container) cacerola f (**b**) Culin guisado m

cassette [kə'set] n cassette f; **c. recorder** cassette m

cast [kɑ:st] 1 vt (pt & pp **cast**) (**a**) (net, fishing line) echar, arrojar; (light) proyectar; (glance) lanzar; (anchor) echar; (vote) emitir; (skin) mudar (**b**) Fig **to c. doubts on sth** poner algo en duda; **to c. suspicion on sb** levantar sospechas sobre algn (**c**) (metal) moldear; **c. iron** hierro fundido (**d**) Th (play) hacer el reparto de
2 n (**a**) (mould) molde m; (product) pieza f (**b**) Med (**plaster**) **c.** escayola f (**c**) Th reparto m
▶**cast off** vi Naut soltar (las) amarras

castanets [kæstə'nets] npl castañuelas fpl

castaway ['kɑ:stəweɪ] n náufrago(a) m,f

caste [kɑ:st] n casta f

caster ['kɑ:stə(r)] n **c. sugar** azúcar m or f extrafino(a)

Castile [kæ'sti:l] n Castilla

Castilian [kæ'stɪlɪən] 1 adj castellano(a)
2 n C. (**Spanish**) (language) castellano m

casting ['kɑ:stɪŋ] n **c. vote** voto m de calidad

cast-iron ['kɑ:staɪən] adj de hierro fundido

castle ['kɑ:səl] 1 n (**a**) castillo m (**b**) (in chess) torre f
2 vi (in chess) enrocar

castor[1] ['kɑ:stə(r)] n **c. oil** aceite m de ricino

castor[2] ['kɑ:stə(r)] n (on furniture) ruedecilla f

castrate [kæ'streɪt] vt castrar

casual ['kæʒjʊəl] adj (**a**) (meeting etc) fortuito(a) (**b**) (worker) eventual (**c**) (clothes) (de) sport (**d**) (visit) de paso (**e**) (person, attitude) despreocupado(a), informal

casualty ['kæʒjʊəltɪ] n (**a**) Mil baja f; **casualties** pérdidas fpl (**b**) (injured) herido(a) m,f

> 📖 Note that the Spanish word **casualidad** is a false friend and is never a translation for the English word **casualty**. In Spanish, **casualidad** means "chance, coincidence".

cat [kæt] n gato(a) m,f; Fig **to let the c. out of the bag** descubrir el pastel

Catalan ['kætələn] **1** adj catalán(ana)
2 n (**a**) (person) catalán(ana) m,f (**b**) (language) catalán m

catalogue, US **catalog** ['kætəlɒg] **1** n catálogo m
2 vt catalogar

Catalonia [kætə'ləʊnɪə] n Cataluña

catalyst ['kætəlɪst] n catalizador m

catapult ['kætəpʌlt] n Br tirachinas m inv

catarrh [kə'tɑː(r)] n catarro m

catastrophe [kə'tæstrəfɪ] n catástrofe f

catastrophic [kætə'strɒfɪk] adj catastrófico(a)

catch [kætʃ] **1** vt (pt & pp **caught**) (**a**) (ball, thief) coger; (fish) pescar; (mouse etc) atrapar; (train, bus) coger, Am agarrar; **to c. a cold** coger un resfriado; **to c. fire** (log) prenderse; (building) incendiarse; **to c. hold of** agarrar; **to c. sb's eye** captar la atención de algn; **to c. sight of** entrever
(**b**) (surprise) pillar, sorprender
(**c**) (hear) entender
(**d**) **to c. one's breath** (hold) sostener la respiración; (recover) recuperar el aliento
2 vi (sleeve etc) engancharse (**on** en); (fire) encenderse
3 n (**a**) (of ball) parada f; (of fish) presa f (**b**) (on door) pestillo m (**c**) (drawback) pega f, **c. question** pregunta f con pega
(**d**) **c. phrase** slogan m
▶ **catch on** vi Fam (**a**) (become popular) ganar popularidad (**b**) (understand) caer en la cuenta
▶ **catch out** vt sep Fam **to c. sb out** pillar a algn cometiendo una falta
▶ **catch up** vi (**a**) **to c. up with sb** (reach) alcanzar a algn (**b**) (with news) ponerse al corriente (**on** de); **to c. up on sleep** recuperar el sueño perdido; **to c. up with work** ponerse al día de trabajo

catching ['kætʃɪŋ] adj (disease) contagioso(a)

catchment ['kætʃmənt] n **c. area** zona f de captación

catchword ['kætʃwɜːd] n lema m

catchy ['kætʃɪ] adj (**catchier**, **catchiest**) Fam (tune) pegadizo(a)

categoric(al) [kætɪ'gɒrɪk(əl)] adj categórico(a)

categorize ['kætɪgəraɪz] vt clasificar

category ['kætɪgərɪ] n categoría f

cater ['keɪtə(r)] vi (**a**) **to c. for** (wedding etc) proveer comida para (**b**) **to c. for** (taste) atender a

caterer ['keɪtərə(r)] n proveedor(a) m,f

catering ['keɪtərɪŋ] n abastecimiento m (de comidas por encargo)

caterpillar ['kætəpɪlə(r)] n (**a**) oruga f (**b**) **c. (tractor)** tractor m de oruga

cathedral [kə'θiːdrəl] n catedral f

Catholic ['kæθəlɪk] adj & n católico(a) (m,f)

catholic ['kæθəlɪk] adj católico(a)

Catholicism [kə'θɒlɪsɪzəm] n catolicismo m

cat's-eye® ['kætsaɪ] n Br captafaro m, = baliza reflectante en la calzada

cattle ['kætəl] npl ganado m (vacuno)

catty ['kætɪ] adj (**cattier**, **cattiest**) Fam (remark) malintencionado(a); (person) malicioso(a)

catwalk ['kætwɔːk] n pasarela f

Caucasian [kɔː'keɪzɪən] adj & n caucásico(a) (m,f), blanco(a) (m,f)

caucus ['kɔːkəs] n comité m central, ejecutiva f

caught [kɔːt] pt & pp of **catch**

cauliflower ['kɒlɪflaʊə(r)] n coliflor f

cause [kɔːz] **1** n (**a**) (origin) causa f (**b**) (reason) motivo m (**c**) **for a good c.** por una buena causa
2 vt causar; **to c. sb to do sth** hacer que algn haga algo

caustic ['kɔːstɪk] adj cáustico(a); Fig mordaz

caution ['kɔːʃən] **1** n (**a**) (care) cautela f, prudencia f (**b**) (warning) aviso m, advertencia f (**c**) Br Jur reprensión f
2 vt advertir, amonestar

cautious ['kɔːʃəs] adj cauteloso(a), prudente

cavalcade [kævəl'keɪd] n cabalgata f

cavalier [kævə'lɪə(r)] **1** adj arrogante
2 n caballero m

cavalry ['kævəlrɪ] n caballería f

cave [keɪv] n cueva f
▶ **cave in** vi (roof etc) derrumbarse, hundirse

caveman ['keɪvmæn] n hombre m de las cavernas

cavern ['kævən] n caverna f

caviar(e) ['kævɪɑː(r)] n caviar m

cavity ['kævɪtɪ] n (a) (hole) cavidad f (b) (in tooth) caries f inv

cavort [kə'vɔːt] vi retozar, brincar

CB [siː'biː] (abbr **Citizens' Band**) banda ciudadana

CBI [siːbiː'aɪ] n Br (abbr **Confederation of British Industry**) ≃ CEOE f

cc [siː'siː] (abbr **cubic centimetre(s)**) cc

CD [siː'diː] n (abbr **compact disc**) CD m; **CD player** (lector m or reproductor m de) CD m

CD-ROM [siːdiː'rɒm] n Comput (abbr **compact disc read-only memory**) CD-ROM m

cease [siːs] 1 vt cesar; **to c. doing** or **to do sth** dejar de hacer algo
　2 vi terminar

cease-fire [siːs'faɪə(r)] n alto m el fuego

ceaseless ['siːslɪs] adj incesante

cedar ['siːdə(r)] n cedro m

cede [siːd] vt ceder

ceiling ['siːlɪŋ] n techo m

celebrate ['selɪbreɪt] 1 vt (occasion) celebrar
　2 vi divertirse

celebrated ['selɪbreɪtɪd] adj célebre

celebration [selɪ'breɪʃən] n (a) celebración f (b) **celebrations** festividades fpl

celebrity [sɪ'lebrɪtɪ] n celebridad f

celery ['selərɪ] n apio m

celibate ['selɪbɪt] adj & n célibe (mf)

cell [sel] n (a) (in prison) celda f (b) Biol & Pol célula f (c) Elec pila f

cellar ['selə(r)] n sótano m; (for wine) bodega f

cello ['tʃeləʊ] n violoncelo m

cellophane® ['seləfeɪn] n Br celofán m

celluloid ['seljʊlɔɪd] n celuloide m

cellulose ['seljʊləʊs] n celulosa f

Celsius ['selsɪəs] adj Celsio

Celt [kelt, selt] n celta mf

Celtic ['keltɪk, 'seltɪk] 1 n (language) celta m
　2 adj celta

cement [sɪ'ment] 1 n cemento m; **c. mixer** hormigonera f
　2 vt Constr unir con cemento; Fig (friendship) cimentar

cemetery ['semɪtrɪ] n cementerio m

censor ['sensə(r)] 1 n censor(a) m,f
　2 vt censurar

censorship ['sensəʃɪp] n censura f

censure ['senʃə(r)] 1 n censura f
　2 vt censurar

census ['sensəs] n censo m

cent [sent] n (a) centavo m, céntimo m (b) **per c.** por ciento

centenary [sen'tiːnərɪ] n centenario m

center ['sentər] n & vt US = **centre**

centigrade ['sentɪgreɪd] adj centígrado(a)

centilitre, US **centiliter** ['sentɪliːtə(r)] n centilitro m

centimetre, US **centimeter** ['sentɪmiːtə(r)] n centímetro m

centipede ['sentɪpiːd] n ciempiés m inv

central ['sentrəl] adj central; **c. heating** calefacción f central; **C. America** Centroamérica; **C. American** centroamericano(a) m,f; Br **c. reservation** (on motorway) mediana f, Col, Méx camellón m

centralize ['sentrəlaɪz] vt centralizar

centrally ['sentrəlɪ] adv **c. heated** con calefacción central; **c. situated** céntrico(a)

centre ['sentə(r)] 1 n centro m; **town c.** centro de la ciudad; Ftb **c. forward** delantero centro; Ftb **c. half** medio centro; Pol **c. party** partido m centrista; **sports c.** centro deportivo
　2 vt (attention etc) centrar (**on** en)

century ['sentʃərɪ] n siglo m; **the nineteenth c.** el siglo diecinueve

ceramic [sɪ'ræmɪk] 1 n cerámica f
　2 adj de cerámica

ceramics [sɪ'ræmɪks] n sing cerámica f

cereal ['sɪərɪəl] n cereal m

cerebral ['serɪbrəl, sɪ'riːbrəl] adj cerebral; **c. palsy** parálisis f cerebral

ceremony ['serɪmənɪ] n ceremonia f

certain ['sɜːtən] 1 adj (a) (sure) seguro(a); **to be c.** estar seguro(a); **to make c. of sth** asegurarse de algo (b) **to a c. extent** hasta cierto punto (c) (not known) cierto(a); **a c. Miss Ward** una tal señorita Ward (d) (true) cierto(a)
　2 adv **for c.** a ciencia cierta

certainly ['sɜːtənlɪ] adv desde luego; **c. not** de ninguna manera

certainty ['sɜːtəntɪ] n certeza f; (assurance) seguridad f

certificate [sə'tɪfɪkɪt] n certificado m; Educ diploma m

certified ['sɜːtɪfaɪd] adj certificado(a); (copy) compulsado(a); US **c. public accountant** censor(a) m,f jurado(a) de cuentas, auditor(a) m,f, Am contador(a) m,f público(a)

certify ['sɜːtɪfaɪ] vt certificar

cervical ['sɜːvɪkəl, sə'vaɪkəl] adj **c. cancer** cáncer m del útero; **c. smear** frotis m cervical

cervix ['sɜːvɪks] n (a) (uterus) cuello m del útero (b) (neck) cerviz f, cuello m

cessation [se'seɪʃən] n cese m

cesspit ['sespɪt] n pozo negro

Ceylon [sɪ'lɒn] n Ceilán

cf [siːf] (abbr confer, compare) cf., cfr.

chafe [tʃeɪf] 1 vt (make sore) rozar

2 vi (skin) irritarse; (item of clothing) rozar

chaffinch ['tʃæfɪntʃ] n pinzón m vulgar

chagrin ['ʃægrɪn] n disgusto m, desilusión f

chain [tʃeɪn] 1 n cadena f; Fig (of events) serie f; **c. of mountains** cordillera f; **c. reaction** reacción f en cadena; **c. saw** sierra mecánica

2 vt **to c. (up)** encadenar

chain-smoke ['tʃeɪnsməʊk] vi fumar un pitillo tras otro

chair [tʃeə(r)] 1 n (a) silla f; (with arms) sillón m; **c. lift** telesilla m (b) (position) presidencia f; Univ cátedra f

2 vt presidir

chairman ['tʃeəmən] n presidente m

chairperson ['tʃeəpɜːsən] n presidente(a) m/f

chalet ['ʃæleɪ] n chalet m, chalé m

chalk [tʃɔːk] n (for writing) tiza f

► **chalk up** vt sep Fam (victory etc) apuntarse

challenge ['tʃælɪndʒ] 1 vt (a) retar, desafiar; **to c. sb to do sth** retar a algn a que haga algo (b) (authority etc) poner a prueba; (statement) poner en duda (c) Mil dar el alto a

2 n (a) reto m, desafío m (b) Mil quién vive m

challenging ['tʃælɪndʒɪŋ] adj (idea) desafiante; (task) que presenta un desafío

chamber ['tʃeɪmbə(r)] n (a) (hall) cámara f; **C. of Commerce** Cámara de Comercio (b) Mus **c. music** música f de cámara (c) Br Jur **chambers** gabinete m

chambermaid ['tʃeɪmbəmeɪd] n camarera f

chameleon [kə'miːlɪən] n camaleón m

champagne [ʃæm'peɪn] n (French) champán m; (from Catalonia) cava m

champion ['tʃæmpɪən] n campeón(ona) m/f; Fig **c. of human rights** defensor(a) m/f de los derechos humanos

championship ['tʃæmpɪənʃɪp] n campeonato m

chance [tʃɑːns] 1 n (a) (fortune) casualidad f, azar m; **by c.** por casualidad; **to take a c.** arriesgarse; **c. meeting** encuentro m casual (b) (likelihood) posibilidad f; **(the) chances are that ...** lo más posible

es que ... (c) (opportunity) oportunidad f

2 vt arriesgar

► **chance upon** vt insep encontrar por casualidad

chancellor ['tʃɑːnsələ(r)] n (a) (head of state, in embassy) canciller m (b) Br Univ rector(a) m/f (c) Br **C. of the Exchequer** ≃ ministro(a) m/f de Hacienda

chandelier [ʃændɪ'lɪə(r)] n araña f (de luces)

change [tʃeɪndʒ] 1 vt cambiar; **to c. gear** cambiar de marcha; **to c. one's mind/the subject** cambiar de opinión/de tema; **to c. trains** hacer transbordo; **to get changed** cambiarse de ropa; Fig **to c. hands** cambiar de dueño(a)

2 vi cambiar, cambiarse; **to c. for the better/worse** mejorar/empeorar; **to c. into** convertirse en

3 n (a) cambio m; **for a c.** para variar; **c. of heart** cambio de parecer; **c. of scene** cambio de aires (b) (money) cambio m; (after purchase) vuelta f; **small c.** suelto m

► **change over** vi cambiarse

changeable ['tʃeɪndʒəbəl] adj (weather) variable; (person) inconstante

changeover ['tʃeɪndʒəʊvə(r)] n conversión f

changing ['tʃeɪndʒɪŋ] 1 n (a) **c. room** vestuario m (b) Mil relevo m (de la guardia)

2 adj cambiante

channel ['tʃænəl] 1 n (a) Geog canal m; (of river) cauce m; **the C. Islands** las Islas Anglonormandas; **the English C.** el Canal de la Mancha (b) (administrative) vía f (c) TV & Rad canal m, cadena f

2 vt Fig (ideas etc) canalizar, encauzar

chant [tʃɑːnt] 1 n Rel cántico m; (of demonstrators) slogan m

2 vt & vi Rel cantar; (demonstrators) corear

chaos ['keɪɒs] n caos m

chaotic [keɪ'ɒtɪk] adj caótico(a)

chap [tʃæp] n Fam chico m, tío m

chapel ['tʃæpəl] n capilla f

chaperon(e) ['ʃæpərəʊn] n carabina f

chaplain ['tʃæplɪn] n capellán m

chapter ['tʃæptə(r)] n (a) capítulo m (b) Rel cabildo m

char [tʃɑː(r)] vt chamuscar, carbonizar

character ['kærɪktə(r)] n (a) carácter m (b) Fam (person) tipo m (c) Th personaje m

characteristic [kærɪktə'rɪstɪk] 1 n característica f

2 adj característico(a)

characterize ['kærıktəraız] *vt* caracterizar

charcoal ['tʃɑːkəʊl] *n* carbón *m* vegetal; *Art* **c. drawing** carboncillo *m*; **c. grey** gris marengo *or* oscuro

charge [tʃɑːdʒ] **1** *vt* (**a**) cobrar; **c. it to my account** cárguelo en mi cuenta (**b**) **to c. sb with a crime** acusar a algn de un crimen (**c**) *Mil* cargar contra (**d**) *Elec* cargar

2 *vi Elec & Mil* cargar; **to c. about** andar a lo loco

3 *n* (**a**) (*cost*) precio *m*; **bank charges** comisión *f*; **free of c.** gratis; **service c.** servicio *m*; **c. account** cuenta *f* corriente (**b**) **to be in c. of** estar a cargo de; **to take c. of** hacerse cargo de (**c**) *Jur* cargo *m*, acusación *f* (**d**) (*explosive*) carga explosiva (**e**) *Elec* carga *f*

charged [tʃɑːdʒd] *adj Fig* emotivo(a)

charismatic [kærız'mætık] *adj* carismático(a)

charitable ['tʃærıtəbəl] *adj* (*person*) caritativo(a); (*organization*) benéfico(a)

charity ['tʃærıtı] *n* caridad *f*; (*organization*) institución benéfica

charlady ['tʃɑːleıdı] *n Br* mujer *f* de la limpieza

charlatan ['ʃɑːlətən] *n* (*doctor*) curandero(a) *m,f*

charm [tʃɑːm] **1** *n* (**a**) (*quality*) encanto *m* (**b**) (*spell*) hechizo *m*; **lucky c.** amuleto *m*
2 *vt* encantar

charming ['tʃɑːmıŋ] *adj* encantador(a)

chart [tʃɑːt] **1** *n* (**a**) (*giving information*) tabla *f*; (*graph*) gráfico *m* (**b**) (*map*) carta *f* de navegación (**c**) *Mus* **the charts** la lista de éxitos
2 *vt Av & Naut* (*on map*) trazar

charter ['tʃɑːtə(r)] **1** *n* (**a**) (*of institution*) estatutos *mpl*; (*of rights*) carta *f* (**b**) **c. flight** vuelo *m* chárter
2 *vt* (*plane, boat*) fletar

chartered accountant [tʃɑːtəd-ə'kaʊntənt] *n Br* censor(a) *m,f* jurado(a) de cuentas, *Am* contador(a) *m,f* público(a)

chase [tʃeıs] **1** *vt* perseguir; (*hunt*) cazar
2 *n* persecución *f*, (*hunt*) caza *f*

chasm ['kæzəm] *n Geog* sima *f*; *Fig* abismo *m*

chassis ['ʃæsı] *n* chasis *m inv*

chastise [tʃæs'taız] *vt* castigar

chastity ['tʃæstıtı] *n* castidad *f*

chat [tʃæt] **1** *n* (**a**) (*informal conversation*) charla *f*; *Br* **c. show** coloquio *m* (**b**) *Comput* charla *f*; **c. room** sala *f* de conversación
2 *vi* (**a**) (*talk informally*) charlar (**b**)

Comput charlar (**to** *or* **with** con)
▸**chat up** *vt sep Br Fam* **to chat sb up** (intentar) ligar con algn

chatter ['tʃætə(r)] **1** *vi* (*person*) parlotear; (*bird*) piar; (*teeth*) castañetear
2 *n* (*of person*) parloteo *m*; (*of birds*) gorjeo *m*; (*of teeth*) castañeteo *m*

chatterbox ['tʃætəbɒks] *n Fam* parlanchín(ina) *m,f*

chatty ['tʃætı] *adj* (**chattier, chattiest**) hablador(a)

chauffeur ['ʃəʊfə(r), ʃəʊ'fɜː(r)] *n* chófer *m*

chauvinism ['ʃəʊvınızəm] *n* chovinismo *m*; **male c.** machismo *m*

chauvinist ['ʃəʊvınıst] *adj & n* chovinista (*mf*); **male c.** machista *m*

cheap [tʃiːp] **1** *adj* barato(a); (*fare*) económico(a); (*joke*) de mal gusto; (*contemptible*) bajo(a); *Fam* **dirt c.** tirado(a)
2 *n Br Fam* **on the c.** en plan barato
3 *adv* barato

cheapen ['tʃiːpən] *vt Fig* degradar

cheaply ['tʃiːplı] *adv* barato, en plan económico

cheat [tʃiːt] **1** *vt* engañar; **to c. sb out of sth** estafar algo a algn
2 *vi* (**a**) (*at games*) hacer trampa; (*in exam etc*) copiar(se) (**b**) *Fam* (*husband, wife*) poner cuernos (**on** a)
3 *n* (*trickster*) tramposo(a) *m,f*

check [tʃek] **1** *vt* (**a**) repasar; (*facts*) comprobar; (*tickets*) controlar; (*tyres, oil*) revisar (**b**) (*impulse*) refrenar; (*growth*) retardar (**c**) (*stop*) detener (**d**) (*in chess*) dar jaque a
2 *vi* comprobar
3 *n* (**a**) (*of documents etc*) revisión *f*; (*of facts*) comprobación *f* (**b**) (*in chess*) jaque *m* (**c**) (*pattern*) cuadro *m* (**d**) **to keep in c.** (*feelings*) contener; (*enemy*) mantener a raya (**e**) *US* = **cheque**
▸**check in** *vi* (*at airport*) facturar; (*at hotel*) registrarse (**at** en)
▸**check out 1** *vi* (*of hotel*) dejar el hotel
2 *vt sep* (*facts*) verificar
▸**check up** *vi* **to c. up on sb** hacer averiguaciones sobre algn; **to c. up on sth** comprobar algo

checked [tʃekt] *adj* a cuadros

checker ['tʃekər] *n US* (*cashier*) cajero(a) *m,f*

checkered ['tʃekərd] *adj US* = **chequered**

checkers ['tʃekərz] *n sing US* (*game*) damas *fpl*

check-in ['tʃekın] *n* **c. desk** (*at airport*) mostrador *m* de facturación

checkmate ['tʃekmeɪt] **1** n jaque mate m
2 vt dar (jaque) mate a; *Fig* poner en un callejón sin salida

checkout ['tʃekaʊt] n *(counter)* caja f

checkpoint ['tʃekpɔɪnt] n control m

checkroom ['tʃekruːm] n *US (for coats, hats)* guardarropa m; *(for luggage)* consigna f

checkup ['tʃekʌp] n *Med* chequeo m, examen médico

cheek [tʃiːk] n **(a)** mejilla f **(b)** *Fam (nerve)* cara f; **what c.!** ¡vaya jeta!

cheekbone ['tʃiːkbəʊn] n pómulo m

cheeky ['tʃiːkɪ] adj **(cheekier, cheekiest)** *Fam* fresco(a), descarado(a)

cheep [tʃiːp] **1** n *(of bird)* pío m
2 vi piar

cheer [tʃɪə(r)] **1** vi aplaudir, aclamar
2 vt **(a)** *(applaud)* vitorear, aclamar **(b)** *(make hopeful)* animar
3 n viva m; **cheers** aplausos mpl; *Fam* **cheers!** *(thank you)* ¡gracias!; *(before drinking)* ¡salud!
▸ **cheer up 1** vi animarse
2 vt sep **to c. sb up** alegrar *or* animar a algn

cheerful ['tʃɪəfʊl] adj alegre

cheerio [tʃɪərɪ'əʊ] interj *Br Fam* ¡hasta luego!

cheese [tʃiːz] n queso m

cheesecake ['tʃiːzkeɪk] n tarta f de queso

cheetah ['tʃiːtə] n guepardo m

chef [ʃef] n chef m

chemical ['kemɪkəl] **1** n sustancia química, producto químico
2 adj químico(a)

chemist ['kemɪst] n **(a)** químico(a) m,f **(b)** *Br* **c.'s (shop)** farmacia f; **(dispensing) c.** farmacéutico(a) m,f

chemistry ['kemɪstrɪ] n química f

cheque [tʃek] n cheque m; **to pay by c.** pagar con (un) cheque; **c. book** talonario m (de cheques); **c. card** tarjeta f de identificación bancaria

chequered ['tʃekəd] adj a cuadros; *Fig* **a c. career** una carrera con altibajos

cherish ['tʃerɪʃ] vt **(a)** *(person)* tenerle mucho cariño a **(b)** *Fig (hopes etc)* abrigar

cherry ['tʃerɪ] n cereza f

chess [tʃes] n ajedrez m

chessboard ['tʃesbɔːd] n tablero m de ajedrez

chesspiece ['tʃespiːs] n pieza f de ajedrez

chest [tʃest] n **(a)** *Anat* pecho m **(b)** *(for linen)* arca f; *(for valuables)* cofre m; **c. of drawers** cómoda f

chestnut ['tʃesnʌt] n *(tree, colour)* castaño m; *(nut)* castaña f

chew [tʃuː] vt masticar, mascar

chewing gum ['tʃuːɪŋɡʌm] n chicle m

chic [ʃiːk] adj elegante

chick [tʃɪk] n **(a)** *(young chicken)* pollito m **(b)** *Fam (woman)* nena f, *Arg* piba f, *Méx* chava f

chicken ['tʃɪkɪn] **1** n **(a)** pollo m **(b)** *Fam (coward)* gallina mf
2 vi *Fam* **to c. out** rajarse (por miedo)

chickenpox ['tʃɪkɪnpɒks] n varicela f

chickpea ['tʃɪkpiː] n garbanzo m

chicory ['tʃɪkərɪ] n achicoria f

chief [tʃiːf] **1** n jefe m
2 adj principal

chiefly ['tʃiːflɪ] adv *(above all)* sobre todo; *(mainly)* principalmente

chiffon ['ʃɪfɒn] n gasa f

chilblain ['tʃɪlbleɪn] n sabañón m

child [tʃaɪld] n *(pl* **children***)* niño(a) m,f; *(son)* hijo m; *(daughter)* hija f; **c. minder** = persona que cuida niños en su propia casa

childbirth ['tʃaɪldbɜːθ] n parto m

childhood ['tʃaɪldhʊd] n infancia f, niñez f

childish ['tʃaɪldɪʃ] adj pueril, aniñado(a)

childlike ['tʃaɪldlaɪk] adj infantil

children ['tʃɪldrən] pl of **child**

Chile ['tʃɪlɪ] n Chile

Chilean ['tʃɪlɪən] adj & n chileno(a) (m,f)

chili ['tʃɪlɪ] n = **chilli**

chill [tʃɪl] **1** n **(a)** *Med* resfriado m **(b)** *(coldness)* fresco m
2 adj frío(a)
3 vt *(meat)* refrigerar; *(wine)* enfriar

chilli ['tʃɪlɪ] n chile m

chilly ['tʃɪlɪ] adj **(chillier, chilliest)** frío(a)

chime [tʃaɪm] **1** n *(peal)* campanada f
2 vt **to c. five o'clock** *(of clock)* dar las cinco
3 vi sonar
▸ **chime in** vi *Fam* intervenir

chimney ['tʃɪmnɪ] n chimenea f; **c. sweep** deshollinador m

chimpanzee [tʃɪmpæn'ziː] n chimpancé m

chin [tʃɪn] n barbilla f, mentón m; **double c.** papada f

China ['tʃaɪnə] n China

china ['tʃaɪnə] n loza f, porcelana f

> 🖉 Note that the Spanish word **china** is a false friend and is never a translation for the English word **china**. In Spanish, **china** means "pebble, small stone".

Chinese [tʃaɪ'niːz] **1** adj chino(a)

2 *n* (**a**) *(person)* chino(a) *m,f* (**b**) *(language)* chino *m*

chink¹ [tʃɪŋk] *n* *(opening)* resquicio *m*; *(crack)* grieta *f*

chink² [tʃɪŋk] **1** *vi* tintinear
2 *n* tintineo *m*

chip [tʃɪp] **1** *n* (**a**) *(of wood)* astilla *f*; *(of stone)* lasca *f*; *(in cup)* mella *f* (**b**) *Br Culin* **chips** patatas *or Am* papas fritas; *US* (**potato**) **chips** *(crisps)* patatas *or Am* papas fritas *(de bolsa)* (**c**) *Comput* chip *m* (**d**) *(in gambling)* ficha *f*
2 *vt* *(wood)* astillar; *(stone)* resquebrajar; *(china, glass)* mellar
3 *vi* *(wood)* astillarse; *(china, glass)* mellarse; *(paint)* desconcharse
▸ **chip in** *vi Fam* (**a**) *(with money)* poner algo (de dinero)

chiropodist [kɪˈrɒpədɪst] *n* pedicuro(a) *m,f*

chirp [tʃɜːp] *vi* *(birds)* gorjear

chisel [ˈtʃɪzəl] *n* cincel *m*

chit [tʃɪt] *n* nota *f*; *(small invoice)* vale *m*

chitchat [ˈtʃɪttʃæt] *n Fam* palique *m*

chivalry [ˈʃɪvəlrɪ] *n* caballerosidad *f*

chives [tʃaɪvz] *npl* cebolleta *f*

chlorine [ˈklɔːriːn] *n* cloro *m*

chock-a-block [tʃɒkəˈblɒk], **chock-full** [tʃɒkˈfʊl] *adj Fam* (lleno(a)) hasta los topes

chocolate [ˈtʃɒkəlɪt] **1** *n* chocolate *m*; **chocolates** bombones *mpl*
2 *adj* de chocolate

choice [tʃɔɪs] **1** *n* elección *f*; **a wide c.** un gran surtido; **by c.** por gusto
2 *adj* selecto(a)

choir [ˈkwaɪə(r)] *n* coro *m*, coral *f*

choirboy [ˈkwaɪəbɔɪ] *n* niño *m* de coro

choke [tʃəʊk] **1** *vt* (**a**) *(person)* ahogar (**b**) *(obstruct)* obstruir
2 *vi* ahogarse; **to c. on food** atragantarse con la comida
3 *n Aut* estárter *m*
▸ **choke back** *vt sep* *(emotions)* tragarse

cholera [ˈkɒlərə] *n* cólera *m*

cholesterol [kəˈlestərɒl] *n* colesterol *m*

choose [tʃuːz] **1** *vt* *(pt* chose; *pp* chosen*)* escoger, elegir; *(decide on)* optar por
2 *vi* escoger, elegir

choos(e)y [ˈtʃuːzɪ] *adj* (**choosier, choosiest**) *Fam* exigente

chop [tʃɒp] **1** *vt* (**a**) *(wood)* cortar; *(tree)* talar (**b**) *Culin* cortar a pedacitos
2 *n* (**a**) *(blow)* tajo *m*; *(with axe)* hachazo *m* (**b**) *Culin* chuleta *f*

chopper [ˈtʃɒpə(r)] *n Fam* helicóptero *m*

choppy [ˈtʃɒpɪ] *adj* (**choppier, choppiest**) *(sea)* picado(a)

chopsticks [ˈtʃɒpstɪks] *npl* palillos *mpl*

chord [kɔːd] *n Mus* acorde *m*; *Fig* **it strikes a c.** (me) suena

chore [tʃɔː(r)] *n* quehacer *m*, tarea *f*

chortle [ˈtʃɔːtəl] *vi* reír con ganas

chorus [ˈkɔːrəs] *n Mus & Th* coro *m*; *(in a song)* estribillo *m*; **c. girl** corista *f*

chose [tʃəʊz] *pt of* **choose**

chosen [ˈtʃəʊzən] *pp of* **choose**

Christ [kraɪst] *n* Cristo *m*, Jesucristo *m*

christen [ˈkrɪsən] *vt* bautizar

christening [ˈkrɪsənɪŋ] *n* bautizo *m*

Christian [ˈkrɪstʃən] **1** *adj* cristiano(a); **c. name** nombre *m* de pila
2 *n* cristiano(a) *m,f*

Christianity [krɪstɪˈænɪtɪ] *n* cristianismo *m*

Christmas [ˈkrɪsməs] *n* Navidad *f*; **merry C.!** ¡feliz Navidad!; **C. carol** villancico *m*; **C. Day** día *m* de Navidad; **C. Eve** Nochebuena *f*

chrome [krəʊm] *n* cromo *m*

chromium [ˈkrəʊmɪəm] *n* cromo *m*; **c. plating** cromado *m*

chromosome [ˈkrəʊməsəʊm] *n* cromosoma *m*

chronic [ˈkrɒnɪk] *adj* crónico(a)

chronicle [ˈkrɒnɪkəl] **1** *n* crónica *f*
2 *vt* hacer la crónica de

chronological [krɒnəˈlɒdʒɪkəl] *adj* cronológico(a)

chrysanthemum [krɪˈsænθəməm] *n* crisantemo *m*

chubby [ˈtʃʌbɪ] *adj* (**chubbier, chubbiest**) rellenito(a)

chuck [tʃʌk] *vt Fam* tirar; **to c. one's job in** *or* **up** dejar el trabajo; **to c. sb out** echar a algn; **to c. sth away** *or* **out** tirar algo

chuckle [ˈtʃʌkəl] **1** *vi* reír entre dientes
2 *n* sonrisita *f*

chug [tʃʌg] *vi* traquetear

chum [tʃʌm] *n* compinche *mf*, compañero(a) *m,f*

chunk [tʃʌŋk] *n Fam* cacho *m*, pedazo *m*

church [tʃɜːtʃ] *n* iglesia *f*; **to go to c.** ir a misa; **C. of England** Iglesia Anglicana

churchyard [ˈtʃɜːtʃjɑːd] *n* cementerio *m*, campo santo

churlish [ˈtʃɜːlɪʃ] *adj* grosero(a)

churn [tʃɜːn] **1** *n* *(for butter)* mantequera *f*; *Br (for milk)* lechera *f*
2 *vt* *(butter)* hacer
3 *vi* revolverse, agitarse
▸ **churn out** *vt sep Fam* producir en serie

chute [ʃuːt] *n* *(channel)* conducto *m*; *(slide)* tobogán *m*

chutney [ˈtʃʌtnɪ] *n* conserva *f* (de frutas) picante

CIA [si:aɪ'eɪ] *n US* (*abbr* **Central Intelligence Agency**) CIA *f*

CID [si:aɪ'di:] *n Br* (*abbr* **Criminal Investigation Department**) = policía judicial británica

cider ['saɪdə(r)] *n* sidra *f*

cigar [sɪ'gɑ:(r)] *n* puro *m*

cigarette [sɪgə'ret] *n* cigarrillo *m*; **c. case** pitillera *f*; **c. end** colilla *f*; **c. holder** boquilla *f*; **c. lighter** mechero *m*

Cinderella [sɪndə'relə] *n* Cenicienta *f*

cine camera ['sɪnɪkæmərə] *n Br* cámara cinematográfica

cinema ['sɪnɪmə] *n* (**a**) *Br* (*building*) cine *m* (**b**) (*art*) cine *m*

cinnamon ['sɪnəmən] *n* canela *f*

cipher ['saɪfə(r)] *n* (*numeral*) cifra *f*

circle ['sɜ:kəl] **1** *n* (**a**) (*of people*) círculo *m*; (*of people*) corro *m*; **in business circles** en el mundo de los negocios (**b**) *Th* anfiteatro *m*
2 *vt* (*surround*) rodear; (*move round*) dar la vuelta a
3 *vi* dar vueltas

circuit ['sɜ:kɪt] *n* (**a**) (*journey*) recorrido *m* (**b**) *Elec* circuito *m* (**c**) *Sport* (*events*) liga *f*; *Br* (*track*) circuito *m* (**d**) *Br Jur* **c. judge** juez *mf* de distrito

circular ['sɜ:kjʊlə(r)] *adj & n* circular (*f*)

circulate ['sɜ:kjʊleɪt] **1** *vt* (*news*) hacer circular
2 *vi* circular

circulation [sɜ:kjʊ'leɪʃən] *n* (**a**) (*of blood*) circulación *f* (**b**) (*of newspaper*) tirada *f*

circumcise ['sɜ:kəmsaɪz] *vt* circuncidar

circumference [sə'kʌmfərəns] *n* circunferencia *f*

circumspect ['sɜ:kəmspekt] *adj* prudente

circumstance ['sɜ:kəmstəns] *n* (*usu pl*) circunstancia *f*; **under no circumstances** en ningún caso; **economic circumstances** situación económica

circumvent [sɜ:kəm'vent] *vt Fig* burlar

circus ['sɜ:kəs] *n* circo *m*

cirrhosis [sɪ'rəʊsɪs] *n* cirrosis *f*

CIS [si:aɪ'es] *n* (*abbr* **Commonwealth of Independent States**) CEI *f*

cistern ['sɪstən] *n* cisterna *f*

cite [saɪt] *vt* (*quote*) citar

citizen ['sɪtɪzən] *n* ciudadano(a) *m,f*

citizenship ['sɪtɪzənʃɪp] *n* ciudadanía *f*

citrus ['sɪtrəs] *adj* **c. fruits** agrios *mpl*

city ['sɪtɪ] *n* (**a**) ciudad *f*; *US* **c. council** ayuntamiento *m*; *US* **c. hall** ayuntamiento (**b**) *Fin* **the C.** = el centro financiero de Londres

civic ['sɪvɪk] *adj* cívico(a); *Br* **c. centre** centro cívico; **c. duties** obligaciones cívicas

civil ['sɪvəl] *adj* (**a**) civil; **c. defence** defensa *f* civil; **c. rights** derechos *mpl* civiles; **c. servant** funcionario(a) *m,f*; *Pol* **c. service** administración pública (**b**) (*polite*) cortés, educado(a)

civilian [sɪ'vɪljən] *adj & n* civil (*mf*); **c. clothing** traje *m* de paisano

civilization [sɪvɪlaɪ'zeɪʃən] *n* civilización *f*

civilized ['sɪvɪlaɪzd] *adj* civilizado(a)

clad [klæd] **1** *adj Literary* vestido(a)
2 *pt & pp of* **clothe**

claim [kleɪm] **1** *vt* (**a**) (*benefits, rights*) reclamar; *Jur* (*compensation*) exigir (**b**) (*assert*) afirmar
2 *n* (**a**) (*demand*) reclamación *f*; *Jur* demanda *f*; **to put in a c.** reclamar una indemnización (**b**) (*right*) derecho *m* (**c**) (*assertion*) pretensión *f*

claimant ['kleɪmənt] *n Jur* demandante *mf*

clairvoyant [kleə'vɔɪənt] *n* clarividente *mf*

clam [klæm] *n* almeja *f*
► **clam up** *vi Fam* callarse

clamber ['klæmbə(r)] *vi* trepar (**over** por)

clammy ['klæmɪ] *adj* (**clammier, clammiest**) (*weather*) bochornoso(a); (*hand*) pegajoso(a)

clamour, *US* **clamor** ['klæmə(r)] **1** *n* clamor *m*
2 *vi* clamar; **to c. for** pedir a gritos

clamp [klæmp] **1** *n* (*for carpentry*) tornillo *m* de banco; *Tech* abrazadera *f*; **wheel c.** cepo *m*
2 *vt* sujetar con abrazaderas
► **clamp down on** *vt insep* aumentar los esfuerzos contra

clan [klæn] *n* clan *m*

clandestine [klæn'destɪn] *adj* clandestino(a)

clang [klæŋ] **1** *vi* sonar
2 *n* sonido metálico

clap [klæp] *vi* aplaudir
2 *n* (**a**) palmada *f* (**b**) **a c. of thunder** un trueno

clapping ['klæpɪŋ] *n* aplausos *mpl*

claret ['klærət] *n Br* (*wine*) clarete *m*; (*colour*) burdeos *m*

clarify ['klærɪfaɪ] *vt* aclarar

clarinet [klærɪ'net] *n* clarinete *m*

clarity ['klærɪtɪ] *n* claridad *f*

clash [klæʃ] **1** *vi* (**a**) (*cymbals*) sonar; (*swords*) chocar; *Fig* (*disagree*) estar en desacuerdo (**b**) *(colours)* desentonar (**c**) *(dates)* coincidir

2 *n* (**a**) *(sound)* sonido *m* (**b**) *(fight)* choque *m*; *Fig (conflict)* conflicto *m*

clasp [klɑːsp] **1** *n* (**a**) *(on belt)* cierre *m*; *(on necklace)* broche *m* (**b**) *(grasp)* apretón *m*; **c. knife** navaja *f*

2 *vt (object)* agarrar; **to c. hands** juntar las manos

class [klɑːs] **1** *n* clase *f*; **c. struggle** lucha *f* de clases; *US Educ* **c. of '84** promoción *f* de 1984; *Rail* **second c. ticket** billete *m* de segunda (clase)

2 *vt* clasificar

classic ['klæsɪk] **1** *adj* clásico(a)

2 *n* (**a**) *(author)* autor clásico; *(work)* obra clásica (**b**) **the classics** *(literature)* las obras clásicas; **classics** *(languages)* clásicas *fpl*

classical ['klæsɪkəl] *adj* clásico(a)

classified ['klæsɪfaɪd] *adj (information)* secreto(a); **c. advertisements** anuncios *mpl* por palabras

classify ['klæsɪfaɪ] *vt* clasificar

classless ['klɑːslɪs] *adj* sin clases

classmate ['klɑːsmeɪt] *n* compañero(a) *m,f* de clase

classroom ['klɑːsruːm] *n* aula *f*, clase *f*

clatter ['klætə(r)] **1** *vi* hacer ruido; *(things falling)* hacer estrépito

2 *n* ruido *m*, estrépito *m*

clause [klɔːz] *n* (**a**) *Jur* cláusula *f* (**b**) *Ling* oración *f*

claw [klɔː] **1** *n (of bird, lion)* garra *f*; *(of cat)* uña *f*, *(of crab)* pinza *f*

2 *vt* agarrar, arañar; *(tear)* desgarrar

▸ **claw at** *vt insep* agarrar, arañar

clay [kleɪ] *n* arcilla *f*; **c. pigeon shooting** tiro *m* al plato

clean [kliːn] **1** *adj* (**a**) limpio(a) (**b**) *(unmarked, pure)* sin defecto; **a c. copy** una copia en limpio; **to have a c. record** no tener antecedentes (penales) (**c**) *(not obscene)* decente (**d**) *Fig* **to make a c. sweep of** it arrasar

2 *adv* (**a**) **to play c.** jugar limpio; *Fam* **to come c.** confesarlo todo (**b**) *Fam* por completo; **it went c. through the middle** pasó justo por el medio

3 *vt (room)* limpiar; **to c. one's teeth** lavarse los dientes

▸ **clean out** *vt sep (room)* limpiar a fondo

▸ **clean up** *vt sep & vi* limpiar

clean-cut ['kliːnˈkʌt] *adj (person)* limpio(a), pulcro(a)

cleaner ['kliːnə(r)] *n* limpiador(a) *m,f*

cleaning ['kliːnɪŋ] *n* limpieza *f*

cleanliness ['klenlɪnɪs] *n* limpieza *f*

cleanse [klenz] *vt* limpiar

cleansing ['klenzɪŋ] *n* **c. lotion** leche limpiadora

clear [klɪə(r)] **1** *adj* (**a**) claro(a); *(road, day)* despejado(a); **c. conscience** conciencia tranquila (**b**) *(obvious)* claro(a); **to make sth c.** aclarar algo (**c**) *(majority)* absoluto(a); *(profit)* neto(a); **three c. days** tres días completos (**d**) *(free)* libre

2 *adv* (**a**) *Fig* **loud and c.** claramente (**b**) **stand c.!** ¡apártese!; **to stay c. of** evitar

3 *vt (room)* vaciar; *Com* liquidar; **to c. one's throat** aclararse la garganta; **to c. the table** quitar la mesa (**b**) *(authorize)* autorizar (**c**) *(hurdle)* salvar (**d**) **to c. sb of a charge** exculpar a algn de un delito

4 *vi (sky)* despejarse

▸ **clear away** *vt sep* quitar

▸ **clear off** *vi Fam* largarse; **c. off!** ¡largo!

▸ **clear out** *vt sep (room)* limpiar a fondo; *(cupboard)* vaciar

▸ **clear up** *vt sep* (**a**) *(tidy)* recoger; *(arrange)* ordenar (**b**) *(mystery)* resolver; *(misunderstanding)* aclarar

2 *vi (weather)* despejarse; *(problem)* desaparecer

clearance ['klɪərəns] *n* (**a**) *(of area)* despeje *m*; *Com* **c. sale** liquidación *f* (de existencias) (**b**) *(space)* espacio *m* libre (**c**) *(authorization)* autorización *f*

clear-cut [klɪəˈkʌt] *adj* claro(a)

clearing ['klɪərɪŋ] *n* (**a**) *(in wood)* claro *m* (**b**) *(of rubbish)* limpieza *f* (**c**) *(of cheque)* compensación *f*

clearly ['klɪəlɪ] *adv* (**a**) claramente (**b**) *(at start of sentence)* evidentemente

clearway ['klɪəweɪ] *n Br* = carretera donde está prohibido parar

cleaver ['kliːvə(r)] *n* cuchillo *m* de carnicero

clef [klef] *n* clave *f*; **bass/treble c.** clave de fa/de sol

cleft [kleft] *n* hendidura *f*, grieta *f*

clementine ['kleməntaɪn] *n* clementina *f*

clench [klentʃ] *vt (teeth, fist)* apretar

clergy ['klɜːdʒɪ] *n* clero *m*

clergyman ['klɜːdʒɪmən] *n* clérigo *m*

clerical ['klerɪkəl] *adj* (**a**) *Rel* clerical (**b**) *(staff, work)* de oficina

clerk [klɑːk, *US* klɜːrk] *n* (**a**) *(office worker)* oficinista *mf*; *(civil servant)* funcionario(a) *m,f* (**b**) *US Com* dependiente(a) *m,f*, vendedor(a) *m,f*

clever ['klevə(r)] *adj* (**a**) *(person)* inteligente, listo(a); **to be c. at sth** tener aptitud para algo; *Fam* **c. Dick** sabiondo(a) *m,f* (**b**) *(argument)* ingenioso(a)

cliché ['kliːʃeɪ] n cliché m

click [klɪk] **1** n (sound) clic m

  2 vt (tongue) chasquear

  3 vi **it didn't c.** (I didn't realize) no me di cuenta

client ['klaɪənt] n cliente mf

clientele [kliːɒn'tel] n clientela f

cliff [klɪf] n acantilado m

climate ['klaɪmɪt] n clima m

climax ['klaɪmæks] n (a) (peak) clímax m, punto m culminante (b) (sexual) orgasmo m

climb [klaɪm] **1** vt (ladder) subir a; (mountain) escalar; (tree) trepar a

  2 vi (plants) trepar; Av subir; Fig (socially) ascender

  3 n subida f, ascensión f

  ▸ **climb down** vi bajar; Fig volverse atrás

climber ['klaɪmə(r)] n alpinista mf, Am andinista mf

climbing ['klaɪmɪŋ] n Sport montañismo m, alpinismo m, Am andinismo m

clinch [klɪntʃ] **1** vt resolver; (deal) cerrar

  2 n Fam abrazo apasionado

cling [klɪŋ] vi (pt & pp clung) (hang on) agarrarse; (clothes) ajustarse; (smell) pegarse; **to c. together** unirse

clinic ['klɪnɪk] n (in state hospital) ambulatorio m; (specialized) clínica f

clinical ['klɪnɪkəl] adj Med clínico(a) (b) (detached) frío(a)

clink [klɪŋk] **1** vi tintinear

  2 n tintineo m

clip¹ [klɪp] **1** vt (cut) cortar; (ticket) picar

  2 n (a) (of film) extracto m (b) (with scissors) tijeretada f

clip² [klɪp] **1** n (for hair) pasador m; (for paper) clip m, sujetapapeles m inv; (brooch) clip

  2 vt sujetar

clippers ['klɪpəz] npl (for hair) maquinilla f para rapar; (for nails) cortaúñas m inv; (for hedge) tijeras fpl de podar

clipping ['klɪpɪŋ] n recorte m

clique [kliːk] n Pej camarilla f

cloak [kləʊk] **1** n (garment) capa f

  2 vt encubrir

cloakroom ['kləʊkruːm] n guardarropa m; Euph (toilets) servicios mpl

clock [klɒk] **1** n reloj m

  2 vt (race) cronometrar

  ▸ **clock in, clock on** vi fichar

  ▸ **clock off, clock out** vi fichar a la salida

  ▸ **clock up** vt sep (mileage) hacer

clockwise ['klɒkwaɪz] adj & adv en el sentido de las agujas del reloj

clockwork ['klɒkwɜːk] n mecanismo m; **c. toy** juguete m de cuerda

clog [klɒg] **1** vt obstruir; (pipe) atascar; **to get clogged up** atascarse

  2 n (footwear) zueco m

cloister ['klɔɪstə(r)] n claustro m

close¹ [kləʊs] **1** adj (a) (in space, time) cercano(a); (print, weave) compacto(a); (encounter) cara a cara; (contact) directo(a); **c. to** cerca de; **c. together** juntos(as); Fig **we had a c. shave** nos libramos por los pelos (b) (relationship) estrecho(a); (friend) íntimo(a) (c) (inspection) detallado(a); (watch) atento(a) (d) (contest) reñido(a); **a c. resemblance** un gran parecido (e) (air) cargado(a); (weather) bochornoso(a) (f) (secretive) reservado(a) (g) **c. season** (in hunting) veda f

  2 adv cerca; **they live c. by** or **c. at hand** viven cerca; **to stand c. together** estar apretados(as)

close² [kləʊz] **1** vt (a) cerrar; **closing time** hora f de cierre (b) (end) concluir, terminar; (meeting) levantar

  2 vi (a) (shut) cerrar, cerrarse (b) (end) concluirse, terminarse

  3 n fin m, final m

  ▸ **close down** vi (business) cerrar para siempre; Rad & TV cerrar

  ▸ **close in** vi **to c. in on sb** rodear a algn

closed [kləʊzd] adj cerrado(a); Ind **c. shop** = empresa que emplea solamente a miembros de un sindicato

close-knit [kləʊs'nɪt] adj Fig unido(a)

closely ['kləʊslɪ] adv (a) (tightly) estrechamente, muy; **c. contested** muy reñido(a); **they are c. related** (people) son parientes próximos (b) (attentively) con atención; **to follow (events) c.** seguir de cerca (los acontecimientos)

closet ['klɒzɪt] n US armario m

close-up ['kləʊsʌp] n primer plano m

closure ['kləʊʒə(r)] n cierre m

clot [klɒt] **1** n (a) (of blood) coágulo m; Med **c. on the brain** embolia f cerebral (b) Br Fam tonto(a) m,f

  2 vi coagularse

cloth [klɒθ] n tela f, paño m; (rag) trapo m; (tablecloth) mantel m

clothe [kləʊð] vt (pt & pp clothed or clad) vestir (in or with de); Fig revestir, cubrir (in or with de)

clothes [kləʊðz] npl ropa f, vestidos mpl; **c. brush** cepillo m de la ropa; **c. hanger** percha f; **c. horse** tendedero m plegable; **c. line** tendedero m; **c. peg** or US **pin** pinza f

clothing ['kləʊðɪŋ] n ropa f

cloud [klaʊd] **1** n nube f

2 *vt* nublar; *Fig* **to c. the issue** complicar el asunto

3 *vi* **to c. over** nublarse

cloudy ['klaʊdɪ] *adj* (**cloudier, cloudiest**) (a) *(sky)* nublado(a) (b) *(liquid)* turbio(a)

clout [klaʊt] *Fam* **1** *n* (a) *(blow)* tortazo *m* (b) *(influence)* influencia *f*

2 *vt* dar un tortazo a

clove¹ [kləʊv] *n (spice)* clavo *m*

clove² [kləʊv] *n (of garlic)* diente *m*

clover ['kləʊvə(r)] *n* trébol *m*

clown [klaʊn] **1** *n* payaso *m*

2 *vi* **to c. (about** *or* **around)** hacer el payaso

cloying ['klɔɪɪŋ] *adj* empalagoso(a)

club [klʌb] **1** *n* (a) *(society)* club *m*; **sports c.** club deportivo (b) *(heavy stick)* garrote *m*, porra *f*; *(in golf)* palo *m* (c) *Cards* trébol *m* (d) *Culin* **c. sandwich** sándwich *m* doble; *US* **c. soda** soda *f*

2 *vt* aporrear

3 *vi* **to c. together** pagar entre varios

clubhouse ['klʌbhaʊs] *n* sede *f* de un club

cluck [klʌk] **1** *n* cloqueo *m*

2 *vi* cloquear

clue [kluː] *n (sign)* indicio *m*; *(to mystery)* pista *f*; *(in crossword)* clave *f*; *Fam* **I haven't a c.** no tengo ni idea

clump [klʌmp] *n (of trees)* grupo *m*; *(of plants)* mata *f*

clumsy ['klʌmzɪ] *adj* (**clumsier, clumsiest**) desmañado(a), torpe; *(awkward)* tosco(a)

clung [klʌŋ] *pt & pp of* **cling**

cluster ['klʌstə(r)] **1** *n* grupo *m*, *(of grapes)* racimo *m*

2 *vi* agruparse

clutch [klʌtʃ] **1** *vt* agarrar

2 *vi Fig* **to c. at straws** aferrarse a cualquier cosa

3 *n* (a) *Aut* embrague *m* (b) *Fig* **to fall into sb's clutches** caer en las garras de algn

clutter ['klʌtə(r)] *vt* **to c. (up)** llenar, atestar

cm *(abbr* **centimetre(s))** cm

CND [siːen'diː] *n Br (abbr* **Campaign for Nuclear Disarmament)** = organización británica en favor del desarme nuclear

Co (a) *Com (abbr* **Company)** Cía. (b) *abbr* **County**

c/o [siː'əʊ] *(abbr* **care of)** en el domicilio de

coach [kəʊtʃ] **1** *n* (a) *Aut* autocar *m*; *(carriage)* carruaje *m*; **c. tour** excursión *f* en autocar (b) *Rail* coche *m*, vagón *m* (c) *Sport* entrenador(a) *m,f*

2 *vt Sport* entrenar; *Educ* dar clases particulares a

coagulate [kəʊˈægjʊleɪt] *vi* coagularse

coal [kəʊl] *n* carbón *m*, hulla *f*; **c. bunker** carbonera *f*; **c. merchant** carbonero *m*; **c. mine** mina *f* de carbón

coalfield ['kəʊlfiːld] *n* yacimiento *m* de carbón

coalition [kəʊə'lɪʃən] *n* coalición *f*

coarse [kɔːs] *adj (material)* basto(a); *(skin)* áspero(a); *(language)* grosero(a), ordinario(a)

coast [kəʊst] **1** *n* costa *f*, litoral *m*; *Fam Fig* **the c. is clear** no hay moros en la costa

2 *vi Aut* ir en punto muerto

coastal ['kəʊstəl] *adj* costero(a)

coaster ['kəʊstə(r)] *n (mat)* salvamanteles *m inv*

coastguard ['kəʊstgɑːd] *n* guardacostas *m inv*

coastline ['kəʊstlaɪn] *n* litoral *m*, costa *f*

coat [kəʊt] **1** *n* (a) *(overcoat)* abrigo *m*; *(short)* chaquetón *m*; **c. hanger** percha *f* (b) *(of animal)* pelo *m* (c) *(of paint)* mano *f*, capa *f* (d) **c. of arms** escudo *m* de armas

2 *vt* cubrir (**with** de); *(with liquid)* bañar (**with** en)

coating ['kəʊtɪŋ] *n* capa *f*, baño *m*

coax [kəʊks] *vt* engatusar

cob [kɒb] *n* mazorca *f*

cobble ['kɒbəl] *n* adoquín *m*

cobbler ['kɒblə(r)] *n* zapatero *m*

cobweb ['kɒbweb] *n* telaraña *f*

cocaine [kə'keɪn] *n* cocaína *f*

cock [kɒk] **1** *n* (a) *Orn* gallo *m*; *(male bird)* macho *m* (b) *(on gun)* percutor *m* (c) *Vulg (penis)* polla *f*

2 *vt (gun)* amartillar; *(ears)* erguir

► **cock up** *vt sep Br very Fam* chapucear

cocker ['kɒkə(r)] *n* **c. spaniel** cocker *m*

cockerel ['kɒkərəl] *n* gallo *m* joven

cockeyed ['kɒkaɪd] *adj Fam (lopsided)* torcido(a); *(scheme)* disparatado(a)

cockle ['kɒkəl] *n* berberecho *m*

cockney ['kɒknɪ] **1** *adj* = del East End londinense

2 *n* = persona del East End londinense

cockpit ['kɒkpɪt] *n* cabina *f* del piloto

cockroach ['kɒkrəʊtʃ] *n* cucaracha *f*

cocktail ['kɒkteɪl] *n* cóctel *m*; **c. lounge** bar *m*; **c. party** cóctel; **prawn c.** cóctel de gambas; **Molotov c.** cóctel Molotov

cocky ['kɒkɪ] *adj* (**cockier, cockiest**) *Fam* creído(a)

cocoa ['kəʊkəʊ] *n* cacao *m*

coconut ['kəʊkənʌt] *n* coco *m*

cocoon [kə'kuːn] *n* capullo *m*

COD [si:əʊ'di:] *Br* (*abbr* **cash on delivery**) CAE

cod [kɒd] *n* bacalao *m*; **c. liver oil** aceite *m* de hígado de bacalao

code [kəʊd] **1** *n* código *m*; (*symbol*) clave *f*; *Tel* prefijo *m*
2 *vt* (*message*) cifrar, poner en clave

co-ed [kəʊ'ed] *Fam* **1** *adj* mixto(a)
2 *n* colegio mixto

coerce [kəʊ'ɜːs] *vt* coaccionar

coercion [kəʊ'ɜːʃən] *n* coacción *f*

coexist [kəʊɪg'zɪst] *vi* coexistir

coffee ['kɒfɪ] *n* café *m*; **c. bar/shop** cafetería *f*; **c. break** descanso *m*; **c. table** mesita *f* de café

coffeepot ['kɒfɪpɒt] *n* cafetera *f*

coffer ['kɒfə(r)] *n* arca *f*

coffin ['kɒfɪn] *n* ataúd *m*

cog [kɒg] *n* diente *m*

cognac ['kɒnjæk] *n* coñac *m*

coherent [kəʊ'hɪərənt] *adj* coherente

coil [kɔɪl] **1** *vt* **to c. (up)** enrollar
2 *vi* enroscarse
3 *n* (a) (*loop*) vuelta *f*; (*of rope*) rollo *m*; (*of hair*) rizo *m* (b) (*contraceptive*) espiral *f* (c) *Elec* carrete *m*, bobina *f*

coin [kɔɪn] **1** *n* moneda *f*
2 *vt* (a) (*money*) acuñar (b) *Fig* **to c. a phrase** por así decirlo

coinage ['kɔɪnɪdʒ] *n* moneda *f*, sistema monetario

coincide [kəʊɪn'saɪd] *vi* coincidir (**with** con)

coincidence [kəʊ'ɪnsɪdəns] *n* coincidencia *f*

coincidental [kəʊɪnsɪ'dentəl] *adj* casual

coincidentally [kəʊɪnsɪ'dentəlɪ] *adv* por casualidad *or* coincidencia

Coke® [kəʊk] *n Fam* Coca-Cola® *f*

coke [kəʊk] *n* (*coal*) coque *m*

colander ['kɒləndə(r)] *n* colador *m*

cold [kəʊld] **1** *adj* frío(a); **I'm c.** tengo frío; **it's c.** (*weather*) hace frío; (*thing*) está frío(a); *Fig* **to get c. feet (about doing sth)** entrarle miedo a algn (de hacer algo); **c. cream** crema *f* hidratante; *Fig* **it leaves me c.** no me dice nada; **c. war** guerra fría
2 *n* (a) frío *m* (b) *Med* resfriado *m*; **to catch a c.** resfriarse, acatarrarse; **to have a c.** estar resfriado(a); **c. sore** herpes *m* (en el labio)

cold-blooded [kəʊld'blʌdɪd] *adj* (a) (*animal*) de sangre fría (b) *Fig* (*person*) frío(a); (*crime*) a sangre fría

coleslaw ['kəʊlslɔː] *n* ensalada *f* de col

collaborate [kə'læbəreɪt] *vi* colaborar (**with** con)

collaborator [kə'læbəreɪtə(r)] *n Pol* colaboracionista *mf*

collapse [kə'læps] **1** *vi* (*break down*) derrumbarse; (*cave in*) hundirse; *Fig* (*prices*) caer en picado; *Med* sufrir un colapso
2 *vt* (*table*) plegar
3 *n* (*breaking down*) derrumbamiento *m*; (*caving in*) hundimiento *m*; *Med* colapso *m*

collapsible [kə'læpsəbəl] *adj* plegable

collar ['kɒlə(r)] **1** *n* (*of garment*) cuello *m*; (*for dog*) collar *m*
2 *vt Fam* pescar, agarrar

collarbone ['kɒləbəʊn] *n* clavícula *f*

collateral [kɒ'lætərəl] **1** *n Fin* garantía subsidiaria
2 *adj* colateral

colleague ['kɒliːg] *n* colega *mf*

collect [kə'lekt] **1** *vt* (a) (*gather*) recoger (b) (*stamps etc*) coleccionar (c) (*taxes*) recaudar
2 *vi* (a) (*people*) reunirse (b) (*for charity*) hacer una colecta (**for** para)
3 *adj US* **c. call** llamada *f or Am* llamado *m* a cobro revertido
4 *adv US Tel* **to call c.** llamar a cobro revertido

collection [kə'lekʃən] *n* (a) (*of mail*) recogida *f*; (*of money*) colecta *f* (b) (*of stamps*) colección *f* (c) (*of taxes*) recaudación *f* (d) (*of people*) grupo *m*

collective [kə'lektɪv] **1** *adj* colectivo(a); **c. bargaining** negociación colectiva
2 *n* colectivo *m*

collector [kə'lektə(r)] *n* (a) (*of stamps*) coleccionista *mf* (b) **tax c.** recaudador(a) *m,f* (de impuestos)

college ['kɒlɪdʒ] *n* colegio *m*; (*of university*) colegio mayor; *US* (*university*) universidad *f*

collide [kə'laɪd] *vi* chocar, colisionar

collie ['kɒlɪ] *n* perro *m* pastor escocés

colliery ['kɒljərɪ] *n Br* mina *f* de carbón

collision [kə'lɪʒən] *n* choque *m*

colloquial [kə'ləʊkwɪəl] *adj* coloquial

collusion [kə'luːʒən] *n* conspiración *f*

cologne [kə'ləʊn] *n* (agua *f* de) colonia *f*

Colombia [kə'lɒmbɪə] *n* Colombia

Colombian [kə'lɒmbɪən] *adj & n* colombiano(a) (*m,f*)

colon¹ ['kəʊlən] *n Typ* dos puntos *mpl*

colon² ['kəʊlən] *n Anat* colon *m*

colonel ['kɜːnəl] *n* coronel *m*

colonial [kə'ləʊnɪəl] *adj* colonial

colonize ['kɒlənaɪz] *vt* colonizar

colony ['kɒlənɪ] *n* colonia *f*

color ['kʌlər] *n, vt & vi US* = **colour**

colossal [kə'lɒsəl] *adj* colosal

colour ['kʌlə(r)] **1** *n* (**a**) color *m*; **what c. is it?** ¿de qué color es?; **c. film/television** película *f*/televisión *f* en color; **c. scheme** combinación *f* de colores (**b**) *(race)* color *m*; **c. bar** discriminación *f* racial (**c**) **colours** *Br Sport* colores *mpl*; *Mil (flag)* bandera *f*

2 *vt* colorear

3 *vi* **to c. (up)** ruborizarse

colour-blind ['kʌləblaɪnd] *adj* daltónico(a)

Coloured ['kʌləd] *adj* de color

coloured ['kʌləd] *adj (photograph)* en color

> 🖉 Note that the Spanish word **colorado** is a false friend and is never a translation for the English word **coloured**. In Spanish, **colorado** means "red".

colourful ['kʌləfʊl] *adj* (**a**) con muchos colores (**b**) *Fig* lleno(a) de color; *(person)* pintoresco(a)

colouring ['kʌlərɪŋ] *n (colour)* colorido *m*

colourless ['kʌləlɪs] *adj* incoloro(a); *Fig* soso(a)

colt [kəʊlt] *n* potro *m*

column ['kɒləm] *n* columna *f*

columnist ['kɒləmnɪst] *n* columnista *mf*

coma ['kəʊmə] *n* coma *m*; **to go into a c.** entrar en coma

comb [kəʊm] **1** *n* peine *m*

2 *vt* peinar; **to c. one's hair** peinarse

combat ['kɒmbæt] **1** *n* combate *m*

2 *vt (enemy, disease)* combatir

3 *vi* combatir (**against** contra)

combination [kɒmbɪ'neɪʃən] *n* combinación *f*

combine 1 *vt* [kəm'baɪn] combinar

2 *vi* combinarse; *(companies)* asociarse

3 *n* ['kɒmbaɪn] (**a**) *Com* asociación *f* (**b**) **c. harvester** cosechadora *f*

combustion [kəm'bʌstʃən] *n* combustión *f*

come [kʌm] *vi (pt* **came**; *pp* **come**) (**a**) venir; *(arrive)* llegar; **coming!** ¡voy!; **to c. and go** ir y venir; *Fig* **in years to c.** en el futuro

(**b**) **to c. apart/undone** desatarse/soltarse

(**c**) *(happen)* suceder; **that's what comes of being too impatient** es lo que pasa por ser demasiado impaciente; *Fam* **how c.?** ¿y eso?

(**d**) **I came to believe that ...** llegué a creer que ...

(**e**) *Fig* **c. what may** pase lo que pase

(**f**) *very Fam (have orgasm)* correrse

▸ **come about** *vi* ocurrir, suceder

▸ **come across 1** *vt insep (thing)* encontrar por casualidad; **to c. across sb** tropezar con algn

2 *vi Fig* **to c. across well** causar buena impresión

▸ **come along** *vi* (**a**) *(arrive)* venir; **c. along!** ¡venga! (**b**) *(make progress)* progresar

▸ **come away** *vi (leave)* salir; *(part)* desprenderse (**from** de)

▸ **come back** *vi (return)* volver

▸ **come before** *vt insep* (**a**) preceder (**b**) *(court)* comparecer ante

▸ **come by** *vt insep* adquirir

▸ **come down** *vi* bajar; *(rain)* caer; *(building)* ser derribado(a); **to c. down with the flu** coger la gripe

▸ **come forward** *vi (advance)* avanzar; *(volunteer)* ofrecerse

▸ **come in** *vi* (**a**) *(enter)* entrar; **c. in!** ¡pase! (**b**) *(arrive) (train)* llegar; *(tide)* subir; *Fam Fig* **where do I c. in?** y yo ¿qué pinto? (**c**) **to c. in handy** venir bien (**d**) **to c. in for** ser objeto de

▸ **come into** *vt insep* (**a**) *(enter)* entrar en (**b**) *(inherit)* heredar

▸ **come off 1** *vt insep (fall from)* caerse de; *Fam* **c. off it!** ¡venga ya!

2 *vi* (**a**) *(fall)* caerse; *(stain)* quitarse; *(button)* caerse (**b**) *Fam (take place)* pasar; *(succeed)* salir bien; **to c. off badly** salir mal

▸ **come on** *vi* (**a**) **c. on!** *(hurry)* ¡venga! (**b**) *(make progress)* progresar (**c**) *(rain, illness)* comenzar

▸ **come out** *vi* (**a**) salir (**of** de); *(book)* aparecer; *(product)* estrenarse; *(facts)* revelarse (**b**) *(stain)* quitarse; *(colour)* desteñir (**c**) **to c. out against/in favour of sth** declararse en contra/a favor de algo; *Br Ind* **to c. out (on strike)** declararse en huelga (**d**) *(turn out)* salir

▸ **come over 1** *vi* venir

2 *vt insep* (**a**) *(hill)* aparecer en lo alto de (**b**) *Fam* **what's c. over you?** ¿qué te pasa?

▸ **come round 1** *vt insep (corner)* dar la vuelta a

2 *vi* (**a**) *(visit)* venir (**b**) *(regain consciousness)* volver en sí (**c**) **to c. round to sb's way of thinking** dejarse convencer por algn

▸ **come through 1** *vt insep* (**a**) *(cross)* cruzar (**b**) *(illness)* recuperarse de; *(accident)* sobrevivir

2 *vi (message)* llegar

▸ **come to 1** *vi (regain consciousness)* volver en sí

2 *vt insep* (**a**) *Fig* to c. to one's senses recobrar la razón (**b**) *(amount to)* costar (**c**) *(arrive at)* llegar a; **to c. to an end** terminar; *Fam* **c. to that** a propósito

▶**come under** *vt insep Fig* **to c. under fire from sb** ser criticado(a) por algn

▶**come up** *vi* (**a**) *(rise)* subir; *(approach)* acercarse (**to** a) (**b**) *(difficulty, question)* surgir; **to c. up with a solution** encontrar una solución; **to c. up against problems** encontrarse con problemas (**c**) *(sun)* salir (**d**) **to c. up to** igualar; **to c. up to sb's expectations** satisfacer a algn (**e**) *Fam* **three chips, coming up!** ¡van tres de patatas fritas!

▶**come upon** *vt insep* = **come across**

comeback ['kʌmbæk] *n Fam* (**a**) *(of person)* reaparición *f*; **to make a c.** reaparecer (**b**) *(answer)* réplica *f*

comedian [kə'miːdɪən] *n* cómico *m*

comedienne [kəmiːdɪ'en] *n* cómica *f*

comedown ['kʌmdaʊn] *n Fam* desilusión *f*, revés *m*

comedy ['kɒmɪdɪ] *n* comedia *f*

comet ['kɒmɪt] *n* cometa *m*

comeuppance [kʌm'ʌpəns] *n Fam* **to get one's c.** llevarse su merecido

comfort ['kʌmfət] **1** *n* (**a**) comodidad *f*; *US* **c. station** servicios *mpl* (**b**) *(consolation)* consuelo *m*; **to take c. in** *or* **from sth** consolarse con algo

2 *vt* consolar

comfortable ['kʌmfətəbəl] *adj (chair, person, margin)* cómodo(a); *(temperature)* agradable

comfortably ['kʌmfətəblɪ] *adv (win)* con facilidad; **to be c. off** vivir cómodamente

comforter ['kʌmfətə(r)] *n* (**a**) *Br (scarf)* bufanda *f* (**b**) *(for baby)* chupete *m* (**c**) *US (quilt)* edredón *m*

comforting ['kʌmfətɪŋ] *adj* consolador(a)

comic ['kɒmɪk] **1** *adj* cómico(a); **c. strip** tira cómica, historieta *f*

2 *n* (**a**) *(person)* cómico(a) *m,f* (**b**) *Press* tebeo *m*, comic *m*

coming ['kʌmɪŋ] **1** *adj (year)* próximo(a); *(generation)* futuro(a)

2 *n* venida *f*, llegada *f*; **comings and goings** idas *fpl* y venidas; *Fig* **c. and going** ajetreo *m*

comma ['kɒmə] *n* coma *f*

command [kə'mɑːnd] **1** *vt* (**a**) mandar (**b**) *(respect)* infundir; *(sympathy)* merecer; *(money etc)* disponer de

2 *n* (**a**) *(order)* orden *f*; *(authority)* mando *m*; **to be at sb's c.** estar a las órdenes

de algn (**b**) *(of language)* dominio *m* (**c**) *(disposal)* disposición *f* (**d**) *Comput* comando *m*, instrucción *f*

commandeer [kɒmən'dɪə(r)] *vt* requisar

commander [kə'mɑːndə(r)] *n* comandante *m*

commanding [kə'mɑːndɪŋ] *adj* dominante; *Mil* **c. officer** comandante *m*

commandment [kə'mɑːndmənt] *n* mandamiento *m*

commando [kə'mɑːndəʊ] *n* comando *m*

commemorate [kə'meməreɪt] *vt* conmemorar

commence [kə'mens] *vt & vi Fml* comenzar

commend [kə'mend] *vt* (**a**) *(praise)* alabar, elogiar (**b**) *(entrust)* encomendar (**c**) *(recommend)* recomendar

commensurate [kə'menʃərɪt] *adj* proporcional; **c. to** *or* **with** en proporción con

comment ['kɒment] **1** *n* comentario *m*; **no c.** sin comentario

2 *vi* hacer comentarios

commentary ['kɒməntərɪ] *n* comentario *m*

commentator ['kɒmənteɪtə(r)] *n* comentarista *mf*

commerce ['kɒmɜːs] *n* comercio *m*

commercial [kə'mɜːʃəl] **1** *adj* comercial; *TV* **c. break** corte publicitario

2 *n TV* anuncio *m*

commiserate [kə'mɪzəreɪt] *vi* compadecerse (**with** de)

commission [kə'mɪʃən] **1** *n* (**a**) *Mil* despacho *m* (de oficial); **out of c.** fuera de servicio (**b**) *(of inquiry)* comisión *f*; *(job)* encargo *m* (**c**) *(payment)* comisión *f*

2 *vt* (**a**) *Mil* nombrar (**b**) *(order)* encargar (**c**) *Naut* poner en servicio

commissionaire [kəmɪʃə'neə(r)] *n Br* portero *m*

commissioner [kə'mɪʃənə(r)] *n (official)* comisario *m*; **c. of police** comisario de policía

commit [kə'mɪt] *vt* (**a**) *(crime)* cometer; **to c. suicide** suicidarse (**b**) **to c. oneself (to do sth)** comprometerse (a hacer algo) (**c**) **to c. sth to sb's care** confiar algo a algn

commitment [kə'mɪtmənt] *n* compromiso *m*

committee [kə'mɪtɪ] *n* comisión *f*, comité *m*

commode [kə'məʊd] *n (chair)* silla *f* con orinal; *(chest of drawers)* cómoda *f*

commodity [kə'mɒdɪtɪ] *n* producto *m* básico

🖉 Note that the Spanish word **comodidad** is a false friend and is never a translation for the English word **commodity**. In Spanish, **comodidad** means "comfort, convenience".

common ['kɒmən] **1** adj (**a**) común; **that's c. knowledge** eso lo sabe todo el mundo; **c. law** derecho consuetudinario; **C. Market** Mercado m Común; Br **c. room** sala f de profesores/de estudiantes (**b**) (ordinary) corriente (**c**) (vulgar) ordinario(a), maleducado(a)
2 n (land) campo m or terreno m comunal

commonplace ['kɒmənpleɪs] adj corriente

Commons ['kɒmənz] npl Br **the (House of) C.** (la Cámara de) los Comunes

Commonwealth ['kɒmənwelθ] n Br **the C.** la Commonwealth; **C. of Independent States** Comunidad f de Estados Independientes

commotion [kə'məʊʃən] n alboroto m

commune¹ [kə'mju:n] vi (converse) conversar íntimamente; (with nature) estar en comunión (**with** con)

commune² ['kɒmju:n] n comuna f

communicate [kə'mju:nɪkeɪt] **1** vi comunicarse (**with** con)
2 vt comunicar

communication [kəmju:nɪ'keɪʃən] n (**a**) comunicación f (**b**) Br Rail **c. cord** timbre m de alarma

communion [kə'mju:nɪən] n comunión f; **to take c.** comulgar

communiqué [kə'mju:nɪkeɪ] n comunicado m oficial

communism ['kɒmjʊnɪzəm] n comunismo m

communist ['kɒmjʊnɪst] adj & n comunista (mf)

community [kə'mju:nɪtɪ] n comunidad f; (people) colectividad f; **c. centre** centro m social

commute [kə'mju:t] **1** vi = viajar diariamente al lugar de trabajo
2 vt Jur conmutar

commuter [kə'mju:tə(r)] n = persona que viaja diariamente al lugar de trabajo

compact¹ 1 adj [kəm'pækt] compacto(a); (style) conciso(a)
2 n ['kɒmpækt] (for powder) polvera f

compact² ['kɒmpækt] n Pol pacto m

compact disc ['kɒmpækt'dɪsk] n disco compacto

companion [kəm'pænjən] n compañero(a) m,f

companionship [kəm'pænjənʃɪp] n compañerismo m

company ['kʌmpənɪ] n (**a**) compañía f; **to keep sb c.** hacer compañía a algn (**b**) Com empresa f, compañía f

comparable ['kɒmpərəbəl] adj comparable (**to** or **with** con)

comparative [kəm'pærətɪv] **1** adj comparativo(a); (relative) relativo(a)
2 n Ling comparativo m

comparatively [kəm'pærətɪvlɪ] adv relativamente

compare [kəm'peə(r)] **1** vt comparar (**to** or **with** con); **(as) compared with** en comparación con
2 vi compararse

comparison [kəm'pærɪsən] n comparación f; **by c.** en comparación; **there's no c.** no se puede comparar

compartment [kəm'pɑ:tmənt] n (section) compartimiento m; Rail departamento m

compass ['kʌmpəs] n (**a**) brújula f (**b**) **(pair of) compasses** compás m (**c**) Fig (range) límites mpl

compassion [kəm'pæʃən] n compasión f

compassionate [kəm'pæʃənət] adj compasivo(a)

compatible [kəm'pætəbəl] adj compatible

compel [kəm'pel] vt (**a**) (oblige) obligar; **to c. sb to do sth** obligar a algn a hacer algo (**b**) (admiration) despertar

compelling [kəm'pelɪŋ] adj irresistible

compensate ['kɒmpənseɪt] **1** vt compensar; **to c. sb for sth** indemnizar a algn de algo
2 vi compensar

compensation [kɒmpən'seɪʃən] n compensación f; (for loss) indemnización f

compere ['kɒmpeə(r)] n Br animador(a) m,f

compete [kəm'pi:t] vi competir

competence ['kɒmpɪtəns] n (**a**) (ability) aptitud f (**b**) (of court etc) competencia f

competent ['kɒmpɪtənt] adj competente

competition [kɒmpɪ'tɪʃən] n (**a**) (contest) concurso m (**b**) Com competencia f

competitive [kəm'petɪtɪv] adj competitivo(a)

competitor [kəm'petɪtə(r)] n competidor(a) m,f

compilation [kɒmpɪ'leɪʃən] n recopilación f

compile [kəm'paɪl] vt compilar, recopilar

complacency [kəm'pleɪsənsɪ] n autocomplacencia f

📝 Note that the Spanish word **complacencia** is a false friend and is never a translation for the English word **complacency**. In Spanish, **complacencia** means "satisfaction, indulgence".

complacent [kəm'pleɪsənt] *adj* autocomplaciente

complain [kəm'pleɪn] *vi* quejarse (**of/about** de)

complaint [kəm'pleɪnt] *n* (**a**) queja *f*; *Com* reclamación *f* (**b**) *Jur* demanda *f* (**c**) *Med* enfermedad *f*

complement ['kɒmplɪmənt] **1** *n* (**a**) complemento *m* (**b**) *Naut* dotación *f*
2 *vt* complementar

complementary [kɒmplɪ'mentərɪ] *adj* complementario(a)

complete [kəm'pliːt] **1** *adj* (**a**) *(entire)* completo(a) (**b**) *(absolute)* total
2 *vt* completar; **to c. a form** rellenar un formulario

completely [kəm'pliːtlɪ] *adv* completamente, por completo

completion [kəm'pliːʃən] *n* terminación *f*; **near c.** casi terminado(a); **on c.** en cuanto se termine

complex ['kɒmpleks] **1** *adj* complejo(a)
2 *n* complejo *m*; **inferiority c.** complejo de inferioridad

complexion [kəm'plekʃən] *n* tez *f*; *Fig* aspecto *m*

📝 Note that the Spanish word **complexión** is a false friend and is never a translation for the English word **complexion**. In Spanish, **complexión** means "build".

compliance [kəm'plaɪəns] *n* conformidad *f*; **in c. with** de acuerdo con

complicate ['kɒmplɪkeɪt] *vt* complicar

complicated ['kɒmplɪkeɪtɪd] *adj* complicado(a)

complication [kɒmplɪ'keɪʃən] *n* complicación *f*

complicity [kəm'plɪsɪtɪ] *n* complicidad *f*

compliment 1 *n* ['kɒmplɪmənt] (**a**) cumplido *m*; **to pay sb a c.** hacerle un cumplido a algn (**b**) **compliments** saludos *mpl*
2 *vt* ['kɒmplɪment] felicitar; **to c. sb on sth** felicitar a algn por algo

complimentary [kɒmplɪ'mentərɪ] *adj* (**a**) *(praising)* elogioso(a) (**b**) *(free)* gratis

comply [kəm'plaɪ] *vi* obedecer; **to c. with** *(order)* cumplir con; *(request)* acceder a

component [kəm'pəʊnənt] **1** *n* componente *m*
2 *adj* componente; **c. part** parte *f*

compose [kəm'pəʊz] *vt & vi* (**a**) componer; **to be composed of** componerse de (**b**) **to c. oneself** calmarse

composed [kəm'pəʊzd] *adj (calm)* sereno(a)

composer [kəm'pəʊzə(r)] *n* compositor(a) *m,f*

composite ['kɒmpəzɪt] *adj* compuesto(a)

composition [kɒmpə'zɪʃən] *n* composición *f*; *(essay)* redacción *f*

compost ['kɒmpɒst] *n* abono *m*

composure [kəm'pəʊʒə(r)] *n* calma *f*, serenidad *f*

compound¹ ['kɒmpaʊnd] **1** *n* compuesto *m*
2 *adj* compuesto(a); *(fracture)* complicado(a)
3 *vt* [kəm'paʊnd] *(problem)* agravar

compound² ['kɒmpaʊnd] *n (enclosure)* recinto *m*

comprehend [kɒmprɪ'hend] *vt* comprender

comprehensible [kɒmprɪ'hensəbəl] *adj* comprensible

comprehension [kɒmprɪ'henʃən] *n* comprensión *f*

comprehensive [kɒmprɪ'hensɪv] *adj* (**a**) *(knowledge)* amplio(a); *(study)* detallado(a) (**b**) *Ins* a todo riesgo (**c**) *Br* **c. school** ≃ instituto *m* de segunda enseñanza

📝 Note that the Spanish word **comprensivo** is a false friend and is never a translation for the English word **comprehensive**. In Spanish, **comprensivo** means "understanding".

compress 1 *vt* [kəm'pres] comprimir
2 *n* ['kɒmpres] compresa *f*

comprise [kəm'praɪz] *vt* comprender; *(consist of)* constar de

compromise ['kɒmprəmaɪz] **1** *n* solución *f* negociada; **to reach a c.** llegar a un acuerdo
2 *vi (two people)* llegar a un acuerdo; *(individual)* transigir
3 *vt (person)* comprometer

📝 Note that the Spanish word **compromiso** is a false friend and is never a translation for the English word **compromise**. In Spanish, **compromiso** means "obligation, commitment, agreement".

compulsion [kəm'pʌlʃən] *n* obligación *f*

compulsive [kəm'pʌlsɪv] *adj* compulsivo(a)

compulsory [kəm'pʌlsərɪ] *adj* obligatorio(a)

computer [kəm'pju:tə(r)] *n* ordenador *m*, *Am* computadora *f*; **c. programmer** programador(a) *m,f* de ordenadores; **c. science** informática *f*; **personal c.** ordenador personal, *Am* computadora personal

computerize [kəm'pju:təraɪz] *vt* informatizar

computing [kəm'pju:tɪŋ] *n* informática *f*

comrade ['kɒmreɪd] *n* (**a**) *(companion)* compañero(a) *m,f* (**b**) *Pol* camarada *mf*

comradeship ['kɒmreɪdʃɪp] *n* camaradería *f*

con [kɒn] *Fam* **1** *vt* estafar, timar
2 *n* estafa *f*, camelo *m*; **c. man** estafador *m*

concave ['kɒnkeɪv] *adj* cóncavo(a)

conceal [kən'si:l] *vt* ocultar; *(emotions)* disimular

concede [kən'si:d] *vt* conceder

conceit [kən'si:t] *n* presunción *f*, vanidad *f*

conceited [kən'si:tɪd] *adj* presuntuoso(a)

conceivable [kən'si:vəbəl] *adj* concebible

conceive [kən'si:v] *vt & vi* concebir

concentrate ['kɒnsəntreɪt] **1** *vt* concentrar
2 *vi* **to c. on sth** concentrarse en algo

concentration [kɒnsən'treɪʃən] *n* concentración *f*; **c. camp** campo *m* de concentración

concept ['kɒnsept] *n* concepto *m*

conception [kən'sepʃən] *n Med* concepción *f*; *(understanding)* concepto *m*, idea *f*

concern [kən'sɜ:n] **1** *vt* (**a**) concernir, afectar; **as far as I'm concerned** por lo que a mí se refiere (**b**) *(worry)* preocupar
2 *n* (**a**) **it's no c. of mine** no es asunto mío (**b**) *(worry)* preocupación *f* (**c**) *Com* negocio *m*

concerned [kən'sɜ:nd] *adj* (**a**) *(affected)* afectado(a) (**b**) *(worried)* preocupado(a) (**about** por)

concerning [kən'sɜ:nɪŋ] *prep* con respecto a, en cuanto a

concert ['kɒnsət, 'kɒnsɜ:t] *n Mus* concierto *m*; **c. hall** sala *f* de conciertos

concerted [kən'sɜ:tɪd] *adj* concertado(a)

concertina [kɒnsə'ti:nə] *n* concertina *f*

concerto [kən'tʃɜ:təʊ] *n* concierto *m*

concession [kən'seʃən] *n* (**a**) concesión *f*; **tax c.** privilegio *m* fiscal (**b**) *Com* reducción *f*

concise [kən'saɪs] *adj* conciso(a)

conclude [kən'klu:d] *vt & vi* concluir

conclusion [kən'klu:ʒən] *n* conclusión *f*; **to reach a c.** llegar a una conclusión

conclusive [kən'klu:sɪv] *adj* concluyente

concoct [kən'kɒkt] *vt* *(dish)* confeccionar; *Fig (plan)* fraguar; *(excuse)* inventar

concoction [kən'kɒkʃən] *n* *(mixture)* mezcolanza *f*; *Pej (brew)* brebaje *m*

concourse ['kɒŋkɔ:s] *n* explanada *f*

> 🖉 Note that the Spanish word **concurso** is a false friend and is never a translation for the English word **concourse**. In Spanish, **concurso** means "competition, contest".

concrete ['kɒnkri:t] **1** *n* hormigón *m*; **c. mixer** hormigonera *f*
2 *adj* (**a**) *(definite)* concreto(a) (**b**) *(made of concrete)* de hormigón

concur [kən'kɜ:(r)] *vi* (**a**) **to c. with** *(agree)* estar de acuerdo con (**b**) *(coincide)* coincidir

concurrent [kən'kʌrənt] *adj* simultáneo(a)

concussion [kən'kʌʃən] *n* conmoción *f* cerebral

condemn [kən'dem] *vt* condenar

condemnation [kɒndem'neɪʃən] *n* condena *f*

condensation [kɒnden'seɪʃən] *n* condensación *f*

condense [kən'dens] **1** *vt* condensar
2 *vi* condensarse

condensed [kən'denst] *adj* **c. milk** leche condensada

condescending [kɒndɪ'sendɪŋ] *adj* condescendiente

condition [kən'dɪʃən] **1** *n* condición *f*; **to be in good c.** estar en buen estado; **on c. that ...** a condición de que ...; **on one c.** con una condición; **heart c.** enfermedad cardíaca; **conditions** *(circumstances)* circunstancias *fpl*
2 *vt* condicionar

conditional [kən'dɪʃənəl] *adj* condicional

conditioner [kən'dɪʃənə(r)] *n* acondicionador *m*

condolences [kən'dəʊlənsɪz] *npl* pésame *m*; **please accept my c.** le acompaño en el sentimiento

condom ['kɒndəm] *n* preservativo *m*

condominium [kɒndə'mɪnɪəm] *n US* *(building)* = bloque de apartamentos poseídos por diferentes propietarios; *(apartment)* apartamento *m*, piso *m* (en propiedad)

condone [kən'dəʊn] *vt* perdonar, consentir

condor ['kɒndɔ:(r)] *n* cóndor *m*

conducive [kən'dju:sɪv] *adj* conducente

conduct 1 *n* ['kɒndʌkt] *(behaviour)*

conducta *f*, comportamiento *m*

2 *vt* [kən'dʌkt] *(lead)* guiar; *(business, orchestra)* dirigir; **conducted tour** visita acompañada; **to c. oneself** comportarse

3 *vi Mus* dirigir

conductor [kən'dʌktə(r)] *n* **(a)** *Br (on bus)* cobrador *m* **(b)** *US Rail* revisor(a) *m,f* **(c)** *Mus* director(a) *m,f* **(d)** *Phys* conductor *m*

conductress [kən'dʌktrɪs] *n (on bus)* cobradora *f*

cone [kəʊn] *n* **(a)** cono *m*; **ice-cream c.** cucurucho *m* **(b)** *Bot* piña *f*

confectioner [kən'fekʃənə(r)] *n* confitero(a) *m,f*; **c.'s (shop)** confitería *f*

confectionery [kən'fekʃənɪ] *n* dulces *mpl*

confederate [kən'fedərɪt] **1** *adj* confederado(a)

2 *n* confederado(a) *m,f*; *Jur* cómplice *mf*

confer [kən'fɜː(r)] **1** *vt* **to c. a title on sb** conferir un título a algn

2 *vi* consultar

conference ['kɒnfərəns] *n* conferencia *f*

confess [kən'fes] **1** *vi* confesar; *Rel* confesarse

2 *vt* confesar

confession [kən'feʃən] *n* confesión *f*

confessional [kən'feʃənəl] *n* confesionario *m*

confetti [kən'fetɪ] *n* confeti *m*

confide [kən'faɪd] *vi* **to c. in sb** confiar en algn

confidence ['kɒnfɪdəns] *n* **(a)** confianza *f*; **vote of c./no c.** voto *m* de confianza/de censura; **c. trick** camelo *m* **(b)** *(secret)* confidencia *f*; **in c.** en confianza

confident ['kɒnfɪdənt] *adj* seguro(a)

confidential [kɒnfɪ'denʃəl] *adj (secret)* confidencial; *(entrusted)* de confianza

confine [kən'faɪn] *vt* encerrar; *Fig* limitar

confinement [kən'faɪnmənt] *n* **(a)** *(prison)* prisión *f*; **to be in solitary c.** estar incomunicado(a) **(b)** *Med* parto *m*

confirm [kən'fɜːm] *vt* confirmar

confirmation [kɒnfə'meɪʃən] *n* confirmación *f*

confirmed [kən'fɜːmd] *adj* empedernido(a)

confiscate ['kɒnfɪskeɪt] *vt* confiscar

conflict 1 *n* ['kɒnflɪkt] conflicto *m*

2 *vi* [kən'flɪkt] chocar (**with** con)

conflicting [kən'flɪktɪŋ] *adj* contradictorio(a)

conform [kən'fɔːm] *vi* conformarse; **to c. to** *or* **with** *(customs)* amoldarse a; *(rules)* someterse a

confound [kən'faʊnd] *vt* confundir, desconcertar

confront [kən'frʌnt] *vt* hacer frente a

confrontation [kɒnfrʌn'teɪʃən] *n* confrontación *f*

confuse [kən'fjuːz] *vt (person)* despistar; *(thing)* confundir (**with** con); **to get confused** confundirse

confused [kən'fjuːzd] *adj (person)* confundido(a); *(mind, ideas)* confuso(a)

confusing [kən'fjuːzɪŋ] *adj* confuso(a)

confusion [kən'fjuːʒən] *n* confusión *f*

congeal [kən'dʒiːl] *vi* coagularse

congenial [kən'dʒiːnɪəl] *adj* agradable

congenital [kən'dʒenɪtəl] *adj* congénito(a)

congested [kən'dʒestɪd] *adj* **(a)** *(street)* repleto(a) de gente; *(city)* superpoblado(a) **(b)** *Med* congestionado(a)

congestion [kən'dʒestʃən] *n* congestión *f*

conglomeration [kənglɒmə'reɪʃən] *n* conglomeración *f*

congratulate [kən'grætjʊleɪt] *vt* felicitar

congratulations [kəngrætjʊ'leɪʃənz] *npl* felicitaciones *fpl*; **c.!** ¡enhorabuena!

congregate ['kɒŋgrɪgeɪt] *vi* congregarse

congregation [kɒŋgrɪ'geɪʃən] *n (group)* congregación *f*; *Rel* fieles *mpl*

congress ['kɒŋgres] *n* **(a)** *(conference)* congreso *m* **(b)** *US Pol* **C.** el Congreso *(de los Estados Unidos)*

Congressman ['kɒŋgresmən] *n US Pol* congresista *m*, *Am* congresal *m*

Congresswoman ['kɒŋgreswʊmən] *n US Pol* congresista *f*, *Am* congresal *f*

conifer ['kɒnɪfə(r)] *n* conífera *f*

conjecture [kən'dʒektʃə(r)] **1** *n* conjetura *f*

2 *vt* conjeturar

3 *vi* hacer conjeturas

conjugal ['kɒndʒʊgəl] *adj* conyugal

conjugate ['kɒndʒʊgeɪt] *vt* conjugar

conjunction [kən'dʒʌŋkʃən] *n* conjunción *f*; *Fig* **in c. with** conjuntamente con

conjunctivitis [kəndʒʌŋktɪ'vaɪtɪs] *n* conjuntivitis *f*

conjure ['kʌndʒə(r)] **1** *vt* **to c. (up)** *(magician)* hacer aparecer; *(memories)* evocar

2 *vi* hacer juegos de manos

conjurer ['kʌndʒərə(r)] *n* prestidigitador(a) *m,f*

conker ['kɒŋkə(r)] *n Fam* castaña *f*

connect [kə'nekt] **1** *vt* **(a)** *(join)* juntar, unir; *(wires)* empalmar; *Fig* **to be connected by marriage** estar emparentado(a) por matrimonio **(b)** *(install)* instalar; *Elec*

conectar (**c**) *Tel* (*person*) poner (**d**) *Fig* (*associate*) asociar

   2 *vi* unirse; (*rooms*) comunicarse; (*train, flight*) enlazar *or* empalmar (**with** con)

connected [kə'nektɪd] *adj* unido(a); (*events*) relacionado(a); *Fig* **to be well c.** (*person*) (*socially*) estar bien relacionado(a)

connection [kə'nekʃən] *n* (**a**) (*joint*) juntura *f*, unión *f*; *Elec* conexión *f*; *Tel* instalación *f* (**b**) *Rail* correspondencia *f* (**c**) *Fig* (*of ideas*) relación *f*; **in c. with** (*regarding*) con respecto a (**d**) (*person*) contacto *m*

connive [kə'naɪv] *vi* **to c. at** hacer la vista gorda con

connoisseur [kɒnɪ'sɜː(r)] *n* conocedor(a) *m,f*

connotation [kɒnə'teɪʃən] *n* connotación *f*

conquer ['kɒŋkə(r)] *vt* (*enemy, bad habit*) vencer; (*country*) conquistar

conqueror ['kɒŋkərə(r)] *n* conquistador *m*

conquest ['kɒŋkwest] *n* conquista *f*

conscience ['kɒnʃəns] *n* conciencia *f*; **to have a clear c.** tener la conciencia tranquila; **to have a guilty c.** sentirse culpable

conscientious [kɒnʃɪ'enʃəs] *adj* concienzudo(a); **c. objector** objetor(a) *m,f* de conciencia

conscious ['kɒnʃəs] *adj* (*aware*) consciente; (*choice etc*) deliberado(a)

consciousness ['kɒnʃəsnɪs] *n Med* conocimiento *m*; (*awareness*) consciencia *f*

conscript ['kɒnskrɪpt] *n* recluta *m*

conscription [kən'skrɪpʃən] *n* servicio *m* militar obligatorio

consecrate ['kɒnsɪkreɪt] *vt* consagrar

consecutive [kən'sekjʊtɪv] *adj* consecutivo(a)

consensus [kən'sensəs] *n* consenso *m*

consent [kən'sent] **1** *n* consentimiento *m*; **by common c.** de común acuerdo

   2 *vi* consentir (**to** en)

consequence ['kɒnsɪkwəns] *n* consecuencia *f*

consequent ['kɒnsɪkwənt] *adj* consiguiente

consequently ['kɒnsɪkwəntlɪ] *adv* por consiguiente

conservation [kɒnsə'veɪʃən] *n* conservación *f*

conservative [kən'sɜːvətɪv] **1** *adj* cauteloso(a)

   2 *adj & n Pol* **C.** conservador(a) (*m,f*)

conservatory [kən'sɜːvətrɪ] *n* (**a**) (*greenhouse*) invernadero *m* (**b**) *Mus* conservatorio *m*

conserve **1** *vt* [kən'sɜːv] conservar

   2 *n* ['kɒnsɜːv] conserva *f*

consider [kən'sɪdə(r)] *vt* (**a**) (*ponder on, regard*) considerar; **to c. doing sth** pensar hacer algo (**b**) (*keep in mind*) tener en cuenta

considerable [kən'sɪdərəbəl] *adj* considerable

considerably [kən'sɪdərəblɪ] *adv* bastante

considerate [kən'sɪdərɪt] *adj* considerado(a)

consideration [kənsɪdə'reɪʃən] *n* consideración *f*; **without due c.** sin reflexión

considering [kən'sɪdərɪŋ] *prep* teniendo en cuenta

consign [kən'saɪn] *vt Com* consignar; *Fig* entregar

consignment [kən'saɪnmənt] *n* envío *m*

consist [kən'sɪst] *vi* **to c. of** consistir en

consistency [kən'sɪstənsɪ] *n* (**a**) (*of actions*) consecuencia *f* (**b**) (*of mixture*) consistencia *f*

consistent [kən'sɪstənt] *adj* consecuente; **c. with** de acuerdo con

> 📝 Note that the Spanish word **consistente** is a false friend and is never a translation for the English word **consistent**. In Spanish, **consistente** means "firm, solid, sound".

consolation [kɒnsə'leɪʃən] *n* consuelo *m*; **c. prize** premio *m* de consolación

console¹ [kən'səʊl] *vt* consolar

console² ['kɒnsəʊl] *n* consola *f*

consolidate [kən'sɒlɪdeɪt] **1** *vt* consolidar

   2 *vi* consolidarse

consonant ['kɒnsənənt] *n* consonante *f*

consortium [kən'sɔːtɪəm] *n* consorcio *m*

conspicuous [kən'spɪkjʊəs] *adj* (*striking*) llamativo(a); (*easily seen*) visible; (*mistake*) evidente

conspiracy [kən'spɪrəsɪ] *n* conjura *f*

conspire [kən'spaɪə(r)] *vi* conspirar

constable ['kʌnstəbəl] *n* policía *m*, guardia *m*; **chief c.** jefe *m* de policía

constabulary [kən'stæbjʊlərɪ] *n Br* comisaría *f*

constant ['kɒnstənt] **1** *adj* constante; (*continuous*) incesante; (*loyal*) fiel, leal

   2 *n* constante *f*

constellation [kɒnstɪ'leɪʃən] *n* constelación *f*

consternation [kɒnstə'neɪʃən] *n* consternación *f*

constipated [ˈkɒnstɪpeɪtɪd] *adj* **to be c.** estar estreñido(a)

> *ℓ* Note that the Spanish word **constipado** is a false friend and is never a translation for the English word **constipated**. In Spanish, **constipado** means both "cold, chill" and "suffering from a cold".

constipation [kɒnstɪˈpeɪʃən] *n* estreñimiento *m*

constituency [kənˈstɪtjʊənsɪ] *n* circunscripción *f* electoral

constituent [kənˈstɪtjʊənt] **1** *adj (component)* constituyente

2 *n* (**a**) *(part)* componente *m* (**b**) *Pol* votante *mf*

constitute [ˈkɒnstɪtjuːt] *vt* constituir

constitution [kɒnstɪˈtjuːʃən] *n* constitución *f*

constitutional [kɒnstɪˈtjuːʃənəl] *adj* constitucional

constrained [kənˈstreɪnd] *adj* **to feel c. to do sth** sentirse obligado(a) a hacer algo

constraint [kənˈstreɪnt] *n* coacción *f*; **to feel c. in sb's presence** sentirse cohibido(a) ante algn

construct [kənˈstrʌkt] *vt* construir

construction [kənˈstrʌkʃən] *n* construcción *f*

constructive [kənˈstrʌktɪv] *adj* constructivo(a)

construe [kənˈstruː] *vt* interpretar

> *ℓ* Note that the Spanish verb **construir** is a false friend and is never a translation for the English verb **to construe**. In Spanish, **construir** means "to build, to manufacture".

consul [ˈkɒnsəl] *n* cónsul *mf*

consulate [ˈkɒnsjʊlɪt] *n* consulado *m*

consult [kənˈsʌlt] *vt & vi* consultar (**about** sobre)

consultant [kənˈsʌltənt] *n Med* especialista *mf*; *Com & Ind* asesor(a) *m,f*

consultation [kɒnsəlˈteɪʃən] *n* consulta *f*

consulting [kənˈsʌltɪŋ] *adj* **c. room** consulta *f*

consume [kənˈsjuːm] *vt* consumir

consumer [kənˈsjuːmə(r)] *n* consumidor(a) *m,f*; **c. goods** bienes *mpl* de consumo

consummate 1 *vt* [ˈkɒnsəmeɪt] consumar

2 *adj* [ˈkɒnsəmɪt] consumado(a)

consumption [kənˈsʌmpʃən] *n* (**a**) *(of food)* consumo *m*; **fit for c.** apto(a) para el consumo (**b**) *Med* tisis *f*

cont. *(abbr* **continued**) sigue

contact [ˈkɒntækt] **1** *n* contacto *m*; **c. lenses** lentes *fpl* de contacto

2 *vt* ponerse en contacto con

contagious [kənˈteɪdʒəs] *adj* contagioso(a)

contain [kənˈteɪn] *vt* contener; **to c. oneself** contenerse

container [kənˈteɪnə(r)] *n* (**a**) *(box, package)* recipiente *m*; *(bottle)* envase *m* (**b**) *Naut* contenedor *m*

contaminate [kənˈtæmɪneɪt] *vt* contaminar

contamination [kəntæmɪˈneɪʃən] *n* contaminación *f*

contd. *(abbr* **continued**) sigue

contemplate [ˈkɒntempleɪt] *vt* (**a**) *(consider)* considerar, pensar en (**b**) *(look at)* contemplar

contemporary [kənˈtemprərɪ] *adj & n* contemporáneo(a) *(m,f)*

contempt [kənˈtempt] *n* desprecio *m*; **to hold in c.** despreciar; **c. of court** desacato *m* a los tribunales

contemptible [kənˈtemptəbəl] *adj* despreciable

contemptuous [kənˈtemptjʊəs] *adj* despectivo(a)

contend [kənˈtend] **1** *vi* competir; *Fig* **there are many problems to c. with** se han planteado muchos problemas

2 *vt* afirmar

contender [kənˈtendə(r)] *n* contendiente *mf*

content[1] [ˈkɒntent] *n* contenido *m*; **table of contents** índice *m* de materias

content[2] [kənˈtent] **1** *adj* contento(a)

2 *vt* contentar

3 *n* contento *m*; **to one's heart's c.** todo lo que uno quiera

contented [kənˈtentɪd] *adj* contento(a), satisfecho(a)

contention [kənˈtenʃən] *n* (**a**) *(dispute)* controversia *f* (**b**) *(point)* punto *m* de vista

contentment [kənˈtentmənt] *n* contento *m*

contest 1 *n* [ˈkɒntest] concurso *m*; *Sport* prueba *f*

2 *vt* [kənˈtest] (**a**) *(matter)* rebatir; *(verdict)* impugnar; *Fig (will)* disputar (**b**) *Pol (seat)* luchar por

contestant [kənˈtestənt] *n* concursante *mf*

context [ˈkɒntekst] *n* contexto *m*

continent [ˈkɒntɪnənt] *n* continente *m*; **(on) the C.** (en) Europa

continental [kɒntɪˈnentəl] *adj* (**a**) continental; **c. shelf** plataforma *f* continental (**b**) *Br* **C.** europeo(a); **c. quilt** edredón *m* de pluma

contingency [kən'tındʒənsɪ] *n* contingencia *f*; **c. plans** planes *mpl* para casos de emergencia

contingent [kən'tındʒənt] *adj* & *n* contingente *(m)*

continual [kən'tınjʊəl] *adj* continuo(a), constante

continuation [kəntınjʊ'eɪʃən] *n (sequel etc)* continuación *f*; *(extension)* prolongación *f*

continue [kən'tınju:] *vt* & *vi* continuar, seguir; **to c. to do sth** seguir *or* continuar haciendo algo

continuous [kən'tınjʊəs] *adj* continuo(a)

contort [kən'tɔ:t] *vt* retorcer

contortion [kən'tɔ:ʃən] *n* contorsión *f*

contour ['kɒntʊə(r)] *n* contorno *m*; **c. line** línea *f* de nivel

contraband ['kɒntrəbænd] *n* contrabando *m*

contraception [kɒntrə'sepʃən] *n* anticoncepción *f*

contraceptive [kɒntrə'septɪv] *adj* & *n* anticonceptivo *(m)*

contract 1 *vi* [kən'trækt] *Phys* contraerse
2 *vt* (**a**) contraer (**b**) **to c. to do sth** *(make agreement)* comprometerse por contrato a hacer algo
3 *n* ['kɒntrækt] contrato *m*; **to enter into a c.** hacer un contrato

contraction [kən'trækʃən] *n* contracción *f*

contractor [kən'træktə(r)] *n* contratista *mf*

contradict [kɒntrə'dɪkt] *vt* contradecir

contradiction [kɒntrə'dɪkʃən] *n* contradicción *f*; **it's a c. in terms** no tiene lógica

contradictory [kɒntrə'dɪktərɪ] *adj* contradictorio(a)

contraption [kən'træpʃən] *n Fam* cacharro *m*

contrary ['kɒntrərɪ] **1** *adj* (**a**) *(opposite)* contrario(a) (**b**) [kən'treərɪ] *(awkward)* terco(a)
2 *n* **on the c.** todo lo contrario; **unless I tell you to the c.** a menos que te diga lo contrario
3 *adv* **c. to** en contra de

contrast 1 *vi* [kən'trɑ:st] contrastar
2 *n* ['kɒntrɑ:st] contraste *m*

contrasting [kən'trɑ:stıŋ] *adj* opuesto(a)

contravene [kɒntrə'vi:n] *vt* contravenir

contribute [kən'trɪbju:t] **1** *vt (money)* contribuir con; *(ideas, information)* aportar

2 *vi* (**a**) contribuir; *(in discussion)* participar (**b**) *Press* colaborar (**to** en)

contribution [kɒntrɪ'bju:ʃən] *n* (**a**) *(of money)* contribución *f*; *(of ideas etc)* aportación *f* (**b**) *Press* colaboración *f*

contributor [kən'trɪbjʊtə(r)] *n (to newspaper)* colaborador(a) *m,f*

contrive [kən'traɪv] *vt* inventar, idear; **to c. to do sth** buscar la forma de hacer algo

contrived [kən'traɪvd] *adj* artificial, forzado(a)

control [kən'trəʊl] **1** *vt* controlar; *(person, animal)* dominar; *(vehicle)* manejar; **to c. one's temper** controlarse
2 *n* (**a**) *(power)* control *m*, dominio *m*; *(authority)* autoridad *f*; **out of c.** fuera de control; **to be in c.** estar al mando; **to be under c.** *(situation)* estar bajo control; **to go out of c.** descontrolarse; **to lose c.** perder los estribos (**b**) *Aut & Av (device)* mando *m*; *Rad & TV* botón *m* de control; **c. panel** tablero *m* de instrumentos; **c. room** sala *f* de control; *Av* **c. tower** torre *f* de control

controversial [kɒntrə'vɜ:ʃəl] *adj* controvertido(a), polémico(a)

controversy ['kɒntrəvɜ:sɪ, kən'trɒvəsɪ] *n* polémica *f*

conurbation [kɒnɜ:'beɪʃən] *n* conurbación *f*

convalesce [kɒnvə'les] *vi* convalecer

convalescence [kɒnvə'lesəns] *n* convalecencia *f*

convalescent [kɒnvə'lesənt] *adj* convaleciente; **c. home** clínica *f* de reposo

convene [kən'vi:n] **1** *vt* convocar
2 *vi* reunirse

convenience [kən'vi:nɪəns] *n* conveniencia *f*, comodidad *f*; **all modern conveniences** todas las comodidades; **at your c.** cuando le convenga; **c. food** comida precocinada; *Br Euph* **public conveniences** aseos públicos

convenient [kən'vi:nɪənt] *adj (time, arrangement)* conveniente, oportuno(a); *(place)* bien situado(a)

convent ['kɒnvənt] *n* convento *m*

convention [kən'venʃən] *n* convención *f*

conventional [kən'venʃənəl] *adj* clásico(a); *(behaviour)* convencional

converge [kən'vɜ:dʒ] *vi* convergir

conversant [kən'vɜ:sənt] *adj Fml* **to be c. with a subject** ser versado(a) en una materia

conversation [kɒnvə'seɪʃən] *n* conversación *f*

conversational [kɒnvə'seɪʃənəl] *adj* coloquial

converse¹ [kən'vɜːs] *vi* conversar

converse² [kən'vɜːs] *n* **the c.** lo opuesto

conversely ['kɒnvɜːslɪ] *adv* a la inversa

conversion [kən'vɜːʃən] *n* *Math & Rel* conversión *f* (**to** a; **into** en)

convert **1** *vt* [kən'vɜːt] convertir
2 *n* ['kɒnvɜːt] converso(a) *m,f*

convertible [kən'vɜːtəbəl] **1** *adj* convertible
2 *n* *Aut* descapotable *m*

convex ['kɒnveks, kɒn'veks] *adj* convexo(a)

convey [kən'veɪ] *vt* (**a**) *(carry)* transportar (**b**) *(sound)* transmitir; *(idea)* comunicar

conveyor [kən'veɪə(r)] *n* **c. belt** cinta transportadora

convict **1** *vt* [kən'vɪkt] declarar culpable a, condenar
2 *n* ['kɒnvɪkt] presidiario(a) *m,f*

conviction [kən'vɪkʃən] *n* (**a**) *(belief)* creencia *f*, convicción *f* (**b**) *Jur* condena *f*

convince [kən'vɪns] *vt* convencer

convincing [kən'vɪnsɪŋ] *adj* convincente

convoluted ['kɒnvəluːtɪd] *adj* intrincado(a)

convoy ['kɒnvɔɪ] *n* convoy *m*

convulse [kən'vʌls] *vt* convulsionar; *Fam* **to be convulsed with laughter** troncharse de risa

convulsion [kən'vʌlʃən] *n* convulsión *f*

coo [kuː] *vi* *(pigeon)* arrullar

cook [kʊk] **1** *vt* cocinar, guisar; *(dinner)* preparar; *Fam* **to c. the books** falsificar las cuentas
2 *vi* *(person)* cocinar, guisar; *(food)* cocerse
3 *n* cocinero(a) *m,f*

cookbook ['kʊkbʊk] *n* *US* libro *m* de cocina

cooker ['kʊkə(r)] *n* cocina *f*

cookery ['kʊkərɪ] *n* cocina *f*; **c. book** libro *m* de cocina

cookie ['kʊkɪ] *n* *US* galleta *f*

cooking ['kʊkɪŋ] *n* cocina *f*

cool [kuːl] **1** *adj* (**a**) fresco(a); **it's c.** *(weather)* hace fresquito (**b**) *Fig (calm)* tranquilo(a); *(reserved)* frío(a)
2 *n* (**a**) *(coolness)* fresco *m* (**b**) *Fam* **to lose one's c.** perder la calma
3 *vt* *(air)* refrescar; *(drink)* enfriar
4 *adv* *Fam* **to play it c.** hacer como si nada
► **cool down, cool off** *vi* *Fig* calmarse; *(feelings)* enfriarse

coolness ['kuːlnɪs] *n* (**a**) *Fig (calmness)* calma *f*; *(composure)* aplomo *m* (**b**) *Fam (nerve, cheek)* frescura *f*

coop [kuːp] **1** *n* gallinero *m*
2 *vt* **to c. (up)** encerrar

co-operate [kəʊ'ɒpəreɪt] *vi* cooperar

co-operation [kəʊɒpə'reɪʃən] *n* cooperación *f*

co-operative [kəʊ'ɒpərətɪv] **1** *adj* *(helpful)* cooperador(a)
2 *n* cooperativa *f*

co-ordinate **1** *vt* [kəʊ'ɔːdɪneɪt] coordinar
2 *n* [kəʊ'ɔːdɪnɪt] (**a**) *Math* coordenada *f*
(**b**) **co-ordinates** *(clothes)* conjunto *m*

co-ordination [kəʊɔːdɪ'neɪʃən] *n* coordinación *f*

cop [kɒp] *Fam* **1** *n* *(policeman)* poli *m*
2 *vt* **you'll c. it** te vas a ganar una buena
► **cop out** *vi* rajarse

cope [kəʊp] *vi* arreglárselas; **to c. with** *(person, work)* poder con; *(problem)* hacer frente a

Copenhagen [kəʊpən'heɪɡən] *n* Copenhague

copious ['kəʊpɪəs] *adj* copioso(a), abundante

copper¹ ['kɒpə(r)] **1** *n* *(metal)* cobre *m*
2 *adj* *(colour)* cobrizo(a)

copper² ['kɒpə(r)] *n* *Fam* poli *mf*

coppice ['kɒpɪs], **copse** [kɒps] *n* arboleda *f*, bosquecillo *m*

copulate ['kɒpjʊleɪt] *vi* copular

copy ['kɒpɪ] **1** *n* (**a**) copia *f* (**b**) *(of book)* ejemplar *m*
2 *vt & vi* copiar

copycat ['kɒpɪkæt] *n* *Fam* copión(ona) *m,f*

copyright ['kɒpɪraɪt] *n* derechos *mpl* de autor

coral ['kɒrəl] *n* coral *m*; **c. reef** arrecife *m* de coral

cord [kɔːd] *n* (**a**) *(string)* cuerda *f*; *Elec* cordón *m* (**b**) *Tex (corduroy)* pana *f*; **cords** pantalones *mpl* de pana

cordial ['kɔːdɪəl] **1** *adj* cordial
2 *n* licor *m*

cordon ['kɔːdən] **1** *n* cordón *m*
2 *vt* **to c. off a street** acordonar una calle

corduroy ['kɔːdərɔɪ] *n* pana *f*

core [kɔː(r)] **1** *n* *(of fruit)* corazón *m*; *Elec* núcleo *m*; *Fig* **the hard c.** los incondicionales
2 *vt* quitarle el corazón a

coriander [kɒrɪ'ændə(r)] *n* culantro *m*

cork [kɔːk] *n* corcho *m*; **c. oak** alcornoque *m*

corkscrew ['kɔːkskruː] *n* sacacorchos *m inv*

corn¹ [kɔːn] *n* cereal *m*; *(grain)* granos *mpl*; *(maize)* maíz *m*; **c. on the cob**

mazorca f de maíz or Andes, RP choclo, Méx elote m

corn² [kɔːn] n Med callo m

corncob ['kɔːnkɒb] n mazorca f

cornea ['kɔːnɪə] n córnea f

corner ['kɔːnə(r)] 1 n (a) (of street) esquina f; (bend in road) curva f; **round the c.** a la vuelta de la esquina; Ftb **c. kick** córner m; **c. shop** tienda pequeña de barrio (b) (of room) rincón m

2 vt (a) (enemy) arrinconar (b) Com acaparar

3 vi Aut tomar una curva

cornerstone ['kɔːnəstəʊn] n piedra f angular

cornet ['kɔːnɪt] n (a) Mus corneta f (b) Br (for ice cream) cucurucho m

cornflakes ['kɔːnfleɪks] npl copos mpl de maíz, cornflakes mpl

cornflour ['kɔːnflaʊə(r)], US **cornstarch** ['kɔːnstɑːrtʃ] n harina f de maíz

Cornwall ['kɔːnwəl] n Cornualles

corny ['kɔːnɪ] adj (**cornier, corniest**) Fam gastado(a)

corollary [kə'rɒlərɪ] n corolario m

coronary ['kɒrənərɪ] adj coronario(a); **c. thrombosis** trombosis coronaria

coronation [kɒrə'neɪʃən] n coronación f

coroner ['kɒrənə(r)] n juez mf de instrucción

corporal¹ ['kɔːpərəl] adj corporal; **c. punishment** castigo m corporal

corporal² ['kɔːpərəl] n Mil cabo m

corporate ['kɔːpərɪt] adj corporativo(a)

corporation [kɔːpə'reɪʃən] n (a) (business) sociedad anónima (b) (of city) ayuntamiento m

corps [kɔː(r)] n (pl **corps** [kɔːz]) cuerpo m

corpse [kɔːps] n cadáver m

corpulent ['kɔːpjʊlənt] adj corpulento(a)

corpuscle ['kɔːpʌsəl] n corpúsculo m

corral [kə'rɑːl] n US corral m

correct [kə'rekt] 1 vt (a) (mistake) corregir (b) (child) reprender

2 adj correcto(a), exacto(a); (behaviour) formal

correction [kə'rekʃən] n corrección f

correlation [kɒrə'leɪʃən] n correlación f

correspond [kɒrɪ'spɒnd] vi (a) corresponder; **to c. to** equivaler a (b) (by letter) escribirse

correspondence [kɒrɪ'spɒndəns] n correspondencia f; **c. course** curso m por correspondencia

correspondent [kɒrɪ'spɒndənt] n Press corresponsal mf; **special c.** enviado(a) m,f especial

corridor ['kɒrɪdɔː(r)] n pasillo m

corroborate [kə'rɒbəreɪt] vt corroborar

corrode [kə'rəʊd] 1 vt corroer

2 vi corroerse

corrosion [kə'rəʊʒən] n corrosión f

corrugated ['kɒrʊgeɪtɪd] adj **c. iron** hierro ondulado

corrupt [kə'rʌpt] 1 adj (person) corrompido(a), corrupto(a); (actions) deshonesto(a)

2 vt & vi corromper

corruption [kə'rʌpʃən] n corrupción f

corset ['kɔːsɪt] n (garment) faja f

Corsica ['kɔːsɪkə] n Córcega

cortège [kɔː'teɪʒ] n cortejo m, comitiva f

cosh [kɒʃ] n Br porra f

cosmetic [kɒz'metɪk] 1 n cosmético m

2 adj cosmético(a); **c. surgery** cirugía plástica

cosmic ['kɒzmɪk] adj cósmico(a)

cosmonaut ['kɒzmənɔːt] n cosmonauta mf

cosmopolitan [kɒzmə'pɒlɪtən] adj cosmopolita

cosset ['kɒsɪt] vt mimar

cost [kɒst] 1 n (price) precio m, coste m; **c. of living** coste de la vida; **to count the c.** considerar las desventajas; **at all costs** a toda costa

2 vt & vi (pt & pp **cost**) costar, valer; **how much does it c.?** ¿cuánto cuesta?; **whatever it costs** cueste lo que cueste

3 vt (pt & pp **costed**) Com & Ind calcular el coste de

co-star ['kəʊstɑː(r)] n Cin & Th coprotagonista mf

Costa Rica [kɒstə'riːkə] n Costa Rica

Costa Rican [kɒstə'riːkən] adj & n costarricense (mf)

cost-effective [kɒstɪ'fektɪv] adj rentable

costly ['kɒstlɪ] adj (**costlier, costliest**) costoso(a)

costume ['kɒstjuːm] n traje m; **swimming c.** bañador m; **c. jewellery** bisutería f

cosy ['kəʊzɪ] adj (**cosier, cosiest**) (atmosphere) acogedor(a); (bed) calentito(a); **it's c. in here** aquí se está bien

cot [kɒt] n (a) Br (for child) cuna f (b) US (folding bed) catre m, cama f plegable

cottage ['kɒtɪdʒ] n casa f de campo; **c. cheese** queso fresco; **c. industry** industria casera; Br **c. pie** = pastel de carne picada con puré de patatas or Am papas

cotton ['kɒtən] n (a) Bot algodonero m; Tex algodón m; Br **c. wool**, US **absorbent c.** algodón hidrófilo (b) (thread) hilo m

▸ **cotton on** vi Fam **to c. on to sth** caer en la cuenta de algo

couch [kaʊtʃ] *n* sofá *m*; *(in surgery)* camilla *f*

couchette [kuːˈʃet] *n Rail* litera *f*

cough [kɒf] **1** *vi* toser

2 *n* tos *f*; **c. drop** pastilla *f* para la tos; **mixture** jarabe *m* para la tos

▶ **cough up** *vt sep Fam* **to c. up the money** soltar la pasta

could [kʊd] *v aux see* **can¹**

council [ˈkaʊnsəl] *n (body)* consejo *m*; *Br* **c. house** vivienda *f* de protección oficial; **town c.** consejo municipal, ayuntamiento *m*

councillor, *US* **councilor** [ˈkaʊnsələ(r)] *n* concejal *mf*

counsel [ˈkaʊnsəl] **1** *n (a) (advice)* consejo *m* **(b)** *Jur* abogado(a) *m,f*

2 *vt* aconsejar

counsellor, *US* **counselor** [ˈkaʊnsələ(r)] *n (a) (adviser)* asesor(a) *m,f* **(b)** *US Jur* abogado(a) *m,f*

count¹ [kaʊnt] **1** *vt (a)* contar **(b)** *Fig* **to c. oneself lucky** considerarse afortunado(a)

2 *vi* contar; **that doesn't c.** eso no vale; **to c. to ten** contar hasta diez

3 *n (a)* cuenta *f*, *(total)* recuento *m* **(b)** *Jur* cargo *m*

▶ **count on** *vt insep* contar con

count² [kaʊnt] *n (nobleman)* conde *m*

countdown [ˈkaʊntdaʊn] *n* cuenta *f* atrás

countenance [ˈkaʊntɪnəns] **1** *n* semblante *m*, rostro *m*

2 *vt* aprobar

counter¹ [ˈkaʊntə(r)] *n (a) (in shop)* mostrador *m*; *(in bank)* ventanilla *f* **(b)** *(in board games)* ficha *f*

counter² [ˈkaʊntə(r)] *n* contador *m*

counter³ [ˈkaʊntə(r)] **1** *adv* **c. to** en contra de

2 *vt (attack)* contestar a; *(trend)* contrarrestar

3 *vi* contestar

counteract [kaʊntərˈækt] *vt* contrarrestar

counterattack [ˈkaʊntərətæk] *n* contraataque *m*

counter-clockwise [ˈkaʊntəˈklɒkwaɪz] *adv US* en sentido opuesto al de las agujas del reloj

counterfeit [ˈkaʊntəfɪt] **1** *adj* falsificado(a); **c. coin** moneda falsa

2 *n* falsificación *f*

3 *vt* falsificar

counterfoil [ˈkaʊntəfɔɪl] *n Br (of cheque)* matriz *f*

countermand [kaʊntəˈmɑːnd] *vt (command)* revocar; *Com (order)* anular

counterpart [ˈkaʊntəpɑːt] *n* homólogo(a) *m,f*

counterproductive [kaʊntəprəˈdʌktɪv] *adj* contraproducente

countersign [ˈkaʊntəsaɪn] *vt* refrendar

countess [ˈkaʊntɪs] *n* condesa *f*

countless [ˈkaʊntlɪs] *adj* innumerable, incontable

country [ˈkʌntrɪ] *n (a) (state)* país *m*; **native c.** patria *f* **(b)** *(rural area)* campo *m*; **c. dancing** baile *m* popular

countryman [ˈkʌntrɪmən] *n (a) (rural)* hombre *m* del campo **(b)** *(compatriot)* compatriota *m*

countryside [ˈkʌntrɪsaɪd] *n (area)* campo *m*; *(scenery)* paisaje *m*

county [ˈkaʊntɪ] *n* condado *m*

coup [kuː] *n (pl coups* [kuːz]*)* golpe *m*; **c. d'eˋtat** golpe de estado

couple [ˈkʌpəl] **1** *n (a) (of people)* pareja *f*; **a married c.** un matrimonio **(b)** *(of things)* par *m*; *Fam* **a c. of times** un par de veces

2 *vt (wagons)* enganchar

coupling [ˈkʌplɪŋ] *n Rail* enganche *m*

coupon [ˈkuːpɒn] *n (a)* cupón *m* **(b)** *Br Ftb* quiniela *f*

courage [ˈkʌrɪdʒ] *n* coraje *m*, valentía *f*

courageous [kəˈreɪdʒəs] *adj* valeroso(a), valiente

courgette [kʊəˈʒet] *n Br* calabacín *m*, *CSur* zapallito *m*

courier [ˈkʊrɪə(r)] *n (a) (messenger)* mensajero(a) *m,f* **(b)** *(guide)* guía *mf* turístico(a)

course [kɔːs] *n (a) (of river)* curso *m*; *Naut & Av* rumbo *m* **(b)** *Fig* desarrollo *m*; **in the c. of construction** en vías de construcción; **in the c. of time** con el tiempo **(c)** *(series)* ciclo *m*; **a c. of treatment** un tratamiento **(d)** *Educ* curso *m*; *Univ* asignatura *f* **(e)** *(for golf)* campo *m*; *(for horseracing)* hipódromo *m* **(f)** *Culin* plato *m* **(g)** **of c.** claro, por supuesto; **of c. not!** ¡claro que no!

court [kɔːt] **1** *n (a)* *Jur* tribunal *m*; **c. martial** consejo *m* de guerra; **c. order** orden *f* judicial **(b)** *(royal)* corte *f* **(c)** *Sport* pista *f*, cancha *f*

2 *vt (woman)* hacer la corte a; *Fig* **to c. danger** buscar el peligro; *Fig* **to c. disaster** exponerse al desastre

3 *vi (couple)* tener relaciones

courteous [ˈkɜːtɪəs] *adj* cortés

courtesy [ˈkɜːtɪsɪ] *n (a)* cortesía *f*, educación *f* **(b)** **by c. of** por cortesía de

courthouse [ˈkɔːthaʊs] *n US* palacio *m* de justicia

courtier ['kɔːtɪə(r)] n cortesano(a) m,f
court-martial [kɔːt'mɑːʃəl] vt someter a consejo de guerra
courtroom ['kɔːtruːm] n sala f de justicia
courtyard ['kɔːtjɑːd] n patio m
cousin ['kʌzən] n primo(a) m,f; **first c.** primo(a) hermano(a)
cove [kəʊv] n cala f, ensenada f
covenant ['kʌvənənt] n convenio m, pacto m
cover ['kʌvə(r)] **1** vt (a) cubrir (**with** de); (furniture) revestir (**with** de); (with lid) tapar
   (b) (hide) disimular
   (c) (protect) abrigar
   (d) (distance) recorrer
   (e) Press investigar
   (f) (deal with) abarcar
   (g) (include) incluir
   (h) Sport marcar
   2 vi **to c. for sb** sustituir a algn
   3 n (a) cubierta f; (lid) tapa f; (on bed) manta f, Am frazada f, cobija f, (of chair etc) funda f
   (b) (of book) tapa f; (of magazine) portada f; **c. girl** modelo f de revista
   (c) (in restaurant) cubierto m
   (d) **under separate c.** por separado
   (e) Ins **full c.** cobertura completa; Br **c. note** seguro m provisional
   (f) (protection) abrigo m; **to take c.** abrigarse; **under c.** al abrigo; (indoors) bajo techo
► **cover up 1** vt sep (a) cubrir (b) (crime) encubrir
   2 vi (a) (person) abrigarse (b) **to c. up for sb** encubrir a algn
coverage ['kʌvərɪdʒ] n cobertura f
coveralls ['kʌvərɔːlz] npl US mono m
covering ['kʌvərɪŋ] **1** n cubierta f, envoltura f
   2 adj (letter) explicatorio(a)
covert ['kʌvət] adj disimulado(a), secreto(a)
cover-up ['kʌvərʌp] n encubrimiento m
covet ['kʌvɪt] vt codiciar
cow¹ [kaʊ] n vaca f, Pej (woman) arpía f, bruja f
cow² [kaʊ] vt intimidar
coward ['kaʊəd] n cobarde mf
cowardice ['kaʊədɪs] n cobardía f
cowardly ['kaʊədlɪ] adj cobarde
cowboy ['kaʊbɔɪ] n vaquero m
cower ['kaʊə(r)] vi (with fear) encogerse
cox [kɒks] n timonel m
coy [kɔɪ] adj (shy) tímido(a); (demure) coquetón(ona)
cozy ['kəʊzɪ] adj US = **cosy**

crab [kræb] n (a) cangrejo m (b) **c. apple** manzana f silvestre
crack [kræk] **1** vt (a) (cup) partir; (bone) fracturar; (nut) cascar; (safe) forzar (b) (whip) hacer restallar (c) Fam (problem) dar con la solución de; (joke) contar
   2 vi (a) (glass) partirse; (wall) agrietarse (b) (whip) restallar (c) Fam **to get cracking on sth** ponerse a hacer algo
   3 n (a) (in cup) raja f; (in wall, ground) grieta f (b) (of whip) restallido m; (of gun) detonación f (c) Fam (blow) golpetazo m (d) Fam **to have a c. at sth** (attempt) intentar hacer algo (e) Fam (wisecrack) réplica aguda (f) Fam (drug) crack m
   4 adj Fam de primera
► **crack down on** vt insep atajar con mano dura
► **crack up** vi Fam Fig (go mad) desquiciarse; (with laughter) partirse de risa
cracker ['krækə(r)] n (a) (biscuit) galleta salada f (b) (firework) petardo m
crackle ['krækəl] vi crujir; (fire) crepitar
cradle ['kreɪdəl] n (baby's) cuna f
craft [krɑːft] n (a) (occupation) oficio m; (art) arte m; (skill) destreza f (b) (cunning) maña f (c) Naut embarcación f
craftsman ['krɑːftsmən] n artesano m
craftsmanship ['krɑːftsmənʃɪp] n arte f
crafty ['krɑːftɪ] adj (**craftier, craftiest**) astuto(a)
crag [kræg] n peña f, peñasco m
cram [kræm] **1** vt atiborrar; **crammed with** atestado(a) de
   2 vi Fam Educ empollar
cramp¹ [kræmp] n Med calambre m; **cramps** retortijones mpl
cramp² [kræmp] vt (development etc) poner trabas a
cramped [kræmpt] adj atestado(a); (writing) apretado(a)
cranberry ['krænbərɪ] n arándano m
crane [kreɪn] **1** n (a) Zool grulla f común (b) (device) grúa f
   2 vt estirar
crank [kræŋk] n (a) Tech manivela f (b) Fam (eccentric) tío raro
crankshaft ['kræŋkʃɑːft] n árbol m del cigüeñal
cranny ['krænɪ] n Fig **in every nook and c.** en todos los rincones
crap [kræp] n Fam mierda f
crash [kræʃ] **1** vt **to c. one's car** tener un accidente con el coche
   2 vi (a) (car, plane) estrellarse; (collide) chocar; **to c. into** estrellarse contra (b) Com quebrar
   3 n (a) (noise) estrépito m (b) (collision)

choque *m*; **car/plane c.** accidente *m* de coche/avión; *Fig* **c. course** curso intensivo; **c. helmet** casco *m* protector (**c**) *Com* quiebra *f*

crash-land [kræʃ'lænd] *vi* hacer un aterrizaje forzoso

crass [kræs] *adj* (*person*) grosero(a); (*error*) garrafal

crate [kreɪt] *n* caja *f*, cajón *m* (*para embalaje*)

crater ['kreɪtə(r)] *n* cráter *m*

cravat [krə'væt] *n* pañuelo *m* (*de hombre*)

crave [kreɪv] *vi* **to c. for sth** ansiar algo

craving ['kreɪvɪŋ] *n* ansia *f*; (*in pregnancy*) antojo *m*

crawfish ['krɔːfɪʃ] *n* langosta *f*

crawl [krɔːl] 1 *vi* (*baby*) gatear; (*vehicle*) avanzar lentamente; *Fig* **to c. to sb** arrastrarse a los pies de algn
2 *n* (*swimming*) crol *m*

crayfish ['kreɪfɪʃ] *n* cangrejo *m* de río

crayon ['kreɪɒn] *n* cera *f*

craze [kreɪz] *n* manía *f*; (*fashion*) moda *f*; **it's the latest c.** es el último grito

crazy ['kreɪzɪ] *adj* (**crazier, craziest**) *Fam* loco(a), chalado(a); *Br* **c. paving** pavimento *m* en mosaico

creak [kriːk] *vi* (*floor*) crujir; (*hinge*) chirriar

cream [kriːm] 1 *n* (**a**) (*of milk*) nata *f*, **c.-coloured** color crema; *Fig* **the c.** la flor y nata; **c. cheese** queso *m* crema (**b**) (*cosmetic*) crema *f*
2 *vt* (**a**) (*milk*) desnatar (**b**) *Culin* batir; **creamed potatoes** puré *m* de patatas *or Am* papas

creamy ['kriːmɪ] *adj* (**creamier, creamiest**) cremoso(a)

crease [kriːs] 1 *n* (*wrinkle*) arruga *f*; (*fold*) pliegue *m*; (*on trousers*) raya *f*
2 *vt* (*clothes*) arrugar
3 *vi* arrugarse

create [kriː'eɪt] *vt* crear

creation [kriː'eɪʃən] *n* creación *f*

creative [kriː'eɪtɪv] *adj* (*person*) creativo(a)

creativity [kriːeɪ'trɪvɪtɪ] *n* creatividad *f*

creator [kriː'eɪtə(r)] *n* creador(a) *m,f*

creature ['kriːtʃə(r)] *n* (*animal*) criatura *f*

crèche [kreɪʃ, kreʃ] *n* guardería *f*

credence ['kriːdəns] *n* **to give c. to** dar crédito a

credentials [krɪ'denʃəlz] *npl* credenciales *fpl*

credible ['kredɪbəl] *adj* creíble

credit ['kredɪt] 1 *n* (**a**) *Com* crédito *m*; **on c. a** crédito; **c. card** tarjeta *f* de crédito (**b**) **to give c. to sb for sth** reconocer algo a

algn (**c**) (*benefit*) honor *m*; **to be a c. to** hacer honor a (**d**) *Cin & TV* **credits** créditos *mpl*
2 *vt* (**a**) *Com* abonar (**b**) (*believe*) creer (**c**) *Fig* atribuir; **he is credited with having** se le atribuye haber

creditor ['kredɪtə(r)] *n* acreedor(a) *m,f*

creed [kriːd] *n* credo *m*

creek [kriːk] *n* (**a**) *Br* cala *f* (**b**) *US & Austral* riachuelo *m*

creep [kriːp] 1 *vi* (*pt & pp* **crept**) andar silenciosamente; (*insect*) arrastrarse; (*plant*) trepar; **to c. up on sb** sorprender a algn
2 *n* *Fam* (*person*) pelotillero(a) *m,f*

creeper ['kriːpə(r)] *n* *Bot* trepadora *f*

creepy ['kriːpɪ] *adj* (**creepier, creepiest**) *Fam* espeluznante

cremate [krɪ'meɪt] *vt* incinerar

crematorium [kremə'tɔːrɪəm] *n* crematorio *m*

crêpe [kreɪp] *n* (**a**) *Tex* crepé *m* (**b**) **c. paper** papel *m* crespón

crept [krept] *pt & pp of* **creep**

crescendo [krɪ'ʃendəʊ] *n* crescendo *m*

crescent ['kresənt] *n* (*in shape*) medialuna *f*; *Br* (*street*) calle *f* en medialuna
2 *adj* creciente

cress [kres] *n* berro *m*

crest [krest] *n* (**a**) (*of cock, wave*) cresta *f*; (*on helmet*) penacho *m*; (*of hill*) cima *f* (**b**) (*heraldic*) blasón *m*

crestfallen ['krestfɔːlən] *adj* abatido(a)

Crete [kriːt] *n* Creta

cretin ['kretɪn] *n* cretino(a) *m,f*

crevasse [krɪ'væs] *n* grieta *f*, fisura *f*

crevice ['krevɪs] *n* grieta *f*, hendedura *f*

crew [kruː] *n* *Av & Naut* tripulación *f*; **c. cut** corte *m* al rape; **c.-neck sweater** jersey *m* con cuello redondo

crib [krɪb] 1 *n* (**a**) (*manger*) pesebre *m* (**b**) (*for baby*) cuna *f* (**c**) *Fam* (*in exam*) chuleta *f*, *Arg* machete *m*, *Col, Méx* acordeón *m*
2 *vt* *Fam* (**a**) (*copy*) copiar (**b**) (*steal*) quitar

crick [krɪk] *n* *Fam* **a c. in the neck** una tortícolis

cricket¹ ['krɪkɪt] *n* (*insect*) grillo *m*

cricket² ['krɪkɪt] *n* *Sport* cricket *m*

crikey ['kraɪkɪ] *interj* *Fam Old-fashioned* ¡caramba!

crime [kraɪm] *n* delincuencia *f*; (*offence*) delito *m*

criminal ['krɪmɪnəl] *adj & n* criminal (*mf*); **c. law** derecho *m* penal; **c. record** antecedentes *mpl* penales

crimson ['krɪmzən] *adj & n* carmesí (*m*)

cringe [krɪndʒ] *vi* abatirse, encogerse

crinkle ['krɪŋkəl] *vt* fruncir, arrugar

cripple ['krɪpəl] **1** *n* lisiado(a) *m,f*, mutilado(a) *m,f*

2 *vt* mutilar, dejar cojo(a); *Fig* paralizar

crisis ['kraɪsɪs] *n* (*pl* **crises** ['kraɪsiːz]) crisis *f inv*

crisp [krɪsp] **1** *adj* crujiente; (*lettuce*) fresco(a); (*banknote*) nuevo(a); (*weather*) frío(a) y seco(a); *Fig* (*style*) directo(a)

2 *n Br* (**potato**) **c.** patata *or Am* papa frita

crisscross ['krɪskrɒs] *n* líneas entrecruzadas

criterion [kraɪ'tɪərɪən] *n* (*pl* **criteria** [kraɪ'tɪərɪə]) criterio *m*

critic ['krɪtɪk] *n Art & Th* crítico(a) *m,f*

critical ['krɪtɪkəl] *adj* crítico(a)

critically ['krɪtɪkəlɪ] *adv* críticamente; **c. ill** gravemente enfermo(a)

criticism ['krɪtɪsɪzəm] *n* crítica *f*

criticize ['krɪtɪsaɪz] *vt* criticar

croak [krəʊk] *vi* (*frog*) croar; (*raven*) graznar; (*person*) hablar con voz ronca

Croat ['krəʊæt] **1** *adj* croata

2 *n* (**a**) (*person*) croata *mf* (**b**) (*language*) croata *m*

Croatia [krəʊ'eɪʃə] *n* Croacia

Croatian [krəʊ'eɪʃən] *adj & n* = **Croat**

crochet ['krəʊʃeɪ] *n* ganchillo *m*

crockery ['krɒkərɪ] *n* loza *f*

crocodile ['krɒkədaɪl] *n* cocodrilo *m*

crocus ['krəʊkəs] *n* azafrán *m*

crony ['krəʊnɪ] *n* compinche *mf*

crook [krʊk] **1** *n* (**a**) (*of shepherd*) cayado *m* (**b**) *Fam* caco *m*

2 *vt* (*arm*) doblar

crooked ['krʊkɪd] *adj* (**a**) (*stick, picture*) torcido(a); (*path*) tortuoso(a) (**b**) *Fam* (*dishonest*) deshonesto(a)

crop [krɒp] **1** *n* (**a**) (*cultivo m*; (*harvest*) cosecha *f*; (*of hair*) mata *f* (**b**) (*whip*) fusta *f*

2 *vt* (*hair*) rapar; (*grass*) cortar

► **crop up** *vi Fam* surgir, presentarse

croquet ['krəʊkeɪ] *n* croquet *m*

cross [krɒs] **1** *n* (**a**) cruz *f* (**b**) (*breeds*) cruce *m* (**c**) **c. section** sección *f* transversal

2 *vt* (**a**) cruzar (**b**) *Rel* **to c. oneself** hacer la señal de la cruz; *Fam* **c. my heart!** ¡te lo juro! (**c**) (*thwart*) contrariar

3 *vi* cruzar; (*roads*) cruzarse; **to c. over** cruzar

4 *adj* (**a**) *Fig* **they are at c. purposes** hay un malentendido entre ellos (**b**) (*angry*) enfadado(a)

► **cross off, cross out** *vt sep* tachar, rayar

crossbar ['krɒsbɑː(r)] *n* travesaño *m*

cross-country **1** *adj* ['krɒskʌntrɪ] **c. race** cros *m*

2 *adv* [krɒs'kʌntrɪ] campo través

cross-examine [krɒsɪg'zæmɪn] *vt* interrogar

cross-eyed ['krɒsaɪd] *adj* bizco(a)

crossfire ['krɒsfaɪə(r)] *n* fuego cruzado

crossing ['krɒsɪŋ] *n* cruce *m*; **pedestrian c.** paso *m* de peatones; **sea c.** travesía *f*

cross-legged [krɒs'leg(ɪ)d] *adj* con las piernas cruzadas

cross-reference [krɒs'refərəns] *n* remisión *f*

crossroads ['krɒsrəʊdz] *n* cruce *m*; *Fig* encrucijada *f*

crosswalk ['krɒswɔːk] *n US* paso *m* de peatones

crosswind ['krɒswɪnd] *n* viento *m* lateral

crossword ['krɒswɜːd] *n* **c. (puzzle)** crucigrama *m*

crotch [krɒtʃ] *n* entrepierna *f*

crotchet ['krɒtʃɪt] *n Br Mus* negra *f*

crotchety ['krɒtʃɪtɪ] *adj Fam* gruñón(ona)

crouch [kraʊtʃ] *vi* **to c. (down)** agacharse

crow¹ [krəʊ] *n* cuervo *m*; *Fig* **as the c. flies** en línea recta; **c.'s-feet** patas *fpl* de gallo

crow² [krəʊ] **1** *vi* (**a**) (*cock*) cantar; *Fig* **to c. over sth** jactarse de algo (**b**) (*baby*) balbucir

2 *n* (*of cock*) canto *m*

crowbar ['krəʊbɑː(r)] *n* palanca *f*

crowd [kraʊd] **1** *n* muchedumbre *f*; *Fam* (*gang*) pandilla *f*; **the c.** el populacho

2 *vt* (*streets*) llenar

3 *vi* apiñarse; **to c. in/out** entrar/salir en tropel

crowded ['kraʊdɪd] *adj* atestado(a), lleno(a)

crown [kraʊn] **1** *n* (**a**) corona *f*; (*garland*) guirnalda *f*; **the c. jewels** las joyas de la corona; *Br Jur* **C. court** tribunal *m* superior; **C. Prince** príncipe heredero (**b**) *Anat* coronilla *f*; (*of hat, tree*) copa *f*

2 *vt* coronar; *Fam Fig* **to c. it all** y para más inri

crucial ['kruːʃəl] *adj* decisivo(a)

crucifix ['kruːsɪfɪks] *n* crucifijo *m*

crucifixion [kruːsɪ'fɪkʃən] *n* crucifixión *f*

crucify ['kruːsɪfaɪ] *vt* crucificar

crude [kruːd] *adj* (**a**) (*manners, style*) tosco(a), grosero(a); (*tool*) primitivo(a) (**b**) **c. oil** crudo *m*

cruel [krʊəl] *adj* cruel (**to** con)

cruelty ['krʊəltɪ] *n* crueldad *f* (**to** hacia)

cruet ['kruːɪt] *n* **c. set** vinagreras *fpl*

cruise [kruːz] *vi* (**a**) *Naut* hacer un crucero (**b**) *Aut* viajar a velocidad constante;

Av viajar a velocidad de crucero

2 *n* (**a**) *Naut* crucero *m* (**b**) **c. missile** misil teledirigido

cruiser ['kru:zə(r)] *n* (barco *m*) crucero *m*

crumb [krʌm] *n* miga *f*, migaja *f*

crumble ['krʌmbəl] **1** *vt* desmigar

2 *vi* (*wall*) desmoronarse; *Fig* (*hopes*) desvanecerse

crumbly ['krʌmblɪ] *adj* (**crumblier, crumbliest**) que se desmigaja

crumpet ['krʌmpɪt] *n Br* = clase de crepe grueso que se puede tostar

crumple ['krʌmpəl] *vt* arrugar

crunch [krʌntʃ] **1** *vt* (*food*) ronchar; (*with feet*) hacer crujir

2 *n Fam* **when it comes to the c.** a la hora de la verdad

crunchy ['krʌntʃɪ] *adj* (**crunchier, crunchiest**) crujiente

crusade [kru:'seɪd] *n* cruzada *f*

crush [krʌʃ] **1** *vt* aplastar; (*wrinkle*) arrugar; (*grind*) moler; (*squeeze*) exprimir

2 *n* (**a**) (*of people*) gentío *m* (**b**) **orange c.** naranjada *f*

crushing ['krʌʃɪŋ] *adj Fig* (*defeat, reply*) aplastante

crust [krʌst] *n* corteza *f*

crutch [krʌtʃ] *n Med* muleta *f*; *Fig* apoyo *m*

crux [krʌks] *n* **the c. of the matter** el quid de la cuestión

cry [kraɪ] **1** *vi* (*pt & pp* **cried**) (**a**) gritar (**b**) (*weep*) llorar

2 *vt* gritar; *Fig* **to c. wolf** dar una falsa alarma

3 *n* (**a**) grito *m* (**b**) (*weep*) llanto *m*

► **cry off** *vi Fam* rajarse

► **cry out** *vi* gritar; **to c. out for sth** pedir algo a gritos

crying ['kraɪɪŋ] *adj* **it's a c. shame** es una vergüenza

cryptic ['krɪptɪk] *adj* enigmático(a)

crystal ['krɪstəl] *n* cristal *m*

crystal-clear [krɪstəl'klɪə(r)] *adj* claro(a) como el agua

crystallize ['krɪstəlaɪz] **1** *vt* cristalizar

2 *vi* cristalizarse

cub [kʌb] *n* (**a**) (*animal*) cachorro *m* (**b**) (*junior scout*) niño *m* explorador

Cuba ['kju:bə] *n* Cuba

Cuban ['kju:bən] *adj & n* cubano(a) (*m,f*)

cubbyhole ['kʌbɪhəʊl] *n* cuchitril *m*

cube [kju:b] **1** *n* cubo *m*; (*of sugar*) terrón *m*; **c. root** raíz cúbica

2 *vt Math* elevar al cubo

cubic ['kju:bɪk] *adj* cúbico(a)

cubicle ['kju:bɪkəl] *n* cubículo *m*; (*at swimming pool*) caseta *f*

cuckoo ['kʊku:] **1** *n* cuco *m*; **c. clock** reloj *m* de cuco

2 *adj Fam* lelo(a)

cucumber ['kju:kʌmbə(r)] *n* pepino *m*

cuddle ['kʌdəl] **1** *vt* abrazar

2 *vi* abrazarse

cuddly ['kʌdlɪ] *adj* **c. toy** muñeco *m* de peluche

cue¹ [kju:] *n Th* pie *m*

cue² [kju:] *n* (*in billiards*) taco *m*; **c. ball** bola blanca

cuff¹ [kʌf] *n* (*of sleeve*) puño *m*; *US* (*of trousers*) dobladillo *m*; *Fig* **to do sth off the c.** improvisar algo

cuff² [kʌf] **1** *vt* abofetear

2 *n* bofetada *f*

cufflinks ['kʌflɪŋks] *npl* gemelos *mpl*

cul-de-sac ['kʌldəsæk] *n* callejón *m* sin salida

cull [kʌl] *vt* (**a**) (*choose*) escoger (**b**) (*animals*) eliminar

culminate ['kʌlmɪneɪt] *vi* **to c. in** terminar en

culmination [kʌlmɪ'neɪʃən] *n* culminación *f*, punto *m* culminante

culottes [kju:'lɒts] *npl* falda-pantalón *f*

culprit ['kʌlprɪt] *n* culpable *mf*

cult [kʌlt] *n* culto *m*; **c. figure** ídolo *m*

cultivate ['kʌltɪveɪt] *vt* cultivar

cultivated ['kʌltɪveɪtɪd] *adj* (*person*) culto(a)

cultivation [kʌltɪ'veɪʃən] *n* cultivo *m* (de la tierra)

cultural ['kʌltʃərəl] *adj* cultural

culture ['kʌltʃə(r)] *n* cultura *f*

cultured ['kʌltʃəd] *adj* = **cultivated**

cumbersome ['kʌmbəsəm] *adj* (*awkward*) incómodo(a); (*bulky*) voluminoso(a)

cum(m)in ['kʌmɪn] *n* comino *m*

cumulative ['kju:mjʊlətɪv] *adj* acumulativo(a)

cunning ['kʌnɪŋ] **1** *adj* astuto(a)

2 *n* astucia *f*

cup [kʌp] **1** *n* taza *f*; *Sport* copa *f*; **C. Final** final *f* de copa; **c. tie** partido *m* de copa

2 *vt* (*hands*) ahuecar

cupboard ['kʌbəd] *n* armario *m*; (*on wall*) alacena *f*

curate ['kjʊərɪt] *n* cura *m* coadjutor

curator [kjʊə'reɪtə(r)] *n* conservador(a) *m,f*

curb [kɜ:b] **1** *n* (**a**) (*limit*) freno *m* (**b**) *US* (*kerb*) bordillo *m*

2 *vt* (*horse*) refrenar; *Fig* (*public spending*) contener

curd [kɜ:d] *n* cuajada *f*

curdle ['kɜ:dəl] *vi* cuajarse

cure [kjʊə(r)] **1** vt curar
   2 n (remedy) cura f, remedio m
curfew ['kɜːfjuː] n toque m de queda
curiosity [kjʊərɪ'ɒsɪtɪ] n curiosidad f
curious ['kjʊərɪəs] adj (a) (inquisitive)
   curioso(a) (b) (odd) extraño(a)
curl [kɜːl] **1** vt (hair) rizar; (lip) fruncir
   2 vi rizarse
   3 n (of hair) rizo m; (of smoke) espiral f
   ▶ **curl up** vi enroscarse
curly ['kɜːlɪ] adj (**curlier, curliest**) riza-
   do(a)
currant ['kʌrənt] n pasa f (de Corinto)
currency ['kʌrənsɪ] n (a) moneda f;
   foreign c. divisa f (b) **to gain c.** cobrar
   fuerza
current ['kʌrənt] **1** adj (a) (opinion) general; (word) en uso; (year) en curso; **c.
   account** cuenta f corriente; **c. affairs** actualidad f (política); Fin **c. assets** activo m
   disponible (b) **the c. issue** (of magazine,
   newspaper) el último número
   2 n corriente f
currently ['kʌrəntlɪ] adv actualmente
curriculum [kə'rɪkjʊləm] n (pl **curricula**
   [kə'rɪkjʊlə]) plan m de estudios; **c. vitae**
   curriculum m (vitae)
curry¹ ['kʌrɪ] n curry m; **chicken c.** pollo
   m al curry
curry² ['kʌrɪ] vt **to c. favour with** congraciarse con
curse [kɜːs] **1** n maldición f, (oath) palabrota f, Fig azote m
   2 vt maldecir
   3 vi blasfemar
cursor ['kɜːsə(r)] n cursor m
cursory ['kɜːsərɪ] adj rápido(a)
curt [kɜːt] adj brusco(a), seco(a)
curtail [kɜː'teɪl] vt (expenses) reducir;
   (text) acortar
curtain ['kɜːtən] n cortina f, Th telón m;
   Fig velo m
curts(e)y ['kɜːtsɪ] **1** n reverencia f
   2 vi hacer una reverencia (**to** a)
curve [kɜːv] **1** n curva f
   2 vt encorvar
   3 vi torcerse, describir una curva
cushion ['kʊʃən] **1** n cojín m; (large)
   almohadón m; (of billiard table) banda f
   2 vt Fig amortiguar; (person) proteger
cushy ['kʊʃɪ] adj (**cushier, cushiest**) Fam
   cómodo(a)
custard ['kʌstəd] n natillas fpl; **c. powder**
   polvos mpl para natillas
custodian [kʌ'stəʊdɪən] n conserje mf,
   guarda mf
custody ['kʌstədɪ] n custodia f; **to take
   into c.** detener

custom ['kʌstəm] n (a) (habit) costumbre f (b) Com clientela f
customary ['kʌstəmərɪ] adj habitual
customer ['kʌstəmə(r)] n cliente mf
customize ['kʌstəmaɪz] vt hacer por encargo
custom-made [kʌstəm'meɪd] adj he-
   cho(a) a la medida
customs ['kʌstəmz] n sing or pl aduana f,
   c. duty derechos mpl de aduana; **c. officer** agente mf de aduana
cut [kʌt] **1** vt (pt & pp **cut**) (a) cortar;
   (stone) tallar; (record) grabar; **he's cutting
   a tooth** le está saliendo un diente; **to c.
   one's finger** cortarse el dedo; Fig **to c. a
   long story short** en resumidas cuentas;
   Fig **to c. corners** recortar presupuestos
   (b) (reduce) reducir
   (c) (divide up) dividir (**into** en)
   2 n (a) corte m; (in skin) cortadura f,
   (wound) herida f, (with knife) cuchillada f
   (b) (of meat) clase f de carne
   (c) (reduction) reducción f
   (d) Fig **to be a c. above sb** estar por
   encima de algn
   3 adj cortado(a); (price) reducido(a); Fig
   c. and dried convenido(a) de antemano;
   c. glass cristal tallado
   4 vi cortar; Fam Fig **to c. loose**
   romper con todo
   (b) Cin **c.!** ¡corten!
   ▶ **cut back** vt sep (expenses) reducir; (production) disminuir
   ▶ **cut down 1** vt sep (tree) talar
   2 vt insep **to c. down on** reducir
   ▶ **cut in** vi (driver) adelantar bruscamente
   ▶ **cut off** vt sep (water etc) cortar; (place)
   aislar; (heir) excluir; Tel **I've been c. off**
   me han cortado (la comunicación)
   ▶ **cut out 1** vt sep (a) (from newspaper)
   recortar; (person) **to be c. out for sth**
   estar hecho(a) para algo (b) (delete) suprimir
   2 vi (engine) calarse
   ▶ **cut up** vt sep cortar en pedazos
cutback ['kʌtbæk] n reducción f (**in**
   de)
cute [kjuːt] adj mono(a), lindo(a); US Fam
   Pej listillo(a)
cuticle ['kjuːtɪkəl] n cutícula f
cutlery ['kʌtlərɪ] n cubiertos mpl
cutlet ['kʌtlɪt] n chuleta f
cut-price [kʌt'praɪs] adj (article) a precio
   rebajado
cutthroat ['kʌtθrəʊt] **1** n asesino(a) m,f,
   matón m
   2 adj (cruel) cruel; (competition) feroz
cutting ['kʌtɪŋ] **1** n (from newspaper)

recorte *m*; *Rail* tajo *m*
  2 *adj* cortante; *(remark)* mordaz
CV, cv [si:'vi:] *n* *(abbr* **curriculum vitae**)
  CV *m*
cwt. *(abbr* **hundredweight**) *(metric)* 50
  kg; *(imperial) Br* = 50,8 kg; *US* = 45,36 kg
cyanide ['saɪənaɪd] *n* cianuro *m*
cybercafe ['saɪbəkæfeɪ] *n* *Comput* cibercafé *m*
cyberspace ['saɪbəspeɪs] *n* *Comput* ciberespacio *m*
cycle ['saɪkəl] **1** *n* (**a**) ciclo *m* (**b**) *(bicycle)*
  bicicleta *f*; *(motorcycle)* moto *f*
  2 *vi* ir en bicicleta
cycling ['saɪklɪŋ] *n* ciclismo *m*
cyclist ['saɪklɪst] *n* ciclista *mf*
cyclone ['saɪkləʊn] *n* ciclón *m*
cygnet ['sɪgnɪt] *n* pollo *m* de cisne
cylinder ['sɪlɪndə(r)] *n* (**a**) cilindro *m* (**b**)
  (for gas) bombona *f*
cymbal ['sɪmbəl] *n* címbalo *m*, platillo *m*
cynic ['sɪnɪk] *n* descreído(a) *m,f*, suspicaz *mf*

> ♪ Note that the Spanish word **cínico** is a
> false friend and is never a translation for
> the English word **cynic**. In Spanish, **cínico**
> means "shameless person".

cynical ['sɪnɪkəl] *adj* (**a**) *(sceptical)* des-
  creído(a), suspicaz (**b**) *(unscrupulous)*
  desaprensivo(a), sin escrúpulos

> ♪ Note that the Spanish word **cínico** is a
> false friend and is never a translation for
> the English word **cynical**. In Spanish, **cínico**
> means "shameless".

cynicism ['sɪnɪsɪzəm] *n* descreimiento *m*,
  suspicacia *f*

> ♪ Note that the Spanish word **cinismo** is a
> false friend and is never a translation for the
> English word **cynicism**. In Spanish, **cinismo**
> means "shamelessness".

cypress ['saɪprəs] *n* ciprés *m*
Cypriot ['sɪprɪət] *adj & n* chipriota *(mf)*
Cyprus ['saɪprəs] *n* Chipre
cyst [sɪst] *n* quiste *m*
cystitis [sɪ'staɪtɪs] *n* cistitis *f*
Czech [tʃek] **1** *adj* checo(a); **the C. Republic** la República Checa
  2 *n* (**a**) *(person)* checo(a) *m,f* (**b**) *(language)* checo *m*
Czechoslovakia [tʃekəʊslə'vækɪə] *n*
  Checoslovaquia

D

D, d [diː] *n* (**a**) *(the letter)* D, d *f* (**b**) *Mus* D re *m*

D.A. [diː'eɪ] *n US* (*abbr* **district attorney**) fiscal *mf* (del distrito)

dab [dæb] **1** *n* *(small quantity)* toque *m*

2 *vt* (**a**) *(apply)* aplicar (**b**) *(touch lightly)* tocar ligeramente

dabble ['dæbəl] *vi* **to d. in politics** meterse en política

dachshund ['dækshʊnd] *n* perro *m* salchicha

dad [dæd], **daddy** ['dædɪ] *n Fam* papá *m*, papi *m*

daddy-longlegs [dædɪ'lɒŋlegz] *n inv Fam* (**a**) *Br (cranefly)* típula *f* (**b**) *US (spider)* segador *m*

daffodil ['dæfədɪl] *n* narciso *m*

daft [dɑːft] *adj Br Fam* chalado(a); *(idea)* tonto(a)

dagger ['dægə(r)] *n* puñal *m*, daga *f*

dahlia ['deɪlɪə] *n* dalia *f*

daily ['deɪlɪ] **1** *adj* diario(a), cotidiano(a)

2 *adv* diariamente; **three times d.** tres veces al día

3 *n* (**a**) *(newspaper)* diario *m* (**b**) *Br Fam (cleaning lady)* asistenta *f*

dainty ['deɪntɪ] *adj* (**daintier, daintiest**) *(flower)* delicado(a); *(child)* precioso(a); *(food)* exquisito(a)

dairy ['deərɪ] *n* *(on farm)* vaquería *f*; *(shop)* lechería *f*; **d. farming** industria lechera; **d. produce** productos lácteos

dais ['deɪɪs] *n* *(in hall)* tarima *f*; *(in ceremony)* estrado *m*

daisy ['deɪzɪ] *n* margarita *f*

daisywheel ['deɪzɪwiːl] *n* *(printer)* margarita *f*

dale [deɪl] *n* valle *m*, hondonada *f*

Dalmatian [dæl'meɪʃən] *n* (perro *m*) dálmata *m*

dam [dæm] **1** *n* *(barrier)* dique *m*; *(lake)* presa *f*

2 *vt* *(water)* represar

▸ **dam up** *vt sep Fig (emotion)* contener

damage ['dæmɪdʒ] **1** *n* (**a**) daño *m*; *(to health, reputation)* perjuicio *m*; *(to relationship)* deterioro *m* (**b**) *Jur* **damages** daños *mpl* y perjuicios *mpl*

2 *vt* *(harm)* dañar, hacer daño a; *(spoil)* estropear; *(undermine)* perjudicar

damaging ['dæmɪdʒɪŋ] *adj* perjudicial

damn [dæm] **1** *vt* condenar

2 *interj Fam* **d. (it)!** ¡maldito(a) sea!; **well, I'll be damned!** ¡vaya por Dios!

3 *n Fam* **I don't give a d.** me importa un bledo

4 *adj Fam* maldito(a)

5 *adv Fam* muy, sumamente

damned [dæmd] *adj & adv* = **damn**

damnedest ['dæmdɪst] *n Fam* **to do one's d. to ...** hacer todo lo posible para ...

damning ['dæmɪŋ] *adj (evidence)* irrefutable; *(criticism)* mordaz

damp [dæmp] **1** *adj* húmedo(a); *(wet)* mojado(a)

2 *n* humedad *f*

3 *vt* (**a**) *(for ironing)* humedecer (**b**) **to d. (down)** *(fire)* sofocar; *Fig (violence)* frenar

dampen ['dæmpən] *vt* humedecer; *Fig* frenar

damper ['dæmpə(r)] *n Fig* **to put a d. on sth** poner freno a algo

damsel ['dæmzəl] *n Literary* doncella *f*

damson ['dæmzən] *n* ciruela damascena

dance [dɑːns] **1** *n* baile *m*; *(classical, tribal)* danza *f*; **d. band** orquesta *f* de baile; **d. floor** pista *f* de baile; **d. hall** salón *m* de baile

2 *vi & vt* bailar

dancer ['dɑːnsə(r)] *n* *(by profession)* bailarín(ina) *m,f*

dandelion ['dændɪlaɪən] *n* diente *m* de león

dandruff ['dændrəf] *n* caspa *f*

Dane [deɪn] *n* danés(esa) *m,f*

danger ['deɪndʒə(r)] *n* (**a**) *(risk)* riesgo *m*; *(of war etc)* amenaza *f* (**b**) *(peril)* peligro *m*; **d. (sign)** peligro; **out of d.** fuera de peligro

dangerous ['deɪndʒərəs] *adj* peligroso(a); *(risky)* arriesgado(a); *(harmful)* nocivo(a); *(illness)* grave

dangerously ['deɪndʒərəslɪ] *adv* peligrosamente

dangle ['dæŋgəl] **1** *vi* *(hang)* colgar; *(swing)* balancearse

2 *vt (legs)* colgar; *(bait)* dejar colgado(a);

(swing) balancear en el aire

Danish ['deɪnɪʃ] **1** *adj* danés(esa); **D. pastry** pastel *m* de hojaldre

2 *n (language)* danés *m*

dapper ['dæpə(r)] *adj* pulcro(a)

dappled ['dæpəld] *adj (shade)* moteado(a)

dare [deə(r)] **1** *vi* atreverse, osar; **he doesn't d. be late** no se atreve a llegar tarde; **how d. you!** ¿cómo te atreves?; *esp Br* **I d. say** quizás; *Ironic* ya (lo creo)

2 *vt (challenge)* desafiar

3 *n* desafío *m*

daredevil ['deədevəl] *adj & n* atrevido(a) *(m,f)*, temerario(a) *(m,f)*

daring ['deərɪŋ] **1** *adj* **(a)** *(bold)* audaz, osado(a) **(b)** *(clothes)* atrevido(a)

2 *n* atrevimiento *m*, osadía *f*

dark [dɑːk] **1** *adj* **(a)** *(room, colour)* oscuro(a); *(hair, complexion)* moreno(a); *(eyes, future)* negro(a) **(b)** *Fig (gloomy)* triste **(c)** *Fig* **to be a d. horse** ser una incógnita; *(discreet)* ser una caja de sorpresas **(d)** *Fig (sinister)* siniestro(a)

2 *n* **(a)** *(darkness)* oscuridad *f*, tinieblas *fpl*; **after d.** después del anochecer **(b)** *Fig* **to be in the d. (about)** estar a oscuras (sobre)

darken ['dɑːkən] **1** *vt (sky)* oscurecer; *(colour)* hacer más oscuro(a)

2 *vi* oscurecerse; *(sky)* nublarse; *Fig (face)* ensombrecerse

darkness ['dɑːknɪs] *n* oscuridad *f*, tinieblas *fpl*

darkroom ['dɑːkruːm] *n* cuarto oscuro

darling ['dɑːlɪŋ] *adj & n* querido(a) *(m,f)*

darn [dɑːn] **1** *vt* zurcir

2 *n* zurcido *m*

dart [dɑːt] **1** *n* **(a)** *(missile)* dardo *m* **(b) darts** *sing* dardos *mpl*

2 *vi (fly about)* revolotear; **to d. in/out** entrar/salir corriendo

dartboard ['dɑːtbɔːd] *n* diana *f*

dash [dæʃ] **1** *n* **(a)** *(rush)* carrera *f* **(b)** *esp US (race)* sprint *m* **(c)** *(small amount)* poquito *m*; *(of salt)* pizca *f*; *(of liquid)* gota *f* **(d)** *Typ* guión largo; *(hyphen)* guión **(e)** *(vitality)* brío *m*

2 *vt* **(a)** *(throw)* arrojar **(b)** *(smash)* estrellar; **to d. sb's hopes** desvanecer las esperanzas de algn

3 *vi (rush)* correr; **to d. around** correr de un lado a otro; **to d. out** salir corriendo; *Fam* **I must d.!** ¡me voy pitando!

▶ **dash off** *vi* salir corriendo

dashboard ['dæʃbɔːd] *n Aut* salpicadero *m*

dashing ['dæʃɪŋ] *adj (appearance)* garboso(a)

data ['deɪtə, 'dɑːtə] *npl* datos *mpl*; **d. bank** *or* **base** banco *m* de datos; **d. processing** *(act)* proceso *m* de datos; *(science)* informática *f*; **d. protection act** ley *f* de informática

date¹ [deɪt] **1** *n* **(a)** *(time)* fecha *f*; **what's the d. today?** ¿qué día es hoy?; **out of d.** *(ideas)* anticuado(a); *(expression)* desusado(a); *(invalid)* caducado(a); **to d.** hasta la fecha; *Fig* **to be up to d.** estar al día; **d. of birth** fecha de nacimiento **(b)** *(social event)* compromiso *m*; *Fam (with girl, boy)* cita *f* **(c)** *US Fam (person dated)* ligue *m*

2 *vt (ruins)* datar

3 *vi (ideas)* quedar anticuado(a)

▶ **date back to, date from** *vt insep* remontar a, datar de

date² [deɪt] *n (fruit)* dátil *m*; **d. palm** datilera *f*

dated ['deɪtɪd] *adj (idea)* anticuado(a); *(fashion)* pasado(a) de moda; *(expression)* desusado(a)

daub [dɔːb] *vt* embadurnar; *(with oil, grease)* untar

daughter ['dɔːtə(r)] *n* hija *f*

daughter-in-law ['dɔːtərɪnlɔː] *n* nuera *f*, hija política

daunting ['dɔːntɪŋ] *adj* desalentador(a)

dawdle ['dɔːdəl] *vi Fam (walk slowly)* andar despacio; *(waste time)* perder el tiempo

dawn [dɔːn] **1** *n* alba *f*, amanecer *m*

2 *vi* **(a)** *(day)* amanecer **(b)** *Fig (age, hope)* comenzar **(c)** *Fig* **suddenly it dawned on him that ...** de repente cayó en la cuenta de que ...

day [deɪ] *n* **(a)** *(time)* día *m*; **d. in, d. out** día tras día; **d. by d.** diariamente; **good d.!** ¡buenos días!; **once a d.** una vez al día; **one of these days** un día de éstos; **(on) the next** *or* **following d.** el *or* al día siguiente; **the d. after tomorrow** pasado mañana; **the d. before yesterday** anteayer; **the other d.** el otro día; *Fig* **to live from d. to d.** vivir al día; *Fig* **to win the d.** llevarse la palma; *Fam* **to call it a d.** *(finish)* dar por acabado un trabajo; *(give up)* darse por vencido(a); *Fam* **to make sb's d.** alegrarle a algn el día; *Br Rail* **d. return** *(ticket)* billete *m* de ida y vuelta para el mismo día; **d. trip** excursión *f* de un día

(b) *(daylight)* día *m*; **by d.** de día; **d. and night** de día y de noche; *Br* **d. shift** turno *m* de día

(c) *(period of work)* jornada *f*; **an eight-hour d.** una jornada de ocho horas; **paid**

by the d. pagado(a) a jornal; **d. off** día de fiesta; **I'll take a d. off tomorrow** mañana me tomaré el día libre

   (**d**) *(era)* época *f*; **in those days** en aquellos tiempos; **these days, in this d. and age** hoy (en) día

daybreak ['deɪbreɪk] *n* amanecer *m*

daydream ['deɪdriːm] **1** *n* ensueño *m*; *(vain hope)* fantasía *f*

   2 *vi* soñar despierto(a); *(hope vainly)* hacerse ilusiones

daylight ['deɪlaɪt] *n* luz *f* del día; **in broad d.** en pleno día; **to scare the (living) daylights out of sb** pegarle a algn un susto de muerte

daytime ['deɪtaɪm] *n* día *m*; **in the d.** de día

day-to-day ['deɪtədeɪ] *adj* cotidiano(a), diario(a)

daze [deɪz] *n* aturdimiento *m*; **in a d.** aturdido(a)

dazed [deɪzd] *adj* aturdido(a), atontado(a)

dazzle ['dæzəl] *vt* deslumbrar

D-day ['diːdeɪ] *n* día *m* D

deacon ['diːkən] *n* diácono *m*

dead [ded] **1** *adj* (**a**) muerto(a); **he was shot d.** le mataron a tiros; **to be d.** estar muerto(a); *Fam Fig* **over my d. body!** ¡sobre mi cadáver!; **d. man** muerto *m*

   (**b**) *(machine)* averiado(a); *(phone)* cortado(a)

   (**c**) *(numb)* entumecido(a); *(limb)* adormecido(a); **my leg's gone d.** se me ha dormido la pierna

   (**d**) *(silence, secrecy)* total; **d. end** callejón *m* sin salida; *Sport* **d. heat** empate *m*; *Fam* **d. loss** inútil *m*, birria *f*

   2 *adv* (**a**) *(exactly)* justo; **d. on time** a la hora en punto

   (**b**) **to stop d.** pararse en seco

   (**c**) *(very)* muy; *Fam* **d. beat, d. tired** rendido(a); *Fam* **it's d. easy!** ¡está chupado(a)!; *Aut* **d. slow** *(sign)* al paso; *Fam* **you're d. right** tienes toda la razón

   3 *n* (**a**) **the d.** *pl* los muertos

   (**b**) **at d. of night** a altas horas de la noche

deaden ['dedən] *vt (impact, noise)* amortiguar; *Fig (pain, feeling)* calmar, aliviar

deadline ['dedlaɪn] *n (date)* fecha *f* tope; *(time)* hora *f* tope; **we have to meet the d.** tenemos que hacerlo dentro del plazo

deadlock ['dedlɒk] *n* punto muerto

deadly ['dedlɪ] **1** *adj* (**deadlier, deadliest**) mortal; *(weapon)* mortífero(a); *(aim)* certero(a)

   2 *adv (extremely)* terriblemente, sumamente

deadpan ['dedpæn] *adj Fam (face)* sin expresión; *(humour)* guasón(ona)

deaf [def] **1** *adj* sordo(a); *Fig* **to turn a d. ear** hacerse el sordo; **d. mute** sordomudo(a) *m,f*

   2 *npl* **the d.** los sordos; **the d. and dumb** los sordomudos

deafen ['defən] *vt* ensordecer

deafening ['defənɪŋ] *adj* ensordecedor(a)

deafness ['defnɪs] *n* sordera *f*

deal [diːl] **1** *n* (**a**) *Com & Pol* trato *m*, pacto *m*; **business d.** negocio *m*, transacción *f*; **to do a d. with sb** *(transaction)* cerrar un trato con algn; *(agreement)* pactar algo con algn; *Fam* **it's a d.!** ¡trato hecho! (**b**) *(amount)* cantidad *f*; **a good d. of criticism** muchas críticas; **a good d. slower** mucho más despacio (**c**) *Cards* reparto *m*

   2 *vt* (*pt & pp* **dealt**) (**a**) *Cards* dar (**to** a) (**b**) **to d. sb a blow** asestarle un golpe a algn

   ▶**deal in** *vt insep (goods)* comerciar en, tratar en; *(drugs)* traficar con

   ▶**deal out** *vt sep* repartir

   ▶**deal with** *vt insep (firm, person)* tratar con; *(subject, problem)* abordar, ocuparse de; *(in book etc)* tratar de

dealer ['diːlə(r)] *n* (**a**) *Com (in goods)* comerciante *mf*; *(in drugs)* traficante *mf* (**b**) *Cards* repartidor(a) *m,f*

dealings ['diːlɪŋz] *npl* (**a**) *(relations)* trato *m* (**b**) *Com* negocios *mpl*

dealt [delt] *pt & pp* of **deal**

dean [diːn] *n* (**a**) *Rel* deán *m* (**b**) *Univ* decano *m*

dear [dɪə(r)] **1** *adj* (**a**) *(loved)* querido(a); **to hold sth/sb d.** apreciar mucho algo/a algn (**b**) *(in letter)* Querido(a); *Fam* **D. Andrew** Querido Andrew; *Fml* **D. Madam** Estimada señora; *Fml* **D. Sir(s)** Muy señor(es) mío(s) (**c**) **it is very d. to me** *(precious)* le tengo un gran cariño (**d**) *Br (expensive)* caro(a)

   2 *n* querido(a) *m,f*; **my d.** mi vida

   3 *interj* **oh d.!, d. me!** *(surprise)* ¡caramba!; *(disappointment)* ¡qué pena!

dearly ['dɪəlɪ] *adv* muchísimo; *Fig* **he paid d. for his mistake** su error le costó caro

dearth [dɜːθ] *n Fml* escasez *f*

death [deθ] *n* (**a**) muerte *f*; *Fml* fallecimiento *m*; **to put sb to d.** dar muerte a algn; *Fam* **to be bored to d.** aburrirse como una ostra; *Fam* **to be scared to d.** estar muerto(a) de miedo; *Fam Fig* **to be**

sick to d. of estar hasta la coronilla de; **d. certificate** certificado *m* de defunción; **d. penalty**, **d. sentence** pena *f* de muerte; **d. rate** índice *m* de mortalidad; **d. squad** escuadrón *m* de la muerte (**b**) *Fig (end)* fin *m*

deathbed ['deθbed] *n* **to be on one's d.** estar en el lecho de muerte

deathly ['deθlɪ] *adj* (**deathlier, deathliest**) *(silence)* sepulcral; **d. pale** pálido(a) como un muerto

debacle [deɪ'bɑːkəl] *n* debacle *f*

debar [dɪ'bɑː(r)] *vt Fml* excluir, prohibir

debase [dɪ'beɪs] *vt Fig* envilecer; **to d. oneself** humillarse

debatable [dɪ'beɪtəbəl] *adj* discutible

debate [dɪ'beɪt] **1** *n* debate *m*; **a heated d.** una discusión acalorada
2 *vt* (**a**) *(discuss)* discutir (**b**) *(wonder about)* dar vueltas a
3 *vi* discutir

debateable dɪ'beɪtəbəl] *adj* = **debatable**

debauchery [dɪ'bɔːtʃərɪ] *n* libertinaje *m*

debilitating [dɪ'bɪlɪteɪtɪŋ] *adj* debilitante; *(heat, climate)* agotador(a)

debit ['debɪt] **1** *n* débito *m*; **d. balance** saldo negativo
2 *vt* **d. Mr Jones with £20** cargar la suma de 20 libras en la cuenta del Sr. Jones

debris ['debriː, 'deɪbriː] *n sing* escombros *mpl*

debt [det] *n* deuda *f*; **to be deeply in d.** estar cargado(a) de deudas; *Fig* **to be in sb's d.** estar en deuda con algn

debtor ['detə(r)] *n* deudor(a) *m,f*

debug [diː'bʌg] *vt Comput* eliminar fallos de

debunk [diː'bʌŋk] *vt Fam* desacreditar, desprestigiar

debut ['debjuː, 'deɪbjuː] *n* debut *m*; **to make one's d.** debutar

debutante ['debjʊtɑːnt] *n* debutante *f*

decade [de'keɪd, 'dekeɪd] *n* decenio *m*, década *f*

decadence ['dekədəns] *n* decadencia *f*

decadent ['dekədənt] *adj* decadente

decaffeinated [diː'kæfɪneɪtɪd] *adj* descafeinado(a)

decanter [dɪ'kæntə(r)] *n* jarra *f*, jarro *m*

decapitate [dɪ'kæpɪteɪt] *vt* decapitar

decay [dɪ'keɪ] **1** *n* (*of food, body*) descomposición *f*, *(of teeth)* caries *f inv*; *(of buildings)* desmoronamiento *m*; *Fig* decadencia *f*
2 *vi* descomponerse; *(teeth)* cariarse; *(building)* deteriorarse; *Fig* corromperse

deceased [dɪ'siːst] *adj Fml* difunto(a), fallecido(a)

deceit [dɪ'siːt] *n* (**a**) *(dishonesty)* falta *f* de honradez, falsedad *f* (**b**) *(trick)* engaño *m*, mentira *f*

deceitful [dɪ'siːtfʊl] *adj* falso(a)

deceive [dɪ'siːv] *vt (mislead)* engañar; *(lie to)* mentir

December [dɪ'sembə(r)] *n* diciembre *m*

decency ['diːsənsɪ] *n* decencia *f*; *(modesty)* pudor *m*; *(morality)* moralidad *f*

decent ['diːsənt] *adj* decente; *(person)* honrado(a); *Fam (kind)* simpático(a)

decentralize [diː'sentrəlaɪz] *vt* descentralizar

deception [dɪ'sepʃən] *n* engaño *m*

> 🖉 Note that the Spanish word **decepción** is a false friend and is never a translation for the English word **deception**. In Spanish, **decepción** means "disappointment".

deceptive [dɪ'septɪv] *adj* engañoso(a)

deceptively [dɪ'septɪvlɪ] *adv* **it looks d. simple** parece engañosamente sencillo(a)

decibel ['desɪbel] *n* decibelio *m*

decide [dɪ'saɪd] **1** *vt* (**a**) *(decide)*; **to d. to do sth** decidir hacer algo (**b**) *(matter, question)* resolver, determinar
2 *vi (reach decision)* decidirse; **to d. against sth** decidirse en contra de algo
▸ **decide on** *vt insep (choose)* optar por

decided [dɪ'saɪdɪd] *adj* (**a**) *(noticeable)* marcado(a) (**b**) *(resolute)* decidido(a); *(views)* categórico(a)

decidedly [dɪ'saɪdɪdlɪ] *adv Fml* (**a**) *(clearly)* indudablemente (**b**) *(resolutely)* decididamente

deciding [dɪ'saɪdɪŋ] *adj* decisivo(a)

deciduous [dɪ'sɪdjʊəs] *adj* de hoja caduca

decimal ['desɪməl] **1** *adj* decimal; **d. point** coma *f* (de fracción decimal)
2 *n* decimal *m*

decimate ['desɪmeɪt] *vt* diezmar

decipher [dɪ'saɪfə(r)] *vt* descifrar

decision [dɪ'sɪʒən] *n* (**a**) decisión *f*; *Jur* fallo *m*; **to come to a d.** llegar a una decisión; **to make a d.** tomar una decisión (**b**) *(resolution)* resolución *f*

decisive [dɪ'saɪsɪv] *adj* (**a**) *(resolute)* decidido(a), resuelto(a) (**b**) *(conclusive)* decisivo(a)

deck [dek] **1** *n* (**a**) *(of ship)* cubierta *f*; **on/below d.** en/bajo cubierta; **d. chair** tumbona *f* (**b**) *(of bus)* piso *m*; **top d.** piso de arriba (**c**) *esp US (of cards)* baraja *f* (**d**) *(of record player)* plato *m*
2 *vt* **to d. out** adornar

declaration [deklə'reɪʃən] *n* declaración *f*

declare [dɪ'kleə(r)] *vt* declarar; *(winner, innocence)* proclamar; *(decision)* manifestar

declared [dɪ'kleəd] *adj (opponent)* declarado(a); *(intention)* manifiesto(a)

decline [dɪ'klaɪn] **1** *n* (**a**) *(decrease)* disminución *f* (**b**) *(deterioration)* deterioro *m*; *(of health)* empeoramiento *m*; **to fall into d.** empezar a decaer

 2 *vi* (**a**) *(decrease)* disminuir; *(amount)* bajar; *(business)* decaer (**b**) *(deteriorate)* deteriorarse; *(health)* empeorar (**c**) *(refuse)* negarse

 3 *vt* (**a**) *(refuse)* rechazar (**b**) *Ling* declinar

declutch [dɪ'klʌtʃ] *vi* soltar el embrague

decode [di:'kəʊd] *vt* descifrar

decompose [di:kəm'pəʊz] *vi* descomponerse

décor ['deɪkɔ:(r)] *n* decoración *f*; *Th* decorado *m*

decorate ['dekəreɪt] *vt* (**a**) *(adorn)* decorar, adornar (**with** con) (**b**) *(paint)* pintar; *(wallpaper)* empapelar (**c**) *(honour)* condecorar

decoration [dekə'reɪʃən] *n* (**a**) *(decor)* decoración *f*; **Christmas decorations** adornos navideños (**b**) *(medal)* condecoración *f*

decorative ['dekərətɪv] *adj* decorativo(a)

decorator ['dekəreɪtə(r)] *n* decorador(a) *m,f*; *(painter)* pintor(a) *m,f*; *(paperhanger)* empapelador(a) *m,f*

decorum [dɪ'kɔ:rəm] *n* decoro *m*

decoy ['di:kɔɪ] *n Fig* señuelo *m*

decrease 1 *n* ['di:kri:s] disminución *f*; *(in speed, size, price)* reducción *f*

 2 *vi* [dɪ'kri:s] disminuir; *(strength)* menguar; *(price, temperature)* bajar; *(speed, size)* reducir

 3 *vt* disminuir, reducir; *(price, temperature)* bajar

decree [dɪ'kri:] **1** *n* (**a**) *Pol & Rel* decreto *m* (**b**) *esp US Jur* sentencia *f*; **d. absolute** sentencia definitiva de divorcio; **d. nisi** sentencia provisional de divorcio

 2 *vt Pol & Rel* decretar, pronunciar

decrepit [dɪ'krepɪt] *adj* decrépito(a)

dedicate ['dedɪkeɪt] *vt* consagrar, dedicar

dedicated ['dedɪkeɪtɪd] *adj* ardiente; **d. to** entregado(a) a

dedication [dedɪ'keɪʃən] *n (act)* dedicación *f*; *(commitment)* entrega *f*; *(in book)* dedicatoria *f*

deduce [dɪ'dju:s] *vt* deducir (**from** de)

deduct [dɪ'dʌkt] *vt* descontar (**from** de)

deduction [dɪ'dʌkʃən] *n* (**a**) *(conclusion)* conclusión *f* (**b**) *(subtraction)* descuento *m*

deed [di:d] *n* (**a**) *(act)* acto *m*; *(feat)* hazaña *f*; *Jur* escritura *f*; **title deeds** título *m* de propiedad

deem [di:m] *vt Fml* estimar

deep [di:p] **1** *adj* (**a**) profundo(a); *(breath, sigh)* hondo(a); **it's 10 m d.** tiene 10 m de profundidad (**b**) *(voice)* grave; *(shame)* grande; *(interest)* vivo(a) (**c**) *(colour)* oscuro(a) (**d**) *(serious)* grave

 2 *adv* **to dig d.** cavar hondo; **to be d. in thought** estar absorto(a); **to look d. into sb's eyes** penetrar a algn con la mirada; *Fig* **nine d.** de nueve en fondo

deepen ['di:pən] **1** *vt (well)* profundizar, ahondar; *Fig (knowledge)* aumentar

 2 *vi (river etc)* hacerse más hondo *or* profundo; *Fig (knowledge)* aumentar; *(colour, emotion)* intensificarse; *(sound, voice)* hacerse más grave

deep-freeze [di:p'fri:z] **1** *n* congelador *m*
 2 *vt* congelar

deep-fry [di:p'fraɪ] *vt* freír en mucho aceite

deeply ['di:plɪ] *adv* profundamente; *(breathe)* hondo; **to be d. in debt** estar cargado(a) de deudas

deep-rooted [di:p'ru:tɪd] *adj Fig* arraigado(a)

deep-seated [di:p'si:tɪd] *adj Fig* arraigado(a)

deep-set [di:p'set] *adj (eyes)* hundido(a)

deer [dɪə(r)] *n inv* ciervo *m*

deface [dɪ'feɪs] *vt (book, poster)* garabatear

de facto [deɪ'fæktəʊ] *adj & adv Fml* de hecho

defamation [defə'meɪʃən] *n* difamación *f*

default [dɪ'fɔ:lt] **1** *vi* (**a**) *(not act)* faltar a sus compromisos (**b**) *Jur* estar en rebeldía (**c**) *(not pay)* suspender pagos

 2 *n* (**a**) *(failure to act)* omisión *f* (**b**) *(failure to pay)* incumplimiento *m* de pago (**c**) *Jur* rebeldía *f*; **in d. of** a falta de; **to win by d.** ganar por incomparecencia del adversario

defaulter [dɪ'fɔ:ltə(r)] *n (on loan)* moroso(a) *m,f*; *Jur & Mil* rebelde *mf*

defeat [dɪ'fi:t] **1** *vt* (**a**) derrotar, vencer; *(motion)* rechazar (**b**) *Fig* frustrar

 2 *n* (**a**) *(of army, team)* derrota *f*; *(of motion)* rechazo *m* (**b**) *Fig* fracaso *m*

defeatist [dɪ'fiːtɪst] *adj & n* derrotista *(mf)*

defect 1 *n* ['diːfekt] defecto *m*; *(flaw)* desperfecto *m*
2 *vi* [dɪ'fekt] desertar (**from** de); *(from country)* huir

defective [dɪ'fektɪv] *adj (faulty)* defectuoso(a); *(flawed)* con desperfectos; *(lacking)* incompleto(a)

defector [dɪ'fektə(r)] *n Pol* tránsfuga *mf*, trásfuga *mf*

defence [dɪ'fens] *n* (**a**) defensa *f*; **the Ministry of D.** el Ministerio de Defensa; **to come to sb's d.** salir en defensa de algn (**b**) *usu sing Jur* defensa *f* (**c**) *Sport* [*Br* dɪ'fens, *US* 'diːfens] **the d.** la defensa

defenceless [dɪ'fenslɪs] *adj* indefenso(a)

defend [dɪ'fend] *vt* defender

defendant [dɪ'fendənt] *n Jur* acusado(a) *m,f*

defender [dɪ'fendə(r)] *n* defensor(a) *m,f*; *Sport* defensa *mf*

defending [dɪ'fendɪŋ] *adj Sport* defensor(a); **d. champion** campeón(ona) *m,f* titular

defense [dɪ'fens, 'diːfens] *n US* = **defence**

defensive [dɪ'fensɪv] **1** *adj* defensivo(a)
2 *n* **to be on the d.** estar a la defensiva

defer[1] [dɪ'fɜː(r)] *vt* aplazar, retrasar

defer[2] [dɪ'fɜː(r)] *vi* **to d. to** deferir a

deference ['defərəns] *n Fml* deferencia *f*, respeto *m*; **out of** *or* **in d. to** por respeto *or* por deferencia a

defiance [dɪ'faɪəns] *n* (**a**) *(challenge)* desafío *m*; **in d. of** a despecho de (**b**) *(resistance)* resistencia *f*

defiant [dɪ'faɪənt] *adj (challenging)* desafiante; *(bold)* insolente

deficiency [dɪ'fɪʃənsɪ] *n* (**a**) *(lack)* falta *f*, carencia *f* (**b**) *(shortcoming)* defecto *m*

deficient [dɪ'fɪʃənt] *adj* deficiente; **to be d. in sth** carecer de algo

deficit ['defɪsɪt] *n* déficit *m*

defile [dɪ'faɪl] *vt Fml* (**a**) *(mind)* corromper; *(honour)* manchar; *(woman)* deshonrar (**b**) *(desecrate)* profanar

define [dɪ'faɪn] *vt* definir; *(duties, powers)* delimitar

definite ['defɪnɪt] *adj* (**a**) *(clear)* claro(a); *(progress)* notable (**b**) *(date, place)* determinado(a); **is it d.?** ¿es seguro?

definitely ['defɪnɪtlɪ] **1** *adv* sin duda; **he was d. drunk** no cabe duda de que estaba borracho
2 *interj* ¡desde luego!

definition [defɪ'nɪʃən] *n* definición *f*; **by d.** por definición

definitive [dɪ'fɪnɪtɪv] *adj* definitivo(a)

deflate [dɪ'fleɪt] *vt* (**a**) *(tyre etc)* desinflar (**b**) *Fig* rebajar; **to d. sb** hacer bajar los humos a algn (**c**) **to d. the economy** tomar medidas deflacionistas

deflationary [dɪ'fleɪʃənərɪ] *adj Econ* deflacionista

deflect [dɪ'flekt] *vt* desviar

deflection [dɪ'flekʃən] *n* desviación *f*

deforestation [diːfɒrɪ'steɪʃən] *n* deforestación *f*

deformed [dɪ'fɔːmd] *adj* deforme

deformity [dɪ'fɔːmɪtɪ] *n* deformidad *f*

defraud [dɪ'frɔːd] *vt* estafar

defrost [diː'frɒst] *vt* (**a**) *(freezer, food)* descongelar (**b**) *US (windscreen)* desempañar

deft [deft] *adj* hábil, diestro(a)

defunct [dɪ'fʌŋkt] *adj (person)* difunto(a); *(thing)* en desuso

defuse [diː'fjuːz] *vt (bomb)* desactivar; *Fig* **to d. a situation** reducir la tensión de una situación

defy [dɪ'faɪ] *vt* (**a**) *(person)* desafiar; *(law, order)* contravenir (**b**) *(challenge)* retar, desafiar

degenerate 1 *vi* [dɪ'dʒenəreɪt] degenerar (**into** en)
2 *adj & n* [dɪ'dʒenərɪt] degenerado(a) *(m,f)*

degrading [dɪ'greɪdɪŋ] *adj* degradante

degree [dɪ'griː] *n* (**a**) grado *m*; **to some d.** hasta cierto punto (**b**) *(stage)* etapa *f*; **by degrees** poco a poco (**c**) *(qualification)* título *m*; *(doctorate)* doctorado *m*; **to have a d. in science** ser licenciado(a) en ciencias

dehydrated [diːhaɪ'dreɪtɪd] *adj (person)* deshidratado(a); *(vegetables)* seco(a)

de-ice [diː'aɪs] *vt* quitar el hielo a, deshelar

de-icer [diː'aɪsə(r)] *n* anticongelante *m*

deign [deɪn] *vi* dignarse

deity ['deɪɪtɪ] *n* deidad *f*

dejected [dɪ'dʒektɪd] *adj* desalentado(a), abatido(a)

delay [dɪ'leɪ] **1** *vt* (**a**) *(flight, train)* retrasar; *(person)* entretener; **delayed action** acción retardada (**b**) *(postpone)* aplazar
2 *vi* **don't d.** no lo deje para más tarde
3 *n* retraso *m*

delectable [dɪ'lektəbəl] *adj* delicioso(a)

delegate 1 *n* ['delɪgɪt] delegado(a) *m,f*
2 *vt* ['delɪgeɪt] delegar (**to** en); **to d. sb to do sth** encargar a algn que haga algo

delegation [delɪ'geɪʃən] *n* delegación *f*

delete [dɪ'liːt] *vt* tachar, suprimir

deliberate 1 *adj* [dɪ'lɪbərɪt] *(intentional)*

deliberado(a), intencionado(a); *(studied)*
premeditado(a); *(careful)* prudente; *(unhurried)* pausado(a)
  2 *vt* [dɪ'lɪbəreɪt] deliberar
  3 *vi* deliberar (**on** or **about** sobre);
deliberately [dɪ'lɪbərɪtlɪ] *adv (intentionally)* a propósito; *(unhurriedly)* pausadamente
deliberation [dɪlɪbə'reɪʃən] *n* (**a**) *esp pl (consideration)* deliberación *f* (**b**) *(care)* cuidado *m; (unhurriedness)* pausa *f*
delicacy ['delɪkəsɪ] *n* (**a**) delicadeza *f* (**b**) *(food)* manjar *m* (exquisito)
delicate ['delɪkɪt] *adj* delicado(a); *(handiwork)* fino(a); *(instrument)* sensible; *(flavour)* sutil
delicious [dɪ'lɪʃəs] *adj* delicioso(a)
delight [dɪ'laɪt] **1** *n* (**a**) *(pleasure)* placer *m;* **he took d. in it** le encantó (**b**) *(source of pleasure)* encanto *m,* delicia *f*
  2 *vt* encantar
delighted [dɪ'laɪtɪd] *adj* encantado(a); *(smile)* de alegría; **I'm d. to see you** me alegro mucho de verte
delightful [dɪ'laɪtfʊl] *adj* encantador(a); *(view, person)* muy agradable; *(meal, weather)* delicioso(a)
delinquency [dɪ'lɪŋkwənsɪ] *n* delincuencia *f;* **juvenile d.** delincuencia juvenil
delinquent [dɪ'lɪŋkwənt] *adj & n* delincuente *(mf)*
delirious [dɪ'lɪrɪəs] *adj* delirante
deliver [dɪ'lɪvə(r)] *vt* (**a**) *(goods)* repartir, entregar; *(message)* dar; *(order)* despachar; *Fig* **to d. the goods** cumplir con la obligación (**b**) *(blow)* asestar; *(speech, verdict)* pronunciar (**c**) *Med* ayudar en el nacimiento de (**d**) *Fml (rescue)* liberar
delivery [dɪ'lɪvərɪ] *n* (**a**) *(of goods)* reparto *m,* entrega *f;* **to take d. of an order** recibir un pedido; **d. note** albarán *m* de entrega; *Br* **d. van** furgoneta *f* de reparto (**b**) *(of speech)* declamación *f* (**c**) *(of baby)* parto *m*
delta ['deltə] *n Geog* delta *m*
delude [dɪ'luːd] *vt* engañar; **don't d. yourself** no te hagas ilusiones
deluge ['deljuːdʒ] **1** *n (flood)* inundación *f; (rain)* diluvio *m; Fig (of letters etc)* avalancha *f*
  2 *vt Fml* inundar
delusion [dɪ'luːʒən] *n* (**a**) *(state, act)* engaño *m* (**b**) *(false belief)* ilusión *f* (vana); **delusions of grandeur** delirios *mpl* de grandeza
de luxe [də'lʌks, də'lʊks] *adj* de lujo *inv*
delve [delv] *vi* **to d. into** *(pocket)* hurgar

en; *(subject)* profundizar en
demand [dɪ'mɑːnd] **1** *n* (**a**) solicitud *f; (for pay rise, rights)* reclamación *f; (need)* necesidad *f;* **on d.** a petición (**b**) *(claim)* exigencia *f;* **to be in d.** ser solicitado(a) (**c**) *Econ* demanda *f*
  2 *vt* (**a**) exigir; *(rights)* reclamar; **to d. that ...** insistir en que ... (+ *subj*) (**b**) *(need)* requerir
demanding [dɪ'mɑːndɪŋ] *adj* (**a**) *(person)* exigente (**b**) *(job)* agotador(a)
demean [dɪ'miːn] *vt Fml* **to d. oneself** rebajarse
demeaning [dɪ'miːnɪŋ] *adj Fml* humillante
demeanour, *US* **demeanor** [dɪ'miːnə(r)] *n Fml* (**a**) *(behaviour)* comportamiento *m,* conducta *f* (**b**) *(bearing)* porte *m*
demented [dɪ'mentɪd] *adj Med* demente; *Fam* loco(a)
demise [dɪ'maɪz] *n Fml (death)* fallecimiento *m; Fig (of institution)* desaparición *f; (of ambition etc)* fracaso *m*
demist [diː'mɪst] *vt Aut* desempañar
demo ['deməʊ] *n Fam* manifestación *f;* **d. tape** maqueta *f*
demobilize [diː'məʊbɪlaɪz] *vt* desmovilizar
democracy [dɪ'mɒkrəsɪ] *n* democracia *f*
democrat ['deməkræt] *n* demócrata *mf; Pol* **Christian D.** democratacristiano(a) *m,f;* **Social D.** socialdemócrata *mf*
democratic [demə'krætɪk] *adj* democrático(a); *US Pol* **D. party** partido *m* demócrata
demographic [demə'græfɪk] *adj* demográfico(a)
demolish [dɪ'mɒlɪʃ] *vt (building)* derribar, demoler; *Fig (theory, proposal)* echar por tierra
demolition [demə'lɪʃən] *n* demolición *f*
demon ['diːmən] *n* demonio *m*
demonstrate ['demənstreɪt] **1** *vt* demostrar
  2 *vi Pol* manifestarse
demonstration [demən'streɪʃən] *n* (**a**) *(proof)* demostración *f,* prueba *f* (**b**) *(explanation)* explicación *f* (**c**) *Pol* manifestación *f*
demonstrative [dɪ'mɒnstrətɪv] *adj* expresivo(a)
demonstrator ['demənstreɪtə(r)] *n* manifestante *mf*
demoralize [dɪ'mɒrəlaɪz] *vt* desmoralizar
demoralizing [dɪ'mɒrəlaɪzɪŋ] *adj* desmoralizador(a), desmoralizante

demote [dɪ'məʊt] *vt* rebajar de graduación a

demure [dɪ'mjʊə(r)] *adj (person)* recatado(a)

den [den] *n* (a) *(of animal)* guarida *f* (b) *Fam (study)* estudio *m*

denial [dɪ'naɪəl] *n* (a) *(of charge)* desmentido *m* (b) *(of rights)* denegación *f*; *(of request)* negativa *f*

denim ['denɪm] *n* dril *m*; **d. skirt** falda tejana; **denims** tejanos *mpl*, vaqueros *mpl*

Denmark ['denmɑːk] *n* Dinamarca

denomination [dɪnɒmɪ'neɪʃən] *n* (a) *Rel* confesión *f* (b) *Fin (of coins)* valor *m*

denominator [dɪ'nɒmɪneɪtə(r)] *n* denominador *m*

denote [dɪ'nəʊt] *vt (show)* indicar; *(mean)* significar

denounce [dɪ'naʊns] *vt* denunciar; *(criticize)* censurar

dense [dens] *adj* (a) denso(a); *(crowd)* numeroso(a) (b) *Fam (stupid)* torpe

densely ['densli] *adv* densamente

density ['densɪtɪ] *n* densidad *f*

dent [dent] **1** *n* abolladura *f*
2 *vt (car)* abollar

dental ['dentəl] *adj* dental; **d. floss** hilo *m* dental; **d. surgeon** odontólogo(a) *m,f*; **d. surgery** *(place)* clínica *f* dental; *(treatment)* cirugía *f* dental

dentist ['dentɪst] *n* dentista *mf*

dentistry ['dentɪstrɪ] *n* odontología *f*

denture ['dentʃə(r)] *n (usu pl)* dentadura postiza

denunciation [dɪnʌnsɪ'eɪʃən] *n* denuncia *f*, condena *f*

deny [dɪ'naɪ] *vt* (a) *(repudiate)* negar; *(rumour, report)* desmentir; *(charge)* rechazar (b) *(refuse)* negar

deodorant [diː'əʊdərənt] *n* desodorante *m*

depart [dɪ'pɑːt] *vi* marcharse, irse; *Fig (from subject)* desviarse (**from** de)

department [dɪ'pɑːtmənt] *n* sección *f*; *(in university)* departamento *m*; *(in government)* ministerio *m*; **d. store** grandes almacenes *mpl*; *US* **D. of the Interior** Ministerio *m* del Interior

departure [dɪ'pɑːtʃə(r)] *n* partida *f*; *Av & Rail* salida *f*; *Av* **d. lounge** sala *f* de embarque

depend [dɪ'pend] **1** *vi (rely)* fiarse (**on** or **upon** de)
2 *v impers (be determined by)* depender (**on** or **upon** de); **it depends on the weather** según el tiempo que haga; **that depends** según

dependable [dɪ'pendəbəl] *adj (person)*

responsable, fiable; *(income)* seguro(a); *(machine)* fiable

dependant, *US* **dependent** [dɪ'pendənt] *n* dependiente *mf*

dependence [dɪ'pendəns] *n* dependencia *f*

dependent [dɪ'pendənt] **1** *adj* dependiente; **to be d. on sth** depender de algo
2 *n US* = **dependant**

depict [dɪ'pɪkt] *vt Art* representar; *Fig* describir

deplete [dɪ'pliːt] *vt* reducir

deplorable [dɪ'plɔːrəbəl] *adj* lamentable

deplore [dɪ'plɔː(r)] *vt* deplorar

deploy [dɪ'plɔɪ] *vt Mil* desplegar; *Fig* utilizar

depopulate [diː'pɒpjʊleɪt] *vt* despoblar

deport [dɪ'pɔːt] *vt* expulsar (**from** de; **to** a)

deportation [diːpɔː'teɪʃən] *n* expulsión *f*

deportment [dɪ'pɔːtmənt] *n Fml* porte *m*

depose [dɪ'pəʊz] *vt* deponer

deposit [dɪ'pɒzɪt] **1** *n* (a) sedimento *m*; *Min* yacimiento *m*; *(in wine)* poso *m* (b) *(in bank)* depósito *m*; **d. account** cuenta *f* de ahorros (c) *Com (on purchase)* señal *f*; *(on rented car, flat)* depósito *m*; *(on house)* entrada *f*
2 *vt* depositar; *(into account)* ingresar

deposition [depə'zɪʃən] *n* (a) *(of leader)* destitución *f* (b) *Jur (of witness)* declaración *f*

depositor [dɪ'pɒzɪtə(r)] *n* depositante *mf*

depot ['depəʊ] *n* almacén *m*; *Mil* depósito *m*; *(bus garage)* garaje *m* (de autobuses); *US (bus station)* estación *f* de autobuses

depraved [dɪ'preɪvd] *adj (person)* depravado(a)

deprecate ['deprɪkeɪt] *vt* desaprobar, censurar

depreciate [dɪ'priːʃɪeɪt] *vi* depreciarse

depreciation [dɪpriːʃɪ'eɪʃən] *n* depreciación *f*

depress [dɪ'pres] *vt* (a) *(person)* deprimir (b) *Econ (profits)* reducir; *(trade)* dificultar (c) *Fml (switch, lever etc)* presionar; *(clutch, piano pedal)* pisar

depressed [dɪ'prest] *adj* (a) *(person)* deprimido(a); **to get d.** deprimirse (b) *(market)* en crisis (c) *(surface)* hundido(a)

depressing [dɪ'presɪŋ] *adj* deprimente

depression [dɪ'preʃən] *n* depresión *f*

deprivation [deprɪ'veɪʃən] *n (hardship)* privación *f*; *(loss)* pérdida *f*

deprive [dɪ'praɪv] *vt* privar (**of** de)

deprived [dɪ'praɪvd] *adj* necesitado(a)

dept (*abbr* **department**) dpt, dpto

depth [depθ] *n* (**a**) profundidad *f* (**b**) *Fig (of emotion)* intensidad *f*; *(of thought)* complejidad *f*; **to be in the depths of despair** estar completamente desesperado(a); **in d.** a fondo

deputation [depjʊˈteɪʃən] *n* delegación *f*

deputy [ˈdepjʊtɪ] *n* (**a**) *(substitute)* suplente *mf*; **d. chairman** vicepresidente *m*; **d. head** subdirector(a) *m,f* (**b**) *Pol* diputado(a) *m,f*

derail [dɪˈreɪl] *vt* hacer descarrilar

deranged [dɪˈreɪndʒd] *adj* trastornado(a)

derby *n* (**a**) [ˈdɑːbɪ] *Sport* prueba *f* (**b**) [ˈdɜːrbɪ] *US* sombrero hongo

derelict [ˈderɪlɪkt] *adj* abandonado(a), en ruinas

deride [dɪˈraɪd] *vt* ridiculizar, burlarse de

derisive [dɪˈraɪsɪv] *adj* burlón(ona)

derisory [dɪˈraɪsərɪ] *adj* irrisorio(a)

derivative [dɪˈrɪvətɪv] **1** *adj (art, writing)* sin originalidad
2 *n (of word, substance)* derivado *m*

derive [dɪˈraɪv] **1** *vt* sacar
2 *vi (word)* derivarse (**from** de); *(skill)* provenir (**from** de)

derogatory [dɪˈrɒgətərɪ] *adj (remark, article)* despectivo(a); *(meaning)* peyorativo(a)

derrick [ˈderɪk] *n* torre *f* de perforación

descend [dɪˈsend] **1** *vi* descender; **to d. from** *(be related to)* descender de
2 *vt (stairs)* bajar

descendant [dɪˈsendənt] *n* descendiente *mf*

descent [dɪˈsent] *n* (**a**) descenso *m* (**b**) *Fig (into madness, poverty)* caída *f* (**c**) *(slope)* declive *m* (**d**) *(ancestry)* ascendencia *f*

describe [dɪˈskraɪb] *vt* (**a**) describir (**b**) *(circle)* trazar

description [dɪˈskrɪpʃən] *n* (**a**) descripción *f*; **to defy d.** superar la descripción (**b**) *(type)* clase *f*

desecrate [ˈdesɪkreɪt] *vt* profanar

desert[1] [ˈdezət] *n* desierto *m*

desert[2] [dɪˈzɜːt] **1** *vt (place, family)* abandonar
2 *vi Mil* desertar (**from** de)

deserter [dɪˈzɜːtə(r)] *n* desertor(a) *m,f*

desertion [dɪˈzɜːʃən] *n* abandono *m*; *Pol* defección *f*; *Mil* deserción *f*

deserts [dɪˈzɜːts] *npl* **to get one's just d.** llevarse su merecido

deserve [dɪˈzɜːv] *vt (rest, punishment)* merecer; *(prize, praise)* ser digno(a) de

deservedly [dɪˈzɜːvɪdlɪ] *adv* con (toda) razón

deserving [dɪˈzɜːvɪŋ] *adj (person)* de valía; *(cause)* meritorio(a)

design [dɪˈzaɪn] **1** *n* (**a**) diseño *m* (**b**) *(drawing, blueprint)* plano *m* (**c**) *(layout)* disposición *f* (**d**) *(pattern)* dibujo *m* (**e**) *Fig (scheme)* intención *f*; **by d.** a propósito; *Fam* **to have designs on** tener puestas las miras en
2 *vt* diseñar

designate 1 *vt* [ˈdezɪgneɪt] (**a**) *(appoint)* designar, nombrar (**b**) *Fml (boundary)* señalar
2 *adj* [ˈdezɪgnɪt] designado(a)

designer [dɪˈzaɪnə(r)] *n Art* diseñador(a) *m,f*; **d. jeans** pantalones *mpl* de marca

desirable [dɪˈzaɪərəbəl] *adj* deseable; *(asset, offer)* atractivo(a)

desire [dɪˈzaɪə(r)] **1** *n* deseo *m*; **I haven't the slightest d. to go** no me apetece nada ir
2 *vt* desear

desist [dɪˈzɪst] *vi Fml* desistir (**from** de)

desk [desk] *n (in school)* pupitre *m*; *(in office)* escritorio *m*; *US* **d. clerk** recepcionista *mf*; **d. job** trabajo *m* de oficina; **news d.** redacción *f*; **reception d.** recepción *f*

desktop [ˈdesktɒp] *n Comput* escritorio *m*; **d. computer** ordenador *m* de sobremesa, *Am* computadora *f* de mesa; **d. publishing** autoedición *f*

desolate [ˈdesəlɪt] *adj* (**a**) *(uninhabited)* desierto(a); *(barren)* yermo(a) (**b**) *(person)* desconsolado(a)

desolation [desəˈleɪʃən] *n* (**a**) *(of place)* desolación *f*; *(by destruction)* asolamiento *m* (**b**) *(of person)* desconsuelo *m*

despair [dɪˈspeə(r)] **1** *n* desesperación *f*; **to drive sb to d.** desesperar a algn
2 *vi* desesperar(se) (**of** de)

despairing [dɪˈspeərɪŋ] *adj* desesperado(a)

despatch [dɪˈspætʃ] *n & vt* = **dispatch**

desperate [ˈdespərɪt] *adj* (**a**) desesperado(a); *(struggle)* encarnizado(a) (**b**) *(need)* apremiante

desperately [ˈdespərɪtlɪ] *adv (recklessly)* desesperadamente; *(struggle)* encarnizadamente; *(ill)* gravemente; *(in love)* locamente; *(difficult)* sumamente

desperation [despəˈreɪʃən] *n* desesperación *f*; **in d.** a la desesperada

despicable [dɪˈspɪkəbəl] *adj* despreciable; *(behaviour)* indigno(a)

despise [dɪˈspaɪz] *vt* despreciar, menospreciar

despite [dɪˈspaɪt] *prep Fml* a pesar de

despondent [dɪˈspɒndənt] *adj* abatido(a)

despot [ˈdespɒt] n déspota mf

dessert [dɪˈzɜːt] n postre m; **d. wine** vino m dulce

dessertspoon [dɪˈzɜːtspuːn] n (a) cuchara f de postre (b) **dessertspoon(ful)** (measure) cucharada f de postre

destination [destɪˈneɪʃən] n destino m

destined [ˈdestɪnd] adj (a) **d. to fail** condenado(a) al fracaso (b) (bound) con destino (**for** a)

destiny [ˈdestɪnɪ] n destino m

destitute [ˈdestɪtjuːt] adj indigente

destroy [dɪˈstrɔɪ] vt destruir; (vehicle, old furniture) destrozar

destroyer [dɪˈstrɔɪə(r)] n Naut destructor m

destruction [dɪˈstrʌkʃən] n destrucción f, Fig ruina f

destructive [dɪˈstrʌktɪv] adj (gale etc) destructor(a); (tendency, criticism) destructivo(a)

detach [dɪˈtætʃ] vt (remove) separar

detachable [dɪˈtætʃəbəl] adj separable (**from** de)

detached [dɪˈtætʃt] adj (a) (separated) separado(a); **d. house** casa f independiente (b) (impartial) objetivo(a)

detachment [dɪˈtætʃmənt] n (a) (impartiality) objetividad f; (aloofness) desapego m (b) Mil destacamento m

detail [ˈdiːteɪl] **1** n (a) detalle m, pormenor m; **without going into detail(s)** sin entrar en detalles; **details** (information) información f (b) Mil destacamento m

2 vt (a) (list) detallar, enumerar (b) Mil (appoint) destacar

detailed [ˈdiːteɪld] adj detallado(a), minucioso(a)

detain [dɪˈteɪn] vt (a) Jur detener (b) (delay) retener

detainee [diːteɪˈniː] n Pol preso(a) m,f

detect [dɪˈtekt] vt (a) (error, movement) advertir; (difference) notar; (smell, sound) percibir (b) (discover) descubrir; (enemy ship) detectar; (position) localizar

detection [dɪˈtekʃən] n (a) descubrimiento m; (of smell, sound) percepción f (b) (discovery) (of enemy ship) detección f

detective [dɪˈtektɪv] n detective mf; **d. story** novela policíaca

detector [dɪˈtektə(r)] n aparato m detector

detention [dɪˈtenʃən] n (of suspect etc) detención f, arresto m; Educ **to get d.** quedarse castigado(a)

deter [dɪˈtɜː(r)] vt (dissuade) disuadir (**from** de); (stop) impedir

detergent [dɪˈtɜːdʒənt] n detergente m

deteriorate [dɪˈtɪərɪəreɪt] vi deteriorarse

deterioration [dɪtɪərɪəˈreɪʃən] n empeoramiento m; (of substance, friendship) deterioro m

determination [dɪtɜːmɪˈneɪʃən] n (resolution) resolución f

determine [dɪˈtɜːmɪn] vt determinar

determined [dɪˈtɜːmɪnd] adj (person) decidido(a); (effort) enérgico(a)

deterrent [dɪˈterənt] **1** adj disuasivo(a) **2** n fuerza disuasoria

detest [dɪˈtest] vt detestar, odiar

detonate [ˈdetəneɪt] vt & vi detonar

detonation [detəˈneɪʃən] n detonación f

detour [ˈdiːtʊə(r)] n desvío m

detract [dɪˈtrækt] vi quitar mérito (**from** a)

detractor [dɪˈtræktə(r)] n detractor(a) m,f

detriment [ˈdetrɪmənt] n perjuicio m (**to** de)

detrimental [detrɪˈmentəl] adj perjudicial (**to** para)

deuce [djuːs] n (in tennis) cuarenta iguales mpl

devaluation [diːvæljuːˈeɪʃən] n devaluación f

devastate [ˈdevəsteɪt] vt (city, area) asolar; Fig (person) desolar

devastating [ˈdevəsteɪtɪŋ] adj (fire) devastador(a); (wind, flood) arrollador(a)

devastation [devəˈsteɪʃən] n asolación f

develop [dɪˈveləp] **1** vt (a) desarrollar; (trade) fomentar; (skill) perfeccionar; (plan) elaborar; (habit) contraer; (interest) mostrar (b) (natural resources) aprovechar; Constr (site) urbanizar (c) Phot revelar

2 vi (a) (body, industry) desarrollarse; (system) perfeccionarse; (interest) crecer (b) (appear) crearse; (evolve) evolucionar

developer [dɪˈveləpə(r)] n (property) **d.** inmobiliaria f

development [dɪˈveləpmənt] n (a) desarrollo m; (of trade) fomento m; (of skill) perfección f; (of character) formación f; **aid** ayuda f al desarrollo (b) (advance) avance m (c) **there are no new developments** no hay ninguna novedad (d) (exploitation) explotación f (e) Constr urbanización f

deviate [ˈdiːvieɪt] vi desviarse (**from** de)

deviation [diːvɪˈeɪʃən] n (from norm, route) desviación f (**from** de); (from truth) alejamiento m

device [dɪ'vaɪs] *n* (**a**) aparato *m*; *(mechanism)* mecanismo *m* (**b**) *(trick, scheme)* ardid *m*

devil ['devəl] *n* diablo *m*, demonio *m*; **d.'s advocate** abogado(a) *m,f* del diablo; *Fam* **where the d. did you put it?** ¿dónde demonios lo pusiste?; **you lucky d.!** ¡vaya suerte que tienes!

devious ['diːvɪəs] *adj* (**a**) *(winding)* tortuoso(a) (**b**) *Pej (person)* taimado(a)

devise [dɪ'vaɪz] *vt* idear, concebir

devoid [dɪ'vɔɪd] *adj* desprovisto(a) (**of** de)

devolution [diːvə'luːʃən] *n Pol* = transmisión de poderes a las regiones

devote [dɪ'vəʊt] *vt* dedicar; **she devoted her life to helping the poor** consagró su vida a la ayuda de los pobres

devoted [dɪ'vəʊtɪd] *adj* fiel, leal (**to** a)

devotee [devə'tiː] *n* *(of religion)* devoto(a) *m,f*; *(of theatre, sport)* aficionado(a) *m,f*; *Pol* partidario(a) *m,f*

devotion [dɪ'vəʊʃən] *n* devoción *f*; *(to cause)* dedicación *f*

devour [dɪ'vaʊə(r)] *vt* devorar

devout [dɪ'vaʊt] *adj* devoto(a)

dew [djuː] *n* rocío *m*

dexterity [dek'sterɪtɪ] *n* destreza *f*

dext(e)rous ['dekstrəs] *adj* diestro(a)

diabetes [daɪə'biːtiːz, daɪə'biːtɪs] *n* diabetes *f*

diabetic [daɪə'betɪk] *adj & n* diabético(a) *(m,f)*

diabolical [daɪə'bɒlɪkəl] *adj* (**a**) *(evil)* diabólico(a) (**b**) *Fam (unbearable)* espantoso(a)

diagnose ['daɪəgnəʊz] *vt* diagnosticar

diagnosis [daɪəg'nəʊsɪs] *n* (*pl* **diagnoses** [daɪəg'nəʊsiːz]) diagnóstico *m*

diagonal [daɪ'ægənəl] *adj & n* diagonal *(f)*

diagonally [daɪ'ægənəlɪ] *adv* en diagonal, diagonalmente

diagram ['daɪəgræm] *n* diagrama *m*; *(of process, system)* esquema *m*; *(of workings)* gráfico *m*

dial ['daɪəl, daɪl] **1** *n (of clock)* esfera *f*; *(of radio)* cuadrante *m*; *(of telephone)* disco *m*; *(of machine)* botón *m* selector
  2 *vt & vi Tel* marcar; *Br* **dialling** or *US* **d. code** prefijo *m*; *Br* **dialling** or *US* **d. tone** señal *f* de marcar

dialect ['daɪəlekt] *n* dialecto *m*

dialogue, *US* **dialog** ['daɪəlɒg] *n* diálogo *m*

diameter [daɪ'æmɪtə(r)] *n* diámetro *m*

diametrically [daɪə'metrɪkəlɪ] *adv* diametralmente

diamond ['daɪəmənd] *n* (**a**) diamante *m* (**b**) *(shape)* rombo *m*

diaper ['daɪəpə(r)] *n US* pañal *m*

diaphragm ['daɪəfræm] *n* diafragma *m*

diarrhoea, *US* **diarrhea** [daɪə'rɪə] *n* diarrea *f*

diary ['daɪərɪ] *n* (**a**) diario *m*; **to keep a d.** llevar un diario (**b**) *Br (for appointments)* agenda *f*

dice [daɪs] **1** *n (pl* **dice**) dado *m*
  2 *vt Culin* cortar en cuadritos

dichotomy [daɪ'kɒtəmɪ] *n* dicotomía *f*

dictate 1 *vt* [dɪk'teɪt] *(letter, order)* dictar
  2 *vi* **to d. to sb** dar órdenes a algn
  3 *n* ['dɪkteɪt] *Fig* **the dictates of conscience** los dictados de la conciencia

dictation [dɪk'teɪʃən] *n* dictado *m*

dictator [dɪk'teɪtə(r)] *n* dictador(a) *m,f*

dictatorship [dɪk'teɪtəʃɪp] *n* dictadura *f*

diction ['dɪkʃən] *n* dicción *f*

dictionary ['dɪkʃənərɪ] *n* diccionario *m*

did [dɪd] *pt of* **do**

die [daɪ] *vi* (**a**) morir, morirse; *Fam Fig* **to be dying for sth/to do sth** morirse por algo/de ganas de hacer algo (**b**) *Fig (flame)* extinguirse; *Fig* **to d. hard** *(habit)* tardar en desaparecer (**c**) *(engine)* calarse; *(battery)* agotarse
  ▸ **die away** *vi* desvanecerse
  ▸ **die down** *vi (fire)* extinguirse; *(wind)* amainar; *(noise, excitement)* disminuir
  ▸ **die off** *vi* morir uno por uno
  ▸ **die out** *vi* extinguirse

die-hard ['daɪhɑːd] *n* reaccionario(a) *m,f*

diesel ['diːzəl] *n* (**a**) *(oil)* gasoil *m*; **d. engine** motor *m* diesel (**b**) *Fam (vehicle)* vehículo *m* diesel

diet ['daɪət] **1** *n (normal food)* dieta *f*; *(selected food)* régimen *m*; **to be on a d.** estar a régimen
  2 *vi* estar a régimen

dietician [daɪə'tɪʃən] *n* especialista *mf* en dietética

differ ['dɪfə(r)] *vi (be unlike)* ser distinto(a); *(disagree)* discrepar

difference ['dɪfərəns] *n* (**a**) *(dissimilarity)* diferencia *f*; **it makes no d. (to me)** (me) da igual; **what d. does it make?** ¿qué más da? (**b**) *(disagreement)* desacuerdo *m*

different ['dɪfərənt] *adj* diferente, distinto(a); **you look d.** pareces otro(a)

differentiate [dɪfə'renʃɪeɪt] **1** *vt* distinguir, diferenciar (**from** de)
  2 *vi* distinguir (**between** entre)

differently ['dɪfərəntlɪ] *adv* de otra manera

difficult ['dɪfɪkəlt] *adj* difícil

difficulty ['dɪfɪkəltɪ] *n* dificultad *f*; *(problem)* problema *m*; **to be in difficulties** estar en un apuro

diffident ['dɪfɪdənt] *adj* tímido(a)

diffuse 1 *adj* [dɪ'fju:s] *(light)* difuso(a); *Fig* vago(a)
   2 *vt* [dɪ'fju:z] difundir; *(heat)* desprender

dig [dɪg] **1** *n* **(a)** *(poke)* codazo *m* **(b)** *Fam (gibe)* pulla *f* **(c)** *(archaeological)* excavación *f* **(d)** *Br* **digs** *(lodgings)* alojamiento *m*; *(room)* habitación *f* alquilada
   2 *vt* *(pt & pp* **dug)** **(a)** *(earth)* cavar; *(tunnel)* excavar **(b)** *Fam Fig* **to d. one's heels in** mantenerse en sus trece
   3 *vi (person)* cavar; *(animal)* escarbar; *(excavate)* excavar
   ▸ **dig in** *vi Mil* atrincherarse
   ▸ **dig out** *vt sep Fig (old suit)* sacar; *(information)* descubrir
   ▸ **dig up** *vt sep (weeds)* arrancar; *(buried object)* desenterrar; *(road)* levantar; *Fig* sacar a relucir

digest 1 *n* ['daɪdʒest] *(summary)* resumen *m*
   2 *vt* [dɪ'dʒest] *(food)* digerir; *Fig (facts)* asimilar

digestion [dɪ'dʒestʃən] *n* digestión *f*

digestive [dɪ'dʒestɪv] *adj* digestivo(a); *Br* **d. biscuit** galleta *f* integral

digger ['dɪgə(r)] *n* excavadora *f*

digit ['dɪdʒɪt] *n* **(a)** *Math* dígito *m* **(b)** *Fml Anat* dedo *m*

digital ['dɪdʒɪtəl] *adj* digital; **d. television** televisión *f* digital

dignified ['dɪgnɪfaɪd] *adj (manner)* solemne, serio(a); *(appearance)* majestuoso(a)

dignitary ['dɪgnɪtərɪ] *n* dignatario *m*

dignity ['dɪgnɪtɪ] *n* dignidad *f*

digress [daɪ'gres] *vi* apartarse del tema

dike [daɪk] *n US* = **dyke**

dilapidated [dɪ'læpɪdeɪtɪd] *adj* en mal estado

dilemma [dɪ'lemə, daɪ'lemə] *n* dilema *m*

diligent ['dɪlɪdʒənt] *adj (worker)* diligente; *(inquiries, search)* esmerado(a)

dilute [daɪ'lu:t] **1** *vt* diluir; *(wine, milk)* aguar; *Fig (effect, influence)* atenuar
   2 *vi* diluirse

dim [dɪm] **1** *adj* **(dimmer, dimmest)** **(a)** *(light)* débil, tenue; *(room)* oscuro(a); *(outline)* borroso(a); *(eyesight)* defectuoso(a); *Fig (memory)* vago(a); *Fig (future)* sombrío(a) **(b)** *Fam (stupid)* torpe
   2 *vt (light)* bajar
   3 *vi (light)* bajarse; *(sight)* nublarse; *Fig (joy)* extinguirse

dime [daɪm] *n US* moneda *f* de 10 centavos

dimension [daɪ'menʃən] *n* dimensión *f*

diminish [dɪ'mɪnɪʃ] *vt & vi* disminuir

diminutive [dɪ'mɪnjʊtɪv] **1** *adj* diminuto(a)
   2 *n Ling* diminutivo *m*

dimly ['dɪmlɪ] *adv* vagamente

dimmer ['dɪmə(r)] *n* **d. (switch)** regulador *m* de voltaje

dimple ['dɪmpəl] *n* hoyuelo *m*

din [dɪn] *n (of crowd)* alboroto *m*; *(of machinery)* estruendo *m*

dine [daɪn] *vi Fml* cenar; **to d. out** cenar fuera

diner ['daɪnə(r)] *n* **(a)** *(person)* comensal *mf* **(b)** *US (restaurant)* restaurante barato

dinghy ['dɪŋɪ] *n* bote *m*; **(rubber) d.** bote neumático

dingy ['dɪndʒɪ] *adj* **(dingier, dingiest)** **(a)** *(dark)* oscuro(a) **(b)** *(dirty)* sucio(a) **(c)** *(colour)* desteñido(a)

dining car ['daɪnɪŋkɑ:(r)] *n* vagón *m* restaurante

dining room ['daɪnɪŋru:m] *n* comedor *m*

dinner ['dɪnə(r)] *n (at midday)* comida *f*; *(in evening)* cena *f*; **d. jacket** smoking *m*; **d. service** vajilla *f*; **d. table** mesa *f* de comedor

dinosaur ['daɪnəsɔ:(r)] *n* dinosaurio *m*

dint [dɪnt] *n* **by d. of** a fuerza de

diocese ['daɪəsɪs] *n* diócesis *f inv*

dioxide [daɪ'ɒksaɪd] *n* bióxido *m*

dip [dɪp] **1** *n* **(a)** *Fam (bathe)* chapuzón *m* **(b)** *(of road)* pendiente *f*; *(in ground)* depresión *f* **(c)** *Culin* salsa *f*
   2 *vt* **(a)** bañar; *(spoon, hand)* meter **(b)** *Br Aut* **to d. one's lights** poner luces de cruce
   3 *vi (road)* bajar
   ▸ **dip into** *vt insep* **(a)** *(savings)* echar mano de **(b)** *(book)* hojear

diphthong ['dɪfθɒŋ] *n* diptongo *m*

diploma [dɪ'pləʊmə] *n* diploma *m*

diplomacy [dɪ'pləʊməsɪ] *n* diplomacia *f*

diplomat ['dɪpləmæt] *n* diplomático(a) *m,f*

diplomatic [dɪplə'mætɪk] *adj* diplomático(a)

dipstick ['dɪpstɪk] *n* indicador *m* de nivel del aceite

dire ['daɪə(r)] *adj (urgent)* extremo(a); *(serious)* grave

direct [dɪ'rekt, 'daɪrekt] **1** *adj* **(a)** directo(a); **d. current** corriente continua **(b)** **the d. opposite** todo lo contrario
   2 *adv* directamente
   3 *vt* **(a)** dirigir; **can you d. me to a bank?**

¿me puede indicar dónde hay un banco? (**b**) *Fml (order)* mandar

direction [dɪˈrekʃən, daɪˈrekʃən] *n* (**a**) dirección *f*; **sense of d.** sentido *m* de la orientación (**b**) **directions** *(to place)* señas *fpl*; **directions for use** modo *m* de empleo (**c**) *Th* puesta *f* en escena

directive [dɪˈrektɪv, daɪˈrektɪv] *n* directiva *f*

directly [dɪˈrektlɪ, daɪˈrektlɪ] **1** *adv* (**a**) *(above etc)* exactamente, justo (**b**) *(speak)* francamente (**c**) *(descend)* directamente (**d**) *(come)* en seguida
2 *conj Fam* en cuanto

director [dɪˈrektə(r), daɪˈrektə(r)] *n* director(a) *m,f*

directory [dɪˈrektərɪ, daɪˈrektərɪ] *n Tel* guía telefónica; **d. enquiries** (servicio *m* de) información *f*

dirt [dɜːt] *n* suciedad *f*

dirt-cheap [dɜːtˈtʃiːp] *adv* & *adj Fam* tirado(a)

dirty [ˈdɜːtɪ] **1** *adj* (**dirtier, dirtiest**) (**a**) sucio(a) (**b**) **to give sb a d. look** fulminar a algn con la mirada (**c**) *(joke)* verde; *(mind)* pervertido(a); **d. word** palabrota *f*; **d. old man** viejo *m* verde
2 *vt* ensuciar

disability [dɪsəˈbɪlɪtɪ] *n* incapacidad *f*, discapacidad *f*; **d. pension** pensión *f* por invalidez

disabled [dɪsˈeɪbəld] **1** *adj* minusválido(a)
2 *npl* **the d.** los minusválidos

disadvantage [dɪsədˈvɑːntɪdʒ] *n* desventaja *f*; *(obstacle)* inconveniente *m*

disaffection [dɪsəˈfekʃən] *n* descontento *m*

disagree [dɪsəˈgriː] *vi* (**a**) *(differ)* no estar de acuerdo (**with** con); **to d. on** *or* **over sth** reñir por algo (**b**) *(not match)* discrepar (**with** *or* con) (**c**) **garlic disagrees with me** el ajo no me sienta bien

disagreeable [dɪsəˈgriːəbəl] *adj* desagradable

disagreement [dɪsəˈgriːmənt] *n* (**a**) desacuerdo *m*; *(argument)* riña *f* (**b**) *(non-correspondence)* discrepancia *f*

disallow [dɪsəˈlaʊ] *vt (goal)* anular; *(objection)* rechazar

disappear [dɪsəˈpɪə(r)] *vi* desaparecer

disappearance [dɪsəˈpɪərəns] *n* desaparición *f*

disappoint [dɪsəˈpɔɪnt] *vt (person)* decepcionar, defraudar; *(hope, ambition)* frustrar

disappointed [dɪsəˈpɔɪntɪd] *adj* decepcionado(a)

disappointing [dɪsəˈpɔɪntɪŋ] *adj* decepcionante

disappointment [dɪsəˈpɔɪntmənt] *n* decepción *f*

disapproval [dɪsəˈpruːvəl] *n* desaprobación *f*

disapprove [dɪsəˈpruːv] *vi* **to d. of** desaprobar

disarm [dɪsˈɑːm] **1** *vt* desarmar
2 *vi* desarmarse

disarmament [dɪsˈɑːməmənt] *n* desarme *m*

disarray [dɪsəˈreɪ] *n Fml* **in d.** *(room, papers)* en desorden; *(hair)* desarreglado(a); *(thoughts)* confuso(a)

disaster [dɪˈzɑːstə(r)] *n* desastre *m*

disastrous [dɪˈzɑːstrəs] *adj* desastroso(a)

disband [dɪsˈbænd] **1** *vt* disolver
2 *vi* disolverse

disbelief [dɪsbɪˈliːf] *n* incredulidad *f*

disc [dɪsk] *n* disco *m*; *Comput* disquete *m*; **d. jockey** disc-jockey *mf*, pinchadiscos *mf inv*

discard [dɪsˈkɑːd] *vt (old things)* deshacerse de; *(plan)* descartar

discern [dɪˈsɜːn] *vt (shape, difference)* percibir; *(truth)* darse cuenta de

discerning [dɪˈsɜːnɪŋ] *adj (person)* perspicaz; *(taste)* refinado(a)

discharge *Fml* **1** *vt* [dɪsˈtʃɑːdʒ] (**a**) *(smoke)* emitir; *(liquid)* echar; *(cargo)* descargar (**b**) *(prisoner)* soltar; *(patient)* dar de alta a; *(soldier)* licenciar; *(employee)* despedir (**c**) *(debt)* saldar (**d**) *(fulfil)* cumplir
2 *n* [ˈdɪstʃɑːdʒ] (**a**) *(of current, load)* descarga *f*; *(of gases)* escape *m* (**b**) *(of prisoner)* liberación *f*; *(of patient)* alta *f*; *(of soldier)* licencia *f* (**c**) *(of debt)* descargo *m* (**d**) *(of duty)* cumplimiento *m*

disciple [dɪˈsaɪpəl] *n* discípulo(a) *m,f*

discipline [ˈdɪsɪplɪn] **1** *n* disciplina *f*
2 *vt (child)* castigar; *(worker)* sancionar; *(official)* expedientar

disclaim [dɪsˈkleɪm] *vt Fml* negar tener

disclose [dɪsˈkləʊz] *vt* revelar

disclosure [dɪsˈkləʊʒə(r)] *n* revelación *f*

disco [ˈdɪskəʊ] *n Fam (abbr* **discotheque**) disco *f*

discolour, *US* **discolor** [dɪsˈkʌlə(r)] *vt* descolorir

discomfort [dɪsˈkʌmfət] *n* (**a**) *(lack of comfort)* incomodidad *f* (**b**) *(pain)* malestar *m* (**c**) *(unease)* inquietud *f*

disconcert [dɪskənˈsɜːt] *vt* desconcertar

disconcerting [dɪskənˈsɜːtɪŋ] *adj* desconcertante

disconnect [dɪskə'nekt] *vt* desconectar (**from** de); *(gas, electricity)* cortar

disconnected [dɪskə'nektɪd] *adj* inconexo(a)

disconsolate [dɪs'kɒnsəlɪt] *adj* desconsolado(a)

discontent [dɪskən'tent] *n* descontento *m*

discontented [dɪskən'tentɪd] *adj* descontento(a)

discontinue [dɪskən'tɪnjuː] *vt Fml* abandonar; *(work)* interrumpir

discord ['dɪskɔːd] *n* (**a**) *Fml* discordia *f* (**b**) *Mus* disonancia *f*

discordant [dɪs'kɔːdənt] *adj* discordante

discotheque ['dɪskətek] *n* discoteca *f*

discount 1 *n* ['dɪskaʊnt] descuento *m*
2 *vt* [dɪs'kaʊnt] (**a**) *(price)* rebajar (**b**) *(view, suggestion)* descartar

discourage [dɪs'kʌrɪdʒ] *vt (dishearten)* desanimar; *(advances)* rechazar

discouraging [dɪs'kʌrɪdʒɪŋ] *adj* desalentador(a)

discover [dɪ'skʌvə(r)] *vt* descubrir; *(missing person, object)* encontrar

discovery [dɪ'skʌvərɪ] *n* descubrimiento *m*

discredit [dɪs'kredɪt] 1 *n* descrédito *m*
2 *vt (person, régime)* desacreditar; *(theory)* poner en duda

discreet [dɪ'skriːt] *adj* discreto(a); *(distance, silence)* prudente; *(hat, house)* modesto(a)

discrepancy [dɪ'skrepənsɪ] *n* diferencia *f*

discretion [dɪ'skreʃən] *n* discreción *f*; *(prudence)* prudencia *f*; **at the d. of ...** a juicio de ...

discriminate [dɪ'skrɪmɪneɪt] *vi* discriminar (**between** entre); **to d. against sth/sb** discriminar algo/a algn

discriminating [dɪ'skrɪmɪneɪtɪŋ] *adj (person)* entendido(a); *(taste)* refinado(a)

discrimination [dɪskrɪmɪ'neɪʃən] *n* (**a**) *(bias)* discriminación *f* (**b**) *(distinction)* diferenciación *f*

discuss [dɪ'skʌs] *vt* discutir; *(in writing)* tratar de

discussion [dɪ'skʌʃən] *n* discusión *f*

disdain [dɪs'deɪn] *Fml* 1 *n* desdén *m*
2 *vt* desdeñar

disdainful [dɪs'deɪnfʊl] *adj Fml* desdeñoso(a)

disease [dɪ'ziːz] *n* enfermedad *f*; *Fig* mal *m*

disembark [dɪsɪm'bɑːk] *vt & vi* desembarcar

disenchanted [dɪsɪn'tʃɑːntɪd] *adj* desencantado(a), desilusionado(a)

disengage [dɪsɪn'geɪdʒ] *vt* soltar; *Aut* **to d. the clutch** soltar el embrague, desembragar

disentangle [dɪsɪn'tæŋgəl] *vt* desenredar

disfigure [dɪs'fɪgə(r)] *vt* desfigurar

disgrace [dɪs'greɪs] 1 *n* (**a**) *(disfavour)* desgracia *f*; **to be in d.** estar desacreditado(a); **to fall into d.** caer en desgracia (**b**) *(shame)* vergüenza *f*, escándalo *m*
2 *vt* deshonrar, desacreditar

disgraceful [dɪs'greɪsfʊl] *adj* vergonzoso(a)

disgruntled [dɪs'grʌntəld] *adj* contrariado(a), disgustado(a)

disguise [dɪs'gaɪz] 1 *n* disfraz *m*; **in d.** disfrazado(a)
2 *vt* (**a**) *(person)* disfrazar (**as** de) (**b**) *(feelings)* disimular

disgust [dɪs'gʌst] 1 *n* (**a**) *(loathing)* repugnancia *f*, asco *m* (**b**) *(strong disapproval)* indignación *f*
2 *vt* (**a**) *(revolt)* repugnar, dar asco a (**b**) *(offend)* indignar

---

⚠ Note that the Spanish words **disgusto** and **disgustar** are false friends and are never a translation for the English word **disgust**. In Spanish, **disgusto** means "annoyance, trouble", and **disgustar** means "to upset".

---

disgusting [dɪs'gʌstɪŋ] *adj* asqueroso(a), repugnante; *(behaviour, state of affairs)* intolerable

dish [dɪʃ] *n (for serving)* fuente *f*; *(course)* plato *m*; **to wash** or **do the dishes** fregar los platos

▸ **dish out** *vt sep Fam (food)* servir; *(books, advice)* repartir; **to d. it out (to sb)** *(criticize)* criticar (a algn)

▸ **dish up** *vt sep (meal)* servir

dishcloth ['dɪʃklɒθ] *n* trapo *m* de fregar

dishearten [dɪs'hɑːtən] *vt* desanimar

dishevelled, *US* **disheveled** [dɪ'ʃevəld] *adj (hair)* despeinado(a); *(appearance)* desaliñado(a)

dishonest [dɪs'ɒnɪst] *adj (person)* poco honrado(a); *(means)* fraudulento(a)

dishonesty [dɪs'ɒnɪstɪ] *n (of person)* falta *f* de honradez

dishonour, *US* **dishonor** [dɪs'ɒnə(r)] 1 *n Fml* deshonra *f*
2 *vt (name)* deshonrar

dishonourable, *US* **dishonorable** [dɪs'ɒnərəbəl] *adj* deshonroso(a)

dishtowel ['dɪʃtaʊəl] *n US* trapo *m* de cocina

dishwasher ['dɪʃwɒʃə(r)] *n* lavaplatos *m*

inv; *(person)* lavaplatos *mf inv*

disillusion [dɪsɪ'luːʒən] *vt* desilusionar

disincentive [dɪsɪn'sentɪv] *n* freno *m*

disinfect [dɪsɪn'fekt] *vt* desinfectar

disinfectant [dɪsɪn'fektənt] *n* desinfectante *m*

disinherit [dɪsɪn'herɪt] *vt* desheredar

disintegrate [dɪs'ɪntɪɡreɪt] *vi* desintegrarse

disintegration [dɪsɪntɪ'ɡreɪʃən] *n* desintegración *f*

disinterested [dɪs'ɪntrɪstɪd] *adj* desinteresado(a)

disjointed [dɪs'dʒɔɪntɪd] *adj* inconexo(a)

disk [dɪsk] *n US* disco *m*; *Comput* disquete *m*; **on d.** en disco; **d. drive** disquetera *f*, disketera *f*

diskette [dɪs'ket] *n Comput* disquete *m*

dislike [dɪs'laɪk] **1** *n* antipatía *f*, aversión *f* (**of** a *or* hacia)
2 *vt* tener antipatía *or* aversión a *or* hacia

dislocate ['dɪsləkeɪt] *vt* (joint) dislocar

dislodge [dɪs'lɒdʒ] *vt* sacar

disloyal [dɪs'lɔɪəl] *adj* desleal

dismal ['dɪzməl] *adj* (**a**) *(prospect)* sombrío(a); *(place, weather)* deprimente; *(person)* triste (**b**) *(failure)* lamentable

dismantle [dɪs'mæntəl] *vt* desmontar

dismay [dɪs'meɪ] **1** *n* consternación *f*
2 *vt* consternar

dismiss [dɪs'mɪs] *vt* (**a**) *(idea)* descartar (**b**) *(employee)* despedir; *(official)* destituir (**c**) **to d. sb** *(from room, presence)* dar permiso a algn para retirarse (**d**) *(reject)* rechazar; *Jur* desestimar; *(case)* sobreseer

dismissal [dɪs'mɪsəl] *n* (**a**) *(of employee)* despido *m*; *(of official)* destitución *f* (**b**) *(of claim)* rechazo *m*; *Jur* desestimación *f*

dismount [dɪs'maʊnt] *vi Fml* apearse (**from** de)

disobedience [dɪsə'biːdɪəns] *n* desobediencia *f*

disobedient [dɪsə'biːdɪənt] *adj* desobediente

disobey [dɪsə'beɪ] *vt & vi* desobedecer; *(law)* violar

disorder [dɪs'ɔːdə(r)] *n* (**a**) *(untidiness)* desorden *m* (**b**) *(riot)* disturbio *m* (**c**) *(of organ, mind)* trastorno *m*; *(of speech)* defecto *m*

disorderly [dɪs'ɔːdəlɪ] *adj* (**a**) *(untidy)* desordenado(a) (**b**) *(meeting)* alborotado(a); *(conduct)* escandaloso(a)

disorganized [dɪs'ɔːɡənaɪzd] *adj* desorganizado(a)

disorient [dɪs'ɔːrɪənt], **disorientate** [dɪs'ɔːrɪənteɪt] *vt* desorientar

disown [dɪs'əʊn] *vt* desconocer

disparaging [dɪ'spærɪdʒɪŋ] *adj* despectivo(a)

disparity [dɪ'spærɪtɪ] *n Fml* disparidad *f*

dispassionate [dɪ'spæʃənɪt] *adj* desapasionado(a)

dispatch [dɪ'spætʃ] **1** *n* (**a**) *(official message)* despacho *m*; *(journalist's report)* reportaje *m*; *(military message)* parte *m* (**b**) *(of mail)* envío *m*; *(of goods)* consignación *f*
2 *vt* (**a**) *(mail)* enviar; *(goods)* expedir (**b**) *Fam (food)* zamparse; *(job)* despachar

dispel [dɪ'spel] *vt* disipar

dispensary [dɪ'spensərɪ] *n* dispensario *m*

dispense [dɪ'spens] *vt (supplies)* repartir; *(justice)* administrar
▸**dispense with** *vt insep (do without)* prescindir de

dispenser [dɪ'spensə(r)] *n* máquina expendedora; **cash d.** cajero automático; **soap d.** dosificador *m* de jabón

dispensing chemist [dɪspensɪŋ'kemɪst] *n Br* farmacéutico(a) *m,f*

dispersal [dɪ'spɜːsəl] *n* dispersión *f*

disperse [dɪ'spɜːs] **1** *vt* dispersar
2 *vi* dispersarse; *(fog)* disiparse

dispirited [dɪ'spɪrɪtɪd] *adj* abatido(a)

displace [dɪs'pleɪs] *vt* (**a**) desplazar; **displaced person** desterrado(a) *m,f* (**b**) *(supplant)* sustituir

display [dɪ'spleɪ] **1** *n (exhibition)* exposición *f*; *Comput* visualización *f*; *(of feelings, skills)* demostración *f*; *(of force)* despliegue *m*; **d. window** escaparate *m*; **military d.** desfile *m* militar
2 *vt* (**a**) mostrar; *(goods)* exponer; *Comput* visualizar (**b**) *(feelings)* manifestar

displease [dɪs'pliːz] *vt* disgustar; *(offend)* ofender

displeasure [dɪs'pleʒə(r)] *n* disgusto *m*

disposable [dɪ'spəʊzəbəl] *adj* (**a**) *(throwaway)* desechable (**b**) *(available)* disponible

disposal [dɪ'spəʊzəl] *n* (**a**) *(removal)* eliminación *f* (**b**) *(availability)* disponibilidad *f*; **at my d.** a mi disposición (**c**) *Fml (arrangement)* disposición *f* (**d**) *(sale)* venta *f*; *(of property)* traspaso *m*

dispose [dɪ'spəʊz] **1** *vi* **to d. of** (**a**) *(remove)* eliminar; *(rubbish)* tirar; *(unwanted object)* deshacerse de; *(matter)* resolver; *(sell)* vender; *(property)* traspasar
2 *vt Fml (arrange)* disponer

disposed [dɪ'spəʊzd] *adj (inclined)* dispuesto(a)

disposition [dɪspə'zɪʃən] *n* (**a**) *(temperament)* genio *m* (**b**) *Fml (arrangement)* disposición *f*

disproportionate [dɪsprə'pɔːʃənɪt] *adj* desproporcionado(a) (**to** a)

disprove [dɪs'pruːv] *vt* refutar

dispute 1 *n* ['dɪspjuːt] *(disagreement)* discusión *f; (quarrel)* disputa *f;* **industrial d.** conflicto *m* laboral

2 *vt* [dɪ'spjuːt] *(claim)* refutar; *(territory)* disputar; *(matter)* discutir

3 *vi* discutir (**about** *or* **over** de *or* sobre)

disqualify [dɪs'kwɒlɪfaɪ] *vt* (**a**) *Sport* descalificar (**b**) *(make ineligible)* incapacitar

disquiet [dɪs'kwaɪət] *n* preocupación *f,* inquietud *f*

disregard [dɪsrɪ'gɑːd] **1** *n* indiferencia *f; (for safety)* despreocupación *f*

2 *vt* descuidar; *(ignore)* ignorar

disrepair [dɪsrɪ'peə(r)] *n* mal estado *m;* **in (a state of) d.** en mal estado; **to fall into d.** deteriorarse

disreputable [dɪs'repjʊtəbəl] *adj (person, area)* de mala fama; *(behaviour)* vergonzoso(a)

disrepute [dɪsrɪ'pjuːt] *n* mala fama, oprobio *m*

disrespectful [dɪsrɪ'spektfʊl] *adj* irrespetuoso(a)

disrupt [dɪs'rʌpt] *vt (meeting, traffic)* interrumpir; *(schedule etc)* desbaratar

disruption [dɪs'rʌpʃən] *n (of meeting, traffic)* interrupción *f; (of schedule etc)* desbaratamiento *m*

dissatisfaction [dɪssætɪs'fækʃən] *n* descontento *m,* insatisfacción *f*

dissatisfied [dɪs'sætɪsfaɪd] *adj* descontento(a)

dissect [dɪ'sekt, daɪ'sekt] *vt* disecar

disseminate [dɪ'semɪneɪt] *vt Fml* diseminar, difundir

dissent [dɪ'sent] **1** *n* disentimiento *m*

2 *vi* disentir

dissertation [dɪsə'teɪʃən] *n* disertación *f; Univ* tesina *f* (mf)

disservice [dɪs'sɜːvɪs] *n* perjuicio *m;* **to do sth/sb a d.** perjudicar algo/a algn

dissident ['dɪsɪdənt] *adj & n* disidente (mf)

dissimilar [dɪ'sɪmɪlə(r)] *adj* distinto(a)

dissipate ['dɪsɪpeɪt] **1** *vt* (**a**) disipar (**b**) *(waste)* derrochar

2 *vi* disiparse

dissociate [dɪ'səʊʃɪeɪt] *vt* **to d. oneself** distanciarse

dissolute ['dɪsəluːt] *adj* disoluto(a)

dissolution [dɪsə'luːʃən] *n* disolución *f; (of agreement)* rescisión *f*

dissolve [dɪ'zɒlv] **1** *vt* disolver

2 *vi* disolverse

dissuade [dɪ'sweɪd] *vt* disuadir (**from** de)

distance ['dɪstəns] **1** *n* distancia *f;* **in the d.** a lo lejos; *Fam* **to stay the d.** completar la prueba

2 *vt* **to d. oneself (from)** distanciarse (de)

distant ['dɪstənt] *adj* (**a**) *(place, time)* lejano(a); *(look)* distraído(a) (**b**) *(aloof)* distante, frío(a)

distaste [dɪs'teɪst] *n* aversión *f*

distasteful [dɪs'teɪstfʊl] *adj* desagradable

distend [dɪ'stend] *Fml* **1** *vt* dilatar

2 *vi* dilatarse

distil, *US* **distill** [dɪ'stɪl] *vt* destilar

distillery [dɪ'stɪlərɪ] *n* destilería *f*

distinct [dɪ'stɪŋkt] *adj* (**a**) *(different)* diferente; **as d. from** a diferencia de (**b**) *(smell, change)* marcado(a); *(idea, intention)* claro(a)

distinction [dɪ'stɪŋkʃən] *n* (**a**) *(difference)* diferencia *f* (**b**) *(excellence)* distinción *f* (**c**) *Educ* sobresaliente *m*

distinctive [dɪ'stɪŋktɪv] *adj* distintivo(a)

distinguish [dɪ'stɪŋgwɪʃ] *vt* distinguir

distinguished [dɪ'stɪŋgwɪʃt] *adj* distinguido(a)

distinguishing [dɪ'stɪŋgwɪʃɪŋ] *adj* distintivo(a), característico(a)

distort [dɪ'stɔːt] *vt (misrepresent)* deformar; *(words)* tergiversar

distortion [dɪ'stɔːʃən] *n* deformación *f; (of sound, image)* distorsión *f*

distract [dɪ'strækt] *vt* distraer

distracted [dɪ'stræktɪd] *adj* distraído(a)

distraction [dɪ'strækʃən] *n (interruption)* distracción *f; (confusion)* confusión *f;* **to drive sb to d.** sacar a algn de quicio

distraught [dɪ'strɔːt] *adj (anguished)* afligido(a)

distress [dɪ'stres] **1** *n (mental)* angustia *f; (physical)* dolor *m;* **d. signal** señal *f* de socorro

2 *vt (upset)* apenar

distressing [dɪ'stresɪŋ] *adj* penoso(a)

distribute [dɪ'strɪbjuːt] *vt* distribuir, repartir

distribution [dɪstrɪ'bjuːʃən] *n* distribución *f*

distributor [dɪ'strɪbjʊtə(r)] *n* (**a**) *Com* distribuidor(a) *m,f* (**b**) *Aut* delco *m*

district ['dɪstrɪkt] *n (of country)* región *f;*

(of town) barrio *m*; *US* **d. attorney** fiscal *m*; **d. council** corporación *f* local; **d. nurse** practicante *mf*

distrust [dɪs'trʌst] **1** *n* recelo *m*
2 *vt* desconfiar de

disturb [dɪ'stɜːb] *vt* (a) *(inconvenience)* molestar (b) *(silence)* romper; *(sleep)* interrumpir (c) *(worry)* perturbar (d) *(papers)* desordenar

disturbance [dɪ'stɜːbəns] *n* (a) *(of routine)* alteración *f* (b) *(commotion)* disturbio *m*, alboroto *m*

disturbed [dɪ'stɜːbd] *adj (mentally)* inestable

disturbing [dɪ'stɜːbɪŋ] *adj* inquietante

disuse [dɪs'juːs] *n* desuso *m*

disused [dɪs'juːzd] *adj* abandonado(a)

ditch [dɪtʃ] **1** *n* zanja *f*; *(at roadside)* cuneta *f*; *(for irrigation)* acequia *f*
2 *vt Fam (plan, friend)* abandonar

dither ['dɪðə(r)] *vi Br Fam* vacilar, titubear

ditto ['dɪtəʊ] *adv* ídem, lo mismo

dive [daɪv] **1** *n* (a) *(into water)* salto *m* de cabeza; *(of submarine)* inmersión *f*; *(of plane)* picado *m*; *Sport* salto (b) *Fam (bar)* antro *m*
2 *vi* (a) *(from poolside, diving board)* tirarse de cabeza; *(submarine)* sumergirse; *(plane)* bajar en picado; *Sport* saltar (b) *(move quickly)* **he dived for the phone** se precipitó hacia el teléfono

diver ['daɪvə(r)] *n (person)* buceador(a) *m,f*; *(professional)* buzo *m*; *Sport* saltador(a) *m,f*

diverge [daɪ'vɜːdʒ] *vi* divergir

diverse [daɪ'vɜːs] *adj (varied)* diverso(a), variado(a); *(different)* distinto(a), diferente

diversion [daɪ'vɜːʃən] *n* (a) *(distraction)* distracción *f* (b) *Br (detour)* desvío *m*

divert [daɪ'vɜːt] *vt* desviar

divide [dɪ'vaɪd] **1** *vt* dividir
2 *vi (road, stream)* bifurcarse
3 *n* división *f*, diferencia *f*

dividend ['dɪvɪdend] *n Com* dividendo *m*; *Fig* beneficio *m*

divine [dɪ'vaɪn] *adj* divino(a)

diving board ['daɪvɪŋbɔːd] *n* trampolín *m*

divinity [dɪ'vɪnɪtɪ] *n* (a) *divinidad* *f* (b) *(subject)* teología *f*

division [dɪ'vɪʒən] *n* (a) *división* *f* (b) *(sharing)* reparto *m* (c) *(of organization)* sección *f*

divorce [dɪ'vɔːs] **1** *n* divorcio *m*
2 *vt* **she divorced him** se divorció de él
3 *vi* divorciarse

divorcé [dɪ'vɔːseɪ], **divorcée** [dɪvɔː'siː] *n* divorciado(a) *m,f*

divulge [daɪ'vʌldʒ] *vt Fml* divulgar, revelar

DIY [diːaɪ'waɪ] *n Br (abbr* **do-it-yourself**) bricolaje *m*

dizziness ['dɪzɪnɪs] *n* vértigo *m*

dizzy ['dɪzɪ] *adj* (**dizzier, dizziest**) (a) *(person) (unwell)* mareado(a) (b) *(height, pace)* vertiginoso(a)

DJ ['diːdʒeɪ] *n Fam (abbr* **disc jockey**) pinchadiscos *mf inv*, disc-jockey *mf*

DNA [diːen'eɪ] *n (abbr* **deoxyribonucleic acid**) ADN *m*

do [duː, *unstressed* dʊ, də] **1** *v aux*

> En el inglés hablado, y en el escrito en estilo coloquial, las formas negativas **do not**, **does not** y **did not** se transforman en **don't**, **doesn't** y **didn't**.

(3rd person sing pres **does**; *pt* **did**; *pp* **done**) (a) *(in negatives and questions) (not translated in Spanish)* **do you want some coffee?** ¿quieres café?; **do you drive?** ¿tienes carnet de conducir?; **don't you want to come?** ¿no quieres venir?; **he doesn't smoke** no fuma

(b) *(emphatic) (not translated in Spanish)* **do come with us!** ¡ánimo, vente con nosotros!; I **do like your bag** me encanta tu bolso

(c) *(substituting main verb in sentence) (not translated in Spanish)* **I don't believe him** – neither do I no le creo – yo tampoco; **I'll go if you do** si vas tú, voy yo; **I think it's dear, but he doesn't** a mí me parece caro pero a él no; **who went?** – **I did** ¿quién asistió? – yo

(d) *(in question tags)* **he refused, didn't he?** dijo que no, ¿verdad?; **I don't like it, do you?** a mí no me gusta, ¿y a ti?

2 *vt* (a) hacer; *(task)* realizar; *(duty)* cumplir con; **to do one's best** hacer todo lo posible; **to do sth again** volver a hacer algo; **to do sth for sb** hacer algo por algn; **to do the cooking/cleaning** cocinar/limpiar; **to do the dishes** lavar los platos; **what can I do for you?** ¿en qué puedo servirle?; **what do you do (for a living)?** ¿a qué te dedicas?; **what's to be done?** ¿qué se puede hacer?; *Fam* **he's done it!** ¡lo ha conseguido!

(b) **do you do sportswear?** *(make, offer)* ¿(aquí) tienen ropa de deporte?

(c) *(distance) (speed)* **we were doing 80** íbamos a 80; **this car can do 120** este coche puede alcanzar los 120

Do, unido a muchos nombres, expresa actividades, como **to do the gardening**, **to do the ironing**, etc. En este diccionario, estas estructuras se encuentran bajo los nombres respectivos.

3 *vi* (**a**) *(act)* hacer; **do as I tell you** haz lo que te digo; **you did right** hiciste bien
(**b**) **he did badly in the exams** los exámenes le salieron mal; **how are you doing?** ¿qué tal?; **how do you do?** *(greeting)* ¿cómo está usted?; *(answer)* mucho gusto; **to do well** *(person)* tener éxito; *(business)* ir bien
(**c**) **£5 will do** *(suffice)* con 5 libras será suficiente; *Fam* **that will do!** ¡basta ya!
(**d**) **this cushion will do as a pillow** *(be suitable)* este cojín servirá de almohada; **this won't do** esto no puede ser

4 *n Fam* (**a**) *Br (party)* fiesta *f*; *(event)* ceremonia *f*
(**b**) **do's and don'ts** reglas *fpl* de conducta
▸ **do away with** *vt insep* (**a**) *(abolish)* abolir; *(discard)* deshacerse de (**b**) *(kill)* asesinar
▸ **do down** *vt sep Fam (humiliate)* hacer quedar mal
▸ **do for** *vt insep Fam (destroy, ruin)* arruinar; *Fig* **I'm done for if I don't finish this** estoy perdido(a) si no acabo esto
▸ **do in** *vt sep Fam* (**a**) *(kill)* cargarse (**b**) **I'm done in** *(exhausted)* estoy hecho(a) polvo
▸ **do over** *vt sep Fam* (**a**) *US (repeat)* repetir (**b**) *Br (thrash)* dar una paliza a
▸ **do up** *vt sep* (**a**) *(wrap)* envolver (**b**) *(belt etc)* abrochar; *(laces)* atar (**c**) *(dress up)* arreglar (**d**) *Fam (redecorate)* renovar
▸ **do with** *vt insep* (**a**) **I could do with a rest** *(need)* un descanso no me vendría nada mal (**b**) **to have** *or* **be to do with** *(concern)* tener que ver con
▸ **do without** *vt insep* pasar sin, prescindir de

docile ['dəʊsaɪl] *adj* dócil; *(animal)* manso(a)

dock¹ [dɒk] **1** *n Naut* **the docks** el muelle
2 *vi* (**a**) *(ship)* atracar (**b**) *(spacecraft)* acoplarse

dock² [dɒk] *vt (reduce)* descontar

dock³ [dɒk] *n Jur* banquillo *m* (de los acusados)

docker ['dɒkə(r)] *n* estibador *m*

dockland ['dɒklænd] *n* zona *f* del puerto

dockyard ['dɒkjɑːd] *n* astillero *m*

doctor ['dɒktə(r)] **1** *n* (**a**) *Med* médico *m,f* (**b**) *Univ* doctor(a) *m,f*; **D. of Law** doctor en derecho

2 *vt Pej (figures)* falsificar; *(text)* arreglar; *(drink etc)* adulterar

doctorate ['dɒktərɪt] *n* doctorado *m*

doctrine ['dɒktrɪn] *n* doctrina *f*

document ['dɒkjʊmənt] **1** *n* documento *m*; **documents** documentación *f*
2 *vt* documentar

documentary [dɒkjʊ'mentərɪ] *adj & n* documental *(m)*

dodge [dɒdʒ] **1** *vt* (**a**) *(blow)* esquivar; *(pursuer)* despistar; *Fig* eludir (**b**) *Fam* **to d. one's taxes** engañar a Hacienda
2 *vi (move aside)* echarse a un lado
3 *n* (**a**) *(movement)* regate *m* (**b**) *Fam (trick)* truco *m*

Dodgem® ['dɒdʒəm] *n Br* **D. (car)** coche *m* de choque

dodgy ['dɒdʒɪ] *adj* (**dodgier, dodgiest**) *Br Fam (risky)* arriesgado(a); *(tricky)* difícil; *(dishonest, not working properly)* chungo(a)

doe [dəʊ] *n (of deer)* gama *f*; *(of rabbit)* coneja *f*

does [dʌz] *3rd person sing pres of* **do**

doesn't ['dʌzənt] = **does not**

dog [dɒg] **1** *n* (**a**) *(perro(a) m,f; Fam Fig* **a d.'s life** una vida de perros; **d. collar** *(of dog)* collar *m* de perro; *Fam Rel* alzacuello *m* (**b**) *(male canine)* macho *m*; *(fox)* zorro *m*; *(wolf)* lobo *m* (**c**) *Fam* **dirty d.** canalla *m* (**d**) *US Fam (disappointment)* desastre *m*
2 *vt* acosar; **to d. sb's footsteps** seguir los pasos de algn; *Fig* **dogged by bad luck** perseguido(a) por la mala suerte

dog-eared ['dɒgɪəd] *adj (book)* con los bordes de las páginas doblados; *(shabby)* sobado(a)

dogged ['dɒgɪd] *adj* obstinado(a), tenaz

doghouse ['dɒghaʊs] *n US Fam* perrera *f*; *Fig* **to be in the d.** estar castigado(a)

dogma ['dɒgmə] *n* dogma *m*

dogmatic [dɒg'mætɪk] *adj* dogmático(a)

dogsbody ['dɒgzbɒdɪ] *n Br Fam (drudge)* burro *m* de carga

doh [dəʊ] *n Mus* do *m*

doing ['duːɪŋ] *n* (**a**) *(action)* obra *f*; **it was none of my d.** yo no tuve nada que ver; *Fig* **it took some d.** costó trabajo hacerlo (**b**) **doings** *(activities)* actividades *fpl*

do-it-yourself [duːɪtjə'self] *n* bricolaje *m*

doldrums ['dɒldrəmz] *npl Fam Fig* **to be in the d.** *(person)* estar abatido(a); *(trade)* estar estancado(a)

dole [dəʊl] *Fam* **1** *n Br* **the d.** el paro; **to be on the d.** cobrar el paro; **to go on the d.**

apuntarse al paro; *Fig* **d. queue** los parados

2 *vt* **to d. (out)** repartir

doleful ['dəʊlfʊl] *adj* triste, afligido(a)

doll [dɒl] **1** *n* (**a**) *(toy)* muñeca *f* (**b**) *US Fam (girl)* muñeca *f*

2 *vt Fam* **to d. oneself up** ponerse guapa

dollar ['dɒlə(r)] *n* dólar *m*

dolphin ['dɒlfɪn] *n* delfín *m*

domain [də'meɪn] *n* (**a**) *(sphere)* campo *m*, esfera *f*; **that's not my d.** no es de mi competencia (**b**) *(territory)* dominio *m* (**c**) *Comput* dominio *m*; **d. name** nombre *m* de dominio

dome [dəʊm] *n (roof)* cúpula *f*; *(ceiling)* bóveda *f*

domestic [də'mestɪk] *adj* (**a**) *(appliance, pet)* doméstico(a); **d. science** economía doméstica (**b**) *(home-loving)* casero(a) (**c**) *(flight, news)* nacional; *(trade, policy)* interior

domesticate [də'mestɪkeɪt] *vt (make home-loving)* volver hogareño(a) *or* casero(a)

domicile ['dɒmɪsaɪl] *n* domicilio *m*

dominant ['dɒmɪnənt] *adj* dominante

dominate ['dɒmɪneɪt] *vt & vi* dominar

domineering [dɒmɪ'nɪərɪŋ] *adj* dominante

Dominican [də'mɪnɪkən] *adj & n (of Dominica)* dominicano(a) *(m,f)*; **D. Republic** República Dominicana

dominion [də'mɪnjən] *n* dominio *m*

domino ['dɒmɪnəʊ] *n (pl dominoes) (piece)* ficha *f* de dominó; **dominoes** *(game)* dominó *m*

don [dɒn] *n Br Univ* catedrático(a) *m,f*

donate [dəʊ'neɪt] *vt* donar

donation [dəʊ'neɪʃən] *n* donativo *m*

done [dʌn] **1** *adj* (**a**) *(finished)* terminado(a); **it's over and d. with** se acabó (**b**) *Fam (tired)* rendido(a) (**c**) *(meat)* hecho(a); *(vegetables)* cocido(a)

2 *pp* of **do**

donkey ['dɒŋkɪ] *n* burro(a) *m,f*

donor ['dəʊnə(r)] *n* donante *f*

don't [dəʊnt] = **do not**

donut ['dəʊnʌt] *n US* dónut® *m*

doodle ['du:dəl] *vi Fam (write)* garabatear; *(draw)* hacer dibujos

doom [du:m] **1** *n (fate)* destino *m* (funesto); *(ruin)* perdición *f*, *(death)* muerte *f*

2 *vt usu pass (destine)* destinar; **doomed to failure** condenado(a) al fracaso

doomsday ['du:mzdeɪ] *n* día *m* del juicio final

door [dɔ:(r)] *n* puerta *f*; **front/back d.** puerta principal/trasera; *Fig* **behind**

closed doors a puerta cerrada; **d. handle** manilla *f* (de la puerta); **d. knocker** picaporte *m*; **next d. (to)** (en) la casa de al lado (de)

doorbell ['dɔ:bel] *n* timbre *m* (de la puerta)

doorknob ['dɔ:nɒb] *n* pomo *m*

doorman ['dɔ:mən] *n* portero *m*

doormat ['dɔ:mæt] *n* felpudo *m*, esterilla *f*, *Fam Fig (person)* trapo *m*

doorstep ['dɔ:step] *n* peldaño *m*; *Fig* **on one's d.** a la vuelta de la esquina

door-to-door ['dɔ:tə'dɔ:(r)] *adj* a domicilio

doorway ['dɔ:weɪ] *n* portal *m*, entrada *f*

dope [dəʊp] **1** *n* (**a**) *Fam (drug)* chocolate *m* (**b**) *Fam (person)* imbécil *mf*

2 *vt (food, drink)* adulterar con drogas; *Sport* dopar

dop(e)y ['dəʊpɪ] *adj* (**dopier, dopiest**) *Fam* (**a**) *(sleepy)* medio dormido(a); *(fuddled)* atontado(a) (**b**) *Fam (silly)* torpe

dork [dɔ:k] *n US Fam* petardo(a) *m,f*

dormant ['dɔ:mənt] *adj* inactivo(a); *Fig (rivalry)* latente

dormitory ['dɔ:mɪtərɪ] *n* (**a**) *(in school)* dormitorio *m* (**b**) *US (in university)* colegio *m* mayor

dosage ['dəʊsɪdʒ] *n Fml (amount)* dosis *f inv*

dose [dəʊs] **1** *n* dosis *f inv*

2 *vt (patient)* medicar

doss [dɒs] *vi Br Fam* sobar

dosshouse ['dɒshaʊs] *n Br Fam* pensión *f* de mala muerte

dossier ['dɒsɪeɪ] *n* expediente *m*

dot [dɒt] **1** *n* punto *m*; **on the d.** en punto; *Comput* **d. matrix printer** impresora *f* matricial *or* de agujas

2 *vt* (**a**) *Fam* **to d. one's i's and cross one's t's** poner los puntos sobre las íes (**b**) *(scatter)* esparcir, salpicar

dote [dəʊt] *vi* **to d. on sb** chochear con algn

double ['dʌbəl] **1** *adj* doble; **it's d. the price** cuesta dos veces más; **d. bass** contrabajo *m*; **d. bed** cama *f* de matrimonio; **d. bill** programa *m* doble; *Br* **d. cream** nata *f* para montar; **d. glazing** ventana *f* doble

2 *adv* doble; **folded d.** doblado(a) por la mitad

3 *n* (**a**) *(vivo retrato m; Cin & Th doble m* (**b**) **to earn d.** ganar el doble; *Fam* **at** *or* **on the d.** corriendo (**c**) **doubles** *(in chess)* (partido *m* de) dobles *mpl*

4 *vt* doblar; *Fig (efforts)* redoblar

5 *vi* (**a**) *(increase)* doblarse (**b**) **to d. as** *(serve)* hacer las veces de

▸**double back** *vi* **to d. back on one's tracks** volver sobre sus pasos

▸**double up 1** *vt sep (bend)* doblar

2 *vi* (**a**) *(bend)* doblarse (**b**) *(share room)* compartir la habitación (**with** con)

double-barrelled ['dʌbəlbærəld] *adj* (**a**) *(gun)* de dos cañones (**b**) *Br (surname)* compuesto(a)

double-breasted ['dʌbəlbrestɪd] *adj* cruzado(a)

double-check [dʌbəl't∫ek] *vt & vi* repasar dos veces

double-cross [dʌbəl'krɒs] *Fam* **1** *vt* engañar, traicionar

2 *n* engaño *m*, traición *f*

double-decker [dʌbəl'dekə(r)] *n Br* **d. (bus)** autobús *m* de dos pisos

double-edged ['dʌbəledʒd] *adj* de doble filo

doubt [daʊt] **1** *n* duda *f*; **beyond (all) d.** sin duda alguna; **no d.** sin duda; **there's no d. about it** no cabe la menor duda; **to be in d. about sth** dudar algo; **to be open to d.** *(fact)* ser dudoso(a); *(outcome)* ser incierto(a)

2 *vt* (**a**) *(distrust)* desconfiar de (**b**) *(not be sure of)* dudar; **I d. if** *or* **whether he'll come** dudo que venga

doubtful ['daʊtfʊl] *adj* (**a**) *(future)* dudoso(a), *(look)* dubitativo(a); **I'm a bit d. about it** no me convence del todo; (**b**) *(questionable)* sospechoso(a)

doubtless ['daʊtlɪs] *adv* sin duda, seguramente

dough [dəʊ] *n* (**a**) *(for bread)* masa *f*; *(for pastries)* pasta *f* (**b**) *Fam (money)* pasta *f*

doughnut ['dəʊnʌt] *n* rosquilla *f*, dónut® *m*

douse [daʊs] *vt* (**a**) *(soak)* mojar (**b**) *(extinguish)* apagar

dove [dʌv] *n* paloma *f*

dovetail ['dʌvteɪl] *vt Fig (plans)* sincronizar

dowdy ['daʊdɪ] *adj* (**dowdier, dowdiest**) poco elegante

down¹ [daʊn] **1** *prep* (**a**) *(to or at a lower level)* **d. the river** río abajo; **to go d. the road** bajar la calle

(**b**) *(along)* por

2 *adv* (**a**) *(to lower level)* (hacia) abajo; *(to floor)* al suelo; *(to ground)* a tierra; **to fall d.** caerse; **to go d.** *(price, person)* bajar; *(sun)* ponerse

(**b**) *(at lower level)* abajo; **d. there** allí abajo; **face d.** boca abajo; *Fig* **to be d. with a cold** estar resfriado(a); *Fam Fig* **to feel d.** estar deprimido(a); *Fam Fig* **d. under** en/a Australia y Nueva Zelanda

(**c**) **I'm d. to my last stamp** no me queda más que un solo sello; **sales are d. by 5 percent** las ventas han bajado un 5 por ciento

(**d**) **to take sth d.** *(in writing)* apuntar algo

(**e**) **d. through the ages** a través de los siglos

3 *adj (payment)* al contado; *(on property)* de entrada

4 *vt Fam (drink)* tomarse de un trago; *(food)* zamparse

5 *n* **ups and downs** altibajos *mpl*

6 *interj* **d. with taxes!** ¡abajo los impuestos!

down² [daʊn] *n* (**a**) *(on bird)* plumón *m* (**b**) *(on cheek, peach)* pelusa *f*; *(on body)* vello *m*

down-and-out ['daʊnən'aʊt] **1** *adj* en las últimas

2 *n* vagabundo(a) *m,f*

downbeat ['daʊnbiːt] *adj Fam (gloomy)* deprimido(a)

downcast ['daʊnkɑːst] *adj* abatido(a)

downfall ['daʊnfɔːl] *n (of regime)* caída *f*; *(of person)* perdición *f*

downgrade ['daʊngreɪd] *vt* degradar

downhearted [daʊn'hɑːtɪd] *adj* desalentado(a)

downhill [daʊn'hɪl] **1** *adj (skiing)* de descenso; *Fam* **after his first exam, the rest were all d.** después del primer examen, los demás le fueron sobre ruedas

2 *adv* **to go d.** ir cuesta abajo; *Fig (standards)* deteriorarse

download ['daʊn'ləʊd] *vt Comput* bajar, descargar

down-market [daʊn'mɑːkɪt] **1** *adj* barato(a)

2 *adv* **to move d.** *(of company)* producir artículos más asequibles

downpour ['daʊnpɔː(r)] *n* chaparrón *m*

downright ['daʊnraɪt] *Fam* **1** *adj (blunt)* tajante; *(categorical)* categórico(a); **it's a d. lie** es una mentira y gorda

2 *adv (totally)* completamente

downsizing ['daʊnsaɪzɪŋ] *n Com* reajuste *m* de plantillas

downstairs 1 *adv* [daʊn'steəz] abajo; *(to ground floor)* a la planta baja; **to go d.** bajar la escalera

2 *adj* ['daʊnsteəz] *(on ground floor)* de la planta baja

downstream [daʊn'striːm] *adv* río abajo

down-to-earth [daʊntʊ'ɜːθ] *adj* realista

downtown [daʊn'taʊn] *adv US* en el centro (de la ciudad)

downturn ['daʊntɜːn] *n* baja *f*

downward ['daʊnwəd] **1** *adj (slope)* descendente; *(look)* hacia abajo; *Fin (tendency)* a la baja

  2 *adv* = **downwards**

downwards ['daʊnwədz] *adv* hacia abajo

dowry ['daʊərɪ] *n* dote *f*

doz *(abbr* **dozen)** docena *f*

doze [dəʊz] **1** *vi* dormitar

  2 *n* cabezada *f*; **to have a d.** echar una cabezada

  ▸ **doze off** *vi* quedarse dormido(a)

dozen ['dʌzən] *n* docena *f*; **half a d./a d. eggs** media docena/una docena de huevos; *Fam* **dozens of** un montón de

Dr *(abbr* **Doctor)** Dr., Dra.

drab [dræb] *adj* **(drabber, drabbest)** **(a)** *(ugly)* feo(a); *(dreary)* monótono(a), gris **(b)** *(colour)* pardo(a)

draft [drɑːft] **1** *n* **(a)** borrador *m* **(b)** *(bill of exchange)* giro *m* **(c)** *US* servicio militar obligatorio **(d)** *US* = **draught**

  2 *vt* **(a)** hacer un borrador de **(b)** *US Mil* reclutar

draftsman ['drɑːftsmən] *n US* = **draughtsman**

drag [dræg] **1** *vt* **(a)** *(pull)* arrastrar; *Fig* **to d. one's heels (over sth)** dar largas (a algo) **(b)** *(lake)* rastrear

  2 *vi* **(a)** *(trail)* arrastrarse **(b)** *(person)* rezagarse

  3 *n* **(a)** *Tech* resistencia *f* (aerodinámica) **(b)** *Fam (nuisance)* lata *f* **(c)** *Fam (on cigarette)* calada *f* **(d)** *Fam* **to be in d.** ir vestido de mujer **(e)** *US Fam* **the main d.** la calle mayor *or* principal

  ▸ **drag along** *vt sep* llevarse arrastrando

  ▸ **drag on** *vi (war, strike)* hacerse interminable

  ▸ **drag out** *vt sep (speech etc)* alargar

dragon ['drægən] *n* dragón *m*

dragonfly ['drægənflaɪ] *n* libélula *f*

drain [dreɪn] **1** *n* **(a)** *(for water)* desagüe *m*; *(for sewage)* alcantarilla *f* **(b)** *(grating)* sumidero *m* **(c)** *Fig* **the boys are a d. on her strength** los niños la dejan agotada

  2 *vt* **(a)** *(marsh etc)* avenar; *(reservoir)* desecar **(b)** *(crockery)* escurrir **(c)** *(empty) (glass)* apurar; *Fig (capital etc)* agotar

  3 *vi* **(a)** *(crockery)* escurrirse **(b)** **to d. (away)** *(liquid)* irse

drainage ['dreɪnɪdʒ] *n (of marsh)* drenaje *m*; *(of reservoir, building)* desagüe *m*; *(of town)* alcantarillado *m*

drainpipe ['dreɪnpaɪp] *n* tubo *m* de desagüe

dram [dræm] *n Fam* trago *m (de whisky)*

drama ['drɑːmə] *n* **(a)** *(play)* obra *f* de teatro; *Fig* drama *m* **(b)** *(subject)* teatro *m*

dramatic [drə'mætɪk] *adj* **(a)** *(change)* impresionante; *(moment)* emocionante **(b)** *Th* dramático(a), teatral

dramatist ['dræmətɪst] *n* dramaturgo(a) *m,f*

dramatization [dræmətaɪ'zeɪʃən] *n* adaptación *f* teatral

dramatize ['dræmətaɪz] *vt* **(a)** *(adapt)* hacer una adaptación teatral de **(b)** *(exaggerate)* dramatizar

drank [dræŋk] *pt of* **drink**

drape [dreɪp] **1** *vt* **to d. sth over sth** colgar algo sobre algo; **draped with** cubierto(a) de

  2 *n* **(a)** *(of fabric)* caída *f* **(b)** *US* cortina *f*

draper ['dreɪpə(r)] *n Br* pañero(a) *m,f*

drastic ['dræstɪk] *adj* **(a)** *(measures)* drástico(a), severo(a) **(b)** *(change)* radical

draught [drɑːft] **1** *n* **(a)** *(of cold air)* corriente *f* (de aire) **(b)** *(of liquid)* trago *m* **(c)** **d. (beer)** cerveza *f* de barril **(d)** *Br* **draughts** *(game)* damas *fpl* **(e)** *Naut* calado *m*

  2 *adj (animal)* de tiro

draughtboard ['drɑːftbɔːd] *n Br* tablero *m* de damas

draughtsman ['drɑːftsmən] *n* delineante *mf*

draw [drɔː] **1** *vt (pt* **drew**; *pp* **drawn)** **(a)** *(picture)* dibujar; *(line)* trazar

  (b) *(pull)* tirar de; *(train, carriage)* arrastrar; *(curtains) (open)* descorrer; *(close)* correr; *(blinds)* bajar

  (c) *(remove)* sacar; *(salary)* cobrar; *(cheque)* librar

  (d) *(attract)* atraer; *(attention)* llamar

  (e) *Fig (strength)* sacar

  (f) **to d. breath** respirar

  (g) **to d. lots** echar a suertes

  (h) *(comparison)* hacer; *(conclusion)* sacar

  2 *vi* **(a)** *(sketch)* dibujar

  (b) *(move)* **the train drew into/out of the station** el tren entró en/salió de la estación; **to d. apart (from)** separarse (de); **to d. to an end** acabarse

  (c) *Sport* **they drew two all** empataron a dos

  3 *n* **(a)** *(raffle)* sorteo *m*

  (b) *Sport* empate *m*

  (c) *Fig (attraction)* atracción *f*

  ▸ **draw in** *vi (days)* acortarse

▸**draw on** *vt insep (savings)* recurrir a; *(experience)* aprovecharse de

▸**draw out** *vt sep* (**a**) *(make long)* alargar (**b**) *(encourage to speak)* desatar la lengua a (**c**) *(from pocket, drawer etc)* sacar

▸**draw up** *vt sep (contract)* preparar; *(plan)* esbozar

drawback ['drɔːbæk] *n* desventaja *f*, inconveniente *m*

drawbridge ['drɔːbrɪdʒ] *n* puente levadizo

drawer ['drɔːə(r)] *n* cajón *m*

drawing ['drɔːɪŋ] *n* dibujo *m; Fam Fig* **to go back to the d. board** volver a empezar; *Br* **d. pin** chincheta *f; Fml* **d. room** sala *f* de estar

drawl [drɔːl] **1** *vi* hablar arrastrando las palabras

2 *n* voz cansina; *US* **a Southern d.** un acento sureño

drawn [drɔːn] **1** *adj (tired)* ojeroso(a)

2 *pp of* **draw**

dread [dred] **1** *vt* temer a, tener pavor a

2 *n* temor *m*

dreadful ['dredfʊl] *adj* (**a**) *(shocking)* espantoso(a) (**b**) *Fam (awful)* fatal; **how d.!** ¡qué horror!

dreadfully ['dredfʊlɪ] *adv Fam (horribly)* terriblemente; *(very)* muy, sumamente

dream [driːm] **1** *n* (**a**) sueño *m* (**b**) *(daydream)* ensueño *m* (**c**) *Fam (marvel)* maravilla *f*

2 *vt (pt & pp* **dreamed** *or* **dreamt**) soñar

3 *vi* soñar (**of** *or* **about** con)

dreamer ['driːmə(r)] *n* soñador(a) *m,f*

dreamt [dremt] *pt & pp of* **dream**

dreamy [driːmɪ] *adj* (**dreamier, dreamiest**) *(absent-minded)* distraído(a); *(wonderful)* de ensueño

dreary ['drɪərɪ] *adj* (**drearier, dreariest**) (**a**) *(gloomy)* triste (**b**) *Fam (boring)* aburrido(a), pesado(a)

dredge [dredʒ] *vt & vi* dragar, rastrear

▸**dredge up** *vt sep* (**a**) *(body)* sacar del agua (**b**) *Fam Fig* sacar a relucir

dregs [dregz] *npl* poso *m*

drench [drentʃ] *vt* empapar

dress [dres] **1** *n* (**a**) *(frock)* vestido *m* (**b**) *(clothing)* ropa *f;* **d. rehearsal** ensayo *m* general; **d. shirt** camisa *f* de etiqueta

2 *vt* (**a**) *(person)* vestir; **he was dressed in a grey suit** llevaba (puesto) un traje gris (**b**) *(salad)* aliñar (**c**) *(wound)* vendar

3 *vi* vestirse

▸**dress up 1** *vi* (**a**) *(in disguise)* disfrazarse (**as** de) (**b**) *(in best clothes)* vestirse elegante

2 *vt sep Fig* disfrazar

dresser ['dresə(r)] *n* (**a**) *Br (in kitchen)* aparador *m* (**b**) *US (in bedroom)* tocador *m* (**c**) *Th* ayudante *mf* de camerino

dressing ['dresɪŋ] *n* (**a**) *(bandage)* vendaje *m* (**b**) *(salad)* **d.** aliño *m* (**c**) **d. gown** bata *f;* **d. room** *Th* camerino *m; Sport* vestuario *m;* **d. table** tocador *m*

dressmaker ['dresmeɪkə(r)] *n* modista *mf*

dressy ['dresɪ] *adj* (**dressier, dressiest**) vistoso(a)

drew [druː] *pt of* **draw**

dribble ['drɪbəl] **1** *vi* (**a**) *(baby)* babear (**b**) *(liquid)* gotear

2 *vt Sport (ball)* driblar

3 *n (saliva)* saliva *f;* *(of water, blood)* gotas *fpl*

dried [draɪd] *adj (fruit)* seco(a); *(milk)* en polvo

drier ['draɪə(r)] *n* = **dryer**

drift [drɪft] **1** *vi* (**a**) *(boat)* ir a la deriva; *Fig (person)* ir sin rumbo, vagar; **they drifted away** se marcharon poco a poco (**b**) *(snow)* amontonarse

2 *n* (**a**) *(flow)* flujo *m* (**b**) *(of snow)* ventisquero *m;* *(of sand)* montón *m* (**c**) *Fig (meaning)* idea *f*

driftwood ['drɪftwʊd] *n* madera *f* flotante

drill [drɪl] **1** *n* (**a**) *(hand tool)* taladro *m; Min* barrena *f;* **dentist's d.** fresa *f;* **pneumatic d.** martillo neumático (**b**) *esp Mil* instrucción *f*

2 *vt* (**a**) *(wood etc)* taladrar (**b**) *(soldiers, children)* instruir

3 *vi (by hand)* taladrar; *(for oil, coal)* perforar, sondar

drink [drɪŋk] **1** *vt (pt* **drank**; *pp* **drunk**) beber

2 *vi* beber; **to have sth to d.** tomarse algo; **to d. to sth/sb** brindar por algo/algn

3 *n* bebida *f;* *(alcoholic)* copa *f*

drinker ['drɪŋkə(r)] *n* bebedor(a) *m,f*

drinking ['drɪŋkɪŋ] *n* **d. water** agua *f* potable

drip [drɪp] **1** *n* (**a**) *(drop)* goteo *m* (**b**) *Med* gota a gota *m inv* (**c**) *Fam (person)* necio(a) *m,f*

2 *vi* gotear; **he was dripping with sweat** el sudor le caía a gotas

drip-dry ['drɪp'draɪ] *adj* que no necesita planchado

dripping ['drɪpɪŋ] *n Culin* pringue *f*

drive [draɪv] **1** *vt (pt* **drove**; *pp* **driven**) (**a**) *(vehicle)* conducir, *Am* manejar; *(person)* llevar

(**b**) *(power)* impulsar

(**c**) *(enemy)* acosar; *(ball)* mandar (**d**) *(stake)* hincar; *(nail)* clavar (**e**) *(compel)* forzar, obligar; **to d. sb mad** volver loco(a) a algn (**f**) **to d. (off)** rechazar

2 *vi Aut* conducir, *Am* manejar

3 *n* (**a**) *(trip)* paseo *m* en coche; **to go for a d.** dar una vuelta en coche (**b**) *(to house)* camino *m* de entrada (**c**) *(transmission)* transmisión *f*; *Aut* tracción *f*; *Aut* **left-hand d.** conducción *f* por la izquierda (**d**) *(in golf)* golpe *m* inicial (**e**) *(campaign)* campaña *f* (**f**) *(need)* necesidad *f*; *(energy)* energía *f*, vigor *m*; **sex d.** instinto *m* sexual (**g**) *Comput* unidad *f* de disco

drive-in ['draɪvɪn] *n US (cinema)* autocine *m*

driven ['drɪvən] *pp of* **drive**

driver ['draɪvə(r)] *n (of car, bus)* conductor(a) *m,f*; *(of train)* maquinista *mf*; *(of lorry)* camionero(a) *m,f*; *(of racing car)* piloto *mf*; *US* **d.'s license** carnet *m* de conducir

driveway ['draɪvweɪ] *n (to house)* camino *m* de entrada

driving ['draɪvɪŋ] **1** *n Br* **d. licence** carnet *m* de conducir; **d. school** autoescuela *f*; **d. test** examen *m* de conducir

2 *adj* (**a**) *(rain)* intenso(a) (**b**) **d. force** fuerza *f* motriz

drizzle ['drɪzəl] **1** *n* llovizna *f*

2 *vi* lloviznar

droll [drəʊl] *adj* gracioso(a)

dromedary ['drɒmədərɪ] *n* dromedario *m*

drone [drəʊn] *vi (bee etc)* zumbar

droop [druːp] *vi (flower)* marchitarse; *(eyelids)* caerse

drop [drɒp] **1** *n* (**a**) *(of liquid)* gota *f*; **eye drops** colirio *m* (**b**) *(sweet)* pastilla *f* (**c**) *(descent)* desnivel *m* (**d**) *(in price)* bajada *f*; *(in temperature)* descenso *m*

2 *vt* (**a**) *(let fall)* dejar caer; *(lower)* bajar; *(reduce)* disminuir; **to d. a hint** soltar una indirecta (**b**) *(abandon)* *(subject, charge etc)* abandonar, dejar; *Sport* **he was dropped from the team** le echaron del equipo (**c**) *(omit)* *(spoken syllable)* comerse

3 *vi (object)* caerse; *(person)* tirarse; *(voice, price, temperature)* bajar; *(wind)* amainar; *(speed)* disminuir

▸ **drop by, drop in** *vi Fam (visit)* pasarse (**at** por)

▸ **drop off 1** *vi Fam (fall asleep)* quedarse dormido(a)

2 *vt sep (deliver)* dejar

▸ **drop out** *vi (from college)* dejar los estudios; *(from society)* marginarse; *(from competition)* retirarse

▸ **drop round** *vi Fam* = **drop by**

dropout ['drɒpaʊt] *n Fam Pej* automarginado(a) *m,f*

dropper ['drɒpə(r)] *n* cuentagotas *m inv*

droppings ['drɒpɪŋz] *npl* excrementos *mpl*

drought [draʊt] *n* sequía *f*

drove [drəʊv] **1** *n (of cattle)* manada *f*

2 *pt of* **drive**

drown [draʊn] **1** *vt* (**a**) ahogar (**b**) *(place)* inundar

2 *vi* ahogarse; **he (was) drowned** murió ahogado

drowsy ['draʊzɪ] *adj* (**drowsier, drowsiest**) soñoliento(a); **to feel d.** tener sueño

drudgery ['drʌdʒərɪ] *n* trabajo duro y pesado

drug [drʌg] **1** *n* (**a**) *(medicine)* medicamento *m* (**b**) *(narcotic)* droga *f*, estupefaciente *m*; **to be on drugs** drogarse; **d. addict** drogadicto(a) *m,f*; **d. addiction** drogadicción *f*; **d. squad** brigada *f* antidroga

2 *vt (person)* drogar; *(food, drink)* adulterar con drogas

druggist ['drʌgɪst] *n US* farmacéutico(a) *m,f*

drugstore ['drʌgstɔːr] *n US* = establecimiento donde se compran medicamentos, periódicos, etc.

drum [drʌm] **1** *n* (**a**) tambor *m*; **to play the drums** tocar la batería (**b**) *(container)* bidón *m*

2 *vi Fig (with fingers)* tabalear

3 *vt Fig* **to d. sth into sb** enseñar algo a algn a machamartillo

▸ **drum up** *vt sep Fam* solicitar

drummer ['drʌmə(r)] *n (in band)* tambor *mf*; *(in pop group)* batería *mf*

drumstick ['drʌmstɪk] *n* (**a**) *Mus* baqueta *f* (**b**) *(chicken leg)* muslo *m*

drunk [drʌŋk] **1** *adj* borracho(a); **to get d.** emborracharse ·

2 *n* borracho(a) *m,f*

3 *pp of* **drink**

drunkard ['drʌŋkəd] *n* borracho(a) *m,f*

dry [draɪ] **1** *adj* (**drier, driest** *or* **dryer, dryest**) (**a**) seco(a); *US* **d. goods store** mercería *f*, tienda *f* de confección (**b**) *(wry)* socarrón(ona)

2 *vt* (*pt & pp* **dried**) secar

3 *vi* to d. (off) secarse

dry-clean [draɪ'kliːn] *vt* limpiar *or* lavar en seco

dryer ['draɪə(r)] *n* secadora *f*

dub¹ [dʌb] *vt* (*subtitle*) doblar (**into** a)

dub² [dʌb] *vt* (**a**) (*give nickname to*) apodar (**b**) (*knight*) armar

dubious ['djuːbɪəs] *adj* (**a**) (*morals etc*) dudoso(a); (*compliment*) equívoco(a) (**b**) (*doubting*) indeciso(a)

Dublin ['dʌblɪn] *n* Dublín

duchess ['dʌtʃɪs] *n* duquesa *f*

duck¹ [dʌk] *n* pato(a) *m,f*; Culin pato *m*

duck² [dʌk] **1** *vt* (**a**) (*submerge*) dar una ahogadilla a (**b**) (*evade*) esquivar

2 *vi* (**a**) (*evade blow*) esquivar (**b**) Fam to **d. (out)** rajarse

duckling ['dʌklɪŋ] *n* patito *m*

duct [dʌkt] *n* (*for fuel etc*) conducto *m*; Anat canal *m*

dud [dʌd] Fam **1** *adj* (**a**) (*useless*) inútil; (*defective*) estropeado(a) (**b**) (*banknote*) falso(a); (*cheque*) sin fondos

2 *n* (*useless thing*) engañifa *f*; (*person*) desastre *m*

dude [duːd] *n US Fam* (*man*) tipo *m*, tío *m*

due [djuː] **1** *adj* (**a**) (*expected*) esperado(a); **the train is d. (to arrive) at ten** el tren debe llegar a las diez (**b**) Fml (*proper*) debido(a); **in d. course** a su debido tiempo (**c**) (*owing*) pagadero(a); **how much are you d.?** (*owed*) ¿cuánto te deben? (**d**) **to be d. to** (*caused by*) deberse a; **d. to** (*because of*) debido de

2 *adv* (*north etc*) derecho hacia

3 *n* (**a**) **to give sb their d.** dar a algn su merecido (**b**) **dues** (*fee*) cuota *f*

duel ['djuːəl] *n* duelo *m*

duet [djuː'et] *n* dúo *m*

duffel ['dʌfəl] *n* **d. bag** petate *m*; **d. coat** trenca *f*

dug [dʌg] *pt & pp of* **dig**

duke [djuːk] *n* duque *m*

dull [dʌl] **1** *adj* (**a**) (*boring*) pesado(a); (*place*) sin interés (**b**) (*light*) apagado(a); (*weather*) gris (**c**) (*sound, ache*) sordo(a) (**d**) Fig (*slow-witted*) torpe

2 *vt* (**a**) (*pain*) aliviar (**b**) Fig (*faculty*) embotar

duly ['djuːlɪ] *adv* Fml (*properly*) debidamente; (*as expected*) como era de esperar; (*in due course*) a su debido tiempo

dumb [dʌm] **1** *adj* (**a**) Med mudo(a) (**b**) Fam (*stupid*) tonto(a)

2 *npl* **the d.** los mudos

dumbbell ['dʌmbel] *n Sport* pesa *f*

dumbfounded [dʌm'faʊndɪd], **dumbstruck** ['dʌmstrʌk] *adj* pasmado(a)

dummy ['dʌmɪ] *n* (**a**) (*sham*) imitación *f* (**b**) (*in shop window*) maniquí *m*; (*of ventriloquist*) muñeco *m* (**c**) Br (*for baby*) chupete *m*

dump [dʌmp] **1** *n* (**a**) (*tip*) vertedero *m*; (*for old cars*) cementerio *m* (de coches) (**b**) Fam Pej (*place*) estercolero *m*; (*town*) poblacho *m*; (*dwelling*) tugurio *m* (**c**) Mil depósito *m*

2 *vt* (**a**) (*rubbish*) verter; (*truck contents*) descargar (**b**) (*person*) dejar; Com inundar el mercado con (**c**) Comput (*transfer*) copiar de memoria interna

dumping ['dʌmpɪŋ] *n* vertido *m*

dumpling ['dʌmplɪŋ] *n* Culin = bola de masa hervida

dumpy ['dʌmpɪ] *adj* (**dumpier, dumpiest**) Fam rechoncho(a)

dunce [dʌns] *n* Fam tonto(a) *m,f*

dune [djuːn] *n* (**sand**) d. duna *f*

dung [dʌŋ] *n* estiércol *m*

dungarees ['dʌŋgə'riːz] *npl* mono *m*

dungeon ['dʌndʒən] *n* calabozo *m*, mazmorra *f*

duo ['djuːəʊ] *n Mus* dúo *m*; Fam pareja *f*

dupe [djuːp] **1** *vt* engañar

2 *n* ingenuo(a) *m,f*

duplex ['djuːpleks] *n US* (*house*) casa adosada; **d. apartment** dúplex *m inv*

duplicate 1 *vt* ['djuːplɪkeɪt] (**a**) (*copy*) duplicar; (*film, tape*) reproducir (**b**) (*repeat*) repetir

2 *n* ['djuːplɪkɪt] duplicado *m*; **in d.** por duplicado

durable ['djʊərəbəl] *adj* duradero(a)

duration [djʊ'reɪʃən] *n Fml* duración *f*

duress [djʊ'res] *n Fml* coacción *f*

📖 Note that the Spanish word **dureza** is a false friend and is never a translation for the English word **duress**. In Spanish, **dureza** means "hardness, harshness".

---

during ['djʊərɪŋ] *prep* durante

dusk [dʌsk] *n Fml* crepúsculo *m*; **at d.** al anochecer

dust [dʌst] **1** *n* polvo *m*; **d. cloud** polvareda *f*; **d. jacket** sobrecubierta *f*

2 *vt* (**a**) (*furniture*) quitar el polvo a (**b**) (*cake*) espolvorear

dustbin ['dʌstbɪn] *n Br* cubo *m* de la basura

dustcart ['dʌstkɑːt] *n Br* camión *m* de la basura

duster ['dʌstə(r)] *n* (*for housework*) trapo *m or* paño *m* (del polvo); **feather d.** plumero *m*

dustman ['dʌstmən] *n Br* basurero *m*

dustpan ['dʌstpæn] *n* recogedor *m*

dusty ['dʌstɪ] *adj* (**dustier, dustiest**) polvoriento(a)

Dutch [dʌtʃ] **1** *adj* holandés(esa); *Fig* D. cap diafragma *m*

2 *n* (**a**) *pl* **the** D. los holandeses (**b**) *(language)* holandés *m*; **it's double D. to me** me suena a chino

3 *adv Fig* **to go** D. pagar cada uno lo suyo

Dutchman ['dʌtʃmən] *n* holandés *m*

Dutchwoman ['dʌtʃwʊmən] *n* holandesa *f*

duty ['djuːtɪ] *n* (**a**) deber *m*; **to do one's d.** cumplir con su deber (**b**) *(task)* función *f* (**c**) **to be on d.** estar de servicio; *Med & Mil* estar de guardia; **d. chemist** farmacia *f* de guardia (**d**) *(tax)* impuesto *m*; **customs d.** derechos *mpl* de aduana

duty-free [djuːtɪˈfriː] **1** *adj* libre de impuestos

2 *adv* sin pagar impuestos

3 *n* duty-free *m*

duvet ['duːveɪ] *n* edredón *m*

DVD [diːviːˈdiː] *n Comput* (*abbr* **Digital Versatile Disk, Digital Video Disk**) DVD *m*

dwarf [dwɔːf] **1** *n* (*pl* **dwarves** [dwɔːvz]) *(person)* enano(a) *m,f*

2 *vt* hacer parecer pequeño(a) a

dwell [dwel] *vi* (*pt & pp* **dwelt**) *Fml* morar
▸ **dwell on** *vt insep* hablar extensamente de; **let's not d. on it** olvidémoslo

dwelling ['dwelɪŋ] *n Fml & Hum* morada *f*, vivienda *f*

dwelt [dwelt] *pt & pp of* **dwell**

dwindle ['dwɪndəl] *vi* menguar, disminuir

dye [daɪ] **1** *n* tinte *m*

2 *vt* (*pres p* **dyeing**; *pt & pp* **dyed**) teñir; **to d. one's hair black** teñirse el pelo de negro

dying ['daɪɪŋ] *adj (person)* moribundo(a), agonizante; *Fig (custom)* en vías de desaparición

dyke [daɪk] *n* (**a**) *(bank)* dique *m*; *(causeway)* terraplén *m* (**b**) *very Fam Pej* tortillera *f*

dynamic [daɪˈnæmɪk] *adj* dinámico(a)

dynamics [daɪˈnæmɪks] *n sing* dinámica *f*

dynamism ['daɪnəmɪzəm] *n* dinamismo *m*

dynamite ['daɪnəmaɪt] *n* dinamita *f*

dynamo ['daɪnəməʊ] *n* dínamo *f*

dynasty ['dɪnəstɪ] *n* dinastía *f*

dysentery ['dɪsəntrɪ] *n* disentería *f*

dyslexia [dɪsˈleksɪə] *n* dislexia *f*

E, e [iː] *n* (**a**) *(the letter)* E, e *f* (**b**) *Mus* E mi *m*
E [iː] *n* (**a**) *(abbr* **East)** E (**b**) *Fam (abbr* **ecstasy)** *(drug)* éxtasis *m inv*
each [iːtʃ] **1** *adj* cada; **e. day/month** todos los días/meses; **e. person** cada cual; **e. time I see him** cada vez que lo veo
   2 *pron* (**a**) cada uno(a); **£2 e.** 2 libras cada uno; **we bought one e.** nos compramos uno cada uno (**b**) **e. other** el uno al otro; **they hate e. other** se odian
eager ['iːgə(r)] *adj (anxious)* impaciente; *(desirous)* deseoso(a); **e. to begin** impaciente por empezar; **to be e. for success** codiciar el éxito
eagerly ['iːgəlɪ] *adv (anxiously)* con impaciencia; *(keenly)* con ilusión
eagle ['iːgəl] *n* águila *f*
ear [ɪə(r)] *n* (**a**) oreja *f*; *(sense of hearing)* oído *m* (**b**) *(of corn etc)* espiga *f*
earache ['ɪəreɪk] *n* dolor *m* de oídos
eardrum ['ɪədrʌm] *n* tímpano *m*
earl [ɜːl] *n* conde *m*
earlobe ['ɪələʊb] *n* lóbulo *m*
early ['ɜːlɪ] *(earlier, earliest)* **1** *adj* (**a**) *(before the usual time)* temprano(a); **to have an e. night** acostarse pronto; **you're e.!** ¡qué pronto has venido!
   (**b**) *(at first stage, period)* **at an e. age** siendo joven; **in e. July** a principios de julio; **e. work** obra de juventud; **in her e. forties** a los cuarenta y pocos; **it's still e. days** aún es pronto
   (**c**) *(in the near future)* **an e. reply** una respuesta pronta; **at the earliest** cuanto antes
   2 *adv* (**a**) *(before the expected time)* temprano, pronto; **earlier on** antes; **five minutes e.** con cinco minutos de adelanto; **to leave e.** irse pronto
   (**b**) *(near the beginning)* **as e. as 1914** ya en 1914; **as e. as possible** tan pronto como sea posible; **to book e.** reservar con tiempo; **e. on** temprano
earmark ['ɪəmɑːk] *vt* destinar (**for** para or a)
earn [ɜːn] *vt* (**a**) *(money)* ganar; **to e. one's living** ganarse la vida (**b**) *(reputation)* ganarse (**c**) **to e. interest** cobrar interés or intereses

earnest ['ɜːnɪst] **1** *adj* serio(a), formal
   2 *n* **in e.** de veras, en serio
earnings ['ɜːnɪŋz] *npl* ingresos *mpl*
earring ['ɪərɪŋ] *n* pendiente *m*
earshot ['ɪəʃɒt] *n* **out of e.** fuera del alcance del oído; **within e.** al alcance del oído
earth [ɜːθ] **1** *n* (**a**) tierra *f*; *Fig* **to be down to e.** ser práctico; *Fam* **where/why on e. ...?** ¿pero dónde/por qué demonios ...? (**b**) *Br Elec* toma *f* de tierra
   2 *vt Br Elec* conectar a tierra
earthenware ['ɜːðənweə(r)] **1** *n* loza *f*
   2 *adj* de barro
earthquake ['ɜːθkweɪk] *n* terremoto *m*
earthshattering ['ɜːθʃætərɪŋ] *adj* trascendental; **e. news** noticia bomba
earthworm ['ɜːθwɜːm] *n* lombriz *f* de tierra
earthy ['ɜːθɪ] *adj (earthier, earthiest)* (**a**) *(taste)* terroso(a) (**b**) *(bawdy)* tosco(a)
earwig ['ɪəwɪg] *n* tijereta *f*
ease [iːz] **1** *n* (**a**) *(freedom from discomfort)* tranquilidad *f*; *Mil* posición *f* de descanso; **at e.** relajado(a) (**b**) *(lack of difficulty)* facilidad *f* (**c**) *(affluence)* comodidad *f* (**d**) **e. of manner** naturalidad *f*
   2 *vt* (**a**) *(pain)* aliviar (**b**) *(move gently)* deslizar con cuidado
   ▸ **ease off, ease up** *vi* (**a**) *(decrease)* disminuir (**b**) *(slow down)* ir más despacio
easel ['iːzəl] *n* caballete *m*
easily ['iːzɪlɪ] *adv* fácilmente; **e. the best** con mucho el mejor
east [iːst] **1** *n* este *m*; **the Middle E.** el Oriente Medio
   2 *adj* del este, oriental; **E. Germany** Alemania Oriental
   3 *adv* al *or* hacia el este
Easter ['iːstə(r)] *n* Semana Santa, Pascua *f*; **E. egg** huevo *m* de Pascua; **E. Sunday** Domingo *m* de Resurrección
easterly ['iːstəlɪ] *adj (from the east)* del este; *(to the east)* hacia al este
eastern ['iːstən] *adj* oriental, del este
eastward(s) ['iːstwəd(z)] *adv* hacia el este

easy ['iːzɪ] (**easier, easiest**) **1** *adj* (**a**) *(simple)* fácil, sencillo(a) (**b**) *(unworried, comfortable)* cómodo(a), tranquilo(a); *Fam* **I'm e.!** ¡me da lo mismo!; **e. chair** butacón *m*

2 *adv* **go e. on the wine** no te pases con el vino; *Fam* **to take things e.** tomarse las cosas con calma; *Fam* **take it e.!** ¡tranquilo!

easy-going [iːzɪ'gəʊɪŋ] *adj (calm)* tranquilo(a); *(lax)* despreocupado(a); *(undemanding)* poco exigente

eat [iːt] *vt* (*pt* **ate** [et, eɪt]; *pp* **eaten**) comer
▸**eat away** *vt sep* desgastar; *(metal)* corroer
▸**eat into** *vt insep* (**a**) *(wood)* roer (**b**) *Fig (savings)* consumir
▸**eat out** *vi* comer fuera
▸**eat up** *vt sep* (**a**) *(meal)* terminar (**b**) *Fig (petrol)* consumir; *(miles)* recorrer rápidamente

eatable ['iːtəbəl] *adj* comestible

eaten ['iːtən] *pp of* **eat**

eau de Cologne [əʊdəkə'ləʊn] *n* colonia *f*

eaves [iːvz] *npl* alero *m*

eavesdrop ['iːvzdrɒp] *vi* escuchar disimuladamente

ebb [eb] **1** *n* reflujo *m*; **e. and flow** flujo y reflujo; *Fig* **to be at a low e.** estar decaído
2 *vi* (**a**) *(tide)* bajar; **to e. and flow** subir y bajar (**b**) *Fig* **to e. away** decaer

ebony ['ebənɪ] **1** *n* ébano *m*
2 *adj* de ébano

eccentric [ɪk'sentrɪk] *adj & n* excéntrico(a) *(m,f)*

ecclesiastic [ɪkliːzɪ'æstɪk] *adj & n* eclesiástico(a) *(m,f)*

echelon ['eʃəlɒn] *n* escalafón *m*

echo ['ekəʊ] **1** *n* (*pl* **echoes**) eco *m*
2 *vt (repeat)* repetir
3 *vi* resonar, hacer eco

eclectic [ɪ'klektɪk] *adj* ecléctico(a)

eclipse [ɪ'klɪps] **1** *n* eclipse *m*
2 *vt* eclipsar

ecological [iːkə'lɒdʒɪkəl] *adj* ecológico(a)

ecology [ɪ'kɒlədʒɪ] *n* ecología *f*

e-commerce [iː'kɒmɜːs] *n* comercio electrónico

economic [iːkə'nɒmɪk] *adj* económico(a); *(profitable)* rentable

economical [iːkə'nɒmɪkəl] *adj* económico(a)

economics [iːkə'nɒmɪks] *n sing (science)* economía *f*; *Educ* (ciencias *fpl*) económicas *fpl*

economist [ɪ'kɒnəmɪst] *n* economista *mf*

economize [ɪ'kɒnəmaɪz] *vi* economizar

economy [ɪ'kɒnəmɪ] *n* (**a**) *Pol* **the e.** la economía *f* (**b**) *(saving)* ahorro *m*; **e. class** clase *f* turista

ecosystem ['iːkəʊsɪstəm] *n* ecosistema *m*

ecotax ['iːkəʊtæks] *n* ecotasa *f*

ecotourism ['iːkəʊtʊːrɪzəm] *n* ecoturismo *m*

ecstasy ['ekstəsɪ] *n* éxtasis *m*

ecstatic [ek'stætɪk] *adj* extático(a)

Ecuador ['ekwədɔː(r)] *n* Ecuador *m*

eczema ['eksɪmə] *n* eczema *m*

eddy ['edɪ] **1** *n* remolino *m*
2 *vi* arremolinarse

edge [edʒ] **1** *n* borde *m*; *(of knife)* filo *m*; *(of coin)* canto *m*; *(of water)* orilla *f*; **on the e. of town** en las afueras de la ciudad; **to have the e. on sb** llevar ventaja a algn; *Fig* **to be on e.** tener los nervios de punta
2 *vt Sewing* ribetear
3 *vi* **to e. closer** acercarse lentamente; **to e. forward** avanzar poco a poco

edgeways ['edʒweɪz], **edgewise** ['edʒwaɪz] *adv* de lado; *Fig* **I couldn't get a word in e.** no pude decir ni pío

edging ['edʒɪŋ] *n* borde *m*; *Sewing* ribete *m*

edgy ['edʒɪ] *adj* (**edgier, edgiest**) nervioso(a)

edible ['edɪbəl] *adj* comestible

edict ['iːdɪkt] *n Hist* edicto *m*; *Jur* decreto *m*

Edinburgh ['edɪnbrə] *n* Edimburgo

edit ['edɪt] *vt* (**a**) *(prepare for printing)* preparar para la imprenta (**b**) *(rewrite)* corregir; **to e. sth out** suprimir algo (**c**) *Press* ser redactor(a) de (**d**) *Cin, Rad & TV* montar; *(cut)* cortar

edition [ɪ'dɪʃən] *n* edición *f*

editor ['edɪtə(r)] *n (of book)* editor(a) *m,f*; *Press* redactor(a) *m,f*; *Cin & TV* montador(a) *m,f*

editorial [edɪ'tɔːrɪəl] **1** *adj* editorial; **e. staff** redacción *f*
2 *n* editorial *m*

educate ['edjʊkeɪt] *vt* educar

educated ['edjʊkeɪtɪd] *adj* culto(a)

education [edjʊ'keɪʃən] *n* (**a**) *(schooling)* enseñanza *f*; **adult e.** educación *f* de adultos; **Ministry of E.** Ministerio *m* de Educación (**b**) *(training)* formación *f* (**c**) *(studies)* estudios *mpl* (**d**) *(culture)* cultura *f*

educational [edjʊ'keɪʃənəl] *adj* educativo(a), educacional

eel [iːl] *n* anguila *f*

eerie [ˈɪərɪ] adj (**eerier, eeriest**) siniestro(a)

efface [ɪˈfeɪs] vt borrar

effect [ɪˈfekt] **1** n (**a**) efecto m; **in e.** efectivamente; **to come into e.** entrar en vigor; **to have an e. on** afectar a; **to no e.** sin resultado alguno; **to take e.** (drug) surtir efecto; (law) entrar en vigor (b) (impression) impresión f (**c**) **effects** (possessions) efectos mpl

2 vt Fml provocar

effective [ɪˈfektɪv] adj (**a**) (successful) eficaz (**b**) (real) efectivo(a) (**c**) (impressive) impresionante

effectively [ɪˈfektɪvlɪ] adv (**a**) (successfully) eficazmente (**b**) (in fact) en efecto

effeminate [ɪˈfemɪnɪt] adj afeminado(a)

effervescent [efəˈvesənt] adj efervescente

efficiency [ɪˈfɪʃənsɪ] n (of person) eficacia f, (of machine) rendimiento m

efficient [ɪˈfɪʃənt] adj eficaz, eficiente; (machine) de buen rendimiento

effigy [ˈefɪdʒɪ] n efigie f

effluent [ˈefluənt] n vertidos mpl

effort [ˈefət] n (**a**) esfuerzo m; **to make an e.** hacer un esfuerzo, esforzarse (**b**) (attempt) intento m

effortless [ˈefətlɪs] adj sin esfuerzo

effrontery [ɪˈfrʌntərɪ] n desfachatez f

effusive [ɪˈfjuːsɪv] adj efusivo(a)

eg [iːˈdʒiː] (abbr **exempli gratia**) p. ej.

egalitarian [ɪɡælɪˈteərɪən] adj igualitario(a)

egg [eɡ] **1** n huevo m; Fam Fig **to put all one's eggs in one basket** jugárselo todo a una carta; **e. cup** huevera f; **e. timer** reloj m de arena; **e. white** clara f de huevo

2 vt **to e. sb on (to do sth)** empujar a algn (a hacer algo)

eggplant [ˈeɡplɑːnt] n US berenjena f

eggshell [ˈeɡʃel] n cáscara f de huevo

ego [ˈiːɡəʊ, ˈeɡəʊ] n (**a**) ego m; Fam **e. trip** autobombo m (**b**) Fam amor propio

egocentric(al) [iːɡəʊˈsentrɪk(əl)] adj egocéntrico(a)

egoism [ˈiːɡəʊɪzəm] n egoísmo m

egoist [ˈiːɡəʊɪst] n egoísta mf

egotistic(al) [iːɡəʊˈtɪstɪk(əl)] adj egotista

Egypt [ˈiːdʒɪpt] n Egipto

Egyptian [ɪˈdʒɪpʃən] adj & n egipcio(a) (m,f)

eiderdown [ˈaɪdədaʊn] n edredón m

eight [eɪt] adj & n ocho (m inv)

eighteen [eɪˈtiːn] adj & n dieciocho (m inv)

eighteenth [eɪˈtiːnθ] **1** adj & n decimoctavo (m,f)

2 n (fraction) decimoctavo m

eighth [eɪtθ] **1** adj & n octavo(a) (m,f)

2 n (fraction) octavo m

eighty [ˈeɪtɪ] adj & n ochenta (m inv)

Eire [ˈeərə] n Eire

either [ˈaɪðə(r), ˈiːðə(r)] **1** pron (**a**) (affirmative) cualquiera; **e. of them** cualquiera de los dos; **e. of us** cualquiera de nosotros dos (**b**) (negative) ninguno/ninguna, ni el uno ni el otro/ni la una ni la otra; **I don't want e. of them** no quiero ninguno de los dos

2 adj (both) cada, los dos/las dos; **on e. side** en ambos lados; **in e. case** en cualquier de los dos casos

3 conj o; **e. ... or ...** o ... o ...; **e. Friday or Saturday** o (bien) el viernes o el sábado

4 adv (after negative) tampoco; **I don't want to do it e.** yo tampoco quiero hacerlo

ejaculate [ɪˈdʒækjʊleɪt] vi (man) eyacular

eject [ɪˈdʒekt] **1** vt expulsar

2 vi Av eyectarse

eke [iːk] vt **to e. out a living** ganarse la vida a duras penas

elaborate 1 vt [ɪˈlæbəreɪt] (**a**) (devise) elaborar (**b**) (explain) explicar detalladamente

2 vi explicarse; **to e. on sth** explicar algo con más detalles

3 adj [ɪˈlæbərɪt] (**a**) (complicated) complicado(a) (**b**) (detailed) detallado(a); (style) esmerado(a)

elapse [ɪˈlæps] vi transcurrir, pasar

elastic [ɪˈlæstɪk] **1** adj elástico(a); Fig flexible; **e. band** goma elástica

2 n elástico m

Elastoplast® [ɪˈlɑːstəplɑːst] n tirita f, Am curita f

elated [ɪˈleɪtɪd] adj eufórico(a)

elation [ɪˈleɪʃən] n regocijo m

elbow [ˈelbəʊ] **1** n (**a**) codo m; Fig **e. room** espacio m (**b**) (bend) recodo m

2 vt **to e. sb** dar un codazo a algn

elder¹ [ˈeldə(r)] **1** adj mayor

2 n **the elders** los ancianos

elder² [ˈeldə(r)] n Bot saúco m

elderly [ˈeldəlɪ] **1** adj anciano(a)

2 npl **the e.** los ancianos

eldest [ˈeldɪst] **1** adj mayor

2 n **the e.** el/la mayor

elect [ɪˈlekt] **1** vt (**a**) Pol elegir (**b**) **to e. to do sth** (choose) decidir hacer algo

2 adj **the president e.** el presidente electo

election [ɪˈlekʃən] **1** *n* elección *f*; **general e.** elecciones *fpl* generales
2 *adj* electoral

electioneering [ɪlekʃəˈnɪərɪŋ] *n* electoralismo *m*

elector [ɪˈlektə(r)] *n* elector(a) *m,f*

electoral [ɪˈlektərəl] *adj* electoral

electorate [ɪˈlektərɪt] *n* electorado *m*

electric [ɪˈlektrɪk] *adj* (**a**) eléctrico(a); **e. blanket** manta eléctrica, *Am* frazada eléctrica; **e. chair** silla eléctrica; **e. shock** electrochoque *m* (**b**) *Fig* electrizante

electrical [ɪˈlektrɪkəl] *adj* eléctrico(a)

electrician [ɪlekˈtrɪʃən] *n* electricista *mf*

electricity [ɪlekˈtrɪsɪtɪ] *n* electricidad *f*; **e. bill** recibo *m* de la luz

electrify [ɪˈlektrɪfaɪ] *vt* (**a**) *(railway line)* electrificar (**b**) *Fig (excite)* electrizar

electrocute [ɪˈlektrəkjuːt] *vt* electrocutar

electron [ɪˈlektrɒn] *n* electrón *m*

electronic [ɪlekˈtrɒnɪk] *adj* electrónico(a); **e. banking** banca electrónica, telebanca *f*

electronics [ɪlekˈtrɒnɪks] **1** *n sing (science)* electrónica *f*
2 *npl (of machine)* componentes *mpl* electrónicos

elegant [ˈelɪgənt] *adj* elegante

element [ˈelɪmənt] *n* (**a**) elemento *m* (**b**) *(part)* parte *f* (**c**) *(electrical)* resistencia *f* (**d**) *Fam Fig* **to be in one's e.** estar en su salsa

elementary [elɪˈmentərɪ] *adj (basic)* elemental; *(not developed)* rudimentario(a); *(easy)* fácil; *US* **e. school** escuela primaria

elephant [ˈelɪfənt] *n* elefante *m*

elevate [ˈelɪveɪt] *vt* elevar; *(in rank)* ascender

elevation [elɪˈveɪʃən] *n* (**a**) elevación *f* (**b**) *Archit* alzado *m* (**c**) *(above sea level)* altitud *f*

elevator [ˈelɪveɪtər] *n US* ascensor *m*

eleven [ɪˈlevən] *adj & n* once *(m inv)*

elevenses [ɪˈlevənzɪz] *npl Fam* bocadillo *m* de las once

eleventh [ɪˈlevənθ] **1** *adj & n* undécimo(a) *(m,f)*
2 *n (fraction)* undécimo *m*

elicit [ɪˈlɪsɪt] *vt* obtener

eligible [ˈelɪdʒəbəl] *adj* apto(a); **he isn't e. to vote** no tiene derecho al voto

eliminate [ɪˈlɪmɪneɪt] *vt* eliminar

elite [ɪˈliːt] *n* elite *f*

elitist [ɪˈliːtɪst] *adj* elitista

elm [elm] *n* olmo *m*

elocution [eləˈkjuːʃən] *n* elocución *f*

elongate [ˈiːlɒŋgeɪt] *vt* alargar

elope [ɪˈləʊp] *vi* fugarse para casarse

eloquent [ˈeləkwənt] *adj* elocuente

else [els] *adv* (**a**) **anyone e.** alguien más; **anything e.?** ¿algo más?; **everything e.** todo lo demás; **no one e.** nadie más; **someone e.** otro(a); **something e.** otra cosa, algo más; **somewhere e.** en otra parte; **what e.?** ¿qué más?; **where e.?** ¿en qué otro sitio? (**b**) **or e.** *(otherwise)* si no

elsewhere [elsˈweə(r)] *adv* en otra parte

elucidate [ɪˈluːsɪdeɪt] *vt* aclarar

elude [ɪˈluːd] *vt* (**a**) *(escape)* eludir; **his name eludes me** no consigo acordarme de su nombre (**b**) *(avoid)* esquivar

elusive [ɪˈluːsɪv] *adj* esquivo(a); *(evasive)* evasivo(a)

emaciated [ɪˈmeɪsɪeɪtɪd] *adj* demacrado(a)

e-mail [ˈiːmeɪl] *Comput* **1** *n (system)* correo *m* electrónico; *(message)* (mensaje *m* por) correo electrónico; **e. address** dirección *f* de correo electrónico
2 *vt (person)* enviar un correo electrónico a; *(file)* enviar por correo electrónico

emanate [ˈeməneɪt] *vi* provenir (**from** de)

emancipate [ɪˈmænsɪpeɪt] *vt* emancipar

emancipation [ɪmænsɪˈpeɪʃən] *n* emancipación *f*

embankment [ɪmˈbæŋkmənt] *n* (**a**) *(made of earth)* terraplén *m* (**b**) *(of river)* dique *m*

embargo [emˈbɑːgəʊ] *n (pl embargoes)* embargo *m*

embark [emˈbɑːk] **1** *vt (merchandise)* embarcar
2 *vi* embarcar, embarcarse; *Fig* **to e. upon** emprender; *(sth difficult)* embarcarse en

embarkation [embɑːˈkeɪʃən] *n* embarque *m*

embarrass [ɪmˈbærəs] *vt* avergonzar, *Andes, CAm, Carib, Méx* apenar

embarrassed [ɪmˈbærəst] *adj* avergonzado(a), *Andes, CAm, Carib, Méx* apenado(a)

> 🖉 Note that the Spanish word **embarazado** is a false friend and is never a translation for the English word **embarrassed**. In Spanish, **embarazado** means "pregnant".

embarrassing [ɪmˈbærəsɪŋ] *adj* embarazoso(a), *Andes, CAm, Carib, Méx* penoso(a)

embarrassment [ɪmˈbærəsmənt] *n* vergüenza *f*, *Andes, CAm, Carib, Méx* pena *f*

embassy [ˈembəsɪ] *n* embajada *f*

embed [ɪm'bed] vt (jewels) incrustar; Fig grabar

embellish [ɪm'belɪʃ] vt embellecer; (story) exagerar

ember ['embə(r)] n ascua f, rescoldo m

embezzle [ɪm'bezəl] vt desfalcar, malversar

embezzlement [ɪm'bezəlmənt] n malversación f

embitter [ɪm'bɪtə(r)] vt amargar

embittered [ɪm'bɪtəd] adj amargado(a), resentido(a)

emblem ['embləm] n emblema m

embody [ɪm'bɒdɪ] vt (a) (include) abarcar (b) (personify) encarnar

embossed [ɪm'bɒst] adj en relieve

embrace [ɪm'breɪs] 1 vt (a) abrazar (b) (accept) adoptar (c) (include) abarcar
  2 vi abrazarse
  3 n abrazo m

embroider [ɪm'brɔɪdə(r)] vt (a) Sewing bordar (b) Fig (story, truth) adornar, embellecer

embroidery [ɪm'brɔɪdərɪ] n bordado m

embryo ['embrɪəʊ] n embrión m

emerald ['emərəld] n esmeralda f

emerge [ɪ'mɜːdʒ] vi salir; (problem) surgir; **it emerged that ...** resultó que ...

emergence [ɪ'mɜːdʒəns] n aparición f

emergency [ɪ'mɜːdʒənsɪ] n emergencia f; Med urgencia f; **in an e.** en caso de emergencia; **e. exit** salida f de emergencia; **e. landing** aterrizaje forzoso; US **e. measures** medidas fpl de urgencia; US **e. room** sala f de urgencias; Aut **e. stop** frenazo m en seco; Pol **state of e.** estado m de excepción

emery ['emərɪ] **n e. board** lima f de uñas

emigrant ['emɪgrənt] n emigrante mf

emigrate ['emɪgreɪt] vi emigrar

emigration [emɪ'greɪʃən] n emigración f

eminent ['emɪnənt] adj eminente

emission [ɪ'mɪʃən] n emisión f

emit [ɪ'mɪt] vt (signals) emitir; (smells) despedir; (sound) producir

emotion [ɪ'məʊʃən] n emoción f

emotional [ɪ'məʊʃənəl] adj (a) emocional (b) (moving) conmovedor(a)

emotive [ɪ'məʊtɪv] adj emotivo(a)

emperor ['empərə(r)] n emperador m

emphasis ['emfəsɪs] n (pl **emphases** ['emfəsiːz]) énfasis m; **to place e. on sth** hacer hincapié en algo

emphasize ['emfəsaɪz] vt subrayar, hacer hincapié en; (insist) insistir; (highlight) hacer resaltar

emphatic [em'fætɪk] adj (forceful) enfático(a); (convinced) categórico(a)

emphatically [em'fætɪklɪ] adv categóricamente

empire ['empaɪə(r)] n imperio m

employ [ɪm'plɔɪ] vt emplear; (time) ocupar

employee [em'plɔɪiː, emplɔɪ'iː] n empleado(a) m,f

employer [ɪm'plɔɪə(r)] n patrón(ona) m,f

employment [ɪm'plɔɪmənt] n empleo m; **e. agency** agencia f de colocaciones; **full e.** pleno empleo

empower [ɪm'paʊə(r)] vt autorizar

empress ['emprɪs] n emperatriz f

emptiness ['emptɪnɪs] n vacío m

empty ['emptɪ] 1 adj (**emptier, emptiest**) vacío(a); **an e. house** una casa deshabitada; **e. promises** promesas fpl vanas
  2 vt vaciar
  3 vi (a) vaciarse (b) (river) desembocar (into en)
  4 npl **empties** envases vacíos

empty-handed [emptɪ'hændɪd] adj con las manos vacías

EMU [iːem'juː] n Fin (abbr **Economic and Monetary Union**) UEM f

emulate ['emjʊleɪt] vt emular

emulsion [ɪ'mʌlʃən] n emulsión f; **e. paint** pintura f mate

enable [ɪn'eɪbəl] vt permitir

enact [ɪ'nækt] vt (play) representar; (law) promulgar

enamel [ɪ'næməl] n esmalte m

enamoured, US **enamored** [ɪ'næməd] adj **to be e. of** estar enamorado(a) de; **I'm not greatly e. of the idea** no me entusiasma la idea

encase [ɪn'keɪs] vt **encased in** revestido de

enchant [ɪn'tʃɑːnt] vt encantar

enchanting [ɪn'tʃɑːntɪŋ] adj encantador(a)

encircle [ɪn'sɜːkəl] vt rodear

enclave ['enkleɪv] n enclave m

enclose [ɪn'kləʊz] vt (a) (surround) rodear (b) (fence in) cercar (c) (in envelope) adjuntar; **please find enclosed** le enviamos adjunto

enclosure [ɪn'kləʊʒə(r)] n (a) (fenced area) cercado m (b) (in envelope) documento adjunto (c) (of racecourse) recinto m

encompass [ɪn'kʌmpəs] vt abarcar

encore ['ɒŋkɔː(r)] 1 interj ¡otra!, ¡bis!
  2 n repetición f, bis m

encounter [ɪn'kaʊntə(r)] 1 n (meeting) encuentro m
  2 vt encontrar, encontrarse con; (problems) tropezar con

encourage [ɪn'kʌrɪdʒ] *vt* (**a**) *(person)* animar (**b**) *(tourism, trade)* fomentar

encouragement [ɪn'kʌrɪdʒmənt] *n* estímulo *m*

encroach [ɪn'krəʊtʃ] *vi* **to e. on** *(territory)* invadir; *(rights)* usurpar; *(time, freedom)* quitar

encrusted [ɪn'krʌstɪd] *adj* incrustado(a) (**with** de)

encumber [ɪn'kʌmbə(r)] *vt* estorbar; *(with debts)* gravar

encyclop(a)edia [ensaɪkləʊ'piːdɪə] *n* enciclopedia *f*

end [end] **1** *n* (**a**) *(of stick)* punta *f*; *(of street)* final *m*; *(of table)* extremo *m*; *Fig* **to make ends meet** llegar a final de mes; *Fig* **it makes my hair stand on e.** me pone el pelo de punta (**b**) *(conclusion)* fin *m*, final *m*; **in the e.** al final; **for hours on e.** hora tras hora; **no e. of** un sinfín de; **to bring an e. to sth** poner fin a algo; **to put an e. to** acabar con (**c**) *(aim)* objetivo *m*, fin *m*; **to no e.** en vano

  2 *vt* acabar, terminar

  3 *vi* acabarse, terminarse

▶ **end up** *vi* terminar; **it ended up in the dustbin** fue a parar al cubo de la basura; **to e. up doing sth** terminar por hacer algo

endanger [ɪn'deɪndʒə(r)] *vt* poner en peligro

endangered [ɪn'deɪndʒəd] *adj* en peligro

endearing [ɪn'dɪərɪŋ] *adj* simpático(a)

endeavour, *US* **endeavor** [ɪn'devə(r)] **1** *n* esfuerzo *m*

  2 *vt* intentar, procurar

ending ['endɪŋ] *n* final *m*

endive ['endaɪv] *n Bot* (**a**) *(curly)* escarola *f* (**b**) *esp US (chicory)* endibia *f*

endless ['endlɪs] *adj* interminable

endorse [ɪn'dɔːs] *vt* (**a**) *Fin* endosar (**b**) *(approve)* aprobar; *(support)* apoyar

endorsement [ɪn'dɔːsmənt] *n* (**a**) *Fin* endoso *m* (**b**) *Aut* nota *f* de sanción (**c**) *(approval)* aprobación *f*

endow [ɪn'daʊ] *vt* dotar; **to be endowed with** estar dotado(a) de

endurance [ɪn'djʊərəns] *n* resistencia *f*

endure [ɪn'djʊə(r)] **1** *vt* *(bear)* aguantar, soportar

  2 *vi* perdurar

enemy ['enəmɪ] *adj & n* enemigo(a) *(m,f)*

energetic [enə'dʒetɪk] *adj* enérgico(a)

energy ['enədʒɪ] *n* energía *f*

enforce [ɪn'fɔːs] *vt* *(law)* hacer cumplir

enforcement [ɪn'fɔːsmənt] *n* aplicación *f*

engage [ɪn'geɪdʒ] *vt* (**a**) *(hire)* contratar (**b**) *(attention)* llamar (**c**) *(in conversation)* entablar (**d**) *Tech* engranar; *Aut* **to e. the clutch** pisar el embrague

engaged [ɪn'geɪdʒd] *adj* (**a**) *(betrothed)* prometido(a); **to get e.** prometerse (**b**) *(busy)* ocupado(a); *Br Tel* **it's e.** está comunicando

engagement [ɪn'geɪdʒmənt] *n* (**a**) *(betrothal)* petición *f* de mano; *(period)* noviazgo *m*; **e. ring** anillo *m* de compromiso (**b**) *(appointment)* cita *f* (**c**) *Mil* combate *m*

engaging [ɪn'geɪdʒɪŋ] *adj* simpático(a), agradable

engender [ɪn'dʒendə(r)] *vt* engendrar

engine ['endʒɪn] *n* motor *m*; *Rail* locomotora *f*; **e. room** sala *f* de máquinas; **e. driver** maquinista *mf*

engineer [endʒɪ'nɪə(r)] **1** *n* (**a**) ingeniero(a) *m,f*; **civil e.** ingeniero de caminos (**b**) *US Rail* maquinista *mf*

  2 *vt Fig (contrive)* maquinar

engineering [endʒɪ'nɪərɪŋ] *n* ingeniería *f*; **electrical e.** electrotecnia *f*; **civil e.** ingeniería civil

England ['ɪŋglənd] *n* Inglaterra *f*

English ['ɪŋglɪʃ] **1** *adj* inglés(esa)

  2 *n* (**a**) *(language)* inglés *m* (**b**) *pl* **the E.** los ingleses

Englishman ['ɪŋglɪʃmən] *n* inglés *m*

English-speaking ['ɪŋglɪʃspiːkɪŋ] *adj* de habla inglesa

Englishwoman ['ɪŋglɪʃwʊmən] *n* inglesa *f*

engraving [ɪn'greɪvɪŋ] *n* grabado *m*

engrossed [ɪn'grəʊst] *adj* absorto(a) (**in** en)

engulf [ɪn'gʌlf] *vt* tragarse

enhance [ɪn'hɑːns] *vt* *(beauty)* realzar; *(power, chances)* aumentar

enigma [ɪ'nɪgmə] *n* enigma *m*

enjoy [ɪn'dʒɔɪ] *vt* (**a**) disfrutar de; **to e. oneself** pasarlo bien (**b**) *(benefit from)* gozar de

enjoyable [ɪn'dʒɔɪəbəl] *adj* agradable; *(amusing)* divertido(a)

enjoyment [ɪn'dʒɔɪmənt] *n* placer *m*, gusto *m*

enlarge [ɪn'lɑːdʒ] **1** *vt* extender, ampliar; *Phot* ampliar

  2 *vi* **to e. upon a subject** extenderse sobre un tema

enlargement [ɪn'lɑːdʒmənt] *n Phot* ampliación *f*

enlighten [ɪn'laɪtən] *vt* iluminar

enlightened [ɪn'laɪtənd] *adj* (**a**) *(learned)* culto(a); *(informed)* bien informado(a) (**b**) *Hist* ilustrado(a)

enlightenment [ɪn'laɪtənmənt] *n* the Age of E. el Siglo de las Luces

enlist [ɪn'lɪst] **1** *vt Mil* reclutar; **to e. sb's help** conseguir ayuda de algn
 2 *vi Mil* alistarse

enmity ['enmɪtɪ] *n* enemistad *f*, hostilidad *f*

enormous [ɪ'nɔːməs] *adj* enorme

enormously [ɪ'nɔːməslɪ] *adv* enormemente; **I enjoyed myself e.** lo pasé genial

enough [ɪ'nʌf] **1** *adj* bastante, suficiente; **e. books** bastantes libros; **e. money** bastante dinero; **have we got e. petrol?** ¿tenemos suficiente gasolina?
 2 *adv* bastante; **oddly e. ...** lo curioso es que ...; **sure e.** en efecto
 3 *pron* lo bastante, lo suficiente; **e. to live on** lo suficiente para vivir; **it isn't e.** no basta; **more than e.** más que suficiente; **Fam e. is e.!** ¡ya está!; **Fam I've had e.!** ¡estoy harto!

enquire [ɪn'kwaɪə(r)] *vi* preguntar

enquiry [ɪn'kwaɪərɪ] *n* **(a)** *(question)* pregunta *f*; **to make an e.** preguntar; **enquiries** información *f* **(b)** *(investigation)* investigación *f*

enrage [ɪn'reɪdʒ] *vt* enfurecer

enrich [ɪn'rɪtʃ] *vt* enriquecer

enrol, *US* **enroll** [ɪn'rəʊl] **1** *vt* matricular, inscribir
 2 *vi* matricularse, inscribirse

🖉 Note that the Spanish verb **enrollar** is a false friend and is never a translation for the English verb to **enrol**. In Spanish, **enrollar** means "to roll up".

---

enrolment [ɪn'rəʊlmənt] *n* matrícula *f*

en route [ɒn'ruːt] *adv* en or por el camino

ensign ['ensaɪn] *n* **(a)** *(flag)* bandera *f*; *Naut* pabellón *m* **(b)** *US (naval officer)* alférez *m* de fragata

enslave [ɪn'sleɪv] *vt* esclavizar

ensue [ɪn'sjuː] *vi* **(a)** *(follow)* seguir **(b)** *(result)* resultar **(from** de)

ensure [ɪn'ʃʊə(r)] *vt* asegurar

entail [ɪn'teɪl] *vt (involve)* suponer

entangle [ɪn'tæŋgəl] *vt* enredar

enter ['entə(r)] **1** *vt* **(a)** *(go into)* entrar en; *Fig (join)* ingresar en **(b)** *(write down)* apuntar, anotar **(c)** **to e. one's name for a course** *(register)* matricularse en un curso **(d)** *Comput* dar entrada a
 2 *vi* entrar
 ▸ **enter into** *vt insep* **(a)** *(agreement)* firmar; *(negotiations)* iniciar; *(bargain)* cerrar **(b)** *(relations)* establecer; *(conversation)* entablar

enterprise ['entəpraɪz] *n* empresa *f*; **free e.** libre empresa; **private e.** iniciativa privada; *(as a whole)* el sector privado; **public e.** el sector público

enterprising ['entəpraɪzɪŋ] *adj* emprendedor(a)

entertain [entə'teɪn] **1** *vt* **(a)** *(amuse)* divertir **(b)** *(consider)* considerar; **to e. an idea** abrigar una idea
 2 *vi* tener invitados

entertainer [entə'teɪnə(r)] *n* artista *mf*

entertaining [entə'teɪnɪŋ] *adj* divertido(a)

entertainment [entə'teɪnmənt] *n* **(a)** diversión *f* **(b)** *Th* espectáculo *m*

enthralling [ɪn'θrɔːlɪŋ] *adj* fascinante

enthuse [ɪn'θjuːz] *vi* entusiasmarse **(over** por)

enthusiasm [ɪn'θjuːzɪæzəm] *n* entusiasmo *m*

enthusiast [ɪn'θjuːzɪæst] *n* entusiasta *mf*

enthusiastic [ɪnθjuːzɪ'æstɪk] *adj* entusiasta; *(praise)* caluroso(a); **to be e. about sth** entusiasmarse por algo

entice [ɪn'taɪs] *vt* seducir, atraer

enticing [ɪn'taɪsɪŋ] *adj* atractivo(a), tentador(a)

entire [ɪn'taɪə(r)] *adj* entero(a), todo(a)

entirely [ɪn'taɪəlɪ] *adv* **(a)** *(completely)* totalmente **(b)** *(solely)* exclusivamente

entirety [ɪn'taɪərɪtɪ] *n* **in its e.** en su totalidad

entitle [ɪn'taɪtəl] *vt* **(a)** dar derecho a; **to be entitled to** tener derecho a **(b)** *(book etc)* titular

entity ['entɪtɪ] *n* entidad *f*

entourage [ɒntʊ'rɑːʒ] *n* séquito *m*

entrails ['entreɪlz] *npl* tripas *fpl*; *Fig* entrañas *fpl*

entrance¹ ['entrəns] *n* **(a)** entrada *f*; **e. fee** *(to museum etc)* entrada; *(to organization)* cuota *f* **(b)** *(admission)* ingreso *m*; **e. examination** examen *m* de ingreso

entrance² [ɪn'trɑːns] *vt* encantar

entrant ['entrənt] *n (in competition)* participante *mf*; *(applicant)* aspirante *mf*

entreat [ɪn'triːt] *vt Fml* suplicar, rogar

entrée ['ɒntreɪ] *n Br (first course)* entrada *f*, primer plato *m*; *US (main course)* plato principal

entrenched [ɪn'trentʃt] *adj* firmemente enraizado(a)

entrepreneur [ɒntrəprə'nɜː(r)] *n* empresario(a) *m,f*

entrust [ɪn'trʌst] *vt* encargar **(with** de); **to e. sth to sb** dejar algo al cuidado de algn

entry ['entrɪ] *n* **(a)** *(entrance)* entrada *f*;

no e. *(sign)* dirección prohibida (**b**) *(in competition)* participante *mf*

enumerate [ɪ'njuːməreɪt] *vt* enumerar

enunciate [ɪ'nʌnsɪeɪt] *vt (words)* articular; *(ideas)* formular

envelop [ɪn'veləp] *vt* envolver

envelope ['envələʊp] *n* sobre *m*

envious ['envɪəs] *adj* envidioso(a); **to feel e.** tener envidia

environment [ɪn'vaɪərənmənt] *n* medio *m* ambiente

environmental [ɪnvaɪərən'mentəl] *adj* medioambiental

environmentally [ɪnvaɪərən'mentəlɪ] *adv* ecológicamente; **e. friendly** ecológico(a), que no daña el medio ambiente

envisage [ɪn'vɪzɪdʒ] *vt (imagine)* imaginarse; *(foresee)* prever

envoy ['envɔɪ] *n* enviado(a) *m,f*

envy ['envɪ] **1** *n* envidia *f*
2 *vt* envidiar, tener envidia de

enzyme ['enzaɪm] *n* enzima *m*

ephemeral [ɪ'femərəl] *adj* efímero(a)

epic ['epɪk] **1** *n* epopeya *f*
2 *adj* épico(a)

epidemic [epɪ'demɪk] *n* epidemia *f; Fig (of crime etc)* ola *f*

epilepsy ['epɪlepsɪ] *n* epilepsia *f*

epilogue, *US* **epilog** ['epɪlɒg] *n* epílogo *m*

episode ['epɪsəʊd] *n* episodio *m*

epistle [ɪ'pɪsəl] *n* epístola *f*

epitaph ['epɪtɑːf] *n* epitafio *m*

epitome [ɪ'pɪtəmɪ] *n Fml* personificación *f*

epitomize [ɪ'pɪtəmaɪz] *vt Fml* personificar

epoch ['iːpɒk] *n* época *f*

equable ['ekwəbəl] *adj* (**a**) *(person)* ecuánime (**b**) *(climate)* uniforme

equal ['iːkwəl] **1** *adj* igual; **to be e. to the occasion** estar a la altura de las circunstancias; **e. pay** igualdad *f* de salarios
2 *n* igual *mf*; **to treat sb as an e.** tratar a algn de igual a igual
3 *vt* (**a**) *Math* equivaler (**b**) *(match)* igualar

equality [iː'kwɒlɪtɪ] *n* igualdad *f*

equalize ['iːkwəlaɪz] **1** *vi Ftb* empatar
2 *vt* igualar

equalizer ['iːkwəlaɪzə(r)] *n Ftb* gol *m* del empate; *(of sound)* ecualizador *m*

equally ['iːkwəlɪ] *adv* igualmente; **e. pretty** igual de bonito; **to share sth e.** dividir algo en partes iguales

equanimity [ekwə'nɪmɪtɪ] *n* ecuanimidad *f*

equate [ɪ'kweɪt] *vt* equiparar, comparar (**to** con)

equation [ɪ'kweɪʒən, ɪ'kweɪʃən] *n Math* ecuación *f*

equator [ɪ'kweɪtə(r)] *n* ecuador *m*

equatorial [ekwə'tɔːrɪəl] *adj* ecuatorial

equestrian [ɪ'kwestrɪən] *adj* ecuestre

equilibrium [iːkwɪ'lɪbrɪəm] *n* equilibrio *m*

equinox ['iːkwɪnɒks] *n* equinoccio *m*

equip [ɪ'kwɪp] *vt (with tools, machines)* equipar; *(with food)* proveer

equipment [ɪ'kwɪpmənt] *n (materials)* equipo *m*; **office e.** material *m* de oficina

equipped [ɪ'kwɪpt] *adj (with tools, machines)* equipado(a); *(with skills)* dotado(a)

equitable ['ekwɪtəbəl] *adj* equitativo(a)

equities ['ekwɪtɪz] *npl* acciones ordinarias

equivalent [ɪ'kwɪvələnt] *adj & n* equivalente *(m)*; **to be e. to** equivaler a, ser equivalente a

equivocal [ɪ'kwɪvəkəl] *adj* equívoco(a)

era ['ɪərə] *n* era *f*

eradicate [ɪ'rædɪkeɪt] *vt* erradicar

erase [ɪ'reɪz] *vt* borrar

eraser [*Br* ɪ'reɪzə(r), *US* ɪ'reɪsər] *n* goma *f* de borrar

erect [ɪ'rekt] **1** *adj* (**a**) *(upright)* erguido(a) (**b**) *(penis)* erecto(a)
2 *vt (monument)* levantar, eregir

erection [ɪ'rekʃən] *n* (**a**) *(of building)* construcción *f* (**b**) *(penis)* erección *f*

ermine ['ɜːmɪn] *n* armiño *m*

erode [ɪ'rəʊd] *vt* (**a**) *(rock, soil)* erosionar (**b**) *(metal)* corroer, desgastar; *Fig (power, confidence)* hacer perder

erosion [ɪ'rəʊʒən] *n Geol* erosión *f*

erotic [ɪ'rɒtɪk] *adj* erótico(a)

err [ɜː(r)] *vi* errar; **to e. on the side of caution** pecar de prudente

errand ['erənd] *n* recado *m*; **e. boy** recadero *m*

erratic [ɪ'rætɪk] *adj (performance, behaviour)* irregular; *(weather)* muy variable; *(person)* caprichoso(a)

erroneous [ɪ'rəʊnɪəs] *adj* erróneo(a)

error ['erə(r)] *n* error *m*, equivocación *f*

erupt [ɪ'rʌpt] *vi* (**a**) *(volcano)* entrar en erupción; *(violence)* estallar (**b**) **his skin erupted in a rash** le salió una erupción

eruption [ɪ'rʌpʃən] *n* erupción *f*

escalate ['eskəleɪt] *vi (war)* intensificarse; *(prices)* aumentar; *(change)* convertirse (**into** en)

escalation [eskə'leɪʃən] *n (of war)* intensificación *f*, escalada *f*; *(of prices)* subida *f*

escalator ['eskəleɪtə(r)] *n* escalera mecánica

> ♪ Note that the Spanish word **escalador** is a false friend and is never a translation for the English word **escalator**. In Spanish, **escalador** means "climber, mountaineer".

escalope ['eskɒlɒp] *n* escalope *m*
escapade ['eskəpeɪd] *n* aventura *f*

> ♪ Note that the Spanish word **escapada** is a false friend and is never a translation for the English word **escapade**. In Spanish, **escapada** means both "escape" and "quick trip".

escape [ɪ'skeɪp] **1** *n* huída *f*, fuga *f*; *(of gas)* escape *m*; **e. route** vía *f* de escape
  2 *vi* escaparse
  3 *vt* (**a**) *(avoid)* evitar, huir de; **to e. punishment** librarse del castigo (**b**) *Fig* **his name escapes me** no recuerdo su nombre
escapism [ɪ'skeɪpɪzəm] *n* evasión *f*
escort 1 *n* ['eskɔːt] (**a**) *(companion)* acompañante *mf* (**b**) *Mil* escolta *f*
  2 *vt* [ɪ'skɔːt] (**a**) *(accompany)* acompañar (**b**) *(protect)* escoltar
Eskimo ['eskɪməʊ] *adj & n* esquimal *(mf)*
esoteric [esəʊ'terɪk] *adj* esotérico(a)
especial [ɪ'speʃəl] *adj* especial
especially [ɪ'speʃəlɪ] *adv* especialmente, sobre todo
espionage ['espɪənɑːʒ] *n* espionaje *m*
esplanade [esplə'neɪd] *n* paseo marítimo
espouse [ɪ'spaʊz] *vt Fml (cause)* abrazar, adoptar
espresso [e'spresəʊ] *n* **e. (coffee)** café *m* exprés
esquire [ɪ'skwaɪə(r)] *n Br* señor *m*; **Timothy Whiteman E.** Sr. Don Timothy Whiteman
essay ['eseɪ] *n Educ* redacción *f*
essence ['esəns] *n* esencia *f*; **in e.** esencialmente
essential [ɪ'senʃəl] **1** *adj* esencial, imprescindible
  2 *n* necesidad básica; **the essentials** lo fundamental
essentially [ɪ'senʃəlɪ] *adv* esencialmente
establish [ɪ'stæblɪʃ] *vt* (**a**) *(found)* establecer; *(business)* montar (**b**) *Jur* **to e. a fact** probar un hecho; **to e. the truth** demostrar la verdad
established [ɪ'stæblɪʃt] *adj (person)* establecido(a); *(fact)* conocido(a)
establishment [ɪ'stæblɪʃmənt] *n* establecimiento *m*; **the E.** el sistema
estate [ɪ'steɪt] *n* (**a**) *(land)* finca *f*; *Br* **e.**

agent agente *mf* inmobiliario(a); *Br* **e. car** coche *m* modelo familiar (**b**) *(housing)* **e. zone** urbanizada (**c**) *(property)* bienes *mpl* (**d**) *(inheritance)* herencia *f*
esteem [ɪ'stiːm] **1** *n* **to hold sb in great e.** apreciar mucho a algn
  2 *vt* estimar
esthetic [es'θetɪk] *adj US* estético(a)
estimate 1 *n* ['estɪmɪt] *(calculation)* cálculo *m*; *(likely cost of work)* presupuesto *m*; **rough e.** cálculo aproximado
  2 *vt* ['estɪmeɪt] calcular; *Fig* pensar, creer
estimation [estɪ'meɪʃən] *n* (**a**) *(opinion)* juicio *m*, opinión *f* (**b**) *(esteem)* estima *f*
Estonia [e'stəʊnɪə] *n* Estonia
Estonian [e'stəʊnɪən] **1** *adj* estonio(a)
  2 *n* (**a**) *(person)* estonio(a) *m,f* (**b**) *(language)* estonio *m*
estrange [ɪ'streɪndʒ] *vt* **to become estranged (from)** alejarse (de)
Estremadura [estreɪmə'dʊrə] *n* Extremadura
estuary ['estjʊərɪ] *n* estuario *m*
etching ['etʃɪŋ] *n* aguafuerte *m*
eternal [ɪ'tɜːnəl] *adj* eterno(a), incesante; **e. triangle** triángulo amoroso
eternity [ɪ'tɜːnɪtɪ] *n* eternidad *f*
ether ['iːθə(r)] *n* éter *m*
ethereal [ɪ'θɪərɪəl] *adj* etéreo(a)
ethical ['eθɪkəl] *adj* ético(a)
ethics ['eθɪks] *n* ética *f*
Ethiopia [iːθɪ'əʊpɪə] *n* Etiopía
ethnic ['eθnɪk] *adj* étnico(a)
ethos ['iːθɒs] *n* carácter distintivo
etiquette ['etɪket] *n* protocolo *m*, etiqueta *f*
etymology [etɪ'mɒlədʒɪ] *n* etimología *f*
EU [iː'juː] *n (abbr* **European Union)** UE *f*
eucalyptus [juːkə'lɪptəs] *n* eucalipto *m*
euphemism ['juːfɪmɪzəm] *n* eufemismo *m*
euphoria [juː'fɔːrɪə] *n* euforia *f*
euro ['jʊərəʊ] *n (pl* **euros)** *(European currency)* euro *m*
Eurocheque ['jʊərəʊtʃek] *n* eurocheque *m*
Eurocrat ['jʊərəʊkræt] *n* eurócrata *mf*
Euro-MP ['jʊərəʊempiː] *n* eurodiputado(a) *m,f*
Europe ['jʊərəp] *n* Europa
European [jʊərə'piːən] *adj & n* europeo(a) *(m,f)*; **E. Economic Community** Comunidad Económica Europea
Eurosceptic ['jʊərəʊskeptɪk] *n Br* euroescéptico(a) *m,f*
euthanasia [juːθə'neɪzɪə] *n* eutanasia *f*
evacuate [ɪ'vækjʊeɪt] *vt* evacuar

evacuation [ɪvækjʊ'eɪʃən] n evacuación f

evade [ɪ'veɪd] vt evadir

evaluate [ɪ'væljʊeɪt] vt evaluar

evaluation [ɪvæljʊ'eɪʃən] n evaluación f

evangelical [iːvæn'dʒelɪkəl] adj evangélico(a)

evangelist [ɪ'vændʒɪlɪst] n evangelista mf

evaporate [ɪ'væpəreɪt] **1** vt evaporar; **evaporated milk** leche condensada sin endulzar
2 vi evaporarse; Fig desvanecerse

evasion [ɪ'veɪʒən] n (a) evasión f (b) (evasive answer) evasiva f

evasive [ɪ'veɪsɪv] adj evasivo(a)

eve [iːv] n víspera f; **on the e. of** en vísperas de

even ['iːvən] **1** adj (a) (smooth) liso(a); (level) llano(a)
(b) (regular) uniforme
(c) (equally balanced) igual; Sport **to be e. if** empatados(as); **to get e. with sb** desquitarse con algn
(d) (number) par
(e) (at the same level) a nivel
(f) (quantity) exacto(a)
2 adv (a) incluso, hasta, aun; **e. now** incluso ahora; **e. so** aun así; **e. the children knew** hasta los niños lo sabían
(b) (negative) ni siquiera; **she can't e. write her name** ni siquiera sabe escribir su nombre; **without e. speaking** sin hablar siquiera
(c) (before comparative) aun, todavía; **e. worse** aun peor
(d) **e. as** mientras; **e. if** incluso si; **e. though** aunque
3 vt igualar

evening ['iːvnɪŋ] n (a) (early) tarde f; (late) noche f; **in the e.** por la tarde; **tomorrow e.** mañana por la tarde; **e. class** clase nocturna; **e. dress** (for man) traje m de etiqueta; (for woman) traje de noche; **e. paper** periódico vespertino (b) (greeting) **good e.!** (early) ¡buenas tardes!; (late) ¡buenas noches!

event [ɪ'vent] n (a) (happening) suceso m, acontecimiento m (b) (case) caso m; **at all events** en todo caso; **in the e. of fire** en caso de incendio (c) Sport prueba f

eventful [ɪ'ventfʊl] adj **an e. day** (busy) un día agitado; (memorable) un día memorable

eventual [ɪ'ventʃʊəl] adj (ultimate) final; (resulting) consiguiente

📝 Note that the Spanish word **eventual** is a false friend and is never a translation for the English word **eventual**. In Spanish, **eventual** means both "possible" and "temporary".

eventuality [ɪventʃʊ'ælɪtɪ] n eventualidad f

eventually [ɪ'ventʃʊəlɪ] adv finalmente

📝 Note that the Spanish word **eventualmente** is a false friend and is never a translation for the English word **eventually**. In Spanish, **eventualmente** means both "by chance" and "possibly".

ever ['evə(r)] adv (a) nunca, jamás; **stronger than e.** más fuerte que nunca (b) (interrogative) alguna vez; **have you e. been there?** ¿has estado allí alguna vez? (c) (always) siempre; **for e.** para siempre; **for e. and e.** para siempre jamás (d) (emphasis) **how e. did you manage it?** ¿cómo diablos lo conseguiste?; **why e. not?** ¿por qué no?; Fam **e. so expensive** tan carísimo; **e. such a lot of money** tantísimo dinero; **thank you e. so much** muchísimas gracias

evergreen ['evəgriːn] **1** adj de hoja perenne
2 n árbol m/planta f de hoja perenne

everlasting [evə'lɑːstɪŋ] adj eterno(a)

evermore [evə'mɔː(r)] adv **for e.** para siempre jamás

every ['evrɪ] adj (a) (each) cada; **e. now and then** de vez en cuando; **e. day** todos los días; **e. other day** cada dos días; **e. one of you** todos(as) vosotros(as); **e. citizen** todo ciudadano (b) **you had e. right to be angry** tenías toda la razón para estar enfadado

everybody ['evrɪbɒdɪ] pron todo el mundo, todos(as)

everyday ['evrɪdeɪ] adj diario(a), de todos los días; **an e. occurrence** un suceso cotidiano

everyone ['evrɪwʌn] pron todo el mundo, todos(as)

everyplace ['evrɪpleɪs] adv US = everywhere

everything ['evrɪθɪŋ] pron todo; **he eats e.** come de todo; **she means e. to me** ella lo es todo para mí

everywhere ['evrɪweə(r)] adv en todas partes, por todas partes

evict [ɪ'vɪkt] vt desahuciar

evidence ['evɪdəns] n (a) (proof) evidencia f (b) Jur testimonio m; **to give e.** prestar declaración (c) (sign) indicio m, señal f; **to be in e.** dejarse notar

evident ['evɪdənt] *adj* evidente, manifiesto(a)

evidently ['evɪdəntlɪ] *adv* evidentemente, al parecer

evil ['iːvəl] **1** *adj (wicked)* malo(a), malvado(a); *(harmful)* nocivo(a); *(unfortunate)* aciago(a)

2 *n* mal *m*

evocative [ɪ'vɒkətɪv] *adj* evocador(a)

evoke [ɪ'vəʊk] *vt* evocar

evolution [iːvə'luːʃən] *n* evolución f; *Biol* desarrollo *m*

evolve [ɪ'vɒlv] **1** *vi (species)* evolucionar; *(ideas)* desarrollarse

2 *vt* desarrollar

ewe [juː] *n* oveja f

ex [eks] *n* **her ex** su ex marido; **his ex** su ex mujer

ex- [eks] *pref* ex, antiguo(a); **ex-minister** ex ministro *m*

exacerbate [ɪg'zæsəbeɪt] *vt* exacerbar

exact [ɪg'zækt] **1** *adj (accurate)* exacto(a); *(definition)* preciso(a); **this e. spot** ese mismo lugar

2 *vt* exigir

exacting [ɪg'zæktɪŋ] *adj* exigente

exactly [ɪg'zæktlɪ] *adv* exactamente; precisamente; **e.!** ¡exacto!

exaggerate [ɪg'zædʒəreɪt] *vi & vt* exagerar

exaggeration [ɪgzædʒə'reɪʃən] *n* exageración f

exalt [ɪg'zɔːlt] *vt Fml* exaltar

exam [ɪg'zæm] *n Fam* examen *m*

examination [ɪgzæmɪ'neɪʃən] *n* (a) *Educ* examen *m*; **to sit an e.** hacer un examen (b) *Med* reconocimiento *m* (c) *Jur* interrogatorio *m*

examine [ɪg'zæmɪn] *vt Educ* examinar; *(customs)* registrar; *Med* hacer un reconocimiento médico a; *Jur* interrogar

examiner [ɪg'zæmɪnə(r)] *n* examinador(a) *m,f*

example [ɪg'zɑːmpəl] *n* ejemplo *m*; *(specimen)* ejemplar *m*; **for e.** por ejemplo

exasperate [ɪg'zɑːspəreɪt] *vt* exasperar

exasperation [ɪgzɑːspə'reɪʃən] *n* exasperación f

excavate ['ekskəveɪt] *vt* excavar

excavation [ekskə'veɪʃən] *n* excavación f

exceed [ek'siːd] *vt* exceder, sobrepasar

exceedingly [ek'siːdɪŋlɪ] *adv* extremadamente, sumamente

excel [ɪk'sel] **1** *vi* sobresalir

2 *vt* superar

excellency ['eksələnsɪ] *n* **His E.** Su Excelencia

excellent ['eksələnt] *adj* excelente

except [ɪk'sept] **1** *prep* excepto, salvo; **e. for the little ones** excepto los pequeños; **e. that ...** salvo que ...

2 *vt* exceptuar

exception [ɪk'sepʃən] *n* (a) excepción f; **with the e. of** a excepción de; **without e.** sin excepción (b) *(objection)* objeción f; **to take e. to sth** ofenderse por algo

exceptional [ɪk'sepʃənəl] *adj* excepcional

excerpt ['eksɜːpt] *n* extracto *m*

excess **1** *n* [ɪk'ses] exceso *m*

2 *adj* ['ekses] excedente; **e. baggage** exceso *m* de equipaje; **e. fare** suplemento *m*

excessive [ɪk'sesɪv] *adj* excesivo(a)

excessively [ɪk'sesɪvlɪ] *adv* excesivamente, en exceso

exchange [ɪks'tʃeɪndʒ] **1** *n* (a) cambio *m*; **e. of ideas** intercambio *m* de ideas; **in e. for** a cambio de (b) *Fin* **e. rate** tipo *m* de cambio (c) **(telephone) e.** central telefónica

2 *vt* (a) intercambiar; **to e. blows** golpearse (b) *(prisoners)* canjear

exchequer [ɪks'tʃekə(r)] *n Br* **the E.** Hacienda f; **Chancellor of the E.** Ministro *m* de Hacienda

excise ['eksaɪz] *n* impuesto *m* sobre el consumo; **e. duty** derechos *mpl* de aduana

excitable [ɪk'saɪtəbəl] *adj* excitable

excite [ɪk'saɪt] *vt (stimulate)* excitar; *(move)* emocionar; *(enthuse)* entusiasmar; *(arouse)* provocar

excitement [ɪk'saɪtmənt] *n (stimulation)* excitación f; *(emotion)* emoción f; *(commotion)* agitación f

exciting [ɪk'saɪtɪŋ] *adj* apasionante, emocionante

exclaim [ɪk'skleɪm] **1** *vi* exclamar

2 *vt* gritar

exclamation [eksklə'meɪʃən] *n* exclamación f; **e.** *Br* **mark** *or US* **point** signo *m* de admiración

exclude [ɪk'skluːd] *vt* excluir; *(from club)* no admitir

excluding [ɪk'skluːdɪŋ] *prep* excepto

exclusion [ɪk'skluːʒən] *n* exclusión f

exclusive [ɪk'skluːsɪv] **1** *adj* exclusivo(a); *(neighbourhood)* selecto(a); *(club)* cerrado(a)

2 *n Press* exclusiva f

exclusively [ɪk'skluːsɪvlɪ] *adv* exclusivamente

excommunicate [ekskə'mjuːnɪkeɪt] *vt* excomulgar

excrement ['ekskrɪmənt] n excremento m

excruciating [ɪk'skruːʃɪeɪtɪŋ] adj insoportable

excruciatingly [ɪk'skruːʃɪeɪtɪŋlɪ] adv horriblemente

excursion [ɪk'skɜːʃən] n excursión f

excusable [ɪk'skjuːzəbəl] adj perdonable

excuse 1 vt [ɪk'skjuːz] (**a**) perdonar, disculpar; **e. me!** (to attract attention) ¡perdón!, ¡oiga (por favor)!; (when trying to get past) con permiso; **may I be excused for a moment?** ¿puedo salir un momento? (**b**) (exempt) dispensar (**c**) (justify) justificar

2 n [ɪk'skjuːs] excusa f; **to make an e.** dar excusas

ex-directory [eksdɪ'rektərɪ] adj Br Tel = que no se encuentra en la guía telefónica

execute ['eksɪkjuːt] vt (**a**) (order) cumplir; (task) realizar (**b**) Jur cumplir (**c**) (person) ejecutar

execution [eksɪ'kjuːʃən] n (**a**) (of order) cumplimiento m; (of task) realización f (**b**) Jur cumplimiento m (**c**) (of person) ejecución f

executioner [eksɪ'kjuːʃənə(r)] n verdugo m

executive [ɪg'zekjʊtɪv] 1 adj ejecutivo(a) 2 n ejecutivo(a) m,f

executor [ɪg'zekjʊtə(r)] n albacea m

exemplary [ɪg'zemplərɪ] adj ejemplar

exemplify [ɪg'zemplɪfaɪ] vt ejemplificar

exempt [ɪg'zempt] 1 vt eximir (**from** de) 2 adj exento(a); **e. from tax** libre de impuesto

exemption [ɪg'zempʃən] n exención f

exercise ['eksəsaɪz] 1 n ejercicio m; **e. book** cuaderno m

2 vt (**a**) (rights, duties) ejercer (**b**) (dog) sacar de paseo

3 vi hacer ejercicio

exert [ɪg'zɜːt] vt (influence) ejercer; **to e. oneself** esforzarse

exertion [ɪg'zɜːʃən] n esfuerzo m

exhale [eks'heɪl] 1 vt (breathe) exhalar 2 vi espirar

exhaust [ɪg'zɔːst] 1 vt agotar

2 n (gas) gases mpl de combustión; **e. pipe** tubo m de escape

exhausted [ɪg'zɔːstɪd] adj agotado(a)

exhaustion [ɪg'zɔːstʃən] n agotamiento m

exhaustive [ɪg'zɔːstɪv] adj exhaustivo(a)

exhibit [ɪg'zɪbɪt] 1 n Art objeto expuesto; Jur prueba f instrumental

2 vt Art exponer; (surprise etc) mostrar

exhibition [eksɪ'bɪʃən] n exposición f

exhibitionist [eksɪ'bɪʃənɪst] adj & n exhibicionista (mf)

exhilarating [ɪg'zɪləreɪtɪŋ] adj estimulante

exhilaration [ɪgzɪlə'reɪʃən] n regocijo m

exhume [eks'hjuːm] vt exhumar

exile ['eksaɪl] 1 n (**a**) (banishment) exilio m (**b**) (person) exiliado(a) m,f

2 vt exiliar

exist [ɪg'zɪst] vi existir; (have little money) malvivir

existence [ɪg'zɪstəns] n existencia f

existing [ɪg'zɪstɪŋ] adj existente, actual

exit ['eksɪt] 1 n (**a**) salida f (**b**) Th mutis m 2 vi Th hacer mutis

> ♬ Note that the Spanish word **éxito** is a false friend and is never a translation for the English word **exit**. In Spanish, **éxito** means "success".

exodus ['eksədəs] n éxodo m

exonerate [ɪg'zɒnəreɪt] vt Fml exonerar (**from** de)

exorbitant [ɪg'zɔːbɪtənt] adj exorbitante, desorbitado(a)

exotic [ɪg'zɒtɪk] adj exótico(a)

expand [ɪk'spænd] 1 vt (enlarge) ampliar; (gas, metal) dilatar

2 vi (grow) ampliarse; (metal) dilatarse; (become more friendly) abrirse

▸ **expand on** vt insep ampliar

expanse [ɪk'spæns] n extensión f

expansion [ɪk'spænʃən] n (in size) expansión f; (of gas, metal) dilatación f

expatriate 1 adj & n [eks'pætrɪɪt] expatriado(a) (m,f)

2 vt [eks'pætrɪeɪt] expatriar

expect [ɪk'spekt] 1 vt (**a**) (anticipate) esperar; **I half-expected that to happen** suponía que iba a ocurrir (**b**) (demand) contar con (**c**) (suppose) suponer

2 vi Fam **to be expecting** estar embarazada

expectancy [ɪk'spektənsɪ] n expectación f

expectant [ɪk'spektənt] adj ilusionado(a); **e. mother** mujer embarazada

expectation [ekspek'teɪʃən] n esperanza f; **contrary to e.** contrariamente a lo que se esperaba

expedient [ɪk'spiːdɪənt] 1 adj conveniente, oportuno(a)

2 n expediente m, recurso m

expedition [ekspɪ'dɪʃən] n expedición f

expel [ɪk'spel] vt expulsar

expend [ɪk'spend] vt gastar

expendable [ɪk'spendəbəl] adj prescindible

expenditure [ɪk'spendɪtʃə(r)] *n* desembolso *m*

expense [ɪk'spens] *n* gasto *m*; **all expenses paid** con todos los gastos pagados; **to spare no e.** no escatimar gastos; *Fig* **at the e. of** a costa de; **e. account** cuenta *f* de gastos de representación

expensive [ɪk'spensɪv] *adj* caro(a), costoso(a)

experience [ɪk'spɪərɪəns] **1** *n* experiencia *f*

2 *vt* (*sensation*) experimentar; (*difficulty, loss*) sufrir

experienced [ɪk'spɪərɪənst] *adj* experimentado(a)

experiment [ɪk'sperɪmənt] **1** *n* experimento *m*

2 *vi* experimentar, hacer experimentos (**on** *or* **with** con)

experimental [ɪksperɪ'mentəl] *adj* experimental

expert ['ekspɜːt] **1** *adj* experto(a)

2 *n* experto(a) *m,f*, especialista *mf*

expertise [ekspɜː'tiːz] *n* pericia *f*

expire [ɪk'spaɪə(r)] *vi* (**a**) (*die*) expirar; (*mandate*) terminar (**b**) *Com & Ins* vencer; (*ticket*) caducar

expiry [ɪk'spaɪərɪ] *n* vencimiento *m*; **e. date** fecha *f* de caducidad

explain [ɪk'spleɪn] **1** *vt* explicar; (*clarify*) aclarar; **to e. oneself** justificarse

2 *vi* explicarse

explanation [eksplə'neɪʃən] *n* explicación *f*; (*clarification*) aclaración *f*

explanatory [ɪk'splænətərɪ] *adj* explicativo(a), aclaratorio(a)

explicit [ɪk'splɪsɪt] *adj* explícito(a)

explode [ɪk'spləʊd] **1** *vt* (**a**) (*bomb*) hacer explotar (**b**) *Fig* (*theory*) echar por tierra

2 *vi* (*bomb*) estallar, explotar; *Fig* **to e. with** *or* **in anger** montar en cólera

exploit 1 *n* ['eksplɔɪt] proeza *f*, hazaña *f*

2 *vt* [ek'splɔɪt] explotar

exploitation [eksplɔɪ'teɪʃən] *n* explotación *f*

exploratory [ek'splɒrətərɪ] *adj* exploratorio(a)

explore [ɪk'splɔː(r)] *vt* explorar

explorer [ɪk'splɔːrə(r)] *n* explorador(a) *m,f*

explosion [ɪk'spləʊʒən] *n* explosión *f*

explosive [ɪk'spləʊsɪv] **1** *adj* explosivo(a); **e. issue** asunto delicado

2 *n* explosivo *m*

exponent [ɪk'spəʊnənt] *n* exponente *m*; (*supporter*) defensor(a) *m,f*

export 1 *vt* [ɪk'spɔːt] exportar

2 *n* ['ekspɔːt] (**a**) (*trade*) exportación *f*

(**b**) (*commodity*) artículo *m* de exportación

exporter [ek'spɔːtə(r)] *n* exportador(a) *m,f*

expose [ɪk'spəʊz] *vt* (*uncover*) exponer; (*secret*) revelar; (*plot*) descubrir; **to e. oneself** exhibirse desnudo

exposed [ɪk'spəʊzd] *adj* expuesto(a)

exposure [ɪk'spəʊʒə(r)] *n* (**a**) (*to light, cold, heat*) exposición *f*; **to die of e.** morir de frío (**b**) *Phot* fotografía *f*; **e. meter** fotómetro *m* (**c**) (*of criminal*) descubrimiento *m*

expound [ɪk'spaʊnd] *vt* exponer

express [ɪk'spres] **1** *adj* (**a**) (*explicit*) expreso(a) (**b**) *Br* (*letter*) urgente; **e. train** expreso *m*

2 *n* *Rail* expreso *m*

3 *vt* expresar

4 *adv* **send it e.** mándalo urgente

expression [ɪk'spreʃən] *n* expresión *f*

expressly [ɪk'spreslɪ] *adv* *Fml* expresamente

expressway [ɪk'spresweɪ] *n* *US* autopista *f*

expulsion [ɪk'spʌlʃən] *n* expulsión *f*

exquisite [ɪk'skwɪzɪt] *adj* exquisito(a)

extend [ɪk'stend] **1** *vt* (**a**) (*enlarge*) ampliar; (*lengthen*) alargar; (*increase*) aumentar; *Fig* **the prohibition was extended to cover cigarettes** extendieron la prohibición a los cigarrillos (**b**) (*give*) rendir, dar; **to e. a welcome to sb** recibir a algn (**c**) (*prolong*) prolongar

2 *vi* (**a**) (*stretch*) extenderse (**b**) (*last*) prolongarse

extension [ɪk'stenʃən] *n* (**a**) extensión *f*; (*of time*) prórroga *f* (**b**) *Constr* anexo *m*

extensive [ɪk'stensɪv] *adj* extenso(a)

extent [ɪk'stent] *n* (**a**) (*area*) extensión *f* (**b**) **to some e.** hasta cierto punto; **to a large e.** en gran parte; **to a lesser e.** en menor grado; **to such an e.** hasta tal punto

extenuating [ɪk'stenjʊeɪtɪŋ] *adj* atenuante

exterior [ɪk'stɪərɪə(r)] **1** *adj* exterior, externo(a)

2 *n* exterior *m*

exterminate [ɪk'stɜːmɪneɪt] *vt* exterminar

extermination [ɪkstɜːmɪ'neɪʃən] *n* exterminación *f*, exterminio *m*

external [ɪk'stɜːnəl] *adj* externo(a), exterior

extinct [ɪk'stɪŋkt] *adj* extinguido(a)

extinction [ɪk'stɪŋkʃən] *n* extinción *f*

extinguish [ɪk'stɪŋgwɪʃ] *vt* extinguir, apagar

extinguisher [ɪk'stɪŋgwɪʃə(r)] *n* extintor *m*

extol, *US* **extoll** [ɪk'stəʊl] *vt* ensalzar, alabar

extort [ɪk'stɔːt] *vt* arrancar; *(money)* sacar

extortion [ɪk'stɔːʃən] *n* extorsión *f*

extortionate [ɪk'stɔːʃənɪt] *adj* desorbitado(a)

extra ['ekstrə] **1** *adj* extra; *(spare)* de sobra; **e. time** *(in soccer match)* prórroga *f*
   2 *adv* extra; **e. fine** extra fino
   3 *n (additional charge)* suplemento *m*; *Cin* extra *mf*; *(newspaper)* edición *f* especial

extract 1 *n* ['ekstrækt] extracto *m*
   2 *vt* [ɪk'strækt] *(tooth, information)* extraer; *(confession)* arrancar

extraction [ɪk'strækʃən] *n* extracción *f*

extracurricular [ekstrəkə'rɪkjʊlə(r)] *adj* extracurricular

extradite ['ekstrədaɪt] *vt* extraditar

extramarital [ekstrə'mærɪtəl] *adj* extramatrimonial

extramural [ekstrə'mjʊərəl] *adj* **e. course** = curso para estudiantes libres

extraordinary [ɪk'strɔːdənərɪ] *adj (meeting)* extraordinario(a); *(behaviour etc)* extraño(a)

extravagance [ɪk'strævəgəns] *n (with money)* derroche *m*; *(of behaviour)* extravagancia *f*

extravagant [ɪk'strævəgənt] *adj (wasteful)* derrochador(a); *(excessive)* exagerado(a); *(luxurious)* lujoso(a)

extreme [ɪk'striːm] **1** *adj* extremo(a); **an e. case** un caso excepcional; **to hold e. views** tener opiniones radicales
   2 *n* extremo *m*; **in the e.** en sumo grado

extremely [ɪk'striːmlɪ] *adv* extremadamente; **I'm e. sorry** lo siento de veras

extremist [ɪk'striːmɪst] *n* extremista *mf*

extremity [ɪk'stremɪtɪ] *n* extremidad *f*

extricate ['ekstrɪkeɪt] *vt* sacar; **to e. oneself (from)** lograr salir (de)

extrovert ['ekstrəvɜːt] *adj & n* extrovertido(a) *(m,f)*

exuberant [ɪg'zjuːbərənt] *adj* exuberante

exude [ɪg'zjuːd] *vt & vi (moisture, sap)* exudar; *Fig* rebosar

exultant [ɪg'zʌltənt] *adj* jubiloso(a)

eye [aɪ] **1** *n* ojo *m*; *Fig* **I couldn't believe my eyes** no podía creerlo; *Fig* **in the eyes of** según; *Fig* **not to take one's eyes off sb/sth** no quitar la vista de encima a algn/algo; *Fig* **to catch sb's e.** llamar la atención a algn; *Fig* **to have an e. for** tener buen ojo para; *Fig* **to make eyes at sb** echar miraditas a algn; *Fig* **to see e. to e. with sb** estar de acuerdo con algn; *Fig* **to turn a blind e. (to)** hacer la vista gorda (a); *Fig* **with an e. to** con miras a; **to keep an e. on sb/sth** vigilar a algn/algo; **to keep an e. out for** estar pendiente de; **black e.** ojo morado; *US* **e. doctor** óptico(a) *m,f*
   2 *vt* observar

eyeball ['aɪbɔːl] *n* globo *m* ocular

eyebrow ['aɪbraʊ] *n* ceja *f*

eyecatching ['aɪkætʃɪŋ] *adj* llamativo(a)

eye-drops ['aɪdrɒps] *npl (medicine)* colirio *m*

eyeglasses ['aɪglɑːsɪz] *npl US (spectacles)* gafas *fpl*, *Am* lentes *mpl*, anteojos *mpl*

eyelash ['aɪlæʃ] *n* pestaña *f*

eyelid ['aɪlɪd] *n* párpado *m*

eyeliner ['aɪlaɪnə(r)] *n* lápiz *m* de ojos

eye-opener ['aɪəʊpənə(r)] *n* revelación *f*, gran sorpresa *f*

eyeshadow ['aɪʃædəʊ] *n* sombra *f* de ojos

eyesight ['aɪsaɪt] *n* vista *f*

eyesore ['aɪsɔː(r)] *n* monstruosidad *f*

eyestrain ['aɪstreɪm] *n* vista cansada

eyewash ['aɪwɒʃ] *n* colirio *m*; *Fig* **it's all e.** eso son disparates

eyewitness ['aɪwɪtnɪs] *n* testigo *mf* ocular

F, f [ef] *n* (**a**) *(the letter)* F, f *f* (**b**) *Mus* F fa *m*
F [ef] *(abbr Fahrenheit)* F
fable ['feɪbəl] *n* fábula *f*
fabric ['fæbrɪk] *n* (**a**) *Tex* tejido *m* (**b**) *Constr* estructura *f*

> 🖉 Note that the Spanish word **fábrica** is a false friend and is never a translation for the English word **fabric**. In Spanish, **fábrica** means "factory".

fabricate ['fæbrɪkeɪt] *vt* fabricar
fabrication [fæbrɪ'keɪʃən] *n Fig* fabricación *f*
fabulous ['fæbjʊləs] *adj* fabuloso(a)
façade [fə'sɑːd, fæ'sɑːd] *n* fachada *f*
face [feɪs] **1** *n* (**a**) cara *f*, rostro *m*; **f. to f.** cara a cara; **I told him to his f.** se lo dije en la cara; **she slammed the door in my f.** me dió con la puerta en las narices; **to look sb in the f.** mirarle a algn a la cara; **f. cloth** paño *m*; **f. cream** crema *f* facial; **f. pack** mascarilla *f* facial
  (**b**) *(expression)* cara *f*, expresión *f*; **to pull a long f.** poner cara larga; **to pull faces** hacer muecas
  (**c**) *(surface)* superficie *f*; *(of card, coin)* cara *f*; *(of watch)* esfera *f*; **f. down/up** boca abajo/arriba; *Fig* **in the f. of danger** ante el peligro; **f. value** valor *m* nominal; **to take sth at f. value** entender algo sólo en su sentido literal
  (**d**) *(appearance)* aspecto *m*; **on the f. of it** a primera vista; **to lose f.** desprestigiarse; **to save f.** salvar las apariencias
  2 *vt* (**a**) *(look on to)* dar a; *(be opposite)* estar enfrente de
  (**b**) **to f. the wall/window** *(of person)* estar de cara a la pared/ventana
  (**c**) *(problem)* hacer frente a; **let's f. it** hay que reconocerlo; **to f. up to** hacer cara a
  (**d**) *(tolerate)* soportar, aguantar
  3 *vi* **to f. on to** dar a; **to f. towards** mirar hacia; **f. this way** vuélvase de este lado
facelift ['feɪslɪft] *n Med* lifting *m*; *Fig* renovación *f*
facet ['fæsɪt] *n* faceta *f*
facetious [fə'siːʃəs] *adj* bromista

facial ['feɪʃəl] *adj* facial
facile ['fæsaɪl] *adj* superficial
facilitate [fə'sɪlɪteɪt] *vt* facilitar
facility [fə'sɪlɪtɪ] *n* (**a**) *(ease)* facilidad *f* (**b**) **facilities** *(means)* facilidades *fpl*; **credit facilities** facilidades de crédito (**c**) **facilities** *(rooms, equipment)* instalaciones *fpl*; **cooking facilities** derecho *m* a cocina
facing ['feɪsɪŋ] *adj* de enfrente
facsimile [fæk'sɪmɪlɪ] *n* (**a**) *(copy)* facsímil *m* (**b**) *(message)* telefax *m* (**c**) *(machine)* facsímil *m*
fact [fækt] *n* hecho *m*; **as a matter of f.** de hecho; **the f. that he confessed** el hecho de que confesara; **in f.** en realidad
fact-finding ['fæktfaɪndɪŋ] *adj* investigador(a)
faction ['fækʃən] *n (group)* facción *f*
factor ['fæktə(r)] *n* factor *m*
factory ['fæktərɪ] *n* fábrica *f*
factual ['fæktʃʊəl] *adj* **a f. error** un error de hecho
faculty ['fækəltɪ] *n* (**a**) facultad *f* (**b**) *US Univ* profesorado *m*, cuerpo *m* docente
fad [fæd] *n Fam (craze)* moda pasajera; *(whim)* capricho *m*
fade [feɪd] *vi (colour)* desteñirse; *(flower)* marchitarse; *(light)* apagarse
▸ **fade away** *vi* desvanecerse
▸ **fade in, fade out** *vt sep Cin & TV* fundir
faded ['feɪdɪd] *adj (colour)* desteñido(a); *(flower)* marchito(a)
fag [fæg] *n* (**a**) *Br Fam (cigarette)* pitillo *m* (**b**) *US very Fam (homosexual)* marica *m*
faggot ['fægət] *n* (**a**) *Br (meatball)* albóndiga *f* (**b**) *US very Fam (homosexual)* maricón *m*
fail [feɪl] **1** *n* (**a**) *Educ* suspenso *m* (**b**) **without f.** sin falta
  2 *vt* (**a**) **don't f. me** no me falles; **words f. me** no encuentro palabras (**b**) *(exam)* suspender (**c**) *(to be unable)* no lograr; **he failed to score** no logró marcar (**d**) *(neglect)* dejar de; **don't f. to come** no deje de venir
  3 *vi* (**a**) *(show, film)* fracasar; *(brakes)* fallar (**b**) *(business)* quebrar; *Educ* suspender (**c**) *(of health)* deteriorarse

failing ['feɪlɪŋ] **1** *n* (**a**) *(shortcoming)* defecto *m* (**b**) *(weakness)* punto *m* débil
　2 *prep* a falta de

failure ['feɪljə(r)] *n* (**a**) *fracaso m* (**b**) *Com* quiebra *f* (**c**) *Educ* suspenso *m* (**d**) *(person)* fracasado(a) *m,f* (**e**) *(breakdown)* avería *f*; **brake f.** fallo *m* de los frenos; **power f.** apagón *m*; *Med* **heart f.** paro cardíaco (**f**) **her f. to answer** *(neglect)* el hecho de que no contestara

faint [feɪnt] **1** *adj* (**a**) *(sound)* débil; *(colour)* pálido(a); *(outline)* borroso(a); *(recollection)* vago(a); **I haven't the faintest idea** no tengo la más mínima idea (**b**) *(giddy)* mareado(a)
　2 *n* desmayo *m*
　3 *vi* desmayarse

faint-hearted [feɪnt'hɑːtɪd] *adj* temeroso(a)

fair¹ [feə(r)] **1** *adj* (**a**) *(impartial)* imparcial; *(just)* justo(a); **it's not f.** no hay derecho; *Fam* **f. enough!** ¡vale!; **f. trade** comercio justo (**b**) *(hair)* rubio(a) (**c**) *(weather)* bueno(a) (**d**) *(beautiful)* bello(a) (**e**) **a f. number** un buen número; **he has a f. chance** tiene bastantes probabilidades
　2 *adv* **to play f.** jugar limpio

fair² [feə(r)] *n* feria *f*; **trade f.** feria de muestras

fairground ['feəgraʊnd] *n* real *m* de la feria

fairly ['feəlɪ] *adv* (**a**) *(justly)* justamente (**b**) *(moderately)* bastante

fairness ['feənɪs] *n* justicia *f*, equidad *f*; **in all f.** para ser justo(a)

fairy ['feərɪ] *n* (**a**) hada *f*; **f. godmother** hada madrina, *f.* **tale** cuento *m* de hadas (**b**) *Fam Pej* marica *m*

fait accompli [feɪtə'kɒmpliː] *n Fml* hecho consumado

faith [feɪθ] *n* (**a**) *Rel* fe *f* (**b**) *(trust)* confianza *f*; **in good f.** de buena fe

faithful ['feɪθful] **1** *adj* fiel
　2 *npl* **the f.** los fieles

faithfully ['feɪθfulɪ] *adv* fielmente; **yours f.** *(in letter)* le saluda atentamente

fake [feɪk] **1** *adj* falso(a)
　2 *n* (**a**) *(object)* falsificación *f* (**b**) *(person)* impostor(a) *m,f*
　3 *vt* (**a**) *(forge)* falsificar (**b**) *(feign)* fingir
　4 *vi* *(pretend)* fingir

falcon ['fɔːlkən] *n* halcón *m*

Falklands ['fɔːlkləndz] *npl* **the F.** las (Islas) Malvinas

fall [fɔːl] **1** *n* (**a**) *caída f* (**b**) *(of rock)* desprendimiento *m*; **f. of snow** nevada *f* (**c**) *(decrease)* baja *f* (**d**) *US* otoño *m* (**e**)

(usu pl) cascada *f*; **Niagara Falls** las cataratas del Niágara
　2 *vi* (*pt* **fell**; *pp* **fallen**) (**a**) caer, caerse; **they f. into two categories** se dividen en dos categorías; *Fig* **night was falling** anochecía; *Fig* **to f. into line** aceptar las reglas; *Fig* **to f. short (of)** no alcanzar (**b**) *(in battle)* caer (**c**) *(temperature, prices)* bajar (**d**) **to f. asleep** dormirse; **to f. ill** caer enfermo(a); **to f. in love** enamorarse
　▸ **fall back** *vi* replegarse
　▸ **fall back on** *vt insep* echar mano a, recurrir a
　▸ **fall behind** *vi* *(in race)* quedarse atrás; **to f. behind with one's work** retrasarse en el trabajo
　▸ **fall down** *vi* (**a**) *(picture etc)* caerse (**b**) *(building)* derrumbarse (**c**) *(argument)* fallar
　▸ **fall for** *vt insep* (**a**) *(person)* enamorarse de (**b**) *(trick)* dejarse engañar por
　▸ **fall in** *vi* (**a**) *(roof)* desplomarse (**b**) *Mil* formar filas
　▸ **fall off** **1** *vi* (**a**) *(drop off)* caerse (**b**) *(part)* desprenderse (**c**) *(diminish)* disminuir
　　2 *vt insep* **to f. off sth** caerse de algo
　▸ **fall out** *vi* (**a**) *(hair)* caerse (**b**) *Mil* romper filas (**c**) *(quarrel)* pelearse
　▸ **fall over** *vi* caerse
　▸ **fall through** *vi* *(plan)* fracasar

fallacy ['fæləsɪ] *n* falacia *f*

fallen ['fɔːlən] *pp of* **fall**

fallible ['fælɪbəl] *adj* falible

fall-out ['fɔːlaʊt] *n* **(radioactive) f.** lluvia radioactiva; **f. shelter** refugio antiatómico

fallow ['fæləʊ] *adj Agr* en barbecho

false [fɔːls] *adj* falso(a); **f. step** paso *m* en falso; **f. start** salida nula; **f. teeth** dentadura postiza; **f. alarm** falsa alarma

falsehood ['fɔːlshʊd] *n* falsedad *f*

falsify ['fɔːlsɪfaɪ] *vt* *(records, accounts)* falsificar; *(story)* falsear

falter ['fɔːltə(r)] *vi* vacilar; *(voice)* fallar

faltering ['fɔːltərɪŋ] *adj* vacilante

fame [feɪm] *n* fama *f*

familiar [fə'mɪlɪə(r)] *adj* (**a**) *(common)* familiar, conocido(a); **his face is f.** su cara me suena (**b**) *(aware, knowledgeable)* enterado(a), al corriente (**with** de) (**c**) **to be on f. terms with sb** *(know well)* tener confianza con algn

familiarity [fəmɪlɪ'ærɪtɪ] *n* (**a**) *(awareness, knowledge)* familiaridad *f* (**with** con) (**b**) *(intimacy)* confianza *f*

familiarize [fə'mɪljəraɪz] *vt* (**a**) *(become acquainted)* familiarizar (**with** con); **to f.**

oneself with sth familiarizarse con algo (**b**) *(make widely known)* popularizar

family ['fæmɪlɪ] *n* familia *f*; **f. allowance** subsidio *m* familiar; **f. doctor** médico *m* de cabecera; **f. man** hombre hogareño; **f. planning** planificación *f* familiar; **f. tree** árbol genealógico

famine ['fæmɪn] *n* hambre *f*, escasez *f* de alimentos

famished ['fæmɪʃt] *adj Fam* muerto(a) de hambre

famous ['feɪməs] *adj* célebre, famoso(a) (**for** por)

famously ['feɪməslɪ] *adv Fam* estupendamente

fan [fæn] **1** *n* (**a**) abanico *m*; *Elec* ventilador *m* (**b**) *(person)* aficionado(a) *m,f*, *(of pop star etc)* fan *mf*; **f. club** club *m* de fans; **football f.** hincha *mf*
2 *vt* (**a**) abanicar (**b**) *(fire, passions)* avivar
▸**fan out** *vi (troops)* desplegarse en abanico

fanatic [fə'nætɪk] *adj & n* fanático(a) *(m,f)*

fanatical [fə'nætɪkəl] *adj* fanático(a)

fanciful ['fænsɪfəl] *adj* (**a**) *(person)* caprichoso(a) (**b**) *(idea)* fantástico(a)

fancy ['fænsɪ] **1** *adj (fancier, fanciest)* de fantasía; **f. dress** disfraz *m*; **f. dress ball** baile *m* de disfraces; **f. prices** precios *mpl* exorbitantes
2 *n* (**a**) *(imagination)* fantasía *f* (**b**) *(whim)* capricho *m*, antojo *m*; **to take a f. to sb** cogerle cariño a algn; **to take a f. to sth** encapricharse con algo; **what takes your f.?** ¿qué se le antoja?
3 *vt* (**a**) *(imagine)* imaginarse; *Fam* **f. that!** ¡fíjate!; *Fam* **f. seeing you here!** ¡qué casualidad verte por aquí! (**b**) *(like, want)* apetecer; **do you f. a drink?** ¿te apetece una copa?; *Fam* **I f. her** ella me gusta; *Fam* **to f. oneself** ser creído(a) *or* presumido(a)

fanfare ['fænfeə(r)] *n* fanfarria *f*

fang [fæŋ] *n* colmillo *m*

fanny ['fænɪ] *n* (**a**) *US Fam (buttocks)* culo *m*, *Am* cola *f* (**b**) *Br Vulg (vagina)* coño *m*, *Andes, RP* concha *f*

fantasize ['fæntəsaɪz] *vi* fantasear

fantastic [fæn'tæstɪk] *adj* fantástico(a)

fantasy ['fæntəsɪ] *n* fantasía *f*

far [fɑː(r)] (**farther** *or* **further, farthest** *or* **furthest**) **1** *adj* (**a**) *(distant)* lejano(a); **the F. East** el Lejano Oriente (**b**) **at the f. end** en el otro extremo (**c**) **the f. left** la extrema izquierda
2 *adv* (**a**) *(distant)* lejos; **f. and wide** por

todas partes; **f. off** a lo lejos; **farther back** más atrás; **farther north** más al norte; **how f. is it to Cardiff?** ¿cuánto hay de aquí a Cardiff?; *Fig* **as f. as I can** lo que puedo; **as f. as I know** que yo sepa; **as f. as possible** en lo posible; *Fig* **f. from complaining, he seemed pleased** lejos de quejarse, parecía contento; *Fig* **he went so f. as to swear** llegó a jurar; *Fig* **I'm f. from satisfied** no estoy satisfecho(a) ni mucho menos; *Fig* **in so f. as ...** en la medida en que ...; *Fam* **to go too f.** pasarse de la raya
(**b**) *(in time)* **as f. back as the fifties** ya en los años cincuenta; **f. into the night** hasta muy entrada la noche; **so f.** hasta ahora
(**c**) *(much)* mucho; **by f.** con mucho; **f. cleverer** mucho más listo(a); **f. too much** demasiado; **you're not f. wrong** casi aciertas

faraway ['fɑːrəweɪ] *adj* lejano(a), remoto(a)

farce [fɑːs] *n* farsa *f*

farcical ['fɑːsɪkəl] *adj* absurdo(a)

fare [feə(r)] **1** *n* (**a**) *(ticket price)* tarifa *f*, precio *m* del billete; *(for boat)* pasaje *m*; **half f.** media tarifa (**b**) *(passenger)* pasajero(a) *m,f* (**c**) *(food)* comida *f*
2 *vi* **how did you f.?** ¿qué tal te fue?

farewell [feə'wel] **1** *interj Literary* ¡adiós!
2 *n* despedida *f*

far-fetched [fɑː'fetʃt] *adj* rebuscado(a)

farm [fɑːm] **1** *n* granja *f*, *Am* hacienda *f*
2 *vt* cultivar, labrar
▸**farm out** *vt sep* encargar fuera

farmer ['fɑːmə(r)] *n* granjero(a) *m,f*, *Am* hacendado(a) *m,f*

farmhand ['fɑːmhænd] *n* peón *m*, labriego(a) *m,f*

farmhouse ['fɑːmhaʊs] *n* granja *f*, *Am* hacienda *f*

farming ['fɑːmɪŋ] **1** *n* (**a**) *(agriculture)* agricultura *f* (**b**) *(of land)* cultivo *m*, labranza *f*
2 *adj* agrícola

farmyard ['fɑːmjɑːd] *n* corral *m*

far-reaching [fɑː'riːtʃɪŋ] *adj* de gran alcance

far-sighted [fɑː'saɪtɪd] *adj* (**a**) *(person)* con visión de futuro (**b**) *(plan)* con miras al futuro

fart [fɑːt] *Fam* **1** *n* pedo *m*
2 *vi* echarse un pedo

farther ['fɑːðə(r)] *adj & adv comp of* **far**

farthest ['fɑːðɪst] *adj & adv superl of* **far**

fascinate ['fæsɪneɪt] *vt* fascinar

fascinating ['fæsɪneɪtɪŋ] *adj* fascinante

fascination [fæsɪ'neɪʃən] n fascinación f

fascism ['fæʃɪzəm] n fascismo m

fascist ['fæʃɪst] adj & n fascista (mf)

fashion ['fæʃən] 1 n (a) (manner) manera f, modo m; **after a f.** más o menos (b) (latest style) moda f; **to go/be out of f.** pasar/no estar de moda; **f. designer** diseñador(a) m,f de modas; **f. parade** desfile m de modelos

2 vt (metal) labrar; (clay) formar

fashionable ['fæʃənəbəl] adj (a) de moda (b) (area, hotel) elegante

fast¹ [fɑːst] 1 adj (a) (quick) rápido(a); **hard and f. rules** reglas estrictas (c) (clock) adelantado(a)

2 adv (a) rápidamente, deprisa; **how f.?** ¿a qué velocidad? (b) (securely) firmemente; **f. asleep** profundamente dormido(a)

fast² [fɑːst] 1 n ayuno m

2 vi ayunar

fasten ['fɑːsən] 1 vt (a) (attach) sujetar; (fix) fijar (b) (belt) abrochar; (bag) asegurar; (shoelaces) atar

2 vi (dress) abrocharse

fastener ['fɑːsənə(r)] n cierre m

fastidious [fæ'stɪdɪəs] adj quisquilloso(a)

fat [fæt] 1 adj (fatter, fattest) (a) gordo(a) (b) (book, file) grueso(a) (c) (meat) que tiene mucha grasa

2 n grasa f; **cooking f.** manteca f de cerdo

fatal ['feɪtəl] adj (a) (accident, illness) mortal (b) (ill-fated) fatal, funesto(a) (c) (fateful) fatídico(a)

fatalistic [feɪtə'lɪstɪk] adj fatalista

fatality [fə'tælɪti] n víctima f mortal

> ℓ Note that the Spanish word **fatalidad** is a false friend and is never a translation for the English word **fatality**. In Spanish, **fatalidad** means both "fate" and "misfortune".

fatally ['feɪtəlɪ] adv **f. wounded** mortalmente herido(a)

fate [feɪt] n destino m, suerte f

fateful ['feɪtfʊl] adj fatídico(a), aciago(a)

father ['fɑːðə(r)] n (a) padre m; **my f. and mother** mis padres; **F. Christmas** Papá m Noel (b) Rel padre m

father-in-law ['fɑːðərɪnlɔː] n suegro m

fatherland ['fɑːðəlænd] n patria f

fatherly ['fɑːðəlɪ] adj paternal

fathom ['fæðəm] 1 n Naut braza f

2 vt comprender

▸**fathom out** vt sep comprobar; **I can't f. it out** no me lo explico

fatigue [fə'tiːg] n (a) (tiredness) fatiga f (b) Mil faena f; **f. dress** traje m de faena

fatten ['fætən] vt engordar

fattening ['fætənɪŋ] adj que engorda

fatty ['fætɪ] 1 adj (food) graso(a); Anat (tissue) adiposo(a)

2 n Fam (person) gordinflón(ona) m,f

fatuous ['fætjʊəs] adj necio(a)

faucet ['fɔːsɪt] n US grifo m, Chile, Méx llave f, RP canilla f

fault [fɔːlt] 1 n (a) (defect) defecto m (b) (in merchandise) desperfecto m; **to find f. with** poner reparos a (c) (blame) culpa f; **to be at f.** tener la culpa (d) (mistake) error m (e) Geol falla f (f) (in tennis) falta f

2 vt criticar

faultless ['fɔːltlɪs] adj intachable

faulty ['fɔːltɪ] adj defectuoso(a)

fauna ['fɔːnə] n fauna f

faux pas [fəʊ'pɑː] n (pl **faux pas**) Fml (mistake) paso m en falso; (blunder) metedura f de pata

favour, US favor ['feɪvə(r)] 1 n (a) favor m; **in f. of** a favor de; **to be in f. with sb** gozar del favor de algn; **to ask sb a f.** pedirle un favor a algn (b) **1–0 in our f.** (advantage) 1-0 a favor nuestro

2 vt (a) (person) favorecer a (b) (approve) estar a favor de

favourable ['feɪvərəbəl] adj favorable

favourite ['feɪvərɪt] adj & n favorito(a) (m,f)

favouritism ['feɪvərɪtɪzəm] n favoritismo m

fawn¹ [fɔːn] 1 adj (de) color café claro

2 n (a) Zool cervato m (b) color m café claro

fawn² [fɔːn] vi adular (**on** a)

fax [fæks] 1 n (machine, message) fax m; **f. modem** modem m fax

2 vt mandar por fax

fear [fɪə(r)] 1 n miedo m, temor m; **for f. of** por temor a; Fam **no f.!** ¡ni pensarlo!

2 vt temer; **I f. it's too late** me temo que ya es tarde

3 vi temer (**for** por)

fearful ['fɪəfʊl] adj (a) (person) temeroso(a) (b) (frightening) espantoso(a)

fearless ['fɪəlɪs] adj intrépido(a)

feasibility [fiːzə'bɪlɪtɪ] n viabilidad f

feasible ['fiːzəbəl] adj (practicable) factible; (possible) viable

feast [fiːst] n (a) banquete m; Fam comilona f (b) Rel **f. day** fiesta f de guardar

feat [fiːt] n hazaña f

feather ['feðə(r)] 1 n pluma f; **f. duster** plumero m

2 vt Fam **to f. one's nest** hacer su agosto

feature ['fiːtʃə(r)] **1** n (a) (of face) rasgo m, facción f (b) (characteristic) característica f (c) **f. film** largometraje m (d) Press crónica f especial

2 vt (a) poner de relieve (b) Cin tener como protagonista a

3 vi figurar

February ['februəri] n febrero m

fed [fed] **1** adj Fam **f. up (with)** harto(a) (de)

2 pt & pp of **feed**

federal ['fedərəl] adj federal

federation [fedə'reɪʃən] n federación f

fee [fiː] n (of lawyer, doctor) honorarios mpl; Ftb **transfer f.** prima f de traslado; Univ **tuition fees** derechos mpl de matrícula

feeble ['fiːbəl] adj débil

feed [fiːd] **1** vt (pt & pp **fed**) (a) (give food to) dar de comer a; Fig (fire) alimentar; **to f. a baby** (breast-feed) amamantar a un bebé; (with bottle) dar el biberón a un bebé (b) Elec alimentar (c) (insert) introducir

2 vi (cows, sheep) pacer; **to f. on sth** (person) comer algo

3 n (a) (food) comida f; **cattle f.** pienso m (b) Tech alimentación f

▸ **feed up** vt sep cebar

feedback ['fiːdbæk] n (a) Tech feedback m (b) Fig reacción f

feeder ['fiːdə(r)] n Tech alimentador m

feeding ['fiːdɪŋ] n **f. bottle** biberón m

feel [fiːl] **1** vi (pt & pp **felt**) (a) (emotion, sensation) sentir; **how do you f.?** ¿qué tal te encuentras?; **I f. bad about it** me da pena; **I f. (sorry) for him** le compadezco; **to f. happy/uncomfortable** sentirse feliz/incómodo; **to f. cold/sleepy** tener frío/sueño; Fam **to f. up to (doing)** sth sentirse con ánimos para hacer algo

(b) (seem) your hand feels cold tienes la mano fría; **it feels like summer** parece verano

(c) (opinion) opinar; **I f. sure that ...** estoy seguro(a) de que ...

(d) **I f. like an ice cream** me apetece un helado; **to f. like doing sth** tener ganas de hacer algo

2 vt (a) (touch) tocar

(b) **she feels a failure** se siente inútil

(c) (notice, be aware of) notar

3 n (a) (touch, sensation) tacto m; Fig **to get the f. for sth** cogerle el truco a algo

(b) (atmosphere) ambiente m

▸ **feel for** vt insep (a) (search for) buscar (b) (have sympathy for) compadecer

feeler ['fiːlə(r)] n (of insect) antena f; Fig

to put one's feelers out tantear el terreno

feeling ['fiːlɪŋ] **1** n (a) (emotion) sentimiento m; **ill f.** rencor m (b) (compassion) compasión f (c) **I had the f. that ...** (impression) tuve la impresión de que ... (d) (sensitivity) sensibilidad f (e) (opinion) opinión f; **to express one's feelings** expresar sus opiniones

2 adj sensible, compasivo(a)

feet [fiːt] pl of **foot**

feign [feɪn] vt fingir

feint [feɪnt] Sport **1** n finta f

2 vi fintar

fell¹ [fel] pt of **fall**

fell² [fel] vt (trees) talar; Fig (enemy) derribar

fellow ['feləʊ] n (a) (companion) compañero(a) m,f; **f. citizen** conciudadano(a) m,f; **f. countryman/countrywoman** compatriota mf; **f. men** prójimos mpl; **f. passenger/student** compañero(a) m,f de viaje/estudios (b) Fam (chap) tipo m, tío m (c) (of society) socio(a) m,f

fellowship ['feləʊʃɪp] n (a) (comradeship) camaradería f (b) Univ beca f de investigación

felony ['feləni] n crimen m, delito m mayor

felt¹ [felt] pt & pp of **feel**

felt² [felt] n Tex fieltro m

felt-tip(ped) ['felttɪp(t)] adj **f. pen** rotulador m

female ['fiːmeɪl] **1** adj (a) Zool hembra (b) femenino(a)

2 n (a) Zool hembra f (b) (woman) mujer f; (girl) chica f

feminine ['femɪnɪn] adj femenino(a)

feminism ['femɪnɪzəm] n feminismo m

feminist ['femɪnɪst] adj & n feminista (mf)

fence [fens] **1** n cerca f, valla f; Fig **to sit on the f.** ver los toros desde la barrera

2 vi Sport practicar la esgrima

▸ **fence in** vt sep meter en un cercado

fencing ['fensɪŋ] n Sport esgrima f

fend [fend] vi **to f. for oneself** valerse por sí mismo

▸ **fend off** vt sep (blow) parar; (question) rehuir; (attack) rechazar

fender ['fendə(r)] n (a) (fireplace) pantalla f (b) US Aut guardabarros mpl (c) Naut defensa f

ferment 1 n ['fɜːment] Fig **in a state of f.** agitado(a)

2 vt & vi [fə'ment] fermentar

fern [fɜːn] n helecho m

ferocious [fə'rəʊʃəs] adj feroz

ferocity [fə'rɒsɪtɪ] n ferocidad f

ferret ['ferɪt] **1** n hurón m
2 vi huronear, husmear
▸ **ferret out** vt sep descubrir
ferry ['ferɪ] **1** n **(a)** (small) barca f de pasaje **(b)** (large, for cars) transbordador m, ferry m
2 vt transportar
fertile ['fɜːtaɪl] adj fértil
fertility [fə'tɪlɪtɪ] n (of soil) fertilidad f
fertilize ['fɜːtɪlaɪz] vt **(a)** (soil) abonar **(b)** (egg) fecundar
fertilizer ['fɜːtɪlaɪzə(r)] n abono m
fervent ['fɜːvənt] adj ferviente
fervour, US **fervor** ['fɜːvə(r)] n fervor m
fester ['festə(r)] vi supurar
festival ['festɪvəl] n (event) festival m; (celebration) fiesta f
festive ['festɪv] adj festivo(a); **the f. season** las fiestas de Navidad
festivity [fe'stɪvɪtɪ] n **the festivities** las fiestas
festoon [fe'stuːn] vt adornar
fetch [fetʃ] vt **(a)** (go for) ir a buscar **(b)** (bring) traer **(c)** **how much did it f.?** (sell for) ¿por cuánto se vendió?
fetching ['fetʃɪŋ] adj atractivo(a)
fete [feɪt] **1** n fiesta f
2 vt festejar
fetish ['fetɪʃ, 'fiːtɪʃ] n fetiche m
fetus ['fiːtəs] n US = **foetus**
feud [fjuːd] **1** n enemistad duradera
2 vi pelear
feudal ['fjuːdəl] adj feudal
fever ['fiːvə(r)] n fiebre f
feverish ['fiːvərɪʃ] adj febril
few [fjuː] **1** adj **(a)** (not many) pocos(as); **as f. as** solamente **(b)** (some) algunos(as), unos(as) cuantos(as); **a f. books** unos or algunos libros; **she has fewer books than I thought** tiene menos libros de lo que pensaba; **for the past f. years** durante estos últimos años; **in the next f. days** dentro de unos días; **quite a f.** bastantes
2 pron **(a)** (not many) pocos(as); **there are too f.** no hay suficientes; **the fewer the better** cuantos menos mejor **(b)** a **f.** (some) algunos(as), unos(as) cuantos(as); **the chosen f.** los elegidos; **who has the fewest?** ¿quién tiene menos?
fiancé [fɪ'ɒnseɪ] n prometido m
fiancée [fɪ'ɒnseɪ] n prometida f
fiasco [fɪ'æskəʊ] n fiasco m
fib [fɪb] Fam **1** n trola f
2 vi contar trolas
fibre, US **fiber** ['faɪbə(r)] n fibra f
fibreglass, US **fiberglass** ['faɪbəglɑːs] n fibra f de vidrio

fickle ['fɪkəl] adj inconstante, voluble
fiction ['fɪkʃən] n ficción f
fictional ['fɪkʃənəl] adj **(a)** Lit novelesco(a) **(b)** (imaginative) ficticio(a)
fictitious [fɪk'tɪʃəs] adj ficticio(a)
fiddle ['fɪdəl] Fam **1** n **(a)** Mus violín m **(b)** (shady deal) trampa f
2 vt estafar; (accounts) falsificar
3 vi juguetear (**with** con)
▸ **fiddle about** vi perder tiempo
fiddly ['fɪdlɪ] adj Fam laborioso(a)
fidelity [fɪ'delɪtɪ] n fidelidad f
fidget ['fɪdʒɪt] vi **(a)** moverse; **stop fidgeting!** ¡estáte quieto! **(b)** jugar (**with** con)
field [fiːld] **1** n **(a)** campo m; **f. glasses** gemelos mpl; **f. marshal** mariscal m de campo **(b)** Geol & Min yacimiento m **(c)** **f. trip** viaje m de estudios; **f. work** trabajo m de campo
2 vt Sport **(a)** (ball) parar y devolver **(b)** (team) presentar
fiend [fiːnd] n demonio m; Fam (fanatic) fanático(a) m,f
fiendish ['fiːndɪʃ] adj Fam diabólico(a)
fierce [fɪəs] adj **(a)** (animal) feroz; (argument) acalorado(a); (heat, competition) intenso(a); (wind) violento(a)
fiery ['faɪərɪ] adj (temper) fogoso(a); (speech) acalorado(a); (colour) encendido(a)
fifteen [fɪf'tiːn] adj & n quince (m inv)
fifteenth [fɪf'tiːnθ] **1** adj & n decimoquinto(a) (m,f)
2 n (fraction) quinzavo m
fifth [fɪfθ] **1** adj & n quinto(a) (m,f)
2 n (fraction) quinto m
fifty ['fɪftɪ] adj & n cincuenta (m inv)
fifty-fifty ['fɪftɪ'fɪftɪ] Fam **1** adj **a f. chance** una probabilidad del cincuenta por ciento
2 adv **to go f.** ir a medias
fig¹ [fɪg] n (fruit) higo m
fig² [fɪg] (abbr **figure**) fig
fight [faɪt] **1** vt (pt & pp **fought**) **(a)** pelear(se) con, luchar con; (of boxer) enfrentarse a, luchar con; (of bullfighter) lidiar; Fig (corruption) combatir **(b)** (battle) librar; (war) hacer **(c)** (decision) recurrir contra
2 vi **(a)** pelear(se), luchar **(b)** (quarrel) reñir; **to f. over sth** disputarse la posesión de algo **(c)** Fig (struggle) luchar (**for/against** por/contra)
3 n **(a)** pelea f, lucha f; (in boxing) combate m **(b)** (quarrel) riña f **(c)** Fig (struggle) lucha f **(d)** (spirit) combatividad f

► **fight back 1** *vt sep (tears)* contener
2 *vi* contraatacar

► **fight off** *vt sep* (**a**) *(attack)* rechazar (**b**) *(illness)* cortar

► **fight out** *vt sep* discutir

fighter ['faɪtə(r)] ʀ (**a**) *(person)* combatiente *mf; (in boxing)* púgil *m* (**b**) *Fig* luchador(a) *m,f;* **f. plane** (avión *m* de) caza *m;* **f. bomber** cazabombardero *m*

fighting ['faɪtɪŋ] **1** *adj* **he's got a f. chance** tiene verdaderas posibilidades
2 *n* lucha *f*

figment ['fɪgmənt] *n* **it's a f. of your imagination** es un producto de tu imaginación

figurative ['fɪgərətɪv] *adj* figurado(a)

figure ['fɪgə(r), *US* 'fɪgjər] **1** *n* (**a**) *(form, outline)* forma *f*, silueta *f* (**b**) *(shape, statue, character)* figura *f;* **she has a good f.** tiene buen tipo; *Br* **f. of eight,** *US* **f. eight** ocho *m* (**c**) *(in book)* dibujo *m* (**d**) **f. of speech** figura retórica (**e**) *Math* cifra *f*
2 *vt US Fam* imaginarse
3 *vi* (**a**) *(appear)* figurar (**b**) *US Fam* **that figures** eso tiene sentido

► **figure out** *vt sep Fam* comprender; **I can't f. it out** no me lo explico

figurehead ['fɪgəhed] *n Fig* figura decorativa

filament ['fɪləmənt] *n* filamento *m*

filch [fɪltʃ] *vt Fam* mangar, birlar

file [faɪl] **1** *n* (**a**) *(tool)* lima *f* (**b**) *(folder)* carpeta *f* (**c**) *(archive, of computer)* archivo *m;* **on f.** archivado(a) (**d**) *(line)* fila *f;* **in single f.** en fila india
2 *vt* (**a**) *(smooth)* limar (**b**) *(put away)* archivar
3 *vi* **to f. past** desfilar

filing ['faɪlɪŋ] *n* clasificación *f;* **f. cabinet** archivador *m; (for cards)* fichero *m*

Filipino [fɪlɪ'piːnəʊ] *n* filipino(a) *m,f*

fill [fɪl] **1** *vt* (**a**) *(space, time)* llenar (**with** de) (**b**) *(post, requirements)* cubrir (**c**) *Culin* rellenar
2 *vi* llenarse (**with** de)
3 *n* **to eat one's f.** comer hasta hartarse

► **fill in 1** *vt sep* (**a**) *(space, form)* rellenar (**b**) *Fam (inform)* poner al corriente (**on** de) (**c**) *(time)* pasar
2 *vi* **to f. in for sb** sustituir a algn

► **fill out 1** *vt sep US (form)* llenar
2 *vi Fam* engordar

► **fill up 1** *vt sep* llenar hasta arriba; *Fam Aut* **f. her up!** ¡llénelo!
2 *vi* llenarse

fillet ['fɪlɪt] *n* filete *m;* **f. steak** filete *m*

filling ['fɪlɪŋ] **1** *adj* que llena mucho
2 *n* (**a**) *(stuffing)* relleno *m* (**b**) *(in tooth)*

empaste *m* (**c**) *Br* **f. station** gasolinera *f,* estación *f* de servicio, *Andes, Ven* bomba *f, Méx* gasolinería *f, Perú* grifo *m*

fillip ['fɪlɪp] *n Fam* estímulo *m*

film [fɪlm] **1** *n* (**a**) *Cin & Phot* película *f;* **f. star** estrella *f* de cine (**b**) *(layer)* capa *f*
2 *vt Cin* filmar
3 *vi Cin* rodar

film-strip ['fɪlmstrɪp] *n* cortometraje *m*

filter ['fɪltə(r)] **1** *n* filtro *m; Aut* **f. lane** carril *m* de acceso
2 *vt* filtrar
3 *vi Aut* **to f. to the right** girar a la derecha

► **filter through** *vi Fig* filtrarse (**to** a)

filter-tip ['fɪltətɪp] *n (cigarette)* cigarrillo *m* con filtro

filth [fɪlθ] *n (dirt)* porquería *f; Fig* porquerías *fpl*

filthy ['fɪlθɪ] *adj* (**filthier, filthiest**) (**a**) *(dirty)* asqueroso(a) (**b**) *(obscene)* obsceno(a)

fin [fɪn] *n Zool & Av* aleta *f*

final ['faɪnəl] **1** *adj* (**a**) *(last)* último(a), final (**b**) *(definitive)* definitivo(a)
2 *n* (**a**) *Sport* final *f* (**b**) *Univ* **finals** exámenes *mpl* de fin de carrera

finale [fɪ'nɑːlɪ] *n* final *m*

finalist ['faɪnəlɪst] *n* finalista *mf*

finalize ['faɪnəlaɪz] *vt* ultimar; *(date)* fijar

finally ['faɪnəlɪ] *adv (lastly)* por último; *(at last)* por fin

finance ['faɪnæns, fɪ'næns] **1** *n* (**a**) *(business)* finanzas *fpl* (**b**) **finances** fondos *mpl*
2 *vt* financiar

financial [faɪ'nænʃəl, fɪ'nænʃəl] *adj* financiero(a); **f. crisis** crisis económica; **f. year** año económico

financier [faɪ'nænsɪə(r), fɪ'nænsɪə(r)] *n* financiero(a) *m,f*

finch [fɪntʃ] *n* pinzón *m*

find [faɪnd] **1** *vt (pt & pp* **found**) (**a**) *(locate)* encontrar (**b**) *(think)* encontrar (**c**) **this found its way into my bag** esto vino a parar a mi bolso (**d**) *(discover)* descubrir; **it has been found that ...** se ha comprobado que ... (**e**) *Jur* **to f. sb guilty/not guilty** declarar culpable/inocente a algn (**f**) **I can't f. the courage to tell him** no tengo valor para decírselo; **I found it impossible to get away** me resultó imposible irme
2 *n* hallazgo *m*

► **find out 1** *vt sep* (**a**) *(inquire)* averiguar (**b**) *(discover)* descubrir
2 *vi* (**a**) **to f. out about sth** informarse sobre algo (**b**) *(discover)* enterarse

findings ['faɪndɪŋz] *npl* conclusiones *fpl*

fine¹ [faɪn] **1** n multa f
　2 vt multar

fine² [faɪn] **1** adj (**a**) (delicate etc) fino(a)
(**b**) (subtle) sutil (**c**) (excellent) excelente
(**d**) (weather) bueno(a); **it was f.** hacía
buen tiempo (**e**) **the f. arts** las bellas
artes (**f**) (all right) bien
　2 adv Fam muy bien
　3 interj ¡vale!

finely ['faɪnlɪ] adv (**a**) finamente; **f.
chopped** picado fino (**b**) **f. tuned** a
punto

finery ['faɪnərɪ] n galas fpl

finesse [fɪ'nes] n (delicacy) finura f;
(cunning) astucia f; (tact) sutileza f

finger ['fɪŋgə(r)] **1** n dedo m (de la mano);
Fam **to keep one's fingers crossed** esperar que todo salga bien; Fam **you've put
your f. on it** has dado en el clavo; **middle
f.** dedo corazón
　2 vt tocar; Pej manosear

fingernail ['fɪŋgəneɪl] n uña f

fingerprint ['fɪŋgəprɪnt] n huella f dactilar

fingertip ['fɪŋgətɪp] n punta f or yema f
del dedo

finicky ['fɪnɪkɪ] adj (person) quisquillo-
so(a)

finish ['fɪnɪʃ] **1** n (**a**) fin m; (of race)
llegada f (**b**) (surface) acabado m
　2 vt (**a**) (complete) acabar, terminar; **to f.
doing sth** terminar de hacer algo (**b**) (use
up) agotar
　3 vi acabar, terminar; **to f. second** quedar el segundo
　▸ **finish off** vt sep (**a**) (complete) terminar
completamente (**b**) Fam (kill) rematar
　▸ **finish up** **1** vt sep acabar, agotar
　2 vi **to f. up in jail** ir a parar a la cárcel

finished ['fɪnɪʃt] adj (**a**) (product) aca-
bado(a) (**b**) Fam (exhausted) rendido(a)

finishing ['fɪnɪʃɪŋ] adj **to put the f.
touch(es) to sth** darle los últimos toques
a algo; **f. line** (línea f de) meta f; **f. school**
= escuela privada de modales para se-
ñoritas

finite ['faɪnaɪt] adj finito(a); (verb) conju-
gable

Finland ['fɪnlənd] n Finlandia

Finn [fɪn] n finlandés(esa) m,f

Finnish ['fɪnɪʃ] **1** adj finlandés(esa)
　2 n (language) finlandés m

fir [fɜ:(r)] n abeto m

fire ['faɪə(r)] **1** n (**a**) fuego m (**b**) (accident
etc) incendio m; **to be on f.** estar en
llamas; **to catch f.** incendiarse; **f. alarm**
alarma f de incendios; Br **f. brigade**, US **f.
department** (cuerpo m de) bomberos

mpl; **f. engine** coche m de bomberos; **f.
escape** escalera f de incendios; **f. exit**
salida f de emergencia; **f. extinguisher**
extintor m; **f. fighting** extinción f de
incendios; **f. station** parque m de bomberos (**c**) (heater) estufa f (**d**) Mil fuego m;
to open f. abrir fuego; Fig **to come under
f.** ser el blanco de las críticas
　2 vt (**a**) (gun) disparar (**at** a); (rocket)
lanzar; Fig **to f. questions at sb** bombardear a algn a preguntas (**b**) Fam (dismiss)
despedir
　3 vi (shoot) disparar (**at** sobre)

firearm ['faɪərɑ:m] n arma f de fuego

fire-fighter ['faɪəfaɪtə(r)] n US bombero
m

fireman ['faɪəmən] n bombero m

fireplace ['faɪəpleɪs] n chimenea f;
(hearth) hogar m

fireside ['faɪəsaɪd] n hogar m; **by the f.** al
calor de la lumbre

firewood ['faɪəwʊd] n leña f

fireworks ['faɪəwɜ:ks] npl fuegos mpl
artificiales

firing ['faɪərɪŋ] n Mil tiroteo m; **f. line**
línea f de fuego; **f. squad** pelotón m de
fusilamiento

firm [fɜ:m] **1** adj firme; **to be f. with sb**
(strict) tratar a algn con firmeza
　2 n Com empresa f, firma f

firmly ['fɜ:mlɪ] adv firmemente

firmness ['fɜ:mnɪs] n firmeza f

first [fɜ:st] **1** adj primero(a); (before masculine singular noun) primer; **Charles the
F.** Carlos Primero; **for the f. time** por
primera vez; **in the f. place** en primer
lugar; **f. aid** primeros auxilios; **f. aid box**
botiquín m; **f. floor** primer piso, US planta baja; **f. name** nombre m de pila
　2 adv (before anything else) primero; **f.
and foremost** ante todo; **f. of all** en
primer lugar
　3 n (**a**) **the f.** el primero/la primera; **the
f. of April** el uno or el primero de abril (**b**)
at f. al principio; **from the (very) f.** desde
el principio (**c**) Aut primera f (**d**) Univ **to
get a f.** sacar un sobresaliente

first-class ['fɜ:st'klɑ:s] **1** adj de primera
clase
　2 adv **to travel f.** viajar en primera

first-hand ['fɜ:st'hænd] adv & adj de
primera mano

firstly ['fɜ:stlɪ] adv en primer lugar

first-rate ['fɜ:streɪt] adj de primera

fiscal ['fɪskəl] adj fiscal

fish [fɪʃ] **1** n (pl fish) (**a**) pez m; **f. shop**
pescadería f (**b**) Culin pescado m; **f. and
chips** = pescado frito con patatas or Am

papas fritas; **f.** *Br* **finger** *or US* **stick** palito *m* de pescado

2 *vi* pescar; *Fig* **to f. in one's pocket for sth** buscar algo en el bolsillo

fishbone ['fɪʃbəʊn] *n* espina *f*, raspa *f*

fisherman ['fɪʃəmən] *n* pescador *m*

fishfinger [fɪʃ'fɪŋgə(r)] *n* palito *m* de pescado

fishing ['fɪʃɪŋ] *n* pesca *f*; **to go f.** ir de pesca; **f. net** red *f* de pesca; **f. rod** caña *f* de pescar; **f. tackle** aparejo *m* de pescar

fishmonger ['fɪʃmʌŋgə(r)] *n Br* pescadero(a) *m,f*; **fishmonger's (shop)** pescadería *f*

fishy ['fɪʃɪ] *adj* (**fishier, fishiest**) de pescado; *Fam Fig* **there's something f. going on** aquí hay gato encerrado

fist [fɪst] *n* puño *m*

fit¹ [fɪt] **1** *vt* (**a**) ir bien a; **that suit doesn't f. you** ese traje no te entalla

(**b**) *Sewing* probar

(**c**) **the key doesn't f. the lock** la llave no es de esta cerradura

(**d**) (*install*) colocar; **a car fitted with a radio** un coche provisto de radio

(**e**) *Fig* **she doesn't f. the description** no responde a la descripción

2 *vi* (**a**) (*be of right size*) caber

(**b**) (*facts etc*) cuadrar

3 *adj* (**a**) (*suitable*) apto(a), adecuado(a) (**for** para); **are you f. to drive?** ¿estás en condiciones de conducir?

(**b**) (*healthy*) en (plena) forma; **to keep f.** mantenerse en forma

4 *n* ajuste *m*; *Sewing* corte *m*; **to be a good f.** encajar bien

► **fit in 1** *vi* (**a**) he didn't **f. in with his colleagues** no encajó con sus compañeros de trabajo (**b**) (*tally*) cuadrar (**with** con)

2 *vt sep* (*find time for*) encontrar un hueco para

► **fit out** *vt sep* equipar

fit² [fɪt] *n* (**a**) *Med* ataque *m* (**b**) *Fig* arrebato *m*; **f. of anger** arranque *m* de cólera; *Fig* **by fits and starts** a trompicones

fitful ['fɪtfʊl] *adj* discontinuo(a)

fitness ['fɪtnɪs] *n* (**a**) (*aptitude*) aptitud *f*, capacidad *f* (**b**) (*health*) (buen) estado físico

fitted ['fɪtɪd] *adj* empotrado(a); **f. carpet** moqueta *f*; **f. cupboard** armario empotrado

fitter ['fɪtə(r)] *n* ajustador(a) *m,f*

fitting ['fɪtɪŋ] **1** *adj* apropiado(a)

2 *n* (**a**) (*of dress*) prueba *f*; **f. room** probador *m* (**b**) (*usu pl*) accesorio *m*;

light fittings apliques eléctricos

five [faɪv] *adj & n* cinco (*m inv*)

fiver ['faɪvə(r)] *n Fam* billete *m* de 5 libras/dólares

fix [fɪks] **1** *n* (**a**) *Fam* **to be in a f.** estar en un apuro (**b**) *Fam* (*drugs*) chute *m*

2 *vt* (**a**) (*fasten*) fijar, asegurar (**b**) (*date, price*) fijar; (*limit*) señalar (**c**) **he'll f. it with the boss** (*arrange*) se las arreglará con el jefe (**d**) (*repair*) arreglar (**e**) *US* (*food, drink*) preparar

► **fix up** *vt sep* (*arrange*) arreglar; **to f. sb up with sth** proveer a algn de algo

fixation [fɪk'seɪʃən] *n* idea fija

fixed [fɪkst] *adj* (**a**) fijo(a) (**b**) *Fam* (*match etc*) amañado(a)

fixture ['fɪkstʃə(r)] *n* (**a**) *Sport* encuentro *m* (**b**) **fixtures** (*in building*) accesorios *mpl*

fizz [fɪz] **1** *n* burbujeo *m*

2 *vi* burbujear

► **fizzle out** ['fɪzəl] *vi* quedar en nada

fizzy ['fɪzɪ] *adj* (**fizzier, fizziest**) (*water*) con gas

flabbergasted ['flæbəgɑːstɪd] *adj* pasmado(a)

flabby ['flæbɪ] *adj* (**flabbier, flabbiest**) fofo(a)

flag [flæg] **1** *n* bandera *f*; *Naut* pabellón *m*

2 *vt Fig* **to f. down a car** hacer señales a un coche para que pare

3 *vi* (*interest*) decaer; (*conversation*) languidecer

flagpole ['flægpəʊl] *n* asta *f* de bandera

flagrant ['fleɪgrənt] *adj* flagrante

flagship ['flægʃɪp] *n* buque *m* insignia

flagstone ['flægstəʊn] *n* losa *f*

flair [fleə(r)] *n* facilidad *f*

flak [flæk] *n* (**a**) *Mil* fuego antiaéreo (**b**) *Fam* críticas *fpl*

flake [fleɪk] **1** *n* (*of snow*) copo *m*; (*of skin, soap*) escama *f*; (*of paint*) desconchón *m*

2 *vi* (*skin*) descamarse; (*paint*) desconcharse

flamboyant [flæm'bɔɪənt] *adj* extravagante

flame [fleɪm] *n* (**a**) (*of fire*) llama *f*; **to go up in flames** incendiarse (**b**) *Comput* llamarada *f*, = mensaje ofensivo

flameproof ['fleɪmpruːf] *adj* ininflamable

flamingo [flə'mɪŋgəʊ] *n* flamenco *m*

flammable ['flæməbəl] *adj* inflamable

flan [flæn] *n* tarta *f*; **fruit f.** tarta de fruta

♪ Note that the Spanish word **flan** is a false friend and is never a translation for the English word **flan**. In Spanish, **flan** means "crème caramel".

flank [flæŋk] **1** n (**a**) (of animal) ijada f (**b**) Mil flanco m
2 vt flanquear

flannel ['flænəl] n (**a**) Tex franela f (**b**) Br (face cloth) toallita f

flap [flæp] **1** vt (wings, arms) batir
2 vi (wings) aletear; (flag) ondear
3 n (**a**) (of envelope, pocket) solapa f; (of tent) faldón m (**b**) (of wing) aletazo m (**c**) Fam **to get into a f.** ponerse nervioso(a)

flare [fleə(r)] **1** n (**a**) (flame) llamarada f (**b**) Mil & Naut bengala f
2 vi **to f. (up)** (fire) llamear; Fig (person) encolerizarse; (trouble) estallar

flared [fleəd] adj (trousers etc) acampanado(a)

flash [flæʃ] **1** n (**a**) (of light) destello m; (of lightning) relámpago m; Fig **in a f.** en un santiamén; Fig **a f. in the pan** un éxito fugaz (**b**) **news f.** noticia f de última hora (**c**) Phot flash m
2 adj Fam chulo(a)
3 vt (**a**) (torch) dirigir (**b**) Rad & TV transmitir (**c**) **he flashed his card** enseñó rápidamente su carnet
4 vi (**a**) (light) destellar (**b**) **a car flashed past** un coche pasó como un rayo

flashback ['flæʃbæk] n flashback m

flashcube ['flæʃkjuːb] n cubo m flash

flashlight ['flæʃlaɪt] n US linterna f

flashy ['flæʃɪ] adj (flashier, flashiest) Fam chillón(ona)

flask [flɑːsk, flæsk] n frasco m; (Thermos®) f. termo m

flat [flæt] **1** adj (flatter, flattest) (**a**) (surface) llano(a) (**b**) (beer) sin gas (**c**) (battery) descargado(a); (tyre) desinflado(a) (**d**) (rate) fijo(a) (**e**) (categorical) rotundo(a) (**f**) (dull) soso(a) (**g**) Mus **B f.** si m bemol
2 adv (**a**) **to fall f. on one's face** caerse de bruces (**b**) **in ten seconds f.** en diez segundos justos (**c**) Fam **to go f. out** ir a todo gas
3 n (**a**) (apartment) piso m (**b**) US Aut pinchazo m (**c**) **mud flats** marismas fpl

flatly ['flætlɪ] adv rotundamente

flatmate ['flætmeɪt] n Br compañero(a) m,f de piso

flatten ['flætən] vt (**a**) (make level) allanar (**b**) (crush) aplastar

flatter ['flætə(r)] vt (**a**) adular, halagar (**b**) (clothes, portrait) favorecer (**c**) **to f. oneself** hacerse ilusiones

flattering ['flætərɪŋ] adj (**a**) (words) halagador(a) (**b**) (dress, portrait) favorecedor(a)

flattery ['flætərɪ] n adulación f, halago m

flaunt [flɔːnt] vt hacer alarde de

flavour, US **flavor** ['fleɪvə(r)] **1** n sabor m
2 vt Culin sazonar (with con)

flavoured, US **flavored** ['fleɪvəd] adj **strawberry f.** con sabor a fresa, Bol, CSur, Ecuad frutilla

flavouring, US **flavoring** ['fleɪvərɪŋ] n condimento m; **artificial f.** aroma m artificial

flaw [flɔː] n (failing) defecto m; (fault) desperfecto m

flawless ['flɔːlɪs] adj perfecto(a)

flax [flæks] n lino m

flaxen ['flæksən] adj (hair) rubio pajizo

flea [fliː] n pulga f; **f. market** rastro m

fleck [flek] n (speck) mota f, punto m

fled [fled] pt & pp of **flee**

fledg(e)ling ['fledʒlɪŋ] adj Fig novato(a)

flee [fliː] **1** vt (pt & pp **fled**) huir de
2 vi huir (from de)

fleece [fliːs] **1** n (**a**) (sheep's coat) lana f (**b**) (sheared) vellón m
2 vt Fam (cheat) sangrar

fleet [fliːt] n flota f

fleeting ['fliːtɪŋ] adj fugaz

Flemish ['flemɪʃ] **1** adj flamenco(a)
2 n (language) flamenco m

flesh [fleʃ] n (**a**) carne f; Fig **in the f.** en persona; Fig **to be of f. and blood** ser de carne y hueso; **f. wound** herida f superficial (**b**) (of fruit) pulpa f

flew [fluː] pt of **fly**

flex [fleks] **1** n Br Elec cable m
2 vt (muscles) flexionar

flexibility [fleksɪ'bɪlɪtɪ] n flexibilidad f

flexible ['fleksɪbəl] adj flexible

flick [flɪk] **1** n movimiento rápido; (of finger) capirotazo m
2 vt (with finger) dar un capirotazo a
▸ flick through vt insep (book) hojear

flicker ['flɪkə(r)] **1** n (**a**) parpadeo m; (of light) titileo m (**b**) Fig **a f. of hope** un destello de esperanza
2 vi (eyes) parpadear; (flame) vacilar

flier ['flaɪə(r)] n aviador(a) m,f

flight [flaɪt] n (**a**) vuelo m; **f. path** trayectoria f de vuelo; **f. recorder** registrador m de vuelo (**b**) (of ball) trayectoria f (**c**) (escape) huida f, fuga f; **to take f.** darse a la fuga (**d**) (of stairs) tramo m

flight-deck ['flaɪtdek] n (cockpit) cabina f del piloto

flimsy ['flɪmzɪ] adj (flimsier, flimsiest) (cloth) ligero(a); (paper) fino(a); (structure) poco sólido(a); (excuse) poco convincente

flinch [flɪntʃ] vi (wince) estremecerse

fling [flɪŋ] **1** vt (pt & pp **flung**) arrojar

2 *n Fam* **to have a f.** echar una cana al aire

flint [flɪnt] *n* (a) *(stone)* pedernal *m* (b) *(in lighter)* piedra *f* de mechero

flip [flɪp] **1** *n (flick)* capirotazo *m*; **f. chart** flip chart *m*, pizarra *f* de conferencia *(con bloc)*
2 *vt (toss)* tirar (al aire); **to f. a coin** echar a cara o cruz

flip-flop [ˈflɪpflɒp] *n* (a) *Comput* báscula *f* biestable (b) *Br (footwear)* chancla *f*

flippant [ˈflɪpənt] *adj* frívolo(a)

flipper [ˈflɪpə(r)] *n* aleta *f*

flirt [flɜːt] **1** *n* coqueto(a) *m,f*
2 *vi* flirtear, coquetear; **to f. with death** jugar con la muerte

flirtation [flɜːˈteɪʃən] *n* flirteo *m*, coqueteo *m*

flit [flɪt] *vi* revolotear

float [fləʊt] **1** *n* (a) flotador *m* (b) *(money)* cambio *m* (c) *(in procession)* carroza *f*
2 *vt* (a) poner a flote (b) *(shares)* emitir; *(currency, business)* hacer flotar
3 *vi* flotar

floating [ˈfləʊtɪŋ] *adj* flotante; *(voter)* indeciso(a)

flock [flɒk] **1** *n Zool* rebaño *m*; *Orn* bandada *f*; *Rel* grey *f*; *(crowd)* multitud *f*
2 *vi* acudir en masa

flog [flɒg] *vt* (a) azotar; *Fam Fig* **flogged to death** *(idea)* trillado(a) (b) *Fam (sell)* vender

flood [flʌd] **1** *n* inundación *f*; *(of river)* riada *f*; *Fig* torrente *m*
2 *vt* inundar
3 *vi (river)* desbordarse; *Fig* **to f. in** entrar a raudales

flooding [ˈflʌdɪŋ] *n* inundaciones *fpl*

floodlight [ˈflʌdlaɪt] *n* foco *m*

floor [flɔː(r)] **1** *n* (a) *(of room)* suelo *m*; **dance f.** pista *f* de baile (b) *(of ocean, forest)* fondo *m* (c) *(storey)* piso *m*; **first f.** *Br* primer piso, *US* planta baja; *Br* **ground f.** planta baja
2 *vt Fig* dejar perplejo(a)

floorboard [ˈflɔːbɔːd] *n* tabla *f* (del suelo)

flop [flɒp] **1** *n Fam* fracaso *m*
2 *vi* (a) **to f. down on the bed** tumbarse en la cama (b) *Fam* fracasar

floppy [ˈflɒpɪ] *adj* **(floppier, floppiest)** flojo(a); *Comput* **f. disk** disco *m* flexible

flora [ˈflɔːrə] *n* flora *f*

florid [ˈflɒrɪd] *adj (style)* florido(a)

florist [ˈflɒrɪst] *n* florista *mf*; **f.'s shop** floristería *f*

flounce[1] [flaʊns] *vi* **to f. in/out** entrar/salir airadamente

flounce[2] [flaʊns] *n Sewing* volante *m*

flounder[1] [ˈflaʊndə(r)] *n (fish)* platija *f*

flounder[2] [ˈflaʊndə(r)] *vi* (a) *(struggle)* forcejear; *Fig* enredarse (b) *(be at a loss)* no saber que decir *or* hacer

flour [ˈflaʊə(r)] *n* harina *f*

flourish [ˈflʌrɪʃ] **1** *n* (a) *(gesture)* ademán *m* (teatral) (b) *(under signature)* rúbrica *f*
2 *vt (brandish)* agitar
3 *vi (thrive)* florecer; *(plant)* crecer

flourishing [ˈflʌrɪʃɪŋ] *adj* floreciente

flout [flaʊt] *vt Jur* desacatar

flow [fləʊ] **1** *n* flujo *m*; *(of river)* corriente *f*; *(of traffic)* circulación *f*; *(of capital)* movimiento *m*; *(of people, goods)* afluencia *f*; **f. chart** diagrama *m* de flujo; *Comput* organigrama *m*
2 *vi (blood, river)* fluir; *(sea)* subir; *(traffic)* circular

flower [ˈflaʊə(r)] **1** *n* flor *f*; **f. bed** arriate *m*
2 *vi* florecer

flowerpot [ˈflaʊəpɒt] *n* maceta *f*

flowery [ˈflaʊərɪ] *adj Fig* florido(a)

flowing [ˈfləʊɪŋ] *adj (hair)* suelto(a); *(dress)* de mucho vuelo; *(style)* fluido(a); *(shape, movement)* natural

flown [fləʊn] *pp of* **fly**

flu [fluː] *n (abbr* **influenza***)* gripe *f*

fluctuate [ˈflʌktjʊeɪt] *vi* fluctuar

fluctuation [flʌktjʊˈeɪʃən] *n* fluctuación *f*

flue [fluː] *n* conducto *m* de humos; *(chimney)* cañón *m*

fluent [ˈfluːənt] *adj* (a) **he speaks f. German** habla el alemán con soltura (b) *(eloquent)* fluido(a)

fluff [flʌf] **1** *n (down)* pelusa *f*
2 *vt Fam* **to f. sth** hacer algo mal

fluffy [ˈflʌfɪ] *adj* **(fluffier, fluffiest)** *(pillow)* mullido(a); *(toy)* de peluche; *(cake)* esponjoso(a)

fluid [ˈfluːɪd] **1** *adj (movement)* natural; *(style, prose)* fluido(a); *(situation)* incierto(a)
2 *n* fluido *m*, líquido *m*

fluke [fluːk] *n Fam* chiripa *f*; **by a f.** por chiripa

flummox [ˈflʌməks] *vt Fam* desconcertar

flung [flʌŋ] *pt & pp of* **fling**

flunk [flʌŋk] *vt & vi US Fam* catear

fluorescent [flʊəˈresənt] *adj* fluorescente

fluoride [ˈflʊəraɪd] *n* fluoruro *m*

flurry [ˈflʌrɪ] *n* (a) *(of wind)* ráfaga *f*; *(of snow)* nevasca *f* (b) *Fig (bustle)* agitación *f*

flush [flʌʃ] **1** *adj* **f. with** *(level)* a ras de
2 *n (blush)* rubor *m*

3 vt **to f. the lavatory** tirar de la cadena
4 vi (**a**) **the loo won't f.** la cisterna del wáter no funciona (**b**) (blush) ruborizarse

flushed [flʌʃt] adj (cheeks) rojo(a), encendido(a); Fig **f. with success** emocionado(a) ante el éxito

fluster ['flʌstə(r)] vt **to get flustered** ponerse nervioso(a)

flute [fluːt] n flauta f

flutist ['fluːtɪst] n US Mus flautista mf

flutter ['flʌtə(r)] **1** vi (leaves, birds) revolotear; (flag) ondear
2 n Fam (bet, gambling) apuesta pequeña

flux [flʌks] n (flow) flujo m; (instability) inestabilidad f; Fig **to be in a state of f.** estar cambiando constantemente

fly¹ [flaɪ] **1** vt (pt **flew**; pp **flown**) (**a**) Av pilotar (**b**) (merchandise, troops) transportar (**c**) (distance) recorrer (**d**) (kite) hacer volar
2 vi (**a**) (bird, plane) volar (**b**) (go by plane) ir en avión (**c**) (flag) ondear (**d**) **to f. into a rage** montar en cólera (**e**) **the train flew past** el tren pasó volando (**f**) Fam **to go flying** (fall) caerse
3 npl **flies** bragueta f

fly² [flaɪ] n (insect) mosca f; **f. spray** spray m matamoscas

flying ['flaɪɪŋ] **1** adj volador(a); (rapid) rápido(a); **a f. visit** una visita relámpago; Fig **to come out of an affair with f. colours** salir airoso(a) de un asunto; Fig **to get off to a f. start** empezar con buen pie; **f. picket** piquete m (informativo); **f. saucer** platillo m volante
2 n (**a**) (action) vuelo m (**b**) (aviation) aviación f

flyleaf ['flaɪliːf] n (of book) guarda f

flyover ['flaɪəʊvə(r)] n Br paso elevado

flypast ['flaɪpɑːst] n Br Av desfile aéreo

flyweight ['flaɪweɪt] n (in boxing) peso m mosca

foal [fəʊl] n potro(a) m,f

foam [fəʊm] **1** n espuma f; **f. bath** espuma de baño; **f. rubber** goma espuma
2 vi hacer espuma

fob [fɒb] n (chain) cadena f (de reloj)
► **fob off** vt sep Fam **he fobbed off his old radio on a stranger** le colocó su radio vieja a un desconocido; **to f. sb off with excuses** darle largas a algn

focus ['fəʊkəs] **1** vt centrarse (**on** en)
2 vi enfocar; **to f. on sth** Phot enfocar algo; Fig centrarse en algo
3 n (pl **focuses**) foco m; **to be in f./out of f.** estar enfocado(a)/desenfocado(a);

Com & Pol **f. group** grupo m muestra

fodder ['fɒdə(r)] n pienso m

foe [fəʊ] n Fml enemigo(a) m,f

foetus ['fiːtəs] n feto m

fog [fɒg] n niebla f; (at sea) bruma f

fogey ['fəʊgɪ] n Fam **old f.** cascarrabias mf inv

foggy ['fɒgɪ] adj (**foggier, foggiest**) **it is f.** hay niebla; Fam **I haven't the foggiest (idea)** no tengo la más mínima idea

foghorn ['fɒghɔːn] n sirena f (de niebla)

foglamp ['fɒglæmp], US **foglight** ['fɒglaɪt] n faro m antiniebla

foil [fɔɪl] **1** n (**a**) **aluminium f.** papel m de aluminio (**b**) (in fencing) florete m
2 vt (plot) desbaratar

fold [fəʊld] **1** n (crease) pliegue m
2 vt plegar, doblar; **to f. one's arms** cruzar los brazos
3 vi **to f. (up)** (chair etc) plegarse; Com quebrar

folder ['fəʊldə(r)] n carpeta f

folding ['fəʊldɪŋ] adj (chair etc) plegable

foliage ['fəʊlɪdʒ] n follaje m

folk [fəʊk] **1** npl (people) gente f (**b**) Fam **folks** (family) padres mpl; **one's folks** la familia
2 adj popular; **f. music** música f folk; **f. song** canción f popular

folklore ['fəʊklɔː(r)] n folklore m

follow ['fɒləʊ] **1** vt seguir; (pursue) perseguir; (understand) comprender; (way of life) llevar
2 vi (**a**) (come after) seguir; **as follows** como sigue (**b**) (result) resultar; **that doesn't f.** eso no es lógico (**c**) (understand) entender
► **follow through, follow up** vt sep (idea) llevar a cabo; (clue) investigar

follower ['fɒləʊə(r)] n seguidor(a) m,f

following ['fɒləʊɪŋ] **1** adj siguiente
2 n seguidores mpl

folly ['fɒlɪ] n locura f, desatino m

fond [fɒnd] adj (loving) cariñoso(a); **to be f. of sb** tenerle mucho cariño a algn; **to be f. of doing sth** ser aficionado(a) a hacer algo

fondle ['fɒndəl] vt acariciar

fondness ['fɒndnɪs] n (love) cariño m (**for** a); (liking) afición f (**for** a)

font [fɒnt] n Rel pila f

food [fuːd] n comida f; **f. chain** cadena trófica; **f. poisoning** intoxicación alimenticia

foodstuffs ['fuːdstʌfs] npl productos alimenticios

fool [fuːl] **1** n (**a**) tonto(a) m,f, imbécil mf; **to make a f. of sb** poner a algn en ridículo; **to play the f.** hacer el tonto (**b**) *Culin* ≃ mousse *f* de fruta

2 *vt* *(deceive)* engañar

3 *vi* *(joke)* bromear; **to f. about** or **around** hacer el tonto

foolhardy ['fuːlhɑːdɪ] *adj* (**foolhardier, foolhardiest**) temerario(a); *(person)* intrépido(a)

foolish ['fuːlɪʃ] *adj* estúpido(a)

foolproof ['fuːlpruːf] *adj* infalible

foot [fut] **1** *n* (*pl* **feet**) pie *m*; *Zool* pata *f*; **on f.** a pie, andando; *Fig* **to find one's feet** acostumbrarse; *Fam Fig* **to put one's f. down** *(control)* imponerse; *(in car)* pisar a fondo; *Fam Fig* **to put one's f. in it** meter la pata; *Fam Fig* **to put one's feet up** descansar

2 *vt* **to f. the bill** *(pay)* pagar la cuenta

footage ['fʊtɪdʒ] *n* *Cin* metraje *m*

football ['fʊtbɔːl] *n* (**a**) *(soccer)* fútbol *m*; **bar f.** futbolín *m*; **f. ground** campo *m* de fútbol; **f. match** partido *m* de fútbol; **f. pools** quinielas *fpl* (**b**) *(ball)* balón *m*

footballer ['fʊtbɔːlə(r)] *n* futbolista *mf*

footbridge ['fʊtbrɪdʒ] *n* puente *m* para peatones

foothills ['fʊthɪlz] *npl* estribaciones *fpl*

foothold ['fʊthəʊld] *n* *Fig* **to gain a f.** afianzarse en una posición

footing ['fʊtɪŋ] *n* **to lose one's f.** perder el equilibrio; **on a friendly f.** en plan amistoso; **on an equal f.** en pie de igualdad

footlights ['fʊtlaɪts] *npl* candilejas *fpl*

footman ['fʊtmən] *n* lacayo *m*

footnote ['fʊtnəʊt] *n* nota *f* a pie de página

footpath ['fʊtpɑːθ] *n* *(track)* sendero *m*

footprint ['fʊtprɪnt] *n* pisada *f*

footsore ['fʊtsɔː(r)] *adj* con los pies doloridos

footstep ['fʊtstep] *n* paso *m*

footwear ['fʊtweə(r)] *n* calzado *m*

for [fɔː(r), *unstressed* fə(r)] **1** *prep* (**a**) *(intended)* para; **curtains f. the bedroom** cortinas para el dormitorio; **f. sale** en venta; **it's time f. bed** es hora de acostarse

(**b**) *(representing)* por; **a cheque f. £10** un cheque de 10 libras; **J f. John** J de John; **what's the Spanish f. "rivet"?** ¿cómo se dice "rivet" en español?

(**c**) *(purpose)* para; **it's good f. the digestion** es bueno para la digestión; **what's this f.?** ¿para qué sirve esto?

(**d**) *(because of)* por; **famous f. its cuisine** famoso(a) por su cocina; **to jump f. joy** saltar de alegría

(**e**) *(on behalf of)* por; **the campaign f.**

peace la campaña por la paz; **will you do it f. me?** ¿lo harás por mí?

(**f**) *(during)* por, durante; **I lent it to her f. a year** se lo presté por un año; **I shall stay f. two weeks** me quedaré dos semanas; **I was ill f. a month** estuve enfermo(a) durante un mes; **I've been here f. three months** hace tres meses que estoy aquí

(**g**) *(distance)* **I walked f. 10 km** caminé 10 km

(**h**) *(at a point in time)* para; **I can do it f. next Monday** puedo hacerlo para el lunes que viene; **f. the last time** por última vez

(**i**) *(destination)* para

(**j**) *(amount of money)* por; **I got the car f. £500** conseguí el coche por 500 libras

(**k**) *(in favour of)* a favor de; **are you f. or against?** ¿estás a favor o en contra?; **to vote f. sb** votar a algn

(**l**) *(to obtain)* para; **to run f. the bus** correr para coger al autobús; **to send sb f. water** mandar a algn a por agua

(**m**) *(with respect to)* en cuanto a; **as f. him** en cuanto a él; **f. all I care** por mí; **f. all I know** que yo sepa; **f. one thing** para empezar

(**n**) *(despite)* a pesar de; **f. all that** aún así; **he's tall f. his age** está muy alto para su edad

(**o**) *(instead of)* por; **can you go f. me?** ¿puede ir por mí?

(**p**) *(towards)* hacia, por; **affection f. sb** cariño hacia algn; **his love f. you** su amor por ti

(**q**) *(as)* por; **to leave sb f. dead** dar a algn por muerto(a); **what do you use f. fuel?** ¿qué utilizan como combustible?

(**r**) *(in exchange)* por; **to exchange one thing f. another** cambiar una cosa por otra; **how much did you sell it f.?** ¿por cuánto lo vendiste?

(**s**) (+ *object* + *infin*) **there's no reason f. us to quarrel** no hay motivo para que riñamos; **it's time f. you to go** es hora de que os marchéis; **it's easy f. him to say that** le es fácil decir eso

2 *conj* *(since, as)* ya que, puesto que

forage ['fɒrɪdʒ] **1** *n* forraje *m*

2 *vi* hurgar

foray ['fɒreɪ] *n* incursión *f*

forbade [fə'beɪd] *pt of* **forbid**

forbearance [fɔː'beərəns] *n* paciencia *f*

forbid [fə'bɪd] *vt* (*pt* **forbade** [fə'beɪd], *pp* **forbidden** [fə'bɪdən]) prohibir; **to f. sb to do sth** prohibirle a algn hacer algo

forbidding [fə'bɪdɪŋ] *adj* *(stern)* severo(a); *(bleak)* inhóspito(a)

force [fɔːs] **1** *n* (**a**) fuerza *f*; **by f.** por la fuerza; **to come into f.** entrar en vigor (**b**) *Mil* cuerpo *m*; **the (armed) forces** las fuerzas armadas; **the police f.** la policía
2 *vt* forzar; **to f. sb to do sth** forzar a algn a hacer algo

forced [fɔːst] *adj* forzado(a); **f. landing** aterrizaje forzoso

force-feed ['fɔːsfiːd] *vt* alimentar a la fuerza

forceful ['fɔːsfʊl] *adj* (**a**) *(person)* enérgico(a) (**b**) *(argument)* convincente

forceps ['fɔːseps] *npl* fórceps *m*

forcible ['fɔːsəbəl] *adj* **f. entry** allanamiento *m* de morada

forcibly ['fɔːsəblɪ] *adv* a *or* por la fuerza

ford [fɔːd] **1** *n* vado *m*
2 *vt* vadear

fore [fɔː(r)] *n Fig* **to come to the f.** empezar a destacar

forearm ['fɔːrɑːm] *n* antebrazo *m*

foreboding [fɔː'bəʊdɪŋ] *n* presentimiento *m*

forecast ['fɔːkɑːst] **1** *n* pronóstico *m*
2 *vt* *(pt & pp* **forecast** *or* **forecasted**) pronosticar

forecourt ['fɔːkɔːt] *n (of garage)* área *f* de servicio

forefathers ['fɔːfɑːðəz] *npl* antepasados *mpl*

forefront ['fɔːfrʌnt] *n* **in the f.** a la vanguardia

forego [fɔː'gəʊ] *vt (pt* **forewent**; *pp* **foregone** [fɔː'gɒn]) *Fml* sacrificar

foregone ['fɔːgɒn] *adj* **a f. conclusion** un resultado inevitable

foreground ['fɔːgraʊnd] *n* primer plano *m*

forehead ['fɒrɪd, 'fɔːhed] *n* frente *f*

foreign ['fɒrɪn] *adj* extranjero(a); *(trade, policy)* exterior; **f. exchange** divisas *fpl*; **the F. Office** el Ministerio de Asuntos Exteriores; **f. body** cuerpo extraño

foreigner ['fɒrɪnə(r)] *n* extranjero(a) *m,f*

foreman ['fɔːmən] *n* (**a**) *Ind* capataz *m* (**b**) *Jur* presidente *m* del jurado

foremost ['fɔːməʊst] *adj* principal; **first and f.** ante todo

forename ['fɔːneɪm] *n* nombre *m* de pila

forensic [fə'rensɪk] *adj* forense

forerunner ['fɔːrʌnə(r)] *n* precursor(a) *m,f*

foresee [fɔː'siː] *vt (pt* **foresaw** [fɔː'sɔː]; *pp* **foreseen**) prever

foreseeable [fɔː'siːəbəl] *adj* previsible; **in the f. future** en un futuro próximo

foreseen [fɔː'siːn] *pp of* **foresee**

foreshadow [fɔː'ʃædəʊ] *vt* presagiar

foresight ['fɔːsaɪt] *n* previsión *f*

forest ['fɒrɪst] *n* bosque *m*

forestall [fɔː'stɔːl] *vt (plan)* anticiparse a; *(danger)* prevenir

forestry ['fɒrɪstrɪ] *n* silvicultura *f*

foretaste ['fɔːteɪst] *n* anticipo *m* (**of** de)

foretell [fɔː'tel] *vt (pt & pp* **foretold** [fɔː'təʊld]) presagiar

forever [fə'revə(r)] *adv* (**a**) *(eternally)* siempre (**b**) *(for good)* para siempre (**c**) *Fam (ages)* siglos *mpl*

forewent [fɔː'went] *pt of* **forego**

foreword ['fɔːwɜːd] *n* prefacio *m*

forfeit ['fɔːfɪt] **1** *n (penalty)* pena *f*; *(in games)* prenda *f*
2 *vt* perder

forgave [fə'geɪv] *pt of* **forgive**

forge [fɔːdʒ] **1** *n* (**a**) *(furnace)* fragua *f* (**b**) *(blacksmith's)* herrería *f*
2 *vt* (**a**) *(counterfeit)* falsificar (**b**) *(metal)* forjar
3 *vi* **to f. ahead** hacer grandes progresos

forger ['fɔːdʒə(r)] *n* falsificador(a) *m,f*

forgery ['fɔːdʒərɪ] *n* falsificación *f*

forget [fə'get] **1** *vt (pt* **forgot**; *pp* **forgotten**) olvidar, olvidarse de; **I forgot to close the window** se me olvidó cerrar *or* me olvidé de cerrar la ventana; **I've forgotten my key** he olvidado la llave
2 *vi* olvidarse

forgetful [fə'getfʊl] *adj* olvidadizo(a)

forget-me-not [fə'getmɪnɒt] *n* nomeolvides *f inv*

forgive [fə'gɪv] *vt (pt* **forgave**; *pp* **forgiven** [fə'gɪvən]) perdonar; **to f. sb for sth** perdonarle algo a algn

forgiveness [fə'gɪvnɪs] *n* perdón *m*

forgo [fɔː'gəʊ] *vt Fml* = **forego**

forgot [fə'gɒt] *pt of* **forget**

forgotten [fə'gɒtən] *pp of* **forget**

fork [fɔːk] **1** *n* (**a**) *Agr* horca *f* (**b**) *(cutlery)* tenedor *m* (**c**) *(in road)* bifurcación *f*
2 *vi (roads)* bifurcarse
▸ **fork out** *vt sep Fam (money)* soltar

fork-lift truck [fɔːklɪft'trʌk] *n* carretilla *f* elevadora de horquilla

forlorn [fə'lɔːn] *adj (forsaken)* abandonado(a); *(desolate)* triste; *(without hope)* desesperado(a)

form [fɔːm] **1** *n* (**a**) *(shape)* forma *f* (**b**) *(type)* clase *f* (**c**) **for f.'s sake** para guardar las formas (**d**) *(document)* formulario *m* (**e**) **on/on top/off f.** en/en plena/en baja forma (**f**) *Br Educ* clase *f*; **the first f.** el primer curso
2 *vt* formar; **to f. an impression** formarse una impresión
3 *vi* formarse

formal ['fɔːməl] *adj* (**a**) *(official)* oficial;

a f. application una solicitud en forma (b) (party, dress) de etiqueta (c) (ordered) formal (d) (person) formalista
formality [fɔː'mælɪtɪ] n formalidad f
formally ['fɔːməlɪ] adv oficialmente
format ['fɔːmæt] **1** n formato m
2 vt Comput formatear
formation [fɔː'meɪʃən] n formación f
formative ['fɔːmətɪv] adj formativo(a)
former ['fɔːmə(r)] adj (a) (time) anterior (b) (one-time) antiguo(a); (person) ex; the f. champion el excampeón (c) (first) aquél/aquélla; Peter and Lisa came, the f. wearing a hat vinieron Peter y Lisa, aquél llevaba sombrero
formerly ['fɔːməlɪ] adv antiguamente
formidable ['fɔːmɪdəbəl] adj (prodigious) formidable; (daunting) terrible
formula ['fɔːmjʊlə] n fórmula f
forsake [fə'seɪk] vt (pt forsook [fə'sʊk]; pp forsaken [fə'seɪkən]) Literary (a) (abandon, desert) abandonar (b) (give up) renunciar a
fort [fɔːt] n fortaleza f
forte ['fɔːteɪ] n fuerte m
forth [fɔːθ] adv Fml and so f. y así sucesivamente; to go back and f. ir de acá para allá
forthcoming [fɔːθ'kʌmɪŋ] adj (a) (event) próximo(a) (b) no money was f. no hubo oferta de dinero (c) (communicative) comunicativo(a)
forthright ['fɔːθraɪt] adj franco(a)
fortify ['fɔːtɪfaɪ] vt fortificar
fortitude ['fɔːtɪtjuːd] n fortaleza f, fuerza f
fortnight ['fɔːtnaɪt] n Br quincena f
fortnightly ['fɔːtnaɪtlɪ] Br **1** adj quincenal
2 adv cada quince días
fortress ['fɔːtrɪs] n fortaleza f
fortunate ['fɔːtʃənɪt] adj afortunado(a); it was f. that he came fue una suerte que viniera
fortunately ['fɔːtʃənɪtlɪ] adv afortunadamente
fortune ['fɔːtʃən] n (a) (luck, fate) suerte f; to tell sb's f. echar la buenaventura a algn (b) (money) fortuna f
fortune-teller ['fɔːtʃəntelə(r)] n adivino(a) m,f
forty ['fɔːtɪ] adj & n cuarenta (m inv)
forum ['fɔːrəm] n foro m
forward ['fɔːwəd] **1** adv (a) (also forwards) (direction and movement) hacia adelante (b) Fig to come f. ofrecerse (c) from this day f. de ahora en adelante
2 adj (a) (movement) hacia adelante;

(position) delantero(a) (b) (person) fresco(a)
3 n Sport delantero(a) m,f
4 vt (a) (send on) remitir (b) Fml (send goods) expedir (c) Fml (further) fomentar
fossil ['fɒsəl] n fósil m; f. fuel combustible m fósil
foster ['fɒstə(r)] **1** vt (a) (child) criar (b) Fml (hopes) abrigar; (relations) fomentar
2 adj f. child hijo(a) adoptivo(a); f. father padre adoptivo; f. mother madre adoptiva; f. parents padres adoptivos
fought [fɔːt] pt & pp of fight
foul [faʊl] **1** adj (a) (smell) fétido(a); (taste) asqueroso(a) (b) (deed) atroz; (weather) de perros (c) (language) grosero(a) (d) to fall f. of tener problemas con; Sport f. play juego sucio; Jur f. play is suspected se sospecha que se haya cometido un acto criminal
2 n Sport falta f
3 vt (a) (dirty) ensuciar; (air) contaminar (b) Sport cometer una falta contra
found[1] [faʊnd] pt & pp of find
found[2] [faʊnd] vt (establish) fundar
foundation [faʊn'deɪʃən] n (a) (establishment) fundación f (b) (basis) fundamento m (c) f. (cream) maquillaje m de fondo (d) Constr foundations cimientos mpl
founder[1] ['faʊndə(r)] n fundador(a) m,f
founder[2] ['faʊndə(r)] vi (a) Fml (sink) hundirse (b) Fig (plan, hopes) fracasar
foundry ['faʊndrɪ] n fundición f
fountain ['faʊntɪn] n (structure) fuente f; (jet) surtidor m; f. pen pluma estilográfica, CSur lapicera f fuente, Perú lapicero m
four [fɔː(r)] adj & n cuatro (m inv); on all fours a gatas
four-door ['fɔːdɔː(r)] adj Aut de cuatro puertas
four-poster [fɔː'pəʊstə(r)] adj & n f. (bed) cama f con dosel
foursome ['fɔːsəm] n grupo m de cuatro personas
fourteen [fɔː'tiːn] adj & n catorce (m inv)
fourteenth [fɔː'tiːnθ] **1** adj & n decimocuarto(a) (m,f)
2 n (fraction) catorceavo m
fourth [fɔːθ] **1** adj & n cuarto(a) (m,f)
2 n (a) (fraction) cuarto m (b) Aut cuarta f (velocidad)
fowl [faʊl] n (pl fowl) ave f de corral
fox [fɒks] **1** n zorro(a) m,f
2 vt (a) (perplex) dejar perplejo(a) (b) (deceive) engañar
foyer ['fɔɪeɪ,'fɔɪə(r)] n vestíbulo m

fracas ['frækɑː] n gresca f, refriega f

> 🖉 Note that the Spanish word **fracaso** is a false friend and is never a translation for the English word **fracas**. In Spanish, **fracaso** means "failure".

fraction ['frækʃən] n fracción f

fracture ['fræktʃə(r)] **1** n fractura f .
2 vt fracturar

fragile ['frædʒaɪl] adj frágil

fragment ['frægmənt] n fragmento m

fragrance ['freɪgrəns] n fragancia f, perfume m

fragrant ['freɪgrənt] adj fragante, aromático(a)

frail [freɪl] adj frágil, delicado(a)

frame [freɪm] **1** n (a) (of window, door, picture) marco m; (of machine) armazón m; (of bicycle) cuadro m; (of spectacles) montura f; Fig **f. of mind** estado m de ánimo (b) (in Cine & TV) fotograma m
2 vt (a) (picture) enmarcar (b) (question) formular (c) Fam (innocent person) incriminar

framework ['freɪmwɜːk] n Fig **within the f. of ...** dentro del marco de ...

franc [fræŋk] n franco m

France [frɑːns] n Francia f

franchise ['fræntʃaɪz] n (a) Pol derecho m al voto (b) Com concesión f, licencia f

frank [fræŋk] **1** adj franco(a)
2 vt (mail) franquear

frankly ['fræŋklɪ] adv francamente

frankness ['fræŋknɪs] n franqueza f

frantic ['fræntɪk] adj (anxious) desesperado(a); (hectic) frenético(a)

fraternal [frə'tɜːnəl] adj fraterno(a)

fraternity [frə'tɜːnɪtɪ] n (society) asociación f; Rel cofradía f; US Univ club m de estudiantes

fraud [frɔːd] n (a) fraude m (b) (person) *impostor(a) m,f

fraught [frɔːt] adj (a) (full) cargado(a) (with de) (b) (tense) nervioso(a)

fray¹ [freɪ] vi (a) (cloth) deshilacharse (b) (nerves) crisparse; **his temper frequently frayed** se irritaba a menudo

fray² [freɪ] n combate m

freak [friːk] **1** n (a) (monster) monstruo m (b) Fam (eccentric) estrafalario(a) m,f (c) Fam (fan) fanático(a) m,f
2 adj (a) (unexpected) inesperado(a) (b) (unusual) insólito(a)

freckle ['frekəl] n peca f

free [friː] **1** adj (a) (at liberty) libre; **to set sb f.** poner en libertad a algn; **f. kick** tiro m libre; **f. speech** libertad f de expresión; **f. will** libre albedrío m; **f. trade** libre cambio m;

f. time tiempo m libre (b) **f. (of charge)** (gratis) gratuito(a); **f. gift** obsequio m (c) (generous) generoso(a)
2 adv (a) **(for) f.** gratis (b) (loose) suelto(a)
3 vt (a) (liberate) poner en libertad (b) (let loose, work loose) soltar (c) (untie) desatar (d) (exempt) eximir (from de)

freedom ['friːdəm] n (a) (liberty) libertad f; **f. of the press** libertad de prensa (b) (exemption) exención f

free-for-all ['friːfərɔːl] n pelea f

freehold ['friːhəʊld] adj en propiedad absoluta

freelance ['friːlɑːns] adj independiente

freely ['friːlɪ] adv (a) libremente (b) (openly) abiertamente

freemason ['friːmeɪsən] n francmasón m

free-range ['friːreɪndʒ] adj Br de granja

free-style ['friːstaɪl] n estilo m libre

freeway ['friːweɪ] n US autopista f

freewheel [friː'wiːl] vi ir en punto muerto

freeze [friːz] **1** vt (pt froze; pp frozen) congelar
2 n Met helada f; **price f.** congelación f de precios; TV & Cin **f. frame** imagen congelada
3 vi (liquid) helarse; (food) congelarse

freeze-dried ['friːzdraɪd] adj liofilizado(a)

freezer ['friːzə(r)] n congelador m

freezing ['friːzɪŋ] adj (a) glacial (b) **f. point** punto m de congelación; **above/below f. point** sobre/bajo cero

freight [freɪt] n (a) (transport) transporte m (b) (goods, price) flete m; US **f. car** vagón m; US **f. elevator** montacargas m inv; **f. train** tren m de mercancías

French [frentʃ] **1** adj francés(esa); **F. bean** judía f verde, Bol, RP chaucha f, CAm ejote m, Col, Cuba habichuela f, Chile poroto m verde, Ven vainita f; **F. dressing** vinagreta f; US **F. fries** patatas fpl or Am papas fpl fritas; **F. window** puerta f vidriera
2 n (a) (language) francés m (b) pl **the F.** los franceses

Frenchman ['frentʃmən] n francés m

Frenchwoman ['frentʃwʊmən] n francesa f

frenetic [frɪ'netɪk] adj frenético(a)

frenzy ['frenzɪ] n frenesí m

frequency ['friːkwənsɪ] n frecuencia f

frequent 1 adj ['friːkwənt] frecuente
2 vt [frɪ'kwent] frecuentar

frequently ['friːkwəntlɪ] adv frecuentemente, a menudo

fresh [freʃ] adj (**a**) fresco(a); **f. water** agua f dulce; **f. bread** pan del día (**b**) (new) nuevo(a); **open a f. packet** abre otro paquete (**c**) (air) puro(a); **in the f. air** al aire libre (**d**) US Fam (cheeky) fresco(a)

freshen ['freʃən] vi (wind) refrescar
► **freshen up** vi asearse

fresher ['freʃə(r)] n Univ estudiante mf de primer año, novato(a) m,f

freshly ['freʃlɪ] adv recién, recientemente

freshman ['freʃmən] n US = fresher

freshness ['freʃnɪs] n frescura f

freshwater ['freʃwɔːtə(r)] adj de agua dulce

fret [fret] vi preocuparse (about por)

FRG [efɑː'dʒiː] n Hist (abbr Federal Republic of Germany) RFA f

friar ['fraɪə(r)] n fraile m

friction ['frɪkʃən] n fricción f

Friday ['fraɪdɪ] n viernes m

fridge [frɪdʒ] n nevera f, frigorífico m, Andes frigider m, RP heladera f

friend [frend] n amigo(a) m,f; **a f. of mine** un(a) amigo(a) mío(a); **to make friends with sb** hacerse amigo(a) de algn; **to make friends again** hacer las paces

friendliness ['frendlɪnɪs] n amabilidad f, simpatía f

friendly ['frendlɪ] adj (**friendlier, friendliest**) (person) simpático(a); (atmosphere) acogedor(a); **f. advice** consejo m de amigo; **f. nation** nación amiga

friendship ['frendʃɪp] n amistad f

frieze [friːz] n friso m

frigate ['frɪgɪt] n fragata f

fright [fraɪt] n (**a**) (fear) miedo m; **to take f.** asustarse (**b**) (shock) susto m; **to get a f.** pegarse un susto

frighten ['fraɪtən] vt asustar
► **frighten away, frighten off** vt sep ahuyentar

frightened ['fraɪtənd] adj asustado(a); **to be f. of sb** tenerle miedo a algn

frightening ['fraɪtənɪŋ] adj espantoso(a)

frightful ['fraɪtfʊl] adj espantoso(a), horroroso(a)

frightfully ['fraɪtfʊlɪ] adv tremendamente, terriblemente

frigid ['frɪdʒɪd] adj frígido(a)

frill [frɪl] n (on dress) volante m; Fig **frills** (decorations) adornos mpl

fringe [frɪndʒ] n (**a**) Br (of hair) flequillo m, Am cerquillo m (**b**) (edge) borde m; Fig **on the f. of society** al margen de la

sociedad; **f. theatre** teatro m experimental; **f. benefits** extras mpl

Frisbee® ['frɪzbɪ] n platillo m

frisk [frɪsk] vt Fam (search) registrar

frisky ['frɪskɪ] adj (**friskier, friskiest**) (**a**) (children, animals) juguetón(ona) (**b**) (adult) vivo(a)

fritter ['frɪtə(r)] n buñuelo m
► **fritter away** vt sep malgastar

frivolous ['frɪvələs] adj frívolo(a)

frizzy ['frɪzɪ] adj (**frizzier, frizziest**) crespo(a)

frock [frɒk] n vestido m; **f. coat** levita f

frog [frɒg] n rana f; **frogs' legs** ancas fpl de rana; Fig **to have a f. in one's throat** tener carraspera

frogman ['frɒgmən] n hombre m rana

frolic ['frɒlɪk] vi retozar, juguetear

from [frɒm, unstressed frəm] prep (**a**) (time) desde, a partir de; **f. now on** a partir de ahora; **f. Monday to Friday** de lunes a viernes; **f. the 8th to the 17th** desde el 8 hasta el 17; **f. time to time** de vez en cuando

(**b**) (price, number) desde, de; **dresses f. £5** vestidos desde 5 libras; **a number f. one to ten** un número del uno a diez

(**c**) (origin) de; **a letter f. her father** una carta de su padre; **f. English into Spanish** del inglés al español; **he's f. Malaga** es de Málaga; **the train f. Bilbao** el tren procedente de Bilbao; **to go f. door to door** ir de puerta en puerta; **her eyes were red f. crying** tenía los ojos rojos de llorar

(**d**) (distance) de; **the town is 4 miles f. the coast** el pueblo está a 4 millas de la costa

(**e**) (out of) de; **bread is made f. flour** el pan se hace con harina

(**f**) (remove, subtract) a; **he took the book f. the child** le quitó el libro al niño; **take three f. five** restar tres a cinco

(**g**) (according to) según, por; **f. what the author said** según lo que dijo el autor; **speaking f. my own experience** hablando por experiencia propia

(**h**) (position) desde, de; **f. here** desde aquí

(**i**) **can you tell margarine f. butter?** ¿puedes distinguir entre la margarina y la mantequilla?

front [frʌnt] **1** n (**a**) parte delantera; **in f. (of)** delante (de) (**b**) (of building) fachada f (**c**) Mil, Pol & Met frente m (**d**) (seaside) paseo marítimo (**e**) Fig **she put on a brave f.** hizo de tripas corazón

2 adj delantero(a), de delante; Pol **f. bench** = primera fila de escaños donde se sientan los ministros del Gobierno o de la Oposición; **f. door** puerta *f* principal; **f. room** salón *m*; **f. seat** asiento *m* de delante

frontier ['frʌntɪə(r)] *n* frontera *f*

front-page ['frʌntpeɪdʒ] *adj* de primera página

frost [frɒst] **1** *n* (**a**) *(covering)* escarcha *f* (**b**) *(freezing)* helada *f*

  2 *vt US Culin* recubrir con azúcar glas

  ▶ **frost over** *vi* escarchar

frostbite ['frɒstbaɪt] *n* congelación *f*

frosted ['frɒstɪd] *adj* (**a**) *(glass)* esmerilado(a) (**b**) *US Culin* recubierto(a) de azúcar glas

frosty ['frɒstɪ] *adj* (**frostier, frostiest**) (**a**) **it will be a f. night tonight** esta noche habrá helada (**b**) *Fig* glacial

froth [frɒθ] **1** *n* espuma *f*; *(from mouth)* espumarajos *mpl*

  2 *vi* espumar

frothy ['frɒθɪ] *adj* (**frothier, frothiest**) espumoso(a)

frown [fraʊn] *vi* fruncir el ceño

  ▶ **frown upon** *vt insep* desaprobar

froze [frəʊz] *pt of* **freeze**

frozen ['frəʊzən] **1** *adj (liquid, feet etc)* helado(a); *(food)* congelado(a)

  2 *pp of* **freeze**

frugal ['fruːgəl] *adj* frugal

fruit [fruːt] *n* (**a**) *Bot* fruto *m* (**b**) *(apple, orange etc)* fruta *f*; **f. cake** pastel *m* con fruto seco; **f. machine** máquina *f* tragaperras; **f. salad** macedonia *f* de frutas (**c**) **fruits** *(rewards)* frutos *mpl*

fruitful ['fruːtfʊl] *adj Fig* provechoso(a)

fruition [fruːˈɪʃən] *n Fml* **to come to f.** realizarse

frustrate [frʌˈstreɪt] *vt* frustrar

frustrated [frʌˈstreɪtɪd] *adj* frustrado(a)

frustration [frʌˈstreɪʃən] *n* frustración *f*

fry¹ [fraɪ] **1** *vt (pt & pp* **fried**) freír

  2 *vi Fig* asarse

fry² [fraɪ] *npl* **small f.** gente *f* de poca monta

frying pan ['fraɪŋpæn], *US* **fry-pan** ['fraɪpæn] *n* sartén *f*

ft *(abbr* **foot**) pie *m*; *(abbr* **feet**) pies *mpl*

fuck [fʌk] *vt & vi Vulg* joder; **f. (it)!** ¡joder!

  ▶ **fuck off** *vi Vulg* **f. off!** ¡vete a la mierda!

  ▶ **fuck up** *vt sep Vulg* joder

fucking ['fʌkɪŋ] *Vulg* **1** *adj* **f. idiot!** ¡gilipollas!; **where are my f. keys?** ¿dónde coño están las llaves?

  2 *adv* **a f. good film** una película de puta madre

fuddy-duddy ['fʌdɪdʌdɪ] *n Fam* **an old f.** un carcamal *or Am* carcamán

fudge [fʌdʒ] **1** *n Culin* = dulce hecho con azúcar, leche y mantequilla

  2 *vt (figures)* amañar

fuel ['fjʊəl] **1** *n* combustible *m*; *(for engines)* carburante *m*; **f. tank** depósito *m* de combustible

  2 *vt Fig (ambition)* estimular; *(difficult situation)* empeorar

fugitive ['fjuːdʒɪtɪv] *n Fml* fugitivo(a) *m,f*

fulfil, *US* **fulfill** [fʊlˈfɪl] *vt* (**a**) *(task, ambition)* realizar; *(promise)* cumplir; *(role)* desempeñar (**b**) *(wishes)* satisfacer

fulfilment, *US* **fulfillment** [fʊlˈfɪlmənt] *n* (**a**) *(of ambition)* realización *f* (**b**) *(of duty, promise)* cumplimiento *m*

full [fʊl] **1** *adj* (**a**) lleno(a); **f. of** lleno(a) de; **I'm f. (up)** no puedo más (**b**) *(complete)* completo(a); **at f. speed** a toda velocidad; **f. text** texto íntegro; *Fam* **in f. swing** en plena marcha; **f. board** pensión completa; **f. employment** pleno empleo; **f. house** lleno total; **f. moon** luna llena; **f. stop** punto *m*

  2 *n* **in f.** en su totalidad; **name in f.** nombre y apellidos completos

  3 *adv* **f. well** perfectamente

full-blown ['fʊlbləʊn] *adj* auténtico(a)

full-fledged ['fʊlfledʒd] *adj US =* **fully-fledged**

fullness ['fʊlnɪs] *n* **in the f. of time** con el tiempo

full-scale ['fʊlskeɪl] *adj* (**a**) *(model)* de tamaño natural (**b**) **f. search** registro *m* a fondo; **f. war** guerra generalizada *or* total

full-time [fʊlˈtaɪm] **1** *adj* de jornada completa

  2 *adv* **to work f.** trabajar a tiempo completo

fully ['fʊlɪ] *adv* completamente

fully-fledged ['fʊlɪfledʒd] *adj* hecho(a) y derecho(a)

fulsome ['fʊlsəm] *adj* excesivo(a), exagerado(a)

fumble ['fʌmbəl] *vi* hurgar; **to f. for sth** buscar algo a tientas; **to f. with sth** manejar algo con torpeza

fume [fjuːm] **1** *n (usu pl)* humo *m*

  2 *vi* despedir humo

> 🖉 Note that the Spanish verb **fumar** is a false friend and is never a translation for the English verb **to fume**. In Spanish, **fumar** means "to smoke".

fun [fʌn] **1** *n (amusement)* diversión *f*; **in** *or* **for f.** en broma; **to have f.** divertirse, pasarlo bien; **to make f. of sb** reírse de algn

  2 *adj* divertido(a)

function ['fʌŋkʃən] **1** *n* (**a**) función *f* (**b**) *(ceremony)* acto *m*; *(party)* recepción *f*
2 *vi* funcionar

functional ['fʌŋkʃənəl] *adj* funcional

fund [fʌnd] **1** *n* (**a**) *Com* fondo *m* (**b**) **funds** fondos *mpl*
2 *vt (finance)* financiar

📖 Note that the Spanish verb **fundar** is a false friend and is never a translation for the English verb **to fund**. In Spanish, **fundar** means "to found".

fundamental [fʌndəˈmentəl] **1** *adj* fundamental
2 *npl* **fundamentals** los fundamentos

funeral ['fjuːnərəl] *n* funeral *m*; *US* **f. home** funeraria *f*; **f. march** marcha *f* fúnebre; *Br* **f. parlour** funeraria; **f. service** misa *f* de cuerpo presente

funfair ['fʌnfeə(r)] *n Br* parque *m* de atracciones

fungus ['fʌŋgəs] *n* (*pl* **fungi** ['fʌŋgaɪ]) (**a**) *Bot* hongo *m* (**b**) *Med* fungo *m*

funnel ['fʌnəl] **1** *n* (**a**) *(for liquids)* embudo *m* (**b**) *Naut* chimenea *f*
2 *vt Fig (funds, energy)* encauzar

funnily ['fʌnɪlɪ] *adv Fam* **f. enough** aunque parezca extraño

funny ['fʌnɪ] *adj* (**funnier, funniest**) (**a**) *(peculiar)* raro(a), extraño(a); **that's f.!** ¡qué raro! (**b**) *(amusing)* divertido(a), gracioso(a); **I found it very f.** me hizo mucha gracia (**c**) *Fam (ill)* mal (**d**) *Fam (dishonest)* dudoso(a)

fur [fɜː(r)] **1** *n* (**a**) *(of living animal)* pelo *m* (**b**) *(of dead animal)* piel *f* (**c**) *(in kettle, on tongue)* sarro *m*
2 *adj* de piel; **f. coat** abrigo *m* de pieles

furious ['fjʊərɪəs] *adj* (**a**) *(angry)* furioso(a) (**b**) *(vigorous)* violento(a)

furlong ['fɜːlɒŋ] *n (measurement)* = aprox 201 m

furnace ['fɜːnɪs] *n* horno *m*

furnish ['fɜːnɪʃ] *vt* (**a**) *(house)* amueblar (**b**) *Fml (food)* suministrar; *(details)* facilitar

furnishings ['fɜːnɪʃɪŋz] *npl* (**a**) muebles *mpl* (**b**) *(fittings)* accesorios *mpl*

furniture ['fɜːnɪtʃə(r)] *n* muebles *mpl*; **a piece of f.** un mueble

furrow ['fʌrəʊ] *n Agr* surco *m*; *(on forehead)* arruga *f*

furry ['fɜːrɪ] *adj* (**furrier, furriest**) (**a**) *(hairy)* peludo(a) (**b**) *(tongue, kettle)* sarroso(a)

further ['fɜːðə(r)] **1** *adj* (*comp* of **far**) (**a**) *(new)* nuevo(a); **until f. notice** hasta nuevo aviso (**b**) *(additional)* otro(a), adicional (**c**) *(later)* posterior; **f. education** estudios *mpl* superiores
2 *adv* (**a**) *(more)* más; **f. back** más atrás; **f. along** más adelante; **she heard nothing f.** no volvió a saber nada más (**b**) *Fml* **f. to your letter of the 9th** con referencia a su carta del 9 del corriente (**c**) *Fml (besides)* además
3 *vt* fomentar

furthermore [fɜːðəˈmɔː(r)] *adv Fml* además

furthest ['fɜːðɪst] *adj* (*superl* of **far**) más lejano(a)

furtive ['fɜːtɪv] *adj* furtivo(a)

fury ['fjʊərɪ] *n* furia *f*, furor *m*

fuse [fjuːz] **1** *n* (**a**) *Elec* fusible *m*; **f. box** caja *f* de fusibles (**b**) *(of bomb)* mecha *f*
2 *vi* (**a**) *Elec* **the lights fused** se fundieron los plomos (**b**) *Fig (merge)* fusionarse (**c**) *(melt)* fundirse
3 *vt* (**a**) *Elec* fundir los plomos de (**b**) *Fig (merge)* fusionar (**c**) *(melt)* fundir

fuselage ['fjuːzɪlɑːʒ] *n* fuselaje *m*

fuss [fʌs] **1** *n (commotion)* jaleo *m*; **to kick up a f.** armar un escándalo; **stop making a f. (complaining)** deja ya de quejarte; **to make a f. of (pay attention to)** mimar a
2 *vi* preocuparse (**about** por)

fussy ['fʌsɪ] *adj* (**fussier, fussiest**) exigente; *(nitpicking)* quisquilloso(a)

futile ['fjuːtaɪl] *adj* inútil, vano(a)

futility [fjuːˈtɪlɪtɪ] *n* inutilidad *f*

future ['fjuːtʃə(r)] **1** *n* futuro *m*, porvenir *m*; **in the near f.** en un futuro próximo; **in f.** de aquí en adelante
2 *adj* futuro(a)

futuristic [fjuːtʃəˈrɪstɪk] *adj* futurista

fuze [fjuːz] *n, vi & vt US* = **fuse**

fuzzy ['fʌzɪ] *adj* (**fuzzier, fuzziest**) (**a**) *(hair)* muy rizado(a) (**b**) *(blurred)* borroso(a)

G, g [dʒiː] *n* (**a**) *(the letter)* G, g *f* (**b**) *Mus* G sol *m*

G [dʒiː] *adj US Cin* ≃ (apta) para todos los públicos

g *(abbr* **gramme**) g

gabble ['gæbəl] **1** *n* chapurreo *m*
2 *vi* hablar atropelladamente

gable ['geɪbəl] *n* aguilón *m*

gadget ['gædʒɪt] *n* artilugio *m*, aparato *m*

Gaelic ['geɪlɪk] **1** *adj* gaélico(a)
2 *n (language)* gaélico *m*

gaffe [gæf] *n* metedura *f* de pata, desliz *m*; **to make a g.** meter la pata, patinar

> 🖉 Note that the Spanish word **gafe** is a false friend and is never a translation for the English word **gaffe**. In Spanish, **gafe** means "jinxed person".

gag [gæg] **1** *n* (**a**) mordaza *f* (**b**) *Fam (joke)* chiste *m*
2 *vt* amordazar

gage [geɪdʒ] *n & vt US* = **gauge**

gaiety ['geɪətɪ] *n* regocijo *m*

gaily ['geɪlɪ] *adv* alegremente

gain [geɪn] **1** *n* ganancia *f*, beneficio *m*; *(increase)* aumento *m*
2 *vt* ganar; *Fig* **to g. ground** ganar terreno; **to g. speed** ganar velocidad, acelerar; **to g. weight** aumentar de peso

gait [geɪt] *n* (manera *f* de) andar *m*

gal (*pl* **gal** *or* **gals**) *(abbr* **gallon**) galón *m*

gala ['gɑːlə, 'geɪlə] *n* gala *f*, fiesta *f*

galaxy ['gæləksɪ] *n* galaxia *f*

gale [geɪl] *n* vendaval *m*

Galicia [gə'lɪʃə] *n* Galicia

Galician [gə'lɪʃən, gə'lɪʃən] **1** *adj* gallego(a)
2 *n* (**a**) *(person)* gallego(a) *m,f* (**b**) *(language)* gallego *m*

gall [gɔːl] **1** *n Fam* descaro *m*
2 *vt* molestar, irritar

gallant ['gælənt] *adj (brave)* valiente; *(also* [gə'lænt]) *(chivalrous)* galante

gallantry ['gæləntrɪ] *n (bravery)* gallardía *f*; *(politeness)* galantería *f*

galleon ['gælɪən] *n* galeón *m*

gallery ['gælərɪ] *n* (**a**) galería *f* (**b**) *Th* gallinero *m* (**c**) *(court)* tribuna *f*

galley ['gælɪ] *n* (**a**) *(ship)* galera *f*; **g. slave** galeote *m* (**b**) *(kitchen)* cocina *f*

Gallicism ['gælɪsɪzəm] *n* galicismo *m*

gallivant ['gælɪvænt] *vi Fam* callejear

gallon ['gælən] *n* galón *m* *(Br = 4,55 l; US = 3,79 l)*

gallop ['gæləp] **1** *n* galope *m*
2 *vi* galopar

gallows ['gæləʊz] *n sing* horca *f*, patíbulo *m*

gallstone ['gɔːlstəʊn] *n* cálculo *m* biliar

galore [gə'lɔː(r)] *adv Fam* en cantidad, en abundancia

galvanize ['gælvənaɪz] *vt (metal)* galvanizar; *Fig* **to g. sb into action** galvanizar a algn

galvanized ['gælvənaɪzd] *adj* galvanizado(a)

gambit ['gæmbɪt] *n (in chess)* gambito *m*; *Fig* táctica *f*

gamble ['gæmbəl] **1** *n (risk)* riesgo *m*; *(risky undertaking)* empresa arriesgada; *(bet)* apuesta *f*
2 *vi (bet)* jugar; *(take a risk)* arriesgarse

gambler ['gæmblə(r)] *n* jugador(a) *m,f*

gambling ['gæmblɪŋ] *n* juego *m*

gambol ['gæmbəl] *vi* brincar

game [geɪm] **1** *n* (**a**) juego *m*; **g. of chance** juego de azar (**b**) *(match)* partido *m*; *(of bridge)* partida *f* (**c**) **games** *Sport* juegos *mpl; Br Educ* educación física (**d**) *(hunting)* caza *f*; *Fig* presa *f*, **g. reserve** coto *m* de caza
2 *adj* **g. for anything** dispuesto(a) a todo

gamekeeper ['geɪmkiːpə(r)] *n* guardabosque *mf*

gamely ['geɪmlɪ] *adv* resueltamente

gammon ['gæmən] *n Br* jamón ahumado *or* curado

gamut ['gæmət] *n* gama *f*; **to run the g. of ...** experimentar todas las posibilidades de ...

gang [gæŋ] *n (of criminals)* banda *f*, *(of youths)* pandilla *f*; *(of workers)* cuadrilla *f*
▸ **gang up** *vi Fam* confabularse (**on** contra)

gangplank ['gæŋplæŋk] *n* plancha *f*

gangrene ['gæŋgriːn] *n* gangrena *f*

gangster ['gæŋstə(r)] n gángster m

gangway ['gæŋweɪ] n Naut pasarela f; Th pasillo m

gantry ['gæntrɪ] n puente m transversal

gaol [dʒeɪl] n & vt Br = jail

gap [gæp] n (a) abertura f, hueco m; (blank space) blanco m; (in traffic) claro m; **to bridge a g.** rellenar un hueco (b) (in time) intervalo m; (emptiness) vacío m (c) (gulf) diferencia f (d) (deficiency) laguna f

gape [geɪp] vi (person) quedarse boquiabierto(a), mirar boquiabierto(a); (thing) estar abierto(a)

gaping ['geɪpɪŋ] adj Fig profundo(a)

garage ['gærɑːʒ, 'gærɪdʒ] n garaje m; (for repairs) taller mecánico; (filling station) gasolina f, estación f de servicio, Andes, Ven bomba f, Méx gasolinería f, Perú grifo m

garbage ['gɑːbɪdʒ] n US basura f; Fig tonterías fpl; **g. can** cubo m de la basura; **g. dump** vertedero m; **g. man** basurero m; **g. truck** camión m de la basura

garbled ['gɑːbəld] adj embrollado(a); **g. account** relato confuso

garden ['gɑːdən] n jardín m; **g. centre** centro m de jardinería; **g. party** recepción f al aire libre

gardener ['gɑːdənə(r)] n jardinero(a) m,f

gardenia [gɑːˈdiːnɪə] n gardenia f

gardening ['gɑːdənɪŋ] n jardinería f; **his mother does the g.** su madre es la que cuida el jardín

gargle ['gɑːgəl] vi hacer gárgaras

gargoyle ['gɑːgɔɪl] n gárgola f

garish ['geərɪʃ] adj chillón(ona)

garland ['gɑːlənd] n guirnalda f

garlic ['gɑːlɪk] n ajo m

garment ['gɑːmənt] n prenda f

garnish ['gɑːnɪʃ] vt guarnecer

garrison ['gærɪsən] n guarnición f

garrulous ['gærələs] adj locuaz

garter ['gɑːtə(r)] n liga f

gas [gæs] **1** n (a) gas m; **g. chamber** cámara f de gas; **g. cooker** cocina f de gas; **g. fire** estufa f de gas; **g. mask** careta f antigás; **g. ring** hornillo m de gas (b) US gasolina f, RP nafta f; **g. pump** surtidor m de gasolina; **g. station** gasolinera f, estación f de servicio, Andes, Ven bomba f, Méx gasolinería f, Perú grifo m; **g. tank** depósito m de la gasolina

2 vt (asphyxiate) asfixiar con gas

3 vi Fam (talk) charlotear

gash [gæʃ] **1** n herida profunda

2 vt hacer un corte en; **he gashed his forehead** se hizo una herida en la frente

gasket ['gæskɪt] n junta f

gasoline ['gæsəliːn] n US gasolina f

gasp [gɑːsp] **1** n (cry) grito sordo; (breath) bocanada f, Fig **to be at one's last g.** estar en las últimas

2 vi (in surprise) quedar boquiabierto(a); (breathe) jadear

gassy ['gæsɪ] adj (gassier, gassiest) gaseoso(a)

gastric ['gæstrɪk] adj gástrico(a)

gastronomic [gæstrəˈnɒmɪk] adj gastronómico(a)

gate [geɪt] n (a) puerta f (b) (at football ground) entrada f; **g. (money)** taquilla f (c) (attendance) entrada f

gateau ['gætəʊ] n (pl gateaux ['gætəʊz]) pastel m con nata

gatecrash ['geɪtkræʃ] **1** vt colarse en

2 vi colarse

gateway ['geɪtweɪ] n puerta f; Fig pasarte m

gather ['gæðə(r)] **1** vt (a) (collect) juntar; (pick) coger; (pick up) recoger (b) (bring together) reunir (c) (harvest) cosechar (d) **to g. speed** ir ganando velocidad; **to g. strength** cobrar fuerzas (e) (understand) suponer; **I g. that ...** tengo entendido que ... (f) Sewing fruncir

2 vi (a) (come together) reunirse (b) (form) formarse

▸ **gather round** vi agruparse

gathering ['gæðərɪŋ] **1** adj creciente

2 n reunión f

gauche [gəʊʃ] adj (clumsy) torpe; (tactless) sin tacto

gaudy ['gɔːdɪ] adj (gaudier, gaudiest) chillón(ona)

gauge [geɪdʒ] **1** n (a) medida f estándar; (of gun, wire) calibre m (b) Rail ancho m de vía (c) (calibrator) indicador m (d) Fig (indication) indicación f

2 vt (a) (measure) medir, calibrar (b) Fig (judge) juzgar

gaunt [gɔːnt] adj (lean) demacrado(a); (desolate) lúgubre

gauntlet ['gɔːntlɪt] n guantelete m; Fig **to run the g. of ...** estar sometido(a) a ...; Fig **to throw down the g.** arrojar el guante

gauze [gɔːz] n gasa f

gave [geɪv] pt of give

gawky ['gɔːkɪ] adj (gawkier, gawkiest) desgarbado(a)

gay [geɪ] adj (a) (homosexual) gay (b) (happy) alegre

gaze [geɪz] **1** n mirada fija

2 vi mirar fijamente

gazelle [gəˈzel] n gacela f

gazette [gəˈzet] n gaceta f; US periódico m

gazump [gəˈzʌmp] vi Br Fam = romper

un compromiso de venta para vender a un precio más alto

GB [dʒiː'biː] (*abbr* **Great Britain**) GB

GCE [dʒiːsiː'iː] *n Br Formerly* (*abbr* **General Certificate of Education (A-Level)**) = certificado de enseñanza secundaria

GCSE [dʒiːsiːes'iː] *n Br* (*abbr* **General Certificate of Secondary Education**) = certificado de enseñanza secundaria

GDP [dʒiːdiː'piː] *n* (*abbr* **gross domestic product**) PIB *m*

GDR [dʒiːdiːˈɑː(r)] *n Hist* (*abbr* **German Democratic Republic**) RDA *f*

gear [ɡɪə(r)] **1** *n* (**a**) (*equipment*) equipo *m* (**b**) *Fam* (*belongings*) bártulos *mpl* (**c**) *Fam* (*clothing*) ropa *f* (**d**) *Tech* engranaje *m* (**e**) *Aut* velocidad *f*, marcha *f*; **first g.** primera *f* (velocidad *f*); **g. lever** *or US* **shift** palanca *f* de cambio
   2 *vt* ajustar, adaptar

gearbox ['ɡɪəbɒks] *n* caja *f* de cambios

gearstick ['ɡɪəstɪk], *US* **gearshift** ['ɡɪəʃɪft] *n* palanca *f* de cambio

gee [dʒiː] *interj US* ¡caramba!

geese [ɡiːs] *pl of* **goose**

gel [dʒel] **1** *n* gel *m*; (*for hair*) gomina *f*
   2 *vi Fig* (*ideas etc*) cuajar
   3 *vt* (*hair*) engominar

gelatin ['dʒelətɪn] *n* gelatina *f*

gelignite ['dʒelɪɡnaɪt] *n* gelignita *f*

gem [dʒem] *n* piedra preciosa; *Fig* (*person*) joya *f*

Gemini ['dʒemɪnaɪ] *n* Géminis *m*

gen [dʒen] *n Fam* **to get the g. on sth** informarse sobre algo

gender ['dʒendə(r)] *n* género *m*

gene [dʒiːn] *n* gene *m*, gen *m*

general ['dʒenərəl] **1** *adj* general; **g. knowledge** conocimientos *mpl* generales; **in g.** en general; **the g. public** el público; **g. practitioner** médico *m* de cabecera
   2 *n Mil* general *m*; *US* **g. of the army** mariscal *m* de campo

generalization [dʒenərəlaɪ'zeɪʃən] *n* generalización *f*

generalize ['dʒenərəlaɪz] *vt & vi* generalizar

generally ['dʒenərəlɪ] *adv* generalmente, en general

generate ['dʒenəreɪt] *vt* generar

generation [dʒenə'reɪʃən] *n* generación *f*; **g. gap** abismo *m* or conflicto *m* generacional

generator ['dʒenəreɪtə(r)] *n* generador *m*

generosity [dʒenə'rɒsɪtɪ] *n* generosidad *f*

generous ['dʒenərəs] *adj* generoso(a); (*plentiful*) copioso(a)

genetic [dʒɪ'netɪk] *adj* genético(a); **g. engineering** ingeniería genética

genetically [dʒɪ'netɪklɪ] *adv* **g. modified** (*plant, food*) modificado(a) genéticamente

genetics [dʒɪ'netɪks] *n sing* genética *f*

Geneva [dʒɪ'niːvə] *n* Ginebra

genial ['dʒiːnɪəl, 'dʒiːnjəl] *adj* cordial, amable

> 🖊 Note that the Spanish word **genial** is a false friend and is never a translation for the English word **genial**. In Spanish, **genial** means both "brilliant" and "terrific".

genie ['dʒiːnɪ] *n* duende *m*, genio *m*

genitals ['dʒenɪtəlz] *npl* órganos *mpl* genitales

genius ['dʒiːnjəs, 'dʒiːnɪəs] *n* (**a**) (*person*) genio *m* (**b**) (*gift*) don *m*

genre ['ʒɑːnrə] *n* género *m*

gent [dʒent] *n Fam* (*abbr* **gentleman**) señor *m*, caballero *m*; **the gents** los servicios (de caballeros)

genteel [dʒen'tiːl] *adj* fino(a), distinguido(a)

> 🖊 Note that the Spanish word **gentil** is a false friend and is never a translation for the English word **genteel**. In Spanish, **gentil** means "kind" and "pagan".

gentle ['dʒentəl] *adj* dulce, tierno(a); (*breeze*) suave

gentleman ['dʒentəlmən] *n* caballero ; *bm*; **g.'s agreement** pacto *m* de caballeros

gently ['dʒentlɪ] *adv* con cuidado

gentry ['dʒentrɪ] *n* pequeña nobleza, alta burguesía

genuine ['dʒenjʊɪn] *adj* auténtico(a), genuino(a); (*sincere*) sincero(a)

genuinely ['dʒenjʊɪnlɪ] *adv* auténticamente

geographic(al) [dʒɪə'ɡræfɪk(əl)] *adj* geográfico(a)

geography [dʒɪ'ɒɡrəfɪ, 'dʒɒɡrəfɪ] *n* geografía *f*

geologic(al) [dʒɪə'lɒdʒɪk(əl)] *adj* geológico(a)

geology [dʒɪ'ɒlədʒɪ] *n* geología *f*

geometric(al) [dʒɪə'metrɪk(əl)] *adj* geométrico(a)

geometry [dʒɪ'ɒmɪtrɪ] *n* geometría *f*

geopolitical [dʒiːəʊpə'lɪtɪkəl] *adj* geopolítico(a)

geranium [dʒɪ'reɪnɪəm] *n* geranio *m*

geriatric [dʒerɪ'ætrɪk] *adj* geriátrico(a)

germ [dʒɜːm] *n* (**a**) *Biol & Fig* germen *m*
(**b**) *Med* microbio *m*

German [ˈdʒɜːmən] **1** *adj* alemán(ana);
G. measles rubeola *f*
2 *n* (**a**) alemán(ana) *m,f* (**b**) *(language)*
alemán *m*

Germany [ˈdʒɜːmənɪ] *n* Alemania

germinate [ˈdʒɜːmɪneɪt] *vi* germinar

gestation [dʒeˈsteɪʃən] *n* gestación *f*

gesticulate [dʒeˈstɪkjʊleɪt] *vi* gesticular

gesture [ˈdʒestʃə(r)] **1** *n* gesto *m*, ademán *m*; **it's an empty g.** es pura formalidad
2 *vi* gesticular, hacer gestos

get [get] **1** *vt* (*pt & pp* **got**; *pp US also*
gotten) (**a**) *(obtain)* obtener, conseguir;
to g. one's own way salirse con la suya
(**b**) *(earn)* ganar
(**c**) *(fetch) (something)* traer; *(somebody)*
ir a por; **g. the police!** ¡llama a la policía!;
Tel **me Mr Brown** póngame con el Sr.
Brown
(**d**) *(receive)* recibir; *Fam* **he got the sack**
le despidieron
(**e**) *(bus, train, thief etc)* coger; *Am* agarrar
(**f**) *(prepare)* preparar; **can I g. you
something to eat?** ¿quieres comer algo?
(**g**) *(ask)* pedir; **g. him to call me** dile que
me llame
(**h**) **to g. sb to agree to sth** conseguir
que algn acepte algo
(**i**) **when did you g. the house painted?**
¿cuándo os pintaron la casa?; **to g. one's
hair cut** cortarse el pelo
(**j**) **they got him in the chest** le dieron en
el pecho
(**k**) **have got, have got to** *see* **have**
(**l**) *Fam (understand)* entender
(**m**) *(record) (in writing)* apuntar; *(on
tape)* grabar
2 *vi* (**a**) *(become)* ponerse; **to g. dark**
anochecer; **to g. dressed** vestirse; **to g.
drunk** emborracharse; **to g. late** hacerse
tarde; **to g. married** casarse; **to g. used to
doing sth** acostumbrarse a hacer algo; **to
g. paid** cobrar
(**b**) *Fig* **we are not getting anywhere** así
no vamos a ninguna parte
(**c**) *(arrive)* llegar
(**d**) **to g. to** *(come to)* llegar a; **to g. to
know sb** llegar a conocer a algn

▸ **get about** *vi (person)* salir; *(news)* difundirse

▸ **get across** *vt sep (idea etc)* hacer
comprender

▸ **get ahead** *vi* progresar

▸ **get along** *vi* (**a**) *(leave)* marcharse (**b**)

(manage) arreglárselas (**c**) *(two people)*
llevarse bien

▸ **get around** *vi (person)* salir; *(travel)*
viajar; *(news)* difundirse

▸ **get at** *vt insep* (**a**) *(reach)* alcanzar (**b**)
(ascertain) descubrir (**c**) *(insinuate)* insinuar; **what are you getting at?** ¿a dónde
quieres llegar? (**d**) *(criticize)* criticar

▸ **get away** *vi* escaparse

▸ **get away with** *vt insep* salir impune de

▸ **get back 1** *vi* (**a**) *(return)* regresar, volver
(**b**) **g. back!** *(move backwards)* ¡atrás!
2 *vt sep (recover)* recuperar; *Fam* **to g.
one's own back on sb** vengarse de algn

▸ **get by** *vi* (**a**) *(manage)* arreglárselas;
she can g. by in French sabe defenderse
en francés (**b**) *(pass)* pasar

▸ **get down 1** *vt sep (depress)* deprimir
2 *vi (descend)* bajar

▸ **get down to** *vt insep* ponerse a; **to g.
down to the facts** ir al grano

▸ **get in 1** *vi* (**a**) *(arrive)* llegar (**b**) *Pol* ser
elegido(a)
2 *vt sep* (**a**) *(buy)* comprar (**b**) *(collect)*
recoger; *Fam* **he couldn't g. a word in
edgeways** no pudo decir ni pío

▸ **get into** *vt insep* *Fig* **to g. into bad
habits** adquirir malas costumbres; **to g.
into trouble** meterse en un lío

▸ **get off 1** *vt insep (bus etc)* bajarse de
2 *vt sep (remove)* quitarse
3 *vi* (**a**) *bajarse*; *Fam* **g. off!** ¡fuera! (**b**) **to
g. off to a good start** *(begin)* empezar
bien (**c**) *(escape)* escaparse; **to g. off
lightly** salir bien librado(a)

▸ **get off with** *vt insep* *Fam* ligar

▸ **get on 1** *vt insep (board)* subir a
2 *vi* (**a**) *(board)* subirse (**b**) *(make progress)* hacer progresos; **how are you
getting on?** ¿cómo te van las cosas? (**c**)
to g. on (well) (with sb) llevarse bien
(con algn) (**d**) *(continue)* seguir; **to g. on
with one's work** seguir trabajando (**e**)
it's getting on for eleven son casi las
once; **time's getting on** se está haciendo
tarde

▸ **get on to** *vt insep* (**a**) *(find a person)*
localizar; *(find out)* descubrir (**b**) *(continue)* pasar a

▸ **get out 1** *vt sep (object)* sacar
2 *vi* (**a**) *(room etc)* salir (**of** de); *(train)*
bajar (**of** de) (**b**) *(escape)* escaparse (**of**
de); **to g. out of an obligation** librarse de
un compromiso (**c**) *(news)* difundirse;
(secret) hacerse público

▸ **get over 1** *vt insep* (**a**) *(illness)* recuperarse de; **I can't g. over him** no le puedo
olvidar (**b**) *(difficulty)* vencer

2 *vt sep (convey)* hacer comprender

▸ **get round** *vt insep* (**a**) *(problem)* salvar; *(difficulty)* vencer (**b**) *(rule)* soslayar (**c**) *(win over)* persuadir

▸ **get round to** *vt insep* **if I g. round to it** si tengo tiempo

▸ **get through 1** *vi* (**a**) *(message)* llegar (**b**) *Educ* aprobar (**c**) *Tel* **to g. through to sb** conseguir comunicar con algn

2 *vt insep* (**a**) **to g. through a lot of work** trabajar mucho (**b**) *(consume)* consumir (**c**) *Educ* aprobar

▸ **get together 1** *vi (people)* juntarse, reunirse

2 *vt sep (people)* juntar, reunir

▸ **get up 1** *vi (rise)* levantarse

2 *vt sep* (**a**) *(wake)* despertar (**b**) *(disguise)* **to g. oneself up as ...** disfrazarse de ...

▸ **get up to** *vt insep* hacer; **to g. up to mischief** hacer de las suyas

getaway ['getəweɪ] *n* fuga *f*; **to make one's g.** fugarse

get-together ['getəgeðə(r)] *n* reunión *f*

geyser ['giːzə(r), *US* 'gaɪzər] *n* (**a**) *Geog* géiser *m* (**b**) *(water heater)* calentador *m* de agua

ghastly ['gɑːstlɪ] *adj* (**ghastlier, ghastliest**) horrible, espantoso(a)

gherkin ['gɜːkɪn] *n* pepinillo *m*

ghetto ['getəʊ] *n* gueto *m*

ghost [gəʊst] *n* fantasma *m*; **g. story** cuento *m* de fantasmas; **g. town** pueblo *m* fantasma

ghost-writer ['gəʊstraɪtə(r)] *n* negro(a) *m,f*

ghoulish ['guːlɪʃ] *adj* macabro(a)

giant ['dʒaɪənt] *adj & n* gigante *(m)*

gibberish ['dʒɪbərɪʃ] *n* galimatías *m inv*

gibe [dʒaɪb] **1** *n* mofa *f*

2 *vi* mofarse (**at** de)

giblets ['dʒɪblɪts] *npl* menudillos *mpl*

Gibraltar [dʒɪ'brɔːltə(r)] *n* Gibraltar

Gibraltarian [dʒɪbrɔːl'teərɪən] *adj & n* gibraltareño(a) *(m,f)*

giddiness ['gɪdɪnɪs] *n* mareo *m*; *(vertigo)* vértigo *m*

giddy ['gɪdɪ] *adj* (**giddier, giddiest**) mareado(a); **it makes me g.** me da vértigo; **to feel g.** sentirse mareado(a)

gift [gɪft] *n* (**a**) regalo *m*; *Com* obsequio *m*; **g. token** vale *m* (**b**) *(talent)* don *m*; **to have a g. for music** estar muy dotado(a) para la música

gifted ['gɪftɪd] *adj* dotado(a)

gig [gɪg] *n Fam Mus* actuación *f*

gigantic [dʒaɪ'gæntɪk] *adj* gigantesco(a)

giggle ['gɪgəl] **1** *n* (**a**) risita *f* (**b**) *(lark)* broma *f*, diversión *f*

2 *vi* reírse tontamente

gild [gɪld] *vt* dorar

gill[1] [dʒɪl] *n (liquid measure)* = 0,142 l

gill[2] [gɪl] *n (of fish)* branquia *f*, agalla *f*

gilt [gɪlt] **1** *adj* dorado(a)

2 *n (colour)* dorado *m*

gilt-edged ['gɪltedʒd] *adj* **g. securities** valores *mpl* de máxima garantía

gimmick ['gɪmɪk] *n* truco *m*; *(in advertising)* reclamo *m*

gin [dʒɪn] *n* ginebra *f*; **g. and tonic** gin tonic *m*

ginger ['dʒɪndʒə(r)] **1** *n* jengibre *m*; **g. ale** ginger ale *m*

2 *adj* (**a**) de jengibre (**b**) *(hair)* pelirrojo(a)

gingerbread ['dʒɪndʒəbred] *n* pan *m* de jengibre

gingerly ['dʒɪndʒəlɪ] *adv* cautelosamente

gipsy ['dʒɪpsɪ] *adj & n* gitano(a) *(m,f)*

giraffe [dʒɪ'rɑːf] *n* jirafa *f*

girder ['gɜːdə(r)] *n* viga *f*

girdle ['gɜːdəl] *n* faja *f*

girl [gɜːl] *n* (**a**) chica *f*, joven *f*, *(child)* niña *f*; **g. guide**, *US* **g. scout** exploradora *f* (**b**) *(daughter)* hija *f* (**c**) *(sweetheart)* novia *f*

girlfriend ['gɜːlfrend] *n* (**a**) *(lover)* novia *f* (**b**) *(female friend)* amiga *f*

girlhood ['gɜːlhʊd] *n* niñez *f*

girlish ['gɜːlɪʃ] *adj* (**a**) de niña (**b**) *(effeminate)* afeminado(a)

giro ['dʒaɪrəʊ] *n Br* giro *m* (postal); **g. (cheque)** cheque *m* de giros postales

gist [dʒɪst] *n* esencia *f*; **did you get the g. of what he was saying?** ¿cogiste la idea de lo que decía?

give [gɪv] **1** *n (elasticity)* elasticidad *f*

2 *vt (pt* **gave**; *pp* **given**) (**a**) dar; **to g. sth to sb** dar algo a algn; **to g. a start** pegar un salto; **to g. sb a present** regalar algo a algn

(**b**) *(provide)* suministrar; **to g. sb sth to eat** dar de comer a algn

(**c**) *(pay)* pagar

(**d**) *(concert)* dar; *(speech)* pronunciar

(**e**) *(dedicate)* dedicar

(**f**) *(grant)* otorgar; **to g. sb one's attention** prestar atención a algn

(**g**) **to g. sb to understand that ...** dar a entender a algn que ...

(**h**) *(yield)* ceder; **to g. way** *Aut* ceder el paso; *Fig* ceder; *(of legs)* flaquear

3 *vi* (**a**) **to g. as good as one gets** devolver golpe por golpe

(**b**) *(yield)* ceder; *(fabric)* dar de sí

▸ **give away** *vt sep* (**a**) repartir; *(present)* regalar (**b**) *(disclose)* revelar; **to g. the game away** descubrir el pastel (**c**) *(betray)* traicionar

▸ **give back** *vt sep* devolver

▸ **give in 1** *vi* (**a**) *(admit defeat)* darse por vencido(a); *(surrender)* rendirse (**b**) **to g. in to** ceder ante

2 *vt sep* *(hand in)* entregar

▸ **give off** *vt sep* *(smell etc)* despedir

▸ **give out** *vt sep* distribuir, repartir

▸ **give over 1** *vt sep* *(hand over)* entregar; *(devote)* dedicar

2 *vi Fam* **g. over!** ¡basta ya!

▸ **give up 1** *vt sep* (**a**) *(idea)* abandonar; **to g. up smoking** dejar de fumar (**b**) *(betray)* traicionar (**c**) *(hand over)* entregar; **to g. oneself up** entregarse

2 *(admit defeat)* darse por vencido(a), rendirse

▸ **give up on** *vt insep* darse por vencido con

given ['gɪvən] **1** *adj* (**a**) *(particular)* dado(a); **at a g. time** en un momento dado (**b**) **g. to** dado(a) a

2 *conj* (**a**) *(considering)* dado(a) (**b**) *(if)* si

3 *pp of* **give**

glacial ['gleɪsɪəl] *adj* (**a**) *Geol* glaciar (**b**) *(icy)* glacial; *Fig* **g. look** mirada *f* glacial

glacier ['glæsɪə(r)] *n* glaciar *m*

glad [glæd] *adj* (**gladder, gladdest**) contento(a); *(happy)* alegre; **he'll be only too g. to help you** tendrá mucho gusto en ayudarle; **to be g.** alegrarse

gladiator ['glædɪeɪtə(r)] *n Hist* gladiador *m*

gladly ['glædlɪ] *adv* con mucho gusto

glamor ['glæmər] *n US* = **glamour**

glamorous ['glæmərəs] *adj* atractivo(a), encantador(a)

glamour ['glæmə(r)] *n* atractivo *m*; *(charm)* encanto *m*; **a g. girl** una belleza

glance [glɑːns] **1** *n* mirada *f*, vistazo *m*; **at a g.** de un vistazo; **at first g.** a primera vista

2 *vi* echar un vistazo (**at** a)

▸ **glance off** *vt insep (of ball etc)* rebotar de

glancing ['glɑːnsɪŋ] *adj (blow)* oblicuo(a)

gland [glænd] *n* glándula *f*

glandular ['glændjʊlə(r)] *adj* glandular; **g. fever** mononucleosis infecciosa

glare [gleə(r)] **1** *n (light)* luz *f* deslumbrante; *(dazzle)* deslumbramiento *m*; *(look)* mirada *f* feroz

2 *vi (dazzle)* deslumbrar; *(look)* lanzar

una mirada furiosa (**at** a)

glaring ['gleərɪŋ] *adj (light)* deslumbrante; *(colour)* chillón(ona); *(obvious)* evidente

glass [glɑːs] *n* (**a**) *(material)* vidrio *m*; **pane of g.** cristal *m* (**b**) *(drinking vessel)* vaso *m*; **wine g.** copa *f* (para vino) (**c**) **glasses** gafas *fpl*, *Am* lentes *mpl*, anteojos *mpl*; **to wear glasses** llevar gafas *or Am* lentes *or* anteojos

glasshouse ['glɑːshaʊs] *n* invernadero *m*

glassware ['glɑːsweə(r)] *n* cristalería *f*

glassy ['glɑːsɪ] *adj* (**glassier, glassiest**) *(water)* cristalino(a); *(eyes)* vidrioso(a)

glaze [gleɪz] **1** *n (varnish)* barniz *m*; *(for pottery)* vidriado *m*

2 *vt* (**a**) *(windows)* acristalar; (**b**) *(varnish)* barnizar; *(ceramics)* vidriar (**c**) *Culin* glasear

glazed [gleɪzd] *adj (eyes)* de mirada ausente

glazier ['gleɪzɪə(r)] *n* vidriero(a) *m,f*

gleam [gliːm] **1** *n* (**a**) *(glimmer)* destello *m* (**b**) *Fig (glimmer)* rayo *m*

2 *vi* brillar, relucir

gleaming ['gliːmɪŋ] *adj* brillante, reluciente

glean [gliːn] *vt Fig* recoger, cosechar

glee [gliː] *n* gozo *m*

gleeful ['gliːfʊl] *adj* gozoso(a)

glen [glen] *n* cañada *f*

glib [glɪb] *adj* (**glibber, glibbest**) *Pej* de mucha labia

glide [glaɪd] *vi* (**a**) *(slip, slide)* deslizarse (**b**) *Av* planear

glider ['glaɪdə(r)] *n* planeador *m*

gliding ['glaɪdɪŋ] *n* vuelo *m* sin motor

glimmer ['glɪmə(r)] *n* (**a**) *(light)* luz *f* tenue (**b**) *Fig (trace)* destello *m*

glimpse [glɪmps] **1** *n* atisbo *m*

2 *vt* atisbar

glint [glɪnt] **1** *n* destello *m*, centelleo *m*; **he had a g. in his eye** le brillaban los ojos

2 *vi* destellar, centellear

glisten ['glɪsən] *vi* relucir, brillar

glitter ['glɪtə(r)] **1** *n* brillo *m*

2 *vi* relucir

gloat [gləʊt] *vi* jactarse; **to g. over another's misfortune** recrearse con la desgracia de otro

global ['gləʊbəl] *adj* (**a**) *(of the world)* mundial (**b**) *(overall)* global

globe [gləʊb] *n* globo *m*, esfera *f*

gloom [gluːm] *n (obscurity)* penumbra *f*; *(melancholy)* melancolía *f*; *(despair)* desolación *f*

gloomy ['gluːmɪ] *adj* (**gloomier, gloomiest**) *(dark)* oscuro(a); *(weather)* gris;

(dismal) deprimente; *(despairing)* pesimista; *(sad)* triste

glorify ['glɔːrɪfaɪ] *vt* glorificar

glorious ['glɔːrɪəs] *adj (momentous)* glorioso(a); *(splendid)* magnífico(a), espléndido(a)

glory ['glɔːrɪ] *n* gloria *f*, *Fig (splendour)* esplendor *m*; *Fig (triumph)* triunfo *m*

gloss [glɒs] **1** *n* (**a**) *(explanation)* glosa *f* (**b**) *(sheen)* brillo *m*; **g. (paint)** pintura *f* brillante

　　2 *vi* glosar

▸ **gloss over** *vt insep Fig* encubrir

glossary ['glɒsərɪ] *n* glosario *m*

glossy ['glɒsɪ] *adj* (**glossier, glossiest**) lustroso(a); **g. magazine** revista *f* de lujo

glove [glʌv] *n* guante *m*; *Aut* **g. compartment** guantera *f*

glow [gləʊ] **1** *n* brillo *m*; *(of fire)* incandescencia *f*; *(of sun)* arrebol *m*, *(heat)* calor *m*; *(light)* luz *f*; *(in cheeks)* rubor *m*

　　2 *vi* brillar; *(fire)* arder; *Fig* rebosar de

glower ['glaʊə(r)] *vi* poner cara de enfadado(a)

glowing ['gləʊɪŋ] *adj* (**a**) *(fire)* incandescente; *(colour)* vivo(a); *(light)* brillante (**b**) *(cheeks)* encendido(a) (**c**) *Fig (report)* entusiasta

glucose ['gluːkəʊz] *n* glucosa *f*

glue [gluː] **1** *n* pegamento *m*, cola *f*

　　2 *vt* pegar (**to** a)

glum [glʌm] *adj* (**glummer, glummest**) alicaído(a)

glut [glʌt] *n* superabundancia *f*, exceso *m*

glutton ['glʌtən] *n* glotón(ona) *m,f*; *Fam Fig* **you're a g. for punishment** eres masoquista

GM [dʒiː'em] *adj* (*abbr* **genetically modified**) transgénico(a), modificado(a) genéticamente; **GM food** (alimentos) transgénicos

GMO [dʒiːem'əʊ] *n* (*abbr* **genetically modified organism**) OMG *m*

GMT [dʒiːem'tiː] *n* (*abbr* **Greenwich Mean Time**) hora *f* del meridiano de Greenwich

gnarled [nɑːld] *adj* nudoso(a)

gnash [næʃ] *vt* rechinar

gnat [næt] *n* mosquito *m*

gnaw [nɔː] *vt & vi (chew)* roer

gnome [nəʊm] *n* gnomo *m*

GNP [dʒiːen'piː] *n* (*abbr* **gross national product**) PNB *m*

go [gəʊ] **1** *vi* (*3rd person sing pres* **goes**; *pt* **went**; *pp* **gone**) (**a**) ir; **to go by car/on foot** ir en coche/a pie; **to go for a walk** (ir a) dar un paseo; **to g. on a journey** ir de viaje; **to go shopping** ir de compras; *Fig* **to go too far** pasarse (de la raya)

(**b**) *(depart)* irse, marcharse; *(bus)* salir

(**c**) *(disappear)* desaparecer

(**d**) *(function)* funcionar; *Fig* **to get things going** poner las cosas en marcha

(**e**) *(sell)* venderse; **shoes going cheap** zapatos a precios de rebaja

(**f**) *(become)* quedarse, volverse; **to go blind** quedarse ciego(a); **to go mad** volverse loco(a)

(**g**) *(progress)* ir, marchar; **everything went well** todo salió bien; **how's it going?** ¿qué tal (te van las cosas)?

(**h**) **to be going to** *(in the future)* ir a; *(on the point of)* estar a punto de

(**i**) *(fit)* caber

(**j**) *(be kept)* guardarse

(**k**) *(be available)* quedar; **I'll take whatever's going** me conformo con lo que hay

(**l**) *(be acceptable)* valer; **anything goes** todo vale

(**m**) *(break)* romperse; *(yield)* ceder

(**n**) **how does that song go?** ¿cómo es aquella canción?

(**o**) *(time)* pasar; **there are only two weeks to go** sólo quedan dos semanas

(**p**) *(be inherited)* pasar (**to** a)

(**q**) *(say)* decir; **as the saying goes** según el dicho

(**r**) **to let sth go** soltar algo

　　2 *vt* (**a**) *(travel)* hacer, recorrer

(**b**) **to go it alone** apañárselas solo

　　3 *n* (**a**) *(energy)* energía *f*, dinamismo *m*

(**b**) *(try)* intento *m*; **to have a go at sth** probar suerte con algo

(**c**) *(turn)* turno *m*; **it's your go** te toca a ti

(**d**) **to make a go of sth** tener éxito en algo

(**e**) **I knew from the word go** lo sabía desde el principio

(**f**) **to have a go at sb** criticar a algn

▸ **go about 1** *vt insep* (**a**) *(task)* emprender; **how do you go about it?** ¿cómo hay que hacerlo? (**b**) **to go about one's business** ocuparse de sus asuntos

　　2 *vi* *(rumour)* correr

▸ **go after** *vt insep (pursue)* andar tras

▸ **go against** *vt insep (oppose)* ir en contra de; *(verdict)* ser desfavorable a

▸ **go ahead** *vi* (**a**) *(proceed)* proceder (**b**) **we'll go on ahead** iremos delante

▸ **go along 1** *vt insep (street)* pasar por

　　2 *vi (progress)* progresar

▸ **go along with** *vt insep* (**a**) *(agree with)* estar de acuerdo con (**b**) *(accompany)* acompañar

▸ **go around** *vi* (**a**) *(rumour)* correr (**b**) **there's enough to go around** hay para todos

▸**go away** *vi* marcharse
▸**go back** *vi* (**a**) *(return)* volver, regresar (**b**) *Fig* **to go back to** *(date from)* datar de
▸**go back on** *vt insep* **to go back on one's word** faltar a su palabra
▸**go back to** *vt insep* volver a
▸**go by** *vi* pasar; **as time goes by** con el tiempo
▸**go down** *vi* (**a**) *(descend)* bajar; *(sun)* ponerse; *(ship)* hundirse (**b**) *(diminish)* disminuir; *(temperature)* bajar (**c**) *(be received)* ser acogido(a)
▸**go down with** *vt insep (contract)* coger
▸**go for** *vt insep* (**a**) *(attack)* lanzarse sobre; *Fam Fig* **go for it!** ¡a por ello! (**b**) *(fetch)* ir por (**c**) *Fam (like)* gustar
▸**go in** *vi* entrar
▸**go in for** *vt insep (exam)* presentarse a; *(hobby)* dedicarse a
▸**go into** *vt insep* (**a**) *(enter)* entrar en; **to go into journalism** dedicarse al periodismo (**b**) *(study)* examinar; *(matter)* investigar (**c**) *(energy, money)* invertir en
▸**go off 1** *vi* (**a**) *(leave)* irse, marcharse (**b**) *(bomb)* explotar; *(gun)* dispararse; *(alarm)* sonar (**c**) *(food)* pasarse (**d**) *(event)* resultar
2 *vt insep Fam* **to go off sth** perder el gusto *or* el interés por algo
▸**go on** *vi* (**a**) *(continue)* seguir, continuar; **to go on talking** seguir hablando; *Fam* **to go on and on about sth** no parar de hablar sobre algo; *(complain)* quejarse constantemente de algo (**b**) *(happen)* pasar, ocurrir (**c**) *(time)* transcurrir, pasar (**d**) *(light)* encenderse
▸**go out** *vi* (**a**) *(leave)* salir; **to go out for a meal** comer *or* cenar fuera (**b**) *(boy and girl)* salir juntos (**c**) *(fire, light)* apagarse (**d**) *(tide)* bajar (**e**) *TV & Rad* transmitirse (**f**) **to go (all) out** ir a por todas (**g**) *(in competition)* perder la eliminatoria
▸**go over** *vt insep (revise)* repasar
▸**go over to** *vt insep* (**a**) acercarse a; **to go over to the enemy** pasarse al enemigo (**b**) *(switch to)* pasar a
▸**go round** *vi* (**a**) *(revolve)* dar vueltas (**b**) **to go round to sb's house** pasar por casa de algn
▸**go through 1** *vi (bill)* ser aprobado(a)
2 *vt insep* (**a**) *(examine)* examinar; *(search)* registrar (**b**) *(rehearse)* ensayar (**c**) *(spend)* gastar (**d**) *(list etc)* explicar (**e**) *(endure)* sufrir
▸**go through with** *vt insep* llevar a cabo
▸**go under** *vi* (**a**) *(ship)* hundirse (**b**) *(business)* fracasar
▸**go up** *vi* (**a**) *(price etc)* subir (**b**) **to go up**

to sb acercarse a algn (**c**) *(in a lift)* subir (**d**) **to go up in flames** quemarse (**e**) *Sport (be promoted)* subir
▸**go with** *vt insep* (**a**) *(accompany)* ir con (**b**) *(colours)* hacer juego con
▸**go without 1** *vt insep* (**a**) pasarse sin, prescindir de (**b**) *Fam* **that goes without saying** eso es evidente
2 *vi (not have)* aguantarse sin nada
goad [gəʊd] *vt* aguijonear
go-ahead ['gəʊəhed] *n Fam* **to give sb the g.** dar luz verde a algn
goal [gəʊl] *n* (**a**) *Sport* gol *m*; **g. kick** saque *m* de puerta; **g. post** poste *m*; **g. scorer** goleador(a) *m,f* (**b**) *(aim, objective)* meta *f*, objetivo *m*
goalkeeper ['gəʊlkiːpə(r)] *n* portero(a) *m,f*
goat [gəʊt] *n (female)* cabra *f*; *(male)* macho cabrío
gob [gɒb] *n Br Fam* boca *f*
gobble ['gɒbəl] *vt* engullir
go-between ['gəʊbɪtwiːn] *n* intermediario(a) *m,f*
goblet ['gɒblɪt] *n* copa *f*
god [gɒd] *n* dios *m*; **for G.'s sake!** ¡por Dios!; **G.** Dios; **(my) G.!** ¡Dios mío!; **G. forbid!** ¡Dios no lo quiera!; **G. only knows** sabe Dios
godchild ['gɒdtʃaɪld] *n* ahijado(a) *m,f*
goddam(n) ['gɒdæm] *US Fam* **1** *adj* maldito(a), dichoso(a), *Méx* pinche
2 *adv* **that was g. stupid!** ¡eso fue una auténtica estupidez!
goddaughter ['gɒdɔːtə(r)] *n* ahijada *f*
goddess ['gɒdɪs] *n* diosa *f*
godfather ['gɒdfɑːðə(r)] *n* padrino *m*
godforsaken ['gɒdfəseɪkən] *adj (place)* remoto(a)
godmother ['gɒdmʌðə(r)] *n* madrina *f*
godparents ['gɒdpeərənts] *npl* padrinos *mpl*
godsend ['gɒdsend] *n* regalo inesperado
godson ['gɒdsʌn] *n* ahijado *m*
goggles ['gɒgəlz] *npl* gafas *fpl* protectoras, *CSur* antiparras *fpl*
going ['gəʊɪŋ] **1** *adj* (**a**) *(price)* corriente; **the g. rate** el precio medio (**b**) **a g. concern** un negocio que marcha bien (**c**) **to get** *or* **be g.** marcharse (**d**) **to keep g.** resistir
2 *n* (**a**) **that was good g.!** ¡qué rápido! (**b**) *Fig* **to get out while the g. is good** retirarse antes que sea demasiado tarde
goings-on [gəʊɪŋz'ɒn] *npl Fam* tejemanejes *mpl*
go-kart ['gəʊkɑːt] *n Sport* kart *m*
gold [gəʊld] **1** *n* oro *m*; **g. leaf** pan *m* de

oro; **g. medal** medalla *f* de oro; **g. mine** mina *f* de oro

2 *adj* de oro; *(colour)* oro, dorado(a)

golden ['gəʊldən] *adj* de oro; *(colour)* dorado(a); **Fig a g. opportunity** una excelente oportunidad; *Orn* **g. eagle** águila *f* real; *Fig* **g. handshake** indemnización *f* por despido; **g. wedding** bodas *fpl* de oro

goldfish ['gəʊldfɪʃ] *n* pez *m* de colores

gold-plated [gəʊld'pleɪtɪd] *adj* chapado(a) en oro

goldsmith ['gəʊldsmɪθ] *n* orfebre *m*

golf [gɒlf] *n* golf *m*; **g. ball** pelota *f* de golf; **g. club** *(stick)* palo *m* de golf; *(place)* club *m* de golf; **g. course** campo *m* de golf

golfer ['gɒlfə(r)] *n* golfista *mf*

golly ['gɒlɪ] *interj* ¡vaya!

gone [gɒn] **1** *adj* desaparecido(a)

2 *pp* of **go**

gong [gɒŋ] *n* gong *m*

good [gʊd] **1** *adj* (**better**, **best**) (**a**) *(before noun)* buen(a); *(after noun)* bueno(a); **a g. book** un buen libro; **g. afternoon/evening** buenas tardes; **g. morning** buenos días; **g. night** buenas noches; **it looks g.** tiene buena pinta; **to be as g. as new** estar como nuevo(a); **to feel g.** sentirse bien; **to have a g. time** pasarlo bien; **to smell g.** oler bien; **G. Friday** Viernes *m* Santo

(**b**) *(kind)* amable; *(generous)* generoso(a)

(**c**) *(healthy)* sano(a)

(**d**) *(morally correct)* correcto(a); **be g.!** ¡pórtate bien!

(**e**) **he's g. at languages** tiene facilidad para los idiomas

(**f**) *(attractive)* bonito(a); **red looks g. on you** el rojo te favorece mucho; **g. looks** atractivo *m*, belleza *f*

(**g**) **it's as g. as an offer** equivale a una oferta; **it's as g. a way as any** es una manera como otra cualquiera

(**h**) *(at least)* como mínimo

(**i**) *(sufficient)* bastante

(**j**) **to make g.** *(injustice)* reparar; *(loss)* compensar; *(succeed in life)* triunfar

(**k**) *(reliable)* de confianza

(**l**) *(propitious)* propicio(a)

(**m**) **she comes from a g. family** es de buena familia

(**n**) *(character)* agradable; **he's in a g. mood** está de buen humor

2 *n* (**a**) bien *m*; **g. and evil** el bien y el mal; **to do g.** hacer el bien

(**b**) *(advantage)* bien *m*, provecho *m*; **for your own g.** para tu propio bien; **it's no g. waiting** no sirve de nada esperar; **it**

will do you g. te hará bien

(**c**) **goods** *(possessions)* bienes *mpl*

(**d**) *Com* **goods** artículos *mpl*, géneros *mpl*; **goods train** tren *m* de mercancías

3 *adv* **she's gone for g.** se ha ido para siempre

4 *interj* ¡muy bien!

goodbye [gʊd'baɪ] **1** *interj* ¡adiós!

2 *n* adiós *m*, despedida *f*; **to say g. to sb** despedirse de algn

good-for-nothing ['gʊdfənʌθɪŋ] *adj* & *n* inútil *(mf)*

good-hearted [gʊd'hɑːtɪd] *adj* de buen corazón

good-looking [gʊd'lʊkɪŋ] *adj* guapo(a)

good-natured [gʊd'neɪtʃəd] *adj* amable, bondadoso(a)

goodness ['gʊdnɪs] *n* bondad *f*; **my g.!** ¡Dios mío!; **thank g.!** ¡gracias a Dios!; **for g. sake!** ¡por Dios!

good-tempered [gʊd'tempəd] *adj* apacible

goodwill [gʊd'wɪl] *n* (**a**) buena voluntad *f* (**b**) *Com (reputation)* buen nombre *m*

goof [guːf] *US Fam* **1** *n* metedura *f* or *Am* metida *f* de pata

2 *vi* meter la pata

goose [guːs] *n* (*pl* **geese**) ganso *m*, oca *f*

gooseberry ['gʊzbərɪ, 'guːsbərɪ] *n* uva espina, grosella espinosa; *Fam* **to play g.** hacer de carabina

gooseflesh ['guːsfleʃ] *n*, **goosepimples** ['guːspɪmpəlz] *npl* carne *f* de gallina

goose-step ['guːsstep] *vi* ir a paso de la oca

gore¹ [gɔː(r)] *n* sangre derramada

gore² [gɔː(r)] *vt (of bull)* cornear, dar cornadas a

gorge [gɔːdʒ] **1** *n* desfiladero *m*

2 *vt* & *vi* **to g. (oneself) (on)** atiborrarse (de)

gorgeous ['gɔːdʒəs] *adj* magnífico(a), estupendo(a); *(person)* atractivo(a), guapo(a)

gorilla [gə'rɪlə] *n* gorila *m*

gorse [gɔːs] *n* aulaga *f*

gory ['gɔːrɪ] *adj* (**gorier**, **goriest**) sangriento(a)

gosh [gɒʃ] *interj Fam* ¡cielos!, ¡caray!

go-slow [gəʊ'sləʊ] *n* huelga *f* de celo

gospel ['gɒspəl] *n* **the G.** el Evangelio; *Fam* **it's the g. truth** es la pura verdad

gossip ['gɒsɪp] **1** *n* (**a**) *(rumour)* cotilleo *m*; **g. column** ecos *mpl* de sociedad (**b**) *(person)* chismoso(a) *m,f*, cotilla *mf*

2 *vi (natter)* cotillear, chismorrear

got [gɒt] *pt* & *pp* of **get**

Gothic ['gɒθɪk] *adj* gótico(a)

gotten ['gɒtən] *US pp of* **get**

gourmet ['gʊəmeɪ] *n* gourmet *mf*

gout [gaʊt] *n* gota *f*

govern ['gʌvən] *vt* (a) gobernar (b) *(determine)* determinar

governess ['gʌvənɪs] *n* institutriz *f*

governing ['gʌvənɪŋ] *adj* gobernante; **g. body** consejo *m* de administración

government ['gʌvənmənt] *n* gobierno *m*

governmental [gʌvən'mentəl] *adj* gubernamental

governor ['gʌvənə(r)] *n (ruler)* gobernador(a) *m,f*, *(of prison)* director(a) *m,f*, *(of school)* administrador(a) *m,f*

gown [gaʊn] *n (dress)* vestido largo; *Jur & Univ* toga *f*

GP [dʒiː'piː] *n (abbr* **general practitioner)** médico(a) *m,f* de familia *or* de cabecera

GPO [dʒiːpiː'əʊ] *n Br Formerly (abbr* **General Post Office)** ≃ (Administración *f* Central de) Correos *mpl*

grab [græb] **1** *n* agarrón *m*; *Fam* **to be up for grabs** estar disponible

2 *vt* (a) agarrar; **to g. hold of sb** agarrarse a algn (b) *Fig* **g. a bottle of wine** píllate una botella de vino (c) *Fig* **how does that g. you?** ¿qué te parece?

grace [greɪs] **1** *n* (a) gracia *f*; *Fig* **to fall from g.** caer en desgracia (b) **to say g.** bendecir la mesa (c) **to do sth with good g.** hacer algo de buena gana (d) **five days' g.** *(reprieve)* un plazo de cinco días (e) *(elegance)* elegancia *f* (f) **Your G.** (Su) Excelencia

2 *vt* (a) *(adorn)* adornar (b) *(honour)* honrar

graceful ['greɪsfʊl] *adj* elegante; *(movement)* garboso(a)

gracefully ['greɪsfʊlɪ] *adv* (a) *(beautifully)* con gracia, con elegancia (b) *(accept)* con cortesía

gracious ['greɪʃəs] **1** *adj* (a) *(elegant)* elegante (b) *(courteous)* cortés (c) *(kind)* amable

2 *interj* **good g. (me)!, goodness g.!** ¡santo cielo!

grade [greɪd] **1** *n* (a) *(quality)* grado *m*; *(rank)* categoría *f*; *Mil* rango *m* (b) *US Educ (mark)* nota *f* (c) *US Educ (class)* clase *f*; **g. school** escuela primaria (d) *(level)* nivel *m*; **to make the g.** llegar al nivel deseado (e) *US (slope)* pendiente *f* (f) *US* **g. crossing** paso *m* a nivel

2 *vt* clasificar

gradient ['greɪdɪənt] *n (graph)* declive *m*; *(hill)* cuesta *f*, pendiente *f*

gradual ['grædjʊəl] *adj* gradual, progresivo(a)

gradually ['grædjʊəlɪ] *adv* poco a poco

graduate 1 *n* ['grædjʊət] *Educ* titulado(a) *m,f*; *Univ* licenciado(a) *m,f*; *US* **g. school** escuela *f* para graduados

2 *vi* ['grædjʊeɪt] (a) *Educ* sacarse el título; *Univ* licenciarse (**in** en) (b) **to g. to** pasar a (c) *US (from high school)* ≃ sacar el bachillerato

graduation [grædjʊ'eɪʃən] *n* graduación *f*; *Univ* **g. ceremony** ceremonia *f* de entrega de los títulos

graffiti [grə'fiːtiː] *npl* grafiti *mpl*

graft [grɑːft] **1** *n* (a) *Med* injerto *m* (b) *Fam (work)* trabajo *m* (c) *US (bribery)* soborno *m*

2 *vt Med* injertar (**on to** en)

3 *vi Fam* trabajar duro

grain [greɪn] *n* (a) *(cereals)* cereales *mpl* (b) *(particle)* grano *m*; *Fig* **there's not a g. of truth in it** no tiene ni pizca de verdad (c) *(in wood)* fibra *f*; *(in stone)* veta *f*; *(in leather)* flor *f*; *Fig* **to go against the g.** ir a contrapelo

gram [græm] *n* gramo *m*

grammar ['græmə(r)] *n* gramática *f*; **g. (book)** libro *m* de gramática; *Br* **g. school** = instituto estatal de segunda enseñanza al que se ingresa por examen selectivo

grammatical [grə'mætɪkəl] *adj* gramatical

gramme [græm] *n* gramo *m*

gramophone ['græməfəʊn] *n* gramófono *m*

granary ['grænərɪ] *n* granero *m*

grand [grænd] **1** *adj* (a) grande; *(before singular noun)* gran; **g. piano** piano *m* de cola; **G. Prix** Gran Premio *m* (b) *(splendid)* grandioso(a), magnífico(a); *(impressive)* impresionante (c) **g. total** total *m* (d) *Fam (wonderful)* estupendo(a)

2 *n Fam* mil libras *fpl*; *US* mil dólares *mpl*

grandchild ['græntʃaɪld] *n* nieto(a) *m,f*

granddad ['grændæd] *n Fam* abuelo *m*

granddaughter ['grændɔːtə(r)] *n* nieta *f*

grandeur ['grændʒə(r)] *n* grandeza *f*, grandiosidad *f*

grandfather ['grænfɑːðə(r)] *n* abuelo *m*; **g. clock** reloj *m* de caja

grandiose ['grændɪəʊs] *adj* grandioso(a)

grandma ['grænmɑː] *n Fam* abuelita *f*

grandmother ['grænmʌðə(r)] *n* abuela *f*

grandpa ['grænpɑː] *n Fam* abuelito *m*

grandparents ['grænpeərənts] *npl* abuelos *mpl*

grandson ['grænsʌn] *n* nieto *m*

grandstand ['grænstænd] *n* tribuna *f*

granite ['grænɪt] *n* granito *m*

granny ['grænɪ] *n Fam* abuelita *f*

grant [grɑːnt] **1** *vt* (**a**) *(allow)* conceder, otorgar (**b**) *(admit)* admitir; **to take sb for granted** no apreciar a algn en lo que vale; **to take sth for granted** dar algo por sentado

2 *n Educ* beca *f*; *(subsidy)* subvención *f*

granulated ['grænjʊleɪtd] *adj* granulado(a)

granule ['grænjuːl] *n* gránulo *m*

grape [greɪp] *n* uva *f*; **g. juice** mosto *m*

grapefruit ['greɪpfruːt] *n* pomelo *m*

grapevine ['greɪpvaɪn] *n Bot* vid *f*; *(against wall)* parra *f*; *Fam* **I heard it on** *or* **through the g.** me enteré por ahí

graph [grɑːf, græf] *n* gráfica *f*

graphic ['græfɪk] *adj* gráfico(a); **g. arts** artes gráficas; **g. designer** grafista *mf*

graphics ['græfɪks] *n* (**a**) *(study)* grafismo *m* (**b**) *pl Comput* gráficas *fpl*

grapple ['græpəl] **1** *vi* *(struggle)* luchar cuerpo a cuerpo (**with** con); *Fig* **to g. with a problem** intentar resolver un problema

2 *n* *(hook)* garfio *m*

grasp [grɑːsp] **1** *vt* (**a**) agarrar (**b**) *(understand)* comprender

2 *n* (**a**) *(grip)* agarrón *m* (**b**) *(understanding)* comprensión *f*; **within sb's g.** al alcance de algn

grasping ['grɑːspɪŋ] *adj* avaro(a)

grass [grɑːs] **1** *n* (**a**) hierba *f*; *(lawn)* césped *m*; *(pasture)* pasto *m*; **keep off the g.** *(sign)* prohibido pisar el césped; **g. court** pista *f* de hierba; **g. roots** base *f*; **g. snake** culebra *f* (**b**) *Fam (drug)* hierba *f* (**c**) *Br Fam (informer)* soplón(ona) *m,f*, chivato(a) *m,f*

2 *vi Br Fam* chivarse (**on** a)

▸ **grass over** *vi* cubrirse de hierba

grasshopper ['grɑːshɒpə(r)] *n* saltamontes *m inv*

grassland ['grɑːslænd] *n* pradera *f*

grass-roots ['grɑːsruːts] *adj* de base; **at g. level** a nivel popular

grassy ['grɑːsɪ] *adj* (**grassier, grassiest**) cubierto(a) de hierba

grate¹ [greɪt] **1** *vt Culin* rallar

2 *vi* chirriar

grate² [greɪt] *n* (**a**) *(in fireplace)* rejilla *f* (**b**) *(fireplace)* chimenea *f* (**c**) *Constr* rejilla *f*, reja *f*

grateful ['greɪtfʊl] *adj* agradecido(a); **to be g. for** agradecer

grater ['greɪtə(r)] *n Culin* rallador *m*

gratification [grætɪfɪ'keɪʃən] *n (pleasure)* placer *m*, satisfacción *f*

gratify ['grætɪfaɪ] *vt* (**a**) *(please)* complacer (**b**) *(yield to)* sucumbir a

gratifying ['grætɪfaɪŋ] *adj* grato(a)

grating¹ ['greɪtɪŋ] *n* rejilla *f*, reja *f*

grating² ['greɪtɪŋ] *adj* chirriante; *(tone)* áspero(a)

gratis ['greɪtɪs, 'grætɪs] *adv* gratis

gratitude ['grætɪtjuːd] *n* agradecimiento *m*

gratuitous [grə'tjuːɪtəs] *adj* gratuito(a)

gratuity [grə'tjuːɪtɪ] *n* gratificación *f*

grave¹ [greɪv] *n* sepultura *f*, tumba *f*

grave² [greɪv] *adj* *(look etc)* serio(a); *(situation)* grave

gravel ['grævəl] *n* grava *f*, gravilla *f*

gravestone ['greɪvstəʊn] *n* lápida *f* sepulcral

graveyard ['greɪvjɑːd] *n* cementerio *m*

gravity ['grævɪtɪ] *n* gravedad *f*

gravy ['greɪvɪ] *n* salsa *f*, jugo *m* (de la carne)

gray [greɪ] *adj & n US* = **grey**

graze¹ [greɪz] *vi* pacer, pastar

graze² [greɪz] **1** *vt* *(scratch)* rasguñar; *(brush against)* rozar

2 *n* rasguño *m*

grease [griːs, griːz] **1** *n* grasa *f*

2 *vt* engrasar

greaseproof ['griːspruːf] *adj* **g. paper** papel graso

greasy ['griːsɪ, 'griːzɪ] *adj* (**greasier, greasiest**) (**a**) *(oily)* grasiento(a); *(hair, food)* graso(a) (**b**) *(slippery)* resbaladizo(a) (**c**) *Fam (ingratiating)* pelotillero(a)

great [greɪt] **1** *adj* (**a**) grande; *(before singular noun)* gran; *(pain, heat)* fuerte; **a g. many** muchos(as); **G. Britain** Gran Bretaña; *Br* **G. Bear** Osa *f* Mayor (**b**) *Fam (excellent)* estupendo(a), magnífico(a); **to have a g. time** pasarlo en grande

2 *adv Fam* muy bien, estupendamente

great-aunt [greɪt'ɑːnt] *n* tía abuela

great-grandchild [greɪt'grænt∫aɪld] *n* bisnieto(a) *m,f*

great-grandfather [greɪt'grænfɑːðə(r)] *n* bisabuelo *m*

great-grandmother [greɪt'grænmʌðə(r)] *n* bisabuela *f*

greatly ['greɪtlɪ] *adv* muy, mucho

greatness ['greɪtnɪs] *n* grandeza *f*

great-uncle [greɪt'ʌŋkəl] *n* tío abuelo

Greece [griːs] *n* Grecia

greed [griːd], **greediness** ['griːdɪnɪs] *n (for food)* gula *f*; *(for money)* codicia *f*, avaricia *f*

greedy ['griːdɪ] *adj* (**greedier, greediest**) *(for food)* glotón(ona); *(for money)* codicioso(a) (**for** de)

Greek [gri:k] **1** *adj* griego(a)
2 *n* (**a**) *(person)* griego(a) *m,f* (**b**) *(language)* griego *m*

green [gri:n] **1** *n* (**a**) *(colour)* verde *m* (**b**) *(in golf)* campo *m*; **village g.** plaza *f* (del pueblo) (**c**) **greens** verdura *f*, verduras *fpl*
2 *adj* (**a**) verde; **g. bean** judía *f* verde, *Bol, RP* chaucha *f*, *CAm* ejote *m*, *Col, Cuba* habichuela *f*, *Chile* poroto *m* verde, *Ven* vainita *f*; **g. belt** zona *f* verde; *US* **g. card** *(work permit)* permiso *m* de trabajo; **g. pepper** pimiento *m* verde; **she was g. with envy** se la comía la envidia (**b**) *(inexperienced)* verde, novato(a); *(gullible)* crédulo(a) (**c**) *Pol* **G. Party** Partido *m* Verde

greenery ['gri:nəri] *n* follaje *m*

greenfly ['gri:nflaɪ] *n* pulgón *m*

greengage ['gri:ngeɪdʒ] *n* ciruela claudia

greengrocer ['gri:ngrəʊsə(r)] *n Br* verdulero(a) *m,f*

greenhouse ['gri:nhaʊs] *n* invernadero *m*; **g. effect** efecto invernadero

greenish ['gri:nɪʃ] *adj* verdoso(a)

Greenland ['gri:nlənd] *n* Groenlandia

greet [gri:t] *vt (wave at)* saludar; *(receive)* recibir; *(welcome)* dar la bienvenida a

greeting ['gri:tɪŋ] *n* saludo *m*; **greetings card** tarjeta *f* de felicitación (**b**) *(reception)* recibimiento *m*; *(welcome)* bienvenida *f*

gregarious [grɪˈgeərɪəs] *adj* gregario(a), sociable

Grenada [greˈneɪdə] *n* Granada

grenade [grəˈneɪd] *n* granada *f*

grew [gru:] *pt of* **grow**

grey [greɪ] **1** *adj (colour)* gris; *(hair)* cano(a); *(sky)* nublado(a); **g. matter** materia *f* gris
2 *n* (**a**) *(colour)* gris *m* (**b**) *(horse)* caballo tordo

grey-haired ['greɪheəd] *adj* canoso(a)

greyhound ['greɪhaʊnd] *n* galgo *m*

greyish ['greɪɪʃ] *adj* grisáceo(a)

grid [grɪd] *n* (**a**) *(on map)* cuadrícula *f* (**b**) *(of electricity etc)* red *f* nacional (**c**) = **gridiron**

gridiron ['grɪdaɪən] *n Culin* parrilla *f*

grief [gri:f] *n* dolor *m*, pena *f*; *Fam* **to come to g.** *(car, driver)* sufrir un accidente; *(plans)* irse al traste

grievance ['gri:vəns] *n (wrong)* agravio *m*; *(resentment)* queja *f*

grieve [gri:v] **1** *vt* apenar, dar pena a
2 *vi* apenarse, afligirse; **to g. for sb** llorar la muerte de algn

grievous ['gri:vəs] *adj (offence)* grave; **g.**

bodily harm lesiones *fpl* corporales graves

grill [grɪl] **1** *vt* (**a**) *Culin* asar a la parrilla (**b**) *Fam (interrogate)* interrogar duramente
2 *n* parrilla *f*; *(dish)* parrillada *f*

grill(e) [grɪl] *n (grating)* reja *f*

grim [grɪm] *adj* (**grimmer, grimmest**) (**a**) *(sinister)* macabro(a); *(landscape)* lúgubre; *(smile)* sardónico(a) (**b**) *(manner)* severo(a); *(person)* ceñudo(a) (**c**) *(resolute)* inexorable (**d**) *Fam (unpleasant)* desagradable; **g. reality** la dura realidad

grimace [grɪˈmeɪs] **1** *n* mueca *f*
2 *vi* hacer una mueca

grimy ['graɪmɪ] *adj* (**grimier, grimiest**) mugriento(a)

grin [grɪn] **1** *vi* sonreír abiertamente
2 *n* sonrisa abierta

grind [graɪnd] **1** *vt (pt & pp ground) (mill)* moler; *(crush)* triturar; *(sharpen)* afilar; *US (meat)* picar; **to g. one's teeth** hacer rechinar los dientes
2 *vi* (**a**) rechinar; *Fig* **to g. to a halt** *(vehicle)* pararse lentamente; *(production etc)* pararse poco a poco (**b**) *US Fam* empollar
3 *n* (**a**) *Fam* **the daily g.** la rutina cotidiana; **what a g.!** ¡qué rollo! (**b**) *US Fam (studious pupil)* empollón(ona) *m,f*
▶ **grind down** *vt sep Fig* **to g. down the opposition** acabar con la oposición

grip [grɪp] **1** *n* (**a**) *(hold)* agarrón *m*; *(handshake)* apretón *m*; *(of tyre)* adherencia *f*; **get a g. on yourself!** ¡tranquilízate!; **to get to grips with a problem** superar un problema (**b**) *(handle)* asidero *m* (**c**) *(travel bag)* maletín *m* (**d**) *(hairgrip)* pasador *m*
2 *vt* (**a**) agarrar, asir; *(hand)* apretar (**b**) *Fig (of film, story)* captar la atención de; **to be gripped by fear** ser presa del miedo

gripe [graɪp] **1** *vi Fam (complain)* quejarse
2 *n* (**a**) *Med (pain)* retortijón *m* (**b**) *Fam (complaint)* queja *f*

gripping ['grɪpɪŋ] *adj (film, story)* apasionante

grisly ['grɪzlɪ] *adj* (**grislier, grisliest**) espeluznante

gristle ['grɪsəl] *n* cartílago *m*, ternilla *f*

grit [grɪt] **1** *n* (**a**) *(gravel)* grava *f* (**b**) *Fam (courage)* valor *m*
2 *vt Fig* **to g. one's teeth** apretar los dientes

gritty ['grɪtɪ] *adj* (**grittier, grittiest**) valiente

grizzly ['grɪzlɪ] *adj* **g. bear** oso pardo

groan [grəʊn] **1** n (**a**) (of pain) gemido m (**b**) Fam (of disapproval) gruñido m
　　2 vi (**a**) (in pain) gemir (**b**) Fam (complain) quejarse (**about** de)

grocer ['grəʊsə(r)] n tendero(a) m,f; **g.'s (shop)** tienda f de comestibles, CSur almacén m, Andes, CAm, Méx tienda f de abarrotes

groceries ['grəʊsərɪz] npl comestibles mpl

grocery ['grəʊsərɪ] n (shop) tienda f de ultramarinos; US **g. store** supermercado m

groggy ['grɒgɪ] adj (**groggier, groggiest**) Fam (boxer) grogui; Fig (unsteady) atontado(a); (weak) débil

groin [grɔɪn] n ingle f

groom [gruːm] **1** n (**a**) (of horse) mozo m de cuadra (**b**) (bridegroom) novio m
　　2 vt (horse) almohazar; (clothes, appearance) cuidar

groove [gruːv] n (furrow etc) ranura f; (of record) surco m

grope [grəʊp] vi (**a**) (search about) andar a tientas; **to g. for sth** buscar algo a tientas (**b**) Fam (fondle) meter mano

gross [grəʊs] **1** adj (**a**) grosero(a); (joke) verde (**b**) (fat) obeso(a) (**c**) (flagrant) flagrante; (ignorance) craso(a) (**d**) Com & Econ bruto(a); **g. national product** producto nacional bruto
　　2 vt Com recaudar (en bruto)

grossly ['grəʊslɪ] adv enormemente

grotesque [grəʊ'tesk] adj grotesco(a)

grotto ['grɒtəʊ] n gruta f

ground¹ [graʊnd] **1** n (**a**) suelo m, tierra f; **at g. level** al nivel del suelo; Av **to get off the g.** despegar; Av **g. control** control m de tierra; Av **g. floor** planta baja; Av **g. staff** personal m de tierra; Fig **g. swell** marejada f (**b**) (terrain) terreno m; **to gain/lose g.** ganar/perder terreno; Fig **to stand one's g.** mantenerse firme; **football g.** campo m de fútbol (**c**) US Elec toma f de tierra (**d**) **grounds** (gardens) jardines mpl (**e**) **grounds** (reason) motivo m (**f**) **grounds** (sediment) poso m
　　2 vt (**a**) Av obligar a quedarse en tierra; Naut varar (**b**) US Elec conectar con tierra

ground² [graʊnd] **1** adj (coffee) molido(a); US (meat) picado(a)
　　2 pt & pp of **grind**

grounding ['graʊndɪŋ] n base f; **to have a good g. in** tener buenos conocimientos de

groundless ['graʊndlɪs] adj infundado(a)

groundsheet ['graʊndʃiːt] n tela f impermeable

groundsman ['graʊndzmən] n encargado m de campo

groundwork ['graʊndwɜːk] n trabajo preparatorio

group [gruːp] **1** n grupo m, conjunto m
　　2 vt agrupar, juntar (**into** en)
　　3 vi **to g. (together)** agruparse, juntarse

grouse¹ [graʊs] n Orn urogallo m

grouse² [graʊs] Fam **1** vi quejarse (**about** de)
　　2 n queja f

grove [grəʊv] n arboleda f

grovel ['grɒvəl] vi humillarse (**to** ante); (crawl) arrastrarse (**to** ante)

grow [grəʊ] **1** vt (pt **grew**; pp **grown**) (cultivate) cultivar; **to g. a beard** dejarse (crecer) la barba
　　2 vi (**a**) crecer; (increase) aumentar (**b**) (become) hacerse, volverse; **to g. accustomed to** acostumbrarse a; **to g. dark** oscurecer; **to g. old** envejecer
　　▸ **grow out of** vt insep (**a**) **he's grown out of his shirt** se le ha quedado pequeña la camisa (**b**) Fig (phase etc) superar
　　▸ **grow up** vi crecer, hacerse mayor

grower ['grəʊə(r)] n cultivador(a) m,f

growing ['grəʊɪŋ] adj (child) que crece; (problem etc) creciente; **he's a g. boy** está dando el estirón

growl [graʊl] **1** vi gruñir
　　2 n gruñido m

grown [grəʊn] **1** adj crecido(a), adulto(a)
　　2 pp of **grow**

grown-up ['grəʊnʌp] adj & n adulto(a) (m,f); **the grown-ups** los mayores

growth [grəʊθ] n (**a**) crecimiento m; (increase) aumento m; (development) desarrollo m (**b**) Med bulto m

grub [grʌb] n (**a**) (larva) gusano m (**b**) Fam (food) papeo m

grubby ['grʌbɪ] adj (**grubbier, grubbiest**) sucio(a)

grudge [grʌdʒ] **1** n rencor m; **to bear sb a g.** guardar rencor a algn
　　2 vt (give unwillingly) dar a regañadientes; **he grudges me my success** me envidia el éxito

grudgingly ['grʌdʒɪŋlɪ] adv a regañadientes

gruelling, US **grueling** ['gruːəlɪŋ] adj penoso(a)

gruesome ['gruːsəm] adj espantoso(a), horrible

gruff [grʌf] adj (manner) brusco(a); (voice) áspero(a)

grumble ['grʌmbəl] **1** vi refunfuñar
　　2 n queja f

grumpy ['grʌmpɪ] adj (**grumpier, grumpiest**) gruñón(ona)

grunt [grʌnt] **1** vi gruñir
2 n gruñido m

guarantee [gærən'tiː] **1** n garantía f; (certificate) certificado m de garantía
2 vt garantizar; (assure) asegurar

guard [gɑːd] **1** vt (a) (protect) defender, proteger; (keep watch over) vigilar (b) (control) guardar
2 vi protegerse (**against** de or contra)
3 n (a) **to be on one's g.** estar en guardia; **to catch sb off his g.** coger desprevenido a algn (b) (sentry) guardia mf; **g. of honour** guardia de honor; **to stand g.** montar la guardia; **g. dog** perro m guardián (c) Br Rail jefe m del tren; **g.'s van** furgón m de cola (d) (on machine) dispositivo m de seguridad; **fire g.** pantalla f

guarded ['gɑːdɪd] adj cauteloso(a), precavido(a)

guardhouse ['gɑːdhaʊs] n Mil (a) (headquarters) cuerpo m de guardia (b) (prison) prisión f militar

guardian ['gɑːdɪən] n (a) guardián(ana) m,f; **g. angel** ángel m de la guarda (b) Jur (of minor) tutor(a) m,f

Guatemala [gwɑːtə'mɑːlə] n Guatemala

Guatemalan [gwɑːtə'mɑːlən] adj & n guatemalteco(a) m,f

guava ['gwɑːvə] n Bot guayaba f; **g. tree** guayabo m

guer(r)illa [gə'rɪlə] n guerrillero(a) m,f; **g. warfare** guerra f de guerrillas

guess [ges] **1** vt & vi (a) adivinar; **I guessed as much** me lo imaginaba, me lo suponía; **to g. right/wrong** acertar/no acertar (b) US Fam pensar, suponer; **I g. so** supongo que sí
2 n conjetura f; (estimate) cálculo m; **at a rough g.** a ojo de buen cubero; **to have** or **make a g.** intentar adivinar

guesswork ['geswɜːk] n conjetura f

guest [gest] n (at home) invitado(a) m,f; (in hotel) cliente(a) m,f, huésped(a) m,f; **g. artist** artista mf invitado(a); **g. room** cuarto m de los invitados

guesthouse ['gesthaʊs] n casa f de huéspedes

guffaw [gʌ'fɔː] vi reírse a carcajadas

guidance ['gaɪdəns] n orientación f, consejos mpl; **for your g.** a título de información

guide [gaɪd] **1** vt guiar, dirigir
2 n (a) (person) guía mf; Br **girl g.** exploradora f; **g. dog** perro lazarillo (b) (guidebook) guía f

guidebook ['gaɪdbʊk] n guía f

guided ['gaɪdɪd] adj dirigido(a); **g. tour** visita con guía; **g. missile** misil teledirigido

guideline ['gaɪdlaɪn] n pauta f

guild [gɪld] n gremio m

guile [gaɪl] n astucia f

guillotine ['gɪlətiːn] n guillotina f

guilt [gɪlt] n (a) culpa f (b) Jur culpabilidad f

guilty ['gɪltɪ] adj (**guiltier, guiltiest**) culpable (**of** de); **to have a g. conscience** remorderle a uno la conciencia

guinea¹ ['gɪnɪ] n **g. pig** conejillo m de Indias, cobayo m; Fig **to act as a g. pig** servir de conejillo de Indias

guinea² ['gɪnɪ] n (coin) guinea f (= 21 chelines)

guise [gaɪz] n **under the g. of** so pretexto de

guitar [gɪ'tɑː(r)] n guitarra f

guitarist [gɪ'tɑːrɪst] n guitarrista mf

gulf [gʌlf] n (a) golfo m; **G. of Mexico** Golfo de Méjico; **G. Stream** corriente f del Golfo de Méjico; **the G. War** la guerra del Golfo (b) Fig abismo m

gull [gʌl] n gaviota f

gulley ['gʌlɪ] n = **gully**

gullible ['gʌləbəl] adj crédulo(a)

gully ['gʌlɪ] n barranco m, hondonada f

gulp [gʌlp] **1** n trago m
2 vt tragar; **to g. sth down** (drink) tomarse algo de un trago; (food) engullir algo
3 vi (a) (swallow air) tragar aire (b) Fig (with fear) tragar saliva

gum¹ [gʌm] **1** n goma f
2 vt pegar con goma

gum² [gʌm] n Anat encía f

gumboots ['gʌmbuːts] npl botas fpl de agua

gun [gʌn] n arma f de fuego; (handgun) pistola f, revólver m; (rifle) fusil m, escopeta f; (cannon) cañón m; Fam **the big guns** los peces gordos
▸ **gun down** vt sep matar a tiros

gunboat ['gʌnbəʊt] n cañonero m

gunfire ['gʌnfaɪə(r)] n tiros mpl

gunman ['gʌnmən] n pistolero m, gángster m

gunpoint ['gʌnpɔɪnt] n **at g.** a punta de pistola

gunpowder ['gʌnpaʊdə(r)] n pólvora f

gunrunner ['gʌnrʌnə(r)] n traficante mf de armas

gunshot ['gʌnʃɒt] n disparo m, tiro m

gunsmith ['gʌnsmɪθ] n armero m

gurgle ['gɜːgəl] vi (baby) gorjear; (liquid) gorgotear; (stream) murmurar

guru ['gʊruː, 'guːruː] n gurú m
gush [gʌʃ] **1** vi (a) brotar (b) Fig to g.
over sb enjabonar a algn
   2 n (of water) chorro m; (of words) torrente m
gushing ['gʌʃɪŋ] adj Fig (person) efusi-
vo(a)
gusset ['gʌsɪt] n escudete m
gust [gʌst] n (of wind) ráfaga f, racha f
gusto ['gʌstəʊ] n entusiasmo m
gut [gʌt] **1** n (a) Anat intestino m (b)
(catgut) cuerda f de tripa (c) **guts** (entrails) tripas fpl; Fam **to have guts** tener
agallas
   2 vt (a) (fish) destripar (b) (destroy)
destruir por dentro
   3 adj Fam **g. reaction** reacción f
visceral
gutter ['gʌtə(r)] n (in street) arroyo m; (on

roof) canalón m; Fig **g. press** prensa
amarilla
guttural ['gʌtərəl] adj gutural
guy¹ [gaɪ] n Fam tipo m, tío m
guy² [gaɪ] n (rope) viento m, cuerda f
guzzle ['gʌzəl] vt & vi Fam (food etc)
zamparse; (car) tragar mucho
gym [dʒɪm] Fam (a) (gymnasium) gimnasio m (b) (gymnastics) gimnasia f; **g.
shoes** zapatillas fpl de deporte
gymnasium [dʒɪm'neɪzɪəm] n gimnasio
m
gymnast ['dʒɪmnæst] n gimnasta mf
gymnastics [dʒɪm'næstɪks] n sing gimnasia f
gynaecologist, US **gynecologist**
[gaɪnɪ'kɒlədʒɪst] n ginecólogo(a) m,f
gypsy ['dʒɪpsɪ] adj & n gitano(a) (m,f)
gyrate [dʒaɪ'reɪt] vi girar

H

H, h [eɪtʃ] n (the letter) H, h f
haberdashery [hæbə'dæʃərɪ] n (a) Br artículos mpl de mercería (b) US ropa masculina
habit ['hæbɪt] n (a) costumbre f (b) (garment) hábito m
habitable ['hæbɪtəbəl] adj habitable
habitat ['hæbɪtæt] n hábitat m
habitual [hə'bɪtjʊəl] adj habitual; (drinker, liar) empedernido(a)
habitually [hə'bɪtjʊəlɪ] adv por costumbre
hack¹ [hæk] **1** n (cut) corte m; (with an axe) hachazo m
2 vt (with knife, axe) cortar; (kick) dar un puntapié a
hack² [hæk] n Fam (writer) escritorzuelo(a) m,f; (journalist) gacetillero(a) m,f
hackneyed ['hæknɪd] adj trillado(a)
hacksaw ['hæksɔ:] n sierra f para metales
had [hæd] pt & pp of have
haddock ['hædək] n abadejo m
haemophilia [hi:mə'fɪlɪə] n hemofilia f
haemophiliac [hi:mə'fɪlɪæk] adj & n hemofílico(a) (m,f)
haemorrhage ['hemərɪdʒ] n hemorragia f
haemorrhoids ['hemərɔɪdz] npl hemorroides fpl
hag [hæg] n Pej bruja f, arpía f
haggard ['hægəd] adj ojeroso(a)
haggle ['hægəl] vi regatear
Hague [heɪg] n The H. La Haya
hail¹ [heɪl] **1** n granizo m; Fig **a h. of bullets/insults** una lluvia de balas/insultos
2 vi granizar
hail² [heɪl] **1** vt (a) (taxi etc) parar (b) (acclaim) aclamar
2 vi **to h. from** (originate) ser nativo(a) de
hailstone ['heɪlstəʊn] n granizo m
hailstorm ['heɪlstɔ:m] n granizada f
hair [heə(r)] n (strand) pelo m, cabello m; (mass) pelo, cabellos mpl; (on arm, leg) vello m; **to have long h.** tener el pelo largo
hairbrush ['heəbrʌʃ] n cepillo m (para el pelo)

haircut ['heəkʌt] n corte m de pelo; **to have a h.** cortarse el pelo
hairdo ['heədu:] n Fam peinado m
hairdresser ['heədresə(r)] n peluquero(a) m,f; **h.'s (shop)** peluquería f
hairdryer, hairdrier ['heədraɪə(r)] n secador m (de pelo)
hairgrip ['heəgrɪp] n Br horquilla f
hairline ['heəlaɪn] **1** adj muy fino(a)
2 n nacimiento m del pelo; **receding h.** entradas fpl
hairnet ['heənet] n redecilla f
hairpiece ['heəpi:s] n postizo m
hairpin ['heəpɪn] n horquilla f; **h. bend** curva muy cerrada
hair-raising ['heəreɪzɪŋ] adj espeluznante
hair-remover ['heərɪmu:və(r)] n depilatorio m
hairspray ['heəspreɪ] n laca f (para el pelo)
hairstyle ['heəstaɪl] n peinado m, corte m de pelo
hairy ['heərɪ] adj (hairier, hairiest) (a) (with hair) peludo(a) (b) Fig (frightening) enervante, espantoso(a)
hake [heɪk] n merluza f; (young) pescadilla f
half [hɑ:f] **1** n (pl halves) mitad f; Sport (period) tiempo m; **he's four and a h.** tiene cuatro años y medio; **to cut in h.** cortar por la mitad
2 adj medio(a); **h. a dozen/an hour** media docena/hora; **h. board** media pensión; **h. fare** media tarifa; **h. term** medio trimestre; **h. year** semestre m
3 adv medio, a medias; **h. asleep** medio dormido(a)
half-caste ['hɑ:fkɑ:st] adj & n mestizo(a) (m,f)
half-day [hɑ:f 'deɪ] n media jornada
half-hearted [hɑ:f 'hɑ:tɪd] adj poco entusiasta
half-hour [hɑ:f 'aʊə(r)] n media hora
half-life [hɑ:f'laɪf] n media vida
half-mast [hɑ:f 'mɑ:st] n **at h.** a media asta
half-price [hɑ:f 'praɪs] adv a mitad de precio

half-time ['hɑːf'taɪm] *n* descanso *m*

half-way ['hɑːfweɪ] **1** *adj* intermedio(a)
  2 halfway [hɑːf'weɪ] *adv* a medio camino, a mitad de camino

half-yearly ['hɑːfjɪəlɪ] *adj* semestral

halibut ['hælɪbət] *n* mero *m*

hall [hɔːl] *n* (a) *(lobby)* vestíbulo *m* (b) *(building)* sala *f; Univ* **h. of residence** colegio *m* mayor

hallmark ['hɔːlmɑːk] *n* (a) *(on gold, silver)* contraste *m* (b) *Fig* sello *m*

hallo [hə'ləʊ] *interj* ¡hola!

hallowed ['hæləʊd] *adj* santificado(a)

Hallowe('en [hæləʊ'iːn] *n* víspera *f* de Todos los Santos

hallucinate [hə'luːsɪneɪt] *vi* alucinar

hallucination [həluːsɪ'neɪʃən] *n* alucinación *f*

hallucinogenic [həluːsɪnəʊ'dʒenɪk] *adj* alucinógeno(a)

hallway ['hɔːlweɪ] *n* vestíbulo *m*

halo ['heɪləʊ] *n* (a) *Rel* aureola *f* (b) *Astron* halo *m*

halt [hɔːlt] **1** *n (stop)* alto *m*, parada *f;* **to call a h. to sth** poner fin a algo
  2 *vt* parar
  3 *vi* pararse

halting ['hɔːltɪŋ] *adj* vacilante

halve [hɑːv] *vt* (a) partir por la mitad; *(reduce by half)* reducir a la mitad (b) *(share)* compartir

halves [hɑːvz] *pl of* **half**

ham [hæm] *n* jamón *m;* **boiled h.** jamón de York; **Parma** *or* **cured h.** jamón serrano

hamburger ['hæmbɜːgə(r)] *n* hamburguesa *f*

hamlet ['hæmlɪt] *n* aldea *f*

hammer ['hæmə(r)] **1** *n* (a) martillo *m;* **the h. and sickle** la hoz y el martillo (b) *(of gun)* percursor *m* (c) *Sport* lanzamiento *m* de martillo
  2 *vt* (a) martillar; *(nail)* clavar; *Fig* **to h. home** insistir sobre (b) *Fam (defeat)* dar una paliza a
  3 *vi* martillar, dar golpes

hammering ['hæmərɪŋ] *n Fam* paliza *f*

hammock ['hæmək] *n* hamaca *f; Naut* coy *m*

hamper¹ ['hæmpə(r)] *n* cesta *f*

hamper² ['hæmpə(r)] *vt* estorbar, dificultar

hamster ['hæmstə(r)] *n* hámster *m*

hamstring ['hæmstrɪŋ] *n* tendón *m* de la corva

hand [hænd] **1** *n* (a) mano *f;* **by h.** a mano; **(close) at h.** a mano; **hands up!** ¡manos arriba!; **on the one/other h.** por una/otra parte; *Fig* **to get out of h.** descontrolarse;

Fig **to be on h.** estar a mano; *Fig* **to have a h. in** intervenir en; *Fig* **to have time in h.** sobrarle a uno tiempo; *Fig* **to wash one's hands of sth** lavarse las manos de algo; *Fig* **to give sb a h.** echarle una mano a algn; **h. grenade** granada *f* de mano
  (b) *(worker)* trabajador(a) *m,f; Naut* tripulante *m*
  (c) *(of clock)* aguja *f*
  (d) **to give sb a big h.** *(applause)* dedicar a algn una gran ovación
  (e) *(handwriting)* letra *f*
  2 *vt (give)* dar, entregar; *Fam Fig* **I have to h. it to you** tengo que reconocerlo
  ▸ **hand back** *vt sep* devolver
  ▸ **hand down** *vt sep* dejar en herencia
  ▸ **hand in** *vt sep (homework)* entregar; *(resignation)* presentar
  ▸ **hand out** *vt sep* repartir
  ▸ **hand over** *vt sep* entregar
  ▸ **hand round** *vt sep* repartir

handbag ['hændbæg] *n Br* bolso *m*, cartera *f, Méx* bolsa *f*

handball ['hændbɔːl] *n Sport* balonmano *m*

handbook ['hændbʊk] *n* manual *m*

handbrake ['hændbreɪk] *n* freno *m* de mano

handcuff ['hændkʌf] **1** *vt* esposar
  2 *npl* **handcuffs** esposas *fpl*

handful ['hændfʊl] *n* puñado *m*

handicap ['hændɪkæp] **1** *n* (a) *Med* minusvalía *f* (b) *Sport* hándicap *m*, desventaja *f*
  2 *vt* impedir

handicapped ['hændɪkæpt] *adj* (a) *(physically)* minusválido(a); *(mentally)* retrasado(a) (b) *Sport* en desventaja (c) *Fig* desfavorecido(a)

handicraft ['hændɪkrɑːft] *n* artesanía *f*

handiwork ['hændɪwɜːk] *n (work)* obra *f; (craft)* artesanía *f*

handkerchief ['hæŋkətʃiːf] *n* pañuelo *m*

handle ['hændəl] **1** *n (of knife)* mango *m; (of cup)* asa *f; (of door)* pomo *m; (of lever)* palanca *f; (of drawer)* tirador *m*
  2 *vt* (a) manejar; **h. with care** *(sign)* frágil (b) *(problem)* encargarse de; *(people)* tratar; *Fam (put up with)* soportar
  3 *vi (car)* comportarse

handlebar ['hændəlbɑː(r)] *n* manillar *m*

handmade [hænd'meɪd] *adj* hecho(a) a mano

hand-out ['hændaʊt] *n* (a) *(leaflet)* folleto *m; Press* nota *f* de prensa (b) *(charity)* limosna *f*

hand-picked [hænd'pɪkt] *adj* selecto(a)

handrail ['hændreɪl] *n* pasamanos *m inv*

handshake ['hændʃeɪk] *n* apretón *m* de manos

handsome ['hænsəm] *adj* (a) *(person)* guapo(a) (b) *(substantial)* considerable

handwriting ['hændraɪtɪŋ] *n* letra *f*

handy ['hændɪ] *adj* (**handier, handiest**) (a) *(useful)* útil, práctico(a); *(nearby)* a mano (b) *(dextrous)* diestro(a)

hang [hæŋ] **1** *vt* (*pt & pp* **hung**) (a) *(head)* colgar (b) *(head)* bajar (c) (*pt* **hanged**) ahorcar
2 *vi* (a) colgar (**from** de); *(in air)* flotar (b) *(criminal)* ser ahorcado(a); **to h. one-self** ahorcarse
▸ **hang about** *vi Fam* (a) perder el tiempo (b) *(wait)* esperar
▸ **hang around** *vi Fam* (a) esperar (b) frecuentar; **where does he h. around?** ¿a qué lugares suele ir?
▸ **hang on** *vi* (a) agarrarse (b) *(wait)* esperar
▸ **hang out 1** *vt sep (washing)* tender
2 *vi Fam (frequent)* frecuentar
▸ **hang round** *vi Fam* = **hang about**
▸ **hang together** *vi (ideas)* ser coherente
▸ **hang up** *vt sep (picture, telephone)* colgar

hangar ['hæŋə(r)] *n* hangar *m*

hanger ['hæŋə(r)] *n* percha *f*

hang-glider ['hæŋglaɪdə(r)] *n* ala delta

hang-gliding ['hæŋglaɪdɪŋ] *n* vuelo *m* libre

hangman ['hæŋmən] *n* verdugo *m*

hangover ['hæŋəʊvə(r)] *n* resaca *f*

hang-up ['hæŋʌp] *n Fam (complex)* complejo *m*

hanker ['hæŋkə(r)] *vi* **to h. after sth** anhelar algo

hankie, hanky ['hæŋkɪ] *n Fam* pañuelo *m*

haphazard [hæp'hæzəd] *adj* caótico(a), desordenado(a)

happen ['hæpən] *vi* suceder, ocurrir; **it so happens that** lo que pasa es que; **if you h. to see my friend** si por casualidad ves a mi amigo

happening ['hæpənɪŋ] *n* acontecimiento *m*

happily ['hæpɪlɪ] *adv (with pleasure)* felizmente; *(fortunately)* afortunadamente

happiness ['hæpɪnɪs] *n* felicidad *f*

happy ['hæpɪ] *adj* (**happier, happiest**) *(cheerful)* feliz, contento(a); *(fortunate)* afortunado(a); **h. birthday!** ¡feliz cumpleaños!

happy-go-lucky [hæpɪgəʊ'lʌkɪ] *adj* despreocupado(a); **a h. fellow** un viva la virgen

harangue [hə'ræŋ] **1** *vt* arengar
2 *n* arenga *f*

harass ['hærəs] *vt* acosar

harassment ['hærəsmənt, hə'ræsmənt] *n* hostigamiento *m*, acoso *m*

harbour, *US* **harbor** ['hɑːbə(r)] **1** *n* puerto *m*
2 *vt* (a) *(criminal)* encubrir (b) *(doubts)* abrigar

hard [hɑːd] **1** *adj* (a) *(solid)* duro(a); *(solid)* sólido(a); **h. court** pista (de tenis) rápida; *Comput* **h. disk** disco duro; *Br Aut* **h. shoulder** arcén *m*, *Andes* berma *f*, *Méx* acotamiento *m*, *RP* banquina *f*, *Ven* hombrillo *m*
(b) *(difficult)* difícil; **h. of hearing** duro(a) de oído; *Fam Fig* **to be h. up** estar sin blanca
(c) *(harsh)* severo(a); *(strict)* estricto(a); **to take a h. line** tomar medidas severas; **h. drugs** droga dura; *Pol* **h. left** extrema izquierda; **h. porn** pornografía dura; **h. sell** promoción *f* de venta agresiva
(d) **a h. drinker** un bebedor inveterado; **a h. worker** un trabajador concienzudo
(e) **h. luck!** ¡mala suerte!
(f) **h. evidence** pruebas definitivas; *Com* **h. cash** dinero *m* en metálico; **h. currency** divisa *f* fuerte
2 *adv* (a) *(hit)* fuerte
(b) *(work)* mucho, concienzudamente; *Fig* **to be h. on sb's heels** pisar los talones a algn
(c) **to be h. done by** ser tratado(a) injustamente

hardback ['hɑːdbæk] *n* edición *f* de tapas duras

hard-boiled ['hɑːdbɔɪld] *adj* duro(a)

hard-core ['hɑːdkɔː(r)] *adj* irreductible

harden ['hɑːdən] **1** *vt* endurecer
2 *vi* endurecerse

hardened ['hɑːdənd] *adj Fig* habitual

hard-headed [hɑːd'hedɪd] *adj* realista

hard-hearted [hɑːd'hɑːtɪd] *adj* insensible

hardliner [hɑːd'laɪnə(r)] *n* duro(a) *m,f*

hardly ['hɑːdlɪ] *adv* apenas; **h. anyone/ ever** casi nadie/nunca; **he had h. begun when ...** apenas había comenzado cuando ...; **I can h. believe it** apenas lo puedo creer

hardship ['hɑːdʃɪp] *n* privación *f*, apuro *m*

hardware ['hɑːdweə(r)] *n* (a) *(goods)* ferretería *f*; **h. shop** ferretería (b) *Comput* hardware *m*

hardwearing [hɑːd'weərɪŋ] *adj* duradero(a)

hardworking ['hɑːdwɜːkɪŋ] *adj* muy trabajador(a)

hardy ['hɑːdɪ] *adj* (**hardier, hardiest**) *(person)* robusto(a), fuerte; *(plant)* resistente

hare [heə(r)] **1** *n* liebre *f*
　2 *vi* correr muy de prisa

haricot ['hærɪkəʊ] *n* **h. (bean)** alubia *f*

harm [hɑːm] **1** *n* daño *m*, perjuicio *m*; **to be out of h.'s way** estar a salvo
　2 *vt* hacer daño a, perjudicar

harmful ['hɑːmfʊl] *adj* perjudicial (**to** para)

harmless ['hɑːmlɪs] *adj* inofensivo(a)

harmonica [hɑːˈmɒnɪkə] *n* armónica *f*

harmonize ['hɑːmənaɪz] *vt & vi* armonizar

harmony ['hɑːmənɪ] *n* armonía *f*

harness ['hɑːnɪs] **1** *n* *(for horse)* arreos *mpl*
　2 *vt* **(a)** *(horse)* enjaezar **(b)** *Fig (resources etc)* aprovechar

harp [hɑːp] *n* arpa *f*
　► **harp on** *vi* Fam hablar sin parar

harpoon [hɑːˈpuːn] **1** *n* arpón *m*
　2 *vt* arponear

harrowing ['hærəʊɪŋ] *adj* angustioso(a)

harsh [hɑːʃ] *adj* severo(a); *(voice)* áspero(a); *(sound)* discordante

harvest ['hɑːvɪst] **1** *n* cosecha *f*, *(of grapes)* vendimia *f*
　2 *vt* cosechar, recoger

harvester ['hɑːvɪstə(r)] *n* **(a)** *(person)* segador(a) *m,f* **(b)** *(machine)* cosechadora *f*

has [hæz] *3rd person sing pres of* **have**

hash¹ [hæʃ] *n Culin* sofrito *m* de carne; *Fam Fig* **to make a h. of sth** estropear algo

hash² [hæʃ] *n Fam* hachís *m*

hashish ['hæʃɪʃ] *n* hachís *m*

hassle ['hæsəl] *Fam* **1** *n* **(a)** *(nuisance)* rollo *m* **(b)** *(problem)* lío *m* **(c)** *(wrangle)* bronca *f*
　2 *vt* fastidiar

haste [heɪst] *n Fml* prisa *f*; **to make h.** darse prisa

hasten ['heɪsən] *vi* apresurarse

hastily ['heɪstɪlɪ] *adv (quickly)* de prisa

hasty ['heɪstɪ] *adj* (**hastier, hastiest**) apresurado(a); *(rash)* precipitado(a)

hat [hæt] *n* sombrero *m*

hatch¹ [hætʃ] *n* escotilla *f*; **serving h.** ventanilla *f*

hatch² [hætʃ] *vt* **(a)** *(eggs)* empollar **(b)** *Fig (plan)* tramar
　► **hatch out** *vi* salirse del huevo

hatchback ['hætʃbæk] *n* coche *m* de 3/5 puertas

hatchet ['hætʃɪt] *n* hacha *f*; *Fam* **h. man** matón *m*

hate [heɪt] **1** *n* odio *m*
　2 *vt* odiar

hateful ['heɪtfʊl] *adj* odioso(a)

hatred ['heɪtrɪd] *n* odio *m*

haughty ['hɔːtɪ] *adj* (**haughtier, haughtiest**) altanero(a), arrogante

haul [hɔːl] **1** *n* **(a)** *(journey)* trayecto *m* **(b)** *(of fish)* redada *f* **(c)** *(loot)* botín *m*
　2 *vt* **(a)** tirar; *(drag)* arrastrar **(b)** *(transport)* acarrear
　► **haul up** *vt sep Fam (to court)* llevar

haulage ['hɔːlɪdʒ] *n* transporte *m*

haulier ['hɔːljə(r)] *n* transportista *mf*

haunch [hɔːntʃ] *n* cadera *f*; *Culin* pernil *m*

haunt [hɔːnt] **1** *n* guarida *f*
　2 *vt* **(a)** *(of ghost)* aparecerse en **(b)** *Fig* atormentar **(c)** *(frequent)* frecuentar

haunted ['hɔːntɪd] *adj* encantado(a), embrujado(a)

Havana [həˈvænə] *n* La Habana; **H. cigar** habano *m*

have [hæv]

En el inglés hablado, y en el escrito en estilo coloquial, el verbo auxiliar **have** se contrae de forma que **I have** se transforma en **I've**, **he/she/it has** se transforman en **he's/she's/it's** y **you/we/they have** se transforman en **you've/we've/they've**. Las formas de pasado **I/you/he** *etc* **had** se transforman en **I'd, you'd, he'd** *etc*. Las formas negativas **has not, have not** y **had not** se transforman en **hasn't, haven't** y **hadn't**.

---

1 *vt* (*3rd person sing pres* **has**; *pt & pp* **had**)
　(a) *(possess)* tener; **h. you got a car?** ¿tienes coche?
　(b) *(get, experience, suffer)* tener; **to h. a holiday** tomarse unas vacaciones
　(c) *(partake of)* tomar; **to h. a cigarette** fumarse un cigarrillo; **to h. breakfast/lunch/tea/dinner** desayunar/comer/merendar/cenar
　(d) **to h. a bath/shave** bañarse/afeitarse; **to h. a nap** echar la siesta
　(e) **to h. to** *(obligation)* tener que, deber
　(f) *(make happen)* hacer que; **I'll h. someone come round** haré que venga alguien
　(g) *(receive)* recibir; **to h. people round** invitar a gente
　(h) **can I h. your pen a moment?** *(borrow)* ¿me dejas tu bolígrafo un momento?
　(i) *(party, meeting)* hacer, celebrar
　(j) **to h. a baby** tener un niño

(**k**) **we won't h. it** *(allow)* no lo consentiremos

(**l**) *(hold)* tener; *Fig* **to h. sth against sb** tener algo en contra de algn

(**m**) **legend has it that ...** según la leyenda ...

(**n**) *Fam (deceive)* engañar

(**o**) **you'd better stay** más vale que te quedes

2 *v aux* (**a**) *(compound)* haber; **I had been waiting for half an hour** hacía media hora que esperaba; **he hasn't eaten yet** no ha comido aún; **she had broken the window** había roto el cristal; **we h. lived here for ten years** hace diez años que vivimos aquí; **so I h.!** *(emphatic)* ¡ay, sí!, es verdad; **yes I h.!** ¡que sí!

(**b**) *(tag questions)* **you haven't seen my book, h. you?** no has visto mi libro, ¿verdad?; **he's been to France, hasn't he?** ha estado en Francia, ¿verdad? *or* ¿no?

(**c**) *(have + just)* acabar de

▸ **have on** *vt sep* (**a**) *(wear)* vestir (**b**) *Fam* **to h. sb on** tomarle el pelo a algn

▸ **have out** *vt sep Fam* **to h. it out with sb** ajustar cuentas con algn

▸ **have over** *vt sep (invite)* recibir

haven ['heɪvən] *n* puerto *m*; *Fig* refugio *m*

haversack ['hævəsæk] *n* mochila *f*

havoc ['hævək] *n* **to play h. with** hacer estragos en

hawk [hɔːk] *n Orn & Pol* halcón *m*

hawker ['hɔːkə(r)] *n* vendedor(a) *m,f* ambulante

hawthorn ['hɔːθɔːn] *n* espino *m* albar

hay [heɪ] *n* heno *m*; **h. fever** fiebre *f* del heno

haystack ['heɪstæk] *n* almiar *m*

haywire ['heɪwaɪə(r)] *adj Fam* en desorden; **to go h.** *(machine etc)* estropearse; *(person)* volverse loco(a)

hazard ['hæzəd] **1** *n* peligro *m*, riesgo *m*; *(in golf)* obstáculo *m*

2 *vt Fml* arriesgar; **to h. a guess** intentar adivinar

hazardous ['hæzədəs] *adj* arriesgado(a), peligroso(a)

haze [heɪz] *n (mist)* neblina *f*; *Fig (blur)* confusión *f*

hazel ['heɪzəl] *adj* (de color) avellana

hazelnut ['heɪzəlnʌt] *n* avellana *f*

hazy ['heɪzɪ] *adj* (**hazier, haziest**) nebuloso(a)

he [hiː] *pers pron* él *(usually omitted in Spanish, except for contrast)*; **he did it** ha sido él; **he who** el que

head [hed] **1** *n* (**a**) cabeza *f*; *(mind)* mente *f*; *Fig* **£3 a h.** 3 libras por cabeza; *Fig* **to be** **h. over heels in love** estar locamente enamorado(a); *Fig* **to keep one's h.** mantener la calma; *Fig* **to lose one's h.** perder la cabeza; **success went to his h.** se le subió el éxito a la cabeza; *Fig* **to come to a h.** llegar a un momento decisivo

(**b**) *(of nail)* cabeza *f*; *(of beer)* espuma *f*; *(of tape recorder)* cabezal *m*; *(of steam)* presión *f*; *Fig* **to come to a h.** llegar a un momento decisivo

(**c**) *(boss)* cabeza *m*; *(of company)* director(a) *m,f*, **h. teacher** director(a) *m,f*

(**d**) *(of coin)* cara *f*; **heads or tails** cara o cruz

2 *adj* principal; **h. office** oficina *f* central

3 *vt* (**a**) *(list etc)* encabezar

(**b**) *Ftb* cabecear

▸ **head for** *vt insep* dirigirse hacia

▸ **head off 1** *vi* irse

2 *vt sep (avert)* evitar

headache ['hedeɪk] *n* dolor *m* de cabeza; *Fig* quebradero *m* de cabeza

headcheese ['hedtʃiːz] *n US* queso *m* de cerdo

header ['hedə(r)] *n Ftb* cabezazo *m*

head-first [hed'fɜːst] *adv* de cabeza

head-hunter ['hedhʌntə(r)] *n Fig* cazatalentos *mf inv*

heading ['hedɪŋ] *n* título *m*; *(of letter)* membrete *m*

headlamp ['hedlæmp] *n* faro *m*

headland ['hedlənd] *n* punta *f*, cabo *m*

headlight ['hedlaɪt] *n* faro *m*

headline ['hedlaɪn] *n* titular *m*; **the headlines** *(on radio, TV)* los titulares

headlong ['hedlɒŋ] *adj & adv* de cabeza; **to rush h. into sth** lanzarse a hacer algo sin pensar

headmaster [hed'mɑːstə(r)] *n* director *m*

headmistress [hed'mɪstrɪs] *n* directora *f*

head-on ['hedɒn] *adj* **a h. collision** un choque frontal

headphones ['hedfəʊnz] *npl* auriculares *mpl*

headquarters ['hedkwɔːtəz] *npl* (**a**) oficina *f* central, sede *f* (**b**) *Mil* cuartel *m* general

headrest ['hedrest] *n Aut* apoyacabezas *m*

headroom ['hedruːm] *n* altura *f* libre

headscarf ['hedskɑːf] *n* pañuelo *m*

headstrong ['hedstrɒŋ] *adj* testarudo(a)

headway ['hedweɪ] *n* **to make h.** avanzar, progresar

headwind ['hedwɪnd] *n* viento *m* de proa

heady ['hedɪ] *adj* (**headier, headiest**) embriagador(a)

heal [hiːl] **1** *vi* cicatrizar

2 *vt (wound)* curar

health [helθ] *n* salud *f*; *Fig* prosperidad *f*; **to be in good/bad h.** estar bien/mal de salud; **your good h.!** ¡salud!; **h. foods** alimentos *mpl* naturales; **h. food shop** tienda *f* de alimentos naturales; *Br* **H. Service** ≃ Insalud *m*

healthy ['helθɪ] *adj* (**healthier, healthiest**) sano(a); *(good for health)* saludable; *(thriving)* próspero(a)

heap [hi:p] **1** *n* montón *m*

2 *vt* amontonar; *Fig* **to h. praise on sb** colmar a algn de alabanzas; **a heaped spoonful** una cucharada colmada

hear [hɪə(r)] **1** *vt (pt & pp heard* [hɜːd]*)* **(a)** oír **(b)** *(listen to)* escuchar **(c) I won't h.** of it! ¡ni hablar! **(d)** *(find out)* enterarse de **(e)** *Jur* ver; *(evidence)* oír

2 *vi* **to h. from sb** tener noticias de algn

hearing ['hɪərɪŋ] *n* **(a)** oído *m*; **h. aid** audífono *m* **(b)** *Jur* audiencia *f*; *Fig* **to give sb a fair h.** escuchar a algn

hearsay ['hɪəseɪ] *n* rumores *mpl*

hearse [hɜːs] *n* coche *m* fúnebre

heart [hɑːt] *n* **(a)** corazón *m*; **h. attack** infarto *m* de miocardio; **h. transplant** trasplante *m* de corazón; **a broken h.** un corazón roto; **at h.** en el fondo; **to take sth to h.** tomarse algo a pecho; **to have a good h.** *(be kind)* tener buen corazón **(b)** *(courage)* valor *m*; **his h. wasn't in it** no ponía interés en ello; **to lose h.** desanimarse **(c)** *(core)* meollo *m*, *(of lettuce)* cogollo *m*

heartbeat ['hɑːtbiːt] *n* latido *m* del corazón

heart-breaking ['hɑːtbreɪkɪŋ] *adj* desgarrador(a)

heart-broken ['hɑːtbrəʊkən] *adj* hundido(a); **he's h.** tiene el corazón destrozado

heartburn ['hɑːtbɜːn] *n* acedía *f*

heartening ['hɑːtənɪŋ] *adj* alentador(a)

heartfelt ['hɑːtfelt] *adj* sincero(a)

hearth [hɑːθ] *n* **(a)** *(fireplace)* chimenea *f* **(b)** *Fml (home)* hogar *m*

heartless ['hɑːtlɪs] *adj* cruel, insensible

heart-throb ['hɑːtθrɒb] *n* ídolo *m*

hearty ['hɑːtɪ] *adj* (**heartier, heartiest**) *(person)* francote; *(meal)* abundante; *(welcome)* cordial; **to have a h. appetite** ser de buen comer

heat [hiːt] **1** *n* **(a)** calor *m* **(b)** *Sport* eliminatoria *f* **(c)** *Zool* **on h.** en celo

2 *vt* calentar

▸ heat up *vi* **(a)** *(warm up)* calentarse **(b)** *(increase excitement)* acalorarse

heated ['hiːtɪd] *adj Fig (argument)* acalorado(a)

heater ['hiːtə(r)] *n* calentador *m*

heath [hiːθ] *n (land)* brezal *m*

heathen ['hiːðən] *adj & n* pagano(a) *(m,f)*

heather ['heðə(r)] *n* brezo *m*

heating ['hiːtɪŋ] *n* calefacción *f*

heatwave ['hiːtweɪv] *n* ola *f* de calor

heave [hiːv] **1** *n (pull)* tirón *m*; *(push)* empujón *m*

2 *vt* **(a)** *(lift)* levantar; *(haul)* tirar; *(push)* empujar **(b)** *(throw)* arrojar

3 *vi* subir y bajar

heaven ['hevən] **1** *n* **(a)** cielo *m*; **for h.'s sake!** ¡por Dios!; **h. on earth** un paraíso en la tierra **(b)** *heavens* cielo *m*

2 *interj* **good heavens!** ¡por Dios!

heavenly ['hevənlɪ] *adj* celestial

heavily ['hevɪlɪ] *adv* **it rained h.** llovió mucho; **to sleep h.** dormir profundamente

heavy ['hevɪ] **1** *adj* (**heavier, heaviest**) pesado(a); *(rain, meal)* fuerte; *(traffic)* denso(a); *(loss)* grande; **h. going** duro(a); **is it h.?** ¿pesa mucho?; **a h. drinker/ smoker** un(a) bebedor(a)/fumador(a) empedernido(a); *Mus* **h. metal** heavy metal *m*

2 *n Fam* gorila *m*

heavyweight ['hevɪweɪt] *n* peso pesado

Hebrew ['hiːbruː] **1** *adj* hebreo(a)

2 *n (language)* hebreo *m*

Hebrides ['hebrɪdiːz] *npl* **the H.** las (Islas) Hébridas

heckle ['hekəl] *vt* interrumpir

heckler ['heklə(r)] *n* altercador(a) *m,f*

hectare ['hektɑː(r)] *n* hectárea *f*

hectic ['hektɪk] *adj* agitado(a)

hedge [hedʒ] **1** *n* seto *m*

2 *vt* cercar con un seto; *Fig* **to h. one's bets** cubrirse

hedgehog ['hedʒhɒg] *n* erizo *m*

hedgerow ['hedʒrəʊ] *n* seto vivo

heed [hiːd] *n* **to take h. of** hacer caso de

heedless ['hiːdlɪs] *adj* desatento(a)

heel [hiːl] *n (of foot)* talón *m*; *(of shoe)* tacón *m*; *(of palm)* pulpejo *m*; *Fig* **to be on sb's heels** pisarle los talones a algn; **high heels** zapatos *mpl* de tacón alto

heeled [hiːld] *adj Fam Fig* **well-h.** adinerado(a)

hefty ['heftɪ] *adj* (**heftier, heftiest**) **(a)** *(person)* fornido(a); *(package)* pesado(a) **(b)** *(large)* grande

height [haɪt] *n* **(a)** altura *f*; *(of person)* estatura *f*; *Av* **to gain/lose h.** subir/bajar; **what h. are you?** ¿cuánto mides?; *Fig* **the h. of ignorance** el colmo de la ignorancia **(b)** *Geog* cumbre *f*

heighten ['haɪtən] *vt (intensify)* realzar; *(increase)* aumentar

heir [eə(r)] *n* heredero *m*

heiress ['eərɪs] *n* heredera *f*

heirloom ['eəlu:m] *n* reliquia *f*/joya *f* de familia

held [held] *pt & pp of* **hold**

helicopter ['helɪkɒptə(r)] *n* helicóptero *m*

helium ['hi:lɪəm] *n* helio *m*

hell [hel] *n* infierno *m*; *Fam* **what the h. are you doing?** ¿qué diablos estás haciendo?; *Fam* **go to h.!** ¡vete a hacer puñetas!; *Fam* **a h. of a party** una fiesta estupenda; *Fam* **she's had a h. of a day** ha tenido un día fatal

hellish ['helɪʃ] *adj Fam* infernal

hello [hə'ləʊ, he'ləʊ] *interj* ¡hola!; *Tel* ¡diga!; *(showing surprise)* ¡hala!

helm [helm] *n* timón *m*; **to be at the h.** llevar el timón

helmet ['helmɪt] *n* casco *m*

help [help] **1** *n* (a) ayuda *f*; **h.!** ¡socorro! (b) **(daily) h.** asistenta *f*
2 *vt* (a) ayudar; **can I h. you?** *(in shop)* ¿qué desea? (b) *(alleviate)* aliviar (c) **h. yourself!** *(to food etc)* ¡sírvete! (d) *(avoid)* evitar; **I can't h. it** no lo puedo remediar
▸ **help out** *vt sep* **to h. sb out** echarle una mano a algn

helper ['helpə(r)] *n* ayudante(a) *m,f*

helpful ['helpfʊl] *adj (person)* amable; *(thing)* útil

helping ['helpɪŋ] *n* ración *f*; **who wants a second h.?** ¿quién quiere repetir?

helpless ['helplɪs] *adj (defenceless)* desamparado(a); *(powerless)* incapaz

helplessly ['helplɪslɪ] *adv* inútilmente, en vano

helter-skelter [heltə'skeltə(r)] **1** *n* tobogán *m*
2 *adj* atropellado(a)
3 *adv* atropelladamente

hem [hem] **1** *n Sewing* dobladillo *m*
2 *vt Sewing* hacer un dobladillo a
▸ **hem in** *vt sep* cercar, rodear

hemisphere ['hemɪsfɪə(r)] *n* hemisferio *m*

hemophilia [hi:məʊ'fɪlɪə] *n US* = **haemophilia**

hemophiliac [hi:məʊ'fɪlɪæk] *adj & n* = **haemophiliac**

hemorrhage ['hemərɪdʒ] *n US* = **haemorrhage**

hen [hen] *n* gallina *f*; *Fam* **h. party** reunión *f* de mujeres

hence [hens] *adv Fml* (a) **six months h.** *(from now)* de aquí a seis meses (b) *(consequently)* por lo tanto

henceforth [hens'fɔ:θ] *adv Fml* de ahora en adelante

henchman ['hentʃmən] *n Pej* secuaz *m*

henna ['henə] *n Bot* alheña *f*; *(dye)* henna *f*

henpecked ['henpekt] *adj Fam* **a h. husband** un calzonazos

hepatitis [hepə'taɪtɪs] *n* hepatitis *f*

her [hɜ:(r), *unstressed* hə(r)] **1** *poss adj* *(one thing)* su; *(more than one)* sus; *(to distinguish)* de ella; **are they h. books or his?** ¿los libros son de ella o de él?; **she has cut h. finger** se ha cortado el dedo
2 *pron* (a) *(direct object)* la; **I saw h. recently** la vi hace poco (b) *(indirect object)* le; *(with other third person pronouns)* se; **he gave h. money** le dio dinero; **they handed it to h.** se lo entregaron (c) *(after prep)* ella; **for h.** para ella (d) *(as subject) Fam* ella; **look, it's h.!** ¡mira, es ella!

herald ['herəld] **1** *n* heraldo *m*
2 *vt* anunciar

heraldry ['herəldrɪ] *n* heráldica *f*

herb [hɜ:b, *US* ɜ:rb] *n* hierba *f*; **h. tea** infusión *f*

herbal ['hɜ:bəl] *adj* herbario(a); **h. remedies** curas *fpl* de hierbas

herd [hɜ:d] *n (of cattle)* manada *f*; *(of goats)* rebaño *m*; *Fig (large group)* multitud *f*

here [hɪə(r)] **1** *adv* aquí; **come h.** ven aquí; **h.!** ¡presente!; **h. goes!** ¡vamos a ver!; **here's to success!** ¡brindemos por el éxito!; **h. you are!** ¡toma!
2 *interj* **look h., you can't do that!** ¡oiga, que no se permite hacer eso!

hereafter [hɪər'ɑ:ftə(r)] *Fml* **1** *adv* de ahora en adelante
2 *n* **the h.** la otra vida, el más allá

hereby [hɪə'baɪ] *adv Fml* por la presente

hereditary [hɪ'redɪtərɪ] *adj* hereditario(a)

heresy ['herəsɪ] *n* herejía *f*

heretic ['herətɪk] *n* hereje *mf*

heritage ['herɪtɪdʒ] *n* patrimonio *m*; *Jur* herencia *f*

hermetically [hɜ:'metɪklɪ] *adv* **h. sealed** herméticamente cerrado(a)

hermit ['hɜ:mɪt] *n* ermitaño(a) *m,f*

> 🖉 Note that the Spanish word **ermita** is a false friend and is never a translation for the English word **hermit**. In Spanish, **ermita** means "hermitage".

hermitage ['hɜ:mɪtɪdʒ] *n* ermita *f*

hernia ['hɜ:nɪə] *n* hernia *f*

hero ['hɪərəʊ] *n (pl* **heroes***)* héroe *m*; *(in*

novel) protagonista *m*; **h. worship** idolatría *f*

heroic [hɪˈrəʊɪk] *adj* heroico(a)

heroin [ˈherəʊɪn] *n* heroína *f*

heroine [ˈherəʊɪn] *n* heroína *f*; *(in novel)* protagonista *f*

heron [ˈherən] *n* garza *f*

herring [ˈherɪŋ] *n* arenque *m*

hers [hɜːz] *poss pron* (a) *(attribute) (one thing)* suyo(a); *(more than one)* suyos(as); *(to distinguish)* de ella; **they are h., not his** son de ella, no de él (b) *(noun reference) (one thing)* el suyo/la suya; *(more than one)* los suyos/las suyas; **my car is blue and h. is red** mi coche es azul y el suyo es rojo

herself [hɜːˈself] *pers pron* (a) *(reflexive)* se; **she dressed h.** se vistió (b) *(alone)* ella misma; **she was by h.** estaba sola (c) *(emphatic)* **she told me so h.** eso dijo ella

hesitant [ˈhezɪtənt] *adj* vacilante

hesitate [ˈhezɪteɪt] *vi* vacilar

hesitation [hezɪˈteɪʃən] *n* indecisión *f*

heterogeneous [hetərəʊˈdʒiːnɪəs] *adj* heterogéneo(a)

heterosexual [hetərəʊˈseksjʊəl] *adj & n* heterosexual *(mf)*

hey [heɪ] *interj* ¡oye!, ¡oiga!

heyday [ˈheɪdeɪ] *n* auge *m*, apogeo *m*

HGV [eɪtʃdʒiːˈviː] *n Br (abbr* **heavy goods vehicle***)* vehículo *m* de carga pesada

hi [haɪ] *interj Fam* ¡hola!

hiatus [haɪˈeɪtəs] *n Fml* laguna *f*

hibernate [ˈhaɪbəneɪt] *vi* hibernar

hibernation [haɪbəˈneɪʃən] *n* hibernación *f*

hibiscus [haɪˈbɪskəs] *n* hibisco *m*

hiccup, hiccough [ˈhɪkʌp] *n* hipo *m*; *Fam (minor problem)* problemilla *m*; **to have hiccups** tener hipo

hide¹ [haɪd] **1** *vt (pt* **hid** [hɪd]; *pp* **hidden** [ˈhɪdən]) *(conceal)* esconder; *(obscure)* ocultar

2 *vi* esconderse, ocultarse

3 *n* puesto *m*

hide² [haɪd] *n (of animal)* piel *f*

hide-and-seek [haɪdənˈsiːk] *n* escondite *m*

hideous [ˈhɪdɪəs] *adj (horrific)* horroroso(a); *(extremely ugly)* espantoso(a)

hide-out [ˈhaɪdaʊt] *n* escondrijo *m*, guarida *f*

hiding¹ [ˈhaɪdɪŋ] *n* **to go into h.** esconderse

hiding² [ˈhaɪdɪŋ] *n Fam* paliza *f*

hierarchy [ˈhaɪərɑːkɪ] *n* jerarquía *f*

hi-fi [ˈhaɪfaɪ] *n* hifi *m*; **h. equipment** equipo *m* de alta fidelidad

high [haɪ] **1** *adj* (a) *alto(a)*; **how h. is that wall?** ¿qué altura tiene esa pared?; **it's 3 feet h.** tiene 3 pies de alto; **h. chair** silla alta para niños; **h. jump** salto *m* de altura (b) *(elevated)* elevado(a); **h. blood pressure** tensión alta; **h. prices** precios elevados; **to be in h. spirits** estar de buen humor (c) *(important)* importante; **h. wind** viento *m* fuerte; **to have a h. opinion of sb** tener muy buena opinión de algn; **H. Court** Tribunal Supremo; **h. fidelity** alta fidelidad; **h. road** carretera *f* principal; **h. school** instituto *m* de enseñanza media; **the H. Street** la Calle Mayor (d) *Fam (drugged)* colocado(a)

2 *adv* alto; **to fly h.** volar a gran altura

3 *n (high point)* punto máximo

highbrow [ˈhaɪbraʊ] *adj & n* intelectual *(mf)*

high-class [ˈhaɪklɑːs] *adj* de alta categoría

higher [ˈhaɪə(r)] **1** *adj* superior; **h. education** enseñanza *f* superior

2 *n Scot Educ* **H.** = examen final de los estudios preuniversitarios

high-five [ˈhaɪfaɪv] *n US Fam* palmada *f* en el aire *(saludo entre dos)*

high-flier, high-flyer [haɪˈflaɪə(r)] *n Fig* = persona dotada y ambiciosa

high-handed [haɪˈhændɪd] *adj* despótico(a)

high-heeled [ˈhaɪhiːld] *adj* de tacón alto

highlands [ˈhaɪləndz] *npl* tierras altas

highlight [ˈhaɪlaɪt] **1** *n* (a) *(in hair)* reflejo *m* (b) *(of event)* atracción *f* principal

2 *vt* (a) hacer resaltar (b) *(text)* marcar con un rotulador fosforescente

highly [ˈhaɪlɪ] *adv (very)* sumamente; **to speak h. of sb** hablar muy bien de algn

highly-strung [haɪlɪˈstrʌŋ] *adj* muy nervioso(a)

Highness [ˈhaɪnɪs] *n* alteza *mf*; **Your H.** Su Alteza

high-pitched [ˈhaɪpɪtʃt] *adj* estridente

high-powered [ˈhaɪpaʊəd] *adj (person)* dinámico(a)

high-ranking [ˈhaɪræŋkɪŋ] *adj* **h. official** alto funcionario

high-rise [ˈhaɪraɪz] *adj* **h. building** rascacielos *m inv*

high-speed [ˈhaɪspiːd] *adj* **h. lens** objetivo ultrarrápido; **h. train** tren *m* de alta velocidad

highway [ˈhaɪweɪ] *n US* carretera *f*, autopista *f*; *Br* **H. Code** código *m* de la circulación

highwayman [ˈhaɪweɪmən] *n* salteador *m* de caminos

hijack ['haɪdʒæk] **1** vt secuestrar
2 n secuestro m

hijacker ['haɪdʒækə(r)] n secuestrador(a) m,f; (of planes) pirata mf del aire

hike [haɪk] **1** n (**a**) (walk) excursión f (**b**) **price h.** aumento m de precio
2 vi ir de excursión

hiker ['haɪkə(r)] n excursionista mf

hilarious [hɪ'leərɪəs] adj graciosísimo(a)

hill [hɪl] n colina f; (slope) cuesta f

hillside ['hɪlsaɪd] n ladera f

hilltop ['hɪltɒp] n cima f de una colina

hilly ['hɪlɪ] adj (**hillier, hilliest**) accidentado(a)

hilt [hɪlt] n puño m, empuñadura f; **I'll support you up to the h.** te daré mi apoyo total

him [hɪm] pron (**a**) (direct object) lo, le; **hit h.!** ¡pégale!; **she loves h.** lo quiere (**b**) (indirect object) le; (with other third person pronouns) se; **give h. the money** dale el dinero; **give it to h.** dáselo (**c**) (after prep) él; **it's not like h. to say that** no es propio de él decir eso (**d**) Fam (as subject) él; **it's h.** es él

himself [hɪm'self] pers pron (**a**) (reflexive) se; **he hurt h.** se hizo daño (**b**) (alone) solo, por sí mismo; **by h.** solo (**c**) (emphatic) él mismo

hind¹ [haɪnd] adj trasero(a); **h. legs** patas traseras

hind² [haɪnd] n Zool cierva f

hinder ['hɪndə(r)] vt dificultar, estorbar; **to h. sb from doing sth** impedir a algn hacer algo

hindrance ['hɪndrəns] n estorbo m

hindsight ['haɪndsaɪt] n retrospectiva f

Hindu [hɪn'du:, 'hɪndu:] adj & n hindú (mf)

Hinduism ['hɪndʊɪzəm] n hinduismo m

hinge [hɪndʒ] **1** n bisagra f; Fig eje m
2 vt engoznar
▶ **hinge on** vt insep depender de

hint [hɪnt] **1** n (**a**) indirecta f; **to take the h.** coger la indirecta (**b**) (clue) pista f (**c**) (trace) pizca f (**d**) (advice) consejo m
2 vi (**a**) lanzar indirectas (**b**) (imply) insinuar algo

hip¹ [hɪp] n cadera f; **h. flask** petaca f

hip² [hɪp] adj Fam en la onda

hippie ['hɪpɪ] adj & n Fam hippy (mf)

hippopotamus [hɪpə'pɒtəməs] n hipopótamo m

hire ['haɪə(r)] **1** n alquiler m; **bicycles for h.** se alquilan bicicletas; **taxi for h.** taxi m libre; **h. purchase** compra f a plazos
2 vt (**a**) (rent) alquilar, Méx rentar (**b**) (employ) contratar

▶ **hire out** vt sep (car) alquilar, Méx rentar; (people) contratar

his [hɪz] **1** poss adj (one thing) su; (more than one) sus; (to distinguish) de él; **he washed h. face** se lavó la cara; **is it h. dog or hers?** ¿el perro es de él o de ella?
2 poss pron (**a**) (attribute) (one thing) suyo(a); (more than one) suyos(as); (to distinguish) de él (**b**) (noun reference) (one thing) el suyo/la suya; (more than one) los suyos/las suyas; **my car is blue and h. is red** mi coche es azul y el suyo es rojo

Hispanic [hɪ'spænɪk] **1** adj hispánico(a)
2 n US hispano(a) m,f, latino(a) m,f

hiss [hɪs] **1** n siseo m; Th silbido m
2 vt & vi silbar

historian [hɪ'stɔ:rɪən] n historiador(a) m,f

historic [hɪ'stɒrɪk] adj histórico(a)

historical [hɪ'stɒrɪkəl] adj histórico(a); **h. novel** novela histórica

history ['hɪstərɪ] n historia f

hit [hɪt] **1** n (**a**) (blow) golpe m; direct h. impacto directo; Fam **h. list** lista negra; Fam **h. man** asesino m a sueldo (**b**) (success) éxito m; **h. parade** lista f de éxitos (**c**) Comput (visit to web site) acceso m, visita f
2 vt (pt & pp **hit**) (**a**) (strike) golpear, pegar; **he was h. in the leg** le dieron en la pierna; **the car h. the kerb** el coche chocó contra el bordillo; Fam Fig **to h. the roof** poner el grito en el cielo (**b**) (affect) afectar (**c**) **to h. the headlines** ser noticia
▶ **hit back** vi (reply to criticism) replicar
▶ **hit on** vt insep dar con; **we h. on the idea of ...** se nos ocurrió la idea de ...
▶ **hit out** vi **to h. out at sb** atacar a algn
▶ **hit upon** vt insep = hit on

hit-and-run [hɪtən'rʌn] adj **h. driver** = conductor que atropella a algn y no para

hitch [hɪtʃ] **1** n dificultad f
2 vt (fasten) atar
3 vi Fam (hitch-hike) hacer autostop
▶ **hitch up** vt sep remangarse

hitch-hike ['hɪtʃhaɪk] vi hacer autostop or dedo

hitch-hiker ['hɪtʃhaɪkə(r)] n autostopista mf

hitherto [hɪðə'tu:] adv Fml hasta la fecha

HIV [eɪtʃaɪ'vi:] n (abbr **human immunodeficiency virus**) VIH m; **to be diagnosed HIV positive/negative** dar seropositivo(a)/seronegativo(a) en la prueba del SIDA

hive [haɪv] n colmena f; Fig lugar muy activo

HM (*abbr His/Her Majesty*) SM

hoard [hɔːd] **1** *n* (*provisions*) reservas *fpl*; (*money etc*) tesoro *m*
  2 *vt* (*objects*) acumular; (*money*) atesorar

hoarding ['hɔːdɪŋ] *n* (*temporary fence*) valla *f*; *Br* (*billboard*) valla publicitaria

hoarfrost ['hɔːfrɒst] *n* escarcha *f*

hoarse [hɔːs] *adj* ronco(a); **to be h.** tener la voz ronca

hoax [həʊks] *n* (*joke*) broma pesada; (*trick*) engaño *m*

hob [hɒb] *n* (*of cooker*) encimera *f*

hobble ['hɒbəl] *vi* cojear

hobby ['hɒbɪ] *n* pasatiempo *m*, afición *f*

hobbyhorse ['hɒbɪhɔːs] *n* (*toy*) caballito *m* de juguete; *Fig* (*fixed idea*) idea fija, manía *f*

hobo ['həʊbəʊ] *n US* vagabundo(a) *m,f*

hockey ['hɒkɪ] *n* hockey *m*

hog [hɒg] **1** *n* cerdo *m*, puerco *m*; *Fam* **to go the whole h.** liarse la manta a la cabeza
  2 *vt Fam* acaparar

hoist [hɔɪst] **1** *n* (*crane*) grúa *f*; (*lift*) montacargas *m inv*
  2 *vt* levantar, subir; **to h. the flag** izar la bandera

hold [həʊld] **1** *vt* (*pt & pp* **held**) (**a**) (*keep in hand*) aguantar, tener (en la mano); (*grip*) agarrar; (*support*) (*weight*) soportar; (*opinion*) mantener; **to h. sb** abrazar a algn; **to h. sb's hand** cogerle la mano a algn; *Fig* **she can h. her own in French** se defiende en francés
  (**b**) (*contain*) dar cabida a; **the jug holds a litre** en la jarra cabe un litro
  (**c**) (*meeting*) celebrar; (*conversation*) mantener
  (**d**) (*reserve*) guardar
  (**e**) **to h. office** ocupar un puesto
  (**f**) (*consider*) considerar
  (**g**) **he was held for two hours at the police station** estuvo detenido durante dos horas en la comisaría; **to h. one's breath** contener la respiración; **to h. sb hostage** retener a algn como rehén
  (**h**) *Tel* **to h. the line** no colgar
  2 *vi* (**a**) (*rope*) aguantar
  (**b**) *Fig* (*offer*) ser válido(a)
  3 *n* (**a**) **to get h. of** (*grip*) coger, agarrar; *Fig* localizar; **can you get h. of a newspaper?** ¿puedes conseguir un periódico?
  (**b**) (*control*) control *m*
  (**c**) *Naut* bodega *f*
  (**d**) (*in wrestling*) llave *f*

▶ **hold back 1** *vt sep* (*crowd*) contener; (*feelings*) reprimir; (*truth*) ocultar; **I don't**

want to h. you back (*delay*) no quiero entretenerte
  2 *vi* (*hesitate*) vacilar

▶ **hold down** *vt sep* (**a**) (*control*) dominar (**b**) *Fam* (*job*) desempeñar

▶ **hold off** *vt sep* mantener a distancia

▶ **hold on 1** *vi* (**a**) (*keep a firm grasp*) agarrarse bien (**b**) (*wait*) esperar; *Tel* **h. on!** ¡no cuelgue!

▶ **hold out 1** *vt sep* (*hand*) tender
  2 *vi* (**a**) (*last*) (*things*) durar; (*person*) resistir (**b**) **to h. out for** insistir en

▶ **hold up** *vt sep* (**a**) (*rob*) (*train*) asaltar; (*bank*) atracar (**b**) (*delay*) retrasar; **we were held up for half an hour** sufrimos media hora de retraso (**c**) (*raise*) levantar (**d**) (*support*) apuntalar

holdall ['həʊldɔːl] *n Br* bolsa *f* de viaje

holder ['həʊldə(r)] *n* (**a**) (*receptacle*) recipiente *m* (**b**) (*owner*) poseedor(a) *m,f*; (*bearer*) portador(a) *m,f*; (*of passport*) titular *mf*; **record h.** plusmarquista *mf*

holding ['həʊldɪŋ] *n* (**a**) (*property*) propiedad *f* (**b**) *Fin* valor *m* en cartera; **h. company** holding *m*

hold-up ['həʊldʌp] *n* (**a**) (*robbery*) atraco *m* (**b**) (*delay*) retraso *m*; (*in traffic*) atasco *m*

hole [həʊl] *n* (**a**) agujero *m*; (*large*) hoyo *m*; (*in the road*) bache *m* (**b**) (*in golf*) hoyo *m* (**c**) *Fam* (*of place*) antro *m*

holiday ['hɒlɪdeɪ] **1** *n* (*one day*) día *m* de fiesta; *Br* (*several days*) vacaciones *fpl*; **to be/go on h.** estar/ir de vacaciones; **h. resort** lugar turístico
  2 *vi Br* pasar las vacaciones; (*in summer*) veranear

holiday-maker ['hɒlɪdeɪmeɪkə(r)] *n Br* turista *mf*; (*in summer*) veraneante *mf*

holiness ['həʊlɪnɪs] *n* santidad *f*

Holland ['hɒlənd] *n* Holanda

hollow ['hɒləʊ] **1** *adj* (**a**) hueco(a) (**b**) (*cheeks, eyes*) hundido(a) (**c**) *Fig* (*insincere*) falso(a); (*empty*) vacío(a)
  2 *n* hueco *m*; *Geog* hondonada *f*
  3 *vt* **to h. (out)** hacer un hueco en

holly ['hɒlɪ] *n* acebo *m*

holocaust ['hɒləkɔːst] *n* holocausto *m*

holster ['həʊlstə(r)] *n* pistolera *f*

holy ['həʊlɪ] *adj* sagrado(a), santo(a); (*blessed*) bendito(a); **H. Ghost** Espíritu Santo; **H. Land** Tierra Santa; **H. See** Santa Sede

homage ['hɒmɪdʒ] *n* homenaje *m*; **to pay h. to sb** rendir homenaje a algn

home [həʊm] **1** *n* (**a**) casa *f*, hogar *m*; **at h.** en casa; *Fig* **make yourself at h.!** ¡estás en tu casa!; *Fig* **to feel at h.** estar a gusto;

h. banking telebanco *m*; *Comput* **h. page** *(initial page)* portada *f*, página *f* inicial *or* de inicio; *(personal page)* página personal; **h. shopping** telecompra *f*; **h. shopping channel** teletienda *f*

　(**b**) *(institution)* asilo *m*; **old people's h.** asilo de ancianos

　(**c**) *(country)* patria *f*

　(**d**) *Sport* **to play at h.** jugar en casa; *US* **h. base** *(in baseball)* base *f* del bateador; **h. run** carrera completa

　2 *adj* (**a**) *(domestic)* del hogar; *Br* **h. help** asistenta *f*

　(**b**) *Pol* interior; **h. affairs** asuntos *mpl* interiores; *Br* **H. Office** Ministerio *m* del Interior; *Br* **H. Secretary** Ministro(a) *m,f* del Interior

　(**c**) *(native)* natal

　3 *adv* en casa; **to go h.** irse a casa; **to leave h.** irse de casa

homeland ['hǝʊmlænd] *n* patria *f*; *(birthplace)* tierra *f* natal

homeless ['hǝʊmlɪs] **1** *adj* sin techo

　2 *npl* **the h.** los sin techo

homely ['hǝʊmlɪ] *adj* (**homelier, homeliest**) (**a**) *Br (person)* casero(a); *(atmosphere)* familiar (**b**) *US (unattractive)* sin atractivo

home-made ['hǝʊmmeɪd] *adj* casero(a)

homeopathy [hǝʊmɪ'ɒpǝθɪ] *n US* = **homeopathy**

homesick ['hǝʊmsɪk] *adj* **to be h.** tener morriña

homeward(s) ['hǝʊmwǝd(z)] *adv* hacia casa

homework ['hǝʊmwɜːk] *n* deberes *mpl*

homey ['hǝʊmɪ] *adj US Fam* hogareño(a)

homicide ['hɒmɪsaɪd] *n* homicidio *m*

homing ['hǝʊmɪŋ] *adj* (**a**) **h. device** cabeza buscadora (**b**) **h. pigeon** paloma mensajera

homoeopathy [hǝʊmɪ'ɒpǝθɪ] *n* homeopatía *f*

homogeneous [hɒmǝ'dʒiːnɪǝs] *adj* homogéneo(a)

homosexual [hǝʊmǝʊ'seksjʊǝl] *adj & n* homosexual *(mf)*

Honduran [hɒn'djʊǝrǝn] *adj & n* hondureño(a) *(m,f)*

Honduras [hɒn'djʊǝrǝs] *n* Honduras

honest ['ɒnɪst] *adj* honrado(a); *(sincere)* sincero(a), franco(a); *(fair)* justo(a); **the h. truth** la pura verdad

honestly ['ɒnɪstlɪ] *adv* honradamente; *(question)* ¿de verdad?; *(exclamation)* ¡hay que ver!; **h., it doesn't matter** de verdad, no tiene importancia

honesty ['ɒnɪstɪ] *n* honradez *f*

honey ['hʌnɪ] *n* miel *f*; *US Fam (endearment)* cariño *m*

honeycomb ['hʌnɪkǝʊm] *n* panal *m*

honeymoon ['hʌnɪmuːn] *n* luna *f* de miel

honeysuckle ['hʌnɪsʌkǝl] *n* madreselva *f*

honk [hɒŋk] *vi Aut* tocar la bocina

honor ['ɒnǝr] *n & vt US* = **honour**

honorary ['ɒnǝrǝrɪ] *adj (member)* honorario(a); *(duties)* honorífico(a)

honour ['ɒnǝ(r)] **1** *n* (**a**) honor *m* (**b**) *US Jur* **Her H./His H./Your H.** Su Señoría *f* (**c**) *Mil* **honours** honores *mpl* (**d**) **Honours degree** licenciatura *f* superior

　2 *vt* (**a**) *(respect)* honrar (**b**) *(obligation)* cumplir con

honourable ['ɒnǝrǝbǝl] *adj (person)* honrado(a); *(action)* honroso(a)

hood [hʊd] *n* (**a**) *(of garment)* capucha *f* (**b**) *(of car)* capota *f*; *US (bonnet)* capó *m* (**c**) *US Fam (gangster)* matón(ona) *m,f*

hoodlum ['huːdlǝm] *n* matón *m*

hoodwink ['hʊdwɪŋk] *vt* engañar

hoof [huːf] *n* (*pl* **hoofs** *or* **hooves**) *(of horse)* casco *m*; *(of cow, sheep)* pezuña *f*

hook [hʊk] **1** *n* (**a**) gancho *m*; *(in fishing)* anzuelo *m*; *Sewing* **hooks and eyes** corchetes *mpl*; **to take the phone off the h.** descolgar el teléfono (**b**) *(in boxing)* gancho *m*

　2 *vt* enganchar

▸ **hook up** *vt sep & vi Rad, TV & Comput* conectar (**with** con)

hooked [hʊkt] *adj* (**a**) *(nose)* aguileño(a) (**b**) *Fam (addicted)* enganchado(a) (**on** a); **to get h.** engancharse

hooker ['hʊkǝ(r)] *n US Fam (prostitute)* fulana *f*, puta *f*

hookey ['hʊkɪ] *n US Fam* **to play h.** hacer novillos

hook-up ['hʊkʌp] *n* (**a**) *Comput* conexión *f* (**b**) *Rad & TV* emisión *f* múltiple

hooky ['hʊkɪ] *n US Fam* = **hookey**

hooligan ['huːlɪgǝn] *n Fam* gamberro(a) *m,f*

hoop [huːp] *n* aro *m*; *(of barrel)* fleje *m*

hooray [huː'reɪ] *interj* ¡hurra!

hoot [huːt] **1** *n* (**a**) ululato *m*; *Fam* **hoots of laughter** carcajadas *fpl*; *Fam* **I don't care a h.** me importa un pepino (**b**) *(of car horn)* bocinazo *m*

　2 *vi* (**a**) *(owl)* ulular (**b**) *(car)* dar un bocinazo; *(train)* silbar; *(siren)* pitar

hooter ['huːtǝ(r)] *n esp Br (of car)* bocina *f*; *(siren)* sirena *f*

Hoover® ['huːvǝ(r)] *Br* **1** *n* aspiradora *f*

　2 *vt* **to h.** pasar la aspiradora por

hooves [huːvz] *pl of* hoof

hop¹ [hɒp] **1** *vi* saltar; **to h. on one leg** andar a la pata coja

2 *n (small jump)* brinco *m*

hop² [hɒp] *n Bot* lúpulo *m*

hope [həʊp] **1** *n* esperanza *f; (false)* ilusión *f;* **to have little h. of doing sth** tener pocas posibilidades de hacer algo

2 *vt & vi* esperar; **I h. so/not** espero que sí/no; **we h. you're well** esperamos que estés bien

hopeful [ˈhəʊpfʊl] *adj (confident)* optimista; *(promising)* prometedor(a)

hopefully [ˈhəʊpfʊlɪ] *adv* **(a)** *(confidently)* con optimismo **(b)** **h. the weather will be fine** *(it is hoped)* esperemos que haga buen tiempo

hopeless [ˈhəʊplɪs] *adj* desesperado(a); *Fam* **to be h. at sports** ser negado(a) para los deportes

hopelessly [ˈhəʊplɪslɪ] *adv* desesperadamente; **h. lost** completamente perdido(a)

horde [hɔːd] *n* multitud *f*

horizon [həˈraɪzən] *n* horizonte *m*

horizontal [hɒrɪˈzɒntəl] *adj* horizontal

hormone [ˈhɔːməʊn] *n* hormona *f*

horn [hɔːn] *n* **(a)** cuerno *m* **(b)** *Fam Mus* trompeta *f;* **French h.** trompa *f;* **hunting h.** cuerno *m* de caza **(c)** *Aut* bocina *f*

hornet [ˈhɔːnɪt] *n* avispón *m*

horny [ˈhɔːnɪ] *adj* **(hornier, horniest) (a)** *(hands)* calloso(a) **(b)** *very Fam (sexually aroused)* caliente, cachondo(a)

horoscope [ˈhɒrəskəʊp] *n* horóscopo *m*

horrendous [hɒˈrendəs] *adj* horrendo(a)

horrible [ˈhɒrəbəl] *adj* horrible

horrid [ˈhɒrɪd] *adj* horrible

horrific [həˈrɪfɪk] *adj* horrendo(a)

horrify [ˈhɒrɪfaɪ] *vt* horrorizar

horror [ˈhɒrə(r)] *n* horror *m; Fam* **a little h.** un diablillo; **h. film** película *f* de miedo *or* de terror

hors d'oeuvre [ɔːˈdɜːvr] *n (pl* **hors d'oeuvres)** entremés *m*

horse [hɔːs] *n* **(a)** caballo *m;* **h. race** carrera *f* de caballos **(b)** *(in gymnastics)* potro *m* **(c)** *Tech* caballete *m* **(d)** **h. chestnut** *(tree)* castaño *m* de Indias

horseback [ˈhɔːsbæk] *n* **on h.** a caballo; *US* **h. riding** equitación *f*

horseman [ˈhɔːsmən] *n* jinete *m*

horseplay [ˈhɔːspleɪ] *n* payasadas *fpl*

horsepower [ˈhɔːspaʊə(r)] *n* caballo *m* (de vapor)

horseradish [ˈhɔːsrædɪʃ] *n* rábano rusticano

horseshoe [ˈhɔːsʃuː] *n* herradura *f*

horsewoman [ˈhɔːswʊmən] *n* amazona *f*

horticulture [ˈhɔːtɪkʌltʃə(r)] *n* horticultura *f*

hose [həʊz] *n (pipe)* manguera *f*

hosiery [ˈhəʊzɪərɪ] *n* medias *fpl* y calcetines *mpl*

hospice [ˈhɒspɪs] *n* residencia *f* para enfermos terminales

hospitable [ˈhɒspɪtəbəl, hɒˈspɪtəbəl] *adj* hospitalario(a); **h. atmosphere** ambiente acogedor

hospital [ˈhɒspɪtəl] *n* hospital *m*

hospitality [hɒspɪˈtælɪtɪ] *n* hospitalidad *f*

Host [həʊst] *n Rel* hostia *f*

host¹ [həʊst] **1** *n* **(a)** *(at home)* anfitrión *m* **(b)** *Th & TV* presentador *m* **(c)** *Biol* huésped *m*

2 *vt Th & TV* presentar

host² [həʊst] *n (large number)* montón *m*

hostage [ˈhɒstɪdʒ] *n* rehén *m*

hostel [ˈhɒstəl] *n* hostal *m*

hostess [ˈhəʊstɪs] *n* **(a)** *(at home etc)* anfitriona *f* **(b)** *Th & TV* presentadora *f* **(c)** **(air) h.** azafata *f*

hostile [ˈhɒstaɪl] *adj* hostil

hostility [hɒˈstɪlɪtɪ] *n* hostilidad *f*

hot [hɒt] *adj* **(hotter, hottest) (a)** caliente; *Fig* **h. line** teléfono rojo; **h. spot** *(nightclub)* club nocturno **(b)** *(weather)* caluroso(a); **it's very h.** hace mucho calor; **to feel h.** tener calor **(c)** *(spicy)* picante; **h. dog** perrito *m* caliente **(d)** *(temper)* fuerte **(e)** *Fam (fresh)* de última hora **(f)** *Fam (good)* bueno(a); **it's not so h.** no es nada del otro mundo **(g)** *(popular)* popular **(h)** *(dangerous)* peligroso(a); *Fig* **to get oneself into h. water** meterse en un lío; *Fam* **h. seat** primera fila

► hot up *vi Fam* **things are hotting up** la cosa se está poniendo al rojo vivo

hotbed [ˈhɒtbed] *n Fig* hervidero *m*

hotel [həʊˈtel] *n* hotel *m*

hotelier [həʊˈteljeɪ] *n* hotelero(a) *m,f*

hot-headed [hɒtˈhedɪd] *adj* impetuoso(a)

hothouse [ˈhɒthaʊs] *n* invernadero *m*

hotplate [ˈhɒtpleɪt] *n (cooker)* placa *f* de cocina; *(to keep food warm)* calientaplatos *m inv*

hotshot [ˈhɒtʃɒt] *n Fam* as *m*

hot-water [hɒtˈwɔːtə(r)] *adj* **h. bottle** bolsa *f* de agua caliente

hound [haʊnd] **1** *n* perro *m* de caza

2 *vt* acosar

hour [ˈaʊə(r)] *n* hora *f;* **60 miles an h.** 60 millas por hora; **by the h.** por horas; **h. hand** manecilla *f*

hourly [ˈaʊəlɪ] **1** adj cada hora
 2 adv por horas
house 1 n [haʊs] (**a**) casa f; **at my h.** en mi casa; Fig **on the h.** cortesía de la casa; **h. arrest** arresto domiciliario; **h. plant** planta f de interior (**b**) Pol **H. of Commons** Cámara f de los Comunes; **H. of Lords** Cámara f de los Lores; US **H. of Representatives** Cámara de Representantes; **Houses of Parliament** Parlamento m (**c**) (company) empresa f; **publishing h.** editorial f (**d**) Th sala f
 2 vt [haʊz] alojar; (store) guardar
houseboat [ˈhaʊsbəʊt] n casa f flotante
housebreaking [ˈhaʊsbreɪkɪŋ] n allanamiento m de morada
housebroken [ˈhaʊsbrəʊkən] adj US (pet) = que ya ha aprendido a no hacer sus necesidades en casa
housecoat [ˈhaʊskəʊt] n bata f
household [ˈhaʊshəʊld] n hogar m; **h. products** productos domésticos
housekeeper [ˈhaʊskiːpə(r)] n ama f de llaves
housekeeping [ˈhaʊskiːpɪŋ] n administración doméstica; **h. money** dinero m para los gastos domésticos
house-train [ˈhaʊstreɪn] vt (pet) educar
house-warming [ˈhaʊswɔːmɪŋ] n **h. (party)** = fiesta que se da al estrenar casa
housewife [ˈhaʊswaɪf] n ama f de casa
housework [ˈhaʊswɜːk] n trabajo doméstico
housing [ˈhaʊzɪŋ] n vivienda f; **h. estate** urbanización f
hovel [ˈhʌvəl, ˈhɒvəl] n casucha f
hover [ˈhɒvə(r)] vi (bird) cernerse; (aircraft) permanecer inmóvil (en el aire)
hovercraft [ˈhɒvəkrɑːft] n aerodeslizador m
how [haʊ] adv (**a**) (direct question) ¿cómo?; **h. are you?** ¿cómo estás?; Fam **h. come?** ¿por qué? (**b**) (indirect question) cómo; **I don't know h. to tell you** no sé cómo decírtelo (**c**) (very) qué; **h. funny!** ¡qué divertido! (**d**) (suggestion) **h. about going to the cinema?** ¿te apetece ir al cine?; **h. about a stroll?** ¿qué te parece un paseo? (**e**) (quantity) cuánto; **h. old is she?** ¿cuántos años tiene?; **h. tall are you?** ¿cuánto mides? (**f**) **h. many?** ¿cuántos(as)?; **h. much?** ¿cuánto(a)?; **I don't know h. many people there were** no sé cuánta gente había
however [haʊˈevə(r)] adv (**a**) (nevertheless) no obstante, sin embargo (**b**) (with adjective) **h. difficult it may be** por difícil que sea; **h. much** por mucho que (+ subj)

howl [haʊl] **1** n aullido m
 2 vi aullar
howler [ˈhaʊlə(r)] n Fam despiste m
HP, hp [eɪtʃˈpiː] n (**a**) Br (abbr hire purchase) compra f a plazos (**b**) (abbr horsepower) cv mpl
HQ [eɪtʃˈkjuː] n (abbr headquarters) sede f, central f
hub [hʌb] n Aut cubo m; Fig eje m
hubbub [ˈhʌbʌb] n alboroto m
hubcap [ˈhʌbkæp] n Aut tapacubos m inv
huddle [ˈhʌdəl] **1** n grupo m
 2 vi **to h. (up** or **together)** acurrucarse
hue¹ [hjuː] n (colour) tinte m; (shade) matiz m
hue² [hjuː] n **h. and cry** fuerte protesta f
huff [hʌf] n **to be in a h.** estar de mala uva
hug [hʌg] **1** vt abrazar
 2 n abrazo m
huge [hjuːdʒ] adj enorme
hugely [ˈhjuːdʒlɪ] adv enormemente
hulk [hʌlk] n (**a**) Naut casco m (**b**) (thing, person) armatoste m
hull [hʌl] n Naut casco m
hullabal(l)oo [hʌləbəˈluː] n Fam follón m
hullo [hʌˈləʊ] interj Br ¡hola!
hum [hʌm] **1** vt (tune) tararear
 2 vi (bees, engine) zumbar; (sing) tararear
 3 n (of bees) zumbido m
human [ˈhjuːmən] **1** adj humano(a); **h. race** raza humana; **h. being** ser humano
 2 n ser humano
humane [hjuːˈmeɪn] adj humano(a)
humanitarian [hjuːmænɪˈteərɪən] adj humanitario(a)
humanity [hjuːˈmænɪtɪ] n (**a**) humanidad f (**b**) Univ **the humanities** las humanidades
humble [ˈhʌmbəl] **1** adj humilde
 2 vt humillar
humbug [ˈhʌmbʌg] n (**a**) Fam tonterías fpl (**b**) Br (mint) **h.** caramelo m de menta
humdrum [ˈhʌmdrʌm] adj monótono(a), aburrido(a)
humid [ˈhjuːmɪd] adj húmedo(a)
humidity [hjuːˈmɪdɪtɪ] n humedad f
humiliate [hjuːˈmɪlɪeɪt] vt humillar
humiliation [hjuːmɪlɪˈeɪʃən] n humillación f
humility [hjuːˈmɪlɪtɪ] n humildad f
humor [ˈhjuːmə(r)] n US = **humour**
humorous [ˈhjuːmərəs] adj (writer) humorístico(a); (person, story) gracioso(a), divertido(a)
humour [ˈhjuːmə(r)] **1** n humor m
 2 vt seguir la corriente a
hump [hʌmp] **1** n (**a**) (on back) joroba f

(**b**) *(small hill)* montículo *m*
2 *vt Br Fam (carry)* cargar (a la espalda)
humus ['hju:məs] *n* mantillo *m*, humus *m*
hunch [hʌntʃ] *n Fam* corazonada *f*
hunchback ['hʌntʃbæk] *n* jorobado(a) *m,f*
hundred ['hʌndrəd] **1** *n* cien *m*, ciento *m*; *(rough number)* centenar *m*; **a h. and twenty-five** ciento veinticinco; **five h.** quinientos
    2 *adj* cien; **a h. people** cien personas; **a h. percent** cien por cien; **two h. chairs** doscientas sillas
hundredth ['hʌndrədθ] *adj & n* centésimo(a) *(m,f)*
hundredweight ['hʌndrədweɪt] *n Br* = 50,8 kg; *US* = 45,36 kg
hung [hʌŋ] **1** *adj Fam* (**a**) **h. over** con resaca (**b**) **h. up** acomplejado(a)
    2 *pt & pp of* **hang**
Hungarian [hʌŋ'geərɪən] *adj & n* húngaro(a) *(m,f)*
Hungary ['hʌŋgərɪ] *n* Hungría
hunger ['hʌŋgə(r)] **1** *n* hambre *f*; **h. strike** huelga *f* de hambre
    2 *vi Fig* tener hambre (**for** de)
hungry ['hʌŋgrɪ] *adj* (**hungrier, hungriest**) hambriento(a); **to be h.** tener hambre; **to go h.** pasar hambre
hunk [hʌŋk] *n* (**a**) *(piece)* buen pedazo *m* (**b**) *Fam (man)* machote *m*
hunt [hʌnt] **1** *vt* cazar
    2 *vi (for game)* cazar; *(search)* buscar
    3 *n* caza *f*; *(search)* búsqueda *f*
    ▶ **hunt down** *vt sep* perseguir
hunter ['hʌntə(r)] *n* cazador(a) *m,f*
hunting ['hʌntɪŋ] *n* caza *f*; *(expedition)* cacería *f*
hurdle ['hɜːdəl] *n Sport* valla *f*; *Fig* obstáculo *m*
hurl [hɜːl] *vt* arrojar, lanzar
hurrah [hʊ'rɑː], **hurray** [hʊ'reɪ] *interj* ¡hurra!; **h. for John!** ¡viva John!
hurricane ['hʌrɪkən, 'hʌrɪkeɪn] *n* huracán *m*
hurried ['hʌrɪd] *adj* apresurado(a); *(action etc)* hecho(a) de prisa
hurriedly ['hʌrɪdlɪ] *adv* deprisa, apresuradamente
hurry ['hʌrɪ] **1** *vi* darse prisa
    2 *vt* meter prisa a
    3 *n* **to be in a h.** tener prisa
hurt [hɜːt] **1** *vt* (*pt & pp* **hurt**) hacer daño a; *(wound)* herir; *(feelings)* ofender
    2 *vi* doler; **my arm hurts** me duele el brazo; *Fam* **it doesn't h. to go out once in a while** no viene mal salir de vez en cuando

3 *adj (physically)* herido(a); *(mentally)* dolido(a)
hurtful ['hɜːtfʊl] *adj* hiriente
hurtle ['hɜːtəl] *vi* lanzarse; **to h. down** desplomarse
husband ['hʌzbənd] *n* marido *m*, esposo *m*
hush [hʌʃ] **1** *vt* callar; **to h. sth up** echar tierra a un asunto
    2 *n* silencio *m*
    3 *interj* ¡silencio!
hush-hush [hʌʃ'hʌʃ] *adj Fam* confidencial
husky¹ ['hʌskɪ] *adj* (**huskier, huskiest**) ronco(a)
husky² ['hʌskɪ] *n (dog)* perro *m* esquimal
hustings ['hʌstɪŋz] *npl Pol* (**a**) *(platform)* tribuna *f* electoral (**b**) *(election)* elecciones *fpl*
hustle ['hʌsəl] **1** *vt* (**a**) *(jostle)* empujar (**b**) *Fam* meter prisa a
    2 *n* bullicio *m*; **h. and bustle** ajetreo *m*
hut [hʌt] *n* cabaña *f*, *(shed)* cobertizo *m*; *Mil* barraca *f*
hutch [hʌtʃ] *n* jaula *f*; **rabbit h.** conejera *f*
hyacinth ['haɪəsɪnθ] *n* jacinto *m*
hybrid ['haɪbrɪd] *adj & n* híbrido(a) *(m,f)*
hydrant ['haɪdrənt] *n* **fire h.** boca *f* de incendio
hydraulic [haɪ'drɒlɪk] *adj* hidráulico(a)
hydrocarbon [haɪdrəʊ'kɑːbən] *n* hidrocarburo *m*
hydrochloric [haɪdrəʊ'klɒrɪk] *adj* **h. acid** ácido clorhídrico
hydroelectric [haɪdrəʊɪ'lektrɪk] *adj* hidroeléctrico(a)
hydrofoil ['haɪdrəfɔɪl] *n* hidroala *f*
hydrogen ['haɪdrədʒən] *n* hidrógeno *m*
hydroplane ['haɪdrəpleɪn] *n US (seaplane)* hidroavión *m*
hyena [haɪ'iːnə] *n* hiena *f*
hygiene ['haɪdʒiːn] *n* higiene *f*
hygienic [haɪ'dʒiːnɪk] *adj* higiénico(a)
hymn [hɪm] *n* himno *m*; **h. book** cantoral *m*
hype [haɪp] *n Fam* campaña publicitaria, movida *f*
hyper- ['haɪpə(r)] *pref* hiper-; **hyperactive** hiperactivo(a)
hypermarket ['haɪpəmɑːkɪt] *n Br* hipermercado *m*
hypersensitive [haɪpə'sensɪtɪv] *adj* hipersensible
hyphen ['haɪfən] *n* guión *m*
hypnosis [hɪp'nəʊsɪs] *n* hipnosis *f*
hypnotist ['hɪpnətɪst] *n* hipnotizador(a) *m,f*

hypnotize ['hɪpnətaɪz] *vt* hipnotizar

hypochondriac [haɪpə'kɒndrɪæk] *adj & n* hipocondríaco(a) *(m,f)*

hypocrisy [hɪ'pɒkrəsɪ] *n* hipocresía *f*

hypocrite ['hɪpəkrɪt] *n* hipócrita *mf*

hypocritical [hɪpə'krɪtɪkəl] *adj* hipócrita

hypodermic [haɪpə'dɜːmɪk] *adj Med* hipodérmico(a); **h. needle** aguja hipodérmica

hypothesis [haɪ'pɒθɪsɪs] *n* (*pl* **hypotheses** [haɪ'pɒθɪsiːz]) hipótesis *f*

hypothetic(al) [haɪpə'θetɪk(əl)] *adj* hipotético(a)

hysteria [hɪ'stɪərɪə] *n* histeria *f*

hysterical [hɪ'sterɪkəl] *adj* histérico(a)

hysterics [hɪ'sterɪks] *npl* (**a**) ataque *m* de histeria (**b**) *Fam (of laughter)* ataque *m* de risa

I

I, i [aɪ] *n (the letter)* I, i *f*

I [aɪ] *pers pron* yo *(usually omitted in Spanish, except for contrast)*; **I know her** (yo) la conozco

ICBM [aɪsiːbiːˈem] *n (abbr intercontinental ballistic missile)* misil *m* balístico intercontinental

ice [aɪs] **1** *n* hielo *m*; **i. axe** pico *m* (de alpinista); **i. cream** helado *m*; **i. cube** cubito *m* de hielo; **i. hockey** hockey *m* sobre hielo; *Br* **i. lolly** polo *m*; **i. rink** pista *f* de patinaje; **i. skate** patín *m* de cuchilla

2 *vt (cake)* alcorzar

▸ **ice over, ice up** *vi (pond etc)* helarse; *(windscreen, plane wings)* cubrirse de hielo

iceberg [ˈaɪsbɜːɡ] *n* iceberg *m*

icebox [ˈaɪsbɒks] *n* **(a)** *(compartment of fridge)* congelador *m* **(b)** *US (fridge)* nevera *f*, frigorífico *m*, *Andes* frigider *m*, *RP* heladera *f*

icecap [ˈaɪskæp] *n* casquete *m* glaciar

Iceland [ˈaɪslənd] *n* Islandia

ice-skating [ˈaɪsskeɪtɪŋ] *n* patinaje *m* sobre hielo

icicle [ˈaɪsɪkəl] *n* carámbano *m*

icing [ˈaɪsɪŋ] *n* alcorza *f*; **i. sugar** azúcar *m* glas

icon [ˈaɪkɒn] *n* icono *m*

icy [ˈaɪsɪ] *adj* (**icier, iciest**) *(road etc)* helado(a); *(Fig (smile)* glacial

ID [aɪˈdiː] *n US* documentación *f*; **ID card** DNI *m*

I'd [aɪd] = I would; I had

idea [aɪˈdɪə] *n* **(a)** idea *f* **(b)** *(aim)* intención *f* **(c)** *(impression)* impresión *f*

ideal [aɪˈdɪəl] *adj & n* ideal *(m)*

idealist [aɪˈdɪəlɪst] *n* idealista *mf*

idealistic [aɪdɪəˈlɪstɪk] *adj* idealista

idealize [aɪˈdɪəlaɪz] *vt* idealizar

ideally [aɪˈdɪəlɪ] *adv* **(a)** *(perfectly)* perfectamente **(b)** *(in the best conditions)* de ser posible

identical [aɪˈdentɪkəl] *adj* idéntico(a)

identification [aɪdentɪfɪˈkeɪʃən] *n* **(a)** identificación *f* **(b)** *(papers)* documentación *f*

identify [aɪˈdentɪfaɪ] **1** *vt (body)* identificar; *(cause)* descubrir

2 *vi* identificarse (**with** con)

Identikit® [aɪˈdentɪkɪt] *n* **I. picture** retrato *m* robot

identity [aɪˈdentɪtɪ] *n* identidad *f*; **i. card** carné *m* de identidad; **proof of i.** prueba *f* de identidad

ideological [aɪdɪəˈlɒdʒɪkəl] *adj* ideológico(a)

ideology [aɪdɪˈɒlədʒɪ] *n* ideología *f*

idiom [ˈɪdɪəm] *n* modismo *m*; *Fig (style)* lenguaje *m*

idiomatic [ɪdɪəˈmætɪk] *adj* idiomático(a)

idiosyncrasy [ɪdɪəˈsɪŋkrəsɪ] *n* idiosincrasia *f*

idiot [ˈɪdɪət] *n* idiota *mf*, tonto(a) *m,f*

idiotic [ɪdɪˈɒtɪk] *adj (behaviour)* idiota, tonto(a); *(joke, plan)* estúpido(a)

idle [ˈaɪdəl] **1** *adj* holgazán(ana); *(not working) (person)* desempleado(a); *(machinery)* parado(a); *(gossip)* frívolo(a); *(threat)* vano(a)

2 *vi (engine)* funcionar en vacío

▸ **idle away** *vt sep (time)* desperdiciar

idleness [ˈaɪdəlnɪs] *n (laziness)* holgazanería *f*; *(unemployment)* desempleo *m*; *(stoppage)* paro *m*

idol [ˈaɪdəl] *n* ídolo *m*

idolize [ˈaɪdəlaɪz] *vt* idolatrar

idyllic [ɪˈdɪlɪk] *adj* idílico(a)

i.e. *(abbr id est)* i.e.

if [ɪf] **1** *conj (a)* si; **if at all** si acaso; **rarely, if ever** raras veces; **if I were rich** si fuera rico(a); **if necessary** (en) caso de que sea necesario; **if not** si no; **if so** de ser así; **if I were you** yo en tu lugar **(b)** *(whenever)* si; **if you need help, ask** siempre que necesites ayuda, pídela **(c)** *(although)* aunque, si bien **(d)** *(exclamations)* **if only I'd known!** ¡de haberlo sabido!; **if only she were here!** ¡ojalá estuviera aquí!

2 *n* **ifs and buts** pegas *fpl*

igloo [ˈɪɡluː] *n* iglú *m*

ignite [ɪɡˈnaɪt] **1** *vt* encender

2 *vi* encenderse

ignition [ɪɡˈnɪʃən] *n* ignición *f*; *Aut* encendido *m*; **i. key** llave *f* de contacto

ignorance [ˈɪɡnərəns] *n* ignorancia *f*

ignorant [ˈɪɡnərənt] *adj* ignorante (**of** de); **to be i. of the facts** ignorar *or* desconocer los hechos

ignore [ɪɡ'nɔː(r)] vt (warning, remark) no hacer caso de; (behaviour, fact) pasar por alto

ill [ɪl] **1** adj (**a**) enfermo(a); **to be taken i.** caer enfermo(a); **to feel i.** encontrarse mal (**b**) (bad) malo(a); **i. feeling** resentimiento m; **i. will** mala voluntad
2 n mal m
3 adv difícilmente

I'll [aɪl] = **I shall**; **I will**

ill-advised [ɪləd'vaɪzd] adj (person) imprudente; (act) desatinado(a); **you'd be i. to go** harías mal en ir

ill-disposed [ɪldɪ'spəʊzd] adj poco dispuesto(a)

illegal [ɪ'liːɡəl] adj ilegal

illegible [ɪ'ledʒɪbəl] adj ilegible

illegitimate [ɪlɪ'dʒɪtɪmɪt] adj ilegítimo(a)

ill-fated [ɪl'feɪtɪd] adj abocado(a) al fracaso

ill-founded [ɪl'faʊndɪd] adj infundado(a)

illicit [ɪ'lɪsɪt] adj ilícito(a)

illiteracy [ɪ'lɪtərəsɪ] n analfabetismo m

illiterate [ɪ'lɪtərɪt] adj (person) analfabeto(a); Fam (uneducated) inculto(a)

illness ['ɪlnɪs] n enfermedad f

illogical [ɪ'lɒdʒɪkəl] adj ilógico(a)

ill-treat [ɪl'triːt] vt maltratar

illuminate [ɪ'luːmɪneɪt] vt (**a**) (light up) iluminar, alumbrar; Fig (clarify) aclarar (**b**) (manuscript) iluminar

illuminating [ɪ'luːmɪneɪtɪŋ] adj (experience, book) instructivo(a); (remark) revelador(a)

illumination [ɪluːmɪ'neɪʃən] n (**a**) iluminación f; Fig (clarification) aclaración f (**b**) Br **illuminations** iluminación f

illusion [i'luːʒən] n ilusión f; **to be under the i. that ...** engañarse pensando que ...

illusory [ɪ'luːsərɪ] adj ilusorio(a)

illustrate ['ɪləstreɪt] vt ilustrar

illustration [ɪlə'streɪʃən] n ilustración f; (example) ejemplo m

illustrious [ɪ'lʌstrɪəs] adj ilustre

I'm [aɪm] = **I am**

image ['ɪmɪdʒ] n imagen f

imagery ['ɪmɪdʒərɪ] n Lit imágenes fpl

imaginary [ɪ'mædʒɪnərɪ] adj imaginario(a)

imagination [ɪmædʒɪ'neɪʃən] n imaginación f; (inventiveness) inventiva f

imaginative [ɪ'mædʒɪnətɪv] adj imaginativo(a)

imagine [ɪ'mædʒɪn] vt (visualize) imaginar; (think) suponer, imaginarse; **just i.!** ¡imagínate!

imbalance [ɪm'bæləns] n desequilibrio m

imbecile ['ɪmbɪsiːl] n imbécil mf

imitate ['ɪmɪteɪt] vt imitar

imitation [ɪmɪ'teɪʃən] **1** n imitación f, copia f; Pej remedo m
2 adj de imitación

immaculate [ɪ'mækjʊlɪt] adj (clean) inmaculado(a); (tidy) perfectamente ordenado(a); (clothes) impecable; (work) perfecto(a); **the I. Conception** la Inmaculada Concepción

immaterial [ɪmə'tɪərɪəl] adj irrelevante; **it's i. to me whether ...** me trae sin cuidado si ...

immature [ɪmə'tjʊə(r)] adj inmaduro(a)

immediate [ɪ'miːdɪət] adj (**a**) inmediato(a); (urgent) urgente (**b**) (close) cercano(a); (danger) inminente (**c**) (cause) primero(a)

immediately [ɪ'miːdɪətlɪ] **1** adv (**a**) inmediatamente (**b**) (directly) directamente
2 conj en cuanto

immense [ɪ'mens] adj inmenso(a), enorme

immensely [ɪ'menslɪ] adv (rich) enormemente; (interesting, difficult) sumamente

immerse [ɪ'mɜːs] vt sumergir (**in** en); Fig **to be immersed in sth** estar absorto(a) en algo

immersion [ɪ'mɜːʃən] n inmersión f; Br **i. heater** calentador m de inmersión; **i. course** cursillo intensivo

immigrant ['ɪmɪɡrənt] adj & n inmigrante (mf)

immigration [ɪmɪ'ɡreɪʃən] n inmigración f

imminent ['ɪmɪnənt] adj inminente

immobile [ɪ'məʊbaɪl] adj inmóvil

immobilize [ɪ'məʊbɪlaɪz] vt inmovilizar

immodest [ɪ'mɒdɪst] adj indecente

immoral [ɪ'mɒrəl] adj inmoral

immortal [ɪ'mɔːtəl] adj inmortal

immortality [ɪmɔː'tælɪtɪ] n inmortalidad f

immortalize [ɪ'mɔːtəlaɪz] vt inmortalizar

immune [ɪ'mjuːn] adj inmune; (exempt) exento(a)

immunity [ɪ'mjuːnɪtɪ] n inmunidad f

immunize ['ɪmjʊnaɪz] vt inmunizar (**against** contra)

impact ['ɪmpækt] n impacto m; (crash) choque m

impair [ɪm'peə(r)] vt perjudicar; (sight etc) dañar

impart [ɪm'pɑːt] vt Fml (news) comunicar; (knowledge) transmitir

impartial [ɪm'pɑːʃəl] adj imparcial

impassable [ɪm'pɑːsəbəl] adj (road, ground) intransitable; (barrier) infranqueable

impasse [æm'pɑːs] n punto muerto

impassive [ɪm'pæsɪv] adj impasible

impatience [ɪm'peɪʃəns] n impaciencia f

impatient [ɪm'peɪʃənt] adj impaciente; (fretful) irritable; **to get i.** perder la paciencia

impeccable [ɪm'pekəbəl] adj impecable

impede [ɪm'piːd] vt (prevent) impedir; (hinder) estorbar; (obstruct) poner trabas a

impediment [ɪm'pedɪmənt] n impedimento m; (obstacle) estorbo m; **speech i.** defecto m del habla

impending [ɪm'pendɪŋ] adj Fml inminente

impenetrable [ɪm'penɪtrəbəl] adj impenetrable; Fig (mystery, thoughts) insondable

imperative [ɪm'perətɪv] **1** adj Fml imperativo(a); (tone) imperioso(a); (urgent) urgente
   2 n Ling imperativo m

imperceptible [ɪmpə'septəbəl] adj imperceptible

imperfect [ɪm'pɜːfɪkt] **1** adj imperfecto(a); (goods) defectuoso(a)
   2 n Ling imperfecto m

imperfection [ɪmpə'fekʃən] n defecto m

imperial [ɪm'pɪərɪəl] adj (a) imperial (b) (measure) **i. gallon** galón británico (aprox 4,546 l)

imperialism [ɪm'pɪərɪəlɪzəm] n imperialismo m

imperialist [ɪm'pɪərɪəlɪst] adj & n imperialista (mf)

imperious [ɪm'pɪərɪəs] adj imperioso(a)

impersonal [ɪm'pɜːsənəl] adj impersonal

impersonate [ɪm'pɜːsəneɪt] vt hacerse pasar por; (famous people) imitar

impersonation [ɪmpɜːsə'neɪʃən] n imitación f

impertinent [ɪm'pɜːtɪnənt] adj impertinente

impervious [ɪm'pɜːvɪəs] adj (rock) impermeable; Fig **to be i. to reason** no atender a razones

impetuous [ɪm'petjʊəs] adj impetuoso(a)

impetus ['ɪmpɪtəs] n ímpetu m; Fig impulso m

impinge [ɪm'pɪndʒ] vi Fml afectar (**on** a)

implant Med **1** vt [ɪm'plɑːnt] implantar
   2 n ['ɪmplɑːnt] implantación f

implement 1 n ['ɪmplɪmənt] (tool) herramienta f; (instrument) instrumento m; **farm implements** aperos mpl de labranza
   2 vt ['ɪmplɪment] (decision, plan) llevar a cabo; (law, policy) aplicar

implicate ['ɪmplɪkeɪt] vt implicar (**in** en)

implication [ɪmplɪ'keɪʃən] n implicación f; (consequence) consecuencia f

implicit [ɪm'plɪsɪt] adj (implied) implícito(a); (trust) absoluto(a); (faith) incondicional

implore [ɪm'plɔː(r)] vt implorar, suplicar

imply [ɪm'plaɪ] vt (**a**) (involve) implicar (**b**) (hint) dar a entender; (mean) significar

impolite [ɪmpə'laɪt] adj maleducado(a)

import 1 n ['ɪmpɔːt] (**a**) Com (usu pl) importación f; **i. duty** derechos mpl de importación (**b**) Fml (meaning) sentido m
   2 vt [ɪm'pɔːt] Com importar

importance [ɪm'pɔːtəns] n importancia f; (standing) envergadura f; **of little i.** de poca monta

important [ɪm'pɔːtənt] adj importante; **it's not i.** no importa

importer [ɪm'pɔːtə(r)] n Com importador(a) m,f

impose [ɪm'pəʊz] **1** vt imponer (**on** or **upon** a)
   2 vt **to i. on** or **upon** (take advantage of) abusar de

imposing [ɪm'pəʊzɪŋ] adj imponente, impresionante

imposition [ɪmpə'zɪʃən] n (of tax etc) imposición f; (unfair demand) abuso m; **would it be an i. if ...?** ¿le molestaría si ...?

impossibility [ɪmpɒsə'bɪlɪtɪ] n imposibilidad f

impossible [ɪm'pɒsəbəl] **1** adj imposible; (person) insoportable
   2 n **to do the i.** hacer lo imposible

impossibly [ɪm'pɒsəblɪ] adv de manera insoportable; **i. difficult** de una dificultad insuperable

impostor [ɪm'pɒstə(r)] n impostor(a) m,f

impotent ['ɪmpətənt] adj impotente

impound [ɪm'paʊnd] vt incautarse de

impoverished [ɪm'pɒvərɪʃt] adj (person, country) empobrecido(a); (soil) agotado(a)

impracticable [ɪm'præktɪkəbəl] adj impracticable, irrealizable

impractical [ɪm'præktɪkəl] adj (person) poco práctico(a); (project, solution etc) poco viable

imprecise [ɪmprɪ'saɪs] adj impreciso(a)

impregnable [ɪmˈpregnəbəl] *adj* inexpugnable

impregnate [ˈɪmpregneɪt] *vt* (**a**) *(soak)* impregnar (**with** de) (**b**) *Fml (fertilize)* fecundar

impress [ɪmˈpres] *vt* (**a**) impresionar; **to i. sb favourably/unfavourably** dar a algn buena/mala impresión (**b**) *(mark)* imprimir (**on** en); *(pattern)* estampar (**on** en); *Fig* **to i. sth on sb** convencer a algn de la importancia de algo

impression [ɪmˈpreʃən] *n* (**a**) impresión *f*; **to be under the i. that ...** tener la impresión de que ...; **to give the i. of ...** dar la impresión de ... (**b**) *(imprint)* marca *f*; *(in snow)* huella *f* (**c**) *(imitation)* imitación *f*

impressionist [ɪmˈpreʃənɪst] *adj & n* impresionista *(mf)*

impressive [ɪmˈpresɪv] *adj* impresionante

imprint 1 *vt* [ɪmˈprɪnt] *(mark)* dejar huella (**on** en)
2 *n* [ˈɪmprɪnt] (**a**) *(mark)* marca *f*; *(left by foot etc)* huella *f* (**b**) *(publisher's name)* pie *m* de imprenta

imprison [ɪmˈprɪzən] *vt* encarcelar

imprisonment [ɪmˈprɪzənmənt] *n* encarcelamiento *m*

improbable [ɪmˈprɒbəbəl] *adj (event)* improbable; *(story)* inverosímil

impromptu [ɪmˈprɒmptjuː] **1** *adj (speech)* improvisado(a); *(visit)* imprevisto(a)
2 *adv* de improviso

improper [ɪmˈprɒpə(r)] *adj* (**a**) impropio(a); *(method)* inadecuado(a) (**b**) *(indecent)* indecente; *(behaviour)* deshonesto(a) (**c**) *(wrong)* incorrecto(a)

improve [ɪmˈpruːv] **1** *vt* mejorar; *(knowledge)* perfeccionar; *(mind)* cultivar; *(increase)* aumentar
2 *vi* mejorarse; *(increase)* aumentar
▶ **improve on** *vt insep* superar; *(offer, bid)* sobrepujar

improvement [ɪmˈpruːvmənt] *n* mejora *f*; *(in skill)* perfeccionamiento *m*; *(increase)* aumento *m*

improvise [ˈɪmprəvaɪz] *vt & vi* improvisar

imprudent [ɪmˈpruːdənt] *adj* imprudente

impudence [ˈɪmpjʊdəns] *n* insolencia *f*

impudent [ˈɪmpjʊdənt] *adj* insolente

impulse [ˈɪmpʌls] *n* impulso *m*; **to act on (an) i.** dejarse llevar por un impulso

impulsive [ɪmˈpʌlsɪv] *adj* irreflexivo(a)

impunity [ɪmˈpjuːnɪti] *n* impunidad *f*

impure [ɪmˈpjʊə(r)] *adj* (**a**) *(act)* impuro(a); *(thought)* impúdico(a) (**b**) *(air)* contaminado(a)

impurity [ɪmˈpjʊərɪti] *n* (**a**) *(of act)* deshonestidad *f* (**b**) *(usu pl) (in air, substance)* impureza *f*

in [ɪn] **1** *prep* (**a**) *(place)* en; *(within)* dentro de; **in bed** en la cama; **in England/Brazil/China** en Inglaterra/Brasil/China; **in prison** en la cárcel; **in the distance** a lo lejos
(**b**) *(motion)* en; **I threw it in the fire** lo eché al fuego; **she arrived in Paris** llegó a París
(**c**) *(time) (during)* en, durante; **I haven't seen her in years** hace años que no la veo; **in May/1945** en mayo/1945; **in spring** en primavera; **in the daytime** durante el día; **in the morning** por la mañana; **at ten in the morning** a las diez de la mañana
(**d**) *(time) (within)* dentro de; **I arrived in time** llegué a tiempo
(**e**) *(time) (after)* al cabo de
(**f**) *(manner)* en; **in alphabetical order** en orden alfabético; **in a loud/quiet voice** en voz alta/baja; **in fashion** de moda; **in French** en francés; **in an odd way** de una manera rara; **in writing** por escrito; **write in pencil** escribe con lápiz
(**g**) *(wearing)* en; **dressed in blue** vestido(a) de azul; **in uniform** de uniforme
(**h**) *(weather etc)* a, en; **in the rain** bajo la lluvia; **in the sun** al sol; **in darkness** en la oscuridad; **in daylight** a la luz del día; **in the shade** a la sombra
(**i**) *(state, emotion)* en; **carved in wood** tallado(a) en madera; **in bloom/danger/public/silence** en flor/peligro/público/silencio; **in love** enamorado(a); **in tears** llorando
(**j**) *(ratio, numbers)* de; **cut in half** cortado(a) por la mitad; **in threes** de tres en tres; **one in six** uno de cada seis; **2 m in length** 2 m de largo
(**k**) *(profession)* en; **to be in insurance** trabajar en seguros
(**l**) *(person)* en; **he has it in him to win** es capaz de ganar
(**m**) *(after superlative)* de; **the smallest car in the world** el coche más pequeño del mundo
(**n**) *(before present participle)* **in behaving this way** con su comportamiento; **in so doing** con ello
(**o**) *(phrases)* **in all** en total; **in itself/himself/herself** en sí; **in that ...** dado que ...

2 *adv* **in here/there** aquí/allí dentro; **let's go in** vamos adentro; **to be in** *(at home)* estar (en casa); *(at work)* estar; *(tide)* estar alta; *Fam (in fashion)* estar de moda; **the bus is in** el autobús ha llegado; **to invite sb in** invitar a algn a entrar; *Fam* **to be in on sth** estar enterado(a) de algo; *Fam* **we're in for a storm** vamos a tener tormenta

3 *adj Fam* (**a**) *(fashionable) (place)* de moda; *(clothes)* del último grito
  (**b**) **an in joke** una broma privada

4 *n Fam* **ins and outs** detalles *mpl*

inability [ɪnə'bɪlɪtɪ] *n* incapacidad *f*

inaccessible [ɪnæk'sesəbəl] *adj* inaccesible

inaccurate [ɪn'ækjʊrɪt] *adj* inexacto(a); *(statement)* erróneo(a); *(figures, total)* incorrecto(a)

inactivity [ɪnæk'tɪvɪtɪ] *n* inactividad *f*

inadequate [ɪn'ædɪkwɪt] *adj* (**a**) *(lacking)* insuficiente (**b**) *(not capable)* incapaz; *(unsuitable)* inadecuado(a) (**c**) *(defective)* defectuoso(a)

inadvertent [ɪnəd'vɜːtənt] *adj* involuntario(a)

inadvertently [ɪnəd'vɜːtəntlɪ] *adv* involuntariamente

inadvisable [ɪnəd'vaɪzəbəl] *adj* imprudente

inane [ɪ'neɪn] *adj* necio(a), fatuo(a)

inanimate [ɪn'ænɪmɪt] *adj* inanimado(a)

inappropriate [ɪnə'prəʊprɪɪt] *adj* inoportuno(a); *(behaviour)* poco apropiado(a)

inarticulate [ɪnɑː'tɪkjʊlɪt] *adj* *(cry, sound)* inarticulado(a); *(words)* mal pronunciado(a)

inasmuch as [ɪnəz'mʌtʃəz] *conj Fml* (**a**) *(since)* puesto que, ya que (**b**) *(in so far as)* en la medida en que

inattentive [ɪnə'tentɪv] *adj* desatento(a)

inaudible [ɪn'ɔːdəbəl] *adj* inaudible

inaugural [ɪn'ɔːgjʊrəl] *adj* inaugural

inaugurate [ɪn'ɔːgjʊreɪt] *vt (building)* inaugurar; *(president)* investir

inauguration [ɪnɔːgjʊ'reɪʃən] *n* *(of building)* inauguración *f*; *(of president)* investidura *f*

inauspicious [ɪnɔː'spɪʃəs] *adj* *(start)* poco prometedor(a); *(circumstances)* desfavorable

inborn ['ɪnbɔːn] *adj* innato(a)

inbred ['ɪnbred] *adj* (**a**) *(quality)* innato(a) (**b**) *(family)* endogámico(a)

Inc, inc *US Com* (*abbr* **Incorporated**) ≃ S.A.

incalculable [ɪn'kælkjʊləbəl] *adj* incalculable

incapable [ɪn'keɪpəbəl] *adj* incapaz

incapacitate [ɪnkə'pæsɪteɪt] *vt Fml* incapacitar

incapacity [ɪnkə'pæsɪtɪ] *n* incapacidad *f*

incarcerate [ɪn'kɑːsəreɪt] *vt Fml* encarcelar

incarnation [ɪnkɑː'neɪʃən] *n* encarnación *f*

incendiary [ɪn'sendɪərɪ] **1** *adj* incendiario(a)

  2 *n* bomba incendiaria

incense¹ ['ɪnsens] *n* incienso *m*

incense² [ɪn'sens] *vt* enfurecer, sacar de quicio

incentive [ɪn'sentɪv] *n* incentivo *m*

incessant [ɪn'sesənt] *adj* incesante; *(demands)* constante

incessantly [ɪn'sesəntlɪ] *adv* sin cesar

incest ['ɪnsest] *n* incesto *m*

inch [ɪntʃ] *n* pulgada *f (aprox 2,54 cm)*; *Fig* **i. by i.** poco a poco; *Fig* **she wouldn't give an i.** no quería ceder ni un ápice
  ▸ **inch forward** *vt sep & vi* avanzar poco a poco

incidence ['ɪnsɪdəns] *n* frecuencia *f*

incident ['ɪnsɪdənt] *n* incidente *m*

incidental [ɪnsɪ'dentəl] *adj* *(accessory)* incidental, accesorio(a); *(risk)* inherente (**to** a); **i. music** música *f* de fondo

incidentally [ɪnsɪ'dentəlɪ] *adv* a propósito

incinerator [ɪn'sɪnəreɪtə(r)] *n* incinerador *m*

incipient [ɪn'sɪpɪənt] *adj Fml* incipiente

incision [ɪn'sɪʒən] *n* incisión *f*

incisive [ɪn'saɪsɪv] *adj (comment)* incisivo(a); *(reply)* tajante; *(mind)* penetrante

incite [ɪn'saɪt] *vt* incitar; **to i. sb to do sth** incitar a algn a hacer algo

inclination [ɪnklɪ'neɪʃən] *n* inclinación *f*; **my i. is to stay** yo prefiero quedarme

incline [ɪn'klaɪn] **1** *vt* (**a**) **I'm inclined to believe him** me inclino a creerlo; **if you feel so inclined** si quieres; **she's inclined to be aggressive** tiende a ser agresiva (**b**) *(head etc)* inclinar
  2 *vi (slope)* inclinarse
  3 *n* ['ɪnklaɪn] *(slope)* pendiente *f*; **steep i.** cuesta empinada

include [ɪn'kluːd] *vt* incluir (**in** en); *(in price)* comprender (**in** en); *(in list)* figurar (**in** en)

including [ɪn'kluːdɪŋ] *prep* incluso, inclusive

inclusion [ɪn'kluːʒən] *n* inclusión *f*

inclusive [ɪn'kluːsɪv] *adj* inclusivo(a); **pages 6 to 10 i.** de la página 6 a la 10, ambas inclusive; **the rent is i. of bills** el alquiler incluye las facturas

incognito [ɪnkɒgˈniːtəʊ] *adv* de incógnito

incoherent [ɪnkəʊˈhɪərənt] *adj* incoherente

income [ˈɪnkʌm] *n* ingresos *mpl*; *(from investment)* réditos *mpl*; **i. tax** impuesto *m* sobre la renta; **i. tax return** declaración *f* de la renta

incoming [ˈɪnkʌmɪŋ] *adj (flight, train)* de llegada; *(tide)* ascendente; *(mail, message, call)* recibido(a)

incomparable [ɪnˈkɒmpərəbəl] *adj* incomparable, sin par

incompatible [ɪnkəmˈpætəbəl] *adj* incompatible (**with** con)

incompetence [ɪnˈkɒmpɪtəns] *n* incompetencia *f*

incompetent [ɪnˈkɒmpɪtənt] *adj* incompetente

incomplete [ɪnkəmˈpliːt] *adj* incompleto(a)

incomprehensible [ɪnkɒmprɪˈhensəbəl] *adj* incomprensible

inconceivable [ɪnkənˈsiːvəbəl] *adj* inconcebible

inconclusive [ɪnkənˈkluːsɪv] *adj (vote)* no decisivo(a); *(proof)* no concluyente

incongruous [ɪnˈkɒŋgrʊəs] *adj* incongruente

inconsiderate [ɪnkənˈsɪdərɪt] *adj* desconsiderado(a); **how i. of you!** ¡qué falta de consideración por tu parte!

inconsistency [ɪnkənˈsɪstənsɪ] *n* inconsecuencia *f*, *(contradiction)* contradicción *f*

inconsistent [ɪnkənˈsɪstənt] *adj* inconsecuente; *(contradictory)* contradictorio(a); **your evidence is i. with the facts** su testimonio no concuerda con los hechos

inconspicuous [ɪnkənˈspɪkjʊəs] *adj* que pasa desapercibido(a); *(discreet)* discreto(a)

incontrovertible [ɪnkɒntrəˈvɜːtəbəl] *adj Fml* incontrovertible

inconvenience [ɪnkənˈviːnɪəns] **1** *n* inconveniente *f*; *(annoyance)* molestia *f*
 2 *vt (annoy)* molestar; *(cause difficulty to)* incomodar

inconvenient [ɪnkənˈviːnɪənt] *adj* molesto(a); *(time)* inoportuno(a); *(design)* poco práctico(a)

incorporate [ɪnˈkɔːpəreɪt] *vt* incorporar (**in** *or* **into** a); *(include)* incluir; *(contain)* contener

incorporated [ɪnˈkɔːpəreɪtɪd] *adj US Com* **i. company** sociedad anónima

incorrect [ɪnkəˈrekt] *adj* incorrecto(a)

incorrigible [ɪnˈkɒrɪdʒəbəl] *adj* incorregible

increase 1 *n* [ˈɪnkriːs] aumento *m*; *(in number)* incremento *m*; *(in price etc)* subida *f*
 2 *vt* [ɪnˈkriːs] aumentar; *(price etc)* subir
 3 *vi* aumentar

increasing [ɪnˈkriːsɪŋ] *adj* creciente

increasingly [ɪnˈkriːsɪŋlɪ] *adv* cada vez más

incredible [ɪnˈkredəbəl] *adj* increíble

incredulous [ɪnˈkredjʊləs] *adj* incrédulo(a)

increment [ˈɪnkrɪmənt] *n* incremento *m*

incriminate [ɪnˈkrɪmɪneɪt] *vt* incriminar

incriminating [ɪnˈkrɪmɪneɪtɪŋ] *adj* incriminatorio(a)

incubation [ɪnkjʊˈbeɪʃən] *n* incubación *f*

incubator [ˈɪnkjʊbeɪtə(r)] *n* incubadora *f*

incumbent [ɪnˈkʌmbənt] **1** *n* titular *mf*
 2 *adj Fml* **to be i. on sb to do sth** ser la obligación de algn hacer algo

incur [ɪnˈkɜː(r)] *vt (blame)* incurrir en; *(risk)* correr; *(debt)* contraer; *(loss)* sufrir

incurable [ɪnˈkjʊərəbəl] *adj* incurable

indebted [ɪnˈdetɪd] *adj* endeudado(a); *Fig (grateful)* agradecido(a); *Fig* **to be i. to sb** estar en deuda con algn

indecent [ɪnˈdiːsənt] *adj* indecente; **i. assault** atentado *m* contra el pudor; **i. exposure** exhibicionismo *m*

indecision [ɪndɪˈsɪʒən] *n* indecisión *f*

indecisive [ɪndɪˈsaɪsɪv] *adj (person)* indeciso(a); *(evidence)* poco concluyente; *(victory)* no decisivo(a)

indeed [ɪnˈdiːd] *adv* (**a**) *Fml (in fact)* efectivamente, en realidad (**b**) **I'm very sorry i.** lo siento de veras; **it's very hard i.** es verdaderamente difícil; **thank you very much i.** muchísimas gracias

indefinite [ɪnˈdefɪnɪt] *adj* indefinido(a)

indelible [ɪnˈdeləbəl] *adj* indeleble

indemnify [ɪnˈdemnɪfaɪ] *vt* indemnizar (**for** por)

indemnity [ɪnˈdemnɪtɪ] *n* (**a**) *(insurance)* indemnidad *f* (**b**) *(compensation)* indemnización *f*

indentation [ɪndenˈteɪʃən] *n* (**a**) *Typ* sangría *f* (**b**) *(of edge)* muesca *f*; *(of surface)* depresión *f*

independence [ɪndɪˈpendəns] *n* independencia *f*; *US* **I. Day** día *m* de la Independencia *(4 julio)*

independent [ɪndɪˈpendənt] *adj* independiente; *Br* **i. school** = colegio no subvencionado por el estado; **to become i.** independizarse

in-depth [ˈɪndepθ] *adj* minucioso(a), exhaustivo(a)

indestructible [ɪndɪˈstrʌktəbəl] *adj* indestructible

indeterminate [ɪndɪˈtɜːmɪnɪt] *adj* indeterminado(a)

index [ˈɪndeks] **1** *n* (*pl* **indexes** *or* **indices**) (**a**) (*in book*) índice *m*; (*in library*) catálogo *m*; **i. card** ficha *f* (**b**) *Math* exponente *m*; *Econ* índice *m* (**c**) **i. finger** dedo *m* índice
2 *vt* catalogar

index-linked [ˈɪndekslɪŋkt] *adj* sujeto(a) al aumento de la inflación

India [ˈɪndɪə] *n* (la) India

Indian [ˈɪndɪən] *adj & n* (*of America*) indio(a) (*m,f*); (*of India*) hindú (*mf*); **I. Ocean** Océano Índico; **I. Summer** veranillo *m* de San Martín

indicate [ˈɪndɪkeɪt] **1** *vt* indicar
2 *vi* *Aut* poner el intermitente

indication [ɪndɪˈkeɪʃən] *n* indicio *m*

indicative [ɪnˈdɪkətɪv] **1** *adj* indicativo(a)
2 *n* *Ling* indicativo *m*

indicator [ˈɪndɪkeɪtə(r)] *n* indicador *m*; *Br Aut* intermitente *m*

indices [ˈɪndɪsiːz] *pl of* **index**

indict [ɪnˈdaɪt] *vt* acusar (**for** de)

indictment [ɪnˈdaɪtmənt] *n* *Jur* acusación *f*; *Fig* **a damning i. of his books** una crítica feroz de sus libros

indifference [ɪnˈdɪfərəns] *n* indiferencia *f*

indifferent [ɪnˈdɪfərənt] *adj* (**a**) (*uninterested*) indiferente (**b**) (*mediocre*) regular

indigenous [ɪnˈdɪdʒɪnəs] *adj* indígena

indigestion [ɪndɪˈdʒestʃən] *n* indigestión *f*; **to suffer from i.** tener un empacho

indignant [ɪnˈdɪgnənt] *adj* indignado(a); (*look*) de indignación; **to get i. about sth** indignarse por algo

indignity [ɪnˈdɪgnɪtɪ] *n* indignidad *f*

indigo [ˈɪndɪgəʊ] **1** *n* añil *m*
2 *adj* (*de color*) añil

indirect [ɪndɪˈrekt, ɪndaɪˈrekt] *adj* indirecto(a)

indiscreet [ɪndɪˈskriːt] *adj* indiscreto(a)

indiscretion [ɪndɪˈskreʃən] *n* indiscreción *f*

indiscriminate [ɪndɪˈskrɪmɪnɪt] *adj* (*punishment, shooting*) indiscriminado(a); (*praise, reading*) sin criterio

indispensable [ɪndɪˈspensəbəl] *adj* indispensable, imprescindible

indisposed [ɪndɪˈspəʊzd] *adj* *Fml* indispuesto(a)

indisputable [ɪndɪˈspjuːtəbəl] *adj* indiscutible, incontestable

indistinct [ɪndɪˈstɪŋkt] *adj* indistinto(a); (*memory*) confuso(a), vago(a); (*shape etc*) borroso(a)

indistinguishable [ɪndɪˈstɪŋgwɪʃəbəl] *adj* indistinguible

individual [ɪndɪˈvɪdʒʊəl] **1** *adj* (**a**) (*separate*) individual; (*for one*) particular; (*personal*) personal (**b**) (*characteristic*) particular; (*original*) original
2 *n* (*person*) individuo *m*; **private i.** particular *m*

individualist [ɪndɪˈvɪdʒʊəlɪst] *n* individualista *mf*

indoctrinate [ɪnˈdɒktrɪneɪt] *vt* adoctrinar

indoctrination [ɪndɒktrɪˈneɪʃən] *n* adoctrinamiento *m*

indolent [ˈɪndələnt] *adj* *Fml* indolente

Indonesia [ɪndəʊˈniːzɪə] *n* Indonesia

Indonesian [ɪndəʊˈniːzɪən] **1** *adj* indonesio(a)
2 *n* (**a**) (*person*) indonesio(a) *m,f* (**b**) (*language*) indonesio *m*

indoor [ˈɪndɔː(r)] *adj* (*plant*) de interior; **i. football** fútbol *m* sala; **i. pool** piscina cubierta

indoors [ɪnˈdɔːz] *adv* (*inside*) dentro (de casa); (*at home*) en casa; **let's go i.** vamos adentro

induce [ɪnˈdjuːs] *vt* (**a**) (*persuade*) inducir, persuadir (**b**) (*cause*) producir; *Med* (*labour*) provocar

inducement [ɪnˈdjuːsmənt] *n* incentivo *m*, aliciente *m*

induction [ɪnˈdʌkʃən] *n* (**a**) *Med* (*of labour*) provocación *f* (**b**) *Elec* inducción *f* (**c**) *Educ* introducción *f*

indulge [ɪnˈdʌldʒ] **1** *vt* (**a**) (*child*) consentir; (*person*) complacer; **to i. oneself** darse gusto (**b**) (*whim*) ceder a, satisfacer
2 *vi* darse el gusto (**in** de)

indulgence [ɪnˈdʌldʒəns] *n* (**a**) (*of child*) mimo *m*; (*of attitude*) indulgencia *f* (**b**) (*of whim*) satisfacción *f*

indulgent [ɪnˈdʌldʒənt] *adj* indulgente

industrial [ɪnˈdʌstrɪəl] *adj* industrial; (*accident*) laboral; (*disease*) profesional; *Br* **to take i. action** declararse en huelga; *Br* **i. dispute** conflicto *m* laboral; **i.** *Br* **estate** *or* *US* **park** polígono *m* industrial; **i. relations** relaciones *fpl* laborales

industrialist [ɪnˈdʌstrɪəlɪst] *n* industrial *mf*

industrialize [ɪnˈdʌstrɪəlaɪz] *vt* industrializar; **to become industrialized** industrializarse

industrious [ɪnˈdʌstrɪəs] *adj* trabajador(a)

industry ['ɪndəstrɪ] n (**a**) industria f (**b**) (*diligence*) aplicación f

inebriated [ɪn'iːbrɪeɪtɪd] adj embriagado(a)

inedible [ɪn'edəbəl] adj incomible

ineffective [ɪnɪ'fektɪv] adj ineficaz

ineffectual [ɪnɪ'fektʃʊəl] adj (*aim, protest*) ineficaz; (*person*) incompetente

inefficiency [ɪnɪ'fɪʃənsɪ] n ineficacia f; (*of person*) incompetencia f

inefficient [ɪnɪ'fɪʃənt] adj ineficaz; (*person*) inepto(a)

ineligible [ɪn'elɪdʒəbəl] adj no apto(a) (**for** para)

inept [ɪn'ept] adj (*person*) inepto(a); (*remark*) estúpido(a)

inequality [ɪnɪ'kwɒlɪtɪ] n desigualdad f

inert [ɪn'ɜːt] adj inerte

inertia [ɪn'ɜːʃə] n inercia f

inescapable [ɪnɪ'skeɪpəbəl] adj ineludible

inevitability [ɪnevɪtə'bɪlɪtɪ] n inevitabilidad f

inevitable [ɪn'evɪtəbəl] adj inevitable

inexcusable [ɪnɪk'skjuːzəbəl] adj inexcusable, imperdonable

inexhaustible [ɪnɪg'zɔːstəbəl] adj inagotable

inexorable [ɪn'eksərəbəl] adj Fml inexorable

inexpensive [ɪnɪk'spensɪv] adj económico(a)

inexperience [ɪnɪk'spɪərɪəns] n inexperiencia f

inexperienced [ɪnɪk'spɪərɪənst] adj inexperto(a)

inexplicable [ɪnɪk'splɪkəbəl] adj inexplicable

infallible [ɪn'fæləbəl] adj infalible

infamous ['ɪnfəməs] adj infame

infancy ['ɪnfənsɪ] n infancia f

infant ['ɪnfənt] n niño(a) m,f; Br **i. school** parvulario m

infantile ['ɪnfəntaɪl] adj infantil

infantry ['ɪnfəntrɪ] n infantería f

infatuated [ɪn'fætjʊeɪtɪd] adj encaprichado(a)

infatuation [ɪnfætjʊ'eɪʃən] n encaprichamiento m

infect [ɪn'fekt] vt (*cut*) infectar; (*water*) contaminar; (*person*) contagiar

infection [ɪn'fekʃən] n (*of cut*) infección f; (*of water*) contaminación f; (*with illness*) contagio m

infectious [ɪn'fekʃəs] adj (*disease*) infeccioso(a); Fig contagioso(a)

infer [ɪn'fɜː(r)] vt inferir (**from** de)

inference ['ɪnfərəns] n inferencia f

inferior [ɪn'fɪərɪə(r)] **1** adj inferior (**to** a)
2 n Pej inferior mf

inferiority [ɪnfɪərɪ'ɒrɪtɪ] n inferioridad f

inferno [ɪn'fɜːnəʊ] n Literary infierno m; Fig **the house was a raging i.** la casa ardía en llamas

infertile [ɪn'fɜːtaɪl] adj estéril

infertility [ɪnfə'tɪlɪtɪ] n esterilidad f

infest [ɪn'fest] vt infestar, plagar (**with** de)

infighting ['ɪnfaɪtɪŋ] n Fig luchas fpl internas

infiltrate ['ɪnfɪltreɪt] vt infiltrarse (**into** en)

infinite ['ɪnfɪnɪt] adj infinito(a)

infinitive [ɪn'fɪnɪtɪv] n infinitivo m

infinity [ɪn'fɪnɪtɪ] n infinidad f; Math infinito m

infirm [ɪn'fɜːm] **1** adj (*ailing*) enfermizo(a); (*weak*) débil
2 npl **the i.** los inválidos

infirmary [ɪn'fɜːmərɪ] n hospital m

infirmity [ɪn'fɜːmɪtɪ] n Fml (*ailment*) enfermedad f; (*weakness*) debilidad f

inflame [ɪn'fleɪm] vt (*passion*) encender; (*curiosity*) avivar; (*crowd*) excitar; **to be inflamed with rage** rabiar

inflamed [ɪn'fleɪmd] adj inflamado(a); **to become i.** inflamarse

inflammable [ɪn'flæməbəl] adj (*material*) inflamable; Fig (*situation*) explosivo(a)

inflammation [ɪnflə'meɪʃən] n inflamación f

inflatable [ɪn'fleɪtəbəl] adj inflable

inflate [ɪn'fleɪt] **1** vt inflar
2 vi inflarse

inflated [ɪn'fleɪtɪd] adj (**a**) Fig (*prices*) inflacionista (**b**) Pej (*view, idea*) exagerado(a)

inflation [ɪn'fleɪʃən] n inflación f

inflexible [ɪn'fleksəbəl] adj inflexible

inflict [ɪn'flɪkt] vt (*blow*) asestar (**on** a); (*damage*) causar (**on** a); (*defeat*) infligir (**on** a)

in-flight ['ɪnflaɪt] adj durante el vuelo

influence ['ɪnflʊəns] **1** n influencia f; Fam **to be under the i.** llevar una copa de más
2 vt influir en

influential [ɪnflʊ'enʃəl] adj influyente

influenza [ɪnflʊ'enzə] n gripe f

influx ['ɪnflʌks] n afluencia f

inform [ɪn'fɔːm] **1** vt informar (**of** or **about** de or sobre); (*police*) avisar (**of** or **about** de)
2 vi **to i. against** or **on** denunciar

informal [ɪn'fɔːməl] adj (**a**) (*occasion, behaviour*) informal; (*language, treatment*) familiar (**b**) *(unofficial)* no oficial

informality [ɪnfɔːˈmælɪtɪ] *n (of occasion, behaviour)* sencillez *f*; *(of treatment)* familiaridad *f*

informant [ɪnˈfɔːmənt] *n* informante *mf*

information [ɪnfəˈmeɪʃən] *u* información *f*; *(details)* detalles *mpl*; *(facts)* datos *mpl*; *(knowledge)* conocimientos *mpl*; *(news)* noticias *fpl*; **a piece of i.** un dato; **i. bureau** centro *m* de información; **i. (super)highway** autopista *f* de la información; **i. technology** informática *f*

informative [ɪnˈfɔːmətɪv] *adj* informativo(a)

informed [ɪnˈfɔːmd] *adj* enterado(a); **keep me i.** téngame al corriente

informer [ɪnˈfɔːmə(r)] *n* delator(a) *m,f*, *(to the police)* soplón(ona) *m,f*

infrared [ɪnfrəˈred] *adj* infrarrojo(a)

infrastructure [ˈɪnfrəstrʌktʃə(r)] *n* infraestructura *f*

infringe [ɪnˈfrɪndʒ] **1** *vt (law, rule)* infringir; *(copyright)* no respetar

2 *vi* **to i. on** or **upon** *(rights)* violar; *(privacy)* invadir

infringement [ɪnˈfrɪndʒmənt] *n (of law, rule)* infracción *f*; *(of rights)* violación *f*

infuriate [ɪnˈfjʊərɪeɪt] *vt* poner furioso(a)

infuriating [ɪnˈfjʊərɪeɪtɪŋ] *adj* exasperante

infusion [ɪnˈfjuːʒən] *n* infusión *f*

ingenious [ɪnˈdʒiːnɪəs] *adj* ingenioso(a)

ingenuity [ɪndʒɪˈnjuːɪtɪ] *n* ingenio *m*

ingenuous [ɪnˈdʒenjʊəs] *adj* ingenuo(a)

ingot [ˈɪŋɡət] *n* lingote *m*

ingrained [ɪnˈɡreɪnd] *adj* Fig arraigado(a)

ingratiate [ɪnˈɡreɪʃɪeɪt] *vt Pej* **to i. oneself with sb** congraciarse con algn

ingratiating [ɪnˈɡreɪʃɪeɪtɪŋ] *adj* zalamero(a)

ingratitude [ɪnˈɡrætɪtjuːd] *n* ingratitud *f*

ingredient [ɪnˈɡriːdɪənt] *n* ingrediente *m*

inhabit [ɪnˈhæbɪt] *vt* vivir en, ocupar

inhabitable [ɪnˈhæbɪtəbəl] *adj* habitable

> *Note that the Spanish word* **inhabitable** *is a false friend and is never a translation for the English word* **inhabitable**. *In Spanish,* **inhabitable** *means "uninhabitable".*

inhabitant [ɪnˈhæbɪtənt] *n* habitante *mf*

inhale [ɪnˈheɪl] **1** *vt (gas)* inhalar; *(air)* aspirar

2 *vi* aspirar; *(smoker)* tragar el humo

inherent [ɪnˈhɪərənt] *adj* inherente

inherit [ɪnˈherɪt] *vt* heredar (**from** de)

inheritance [ɪnˈherɪtəns] *n* herencia *f*

inhibit [ɪnˈhɪbɪt] *vt (freedom)* limitar;

(person) cohibir; **to i. sb from doing sth** impedir a algn hacer algo

inhibited [ɪnˈhɪbɪtɪd] *adj* cohibido(a)

inhibition [ɪnhɪˈbɪʃən] *n* cohibición *f*

inhospitable [ɪnhɒˈspɪtəbəl] *adj* inhospitalario(a); *(climate, place)* inhóspito(a)

inhuman [ɪnˈhjuːmən] *adj* inhumano(a)

iniquity [ɪˈnɪkwɪtɪ] *n Fml* iniquidad *f*

initial [ɪˈnɪʃəl] **1** *adj* inicial, primero(a)

2 *n* **(a)** inicial *f* **(b) initials** *(of name)* iniciales *fpl*; *(of abbreviation)* siglas *fpl*

3 *vt* firmar con las iniciales

initially [ɪˈnɪʃəlɪ] *adv* al principio

initiate [ɪˈnɪʃɪeɪt] *vt* **(a)** iniciar; *(reform)* promover; *(lawsuit)* entablar **(b)** *(into society)* admitir (**into** en); *(into knowledge)* iniciar (**into** en)

initiation [ɪnɪʃɪˈeɪʃən] *n* **(a)** *(start)* principio *m* **(b)** *(admission)* iniciación *f*

initiative [ɪˈnɪʃətɪv] *n* iniciativa *f*

inject [ɪnˈdʒekt] *vt* **(a)** *(drug etc)* inyectar **(b)** *Fig (capital)* invertir; *(life, hope)* infundir

injection [ɪnˈdʒekʃən] *n* **(a)** inyección *f* **(b)** *Fig (of capital)* inversión *f*

injunction [ɪnˈdʒʌŋkʃən] *n* interdicto *m*

injure [ˈɪndʒə(r)] *vt* herir; **to i. oneself** hacerse daño; *Fig (health, reputation)* perjudicar

injured [ˈɪndʒəd] **1** *adj* herido(a); *Fig (look, tone)* ofendido(a)

2 *npl* **the i.** los heridos

injury [ˈɪndʒərɪ] *n (hurt)* herida *f*; *Fig (harm)* daño *m*; *Sport* **i. time** (tiempo *m* de) descuento *m*

injustice [ɪnˈdʒʌstɪs] *n* injusticia *f*

ink [ɪŋk] *n* tinta *f*; **invisible i.** tinta simpática

inkjet printer [ˈɪŋkdʒet ˈprɪntə(r)] *n Comput* impresora *f* de chorro de tinta

inkling [ˈɪŋklɪŋ] *n (idea)* idea *f*; *(suspicion)* sospecha *f*; *(sign)* señal *f*

inkwell [ˈɪŋkwel] *n* tintero *m*

inlaid [ɪnˈleɪd] *adj (wood)* taraceado(a); *(ivory, gems)* incrustado(a)

inland 1 *adj* [ˈɪnlənd] (del) interior; *Br* **I. Revenue** Hacienda *f*

2 *adv* [ɪnˈlænd] *(travel)* tierra adentro

in-laws [ˈɪnlɔːz] *npl Fam* familia *f* política

inlet [ˈɪnlet] *n* **(a)** *(in coastline)* ensenada *f*, cala *f* **(b)** *(in pipe, machine)* entrada *f*, admisión *f*

inline [ˈɪnlaɪn] *adj* **i. skates** patines *mpl* en línea

inmate [ˈɪnmeɪt] *n (of prison)* preso(a) *m,f*, *(of hospital)* enfermo(a) *m,f*, *(of asylum, camp)* internado(a) *m,f*

inn [ɪn] *n (with lodging)* posada *f*, mesón *m*

innate [ɪ'neɪt] *adj* innato(a)

inner ['mə(r)] *adj* (**a**) *(region)* interior; *(structure)* interno(a); **i. city** zona urbana desfavorecida; **i. tube** cámara *f* de aire (**b**) *Fig (thoughts)* íntimo(a); *(peace etc)* interior

innermost ['məməʊst] *adj (room)* más interior; *Fig (thoughts)* más íntimo(a)

innings ['ɪnɪŋz] *npl (in cricket)* entrada *f*, turno *m*

innocence ['məsəns] *n* inocencia *f*

innocent ['məsənt] *adj & n* inocente *(mf)*

innocuous [ɪ'nɒkjʊəs] *adj* inocuo(a)

innovation [mə'veɪʃən] *n* novedad *f*

innuendo [ɪnjʊ'endəʊ] *n* indirecta *f*

inoculate [ɪ'nɒkjʊleɪt] *vt* inocular

inoculation [ɪnɒkjʊ'leɪʃən] *n* inoculación *f*

inoffensive [mə'fensɪv] *adj* inofensivo(a)

inopportune [ɪn'ɒpətjuːn, ɪnɒpə'tjuːn] *adj* inoportuno(a)

inordinate [ɪ'nɔːdɪnɪt] *adj* desmesurado(a)

inpatient ['ɪnpeɪʃənt] *n* interno(a) *m,f*

input ['ɪnpʊt] *n (of resources)* inversión *f*; *(of power)* entrada *f*; *Comput (of data)* input *m*, entrada

inquest ['ɪnkwest] *n* investigación *f* judicial

inquire [ɪn'kwaɪə(r)] **1** *vt* preguntar; *(find out)* averiguar

2 *vi* preguntar (**about** por); *(find out)* informarse (**about** de)

▶ **inquire after** *vt insep* preguntar por

▶ **inquire into** *vt insep* investigar, indagar

inquiry [ɪn'kwaɪərɪ] *n* (**a**) pregunta *f*; **inquiries** *(sign)* información (**b**) *(investigation)* investigación *f*

inquisitive [ɪn'kwɪzɪtɪv] *adj (curious)* curioso(a); *(questioning)* preguntón(ona)

inroads ['ɪnrəʊdz] *npl* **the firm is making i. into the market** la empresa está ganando terreno en el mercado; **to make i. into one's capital** reducir su capital

insane [ɪn'seɪn] *adj* loco(a); *(act)* insensato(a); *Fig* **to drive sb i.** volver loco(a) a algn

insanity [ɪn'sænɪtɪ] *n* demencia *f*, locura *f*

insatiable [ɪn'seɪʃəbəl] *adj* insaciable

inscribe [ɪn'skraɪb] *vt Fml* inscribir; *(book)* dedicar

inscription [ɪn'skrɪpʃən] *n (on stone, coin)* inscripción *f*; *(in book, on photo)* dedicatoria *f*

inscrutable [ɪn'skruːtəbəl] *adj* inescrutable, insondable

insect ['ɪnsekt] *n* insecto *m*; **i. bite** picadura *f*

insecticide [ɪn'sektɪsaɪd] *n* insecticida *m*

insecure [ɪnsɪ'kjʊə(r)] *adj* inseguro(a)

insecurity [ɪnsɪ'kjʊərɪtɪ] *n* inseguridad *f*

insemination [ɪnsemɪ'neɪʃən] *n* inseminación *f*

insensible [ɪn'sensəbəl] *adj Fml* inconsciente

insensitive [ɪn'sensɪtɪv] *adj* insensible

inseparable [ɪn'sepərəbəl] *adj* inseparable

insert 1 *n* ['ɪnsɜːt] encarte *m*

2 *vt* [ɪn'sɜːt] introducir

insertion [ɪn'sɜːʃən] *n* introducción *f*; *(of clause, text)* inserción *f*

inshore 1 *adj* ['ɪnʃɔː(r)] *(fishing)* de bajura

2 *adv* [ɪn'ʃɔː(r)] cerca de la costa

inside [ɪn'saɪd] **1** *n* (**a**) interior *m*; **on the i.** por dentro; **to turn sth i. out** volver algo al revés (**b**) *Fam* **insides** tripas *fpl*

2 ['ɪnsaɪd] *adj* interior; *Sport* **i. forward** interior *mf*; *Aut* **i. lane** carril *m* interior

3 *adv* (*be*) dentro, adentro; *(run etc)* (hacia) adentro; **to come i.** entrar; *Br Fam* **he spent a year i.** pasó un año en chirona

4 *prep* (**a**) *(place)* dentro de (**b**) *Fam* **i. (of)** *(time)* en menos de

insider [ɪn'saɪdə(r)] *n* **i. dealing** = uso indebido de información privilegiada y confidencial para operaciones comerciales

insidious [ɪn'sɪdɪəs] *adj* insidioso(a)

insight ['ɪnsaɪt] *n* perspicacia *f*

insignia [ɪn'sɪgnɪə] *n inv* insignia *f*

insignificant [ɪnsɪg'nɪfɪkənt] *adj* insignificante

insincere [ɪnsɪn'sɪə(r)] *adj* poco sincero(a)

insinuate [ɪn'sɪnjʊeɪt] *vt* insinuar

insipid [ɪn'sɪpɪd] *adj* soso(a), insulso(a)

insist [ɪn'sɪst] **1** *vi* insistir (**on** en); *(argue)* obstinarse (**on** en)

2 *vt* **to i. that ...** insistir en que ...

insistence [ɪn'sɪstəns] *n* insistencia *f*

insistent [ɪn'sɪstənt] *adj* insistente

in so far as [ɪnsəʊ'fɑːrəz] *adv* en tanto que

insole ['ɪnsəʊl] *n (of shoe)* plantilla *f*

insolent ['ɪnsələnt] *adj* insolente

insoluble [ɪn'sɒljʊbəl] *adj* insoluble

insomnia [ɪn'sɒmnɪə] *n* insomnio *m*

insomniac [ɪn'sɒmnɪæk] *n* insomne *mf*

inspect [ɪn'spekt] *vt* inspeccionar, examinar; *(troops)* pasar revista a

inspection [ɪnˈspekʃən] *n* inspección *f*; *(of troops)* revista *f*

inspector [ɪnˈspektə(r)] *n* inspector(a) *m,f*; *(on bus, train)* revisor(a) *m,f*

inspiration [ɪnspɪˈreɪʃən] *n* inspiración *f*; **to get i. from sb/sth** inspirarse en algn/algo

inspire [ɪnˈspaɪə(r)] *vt* (**a**) inspirar; **to i. respect in sb** infundir respeto a algn (**b**) **to i. sb to do sth** animar a algn a hacer algo

inspired [ɪnˈspaɪəd] *adj* inspirado(a)

instability [ɪnstəˈbɪlɪtɪ] *n* inestabilidad *f*

install, *US* **instal** [ɪnˈstɔːl] *vt* instalar

installation [ɪnstəˈleɪʃən] *n* instalación *f*

instalment, *US* **installment** [ɪnˈstɔːlmənt] *n* (**a**) *(of payment)* plazo *m*; **to pay by instalments** pagar a plazos; *US* **i. plan** venta *f*/compra *f* a plazos (**b**) *(of novel, programme)* entrega *f*; *(of journal)* fascículo *m*

instance [ˈɪnstəns] *n* caso *m*, ejemplo *m*; **for i.** por ejemplo; **in the first i.** en primer lugar

> ♪ Note that the Spanish word **instancia** is a false friend and is never a translation for the English word **instance**. In Spanish, **instancia** means "request".

instant [ˈɪnstənt] **1** *n (moment)* instante *m*, momento *m*; **in an i.** en un instante

   2 *adj* inmediato(a); *(coffee, meal)* instantáneo(a)

instantly [ˈɪnstəntlɪ] *adv* inmediatamente

instead [ɪnˈsted] **1** *adv* en cambio

   2 *prep* **i. of** en vez de, en lugar de

instep [ˈɪnstep] *n* empeine *m*

instigation [ɪnstɪˈgeɪʃən] *n* instigación *f*

instil, *US* **instill** [ɪnˈstɪl] *vt (idea, habit)* inculcar (**in** a *or* en); *(courage, respect)* infundir (**in** a)

instinct [ˈɪnstɪŋkt] *n* instinto *m*

instinctive [ɪnˈstɪŋktɪv] *adj* instintivo(a)

institute [ˈɪnstɪtjuːt] **1** *n* instituto *m*; *(centre)* centro *m*; *(professional body)* colegio *m*

   2 *vt* *Fml* (**a**) *(system)* establecer (**b**) *(start)* iniciar; *(proceedings)* entablar

institution [ɪnstɪˈtjuːʃən] *n* (**a**) institución *f* (**b**) *(home)* asilo *m*; *(asylum)* manicomio *m*

instruct [ɪnˈstrʌkt] *vt* instruir; *(order)* mandar; **I am instructed to say that ...** me han encargado decir que ...

instruction [ɪnˈstrʌkʃən] *n* (**a**) instrucción *f* (**b**) **instructions** instrucciones *fpl*; **instructions for use** modo de empleo

instructive [ɪnˈstrʌktɪv] *adj* instructivo(a)

instructor [ɪnˈstrʌktə(r)] *n* instructor(a) *m,f*; *(of driving)* profesor(a) *m,f*

instrument [ˈɪnstrəmənt] *n* instrumento *m*; **i. panel** tablero *m* de mandos

instrumental [ɪnstrəˈmentəl] *adj* (**a**) *Mus* instrumental (**b**) **to be i. in sth** contribuir decisivamente a algo

insubordinate [ɪnsəˈbɔːdɪnɪt] *adj* insubordinado(a)

insubstantial [ɪnsəbˈstænʃəl] *adj* insubstancial; *(structure)* poco sólido(a)

insufferable [ɪnˈsʌfərəbəl] *adj* insoportable

insufficient [ɪnsəˈfɪʃənt] *adj* insuficiente

insular [ˈɪnsjʊlə(r)] *adj* (**a**) *Geog* insular (**b**) *Fig Pej* estrecho(a) de miras

insulate [ˈɪnsjʊleɪt] *vt* aislar (**against** *or* **from** de)

insulating tape [ˈɪnsjʊleɪtɪŋteɪp] *n* cinta *f* aislante

insulation [ɪnsjʊˈleɪʃən] *n* aislamiento *m*

insulin [ˈɪnsjʊlɪn] *n* insulina *f*

insult 1 *n* [ˈɪnsʌlt] *(words)* insulto *m*; *(action)* afrenta *f*, ofensa *f*

   2 *vt* [ɪnˈsʌlt] insultar, ofender

insulting [ɪnˈsʌltɪŋ] *adj* insultante, ofensivo(a)

insuperable [ɪnˈsuːpərəbəl] *adj* insuperable

insurance [ɪnˈʃʊərəns] *n* seguro *m*; **fire i.** seguro contra incendios; **i. broker** agente *mf* de seguros; **i. company** compañía *f* de seguros; **i. policy** póliza *f* (de seguros); **private health i.** seguro médico privado

insure [ɪnˈʃʊə(r)] *vt* asegurar (**against** contra)

insurgent [ɪnˈsɜːdʒənt] *adj & n* insurrecto(a) *(m,f)*

insurmountable [ɪnsəˈmaʊntəbəl] *adj (problem etc)* insuperable; *(barrier)* infranqueable

intact [ɪnˈtækt] *adj* intacto(a)

intake [ˈɪnteɪk] *n* (**a**) *(of air, water)* entrada *f*; *(of electricity etc)* toma *f* (**b**) *(of food, calories)* consumo *m* (**c**) *(of students, recruits)* número *m* de admitidos

integral [ˈɪntɪgrəl] **1** *adj* (**a**) *(intrinsic)* integrante (**b**) *(whole)* íntegro(a) (**c**) *Math* integral

   2 *n Math* integral *f*

integrate [ˈɪntɪgreɪt] **1** *vt* integrar

   2 *vi* integrarse

integration [ɪntɪˈgreɪʃən] *n* integración *f*

integrity [ɪnˈtegrɪtɪ] *n* integridad *f*, honradez *f*

intellect [ˈɪntɪlekt] *n* intelecto *m*

intellectual [ɪntɪˈlektʃʊəl] *adj & n* intelectual *(mf)*

intelligence [ɪnˈtelɪdʒəns] *n* (a) inteligencia *f* (b) *(information)* información *f*

intelligent [ɪnˈtelɪdʒənt] *adj* inteligente

intelligentsia [ɪntelɪˈdʒentsɪə] *n* intelectualidad *f*

intelligible [ɪnˈtelɪdʒəbəl] *adj* inteligible

intend [ɪnˈtend] *vt* (a) *(mean)* tener la intención de (b) **to i. sth for sb** destinar algo a algn

intended [ɪnˈtendɪd] *adj (planned)* previsto(a)

intense [ɪnˈtens] *adj* intenso(a); *(person)* muy serio(a)

intensely [ɪnˈtenslɪ] *adv (extremely)* enormemente, sumamente

intensify [ɪnˈtensɪfaɪ] *vt (search)* intensificar; *(effort)* redoblar; *(production, pollution)* aumentar

intensity [ɪnˈtensɪtɪ] *n* intensidad *f*

intensive [ɪnˈtensɪv] *adj* intensivo(a); *Med* **i. care unit** unidad *f* de vigilancia intensiva

intent [ɪnˈtent] **1** *adj (absorbed)* absorto(a); *(gaze etc)* atento(a); **to be i. on doing sth** estar resuelto(a) a hacer algo
2 *n Fml* intención *f*, propósito *m*; **to all intents and purposes** a todos los efectos

intention [ɪnˈtenʃən] *n* intención *f*

intentional [ɪnˈtenʃənəl] *adj* deliberado(a)

intentionally [ɪnˈtenʃənəlɪ] *adv* a propósito

interact [ɪntərˈækt] *vi (people)* interrelacionarse

interaction [ɪntərˈækʃən] *n* interacción *f*

interactive [ɪntərˈæktɪv] *adj* interactivo(a)

intercede [ɪntəˈsiːd] *vi* interceder (**with** ante)

intercept [ɪntəˈsept] *vt* interceptar

interchange 1 *n* [ˈɪntətʃeɪndʒ] (a) *(exchange)* intercambio *m* (b) *(on motorway)* cruce *m*
2 *vt* [ɪntəˈtʃeɪndʒ] intercambiar (**with** con)

interchangeable [ɪntəˈtʃeɪndʒəbəl] *adj* intercambiable

intercity [ɪntəˈsɪtɪ] *adj Rail* de largo recorrido

intercom [ˈɪntəkɒm] *n* portero automático

intercontinental [ɪntəkɒntɪˈnentəl] *adj* **i. ballistic missile** misil balístico intercontinental

intercourse [ˈɪntəkɔːs] *n* (a) *(dealings)* trato *m* (b) *(sexual)* relaciones *fpl* sexuales

interest [ˈɪntrɪst] **1** *n* (a) interés *m* (b) *(advantage)* provecho *m*; **in the i. of** en pro de (c) *Com (share)* participación *f* (d) *Fin* interés *m*; **i. rate** tipo *m* de interés
2 *vt* interesar; **he's interested in politics** le interesa la política

interesting [ˈɪntrɪstɪŋ] *adj* interesante

interface [ˈɪntəfeɪs] *n* interface *f*

interfere [ɪntəˈfɪə(r)] *vi* (a) *(meddle)* entrometerse (**in** en); **to i. with** *(hinder)* dificultar; *(spoil)* estropear; *(prevent)* impedir (b) *Rad & TV* interferir (**with** con)

interference [ɪntəˈfɪərəns] *n (meddling)* intromisión *f*; *(hindrance)* estorbo *m*; *Rad & TV* interferencia *f*

interim [ˈɪntərɪm] **1** *n Fml* **in the i.** en el ínterin
2 *adj* interino(a), provisional

interior [ɪnˈtɪərɪə(r)] **1** *adj* interior
2 *n* interior *m*; **i. design** diseño *m* de interiores

interlock [ɪntəˈlɒk] *vi* encajarse; *(fingers)* entrelazarse; *(cogs)* engranarse

interloper [ˈɪntələʊpə(r)] *n* intruso(a) *m,f*

interlude [ˈɪntəluːd] *n (break)* intervalo *m*; *Cin & Th* intermedio *m*; *Mus* interludio *m*

intermediary [ɪntəˈmiːdɪərɪ] *n* intermediario(a) *m,f*

intermediate [ɪntəˈmiːdɪɪt] *adj* intermedio(a)

interminable [ɪnˈtɜːmɪnəbəl] *adj* interminable

intermission [ɪntəˈmɪʃən] *n Cin & Th* intermedio *m*

intermittent [ɪntəˈmɪtənt] *adj* intermitente

intern 1 *vt* [ɪnˈtɜːn] internar
2 *n* [ˈɪntɜːn] *US Med* interno(a) *m,f*

internal [ɪnˈtɜːnəl] *adj* interior; *(dispute, injury)* interno(a); *US* **I. Revenue Service** ≃ Hacienda *f*

internally [ɪnˈtɜːnəlɪ] *adv* interiormente; **not to be taken i.** *(on medicine)* uso externo

international [ɪntəˈnæʃənəl] **1** *adj* internacional
2 *n Sport (player)* internacional *mf*; *(match)* partido *m* internacional

Internet [ˈɪntənet] *n Comput* **the I.** Internet; **it's on the I.** está en Internet; **I. access provider** proveedor *m* de acceso a Internet; **I. service provider** proveedor *m* de (acceso a) Internet

interplay [ˈɪntəpleɪ] *n* interacción *f*

interpret [ɪnˈtɜːprɪt] **1** *vt* interpretar
2 *vi* actuar de intérprete

interpretation [ɪntɜ:prɪˈteɪʃən] *n* interpretación *f*

interpreter [ɪnˈtɜ:prɪtə(r)] *n* intérprete *mf*

interrelated [ɪntərɪˈleɪtɪd] *adj* estrechamente relacionado(a)

interrogate [ɪnˈterəgeɪt] *vt* interrogar

interrogation [ɪnterəˈgeɪʃən] *n* interrogatorio *m*

interrogative [ɪntəˈrɒgətɪv] *Ling* **1** *adj* interrogativo(a)
 2 *n (word)* palabra interrogativa

interrupt [ɪntəˈrʌpt] *vt & vi* interrumpir

interruption [ɪntəˈrʌpʃən] *n* interrupción *f*

intersect [ɪntəˈsekt] **1** *vt* cruzar
 2 *vi* cruzarse

intersection [ɪntəˈsekʃən] *n* **(a)** *(crossroads)* cruce *m* **(b)** *(of two lines)* intersección *f*

intersperse [ɪntəˈspɜ:s] *vt* esparcir

intertwine [ɪntəˈtwaɪn] **1** *vt* entrelazar **(with** con**)**
 2 *vi* entrelazarse **(with** con**)**

interval [ˈɪntəvəl] *n* **(a)** *(of time, space)* intervalo *m*; **at intervals** *(time, space)* a intervalos; *(time)* de vez en cuando **(b)** *Br Cin & Th* intermedio *m*

intervene [ɪntəˈvi:n] *vi* **(a)** *(person)* intervenir **(in** en**) (b)** *(event)* sobrevenir **(c)** *(time)* transcurrir

intervention [ɪntəˈvenʃən] *n* intervención *f*

interview [ˈɪntəvju:] **1** *n* entrevista *f*; **to give an i.** conceder una entrevista
 2 *vt* entrevistar

interviewer [ˈɪntəvju:ə(r)] *n* entrevistador(a) *m,f*

intestine [ɪnˈtestɪn] *n (usu pl)* intestino *m*; **large/small i.** intestino grueso/delgado

intimacy [ˈɪntɪməsɪ] *n (closeness)* intimidad *f*; *Euph (sex)* relación íntima; **intimacies** intimidades *fpl*

intimate¹ [ˈɪntɪmɪt] *adj* íntimo(a); *(knowledge)* profundo(a)

intimate² [ˈɪntɪmeɪt] *vt Fml* dar a entender

intimidate [ɪnˈtɪmɪdeɪt] *vt* intimidar

intimidating [ɪnˈtɪmɪdeɪtɪŋ] *adj* atemorizante

into [ˈɪntu:, *unstressed* ˈɪntə] *prep* **(a)** *(motion)* en, a, con; **he fell i. the water** se cayó al agua; **I bumped i. a friend** me topé con un amigo; **to get i. a car** subir a un coche; **to go i. a house** entrar en una casa **(b)** *(state)* en, a; **he grew i. a man** se hizo un hombre; **to burst i. tears** echarse

a llorar; **to change pounds i. pesetas** cambiar libras en *or* por pesetas; **to translate sth i. French** traducir algo al francés **(c)** **to work i. the night** trabajar hasta muy avanzada la noche **(d)** **to divide sth i. three** dividir algo en tres **(e)** *Fam* **to be i. sth** ser aficionado(a) a algo

intolerable [ɪnˈtɒlərəbəl] *adj* intolerable

intolerant [ɪnˈtɒlərənt] *adj* intolerante

intonation [ɪntəˈneɪʃən] *n* entonación *f*

intoxicated [ɪnˈtɒksɪkeɪtɪd] *adj* borracho(a)

> 🖉 Note that the Spanish word **intoxicado** is a false friend and is never a translation for the English word **intoxicated**. In Spanish, **intoxicado** means "poisoned".

intoxicating [ɪnˈtɒksɪkeɪtɪŋ] *adj* embriagador(a); **i. liquor** bebida alcohólica

intoxication [ɪntɒksɪˈkeɪʃən] *n* embriaguez *f*

> 🖉 Note that the Spanish word **intoxicación** is a false friend and is never a translation for the English word **intoxication**. In Spanish, **intoxicación** means "poisoning".

intractable [ɪnˈtræktəbəl] *adj Fml (person)* intratable; *(problem)* insoluble

intranet [ˈɪntrənet] *n Comput* intranet *f*

intransigent [ɪnˈtrænsɪdʒənt] *adj Fml* intransigente, intolerante

intransitive [ɪnˈtrænsɪtɪv] *adj* intransitivo(a)

intravenous [ɪntrəˈvi:nəs] *adj* intravenoso(a)

in-tray [ˈɪntreɪ] *n* bandeja *f* de asuntos pendientes

intrepid [ɪnˈtrepɪd] *adj* intrépido(a), audaz

intricate [ˈɪntrɪkɪt] *adj* intrincado(a)

intrigue **1** *n* [ɪnˈtri:g, ˈɪntri:g] intriga *f*
 2 *vt* [ɪnˈtri:g] intrigar
 3 *vi* intrigar, conspirar

intriguing [ɪnˈtri:gɪŋ] *adj* intrigante

intrinsic [ɪnˈtrɪnsɪk] *adj Fml* intrínseco(a)

introduce [ɪntrəˈdju:s] *vt* **(a)** *(person, programme)* presentar **(to** a**) (b)** *(bring in)* introducir **(into** *or* **to** en**)**; *Com* lanzar **(into** *or* **to** a**)**; *(topic)* proponer

introduction [ɪntrəˈdʌkʃən] *n* **(a)** *(of person, programme)* presentación *f*; *(in book)* introducción *f* **(b)** *(bringing in)* introducción *f*; *Com (of product)* lanzamiento *m*

introductory [ɪntrəˈdʌktərɪ] *adj* introductorio(a); *(remarks)* preliminar; *Com* de lanzamiento

introspective [ɪntrə'spektɪv] *adj* introspectivo(a)

introvert ['ɪntrəvɜːt] *n* introvertido(a) *m,f*

intrude [ɪn'truːd] *vi* entrometerse (**into** *or* **on** en); *(disturb)* molestar

intruder [ɪn'truːdə(r)] *n* intruso(a) *m,f*

intrusion [ɪn'truːʒən] *n* incursión *f*

intuition [ɪntjʊ'ɪʃən] *n* intuición *f*

inundate ['ɪnʌndeɪt] *vt* inundar (**with** de)

invade [ɪn'veɪd] *vt* invadir

invader [ɪn'veɪdə(r)] *n* invasor(a) *m,f*

invalid[1] ['ɪnvəlɪd] *n (disabled person)* minusválido(a) *m,f*; *(sick person)* enfermo(a) *m,f*

invalid[2] [ɪn'vælɪd] *adj* inválido(a), nulo(a)

invalidate [ɪn'vælɪdeɪt] *vt* invalidar

invaluable [ɪn'væljʊəbəl] *adj* inestimable

invariable [ɪn'veərɪəbəl] *adj* invariable

invasion [ɪn'veɪʒən] *n* invasión *f*

invent [ɪn'vent] *vt* inventar

invention [ɪn'venʃən] *n* invento *m*; *(creativity)* inventiva *f*; *(lie)* mentira *f*

inventive [ɪn'ventɪv] *adj* inventivo(a)

inventor [ɪn'ventə(r)] *n* inventor(a) *m,f*

inventory ['ɪnvəntərɪ] *n* inventario *m*

invert [ɪn'vɜːt] *vt* invertir

invertebrate [ɪn'vɜːtɪbrɪt] **1** *adj* invertebrado(a)
2 *n* invertebrado *m*

inverted [ɪn'vɜːtɪd] *adj* (**in**) **i. commas** (entre) comillas *fpl*

invest [ɪn'vest] **1** *vt* invertir (**in** en); **to i. sb with sth** conferir algo a algn
2 *vi* invertir (**in** en)

investigate [ɪn'vestɪgeɪt] *vt (crime, subject)* investigar; *(cause, possibility)* estudiar

investigation [ɪnvestɪ'geɪʃən] *n (of crime)* investigación *f*; *(of cause)* examen *m*

investigator [ɪn'vestɪgeɪtə(r)] *n* investigador(a) *m,f*; **private i.** detective privado

investment [ɪn'vestmənt] *n* inversión *f*

investor [ɪn'vestə(r)] *n* inversor(a) *m,f*

inveterate [ɪn'vetərɪt] *adj* empedernido(a)

invidious [ɪn'vɪdɪəs] *adj (task)* ingrato(a); *(comparison)* injusto(a)

⚠ Note that the Spanish word **envidioso** is a false friend and is never a translation for the English word **invidious**. In Spanish, **envidioso** means "envious".

---

invigilator [ɪn'vɪdʒɪleɪtə(r)] *n Br* vigilante *mf*

invigorating [ɪn'vɪgəreɪtɪŋ] *adj* vigorizante

invincible [ɪn'vɪnsəbəl] *adj* invencible

invisible [ɪn'vɪzəbəl] *adj* invisible

invitation [ɪnvɪ'teɪʃən] *n* invitación *f*

invite [ɪn'vaɪt] *vt* (**a**) invitar (**to** a) (**b**) *(comments etc)* solicitar; *(criticism)* provocar; **to i. trouble** buscarse problemas

inviting [ɪn'vaɪtɪŋ] *adj (attractive)* atractivo(a); *(food)* apetitoso(a)

invoice ['ɪnvɔɪs] **1** *n* factura *f*
2 *vt* facturar

invoke [ɪn'vəʊk] *vt Fml* invocar

involuntary [ɪn'vɒləntərɪ] *adj* involuntario(a)

involve [ɪn'vɒlv] *vt* (**a**) *(concern)* implicar (**in** en); **the issues involved** las cuestiones en juego; **to be involved in an accident** sufrir un accidente (**b**) *(entail)* suponer, implicar; *(trouble, risk)* acarrear

involved [ɪn'vɒlvd] *adj (complicated)* complicado(a), *Fam (romantically attached)* enredado(a), liado(a)

involvement [ɪn'vɒlvmənt] *n (participation)* participación *f*; *(in crime)* implicación *f*

inward ['ɪnwəd] **1** *adj* interior
2 *adv* = inwards

inwardly ['ɪnwədlɪ] *adv* interiormente, por dentro

inwards ['ɪnwədz] *adv* hacia dentro

in-your-face ['ɪnjə'feɪs] *adj Fam (style)* descarado(a); *(movie, advert)* impactante, fuerte

iodine ['aɪədiːn] *n* yodo *m*

iota [aɪ'əʊtə] *n* pizca *f*, ápice *m*

IOU [aɪəʊ'juː] *n (abbr* **I owe you**) pagaré *m*

IQ [aɪ'kjuː] *n (abbr* **intelligence quotient**) CI *m*

IRA [aɪɑː'reɪ] *n (abbr* **Irish Republican Army**) IRA *m*

Iran [ɪ'rɑːn] *n* Irán *m*

Iranian [ɪ'reɪnɪən] *adj & n* iraní *(mf)*

Iraq [ɪ'rɑːk] *n* Irak *m*

Iraqi [ɪ'rɑːkɪ] *adj & n* iraquí *(mf)*

irascible [ɪ'ræsɪbəl] *adj Fml* irascible

irate [aɪ'reɪt] *adj* airado(a), furioso(a)

Ireland ['aɪələnd] *n* Irlanda; **Republic of I.** República de Irlanda

iris ['aɪərɪs] *n* (**a**) *Anat* iris *m inv* (**b**) *Bot* lirio *m*

Irish ['aɪrɪʃ] **1** *adj* irlandés(esa); **I. coffee** café *m* irlandés; **I. Sea** Mar *m* de Irlanda
2 *n* (**a**) *(language)* irlandés *m* (**b**) *pl* **the I.** los irlandeses

Irishman ['aɪrɪʃmən] *n* irlandés *m*

Irishwoman ['aɪrɪʃwʊmən] *n* irlandesa *f*

irksome ['ɜːksəm] *adj* fastidioso(a)

iron ['aɪən] **1** *n* (**a**) hierro *m*; **the i. and steel industry** la industria siderúrgica; **I. Curtain** Telón *m* de Acero; **i. ore** mineral *m* de hierro (**b**) *(for clothes)* plancha *f* (**c**) *(for golf)* hierro *m* (**d**) **irons** *(chains)* grillos *mpl*
2 *vt (clothes)* planchar
▸ **iron out** *vt sep* (**a**) *(crease)* planchar (**b**) *Fam Fig (problem)* resolver

ironic(al) [aɪ'rɒnɪk(əl)] *adj* irónico(a)

ironing ['aɪənɪŋ] *n* (**a**) **to do the i.** planchar; **i. board** mesa *f* de la plancha (**b**) *(clothes to be ironed)* ropa *f* para planchar; *(clothes ironed)* ropa planchada

ironmonger ['aɪənmʌŋgə(r)] *n Br* ferretero(a) *m,f*; **i.'s (shop)** ferretería *f*

irony ['aɪrənɪ] *n* ironía *f*

irrational [ɪ'ræʃənəl] *adj* irracional

irreconcilable [ɪrekən'saɪləbəl] *adj* irreconciliable

irrefutable [ɪrɪ'fjuːtəbəl] *adj Fml* irrefutable

irregular [ɪ'regjʊlə(r)] *adj* (**a**) irregular; *(abnormal)* anormal (**b**) *(uneven)* desigual

irrelevant [ɪ'reləvənt] *adj* no pertinente

irreparable [ɪ'repərəbəl] *adj* irreparable

irreplaceable [ɪrɪ'pleɪsəbəl] *adj* irremplazable

irrepressible [ɪrɪ'presəbəl] *adj* incontenible

irresistible [ɪrɪ'zɪstəbəl] *adj* irresistible

irresolute [ɪ'rezəluːt] *adj Fml* indeciso(a)

irrespective [ɪrɪ'spektɪv] *adj* **i. of** sin tener en cuenta

irresponsible [ɪrɪ'spɒnsəbəl] *adj* irresponsable

irreverent [ɪ'revərənt] *adj* irreverente

irrevocable [ɪ'revəkəbəl] *adj* irrevocable

irrigate ['ɪrɪgeɪt] *vt* regar

irrigation [ɪrɪ'geɪʃən] *n* riego *m*; **i. channel** acequia *f*; **i. system** sistema *m* de regadío

irritable ['ɪrɪtəbəl] *adj* irritable

irritate ['ɪrɪteɪt] *vt (annoy)* fastidiar; *Med* irritar

irritating ['ɪrɪteɪtɪŋ] *adj* irritante

irritation [ɪrɪ'teɪʃən] *n* (**a**) *(annoyance)* fastidio *m*; *(ill humour)* mal humor *m* (**b**) *Med* irritación *f*

is [ɪz] *3rd person sing pres of* **be**

Islam ['ɪzlɑːm] *n* Islam *m*

Islamic [ɪz'læmɪk] *adj* islámico(a)

island ['aɪlənd] *n* isla *f*; **(traffic) i.** isleta *f*

islander ['aɪləndə(r)] *n* isleño(a) *m,f*

isle [aɪl] *n* isla *f*

isn't ['ɪzənt] = **is not**

isolate ['aɪsəleɪt] *vt* aislar (**from** de)

isolated ['aɪsəleɪtɪd] *adj* aislado(a)

isolation [aɪsə'leɪʃən] *n* aislamiento *m*

ISP [aɪes'piː] *n Comput (abbr* **Internet Service Provider)** PSI *m*

Israel ['ɪzreɪəl] *n* Israel

Israeli [ɪz'reɪlɪ] *adj & n* israelí *(mf)*

issue ['ɪʃuː] **1** *n* (**a**) *(matter)* cuestión *f*; **to take i. with sb (over sth)** manifestar su desacuerdo con algn (en algo) (**b**) *(of banknotes etc)* emisión *f*; *(of passport)* expedición *f* (**c**) *(of journal etc)* ejemplar *m* (**d**) *(of supplies)* reparto *m* (**e**) *Fml (outcome)* resultado *m* (**f**) *Jur (offspring)* descendencia *f*
2 *vt* (**a**) *(book)* publicar; *(banknotes etc)* emitir; *(passport)* expedir (**b**) *(supplies)* repartir (**c**) *(order, instructions)* dar; *(warrant)* dictar
3 *vi Fml (blood)* brotar (**from** de); *(smoke)* salir (**from** de)

isthmus ['ɪsməs] *n* istmo *m*

it [ɪt] *pers pron* (**a**) *(subject)* él/ella/ello *(usually omitted in Spanish, except for contrast)*; **it's here** está aquí
(**b**) *(direct object)* lo/la; **I don't believe it** no me lo creo; **I liked the house and bought it** me gustó la casa y la compré
(**c**) *(indirect object)* le; **give it a kick** dale una patada
(**d**) *(after prep)* él/ella/ello; **I saw the beach and ran towards it** vi la playa y fui corriendo hacia ella; **we'll talk about it later** ya hablaremos de ello
(**e**) *(abstract)* ello; **let's get down to it!** ¡vamos a ello!
(**f**) *(impersonal)* **it's late** es tarde; **it's me** soy yo; **it's raining** está lloviendo; **it's said that ...** se dice que ...; **it's 2 miles to town** hay 2 millas de aquí al pueblo; **that's it!** *(agreeing)* ¡precisamente!; *(finishing)* ¡se acabó!; **this is it!** ¡ha llegado la hora!; **who is it?** ¿quién es?

Italian [ɪ'tæljən] **1** *adj* italiano(a)
2 *n* (**a**) *(person)* italiano(a) *m,f* (**b**) *(language)* italiano *m*

italic [ɪ'tælɪk] *n* cursiva *f*

Italy ['ɪtəlɪ] *n* Italia

itch [ɪtʃ] **1** *n* picor *m*; *Fig* **an i. to travel** unas ganas locas de viajar
2 *vi* (**a**) *(skin)* picar (**b**) *Fig* anhelar; *Fam* **to be itching to do sth** tener muchas ganas de hacer algo

itchy ['ɪtʃɪ] *adj* **(itchier, itchiest)** que pica

item ['aɪtəm] *n* (**a**) *(in list)* artículo *m*; *(in collection)* pieza *f*; **i. of clothing** prenda *f* de vestir (**b**) *(on agenda)* asunto *m*; *(in show)* número *m*; **news i.** noticia *f*

itemize ['aɪtəmaɪz] *vt* detallar

itinerant [ɪ'tɪnərənt] *adj Fml* itinerante
itinerary [aɪ'tɪnərərɪ] *n* itinerario *m*
it'll ['ɪtəl] = **it will**
its [ɪts] *poss adj (one thing)* su; *(more than one)* sus
itself [ɪt'self] *pers pron* (**a**) *(reflexive)* se; **the cat scratched i.** el gato se arañó (**b**) *(emphatic)* él mismo/ella misma/ello mismo; *(after prep)* sí (mismo(a)); **in i.** en sí

ITV [aɪtiː'viː] *n Br (abbr* **Independent Television***)* = canal privado de televisión británico
IUD [aɪjuː'diː] *n (abbr* **intrauterine (contraceptive) device***)* DIU *m*
IVF [aɪviː'ef] *n Med (abbr* **in vitro fertilization***)* fertilización *f* in vitro
ivory ['aɪvərɪ] *n* marfil *m*
ivy ['aɪvɪ] *n* hiedra *f*

J

J, j [dʒeɪ] n (the letter) J, j f
jab [dʒæb] **1** n pinchazo m; (poke) golpe
seco
   2 vt pinchar; (with fist) dar un puñetazo
a
jabber ['dʒæbə(r)] vi Fam (chatter) charlotear; (speak quickly) hablar atropelladamente
jack [dʒæk] n (**a**) Aut gato m (**b**) Cards
sota f (**c**) (bowls) boliche m
▸**jack in** vt sep Br Fam dejar
▸**jack up** vt sep Aut levantar (con el gato);
Fig (prices) aumentar
jackal ['dʒækɔːl] n chacal m
jackdaw ['dʒækdɔː] n Orn grajilla f
jacket ['dʒækɪt] n (**a**) chaqueta f, (of suit)
americana f, (bomber jacket) cazadora f
(**b**) (of book) sobrecubierta f, US (of record) funda f (**c**) **j. potatoes** patatas fpl or
Am papas fpl al horno
jack-knife ['dʒæknaɪf] **1** n navaja f
   2 vi colear
jack-of-all-trades [dʒækəv'ɔːltreɪdz] n
persona f mañosa or de muchos oficios
jackpot ['dʒækpɒt] n (premio m) gordo m
Jacuzzi® [dʒə'kuːzɪ] n jacuzzi® m
jade [dʒeɪd] n jade m
jaded ['dʒeɪdɪd] adj (tired) agotado(a);
(palate) hastiado(a)
jagged ['dʒægɪd] adj dentado(a)
jaguar ['dʒægjʊə(r)] n jaguar m
jail [dʒeɪl] **1** n cárcel f, prisión f
   2 vt encarcelar
jailbreak ['dʒeɪlbreɪk] n fuga f, evasión f
jailer ['dʒeɪlə(r)] n carcelero(a) m,f
jam¹ [dʒæm] n Culin mermelada f
jam² [dʒæm] **1** n (**a**) (blockage) atasco m;
Fam (fix) apuro m (**b**) Mus improvisación f
   2 vt (**a**) (cram) meter a la fuerza (**b**)
(block) atascar; Rad interferir
   3 vi (door) atrancarse; (brakes) agarrotarse
Jamaica [dʒə'meɪkə] n Jamaica
jam-packed [dʒæm'pækt] adj Fam (with
people) atestado(a); (with things) atibo-
rrado(a)
jangle ['dʒæŋgəl] vi tintinear
janitor ['dʒænɪtə(r)] n portero m, conserje m

January ['dʒænjʊərɪ] n enero m
Japan [dʒə'pæn] n (el) Japón
Japanese [dʒæpə'niːz] **1** adj japonés(e-
sa)
   2 n (person) japonés(esa) m,f, (language) japonés m
jar¹ [dʒɑː(r)] n (glass) tarro m; (earthenware) tinaja f, (jug) jarra f; Br Fam **to have
a j.** tomar una copa
jar² [dʒɑː(r)] vi (sounds) chirriar; (appearance) chocar; (colours) desentonar; Fig
to j. on one's nerves ponerle a uno los
nervios de punta
jargon ['dʒɑːgən] n jerga f, argot m
jasmin(e) ['dʒæzmɪn] n jazmín m
jaundice ['dʒɔːndɪs] n ictericia f
jaundiced ['dʒɔːndɪst] adj Med ictéri-
co(a); Fig (bitter) amargado(a)
jaunt [dʒɔːnt] n (walk) paseo m; (trip)
excursión f
jaunty ['dʒɔːntɪ] adj (jauntier, jauntiest)
(sprightly) garboso(a); (lively) vivaz
javelin ['dʒævəlɪn] n jabalina f
jaw [dʒɔː] **1** n mandíbula f
   2 vi Fam estar de palique
jay [dʒeɪ] n Orn arrendajo m (común)
jaywalker ['dʒeɪwɔːkə(r)] n peatón m
imprudente
jazz [dʒæz] n jazz m
▸**jazz up** vt sep alegrar; (premises) arreglar
jazzy ['dʒæzɪ] adj (jazzier, jazziest) Fam
(showy) llamativo(a); (brightly coloured)
de colores chillones
jealous ['dʒeləs] adj celoso(a); (envious)
envidioso(a); **to be j. of ...** tener celos de
...
jealousy ['dʒeləsɪ] n celos mpl; (envy)
envidia f
jeans [dʒiːnz] npl vaqueros mpl, tejanos
mpl
Jeep® [dʒiːp] n jeep m, todo terreno m inv
jeer [dʒɪə(r)] **1** n (boo) abucheo m;
(mocking) mofa f
   2 vi (boo) abuchear; (mock) burlarse
jeering ['dʒɪərɪŋ] adj burlón(ona)
Jehovah [dʒɪ'həʊvə] n **J.'s Witness** testigo
mf de Jehová
Jell-O®, jello ['dʒeləʊ] n US gelatina f

jelly ['dʒelɪ] *n* gelatina *f*

jellyfish ['dʒelɪfɪʃ] *n* medusa *f*

jeopardize ['dʒepədaɪz] *vt* poner en peligro; *(agreement etc)* comprometer

jeopardy ['dʒepədɪ] *n* riesgo *m*, peligro *m*

jerk [dʒɜːk] **1** *n* (**a**) *(jolt)* sacudida *f*, *(pull)* tirón *m* (**b**) *Pej (idiot)* imbécil *mf*
2 *vt (shake)* sacudir; *(pull)* dar un tirón a
3 *vi (move suddenly)* dar una sacudida; **the car jerked forward** el coche avanzaba a tirones

jerkin ['dʒɜːkɪn] *n* chaleco *m*

jersey ['dʒɜːzɪ] *n* jersey *m*, suéter *m*, pulóver *m*, *Andes* chompa *f*, *Urug* buzo *m*

jest [dʒest] **1** *n* broma *f*
2 *vi* bromear

Jesuit ['dʒezjʊɪt] *adj & n* jesuita *(m)*

Jesus ['dʒiːzəs] *n* Jesús *m*; **J. Christ** Jesucristo *m*

jet¹ [dʒet] **1** *n* (**a**) *(stream of water)* chorro *m* (**b**) *(spout)* surtidor *m* (**c**) *Av* reactor *m*; **j. engine** reactor; **j. lag** = cansancio debido al desfase horario; **j. ski** moto náutica *or* acuática
2 *vi Fam* volar

jet² [dʒet] *n* **j. black** negro(a) como el azabache

jet-set ['dʒetset] *n* **the j.** la alta sociedad, la jet

jettison ['dʒetɪsən] *vt* echar al mar; *Fig* deshacerse de; *(project etc)* abandonar

jetty ['dʒetɪ] *n* muelle *m*, malecón *m*

Jew [dʒuː] *n* judío(a) *m,f*

jewel ['dʒuːəl] *n* joya *f*; *(stone)* piedra preciosa; *(in watch)* rubí *m*; *Fig (person)* joya

jeweller, jeweler ['dʒuːələ(r)] *n* joyero(a) *m,f*; **j.'s (shop)** joyería *f*

jewellery, jewelry ['dʒuːəlrɪ] *n* joyas *fpl*, alhajas *fpl*

Jewess ['dʒuːɪs] *n* judía *f*

Jewish ['dʒuːɪʃ] *adj* judío(a)

jibe [dʒaɪb] *n & vi* = **gibe**

jiffy ['dʒɪfɪ] *n Fam* momento *m*; **in a j.** en un santiamén; **just a j.!** ¡un momento!

jig [dʒɪg] *n Mus* giga *f*

jigsaw ['dʒɪgsɔː] *n (puzzle)* rompecabezas *m inv*

jilt [dʒɪlt] *vt Fam* dejar plantado(a)

jingle ['dʒɪŋgəl] **1** *n Rad & TV* = canción que acompaña un anuncio
2 *vi* tintinear

jingoistic [dʒɪŋgəʊ'ɪstɪk] *adj* patriotero(a)

jinx [dʒɪŋks] **1** *n (person)* gafe *mf*
2 *vt* gafar

jitters ['dʒɪtəz] *npl Fam* **to get the j.** tener canguelo

jive [dʒaɪv] **1** *n* swing *m*
2 *vi* bailar el swing

job [dʒɒb] *n* (**a**) trabajo *m*; *(task)* tarea *f*; **to give sth up as a bad j.** darse por vencido(a); *Fam* **just the j.!** ¡me viene de perlas! (**b**) *(occupation)* (puesto *m* de) trabajo *m*, empleo *m*; *(trade)* oficio *m*; *Br Fam* **jobs for the boys** enchufismo *m*; **US j. office** oficina *f* de empleo; **j. hunting** búsqueda *f* de empleo; **j. sharing** trabajo compartido a tiempo parcial (**c**) *Fam* **we had a j. to ...** nos costó (trabajo) ... (**d**) *(duty)* deber *m* (**e**) *Fam* **it's a good j. that ...** menos mal que ...

Jobcentre ['dʒɒbsentə(r)] *n Br* oficina *f* de empleo

jobless ['dʒɒblɪs] *adj* parado(a)

jockey ['dʒɒkɪ] **1** *n* jinete *m*, jockey *m*
2 *vi* **to j. for position** luchar para conseguir una posición aventajada

jocular ['dʒɒkjʊlə(r)] *adj* jocoso(a)

jog [dʒɒg] **1** *n* trote *m*
2 *vt* empujar; *Fig (memory)* refrescar
3 *vi Sport* hacer footing; *Fig* **to j. along** *(progress slowly)* avanzar poco a poco; *(manage)* ir tirando

jogging ['dʒɒgɪŋ] *n* footing *m*

john [dʒɒn] *n US Fam* **the j.** *(lavatory)* el váter

join [dʒɔɪn] **1** *vt* (**a**) juntar; **to j. forces with sb** unir fuerzas con algn (**b**) *(road)* empalmar con; *(river)* desembocar en (**c**) *(meet)* reunirse con (**d**) *(group)* unirse a; *(institution)* entrar; *(army)* alistarse a (**e**) *(party)* afiliarse a; *(club)* hacerse socio(a) de
2 *vi* (**a**) unirse (**b**) *(roads)* empalmar; *(rivers)* confluir (**c**) *(become member of political party)* afiliarse; *(become member of club)* hacerse socio(a)
3 *n* juntura *f*
▶ **join in** *vi* participar, tomar parte; *(debate)* intervenir
2 *vt insep* participar en, tomar parte en
▶ **join up** *vt sep* juntar
2 *vi (of roads)* unirse; *Mil* alistarse

joiner ['dʒɔɪnə(r)] *n Br* carpintero(a) *m,f*

joinery ['dʒɔɪnərɪ] *n* carpintería *f*

joint [dʒɔɪnt] **1** *n* (**a**) juntura *f*, unión *f*; *Tech & Anat* articulación *f*; **out of j.** dislocado(a) (**b**) *Culin* = corte de carne para asar; *(once roasted)* asado *m* (**c**) *Fam (nightclub etc)* garito *m* (**d**) *Fam (drug)* porro *m*
2 *adj* colectivo(a); **j. (bank) account** cuenta conjunta; **j. venture** empresa conjunta

jointly ['dʒɔɪntlɪ] *adv* conjuntamente, en común

joist [dʒɔɪst] *n* vigueta *f*

joke [dʒəʊk] **1** *n* (**a**) chiste *m*; (*prank*) broma *f*; **to play a j. on sb** gastarle una broma a algn; **to tell a j.** contar un chiste (**b**) *Fam (person)* hazmerreír *m*, payaso(a) *m,f*; **to be a j.** (*of thing*) ser de chiste
2 *vi* estar de broma; **you must be joking!** ¡no hablarás en serio!

joker ['dʒəʊkə(r)] *n* (**a**) bromista *mf* (**b**) *Cards* comodín *m*

jolly ['dʒɒlɪ] **1** *adj* (**jollier, jolliest**) alegre
2 *adv Fam (very)* muy; **she played j. well** jugó muy bien

jolt [dʒəʊlt] **1** *n* (**a**) sacudida *f*; (*pull*) tirón *m* (**b**) *Fig (fright)* susto *m*
2 *vi* moverse a sacudidas
3 *vt* sacudir

Jordan ['dʒɔːdən] *n* (**a**) (*river*) Jordán *m* (**b**) (*country*) Jordania

joss-stick ['dʒɒsstɪk] *n* varita *f* de incienso

jostle ['dʒɒsəl] **1** *vi* dar empujones
2 *vt* dar empujones a

jot [dʒɒt] *n* jota *f*, pizca *f*; **not a j.** ni jota
▸ **jot down** *vt sep* apuntar

jotter ['dʒɒtə(r)] *n Br* bloc *m*

journal ['dʒɜːnəl] *n* (**a**) revista *f* (**b**) (*diary*) diario *m* (**c**) (*newspaper*) periódico *m*

> 🖉 Note that the Spanish word **jornal** is a false friend and is never a translation for the English word **journal**. In Spanish, **jornal** means "day's wage".

journalism ['dʒɜːnəlɪzəm] *n* periodismo *m*

journalist ['dʒɜːnəlɪst] *n* periodista *mf*

journey ['dʒɜːnɪ] **1** *n* viaje *m*; (*distance*) trayecto *m*
2 *vi Fml* viajar

jovial ['dʒəʊvɪəl] *adj* jovial

jowl [dʒaʊl] *n* quijada *f*

joy [dʒɔɪ] *n* alegría *f*, (*pleasure*) placer *m*

joyful ['dʒɔɪfʊl] *adj* alegre, contento(a)

joyride ['dʒɔɪəs] *adj Literary* alegre

joyride ['dʒɔɪraɪd] *n Fam* = paseo en un coche robado

joystick ['dʒɔɪstɪk] *n Av* palanca *f* de mando; (*of video game*) joystick *m*

JP [dʒeɪ'piː] *n Br Law* (*abbr* **Justice of the Peace**) juez *mf* de paz

Jr (*abbr* **Junior**) **Neil Smith, Jr** Neil Smith, hijo

jubilant ['dʒuːbɪlənt] *adj* jubiloso(a)

jubilation [dʒuːbɪ'leɪʃən] *n* júbilo *m*

jubilee ['dʒuːbɪliː] *n* festejos *mpl*; **golden j.** quincuagésimo aniversario

judge [dʒʌdʒ] **1** *n* juez *mf*, jueza *f*; (*in competition*) jurado *m*
2 *vt* (**a**) *Jur* juzgar (**b**) (*estimate*) considerar (**c**) (*competition*) actuar de juez de (**d**) (*assess*) juzgar
3 *vi* juzgar; **judging from what you say** a juzgar por lo que dices

judg(e)ment ['dʒʌdʒmənt] *n* (**a**) *Jur* sentencia *f*, fallo *m*; **to pass j.** dictar sentencia (**b**) (*opinion*) juicio *m*; **to pass j. (on)** opinar (sobre); **to reserve j. (on)** no opinar (sobre) (**c**) (*ability*) buen juicio *m* (**d**) (*trial*) juicio *m*

judicial [dʒuː'dɪʃəl] *adj* judicial

judiciary [dʒuː'dɪʃərɪ] *n* magistratura *f*

judicious [dʒuː'dɪʃəs] *adj Fml* juicioso(a)

judo ['dʒuːdəʊ] *n* judo *m*

jug [dʒʌg] *n Br* jarra *f*; **milk j.** jarra de leche

juggernaut ['dʒʌgənɔːt] *n Br* camión pesado

juggle ['dʒʌgəl] *vi* (*perform*) hacer juegos malabares (**with** con); *Fig (responsibilities)* ajustar

juggler ['dʒʌglə(r)] *n* malabarista *mf*

juice [dʒuːs] *n* jugo *m*; (*of citrus fruits*) zumo *m*

juicy ['dʒuːsɪ] *adj* (**juicier, juiciest**) (**a**) jugoso(a) (**b**) *Fam Fig* picante

jukebox ['dʒuːkbɒks] *n* rocola *f*

July [dʒuː'laɪ, dʒə'laɪ] *n* julio *m*

jumble ['dʒʌmbəl] **1** *n* revoltijo *m*; **j. sale** mercadillo *m* de caridad
2 *vt* revolver

jumbo ['dʒʌmbəʊ] *n* **j. (jet)** jumbo *m*

jump [dʒʌmp] **1** *n* salto *m*; (*sudden increase*) subida repentina; **j. leads** cables *mpl* de emergencia; **j. suit** mono *m*
2 *vi* (**a**) saltar, dar un salto; *Fig* **to j. to conclusions** sacar conclusiones precipitadas (**b**) *Fig (start)* sobresaltarse (**c**) (*increase*) aumentar de golpe
3 *vt* saltar; *Fam Fig* **to j. the gun** precipitarse; **to j. the lights** saltarse el semáforo; *Br* **to j. the queue** colarse; *US* **to j. rope** saltar a la comba
▸ **jump at** *vt insep* aceptar sin pensarlo

jumper ['dʒʌmpə(r)] *n* (**a**) *Br (sweater)* jersey *m*, suéter *m*, pulóver *m*, *Andes* chompa *f*, *Urug* buzo *m* (**b**) *US (dress)* pichi *m*, falda *f* con peto (**c**) *US Aut* **j. cables** cables *mpl* de emergencia

jumpy ['dʒʌmpɪ] *adj* (**jumpier, jumpiest**) *Fam* nervioso(a)

junction ['dʒʌŋkʃən] *n* (*of roads*) cruce *m*; *Rail & Elec* empalme *m*

juncture ['dʒʌŋktʃə(r)] *n Fml* **at this j.** en esta coyuntura

June [dʒuːn] *n* junio *m*

jungle ['dʒʌŋgəl] *n* jungla *f*, selva *f*; *Fig* laberinto *m*; **the concrete j.** la jungla de asfalto

junior ['dʒuːnjə(r)] **1** *adj* (a) *(son of)* hijo; **David Hughes J.** David Hughes hijo (b) *US* **j. high (school)** *(between 11 and 15)* escuela secundaria; *Br* **j. school** *(between 7 and 11)* escuela primaria; **j. team** equipo *m* juvenil (c) *(lower in rank)* subalterno(a)

2 *n* (a) *(person of lower rank)* subalterno(a) *m,f* (b) *(younger person)* menor *mf*

junk [dʒʌŋk] *n* (a) *Fam* trastos *mpl*; **j. food** comida basura; **j. mail** propaganda *f* (por correo); **j. shop** tienda *f* de segunda mano (b) *(boat)* junco *m*

junkie ['dʒʌŋkɪ] *n Fam* yonqui *mf*

junkman ['dʒʌŋkmæn] *n US* trapero(a) *m,f*

junta ['dʒʌntə, *US* 'hʊntə] *n* junta *f* militar

jurisdiction [dʒʊərɪs'dɪkʃən] *n Fml* jurisdicción *f*

juror ['dʒʊərə(r)] *n* jurado(a) *m,f*

jury ['dʒʊərɪ] *n* jurado *m*

just [dʒʌst] **1** *adj (fair)* justo(a); *Fml (well-founded)* justificado(a)

2 *adv* (a) **he had j. arrived** acababa de llegar

(b) *(at this very moment)* ahora mismo, en este momento; **he was j. leaving when Rosa arrived** estaba a punto de salir cuando llegó Rosa; **I'm j. coming!** ¡ya voy!; **j. as ... cuando ...**, justo al ...; **j. as I** thought me lo figuraba

(c) *(only)* solamente; **j. in case** por si acaso; **j. a minute!** ¡un momento!

(d) *(barely)* por poco; **I only j. caught the bus** cogí el autobús por los pelos; **j. about** casi; **j. enough** justo lo suficiente

(e) *(emphatic)* **it's j. fantastic!** ¡es sencillamente fantástico!; **you'll j. have to wait** tendrás que esperar

(f) *(exactly)* exactamente, justo; **that's j. it!** ¡precisamente!

(g) *(equally)* **j. as fast as** tan rápido como

justice ['dʒʌstɪs] *n* (a) justicia *f*; **he was brought to j.** lo llevaron ante los tribunales; **you didn't do yourself j.** no diste lo mejor de ti (b) *US (judge)* juez *mf*; *Br* **J. of the Peace** juez de paz

justifiable ['dʒʌstɪfaɪəbəl] *adj* justificable

justification [dʒʌstɪfɪ'keɪʃən] *n* justificación *f*

justified ['dʒʌstɪfaɪd] *adj* **to be j. in doing sth** tener razón en hacer algo

justify ['dʒʌstɪfaɪ] *vt* justificar

jut [dʒʌt] *vi* sobresalir; **to j. out over** proyectarse sobre

juvenile ['dʒuːvənaɪl] **1** *adj* (a) juvenil; **j. court** tribunal *m* de menores; **j. delinquent** delincuente *mf* juvenil (b) *(immature)* infantil

2 *n* menor *mf*, joven *mf*

juxtapose [dʒʌkstə'pəʊz] *vt* yuxtaponer

K, k [keɪ] n (the letter) K, k f

kaleidoscope [kə'laɪdəskəʊp] n caleidoscopio m

Kampuchea [kæmpʊ'tʃɪə] n Kampuchea

kangaroo [kæŋgə'ruː] n canguro m

karat ['kærət] n US quilate m

karate [kə'rɑːtɪ] n kárate m

kebab [kə'bæb] n Culin pincho moruno, brocheta f

keel [kiːl] n quilla f; Fig to be on an even k. estar en calma
▸ **keel over** vi Fam desmayarse

keen [kiːn] adj (a) (eager) entusiasta (b) (intense) profundo(a) (c) (mind, senses) agudo(a); (look) penetrante; (blade) afilado(a); (competition) fuerte

keep [kiːp] 1 n (a) to earn one's k. ganarse el pan
(b) (tower) torreón m
(c) Fam for keeps para siempre
2 vt (pt & pp kept) (a) guardar; to k. one's room tidy mantener su cuarto limpio; to k. sb informed tener a algn al corriente; to k. sth in mind tener algo en cuenta
(b) (not give back) quedarse con
(c) (detain) detener; to k. sb waiting hacer esperar a algn
(d) (maintain) mantener; (animals) criar
(e) (the law) observar; (a promise) cumplir
(f) (a secret) guardar
(g) (diary, accounts) llevar
(h) (prevent) to k. sb from doing sth impedir a algn hacer algo
(i) (own, manage) tener; (shop, hotel) llevar
(j) (stock) tener
3 vi (a) (remain) seguir; k. still! ¡estáte quieto(a)!; to k. fit mantenerse en forma; to k. going seguir adelante; to k. in touch no perder el contacto
(b) (do frequently) no dejar de; she keeps forgetting her keys siempre se olvida las llaves
(c) (food) conservarse
▸ **keep at** vt insep perseverar en
▸ **keep away** 1 vt sep mantener a distancia

2 vi mantenerse a distancia
▸ **keep back** vt sep (information) ocultar, callar; (money etc) retener
▸ **keep down** vt sep to k. prices down mantener los precios bajos
▸ **keep off** vt insep k. off the grass (sign) prohibido pisar la hierba
▸ **keep on** 1 vt sep (a) (clothes etc) no quitarse; to k. an eye on sth/sb vigilar algo/a algn (b) (continue to employ) no despedir a
2 vi (continue to do) seguir
▸ **keep out** 1 vt sep no dejar pasar
2 vi no entrar; k. out! (sign) ¡prohibida la entrada!
▸ **keep to** vt insep (subject) limitarse a; to k. to one's room quedarse en el cuarto; k. to the point! ¡cíñete a la cuestión!; to k. to the left circular por la izquierda
▸ **keep up** vt sep (a) mantener; to k. up appearances guardar las apariencias (b) k. it up! ¡sigue así! (c) (prevent from sleeping) mantener despierto(a)
▸ **keep up with** vt insep to k. up with the times estar al día

keeper ['kiːpə(r)] n (in zoo) guarda mf; (in record office) archivero(a) m,f; (in museum) conservador(a) m,f

keeping ['kiːpɪŋ] n (a) (care) cuidado m (b) in k. with en armonía con; out of k. with en desacuerdo con

keepsake ['kiːpseɪk] n recuerdo m

keg [keg] n barril m

kennel ['kenəl] n caseta f para perros; kennels hotel m de perros

Kenya ['kenjə, 'kiːnjə] n Kenia

Kenyan ['kenjən, 'kiːnjən] adj & n keniano(a) (m,f)

kept [kept] pt & pp of keep

kerb [kɜːb] n Br bordillo m

kernel ['kɜːnəl] n (of fruit, nut) pepita f; (of wheat) grano m; Fig meollo m

kerosene, kerosine ['kerəsiːn] n US queroseno m

ketchup ['ketʃəp] n ketchup m, salsa f de tomate

kettle ['ketəl] n hervidor m; that's a different k. of fish eso es harina de otro costal

key [kiː] **1** n **(a)** *(for lock)* llave f; **k. ring** llavero m **(b)** *(to code)* clave f **(c)** *(of piano, typewriter)* tecla f **(d)** *Mus* tono m

2 adj clave; *Br Educ* **k. stage** etapa educativa

3 vt *Comput* teclear

▶ **key in** vt sep *Comput* introducir

keyboard ['kiːbɔːd] n teclado m

keyed up [kiːd'ʌp] adj nervioso(a)

keyhole ['kiːhəʊl] n ojo m de la cerradura

keynote ['kiːnəʊt] n *Mus* tónica f; *Fig* nota f dominante

kg *(abbr* **kilogram(s))** kg

khaki ['kɑːkɪ] adj & n caqui *(m)*

kick [kɪk] **1** n **(a)** *(from person)* patada f, puntapié m; *(from horse etc)* coz f; *(from gun)* culatazo m **(b)** *Fam* **I get a k. out of it** eso me encanta; **to do sth for kicks** hacer algo por gusto

2 vi *(animal)* cocear; *(person)* dar patadas; *(gun)* dar un culatazo

3 vt dar un puntapié a

▶ **kick off** vi *Fam* empezar; *Ftb* sacar

▶ **kick out** vt sep echar a patadas

▶ **kick up** vt insep *Fam (fuss)* armar

kick-off ['kɪkɒf] n *Ftb* saque m inicial

kid¹ [kɪd] n **(a)** *Zool* cabrito m; *Fig* **to handle sb with k. gloves** tratar a algn con guante blanco **(b)** *Fam* niño(a) m,f, chiquillo(a) m,f; **the kids** los críos

kid² [kɪd] **1** vi *Fam* tomar el pelo; **no kidding!** ¡va en serio!

2 vt tomar el pelo a; **to k. oneself** *(fool)* hacerse ilusiones

kidnap ['kɪdnæp] vt secuestrar

kidnapper ['kɪdnæpə(r)] n secuestrador(a) m,f

kidnapping ['kɪdnæpɪŋ] n secuestro m

kidney ['kɪdnɪ] n riñón m

kill [kɪl] vt matar; *Fig* **to k. time** pasar el rato; *Fam* **my feet are killing me!** ¡cómo me duelen los pies!

▶ **kill off** vt sep exterminar

killer ['kɪlə(r)] n asesino(a) m,f; **k. whale** orca f

killing ['kɪlɪŋ] n asesinato m; *Fig* **to make a k.** forrarse de dinero

killjoy ['kɪldʒɔɪ] n aguafiestas mf inv

kiln [kɪln] n horno m

kilo ['kiːləʊ] n kilo m

kilogram(me) ['kɪləʊgræm] n kilogramo m

kilometre, *US* **kilometer** [kɪ'lɒmɪtə(r)] n kilómetro m

kilowatt ['kɪləʊwɒt] n kilovatio m

kilt [kɪlt] n falda escocesa, kilt m

kin [kɪn] n familiares mpl, parientes mpl

kind¹ [kaɪnd] **1** n tipo m, clase f; **they are two of a k.** son tal para cual; **in k.** *(payment)* en especie; *(treatment)* con la misma moneda

2 adv *Fam* **k. of** en cierta manera

kind² ['kaɪnd] adj amable, simpático(a); *Fml* **would you be so k. as to ...?** ¿me haría usted el favor de ...?

kindergarten ['kɪndəgɑːtən] n jardín m de infancia

kind-hearted [kaɪnd'hɑːtɪd] adj bondadoso(a)

kindle ['kɪndəl] vt encender

kindly ['kaɪndlɪ] **1** adj **(kindlier, kindliest)** amable, bondadoso(a)

2 adv *Fml (please)* por favor; **k. remit a cheque** sírvase enviar cheque; **to look k. on** aprobar

kindness ['kaɪndnɪs] n bondad f, amabilidad f

kindred ['kɪndrɪd] adj **k. spirits** almas gemelas

kinetic [kɪ'netɪk] adj cinético(a)

king [kɪŋ] n rey m; *(draughts)* dama f

kingdom ['kɪŋdəm] n reino m

kingfisher ['kɪŋfɪʃə(r)] n *Orn* martín m pescador

king-size ['kɪŋsaɪz] adj extralargo(a)

kink [kɪŋk] n *(in rope)* coca f; *(in hair)* rizo m

kinky ['kɪŋkɪ] adj **(kinkier, kinkiest)** *Fam* raro(a); *(sexually)* pervertido(a)

kiosk ['kiːɒsk] n quiosco m

kiss [kɪs] **1** n beso m

2 vt besar

3 vi besarse

kit [kɪt] n **(a)** *(gear)* equipo m; *Mil* avíos mpl **(b)** *(clothing)* ropa f **(c)** *(toy model)* maqueta f

▶ **kit out** vt sep equipar

kitchen ['kɪtʃɪn] n cocina f; **k. sink** fregadero m

kite [kaɪt] n **(a)** *(toy)* cometa f **(b)** *Orn* milano m

kitten ['kɪtən] n gatito(a) m,f

kitty ['kɪtɪ] n *(money)* fondo m común; *Cards* bote m

kiwi ['kiːwiː] n *Bot & Orn* kiwi m

km *(pl* **km** *or* **kms)** *(abbr* **kilometre(s))** km

knack [næk] n **to get the k. of doing sth** cogerle el truquillo a algo

knapsack ['næpsæk] n mochila f

knead [niːd] vt dar masaje a; *(bread etc)* amasar

knee [niː] **1** n rodilla f

2 vt dar un rodillazo a

kneecap ['niːkæp] **1** n rótula f

2 vt romper la rótula a

kneel [niːl] *vi* (*pt & pp* **knelt**) **to k. (down)** arrodillarse

knell [nel] *n Literary* toque *m* de difuntos

knelt [nelt] *pt & pp of* **kneel**

knew [njuː] *pt of* **know**

knickers ['nɪkəz] *npl Br* bragas *fpl*

knife [naɪf] **1** *n* (*pl* **knives**) cuchillo *m*
2 *vt* apuñalar, dar una puñalada a

knight [naɪt] **1** *n Hist* caballero *m*; (*in chess*) caballo *m*
2 *vt* armar caballero

knighthood ['naɪthʊd] *n* (*rank*) título *m* de caballero

knit [nɪt] **1** *vt* (*pt & pp* **knitted** *or* **knit**) (**a**) tejer (**b**) **to k. (together)** (*join*) juntar; *Fig* **to k. one's brow** fruncir el ceño
2 *vi* (**a**) tejer, hacer punto (**b**) (*bone*) soldarse

knitting ['nɪtɪŋ] *n* punto *m*; **k. machine** máquina *f* de tejer; **k. needle** aguja *f* de tejer

knitwear ['nɪtweə(r)] *n* géneros *mpl* de punto

knives [naɪvz] *pl of* **knife**

knob [nɒb] *n* (**a**) (*of stick*) puño *m*; (*of drawer*) tirador *m*; (*button*) botón *m* (**b**) (*small portion*) trozo *m*

knock [nɒk] **1** *n* golpe *m*; *Fig* revés *m*
2 *vt* (**a**) golpear (**b**) *Fam* (*criticize*) criticar
3 *vi* chocar (**against** *or* **into** contra); (*at door*) llamar (**at** a)
▸ **knock down** *vt sep* (**a**) (*demolish*) derribar (**b**) *Aut* atropellar (**c**) (*price*) rebajar
▸ **knock off 1** *vt sep* (**a**) tirar (**b**) *Fam* (*steal*) birlar (**c**) *Fam* (*kill*) liquidar
2 *vi Fam* **they k. off at five** se piran a las cinco
▸ **knock out** *vt sep* (**a**) (*make unconscious*) dejar sin conocimiento; (*in boxing*) poner fuera de combate, derrotar por K.O. (**b**) (*surprise*) dejar pasmado(a)
▸ **knock over** *vt sep* (*cup*) volcar; (*with car*) atropellar

knocker ['nɒkə(r)] *n* (*on door*) aldaba *f*

knock-kneed [nɒk'niːd] *adj* patizambo(a)

knockout ['nɒkaʊt] *n* (**a**) (*in boxing*) K.O. *m*, knock-out *m* (**b**) *Fam* maravilla *f*

knot [nɒt] **1** *n* nudo *m*; (*group*) grupo *m*
2 *vt* anudar

knotty ['nɒtɪ] *adj* (**knottier, knottiest**) nudoso(a); *Fig* **a k. problem** un problema espinoso

know [nəʊ] *vt & vi* (*pt* **knew**; *pp* **known**) (**a**) saber; **as far as I k.** que yo sepa; **she knows how to ski** sabe esquiar; **to get to k. sth** enterarse de algo; **to let sb k.** avisar al algn (**b**) (*be acquainted with*) conocer; **we got to k. each other at the party** nos conocimos en la fiesta

know-all ['nəʊɔːl] *n Fam* sabelotodo *mf*

know-how ['nəʊhaʊ] *n Fam* conocimiento práctico

knowing ['nəʊɪŋ] *adj* (*deliberate*) deliberado(a); **a k. smile** una sonrisa de complicidad

knowingly ['nəʊɪŋlɪ] *adv* (*shrewdly*) a sabiendas; (*deliberately*) deliberadamente

knowledge ['nɒlɪdʒ] *n* (**a**) conocimiento *m*; **without my k.** sin saberlo yo (**b**) (*learning*) conocimientos *mpl*

knowledgeable ['nɒlɪdʒəbəl] *adj* erudito(a); **k. about** muy entendido(a) en

known [nəʊn] **1** *adj* conocido(a)
2 *pp of* **know**

knuckle ['nʌkəl] *n Anat* nudillo *m*; *Culin* hueso *m*
▸ **knuckle down** *vi Fam* ponerse a trabajar en serio

KO [keɪ'əʊ] *n Fam* (*abbr* **knockout**) K.O. *m*

Koran [kɔː'rɑːn] *n* Corán *m*

Korea [kə'rɪə] *n* Corea

Korean [kə'rɪən] *adj & n* coreano(a) (*m,f*)

Kurd [kɜːd] *n* curdo(a) *m,f*

Kuwait [kʊ'weɪt] *n* Kuwait

L

L, l [el] *n (the letter)* L, l *f*

lab [læb] *n Fam (abbr* **laboratory**) laboratorio *m*

label ['leɪbəl] **1** *n* etiqueta *f*; **record l.** ≃ casa discográfica
2 *vt* poner etiqueta a

labor ['leɪbər] *n, adj, vt & vi US =* **labour**

laboratory [lə'bɒrətərɪ, *US* 'læbrətɔːrɪ] *n* laboratorio *m*

laborious [lə'bɔːrɪəs] *adj* penoso(a)

labour ['leɪbə(r)] **1** *n* **(a)** *(work)* trabajo *m*; *(task)* tarea *f* **(b)** *(workforce)* mano *f* de obra **(c) labours** esfuerzos *mpl* **(d) the L. Party** el Partido Laborista **(e)** *(childbirth)* parto *m*; **to be in l.** estar de parto
2 *adj* laboral
3 *vt (stress, linger on)* machacar; *(a point)* insistir en
4 *vi* **(a)** *(work)* trabajar (duro) **(b)** *(move with difficulty)* avanzar penosamente

laboured ['leɪbəd] *adj (breathing)* fatigoso(a); *(style)* forzado(a)

labourer ['leɪbərə(r)] *n* peón *m*; **farm l.** peón *m* agrícola

labour-saving ['leɪbəseɪvɪŋ] *adj* **l. devices** electrodomésticos *mpl*

labyrinth ['læbərɪnθ] *n* laberinto *m*

lace [leɪs] **1** *n* **(a)** *(fabric)* encaje *m* **(b) laces** cordones *mpl*
2 *vt* **(a)** *(shoes)* atar (los cordones de) **(b)** *(add spirits to)* echar licor a
▸ **lace up** *vt sep* atar con cordones

lacerate ['læsəreɪt] *vt* lacerar

lack [læk] **1** *n* falta *f*, escasez *f*; **for l. of** por falta de
2 *vt* carecer de
3 *vi* carecer (**in** de)

lackadaisical [lækə'deɪzɪkəl] *adj (lazy)* perezoso(a); *(indifferent)* indiferente

lacklustre, *US* **lackluster** ['læklʌstə(r)] *adj (eyes)* apagado(a); *(performance)* anodino(a)

laconic [lə'kɒnɪk] *adj* lacónico(a)

lacquer ['lækə(r)] **1** *n* laca *f*
2 *vt (hair)* poner laca en

lad [læd] *n Fam* chaval *m*, muchacho *m*; *Fam* **the lads** los amigotes; **(stable) l.** mozo *m* de cuadra

ladder ['lædə(r)] **1** *n* **(a)** escalera *f* (de mano); *Fig* escala *f* **(b)** *(in stocking)* carrera *f*
2 *vt* **I've laddered my stocking** me he hecho una carrera en las medias

laden ['leɪdən] *adj* cargado(a) (**with** de)

ladle ['leɪdəl] *n* cucharón *m*

lady ['leɪdɪ] *n* señora *f*; *Pol* **First L.** primera dama; **Ladies** *(sign on WC)* Señoras; **ladies and gentlemen!** ¡señoras y señores!; **L. Brown** Lady Brown

ladybird ['leɪdɪbɜːd], *US* **ladybug** ['leɪdɪbʌg] *n* mariquita *f*

lady-in-waiting [leɪdɪɪn'weɪtɪŋ] *n* dama *f* de honor

ladylike ['leɪdɪlaɪk] *adj* elegante

ladyship ['leɪdɪʃɪp] *n* **her l./your l.** su señoría

lag [læg] **1** *n* **time l.** demora *f*
2 *vi* **to l. (behind)** quedarse atrás, retrasarse
3 *vt Tech* revestir

lager ['lɑːgə(r)] *n* cerveza rubia

lagoon [lə'guːn] *n* laguna *f*

laid [leɪd] *pt & pp of* **lay**

laid-back [leɪd'bæk] *adj Fam* tranquilo(a)

lain [leɪn] *pp of* **lie²**

lair [leə(r)] *n* guarida *f*

lake [leɪk] *n* lago *m*

lamb [læm] *n* cordero *m*; *(meat)* carne *f* de cordero; **l. chop** chuleta *f* de cordero; **l.'s wool** lana *f* de cordero

lame [leɪm] *adj* **(a)** cojo(a) **(b)** *Fig (excuse)* poco convincente; *(argument)* flojo(a)

lament [lə'ment] **1** *n Mus* elegia *f*
2 *vt (death)* llorar, lamentar
3 *vi* llorar (**for** a), lamentarse (**over** de)

lamentable ['læməntəbəl] *adj* lamentable

laminated ['læmɪneɪtɪd] *adj (metal)* laminado(a); *(glass)* inastillable; *(paper)* plastificado(a)

lamp [læmp] *n* lámpara *f*; *Aut* faro *m*

lampoon [læm'puːn] **1** *n* sátira *f*
2 *vt* satirizar

lamp-post ['læmppəʊst] *n* farola *f*

lampshade ['læmpʃeɪd] *n* pantalla *f*

lance [lɑːns] **1** *n* lanza *f*; *Br Mil* **l. corporal**

cabo interino; *Med* lanceta *f*
2 *vt Med* abrir con lanceta

> ℓ Note that the Spanish word **lance** is a
> false friend and is never a translation for
> the English word **lance**. In Spanish, **lance**
> means "event, incident".

land [lænd] **1** *n* (**a**) *(soil)* tierra *f*; *(soil)* suelo *m*;
by l. por tierra; **farm l.** tierras *fpl* de
cultivo (**b**) *(country)* país *m* (**c**) *(property)*
tierras *fpl*; *(estate)* finca *f*; **piece of l.**
terreno *m*
2 *vt* (**a**) *(plane)* hacer aterrizar (**b**) *(disembark)* desembarcar (**c**) *(fish)* pescar
(**d**) *Fam (obtain)* conseguir; *(contract)*
ganar (**e**) *Fam* **she got landed with the
responsibility** tuvo que cargar con la
responsabilidad (**f**) *Fam (blow)* asestar
3 *vi* (**a**) *(plane)* aterrizar (**b**) *(disembark)*
desembarcar (**c**) *(after falling)* caer (**in**
sobre)
► land up *vi Fam* ir a parar

landing ['lændɪŋ] *n* (**a**) *(of staircase)* rellano *m* (**b**) *(of plane)* aterrizaje *m*; **l. strip**
pista *f* de aterrizaje (**c**) *(of passengers)*
desembarco *m*; **l. stage** desembarcadero
m

landlady ['lændleɪdɪ] *n* *(of flat)* dueña *f*,
propietaria *f*; *(of boarding house)* patrona
f; *(of pub)* dueña

landlord ['lændlɔːd] *n* *(of flat)* dueño *m*,
propietario *m*; *(of pub)* patrón *m*, dueño

landmark ['lændmɑːk] *n* (**a**) señal *f*,
marca *f*; *(well-known place)* lugar muy
conocido (**b**) *Fig* hito *m*

landowner ['lændəʊnə(r)] *n* terrateniente *mf*

landscape ['lændskeɪp] **1** *n* paisaje *m*
2 *vt* ajardinar

landslide ['lændslaɪd] *n* desprendimiento *m* de tierras; **l. victory** victoria arrolladora

lane [leɪn] *n* *(in country)* camino *m*; *(in
town)* callejón *m*; *(of motorway)* carril *m*;
Sport calle *f*; *Naut* ruta *f*

language ['læŋgwɪdʒ] *n* (**a**) lenguaje *m*;
bad l. palabrotas *fpl* (**b**) *(of a country)*
idioma *m*, lengua *f*; **l. laboratory** laboratorio *m* de idiomas; **l. school** academia *f*
de idiomas

languid ['læŋgwɪd] *adj* lánguido(a)

languish ['læŋgwɪʃ] *vi* languidecer;
(project, plan etc) quedar abandonado(a); *(in prison)* pudrirse

lank [læŋk] *adj (hair)* lacio(a)

lanky ['læŋkɪ] *adj* (**lankier, lankiest**) larguirucho(a)

lantern ['læntən] *n* farol *m*

lap¹ [læp] *n Anat* regazo *m*

lap² [læp] **1** *n* (*circuit*) vuelta *f*; *Fig* etapa *f*
2 *vt (overtake)* doblar

lap³ [læp] **1** *vt* (*pt & pp* **lapped**) *(of cat)*
beber a lengüetadas
2 *vi (waves)* lamer, besar
► lap up *vt sep* (**a**) *(of cat)* beber a lengüetadas (**b**) *Fig (wallow in)* disfrutar con;
(flattery) recibir con estusiasmo (**c**) *Fig
(believe)* tragar

lapel [lə'pel] *n* solapa *f*

Lapland ['læplænd] *n* Laponia

lapse [læps] **1** *n* (**a**) *(of time)* lapso *m* (**b**)
(error) error *m*, desliz *m*; *(of memory)* fallo
m
2 *vi* (**a**) *(time)* pasar, transcurrir (**b**)
(expire) caducar (**c**) *(err)* cometer un
error; *(fall back)* caer (**into** en) (**d**) *Rel*
perder la fe

larceny ['lɑːsənɪ] *n Br* latrocinio *m*; *US*
hurto *m*

larch [lɑːtʃ] *n* alerce *m*

lard [lɑːd] *n* manteca *f* de cerdo

larder ['lɑːdə(r)] *n* despensa *f*

large [lɑːdʒ] **1** *adj* grande; *(amount)* importante; *(extensive)* amplio(a); **by and l.**
por lo general
2 *n* **to be at l.** andar suelto(a); **the public
at l.** el público en general

> ℓ Note that the Spanish word **largo** is a
> false friend and is never a translation for
> the English word **large**. In Spanish, **largo**
> means "long".

largely ['lɑːdʒlɪ] *adv (mainly)* en gran
parte; *(chiefly)* principalmente

large-scale ['lɑːdʒskeɪl] *adj (project,
problem etc)* de gran envergadura; *(map)*
a gran escala

lark¹ [lɑːk] *n Orn* alondra *f*

lark² [lɑːk] *n Fam (joke)* broma *f*; **what a
l.!** ¡qué risa!
► lark about, lark around *vi Fam* hacer el
tonto

larva ['lɑːvə] *n* larva *f*

laryngitis [lærɪn'dʒaɪtɪs] *n* laringitis *f*

larynx ['lærɪŋks] *n Anat* laringe *f*

laser ['leɪzə(r)] *n* láser *m*; **l. printer** impresora *f* láser

lash [læʃ] **1** *n* (**a**) *(eyelash)* pestaña *f* (**b**)
(blow with whip) latigazo *m*
2 *vt* (**a**) *(beat)* azotar (**b**) *(rain)* azotar
(**c**) *(tie)* atar
► lash out *vi* (**a**) *(with fists)* repartir golpes a diestro y siniestro; *(verbally)* criticar (**at** a) (**b**) *Fam (spend money)* tirar la
casa por la ventana

lass [læs] *n Fam* chavala *f*, muchacha *f*

lasso [læ'su:] **1** n lazo m
2 vt coger con el lazo
last [lɑːst] **1** adj (**a**) (final) último(a), final;
Fam **the l. straw** el colmo (**b**) (most recent) último(a) (**c**) (past) pasado(a); (previous) anterior; **l. but one** penúltimo(a); **l. month** el mes pasado; **l. night** anoche; **the night before l.** anteanoche
2 adv (**a**) **when I l. saw her** la última vez que la vi (**b**) (at the end) en último lugar; (in race etc) último; **at (long) l.** por fin; **l. but not least** el último en orden pero no en importancia
3 n **the l.** el último/la última
4 vi (**a**) (time) durar; (hold out) aguantar (**b**) (be enough for) llegar, alcanzar
last-ditch ['lɑːstdɪtʃ] adj (effort, attempt) último(a) y desesperado(a)
lasting ['lɑːstɪŋ] adj duradero(a)
lastly ['lɑːstlɪ] adv por último, finalmente
last-minute ['lɑːstmɪnɪt] adj de última hora
latch [lætʃ] n picaporte m, pestillo m
late [leɪt] **1** adj (**a**) (not on time) tardío(a); (hour) avanzado(a); **to be five minutes l.** llegar con cinco minutos de retraso (**b**) (far on in time) tarde; **in l. autumn** a finales del otoño; **in l. afternoon** a última hora de la tarde; **she's in her l. twenties** ronda los treinta (**c**) (dead) difunto(a)
2 adv (**a**) (not on time) tarde; **to arrive l.** llegar tarde (**b**) (far on in time) tarde; **l. at night** a altas horas de la noche; **l. in life** a una edad avanzada (**c**) **as l. as 1950** todavía en 1950; **of l.** últimamente
latecomer ['leɪtkʌmə(r)] n tardón(ona) m,f
lately ['leɪtlɪ] adv últimamente, recientemente
latent ['leɪtənt] adj (**a**) latente (**b**) (desire) oculto(a)
later ['leɪtə(r)] **1** adj (**a**) (subsequent) más tarde; **in her l. novels** en sus novelas posteriores (**b**) (more recent) más reciente
2 adv más tarde, después; **l. on** más adelante, más tarde
lateral ['lætərəl] adj lateral
latest ['leɪtɪst] **1** adj (superl of late) (most recent) último(a), más reciente
2 n **the l.** lo último; **have you heard the l.?** ¿te enteraste de lo último?; **Friday at the l.** el viernes a más tardar
lathe [leɪð] n Tech torno m
lather ['lɑːðə(r)] **1** n (of soap) espuma f; (horse's sweat) sudor m
2 vt (with soap) enjabonar

Latin ['lætɪn] **1** adj & n latino(a) (m,f); **L. America** América Latina, Latinoamérica; **L. American** latinoamericano(a) (m,f)
2 n (language) latín m
latitude ['lætɪtjuːd] n latitud f
latrine [lə'triːn] n letrina f
latter ['lætə(r)] **1** adj (**a**) (last) último(a) (**b**) (second of two) segundo(a)
2 pron éste(a); **the former ... the l.** aquél ... éste/aquélla ... ésta
lattice ['lætɪs] n enrejado m, rejilla f
laudable ['lɔːdəbl] adj loable
laugh [lɑːf] **1** n risa f; (guffaw) carcajada f; **for a l.** para divertirse
2 vi reír, reírse
► **laugh at** vt insep **to l. at sb/sth** reírse de algn/algo
► **laugh about** vt insep **to l. about sb/sth** reírse de algn/algo
► **laugh off** vt sep tomar a risa
laughable ['lɑːfəbl] adj (situation, suggestion) ridículo(a); (amount, offer) irrisorio(a)
laughing-stock ['lɑːfɪŋstɒk] n hazmerreír m inv
laughter ['lɑːftə(r)] n risa f
launch [lɔːntʃ] **1** n (**a**) (vessel) lancha f (**b**) = **launching**
2 vt (**a**) (attack, rocket, new product) lanzar (**b**) (ship) botar (**c**) (film, play) estrenar (**d**) (company) fundar (**e**) Fig (scheme) iniciar
launching ['lɔːntʃɪŋ] n (**a**) (of rocket, new product) lanzamiento m (**b**) (of ship) botadura f (**c**) (of film, play) estreno m (**d**) (of new company) fundación f
launchpad ['lɔːntʃpæd] n plataforma f de lanzamiento
launder ['lɔːndə(r)] vt lavar y planchar; Fig (money) blanquear
launderette [lɔːndə'ret], US **Laundromat®** ['lɔːndrəmæt] n lavandería automática
laundry ['lɔːndrɪ] n (**a**) (place) lavandería f (**b**) (dirty clothes) ropa sucia; **to do the l.** lavar la ropa
laurel ['lɒrəl] n laurel m; Fam Fig **to rest on one's laurels** dormirse en los laureles
lava ['lɑːvə] n lava f
lavatory ['lævətərɪ] n (**a**) excusado m, retrete m (**b**) (room) baño m; **public l.** servicios mpl, aseos mpl
lavender ['lævəndə(r)] n lavanda f
lavish ['lævɪʃ] **1** adj (**a**) (generous) pródigo(a) (**b**) (abundant) abundante (**c**) (luxurious) lujoso(a)
2 vt **to l. praise on sb** colmar de alabanzas a alguien; **to l. attention on sb**

prodigarse en atenciones con alguien

law [lɔ:] n (**a**) ley f; **by l.** según la ley; **l. and order** el orden público; **to lay down the l.** dictar la ley (**b**) (as subject) derecho m; **l. court** tribunal m de justicia (**c**) Fam **the l.** los maderos

law-abiding ['lɔːəbaɪdɪŋ] adj respetuoso(a) de la ley

lawful ['lɔːfʊl] adj legal; (permitted by law) lícito(a); (legitimate) legítimo(a)

lawn [lɔːn] n césped m; **l. tennis** tenis m sobre hierba

lawnmower ['lɔːnməʊə(r)] n cortacésped m

lawsuit ['lɔːsjuːt] n pleito m

lawyer ['lɔːjə(r)] n abogado(a) m,f; **l.'s office** bufete m de abogados

lax [læks] adj (not strict) relajado(a); (not demanding) poco exigente; (careless) descuidado(a)

laxative ['læksətɪv] adj & n laxante (m)

laxity ['læksɪtɪ] n relajamiento m; (carelessness) descuido m; (negligence) negligencia f

lay¹ [leɪ] adj (**a**) Rel laico(a) (**b**) (nonspecialist) lego(a)

lay² [leɪ] vt (pt & pp laid) (**a**) (place) poner, colocar; (cable, trap) tender; (foundations) echar (**b**) (fire) preparar; (table) poner (**c**) (leave) dejar (**d**) (eggs) poner (**e**) very Fam (have sex with) follar (**f**) (set down) asentar; (blame) echar
► **lay aside** vt sep dejar a un lado
► **lay by** vt sep (save) guardar; (money) ahorrar
► **lay down** vt sep (**a**) (put down) poner; (let go) dejar; **to l. down one's arms** rendir las armas (**b**) (plan) formular (**c**) (establish) fijar, imponer; (principles) sentar
► **lay into** vt insep Fam (physically) dar una paliza a; (verbally) arremeter contra
► **lay off 1** vt sep (dismiss) despedir
2 vt insep Fam dejar en paz
3 vt l. off! ¡para ya!
► **lay on** vt sep (**a**) (provide) proveer de; (food) preparar (**b**) (spread) aplicar; Fam **to l. it on (thick)** cargar las tintas
► **lay out** vt sep (**a**) (open out) extender (**b**) (arrange) disponer (**c**) (ideas) exponer (**d**) (plan) trazar (**e**) Fam (spend) gastar (**f**) Fam (knock out) derribar
► **lay up** vt sep (**a**) (store) guardar (**b**) (accumulate) almacenar (**c**) Fam **to be laid up** tener que guardar cama

lay³ [leɪ] pt of **lie²**

layabout ['leɪəbaʊt] n Fam vago(a) m,f

lay-by ['leɪbaɪ] n área f de descanso

layer ['leɪə(r)] n capa f

layman ['leɪmən] n lego(a) m,f

layout ['leɪaʊt] n (arrangement) disposición f, (presentation) presentación f; Typ composición f; (plan) diseño m, trazado m

laze [leɪz] vi holgazanear, gandulear

laziness ['leɪzɪnɪs] n pereza f, holgazanería f

lazy ['leɪzɪ] adj (**lazier, laziest**) perezoso(a), holgazán(ana); **at a l. pace** a paso lento

lb (abbr **pound**) libra f

lead¹ [led] n (**a**) (metal) plomo m (**b**) (in pencil) mina f

lead² [liːd] **1** n (**a**) (front position) delantera f; (advantage) ventaja f; **to take the l.** (in race) tomar la delantera; (score) adelantarse
(**b**) (clue) pista f
(**c**) Th primer papel m; **l. singer** cantante mf principal
(**d**) (leash) correa f
(**e**) Elec cable m
2 vt (pt & pp led) (**a**) (conduct) llevar, conducir
(**b**) (be the leader of) dirigir, encabezar
(**c**) (influence) llevar a; **this leads me to believe that** esto me lleva a creer que; **she's easily led** se deja llevar fácilmente
(**d**) (life) llevar
3 vi (**a**) (road) llevar, conducir (**to** a)
(**b**) (go first) ir delante; (in race) llevar la delantera
(**c**) **to l. to** llevar a
► **lead away** vt sep llevar
► **lead on 1** vi (go ahead) ir adelante
2 vt sep (deceive) engañar, timar
► **lead up to** vt insep llevar a

leaden ['ledən] adj (sky) plomizo(a); (food) pesado(a)

leader ['liːdə(r)] n (**a**) jefe(a) m,f, líder mf; (in race) líder (**b**) Press editorial m, artículo m de fondo

leadership ['liːdəʃɪp] n (**a**) (command) dirección f, mando m; Pol liderazgo m (**b**) (leaders) dirigentes mpl, cúpula f

lead-free ['ledfriː] adj sin plomo

leading ['liːdɪŋ] adj (**a**) (main) principal (**b**) (outstanding) destacado(a)

leaf [liːf] n (pl **leaves**) hoja f; **to turn over a new l.** hacer borrón y cuenta nueva
► **leaf through** vt insep hojear

leaflet ['liːflɪt] n folleto m

league [liːg] n (**a**) (alliance) alianza f; (association) sociedad f; Fam **to be in l. with sb** estar conchabado(a) con algn (**b**) Sport liga f

leak [liːk] **1** n (**a**) (hole) agujero m; (in

roof) gotera *f* (**b**) *(of gas, liquid)* fuga *f*, escape *m*; *(of information)* filtración *f*

2 *vi* (**a**) *(container)* tener un agujero; *(pipe)* tener un escape; *(roof)* gotear; *(boat)* hacer agua (**b**) *(gas, liquid)* escaparse; *(information)* filtrarse; *(news)* trascender

3 *vt (information)* filtrar (**to** a)

leaky ['li:kɪ] *adj* (**leakier, leakiest**) *(container)* agujereado(a); *(roof)* que tiene goteras; *(ship)* que hace agua

lean¹ [li:n] *adj (meat)* magro(a); *(person)* flaco(a); *(harvest)* escaso(a)

lean² [li:n] **1** *vi* (**a**) *(go away from)* abandonar; (**b**) **to l. on/against** apoyarse en/contra; *Fig* **to l. on sb** *(pressurize)* presionar a algn; *(depend)* depender de algn

2 *vt* apoyar (**on** en)
▶ **lean back** *vi* reclinarse
▶ **lean forward** *vi* inclinarse hacia delante
▶ **lean out** *vi* asomarse
▶ **lean over** *vi* inclinarse

leaning ['li:nɪŋ] **1** *adj* inclinado(a)

2 *n Fig (tendency)* inclinación *f*, tendencia *f*

leant [lent] *pt & pp of* **lean**

lean-to ['li:ntu:] *n (hut)* cobertizo *m*

leap [li:p] **1** *n (jump)* salto *m; Fig* paso *m*; **l. year** año bisiesto

2 *vi (pt & pp* **leaped** *or* **leapt)** saltar; *Fig* **her heart leapt** su corazón dio un vuelco
▶ **leap at** *vt insep Fig (chance)* no dejar escapar

leapfrog ['li:pfrɒg] *n* pídola *f*

leapt [lept] *pt & pp of* **leap**

learn [lɜ:n] **1** *vt (pt & pp* **learned** *or* **learnt)** (**a**) aprender; **to l. (how) to ski** aprender a esquiar (**b**) **to l. that** enterarse de que

2 *vi* (**a**) aprender (**b**) **to l. about** *or* **of** *(find out)* enterarse de

learned ['lɜ:nɪd] *adj* erudito(a)

learner ['lɜ:nə(r)] *n (beginner)* principiante *mf*; **l. driver** aprendiz(a) *m,f* de conductor

learning ['lɜ:nɪŋ] *n (knowledge)* conocimientos *mpl; (erudition)* saber *m*

learnt [lɜ:nt] *pt & pp of* **learn**

lease [li:s] **1** *n* contrato *m* de arrendamiento; *Fig* **to give sb a new l.** *Br of or US* **on life** dar nueva vida a algn

2 *vt* arrendar

leasehold ['li:shəʊld] **1** *n* derechos *mpl* de arrendamiento

2 *adj (property)* arrendado(a)

leash [li:ʃ] *n* correa *f*

least [li:st] *(superl of* **little)** **1** *adj* menor,

mínimo(a); **he has the l. time** él es quien menos tiempo tiene

2 *adv* menos; **l. of all him** él menos que nadie

3 *n* **the l.** lo menos; **at l.** por lo menos, al menos; **not in the l.!** ¡en absoluto!; **to say the l.** por no decir más

leather ['leðə(r)] **1** *n* piel *f*, cuero *m*

2 *adj* de piel

leave¹ [li:v] **1** *vt (pt & pp* **left)** (**a**) dejar; *(go away from)* abandonar; *(go out of)* salir de (**b**) **l. him alone!** ¡déjale en paz!; *Fam* **l. it to me** yo me encargo (**c**) *(bequeath)* legar (**d**) *(forget)* dejarse, olvidarse (**e**) **I have two biscuits left** me quedan dos galletas (**f**) **to be left over** sobrar

2 *vi (go away)* irse, marcharse; *(go out)* salir; **the train leaves in five minutes** el tren sale dentro de cinco minutos
▶ **leave behind** *vt sep* (**a**) dejar atrás (**b**) *(forget)* olvidarse
▶ **leave on** *vt sep (clothes)* dejar puesto(a) (**b**) *(lights, radio)* dejar encendido(a)
▶ **leave out** *vt sep (omit)* omitir; *Fig* **to feel left out** sentirse excluido(a)

leave² [li:v] *n* (**a**) *(permission)* permiso *m* (**b**) *(time off)* vacaciones *fpl; Mil* **on l.** de permiso; **l. of absence** excedencia *f* (**c**) **to take one's l. of sb** despedirse de algn

leaves [li:vz] *pl of* **leaf**

Lebanon ['lebənən] *n* **(the) L.** (el) Líbano

lecherous ['letʃərəs] *adj* lascivo(a)

lecture ['lektʃə(r)] **1** *n* (**a**) conferencia *f; Univ* clase *f*; **to give a l.** dar una conferencia (sobre); **l. hall, l. room, l. theatre** sala *f* de conferencias; *Univ* aula *f* (**b**) *(rebuke)* sermón *m*

2 *vi* dar una conferencia; *Univ* dar clases

3 *vt (reproach)* sermonear

lecturer ['lektʃərə(r)] *n* conferenciante *mf; Univ* profesor(a) *m,f*

led [led] *pt & pp of* **lead**

ledge [ledʒ] *n* (**a**) *(shelf)* repisa *f; (of window)* alféizar *m* (**b**) *(on mountain)* saliente *m*

ledger ['ledʒə(r)] *n* libro *m* mayor

lee [li:] *n* (**a**) *Naut* sotavento *m* (**b**) *Fig* abrigo *m*

leech [li:tʃ] *n* sanguijuela *f*

leek [li:k] *n* puerro *m*

leer [lɪə(r)] *vi* mirar con lascivia

leeway ['li:weɪ] *n* libertad *f*; **this gives me a certain amount of l.** esto me da cierto margen de libertad

left¹ [left] **1** *adj* izquierdo(a); *Pol* **l. wing** izquierda *f*

2 *adv* a la izquierda

3 n (**a**) izquierda f; **on the l.** a mano izquierda (**b**) Pol **to be on the l.** ser de izquierdas

left² [left] pt & pp of **leave**

left-hand ['lefthænd] adj **l. drive** con el volante a la izquierda; **on the l. side** a mano izquierda

left-handed [left'hændɪd] adj zurdo(a)

left-luggage [left'lʌgɪdʒ] n Br **l. office** consigna f

leftovers ['leftəʊvəz] npl sobras fpl

left-wing ['leftwɪŋ] adj de izquierdas, izquierdista

leg [leg] n (**a**) (of person) pierna f; (of animal, table) pata f; Culin (of lamb) pierna; (of trousers) pernera f (**b**) (stage) etapa f

legacy ['legəsɪ] n herencia f, legado m

legal ['liːgəl] adj (**a**) legal; (permitted by law) lícito(a); **l. tender** moneda f de curso legal (**b**) (relating to the law) jurídico(a); **l. aid** asesoramiento jurídico gratuito; **l. dispute** contencioso m; US **l. holiday** fiesta f nacional

legalize ['liːgəlaɪz] vt legalizar

legally ['liːgəlɪ] adv legalmente

legend ['ledʒənd] n leyenda f

legendary ['ledʒəndərɪ] adj legendario(a)

leggings ['legɪŋz] npl polainas fpl

legible ['ledʒəbəl] adj legible

legion ['liːdʒən] n legión f

legislation [ledʒɪs'leɪʃən] n legislación f

legislative ['ledʒɪslətɪv] adj legislativo(a)

legislator ['ledʒɪsleɪtə(r)] n legislador(a) m,f

legislature ['ledʒɪsleɪtʃə(r)] n asamblea legislativa

legitimate [lɪ'dʒɪtɪmɪt] adj legítimo(a)

legroom ['legruːm] n espacio m para las piernas

leisure ['leʒə(r), US 'liːʒər] n ocio m, tiempo m libre; **at l.** con calma; **do it at your l.** hazlo cuando tengas tiempo; **l. activities** pasatiempos mpl; **l. centre** centro recreativo

leisurely ['leʒəlɪ, US 'liːʒərlɪ] adj (unhurried) tranquilo(a); (slow) lento(a)

lemon ['lemən] n limón m; **l. curd** crema f de limón; **l. juice** zumo m de limón; **l. tea** té m con limón

lemonade [lemə'neɪd] n limonada f

lend [lend] vt (pt & pp **lent**) prestar; **to l. oneself/itself to sth** prestarse a or para algo

lending ['lendɪŋ] n **l. library** biblioteca f pública

length [leŋθ, leŋθ] n (**a**) longitud f, largo m; **it is 5 m in l.** tiene 5 m de largo (**b**) (duration) duración f (**c**) (of string) trozo m; (of cloth) retal m (**d**) (of swimming pool) largo m; Fig **to go to any lengths to achieve sth** hacer lo que sea para conseguir algo (**e**) **at l.** (finally) finalmente; (in depth) a fondo

lengthen ['leŋθən, 'leŋθən] **1** vt alargar; (lifetime) prolongar

2 vi alargarse; (lifetime) prolongarse

lengthways ['leŋθweɪz] adv a lo largo

lengthy ['leŋθɪ, 'leŋθɪ] (lengthier, lengthiest) largo(a); (film, illness) de larga duración; (meeting, discussion) prolongado(a)

lenient ['liːnɪənt] adj indulgente

lens [lenz] n (of eye) cristalino m; (of spectacles) lente f, Phot objetivo m

Lent [lent] n Cuaresma f

lent [lent] pt & pp of **lend**

lentil ['lentɪl] n lenteja f

Leo ['liːəʊ] n Leo m

leopard ['lepəd] n leopardo m

leotard ['liːətɑːd] n leotardo m

leper ['lepə(r)] n leproso(a) m,f

leprosy ['leprəsɪ] n lepra f

lesbian ['lezbɪən] adj & n lesbiana (f)

less [les] **1** adj (comp of **little**) menos

2 pron menos; **the l. said about it, the better** cuanto menos se hable de eso mejor

3 adv menos; **l. and l.** cada vez menos; **still l.** menos aún

4 prep menos; **a year l. two days** un año menos dos días

lessen ['lesən] vt & vi disminuir

lesser ['lesə(r)] adj menor; **to a l. extent** en menor grado

lesson ['lesən] n (**a**) clase f; (in book) lección f; **Spanish lessons** clases de español (**b**) Rel lectura f

lest [lest] conj Fml (**a**) para (que) no; **l. we forget** para que no lo olvidemos (**b**) (for fear that) por miedo a que

let [let] **1** vt (pt & pp **let**) (**a**) dejar, permitir; **to l. go of sth** soltar algo; **to l. sb know** avisar a algn; Fig **to l. oneself go** dejarse ir (**b**) (rent out) alquilar, Méx rentar; **to l.** (sign) se alquila (**c**) **l. alone** ni mucho menos

2 v aux **l. him wait** que espere; **l. me go!** ¡suéltame!; **l.'s go!** ¡vamos!, ¡vámonos!; **l.'s see** a ver

▸ **let down** vt sep (**a**) (lower) bajar; (lengthen) alargar; Fam Fig **to l. one's hair down** desmelenarse (**b**) (deflate) desinflar (**c**) (fail) fallar, defraudar

▸ **let in** *vt sep* (**a**) *(admit)* dejar entrar (**b**) **to l. oneself in for** meterse en

▸ **let off** *vt sep* (**a**) *(bomb)* hacer explotar; *(fireworks)* hacer estallar (**b**) *(liquid, air)* soltar (**c**) *Fam* **to l. sb off** *(pardon)* perdonar

▸ **let on** *vi Fam* **don't l. on** *(reveal information)* no se lo digas

▸ **let out** *vt sep* (**a**) *(release)* soltar; *(news)* divulgar; *(secret)* revelar (**b**) *(air, water)* dejar salir (**c**) *(cry)* soltar (**d**) *Sewing* ensanchar

▸ **let up** *vi* cesar, parar

letdown ['letdaʊn] *n* decepción *f*

lethal ['liːθəl] *adj* letal

lethargic [lɪ'θɑːdʒɪk] *adj* aletargado(a)

letter ['letə(r)] *n* (**a**) *(of alphabet)* letra *f*; *Fig* **to the l.** al pie de la letra (**b**) *(written message)* carta *f*; *Br* **l. box** buzón *m*; *Com* **l. of credit** carta de crédito

letterhead ['letəhed] *n* membrete *m*

lettering ['letərɪŋ] *n* rótulo *m*

lettuce ['letɪs] *n* lechuga *f*

let-up ['letʌp] *n Fam* descanso *m*, respiro *m*

leukaemia, *US* **leukemia** [luː'kiːmɪə] *n* leucemia *f*

level ['levəl] **1** *adj* (**a**) *(flat)* llano(a); *(even)* nivelado(a); *(equal)* igual, parejo(a); **a l. spoonful of** una cucharada rasa de; **to be l. with** estar a nivel de; *Br* **l. crossing** paso *m* a nivel (**b**) *(steady)* estable; *(tone)* uniforme

2 *vt* (**a**) nivelar, allanar (**b**) *(building)* arrasar (**c**) *(stare, criticism)* dirigir

3 *n* nivel *m*; **to be on a l. with** estar al mismo nivel que; *Fam* **to be on the l.** *(be honest)* ser de fiar; *(be truthful)* decir la verdad

▸ **level off, level out** *vi* estabilizarse

▸ **level with** *vt insep Fam* ser franco(a) con

level-headed [levəl'hedɪd] *adj* sensato(a)

lever ['liːvə(r)] **1** *n* palanca *f*

2 *vt* apalancar; **to l. sth out** sacar algo con palanca

leverage ['liːvərɪdʒ] *n Fig* influencia *f*

levy ['levɪ] **1** *vt* *(tax)* recaudar; *(fine)* imponer

2 *n* *(of tax)* recaudación *f*; *(of fine)* imposición *f*

lewd [luːd] *adj* *(person)* lascivo(a); *(story)* obsceno(a)

liability [laɪə'bɪlɪtɪ] *n* (**a**) *Jur* responsabilidad *f* (**b**) *(handicap)* estorbo *m* (**c**) *Fin* **liabilities** pasivo *m*

liable ['laɪəbəl] *adj* (**a**) *Jur* responsable; *(susceptible)* sujeto(a); **to be l. for** ser responsable de (**b**) **to be l. to do sth** ser propenso(a) a hacer algo; **it's l. to happen** es muy probable que (así) suceda

liaise [liː'eɪz] *vi* comunicarse (**with** con)

liaison [liː'eɪzɒn] *n* (**a**) enlace *m*; **l. officer** oficial *mf* de enlace (**b**) *(love affair)* amorío *m*

liar ['laɪə(r)] *n* mentiroso(a) *m,f*, embustero(a) *m,f*

libel ['laɪbəl] **1** *n* libelo *m*

2 *vt* difamar, calumniar

liberal ['lɪbərəl] **1** *adj* (**a**) liberal; **L. Party** Partido *m* Liberal (**b**) *(abundant)* abundante

2 *n Pol* **L.** liberal *mf*

liberate ['lɪbəreɪt] *vt* liberar; *(prisoner etc)* poner en libertad; **liberated woman** mujer liberada

liberation [lɪbə'reɪʃən] *n* liberación *f*

liberty ['lɪbətɪ] *n* libertad *f*; **to be at l. to say sth** ser libre de decir algo; **to take liberties** tomarse libertades

Libra ['liːbrə] *n* Libra *f*

librarian [laɪ'breərɪən] *n* bibliotecario(a) *m,f*

> 🔍 Note that the Spanish word **librero** is a false friend and is never a translation for the English word **librarian**. In Spanish, **librero** means "bookseller".

library ['laɪbrərɪ] *n* biblioteca *f*

> 🔍 Note that the Spanish word **librería** is a false friend and is never a translation for the English word **library**. In Spanish, **librería** means "bookshop".

Libya ['lɪbɪə] *n* Libia

Libyan ['lɪbɪən] *adj & n* libio(a) *(m,f)*

lice [laɪs] *pl of* **louse**

licence ['laɪsəns] *n* (**a**) *(permit)* licencia *f*, permiso *m*; *Aut* **l. number** matrícula *f*; *US* **l. plate** (placa *f* de la) matrícula (**b**) *(freedom)* libertad *f*, *(excessive freedom)* libertinaje *m*

license ['laɪsəns] **1** *vt* dar licencia a, autorizar

2 *n US* = **licence**

licensed ['laɪsənst] *adj* autorizado(a); **l. premises** = local autorizado para la venta de bebidas alcohólicas

licentious [laɪ'senʃəs] *adj* licencioso(a)

lichen ['laɪkən, 'lɪtʃən] *n* liquen *m*

lick [lɪk] **1** *vt* lamer; **to l. one's lips** relamerse

2 *n* lamedura *f*; *Fam* **a l. of paint** una mano de pintura

licorice ['lɪkərɪs, 'lɪkərɪʃ] *n US* = **liquorice**

lid [lɪd] *n* (**a**) *(cover)* tapa *f* (**b**) *(of eye)* párpado *m*

lie¹ [laɪ] **1** *vi* mentir
2 *n* mentira *f*

lie² [laɪ] **1** *vi* (*pt* lay; *pp* lain) (**a**) *(act)* echarse, acostarse; *(state)* estar echado(a), estar acostado(a); *(be buried)* yacer (**b**) *(be situated)* encontrarse, hallarse; **the valley lay before us** el valle se extendía ante nosotros (**c**) *(remain)* quedarse
2 *n (position)* situación *f*; *(direction)* orientación *f*
▶ **lie about, lie around** *vi (person)* estar tumbado(a); *(things)* estar tirado(a)
▶ **lie down** *vi* acostarse, echarse

lie-in ['laɪɪn] *n Fam* **to have a l.** levantarse tarde

lieu [ljuː, luː] *n* **in l. of** en lugar de

lieutenant [lef'tenənt, *US* luː'tenənt] *n* (**a**) *Mil* teniente *m* (**b**) *(non-military)* lugarteniente *m*

life [laɪf] *n (pl* lives) (**a**) vida *f*; **to come to l.** cobrar vida; **to take one's own l.** suicidarse; *Fam* **how's l.?** ¿qué tal?; **l. belt** cinturón *m* salvavidas; **l. imprisonment** cadena perpetua; **l. insurance** seguro *m* de vida; **l. jacket** chaleco *m* salvavidas; **l. style** estilo *m* de vida; **l. story** biografía *f* (**b**) *(liveliness)* vitalidad *f*; *Fam Fig* **to be the l. and soul of the party** ser el alma de la fiesta

lifeboat ['laɪfbəʊt] *n (on ship)* bote *m* salvavidas; *(on shore)* lancha *f* de socorro

lifeguard ['laɪfgɑːd] *n* socorrista *mf*

lifeless ['laɪflɪs] *adj* sin vida

lifelike ['laɪflaɪk] *adj* natural; *(portrait)* fiel

lifeline ['laɪflaɪn] *n Fig* cordón *m* umbilical

lifelong ['laɪflɒŋ] *adj* de toda la vida

life-size(d) ['laɪfsaɪz(d)] *adj* (de) tamaño natural

lifetime ['laɪftaɪm] *n* vida *f*; **in his l.** durante su vida; **it's the chance of a l.** es una ocasión única

lift [lɪft] **1** *vt* (**a**) levantar; *(head etc)* alzar; *(pick up)* coger (**b**) *(troops)* transportar (**c**) *Fam (steal)* birlar; *(plagiarize)* plagiar
2 *vi (clouds, mist)* disiparse
3 *n* (**a**) *Br (elevator)* ascensor *m* (**b**) **to give sb a l.** llevar a algn en coche (**c**) *Fig (boost)* estímulo *m*
▶ **lift up** *vt sep* levantar, alzar

lift-off ['lɪftɒf] *n* despegue *m*

light¹ [laɪt] **1** *n* (**a**) luz *f*; *Fig* **in the l. of** en vista de; *Fig* **to bring sth to l.** sacar algo a la luz; *Fig* **to come to l.** salir a la luz; **l.**

bulb bombilla *f*; **l. meter** fotómetro *m*; **l. pen** lápiz óptico; **l. switch** interruptor *m* de la luz; **l. year** año *m* luz (**b**) *(lamp)* luz *f*, lámpara *f*; *(traffic light)* semáforo *m*; *(headlight)* faro *m* (**c**) *(flame)* lumbre *f*; **to set l. to sth** prender fuego a algo; *Fam* **have you got a l.?** ¿tiene fuego?
2 *vt (pt & pp* lighted *or* lit) (**a**) *(illuminate)* iluminar, alumbrar (**b**) *(ignite)* encender
3 *adj* claro(a); *(hair)* rubio(a)
▶ **light up 1** *vt sep* iluminar, alumbrar
2 *vi* (**a**) iluminarse (**b**) *Fam* encender un cigarrillo

light² [laɪt] **1** *adj* ligero(a); *(rain)* fino(a); *(breeze)* suave; *Fig (sentence etc)* leve; *Fig* **to make l. of sth** dar poca importancia a algo
2 *adv* **to travel l.** ir ligero(a) de equipaje

lighten¹ ['laɪtən] **1** *vt* (**a**) *(colour)* aclarar (**b**) *(illuminate)* iluminar
2 *vi* aclararse

lighten² ['laɪtən] *vt* (**a**) *(weight)* aligerar (**b**) *Fig (mitigate)* aliviar; *(heart)* alegrar

lighter¹ ['laɪtə(r)] *n (cigarette)* **l.** encendedor *m*, mechero *m*

light-headed [laɪt'hedɪd] *adj* (**a**) *(dizzy)* mareado(a) (**b**) *(frivolous)* frívolo(a)

light-hearted [laɪt'hɑːtɪd] *adj* alegre

lighthouse ['laɪthaʊs] *n* faro *m*

lighting ['laɪtɪŋ] *n* (**a**) *(act)* iluminación *f* (**b**) *(system)* alumbrado *m*

lightly ['laɪtlɪ] *adv* (**a**) ligeramente (**b**) **to get off l.** salir casi indemne

lightness¹ ['laɪtnɪs] *n* luminosidad *f*, claridad *f*

lightness² ['laɪtnɪs] *n (of weight)* ligereza *f*

lightning ['laɪtnɪŋ] *n (flash)* relámpago *m*; *(stroke)* rayo *m*; **l. conductor** *or* **rod** pararrayos *m inv*; **l. strike** huelga *f* relámpago

lightweight ['laɪtweɪt] *adj (suit etc)* ligero(a); *(boxer)* de peso ligero; *Fig (person)* light

like¹ [laɪk] **1** *adj* (**a**) parecido(a), semejante (**b**) *(equal)* igual
2 *adv* (**as**) **l. as not** a lo mejor
3 *prep* (**a**) *(similar to)* como, parecido(a) a; *(the same as)* igual que; **it's not l. her to do that** no es propio de ella hacer eso; **I've never seen anything l. it** nunca he visto cosa igual; **l. that** así; **people l. that** ese tipo de gente; **what's he l.?** ¿cómo es?; *Fam* **that's more l. it!** ¡así se hace! (**b**) **to feel l.** *(want)* tener ganas de; **I feel l. a change** me apetece un cambio
4 *n* **brushes, combs and the l.** cepillos,

peines y cosas por el estilo

like² [laɪk] **1** vt (**a**) **do you l. chocolate?** ¿te gusta el chocolate?; **he likes dancing** le gusta bailar; **she likes children** le gustan los niños (**b**) (want) querer; **whether you l. it or not** quieras o no (quieras); **would you l. a drink?** ¿te apetece tomar algo?

2 vi querer, gustar; **as you l.** como quieras; **whenever you l.** cuando quieras

3 n gusto m

likeable ['laɪkəbəl] adj simpático(a)

likelihood ['laɪklɪhʊd] n probabilidad f

likely ['laɪklɪ] **1** adj (likelier, likeliest) probable; **he's l. to cause trouble** es probable que cause problemas; **where are you l. to be this afternoon?** ¿dónde piensas estar esta tarde?

2 adv probablemente; **not l.!** ¡ni hablar!

likeness ['laɪknɪs] n (**a**) semejanza f, parecido m (**b**) (portrait) retrato m

likewise ['laɪkwaɪz] adv (**a**) (also) también, asimismo (**b**) (the same) lo mismo, igual

liking ['laɪkɪŋ] n (for thing) afición f; (for person) simpatía f; (for friend) cariño m; **to take a l. to sth** cogerle el gusto a algo; **to take a l. to sb** coger cariño a algn

lilac ['laɪlək] **1** n (**a**) Bot lila f (**b**) (colour) lila m

2 adj lila, de color lila

lilt [lɪlt] n melodía f

lily ['lɪlɪ] n lirio m, azucena f; **l. of the valley** lirio de los valles

limb [lɪm] n miembro m; Fig **to be out on a l.** (in danger) estar en peligro; Br (isolated) estar aislado(a)

▸ limber up ['lɪmbə(r)] vi Sport entrar en calor; Fig prepararse (for para)

limbo ['lɪmbəʊ] n limbo m; Fig olvido m; **to be in l.** caer en el olvido

lime¹ [laɪm] n Chem cal f

lime² [laɪm] n (fruit) lima f; (tree) limero m

limelight ['laɪmlaɪt] n Fig **to be in the l.** estar en el candelero

limerick ['lɪmərɪk] n quintilla humorística

limestone ['laɪmstəʊn] n piedra caliza

limit ['lɪmɪt] **1** n límite m; (maximum) máximo m; (minimum) mínimo m

2 vt (restrict) limitar

limitation [lɪmɪ'teɪʃən] n limitación f

limited ['lɪmɪtɪd] adj limitado(a); **l. edition** edición limitada; Br **l. (liability) company** sociedad anónima

limitless ['lɪmɪtlɪs] adj ilimitado(a)

limousine ['lɪməzi:n, lɪmə'zi:n] n limusina f

limp¹ [lɪmp] **1** vi cojear

2 n cojera f

limp² [lɪmp] adj (**a**) (floppy) flojo(a) (**b**) (weak) débil

limpet ['lɪmpɪt] n lapa f

linchpin ['lɪntʃpɪn] n Tech pezonera f; Fig eje m

line¹ [laɪn] n (**a**) línea f; (straight) raya f; **to be on the right lines** ir por buen camino; US **State l.** límite m de un Estado

(**b**) (of writing) renglón m; (of poetry) verso m; Th **to learn one's lines** aprenderse el papel

(**c**) (row) fila f; (of trees) hilera f; US (queue) cola f; Mil **l. of fire** línea f de fuego; Mil **to be in the front l.** estar en primera línea; Fig **to be in l. (with)** coincidir (con); Fam **to bring sb into l.** pararle los pies a algn; US **to stand in l.** (queue) hacer cola; Fam **to step out of l.** salirse de las reglas; Fig **sth along these lines** algo por el estilo; **l. dancing** = baile al ritmo de música country en el que los participantes se colocan en hileras y se mueven todos al mismo tiempo dando los mismos pasos

(**d**) (rope) cuerda f; (wire) cable m; **fishing l.** sedal m

(**e**) Tel línea f; **hold the l.!** ¡no cuelgue!

(**f**) Br Rail vía f

(**g**) (range of goods) surtido m; **a new l.** una nueva línea

(**h**) (of descent) linaje m

line² [laɪn] vt (pipe etc) revestir; Sewing forrar; Fam **to l. one's pockets** forrarse

▸ line up 1 vt sep (**a**) (arrange in rows) poner en fila (**b**) **he has something lined up for this evening** tiene algo organizado para esta noche

2 vi (people) ponerse en fila; (troops) formar; (in queue) hacer cola

linear ['lɪnɪə(r)] adj lineal

lined [laɪnd] adj (**a**) (paper) rayado(a); (face) arrugado(a) (**b**) (garment) forrado(a)

linen ['lɪnɪn] n (**a**) (cloth) lino m (**b**) (clothes) ropa f; (sheets etc) ropa blanca

liner ['laɪnə(r)] n transatlántico m

linesman ['laɪnzmən] n Sport juez m de línea

line-up ['laɪnʌp] n Sport alineación f

linger ['lɪŋgə(r)] vi tardar; (dawdle) rezagarse; (smell, doubt) persistir; Fig (memory) perdurar

lingerie ['lænʒəri:] n Fml ropa f interior (de mujer)

lingering ['lɪŋgərɪŋ] adj (doubt) persistente; (look) fijo(a)

lingo ['lɪŋgəʊ] n (pl **lingoes**) Fam (a) (language) lengua f, idioma m (b) (jargon) jerga f

linguist ['lɪŋgwɪst] n lingüista mf; **he's a good l.** se le dan bien los idiomas

linguistic [lɪŋ'gwɪstɪk] adj lingüístico(a)

linguistics [lɪŋ'gwɪstɪks] n sing lingüística f

lining ['laɪnɪŋ] n forro m

link [lɪŋk] **1** n (a) (of chain) eslabón m (b) (connection) conexión f; Fig vínculo m; **rail l.** enlace ferroviario (c) **links** campo m de golf

    2 vt unir

▸ **link up** vi unirse; (meet) encontrarse; (spaceships) acoplarse

link-up ['lɪŋkʌp] n Tel & TV conexión f; (meeting) encuentro m; (of spaceships) acoplamiento m

lino ['laɪnəʊ] n Fam linóleo m

linoleum [lɪ'nəʊlɪəm] n linóleo m, linóleum m

lion ['laɪən] n león m

lioness ['laɪənɪs] n leona f

lip [lɪp] n (a) labio m (b) (of jug) pico m

lip-read ['lɪpriːd] vt & vi leer en los labios

lip-service ['lɪpsɜːvɪs] n palabrería f

lipstick ['lɪpstɪk] n lápiz m de labios

liqueur [lɪ'kjʊə(r)] n licor m

liquid ['lɪkwɪd] adj & n líquido(a) (m)

liquidate ['lɪkwɪdeɪt] vt liquidar

liquidation [lɪkwɪ'deɪʃən] n liquidación f; **to go into l.** entrar en liquidación

liquidize ['lɪkwɪdaɪz] vt licuar

liquidizer ['lɪkwɪdaɪzə(r)] n licuadora f

liquor ['lɪkər] n US alcohol m, bebidas alcohólicas; **l. store** tienda f de bebidas alcohólicas

liquorice ['lɪkərɪs, 'lɪkərɪʃ] n regaliz m

Lisbon ['lɪzbən] n Lisboa

lisp [lɪsp] **1** n ceceo m

    2 vi cecear

list¹ [lɪst] **1** n lista f; (catalogue) catálogo m

    2 vt (make a list of) hacer una lista de; (put on a list) poner en una lista; **it is not listed** no figura en la lista

list² [lɪst] Naut **1** n escora f

    2 vi escorar

listen ['lɪsən] vi escuchar; (pay attention) prestar atención

▸ **listen out for** vt insep estar atento(a) a

listener ['lɪsənə(r)] n oyente mf

listless ['lɪstlɪs] adj apático(a)

lit [lɪt] pt & pp of **light**

liter ['liːtər] n US = **litre**

literacy ['lɪtərəsɪ] n alfabetización f

literal ['lɪtərəl] adj literal

literally ['lɪtərəlɪ] adv literalmente

literary ['lɪtərərɪ] adj literario(a)

literate ['lɪtərɪt] adj alfabetizado(a)

> 🖉 Note that the Spanish word **literato** is a false friend and is never a translation for the English word **literate**. In Spanish, **literato** means "writer, author."

literature ['lɪtərətʃə(r)] n (a) literatura f (b) Fam (documentation) folleto informativo

lithe [laɪð] adj Fml ágil

Lithuania [lɪθjʊ'eɪnɪə] n Lituania

Lithuanian [lɪθjʊ'eɪnɪən] **1** adj lituano(a)

    2 n (person) lituano(a) m,f; (language) lituano m

litigation [lɪtɪ'geɪʃən] n litigio m

litmus ['lɪtməs] n Fig **l. test** prueba f contundente

litre ['liːtə(r)] n litro m

litter ['lɪtə(r)] **1** n (a) (rubbish) basura f; (papers) papeles mpl; **l. bin** papelera f (b) (offspring) camada f

    2 vt ensuciar

littered ['lɪtəd] adj cubierto(a) (with de)

little ['lɪtəl] **1** adj (a) pequeño(a); **a l. dog** un perrito; **a l. house** una casita; **l. finger** dedo m meñique; **L.** Br **Bear** or US **Dipper** Osa f Menor (b) (not much) poco(a); **a l. cheese** un poco de queso

    2 pron poco m; **save me a l.** guárdame un poco

    3 adv poco; **l. by l.** poco a poco; **as l. as possible** lo menos posible; **they were a l. surprised** se quedaron algo sorprendidos

live¹ [lɪv] **1** vi vivir; **long l. the King!** ¡viva el Rey!

    2 vt vivir; **to l. an interesting life** vivir una vida interesante

▸ **live down** vt sep conseguir que se olvide

▸ **live for** vt insep vivir para

▸ **live off** vt insep vivir de

▸ **live on 1** vt insep (food, money) vivir de **2** vi (memory) persistir

▸ **live through** vt insep vivir durante

▸ **live together** vi vivir juntos

▸ **live up** vt sep Fam **to l. it up** pegarse la gran vida

▸ **live up to** vt insep (promises) cumplir con; **it didn't l. up to expectations** no fue lo que se esperaba

▸ **live with** vt insep (a) vivir con (b) Fig (accept) aceptar

live² [laɪv] adj (a) (living) vivo(a) (b) TV & Rad en directo, en vivo (c) (ammunition) real; (bomb) sin explotar; Elec con corriente; Fam **he's a real l. wire!** ¡éste no para nunca!

livelihood ['laɪvlɪhʊd] *n* sustento *m*

lively ['laɪvlɪ] *adj* (**livelier, liveliest**) *(person)* vivo(a); *(place)* animado(a); *Fig (interest)* entusiástico(a)

liven ['laɪvən] *vt* **to l. (up)** animar

liver ['lɪvə(r)] *n* hígado *m*

livery ['lɪvərɪ] *n* librea *f*

lives [laɪvz] *pl of* **life**

livestock ['laɪvstɒk] *n* ganado *m*

livid ['lɪvɪd] *adj* lívido(a); *Fam (angry)* furioso(a)

living ['lɪvɪŋ] **1** *adj* vivo(a)

2 *n* vida *f*; **l. conditions** condiciones *fpl* de vida; **l. expenses** dietas *fpl*; **to earn or make one's l.** ganarse la vida; **l. room** sala *f* de estar; **l. standards** nivel *m* de vida; **l. wage** sueldo mínimo

lizard ['lɪzəd] *n (large)* lagarto *m*; *(small)* lagartija *f*

llama ['lɑːmə] *n* llama *f*

load [ləʊd] **1** *n (cargo)* carga *f*; *(weight)* peso *m*; *Elec & Tech* carga; *Fam* **loads (of)** montones de; *Fam* **that's a l. of rubbish!** ¡no son más que tonterías!

2 *vt* cargar

▸ **load up** *vi & vt sep* cargar

loaded ['ləʊdɪd] *adj* (**a**) cargado(a) (**with** de); *Fig* **a l. question** una pregunta intencionada (**b**) *Fam* **to be l.** *(rich)* estar forrado(a) (**c**) *(dice)* trucado(a)

loading ['ləʊdɪŋ] *n* carga *f*; **l. bay** cargadero *m*

loaf¹ [ləʊf] *n (pl* **loaves**) pan *m*; *(French stick)* barra *f* de pan; *(sliced)* pan de molde

loaf² [ləʊf] *vi* **to l. (about or around)** holgazanear

loan [ləʊn] **1** *n* préstamo *m*; *Fin* empréstito *m*; **on l.** prestado(a); *(footballer)* cedido(a)

2 *vt* prestar

loath [ləʊθ] *adj* **to be l. to do sth** ser reacio(a) a hacer algo

loathe [ləʊð] *vt* aborrecer, odiar

loathing ['ləʊðɪŋ] *n* aborrecimiento *m*, odio *m*

loathsome ['ləʊðsəm] *adj* odioso(a), repugnante

loaves [ləʊvz] *pl of* **loaf**

lobby ['lɒbɪ] **1** *n* (**a**) *(hall)* vestíbulo *m* (**b**) *(pressure group)* grupo *m* de presión, lobby *m*

2 *vt* presionar

3 *vi* ejercer presiones

lobe [ləʊb] *n* lóbulo *m*

lobster ['lɒbstə(r)] *n* langosta *f*

local ['ləʊkəl] **1** *adj* local; *(person)* del pueblo; *Med* **l. anaesthetic** anestesia *f* local; *Tel* **l. call** llamada urbana; **l. government** gobierno *m* municipal

2 *n Fam* (**a**) **the locals** los vecinos (**b**) *Br (pub)* bar *m* del barrio

locality [ləʊ'kælɪtɪ] *n* localidad *f*

locally ['ləʊkəlɪ] *adv* en *or* de la localidad

locate [ləʊ'keɪt] *vt (situate)* situar, ubicar; *(find)* localizar

location [ləʊ'keɪʃən] *n* (**a**) lugar *m*, situación *f* (**b**) *Cin* **l. shots** exteriores *mpl*; **they're on l. in Australia** están rodando en Australia

loch [lɒx, lɒk] *n Scot* lago *m*

lock¹ [lɒk] **1** *n* (**a**) *(on door etc)* cerradura *f*; *(bolt)* cerrojo *m*; *(padlock)* candado *m* (**b**) *(on canal)* esclusa *f*

2 *vt* cerrar con llave/cerrojo/candado

3 *vi (door etc)* cerrarse; *(wheels)* trabarse

▸ **lock up** *vt sep (house)* cerrar; *(jail)* meter en la cárcel

lock² [lɒk] *n Literary (of hair)* mechón *m*

locker ['lɒkə(r)] *n (cupboard)* armario ropero; *US* **l. room** vestuario *m* con armarios roperos

locket ['lɒkɪt] *n* medallón *m*

lockout ['lɒkaʊt] *n* cierre *m* patronal

locksmith ['lɒksmɪθ] *n* cerrajero *m*

lockup ['lɒkʌp] *n (garage)* garaje alejado de la casa; *US (prison)* cárcel *f*

loco ['ləʊkəʊ] *adj US Fam* pirado(a)

locomotive [ləʊkə'məʊtɪv] *n* locomotora *f*

locust ['ləʊkəst] *n* langosta *f*

lodge [lɒdʒ] **1** *n* (**a**) *(gamekeeper's)* casa *f* del guarda; *(porter's)* portería *f*; *(hunter's)* refugio *m* (**b**) *(masonic)* logia *f* (**c**) *(beaver's den)* madriguera *f*

2 *vt* (**a**) *(accommodate)* alojar (**b**) *(complaint)* presentar

3 *vi* (**a**) *(live)* alojarse (**b**) *(get stuck)* meterse (**in** en)

lodger ['lɒdʒə(r)] *n* huésped(a) *m,f*

lodging ['lɒdʒɪŋ] *n* alojamiento *m*; **l. house** casa *f* de huéspedes

loft [lɒft] *n* desván *m*

lofty ['lɒftɪ] *adj* (**loftier, loftiest**) *Literary (high)* alto(a); *Pej (haughty)* altivo(a)

log [lɒg] **1** *n* (**a**) *(for fuel)* leño *m*; **l. cabin** cabaña *f* de troncos (**b**) *Naut* diario *m* de a bordo

2 *vt (record)* registrar

▸ **log in, log on** *vi Comput* entrar (en sistema)

▸ **log out, log off** *vi Comput* salir (del sistema)

logarithm ['lɒgərɪðəm] *n* logaritmo *m*

log-book ['lɒgbʊk] *n Naut* diario *m* de a

bordo; *Av* diario de vuelo; *Aut* documentación *f* (del coche)

loggerheads ['lɒgəhedz] *npl* **to be at l. with sb** estar a mal con algn

logic ['lɒdʒɪk] *n* lógica *f*

logical ['lɒdʒɪkəl] *adj* lógico(a)

logistics [lə'dʒɪstɪks] *npl* logística *f*

logo ['ləʊgəʊ] *n* logotipo *m*

loin [lɔɪn] *n (of animal)* ijada *f; Culin (of pork)* lomo *m; (of beef)* solomillo *m*

loiter ['lɔɪtə(r)] *vi (hang about)* holgazanear; *(lag behind)* rezagarse; *(prowl)* merodear

loll [lɒl] *vi (tongue, head)* colgar
▸ **loll about, loll around** *vi* repantigarse

lollipop ['lɒlɪpɒp] *n* pirulí *m*, chupachup® *m*; **ice(d) l.** polo *m; Br Fam* **lady/ man** = guardia que para el tráfico para que crucen los colegiales

lolly ['lɒlɪ] *n Fam* **(a)** *(sweet)* pirulí *m*, chupachup® *m*; **ice(d) l.** polo *m* **(b)** *Fam (money)* pasta *f*

London ['lʌndən] *n* Londres

Londoner ['lʌndənə(r)] *n* londinense *mf*

lone [ləʊn] *adj (solitary)* solitario(a); *(single)* solo(a)

loneliness ['ləʊnlɪnɪs] *n* soledad *f*

lonely ['ləʊnlɪ] *adj* **(lonelier, loneliest)** solo(a), solitario(a)

long¹ [lɒŋ] **1** *adj* **(a)** *(size)* largo(a); **how l. is the table?** ¿cuánto tiene de largo la mesa?; **it's 3 m l.** tiene 3 m de largo; **l. jump** salto *m* de longitud **(b)** *(time)* mucho(a); **at l. last** por fin; **how l. is the film?** ¿cuánto tiempo dura la película?

2 *adv* mucho, mucho tiempo; **all day l.** todo el día; **as l. as the exhibition lasts** mientras dure la exposición; **as l. as** *or* **so l. as you don't mind** con tal de que no te importe; **before l.** dentro de poco; **how l. have you been here?** ¿cuánto tiempo llevas aquí?

long² [lɒŋ] *vi* añorar; **to l. for** anhelar

long-distance ['lɒŋdɪstəns] *adj* de larga distancia; **l. call** conferencia interurbana; **l. runner** corredor(a) *m,f* de fondo

longhand ['lɒŋhænd] *n* escritura *f* a mano

longing ['lɒŋɪŋ] *n (desire)* anhelo *m*; *(nostalgia)* nostalgia *f*

longitude ['lɒndʒɪtjuːd] *n* longitud *f*

long-playing ['lɒŋpleɪɪŋ] *adj* de larga duración; **l. record** elepé *m*

long-range ['lɒŋreɪndʒ] *adj (missile etc)* de largo alcance; *(weather forecast)* de largo plazo

long-sighted [lɒŋ'saɪtɪd] *adj* **(a)** *Med* présbita **(b)** *Fig* previsor(a)

long-standing ['lɒŋstændɪŋ] *adj* antiguo(a), de mucho tiempo

long-suffering ['lɒŋsʌfərɪŋ] *adj* sufrido(a)

long-term ['lɒŋtɜːm] *adj* a largo plazo

long-winded [lɒŋ'wɪndɪd] *adj* prolijo(a)

loo [luː] *n Br Fam* váter *m*

look [lʊk] **1** *n* **(a)** *(glance)* mirada *f*; **to take a l. at** *(peep)* echar un vistazo a; *(examine)* examinar **(b)** *(appearance)* aspecto *m*, apariencia *f*; **I don't like the l. of it** me da mala espina **(c)** *(fashion)* moda *f* **(d)** **(good) looks** belleza *f*

2 *vi* **(a)** mirar **(b)** *(seem)* parecer; **he looks well** tiene buena cara; **it looks delicious** tiene un aspecto buenísimo; **she looks like her father** *(resembles)* se parece a su padre

3 *vt* mirar
▸ **look after** *vt insep* cuidar a, ocuparse de
▸ **look at** *vt insep* mirar; *Fig* **whichever way you l. at it** desde cualquier punto de vista
▸ **look away** *vi* apartar la mirada
▸ **look back** *vi* **(a)** mirar hacia atrás; *Fig* **since then he has never looked back** desde entonces ha ido prosperando **(b)** *(remember)* recordar
▸ **look down** *vi Fig* **to l. down on sth/sb** despreciar algo/a algn
▸ **look for** *vt insep* buscar
▸ **look forward to** *vt insep* esperar con ansia; **I l. forward to hearing from you** *(in letter)* espero noticias suyas
▸ **look into** *vt insep* examinar, investigar
▸ **look on 1** *vt insep (consider)* considerar
2 *vi* quedarse mirando
▸ **look onto** *vt insep* dar a
▸ **look out** *vi* **(a)** **the bedroom looks out onto the garden** el dormitorio da al jardín **(b)** **l. out!** *(take care)* ¡cuidado!, ¡ojo!
▸ **look over** *vt sep (examine)* revisar; *(place)* inspeccionar
▸ **look round 1** *vi* mirar alrededor; *(turn head)* volver la cabeza
2 *vt insep (house, shop)* ver
▸ **look through** *vt insep* **(a)** *(window)* mirar por **(b)** *(leaf through)* hojear; *(examine)* revisar; *(check)* registrar
▸ **look to** *vt insep* **(a)** *(take care of)* velar por **(b)** *(turn to)* recurrir a
▸ **look up 1** *vi* **(a)** *(glance upwards)* alzar la vista **(b)** *Fam (improve)* mejorar
2 *vt sep* **(a)** *(look for)* buscar **(b)** *(visit)* ir a visitar
▸ **look upon** *vt insep* considerar
▸ **look up to** *vt insep (person)* respetar

lookout ['lʊkaʊt] n (person) centinela mf; (place) mirador m; **to be on the l. for** estar al acecho de; Fam **that's his l.!** ¡eso es asunto suyo!

loom¹ [luːm] n telar m

loom² [luːm] vi alzarse; Fig (threaten) amenazar

loony ['luːnɪ] adj (**loonier, looniest**) Fam loco(a)

loop [luːp] **1** n (a) lazo m (b) Comput bucle m
2 vt (a) encordar (b) Av **to l. the loop** rizar el rizo

loophole ['luːphəʊl] n Fig escapatoria f

loose [luːs] adj (a) (not secure) flojo(a); (papers, hair, clothes) suelto(a); (tongue) desatado(a); (baggy) holgado(a); **to set sb l.** soltar a algn; Fam **to be at a l. end** no saber qué hacer (b) (not packaged) a granel; **l. tobacco** tabaco m en hebras; **l. change** suelto m (c) (not exact) vago(a); (translation) libre (d) (lax) relajado(a); **a l. woman** una mujer fácil

loosely ['luːslɪ] adv (a) (approximately) aproximadamente (b) (vaguely) vagamente

loosen ['luːsən] **1** vt aflojar; (belt) desabrochar; Fig (restrictions) flexibilizar
2 vi (slacken) aflojarse

loot [luːt] **1** n botín m
2 vt saquear

lop [lɒp] vt podar
► **lop off** vt sep cortar

lope [ləʊp] vi andar a zancadas

lopsided [lɒp'saɪdɪd] adj ladeado(a)

lord [lɔːd] n (a) señor m; (British peer) lord m; **the House of Lords** la Cámara de los Lores; **the L. Mayor** el señor alcalde (b) Rel **the L.** El Señor; **good L.!** ¡Dios mío!; **the L.'s Prayer** el Padrenuestro (c) (judge) señoría mf

lordship ['lɔːdʃɪp] n Br **his l./your l.** su señoría

lorry ['lɒrɪ] n Br camión m; **l. driver** camionero(a) m,f; **l. load** carga f

lose [luːz] vt (pt & pp **lost**) perder; **to l. time** (of clock) atrasarse
2 vi perder; **to l. to sb** perder contra algn; **to l. out** salir perdiendo

loser ['luːzə(r)] n perdedor(a) m,f

loss [lɒs] n pérdida f; **to make a l.** perder; Fig **to be at a l. for words** quedarse de una pieza; **to be at a l. what to do** no saber qué hacer

lost [lɒst] **1** adj (a) perdido(a); **to get l.** perderse; Fam **get l.!** ¡vete a la porra!; **l. property office,** US **l. and found department** oficina f de objetos perdidos (b)

(disoriented) desorientado(a); (distracted) distraído(a); **l. in thought** ensimismado(a)
2 pt & pp of **lose**

lot [lɒt] n (a) (fate) suerte f (b) **to cast lots for sth** echar algo a suertes (c) US (plot of land) parcela f (d) (in an auction) lote m (e) (everything) todo m; **he ate the l.** se lo comió todo (f) **a l. of** (much) mucho(a); (many) muchos(as); **he feels a l. better** se encuentra mucho mejor; **she reads a l.** lee mucho; Fam **lots of** montones de, cantidad

lotion ['ləʊʃən] n loción f

lottery ['lɒtərɪ] n lotería f; **l. ticket** ≃ décimo m de lotería

loud [laʊd] **1** adj (a) (voice) alto(a); (noise) fuerte; (laugh) estrepitoso(a); (applause) clamoroso(a); (protests, party) ruidoso(a) (b) (flashy) chillón(ona) (c) (vulgar) hortera
2 adv **to read/think out l.** leer/pensar en voz alta

loud-hailer [laʊd'heɪlə(r)] n megáfono m

loudspeaker [laʊd'spiːkə(r)] n altavoz m

lounge [laʊndʒ] **1** n Br salón m, sala f de estar
2 vi hacer el vago

louse [laʊs] n (pl **lice**) piojo m

lousy ['laʊzɪ] adj (**lousier, lousiest**) Fam fatal; **a l. trick** una cochinada

lout [laʊt] n gamberro m

lovable ['lʌvəbəl] adj adorable

love [lʌv] **1** n (a) amor m (**for** por); (passion) pasión f (**for** por); **to be in l. with sb** estar enamorado(a) de algn; **to fall in l.** enamorarse; **to make l.** hacer el amor; **(with) l. (from) Mary** (in letter) un abrazo, Mary; **l. affair** amorío m; **l. letter/story** carta f/historia f de amor; **l. life** vida f sentimental (b) (person) amor m, cariño m; Fam chato(a) m,f; **my l.** mi amor (c) (in tennis) **forty l.** cuarenta a cero
2 vt (person) querer a, amar a; **he loves cooking/football** le encanta cocinar/el fútbol

lovely ['lʌvlɪ] adj (**lovelier, loveliest**) (charming) encantador(a); (beautiful) hermoso(a), precioso(a); (delicious) riquísimo(a)

lover ['lʌvə(r)] n (a) (sexual partner) amante mf (b) (enthusiast) aficionado(a) m,f, amigo(a) m,f

loving ['lʌvɪŋ] adj cariñoso(a)

low¹ [ləʊ] **1** adj (a) bajo(a); (neckline) escotado(a); **the L. Countries** los Países Bajos (b) (in quantity) bajo(a) (c) (poor) pobre (**d**) (*battery*) gastado(a); **l. frequency** baja frecuencia (**e**) **to feel l.** sentirse deprimido(a) (**f**) (*reprehensible*) malo(a)

2 *adv* bajo

3 *n* (**a**) Met área *f* de baja presión (**b**) (*low point*) punto más bajo; **to reach an all-time l.** tocar fondo

low² [ləʊ] *vi* (*cow*) mugir

lowdown ['ləʊdaʊn] *n* Fam pormenores *mpl*

lower ['ləʊə(r)] **1** *adj* (*comp of* **low**) inferior; Typ **l. case** minúscula *f*; **l. class** clase baja

2 *adv* comp of **low**

3 *vt* bajar; (*flag*) arriar; (*reduce*) reducir; (*price*) rebajar

lower-class ['ləʊəklɑːs] *adj* de clase baja

lowest ['ləʊɪst] **1** *adj* (*superl of* **low**) más bajo(a); (*price, speed*) mínimo(a)

2 *n* **at the l.** como mínimo

low-key [ləʊ'kiː] *adj* sin ceremonia

lowlands ['ləʊləndz] *npl* tierras bajas

lowly ['ləʊlɪ] *adj* (**lowlier, lowliest**) humilde

low-necked ['ləʊnekt] *adj* escotado(a)

loyal ['lɔɪəl] *adj* leal, fiel

loyalty ['lɔɪəltɪ] *n* lealtad *f*, fidelidad *f*

lozenge ['lɒzɪndʒ] *n* pastilla *f*

LP [el'piː] *n* (*abbr* **long-playing record**) LP *m*

L-plate ['elpleɪt] *n* Br placa *f* de la "L"

LSD [eles'diː] *n* (*abbr* **lysergic acid diethylamide**) LSD *m*

Ltd Br Com (*abbr* **Limited (Liability)**) ≃ S.A.

lubricant ['luːbrɪkənt] *n* lubricante *m*

lubricate ['luːbrɪkeɪt] *vt* lubricar; (*engine*) engrasar

lubrication [luːbrɪ'keɪʃən] *n* engrase *m*

lucid ['luːsɪd] *adj* lúcido(a)

luck [lʌk] *n* suerte *f*; **bad l.!** ¡mala suerte!; **good l.!** ¡(buena) suerte!; **to be in l.** estar de suerte; **to be out of l.** no tener suerte; Fig **to push one's l.** tentar la suerte; Fig **to try one's l.** probar fortuna

luckily ['lʌkɪlɪ] *adv* por suerte, afortunadamente

lucky ['lʌkɪ] *adj* (**luckier, luckiest**) (*person*) afortunado(a); (*day*) de suerte; (*move*) oportuno(a); (*charm*) de la suerte; **a l. break** una oportunidad

lucrative ['luːkrətɪv] *adj* lucrativo(a)

ludicrous ['luːdɪkrəs] *adj* absurdo(a), ridículo(a)

lug [lʌg] *vt* Fam arrastrar

luggage ['lʌgɪdʒ] *n* equipaje *m*; **l. rack** Aut baca *f*; Rail portaequipajes *m inv*

lukewarm ['luːkwɔːm] *adj* (*water etc*) tibio(a); Fig (*reception etc*) poco entusiasta

lull [lʌl] **1** *n* (*in storm*) calma chicha; (*in fighting*) tregua *f*

2 *vt* (*cause to sleep*) adormecer; **to l. sb into a false sense of security** infundir una falsa seguridad a algn

lullaby ['lʌləbaɪ] *n* canción *f* de cuna, nana *f*

lumbago [lʌm'beɪgəʊ] *n* lumbago *m*

lumber ['lʌmbə(r)] **1** *n* (**a**) Br (*junk*) trastos viejos (**b**) US (*timber*) maderos *mpl*

2 *vt* Fam cargar (**with** de)

lumberjack ['lʌmbədʒæk] *n* leñador *m*

luminous ['luːmɪnəs] *adj* luminoso(a)

lump [lʌmp] **1** *n* (*of coal etc*) trozo *m*; (*of sugar, earth*) terrón *m*; (*in sauce*) grumo *m*; (*swelling*) bulto *m*; Fam Fig (*in throat*) nudo *m*; **l. sum** cantidad *f* global

2 *vt* Fam (*endure*) aguantar

▸ **lump together** *vt sep* apelotonar

lumpy ['lʌmpɪ] *adj* (**lumpier, lumpiest**) (*bed*) lleno(a) de bultos; (*sauce*) grumoso(a)

lunacy ['luːnəsɪ] *n* locura *f*

lunar ['luːnə(r)] *adj* lunar

lunatic ['luːnətɪk] *adj & n* loco(a) (*m,f*); **l. asylum** manicomio *m*

lunch [lʌntʃ] **1** *n* comida *f*, almuerzo *m*; **l. hour** hora *f* de comer

2 *vi* comer, almorzar

luncheon ['lʌntʃən] *n* Old-fashioned Fml almuerzo *m*; **l. voucher** vale *m* de comida; (**pork**) **l. meat** carne *f* de cerdo troceada, chopped *m*

lunchtime ['lʌntʃtaɪm] *n* hora *f* de comer

lung [lʌŋ] *n* pulmón *m*

lunge [lʌndʒ] **1** *n* arremetida *f*

2 *vi* **to l. (forward)** arremeter; **to l. (out) at sb** arremeter contra algn

lurch [lɜːtʃ] **1** *n* (**a**) (*of vehicle*) sacudida *f*; (*of person*) tambaleo *m* (**b**) Fam **to leave sb in the l.** dejar a algn en la cuneta

2 *vi* (*vehicle*) dar sacudidas; (*person*) tambalearse

lure [lʊə(r)] **1** *n* (*decoy*) señuelo *m*; (*bait*) cebo *m*; Fig (*charm*) aliciente *m*

2 *vt* atraer con engaños

lurid ['lʊərɪd] *adj* (**a**) (*gruesome*) espeluznante; (*sensational*) sensacionalista (**b**) (*gaudy*) chillón(ona)

lurk [lɜːk] *vi* (*lie in wait*) estar al acecho; (*hide*) esconderse

luscious ['lʌʃəs] *adj* (*food*) delicioso(a)

lush [lʌʃ] *adj* (*vegetation*) exuberante

lust [lʌst] **1** *n (sexual desire)* lujuria *f*; *(craving)* ansia *f*; *(greed)* codicia *f*
  2 *vi* **to l. after sth/sb** codiciar algo/ desear a algn
lustre, *US* **luster** [ˈlʌstə(r)] *n* lustre *m*
lusty [ˈlʌstɪ] *adj* (**lustier, lustiest**) robusto(a)
lute [luːt] *n* laúd *m*
Luxembourg [ˈlʌksəmbɜːg] *n* Luxemburgo
luxuriant [lʌgˈzjʊərɪənt] *adj (plants)* exuberante; *(hair etc)* abundante
luxurious [lʌgˈzjʊərɪəs]. *adj* lujoso(a)
luxury [ˈlʌkʃərɪ] *n* lujo *m*; **l. flat** piso *m* de lujo

> 🖉 Note that the Spanish word **lujuria** is a false friend and is never a translation for the English word **luxury**. In Spanish, **lujuria** means "lust".

lychee [ˈlaɪtʃiː] *n* lichi *m*
lying [ˈlaɪɪŋ] **1** *adj* mentiroso(a)
  2 *n* mentiras *fpl*
lynch [lɪntʃ] *vt* linchar
lyre [laɪə(r)] *n Mus* lira *f*
lyric [ˈlɪrɪk] **1** *adj* lírico(a)
  2 *n* (**a**) *(poem)* poema lírico (**b**) **lyrics** *(words of song)* letra *f*
lyrical [ˈlɪrɪkəl] *adj* lírico(a)

M, m [em] *n (the letter)* M, m *f*

m (**a**) *(abbr* **metre(s))** m (**b**) *(abbr* **million(s))** m

mac [mæk] *n Br Fam (raincoat)* impermeable *m*, gabardina *f*

macabre [mə'kɑ:brə] *adj* macabro(a)

mac(c)aroni [mækə'rəʊnɪ] *n* macarrones *mpl*

mace¹ [meɪs] *n (club, ceremonial staff)* maza *f*

mace² [meɪs] *n (spice)* macis *f inv*

machine [mə'ʃiːn] **1** *n* máquina *f*; **m. gun** ametralladora *f*, **m. language** lenguaje *m* máquina

2 *vt* trabajar a máquina

machine-gun [mə'ʃiːngʌn] *vt* ametrallar

machine-readable [mə'ʃiːn'riːdəbəl] *adj Comput* para ser leído(a) por ordenador *or Am* computadora

machinery [mə'ʃiːnərɪ] *n (machines)* maquinaria *f*, *(workings of machine)* mecanismo *m*; *Fig* **the bureaucratic m.** la maquinaria burocrática

macintosh 'mækɪntɒʃ *n* = **mackintosh**

mackerel ['mækrəl] *n (pl* **mackerel)** caballa *f*

mackintosh ['mækɪntɒʃ] *n* impermeable *m*

macroeconomics [mækrəʊi:kə'nɒmɪks] *n sing* macroeconomía *f*

mad [mæd] *adj* (**madder, maddest**) (**a**) loco(a); *(animal)* furioso(a); *(dog)* rabioso(a); **to be m.** estar loco(a); **to drive sb m.** volver loco(a) a algn; **to go m.** volverse loco(a); **you must be m.!** ¿estás loco?; *Fam* **m. cow disease** el mal de las vacas locas (**b**) *(idea, plan)* disparatado(a) (**c**) *Fam* **to be m. about sth/sb** estar loco(a) por algo/algn (**d**) *esp US Fam* **to be m. at sb** estar enfadado(a) con algn (**e**) *(gallop, race etc)* desenfrenado(a)

madam ['mædəm] *n* (**a**) señora *f*; **Dear M.** *(in letter)* Muy señora mía, Estimada señora (**b**) *(of brothel)* madam *f*

madden ['mædən] *vt* volver loco(a)

maddening ['mædənɪŋ] *adj* exasperante

made [meɪd] *pt & pp of* **make**

Madeira [mə'dɪərə] *n* (**a**) *(island)* Madeira (**b**) *(wine)* madeira *m*; **M. cake** bizcocho *m*

made-to-measure ['meɪdtə'meʒə(r)] *adj* hecho(a) a (la) medida

made-up ['meɪdʌp] *adj* (**a**) *(face, person)* maquillado(a); *(eyes, lips)* pintado(a) (**b**) *(story, excuse)* inventado(a)

madly ['mædlɪ] *adv Fam (extremely)* terriblemente; **to be m. in love with sb** estar locamente enamorado(a) de algn

madman ['mædmən] *n* loco *m*

madness ['mædnɪs] *n* locura *f*

Madrid [mə'drɪd] *n* Madrid

Mafia ['mæfɪə] *n* mafia *f*

magazine [mægə'ziːn] *n* (**a**) *(periodical)* revista *f* (**b**) *(in rifle)* recámara *f* (**c**) *Mil (storehouse)* almacén *m*; *(for explosives)* polvorín *m*

maggot ['mægət] *n* larva *f*, gusano *m*

magic ['mædʒɪk] **1** *n* magia *f*

2 *adj* (**a**) mágico(a); **m. wand** varita mágica (**b**) *Fam (wonderful)* estupendo(a)

magical ['mædʒɪkəl] *adj* mágico(a)

magician [mə'dʒɪʃən] *n* (**a**) *(wizard)* mago(a) *m*, *f* (**b**) *(conjurer)* prestidigitador(a) *m*, *f*

magistrate ['mædʒɪstreɪt] *n* juez *mf* de primera instancia; **magistrates' court** juzgado *m* de primera instancia

magnanimous [mæg'nænɪməs] *adj* magnánimo(a)

magnet ['mægnɪt] *n* imán *m*

magnetic [mæg'netɪk] *adj* magnético(a); *Fig (personality)* carismático(a); **m. tape** cinta magnetofónica

magnetism ['mægnɪtɪzəm] *n* magnetismo *m*

magnificence [mæg'nɪfɪsəns] *n* magnificencia *f*

magnificent [mæg'nɪfɪsənt] *adj* magnífico(a)

magnify ['mægnɪfaɪ] *vt* (**a**) *(enlarge)* aumentar (**b**) *Fig (exaggerate)* exagerar

magnifying glass ['mægnɪfaɪŋɡlɑːs] *n* lupa *f*

magnitude ['mægnɪtjuːd] *n* magnitud *f*

magpie ['mægpaɪ] *n* urraca *f*

mahogany [mə'hɒgənɪ] **1** n caoba f
2 adj de caoba

maid [meɪd] n (**a**) criada f, Andes, RP mucama f (**b**) Pej old m. solterona f

maiden ['meɪdən] **1** n Literary doncella f
2 adj (**a**) (unmarried) soltera; **m. aunt** tía soltera; **m. name** apellido m de soltera (**b**) (voyage, flight) inaugural

mail [meɪl] **1** n correo m; **by m.** por correo; **m. order** venta f por correo; **m. train** tren m correo
2 vt (post) echar al buzón; (send) enviar por correo

mailbox ['meɪlbɒks] n US buzón m

mailing list ['meɪlɪŋlɪst] n lista f de direcciones

mailman ['meɪlmæn] n US cartero m

maim [meɪm] vt lisiar

main [meɪn] **1** adj (problem, door etc) principal; (square, mast, sail) mayor; (office) central; **the m. thing is to keep calm** lo esencial es mantener la calma; Culin **m. course** plato m principal; **m. road** carretera f principal; US **M. Street** la Calle Mayor
2 n (**a**) (pipe, wire) conducto m principal; **the mains** (water or gas system) la cañería maestra; Elec la red eléctrica; **a radio that works on battery or mains** una radio que funciona con pilas o con corriente (**b**) **in the m.** por regla general

mainframe ['meɪnfreɪm] n **m. computer** computer or Am ordenadora f central

mainland ['meɪnlənd] n continente m

mainly ['meɪnlɪ] adv principalmente, sobre todo; (for the most part) en su mayoría

mainstay ['meɪnsteɪ] n Fig sustento m, sostén m

mainstream ['meɪnstriːm] n corriente f principal

maintain [meɪn'teɪn] vt mantener; (conversation) sostener; (silence, appearances) guardar; (road, machine) conservar en buen estado

maintenance ['meɪntənəns] n (**a**) mantenimiento m (**b**) (divorce allowance) pensión f

maisonette [meɪzə'net] n Br dúplex m

maître d' ['meɪtrə'diː] n US maître mf

maize [meɪz] n maíz m

majestic [mə'dʒestɪk] adj majestuoso(a)

majesty ['mædʒɪstɪ] n majestad f

major ['meɪdʒə(r)] **1** adj (**a**) principal, mayor; (contribution, operation) importante (**b**) Mus mayor
2 n (**a**) Mil comandante m (**b**) US Univ especialidad f

3 vi US Univ **to m. in** especializarse en

Majorca [mə'jɔːkə] n Mallorca

Majorcan [mə'jɔːkən] adj & n mallorquín(ina) (m,f)

majority [mə'dʒɒrɪtɪ] n mayoría f; **to be in the m.** ser (la) mayoría

make [meɪk] (pt & pp made) **1** vt (**a**) hacer; (manufacture) fabricar; (create) crear; (clothes, curtains) confeccionar; (meal) preparar; (payment) efectuar; (speech) pronunciar; (decision) tomar; (mistake) cometer; **to be made of** ser de; **to m. a noise** hacer ruido
(**b**) (render) poner, volver; (convert) convertir (into en); (appoint) nombrar; **he made it clear that ...** dejó claro que ...
(**c**) (force, compel) obligar; (cause) causar; **to m. do with sth** arreglárselas con algo
(**d**) (earn) ganar; **to m. a living** ganarse la vida; **to m. a name for oneself** hacerse famoso(a); Fig **to m. the best of sth** sacar partido de algo
(**e**) **7 and 5 m. 12** 7 y 5 son 12
(**f**) (calculate, reckon) calcular; **what time do you m. it?** ¿qué hora tienes?
(**g**) (think) opinar; **I don't know what to m. of it** no sé qué pensar de eso; **it doesn't m. sense** no tiene sentido
(**h**) (achieve) alcanzar, conseguir
(**i**) **it will m. or break her** será su consagración o su ruina
(**j**) **to m. a fresh start** volver a empezar
2 vi (**a**) hacer; **to m. sure of sth** asegurarse de algo
(**b**) **she made as if to leave** hizo como si quisiera marcharse
3 n (**a**) (brand) marca f
(**b**) Fam **to be on the m.** andar tras el dinero
►**make for** vt insep (**a**) (move towards) dirigirse hacia; (attack) atacar a (**b**) **this makes for less work** esto ahorra trabajo
►**make out 1** vt sep (**a**) (list, receipt) hacer; (cheque) extender (**b**) (perceive) distinguir; (writing) descifrar (**c**) (understand) entender (**d**) (claim) pretender (**e**) **to m. out a case for doing sth** exponer los argumentos para hacer algo
2 vi **how did you m. out?** ¿qué tal te fue?
►**make up 1** vt sep (**a**) (parcel, list) hacer; (prescription) preparar; (assemble) montar (**b**) (story) inventar (**c**) (apply cosmetics to) maquillar; (one's face) maquillarse (**d**) (loss) compensar; (lost time) recuperar (**e**) (constitute) componer (**f**) **to m. it up (with sb)** hacer las

paces (con algn) **(g) to m. up one's mind** decidirse

2 *vi* maquillarse

▸ **make up to 1** *vt insep Br Fam* **to m. up to sb** congraciarse con algn

2 *vt sep* **to m. it up to sb for sth** compensar a algn por algo

make-believe ['meɪkbɪliːv] *n (fantasy)* fantasía *f; (pretence)* fingimiento *m;* **to live in a world of m.** vivir en un mundo de ensueño

maker ['meɪkə(r)] *n* fabricante *mf*

makeshift ['meɪkʃɪft] *adj (improvised)* improvisado(a); *(temporary)* provisional

make-up ['meɪkʌp] *n* **(a)** *(cosmetics)* maquillaje *m;* **m. remover** desmaquillador *m* **(b)** *(composition)* composición *f, (character)* carácter *m*

making ['meɪkɪŋ] *n* **(a)** *(manufacture)* fabricación *f; (preparation)* preparación *f* **(b) he has the makings of a politician** tiene madera de político

malaise [mæˈleɪz] *n* malestar *m*

malaria [məˈleərɪə] *n* malaria *f*

Malay [məˈleɪ] **1** *adj* malayo(a)

2 *n* **(a)** *(person)* malayo(a) *m,f* **(b)** *(language)* malayo *m*

Malaysia [məˈleɪzɪə] *n* Malasia

male [meɪl] **1** *adj (animal, plant)* macho; *(person)* varón; *(sex)* masculino; *Pej* **m. chauvinism** machismo *m*

2 *n (person)* varón *m; (animal, plant)* macho *m*

malevolent [məˈlevələnt] *adj* malévolo(a)

malfunction [mælˈfʌŋkʃən] **1** *n* mal funcionamiento *m*

2 *vi* funcionar mal

malice ['mælɪs] *n* malicia *f; Jur* **with m. aforethought** con premeditación

malicious [məˈlɪʃəs] *adj* malévolo(a)

malign [məˈlaɪn] **1** *adj* maligno(a); *(influence)* perjudicial

2 *vt* calumniar, difamar

malignant [məˈlɪgnənt] *adj* **(a)** *(person)* malvado(a) **(b)** *Med* maligno(a)

mall [mɔːl] *n US* centro *m* comercial

malleable ['mælɪəbəl] *adj* maleable

mallet ['mælɪt] *n* mazo *m*

malnutrition [mælnjuːˈtrɪʃən] *n* desnutrición *f*

malpractice [mælˈpræktɪs] *n* procedimiento *m* ilegal; *Med* negligencia *f*

malt [mɔːlt] *n* malta *f*

Malta ['mɔːltə] *n* Malta

mammal ['mæməl] *n* mamífero *m*

mammary ['mæmərɪ] *adj* **m. gland** mama *f*

mammoth ['mæməθ] **1** *n Zool* mamut *m*

2 *adj* gigantesco(a)

man [mæn] **1** *n (pl* **men) (a)** hombre *m;* **old m.** viejo *m;* **young m.** joven *m; Fig* **he's a m. of his word** es hombre de palabra; *Fig* **the m. in the street** el hombre de la calle; **m. Friday** factótum *m; Fam* **dirty old m.** viejo verde **(b)** *(humanity)* el hombre **(c)** *(husband)* marido *m; (partner)* pareja *f* **(d) our m. in Madrid** nuestro representante en Madrid **(e)** *(in chess)* pieza *f*

2 *vt (boat, plane)* tripular; *(post)* servir; **manned flight** vuelo tripulado

manage ['mænɪdʒ] **1** *vt* **(a)** *(company, household)* llevar; *(money, affairs, person)* manejar **(b)** *(succeed)* conseguir; **to m. to do sth** lograr hacer algo

2 *vi (cope physically)* poder; *(esp financially)* arreglárselas; **we're managing** vamos tirando

manageable ['mænɪdʒəbəl] *adj* manejable

management ['mænɪdʒmənt] *n* dirección *f*

manager ['mænɪdʒə(r)] *n* **(a)** *(of company, bank)* director(a) *m,f; (head of department)* jefe(a) *m,f* **(b)** *(of pop group etc)* mánager *m* **(c)** *Sport* entrenador *m*

manageress [mænɪdʒəˈres] *n (of shop, restaurant)* encargada *f; (of company)* directora *f*

managerial [mænɪˈdʒɪərɪəl] *adj* directivo(a)

managing ['mænɪdʒɪŋ] *adj* directivo(a); **m. director** director(a) *m,f* gerente

mandarin ['mændərɪn] *n* **m. (orange)** mandarina *f*

mandate ['mændeɪt] *n* mandato *m*

mandatory ['mændətərɪ] *adj Fml* obligatorio(a)

mane [meɪn] *n (of horse)* crin *f; (of lion)* melena *f*

maneuver [məˈnuːvər] *n, vt & vi US* = **manoeuvre**

manfully ['mænfʊlɪ] *adv* valientemente

manger ['meɪndʒə(r)] *n* pesebre *m*

mangle¹ ['mæŋgəl] *n (for wringing)* rodillo *m*

mangle² ['mæŋgəl] *vt (crush)* aplastar; *(destroy by cutting)* despedazar

mango ['mæŋgəʊ] *n (pl* **mangoes)** mango *m*

mangy ['meɪndʒɪ] *adj* **(mangier, mangiest)** *(animal)* sarnoso(a); *Fam (carpet)* raído(a)

manhandle ['mænhændəl] *vt* maltratar

manhole ['mænhəʊl] *n* boca *f* de acceso

manhood ['mænhʊd] *n* **(a)** *(age)* mayoría

f de edad; **to reach m.** llegar a la edad viril (**b**) *(manly qualities)* virilidad *f*

mania ['meɪnɪə] *n* manía *f*

maniac ['meɪnɪæk] *n* maníaco(a) *m,f*; *Fam* loco(a) *m,f*

manic ['mænɪk] *adj* maníaco(a)

manic-depressive ['mænɪkdɪ'presɪv] *adj & n* maníaco(a) *(m,f)* depresivo(a)

manicure ['mænɪkjʊə(r)] **1** *n* manicura *f*
2 *vt* **to m. one's nails** hacerse la manicura

manifest ['mænɪfest] *Fml* **1** *adj* manifiesto(à)
2 *vt* manifestar

manifesto [mænɪ'festəʊ] *n* programa *m* electoral

manifold ['mænɪfəʊld] *adj Fml (many)* múltiples; *(varied)* diversos(as)

manipulate [mə'nɪpjʊleɪt] *vt* (**a**) manipular (**b**) *Fig (accounts etc)* falsificar

mankind [mæn'kaɪnd] *n* la humanidad, el género humano

manly ['mænlɪ] *adj* (**manlier, manliest**) varonil, viril

man-made ['mænmeɪd] *adj (lake)* artificial; *(fibres, fabric)* sintético(a)

manner ['mænə(r)] *n* (**a**) *(way, method)* manera *f*, modo *m*; **in this m.** de esta manera (**b**) *(way of behaving)* forma *f* de ser (**c**) *Fml (type, class)* clase *f* (**d**) *(etiquette)* (**good**) **manners** buenos modales; **bad manners** falta *f* de educación

mannerism ['mænərɪzəm] *n (gesture)* gesto *m*; *(affectation)* amaneramiento *m*

manoeuvre [mə'nuːvə(r)] **1** *n* maniobra *f*
2 *vt* maniobrar; *(person)* manejar
3 *vi* maniobrar

manor ['mænə(r)] *n* **m. house** casa solariega

manpower ['mænpaʊə(r)] *n* mano *f* de obra

mansion ['mænʃən] *n* casa *f* grande; *(in country)* casa solariega

manslaughter ['mænslɔːtə(r)] *n* homicidio involuntario

mantelpiece ['mæntəlpiːs] *n (shelf)* repisa *f* de chimenea; *(fireplace)* chimenea *f*

mantle ['mæntəl] *n Fig (of snow)* manto *m*, capa *f*

⌀ Note that the Spanish word **mantel** is a false friend and is never a translation for the English word **mantle**. In Spanish, **mantel** means "tablecloth".

---

manual ['mænjʊəl] *adj & n* manual *(m)*

manufacture [mænjʊ'fæktʃə(r)] **1** *vt* fabricar
2 *n* fabricación *f*

manufacturer [mænjʊ'fæktʃərə(r)] *n* fabricante *mf*

manure [mə'njʊə(r)] *n* abono *m*, estiércol *m*

manuscript ['mænjʊskrɪpt] *n* manuscrito *m*

many ['menɪ] **1** *adj* (**more, most**) mucho(a)/muchos(as); **a great m.** muchísimos(as); **as m. ... as ...** tantos(as) ... como ...; **how m. days?** ¿cuántos días?; **m. a time** muchas veces; **so m. flowers!** ¡cuántas flores!; **too m.** demasiados(as)
2 *pron* muchos(as)

map [mæp] **1** *n (of country)* mapa *m*; *(of town, bus route)* plano *m*
2 *vt* trazar un mapa de
► map out *vt sep (route)* trazar en un mapa; *Fig (future etc)* planear

maple ['meɪpəl] *n* arce *m*

mar [mɑː(r)] *vt* estropear; **to m. sb's enjoyment** aguarle la fiesta a algn

marathon ['mærəθən] *n* maratón *m*

marble ['mɑːbəl] **1** *n* (**a**) *(stone)* mármol *m* (**b**) *(glass ball)* canica *f*
2 *adj* de mármol

March [mɑːtʃ] *n* marzo *m*

march [mɑːtʃ] **1** *n* (**a**) *Mil* marcha *f*; *Fig* **to steal a m. on sb** tomar la delantera a algn; **m. past** desfile *m* (**b**) *(demonstration)* manifestación *f*
2 *vi* (**a**) marchar (**b**) *(demonstrate)* manifestarse
3 *vt Mil* hacer marchar

mare [meə(r)] *n* yegua *f*

margarine [mɑːdʒə'riːn] *n* margarina *f*

margin ['mɑːdʒɪn] *n* margen *m*; *Fig* **to win by a narrow m.** ganar por escaso margen; **m. of error** *(in statistics)* margen de error

marginal ['mɑːdʒɪnəl] *adj* marginal; *Pol* **m. seat** escaño *m* pendiente

marginally ['mɑːdʒɪnəlɪ] *adv* ligeramente

marigold ['mærɪgəʊld] *n* caléndula *f*

marijuana, marihuana [mærɪ'hwɑːnə] *n* marihuana *f*, marijuana *f*

marinate ['mærɪneɪt] *vt* adobar

marine [mə'riːn] **1** *adj* marino(a)
2 *n* soldado *m* de infantería de marina; *Br* **the Marines,** *US* **the M. Corps** la infantería de marina

marital ['mærɪtəl] *adj* matrimonial; **m. status** estado *m* civil

maritime ['mærɪtaɪm] *adj* marítimo(a)

marjoram ['mɑːdʒərəm] *n* mejorana *f*

mark¹ [mɑːk] **1** *n* (**a**) *(left by blow etc)* señal *f*; *(stain)* mancha *f*; *Fig* **to make one's m.** distinguirse (**b**) *(sign, token)* señal *f; (indication)* indicio *m* (**c**) *Br (in exam etc)* nota *f;* **to get high marks** sacar buenas notas (**d**) *Fig* **to hit the m.** dar en el clavo; *Fig* **to be wide of the m.** estar lejos de la verdad

2 *vt* (**a**) *(stain)* manchar (**b**) *(with tick, cross)* señalar (**c**) *(exam)* corregir; *(student)* dar notas a (**d**) **10 percent off marked price** *(sign)* descuento del 10 por ciento sobre el precio indicado (**e**) **m. my words** fíjate en lo que te digo (**f**) *Sport* marcar (**g**) **to m. time** *Mil* marcar el paso; *Fig* hacer tiempo

▸ **mark out** *vt sep* (**a**) *(area)* delimitar (**b**) **to m. sb out for** destinar a algn a

mark² [mɑːk] *n (unit of currency)* marco *m*

marked [mɑːkt] *adj (noticeable)* marcado(a), acusado(a)

marker ['mɑːkə(r)] *n* (**a**) *(bookmark)* registro *m* (**b**) *Sport* marcador(a) *m,f* (**c**) *(pen)* rotulador *m* fluorescente

market ['mɑːkɪt] **1** *n* mercado *m;* **on the m.** en venta; **m. forces** tendencias *fpl* del mercado; *Br* **m. garden** *(small)* huerto *m; (large)* huerta *f; Br* **m. gardener** hortelano(a) *m,f;* **m. price** precio *m* de mercado; **m. research** estudio *m* de mercado

2 *vt (sell)* poner en venta; *(promote)* promocionar

marketable ['mɑːkɪtəbəl] *adj* comerciable

marketing ['mɑːkɪtɪŋ] *n* marketing *m,* mercadotecnia *f*

marketplace ['mɑːkɪtpleɪs] *n* mercado *m*

marksman ['mɑːksmən] *n* tirador *m*

marmalade ['mɑːməleɪd] *n* mermelada *f (de cítricos)*

maroon [mə'ruːn] *adj (de color)* granate

marooned [mə'ruːnd] *adj* bloqueado(a)

marquee [mɑː'kiː] *n* (**a**) *Br (tent)* carpa *f* (**b**) *US (of building)* marquesina *f*

marquess, marquis ['mɑːkwɪs] *n* marqués *m*

marriage ['mærɪdʒ] *n (state)* matrimonio *m; (wedding)* boda *f;* **m. bureau** agencia *f* matrimonial; **m. certificate** certificado *m* de matrimonio

married ['mærɪd] *adj* casado(a); **m. life** vida *f* conyugal

marrow ['mærəʊ] *n* (**a**) **(bone) m.** médula *f* (**b**) **(vegetable) m.** calabacín *m*

marry ['mærɪ] *vt (take in marriage)* casarse con; *(give in marriage)* casar (**to** con); *(unite in marriage)* casar; **to get married** casarse

Mars [mɑːz] *n* Marte *m*

marsh [mɑːʃ] *n* pantano *m;* **salt m.** marisma *f*

marshal ['mɑːʃəl] **1** *n* (**a**) *Mil* mariscal *m* (**b**) *Br (at sports event etc)* oficial *mf* (**c**) *US (sheriff)* alguacil *m* (**d**) *US (of police or fire department)* jefe *m*

2 *vt* (**a**) *Mil* formar (**b**) *(facts etc)* ordenar

marshy ['mɑːʃɪ] *adj* (**marshier, marshiest**) pantanoso(a)

martial ['mɑːʃəl] *adj* marcial; **m. arts** artes *fpl* marciales; **m. law** ley *f* marcial

Martian ['mɑːʃən] *adj & n* marciano(a) *(m,f)*

martyr ['mɑːtə(r)] **1** *n* mártir *mf*

2 *vt* martirizar

martyrdom ['mɑːtədəm] *n* martirio *m*

marvel ['mɑːvəl] **1** *n* maravilla *f*

2 *vi* **to m. at** maravillarse de

marvellous, *US* **marvelous** ['mɑːvələs] *adj* maravilloso(a)

Marxism ['mɑːksɪzəm] *n* marxismo *m*

Marxist ['mɑːksɪst] *adj & n* marxista *(mf)*

marzipan ['mɑːzɪpæn] *n* mazapán *m*

mascara [mæ'skɑːrə] *n* rímel *m*

> 🖉 Note that the Spanish word **máscara** is a false friend and is never a translation for the English word **mascara**. In Spanish, **máscara** means "mask".

mascot ['mæskət] *n* mascota *f*

masculine ['mæskjʊlɪn] *adj* masculino(a); *(woman)* hombruna

mash [mæʃ] **1** *n (for animals)* afrecho *m*

2 *vt* **to m. (up)** machacar; **mashed potatoes** puré *m* de patatas *or Am* papas

mask [mɑːsk] **1** *n* (**a**) *(mask)* máscara *f; (of doctor, dentist etc)* mascarilla *f*

2 *vt* enmascarar; *Fig (conceal)* ocultar *(from* de*)*

masochist ['mæsəkɪst] *adj & n* masoquista *(mf)*

mason ['meɪsən] *n* (**a**) *(builder)* albañil *m* (**b**) *(freemason)* masón *m,* francmasón *m*

masonic [mə'sɒnɪk] *adj* masónico(a)

masonry ['meɪsənrɪ] *n (stonework)* albañilería *f*

masquerade [mæskə'reɪd] **1** *n (pretence)* farsa *f*

2 *vi* **to m. as** hacerse pasar por

mass¹ [mæs] *n Rel* misa *f;* **to say m.** decir misa

mass² [mæs] **1** *n* (**a**) masa *f* (**b**) *(large quantity)* montón *m; (of people)* multitud *f* (**c**) **the masses** las masas

2 *adj* masivo(a); **m. media** medios *mpl* de comunicación (de masas); **m. production** fabricación *f* en serie

3 *vi (people)* congregarse; *Mil* concentrarse

massacre ['mæsəkə(r)] **1** n masacre f
2 vt masacrar

massage ['mæsɑːʒ, mə'sɑːdʒ] **1** n masaje m
2 vt (**a**) dar masajes a (**b**) Fig (figures) amañar

masseur [mæ'sɜː(r)] n masajista m

masseuse [mæ'sɜːz] n masajista f

massive ['mæsɪv] adj enorme; (heart attack) grave

mast [mɑːst] n (**a**) Naut mástil m (**b**) Rad & TV torre f

master ['mɑːstə(r)] **1** n (**a**) (of dog, servant) amo m; (of household) señor m (**b**) Br (teacher) profesor m (**c**) Univ **m.'s degree** ≃ máster m (**d**) (expert) maestro m (**e**) (boy) **M. James Brown** el señor James Brown
2 adj (**a**) **m. copy** original m; **m. key** llave f maestra (**b**) (expert) maestro(a)
3 vt (**a**) (person, situation) dominar (**b**) (subject, skill) llegar a dominar

masterful ['mɑːstəfʊl] adj autoritario(a); (imperious) imperioso(a); (personality) dominante

masterly ['mɑːstəlɪ] adj magistral

mastermind ['mɑːstəmaɪnd] **1** n (person) cerebro m
2 vt ser el cerebro de

masterpiece ['mɑːstəpiːs] n obra f maestra

mastery ['mɑːstərɪ] n (**a**) (control) dominio m (**of** de) (**b**) (skill, expertise) maestría f

masturbate ['mæstəbeɪt] vi masturbarse

mat¹ [mæt] n (rug) alfombrilla f; (doormat) felpudo m; (rush mat) estera f; Sport colchoneta f

mat² [mæt] adj mate

match¹ [mætʃ] n cerilla f, fósforo m

match² [mætʃ] **1** n (**a**) Sport partido m; (in boxing) combate m (**b**) Fig **to meet one's m.** (equal) encontrar uno la horma de su zapato
2 vt (**a**) (equal, be the equal of) igualar (**b**) (be in harmony with) armonizar; **they are well matched** (teams) van iguales; (couple) hacen buena pareja (**c**) (colours, clothes) hacer juego con; (pair of socks, gloves) ser el compañero de
3 vi (harmonize) hacer juego

matchbox ['mætʃbɒks] n caja f de cerillas

matching ['mætʃɪŋ] adj que hace juego

mate [meɪt] **1** n (**a**) (at school, work) compañero(a) m,f, colega mf; Br Fam (friend) amigo(a) m,f (**b**) Zool (male) macho m; (female) hembra f (**c**) (assistant)

ayudante mf (**d**) Naut **first/second m.** primer/segundo oficial
2 vt Zool aparear
3 vi Zool aparearse

material [mə'tɪərɪəl] **1** n (**a**) (substance) materia f (**b**) (cloth) tejido m, tela f (**c**) (information) material m (**d**) **materials** (ingredients, equipment) materiales mpl
2 adj (**a**) substancial (**b**) (not spiritual) material

materialistic [mətɪərɪə'lɪstɪk] adj materialista

materialize [mə'tɪərɪəlaɪz] vi (**a**) (hopes) realizarse; (plan, idea) concretarse (**b**) (show up) presentarse

maternal [mə'tɜːnəl] adj maternal; (uncle etc) materno(a)

maternity [mə'tɜːnɪtɪ] n maternidad f; **m. dress** vestido m premamá; **m. hospital** maternidad f

math [mæθ] n US = **maths**

mathematical [mæθə'mætɪkəl] adj matemático(a)

mathematician [mæθəmə'tɪʃən] n matemático(a) m,f

mathematics [mæθə'mætɪks] n sing matemáticas fpl

maths [mæθs] n sing Fam matemáticas fpl

matinée ['mætɪneɪ] n Cin sesión f de tarde; Th función f de tarde

mating ['meɪtɪŋ] n apareamiento m; **m. call** reclamo m; **m. season** época f de celo

matrices ['meɪtrɪsiːz] pl of **matrix**

matriculation [mətrɪkjʊ'leɪʃən] n Univ matriculación f

matrimonial [mætrɪ'məʊnɪəl] adj matrimonial

matrimony ['mætrɪmənɪ] n matrimonio m; (married life) vida f conyugal

matrix ['meɪtrɪks] n (pl **matrices**) matriz f

matron ['meɪtrən] n (in hospital) enfermera f jefe

matronly ['meɪtrənlɪ] adj madura y recia

matt [mæt] adj mate

matted ['mætɪd] adj enmarañado(a)

matter ['mætə(r)] **1** n (**a**) (affair, question) asunto m; **as a m. of course** por rutina; **as a m. of fact** en realidad; **that's another m.** eso es otra cosa (**b**) (problem) **what's the m.?** ¿qué pasa? (**c**) no **m. what he does** haga lo que haga; **no m. when** no importa cuando; **no m. where you go** dondequiera que vayas; **no m. how clever he is** por muy inteligente que sea; **no m. how** como sea (**d**) (substance) materia f, sustancia f (**e**) (content) contenido m;

(subject) tema *m* (**f**) *Med (pus)* pus *m*

  2 *vi* importar; **it doesn't m.** no importa, da igual

matter-of-fact ['mætərəv'fækt] *adj* *(person)* práctico(a); *(account)* realista; *(style)* prosaico(a)

mattress ['mætrɪs] *n* colchón *f*

mature [mə'tʃʊə(r)] **1** *adj* maduro(a); *Fin* vencido(a)

  2 *vi* madurar; *Fin* vencer

  3 *vt* madurar

maturity [mə'tʃʊərɪtɪ] *n* madurez *f*

maul [mɔːl] *vt* (**a**) *(wound)* agredir (**b**) *(handle roughly)* maltratar (**c**) *(touch in unpleasant way)* sobar

mauve [məʊv] *adj & n* malva (*m*)

max [mæks] *n (abbr* **maximum**) máx

maxim ['mæksɪm] *n* máxima *f*

maxima ['mæksɪmə] *pl of* **maximum**

maximize ['mæksɪmaɪz] *vt* maximizar

maximum ['mæksɪməm] **1** *n (pl* **maxima**) máximo *m*

  2 *adj* máximo(a)

May [meɪ] *n* mayo *m*; **M. Day** el Primero *or* el Uno de Mayo

may [meɪ] *v aux (pt* **might**)

En el inglés hablado, y en el escrito en estilo coloquial, la forma negativa **might not** se transforma en **mightn't**. La forma **might have** se transforma en **might've**.

(**a**) *(expressing possibility)* poder, ser posible; **be that as it m.** sea como sea; **come what m.** pase lo que pase; **he m.** *or* **might come** puede que venga; **you m.** *or* **might as well stay** más vale que te quedes (**b**) *(permission)* poder; **m. I?** ¿me permite?; **you~m. smoke** pueden fumar (**c**) *(wish)* ojalá (+ *subj);* **m. you always be happy!** ¡ojalá seas siempre feliz!

maybe ['meɪbiː] *adv* quizá(s), tal vez

mayhem ['meɪhem] *n (disturbance)* alboroto *m;* *(havoc)* estragos *mpl*

mayonnaise [meɪə'neɪz] *n* mayonesa *f,* mahonesa *f*

mayor [meə(r)] *n (man)* alcalde *m; (woman)* alcaldesa *f*

mayoress ['meərɪs] *n* alcaldesa *f*

maze [meɪz] *n* laberinto *m*

MD [em'diː] *n* (**a**) *(abbr* **Doctor of Medicine**) Dr. en Medicina (**b**) *Fam (abbr* **Managing Director**) director(a) *m,f* gerente

me [miː, *unstressed* mɪ] *pron* (**a**) *(as object)* me; **he gave it to me** me lo dio; **listen to me** escúchame; **she knows me** me conoce (**b**) *(after prep)* mí; **it's for me** es para mí; **with me** conmigo (**c**) *(emphatic)*

yo; **it's me** soy yo; **what about me?** ¿y yo, qué?

meadow ['medəʊ] *n* prado *m,* pradera *f*

meagre, *US* **meager** ['miːgə(r)] *adj* exiguo(a)

meal¹ [miːl] *n (flour)* harina *f*

meal² [miːl] *n (food)* comida *f*

mealtime ['miːltaɪm] *n* hora *f* de comer

mean¹ [miːn] *vt (pt & pp* **meant**) (**a**) *(signify)* significar, querer decir; **what do you m. by that?** ¿qué quieres decir con eso? (**b**) *(intend)* pensar, tener la intención de; **I m. it** (te) lo digo en serio; **she was meant to arrive on the 7th** tenía que *or* debía llegar el día 7; **they m. well** tienen buenas intenciones; **she didn't m. to do it** lo hizo sin querer (**c**) *(entail)* suponer (**d**) *(refer to)* referirse a (**e**) *(destine)* destinar (**for** a *or* para)

mean² [miːn] *adj* (**meaner, meanest**) (**a**) *(miserly)* tacaño(a) (**b**) *(unkind)* malo(a); *(petty)* mezquino(a); *US (bad-tempered)* malhumorado(a); **to be m. to sb** tratar mal a algn (**c**) *(inferior)* mediocre; *(origins)* humilde (**d**) **it was no m. feat** fue toda una hazaña

mean³ [miːn] **1** *adj (average)* medio(a)

  2 *n (average)* promedio *m; Math* media *f*

meander [mɪ'ændə(r)] *vi (river)* serpentear; *(person)* vagar; *Fig (digress)* divagar

meaning ['miːnɪŋ] *n* sentido *m,* significado *m*

meaningful ['miːnɪŋfʊl] *adj* significativo(a)

meaningless ['miːnɪŋlɪs] *adj* sin sentido

meanness ['miːnnɪs] *n* (**a**) *(miserliness)* tacañería *f* (**b**) *(nastiness)* maldad *f*

means [miːnz] *n* (**a**) *sing or pl (method)* medio *m,* manera *f;* **by m. of** por medio de, mediante (**b**) *pl (resources, wealth)* medios *mpl* (de vida), recursos *mpl* (económicos); **to live beyond one's m.** vivir por encima de sus posibilidades (**c**) **by all m.!** ¡por supuesto!; **by no m.** de ninguna manera

meant [ment] *pt & pp of* **mean**

meantime ['miːntaɪm] **1** *adv* mientras tanto

  2 in the m. mientras tanto

meanwhile ['miːnwaɪl] *adv* mientras tanto

measles ['miːzəlz] *n sing* sarampión *m*

measure ['meʒə(r)] **1** *n* (**a**) *(action, step)* medida *f* (**b**) *(ruler)* regla *f* (**c**) **in some m.** hasta cierto punto (**d**) *Mus* compás *m*

  2 *vt (object, area)* medir; *(person)* tomar las medidas de

📝 Note that the Spanish word **mesura** is a false friend and is never a translation for the English word **measure**. In Spanish, **mesura** means "moderation, restraint".

▸**measure up** *vi* to m. up (to sth) estar a la altura (de algo)

measurement ['meʒəmənt] *n* medida *f*

meat [mi:t] *n* carne *f*; *Culin* m. pie empanada *f* de carne

meatball ['mi:tbɔ:l] *n* albóndiga *f*

meaty ['mi:tɪ] *adj* (**meatier, meatiest**) (**a**) carnoso(a) (**b**) *Fig* (*story*) jugoso(a)

Mecca ['mekə] *n* la Meca

mechanic [mɪ'kænɪk] *n* (*person*) mecánico(a) *m,f*

mechanical [mɪ'kænɪkəl] *adj* mecánico(a)

mechanics [mɪ'kænɪks] **1** *n sing* (*science*) mecánica *f*
2 *npl* (*technical aspects*) mecanismo *m*

mechanism ['mekənɪzəm] *n* mecanismo *m*

medal ['medəl] *n* medalla *f*

medallion [mɪ'dæljən] *n* medallón *m*

medallist, *US* **medalist** ['medəlɪst] *n* medalla *f*

meddle ['medəl] *vi* entrometerse (**in** en); to m. with sth manosear algo

media ['mi:dɪə] *npl* medios *mpl* de comunicación; **m. coverage** cobertura periodística

📝 Note that the Spanish word **media** is a false friend and is never a translation for the English word **media**. In Spanish, **media** means both "stocking, sock" and "average".

median ['mi:dɪən] **1** *adj* mediano(a); *US Aut* m. (**strip**) mediana *f*, *Col, Méx* camellón *m*
2 *n Geom* mediana *f*; *Math* valor mediano

mediate ['mi:dɪeɪt] *vi* mediar

mediator ['mi:dɪeɪtə(r)] *n* mediador(a) *m,f*

Medicaid ['medɪkeɪd] *n* (*in US*) = seguro médico estatal para personas con renta baja

medical ['medɪkəl] **1** *adj* (*treatment*) médico(a); (*book*) de medicina
2 *n Fam* reconocimiento médico

Medicare ['medɪkeə(r)] *n* (*in US*) = seguro médico para ancianos y algunos discapacitados

medicated ['medɪkeɪtɪd] *adj* medicinal

medicine ['medɪsɪn] *n* (*science*) medicina *f*; (*drugs etc*) medicamento *m*

medieval [medɪ'i:vəl] *adj* medieval

mediocre [mi:dɪ'əʊkə(r)] *adj* mediocre

meditate ['medɪteɪt] *vi* meditar (**on** sobre)

meditation [medɪ'teɪʃən] *n* meditación *f*

Mediterranean [medɪtə'reɪnɪən] **1** *adj* mediterráneo(a)
2 n **the M.** el Mediterráneo

medium ['mi:dɪəm] **1** *adj* (*average*) mediano(a); *Rad* m. wave onda media
2 *n* (**a**) (*pl* **media**) (*means*) medio *m* (**b**) (*pl* **mediums**) (*spiritualist*) médium *mf*

medley ['medlɪ] *n* (*mixture*) mezcla *f*; *Mus* popurrí *m*

meek [mi:k] *adj* manso(a), sumiso(a); (*humble*) humilde

meet [mi:t] **1** *vt* (*pt & pp* **met**) (**a**) (*by chance*) encontrar, encontrarse con; (*by arrangement*) reunirse con; (*in formal meeting*) entrevistarse con
(**b**) (*get to know*) conocer; **I'd like you to m. my mother** quiero presentarte a mi madre; **the first time I met him** cuando lo conocí; **pleased to m. you!** ¡mucho gusto!
(**c**) (*await arrival of*) esperar; (*collect*) ir a buscar
(**d**) (*danger*) encontrar; (*opponent*) enfrentarse con
(**e**) (*satisfy*) satisfacer; (*obligations*) cumplir con; (*expenses*) hacer frente a
2 *vi* (*by chance*) encontrarse; (*by arrangement*) reunirse; (*formal meeting*) entrevistarse; (*get to know each other*) conocerse; *Sport* enfrentarse; (*join*) unirse; (*rivers*) confluir; **their eyes met** cruzaron las miradas
3 *n* (*sports event*) encuentro *m*; (*in athletics*) reunión *f* atlética
▸**meet with** *vt insep* (*difficulty*) tropezar con; (*loss*) sufrir; (*success*) tener; *esp US* (*person*) reunirse con

meeting ['mi:tɪŋ] *n* (*chance encounter*) encuentro *m*; (*prearranged*) cita *f*; (*formal*) entrevista *f*; (*of committee etc*) reunión *f*; (*of assembly*) sesión *f*; (*of shareholders*) junta *f*; (*rally*) mitin *m*; *Sport* encuentro *m*; (*of rivers*) confluencia *f*

mega ['megə] *adj Fam* (*excellent*) genial, guay, *Andes, CAm, Carib, Méx* chévere, *RP* bárbaro

megabyte ['megəbaɪt] *n Comput* megabyte *m*

megaphone ['megəfəʊn] *n* megáfono *m*

melancholy ['melənkəlɪ] **1** *n* melancolía *f*
2 *adj* melancólico(a)

Melilla [me'li:jə] *n* Melilla

mellow ['meləʊ] **1** *adj* maduro(a); (*wine*)

añejo(a); *(colour, voice)* suave; *(person)* apacible

2 *vi (fruit)* madurar; *(colour, voice)* suavizarse

melodramatic [melədrə'mætɪk] *adj* melodramático(a)

melody ['melədɪ] *n* melodía *f*

melon ['melən] *n* melón *m*

melt [melt] **1** *vt (metal)* fundir; *Fig (sb's heart)* ablandar

2 *vi (snow)* derretirse; *(metal)* fundirse; *Fig* ablandarse

▸ **melt away** *vi (snow)* derretirse; *Fig (money)* desaparecer; *Fig (confidence)* desvanecerse

▸ **melt down** *vt sep (metal)* fundir

melting ['meltɪŋ] *n* fundición *f*; **m. point** punto *m* de fusión; **m. pot** crisol *m*

member ['membə(r)] *n* miembro *mf*; *(of a society)* socio(a) *m,f*; *(of party, union)* afiliado(a) *m,f*; *US* **M. of Congress** congresista *mf*; *Br* **M. of Parliament** diputado(a) *m,f*

membership ['membəʃɪp] *n (state)* calidad *f* de socio; *(entry)* ingreso *m*; *Pol* afiliación *f*; *(number of members)* número *m* de socios; **m. card** carnet *m* de socio

memento [mə'mentəʊ] *n* recuerdo *m*

memo ['meməʊ] *n (official note)* memorándum *m*; *(personal note)* nota *f*, apunte *m*

memoirs ['memwɑːz] *npl* memorias *fpl*

memorable ['memərəbəl] *adj* memorable

memorandum [memə'rændəm] *n (pl* **memoranda)** *(official note)* memorándum *m*; *(personal note)* nota *f*, apunte *m*

memorial [mɪ'mɔːrɪəl] **1** *adj (plaque etc)* conmemorativo(a)

2 *n* monumento conmemorativo

memorize ['meməraɪz] *vt* memorizar, aprender de memoria

memory ['memərɪ] *n* memoria *f*; *(recollection)* recuerdo *m*

men [men] *pl of* **man**

menace ['menɪs] **1** *n (threat)* amenaza *f*; *(danger)* peligro *m*; *Fam (person)* pesado(a) *m,f*

2 *vt* amenazar

menacing ['menɪsɪŋ] *adj* amenazador(a)

menagerie [mɪ'nædʒərɪ] *n* casa *f* de fieras

mend [mend] **1** *vt* reparar, arreglar; *(clothes)* remendar; *(socks etc)* zurcir

2 *vi (ill person)* reponerse

3 *n (patch)* remiendo *m*; *(darn)* zurcido *m*; *Fig* **to be on the m.** ir mejorando

mending ['mendɪŋ] *n (repair)* reparación

f; *(darning)* zurcido *m*; *(clothes for mending)* ropa *f* para remendar

menial ['miːnɪəl] *adj (task)* servil, bajo(a)

menopause ['menəpɔːz] *n* menopausia *f*

menstrual ['menstrʊəl] *adj* menstrual

menstruation [menstrʊ'eɪʃən] *n* menstruación *f*

mental ['mentəl] *adj* (**a**) mental; **m. home, m. hospital** hospital psiquiátrico; **m. illness** enfermedad *f* mental (**b**) *Fam (crazy)* chalado(a)

mentality [men'tælɪtɪ] *n* mentalidad *f*

mentally ['mentəlɪ] *adv* **m. ill** enfermo(a) mental; **to be m. handicapped** ser un(a) disminuido(a) psíquico(a)

mention ['menʃən] **1** *n* mención *f*

2 *vt* mencionar; **don't m. it!** ¡de nada!

mentor ['mentɔː(r)] *n* mentor *m*

menu ['menjuː] *n* (**a**) *(card)* carta *f*; *(fixed meal)* menú *m*; **today's m.** menú del día (**b**) *Comput* menú *m*

MEP [emiː'piː] *n (abbr* **Member of the European Parliament**) eurodiputado(a) *m,f*

mercenary ['mɜːsɪnərɪ] *adj & n* mercenario(a) *(m,f)*

merchandise ['mɜːtʃəndaɪz] *n* mercancías *fpl*, géneros *mpl*

merchant ['mɜːtʃənt] *n Com & Fin* comerciante *mf*; *(retailer)* detallista *mf*; **m. bank** banco *m* comercial; **m. navy** marina *f* mercante

merciful ['mɜːsɪfʊl] *adj* clemente, compasivo(a) (**towards** con)

merciless ['mɜːsɪlɪs] *adj* despiadado(a)

Mercury ['mɜːkjʊrɪ] *n* Mercurio *m*

mercury ['mɜːkjʊrɪ] *n* mercurio *m*

mercy ['mɜːsɪ] *n* misericordia *f*, compasión *f*; **at the m. of** a la merced de; **to have m. on** tener compasión de

mere [mɪə(r)] *adj* mero(a), simple

merely ['mɪəlɪ] *adv* simplemente

merge [mɜːdʒ] **1** *vt (blend)* unir (**with** con); *Com* fusionar

2 *vi* unirse; *(roads)* empalmar; *Com* fusionarse

merger ['mɜːdʒə(r)] *n Com* fusión *f*

meringue [mə'ræŋ] *n* merengue *m*

merit ['merɪt] **1** *n (of person)* mérito *m*; *(of plan etc)* ventaja *f*

2 *vt* merecer

mermaid ['mɜːmeɪd] *n* sirena *f*

merry ['merɪ] *adj* (**merrier, merriest**) alegre; *Fam (tipsy)* achispado(a); **m. Christmas!** ¡felices Navidades!

merry-go-round ['merɪgəʊraʊnd] *n* tiovivo *m*

mesh [meʃ] **1** *n Tex* malla *f*; *Tech* engranaje *m*; *Fig* red *f*
2 *vt Tech* engranar
mesmerize ['mezməraɪz] *vt* hipnotizar
mess [mes] **1** *n* (**a**) *(confusion)* confusión *f*; *(disorder)* desorden *m*; **to be in a m.** *(of room etc)* estar desordenado(a) (**b**) *(in life, affairs)* lío *m*; **to get into a m.** meterse en un lío (**c**) *(dirt)* suciedad *f* (**d**) *Mil (food)* rancho *m* (**e**) *Mil (room)* comedor *m*
▶**mess about, mess around** *Fam* **1** *vt sep* fastidiar
2 *vi* (**a**) *(act the fool)* hacer el primo; *(idle)* gandulear; *(kill time)* pasar el rato
▶**mess about with** *vt insep Fam (fiddle with)* manosear; **to m. about with sb** tener un lío con algn
▶**mess up** *vt sep Fam (make untidy)* desordenar; *(dirty)* ensuciar; *(spoil)* estropear
message ['mesɪdʒ] *n (communication)* recado *m*; *(of story etc)* mensaje *m*; *Fam* **to get the m.** comprender
messenger ['mesɪndʒə(r)] *n* mensajero(a) *m,f*
Messrs ['mesəz] *npl (abbr* **Messieurs)** Sres.
messy ['mesɪ] *adj* (**messier, messiest**) *(untidy)* desordenado(a); *(confused)* enredado(a); *(dirty)* sucio(a)
met [met] *pt & pp of* **meet**
metabolism [me'tæbəlɪzəm] *n* metabolismo *m*
metal ['metəl] **1** *n* metal *m*
2 *adj* metálico(a)
metallic [mɪ'tælɪk] *adj* metálico(a); **m. blue** azul metalizado
metallurgy [me'tælədʒɪ] *n* metalurgia *f*
metalwork ['metəlwɜːk] *n (craft)* metalistería *f*; *(objects)* objetos *mpl* de metal
metaphor ['metəfə(r)] *n* metáfora *f*
mete [miːt] *vt* **to m. out** imponer
meteor ['miːtɪə(r)] *n* bólido *m*
meteoric [miːtɪ'ɒrɪk] *adj* meteórico(a)
meteorite ['miːtɪəraɪt] *n* meteorito *m*
meteorology [miːtɪə'rɒlədʒɪ] *n* meteorología *f*
meter[1] ['miːtə(r)] *n* contador *m*
meter[2] ['miːtər] *n US* = **metre**
method ['meθəd] *n* método *m*
methodical [mɪ'θɒdɪkəl] *adj* metódico(a)
Methodist ['meθədɪst] *adj & n* metodista *(mf)*
meths [meθs] *n sing Br Fam* alcohol *m* de quemar
methylated spirits ['meθɪleɪtɪd'spɪrɪts]

n alcohol metilado *or* desnaturalizado
meticulous [mə'tɪkjʊləs] *adj* meticuloso(a)
metre ['miːtə(r)] *n* metro *m*
metric ['metrɪk] *adj* métrico(a)
metropolis [mɪ'trɒpəlɪs] *n* metrópoli *f*
metropolitan [metrə'pɒlɪtən] *adj* metropolitano(a)
mettle ['metəl] *n* valor *m*
mew [mjuː] *vi (cat)* maullar
mews [mjuːz] *n sing (street)* callejuela *f*; **m. flat** = apartamento de lujo en unas caballerizas reconvertidas
Mexican ['meksɪkən] *adj & n* mejicano(a) *(m,f)*, mexicano(a) *(m,f)*
Mexico ['meksɪkəʊ] *n* Méjico, México
miaow [miːaʊ] **1** *vi* maullar
2 *n* maullido *m*
mice [maɪs] *pl of* **mouse**
mickey ['mɪkɪ] *n Fam* **to take the m. (out of sb)** tomar el pelo (a algn)
microbe ['maɪkrəʊb] *n* microbio *m*
microchip ['maɪkrəʊtʃɪp] *n* microplaqueta *f*, microchip *m*
microcomputer ['maɪkrəʊkəm'pjuːtə(r)] *n* microordenador *m*
microcosm ['maɪkrəʊkɒzəm] *n* microcosmo *m*
microfilm ['maɪkrəʊfɪlm] *n* microfilm *m*
microphone ['maɪkrəfəʊn] *n* micrófono *m*
microprocessor [maɪkrəʊ'prəʊsesə(r)] *n* microprocesador *m*
microscope ['maɪkrəskəʊp] *n* microscopio *m*
microwave ['maɪkrəʊweɪv] *n* microonda *f*; **m. (oven)** (horno *m*) microondas *m inv*
mid [mɪd] *adj* (**in**) **m. afternoon** a media tarde; (**in**) **m. April** a mediados de abril; **to be in one's m. thirties** tener unos treinta y cinco años
midair **1** *adj* ['mɪdeə(r)] *(collision, explosion)* en el aire
2 *n* [mɪd'eə(r)] *Fig* **to leave sth in m.** dejar algo en el aire
midday **1** *n* [mɪd'deɪ] mediodía *m*
2 *adj* ['mɪddeɪ] de mediodía
middle ['mɪdəl] **1** *adj* de en medio; **m. age** mediana edad; **the M. Ages** la Edad Media; **the m. class** la clase media
2 *n* (**a**) centro *m*, medio *m*; **in the m. of** en medio de; **in the m. of winter** en pleno invierno; *Fam* **in the m. of nowhere** en el quinto pino (**b**) *Fam (waist)* cintura *f*
middle-aged [mɪdəl'eɪdʒd] *adj* de mediana edad
middle-class [mɪdəl'klɑːs] *adj* de clase media

middleman ['mɪdəlmæn] *n* intermediario *m*

middleweight ['mɪdəlweɪt] *n* peso medio

middling ['mɪdlɪŋ] *adj* mediano(a)

midfielder [mɪd'fiːldə(r)] *n Sport* centrocampista *mf*

midge [mɪdʒ] *n* mosca enana

midget ['mɪdʒɪt] *n* enano(a) *m,f*

Midlands ['mɪdləndz] *npl* **the M.** = la región central de Inglaterra

midnight ['mɪdnaɪt] *n* medianoche *f*

midst [mɪdst] *n* **in the m. of** en medio de

midsummer [mɪd'sʌmə(r)] *n* pleno verano; **M.'s Day** Día *m* de San Juan (*24 de junio*)

midway ['mɪdweɪ] *adv* a medio camino

midweek 1 *adv* [mɪd'wiːk] entre semana
2 *adj* ['mɪdwiːk] de entre semana

midwife ['mɪdwaɪf] *n* comadrona *f*, partera *f*

midwifery ['mɪdwɪfərɪ] *n* obstetricia *f*

midwinter [mɪd'wɪntə(r)] *n* pleno invierno *m*

might¹ [maɪt] *v aux see* **may**

might² [maɪt] *n Fml* fuerza *f*, poder *m*

mighty ['maɪtɪ] **1** *adj* (**mightier, mightiest**) (*strong*) fuerte; (*powerful*) poderoso(a); (*great*) enorme
2 *adv US Fam* cantidad de, muy

migraine ['miːgreɪn, 'maɪgreɪn] *n* jaqueca *f*

migrant ['maɪgrənt] **1** *adj* migratorio(a)
2 *n* (*person*) emigrante *mf*; (*bird*) ave migratoria

migrate [maɪ'greɪt] *vi* emigrar

migration [maɪ'greɪʃən] *n* migración *f*

mike [maɪk] *n Fam* micro *m*

mild [maɪld] *adj* (*person, character*) apacible; (*climate*) templado(a); (*punishment*) leve; (*tobacco, taste*) suave

mildew ['mɪldjuː] *n* moho *m*; (*on plants*) añublo *m*

mildly ['maɪldlɪ] *adv* (*softly, gently*) suavemente; (*slightly*) ligeramente; **and that's putting it m.** y esto es decir poco

mildness ['maɪldnɪs] *n* (*of character*) apacibilidad *f*; (*of climate, taste*) suavidad *f*; (*of punishment*) levedad *f*

mile [maɪl] *n* milla *f*; *Fam* **miles better** muchísimo mejor

mileage ['maɪlɪdʒ] *n* kilometraje *m*

milestone ['maɪlstəʊn] *n* hito *m*

milieu ['miːljɜː] *n* medio *m* ambiente

militant ['mɪlɪtənt] *adj & n* militante (*mf*)

military ['mɪlɪtərɪ] *adj* militar; **to do one's m. service** hacer el servicio militar

militia [mɪ'lɪʃə] *n* milicia *f*

milk [mɪlk] **1** *n* leche *f*; **m. chocolate** chocolate *m* con leche; **m. shake** batido *m*
2 *vt* (**a**) (*cow, goat*) ordeñar (**b**) *Fam* **they milked him of all his money** le sangraron hasta la última peseta

milkman ['mɪlkmən] *n* lechero *m*

milky ['mɪlkɪ] *adj* (**milkier, milkiest**) lechoso(a); (*colour*) pálido(a); **M. Way** Vía Láctea

mill [mɪl] **1** *n* (*grinder*) molino *m*; (*for coffee*) molinillo *m*; (*factory*) fábrica *f*; **cotton m.** hilandería *f*
2 *vt* moler

▸ **mill about, mill around** *vi* arremolinarse

millennium [mɪ'lenɪəm] *n* (*pl* **millenniums** *or* **millennia** [mɪ'lenɪə]) milenio *m*

miller ['mɪlə(r)] *n* molinero(a) *m,f*

millet ['mɪlɪt] *n* mijo *m*

milligram(me) ['mɪlɪgræm] *n* miligramo *m*

millilitre, *US* **milliliter** ['mɪlɪliːtə(r)] *n* mililitro *m*

millimetre, *US* **millimeter** ['mɪlɪmiːtə(r)] *n* milímetro *m*

milliner ['mɪlɪnə(r)] *n* sombrerero(a) *m,f*

millinery ['mɪlɪnərɪ] *n* sombreros *mpl* de señora

million ['mɪljən] *n* millón *m*

millionaire [mɪljə'neə(r)] *n* millonario(a) *m,f*

millstone ['mɪlstəʊn] *n* muela *f*; *Fig* carga *f*

mime [maɪm] **1** *n* (*art*) mímica *f*; (*play*) pantomima *f*
2 *vt* representar con gestos

> 🖉 Note that the Spanish verb **mimar** is a false friend and is never a translation for the English verb to **mime**. In Spanish, **mimar** means "to spoil, to pamper".

mimic ['mɪmɪk] **1** *adj & n* mímico(a) (*m,f*)
2 *vt* imitar

mimicry ['mɪmɪkrɪ] *n* imitación *f*

minaret ['mɪnəret] *n* alminar *m*, minarete *m*

mince [mɪns] **1** *n Br* (*meat*) carne picada; **m. pie** (*containing meat*) = especie de empanada de carne picada; (*containing fruit*) pastel *m* de picadillo de fruta
2 *vt* picar; *Fig* **he doesn't m. his words** no tiene pelos en la lengua
3 *vi* (*walk*) **to m. (along)** andar con pasos menuditos

mincemeat ['mɪnsmiːt] *n* (*dried fruit*) conserva *f* de picadillo de fruta; (*meat*) carne picada

mincer ['mɪnsə(r)] *n* picadora *f* de carne

mind [maɪnd] **1** n (**a**) *(intellect)* mente f; *(brain)* cabeza f; **what kind of car do you have in m.?** ¿en qué clase de coche estás pensando?; **to lose one's m.** perder el juicio; **it slipped my m.** lo olvidé por completo; **to call sth to m.** recordar algo
(**b**) *(opinion)* **to be in two minds (about sth)** estar indeciso(a) (acerca de algo); **to my m.** a mi parecer
2 vt (**a**) *(child)* cuidar; *(house)* vigilar; *(be careful of)* tener cuidado con; **m. the step!** ¡ojo con el escalón!; **m. your own business!** ¡no te metas donde no te llaman!
(**b**) *(object to)* tener inconveniente en; **I wouldn't m. a cup of coffee** me vendría bien un café; **never m.** no importa
3 vi (**a**) **m. you, he is fifty** ten en cuenta que tiene cincuenta años
(**b**) *(object)* importar; **do you m. if I open the window?** ¿le importa que abra la ventana?

minder ['maɪndə(r)] n Fam *(bodyguard)* guardaespaldas m inv, *(for child)* niñera f; *(babysitter)* canguro mf

mindful ['maɪndfʊl] adj consciente

mindless ['maɪndlɪs] adj *(task)* de autómata; *(violence)* injustificable

mine¹ [maɪn] poss pron (el) mío/(la) mía/(los) míos, (las) mías, lo mío; **a friend of m.** un amigo mío; **these gloves are m.** estos guantes son míos; **which is ▸m.?** ¿cuál es el mío?

mine² [maɪn] **1** n mina f; Fig **a m. of information** un pozo de información
2 vt *(coal etc)* extraer; Mil minar

minefield ['maɪnfiːld] n campo m de minas

miner ['maɪnə(r)] n minero(a) m,f

mineral ['mɪnərəl] **1** adj mineral; **m. water** agua f mineral
2 n mineral m

minesweeper ['maɪnswiːpə(r)] n dragaminas m inv

mingle ['mɪŋgəl] vi mezclarse

miniature ['mɪnɪtʃə(r)] **1** n miniatura f
2 adj *(railway)* en miniatura; *(camera, garden)* diminuto(a)

minibus ['mɪnɪbʌs] n microbús m

minim ['mɪnɪm] n Mus blanca f

minimal ['mɪnɪməl] adj mínimo(a)

minimum ['mɪnɪməm] **1** adj mínimo(a); **m. wage** salario mínimo
2 n mínimo m

mining ['maɪnɪŋ] **1** n minería f, explotación f de minas; Mil & Naut minado m
2 adj minero(a)

miniskirt ['mɪnɪskɜːt] n minifalda f

minister ['mɪnɪstə(r)] **1** n ministro(a) m,f; Rel pastor(a) m,f
2 vi **to m. to sb** atender a algn

ministerial [mɪnɪ'stɪərɪəl] adj Pol ministerial

ministry ['mɪnɪstrɪ] n Pol ministerio m; Rel sacerdocio m

mink [mɪŋk] n visón m; **m. coat** abrigo m de visón

minnow ['mɪnəʊ] n piscardo m

minor ['maɪnə(r)] **1** adj *(lesser)* menor; *(unimportant)* sin importancia; *(role)* secundario(a); Mus menor
2 n Jur menor mf de edad

Minorca [mɪ'nɔːkə] n Menorca

minority [maɪ'nɒrɪtɪ] n minoría f; **to be in the m.** ser (la) minoría; Pol **m. party** partido minoritario

mint¹ [mɪnt] **1** n Fin **the M.** la Casa de la Moneda; **in m. condition** en perfecto estado
2 vt *(coin, words)* acuñar

mint² [mɪnt] n Bot menta f; *(sweet)* pastilla f de menta

minus ['maɪnəs] **1** prep **5 m. 3** 5 menos 3; **m. 10 degrees** 10 grados bajo cero
2 adj negativo(a)
3 n **m. (sign)** signo m (de) menos

minute¹ ['mɪnɪt] n (**a**) *(minute)* minuto m; **at the last m.** a última hora; **just a m.** (espera) un momento; **this very m.** ahora mismo
(**b**) **minutes** *(notes)* el acta

minute² [maɪ'njuːt] adj *(tiny)* diminuto(a); *(examination)* minucioso(a)

miracle ['mɪrəkəl] n milagro m

miraculous [mɪ'rækjʊləs] adj milagroso(a)

mirage [mɪ'rɑːʒ] n espejismo m

mire [maɪə(r)] n fango m, lodo m; *(muddy place)* lodazal m

mirror ['mɪrə(r)] **1** n espejo m; Fig reflejo m; **rear-view m.** retrovisor m; **m. image** réplica f
2 vt reflejar

mirth [mɜːθ] n alegría f; *(laughter)* risas fpl

misadventure [mɪsəd'ventʃə(r)] n desgracia f; **death by m.** muerte f accidental

misanthropist [mɪ'zænθrəpɪst] n misántropo(a) m,f

misapprehension [mɪsæprɪ'henʃən] n malentendido m

misbehave [mɪsbɪ'heɪv] vi portarse mal

miscalculate [mɪs'kælkjʊleɪt] vt & vi calcular mal

miscarriage ['mɪskærɪdʒ] n Med aborto m (espontáneo); **m. of justice** error m judicial

223

miscellaneous ► mistrust

miscellaneous [mɪsɪˈleɪnɪəs] *adj* variado(a); **m. expenses** gastos diversos

mischief [ˈmɪstʃɪf] *n (naughtiness)* travesura *f*; *Fml (evil)* malicia *f*; *Fam (harm)* daño *m*; **to get up to m.** hacer travesuras

mischievous [ˈmɪstʃɪvəs] *adj (naughty)* travieso(a); *(playful)* juguetón(ona); *Fml (wicked)* malicioso(a)

misconception [mɪskənˈsepʃən] *n* concepto erróneo

misconduct [mɪsˈkɒndʌkt] *n* mala conducta; **professional m.** error *m* profesional

misconstrue [mɪskənˈstruː] *vt* interpretar mal

miscount [mɪsˈkaʊnt] *vt (votes etc)* contar mal

misdeed [mɪsˈdiːd] *n* fechoría *f*

misdemeanour, *US* **misdemeanor** [mɪsdɪˈmiːnə(r)] *n (misdeed)* fechoría *f*; *Jur* delito *m* menor

miser [ˈmaɪzə(r)] *n* avaro(a) *m,f*

miserable [ˈmɪzərəbəl] *adj (sad)* triste; *(unfortunate)* desgraciado(a); *(wretched)* miserable

miserly [ˈmaɪzəlɪ] *adj* avaro(a), tacaño(a)

misery [ˈmɪzərɪ] *n (sadness)* tristeza *f*; *(wretchedness)* desgracia *f*; *(suffering)* sufrimiento *m*; *(poverty)* miseria *f*; *Fam (person)* aguafiestas *mf*

misfire [mɪsˈfaɪə(r)] *vi (engine, plan etc)* fallar

misfit [ˈmɪsfɪt] *n (person)* inadaptado(a) *m,f*

misfortune [mɪsˈfɔːtʃən] *n* desgracia *f*

misgiving [mɪsˈɡɪvɪŋ] *n (doubt)* recelo *m*; *(fear)* temor *m*

misguided [mɪsˈɡaɪdɪd] *adj* equivocado(a)

mishandle [mɪsˈhændəl] *vt* llevar *or* manejar mal

mishap [ˈmɪshæp] *n* contratiempo *m*

misinform [mɪsɪnˈfɔːm] *vt* informar mal

misinterpret [mɪsɪnˈtɜːprɪt] *vt* interpretar mal

misjudge [mɪsˈdʒʌdʒ] *vt* juzgar mal

mislay [mɪsˈleɪ] *vt* extraviar

mislead [mɪsˈliːd] *vt* despistar; *(deliberately)* engañar

misleading [mɪsˈliːdɪŋ] *adj (erroneous)* erróneo(a); *(deliberately)* engañoso(a)

mismanagement [mɪsˈmænɪdʒmənt] *n* mala administración *f*

misnomer [mɪsˈnəʊmə(r)] *n* nombre equivocado

misogynist [mɪˈsɒdʒɪnɪst] *n* misógino(a) *m,f*

misplace [mɪsˈpleɪs] *vt (trust)* encauzar mal; *(book, spectacles etc)* extraviar

misprint [ˈmɪsprɪnt] *n* errata *f*, error *m* de imprenta

misrepresent [mɪsreprɪˈzent] *vt (facts)* desvirtuar; *(words)* tergiversar

miss¹ [mɪs] *n* señorita *f*

miss² [mɪs] **1** *n (throw etc)* fallo *m*; *Fam* **to give sth a m.** pasar de algo

2 *vt* (**a**) *(when throwing)* fallar; *(when shooting)* errar (**b**) *(train etc)* perder; *(opportunity)* dejar pasar; **you have missed the point** no has captado la idea; *Fig* **to m. the boat** perder el tren (**c**) *(omit)* saltarse (**d**) **I m. you** te echo de menos

3 *vi (when throwing)* fallar; *(when shooting)* errar; **is anything missing?** ¿falta algo?

► **miss out 1** *vt sep (omit)* saltarse; *(on purpose)* pasar por alto

2 *vt insep* **to m. out on** perderse

misshapen [mɪsˈʃeɪpən] *adj* deforme

missile [ˈmɪsaɪl, *US* ˈmɪsəl] *n Mil* misil *m*; *(object thrown)* proyectil *m*

missing [ˈmɪsɪŋ] *adj (object)* perdido(a); *(person)* desaparecido(a); *(from meeting etc)* ausente; **m. person** desaparecido(a) *m,f*; **three cups are m.** faltan tres tazas

mission [ˈmɪʃən] *n* misión *f*

missionary [ˈmɪʃənərɪ] *n* misionero(a) *m,f*

misspent [ˈmɪsspent] *adj (youth)* malgastado(a)

mist [mɪst] **1** *n* neblina *f*; *(thick)* niebla *f*; *(at sea)* bruma *f*

2 *vi* **to m. over** *or* **up** *(countryside)* cubrirse de neblina; *(window etc)* empañarse

mistake [mɪˈsteɪk] **1** *n* error *m*; **by m.** por equivocación; **I hurt him by m.** le golpeé sin querer; **to make a m.** equivocarse, cometer un error

2 *vt (pt* mistook; *pp* mistaken) *(meaning)* malentender; **to m. Jack for Bill** confundir a Jack con Bill

mistaken [mɪˈsteɪkən] *adj* equivocado(a), erróneo(a); **you are m.** estás equivocado(a)

mister [ˈmɪstə(r)] *n* señor *m*

mistletoe [ˈmɪsltəʊ] *n* muérdago *m*

mistook [mɪˈstʊk] *pt of* mistake

mistreat [mɪsˈtriːt] *vt* tratar mal

mistress [ˈmɪstrɪs] *n (of house)* señora *f*, ama *f*; *(lover)* amante *f*; *Educ (primary school)* maestra *f*; *(secondary school)* profesora *f*

mistrust [mɪsˈtrʌst] **1** *n* recelo *m*
2 *vt* desconfiar de

misty ['mɪstɪ] adj (mistier, mistiest) (day) de niebla; (window etc) empañado(a)

misunderstand [mɪsʌndə'stænd] vt & vi malentender

misunderstanding [mɪsʌndə'stændɪŋ] n malentendido m; (disagreement) desavenencia f

misuse 1 n [mɪs'juːs] mal uso m; (of funds) malversación f; (of power) abuso m
2 vt [mɪs'juːz] emplear mal; (funds) malversar; (power) abusar de

miter ['maɪtər] n US = mitre

mitigate ['mɪtɪgeɪt] vt atenuar

mitigating ['mɪtɪgeɪtɪŋ] adj m. circumstances circunstancias fpl atenuantes

mitre ['maɪtə(r)] n mitra f

mitten ['mɪtən] n manopla f; (fingerless) mitón m

mix [mɪks] **1** n mezcla f
2 vt mezclar
3 vi (blend) mezclarse (with con); (go well together) ir bien juntos
▸ mix up vt sep (confuse) confundir (with con); (papers) revolver; to be mixed up in sth estar involucrado(a) en algo

mixed [mɪkst] adj (assorted) surtido(a); (varied) variado(a); (school) mixto(a); (feelings) contradictorio(a)

mixed-up [mɪkst'ʌp] adj (objects, papers etc) revuelto(a); (person) confuso(a)

mixer ['mɪksə(r)] n (a) Culin batidora f (b) to be a good m. (person) tener don de gentes

mixture ['mɪkstʃə(r)] n mezcla f

mix-up ['mɪksʌp] n Fam confusión f, lío m

mm (abbr millimetre(s)) mm

moan [məʊn] **1** n (groan) gemido m, quejido m
2 vi (groan) gemir; (complain) quejarse (about de)

moat [məʊt] n foso m

mob [mɒb] **1** n multitud f; (riff-raff) gentuza f; the m. el populacho
2 vt acosar

mobile ['məʊbaɪl, US 'məʊbəl] **1** adj móvil; **m. home** caravana f; **m. phone** teléfono m móvil, Am teléfono m celular
2 n (a) (hanging ornament) móvil m (b) Fam (mobile phone) móvil m, Am celular m

mobility [məʊ'bɪlɪtɪ] n movilidad f

mobilize ['məʊbɪlaɪz] vt movilizar

mock [mɒk] **1** adj (sympathy etc) fingido(a); (objects) de imitación
2 vt (make fun of) burlarse de
3 vi burlarse (at de)

mockery ['mɒkərɪ] n burla f

mode [məʊd] n (manner) modo m, estilo m; (fashion) moda f

model ['mɒdəl] **1** n modelo m; (fashion model) modelo mf; (scale) m. maqueta f
2 adj (railway) en miniatura; (pupil) ejemplar; (school) modelo
3 vt (clay etc) modelar; (clothes) presentar
4 vi (make models) modelar; (work as model) trabajar de modelo

modem ['məʊdem] n Comput modem m

moderate¹ ['mɒdərɪt] **1** adj moderado(a); (reasonable) razonable; (average) regular; (ability) mediocre
2 n Pol moderado(a) m,f

moderate² ['mɒdəreɪt] **1** vt moderar
2 vi moderarse; (wind) calmarse; (in debate) arbitrar

moderately ['mɒdərɪtlɪ] adv medianamente

moderation [mɒdə'reɪʃən] n moderación f; in m. con moderación

modern ['mɒdən] adj moderno(a); (history) contemporáneo(a); **m. languages** lenguas modernas

modernize ['mɒdənaɪz] vt modernizar

modest ['mɒdɪst] adj modesto(a); (chaste) púdico(a); (price) módico(a); (success) discreto(a)

modesty ['mɒdɪstɪ] n (humility) modestia f; (chastity) pudor m

modification [mɒdɪfɪ'keɪʃən] n modificación f

modify ['mɒdɪfaɪ] vt modificar

module ['mɒdjuːl] n módulo m

mogul ['məʊgʌl] n magnate m

mohair ['məʊheə(r)] **1** n mohair m
2 adj de mohair

moist [mɔɪst] adj húmedo(a)

moisten ['mɔɪsən] vt humedecer

moisture ['mɔɪstʃə(r)] n humedad f

moisturizer ['mɔɪstʃəraɪzə(r)] n crema f or leche f hidratante

molar ['məʊlə(r)] n muela f

molasses [mə'læsɪz] n sing melaza f

mold¹ [məʊld] n US = mould¹

mold² [məʊld] n & vt US = mould²

molder ['məʊldər] vi US = moulder

molding ['məʊldɪŋ] n US = moulding

moldy ['məʊldɪ] adj US = mouldy

mole¹ [məʊl] n (beauty spot) lunar m

mole² [məʊl] n (animal) topo m

molecule ['mɒlɪkjuːl] n molécula f

molest [mə'lest] vt importunar; (sexually assault) acosar (sexualmente)

mollycoddle ['mɒlɪkɒdəl] vt Fam mimar, consentir

molt [məʊlt] vi US = moult

molten ['məʊltən] *adj* fundido(a); *(lava)* líquido(a)

mom [mɒm] *n US Fam* mamá *f*

moment ['məʊmənt] *n* momento *m*; **at the m.** en este momento; **for the m.** de momento; **in a m.** dentro de un momento; **at any m.** de un momento a otro

momentarily ['məʊməntərɪlɪ] *adv* momentáneamente; *US (soon)* dentro de poco

momentary ['məʊməntərɪ] *adj* momentáneo(a)

momentous [məʊ'mentəs] *adj* trascendental

momentum [məʊ'mentəm] *n Phys* momento *m*; *(speed)* velocidad *f*; *Fig* **to gather m.** cobrar velocidad

mommy ['mɒmɪ] *n US Fam* mamá *f*

Monaco ['mɒnəkəʊ] *n* Mónaco

monarch ['mɒnək] *n* monarca *m*

monarchy ['mɒnəkɪ] *n* monarquía *f*

monastery ['mɒnəstərɪ] *n* monasterio *m*

Monday ['mʌndɪ] *n* lunes *m*

monetarism ['mʌnɪtərɪzəm] *n* monetarismo *m*

monetary ['mʌnɪtərɪ] *adj* monetario(a)

money ['mʌnɪ] *n* dinero *m*; *(currency)* moneda *f*; **to make m.** ganar dinero; **to put m. on** apostar por

moneylender ['mʌnɪlendə(r)] *n* prestamista *mf*

money-spinner ['mʌnɪspɪnə(r)] *n Fam* negocio *m* rentable

Mongolia [mɒn'gəʊlɪə] *n* Mongolia

mongolism ['mɒŋgəlɪzəm] *n* mongolismo *m*

mongrel ['mʌŋgrəl] *n* perro mestizo

monitor ['mɒnɪtə(r)] **1** *n (screen)* monitor *m*; *Educ* delegado(a) *m,f*
    2 *vt (check)* controlar; *(progress, events)* seguir de cerca

monk [mʌŋk] *n* monje *m*

monkey ['mʌŋkɪ] *n* mono *m*; **m. nut** cacahuete *m*, maní *m*, *Méx* cacahuate *m*; **m. wrench** llave inglesa

monochrome ['mɒnəkrəʊm] *adj* monocromo(a); *(television, photo)* en blanco y negro

monocle ['mɒnəkəl] *n* monóculo *m*

monologue, *US* **monolog** ['mɒnəlɒg] *n* monólogo *m*

monopolize [mə'nɒpəlaɪz] *vt Fin* monopolizar; *(attention etc)* acaparar

monopoly [mə'nɒpəlɪ] *n* monopolio *m*

monotone ['mɒnətəʊn] *n* **in a m.** con una voz monótona

monotonous [mə'nɒtənəs] *adj* monótono(a)

monotony [mə'nɒtənɪ] *n* monotonía *f*

monsoon [mɒn'suːn] *n* monzón *m*

monster ['mɒnstə(r)] *n* monstruo *m*

monstrosity [mɒn'strɒsɪtɪ] *n* monstruosidad *f*

monstrous ['mɒnstrəs] *adj (huge)* enorme; *(hideous)* monstruoso(a); *(outrageous)* escandaloso(a)

montage ['mɒntɑːʒ] *n* montaje *m*

month [mʌnθ] *n* mes *m*

monthly ['mʌnθlɪ] **1** *adj* mensual; **m. instalment** mensualidad *f*
    2 *n (periodical)* revista *f* mensual
    3 *adv* mensualmente, cada mes

monument ['mɒnjʊmənt] *n* monumento *m*

monumental [mɒnjʊ'mentəl] *adj* monumental; *Fam (huge)* enorme

moo [muː] **1** *n* mugido *m*
    2 *vi* mugir

mooch [muːtʃ] *Fam.* **1** *vi* **to m. around** vagar, dar vueltas
    2 *vt* **to m. sth off sb** *(cadge)* gorronearle algo a algn

mood [muːd] *n* humor *m*; **to be in a good/bad m.** estar de buen/mal humor; **to be in the m. for (doing) sth** estar de humor para (hacer) algo

moody ['muːdɪ] *adj (moodier, moodiest) (changeable)* de humor variable; *(bad-tempered)* malhumorado(a)

moon [muːn] *n* luna *f*; *Fam* **over the m.** en el séptimo cielo

moonlight ['muːnlaɪt] *n* luz *f* de la luna

moonlighting ['muːnlaɪtɪŋ] *n Fam* pluriempleo *m*

moonlit ['muːnlɪt] *adj (night)* de luna

Moor [mʊə(r)] *n* moro(a) *m,f*

moor[1] [mʊə(r)] *n (heath)* páramo *m*

moor[2] [mʊə(r)] *vt Naut* amarrar

Moorish ['mʊərɪʃ] *adj* moro(a)

moorland ['mʊələnd] *n* páramo *m*

moose [muːs] *n (pl* **moose**) alce *m*

moot [muːt] *adj* **it's a m. point** es discutible

mop [mɒp] **1** *n (for floor)* fregona *f*; *Fam* **m. of hair** melena *f*
    2 *vt* fregar
   ▸ **mop up** *vt sep (liquids)* enjugar; *(enemy forces)* acabar con

mope [məʊp] *vi* estar alicaído(a)
   ▸ **mope about, mope around** *vi* andar abatido(a)

moped ['məʊped] *n* ciclomotor *m*, vespa *f*

moral ['mɒrəl] **1** *adj* moral
    2 *n* moraleja *f*; **morals** moral *f*, moralidad *f*

morale [mə'rɑːl] *n* moral *f*, estado *m* de ánimo

morality [mə'rælɪtɪ] *n* moralidad *f*

morass [mə'ræs] *n* pantano *m*; *Fig* lío *m*

moratorium [mɒrə'tɔːrɪəm] *n* moratoria *f* (**on** en)

morbid ['mɔːbɪd] *adj Med* mórbido(a); (*mind*) morboso(a)

more [mɔː(r)] **1** *adj* más; **is there any m. tea?** ¿queda más té?; **I've no m. money** no me queda más dinero; **m. tourists** más turistas

2 *pron* más; **how many m.?** ¿cuántos más?; **I need some m.** necesito más; **it's m. than enough** es más que suficiente; **many/much m.** muchos(as)/mucho más; **m. than a hundred** más de cien; **the m. he has, the m. he wants** cuanto más tiene más quiere; **and what is m.** y lo que es más

3 *adv* más; **I won't do it any m.** no lo volveré a hacer; **she doesn't live here any m.** ya no vive aquí; **m. and m. difficult** cada vez más difícil; **m. or less** más o menos; **once m.** una vez más

moreover [mɔː'rəʊvə(r)] *adv* además

morgue [mɔːg] *n* depósito *m* de cadáveres

morning ['mɔːnɪŋ] **1** *n* mañana *f*; (*before dawn*) madrugada *f*; **in the m.** por la mañana; **on Monday mornings** los lunes por la mañana; **tomorrow m.** mañana por la mañana

2 *adj* matutino(a)

Moroccan [mə'rɒkən] *adj & n* marroquí (*mf*)

Morocco [mə'rɒkəʊ] *n* Marruecos

moron ['mɔːrɒn] *n Fam* imbécil *mf*

morose [mə'rəʊs] *adj* hosco(a), huraño(a)

> ♪ Note that the Spanish word **moroso** is a false friend and is never a translation for the English word **morose**. In Spanish, **moroso** means "bad debtor".

morphine ['mɔːfiːn] *n* morfina *f*

Morse [mɔːs] *n* **M. (code)** (alfabeto *m*) Morse *m*

morsel ['mɔːsəl] *n* (*of food*) bocado *m*; *Fig* trozo *m*

mortal ['mɔːtəl] **1** *adj* mortal

2 *n* mortal *mf*

mortality [mɔː'tælɪtɪ] *n* mortalidad *f*

mortally ['mɔːtəlɪ] *adv* mortalmente; **m. wounded** herido(a) de muerte

mortar ['mɔːtə(r)] *n* mortero *m*

mortgage ['mɔːgɪdʒ] **1** *n* hipoteca *f*

2 *vt* hipotecar

mortician [mɔː'tɪʃən] *n US* (*undertaker*) encargado(a) *m,f* de funeraria

mortify ['mɔːtɪfaɪ] *vt* mortificar; *Fam* **I was mortified** me sentí avergonzado(a)

mortuary ['mɔːtʃʊərɪ] *n* depósito *m* de cadáveres

mosaic [mə'zeɪk] *n* mosaico *m*

Moscow ['mɒskəʊ, *US* 'mɒskaʊ] *n* Moscú

Moslem ['mɒzləm] *adj & n* musulmán(a-na) (*m,f*)

mosque [mɒsk] *n* mezquita *f*

mosquito [mɒs'kiːtəʊ] *n* (*pl* **mosquitoes**) mosquito *m*; **m. net** mosquitero *m*

moss [mɒs] *n* musgo *m*

most [məʊst] **1** *adj* (*superl of* **much**, **many**) (**a**) (*greatest in quantity etc*) más; **this house suffered (the) m. damage** esta casa fue la más afectada; **who made (the) m. mistakes?** ¿quién cometió más errores?

(**b**) (*the majority of*) la mayoría de, la mayor parte de; **for the m. part** por lo general; **m. of the time** la mayor parte del tiempo; **m. people** la mayoría de la gente

2 *pron* (*greatest part*) la mayor parte; (*greatest number*) lo máximo, lo más; (*the majority of people*) la mayoría; **at the (very) m.** como máximo; **to make the m. of sth** aprovechar algo al máximo

3 *adv* (*superl of* **much**) (**a**) más; **the m. intelligent student** el estudiante más inteligente; **what I like m.** lo que más me gusta

(**b**) (*very*) muy; **m. likely** muy probablemente; **m. of all** sobre todo

mostly ['məʊstlɪ] *adv* (*chiefly*) en su mayor parte; (*generally*) generalmente; (*usually*) normalmente

MOT [eməʊ'tiː] *n Br* (*abbr* **Ministry of Transport**) **M. test** inspección técnica de vehículos, ≃ ITV

motel [məʊ'tel] *n* motel *m*

moth [mɒθ] *n* mariposa nocturna; **clothes m.** polilla *f*

mother ['mʌðə(r)] **1** *n* madre *f*; **unmarried m.** madre soltera; **M.'s Day** Día *m* de la Madre; **m. tongue** lengua materna

2 *vt* cuidar maternalmente

motherhood ['mʌðəhʊd] *n* maternidad *f*

mother-in-law ['mʌðərɪnlɔː] *n* suegra *f*

motherly ['mʌðəlɪ] *adj* maternal

mother-of-pearl [mʌðərəv'pɜːl] *n* madreperla *f*, nácar *m*

mother-to-be [mʌðətə'biː] *n* futura madre

motif [məʊ'tiːf] *n Art & Mus* motivo *m*; (*embroidered etc*) adorno *m*; *Fig* (*main subject*) tema *m*

motion ['məʊʃən] **1** *n (movement)* movimiento *m; (gesture)* ademán *m; (proposal)* moción *f*

2 *vt & vi* hacer señas; **to m. (to) sb to do sth** hacer señas a algn para que haga algo

motionless ['məʊʃənlɪs] *adj* inmóvil

motivate ['məʊtɪveɪt] *vt* motivar

motivation [məʊtɪ'veɪʃən] *n* motivación *f*

motive ['məʊtɪv] **1** *adj (force)* motriz

2 *n (reason)* motivo *m; Jur* móvil *m;* **with the best of motives** con la mejor intención

motley ['mɒtlɪ] *adj* (**motlier, motliest**) *(multicoloured)* abigarrado(a); *(varied)* variado(a)

motor ['məʊtə(r)] *n (engine)* motor *m; Fam (car)* máquina *f;* **m. racing** carreras *fpl* de coches

motorbike ['məʊtəbaɪk] *n Fam* motocicleta *f,* moto *f*

motorboat ['məʊtəbəʊt] *n* (lancha) motora *f*

motorcar ['məʊtəkaː(r)] *n* coche *m,* automóvil *m*

motorcycle ['məʊtəsaɪkəl] *n* motocicleta *f*

motorcyclist ['məʊtəsaɪklɪst] *n* motociclista *mf*

motoring ['məʊtərɪŋ] *n* automovilismo *m*

motorist ['məʊtərɪst] *n* automovilista *mf*

motorway ['məʊtəweɪ] *n Br* autopista *f*

mottled ['mɒtəld] *adj (skin, animal)* con manchas; *(surface)* moteado(a)

motto ['mɒtəʊ] *n* lema *m*

mould[1] [məʊld] *n (fungus)* moho *m*

mould[2] [məʊld] **1** *n* molde *m*

2 *vt* moldear; *(clay)* modelar

moulder ['məʊldə(r)] *vi* **to m. (away)** desmoronarse

moulding ['məʊldɪŋ] *n* moldura *f*

mouldy ['məʊldɪ] *adj* (**mouldier, mouldiest**) mohoso(a); **to go m.** enmohecerse

moult [məʊlt] *vi* mudar

mound [maʊnd] *n* montón *m; (small hill)* montículo *m*

mount[1] [maʊnt] *n* monte *m;* **M. Everest** (Monte) Everest *m*

mount[2] [maʊnt] **1** *n (horse)* montura *f; (support)* soporte *m,* base *f; (for photograph)* marco *m; (for jewel)* engaste *m*

2 *vt (horse)* subirse or montar a; *(campaign)* organizar; *(photograph)* enmarcar; *(jewel)* engastar

3 *vi (go up)* subir; *(get on horse, bike)* montar; *(increase)* subir

▸ **mount up** *vi (accumulate)* acumularse

mountain ['maʊntɪn] **1** *n* montaña *f; Fig (pile)* montón *m*

2 *adj* de montaña, montañés(esa); **m. bike** bicicleta *f* de montaña; **m. range** sierra *f,* cordillera *f*

mountaineer [maʊntɪ'nɪə(r)] *n* alpinista *mf, Am* andinista *mf*

mountaineering [maʊntɪ'nɪərɪŋ] *n* alpinismo *m, Am* andinismo *m*

mountainous ['maʊntɪnəs] *adj* montañoso(a)

mourn [mɔːn] *vt & vi* **to m. (for) sb** llorar la muerte de algn

mourner ['mɔːnə(r)] *n* doliente *mf*

mournful ['mɔːnfʊl] *adj* triste; *(voice)* lúgubre

mourning ['mɔːnɪŋ] *n* luto *m;* **in m.** de luto

mouse [maʊs] *n (pl* **mice**) *also Comput* ratón *m*

mousetrap ['maʊstræp] *n* ratonera *f*

mousse [muːs] *n Culin* mousse *f; (for hair)* **(styling) m.** espuma *f* (moldeadora)

moustache [mə'staːʃ] *n* bigote *m*

mousy ['maʊsɪ] *adj* (**mousier, mousiest**) *(colour)* pardusco(a); *(hair)* castaño claro; *(shy)* tímido(a)

mouth [maʊθ] **1** *n (pl* **mouths** [maʊðz]) (**a**) boca *f; Fam* **down in the m.** deprimido(a) (**b**) *(of cave etc)* entrada *f; (of river)* desembocadura *f*

2 *vt* [maʊð] pronunciar; *(insults)* proferir

mouthful ['maʊθfʊl] *n (of food)* bocado *m; (of drink)* sorbo *m;* **to be a bit of a m.** ser difícil de pronunciar

mouth organ ['maʊθɔːgən] *n* armónica *f*

mouthpiece ['maʊθpiːs] *n Mus* boquilla *f; (of telephone)* micrófono *m; Fig (spokesman)* portavoz *m*

mouthwash ['maʊθwɒʃ] *n* elixir *m,* enjuague *m* bucal

mouthwatering ['maʊθwɔːtərɪŋ] *adj* muy apetitoso(a), que le hace a uno la boca agua

movable ['muːvəbəl] *adj* movible, móvil

move [muːv] **1** *n* (**a**) *(movement)* movimiento *m;* **to be on the m.** estar en marcha; **we must make a m.** debemos irnos ya; *Fam* **get a m. on!** ¡date prisa!

(**b**) *(in game)* jugada *f; (turn)* turno *m*

(**c**) *(course of action)* medida *f;* **to make the first m.** dar el primer paso

(**d**) *(to new home)* mudanza *f; (to new job)* traslado *m*

2 *vt* (**a**) mover; *(furniture etc)* cambiar de

sitio; *(transfer)* trasladar; **to m. house** mudarse (de casa)

(**b**) *(in game)* mover

(**c**) *(motivate)* inducir; *(persuade)* persuadir; **I won't be moved** no me harán cambiar de parecer

(**d**) *(affect emotionally)* conmover

(**e**) *(resolution etc)* proponer

3 *vi* (**a**) *(change position)* moverse, desplazarse; *(change house)* mudarse (de casa); *(change post)* trasladarse; **m. out of the way!** ¡quítate de en medio!

(**b**) *(train etc)* estar en marcha; **to start moving** ponerse en marcha

(**c**) *(travel)* ir

(**d**) *(leave)* irse, marcharse

(**e**) *(in game)* hacer una jugada

(**f**) *(take action)* tomar medidas

▸ **move about 1** *vt sep* cambiar de sitio

2 *vi (be restless)* ir y venir; *(travel)* viajar de un lugar a otro

▸ **move along 1** *vt sep (move forward)* hacer avanzar; *(keep moving)* hacer circular

2 *vi (move forward)* avanzar; *(keep moving)* circular; **m. along!** *(to person on bench)* ¡haz sitio!

▸ **move around** *vt sep & vi* = **move about**

▸ **move away 1** *vt sep* alejar, apartar (**from** de)

2 *vi (move aside)* alejarse, apartarse; *(leave)* irse; *(change house)* mudarse (de casa)

▸ **move back 1** *vt sep (to original place)* volver

2 *vi (withdraw)* retirarse; *(to original place)* volver

▸ **move forward 1** *vt sep* avanzar; *(clock)* adelantar

2 *vi* avanzar, adelantarse

▸ **move in** *vi (into new home)* instalarse

▸ **move off** *vi (go away)* irse, marcharse; *(train)* salir

▸ **move on** *vi (keep moving)* circular; *(go forward)* avanzar; *(time)* transcurrir

▸ **move out** *vi (leave)* irse, marcharse; *(leave house)* mudarse

▸ **move over** *vi* correrse

▸ **move up** *vi (go up)* subir; *Fig (be promoted)* ser ascendido(a), ascender; *(move along)* correrse, hacer sitio

movement ['mu:vmənt] *n* (**a**) movimiento *m; (gesture)* gesto *m*, ademán *m* (**b**) *(of goods)* transporte *m; (of employees)* traslado *m* (**c**) *(trend)* corriente *f* (**d**) *(of machine)* mecanismo *m* (**e**) *(of goods, capital)* circulación *f*

movie ['mu:vɪ] *n* película *f;* **to go to the** movies ir al cine; **m. star** estrella *f* de cine; *US* **m. theater** cine *m*

moving ['mu:vɪŋ] *adj (that moves)* móvil; *(car etc)* en marcha; *Fig (touching)* conmovedor(a)

mow [məʊ] *vt (pt* mowed; *pp* mown *or* mowed) *(lawn)* cortar; *(corn, wheat)* segar; *Fig* **to m. down** segar

mower ['məʊə(r)] *n* cortacésped *m*

mown [məʊn] *pp of* mow

MP [em'pi:] *n Br Pol (abbr* Member of Parliament) diputado(a) *m,f*

mph [empi:'eɪtʃ] *(abbr* miles per hour) millas *fpl* por hora

MPhil [em'fɪl] *n (abbr* Master of Philosophy) = curso de posgrado de dos años de duración, superior a un máster e inferior a un doctorado

Mr ['mɪstə(r)] *(abbr* Mister) Sr

Mrs ['mɪsɪz] *(abbr* Missus) Sra

Ms [məz] *n* Sra/Srta

> **Ms** es el equivalente femenino de **Mr**, y se utiliza para dirigirse a una mujer sin precisar su estado civil.

MSc [emes'si:] *n (abbr* Master of Science) máster *m* en Ciencias

much [mʌtʃ] **1** *adj* mucho(a); **as m. ... as** tanto(a) ... como; **how m. chocolate?** ¿cuánto chocolate?; **m. admiration** mucha admiración; **so m.** tanto(a)

2 *adv* mucho; **as m. as** tanto como; **as m. as possible** todo lo posible; **how m.?** ¿cuánto?; **how m. is it?** ¿cuánto es?, ¿cuánto vale?; **m. better** mucho mejor; **m. more** mucho más; **so m. the better!** ¡tanto mejor!; **thank you very m.** muchísimas gracias; **they are m. the same** son más o menos iguales; **too m.** demasiado; **without so m. as** sin siquiera

3 *pron* mucho; **I thought as m.** lo suponía; **m. of the town was destroyed** gran parte de la ciudad quedó destruida; **m. remains to be done** queda mucho por hacer

muck [mʌk] *n (dirt)* suciedad *f; (mud)* lodo *m; Fig* porquería *f*

▸ **muck about, muck around** *Fam* **1** *vi (idle)* perder el tiempo; *(play the fool)* hacer el tonto

2 *vt sep* **to m. sb about** fastidiar a algn

▸ **muck up** *vt sep (dirty)* ensuciar; *Fig (spoil)* echar a perder

mucky ['mʌkɪ] *adj (*muckier, muckiest*)* sucio(a)

mucus ['mju:kəs] *n* moco *m*, mucosidad *f*

mud [mʌd] *n* lodo *m*, barro *m; (thick)* fango *m; Fig* **to sling m. at sb** poner a algn por los suelos; **m. flat** marisma *f*

muddle ['mʌdəl] **1** *n* desorden *m*; *Fig (mix-up)* embrollo *m*, lío *m*; **to get into a m.** hacerse un lío

2 *vt* confundir

► **muddle through** *vi* arreglárselas, ingeniárselas

► **muddle up** *vt sep* confundir

muddy ['mʌdɪ] *adj* (**muddier, muddiest**) *(lane)* fangoso(a); *(hands)* cubierto(a) de lodo; *(liquid)* turbio(a)

mudguard ['mʌdgɑːd] *n Br* guardabarros *m inv*

muff[1] [mʌf] *n* manguito *m*; **ear muffs** orejeras *fpl*

muff[2] [mʌf] *vt Fam* pifiar; **to m. it (up)** estropearlo

muffin ['mʌfɪn] *n* panecillo *m*

muffle ['mʌfəl] *vt (sound)* amortiguar; **to m. (up)** *(person)* abrigar

muffler ['mʌflə(r)] *n US Aut* silenciador *m*

mug[1] [mʌg] *n (large cup)* tazón *m*; *(beer tankard)* jarra *f*

mug[2] [mʌg] **1** *n Fam (fool)* tonto(a) *m,f*; *(face)* jeta *f*

2 *vt* atracar, asaltar

mugging ['mʌgɪŋ] *n* asalto *m*

muggy ['mʌgɪ] *adj* (**muggier, muggiest**) bochornoso(a)

mule [mjuːl] *n* mulo(a) *m,f*

mull [mʌl] *vt* **mulled wine** = vino caliente con especias

► **mull over** *vt sep* **to m. over sth** reflexionar sobre algo

multicoloured, *US* **multicolored** ['mʌltɪkʌləd] *adj* multicolor

multinational [mʌltɪ'næʃənəl] *adj & n* multinacional *(f)*

multiple ['mʌltɪpəl] **1** *adj* múltiple; **m. sclerosis** esclerosis *f* múltiple

2 *n* múltiplo *m*

multiplication [mʌltɪplɪ'keɪʃən] *n* multiplicación *f*; **m. sign** signo *m* de multiplicar

multiply ['mʌltɪplaɪ] **1** *vt* multiplicar (**by** por)

2 *vi* multiplicarse

multipurpose [mʌltɪ'pɜːpəs] *adj* multiuso *inv*

multistorey [mʌltɪ'stɔːrɪ] *adj (building)* de varios pisos; **m. car park** parking *m* de varias plantas

multitude ['mʌltɪtjuːd] *n* multitud *f*, muchedumbre *f*

mum[1] [mʌm] *n Fam* mamá *f*

mum[2] [mʌm] *adj* **to keep m.** no decir ni pío

mumble ['mʌmbəl] **1** *vi* hablar entre dientes

2 *vt* decir entre dientes

mumbo-jumbo ['mʌmbəʊ'dʒʌmbəʊ] *n (nonsense)* palabrería *f*, monsergas *fpl*

mummy[1] ['mʌmɪ] *n Fam (mother)* mamá *f*, mami *f*

mummy[2] ['mʌmɪ] *n (body)* momia *f*

mumps [mʌmps] *n sing* paperas *fpl*

munch [mʌntʃ] *vt & vi* mascar

mundane [mʌn'deɪn] *adj Pej (ordinary)* prosaico(a); *(job, life)* rutinario(a)

> 🖋 Note that the Spanish word **mundano** is a false friend and is never a translation for the English word **mundane**. In Spanish, **mundano** means "worldly".

---

municipal [mjuː'nɪsɪpəl] *adj* municipal

municipality [mjuːnɪsɪ'pælɪtɪ] *n* municipio *m*

mural ['mjʊərəl] *adj & n* mural *(m)*

Murcia [muː'siːə] *n* Murcia

murder ['mɜːdə(r)] **1** *n* asesinato *m*, homicidio *m*

2 *vt* asesinar

murderer ['mɜːdərə(r)] *n* asesino(a) *m,f*

murderess ['mɜːdərɪs] *n* asesina *f*

murderous ['mɜːdərəs] *adj* homicida

murky ['mɜːkɪ] *adj* (**murkier, murkiest**) oscuro(a); *(water)* turbio(a)

murmur ['mɜːmə(r)] **1** *n* murmullo *m*; *(of traffic)* ruido *m*; *(complaint)* queja *f*

2 *vt & vi* murmurar

muscle ['mʌsəl] **1** *n* músculo *m*

2 *vi Fam* **to m. in on sth** entrometerse en asuntos ajenos

muscular ['mʌskjʊlə(r)] *adj (pain, tissue)* muscular; *(person)* musculoso(a)

Muse [mjuːz] *n (in mythology)* musa *f*

muse [mjuːz] *vi* **to m. on** *or* **about sth** meditar algo

museum [mjuː'zɪəm] *n* museo *m*

mushroom ['mʌʃruːm] **1** *n* seta *f*, hongo *m*; *Culin* champiñón *m*

2 *vi Fig* crecer de la noche a la mañana

music ['mjuːzɪk] *n* música *f*; **m. hall** teatro *m* de variedades; **m. library** fonoteca *f*; *Psy* **m. therapy** musicoterapia *f*

musical ['mjuːzɪkəl] **1** *adj* musical; **to be m.** estar dotado(a) para la música

2 *n* musical *m*

musician [mjuː'zɪʃən] *n* músico(a) *m,f*

Muslim ['mʊzlɪm] *adj & n* musulmán(a-na) *(m,f)*

muslin ['mʌzlɪn] *n* muselina *f*

mussel ['mʌsəl] *n* mejillón *m*

must [mʌst] **1** *v aux* **(a)** *(obligation)* deber, tener que; **you m. arrive on time**

tienes que *or* debes llegar a la hora (**b**) *(probability)* deber de; **he m. be ill** debe de estar enfermo

2 *n Fam* **to be a m.** ser imprescindible

mustache ['mʌstæʃ] *n US* bigote *m*

mustard ['mʌstəd] *n* mostaza *f*

muster ['mʌstə(r)] **1** *vt Fig* **to m. (up) courage** cobrar fuerzas

2 *vi* reunirse, juntarse

mustn't ['mʌsənt] = **must not**

musty ['mʌstɪ] *adj* (**mustier, mustiest**) que huele a cerrado *or* a humedad

mute ['mju:t] **1** *adj* mudo(a)

2 *n (person)* mudo(a) *m,f; Mus* sordina *f*

muted ['mju:tɪd] *adj (sound)* sordo(a); *(colour)* suave

mutilate ['mju:tɪleɪt] *vt* mutilar

mutiny ['mju:tɪnɪ] **1** *n* motín *m*

2 *vi* amotinarse

mutter ['mʌtə(r)] **1** *n (mumble)* murmullo *m*

2 *vt* murmurar, decir entre dientes

3 *vi (angrily)* refunfuñar

mutton ['mʌtən] *n* (carne *f* de) cordero *m*

mutual ['mju:tʃʊəl] *adj* mutuo(a); *(shared)* común

Muzak® ['mju:zæk] *n* música *f* de super-mercado

muzzle ['mʌzəl] **1** *n (snout)* hocico *m; (for dog)* bozal *m; (of gun)* boca *f*

2 *vt (dog)* abozalar; *Fig* amordazar

my [maɪ]. *poss adj* mi; **my cousins** mis primos; **my father** mi padre; **one of my friends** un amigo mío; **I washed my hair** me lavé el pelo; **I twisted my ankle** me torcí el tobillo

myriad ['mɪrɪəd] *n Literary* miríada *f*

myself [maɪ'self] *pers pron* (**a**) *(emphatic)* yo mismo(a); **my husband and m.** mi marido y yo (**b**) *(reflexive)* me; **I hurt m.** me hice daño (**c**) *(after prep)* mí (mis-mo(a))

mysterious [mɪ'stɪərɪəs] *adj* misterio-so(a)

mystery ['mɪstərɪ] *n* misterio *m*

mystical ['mɪstɪkəl] *adj* místico(a)

mystify ['mɪstɪfaɪ] *vt* dejar perplejo(a)

mystique [mɪ'sti:k] *n* mística *f*

myth [mɪθ] *n* mito *m*; **it's a complete m.** es pura fantasía

mythology [mɪ'θɒlədʒɪ] *n* mitología *f*

N, n [en] *n (the letter)* N, n *f*

N (*abbr* **North**) N

nab [næb] *vt Fam* pillar

naff [næf] *adj Br Fam* (**a**) *(tasteless)* hortera, cutre (**b**) *(for emphasis)* **n. all** nada de nada

NAFTA ['næftə] *n* (*abbr* **North American Free Trade Agreement**) NAFTA *f*, TLC *m*

nag [næg] **1** *vt* dar la tabarra a; **to n. sb to do sth** dar la tabarra a algn para que haga algo

2 *vi* quejarse

nagging ['nægɪŋ] *adj (persistent)* continuo(a)

nail [neɪl] **1** *n* (**a**) *(of finger, toe)* uña *f*; **n. clippers** cortaúñas *m inv*; **n. polish** *or* **varnish** esmalte *m or* laca *f* de uñas (**b**) *(metal)* clavo *m*; *Fig* **to hit the n. on the head** dar en el clavo

2 *vt* (**a**) clavar (**b**) *Fam (catch, trap)* pillar, coger

nailbrush ['neɪlbrʌʃ] *n* cepillo *m* de uñas

nailfile ['neɪlfaɪl] *n* lima *f* de uñas

nail-scissors ['neɪlsɪzəz] *npl* tijeras *fpl* de uñas

naïve [naɪ'iːv] *adj* ingenuo(a)

naked ['neɪkɪd] *adj* desnudo(a); *(flame)* sin protección; **the n. truth** la pura verdad

name [neɪm] **1** *n* (**a**) nombre *m*; *(surname)* apellido *m*; **what's your n.?** ¿cómo te llamas?; **to call sb names** poner verde a algn (**b**) *(reputation)* reputación *f*; **to have a bad/good n.** tener mala/buena reputación; **to make a n. for oneself** hacerse famoso(a)

2 *vt* (**a**) llamar; **to n. sb after** *or US* **for sb** poner a algn el nombre de algn (**b**) *(appoint)* nombrar (**c**) *(refer to)* mencionar

nameless ['neɪmlɪs] *adj* anónimo(a); **to remain n.** permanecer en el anonimato

namely ['neɪmlɪ] *adv* a saber

namesake ['neɪmseɪk] *n* tocayo(a) *m,f*

nanny ['nænɪ] *n* niñera *f*

nap [næp] **1** *n (sleep)* siesta *f*; **to have a n.** echar la *or* una siesta

2 *vi Fig* **to catch sb napping** coger a algn desprevenido(a)

napalm ['neɪpɑːm] *n* napalm *m*

nape [neɪp] *n* nuca *f*, cogote *m*

napkin ['næpkɪn] *n (table)* **n.** servilleta *f*

Naples ['neɪpəlz] *n* Nápoles

nappy ['næpɪ] *n Br* pañal *m*

narcissus [nɑː'sɪsəs] *n Bot* narciso *m*

narcotic [nɑː'kɒtɪk] **1** *adj* narcótico(a)

2 *n (usu pl)* narcótico *m*, estupefaciente *m*

narrate [nə'reɪt] *vt* narrar, relatar

narration [nə'reɪʃən] *n* narración *f*, relato *m*

narrative ['nærətɪv] **1** *n Lit* narrativa *f*; *(story)* narración *f*

2 *adj* narrativo(a)

narrator [nə'reɪtə(r)] *n* narrador(a) *m,f*

narrow ['nærəʊ] **1** *adj* (**a**) *(passage, road etc)* estrecho(a), angosto(a) (**b**) *(restricted)* reducido(a); *(sense)* estricto(a); **to have a n. escape** librarse por los pelos

2 *vi* estrecharse

narrowly ['nærəʊlɪ] *adv* (**a**) *(closely)* de cerca (**b**) *(by a small margin)* por poco

▸**narrow down 1** *vt sep* reducir, limitar

2 *vi* **to n. down to** reducirse a

narrow-minded ['nærəʊ'maɪndɪd] *adj* de miras estrechas

nasal ['neɪzəl] *adj* nasal; *(voice)* gangoso(a)

nastiness ['nɑːstɪnɪs] *n* (**a**) *(unpleasantness)* carácter *m* desagradable (**b**) *(maliciousness)* mala intención

nasty ['nɑːstɪ] *adj* (**nastier, nastiest**) (**a**) *(person)* desagradable; **a n. business** un asunto feo; **a n. trick** una mala jugada *or* pasada; **cheap and n.** hortera; **to turn n.** *(of weather, situation)* ponerse feo(a) (**b**) *(unfriendly)* antipático(a); *(malicious)* mal intencionado(a); *Fam* **he's a n. piece of work** es un asco de tío (**c**) *(dirty)* sucio(a), asqueroso(a) (**d**) *(illness, accident)* grave

nation ['neɪʃən] *n* nación *f*

national ['næʃənəl] **1** *adj* nacional; **n. anthem** himno *m* nacional; **n. insurance** seguridad *f* social; *Br Mil* **n. service** servicio *m* militar

2 *n* súbdito(a) *m,f*

nationalism ['næʃnəlɪzəm] *n* nacionalismo *m*

nationalist [ˈnæʃnəlɪst] *adj & n* nacionalista *(mf)*

nationality [næʃəˈnælɪtɪ] *n* nacionalidad *f*

nationalization [næʃnəlaɪˈzeɪʃən] *n* nacionalización *f*

nationalize [ˈnæʃnəlaɪz] *vt* nacionalizar

nationwide [ˈneɪʃənwaɪd] *adj* de ámbito nacional

native [ˈneɪtɪv] **1** *adj* (a) *(place)* natal; **n. land** patria *f*; **n. language** lengua materna (b) *(innate)* innato(a) (c) *(plant, animal)* originario(a) (**to** de)
2 *n* nativo(a) *m,f*, natural *mf*; *(original inhabitant)* indígena *mf*

NATO, Nato [ˈneɪtəʊ] *n (abbr* **North Atlantic Treaty Organization)** OTAN *f*

natter [ˈnætə(r)] *Fam* **1** *vi* charlar
2 *n* charla *f*

natural [ˈnætʃərəl] **1** *adj* (a) *natural* (b) *(normal)* normal; **it's only n. that ...** es lógico que ... (c) *(born)* nato(a)
2 *n* (a) **she's a n. for the job** es la persona ideal para el trabajo (b) *Mus* becuadro *m*

naturalize [ˈnætʃərəlaɪz] *vt* **to become naturalized** naturalizarse

naturally [ˈnætʃərəlɪ] *adv* (a) *(of course)* naturalmente (b) *(by nature)* por naturaleza (c) *(in a relaxed manner)* con naturalidad

nature [ˈneɪtʃə(r)] *n* (a) naturaleza *f* (b) *(character)* naturaleza *f*, carácter *m*; **by n.** por naturaleza; **human n.** la naturaleza humana (c) *(sort, kind)* índole *f*, clase *f*

naught [nɔːt] *n Literary* nada *f*; **to come to n.** fracasar

naughtily [ˈnɔːtɪlɪ] *adv* **to behave n.** portarse mal

naughty [ˈnɔːtɪ] *adj* (**naughtier, naughtiest**) (a) *(child)* travieso(a) (b) *(joke, story)* atrevido(a), picante

nausea [ˈnɔːzɪə] *n Med (sickness)* náusea *f*

nauseate [ˈnɔːzɪeɪt] *vt (disgust)* dar asco a

nauseating [ˈnɔːzɪeɪtɪŋ] *adj* nauseabundo(a)

nautical [ˈnɔːtɪkəl] *adj* náutico(a); **n. mile** milla marítima

naval [ˈneɪvəl] *adj* naval; **n. officer** oficial *mf* de marina; **n. power** potencia marítima *or* naval

Navarre [nəˈvɑː(r)] *n* Navarra

nave [neɪv] *n Archit* nave *f*

navel [ˈneɪvəl] *n Anat* ombligo *m*

navigate [ˈnævɪgeɪt] **1** *vt (river)* navegar por; *Naut (ship)* ▸ gobernar

2 *vi* navegar; *(in driving)* indicar la dirección

navigation [nævɪˈgeɪʃən] *n Naut* navegación *f*

navigator [ˈnævɪgeɪtə(r)] *n* (a) *Naut* navegante *mf*, oficial *mf* de derrota (b) *Aut & Av* copiloto *mf*

navvy [ˈnævɪ] *n Br Fam* peón *m*

navy [ˈneɪvɪ] *n* marina *f*; **n. blue** azul marino

Nazi [ˈnɑːtsɪ] *adj & n* nazi *(mf)*

Nazism [ˈnɑːtsɪzəm] *n* nazismo *m*

NB, nb [enˈbiː] *(abbr* **nota bene)** N.B.

neap [niːp] *n (tide)* marea muerta

near [nɪə(r)] **1** *adj (in space)* cercano(a); *(in time)* próximo(a); **in the n. future** en un futuro próximo; **it was a n. thing** poco faltó
2 *adv (in space)* cerca; **n. and far** por todas partes; **that's n. enough** (ya) vale, está bien
3 *prep* cerca de; **n. the end of the film** hacia el final de la película
4 *vt* acercarse a

nearby [nɪəˈbaɪ] **1** *adj* cercano(a)
2 *adv* cerca

nearly [ˈnɪəlɪ] *adv* casi; **very n.** casi, casi; **we haven't n. enough** no alcanza ni con mucho

nearside [ˈnɪəsaɪd] *n Aut (with left-hand drive)* lado izquierdo; *(with right-hand drive)* lado derecho

near-sighted [nɪəˈsaɪtɪd] *adj* miope

neat [niːt] *adj* (a) *(room, habits etc)* ordenado(a); *(handwriting)* claro(a); *(appearance)* pulcro(a) (b) *(idea)* ingenioso(a) (c) *(whisky etc)* solo(a) (d) *US Fam (fine)* chulísimo(a)

neatly [ˈniːtlɪ] *adv* (a) *(carefully)* cuidadosamente (b) *(cleverly)* hábilmente

necessarily [nesɪˈserəlɪ] *adv* necesariamente, por fuerza

necessary [ˈnesɪsərɪ] **1** *adj* (a) *(essential)* necesario(a); **to do what is n.** hacer lo que haga falta; **if n.** si es preciso (b) *(unavoidable)* inevitable
2 *n* **the n.** lo necesario

necessitate [nɪˈsesɪteɪt] *vt* necesitar, exigir

necessity [nɪˈsesɪtɪ] *n* (a) necesidad *f*; **out of n.** por necesidad (b) *(article)* requisito *m* indispensable; **necessities** artículos *mpl* de primera necesidad

neck [nek] *n* (a) *(of person)* cuello *m*; *(of animal)* pescuezo *m*; **to be n. and n.** ir parejos; **to be up to one's n. in debt** estar hasta el cuello de deudas; **to risk one's n.** jugarse el tipo; **to stick one's n. out** arriesgarse; **to**

win/lose by a n. *(in horse racing)* ganar/perder por una cabeza; **low n.** escote bajo

2 *vi Fam* magrearse

necklace ['neklɪs] *n* collar *m*

neckline ['neklaɪn] *n (of dress)* escote *m*

necktie ['nektaɪ] *n US* corbata *f*

nectar ['nektə(r)] *n* néctar *m*

nectarine ['nektəriːn] *n* nectarina *f*

née [neɪ] *adj* n. Brown de soltera Brown

need [niːd] 1 *n* (a) necesidad *f*; **if n. be** si fuera necesario; **there's no n. for you to do that** no hace falta que hagas eso (b) *(poverty)* indigencia *f*; **to be in n.** estar necesitado; **to help a friend in n.** sacar a un amigo de un apuro

2 *vt* (a) necesitar; *Ironic* **that's all I n.** sólo me faltaba eso (b) *(action, solution etc)* requerir, exigir

3 *v aux* tener que, deber; **n. he go?** ¿tiene que ir?; **you needn't wait** no hace falta que esperes

Cuando se emplea como verbo modal sólo existe una forma, y los auxiliares **do/does** no se usan: **he need only worry about himself**; **need she go?**; **it needn't matter.**

needle ['niːdəl] 1 *n* (a) *(for sewing, knitting)* aguja *f* (b) *Bot* hoja *f* (c) *Br Fam* **to get the n.** picarse

2 *vt Fam* pinchar

needless ['niːdlɪs] *adj* innecesario(a); **n. to say** huelga decir

needlessly ['niːdlɪslɪ] *adv* innecesariamente

needlework ['niːdəlwɜːk] *n (sewing)* costura *f*; *(embroidery)* bordado *m*

needy ['niːdɪ] *adj* **(needier, neediest)** necesitado(a)

negate [nɪ'ɡeɪt] *vt* (a) *(deny)* negar (b) *(nullify)* anular

negative ['neɡətɪv] 1 *adj* negativo(a)

2 *n* (a) *Ling* negación *f* (b) *Phot* negativo *m*

neglect [nɪ'ɡlekt] 1 *vt* (a) *(child, duty etc)* descuidar, desatender (b) **to n. to do sth** *(omit to do)* no hacer algo

2 *n* dejadez *f*; **n. of duty** incumplimiento *m* del deber

neglectful [nɪ'ɡlektfʊl] *adj* descuidado(a), negligente

negligée ['neɡlɪʒeɪ] *n* salto *m* de cama

negligence ['neɡlɪdʒəns] *n* negligencia *f*, descuido *m*

negligent ['neɡlɪdʒənt] *adj* negligente, descuidado(a)

negligible ['neɡlɪdʒɪbəl] *adj* insignificante

negotiate [nɪ'ɡəʊʃɪeɪt] 1 *vt* (a) *(contract)* negociar (b) *Fig (obstacle)* salvar, franquear

2 *vi* negociar

negotiation [nɪɡəʊʃɪ'eɪʃən] *n* negociación *f*

negro ['niːɡrəʊ] *n (pl negroes)* negro(a) *m,f*

neigh [neɪ] 1 *n* relincho *m*

2 *vi* relinchar

neighbour, *US* **neighbor** ['neɪbə(r)] *n* vecino(a) *m,f*; *Rel* prójimo *m*

neighbourhood, *US* **neighborhood** ['neɪbəhʊd] *n (district)* vecindad *f*, barrio *m*; *(people)* vecindario *m*

neighbouring, *US* **neighboring** ['neɪbərɪŋ] *adj* vecino(a)

neither ['naɪðə(r), 'niːðə(r)] 1 *adj & pron* ninguno de los dos/ninguna de las dos

2 *adv & conj* (a) ni; **n. ... nor** ni ... ni; *Fig* **it's n. here nor there** no viene al caso (b) tampoco; **she was not there and n. was her sister** ella no estaba, ni su hermana tampoco

neon ['niːɒn] *n* neón *m*; **n. light** luz *f* de neón

nephew ['nefjuː] *n* sobrino *m*

nerd [nɜːd] *n Fam* (a) *(boring person)* petardo(a) *m,f*, plasta *mf*, *Méx* sangrón(ona) *m,f*, *RP* nerd *mf* (b) *(as insult)* bobo(a) *m,f*, memo(a) *m,f*

nerve [nɜːv] *n* (a) *Anat* nervio *m*; **to get on sb's nerves** poner los nervios de punta a algn; **n. gas** gas nervioso (b) *(courage)* valor *m* (c) *Fam (cheek)* cara *f*, descaro *m*; **what a n.!** ¡qué cara!

nerve-racking ['nɜːvrækɪŋ] *adj* crispante, exasperante

nervous ['nɜːvəs] *adj* (a) nervioso(a); **n. breakdown** depresión nerviosa (b) *(afraid)* miedoso(a) (c) *(timid)* tímido(a)

nest [nest] 1 *n Orn* nido *m*; *(hen's)* nidal *m*; *(animal's)* madriguera *f*, *Fig* **n. egg** ahorros *mpl*

2 *vi (birds)* anidar

nestle ['nesəl] 1 *vt* recostar

2 *vi (settle comfortably)* acomodarse

Net [net] *n Fam Comput* **the N.** *(Internet)* la Red; **N. user** internauta *mf*

net¹ [net] *n* red *f*; *Br* **n. curtains** visillos *mpl*

net² [net] 1 *adj* neto(a); **n. weight** peso neto

2 *vt (earn)* ganar neto

netball ['netbɔːl] *n Sport* baloncesto femenino

Netherlands ['neðələndz] *npl* **the N.** los Países Bajos

netting ['netɪŋ] *n* redes *fpl*, malla *f*

nettle ['netəl] **1** *n Bot* ortiga *f*
2 *vt Fam* irritar

network ['netwɜːk] **1** *n* red *f*
2 *vi (establish contacts)* establecer contactos

neurosis [njʊˈrəʊsɪs] *n* neurosis *f*

neurotic [njʊˈrɒtɪk] *adj & n* neurótico(a) *(m,f)*

neuter ['njuːtə(r)] **1** *adj* neutro(a)
2 *n Ling* neutro *m*
3 *vt (geld)* castrar

neutral ['njuːtrəl] **1** *adj* neutro(a); *Pol* **to remain n.** permanecer neutral
2 *n Aut* punto muerto

neutrality [njuːˈtrælɪtɪ] *n* neutralidad *f*

neutralize ['njuːtrəlaɪz] *vt* neutralizar

neutron ['njuːtrɒn] *n Phys* neutrón *m*; **n. bomb** bomba *f* de neutrones

never ['nevə(r)] *adv* nunca, jamás; **he n. complains** nunca se queja, no se queja nunca; **n. again** nunca (ja)más; **n. in all my life** jamás en la vida; *Fam* **n. mind** da igual, no me importa; *Fam* **well, I n. (did)!** ¡no me digas!

never-ending ['nevər'endɪŋ] *adj* sin fin, interminable

nevertheless [nevəðə'les] *adv* sin embargo, no obstante

new [njuː] *adj* nuevo(a); **as good as n.** como nuevo; **n. baby** recién nacido *m*; **n. moon** luna nueva; **N. Year** Año nuevo; **N. Year's Eve** Nochevieja *f*; **N. York** Nueva York; **N. Zealand** Nueva Zelanda

newborn ['njuːbɔːn] *adj* recién nacido(a)

newcomer ['njuːkʌmə(r)] *n* recién llegado(a) *m,f*; *(to job etc)* nuevo(a) *m,f*

newfangled ['njuːfæŋgəld] *adj* novedoso(a)

newly ['njuːlɪ] *adv* recién, recientemente

newlywed ['njuːlɪwed] *n* recién casado(a) *m,f*

news [njuːz] *n sing* noticias *fpl*; **a piece of n.** una noticia; *Fam* **it's n. to me** ahora me entero; **n. agency** agencia *f* de información; *US* **n. in brief** avance informativo; **n. bulletin** boletín informativo; **n. clipping** recorte *m* de periódico; **n. summary** avance informativo;

newsagent ['njuːzeɪdʒənt] *n* vendedor(a) *m,f* de periódicos

newsflash ['njuːzflæʃ] *n* noticia *f* de última hora

newsgroup ['njuːzgruːp] *n Comput* grupo *m* de noticias

newsletter ['njuːzletə(r)] *n* hoja informativa

newspaper ['njuːzpeɪpə(r)] *n* periódico *m*, diario *m*

newsprint ['njuːzprɪnt] *n* papel *m* de periódico

newsreader ['njuːzriːdə(r)] *n TV & Rad* presentador(a) *m,f* de los informativos

newsreel ['njuːzriːl] *n* noticiario *m*

news-stand ['njuːzstænd] *n* quiosco *m* de periódicos

newt [njuːt] *n Zool* tritón *m*

next [nekst] **1** *adj* **(a)** *(in place)* de al lado **(b)** *(in time)* próximo(a); **the n. day** el día siguiente; **n. Friday** el viernes que viene; **n. time** la próxima vez; **the week after n.** dentro de dos semanas **(c)** *(in order)* siguiente, próximo(a); **n. of kin** pariente *m* más cercano
2 *adv* después, luego; **what shall we do n.?** ¿qué hacemos ahora?
3 *prep* **n. to** al lado de, junto a; **n. to nothing** casi nada

next-door 1 *adj* ['neksdɔː(r)] de al lado; **our n. neighbour** el vecino/la vecina de al lado
2 *adv* [neks'dɔː(r)] al lado

NHS [eneɪtʃ'es] *n Br (abbr* **National Health Service)** Seguridad *f* Social

nib [nɪb] *n* plumilla *f*

nibble ['nɪbəl] *vt & vi* mordisquear

nice [naɪs] *adj* **(a)** *(person)* simpático(a); *(thing)* agradable; **n. and cool** fresquito(a); **to smell/taste n.** oler/saber bien **(b)** *(nice-looking)* bonito(a), *Am* lindo(a) **(c)** *Ironic* menudo(a); **a n. mess you've made!** ¡menudo lío has hecho! **(d)** *Fml (subtle)* sutil

nicely ['naɪslɪ] *adv* muy bien

niche [niːʃ] *n* **(a)** hornacina *f*, nicho *m* **(b)** *Fig* hueco *m*

nick [nɪk] **1** *n* **(a)** *(notch)* muesca *f*; *(cut)* herida pequeña; *Fam* **in the n. of time** en el momento preciso **(b)** *Br Fam* **the n.** *(prison)* chirona *f*
2 *vt Br Fam* **(a)** *(steal)* birlar **(b)** *(arrest)* pillar

nickel ['nɪkəl] *n* **(a)** níquel *m*; **n. silver** alpaca *f* **(b)** *US* moneda *f* de 5 centavos

nickname ['nɪkneɪm] **1** *n* apodo *m*
2 *vt* apodar

nicotine ['nɪkətiːn] *n* nicotina *f*

niece [niːs] *n* sobrina *f*

nifty ['nɪftɪ] *adj* **(niftier, niftiest)** **(a)** *(quick)* rápido(a); *(agile)* ágil **(b)** *(ingenious)* ingenioso(a)

Nigeria [naɪˈdʒɪərɪə] *n* Nigeria

nigger ['nɪgə(r)] *n Fam Pej* negro(a) *m,f*

niggling ['nɪgəlɪŋ] *adj (trifling)* insignificante; *(irritating)* molesto(a)

night [naɪt] *n* noche *f*; **at n.** de noche; **at twelve o'clock at n.** a las doce de la noche; **last n.** anoche; **to have a n. out** salir por la noche; **n. life** vida nocturna; *Fam* **n. owl** trasnochador(a) *m,f*; **n. school** escuela nocturna; **n. shift** turno *m* de noche

nightclub ['naɪtklʌb] *n* sala *f* de fiestas; *(disco)* discoteca *f*

nightdress ['naɪtdres] *n* camisón *m*

nightfall ['naɪtfɔːl] *n* anochecer *m*

nightgown ['naɪtgaʊn] *n* camisón *m*

nightingale ['naɪtɪŋgeɪl] *n* ruiseñor *m*

nightly ['naɪtlɪ] **1** *adj* de cada noche **2** *adv* todas las noches

nightmare ['naɪtmeə(r)] *n* pesadilla *f*

nightshade ['naɪtʃeɪd] *n Bot* **deadly n.** belladona *f*

night-time ['naɪttaɪm] *n* noche *f*; **at n.** por la noche

nil [nɪl] *n* nada *f*; *Sport* cero *m*; **two n.** dos a cero

Nile [naɪl] *n* the N. el Nilo

nimble ['nɪmbəl] *adj* ágil, rápido(a)

nine [naɪn] *adj & n* nueve *(m inv)*; *Fam* **dressed up to the nines** de punta en blanco

nineteen [naɪn'tiːn] *adj & n* diecinueve *(m inv)*

nineteenth [naɪn'tiːnθ] *adj* decimonoveno(a)

ninety ['naɪntɪ] *adj & n* noventa *(m inv)*

ninth [naɪnθ] **1** *adj & n* noveno(a) *(m,f)* **2** *n (fraction)* noveno *m*

nip [nɪp] **1** *vt* (a) *(pinch)* pellizcar (b) *(bite)* morder; **to n. sth in the bud** cortar algo de raíz **2** *n* (a) *(pinch)* pellizco *m* (b) *(bite)* mordisco *m*

nipple ['nɪpəl] *n* (a) *Anat (female)* pezón *m*; *(male)* tetilla *f* (b) *US (on baby's bottle)* tetilla *f*, tetina *f*

nippy ['nɪpɪ] *adj (nippier, nippiest) Fam* (a) *Br (quick)* rápido(a) (b) *(cold)* fresquito(a)

nit [nɪt] *n* liendre *f*

nitrogen ['naɪtrədʒən] *n Chem* nitrógeno *m*

nitroglycerin(e) [naɪtrəʊ'glɪsəriːn] *n Chem* nitroglicerina *f*

nitty-gritty [nɪtɪ'grɪtɪ] *n Fam* **to get down to the n.** ir al grano

nitwit ['nɪtwɪt] *n Fam* imbécil *mf*

no [nəʊ] **1** *adv* no; **come here! – no!** ¡ven aquí! – ¡no!; **no longer** ya no; **no less than** no menos de

2 *adj* ninguno(a); **she has no children** no tiene hijos; **I have no idea** no tengo (ni) idea; **it's no good** *or* **use** no vale la pena; *Aut* **no parking** *(sign)* prohibido aparcar; **no sensible person** ninguna persona razonable; *Fam* **no way!** ¡ni hablar!

3 *n* no *m*; **she won't take no for an answer** no para hasta salirse con la suya; **to say no** decir que no

no. *(pl nos.) (abbr* **number)** n, núm.

nobility [nəʊ'bɪlɪtɪ] *n* nobleza *f*

noble ['nəʊbəl] *adj* noble

nobleman ['nəʊbəlmən] *n* noble *m*

noblewoman ['nəʊbəlwʊmən] *n* noble *f*

nobody ['nəʊbədɪ] **1** *pron* nadie; **there was n. there** no había nadie; **n. else** nadie más

2 *n* nadie *m*; **he's a n.** es un don nadie

nocturnal [nɒk'tɜːnəl] *adj* nocturno(a)

nod [nɒd] **1** *n (of greeting)* saludo *m (con la cabeza)*; *(of agreement)* señal *f* de asentimiento

2 *vi (greet)* saludar con la cabeza; *(agree)* asentir con la cabeza

▸ **nod off** *vi* dormirse

3 *vt* **to n. one's head** inclinar la cabeza

no-go ['nəʊ'gəʊ] *adj* **n. area** zona prohibida

noise [nɔɪz] *n* ruido *m*; **to make a n.** hacer ruido

noiseless ['nɔɪzlɪs] *adj* silencioso(a), sin ruido

noisy ['nɔɪzɪ] *adj* (**noisier, noisiest**) ruidoso(a)

nomad ['nəʊmæd] *n* nómada *mf*

no-man's-land ['nəʊmænzlænd] *n* tierra *f* de nadie

nominal ['nɒmɪnəl] *adj* nominal; *(payment, rent)* simbólico(a)

nominate ['nɒmɪneɪt] *vt* (a) *(propose)* designar, proponer (b) *(appoint)* nombrar

nomination [nɒmɪ'neɪʃən] *n* (a) *(proposal)* propuesta *f* (b) *(appointment)* nombramiento *m*

nominative ['nɒmɪnətɪv] *n* nominativo *m*

nominee [nɒmɪ'niː] *n* persona propuesta

non- [nɒn] *pref* no

non-aggression [nɒnə'greʃən] *n Pol* no agresión *f*; **n. pact** pacto *m* de no agresión

non-alcoholic [nɒnælkə'hɒlɪk] *adj* sin alcohol

non-aligned [nɒnə'laɪnd] *adj Pol* no alineado(a)

nonchalant ['nɒnʃələnt] *adj (indifferent)*

indiferente; *(calm)* imperturbable, impasible

noncommittal [ˈnɒnkəmɪtəl] *adj (person)* evasivo(a); *(answer)* que no compromete (a nada)

nonconformist [ˈnɒnkənˈfɔːmɪst] *n* inconformista *mf*

nondescript [ˈnɒndɪskrɪpt] *adj* indescriptible; *(uninteresting)* soso(a)

none [nʌn] **1** *pron* ninguno(a); **I know n. of them** no conozco a ninguno de ellos; **n. at all** nada en absoluto; **n. other than ...** nada menos que ...

2 *adv* de ningún modo; **she's n. the worse for it** no se ha visto afectada *or* perjudicada por ello; **n. too soon** a buena hora

nonentity [nɒˈnentɪtɪ] *n (person)* cero *m* a la izquierda

nonetheless [nʌnðəˈles] *adv* no obstante, sin embargo

nonevent [nɒnɪˈvent] *n* fracaso *m*

nonexistent [nɒnɪɡˈzɪstənt] *adj* inexistente

nonfiction [nɒnˈfɪkʃən] *n* no ficción *f*

no-nonsense [ˈnəʊˈnɒnsəns] *adj (person)* recto(a), serio(a)

nonplussed [nɒnˈplʌst] *adj* perplejo(a)

non-profit(-making) [nɒnˈprɒfɪt(meɪkɪŋ)] *adj* sin fin lucrativo

nonreturnable [nɒnrɪˈtɜːnəbəl] *adj* no retornable

nonsense [ˈnɒnsəns] *n* tonterías *fpl*, disparates *mpl*; **that's n.** eso es absurdo

nonsmoker [nɒnˈsməʊkə(r)] *n* no fumador(a) *m,f*, persona *f* que no fuma

nonstarter [nɒnˈstɑːtə(r)] *n Fig* **to be a n.** *(person)* estar destinado a fracasar; *(plan)* ser irrealizable

nonstick [nɒnˈstɪk] *adj* antiadherente

nonstop [nɒnˈstɒp] **1** *adj* sin parar; *(train)* directo(a)

2 *adv* sin parar

noodles [ˈnuːdəlz] *npl Culin* fideos *mpl*

nook [nʊk] *n* recoveco *m*, rincón *m*

noon [nuːn] *n* mediodía *m*; **at n.** a mediodía

no one [ˈnəʊwʌn] *pron* nadie; **n. came** no vino nadie

noose [nuːs] *n* lazo *m*; *(hangman's)* soga *f*

nor [nɔː(r)] *conj* ni, ni tampoco; **neither ... n. ni ... ni**; **neither you n. I** ni tú ni yo; **n. do I** (ni) yo tampoco

norm [nɔːm] *n* norma *f*

normal [ˈnɔːməl] *adj* normal

normality [nɔːˈmælɪtɪ] *n* normalidad *f*

normally [ˈnɔːməlɪ] *adv* normalmente

Normandy [ˈnɔːməndɪ] *n* Normandía

north [nɔːθ] **1** *n* norte *m*; **the N.** el norte *m*; **N. America** América del Norte, Norteamérica; **N. Korea** Corea del Norte; **N. Pole** Polo *m* Norte; **N. Sea** Mar *m* del Norte

2 *adv* hacia el norte, al norte

3 *adj* del norte; **n. wind** viento *m* del norte

northeast [nɔːθˈiːst] *n* nor(d)este *m*

northerly [ˈnɔːðəlɪ] *adj* norte, del norte

northern [ˈnɔːðən] *adj* del norte, septentrional; **n. hemisphere** hemisferio *m* norte; **N. Ireland** Irlanda del Norte

northerner [ˈnɔːðənə(r)] *n* norteño(a) *m,f*

northward [ˈnɔːθwəd] *adj & adv* hacia el norte

northwest [nɔːθˈwest] *n* noroeste *m*

Norway [ˈnɔːweɪ] *n* Noruega

Norwegian [nɔːˈwiːdʒən] **1** *adj* noruego(a)

2 *n* **(a)** *(person)* noruego(a) *m,f* **(b)** *(language)* noruego *m*

nose [nəʊz] *n* **(a)** nariz *f*; *Fig* **(right) under sb's n.** delante de las propias narices de algn; *Br Fam* **to get up sb's n.** hincharle a algn las narices **(b)** *(sense of smell)* olfato *m* **(c)** *(of car, plane)* morro *m*

▸ **nose about, nose around** *vi* curiosear

nosebleed [ˈnəʊzbliːd] *n* hemorragia *f* nasal

nosedive [ˈnəʊzdaɪv] *Av* **1** *n* picado *m*

2 *vi* descender en picado

nostalgia [nɒˈstældʒɪə] *n* nostalgia *f*

nostalgic [nɒˈstældʒɪk] *adj* nostálgico(a)

nostril [ˈnɒstrɪl] *n Anat* orificio *m* nasal

nosy [ˈnəʊzɪ] *adj (nosier, nosiest) Fam* entrometido(a)

not [nɒt] *adv* no; **he's n. in today** hoy no está; **I'm n. sorry to leave** no siento nada irme; **n. at all** en absoluto; **thank you – n. at all** no hay de qué; **n. one (of them)** thanked me nadie me dio las gracias; **n. that I don't want to come** no es que no quiera ir; **n. too well** bastante mal; **n. without reason** no sin razón; *Fam* **n. likely!** ¡ni hablar!

En el inglés hablado, y en el escrito en estilo coloquial, **not** se contrae después de verbos modales y auxiliares.

notable [ˈnəʊtəbəl] *adj* notable

notably [ˈnəʊtəblɪ] *adv* notablemente

notary [ˈnəʊtərɪ] *n* notario *m*

notch [nɒtʃ] *n* muesca *f*; *(cut)* corte *m*

▸ **notch up** *vt sep Fig* **to n. up a victory** apuntarse una victoria

note [nəʊt] **1** *n* **(a)** *Mus* nota *f*; *Fig* **to strike**

the right n. acertar (**b**) *(on paper)* nota *f* (**c**) **to take** n. **of** *(notice)* prestar atención a (**d**) *(banknote)* billete *m* (de banco) (**e**) **notes** apuntes *mpl*; **to take** n. tomar apuntes

2 *vt* (**a**) *(write down)* apuntar, anotar (**b**) *(notice)* notar, fijarse en

notebook ['nəʊtbʊk] *n* cuaderno *m*, libreta *f*

noted ['nəʊtɪd] *adj* notable, célebre

notepad ['nəʊtpæd] *n* bloc *m* de notas

notepaper ['nəʊtpeɪpə(r)] *n* papel *m* de carta

noteworthy ['nəʊtwɜːðɪ] *adj* digno(a) de mención

nothing ['nʌθɪŋ] **1** *n* nada; **I saw** n. no vi nada; **for** n. *(free of charge)* gratis; **it's** n. no es nada; **it's n. to do with you** no tiene nada que ver contigo; n. **else** nada más; **there's** n. **in it** no es cierto; *Fam* n. **much** poca cosa; *Fam* **there's** n. **to it** es facilísimo

2 *adv* **she looks** n. **like her sister** no se parece en nada a su hermana

notice ['nəʊtɪs] **1** *n* (**a**) *(warning)* aviso *m*; **he gave a month's** n. presentó la dimisión con un mes de antelación; **at short** n. con poca antelación; **until further** n. hasta nuevo aviso; **without** n. sin previo aviso (**b**) *(attention)* atención *f*; **to take no** n. **of sth** no hacer caso de algo; **to take** n. **of sth** prestar atención a algo; **it escaped my** n. se me escapó; **to come to one's** n. llegar al conocimiento de uno (**c**) *(in newspaper etc)* anuncio *m* (**d**) *(sign)* letrero *m*, aviso *m*

2 *vt* darse cuenta de, notar

> *ℐ* Note that the Spanish word **noticia** is a false friend and is never a translation for the English word **notice**. In Spanish, **noticia** means "(piece of) news".

noticeable ['nəʊtɪsəbəl] *adj* que se nota, evidente

noticeboard ['nəʊtɪsbɔːd] *n Br* tablón *m* de anuncios

notification [nəʊtɪfɪ'keɪʃən] *n* aviso *m*

notify ['nəʊtɪfaɪ] *vt* avisar

notion ['nəʊʃən] *n* (**a**) idea *f*, concepto *m* (**b**) *(whim)* capricho *m* (**c**) *US Sewing* **notions** artículos *mpl* de mercería

notorious [nəʊ'tɔːrɪəs] *adj Pej* tristemente célebre

> *ℐ* Note that the Spanish word **notorio** is a false friend and is never a translation for the English word **notorious**. In Spanish, **notorio** means both "obvious" and "famous, well-known".

notwithstanding [nɒtwɪθ'stændɪŋ] **1** *prep* a pesar de

2 *adv* sin embargo, no obstante

nougat ['nuːgɑː] *n* turrón blando

nought [nɔːt] *n* cero *m*; *Br* **noughts and crosses** *(game)* tres en raya *m*

noun [naʊn] *n* nombre *m*, sustantivo *m*

nourish ['nʌrɪʃ] *vt* nutrir; *Fig (hopes)* abrigar

nourishing ['nʌrɪʃɪŋ] *adj* nutritivo(a)

nourishment ['nʌrɪʃmənt] *n* alimentación *f*, nutrición *f*

novel¹ ['nɒvəl] *n* novela *f*

novel² ['nɒvəl] *adj* original, novedoso(a)

novelist ['nɒvəlɪst] *n* novelista *mf*

novelty ['nɒvəltɪ] *n* novedad *f*

November [nəʊ'vembə(r)] *n* noviembre *m*

novice ['nɒvɪs] *n* (**a**) *(beginner)* novato(a) *m,f*, principiante *mf* (**b**) *Rel* novicio(a) *m,f*

now [naʊ] **1** *adv* (**a**) *(at this moment)* ahora; **just** n., **right** n. ahora mismo; **from** n. **on** de ahora en adelante; n. **and then**, n. **and again** de vez en cuando (**b**) *(for events in past)* entonces (**c**) *(at present, these days)* actualmente, hoy (en) día (**d**) *(not related to time)* n. **(then)** ahora bien; n., n.! ¡vamos!, ¡ya está bien!

2 *conj* n. **(that)** ahora que, ya que

3 *n* **until** n. hasta ahora; **he'll be home by** n. ya habrá llegado a casa

nowadays ['naʊədeɪz] *adv* hoy (en) día, actualmente

nowhere ['nəʊweə(r)] *adv* en ninguna parte; **that will get you** n. eso no te servirá de nada; **it's** n. **near ready** no está preparado, ni mucho menos

noxious ['nɒkʃəs] *adj* nocivo(a)

nozzle ['nɒzəl] *n* boca *f*, boquilla *f*

nuance ['njuːɑːns] *n* matiz *m*

nub [nʌb] *n* **the** n. **of the matter** el quid de la cuestión

nuclear ['njuːklɪə(r)] *adj* nuclear; n. **arms** armas *fpl* nucleares; n. **disarmament** desarme *m* nuclear; n. **power** energía *f* nuclear; n. **power station** central *f* nuclear

nucleus ['njuːklɪəs] *n* núcleo *m*

nude [njuːd] **1** *adj* desnudo(a)

2 *n Art & Phot* desnudo *m*; **in the** n. al desnudo

nudge [nʌdʒ] **1** *vt* dar un codazo a

2 *n* codazo *m*

nudist ['njuːdɪst] *adj & n* nudista *(mf)*

nudity ['njuːdɪtɪ] *n* desnudez *f*

nugget ['nʌgɪt] *n Min* pepita *f*; **gold** n. pepita de oro

nuisance ['njuːsəns] *n* (**a**) molestia *f*,

pesadez f; **what a n.!** ¡qué lata! (**b**) (person) pesado(a) m,f

nuke [njuːk] Fam **1** n (bomb) bomba f nuclear or atómica

2 vt atacar con armas nucleares

null [nʌl] adj nulo(a); **n. and void** nulo y sin valor

nullify ['nʌlɪfaɪ] vt anular

numb [nʌm] **1** adj (without feeling) entumecido(a); Fig paralizado(a); **n. with fear** paralizado de miedo

2 vt (with cold) entumecer (de frío); (with anaesthetic) adormecer

number ['nʌmbə(r)] **1** n (**a**) número m; Tel **have you got my n.?** ¿tienes mi (número de) teléfono?; Fam **to look after n. one** barrer para adentro (**b**) (quantity) **a n. of people** varias personas (**c**) Br (of car) matrícula f; **n. plate** (placa f de la) matrícula f

2 vt (**a**) (put a number on) numerar (**b**) (count) contar; **his days are numbered** tiene los días contados

numeral ['njuːmərəl] n número m, cifra f

numerate ['njuːmərət] adj **to be n.** tener un conocimiento básico de matemáticas

numerical [njuːˈmerɪkəl] adj numérico(a)

numerically [njuːˈmerɪkəlɪ] adv numéricamente

numerous ['njuːmərəs] adj numeroso(a)

numismatics [njuːmɪzˈmætɪks] n sing numismática f

nun [nʌn] n monja f

nuptial ['nʌpʃəl] adj nupcial

nurse [nɜːs] **1** n enfermera f; (male) enfermero m; **children's n.** niñera f

2 vt (**a**) (look after) cuidar, atender (**b**) (baby) acunar (**c**) (suckle) amamantar (**d**) Fig (grudge etc) guardar

nursery ['nɜːsərɪ] n (**a**) (institution) guardería f; **n. school** jardín m de infancia (**b**) (in house) cuarto m de los niños; **n. rhyme** poema m infantil (**c**) (garden centre) vivero m

nursing ['nɜːsɪŋ] n **n. home** clínica f

nurture ['nɜːtʃə(r)] vt (animal) alimentar; (feelings) abrigar

nut [nʌt] n (**a**) (fruit) fruto seco; Fig **a tough n. to crack** un hueso duro de roer (**b**) Fam (head) coco m (**c**) Fam (mad person) loco(a) m,f (**d**) Tech tuerca f

nutcracker ['nʌtkrækə(r)] n cascanueces m inv

nutmeg ['nʌtmeg] n nuez moscada

nutrition [njuːˈtrɪʃən] n nutrición f

nutritious [njuːˈtrɪʃəs] adj nutritivo(a), alimenticio(a)

nuts [nʌts] adj Fam chalado(a); **to go n.** volverse loco; **he's n. about motorbikes** las motos le chiflan

nutshell ['nʌtʃel] n cáscara f; Fig **in a n.** en pocas palabras

nylon ['naɪlɒn] **1** n (**a**) (fibre) nilón m, nailon m (**b**) **nylons** medias fpl de nilón

2 adj de nilón

nymph [nɪmf] n ninfa f

nymphomaniac [nɪmfəˈmeɪnɪæk] n ninfómana f

O

O, o [əʊ] n (**a**) (the letter) O, o f (**b**) Math & Tel cero m

oak [əʊk] n roble m

OAP [əʊeɪ'piː] n Br (abbr **old-age pensioner**) pensionista mf, jubilado(a) m,f

oar [ɔː(r)] n remo m

oarsman ['ɔːzmən] n remero m

oasis [əʊ'eɪsɪs] n (pl **oases** [əʊ'eɪsiːz]) oasis m inv

oat [əʊt] n avena f; **rolled oats** copos mpl de avena

oath [əʊθ] n (pl **oaths** [əʊðz]) (**a**) Jur juramento m; **to take an o.** prestar juramento; Fam **on my o.** palabra de honor (**b**) (swearword) palabrota f

oatmeal ['əʊtmiːl] n harina f de avena

obedience [ə'biːdɪəns] n obediencia f

obedient [ə'biːdɪənt] adj obediente

obese [əʊ'biːs] adj obeso(a)

obey [ə'beɪ] vt obedecer; (law) cumplir con

obituary [ə'bɪtjʊərɪ] n necrología f

object¹ ['ɒbdʒɪkt] n (**a**) (thing) objeto m (**b**) (aim, purpose) fin m, objetivo m (**c**) **the o. of criticism** el blanco de las críticas (**d**) (obstacle) inconveniente m (**e**) Ling complemento m

object² [əb'dʒekt] vi oponerse (**to** a); **do you o. to my smoking?** ¿le molesta que fume?

objection [əb'dʒekʃən] n (**a**) objeción f (**b**) (drawback) inconveniente m; **provided there's no o.** si no hay inconveniente

objectionable [əb'dʒekʃənəbəl] adj (unacceptable) inaceptable; (unpleasant) ofensivo(a)

objective [əb'dʒektɪv] **1** adj objetivo(a)
2 n objetivo m

objector [əb'dʒektə(r)] n objetor(a) m,f

obligation [ɒblɪ'geɪʃən] n obligación f; **to be under an o. to sb** estarle muy agradecido(a) a algn

obligatory [ɒ'blɪgətərɪ] adj obligatorio(a)

oblige [ə'blaɪdʒ] vt (**a**) (compel) obligar; **I'm obliged to do it** me veo obligado(a) a hacerlo (**b**) (do a favour for) hacer un favor a (**c**) **to be obliged** (grateful) estar agradecido(a)

obliging [ə'blaɪdʒɪŋ] adj solícito(a)

oblique [ə'bliːk] adj oblicuo(a), inclinado(a); Fig **an o. reference** una alusión indirecta

obliterate [ə'blɪtəreɪt] vt (**a**) (memory) borrar (**b**) (species, race) eliminar; (village) arrasar

oblivion [ə'blɪvɪən] n olvido m; **to sink into o.** caer en el olvido

oblivious [ə'blɪvɪəs] adj inconsciente

oblong ['ɒblɒŋ] **1** adj oblongo(a)
2 n rectángulo m

obnoxious [əb'nɒkʃəs] adj repugnante

oboe ['əʊbəʊ] n oboe m

obscene [əb'siːn] adj obsceno(a)

obscure [əb'skjʊə(r)] **1** adj (**a**) oscuro(a); (vague) vago(a) (**b**) (author, poet etc) desconocido(a)
2 vt (truth) ocultar

obsequious [əb'siːkwɪəs] adj servil

observance [əb'zɜːvəns] n (**a**) observancia f (**b**) Rel **observances** prácticas religiosas

observant [əb'zɜːvənt] adj observador(a)

observation [ɒbzə'veɪʃən] n observación f; (surveillance) vigilancia f

observatory [əb'zɜːvətərɪ] n observatorio m

observe [əb'zɜːv] vt (**a**) observar; (in surveillance) vigilar (**b**) (remark) advertir (**c**) (obey) respetar

observer [əb'zɜːvə(r)] n observador(a) m,f

obsess [əb'ses] vt obsesionar; **to be obsessed (with** or **by)** estar obsesionado(a) (con)

obsession [əb'seʃən] n obsesión f

obsessive [əb'sesɪv] adj obsesivo(a)

obsolete ['ɒbsəliːt, ɒbsə'liːt] adj obsoleto(a)

obstacle ['ɒbstəkəl] n obstáculo m; Fig impedimento m; **o. race** carrera f de obstáculos

obstinate ['ɒbstɪnɪt] adj (**a**) (person) obstinado(a), terco(a) (**b**) (pain) persistente

obstruct [əb'strʌkt] vt (**a**) obstruir; (pipe etc) atascar; (view) tapar (**b**) (hinder) estorbar; *(progress)* dificultar

obstruction [əb'strʌkʃən] *n* (**a**) obstrucción *f* (**b**) *(hindrance)* obstáculo *m*

obtain [əb'teɪn] *vt* obtener, conseguir

obtainable [əb'teɪnəbəl] *adj* obtenible

obtrusive [əb'tru:sɪv] *adj* (**a**) *(interfering)* entrometido(a) (**b**) *(noticeable)* llamativo(a)

obtuse [əb'tju:s] *adj* obtuso(a)

obviate ['ɒbvɪeɪt] *vt Fml* obviar

obvious ['ɒbvɪəs] *adj* obvio(a), evidente

obviously ['ɒbvɪəslɪ] *adv* evidentemente; **o.!** ¡claro!, ¡por supuesto!

occasion [ə'keɪʒən] **1** *n* (**a**) ocasión *f*; **on o.** de vez en cuando; **on the o. of** con motivo de (**b**) *(event)* acontecimiento *m* (**c**) *(cause)* motivo *m*
2 *vt Fml* ocasionar

occasional [ə'keɪʒənəl] *adj* esporádico(a), eventual

occasionally [ə'keɪʒənəlɪ] *adv* de vez en cuando

occupant ['ɒkjʊpənt] *n* ocupante *mf*; *(tenant)* inquilino(a) *m,f*

occupation [ɒkjʊ'peɪʃən] *n* (**a**) *(job, profession)* profesión *f*, ocupación *f* (**b**) *(pastime)* pašatiempo *m* (**c**) *(of building, house, country)* ocupación *f*

occupational [ɒkjʊ'peɪʃənəl] *adj* profesional, laboral; **o. hazards** gajes *mpl* del oficio

occupied ['ɒkjʊpaɪd] *adj* ocupado(a)

occupier ['ɒkjʊpaɪə(r)] *n Br* ocupante *mf*; *(tenant)* inquilino(a) *m,f*

occupy ['ɒkjʊpaɪ] *vt* (**a**) *(live in)* ocupar, habitar (**b**) *(time)* pasar; **to o. one's time in doing sth** dedicar su tiempo a hacer algo (**c**) *(building, factory etc in protest)* tomar posesión de

occur [ə'kɜ:(r)] *vi* (**a**) *(event)* suceder, acaecer; *(change)* producirse (**b**) *(be found)* encontrarse (**c**) **it occurred to me that ...** se me ocurrió que ...

occurrence [ə'kʌrəns] *n* suceso *m*, incidencia *f*

> 🖉 Note that the Spanish word **ocurrencia** is a false friend and is never a translation for the English word **occurrence**. In Spanish, **ocurrencia** means "witty remark" and "bright idea".

ocean ['əʊʃən] *n* océano *m*

ocean-going ['əʊʃəngəʊɪŋ] *adj* de alta mar

ochre, *US* **ocher** ['əʊkə(r)] **1** *n* ocre *m*; **red o.** almagre *m*; **yellow o.** ocre amarillo
2 *adj* (de color) ocre

o'clock [ə'klɒk] *adv* (**it's**) **one o.** (es) la

una; (**it's**) **two o.** (son) las dos

octave ['ɒktɪv] *n* octava *f*

October [ɒk'təʊbə(r)] *n* octubre *m*

octogenarian [ɒktəʊdʒɪ'neərɪən] *adj & n* octogenario(a) *(m,f)*

octopus ['ɒktəpəs] *n* pulpo *m*

OD [əʊ'di:] *(pt & pp* **OD'd** *or* **OD'ed**) *vi Fam* meterse una sobredosis

odd [ɒd] **1** *adj* (**a**) *(strange)* raro(a), extraño(a) (**b**) *(occasional)* esporádico(a); **at o. times** de vez en cuando; **the o. customer** algún que otro cliente; **o. job** trabajillo *m* (**c**) **an o. number** *(not even)* un impar (**d**) *(unpaired)* desparejado(a); **an o. sock** un calcetín suelto; *Fig* **to be the o. man out** estar de más
2 *adv* y pico; **twenty o. people** veinte y pico *or* y tantas personas

oddity ['ɒdɪtɪ] *n* (**a**) *(thing)* curiosidad *f*; *(person)* estrafalario(a) *m,f* (**b**) *(quality)* rareza *f*

oddly ['ɒdlɪ] *adv* extrañamente; **o. enough** por extraño que parezca

odds [ɒdz] *npl* (**a**) *(chances)* probabilidades *fpl*; **he's fighting against the o.** lleva las de perder; **the o. are that ...** lo más probable es que ... (+ *subj*) (**b**) *(in betting)* puntos *mpl* de ventaja; **the o. are five to one** las apuestas están cinco a uno (**c**) *Br* **it makes no o.** da lo mismo; *Fig* **at o. with sb** reñido(a) con algn (**d**) **o. and ends** *(small things)* cositas *fpl*; *(trinkets)* chucherías *fpl*

odds-on ['ɒdzɒn] *adj* seguro(a); **o. favourite** *(horse)* caballo favorito

ode [əʊd] *n* oda *f*

odious ['əʊdɪəs] *adj* repugnante

odour, *US* **odor** ['əʊdə(r)] *n* olor *m*; *(fragrance)* perfume *m*

OECD [əʊi:si:'di:] *n* (*abbr* **Organization for Economic Co-operation and Development**) OCDE *f*

of [ɒv, *unstressed* əv] *prep* (**a**) *(belonging to, part of)* de; **a friend of mine** un amigo mío; **the end of the novel** el final de la novela

(**b**) *(containing)* de; **a bottle of wine** una botella de vino

(**c**) *(origin)* de; **of good family** de buena familia

(**d**) *(by)* de, por; **beloved of all** amado(a) por todos

(**e**) *(quantity)* de; **there are four of us** somos cuatro; **two of them** dos de ellos

(**f**) *(from)* de; **free of** libre de; **south of** al sur de

(**g**) *(material)* de; **a dress (made) of silk** un vestido de seda (**h**) *(apposition)* de; **the city of Lisbon** la ciudad de Lisboa

(**i**) *(characteristic)* de; **that's typical of her** es muy propio de ella; **that's very kind of you** es usted muy amable

(**j**) *(with adj)* de; **hard of hearing** duro(a) de oído

(**k**) *(after superlative)* de; **the thing she wanted most of all** lo que más quería

(**l**) *(cause)* por, de; **because of** a causa de; **of necessity** por necesidad

(**m**) *(concerning, about)* de, sobre; **to dream of sth/sb** soñar con algo/algn; **to think of sb** pensar en algn

(**n**) *(with dates)* de; **the 7th of November** el 7 de noviembre

off [ɒf] **1** *prep* (**a**) *(movement)* de; **she fell o. her horse** se cayó del caballo

(**b**) *(removal)* de; **I'll take sth o. the price for you** se lo rebajaré un poco

(**c**) *(distance, situation)* de; **a few kilometres o. the coast** a unos kilómetros de la costa; **a house o. the road** una casa apartada de la carretera

(**d**) **the ship went o. course** el barco se desvió; **to be o. form** no estar en forma

(**e**) **I'm o. wine** he perdido el gusto al vino

2 *adv* (**a**) **he turned o. the radio** apagó la radio

(**b**) *(absent)* fuera; **I have a day o.** tengo un día libre; **to be o. sick** estar de baja por enfermedad

(**c**) *(completely)* **this will kill o. any germs** esto rematará cualquier germen

(**d**) **his arrival is three days o.** faltan tres días para su llegada; **6 miles o.** a 6 millas

(**e**) **I'm o. to London** me voy a Londres; **she ran o.** se fue corriendo

(**f**) **10 percent o.** un descuento del 10 por ciento; **to take one's shoes o.** quitarse los zapatos

(**g**) **o. and on** de vez en cuando

3 *adj* (**a**) *(gas etc)* apagado(a); *(water)* cortado(a)

(**b**) *(cancelled)* cancelado(a)

(**c**) *(low)* bajo(a); *(unsatisfactory)* malo(a); **on the o. chance** por si acaso; **the o. season** la temporada baja

(**d**) **you're better o. like that** así estás mejor

(**e**) *(gone bad)* (meat, fish) malo(a), pasado(a); *(milk)* agrio(a)

offal ['ɒfəl] *n (of chicken etc)* menudillos *mpl; (of cattle, pigs)* asaduras *fpl*

off-colour, US **off-color** ['ɒf'kʌlə(r)] *adj* (**a**) *Br (ill)* indispuesto(a) (**b**) *(joke, story)* indecente

offence [ə'fens] *n* (**a**) *Jur* delito *m* (**b**) *(insult)* ofensa *f;* **to give o.** ofender; **to take o. at sth** ofenderse por algo (**c**) *Mil (attack)* ofensiva *f*

offend [ə'fend] *vt* ofender

offender [ə'fendə(r)] *n (criminal)* delincuente *mf*

offense [ə'fens] *n US* = **offence**

offensive [ə'fensɪv] **1** *adj* (**a**) *(insulting)* ofensivo(a) (**b**) *(repulsive)* repugnante

2 *n Mil* ofensiva *f;* **to be on the o.** estar a la ofensiva

offer ['ɒfə(r)] **1** *vt* (**a**) ofrecer; **to o. to do a job** ofrecerse para hacer un trabajo (**b**) *(propose)* proponer

2 *n* (**a**) oferta *f; (proposal)* propuesta *f;* **o. of marriage** proposición *f* de matrimonio (**b**) *Com* **on o.** de oferta

offering ['ɒfərɪŋ] *n* (**a**) ofrecimiento *m* (**b**) *Rel* ofrenda *f*

offhand 1 *adj* ['ɒfhænd] *(abrupt)* brusco(a); *(inconsiderate)* descortés

2 *adv* [ɒf'hænd] **I don't know o.** así sin pensarlo, no lo sé

office ['ɒfɪs] *n* (**a**) *(room)* despacho *m; (building)* oficina *f; (of lawyer)* despacho, bufete *m; US (of doctor, dentist)* consulta *f,* **o. hours** horas *fpl* de oficina (**b**) *Br Pol* ministerio *m* (**c**) *US (federal agency)* agencia *f* gubernamental (**d**) *(position)* cargo *m;* **to hold o.** ocupar un cargo (**e**) *Pol* **to be in o.** estar en el poder

officer ['ɒfɪsə(r)] *n* (**a**) *Mil* oficial *mf* (**b**) *(police)* **o.** agente *mf* de policía (**c**) *(government official)* funcionario(a) *m,f* (**d**) *(of company, society)* director(a) *m,f*

official [ə'fɪʃəl] **1** *adj* oficial

2 *n* funcionario(a) *m,f*

officiate [ə'fɪʃɪeɪt] *vi* (**a**) ejercer; **to o. as** ejercer de (**b**) *Rel* oficiar

officious [ə'fɪʃəs] *adj Pej* excesivamente celoso(a) *or* diligente

> ℐ Note that the Spanish word **oficioso** is a false friend and is never a translation for the English word **officious**. In Spanish, **oficioso** means "unofficial".

off-licence ['ɒflaɪsəns] *n Br* tienda *f* de bebidas alcohólicas

off-line ['ɒflaɪn] *adj Comput* desconectado(a)

off-peak [ɒf'piːk] *adj (flight)* de temporada baja; *(rate)* de fuera de las horas punta

off-putting ['ɒfpʊtɪŋ] *adj Br Fam* desconcertante

offset [ɒf'set] *vt (pt & pp* **offset**) *(balance out)* compensar

offshoot ['ɒfʃuːt] n (a) Bot renuevo m (b) Fig (of organization) ramificación f

offshore ['ɒf'ʃɔː(r)] adj (a) (breeze etc) terral (b) (oil rig) costa afuera (c) (overseas) en el extranjero; **o. investment** inversión f en el extranjero

offside 1 adv ['ɒf'saɪd] Ftb fuera de juego 2 n ['ɒfsaɪd] Aut (with left-hand drive) lado derecho; (with right-hand drive) lado izquierdo

offspring ['ɒfsprɪŋ] n (pl offspring) (child) vástago m; (children) progenitura f

offstage [ɒf'steɪdʒ] adj & adv entre bastidores

often ['ɒfən,'ɒftən] adv a menudo, con frecuencia; **every so o.** de vez en cuando

ogle ['əʊgəl] vt & vi to o. (at) sb comerse a algn con los ojos

oh [əʊ] interj ¡oh!, ¡ay!; **oh, my God!** ¡Dios mío!

oil [ɔɪl] 1 n (a) aceite m; **o. lamp** lámpara f de aceite, quinqué m; **o. slick** mancha f de aceite; **olive o.** aceite de oliva (b) (petroleum) petróleo m; **o. rig** plataforma petrolera; **o. tanker** petrolero m (c) (painting) pintura f al óleo; **o. paint** óleo m
2 vt engrasar

oilcan ['ɔɪlkæn] n aceitera f

oilfield ['ɔɪlfiːld] n yacimiento petrolífero

oilskin ['ɔɪlskɪn] n (a) hule m (b) oilskins chubasquero m, impermeable m de hule

oily ['ɔɪlɪ] adj (oilier, oiliest) aceitoso(a), grasiento(a); (hair, skin) graso(a)

ointment ['ɔɪntmənt] n ungüento m, pomada f

O.K., okay [əʊ'keɪ] Fam 1 interj ¡vale!, ¡de acuerdo!
2 adj bien; **is it O.K. if ...?** ¿está bien si ...?
3 vt dar el visto bueno a

old [əʊld] 1 adj (a) viejo(a); **an o. man** un anciano; **o. age** vejez f, **o.-age pensioner** pensionista mf; Br **o. boy** antiguo alumno; **o. hand** veterano(a) m,f; **good o. John!** ¡el bueno de John! (b) **how o. are you?** ¿cuántos años tienes?; **she's five years o.** tiene cinco años (c) (previous) antiguo(a)
2 n of o. de antaño

old-fashioned [əʊld'fæʃənd] adj (outdated) a la antigua; (unfashionable) anticuado(a), pasado(a) de moda

olive ['ɒlɪv] n (a) (tree) olivo m; **o. grove** olivar m (b) (fruit) aceituna f, oliva f (c) (wood) olivo m (d) **o. (green)** (colour) verde m oliva

Olympic [ə'lɪmpɪk] 1 adj olímpico(a); **O.**

Games Juegos Olímpicos
2 npl **the Olympics** las Olimpiadas

omelette, US **omelet** ['ɒmlɪt] n tortilla f; **Spanish o.** tortilla española or de patatas or Am papas

omen ['əʊmen] n presagio m

ominous ['ɒmɪnəs] adj de mal agüero

omission [əʊ'mɪʃən] n omisión f; Fig olvido m

omit [əʊ'mɪt] vt omitir; (accidentally) pasar por alto; (forget) olvidarse (**to** de)

omnipotent [ɒm'nɪpətənt] 1 adj omnipotente
2 n **the O.** el Todopoderoso

on [ɒn] 1 prep (a) (location) sobre, encima de, en; **I hit him on the head** le di un golpe en la cabeza; **it's on the desk** está encima de or sobre el escritorio; **hanging on the wall** colgado de la pared; **on page 4** en la página 4; **have you got any money on you?** ¿llevas dinero?; **the drinks are on me/the house** invito yo/invita la casa (b) (alongside) en; **a town on the coast** un pueblo en la costa (c) (direction) en, a; **on the right** a la derecha; **on the way** en el camino (d) (time) **on 3 April** el 3 de abril; **on a sunny day** un día de sol; **on Monday** el lunes; **on Mondays** los lunes; **on that occasion** en aquella ocasión; **on the following day** al día siguiente; **on time** a tiempo (e) en; **on TV/the radio** en la tele/radio; **to play sth on the piano** tocar algo al piano; **on the phone** al teléfono (f) (at the time of) a; **on his arrival** a su llegada; **on second thoughts** pensándolo bien; **on learning of this** al conocer esto (g) **she lives on bread** vive de pan; **to depend on** depender de (h) (transport) en/a; **on foot** a pie; **on the train/plane/bus** en el tren/avión/autobús; (travel by) en tren/avión/autobús (i) (state, process) en/de; **on holiday** de vacaciones; **she is here on business** está aquí de negocios (j) (regarding) sobre; **a lecture on numismatics** una conferencia sobre numismática; **they congratulated him on his success** le felicitaron por su éxito (k) **on condition that** (subject to) bajo la condición de que (l) (against) contra; **an attack on** un ataque contra (m) **he's on the Times** (working for) trabaja para el Times
2 adv (a) (covering) encima, puesto; **she had a coat on** llevaba puesto un abrigo

(**b**) *Fam* **have you anything on tonight?** ¿tienes algún plan para esta noche?

(**c**) **and so on** y así sucesivamente; **go on!** ¡sigue!; **he talks on and on** habla sin parar; **to work on** seguir trabajando

(**d**) **from that day on** a partir de aquel día; **later on** más tarde

3 *adj Fam* (**a**) **to be on** *(TV, radio, light)* estar encendido(a); *(engine)* estar en marcha; *(film, play)* estar en cartelera; **that film was on last week** pusieron esa película la semana pasada

(**b**) *Th & TV* **you're on!** ¡a escena!

(**c**) *(definitely planned)* previsto(a); **you're on!** ¡trato hecho!

(**d**) **that isn't on** eso no vale

once [wʌns] **1** *adv* (*one time*) una vez; **o. a week** una vez por semana; **o. in a while** de vez en cuando; **o. more** una vez más; **o. or twice** un par de veces; *Fig* **o. and for all** de una vez por todas (**b**) *(formerly)* en otro tiempo; **o. (upon a time) there was ...** érase una vez ... (**c**) **at o.** en seguida, inmediatamente; **don't all speak at o.** no habléis todos a la vez

2 *conj* una vez que (+ *subj*), en cuanto (+ *subj*)

oncoming [ˈɒnkʌmɪŋ] *adj (car, traffic)* que viene en dirección contraria

one [wʌn] **1** *adj* (**a**) un/una; **for o. thing** primero; **you're the o. person who knows** tú eres el único que lo sabe; **the o. and only** el único/la única; **o. and the same** el mismo/la misma

(**b**) *(indefinite)* un/una; **he'll come back o. day** un día volverá

2 *dem pron* **any o.** cualquiera; **that o.** ése/ésa; **this o.** éste/ésta; *(distant)* aquél/aquélla; **the blue ones** los azules/las azules; **the o. on the table** el/la que está encima de la mesa; **the ones that, the ones who** los/las que

3 *indef pron* (**a**) uno(a) *m,f*; **I, for o., am against it** yo, por lo menos, estoy en contra; **I'm not o. to complain** no soy de los que se quejan; **o. at a time** de uno en uno; **o. by o.** uno tras otro; *Fig* **o. and all** todo el mundo

(**b**) *(indefinite person)* uno(a) *m,f*; **o. has to fight** hay que luchar; **o. hopes that will never happen** esperemos que no ocurra; **to break o.'s leg/arm** romperse la pierna/el brazo

(**c**) **o. another** el uno al otro; **they love o. another** se aman

4 *n (digit)* uno *m*; **o. hundred/thousand** cien *m*

one-armed [ˈwʌnɑːmd] *adj Fig* **o.**

bandit máquina *f* tragaperras

one-man [ˈwʌnmæn] *adj* **a o. show** un espectáculo con un solo artista

one-man band [wʌnmænˈbænd] *n* hombre *m* orquesta

one-off [ˈwʌnɒf] *adj Br Fam* único(a), fuera de serie

oneself [wʌnˈself] *pron* (**a**) *(reflexive)* uno(a) mismo(a) *m,f*, sí mismo(a) *m,f*; **to talk to o.** hablar para sí (**b**) *(alone)* uno(a) mismo(a) *m,f*; **by o.** solo(a) (**c**) *(one's usual self)* el/la de siempre

one-sided [wʌnˈsaɪdɪd] *adj (bargain)* desigual; *(judgement)* parcial; *(decision)* unilateral

one-to-one [ˈwʌntəˈwʌn] *adj* **o. tuition** clase *f* individual

one-way [ˈwʌnweɪ] *adj* (**a**) *US (ticket)* de ida (**b**) *(street)* de dirección única

ongoing [ˈɒngəʊɪŋ] *adj* (**a**) *(in progress)* en curso, actual (**b**) *(developing)* en desarrollo

onion [ˈʌnjən] *n* cebolla *f*

on-line [ˈɒnlaɪn] *adj Comput* conectado(a)

onlooker [ˈɒnlʊkə(r)] *n* espectador(a) *m,f*

only [ˈəʊnlɪ] **1** *adj* único(a); **o. son** hijo único

2 *adv* (**a**) solamente, sólo; **staff o.** *(sign)* reservado al personal (**b**) *(not earlier than)* apenas; **he has o. just left** acaba de marcharse hace un momento; **o. yesterday** ayer mismo (**c**) **o. too glad!** ¡con mucho gusto!

3 *conj* pero

onset [ˈɒnset] *n (start)* comienzo *m*

onslaught [ˈɒnslɔːt] *n* embestida *f*

onto [ˈɒntʊ, *unstressed* ˈɒntə] *prep* = **on to**

onus [ˈəʊnəs] *n* responsabilidad *f*

onward [ˈɒnwəd] *adj* hacia adelante

onward(s) [ˈɒnwəd(z)] *adv* a partir de, en adelante; **from this time o.** de ahora en adelante

ooze [uːz] **1** *vi* rezumar

2 *vt* rebosar

opaque [əʊˈpeɪk] *adj* opaco(a)

OPEC [ˈəʊpek] *n (abbr* **Organization of Petroleum-Exporting Countries***)* OPEP *f*

open [ˈəʊpən] **1** *adj* (**a**) abierto(a); **half o.** entreabierto; **wide o.** abierto de par en par; **in the o. air** al aire libre; **to be o. with sb** ser sincero(a) con algn; *Fig* **with o. arms** con los brazos abiertos; **to keep an o. mind** no tener prejuicios; **I am o. to suggestions** acepto cualquier sugerencia; **o. to criticism** susceptible a la crítica;

o. admiration franca admiración; *US* **o. house** fiesta *f* de inauguración de residencia; **an o. question** una cuestión sin resolver; **o. season** *(in hunting)* temporada *f* de caza; *Av & Rail* **o. ticket** billete abierto; *Br* **O. University** Universidad *f* a Distancia; **o. verdict** veredicto inconcluso

(b) *(car etc)* descubierto(a)

(c) *(opposition)* manifiesto(a)

2 *vt* **(a)** abrir; **to o. fire** abrir fuego; *Fig* **to o. one's heart to sb** sincerarse con algn

(b) *(exhibition etc)* inaugurar; *(negotiations, conversation)* entablar

3 *vi* **(a)** abrir, abrirse; **to o. onto** *(of door, window)* dar a

(b) *(start)* empezar; *Th & Cin* estrenarse

4 *n* **(a) in the o.** al aire libre; *Fig* **to bring into the o.** hacer público

(b) *Sport* open *m*

▸ **open out 1** *vt sep* abrir, desplegar

2 *vi (flowers)* abrirse; *(view)* extenderse

▸ **open up 1** *vt sep (market etc)* abrir; *(possibilities)* crear

2 *vi* **(a)** abrirse; *Fam* **o. up!** ¡abre la puerta! **(b)** *(start)* empezar

opener ['əʊpənə(r)] *n* tin *or US* can **o.** abrelatas *m inv*

opening ['əʊpənɪŋ] *n* **(a)** *(act)* apertura *f*; **o. night** noche *f* de estreno; *Br* **o. time** hora *f* de apertura de los bares **(b)** *(beginning)* comienzo *m* **(c)** *(aperture)* abertura *f*; *(gap)* brecha *f* **(d)** *Com* oportunidad *f* **(e)** *(vacancy)* vacante *f*

openly ['əʊpənlɪ] *adv* abiertamente

open-minded [əʊpən'maɪndɪd] *adj* sin prejuicios

openness ['əʊpənnɪs] *n* franqueza *f*

open-plan ['əʊpənplæn] *adj (office)* abierto(a)

opera ['ɒpərə] *n* ópera *f*; **o. house** ópera, teatro *m* de la ópera

operate ['ɒpəreɪt] **1** *vi* **(a)** *(function)* funcionar **(b)** *Med* operar; **to o. on sb for appendicitis** operar a algn de apendicitis

2 *vt* **(a)** *(control)* manejar **(b)** *(business)* dirigir

operatic [ɒpə'rætɪk] *adj* de ópera

operating ['ɒpəreɪtɪŋ] *n* **(a) o. costs** gastos *mpl* de funcionamiento **(b)** *Med* **o. table** mesa *f* de operaciones; **o. theatre** *or US* **room** quirófano *m*

operation [ɒpə'reɪʃən] *n* **(a)** *(of machine)* funcionamiento *m*; *(by person)* manejo *m* **(b)** *Mil* maniobra *f* **(c)** *Med* operación *f*, intervención quirúrgica; **to undergo an o. for** ser operado(a) de

operational [ɒpə'reɪʃənəl] *adj* **(a)** *(ready for use)* operativo(a) **(b)** *Mil* operacional

operative ['ɒpərətɪv] *adj* **(a)** *Jur (in force)* vigente; **to become o.** entrar en vigor **(b)** *(significant)* clave, significativo(a); **the o. word** la palabra clave

operator ['ɒpəreɪtə(r)] *n* **(a)** *Ind* operario(a) *m,f* **(b)** *Tel* operador(a) *m,f* **(c)** *(dealer)* negociante *mf*, agente *mf*; **tour o.** agente de viajes

opinion [ə'pɪnjən] *n* opinión *f*; **in my o.** en mi opinión, a mi juicio; **it's a matter of o.** es cuestión de opiniones; **to have a high o. of sb** tener buen concepto de algn; **o. poll** encuesta *f*, sondeo *m*

opinionated [ə'pɪnjəneɪtɪd] *adj* dogmático(a)

opium ['əʊpɪəm] *n* opio *m*

opponent [ə'pəʊnənt] *n* adversario(a) *m,f*

opportune ['ɒpətjuːn] *adj* oportuno(a)

opportunist [ɒpə'tjuːnɪst] *adj & n* oportunista *(mf)*

opportunity [ɒpə'tjuːnɪtɪ] *n* **(a)** oportunidad *f*, ocasión *f* **(b)** *(prospect)* perspectiva *f*

oppose [ə'pəʊz] *vt* oponerse a

opposed [ə'pəʊzd] *adj* opuesto(a); **to be o. to sth** estar en contra de algo; **as o. to** comparado(a) con

opposing [ə'pəʊzɪŋ] *adj* adversario(a)

opposite ['ɒpəzɪt] **1** *adj* **(a)** *(facing)* de enfrente; *(page)* contiguo(a) **(b)** *(contrary)* opuesto(a), contrario(a); **in the o. direction** en dirección contraria

2 *n* **the o.** lo contrario; **quite the o.!** ¡al contrario!

3 *prep* enfrente de, frente a

4 *adv* enfrente

opposition [ɒpə'zɪʃən] *n* **(a)** oposición *f*; **in o. to** en contra de **(b)** *Pol* **the o.** la oposición

oppress [ə'pres] *vt* oprimir

oppression [ə'preʃən] *n* opresión *f*

oppressive [ə'presɪv] *adj* opresivo(a); *(atmosphere)* agobiante; *(heat)* sofocante

opt [ɒpt] *vi* optar; **to o. for** optar por; **to o. to do sth** optar por hacer algo

▸ **opt out** *vi* retirarse; **to o. out of doing sth** decidir no hacer algo

optical ['ɒptɪkəl] *adj* óptico(a)

optician [ɒp'tɪʃən] *n* óptico(a) *m,f*

optics ['ɒptɪks] *n sing* óptica *f*

optimist ['ɒptɪmɪst] *n* optimista *mf*

optimistic [ɒptɪ'mɪstɪk] *adj* optimista

optimistically [ɒptɪ'mɪstɪkəlɪ] *adv* con optimismo

optimum ['ɒptɪməm] **1** *n* grado óptimo **2** *adj* óptimo(a)

option ['ɒpʃən] *n* opción *f*; **I have no o.**
no tengo más remedio; **to keep one's
options open** no comprometerse; **with
the o.** of con opción a

optional ['ɒpʃənəl] *adj* optativo(a), fa-
cultativo(a); *Educ* **o. subject** (asignatura
f) optativa *f*

opulence ['ɒpjʊləns] *n* opulencia *f*

or [ɔː(r), *unstressed* ə(r)] *conj* (a) o; *(before a word beginning with* **o** *or* **ho**) u; **or
else** si no, o bien; **whether you like it or
not** tanto si te gusta como si no; **either a
bun or a piece of cake** (o) una magdalena
o un trozo de pastel (b) *(with negative)* ni;
he can't read or write no sabe leer ni
escribir; *see* **nor**

oral ['ɔːrəl, 'ɒrəl] **1** *adj* oral
  2 *n* examen *m* oral

orally ['ɔːrəlɪ, 'ɒrəlɪ] *adv* **to be taken o.**
(on medicine) por vía oral

orange ['ɒrɪndʒ] **1** *n* naranja *f*; **o. juice**
zumo *m* or *Am* jugo *m* de naranja
  2 *adj* de color naranja

orator ['ɒrətə(r)] *n* orador(a) *m,f*

oratory ['ɒrətərɪ] *n* oratoria *f*

orbit ['ɔːbɪt] **1** *n Astron* órbita *f*
  2 *vt* girar alrededor de
  3 *vi* girar

orchard ['ɔːtʃəd] *n* huerto *m*

orchestra ['ɔːkɪstrə] *n* orquesta *f*; *US (in
theatre)* platea *f*

orchestral [ɔː'kestrəl] *adj* orquestal

orchid ['ɔːkɪd] *n* orquídea *f*

ordain [ɔː'deɪn] *vt* (a) *Rel* ordenar; **to be
ordained** ordenarse (b) *(decree)* decretar

ordeal [ɔː'diːl] *n* mala experiencia

order ['ɔːdə(r)] **1** *n* (a) *(sequence)* orden
m; **in alphabetical o.** por orden alfabético; **to put in o.** ordenar
  (b) *(condition)* estado *m*; **is your passport in o.?** ¿tienes el pasaporte en regla?;
out of o. *(sign)* averiado(a)
  (c) *(peace)* orden *m*; **to restore o.** rees-
tablecer el orden publico
  (d) *(command)* orden *f*
  (e) *Com* pedido *m*, encargo *m*; **to be on
o.** estar pedido; **to o.** a la medida; **o. form**
hoja *f* de pedido
  (f) *Rel* orden *f*
  (g) **of the highest o.** *(quality)* de primera calidad
  (h) *(kind)* índole *f*, tipo *m*; *Biol* orden *m*
  (i) **in the o. of** del orden de
  (j) **in o. that** para que (+ *subj*), a fin de
que (+ *subj*); **in o. to** (+ *infin*) para (+
infin), a fin de (+ *infin*)
  2 *vt* (a) *(command)* ordenar, mandar; **to
o. sb to do sth** mandar a algn hacer algo

  (b) *Com* pedir, encargar; **to o. a dish**
pedir un plato

orderly ['ɔːdəlɪ] **1** *adj* *(tidy etc)* ordena-
do(a)
  2 *n* (a) *Med* enfermero *m* (b) *Mil* ordenanza *m*

ordinary ['ɔːdənrɪ] **1** *adj* usual, normal;
(average) corriente, común; **the o. citizen**
el ciudadano de a pie
  2 *n* **the o.** lo corriente, lo normal; **out of
the o.** fuera de lo común

ordnance ['ɔːdnəns] *n Br* **O. Survey** =
instituto británico de cartografía

ore [ɔː(r)] *n* mineral *m*

organ ['ɔːgən] *n Mus & Anat etc* órgano *m*

organic [ɔː'gænɪk] *adj* orgánico(a);
(farming, food) biológico(a), ecológi-
co(a)

organism ['ɔːgənɪzəm] *n* organismo *m*

organization [ɔːgənaɪ'zeɪʃən] *n* organización *f*

organize ['ɔːgənaɪz] *vt* organizar

organizer ['ɔːgənaɪzə(r)] *n* organiza-
dor(a) *m,f*

orgasm ['ɔːgæzəm] *n* orgasmo *m*

orgy ['ɔːdʒɪ] *n* orgía *f*

Orient ['ɔːrɪent] *n* **the O.** el Oriente

Oriental [ɔːrɪ'entəl] *adj & n* oriental *(mf)*

origin ['ɒrɪdʒɪn] *n* origen *m*; **country of o.**
país *m* natal *or* de origen

original [ə'rɪdʒɪnəl] **1** *adj* (a) original;
(first) primero(a) (b) *(imaginative)* original
  2 *n* original *m*

originality [ərɪdʒɪ'nælɪtɪ] *n* originalidad
f

originally [ə'rɪdʒɪnəlɪ] *adv* (a) *(at first)*
en un principio (b) *(with imagination)*
con originalidad

originate [ə'rɪdʒɪneɪt] **1** *vt* originar
  2 *vi* **to o. from** *or* **in** tener su origen en

Orkneys ['ɔːknɪz] *npl* **the O.** las (Islas)
Orcadas

ornament ['ɔːnəmənt] *n* ornamento *m*,
adorno *m*

ornamental [ɔːnə'mentəl] *adj* decorati-
vo(a)

ornate [ɔː'neɪt] *adj* vistoso(a)

ornithology [ɔːnɪ'θɒlədʒɪ] *n* ornitología
f

orphan ['ɔːfən] **1** *n* huérfano(a) *m,f*
  2 *vt* **she was orphaned** quedó huérfana

orphanage ['ɔːfənɪdʒ] *n* orfanato *m*

orthodox ['ɔːθədɒks] *adj* ortodoxo(a)

orthodoxy ['ɔːθədɒksɪ] *n* ortodoxia *f*

orthopaedic, *US* **orthopedic** [ɔːθəʊ-
'piːdɪk] *adj* ortopédico(a)

Oscar ['ɒskə(r)] *n* Óscar *m*

oscillate [ˈɒsɪleɪt] *vi* oscilar

ostensible [ɒˈstensɪbəl] *adj* (a) *(apparent)* ostensible (b) *(pretended)* aparente

ostentatious [ɒstenˈteɪʃəs] *adj* ostentoso(a)

osteopath [ˈɒstɪəpæθ] *n* osteópata *mf*

ostracize [ˈɒstrəsaɪz] *vt (from society)* condenar al ostracismo; *(from group)* aislar, excluir

ostrich [ˈɒstrɪtʃ] *n* avestruz *f*

other [ˈʌðə(r)] **1** *adj* (a) otro(a); **every o. day** cada dos días; **on the o. hand** por otra parte; **o. people have seen it** otros lo han visto; **the o. four** los otros cuatro; **the o. one** el otro/la otra; **the o. thing** lo otro (b) **he must be somewhere or o.** debe de estar en alguna parte

2 *pron* otro(a) *m,f*; **many others** otros muchos; **the others** los otros, los demás; **we see each o. quite often** nos vemos con bastante frecuencia

otherwise [ˈʌðəwaɪz] **1** *adv* (a) *(if not)* si no (b) *(differently)* de otra manera (c) *(in other respects)* por lo demás

2 *adj* distinto(a)

OTT [əʊtiːˈtiː] *adj Br Fam (abbr over the top)* exagerado(a)

otter [ˈɒtə(r)] *n* nutria *f*

ought [ɔːt] *v aux*

En el inglés hablado, y en el escrito en estilo coloquial, la forma negativa **ought not** se transforma en **oughtn't**.

(a) *(obligation)* deber; **I thought I o. to tell you** creí que debía decírtelo; **she o. to do it** debería hacerlo (b) *(vague desirability)* tener que, deber; **you o. to see the exhibition** deberías ver la exposición (c) *(expectation)* **he o. to pass the exam** seguramente aprobará el examen; **that o. to do** con eso bastará

ounce [aʊns] *n* onza *f*

our [aʊə(r)] *poss adj* nuestro(a)

ours [aʊəz] *poss pron* (a) (el) nuestro/(la) nuestra (b) **of o.** nuestro(a); **a friend of o.** un amigo nuestro

ourselves [aʊəˈselvz] *pers pron pl* (a) *(reflexive)* nos (b) *(emphatic)* nosotros mismos/nosotras mismas (c) **by o.** a solas

oust [aʊst] *vt* (a) *(from a post)* desbancar (b) *(from property etc)* desalojar

out [aʊt] **1** *adv* (a) *(outside, away)* fuera; **o. there** ahí fuera; **to go o.** salir (b) **I told you straight o.** se lo dije muy claramente; **o. loud** en voz alta (c) **hear me o.** escúchame hasta el final (d) **o. of** *(place)* fuera de; **move o. of the**

way! ¡quítate de en medio!; **o. of danger** fuera de peligro; **to go o. of the room** salir de la habitación; **o. of control** fuera de control; **o. of date** *(expired)* caducado(a); *(old-fashioned)* pasado(a) de moda (e) **o. of** *(cause, motive)* por (f) **o. of** *(made from)* de (g) **o. of** *(short of, without)* sin; **I'm o. of money** se me ha acabado el dinero; **o. of breath** sin aliento (h) **o. of** *(among)* entre; **forty o. of fifty** cuarenta de cada cincuenta; *(in exam etc)* cuarenta sobre cincuenta

2 *adj* (a) **the sun is o.** ha salido el sol (b) *(unfashionable)* pasado(a) de moda (c) *(fire)* apagado(a) (d) *(not working)* estropeado(a) (e) **she's o.** *(not in)* ha salido, no está (f) **to be o. for sth** buscar algo; **to be o. to do sth** pretender hacer algo (g) **the book is just o.** el libro acaba de salir (h) *(inaccurate)* equivocado(a); **to be o. in one's calculations** equivocarse en los cálculos (i) **before the week is o.** antes de que acabe la semana

3 *prep (out of)* por; **he jumped o. of the window** saltó por la ventana

out-and-out [ˈaʊtənaʊt] *adj* redomado(a)

outboard [ˈaʊtbɔːd] *adj* **o. motor** fueraborda *m*

outbreak [ˈaʊtbreɪk] *n (of war)* comienzo *m*; *(of spots)* erupción *f*; *(of disease)* brote *m*; *(of violence)* ola *f*; *(of anger)* arrebato *m*; **at the o. of war** cuando estalló la guerra

outbuilding [ˈaʊtbɪldɪŋ] *n* dependencia *f*

outburst [ˈaʊtbɜːst] *n (of anger)* arrebato *m*; *(of generosity)* arranque *m*

outcast [ˈaʊtkɑːst] *n* marginado(a) *m,f*

outcome [ˈaʊtkʌm] *n* resultado *m*

outcrop [ˈaʊtkrɒp] *n Geol* afloramiento *m*

outcry [ˈaʊtkraɪ] *n* **there was an o.** hubo fuertes protestas

outdated [aʊtˈdeɪtɪd] *adj* anticuado(a), obsoleto(a)

outdo [aʊtˈduː] *vt (pt* **outdid** [aʊtˈdɪd]*; pp* **outdone** [aʊtˈdʌn]*)* **to o. sb** superar a algn

outdoor [ˈaʊtdɔː(r)] *adj* (a) al aire libre (b) *(clothes)* de calle

outdoors [aʊtˈdɔːz] *adv* fuera, al aire libre

outer ['aʊtə(r)] *adj* exterior, externo(a)

outfit ['aʊtfɪt] *n* (a) *(kit, equipment)* equipo *m* (b) *(set of clothes)* conjunto *m* (c) *Fam (group)* grupo *m*

outgoing ['aʊtgəʊɪŋ] **1** *adj* (a) *(departing)* saliente (b) *(sociable)* extrovertido(a)
2 *npl* **outgoings** gastos *mpl*

outgrow [aʊt'grəʊ] *vt* (*pt* **outgrew** [aʊt'gruː]; *pp* **outgrown** [aʊt'grɒn]) **he's outgrowing all his clothes** toda la ropa se le está quedando pequeña; **she'll o. it** se le pasará con la edad

outhouse ['aʊthaʊs] *n* = **outbuilding**

outing ['aʊtɪŋ] *n* excursión *f*

outlandish [aʊt'lændɪʃ] *adj* estrafalario(a)

outlast [aʊt'lɑːst] *vt* durar más que

outlaw ['aʊtlɔː] **1** *n* proscrito(a) *m,f*
2 *vt* prohibir

outlet ['aʊtlet] *n* (a) *(opening)* salida *f* (b) *(for emotions)* válvula *f* de escape (c) *Com* mercado *m* (d) *(for water)* desagüe *m*

outline ['aʊtlaɪn] **1** *n* (a) *(draft)* bosquejo *m* (b) *(outer line)* contorno *m*; *(silhouette)* perfil *m*
2 *vt* (a) *(draw lines of)* perfilar (b) *(summarize)* resumir (c) *(describe roughly)* trazar las líneas generales de

outlive [aʊt'lɪv] *vt* sobrevivir a

outlook ['aʊtlʊk] *n* (a) *(point of view)* punto *m* de vista (b) *(prospect)* perspectiva *f*; *Met* previsión *f*

outlying ['aʊtlaɪɪŋ] *adj (remote)* aislado(a)

outmoded [aʊt'məʊdɪd] *adj* anticuado(a)

outnumber [aʊt'nʌmbə(r)] *vt* exceder en número

out-of-the-way ['aʊtəvðə'weɪ] *adj* (a) *(distant)* apartado(a), aislado(a) (b) *(uncommon)* poco corriente

outpatient ['aʊtpeɪʃənt] *n* paciente externo(a); **outpatients' department** clínica ambulatoria

outpost ['aʊtpəʊst] *n* avanzada *f*

output ['aʊtpʊt] *n* (a) *(production)* producción *f*; *(of machine)* rendimiento *m* (b) *Elec* potencia *f* (c) *Comput* salida *f*

outrage ['aʊtreɪdʒ] **1** *n* ultraje *m*; **it's an o.!** ¡es un escándalo!
2 *vt* **to be outraged by sth** indignarse por algo

outrageous [aʊt'reɪdʒəs] *adj (behaviour)* escandaloso(a); *(clothes)* extravagante; *(price)* exorbitante

outright 1 *adj* ['aʊtraɪt] *(absolute)* absoluto(a)

2 *adv* [aʊt'raɪt] (a) *(completely)* por completo (b) *(directly)* directamente, sin reserva (c) *(immediately)* en el acto

outset ['aʊtset] *n* comienzo *m*, principio *m*

outside 1 *prep* [aʊt'saɪd, 'aʊtsaɪd] (a) *(departing)* fuera de (b) *(beyond)* más allá de (c) *(other than)* aparte de
2 *adj* ['aʊtsaɪd] (a) *(exterior)* exterior, externo(a) (b) *(remote)* remoto(a)
3 *adv* ['aʊtsaɪd] fuera, afuera
4 *n* [aʊt'saɪd, 'aʊtsaɪd] exterior *m*; **on the o.** por fuera; *Fam* **at the o.** como mucho

outsider [aʊt'saɪdə(r)] *n* (a) *(stranger)* extraño(a) *m,f*, forastero(a) *m,f* (b) *Pol* = candidato(a) con pocas posibilidades de ganar

outsize(d) ['aʊtsaɪz(d)] *adj (clothes)* de talla muy grande

outskirts ['aʊtskɜːts] *npl* afueras *fpl*

outsourcing ['aʊtsɔːsɪŋ] *n* *Com* externalización *f*, subcontratación *f*, *Am* tercerización *f*

outspoken [aʊt'spəʊkən] *adj* directo(a), abierto(a)

outstanding [aʊt'stændɪŋ] *adj* (a) *(exceptional)* destacado(a) (b) *(unpaid, unresolved)* pendiente

outstretched [aʊt'stretʃt] *adj* extendido(a)

outward ['aʊtwəd] **1** *adj* (a) *(external)* exterior, externo(a) (b) **the o. journey** el viaje de ida
2 *adv* = **outwards**

outwardly ['aʊtwədlɪ] *adv* aparentemente

outwards ['aʊtwədz] *adv* hacia (a)fuera

outweigh [aʊt'weɪ] *vt* (a) *(prevail over)* prevalecer sobre (b) *(weigh more than)* pesar más que

oval ['əʊvəl] **1** *adj* oval, ovalado(a)
2 *n* óvalo *m*

ovary ['əʊvərɪ] *n* ovario *m*

ovation [əʊ'veɪʃən] *n* ovación *f*

oven ['ʌvən] *n* horno *m*

ovenproof ['ʌvənpruːf] *adj* refractario(a)

over ['əʊvə(r)] **1** *prep* (a) *(above)* encima de
(b) *(on top of)* sobre, encima de
(c) *(across)* al otro lado de; **the bridge o. the river** el puente que cruza el río
(d) *(during)* durante
(e) *(throughout)* por
(f) **all o.** por todo(a); **famous all o. the world** famoso en el mundo entero
(g) *(by the agency of)* por; **o. the phone** por teléfono

(**h**) *(more than)* más de; **men o. twenty-five** hombres mayores de veinticinco años; **o. and above** además de

(**i**) *(recovered from)* recuperado(a) de

2 *adv* (**a**) **o. there** allá; **why don't you come o. tomorrow?** ¿por qué no vienes a casa mañana?

(**b**) *(throughout)* por; **all o.** por todas partes

(**c**) *(more)* más

(**d**) *(again)* otra vez; **o. and o.** *(again)* una y otra vez; **twice o.** dos veces seguidas

(**e**) *(in excess)* de más

3 *adj (finished)* acabado(a); **it's (all) o.** se acabó; **the danger is o.** ha pasado el peligro

overall ['əʊvərɔːl] **1** *adj* total, global

2 *n* (**a**) *Br* guardapolvo *m* (**b**) **overalls** mono *m*

3 *adv* [əʊvə'rɔːl] *(on the whole)* por lo general, en conjunto

overawe [əʊvər'ɔː] *vt* **to be overawed** sobrecogerse

overbearing [əʊvə'beərɪŋ] *adj (domineering)* dominante; *(important)* significativo(a)

overboard ['əʊvəbɔːd] *adv* por la borda; **man o.!** ¡hombre al agua!; *Fam* **to go o.** pasarse

overcast ['əʊvəkɑːst] *adj* nublado(a)

overcharge [əʊvə'tʃɑːdʒ] *vt* (**a**) *(charge too much)* cobrar demasiado (**b**) *(overload)* sobrecargar

overcoat ['əʊvəkəʊt] *n* abrigo *m*

overcome [əʊvə'kʌm] *vt* (**a**) *(conquer)* vencer; **o. by grief** deshecho por el dolor (**b**) *(obstacle)* superar

overconfident [əʊvə'kɒnfɪdənt] *adj* presumido(a), creído(a)

overcrowded [əʊvə'kraʊdɪd] *adj (room)* atestado(a) (de gente); *(country)* superpoblado(a)

overcrowding [əʊvə'kraʊdɪŋ] *n (of prisons etc)* hacinamiento *m*; *(of country)* superpoblación *f*

overdo [əʊvə'duː] *vt (pt* **overdid** [əʊvə'dɪd]; *pp* **overdone** [əʊvə'dʌn]) (**a**) *(carry too far)* exagerar; **don't o. it** no te pases (**b**) *Culin* cocer *or* asar demasiado

overdose ['əʊvədəʊs] *n* sobredosis *f*

overdraft ['əʊvədrɑːft] *n* giro *m* en descubierto; *(amount)* saldo *m* deudor

overdraw [əʊvə'drɔː] *vt* **to be overdrawn** tener la cuenta en descubierto

overdue [əʊvə'djuː] *adj (rent, train etc)* atrasado(a); *(reform)* largamente esperado(a)

overestimate [əʊvər'estɪmeɪt] *vt* sobreestimar

overflow 1 *vi* [əʊvə'fləʊ] *(river)* desbordarse; *(cup etc)* derramarse

2 *n* ['əʊvəfləʊ] *(of river etc)* desbordamiento *m*; **o. pipe** cañería *f* de desagüe

overgrown [əʊvə'grəʊn] *adj* (**a**) *(with grass)* cubierto(a) (de hierba) (**b**) *(in size)* demasiado grande

overhaul 1 *vt* [əʊvə'hɔːl] revisar

2 *n* ['əʊvəhɔːl] revisión *f* y reparación *f*

overhead 1 *adj* ['əʊvəhed] *(por)* encima de la cabeza; **o. cable** cable aéreo

2 *adv* [əʊvə'hed] arriba, por encima de la cabeza

3 *n* ['əʊvəhed] *US* = **overheads**

overheads ['əʊvəhedz] *npl Br* gastos *mpl* generales

overhear [əʊvə'hɪə(r)] *vt (pt & pp* **overheard** [əʊvə'hɜːd]) oír *or* casualidad

overheat [əʊvə'hiːt] *vi* recalentarse

overjoyed [əʊvə'dʒɔɪd] *adj* rebosante de alegría

overlap [əʊvə'læp] *vi* superponerse; *Fig* **our plans o.** nuestros planes coinciden parcialmente

overleaf [əʊvə'liːf] *adv* al dorso

overload 1 *vt* [əʊvə'ləʊd] sobrecargar

2 *n* ['əʊvələʊd] sobrecarga *f*

overlook [əʊvə'lʊk] *vt* (**a**) *(fail to notice)* saltarse (**b**) *(ignore)* no hacer caso de; **we'll o. it this time** esta vez haremos la vista gorda (**c**) *(have a view of)* dar a, tener vista a

overmanning [əʊvə'mænɪŋ] *n Ind* exceso *m* de empleados

overnight 1 *adv* [əʊvə'naɪt] (**a**) *(during the night)* por la noche; **we stayed there o.** pasamos la noche allí (**b**) *(suddenly)* de la noche a la mañana

2 *adj* ['əʊvənaɪt] *(sudden)* repentino(a)

overpass ['əʊvəpɑːs] *n Br* paso *m* elevado

overpay [əʊvə'peɪ] *vt (pt & pp* **overpaid** [əʊvə'peɪd]) pagar demasiado

overpower [əʊvə'paʊə(r)] *vt* (**a**) *(subdue)* dominar (**b**) *(affect strongly)* abrumar

overrate [əʊvə'reɪt] *vt* sobreestimar, supervalorar

override [əʊvə'raɪd] *vt (pt* **overrode**; *pp* **overridden** [əʊvə'rɪdən] (**a**) *(disregard)* hacer caso omiso de (**b**) *(annul, cancel out)* anular (**c**) *(be more important than)* contar más que

overriding [əʊvə'raɪdɪŋ] *adj* principal; *(importance)* primordial; *(need)* imperioso(a)

overrode [əʊvə'rəʊd] *pt of* **override**

overrule [əʊvə'ruːl] *vt* invalidar; *Jur* denegar

overrun [əʊvə'rʌn] *vt* (**a**) *(country)* invadir (**b**) *(allotted time)* excederse de

oversaw [əʊvə'sɔː] *pt of* **oversee**

overseas 1 *adv* [əʊvə'siːz] en ultramar; **to live o.** vivir en el extranjero

　2 *adj* ['əʊvəsiːz] de ultramar; *(person)* extranjero(a); *(trade)* exterior

oversee [əʊvə'siː] *vt* (*pt* **oversaw**; *pp* **overseen** [əʊvə'siːn]) supervisar

overseer ['əʊvəsiːə(r)] *n* supervisor(a) *m,f*; *(foreman)* capataz *m*

overshadow [əʊvə'ʃædəʊ] *vt Fig* eclipsar

overshoot [əʊvə'ʃuːt] *vt* (*pt & pp* **overshot** [əʊvə'ʃɒt]) **to o. a turning** pasarse un cruce; *Fig* **to o. the mark** pasarse de la raya

oversight ['əʊvəsaɪt] *n* descuido *m*

oversleep [əʊvə'sliːp] *vi* (*pt & pp* **overslept** [əʊvə'slept]) quedarse dormido(a)

overspill ['əʊvəspɪl] *n* exceso *m* de población

overstate [əʊvə'steɪt] *vt* exagerar

overstep [əʊvə'step] *vt Fig* **to o. the mark** pasarse de la raya

overt [əʊ'vɜːt] *adj* patente

overtake [əʊvə'teɪk] *vt* (*pt* **overtook**; *pp* **overtaken** [əʊvə'teɪkən]) (**a**) *Br Aut* adelantar (**b**) *(surpass)* superar a (**c**) *(of night)* sorprender

overthrow [əʊvə'θrəʊ] *vt* (*pt* **overthrew** [əʊvə'θruː]; *pp* **overthrown** [əʊvə'θrəʊn]) *(government)* derribar

overtime ['əʊvətaɪm] *n* (**a**) *(work)* horas *fpl* extra (**b**) *US* prórroga *f*

overtone ['əʊvətəʊn] *n* matiz *m*

overtook [əʊvə'tʊk] *pt of* **overtake**

overture ['əʊvətjʊə(r)] *n* (**a**) *Mus* obertura *f*; *Fig (introduction)* introducción *f* (**b**) *(proposal)* propuesta *f*

overturn [əʊvə'tɜːn] *vt & vi* volcar

overweight [əʊvə'weɪt] *adj* demasiado pesado(a)

overwhelm [əʊvə'welm] *vt* (**a**) *(defeat)* aplastar; *(overpower)* abrumar; **I'm overwhelmed** estoy abrumado (**b**) *(with letters, work etc)* inundar

overwhelming [əʊvə'welmɪŋ] *adj (defeat)* aplastante; *(desire etc)* irresistible

overwork [əʊvə'wɜːk] **1** *vi* trabajar demasiado

　2 *vt (person)* forzar; *(excuse etc)* abusar de

overwrought [əʊvə'rɔːt] *adj* (**a**) *(tense)* muy nervioso(a) (**b**) *Literary (too elaborate)* forzado(a)

owe [əʊ] *vt* deber

owing ['əʊɪŋ] *adj* **o. to** debido a, a causa de

owl [aʊl] *n* lechuza *f*, búho *m*

own [əʊn] **1** *adj* propio(a); **it's his o. fault** es culpa suya

　2 *pron* (**a**) **my o./your o./his o.**/etc lo mío/lo tuyo/lo suyo/*etc*; *Fig* **to come into one's o.** realizarse; *Fam* **to get one's o. back** tomarse la revancha (**b**) **on one's o.** *(without help)* uno(a) mismo(a); *(alone)* solo(a)

　3 *vt* poseer, ser dueño(a) de

　▸ **own up** *vi* **to o. up (to sth)** confesar (algo)

owner ['əʊnə(r)] *n* propietario(a) *m,f*, dueño(a) *m,f*

ownership ['əʊnəʃɪp] *n* propiedad *f*, posesión *f*

ox [ɒks] *n* (*pl* **oxen** ['ɒksən]) buey *m*

oxide ['ɒksaɪd] *n Chem* óxido *m*

oxtail ['ɒksteɪl] *n* rabo *m* de buey

oxygen ['ɒksɪdʒən] *n* oxígeno *m*; **o. mask** máscara *f* de oxígeno

oyster ['ɔɪstə(r)] *n* ostra *f*

ozone ['əʊzəʊn] *n* ozono *m*; **o. layer** capa *f* de ozono

P

P, p [pi:] *n (the letter)* P, p *f*

p (**a**) *(pl* **pp)** *(abbr* **page)** pág., p (**b**) [pi:] *Br Fam (abbr* **penny, pence)** penique(s) *m(pl)*

PA [pi:'eɪ] *n Fam* (**a**) *(abbr* **personal assistant)** ayudante *mf* personal (**b**) *(abbr* **public-address (system))** megafonía *f*

p.a. *(abbr* **per annum)** al año

pace [peɪs] **1** *n (step)* paso *m; (speed)* ritmo *m;* **to keep p. with** seguir a; *Fig* avanzar al mismo ritmo que; **to set the p.** marcar el paso; *Fig* marcar la pauta

2 *vi* **to p. up and down** ir de un lado a otro

pacemaker ['peɪsmeɪkə(r)] *n Sport* liebre *f; Med* marcapasos *m inv*

Pacific [pə'sɪfɪk] *adj* **the P. (Ocean)** el (océano) Pacífico

pacifier ['pæsɪfaɪə(r)] *n US (for baby)* chupete *m*

pacifist ['pæsɪfɪst] *adj & n* pacifista *(mf)*

pacify ['pæsɪfaɪ] *vt (person)* calmar; *(country)* pacificar

pack¹ [pæk] **1** *n (parcel)* paquete *m; (bundle)* bulto *m; US (of cigarettes)* paquete; *Br (of cards)* baraja *f; (of hounds)* jauría *f*

2 *vt* (**a**) *(goods)* embalar, envasar; *(in suitcase)* poner; **to p. one's bags** hacer las maletas; *Fig* marcharse (**b**) *(fill)* atestar (**c**) *(press down) (snow)* apretar

3 *vi* (**a**) hacer las maletas; *Fam* **to send sb packing** mandar a paseo a algn (**b**) *(of people)* apiñarse (**into** en)
  ► **pack in** *vt sep Br Fam (give up)* dejar
  ► **pack off** *vt sep Fam* mandar
  ► **pack up** *Fam* **1** *vt sep (give up)* dejar

2 *vi (stop working)* terminar; *(machine etc)* estropearse

pack² [pæk] *vt (meeting)* llenar de partidarios

package ['pækɪdʒ] **1** *n* (**a**) *(parcel)* paquete *m; (bundle)* bulto *m* (**b**) *(of proposals etc)* paquete *m; (agreement)* acuerdo *m;* **p. deal** convenio *m* general; **p. tour** viaje *m* todo incluido

2 *vt (goods)* envasar, embalar

packet ['pækɪt] *n* paquete *m; Fam (fortune)* dineral *m*

packing ['pækɪŋ] *n* embalaje *m;* **p. case** caja *f* de embalar; **to do one's p.** hacer las maletas

pact [pækt] *n* pacto *m*

pad¹ [pæd] **1** *n* (**a**) almohadilla *f; (of paper)* bloc *m,* taco *m* (**b**) **launch p.** plataforma *f* de lanzamiento (**c**) *Fam (flat)* piso *m*

2 *vt (chair)* acolchar
  ► **pad out** *vt sep Fig* meter paja en

pad² [pæd] *vi* **to p. about** *or* **around** andar silenciosamente

padding ['pædɪŋ] *n (material)* relleno *m; Fig (in speech etc)* paja *f*

paddle¹ ['pædəl] **1** *n* (**a**) *(oar)* pala *f;* **p. boat** *or* **steamer** vapor *m* de ruedas (**b**) *US (for table tennis)* pala *f*

2 *vt (boat)* remar con pala en

3 *vi (in boat)* remar con pala

paddle² ['pædəl] *vi* chapotear

paddling pool ['pædlɪŋpu:l] *n Br* piscina *f* para niños

paddock ['pædək] *n* potrero *m; (in race course)* paddock *m*

paddy ['pædɪ] *n* arrozal *m*

padlock ['pædlɒk] **1** *n* candado *m*

2 *vt* cerrar con candado

paediatrician [pi:dɪə'trɪʃən] *n* pediatra *mf*

pagan ['peɪgən] *adj & n* pagano(a) *(m,f)*

page¹ [peɪdʒ] *n* página *f*

page² [peɪdʒ] **1** *n (servant)* paje *m; (of knight)* escudero *m; (at club)* botones *m inv*

2 *vt (call)* llamar por altavoz

pageant ['pædʒənt] *n (show)* espectáculo *m; (procession)* desfile *m; (on horses)* cabalgata *f*

pageantry ['pædʒəntrɪ] *n* pompa *f,* boato *m*

paid [peɪd] **1** *adj* pagado(a); *Fig* **to put p. to sth** acabar con algo

2 *pt & pp of* **pay**

pail [peɪl] *n* cubo *m; (child's)* cubito *m*

pain [peɪn] **1** *n* (**a**) dolor *m; (grief)* sufrimiento *m; Fam* **he's a p. (in the neck)** es un pelmazo; **on p. of death** so pena de muerte (**b**) **to take pains over sth** esmerarse en algo

2 *vt (grieve)* dar pena a

pained [peɪnd] *adj* de reproche

painful ['peɪnfʊl] *adj* doloroso(a); *Fam (very bad)* malísimo(a)

painfully ['peɪnfʊlɪ] *adv* (**a**) **p. shy** lastimosamente tímido(a) (**b**) *Fam* terriblemente

painkiller ['peɪnkɪlə(r)] *n* analgésico *m*

painless ['peɪnlɪs] *adj* sin dolor; *Fig* sin dificultades

painstaking ['peɪnzteɪkɪŋ] *adj (person)* concienzudo(a); *(care, research)* esmerado(a)

paint [peɪnt] **1** *n* pintura *f*
2 *vt* pintar; **to p. sth white** pintar algo de blanco
3 *vi* pintar

paintbrush ['peɪntbrʌʃ] *n Art* pincel *m*; *(for walls)* brocha *f*

painter ['peɪntə(r)] *n* pintor(a) *m,f*

painting ['peɪntɪŋ] *n* cuadro *m*; *(activity)* pintura *f*

paintwork ['peɪntwɜːk] *n* pintura *f*

pair [peə(r)] *n (of gloves, shoes)* par *m*; *(of people, cards)* pareja *f*; **a p. of scissors** unas tijeras; **a p. of trousers** un pantalón, unos pantalones

pajamas [pə'dʒæməz] *npl US* = pyjamas

Pakistan [pɑːkɪ'stɑːn] *n* Paquistán

Pakistani [pɑːkɪ'stɑːnɪ] *adj & n* paquistaní *(mf)*

pal [pæl] *n Fam* amigo(a) *m,f*, colega *mf*

palace ['pælɪs] *n* palacio *m*

palatable ['pælətəbəl] *adj (tasty)* sabroso(a); *Fig* aceptable

palate ['pælɪt] *n* paladar *m*

palatial [pə'leɪʃəl] *adj* suntuoso(a), señorial

palaver [pə'lɑːvə(r)] *n Fam* lío *m*, follón *m*

pale¹ [peɪl] **1** *adj (skin)* pálido(a); *(colour)* claro(a); *(light)* tenue; **to turn p.** palidecer
2 *vi* palidecer

pale² [peɪl] *n Fig* **to be beyond the p.** ser inaceptable

Palestine ['pælɪstaɪn] *n* Palestina

Palestinian [pælɪ'stɪnɪən] *adj & n* palestino(a) *(m,f)*

palette ['pælɪt] *n* paleta *f*; **p. knife** espátula *f*

paling ['peɪlɪŋ] *n* valla *f*

palisade [pælɪ'seɪd] *n* palizada *f*, estacada *f*

pall¹ [pɔːl] *n Fig* manto *m*; *(of smoke)* cortina *f*

pall² [pɔːl] *vi* aburrir; **it never palls** nunca cansa

pallet ['pælɪt] *n* plataforma *f* de carga

pallid ['pælɪd] *adj* pálido(a)

pallor ['pælə(r)] *n* palidez *f*

palm¹ [pɑːm] *n (tree)* palmera *f*; *(leaf)* palma *f*; **date p.** palma datilera; **P. Sunday** domingo *m* de Ramos

palm² [pɑːm] *n Anat* palma *f*
▸ **palm off** *vt sep* **to p. sth off on sb** colocar *or* endosar algo a algn

palmistry ['pɑːmɪstrɪ] *n* quiromancia *f*

palpable ['pælpəbəl] *adj* palpable

palpitate ['pælpɪteɪt] *vi* palpitar

palpitation [pælpɪ'teɪʃən] *n* palpitación *f*

paltry ['pɔːltrɪ] *adj* (**paltrier, paltriest**) insignificante

pamper ['pæmpə(r)] *vt* mimar, consentir

pamphlet ['pæmflɪt] *n* folleto *m*

pan¹ [pæn] **1** *n* (**a**) *(saucepan)* cazuela *f*, cacerola *f* (**b**) *(of scales)* platillo *m* (**c**) *(of lavatory)* taza *f*
2 *vt Fam (criticize)* dejar por los suelos

pan² [pæn] *vi Cin* tomar vistas panorámicas

panacea [pænə'sɪə] *n* panacea *f*

panache [pə'næʃ] *n* garbo *m*, salero *m*

Panama ['pænəmɑː] *n* Panamá; **P. Canal** Canal *m* de Panamá

pancake ['pænkeɪk] *n* crepe *f*

panda ['pændə] *n* panda *m*; *Br* **p. car** coche *m* patrulla

pandemonium [pændɪ'məʊnɪəm] *n* alboroto *m*

pander ['pændə(r)] *vi* **to p. to** *(person)* complacer a; *(wishes)* acceder a

pane [peɪn] *n* cristal *m*, vidrio *m*

panel ['pænəl] *n* (**a**) *(of wall)* panel *m*; *(flat surface)* tabla *f*; *(of instruments)* tablero *m*; *(of ceiling)* artesón *m* (**b**) *(jury)* jurado *m*; *Rad & TV* concursantes *mpl*

panelling, *US* **paneling** ['pænəlɪŋ] *n* paneles *mpl*

pang [pæŋ] *n (of pain, hunger)* punzada *f*; *(of childbirth)* dolores *mpl*; *Fig (of conscience)* remordimiento *m*

panic ['pænɪk] **1** *n* pánico *m*; **to get into a p.** ponerse histérico(a)
2 *vi* aterrarse

panicky ['pænɪkɪ] *adj* asustadizo(a)

panic-stricken ['pænɪkstrɪkən] *adj* aterrado(a)

panorama [pænə'rɑːmə] *n* panorama *m*

pansy ['pænzɪ] *n Bot* pensamiento *m*; *Fam Pej* mariquita *m*

pant [pænt] **1** *n* jadeo *m*
2 *vi* jadear

panther ['pænθə(r)] *n* pantera *f*

panties ['pæntɪz] *npl* bragas *fpl*

📕 Note that the Spanish word **panty** is a false friend and is never a translation for the English word **panties**. In Spanish, **panty** means "(pair of) tights".

---

pantomime ['pæntəmaɪm] *n Th (play)* función *f* musical navideña; *(mime)* pantomima *f*

pantry ['pæntrɪ] *n* despensa *f*

pants [pænts] *npl Br (underpants) (ladies')* bragas *fpl; (men's)* calzoncillos *mpl; US (trousers)* pantalones *mpl,* pantalón *m*

pantyhose ['pæntɪhəʊz] *n US* medias *fpl,* pantis *mpl*

papal ['peɪpəl] *adj* papal

paper ['peɪpə(r)] **1** *n* (**a**) papel *m; Fig* **on p. en teoría; p. money** papel moneda; **writing p.** papel de escribir (**b**) *(exam)* examen *m; (essay)* trabajo *m (escrito)* (**c**) *Pol* libro *m* (**d**) *(newspaper)* periódico *m;* **the papers** la prensa (**e**) **papers** *(documents)* documentos *mpl*

2 *vt* empapelar

paperback ['peɪpəbæk] *n* libro *m* en rústica

paperclip ['peɪpəklɪp] *n* clip *m,* sujetapapeles *m inv*

paperweight ['peɪpəweɪt] *n* pisapapeles *m inv*

paperwork ['peɪpəwɜːk] *n* papeleo *m*

papier-mâché [pæpjeɪ'mæʃeɪ] *n* cartón *m* piedra

paprika ['pæprɪkə] *n* pimentón molido

par [pɑː(r)] *n (parity)* igualdad *f; (in golf)* par *m; Fig* **it's p. for the course** es lo normal en estos casos; *Fig* **to feel below p.** estar en baja forma

parable ['pærəbəl] *n* parábola *f*

paracetamol [pærə'siːtəmɒl] *n* paracetamol *m*

parachute ['pærəʃuːt] **1** *n* paracaídas *m inv*

2 *vi* **to p. (down)** saltar *or* lanzarse en paracaídas

parade [pə'reɪd] **1** *n* desfile *m; Mil* **to be on p.** pasar revista

2 *vt Mil* hacer desfilar; *Fig (flaunt)* hacer alarde de

3 *vi (troops)* pasar revista; *(procession)* desfilar

paradise ['pærədaɪs] *n* paraíso *m*

paradox ['pærədɒks] *n* paradoja *f*

paradoxical [pærə'dɒksɪkəl] *adj* paradójico(a)

paraffin ['pærəfɪn] *n* parafina *f,* **liquid p.** aceite *m* de parafina; **p. lamp** lámpara *f* de petróleo

paragliding ['pærəglaɪdɪŋ] *n* parapente *m*

paragon ['pærəgən] *n* modelo *m*

paragraph ['pærəgrɑːf] *n* párrafo *m*

Paraguay ['pærəgwaɪ] *n* Paraguay

Paraguayan [pærə'gwaɪən] *adj & n* paraguayo(a) *(m,f)*

parallel ['pærəlel] **1** *adj* paralelo(a) (**to** *or* **with** a); *Fig* comparable (**to** *or* **with** a)

2 *n Geog* paralelo *m; Geom* paralela *f; Fig* paralelo

3 *vt Fig* ser paralelo(a) a

paralyse ['pærəlaɪz] *vt* paralizar

paralysis [pə'rælɪsɪs] *n* parálisis *f*

paralyze ['pærəlaɪz] *vt US* = **paralyse**

paramedic [pærə'medɪk] *n* auxiliar *mf* sanitario(a)

parameter [pə'ræmɪtə(r)] *n* parámetro *m*

paramilitary [pærə'mɪlɪtərɪ] *adj* paramilitar

paramount ['pærəmaʊnt] *adj* **of p. importance** de suma importancia

paranoid ['pærənɔɪd] *adj & n* paranoico(a) *(m,f)*

paraphernalia [pærəfə'neɪlɪə] *n* parafernalia *f*

paraphrase ['pærəfreɪz] *vt* parafrasear

parasite ['pærəsaɪt] *n* parásito *m*

parasol ['pærəsɒl] *n* sombrilla *f*

paratrooper ['pærətruːpə(r)] *n* paracaidista *m*

parcel ['pɑːsəl] **1** *n* paquete *m; p.* **bomb** paquete bomba

2 *vt* **to p. up** envolver, empaquetar

parched [pɑːtʃt] *adj (land)* reseco(a); *(lips, mouth)* seco(a); *Fig* **to be p.** estar muerto(a) de sed

parchment ['pɑːtʃmənt] *n* pergamino *m*

pardon ['pɑːdən] **1** *n* perdón *m; Jur* indulto *m;* **I beg your p.** (Usted) perdone; (**I beg your**) **p.?** ¿cómo (dice)?

2 *vt* perdonar; *Jur* indultar; **p. me!** ¡Usted perdone!

parent ['peərənt] *n* **parents** padres *mpl*

📕 Note that the Spanish word **pariente** is a false friend and is never a translation for the English word **parent**. In Spanish, **pariente** means "relative, relation".

---

parental [pə'rentəl] *adj* paternal; **p. guidance** consejos *mpl* paternales

parenthesis [pə'renθɪsɪs] *n (pl* **parentheses** [pə'renθɪsiːz]) paréntesis *m inv;* **in p.** entre paréntesis

pariah [pə'raɪə] *n* paria *mf*

Paris ['pærɪs] *n* París

parish ['pærɪʃ] *n* parroquia *f*

Parisian [pə'rɪzɪən] *adj & n* parisino(a) *(m,f)*

parity ['pærɪtɪ] *n* igualdad *f*; *(of shares)* paridad *f*

park [pɑːk] **1** *n* parque *m*
2 *vt (car)* aparcar, *Carib, Col, Pan* parquear

parking ['pɑːkɪŋ] *n* aparcamiento *m*, estacionamiento *m*; **no p.** *(sign)* prohibido aparcar; *US* **p. lot** parking *m*, aparcamiento *m*; **p. meter** parquímetro *m*; **p. space** aparcamiento *m*

parliament ['pɑːləmənt] *n* parlamento *m*

parliamentary [pɑːlə'mentərɪ] *adj* parlamentario(a)

parlour, *US* **parlor** ['pɑːlə(r)] *n* salón *m*

parochial [pə'rəʊkɪəl] *adj* parroquial; *Pej (narrow-minded)* de miras estrechas

parody ['pærədɪ] *n* parodia *f*

parole [pə'rəʊl] *n Jur* libertad *f* condicional; **on p.** en libertad bajo palabra

parquet ['pɑːkeɪ] *n* **p. floor** suelo *m* de parqué

parrot ['pærət] *n* loro *m*, papagayo *m*

parry ['pærɪ] *vt* parar

parsimonious [pɑːsɪ'məʊnɪəs] *adj* tacaño(a)

parsley ['pɑːslɪ] *n* perejil *m*

parsnip ['pɑːsnɪp] *n* chirivía *f*

parson ['pɑːsən] *n* cura *m*

part [pɑːt] **1** *n* (**a**) parte *f*; *(piece)* trozo *m*; *(episode)* capítulo *m*; *Tech* pieza *f*; **for the most p.** en la mayor parte (**b**) *Cin & Th* papel *m*; **to play a p. in sth** desempeñar un papel en algo; **to take p. in sth** participar en algo (**c**) *(place)* lugar *m*; **in these parts** por estos lugares (**d**) **for my p.** por mi parte; **to take sb's p.** tomar partido por algn; **to take sth in good p.** tomarse bien algo (**e**) *US (in hair)* raya *f*
2 *adj (partial)* parcial; **in p. exchange** como parte del pago
3 *adv (partly)* en parte
4 *vt (separate)* separar; **to p. company with sb** separarse de algn; **to p. one's hair** hacerse la raya (en el pelo)
5 *vi* separarse; *(say goodbye)* despedirse
▶ **part with** *vt insep* separarse de

partial ['pɑːʃəl] *adj* parcial; **to be p. to sth** ser aficionado(a) a algo

participant [pɑː'tɪsɪpənt] *n* participante *mf*; *(in competition)* concursante *mf*

participate [pɑː'tɪsɪpeɪt] *vi* participar (**in** en)

participation [pɑːtɪsɪ'peɪʃən] *n* participación *f*

participle ['pɑːtɪsɪpəl] *n* participio *m*

particle ['pɑːtɪkəl] *n* partícula *f*

particular [pə'tɪkjʊlə(r)] **1** *adj* (**a**) *(special)* particular, especial; **in this p. case** en este caso concreto; **that p. person** esa persona en particular (**b**) *(fussy)* exigente
2 *npl* **particulars** pormenores *mpl*; **to take down sb's particulars** anotar los datos personales de algn

particularly [pə'tɪkjʊləlɪ] *adv* particularmente, especialmente

parting ['pɑːtɪŋ] **1** *n (separation)* separación *f*; *(farewell)* despedida *f*; *Br (in hair)* raya *f*
2 *adj* de despedida

partisan [pɑːtɪ'zæn, 'pɑːtɪzæn] **1** *n Mil* guerrillero(a) *m,f*; *(supporter)* partidario(a) *m,f*
2 *adj (supporter)* a ultranza; *(of party)* partidista

partition [pɑː'tɪʃən] **1** *n (wall)* tabique *m*; *(of country)* partición *f*
2 *vt* dividir

partly ['pɑːtlɪ] *adv* en parte

partner ['pɑːtnə(r)] **1** *n* compañero(a) *m,f*; *(in dancing, tennis)* pareja *f*; *(husband)* marido *m*; *(wife)* mujer *f*; *Com* socio(a) *m,f*
2 *vt* acompañar

partnership ['pɑːtnəʃɪp] *n (relationship)* vida *f* en común; *Com* sociedad *f*

partridge ['pɑːtrɪdʒ] *n* perdiz pardilla

part-time ['pɑːtaɪm] **1** *adj (work etc)* de tiempo parcial
2 *adv* a tiempo parcial

party ['pɑːtɪ] **1** *n* (**a**) *(celebration)* fiesta *f* (**b**) *(group)* grupo *m* (**c**) *Pol* partido *m*; **p. political broadcast** espacio *m* electoral (**d**) *Jur* parte *f*
2 *adj* de fiesta; *Tel* **p. line** línea compartida

pass [pɑːs] **1** *n* (**a**) *(of mountain)* desfiladero *m*
(**b**) *(permit)* permiso *m*; **bus p.** abono *m* de autobús
(**c**) *Sport* pase *m*
(**d**) *Fam* **to make a p. at sb** intentar ligar con algn
2 *vt* (**a**) pasar; *(overtake)* adelantar
(**b**) *(exam, law)* aprobar; *Jur* **to p. sentence** dictar sentencia
3 *vi* (**a**) pasar; *(procession)* desfilar; *(car)* adelantar; *(people)* cruzarse; *Sport* hacer un pase; **we passed on the stairs** nos cruzamos en la escalera
(**b**) *(pain)* remitir; *(opportunity)* perderse; *(time)* pasar
(**c**) *(happen)* ocurrir, pasar

(**d**) (in exam) aprobar

▶**pass away** vi Euph pasar a mejor vida

▶**pass by 1** vt sep pasar de largo
2 vi pasar

▶**pass for** vt insep pasar por

▶**pass off 1** vt sep hacer pasar; **to p. oneself off as sth** hacerse pasar por algo
2 vi (happen) transcurrir

▶**pass on 1** vt sep (hand on) transmitir
2 vi Euph pasar a mejor vida

▶**pass out** vi (faint) desmayarse; Mil graduarse

▶**pass over** vt insep (**a**) (aircraft) volar por (**b**) (disregard) pasar por alto

▶**pass up** vt sep Fam (opportunity) renunciar; (offer) rechazar

passable ['pɑːsəbəl] adj (road) transitable; (acceptable) pasable

passage ['pæsɪdʒ] n (**a**) (alleyway) callejón m; (hallway) pasillo m (**b**) (movement) tránsito m; Naut travesía f (**c**) Mus & Lit pasaje m

passageway ['pæsɪdʒweɪ] n (interior) pasillo m; (exterior) pasaje m

passbook ['pɑːsbʊk] n libreta f de banco

passenger ['pæsɪndʒə(r)] n pasajero(a) m,f

passer-by [pɑːsə'baɪ] n transeúnte mf

passing ['pɑːsɪŋ] **1** n (**a**) (of time) transcurso m; **in p.** de pasada (**b**) (of law) aprobación f
2 adj que pasa; (glance) rápido(a); (thought) pasajero(a)

passion ['pæʃən] n pasión f; **p. fruit** granadilla f

passionate ['pæʃənɪt] adj apasionado(a)

passive ['pæsɪv] adj pasivo(a)

Passover ['pɑːsəʊvə(r)] n Pascua f de los judíos

passport ['pɑːspɔːt] n pasaporte m

password ['pɑːswɜːd] n contraseña f

past [pɑːst] **1** n pasado m; **in the p.** en el pasado; **to have a p.** tener antecedentes
2 adj pasado(a); (former) anterior; **in the p. weeks** en las últimas semanas
3 adv por delante; **to run p.** pasar corriendo
4 prep (beyond) más allá de; (more than) más de; **he's p. forty** pasa de los cuarenta (años); **it's five p. ten** son las diez y cinco; Fam **to be p. it** estar muy carroza

pasta ['pæstə] n pasta f, pastas fpl

paste [peɪst] **1** n pasta f; (glue) engrudo m
2 vt (stick) pegar; (put paste on) engomar

pastel ['pæstəl] adj & n pastel (m)

pasteurized ['pæstʃəraɪzd] adj pasteurizado(a)

pastille ['pæstɪl] n pastilla f

pastime ['pɑːstaɪm] n pasatiempo m

pastor ['pɑːstə(r)] n pastor m

pastoral ['pɑːstərəl] adj pastoral

pastry ['peɪstrɪ] n (dough) pasta f; (cake) pastel m

pasture ['pɑːstʃə(r)] n pasto m

pasty¹ ['pæstɪ] n Culin empanada f, pastel m de carne

pasty² ['peɪstɪ] adj (**pastier, pastiest**) (complexion) pálido(a)

pat [pæt] **1** n (caress) caricia f; (tap) palmadita f; Fig **to give sb a p. on the back** felicitar a algn
2 vt acariciar; **to p. sb on the back** dar a algn una palmadita en la espalda

patch [pætʃ] n (of material) parche m; (of land) terreno m; (of colour) mancha f; Fig **to go through a bad p.** pasar por una mala racha

▶**patch up** vt sep (garment) poner un parche en; **to p. things up** (after argument) limar asperezas

patchwork ['pætʃwɜːk] **1** n labor f de retales
2 adj (quilt etc) hecho(a) con retales distintos

patchy ['pætʃɪ] adj (**patchier, patchiest**) (colour, performance) desigual; (knowledge) incompleto(a)

pâté ['pæteɪ] n paté m

patent¹ ['peɪtənt] **1** n Com patente f
2 adj (obvious) patente, evidente; **p. medicine** específico m
3 vt Com patentar

patent² ['peɪtənt] n **p. (leather)** charol m

patently ['peɪtəntlɪ] adv **it is p. obvious** está clarísimo

paternal [pə'tɜːnəl] adj paternal; (grandmother etc) paterno(a)

paternity [pə'tɜːnɪtɪ] n paternidad f

path [pɑːθ] n camino m, sendero m; (route) ruta f; (of missile) trayectoria f

pathetic [pə'θetɪk] adj (pitiful) patético(a); Fam (hopeless) malísimo(a); **she was a p. sight** daba lástima verla

pathological [pæθə'lɒdʒɪkəl] adj patológico(a)

pathologist [pə'θɒlədʒɪst] n patólogo(a) m,f

pathology [pə'θɒlədʒɪ] n patología f

pathos ['peɪθɒs] n patetismo m

pathway ['pɑːθweɪ] n camino m, sendero m

patience ['peɪʃəns] n (**a**) paciencia f; **to lose one's p. with sb** perder la paciencia con algn (**b**) Br Cards solitario m

patient ['peɪʃənt] **1** adj paciente; **to be p.**

with sb tener paciencia con algn
2 *n Med* paciente *mf*

patio ['pætɪəʊ] *n* patio *m*

patriotic [pætrɪ'ɒtɪk] *adj (person)* patriota; *(speech, act)* patriótico(a)

patrol [pə'trəʊl] **1** *n* patrulla *f*; **p. car** coche *m* patrulla
2 *vt* patrullar por

patrolman [pə'trəʊlmən] *n US* policía *m*

patron ['peɪtrən] *n* (**a**) *(of charity)* patrocinador(a) *m,f*; *(of arts)* mecenas *m inv*; **p. saint** (santo(a) *m,f*) patrón(ona) *m,f* (**b**) *(customer)* cliente(a) *m,f* habitual

patronize ['pætrənaɪz] *vt* (**a**) *(arts)* fomentar; *(shop)* ser cliente(a) *m,f* habitual de; *(club etc)* frecuentar (**b**) *Pej (person)* tratar con condescendencia

patronizing ['pætrənaɪzɪŋ] *adj Pej* condescendiente

patter¹ ['pætə(r)] **1** *n (of rain)* repiqueteo *m*; *(of feet)* pasito *m*
2 *vi (rain)* repiquetear; *(feet)* hacer ruido sordo

patter² ['pætə(r)] *n Fam* labia *f*; *(of salesman)* discursillo preparado

pattern ['pætən] *n Sewing* patrón *m*; *(design)* dibujo *m*; *(on material)* estampado *m*; *Fig (of behaviour)* modelo *m*

paunch [pɔːntʃ] *n* panza *f*

pauper ['pɔːpə(r)] *n* pobre *mf*

pause [pɔːz] **1** *n* pausa *f*; *(silence)* silencio *m*
2 *vi* hacer una pausa; *(be silent)* callarse

pave [peɪv] *vt* pavimentar; *(with stones)* empedrar; *Fig* **to p. the way for sb/sth** preparar el terreno para algn/algo

pavement ['peɪvmənt] *n* (**a**) *Br (beside road)* acera *f*, *CSur*, *Perú* vereda *f*, *CAm*, *Méx* banqueta *f* (**b**) *US (roadway)* calzada *f*, pavimento *m*

pavilion [pə'vɪljən] *n* pabellón *m*; *Br Sport (changing rooms)* vestuarios *mpl*

paving ['peɪvɪŋ] *n (on road)* pavimento *m*; *(on floor)* enlosado *m*; *(with stones)* empedrado *m*; **p. stone** losa *f*

paw [pɔː] **1** *n (of foot)* pata *f*; *(of cat)* garra *f*, *(of lion)* zarpa *f*
2 *vt (of lion)* dar zarpazos a; *Pej (of person)* manosear, sobar

pawn¹ [pɔːn] *n (in chess)* peón *m*; *Fig* **to be sb's p.** ser el juguete de algn

pawn² [pɔːn] *vt* empeñar

pawnbroker ['pɔːnbrəʊkə(r)] *n* prestamista *mf*

pawnshop ['pɔːnʃɒp] *n* casa *f* de empeños

pay [peɪ] **1** *n (wages)* paga *f*, sueldo *m*; **p.**

Br **packet** *or US* **envelope** sobre *m* de la paga; **p. rise** aumento *m* del sueldo; **p. slip** nómina *f*
2 *vt (pt & pp paid)* (**a**) pagar; **to be** *or* **get paid** cobrar (**b**) *(attention)* prestar; *(homage)* rendir; *(visit)* hacer; **to p. sb a compliment** halagar a algn (**c**) *(be profitable for)* compensar
3 *vi* (**a**) pagar; **to p. for sth** pagar (por) algo (**b**) *(be profitable)* ser rentable
▸ **pay back** *vt sep* reembolsar; *Fig* **to p. sb back** vengarse de algn
▸ **pay in** *vt sep (money)* ingresar
▸ **pay off 1** *vt sep (debt)* liquidar; *(mortgage)* cancelar
2 *vi (be successful)* dar resultado
▸ **pay out** *vt sep (spend)* gastar (**on** en)
▸ **pay up** *vi* pagar

payable ['peɪəbəl] *adj* pagadero(a)

payday ['peɪdeɪ] *n* día *m* de pago

payee [peɪ'iː] *n* portador(a) *m,f*

payment ['peɪmənt] *n* pago *m*; *(of cheque)* cobro *m*; **advance p.** anticipo *m*; **down p.** entrada *f*; **monthly p.** mensualidad *f*

payoff ['peɪɒf] *n (reward)* recompensa *f*; *Fam (bribe)* soborno *m*

pay-per-view ['peɪpə'vjuː] *n* pago *m* por visión

payroll ['peɪrəʊl] *n* nómina *f*

PC ['piː'siː] **1** *n* (**a**) *Br (abbr* **Police Constable***)* agente *mf* de policía (**b**) *(abbr* **personal computer***)* PC *m*
2 *adj (abbr* **politically correct***)* políticamente correcto(a)

pc *(abbr* **per cent***)* p.c.

PE ['piː'iː] *n Sch (abbr* **physical education***)* educación *f* física

pea [piː] *n* guisante *m*, *Andes*, *Carib*, *RP* arveja *f*, *CAm*, *Méx* chícharo *m*

peace [piːs] *n (calm)* tranquilidad *f*; **at** *or* **in p.** en paz; **p. and quiet** tranquilidad; **to make p.** hacer las paces; *(of countries)* firmar la paz

peaceable ['piːsəbəl] *adj* pacífico(a)

peaceful ['piːsfʊl] *adj (demonstration)* pacífico(a); *(place)* tranquilo(a)

peace-keeping ['piːskiːpɪŋ] *adj* pacificador(a); **p. forces** fuerzas *fpl* de pacificación

peach [piːtʃ] *n* melocotón *m*, *Am* durazno *m*

peacock ['piːkɒk] *n* pavo *m* real

peak [piːk] *n (of cap)* visera *f*; *(of mountain)* pico *m*; *(summit)* cima *f*; *Fig* cumbre *f*; **p. hours** horas *fpl* punta; **p. period** horas de mayor consumo; **p. season** temporada alta

peal [piːl] *n (of bells)* repique *m*; **p. of thunder** trueno *m*; **peals of laughter** carcajadas *fpl*

peanut ['piːnʌt] *n* cacahuete *m*, maní *m*, *Méx* cacahuate *m*; **p. butter** mantequilla *f or* manteca *f* de cacahuete, maní, *Méx* cacahuate

pear [peə(r)] *n* pera *f*

pearl [pɜːl] *n* perla *f*

peasant ['pezənt] *adj & n* campesino(a) *(m,f)*

peat [piːt] *n* turba *f*; **p. bog** turbera *f*

pebble ['pebəl] *n* guijarro *m*; *(small)* china *f*

pecan [pɪ'kæn] *n (nut)* pacana *f*

peck [pek] **1** *n (of bird)* picotazo *m*; *Fam (kiss)* besito *m*
   2 *vt (bird)* picotear; *Fam (kiss)* dar un besito a
   3 *vi* **to p. at one's food** picar la comida

pecking order ['pekɪŋɔːdə(r)] *n Fig* jerarquía *f*

peckish ['pekɪʃ] *adj Fam* **to feel p.** empezar a tener hambre

peculiar [pɪ'kjuːlɪə(r)] *adj (odd)* extraño(a); *(particular)* característico(a)

peculiarity [pɪkjuːlɪ'ærɪtɪ] *n (oddity)* rareza *f*, *(characteristic)* característica *f*, peculiaridad *f*

pedal ['pedəl] **1** *n* pedal *m*
   2 *vi* pedalear

pedantic [pɪ'dæntɪk] *adj* pedante

peddle ['pedəl] *vt & vi Com* vender de puerta en puerta; **to p. drugs** traficar con drogas

peddler ['pedlə(r)] *n (of drugs)* traficante *mf*

pedestal ['pedɪstəl] *n* pedestal *m*; *Fig* **to put sb on a p.** poner a algn sobre un pedestal

pedestrian [pɪ'destrɪən] **1** *n* peatón(ona) *m,f*; **p. crossing** paso *m* de peatones
   2 *adj Pej* prosaico(a)

pediatrician [piːdɪə'trɪʃən] *n US* = **paediatrician**

pedigree ['pedɪgriː] **1** *n* linaje *m*; *(family tree)* árbol genealógico; *(of animal)* pedigrí *m*
   2 *adj (animal)* de raza

pee [piː] *Fam* **1** *n* pis *m*
   2 *vi* hacer pis

peek [piːk] **1** *n* ojeada *f*
   2 *vi* **to p. at sth** mirar algo a hurtadillas

peel [piːl] **1** *n (of orange, lemon)* cáscara *f*
   2 *vt (fruit)* pelar
   3 *vi (paint)* desconcharse; *(wallpaper)* despegarse; *(skin)* pelarse

peeler ['piːlə(r)] *n* **potato p.** pelapatatas *m inv*

peelings ['piːlɪŋz] *npl* peladuras *fpl*, mondaduras *fpl*

peep¹ [piːp] *n (sound)* pío *m*

peep² [piːp] **1** *n (glance)* ojeada *f*; *(furtive look)* mirada furtiva
   2 *vi* **to p. at sth** echar una ojeada a algo; **to p. out from behind sth** dejarse ver detrás de algo

peephole ['piːphəʊl] *n* mirilla *f*

peer¹ [pɪə(r)] *n (noble)* par *m*; *(equal)* igual *mf*; **p. group** grupo parejo

peer² [pɪə(r)] *vi* mirar detenidamente; *(shortsightedly)* mirar con ojos de miope

peerage ['pɪərɪdʒ] *n* título *m* de nobleza

peeved [piːvd] *adj Fam* fastidiado(a), de mal humor

peevish ['piːvɪʃ] *adj* malhumorado(a)

peg [peg] **1** *n* clavija *f*; *(for coat, hat)* percha *f*
   2 *vt (clothes)* tender; *(prices)* fijar

pejorative [pɪ'dʒɒrətɪv] *adj* peyorativo(a)

Pekinese [piːkə'niːz] *adj & n* pequinés(esa) *(m,f)*

Peking [piː'kɪŋ] *n* Pekín *m*

pelican ['pelɪkən] *n* pelícano *m*; *Br* **p. crossing** paso *m* de peatones

pellet ['pelɪt] *n* bolita *f*, *(for gun)* perdigón *m*

pelt¹ [pelt] *n (skin)* pellejo *m*

pelt² [pelt] **1** *vt* **to p. sb with sth** tirar algo a algn
   2 *vi Fam* **(a) it's pelting (down)** *(raining)* llueve a cántaros **(b) to p. along** *(rush)* correr a toda prisa

pelvis ['pelvɪs] *n* pelvis *f*

pen¹ [pen] **1** *n* pluma *f*, *RP* birome *f*
   2 *vt* escribir

pen² [pen] **1** *n (enclosure)* corral *m*; *(for sheep)* redil *m*; *(for children)* corralito *m*
   2 *vt* **to p. in** acorralar

penal ['piːnəl] *adj* penal

penalize ['piːnəlaɪz] *vt* castigar; *Sport* penalizar

penalty ['penəltɪ] *n (punishment)* pena *f*; *Sport* castigo *m*; *Ftb* penalti *m*; **to pay the p. for sth** cargar con las consecuencias de algo; **p. area** área *f* de castigo

penance ['penəns] *n* penitencia *f*

pence [pens] *pl of* **penny**

pencil ['pensəl] *n* lápiz *m*; **p. case** estuche *m* de lápices; **p. sharpener** sacapuntas *m inv*

pendant ['pendənt] *n* colgante *m*

pending ['pendɪŋ] **1** *adj* pendiente
   2 *prep* a la espera de; **p. a decision** *(until)*

hasta que se tome una decisión

pendulum ['pendjʊləm] n péndulo m

penetrate ['penɪtreɪt] **1** vt penetrar; Fig adentrarse en

  2 vi atravesar; (get inside) penetrar

penetrating ['penɪtreɪtɪŋ] adj (look) penetrante; (mind) perspicaz; (sound) agudo(a)

penfriend ['penfrend] n amigo(a) m,f por carta

penguin ['peŋgwɪn] n pingüino m

penicillin [penɪ'sɪlɪn] n penicilina f

peninsula [pɪ'nɪnsjʊlə] n península f

penis ['piːnɪs] n pene m

penitent ['penɪtənt] adj Rel penitente; (repentant) arrepentido(a)

penitentiary [penɪ'tenʃərɪ] n US cárcel f, penal m

penknife ['pennaɪf] n navaja f, cortaplumas m inv

penniless ['penɪlɪs] adj sin dinero

penny ['penɪ] n (pl pennies, pence) Br penique m; US centavo m

penpal ['penpæl] n US = penfriend

pension ['penʃən] n pensión f; retirement p. jubilación f

pensioner ['penʃənə(r)] n jubilado(a) m,f

pensive ['pensɪv] adj pensativo(a)

pentagon ['pentəgɒn] n US Pol the P. el Pentágono

Pentecost ['pentɪkɒst] n Pentecostés m

penthouse ['penthaʊs] n ático m

pent-up ['pentʌp] adj reprimido(a)

penultimate [pɪ'nʌltɪmɪt] adj penúltimo(a)

people ['piːpəl] npl (a) gente f; (individuals) personas fpl; many p. mucha gente; old p.'s home asilo m de ancianos; p. say that ... se dice que ...; some p. algunas personas (b) (citizens) ciudadanos mpl; (inhabitants) habitantes mpl; the p. el pueblo m, nación f

pep [pep] n Fam ánimo m, energía f; p. talk discurso m enardecedor

  ▸ **pep up** vt sep Fam animar

pepper ['pepə(r)] **1** n (a) (spice) pimienta f; (fruit) pimiento m; black p. pimienta negra; p. pot pimentero m; red/green p. pimiento rojo/verde; p. mill molinillo m de pimienta

  2 vt Fig peppered with salpicado(a) de

peppermint ['pepəmɪnt] n menta f; (sweet) pastilla f de menta

per [pɜː(r)] prep por; five times p. week cinco veces a la semana; p. cent por

ciento; p. day/annum al or por día/año; p. capita per cápita

perceive [pə'siːv] vt (see) percibir

percentage [pə'sentɪdʒ] n porcentaje m

perceptible [pə'septəbl] adj (visible) perceptible; (sound) audible; (improvement) sensible

perception [pə'sepʃən] n percepción f

perceptive [pə'septɪv] adj perspicaz

perch¹ [pɜːtʃ] n (fish) perca f

perch² [pɜːtʃ] **1** n (for bird) percha f

  2 vi (bird) posarse (on en)

percolate ['pɜːkəleɪt] **1** vt filtrar; percolated coffee café m de cafetera

  2 vi filtrarse

percolator ['pɜːkəleɪtə(r)] n cafetera f

percussion [pə'kʌʃən] n percusión f

perennial [pə'renɪəl] adj Bot perenne

perfect 1 adj ['pɜːfɪkt] perfecto(a); he's a p. stranger to us nos es totalmente desconocido; p. tense tiempo perfecto

  2 vt [pə'fekt] perfeccionar

perfection [pə'fekʃən] n perfección f

perfectly ['pɜːfɪktlɪ] adv perfectamente; (absolutely) completamente

perforate ['pɜːfəreɪt] vt perforar

perforation [pɜːfə'reɪʃən] n perforación f; (on stamps etc) perforado m

perform [pə'fɔːm] **1** vt (task) ejecutar, realizar; (piece of music) interpretar; Th representar

  2 vi (machine) funcionar; Mus interpretar; Th actuar

performance [pə'fɔːməns] n (of task) ejecución f, realización f; Mus interpretación f; Th representación f; Sport actuación f; (of machine etc) rendimiento m

performer [pə'fɔːmə(r)] n Mus intérprete mf; Th actor m, actriz f

perfume ['pɜːfjuːm] n perfume m

perfunctory [pə'fʌŋktərɪ] adj superficial

perhaps [pə'hæps, præps] adv tal vez, quizá(s)

peril ['perɪl] n (risk) riesgo m; (danger) peligro m

perilous ['perɪləs] adj (risky) arriesgado(a); (dangerous) peligroso(a)

perilously ['perɪləslɪ] adv peligrosamente

perimeter [pə'rɪmɪtə(r)] n perímetro m

period ['pɪərɪəd] **1** n (a) período m; (stage) etapa f (b) Educ clase f (c) US (full stop) punto m (d) (menstruation) regla f

  2 adj (dress, furniture) de época

periodic [pɪərɪ'ɒdɪk] adj periódico(a)

periodical [pɪərɪ'ɒdɪkəl] **1** adj periódico(a)

  2 n revista f

periodically [pɪərɪ'ɒdɪklɪ] *adv* de vez en cuando

peripheral [pə'rɪfərəl] **1** *adj* periférico(a) **2** *n Comput* unidad periférica

perish ['perɪʃ] *vi* perecer; *(material)* echarse a perder

perishable ['perɪʃəbəl] *adj* perecedero(a)

perjury ['pɜːdʒərɪ] *n* perjurio *m*

perk [pɜːk] *n Fam* extra *m*
▶ **perk up** *vi (person)* animarse; *(after illness)* reponerse

perky ['pɜːkɪ] *adj* (**perkier, perkiest**) animado(a), alegre

perm [pɜːm] **1** *n* permanente *f*
2 *vt* **to have one's hair permed** hacerse la permanente

permanent ['pɜːmənənt] *adj* permanente; *(address, job)* fijo(a)

permeate ['pɜːmɪeɪt] *vt & vi* penetrar; *Fig* extenderse por

permissible [pə'mɪsəbəl] *adj* admisible

permission [pə'mɪʃən] *n* permiso *m*

permissive [pə'mɪsɪv] *adj* permisivo(a)

permit 1 *n* ['pɜːmɪt] permiso *m*; *Com* licencia *f*
2 *vt* [pə'mɪt] **to p. sb to do sth** permitir a algn hacer algo

pernicious [pə'nɪʃəs] *adj* pernicioso(a)

perpendicular [pɜːpən'dɪkjʊlə(r)] **1** *adj* perpendicular; *(cliff)* vertical
2 *n* perpendicular *f*

perpetrate ['pɜːpɪtreɪt] *vt* cometer

perpetual [pə'petʃʊəl] *adj (noise)* continuo(a); *(arguing)* interminable; *(snow)* perpetuo(a)

perplex [pə'pleks] *vt* dejar perplejo(a)

perplexing [pə'pleksɪŋ] *adj* desconcertante

persecute ['pɜːsɪkjuːt] *vt* perseguir; *(harass)* acosar

persecution [pɜːsɪ'kjuːʃən] *n* persecución *f*; *(harassment)* acoso *m*

perseverance [pɜːsɪ'vɪərəns] *n* perseverancia *f*

persevere [pɜːsɪ'vɪə(r)] *vi* perseverar

Persian ['pɜːʒən] *adj* persa; **P. Gulf** golfo Pérsico

persist [pə'sɪst] *vi* empeñarse (**in** en)

persistence [pə'sɪstəns] *n* empeño *m*

persistent [pə'sɪstənt] *adj (person)* perseverante; *(smell etc)* persistente; *(continual)* constante

person ['pɜːsən] *n* (*pl* **people**) persona *f*; *(individual)* individuo *m*; **in p.** en persona

personable ['pɜːsənəbəl] *adj (handsome)* bien parecido(a); *(pleasant)* amable

personal ['pɜːsənəl] (**a**) *adj (private)* personal; *(friend)* íntimo(a); **p. computer** ordenador *m* personal, *Am* computadora *f* personal; **p. column** anuncios *mpl* personales; **p. pronoun** pronombre *m* personal (**b**) *(in person)* en persona; **he will make a p. appearance** estará aquí en persona (**c**) *Pej (comment etc)* indiscreto(a)

personality [pɜːsə'nælɪtɪ] *n* personalidad *f*

personally ['pɜːsənəlɪ] *adv (for my part)* personalmente; *(in person)* en persona

personify [pɜː'sɒnɪfaɪ] *vt* personificar, encarnar

personnel [pɜːsə'nel] *n* personal *m*

perspective [pə'spektɪv] *n* perspectiva *f*

Perspex® ['pɜːspeks] *n* plexiglás® *m*

perspiration [pɜːspə'reɪʃən] *n* transpiración *f*

perspire [pə'spaɪə(r)] *vi* transpirar

persuade [pə'sweɪd] *vt* persuadir; **to p. sb to do sth** persuadir a algn para que haga algo

persuasion [pə'sweɪʒən] *n* persuasión *f*; *(opinion, belief)* credo *m*

persuasive [pə'sweɪsɪv] *adj* persuasivo(a)

pert [pɜːt] *adj* pizpireta, coqueto(a)

pertain [pə'teɪn] *vi* estar relacionado(a) (**to** con)

pertinent ['pɜːtɪnənt] *adj (relevant)* pertinente; **p. to** relacionado(a) con, a propósito de

perturbing [pə'tɜːbɪŋ] *adj* inquietante

Peru [pə'ruː] *n* Perú

peruse [pə'ruːz] *vt Fml* leer

Peruvian [pə'ruːvɪən] *adj & n* peruano(a) (*m,f*)

pervade [pɜː'veɪd] *vt (of smell)* penetrar; *(of light)* difundirse por; *Fig (of influence)* extenderse por

pervasive [pɜː'veɪsɪv] *adj (smell)* penetrante; *(influence)* extendido(a)

perverse [pə'vɜːs] *adj (wicked)* perverso(a); *(contrary)* contrario(a) a todo

perversion [pə'vɜːʃən] *n Med & Psy* perversión *f*; *(of justice, truth)* desvirtuación *f*

pervert 1 *n* ['pɜːvɜːt] *Med* pervertido(a) *m,f* (sexual)
2 *vt* [pə'vɜːt] pervertir; *(justice, truth)* desvirtuar

pessimist ['pesɪmɪst] *n* pesimista *mf*

pessimistic [pesɪ'mɪstɪk] *adj* pesimista

pest [pest] *n* (**a**) *Zool* animal nocivo; *Bot* planta nociva (**b**) *Fam (person)* pelma *mf*; *(thing)* lata *f*

pester ['pestə(r)] *vt* molestar, fastidiar

pet [pet] **1** n (**a**) animal doméstico (**b**) (favourite) preferido(a) m,f; Fam cariño m

2 adj (favourite) preferido(a)

3 vt acariciar

4 vi (sexually) besuquearse

petal ['petəl] n pétalo m

peter ['piːtə(r)] vi to p. out agotarse

petite [pə'tiːt] adj menuda, chiquita

petition [pɪ'tɪʃən] n petición f

petrify ['petrɪfaɪ] vt Literary petrificar; Fig they were petrified se quedaron de piedra

petrol ['petrəl] n Br gasolina f, RP nafta f; **p. can** bidón m de gasolina; **p. pump** surtidor m de gasolina; **p. station** gasolinera f, estación f de servicio, Andes, Ven bomba f, Méx gasolinería f, Perú grifo m; **p. tank** depósito m de gasolina

> 🖉 Note that the Spanish word **petróleo** is a false friend and is never a translation for the English word **petrol**. In Spanish, **petróleo** means "oil, petroleum".

petroleum [pə'trəʊliəm] n petróleo m

petticoat ['petɪkəʊt] n enaguas fpl

petty ['petɪ] adj (pettier, pettiest) (trivial) insignificante; (small-minded) mezquino(a); **p. cash** dinero m para gastos pequeños; Naut **p. officer** sargento m de marina

petulant ['petjʊlənt] adj malhumorado(a)

> 🖉 Note that the Spanish word **petulante** is a false friend and is never a translation for the English word **petulant**. In Spanish, **petulante** means "opinionated, arrogant".

pew [pjuː] n banco m de iglesia; Fam take a p.! ¡siéntate!

pewter ['pjuːtə(r)] n peltre m

phantom ['fæntəm] adj & n fantasma (m)

pharmaceutical [fɑːmə'sjuːtɪkəl] adj farmacéutico(a)

pharmacist ['fɑːməsɪst] n farmacéutico(a) m,f

pharmacy ['fɑːməsɪ] n farmacia f

phase [feɪz] **1** n fase f

2 vt to p. sth in/out introducir/retirar algo progresivamente

PhD [piːeɪtʃ'diː] n (abbr **Doctor of Philosophy**) (person) Doctor(a) m,f en Filosofía

pheasant ['fezənt] n faisán m (vulgar)

phenomena [fɪ'nɒmɪnə] pl of phenomenon

phenomenal [fɪ'nɒmɪnəl] adj fenomenal

phenomenon [fɪ'nɒmɪnən] n (pl phenomena) fenómeno m

phial [faɪəl] n frasco m

philanthropist [fɪ'lænθrəpɪst] n filántropo(a) m,f

philately [fɪ'lætəlɪ] n filatelia f

Philippines ['fɪlɪpiːnz] npl the P. las (Islas) Filipinas

philosopher [fɪ'lɒsəfə(r)] n filósofo(a) m,f

philosophical [fɪlə'sɒfɪkəl] adj filosófico(a)

philosophy [fɪ'lɒsəfɪ] n filosofía f

phlegm [flem] n flema f

phlegmatic [fleg'mætɪk] adj flemático(a)

phobia ['fəʊbɪə] n fobia f

phone [fəʊn] n = telephone

phone-in ['fəʊnɪn] n Fam = programa de radio o televisión con línea telefónica abierta

phonetic [fə'netɪk] **1** adj fonético(a)

2 n phonetics fonética f

phoney ['fəʊnɪ] **1** adj (phonier, phoniest) (thing) falso(a); (person) farsante

2 n (person) farsante mf

phonograph ['fəʊnəgrɑːf] n US tocadiscos m inv

phosphate ['fɒsfeɪt] n fosfato m

photo ['fəʊtəʊ] n foto f

photocopier ['fəʊtəʊkɒpɪə(r)] n fotocopiadora f

photocopy ['fəʊtəʊkɒpɪ] **1** n fotocopia f

2 vt fotocopiar

photogenic [fəʊtəʊ'dʒenɪk] adj fotogénico(a)

photograph ['fəʊtəgræf, 'fəʊtəgrɑːf] **1** n fotografía f; **black and white/colour p.** fotografía en blanco y negro/en color

2 vt fotografiar

photographer [fə'tɒgrəfə(r)] n fotógrafo(a) m,f

photography [fə'tɒgrəfɪ] n fotografía f

phrase [freɪz] **1** n frase f; **p. book** libro m de frases

2 vt expresar

physical ['fɪzɪkəl] adj físico(a); **p. education** educación física

physically ['fɪzɪkəlɪ] adv físicamente; **p. handicapped** minusválido(a); **to be p. fit** estar en forma

physician [fɪ'zɪʃən] n médico(a) m,f

physicist ['fɪzɪsɪst] n físico(a) m,f

physics ['fɪzɪks] n sing física f

physiological [fɪzɪə'lɒdʒɪkəl] adj fisiológico(a)

physiotherapist [fɪzɪəʊ'θerəpɪst] n fisioterapeuta mf

physique [fɪ'ziːk] n físico m

pianist ['pɪənɪst] n pianista mf

piano [pɪ'ænəʊ] n piano m

piccolo ['pɪkələʊ] n flautín m

pick [pɪk] **1** n (**a**) (tool) pico m, piqueta f (**b**) **take your p.** (choice) elige el que quieras

2 vt (**a**) (choose) escoger; (team) seleccionar (**b**) (flowers, fruit) coger, recoger (**c**) (scratch) hurgar; **to p. one's nose** hurgarse la nariz; **to p. one's teeth** mondarse los dientes (**d**) **to p. sb's pocket** robar algo del bolsillo de algn (**e**) (lock) forzar

3 vi **to p. at one's food** comer sin ganas

▸ **pick off** vt sep (**a**) (remove) quitar (**b**) (shoot) matar uno a uno

▸ **pick on** vt insep (persecute) meterse con

▸ **pick out** vt sep (choose) elegir; (distinguish) distinguir; (identify) identificar

▸ **pick up 1** vt sep (**a**) (object on floor) recoger; (telephone) descolgar; **to p. oneself up** levantarse (**b**) Fig reponerse (**b**) (collect) recoger; (shopping, person) buscar; **to p. up speed** ganar velocidad (**c**) (acquire) conseguir; (learn) aprender

2 vi (improve) mejorarse, ir mejorando; (prices) subir

pickaxe, US **pickax** ['pɪkæks] n piqueta f

picket ['pɪkɪt] **1** n piquete m; **p. line** piquete

2 vt piquetear

3 vi hacer piquete

pickle ['pɪkəl] **1** n (**a**) Br Culin salsa f picante (**b**) Fam (mess) lío m, apuro m

2 vt Culin conservar en adobo or escabeche; **pickled onions** cebollas fpl en vinagre

pick-me-up ['pɪkmɪʌp] n Fam reconstituyente m, tónico m

pickpocket ['pɪkpɒkɪt] n carterista mf

pick-up ['pɪkʌp] n **p. (arm)** (on record player) brazo m; **p. (truck)** furgoneta f

picnic ['pɪknɪk] **1** n comida f de campo, picnic m

2 vi hacer una comida de campo

pictorial [pɪk'tɔːrɪəl] adj ilustrado(a)

picture ['pɪktʃə(r)] **1** n (**a**) (painting) cuadro m; (drawing) dibujo m; (portrait) retrato m; (photo) foto f; (illustration) ilustración f; **p. book** libro ilustrado; **p. postcard** tarjeta f postal (**b**) TV imagen f; Cin película f; **to go to the pictures** ir al cine

2 vt (imagine) imaginarse

picturesque [pɪktʃə'resk] adj pintoresco(a)

pie [paɪ] n (of fruit) tarta f, pastel m; (of meat etc) pastel, empanada f; (pasty) empanadilla f

piece [piːs] n (**a**) (of food) pedazo m, trozo m; (of paper) trozo; (part) pieza f; **a p. of advice** un consejo; **a p. of furniture** un mueble; **a p. of land** una parcela; **a p. of news** una noticia; **to break sth into pieces** hacer algo pedazos; Fig **to go to pieces** perder el control (de sí mismo) (**b**) Lit & Mus obra f, pieza f (**c**) (coin) moneda f (**d**) (in chess) pieza f; (in draughts) ficha f

▸ **piece together** vt sep (facts) reconstruir; (jigsaw) hacer

piecemeal ['piːsmiːl] adv (by degrees) poco a poco, a etapas; (unsystematically) desordenadamente

piecework ['piːswɜːk] n trabajo m a destajo; **to be on p.** trabajar a destajo

pier [pɪə(r)] n embarcadero m, muelle m; (promenade) = paseo de madera que entra en el mar

pierce [pɪəs] vt perforar; (penetrate) penetrar

piercing ['pɪəsɪŋ] adj (sound etc) penetrante

piety ['paɪtɪ] n piedad f

pig [pɪg] n (**a**) cerdo m (**b**) Fam (person) cochino m; (glutton) tragón(ona) m,f (**c**) Fam Pej (policeman) madero m

pigeon ['pɪdʒɪn] n paloma f; Culin & Sport pichón m

pigeonhole ['pɪdʒɪnhəʊl] n casilla f

piggy ['pɪgɪ] n **p. bank** = hucha en forma de cerdito

pigheaded [pɪg'hedɪd] adj terco(a), cabezota

piglet ['pɪglɪt] n cerdito m, lechón m

pigment ['pɪgmənt] n pigmento m

pigskin ['pɪgskɪn] n piel f de cerdo

pigsty ['pɪgstaɪ] n pocilga f

pigtail ['pɪgteɪl] n trenza f, (bullfighter's) coleta f

pike [paɪk] n (fish) lucio m

pilchard ['pɪltʃəd] n sardina f

pile¹ [paɪl] **1** n montón m

2 vt amontonar

3 vi **to p. into** apiñarse en; **to p. on/off a bus** subir a/bajar de un autobús en tropel

▸ **pile up 1** vt sep (things) amontonar; (riches, debts) acumular

2 vi amontonarse

pile² [paɪl] n (on carpet) pelo m; **thick p.** pelo largo

piles [paɪlz] npl Med almorranas fpl, hemorroides fpl

pile-up ['paɪlʌp] n Aut choque m en cadena

pilfer ['pɪlfə(r)] vt & vi hurtar

pilgrim ['pɪlgrɪm] n peregrino(a) m,f

pilgrimage ['pɪlgrɪmɪdʒ] n peregrinación f

pill [pɪl] n píldora f, pastilla f; **to be on the p.** estar tomando la píldora (anticonceptiva)

pillage ['pɪlɪdʒ] vt & vi pillar, saquear

pillar ['pɪlə(r)] n pilar m, columna f; Br **p. box** buzón m

pillion ['pɪljən] n asiento trasero (de una moto)

pillow ['pɪləʊ] n almohada f

pillowcase ['pɪləʊkeɪs] n funda f de almohada

pilot ['paɪlət] 1 n piloto m
2 adj (trial) piloto inv; **p. light** piloto m; **p. scheme** proyecto piloto
3 vt pilotar

pimp [pɪmp] n chulo m

pimple ['pɪmpəl] n grano m, espinilla f

PIN [pɪn] n (abbr personal identification number) P. (number) PIN m

pin [pɪn] 1 n alfiler m; Tech clavija f; (wooden) espiga f; (in plug) polo m; (in bowling) bolo m; US (brooch) broche m; **pins and needles** hormigueo m
2 vt (on board) clavar con chinchetas; (garment etc) sujetar con alfileres; **to p. sb against a wall** tener a algn contra una pared; Fig **to p. one's hopes on sth** poner sus esperanzas en algo; Fam **to p. a crime on sb** endosar un delito a algn
▶ **pin down** vt sep Fig **to p. sb down** hacer que algn se comprometa

pinafore ['pɪnəfɔː(r)] n (apron) delantal m; **p. dress** pichi m

pinball ['pɪnbɔːl] n flipper m, máquina f de pelcaza

pincers ['pɪnsəz] npl (on crab) pinzas fpl; (tool) tenazas fpl

pinch [pɪntʃ] 1 n (nip) pellizco m; Fig Br **at** or US **in a p.** en caso de apuro; **a p. of salt** una pizca de sal
2 vt pellizcar; Fam (steal) birlar
3 vi (shoes) apretar

> 🖉 Note that the Spanish verb **pinchar** is a false friend and is never a translation for the English verb **to pinch**. In Spanish, **pinchar** means "to prick, to puncture".

pincushion ['pɪnkʊʃən] n acerico m

pine¹ [paɪn] n (tree) pino m; **p. cone** piña f

pine² [paɪn] vi **to p. (away)** consumirse, morirse de pena; **to p. for sth/sb** añorar algo/a algn

pineapple ['paɪnæpəl] n piña f

ping [pɪŋ] n sonido metálico; (of bullet) silbido m

Ping-Pong® ['pɪŋpɒŋ] n ping-pong® m

pink [pɪŋk] 1 n (colour) rosa m; Bot clavel m
2 adj (colour) rosa inv; Pol Fam rojillo(a)

pinnacle ['pɪnəkəl] n (of building) pináculo m; (of mountain) cima f, pico m; Fig (of success) cumbre f

pinpoint ['pɪnpɔɪnt] vt señalar

pinstripe ['pɪnstraɪp] adj a rayas

pint [paɪnt] n pinta f; Br Fam **a p. (of beer)** una pinta (de cerveza)

pioneer [paɪə'nɪə(r)] 1 n (settler) pionero(a) m,f; (forerunner) precursor(a) m,f
2 vt ser pionero(a) en

pious ['paɪəs] adj piadoso(a), devoto(a); Pej beato(a)

pip¹ [pɪp] n (seed) pepita f

pip² [pɪp] n (sound) señal f (corta); (on dice) punto m

pipe [paɪp] 1 n (a) conducto m, tubería f; (of organ) caramillo m; Fam **the pipes** (bagpipes) la gaita (b) (for smoking) pipa f; **p. cleaner** limpiapipas m inv; Fig **p. dream** sueño m imposible
2 vt (water) llevar por tubería; (oil) transportar por oleoducto; **piped music** hilo m musical
▶ **pipe down** vi Fam callarse
▶ **pipe up** vi Fam hacerse oír

pipeline ['paɪplaɪn] n tubería f, cañería f; (for gas) gasoducto m; (for oil) oleoducto m

piper ['paɪpə(r)] n gaitero(a) m,f

piping ['paɪpɪŋ] 1 n (for water, gas etc) tubería f, cañería f
2 adj **p. hot** bien caliente

piquant ['piːkənt] adj picante; (fig) intrigante

pique [piːk] 1 n enojo m
2 vt herir

pirate ['paɪrɪt] n pirata m; **p. edition** edición f pirata; **p. radio** emisora f pirata; **p. ship** barco m pirata

pirouette [pɪrʊ'et] 1 n pirueta f
2 vi hacer piruetas

Pisces ['paɪsiːz] n Piscis m

piss [pɪs] very Fam 1 vi mear
2 n meada f

pissed [pɪst] adj very Fam (a) Br (drunk) borracho(a) (b) US (angry) cabreado(a)

pistachio [pɪs'tɑːʃɪəʊ] n (nut) pistacho m

pistol ['pɪstəl] n pistola f

piston ['pɪstən] n pistón m

pit¹ [pɪt] 1 n hoyo m; (large) hoya f; (coal mine) mina f de carbón; Th platea f; (in motor racing) foso m, box m
2 vt **to p. one's wits against sb** medirse con algn

pit² [pɪt] n *(of cherry)* hueso m, pipo m; *US (of peach, plum)* hueso

pitch¹ [pɪtʃ] **1** vt (a) *Mus (sound)* entonar (b) *(throw)* lanzar, arrojar (c) *(tent)* armar

2 vi *(ship)* cabecear; **to p. forward** caerse hacia adelante

3 n (a) *Mus (of sound)* tono m (b) *Sport* campo m, cancha f (c) *(in market etc)* puesto m (d) *(throw)* lanzamiento m

pitch² [pɪtʃ] n *(tar)* brea f, pez f

pitch-black [pɪtʃˈblæk], **pitch-dark** [pɪtʃˈdɑːk] adj negro(a) como la boca del lobo

pitched [pɪtʃt] adj **p. battle** batalla f campal

pitcher [ˈpɪtʃə(r)] n *(container)* cántaro m, jarro m

pitchfork [ˈpɪtʃfɔːk] n horca f

piteous [ˈpɪtɪəs] adj lastimoso(a)

pitfall [ˈpɪtfɔːl] n dificultad f, obstáculo m

pith [pɪθ] n *(of orange)* piel blanca; *Fig* meollo m

pithy [ˈpɪθɪ] adj **(pithier, pithiest)** *Fig* contundente

pitiful [ˈpɪtɪfʊl] adj *(producing pity)* lastimoso(a), *(terrible)* lamentable

pitiless [ˈpɪtɪlɪs] adj despiadado(a), implacable

pittance [ˈpɪtəns] n miseria f

pity [ˈpɪtɪ] **1** n (a) *(compassion)* compasión f, piedad f; **to take p. on sb** compadecerse de algn (b) *(shame)* lástima f, pena f; **what a p.!** ¡qué pena!, ¡qué lástima!

2 vt compadecerse de; **I p. them** me dan pena

pivot [ˈpɪvət] **1** n pivote m

2 vi girar sobre su eje

pizza [ˈpiːtsə] n pizza f; **p. parlour** pizzería f

placard [ˈplækɑːd] n pancarta f

placate [pləˈkeɪt] vt aplacar, apaciguar

place [pleɪs] **1** n (a) sitio m, lugar m; **to be in/out of p.** estar en/fuera de su sitio; **to take p.** tener lugar

(b) *(seat)* sitio m; *(on bus)* asiento m; *(at university)* plaza m; **to change places with sb** intercambiar el sitio con algn; **to feel out of p.** encontrarse fuera de lugar; **to take sb's p.** sustituir a algn

(c) *(position on scale)* posición f; *(social position)* rango m; **in the first p.** en primer lugar; **to take first p.** ganar el primer lugar

(d) *(house)* casa f; *(building)* lugar m; **we're going to his p.** vamos a su casa

2 vt (a) poner, colocar; **to p. a bet** hacer una apuesta; **to p. an order with sb** hacer un pedido a algn

(b) *(face, person)* recordar; *(in job)* colocar en un empleo

placid [ˈplæsɪd] adj apacible

plagiarize [ˈpleɪdʒəraɪz] vt plagiar

plague [pleɪg] **1** n *(of insects)* plaga f; *Med* peste f

2 vt **to p. sb with requests** acosar a algn a peticiones

plaice [pleɪs] n *(pl* plaice*) (fish)* platija f

plaid [plæd, pleɪd] n *(cloth)* tejido m escocés

plain [pleɪn] **1** adj (a) *(clear)* claro(a), evidente; *Fig* **he likes p. speaking** le gusta hablar con franqueza (b) *(simple)* sencillo(a); *(chocolate)* amargo(a); *(flour)* sin levadura; **in p. clothes** vestido(a) de paisano; **the p. truth** la verdad lisa y llana (c) *(unattractive)* poco atractivo(a)

2 n *Geog* llanura f, llano m

plainly [ˈpleɪnlɪ] adv claramente; *(simply)* sencillamente; **to speak p.** hablar con franqueza

plaintiff [ˈpleɪntɪf] n demandante mf

plaintive [ˈpleɪntɪv] adj lastimero(a)

plait [plæt] **1** n trenza f

2 vt trenzar

plan [plæn] **1** n *(scheme)* plan m, proyecto m; *(drawing)* plano m

2 vt (a) *(for future)* planear, proyectar; *(economy)* planificar (b) *(intend)* pensar, tener la intención de; **it wasn't planned** no estaba previsto

3 vi hacer planes; **to p. on doing sth** tener la intención de hacer algo

plane¹ [pleɪn] **1** n (a) *Math* plano m; *Fig* nivel m (b) *Fam Av* avión m

2 adj *Geom* plano(a)

3 vi *(glide)* planear

plane² [pleɪn] **1** n *(tool)* cepillo m

2 vt cepillar

plane³ [pleɪn] n *Bot* **p. (tree)** plátano m

planet [ˈplænɪt] n planeta m

plank [plæŋk] n tabla f, tablón m

planner [ˈplænə(r)] n planificador(a) m,f

planning [ˈplænɪŋ] n planificación f; **family p.** planificación familiar; **p. permission** permiso m de obras

plant¹ [plɑːnt] **1** n planta f

2 vt *(flowers)* plantar; *(seeds)* sembrar; *(bomb)* colocar

plant² [plɑːnt] n *(factory)* planta f, fábrica f; *(machinery)* maquinaria f

plantation [plænˈteɪʃən] n plantación f

plaque [plæk] n placa f; *(on teeth)* sarro m

plaster [ˈplɑːstə(r)] **1** n *Constr* yeso m;

Med escayola *f; Br* **sticking p.** esparadrapo *m,* tirita® *f, Am* curita *f;* **p. of Paris** yeso mate

2 *vt Constr* enyesar; *Fig (cover)* cubrir (**with** de)

plastered ['plɑːstəd] *adj Fam* borracho(a), trompa

plasterer ['plɑːstərə(r)] *n* yesero(a) *m,f*

plastic ['plæstɪk] **1** *n* plástico *m*

2 *adj (cup; bag)* de plástico; **p. surgery** cirugía plástica

Plasticine® ['plæstɪsiːn] *n* plastilina® *f*

plate [pleɪt] **1** *n* (a) plato *m* (b) *(sheet)* placa *f;* **gold p.** chapa *f* de oro; **p. glass** vidrio cilindrado (c) *(in book)* grabado *m,* lámina *f*

2 *vt* chapar

plateau ['plætəʊ] *n* meseta *f*

platform ['plætfɔːm] *n* (a) plataforma *f; (stage)* estrado *m; (at meeting)* tribuna *f* (b) *Rail* andén *m;* **p. ticket** billete *m* de andén (c) *Pol (programme)* programa *m*

platinum ['plætɪnəm] *n* platino *m*

platitude ['plætɪtjuːd] *n* lugar *m* común, tópico *m*

platoon [plə'tuːn] *n Mil* pelotón *m*

platter ['plætə(r)] *n* fuente *f*

plausible ['plɔːzəbəl] *adj* plausible

play [pleɪ] **1** *vt* (a) *(game)* jugar a

(b) *Sport (position)* jugar de; *(team)* jugar contra; **to p. a shot** *(in golf, tennis)* golpear

(c) *(instrument, tune)* tocar; **to p. a record** poner un disco

(d) *Th (part)* hacer (el papel) de; *(play)* representar; *Fig* **to p. a part in sth** participar en algo; *Fig* **to p. the fool** hacer el tonto

2 *vi* (a) *(children)* jugar (**with** con); *(animals)* juguetear

(b) *Sport* jugar; **to p. fair** jugar limpio; *Fig* **to p. for time** tratar de ganar tiempo

(c) *(joke)* bromear

(d) *Mus* tocar; *(instrument)* sonar

3 *n* (a) *Th* obra *f* de teatro

(b) *Sport* juego *m;* **fair/foul p.** juego limpio/sucio

(c) *Tech & Fig (movement)* juego *m; Fig* **to bring sth into p.** poner algo en juego; **a p. on words** un juego de palabras

▸ **play around** *vi (waste time)* gandulear; *(be unfaithful)* tener líos

▸ **play down** *vt sep* minimizar, quitar importancia a

▸ **play on** *vt insep (take advantage of)* aprovecharse de; *(nerves etc)* exacerbar

▸ **play up 1** *vt sep (annoy)* dar la lata a, fastidiar

2 *vi (child etc)* dar guerra

playboy ['pleɪbɔɪ] *n* playboy *m*

player ['pleɪə(r)] *n Sport* jugador(a) *m,f; Mus* músico(a) *m,f; Th (man)* actor *m; (woman)* actriz *f*

playful ['pleɪfʊl] *adj* juguetón(ona)

playground ['pleɪgraʊnd] *n* patio *m* de recreo

playgroup ['pleɪgruːp] *n* jardín *m* de infancia

playing ['pleɪɪŋ] *n* juego *m;* **p. card** carta *f,* naipe *m;* **p. field** campo *m* de deportes

playmate ['pleɪmeɪt] *n* compañero(a) *m,f* de juego

play-off ['pleɪɒf] *n Sport* partido *m* de desempate

playpen ['pleɪpen] *n* corralito *m* or parque *m* (de niños)

playschool ['pleɪskuːl] *n* jardín *m* de infancia

plaything ['pleɪθɪŋ] *n* juguete *m*

playwright ['pleɪraɪt] *n* dramaturgo(a) *m,f*

PLC, plc [piːel'siː] *n Br (abbr* **public limited company)** ≃ S.A.

plea [pliː] *n* (a) *(request)* petición *f,* súplica *f; (excuse)* pretexto *m,* disculpa *f* (b) *Jur* alegato *m*

plead [pliːd] **1** *vt* (a) *Jur & Fig* **to p. sb's cause** defender la causa de algn (b) **to p. ignorance** *(give as excuse)* alegar ignorancia

2 *vi (beg)* rogar, suplicar; **to p. with sb to do sth** suplicar a algn que haga algo (b) *Jur* **to p. guilty/not guilty** declararse culpable/inocente

pleasant ['plezənt] *adj* agradable

pleasantry ['plezəntrɪ] *n* cumplido *m*

please [pliːz] **1** *vt (give pleasure to)* agradar, complacer; *(satisfy)* satisfacer; *Fam* **p. yourself** como quieras

2 *vi* complacer; *(give satisfaction)* satisfacer; **easy/hard to p.** poco/muy exigente

3 *adv* por favor; **may I? − p. do** ¿me permite? − desde luego; **p. do not smoke** *(sign)* se ruega no fumar; **yes, p.** sí, por favor

pleased [pliːzd] *adj (happy)* contento(a); *(satisfied)* satisfecho(a); **p. to meet you!** ¡encantado(a)!, ¡mucho gusto!; **to be p. about sth** alegrarse de algo

pleasing ['pliːzɪŋ] *adj (pleasant)* agradable, grato(a); *(satisfactory)* satisfactorio(a)

pleasure ['pleʒə(r)] *n* placer *m;* **it's a p. to talk to him** da gusto hablar con él; **to take great p. in doing sth** disfrutar mucho haciendo algo; **with p.** con mucho gusto

pleat [pliːt] **1** n pliegue m

2 vt hacer pliegues en

pledge [pledʒ] **1** n promesa f; (token of love etc) señal f; (guarantee) prenda f

2 vt (promise) prometer; (pawn) empeñar

plentiful ['plentɪfʊl] adj abundante

plenty ['plentɪ] n abundancia f; **p. of books** muchos libros; **p. of time** tiempo de sobra; **we've got p.** tenemos de sobra

Plexiglas® ['pleksɪglɑːs] n US plexiglás® m

pliable ['plaɪəbəl] adj flexible

pliers ['plaɪəz] npl alicates mpl, tenazas fpl

plight [plaɪt] n situación f grave

plimsolls ['plɪmsəlz] npl Br zapatos mpl de tenis

plinth [plɪnθ] n plinto m

plod [plɒd] vi andar con paso pesado; Fig **to p. on** perseverar; Fig **to p. through a report** estudiar laboriosamente un informe

plodder ['plɒdə(r)] n trabajador(a) m,f/ estudiante mf tenaz

plonk¹ [plɒŋk] n vt Fam dejar caer

plonk² [plɒŋk] n Br Fam (wine) vinazo m

plot¹ [plɒt] **1** n (a) (conspiracy) complot m (b) Th & Lit (story) argumento m, trama f

2 vt (a) (course, route) trazar (b) (scheme) fraguar

3 vi conspirar, tramar

plot² [plɒt] n Agr terreno m; (for building) solar m; **vegetable p.** campo m de hortalizas

plough [plaʊ] **1** n arado m

2 vt arar

3 vi Fig **the car ploughed through the fencing** el coche atravesó la valla; **to p. into sth** chocar contra algo; Fig **to p. through a book** leer un libro con dificultad

▸ **plough back** vt sep (profits) reinvertir

plow [plaʊ] n, vt & vi US = **plough**

ploy [plɔɪ] n estratagema f

pluck [plʌk] **1** vt (a) arrancar (**out of** de) (b) (flowers) coger (c) (chicken) desplumar (d) (guitar) puntear

2 n (courage) valor m, ánimo m

▸ **pluck up** vt sep **to p. up courage** armarse de valor

plucky ['plʌkɪ] adj (**pluckier, pluckiest**) valiente

plug [plʌg] **1** n (a) (in bath etc) tapón m (b) Elec enchufe m, clavija f; **two-/three-pin p.** clavija bipolar/tripolar

2 vt (a) (hole) tapar (b) Fam (publicize) dar publicidad a; (idea etc) hacer hincapié en

▸ **plug in** vt sep & vi enchufar

plum [plʌm] n (fruit) ciruela f, Fig **a p. job** un chollo

plumage ['pluːmɪdʒ] n plumaje m

plumb [plʌm] **1** n plomo m; **p. line** plomada f

2 adj vertical

3 adv Fam **p. in the middle** justo en medio; US **he's p. crazy** está completamente loco

4 vt Fig **to p. the depths** tocar fondo

plumber ['plʌmə(r)] n fontanero(a) m,f

plumbing ['plʌmɪŋ] n (occupation) fontanería f; (system) tuberías fpl, cañerías fpl

plume [pluːm] n penacho m

plummet ['plʌmɪt] vi (bird, plane) caer en picado; Fig (prices) bajar vertiginosamente; (morale) caer a plomo

plump¹ [plʌmp] adj (person) relleno(a); (baby) rechoncho(a)

plump² [plʌmp] vi **to p. for sth** optar por algo

▸ **plump down** vt sep dejar caer

▸ **plump up** vt sep (cushions) ahuecar

plunder ['plʌndə(r)] **1** vt saquear

2 n (action) saqueo m, pillaje m; (loot) botín m

plunge [plʌndʒ] **1** vt (immerse) sumergir; (thrust) arrojar

2 vi (dive) lanzarse, zambullirse; Fig (fall) caer, hundirse; (prices) desplomarse

3 n (dive) zambullida f, Fig (fall) desplome m; **to take the p.** dar el paso decisivo

plunger ['plʌndʒə(r)] n Tech émbolo m; (for pipes) desatascador m

pluperfect [pluːˈpɜːfɪkt] n pluscuamperfecto m

plural ['plʊərəl] adj & n plural (m)

plus [plʌs] **1** prep más; **three p. four makes seven** tres más cuatro hacen siete

2 n Math signo m más; Fig (advantage) ventaja f

plush [plʌʃ] **1** n felpa f

2 adj Fam lujoso(a)

plutonium [pluːˈtəʊnɪəm] n plutonio m

ply [plaɪ] **1** vt **to p. one's trade** ejercer su oficio; **to p. sb with drinks** no parar de ofrecer copas a algn

2 vi (ship) ir y venir; **to p. for hire** ir en busca de clientes

plywood ['plaɪwʊd] n madera contrachapada

PM [piː'em] *n Br* (*abbr* **Prime Minister**) primer(a) ministro(a) *m,f*

p.m. [piː'em] (*abbr* **post meridiem**) después del mediodía; **at 2 p.m.** a las dos de la tarde

PMT [piːem'tiː] *n* (*abbr* **premenstrual tension**) tensión *f* premenstrual

pneumatic [njʊ'mætɪk] *adj* neumático(a)

pneumonia [njuː'məʊnɪə] *n* pulmonía *f*

PO [piː'əʊ] *n* (*abbr* **Post Office**) oficina *f* de correos; **PO Box** apartado *m* de correos, *CAm, Carib, Méx* casilla *f* postal, *Andes, RP* casilla de correos

poach¹ [pəʊtʃ] *vt* (**a**) **to p. fish/game** pescar/cazar furtivamente (**b**) *Fam Fig* (*steal*) birlar

poach² [pəʊtʃ] *vt Culin* (*egg*) escalfar; (*fish*) hervir

poacher ['pəʊtʃə(r)] *n* pescador/cazador furtivo

pocket ['pɒkɪt] **1** *n* (**a**) bolsillo *m*; *Fig* **to be £10 in/out of p.** salir ganando/perdiendo 10 libras; **p. money** dinero *m* de bolsillo (**b**) (*of air*) bolsa *f* (**c**) (*of resistance*) foco *m*

2 *vt* (*money*) embolsar

pocketbook ['pɒkɪtbʊk] *n US* bolso *m*

pocketknife ['pɒkɪtnaɪf] *n* navaja *f*

pod [pɒd] *n* vaina *f*

podgy ['pɒdʒɪ] *adj* (**podgier, podgiest**) gordinflón(ona), regordete

podiatrist [pə'daɪətrɪst] *n US* pedicuro(a) *m,f*

podium ['pəʊdɪəm] *n* podio *m*

poem ['pəʊɪm] *n* poema *m*

poet ['pəʊɪt] *n* poeta *mf*

poetic [pəʊ'etɪk] *adj* poético(a)

poetry ['pəʊɪtrɪ] *n* poesía *f*

poignant ['pɔɪnjənt] *adj* conmovedor(a)

point [pɔɪnt] **1** *n* (**a**) (*sharp end*) punta *f*

(**b**) (*place*) punto *m*; *Fig* **p. of no return** punto sin retorno

(**c**) (*quality*) **good/bad p.** cualidad buena/mala; **weak/strong p.** punto débil/fuerte

(**d**) (*moment*) **at that p.** en aquel momento; **from that p. onwards** desde entonces; **to be on the p. of doing sth** estar a punto de hacer algo

(**e**) (*score*) punto *m*, tanto *m*; **to win on points** ganar por puntos; **match p.** (*in tennis*) pelota *f* de match

(**f**) (*in argument*) punto *m*; **to make one's p.** insistir en el argumento; **I take your p.** entiendo lo que quieres decir

(**g**) (*purpose*) propósito *m*; **I don't see the p.** no veo el sentido; **that isn't the p.,**

it's beside the p. eso no viene al caso; **there's no p. in going** no merece la pena ir; **to come to the p.** llegar al meollo de la cuestión

(**h**) (*on scale*) punto *m*; (*in share index*) entero *m*; **six p. three** seis coma tres; *Fig* **up to a p.** hasta cierto punto

(**i**) *Geog* punta *f*

(**j**) **power p.** toma *f* de corriente

(**k**) **points** *Aut* platinos *mpl*; *Rail* agujas *fpl*

2 *vt* (*way etc*) señalar, indicar; **to p. a gun at sb** apuntar a algn con una pistola

3 *vi* señalar, indicar; **to p. at sth/sb** señalar algo/a algn con el dedo

▸ **point out** *vt sep* indicar, señalar; (*mention*) hacer resaltar

point-blank ['pɔɪnt'blæŋk] **1** *adj* a quemarropa; (*refusal*) rotundo(a)

2 *adv* (*shoot*) a quemarropa; (*refuse*) rotundamente

pointed ['pɔɪntɪd] *adj* (*sharp*) puntiagudo(a); *Fig* (*comment*) intencionado(a); (*cutting*) mordaz

pointedly ['pɔɪntɪdlɪ] *adv Fig* (*significantly*) con intención; (*cuttingly*) con mordacidad

pointer ['pɔɪntə(r)] *n* (**a**) (*indicator*) indicador *m*, aguja *f*; (*for map*) puntero *m* (**b**) (*dog*) perro *m* de muestra

pointless ['pɔɪntlɪs] *adj* sin sentido

poise [pɔɪz] **1** *n* (*bearing*) porte *m*; (*self-assurance*) aplomo *m*

2 *vt Fig* **to be poised to do sth** estar listo(a) para hacer algo

poison ['pɔɪzən] **1** *n* veneno *m*

2 *vt* envenenar

poisoning ['pɔɪzənɪŋ] *n* envenenamiento *m*; (*by food etc*) intoxicación *f*

poisonous ['pɔɪzənəs] *adj* (*plant, snake*) venenoso(a); (*gas*) tóxico(a); *Fig* (*rumour*) pernicioso(a)

poke [pəʊk] *vt* (*with finger or stick*) dar con la punta del dedo/del bastón a; **to p. one's head out** asomar la cabeza; **to p. the fire** atizar el fuego

▸ **poke about, poke around** *vi* fisgonear, hurgar

▸ **poke out** *vt sep* (*eye*) sacar

poker¹ ['pəʊkə(r)] *n* (*for fire*) atizador *m*

poker² ['pəʊkə(r)] *n Cards* póquer *m*

poker-faced ['pəʊkəfeɪst] *adj Fam* de cara impasible

poky ['pəʊkɪ] *adj* (**pokier, pokiest**) *Fam Pej* minúsculo(a); **a p. little room** un cuartucho

Poland ['pəʊlənd] *n* Polonia

polar ['pəʊlə(r)] *adj* polar; **p. bear** oso *m* polar

Pole [pəʊl] *n* polaco(a) *m,f*

pole¹ [pəʊl] *n* palo *m*; **p. vault** salto *m* con pértiga

pole² [pəʊl] *n Geog* polo *m*; *Fig* **to be poles apart** ser polos opuestos

police [pə'liːs] *n* policía *f*; **p. car** coche *m* patrulla; **p. constable** policía *m*; **p. force** cuerpo *m* de policía; **p. record** antecedentes *mpl* penales; **p. state** estado *m* policial; **p. station** comisaría *f*
2 *vt* vigilar

policeman [pə'liːsmən] *n* policía *m*

policewoman [pə'liːswʊmən] *n* (mujer *f*) policía *f*

policy ['pɒlɪsɪ] *n Pol* política *f*; (of company) norma *f*, principio *m*; *Ins* póliza *f* (de seguros)

polio ['pəʊlɪəʊ] *n* poliomielitis *f*

Polish ['pəʊlɪʃ] 1 *adj* polaco(a)
2 *n* (a) **the P.** los polacos (b) *(language)* polaco *m*

polish ['pɒlɪʃ] 1 *vt* pulir; *(furniture)* encerar; *(shoes)* limpiar; *(silver)* sacar brillo a
2 *n* (a) *(for furniture)* cera *f*, *(for shoes)* betún *m*; *(for nails)* esmalte *m* (b) *(shine)* brillo *m*; *Fig (refinement)* refinamiento *m*
▸ **polish off** *vt sep Fam (work)* despachar; *(food)* zamparse
▸ **polish up** *vt sep Fig* perfeccionar

polished ['pɒlɪʃt] *adj Fig (manners)* refinado(a); *(style)* pulido(a); *(performance)* impecable

polite [pə'laɪt] *adj* educado(a)

politeness [pə'laɪtnɪs] *n* educación *f*

politic ['pɒlɪtɪk] *adj* prudente

political [pə'lɪtɪkəl] *adj* político(a)

politically [pə'lɪtɪklɪ] *adv* políticamente; **p. correct** políticamente correcto(a)

politician [pɒlɪ'tɪʃən] *n* político(a) *m,f*

politics ['pɒlɪtɪks] *n sing* política *f*

polka ['pɒlkə] *n (dance)* polca *f*; **p. dot** lunar *m*

poll [pəʊl] 1 *n* (a) votación *f*; **the polls** las elecciones; **to go to the polls** acudir a las urnas (b) *(survey)* encuesta *f*
2 *vt (votes)* obtener

pollen ['pɒlən] *n* polen *m*

polling ['pəʊlɪŋ] *n* votación *f*; **p. booth** cabina *f* electoral; **p. station** colegio *m* electoral

pollute [pə'luːt] *vt* contaminar

pollution [pə'luːʃən] *n* contaminación *f*, polución *f*; **environmental p.** contaminación ambiental

polo ['pəʊləʊ] *n Sport* polo *m*; **p. neck (sweater)** jersey *m* de cuello vuelto

polyester [pɒlɪ'estə(r)] *n* poliéster *m*

polyethylene [pɒlɪ'eθəliːn] *n US* polietileno *m*

polymer ['pɒlɪmə(r)] *n Chem* polímero *m*

Polynesia [pɒlɪ'niːʒɪə] *n* Polinesia

polystyrene [pɒlɪ'staɪriːn] *n* poliestireno *m*

polytechnic [pɒlɪ'teknɪk] *n* escuela politécnica, politécnico *m*

polythene ['pɒlɪθiːn] *n Br* polietileno *m*

pomegranate ['pɒmɪgrænɪt] *n* granada *f*

pomp [pɒmp] *n* pompa *f*

pompom ['pɒmpɒm], **pompon** ['pɒmpɒn] *n* borla *f*, pompón *m*

pompous ['pɒmpəs] *adj (person)* presumido(a); *(speech)* rimbombante

pond [pɒnd] *n* estanque *m*

ponder ['pɒndə(r)] 1 *vt* considerar
2 *vi* **to p. over sth** meditar sobre algo

ponderous ['pɒndərəs] *adj* pesado(a)

pong [pɒŋ] *n Br Fam* hedor *m*

pontoon¹ [pɒn'tuːn] *n Constr* pontón *m*

pontoon² [pɒn'tuːn] *n Cards* veintiuna *f*

pony ['pəʊnɪ] *n* poney *m*

ponytail ['pəʊnɪteɪl] *n* cola *f* de caballo

poodle ['puːdəl] *n* caniche *m*

poof [pʊf] *n Br Fam Pej* marica *m*

pool¹ [puːl] *n (of water, oil etc)* charco *m*; *(pond)* estanque *m*; *(in river)* pozo *m*; **swimming p.** piscina *f*

pool² [puːl] 1 *n* (a) *(common fund)* fondo *m* común (b) **typing p.** servicio *m* de mecanografía (c) *US (snooker)* billar americano (d) *Br* **football pools** quinielas *fpl*
2 *vt (funds)* reunir; *(ideas, resources)* juntar

poor [pʊə(r)] 1 *adj* pobre; *(quality)* malo(a); *Fam* **you p. thing!** ¡pobrecito!
2 *npl* **the p.** los pobres

poorly ['pʊəlɪ] 1 *adv (badly)* mal
2 *adj (poorlier, poorliest)* *(ill)* mal, malo(a)

pop [pɒp] 1 *vt (burst)* hacer reventar; *(cork)* hacer saltar
2 *vi (burst)* reventar; *(cork)* saltar; *Fam* **I'm just popping over to Ian's** voy un momento a casa de Ian
3 *n* (a) *(noise)* pequeña explosión (b) *Fam (drink)* gaseosa *f* (c) *US Fam (father)* papá *m* (d) *Fam Mus* música *f* pop; **p. singer** cantante *mf* pop
▸ **pop in** *vi Fam* entrar un momento, pasar

popcorn ['pɒpkɔːn] *n* palomitas *fpl*

Pope [pəʊp] *n* **the P.** el Papa

poplar ['pɒplə(r)] *n* álamo *m*

poppy ['pɒpɪ] *n* amapola *f*

Popsicle® [ˈpɒpsɪkəl] *n US* polo *m*

populace [ˈpɒpjʊləs] *n (people)* pueblo *m*

popular [ˈpɒpjʊlə(r)] *adj* popular; *(fashionable)* de moda; *(common)* corriente

popularity [pɒpjʊˈlærɪtɪ] *n* popularidad *f*

popularize [ˈpɒpjʊləraɪz] *vt* popularizar

populate [ˈpɒpjʊleɪt] *vt* poblar

population [pɒpjʊˈleɪʃən] *n* población *f*; **the p. explosion** la explosión demográfica

porcelain [ˈpɔːsəlɪn] *n* porcelana *f*

porch [pɔːtʃ] *n (of church)* pórtico *m*; *(of house)* porche *m*, entrada *f*; *US (veranda)* terraza *f*

porcupine [ˈpɔːkjʊpaɪn] *n* puerco *m* espín

pore¹ [pɔː(r)] *vi* **to p. over sth** leer *or* estudiar algo detenidamente

pore² [pɔː(r)] *n Anat* poro *m*

pork [pɔːk] *n* carne *f* de cerdo

pornography [pɔːˈnɒgrəfɪ] *n* pornografía *f*

porous [ˈpɔːrəs] *adj* poroso(a)

porpoise [ˈpɔːpəs] *n* marsopa *f*

porridge [ˈpɒrɪdʒ] *n* gachas *fpl* de avena

port¹ [pɔːt] *n (harbour)* puerto *m*; **p. of call** puerto de escala

port² [pɔːt] *n Naut & Av* babor *m*

port³ [pɔːt] *n (wine)* vino *m* de Oporto, oporto *m*

portable [ˈpɔːtəbəl] *adj* portátil

portal [ˈpɔːtəl] *n Comput (web page)* portal *m*

portent [ˈpɔːtent] *n Fml* augurio *m*

porter [ˈpɔːtə(r)] *n (in hotel etc)* portero(a) *m,f*; *Rail* mozo *m* de estación; *US* mozo de los coches-cama

portfolio [pɔːtˈfəʊlɪəʊ] *n (file)* carpeta *f*; *(of artist, politician)* cartera *f*

porthole [ˈpɔːthəʊl] *n* portilla *f*

portion [ˈpɔːʃən] *n (part, piece)* parte *f*, porción *f*; *(of food)* ración *f*

▸ **portion out** *vt sep* repartir

portly [ˈpɔːtlɪ] *adj* (**portlier**, **portliest**) corpulento(a)

portrait [ˈpɔːtreɪt] *n* retrato *m*

portray [pɔːˈtreɪ] *vt (paint portrait of)* retratar; *(describe)* describir; *Th* representar

Portugal [ˈpɔːtjʊgəl] *n* Portugal

Portuguese [pɔːtjʊˈgiːz] **1** *adj* portugués(esa)

2 *n (person)* portugués(esa) *m,f*; *(language)* portugués *m*

pose [pəʊz] **1** *vt (problem)* plantear; *(threat)* representar

2 *vi (for painting)* posar; *Pej (behave affectedly)* hacer pose; **to p. as** hacerse pasar por

3 *n (stance)* postura *f*, *Pej (affectation)* pose *f*

posh [pɒʃ] *adj Br Fam* elegante, de lujo; *(person)* presumido(a); *(accent)* de clase alta

position [pəˈzɪʃən] **1** *n* (a) posición *f*; *(location)* situación *f*; *(rank)* rango *m*; **to be in a p. to do sth** estar en condiciones de hacer algo (b) *(opinion)* postura *f* (c) *(job)* puesto *m*

2 *vt* colocar

positive [ˈpɒzɪtɪv] *adj* positivo(a); *(sign)* favorable; *(proof)* incontrovertible; *(sure)* seguro(a); *Fam (absolute)* auténtico(a)

possess [pəˈzes] *vt* poseer; *(of fear)* apoderarse de

possessed [pəˈzest] *adj* poseído(a)

possession [pəˈzeʃən] *n* posesión *f*; **possessions** bienes *mpl*

possessive [pəˈzesɪv] *adj* posesivo(a)

possibility [pɒsɪˈbɪlɪtɪ] *n* posibilidad *f*; **possibilities** *(potential)* potencial *m*

possible [ˈpɒsɪbəl] *adj* posible; **as much as p.** todo lo posible; **as often as p.** cuanto más mejor; **as soon as p.** cuanto antes

possibly [ˈpɒsɪblɪ] *adv* posiblemente; *(perhaps)* tal vez, quizás; **I can't p. come** no puedo venir de ninguna manera

post¹ [pəʊst] **1** *n (of wood)* poste *m*

2 *vt (fix)* fijar

post² [pəʊst] **1** *n (job)* puesto *m*; *US* **trading p.** factoría *f*

2 *vt* enviar

post³ [pəʊst] *Br* **1** *n (mail)* correo *m*; **by p.** por correo; **p. office** oficina *f* de correos; **P. Office Box** apartado *m* de correos

2 *vt (letter)* echar al correo; **to p. sth to sb** mandar algo por correo a algn

postage [ˈpəʊstɪdʒ] *n* franqueo *m*

postal [ˈpəʊstəl] *adj* postal, de correos; *Br* **p. code** código *m* postal **p. order** giro *m* postal; **p. vote** voto *m* por correo

postbox [ˈpəʊstbɒks] *n Br* buzón *m*

postcard [ˈpəʊstkɑːd] *n (tarjeta f)* postal *f*

postcode [ˈpəʊstkəʊd] *n Br* código *m* postal

postdate [pəʊstˈdeɪt] *vt (cheque)* extender con fecha posterior

poster [ˈpəʊstə(r)] *n* póster *m*; *(advertising)* cartel *m*

posterior [pɒˈstɪərɪə(r)] **1** *n Hum* trasero *m*, pompis *m*

2 *adj* posterior

posterity [pɒˈsterɪtɪ] *n* posteridad *f*

postgraduate [pəʊst'grædjʊɪt] **1** *n* posgraduado(a) *m,f*
2 *adj* de posgraduado
posthumous ['pɒstjʊməs] *adj* póstumo(a)
postman ['pəʊstmən] *n Br* cartero *m*
postmark ['pəʊstmɑːk] *n* matasellos *m inv*
postmaster ['pəʊstmɑːstə(r)] *n* administrador *m* de correos; **p. general** director *m* general de correos
postmortem [pəʊst'mɔːtəm] *n* autopsia *f*
postpone [pəs'pəʊn] *vt* aplazar
postscript ['pəʊsskrɪpt] *n* posdata *f*
posture ['pɒstʃə(r)] **1** *n* postura *f*; *(affected)* pose *f*
2 *vi* adoptar una pose
postwar ['pəʊstwɔː(r)] *adj* de la posguerra
posy ['pəʊzɪ] *n* ramillete *m*
pot [pɒt] **1** *n (container)* tarro *m*, pote *m*; *(for cooking)* olla *f*; *(for flowers)* maceta *f*; *Fam* **to go to p.** irse al traste; **p. shot** tiro *m* al azar
2 *vt (plant)* poner en una maceta
potassium [pə'tæsɪəm] *n* potasio *m*
potato [pə'teɪtəʊ] *n (pl potatoes)* patata *f*, *Am* papa *f*
potent ['pəʊtənt] *adj* potente
potential [pə'tenʃəl] **1** *adj* potencial, posible
2 *n* potencial *m*
potentially [pə'tenʃəlɪ] *adv* en potencia
pothole ['pɒthəʊl] *n Geol* cueva *f*; *(in road)* bache *m*
potholing ['pɒthəʊlɪŋ] *n Br* espeleología *f*
potion ['pəʊʃən] *n* poción *f*, pócima *f*
potluck [pɒt'lʌk] *n Fam* **to take p.** conformarse con lo que haya
potted ['pɒtɪd] *adj (food)* en conserva; *(plant)* en maceta *or* tiesto
potter¹ ['pɒtə(r)] *n* alfarero(a) *m,f*
potter² ['pɒtə(r)] *vi Br* **to p. about** *or* **around** entretenerse
pottery ['pɒtərɪ] *n (craft, place)* alfarería *f*; *(objects)* cerámica *f*
potty¹ ['pɒtɪ] *adj* **(pottier, pottiest)** *Br Fam* chiflado(a)
potty² ['pɒtɪ] *n Fam* orinal *m*
pouch [paʊtʃ] *n* **(a)** bolsa pequeña; *(for ammunition)* morral *m*; *(for tobacco)* petaca *f* **(b)** *Zool* bolsa *f* abdominal
poultry ['pəʊltrɪ] *n (live)* aves *fpl* de corral; *(food)* pollos *mpl*
pounce [paʊns] *vi* **to p. on** abalanzarse encima de

pound¹ [paʊnd] **1** *vt (strike)* aporrear
2 *vi (heart)* palpitar; *(walk heavily)* andar con paso pesado
pound² [paʊnd] *n (money, weight)* libra *f*
pound³ [paʊnd] *n (for dogs)* perrera *f*; *(for cars)* depósito *m* de coches
pour [pɔː(r)] **1** *vt* echar, verter; **to p. sb a drink** servirle una copa a algn
2 *vi* correr, fluir; **it's pouring with rain** está lloviendo a cántaros
▸ **pour out** *vt sep* echar, verter; *Fig* **to p. one's heart out to sb** desahogarse con algn
pouring ['pɔːrɪŋ] *adj (rain)* torrencial
pout [paʊt] **1** *vi* hacer pucheros
2 *n* puchero *m*
poverty ['pɒvətɪ] *n* pobreza *f*
poverty-stricken ['pɒvətɪstrɪkən] *adj* necesitado(a); **to be p.** vivir en la miseria
powder ['paʊdə(r)] **1** *n* polvo *m*; **p. compact** polvera *f*; **p. keg** polvorín *m*; **p. puff** borla *f*; **p. room** servicios *mpl* de señoras
2 *vt* **to p. one's nose** ponerse polvos en la cara; *Euph* ir a los servicios *or* al tocador
powdered ['paʊdəd] *adj (milk)* en polvo
power ['paʊə(r)] **1** *n* **(a)** fuerza *f*; *(energy)* energía *f*; *Elec* **to cut off the p.** cortar la corriente; **p. point** enchufe *m*; **p. station** central eléctrica **(b)** *(ability)* poder *m* **(c)** *(authority)* poder *m*; *(nation)* potencia *f*; *(influence)* influencia *f*; **to be in p.** estar en el poder; *Pol* **to come into p.** subir al poder; **the p. of veto** el derecho de veto **(d)** *Tech* potencia *f*; *(output)* rendimiento *m*
2 *vt* propulsar, impulsar
powerboat ['paʊəbəʊt] *n* lancha *f* (motora)
powerful ['paʊəfʊl] *adj (strong)* fuerte; *(influential)* poderoso(a); *(remedy)* eficaz; *(engine, machine)* potente; *(emotion)* fuerte; *(speech)* conmovedor(a)
powerless ['paʊəlɪs] *adj* impotente, ineficaz
pp *(abbr pages)* págs., pp
PR [piː'ɑː(r)] *(abbr* **public relations***)* relaciones *fpl* públicas
practicable ['præktɪkəbəl] *adj* factible
practical ['præktɪkəl] *adj* práctico(a); *(useful)* útil; *(sensible)* adecuado(a)
practicality [præktɪ'kælɪtɪ] *n (of suggestion, plan)* factibilidad *f*; **practicalities** detalles prácticos
practically ['præktɪkəlɪ] *adv (almost)* casi
practice ['præktɪs] **1** *n* **(a)** *(habit)* costumbre *f* **(b)** *(exercise)* práctica *f*; *Sport*

entrenamiento *m*; *Mus* ensayo *m*; **to be out of p.** no estar en forma (**c**) *(way of doing sth)* práctica *f*; **in p.** en la práctica; **to put sth into p.** poner algo en práctica (**d**) *(of profession)* ejercicio *m* (**e**) *(place) (of doctors)* consultorio *m*; *(of lawyers)* bufete *m* (**f**) *(clients) (of doctors)* pacientes *mpl*; *(of lawyers)* clientela *f*

2 *vt & vi US* = **practise**

practicing ['præktɪsɪŋ] *adj US* = **practising**

practise ['præktɪs] **1** *vt* practicar; *(method)* seguir; *(principle)* poner en práctica; *Mus* ensayar; *(profession)* ejercer

2 *vi* practicar; *Sport* entrenar; *Mus* ensayar; *(doctor)* practicar; *(lawyer)* ejercer

practising ['præktɪsɪŋ] *adj (doctor etc)* en ejercicio; *(Christian etc)* practicante

practitioner [præk'tɪʃənə(r)] *n Br Med* **general p.** médico(a) *m,f* de cabecera; **medical p.** médico(a) *m,f*

pragmatic [præg'mætɪk] *adj* pragmático(a)

prairie ['preərɪ] *n* pradera *f*; *US* llanura *f*

praise [preɪz] **1** *n* alabanza *f*

2 *vt* alabar, elogiar

praiseworthy ['preɪzwɜːðɪ] *adj* loable

pram [præm] *n Br* cochecito *m* de niño

prance [prɑːns] *vi (horse)* encabritarse; **to p. about** *(person)* pegar brincos

prank [præŋk] *n* broma *f*; *(of child)* travesura *f*

prat [præt] *n Br Fam* soplagaitas *mf inv*, *Am* pendejo(a) *m,f*

prawn [prɔːn] *n* gamba *f*

pray [preɪ] *vi* rezar, orar

prayer [preə(r)] *n* rezo *m*, oración *f*; *(entreaty)* súplica *f*; **p. book** misal *m*

preach [priːtʃ] *vi* predicar

preacher ['priːtʃə(r)] *n* predicador(a) *m,f*

precarious [prɪ'keərɪəs] *adj* precario(a)

precaution [prɪ'kɔːʃən] *n* precaución *f*

precede [prɪ'siːd] *vt* preceder

precedence ['presɪdəns] *n* preferencia *f*, prioridad *f*; **to take p. over sth/sb** tener prioridad sobre algo/algn

precedent ['presɪdənt] *n* precedente *m*

preceding [prɪ'siːdɪŋ] *adj* precedente

precinct ['priːsɪŋkt] *n* (**a**) *(area)* recinto *m*; **pedestrian/shopping p.** zona *f* peatonal/comercial (**b**) *US (administrative, police division)* distrito *m*; *(police station)* comisaría *f* (de policía)

> Note that the Spanish word **precinto** is a false friend and is never a translation for the English word **precinct**. In Spanish, **precinto** means "seal".

precious ['preʃəs] **1** *adj* precioso(a); **p. stones** piedras preciosas

2 *adv Fam* **p. little/few** muy poco/pocos

precipice ['presɪpɪs] *n* precipicio *m*

precipitate 1 *vt* [prɪ'sɪpɪteɪt] precipitar; *Fig* arrojar

2 *adj* [prɪ'sɪpɪtət] precipitado(a)

precise [prɪ'saɪs] *adj* preciso(a), exacto(a); *(meticulous)* meticuloso(a)

precisely [prɪ'saɪslɪ] *adv (exactly)* precisamente, exactamente; **p.!** ¡eso es!, ¡exacto!

precision [prɪ'sɪʒən] *n* precisión *f*

preclude [prɪ'kluːd] *vt* excluir; *(misunderstanding)* evitar

precocious [prɪ'kəʊʃəs] *adj* precoz

preconceived [priːkən'siːvd] *adj* preconcebido(a)

precondition [priːkən'dɪʃən] *n* condición previa

precursor [priː'kɜːsə(r)] *n* precursor(a) *m,f*

predator ['predətə(r)] *n* depredador *m*

predecessor ['priːdɪsesə(r)] *n* antecesor(a) *m,f*

predetermine [priːdɪ'tɜːmɪn] *vt* predeterminar

predicament [prɪ'dɪkəmənt] *n* apuro *m*, aprieto *m*

predict [prɪ'dɪkt] *vt* predecir, pronosticar

predictable [prɪ'dɪktəbəl] *adj* previsible

prediction [prɪ'dɪkʃən] *n* pronóstico *m*

predispose [priːdɪ'spəʊz] *vt* **to be predisposed to doing sth** estar predispuesto(a) a hacer algo

predominant [prɪ'dɒmɪnənt] *adj* predominante

predominantly [prɪ'dɒmɪnəntlɪ] *adv* en su mayoría

predominate [prɪ'dɒmɪneɪt] *vi* predominar

pre-empt [prɪ'empt] *vt* adelantarse a

preen [priːn] *vt* **to p. oneself** *(of bird)* arreglarse las plumas; *Fig (of person)* pavonearse

prefab ['priːfæb] *n Br Fam (house)* casa prefabricada

prefabricated [priː'fæbrɪkeɪtɪd] *adj* prefabricado(a)

preface ['prefɪs] **1** *n* prefacio *m*

2 *vt* prologar

prefect ['priːfekt] *n Br Educ* monitor(a) *m,f*

prefer [prɪ'fɜː(r)] *vt* preferir; **I p. coffee to tea** prefiero el café al té

preferable ['prefərəbəl] *adj* preferible (**to** a)

preferably ['prefərəblɪ] adv preferentemente

preference ['prefərəns] n preferencia f; (priority) prioridad f; **to give p. to sth** dar prioridad a algo

preferential [prefə'renʃəl] adj preferente

prefix ['pri:fɪks] n prefijo m

pregnancy ['pregnənsɪ] n embarazo m

pregnant ['pregnənt] adj (woman) embarazada; (animal) preñada; Fig **a p. pause** una pausa cargada de significado

prehistoric(al) [pri:hɪ'stɒrɪk(əl)] adj prehistórico(a)

prejudice ['predʒʊdɪs] 1 n (bias) prejuicio m; (harm) perjuicio m
2 vt (bias) predisponer; (harm) perjudicar

prejudiced ['predʒʊdɪst] adj parcial; **to be p. against/in favour of** estar predispuesto(a) en contra/a favor de

preliminary [prɪ'lɪmɪnərɪ] 1 adj preliminar; Sport (round) eliminatorio(a)
2 n preliminaries preliminares mpl

prelude ['prelju:d] n preludio m

premarital [pri:'mærɪtəl] adj prematrimonial

premature [premə'tjʊə(r), 'premətjʊə(r)] adj prematuro(a)

prematurely [premə'tjʊəlɪ, 'premətjʊəlɪ] adv antes de tiempo

premeditate [prɪ'medɪteɪt] vt (crime) premeditar

premenstrual [pri:'menstrʊəl] adj **p. tension** tensión f premenstrual

premier ['premjə(r)] 1 n Pol primer(a) ministro(a) m,f
2 adj primer, primero(a)

premiere ['premɪeə(r)] n Cin estreno m

premise ['premɪs] n premisa f

premises ['premɪsɪz] npl local m; **on the p.** en el local

premium ['pri:mɪəm] n Com, Fin & Ind prima f; **to be at a p.** tener sobreprecio; Fig estar muy solicitado(a); Br **p. bonds** = bonos numerados emitidos por el Gobierno británico, cuyo comprador entra en un sorteo mensual de premios en metálico

premonition [premə'nɪʃən] n presentimiento m

preoccupied [pri:'ɒkjʊpaɪd] adj preocupado(a); **to be p. with sth** preocuparse por algo

prep [prep] n Br Fam deberes mpl; **p. school** = colegio privado para alumnos de entre 7 y 13 años

prepacked [pri:'pækt] adj empaquetado(a)

prepaid [pri:'peɪd] adj con el porte pagado

preparation [prepə'reɪʃən] n preparación f; (plan) preparativo m

preparatory [prɪ'pærətərɪ] adj preparatorio(a), preliminar; **p. school** Br = colegio privado para alumnos de entre 7 y 13 años; US = escuela secundaria privada

prepare [prɪ'peə(r)] 1 vt preparar; **to p. to do sth** prepararse para hacer algo
2 vi prepararse (**for** para)

prepared [prɪ'peəd] adj (ready) preparado(a); **to be p. to do sth** (willing) estar dispuesto(a) a hacer algo

preponderance [prɪ'pɒndərəns] n preponderancia f

preposition [prepə'zɪʃən] n preposición f

preposterous [prɪ'pɒstərəs] adj absurdo(a), ridículo(a)

prerequisite [pri:'rekwɪzɪt] n condición f previa

prerogative [prɪ'rɒgətɪv] n prerrogativa f

preschool [pri:'sku:l] adj preescolar

prescribe [prɪ'skraɪb] vt (set down) prescribir; Med recetar; Fig (recommend) recomendar

prescription [prɪ'skrɪpʃən] n Med receta f

presence ['prezəns] n presencia f; (attendance) asistencia f; Fig **p. of mind** presencia de ánimo

present¹ ['prezənt] 1 adj (a) (in attendance) presente; Ling **p. tense** (tiempo m) presente m; **to be p. at** estar presente en (b) (current) actual
2 n (time) presente m, actualidad f; **at p.** actualmente; **for the p.** de momento; **up to the p.** hasta ahora

present² 1 vt [prɪ'zent] (a) (give as gift) regalar; (medals, prizes etc) entregar; **to p. sb with sth** obsequiar a algn con algo (b) (report etc) presentar; (opportunity) ofrecer; (problems) plantear (c) (introduce) (person, programme) presentar
2 n ['prezənt] (gift) regalo m; (formal) obsequio m

presentable [prɪ'zentəbəl] adj presentable; **to make oneself p.** arreglarse

presentation [prezən'teɪʃən] n (a) presentación f; **p. ceremony** ceremonia f de entrega (b) Rad & TV representación f

present-day ['prezəntdeɪ] adj actual, de hoy en día

presenter [prɪ'zentə(r)] n Rad locutor(a) m,f; TV presentador(a) m,f

presently ['prezntlɪ] *adv (soon)* dentro de poco; *US (now)* ahora

preservation [prezə'veɪʃən] *n* conservación *f*

preservative [prɪ'zɜ:vətɪv] *n* conservante *m*

preserve [prɪ'zɜ:v] **1** *vt* (**a**) *(keep)* mantener (**b**) Culin conservar

2 *n* (**a**) *(hunting)* coto *m* (**b**) Culin conserva *f*

preside [prɪ'zaɪd] *vi* presidir

president ['prezɪdənt] *n* Pol presidente(a) *m,f*; *US Com* director(a) *m,f*, gerente *mf*

presidential [prezɪ'denʃəl] *adj* presidencial

press [pres] **1** *vt* (**a**) apretar; *(button)* pulsar; *(grapes)* pisar; *(trousers etc)* planchar

(**b**) *(urge)* presionar; **to p. sb to do sth** acosar a algn para que haga algo

2 *vi* (**a**) *(push)* apretar; **to p. against sb/ sth** apretarse contra algn/algo; **to p. (down) on sth** hacer presión sobre algo

(**b**) *(urge)* apremiar; **time presses** el tiempo apremia

3 *n* (**a**) **p. stud** botón *m* de presión

(**b**) *(machine)* prensa *f*; **to go to p.** *(of newspaper)* entrar en prensa

(**c**) *Press* prensa *f*; **the p.** la prensa; **to get a good/bad p.** tener buena/mala prensa; **p. agency** agencia *f* de prensa; **p. conference** rueda *f* de prensa; **p. cutting** recorte *m* de prensa

▸ **press on** *vi* seguir adelante

pressed [prest] *adj* **to be (hard) p. for** andar escaso(a) de; **I'd be hard p. to do it** me costaría mucho hacerlo

pressing ['presɪŋ] *adj* apremiante, urgente

press-up ['presʌp] *n Br* flexión *f* (de brazos)

pressure ['preʃə(r)] *n* presión *f*; *Med & Met* **high/low p.** altas/bajas presiones; **p. cooker** olla *f* a presión; **p. gauge** manómetro *m*; *Fig* **to bring p. (to bear) on sb** ejercer presión sobre algn

pressurize ['preʃəraɪz] *vt Fig* presionar; **pressurized cabin** cabina presurizada

prestige [pre'sti:ʒ] *n* prestigio *m*

presumably [prɪ'zju:məblɪ] *adv* es de suponer que

presume [prɪ'zju:m] **1** *vt* suponer, presumir

2 *vi (suppose)* suponer; **we p. so/not** suponemos que sí/no

presumption [prɪ'zʌmpʃən] *n* (**a**) *(supposition)* suposición *f* (**b**) *(boldness)* osadía *f*; *(conceit)* presunción *f*

presumptuous [prɪ'zʌmptjʊəs] *adj* impertinente

> 🖋 Note that the Spanish word **presuntuoso** is a false friend and is never a translation for the English word **presumptuous**. In Spanish, **presuntuoso** means "vain" and "pretentious".

presuppose [pri:sə'pəʊz] *vt* presuponer

pretence [prɪ'tens] *n* (**a**) *(deception)* fingimiento *m*; **false pretences** estafa *f*; **under the p. of** so pretexto de (**b**) *(claim)* pretensión *f*

pretend [prɪ'tend] **1** *vt (feign)* fingir, aparentar; *(claim)* pretender

2 *vi (feign)* fingir

pretense [prɪ'tens] *n US* = **pretence**

pretention [prɪ'tenʃən] *n* pretensión *f*

pretentious [prɪ'tenʃəs] *adj* presuntuoso(a), pretencioso(a)

pretext ['pri:tekst] *n* pretexto *m*; **on the p. of** so pretexto de

pretty ['prɪtɪ] **1** *adj* (**prettier, prettiest**) bonito(a), guapo(a)

2 *adv Fam* bastante; **p. much the same** más o menos lo mismo

prevail [prɪ'veɪl] *vi* (**a**) predominar (**b**) *(win through)* prevalecer (**c**) **to p. upon** or **on sb to do sth** *(persuade)* persuadir or convencer a algn para que haga algo

prevailing [prɪ'veɪlɪŋ] *adj (wind)* predominante; *(opinion)* general; *(condition, fashion)* actual

prevalent ['prevələnt] *adj* predominante; *(illness)* extendido(a)

prevaricate [prɪ'værɪkeɪt] *vi* andar con ambages

prevent [prɪ'vent] *vt* impedir; *(accident)* evitar; *(illness)* prevenir; **to p. sb from doing sth** impedir a algn hacer algo; **to p. sth from happening** evitar que pase algo

prevention [prɪ'venʃən] *n* prevención *f*

preventive [prɪ'ventɪv] *adj* preventivo(a)

preview ['pri:vju:] *n (of film etc)* preestreno *m*

previous ['pri:vɪəs] **1** *adj* anterior, previo(a); **p. conviction** antecedente *m* penal

2 *adv* **p. to going** antes de ir

previously ['pri:vɪəslɪ] *adv* anteriormente, previamente

prewar ['pri:wɔ:(r)] *adj* de antes de la guerra

prey [preɪ] **1** *n* presa *f*; *Fig* víctima *f*

2 *vi* **to p. on** alimentarse de

price [praɪs] **1** *n* precio *m*; **what p. is that**

coat? ¿cuánto cuesta el abrigo?; **p. list** lista *f* de precios; **p. tag** etiqueta *f*

2 *vt* (*put price on*) poner un precio a; (*value*) valorar

priceless ['praɪslɪs] *adj* que no tiene precio

prick [prɪk] **1** *vt* picar; **to p. one's finger** pincharse el dedo; *Fig* **to p. up one's ears** aguzar el oído

2 *n* (**a**) (*with pin*) pinchazo *m* (**b**) *very Fam* (*penis*) polla *f* (**c**) *very Fam Pej* (*person*) gilipollas *mf inv*

prickle ['prɪkəl] **1** *n* espina *f*; (*spike*) pincho *m*; (*sensation*) picor *m*

2 *vt* & *vi* pinchar, picar

prickly ['prɪklɪ] *adj* (**pricklier, prickliest**) espinoso(a); *Fig* (*touchy*) enojadizo(a); **p. heat** = sarpullido por causa del calor; **p. pear** higo chumbo

pride [praɪd] **1** *n* orgullo *m*; (*arrogance*) soberbia *f*; **to take p. in sth** enorgullecerse de algo

2 *vt* **to p. oneself on** enorgullecerse de

priest [priːst] *n* sacerdote *m*, cura *m*

priestess ['priːstɪs] *n* sacerdotisa *f*

priesthood ['priːsthʊd] *n* (*clergy*) clero *m*; (*office*) sacerdocio *m*

prig [prɪg] *n* gazmoño(a) *m,f*, mojigato(a) *m,f*

prim [prɪm] *adj* (**primmer, primmest**) **p. (and proper)** remilgado(a)

primaeval [praɪˈmiːvəl] *adj* primitivo(a)

primarily ['praɪmərɪlɪ] *adv* ante todo

primary ['praɪmərɪ] **1** *adj* fundamental, principal; **of p. importance** primordial; **p. colour** color primario; **p. education/school** enseñanza/escuela primaria

2 *n US Pol* (*elección f*) primaria *f*

primate¹ ['praɪmeɪt] *n Rel* primado *m*

primate² ['praɪmeɪt] *n Zool* primate *m*

prime [praɪm] **1** *adj* (**a**) principal; (*major*) primordial; **P. Minister** primer(a) ministro(a) *m,f* (**b**) (*first-rate*) de primera; **p. number** número primo

2 *n* **in the p. of life** en la flor de la vida

3 *vt* (*pump, engine*) cebar; (*surface*) imprimar; *Fig* (*prepare*) preparar

primer¹ ['praɪmə(r)] *n* (*textbook*) cartilla *f*

primer² ['praɪmə(r)] *n* (*paint*) imprimación *f*

primeval [praɪˈmiːvəl] *adj* = **primaeval**

primitive ['prɪmɪtɪv] *adj* primitivo(a); (*method, tool*) rudimentario(a)

primrose ['prɪmrəʊz] *n* primavera *f*

Primus® ['praɪməs] *n* hornillo *m* de camping

prince [prɪns] *n* príncipe *m*; **P. Charming** Príncipe Azul

princess [prɪnˈses] *n* princesa *f*

principal ['prɪnsɪpəl] **1** *adj* principal

2 *n Educ* director(a) *m,f*; *Th* (*in play*) protagonista *mf* principal

principle ['prɪnsɪpəl] *n* principio *m*; **in p.** en principio; **on p.** por principio

print [prɪnt] **1** *vt* (**a**) imprimir; (*publish*) publicar; *Fig* grabar; **printed matter** impresos *mpl* (**b**) (*write*) escribir con letra de imprenta

2 *n* (**a**) (*of hand, foot*) huella *f* (**b**) (*written text*) letra *f*; **out of p.** agotado(a) (**c**) *Tex* estampado *m*; **p. skirt** falda estampada (**d**) *Art* grabado *m*; *Phot* copia *f*

▸ **print out** *vt sep Comput* imprimir

printer ['prɪntə(r)] *n* (*person*) impresor(a) *m,f*; (*machine*) impresora *f*

printing ['prɪntɪŋ] *n* (*industry*) imprenta *f*; (*process*) impresión *f*; (*print run*) tirada *f*; **p. press** prensa *f*

print-out ['prɪntaʊt] *n Comput* impresión *f*; (*copy*) copia impresa

prior ['praɪə(r)] *adj* previo(a), anterior; **p. to leaving** antes de salir

priority [praɪˈɒrɪtɪ] *n* prioridad *f*

prise [praɪz] *vt* **to p. sth open** abrir algo con palanca; **to p. sth off** arrancar algo

prism ['prɪzəm] *n* prisma *f*

prison ['prɪzən] *n* cárcel *f*, prisión *f*

prisoner ['prɪzənə(r)] *n* preso(a) *m,f*; **to hold sb p.** detener a algn; **p. of war** prisionero(a) *m,f* de guerra

privacy ['praɪvəsɪ, 'prɪvəsɪ] *n* intimidad *f*

private ['praɪvɪt] **1** *adj* privado(a); (*secretary*) particular; (*matter*) personal; (*letter*) confidencial; **one's p. life** la vida privada de uno; **p.** (*notice*) (*on road*) carretera privada; (*on gate*) propiedad privada; (*on envelope*) confidencial; **p. detective**, *Fam* **p. eye** detective *mf* privado(a); **p. school** escuela privada

2 *n Mil* soldado raso

privately ['praɪvɪtlɪ] *adv* en privado; (*personally*) personalmente

privet ['prɪvɪt] *n* alheña *f*

privilege ['prɪvɪlɪdʒ] *n* privilegio *m*

privileged ['prɪvɪlɪdʒd] *adj* privilegiado(a)

privy ['prɪvɪ] **1** *adj Br* **P. Council** Consejo Privado; **to be p. to sth** estar enterado(a) de algo

2 *n* (*lavatory*) retrete *m*

prize [praɪz] **1** *n* premio *m*

2 *adj* (*first-class*) de primera (categoría *or* clase)

3 *vt* (*value*) apreciar, valorar

prize-giving ['praɪzgɪvɪŋ] *n* distribución *f* de premios

prizewinner ['praɪzwɪnə(r)] *n* premiado(a) *m,f*

pro¹ [prəʊ] *n* pro *m*; **the pros and cons of an issue** los pros y los contras de una cuestión

pro² [prəʊ] *n Fam* profesional *mf*

pro- [prəʊ] *pref (in favour of)* pro-

probability [prɒbə'bɪlɪtɪ] *n* probabilidad *f*

probable ['prɒbəbəl] *adj* probable

probably ['prɒbəblɪ] *adv* probablemente

probation [prə'beɪʃən] *n Jur* **to be on p.** estar en libertad condicional; **to be on two months' p.** *(at work)* trabajar dos meses de prueba

probe [prəʊb] **1** *n Med & (in outer space)* sonda *f*; *(investigation)* sondeo *m*

  2 *vt Med* sondar; *(investigate)* investigar
  ▸ **probe into** *vt insep* investigar

problem ['prɒbləm] *n* problema *m*

problematic(al) [prɒblə'mætɪk(əl)] *adj* problemático(a); **it's p.** tiene sus problemas

procedure [prə'si:dʒə(r)] *n* procedimiento *m*; *(legal, business)* gestión *f*, trámite *m*

proceed [prə'si:d] *vi* seguir, proceder; **to p. to do sth** ponerse a hacer algo; **to p. to the next matter** pasar a la siguiente cuestión

proceedings [prə'si:dɪŋz] *npl (of meeting)* actas *fpl*; *(measures)* medidas *fpl*; *Jur* proceso *m*

proceeds ['prəʊsi:dz] *npl* ganancias *fpl*

process ['prəʊsəs] **1** *n* proceso *m*; *(method)* método *m*, sistema *m*; **in the p. of** en vías de

  2 *vt (information)* tramitar; *(food)* tratar; *Comput* procesar

processing ['prəʊsesɪŋ] *n (of information)* evaluación *f*; *Comput* tratamiento *m*

procession [prə'seʃən] *n* desfile *m*; *Rel* procesión *f*

proclaim [prə'kleɪm] *vt* proclamar, declarar

proclamation [prɒklə'meɪʃən] *n* proclamación *f*

procrastinate [prəʊ'kræstɪneɪt] *vi* dejar las cosas para después

procure [prə'kjʊə(r)] *vt* conseguir, procurarse

prod [prɒd] *vt (with stick etc)* golpear; *(push)* empujar

prodigal ['prɒdɪgəl] *adj* pródigo(a)

prodigious [prə'dɪdʒəs] *adj* prodigioso(a)

prodigy ['prɒdɪdʒɪ] *n* prodigio *m*

produce 1 *vt* [prə'dju:s] **(a)** producir; *Ind* fabricar **(b)** *Th* dirigir; *Rad & TV* realizar; *Cin* producir **(c)** *(give birth to)* dar a luz a **(d)** *(document)* enseñar; *(bring out)* sacar

  2 *n* ['prɒdju:s] productos *mpl*; **p. of Spain** producto *m* de España

producer [prə'dju:sə(r)] *n* **(a)** productor(a) *m,f*; *Ind* fabricante *mf* **(b)** *Th* director(a) *m,f* de escena; *Rad & TV* realizador(a) *m,f*; *Cin* productor(a) *m,f*

product ['prɒdʌkt] *n* producto *m*

production [prə'dʌkʃən] *n* **(a)** producción *f*; *Ind* fabricación *f* **(b)** *Th* representación *f*; *Rad & TV* realización *f*; *Cin* producción *f*; **p. line** cadena *f* de montaje

productive [prə'dʌktɪv] *adj* productivo(a)

productivity [prɒdʌk'tɪvɪtɪ] *n* productividad *f*

profane [prə'feɪn] *adj (secular)* profano(a); *(language)* blasfemo(a)

profess [prə'fes] *vt (faith)* profesar; *(opinion)* expresar; *(claim)* pretender

profession [prə'feʃən] *n* profesión *f*

professional [prə'feʃənəl] **1** *adj* profesional; *(soldier)* de profesión; *(polished)* de gran calidad

  2 *n* profesional *mf*

professor [prə'fesə(r)] *n Univ Br* catedrático(a) *m,f*; *US* profesor(a) *m,f*

proficiency [prə'fɪʃənsɪ] *n (in language)* capacidad *f*; *(in skill)* pericia *f*

proficient [prə'fɪʃənt] *adj (in language)* experto(a); *(in skill)* hábil

profile ['prəʊfaɪl] *n* perfil *m*; **in p.** de perfil

profit ['prɒfɪt] **1** *n* **(a)** beneficio *m*, ganancia *f*; **to make a p. on** sacar beneficios de **(b)** *Fml (benefit)* provecho *m*

  2 *vi Fig* sacar provecho; **to p. from** aprovecharse de

profitability [prɒfɪtə'bɪlɪtɪ] *n* rentabilidad *f*

profitable ['prɒfɪtəbəl] *adj Com* rentable; *Fig (worthwhile)* provechoso(a)

profiteer [prɒfɪ'tɪə(r)] **1** *n* especulador(a) *m,f*

  2 *vi* obtener beneficios excesivos

profound [prə'faʊnd] *adj* profundo(a)

profuse [prə'fju:s] *adj* profuso(a), abundante

profusely [prə'fju:slɪ] *adv* con profusión; **to sweat p.** sudar mucho

profusion [prə'fju:ʒən] *n* profusión *f*, abundancia *f*

prognosis [prɒg'nəʊsɪs] *n Med* pronóstico *m*; *Fig (prediction)* augurio *m*

program ['prəʊɡræm] *Comput* **1** *n* programa *m*
  2 *vi* & *vt* programar
  3 *US* = **programme**

programer ['prəʊɡræmər] *n US* = **programmer**

programme ['prəʊɡræm] **1** *n* programa *m*; *(plan)* plan *m*
  2 *vt* (**a**) *(plan)* planear, planificar (**b**) *(computer)* programar

programmer ['prəʊɡræmə(r)] *n* programador(a) *m,f*

progress 1 *n* ['prəʊɡres] progreso *m*; *(development)* desarrollo *m*; *Med* mejora *f*; **to make p.** hacer progresos; **in p.** en curso
  2 *vi* [prəʊ'ɡres] avanzar; *(develop)* desarrollar; *(improve)* hacer progresos; *Med* mejorar

progressive [prə'ɡresɪv] *adj (increasing)* progresivo(a); *Pol* progresista

progressively [prə'ɡresɪvlɪ] *adv* progresivamente

prohibit [prə'hɪbɪt] *vt* prohibir; **to p. sb from doing sth** prohibir a algn hacer algo

prohibitive [prə'hɪbɪtɪv] *adj* prohibitivo(a)

project 1 *n* ['prɒdʒekt] proyecto *m*; *(plan)* plan *m*; *Educ* trabajo *m*; *US* **(housing) p.** = urbanización con viviendas de protección oficial
  2 *vt* [prə'dʒekt] proyectar, planear
  3 *vi (stick out)* sobresalir

projectile [prə'dʒektaɪl] *n Fml* proyectil *m*

projection [prə'dʒekʃən] *n* (**a**) *(overhang)* saliente *m* (**b**) *Cin* proyección *f* (**c**) *(forecast)* proyección *f*

projector [prə'dʒektə(r)] *n Cin* proyector *m*

proletariat [prəʊlɪ'eərɪət] *n* proletariado *m*

prolific [prə'lɪfɪk] *adj* prolífico(a)

prologue ['prəʊlɒɡ] *n* prólogo *m*

prolong [prə'lɒŋ] *vt* prolongar

prom [prɒm] *n Br Fam (seafront)* paseo marítimo; *Br (concert)* = concierto sinfónico en que parte del público está de pie; *US (school dance)* = baile de fin de curso

promenade [prɒmə'nɑːd] **1** *n (at seaside)* paseo marítimo
  2 *vi* pasearse

prominence ['prɒmɪnəns] *n* prominencia *f*; *Fig (importance)* importancia *f*

prominent ['prɒmɪnənt] *adj (standing out)* saliente; *Fig (important)* importante; *(famous)* eminente

promiscuous [prə'mɪskjʊəs] *adj* promiscuo(a)

promise ['prɒmɪs] **1** *n* promesa *f*; **to show p.** ser prometedor(a)
  2 *vt* & *vi* prometer

promising ['prɒmɪsɪŋ] *adj* prometedor(a)

promontory ['prɒməntərɪ] *n* promontorio *m*

promote [prə'məʊt] *vt* ascender; *(product)* promocionar; *(ideas)* fomentar; *Ftb* **they've been promoted** han subido

promoter [prə'məʊtə(r)] *n* promotor(a) *m,f*

promotion [prə'məʊʃən] *n (in rank)* promoción *f*, ascenso *m*; *(of product)* promoción; *(of arts etc)* fomento *m*

prompt ['prɒmpt] **1** *adj (quick)* rápido(a); *(punctual)* puntual
  2 *adv* **at two o'clock p.** a las dos en punto
  3 *vt* (**a**) *(motivate)* incitar; **to p. sb to do sth** instar a algn a hacer algo (**b**) *(actor)* apuntar

promptly [prɒmptlɪ] *adv (quickly)* rápidamente; *(punctually)* puntualmente

prone [prəʊn] *adj* (**a**) **to be p. to do sth** ser propenso(a) a hacer algo (**b**) *Fml (face down)* boca abajo

prong [prɒŋ] *n* punta *f*, diente *m*

pronoun ['prəʊnaʊn] *n* pronombre *m*

pronounce [prə'naʊns] **1** *vt* pronunciar; *Fml (declare)* declarar
  2 *vi Fml* **to p. on sth** opinar sobre algo

pronounced [prə'naʊnst] *adj* pronunciado(a)

pronouncement [prə'naʊnsmənt] *n Fml* declaración *f*

pronunciation [prənʌnsɪ'eɪʃən] *n* pronunciación *f*

proof [pruːf] **1** *n* prueba *f*
  2 *adj* (**a**) *(secure)* a prueba de (**b**) **this rum is 70 percent p.** este ron tiene 70 grados
  3 *vt* impermeabilizar

prop¹ [prɒp] **1** *n (support)* puntal *m*; *Fig* sostén *m*
  2 *vt (support)* apoyar; *Fig* sostener
  ▸ **prop up** *vt sep* apoyar

prop² [prɒp] *n Fam Th* accesorio *m*

propaganda [prɒpə'ɡændə] *n* propaganda *f*

propel [prə'pel] *vt* propulsar

propeller [prə'pelə(r)] *n* hélice *f*

propelling pencil [prə'pelɪŋ'pensəl] *n* portaminas *m inv*

propensity [prə'pensɪtɪ] *n Fml* propensión *f*

proper ['prɒpə(r)] *adj* (**a**) adecuado(a),

correcto(a); **the p. time** el momento
oportuno (**b**) *(real)* real, auténtico(a);
(actual, exact) propiamente dicho(a) (**c**)
(characteristic) propio(a); *Ling* **p. noun**
nombre propio

properly ['prɒpəlɪ] *adv (suitably, correctly, decently)* correctamente; **it wasn't
p. closed** no estaba bien cerrado(a); **she
refused, quite p.** se negó, y con razón

property ['prɒpətɪ] *n* (**a**) *(quality)* propiedad *f* (**b**) *(possession)* propiedad *f*,
posesión *f*; **personal p.** bienes *mpl*; **public
p.** dominio público (**c**) *(estate)* finca *f*

prophecy ['prɒfɪsɪ] *n* profecía *f*

prophesy ['prɒfɪsaɪ] *vt (predict)* predecir; *Rel* profetizar

prophet ['prɒfɪt] *n* profeta *mf*

proportion [prə'pɔːʃən] *n* proporción *f*;
(part, quantity) parte *f*; **in p. to** *or* **with** en
proporción a

proportional [prə'pɔːʃənəl] *adj* proporcional (**to a**); *Pol* **p. representation** representación *f* proporcional

proportionate [prə'pɔːʃənɪt] *adj* proporcional

proposal [prə'pəʊz] *n* propuesta *f*;
(suggestion) sugerencia *f*; **p. of marriage**
propuesta de matrimonio

propose [prə'pəʊz] **1** *vt* proponer; *(suggest)* sugerir; *Fml (intend)* tener la intención de
2 *vi* declararse

proposition [prɒpə'zɪʃən] *n* propuesta *f*;
Math proposición *f*

proprietor [prə'praɪətə(r)] *n* propieta-
rio(a) *m,f*

propriety [prə'praɪtɪ] *n (decency)* decoro *m*

propulsion [prə'pʌlʃən] *n* propulsión *f*

prosaic [prəʊ'zeɪɪk] *adj* prosaico(a)

prose [prəʊz] *n Lit* prosa *f*; *Educ* texto *m*
para traducir

prosecute ['prɒsɪkjuːt] *vt* procesar

prosecution [prɒsɪ'kjuːʃən] *n (action)*
proceso *m*, juicio *m*; **the p.** la acusación

prosecutor ['prɒsɪkjuːtə(r)] *n* acusa-
dor(a) *m,f*

prospect 1 *n* ['prɒspekt] *(outlook)* perspectiva *f*; *(hope)* esperanza *f*; **the job has
prospects** es un trabajo con porvenir
2 *vt* [prə'spekt] explorar
3 *vi* **to p. for gold/oil** buscar oro/petró-
leo

prospective [prə'spektɪv] *adj (future)*
futuro(a); *(possible)* eventual, probable

prospector [prə'spektə(r)] *n* **gold p.** bus-
cador(a) *m,f* del oro

prospectus [prə'spektəs] *n* prospecto *m*

prosper ['prɒspə(r)] *vi* prosperar

prosperity [prɒ'sperɪtɪ] *n* prosperidad *f*

prosperous ['prɒspərəs] *adj* próspero(a)

prostitute ['prɒstɪtjuːt] *n* prostituta *f*

prostitution [prɒstɪ'tjuːʃən] *n* prostitución *f*

prostrate ['prɒstreɪt] *adj (face down)* boca abajo; **p. with grief** deshecho(a) de
dolor

protagonist [prəʊ'tægənɪst] *n* protagonista *mf*

protect [prə'tekt] *vt* proteger; *(interests
etc)* salvaguardar; **to p. sb from sth** proteger a algn de algo

protection [prə'tekʃən] *n* protección *f*

protective [prə'tektɪv] *adj* protector(a)

protégé ['prɒtəʒeɪ] *n* protegido *m*

protégée ['prɒtəʒeɪ] *n* protegida *f*

protein ['prəʊtiːn] *n* proteína *f*

protest 1 *n* ['prəʊtest] protesta *f*;
(complaint) queja *f*
2 *vt* [prə'test] *US* protestar en contra de
3 *vi Br* protestar

Protestant ['prɒtɪstənt] *adj & n* protestante *(mf)*

protester [prə'testə(r)] *n* manifestante
mf

protocol ['prəʊtəkɒl] *n* protocolo *m*

prototype ['prəʊtətaɪp] *n* prototipo *m*

protracted [prə'træktɪd] *adj* prolonga-
do(a)

protrude [prə'truːd] *vi Fml* sobresalir

protuberance [prə'tjuːbərəns] *n Fml*
protuberancia *f*

proud [praʊd] *adj* orgulloso(a); *(arrogant)* soberbio(a)

prove [pruːv] *vt* (**a**) probar, demostrar;
Math comprobar; **to p. oneself** dar pruebas de valor (**b**) **it proved to be disastrous** *(turned out)* resultó ser
desastroso(a)

proverb ['prɒvɜːb] *n* refrán *m*, proverbio
m

provide [prə'vaɪd] **1** *vt* proporcionar;
(supplies) suministrar, proveer
2 *vi* proveer; **to p. for sb** mantener a
algn

provided [prə'vaɪdɪd] *conj* **p. (that)** con
tal de que

providing [prə'vaɪdɪŋ] *conj* = **provided**

province ['prɒvɪns] *n* provincia *f*; *Fig
(field of knowledge)* campo *m*

provincial [prə'vɪnʃəl] **1** *adj* provincial;
Pej provinciano(a)
2 *n Pej (person)* provinciano(a) *m,f*

provision [prə'vɪʒən] *n* provisión *f*; *(supply)* suministro *m*; **provisions** *(food)* provisiones *fpl*, víveres *mpl*

provisional [prəˈvɪʒənəl] *adj* provisional

proviso [prəˈvaɪzəʊ] *n* with the p. that a condición de que

provocation [prɒvəˈkeɪʃən] *n* provocación *f*

provocative [prəˈvɒkətɪv] *adj* provocador(a); *(flirtatious)* provocativo(a)

provoke [prəˈvəʊk] *vt* provocar

prow [praʊ] *n* proa *f*

prowess [ˈpraʊɪs] *n* destreza *f*

prowl [praʊl] **1** *n* merodeo *m*; **to be on the p.** merodear, rondar

2 *vi* merodear; *Fam* **to p. about** *or* **around** rondar

prowler [ˈpraʊlə(r)] *n Fam* merodeador *m*

proximity [prɒkˈsɪmɪtɪ] *n* proximidad *f*, **in p. to, in the p. of** cerca de

proxy [ˈprɒksɪ] *n Jur (power)* poderes *mpl*; *(person)* apoderado(a) *m,f*; **by p.** por poderes

prudence [ˈpruːdəns] *n* prudencia *f*

prudent [ˈpruːdənt] *adj* prudente

prudish [ˈpruːdɪʃ] *adj* remilgado(a)

prune¹ [pruːn] *n* ciruela pasa

prune² [pruːn] *vt (roses etc)* podar; *Fig* acortar

pry [praɪ] *vi* curiosear, husmear; **to p. into sb's affairs** meterse en asuntos ajenos

PS, ps [piːˈes] *(abbr postscript)* P.S., P.D.

psalm [sɑːm] *n* salmo *m*

pseudo- [ˈsjuːdəʊ] *pref* pseudo-, seudo-

pseudonym [ˈsjuːdənɪm] *n* (p)seudónimo *m*

psyche [ˈsaɪkɪ] *n* psique *f*

psychiatric [saɪkɪˈætrɪk] *adj* psiquiátrico(a)

psychiatrist [saɪˈkaɪətrɪst] *n* psiquiatra *mf*

psychiatry [saɪˈkaɪətrɪ] *n* psiquiatría *f*

psychic [ˈsaɪkɪk] **1** *adj* psíquico(a)

2 *n* médium *mf*

psychoanalysis [saɪkəʊəˈnælɪsɪs] *n* psicoanálisis *f*

psychoanalyst [saɪkəʊˈænəlɪst] *n* psicoanalista *mf*

psychological [saɪkəˈlɒdʒɪkəl] *adj* psicológico(a)

psychologist [saɪˈkɒlədʒɪst] *n* psicólogo(a) *m,f*

psychology [saɪˈkɒlədʒɪ] *n* psicología *f*

psychopath [ˈsaɪkəʊpæθ] *n* psicópata *mf*

psychotherapist [ˈsaɪkəʊˈθerəpɪst] *n* psicoterapeuta *mf*

psychotherapy [ˈsaɪkəʊˈθerəpɪ] *n* psicoterapia *f*

psychotic [saɪˈkɒtɪk] *adj & n* psicótico(a) *(m,f)*

PT [piːˈtiː] *n (abbr physical training)* educación *f* física

PTA [piːtiːˈeɪ] *n (abbr Parent-Teacher Association)* = asociación de padres de alumnos y profesores, ≃ APA *f*

PTO, pto [piːtiːˈəʊ] *(abbr please turn over)* sigue

pub [pʌb] *n Br Fam* bar *m*, pub *m*

puberty [ˈpjuːbətɪ] *n* pubertad *f*

pubic [ˈpjuːbɪk] *adj* púbico(a)

public [ˈpʌblɪk] **1** *adj* público(a); **to make sth p.** hacer público algo; *Com* **to go p.** *(of company)* pasar a cotizar en Bolsa; **p. company** empresa pública; **p. convenience** servicios *mpl*, aseos *mpl*; **p. holiday** fiesta *f* nacional; *Br* **p. house** pub *m*, taberna *f*; *Br* **p. limited company** sociedad anónima; **p. opinion** opinión pública; *Br* **p. prosecutor** fiscal *m*; **p. relations** relaciones públicas; **p. school** *Br* colegio privado; *US* colegio público; **p. transport** transporte público

2 *n* **the p.** el público; **in p.** en público

public-address system [ˈpʌblɪkəˈdresssɪstəm] *n* megafonía *f*

publican [ˈpʌblɪkən] *n* tabernero(a) *m,f*

publication [pʌblɪˈkeɪʃən] *n* publicación *f*

publicity [pʌˈblɪsɪtɪ] *n* publicidad *f*

publicize [ˈpʌblɪsaɪz] *vt (make public)* hacer público(a); *(advertise)* hacer publicidad a

public-spirited [pʌblɪkˈspɪrɪtɪd] *adj* de espíritu cívico

publish [ˈpʌblɪʃ] *vt* publicar, editar

publisher [ˈpʌblɪʃə(r)] *n (person)* editor(a) *m,f*; *(firm)* (casa *f*) editorial *f*

publishing [ˈpʌblɪʃɪŋ] *n (business)* industria *f* editorial; **p. company** *or* **house** casa *f* editorial

pucker [ˈpʌkə(r)] *vt (lips, brow)* fruncir, arrugar

pudding [ˈpʊdɪŋ] *n Culin* pudín *m*; *(dessert)* postre *m*; **Christmas p.** = pudín a base de frutos secos típico de Navidad; **p. basin** cuenco *m*; **steamed p.** budín *m*

puddle [ˈpʌdəl] *n* charco *m*

Puerto Rican [ˈpweətəʊˈriːkən] *adj & n* portorriqueño(a) *(m,f)*, puertorriqueño(a) *(m,f)*

Puerto Rico [ˈpweətəʊˈriːkəʊ] *n* Puerto Rico

puff [pʌf] **1** *n (of wind)* racha *f*; *(of smoke)* bocanada *f*; **p. pastry** pasta *f* de hojaldre

2 *vi (person)* jadear, resoplar; *(train)* echar humo; **to p. on one's pipe** chupar la pipa

3 *vt (cigarette)* dar una calada a
▸ **puff up** *vi* hincharse
puffy ['pʌfɪ] *adj* (**puffier, puffiest**) hinchado(a)
pugnacious [pʌg'neɪʃəs] *adj* belicoso(a)
pull [pʊl] **1** *n* (**a**) **to give sth a p.** *(tug)* dar un tirón a algo (**b**) *(of engine)* tracción *f*; *Fig (attraction)* atracción *f*; *(influence)* enchufe *m*

2 *vt* (**a**) *(tug)* dar un tirón a; **to p. a muscle** sufrir un tirón en un músculo; **to p. the trigger** apretar el gatillo; **to p. to pieces** hacer pedazos; *Fig* poner algo por los suelos; *Fig* **to p. sb's leg** tomar el pelo a algn (**b**) *(draw)* tirar, arrastrar; *Fig* **to p. one's weight** hacer su parte del trabajo (**c**) *(draw out)* sacar (**d**) *Fam (people)* atraer

3 *vi (drag)* tirar; **to p. alongside sb** acercarse a algn
▸ **pull apart** *vt sep* desmontar; *Fig (criticize)* poner por los suelos
▸ **pull down** *vt sep (building)* derribar
▸ **pull in** *vt sep (crowds)* atraer
2 *vi (train)* entrar en la estación; *(stop)* parar
▸ **pull off 1** *vt sep Fam (carry out)* llevar a cabo
2 *vi (vehicle)* arrancar
▸ **pull out 1** *vt sep (withdraw)* retirar
2 *vi Aut* **to p. out to overtake** salir para adelantar
▸ **pull over** *vi* hacerse a un lado
▸ **pull through** *vi* reponerse, restablecerse
▸ **pull together** *vt sep* **to p. oneself together** calmarse
▸ **pull up** *vt sep* (**a**) *(uproot)* desarraigar; **to p. up one's socks** subirse los calcetines; *Fig* espabilarse (**b**) *(chair)* acercar
2 *vi (stop)* pararse
pulley ['pʊlɪ] *n* polea *f*
pullover ['pʊləʊvə(r)] *n* jersey *m*, suéter *m*, pulóver *m*, *Andes* chompa *f*, *Urug* buzo *m*
pulp [pʌlp] **1** *n (of paper, wood)* pasta *f*; *(of fruit)* pulpa *f*; *Fam Fig (book etc)* basura *f*
2 *vt* reducir a pulpa
pulpit ['pʊlpɪt] *n* púlpito *m*
pulsate [pʌl'seɪt] *vi* vibrar, palpitar
pulse¹ [pʌls] *n Anat* pulso *m*
pulse² [pʌls] *n Bot & Culin* legumbre *f*
pumice ['pʌmɪs] *n* **p. (stone)** piedra *f* pómez
pummel ['pʌməl] *vt* aporrear
pump¹ [pʌmp] **1** *n* bomba *f*
2 *vt* bombear; **to p. sth in/out** meter/

sacar algo con una bomba; *Fam Fig* **to p. sb for information** sonsacar información a algn
▸ **pump out** *vt sep (empty)* vaciar
▸ **pump up** *vt sep (tyre)* inflar
pump² [pʌmp] *n (shoe)* zapatilla *f*
pumpkin ['pʌmpkɪn] *n* calabaza *f*
pun [pʌn] *n* juego *m* de palabras
punch¹ [pʌntʃ] **1** *n (for making holes)* perforadora *f*; *(for tickets)* taladradora *f*; *(for leather etc)* punzón *m*
2 *vt (make hole in)* perforar; *(ticket)* picar; *(leather)* punzar
punch² [pʌntʃ] **1** *n (blow)* puñetazo *m*; *(in boxing)* pegada *f*; *Fig* **it lacks p.** le falta fuerza; **p. line** remate *m* (de un chiste)
2 *vt (with fist)* dar un puñetazo a
punch³ [pʌntʃ] *n (drink)* ponche *m*
punch-up ['pʌntʃʌp] *n Fam* pelea *f*
punctual ['pʌŋktjʊəl] *adj* puntual
punctuate ['pʌŋktjʊeɪt] *vt* puntuar; *Fig* salpicar
punctuation [pʌŋktjʊ'eɪʃən] *n* puntuación *f*
puncture ['pʌŋktʃə(r)] **1** *n* pinchazo *m*
2 *vt (tyre)* pinchar
pundit ['pʌndɪt] *n Fam* experto(a) *m,f*
pungent ['pʌndʒənt] *adj (smell)* acre; *(taste)* fuerte
punish ['pʌnɪʃ] *vt* castigar
punishable ['pʌnɪʃəbəl] *adj* castigable, punible
punishment ['pʌnɪʃmənt] *n* castigo *m*
punk [pʌŋk] *n Fam* (**a**) punk *mf*; **p. music** música *f* punk (**b**) *US* mamón *m*
punt [pʌnt] **1** *n (boat)* batea *f*
2 *vi* ir en batea
punter ['pʌntə(r)] *n Br (gambler)* jugador(a) *m,f*; *(customer)* cliente(a) *m,f*
puny ['pjuːnɪ] *adj* (**punier, puniest**) enclenque, endeble
pup [pʌp] *n* cachorro(a) *m,f*
pupil¹ ['pjuːpəl] *n Educ* alumno(a) *m,f*
pupil² ['pjuːpəl] *n Anat* pupila *f*
puppet ['pʌpɪt] *n* títere *m*
puppy ['pʌpɪ] *n* cachorro(a) *m,f*, perrito *m*
purchase ['pɜːtʃɪs] **1** *n* compra *f*
2 *vt* comprar; **purchasing power** poder adquisitivo
purchaser ['pɜːtʃɪsə(r)] *n* comprador(a) *m,f*
pure [pjʊə(r)] *adj* puro(a)
purée ['pjʊəreɪ] *n* puré *m*
purely [pjʊəlɪ] *adv* simplemente
purge [pɜːdʒ] **1** *n* purga *f*
2 *vt* purgar
purify ['pjʊərɪfaɪ] *vt* purificar

purl [pɜːl] *vt (in knitting)* hacer punto del revés

purple ['pɜːpəl] *adj* morado(a), purpúreo(a); **to go p. (in the face)** ponerse morado(a)

purport [pɜː'pɔːt] *vi Fml* pretender; **to p. to be sth** pretender ser algo

purpose ['pɜːpəs] *n* (a) propósito *m*, intención *f*; **on p.** a propósito (b) *(use)* utilidad *f*

purposeful ['pɜːpəsfʊl] *adj (resolute)* decidido(a), resoluto(a)

purr [pɜː(r)] *vi (cat)* ronronear; *(engine)* zumbar

purse [pɜːs] **1** *n Br* monedero *m*; *US (bag)* bolso *m*, cartera *f*, *Méx* bolsa *f*; *(prize money)* premio *m* en metálico
2 *vt* **to p. one's lips** apretarse los labios

purser ['pɜːsə(r)] *n* contador(a) *m,f*

pursue [pə'sjuː] *vt (criminal)* perseguir; *(person)* seguir; *(pleasure)* buscar; *(career)* ejercer

pursuer [pə'sjuːə(r)] *n Fml* perseguidor(a) *m,f*

pursuit [pə'sjuːt] *n (of criminal)* persecución *f*, *(of animal)* caza *f*, *(of pleasure)* búsqueda *f*; *(pastime)* pasatiempo *m*

purveyor [pə'veɪə(r)] *n Fml* proveedor(a) *m,f*

pus [pʌs] *n* pus *m*

push [pʊʃ] **1** *n* empujón *m*; *Fig (drive)* brío *m*, dinamismo *m*
2 *vt* (a) empujar; *(button)* pulsar, apretar; **to p. one's finger into a hole** meter el dedo en un agujero (b) *Fig (pressurize)* instar; *(harass)* acosar; *Fam* **to be (hard) pushed for time** andar justo(a) de tiempo (c) *Fam (product)* promover; **to p. drugs** pasar droga
3 *vi* empujar
▸ **push aside** *vt sep (object)* apartar
▸ **push in** *vi* colarse
▸ **push off** *vi (in boat)* desatracar; *Fam* **p. off!** ¡lárgate!
▸ **push on** *vi (continue)* seguir adelante
▸ **push through** *vt sep* abrirse paso entre

pushchair ['pʊʃtʃeə(r)] *n Br* sillita *f* (de ruedas)

pusher ['pʊʃə(r)] *n Fam (of drugs)* camello *m*

pushover ['pʊʃəʊvə(r)] *n Fam* **it's a p.** está chupado; **she's a p.** es un ligue fácil

push-up ['pʊʃʌp] *n* flexión *f* (de brazos)

pushy ['pʊʃɪ] *adj* (**pushier, pushiest**) *Fam* agresivo(a)

puss [pʊs], **pussy** ['pʊsɪ] *n Fam* minino *m*

put [pʊt] **1** *vt* (*pt & pp* **put**) (a) poner; *(place)* colocar; *(insert)* meter; **to p. to**

bed acostar a; **to p. a picture up on the wall** colgar un cuadro en la pared; **to p. a stop to sth** poner término a algo; *Fig* **to p. one's foot in it** meter la pata
(b) *(present)* presentar, exponer; **to p. a question to sb** hacer una pregunta a algn
(c) *(express)* expresar, decir; **to p. it mildly** y me quedo corto; **to p. sth simply** explicar algo de manera sencilla
(d) *(estimate)* calcular
(e) *(money)* ingresar; *(invest)* invertir
2 *vi Naut* **to p. to sea** zarpar
3 *adv* **to stay p.** quedarse quieto(a)
▸ **put about** *vt sep (rumour)* hacer correr
▸ **put across** *vt sep (idea etc)* comunicar
▸ **put aside** *vt sep (money)* ahorrar; *(time)* reservar
▸ **put away** *vt sep (tidy away)* recoger; *Fam (eat)* zamparse; *(save money)* ahorrar
▸ **put back** *vt sep (postpone)* aplazar; **to p. the clock back** retrasar la hora
▸ **put by** *vt sep (money)* ahorrar
▸ **put down** *vt sep (set down)* dejar; *(suppress)* sofocar; *(humiliate)* humillar; *(criticize)* criticar; *(animal)* provocar la muerte de; *(write down)* apuntar
▸ **put down to** *vt sep* achacar a
▸ **put forward** *vt sep (theory)* exponer; *(proposal)* hacer; **to p. one's name forward for sth** presentarse como candidato(a) para algo
▸ **put in 1** *vt sep (install)* instalar; *(complaint, request)* presentar; *(time)* pasar
2 *vi Naut* hacer escala (**at** en)
▸ **put off** *vt sep (postpone)* aplazar; **to p. sb off (doing) sth** *(dissuade)* disuadir a algn de (hacer) algo
▸ **put on** *vt sep (clothes)* poner, ponerse; *(show)* montar; *(concert)* dar; *(switch on) (radio)* poner; *(light)* encender; *(water, gas)* abrir; **to p. on weight** aumentar de peso; **to p. on the brakes** frenar; *Fig* **to p. on a straight face** poner cara de serio(a)
▸ **put out** *vt sep (light, fire)* apagar; *(place outside)* sacar; *(extend) (arm)* extender; *(tongue)* sacar; *(hand)* tender; *(spread) (rumour)* hacer correr; *(annoy)* molestar; *(inconvenience)* incordiar; *(anger)* **to be p. out by sth** enojarse por algo
▸ **put through** *vt sep Tel* **p. me through to Pat, please** póngame con Pat, por favor
▸ **put together** *vt sep (join)* unir, reunir; *(assemble)* armar, montar
▸ **put up** *vt sep (raise)* levantar, subir; *(picture)* colocar; *(curtains)* colgar; *(building)* construir; *(tent)* armar; *(prices)*

subir, aumentar; *(accommodate)* alojar, hospedar; **to p. up a fight** ofrecer resistencia

▸ **put up to** *vt sep* **to p. sb up to sth** incitar a algn a hacer algo

▸ **put up with** *vt insep* aguantar, soportar

putrid ['pjuːtrɪd] *adj Fml* putrefacto(a)

putt [pʌt] **1** *n* tiro *m* al hoyo

2 *vt & vi* tirar al hoyo

putting ['pʌtɪŋ] *n* **p. green** minigolf *m*

putty ['pʌtɪ] *n* masilla *f*

puzzle ['pʌzəl] **1** *n* rompecabezas *m inv*; *(crossword)* crucigrama *m*; *Fig (mystery)* misterio *m*

2 *vt* dejar perplejo(a); **to be puzzled about sth** no entender algo

▸ **puzzle over** *vt insep* **to p. over sth** dar vueltas a algo (en la cabeza)

puzzling ['pʌzlɪŋ] *adj* extraño(a), curioso(a)

PVC [piːviːˈsiː] *n (abbr* **polyvinyl chloride**) PVC *m*

pygmy ['pɪgmɪ] *n* pigmeo(a) *m,f; Fig* enano(a) *m,f*

pyjamas [pəˈdʒɑːməz] *npl* pijama *m*

pylon ['paɪlən] *n* torre *f* (de conducción eléctrica)

pyramid ['pɪrəmɪd] *n* pirámide *f*

Pyrenees [pɪrəˈniːz] *npl* **the P.** los Pirineos

Pyrex® ['paɪreks] *n* pírex® *m*

python ['paɪθən] *n* pitón *m*

Q, q [kjuː] *n (the letter)* Q, q *f*

quack [kwæk] **1** *n* (**a**) *(of duck)* graznido *m* (**b**) *Fam (doctor)* curandero(a) *m,f*
2 *vi* graznar

quad [kwɒd] *n Fam* (**a**) *Br (of school, university)* patio *m* interior (**b**) *(quadruplet)* cuatrillizo(a) *m,f*

quadrangle ['kwɒdræŋgəl] *n* (**a**) *Geom* cuadrángulo *m* (**b**) *(courtyard)* patio *m* interior

quadruple ['kwɒdrʊpəl, kwɒ'druːpəl] **1** *n* cuádruplo *m*
2 *adj* cuádruple
3 *vt* cuadruplicar
4 *vi* cuadruplicarse

quadruplet ['kwɒdrʊplɪt, kwɒ'druːplɪt] *n* cuatrillizo(a) *m,f*

quagmire ['kwægmaɪə(r), 'kwɒgmaɪə(r)] *n (land)* cenagal *m*

quail[1] [kweɪl] *n Orn* codorniz *f*
quail[2] [kweɪl] *vi Fig* encogerse

quaint [kweɪnt] *adj (picturesque)* pintoresco(a); *(original)* singular

quake [kweɪk] **1** *vi* temblar
2 *n Fam* temblor *m* de tierra

Quaker ['kweɪkə(r)] *n* cuáquero(a) *m,f*

qualification [kwɒlɪfɪ'keɪʃən] *n* (**a**) *(ability)* aptitud *f* (**b**) *(requirement)* requisito *m* (**c**) *(diploma etc)* título *m* (**d**) *(reservation)* reserva *f*

qualified ['kwɒlɪfaɪd] *adj* (**a**) capacitado(a); **q. teacher** profesor titulado (**b**) **q. approval** *(modified)* aprobación *f* condicional

qualify ['kwɒlɪfaɪ] **1** *vt* (**a**) *(entitle)* capacitar (**b**) *(modify)* modificar; *(statement)* matizar; *Ling* calificar
2 *vi* (**a**) **to q. as** *(doctor etc)* sacar el título de; **when did you q.?** ¿cuándo terminaste la carrera? (**b**) *(in competition)* quedar clasificado(a)

qualifying ['kwɒlɪfaɪɪŋ] *adj (round, exam)* eliminatorio(a)

quality ['kwɒlɪtɪ] *n* (**a**) *(excellence)* calidad *f*; **q. control** control *m* de calidad; *Br* **q. newspapers** prensa *f* no sensacionalista (**b**) *(attribute)* cualidad *f*

qualm [kwɑːm] *n* (**a**) *(scruple)* escrúpulo *m* (**b**) *(doubt)* duda *f*

quandary ['kwɒndərɪ, 'kwɒndrɪ] *n* **to be in a q.** estar en un dilema

quango ['kwæŋgəʊ] *n* = organización semi-autónoma paralela

quantity ['kwɒntɪtɪ] *n* cantidad *f*

quarantine ['kwɒrəntiːn] *n* cuarentena *f*

quarrel ['kwɒrəl] **1** *n (argument)* riña *f*, pelea *f*; *(disagreement)* desacuerdo *m*
2 *vi (argue)* pelearse, reñir; **to q. with sth** discrepar de algo

quarrelsome ['kwɒrəlsəm] *adj* camorrista

quarry[1] ['kwɒrɪ] *Min* **1** *n* cantera *f*
2 *vt* extraer

quarry[2] ['kwɒrɪ] *n* presa *f*

quart [kwɔːt] *n (measurement)* = cuarto de galón *(Br = 1,13 l; US = 0,94 l)*

quarter ['kwɔːtə(r)] **1** *n* (**a**) cuarto *m*, cuarta parte; **a q. of an hour** un cuarto de hora; **a q. of a cake** la cuarta parte de un pastel
(**b**) **it's a q.** *Br* **to** *or US* **of three** son las tres menos cuarto; **it's a q.** *Br* **past** *or US* **after six** son las seis y cuarto
(**c**) *(three months)* trimestre *m*
(**d**) *Br (weight)* cuarto *m* de libra
(**e**) *US (coin)* cuarto *m* (de dólar)
(**f**) *(district)* barrio *m*
(**g**) **there was criticism from all quarters** *(areas, people)* todos lo criticaron
(**h**) *(of moon)* cuarto *m*
(**i**) **quarters** *(lodgings)* alojamiento *m*; *Mil* **officers' quarters** residencia *f* de oficiales; **at close quarters** muy cerca
(**j**) *US Mus* **q. note** negra *f*
2 *vt* (**a**) *(cut into quarters)* dividir en cuartos
(**b**) *(accommodate)* alojar

quarterfinal ['kwɔːtəfaɪnəl] *n Sport* cuarto *m* de final

quarterly ['kwɔːtəlɪ] **1** *adj* trimestral
2 *n* publicación *f* trimestral
3 *adv* trimestralmente

quartermaster ['kwɔːtəmɑːstə(r)] *n* (**a**) *Mil* oficial *m* de intendencia (**b**) *Naut* cabo *m* de la Marina

quartet(te) [kwɔː'tet] *n* cuarteto *m*

quartz [kwɔːts] *n* cuarzo *m*; **q. watch** reloj *m* de cuarzo

quash [kwɒʃ] *vt Jur* anular; *(uprising)* aplastar

quasi ['kwɑːzɪ, 'kweɪzaɪ, 'kweɪsaɪ] *pref* cuasi

quaver ['kweɪvə(r)] **1** *n* (**a**) *Mus* corchea *f* (**b**) *(in voice)* temblor *m*
2 *vi (voice)* temblar

quay(side) ['kiː(saɪd)] *n* muelle *m*

queasy ['kwiːzɪ] *adj* (**queasier, queasiest**) **to feel q.** *(ill)* tener náuseas

queen [kwiːn] *n* (**a**) reina *f* (**b**) *Fam Pej* loca *f*, marica *f*

queer [kwɪə(r)] **1** *adj* (**a**) *(strange)* extraño(a), raro(a) (**b**) *Fam (mad)* loco(a) (**c**) *Fam (unwell)* mareado(a) (**d**) *Fam Pej* maricón
2 *n Fam Pej* marica *m*, maricón *m*

quell [kwel] *vt* reprimir

quench [kwentʃ] *vt* apagar

querulous ['kwerʊləs, 'kwerjʊləs] *adj Fml* quejumbroso(a)

query ['kwɪərɪ] **1** *n (question)* pregunta *f*
2 *vt (ask questions about)* preguntar acerca de; *(have doubts about)* poner en duda

quest [kwest] *n Literary* búsqueda *f*, busca *f*

question ['kwestʃən] **1** *n* (**a**) *(interrogative)* pregunta *f*; **to ask sb a q.** hacer una pregunta a algn; **he did it without q.** lo hizo sin rechistar; **q. mark** signo *m* de interrogación; *Fig* interrogante *m* (**b**) *(problem, issue)* asunto *m*, cuestión *f*; **it's a q. of two hours** es cuestión de dos horas (**c**) *(doubt)* duda *f*; **beyond q.** fuera de duda; **in q.** en duda; **to call sth into q.** poner algo en duda (**d**) *(out of the q.)* imposible; **that's out of the q.!** ¡ni hablar! (**e**) *Educ* problema *m*
2 *vt (ask questions of)* hacer preguntas a; *(interrogate)* interrogar; *(query)* poner en duda

questionable ['kwestʃənəbəl] *adj (doubtful)* dudoso(a); *(debatable)* discutible

questionnaire [kwestʃə'neə(r)] *n* cuestionario *m*

queue [kjuː] *Br* **1** *n* cola *f*
2 *vi* **to q. (up)** hacer cola

quibble ['kwɪbəl] **1** *n* pega *f*
2 *vi* poner pegas (**with** a); *Fam* buscarle tres pies al gato

quiche [kiːʃ] *n* quiche *m* or *f*

quick [kwɪk] *adj* (**a**) *(fast)* rápido(a); **a q. look** un vistazo; **a q. snack** un bocado; **be q.!** ¡date prisa! (**b**) *(clever)* espabilado(a);

(wit) agudo(a) (**c**) **she has a q. temper** se enfada con nada

quicken ['kwɪkən] **1** *vt* acelerar; **to q. one's pace** acelerar el paso
2 *vi (speed up)* acelerarse

quickly ['kwɪklɪ] *adv* rápidamente, de prisa

quickness ['kwɪknɪs] *n* (**a**) *(speed)* rapidez *f* (**b**) *(of wit)* agudeza *f*, viveza *f*

quicksand ['kwɪksænd] *n* arenas movedizas

quicksilver ['kwɪksɪlvə(r)] *n* mercurio *m*

quick-witted [kwɪk'wɪtɪd] *adj* agudo(a)

quid [kwɪd] *n (pl* quid*)* *Br Fam* libra *f* (esterlina)

quiet ['kwaɪət] **1** *n* (**a**) *(silence)* silencio *m* (**b**) *(calm)* tranquilidad *f*
2 *adj* (**a**) *(silent)* silencioso(a); *(street)* tranquilo(a); **a q. voice** una voz suave; **keep q.!** ¡silencio! (**b**) *(calm)* tranquilo(a) (**c**) *Com & Fin* **business is q. today** hoy hay poco negocio (**d**) *(person)* reservado(a) (**e**) *(secret)* confidencial (**f**) *(not showy) (clothes)* sobrio(a); *(colours)* apagado(a) (**g**) *(ceremony, dinner)* íntimo(a)
2 *vt US* calmar
3 *vi US* calmarse

quieten ['kwaɪətən] **1** *vt (silence)* callar; *(calm)* calmar
2 *vi (silence)* callarse; *(calm)* calmarse
▸ **quieten down** *Br* **1** *vt sep* calmar
2 *vi* calmarse

quietly ['kwaɪətlɪ] *adv* (**a**) *(silently)* silenciosamente; **he spoke q.** habló en voz baja (**b**) *(calmly)* tranquilamente (**c**) *(discreetly)* discretamente

quietness ['kwaɪətnɪs] *n* (**a**) *(silence)* silencio *m* (**b**) *(calm)* tranquilidad *f*

quill [kwɪl] *n (feather, pen)* pluma *f*; *(of porcupine)* púa *f*

quilt [kwɪlt] **1** *n* edredón *m*
2 *vt* acolchar

quin [kwɪn] *n Fam* quintillizo(a) *m,f*

quinine ['kwɪniːn, *US* 'kwaɪnaɪn] *n* quinina *f*

quint [kwɪnt] *n Fam US* = quin

quintessential [kwɪntɪ'senʃəl] *adj* fundamental

quintet(te) [kwɪn'tet] *n* quinteto *m*

quintuple ['kwɪntjʊpəl, kwɪn'tjuːpəl] **1** *adj* quíntuplo(a)
2 *n* quíntuplo *m*
3 *vt* quintuplicar

quintuplet ['kwɪntjʊplɪt, kwɪn'tjuːplɪt] *n* quintillizo(a) *m,f*

quip [kwɪp] **1** *n* salida *f*; *(joke)* chiste *m*
2 *vi* bromear

quirk [kwɜːk] *n* (**a**) *(peculiarity)* manía *f*

(**b**) *(of fate)* arbitrariedad *f*

quit [kwɪt] **1** *vt* (*pt & pp* **quitted** *or* **quit**) (**a**) *(leave)* dejar, abandonar (**b**) **q. making that noise!** ¡dejá de hacer ese ruido!

2 *vi* (**a**) *(go)* irse; *(give up)* dimitir (**b**) *(cease)* dejar de hacer algo

3 *adj* **let's call it quits** dejémoslo estar

> 🖉 Note that the Spanish verb **quitar** is a false friend and is never a translation for the English verb **to quit**. In Spanish, **quitar** means both "to remove" and "to take away".

quite [kwaɪt] *adv* (**a**) *(entirely)* totalmente; **she's q. right** tiene toda la razón (**b**) *(rather)* bastante; **q. a few** bastantes; **q. a while** un buen rato; **q. often** con bastante frecuencia; **that's q. enough!** ¡ya está bien! (**c**) **he's q. a character** es un tipo original; **it's q. something** es increíble (**d**) *(exactly)* exactamente; **q.**

(**so**)**!** ¡en efecto!, ¡exacto!

quiver¹ ['kwɪvə(r)] *vi* temblar

quiver² ['kwɪvə(r)] *n (for arrows)* aljaba *f*, carcaj *m*

quiz [kwɪz] **1** *n Rad & TV* **q. show** concurso *m*

2 *vt* hacer preguntas a

quizzical ['kwɪzɪkəl] *adj* (**a**) *(bemused)* burlón(ona) (**b**) *(enquiring)* curioso(a)

quota ['kwəʊtə] *n* (**a**) *(proportional share)* cuota *f*, parte *f* (**b**) *(prescribed amount, number)* cupo *m*

quotation [kwəʊ'teɪʃən] *n* (**a**) *Lit* cita *f*; **q. marks** comillas *fpl* (**b**) *Fin* cotización *f*

quote [kwəʊt] **1** *vt* (**a**) *(cite)* citar (**b**) *Com* **to q. a price** dar un presupuesto (**c**) *Fin* cotizar

2 *n* (**a**) *Lit* cita *f* (**b**) *Com* presupuesto *m*

quotient ['kwəʊʃənt] *n* cociente *m*

R, r [ɑː(r)] *n (the letter)* R, r *f*

rabbi ['ræbaɪ] *n* rabí *m*, rabino *m*

rabbit ['ræbɪt] **1** *n* conejo(a) *m,f*; **r. hutch** conejera *f*

  2 *vi Fam* **to r. (on)** enrollarse

rabble ['ræbəl] *n Pej* **the r.** el populacho

rabies ['reɪbiːz] *n* rabia *f*

RAC [ɑːreɪˈsiː] *n Br (abbr* **Royal Automobile Club)** = organización británica de ayuda al automovilista, ≃ RACE *m*

race¹ [reɪs] **1** *n* **(a)** *Sport* carrera *f* **(b)** *Br* **the races** las carreras (de caballos)

  2 *vt* **(a) I'll r. you!** ¡te echo una carrera! **(b)** *(car, horse)* hacer correr **(c)** *(engine)* acelerar

  3 *vi (go quickly)* correr; *(pulse)* acelerarse

race² [reɪs] *n (people)* raza *f*

racecourse ['reɪskɔːs] *n Br* hipódromo *m*

racehorse ['reɪshɔːs] *n* caballo *m* de carreras

racer ['reɪsə(r)] *n Sport* **(a)** *(person)* corredor(a) *m,f* **(b)** *(bicycle)* bicicleta *f* de carreras; *(car)* coche *m* de carreras

racetrack ['reɪstræk] *n (for cars, people, bikes)* pista *f*; *US (for horses)* hipódromo *m*

racial ['reɪʃəl] *adj* racial

racing ['reɪsɪŋ] **1** *n* carreras *fpl*

  2 *adj* de carreras; **r. car/bike** coche *m*/moto *f* de carreras

racism ['reɪsɪzəm] *n* racismo *m*

racist ['reɪsɪst] *adj & n* racista *(mf)*

rack [ræk] **1** *n (a) (shelf)* estante *m*; *(for clothes)* percha *f*; **luggage r.** portaequipajes *m inv*; **roof r.** baca *f* **(b)** *(for torture)* potro *m*

  2 *vt Literary (torment)* atormentar; *Fam Fig* **to r. one's brains** devanarse los sesos

racket¹ ['rækɪt] *n (a) (din)* ruido *m*, jaleo *m* **(b)** *(swindle)* timo *m*; *(shady business)* chanchullo *m*

racket² ['rækɪt] *n Sport* raqueta *f*

racquet ['rækɪt] *n* = **racket²**

racy ['reɪsɪ] *adj (racier, raciest) (lively)* vivo(a); *(risqué)* atrevido(a)

radar ['reɪdɑː(r)] *n* radar *m*

radiance ['reɪdɪəns] *n* resplandor *m*

radiant ['reɪdɪənt] *adj* radiante, resplandeciente

radiate ['reɪdɪeɪt] *vt* irradiar; *Fig* **she radiated happiness** rebosaba de alegría

radiation [reɪdɪˈeɪʃən] *n* radiación *f*

radiator ['reɪdɪeɪtə(r)] *n* radiador *m*

radical ['rædɪkəl] *adj* radical

radio ['reɪdɪəʊ] *n* radio *f*; **on the r.** en or por la radio; **r. station** emisora *f* (de radio)

radioactive [reɪdɪəʊˈæktɪv] *adj* radiactivo(a)

radio-controlled [reɪdɪəʊkənˈtrəʊld] *adj* teledirigido(a)

radiography [reɪdɪˈɒɡrəfɪ] *n* radiografía *f*

radiology [reɪdɪˈɒlədʒɪ] *n* radiología *f*

radiotherapy [reɪdɪəʊˈθerəpɪ] *n* radioterapia *f*

radish ['rædɪʃ] *n* rábano *m*

radius ['reɪdɪəs] *n* radio *m*; **within a r. of** en un radio de

RAF [ɑːreɪˈef] *n Br (abbr* **Royal Air Force)** = fuerzas aéreas británicas

raffle ['ræfəl] **1** *n* rifa *f*

  2 *vt* rifar

raft [rɑːft] *n* balsa *f*

rafter ['rɑːftə(r)] *n* viga *f* de madera

rag¹ [ræɡ] *n (a) (torn piece)* harapo *m*; **r. doll** muñeca *f* de trapo **(b)** *(for cleaning)* trapo *m* **(c)** *Fam* **rags** *(clothes)* trapos *mpl* **(d)** *Pej Press* periodicucho *m*

rag² [ræɡ] **1** *n Br Univ* función benéfica

  2 *vt* gastar bromas a

rag-and-bone ['ræɡənˈbəʊn] *adj Br* **r. man** trapero *m*

rage [reɪdʒ] **1** *n (a) (fury)* cólera *f* **(b)** *Fam* **it's all the r.** hace furor

  2 *vi* **(a)** *(person)* rabiar, estar furioso(a) **(b)** *Fig (storm, sea)* rugir; *(wind)* bramar

ragged ['ræɡɪd] *adj* **(a)** *(clothes)* hecho(a) jirones **(b)** *(person)* harapiento(a) **(c)** *(edge)* mellado(a) **(d)** *Fig (uneven)* desigual

raging ['reɪdʒɪŋ] *adj* **(a)** *(angry)* furioso(a) **(b)** *Fig (sea)* embravecido(a) **(c)** *(intense)* feroz; *(storm)* violento(a)

raid [reɪd] **1** *n Mil* incursión *f*; *(by police)* redada *f*; *(robbery etc)* atraco *m*

  2 *vt Mil* hacer una incursión en; *(police)*

hacer una redada en; *(rob)* asaltar; *Fam*
to r. the larder vaciar la despensa
raider ['reɪdə(r)] *n (invader)* invasor(a)
m,f
rail [reɪl] *n* **(a)** barra *f* **(b)** *(railing)* barandilla *f* **(c)** *Rail* carril *f*; **by r.** *(send sth)* por
ferrocarril; *(travel)* en tren
railcard ['reɪlkɑːd] *n Br* abono *m*
railing ['reɪlɪŋ] *n (usu pl)* verja *f*
railroad ['reɪlrəʊd] *n US* ferrocarril *m*
railway ['reɪlweɪ] *n Br* ferrocarril *m*; **r.
line, r. track** vía férrea; **r. station** estación
f de ferrocarril
railwayman ['reɪlweɪmən] *n Br* ferroviario *m*
rain [reɪn] **1** *n* lluvia *f*; **in the r.** bajo la
lluvia
  2 *vi* llover; **it's raining** llueve
rainbow ['reɪnbəʊ] *n* arco *m* iris
raincoat ['reɪnkəʊt] *n* impermeable *m*
raindrop ['reɪndrɒp] *n* gota *f* de lluvia
rainfall ['reɪnfɔːl] *n (falling of rain)* precipitación *f*; *(amount)* pluviosidad *f*
rainforest ['reɪnfɒrɪst] *n* selva *f* tropical
rainy ['reɪnɪ] *adj* **(rainier, rainiest)** lluvio-
so(a)
raise [reɪz] **1** *n US* aumento *m* (de sueldo)
  2 *vt* **(a)** levantar; *(glass)* brindar; *(voice)*
subir; *(building)* erigir **(b)** *(prices)* aumentar **(c)** *(money, help)* reunir **(d)** *(issue)* plantear **(e)** *(crops, children)* criar
(f) *Rad* comunicar con **(g)** *(standards)*
mejorar **(h)** *(laugh)* provocar
raisin ['reɪzən] *n* pasa *f*
rake¹ [reɪk] **1** *n (garden tool)* rastrillo *m*;
(for fire) hurgón *m*
  2 *vt (leaves)* rastrillar; *(fire)* hurgar; *(with
machine gun)* barrer
rake² [reɪk] *n (dissolute man)* calavera *m*,
libertino *m*
rally ['rælɪ] **1** *n* **(a)** *(gathering)* reunión *f*;
Pol mitin *m* **(b)** *Aut* rallye *m* **(c)** *(in tennis)*
jugada *f*
  2 *vt (support)* reunir
  3 *vi* recuperarse
  ▸ **rally round** *vi* formar una piña
RAM [ræm] *n Comput (abbr* **random access memory)** RAM *f*
ram [ræm] **1** *n* **(a)** *Zool* carnero *m* **(b)** *Tech*
maza *f*
  2 *vt* **(a)** *(drive into place)* hincar; *(cram)*
embutir; *Fam* **to r. sth home** hacer algo
patente **(b)** *(crash into)* chocar con
ramble ['ræmbəl] **1** *n (walk)* caminata *f*
  2 *vi* **(a)** *(walk)* hacer una excursión a pie
(b) *Fig (digress)* divagar
rambler ['ræmblə(r)] *n* **(a)** *(person)* excursionista *mf* **(b)** *Bot* rosal *m* trepador

rambling ['ræmblɪŋ] *adj* **(a)** *(incoherent)*
incoherente **(b)** *(house)* laberíntico(a)
(c) *Bot* trepador(a)
ramp [ræmp] *n* **(a)** rampa *f* **(b)** *Av (movable stairway)* escalerilla *f*
rampage **1** *n* ['ræmpeɪdʒ] **to be on the r.**
desmandarse
  2 *vi* [ræm'peɪdʒ] **to r. about** comportarse como un loco
rampant ['ræmpənt] *adj* incontrola-
do(a); **corruption is r.** la corrupción está
muy extendida
rampart ['ræmpɑːt] *n* muralla *f*
ramshackle ['ræmʃækəl] *adj* destartala-
do(a)
ran [ræn] *pt of* **run**
ranch [rɑːntʃ] *n US* rancho *m*, hacienda *f*
rancher ['rɑːntʃə(r)] *n US* ranchero(a)
m,f
rancid ['rænsɪd] *adj* rancio(a)
rancour, *US* **rancor** ['ræŋkə(r)] *n Fml*
rencor *m*
R & D [ɑːrən'diː] *n (abbr* **Research and
Development)** I+D
random ['rændəm] **1** *n* **at r.** al azar
  2 *adj* fortuito(a); **r. selection** selección
hecha al azar
randy ['rændɪ] *adj* **(randier, randiest)** *Br
Fam* cachondo(a), caliente
rang [ræŋ] *pt of* **ring**
range [reɪndʒ] **1** *n* **(a)** *(of mountains)*
cordillera *f*, sierra *f* **(b)** *US (open land)*
pradera *f* **(c)** *(choice)* surtido *m*; *(of products)* gama *f* **(d)** *Mus* registro *m* **(e)**
firing r. campo *m* de tiro **(f)** *(of missile)*
alcance *m*; **at close r.** de cerca; **long-/
short-r. missiles** misiles *mpl* de largo/
corto alcance **(g)** *Culin* cocina *f* de carbón
  2 *vi (extend)* extenderse **(to** hasta);
prices r. from £5 to £20 pounds los precios oscilan entre 5 y 20 libras
  3 *vt Literary (wander)* vagar por
ranger ['reɪndʒə(r)] *n* **(a)** *(forest)* **r.** guar-
dabosques *mf inv* **(b)** *US (mounted policeman)* policía montado
rank¹ [ræŋk] **1** *n* **(a)** *Mil (row)* fila *f*; **the
ranks** los soldados rasos; **the r. and file**
base **(b)** *(position in army)* graduación *f*;
(in society) rango *m* **(c)** **(taxi) r.** parada *f*
de taxis
  2 *vt (classify)* clasificar
  3 *vi (figure)* figurar; **to r. above/below
sb** figurar por encima/debajo de algn; **to
r. with** estar al mismo nivel que
rank² [ræŋk] *adj Fml* **(a)** *(vegetation)*
exuberante **(b)** *(foul-smelling)* fétido(a)
(c) *(thorough)* total, absoluto(a)

ransack ['rænsæk] *vt (plunder)* saquear; *(rummage in)* registrar

ransom ['rænsəm] *n* rescate *m*; **to hold sb to r.** pedir rescate por algn; *Fig* poner a algn entre la espada y la pared

rant [rænt] *vi* vociferar; *Fam* **to r. and rave** pegar gritos

rap [ræp] **1** *n* (**a**) *(blow)* golpe *m* seco; *(on door)* golpecito *m* (**b**) *Mus* rap *m*

　　2 *vt & vi (knock)* golpear

rape¹ [reɪp] *Jur* **1** *n* violación *f*

　　2 *vt* violar

rape² [reɪp] *n Bot* colza *f*

rapeseed ['reɪpsiːd] *n* **r. oil** aceite *m* de colza

rapid ['ræpɪd] **1** *adj* rápido(a)

　　2 *n* **rapids** *(in river)* rápidos *mpl*

rapidity [rə'pɪdɪtɪ] *n* rapidez *f*

rapist ['reɪpɪst] *n* violador(a) *m,f*

rapport [ræ'pɔː(r)] *n* compenetración *f*

rapture ['ræptʃə(r)] *n* éxtasis *m*

rapturous ['ræptʃərəs] *adj* muy entusiasta

rare¹ [reə(r)] *adj* raro(a), poco común

rare² [reə(r)] *adj (steak)* poco hecho(a)

rarefied ['reərɪfaɪd] *adj* enrarecido(a)

rarely ['reəlɪ] *adv* raras veces

raring ['reərɪŋ] *adj Fam* **to be r. to do sth** morirse de ganas de hacer algo

rarity ['reərɪtɪ] *n* rareza *f*

rascal ['rɑːskəl] *n* granuja *mf*

rash¹ [ræʃ] *n* (**a**) *Med* erupción *f*, sarpullido *m* (**b**) *Fig (of robberies etc)* racha *f*

rash² [ræʃ] *adj (reckless)* impetuoso(a); *(words, actions)* precipitado(a), imprudente

rasher ['ræʃə(r)] *n* loncha *f*

raspberry ['rɑːzbərɪ] *n* frambuesa *f*

rasping ['rɑːspɪŋ] *adj* áspero(a)

rat [ræt] *n* (**a**) *(animal)* rata *f*; **r. poison** raticida *m* (**b**) *US Fam (informer)* soplón(ona) *m,f*, chivato(a) *m,f*

rate [reɪt] **1** *n* (**a**) *(ratio)* índice *m*, tasa *f*; **at any r.** *(at least)* al menos; *(anyway)* en cualquier caso (**b**) *(cost)* precio *m*; *Fin (of interest, exchange)* tipo *m* (**c**) **at the r. of** *(speed)* a la velocidad de; *(quantity)* a razón de (**d**) **first r.** de primera categoría (**e**) *Br* **rates** impuestos *mpl* municipales

　　2 *vt* (**a**) *(estimate)* estimar (**b**) *(evaluate)* tasar (**c**) *(consider)* considerar

rateable ['reɪtəbəl] *adj Br* **r. value** valor *m* catastral

ratepayer ['reɪtpeɪə(r)] *n Br* contribuyente *mf*

rather ['rɑːðə(r)] *adv* (**a**) *(quite)* más bien, bastante; *(very much so)* muy (**b**) *(more accurately)* mejor dicho; **r. than**

(instead of) en vez de; *(more than)* más que (**c**) **she would r. stay here** *(prefer to)* prefiere quedarse aquí

ratify ['rætɪfaɪ] *vt* ratificar

rating ['reɪtɪŋ] *n* (**a**) *(valuation)* tasación *f*; *(score)* valoración *f* (**b**) *TV* **(programme) ratings** índice *m* de audiencia (**c**) *Naut* marinero *m* sin graduación

ratio ['reɪʃɪəʊ] *n* razón *f*; **in the r. of** a razón de

ration ['ræʃən] **1** *n* (**a**) *(allowance)* ración *f* (**b**) **rations** víveres *mpl*

　　2 *vt* racionar

rational ['ræʃənəl] *adj* racional

rationale [ræʃə'nɑːl] *n* base *f*

rationalize ['ræʃənəlaɪz] *vt* racionalizar

rattle ['rætəl] **1** *n* (**a**) *(of train, cart)* traqueteo *m*; *(of metal)* repiqueteo *m*; *(of glass)* tintineo *m* (**b**) *(toy)* sonajero *m*; *(instrument)* carraca *f*

　　2 *vt* (**a**) *(keys etc)* hacer sonar (**b**) *Fam (unsettle)* poner nervioso(a)

　　3 *vi* sonar; *(metal)* repiquetear; *(glass)* tintinear

rattlesnake ['rætəlsneɪk] *n* serpiente *f* de cascabel

raucous ['rɔːkəs] *adj* estridente

ravage ['rævɪdʒ] *Fml* **1** *n (usu pl)* estragos *mpl*

　　2 *vt* asolar, devastar

rave [reɪv] **1** *vi* (**a**) *(be delirious)* delirar (**b**) *(be angry)* enfurecerse (**at** con) (**c**) *Fam (show enthusiasm)* entusiasmarse (**about** por)

　　2 *n Fam* **r. review** crítica *f* muy favorable

raven ['reɪvən] *n* cuervo *m*

ravenous ['rævənəs] *adj* **I'm r.** tengo un hambre que no veo

ravine [rə'viːn] *n* barranco *m*

raving ['reɪvɪŋ] *n Fam* **r. mad** loco(a) de atar

ravishing ['rævɪʃɪŋ] *adj (person)* encantador(a)

raw [rɔː] *adj* (**a**) *(uncooked)* crudo(a) (**b**) *(not processed)* bruto(a); *(alcohol)* puro(a); **r. material** materia prima (**c**) *(emotion)* instintivo(a) (**d**) *(weather)* crudo(a) (**e**) **r. deal** trato injusto (**f**) *(wound)* abierto(a); **r. flesh** carne viva (**g**) *US (inexperienced)* novato(a) (**h**) *(frank)* franco(a)

ray¹ [reɪ] *n* rayo *m*; *Fig* **r. of hope** rayo de esperanza

ray² [reɪ] *n (fish)* raya *f*

rayon ['reɪɒn] *n* rayón *m*

raze [reɪz] *vt* arrasar

razor ['reɪzə(r)] *n (for shaving)* maquinilla *f* de afeitar; **r. blade** hoja *f* de afeitar

Rd *(abbr* **Road)** calle *f*, c/

re [riː] *prep* respecto a, con referencia a

reach [riːtʃ] **1** *vt* (**a**) *(arrive at)* llegar a (**b**) *(contact)* localizar

2 *vi* alcanzar; **to r. for sth** intentar coger algo; **to r. out** extender la mano

3 *n* (**a**) *(range)* alcance *m*; **out of r.** fuera del alcance; **within r.** al alcance (**b**) *(in boxing)* extensión *f* del brazo (**c**) **reaches** *(on a river)* recta *f*

react [rɪˈækt] *vi* reaccionar

reaction [rɪˈækʃən] *n* reacción *f*

reactor [rɪˈæktə(r)] *n* reactor *m*

read [riːd] **1** *vt* (*pt & pp* **read** [red]) (**a**) leer (**b**) *(decipher)* descifrar (**c**) *(understand)* entender; *(interpret)* interpretar (**d**) *Univ* estudiar (**e**) *(of dial)* marcar (**f**) *(of signpost, text)* decir

2 *vi* leer

▸ **read out** *vt sep* leer en voz alta

readable [ˈriːdəbəl] *adj* (**a**) *(interesting)* interesante (**b**) *(legible)* legible

reader [ˈriːdə(r)] *n* (**a**) lector(a) *m,f* (**b**) *(book)* libro *m* de lectura (**c**) *Br Univ* profesor(a) *m,f* adjunto(a)

readership [ˈriːdəʃɪp] *n Press* lectores *mpl*

readily [ˈredɪlɪ] *adv* (**a**) *(easily)* fácilmente; **r. available** disponible en el acto (**b**) *(willingly)* de buena gana

readiness [ˈredmɪs] *n* (**a**) *(preparedness)* preparación *f* (**b**) *(willingness)* buena disposición

reading [ˈriːdɪŋ] *n* (**a**) lectura *f* (**b**) *Fig* interpretación *f* (**c**) *(of laws, bill)* presentación *f*

readjust [riːəˈdʒʌst] **1** *vt* reajustar

2 *vi (adapt oneself)* adaptarse

ready [ˈredɪ] *adj* (**a**) *(prepared)* listo(a), preparado(a); **r., steady, go!** ¡preparados, listos, ya! (**b**) **r. to** *(about to)* a punto de (**c**) *(to hand)* a mano; **r. cash** dinero *m* en efectivo (**d**) *(willing)* dispuesto(a)

ready-cooked [ˈredɪˈkʊkt] *adj* precocinado(a)

ready-made [ˈredɪˈmeɪd] *adj* confeccionado(a); *(food)* preparado(a)

real [rɪəl] *adj* (**a**) real, verdadero(a); *Fam* **for r.** de veras (**b**) *(genuine)* auténtico(a); **r. leather** piel legítima (**c**) *US Com* **r. estate** bienes *mpl* inmuebles; **r. estate agent** agente inmobiliario

realism [ˈrɪəlɪzəm] *n* realismo *m*

realistic [ˈrɪəlɪstɪk] *adj* realista

reality [rɪˈælɪtɪ] *n* realidad *f*; **in r.** en realidad

realization [rɪələˈzeɪʃən] *n* (**a**) *(understanding)* comprensión *f* (**b**) *(of plan, assets)* realización *f*

realize [ˈrɪəlaɪz] *vt* (**a**) *(become aware of)* darse cuenta de (**b**) *(assets, plan)* realizar

really [ˈrɪəlɪ] *adv* verdaderamente, realmente; **I r. don't know** no lo sé de verdad; **r.?** ¿de veras?

realm [relm] *n (kingdom)* reino *m*; *Fig (field)* terreno *m*

realtor [ˈrɪəltə(r)] *n US* agente *mf* inmobiliario(a)

ream [riːm] *n (of paper)* resma *f*

reap [riːp] *vt Agr* cosechar; *Fig* **to r. the benefits** llevarse los beneficios

reappear [riːəˈpɪə(r)] *vi* reaparecer

reappraisal [riːəˈpreɪzəl] *n* revaluación *f*

rear¹ [rɪə(r)] **1** *n* (**a**) *(back part)* parte *f* de atrás (**b**) *Fam (buttocks)* trasero *m*

2 *adj* trasero(a); **r. entrance** puerta *f* de atrás

rear² [rɪə(r)] **1** *vt* (**a**) *(breed, raise)* criar (**b**) *(lift up)* levantar

2 *vi* **to r. up** *(horse)* encabritarse

rearguard [ˈrɪɑːd] *n* retaguardia *f*

rearmament [riːˈɑːməmənt] *n* rearme *m*

rearrange [riːəˈreɪndʒ] *vt* (**a**) *(furniture)* colocar de otra manera (**b**) *(appointment)* fijar otra fecha para

rear-view [ˈrɪəvjuː] *adj* **r. mirror** (espejo *m*) retrovisor *m*

reason [ˈriːzən] **1** *n* (**a**) motivo *m*, razón *f*; **for no r.** sin razón; **for some r.** por algún motivo (**b**) *(good sense)* razón *f*; **it stands to r.** es lógico; **to listen to r.** atender a razones

2 *vi* (**a**) **to r. with sb** convencer a algn (**b**) *(argue, work out)* razonar

reasonable [ˈriːzənəbəl] *adj* (**a**) *(fair)* razonable (**b**) *(sensible)* sensato(a) (**c**) *(average)* regular

reasonably [ˈriːzənəblɪ] *adv (fairly)* bastante

reasoning [ˈriːzənɪŋ] *n* razonamiento *m*

reassurance [riːəˈʃʊərəns] *n* consuelo *m*

reassure [riːəˈʃʊə(r)] *vt* (**a**) *(comfort)* tranquilizar (**b**) *(restore confidence)* dar confianza a

reassuring [riːəˈʃʊərɪŋ] *adj* consolador(a)

rebate [ˈriːbeɪt] *n* devolución *f*; **tax r.** devolución fiscal

> 🖉 Note that the Spanish verb **rebatir** is a false friend and is never a translation for the English verb **to rebate**. In Spanish, **rebatir** means "to refute".

rebel 1 *adj & n* [ˈrebəl] rebelde *(mf)*

2 *vi* [rɪˈbel] rebelarse, sublevarse (**against** contra)

rebellion [rɪˈbeljən] *n* rebelión *f*

rebellious [rɪ'beljəs] *adj* rebelde

rebound 1 *n* ['riːbaʊnd] *(of ball)* rebote *m*; *Fig* **on the r.** de rebote

  2 *vi* [rɪ'baʊnd] *(ball)* rebotar

rebuff [rɪ'bʌf] **1** *n* desaire *m*

  2 *vt* desairar

rebuild [riː'bɪld] *vt* reconstruir

rebuke [rɪ'bjuːk] **1** *n* reproche *m*

  2 *vt* reprochar

rebut [rɪ'bʌt] *vt* refutar

recalcitrant [rɪ'kælsɪtrənt] *adj Fml* recalcitrante

recall [rɪ'kɔːl] *vt* **(a)** *(soldiers, products)* hacer volver; *(ambassador)* retirar **(b)** *(remember)* recordar

recant [rɪ'kænt] *vi Fml* retractarse

recap **1** *vt & vi* [riː'kæp] resumir; **to r.** en resumen

  2 *n* ['riːkæp] recapitulación *f*

recapitulate [riːkə'pɪtjʊleɪt] *vt & vi Fml* recapitular

recapture [riː'kæptʃə(r)] *vt Fig* recuperar

recd *Com (abbr* **received)** recibido(a)

recede [rɪ'siːd] *vi* retroceder; *(fade)* desvanecerse

receipt [rɪ'siːt] *n* **(a)** *(act)* recepción *f*; **to acknowledge r. of sth** acusar recibo de algo **(b)** *Com (paper)* recibo *m* **(c)** **receipts** *(takings)* recaudación *f*

receive [rɪ'siːv] *vt* **(a)** recibir **(b)** *Jur (stolen goods)* ocultar **(c)** *(welcome)* acoger **(d)** *TV & Rad* captar

receiver [rɪ'siːvə(r)] *n* **(a)** *(person)* receptor(a) *m,f* **(b)** *Jur (of stolen goods)* perista *mf* **(c)** *Br Jur* **official r.** síndico *m* **(d)** *Tel* auricular *m* **(e)** *Rad* receptor *m*

recent ['riːsənt] *adj* reciente; **in r. years** en los últimos años

recently ['riːsəntlɪ] *adv* hace poco, recientemente

receptacle [rɪ'septəkəl] *n* receptáculo *m*

reception [rɪ'sepʃən] *n* **(a)** *(welcome)* acogida *f* **(b)** *(party)* recepción *f*; **wedding r.** banquete *m* de bodas **(c) r. (desk)** recepción *f* **(d)** *Rad & TV* recepción *f*

receptionist [rɪ'sepʃənɪst] *n* recepcionista *mf*

recess ['riːses, 'riːses] *n* **(a)** *(in a wall)* hueco *m* **(b)** *(secret place)* escondrijo *m* **(c)** *US Educ* recreo *m*; *Pol* período *m* de vacaciones

recession [rɪ'seʃən] *n* recesión *f*

recharge [riː'tʃɑːdʒ] *vt (battery)* recargar

rechargeable [riː'tʃɑːdʒəbəl] *adj* recargable

recipe ['resɪpɪ] *n Culin* receta *f*; *Fig* fórmula *f*

recipient [rɪ'sɪpɪənt] *n* receptor(a) *m,f*; *(of letter)* destinatario(a) *m,f*

> 🖉 Note that the Spanish word **recipiente** is a false friend and is never a translation for the English word **recipient**. In Spanish, **recipiente** means "receptacle, container".

reciprocate [rɪ'sɪprəkeɪt] **1** *vt (favour etc)* devolver

  2 *vi* hacer lo mismo

recital [rɪ'saɪtəl] *n* recital *m*

recite [rɪ'saɪt] *vt & vi* recitar

reckless ['reklɪs] *adj (unwise)* imprudente; *(fearless)* temerario(a)

reckon ['rekən] *vt & vi* **(a)** *(calculate)* calcular; *(count)* contar **(b)** *Fam (think)* creer; *(consider)* considerar

▶ **reckon on** *vt insep* contar con

reckoner ['rekənə(r)] *n* **ready r.** tabla *f* de cálculo

reckoning ['rekənɪŋ] *n* cálculo *m*; **by my r. ...** según mis cálculos ...; *Fig* **day of r.** día *m* del juicio final

reclaim [rɪ'kleɪm] *vt* **(a)** *(recover)* recuperar; *(demand back)* reclamar **(b)** *(marshland etc)* recuperar

recline [rɪ'klaɪn] *vi* recostarse, reclinarse

reclining [rɪ'klaɪnɪŋ] *adj* recostado(a); **r. seat** asiento *m* abatible

recluse [rɪ'kluːs] *n* solitario(a) *m,f*

> 🖉 Note that the Spanish word **recluso** is a false friend and is never a translation for the English word **recluse**. In Spanish, **recluso** means "prisoner".

recognition [rekəg'nɪʃən] *n* reconocimiento *m*; *(appreciation)* apreciación *f*; **changed beyond all r.** irreconocible

recognizable [rekəg'naɪzəbəl] *adj* reconocible

recognize ['rekəgnaɪz] *vt* reconocer

recoil **1** *n* ['riːkɔɪl] *(of gun)* culatazo *m*; *(of spring)* aflojamiento *m*

  2 *vi* [rɪ'kɔɪl] **(a)** *(gun)* dar un culatazo; *(spring)* aflojarse **(b)** *(in fear)* espantarse

recollect [rekə'lekt] *vt* recordar

recollection [rekə'lekʃən] *n* recuerdo *m*

> 🖉 Note that the Spanish word **recolección** is a false friend and is never a translation for the English word **recollection**. In Spanish, **recolección** means "harvest, collection".

recommend [rekə'mend] *vt* recomendar

recommendation [rekəmen'deɪʃən] *n* recomendación *f*

recompense ['rekəmpens] **1** *n* recompensa *f*; *Jur* indemnización *f*

  2 *vt* recompensar; *Jur* indemnizar

reconcile ['rekənsaɪl] *vt (two people)* reconciliar; *(two ideas)* conciliar; **to r. oneself to** resignarse a

recondition [ri:kən'dɪʃən] *vt (engine)* revisar

reconnaissance [rɪ'kɒnɪsəns] *n* Mil reconocimiento *m*

reconnoitre, US **reconnoiter** [rekə'nɔɪtə(r)] *vt* Mil reconocer

reconsider [ri:kən'sɪdə(r)] *vt* reconsiderar

reconstruct [ri:kən'strʌkt] *vt* reconstruir

reconstruction [ri:kən'strʌkʃən] *n* reconstrucción *f*

record 1 *n* ['rekɔ:d] (**a**) *(account)* relación *f*; *(of meeting)* actas *fpl*; **off the r.** confidencialmente (**b**) *(document)* documento *m*; **r. of attendance** registro *m* de asistencia; **public records** archivos *mpl* (**c**) *Med* historial médico (**d**) *Mus* disco *m*; **r. player** tocadiscos *m inv* (**e**) *Sport* récord *m*

2 *vt* [rɪ'kɔ:d] (**a**) *(relate)* hacer constar; *(note down)* apuntar (**b**) *(record, voice)* grabar (**c**) *(of thermometer etc)* marcar

recorded [rɪ'kɔ:dɪd] *adj* **r. delivery** correo certificado; **r. message** mensaje grabado

recorder [rɪ'kɔ:də(r)] *n* (**a**) *(person)* registrador(a) *m,f*; *Jur* magistrado(a) *m,f* (**b**) *Mus* flauta *f*

recording [rɪ'kɔ:dɪŋ] *n (registering)* registro *m*; *(recorded music, message etc)* grabación *f*

recount [rɪ'kaʊnt] *vt (tell)* contar

re-count 1 *vi* [ri:'kaʊnt] *Pol* hacer un recuento

2 *n* ['ri:kaʊnt] *Pol* recuento *m*

recoup [rɪ'ku:p] *vt (losses etc)* recuperar

recourse [rɪ'kɔ:s] *n* **to have r. to** recurrir a

recover [rɪ'kʌvə(r)] **1** *vt (items, lost time)* recuperar; *(consciousness)* recobrar

2 *vi (from illness etc)* reponerse

recovery [rɪ'kʌvərɪ] *n* (**a**) *(retrieval)* recuperación *f* (**b**) *(from illness)* restablecimiento *m*

recreation [rekrɪ'eɪʃən] *n* (**a**) diversión *f* (**b**) *Educ (playtime)* recreo *m*; **r. ground** terreno *m* de juegos

recreational [rekrɪ'eɪʃənəl] *adj* recreativo(a)

recrimination [rɪkrɪmɪ'neɪʃən] *n* reproche *m*

recruit [rɪ'kru:t] **1** *n* recluta *m*

2 *vt (soldiers)* reclutar; *(workers)* contratar

recruitment [rɪ'kru:tmənt] *n (of soldiers)* reclutamiento *m*; *(of employees)* contratación *f*

rectangle ['rektæŋgəl] *n* rectángulo *m*

rectangular [rek'tæŋgjʊlə(r)] *adj* rectangular

rectify ['rektɪfaɪ] *vt* rectificar

rector ['rektə(r)] *n* (**a**) *Rel* párroco *m* (**b**) *Scot Educ* director(a) *m,f*

recuperate [rɪ'ku:pəreɪt] *vi* reponerse

recur [rɪ'kɜ:(r)] *vi* repetirse

> ⚠ Note that the Spanish verb **recurrir** is a false friend and is never a translation for the English verb **to recur**. In Spanish, **recurrir** means "to appeal, to resort".

recurrence [rɪ'kʌrəns] *n* repetición *f*, reaparición *f*

recurrent [rɪ'kʌrənt] *adj* constante; *Med* recurrente

recycle [ri:'saɪkəl] *vt* reciclar

recycling [ri:'saɪklɪŋ] *n* reciclaje *m*

red [red] **1** *adj* (**redder, reddest**) rojo(a); **r. light** semáforo *m* en rojo; **r. wine** vino tinto; **to go r.** ponerse colorado(a); **to have r. hair** ser pelirrojo(a); *Fig* **r. herring** truco *m* para despistar; *Fam* **to roll out the r. carpet for sb** recibir a algn con todos los honores; **R. Cross** Cruz Roja; **R. Indian** piel roja *mf*; **R. Riding Hood** Caperucita Roja; **R. Sea** Mar Rojo; **r. tape** papeleo *m*

2 *n* (**a**) *(colour)* rojo *m* (**b**) *Fin* **to be in the r.** estar en números rojos

redcurrant ['redkʌrənt] *n* grosella roja

redden ['redən] **1** *vi (blush)* enrojecerse, ponerse colorado(a)

2 *vt (make red)* teñir de rojo

reddish ['redɪʃ] *adj* rojizo(a)

redeem [rɪ'di:m] *vt* (**a**) *(regain)* recobrar; *(from pawn)* desempeñar; *(voucher)* canjear (**b**) *(debt)* amortizar (**c**) *(film, novel etc)* salvar (**d**) *Rel* redimir; *Fig* **to r. oneself** redimirse

redeeming [rɪ'di:mɪŋ] *adj* compensatorio(a); **his only r. feature** lo único que le salva

redemption [rɪ'dempʃən] *n* Fml (**a**) *(of debt)* amortización *f* (**b**) *Rel* redención *f*; **beyond r.** sin remedio

redeploy [ri:dɪ'plɔɪ] *vt* redistribuir

red-handed [red'hændɪd] *adj* **to catch sb r.** coger a algn con las manos en la masa

redhead ['redhed] *n* pelirrojo(a) *m,f*

red-hot [red'hɒt] *adj* (**a**) candente; **r. news** noticia(s) *f(pl)* de última hora (**b**) *Fam (passionate)* ardiente

redial [ri:'daɪəl] *n* Tel *(facility)* rellamada *f*

redirect [ri:dɪ'rekt] *vt* (**a**) *(funds)* redistribuir (**b**) *(letter)* remitir a la nueva dirección

red-light [red'laɪt] *adj Fam* **r. district** barrio chino

redouble [riː'dʌbəl] *vt* redoblar

redress [rɪ'dres] *Fml* **1** *n* reparación *f*
  2 *vt* reparar

redskin ['redskɪn] *n* piel roja *mf*

reduce [rɪ'djuːs] *vt* (**a**) reducir (**b**) *(in rank)* degradar (**c**) *Culin (sauce)* espesar (**d**) *Med* recomponer

reduction [rɪ'dʌkʃən] *n* reducción *f*; *Com (in purchase price)* descuento *m*, rebaja *f*

redundancy [rɪ'dʌndənsɪ] *n* despido *m*

redundant [rɪ'dʌndənt] *adj* (**a**) *(superfluous)* redundante (**b**) *Ind* **to be made r.** perder el empleo; **to make sb r.** despedir a algn

reed [riːd] *n* (**a**) *Bot* caña *f* (**b**) *Mus* caramillo *m*

reef [riːf] *n* arrecife *m*

reek [riːk] **1** *n* tufo *m*
  2 *vi* apestar

reel [riːl] **1** *n* (**a**) *(spool)* bobina *f*, carrete *m* (**b**) *Scot Mus* danza *f* tradicional
  2 *vi (stagger)* tambalearse

re-elect [riːɪ'lekt] *vt* reelegir

ref [ref] *n* (**a**) *Fam Sport* árbitro *m* (**b**) *Com (abbr reference)* ref

refectory [rɪ'fektərɪ] *n* refectorio *m*

refer [rɪ'fɜː(r)] **1** *vt* mandar, enviar; **to r. a matter to a tribunal** remitir un asunto a un tribunal
  2 *vi* (**a**) *(allude)* referirse, aludir (**to** a) (**b**) **r. to** *(consult)* consultar

referee [refə'riː] **1** *n* (**a**) *Sport* árbitro *m, f* (**b**) *(for job application)* garante *mf*
  2 *vt Sport* arbitrar

reference ['refərəns] *n* (**a**) referencia *f*; **with r. to** referente a, con referencia a; **r. book** libro *m* de consulta; **r. library** biblioteca *f* de consulta (**b**) *(character report)* informe *m*, referencia *f*

referendum [refə'rendəm] *n* referéndum *m*

refill **1** *n* ['riːfɪl] (**a**) *(replacement)* recambio *m*, carga *f* (**b**) *Fam (drink)* otra copa
  2 *vt* [riː'fɪl] rellenar

refine [rɪ'faɪn] *vt* refinar

refined [rɪ'faɪnd] *adj* refinado(a)

refinement [rɪ'faɪnmənt] *n* refinamiento *m*

refinery [rɪ'faɪnərɪ] *n* refinería *f*

reflect [rɪ'flekt] **1** *vt* *(light, attitude)* reflejar
  2 *vi (think)* reflexionar; **to r. on sth** meditar sobre algo

reflection [rɪ'flekʃən] *n* (**a**) *(indication, mirror image)* reflejo *m* (**b**) *(thought)* reflexión *f*; **on r.** pensándolo bien (**c**) *(criticism)* crítica *f*

reflector [rɪ'flektə(r)] *n (of vehicle)* catafaro *m*

reflex ['riːfleks] *n* reflejo *m*

reflexive [rɪ'fleksɪv] *adj* reflexivo(a)

reform [rɪ'fɔːm] **1** *n* reforma *f*; **r. school** reformatorio *m*
  2 *vt* reformar

reformation [refə'meɪʃən] *n* reforma *f*

reformatory [rɪ'fɔːmətərɪ] *n* reformatorio *m*

reformer [rɪ'fɔːmə(r)] *n* reformador(a). *m,f*

refrain [rɪ'freɪn] **1** *n Mus* estribillo *m*; *Fig* lema *m*
  2 *vi* abstenerse (**from** de)

refresh [rɪ'freʃ] *vt* refrescar

refresher [rɪ'freʃə(r)] *n* **r. course** cursillo *m* de reciclaje

refreshing [rɪ'freʃɪŋ] *adj* refrescante; **a r. change** un cambio muy agradable

refreshment [rɪ'freʃmənt] *n* refresco *m*

refrigerator [rɪ'frɪdʒəreɪtə(r)] *n* nevera *f*, frigorífico *m*, *Andes* frigider *m*, *RP* heladera *f*

refuel [riː'fjuːəl] *vi* repostar combustible

refuge ['refjuːdʒ] *n* refugio *m*, cobijo *m*; **to take r.** refugiarse

refugee [refjʊ'dʒiː] *n* refugiado(a) *m,f*

refund **1** *n* ['riːfʌnd] reembolso *m*
  2 *vt* [rɪ'fʌnd] reembolsar, devolver

refurbish [riː'fɜːbɪʃ] *vt* redecorar

refusal [rɪ'fjuːzəl] *n* negativa *f*; **to have first r. on sth** tener la primera opción en algo

refuse¹ [rɪ'fjuːz] **1** *vt* rechazar; **to r. sb sth** negar algo a algn
  2 *vi* negarse

refuse² ['refjuːs] *n* basura *f*; **r. collector** basurero *m*

refute [rɪ'fjuːt] *vt* refutar, rebatir

regain [rɪ'geɪn] *vt* recuperar; *(consciousness)* recobrar

regal ['riːgəl] *adj* regio(a)

regard [rɪ'gɑːd] **1** *n* (**a**) *(concern)* consideración *f*, respeto *m*; **with r. to** respecto a (**b**) *(esteem)* estima *f* (**c**) **regards** *(good wishes)* recuerdos *mpl*; **give him my regards** dale recuerdos de mi parte
  2 *vt* (**a**) *(consider)* considerar (**b**) **as regards** *(regarding)* respecto a

regarding [rɪ'gɑːdɪŋ] *prep* respecto a

regardless [rɪ'gɑːdlɪs] **1** *prep* **r. of** sin tener en cuenta; **r. of the outcome** pase lo que pase
  2 *adv* a toda costa

regime [reɪ'ʒiːm] *n* régimen *m*

regiment ['redʒɪmənt] **1** n regimiento m
2 vt regimentar

regimental [redʒɪ'mentəl] adj del regimiento

region ['riːdʒən] n (a) región f (b) **in the r. of** aproximadamente

regional ['riːdʒənəl] adj regional

regionalism ['riːdʒənəlɪzəm] n regionalismo m

register ['redʒɪstə(r)] **1** n registro m
2 vt (a) (record) registrar (b) (letter) certificar (c) (show) mostrar; **his face registered fear** en su rostro se reflejaba el miedo
3 vi (for course) inscribirse; Univ matricularse

registered ['redʒɪstəd] adj certificado(a); **r. letter** carta certificada; **r. trademark** marca registrada

registrar [redʒɪ'straː(r), 'redʒɪstraː(r)] n (a) (record keeper) registrador(a) m,f (b) Br Med interno(a) m,f (c) Univ secretario(a) m,f general

registration [redʒɪ'streɪʃən] n inscripción f; Univ matrícula f; Br Aut **r. number** matrícula f

registry ['redʒɪstrɪ] n registro m; **to get married in a r. office** casarse por lo civil; **r. office** registro civil

regret [rɪ'gret] **1** n (remorse) remordimiento m; (sadness) pesar m; **regrets** (excuses) excusas fpl; **to have no regrets** no arrepentirse de nada
2 vt arrepentirse de, lamentar

regretful [rɪ'gretfʊl] adj arrepentido(a)

regrettable [rɪ'gretəbəl] adj lamentable

regroup [riː'gruːp] **1** vt reagrupar
2 vi reagruparse

regular ['regjʊlə(r)] **1** adj (a) regular (b) (usual) normal (c) (staff) permanente (d) (frequent) frecuente (e) **r. army** tropas fpl regulares (f) US Fam **a r. guy** un tío legal, Am un tipo derecho
2 n (a) (customer) cliente mf habitual (b) Mil militar m de carrera

regularity [regjʊ'lærɪtɪ] n regularidad f

regularly ['regjʊləlɪ] adv con regularidad

regulate ['regjʊleɪt] vt regular

regulation [regjʊ'leɪʃən] **1** n (a) (control) regulación f (b) (rule) regla f
2 adj reglamentario(a)

rehabilitation [riːəbɪlɪ'teɪʃən] n rehabilitación f; **r. centre** centro m de reinserción

rehearsal [rɪ'hɜːsəl] n ensayo m

rehearse [rɪ'hɜːs] vt & vi ensayar

reign [reɪn] **1** n reinado m
2 vi reinar

reigning ['reɪnɪŋ] adj **r. champion** campeón m actual

reimburse [riːɪm'bɜːs] vt reembolsar

rein [reɪn] n (for horse) rienda f; Fig **he gave free r. to his emotions** dio rienda suelta a sus emociones

reindeer ['reɪndɪə(r)] n reno m

reinforce [riːɪn'fɔːs] vt (strengthen) reforzar; (support) apoyar; **reinforced concrete** hormigón armado

reinforcement [riːɪn'fɔːsmənt] n (a) refuerzo m; Constr armazón m (b) Mil **reinforcements** refuerzos mpl

reinstate [riːɪn'steɪt] vt (to job) reincorporar

reiterate [riː'ɪtəreɪt] vt & vi reiterar

reject 1 n ['riːdʒekt] (a) desecho m (b) Com **rejects** artículos defectuosos
2 vt [rɪ'dʒekt] rechazar

rejection [rɪ'dʒekʃən] n rechazo m

rejoice [rɪ'dʒɔɪs] vi regocijarse (**at** or **over** de)

rejuvenate [rɪ'dʒuːvɪneɪt] vt rejuvenecer; Fig revitalizar

relapse [rɪ'læps] **1** n (a) Med recaída f; **to have a r.** sufrir una recaída (b) (into crime, alcoholism) reincidencia f
2 vi recaer

relate [rɪ'leɪt] **1** vt (a) (connect) relacionar (b) (tell) relatar
2 vi relacionarse

related [rɪ'leɪtɪd] adj (a) (linked) relacionado(a) (**to** con) (b) **to be r. to sb** ser pariente de algn

relation [rɪ'leɪʃən] n (a) (link) relación f; **in** or **with r. to** respecto a; **it bears no r. to what we said** no tiene nada que ver con lo que dijimos (b) (member of family) pariente(a) m,f

relationship [rɪ'leɪʃənʃɪp] n (a) (link) relación f (b) (between people) relaciones fpl; **to have a good/bad r. with sb** llevarse bien/mal con algn

relative ['relətɪv] **1** n pariente mf
2 adj relativo(a)

relatively ['relətɪvlɪ] adv relativamente

relax [rɪ'læks] **1** vt (muscles, rules) relajar
2 vi relajarse

relaxation [riːlæk'seɪʃən] n (a) (rest) descanso m, relajación f (b) (of rules) relajación f (c) (pastime) distracción f

relaxed [rɪ'lækst] adj relajado(a); (peaceful) tranquilo(a)

relaxing [rɪ'læksɪŋ] adj relajante

relay 1 n ['riːleɪ] (a) relevo m; **r. (race)** carrera f de relevos (b) Rad & TV retransmisión f

2 *vt* [rɪ'leɪ] (**a**) *(pass on)* difundir (**b**) *Rad & TV* retransmitir

release [rɪ'liːs] **1** *n* (**a**) *(of prisoner)* liberación *f*, puesta *f* en libertad; *(of gas)* escape *m* (**b**) *Com* puesta *f* en venta (**c**) *Cin* estreno *m* (**d**) *(record)* disco *m* (**e**) *Press* comunicado *m*
2 *vt* (**a**) *(let go)* soltar; *(prisoner)* poner en libertad; *(gas)* despedir (**b**) *Com* poner en venta (**c**) *Cin* estrenar (**d**) *(record)* editar (**e**) *(publish)* publicar

relegate ['relɪgeɪt] *vt* (**a**) relegar (**b**) *Ftb* **to be relegated** bajar a una división inferior

relent [rɪ'lent] *vi* ceder; *(storm)* aplacarse

relentless [rɪ'lentlɪs] *adj* implacable

relevant ['reləvənt] *adj* pertinente (**to** a); **it is not r.** no viene al caso

> *Note that the Spanish word **relevante** is a false friend and is never a translation for the English word **relevant**. In Spanish, **relevante** means "outstanding, important".*

reliability [rɪlaɪə'bɪlɪtɪ] *n* (**a**) *(of person)* formalidad *f* (**b**) *(of car, machine)* fiabilidad *f*

reliable [rɪ'laɪəbəl] *adj (person)* de fiar; **a r. car** un coche seguro; **a r. source** una fuente fidedigna

reliably [rɪ'laɪəblɪ] *adv* **to be r. informed that** saber de buena tinta que

reliant [rɪ'laɪənt] *adj* **to be r. on** depender de

relic ['relɪk] *n* (**a**) *Rel* reliquia *f* (**b**) *(reminder of past)* vestigio *m*

relief [rɪ'liːf] *n* (**a**) alivio *m* (**b**) *(help)* auxilio *m*, ayuda *f*; *US* **to be on r.** cobrar un subsidio (**c**) *Art & Geog* relieve *m*

relieve [rɪ'liːv] *vt* (**a**) aliviar; *(monotony)* romper (**b**) *(take over from)* relevar (**c**) *Euph* **to r. oneself** hacer sus necesidades (**d**) **to r. sb of sth** coger algo a algn

relieved [rɪ'liːvd] *adj* aliviado(a), tranquilizado(a)

religion [rɪ'lɪdʒən] *n* religión *f*

religious [rɪ'lɪdʒəs] *adj* religioso(a)

relinquish [rɪ'lɪŋkwɪʃ] *vt* renunciar a; **to r. one's hold on sth** soltar algo

relish ['relɪʃ] **1** *n* (**a**) *(enjoyment)* deleite *m* (**b**) *Culin* condimento *m*
2 *vt* agradar

relocate [riːləʊ'keɪt] *vt* trasladar

reluctance [rɪ'lʌktəns] *n* desgana *f*

reluctant [rɪ'lʌktənt] *adj* reacio(a); **to be r. to do sth** estar poco dispuesto(a) a hacer algo

reluctantly [rɪ'lʌktəntlɪ] *adv* de mala gana, a regañadientes

rely [rɪ'laɪ] *vi* contar (**on** con), confiar (**on** en)

remain [rɪ'meɪn] **1** *vi* (**a**) *(stay)* permanecer, quedarse (**b**) *(be left)* quedar; **it remains to be seen** está por ver
2 *npl* **remains** restos *mpl*

remainder [rɪ'meɪndə(r)] *n* resto *m*

remaining [rɪ'meɪnɪŋ] *adj* restante

remand [rɪ'mɑːnd] *Jur* **1** *vt* remitir; **remanded in custody** en prevención
2 *n* detención *f*; **on r.** detenido(a)

remark [rɪ'mɑːk] **1** *n* comentario *m*
2 *vt* comentar, observar

> *Note that the Spanish verb **remarcar** is a false friend and is never a translation for the English verb **to remark**. In Spanish, **remarcar** means "to stress, to underline".*

remarkable [rɪ'mɑːkəbəl] *adj* extraordinario(a); *(strange)* curioso(a)

remedial [rɪ'miːdɪəl] *adj* reparador(a); **r. classes** clases *fpl* para niños atrasados en los estudios

remedy ['remɪdɪ] **1** *n* remedio *m*
2 *vt* remediar

remember [rɪ'membə(r)] **1** *vt* (**a**) acordarse de, recordar (**b**) **r. me to your mother** dale recuerdos a tu madre
2 *vi* acordarse, recordar; **I don't r.** no me acuerdo

remembrance [rɪ'membrəns] *n* **in r. of** en recuerdo de; *Br* **R. Day** *or* **Sunday** = día en que se conmemora el armisticio de 1918

remind [rɪ'maɪnd] *vt* recordar; **r. me to do it** recuérdame que lo haga; **she reminds me of your sister** me recuerda a tu hermana; **that reminds me** ahora que me acuerdo

reminder [rɪ'maɪndə(r)] *n* recordatorio *m*, aviso *m*

reminisce [remɪ'nɪs] *vi* rememorar

reminiscent [remɪ'nɪsənt] *adj Fml* nostálgico(a); **to be r. of** recordar

remiss [rɪ'mɪs] *adj (negligent)* descuidado(a)

remission [rɪ'mɪʃən] *n* (**a**) *Med* remisión *f* (**b**) *Jur* perdón *m*

remit [rɪ'mɪt] *vt* (**a**) *(send)* remitir (**b**) *Jur* referir a otro tribunal

remittance [rɪ'mɪtəns] *n* (**a**) *(sending)* envío *m* (**b**) *(payment)* giro *m*, pago *m*

remnant ['remnənt] *n* resto *m*; **remnants** *(of cloth)* retales *mpl*

remould ['riːməʊld] *n US* = **remould**

remorse [rɪ'mɔːs] *n* remordimiento *m*

remorseful [rɪ'mɔːsfʌl] *adj* lleno(a) de remordimiento

remorseless [rɪ'mɔːslɪs] *adj* despiadado(a)

remote [rɪ'məʊt] *adj* (**a**) *(far away)* remoto(a); **r. control** mando *m* a distancia (**b**) *(isolated)* aislado(a) (**c**) *(possibility)* remoto(a); **I haven't the remotest idea** no tengo la más mínima idea

remote-controlled [rɪ'məʊtkən'trəʊld] *adj* teledirigido(a)

remotely [rɪ'məʊtlɪ] *adv* (**a**) *(vaguely)* vagamente (**b**) *(distantly)* en lugar aislado

remould ['riːməʊld] *n Aut* neumático recauchutado

removable [rɪ'muːvəbəl] *adj* *(detachable)* que se puede quitar

removal [rɪ'muːvəl] *n* (**a**) *(moving house)* mudanza *f*; **r. van** camión *m* de mudanzas (**b**) *(of stain etc)* eliminación *f*

remove [rɪ'muːv] *vt* (**move**) quitar; **to r. one's make-up** desmaquillarse; **to r. one's name from a list** tachar su nombre de una lista (**b**) *(from office)* despedir

> *ℓ* Note that the Spanish verb **remover** is a false friend and is never a translation for the English verb **to remove**. In Spanish, **remover** means "to move over, to turn over, to stir".

removed [rɪ'muːvd] *adj* **far r. from** muy diferente de

remover [rɪ'muːvə(r)] *n* **make-up r.** desmaquillador *m*; **nail varnish r.** quitaesmalte *m*; **stain r.** quitamanchas *m inv*

remuneration [rɪmjuːnə'reɪʃən] *n Fml* remuneración *f*

renaissance [rə'neɪsəns] **1** *n* renacimiento *m*; **the R.** el Renacimiento

2 *adj* renacentista

rend [rend] *vt* (*pt & pp* **rent**) *Fml* rasgar

render ['rendə(r)] *vt Fml* (**a**) *(give)* dar (**b**) *(make)* hacer (**c**) *Com* presentar (**d**) *(translate)* traducir

rendering ['rendərɪŋ] *n* (**a**) *(of song, piece of music)* interpretación *f* (**b**) *(translation)* traducción *f*

rendezvous ['rɒndɪvuː] **1** *n* (**a**) *(meeting)* cita *f* (**b**) *(place)* lugar *m* de reunión

2 *vi* reunirse

renegade ['renɪgeɪd] *n* renegado(a) *m,f*

renew [rɪ'njuː] *vt* *(contract etc)* renovar; *(talks etc)* reanudar; **with renewed vigour** con renovadas fuerzas

renewal [rɪ'njuːəl] *n* *(of contract etc)* renovación *f*; *(of talks etc)* reanudación *f*

renounce [rɪ'naʊns] *vt Fml* renunciar

renovate ['renəveɪt] *vt* renovar, hacer reformas en

renown [rɪ'naʊn] *n* renombre *m*

renowned [rɪ'naʊnd] *adj* renombrado(a)

rent [rent] **1** *n* (**a**) *(for building, car, TV)* alquiler *m* (**b**) *(for land)* arriendo *m*

2 *vt* (**a**) *(building, car, TV)* alquilar, *Méx* rentar (**b**) *(land)* arrendar

3 *pt & pp* of **rend**

rental ['rentəl] *n* *(of house etc)* alquiler *m*

renunciation [rɪnʌnsɪ'eɪʃən] *n Fml* renuncia *f*

reorganize [riː'ɔːgənaɪz] *vt* reorganizar

rep [rep] *n Fam* (**a**) *Com* representante *mf* (**b**) *Th* teatro *m* de repertorio

repaid [riː'peɪd] *pt & pp* of **repay**

repair [rɪ'peə(r)] **1** *n* reparación *f*, arreglo *m*; **in good/bad r.** en buen/mal estado

2 *vt* (**a**) *(make amends for)* reparar (**b**) *(clothes)* remendar (**b**) *(make amends for)* reparar

repartee [repɑː'tiː] *n* réplica aguda

repatriate [riː'pætrɪeɪt] *vt* repatriar

repay [riː'peɪ] *vt* (*pt & pp* **repaid**) devolver; **to r. a debt** liquidar una deuda; **to r. a kindness** devolver un favor

repayment [riː'peɪmənt] *n* pago *m*

repeal [rɪ'piːl] *Jur* **1** *n* revocación *f*

2 *vt* revocar

repeat [rɪ'piːt] **1** *vt* repetir; **to r. oneself** repetirse

2 *n* *(repetition)* repetición *f*; *TV* reposición *f*

repeated [rɪ'piːtɪd] *adj* repetido(a)

repeatedly [rɪ'piːtɪdlɪ] *adv* repetidas veces

repel [rɪ'pel] *vt* (**a**) *(fight off)* repeler (**b**) *(disgust)* repugnar

repellent [rɪ'pelənt] **1** *adj* repelente; **water-r.** impermeable

2 *n* (**insect**) **r.** loción *f* or spray *m* antiinsectos

repent [rɪ'pent] *vt & vi* arrepentirse (de)

repentance [rɪ'pentəns] *n* arrepentimiento *m*

repercussion [riːpə'kʌʃən] *n* *(usu pl)* repercusión *f*

repertoire ['repətwɑː(r)] *n* repertorio *m*

repertory ['repətərɪ] *n Th* teatro *m* de repertorio

repetition [repɪ'tɪʃən] *n* repetición *f*

repetitive [rɪ'petɪtɪv] *adj* repetitivo(a)

replace [rɪ'pleɪs] *vt* (**a**) *(put back)* volver a poner en su sitio (**b**) *(substitute for)* sustituir, reemplazar

replacement [rɪ'pleɪsmənt] *n* (**a**) *(returning)* reemplazo *m* (**b**) *(person)* sustituto(a) *m,f* (**c**) *(part)* pieza *f* de recambio

replay ['riːpleɪ] *n* repetición *f*

replenish [rɪ'plenɪʃ] *vt* (**a**) *(fill up)* rellenar (**b**) **to r. stocks** reponer las existencias

replete [rɪ'pliːt] *adj Fml* repleto(a)

replica ['replɪkə] *n* réplica *f*

reply [rɪ'plaɪ] **1** *n* respuesta *f*, contestación *f*
  2 *vi* responder, contestar

report [rɪ'pɔːt] **1** *n* (a) informe *m*; **medical r.** parte médico; *Br* **school r.** informe escolar (b) *(piece of news)* noticia *f* (c) *Press, Rad & TV* reportaje *m* (d) *(rumour)* rumor *m* (e) *Fml (of gun)* estampido *m*
  2 *vt* (a) **it is reported that ...** se dice que ... (b) *(tell authorities about)* denunciar (c) *Press* hacer un reportaje sobre
  3 *vi* (a) *(of committee member etc)* hacer un informe (b) *Press* hacer un reportaje (c) *(for duty etc)* presentarse; *Mil* **to r. sick** coger la baja por enfermedad

reported [rɪ'pɔːtɪd] *adj* **r. speech** estilo indirecto

reportedly [rɪ'pɔːtɪdlɪ] *adv Fml* según se dice

reporter [rɪ'pɔːtə(r)] *n* periodista *mf*

repose [rɪ'pəʊz] *Fml* **1** *n* reposo *m*
  2 *vt & vi* reposar

repossess [riːpə'zes] *vt* **our house has been repossessed** el banco ha ejecutado la hipoteca de nuestra casa

reprehensible [reprɪ'hensəbəl] *adj* reprensible, censurable

represent [reprɪ'zent] *vt* representar

representation [reprɪzen'teɪʃən] *n* (a) representación *f* (b) *Fml* **representations** queja *f*

representative [reprɪ'zentətɪv] **1** *adj* representativo(a)
  2 *n* (a) representante *mf* (b) *US Pol* diputado(a) *m,f*

repress [rɪ'pres] *vt* reprimir, contener

repressed [rɪ'prest] *adj* **to be r.** estar reprimido(a)

repression [rɪ'preʃən] *n* represión *f*

repressive [rɪ'presɪv] *adj* represivo(a)

reprieve [rɪ'priːv] **1** *n* (a) *Jur* indulto *m* (b) *Fig* alivio *m*
  2 *vt Jur* indultar

reprimand ['reprɪmaːnd] **1** *n* reprimenda *f*
  2 *vt* reprender

reprisal [rɪ'praɪzəl] *n* represalia *f*

reproach [rɪ'prəʊtʃ] **1** *n* reproche *m*; **beyond r.** intachable
  2 *vt* reprochar

reproachful [rɪ'prəʊtʃfʊl] *adj* reprobador(a)

reproduce [riːprə'djuːs] **1** *vt* reproducir
  2 *vi* reproducirse

reproduction [riːprə'dʌkʃən] *n* reproducción *f*

reproof [rɪ'pruːf] *n Fml* reprobación *f*, censura *f*

reprove [rɪ'pruːv] *vt Fml* reprobar, censurar

reptile ['reptaɪl] *n* reptil *m*

republic [rɪ'pʌblɪk] *n* república *f*

republican [rɪ'pʌblɪkən] *adj & n* republicano(a) *(m,f)*; *US Pol* **R. Party** Partido Republicano

repudiate [rɪ'pjuːdɪeɪt] *vt Fml* (a) *(reject)* rechazar (b) *(not acknowledge)* negarse a reconocer

repugnant [rɪ'pʌgnənt] *adj* repugnante

repulse [rɪ'pʌls] *vt* rechazar

repulsive [rɪ'pʌlsɪv] *adj* repulsivo(a)

reputable ['repjʊtəbəl] *adj (company etc)* acreditado(a); *(person, products)* de toda confianza

reputation [repjʊ'teɪʃən] *n* reputación *f*

repute [rɪ'pjuːt] *n Fml* reputación *f*

reputed [rɪ'pjuːtɪd] *adj* supuesto(a); **to be r. to be** ser considerado(a) como

reputedly [rɪ'pjuːtɪdlɪ] *adv* según se dice

request [rɪ'kwest] **1** *n* petición *f*, solicitud *f*; **available on r.** disponible a petición de los interesados; *Br* **r. stop** *(for bus)* parada *f* discrecional
  2 *vt* pedir, solicitar

require [rɪ'kwaɪə(r)] *vt* (a) *(need)* necesitar, requerir (b) *(demand)* exigir

requirement [rɪ'kwaɪəmənt] *n* (a) *(need)* necesidad *f* (b) *(demand)* requisito *m*

> 🖉 Note that the Spanish word **requerimiento** is a false friend and is never a translation for the English word **requirement**. In Spanish, **requerimiento** means both "entreaty" and "writ, injunction".

requisite ['rekwɪzɪt] *Fml* **1** *adj* requerido(a)
  2 *n* requisito *m*

requisition [rekwɪ'zɪʃən] **1** *n* requisición *f*
  2 *vt* requisar

rescind [rɪ'sɪnd] *vt Fml (contract)* rescindir; *(law)* abrogar

rescue ['reskjuː] **1** *n* rescate *m*; **r. team** equipo *m* de rescate
  2 *vt* rescatar

rescuer ['reskjʊə(r)] *n* rescatador(a) *m,f*

research [rɪ'sɜːtʃ] **1** *n* investigación *f*; **R. and Development** Investigación más Desarrollo
  2 *vt & vi* investigar

researcher [rɪ'sɜːtʃə(r)] *n* investigador(a) *m,f*

resemblance [rɪ'zembləns] *n* semejanza *f*

resemble [rɪ'zembəl] *vt* parecerse a

resent [rɪ'zent] *vt* ofenderse por

resentful [rɪ'zentfʊl] *adj* ofendido(a)

resentment [rɪ'zentmənt] *n* resentimiento *m*

reservation [rezə'veɪʃən] *n* reserva *f*

reserve [rɪ'zɜːv] **1** *n* (a) reserva *f*; **to keep sth in r.** guardar algo de reserva (b) *Sport* suplente *mf* (c) *Mil* **reserves** reservas *fpl*
2 *vt* reservar

reserved [rɪ'zɜːvd] *adj* reservado(a)

reservoir ['rezəvwɑː(r)] *n* embalse *m*, pantano *m*; *Fig* reserva *f*

reshape [riː'ʃeɪp] *vt* rehacer; *Fig* reorganizar

reshuffle [riː'ʃʌfəl] *n Pol* remodelación *f*

reside [rɪ'zaɪd] *vi Fml* residir

residence ['rezɪdəns] *n Fml (home)* residencia *f*; *(address)* domicilio *m*; *(period of time)* permanencia *f*

resident ['rezɪdənt] *adj & n* residente *(mf)*; *US Med* = médico que ha cumplido la residencia y prosigue con su especialización; **to be r. in** estar domiciliado(a) en

residential [rezɪ'denʃəl] *adj* residencial

residual [rɪ'zɪdjʊəl] *adj* residual

residue ['rezɪdjuː] *n* residuo *m*

resign [rɪ'zaɪn] **1** *vt* (a) *(give up)* dimitir (b) **to r. oneself to sth** resignarse a algo
2 *vi (from job)* dimitir

resignation [rezɪg'neɪʃən] *n* (a) *(from a job)* dimisión *f* (b) *(acceptance)* resignación *f*

resigned [rɪ'zaɪnd] *adj* resignado(a)

resilience [rɪ'zɪlɪəns] *n* resistencia *f*

resilient [rɪ'zɪlɪənt] *adj (strong)* resistente

resin ['rezɪn] *n* resina *f*

resist [rɪ'zɪst] **1** *vt* (a) *(not yield to)* resistir (b) *(oppose)* oponerse a
2 *vi* resistir

resistance [rɪ'zɪstəns] *n* resistencia *f*

resit [riː'sɪt] *vt (exam)* volver a presentarse a

resolute ['rezəluːt] *adj* resuelto(a), decidido(a)

resolution [rezə'luːʃən] *n* resolución *f*

resolve [rɪ'zɒlv] **1** *n* resolución *f*
2 *vt* resolver; **to r. to do** resolverse a hacer
3 *vi* resolverse

resonant ['rezənənt] *adj* resonante

resort [rɪ'zɔːt] **1** *n* (a) *(place)* lugar *m* de vacaciones; **tourist r.** centro turístico (b) *(recourse)* recurso *m*; **as a last r.** como último recurso
2 *vi* recurrir (**to** a)

> *Note that the Spanish word* **resorte** *is a false friend and is never a translation for the English word* **resort**. *In Spanish,* **resorte** *means both "spring" and "means".*

resound [rɪ'zaʊnd] *vi* resonar; *Fig* tener resonancia

resounding [rɪ'zaʊndɪŋ] *adj* **a r. failure** un fracaso total; **a r. success** un éxito rotundo

resource [rɪ'sɔːs] *n* recurso *m*

resourceful [rɪ'sɔːsfʊl] *adj* ingenioso(a)

respect [rɪ'spekt] **1** *n* (a) *(deference)* respeto *m*; **to pay one's respects to sb** presentar sus respetos a algn (b) *(relation, reference)* respecto *m*; **in that r.** a ese respecto; **with r. to** con referencia a
2 *vt* respetar

respectable [rɪ'spektəbəl] *adj* respetable; *(clothes)* decente

respectful [rɪ'spektfʊl] *adj* respetuoso(a)

respective [rɪ'spektɪv] *adj* respectivo(a)

respectively [rɪ'spektɪvlɪ] *adv* respectivamente

respite ['respaɪt] *n Fml* respiro *m*

resplendent [rɪ'splendənt] *adj* resplandeciente

respond [rɪ'spɒnd] *vi* responder

response [rɪ'spɒns] *n* (a) *(reply)* respuesta *f* (b) *(reaction)* reacción *f*

responsibility [rɪspɒnsə'bɪlɪtɪ] *n* responsabilidad *f*

responsible [rɪ'spɒnsəbəl] *adj* responsable (**for** de); **to be r. to sb** tener que dar cuentas a algn

responsive [rɪ'spɒnsɪv] *adj* sensible

rest¹ [rest] **1** *n* (a) *(break)* descanso *m*; **r. cure** cura *f* de reposo; *US* **r. room** aseos *mpl* (b) *(peace)* tranquilidad *f*; **at r.** *(object)* inmóvil (c) *(support)* apoyo *m* (d) *Mus* pausa *f*
2 *vt* (a) descansar (b) *(lean)* apoyar; **to r. a ladder against a wall** apoyar una escalera contra una pared
3 *vi* (a) descansar (b) *(be calm)* quedarse tranquilo(a) (c) **it doesn't r. with me** no depende de mí; **we'll let the matter r.** dejémoslo estar

rest² [rest] *n* the **r.** *(remainder)* el resto, lo demás; **the r. of the day** el resto del día; **the r. of the girls** las demás chicas; **the r. of us** los demás

restaurant ['restərɒnt] *n* restaurante *m*; *Rail* **r. car** coche *m* restaurante

restful ['restfʊl] *adj* relajante

restitution [restɪ'tjuːʃən] *n Fml* restitución *f*; **to make r.** restituir

restive ['restɪv] *adj* inquieto(a), nervioso(a)

restless ['restlɪs] *adj* agitado(a), inquieto(a)

restoration [restə'reɪʃən] *n* (**a**) *(giving back)* devolución *f* (**b**) *Br Hist* **the R.** la Restauración (**c**) *(of building, piece of furniture)* restauración *f*

restore [rɪ'stɔː(r)] *vt* (**a**) *(give back)* devolver (**b**) *(re-establish)* restablecer (**c**) *(building etc)* restaurar

restrain [rɪ'streɪn] *vt* contener; **to r. one's anger** reprimir la cólera; **to r. oneself** contenerse

restrained [rɪ'streɪnd] *adj (person)* moderado(a); *(emotion)* contenido(a)

restraint [rɪ'streɪnt] *n* (**a**) *(restriction)* restricción *f*; *(hindrance)* traba *f* (**b**) *(moderation)* moderación *f*

restrict [rɪ'strɪkt] *vt* restringir, limitar

restriction [rɪ'strɪkʃən] *n* restricción *f*, limitación *f*

restrictive [rɪ'strɪktɪv] *adj* restrictivo(a)

result [rɪ'zʌlt] **1** *n* (**a**) resultado *m* (**b**) *(consequence)* consecuencia *f*; **as a r. of** como consecuencia de
2 *vi* (**a**) resultar; **to r. from** resultar de (**b**) **to r. in** causar

resume [rɪ'zjuːm] **1** *vt (journey, work, conversation)* reanudar; *(control)* reasumir
2 *vi* recomenzar

> 🖉 Note that the Spanish verb **resumir** is a false friend and is never a translation for the English verb **to resume**. In Spanish, **resumir** means "to sum up, to summarize".

résumé ['rezjʊmeɪ] *n* (**a**) *(summary)* resumen *m* (**b**) *US (curriculum vitae)* currículum (vitae) *m*

resumption [rɪ'zʌmpʃən] *n* (*of journey, work, conversation)* reanudación *f*

resurface [riː'sɜːfɪs] **1** *vt (road)* rehacer el firme
2 *vi Fig* resurgir

resurgence [rɪ'sɜːdʒəns] *n* resurgimiento *m*

resurrection [rezə'rekʃən] *n* resurrección *f*

resuscitate [rɪ'sʌsɪteɪt] *vt Med* reanimar

retail ['riːteɪl] **1** *n* venta *f* al por menor; **r. outlet** punto *m* de venta; **r. price** precio *m* de venta al público; **R. Price Index** Índice *m* de Precios al Consumo
2 *vt* vender al por menor
3 *vi* venderse al por menor
4 *adv* al por menor

retailer ['riːteɪlə(r)] *n* detallista *mf*

retain [rɪ'teɪn] *vt* (**a**) *(heat)* conservar; *(personal effects)* guardar (**b**) *(water)* retener (**c**) *(facts, information)* recordar (**d**) **to r. the services of a lawyer** contratar a un abogado

retainer [rɪ'teɪnə(r)] *n* (**a**) *(payment)* anticipo *m* sobre los honorarios (**b**) *(servant)* criado(a) *m,f*

retaliate [rɪ'tælɪeɪt] *vi* tomar represalias (**against** contra)

retaliation [rɪtælɪ'eɪʃən] *n* represalias *fpl*; **in r.** en represalia

retarded [rɪ'tɑːdɪd] *adj* retrasado(a)

retch [retʃ] *vi* tener náuseas

retentive [rɪ'tentɪv] *adj* retentivo(a)

rethink ['riːθɪŋk] *n Fam* **to have a r. about sth** volver a reflexionar sobre algo

reticent ['retɪsənt] *adj* reticente

retina ['retɪnə] *n* retina *f*

retinue ['retɪnjuː] *n* séquito *m*

retire [rɪ'taɪə(r)] **1** *vt* jubilar
2 *vi* (**a**) *(stop working)* jubilarse (**b**) *(from race)* retirarse; **to r. for the night** irse a la cama, acostarse

retired [rɪ'taɪəd] *adj* jubilado(a)

retiree [rɪtaɪə'riː] *n US* retirado(a) *m,f*

retirement [rɪ'taɪəmənt] *n* jubilación *f*

retiring [rɪ'taɪərɪŋ] *adj* (**a**) *(reserved)* reservado(a) (**b**) *(official)* saliente

retort [rɪ'tɔːt] **1** *n* réplica *f*
2 *vi* replicar

retrace [riː'treɪs] *vt (recall)* reconstruir; **to r. one's steps** volver sobre sus pasos

retract [rɪ'trækt] **1** *vt (claws)* retraer; *(landing gear)* replegar (**b**) *(statement)* retirar
2 *vi* (**a**) *(claws)* retraerse; *(landing gear)* replegarse (**b**) *Fml* retractarse

retread ['riːtred] *n Aut* neumático recauchutado

retreat [rɪ'triːt] **1** *n* (**a**) *Mil* retirada *f* (**b**) *(shelter)* refugio *m* (**c**) *Rel* retiro *m*
2 *vi* retirarse (**from** de)

retrial ['riːtraɪəl] *n Jur* nuevo juicio

retribution [retrɪ'bjuːʃən] *n* represalias *fpl*

> 🖉 Note that the Spanish word **retribución** is a false friend and is never a translation for the English word **retribution**. In Spanish, **retribución** means "payment, reward".

retrieval [rɪ'triːvəl] *n* recuperación *f*; *Comput* **information r. system** sistema *m* de recuperación de datos

retrieve [rɪ'triːv] *vt (recover)* recuperar; *(of dog)* cobrar; *Comput* recoger (**b**) *(rescue)* salvar

retriever [rɪ'triːvə(r)] *n* perro *m* cazador

retrograde [ˈretrəʊɡreɪd] *adj* retrógrado(a)

retrospect [ˈretrəʊspekt] *n* **in r.** retrospectivamente

retrospective [retrəʊˈspektɪv] **1** *adj* retrospectivo(a)

2 *n Art* (exposición *f*) retrospectiva *f*

return [rɪˈtɜːn] **1** *n* (a) *(of person)* regreso *m*, vuelta *f*; **by r. of post** a vuelta de correo; **in r. for** a cambio de; **many happy returns!** ¡felicidades!; **r. match** partido *m* de vuelta; *Br* **r. (ticket)** billete *m* de ida y vuelta (b) *(of sth borrowed, stolen)* devolución *f* (c) *(profit)* beneficio *m*, ganancia *f* (d) *(interest)* interés *m*

2 *vt* (a) *(give back)* devolver; **r. to sender** *(on envelope)* devuélvase al remitente; **to r. a favour/sb's love** corresponder a un favor/al amor de algn (b) *Br Pol* elegir (c) *Jur (verdict)* pronunciar

3 *vi* (a) *(come or go back)* volver, regresar (b) *(reappear)* reaparecer

returnable [rɪˈtɜːnəbəl] *adj (bottle)* retornable

reunion [riːˈjuːnjən] *n* reunión *f*

reunite [riːjuːˈnaɪt] *vt* **to be reunited with** *(after separation)* reunirse con

rev [rev] *Fam Aut* **1** *n* revolución *f*

2 *vi* **to r. (up)** acelerar el motor

revamp [riːˈvæmp] *vt Fam* modernizar, renovar

reveal [rɪˈviːl] *vt (make known)* revelar; *(show)* dejar ver

revealing [rɪˈviːlɪŋ] *adj* revelador(a)

reveille [rɪˈvælɪ] *n* diana *f*

revel [ˈrevəl] *vi* disfrutar (**in** con); **to r. in doing sth** gozar muchísimo haciendo algo

revelation [revəˈleɪʃən] *n* revelación *f*

revelry [ˈrevəlrɪ] *n* jarana *f*, juerga *f*

revenge [rɪˈvendʒ] *n* venganza *f*; **to take r. on sb for sth** vengarse de algo en algn

revenue [ˈrevɪnjuː] *n* renta *f*

reverberate [rɪˈvɜːbəreɪt] *vi* (a) *(sound)* reverberar (b) *(ideas, news)* resonar

reverberation [rɪvɜːbəˈreɪʃən] *n* resonancia *f*

revere [rɪˈvɪə(r)] *vt* reverenciar

reverence [ˈrevərəns] *n* reverencia *f*

reverend [ˈrevərənd] *Rel* **1** *adj* reverendo(a); **R. Mother** reverenda madre

2 *n (Protestant)* pastor *m*; *(Catholic)* padre *m*

reverie [ˈrevərɪ] *n* ensueño *m*

reversal [rɪˈvɜːsəl] *n* (a) *(of order)* inversión *f* (b) *(of attitude, policy)* cambio *m* total (c) *Jur* revocación *f*

reverse [rɪˈvɜːs] **1** *adj* inverso(a); *Br*

r.-charge call llamada *f or Am* llamado *m* a cobro revertido

2 *n* (a) **quite the r.** todo lo contrario (b) *(other side)* *(of cloth)* revés *m*; *(of coin)* cruz *f*; *(of page)* dorso *m* (c) *Aut* **r. gear** marcha *f* atrás

3 *vt* (a) *(order)* invertir (b) *(turn round)* volver del revés (c) *(change)* cambiar totalmente (d) *Jur* revocar (e) *Br Tel* **to r. the charges** poner una conferencia a cobro revertido

4 *vi Aut* dar marcha atrás

revert [rɪˈvɜːt] *vi* volver (**to** a)

review [rɪˈvjuː] **1** *n* (a) *(examination)* examen *m* (b) *Mil* revista *f* (c) *Press* crítica *f*, reseña *f* (d) *(magazine)* revista *f*

2 *vt* (a) *(examine)* examinar (b) *Mil* **to r. the troops** pasar revista a las tropas (c) *(book etc)* hacer una crítica de

reviewer [rɪˈvjuːə(r)] *n* crítico(a) *m,f*

revile [rɪˈvaɪl] *vt Fml* injuriar

revise [rɪˈvaɪz] *vt* (a) *(look over)* revisar; *(at school)* repasar (b) *(change)* modificar (c) *(proofs)* corregir

revision [rɪˈvɪʒən] *n* (a) revisión *f*; *(at school)* repaso *m* (b) *(change)* modificación *f* (c) *(of proofs)* corrección *f*

revitalize [riːˈvaɪtəlaɪz] *vt* revivificar

revival [rɪˈvaɪvəl] *n* (a) *(of interest)* renacimiento *m*; *(of economy, industry)* reactivación *f*; *(of a country)* resurgimiento *m* (b) *Th* reestreno *m* (c) *Med* reanimación *f*

revive [rɪˈvaɪv] **1** *vt* (a) *(interest)* renovar; *(a law)* restablecer; *(economy, industry)* reactivar; *(hopes)* despertar (b) *Th* reestrenar (c) *Med* reanimar

2 *vi* (a) *(interest, hopes)* renacer (b) *Med* volver en sí

revoke [rɪˈvəʊk] *vt* revocar; *(permission)* suspender

revolt [rɪˈvəʊlt] **1** *n* rebelión *f*, sublevación *f*

2 *vi* rebelarse, sublevarse

3 *vt* repugnar, dar asco a

revolting [rɪˈvəʊltɪŋ] *adj* repugnante

revolution [revəˈluːʃən] *n* revolución *f*

revolutionary [revəˈluːʃənərɪ] *adj & n* revolucionario(a) *(m,f)*

revolve [rɪˈvɒlv] **1** *vi* girar; *Fig* **to r. around** girar en torno a

2 *vt* hacer girar

𝓵 Note that the Spanish verb **revolver** is a false friend and is never a translation for the English verb **to revolve**. In Spanish, **revolver** means "to stir, to mix" and "to mess up".

---

revolver [rɪˈvɒlvə(r)] *n* revólver *m*

revolving [rɪˈvɒlvɪŋ] *adj* giratorio(a)

revue [rɪ'vjuː] n revista f
revulsion [rɪ'vʌlʃən] n repulsión f
reward [rɪ'wɔːd] 1 n recompensa f
   2 vt recompensar
rewarding [rɪ'wɔːdɪŋ] adj provechoso(a)
rewire [riː'waɪə(r)] vt Elec **to r. a house** poner nueva instalación eléctrica a una casa
reword [riː'wɜːd] vt expresar con otras palabras
rewrite [riː'raɪt] vt (pt **rewrote** [riː'rəʊt]; pp **rewritten** [riː'rɪtən]) escribir de nuevo
rhapsody ['ræpsədɪ] n Mus rapsodia f
rhetoric ['retərɪk] n retórica f
rhetorical [rɪ'tɒrɪkəl] adj retórico(a)
rheumatism ['ruːmətɪzəm] n reuma m
rheumatoid ['ruːmətɔɪd] adj **r. arthritis** reuma m articular
Rhine [raɪn] n the **R.** el Rin
rhinoceros [raɪ'nɒsərəs] n rinoceronte m
rhododendron [rəʊdə'dendrən] n rododendro m
Rhone [rəʊn] n the **R.** el Ródano
rhubarb ['ruːbɑːb] n ruibarbo m
rhyme [raɪm] 1 n rima f; (poem) poema m
   2 vi rimar
rhythm ['rɪðəm] n ritmo m
rib¹ [rɪb] n (a) Anat costilla f; **r. cage** caja torácica (b) (in knitting) canalé m (c) (of umbrella) varilla f (d) Bot (of leaf) nervio m
rib² [rɪb] vt Fam burlarse de
ribald ['rɪbəld] adj (humour) verde
ribbon ['rɪbən] n cinta f; (in hair etc) lazo m; **torn to ribbons** hecho(a) jirones
rice [raɪs] n arroz m; **brown r.** arroz integral; **r. paper** papel de arroz; **r. pudding** arroz con leche
rich [rɪtʃ] 1 adj (person, food) rico(a); (soil) fértil; (voice) sonoro(a); (colour) vivo(a)
   2 npl the **r.** los ricos
riches ['rɪtʃɪz] npl riquezas fpl
richly ['rɪtʃlɪ] adv ricamente; **r. deserved** bien merecido(a)
richness ['rɪtʃnɪs] n riqueza f; (of soil) fertilidad f; (of voice) sonoridad f; (of colour) viveza f
rickets ['rɪkɪts] n sing Med raquitismo m
rickety ['rɪkətɪ] adj (chair etc) cojo(a); (car) desvencijado(a)
ricochet ['rɪkəʃeɪ, 'rɪkəʃet] 1 n rebote m
   2 vi rebotar
rid [rɪd] vt (pt & pp rid) librar; **to get r. of sth** deshacerse de algo; **to r. oneself of** librarse de
riddance ['rɪdəns] n Fam **good r.!** ¡ya era hora!

ridden ['rɪdən] pp of ride
riddle¹ ['rɪdəl] n (a) (puzzle) acertijo m, adivinanza f (b) (mystery) enigma m
riddle² ['rɪdəl] vt (with bullets) acribillar
ride [raɪd] 1 n paseo m, vuelta f; **a short bus r.** un corto trayecto en autobús; Fam **to take sb for a r.** tomar el pelo a algn; **horse r.** paseo a caballo
   2 vt (pt **rode**; pp **ridden**) (bicycle, horse) montar en; **can you r. a bike?** ¿sabes montar en bici?
   3 vi (a) (on horse) montar a caballo (b) (travel) (in bus, train etc) viajar (c) Naut **to r. at anchor** estar anclado(a)
   ▸ **ride out** vt sep sobrevivir; **to r. out the storm** capear el temporal
rider ['raɪdə(r)] n (of horse) (man) jinete m; (woman) amazona f; (of bicycle) ciclista mf; (of motorbike) motociclista mf
ridge [rɪdʒ] n (crest of a hill) cresta f; (hillock) loma f; (of roof) caballete m; Met área m
ridicule ['rɪdɪkjuːl] 1 n burla f
   2 vt burlarse de
ridiculous [rɪ'dɪkjʊləs] adj ridículo(a)
riding ['raɪdɪŋ] n equitación f; **r. breeches** pantalones mpl de montar; **r. school** escuela hípica
rife [raɪf] adj abundante; **rumour is r. that ...** corre la voz de que ...; **to be r. with** abundar en
riffraff ['rɪfræf] n Fam chusma f, gentuza f
rifle¹ ['raɪfəl] n fusil m, rifle m; **r. range** campo m de tiro
rifle² ['raɪfəl] vt desvalijar
rift [rɪft] n (a) Geol falla f (b) Fig (in friendship) ruptura f, Pol (in party) escisión f; (quarrel) desavenencia f
rig [rɪg] 1 n (a) Naut aparejo m (b) (oil) **r.** (onshore) torre f de perforación; (offshore) plataforma petrolífera
   2 vt Pej amañar
   ▸ **rig out** vt sep Fam ataviar
   ▸ **rig up** vt sep improvisar
rigging ['rɪgɪŋ] n aparejo m, jarcia f
right [raɪt] 1 adj (a) (not left) derecho(a); **the r. hand** la mano derecha
   (b) (correct) correcto(a); (time) exacto(a); **to be r.** tener razón; **all r.** de acuerdo; **r.?** ¿vale?; **that's r.** eso es; **the r. word** la palabra justa
   (c) (true) cierto(a)
   (d) (suitable) adecuado(a); **the r. time** el momento oportuno
   (e) (proper) apropiado(a)
   (f) Fam (healthy) bien
   (g) Fam (complete) auténtico(a)

(**h**) *(in order)* en orden

(**i**) **r. angle** ángulo recto

2 *n* (**a**) *(right side)* derecha *f*

(**b**) *(right hand)* mano derecha

(**c**) *Pol* **the R.** la derecha

(**d**) *(lawful claim)* derecho *m*; **in one's own** r. por derecho propio; **r. of way** *(across land)* derecho de paso; *(on roads)* prioridad *f*; **civil rights** derechos civiles

(**e**) **r. and wrong** el bien y el mal

3 *adv* (**a**) *(correctly)* bien; **it's just r.** es justo lo que hace falta

(**b**) **r. away** *(immediately)* en seguida

(**c**) *(to the right)* a la derecha; **r. and left** a diestro y siniestro; **to turn r.** girar a la derecha

(**d**) *(directly)* directamente; **go r. on** sigue recto; **r. at the top** en todo lo alto; **r. in the middle** justo en medio; **r. to the end** hasta el final

4 *vt* (**a**) *(correct)* corregir

(**b**) *(put straight)* enderezar

righteous ['raɪtʃəs] *adj (upright)* recto(a)

rightful ['raɪtfʊl] *adj* legítimo(a)

right-hand ['raɪthænd] *adj* derecho(a); **r. drive** conducción *f* por la derecha; **r. side** lado derecho; *Fam* **r. man** brazo derecho

right-handed [raɪt'hændɪd] *adj (person)* que usa la mano derecha; *(tool)* para la mano derecha

rightly ['raɪtlɪ] *adv* debidamente; **and r. so** y con razón

right-wing ['raɪtwɪŋ] *adj* de derechas, derechista

right-winger [raɪt'wɪŋə(r)] *n* derechista *mf*

rigid ['rɪdʒɪd] *adj* rígido(a), inflexible

rigidity [rɪ'dʒɪdɪtɪ] *n* rigidez *f*, inflexibilidad *f*

rigmarole ['rɪgmərəʊl] *n Fam* galimatías *m inv*

rigor ['rɪgər] *n US* = **rigour**

rigorous ['rɪgərəs] *adj* riguroso(a)

rigour ['rɪgə(r)] *n* rigor *m*, severidad *f*

rile [raɪl] *vt Fam* irritar, sacar de quicio

rim [rɪm] *n (edge)* borde *m*; *(of wheel)* llanta *f*; *(of spectacles)* montura *f*

rind [raɪnd] *n (of fruit, cheese)* corteza *f*

ring[1] [rɪŋ] **1** *n* (**a**) *(sound of bell)* toque *m*; *(of doorbell, alarm clock)* timbre *m* (**b**) *Tel* llamada *f*

2 *vt (pt* **rang**; *pp* **rung**) (**a**) *(bell)* tocar; *Fig* **it rings a bell** me suena (**b**) *Br Tel* llamar por teléfono

3 *vi* (**a**) *(bell, phone etc)* sonar (**b**) **my ears are ringing** tengo un pitido en los oídos (**c**) *Tel* llamar

► **ring back** *vt sep Br Tel* volver a llamar

► **ring off** *vi Br Tel* colgar

► **ring out** *vi* resonar

► **ring up** *vt sep Br Tel* llamar por teléfono a

ring[2] [rɪŋ] **1** *n* (**a**) *(metal hoop)* aro *m*; **curtain r.** anilla *f*; **r. binder** carpeta *f* de anillas (**b**) *(for finger)* anillo *m*, sortija *f*; **finger** dedo *m* anular (**c**) *(circle)* círculo *m*; *Br* **r. road** carretera *f* de circunvalación (**d**) **rings** *(in gymnastics)* anillas *fpl*

(**e**) *(group of people)* corro *m*; *(of spies)* red *f*; *(of thieves)* banda *f* (**f**) *(arena)* pista *f*; *(for boxing)* cuadrilátero *m*; *(for bullfights)* ruedo *m*; **circus r.** pista de circo

2 *vt* (**a**) *(bird, animal)* anillar (**b**) *(surround)* rodear

ringing ['rɪŋɪŋ] *n (of bell)* toque *m*, repique *m*; *(in ears)* pitido *m*

ringleader ['rɪŋliːdə(r)] *n* cabecilla *mf*

ringlet ['rɪŋlɪt] *n* tirabuzón *m*

rink [rɪŋk] *n* pista *f*; **ice r.** pista de hielo

rinse [rɪns] **1** *n* (**a**) *(of clothes, hair)* aclarado *m*, enjuague *m*; *(of dishes)* enjuagado *m* (**b**) *(tint for hair)* reflejo *m*

2 *vt* (**a**) aclarar; *(the dishes)* enjuagar (**b**) **to r. one's hair** *(tint)* darse reflejos en el pelo

riot ['raɪət] **1** *n* (**a**) disturbio *m*, motín *m*; **to run r.** desmandarse; **r. police** policía *f* antidisturbios (**b**) *Fig (of colour)* profusión *f*

2 *vi* amotinarse

rioter ['raɪətə(r)] *n* amotinado(a) *m,f*

riotous ['raɪətəs] *adj* (**a**) amotinado(a) (**b**) *(noisy)* bullicioso(a) (**c**) *(unrestrained)* desenfrenado(a)

rip [rɪp] **1** *n (tear)* rasgón *m*

2 *vt* rasgar, rajar; **to r. one's trousers** rajarse los pantalones

3 *vi* rasgarse, rajarse

► **rip off** *vt sep Fam* **to r. sb off** timar a algn

► **rip up** *vt sep* hacer pedacitos

ripcord ['rɪpkɔːd] *n* cuerda *f* de apertura

ripe [raɪp] *adj* (**a**) maduro(a) (**b**) *(ready)* listo(a); **the time is r.** es el momento oportuno

ripen ['raɪpən] *vt & vi* madurar

rip-off ['rɪpɒf] *n Fam* timo *m*

ripple ['rɪpəl] **1** *n* (**a**) *(on water, fabric)* onda *f* (**b**) *(sound)* murmullo *m*

2 *vt (water)* ondular

3 *vi* (**a**) *(water)* ondularse (**b**) *(applause)* extenderse

rise [raɪz] **1** *n* (**a**) *(of slope, hill)* cuesta *f* (**b**) *(of waters)* crecida *f* (**c**) *(in status)* ascenso *m*

(d) (in prices, temperature) subida f; (in wages) aumento m
(e) (in sound) aumento m
(f) to give r. to ocasionar
2 vi (pt **rose**; pp **risen** ['rɪzən]) **(a)** (land etc) elevarse
(b) (waters) crecer; (river) nacer; (tide) subir; (wind) levantarse
(c) (sun, moon) salir
(d) (voice) alzarse
(e) (in rank) ascender
(f) (prices, temperature) subir; (wages) aumentar
(g) (curtain) subir
(h) (from bed) levantarse
(i) (stand up) levantarse; Fig (city, building) erguirse
(j) to r. to a challenge aceptar un reto; **to r. to the occasion** ponerse a la altura de las circunstancias
▸ **rise above** vt insep estar por encima de
▸ **rise up** vi (rebel) sublevarse

rising ['raɪzɪŋ] **1** adj (sun) naciente; (tide) creciente; (prices) en aumento; **r. damp** humedad f
2 n **(a)** (of sun) salida f **(b)** (rebellion) levantamiento m

risk [rɪsk] **1** n riesgo m; **at r.** en peligro; **at your own r.** por su cuenta y riesgo; **to take risks** arriesgarse
2 vt arriesgar; **I'll r. it** correré el riesgo

risky ['rɪskɪ] adj (**riskier, riskiest**) arriesgado(a).

risqué ['rɪskeɪ] adj atrevido(a); (joke) picante

rite [raɪt] n rito m; **the last rites** la extremaunción

ritual ['rɪtjʊəl] adj & n ritual (m)

rival ['raɪvəl] **1** adj & n rival (mf)
2 vt rivalizar con

rivalry ['raɪvəlrɪ] n rivalidad f

river ['rɪvə(r)] n río m; **down/up r.** río abajo/arriba

river-bank ['rɪvəbæŋk] n orilla f, ribera f

river-bed ['rɪvəbed] n lecho m

rivet ['rɪvɪt] **1** n Tech remache m, roblón m
2 vt Tech remachar; Fig cautivar

riveting ['rɪvɪtɪŋ] adj Fig fascinante

roach [rəʊtʃ] n US Fam (cockroach) cucaracha f

road [rəʊd] n **(a)** carretera f; Br **A/B r.** carretera nacional/secundaria; **main r.** carretera principal; **r. accident** accidente m de tráfico; **r. safety** seguridad f vial; **r. sign** señal f de tráfico; **r. Br works** or US **work** obras fpl **(b)** (street) calle f **(c)** (way) camino m

roadblock ['rəʊdblɒk] n control m policial

roadhog ['rəʊdhɒg] n Fam loco(a) m,f del volante, dominguero(a) m,f

roadside ['rəʊdsaɪd] n borde m de la carretera; **r. restaurant/café** restaurante m/cafetería f de carretera

roadway ['rəʊdweɪ] n calzada f

roadworthy ['rəʊdwɜːðɪ] adj (vehicle) en buen estado

roam [rəʊm] **1** vt vagar por, rondar
2 vi vagar

roar [rɔː(r)] **1** n (of lion) rugido m; (of bull, sea, wind) bramido m; (of crowd) clamor m
2 vi (lion, crowd) rugir; (bull, sea, wind) bramar; (crowd) clamar; Fig **to r. with laughter** reírse a carcajadas

roaring ['rɔːrɪŋ] adj Fam Fig **a r. success** un éxito clamoroso; **to do a r. trade** hacer un negocio redondo

roast [rəʊst] **1** adj (meat) asado(a); **r. beef** rosbif m
2 n Culin asado m
3 vt (meat) asar; (coffee, nuts) tostar
4 vi asarse; Fam Fig **I'm roasting** me aso de calor

rob [rɒb] vt robar; (bank) atracar

robber ['rɒbə(r)] n ladrón(ona) m,f; **bank r.** atracador(a) m,f

robbery ['rɒbərɪ] n robo m

robe [rəʊb] n (ceremonial) toga f, (dressing gown) bata f

robin ['rɒbɪn] n petirrojo m

robot ['rəʊbɒt] n robot m

robust [rəʊ'bʌst] adj (sturdy) robusto(a)

rock [rɒk] **1** n **(a)** roca f; Fig **to be on the rocks** (of marriage) estar a punto de fracasar; Fig **whisky on the rocks** whisky m con hielo **(b)** US (stone) piedra f **(c)** Br (sweet) **stick of r.** barra f de caramelo **(d)** Mus música f rock; **r. and roll** rock and roll m
2 vt **(a)** (chair) mecer; (baby) acunar **(b)** (shake) hacer temblar; Fig (shock) conmover
3 vi **(a)** (move to and fro) mecerse **(b)** (shake) vibrar

rock-bottom ['rɒk'bɒtəm] adj bajísimo(a); **r. prices** precios regalados

rockery ['rɒkərɪ] n jardín m de rocas

rocket ['rɒkɪt] **1** n cohete m; **r. launcher** lanzacohetes m inv
2 vi Fam (prices) dispararse

rocking-chair ['rɒkɪŋtʃeə(r)] n mecedora f

rocking-horse ['rɒkɪŋhɔːs] n caballito m de balancín

rocky ['rɒkɪ] *adj* (**rockier, rockiest**) rocoso(a); *Fam Fig* (*unsteady*) inseguro(a); **the R. Mountains** las Montañas Rocosas

rod [rɒd] *n* (*of metal*) barra *f*; (*stick*) vara *f*; **fishing r.** caña *f* de pescar

rode [rəʊd] *pt of* **ride**

rodent ['rəʊdənt] *n* roedor *m*

roe¹ [rəʊ] *n Zool* **r.** (*deer*) corzo(a) *m,f*

roe² [rəʊ] *n* (*fish eggs*) hueva *f*

rogue [rəʊg] *n* granuja *m*

role, rôle [rəʊl] *n* papel *m*; **to play a r.** desempeñar un papel

roll [rəʊl] **1** *n* (**a**) rollo *m*; **r. of banknotes** fajo *m* de billetes; *Fam Fig* **rolls of fat** michelines *mpl* (**b**) (*bread*) **r.** bollo *m* (**c**) (*list of names*) lista *f*, nómina *f*; **to call the r.** pasar lista (**d**) (*movement of ship*) balanceo *m* (**e**) (*of drum*) redoble *m*; (*of 'thunder*) fragor *m*

2 *vt* (**a**) (*ball*) hacer rodar (**b**) (*cigarette*) liar (**c**) (*move*) mover (**d**) (*push*) empujar (**e**) (*lawn, road*) allanar

3 *vi* (**a**) (*ball*) rodar; *Fam* **to be rolling in money** estar forrado(a) (**b**) (*animal*) revolcarse (**c**) (*ship*) balancearse (**d**) (*drum*) redoblar; (*thunder*) retumbar

▶ **roll about, roll around** *vi* rodar (de acá para allá)

▶ **roll by** *vi* (*years*) pasar

▶ **roll in** *vi Fam* (**a**) (*arrive*) llegar (**b**) (*money*) llegar a raudales

▶ **roll over** *vi* dar una vuelta

▶ **roll up 1** *vt sep* enrollar; (*blinds*) subir; **to r. up one's sleeves** (ar)remangarse

2 *vi Fam* (*arrive*) llegar

roll-call ['rəʊlkɔːl] *n* **to have a r.** pasar lista

roller ['rəʊlə(r)] *n* (**a**) *Tech* rodillo *m*; **r. blades** patines *mpl* en línea; **r. coaster** montaña rusa; **r. skates** patines *mpl* (de ruedas) (**b**) (*large wave*) ola *f* grande (**c**) (*for hair*) rulo *m*

rolling ['rəʊlɪŋ] **1** *adj* (**a**) *Rail* **r. stock** material *m* rodante (**b**) (*countryside*) ondulado(a)

2 *n* rodamiento *m*; (*of ground*) apisonamiento *m*; **r. pin** rodillo *m* (de cocina)

ROM [rɒm] *n Comput* (*abbr* **read-only memory**) ROM *f*

Roman ['rəʊmən] *adj & n* romano(a) (*m,f*); **R. Catholic** católico(a) *m,f* (romano(a)); **R. law** derecho romano; **R. numerals** números romanos

Romance [rəʊ'mæns] *adj Ling* románico(a), romance; **R. languages** lenguas románicas

romance [rəʊ'mæns] **1** *n* (**a**) (*tale*) novela romántica (**b**) (*love affair*) aventura

amorosa (**c**) (*romantic quality*) lo romántico

2 *vi* fantasear

Romania [rə'meɪnɪə] *n* Rumanía

Romanian [rə'meɪnɪən] **1** *adj* rumano(a)

2 *n* (*person*) rumano(a) *m,f*; (*language*) rumano *m*

romantic [rəʊ'mæntɪk] *adj & n* romántico(a) (*m,f*)

Rome [rəʊm] *n* Roma

romp [rɒmp] **1** *n* jugueteo *m*

2 *vi* juguetear

rompers ['rɒmpəz] *npl* pelele *m*

roof [ruːf] **1** *n* (*pl* **roofs** [ruːfs, ruːvz]) (**a**) tejado *m*; *Fam Fig* **to go through the r.** (*of prices*) estar por las nubes; (*with anger*) subirse por las paredes (**b**) *Aut* techo *m*; **r. rack** baca *f* (**c**) (*of mouth*) cielo *m*

2 *vt* techar

roofing ['ruːfɪŋ] *n* materiales *mpl* usados para techar

rook [rʊk] *n* (**a**) *Orn* grajo *m* (**b**) (*in chess*) torre *f*

rookie ['rʊkɪ] *n US Fam* (*novice*) novato(a) *m,f*

room [ruːm] *n* (**a**) habitación *f*, cuarto *m*; **single r.** habitación individual; **r. service** servicio *m* de habitación (**b**) (*space*) sitio *m*, espacio *m*; **make r. for me** hazme sitio

rooming-house ['ruːmɪŋhaʊs] *n US* pensión *f*

roommate ['ruːmmeɪt] *n* compañero(a) *m,f* de habitación

roomy ['ruːmɪ] *adj* (**roomier, roomiest**) amplio(a)

roost [ruːst] **1** *n* palo *m*, percha *f*; (**hen**) **r.** gallinero *m*; *Fig* **to rule the r.** llevar la batuta

2 *vi* posarse

rooster ['ruːstə(r)] *n esp US* gallo *m*

root¹ [ruːt] **1** *n* raíz *f*; **to take r.** echar raíces

2 *vt* arraigar

3 *vi* arraigar

▶ **root out, root up** *vt sep* arrancar de raíz

root² [ruːt] *vi* (*search*) buscar; **to r. about** *or* **around for sth** hurgar en busca de algo

root³ [ruːt] *vi Fam* **to r. for a team** animar a un equipo

rope [rəʊp] **1** *n* (**a**) (*thin*) cuerda *f*; (*thick*) soga *f*; *Naut* cabo *m* (**b**) *Fig* **to have sb on the ropes** tener a algn contra las cuerdas; *Fam Fig* **to know the ropes** estar al tanto

2 *vt* (*package*) atar; (*climbers*) encordar

> *Note that the Spanish word* **ropa** *is a false friend and is never a translation for the English word* **rope**. *In Spanish,* **ropa** *means "clothes".*

▸ **rope in** *vt sep Fam* enganchar

▸ **rope off** *vt sep* acordonar

rop(e)y ['rəʊpɪ] *adj* (**ropier, ropiest**) *Br Fam* chungo(a)

rosary ['rəʊzərɪ] *n* rosario *m*

rose¹ [rəʊz] *pt of* **rise**

rose² [rəʊz] *n* (**a**) *Bot* rosa *f*; **r. bed** rosaleda *f*; **r. bush** rosal *m* (**b**) (*colour*) rosa *m* (**c**) (*of watering can*) alcachofa *f*

rosé ['rəʊzeɪ] *n* (vino *m*) rosado *m*

rosebud ['rəʊzbʌd] *n* capullo *m* de rosa

rosemary ['rəʊzmərɪ] *n* romero *m*

rosette [rəʊ'zet] *n* (*of ribbons*) escarapela *f*

roster ['rɒstə(r)] *n* lista *f*

rostrum ['rɒstrəm] *n* estrado *m*

> Note that the Spanish word **rostro** is a false friend and is never a translation for the English word **rostrum**. In Spanish, **rostro** means "face".

---

rosy ['rəʊzɪ] *adj* (**rosier, rosiest**) (**a**) (*complexion*) sonrosado(a) (**b**) *Fig* (*future*) prometedor(a)

rot [rɒt] **1** *n* (**a**) (*decay*) putrefacción *f*; **dry r.** putrefacción de la madera (**b**) *Fam* (*nonsense*) tonterías *fpl*

2 *vt* pudrir

▸ **rot away** *vi* pudrirse

rota ['rəʊtə] *n esp Br* lista *f*

rotary ['rəʊtərɪ] **1** *n US* (*for traffic*) rotonda *f*

2 *adj* rotatorio(a), giratorio(a)

rotate [rəʊ'teɪt] **1** *vt* (**a**) (*revolve*) hacer girar (**b**) (*jobs, crops*) alternar

2 *vi* (*revolve*) girar

rotating [rəʊ'teɪtɪŋ] *adj* rotativo(a)

rotation [rəʊ'teɪʃən] *n* rotación *f*

rote [rəʊt] *n* **by r.** de memoria

rotten ['rɒtən] *adj* (**a**) (*decayed*) podrido(a); (*tooth*) picado(a) (**b**) *Fam* (*very bad*) malísimo(a); *Fam* **I feel r.** me encuentro fatal

rouble ['ruːbəl] *n* rublo *m*

rouge [ruːʒ] **1** *n* colorete *m*

2 *vt* poner colorete a

rough [rʌf] **1** *adj* (**a**) (*surface, skin*) áspero(a); (*terrain*) accidentado(a); (*road*) desigual; (*sea*) agitado(a); (*weather*) tempestuoso(a)

(**b**) (*rude*) grosero(a); (*violent*) violento(a)

(**c**) (*voice*) bronco(a)

(**d**) (*wine*) áspero(a)

(**e**) (*bad*) malo(a); *Fam* **to feel r.** encontrarse fatal

(**f**) (*approximate*) aproximado(a)

(**g**) (*plan etc*) preliminar; **r. draft** borrador *m*; **r. sketch** esbozo *m*

(**h**) (*harsh*) severo(a)

2 *adv* duramente; *Fam Fig* **to sleep r.** dormir a la intemperie

3 *n* (**a**) *Fam* (*person*) matón *m*

(**b**) **the r.** (*in golf*) la hierba alta

4 *vt Fam* **to r. it** vivir sin comodidades

roughage ['rʌfɪdʒ] *n* (*substance*) fibra *f*

rough-and-ready ['rʌfən'redɪ] *adj* improvisado(a)

roughen ['rʌfən] *vt* poner áspero(a)

roughly ['rʌflɪ] *adv* (**a**) (*crudely*) toscamente (**b**) (*clumsily*) torpemente (**c**) (*not gently*) bruscamente (**d**) (*approximately*) aproximadamente

roulette [ruː'let] *n* ruleta *f*

Roumania [ruː'meɪnɪə] *n* = **Romania**

round [raʊnd] **1** *adj* redondo(a); **in r. figures** en números redondos; **r. table** mesa redonda; **r. trip** viaje *m* de ida y vuelta

2 *n* (**a**) (*circle*) círculo *m*

(**b**) (*series*) serie *f*; **r. of talks** ronda *f* de negociaciones

(**c**) (*of ammunition*) cartucho *m*; (*salvo*) salva *f*

(**d**) **a r. of toast** una tostada

(**e**) (*of drinks*) ronda *f*

(**f**) **the daily r.** (*routine*) la rutina diaria

(**g**) (*in golf*) partido *m*; *Cards* partida *f*

(**h**) (*in boxing*) round *m*

(**i**) (*in a competition*) eliminatoria *f*

(**j**) **rounds** (*doctor's*) visita *f*; (*of salesman*) recorrido *m*

3 *adv* **all year r.** durante todo el año; **to invite sb r.** invitar a algn a casa

4 *prep* alrededor de; **r. here** por aquí; **r. the clock** día y noche; **r. the corner** a la vuelta de la esquina

5 *vt* (*turn*) dar la vuelta a

▸ **round off** *vt sep* acabar, concluir

▸ **round on** *vt insep* (*attack*) atacar

▸ **round up** *vt sep* (*cattle*) acorralar, rodear; (*people*) reunir

roundabout ['raʊndəbaʊt] **1** *n* (**a**) (*merry-go-round*) tiovivo *m* (**b**) *Br Aut* rotonda *f*

2 *adj* indirecto(a)

rounders ['raʊndəz] *n Br* = juego parecido al béisbol

roundly ['raʊndlɪ] *adv* completamente, totalmente

round-shouldered ['raʊnd'ʃəʊldəd] *adj* cargado(a) de espaldas

round-trip ['raʊnd'trɪp] *US* **1** *n* billete *m* de ida y vuelta

2 *adj* (*ticket*) de ida y vuelta

round-up ['raʊndʌp] *n* (**a**) (*of cattle*)

rodeo *m*; *(of suspects)* redada *f* (**b**) *(summary)* resumen *m*

rouse [raʊz] *vt* despertar; *(stir up)* suscitar

rousing [ˈraʊzɪŋ] *adj (cheer)* entusiasta; *(applause)* caluroso(a); *(speech, song)* conmovedor(a)

rout [raʊt] **1** *n* aniquilación *f*
2 *vt* aniquilar

route [ruːt] **1** *n* (**a**) ruta *f*; *(of bus)* línea *f*; *Naut* derrota *f*; *Fig* camino *m*; **r. map** mapa *m* de carreteras (**b**) *US* **R.** ≃ carretera *f* nacional
2 *vt* encaminar

routine [ruːˈtiːn] **1** *n* (**a**) rutina *f* (**b**) *Th* número *m*
2 *adj* rutinario(a)

roving [ˈraʊvɪŋ] *adj* errante; **r. reporter** enviado(a) *m,f* especial

row¹ [raʊ] *n* fila *f*, hilera *f*; *Fig* **three times in a r.** tres veces seguidas

row² [raʊ] *vt & vi (in a boat)* remar

row³ [raʊ] **1** *n* (**a**) *(quarrel)* pelea *f*, bronca *f* (**b**) *(noise)* jaleo *m*; *(protest)* escándalo *m*
2 *vi* pelearse

rowboat [ˈraʊbəʊt] *n US* bote *m* de remos

rowdy [ˈraʊdɪ] **1** *adj* (**rowdier, rowdiest**) (**a**) *(noisy)* ruidoso(a); *(disorderly)* alborotador(a) (**b**) *(quarrelsome)* camorrista
2 *n* camorrista

rowing [ˈraʊɪŋ] *n* remo *m*; **r. boat** bote *m* de remos

royal [ˈrɔɪəl] **1** *adj* real; **r. blue** azul marino; **the R. Family** la Familia Real
2 *npl* **the Royals** los miembros de la Familia Real

royally [ˈrɔɪəlɪ] *adv Fig* magníficamente

royalty [ˈrɔɪəltɪ] *n* (**a**) *(royal persons)* miembro(s) *m(pl)* de la Familia Real (**b**) **royalties** derechos *mpl* de autor

RPI [ɑːpiːˈaɪ] *n (abbr* **Retail Price Index)** IPC *m*

rpm [ɑːpiːˈem] *n (abbr* **revolutions per minute)** r.p.m.

RSPCA [ɑːrespiːsiːˈeɪ] *n Br (abbr* **Royal Society for the Prevention of Cruelty to Animals)** ≃ Sociedad *f* Protectora de Animales

RSVP [ɑːresviːˈpiː] *(abbr* **répondez s'il vous plaît)** se ruega contestación, S.R.C.

Rt Hon *Br Pol (abbr* (**the**) **Right Honourable**) su Señoría

rub [rʌb] **1** *n* **to do sth a r.** frotar algo
2 *vt* frotar; *(hard)* restregar; *(massage)* friccionar
3 *vi* rozar (**against** contra)
▸ **rub down** *vt sep* rotar; *(horse)* almohazar; *(surface)* raspar

▸ **rub in** *vt sep* (**a**) *(cream etc)* frotar con (**b**) *Fam* **don't r. it in** no me lo refriegues

▸ **rub off** **1** *vt sep (erase)* borrar
2 *vi* **to r. off on sb** influir en algn

▸ **rub out** *vt sep* borrar

▸ **rub up** *vt sep Fam Fig* **to r. sb up the wrong way** fastidiar a algn

rubber¹ [ˈrʌbə(r)] *n* (**a**) *(substance)* caucho *m*, goma *f*; **r. band** goma; **r. plant** gomero *m*; **r. stamp** tampón *m* (**b**) *Br (eraser)* goma *f* (de borrar) (**c**) *Fam (condom)* goma *f*

rubber² [ˈrʌbə(r)] *n (in bridge)* rubber *m*

rubbery [ˈrʌbərɪ] *adj (elastic)* elástico(a)

rubbish [ˈrʌbɪʃ] *n* (**a**) *Br (refuse)* basura *f*; **r. bin** cubo *m* de la basura; **r. dump** *or* **tip** vertedero *m* (**b**) *Fam (worthless thing)* birria *f* (**c**) *Fam (nonsense)* tonterías *fpl*

rubble [ˈrʌbəl] *n* escombros *mpl*

rubric [ˈruːbrɪk] *n* rúbrica *f*

ruby [ˈruːbɪ] *n* rubí *m*

rucksack [ˈrʌksæk] *n* mochila *f*

ructions [ˈrʌkʃənz] *npl Fam* jaleo *m*

rudder [ˈrʌdə(r)] *n* timón *m*

ruddy [ˈrʌdɪ] *adj* (**ruddier, ruddiest**) *(complexion)* rojizo(a), colorado(a) (**b**) *Br Fam (damned)* maldito(a)

rude [ruːd] *adj* (**a**) *(impolite)* maleducado(a); *(foul-mouthed)* grosero(a); **don't be r. to your mother** no le faltes al respeto a tu madre (**b**) *(abrupt)* **a r. awakening** un despertar repentino

rudimentary [ruːdɪˈmentərɪ] *adj* rudimentario(a)

rudiments [ˈruːdɪmənts] *npl* rudimentos *mpl*

rue [ruː] *vt* arrepentirse de

rueful [ˈruːfəl] *adj (regretful)* arrepentido(a); *(sad)* triste

ruff [rʌf] *n (collar)* gorguera *f*

ruffian [ˈrʌfɪən] *n* canalla *m*

ruffle [ˈrʌfəl] *vt* (**a**) *(water)* agitar (**b**) *(feathers)* encrespar; *(hair)* despeinar (**c**) *Fig (annoy)* hacer perder la calma a

ruffled [ˈrʌfəld] *adj* (**a**) *(hair)* alborotado(a); *(clothes)* en desorden (**b**) *(perturbed)* perturbado(a)

rug [rʌg] *n* alfombra *f*, alfombrilla *f*

rugby [ˈrʌgbɪ] *n* rugby *m*; **r. league** rugby a trece; **r. union** rugby a quince

rugged [ˈrʌgɪd] *adj* (**a**) *(terrain)* accidentado(a) (**b**) *(features)* marcado(a) (**c**) *(character)* vigoroso(a)

rugger [ˈrʌgə(r)] *n Fam* rugby *m*

ruin [ˈruːɪn] **1** *n* (**a**) ruina *f* (**b**) **ruins** ruinas *fpl*, restos *mpl*; **in ruins** en ruinas
2 *vt* arruinar; *(spoil)* estropear

rule [ruːl] **1** *n* (**a**) regla *f*, norma *f*; **to work**

to r. hacer una huelga de celo; **as a r.** por regla general (**b**) *(government)* dominio *m*; *(of monarch)* reinado *m*; **r. of law** imperio *m* de la ley

2 *vt & vi* (**a**) *(govern)* gobernar; *(of monarch)* reinar (**b**) *(decide)* decidir; *(decree)* decretar (**c**) *(draw)* tirar

▸ **rule out** *vt sep* descartar

ruled [ruːld] *adj* rayado(a)

ruler ['ruːlə(r)] *n* (**a**) dirigente *mf*; *(monarch)* soberano(a) *m,f* (**b**) *(for measuring)* regla *f*

ruling ['ruːlɪŋ] **1** *adj (in charge)* dirigente; *Fig (predominant)* predominante; **the r. party** el partido en el poder

2 *n Jur* fallo *m*

rum [rʌm] *n* ron *m*

Rumania [ruːˈmeɪnɪə] *n* = **Romania**

Rumanian [ruːˈmeɪnɪən] *adj & n* = **Romanian**

rumble ['rʌmbəl] **1** *n* (**a**) ruido sordo; *(of thunder)* estruendo *m* (**b**) *(of stomach)* ruido *m*

2 *vi* (**a**) hacer un ruido sordo; *(thunder)* retumbar (**b**) *(stomach etc)* hacer ruidos

ruminate ['ruːmɪneɪt] *vi (chew, ponder)* rumiar

rummage ['rʌmɪdʒ] *vi* revolver (**through** en); *US* **r. sale** *(in store)* = venta de productos discontinuados o sin salida en un almacén; *(for charity)* rastrillo benéfico

rumour, *US* **rumor** ['ruːmə(r)] **1** *n* rumor *m*; **r. has it that ...** se dice que ...

2 *vt* **it is rumoured that** se rumorea que

rump [rʌmp] *n (of animal)* ancas *fpl; Fam Hum (of person)* trasero *m*; **r. steak** filete *m* de lomo

rumpus ['rʌmpəs] *n Fam* jaleo *m*

run [rʌn] **1** *n* (**a**) carrera *f*; **on the r.** fugado(a); **to go for a r.** hacer footing; *Fig* **in the long r.** a largo plazo

(**b**) *(trip)* paseo *m*, vuelta *f*

(**c**) *(sequence)* serie *f*

(**d**) ski **r.** pista *f* de esquí

(**e**) *(demand)* gran demanda *f*; **a r. on** una gran demanda de

(**f**) **to give sb the r. of a house** poner una casa a disposición de algn

(**g**) *(print run)* tirada *f*

(**h**) *(in stocking)* carrera *f*

2 *vt (pt* **ran**; *pp* **run**) (**a**) correr; **to r. a race** correr en una carrera; **to r. errands** hacer recados

(**b**) *(drive)* llevar

(**c**) *(house, business)* llevar; *(company)* dirigir; *(organize)* organizar

(**d**) *(fingers)* pasar

(**e**) **it's a cheap car to r.** *(operate)* es un coche económico; *Comput* **to r. a program** pasar un programa

(**f**) *Press* publicar

3 *vi* (**a**) correr

(**b**) *(colour)* desteñirse

(**c**) *(water, river)* correr; **to leave the tap running** dejar el grifo abierto; *Fam* **your nose is running** se te caen los mocos

(**d**) *(operate) (machine)* funcionar (**on** con); **trains r. every two hours** hay trenes cada dos horas

(**e**) *Naut* **to r. aground** encallar

(**f**) *Pol* **to r. for president** presentarse como candidato a la presidencia

(**g**) **so the story runs** según lo que se dice

(**h**) *(range)* oscilar (**between** entre)

(**i**) **we're running low on milk** nos queda poca leche

(**j**) **shyness runs in the family** la timidez le viene de familia

(**k**) *Cin & Th* estar en cartel

(**l**) *(last)* durar

(**m**) *(stocking)* tener una carrera

▸ **run about** *vi* corretear

▸ **run across** *vt insep (meet)* tropezar con

▸ **run away** *vi* fugarse; *(horse)* desbocarse

▸ **run down 1** *vt insep (stairs)* bajar corriendo

2 *vt sep* (**a**) *(in car)* atropellar (**b**) *(criticize)* criticar

3 *vi (battery)* agotarse; *(clock)* pararse

▸ **run in** *vt sep Aut* rodar

▸ **run into** *vt insep* (**a**) *(room)* entrar corriendo en (**b**) *(people, problems)* tropezar con (**c**) *(crash into)* chocar contra

▸ **run off 1** *vt sep (print)* tirar

2 *vi* escaparse

▸ **run on 1** *vt sep Typ* enlazar

2 *vi (meeting)* continuar

▸ **run out** *vi* (**a**) *(exit)* salir corriendo (**b**) *(come to an end)* agotarse; *(of contract)* vencer; **to r. out of** quedarse sin

▸ **run over 1** *vt sep (in car)* atropellar

2 *vt insep (rehearse)* ensayar

3 *vi (overflow)* rebosar

▸ **run through** *vt insep* (**a**) *(of river)* pasar por (**b**) *(read quickly)* echar un vistazo a (**c**) *(rehearse)* ensayar

▸ **run up** *vt sep* (**a**) *(flag)* izar (**b**) *(debts)* acumular

▸ **run up against** *vt insep* tropezar con

runaway ['rʌnəweɪ] **1** *n* fugitivo(a) *m,f*

2 *adj (person)* huido(a); *(horse)* desbocado(a); *(vehicle)* incontrolado(a); *(inflation)* galopante; *(success)* clamoroso(a)

rundown ['rʌndaʊn] *n Fam* **to give sb a r.** poner a algn al corriente

run-down [rʌn'daʊn] *adj* (a) *(exhausted)* agotado(a) (b) *(dilapidated)* ruinoso(a)

rung¹ [rʌŋ] *pp of* **ring**

rung² [rʌŋ] *n (of ladder)* escalón *m*, peldaño *m*

runner ['rʌnə(r)] *n* (a) *(person)* corredor(a) *m,f*, (b) *(horse)* caballo *m* de carreras (c) *(of skate)* cuchilla *f* (d) *(on table)* tapete *m* (e) **r. bean** judía escarlata

runner-up [rʌnər'ʌp] *n* subcampeón(ona) *m,f*

running ['rʌnɪŋ] **1** *n* (a) **he likes r.** le gusta correr; *Fig* **to be in the r. for sth** tener posibilidades de conseguir algo (b) *(of company)* dirección *f* (c) *(of machine)* funcionamiento *m*

2 *adj* (a) **r. commentary** comentario en directo; **r. costs** gastos *mpl* de mantenimiento; *Pol* **r. mate** candidato *m* a la vicepresidencia; **r. water** agua *f* corriente (b) **three weeks r.** tres semanas seguidas

runny ['rʌnɪ] *adj* (**runnier, runniest**) blando(a); *(egg)* crudo(a); *(butter)* derretido(a); *(nose)* que moquea

run-of-the-mill ['rʌnəvðə'mɪl] *adj* corriente y moliente

runt [rʌnt] *n Fam* enano(a) *m,f*

run-up ['rʌnʌp] *n (to elections)* preliminares *mpl*

runway ['rʌnweɪ] *n Av* pista *f* (de aterrizaje y despegue)

rupee [ruː'piː] *n* rupia *f*

rupture ['rʌptʃə(r)] **1** *n* (a) *Med* hernia *f* (b) *Fig* ruptura *f*

2 *vt* (a) **to r. oneself** herniarse (b) *(break)* romper

rural ['rʊərəl] *adj* rural

ruse [ruːz] *n* ardid *m*, astucia *f*

rush¹ [rʌʃ] *n Bot* junco *m*

rush² [rʌʃ] **1** *n* (a) *(hurry)* prisa *f*; *(hustle and bustle)* ajetreo *m*; **there's no r.** no corre prisa; **r. hour** hora punta (b) *(demand)* demanda *f* (c) *(of wind)* ráfaga *f* (d) *(of water)* torrente *m* (e) *Mil* ataque *m*

2 *vt* (a) *(task)* hacer de prisa; *(person)* meter prisa a; **to r. sb to hospital** llevar a algn urgentemente al hospital (b) *(attack)* abalanzarse sobre; *Mil* tomar por asalto

3 *vi (go quickly)* precipitarse

▸ **rush about** *vi* correr de un lado a otro

▸ **rush into** *vt insep Fig* **to r. into sth** hacer algo sin pensarlo bien

▸ **rush off** *vi* irse corriendo

rusk [rʌsk] *n* = galleta dura para niños ·

Russia ['rʌʃə] *n* Rusia

Russian ['rʌʃən] **1** *adj* ruso(a)

2 *n* (a) *(person)* ruso(a) *m,f* (b) *(language)* ruso *m*

rust [rʌst] **1** *n* (a) *(substance)* herrumbre *f* (b) *(colour)* pardo rojizo

2 *vt* oxidar

3 *vi* oxidarse

rustic ['rʌstɪk] *adj* rústico(a)

rustle ['rʌsəl] **1** *n* crujido *m*

2 *vt (papers etc)* hacer crujir

3 *vi (steal cattle)* robar ganado

rustproof ['rʌstpruːf] *adj* inoxidable

rusty ['rʌstɪ] *adj* (**rustier, rustiest**) oxidado(a); *Fam Fig* **my French is a bit r.** tengo el francés un poco oxidado

rut [rʌt] *n* (a) *(furrow)* surco *m*; *(groove)* ranura *f* (b) *Fig* **to be in a r.** ser esclavo de la rutina (c) *Zool* celo *m*

ruthless ['ruːθlɪs] *adj* despiadado(a)

rye [raɪ] *n* centeno *m*; **r. bread** pan *m* de centeno; **r. grass** ballica *f*; *US* **r. (whiskey)** whisky *m* de centeno

S

S, s [es] *n (the letter)* S, s *f*
Sabbath ['sæbəθ] *n (Jewish)* sábado *m*; *(Christian)* domingo *m*
sabbatical [sə'bætɪkəl] *adj* sabático(a)
sabotage ['sæbətɑːʒ] **1** *n* sabotaje *m*
  2 *vt* sabotear
saccharin ['sækərɪn] *n* sacarina *f*
sachet ['sæʃeɪ] *n* bolsita *f*, sobrecito *m*
sack [sæk] **1** *n* (a) *(bag)* saco *m* (b) *Br Fam* **to get the s.** ser despedido(a); *Fam* **to give sb the s.** despedir a algn
  2 *vt* (a) *Br Fam* despedir (b) *Mil* saquear
sacking ['sækɪŋ] *n Tex* arpillera *f*
sacrament ['sækrəmənt] *n* sacramento *m*
sacred ['seɪkrɪd] *adj* sagrado(a)
sacrifice ['sækrɪfaɪs] **1** *n* sacrificio *m*
  2 *vt* sacrificar
sacrificial [sækrɪ'fɪʃəl] *adj* **s. lamb** chivo expiatorio
sacrilege ['sækrɪlɪdʒ] *n* sacrilegio *m*
sacrosanct ['sækrəʊsæŋkt] *adj* sacrosanto(a)
sad [sæd] *adj* (**sadder, saddest**) triste; **how s.!** ¡qué pena!
sadden ['sædən] *vt* entristecer
saddle ['sædəl] **1** *n (for horse)* silla *f* (de montar); *(of bicycle etc)* sillín *m*
  2 *vt (horse)* ensillar; *Fam* **to s. sb with sth** cargarle a algn con algo
saddlebag ['sædəlbæg] *n* alforja *f*
sadist ['seɪdɪst] *n* sádico(a) *m,f*
sadistic [sə'dɪstɪk] *adj* sádico(a)
sadness ['sædnɪs] *n* tristeza *f*
sadomasochism [seɪdəʊ'mæsəkɪzəm] *n* sadomasoquismo *m*
sae [eseɪ'iː] *n Br (abbr* **stamped addressed envelope**) = sobre franqueado con la dirección del remitente
safari [sə'fɑːrɪ] *n* safari *m*; **s. park** reserva *f*
safe [seɪf] **1** *adj* (a) *(unharmed)* ileso(a); *(out of danger)* a salvo; **s. and sound** sano(a) y salvo(a) (b) *(not dangerous)* inocuo(a) (c) *(secure, sure)* seguro(a); **to be on the s. side** para mayor seguridad; **s. house** *(for spies etc)* piso franco (d) *(driver)* prudente
  2 *n (for money etc)* caja *f* fuerte

safe-conduct [seɪf'kɒndʌkt] *n* salvoconducto *m*
safe-deposit [seɪfdɪ'pɒzɪt] *n* **s. (box)** cámara blindada
safeguard ['seɪfgɑːd] **1** *n (protection)* salvaguarda *f*; *(guarantee)* garantía *f*
  2 *vt* proteger, salvaguardar
safekeeping [seɪf'kiːpɪŋ] *n* custodia *f*
safely ['seɪflɪ] *adv* (a) con toda seguridad (b) **to arrive s.** llegar sin incidentes
safety ['seɪftɪ] *n* seguridad *f*; **s. first!** ¡la seguridad ante todo!; **s. belt** cinturón *m* de seguridad; **s. net** red *f* de protección; **s. pin** imperdible *m*
saffron ['sæfrən] *n* azafrán *m*
sag [sæg] *vi* (a) *(roof)* hundirse; *(wall)* pandear; *(wood, iron)* combarse; *(flesh)* colgar (b) *Fig (spirits)* flaquear
sage¹ [seɪdʒ] **1** *adj (wise)* sabio(a)
  2 *n (person)* sabio(a) *m,f*
sage² [seɪdʒ] *n* salvia *f*
Sagittarius [sædʒɪ'teərɪəs] *n* Sagitario *m*
Sahara [sə'hɑːrə] *n* **the S.** el Sahara
Saharan [sə'hɑːrən] *adj* saharaui, sahariano(a)
said [sed] **1** *adj* dicho(a)
  2 *pt & pp of* **say**
sail [seɪl] **1** *n* (a) *(canvas)* vela *f*; **to set s.** zarpar (b) *(trip)* paseo *m* en barco
  2 *vt (ship)* gobernar; *Literary* navegar
  3 *vi* (a) ir en barco (b) *(set sail)* zarpar
► **sail through** *vt insep Fam* **he sailed through university** en la universidad todo le fue sobre ruedas
sailboat ['seɪlbəʊt] *n US* velero *m*
sailing ['seɪlɪŋ] *n* navegación *f*; *(yachting)* vela *f*; *Fam* **it's all plain s.** es todo coser y cantar; *Br* **s. boat** *or* **ship** velero *m*, barco *m* de vela
sailor ['seɪlə(r)] *n* marinero *m*
saint [seɪnt] *n* santo(a) *m,f*; *(before all masculine names except those beginning* **Do** *or* **To**) San; *(before feminine names)* Santa; **S. Dominic** Santo Domingo; **S. Helen** Santa Elena; **S. John** San Juan; **All Saints' Day** Día *m* de Todos los Santos
saintly ['seɪntlɪ] *adj* (**saintlier, saintliest**) santo(a)
sake [seɪk] *n* **for the s. of** por (el bien de);

for your own s. por tu propio bien

salad ['sæləd] n ensalada f; **potato s.** ensalada de patatas or Am papas; **s. bowl** ensaladera f; **s. cream** salsa f tipo mahonesa; **s. dressing** vinagreta f, aliño m

salami [sə'lɑːmɪ] n salchichón m, salami m

salary ['sælərɪ] n salario m, sueldo m

sale [seɪl] n (a) venta f; **for** or **on s.** en venta; **sales department** departamento m comercial; **sales manager** jefe(a) m,f de ventas (b) (at low prices) rebajas fpl

salesclerk ['seɪlzklɑːk] n US dependiente(a) m,f

salesman ['seɪlzmən] n (a) vendedor m; (in shop) dependiente m (b) (commercial traveller) representante m

salesroom ['seɪlzruːm] n sala f de subastas

saleswoman ['seɪlzwʊmən] n (a) vendedora f; (in shop) dependienta f (b) (commercial traveller) representante f

salient ['seɪlɪənt] adj Fig sobresaliente

saliva [sə'laɪvə] n saliva f

sallow ['sæləʊ] adj cetrino(a)

salmon ['sæmən] 1 n salmón m
2 adj (de color) salmón

salmonella [sælmə'nelə] n Biol & Med (bacteria) salmonela f; (food poisoning) salmonelosis f

salon ['sælɒn] n salón m

saloon [sə'luːn] n (a) (on ship) cámara f (b) US (bar) taberna f, bar m; Br **s. (bar)** bar de lujo (c) (car) turismo m

salt [sɔːlt] 1 n sal f; Fig **to take sth with a pinch of s.** creer algo con reservas; **bath salts** sales de baño; **smelling salts** sales aromáticas
2 adj salado(a)
3 vt (a) (cure) salar (b) (add salt to) echar sal a

saltcellar ['sɔːltselə(r)] n salero m

saltwater ['sɔːltwɔːtə(r)] adj de agua salada

salty ['sɔːltɪ] adj (saltier, saltiest) salado(a)

salubrious [sə'luːbrɪəs] adj salubre, sano(a)

salutary ['sæljʊtərɪ] adj (experience) beneficioso(a); (warning) útil

salute [sə'luːt] 1 n (greeting) saludo m
2 vt (a) Mil saludar (b) Fig (achievement etc) aplaudir
3 vi Mil saludar

salvage ['sælvɪdʒ] 1 n (a) (of ship etc) salvamento m, rescate m (b) (objects recovered) objetos recuperados (c) Jur derecho m de salvamento

2 vt (from ship etc) rescatar

salvation [sæl'veɪʃən] n salvación f; **S. Army** Ejército m de Salvación

Samaritan [sə'mærɪtən] n samaritano(a) m,f; **the Samaritans** ≃ el teléfono de la Esperanza

same [seɪm] 1 adj mismo(a); **at that very s. moment** en ese mismísimo momento; **at the s. time** (simultaneously) al mismo tiempo; (however) sin embargo; **in the s. way** del mismo modo; **the two cars are the s.** los dos coches son iguales

2 pron s. el mismo/la misma/lo mismo; Fam **the s. here** lo mismo digo yo; Fam **the s. to you!** ¡igualmente!

3 adv del mismo modo, igual; **all the s., just the s.** sin embargo, aun así; **it's all the s. to me** (a mí) me da igual or lo mismo

sample ['sɑːmpəl] 1 n muestra f
2 vt (wines) catar; (dish) probar

sanatorium [sænə'tɔːrɪəm] n sanatorio m

sanctimonious [sæŋktɪ'məʊnɪəs] adj beato(a)

sanction ['sæŋkʃən] 1 n (a) (authorization) permiso m (b) (penalty) sanción f (c) Pol **sanctions** sanciones fpl
2 vt sancionar

sanctity ['sæŋktɪtɪ] n (sacredness) santidad f; (of marriage) indisolubilidad f

sanctuary ['sæŋktjʊərɪ] n (a) Rel santuario m (b) Pol asilo m (c) (for birds, animals) reserva f

sand [sænd] 1 n arena f; **s. castle** castillo m de arena; **s. dune** duna f
2 vt **to s. (down)** lijar

sandal ['sændəl] n sandalia f

sandalwood ['sændəlwʊd] n sándalo m

sandbag ['sændbæg] n saco terrero

sandbox ['sændbɒks] n US arenal m

sandpaper ['sændpeɪpə(r)] n papel m de lija

sandpit ['sændpɪt] n Br (in playground etc) arenal m

sandshoe ['sændʃuː] n Br playera f

sandstone ['sændstəʊn] n arenisca f

sandwich ['sænwɪdʒ, 'sænwɪtʃ] 1 n (bread roll) bocadillo m; (sliced bread) sándwich m; Educ **s. course** curso teórico-práctico
2 vt intercalar; **it was sandwiched between two lorries** quedó encajonado entre dos camiones

sandy ['sændɪ] adj (sandier, sandiest) (a) (earth, beach) arenoso(a) (b) (hair) rubio rojizo

sane [seɪn] *adj (not mad)* cuerdo(a); *(sensible)* sensato(a)

> 🖉 Note that the Spanish word **sano** is a false friend and is never a translation for the English word **sane**. In Spanish, **sano** means "healthy".

sang [sæŋ] *pt of* **sing**
sanitarium [sænɪˈteərɪəm] *n US* sanatorio *m*
sanitary [ˈsænɪtərɪ] *adj* sanitario(a); *(hygienic)* higiénico(a); **s.** *Br* **towel** *or US* **napkin** compresa *f*
sanitation [sænɪˈteɪʃən] *n* sanidad *f* (pública); *(plumbing)* sistema *m* de saneamiento
sanity [ˈsænɪtɪ] *n* cordura *f*, juicio *m*; *(good sense)* sensatez *f*

> 🖉 Note that the Spanish word **sanidad** is a false friend and is never a translation for the English word **sanity**. In Spanish, **sanidad** means "health".

sank [sæŋk] *pt of* **sink**
Santa Claus [ˈsæntəˈklɔːz] *n* Papá Noel *m*, San Nicolás *m*
sap¹ [sæp] *n Bot* savia *f*
sap² [sæp] *vt (undermine)* minar; *Fig* agotar
sapling [ˈsæplɪŋ] *n Bot* árbol *m* joven
sapphire [ˈsæfaɪə(r)] *n* zafiro *m*
sarcasm [ˈsɑːkæzm] *n* sarcasmo *m*
sarcastic [sɑːˈkæstɪk] *adj* sarcástico(a)
sardine [sɑːˈdiːn] *n* sardina *f*
Sardinia [sɑːˈdɪnɪə] *n* Cerdeña
sardonic [sɑːˈdɒnɪk] *adj* sardónico(a)
SASE [eseɪes'iː] *n US (abbr* **self-addressed stamped envelope)** = sobre franqueado con la dirección del remitente
sash¹ [sæʃ] *n* faja *f*
sash² [sæʃ] *n* **s. window** ventana *f* de guillotina
sat [sæt] *pt & pp of* **sit**
Satan [ˈseɪtən] *n* Satán *m*, Satanás *m*
satanic [səˈtænɪk] *adj* satánico(a)
satchel [ˈsætʃəl] *n* cartera *f* de colegial
satellite [ˈsætəlaɪt] *n* satélite *m*; **s. dish (aerial)** antena parabólica
satin [ˈsætɪn] *n* satén *m*; **s. finish** (acabado *m*) satinado *m*
satire [ˈsætaɪə(r)] *n* sátira *f*
satirical [səˈtɪrɪkəl] *adj* satírico(a)
satisfaction [sætɪsˈfækʃən] *n* satisfacción *f*
satisfactory [sætɪsˈfæktərɪ] *adj* satisfactorio(a)
satisfied [ˈsætɪsfaɪd] *adj* satisfecho(a)
satisfy [ˈsætɪsfaɪ] *vt* **(a)** satisfacer **(b)**

(fulfil) cumplir con **(c)** *(convince)* convencer
satisfying [ˈsætɪsfaɪɪŋ] *adj* satisfactorio(a); *(pleasing)* agradable; *(meal)* que llena
saturate [ˈsætʃəreɪt] *vt* saturar (**with** de)
Saturday [ˈsætədɪ] *n* sábado *m*
sauce [sɔːs] *n* **(a)** salsa *f* **(b)** *Fam (impudence)* descaro *m*
saucepan [ˈsɔːspən] *n* cacerola *f*, *(large)* olla *f*
saucer [ˈsɔːsə(r)] *n* platillo *m*
saucy [ˈsɔːsɪ] *adj* **(saucier, sauciest)** *Fam* fresco(a)
Saudi Arabia [ˈsaʊdɪəˈreɪbɪə] *n* Arabia *f* Saudita *or* Saudí
Saudi Arabian [ˈsaʊdɪəˈreɪbɪən] *adj & n* saudita *(mf)*, saudí *(mf)*
sauna [ˈsɔːnə] *n* sauna *f*
saunter [ˈsɔːntə(r)] **1** *n* paseo *m*
   2 *vi* pasearse
sausage [ˈsɒsɪdʒ] *n (raw)* salchicha *f*; *(cured)* salchichón *m*; *(spicy)* chorizo *m*; *Fam* **s. dog** perro *m* salchicha; *Br* **s. roll** empanada *f* de carne
sauté [ˈsəʊteɪ] **1** *adj* salteado(a)
   2 *vt* saltear
savage [ˈsævɪdʒ] **1** *adj* **(a)** *(ferocious)* feroz; *(cruel)* cruel; *(violent)* salvaje **(b)** *(primitive)* salvaje
   2 *n* salvaje *mf*
   3 *vt (attack)* embestir; *Fig (criticize)* criticar despiadadamente
save [seɪv] **1** *vt* **(a)** *(rescue)* salvar, rescatar; *Fig* **to s. face** salvar las apariencias **(b)** *(put by)* guardar; *(money, energy, time)* ahorrar; *(food)* almacenar; **it saved him a lot of trouble** le evitó muchos problemas
   2 *vi* **(a)** **to s. (up)** ahorrar **(b)** **to s. on paper** *(economize)* ahorrar papel
   3 *n Ftb* parada *f*
   4 *prep Literary* salvo, excepto
saving [ˈseɪvɪŋ] **1** *n* **(a)** *(of time, money)* ahorro *m* **(b)** **savings** ahorros *mpl*; **savings account** cuenta *f* de ahorros; **savings bank** caja *f* de ahorros
   2 *adj* **it's his only s. grace** es el único mérito que tiene
saviour, *US* **savior** [ˈseɪvjə(r)] *n* salvador(a) *m,f*
savour, *US* **savor** [ˈseɪvə(r)] **1** *n* sabor *m*, gusto *m*
   2 *vi* saborear
savoury, *US* **savory** [ˈseɪvərɪ] *adj (tasty)* sabroso(a); *(salted)* salado(a); *(spicy)* picante
saw¹ [sɔː] **1** *n (tool)* sierra *f*

2 *vt & vi* (*pt* **sawed**; *pp* **sawed** *or* **sawn**) serrar

▸ **saw up** *vt sep* serrar (**into** en)

saw² [sɔː] *pt of* **see**

sawdust ['sɔːdʌst] *n* (a)serrín *m*

sawmill ['sɔːmɪl] *n* aserradero *m*, serrería *f*

sawn [sɔːn] *pp of* **saw**

sawn-off ['sɔːnɒf], *US* **sawed-off** ['sɔːdɒf] *adj* recortado(a); **s. shotgun** escopeta *f* de cañones recortados

saxophone ['sæksəfəʊn] *n* saxofón *m*

say [seɪ] **1** *vt* (*pt & pp* **said**) (a) decir; **it goes without saying that ...** huelga decir que ...; **it is said that ...** se dice que ...; **not to s. ...** por no decir ...; **that is to s.** es decir; **to s. yes/no** decir que sí/no; *Fam* **I s.!** ¡oiga!; **what does the sign s.?** ¿qué pone en el letrero? (b) (*think*) pensar (c) **shall we s. Friday then?** ¿quedamos el viernes, pues?

2 **I have no s. in the matter** no tengo ni voz ni voto en el asunto; **to have one's s.** dar su opinión

saying ['seɪɪŋ] *n* refrán *m*, dicho *m*

scab [skæb] *n* (a)*Med* costra *f* (b) *Fam Pej* esquirol *mf*

scaffold ['skæfəld] *n* (*for execution*) patíbulo *m*

scaffolding ['skæfəldɪŋ] *n Constr* andamio *n*

scald [skɔːld] **1** *n* escaldadura *f*

2 *vt* escaldar

scale¹ [skeɪl] *n* (*of fish, on skin*) escama *f*; (*in boiler*) incrustaciones *fpl*

scale² [skeɪl] **1** *n* (a) escala *f*; **on a large s.** a gran escala; **to s.** a escala; **s. model** maqueta *f* (b) (*extent*) alcance *m* (c) *Mus* escala *f*

2 *vt* (*climb*) escalar

▸ **scale down** *vt sep* (*drawing*) reducir a escala; (*production*) reducir

scales [skeɪlz] *npl* (**pair of**) **s.** (*shop, kitchen*) balanza *f*; (*bathroom*) báscula *f*

scallop ['skɒləp] *n* (a) (*mollusc*) vieira *f* (b) (*shell*) venera *f*

scalp [skælp] **1** *n* cuero cabelludo

2 *vt* arrancar el cuero cabelludo a

scalpel ['skælpəl] *n* bisturí *m*

scamper ['skæmpə(r)] *vi* corretear

scampi ['skæmpɪ] *n* gambas empanadas

scan [skæn] **1** *vt* (a) (*scrutinize*) escrutar; (*horizon*) otear (b) (*glance at*) ojear (c) (*of radar*) explorar

2 *n Med* exploración ultrasónica; (*in gynaecology etc*) ecografía *f*

scandal ['skændəl] *n* (a) escándalo *m*;

what a s.! ¡qué vergüenza! (b) (*gossip*) chismes *mpl*

Scandinavia [skændɪ'neɪvɪə] *n* Escandinavia

Scandinavian [skændɪ'neɪvɪən] *adj & n* escandinavo(a) (*m,f*)

scanner ['skænə(r)] *n Med & Comput* escáner *m*

scant [skænt] *adj* escaso(a)

scanty ['skæntɪ] *adj* (**scantier, scantiest**) escaso(a); (*meal*) insuficiente; (*clothes*) ligero(a)

scapegoat ['skeɪpgəʊt] *n* chivo expiatorio

scar [skɑː(r)] *n* cicatriz *f*

scarce [skeəs] *adj* escaso(a); *Fig* **to make oneself s.** largarse

scarcely ['skeəslɪ] *adv* apenas

scarcity ['skeəsɪtɪ] *n* escasez *f*; (*rarity*) rareza *f*

scare [skeə(r)] **1** *n* (*fright*) susto *m*; (*widespread alarm*) pánico *m*; **bomb s.** amenaza *f* de bomba

2 *vt* asustar, espantar; *Fam* **to be scared stiff** estar muerto(a) de miedo

▸ **scare away, scare off** *vt sep* ahuyentar

scarecrow ['skeəkrəʊ] *n* espantapájaros *m inv*

scarf [skɑːf] *n* (*pl* **scarfs** *or* **scarves**) (*long, woollen*) bufanda *f*; (*square*) pañuelo *m*; (*silk*) fular *m*

scarlet ['skɑːlɪt] **1** *adj* escarlata

2 *n* escarlata *f*; **s. fever** escarlatina *f*

scarves [skɑːvz] *pl of* **scarf**

scathing ['skeɪðɪŋ] *adj* mordaz, cáustico(a)

scatter ['skætə(r)] **1** *vt* (a) (*papers etc*) esparcir, desparramar (b) (*crowd*) dispersar

2 *vi* dispersarse

scatterbrained ['skætəbreɪnd] *adj Fam* ligero(a) de cascos; (*forgetful*) despistado(a)

scattered ['skætəd] *adj* **s. showers** chubascos aislados

scavenger ['skævɪndʒə(r)] *n* (a) (*person*) rebuscador(a) *m,f*, trapero *m* (b) (*animal*) (animal *m*) carroñero(a) *mf*

scenario [sɪ'nɑːrɪəʊ] *n* (a) *Cin* guión *m* (b) (*situation*) situación *f* hipotética

scene [siːn] *n* (a) *Th, Cin & TV* escena *f*; **behind the scenes** entre bastidores (b) (*place*) lugar *m*, escenario *m*; **a change of s.** un cambio de aires (c) (*view*) panorama *m* (d) **to make a s.** (*fuss*) montar un espectáculo

scenery ['siːnərɪ] *n* (a) (*landscape*) paisaje *m* (b)*Th* decorado *m*

scenic ['siːnɪk] *adj (picturesque)* pintoresco(a)

scent [sent] **1** *n* (**a**) *(smell)* olor *m*; *(of food)* aroma *m* (**b**) *(perfume)* perfume *m* (**c**) *(in hunting)* pista *f*
　2 *vt (add perfume to)* perfumar; *(smell)* olfatear; *Fig* presentir

sceptic ['skeptɪk] *n* escéptico(a) *m,f*

sceptical ['skeptɪkəl] *adj* escéptico(a)

scepticism ['skeptɪsɪzəm] *n* escepticismo *m*

sceptre ['septə(r)] *n* cetro *m*

schedule ['ʃedjuːl, *US* 'skedʒʊəl] **1** *n* (**a**) *(plan, agenda)* programa *m*; *(timetable)* horario *m*; **on s.** a la hora (prevista); **to be behind s.** llevar retraso (**b**) *(list)* lista *f*; *(inventory)* inventario *m*
　2 *vt (plan)* programar, fijar

scheduled ['ʃedjuːld, *US* 'skedʒʊəld] *adj* previsto(a), fijo(a); **s. flight** vuelo regular

scheme [skiːm] **1** *n* (**a**) *(plan)* plan *m*; *(project)* proyecto *m*; *(idea)* idea *f*; **colour s.** combinación *f* de colores (**b**) *(plot)* intriga *f*; *(trick)* ardid *m*
　2 *vi (plot)* tramar, intrigar

scheming ['skiːmɪŋ] *adj* intrigante, maquinador(a)

schism ['sɪzəm] *n* cisma *m*

schizophrenic [skɪtsəʊ'frenɪk] *adj & n* esquizofrénico(a) *(m,f)*

scholar ['skɒlə(r)] *n (learned person)* erudito(a) *m,f*; *(pupil)* alumno(a) *m,f*

scholarship ['skɒləʃɪp] *n* (**a**) *(learning)* erudición *f* (**b**) *(grant)* beca *f*; **s. holder** becario(a) *m,f*

school [skuːl] **1** *n* (**a**) escuela *f*, colegio *m*; **drama s.** academia *f* de arte dramático; **of s. age** en edad escolar; **s. year** año *m* escolar (**b**) *US (university)* universidad *f* (**c**) *(university department)* facultad *f* (**d**) *(group of artists)* escuela *f*; **s. of thought** corriente *f* de opinión
　2 *vt (teach)* enseñar; *(train)* formar

schoolbook ['skuːlbʊk] *n* libro *m* de texto

schoolboy ['skuːlbɔɪ] *n* alumno *m*

schoolchild ['skuːltʃaɪld] *n* alumno(a) *m,f*

schooldays ['skuːldeɪz] *npl* años *mpl* de colegio

schoolgirl ['skuːlgɜːl] *n* alumna *f*

schooling ['skuːlɪŋ] *n* educación *f*, estudios *mpl*

schoolmaster ['skuːlmɑːstə(r)] *n* profesor *m*; *(primary school)* maestro *m*

schoolmistress ['skuːlmɪstrɪs] *n* profesora *f*; *(primary school)* maestra *f*

schoolteacher ['skuːltiːtʃə(r)] *n* profesor(a) *m,f*; *(primary school)* maestro(a) *m,f*

schooner ['skuːnə(r)] *n Naut* goleta *f*

sciatica [saɪ'ætɪkə] *n* ciática *f*

science ['saɪəns] *n* ciencia *f*; *(school subject)* ciencias; **s. fiction** ciencia-ficción *f*

scientific [saɪən'tɪfɪk] *adj* científico(a)

scientist ['saɪəntɪst] *n* científico(a) *m,f*

scintillating ['sɪntɪleɪtɪŋ] *adj* brillante

scissors ['sɪzəz] *npl* tijeras *fpl*; **a pair of s.** unas tijeras

scoff[1] [skɒf] *vi (mock)* mofarse (**at** de)

scoff[2] [skɒf] *vt Fam (eat)* zamparse

scold [skəʊld] *vt* regañar, reñir

scone [skəʊn, skɒn] *n* bollo *m*, pastelito *m*

scoop [skuːp] *n* (**a**) *(for flour)* pala *f*; *(for ice cream)* cucharón *m*; *(amount)* palada *f*, cucharada *f* (**b**) *Press* exclusiva *f*
　▶ **scoop out** *vt sep (flour etc)* sacar con pala; *(water) (from boat)* achicar
　▶ **scoop up** *vt sep* recoger

scooter ['skuːtə(r)] *n (child's)* patinete *m*; *(adult's)* Vespa® *f*

scope [skəʊp] *n* (**a**) *(range)* alcance *m*; *(of undertaking)* ámbito *m* (**b**) *(freedom)* libertad *f*

scorch [skɔːtʃ] *vt (singe)* chamuscar

scorching ['skɔːtʃɪŋ] *adj Fam* abrasador(a)

score [skɔː(r)] **1** *n* (**a**) *Sport* tanteo *m*; *Cards & (in golf)* puntuación *f*; *(result)* resultado *m*
　(**b**) *(notch)* muesca *f*
　(**c**) **I have a s. to settle with you** tengo que ajustar las cuentas contigo
　(**d**) **on that s.** a ese respecto
　(**e**) *(twenty)* veintena *f*
　(**f**) *Mus (of opera)* partitura *f*; *(of film)* música *f*
　2 *vt* (**a**) *(goal)* marcar; *(points)* conseguir
　(**b**) *(wood)* hacer una muesca en; *(paper)* rayar
　3 *vi* (**a**) *Sport* marcar un tanto; *Ftb* marcar un gol; *(keep the score)* llevar el marcador
　(**b**) *(have success)* tener éxito (**with** con); *Fam* ligar (**with** con)
　▶ **score out** *vt sep (word etc)* tachar

scoreboard ['skɔːbɔːd] *n* marcador *m*

scorer ['skɔːrə(r)] *n* (**a**) *(goal striker)* goleador *m* (**b**) *(scorekeeper)* encargado(a) *m,f* del marcador

scorn [skɔːn] **1** *n* desprecio *m*
　2 *vt* despreciar

scornful ['skɔːnfʊl] *adj* desdeñoso(a)

Scorpio ['skɔːpɪəʊ] n Escorpión m

scorpion ['skɔːpɪən] n alacrán m, escorpión m

Scot [skɒt] n escocés(esa) m,f

Scotch [skɒtʃ] 1 adj escocés(esa); US **S. tape**® cinta adhesiva, celo® m
2 n (whisky) whisky m escocés

scotch [skɒtʃ] vt (plot) frustrar; (rumour) negar, desmentir

scot-free ['skɒt'friː] adj impune

Scotland ['skɒtlənd] n Escocia

Scots [skɒts] 1 adj escocés(esa)
2 n (dialecto m) escocés m

Scotsman ['skɒtsmən] n escocés m

Scotswoman ['skɒtswʊmən] n escocesa f

Scottish ['skɒtɪʃ] adj escocés(esa)

scoundrel ['skaʊndrəl] n sinvergüenza mf, canalla m

scour¹ [skaʊə(r)] vt (clean) fregar, restregar

scour² [skaʊə(r)] vt (search) (countryside) rastrear; (building) registrar

scourge [skɜːdʒ] n Fig azote m

scout [skaʊt] 1 n Mil explorador(a) m,f; Sport & Cin cazatalentos m inv; **boy s.** boy m scout
2 vi Mil reconocer el terreno; **to s. around for sth** andar en busca de algo

scowl [skaʊl] 1 vi fruncir el ceño; **to s. at sb** mirar a algn con ceño
2 n ceño m

scrabble ['skræbəl] vi escarbar; Fig **to s. around for sth** revolver todo para encontrar algo

scraggy ['skrægɪ] adj (**scraggier, scraggiest**) delgado(a), flacucho(a)

scramble ['skræmbəl] 1 vi trepar; **to s. for** pelearse por; **to s. up a tree** trepar a un árbol
2 vt (a) Culin **scrambled eggs** huevos revueltos (b) Rad & Tel (message) codificar; (broadcast) interferir
3 n (climb) subida f; Fig **it's going to be a s.** (rush) va a ser muy apresurado

scrap¹ [skræp] 1 n (a) (small piece) pedazo m; **there isn't a s. of truth in it** no tiene ni un ápice de verdad; **s. (metal)** chatarra f; **s. dealer** or **merchant** chatarrero(a) m,f; **s. paper** papel m de borrador; **s. yard** (for cars) cementerio m de coches (b) **scraps** restos mpl; (of food) sobras fpl
2 vt (discard) desechar; Fig (idea) descartar

scrap² [skræp] Fam 1 n (fight) pelea f
2 vi pelearse (**with** con)

scrapbook ['skræpbʊk] n álbum m de recortes

scrape [skreɪp] 1 vt (paint, wood) raspar; (knee) arañarse, hacerse un rasguño en
2 vi (make noise) chirriar; (rub) rozar
3 n Fam (trouble) lío m
▸ **scrape through** vi Fam (exam) aprobar por los pelos
▸ **scrape together** vt sep reunir a duras penas

scraper ['skreɪpə(r)] n rasqueta f

scrapheap ['skræphiːp] n (dump) vertedero m

scratch [skrætʃ] 1 n (a) (on skin, paintwork) arañazo m; (on record) raya f (b) (noise) chirrido m (c) Fig **to be up to s.** dar la talla; Fig **to start from s.** partir de cero
2 adj **s. team** equipo improvisado
3 vt (a) (with nail, claw) arañar, rasguñar; (paintwork) rayar (b) (to relieve itching) rascarse

scrawl [skrɔːl] 1 n garabatos mpl
2 vt (message etc) garabatear
3 vi hacer garabatos

scrawny ['skrɔːnɪ] adj (**scrawnier, scrawniest**) flaco(a)

scream [skriːm] 1 n chillido m; **screams of laughter** carcajadas fpl
2 vt (insults etc) gritar
3 vi chillar; **to s. at sb** chillar a algn

scree [skriː] n pedregal m

screech [skriːtʃ] 1 n (of person) chillido m; (of tyres, brakes) chirrido m
2 vi (person) chillar; (tyres) chirriar

screen [skriːn] 1 n (a) (movable partition) biombo m (b) Fig cortina f (c) Cin, TV & Comput pantalla f; **s. test** casting m
2 vt (a) (protect) proteger; (conceal) tapar (b) (sieve) (coal etc) tamizar; Fig (candidates) seleccionar (c) (show) (film) proyectar; (for first time) estrenar (d) Med examinar

screening ['skriːnɪŋ] n (a) (of film) proyección f; (for first time) estreno m (b) Med exploración f

screenplay ['skriːnpleɪ] n guión m

screw [skruː] 1 n (a) tornillo m (b) (propeller) hélice f
2 vt (a) atornillar; **to s. sth down** or **in** or **on** fijar algo con tornillos (b) Vulg joder
▸ **screw up** vt sep (a) (piece of paper) arrugar; (one's face) torcer (b) very Fam (ruin) joder

screwdriver ['skruːdraɪvə(r)] n destornillador m

scribble ['skrɪbəl] 1 n garabatos mpl
2 vt (message etc) garabatear
3 vi hacer garabatos

script [skrɪpt] n (a) (writing) escritura f; (handwriting) letra f; Typ letra cursiva (b) *(in exam)* escrito *m* (**c**) *Cin* guión *m*

Scripture ['skrɪptʃə(r)] *n* **Holy S.** Sagrada Escritura

scroll [skrəʊl] *n* rollo *m* de pergamino

scrounge [skraʊndʒ] *Fam* **1** *vi* gorronear; **to s. (around) for** buscar; **to s. off sb** vivir a costa de algn

2 *vt* gorronear

scrounger ['skraʊndʒə(r)] *n Fam* gorrón(ona) *m,f*

scrub¹ [skrʌb] *n (undergrowth)* maleza *f*

scrub² [skrʌb] **1** *vt* (**a**) frotar (**b**) *Fam (cancel)* borrar

2 *n (cleaning)* fregado *m*

scruff [skrʌf] *n* pescuezo *m*, cogote *m*

scruffy ['skrʌfɪ] *adj* (**scruffier, scruffiest**) *Fam* desaliñado(a)

scrum [skrʌm] *n* melée *f*; **s. half** medio *m* melée

scruple ['skruːpəl] *n* escrúpulo *m*

scrupulous ['skruːpjʊləs] *adj* escrupuloso(a)

scrupulously ['skruːpjʊləslɪ] *adv* **s. honest** sumamente honrado(a)

scrutinize ['skruːtɪnaɪz] *vt* escudriñar

scrutiny ['skruːtɪnɪ] *n* escrutinio *m*

scuff [skʌf] *vt (the floor)* rayar; *(one's feet)* arrastrar

scuffle ['skʌfəl] **1** *n* pelea *f*

2 *vi* pelearse (**with** con)

scullery ['skʌlərɪ] *n* cuarto *m* de pila

sculptor ['skʌlptə(r)] *n* escultor(a) *m,f*

sculpture ['skʌlptʃə(r)] *n* escultura *f*

scum [skʌm] *n* (**a**) *(on liquid)* espuma *f* (**b**) *Fig* escoria *f*

scupper ['skʌpə(r)] *vt Br Fam (plan etc)* desbaratar

scurrilous ['skʌrɪləs] *adj (abusive)* difamatorio(a)

scurry ['skʌrɪ] *vi (run)* corretear; *(hurry)* apresurarse; **to s. away** *or* **off** escabullirse

scuttle¹ ['skʌtəl] *n* cubo *m*; **coal s.** cubo del carbón

scuttle² ['skʌtəl] *vt (ship)* barrenar

scuttle³ ['skʌtəl] *vi* **to s. away** *or* **off** escabullirse

scythe [saɪð] **1** *n* guadaña *f*

2 *vt* guadañar

SDI [esdiː'aɪ] *n (abbr* **Strategic Defence Initiative**) Iniciativa *f* para la Defensa Estratégica

sea [siː] *n* mar *m* or *f*; **by the s.** a orillas del mar; **out at s.** en alta mar; **to go by s.** ir en barco; **to put to s.** zarpar; *Fig* **to be all at s.** estar desorientado(a); **s. breeze** brisa marina; *Fig* **s. change** metamorfosis *f*; **s. level** nivel *m* del mar; **s. lion** león marino; **s. water** agua *f* de mar

seabed ['siːbed] *n* fondo *m* del mar

seaboard ['siːbɔːd] *n US* costa *f*, litoral *m*

seafood ['siːfuːd] *n* mariscos *mpl*

seafront ['siːfrʌnt] *n* paseo marítimo

seagull ['siːgʌl] *n* gaviota *f*

seal¹ [siːl] *n Zool* foca *f*

seal² [siːl] **1** *n* (**a**) *(official stamp)* sello *m* (**b**) *(airtight closure)* cierre hermético; *(on bottle)* precinto *m*

2 *vt* (**a**) *(with official stamp)* sellar; *(with wax)* lacrar (**b**) *(close)* cerrar; *(make airtight)* cerrar herméticamente (**c**) *(determine)* **this sealed his fate** esto decidío su destino

▶ **seal off** *vt sep (pipe etc)* cerrar; *(area)* acordonar

seam [siːm] *n* (**a**) *Sewing* costura *f*; *Tech* juntura *f*; *Fam* **to be bursting at the seams** *(room)* rebosar de gente (**b**) *Geol & Min* veta *f*, filón *m*

seaman ['siːmən] *n* marinero *m*

seamy ['siːmɪ] *adj* (**seamier, seamiest**) *Fig* sórdido(a)

séance ['seɪɑːns] *n* sesión *f* de espiritismo

seaplane ['siːpleɪn] *n* hidroavión *m*

seaport ['siːpɔːt] *n* puerto marítimo

search [sɜːtʃ] **1** *vt (files etc)* buscar en; *(building, suitcase)* registrar; *(person)* cachear; *(one's conscience)* examinar

2 *vi* buscar; **to s. through** registrar

3 *n* búsqueda *f*; *(of building etc)* registro *m*; *(of person)* cacheo *m*; **in s. of** en busca de; *Comput* **s. engine** motor *m* de búsqueda; **s. party** equipo *m* de salvamento; **s. warrant** orden *f* de registro

searching ['sɜːtʃɪŋ] *adj (look)* penetrante; *(question)* indagatorio(a)

searchlight ['sɜːtʃlaɪt] *n* reflector *m*

seashell ['siːʃel] *n* concha marina

seashore ['siːʃɔː(r)] *n (beach)* playa *f*

seasick ['siːsɪk] *adj* mareado(a); **to get s.** marearse

seaside ['siːsaɪd] *n* playa *f*, costa *f*; **s. resort** lugar turístico de veraneo; **s. town** pueblo costero

season¹ ['siːzən] *n* época *f*; *(of year)* estación *f*; *(for sport etc)* temporada *f*; **the busy s.** la temporada alta; **the rainy s.** la estación de lluvias; **in s.** *(fruit)* en sazón; *(animal)* en celo; *Br* **s. ticket** abono *m*

season² ['siːzən] *vt Culin* sazonar

seasonal ['siːzənəl] *adj* estacional

seasoned ['siːzənd] *adj* (**a**) *Culin* sazonado(a) (**b**) *Fig (campaigner)* curtido(a), avezado(a)

seasoning ['siːzənɪŋ] *n* condimento *m*, aderezo *m*

seat [siːt] **1** n (a) asiento m; (place) plaza f; Cin & Th localidad f; **to take a s.** sentarse; Aut **s. belt** cinturón m de seguridad (b) (of cycle) sillín m; Fam (buttocks) trasero m (c) (of power, learning) centro m, sede f (d) Parl escaño m

2 vt (a) (guests etc) sentar (b) (accommodate) tener cabida para

seating [ˈsiːtɪŋ] n asientos mpl; **s. capacity** cabida f, aforo m

seaweed [ˈsiːwiːd] n alga f (marina)

seaworthy [ˈsiːwɜːðɪ] adj en condiciones de navegar

sec [sek] n Fam (abbr **second**) segundo m

secede [sɪˈsiːd] vi separarse (**from** de)

secluded [sɪˈkluːdɪd] adj retirado(a), apartado(a)

second¹ [ˈsekənd] **1** adj segundo(a); **every s. day** cada dos días; **it's the s. highest mountain** es la segunda montaña más alta; **on s. thought(s) ...** pensándolo bien ...; **to have s. thoughts about sth** dudar de algo; **to settle for s. best** conformarse con lo que hay

2 n (a) (in series) segundo(a) m,f; **Charles the S.** Carlos Segundo; **the s. of October** el dos de octubre (b) Aut (gear) segunda f (c) Com **seconds** artículos defectuosos

3 vt (motion) apoyar

4 adv **to come s.** terminar en segundo lugar

second² [ˈsekənd] n (time) segundo m; Fam **in a s.** enseguida; Fam **just a s.!** ¡un momentito!; **s. hand** (of watch, clock) segundero m

secondary [ˈsekəndərɪ] adj secundario(a); Br **s. school** escuela secundaria

second-class [ˈsekəndˈklɑːs] **1** adj de segunda clase

2 adv **to travel s.** viajar en segunda

second-hand [ˈsekəndˈhænd] adj & adv de segunda mano

secondly [ˈsekəndlɪ] adv en segundo lugar

secondment [sɪˈkɒndmənt] n Br traslado m temporal

second-rate [ˈsekəndˈreɪt] adj de segunda categoría

secrecy [ˈsiːkrəsɪ] n secreto m; **in s.** en secreto

secret [ˈsiːkrɪt] **1** adj secreto(a); **to keep sth s.** mantener algo en secreto; **s. ballot** votación secreta

2 n secreto m; Fig clave f; **in s.** en secreto; **to keep a s.** guardar un secreto

secretarial [sekrɪˈteərɪəl] adj de secretario(a)

secretary [ˈsekrətrɪ] n secretario(a) m,f; **S. of State** Br ministro(a) m,f con cartera; US ministro(a) m,f de Asuntos Exteriores

secretion [sɪˈkriːʃən] n secreción f

secretive [ˈsiːkrɪtɪv] adj reservado(a)

secretly [ˈsiːkrɪtlɪ] adv en secreto

sect [sekt] n secta f

sectarian [sekˈteərɪən] adj & n sectario(a) (m,f)

section [ˈsekʃən] n (a) (part) sección f, parte f; (of law) artículo m; (of community) sector m; (of orchestra, department) sección (b) (cut) corte m

sector [ˈsektə(r)] n sector m

secular [ˈsekjʊlə(r)] adj (school, teaching) laico(a); (music, art) profano(a); (priest) seglar, secular

secure [sɪˈkjʊə(r)] **1** adj seguro(a); (window, door) bien cerrado(a); (ladder etc) firme

2 vt (a) (make safe) asegurar (b) (fix) (rope, knot) sujetar, fijar; (object to floor) afianzar; (window, door) cerrar bien (c) (obtain) conseguir, obtener (d) Fin (guarantee) avalar

security [sɪˈkjʊərɪtɪ] n (a) seguridad f; **national s.** seguridad nacional; **S. Council** (of United Nations) Consejo m de Seguridad (b) Fin (guarantee) fianza f; (guarantor) fiador(a) m,f (c) Fin **securities** valores mpl

sedan [sɪˈdæn] n (a) Hist **s. chair** silla f de manos (b) US Aut turismo m

sedate [sɪˈdeɪt] **1** adj sosegado(a)

2 vt sedar

sedation [sɪˈdeɪʃən] n sedación f

sedative [ˈsedətɪv] adj & n sedante (m)

sediment [ˈsedɪmənt] n sedimento m; (of wine) poso m

seduce [sɪˈdjuːs] vt seducir

seduction [sɪˈdʌkʃən] n seducción f

seductive [sɪˈdʌktɪv] adj seductor(a)

see¹ [siː] vt & vi (pt **saw**; pp **seen**) (a) ver; **I'll s. what can be done** veré lo que se puede hacer; **let's s.** a ver; **that remains to be seen** eso queda por ver; **s. page 10** véase la página 10; **s. you (later)/soon!** ¡hasta luego/pronto!

(b) (meet with) ver, tener cita con; **they are seeing each other** (of couple) salen juntos

(c) (visit) ver; **to s. the world** recorrer el mundo

(d) (understand) entender; **as far as I can s.** por lo visto; **I s.** ya veo; **you s., he hasn't got a car** es que no tiene coche, ¿sabes?

(**e**) **he sees himself as a second Caruso** se cree otro Caruso

(**f**) (ensure) asegurarse de (**g**) **to s. sb home** acompañar a algn a casa

▸ **see about** vt insep (deal with) ocuparse de

▸ **see off** vt sep (say goodbye to) despedirse de

▸ **see out** vt sep (**a**) (show out) acompañar hasta la puerta (**b**) (survive) sobrevivir

▸ **see through** 1 vt insep Fam **to s. through sb** verle el plumero a algn

2 vt sep (**a**) **I'll s. you through** puedes contar con mi ayuda; **£20 should s. me through** con 20 libras me las apaño (**b**) **to s. sth through** (carry out) llevar algo a cabo

▸ **see to** vt insep (deal with) ocuparse de

see² [si:] n Rel sede f; **the Holy S.** la Santa Sede

seed [si:d] 1 n (**a**) Bot semilla f; (of fruit) pepita f; **to go to s.** (of plant) granar; Fig (of person) descuidarse (**b**) (in tennis) (player) cabeza mf de serie

2 vt (**a**) (sow with seed) sembrar (**b**) (grapes) despepitar (**c**) (in tennis) preseleccionar

seedling ['si:dlɪŋ] n plantón m

seedy ['si:dɪ] adj (**seedier, seediest**) Fam (bar etc) sórdido(a); (clothes) raído(a); (appearance) desaseado(a)

seeing ['si:ɪŋ] conj **s. that** visto que, dado que

seeing-eye dog ['si:ɪŋaɪ'dɒg] n US perro m lazarillo

seek [si:k] 1 vt (pt & pp **sought**) (**a**) (look for) buscar (**b**) (advice, help) solicitar

2 vt buscar; **to s. to do sth** procurar hacer algo

▸ **seek after** vt insep buscar; **much sought after** (person) muy solicitado(a); (thing) muy cotizado(a)

seem [si:m] vi parecer; **I s. to remember his name was Colin** creo recordar que su nombre era Colin; **it seems to me that** me parece que; **so it seems** eso parece

seeming ['si:mɪŋ] adj aparente

seemingly ['si:mɪŋlɪ] adv aparentemente, según parece

seen [si:n] pp of **see**

seep [si:p] vi **to s. through/into/out** filtrarse por/en/de

seesaw ['si:sɔ:] 1 n balancín m, subibaja m

2 vi (**a**) columpiarse, balancearse (**b**) Fig vacilar, oscilar

seethe [si:ð] vi bullir, hervir; Fig **to s. with anger** rabiar; **to s. with people** rebosar de gente

see-through ['si:θru:] adj transparente

segment ['segmənt] n segmento m; (of orange) gajo m

segregate ['segrɪgeɪt] vt segregar (**from** de)

segregation [segrɪ'geɪʃən] n segregación f

seize [si:z] vt (grab) agarrar, asir; Jur (property, drugs) incautar; (assets) secuestrar; (territory) tomar; (arrest) detener; **to s. an opportunity** aprovechar una ocasión; **to s. power** hacerse con el poder

▸ **seize on** vt insep (chance) agarrar; (idea) aferrarse a

▸ **seize up** vi agarrotarse

seizure ['si:ʒə(r)] n (**a**) Jur (of property, drugs) incautación f; (of newspaper) secuestro m; (arrest) detención f (**b**) Med ataque m (de apoplejía)

seldom ['seldəm] adv rara vez, raramente

select [sɪ'lekt] 1 vt (thing) escoger, elegir; (team) seleccionar

2 adj selecto(a)

selected [sɪ'lektɪd] adj selecto(a), escogido(a); (team, player) seleccionado(a); Lit **s. works** obras escogidas

selection [sɪ'lekʃən] n (choosing) elección f; (people or things chosen) selección f; (range) surtido m

selective [sɪ'lektɪv] adj selectivo(a)

self [self] n (pl **selves**) uno(a) mismo(a), sí mismo(a); Psy **the s.** el yo

self- [self] pref auto-

self-adhesive [selfəd'hi:sɪv] adj autoadhesivo(a)

self-assured [selfə'ʃʊəd] adj seguro(a) de sí mismo(a)

self-catering [self'keɪtərɪŋ] adj sin servicio de comida

self-centred, US self-centered [self'sentəd] adj egocéntrico(a)

self-confessed [selfkən'fest] adj confeso(a)

self-confidence [self'kɒnfɪdəns] n confianza f en sí mismo(a)

self-confident [self'kɒnfɪdənt] adj seguro(a) de sí mismo(a)

self-conscious [self'kɒnʃəs] adj cohibido(a)

self-contained [selfkən'teɪnd] adj (flat) con entrada propia; (person) independiente

self-control [selfkən'trəʊl] n autocontrol m

self-defence, US **self-defense** [self-dɪˈfens] n autodefensa f

self-discipline [selfˈdɪsɪplɪn] n autodisciplina f

self-employed [selfɪmˈplɔɪd] adj (worker) autónomo(a)

self-esteem [selfɪˈstiːm] n amor propio, autoestima f

self-evident [selfˈevɪdənt] adj evidente, patente

self-governing [selfˈgʌvənɪŋ] adj autónomo(a)

self-important [selfɪmˈpɔːtənt] adj engreído(a), presumido(a)

self-indulgent [selfɪnˈdʌldʒənt] adj inmoderado(a)

self-interest [selfˈɪntrɪst] n egoísmo m

selfish [ˈselfɪʃ] adj egoísta

selfishness [ˈselfɪʃnɪs] n egoísmo m

selfless [ˈselflɪs] adj desinteresado(a)

self-made [ˈselfmeɪd] adj **s. man** hombre m que se ha hecho a sí mismo

self-pity [selfˈpɪtɪ] n autocompasión f

self-portrait [selfˈpɔːtreɪt] n autorretrato m

self-possessed [selfpəˈzest] adj sereno(a), dueño(a) de sí mismo(a)

self-preservation [selfprezəˈveɪʃən] n **(instinct of) s.** instinto m de conservación

self-raising [ˈselfreɪzɪŋ] adj **s. flour** harina f con levadura

self-reliant [selfrɪˈlaɪənt] adj autosuficiente

self-respect [selfrɪˈspekt] n amor propio, dignidad f

self-righteous [selfˈraɪtʃəs] adj santurrón(ona)

self-rising [ˈselfraɪzɪŋ] adj US = **self-raising**

self-satisfied [selfˈsætɪsfaɪd] adj satisfecho(a) de sí mismo(a)

self-service [selfˈsɜːvɪs] **1** n (in shop etc) autoservicio m

2 adj de autoservicio

self-sufficient [selfsəˈfɪʃənt] adj autosuficiente

self-taught [selfˈtɔːt] adj autodidacta

sell [sel] **1** vt (pt & pp **sold**) vender

2 vi venderse; **this record is selling well** este disco se vende bien

3 n **hard/soft s.** (in advertising) publicidad agresiva/discreta

▸ **sell off** vt sep vender; (goods) liquidar

▸ **sell out 1** vi **to s. out to the enemy** claudicar ante el enemigo

2 vt sep Com **we're sold out of sugar** se nos ha agotado el azúcar; Th **sold out**

(sign) agotadas las localidades

seller [ˈselə(r)] n vendedor(a) m,f

selling [ˈselɪŋ] n venta f; **s. point** atractivo m comercial; **s. price** precio m de venta

Sellotape® [ˈseləteɪp] **1** n celo® m, cinta adhesiva

2 vt pegar or fijar con celo®

sell-out [ˈselaʊt] n (a) Th éxito m de taquilla (b) (act of disloyalty) claudicación f

selves [selvz] pl of **self**

semaphore [ˈseməfɔː(r)] n semáforo m

semblance [ˈsembləns] n apariencia f; **there was some s. of truth in it** había algo de verdad en ello

semen [ˈsiːmen] n semen m

semester [sɪˈmestə(r)] n semestre m

semi- [ˈsemɪ] pref semi-

semicircle [ˈsemɪsɜːkəl] n semicírculo m

semicolon [semɪˈkəʊlən] n punto y coma m

semiconductor [ˈsemɪkənˈdʌktə(r)] n semiconductor m

semidetached [semɪdɪˈtætʃt] Br **1** adj adosado(a)

2 n chalé adosado, casa adosada

semifinal [semɪˈfaɪnəl] n semifinal f

seminar [ˈsemɪnɑː(r)] n seminario m

seminary [ˈsemɪnərɪ] n seminario m

semitrailer [ˈsemɪtreɪlə(r)] n US camión articulado

semolina [seməˈliːnə] n sémola f

senate [ˈsenɪt] n (a) Pol senado m (b) Univ claustro m

senator [ˈsenətə(r)] n senador(a) m,f

send [send] **1** vt (pt & pp **sent**) (a) (letter) enviar, mandar; (radio signal) transmitir; (rocket, ball) lanzar; **he was sent to prison** lo mandaron a la cárcel; **to s. sth flying** tirar algo (b) **to s. sb mad** (cause to become) volver loco(a) a algn

2 vi **to s. for sb** mandar llamar a algn; **to s. for sth** encargar algo

▸ **send away 1** vt sep (dismiss) despedir

2 vi **to s. away for sth** escribir pidiendo algo

▸ **send back** vt sep (goods etc) devolver; (person) hacer volver

▸ **send in** vt sep (application etc) mandar; (troops) enviar

▸ **send off** vt sep (a) (letter etc) enviar; (goods) despachar (b) Ftb (player) expulsar

▸ **send on** vt sep (luggage) (ahead) facturar; (later) mandar (más tarde)

▸ **send out** vt sep (a) (person) echar (b) (invitations) enviar (c) (emit) emitir

▸ **send up** vt sep (a) hacer subir; (rocket)

lanzar; *(smoke)* echar (**b**) *Br Fam (make fun of) (person)* burlarse de; *(book etc)* satirizar

sender ['sendə(r)] *n* remitente *mf*

sendoff ['sendɒf] *n Fam* despedida *f*

senile ['si:naɪl] *adj* senil

senior ['si:njə(r)] **1** *adj* (**a**) *(in age)* mayor; **William Armstrong S.** William Armstrong padre; **s. citizen** jubilado(a) *m,f* (**b**) *(in rank)* superior; *(with longer service)* más antiguo(a); *Mil* **s. officer** oficial *mf* de alta graduación
   2 *n* (**a**) **she's three years my s.** *(in age)* me lleva tres años (**b**) *US Educ* estudiante *mf* del último curso

seniority [si:nɪ'ɒrɪtɪ] *n* antigüedad *f*

sensation [sen'seɪʃən] *n* sensación *f*; **to be a s.** ser un éxito; **to cause a s.** causar sensación

sensational [sen'seɪʃənəl] *adj (marvellous)* sensacional; *(exaggerated)* sensacionalista

sense [sens] **1** *n* (**a**) *(faculty)* sentido *m*; *(feeling)* sensación *f*; **s. of direction/humour** sentido *m* de la orientación/del humor (**b**) *(wisdom)* sentido *m* común, juicio *m*; **common s.** sentido común (**c**) *(meaning)* sentido *m*; *(of word)* significado *m*; **in a s.** en cierto sentido; **it doesn't make s.** no tiene sentido (**d**) **to come to one's senses** recobrar el juicio
   2 *vt* sentir, percatarse de

senseless ['senslɪs] *adj* (**a**) *(absurd)* insensato(a), absurdo(a) (**b**) *(unconscious)* sin conocimiento

sensibility [sensɪ'bɪlɪtɪ] *n* (**a**) *(sensitivity)* sensibilidad *f* (**b**) **sensibilities** susceptibilidad *f*

sensible ['sensɪbəl] *adj* (**a**) *(wise)* sensato(a) (**b**) *(choice)* acertado(a) (**c**) *(clothes, shoes)* práctico(a), cómodo(a)

> 📝 Note that the Spanish word **sensible** is a false friend and is never a translation for the English word **sensible**. In Spanish, **sensible** means both "sensitive" and "perceptible".

sensitive ['sensɪtɪv] *adj* (**a**) *(person)* sensible; *(touchy)* susceptible (**b**) *(skin)* delicado(a); *(document)* confidencial

sensor ['sensə(r)] *n* sensor *m*

sensual ['sensjʊəl] *adj* sensual

sensuous ['sensjʊəs] *adj* sensual

sent [sent] *pt & pp of* **send**

sentence ['sentəns] **1** *n* (**a**) *(phrase)* frase *f*; *Ling* oración *f* (**b**) *Jur* sentencia *f*; **to pass s. on sb** imponer una pena a algn; **life s.** cadena perpetua
   2 *vt Jur* condenar

sentiment ['sentɪmənt] *n* (**a**) *(sentimentality)* sensiblería *f* (**b**) *(feeling)* sentimiento *m* (**c**) *(opinion)* opinión *f*

sentimental [sentɪ'mentəl] *adj* sentimental

sentry ['sentrɪ] *n* centinela *m*

separate 1 *vt* ['sepəreɪt] separar (**from** de); *(divide)* dividir (**into** en); *(distinguish)* distinguir
   2 *vi* separarse
   3 *adj* ['sepərɪt] separado(a); *(different)* distinto(a); *(entrance)* particular
   4 *npl* **separates** ['sepərɪts] *(clothes)* piezas *fpl*

separately ['sepərɪtlɪ] *adv* por separado

separation [sepə'reɪʃən] *n* separación *f*

separatist ['sepərɪtɪst] *n* separatista *mf*

September [sep'tembə(r)] *n* se(p)tiembre *m*

septic ['septɪk] *adj* séptico(a); **to become s.** *(of wound)* infectarse; **s. tank** fosa séptica

sequel ['si:kwəl] *n* secuela *f*; *(of film etc)* continuación *f*

sequence ['si:kwəns] *n* (**a**) *(order)* secuencia *f*, orden *m* (**b**) *(series)* serie *f*, sucesión *f*; *Cin* **film s.** secuencia *f*

serenade [serɪ'neɪd] *n* serenata *f*

serene [sɪ'ri:n] *adj* sereno(a), tranquilo(a)

sergeant ['sɑːdʒənt] *n Mil* sargento *mf*; *(of police)* ≃ oficial *mf* de policía; **s. major** sargento *mf* mayor

serial ['sɪərɪəl] *n* (**a**) *Rad & TV* serial *m*; *(soap opera)* radionovela *f*, telenovela *f* (**b**) **s. number** número *m* de serie

series ['sɪəriːz] *n (pl* **series***)* serie *f*; *(of books)* colección *f*; *(of concerts, lectures)* ciclo *m*

serious ['sɪərɪəs] *adj* (**a**) *(solemn, earnest)* serio(a); **I am s.** hablo en serio (**b**) *(causing concern)* grave

seriously ['sɪərɪəslɪ] *adv* (**a**) *(in earnest)* en serio (**b**) *(dangerously, severely)* gravemente

seriousness ['sɪərɪəsnɪs] *n* gravedad *f*, seriedad *f*; **in all s.** hablando en serio

sermon ['sɜːmən] *n* sermón *m*

serpent ['sɜːpənt] *n* serpiente *f*

serrated [sɪ'reɪtɪd] *adj* dentado(a)

serum ['sɪərəm] *n* suero *m*

servant ['sɜːvənt] *n (domestic)* criado(a) *m,f*; *Fig* servidor(a) *m,f*

serve [sɜːv] **1** *vt* (**a**) servir (**b**) *(customer)* atender a (**c**) *(in tennis)* servir (**d**) **if my memory serves me right** si mal no recuerdo; **it serves him right** bien merecido lo tiene (**e**) *Fam* **to s. time** cumplir una condena; **to s. one's apprenticeship** hacer el aprendizaje

2 vi (**a**) servir; **to s. on a committee** ser miembro de una comisión (**b**) (in tennis) servir (**c**) (be useful) servir (**as** de)

3 n (in tennis) servicio m

▶ **serve out, serve up** vt sep servir

service ['sɜːvɪs] **1** n (**a**) servicio m; **at your s.!** ¡a sus órdenes!; **how can I be of s. to you?** ¿en qué puedo servirle?; **s. (charge) included** servicio incluido; **s. area** área m de servicio; **s. industry** sector m de servicios; Br **s. lift** montacargas m inv; **s. station** estación f de servicio (**b**) **medical s.** servicios médicos; Mil **the Services** las Fuerzas Armadas; **the train s. to Bristol** la línea de trenes a Bristol (**c**) (maintenance) revisión f (**d**) Rel oficio m; (mass) misa f (**e**) (in tennis) servicio m; **s. line** línea f de saque (**f**) (set of dishes) juego m

2 vt (car, machine) revisar

serviceable ['sɜːvɪsəbəl] adj (**a**) (fit for use) útil, servible (**b**) (practical) práctico(a)

serviceman ['sɜːvɪsmən] n militar m

serviette [sɜːvɪ'et] n Br servilleta f

sesame ['sesəmɪ] n sésamo m

session ['seʃən] n (**a**) sesión f; **to be in s.** estar reunido(a); (of Parliament, court) celebrar una sesión (**b**) Educ (academic year) año académico

set¹ [set] **1** vt (pt & pp **set**) (**a**) (put, place) poner, colocar; (trap) poner (**for** para); **the novel is s. in Moscow** la novela se desarrolla en Moscú; **to s. fire to sth** prender fuego a algo

(**b**) (time, price) fijar; (record) establecer; (trend) imponer

(**c**) (mechanism etc) ajustar; (bone) encajar; **to s. one's watch** poner el reloj en hora

(**d**) (arrange) arreglar; **he s. the words to music** puso música a la letra; **to s. the table** poner la mesa

(**e**) (exam, homework) poner; (example) dar; (precedent) sentar

(**f**) **to s. sail** zarpar; **to s. sb free** poner en libertad a algn; **to s. sth going** poner algo en marcha

(**g**) (pearl, diamond etc) engastar

(**h**) Typ componer

2 vi (**a**) (sun, moon) ponerse

(**b**) (jelly, jam) cuajar; (cement) fraguar; (bone) encajarse

(**c**) **to s. to** (begin) ponerse a

3 n (**a**) **shampoo and s.** lavar y marcar (**b**) (stage) Cin plató m; Th escenario

m; (scenery) decorado m

4 adj (**a**) (task, idea) fijo(a); (date, time) señalado(a); (opinion) inflexible; (smile) rígido(a); (gaze) fijo(a); **s. phrase** frase hecha; **to be s. on doing sth** estar empeñado(a) en hacer algo; **s. square** cartabón m

(**b**) (ready) listo(a)

▶ **set about** vt insep (**a**) (begin) empezar (**b**) (attack) agredir

▶ **set aside** vt sep (time, money) reservar; (differences) dejar de lado

▶ **set back** vt sep (**a**) (delay) retrasar; (hinder) entorpecer (**b**) Fam (cost) costar

▶ **set down** vt sep (luggage etc) dejar (en el suelo); Br (passengers) dejar

▶ **set in** vi (winter, rain) comenzar; **panic s. in** cundió el pánico

▶ **set off 1** vi (depart) salir

2 vt sep (**a**) (bomb) hacer estallar; (burglar alarm) hacer sonar; (reaction) desencadenar (**b**) (enhance) hacer resaltar

▶ **set out 1** vi (**a**) (depart) salir; **to s. out for ...** partir hacia ... (**b**) **to s. out to do sth** proponerse hacer algo

2 vt sep (arrange) disponer; (present) presentar

▶ **set up 1** vt sep (**a**) (position) colocar; (statue, camp) levantar; (tent, stall) montar (**b**) (business etc) establecer; Fam montar; (committee) constituir; Fam **you've been s. up!** ¡te han timado!

2 vi establecerse

set² [set] n (**a**) (series) serie f; (of golf clubs etc) juego m; (of tools) estuche m; (of turbines etc) equipo m; (of books, poems) colección f; (of teeth) dentadura f; **chess s.** juego de ajedrez; **s. of cutlery** cubertería f; **s. of kitchen utensils** batería f de cocina (**b**) (of people) grupo m; Pej (clique) camarilla f (**c**) Math conjunto m (**d**) (in tennis) set m (**e**) TV **s.** televisor m

setback ['setbæk] n revés m, contratiempo m

settee [se'tiː] n sofá m

setting ['setɪŋ] n (**a**) (background) marco m; (of novel, film) escenario m (**b**) (of jewel) engaste m

settle ['setəl] **1** vt (**a**) (put in position) colocar

(**b**) (decide on) acordar; (date, price) fijar; (problem) resolver; (differences) arreglar

(**c**) (debt) pagar; (account) saldar

(**d**) (nerves) calmar; (stomach) asentar

(**e**) Fam (put an end to) acabar con

(**f**) (establish) (person) instalar

(**g**) (colonize) asentarse en

2 *vi* (**a**) *(bird, insect)* posarse; *(dust)* depositarse; *(snow)* cuajar; *(sediment)* precipitarse; *(liquid)* asentarse; **to s. into an armchair** acomodarse en un sillón

(**b**) *(put down roots)* afincarse; *(in a colony)* asentarse

(**c**) *(weather)* serenarse

(**d**) *(child, nerves)* calmarse

(**e**) *(pay)* pagar; **to s. out of court** llegar a un acuerdo amistoso

▸**settle down** *vi* (**a**) *(put down roots)* instalarse; *(marry)* casarse (**b**) **to s. down to work** ponerse a trabajar (**c**) *(child)* calmarse; *(situation)* normalizarse

▸**settle for** *vt insep* conformarse con

▸**settle in** *vi (move in)* instalarse; *(become adapted)* adaptarse

▸**settle up with** *vt sep (pay debt to)* ajustar cuentas con

settlement ['setəlmənt] *n* (**a**) *(agreement)* acuerdo *m* (**b**) *(of debt)* pago *m*; *(of account)* liquidación *f* (**c**) *(dowry)* dote *m* (**d**) *(colonization)* colonización *f* (**e**) *(colony)* asentamiento *m*; *(village)* poblado *m*

settler ['setlə(r)] *n* colono *m*

setup ['setʌp] *n (system)* sistema *m*; *(situation)* situación *f*; *Fam* montaje *m*

seven ['sevən] *adj & n* siete *(m inv)*

seventeen [sevən'ti:n] *adj & n* diecisiete *(m inv)*, diez y siete *(m inv)*

seventeenth [sevən'ti:nθ] **1** *adj & n* decimoséptimo(a) *(m,f)*

2 *n (fraction)* decimoséptima parte

seventh ['sevənθ] **1** *adj & n* séptimo(a) *(m,f)*

2 *n* séptimo *m*

seventy ['sevntɪ] *adj & n* setenta *(m inv)*

sever ['sevə(r)] *vt (cut)* cortar; *Fig (relations)* romper

several ['sevərəl] **1** *adj* (**a**) *(more than a few)* varios(as) (**b**) *(different)* distintos(as)

2 *pron* algunos(as)

severance ['sevərəns] *n (of relations etc)* ruptura *f*; **s. pay** indemnización *f* por despido

severe [sɪ'vɪə(r)] *adj* severo(a); *(climate, blow)* duro(a); *(illness, loss)* grave; *(pain)* intenso(a)

severity [sɪ'verɪtɪ] *n (of persón, criticism, punishment)* severidad *f*; *(of climate)* rigor *m*; *(of illness)* gravedad *f*; *(of pain)* intensidad *f*; *(of style)* austeridad *f*

Seville [sə'vɪl] *n* Sevilla

sew [səʊ] *vt & vi (pt sewed; pp sewed or sewn)* coser

▸**sew up** *vt sep (stitch together)* coser; *(mend)* remendar

sewage ['su:ɪdʒ] *n* aguas *fpl* residuales

sewer ['su:ə(r)] *n* alcantarilla *f*, cloaca *f*

sewerage ['su:ərɪdʒ] *n* alcantarillado *m*

sewing ['səʊɪŋ] *n* costura *f*; **s. machine** máquina *f* de coser

sewn [səʊn] *pp of* **sew**

sex [seks] *n* sexo *m*; **s. education** educación *f* sexual; **to have s. with sb** tener relaciones sexuales con algn; **s. appeal** sex-appeal *m*

sexist ['seksɪst] *adj & n* sexista *(mf)*

sexual ['seksjʊəl] *adj* sexual

sexuality [seksjʊ'ælɪtɪ] *n* sexualidad *f*

sexy ['seksɪ] *adj* (**sexier, sexiest**) *Fam* sexi, erótico(a)

shabby ['ʃæbɪ] *adj* (**shabbier, shabbiest**) (**a**) *(garment)* raído(a); *(house)* desvencijado(a); *(person) (in rags)* harapiento(a); *(unkempt)* desaseado(a) (**b**) *(treatment)* mezquino(a)

shack [ʃæk] *n* choza *f*

shackles ['ʃæklz] *npl* grilletes *mpl*, grillos *mpl*; *Fig* trabas *fpl*

shade [ʃeɪd] **1** *n* (**a**) *(shadow)* sombra *f*; **in the s.** a la sombra (**b**) *(eyeshade)* visera *f*; *(lampshade)* pantalla *f*; *US (blind)* persiana *f* (**c**) *(of colour)* tono *m*, matiz *m*; *Fig (of meaning)* matiz (**d**) *(small amount)* poquito *m* (**e**) *Fam* **shades** gafas *fpl* or *Am* anteojos *mpl* de sol

2 *vt (from sun)* proteger contra el sol

shadow ['ʃædəʊ] **1** *n* (**a**) *(shade)* sombra *f*; *(darkness)* oscuridad *f*; *Fig* **without a s. of a doubt** sin lugar a dudas (**b**) *Br* **the S. Cabinet** el gabinete de la oposición

2 *vt Fig* seguir la pista a

shadowy ['ʃædəʊɪ] *adj (dark)* oscuro(a); *(hazy)* vago(a)

shady ['ʃeɪdɪ] *adj* (**shadier, shadiest**) *(place)* a la sombra; *(suspicious) (person)* sospechoso(a); *(deal)* turbio(a)

shaft [ʃɑ:ft] *n* (**a**) *(of tool, golf club)* mango *m*; *(of lance)* asta *f*; *(of arrow)* astil *m* (**b**) *Tech* eje *m* (**c**) *(of mine)* pozo *m*; *(of lift, elevator)* hueco *m* (**d**) *(beam of light)* rayo *m*

shaggy ['ʃægɪ] *adj* (**shaggier, shaggiest**) *(hairy)* peludo(a); *(long-haired)* melenudo(a); *(beard)* desgreñado(a)

shake [ʃeɪk] **1** *n* sacudida *f*

2 *vt (pt* **shook**; *pp* **shaken** ['ʃeɪkən]) *(carpet etc)* sacudir; *(bottle)* agitar; *(dice)* mover; *(building)* hacer temblar; **the news shook him** la noticia le conmocionó; **to s. hands with sb** estrechar la mano a algn; **to s. one's head** negar con la cabeza

3 vi (person, building) temblar; **to s. with cold** tiritar de frío

▶ **shake off** vt sep (**a**) (dust etc) sacudirse (**b**) Fig (bad habit) librarse de; (cough, cold) quitarse de encima; (pursuer) dar esquinazo a

▶ **shake up** vt sep Fig (shock) trastornar; (reorganize) reorganizar

shake-up ['ʃeɪkʌp] n Fig reorganización f

shaky ['ʃeɪkɪ] adj (**shakier, shakiest**) (hand, voice) tembloroso(a); (step) inseguro(a); (handwriting) temblón(ona)

shall [ʃæl, unstressed ʃəl] v aux

En el inglés hablado, y en el escrito en estilo coloquial, el verbo **shall** se contrae de manera que **I/you/he** etc **shall** se transforman en **I'll/you'll/he'll** etc. La forma negativa **shall not** se transforma en **shan't**.

(**a**) (used to form future tense) (first person only) **I s.** or **I'll buy it** lo compraré; **I s. not** or **I shan't say anything** no diré nada (**b**) (used to form questions) (usu first person) **s. I close the door?** ¿cierro la puerta?; **s. I mend it for you?** ¿quieres que te lo repare?; **s. we go?** ¿nos vamos? (**c**) (emphatic, command, threat) (all persons) **we s. overcome** venceremos; **you s. leave immediately** te irás enseguida

shallow ['ʃæləʊ] adj poco profundo(a); Fig superficial

sham [ʃæm] **1** adj falso(a); (illness etc) fingido(a)

2 n a (pretence) engaño m, farsa f (**b**) (person) fantoche m

3 vt fingir, simular

4 vi fingir

shambles ['ʃæmbəlz] n sing confusión f; **the performance was a s.** la función fue un desastre

shame [ʃeɪm] **1** n (**a**) (embarrassment) vergüenza f; Andes, CAm, Carib, Méx pena f; **to put to s.** (far outdo) eclipsar, sobrepasar (**b**) (pity) pena f, lástima f; **what a s.!** ¡qué pena!, ¡qué lástima!

2 vt avergonzar, Andes, CAm, Carib, Méx apenar; (disgrace) deshonrar

shamefaced ['ʃeɪmfeɪst] adj avergonzado(a), Andes, CAm, Carib, Méx apenado(a)

shameful ['ʃeɪmfʊl] adj vergonzoso(a)

shameless ['ʃeɪmlɪs] adj descarado(a)

shampoo [ʃæm'puː] **1** n champú m

2 vt lavar con champú; **to s. one's hair** lavarse el pelo

shamrock ['ʃæmrɒk] n trébol m

shandy ['ʃændɪ] n Br clara f, cerveza f con gaseosa

shantytown ['ʃæntɪtaʊn] n barrio m de chabolas, Arg villa f miseria, Chile población f callampa, Méx ciudad f perdida, Urug cantegril m, Ven rancho m

shape [ʃeɪp] **1** n (**a**) forma f; (shadow) silueta m; **to take s.** tomar forma (**b**) **in good/bad s.** (condition) en buen/mal estado; **to be in good s.** (health) estar en forma

2 vt dar forma a; (clay) modelar; (stone) tallar; (character) formar; (destiny) determinar; **star-shaped** con forma de estrella

3 vi (also **s. up**) tomar forma; **to s. up well** (events) tomar buen cariz; (person) hacer progresos

shapeless ['ʃeɪplɪs] adj amorfo(a), informe

shapely ['ʃeɪplɪ] adj (**shapelier, shapeliest**) escultural

share ['ʃeə(r)] **1** n (**a**) (portion) parte f (**b**) Fin acción f; **s. index** índice m de la Bolsa; **s. prices** cotizaciones fpl

2 vt (**a**) (divide) dividir (**b**) (have in common) compartir

3 vi compartir

▶ **share out** vt sep repartir

shareholder ['ʃeəhəʊldə(r)] n accionista mf

shark [ʃɑːk] n (**a**) (fish) tiburón m (**b**) Fam (swindler) estafador(a) m,f; **loan s.** usurero(a) m,f

sharp [ʃɑːp] **1** adj (**a**) (razor, knife) afilado(a); (needle, pencil) puntiagudo(a)

(**b**) (angle) agudo(a); (features) anguloso(a); (bend) cerrado(a)

(**c**) (outline) definido(a); (contrast) marcado(a)

(**d**) (observant) perspicaz; (clever) listo(a); (quick-witted) avispado(a); (cunning) astuto(a)

(**e**) (sudden) brusco(a)

(**f**) (pain, cry) agudo(a); (wind) penetrante

(**g**) (sour) acre

(**h**) (criticism) mordaz; (temper) arisco(a); (tone) seco(a)

(**i**) Mus sostenido(a); (out of tune) desafinado(a)

2 adv **at two o'clock s.** (exactly) a las dos en punto

3 n Mus sostenido m

sharpen ['ʃɑːpən] vt (**a**) (knife) afilar; (pencil) sacar punta a (**b**) Fig (desire, intelligence) agudizar

sharpener ['ʃɑːpənə(r)] n (for knife) afilador m; (for pencil) sacapuntas m inv

sharp-eyed [ˈʃɑːpaɪd] *adj* con ojos de lince

sharply [ˈʃɑːplɪ] *adv* (**a**) (*abruptly*) bruscamente (**b**) (*clearly*) marcadamente

shatter [ˈʃætə(r)] **1** *vt* hacer añicos; (*nerves*) destrozar; (*hopes*) frustrar
2 *vi* hacerse añicos

shave [ʃeɪv] **1** *n* afeitado *m*; **to have a s.** afeitarse; *Fig* **to have a close s.** escaparse por los pelos
2 *vt* (*pt* shaved; *pp* shaved *or* shaven [ˈʃeɪvən]) (*person*) afeitar; (*wood*) cepillar
3 *vi* afeitarse

shaver [ˈʃeɪvə(r)] *n* (**electric**) **s.** máquina *f* de afeitar

shaving [ˈʃeɪvɪŋ] *n* (**a**) (*of wood*) viruta *f* (**b**) **s. brush** brocha *f* de afeitar; **s. cream** crema *f* de afeitar; **s. foam** espuma *f* de afeitar

shawl [ʃɔːl] *n* chal *m*

she [ʃiː] *pers pron* ella (*usually omitted in Spanish, except for contrast*)

she- [ʃiː] *pref* (*of animal*) hembra; **s.-cat** gata *f*

sheaf [ʃiːf] *n* (*pl* sheaves) *Agr* gavilla *f*; (*of arrows*) haz *m*; (*of papers, banknotes*) fajo *m*

shear [ʃɪə(r)] **1** *vt* (*pt* sheared; *pp* shorn *or* sheared) (*sheep*) esquilar; **to s. off** cortar
2 *vi* esquilar ovejas

shears [ʃɪəz] *npl* tijeras *fpl* (grandes)

sheath [ʃiːθ] *n* (**a**) (*for sword*) vaina *f*; (*for knife, scissors*) funda *f* (**b**) (*contraceptive*) preservativo *m*

sheaves [ʃiːvz] *pl of* sheaf

shed¹ [ʃed] *n* (*in garden*) cobertizo *m*; (*workmen's hut*) barraca *f*; (*for cattle*) establo *m*; (*in factory*) nave *f*

shed² [ʃed] *vt* (*pt & pp* shed) (**a**) (*clothes*) despojarse de; (*unwanted thing*) deshacerse de; **the snake s. its skin** la serpiente mudó de piel (**b**) (*blood, tears*) derramar

sheen [ʃiːn] *n* brillo *m*

sheep [ʃiːp] *n* (*pl* sheep) oveja *f*

sheepdog [ˈʃiːpdɒg] *n* perro *m* pastor

sheepish [ˈʃiːpɪʃ] *adj* avergonzado(a)

sheepskin [ˈʃiːpskɪn] *n* piel *f* de carnero

sheer [ʃɪə(r)] *adj* (**a**) (*utter*) total, puro(a) (**b**) (*cliff*) escarpado(a); (*drop*) vertical (**c**) (*stockings, cloth*) fino(a)

sheet [ʃiːt] *n* (**a**) (*on bed*) sábana *f* (**b**) (*of paper*) hoja *f*; (*of tin, glass, plastic*) lámina *f*; (*of ice*) capa *f*

sheik(h) [ʃeɪk] *n* jeque *m*

shelf [ʃelf] *n* (*pl* shelves) (*on bookcase*) estante *m*; (*in cupboard*) tabla *f*; **shelves** estantería *f*

shell [ʃel] **1** *n* (**a**) (*of egg, nut*) cáscara *f*; (*of pea*) vaina *f*; (*of tortoise etc*) caparazón *m*; (*of snail etc*) concha *f* (**b**) (*of building*) armazón *m* (**c**) (*mortar etc*) obús *m*, proyectil *m*; (*cartridge*) cartucho *m*; **s. shock** neurosis *f* de guerra
2 *vt* (**a**) (*peas*) desvainar; (*nuts*) pelar (**b**) *Mil* bombardear

shellfish [ˈʃelfɪʃ] *n* (*pl* shellfish) marisco *m*, mariscos *mpl*

shelter [ˈʃeltə(r)] **1** *n* (**a**) (*protection*) abrigo *m*, amparo *m*; **to take s. (from)** refugiarse (de) (**b**) (*place*) refugio *m*; (*for homeless*) asilo *m*; **bus s.** marquesina *f*
2 *vt* (**a**) (*protect*) abrigar, proteger (**b**) (*take into one's home*) ocultar
3 *vi* refugiarse

sheltered [ˈʃeltəd] *adj* (*place*) abrigado(a); **to lead a s. life** vivir apartado(a) del mundo

shelve [ʃelv] *vt Fig* (*postpone*) dar carpetazo a

shelves [ʃelvz] *pl of* shelf

shepherd [ˈʃepəd] **1** *n* pastor *m*; **s.'s pie** = pastel de carne picada con puré de patatas *or Am* papas
2 *vt Fig* **to s. sb in** hacer entrar a algn

sheriff [ˈʃerɪf] *n Br* gobernador *m* civil; *Scot* juez *m* presidente; *US* sheriff *m*

sherry [ˈʃerɪ] *n* jerez *m*

Shetland [ˈʃetlənd] *n* the S. Isles, S. las Islas Shetland; **S. wool** lana *f* Shetland

shield [ʃiːld] **1** *n* (**a**) escudo *m*; (*of policeman*) placa *f* (**b**) (*on machinery*) blindaje *m*
2 *vt* proteger (**from** de)

shift [ʃɪft] **1** *n* (**a**) (*change*) cambio *m*; *US Aut* (**gear**) **s.** cambio de velocidades (**b**) (*period of work, group of workers*) turno *m*; **to be on the day s.** hacer el turno de día
2 *vt* (*change*) cambiar; (*move*) cambiar de sitio, trasladar
3 *vi* (*move*) moverse; (*change place*) cambiar de sitio; (*opinion*) cambiar; (*wind*) cambiar de dirección

shiftless [ˈʃɪftlɪs] *n* perezoso(a), vago(a)

shiftwork [ˈʃɪftwɜːk] *n* trabajo *m* por turnos

shifty [ˈʃɪftɪ] *adj* (**shiftier, shiftiest**) (*look*) furtivo(a); (*person*) sospechoso(a)

shilling [ˈʃɪlɪŋ] *n* chelín *m*

shimmer [ˈʃɪmə(r)] **1** *vi* relucir; (*shine*) brillar
2 *n* luz trémula, reflejo trémulo; (*shining*) brillo *m*

shin [ʃɪn] *n* espinilla *f*; **s. pad** espinillera *f*

shine [ʃaɪn] **1** *vi* (*pt & pp* shone) (**a**) (*light*) brillar; *(metal)* relucir (**b**) *Fig (excel)* sobresalir (**at** en)

2 *vt* (**a**) *(lamp)* dirigir (**b**) *(pt & pp* **shined**) *(polish)* sacar brillo a; *(shoes)* limpiar

3 *n* brillo *m*, lustre *m*

shingle ['ʃɪŋgəl] *n* (**a**) *(pebbles)* guijarros *mpl* (**b**) *(roof tile)* tablilla *f*

shingles ['ʃɪŋgəlz] *n sing Med* herpes *m*

shining ['ʃaɪnɪŋ] *adj Fig (outstanding)* ilustre

shiny ['ʃaɪnɪ] *adj* (**shinier, shiniest**) brillante

ship [ʃɪp] **1** *n* barco *m*, buque *m*

2 *vt* (**a**) *(take on board)* embarcar (**b**) *(transport)* transportar (en barco); *(send)* enviar, mandar

shipbuilding ['ʃɪpbɪldɪŋ] *n* construcción *f* naval

shipment ['ʃɪpmənt] *n* (**a**) *(act)* transporte *m* (**b**) *(load)* consignación *f*, envío *m*

shipper ['ʃɪpə(r)] *n (person)* cargador(a) *m,f*

shipping ['ʃɪpɪŋ] *n* (**a**) *(ships)* barcos *mpl*; **s. lane** vía *f* de navegación (**b**) *(loading)* embarque *m*; *(transporting)* transporte *m* (en barco); **s. company** compañía naviera

shipshape ['ʃɪpʃeɪp] *adj & adv* en perfecto orden

shipwreck ['ʃɪprek] **1** *n* naufragio *m*

2 *vt* **to be shipwrecked** naufragar

shipyard ['ʃɪpjɑːd] *n* astillero *m*

shire [ʃaɪə(r)] *n Br* condado *m*

shirk [ʃɜːk] **1** *vt (duty)* faltar a; *(problem)* eludir

2 *vi* gandulear

shirt [ʃɜːt] *n* camisa *f*; **in s. sleeves** en mangas de camisa; *Fam* **keep your s. on!** ¡no te sulfures!

shit [ʃɪt] *Vulg* **1** *n* mierda *f*; **in the s.** jodido(a)

2 *interj* ¡mierda!

3 *vi* cagar

shiver ['ʃɪvə(r)] **1** *vi (with cold)* tiritar; *(with fear)* temblar, estremecerse

2 *n (with cold, fear)* escalofrío *m*

shoal [ʃəʊl] *n (of fish)* banco *m*

shock [ʃɒk] **1** *n* (**a**) *(jolt)* choque *m*; **s. absorber** amortiguador *m*; **s. wave** onda expansiva (**b**) *(upset)* conmoción *f*; *(scare)* susto *m* (**c**) *Med* shock *m*

2 *vt (upset)* conmover; *(startle)* sobresaltar; *(scandalize)* escandalizar

shocking ['ʃɒkɪŋ] *adj* (**a**) *(causing horror)* espantoso(a); *Fam (very bad)* horroroso(a) (**b**) *(disgraceful)* escandaloso(a) (**c**) **s. pink** rosa chillón

shod [ʃɒd] *pt & pp* of **shoe**

shoddy ['ʃɒdɪ] *adj* (**shoddier, shoddiest**) *(goods)* de mala calidad; *(work)* chapucero(a)

shoe [ʃuː] **1** *n* (**a**) zapato *m*; *(for horse)* herradura *f*; **brake s.** zapata *f*; **s. polish** betún *m*; **s. repair (shop)** remiendo *m* de zapatos; **s. shop**, *US* **s. store** zapatería *f* (**b**) **shoes** calzado *m*

2 *vt (pt & pp* **shod**) *(horse)* herrar

shoebrush ['ʃuːbrʌʃ] *n* cepillo *m* para los zapatos

shoehorn ['ʃuːhɔːn] *n* calzador *m*

shoelace ['ʃuːleɪs] *n* cordón *m* (de zapatos)

shoestring ['ʃuːstrɪŋ] *n Fig* **to do sth on a s.** hacer algo con poquísimo dinero

shone [ʃɒn, *US* ʃəʊn] *pt & pp* of **shine**

shoo [ʃuː] **1** *interj* ¡fuera!

2 *vt* **to s. (away)** espantar

shook [ʃʊk] *pt* of **shake**

shoot [ʃuːt] **1** *n Bot* retoño *m*; *(of vine)* sarmiento *m*

2 *vt (pt & pp* **shot**) (**a**) pegar un tiro a; *(kill)* matar; *(execute)* fusilar; *(hunt)* cazar; **to s. dead** matar a tiros (**b**) *(missile, glance)* lanzar; *(bullet, ball)* disparar (**c**) *(film)* rodar, filmar; *Phot* fotografiar

3 *vi* (**a**) *(with gun)* disparar (**at** sb a algn); **to s. at a target** tirar al blanco; *Ftb* **to s. at the goal** chutar a puerta (**b**) **to s. past** *or* **by** pasar flechado(a)

▸ **shoot down** *vt sep (aircraft)* derribar

▸ **shoot out** *vi (person)* salir disparado(a); *(water)* brotar; *(flames)* salir

▸ **shoot up** *vi* (**a**) *(flames)* salir; *(water)* brotar; *(prices)* dispararse (**b**) *Fam (inject drugs)* chutarse

shooting ['ʃuːtɪŋ] *n* (**a**) *(shots)* tiros *mpl*; *(murder)* asesinato *m*; *(hunting)* caza *f*; **s. star** estrella *f* fugaz (**b**) *(of film)* rodaje *m*

2 *adj (pain)* punzante

shoot-out ['ʃuːtaʊt] *n* tiroteo *m*

shop [ʃɒp] **1** *n* (**a**) tienda *f*; *(large store)* almacén *m*; **s. assistant** dependiente(a) *m,f*; **s. window** escaparate *m* (**b**) *(workshop)* taller *m*; **s. floor** *(place)* planta *f*; *(workers)* obreros *mpl*; **s. steward** enlace *mf* sindical

2 *vi* hacer compras; **to go shopping** ir de compras

shopkeeper ['ʃɒpkiːpə(r)] *n* tendero(a) *m,f*

shoplifter ['ʃɒplɪftə(r)] *n* ladrón(ona) *m,f* (de tiendas)

shopper ['ʃɒpə(r)] *n* comprador(a) *m,f*

shopping ['ʃɒpɪŋ] *n (purchases)* compras *fpl*; **s. bag/basket** bolsa *f*/cesta *f* de

la compra; **s. centre** or **precinct** centro m
comercial
shopsoiled ['ʃɒpsɔild], US **shopworn**
['ʃɒpwɔːn] adj deteriorado(a)
shore [ʃɔː(r)] n (of sea, lake) orilla f; US
(beach) playa f; (coast) costa f; **to go on s.**
desembarcar
  ▸ **shore up** vt sep apuntalar
shorn [ʃɔːn] pp of **shear**
short [ʃɔːt] **1** adj (**a**) corto(a); (not tall)
bajo(a); **in a s. while** dentro de un rato; **in
the s. term** a corto plazo; **s. circuit** cortocircuito m; **s. cut** atajo m; Br **s. list** lista f de
seleccionados; **s. story** relato corto,
cuento m; **s. wave** onda corta
  (**b**) (brief) corto(a), breve; **"Bob" is s. for
"Robert"** "Bob" es el diminutivo de
"Robert"; **for s.** para abreviar; **in s.** en
pocas palabras
  (**c**) **to be s. of breath** faltarle a uno la
respiración; **to be s. of food** andar esca-
so(a) de comida
  (**d**) (curt) brusco(a), seco(a)
  2 adv (**a**) **to pull up s.** pararse en seco
  (**b**) **to cut s.** (holiday) interrumpir;
(meeting) suspender; **we're running s. of
coffee** se nos está acabando el café
  (**c**) **s. of** (except) excepto, menos
  3 n (**a**) Cin cortometraje m
  (**b**) Fam (drink) copa f
  4 vi **to s. (out)** tener un cortocircuito
shortage ['ʃɔːtɪdʒ] n escasez f
shortbread ['ʃɔːtbred] n mantecado m
short-change [ʃɔːt'tʃeɪndʒ] vt **to s. sb** no
devolver el cambio completo a algn; Fig
timar a algn
short-circuit [ʃɔːt'sɜːkɪt] **1** vt provocar
un cortocircuito en
  2 vi tener un cortocircuito
shortcomings ['ʃɔːtkʌmɪŋz] npl defectos mpl
shortcrust ['ʃɔːtkrʌst] n **s. pastry** pasta
brisa
shorten ['ʃɔːtən] vt (skirt, visit) acortar;
(word) abreviar; (text) resumir
shortfall ['ʃɔːtfɔːl] n déficit m
shorthand ['ʃɔːthænd] n taquigrafía f; Br
s. typist taquimecanógrafo(a) m,f
short-list ['ʃɔːtlɪst] vt poner en la lista de
seleccionados
short-lived [ʃɔːt'lɪvd] adj efímero(a)
shortly ['ʃɔːtlɪ] adv (soon) dentro de
poco; **s. after** poco después
short-range [ʃɔːt'reɪndʒ] adj de corto
alcance
shorts [ʃɔːts] npl (**a**) pantalones mpl
cortos; **a pair of s.** un pantalón corto (**b**)
US (underpants) calzoncillos mpl

short-sighted [ʃɔːt'saɪtɪd] adj (person)
miope; Fig (plan etc) sin visión de futuro
short-staffed [ʃɔːt'stɑːft] adj escaso(a)
de personal
short-tempered [ʃɔːt'tempəd] adj de
mal genio
short-term ['ʃɔːttɜːm] adj a corto plazo
shot¹ [ʃɒt] n (**a**) (act, sound) tiro m, disparo m (**b**) (projectile) bala f; (pellets)
perdigones mpl; Fig **he was off like a s.**
salió disparado; Sport **s. put** lanzamiento
m de peso (**c**) (person) tirador(a) m,f (**d**)
Ftb (kick) tiro m (a puerta); (in billiards,
cricket, golf) golpe m (**e**) (attempt) tentativa f; **to have a s. at sth** intentar hacer
algo (f) (injection) inyección f; Fam pinchazo m (**g**) (drink) trago m (**h**) Phot foto
f; Cin toma f
shot² [ʃɒt] pt & pp of **shoot**
shotgun ['ʃɒtgʌn] n escopeta f
should [ʃʊd, unstressed ʃəd] v aux (**a**)
(duty) deber; **all employees s. wear hel-
mets** todos los empleados deben llevar
casco; **he s. have been an architect** debería haber sido arquitecto (**b**) (probability) deber de; **he s. have finished by now**
ya debe de haber acabado; **this s. be
interesting** esto promete ser interesante
(**c**) (conditional use) **if anything strange
s. happen** si pasara algo raro (**d**) **l s. like
to ask a question** quisiera hacer una
pregunta

La forma negativa **should not** se transforma en **shouldn't.**

shoulder ['ʃəʊldə(r)] **1** n (**a**) hombro m;
s. blade omóplato m; **s. strap** (of garment)
tirante m; (of bag) correa f; Br Aut **hard s.**
arcén m, Andes berma f, Méx acotamiento m, RP banquina f, Ven hombrillo m (**b**)
Culin paletilla f (**c**) US Aut arcén m, Andes
berma f; Méx acotamiento m, RP banquina f, Ven hombrillo m
  2 vt Fig (responsibilities) cargar con
shout [ʃaʊt] **1** n grito m
  2 vt gritar
  3 vi gritar; **to s. at sb** gritar a algn
  ▸ **shout down** vt sep abuchear
shouting ['ʃaʊtɪŋ] n gritos mpl, vocerío
m
shove [ʃʌv] **1** n Fam empujón m
  2 vt empujar; **to s. sth into one's pocket**
meterse algo en el bolsillo a empellones
  3 vi empujar; (jostle) dar empellones
  ▸ **shove off** vi Fam largarse
  ▸ **shove up** vi Fam (move along) correrse
shovel ['ʃʌvəl] **1** n pala f; **mechanical s.**
excavadora f

2 *vt* mover con pala *or* a paladas

show [ʃəʊ] **1** *vt* (*pt* **showed**; *pp* **shown** *or* **showed**) (**a**) (*ticket etc*) mostrar; (*painting etc*) exponer; (*film*) poner; (*latest plans etc*) presentar

(**b**) (*display*) demostrar; **to s. oneself to be** comportarse como

(**c**) (*teach*) enseñar; (*explain*) explicar

(**d**) (*temperature, way etc*) indicar; (*profit etc*) registrar

(**e**) (*prove*) demostrar

(**f**) (*conduct*) llevar; **to s. sb in** hacer pasar a algn; **to s. sb to the door** acompañar a algn hasta la puerta

2 *vi* (**a**) (*be visible*) notarse

(**b**) *Fam* (*turn up*) aparecer

(**c**) *Cin* **what's showing?** ¿qué ponen?

3 *n* (**a**) (*display*) demostración *f*

(**b**) (*outward appearance*) apariencia *f*

(**c**) (*exhibition*) exposición *f*; **on s.** expuesto(a); **boat s.** salón náutico; **motor s.** salón del automóvil

(**d**) *Th* (*entertainment*) espectáculo *m*; (*performance*) función *f*; *Rad & TV* programa *m*; **s. business** *or Fam* **biz** el mundo del espectáculo

▸ **show off 1** *vt sep* (**a**) (*highlight*) hacer resaltar (**b**) *Fam* (*flaunt*) hacer alarde de

2 *vi Fam* farolear

▸ **show up 1** *vt sep* (**a**) (*reveal*) sacar a luz; (*highlight*) hacer resaltar (**b**) *Fam* (*embarrass*) dejar en evidencia

2 *vi* (**a**) (*stand out*) destacarse (**b**) *Fam* (*arrive*) aparecer

showdown [ˈʃəʊdaʊn] *n* enfrentamiento *m*

shower [ˈʃaʊə(r)] **1** *n* (**a**) (*rain*) chubasco *m*, chaparrón *m* (**b**) *Fig* (*of stones, blows etc*) lluvia *f* (**c**) (*bath*) ducha *f*, *Col, Méx, Ven* regadera *f*; **to have a s.** ducharse

2 *vt* (**a**) (*spray*) rociar (**b**) *Fig* **to s. gifts/praise on sb** colmar a algn de regalos/elogios

3 *vi* ducharse

showerproof [ˈʃaʊəpruːf] *adj* impermeable

showing [ˈʃəʊɪŋ] *n* (*of film*) proyección *f*

showjumping [ˈʃəʊdʒʌmpɪŋ] *n* hípica *f*

shown [ʃəʊn] *pp* of **show**

show-off [ˈʃəʊɒf] *n Fam* farolero(a) *m,f*

showpiece [ˈʃəʊpiːs] *n* (*in exhibition etc*) obra maestra; *Fig* (*at school etc*) modelo *m*

showroom [ˈʃəʊruːm] *n Com* exposición *f*; *Art* galería *f*

shrank [ʃræŋk] *pt* of **shrink**

shrapnel [ˈʃræpnəl] *n* metralla *f*

shred [ʃred] **1** *n* triza *f*; (*of cloth*) jirón *m*; (*of paper*) tira *f*

2 *vt* (*paper*) hacer trizas; (*vegetables*) rallar

shredder [ˈʃredə(r)] *n* (*for waste paper*) trituradora *f*; (*for vegetables*) rallador *m*

shrew [ʃruː] *n* (**a**) *Zool* musaraña *f* (**b**) *Fig* (*woman*) arpía *f*

shrewd [ʃruːd] *adj* astuto(a); (*clear-sighted*) perspicaz; (*wise*) sabio(a); (*decision*) acertado(a)

shriek [ʃriːk] **1** *n* chillido *m*; **shrieks of laughter** carcajadas *fpl*

2 *vi* chillar

shrill [ʃrɪl] *adj* agudo(a), estridente

shrimp [ʃrɪmp] **1** *n* camarón *m*

2 *vi* pescar camarones

shrine [ʃraɪn] *n* (*tomb*) sepulcro *m*; (*chapel*) capilla *f*; (*holy place*) lugar sagrado

shrink [ʃrɪŋk] **1** *vt* (*pt* **shrank**; *pp* **shrunk**) encoger

2 *vi* (**a**) (*clothes*) encoger(se) (**b**) (*savings*) disminuir (**c**) **to s. (back)** echarse atrás; **to s. from doing sth** no tener valor para hacer algo

2 *n Fam* (*psychiatrist*) psiquiatra *mf*

shrinkage [ˈʃrɪŋkɪdʒ] *n* (**a**) (*of cloth*) encogimiento *m*; (*of metal*) contracción *f* (**b**) (*of savings etc*) disminución *f*

shrink-wrapped [ˈʃrɪŋkræpt] *adj* envuelto(a) en plástico

shrivel [ˈʃrɪvəl] **1** *vt* **to s. (up)** encoger; (*plant*) secar; (*skin*) arrugar

2 *vi* encogerse; (*plant*) secarse; (*skin*) arrugarse

shroud [ʃraʊd] **1** *n Rel* sudario *m*

2 *vt Fig* envolver

Shrove Tuesday [ʃrəʊvˈtjuːzdɪ] *n* martes *m* de carnaval

shrub [ʃrʌb] *n* arbusto *m*

shrubbery [ˈʃrʌbərɪ] *n* arbustos *mpl*

shrug [ʃrʌg] **1** *vt* **to s. one's shoulders** encogerse de hombros

2 *vi* encogerse de hombros

3 *n* encogimiento *m* de hombros

▸ **shrug off** *vt sep* no dejarse desanimar por

shrunk [ʃrʌŋk] *pp* of **shrink**

shudder [ˈʃʌdə(r)] **1** *n* (**a**) escalofrío *m*, estremecimiento *m* (**b**) (*of machinery*) sacudida *f*

2 *vi* (**a**) (*person*) estremecerse (**b**) (*machinery*) dar sacudidas

shuffle [ˈʃʌfəl] **1** *vt* (**a**) (*feet*) arrastrar (**b**) (*papers etc*) revolver; (*cards*) barajar

2 *vi* (**a**) (*walk*) andar arrastrando los pies (**b**) *Cards* barajar

shun [ʃʌn] *vt* (*person*) esquivar; (*responsibility*) rehuir

shunt [ʃʌnt] *vt Rail* cambiar de vía; *Elec* derivar

shut [ʃʌt] **1** *vt (pt & pp* **shut)** cerrar
2 *vi* cerrarse
3 *adj* cerrado(a)
▸ **shut down 1** *vt sep (factory)* cerrar
2 *vi (factory)* cerrar
▸ **shut off** *vt sep (gas, water etc)* cortar
▸ **shut out** *vt sep (a) (lock out)* dejar fuera a **(b)** *(exclude)* excluir
▸ **shut up 1** *vt sep* **(a)** *(close)* cerrar **(b)** *(imprison)* encerrar **(c)** *Fam (silence)* callar
2 *vi Fam (keep quiet)* callarse

shutdown [ʃʌtdaʊn] *n* cierre *m*

shutter [ʃʌtə(r)] *n* **(a)** *(on window)* contraventana *f*, postigo *m* **(b)** *Phot* obturador *m*

shuttle [ʃʌtəl] **1** *n* **(a)** *(in weaving)* lanzadera *f* **(b)** *Av* puente aéreo; **(space) s.** transbordador *m* espacial
2 *vi* ir y venir

shuttlecock [ʃʌtəlkɒk] *n* volante *m*

shy [ʃaɪ] **1** *adj* **(shyer, shyest** *or* **shier, shiest)** *(timid)* tímido(a), *Andes, CAm, Carib, Méx* penoso(a); *(reserved)* reservado(a)
2 *vi (horse)* espantarse **(at** de); *Fig* **to s. away from doing sth** negarse a hacer algo

shyness [ʃaɪnɪs] *n* timidez *f*

Siberia [saɪbɪərɪə] *n* Siberia

sibling [sɪblɪŋ] *n Fml (brother)* hermano *m*; *(sister)* hermana *f*; **siblings** hermanos

Sicily [sɪsɪlɪ] *n* Sicilia

sick [sɪk] *adj* **(a)** *(ill)* enfermo(a); **s. leave** baja *f* por enfermedad; **s. pay** subsidio *m* de enfermedad **(b) to feel s.** *(about to vomit)* tener ganas de devolver; **to be s.** devolver **(c)** *Fam (fed up)* harto(a) **(d)** *Fam (mind, joke)* morboso(a); **s. humour** humor negro

sickbay [sɪkbeɪ] *n* enfermería *f*

sicken [sɪkən] **1** *vt (make ill)* poner enfermo; *(revolt)* dar asco a
2 *vi (fall ill)* enfermar

sickening [sɪkənɪŋ] *adj* nauseabundo(a); *(revolting)* repugnante; *(horrifying)* escalofriante

sickle [sɪkəl] *n* hoz *f*

sickly [sɪklɪ] *adj* **(sicklier, sickliest)** **(a)** *(person)* enfermizo(a) **(b)** *(taste)* empalagoso(a) **(c)** *(smile)* forzado(a)

sickness [sɪknɪs] *n* **(a)** *(illness)* enfermedad *f* **(b)** *(nausea)* náuseas *fpl*

side [saɪd] **1** *n* **(a)** *(of body)* lado *m*; *(of coin etc)* cara *f*; *(of hill)* ladera *f*; **by the s. of** junto a **(b)** *(of body)* costado *m*; *(of animal)* ijar

m; **a s. of bacon** una pieza de tocino; **by my s.** a mi lado; **s. by s.** juntos

(c) *(edge)* borde *m*; *(of lake, river)* orilla *f* **(d)** *Fig (aspect)* aspecto *m* **(e)** *(team)* equipo *m*; *Pol* partido *m*; **she's on our s.** está de nuestro lado; **to take sides with sb** ponerse de parte de algn; **s. dish** plato *m* de guarnición; **s. effect** efecto secundario; **s. entrance** entrada *f* lateral; **s. street** calle *f* lateral
2 *vi* **to s. with sb** ponerse de parte de algn

sideboard [saɪdbɔːd] *n* aparador *m*

sideboards [saɪdbɔːdz], **sideburns** [saɪdbɜːnz] *npl* patillas *fpl*

sidelight [saɪdlaɪt] *n Aut* luz *f* lateral, piloto *m*

sideline [saɪdlaɪn] *n* **(a)** *Sport* línea *f* de banda **(b)** *Com (product)* línea suplementaria; *(job)* empleo suplementario

sidelong [saɪdlɒŋ] *adj* de reojo

side-saddle [saɪdsædəl] **1** *n* silla *f* de amazona
2 *adv* **to ride s.** montar a la inglesa

sideshow [saɪdʃəʊ] *n* atracción secundaria

sidestep [saɪdstep] *vt (issue)* esquivar

sidetrack [saɪdtræk] *vt Fig (person)* despistar

sidewalk [saɪdwɔːk] *n US* acera *f*, *CSur, Perú* vereda *f*, *CAm, Méx* banqueta *f*

sideways [saɪdweɪz] **1** *adj (movement)* lateral; *(look)* de reojo
2 *adv* de lado

siding [saɪdɪŋ] *n Rail* apartadero *m*, vía muerta

sidle [saɪdəl] *vi* **to s. up to sb** acercarse furtivamente a algn

siege [siːdʒ] *n* sitio *m*, cerco *m*; **to lay s. to** sitiar

sieve [sɪv] **1** *n (fine)* tamiz *m*; *(coarse)* criba *f*
2 *vt (fine)* tamizar; *(coarse)* cribar

sift [sɪft] *vt (sieve)* tamizar; *Fig* **to s. through** examinar cuidadosamente

sigh [saɪ] **1** *vi* suspirar
2 *n* suspiro *m*

sight [saɪt] **1** *n* **(a)** *(faculty)* vista *f*; **at first s.** a primera vista; **to catch s. of** divisar; **to know by s.** conocer de vista; **to lose s. of sth/sb** perder algo/a algn de vista **(b)** *(range of vision)* vista *f*; **within s.** a la vista; **to come into s.** aparecer **(c)** *(spectacle)* espectáculo *m* **(d)** *(on gun)* mira *f*; *Fig* **to set one's sights on** tener la mira puesta en **(e) sights** monumentos *mpl*
2 *vt* ver; *(land)* divisar

sightseeing [saɪtsiːɪŋ] *n* turismo *m*; **to go s.** hacer turismo

sign [saɪn] **1** n (**a**) (symbol) signo m (**b**) (gesture) gesto m, seña f; (signal) señal f (**c**) (indication) señal f; (trace) rastro m, huella f; **as a s. of** como muestra de (**d**) (notice) anuncio m; (board) letrero m

2 vt (**a**) (letter etc) firmar (**b**) Ftb fichar

3 vi firmar

▸ **sign on 1** vt sep (worker) contratar

2 vi (worker) firmar un contrato; Br Fam apuntarse al paro; (regularly) firmar en el paro

▸ **sign up 1** vt sep (soldier) reclutar; (worker) contratar

2 vi (soldier) alistarse; (worker) firmar un contrato

signal ['sɪgnəl] **1** n señal f; Rad & TV sintonía f; Rail **s. box** garita f de señales

2 vt (**a**) (message) transmitir por señales (**b**) (direction etc) indicar

3 vi (with hands) hacer señales; (in car) señalar

signalman ['sɪgnəlmən] n guardavía m

signature ['sɪgnɪtʃə(r)] n (name) firma f; Rad & TV **s. tune** sintonía f

signet ['sɪgnɪt] n **s. ring** (anillo m de) sello m

significance [sɪg'nɪfɪkəns] n (meaning) significado m; (importance) importancia f

significant [sɪg'nɪfɪkənt] adj (meaningful) significativo(a); (important) importante

significantly [sɪg'nɪfɪkəntlɪ] adv (markedly) sensiblemente

signify ['sɪgnɪfaɪ] vt (**a**) (mean) significar (**b**) (show, make known) indicar

signpost ['saɪnpəʊst] n poste m indicador

silence ['saɪləns] **1** n silencio m

2 vt acallar; (engine) silenciar

silencer ['saɪlənsə(r)] n (**a**) (on gun) silenciador m (**b**) Br (on car) silenciador m

silent ['saɪlənt] adj silencioso(a); (not talkative) callado(a); (film) mudo(a); **be s.!** ¡cállate!; **to remain s.** guardar silencio

silently ['saɪləntlɪ] adv silenciosamente

silhouette [sɪluː'et] n silueta f

silicon ['sɪlɪkən] n silicio m; **s. chip** chip m (de silicio)

silk [sɪlk] **1** n seda f

2 adj de seda

silky ['sɪlkɪ] adj (silkier, silkiest) (cloth) sedoso(a); (voice etc) aterciopelado(a)

sill [sɪl] n (of window) alféizar m

silly ['sɪlɪ] adj (sillier, silliest) tonto(a)

silo ['saɪləʊ] n silo m

silt [sɪlt] n cieno m

▸ **silt up** vi obstruirse con cieno

silver ['sɪlvə(r)] **1** n (**a**) (metal) plata f (**b**) (coins) monedas fpl (de plata) (**c**) (tableware) vajilla f de plata

2 adj de plata; **s. foil** (tinfoil) papel m de aluminio; **s. paper** papel de plata; **s. wedding** bodas fpl de plata

silver-plated [sɪlvə'pleɪtɪd] adj plateado(a)

silversmith ['sɪlvəsmɪθ] n platero(a) m,f

silverware ['sɪlvəweə(r)] n vajilla f de plata

silvery ['sɪlvərɪ] adj plateado(a)

similar ['sɪmɪlə(r)] adj parecido(a), semejante (**to** a); **to be s.** parecerse

similarity [sɪmɪ'lærɪtɪ] n semejanza f

similarly ['sɪmɪləlɪ] adv (**a**) (as well) igualmente (**b**) (likewise) del mismo modo, asimismo

simile ['sɪmɪlɪ] n símil m

simmer ['sɪmə(r)] **1** vt cocer a fuego lento

2 vi cocerse a fuego lento

▸ **simmer down** vi Fam calmarse

simpering ['sɪmpərɪŋ] adj melindroso(a)

simple ['sɪmpəl] adj (**a**) sencillo(a); **s. interest** interés m simple (**b**) (natural) natural (**c**) (foolish) simple; (naïve) ingenuo(a); (dim) de pocas luces

simplicity [sɪm'plɪsɪtɪ] n (**a**) sencillez f (**b**) (naïveté) ingenuidad f

simplify ['sɪmplɪfaɪ] vt simplificar

simply ['sɪmplɪ] adv (**a**) (plainly) sencillamente (**b**) (only) simplemente, sólo

simulate ['sɪmjʊleɪt] vt simular

simulator ['sɪmjʊleɪtə(r)] n **flight s.** simulador de vuelo

simultaneous [sɪməl'teɪnɪəs] adj simultáneo(a)

simultaneously [sɪməl'teɪnɪəslɪ] adv simultáneamente

sin [sɪn] **1** n pecado m

2 vi pecar

since [sɪns] **1** adv (ever) **s.** desde entonces; **long s.** hace mucho tiempo; **it has s. come out that ...** desde entonces se ha sabido que ...

2 prep desde; **she has been living here s. 1975** vive aquí desde 1975

3 conj (**a**) (time) desde que; **how long is it s. you last saw him?** ¿cuánto tiempo hace que lo viste por última vez? (**b**) (because, as) ya que, puesto que

sincere [sɪn'sɪə(r)] adj sincero(a)

sincerely [sɪn'sɪəlɪ] adv sinceramente; **Yours s.** (in letter) (le saluda) atentamente

sincerity [sɪn'serɪtɪ] n sinceridad f

sinew ['sɪnjuː] n (tendon) tendón m; (in meat) nervio m

sinful ['sɪnfʊl] *adj (person)* pecador(a); *(act, thought)* pecaminoso(a); *Fig (waste etc)* escandaloso(a)

sing [sɪŋ] **1** *vt (pt sang; pp sung)* cantar
2 *vi (person, bird)* cantar; *(kettle, bullets)* silbar

singe [sɪndʒ] *vt* chamuscar

singer ['sɪŋə(r)] *n* cantante *mf*

singing ['sɪŋɪŋ] *n (art)* canto *m*; *(songs)* canciones *fpl*; *(of kettle)* silbido *m*

single ['sɪŋgəl] **1** *adj* **(a)** *(solitary)* solo(a) **(b)** *(only one)* único(a) **(c)** *(not double)* sencillo(a); **s. bed/room** cama *f*/habitación *f* individual **(d)** *(unmarried)* soltero(a)
2 *n* **(a)** *Br Rail* billete *m* or *Am* boleto *m* or *Am* pasaje *m* sencillo or de ida **(b)** *(record)* single *m* **(c)** *Sport* **singles** individuales *mpl*
▸ **single out** *vt sep (choose)* escoger; *(distinguish)* distinguir

single-breasted ['sɪŋgəl'brestɪd] *adj (suit, jacket)* recto(a)

single-handed ['sɪŋgəl'hændɪd] *adj & adv* sin ayuda

single-minded ['sɪŋgəl'maɪndɪd] *adj* resuelto(a)

singlet ['sɪŋglɪt] *n Br* camiseta *f*

singly ['sɪŋglɪ] *adv (individually)* por separado; *(one by one)* uno por uno

singular ['sɪŋgjʊlə(r)] **1** *adj* **(a)** *Ling* singular **(b)** *Fml (outstanding)* excepcional **(c)** *Fml (unique)* único(a)
2 *n Ling* singular *m*

singularly ['sɪŋgjʊləlɪ] *adv* excepcionalmente

sinister ['sɪnɪstə(r)] *adj* siniestro(a)

sink¹ [sɪŋk] *n (in kitchen)* fregadero *m*

sink² [sɪŋk] **1** *vt (pt sank; pp sunk)* **(a)** *(ship)* hundir, echar a pique; *Fig (hopes)* acabar con **(b)** *(hole, well)* cavar; *(post, knife, teeth)* hincar
2 *vi* **(a)** *(ship)* hundirse **(b)** *Fig* **my heart sank** se me cayó el alma a los pies **(c)** *(sun)* ponerse **(d)** **to s. to one's knees** hincarse de rodillas
▸ **sink in** *vi (penetrate)* penetrar; *Fig* **it hasn't sunk in yet** todavía no me he/se ha/*etc* hecho a la idea

sinner ['sɪnə(r)] *n* pecador(a) *m,f*

sinus ['saɪnəs] *n* seno *m* (nasal)

sip [sɪp] **1** *n* sorbo *m*
2 *vt* sorber, beber a sorbos

siphon ['saɪfən] *n* sifón *m*
▸ **siphon off** *vt sep (liquid)* sacar con sifón; *Fig (funds, traffic)* desviar

sir [sɜː(r)] *n Fml* **(a)** señor *m*; **yes, s.** sí, señor **(b)** *(title)* sir; **S. Walter Raleigh** Sir Walter Raleigh

siren ['saɪrən] *n* sirena *f*

sirloin ['sɜːlɔɪn] *n* solomillo *m*

sissy ['sɪsɪ] *n Fam (coward)* miedica *mf*

sister ['sɪstə(r)] *n* **(a)** *(relation)* hermana *f* **(b)** *Br Med* enfermera *f* jefe **(c)** *Rel* hermana *f*; *(before name)* sor

sister-in-law ['sɪstərɪnlɔː] *n* cuñada *f*

sit [sɪt] **1** *vt (pt & pp sat)* **(a)** *(child etc)* sentar (**in/on** en) **(b)** *Br (exam)* presentarse a
2 *vi* **(a)** *(action)* sentarse **(b)** *(be seated)* estar sentado(a) **(c)** *(object)* estar; *(be situated)* hallarse; *(person)* quedarse **(d)** *(assembly)* reunirse
▸ **sit back** *vi* recostarse
▸ **sit down** *vi* sentarse
▸ **sit in on** *vt insep* asistir sin participar a
▸ **sit out** *vt sep* aguantar hasta el final
▸ **sit through** *vt insep* aguantar
▸ **sit up** *vi* **(a)** incorporarse **(b)** *(stay up late)* quedarse levantado(a)

site [saɪt] **1** *n* **(a)** *(area)* lugar *m*; **building s.** solar *m*; *(under construction)* obra *f* **(b)** *(location)* situación *f*; **nuclear testing s.** zona *f* de pruebas nucleares
2 *vt* situar

sit-in ['sɪtɪn] *n Fam (demonstration)* sentada *f*; *(strike)* huelga *f* de brazos caídos

sitting ['sɪtɪŋ] **1** *n (of committee)* sesión *f*; *(in canteen)* turno *m*
2 *adj* **s. room** sala *f* de estar

situated ['sɪtjʊeɪtɪd] *adj* situado(a), ubicado(a)

situation [sɪtjʊ'eɪʃən] *n* **(a)** situación *f* **(b)** *(job)* puesto *m*; *Br* **situations vacant** *(in newspaper)* ofertas de trabajo

six [sɪks] *adj & n* seis *(m inv)*

sixteen [sɪks'tiːn] *adj & n* dieciséis *(m inv)*, diez y seis *(m inv)*

sixteenth [sɪks'tiːnθ] **1** *adj & n* decimosexto(a) *(m,f)*
2 *n (fraction)* dieciseisavo *m*

sixth [sɪksθ] **1** *adj* sexto(a); *Br Educ* **s. form** ≃ COU; **s. former** ≃ estudiante de COU
2 *n* **(a)** *(in series)* sexto(a) *m,f* **(b)** *(fraction)* sexto *m*, sexta parte

sixty ['sɪkstɪ] *adj & n* sesenta *(m inv)*

sizable ['saɪzəbəl] *adj* = sizeable

size [saɪz] *n* tamaño *m*; *(of garment)* talla *f*; *(of shoes)* número *m*; *(of person)* estatura *f*; *(scope)* alcance *m*; **what s. do you take?** *(garment)* ¿qué talla tienes?; *(shoes)* ¿qué número calzas?
▸ **size up** *vt sep (person)* juzgar; *(situation, problem)* evaluar

sizeable ['saɪzəbəl] *adj (building etc)*

(bastante) grande; *(sum)* considerable; *(problem)* importante

sizzle ['sızəl] *vi* chisporrotear

skate¹ [skeɪt] **1** *n* patín *m*
  2 *vi* patinar

skate² [skeɪt] *n (fish)* raya *f*

skateboard ['skeɪtbɔːd] *n* monopatín *m*

skater ['skeɪtə(r)] *n* patinador(a) *m,f*

skating ['skeɪtɪŋ] *n* patinaje *m*; **s. rink** pista *f* de patinaje

skeleton ['skelɪtən] **1** *n* **(a)** esqueleto *m* **(b)** *(of building)* armazón *m* **(c)** *(outline)* esquema *m*
  2 *adj (staff, service)* reducido(a); **s. key** llave maestra

skeptic ['skeptɪk] *n US* = **sceptic**

sketch [sketʃ] **1** *n* **(a)** *(preliminary drawing)* bosquejo *m*, esbozo *m*; *(drawing)* dibujo *m*; *(outline)* esquema *m*; *(rough draft)* boceto *m* **(b)** *Th & TV* sketch *m*
  2 *vt (draw)* dibujar; *(preliminary drawing)* bosquejar, esbozar

sketch-book ['sketʃbʊk], **sketch-pad** ['sketʃpæd] *n* bloc *m* de dibujo

sketchy ['sketʃɪ] *adj* (**sketchier, sketchiest**) *(incomplete)* incompleto(a); *(not detailed)* vago(a)

skewer ['skjʊə(r)] *n* pincho *m*, broqueta *f*

ski [skiː] **1** *n* esquí *m*
  2 *adj* de esquí; **s. boots** botas *fpl* de esquiar; **s. jump** *(action)* salto *m* con esquís; **s. lift** telesquí *m*; *(with seats)* telesilla *f*; **s. pants** pantalón *m* de esquiar; **s. resort** estación *f* de esquí; **s. stick** or **pole** bastón *m* de esquiar
  3 *vi* esquiar; **to go skiing** ir a esquiar

skid [skɪd] **1** *n* patinazo *m*
  2 *vi* patinar

skier ['skiːə(r)] *n* esquiador(a) *m,f*

skiing ['skiːɪŋ] *n* esquí *m*

skilful ['skɪlfʊl] *adj* hábil, diestro(a)

skill [skɪl] *n* **(a)** *(ability)* habilidad *f*, destreza *f*; *(talent)* don *m* **(b)** *(technique)* técnica *f*

skilled [skɪld] *adj* **(a)** *(dextrous)* hábil, diestro(a); *(expert)* experto(a) **(b)** *(worker)* cualificado(a)

skillet ['skɪlɪt] *n US* sartén *f*

skillful ['skɪlfʊl] *adj US* = **skilful**

skim [skɪm] **1** *vt* **(a)** *(milk)* desnatar; **skimmed milk** leche desnatada **(b)** *(brush against)* rozar; **to s. the ground** *(bird, plane)* volar a ras de suelo
  2 *vi Fig* **to s. through a book** hojear un libro

skimp [skɪmp] *vt & vi (food, material)* escatimar; *(work)* chapucear

skimpy ['skɪmpɪ] *adj* (**skimpier,**

skimpiest) *(shorts)* muy corto(a); *(meal)* escaso(a)

skin [skɪn] **1** *n* **(a)** piel *f*; *(of face)* cutis *m*; *(complexion)* tez *f*; **s. cream** crema *f* de belleza **(b)** *(of fruit)* piel *f*; *(of lemon)* cáscara *f*; *(peeling)* mondadura *f* **(c)** *(of sausage)* pellejo *m* **(d)** *(on milk etc)* nata *f*
  2 *vt* **(a)** *(animal)* despellejar **(b)** *(graze)* arañar

skin-deep ['skɪn'diːp] *adj* superficial

skin-diving ['skɪndaɪvɪŋ] *n* buceo *m*, submarinismo *m*

skinhead ['skɪnhed] *n Fam* cabeza *mf* rapada

skinny ['skɪnɪ] *adj* (**skinnier, skinniest**) *Fam* flaco(a)

skin-tight ['skɪntaɪt] *adj (clothing)* muy ajustado(a)

skip¹ [skɪp] **1** *n (jump)* salto *m*, brinco *m*
  2 *vi (jump)* saltar, brincar; *(with rope)* saltar a la comba; *Fig* **to s. over sth** saltarse algo
  3 *vt Fig* saltarse

skip² [skɪp] *n Br (for rubbish)* contenedor *m*

skipper ['skɪpə(r)] *n Naut & Sport Fam* capitán(ana) *m,f*

skipping ['skɪpɪŋ] *n* comba *f*; **s. rope** comba

skirmish ['skɜːmɪʃ] *n* escaramuza *f*

skirt [skɜːt] **1** *n* falda *f*
  2 *vt (town etc)* rodear; *(coast)* bordear; *Fig (problem)* esquivar

skirting ['skɜːtɪŋ] *n Br* **s. (board)** zócalo *m*

skit [skɪt] *n* sátira *f*, parodia *f*

skittle ['skɪtəl] *n* **(a)** *(pin)* bolo *m* **(b) skittles** *(game)* (juego *m* de los) bolos *mpl*, boliche *m*

skive [skaɪv] *vi Br Fam* escaquearse

skulk [skʌlk] *vi (hide)* esconderse; *(prowl)* merodear; *(lie in wait)* estar al acecho

skull [skʌl] *n Anat* cráneo *m*; *Fam* calavera *f*

skunk [skʌŋk] *n* mofeta *f*

sky [skaɪ] *n* cielo *m*; **s. blue** azul *m* celeste

skylight ['skaɪlaɪt] *n* tragaluz *m*, claraboya *f*

skyline ['skaɪlaɪn] *n (of city)* perfil *m*

skyscraper ['skaɪskreɪpə(r)] *n* rascacielos *m inv*

slab [slæb] *n (of stone)* losa *f*; *(of chocolate)* tableta *f*; *(of cake)* trozo *m*

slack [slæk] **1** *adj* **(a)** *(not taut)* flojo(a) **(b)** *(lax)* descuidado(a); *(lazy)* vago(a) **(c)** *(market)* flojo(a); **business is s.** hay poco negocio
  2 *n (in rope)* parte floja

slacken ['slækən] **1** *vt* (a) *(rope)* aflojar (b) *(speed)* reducir

2 *vi* (a) *(rope)* aflojarse; *(wind)* amainar (b) *(trade)* aflojar

▸ **slacken off** *vi* disminuirse

slacks [slæks] *npl* pantalones *mpl* ajustados

slag [slæg] *n* (a) *Min* escoria *f*; **s. heap** escorial *m* (b) *Br very Fam (woman)* puta *f*

▸ **slag off** *vt sep Br* poner verde a

slain [sleɪn] **1** *npl* **the s.** los caídos

2 *pp of* **slay**

slam [slæm] **1** *n (of door)* portazo *m*

2 *vt (bang)* cerrar de golpe; **to s. sth down on the table** soltar algo sobre la mesa de un palmetazo; **to s. the door** dar un portazo; **to s. on the brakes** dar un frenazo

3 *vi (door)* cerrarse de golpe

slander ['slɑːndə(r)] **1** *n* difamación *f*, calumnia *f*

2 *vt* difamar, calumniar

slang [slæŋ] *n* argot *m*, jerga *f*

slant [slɑːnt] **1** *n* (a) *(slope)* inclinación *f*; *(slope)* pendiente *f* (b) *Fig (point of view)* punto *m* de vista

2 *vt Fig (problem etc)* enfocar subjetivamente

3 *vi* inclinarse

slanting ['slɑːntɪŋ] *adj* inclinado(a)

slap [slæp] **1** *n* palmada *f*; *(in face)* bofetada *f*

2 *adv Fam* **he ran s. into the fence** se dio de lleno contra la valla; **s. in the middle of ...** justo en medio de ...

3 *vt* pegar con la mano; *(hit in face)* dar una bofetada a; **to s. sb on the back** dar a algn una palmada en la espalda

slapdash ['slæpdæʃ] *adj Fam* descuidado(a); *(work)* chapucero(a)

slapstick ['slæpstɪk] *n* bufonadas *fpl*, payasadas *fpl*

slap-up ['slæpʌp] *adj Fam* **s. meal** comilona *f*

slash [slæʃ] **1** *n Fam Typ* barra oblicua

2 *vt* (a) *(with knife)* acuchillar; *(with sword)* dar un tajo a (b) *Fig (prices)* rebajar

slat [slæt] *n* tablilla *f*, listón *m*

slate [sleɪt] **1** *n* pizarra *f*; *Fig* **to wipe the s. clean** hacer borrón y cuenta nueva

2 *vt Br Fam* criticar duramente

slaughter ['slɔːtə(r)] **1** *n (of animals)* matanza *f*; *(of people)* carnicería *f*

2 *vt (animals)* matar; *(people)* matar brutalmente; *(in large numbers)* masacrar

slaughterhouse ['slɔːtəhaʊs] *n* matadero *m*

Slav [slɑːv] *adj & n* eslavo(a) *(m,f)*

slave [sleɪv] **1** *n* esclavo(a) *m,f*; **s. trade** trata *f* de esclavos

2 *vi* **to s. (away)** dar el callo

slavery ['sleɪvərɪ] *n* esclavitud *f*

Slavonic [slə'vɒnɪk] *adj* eslavo(a)

slay [sleɪ] *vt (pt* **slew**; *pp* **slain)** matar

sleazy ['sliːzɪ] *adj* (**sleazier, sleaziest**) sórdido(a)

sled [sled] *n US* trineo *m*

2 *vi* ir en trineo

sledge [sledʒ] *n Br* trineo *m*

sledgehammer ['sledʒhæmə(r)] *n* almádena *f*

sleek [sliːk] *adj (hair)* lustroso(a); *(appearance)* impecable

sleep [sliːp] **1** *n* sueño *m*

2 *vi (pt & pp* **slept)** (a) dormir; **to go to s.** dormirse; *Fig* **to send to s.** (hacer) dormir; *Fam* **to s. like a log** dormir como un lirón (b) **my foot has gone to s.** se me ha dormido el pie

▸ **sleep in** *vi Br (oversleep)* quedarse dormido(a); *(have a lie-in)* quedarse en la cama

▸ **sleep with** *vt insep Fam* **to s. with sb** acostarse con algn

sleeper ['sliːpə(r)] *n* (a) *(person)* durmiente *mf*; **to be a heavy s.** tener el sueño pesado (b) *Br Rail (on track)* traviesa *f* (c) *Rail (coach)* coche-cama *m*; *(berth)* litera *f*

sleeping ['sliːpɪŋ] *adj* **s. bag** saco *m* de dormir; **S. Beauty** la Bella durmiente; **s. car** coche-cama *m*; *Br Com* **s. partner** socio(a) *m,f* comanditario(a); **s. pill** somnífero *m*

sleepless ['sliːplɪs] *adj* **to have a s. night** pasar la noche en blanco

sleepwalker ['sliːpwɔːkə(r)] *n* sonámbulo(a) *m,f*

sleepy ['sliːpɪ] *adj* (**sleepier, sleepiest**) soñoliento(a); **to be o feel s.** tener sueño

sleet [sliːt] **1** *n* aguanieve *f*

2 *vi* **it's sleeting** cae aguanieve

sleeve [sliːv] *n (of garment)* manga *f*; *(of record)* funda *f*

sleigh [sleɪ] *n* trineo *m*; **s. bell** cascabel *m*

sleight [slaɪt] *n* **s. of hand** juego *m* de manos

slender ['slendə(r)] *adj* (a) *(thin)* delgado(a) (b) *Fig (hope, chance)* remoto(a)

slept [slept] *pt & pp of* **sleep**

slew [sluː] *pt of* **slay**

slice [slaɪs] **1** *n* (a) *(of bread)* rebanada *f*; *(of ham)* loncha *f*; *(of beef etc)* tajada *f*; *(of* *lemon etc)* rodaja *f; (of cake)* trozo *m* (**b**) *(utensil)* pala *f*

2 *vt (food)* cortar a rebanadas/tajos/rodajas; *(divide)* partir

slick [slɪk] **1** *adj* (**a**) *(programme, show)* logrado(a) (**b**) *(skilful)* hábil, mañoso(a)

2 *n (oil)* s. marea negra

slide [slaɪd] **1** *n* (**a**) *(act)* resbalón *m* (**b**) *(in prices etc)* baja *f* (**c**) *(in playground)* tobogán *m* (**d**) *Phot* diapositiva *f;* **s. projector** proyector *m* de diapositivas (**e**) **s. rule** regla *f* de cálculo (**f**) *Br (for hair)* pasador *m*

2 *vt (pt & pp* **slid** [slɪd]*)* deslizar; *(furniture)* correr

3 *vi (on purpose)* deslizarse; *(slip)* resbalar

sliding ['slaɪdɪŋ] *adj (door, window)* corredizo(a); *Fin* **s. scale** escala *f* móvil

slight [slaɪt] **1** *adj* (**a**) *(small)* pequeño(a); **not in the slightest** en absoluto (**b**) *(build)* menudo(a); *(slim)* delgado(a); *(frail)* delicado(a) (**c**) *(trivial)* leve

2 *n (affront)* desaire *m*

3 *vt* (**a**) *(scorn)* despreciar (**b**) *(snub)* desairar

slightly ['slaɪtlɪ] *adv (a little)* ligeramente, algo

slim [slɪm] **1** *adj* (**slimmer, slimmest**) (**a**) *(person)* delgado(a) (**b**) *Fig (resources)* escaso(a); *(hope, chance)* remoto(a)

2 *vi* adelgazar

slime [slaɪm] *n (mud)* lodo *m,* cieno *m; (of snail)* baba *f*

slimming ['slɪmɪŋ] **1** *adj (diet, pills)* para adelgazar; *(food)* que no engorda

2 *n (process)* adelgazamiento *m*

slimy ['slaɪmɪ] *adj* (**slimier, slimiest**) (**a**) *(muddy)* lodoso(a); *(snail)* baboso(a) (**b**) *Fig (person)* zalamero(a)

sling [slɪŋ] **1** *n* (**a**) *(catapult)* honda *f; (child's)* tirador *m* (**b**) *Med* cabestrillo *m*

2 *vt (pt & pp* **slung**) *(throw)* tirar

slingshot ['slɪŋʃɒt] *n US* tirachinas *m inv*

slink [slɪŋk] *vi (pt & pp* **slunk**) **to s. off** escabullirse

slip [slɪp] **1** *n* (**a**) *(slide)* resbalón *m; Fam Fig* **to give sb the s.** dar esquinazo a algn (**b**) *(mistake)* error *m; (moral)* desliz *m;* **a s. of the tongue** un lapsus linguae (**c**) *(underskirt)* combinación *f* (**d**) *(of paper)* trocito *m*

2 *vi* (**a**) *(slide)* resbalar (**b**) *Med* dislocarse; **slipped disc** vértebra dislocada (**c**) *(move quickly)* ir de prisa (**d**) *(standards etc)* deteriorarse

3 *vt* (**a**) *(slide)* dar a escondidas (**b**) **it slipped my memory** se me fue de la cabeza

▶ **slip away** *vi (person)* escabullirse

▶ **slip off** *vt sep (clothes)* quitarse rápidamente

▶ **slip on** *vt sep (clothes)* ponerse rápidamente

▶ **slip out** *vi* (**a**) *(leave)* salir (**b**) *Fig* **the secret slipped out** se le escapó el secreto

▶ **slip up** *vi Fam (blunder)* cometer un desliz

slipper ['slɪpə(r)] *n* zapatilla *f*

slippery ['slɪpərɪ] *adj* resbaladizo(a)

slip-road ['slɪprəʊd] *n Br* vía *f* de acceso

slipshod ['slɪpʃɒd] *adj* descuidado(a); *(work)* chapucero(a)

slip-up ['slɪpʌp] *n Fam (blunder)* desliz *m*

slipway ['slɪpweɪ] *n* grada *f*

slit [slɪt] **1** *n (opening)* hendidura *f; (cut)* corte *m,* raja *f*

2 *vt (pt & pp* **slit**) cortar, rajar

slither ['slɪðə(r)] *vi* deslizarse

sliver ['slɪvə(r)] *n (of wood, glass)* astilla *f; (of ham)* loncha *f*

slob [slɒb] *n Fam* dejado(a) *m,f*

slog [slɒg] **1** *n Fam* **it was a hard s.** costó un montón

2 *vi* (**a**) *Fam* **to s. away** sudar tinta (**b**) *(walk)* caminar trabajosamente

3 *vt (hit)* golpear fuerte

slogan ['sləʊgən] *n* (e)slogan *m,* lema *m*

slop [slɒp] **1** *vi* **to s. (over)** derramarse; **to s. about** chapotear

2 *vt* derramar

slope [sləʊp] **1** *n (incline)* cuesta *f,* pendiente *f; (up)* subida *f; (down)* bajada *f; (of mountain)* ladera *f; (of roof)* vertiente *f*

2 *vi* inclinarse; **to s. up/down** subir/bajar en pendiente

▶ **slope off** *vi Fam* largarse

sloping ['sləʊpɪŋ] *adj* inclinado(a)

sloppy ['slɒpɪ] *adj* (**sloppier, sloppiest**) *Fam* descuidado(a); *(work)* chapucero(a); *(appearance)* desaliñado(a)

slot [slɒt] **1** *n* (**a**) *(for coin)* ranura *f; (opening)* rendija *f;* **s. machine** *(for gambling)* (máquina *f*) tragaperras *f inv; (vending machine)* distribuidor automático (**b**) *Rad & TV* espacio *m*

2 *vt (place)* meter; *(put in)* introducir

3 *vi* **to s. in** *or* **together** encajar

sloth [sləʊθ] *n Fml (laziness)* pereza *f*

slouch [slaʊtʃ] *vi* andar *or* sentarse con los hombros caídos

Slovakia [sləʊˈvækɪə] *n* Eslovaquia

Slovakian [sləʊˈvækɪən] *adj & n* eslovaco(a) *(m,f)*

Slovene [sləʊˈviːn] **1** *n* (**a**) *(person)* esloveno(a) *m,f* (**b**) *(language)* esloveno *m*

2 *adj* esloveno(a)

Slovenia [sləʊˈviːnɪə] n Eslovenia

slovenly [ˈslʌvənlɪ] adj descuidado(a); (appearance) desaliñado(a); (work) chapucero(a)

slow [sləʊ] 1 adj (a) lento(a); **in s. motion** a cámara lenta; **to be s. to do sth** tardar en hacer algo (b) (clock) atrasado(a) (c) (stupid) lento(a), torpe
2 adv despacio, lentamente
3 vt (car) reducir la marcha de; (progress) retrasar
4 vi **to s. down** or up ir más despacio; (in car) reducir la velocidad

slowly [ˈsləʊlɪ] adv despacio, lentamente

sludge [slʌdʒ] n (mud) fango m, lodo m

slug [slʌg] 1 n (a) Zool babosa f (b) US Fam (bullet) posta f (c) Fam (blow) porrazo m
2 vt Fam (hit) aporrear

sluggish [ˈslʌgɪʃ] adj (a) (river, engine) lento(a); Com flojo(a) (b) (lazy) perezoso(a)

sluice [sluːs] n (waterway) canal m

sluicegate [ˈsluːsgeɪt] n esclusa f

slumber [ˈslʌmbə(r)] Fml 1 n (sleep) sueño m
2 vi dormir

slump [slʌmp] 1 n (a) (drop in sales etc) bajón m (b) (economic depression) crisis económica
2 vi (a) (sales etc) caer de repente; (prices) desplomarse; (the economy) hundirse; Fig (morale) hundirse; (fall) caer

slums [slʌmz] npl barrios bajos

slung [slʌŋ] pt & pp of sling

slunk [slʌŋk] pt & pp of slink

slur [slɜː(r)] 1 n (stigma) mancha f; (slanderous remark) calumnia f
2 vt (word) tragarse

slush [slʌʃ] n (a) (melting snow) nieve medio fundida (b) Fam sentimentalismo m (c) US Fam **s. fund** fondos mpl para sobornos

slut [slʌt] n very Fam Pej (a) (untidy woman) marrana f (b) (whore) fulana f

sly [slaɪ] adj (slyer, slyest or slier, sliest) (a) (cunning) astuto(a) (b) (secretive) furtivo(a) (c) (mischievous) travieso(a) (d) (underhand) malicioso(a)

smack¹ [smæk] 1 n (a) (slap) bofetada f (b) (sharp sound) ruido sonoro
2 vt (a) (slap) dar una bofetada a (b) (hit) golpear; Fig **to s. one's lips** relamerse

smack² [smæk] vi Fig **to s. of** oler a

small [smɔːl] 1 adj (a) pequeño(a); **a s.**

table una mesita; **in s. letters** en minúsculas; **in the s. hours** a altas horas de la noche; **s. ads** anuncios mpl por palabras; Fig **s. print** letra pequeña (b) (in height) bajo(a) (c) (scant) escaso(a); **s. change** cambio m, suelto m (d) (minor) insignificante; **s. businessmen** pequeños comerciantes; **s. talk** charloteo m (e) (increase) ligero(a)
2 n (a) **s. of the back** región f lumbar (b) Br Fam **smalls** (underwear) paños mpl menores

smallholder [ˈsmɔːlhəʊldə(r)] n minifundista mf

smallpox [ˈsmɔːlpɒks] n viruela f

smarmy [ˈsmaːmɪ] adj (smarmier, smarmiest) Fam cobista, zalamero(a)

smart [smaːt] 1 adj (a) (elegant) elegante (b) (clever) listo(a), inteligente; Fam **s. alec(k)** listillo (c) (quick) rápido(a); (pace) ligero(a)
2 vi (a) (sting) picar, escocer (b) Fig sufrir

smarten [ˈsmaːtən] 1 vt **to s. (up)** arreglar
2 vi **to s. (oneself) up** arreglarse

smash [smæʃ] 1 n (a) (loud noise) estrépito m; (collision) choque violento (b) (in tennis) smash m
2 vt (a) (break) romper; (shatter) hacer pedazos; (crush) aplastar (b) (destroy) destrozar; (defeat) aplastar (c) (record) fulminar
3 vi (break) romperse; (shatter) hacerse pedazos; (crash) estrellarse; (in tennis) hacer un mate
▸ **smash up** vt sep Fam (car) hacer pedazos; (place) destrozar

smashing [ˈsmæʃɪŋ] adj Br Fam estupendo(a)

smattering [ˈsmætərɪŋ] n **he had a s. of French** hablaba un poquito de francés

smear [smɪə(r)] 1 n (a) (smudge) mancha f; **s. (test)** citología f (b) Fig (defamation) calumnia f
2 vt (a) (butter etc) untar; (grease) embadurnar (b) (make dirty) manchar (c) Fig (defame) calumniar, difamar

smell [smel] 1 n (a) (sense) olfato m (b) (odour) olor m
2 vt (pt & pp smelled or smelt) oler; Fig olfatear
3 vi oler (of a); **it smells good/like lavender** huele bien/a lavanda; **he smelt of whisky** olía a whisky

smelly [ˈsmelɪ] adj (smellier, smelliest) Fam maloliente, apestoso(a)

smelt¹ [smelt] vt (ore) fundir

smelt² [smelt] pt & pp of smell

smidgen ['smɪdʒən] n Fam pizca f

smile [smaɪl] **1** n sonrisa f

   2 vi sonreír; **to s. at sb** sonreír a algn; **to s. at sth** reírse de algo

smiling ['smaɪlɪŋ] adj sonriente, risueño(a)

smirk [smɜːk] **1** n (conceited) sonrisa satisfecha; (foolish) sonrisa boba

   2 vi (conceitedly) sonreír con satisfacción; (foolishly) sonreír bobamente

smith [smɪθ] n herrero m

smithereens [smɪðə'riːnz] npl **to smash/blow sth to s.** hacer algo añicos

smithy ['smɪðɪ] n herrería f

smitten ['smɪtən] adj Fam **to be s. with sb** estar enamorado(a) de algn

smock [smɒk] n (blouse) blusón m; (worn in pregnancy) blusón de premamá; (overall) bata f

smog [smɒg] n niebla tóxica, smog m

smoke [sməʊk] **1** n humo m; **s. bomb** bomba f de humo; **s. screen** cortina f de humo

   2 vi fumar; (chimney etc) echar humo

   3 vt (a) (tobacco) fumar; **to s. a pipe** fumar en pipa (b) (fish, meat) ahumar

smoked [sməʊkt] adj ahumado(a)

smokeless ['sməʊklɪs] adj **s. fuel** combustible sin humo; **s. zone** zona libre de humos

smoker ['sməʊkə(r)] n (a) (person) fumador(a) m,f (b) Rail vagón m de fumadores

smoking ['sməʊkɪŋ] n **no s.** (sign) prohibido fumar

smoky ['sməʊkɪ] adj (smokier, smokiest) (a) (chimney) humeante; (room) lleno(a) de humo; (atmosphere) cargado(a) (de humo); (taste) ahumado(a) (b) (colour) ahumado(a)

smolder ['sməʊldə(r)] vi US = smoulder

smooth [smuːð] **1** adj (a) (surface) liso(a); (skin) suave; (road) llano(a); (sea) tranquilo(a) (b) (beer, wine) suave (c) (flowing) fluido(a) (d) (flight) tranquilo(a); (transition) sin problemas (e) Pej (slick) zalamero(a)

   2 vt (a) (hair etc) alisar (b) (plane down) limar

   ▸ **smooth out** vt sep (creases) alisar; Fig (difficulties) allanar; (problems) resolver

   ▸ **smooth over** vt sep Fig **to s. things over** limar asperezas

smoothly ['smuːðlɪ] adv sobre ruedas

smother ['smʌðə(r)] vt (a) (asphyxiate) asfixiar; (suffocate) sofocar (b) Fig (cover) cubrir (with de)

smoulder ['sməʊldə(r)] vi (fire) arder sin llama; Fig (passions) arder; **smouldering hatred** odio latente

smudge [smʌdʒ] **1** n (stain) mancha f; (of ink) borrón m

   2 vt manchar; (piece of writing) emborronar

smug [smʌg] adj (smugger, smuggest) engreído(a)

smuggle ['smʌgəl] vt pasar de contrabando

smuggler ['smʌglə(r)] n contrabandista mf

smuggling ['smʌglɪŋ] n contrabando m

smutty ['smʌtɪ] adj (smuttier, smuttiest) Fam obsceno(a); (joke) verde; (book, film etc) pornográfico(a)

snack [snæk] n bocado m; **s. bar** cafetería f

snag [snæg] **1** n (difficulty) pega f, problemilla m

   2 vt (clothing) enganchar

snail [sneɪl] n caracol m

snake [sneɪk] n (big) serpiente f; (small) culebra f

snap [snæp] **1** n (a) (noise) ruido seco; (of branch, fingers) chasquido m (b) (bite) mordisco m (c) Phot (foto f) instantánea f

   2 adj (sudden) repentino(a)

   3 vt (a) (branch etc) partir (en dos) (b) (make noise) **to s. one's fingers** chasquear los dedos; **to s. sth shut** cerrar algo de golpe (c) Phot sacar una foto de

   4 vi (a) (break) romperse (b) (make noise) hacer un ruido seco (c) (whip) chasquear; **to s. shut** cerrarse de golpe (d) **to s. at sb** (dog) intentar morder a algn; Fam (person) regañar a algn

   ▸ **snap off 1** vt sep (branch etc) arrancar

   2 vi (branch etc) separarse

   ▸ **snap up** vt sep Fam **to s. up a bargain** llevarse una ganga

snappy ['snæpɪ] adj (snappier, snappiest) Fam (a) (quick) rápido(a); **look s.!, make it s.!** ¡date prisa! (b) (stylish) elegante (c) (short-tempered) irritable

snapshot ['snæpʃɒt] n (foto f) instantánea f

snare [sneə(r)] **1** n trampa f

   2 vt (animal) cazar con trampa; Fig (person) hacer caer en la trampa

snarl¹ [snɑːl] **1** n gruñido m

   2 vi gruñir

snarl² [snɑːl] **1** n (in wool) maraña f

   2 vt **to s. (up)** (wool) enmarañar; (traffic) atascar; (plans) enredar

snatch [snætʃ] **1** n (a) Fam (theft) robo m; **bag s.** tirón m (b) (fragment) fragmentos mpl

2 vt (**a**) (grab) arrebatar (**b**) Fam (steal) robar; (kidnap) secuestrar

3 vi **to s. at sth** intentar agarrar algo

sneak [sni:k] **1** n Fam chivato(a) m,f

2 (pt & pp **sneaked** or US **snuck**) vt **to s. sth out of a place** sacar algo de un lugar a escondidas

3 vi (**a**) **to s. off** escabullirse; **to s. in/out** entrar/salir a hurtadillas (**b**) Fam **to s. on sb** (tell tales) chivarse de algn

sneaker ['sni:kə(r)] n US playera f

sneaky ['sni:kɪ] adj (**sneakier, sneakiest**) solapado(a)

sneer [snɪə(r)] vi **to s. at** hacer un gesto de desprecio a

sneeze [sni:z] **1** n estornudo m

2 vi estornudar

sniff [snɪf] **1** n (by person) aspiración f; (by dog) husmeo m

2 vt (flower etc) oler; (suspiciously) husmear; (snuff etc) aspirar; (glue) esnifar

3 vi aspirar por la nariz

snigger ['snɪgə(r)] **1** n risa disimulada

2 vi reír disimuladamente; **to s. at sth** burlarse de algo

snip [snɪp] **1** n (**a**) (cut) tijeretada f; (small piece) recorte m (**b**) Br Fam (bargain) ganga f

2 vt cortar a tijeretazos

sniper ['snaɪpə(r)] n francotirador(a) m,f

snippet ['snɪpɪt] n (of cloth, paper) recorte m; (of conversation) fragmento m

snivel ['snɪvəl] vi lloriquear

snivelling ['snɪvəlɪŋ] adj llorón(ona)

snob [snɒb] n (e)snob mf

snobbery ['snɒbərɪ] n (e)snobismo m

snobbish ['snɒbɪʃ] adj (e)snob

snooker ['snu:kə(r)] n snooker m, billar ruso

snoop [snu:p] vi fisgar, fisgonear

snooty ['snu:tɪ] adj (**snootier, snootiest**) Fam (e)snob

snooze [snu:z] Fam **1** n cabezada f

2 vi echar una cabezada

snore [snɔ:(r)] **1** n ronquido m

2 vi roncar

snoring ['snɔ:rɪŋ] n ronquidos mpl

snorkel ['snɔ:kəl] n (of swimmer) tubo m de respiración; (of submarine) esnórquel m

snort [snɔ:t] **1** n resoplido m

2 vi resoplar

snout [snaʊt] n (of animal, gun etc) morro m

snow [snəʊ] **1** n nieve f; **s. shower** nevada f

2 vi nevar; **it's snowing** está nevando

3 vt Fig **to be snowed under with work** estar agobiado(a) de trabajo

snowball ['snəʊbɔ:l] **1** n bola f de nieve

2 vi Fig aumentar rápidamente

snowbound ['snəʊbaʊnd] adj aislado(a) por la nieve

snowdrift ['snəʊdrɪft] n ventisquero m

snowdrop ['snəʊdrɒp] n campanilla f de invierno

snowfall ['snəʊfɔ:l] n nevada f

snowflake ['snəʊfleɪk] n copo m de nieve

snowman ['snəʊmæn] n hombre m de nieve

snowplough, US **snowplow** ['snəʊplaʊ] n quitanieves m inv

snowshoe ['snəʊʃu:] n raqueta f (de nieve)

snowstorm ['snəʊstɔ:m] n nevasca f

snowy ['snəʊɪ] adj (**snowier, snowiest**) (mountain) nevado(a); (climate) nevoso(a); (day) de nieve

Snr (abbr **Senior**) **Neil Smith S.** Neil Smith padre

snub [snʌb] **1** n (of person) desaire m; (of offer) rechazo m

2 vt (person) desairar; (offer) rechazar

snub-nosed ['snʌbnəʊzd] adj de nariz respingona

snuck [snʌk] US pt & pp of **sneak**

snuff [snʌf] n rapé m

snug [snʌg] adj (**snugger, snuggest**) (**a**) (cosy) cómodo(a) (**b**) (tightfitting) ajustado(a)

snuggle ['snʌgəl] vi **to s. down in bed** acurrucarse en la cama; **to s. up to sb** arrimarse a algn

snugly ['snʌglɪ] adv **to fit s.** (clothes) quedar ajustado(a); (object in box etc) encajar

so [səʊ] **1** adv (**a**) (to such an extent) tanto; **he was so tired that ...** estaba tan cansado que ...; **it's so long since ...** hace tanto tiempo que ...; **he isn't so nice as his sister** no es tan agradable como su hermana; Fam **so long!** ¡hasta luego!

(**b**) (degree) tanto; **a week or so** una semana más o menos; **twenty or so** una veintena; **we loved her so (much)** la queríamos tanto; **so many books** tantos libros; Fam **he's ever so handsome!** ¡es tan guapo!; Ironic **so much for that** ¿qué le vamos a hacer?

(**c**) (thus, in this way) así, de esta manera; **and so on, and so forth** y así sucesivamente; **if so** en este caso; **I think/hope so** creo/espero que sí; **I told you so** ya te lo dije; **it so happens that ...** da la casualidad de que ...; **so be it!** ¡así sea!; **so far** hasta ahora *or* allí; **so it seems** eso parece; **so they say** eso dicen; **you're late! – so I am!** ¡llegas tarde! –¡tienes razón!

(d) *(also)* **I'm going to Spain – so am I** voy a España – yo también

2 *conj* (a) *(expresses result)* así que; **so you like England, do you?** ¿así que te gusta Inglaterra, pues?; *Fam* **so what?** ¿y qué?

(b) *(expresses purpose)* para que; **I'll put the key here so (that) everyone can see it** pongo la llave aquí para que todos la vean

soak [səʊk] **1** *vt (washing, food)* remojar; *(cotton, wool)* empapar (**in** en)

2 *vi (washing, food)* estar en remojo

▶ **soak in** *vi* penetrar

▶ **soak up** *vt sep* absorber

soaking ['səʊkɪŋ] *adj (object)* empapado(a); *(person)* calado(a) hasta los huesos

so-and-so ['səʊənsəʊ] *n Fam* **Mr So-and-so** Don Fulano (de tal); *Pej* **an old so-and-so** un viejo imbécil

soap [səʊp] **1** *n* (a) jabón *m*; **s. flakes** jabón en escamas; **s. powder** jabón en polvo (b) *TV* **s. opera** culebrón *m*

2 *vt* enjabonar

soapy ['səʊpɪ] *adj* (**soapier, soapiest**) jabonoso(a); *(hands)* cubierto(a) de jabón

soar [sɔː(r)] *vi (bird, plane)* remontar el vuelo; *Fig (skyscraper)* elevarse; *(hopes, prices)* aumentar

sob [sɒb] **1** *n* sollozo *m*

2 *vi* sollozar

sober ['səʊbə(r)] *adj (not drunk, moderate)* sobrio(a); *(sensible)* sensato(a); *(serious)* serio(a); *(colour)* discreto(a)

▶ **sober up** *vi* **he sobered up** se le pasó la borrachera

so-called ['səʊkɔːld] *adj* supuesto(a), llamado(a)

soccer ['sɒkə(r)] *n* fútbol *m*

sociable ['səʊʃəbəl] *adj (gregarious)* sociable; *(friendly)* amistoso(a)

social ['səʊʃəl] *adj* social; **s. class** clase *f* social; **s. climber** arribista *mf*; **S. Democratic** socialdemócrata; *US* **s. insurance** seguro *m* social; **s. security** seguridad *f* social; **the s. services** los servicios sociales; **s. work** asistencia *f* social; **s. worker** asistente(a) *m,f* social

socialist ['səʊʃəlɪst] *adj & n* socialista *(mf)*

socialite ['səʊʃəlaɪt] *n* vividor(a) *m,f*

socialize ['səʊʃəlaɪz] **1** *vi* alternar, mezclarse con la gente

2 *vt* socializar

socially ['səʊʃəlɪ] *adv* socialmente

society [sə'saɪətɪ] **1** *n* (a) sociedad *f*; **the consumer s.** la sociedad de consumo; **(high) s.** la alta sociedad (b) *(club)* asociación *f* (c) *(companionship)* compañía *f*

2 *adj* de sociedad; **s. column** ecos *mpl* de sociedad

sociologist [səʊsɪ'ɒlədʒɪst] *n* sociólogo(a) *m,f*

sociology [səʊsɪ'ɒlədʒɪ] *n* sociología *f*

sock [sɒk] *n* calcetín *m*, *CSur* zoquete *m*

socket ['sɒkɪt] *n* (a) *(of eye)* cuenca *f* (b) *Elec* enchufe *m*

sod¹ [sɒd] *n Fml (piece of turf)* terrón *m*

sod² [sɒd] *very Fam* **1** *n* (a) *Pej (bastard)* cabrón(ona) *m,f*; **the lazy s.!** ¡qué tío más vago! (b) *(wretch)* desgraciado(a) *m,f*; **the poor s.** el pobrecito (c) **I've done s. all today** hoy no he pegado ni golpe

2 *vt* **s. it!** ¡maldita sea!

soda ['səʊdə] *n* (a) *Chem* sosa *f*; **baking s.** bicarbonato sódico (b) **s. water** soda *f* (c) *US (fizzy drink)* gaseosa *f*

sodden ['sɒdən] *adj* empapado(a)

sodium ['səʊdɪəm] *n* sodio *m*

sofa ['səʊfə] *n* sofá *m*; **s. bed** sofá cama

soft [sɒft] *adj* (a) *(not hard)* blando(a); **s. toy** muñeco *m* de peluche (b) *(skin, colour, hair, light, music)* suave; *(breeze, steps)* ligero(a) (c) *(lenient)* permisivo(a) (d) *(voice)* bajo(a) (e) *(foolish)* lelo(a); **to be a s. touch** ser fácil de engañar (f) **to have a s. spot for sb** tener debilidad por algn (g) *(easy)* fácil; **s. job** chollo *m* (h) *(drink)* no alcohólico(a); **s. drinks** refrescos *mpl* (i) **s. drugs** drogas blandas; **s. porn** pornografía blanda

soften ['sɒfən] **1** *vt (leather, heart)* ablandar; *(skin)* suavizar; *Fig (blow)* amortiguar

2 *vi (leather, heart)* ablandarse; *(skin)* suavizarse

softly ['sɒftlɪ] *adv (gently)* suavemente; *(quietly)* silenciosamente

softness ['sɒftnɪs] *n* (a) blandura *f* (b) *(of hair, skin)* suavidad *f* (c) *(foolishness)* estupidez *f*

software ['sɒftweə(r)] *n Comput* software *m*; **s. package** paquete *m*

soggy ['sɒgɪ] *adj* (**soggier, soggiest**) empapado(a); *(bread)* pastoso(a)

soil [sɔɪl] **1** *n (earth)* tierra *f*

2 *vt (dirty)* ensuciar; *Fig (reputation)* manchar

soiled [sɔɪld] *adj* sucio(a)

solace ['sɒlɪs] *n Fml* consuelo *m*

solar ['səʊlə(r)] *adj* solar

sold [səʊld] *pt & pp of* **sell**

solder [ˈsɒldə(r)] **1** *n* soldadura *f*
2 *vt* soldar
soldier [ˈsəʊldʒə(r)] *n* soldado *m*; *(officer)* militar *m*; **toy s.** soldadito *m* de plomo
► **soldier on** *vi Fig* continuar contra viento y marea
sole¹ [səʊl] *n (of foot)* planta *f*; *(of shoe, sock)* suela *f*
sole² [səʊl] *n (fish)* lenguado *m*
sole³ [səʊl] *adj (only)* único(a)
solemn [ˈsɒləm] *adj* solemne
solicit [səˈlɪsɪt] **1** *vt (request)* solicitar
2 *vi (prostitute)* abordar a los clientes
solicitor [səˈlɪsɪtə(r)] *n* abogado(a) *m,f*; *(for wills)* notario(a) *m,f*
solid [ˈsɒlɪd] **1** *adj* **(a)** *(not liquid)* sólido(a); *(firm)* firme **(b)** *(not hollow, pure) (metal)* macizo(a) **(c)** *(fog etc)* espeso(a); *(of strong material)* resistente; **a man of s. build** un hombre fornido **(d)** *(reliable)* formal **(e)** *(unanimous)* unánime
2 *n* sólido *m*
solidarity [sɒlɪˈdærɪtɪ] *n* solidaridad *f*
solidify [səˈlɪdɪfaɪ] *vi* solidificarse
solidly [ˈsɒlɪdlɪ] *adv* sólidamente; **s. built** *(house etc)* de construcción sólida; **to work s.** trabajar sin descanso
soliloquy [səˈlɪləkwɪ] *n* soliloquio *m*
solitaire [ˈsɒlɪteə(r)] *n* solitario *m*
solitary [ˈsɒlɪtərɪ] *adj* **(a)** *(alone)* solitario(a); *(secluded)* apartado(a) **(b)** *(only)* solo(a)
solitude [ˈsɒlɪtjuːd] *n* soledad *f*
solo [ˈsəʊləʊ] *n* solo *m*
soloist [ˈsəʊləʊɪst] *n* solista *mf*
solstice [ˈsɒlstɪs] *n* solsticio *m*
solution [səˈluːʃən] *n* solución *f*
solve [sɒlv] *vt* resolver, solucionar
solvent [ˈsɒlvənt] *adj & n* solvente (*m*)
sombre, *US* **somber** [ˈsɒmbə(r)] *adj* *(dark)* sombrío(a); *(gloomy)* lúgubre; *(pessimistic)* pesimista
some [sʌm] **1** *adj* **(a)** *(with plural nouns)* unos(as), algunos(as); *(several)* varios(as); *(a few)* unos(as) cuantos(as); **did she bring s. flowers?** ¿trajo flores?; **there were s. roses** había unas rosas; **s. more peas** más guisantes
(b) *(with singular nouns)* algún/alguna; *(a little)* un poco de; **if you need s. help** si necesitas ayuda; **there's s. wine left** queda un poco de vino; **would you like s. coffee?** ¿quiere café?
(c) *(certain)* cierto(a), alguno(a); **in s. ways** en cierto modo; **to s. extent** hasta cierto punto; **s. people say that ...** algunas personas dicen que ...
(d) *(unspecified)* algún/alguna; **for s.**

reason or other por una razón o por otra; **in s. book or other** en algún libro u otro; **s. day** algún día; **s. other time** otro día
(e) *(quite a lot of)* bastante; **it's s. distance away** queda bastante lejos; **s. years ago** hace algunos años
2 *pron* **(a)** *(people)* algunos(as), unos(as); **s. go by bus and s. by train** unos van en autobús y otros en tren
(b) *(objects)* algunos(as); *(a few)* unos(as) cuantos(as); *(a little)* algo, un poco; *(certain ones)* algunos(as)
3 *adv* **s. thirty cars** unos treinta coches
somebody [ˈsʌmbədɪ] *pron* alguien; **s. else** otro(a)
somehow [ˈsʌmhaʊ] *adv* **(a)** *(in some way)* de alguna forma **(b)** *(for some reason)* por alguna razón
someone [ˈsʌmwʌn] *pron* = **somebody**
someplace [ˈsʌmpleɪs] *adv US* = **somewhere**
somersault [ˈsʌməsɔːlt] **1** *n* voltereta *f*; *(by acrobat etc)* salto *m* mortal; *(by car)* vuelta *f* de campana
2 *vi* dar volteretas; *(acrobat etc)* dar un salto mortal; *(car)* dar una vuelta de campana
something [ˈsʌmθɪŋ] *pron & n* algo; **s. to eat/drink** algo de comer/beber; **are you drunk or s.?** ¿estás borracho o qué?; **s. must be done** hay que hacer algo; **she has a certain s.** tiene un no sé qué; **is s. the matter?** ¿le pasa algo?; **s. else** otra cosa; **s. of the kind** algo por el estilo
sometime [ˈsʌmtaɪm] *adv* algún día; **s. last week** un día de la semana pasada; **s. next year** durante el año que viene
sometimes [ˈsʌmtaɪmz] *adv* a veces, de vez en cuando
somewhat [ˈsʌmwɒt] *adv Fml* algo, un tanto
somewhere [ˈsʌmweə(r)] *adv* **(a)** *(in some place)* en alguna parte; *(to some place)* a alguna parte; **s. else** *(in some other place)* en otra parte; *(to some other place)* a otra parte; **s. or other** no sé dónde **(b)** **s. in the region of** *(approximately)* más o menos
son [sʌn] *n* hijo *m*; **eldest/youngest s.** hijo mayor/menor
song [sɒŋ] *n* canción *f*; *(of bird)* canto *m*
songwriter [ˈsɒŋraɪtə(r)] *n* compositor(a) *m,f* (de canciones)
sonic [ˈsɒnɪk] *adj* sónico(a)
son-in-law [ˈsʌnɪnlɔː] *n* yerno *m*
sonnet [ˈsɒnɪt] *n* soneto *m*
sonny [ˈsʌnɪ] *n Fam* hijo *m*, hijito *m*

soon-[suːn] adv (a) (within a short time) pronto, dentro de poco; (quickly) rápidamente; **see you s.!** ¡hasta pronto!; **s. after midnight** poco después de medianoche; **s. afterwards** poco después

(b) **as s. as I arrived** en cuanto llegué; **as s. as possible** cuanto antes

(c) (early) pronto; Fig **don't speak too s.** no cantes victoria

(d) (preference) **I would just as s. stay at home** prefiero quedarme en casa

(e) (indifference) **I would (just) as s. read as watch TV** tanto me da leer como ver la tele

sooner ['suːnə(r)] adv (a) (earlier) más temprano; **s. or later** tarde o temprano; **the s. the better** cuanto antes mejor (b) **no s. had he finished than he fainted** (immediately after) nada más acabar se desmayó (c) **I would s. do it alone** (rather) prefiero hacerlo yo solo

soot [sʊt] n hollín m

soothe [suːð] vt (calm) tranquilizar; (pain) aliviar

sop [sɒp] n (concession) favor m; (bribe) soborno m

▸ **sop up** vt sep empapar

sophisticated [sə'fɪstɪkeɪtɪd] adj sofisticado(a)

sophomore ['sɒfəmɔː(r)] n US Univ = estudiante de segundo curso

soporific [sɒpə'rɪfɪk] adj soporífero(a)

sopping ['sɒpɪŋ] adj Fam **s. (wet)** como una sopa

soppy ['sɒpɪ] adj (soppier, soppiest) Fam sentimentaloide

soprano [sə'prɑːnəʊ] n soprano mf

sorcerer ['sɔːsərə(r)] n brujo m

sorceress ['sɔːsərɪs] n bruja f

sordid ['sɔːdɪd] adj sórdido(a)

sore [sɔː(r)] 1 adj (a) dolorido(a); **to have a s. throat** tener dolor de garganta (b) Fam (angry) enfadado(a); **to feel s. about sth** estar resentido(a) por algo

2 n llaga f

sorely ['sɔːlɪ] adv (very) muy; (a lot) mucho; (deeply) profundamente

sorrow ['sɒrəʊ] n pena f, dolor m

sorrowful ['sɒrəʊfʊl] adj afligido(a)

sorry ['sɒrɪ] 1 adj (sorrier, sorriest) (a) **I feel very s. for her** me da mucha pena (b) (pitiful) triste (c) **to be s. (about sth)** sentir (algo); **I'm s. I'm late** siento llegar tarde

2 interj (a) (apology) ¡perdón! (b) Br (for repetition) ¿cómo?

sort [sɔːt] 1 n (a) (kind) clase f, tipo m; (brand) marca f; **it's a s. of teapot** es una especie de tetera (b) **he is a musician of sorts** tiene algo de músico; **there's an office of sorts** hay una especie de despacho (c) **s. of** en cierto modo

2 vt (classify) clasificar

▸ **sort out** vt sep (a) (classify) clasificar; (put in order) ordenar (b) (problem) arreglar, solucionar

sorting ['sɔːtɪŋ] n **s. office** sala f de batalla

SOS [esəʊ'es] n (abbr save our souls) S.O.S. m

so-so ['səʊsəʊ] adv Fam así así, regular

soufflé ['suːfleɪ] n soufflé m, suflé m

sought [sɔːt] pt & pp of seek

soul [səʊl] n (a) alma f (b) **he's a good s.** (person) es muy buena persona (c) Mus (música f) soul m

soul-destroying ['səʊldɪstrɔɪɪŋ] adj (boring) monótono(a); (demoralizing) desmoralizador(a)

soulful ['səʊlfʊl] adj conmovedor(a)

sound¹ [saʊnd] 1 n sonido m; (noise) ruido m; Fig **I don't like the s. of it** no me gusta nada la idea; **s. barrier** barrera f del sonido; **s. effects** efectos sonoros

2 vt (bell, trumpet) tocar; **to s. the alarm** dar la señal de alarma

3 vi (a) (trumpet, bell, alarm) sonar (b) (give an impression) parecer; **how does it s. to you?** ¿qué te parece?; **it sounds interesting** parece interesante

sound² [saʊnd] 1 adj (a) (healthy) sano(a); (in good condition) en buen estado (b) (safe, dependable) seguro(a); (correct) acertado(a); (logical) lógico(a) (c) (basis etc) sólido(a) (d) (defeat etc) rotundo(a) (e) (sleep) profundo(a)

2 adv **to be s. asleep** estar profundamente dormido(a)

sound³ [saʊnd] vt Naut & Med sondar

▸ **sound out** vt sep sondear

sound⁴ [saʊnd] n Geog estrecho m

sounding ['saʊndɪŋ] n Naut sondeo m

soundproof ['saʊndpruːf] adj insonorizado(a)

soundtrack ['saʊndtræk] n banda sonora

soup [suːp] n sopa f; (thin, clear) caldo m; Fam **in the s.** en un apuro; **s. dish** plato hondo; **s. spoon** cuchara f sopera

sour [saʊə(r)] adj (a) (fruit, wine) agrio(a); (milk) cortado(a); **to go s.** (milk) cortarse; (wine) agriarse; Fig (situation) empeorar (b) Fig (person) amargado(a)

source [sɔːs] n fuente f; (of infection) foco m

south [saʊθ] **1** *n* sur *m*; **in the s. of England** en el sur de Inglaterra; **to the s. of York** al sur de York

2 *adj* del sur; **S. Africa** Sudáfrica; **S. African** sudafricano(a) *(m,f)*; **S. Korea** Corea del Sur; **S. Pole** Polo *m* Sur

3 *adv (location)* al sur; *(direction)* hacia el sur

southeast [saʊθ'iːst] **1** *n* sudeste *m*

2 *adj (location)* al sudeste; *(direction)* hacia el sudeste

southeasterly [saʊθ'iːstəlɪ] *adj* del sudeste

southerly ['sʌðəlɪ] *adj (direction)* hacia el sur; *(point)* al sur; *(wind)* del sur

southern ['sʌðən] *adj* del sur, meridional; **S. Europe** Europa del Sur; **the s. hemisphere** el hemisferio sur

southerner ['sʌðənə(r)] *n* sureño(a) *m,f*

southward ['saʊθwəd] *adj & adv* hacia el sur

southwest [saʊθ'west] **1** *n* suroeste *m*

2 *adj* suroeste

3 *adv (location)* al suroeste; *(direction)* hacia el suroeste

souvenir [suːvə'nɪə(r)] *n* recuerdo *m*, souvenir *m*

sovereign ['sɒvrɪn] **1** *n* **(a)** *(monarch)* soberano(a) *m,f* **(b)** *Hist (coin)* soberano *m*

2 *adj* soberano(a)

soviet ['saʊvɪət] **1** *n* **(a)** *(council)* soviet *m* **(b) the Soviets** los soviéticos

2 *adj* soviético(a); *Hist* **S. Union** Unión Soviética

sow[1] [saʊ] *vt (pt* **sowed**; *pp* **sowed** or **sown)** sembrar

sow[2] [saʊ] *n Zool* cerda *f*

sown [saʊn] *pp of* **sow**

soy [sɔɪ] *n* soja *f*; **s. sauce** salsa *f* de soja

soya ['sɔɪə] *n* soja *f*; **s. bean** semilla *f* de soja

spa [spɑː] *n* balneario *m*

space [speɪs] **1** *n* **(a)** espacio *m*; **s. age** era *f* espacial; **s. shuttle** transbordador *m* espacial; **s. station** estación *f* espacial **(b)** *(room)* sitio *m*; **in a confined s.** en un espacio reducido

2 *vt (also* **s. out)** espaciar, separar

spacecraft ['speɪskrɑːft] *n (pl* **spacecraft)** nave *f* espacial

spaceman ['speɪsmən] *n* astronauta *m*, cosmonauta *m*

spacing ['speɪsɪŋ] *n* **double s.** doble espacio

spacious ['speɪʃəs] *adj* espacioso(a), amplio(a)

spade[1] [speɪd] *n (for digging)* pala *f*

> 🖉 Note that the Spanish word **espada** is a false friend and is never a translation for the English word **spade**. In Spanish, **espada** means "sword".

spade[2] [speɪd] *n Cards* pica *f*

spaghetti [spə'getɪ] *n* espaguetis *mpl*

Spain [speɪn] *n* España

span [spæn] **1** *n (of wing)* envergadura *f*; *(of hand)* palmo *m*; *(of arch)* luz *f*; *(of road)* tramo *m*; *(of time)* lapso *m*; **life s.** vida *f*

2 *vt (river etc)* extenderse sobre, atravesar; *(period of time etc)* abarcar

3 *pt of* **spin**

Spaniard ['spænjəd] *n* español(a) *m,f*

spaniel ['spænjəl] *n* perro *m* de aguas

Spanish ['spænɪʃ] **1** *adj* español(a)

2 *n* **(a) the S.** los españoles **(b)** *(language)* español *m*, castellano *m*

Spanish-speaking ['spænɪʃspiːkɪŋ] *adj* de habla española, hispanohablante

spank [spæŋk] *vt* zurrar

spanner ['spænə(r)] *n* llave *f* (para tuercas); *Br Fam* **to throw a s. in the works** estropear los planes

spar[1] [spɑː(r)] *n Naut* palo *m*, verga *f*

spar[2] [spɑː(r)] *vi* **(a)** *(boxers)* entrenarse **(b)** *(argue)* discutir

spare [speə(r)] **1** *vt* **(a)** *(do without)* prescindir de; **can you s. me ten?** ¿me puedes dejar diez?; **I can't s. the time** no tengo tiempo; **there's none to s.** no sobra nada **(b)** *(begrudge)* escatimar **(c)** *(show mercy to)* perdonar **(d) s. me the details** ahórrate los detalles

2 *adj* **(a)** *(left over)* sobrante; *(surplus)* de sobra, de más; **a s. moment** un momento libre; **s. part** (pieza *f* de) recambio *m*; **s. room** cuarto *m* de los invitados; **s. tyre** *Aut* neumático *m* de recambio; *Br Fam (on body)* michelines *mpl*; **s. wheel** rueda *f* de recambio **(b)** *(thin)* enjuto(a)

3 *n Aut* (pieza *f* de) recambio *m*

sparing ['speərɪŋ] *adj* **to be s. with praise** escatimar elogios; **to be s. with words** ser parco(a) en palabras

sparingly ['speərɪŋlɪ] *adv* en poca cantidad

spark [spɑːk] **1** *n* chispa *f*; *Aut* **s. plug** bujía *f*

2 *vi* echar chispas

▸ **spark off** *vt sep* desatar

sparking ['spɑːkɪŋ] *adj* **s. plug** bujía *f*

sparkle ['spɑːkəl] **1** *vi (diamond, glass)* centellear, destellar; *(eyes)* brillar

2 *n (of diamond, glass)* centelleo *m*,

destello *m*; *(of eyes)* brillo *m*

sparkling ['spɑːklɪŋ] *adj* (**a**) *(diamond, glass)* centelleante; *(eyes)* brillante; **s. wine** vino espumoso (**b**) *Fig (person, conversation)* vivaz

sparrow ['spærəʊ] *n* gorrión *m*

sparse [spɑːs] *adj (thin)* escaso(a); *(scattered)* esparcido(a); *(hair)* ralo(a)

Spartan ['spɑːtən] *adj & n* espartano(a) *(m,f)*

spasm ['spæzəm] *n* (**a**) *Med* espasmo *m*; *(of coughing)* acceso *m* (**b**) *(of anger, activity)* arrebato *m*

spasmodic [spæz'mɒdɪk] *adj* (**a**) *Med* espasmódico(a) (**b**) *(irregular)* irregular

spastic ['spæstɪk] *adj & n Med* espástico(a) *(m,f)*

spat [spæt] *pt & pp of* spit

spate [speɪt] *n* (**a**) *(of letters)* avalancha *f*; *(of words)* torrente *m*; *(of accidents)* racha *f* (**b**) *Br (river)* desbordamiento *m*; **to be in full s.** estar crecido(a)

spatter ['spætə(r)] *vt* salpicar (**with** de)

spatula ['spætjʊlə] *n* espátula *f*

spawn [spɔːn] **1** *n (of fish, frogs)* huevas *fpl*

2 *vi (fish, frogs)* frezar

3 *vt Fig Pej* generar

speak [spiːk] **1** *vt* (*pt* spoke; *pp* spoken) (**a**) *(utter)* decir; **to s. the truth** decir la verdad

(**b**) *(language)* hablar

2 *vi* (**a**) *(gen)* hablar; **roughly speaking** a grandes rasgos; **so to s.** por así decirlo; **speaking of ...** a propósito de ...; **to s. to sb** hablar con algn

(**b**) *(make a speech)* pronunciar un discurso; *(take the floor)* tomar la palabra

(**c**) *Tel* hablar; **speaking!** ¡al habla!; **who's speaking, please?** ¿de parte de quién?

▶ **speak for** *vt insep (person, group)* hablar en nombre de; **it speaks for itself** es evidente

▶ **speak out** *vi* **to s. out against sth** denunciar algo

▶ **speak up** *vi* hablar más fuerte; *Fig* **to s. up for sb** intervenir a favor de algn

speaker ['spiːkə(r)] *n* (**a**) *(in dialogue)* interlocutor(a) *m,f*; *(lecturer)* conferenciante *mf*; (**public**) **s.** orador(a) *m,f* (**b**) *(of language)* hablante *mf* (**c**) *Br Pol* **the S.** el Presidente de la Cámara de los Comunes; *US* **the S. of the House** el Presidente de la Cámara de los Representantes (**d**) *(loudspeaker)* altavoz *m*

spear [spɪə(r)] *n* lanza *f*; *(javelin)* jabalina *f*; *(harpoon)* arpón *m*

spearhead ['spɪəhed] *vt* encabezar

spec [spek] *n Fam* **on s.** sin garantías

special ['speʃəl] **1** *adj* especial; *(specific)* específico(a); *(exceptional)* extraordinario(a); **s. delivery** *(letter)* exprés; *(parcel)* de entrega inmediata; **s. edition** número *m* especial; **s. effects** efectos *mpl* especiales

2 *n Rad & TV* programa *m* especial

specialist ['speʃəlɪst] *n* especialista *mf*

speciality [speʃɪ'ælɪtɪ] *n esp Br* especialidad *f*

specialize ['speʃəlaɪz] *vi* especializarse (**in** en)

specially ['speʃəlɪ] *adv (specifically)* especialmente; *(on purpose)* a propósito

specialty ['speʃəltɪ] *n US* = speciality

species ['spiːʃiːz] *n (pl* species) especie *f*

specific [spɪ'sɪfɪk] *adj* específico(a); *(definite)* concreto(a); *(precise)* preciso(a); **to be s.** concretar

specifically [spɪ'sɪfɪklɪ] *adv (exactly)* específicamente; *(expressly)* expresamente; *(namely)* en concreto

specifications [spesɪfɪ'keɪʃənz] *npl* datos específicos

specify ['spesɪfaɪ] *vt* especificar, precisar

specimen ['spesɪmɪn] *n (sample)* muestra *f*; *(example)* ejemplar *m*; **urine/tissue s.** espécimen de orina/tejido

speck [spek] *n (of dust)* mota *f*; *(stain)* manchita *f*; *(small trace)* pizca *f*

speckled ['spekəld] *adj* moteado(a)

specs [speks] *npl Fam (spectacles)* gafas *fpl*

spectacle ['spektəkəl] *n* (**a**) *(display)* espectáculo *m* (**b**) **spectacles** *(glasses)* gafas *fpl*, *Am* lentes *mpl*, anteojos *mpl*

spectacular [spek'tækjʊlə(r)] **1** *adj* espectacular, impresionante

2 *n Cin & TV* (gran) espectáculo *m*

spectator [spek'teɪtə(r)] *n* espectador(a) *m,f*

spectre, *US* **specter** ['spektə(r)] *n* espectro *m*, fantasma *m*

spectrum ['spektrəm] *n* espectro *m*

speculate ['spekjʊleɪt] *vi* especular

speculation [spekjʊ'leɪʃən] *n* especulación *f*

sped [sped] *pt & pp of* speed

speech [spiːtʃ] *n* (**a**) *(faculty)* habla *f*; *(pronunciation)* pronunciación *f*; **freedom of s.** libertad *f* de expresión (**b**) *(address)* discurso *m*; **to give a s.** pronunciar un discurso (**c**) *Ling* **part of s.** parte *f* de la oración

speechless ['spiːtʃlɪs] *adj* mudo(a), boquiabierto(a)

speed [spiːd] **1** *n* velocidad *f*; *(rapidity)*

rapidez *f*; **at top s.** a toda velocidad; **s. limit** límite *m* de velocidad

2 *vi* (**a**) (*pt & pp* **sped**) (*go fast*) ir corriendo; (*hurry*) apresurarse; **to s. along** (*car etc*) ir a toda velocidad; **to s. past** pasar volando (**b**) (*pt & pp* **speeded**) (*exceed speed limit*) conducir con exceso de velocidad

▸ **speed up 1** *vt sep* acelerar; (*person*) meter prisa a

2 *vi* (*person*) darse prisa

speedboat ['spi:dbəʊt] *n* lancha rápida

speeding ['spi:dɪŋ] *n* exceso *m* de velocidad

speedometer [spɪ'dɒmɪtə(r)] *n* velocímetro *m*

speedway ['spi:dweɪ] *n* (**a**) (*racing*) carreras *fpl* de motos (**b**) (*track*) pista *f* de carreras

speedy ['spi:dɪ] *adj* (**speedier, speediest**) veloz, rápido(a)

spell¹ [spel] (*pt & pp* **spelt** *or* **spelled**) (*letter by letter*) deletrear; *Fig* (*denote*) significar; **how do you s. your name?** ¿cómo se escribe su nombre?

2 *vi* **she can't s.** comete faltas de ortografía

▸ **spell out** *vt sep Fig* explicar con detalle

spell² [spel] *n* (*magical*) hechizo *m*, encanto *m*

spell³ [spel] *n* (**a**) (*period*) período *m*; (*short period*) rato *m*; **Met cold s.** ola *f* de frío (**b**) (*shift*) turno *m*

spellbound ['spelbaʊnd] *adj* hechizado(a), embelesado(a)

spelling ['spelɪŋ] *n* ortografía *f*

spelt [spelt] *pt & pp of* **spell**

spend [spend] *vt* (*pt & pp* **spent**) (**a**) (*money*) gastar (**on** en) (**b**) (*time*) pasar; **to s. time on sth** dedicar tiempo a algo

spending ['spendɪŋ] *n* gastos *mpl*; **s. money** dinero *m* de bolsillo; **s. power** poder adquisitivo

spendthrift ['spendθrɪft] *adj & n* derrochador(a) (*m,f*)

spent [spent] **1** *adj* gastado(a)

2 *pt & pp of* **spend**

sperm [spɜːm] *n* esperma *m*; **s. bank** banco *m* de esperma; **s. whale** cachalote *m*

spew [spju:] *vt* **to s. (up)** vomitar

sphere [sfɪə(r)] *n* esfera *f*

spice [spaɪs] **1** *n* (**a**) especia *f* (**b**) *Fig* sal *f*

2 *vt* (**a**) *Culin* sazonar (**b**) **to s. (up)** (*story etc*) salpimentar

spick-and-span [spɪkən'spæn] *adj* (*very clean*) limpísimo(a); (*well-groomed*) acicalado(a)

spicy ['spaɪsɪ] *adj* (**spicier, spiciest**) (**a**) *Culin* sazonado(a); (*hot*) picante (**b**) *Fig* (*story etc*) picante

spider ['spaɪdə(r)] *n* araña *f*; **s.'s web** telaraña *f*

spike¹ [spaɪk] *n* (*sharp point*) punta *f*; (*metal rod*) pincho *m*; (*on railing*) barrote *m*; *Sport* (*on shoes*) clavo *m*

spike² [spaɪk] *n Bot* espiga *f*

spiky ['spaɪkɪ] *adj* (**spikier, spikiest**) puntiagudo(a); (*hairstyle*) de punta

spill [spɪl] **1** *vt* (*pt & pp* **spilled** *or* **spilt** [spɪlt]) derramar

2 *vi* (*liquid*) derramarse

▸ **spill over** *vi* desbordarse

spin [spɪn] **1** *vt* (*pt* **span** *or* **spun**; *pp* **spun**) (**a**) (*wheel etc*) hacer girar; (*washing*) centrifugar (**b**) (*cotton, wool*) hilar; (*spider's web*) tejer

2 *vi* (*wheel etc*) girar; *Av* caer en barrena; *Aut* patinar

3 *n* (**a**) (*turn*) vuelta *f*, giro *m* (**b**) *Sport* efecto *m* (**c**) *Av* barrena *f*; *Aut* patinazo *m* (**d**) *Br* **to go for a s.** (*ride*) dar una vuelta (**e**) *Pol* (*on news story*) sesgo *m*; **s. doctor** asesor(a) *m,f* político(a) (*para dar buena prensa a un partido o político*)

spinach ['spɪnɪtʃ] *n* espinacas *fpl*

spinal ['spaɪnəl] *adj* espinal, vertebral; **s. column** columna *f* vertebral; **s. cord** médula *f* espinal

spindly ['spɪndlɪ] *adj* (**spindlier, spindliest**) *Fam* (*long-bodied*) larguirucho(a); (*long-legged*) zanquilargo(a)

spin-dryer [spɪn'draɪə(r)] *n* secador centrífugo

spine [spaɪn] *n* (**a**) *Anat* columna *f* vertebral, espinazo *m*; (*of book*) lomo *m* (**b**) *Zool* púa *f*; *Bot* espina *f*

spineless ['spaɪnlɪs] *adj Fig* (*weak*) sin carácter

spinning ['spɪnɪŋ] *n* (**a**) (*of cotton etc*) (*act*) hilado *m*; (*art*) hilandería *f*; **s. wheel** rueca *f* (**b**) **s. top** peonza *f*

spin-off ['spɪnɒf] *n* (*by-product*) derivado *m*; *Fig* efecto secundario

spinster ['spɪnstə(r)] *n* soltera *f*

spiral ['spaɪərəl] **1** *n* espiral *f*

2 *adj* en espiral; **s. staircase** escalera *f* de caracol

spirit¹ ['spɪrɪt] *n* (**a**) (*soul*) espíritu *m*, alma *f*; (*ghost*) fantasma *m* (**b**) (*attitude*) espíritu *m*; (*mood*) humor *m*; **to take sth in the right s.** tomar algo a bien; **community s.** civismo *m* (**c**) (*courage*) valor *m*; (*liveliness*) ánimo *m*; (*vitality*) vigor *m*; **to break sb's s.** quebrar la voluntad de algn (**d**) **spirits** (*mood*) humor *m*; **to be in**

good spirits estar de buen humor; **to be in high/low spirits** estar muy animado/desanimado

spirit² ['spɪrɪt] n (a) Chem alcohol m; **s. level** nivel m de aire (b) **spirits** (alcoholic drinks) licores mpl

spirited ['spɪrɪtɪd] adj (person, attempt) valiente; (horse) fogoso(a); (attack) enérgico(a)

spiritual ['spɪrɪtjʊəl] adj espiritual

spit¹ [spɪt] 1 vt (pt & pp **spat**) escupir

2 vi escupir; Fam **he's the spitting image of his father** es el vivo retrato de su padre

3 n (saliva) saliva f

spit² [spɪt] n Culin asador m

spite [spaɪt] 1 n (a) (ill will) rencor m, ojeriza f (b) **in s. of** a pesar de, pese a; **in s. of the fact that** a pesar de que, pese a que

2 vt (annoy) fastidiar

spiteful ['spaɪtfʊl] adj (person) rencoroso(a); (remark) malévolo(a); (tongue) viperino(a)

spittle ['spɪtəl] n saliva f

spittoon [spɪ'tuːn] n escupidera f

splash [splæʃ] 1 vt salpicar

2 vi (a) **to s. (about)** (in water) chapotear (b) (water etc) salpicar

3 n (a) (noise) chapoteo m (b) (spray) salpicadura f; Fig (of colour) mancha f

► **splash out** vi Fam tirar la casa por la ventana

spleen [spliːn] n Anat bazo m

splendid ['splendɪd] adj espléndido(a)

splendour, US **splendor** ['splendə(r)] n esplendor m

splint [splɪnt] n tablilla f

splinter ['splɪntə(r)] 1 n (wood) astilla f; (bone, stone) esquirla f; (glass) fragmento m; **s. group** grupo m disidente

2 vi (a) (wood etc) astillarse (b) Pol escindirse

split [splɪt] 1 n (a) (crack) grieta f, hendidura f; (tear) desgarrón m; Fig (division) cisma m; Pol escisión f (b) **to do the splits** abrir las piernas en cruz

2 adj partido(a); **in a s. second** en una fracción de segundo; **s. personality** desdoblamiento m de personalidad

3 vt (pt & pp **split**) (a) (crack) agrietar; (cut) partir; (tear) rajar; (atom) desintegrar; Fig **to s. hairs** buscarle tres pies al gato (b) (divide) dividir (c) (share out) repartir (b) Pol escindir

4 vi (a) (crack) agrietarse; (into two parts) partirse (b) (garment) rajarse (c) Pol escindirse

► **split up 1** vt sep (break up) partir; (divide up) dividir; (share out) repartir

2 vi (couple) separarse

splutter ['splʌtə(r)] vi (person) balbucear; (candle, fat) chisporrotear; (engine) petardear

spoil [spɔɪl] 1 vt (pt & pp **spoiled** or **spoilt**) (a) (ruin) estropear, echar a perder (b) (child) mimar a; **to be spoilt for choice** tener demasiadas cosas para elegir

2 vi (food) estropearse

spoilsport ['spɔɪlspɔːt] n Fam aguafiestas mf inv

spoilt [spɔɪlt] 1 adj (a) (food, merchandise) estropeado(a) (b) (child) mimado(a)

2 pt & pp of **spoil**

spoke¹ [spəʊk] pt of **speak**

spoke² [spəʊk] n (of wheel) radio m, rayo m

spoken ['spəʊkən] pp of **speak**

spokesman ['spəʊksmən] n portavoz m

spokeswoman ['spəʊkswʊmən] n portavoz f

sponge [spʌndʒ] 1 n esponja f; Fig **to throw in the s.** arrojar la toalla; Br **s. cake** bizcocho m

2 vt (wash) lavar con esponja

3 vi Fam vivir de gorra

► **sponge off, sponge on** vt insep vivir a costa de

spongy ['spʌndʒɪ] adj (**spongier, spongiest**) esponjoso(a)

sponsor ['spɒnsə(r)] 1 vt patrocinar; Fin avalar; (support) respaldar

2 n patrocinador(a) m,f; Fin avalador(a) m,f

sponsorship ['spɒnsəʃɪp] n patrocinio m; Fin aval m; (support) respaldo m

spontaneous [spɒn'teɪnɪəs] adj espontáneo(a)

spoof [spuːf] n Fam (a) (parody) burla f (b) (hoax) engaño m

spooky ['spuːkɪ] adj (**spookier, spookiest**) Fam espeluznante

spool [spuːl] n bobina f, carrete m

spoon [spuːn] 1 n cuchara f; (small) cucharita f

2 vt sacar con cuchara; (serve) servir con cuchara

spoon-feed ['spuːnfiːd] vt (baby) dar de comer con cuchara a; Fig (spoil) mimar

spoonful ['spuːnfʊl] n cucharada f

sporadic [spə'rædɪk] adj esporádico(a)

sport [spɔːt] 1 n (a) (activity) deporte m (b) Fam **he's a good s.** es buena persona; **be a s.!** ¡sé amable!

2 vt (display) lucir

sporting ['spɔːtɪŋ] adj deportivo(a)

sports [spɔːts] **1** *npl* deportes *mpl*, deporte *m*
2 *adj* **s. car** coche deportivo; **s. jacket** chaqueta *f* (de) sport
sportsman ['spɔːtsmən] *n* deportista *m*
sportsmanlike ['spɔːtsmənlaɪk] *adj* deportivo(a)
sportsmanship ['spɔːtsmənʃɪp] *n* deportividad *f*
sportswear ['spɔːtsweə(r)] *n* (for sport) ropa *f* de deporte; (casual clothes) ropa (de) sport
sportswoman ['spɔːtswʊmən] *n* deportista *f*
sporty ['spɔːtɪ] *adj* (**sportier, sportiest**) *Fam* deportivo(a)
spot [spɒt] **1** *n* (a) (dot) punto *m*; (on fabric) lunar *m*
    (b) (stain) mancha *f*
    (c) (pimple) grano *m*
    (d) (place) sitio *m*, lugar *m*; **on the s.** (person) allí, presente; **to decide sth on the s.** decidir algo en el acto; **s. check** chequeo rápido; *Fig* **weak s.** punto débil; **to be in a tight s.** estar en un apuro; **to put sb on the s.** poner a algn en un aprieto
    (e) *Fam (small amount)* poquito *m*; **a s. of bother** unos problemillas
    (f) *Rad, TV & Th (in show)* espacio *m*; *(advertisement)* spot *m*, anuncio *m*
2 *vt* (notice) darse cuenta de, notar; (see) ver
spotless ['spɒtlɪs] *adj* (very clean) impecable; *Fig (reputation etc)* intachable
spotlight ['spɒtlaɪt] *n* foco *m*; *Aut* faro *m* auxiliar; *Fig* **to be in the s.** ser objeto de la atención pública
spot-on [spɒt'ɒn] *adj Fam* exacto(a)
spotted ['spɒtɪd] *adj* (with dots) con puntos; (fabric) con lunares; (speckled) moteado(a)
spotty ['spɒtɪ] *adj* (**spottier, spottiest**) *Pej* con granos
spouse [spaʊs] *n* cónyuge *mf*
spout [spaʊt] **1** *n* (of jug) pico *m*; (of teapot) pitorro *m*
2 *vt Fam (nonsense)* soltar
3 *vi* **to s. out/up** (liquid) brotar
sprain [spreɪn] **1** *n* esguince *m*
2 *vt* torcer; **to s. one's ankle** torcerse el tobillo
sprang [spræŋ] *pt of* **spring**
sprawl [sprɔːl] **1** *vi* (a) (sit, lie) tumbarse
    (b) (city, plant) extenderse
2 *n* (of city) extensión *f*
spray¹ [spreɪ] **1** *n* (a) (of water) rociada *f*; (from sea) espuma *f*; (from aerosol)

pulverización *f* (b) (aerosol) spray *m*; (for plants) pulverizador *m*; **s. can** aerosol *m*
2 *vt (water)* rociar; (insecticide, perfume) pulverizar
spray² [spreɪ] *n* (of flowers) ramita *f*
spread [spred] **1** *n* (a) extensión *f*; (of ideas) difusión *f*; (of disease, fire) propagación *f*; (of terrorism) generalización *f*
    (b) (range) gama *f*
    (c) (of wings) envergadura *f*
    (d) (for bread) pasta *f*; **cheese s.** queso *m* para untar
    (e) *Fam (large meal)* banquetazo *m*
    (f) *Press* **full-page s.** plana entera; **two-page s.** doble página *f*
2 *vt* (pt & pp **spread**) (a) (unfold) desplegar; (lay out) extender; *Fig* **to s. one's wings** desplegar las alas
    (b) (butter etc) untar
    (c) (news) difundir; (rumour) hacer correr; (disease, fire) propagar; (panic) sembrar
3 *vi* (a) (stretch out) extenderse; (unfold) desplegarse
    (b) (news) difundirse; (rumour) correr; (disease) propagarse
spread-eagled [spred'iːgəld] *adj* despatarrado(a)
spreadsheet ['spredʃiːt] *n Comput* hoja *f* de cálculo
spree [spriː] *n* juerga *f*; **to go on a s.** ir de juerga
sprig [sprɪg] *n* ramita *f*
sprightly ['spraɪtlɪ] *adj* (**sprightlier, sprightliest**) (nimble) ágil; (energetic) enérgico(a); (lively) animado(a)
spring¹ [sprɪŋ] **1** *n* (season) primavera *f*
2 *adj* primaveral; **s. onion** cebolleta *f*; **s. roll** rollo *m* de primavera
spring² [sprɪŋ] **1** *n* (a) (of water) manantial *m*, fuente *f* (b) (of watch etc) resorte *m*; (of mattress) muelle *m*; *Aut* ballesta *f*
2 *vi* (pt **sprang**, pp **sprung**) (a) (jump) saltar; **the lid sprang open** la tapa se abrió de golpe (b) (appear) aparecer (de repente)
3 *vt* (a) **to s. a leak** hacer agua (b) *Fig (news, surprise)* dar de golpe
▸ spring up *vi* aparecer; (plants) brotar; (buildings) elevarse; (problems) surgir
springboard ['sprɪŋbɔːd] *n* trampolín *m*
spring-clean [sprɪŋ'kliːn] *vt* limpiar a fondo
springtime ['sprɪŋtaɪm] *n* primavera *f*
springy ['sprɪŋɪ] *adj* (**springier, springiest**) (bouncy) elástico(a); *Fig (step)* saltarín
sprinkle ['sprɪŋkəl] *vt* (with water) rociar

(with de); *(with sugar)* espolvorear (with de)

sprint [sprɪnt] **1** *n* esprint *m*
  2 *vi* esprintar

sprinter ['sprɪntə(r)] *n* esprínter *mf*, velocista *mf*

sprout [spraʊt] **1** *vi (bud)* brotar; *Fig* crecer rápidamente
  2 *n* **(Brussels) sprouts** coles *fpl* de Bruselas

spruce¹ [spruːs] *n Bot* picea *f*

spruce² [spruːs] *adj (neat)* pulcro(a); *(smart)* apuesto(a)
  ▸ **spruce up** *vt sep* acicalar

sprung [sprʌŋ] *pp of* **spring**

spry [spraɪ] *adj* (**sprier**, **spriest**) *(nimble)* ágil; *(active)* activo(a); *(lively)* vivaz

spun [spʌn] *pt & pp of* **spin**

spur [spɜː(r)] **1** *n* (**a**) *(horse)* espuela *f* (**b**) *Fig (stimulus)* acicate *m*; **on the s. of the moment** sin pensarlo
  2 *vt* (**a**) *(horse)* espolear (**b**) *Fig* incitar

spurious ['spjʊərɪəs] *adj* falso(a), espurio(a)

spurn [spɜːn] *vt Fml* desdeñar, rechazar

spurt [spɜːt] **1** *n* (**a**) *(of liquid)* chorro *m* (**b**) *Fig (of activity etc)* racha *f*; *(effort)* esfuerzo *m*
  2 *vi* (**a**) *(liquid)* chorrear (**b**) *(make an effort)* hacer un último esfuerzo; *(accelerate)* acelerar

spy [spaɪ] **1** *n* espía *mf*
  2 *vt Fml (see)* divisar
  3 *vi* espiar (**on** a)

spyhole ['spaɪhəʊl] *n* mirilla *f*

spying ['spaɪɪŋ] *n* espionaje *m*

squabble ['skwɒbəl] **1** *n* riña *f*, pelea *f*
  2 *vi* reñir, pelearse (**over** *or* **about** por)

squad [skwɒd] *n Mil* pelotón *m*; *(of police)* brigada *f*; *Sport* equipo *m*; **drugs s.** brigada antidroga

squadron ['skwɒdrən] *n Mil* escuadrón *m*; *Av* escuadrilla *f*; *Naut* escuadra *f*

squalid ['skwɒlɪd] *adj (very dirty)* asqueroso(a); *(poor)* miserable; *(motive)* vil

squall¹ [skwɔːl] *n (wind)* ráfaga *f*

squall² [skwɔːl] *vi* chillar, berrear

squalor ['skwɒlə(r)] *n (dirtiness)* mugre *f*; *(poverty)* miseria *f*

squander ['skwɒndə(r)] *vt (money)* derrochar, despilfarrar; *(time)* desperdiciar

square [skweə(r)] **1** *n* (**a**) *(shape)* cuadro *m*; *(on chessboard, crossword)* casilla *f*; *Fig* **we're back to s. one!** ¡volvemos a partir desde cero!
  (**b**) *(in town)* plaza *f*
  (**c**) *Math* cuadrado *m*
  2 *adj* (**a**) *(in shape)* cuadrado(a)

(**b**) *Math* cuadrado(a); **s. metre** metro cuadrado; **s. root** raíz cuadrada
  (**c**) *Fam (fair)* justo(a); **to be s. with sb** *(honest)* ser franco(a) con algn
  (**d**) **a s. meal** una buena comida
  (**e**) *(old-fashioned)* carroza; *(conservative)* carca
  3 *vt* (**a**) *(make square)* cuadrar; **to s. one's shoulders** sacar el pecho
  (**b**) *Math* elevar al cuadrado
  (**c**) *(settle)* arreglar
  4 *vi (agree)* cuadrar (**with** con)

squarely ['skweəlɪ] *adv (directly)* directamente, de lleno

squash¹ [skwɒʃ] **1** *n Br (drink)* concentrado *m*
  2 *vt* (**a**) *(crush)* aplastar (**b**) *Fig (objection)* echar por tierra
  3 *vi (crush)* aplastarse

squash² [skwɒʃ] *n Sport* squash *m*

squash³ [skwɒʃ] *n US (vegetable)* calabacín *m*

squat [skwɒt] **1** *adj (person)* rechoncho(a)
  2 *vi* (**a**) *(crouch)* agacharse, sentarse en cuclillas (**b**) *(in building)* ocupar ilegalmente
  3 *n (building)* edificio *m* ocupado ilegalmente

squatter ['skwɒtə(r)] *n* ocupante *mf* ilegal, okupa *mf*

squawk [skwɔːk] **1** *n* graznido *m*
  2 *vi* graznar

squeak [skwiːk] **1** *n (of mouse)* chillido *m*; *(of hinge, wheel)* chirrido *m*; *(of shoes)* crujido *m*
  2 *vi (mouse)* chillar; *(hinge, wheel)* chirriar, rechinar; *(shoes)* crujir

squeaky ['skwiːkɪ] *adj* (**squeakier**, **squeakiest**) *(hinge)* chirriante; *(voice)* chillón(o-a); *(shoes)* que crujen

squeal [skwiːl] **1** *n (of animal, person)* chillido *m*
  2 *vi* (**a**) *(animal, person)* chillar (**b**) *Fam (inform)* chivarse

squeamish ['skwiːmɪʃ] *adj* muy sensible

squeeze [skwiːz] **1** *vt* apretar; *(lemon etc)* exprimir; *(sponge)* estrujar; **to s. paste out of a tube** sacar pasta de un tubo apretando
  2 *vi* **to s. in** apretujarse
  3 *n* (**a**) *(pressure)* estrujón *m*; **a s. of lemon** unas gotas de limón (**b**) *(of hand)* apretón *m*; *(hug)* abrazo *m*; *(crush)* apiñamiento *m*; **credit s.** reducción *f* de créditos

squelch [skweltʃ] *vi* chapotear

squid [skwɪd] *n* calamar *m*; *(small)* chipirón *m*

squiggle ['skwɪgəl] *n* garabato *m*

squint [skwɪnt] **1** *n* (**a**) bizquera *f*; **to have a s.** ser bizco(a) (**b**) *Fig (quick look)* vistazo *m*

2 *vi* (**a**) ser bizco(a) (**b**) **to s. at sth** *(glance)* echar un vistazo a algo; *(with eyes half-closed)* mirar algo con los ojos entrecerrados

squirm [skwɜːm] *vi* retorcerse; *Fig (feel embarrassed)* sentirse incómodo(a)

squirrel ['skwɪrəl] *n* ardilla *f*

squirt [skwɜːt] **1** *n* (*of liquid*) chorro *m*

2 *vt* lanzar a chorro

3 *vi* **to s. out** salir a chorros

Sr (*abbr* **Senior**) Thomas Smith, Sr Thomas Smith, padre

Sri Lanka [sriː'læŋkə] *n* Sri Lanka

St (**a**) (*abbr* **Saint**) S./Sto./Sta. (**b**) (*abbr* **Street**) c/

st *Br* (*abbr* **stone**) = peso que equivale a 6,348 kg

stab [stæb] **1** *n* (*with knife*) puñalada *f*; (*of pain*) punzada *f*; *Fam Fig* **to have a s. at doing sth** intentar hacer algo

2 *vt* apuñalar

stabbing ['stæbɪŋ] *adj* (*pain*) punzante

stability [stə'bɪlɪtɪ] *n* estabilidad *f*

stable¹ ['steɪbəl] *adj* estable

stable² ['steɪbəl] *n* cuadra *f*, caballeriza *f*

stack [stæk] **1** *n* (*pile*) montón *m*; *Fam* **he's got stacks of money** está forrado

2 *vt* (*pile up*) amontonar, apilar; *Fig* **the odds are stacked against us** todo está en contra nuestra

stadium ['steɪdɪəm] *n* estadio *m*

staff [stɑːf] **1** *n* (**a**) (*personnel*) personal *m*; *Mil* estado *m* mayor; **s. meeting** claustro *m*; *Br* **s. nurse** enfermera cualificada (**b**) (*stick*) bastón *m*; (*of shepherd*) cayado *m*

2 *vt* proveer de personal

staffroom ['stɑːfruːm] *n* sala *f* de profesores

stag [stæg] *n* ciervo *m*, venado *m*; *Fam* **s. party** despedida *f* de soltero

stage [steɪdʒ] **1** *n* (**a**) (*platform*) plataforma *f* (**b**) (*in theatre*) escenario *m*; **s. door** entrada *f* de artistas; **s. fright** miedo escénico; **s. manager** director(a) *m,f* de escena (**c**) (*phase*) (*of development, journey, rocket*) etapa *f*; (*of road, pipeline*) tramo *m*; **at this s. of the negotiations** a estas alturas de las negociaciones; **in stages** por etapas

2 *vt* (**a**) (*play*) poner en escena, montar (**b**) (*arrange*) organizar; (*carry out*) llevar a cabo

stagecoach ['steɪdʒkəʊtʃ] *n* diligencia *f*

stagger ['stægə(r)] **1** *vi* tambalearse

2 *vt* (**a**) (*amaze*) asombrar (**b**) (*hours, work*) escalonar

staggering ['stægərɪŋ] *adj* asombroso(a)

stagnant ['stægnənt] *adj* estancado(a)

stagnate [stæg'neɪt] *vi* estancarse

staid [steɪd] *adj* (*person*) conservador(a); (*manner, clothes*) serio(a), formal

stain [steɪn] **1** *n* (**a**) mancha *f*; **s. remover** quitamanchas *m inv* (**b**) (*dye*) tinte *m*

2 *vt* (**a**) manchar (**b**) (*dye*) teñir

3 *vi* mancharse

stained [steɪnd] *adj* **s. glass window** vidriera *f* de colores

stainless ['steɪnlɪs] *adj* (*steel*) inoxidable

stair [steə(r)] *n* escalón *m*, peldaño *m*; **stairs** escalera *f*

staircase ['steəkeɪs] *n* escalera *f*

stake¹ [steɪk] **1** *n* (*stick*) estaca *f*; (*for plant*) rodrigón *m*; (*post*) poste *m*

2 *vt* **to s. (out)** cercar con estacas

stake² [steɪk] **1** *n* (**a**) (*bet*) apuesta *f*; **the issue at s.** el tema en cuestión; **to be at s.** (*at risk*) estar en juego (**b**) (*investment*) interés *m*

2 *vt* (*bet*) apostar; (*invest*) invertir; **to s. a claim to sth** reivindicar algo

stale [steɪl] *adj* (*food*) pasado(a); (*bread*) duro(a)

stalemate ['steɪlmeɪt] *n* (*in chess*) tablas *fpl*; *Fig* **to reach s.** llegar a un punto muerto

stalk¹ [stɔːk] *n* (*of plant*) tallo *m*; (*of fruit*) rabo *m*

stalk² [stɔːk] **1** *vt* (*of hunter*) cazar al acecho; (*of animal*) acechar

2 *vi* **he stalked out** salió airado

stall¹ [stɔːl] **1** *n* (**a**) (*in market*) puesto *m*; (*at fair*) caseta *f* (**b**) (*stable*) establo *m*; (*stable compartment*) casilla *f* de establo (**c**) *Br Th* **stalls** platea *f*

2 *vt Aut* calar

3 *vi Aut* calarse; *Av* perder velocidad

stall² [stɔːl] *vi* **to s. (for time)** intentar ganar tiempo

stallion ['stæljən] *n* semental *m*

stalwart ['stɔːlwət] *n* incondicional *mf*

stamina ['stæmɪnə] *n* resistencia *f*

stammer ['stæmə(r)] **1** *n* tartamudeo *m*

2 *vi* tartamudear

stamp [stæmp] **1** *n* (**a**) (*postage stamp*) sello *m*; **s. album** álbum *m* de sellos; **s. collector** filatelista *mf*; *Br* **s. duty** póliza *f* (**b**) (*rubber stamp*) tampón *m*; (*for metals*) cuño *m* (**c**) (*with foot*) patada *f*

2 *vt* (**a**) (*with postage stamp*) poner el sello a; *Br* **stamped addressed envelope,**

US **self-addressed stamped envelope** sobre franqueado con la dirección del remitente (**b**) *(with rubber stamp)* sellar (**c**) **to s. one's feet** patear; *(in dancing)* zapatear

3 *vi* patear

📖 Note that the Spanish word **estampa** is a false friend and is never a translation for the English word **stamp**. In Spanish, **estampa** means "print, image".

▸ **stamp out** *vt sep Fig (racism etc)* acabar con; *(rebellion)* sofocar

stampede [stæm'piːd] **1** *n* estampida *f*; *Fig (rush)* desbandada *f*

2 *vi* desbandarse; *Fig (rush)* precipitarse

stance [stæns] *n* postura *f*

stand [stænd] **1** *n* (**a**) *(position)* posición *f*, postura *f*; **to make a s.** resistir

(**b**) *(of lamp, sculpture)* pie *m*

(**c**) *(market stall)* puesto *m*; *(at fair)* caseta *f*; *(at exhibition)* stand *m*; **newspaper s.** quiosco *m*

(**d**) *(platform)* plataforma *f*; *(in stadium)* tribuna *f*, *US (witness box)* estrado *m*

2 *vt (pt & pp* **stood**) (**a**) *(place)* poner, colocar

(**b**) *(tolerate)* aguantar, soportar

(**c**) **to s. one's ground** mantenerse firme

3 *vi* (**a**) *(be upright)* estar de pie; *(get up)* levantarse; *(remain upright)* quedarse de pie; **s. still!** ¡estáte quieto(a)!

(**b**) *(measure)* medir

(**c**) *(be situated)* estar, encontrarse

(**d**) *(remain unchanged)* permanecer

(**e**) *(remain valid)* seguir vigente

(**f**) **as things s.** tal como están las cosas

(**g**) *Pol* presentarse

▸ **stand back** *vi (allow sb to pass)* abrir paso

▸ **stand by 1** *vi* (**a**) *(do nothing)* quedarse sin hacer nada (**b**) *(be ready)* estar listo(a)

2 *vt insep (person)* apoyar a; *(promise)* cumplir con; *(decision)* atenerse a

▸ **stand down** *vi Fig* retirarse

▸ **stand for** *vt insep* (**a**) *(mean)* significar (**b**) *(represent)* representar (**c**) *(tolerate)* aguantar

▸ **stand in** *vi* sustituir

▸ **stand in for** *vt insep* sustituir

▸ **stand out** *vi (mountain etc)* destacarse (**against** contra); *Fig (person)* destacar

▸ **stand up** *vi (get up)* ponerse de pie; *(be standing)* estar de pie; *Fig* **it will s. up to wear and tear** es muy resistente; *Fig* **to s. up for sb** defender a algn; *Fig* **to s. up to sb** hacer frente a algn

standard ['stændəd] **1** *n* (**a**) *(level)* nivel *m*; **s. of living** nivel de vida (**b**) *(criterion)* criterio *m* (**c**) *(norm)* norma *f*, estándar *m* (**d**) *(flag)* estandarte *m*

2 *adj* normal, estándar; **s. lamp** lámpara *f* de pie

standardize ['stændədaɪz] *vt* normalizar

standby ['stændbaɪ] *n* (**a**) *(thing)* recurso *m* (**b**) *(person)* suplente *mf*; **to be on s.** *Mil* estar de retén; *Av* estar en la lista de espera; **s. ticket** billete *m* sin reserva

stand-in ['stændɪn] *n* suplente *mf*; *Cin* doble *mf*

standing ['stændɪŋ] **1** *adj* (**a**) *(not sitting)* de pie; *(upright)* recto(a); **to give sb a s. ovation** ovacionar a algn de pie; **there was s. room only** no quedaban asientos (**b**) *(committee)* permanente; *(invitation)* permanente; *Br* **s. order** pago fijo

2 *n* (**a**) *(social position)* rango *m* (**b**) *(duration)* duración *f*; *(in job)* antigüedad *f*

stand-offish [stænd'ɒfɪʃ] *adj Fam* distante

standpoint ['stændpɔɪnt] *n* punto *m* de vista

standstill ['stændstɪl] *n* **at a s.** *(car, traffic)* parado(a); *(industry)* paralizado(a); **to come to a s.** *(car, traffic)* pararse; *(industry)* paralizarse

stand-up ['stændʌp] *adj* **s. comic** *or* **comedian** = humorista que basa su actuación en contar chistes al público solo desde el escenario

stank [stæŋk] *pt of* **stink**

staple¹ ['steɪpəl] **1** *n (fastener)* grapa *f*

2 *vt* grapar

staple² ['steɪpəl] **1** *adj (food)* básico(a); *(product)* de primera necesidad

2 *n (food)* alimento básico

stapler ['steɪplə(r)] *n* grapadora *f*

star [stɑː(r)] **1** *n* estrella *f*

2 *adj* estelar

3 *vt Cin* tener como protagonista a

4 *vi Cin* **to s. in a film** protagonizar una película

starboard ['stɑːbəd] *n* estribor *m*

starch [stɑːtʃ] **1** *n* almidón *m*

2 *vt* almidonar

stardom ['stɑːdəm] *n* estrellato *m*

stare [steə(r)] **1** *n* mirada fija

2 *vi* mirar fijamente

starfish ['stɑːfɪʃ] *n* estrella *f* de mar

stark [stɑːk] *adj (landscape)* desolado(a); *(décor)* austero(a); **the s. truth** la dura realidad; **s. poverty** la miseria

stark-naked ['stɑːkneɪkɪd] *adj Fam* en cueros

starling ['stɑ:lɪŋ] *n* estornino *m*

starry ['stɑ:rɪ] *adj* (**starrier, starriest**) estrellado(a)

starry-eyed [stɑ:'rɪ'aɪd] *adj* (*idealistic*) idealista; (*in love*) enamorado(a)

start [stɑ:t] **1** *n* (**a**) (*beginning*) principio *m*, comienzo *m*; (*of race*) salida *f*; **at the s.** al principio; **for a s.** para empezar; **from the s.** desde el principio; **to make a fresh s.** volver a empezar

(**b**) (*advantage*) ventaja *f*

(**c**) (*jump*) sobresalto *m*

2 *vt* (**a**) (*begin*) empezar, comenzar; **to s. doing sth** empezar a hacer algo

(**b**) (*cause*) causar, provocar

(**c**) (*found*) fundar; **to s. a business** montar un negocio

(**d**) (*set in motion*) arrancar

3 *vi* (**a**) (*begin*) empezar, comenzar; (*engine*) arrancar; **starting from Monday** a partir de lunes

(**b**) (*take fright*) asustarse, sobresaltarse

▸ **start off** *vi* (**a**) (*begin*) empezar, comenzar; **to s. off by/with** empezar por/con

(**b**) (*leave*) salir, ponerse en camino

▸ **start up 1** *vt sep* (*engine*) arrancar

2 *vi* empezar; (*car*) arrancar

starter ['stɑ:tə(r)] *n* (**a**) *Sport* (*official*) juez *mf* de salida; (*competitor*) competidor(a) *m,f* (**b**) *Aut* motor *m* de arranque (**c**) *Culin* entrada *f*

starting ['stɑ:tɪŋ] *n* **s. block** taco *m* de salida; **s. point** punto *m* de partida; **s. post** línea *f* de salida

startle ['stɑ:təl] *vt* asustar

startling ['stɑ:tlɪŋ] *adj* (**a**) (*frightening*) alarmante (**b**) (*news etc*) asombroso(a); (*coincidence*) extraordinario(a)

starvation [stɑ:'veɪʃən] *n* hambre *f*

starve [stɑ:v] **1** *vt* privar de comida; *Fig* **he was starved of affection** fue privado de cariño

2 *vi* pasar hambre; **to s. to death** morirse de hambre

starving ['stɑ:vɪŋ] *adj* hambriento(a); *Fam* **I'm s.!** ¡estoy muerto(a) de hambre!

state [steɪt] **1** *n* (**a**) estado *m*; **s. of emergency** estado de emergencia; **s. of mind** estado de ánimo; **to be in no fit s. to do sth** no estar en condiciones de hacer algo (**b**) **the States** los Estados Unidos; *US* **s. highway** ≃ carretera *f* nacional; *US* **the S. Department** el Ministerio de Asuntos Exteriores

2 *adj* (**a**) *Pol* estatal; **s. education** enseñanza pública; (**b**) (*ceremonial*) de gala; **s. visit** visita *f* oficial

3 *vt* declarar, afirmar; (*case*) exponer; (*problem*) plantear

stated ['steɪtɪd] *adj* indicado(a)

stately ['steɪtlɪ] *adj* (**statelier, stateliest**) majestuoso(a); **s. home** casa solariega

statement ['steɪtmənt] *n* (**a**) declaración *f*; **official s.** comunicado *m* oficial; *Jur* **to make a s.** prestar declaración (**b**) *Fin* estado *m* de cuenta; **monthly s.** balance *m* mensual

statesman ['steɪtsmən] *n* estadista *m*

static ['stætɪk] **1** *adj* estático(a)

2 *n Rad* ruido *m*

station ['steɪʃən] **1** *n* (**a**) estación *f*; *US* **s. wagon** camioneta *f* (**b**) (*position*) puesto *m* (**c**) (*social standing*) rango *m*

2 *vt* (*place*) colocar; *Mil* apostar

stationary ['steɪʃənərɪ] *adj* (*not moving*) inmóvil; (*unchanging*) estacionario(a)

stationer ['steɪʃənə(r)] *n* papelero(a) *m,f*; **s.'s (shop)** papelería *f*

stationery ['steɪʃənərɪ] *n* (*paper*) papel *m* de escribir; (*pens, ink etc*) artículos *mpl* de escritorio

stationmaster ['steɪʃənmɑ:stə(r)] *n* jefe *m* de estación

statistic [stə'tɪstɪk] *n* estadística *f*

statistical [stə'tɪstɪkəl] *adj* estadístico(a)

statistics [stə'tɪstɪks] **1** *n sing* (*science*) estadística *f*

2 *npl* (*data*) estadísticas *fpl*

statue ['stætju:] *n* estatua *f*

status ['steɪtəs] *n* estado *m*; **social s.** estatus *m*; **s. symbol** signo *m* de prestigio; **s. quo** status quo *m*

statute ['stætju:t] *n* estatuto *m*

statutory ['stætjʊtərɪ] *adj* reglamentario(a); (*offence*) contemplado(a) por la ley; (*right*) legal; (*holiday*) oficial

staunch [stɔ:ntʃ] *adj* incondicional, acérrimo

stave [steɪv] *n Mus* pentagrama *m*

▸ **stave off** *vt sep* (*repel*) rechazar; (*avoid*) evitar; (*delay*) aplazar

stay¹ [steɪ] **1** *n* estancia *f*

2 *vi* (**a**) (*remain*) quedarse, permanecer (**b**) (*reside temporarily*) alojarse; **she's staying with us for a few days** ha venido a pasar unos días con nosotros

3 *vt Fig* **to s. the course** aguantar hasta el final; **staying power** resistencia *f*

▸ **stay in** *vi* quedarse en casa

▸ **stay on** *vi* quedarse

▸ **stay out** *vi* **to s. out all night** no volver a casa en toda la noche

▸ **stay up** *vi* no acostarse

stay² [steɪ] *n* (*rope*) estay *m*, viento *m*

stead [sted] *n* **in sb's s.** en lugar de algn; **to**

stand sb in good s. resultar muy útil a algn

steadfast ['stedfəst, 'stedfɑ:st] *adj* firme

steadily ['stedɪlɪ] *adv* (*improve*) constantemente; (*walk*) con paso seguro; (*gaze*) fijamente; (*rain, work*) sin parar

steady ['stedɪ] **1** *adj* (**steadier, steadiest**) firme, seguro(a); (*gaze*) fijo(a); (*prices*) estable; (*demand, speed*) constante; (*pace*) regular; (*worker*) aplicado(a); **s. job** empleo fijo

2 *vt* (*table etc*) estabilizar; (*nerves*) calmar

3 *vi* (*market*) estabilizarse

steak [steɪk] *n* bistec *m*

steal [sti:l] (*pt* **stole**; *pp* **stolen**) **1** *vt* robar; **to s. a glance at sth** echar una mirada furtiva a algo; **to s. the show** llevarse todos los aplausos

2 *vi* (**a**) (*rob*) robar (**b**) (*move quietly*) moverse con sigilo; **to s. away** escabullirse

stealth [stelθ] *n* sigilo *m*

stealthily ['stelθɪlɪ] *adv* a hurtadillas

stealthy ['stelθɪ] *adj* (**stealthier, stealthiest**) sigiloso(a), furtivo(a)

steam [sti:m] **1** *n* vapor *m*; *Fam* **to let off s.** desahogarse; **s. engine** máquina *f* de vapor

2 *vt Culin* cocer al vapor

3 *vi* (*give off steam*) echar vapor; (*bowl of soup etc*) humear

► **steam up** *vi* (*window etc*) empañarse

steamer ['sti:mə(r)] *n Naut* vapor *m*

steamroller ['sti:mrəʊlə(r)] *n* apisonadora *f*

steamship ['sti:mʃɪp] *n* vapor *m*

steamy ['sti:mɪ] *adj* (**steamier, steamiest**) lleno(a) de vapor

steel [sti:l] **1** *n* acero *m*; **s. industry** industria siderúrgica

2 *vt Fig* **to s. oneself to do sth** armarse de valor para hacer algo

steelworks ['sti:lwɜːks] *npl* acería *f*

steep¹ [sti:p] *adj* (*hill etc*) empinado(a); *Fig* (*price, increase*) excesivo(a)

steep² [sti:p] *vt* (*washing*) remojar; (*food*) poner en remojo

steeple ['sti:pəl] *n* aguja *f*

steeplechase ['sti:pəltʃeɪs] *n* carrera *f* de obstáculos

steer [stɪə(r)] **1** *vt* dirigir; (*car*) conducir; (*ship*) gobernar

2 *vi* (*car*) conducirse; *Fig* **to s. clear of sth** evitar algo

steering ['stɪərɪŋ] *n* dirección *f*; **assisted s.** dirección asistida; **s. wheel** volante *m*

stem [stem] **1** *n* (**a**) (*of plant*) tallo *m*; (*of glass*) pie *m*; (*of pipe*) tubo *m* (**b**) (*of word*) raíz *f*

2 *vi* **to s. from** derivarse de

3 *vt* (*blood*) restañar; (*flood, attack*) contener

stench [stentʃ] *n* hedor *m*

stencil ['stensəl] *n* (**a**) (*for artwork etc*) plantilla *f* (**b**) (*for typing*) cliché *m*

step [step] **1** *n* (**a**) (*step*) paso *m*; (*sound*) pisada *f*; **s. by s.** poco a poco (**b**) (*measure*) medida *f*; **a s. in the right direction** un paso acertado (**c**) (*stair*) peldaño *m*, escalón *m* (**d**) **steps** escalera *f*

2 *vi* dar un paso; **s. this way, please** haga el favor de pasar por aquí; **to s. aside** apartarse

► **step down** *vi* dimitir

► **step forward** *vi* (*volunteer*) ofrecerse

► **step in** *vi* intervenir

► **step up** *vt sep* aumentar

stepbrother ['stepbrʌðə(r)] *n* hermanastro *m*

stepchild ['steptʃaɪld] *n* hijastro(a) *m,f*

stepdaughter ['stepdɔːtə(r)] *n* hijastra *f*

stepfather ['stepfɑːðə(r)] *n* padrastro *m*

stepladder ['steplædə(r)] *n* escalera *f* de tijera

stepmother ['stepmʌðə(r)] *n* madrastra *f*

stepping-stone ['stepɪŋstəʊn] *n* pasadera *f*; *Fig* trampolín *m*

stepsister ['stepsɪstə(r)] *n* hermanastra *f*

stepson ['stepsʌn] *n* hijastro *m*

stereo ['sterɪəʊ] **1** *n* estéreo *m*

2 *adj* estéreo(fónico)(a)

stereotype ['sterɪətaɪp] *n* estereotipo *m*

sterile ['steraɪl] *adj* (*barren*) estéril

sterilize ['sterɪlaɪz] *vt* esterilizar

sterling ['stɜːlɪŋ] **1** *n* libras *fpl* esterlinas; **s. silver** plata *f* de ley; **the pound s.** la libra esterlina

2 *adj* (*person, quality*) excelente

stern¹ [stɜːn] *adj* (*severe*) severo(a)

stern² [stɜːn] *n Naut* popa *f*

steroid ['sterɔɪd] *n* esteroide *m*

stethoscope ['steθəskəʊp] *n* estetoscopio *m*

stew [stju:] **1** *n* estofado *m*, cocido *m*

2 *vt* (*meat*) guisar, estofar; (*fruit*) cocer

steward ['stjʊəd] *n* (*on estate*) administrador *m*; (*on ship*) camarero *m*; (*on plane*) auxiliar *m* de vuelo

stewardess ['stjʊədɪs] *n* (*on ship*) camarera *f*; (*on plane*) azafata *f*

stick¹ [stɪk] *n* (**a**) palo *m*; (*walking stick*) bastón *m*; (*of dynamite*) cartucho *m*; *Fam* **to give sb s.** dar caña a algn (**b**) *Fam* **to live in the sticks** vivir en el quinto pino

stick² [stɪk] **1** *vt* (*pt & pp* **stuck**) (**a**) (*push*) meter; (*knife*) clavar; **he stuck his head out of the window** asomó la cabeza por la ventana (**b**) *Fam* (*put*) meter (**c**) (*with glue etc*) pegar (**d**) *Fam* (*tolerate*) soportar, aguantar

2 *vi* (**a**) (*become attached*) pegarse (**b**) (*window, drawer*) atrancarse; (*machine part*) encasquillarse

▸ **stick at** *vt insep* perseverar en

▸ **stick by** *vt insep* (*friend*) ser fiel a; (*promise*) cumplir con

▸ **stick out 1** *vi* (*project*) sobresalir; (*be noticeable*) resaltar

2 *vt sep* (*tongue*) sacar; *Fig* **to s. one's neck out** jugarse el tipo

▸ **stick to** *vt insep* (*principles*) atenerse a

▸ **stick up 1** *vi* (*project*) sobresalir; (*hair*) ponerse de punta

2 *vt sep* (**a**) (*poster*) fijar (**b**) (*hand etc*) levantar

▸ **stick up for** *vt insep* defender

sticker ['stɪkə(r)] *n* (*label*) etiqueta adhesiva; (*with slogan*) pegatina *f*

sticking-plaster ['stɪkɪŋ'plɑːstə(r)] *n Br* tirita® *f*, *Am* curita *f*

stickler ['stɪklə(r)] *n* meticuloso(a) *m,f*; **to be a s. for detail** ser muy detallista

stick-up ['stɪkʌp] *n US Fam* atraco *m*, asalto *m*

sticky ['stɪkɪ] *adj* (**stickier, stickiest**) pegajoso(a); (*label*) engomado(a); (*weather*) bochornoso(a); *Fam* (*situation*) difícil

stiff [stɪf] **1** *adj* (**a**) rígido(a), tieso(a); (*collar, lock*) duro(a); (*joint*) entumecido(a); (*machine part*) atascado(a); **to have a s. neck** tener tortícolis (**b**) *Fig* (*test*) difícil; (*punishment*) severo(a); (*price*) excesivo(a); (*drink*) fuerte; (*person*) (*unnatural*) estirado(a)

2 *n Fam* (*corpse*) fiambre *m*

stiffen ['stɪfən] **1** *vt* (*fabric*) reforzar; (*collar*) almidonar; *Fig* (*resistance*) fortalecer

2 *vi* (*person*) ponerse tieso(a); (*joints*) entumecerse; *Fig* (*resistance*) fortalecerse

stiffness ['stɪfnɪs] *n* rigidez *f*

stifle ['staɪfəl] **1** *vt* sofocar; (*yawn*) reprimir

2 *vi* ahogarse, sofocarse

stifling ['staɪflɪŋ] *adj* sofocante, agobiante

stigma ['stɪgmə] *n* estigma *m*

stile [staɪl] *n* = escalones para pasar por encima de una valla

stiletto [stɪ'letəʊ] *n* zapato *m* con tacón de aguja

still¹ [stɪl] **1** *adv* (**a**) (*up to this time*) todavía, aún

(**b**) (*with comp adj & adv*) (*even*) aún; **s. colder** aún más frío

(**c**) (*nonetheless*) no obstante, con todo

(**d**) (*however*) sin embargo

(**e**) (*motionless*) quieto; **to stand s.** no moverse

2 *adj* (*calm*) tranquilo(a); (*peaceful*) sosegado(a); (*silent*) silencioso(a); (*motionless*) inmóvil

3 *n Cin* fotograma *m*; *Art* **s. life** naturaleza muerta

4 *vt Fml* (*fears etc*) calmar

still² [stɪl] *n* (*apparatus*) alambique *m*

stillborn ['stɪlbɔːn] *adj* nacido(a) muerto(a)

stillness ['stɪlnɪs] *n* calma *f*; (*silence*) silencio *m*

stilt [stɪlt] *n* zanco *m*

stilted ['stɪltɪd] *adj* afectado(a)

stimulant ['stɪmjʊlənt] *n* estimulante *m*

stimulate ['stɪmjʊleɪt] *vt* estimular

stimulating ['stɪmjʊleɪtɪŋ] *adj* estimulante

stimulus ['stɪmjʊləs] *n* (*pl* **stimuli** ['stɪmjʊlaɪ]) estímulo *m*; *Fig* incentivo *m*

sting [stɪŋ] **1** *n* (*part of bee, wasp*) aguijón *m*; (*wound*) picadura *f*; (*burning*) escozor *m*; *Fig* (*of remorse*) punzada *f*; *Fig* (*of remark*) sarcasmo *m*

2 *vt* (*pt & pp* **stung**) picar; *Fig* (*conscience*) remorder; *Fig* (*remark*) herir en lo vivo

3 *vi* picar

stingy ['stɪndʒɪ] *adj* (**stingier, stingiest**) *Fam* (*person*) tacaño(a); (*amount*) escaso(a); **to be s. with** escatimar

stink [stɪŋk] **1** *n* peste *m*, hedor *m*

2 *vi* (*pt* **stank** *or* **stunk**; *pp* **stunk**) apestar, heder (**of** a)

stinking ['stɪŋkɪŋ] **1** *adj* (*smelly*) apestoso(a); *Fam* **to have a s. cold** tener un catarro bestial

2 *adv Fam* **he's s. rich** está podrido de dinero

stint [stɪnt] **1** *n* (*period*) período *m*, temporada *f*; (*shift*) turno *m*; **he did a two-year s. in the navy** sirvió durante dos años en la Marina

2 *vt* escatimar

stipulate ['stɪpjʊleɪt] *vt* estipular

stipulation [stɪpjʊ'leɪʃən] *n* estipulación *f*

stir [stɜː(r)] **1** *n Fig* revuelo *m*

2 *vt* (**a**) (*liquid*) remover (**b**) (*move*) agitar (**c**) *Fig* (*curiosity, interest*) despertar; (*anger*) provocar

3 *vi* (*move*) rebullirse

▸ **stir up** *vt sep Fig (memories, curiosity)* despertar; *(passions)* excitar; *(anger)* provocar; *(revolt)* fomentar

stirring ['stɜːrɪŋ] *adj* conmovedor(a)

stirrup ['stɪrəp] *n* estribo *m*

stitch [stɪtʃ] **1** *n* (a) *Sewing* puntada *f; (in knitting)* punto *m; Med* punto (de sutura); *Fam* **we were in stitches** nos tronchábamos de risa (b) *(pain)* punzada *f*
2 *vt Sewing* coser; *Med* suturar, dar puntos a

stoat [stəʊt] *n* armiño *m*

stock [stɒk] **1** *n* (a) *(supply)* reserva *f; Com (goods)* existencias *fpl*, stock *m; (selection)* surtido *m*; **out of s.** agotado(a); **to have sth in s.** tener existencias de algo; *Fig* **to take s. of** evaluar
(b) *Fin* capital *m* social; **stocks and shares** acciones *fpl*, valores *mpl*; **S. Exchange** Bolsa *f* (de valores); **s. market** bolsa
(c) *Agr* ganado *m*; **s. farming** ganadería *f*
(d) *Culin* caldo *m*; **s. cube** cubito *m* de caldo
(e) *(descent)* estirpe *f*
2 *adj* (a) *(goods)* corriente
(b) *(excuse, response)* de siempre; *(phrase)* gastado(a)
3 *vt* (a) *(have in stock)* tener existencias de
(b) *(provide)* abastecer, surtir (**with** de); *(cupboard)* llenar (**with** de)
▸ **stock up** *vi* abastecerse (**on** *or* **with** de)

stockbroker ['stɒkbrəʊkə(r)] *n* corredor(a) *m,f* de Bolsa

stockholder ['stɒkhəʊldə(r)] *n US* accionista *mf*

stocking ['stɒkɪŋ] *n* media *f*; **a pair of stockings** unas medias

stockist ['stɒkɪst] *n* distribuidor(a) *m,f*

stockpile ['stɒkpaɪl] **1** *n* reservas *fpl*
2 *vt* almacenar; *(accumulate)* acumular

stocks [stɒks] *npl Hist* cepo *m*

stocktaking ['stɒkteɪkɪŋ] *n Com* inventario *m*

stocky ['stɒkɪ] *adj* (**stockier, stockiest**) *(squat)* rechoncho(a); *(heavily built)* fornido(a)

stodgy ['stɒdʒɪ] *adj* (**stodgier, stodgiest**) *(food)* indigesto(a); *Fig (book, person)* pesado(a)

stoical ['stəʊɪkəl] *adj* estoico(a)

stoke [stəʊk] *vt (poke)* atizar; **to s. (up)** *(feed)* alimentar

stole¹ [stəʊl] *pt of* **steal**

stole² [stəʊl] *n* estola *f*

stolen ['stəʊlən] *pp of* **steal**

stolid ['stɒlɪd] *adj* impasible

stomach ['stʌmək] **1** *n* estómago *m*; **s. ache** dolor *m* de estómago; **s. upset** trastorno gástrico
2 *vt Fig* aguantar

stone [stəʊn] **1** *n* (a) *(piece)* piedra *f; (on grave)* lápida *f; Fig* **at a s.'s throw** a tiro de piedra
(b) *Med* cálculo *m* (c) *(of fruit)* hueso *m*
(d) *(weight)* = 6,348 kg
2 *adj* de piedra; **the S. Age** la Edad de Piedra
3 *vt (kill)* lapidar

stone-cold [stəʊn'kəʊld] *adj* helado(a)

stoned [stəʊnd] *adj Fam (drugged)* colocado(a); *(drunk)* como una cuba

stone-deaf [stəʊn'def] *adj* sordo(a) como una tapia

stonework ['stəʊnwɜːk] *n* mampostería *f*

stony ['stəʊnɪ] *adj* (**stonier, stoniest**) *(ground)* pedregoso(a); *Fig (look, silence)* glacial

stood [stʊd] *pt & pp of* **stand**

stool [stuːl] *n* (a) *(seat)* taburete *m* (b) *Med* heces *fpl*

stoop [stuːp] *vi* (a) *(have a stoop)* andar encorvado(a) (b) *(bend)* **to s. down** inclinarse, agacharse (c) *Fig* **to s. to** rebajarse a; **he wouldn't s. so low** no se rebajaría tanto

stop [stɒp] **1** *n* (a) *(halt)* parada *f*, alto *m*; **to come to a s.** pararse; **to put a s. to sth** poner fin a algo
(b) *(break)* pausa *f; (for refuelling etc)* escala *f*
(c) *(for bus, tram)* parada *f*
(d) *(punctuation mark)* punto *m*
2 *vt* (a) parar; *(conversation)* interrumpir; *(pain, abuse etc)* poner fin a
(b) *(payments)* suspender; *(cheque)* anular
(c) **to s. doing sth** dejar de hacer algo; **s. singing** deja de cantar; **s. it!** ¡basta ya!
(d) *(prevent)* evitar; **to s. sb from doing sth** impedir a algn hacer algo
(e) *(hole)* tapar; *(gap)* rellenar
3 *vi* (a) *(person, moving vehicle)* pararse, detenerse; **my watch has stopped** se me ha parado el reloj; **to s. dead** pararse en seco
(b) *(cease)* acabarse, terminar
(c) *Fam (stay)* pararse
▸ **stop by** *vi Fam* visitar
▸ **stop off** *vi* pararse un rato
▸ **stop over** *vi (spend the night)* pasar la noche; *(for refuelling etc)* hacer escala
▸ **stop up** *vt sep (hole)* tapar

stopgap ['stɒpgæp] *n (thing)* medida *f* provisional; *(person)* sustituto(a) *m,f*

stopover ['stɒpəʊvə(r)] *n* parada *f*; *Av* escala *f*

stoppage ['stɒpɪdʒ] *n* (a) *(of game, payments)* suspensión *f*; *(of work)* paro *m*; *(strike)* huelga *f*, *(deduction)* deducción *f* (b) *(blockage)* obstrucción *f*

stopper ['stɒpə(r)] *n* tapón *m*

stop-press [stɒp'pres] *n* noticias *fpl* de última hora

stopwatch ['stɒpwɒtʃ] *n* cronómetro *m*

storage ['stɔːrɪdʒ] *n* almacenaje *m*, almacenamiento *m*; **s. battery** acumulador *m*; **s. heater** placa acumuladora

store [stɔː(r)] **1** *n* (a) *(stock)* provisión *f*, *Fig (of wisdom)* reserva *f* (b) **stores** víveres *mpl* (c) *(warehouse)* almacén *m* (d) *esp US (shop)* tienda *f*; **department s.** gran almacén *m*
  2 *vt* (a) *(furniture, computer data)* almacenar, *(keep)* guardar (b) **to s. (up)** acumular

storekeeper ['stɔːkiːpə(r)] *n US* tendero(a) *m,f*

storeroom ['stɔːruːm] *n* despensa *f*

storey ['stɔːrɪ] *n* piso *m*

stork [stɔːk] *n* cigüeña *f*

storm [stɔːm] **1** *n* tormenta *f*, *(with wind)* vendaval *m*; *Fig (uproar)* revuelo *m*; *Fig* **she has taken New York by s.** ha cautivado a todo Nueva York
  2 *vt* tomar por asalto
  3 *vi (with rage)* echar pestes

stormy ['stɔːmɪ] *adj* (**stormier, stormiest**) *(weather)* tormentoso(a); *Fig (discussion)* acalorado(a); *(relationship)* tempestuoso(a)

story¹ ['stɔːrɪ] *n* historia *f*, *(tale, account)* relato *m*; *(article)* artículo *m*; *(plot)* trama *f*, *(joke)* chiste *m*; *(rumour)* rumor *m*; **it's a long s.** sería largo de contar; **tall s.** cuento chino

story² ['stɔːrɪ] *n US* = **storey**

storybook ['stɔːrɪbʊk] *n* libro *m* de cuentos

storyteller ['stɔːrɪtelə(r)] *n* cuentista *mf*

stout [staʊt] **1** *adj* (a) *(fat)* gordo(a), corpulento(a) (b) *(strong)* fuerte (c) *(brave)* valiente; *(determined)* firme
  2 *n (beer)* cerveza negra

stoutly ['staʊtlɪ] *adv* resueltamente

stove [stəʊv] *n* (a) *(for heating)* estufa *f* (b) *(cooker)* cocina *f*

stow [stəʊ] *vt* (a) *(cargo)* estibar (b) *(put away)* guardar
  ▸ **stow away** *vi (on ship, plane)* viajar de polizón

stowaway ['stəʊəweɪ] *n* polizón *mf*

straddle ['strædəl] *vt* (a) *(horse etc)* sentarse a horcajadas sobre (b) *Fig (embrace)* abarcar

straggle ['strægəl] *vi* (a) *(lag behind)* rezagarse (b) *(spread untidily)* desparramarse

straggler ['stræglə(r)] *n* rezagado(a) *m,f*

straight [streɪt] **1** *adj* (a) *(not bent)* recto(a), derecho(a); *(hair)* liso(a); **to keep a s. face** contener la risa
  (b) **I work eight hours s.** trabajo ocho horas seguidas
  (c) *(honest)* honrado(a); *(answer)* sincero(a); *(refusal)* rotundo(a); **let's get things s.** pongamos las cosas claras
  (d) *(drink)* solo(a), sin mezcla
  2 *adv* (a) *(in a straight line)* en línea recta
  (b) *(directly)* directamente, derecho; **keep s. ahead** sigue todo recto; **she walked s. in** entró sin llamar
  (c) **s. away** en seguida; **s. off** en el acto
  (d) *(frankly)* francamente
  3 *n Br Sport* **the home s.** la recta final

straighten ['streɪtən] *vt (sth bent)* enderezar, poner derecho(a); *(tie, picture)* poner bien; *(hair)* alisar
  ▸ **straighten out** *vt sep (problem)* resolver

straight-faced ['streɪt'feɪst] *adj* con la cara seria

straightforward [streɪt'fɔːwəd] *adj* (a) *(honest)* honrado(a); *(sincere)* franco(a) (b) *Br (simple)* sencillo(a)

strain¹ [streɪn] **1** *vt* (a) *(rope etc)* estirar; *Fig* crear tensiones en (b) *Med* torcer(se); *(eyes, voice)* forzar; *(heart)* cansar (c) *(liquid)* filtrar; *(vegetables, tea)* colar
  2 *vi (pull)* tirar (**at** de); *Fig* **to s. to do sth** esforzarse por hacer algo
  3 *n* (a) *(tension)* tensión *f*, *(effort)* esfuerzo *m* (b) *(exhaustion)* agotamiento *m* (c) *Med* torcedura *f* (d) *Mus* **strains** son *m*

strain² [streɪn] *n* (a) *(breed)* raza *f* (b) *(streak)* vena *f*

strained ['streɪnd] *adj* (a) *(muscle)* torcido(a); *(eyes)* cansado(a); *(voice)* forzado(a) (b) *(atmosphere)* tenso(a)

strainer ['streɪnə(r)] *n* colador *m*

strait [streɪt] *n* (a) *Geog* estrecho *m* (b) *(usu pl) (difficulty)* aprieto *m*; **in dire straits** en un gran aprieto

straitjacket ['streɪtdʒækɪt] *n* camisa *f* de fuerza

strait-laced [streɪt'leɪst] *adj* remilgado(a)

strand¹ [strænd] *vt Fig (person)* abandonar; **to leave stranded** dejar plantado(a)

strand² [strænd] *n (of thread)* hebra *f*, *(of hair)* pelo *m*

strange ['streɪndʒ] *adj* (**a**) *(unknown)* desconocido(a); *(unfamiliar)* nuevo(a) (**b**) *(odd)* raro(a), extraño(a)

stranger ['streɪndʒə(r)] *n (unknown person)* desconocido(a) *m,f*; *(outsider)* forastero(a) *m,f*

strangle ['stræŋgəl] *vt* estrangular

stranglehold ['stræŋgəlhəʊld] *n* **to have a s. on sb** tener a algn agarrado(a) por el cuello

strangulation [stræŋgjʊ'leɪʃən] *n* estrangulación *f*

strap [stræp] **1** *n (of leather)* correa *f*; *(on bag)* bandolera *f*; *(on dress)* tirante *m*
  2 *vt* atar con correa

strapping ['stræpɪŋ] *adj Fam* fornido(a), robusto(a)

strata ['strɑːtə] *pl of* **stratum**

strategic [strə'tiːdʒɪk] *adj* estratégico(a)

strategy ['strætɪdʒɪ] *n* estrategia *f*

stratosphere ['strætəsfɪə(r)] *n* estratosfera *f*

stratum ['strɑːtəm] *n (pl* **strata***)* estrato *m*

straw [strɔː] *n* (**a**) paja *f*, *Fig* **to clutch at straws** agarrarse a un clavo ardiente; *Fam* **that's the last s.!** ¡eso ya es el colmo! (**b**) *(for drinking)* pajita *f*

strawberry ['strɔːbərɪ] *n* fresa *f*, *Bol, CSur, Ecuad* frutilla *f*; *(large)* fresón *m*

stray [streɪ] **1** *vi (from path)* desviarse; *(get lost)* extraviarse
  2 *n* animal extraviado
  3 *adj (bullet)* perdido(a); *(animal)* callejero(a)

streak [striːk] **1** *n* (**a**) *(line)* raya *f*; **s. of lightning** rayo *m* (**b**) *(in hair)* reflejo *m* (**c**) *Fig (of genius etc)* vena *f*, *Fig (of luck)* racha *f*
  2 *vt* rayar (**with** de)
  3 *vi* **to s. past** pasar como un rayo

stream [striːm] **1** *n* (**a**) *(brook)* arroyo *m*, riachuelo *m* (**b**) *(current)* corriente *f* (**c**) *(of water, air)* flujo *m*; *(of tears)* torrente *m*; *(of blood)* chorro *m*; *(of light)* raudal *m* (**d**) *Fig (of abuse)* sarta *f*; *(of people)* oleada *f* (**e**) *Br Educ* clase *f*
  2 *vt Br Educ* poner en grupos
  3 *vi* (**a**) *(liquid)* correr (**b**) *Fig* **to s. in/ out/past** *(people etc)* entrar/salir/pasar en tropel (**c**) *(hair, banner)* ondear

streamer ['striːmə(r)] *n (paper ribbon)* serpentina *f*

streamlined ['striːmlaɪnd] *adj* (**a**) *(car)* aerodinámico(a) (**b**) *(system, method)* racionalizado(a)

street [striːt] *n* calle *f*; **the man in the s.** el hombre de la calle; **s. map, s. plan** (plano *m*) callejero *m*

streetcar ['striːtkɑː(r)] *n US* tranvía *m*

streetlamp ['striːtlæmp] *n* farol *m*

streetwise ['striːtwaɪz] *adj* espabilado(a)

strength [streŋθ] *n* (**a**) fuerza *f*; *(of rope etc)* resistencia *f*; *(of emotion, colour)* intensidad *f*; *(of alcohol)* graduación *f* (**b**) *(power)* poder *m*; **on the s. of** a base de (**c**) *(ability)* punto *m* fuerte (**d**) **to be at full s./below s.** tener/no tener completo el cupo

strengthen ['streŋθən] **1** *vt* (**a**) reforzar; *(character)* fortalecer (**b**) *(intensify)* intensificar
  2 *vi* (**a**) *(gen)* reforzarse (**b**) *(intensify)* intensificarse

strenuous ['strenjʊəs] *adj* (**a**) *(denial)* enérgico(a); *(effort, life)* intenso(a) (**b**) *(exhausting)* fatigoso(a), cansado(a)

stress [stres] **1** *n* (**a**) *Tech* tensión *f* (**b**) *Med* estrés *m* (**c**) *(emphasis)* hincapié *m*; *(on word)* acento *m*
  2 *vt (emphasize)* subrayar; *(word)* acentuar

stretch [stretʃ] **1** *vt (elastic)* estirar; *(wings)* desplegar
  2 *vi (elastic)* estirarse; *Fig* **my money won't s. to it** mi dinero no me llegará para eso
  3 *n* (**a**) *(length)* trecho *m*, tramo *m* (**b**) *(of land)* extensión *f*; *(of time)* intervalo *m*

  ✎ Note that the Spanish verb **estrechar** is a false friend and is never a translation for the English verb **to stretch**. In Spanish, **estrechar** means "to make narrow, to tighten".

▸ **stretch out 1** *vt sep (arm, hand)* alargar; *(legs)* estirar
  2 *vi* (**a**) *(person)* estirarse (**b**) *(countryside, years etc)* extenderse

stretcher ['stretʃə(r)] *n* camilla *f*

strew [struː] *vt (pt* **strewed**; *pp* **strewed** *or* **strewn** [struːn]*)* esparcir

stricken ['strɪkən] *adj (with grief)* afligido(a); *(with illness)* aquejado(a); *(by disaster etc)* afectado(a); *(damaged)* dañado(a)

strict [strɪkt] *adj* (**a**) estricto(a) (**b**) *(absolute)* absoluto(a)

strictly ['strɪktlɪ] *adv* (**a**) *(categorically)* terminantemente (**b**) *(precisely)* estrictamente; **s. speaking** en sentido estricto

stride [straɪd] **1** *n* zancada *f*, tranco *m*; *Fig (progress)* progresos *mpl*
  2 *vi (pt* **strode**; *pp* **stridden** ['strɪdən]*)* **to s. (along)** andar a zancadas

strident ['straɪdənt] *adj (voice, sound)*

estridente; *(protest etc)* enérgico(a)
strife [straɪf] *n* conflictos *mpl*
strike [straɪk] **1** *vt (pt & pp struck)* **(a)** *(hit)* pegar, golpear
  (b) *(collide with)* chocar contra; *(of bullet, lightning)* alcanzar
  (c) *(match)* encender
  (d) *(pose)* adoptar
  (e) *(bargain)* cerrar; *(balance)* encontrar
  (f) the clock struck three el reloj dio las tres
  (g) *(oil, gold)* descubrir; *Fam* **to s. it lucky/rich** tener suerte/hacerse rico(a)
  (h) *(impress)* impresionar; **it strikes me … me parece …**
  2 *vi* **(a)** *(attack)* atacar; *(disaster)* sobrevenir
  (b) *(clock)* dar la hora
  (c) *(workers)* declararse en huelga
  3 *n* **(a)** *(by workers)* huelga *f*; **on s.** en huelga; **to call a s.** convocar una huelga
  (b) *(of oil, gold)* descubrimiento *m*
  (c) *(blow)* golpe *m*
  (d) *Mil* ataque *m*
  ▸ **strike back** *vi* devolver el golpe
  ▸ **strike down** *vt sep* fulminar, abatir
  ▸ **strike out** *vt sep (cross out)* tachar
  2 *vi* **to s. out at sb** arremeter contra algn
  ▸ **strike up** *vt insep* **(a)** *(friendship)* trabar; *(conversation)* entablar **(b)** *(tune)* empezar a tocar
striker ['straɪkə(r)] *n* **(a)** *(worker)* huelguista *mf* **(b)** *Fam Ftb* marcador(a) *m,f*
striking ['straɪkɪŋ] *adj (eye-catching)* llamativo(a); *(noticeable)* notable; *(impressive)* impresionante
string [strɪŋ] **1** *n* **(a)** *(cord)* cuerda *f*; *Fig* **to pull strings for sb** enchufar a algn; **s. bean** judía *f* verde, *Bol, RP* chaucha *f*, *CAm* ejote *m*, *Col, Cuba* habichuela *f*, *Chile* poroto *m* verde, *Ven* vainita *f* **(b)** *(of events)* cadena *f*; *(of lies)* sarta *f* **(c)** *(of racket, guitar)* cuerda *f*; *Mus* **the strings** los instrumentos de cuerda
  2 *vt (pt & pp strung)* **(a)** *(beads)* ensartar **(b)** *(racket etc)* encordar **(c)** *(beans)* quitar la hebra a
stringent ['strɪndʒənt] *adj* severo(a), estricto(a)
strip¹ [strɪp] **1** *vt* **(a)** *(person)* desnudar; *(bed)* quitar la ropa de; *(paint)* quitar **(b)** *Tech* **to s. (down)** desmontar
  2 *vi (undress)* desnudarse; *(perform striptease)* hacer un striptease
  ▸ **strip off** *vt sep* quitar
  2 *vi (undress)* desnudarse
strip² [strɪp] *n* tira *f*; *(of land)* franja *f*; *(of*

metal) fleje *m*; **s. cartoon** historieta *f*; **s. lighting** alumbrado *m* fluorescente; **to tear sb off a s.** echar una bronca a algn
stripe [straɪp] *n* raya *f*; *Mil* galón *m*
striped [straɪpt] *adj* rayado(a), a rayas
stripper ['strɪpə(r)] *n* artista *mf* de striptease
strive [straɪv] *vi (pt strove; pp striven* ['strɪvən]*)* **to s. to do sth** esforzarse por hacer algo
strobe [strəʊb] *n* **s. lighting** luces estroboscópicas
strode [strəʊd] *pt of* **stride**
stroke [strəʊk] **1** *n* **(a) a s. of luck** un golpe de suerte **(b)** *(in golf, cricket)* golpe *m*; *(in rowing)* remada *f*; *(in swimming)* brazada *f* **(c)** *(of pen)* trazo *m*; *(of brush)* pincelada *f* **(d)** *(caress)* caricia *f* **(e)** *Med* apoplejía *f*
  2 *vt* acariciar
stroll [strəʊl] **1** *vi* dar un paseo
  2 *n* paseo *m*
stroller ['strəʊlə(r)] *n US (for baby)* cochecito *m*
strong [strɒŋ] **1** *adj* **(a)** *(durable)* sólido(a) **(c)** *(firm, resolute)* firme **(d)** *(colour)* intenso(a); *(light)* brillante **(e)** *(incontestable)* convincente **(f) to be twenty s.** contar con veinte miembros
  2 *adv* fuerte; **to be going s.** *(business)* ir fuerte; *(elderly person)* conservarse bien
strongbox ['strɒŋbɒks] *n* caja *f* fuerte
stronghold ['strɒŋhəʊld] *n Mil* fortaleza *f*; *Fig* baluarte *m*
strongly ['strɒŋlɪ] *adv* fuertemente
strongroom ['strɒŋruːm] *n* cámara acorazada
stroppy ['strɒpɪ] *adj (stroppier, stroppiest) Br Fam* de mala uva
strove [strəʊv] *pt of* **strive**
struck [strʌk] *pt & pp of* **strike**
structural ['strʌktʃərəl] *adj* estructural
structure ['strʌktʃə(r)] *n* estructura *f*; *(constructed thing)* construcción *f*; *(building)* edificio *m*
struggle ['strʌgəl] **1** *vi* luchar
  2 *n* lucha *f*; *(physical fight)* pelea *f*
strum [strʌm] *vt (guitar)* rasguear
strung [strʌŋ] *pt & pp of* **string**
strut [strʌt] *vi* pavonearse
stub [stʌb] **1** *n (of cigarette)* colilla *f*; *(of pencil)* cabo *m*; *(of cheque)* matriz *f*
  2 *vt* **(a)** *(strike)* golpear **(b) to s. (out)** apagar
stubble ['stʌbəl] *n (in field)* rastrojo *m*; *(on chin)* barba *f* de tres días
stubborn ['stʌbən] *adj* **(a)** terco(a),

testarudo(a) (**b**) *(stain)* difícil (**c**) *(refusal)* rotundo(a)

stucco ['stʌkəʊ] *n* estuco *m*

stuck [stʌk] *pt & pp of* **stick**

stuck-up [stʌk'ʌp] *adj Fam* creído(a)

stud¹ [stʌd] **1** *n* (on clothing) tachón *m*; *(on football boots)* taco *m*; *(on shirt)* botonadura *f*

  2 *vt (decorate)* tachonar (**with** de); *Fig (dot, cover)* salpicar (**with** de)

stud² [stʌd] *n (horse)* semental *m*

student ['stju:dənt] *n* estudiante *mf*; **s. teacher** profesor(a) *m,f* en prácticas

studio ['stju:dɪəʊ] *n TV & Cin* estudio *m*; *(artist's)* taller *m*; **s. (apartment** *or Br* **flat)** estudio

studious ['stju:dɪəs] *adj* estudioso(a)

studiously ['stju:dɪəslɪ] *adv* cuidadosamente

study ['stʌdɪ] **1** *vt* estudiar; *(facts etc)* examinar, investigar; *(behaviour)* observar

  2 *vi* estudiar; **to s. to be a doctor** estudiar para médico

  3 *n* (**a**) estudio *m*; **s. group** grupo *m* de trabajo (**b**) *(room)* despacho *m*, estudio *m*

stuff [stʌf] **1** *vt* (**a**) *(container)* llenar (**with** de); *Culin* rellenar (**with** con *or* de); *(animal)* disecar (**b**) *(cram)* atiborrar (**with** de)

  2 *n Fam* (**a**) *(substance)* cosa *f* (**b**) *(things)* cosas *fpl*

stuffing ['stʌfɪŋ] *n Culin* relleno *m*

stuffy ['stʌfɪ] *adj* (**stuffier, stuffiest**) (**a**) *(room)* mal ventilado(a); *(atmosphere)* cargado(a) (**b**) *(pompous)* estirado(a); *(narrow-minded)* de miras estrechas

stumble ['stʌmbəl] *vi* tropezar, dar un traspié; *Fig* **to s. across** *or* **on** *or* **upon** tropezar *or* dar con

stumbling ['stʌmblɪŋ] *n* **s. block** escollo *m*

stump [stʌmp] **1** *n* (**a**) *(of pencil)* cabo *m*; *(of tree)* tocón *m*; *(of arm, leg)* muñón *m* (**b**) *(in cricket)* estaca *f*

  2 *vt (puzzle)* confundir; **to be stumped** estar perplejo(a)

stun [stʌn] *vt (of blow)* aturdir; *Fig (of news etc)* sorprender

stung [stʌŋ] *pt & pp of* **sting**

stunk [stʌŋk] *pt & pp of* **stink**

stunning ['stʌnɪŋ] *adj (blow)* duro(a); *(news)* sorprendente; *Fam (woman, outfit)* fenomenal

stunt¹ [stʌnt] *vt (growth)* atrofiar

stunt² [stʌnt] *n* (**a**) *Av* acrobacia *f* (**b**) **publicity s.** truco publicitario (**c**) *Cin*

escena peligrosa; **s. man** doble *m*

stunted ['stʌntɪd] *adj* enano(a), mal desarrollado(a)

stupefy ['stju:pɪfaɪ] *vt (alcohol, drugs)* aturdir; *Fig (news etc)* dejar pasmado(a)

stupendous [stju:'pendəs] *adj (wonderful)* estupendo(a)

stupid ['stju:pɪd] *adj* estúpido(a), imbécil

stupidity [stju:'pɪdɪtɪ] *n* estupidez *f*

stupor ['stju:pə(r)] *n* estupor *m*

sturdy ['stɜ:dɪ] *adj* (**sturdier, sturdiest**) robusto(a), fuerte; *(resistance)* enérgico(a)

stutter ['stʌtə(r)] **1** *vi* tartamudear

  2 *n* tartamudeo *m*

sty [staɪ] *n (pen)* pocilga *f*

sty(e) [staɪ] *n Med* orzuelo *m*

style [staɪl] **1** *n* (**a**) *(manner)* estilo *m*; *(of dress)* modelo *m* (**b**) *(fashion)* moda *f* (**c**) **to live in s.** *(elegance)* vivir a lo grande

  2 *vt (hair)* marcar

stylish ['staɪlɪʃ] *adj* con estilo

stylist ['staɪlɪst] *n (hairdresser)* peluquero(a) *mf*

stylus ['staɪləs] *n (of record player)* aguja *f*

suave [swɑ:v] *adj* amable, afable; *Pej* zalamero(a)

> ✏ Note that the Spanish word **suave** is a false friend and is never a translation for the English word **suave**. In Spanish, **suave** means both "smooth" and "soft".

sub- [sʌb] *n Fam* (**a**) *(to magazine)* suscripción *f*; *(to club)* cuota *f* (**b**) *(substitute)* suplente *mf*

sub- [sʌb] *pref* sub-

subconscious [sʌb'kɒnʃəs] **1** *adj* subconsciente

  2 *n* **the s.** el subconsciente

subcontract [sʌbkən'trækt] *vt* subcontratar

subcontractor [sʌbkən'træktə(r)] *n* subcontratista *mf*

subdivide [sʌbdɪ'vaɪd] *vt* subdividir (**into** en)

subdue [səb'dju:] *vt* (**a**) *(nation, people)* sojuzgar (**b**) *(feelings)* dominar (**c**) *(colour, light)* atenuar

subdued [səb'dju:d] *adj* (**a**) *(person, emotion)* callado(a) (**b**) *(voice, tone)* bajo(a) (**c**) *(light)* tenue; *(colour)* apagado(a)

subject 1 *n* (**a**) *(citizen)* súbdito *m* (**b**) *(topic)* tema *m*; **s. matter** materia *f*; *(contents)* contenido *m* (**c**) *Educ* asignatura *f* (**d**) *Ling* sujeto *m*

  2 *adj* **s. to** *(law, tax)* sujeto(a) a; *(charge)*

expuesto(a) a; *(changes, delays)* susceptible de; *(illness)* propenso(a) a; *(conditional upon)* previo(a)
  3 *vt* [səb'dʒekt] someter
subjective [səb'dʒektɪv] *adj* subjetivo(a)
subjunctive [səb'dʒʌŋktɪv] **1** *adj* subjun-
tivo(a)
  2 *n* subjuntivo *m*
sublet [sʌb'let] *vt & vi* subarrendar
sublime [sə'blaɪm] *adj* sublime
submachine-gun [sʌbmə'ʃiːngʌn] *n*
metralleta *f*
submarine ['sʌbməriːn] *n* submarino *m*
submerge [səb'mɜːdʒ] *vt* sumergir;
(flood) inundar; *Fig* **submerged in ...**
sumido(a) en ...
submission [səb'mɪʃən] *n* **(a)** *(yielding)*
sumisión *f* **(b)** *(of documents)* presentación *f* **(c)** *(report)* informe *m*
submissive [səb'mɪsɪv] *adj* sumiso(a)
submit [səb'mɪt] **1** *vt* **(a)** *(present)* presentar **(b)** *(subject)* someter **(to** a**)**
  2 *vi (surrender)* rendirse
subnormal [sʌb'nɔːməl] *adj* subnormal
subordinate [sə'bɔːdɪnɪt] *adj & n* subor-
dinado(a) *(m,f)*
subpoena [səb'piːnə] *Jur* **1** *n* citación *f*
  2 *vt* citar
subscribe [səb'skraɪb] *vi (magazine)*
suscribirse **(to** a**)**; *(opinion, theory)* adherirse **(to** a**)**
subscriber [səb'skraɪbə(r)] *n* abona-
do(a) *m,f*
subscription [səb'skrɪpʃən] *n (to magazine)* suscripción *f*; *(to club)* cuota *f*
subsequent ['sʌbsɪkwənt] *adj* subsi-
guiente
subsequently ['sʌbsɪkwəntlɪ] *adv* posteriormente
subside [səb'saɪd] *vi (land)* hundirse;
(floodwater) bajar; *(wind, anger)* amainar
subsidence [səb'saɪdəns] *n (of land)*
hundimiento *m*; *(of floodwater)* bajada *f*;
(of wind) amaine *m*
subsidiary [sʌb'sɪdɪərɪ] **1** *adj (role)* se-
cundario(a)
  2 *n Com* sucursal *f*, filial *f*
subsidize ['sʌbsɪdaɪz] *vt* subvencionar
subsidy ['sʌbsɪdɪ] *n* subvención *f*
subsistence [səb'sɪstəns] *n* subsistencia
f
substance ['sʌbstəns] *n* **(a)** sustancia *f*
(b) *(essence)* esencia *f* **(c) a woman of s.**
(wealth) una mujer acaudalada
substantial [səb'stænʃəl] *adj* **(a)** *(solid)*
sólido(a) **(b)** *(sum, loss)* importante; *(difference, improvement)* notable; *(meal)*
abundante

substantiate [səb'stænʃɪeɪt] *vt* respaldar
substitute ['sʌbstɪtjuːt] **1** *vt* sustituir; **to
s. X for Y** sustituir X por Y
  2 *n (person)* suplente *mf*; *(thing)* sucedáneo *m*
subtitle ['sʌbtaɪtəl] *n* subtítulo *m*
subtle ['sʌtəl] *adj* sutil; *(taste)* delica-
do(a); *(remark)* ingenioso(a); *(irony)* fi-
no(a)
subtlety ['sʌtəltɪ] *n* sutileza *f*; *(of remark)*
ingeniosidad *f*; *(of irony, joke)* finura *f*
subtract [səb'trækt] *vt* restar
subtraction [səb'trækʃən] *n* resta *f*
suburb ['sʌbɜːb] *n* barrio periférico; **the
suburbs** las afueras
suburban [sə'bɜːbən] *adj* suburbano(a)
suburbia [sə'bɜːbɪə] *n* barrios residen-
ciales periféricos
subversive [səb'vɜːsɪv] *adj & n* subversi-
vo(a) *(m,f)*
subway ['sʌbweɪ] *n* **(a)** *Br (underpass)*
paso subterráneo **(b)** *US (underground
railway)* metro *m*
succeed [sək'siːd] **1** *vi* **(a)** *(person)* tener
éxito; *(plan)* salir bien; **to s. in doing sth**
conseguir hacer algo **(b)** *(follow after)*
suceder; **to s. to** *(throne)* suceder a
  2 *vt (monarch)* suceder a
succeeding [sək'siːdɪŋ] *adj* sucesivo(a)
success [sək'ses] *n* éxito *m*

> 🖉 Note that the Spanish word **suceso** is a
> false friend and is never a translation for the
> English word **success**. In Spanish, **suceso**
> means both "event" and "incident".

successful [sək'sesfʊl] *adj* de éxito, exi-
toso(a); *(business)* próspero(a); *(marriage)* feliz; **to be s. in doing sth** lograr
hacer algo
successfully [sək'sesfʊlɪ] *adv* con éxito
succession [sək'seʃən] *n* sucesión *f*, serie *f*; **in s.** sucesivamente
successive [sək'sesɪv] *adj* sucesivo(a),
consecutivo(a)
successor [sək'sesə(r)] *n* sucesor(a) *m,f*
succinct [sək'sɪŋkt] *adj* sucinto(a)
succumb [sə'kʌm] *vi* sucumbir **(to** a**)**
such [sʌtʃ] **1** *adj* **(a)** *(of that sort)* tal,
semejante; **artists s. as Monet** artistas
como Monet; **at s. and s. a time** a tal hora;
in s. a way that de tal manera que **(b)** *(so
much, so great)* tanto(a); **he's always in s.
a hurry** siempre anda con tanta prisa;
she was in s. pain sufría tanto
  2 *adv (so very)* tan; **it's s. a long time ago**
hace tanto tiempo; **she's s. a clever wo-
man** es una mujer tan inteligente; **s. a lot
of books** tantos libros; **we had s. good**

weather hizo un tiempo tan bueno
suchlike ['sʌtʃlaɪk] **1** *adj* tal
  2 *pron (things)* cosas *fpl* por el estilo; *(people)* gente *f* por el estilo
suck [sʌk] **1** *vt (by pump)* aspirar; *(liquid)* sorber; *(lollipop, blood)* chupar
  2 *vi (person)* chupar; *(baby)* mamar
  ▸ **suck in** *vt sep (of whirlpool)* tragar
sucker ['sʌkə(r)] *n* **(a)** *Fam* primo(a) *m,f*, bobo(a) *m,f* **(b)** *Zool* ventosa *f*; *Bot* chupón *m*
suckle ['sʌkəl] *vt (mother)* amamantar
suction ['sʌkʃən] *n* succión *f*
sudden ['sʌdən] *adj* **(a)** *(hurried)* súbito(a), repentino(a) **(b)** *(unexpected)* imprevisto(a) **(c)** *(abrupt)* brusco(a); **all of a s.** de repente
suddenly ['sʌdənlɪ] *adv* de repente
suds [sʌdz] *npl* espuma *f* de jabón, jabonaduras *fpl*
sue [su:, sju:] *Jur* **1** *vt* demandar
  2 *vi* presentar una demanda; **to s. for divorce** solicitar el divorcio
suede [sweɪd] *n* ante *m*, gamuza *f*; *(for gloves)* cabritilla *f*
suet ['su:ɪt] *n* sebo *m*
suffer ['sʌfə(r)] **1** *vt* **(a)** sufrir **(b)** *(tolerate)* aguantar, soportar
  2 *vi* sufrir; **to s. from** sufrir de
sufferer ['sʌfərə(r)] *n Med* enfermo(a) *m,f*
suffering ['sʌfərɪŋ] *n (affliction)* sufrimiento *m*; *(pain, torment)* dolor *m*
suffice [sə'faɪs] *vi Fml* bastar, ser suficiente
sufficient [sə'fɪʃənt] *adj* suficiente, bastante
sufficiently [sə'fɪʃəntlɪ] *adv* suficientemente, bastante
suffocate ['sʌfəkeɪt] **1** *vt* asfixiar
  2 *vi* asfixiarse
suffocating ['sʌfəkeɪtɪŋ] *adj (heat)* agobiante, sofocante
suffrage ['sʌfrɪdʒ] *n* sufragio *m*
suffuse [sə'fju:z] *vt Literary* bañar, cubrir (with de)
sugar ['ʃʊgə(r)] **1** *n* azúcar *m or f*; **s. beet** remolacha *f* (azucarera); **s. bowl** azucarero *m*; **s. cane** caña *f* de azúcar
  2 *vt* azucarar, echar azúcar a
sugary ['ʃʊgərɪ] *adj* **(a)** *(like sugar)* azucarado(a) **(b)** *Fig (insincere)* zalamero(a); *(over-sentimental)* sentimentaloide
suggest [sə'dʒest] *vt* **(a)** *(propose)* sugerir **(b)** *(advise)* aconsejar **(c)** *(indicate, imply)* indicar
suggestion [sə'dʒestʃən] *n* **(a)** *(proposal)* sugerencia *f* **(b)** *(trace)* sombra *f*,

(small amount) toque *m*
suggestive [sə'dʒestɪv] *adj* **(a)** *(reminiscent, thought-provoking)* sugerente **(b)** *(remark)* insinuante
suicidal [sju:ɪ'saɪdəl] *adj* suicida
suicide ['sju:ɪsaɪd] *n* suicidio *m*
suit [su:t, sju:t] **1** *n* **(a)** *(clothes)* traje *m* de chaqueta **(b)** *Jur* pleito *m* **(c)** *Cards* palo *m*; *Fig* **to follow s.** seguir el ejemplo
  2 *vt* **(a)** *(be convenient to)* convenir a, venir bien a **(b)** *(be right, appropriate for)* ir bien a; **red really suits you** el rojo te favorece mucho; **they are well suited** están hechos el uno para el otro **(c)** *(adapt)* adaptar a **(d)** *(please)* **s. yourself!** ¡como quieras!
suitable ['sju:təbəl] *adj (convenient)* conveniente; *(appropriate)* adecuado(a); **the most s. woman for the job** la mujer más indicada para el puesto
suitably ['sju:təblɪ] *adv (correctly)* correctamente, con acierto; *(properly)* adecuadamente
suitcase ['su:tkeɪs] *n* maleta *f*, *Méx* petaca *f*, *RP* valija *f*
suite [swɪt] *n* **(a)** *(of furniture)* juego *m* **(b)** *(of hotel rooms, music)* suite *f*
suitor ['sju:tə(r)] *n Literary (wooer)* pretendiente *m*
sulfur ['sʌlfə(r)] *n US* = **sulphur**
sulk [sʌlk] *vi* enfurruñarse
sulky ['sʌlkɪ] *adj (sulkier, sulkiest)* malhumorado(a), enfurruñado(a)
sullen ['sʌlən] *adj* hosco(a); *(sky)* plomizo(a)
sulphur ['sʌlfər] *n* azufre *m*
sulphuric [sʌl'fjʊərɪk] *adj* sulfúrico(a)
sultan ['sʌltən] *n* sultán *m*
sultana [sʌl'tɑːnə] *n (raisin)* pasa *f* de Esmirna
sultry ['sʌltrɪ] *adj (sultrier, sultriest)* **(a)** *(muggy)* bochornoso(a) **(b)** *(seductive)* sensual
sum [sʌm] *n* **(a)** *(arithmetic problem, amount)* suma *f* **(b)** *(total amount)* total *m*; *(of money)* importe *m*
  ▸ **sum up 1** *vt sep* resumir
  2 *vi* resumir; **to s. up ...** en resumidas cuentas ...
summarize ['sʌməraɪz] *vt & vi* resumir
summary ['sʌmərɪ] **1** *n* resumen *m*
  2 *adj* sumario(a)
summer ['sʌmə(r)] **1** *n* verano *m*
  2 *adj (holiday etc)* de verano; *(weather)* veraniego(a); *(resort)* de veraneo
summerhouse ['sʌməhaʊs] *n* cenador *m*, glorieta *f*
summertime ['sʌmətaɪm] *n* verano *m*
summit ['sʌmɪt] *n* **(a)** *(of mountain)* cima

f, cumbre *f* (**b**) *Pol* **s. (meeting)** cumbre *f*

summon ['sʌmən] *vt* (**a**) *(meeting, person)* convocar (**b**) *(aid)* pedir (**c**) *Jur* citar

▸ **summon up** *vt sep (resources)* reunir; **to s. up one's courage** armarse de valor

summons ['sʌmənz] **1** *n sing* (**a**) *(call)* llamada *f*, llamamiento *m* (**b**) *Jur* citación *f* judicial

2 *vt Jur* citar

sumptuous ['sʌmptjʊəs] *adj* suntuoso(a)

sun [sʌn] **1** *n* sol *m*

2 *vt* **to s. oneself** tomar el sol

sunbathe ['sʌnbeɪð] *vi* tomar el sol

sunbed ['sʌnbed] *n (in garden)* tumbona *f*; *(with sunlamp)* solario *m*

sunburn ['sʌnbɜːn] *n (burn)* quemadura *f* de sol

sunburnt ['sʌnbɜːnt] *adj (burnt)* quemado(a) por el sol; *(tanned)* bronceado(a)

Sunday ['sʌndɪ] *n* domingo *m inv*; **S. newspaper** periódico *m* del domingo; **S. school** catequesis *f*

sundial ['sʌndaɪəl] *n* reloj *m* de sol

sundown ['sʌndaʊn] *n US* anochecer *m*

sundry ['sʌndrɪ] **1** *adj* diversos(as), varios(as); *Fam* **all and s.** todos sin excepción

2 *npl Com* **sundries** artículos *mpl* diversos; *(expenses)* gastos diversos

sunflower ['sʌnflaʊə(r)] *n* girasol *m*

sung [sʌŋ] *pp of* **sing**

sunglasses ['sʌnglɑːsɪz] *npl* gafas *fpl* de sol, *Am* lentes *mpl* de sol, anteojos *mpl* de sol

sunk [sʌŋk] *pp of* **sink**

sunlamp ['sʌnlæmp] *n* lámpara *f* solar

sunlight ['sʌnlaɪt] *n* sol *m*, luz *f* del sol

sunlit ['sʌnlɪt] *adj* iluminado(a) por el sol

sunny ['sʌnɪ] *adj* (**sunnier, sunniest**) (**a**) *(day)* de sol; *(place)* soleado(a); **it is s.** hace sol (**b**) *Fig (smile, disposition)* alegre; *(future)* prometedor(a)

sunrise ['sʌnraɪz] *n* salida *f* del sol

sunroof ['sʌnruːf] *n Aut* techo corredizo

sunset ['sʌnset] *n* puesta *f* del sol

sunshade ['sʌnʃeɪd] *n* sombrilla *f*

sunshine ['sʌnʃaɪn] *n* sol *m*, luz *f* del sol

sunstroke ['sʌnstrəʊk] *n* insolación *f*

suntan ['sʌntæn] *n* bronceado *m*; **s. oil** crema protectora; **s. lotion** (aceite *m*) bronceador *m*

super ['suːpə(r)] *adj Fam* fenomenal

super- ['suːpə(r)] *pref* super-, sobre-

superannuation [suːpərænjʊ'eɪʃən] *n Br* jubilación *f*, pensión *f*

superb [sʊ'pɜːb] *adj* espléndido(a)

supercilious [suːpə'sɪlɪəs] *adj (condescending)* altanero(a); *(disdainful)* desdeñoso(a)

superficial [suːpə'fɪʃəl] *adj* superficial

superfluous [suː'pɜːflʊəs] *adj* sobrante, superfluo(a); **to be s.** sobrar

superglue ['suːpəgluː] *n* pegamento rápido

superhuman [suːpə'hjuːmən] *adj* sobrehumano(a)

superimpose [suːpərɪm'pəʊz] *vt* sobreponer

superintendent [suːpərɪn'tendənt] *n* director(a) *m,f*; **police s.** subjefe(a) *m,f* de policía

superior [suː'pɪərɪə(r)] **1** *adj* (**a**) superior (**b**) *(haughty)* altivo(a)

2 *n* superior(a) *m,f*

superiority [suːpɪərɪ'ɒrɪtɪ] *n* superioridad *f*

superlative [suː'pɜːlətɪv] **1** *adj* superlativo(a)

2 *n Ling* superlativo *m*

superman ['suːpəmæn] *n* superhombre *m*, supermán *m*

supermarket ['suːpəmɑːkɪt] *n* supermercado *m*

supernatural [suːpə'nætʃərəl] **1** *adj* sobrenatural

2 *n* **the s.** lo sobrenatural

superpower ['suːpəpaʊə(r)] *n Pol* superpotencia *f*

supersede [suːpə'siːd] *vt Fml* suplantar

supersonic [suːpə'sɒnɪk] *adj* supersónico(a)

superstitious [suːpə'stɪʃəs] *adj* supersticioso(a)

supertanker ['suːpətæŋkə(r)] *n* superpetrolero *m*

supervise ['suːpəvaɪz] *vt* supervisar; *(watch over)* vigilar

supervision [suːpə'vɪʒən] *n* supervisión *f*

supervisor ['suːpəvaɪzə(r)] *n* supervisor(a) *m,f*

supper ['sʌpə(r)] *n* cena *f*; **to have s.** cenar

supplant [sə'plɑːnt] *vt* suplantar

supple ['sʌpəl] *adj* flexible

supplement 1 *n* ['sʌplɪmənt] suplemento *m*

2 *vt* ['sʌplɪmənt] complementar

supplementary [sʌplɪ'mentərɪ] *adj* adicional

supplier [sə'plaɪə(r)] *n* suministrador(a) *m,f*, *Com* proveedor(a) *m,f*

supply [sə'plaɪ] **1** *n* (**a**) suministro *m*; *Com* provisión *f*; *(stock)* surtido *m*; **s. and**

demand oferta f y demanda (**b**) **supplies** (*food*) víveres *mpl*; *Mil* pertrechos *mpl*; **office supplies** material *m* para oficina

2 *vt* (**a**) (*provide*) suministrar (**b**) (*with provisions*) aprovisionar (**c**) (*information*) facilitar (**d**) *Com* surtir

support [sə'pɔːt] **1** *n* (**a**) (*moral*) apoyo *m* (**b**) (*funding*) ayuda económica

2 *vt* (**a**) (*weight etc*) sostener (**b**) *Fig* (*back*) apoyar; (*substantiate*) respaldar (**c**) *Sport* ser (hincha) de (**d**) (*sustain*) mantener; (*feed*) alimentar

supporter [sə'pɔːtə(r)] *n Pol* partidario(a) *m*,*f*; *Sport* hincha *mf*

suppose [sə'pəʊz] *vt* suponer; (*presume*) creer; **I s. not/so** supongo que no/sí; **you're not supposed to smoke in here** no está permitido fumar aquí dentro; **you're supposed to be in bed** deberías estar acostado(a) ya

supposed [sə'pəʊzd] *adj* supuesto(a)

supposedly [sə'pəʊzdlɪ] *adv* teóricamente

suppress [sə'pres] *vt* suprimir; (*feelings, laugh etc*) contener; (*news, truth*) callar; (*revolt*) sofocar

supremacy [sʊ'preməsɪ] *n* supremacía f

supreme [sʊ'priːm] *adj* supremo(a); **with s. indifference** con total indiferencia; *US Law* **S. Court** Tribunal *m* Supremo, *Am* Corte f Suprema

supremely [sʊ'priːmlɪ] *adv* sumamente

surcharge ['sɜːtʃɑːdʒ] *n* recargo *m*

sure [ʃʊə(r)] **1** *adj* (**a**) seguro(a); **I'm s. (that)** ... estoy seguro(a) de que ...; **make s. that it's ready** asegúrate de que esté listo; **s. of oneself** seguro(a) de sí mismo(a) (**b**) *Fam* **s. thing!** ¡claro!; *US* **it s. is cold** qué frío que hace

2 *adv* (**a**) (*of course*) claro (**b**) (*certainly*) seguro (**c**) **s. enough** efectivamente

surely ['ʃʊəlɪ] *adv* (*without a doubt*) sin duda; **s. not!** ¡no puede ser!

surety ['ʃʊərɪtɪ] *n* (**a**) (*sum*) fianza f (**b**) (*person*) fiador(a) *m*,*f*; **to stand s. for sb** ser fiador de algn

surf [sɜːf] **1** *n* (*waves*) oleaje *m*; (*foam*) espuma f

2 *vt Comput* **to s. the Net** navegar por Internet

3 *vi Sport* hacer surf

surface ['sɜːfɪs] **1** *n* superficie f; (*of road*) firme *m*

2 *adj* superficial; **s. area** área f de la superficie; **by s. mail** por vía terrestre *or* marítima

3 *vt* (*road*) revestir

4 *vi* (*submarine etc*) salir a la superficie;

Fam (*wake up*) levantarse

surface-to-air ['sɜːfɪstʊ'eə(r)] *adj* **s. missile** misil *m* tierra-aire

surfboard ['sɜːfbɔːd] *n* tabla f de surf

surfeit ['sɜːfɪt] *n Fml* exceso *m*

surfer ['sɜːfə(r)] *n* surfista *mf*

surfing ['sɜːfɪŋ] *n* surf *m*, surfing *m*

surge [sɜːdʒ] **1** *n* (*growth*) alza f (**b**) (*of sea, sympathy*) oleada f; *Fig* (*of anger, energy*) arranque *m*

2 *vi* **to s. forward** (*people*) avanzar en tropel

surgeon ['sɜːdʒən] *n* cirujano(a) *m*,*f*

surgery ['sɜːdʒərɪ] *n* (**a**) (*operation*) cirugía f (**b**) *Br* (*consulting room*) consultorio *m*; **s. hours** horas *fpl* de consulta

surgical ['sɜːdʒɪkəl] *adj* quirúrgico(a); **s. spirit** alcohol *m* de 90°

surly ['sɜːlɪ] *adj* (**surlier, surliest**) (*bad-tempered*) hosco(a), malhumorado(a); (*rude*) maleducado(a)

surmount [sɜː'maʊnt] *vt* superar, vencer

surname ['sɜːneɪm] *n* apellido *m*

surpass [sɜː'pɑːs] *vt* superar

surplus ['sɜːpləs] **1** *n* (*of goods*) excedente *m*; (*of budget*) superávit *m*

2 *adj* excedente

surprise [sə'praɪz] **1** *n* sorpresa f; **to take sb by s.** coger desprevenido(a) a algn

2 *adj* (*visit*) inesperado(a); **s. attack** ataque *m* sorpresa

3 *vt* sorprender

surprising [sə'praɪzɪŋ] *adj* sorprendente

surprisingly [sə'praɪzɪŋlɪ] *adv* sorprendentemente, de modo sorprendente

surrealist [sə'rɪəlɪst] *adj & n* surrealista (*mf*)

surrender [sə'rendə(r)] **1** *n Mil* rendición f; (*of weapons*) entrega f; *Ins* rescate *m*

2 *vt Mil* rendir; (*right*) renunciar a

3 *vi* (*give in*) rendirse

surreptitious [sʌrəp'tɪʃəs] *adj* subrepticio(a)

surrogate ['sʌrəgɪt] *n Fml* sustituto(a) *m*,*f*; **s. mother** madre f de alquiler

surround [sə'raʊnd] **1** *n* marco *m*, borde *m*

2 *vt* rodear

surrounding [sə'raʊndɪŋ] **1** *adj* circundante

2 *npl* **surroundings** (*of place*) alrededores *mpl*, cercanías *fpl*

surveillance [sɜː'veɪləns] *n* vigilancia f

survey 1 *n* ['sɜːveɪ] (**a**) (*of building*) inspección f, (*of land*) reconocimiento *m* (**b**) (*of trends etc*) encuesta f (**c**) (*overall view*) panorama *m*

2 *vt* [sə'veɪ] (**a**) (*building*) inspeccionar;

(land) medir (**b**) *(trends etc)* hacer una encuesta sobre (**c**) *(look at)* contemplar

surveyor [sə'veɪə(r)] *n* agrimensor(a) *m,f*; **quantity s.** aparejador(a) *m,f*

survival [sə'vaɪvəl] *n* supervivencia *f*

survive [sə'vaɪv] **1** *vi* sobrevivir; *(remain)* perdurar

2 *vt* sobrevivir a

survivor [sə'vaɪvə(r)] *n* superviviente *mf*

susceptible [sə'septəbəl] *adj* (**to attack**) susceptible (**to** a); *(to illness)* propenso(a) (**to** a)

suspect ['sʌspekt] **1** *adj (dubious)* sospechoso(a)

2 *n* sospechoso(a) *m,f*

3 *vt* [sə'spekt] (**a**) *(person)* sospechar (**of** de); *(plot, motives)* recelar de (**b**) *(think likely)* imaginar, creer

suspend [sə'spend] *vt* suspender; *(pupil)* expulsar por un tiempo

suspended [sə'spendɪd] *adj* (**a**) suspendido(a); *Jur* **s. sentence** condena *f* condicional (**b**) *Sport* sancionado(a)

suspender [sə'spendə(r)] *n* (**a**) *Br (for stocking)* liga *f*; **s. belt** liguero *m* (**b**) *US* **suspenders** tirantes *mpl*

suspense [sə'spens] *n* incertidumbre *f*; *Cin & Th* suspense *m*; **to keep sb in s.** mantener a algn en la incertidumbre

suspension [sə'spenʃən] *n* (**a**) suspensión *f* (**b**) *Sport* sanción *f* (**c**) *(of pupil, employee)* expulsión *f* temporal (**d**) **s. bridge** puente *m* colgante

suspicion [sə'spɪʃən] *n* (**a**) sospecha *f*; *(mistrust)* recelo *m*; *(doubt)* duda *f* (**b**) *(trace)* pizca *f*

suspicious [sə'spɪʃəs] *adj* (**a**) *(arousing suspicion)* sospechoso(a) (**b**) *(distrustful)* receloso(a); **to be s. of sb** desconfiar de algn

▸ **suss out** [sʌs] *vt sep Br Fam (person)* calar; *(system)* coger *or Am* agarrar el truco a; **I haven't sussed out how it works yet** todavía no me he enterado de cómo funciona

sustain [sə'steɪn] *vt* (**a**) sostener (**b**) *(nourish)* sustentar (**c**) *Jur (objection)* admitir (**d**) *(injury etc)* sufrir

sustained [sə'steɪnd] *adj* sostenido(a)

sustenance ['sʌstənəns] *n* sustento *m*

swab [swɒb] **1** *n (cotton wool)* algodón *m*; *(for specimen)* frotis *m*

2 *vt (wound)* limpiar

swagger ['swægə(r)] **1** *n* pavoneo *m*

2 *vi* pavonearse

swallow¹ ['swɒləʊ] **1** *n (of drink, food)* trago *m*

2 *vt* (**a**) *(drink, food)* tragar (**b**) *Fig (believe)* tragarse

3 *vi* tragar

▸ **swallow up** *vt sep Fig* (**a**) *(engulf)* tragar (**b**) *(eat up)* consumir

swallow² ['swɒləʊ] *n Orn* golondrina *f*

swam [swæm] *pt of* **swim**

swamp [swɒmp] **1** *n* ciénaga *f*

2 *vt* (**a**) *(boat)* hundir (**b**) *Fig* inundar (**with** *or* **by** de)

swan [swɒn] **1** *n* cisne *m*

2 *vi Fam* **to s. around** pavonearse; **to s. around doing nothing** hacer el vago

swap [swɒp] **1** *n Fam* intercambio *m*

2 *vt* cambiar

▸ **swap round, swap over** *vt sep (switch)* cambiar

swarm [swɔːm] **1** *n* enjambre *m*

2 *vi (bees)* enjambrar; *Fig* **Neath was swarming with tourists** Neath estaba lleno de turistas

swarthy ['swɔːðɪ] *adj* (**swarthier, swarthiest**) moreno(a)

swastika ['swɒstɪkə] *n* esvástica *f*, cruz gamada

swat [swɒt] *vt* aplastar

swathe [sweɪð] *vt (bind up)* envolver

sway [sweɪ] **1** *n (movement)* balanceo *m* (**b**) **to hold s. over sb** dominar a algn

2 *vi* (**a**) *(swing)* balancearse, mecerse (**b**) *(totter)* tambalearse

3 *vt Fig (persuade)* convencer

swear [sweə(r)] **1** *vt* (*pt* **swore**; *pp* **sworn**) *(vow)* jurar; **to s. an oath** prestar juramento

2 *vi* (**a**) *(formally)* jurar, prestar juramento (**b**) *(curse)* soltar tacos, decir palabrotas; *(blaspheme)* jurar; **to s. at sb** echar pestes contra algn

swear-word ['sweəwɜːd] *n* palabrota *f*

sweat [swet] **1** *n (perspiration)* sudor *m*; *Fam (hard work)* trabajo duro

2 *vi (perspire)* sudar; *Fig (work hard)* sudar la gota gorda

3 *vt Fam* **to s. it out** aguantar

sweater ['swetə(r)] *n* suéter *m*

sweatshirt ['swetʃɜːt] *n* sudadera *f*

sweaty ['swetɪ] *adj* (**sweatier, sweatiest**) sudoroso(a)

Swede [swiːd] *n (person)* sueco(a) *m,f*

swede [swiːd] *n Bot* nabo sueco

Sweden ['swiːdən] *n* Suecia *f*

Swedish ['swiːdɪʃ] **1** *adj* sueco(a)

2 *n* (**a**) *(language)* sueco *m* (**b**) **the S.** los suecos

sweep [swiːp] **1** *n* (**a**) *(with broom)* barrido *m*; *Fig* **to make a clean s. of things** hacer tabla rasa (**b**) *(of arm)* gesto amplio (**c**) *(of river, road)* curva *f* (**d**) **(chimney)** s. deshollinador(a) *m,f*

2 *vt* (*pt & pp* **swept**) (**a**) *(floor etc)* barrer (**b**) *(of searchlight)* recorrer; *(minefield)* rastrear (**c**) *(spread throughout)* extenderse por

3 *vi* (**a**) *(with broom)* barrer (**b**) **to s. in/out/past** entrar/salir/pasar rápidamente

▸ **sweep aside** *vt sep* apartar bruscamente; *Fig (objections)* rechazar

▸ **sweep away** *vt sep* (**a**) *(dust)* barrer (**b**) *(of storm)* arrastrar

▸ **sweep up** *vi* barrer

sweeper ['swiːpə(r)] *n* (**a**) *(machine)* barredora *f* (**b**) *Ftb* líbero *m*

sweeping ['swiːpɪŋ] *adj* (**a**) *(broad)* amplio(a); **a s. statement** una declaración demasiado general (**b**) *(victory)* aplastante (**c**) *(reforms, changes etc)* radical

sweet [swiːt] **1** *adj* (**a**) *(to taste)* dulce; *(sugary)* azucarado(a); **to have a s. tooth** ser goloso(a); **s. pea** guisante *m* de olor; **s. shop** confitería *f* (**b**) *(pleasant)* agradable; *(smell)* fragante; *(sound)* melodioso(a) (**c**) *(person, animal)* encantador(a)

2 *n* (**a**) *Br (chocolate)* bombón *m*; **(boiled)** s. caramelo *m* (**b**) *(dessert)* postre *m*

sweet-and-sour ['swiːtən'sauə(r)] *adj* agridulce

sweetcorn ['swiːtkɔːn] *n* maíz tierno

sweeten ['swiːtən] *vt* (**a**) *(tea etc)* azucarar (**b**) *Fig (temper)* aplacar; **to s. the pill** suavizar el golpe

sweetener ['swiːtənə(r)] *n* (for tea, coffee) edulcorante *m*

sweetheart ['swiːthɑːt] *n* (**a**) *(boyfriend)* novio *m*; *(girlfriend)* novia *f* (**b**) *(dear, love)* cariño *m*, amor *m*

sweetness ['swiːtnɪs] *n* dulzura *f*; *(of smell)* fragancia *f*, *(of sound)* suavidad *f*

swell [swel] **1** *n (of sea)* marejada *f*, oleaje *m*

2 *adj US Fam* fenomenal

3 *vi* (*pt* **swelled**; *pp* **swollen**) *(part of body)* hincharse; *(river)* subir

▸ **swell up** *vi* hincharse

swelling ['swelɪŋ] *n* hinchazón *f*, *Med* tumefacción *f*

sweltering ['sweltərɪŋ] *adj* agobiante

swept [swept] *pt & pp of* **sweep**

swerve [swɜːv] **1** *n* (**a**) *(by car)* viraje *m* (**b**) *Sport (by player)* regate *m*

2 *vi* (**a**) *(car)* dar un viraje brusco (**b**) *Sport (player)* dar un regate

swift [swɪft] **1** *adj* rápido(a), veloz

2 *n Orn* vencejo *m* (común)

swiftly ['swɪftlɪ] *adv* rápidamente

swig [swɪg] *Fam* **1** *n* trago *m*

2 *vt* beber a tragos

swill [swɪl] **1** *n* (**a**) *(pig food)* bazofia *f* (**b**) *(rinse)* enjuague *m*

2 *vt* (**a**) *(rinse)* enjuagar (**b**) *Fam (drink)* beber a grandes tragos

▸ **swill out** *vt sep* enjuagar

swim [swɪm] **1** *vi* (*pt* **swam**; *pp* **swum**) nadar; **to go swimming** ir a nadar; *Fam* **my head is swimming** la cabeza me da vueltas

2 *vt (the Channel)* pasar a nado

3 *n* baño *m*; **to go for a s.** ir a nadar *or* bañarse

swimmer ['swɪmə(r)] *n* nadador(a) *m,f*

swimming ['swɪmɪŋ] *n* natación *f*; **s. cap** gorro *m* de baño; **s. costume** traje *m* de baño, bañador *m*; **s. pool** piscina *f*; **s. trunks** bañador

swimsuit ['swɪmsuːt] *n* traje *m* de baño, bañador *m*

swindle ['swɪndəl] **1** *n* estafa *f*

2 *vt* estafar

swindler ['swɪndlə(r)] *n* estafador(a) *m,f*

swine [swaɪn] *n* (**a**) *(pl* **swine**) *(pig)* cerdo *m*, puerco *m* (**b**) *(pl* **swines**) *Fam (person)* canalla *mf*, cochino(a) *m,f*

swing [swɪŋ] **1** *n* (**a**) *(movement)* balanceo *m*, vaivén *m*; *Fig (in votes etc)* viraje *m*; **s. bridge** puente giratorio; **s. door** puerta giratoria (**b**) *(in golf)* swing *m* (**c**) *(plaything)* columpio *m* (**d**) *(rhythm)* ritmo *m*; *(jazz style)* swing *m*; **in full s.** en plena marcha

2 *vi* (*pt & pp* **swung**) (**a**) *(move to and fro)* balancearse; *(arms, legs)* menearse; *(on swing)* columpiarse; **to s. open/shut** abrirse/cerrarse de golpe (**b**) *(turn)* girar; **he swung round** dio media vuelta

3 *vt* (**a**) *(cause to move to and fro)* balancear; *(arms, legs)* menear; *(on swing)* columpiar (**b**) *(turn)* hacer girar; **she swung the sack onto her back** se echó el saco a los hombros

swingeing ['swɪndʒɪŋ] *adj* drástico(a)

swipe [swaɪp] **1** *n* golpe *m*

2 *vt* (**a**) *(hit)* dar un tortazo a (**b**) *Fam (steal)* birlar

swirl [swɜːl] **1** *n* remolino *m*; *(of cream, smoke)* voluta *f*

2 *vi* arremolinarse

swish [swɪʃ] **1** *adj Fam (smart)* elegante

2 *vt (tail)* menear

3 *vi (whip)* dar un chasquido; *(skirt)* crujir

Swiss [swɪs] **1** *adj* suizo(a)
2 *n* (*pl* **Swiss**) (*person*) suizo(a) *m,f*; **the S.** los suizos
switch [swɪtʃ] **1** *n* (**a**) *Elec* interruptor *m* (**b**) (*changeover*) cambio repentino; (*exchange*) intercambio *m* (**c**) (*stick*) vara *f*; (*riding whip*) fusta *f* (**d**) *US Rail* agujas *fpl*
2 *vt* (**a**) (*jobs, direction*) cambiar de (**b**) (*allegiance*) cambiar (**to** por); (*attention*) desviar (**to** hacia)
▸ **switch off** *vt sep* apagar
▸ **switch on** *vt sep* encender
▸ **switch over** *vi* cambiar (**to** a)
switchboard ['swɪtʃbɔːd] *n* centralita *f*
Switzerland ['swɪtsələnd] *n* Suiza
swivel ['swɪvəl] **1** *n* **s. chair** silla giratoria
2 *vt & vi* girar
swollen ['swəʊlən] **1** *adj* (*ankle, face*) hinchado(a); (*river, lake*) crecido(a)
2 *pp of* **swell**
swoon [swuːn] **1** *n* desmayo *m*
2 *vi* desmayarse
swoop [swuːp] **1** *n* (**a**) (*of bird*) calada *f*; (*of plane*) descenso *m* en picado (**b**) (*by police*) redada *f*
2 *vi* (**a**) **to s. down** (*bird*) abalanzarse (**on** sobre); (*plane*) bajar en picado (**b**) (*police*) hacer una redada
swop [swɒp] *n & vt* = **swap**
sword [sɔːd] *n* espada *f*
swordfish ['sɔːdfɪʃ] *n* pez *m* espada
swore [swɔː(r)] *pt of* **swear**
sworn [swɔːn] **1** *adj* jurado(a)
2 *pp of* **swear**
swot [swɒt] *vi Br Fam* empollar
swum [swʌm] *pp of* **swim**
swung [swʌŋ] *pt & pp of* **swing**
sycamore ['sɪkəmɔː(r)] *n* (**a**) *Br* sicomoro *m* (**b**) *US* (*plane tree*) plátano *m*
syllable ['sɪləbəl] *n* sílaba *f*
syllabus ['sɪləbəs] *n* programa *m* de estudios
symbol ['sɪmbəl] *n* símbolo *m*
symbolic [sɪm'bɒlɪk] *adj* simbólico(a)
symbolize ['sɪmbəlaɪz] *vt* simbolizar
symmetry ['sɪmɪtrɪ] *n* simetría *f*
sympathetic [sɪmpə'θetɪk] *adj* (**a**) (*showing pity*) compasivo(a) (**b**) (*understanding*) comprensivo(a); (*kind*) amable

---

🖉 Note that the Spanish word **simpático** is a false friend and is never a translation for the English word **sympathetic**. In Spanish, **simpático** means "nice, likeable".

---

sympathize ['sɪmpəθaɪz] *vi* (**a**) (*show pity*) compadecerse (**with** de) (**b**) (*understand*) comprender
sympathizer ['sɪmpəθaɪzə(r)] *n* simpatizante *mf*
sympathy ['sɪmpəθɪ] *n* (**a**) (*pity*) compasión *f* (**b**) (*condolences*) pésame *m*; **letter of s.** pésame; **to express one's s.** dar el pésame (**c**) (*understanding*) comprensión *f*

🖉 Note that the Spanish word **simpatía** is a false friend and is never a translation for the English word **sympathy**. In Spanish, **simpatía** means "liking, affection".

---

symphony ['sɪmfənɪ] *n* sinfonía *f*
symposium [sɪm'pəʊzɪəm] *n* simposio *m*
symptom ['sɪmptəm] *n* síntoma *m*
symptomatic [sɪmptə'mætɪk] *adj* sintomático(a)
synagogue ['sɪnəgɒg] *n* sinagoga *f*
synchronize ['sɪŋkrənaɪz] *vt* sincronizar
syndicate ['sɪndɪkɪt] *n* corporación *f*; **newspaper s.** sindicato periodístico
syndrome ['sɪndrəʊm] *n* síndrome *m*
synonym ['sɪnənɪm] *n* sinónimo *m*
synopsis [sɪ'nɒpsɪs] *n* sinopsis *f inv*
syntax ['sɪntæks] *n* sintaxis *f inv*
synthesis ['sɪnθɪsɪs] *n* (*pl* **syntheses** ['sɪnθɪsiːz]) síntesis *f inv*
synthesizer ['sɪnθɪsaɪzə(r)] *n* sintetizador *m*
synthetic [sɪn'θetɪk] *adj* sintético(a)
syphilis ['sɪfɪlɪs] *n* sífilis *f*
syphon ['saɪfən] *n* = **siphon**
Syria ['sɪrɪə] *n* Siria
Syrian ['sɪrɪən] *adj & n* sirio(a) (*m,f*)
syringe [sɪ'rɪndʒ] *n* jeringa *f*, jeringuilla *f*
syrup ['sɪrəp] *n* jarabe *m*, almíbar *m*
system ['sɪstəm] *n* sistema *m*; *Fam* **the s.** el orden establecido; *Comput* **systems analyst** analista *mf* de sistemas
systematic [sɪstɪ'mætɪk] *adj* sistemático(a)

T

T, t [tiː] *n (the letter)* T, t *f*

t *(abbr* **ton(s))** tonelada(s) *f(pl)*

ta [tɑː] *interj Br Fam* gracias

tab [tæb] *n* (**a**) *(flap)* lengüeta *f*; *(label)* etiqueta *f*; *Fam* **to keep tabs on sb** vigilar a algn (**b**) *US Fam (bill)* cuenta *f*

tabby ['tæbɪ] *n* **t. (cat)** gato(a) *m,f* romano(a)

table ['teɪbəl] **1** *n* (**a**) mesa *f*; **to lay** or **set the t.** poner la mesa; **t. lamp** lámpara *f* de mesa; **t. mat** salvamanteles *m inv*; **t. tennis** ping-pong® *m*, tenis *m* de mesa; **t. wine** vino *m* de mesa (**b**) *(of figures)* tabla *f*, cuadro *m*; **t. of contents** índice *m* de materias

2 *vt (motion, proposal) Br* presentar; *US* posponer

tablecloth ['teɪbəlklɒθ] *n* mantel *m*

tablespoon ['teɪbəlspuːn] *n* cucharón *m*

tablespoonful ['teɪbəlspuːnfʊl] *n* cucharada *f* grande

tablet ['tæblɪt] *n* (**a**) *Med* pastilla *f* (**b**) *(of stone)* lápida *f* (**c**) *(of soap)* pastilla *f*; *(of chocolate)* tableta *f* (**d**) *US (of writing paper)* bloc *m*

tableware ['teɪbəlweə(r)] *n* vajilla *f*

tabloid ['tæblɔɪd] *n* periódico *m* de pequeño formato; **t. press** prensa sensacionalista

taboo [təˈbuː] *adj & n* tabú *(m)*

tabulate ['tæbjʊleɪt] *vt* disponer en listas

tacit ['tæsɪt] *adj* tácito(a)

taciturn ['tæsɪtɜːn] *adj* taciturno(a)

tack [tæk] **1** *n* (**a**) *(small nail)* tachuela *f* (**b**) *Sewing* hilván *m* (**c**) *Naut (distance)* bordada *f*; *Fig* **to change t.** cambiar de rumbo

2 *vt* (**a**) **to t. sth down** clavar algo con tachuelas (**b**) *Sewing* hilvanar

3 *vi Naut* virar de bordo

▸ **tack on** *vt sep (add)* añadir

tackle ['tækəl] **1** *n* (**a**) *(equipment)* aparejos *mpl*; **fishing t.** aparejos de pescar (**b**) *Sport* placaje *m*; *Ftb* entrada *f*

2 *vt* agarrar; *(task)* emprender; *(problem)* abordar; *Sport* placar; *Ftb* entrar a

tacky[1] ['tækɪ] *adj* (**tackier, tackiest**) pegajoso(a)

tacky[2] ['tækɪ] *adj Fam (shoddy)* cutre

tact [tækt] *n* tacto *m*, diplomacia *f*

tactful ['tæktfʊl] *adj* diplomático(a)

tactic ['tæktɪk] *n* táctica *f*; **tactics** táctica *f*

tactical ['tæktɪkəl] *adj* táctico(a)

tactless ['tæktlɪs] *adj (person)* poco diplomático(a); *(question)* indiscreto(a)

tadpole ['tædpəʊl] *n* renacuajo *m*

taffy ['tæfɪ] *n US* caramelo *m* de melaza

tag [tæg] *n* (**a**) *(label)* etiqueta *f* (**b**) *(saying)* coletilla *f*

▸ **tag along** *vi Fam* pegarse

▸ **tag on** *vt sep (add to end)* añadir

tail [teɪl] **1** *n* (**a**) cola *f*; **t. end** cola (**b**) *(of shirt)* faldón *m*; **to wear tails** ir de frac; **t. coat** frac *m* (**c**) **tails** *(of coin)* cruz *f*

2 *vt Fam (follow)* seguir de cerca

▸ **tail away, tail off** *vi* desvanecerse

tailback ['teɪlbæk] *n Br* caravana *f*

tail-gate ['teɪlgeɪt] **1** *n Aut* puerta trasera

2 *vt US* conducir or *Am* manejar pegado a, pisar los talones a

tailor ['teɪlə(r)] **1** *n* sastre *m*; **t.'s (shop)** sastrería *f*

2 *vt (suit)* confeccionar; *Fig* adaptar

tailor-made [teɪləˈmeɪd] *adj* hecho(a) a la medida

tailwind ['teɪlwɪnd] *n* viento *m* de cola

taint [teɪnt] *vt* contaminar; *Fig* corromper

tainted ['teɪntɪd] *adj* contaminado(a); *(reputation)* manchado(a)

take [teɪk] **1** *vt (pt* **took**; *pp* **taken)** (**a**) tomar, coger; **to t. an opportunity** aprovechar una oportunidad; **to t. hold of sth** agarrar algo; **to t. sth from one's pocket** sacarse algo del bolsillo; **t. your time!** ¡tómate el tiempo que quieras!; **to t. a bath** bañarse; **to t. care (of oneself)** cuidarse; **his car takes six people** caben seis personas en su coche; **is this seat taken?** ¿está ocupado este asiento?; **to t. a decision** tomar una decisión; **to t. a liking/dislike to sb** tomar cariño/antipatía a algn; **to t. a photograph** sacar una fotografía; **t. the first road on the left** coja la primera a la izquierda; **to t. the train** coger el tren

(**b**) *(accept)* aceptar; *(earn)* **to t. so much per week** recaudar tanto por semana

(**c**) *(win)* ganar; *(prize)* llevarse
(**d**) *(eat, drink)* tomar; **to t. drugs** drogarse
(**e**) **she's taking (a degree in) law** estudia derecho; **to t. an exam (in ...)** examinarse (de ...)
(**f**) *(person to a place)* llevar
(**g**) *(endure)* aguantar
(**h**) *(consider)* considerar
(**i**) **I t. it that ...** supongo que ...; **what do you t. me for?** ¿por quién me tomas?
(**j**) *(require)* requerir; **it takes an hour to get there** se tarda una hora en llegar hasta allí
(**k**) **to be taken ill** enfermar
2 *n Cin* toma *f*
▸ **take after** *vt insep* parecerse a
▸ **take apart** *vt sep (machine)* desmontar
▸ **take away** *vt sep* (**a**) *(carry off)* llevarse (**b**) **to t. sth away from sb** quitarle algo a algn (**c**) *Math* restar
▸ **take back** *vt sep* (**a**) *(give back)* devolver; *(receive back)* recuperar (**b**) *(withdraw)* retractarse
▸ **take down** *vt sep* (**a**) *(lower)* bajar (**b**) *(demolish)* derribar (**c**) *(write)* apuntar
▸ **take in** *vt sep* (**a**) *(shelter, lodge)* alojar, acoger (**b**) *Sewing* meter (**c**) *(include)* abarcar (**d**) *(understand)* entender (**e**) *(deceive)* engañar
▸ **take off** *vt sep* (**a**) *(lower)* quitar; **he took off his jacket** se quitó la chaqueta (**b**) *(lead or carry away)* llevarse (**c**) *(deduct)* descontar (**d**) *(imitate)* imitar burlonamente
2 *vi Av* despegar
▸ **take on** *vt sep* (**a**) *(undertake)* encargarse de (**b**) *(acquire)* tomar (**c**) *(employ)* contratar (**d**) *(compete with)* competir con
▸ **take out** *vt sep* sacar, quitar; **he's taking me out to dinner** me ha invitado a cenar fuera
▸ **take over 1** *vt sep Com & Pol* tomar posesión de; **the rebels took over the country** los rebeldes se apoderaron del país
2 *vi* **to t. over from sb** relevar a algn
▸ **take to** *vt insep (become fond of)* coger cariño a; **to t. to drink** darse a la bebida
▸ **take up** *vt sep* (**a**) *Sewing* acortar (**b**) *(accept)* aceptar; *(adopt)* adoptar (**c**) **I've taken up the piano/French** he empezado a tocar el piano/a aprender francés (**d**) *(occupy)* ocupar

takeaway ['teɪkəweɪ] *Br* **1** *n (food)* comida *f* para llevar; *(restaurant)* restaurante *m* que vende comida para llevar
2 *adj (food)* para llevar

take-home pay ['teɪkhəʊm'peɪ] *n* sueldo neto

taken ['teɪkən] *pp of* **take**

takeoff ['teɪkɒf] *n* (**a**) *Av* despegue *m* (**b**) *(imitation)* imitación burlona

takeout ['teɪkaʊt] *US* **1** *n (food)* comida *f* para llevar
2 *adj (food)* para llevar

takeover ['teɪkəʊvə(r)] *n Com* absorción *f*; **military t.** golpe *m* de estado; **t. bid** oferta pública de adquisición, OPA *f*

takings ['teɪkɪŋz] *npl Com* recaudación *f*

talc [tælk] *n* talco *m*

talcum powder ['tælkəmpaʊdə(r)] *n* (polvos *mpl* de) talco *m*

tale [teɪl] *n* cuento *m*; **to tell tales** contar chismes

talent ['tælənt] *n* talento *m*

talented ['tæləntɪd] *adj* dotado(a)

talk [tɔːk] **1** *vi* hablar; *(chat)* charlar; *(gossip)* chismorrear; *Fam* **now you're talking!** ¡eso sí que me interesa!
2 *vt* **to t. nonsense** decir tonterías; **to t. sense** hablar con sentido común; **to t. shop** hablar del trabajo
3 *n* (**a**) *(conversation)* conversación *f* (**b**) *(words)* palabras *fpl*; **he's all t.** no hace más que hablar (**c**) *(rumour)* rumor *m*; *(gossip)* chismes *mpl* (**d**) *(lecture)* charla *f*
▸ **talk into** *vt sep* **to t. sb into sth** convencer a algn para que haga algo
▸ **talk out of** *vt sep* **to t. sb out of sth** disuadir a algn de que haga algo
▸ **talk over** *vt sep* discutir

talkative ['tɔːkətɪv] *adj* hablador(a)

talking ['tɔːkɪŋ] *n* **no t. please!** ¡silencio, por favor!; **t. point** tema *m* de conversación

talking-to ['tɔːkɪŋtuː] *n Fam* bronca *f*

tall [tɔːl] *adj* alto(a); **a tree 10 m t.** un árbol de 10 m (de alto); **how t. are you?** ¿cuánto mides?; *Fig* **that's a t. order** eso es mucho pedir

tally ['tælɪ] **1** *vi* **to t. with sth** corresponderse con algo
2 *n Com* apunte *m*; **to keep a t. of** llevar la cuenta de

talon ['tælən] *n* garra *f*

> *ℓ* Note that the Spanish word **talón** is a false friend and is never a translation for the English word **talon**. In Spanish, **talón** means both "heel" and "cheque".

tambourine [tæmbə'riːn] *n* pandereta *f*

tame [teɪm] **1** *adj* (**a**) *(animal)* domado(a); *(by nature)* manso(a); *(person)* dócil (**b**) *(style)* soso(a)
2 *vt* domar

tamper ['tæmpə(r)] *vi* **to t. with** *(text)* adulterar; *(records, an entry)* falsificar; *(lock)* intentar forzar

tampon ['tæmpɒn] *n* tampón *m*

tan [tæn] **1** *n* (a) *(colour)* marrón rojizo (b) *(of skin)* bronceado *m*
2 *adj (colour)* marrón rojizo
3 *vt* (a) *(leather)* curtir (b) *(skin)* broncear
4 *vi* ponerse moreno(a)

tang [tæŋ] *n* sabor *m* fuerte

tangent ['tændʒənt] *n* tangente *f*; *Fig* **to go off at a t.** salirse por la tangente

tangerine [tændʒə'ri:n] *n* clementina *f*

tangible ['tændʒəbəl] *adj* tangible

tangle ['tæŋgəl] *n (of thread)* maraña *f*; *Fig* lío *m*; *Fig* **to get into a t.** hacerse un lío

tank [tæŋk] *n* (a) *(container)* depósito *m* (b) *Mil* tanque *m*

tanker ['tæŋkə(r)] *n Naut* tanque *m*; *(for oil)* petrolero *m*; *Aut* camión *m* cisterna

Tannoy® ['tænɔɪ] *n* sistema *m* de megafonía

tantalize ['tæntəlaɪz] *vt* atormentar

tantalizing ['tæntəlaɪzɪŋ] *adj* atormentador(a)

tantamount ['tæntəmaʊnt] *adj* **t. to** equivalente a

tantrum ['tæntrəm] *n* rabieta *f*

tap¹ [tæp] **1** *vt* golpear suavemente; *(with hand)* dar una palmadita a
2 *vi* **to t. at the door** llamar suavemente a la puerta
3 *n* golpecito *m*; **t. dancing** claqué *m*

tap² [tæp] **1** *n Br (for water)* grifo *m*, *Chile*, *Méx* llave *f*, *RP* canilla *f*; *Fig* **funds on t.** fondos *mpl* disponibles
2 *vt* (a) *(tree)* sangrar; *Fig* **to t. new markets** explotar nuevos mercados (b) *(phone)* pinchar

tape [teɪp] **1** *n* (a) *(ribbon)* cinta *f*; **sticky t.** cinta adhesiva; **t. measure** cinta métrica (b) *(for recording)* cinta *f* (magnetofónica); **t. recorder** magnetófono *m*, cassette *m*; **t. recording** grabación *f*
2 *vt* (a) *(stick)* pegar (con cinta adhesiva) (b) *(record)* grabar (en cinta)

taper ['teɪpə(r)] **1** *vi* estrecharse; *(to a point)* afilarse
2 *n (candle)* vela *f*
▸ **taper off** *vi* ir disminuyendo

tapestry ['tæpɪstrɪ] *n* tapiz *m*

tapping ['tæpɪŋ] *n* (a) *(of tree)* sangría *f*; *(of resources)* explotación *f* (b) *Tel* intervención *f* ilegal de un teléfono

tar [tɑ:(r)] *n* alquitrán *m*

target ['tɑ:gɪt] *n* (a) *(object aimed at)* blanco *m*; **t. practice** tiro *m* al blanco (b) *(purpose)* meta *f*

tariff ['tærɪf] *n* tarifa *f*, arancel *m*

tarmac® ['tɑ:mæk] **1** *n* (a) *(substance)* alquitrán *m* (b) *Av* pista *f* de aterrizaje
2 *vt* alquitranar

tarnish ['tɑ:nɪʃ] *vt* deslustrar

tarpaulin [tɑ:'pɔ:lɪn] *n* lona *f*

tart¹ [tɑ:t] *n Br Culin* tarta *f*

tart² [tɑ:t] *adj (taste)* ácido(a), agrio(a)

tart³ [tɑ:t] *Fam* **1** *n* puta *f*
2 *vt Br* **to t. oneself up** emperifollarse

tartan ['tɑ:tən] *n* tartán *m*

tartar ['tɑ:tə(r)] *n* (a) *Chem* tártaro *m* (b) *Culin* **t. sauce** salsa tártara

task [tɑ:sk] *n* tarea *f*; **to take sb to t.** reprender a algn; *Mil* **t. force** destacamento *m* (de fuerzas)

tassel ['tæsəl] *n* borla *f*

taste [teɪst] **1** *n* (a) *(sense)* gusto *m*; *(flavour)* sabor *m*; **it has a burnt t.** sabe a quemado (b) *(sample) (of food)* bocado *m*; *(of drink)* trago *m*; **to give sb a t. of his own medicine** pagar a algn con la misma moneda (c) *(liking)* afición *f*; **to have a t. for sth** gustarle a uno algo (d) **in bad t.** de mal gusto; **to have (good) t.** tener (buen) gusto
2 *vt (sample)* probar
3 *vi* **to t. of sth** saber a algo

tasteful ['teɪstfʊl] *adj* de buen gusto

tasteless ['teɪstlɪs] *adj* (a) *(food)* soso(a) (b) *(in bad taste)* de mal gusto

tasty ['teɪstɪ] *adj* (**tastier, tastiest**) sabroso(a)

tattered ['tætəd] *adj* hecho(a) jirones

tatters ['tætəz] *npl* **in t.** hecho(a) jirones

tattoo¹ [tæ'tu:] *n Mil* retreta *f*

tattoo² [tæ'tu:] **1** *vt* tatuar
2 *n (mark)* tatuaje *m*

tatty ['tætɪ] *adj* (**tattier, tattiest**) *Br* en mal estado; *(material, clothing)* raído(a); *(décor)* deslustrado(a)

taught [tɔ:t] *pt & pp of* **teach**

taunt [tɔ:nt] **1** *vt* **to t. sb with sth** echar algo en cara a algn
2 *n* pulla *f*

Taurus ['tɔ:rəs] *n* Tauro *m*

taut [tɔ:t] *adj* tenso(a), tirante

tavern ['tævən] *n* taberna *f*

tawdry ['tɔ:drɪ] *adj* (**tawdrier, tawdriest**) hortera

tawn(e)y ['tɔ:nɪ] *adj* leonado(a), rojizo(a)

tax [tæks] **1** *n* impuesto *m*; **t. free** exento(a) de impuestos; **t. collector** recaudador(a) *m,f* (de impuestos); **t. evasion** evasión *f* fiscal; **t. return** declaración *f* de renta

2 *vt* (**a**) gravar (**b**) *(patience etc)* poner a prueba

taxable ['tæksəbəl] *adj* imponible

taxation [tæk'seɪʃən] *n* impuestos *mpl*

taxi ['tæksɪ] **1** *n* taxi *m*; **t. driver** taxista *mf*; **t.** *Br* **rank** *or US* **stand** parada *f* de taxis

2 *vi* *(aircraft)* rodar por la pista

taxidermy ['tæksɪdɜːmɪ] *n* taxidermia *f*

taxing ['tæksɪŋ] *adj* exigente

taxpayer ['tækspeɪə(r)] *n* contribuyente *mf*

TB [tiː'biː] *n* *(tuberculosis)* tuberculosis *f* *inv*

tea [tiː] *n* (**a**) té *m*; **t. bag** bolsita *f* de té; **t. break** descanso *m*; **t. cosy** cubretetera *f*; **t. leaf** hoja *f* de té; **t. service** *or* **set** juego *m* de té; **t. towel** paño *m* (de cocina) (**b**) *(snack)* merienda *f*; (**high**) **t.** merienda-cena *f*

teach [tiːtʃ] **1** *vt* *(pt & pp* **taught***)* enseñar; *(subject)* dar clases de; **to t. sb (how) to do sth** enseñar a algn a hacer algo; *US* **to t. school** ser profesor(a)

2 *vi* dar clases, ser profesor(a)

teacher ['tiːtʃə(r)] *n* profesor(a) *m,f*; *(in primary school)* maestro(a) *m,f*

teaching ['tiːtʃɪŋ] *n* enseñanza *f*

teacup ['tiːkʌp] *n* taza *f* de té

teak [tiːk] *n* teca *f*

team [tiːm] *n* equipo *m*; *(of oxen)* yunta *f*

team-mate ['tiːmmeɪt] *n* compañero(a) *m,f* de equipo

teamwork ['tiːmwɜːk] *n* trabajo *m* en equipo

teapot ['tiːpɒt] *n* tetera *f*

tear[1] [tɪə(r)] *n* lágrima *f*; **to be in tears** estar llorando; **t. gas** gas lacrimógeno

tear[2] [teə(r)] **1** *vt* *(pt* **tore***; pp* **torn***)* (**a**) rajar, desgarrar (**b**) **to t. sth out of sb's hands** arrancarle algo de las manos a algn

2 *vi* (**a**) *(cloth)* rajarse (**b**) **to t. along** ir a toda velocidad

3 *n* desgarrón *m*; *(in clothes)* rasgón *m*

▸ **tear down** *vt sep* derribar

▸ **tear off** *vt sep* arrancar

▸ **tear out** *vt sep* arrancar

▸ **tear up** *vt sep* (**a**) romper, hacer pedazos (**b**) *(uproot)* arrancar de raiz

tearful ['tɪəfʊl] *adj* lloroso(a)

tearoom ['tiːruːm] *n Br* = **teashop**

tease [tiːz] **1** *vt* tomar el pelo a

2 *n* bromista *mf*

teashop ['tiːʃɒp] *n Br* salón *m* de té

teaspoon ['tiːspuːn] *n* cucharilla *f*

teaspoonful ['tiːspuːnfʊl] *n* cucharadita *f*

teat [tiːt] *n* *(of animal)* teta *f*; *(of bottle)* tetina *f*

teatime ['tiːtaɪm] *n* hora *f* del té

technical ['teknɪkəl] *adj* técnico(a); **t. college** instituto *m* de formación profesional

technicality [teknɪ'kælɪtɪ] *n* detalle técnico

technically ['teknɪkəlɪ] *adv* *(theoretically)* en teoría

technician [tek'nɪʃən] *n* técnico(a) *m,f*

technique [tek'niːk] *n* técnica *f*

technological [teknə'lɒdʒɪkəl] *adj* tecnológico(a)

technology [tek'nɒlədʒɪ] *n* tecnología *f*

teddy bear ['tedɪbeə(r)] *n* oso *m* de felpa

tedious ['tiːdɪəs] *adj* tedioso(a), aburrido(a)

tee [tiː] *n* *(in golf)* tee *m*

teem [tiːm] *vi* **to t. with** rebosar de; *Fam* **it was teeming down** llovía a cántaros

teenage ['tiːneɪdʒ] *adj* adolescente

teenager ['tiːneɪdʒə(r)] *n* adolescente *mf*

teens [tiːnz] *npl* adolescencia *f*

tee-shirt ['tiːʃɜːt] *n* camiseta *f*

teeter ['tiːtə(r)] *vi* balancearse

teeth [tiːθ] *pl of* **tooth**

teethe [tiːð] *vi* echar los dientes

teething ['tiːðɪŋ] *n* **t. ring** chupador *m*; *Fig* **t. troubles** dificultades *fpl* iniciales

teetotaller [tiː'təʊtələ(r)] *n* abstemio(a) *m,f*

telecommunications ['telɪkəmjuːnɪ'keɪʃənz] *n sing* telecomunicaciones *fpl*

telegram ['telɪgræm] *n* telegrama *m*

telegraph ['telɪgrɑːf] **1** *n* telégrafo *m*; **t. pole** poste telegráfico

2 *vt & vi* telegrafiar

telepathy [tɪ'lepəθɪ] *n* telepatía *f*

telephone ['telɪfəʊn] **1** *n* teléfono *m*; **t. banking** telebanca *f*; *Br* **t. booth** *or* **box** cabina *f* (telefónica); **t. call** llamada telefónica; **t. directory** guía telefónica; **t. number** número *m* de teléfono

2 *vt* telefonear, llamar por teléfono

telephonist [tɪ'lefənɪst] *n Br* telefonista *mf*

telephoto ['telɪfəʊtəʊ] *adj* **t. lens** teleobjetivo *m*

teleprinter ['telɪprɪntə(r)] *n* teletipo *m*

telescope ['telɪskəʊp] **1** *n* telescopio *m*

2 *vi* plegarse (como un catalejo)

3 *vt* plegar

telescopic [telɪ'skɒpɪk] *adj* *(umbrella)* plegable

televise ['telɪvaɪz] *vt* televisar

television ['telɪvɪʒən] *n* televisión *f*; **t. programme** programa *m* de televisión; **t. (set)** televisor *m*

teleworker ['telɪwɜːkə(r)] *n* teletrabajador(a) *m,f*

teleworking ['telɪwɜːkɪŋ] *n* teletrabajo *m*

telex ['teleks] **1** *n* télex *m*
2 *vt* enviar por télex

tell [tel] **1** *vt* (*pt & pp* **told**) **(a)** (*say*) decir; (*relate*) contar; (*inform*) comunicar; **to t. lies** mentir; **to t. sb about sth** contarle algo a algn; **you're telling me!** ¡a mí me lo vas a contar! **(b)** (*order*) mandar; **to t. sb to do sth** decir a algn que haga algo **(c)** (*distinguish*) distinguir; **to know how to t. the time** saber decir la hora **(d)** **all told** en total
2 *vi* **(a)** (*reveal*) reflejar **(b) who can t.?** (*know*) ¿quién sabe? **(c)** (*have effect*) notarse; **the pressure is telling on her** está acusando la presión
► **tell off** *vt sep Fam* regañar, reñir

teller ['telə(r)] *n* (*in bank etc*) cajero(a) *m,f*

telling ['telɪŋ] *adj* (*action*) eficaz; (*blow, argument*) contundente

telltale ['telteɪl] *n* chivato(a) *m,f*; **t. signs** señales reveladoras

telly ['telɪ] *n Br Fam* **the t.** la tele

temp [temp] *n Fam* trabajador(a) *m,f* temporal

temper ['tempə(r)] **1** *n* **(a)** (*mood*) humor *m*; **to keep one's t.** no perder la calma; **to lose one's t.** perder los estribos **(b)** (*temperament*) **to have a bad t.** tener (mal) genio
2 *vt* (*in metallurgy*) templar; *Fig* suavizar

temperament ['tempərəmənt] *n* temperamento *m*

temperamental [tempərəmentəl] *adj* temperamental

temperate ['tempərɪt] *adj* **(a)** mesurado(a) **(b)** (*climate*) templado(a)

temperature ['temprɪtʃə(r)] *n* temperatura *f*; **to have a t.** tener fiebre

tempest ['tempɪst] *n* tempestad *f*

temple¹ ['tempəl] *n Archit* templo *m*

temple² ['tempəl] *n Anat* sien *f*

tempo ['tempəʊ] *n* tempo *m*

temporary ['tempərərɪ] *adj* provisional; (*setback, improvement*) momentáneo(a); (*staff*) temporal

tempt [tempt] *vt* tentar; **to t. providence** tentar la suerte; **to t. sb to do sth** incitar a algn a hacer algo

temptation [temp'teɪʃən] *n* tentación *f*

tempting ['temptɪŋ] *adj* tentador(a)

ten [ten] *adj & n* diez (*m inv*)

tenable ['tenəbəl] *adj* (*opinion*) sostenible

tenacious [tɪ'neɪʃəs] *adj* tenaz

tenancy ['tenənsɪ] *n* (*of house*) alquiler *m*; (*of land*) arrendamiento *m*

tenant ['tenənt] *n* (*of house*) inquilino(a) *m,f*; (*of farm*) arrendatario(a) *m,f*

tend¹ [tend] *vi* (*be inclined*) tender, tener tendencia (**to** a)

tend² [tend] *vt* (*care for*) cuidar

tendency ['tendənsɪ] *n* tendencia *f*

tender¹ ['tendə(r)] *adj* (*affectionate*) cariñoso(a); (*compassionate*) compasivo(a); (*meat*) tierno(a)

tender² ['tendə(r)] **1** *vt* ofrecer; **to t. one's resignation** presentar la dimisión
2 *vi Com* **to t. for** sacar a concurso
3 *n* **(a)** *Com* oferta *f* **(b) legal t.** moneda *f* de curso legal

tenderness ['tendənɪs] *n* ternura *f*

tendon ['tendən] *n* tendón *m*

tenement ['tenɪmənt] *n* casa *f* de vecindad

tenet ['tenɪt] *n* principio *m*

tennis ['tenɪs] *n* tenis *m*; **t. ball** pelota *f* de tenis; **t. court** pista *f* de tenis; **t. player** tenista *m,f*; **t. racket** raqueta *f* de tenis; **t. shoe** zapatilla *f* de tenis

tenor ['tenə(r)] *n Mus* tenor *m*

tense¹ [tens] *adj* tenso(a)

tense² [tens] *n Gram* tiempo *m*

tension ['tenʃən] *n* tensión *f*

tent [tent] *n* tienda *f* de campaña; **t. peg** estaca *f*

tentacle ['tentəkəl] *n* tentáculo *m*

tentative ['tentətɪv] *adj* **(a)** (*not definite*) de prueba **(b)** (*hesitant*) indeciso(a)

tenterhooks ['tentəhʊks] *npl Fig* **on t.** sobre ascuas

tenth [tenθ] **1** *adj & n* décimo(a) *(m,f)*
2 *n* (*fraction*) décimo *m*

tenuous ['tenjʊəs] *adj* **(a)** tenue **(b)** (*argument*) flojo(a)

tenure ['tenjʊə(r)] *n* **(a)** (*of office*) ocupación *f* **(b)** (*of property*) arrendamiento *m*

tepid ['tepɪd] *adj* tibio(a)

term [tɜːm] *n* **(a)** (*period*) período *m*; *Educ* trimestre *m*; **t. of office** mandato *m*, legislatura *f*; **in the long/short t.** a largo/corto plazo **(b)** (*word*) término *m*; *Fig* **in terms of money** en cuanto al dinero **(c) terms** (*conditions*) condiciones *fpl*; **to come to terms with** hacerse a la idea de **(d) to be on good/bad terms with sb** tener buenas/malas relaciones con algn
2 *vt* calificar de

terminal ['tɜːmɪnəl] **1** *adj* terminal; **t. cancer** cáncer incurable
2 *n* terminal *f*

terminate ['tɜːmɪneɪt] **1** *vt* terminar; **to t. a pregnancy** abortar
 2 *vi* terminarse

termini ['tɜːmɪnaɪ] *pl of* **terminus**

terminology [tɜːmɪ'nɒlədʒɪ] *n* terminología *f*

terminus ['tɜːmɪnəs] *n* (*pl* **termini**) terminal *m*

terrace ['terəs] *n* (**a**) *Agr* bancal *m* (**b**) *Br* (*of houses*) hilera *f* de casas (**c**) (*patio*) terraza *f* (**d**) *Ftb* the terraces las gradas

terraced ['terəst] *adj Br* **t. houses** casas *fpl* (de estilo uniforme) en hilera

terrain [tə'reɪn] *n* terreno *m*

terrible ['terəbəl] *adj* terrible; *Fig* **I feel t.** (*ill*) me encuentro fatal

terribly ['terəblɪ] *adv* terriblemente

terrier ['terɪə(r)] *n* terrier *m*

terrific [tə'rɪfɪk] *adj* (**a**) *Fam* (*excellent*) fenomenal (**b**) (*extreme*) tremendo(a)

terrify ['terɪfaɪ] *vt* aterrorizar

terrifying ['terɪfaɪɪŋ] *adj* aterrador(a)

territory ['terɪtərɪ] *n* territorio *m*

terror ['terə(r)] *n* terror *m*

terrorism ['terərɪzəm] *n* terrorismo *m*

terrorist ['terərɪst] *adj & n* terrorista (*mf*)

terrorize ['terəraɪz] *vt* aterrorizar

terry ['terɪ] *n* **t. towel** toalla *f* de rizo

terse [tɜːs] *adj* (*curt*) lacónico(a)

test [test] **1** *vt* probar, someter a una prueba; (*analyse*) analizar; *Med* hacer un análisis de
 2 *n* prueba *f*, examen *m*; **to put to the t.** poner a prueba; **to stand the t.** pasar la prueba; **t. match** partido *m* internacional; **t. pilot** piloto *m* de pruebas; **t. tube** probeta *f*; **t.-tube baby** niño *m* probeta

testament ['testəmənt] *n* testamento *m*; **Old/ New T.** Antiguo/Nuevo Testamento

testicle ['testɪkəl] *n* testículo *m*

testify ['testɪfaɪ] **1** *vt* declarar
 2 *vi* Fig **to t. to sth** atestiguar algo

testimonial [testɪ'məʊnɪəl] *n* recomendación *f*

testimony ['testɪmənɪ] *n* testimonio *m*, declaración *f*

tetanus ['tetənəs] *n* tétano(s) *m inv*

tether ['teðə(r)] **1** *n* ronzal *m*; *Fig* **to be at the end of one's t.** estar hasta la coronilla
 2 *vt* (*animal*) atar

Texas ['teksəs] *n* Tejas

text [tekst] *n* texto *m*

textbook ['tekstbʊk] *n* libro *m* de texto

textile ['tekstaɪl] **1** *n* tejido *m*
 2 *adj* textil

texture ['tekstʃə(r)] *n* textura *f*

Thai [taɪ] *adj & n* tailandés(esa) (*m,f*)

Thailand ['taɪlænd] *n* Tailandia

Thames [temz] *n* the **T.** el Támesis

than [ðæn, *unstressed* ðən] *conj* que; (*with numbers*) de; **he's older t. me** es mayor que yo; **I have more/less t. you** tengo más/menos que tú; **more interesting t. we thought** más interesante de lo que creíamos; **more t. once** más de una vez; **more t. ten people** más de diez personas

thank [θæŋk] *vt* agradecer a; **t. you** gracias

thankful ['θæŋkfʊl] *adj* agradecido(a)

thankless ['θæŋklɪs] *adj* (*task*) ingrato(a)

thanks [θæŋks] *npl* gracias *fpl*; **no t.** no gracias; **many t.** muchas gracias; **t. for phoning** gracias por llamar; **t. to** gracias a

thanksgiving [θæŋks'gɪvɪŋ] *n US* **T. Day** Día *m* de Acción de Gracias

that [ðæt, *unstressed* ðət] **1** *dem pron* (*pl* **those**) (**a**) ése *m*, ésa *f*; (*further away*) aquél *m*, aquélla *f*; **this one is new but t. is old** éste es nuevo pero ése es viejo
 (**b**) (*indefinite*) eso; (*remote*) aquello; **after t.** después de eso; **like t.** así; **t.'s right** eso es; **t.'s where I live** allí vivo yo; **what's t.?** ¿qué es eso?; **who's t.?** ¿quién es?
 (**c**) (*with relative*) el/la; **all those I saw** todos los que vi
 2 *dem adj* (*pl* **those**) (*masculine*) ese; (*feminine*) esa; (*further away*) (*masculine*) aquel; (*feminine*) aquella; **at t. time** en aquella época; **t. book** ese/aquel libro; **t. one** ése/aquél
 3 *rel pron* (**a**) (*subject, direct object*) que; **all (t.) you said** todo lo que dijiste; **the letter (t.) I sent you** la carta que te envié
 (**b**) (*governed by preposition*) que, el/la que, los/las que, el/la cual, los/las cuales; **the car (t.) they came in** el coche en el que vinieron
 (**c**) (*when*) que, en que; **the moment (t.) you arrived** el momento en que llegaste

---

El pronombre relativo **that** puede omitirse salvo cuando es sujeto de la oración subordinada.

---

 4 *conj* que; **come here so (t.) I can see you** ven aquí (para) que te vea; **he said (t.) he would come** dijo que vendría

---

La conjunción **that** se puede omitir cuando introduce una oración subordinada.

---

 5 *adv* así de, tanto, tan; **cut off t. much** córteme un trozo así de grande; **I don't think it can be t. old** no creo que sea tan viejo; **we haven't got t. much money**

no tenemos tanto dinero

thatched [θætʃt] *adj* cubierto(a) con paja; **t. cottage** casita *f* con techo de paja; **t. roof** techo *m* de paja

thaw [θɔː] **1** *vt (snow)* derretir; *(food, freezer)* descongelar

2 *vi* descongelarse; *(snow)* derretirse

3 *n* deshielo *m*

the [ðə, *before vowel sound* ðɪ, *emphatic* ðiː] **1** *def art* **(a)** el/la; *pl* los/las; **at/to t.** al/a la; *pl* a los/a las; **of** or **from t.** del/de la; *pl* de los/de las; **t. Alps** los Alpes; **t. right time** la hora exacta; **t. voice of t. people** la voz del pueblo

(b) *(omitted)* **George t. Sixth** Jorge Sexto

(c) **by t. day** al día; **by t. dozen** a docenas

(d) *(with adjectives used as nouns)* **t. elderly** los ancianos

(e) *(indicating kind)* **he's not t. person to do that** no es de los que hacen tales cosas

(f) *(enough)* **he hasn't t. patience to wait** no tiene suficiente paciencia para esperar

2 *adv* **t. more t. merrier** cuantos más mejor; **t. sooner t. better** cuanto antes mejor

theatre, *US* **theater** [ˈθɪətə(r)] *n* teatro *m*

theatre-goer, *US* **theater-goer** [ˈθɪətəgəʊə(r)] *n* aficionado(a) *m,f* al teatro

theatrical [θɪˈætrɪkəl] *adj* teatral

theft [θeft] *n* robo *m*; **petty t.** hurto *m*

their [ðeə(r)] *poss adj (one thing)* su; *(various things)* sus

theirs [ðeəz] *poss pron* (el) suyo/(la) suya; *pl* (los) suyos/(las) suyas

them [ðem, *unstressed* ðəm] *pers pron pl* **(a)** *(direct object)* los/las; *(indirect object)* les; **I know t.** los/las conozco; **I shall tell t. so** se lo diré (a ellos/ellas); **it's t.!** ¡son ellos!; **speak to t.** hábleles **(b)** *(with preposition)* ellos/ellas; **walk in front of t.** camine delante de ellos; **they took the keys away with t.** se llevaron las llaves; **both of t., the two of t.** los dos; **neither of t.** ninguno de los dos; **none of t.** ninguno de ellos

theme [θiːm] *n* tema *m*; **t. tune** sintonía *f*

themselves [ðəmˈselvz] *pers pron pl (as subject)* ellos mismos/ellas mismas, *(as direct or indirect object)* se; *(after a preposition)* sí mismos/sí mismas; **they did it by t.** lo hicieron ellos solos

then [ðen] **1** *adv* **(a)** *(at that time)* entonces; **since t.** desde entonces; **there and t.** en el acto; **till t.** hasta entonces **(b)** *(next, afterwards)* luego **(c)** *(anyway)* de todas

formas **(d)** *(in that case)* entonces; **go t.** pues vete

2 *conj* entonces

3 *adj* **the t. president** el entonces presidente

theology [θɪˈɒlədʒɪ] *n* teología *f*

theoretic(al) [θɪəˈretɪk(əl)] *adj* teórico(a)

theoretically [θɪəˈretɪklɪ] *adv* teóricamente

theory [ˈθɪərɪ] *n* teoría *f*

therapist [ˈθerəpɪst] *n* terapeuta *mf*

therapy [ˈθerəpɪ] *n* terapia *f*

there [ðeə(r), *unstressed* ðə(r)] **1** *adv* **(a)** *(indicating place)* allí, allá; *(nearer speaker)* ahí; **here and t.** acá y allá; **in t.** ahí dentro; **is Peter t.?** ¿está Peter? **(b)** *(emphatic)* **that man t.** aquel hombre **(c)** *(unstressed)* **t. is .../t. are ...** hay...; **t. were many cars** había muchos coches; **t. were six of us** éramos seis **(d)** *(in respect)* **t.'s the difficulty** ahí está la dificultad

2 *interj* **so t.!** ¡ea!; **t., t.** bien, bien

thereabouts [ˈðeərəbaʊts], *US* **thereabout** [ˈðeərəbaʊt] *adv* **in Cambridge or t.** en Cambridge o por allí cerca; **at four o'clock or t.** a las cuatro o así

thereafter [ðeərˈɑːftə(r)] *adv* a partir de entonces

thereby [ˈðeəbaɪ] *adv* por eso *or* ello

therefore [ˈðeəfɔː(r)] *adv* por lo tanto, por eso

thermal [ˈθɜːməl] **1** *adj (spring)* termal; *Phys* térmico(a)

2 *n Met* corriente térmica

thermometer [θəˈmɒmɪtə(r)] *n* termómetro *m*

Thermos® [ˈθɜːməs] *n* **T. (flask)** termo *m*

thermostat [ˈθɜːməstæt] *n* termostato *m*

thesaurus [θɪˈsɔːrəs] *n* diccionario *m* de sinónimos

these [ðiːz] **1** *dem adj pl* estos(as)

2 *dem pron pl* éstos(as); *see* **this**

thesis [ˈθiːsɪs] *n (pl* **theses** [ˈθiːsiːz]) tesis *f inv*

they [ðeɪ] *pron pl* **(a)** ellos/ellas *(usually omitted in Spanish, except for contrast)*; **t. are dancing** están bailando; **t. are rich** son ricos **(b)** *(stressed)* **t. alone** ellos solos; **t. themselves told me** me lo dijeron ellos mismos **(c)** *(with relative)* los/las **(d)** *(indefinite)* **that's what t. say** eso es lo que se dice; **t. say that ...** se dice que ...

thick [θɪk] **1** *adj* **(a)** *(book etc)* grueso(a); **a wall 2 m t.** un muro de 2 m de espesor **(b)** *(dense)* espeso(a) **(c)** *Fam (stupid)* tonto(a)

2 *adv* densamente

3 *n* **to be in the t. of it** estar metido(a) de lleno

thicken ['θɪkən] **1** *vt* espesar

2 *vi* espesarse; *Fig (plot)* complicarse

thickness ['θɪknɪs] *n (of wall etc)* espesor *m*; *(of wire, lips)* grueso *m*; *(of liquid, woodland)* espesura *f*

thickset [θɪk'set] *adj (person)* rechoncho(a)

thick-skinned [θɪk'skɪnd] *adj Fig* poco sensible

thief [θiːf] *n (pl* **thieves** [θiːvz]*)* ladrón(ona) *m,f*

thigh [θaɪ] *n* muslo *m*

thimble ['θɪmbəl] *n* dedal *m*

thin [θɪn] **1** *adj (*thinner, thinnest*)* **(a)** delgado(a); **a t. slice** una loncha fina **(b)** *(hair, vegetation)* ralo(a); *(liquid)* claro(a); *(population)* escaso(a) **(c)** *Fig (voice)* débil; **a t. excuse** un pobre pretexto

2 *vt* **to t. (down)** *(paint)* diluir

thing [θɪŋ] *n* **(a)** cosa *f*; **my things** *(clothing)* mi ropa *f*, *(possessions)* mis cosas *fpl*; **for one t.** en primer lugar; **the t. is ...** resulta que ...; **what with one t. and another** entre unas cosas y otras; **as things are** tal como están las cosas **(b)** **poor little t.!** ¡pobrecito(a)!

think [θɪŋk] **1** *vt (pt & pp* **thought***)* **(a)** *(believe)* pensar, creer; **I t. so/not** creo que sí/no **(b)** **I thought as much** yo me lo imaginaba

2 *vi* **(a)** pensar *(of or* **about** en); **give me time to t.** dame tiempo para reflexionar; **to t. ahead** prevenir **(b)** *(have as opinion)* opinar, pensar; **to t. highly of sb** apreciar a algn; **what do you t.?** ¿a ti qué te parece? **(c)** **just t.!** ¡imagínate!

▸ **think out** *vt sep* meditar; **a carefully thought-out answer** una respuesta razonada

▸ **think over** *vt sep* reflexionar; **we'll have to t. it over** lo tendremos que pensar

▸ **think up** *vt sep* imaginar, idear

thinking ['θɪŋkɪŋ] *adj* racional

think-tank ['θɪŋktæŋk] *n Fam* grupo *m* de expertos

thinly ['θɪnlɪ] *adv* poco, ligeramente

third [θɜːd] **1** *adj* tercero(a); *(before masculine singular noun)* tercer; **(on) the t. of March** el tres de marzo; **the T. World** el Tercer Mundo; **t. party insurance** seguro *m* a terceros

2 *n* **(a)** *(in series)* tercero(a) *m,f* **(b)** *(fraction)* tercio *m*, tercera parte

thirdly ['θɜːdlɪ] *adv* en tercer lugar

third-rate ['θɜːdreɪt] *adj* de calidad inferior

thirst [θɜːst] *n* sed *f*

thirsty ['θɜːstɪ] *adj (*thirstier, thirstiest*)* sediento(a); **to be t.** tener sed

thirteen [θɜː'tiːn] *adj & n* trece *(m inv)*

thirteenth [θɜː'tiːnθ] **1** *adj & n* decimotercero(a) *(m,f)*

2 *n (fraction)* decimotercera parte

thirtieth ['θɜːtɪɪθ] **1** *adj & n* trigésimo(a) *(m,f)*

2 *n (fraction)* trigésima parte

thirty ['θɜːtɪ] *adj & n* treinta *(m inv)*

this [ðɪs] **1** *dem adj (pl* **these***) (masculine)* este; *(feminine)* esta; **t. book/these books** este libro/estos libros; **t. one** éste/ésta

2 *dem pron (pl* **these***)* **(a)** *(indefinite)* esto; **it was like t.** fue así **(b)** *(place)* **t. is where we met** fue aquí donde nos conocimos **(c)** *(time)* **it should have come before t.** debería haber llegado ya **(d)** *(specific person or thing)* éste *m*, ésta *f*; **I prefer these to those** me gustan más éstos que aquéllos; *(introduction)* **t. is Mr Álvarez** le presento al Sr. Álvarez; *Tel* **t. is Julia (speaking)** soy Julia

3 *adv* **he got t. far** llegó hasta aquí; **t. small/big** así de pequeño/grande

thistle ['θɪsəl] *n* cardo *m*

thong [θɒŋ] *n* **(a)** *(for fastening)* correa *f* **(b)** *US & Austral (sandal)* chancla *f*

thorax ['θɔːræks] *n* tórax *m*

thorn [θɔːn] *n* espina *f*

thorough ['θʌrə] *adj (careful)* minucioso(a); *(work)* concienzudo(a); *(knowledge)* profundo(a); **to carry out a t. enquiry into a matter** investigar a fondo un asunto

thoroughbred ['θʌrəbred] **1** *adj (horse)* de pura sangre

2 *n (horse)* pura sangre *mf*

thoroughfare ['θʌrəfeə(r)] *n (road)* carretera *f*, *(street)* calle *f*

thoroughly ['θʌrəlɪ] *adv (carefully)* a fondo; *(wholly)* completamente

those [ðəʊz] **1** *dem pron pl* ésos(as); *(remote)* aquéllos(as); **t. who** los que/las que

2 *dem adj pl* esos(as); *(remote)* aquellos(as); *see* **that**

though [ðəʊ] **1** *conj* **(a)** aunque; **strange t. it may seem** por (muy) extraño que parezca **(b)** *as* **t.** como si; **it looks as t. he's gone** parece que se ha ido

2 *adv* sin embargo

thought [θɔːt] **1** *n* **(a)** *(act of thinking)* pensamiento *m*; **what a tempting t.!** ¡qué

idea más tentadora! (**b**) *(reflection)* reflexión *f* (**c**) **it's the t. that counts** *(intention)* lo que cuenta es la intención
2 *pt & pp of* **think**

thoughtful ['θɔːtfʊl] *adj (pensive)* pensativo(a); *(considerate)* atento(a)

thoughtless ['θɔːtlɪs] *adj (person)* desconsiderado(a); *(action)* irreflexivo(a)

thousand ['θaʊzənd] *adj & n* mil *(m inv)*; **thousands of people** miles de personas

thousandth ['θaʊzənθ] **1** *adj* milésimo(a)
2 *n* (**a**) *(in series)* milésimo(a) *m,f* (**b**) *(fraction)* milésima parte

thrash [θræʃ] **1** *vt* dar una paliza a
2 *vi* **to t. about** *or* **around** agitarse
▸ **thrash out** *vt sep* discutir a fondo

thread [θred] **1** *n* (**a**) hilo *m*; **length of t.** hebra *f* (**b**) *(of screw)* rosca *f*
2 *vt* (**a**) *(needle)* enhebrar (**b**) **to t. one's way (through)** colarse (por)

threadbare ['θredbeə(r)] *adj* raído(a)

threat [θret] *n* amenaza *f*

threaten ['θretən] *vt* amenazar; **to t. to do sth** amenazar con hacer algo

threatening ['θretənɪŋ] *adj* amenazador(a)

threateningly ['θretənɪŋlɪ] *adv* de modo amenazador

three [θriː] *adj & n* tres *(m inv)*

three-dimensional ['θriːdɪ'menʃənəl] *adj* tridimensional

threefold ['θriːfəʊld] **1** *adj* triple
2 *adv* tres veces; **to increase t.** triplicarse

three-piece ['θriːpiːs] *adj* **t. suit** traje *m* de tres piezas; **t. suite** tresillo *m*

three-ply ['θriːplaɪ] *adj* de tres hebras

three-wheeler [θriː'wiːlə(r)] *n Aut* coche *m* de tres ruedas; *(tricycle)* triciclo *m*

thresh [θreʃ] *vt* trillar

threshold ['θreʃəʊld] *n* umbral *m*; *Fig* **to be on the t. of** estar a las puertas *or* en los umbrales de

threw [θruː] *pt of* **throw**

thrifty ['θrɪftɪ] *adj* (**thriftier, thriftiest**) económico(a), ahorrador(a)

thrill [θrɪl] **1** *n* (**a**) *(excitement)* emoción *f* (**b**) *(quiver)* estremecimiento *m*
2 *vt (excite)* emocionar; *(audience)* entusiasmar

thriller ['θrɪlə(r)] *n* novela *f*/película *f* de suspense

thrilling ['θrɪlɪŋ] *adj* emocionante

thrive [θraɪv] *vi* (*pt* **thrived** *or* **throve**; *pp* **thrived** *or* **thriven** ['θrɪvən]) (**a**) *(person)* rebosar de salud (**b**) *Fig (business)* prosperar; **he thrives on it** le viene de maravilla

thriving ['θraɪvɪŋ] *adj Fig* próspero(a)

throat [θrəʊt] *n* garganta *f*

throb [θrɒb] **1** *n (of heart)* latido *m*; *(of machine)* zumbido *m*
2 *vi (heart)* latir; *(machine)* zumbar; **my head is throbbing** me va a estallar la cabeza

throes [θrəʊz] *npl* **to be in one's death t.** estar agonizando; *Fig* **in the t. of ...** en pleno(a) ...

thrombosis [θrɒm'bəʊsɪs] *n Med* trombosis *f inv*

throne [θrəʊn] *n* trono *m*

throng [θrɒŋ] **1** *n* multitud *f*, gentío *m*
2 *vi* apiñarse
3 *vt* atestar

throttle ['θrɒtəl] **1** *n* **t. (valve)** *(of engine)* válvula reguladora
2 *vt (person)* estrangular
▸ **throttle back** *vt sep (engine)* desacelerar

through [θruː] **1** *prep* (**a**) *(place)* a través de, por; **to look t. the window** mirar por la ventana
(**b**) *(time)* a lo largo de; **all t. his life** durante toda su vida; *US* **Tuesday t. Thursday** desde el martes hasta el jueves inclusive
(**c**) *(by means of)* por, mediante; **I learnt of it t.** Jack me enteré por Jack
(**d**) *(because of)* a *or* por causa de; **t. ignorance** por ignorancia
2 *adj* **a t. train** un tren directo; **t. traffic** tránsito *m*
3 *adv* (**a**) *(from one side to the other)* de un lado a otro; **to let sb t.** dejar pasar a algn; *Fig* **socialist/French t. and t.** socialista/francés por los cuatro costados
(**b**) *(finished)* **I'm t. with him** he terminado con él
(**c**) *Tel* **to get t. to sb** comunicar con algn; **you're t.** ¡hablen!

throughout [θruː'aʊt] **1** *prep* por todo(a); **t. the year** durante todo el año
2 *adv (place)* en todas partes; *(time)* todo el tiempo

throve [θrəʊv] *pt of* **thrive**

throw [θrəʊ] **1** *vt* (*pt* **threw**; *pp* **thrown**) (**a**) *(ball)* tirar, arrojar; *(to the ground)* derribar; *(rider)* desmontar; *Fig* **he threw a fit** le dio un ataque; *Fig* **to t. a party** dar una fiesta (**b**) *(disconcert)* desconcertar
2 *n* tiro *m*, lanzamiento *m*; *(in wrestling)* derribo *m*
▸ **throw away** *vt sep (rubbish)* tirar; *(money)* malgastar; *(opportunity)* perder
▸ **throw in** *vt sep* (**a**) tirar; *Sport* sacar de banda; *Fig* **to t. in the towel** arrojar la toalla (**b**) *(include)* añadir; *(in deal)* incluir *(gratis)*

▸ **throw off** vt sep (person, thing) deshacerse de; (clothes) quitarse

▸ **throw out** vt sep (rubbish) tirar; (person) echar

▸ **throw up 1** vt sep (**a**) lanzar al aire (**b**) Constr construir rápidamente
  2 vi Fam vomitar, devolver

throwaway ['θrəʊəweɪ] adj desechable

throw-in ['θrəʊɪn] n Sport saque m de banda

thrown [θrəʊn] pp of throw

thru [θruː] prep, adj & adv US Fam = through

thrush [θrʌʃ] n Orn tordo m, zorzal m

thrust [θrʌst] **1** vt (pt & pp thrust) empujar con fuerza; **he t. a letter into my hand** me puso una carta violentamente en la mano
  2 n (push) empujón m; Av & Phys empuje m

thud [θʌd] n ruido sordo

thug [θʌg] n (lout) gamberro m; (criminal) criminal m

thumb [θʌm] **1** n pulgar m
  2 vt (**a**) manosear (**b**) **to t. a lift** hacer autostop

▸ **thumb through** vt insep (book) hojear

thumbtack ['θʌmtæk] n US chincheta f

thump [θʌmp] **1** n (**a**) (sound) ruido sordo (**b**) (blow) golpazo m; Fam torta f
  2 vt golpear
  3 vi (**a**) **to t. on the table** golpear la mesa (**b**) (heart) latir ruidosamente

thunder ['θʌndə(r)] **1** n trueno m; **t. of applause** estruendo m de aplausos
  2 vi tronar

thunderbolt ['θʌndəbəʊlt] n (lighting) rayo m; Fig (news) bomba f

thunderclap ['θʌndəklæp] n trueno m

thunderous ['θʌndərəs] adj Fig ensordecedor(a)

thunderstorm ['θʌndəstɔːm] n tormenta f

thundery ['θʌndərɪ] adj (weather) tormentoso(a)

Thursday ['θɜːzdɪ] n jueves m

thus [ðʌs] adv así, de esta manera; **and t. ...** así que ...

thwart [θwɔːt] vt frustrar, desbaratar

thyme [taɪm] n tomillo m

thyroid ['θaɪrɔɪd] n tiroides f inv

tiara [tɪ'ɑːrə] n diadema f; Rel tiara f

tic [tɪk] n tic m

tick¹ [tɪk] **1** n (**a**) (sound) tic-tac m (**b**) Br Fam **I'll do it in a t.** ahora mismo lo hago (**c**) (mark) marca f de visto bueno
  2 vi hacer tic-tac
  3 vt marcar

▸ **tick off** vt sep (**a**) (mark) marcar (**b**) Br Fam (reprimand) regañar

▸ **tick over** vi Aut funcionar al ralentí

tick² [tɪk] n (insect) garrapata f

ticket ['tɪkɪt] n (**a**) (for bus etc) billete m, Am boleto m; (for theatre, cinema) entrada f, Méx boleto; (for lottery) décimo m, Am boleto; **t. collector** revisor(a) m,f; **t. office** taquilla f; **t. Br tout** or US **scalper** revendedor m de entradas (**b**) (receipt) recibo m (**c**) (label) etiqueta f (**d**) Aut multa f

tickle ['tɪkəl] **1** vt hacer cosquillas a
  2 vi hacer cosquillas
  3 n cosquillas fpl

ticklish ['tɪklɪʃ] adj **to be t.** tener cosquillas

tick-tack-toe ['tɪktæk'təʊ] n US tres en raya m

tidal ['taɪdəl] adj de la marea; **t. wave** ola f gigante

tidbit ['tɪdbɪt] n US = titbit

tiddlywinks ['tɪdlɪwɪŋks] n sing (game) pulga f

tide [taɪd] n (**a**) marea f; **high/low t.** marea alta/baja (**b**) Fig (of events) curso m; **the t. has turned** han cambiado las cosas; **to go against the t.** ir contra corriente

tidings ['taɪdɪŋz] npl Fml noticias fpl

tidy ['taɪdɪ] **1** adj (tidier, tidiest) (**a**) (room, habits) ordenado(a) (**b**) (appearance) arreglado(a)
  2 vt arreglar; **to t. away** poner en su sitio
  3 vi **to t. (up)** ordenar las cosas

tie [taɪ] **1** vt (shoelaces etc) atar; **to t. a knot** hacer un nudo
  2 vi Sport empatar (**with** con)
  3 n (**a**) (bond) lazo m, vínculo m (**b**) Fig (hindrance) atadura f (**c**) (clothing) corbata f (**d**) Sport (match) partido m; (draw) empate m

▸ **tie down** vt sep sujetar; Fig **to be tied down** estar atado(a); Fig **to t. sb down to a promise** obligar a algn a cumplir una promesa

▸ **tie up** vt sep (**a**) (parcel, dog) atar (**b**) (deal) concluir (**c**) (capital) inmovilizar; Fig **I'm tied up just now** de momento estoy muy ocupado(a)

tiebreaker ['taɪbreɪkə(r)] n tie-break m

tiepin ['taɪpɪn] n alfiler m de corbata

tier [tɪə(r)] n (of seats) fila f; (in stadium) grada f; **four-t. cake** pastel m de cuatro pisos

tiger ['taɪgə(r)] n tigre m

tight [taɪt] **1** adj (**a**) apretado(a); (clothing) ajustado(a); (seal) hermético(a);

my shoes are too t. me aprietan los zapatos; *Fig* **to be in a t. corner** estar en un apuro (**b**) *(scarce)* escaso(a); **money's a bit t.** estamos escasos de dinero (**c**) *(mean)* agarrado(a) (**d**) *Fam (drunk)* borracho(a)

2 *adv* estrechámente; *(seal)* herméticamente; **hold t.** agárrate fuerte; **shut t.** bien cerrado(a); **to sit t.** no moverse de su sitio

tighten ['taɪtən] **1** *vt (screw)* apretar, *(rope)* tensar; *Fig* **to t. (up) restrictions** intensificar las restricciones

2 *vi* apretarse; *(cable)* tensarse

tightfisted [taɪt'fɪstɪd] *adj* tacaño(a)

tightrope ['taɪtrəʊp] *n* cuerda floja; **t. walker** funámbulo(a) *m,f*

tights [taɪts] *npl (thick)* leotardos *mpl*; *(of dancer)* mallas *fpl*; *Br (thin)* medias *fpl*, pantis *mpl*

tile [taɪl] **1** *n (of roof)* teja *f*; *(glazed)* azulejo *m*; *(for floor)* baldosa *f*

2 *vt (roof)* tejar; *(wall)* azulejar; *(floor)* embaldosar

tiled [taɪld] *adj (roof)* de *or* con tejas; *(wall)* revestido(a) de azulejos; *(floor)* embaldosado(a)

till¹ [tɪl] *n (for cash)* caja *f*

till² [tɪl] *vt (field)* labrar, cultivar

till³ [tɪl] **1** *prep* hasta; **from morning t. night** de la mañana a la noche; **t. then** hasta entonces

2 *conj* hasta que

tiller ['tɪlə(r)] *n Naut* caña *f* del timón

tilt [tɪlt] **1** *n* (**a**) *(angle)* inclinación *f* (**b**) **(at) full t.** *(speed)* a toda velocidad

2 *vi* **to t. over** volcarse; **to t. (up)** inclinarse

3 *vt* inclinar

timber ['tɪmbə(r)] *n (wood)* madera *f* (de construcción); *(trees)* árboles *mpl*; **(piece of) t.** viga *f*

time [taɪm] **1** *n* (**a**) tiempo *m*; **all the t.** todo el tiempo; **for some t. (past)** desde hace algún tiempo; **I haven't seen him for a long t.** hace mucho (tiempo) que no lo veo; **in a short t.** en poco tiempo; **in no t.** en un abrir y cerrar de ojos; **in t.** a tiempo; **in three weeks' t.** dentro de tres semanas; **to take one's t. over sth** hacer algo con calma; *Fam* **to do t.** cumplir una condena; **t. bomb** bomba *f* de relojería; **t. limit** límite *m* de tiempo; *(for payment etc)* plazo *m*; **t. switch** interruptor *m* electrónico automático; **t. zone** huso horario

(**b**) *(era)* época *f*, tiempos *mpl*; **a sign of the times** un signo de los tiempos; **to be**

behind the times tener ideas anticuadas

(**c**) *(point in time)* momento *m*; **(at) any t. (you like)** cuando quiera; **at no t.** en ningún momento; **at that t.** (en aquel) entonces; **at the same t.** al mismo tiempo; **at times** a veces; **from t. to t.** de vez en cuando; **he may turn up at any t.** puede llegar en cualquier momento

(**d**) *(time of day)* hora *f*; **and about t. too!** ¡ya era hora!; **in good t.** con anticipación; **on t.** puntualmente; **what's the t.?** ¿qué hora es?

(**e**) **t. of year** época *f* del año

(**f**) **to have a good/bad t.** pasarlo bien/mal

(**g**) *(occasion)* vez *f*; **four at a t.** cuatro a la vez; **next t.** la próxima vez; **several times over** varias veces; **three times running** tres veces seguidas; **t. after t.** una y otra vez

(**h**) *(in multiplication)* **three times four** tres (multiplicado) por cuatro; **four times as big** cuatro veces más grande

(**i**) *Mus* compás *m*; **in t.** al compás

2 *vt* (**a**) *(speech)* calcular la duración de; *Sport (race)* cronometrar

(**b**) *(choose the time of)* escoger el momento oportuno para

time-consuming ['taɪmkənsjuːmɪŋ] *adj* que ocupa mucho tiempo

time-lag ['taɪmlæg] *n* intervalo *m*

timeless ['taɪmlɪs] *adj* eterno(a)

timely ['taɪmlɪ] *adj* (**timelier, timeliest**) oportuno(a)

timer ['taɪmə(r)] *n (device)* temporizador *m*

timetable ['taɪmteɪbəl] *n* horario *m*

timid ['tɪmɪd] *adj* tímido(a)

timing ['taɪmɪŋ] *n* (**a**) *(timeliness)* oportunidad *f*; *(coordination)* coordinación *f*; **your t. was wrong** no calculaste bien (**b**) *Sport* cronometraje *m*

tin [tɪn] **1** *n* (**a**) *(metal)* estaño *m*; **t. plate** hojalata *f* (**b**) *(container)* lata *f*

2 *vt (tins)* enlatar; **tinned food** conservas *fpl*

tinfoil ['tɪnfɔɪl] *n* papel *m* de estaño

tinge [tɪndʒ] **1** *n* tinte *m*, matiz *m*

2 *vt* teñir

tingle ['tɪŋgəl] *vi* **my feet are tingling** siento un hormigueo en los pies

tinker ['tɪŋkə(r)] **1** *n Pej* calderero(a) *mf*

2 *vi* **stop tinkering with the radio** deja de toquetear la radio

tinkle ['tɪŋkəl] *vi* tintinear

tin-opener ['tɪnəʊpənə(r)] *n* abrelatas *m inv*

tinsel ['tɪnsəl] *n* oropel *m*

tint [tɪnt] **1** *n* tinte *m*, matiz *m*
  2 *vt* teñir; **to t. one's hair** teñirse el pelo
tiny ['taɪnɪ] *adj* (**tinier, tiniest**) pequeñito(a); **a t. bit** un poquitín
tip¹ [tɪp] **1** *n* (*end*) punta *f*; (*of cigarette*) colilla *f*; **it's on the t. of my tongue** lo tengo en la punta de la lengua
  2 *vt* poner cantera a; **tipped with steel** con punta de acero
tip² [tɪp] **1** *n* (**a**) (*gratuity*) propina *f* (**b**) (*advice*) consejo *m* (**c**) *Sport* (*racing*) pronóstico *m*
  2 *vt* (**a**) dar una propina a (**b**) *Sport* pronosticar
  ▸ **tip off** *vt sep* (*police*) dar el chivatazo a
tip³ [tɪp] **1** *n Br* **rubbish t.** vertedero *m*
  2 *vt* inclinar; *Br* (*rubbish*) verter
  3 *vi* **to t. (up)** ladearse; (*cart*) bascular
  ▸ **tip over 1** *vt sep* volcar
  2 *vi* volcarse
tipple ['tɪpəl] *Fam* **1** *vi* empinar el codo
  2 *n* bebida alcohólica; **what's your t.?** ¿qué te gusta beber?
tipsy ['tɪpsɪ] *adj* (**tipsier, tipsiest**) contentillo(a)
tiptoe ['tɪptəʊ] **1** *vi* andar de puntillas; **to t. in/out** entrar/salir de puntillas
  2 *n* **on t.** de puntillas
tiptop ['tɪptɒp] *adj Fam* de primera
tire¹ [taɪə(r)] *n US* = **tyre**
tire² [taɪə(r)] **1** *vt* cansar; **to t. sb out** agotar a algn
  2 *vi* cansarse; **to t. of doing sth** cansarse de hacer algo
tired ['taɪəd] *adj* cansado(a); **t. out** rendido(a); **to be t.** estar cansado(a); **to be t. of sth** estar harto(a) de algo
tireless ['taɪəlɪs] *adj* incansable
tiresome ['taɪəsəm] *adj* pesado(a)
tiring ['taɪərɪŋ] *adj* agotador(a)
tissue ['tɪʃuː, 'tɪsjuː] *n* (**a**) *Biol* tejido *m* (**b**) *Tex* tisú *m*; **t. paper** papel *m* de seda (**c**) (*handkerchief*) pañuelo *m* de papel, kleenex® *m*
tit¹ [tɪt] *n* **to give t. for tat** devolver la pelota
tit² [tɪt] *n very Fam* (*breast*) teta *f*
titbit ['tɪtbɪt] *n* golosina *f*
titillate ['tɪtɪleɪt] *vt* excitar
title ['taɪtəl] *n* (**a**) título *m*; *Cin* **credit titles** ficha técnica; **t. page** portada *f*; **t. role** papel *m* principal (**b**) *Jur* título *m*
titter ['tɪtə(r)] **1** *vi* reírse nerviosamente; (*foolishly*) reírse tontamente
  2 *n* risa ahogada; (*foolish*) risilla tonta
titular ['tɪtjʊlə(r)] *adj* titular
TM *n* (*abbr* **trademark**) marca registrada
to [tuː, *unstressed before vowels* tʊ, *before*

consonants tə] **1** *prep* (**a**) (*with place*) a; (*expressing direction*) hacia; **from town to town** de ciudad en ciudad; **he went to France/Japan** fue a Francia/Japón; **I'm going to Mary's** voy a casa de Mary; **it is 30 miles to London** Londres está a 30 millas; **the train to Madrid** el tren de Madrid; **to the east** hacia el este; **to the right** a la derecha; **what school do you go to?** ¿a qué escuela vas?
  (**b**) (*time*) a; **from day to day** de día en día; **from two to four** de dos a cuatro; **ten (minutes) to six** las seis menos diez
  (**c**) (*as far as*) hasta; **accurate to a millimetre** exacto(a) hasta el milímetro
  (**d**) (*with indirect object*) **he gave it to his cousin** se lo dio a su primo; **what's that to you?** ¿qué te importa a ti?
  (**e**) (*towards a person*) **he was very kind to me** se portó muy bien conmigo
  (**f**) (*of*) de; **heir to an estate** heredero *m* de una propiedad; **adviser to the president** consejero *m* del presidente
  (**g**) **to come to sb's assistance** acudir en ayuda de algn; **to everyone's surprise** para sorpresa de todos; **to this end** con este fin
  (**h**) **to the best of my knowledge** que yo sepa
  (**i**) (*compared to*) **that's nothing to what I've seen** eso no es nada en comparación con lo que he visto yo
  (**j**) (*in proportion*) **one house to the square kilometre** una casa por kilómetro cuadrado; **six votes to four** seis votos contra cuatro
  (**k**) (*about*) **what did he say to my suggestion?** ¿qué contestó a mi sugerencia?
  2 *with infin* (**a**) *with simple infinitives* **to** *is not translated but is shown by the verb endings;* **to buy** comprar; **to come** venir
  (**b**) (*in order to*) para; (*with verbs of motion or purpose*) a, por; **he did it to help me** lo hizo para ayudarme; **he stopped to talk** se detuvo a hablar; **he fought to convince them** luchó por convencerlos
  (**c**) *various verbs followed by dependent infinitives take particular prepositions* (a, de, en, por, con, para *etc*) *and others take no preposition; see the entry of the verb in question*
  (**d**) (*with adj and infin*) a, de; **difficult to do** difícil de hacer; **ready to listen** dispuesto(a) a escuchar; **too hot to drink** demasiado caliente para bebérselo
  (**e**) (*with noun and infin*) **the first to complain** el primero en quejarse; **this is**

the time to do it éste es el momento de hacerlo; **to have a great deal to do** tener mucho que hacer

(f) *(expressing following action)* **he awoke to find the light still on** al despertarse encontró la lámpara todavía encendida

(g) *(with verbs of ordering, wishing etc)* **he asked me to do it** me pidió que lo hiciera

(h) *(expressing obligation)* **fifty employees are to go** cincuenta empleados deben ser despedidos; **to have to do sth** tener que hacer algo

(i) *(replacing infin)* **go if you want to** váyase si quiere

3 *adv* **to go to and fro** ir y venir; **to push the door to** encajar la puerta

toad [təʊd] *n* sapo *m*

toadstool ['təʊdstuːl] *n* hongo *m* (venenoso)

toast¹ [təʊst] *Culin* **1** *n* pan tostado; **a slice of t.** una tostada

2 *vt* tostar

toast² [təʊst] **1** *n (drink)* brindis *m inv*; **to drink a t.** to brindar por

2 *vt* brindar por

toaster ['təʊstə(r)] *n* tostador *m* (de pan)

tobacco [tə'bækəʊ] *n* tabaco *m*

tobacconist [tə'bækənɪst] *n Br* estanquero(a) *m,f*; *Br* **t.'s (shop)** estanco *m*

toboggan [tə'bɒgən] *n* tobogán *m*

today [tə'deɪ] **1** *n* hoy *m*

2 *adv* hoy; *(nowadays)* hoy en día; **a week t.** justo dentro de una semana

toddler ['tɒdlə(r)] *n* niño(a) *m,f* que empieza a andar; **the toddlers** los pequeñitos

toddy ['tɒdɪ] *n (drink)* ponche *m*

to-do [tə'duː] *n* lío *m*, jaleo *m*

toe [təʊ] **1** *n* dedo *m* del pie; **big t.** dedo gordo

2 *vt* **to t. the line** conformarse

toenail ['təʊneɪl] *n* uña *f* del dedo del pie

toffee ['tɒfɪ] *n* caramelo *m*

together [tə'geðə(r)] *adv* junto, juntos(as); **all t.** todos juntos; **t. with** junto con; **to bring t.** reunir

toil [tɔɪl] **1** *n* trabajo duro

2 *vi* afanarse, trabajar (duro); **to t. up a hill** subir penosamente una cuesta

toilet ['tɔɪlɪt] *n (a)* wáter *m*, retrete *m*; *(for public)* servicios *mpl*; **t. paper** *or* **tissue** papel higiénico; **t. roll** rollo *m* de papel higiénico *(b)* *(washing etc)* aseo *m* (personal); **t. bag** neceser *m*; **t. soap** jabón *m* de tocador

toiletries ['tɔɪlɪtrɪz] *npl* artículos *mpl* de aseo

token ['təʊkən] **1** *n (a)* *(sign)* señal *f*; **as a t. of respect** en señal de respeto *(b)* *Com* vale *m*; **book t.** vale para comprar libros

2 *adj* simbólico(a)

told [təʊld] *pt & pp of* **tell**

tolerable ['tɒlərəbəl] *adj* tolerable

tolerance ['tɒlərəns] *n* tolerancia *f*

tolerant ['tɒlərənt] *adj* tolerante

tolerate ['tɒləreɪt] *vt* tolerar

toll¹ [təʊl] **1** *vt* tocar

2 *vi* doblar

toll² [təʊl] *n (a)* *Aut* peaje *m (b)* *(loss)* pérdidas *fpl*; **the death t.** el número de víctimas mortales

toll-free [təʊl'friː] *US* **1** *adj* **t. number** (número *m* de) teléfono *m* gratuito

2 *adv (call)* gratuitamente

tomato [tə'mɑːtəʊ, *US* tə'meɪtəʊ] *n (pl* **tomatoes**) tomate *m*; **t. sauce** salsa *f* de tomate

tomb [tuːm] *n* tumba *f*, sepulcro *m*

tomboy ['tɒmbɔɪ] *n* marimacho *f*

tombstone ['tuːmstəʊn] *n* lápida *f* sepulcral

tomcat ['tɒmkæt] *n* gato *m* (macho)

tomorrow [tə'mɒrəʊ] **1** *n* mañana *m*; **the day after t.** pasado mañana; **t. night** mañana por la noche

2 *adv* mañana; **see you t.!** ¡hasta mañana!; **t. week** dentro de ocho días a partir de mañana

ton [tʌn] *n* tonelada *f*, *Fam* **tons of** montones de

tone [təʊn] **1** *n* tono *m*

2 *vi* **to t. (in) with sth** armonizar con algo

► tone down *vt sep* atenuar

tone-deaf ['təʊn'def] *adj* **to be t.** no tener oído

tongs [tɒŋz] *npl (for sugar, hair)* tenacillas *fpl*; **(fire) t.** tenazas *fpl*

tongue [tʌŋ] *n (a)* lengua *f*; *Fig* **to say sth t. in cheek** decir algo con la boca pequeña; *Fig* **t. twister** trabalenguas *m inv (b)* *(of shoe)* lengüeta *f*; *(of bell)* badajo *m*

tongue-tied ['tʌŋtaɪd] *adj* mudo(a) *(por la timidez)*

tonic ['tɒnɪk] **1** *n (a)* *Med* tónico *m (b)* *(drink)* tónica *f*

2 *adj* tónico(a)

tonight [tə'naɪt] *adv & n* esta noche

tonnage ['tʌnɪdʒ] *n (of ship)* tonelaje *m*

tonne [tʌn] *n* = **ton**

tonsil ['tɒnsəl] *n* amígdala *f*; **to have one's tonsils out** ser operado(a) de las amígdalas

tonsillitis [tɒnsɪ'laɪtɪs] *n* amigdalitis *f*

too [tuː] *adv (a)* *(besides)* además *(b)*

(also) también (**c**) *(excessively)* demasiado; **t. much money** demasiado dinero; **£10 t. much** 10 libras de más; **t. frequently** con demasiada frecuencia; **t. old** demasiado viejo

took [tʊk] *pt of* take

tool [tuːl] *n (utensil)* herramienta *f*

toolbox [ˈtuːlbɒks] *n* caja *f* de herramientas

toot [tuːt] *Aut* **1** *vt* tocar
   2 *vi* tocar la bocina

tooth [tuːθ] *n (pl* teeth) (**a**) diente *m*; *(molar)* muela *f*; *Fig* **to fight t. and nail** luchar a brazo partido (**b**) *(of saw)* diente *m*; *(of comb)* púa *f*

toothache [ˈtuːθeɪk] *n* dolor *m* de muelas

toothbrush [ˈtuːθbrʌʃ] *n* cepillo *m* de dientes

toothpaste [ˈtuːθpeɪst] *n* pasta dentífrica

toothpick [ˈtuːθpɪk] *n* mondadientes *m inv*

top¹ [tɒp] **1** *n* (**a**) *(upper part)* parte *f* de arriba; *(of hill)* cumbre *f*, cima *f*; *(of tree)* copa *f*; **from t. to bottom** de arriba a abajo; **on t. of** encima de; *Fig* **on t. of it all ...** para colmo ...; **t. hat** sombrero *m* de copa
   (**b**) *(surface)* superficie *f*
   (**c**) *(of list etc)* cabeza *f*
   (**d**) *(of bottle etc)* tapa *f*, tapón *m*
   (**e**) *(garment)* camiseta *f*
   (**f**) *(best)* lo mejor
   (**g**) *Fig* **at the t. of one's voice** a voz en grito
   2 *adj* (**a**) *(part)* superior, de arriba; **the t. floor** el último piso; **t. coat** *(of paint)* última mano
   (**b**) *(highest)* más alto(a); *Aut* **t. gear** directa *f*
   (**c**) *(best)* mejor
   3 *vt* (**a**) *(place on top of)* coronar
   (**b**) *Th* **to t. the bill** encabezar el reparto
   ▸ **top up** *vt sep* llenar hasta el tope; **to t. up the petrol tank** llenar el depósito; *Fig* **and to t. it all** y para colmo

top² [tɒp] *n (toy)* peonza *f*

topic [ˈtɒpɪk] *n* tema *m*

> 🖋 Note that the Spanish word **tópico** is a false friend and is never a translation for the English word **topic**. In Spanish, **tópico** means "cliché".

topical [ˈtɒpɪkəl] *adj* de actualidad

top-level [ˈtɒplevəl] *adj* de alto nivel

topmost [ˈtɒpməʊst] *adj* (el) más alto/(la) más alta

topple [ˈtɒpəl] **1** *vi (building)* venirse

abajo; **to t. (over)** volcarse
   2 *vt* volcar; *Fig (government)* derrocar

top-secret [ˈtɒpˈsiːkrɪt] *adj* de alto secreto

topsy-turvy [ˈtɒpsɪˈtɜːvɪ] *adj & adv* al revés; *(in confusion)* en desorden, patas arriba

torch [tɔːtʃ] *n (electric)* linterna *f*

tore [tɔː(r)] *pt of* tear

torment 1 *vt* [tɔːˈment] atormentar
   2 *n* [ˈtɔːment] tormento *m*, suplicio *m*

torn [tɔːn] *pp of* tear

tornado [tɔːˈneɪdəʊ] *n* tornado *m*

torpedo [tɔːˈpiːdəʊ] *n* torpedo *m*

torrent [ˈtɒrənt] *n* torrente *m*

torrential [tɒˈrenʃəl] *adj* torrencial

torrid [ˈtɒrɪd] *adj* tórrido(a)

torso [ˈtɔːsəʊ] *n* torso *m*

tortoise [ˈtɔːtəs] *n* tortuga *f* (de tierra)

tortoiseshell [ˈtɔːtəsʃel] *adj* de carey

torture [ˈtɔːtʃə(r)] **1** *vt* torturar; *Fig* atormentar
   2 *n* tortura *f*; *Fig* tormento *m*

Tory [ˈtɔːrɪ] *adj & n Br Pol* conservador(a) *(m,f)*

toss [tɒs] **1** *vt* (**a**) *(ball)* tirar; **to t. a coin** echar a cara o cruz (**b**) *(throw about)* sacudir
   2 *vi* (**a**) **to t. about** agitarse; **to t. and turn** dar vueltas en la cama (**b**) *Sport* **to t. (up)** sortear
   3 *n* (**a**) *(of ball)* lanzamiento *m*; *(of coin)* sorteo *m* (a cara o cruz) (**b**) *(of head)* sacudida *f*

tot¹ [tɒt] *n* (**a**) **(tiny) t.** *(child)* nene(a) *m,f*
   (**b**) *(of whisky etc)* trago *m*

tot² [tɒt] *vt Br* **to t. up** sumar

total [ˈtəʊtəl] **1** *n* total *m*; *(in bill)* importe *m*; **grand t.** suma *f* total
   2 *adj* total
   3 *vt* sumar
   4 *vi* **to t. up to** ascender a

totalitarian [təʊtælɪˈteərɪən] *adj* totalitario(a)

totally [ˈtəʊtəlɪ] *adv* totalmente

tote [təʊt] *n Fam Sport* totalizador *m*

tote bag [ˈtəʊtbæg] *n US* petate *m*

totem [ˈtəʊtəm] *n* tótem *m*

totter [ˈtɒtə(r)] *vi* tambalearse

touch [tʌtʃ] **1** *vt* (**a**) tocar; *Fig* **to t. on a subject** tocar un tema
   (**b**) *(equal)* igualar
   (**c**) *(move)* conmover
   2 *vi* tocarse; *Fig* **it was t. and go whether we caught the train** estuvimos a punto de perder el tren
   3 *n* (**a**) toque *m*
   (**b**) *(sense of touch)* tacto *m*

(c) it was a nice t. of his fue un detalle de su parte; **to put the finishing touches to sth** dar los últimos toques a algo

(d) *(ability)* habilidad *f*

(e) *(contact)* contacto *m*; **to be/get/ keep in t. with sb** estar/ponerse/mantenerse en contacto con algn; **to be out of t. with sth** no estar al tanto de algo

(f) *(small amount)* pizca *f*

(g) *Sport* **in t.** fuera de banda

▶ **touch down** *vi (plane)* aterrizar

▶ **touch off** *vt sep* desencadenar

▶ **touch up** *vt sep (picture)* retocar

touchdown ['tʌtʃdaʊn] *n* (a) *(of plane)* aterrizaje *m*; *(of space capsule)* amerizaje *m* (b) *(in American football)* ensayo *m*

touched [tʌtʃt] *adj* (a) *(moved)* emocionado(a) (b) *Fam (crazy)* tocado(a)

touching ['tʌtʃɪŋ] *adj* conmovedor(a)

touchline ['tʌtʃlaɪn] *n* línea *f* de banda

touchy ['tʌtʃɪ] *adj* (**touchier, touchiest**) *Fam (person)* susceptible; *(subject)* delicado(a)

tough [tʌf] **1** *adj (material, competitor etc)* fuerte, resistente; *(test, criminal, meat)* duro(a); *(punishment)* severo(a); *(problem)* difícil

2 *n (person)* matón *m*

toughen ['tʌfən] *vt* endurecer

toupee ['tu:peɪ] *n* tupé *m*

tour [tʊə(r)] **1** *n* (a) *(journey)* viaje *m*; **package t.** viaje organizado (b) *(of monument etc)* visita *f*; *(of city)* recorrido turístico (c) *Sport & Th* gira *f*; **on t.** de gira

2 *vt* (a) *(country)* viajar por (b) *(building)* visitar (c) *Th* estar de gira en

3 *vi* estar de viaje

tourism ['tʊərɪzəm] *n* turismo *m*

tourist ['tʊərɪst] *n* turista *mf*; **t. centre** centro *m* de información turística; *Av* **t. class** *f* turista

tournament ['tʊənəmənt] *n* torneo *m*

tousled ['taʊzəld] *adj (hair)* despeinado(a)

tout [taʊt] **1** *vt Com* tratar de vender; *(tickets)* revender

2 *vi* = salir a la caza y captura de compradores

3 *n Com* gancho *m*

tow [təʊ] **1** *n* **to take a car in t.** remolcar un coche; *US* **t. truck** grúa *f*

2 *vt* remolcar

towards [tə'wɔːdz, tɔːdz] *prep* (a) *(direction, time)* hacia (b) *(with regard to)* hacia, (para) con; **our duty t. others** nuestro deber para con los demás; **what is your attitude t. religion?** ¿cuál es su actitud respecto a la religión?

towel ['taʊəl] **1** *n* toalla *f*; **hand t.** toallita *f*; **t.** *Br* **rail** *or US* **bar** toallero *m*

2 *vt* **to t. dry** secar con una toalla

towelling ['taʊəlɪŋ] *n* felpa *f*

tower ['taʊə(r)] **1** *n* torre *f*

2 *vi* **to t. over** *or* **above sth** dominar algo

towering ['taʊərɪŋ] *adj* impresionante, enorme

town [taʊn] *n* ciudad *f*; *(small)* pueblo *m*; **to go into t.** ir al centro; *Fam* **to go to t.** tirar la casa por la ventana; **t. council** ayuntamiento *m*; **t. councillor** concejal(a) *m,f*; **t. hall** ayuntamiento *m*; **t. planning** urbanismo *m*

townspeople ['taʊnzpiːpəl] *npl* ciudadanos *mpl*

towpath ['təʊpɑːθ] *n* sendero *m* a lo largo de un canal

towrope ['təʊrəʊp] *n* cable *m* de remolque

toxic ['tɒksɪk] *adj* tóxico(a)

toy [tɔɪ] **1** *n* juguete *m*

2 *vi* **to t. with an idea** acariciar una idea; **to t. with one's food** comer sin gana

toyshop ['tɔɪʃɒp] *n* juguetería *f*

trace [treɪs] **1** *n* (a) *(sign)* indicio *m*, vestigio *m* (b) *(tracks)* huella(s) *f(pl)*

2 *vt* (a) *(drawing)* calcar (b) *(plan)* bosquejar (c) *(locate)* seguir la pista de

tracing ['treɪsɪŋ] *n* **t. paper** papel *m* de calco

track [træk] **1** *n* (a) *(trail)* huellas *fpl*, pista *f*; **to keep/lose t. of sb** no perder/perder de vista a algn

(b) *(pathway)* camino *m*; **to be on the right/wrong t.** ir por el buen/mal camino

(c) *Sport* pista *f*; *(for motor racing)* circuito *m*; *Fig* **t. record** historial *m*

(d) *Rail* vía *f*; *Fig* **he has a one-t. mind** tiene una única obsesión

(e) *(on record, CD)* canción *f*

(f) *US Educ* = cada una de las divisiones del alumnado en grupos por niveles de aptitud

2 *vt* seguir la pista de; *(with radar)* seguir la trayectoria de

▶ **track down** *vt sep (locate)* localizar

tracksuit ['træksuːt] *n* chándal *m*, *Arg* buzo *m*, *Méx* pants *m*, *Urug* jogging *m*, *Ven* mono *m*

tract¹ [trækt] *n (expanse)* extensión *f*

tract² [trækt] *n (treatise)* tratado *m*; *(pamphlet)* folleto *m*

traction ['trækʃən] *n* tracción *f*

tractor ['træktə(r)] *n* tractor *m*

trade [treɪd] **1** *n* (a) *(profession)* oficio *m*; **by t.** de oficio (b) *Com* comercio *m*; **it's good for t.** es bueno para los negocios;

the building t. (la industria de) la construcción; **t. name** nombre *m* comercial; **t. union** sindicato *m*; **t. unionist** sindicalista *mf*

2 *vi* comerciar (**in** en)

3 *vt* **to t. sth for sth** trocar algo por algo

▸ **trade in** *vt sep* dar como entrada

trademark ['treɪdmɑːk] *n* marca *f* (de fábrica); **registered t.** marca registrada

trader ['treɪdə(r)] *n* comerciante *mf*

tradesman ['treɪdzmən] *n (shopkeeper)* tendero *m*

trading ['treɪdɪŋ] *n* comercio *m*; *Br* **t. estate** polígono *m* industrial

tradition [trə'dɪʃən] *n* tradición *f*

traditional [trə'dɪʃənəl] *adj* tradicional

traffic ['træfɪk] 1 *n* (a) *(shop keeper)* tráfico *m*, circulación *f*; *US* **t. circle** rotonda *f*, isleta *f*; **t. jam** atasco *m*; **t. lights** semáforo *m*; *Br* **t. warden** ≃ guardia *mf* urbano(a) (b) *(trade)* tráfico *m*

2 *vi* (*pt & pp* **trafficked**) **to t. in drugs** traficar con droga

trafficker ['træfɪkə(r)] *n* traficante *mf*

tragedy ['trædʒɪdɪ] *n* tragedia *f*

tragic ['trædʒɪk] *adj* trágico(a)

trail [treɪl] 1 *vt* (a) *(drag)* arrastrar (b) *(follow)* rastrear

2 *vi* (a) *(drag)* arrastrarse (b) **to t. behind** rezagarse

3 *n* (a) *(track)* pista *f*, rastro *m* (b) *(path)* senda *f*, camino *m* (c) *(of smoke)* estela *f*

trailer ['treɪlə(r)] *n* (a) *Aut* remolque *m* (b) *US Aut (caravan)* caravana *f* (c) *Cin* trailer *m*, avance *m*

train [treɪn] 1 *n* (a) *Rail* tren *m* (b) *(of vehicles)* convoy *m*; *(of followers)* séquito *m*; *(of events)* serie *f* (c) *(of dress)* cola *f*

2 *vt* (a) *(teach)* formar; *Sport* entrenar; *(animal)* amaestrar; *(voice etc)* educar (b) *(gun)* apuntar (**on** a); *(camera)* enfocar (**on** a)

3 *vi* prepararse; *Sport* entrenarse

trainee [treɪ'niː] *n* aprendiz(a) *m,f*

trainer ['treɪnə(r)] *n* (a) *Sport* entrenador(a) *m,f*; *(of dogs)* amaestrador(a) *m,f*; *(of lions)* domador(a) *m,f* (b) **trainers** *(shoes)* zapatillas *fpl* de deporte

training ['treɪnɪŋ] *n (instruction)* formación *f*; *Sport* entrenamiento *m*; *(of animals)* amaestramiento *m*; *(of lions)* doma *f*; **to go into t.** empezar el entrenamiento; **vocational t.** formación profesional

traipse [treɪps] *vi Fam* vagar

trait [treɪt] *n* rasgo *m*

traitor ['treɪtə(r)] *n* traidor(a) *m,f*

trajectory [trə'dʒektərɪ] *n* trayectoria *f*

tram [træm], **tramcar** ['træmkɑː(r)] *n Br* tranvía *m*

tramp [træmp] 1 *vi* (a) *(travel on foot)* caminar (b) *(walk heavily)* andar con pasos pesados

2 *n (person)* vagabundo(a) *m,f*; *Pej* **she's a t.** es una fulana

> 🖉 Note that the Spanish word **trampa** is a false friend and is never a translation for the English word **tramp**. In Spanish, **trampa** means both "trap" and "trick".

trample ['træmpəl] *vt* **to t. down the grass** pisotear la hierba; **to t. sth underfoot** pisotear algo

trampoline ['træmpəliːn] *n* cama elástica

> 🖉 Note that the Spanish word **trampolín** is a false friend and is never a translation for the English word **trampoline**. In Spanish, **trampolín** means both "diving board" and "ski jump".

trance [trɑːns] *n* trance *m*

tranquil ['træŋkwɪl] *adj* tranquilo(a)

tranquillity [træŋ'kwɪlɪtɪ] *n* tranquilidad *f*

tranquillizer ['træŋkwɪlaɪzə(r)] *n* tranquilizante *m*

transact [træn'zækt] *vt* negociar

transaction [træn'zækʃən] *n (procedure)* tramitación *f*; *(deal)* transacción *f*

transatlantic [trænzət'læntɪk] *adj* transatlántico(a)

transcend [træn'send] *vt* trascender

transcribe [træn'skraɪb] *vt* transcribir

transcript ['trænskrɪpt] *n* transcripción *f*

transcription [træn'skrɪpʃən] *n* transcripción *f*

transfer 1 *vt* [træns'fɜː(r)] trasladar; *(funds)* trasferir; *Jur* ceder; *Ftb* traspasar; *US Rail* hacer transbordo

2 *n* ['trænsfɜː(r)] (a) traslado *m*; *(of funds)* transferencia *f*; *Jur* cesión *f*; *Ftb* traspaso *m* (b) *(picture, design)* calcomanía *f* (c) *US Rail* transbordo *m*

transform [træns'fɔːm] *vt* trasformar

transformation [trænsfə'meɪʃən] *n* trasformación *f*

transfusion [træns'fjuːʒən] *n Med* transfusión *f* (de sangre)

transgenic [trænz'dʒiːnɪk] *adj* transgénico(a)

transgress [trænz'gres] *vi Fml* transgredir

transient ['trænzɪənt] *adj* transitorio(a)

transistor [træn'zɪstə(r)] *n* transistor *m*

transit ['trænzɪt] *n* tránsito *m*; **in t.** de tránsito

transition [træn'zɪʃən] *n* transición *f*
transitive ['trænzɪtɪv] *adj* transitivo(a)
transitory ['trænzɪtərɪ] *adj* transitorio(a)
translate [træns'leɪt] *vt* traducir
translation [træns'leɪʃən] *n* traducción *f*
translator [træns'leɪtə(r)] *n* traductor(a) *m,f*
translucent [trænz'luːsənt] *adj* translúcido(a)
transmission [trænz'mɪʃən] *n* transmisión *f*
transmit [trænz'mɪt] *vt* transmitir
transmitter [trænz'mɪtə(r)] *n Rad (set)* transmisor *m; Rad & TV (station)* emisora *f*
transparency [træns'pærənsɪ] *n Phot* diapositiva *f*
transparent [træns'pærənt] *adj* transparente
transpire [træn'spaɪə(r)] *vi (happen)* ocurrir; **it transpired that ...** ocurrió que ...
transplant 1 *vt* [træns'plɑːnt] trasplantar
2 *n* ['trænsplɑːnt] trasplante *m*
transport 1 *vt* [træns'pɔːt] transportar
2 *n* ['trænspɔːt] transporte *m; t.* **aircraft/ship** avión *m*/buque *m* de transporte; *Br* **t. café** bar *m* de carretera
transportation [trænspɔː'teɪʃən] *n* transporte *m*
transvestite [trænz'vestaɪt] *n Fam* travestí *mf*
trap [træp] **1** *n* trampa *f; t.* **door** trampilla *f; Th* escotillón *m*
2 *vt* atrapar
trapeze [trə'piːz] *n* trapecio *m*
trappings ['træpɪŋz] *npl* parafernalia *f*
trash [træʃ] *n (inferior goods)* bazofia *f; US (rubbish)* basura *f; Fig* **to talk a lot of t.** decir tonterías; *US* **t. can** cubo *m* de la basura
trashy ['træʃɪ] *adj (trashier, trashiest)* de ínfima calidad
trauma ['trɔːmə] *n* trauma *m*
traumatic [trɔː'mætɪk] *adj* traumático(a)
travel ['trævəl] **1** *vi (a)* viajar; **to t. through** recorrer **(b)** *(vehicle, electric current)* ir; *Fig (news)* propagarse
2 *vt* recorrer
3 *n* viajar *m; t.* **agency** agencia *f* de viajes
traveller, *US* **traveler** ['trævələ(r)] *n* viajero(a) *m,f; t.'s Br* **cheque** *or US* **check** cheque *m* de viaje
travelling, *US* **traveling** ['trævəlɪŋ] **1** *adj (salesman)* ambulante
2 *n* viajes *mpl*, (el) viajar *m;* **I'm fond of t.** me gusta viajar; **t. expenses** gastos *mpl* de viaje

travel-sick ['trævəlsɪk] *adj* **to be t.** estar mareado(a)
travesty ['trævɪstɪ] *n* parodia *f* burda

> 🖉 Note that the Spanish word **travesti** is a false friend and is never a translation for the English word **travesty**. In Spanish, **travesti** means "transvestite".

trawler ['trɔːlə(r)] *n* barco *m* de arrastre
tray [treɪ] *n (for food)* bandeja *f; (for letters)* cesta *f (para la correspondencia)*
treacherous ['tretʃərəs] *adj* **(a)** *(person)* traidor(a); *(action)* traicionero(a) **(b)** *(dangerous)* peligroso(a)
treachery ['tretʃərɪ] *n* traición *f*
treacle ['triːkəl] *n Br* melaza *f*
tread [tred] **1** *vi (pt* **trod;** *pp* **trod** *or* **trodden)** pisar; **to t. on** pisar
2 *vt* **(a)** *(step on)* pisar **(b)** **to t. water** mantenerse a flote verticalmente
3 *n* **(a)** *(step)* paso *m; (sound)* ruido *m* de pasos **(b)** *(of tyre)* banda *f* de rodadura
treadmill ['tredmɪl] *n Fig* rutina *f*
treason ['triːzən] *n* traición *f*
treasure ['treʒə(r)] **1** *n* tesoro *m*
2 *vt (keep)* guardar como oro en paño; *(value)* apreciar muchísimo
treasurer ['treʒərə(r)] *n* tesorero(a) *m,f*
treasury ['treʒərɪ] *n Pol Br* **the T.,** *US* **the Department of the T.** ≃ el Ministerio de Hacienda; **T. bill** bono *m* del Tesoro
treat [triːt] **1** *n* **(a)** *(present)* regalo *m* **(b)** *(pleasure)* placer *m*
2 *vt* **(a)** tratar; **to t. badly** maltratar **(b)** *(regard)* considerar **(c)** **he treated them to dinner** les invitó a cenar
treatise ['triːtɪz] *n* tratado *m*
treatment ['triːtmənt] *n* **(a)** *(of person)* trato *m* **(b)** *(of subject, of patient)* tratamiento *m*
treaty ['triːtɪ] *n* tratado *m*
treble ['trebəl] **1** *adj* **(a)** *(triple)* triple **(b)** *Mus* **t. clef** clave *f* de sol; **t. voice** voz *f* tiple
2 *vt* triplicar
3 *vi* triplicarse
tree [triː] *n* árbol *m;* **apple/cherry t.** manzano *m*/cerezo *m*
treetop ['triːtɒp] *n* copa *f*
trek [trek] **1** *n (journey)* viaje *m* (largo y difícil); *Fam (walk)* caminata *f*
2 *vi (pt & pp* **trekked)** hacer un viaje largo y difícil; *Fam (walk)* ir caminando
trellis ['trelɪs] *n* enrejado *m*
tremble ['trembəl] *vi* temblar, estremecerse
trembling ['tremblɪŋ] *adj* tembloroso(a)
tremendous [trɪ'mendəs] *adj (huge)* enorme; *(success)* arrollador(a); *(shock*

etc) tremendo(a); *Fam (marvellous)* estupendo(a)

tremor ['tremə(r)] *n* temblor *m*

trench [trentʃ] *n* **(a)** *(ditch)* zanja *f; Mil* trinchera *f* **(b)** **t. coat** trinchera *f*

trend [trend] **1** *n (tendency)* tendencia *f; (fashion)* moda *f*
　2 *vi* tender (**to** *or* **towards** hacia)

trendy ['trendɪ] *adj* (**trendier, trendiest**) *Fam (person)* moderno(a); *(clothes)* a la última

trepidation [trepɪ'deɪʃən] *n* turbación *f*

trespass ['trespəs] *vi* entrar sin autorización

> 🖉 Note that the Spanish verb **traspasar** is a false friend and is never a translation for the English verb **to trespass**. In Spanish, **traspasar** means "to go through, to cross, to transfer" and "to exceed".

trespasser ['trespəsə(r)] *n* intruso(a) *m,f*

trestle ['tresəl] *n* caballete *m*

trial ['traɪəl] *n* **(a)** *Jur* proceso *m*, juicio *m* **(b)** *(test)* prueba *f*; **on t.** a prueba; **by t. and error** a fuerza de equivocarse **(c)** **trials** *(competition)* concurso *m* **(d)** **trials** *(suffering)* sufrimiento *m*; **trials and tribulations** tribulaciones *fpl*

triangle ['traɪæŋɡəl] *n* triángulo *m*

tribe [traɪb] *n* tribu *f*

tribunal [traɪ'bjuːnəl] *n* tribunal *m*

tributary ['trɪbjʊtərɪ] *n (river)* afluente *m*

tribute ['trɪbjuːt] *n* **(a)** *(payment)* tributo *m* **(b)** *(mark of respect)* homenaje *m*; **to pay t.** to rendir homenaje a

trice [traɪs] *n Fam* **in a t.** en un abrir y cerrar de ojos

trick [trɪk] **1** *n* **(a)** *(ruse)* ardid *m; (dishonest)* engaño *m; (in question)* trampa *f* **(b)** *(practical joke)* broma *f*; **to play a t. on sb** gastarle una broma a algn; *(malicious)* jugar una mala pasada a algn **(c)** *(of magic, knack)* truco *m*; **that'll do the t.!** ¡eso es exactamente lo que hace falta! **(d)** *Cards* baza *f*
　2 *vt* engañar; **to t. sb out of sth** estafar algo a algn

trickery ['trɪkərɪ] *n* engaños *mpl*, trampas *fpl*

trickle ['trɪkəl] **1** *vi* discurrir; *(water)* gotear
　2 *n* hilo *m*

tricky ['trɪkɪ] *adj* (**trickier, trickiest**) *(person)* astuto(a); *(situation, mechanism)* delicado(a)

tricycle ['traɪsɪkəl] *n* triciclo *m*

tried [traɪd] *pt & pp of* **try**

trifle ['traɪfəl] **1** *n* **(a)** *(insignificant thing)*

bagatela *f*; **he's a t. optimistic** es ligeramente optimista **(b)** *Br Culin* = postre de bizcocho, gelatina, frutas y nata
　2 *vi* **to t. with** tomar a la ligera

trifling ['traɪflɪŋ] *adj* insignificante, trivial

trigger ['trɪɡə(r)] **1** *n (of gun)* gatillo *m; (of mechanism)* disparador *m*
　2 *vt* **to t. (off)** desencadenar

trill [trɪl] *n (of music, bird)* trino *m; Ling* vibración *f*

trilogy ['trɪlədʒɪ] *n* trilogía *f*

trim [trɪm] **1** *adj* (**trimmer, trimmest**) *(neat)* aseado(a); **to have a t. figure** tener buen tipo
　2 *vt* **(a)** *(cut)* recortar; *Fig (expenses)* disminuir **(b)** *(decorate)* adornar
　3 *n* **(a)** *(condition)* estado *m; Naut* asiento *m* **(b)** *(cut)* recorte *m*

trimming ['trɪmɪŋ] *n* **(a)** *(cut)* recorte *m* **(b)** *(on clothes)* adorno *m* **(c)** *Culin* **trimmings** guarnición *f*

trinket ['trɪŋkɪt] *n* baratija *f*

trio ['triːəʊ] *n* trío *m*

trip [trɪp] **1** *n* **(a)** *(journey)* viaje *m; (excursion)* excursión *f*; **to go on a t.** ir de excursión **(b)** *Fam* **to be on a t.** *(on drugs)* estar colocado(a)
　2 *vi* **(a)** **to t. (up)** *(stumble)* tropezar (**over** con); *Fig (err)* equivocarse **(b)** **to t. along** ir con paso ligero
　3 *vt* **to t. sb (up)** poner la zancadilla a algn; *Fig* coger *or* pillar a algn

tripe [traɪp] *n* **(a)** *Culin* callos *mpl* **(b)** *Fam* bobadas *fpl*

triple ['trɪpəl] **1** *adj* triple
　2 *vt* triplicar
　3 *vi* triplicarse

triplet ['trɪplɪt] *n* trillizo(a) *m,f*

triplicate ['trɪplɪkɪt] *adj* **in t.** por triplicado

tripod ['traɪpɒd] *n* trípode *m*

trite [traɪt] *adj (sentiment)* banal; *(subject)* trillado(a)

triumph ['traɪəmf] **1** *n* triunfo *m*
　2 *vi* triunfar

triumphant [traɪ'ʌmfənt] *adj* triunfante

trivia ['trɪvɪə] *npl* trivialidades *fpl*

trivial ['trɪvɪəl] *adj* trivial, banal

trod [trɒd] *pt & pp of* **tread**

trodden ['trɒdən] *pp of* **tread**

trolley ['trɒlɪ] *n Br* carro *m*

trombone [trɒm'bəʊn] *n* trombón *m*

troop [truːp] **1** *n* **(a)** *(of people)* grupo *m* **(b)** *Mil* **troops** tropas *fpl*
　2 *vi* **to t. in/out/off** entrar/salir/marcharse en tropel

trooper ['truːpə(r)] *n* **(a)** *(soldier)* soldado

m de caballería (**b**) *US* (*policeman*) policía *mf*

trooping ['truːpɪŋ] *n Br* **t. the colour** = ceremonia de homenaje a la bandera de un regimiento

trophy ['trəʊfɪ] *n* trofeo *m*

tropic ['trɒpɪk] *n* trópico *m*

tropical ['trɒpɪkəl] *adj* tropical

trot [trɒt] **1** *vi* trotar

2 *n* trote *m*; **to go at a t.** ir al trote; *Fam* **on the t.** (*in succession*) seguidos(as)

trouble ['trʌbəl] **1** *n* (**a**) (*misfortune*) desgracia *f*

(**b**) (*problems*) problemas *mpl*; **to be in t.** estar en un lío; **to cause sb t.** ocasionar problemas a algn; **to get sb out of t.** sacar a algn de un apuro; **the t. is that …** lo que pasa es que …

(**c**) (*effort*) esfuerzo *m*; **it's no t.** no es ninguna molestia; **it's not worth the t.** no merece la pena; **to take the t. to do sth** molestarse en hacer algo

(**d**) (*conflict*) conflicto *m*

(**e**) *Med* enfermedad *f*; **to have liver t.** tener problemas de hígado

2 *vt* (**a**) (*affect*) afligir; (*worry*) preocupar; **that doesn't t. him at all** eso lo tiene sin cuidado

(**b**) (*bother*) molestar

3 *vi* molestarse

troubled ['trʌbəld] *adj* agitado(a)

troublemaker ['trʌbəlmeɪkə(r)] *n* alborotador(a) *m,f*

troubleshooter ['trʌbəlʃuːtə(r)] *n Ind* = persona encargada de solucionar problemas

troublesome ['trʌbəlsəm] *adj* molesto(a)

trough [trɒf] *n* (**a**) (**drinking**) **t.** abrevadero *m*; (**feeding**) **t.** pesebre *m* (**b**) (*of wave*) seno *m* (**c**) *Geog & Met* depresión *f*

trounce [traʊns] *vt* dar una paliza a

troupe [truːp] *n Th* compañía *f*

trousers ['traʊzəz] *npl* pantalón *m*, pantalones *mpl*

trousseau ['truːsəʊ] *n* ajuar *m*

trout [traʊt] *n* trucha *f*

trowel ['traʊəl] *n* (**a**) (*builder's*) palustre *m* (**b**) (*for gardening*) desplantador *m*

truant ['truːənt] *n Br* **to play t.** hacer novillos

truce [truːs] *n* tregua *f*

truck¹ [trʌk] *n* (**a**) *Br Rail* vagón *m* (**b**) *Aut* camión *m*; **t. driver** camionero(a) *m,f*; *US* **t. farm** huerta *f*; *US* **t. farmer** hortelano(a) *m,f*

truck² [trʌk] *n* (**a**) **to have no t. with** no

estar dispuesto a tolerar (**b**) *US* verduras *fpl*; **t. farm** huerta *f*; **t. farming** cultivo *m* de hortalizas

truculent ['trʌkjʊlənt] *adj* agresivo(a), airado(a)

> 🖉 Note that the Spanish word **truculento** is a false friend and is never a translation for the English word **truculent**. In Spanish, **truculento** means "horrifying, terrifying".

trudge [trʌdʒ] *vi* caminar con dificultad

true [truː] *adj* (**truer, truest**) (**a**) verdadero(a); **it's t. that …** es verdad que …; **to come t.** cumplirse, hacerse realidad (**b**) (*faithful*) fiel (**c**) (*aim*) acertado(a)

truffle ['trʌfəl] *n* trufa *f*

truly ['truːlɪ] *adv* (**a**) de verdad; **really and t.?** ¿de veras? (**b**) (*faithfully*) fielmente; **yours t.** atentamente

trump [trʌmp] *Cards* **1** *n* triunfo *m*

2 *vt* fallar

trumped-up ['trʌmptʌp] *adj* inventado(a)

trumpet ['trʌmpɪt] *n* trompeta *f*

trumpeting ['trʌmpɪtɪŋ] *n* (*of elephant*) berrido *m*

truncheon ['trʌntʃən] *n Br* porra *f* (*de policía*)

trundle ['trʌndəl] *vi* rodar

trunk [trʌŋk] *n* (**a**) (*of tree, body*) tronco *m* (**b**) (*of elephant*) trompa *f* (**c**) (*luggage*) baúl *m* (**d**) *Br Tel* **t. call** conferencia interurbana; *Br* **t. road** carretera *f* principal (**e**) *US* (*of car*) maletero *m*, *CAm, Méx* cajuela *f*, *RP* baúl *m*

trunks [trʌŋks] *npl* (**bathing**) **t.** bañador *m*

truss [trʌs] **1** *vt* (*tie*) atar

2 *n* (**a**) *Constr* cuchillo *m* de armadura (**b**) *Med* braguero *m*

trust [trʌst] **1** *n* (**a**) (*confianza f*; **breach of t.** abuso *m* de confianza (**b**) *Jur* fideicomiso *m* (**c**) *Fin* trust *m*

2 *vt* (**a**) (*hope*) esperar (**b**) (*rely upon*) fiarse de; **to t. sb with sth** confiar algo a algn

3 *vi* confiar (**in** en)

trusted ['trʌstɪd] *adj* de fiar

trustee [trʌsˈtiː] *n Jur* fideicomisario(a) *m,f*; (*in bankruptcy*) síndico *m*

trustful ['trʌstfʊl], **trusting** ['trʌstɪŋ] *adj* confiado(a)

trustworthy ['trʌstwɜːðɪ] *adj* (*person*) de confianza; (*information*) fidedigno(a)

trusty ['trʌstɪ] *adj* (**trustier, trustiest**) fiel, leal

truth [truːθ] *n* verdad *f*; **to tell the t.** decir la verdad

truthful ['truːθfʊl] *adj (person)* veraz, sincero(a); *(testimony)* verídico(a)

truthfully ['truːθfʊlı] *adv* sinceramente

try [traı] **1** *vt (pt & pp* **tried)** **(a)** *(attempt)* intentar; **to t. to do sth** tratar de *or* intentar hacer algo **(b)** *(test)* probar, ensayar; **to t. sb's patience** poner a prueba la paciencia de algn **(c)** *Jur* juzgar

2 *vi* intentar

3 *n* **(a)** *(attempt)* tentativa *f*, intento *m* **(b)** *Sport* ensayo *m*

▸ **try on** *vt sep (dress)* probarse

▸ **try out** *vt sep* probar

trying ['traııŋ] *adj (person)* molesto(a), pesado(a); **to have a t. time** pasar un mal rato

tsar [zɑː(r)] *n* zar *m*

T-shirt ['tiːʃɜːt] *n* camiseta *f*

tub [tʌb] *n* **(a)** *(container)* tina *f*, cuba *f* **(b)** *(bath)* bañera *f*

tuba ['tjuːbə] *n* tuba *f*

tubby ['tʌbı] *adj* **(tubbier, tubbiest)** rechoncho(a)

tube [tjuːb] *n* **(a)** tubo *m*; *Anat* conducto *m*; *(of bicycle)* cámara *f* (de aire) **(b)** *Br Fam* **the t.** *(underground)* el metro

tuberculosis [tjʊbɜːkjʊˈləʊsɪs] *n* tuberculosis *f*

tubing ['tjuːbɪŋ] *n* tubería *f*; **(piece of) t.** (trozo *m* de) tubo *m*

tubular ['tjuːbjʊlə(r)] *adj* tubular

tuck [tʌk] **1** *vt* **to t. in the bedclothes** remeter la ropa de la cama; **to t. sb in** arropar a algn; **to t. one's shirt into one's trousers** meterse la camisa por dentro (de los pantalones)

2 *n Sewing* pliegue *m*

▸ **tuck in** *vi Fam* devorar

Tuesday ['tjuːzdı] *n* martes *m*

tuft [tʌft] *n (of hair)* mechón *m*

tug [tʌg] **1** *vt (pull at) (haul along)* tirar de; *Naut* remolcar

2 *n* **(a)** *(pull)* tirón *m*; **t. of war** *(game)* lucha *f* de la cuerda; *Fig* lucha encarnizada **(b)** *Naut* remolcador *m*

tugboat ['tʌgbəʊt] *n* remolcador *m*

tuition [tjuːˈɪʃən] *n* instrucción *f*; **private t. fees** honorarios *mpl* **fees** honorarios *mpl*

tulip ['tjuːlɪp] *n* tulipán *m*

tumble ['tʌmbəl] **1** *vi (person)* caerse; *(acrobat)* dar volteretas; *(building)* venirse abajo

2 *vt* volcar

3 *n* **(a)** caída *f* **(b)** **t. dryer** secadora *f*

tumbledown ['tʌmbəldaʊn] *adj* en ruinas

tumbler ['tʌmblə(r)] *n* vaso *m*

tummy ['tʌmı] *n Fam* estómago *m*, barriga *f*

tumour, *US* **tumor** ['tjuːmə(r)] *n* tumor *m*

tumult ['tjuːmʌlt] *n* tumulto *m*

tuna ['tjuːnə] *n* atún *m*, bonito *m*

> 🖉 Note that the Spanish word **tuna** is a false friend and is never a translation for the English word **tuna**. In Spanish, **tuna** means "group of student minstrels".

tune [tjuːn] **1** *n* **(a)** *(melody)* melodía *f*; *Fig* **to change one's t.** cambiar de tono **(b)** *Mus* tono *m*; **in/out of t.** afinado/desafinado; **to sing out of t.** desafinar

2 *vt Mus* afinar

3 *vi Rad & TV* **to t. in to a station** sintonizar una emisora

▸ **tune up** *vi* afinar los instrumentos

tuneful ['tjuːnfʊl] *adj* melodioso(a)

tuner ['tjuːnə(r)] **(a)** *(of pianos)* afinador(a) *m,f* **(b)** *Rad & TV (knob)* sintonizador *m*

tunic ['tjuːnɪk] *n* túnica *f*

tuning ['tjuːnɪŋ] *n* **(a)** *Mus* afinación *f*; **t. fork** diapasón *m* **(b)** *Rad & TV* **t. in** sintonización *f*

Tunisia [tjuːˈnɪzɪə] *n* Túnez

Tunisian [tjuːˈnɪzɪən] *adj & n* tunecino(a) *(m,f)*

tunnel ['tʌnəl] **1** *n* túnel *m*; *Min* galería *f*

2 *vt* **to t. through** abrir un túnel a través de

turban ['tɜːbən] *n* turbante *m*

turbine ['tɜːbaɪn] *n* turbina *f*

turbulent ['tɜːbjʊlənt] *adj* turbulento(a)

tureen [təˈriːn] *n* sopera *f*

turf [tɜːf] *n* **(a)** *(grass)* césped *m*; *(peat)* turba *f* **(b)** *Br* **t. accountant** *(in horse racing)* corredor(a) *m,f* de apuestas

▸ **turf out** *vt sep Br Fam* **to t. sb out** poner a algn de patitas en la calle

Turk [tɜːk] *n* turco(a) *m,f*

Turkey ['tɜːkı] *n* Turquía

turkey ['tɜːkı] *n* pavo *m*

Turkish ['tɜːkıʃ] **1** *adj* turco(a)

2 *n (language)* turco *m*

turmoil ['tɜːmɔıl] *n* confusión *f*

turn [tɜːn] **1** *vt* **(a)** *(rotate)* volver; *(rotate)* girar, hacer girar; **to t. sth inside out** volver algo del revés; **to t. a page** volver una hoja; **to t. one's head/gaze** volver la cabeza/mirada (**towards** hacia); **to t. the corner** doblar la esquina; *Fig* **he's turned forty** ha cumplido los cuarenta **(b)** *(change)* transformar (**into** en) **(c)** *(on lathe)* tornear

2 *vi* **(a)** *(rotate)* girar

(**b**) *(turn round)* volverse, dar la vuelta; **to t. to sb** volverse hacia algn; *Fig (for help)* acudir a algn; **to t. upside down** volcarse; *Fig* **to t. on sb** volverse contra algn

(**c**) *(become)* volverse; **the milk has turned sour** la leche se ha cortado

3 *n* (**a**) *(of wheel)* vuelta *f*; **done to a t.** *(meat)* en su punto

(**b**) *(change of direction)* cambio *m* de dirección; *(in road)* curva *f*; **to take a t. for the better** empezar a mejorar; **left/right t.** giro *m* al izquierdo/a la derecha; *US Aut* **t. signal** intermitente *m*

(**c**) **to do sb a good t.** hacer un favor a algn

(**d**) *Med* ataque *m*

(**e**) *(in game, queue)* turno *m*, vez *f*; **it's your t.** te toca a ti; **to take it in turns to do sth** turnarse para hacer algo

(**f**) *Th* número *m*

(**g**) **t. of phrase** giro *m*

▸ **turn aside 1** *vt sep* desviar

2 *vi* desviarse

▸ **turn away 1** *vt sep (person)* rechazar

2 *vi* volver la cabeza

▸ **turn back 1** *vt sep (person)* hacer retroceder; *(clock)* retrasar

2 *vi* volverse

▸ **turn down** *vt sep* (**a**) *(gas, radio etc)* bajar (**b**) *(reject)* rechazar (**c**) *(fold)* doblar

▸ **turn in** *Fam* **1** *vt sep (person)* entregar a la policía

2 *vi* acostarse

▸ **turn off 1** *vt sep (electricity)* desconectar; *(gas, light)* apagar; *(water)* cerrar

2 *vi* desviarse

▸ **turn on** *vt sep (electricity)* encender; *(tap, gas)* abrir; *(machine)* poner en marcha; *Fam* **it turns me on** me encanta

▸ **turn out 1** *vt sep* (**a**) *(extinguish)* apagar (**b**) *(eject)* echar; *(empty)* vaciar (**c**) *(produce)* producir

2 *vi* (**a**) *(attend)* asistir (**b**) **it turns out that ...** resulta que ...; **things have turned out well** las cosas han salido bien

▸ **turn over 1** *vt sep (turn upside down)* poner al revés; *(page)* dar la vuelta a

2 *vi* volverse

▸ **turn round 1** *vt sep* volver

2 *vi (rotate)* girar, dar vueltas

▸ **turn up 1** *vt sep* (**a**) *(collar)* levantar; **to t. up one's shirt sleeves** arremangarse; **turned-up nose** nariz respingona (**b**) *Rad & TV* subir

2 *vi* (**a**) *Fig* **something is sure to t. up** algo saldrá (**b**) *(arrive)* llegar, presentarse;

nobody turned up nadie se presentó

(**c**) *(attend)* asistir

turning ['tɜːnɪŋ] *n* (**a**) *Fig* **t. point** punto decisivo (**b**) *(in road)* salida *f*

turnip ['tɜːnɪp] *n* nabo *m*

turnout ['tɜːnaʊt] *n* asistencia *f*

turnover ['tɜːnəʊvə(r)] *n Com (sales)* facturación *f*; *(of goods)* movimiento *m*

turnpike ['tɜːnpaɪk] *n US* autopista *f* de peaje

turnstile ['tɜːnstaɪl] *n* torniquete *m*

turntable ['tɜːnteɪbəl] *n (for record)* plato *m (giratorio)*

turn-up ['tɜːnʌp] *n Br* (**a**) *(of trousers)* vuelta *f* (**b**) *Fam Fig* **what a t. for the books!** ¡vaya sorpresa!

turpentine ['tɜːpəntaɪn] *n* (esencia *f* de) trementina *f*

turquoise ['tɜːkwɔɪz] **1** *n (colour, stone)* turquesa *f*

2 *adj* **t. (blue)** azul turquesa

turret ['tʌrɪt] *n* torrecilla *f*

turtle ['tɜːtəl] *n* tortuga *f*, *US (tortoise)* tortuga *f*

turtledove ['tɜːtəldʌv] *n* tórtola *f*

turtleneck ['tɜːtəlnek] *n* **a t. (sweater)** un jersey de cuello alto

tusk [tʌsk] *n* colmillo *m*

tussle ['tʌsəl] *n* pelea *f*, lucha *f*

tutor ['tjuːtə(r)] *n Univ* tutor(a) *m,f*; **private t.** profesor(a) *m,f* particular

tutorial [tjuːˈtɔːrɪəl] *n Univ* tutoría *f*, seminario *m*

tuxedo [tʌkˈsiːdəʊ] *n US* smoking *m*

TV [tiːˈviː] *n (abbr* **television)** televisión *f*

twang [twæŋ] **1** *n* (**a**) *(of instrument)* sonido *m* vibrante (**b**) **nasal t.** gangueo *m*

2 *vt* puntear

3 *vi (string)* vibrar

tweak [twiːk] *vt* pellizcar

tweed [twiːd] *n* cheviot *m*

tweezers ['twiːzəz] *npl* pinzas *fpl*

twelfth [twelfθ] **1** *adj & n* duodécimo(a) *(m,f)*

2 *n (fraction)* duodécimo *m*

twelve [twelv] *adj & n* doce *(m inv)*

twentieth ['twentɪθ] **1** *adj & n* vigésimo(a) *(m,f)*

2 *n (fraction)* vigésimo *m*

twenty ['twentɪ] *adj & n* veinte *(m inv)*

twice [twaɪs] *adv* dos veces; **he's t. as old as I am** tiene el doble de años que yo

twiddle ['twɪdəl] **1** *vt* dar vueltas a; **to t. one's moustache** mesarse el bigote; **to t. one's thumbs** estar mano sobre mano

2 *vi* **to t. with sth** juguetear con algo

twig¹ [twɪg] *n* ramilla *f*

twig² [twɪg] *vi Br Fam* caer en la cuenta

twilight ['twaɪlaɪt] n crepúsculo m

twin [twɪn] **1** n mellizo(a) m,f; **identical twins** gemelos (idénticos); **t. brother/ sister** hermano gemelo/hermana geme-la; **t. beds** camas fpl gemelas
2 vt hermanar

twine [twaɪn] **1** n bramante m
2 vt entretejer
3 vi **to t. round sth** enroscarse alrededor de algo

twinge [twɪndʒ] n (of pain) punzada f; Fig **t. of conscience** remordimiento m

twinkle ['twɪŋkəl] vi (stars) centellear; (eyes) brillar

twinkling ['twɪŋklɪŋ] n (of stars) cente-lleo m; Fig **in the t. of an eye** en un abrir y cerrar de ojos

twirl [twɜːl] **1** vt girar rápidamente
2 vi (spin) girar rápidamente; (dancer) piruetear
3 n (movement) giro rápido; (of dancer) pirueta f

twist [twɪst] **1** vt torcer; (sense) tergiver-sar; **to t. one's ankle** torcerse el tobillo
2 vi (smoke) formar volutas; (path) ser-pentear
3 n (a) (of yarn) torzal m (b) (movement) torsión f; Med torcedura f; Fig **to give a new t. to sth** dar un nuevo enfoque a algo (c) (in road) vuelta f (d) (dance) twist m

twit [twɪt] n Br Fam memo(a) m,f

twitch [twɪtʃ] **1** vt dar un tirón a
2 vi crisparse; **his face twitches** tiene un tic en la cara

twitter ['twɪtə(r)] **1** vi gorjear
2 n gorjeo m

two [tuː] **1** adj dos inv; Fig **to be in** or **of t. minds about sth** estar indeciso(a) res-pecto a algo
2 n dos m inv; Fig **to put t. and t. together** atar cabos

two-faced ['tuːˈfeɪst] adj hipócrita

two-party ['tuːˈpɑːtɪ] adj **t. system** bipar-tidismo m

twopence ['tʌpəns] n Br dos peniques

two-piece ['tuːˈpiːs] **1** adj de dos piezas
2 n (suit) traje m de dos piezas

two-seater ['tuːˈsiːtə(r)] adj & n biplaza (f)

twosome ['tuːsəm] n pareja f

two-time ['tuːtaɪm] vt Fam poner los cuernos a

two-way ['tuːweɪ] adj (a) (street) de dos direcciones (b) **t. radio** aparato m emisor y receptor

tycoon [taɪˈkuːn] n magnate m

type [taɪp] **1** n (a) (kind) tipo m, clase f; (brand) marca f; (of car) modelo m (b) Typ carácter m; (print) caracteres mpl
2 vt & vi escribir a máquina

typecast ['taɪpkɑːst] vt encasillar

typescript ['taɪpskrɪpt] n texto m escrito a máquina

typeset ['taɪpset] vt componer

typesetter ['taɪpsetə(r)] n (a) (person) cajista mf (b) (machine) máquina f para componer tipos

typewriter ['taɪpraɪtə(r)] n máquina f de escribir

typewritten ['taɪprɪtən] adj escrito(a) a máquina

typhoid ['taɪfɔɪd] n **t. (fever)** fiebre tifoi-dea

typhoon [taɪˈfuːn] n tifón m

typical ['tɪpɪkəl] adj típico(a)

typify ['tɪpɪfaɪ] vt tipificar

typing ['taɪpɪŋ] n mecanografía f

typist ['taɪpɪst] n mecanógrafo(a) m,f

tyrannical [tɪˈrænɪkəl] adj tiránico(a)

tyrannize ['tɪrənaɪz] vt tiranizar

tyranny ['tɪrənɪ] n tiranía f

tyrant ['taɪrənt] n tirano(a) m,f

tyre [taɪə(r)] n neumático m; **t. pressure** presión f de los neumáticos

U

U, u [juː] n (the letter) U, u f

U [juː] adj (film) ≃ (apta) para todos los públicos

ubiquity [juːˈbɪkwɪtɪ] n ubicuidad f

udder [ˈʌdə(r)] n ubre f

UFO, ufo [ˈjuːefˈəʊ, ˈjuːfəʊ] n (abbr unidentified flying object) OVNI m

ugh [ʌx] interj ¡uf!, ¡puf!

ugly [ˈʌglɪ] adj (uglier, ugliest) feo(a); (situation) desagradable; Fig u. duckling patito feo

UK [juːˈkeɪ] n (abbr United Kingdom) R.U. m

Ukraine [juːˈkreɪn] n the U. Ucrania

ulcer [ˈʌlsə(r)] n (sore) llaga f; (internal) úlcera f

ulterior [ʌlˈtɪərɪə(r)] adj (motive) oculto(a)

ultimate [ˈʌltɪmɪt] adj (a) (final) último(a); (aim) final (b) (basic) esencial

ultimately [ˈʌltɪmɪtlɪ] adv (a) (finally) finalmente (b) (basically) en el fondo

ultimatum [ʌltɪˈmeɪtəm] n ultimátum m

ultrasound [ˈʌltrəsaʊnd] n ultrasonido m

ultraviolet [ʌltrəˈvaɪəlɪt] adj ultravioleta

umbilical [ʌmˈbɪlɪkəl] adj u. cord cordón m umbilical

umbrella [ʌmˈbrelə] n paraguas m inv

umpire [ˈʌmpaɪə(r)] **1** n árbitro m **2** vt arbitrar

umpteen [ʌmpˈtiːn] adj Fam muchísimos(as), la tira de

umpteenth [ʌmpˈtiːnθ] adj enésimo(a).

UN [juːˈen] n (abbr United Nations (Organization)) ONU f

unabashed [ʌnəˈbæʃt] adj (a) (unperturbed) inmutable, imperturbable (b) (shameless) desvergonzado(a), descarado(a)

unable [ʌnˈeɪbəl] adj incapaz; to be u. to do sth/anything no poder hacer algo/nada

unacceptable [ʌnəkˈseptəbəl] adj inaceptable

unaccompanied [ʌnəˈkʌmpənɪd] adj solo(a)

unaccountable [ʌnəˈkaʊntəbəl] adj inexplicable

unaccounted-for [ʌnəˈkaʊntɪdfɔː(r)] adj to be u. faltar

unaccustomed [ʌnəˈkʌstəmd] adj he's u. to this climate no está muy acostumbrado a este clima

unaffected [ʌnəˈfektɪd] adj (a) no afectado(a) (by por) (b) (indifferent) indiferente (by a) (c) (natural) (person) natural; (style) llano(a)

unaided [ʌnˈeɪdɪd] adj sin ayuda, solo(a)

unanimous [juːˈnænɪməs] adj unánime

unannounced [ʌnəˈnaʊnst] adj sin avisar

unanswered [ʌnˈɑːnsəd] adj sin contestar

unapproachable [ʌnəˈprəʊtʃəbəl] adj inabordable, inaccesible

unarmed [ʌnˈɑːmd] adj desarmado(a)

unashamed [ʌnəˈʃeɪmd] adj desvergonzado(a)

unasked [ʌnˈɑːskt] adv u. (for) (unrequested) no solicitado(a); (spontaneous) espontáneo(a)

unassuming [ʌnəˈsjuːmɪŋ] adj sin pretensiones

unattached [ʌnəˈtætʃt] adj (a) (independent) libre; (loose) suelto(a) (b) (person) soltero(a) y sin compromiso

unattended [ʌnəˈtendɪd] adj (counter etc) desatendido(a); to leave a child u. dejar a un niño solo

unauthorized [ʌnˈɔːθəraɪzd] adj (a) (person) no autorizado(a) (b) (trade etc) ilícito(a), ilegal

unavoidable [ʌnəˈvɔɪdəbəl] adj inevitable; (accident) imprevisible

unaware [ʌnəˈweə(r)] adj to be u. of sth ignorar algo

unawares [ʌnəˈweəz] adv (a) (unexpectedly) desprevenido(a) (b) (without knowing) inconscientemente

unbalanced [ʌnˈbælənst] adj desequilibrado(a)

unbearable [ʌnˈbeərəbəl] adj insoportable

unbeatable [ʌnˈbiːtəbəl] adj (team) invencible; (price, quality) inmejorable

unbelievable [ʌnbɪˈliːvəbəl] adj increíble

unbend [ʌn'bend] *vi Fam Fig* relajarse

unbia(s)sed [ʌn'baɪəst] *adj* imparcial

unborn [ʌn'bɔːn] *adj* sin nacer, nonato(a)

unbreakable [ʌn'breɪkəbəl] *adj* irrompible; *Fig* inquebrantable

unbroken [ʌn'brəʊkən] *adj* (a) *(whole)* intacto(a) (b) *(uninterrupted)* continuo(a) (c) *(record)* imbatido(a)

unbutton [ʌn'bʌtən] *vt* desabrochar

uncalled-for [ʌn'kɔːldfɔː(r)] *adj (inappropriate)* insensato(a); *(unjustified)* inmerecido(a)

uncanny [ʌn'kænɪ] *adj* misterioso(a), extraño(a)

unceasing [ʌn'siːsɪŋ] *adj* incesante

uncertain [ʌn'sɜːtən] *adj* (a) *(not certain)* incierto(a); *(doubtful)* dudoso(a); **in no u. terms** claramente (b) *(hesitant)* indeciso(a)

uncertainty [ʌn'sɜːtəntɪ] *n* incertidumbre *f*

unchanged [ʌn'tʃeɪndʒd] *adj* igual

unchecked [ʌn'tʃekt] *adj* (a) *(unrestrained)* desenfrenado(a) (b) *(not examined)* no comprobado(a)

uncivilized [ʌn'sɪvɪlaɪzd] *adj (tribe)* incivilizado(a), salvaje; *(not cultured)* inculto(a)

uncle ['ʌŋkəl] *n* tío *m*

uncomfortable [ʌn'kʌmftəbəl] *adj* incómodo(a); **to make things u. for** complicarle la vida a

uncommon [ʌn'kɒmən] *adj* (a) *(rare)* poco común; *(unusual)* extraordinario(a) (b) *(excessive)* excesivo(a)

uncommonly [ʌn'kɒmənlɪ] *adv* **not u.** con cierta frecuencia

uncompromising [ʌn'kɒmprəmaɪzɪŋ] *adj* intransigente; **u. honesty** sinceridad absoluta

unconcerned [ʌnkən'sɜːnd] *adj* indiferente (**about** a)

unconditional [ʌnkən'dɪʃənəl] *adj* incondicional; **u. refusal** negativa rotunda

unconnected [ʌnkə'nektɪd] *adj* no relacionado(a)

unconscious [ʌn'kɒnʃəs] **1** *adj* (a) inconsciente (**of** de) (b) *(unintentional)* involuntario(a)

    2 *n* **the u.** el inconsciente

unconsciousness [ʌn'kɒnʃəsnɪs] *n Med* pérdida *f* del conocimiento

uncontested [ʌnkən'testɪd] *adj Pol* **u. seat** escaño *m* ganado sin oposición

uncontrollable [ʌnkən'trəʊləbəl] *adj* incontrolable; *(desire)* irresistible

unconventional [ʌnkən'venʃənəl] *adj* poco convencional, original

uncooperative [ʌnkəʊ'ɒpərətɪv] *adj* poco cooperativo(a)

uncouth [ʌn'kuːθ] *adj (rude)* grosero(a)

uncover [ʌn'kʌvə(r)] *vt* destapar; *Fig* descubrir

undamaged [ʌn'dæmɪdʒd] *adj (article etc)* sin desperfectos; *(person)* indemne; *(reputation)* intacto(a)

undaunted [ʌn'dɔːntɪd] *adj* firme, impávido(a)

undecided [ʌndɪ'saɪdɪd] *adj* (a) *(person)* indeciso(a) (b) *(issue)* pendiente; **it's still u.** está aún por decidir

undefeated [ʌndɪ'fiːtɪd] *adj* invicto(a)

undefined [ʌndɪ'faɪnd] *adj* indeterminado(a)

undeniable [ʌndɪ'naɪəbəl] *adj* innegable

under ['ʌndə(r)] **1** *prep* (a) debajo de; **u. the sun** bajo el sol (b) *(less than)* menos de; **incomes u. £1,000** ingresos inferiores a 1.000 libras; **u. age** menor de edad (c) *(of rank)* de rango inferior a (d) **u. Caesar** bajo César (e) *(subject to)* bajo; **u. arrest** detenido(a); **u. cover** a cubierto; **u. obligation to** en la obligación de; **u. the circumstances** dadas las circunstancias; *Fig* **I was u. the impression that ...** tenía la impresión de que ... (f) *(according to)* según, conforme a

    2 *adv* abajo, debajo

under- ['ʌndə(r)] *pref (below)* sub-, infra-; *(insufficiently)* insuficientemente

underarm ['ʌndərɑːm] **1** *adj* **u. deodorant** desodorante *m* para las axilas

    2 *adv Sport* por debajo del hombro

undercarriage ['ʌndəkærɪdʒ] *n* tren *m* de aterrizaje

undercharge [ʌndə'tʃɑːdʒ] *vt* cobrar menos de lo debido

underclothes ['ʌndəkləʊðz] *npl* ropa *f* interior

undercoat ['ʌndəkəʊt] *n (of paint)* primera mano

undercover [ʌndə'kʌvə(r)] *adj* secreto(a)

undercurrent ['ʌndəkʌrənt] *n* (a) *(in sea)* corriente submarina (b) *Fig* sentimento *m* latente

undercut [ʌndə'kʌt] *vt (pt & pp* **undercut***) Com* vender más barato que

underdeveloped [ʌndədɪ'veləpt] *adj* subdesarrollado(a)

underdog ['ʌndədɒg] *n* desvalido(a) *m,f*

underestimate [ʌndər'estɪmeɪt] *vt* infravalorar

underexposure [ʌndərɪk'spəʊʒə(r)] *n Phot* subexposición *f*

underfed [ʌndə'fed] *adj* subalimentado(a)

underfoot [ʌndə'fʊt] *adv* en el suelo

undergo [ʌndə'gəʊ] *vt* (*pt* **underwent**; *pp* **undergone** [ʌndə'gɒn]) experimentar; *(change)* sufrir; *(test etc)* pasar por

undergraduate [ʌndə'grædjʊɪt] *n* estudiante *mf* universitario(a)

underground ['ʌndəgraʊnd] **1** *adj* subterráneo(a); *Fig* clandestino(a)
  2 *n* (**a**) *Pol* movimiento clandestino (**b**) *Br* **the u.** *(train)* el metro
  3 *adv* [ʌndə'graʊnd] *Fig* **to go u.** pasar a la clandestinidad

undergrowth ['ʌndəgrəʊθ] *n* maleza *f*

underhand 1 *adj* ['ʌndəhænd] *(method)* ilícito(a); *(person)* solapado(a)
  2 *adv* [ʌndə'hænd] bajo cuerda

underline [ʌndə'laɪn] *vt* subrayar

underling ['ʌndəlɪŋ] *n Pej* mandado(a) *m,f*

underlying [ʌndə'laɪɪŋ] *adj (basic)* fundamental

undermine [ʌndə'maɪn] *vt* socavar, minar

underneath [ʌndə'niːθ] **1** *prep* debajo de, bajo
  2 *adv* abajo, debajo
  3 *adj* de abajo
  4 *n* parte *f* inferior

undernourished [ʌndə'nʌrɪʃt] *adj* desnutrido(a)

underpaid [ʌndə'peɪd] *adj* mal pagado(a)

underpass ['ʌndəpɑːs] *n* paso subterráneo

underprivileged [ʌndə'prɪvɪlɪdʒd] **1** *adj* desfavorecido(a)
  2 *npl* **the u.** los menos favorecidos

under-secretary [ʌndə'sekrətərɪ] *n* subsecretario(a) *m,f*

undershirt ['ʌndəʃɜːt] *n US* camiseta *f*

underskirt ['ʌndəskɜːt] *n* combinación *f*

understand [ʌndə'stænd] *vt & vi* (*pt & pp* **understood**) (**a**) *(comprehend)* entender, comprender; **do I make myself understood?** ¿me explico? (**b**) *(assume, believe)* entender; **she gave me to u. that ...** me dio a entender que ... (**c**) *(hear)* tener entendido (**d**) **to u. one another** entenderse

understandable [ʌndə'stændəbəl] *adj* comprensible

understanding [ʌndə'stændɪŋ] **1** *n* (**a**) *(intellectual grasp)* entendimiento *m*, comprensión *f* (**b**) *(interpretation)* interpretación *f* (**c**) *(agreement)* acuerdo *m*

(**d**) **on the u. that ...** a condición de que ...
  2 *adj* comprensivo(a)

understatement [ʌndə'steɪtmənt] *n* **to make an u.** minimizar, subestimar; **to say that the boy is rather clever is an u.** decir que el chico es bastante listo es quedarse corto

understood [ʌndə'stʊd] **1** *adj* (**a**) **I wish it to be u. that ...** que conste que ... (**b**) *(agreed on)* convenido(a) (**c**) *(implied)* sobreentendido(a)
  2 *pt & pp of* **understand**

understudy ['ʌndəstʌdɪ] *n* suplente *mf*

undertake [ʌndə'teɪk] *vt* (*pt* **undertook**; *pp* **undertaken** [ʌndə'teɪkən]) (**a**) *(responsibility)* asumir; *(task, job)* encargarse de (**b**) *(promise)* comprometerse a

undertaker ['ʌndəteɪkə(r)] *n* empresario(a) *m,f* de pompas fúnebres; **u.'s** funeraria *f*

undertaking [ʌndə'teɪkɪŋ] *n* (**a**) *(task)* empresa *f* (**b**) *(promise)* compromiso *m*

undertone ['ʌndətəʊn] *n* **in an u.** en voz baja

undertook [ʌndə'tʊk] *pt of* **undertake**

underwater [ʌndə'wɔːtə(r)] **1** *adj* submarino(a)
  2 *adv* bajo el agua

underwear ['ʌndəweə(r)] *n* ropa *f* interior

underwent [ʌndə'went] *pt of* **undergo**

underworld [ʌndə'wɜːld] *n (criminals)* hampa *f*, bajos fondos

underwrite [ʌndə'raɪt] *vt* (*pt* **underwrote**; *pp* **underwritten**) (**a**) *(guarantee)* garantizar, avalar (**b**) *(insure)* asegurar

underwriter ['ʌndəraɪtə(r)] *n* (**a**) *Fin* suscriptor(a) *m,f* (**b**) *(insurer)* asegurador(a) *m,f*

underwritten [ʌndə'rɪtən] *pp of* **underwrite**

underwrote [ʌndə'rəʊt] *pt of* **underwrite**

undesirable [ʌndɪ'zaɪrəbəl] *adj & n* indeseable *(mf)*

undeterred [ʌndɪ'tɜːd] *adj* sin inmutarse; **u. by** sin arredrarse ante

undid [ʌn'dɪd] *pt of* **undo**

undies ['ʌndɪz] *npl Fam* bragas *fpl*

undignified [ʌn'dɪgnɪfaɪd] *adj (attitude etc)* indecoroso(a)

undisciplined [ʌn'dɪsɪplɪnd] *adj* indisciplinado(a)

undisclosed [ʌndɪs'kləʊzd] *adj* sin revelar

undiscovered [ʌndɪ'skʌvəd] *adj* sin descubrir

undisguised [ʌndɪs'gaɪzd] *adj Fig* no disimulado(a)

undisputed [ʌndɪ'spjuːtɪd] adj (unchallenged) incontestable; (unquestionable) indiscutible

undivided [ʌndɪ'vaɪdɪd] adj to give one's u. attention prestar toda la atención

undo [ʌn'duː] vt (pt undid; pp undone) (a) deshacer; (button) desabrochar (b) (put right) enmendar

undone¹ [ʌn'dʌn] adj (unfinished) inacabado(a)

undone² [ʌn'dʌn] 1 adj (knot etc) deshecho(a); to come u. (shoelace) desatarse; (button, blouse) desabrocharse; (necklace etc) soltarse
2 pp of undo

undoubted [ʌn'daʊtɪd] adj indudable

undress [ʌn'dres] 1 vt desnudar
2 vi desnudarse

undressed [ʌn'drest] adj (naked) desnudo(a)

undue [ʌn'djuː] (a) adj (excessive) excesivo(a) (b) (improper) indebido(a)

undulate ['ʌndjʊleɪt] vi ondular, ondear

unearth [ʌn'ɜːθ] vt desenterrar

unearthly [ʌn'ɜːθlɪ] adj (a) (being) sobrenatural (b) Fam (din) espantoso(a); at an u. hour a una hora intempestiva

uneasy [ʌn'iːzɪ] adj (a) (worried) preocupado(a); (disturbing) inquietante (b) (uncomfortable) incómodo(a)

uneconomic(al) [ʌniːkə'nɒmɪk(əl)] adj poco económico(a)

uneducated [ʌn'edjʊkeɪtɪd] adj inculto(a)

unemployed [ʌnɪm'plɔɪd] 1 adj en paro, parado(a); to be u. estar en paro
2 npl the u. los parados

unemployment [ʌnɪm'plɔɪmənt] n paro m, desempleo m; u. benefit, US u. compensation subsidio m de desempleo

unending [ʌn'endɪŋ] adj interminable

unenviable [ʌn'envɪəbəl] adj poco enviable

unequal [ʌn'iːkwəl] adj desigual

unequivocal [ʌnɪ'kwɪvəkəl] adj inequívoco(a)

uneven [ʌn'iːvən] adj (a) (not level) desigual; (bumpy) accidentado(a) (b) (variable) irregular

uneventful [ʌnɪ'ventfʊl] adj sin acontecimientos

unexceptional [ʌnɪk'sepʃənəl] adj ordinario(a)

unexpected [ʌnɪk'spektɪd] adj (unhoped for) inesperado(a); (event) imprevisto(a)

unfailing [ʌn'feɪlɪŋ] adj indefectible; (incessant) constante; (patience) inagotable

unfair [ʌn'feə(r)] adj injusto(a); Sport sucio(a)

unfaithful [ʌn'feɪθfʊl] adj (friend) desleal; (husband, wife) infiel

unfamiliar [ʌnfə'mɪljə(r)] adj (unknown) desconocido(a); (not conversant) no familiarizado(a) (with con)

unfashionable [ʌn'fæʃənəbəl] adj pasado(a) de moda; (ideas etc) poco popular

unfasten [ʌn'fɑːsən] vt (knot) desatar; (clothing, belt) desabrochar

unfavourable, US **unfavorable** [ʌn'feɪvərəbəl] adj desfavorable; (criticism) adverso(a); (winds) contrario(a)

unfeeling [ʌn'fiːlɪŋ] adj insensible

unfinished [ʌn'fɪnɪʃt] adj inacabado(a); u. business un asunto pendiente

unfit [ʌn'fɪt] adj (a) (thing) inadecuado(a); (person) no apto(a) (for para) (b) (incompetent) incompetente (c) (physically) incapacitado(a); to be u. no estar en forma

unflinching [ʌn'flɪntʃɪŋ] adj (a) (determined) resuelto(a) (b) (fearless) impávido(a)

unfold [ʌn'fəʊld] 1 vt (a) (sheet) desdoblar; (newspaper) abrir (b) (plan, secret) revelar
2 vi (a) (open up) abrirse; (landscape) extenderse (b) (plot) desarrollarse (c) (secret) descubrirse

unforeseen [ʌnfɔː'siːn] adj imprevisto(a)

unforgettable [ʌnfə'getəbəl] adj inolvidable

unforgivable [ʌnfə'gɪvəbəl] adj imperdonable

unfortunate [ʌn'fɔːtʃənɪt] adj (person, event) desgraciado(a); (remark) desafortunado(a); how u.! ¡qué mala suerte!

unfortunately [ʌn'fɔːtʃənɪtlɪ] adv desgraciadamente, por desgracia

unfounded [ʌn'faʊndɪd] adj infundado(a)

unfriendly [ʌn'frendlɪ] adj (unfriendlier, unfriendliest) antipático(a), poco amistoso(a)

unfurl [ʌn'fɜːl] vi desplegarse

unfurnished [ʌn'fɜːnɪʃt] adj sin amueblar

ungainly [ʌn'geɪnlɪ] adj (gait) desgarbado(a)

ungodly [ʌn'gɒdlɪ] adj (ungodlier, ungodliest) (behaviour) impío(a); Fam Fig at an u. hour a una hora intempestiva

ungrateful [ʌn'greɪtfʊl] adj (person) desagradecido(a); (task) ingrato(a)

unguarded [ʌn'gɑːdɪd] *adj* (**a**) *(unprotected)* desatendido(a); *(imprudent)* desprevenido(a) (**b**) *(frank)* franco(a)

unhappiness [ʌn'hæpɪnɪs] *n* (**a**) *(sadness)* tristeza *f* (**b**) *(wretchedness)* desdicha *f*

unhappy [ʌn'hæpɪ] *adj* (**unhappier, unhappiest**) (**a**) *(sad)* triste (**b**) *(wretched)* desgraciado(a), infeliz; *(unfortunate)* desafortunado(a)

unharmed [ʌn'hɑːmd] *adj* ileso(a), indemne

unhealthy [ʌn'helθɪ] *adj* (**unhealthier, unhealthiest**) (**a**) *(ill)* enfermizo(a) (**b**) *(unwholesome)* malsano(a)

unheard [ʌn'hɜːd] *adj* (**a**) **her request went u.** su petición no fue atendida (**b**) **u. of** *(outrageous)* inaudito(a); *(without precedent)* sin precedente

unhesitating [ʌn'hezɪteɪtɪŋ] *adj* resuelto(a)

unhook [ʌn'hʊk] *vt (from hook)* descolgar; *(clothing)* desabrochar

unhurt [ʌn'hɜːt] *adj* ileso(a), indemne

unhygienic [ʌnhaɪ'dʒiːnɪk] *adj* antihigiénico(a)

unidentified [ʌnaɪ'dentɪfaɪd] *adj* **u. flying object** objeto volador no identificado, ovni *m*

unification [juːnɪfɪ'keɪʃən] *n* unificación *f*

uniform ['juːnɪfɔːm] *adj & n* uniforme *(m)*

uniformity [juːnɪ'fɔːmɪtɪ] *n* uniformidad *f*

unify ['juːnɪfaɪ] *vt* unificar

unilateral [juːnɪ'lætərəl] *adj* unilateral

unimportant [ʌnɪm'pɔːtənt] *adj* poco importante

uninformed [ʌnɪn'fɔːmd] *adj (opinion)* sin fundamento

uninhabited [ʌnɪn'hæbɪtɪd] *adj* despoblado(a)

uninhibited [ʌnɪn'hɪbɪtɪd] *adj* sin inhibición

uninspired [ʌnɪn'spaɪəd] *adj (person)* falto(a) de inspiración; *(performance)* insulso(a)

uninspiring [ʌnɪn'spaɪərɪŋ] *adj* que no inspira

unintelligible [ʌnɪn'telɪdʒəbəl] *adj* ininteligible, incomprensible

unintentional [ʌnɪn'tenʃənəl] *adj* involuntario(a)

unintentionally [ʌnɪn'tenʃənəlɪ] *adv* sin querer

uninteresting [ʌn'ɪntrɪstɪŋ] *adj* poco interesante

uninterrupted [ʌnɪntə'rʌptɪd] *adj* ininterrumpido(a)

union ['juːnjən] **1** *n* (**a**) unión *f* (**b**) *(organization)* sindicato *m* (**c**) *US* **the U.** los Estados Unidos; *Br* **U. Jack** bandera *f* del Reino Unido
2 *adj* sindical

unique [juː'niːk] *adj* único(a)

unison ['juːnɪsən] *n Mus* unisonancia *f*; *Fig (harmony)* armonía *f*; **in u.** al unísono

unit ['juːnɪt] *n* (**a**) unidad *f*; **monetary u.** unidad monetaria; *Br Fin* **u. trust** sociedad *f* de inversiones (**b**) *(piece of furniture)* módulo *m*; **kitchen u.** mueble *m* de cocina (**c**) *Tech* grupo *m*; *Comput* **central processing u.** procesador *m* central; **visual display u.** monitor *m* (**d**) *(department)* servicio *m* (**e**) *(team)* equipo *m*

unite [juː'naɪt] **1** *vt* unir
2 *vi* unirse

united [juː'naɪtɪd] *adj* unido(a); **U. Kingdom** Reino Unido; **U. States (of America)** Estados Unidos (de América); **U. Nations** Naciones Unidas

unity ['juːnɪtɪ] *n* unidad *f*; *(harmony)* armonía *f*

universal [juːnɪ'vɜːsəl] *adj* universal

universe ['juːnɪvɜːs] *n* universo *m*

university [juːnɪ'vɜːsɪtɪ] **1** *n* universidad *f*
2 *adj* universitario(a)

unjust [ʌn'dʒʌst] *adj* injusto(a)

unkempt [ʌn'kempt] *adj* descuidado(a); *(hair)* despeinado(a); *(appearance)* desaliñado(a)

unkind [ʌn'kaɪnd] *adj (not nice)* poco amable; *(cruel)* despiadado(a)

unknown [ʌn'nəʊn] **1** *adj* desconocido(a); **u. quantity** incógnita *f*
2 *n* **the u.** lo desconocido

unlawful [ʌn'lɔːfʊl] *adj (not legal)* ilegal

unleash [ʌn'liːʃ] *vt* (**a**) *(dog)* soltar (**b**) *Fig (release)* liberar; *(provoke)* desencadenar

unless [ʌn'les] *conj* a menos que, a no ser que

unlike [ʌn'laɪk] **1** *adj* diferente, distinto(a)
2 *prep* a diferencia de

unlikely [ʌn'laɪklɪ] *adj* (**a**) *(improbable)* poco probable (**b**) *(unusual)* raro(a)

unlimited [ʌn'lɪmɪtɪd] *adj* ilimitado(a)

unlisted [ʌn'lɪstɪd] *adj US Tel* que no se encuentra en la guía telefónica

unload [ʌn'ləʊd] *vt & vi* descargar

unlock [ʌn'lɒk] *vt* abrir (con llave)

unluckily [ʌn'lʌkɪlɪ] *adv* desafortunadamente, por desgracia

unlucky [ʌn'lʌkɪ] *adj* (**unluckier, unluckiest**) *(unfortunate)* desgraciado(a); **to be**

u. *(person)* tener mala suerte; *(thing)* traer mala suerte

unmanageable [ʌn'mænɪdʒəbəl] *adj (people)* ingobernable; *(child, hair)* incontrolable

unmanned [ʌn'mænd] *adj (spacecraft etc)* no tripulado(a)

unmarried [ʌn'mærɪd] *adj* soltero(a)

unmask [ʌn'mɑːsk] *vt Fig (plot)* descubrir

unmistak(e)able [ʌnmɪs'teɪkəbəl] *adj* inconfundible

unmistak(e)ably [ʌnmɪs'teɪkəblɪ] *adv* sin lugar a dudas

unmitigated [ʌn'mɪtɪgeɪtɪd] *adj* (**a**) *(absolute)* absoluto(a); *(liar)* rematado(a) (**b**) *(grief)* profundo(a)

unnamed [ʌn'neɪmd] *adj (anonymous)* anónimo(a)

unnatural [ʌn'nætʃərəl] *adj* (**a**) *(against nature)* antinatural; *(abnormal)* anormal (**b**) *(affected)* afectado(a)

unnecessary [ʌn'nesɪsərɪ] *adj* innecesario(a), inútil; **it's u. to add that ...** sobra añadir que ...

unnoticed [ʌn'nəʊtɪst] *adj* desapercibido(a); **to let sth pass u.** pasar algo por alto

unobserved [ʌnɒb'zɜːvd] *adj* inadvertido(a)

unobtainable [ʌnəb'teɪnəbəl] *adj* inasequible, inalcanzable

unobtrusive [ʌnəb'truːsɪv] *adj* discreto(a)

unoccupied [ʌn'ɒkjʊpaɪd] *adj (house)* desocupado(a); *(seat)* libre

unofficial [ʌnə'fɪʃəl] *adj* no oficial; *Ind* **u. strike** huelga *f* no apoyada por los sindicatos

unorthodox [ʌn'ɔːθədɒks] *adj* (**a**) *(behaviour etc)* poco ortodoxo(a) (**b**) *Rel* heterodoxo(a)

unpack [ʌn'pæk] **1** *vt (boxes)* desembalar; *(suitcase)* deshacer **2** *vi* deshacer la(s) maleta(s)

unpalatable [ʌn'pælətəbəl] *adj* desagradable

unparalleled [ʌn'pærəleld] *adj* (**a**) *(in quality)* incomparable (**b**) *(without precedent)* sin precedente

unpardonable [ʌn'pɑːdənəbəl] *adj* imperdonable

unperturbed [ʌnpə'tɜːbd] *adj* impasible

unpleasant [ʌn'plezənt] *adj* desagradable (**to** con)

unpleasantness [ʌn'plezəntnɪs] *n* disgusto *m*

unplug [ʌn'plʌg] *vt* desenchufar

unpopular [ʌn'pɒpjʊlə(r)] *adj* impopular; **to make oneself u.** ganarse la antipatía de todos

unprecedented [ʌn'presɪdentɪd] *adj* sin precedente

unpredictable [ʌnprɪ'dɪktəbəl] *adj* imprevisible

unprepared [ʌnprɪ'peəd] *adj (speech etc)* improvisado(a); *(person)* desprevenido(a)

unprincipled [ʌn'prɪnsɪpəld] *adj* sin escrúpulos

unprintable [ʌn'prɪntəbəl] *adj (word, comment)* malsonante

unproductive [ʌnprə'dʌktɪv] *adj (inefficient)* improductivo(a); *(fruitless)* infructuoso(a)

unprofessional [ʌnprə'feʃənəl] *adj (unethical)* poco profesional; *(substandard)* de aficionado(a)

unprotected [ʌnprə'tektɪd] *adj* indefenso(a)

unprovoked [ʌnprə'vəʊkt] *adj* gratuito(a)

unpunished [ʌn'pʌnɪʃt] *adj* impune

unqualified [ʌn'kwɒlɪfaɪd] *adj* (**a**) *(without qualification)* sin título; *(incompetent)* incompetente (**b**) *(unconditional)* incondicional; *(denial)* rotundo(a); *(endorsement)* sin reserva; *(success)* total

unquestionable [ʌn'kwestʃənəbəl] *adj* indiscutible

unquestioning [ʌn'kwestʃənɪŋ] *adj* incondicional; *(obedience)* ciego(a)

unravel [ʌn'rævəl] **1** *vt* desenmarañar **2** *vi* desenmarañarse

unreadable [ʌn'riːdəbəl] *adj* (**a**) *(handwriting)* ilegible (**b**) *(book)* imposible de leer

unreal [ʌn'rɪəl] *adj* irreal

unrealistic [ʌnrɪə'lɪstɪk] *adj* poco realista

unreasonable [ʌn'riːzənəbəl] *adj* poco razonable; *(demands)* desmedido(a); *(prices)* exorbitante; *(hour)* inoportuno(a)

unrefined [ʌnrɪ'faɪnd] *adj* (**a**) *(sugar, oil etc)* sin refinar (**b**) *(person)* tosco(a), basto(a)

unrelated [ʌnrɪ'leɪtɪd] *adj (not connected)* no relacionado(a)

unrelenting [ʌnrɪ'lentɪŋ] *adj (behaviour)* implacable; *(struggle)* encarnizado(a)

unreliable [ʌnrɪ'laɪəbəl] *adj* (**a**) *(person)* de poca confianza (**b**) *(information)* que no es de fiar; *(machine)* poco fiable

unrelieved [ʌnrɪ'liːvd] *adj (boredom)* total

unremitting [ʌnrɪ'mɪtɪŋ] *adj* (**a**) *(efforts etc)* incesante (**b**) *(person)* incansable

unrepentant [ʌnrɪ'pentənt] *adj* impenitente

unreserved [ʌnrɪ'zɜ:vd] *adj (praise, support)* sin reserva

unreservedly [ʌnrɪ'zɜ:vɪdlɪ] *adv* sin reserva

unrest [ʌn'rest] *n (social etc)* malestar *m*; **political u.** agitación política

unrivalled, *US* **unrivaled** [ʌn'raɪvəld] *adj* sin par, sin rival

unroll [ʌn'rəʊl] *vt* desenrollar

unruffled [ʌn'rʌfəld] *adj Fig* tranquilo(a)

unruly [ʌn'ru:lɪ] *adj* (**unrulier, unruliest**) (**a**) *(child)* revoltoso(a) (**b**) *(hair)* rebelde

unsafe [ʌn'seɪf] *adj (dangerous)* peligroso(a); *(risky)* inseguro(a); **to feel u.** sentirse expuesto(a)

unsaid [ʌn'sed] *adj* **it's better left u.** más vale no decir nada; **much was left u.** quedó mucho por decir

unsatisfactory [ʌnsætɪs'fæktərɪ] *adj* insatisfactorio(a); **it's most u.** deja mucho que desear

unsavoury, *US* **unsavory** [ʌn'seɪvərɪ] *adj* desagradable

unscathed [ʌn'skeɪðd] *adj* ileso(a), indemne

unscrew [ʌn'skru:] *vt* destornillar

unscrupulous [ʌn'skru:pjʊləs] *adj* sin escrúpulos

unseemly [ʌn'si:mlɪ] *adj* impropio(a)

unseen [ʌn'si:n] **1** *adj* invisible; *(unnoticed)* inadvertido(a)
   2 *n Br Educ* = texto no trabajado en clase

unselfish [ʌn'selfɪʃ] *adj* desinteresado(a)

unsettle [ʌn'setəl] *vt* perturbar

unsettled [ʌn'setəld] *adj* (**a**) *(person)* nervioso(a); *(situation)* inestable (**b**) *(weather)* inestable (**c**) *(matter, debt)* pendiente (**d**) *(land)* sin colonizar

unshaven [ʌn'ʃeɪvən] *adj* sin afeitar

unsightly [ʌn'saɪtlɪ] *adj* feo(a), desagradable

unskilled [ʌn'skɪld] *adj (worker)* no cualificado(a); *(work)* no especializado(a)

unsociable [ʌn'səʊʃəbəl] *adj* insociable, huraño(a)

unsophisticated [ʌnsə'fɪstɪkeɪtɪd] *adj* (**a**) *(naïve)* ingenuo(a) (**b**) *(simple)* poco sofisticado(a)

unsound [ʌn'saʊnd] *adj* (**a**) *(unstable)* inestable; **of u. mind** demente (**b**) *(fallacious)* falso(a)

unspeakable [ʌn'spi:kəbəl] *adj* indecible (**b**) *Fig (evil)* atroz

unspoken [ʌn'spəʊkən] *adj* (**a**) *(tacit)* tácito(a) (**b**) *(feeling)* interior, secreto(a)

unstable [ʌn'steɪbəl] *adj* inestable

unsteady [ʌn'stedɪ] *adj (not firm)* inestable; *(table, chair)* cojo(a); *(hand, voice)* tembloroso(a)

unstinting [ʌn'stɪntɪŋ] *adj* pródigo(a) (**in** en)

unstuck [ʌn'stʌk] *adj* **to come u.** despegarse; *Fig* venirse abajo

unsuccessful [ʌnsək'sesfʊl] *adj* (**a**) *(fruitless)* fracasado(a); *(useless)* vano(a) (**b**) *(businessman etc)* fracasado(a); *(candidate)* derrotado(a); **to be u. at sth** no tener éxito con algo

unsuccessfully [ʌnsək'sesfʊlɪ] *adv* sin éxito, en vano

unsuitable [ʌn'su:təbəl] *adj* (**a**) *(person)* no apto(a) (**b**) *(thing)* inadecuado(a); *(remark)* inoportuno(a); *(time)* inconveniente

unsuited [ʌn'su:tɪd] *adj* (**a**) *(person)* no apto(a); *(thing)* impropio(a) (**to** para) (**b**) *(incompatible)* incompatible

unsure [ʌn'ʃʊə(r)] *adj* poco seguro(a)

unsuspecting [ʌnsə'spektɪŋ] *adj* confiado(a); **he went in u.** entró sin sospechar nada

unswerving [ʌn'swɜ:vɪŋ] *adj* firme

unsympathetic [ʌnsɪmpə'θetɪk] *adj (unfeeling)* impasible; *(not understanding)* poco comprensivo(a)

untapped [ʌn'tæpt] *adj (resource)* sin explotar

untarnished [ʌn'tɑ:nɪʃt] *adj Fig* sin mancha

untenable [ʌn'tenəbəl] *adj* insostenible

unthinkable [ʌn'θɪŋkəbəl] *adj* impensable, inconcebible

untidy [ʌn'taɪdɪ] *adj* (**untidier, untidiest**) *(room, person)* desordenado(a); *(hair)* despeinado(a); *(appearance)* desaseado(a)

untie [ʌn'taɪ] *vt* desatar; *(free)* soltar

until [ʌn'tɪl] **1** *conj* hasta que; **she worked u. she collapsed** trabajó hasta desfallecer; **u. she gets back** hasta que vuelva
   2 *prep* hasta; **u. now** hasta ahora; **u. ten o'clock** hasta las diez; **not u. Monday** hasta el lunes no

untimely [ʌn'taɪmlɪ] *adj* (**a**) *(premature)* prematuro(a) (**b**) *(inopportune)* inoportuno(a); *(hour)* intempestivo(a)

untold [ʌn'təʊld] *adj* (**a**) *(indescribable)* indecible (**b**) *Fig (loss, wealth)* incalculable (**c**) *(not told)* sin contar

untouchable [ʌn'tʌtʃəbəl] *adj & n* intocable (*mf*)

untoward [ʌntə'wɔːd] *adj* (**a**) (*unfortunate*) desafortunado(a) (**b**) (*adverse*) adverso(a)

untrained [ʌn'treɪnd] *adj* (**a**) (*unskilled*) sin preparación profesional (**b**) (*inexpert*) inexperto(a)

untrue [ʌn'truː] *adj* (**a**) (*false*) falso(a) (**b**) (*unfaithful*) infiel (**c**) (*inexact*) inexacto(a)

untrustworthy [ʌn'trʌstwɜːði] *adj* (**a**) (*person*) de poca confianza (**b**) (*source*) no fidedigno(a)

unused [ʌn'juːzd] *adj* (**a**) (*car*) sin usar; (*flat etc*) sin estrenar; (*stamp*) sin matar (**b**) (*not in use*) que ya no se utiliza (**c**) [ʌn'juːst] (*unaccustomed*) desacostumbrado(a) (**to** a)

unusual [ʌn'juːʒʊəl] *adj* (*rare*) insólito(a), poco común; (*original*) original; (*exceptional*) excepcional

unusually [ʌn'juːʒʊəlɪ] *adv* excepcionalmente

unveil [ʌn'veɪl] *vt* descubrir

unwarranted [ʌn'wɒrəntɪd] *adj* injustificado(a); (*remark*) gratuito(a)

unwavering [ʌn'weɪvərɪŋ] *adj* (*loyalty*) constante, firme; (*courage*) inquebrantable

unwelcome [ʌn'welkəm] *adj* (*visitor*) molesto(a); (*visit*) inoportuno(a); *Fig* (*news etc*) desagradable

unwell [ʌn'wel] *adj* malo(a), indispuesto(a)

unwieldy [ʌn'wiːldɪ] *adj* (*difficult to handle*) poco manejable; (*clumsy*) torpe

unwilling [ʌn'wɪlɪŋ] *adj* **to be u. to do sth** no estar dispuesto a hacer algo

unwillingly [ʌn'wɪlɪŋlɪ] *adv* de mala gana

unwind [ʌn'waɪnd] **1** *vt* (*pt & pp* **unwound**) desenrollar

2 *vi* (**a**) desenrollarse (**b**) (*relax*) relajarse

unwise [ʌn'waɪz] *adj* imprudente, desaconsejable

unwitting [ʌn'wɪtɪŋ] *adj* involuntario(a)

unworkable [ʌn'wɜːkəbəl] *adj* (*not feasible*) impracticable; (*suggestion*) irrealizable

unworthy [ʌn'wɜːði] *adj* indigno(a)

unwound [ʌn'waʊnd] *pt & pp of* **unwind**

unwrap [ʌn'ræp] *vt* (*gift*) desenvolver; (*package*) deshacer

unwritten [ʌn'rɪtən] *adj* no escrito(a); (*agreement*) verbal

unyielding [ʌn'jiːldɪŋ] *adj* inflexible

up [ʌp] **1** *prep* (**a**) (*movement*) **to climb up the mountain** escalar la montaña; **to walk up the street** ir calle arriba

(**b**) (*position*) en lo alto de; **further up the street** más adelante (en la misma calle); **halfway up the ladder** a mitad de la escalera

2 *adv* (**a**) (*upwards*) arriba, hacia arriba; (*position*) arriba; **from £10 up** de 10 libras para arriba; **halfway up** a medio camino; **right up (to the top)** hasta arriba (del todo); **to go/come up** subir; **this side up** (*sign*) este lado hacia arriba

(**b**) **the moon is up** ha salido la luna

(**c**) (*towards*) hacia; **to come** *or* **go up to sb** acercarse a algn; **to walk up and down** ir de un lado a otro

(**d**) (*in, to*) **he's up in Yorkshire** está en Yorkshire

(**e**) (*increased*) **bread is up** el pan ha subido

(**f**) **it's up for discussion** se está discutiendo; **up for sale** en venta

(**g**) *Fam* **something's up** pasa algo; **what's up (with you)?** ¿qué pasa (contigo)?

(**h**) **to be up against sth** enfrentarse con algo

(**i**) **up to** (*as far as, until*) hasta; **I can spend up to £5** puedo gastar un máximo de 5 libras; **up to here** hasta aquí; **up to now** hasta ahora

(**j**) **to be up to** (*depend on*) depender de; (*be capable of*) estar a la altura de; **I don't feel up to doing it today** hoy no me encuentro con fuerzas para hacerlo; **it's not up to much** no vale gran cosa

(**k**) **he's up to sth** está tramando algo

3 *adj* (**a**) (*out of bed*) levantado(a)

(**b**) (*finished*) terminado(a); **time's up** (ya) es la hora

4 *vt Fam* aumentar

5 *n Fig* **ups and downs** altibajos *mpl*

up-and-coming ['ʌpən'kʌmɪŋ] *adj* prometedor(a)

upbringing ['ʌpbrɪŋɪŋ] *n* educación *f*

update [ʌp'deɪt] *vt* actualizar, poner al día

upgrade **1** *vt* [ʌp'greɪd] (**a**) (*promote*) ascender (**b**) (*improve*) mejorar la calidad de (**c**) *Comput* (*software, hardware*) actualizar

2 *n* ['ʌpgreɪd] *Comput* actualización *f*

upheaval [ʌp'hiːvəl] *n* trastorno *m*

upheld [ʌp'held] *pt & pp of* **uphold**

uphill 1 *adj* ['ʌphɪl] ascendente; *Fig* arduo(a)

2 *adv* [ʌp'hɪl] cuesta arriba

uphold [ʌp'həʊld] *vt* (*pt & pp* **upheld**) sostener

upholstery [ʌp'həʊlstərɪ] *n* tapizado *m*, tapicería *f*

upkeep ['ʌpkiːp] *n* mantenimiento *m*

up-market ['ʌpmɑːkɪt] *adj* de categoría

upon [ə'pɒn] *prep Fml* en, sobre; **once u. a time ...** érase una vez ...; **u. my word** (mi) palabra de honor

upper ['ʌpə(r)] **1** *adj* (**a**) (*position*) superior; **u. storey** piso de arriba; *Fig* **to have the u. hand** llevar la delantera (**b**) (*in rank*) alto(a); **the u. class** la clase alta; **the U. House** la Cámara Alta
2 *n* (*of shoe*) pala *f*

upper-class ['ʌpə'klæs] *adj* de la clase alta

uppermost ['ʌpəməʊst] *adj* más alto(a); *Fig* **it was u. in my mind** era lo que me preocupaba más

upright ['ʌpraɪt] **1** *adj* (**a**) (*vertical*) vertical (**b**) (*honest*) honrado(a)
2 *adv* derecho
3 *n Ftb* (*post*) poste *m*

uprising ['ʌpraɪzɪŋ] *n* sublevación *f*

uproar ['ʌprɔː(r)] *n* tumulto *m*, alboroto *m*

uproot [ʌp'ruːt] *vt* (*plant*) arrancar de raíz

upset [ʌp'set] **1** *vt* (*pt & pp* **upset**) (**a**) (*overturn*) volcar; (*spill*) derramar (**b**) (*shock*) trastornar; (*worry*) preocupar; (*displease*) disgustar (**c**) (*spoil*) desbaratar (**d**) (*make ill*) sentar mal a
2 *adj* (*shocked*) alterado(a); (*displeased*) disgustado(a); **to have an u. stomach** sentirse mal del estómago
3 *n* ['ʌpset] (**a**) (*reversal*) revés *m* (**b**) *Sport* resultado inesperado

upshot ['ʌpʃɒt] *n* resultado *m*

upside ['ʌpsaɪd] *n* **u. down** al revés

upstage [ʌp'steɪdʒ] *vt Fam* eclipsar

upstairs [ʌp'steəz] **1** *adv* al piso de arriba; **she lives u.** vive en el piso de arriba
2 *n* piso *m* de arriba

upstart ['ʌpstɑːt] *n* advenedizo(a) *m,f*

upstream [ʌp'striːm] *adv* río arriba

uptake ['ʌpteɪk] *n Fam* **to be quick on the u.** cogerlas al vuelo

uptight [ʌp'taɪt] *adj Fam* nervioso(a)

up-to-date [ʌptə'deɪt] *adj* (**a**) (*current*) al día (**b**) (*modern*) moderno(a)

upturn ['ʌptɜːn] *n* mejora *f*

upward ['ʌpwəd] *adj* ascendente

upward(s) ['ʌpwəd(z)] *adv* hacia arriba; **from ten (years) u.** a partir de los diez años; *Fam* **u. of** algo más de

uranium [jʊ'reɪnɪəm] *n* uranio *m*

urban ['ɜːbən] *adj* urbano(a)

urbane [ɜː'beɪn] *adj* urbano(a), cortés

urchin ['ɜːtʃɪn] *n* (**a**) (*child*) pilluelo(a) *m,f* (**b**) **sea u.** erizo *m* de mar

urge [ɜːdʒ] **1** *vt* (**a**) instar; (*plead*) exhortar (**b**) (*advocate*) preconizar; **to u. that sth should be done** insistir en que se haga algo
2 *n* impulso *m*
▸ **urge on** *vt sep* animar a

urgency ['ɜːdʒənsɪ] *n* urgencia *f*

urgent ['ɜːdʒənt] *adj* urgente; (*need, tone*) apremiante

urinal [jʊ'raɪnəl] *n* (*toilet*) urinario *m*; (*bowl*) orinal *m*

urinate ['jʊərɪneɪt] *vi* orinar

urine ['jʊərɪn] *n* orina *f*

URL [juːɑː'rel] *n Comput* (*abbr* **uniform resource locator**) URL *m*

urn [ɜːn] *n* (**a**) urna *f* (**b**) **tea u.** tetera *f* grande

Uruguay ['jʊərəgwaɪ] *n* Uruguay

Uruguayan [jʊərə'gwaɪən] *adj & n* uruguayo(a) *m,f*

US [juː'es] *n* (*abbr* **United States**) EE.UU. *mpl*

us [ʌs, *unstressed* əs] *pers pron* (**a**) (*object*) nos; **let's forget it** olvidémoslo (**b**) (*after prep*) nosotros(as); **both of us** nosotros dos; **he's one of us** es de los nuestros (**c**) (*after v to be*) nosotros(as); **she wouldn't believe it was us** no creía que fuéramos nosotros (**d**) *Fam* me; **give us a kiss!** ¡dame un beso!

USA [juːes'eɪ] *n* (*abbr* **United States of America**) EE.UU. *mpl*

usage ['juːsɪdʒ] *n* (**a**) (*habit, custom*) costumbre *f* (**b**) *Ling* uso *m*

use [juːz] **1** *vt* (**a**) emplear, utilizar; **what is it used for?** ¿para qué sirve?; **to u. force** hacer uso de la fuerza
(**b**) (*consume*) consumir, gastar
(**c**) (*take unfair advantage of*) aprovecharse de
(**d**) *Fam* **I could u. a drink** no me vendría mal un trago
2 *v aux* **used to** ['juːstə] soler, acostumbrar; **where did you u. to live?** ¿dónde vivías (antes)?

> Como verbo auxiliar, aparece siempre en la forma **used to**. Se traduce al español por el verbo principal en pretérito imperfecto, o por el pretérito imperfecto de **soler** más infinitivo.

3 *n* [juːs] (**a**) uso *m*, empleo *m*; (*handling*) manejo *m*; **directions for u.** modo de empleo; **in u.** en uso; **not in u.** (*on* *lift)* no funciona; **ready for u.** listo para usar; **to make (good) u. of sth** aprovechar algo; **to put to good u.** sacar partido de

(**b**) *(application)* aplicación *f*

(**c**) *(usefulness)* utilidad *f*; **it's no u.** es inútil; **what's the u.?** ¿para qué?; *Fam* **it's no u. crying** no sirve de nada llorar; **of u.** útil; **to be of u.** servir

▸ **use up** *vt sep* acabar

used *adj* (**a**) [juːzd] *(second-hand)* usado(a) (**b**) [juːst] **to be u.** to estar acostumbrado(a) a

useful ['juːsfʊl] *adj* útil; *(practical)* práctico(a); **to come in u.** venir bien

usefulness ['juːsfʊlnɪs] *n* utilidad *f*

useless ['juːslɪs] *adj* inútil

user ['juːzə(r)] *n* (**a**) usuario(a) *m,f* (**b**) *Fam (of drugs)* drogadicto(a) *m,f*

usher ['ʌʃə(r)] **1** *n* (**a**) *Cin & Th* acomodador(a) *m,f* (**b**) *(in court etc)* ujier *m*

2 *vt* **to u. in** *Cin & Th* acomodar; *(at home)* hacer pasar; **to u. out** acompañar hasta la puerta

USSR [juːeses'aː(r)] *n Hist (abbr* **Union of Soviet Socialist Republics**) URSS *f*

usual ['juːʒʊəl] **1** *adj* corriente, normal; **as u.** como siempre; **at the u. hour** a la hora habitual; **earlier than u.** más pronto que de costumbre; **the u. problems** los problemas de siempre

2 *n* lo habitual; **out of the u.** fuera de lo común

usually ['juːʒʊəlɪ] *adv* normalmente

usurp [juː'zɜːp] *vt* usurpar

utensil [juː'tensəl] *n* utensilio *m*; **kitchen utensils** batería *f* de cocina

uterus ['juːtərəs] *n* útero *m*

utilitarian [juːtɪlɪ'teərɪən] *adj* (**a**) *(in philosophy)* utilitarista (**b**) *(useful)* utilitario(a)

utility [juː'tɪlɪtɪ] *n* (**a**) utilidad *f*; **u. room** cuarto *m* de planchar; *(for storage)* trascocina *f* (**b**) **(public) u.** empresa *f* de servicio público

utilize ['juːtɪlaɪz] *vt* utilizar

utmost ['ʌtməʊst] **1** *adj* sumo(a); **of the u. importance** de suma importancia

2 *n* máximo *m*; **to do** *or* **try one's u.** hacer todo lo posible; **to the u.** al máximo, à más no poder

utopian [juː'təʊpɪən] *adj* utópico(a)

utter¹ ['ʌtə(r)] *vt (words)* pronunciar; *(sigh)* dar; *(cry, threat)* lanzar

utter² ['ʌtə(r)] *adj* total, completo(a)

utterance ['ʌtərəns] *n* declaración *f*

U-turn ['juːtɜːn] *n* cambio *m* de sentido; *Pol* giro *m* de 180 grados

V, v [viː] *n (the letter)* V, v *f*
V *(abbr* **volt(s))** V
v **(a)** *(abbr* **verse)** v **(b)** *(also* **vs)** *(abbr* **versus)** contra
vacancy ['veɪkənsɪ] *n* **(a)** *(job)* vacante *f* **(b)** *(room)* habitación *f* libre; **no vacancies** *(sign)* completo
vacant ['veɪkənt] *adj* **(a)** *(empty)* vacío(a) **(b)** *(job)* vacante; *Br* **situations v.** *(in newspaper)* ofertas de trabajo **(c)** *(free, not in use)* libre
vacate [və'keɪt] *vt (flat)* desalojar
vacation [və'keɪʃən] *US* **1** *n* vacaciones *fpl*; **on v.** de vacaciones
  2 *vi* pasar las vacaciones (**in/at** en)
vacationer [və'keɪʃənə(r)], **vacationist** [və'keɪʃənɪst] *n US* **summer v.** veraneante *mf*
vaccinate ['væksɪneɪt] *vt* vacunar
vaccine ['væksiːn] *n* vacuna *f*
vacuum ['vækjʊəm] **1** *n* vacío *m*; **v. cleaner** aspiradora *f*; **v. flask** termo *m*
  2 *vt (carpet, room)* pasar la aspiradora por
vacuum-packed ['vækjʊəm'pækt] *adj* envasado(a) al vacío
vagina [və'dʒaɪnə] *n* vagina *f*
vagrant ['veɪɡrənt] *adj & n* vagabundo(a) *(m,f)*
vague [veɪɡ] *adj (imprecise)* vago(a), impreciso(a); *(indistinct)* borroso(a)
vain [veɪn] *adj* **(a)** *(proud)* vanidoso(a), presumido(a) **(b)** *(hopeless)* vano(a); **in v.** en vano
valentine ['væləntaɪn] *n* **(a)** *(card)* = tarjeta que se manda el Día de los Enamorados **(b)** *(sweetheart)* novio(a) *m,f*
valet ['vælɪt, 'væleɪ] *n* ayuda *m* de cámara
valiant ['væljənt] *adj* valiente
valid ['vælɪd] *adj* válido(a); **no longer v.** caducado(a)
valley ['vælɪ] *n* valle *m*
valour, *US* **valor** ['vælə(r)] *n* valor *m*, valentía *f*
valuable ['væljʊəbəl] **1** *adj* valioso(a), de valor
  2 *npl* **valuables** objetos *mpl* de valor

valuation [væljʊ'eɪʃən] *n* **(a)** *(act)* valoración *f* **(b)** *(price)* valor *m*
value ['væljuː] **1** *n* valor *m*; **50 pence is good v.** 50 peniques es un buen precio; **to get good v. for money** sacarle jugo al dinero; **v.-added tax** impuesto *m* sobre el valor añadido
  2 *vt* valorar
valve [vælv] *n* **(a)** *Anat & Tech* válvula *f* **(b)** *Rad* lámpara *f*
vampire ['væmpaɪə(r)] *n* vampiro *m*
van [væn] *n Br* **(a)** *Aut* furgoneta *f* **(b)** *Rail* furgón *m*
vandal ['vændəl] *n* vándalo(a) *m,f*
vandalism ['vændəlɪzəm] *n* vandalismo *m*
vandalize ['vændəlaɪz] *vt* destruir, destrozar
vanguard ['vænɡɑːd] *n* vanguardia *f*
vanilla [və'nɪlə] *n* vainilla *f*
vanish ['vænɪʃ] *vi* desaparecer
vanity ['vænɪtɪ] *n* vanidad *f*; **v. bag** *or* **case** neceser *m*
vantage ['vɑːntɪdʒ] *n* ventaja *f*; **v. point** posición estratégica
vapor ['veɪpər] *n US* = **vapour**
vaporizer ['veɪpəraɪzə(r)] *n (device)* vaporizador *m*; *(spray)* pulverizador *m*
vapour ['veɪpə(r)] *n* vapor *m*; *(on windowpane)* vaho *m*; **v. trail** estela *f* de humo
variable ['veərɪəbəl] *adj & n* variable *(f)*
variance ['veərɪəns] *n Fml* **to be at v.** no concordar; **to be at v. with sb** estar en desacuerdo con algn
variation [veərɪ'eɪʃən] *n* variación *f*
varicose ['værɪkəʊs] *adj* **v. veins** varices *fpl*
varied ['veərɪd] *adj* variado(a), diverso(a)
variety [və'raɪɪtɪ] *n* **(a)** *(diversity)* variedad *f*; *(assortment)* surtido *m*; **for a v. of reasons** por razones diversas **(b)** **v. show** espectáculo *m* de variedades
various ['veərɪəs] *adj* diversos(as), varios(as)
varnish ['vɑːnɪʃ] **1** *n* barniz *m*; *Br* **nail v.** esmalte *m* de uñas
  2 *vt* barnizar; *(nails)* esmaltar
vary ['veərɪ] *vi* variar; **prices v. from £2 to**

£4 los precios oscilan entre 2 y 4 libras; **to v. in size** variar de tamaño

varying ['veəriɪŋ] *adj* **with v. degrees of success** con más o menos éxito

vase [*Br* vɑːz, *US* veɪs] *n* jarrón *m*

> *ℓ* Note that the Spanish word **vaso** is a false friend and is never a translation for the English word **vase**. In Spanish, **vaso** means both "glass" and "vessel".

vasectomy [və'sektəmɪ] *n Med* vasectomía *f*

Vaseline® ['væsɪliːn] *n* vaselina *f*

vast [vɑːst] *adj* vasto(a); *(majority)* inmenso(a)

VAT [viːiːˈtiː, væt] *n* (*abbr* **value-added tax**) IVA *m*

vat [væt] *n* cuba *f*, tina *f*

Vatican ['vætɪkən] *n* **the V.** el Vaticano

vault¹ [vɔːlt] *n* bóveda *f*; *(for wine)* bodega *f*; *(tomb)* cripta *f*; *(of bank)* cámara acorazada

vault² [vɔːlt] **1** *vt & vi* saltar
2 *n* salto *m*

vaunt [vɔːnt] *vt Fml* jactarse de, hacer alarde de

VCR [viːsiːˈɑː(r)] *n* (*abbr* **video cassette recorder**) (aparato *m* de) vídeo *m*

VD [viːˈdiː] *n* (*abbr* **venereal disease**) enfermedad venérea

VDU [viːdiːˈjuː] *n* (*abbr* **visual display unit**) monitor *m*

veal [viːl] *n* ternera *f*

veer [vɪə(r)] *vi (ship)* virar; *(car)* girar

vegan ['viːgən] *n* vegetaliano(a) *m,f*, = vegetariano estricto que no come ningún producto de origen animal

vegeburger ['vedʒɪbɜːgə(r)] *n* hamburguesa vegetariana

vegetable ['vedʒtəbəl] *n (food)* verdura *f*, hortaliza *f*; **v. garden** huerta *f*, huerto *m*

vegetarian [vedʒɪ'teərɪən] *adj & n* vegetariano(a) *(m,f)*

vegetation [vedʒɪ'teɪʃən] *n* vegetación *f*

vehement ['viːɪmənt] *adj* vehemente

vehicle ['viːɪkəl] *n* vehículo *m*

veil [veɪl] **1** *n* velo *m*
2 *vt* velar

vein [veɪn] *n* vena *f*

velocity [vɪ'lɒsɪtɪ] *n* velocidad *f*

velvet ['velvɪt] *n* terciopelo *m*

velvety ['velvɪtɪ] *adj* aterciopelado(a)

vendetta [ven'detə] *n* vendetta *f*

vending ['vendɪŋ] *n* **v. machine** máquina expendedora

vendor ['vendɔː(r)] *n* vendedor(a) *m,f*

veneer [vɪ'nɪə(r)] *n* (a) *(covering)* chapa *f* (b) *Fig* apariencia *f*

venerable ['venərəbəl] *adj* venerable

venereal [vɪ'nɪərɪəl] *adj* venéreo(a)

Venetian [vɪ'niːʃən] *adj & n* veneciano(a) *(m,f)*; **v. blind** persiana *f* graduable

Venezuela [venɪ'zweɪlə] *n* Venezuela

Venezuelan [venɪ'zweɪlən] *adj & n* venezolano(a) *(m,f)*

vengeance ['vendʒəns] *n* venganza *f*; *Fam* **it was raining with a v.** llovía con ganas

Venice ['venɪs] *n* Venecia

venison ['venɪsən] *n* carne *f* de venado

venom ['venəm] *n* veneno *m*

venomous ['venəməs] *adj* venenoso(a); *Fig* **v. tongue** lengua viperina

vent [vent] **1** *n* (a) *(opening)* abertura *f*, orificio *m*; *(grille)* rejilla *f* de ventilación; **air v.** respiradero *m* (b) *(of volcano)* chimenea *f*
2 *vt Fig (feelings)* descargar

ventilate ['ventɪleɪt] *vt* ventilar

ventilation [ventɪ'leɪʃən] *n* ventilación *f*

ventilator ['ventɪleɪtə(r)] *n* ventilador *m*

ventriloquist [ven'trɪləkwɪst] *n* ventrílocuo(a) *m,f*

venture ['ventʃə(r)] **1** *vt* arriesgar, aventurar; **he didn't v. to ask** no se atrevió a preguntarlo
2 *vi* arriesgarse; **to v. out of doors** atreverse a salir
3 *n* empresa arriesgada, aventura *f*; *Com* **business/joint v.** empresa comercial/colectiva

venue ['venjuː] *n* (a) *(meeting place)* lugar *m* de reunión (b) *(for concert etc)* local *m*

Venus ['viːnəs] *n* *(goddess)* Venus *f*; *(planet)* Venus *m*

veranda(h) [və'rændə] *n* porche *m*, terraza *f*

verb [vɜːb] *n* verbo *m*

verbal ['vɜːbəl] *adj* verbal

verbatim [vɜː'beɪtɪm] **1** *adj* textual
2 *adv* textualmente

verbose [vɜː'bəʊs] *adj* pródigo(a) en palabras

verdict ['vɜːdɪkt] *n* (a) *Jur* veredicto *m*, fallo *m* (b) *(opinion)* opinión *f*, juicio *m*

verge [vɜːdʒ] **1** *n* (a) *(margin)* borde *m*; *Fig* **on the v. of** al borde de; *Fig* **to be on the v. of doing sth** estar a punto de hacer algo (b) *Br (of road)* arcén *m*, *Andes* berma *f*, *Méx* acotamiento *m*, *RP* banquina *f*, *Ven* hombrillo *m*
2 *vi* rayar (**on** en)

verification [verɪfɪ'keɪʃən] *n* verificación *f*, comprobación *f*

verify ['verɪfaɪ] *vt* verificar, comprobar

veritable ['verɪtəbəl] *adj* auténtico(a)

vermicelli [vɜːmɪ'tʃelɪ] *n* fideos *mpl*

vermin ['vɜːmɪn] *npl* (**a**) *(animals)* bichos *mpl*, sabandijas *fpl* (**b**) *Fig* gentuza *f*

vermouth ['vɜːməθ] *n* vermú *m*, vermut *m*

verruca [və'ruːkə] *n* verruga *f*

versatile ['vɜːsətaɪl] *adj (person)* polifacético(a); *(object)* versátil

verse [vɜːs] *n* (**a**) *(stanza)* estrofa *f* (**b**) *(poetry)* versos *mpl*, poesía *f* (**c**) *(of song)* copla *f* (**d**) *(of Bible)* versículo *m*

versed [vɜːst] *adj* **to be (well) v. in** ser (muy) versado en

version ['vɜːʃən, 'vɜːʒən] *n* (**a**) versión *f*; **stage v.** adaptación *f* teatral (**b**) *Aut* modelo *m*

versus ['vɜːsəs] *prep* contra

vertebra ['vɜːtɪbrə] *n (pl* **vertebras** *or* **vertebrae** ['vɜːtɪbriː]*)* vértebra *f*

vertical ['vɜːtɪkəl] *adj & n* vertical *(f)*

vertigo ['vɜːtɪgəʊ] *n* vértigo *m*

verve [vɜːv] *n* vigor *m*, brío *m*

very ['verɪ] **1** *adv* (**a**) *(extremely)* muy; **to be v. hungry** tener mucha hambre; **v. much** muchísimo; **v. well** muy bien (**b**) *(emphatic)* **at the v. latest** como máximo; **at the v. least** como mínimo; **the v. best** el mejor de todos; **the v. first/last** el primero/último de todos; **the v. same day** el mismo día

2 *adj* (**a**) **at the v. end/beginning** al final/principio de todo (**b**) *(precise)* **at this v. moment** en este mismo momento; **her v. words** sus palabras exactas; **in the v. middle** justo en medio (**c**) *(mere)* **the v. thought of it!** ¡sólo con pensarlo!

vespers ['vespəz] *npl* vísperas *fpl*

vessel ['vesəl] *n* (**a**) *(container)* vasija *f* (**b**) *Naut* buque *m*, nave *f* (**c**) *Anat & Bot* vaso *m*

vest [vest] **1** *n* (**a**) *Br (undershirt)* camiseta *f* de tirantes (**b**) *US* chaleco *m*

2 *vt Jur* **by the power vested in me ...** por los poderes que se me han conferido ...

vested ['vestɪd] *adj Jur & Fin* **v. interests** derechos adquiridos; *Fig* intereses *mpl* personales

vestibule ['vestɪbjuːl] *n* vestíbulo *m*

vestige ['vestɪdʒ] *n* vestigio *m*

vestry ['vestrɪ] *n* sacristía *f*

vet [vet] **1** *n* veterinario(a) *m,f*

2 *vt Br* someter a investigación, examinar

veteran ['vetərən] *n* (**a**) veterano(a) *m,f* (**b**) *US* **(war) v.** ex combatiente *mf*

veterinarian [vetərɪ'neərɪən] *n US* veterinario(a) *m,f*

veterinary ['vetərɪnərɪ] *adj* veterinario(a); **v. medicine** veterinaria *f*; *Br* **v. surgeon** veterinario(a) *m,f*

veto ['viːtəʊ] **1** *n (pl* **vetoes**) veto *m*

2 *vt Pol* vetar; *(suggestion etc)* descartar

vexed [vekst] *adj* (**a**) *(annoyed)* disgustado(a) (**b**) *(debated)* controvertido(a)

VHF [viːeɪtʃ'ef] *(abbr* **very high frequency**) VHF

via ['vaɪə] *prep* por, vía

viable ['vaɪəbəl] *adj* viable, factible

viaduct ['vaɪədʌkt] *n* viaducto *m*

vibrant ['vaɪbrənt] *adj* (**a**) *(sound)* vibrante (**b**) *Fig (personality)* vital; *(city)* animado(a)

vibrate [vaɪ'breɪt] *vi* vibrar (**with** de)

vibration [vaɪ'breɪʃən] *n* vibración *f*

vicar ['vɪkə(r)] *n* párroco *m*

vicarage ['vɪkərɪdʒ] *n* casa *f* del párroco

vicarious [vɪ'keərɪəs] *adj* experimentado(a) por otro; *(punishment)* sufrido(a) por otro

vice¹ [vaɪs] *n* vicio *m*

vice² [vaɪs] *n Br (tool)* torno *m* de banco

vice- [vaɪs] *pref* vice-; **v.-chancellor** rector(a) *m,f*; **v.-president** vicepresidente(a) *m,f*

vice-chairman [vaɪs'tʃeəmən] *n* vicepresidente *m*

vice versa [vaɪsɪ'vɜːsə] *adv* viceversa

vicinity [vɪ'sɪnɪtɪ] *n (area)* vecindad *f*; **in the v. of** *(geographic location)* cerca de, en las inmediaciones de; *(amount)* alrededor de

vicious ['vɪʃəs] *adj (violent)* violento(a); *(malicious)* malintencionado(a); *(cruel)* cruel; **v. circle** círculo vicioso

victim ['vɪktɪm] *n* víctima *f*

victimize ['vɪktɪmaɪz] *vt* perseguir, tratar injustamente

victor ['vɪktə(r)] *n* vencedor(a) *m,f*

victorious [vɪk'tɔːrɪəs] *adj* victorioso(a)

victory ['vɪktərɪ] *n* victoria *f*

video ['vɪdɪəʊ] *n* vídeo *m*; **v. camera** videocámara *f*; **v. cassette** videocasete *m*; **v. club** videoclub *m*; **v. game** videojuego *m*; **v. (cassette) recorder** vídeo *m*; **v. tape** cinta *f* de vídeo

video-tape ['vɪdɪəʊteɪp] *vt* grabar (en vídeo)

vie [vaɪ] *vi* competir (**against** *or* **with** con)

Vienna [vɪ'enə] *n* Viena

Viennese [vɪə'niːz] *adj & n* vienés(esa) *(m,f)*

Vietnam [vjet'næm] *n* Vietnam

view [vjuː] **1** *n* (**a**) *(sight)* vista *f*, panorama *m*; **in full v.** completamente visible; **on v.** a la vista; **to come into v.** aparecer;

Fig **in v. of the fact that** ... dado que ... **(b)** *(opinion)* opinión *f*; **point of v.** punto *m* de vista; **to take a dim v. of** ver con malos ojos **(c)** *(aim)* fin *m*; **with a v. to** con la intención de

2 *vt* **(a)** *(look at)* mirar; *(house etc)* visitar **(b)** *(consider)* contemplar; *(topic, problem)* enfocar

viewer ['vju:ə(r)] *n* **(a)** *TV* televidente *mf* **(b)** *Phot* visionador *m*

viewfinder ['vju:faɪndə(r)] *n* visor *m*

viewpoint ['vju:pɔɪnt] *n* punto *m* de vista

vigil ['vɪdʒɪl] *n* vigilia *f*

vigilante [vɪdʒɪ'læntɪ] *n* **v. group** patrulla ciudadana

vigorous ['vɪgərəs] *adj* vigoroso(a), enérgico(a)

vigour, *US* **vigor** ['vɪgə(r)] *n* vigor *m*

vile [vaɪl] *adj* **(a)** *(evil)* vil, infame **(b)** *(disgusting)* repugnante **(c)** *Fam (awful)* horrible

vilify ['vɪlɪfaɪ] *vt* denigrar

villa ['vɪlə] *n* **(a)** *(in country)* casa *f* de campo **(b)** *Br* chalet *m*

village ['vɪlɪdʒ] *n (small)* aldea *f*; *(larger)* pueblo *m*

villager ['vɪlɪdʒə(r)] *n* aldeano(a) *m,f*

villain ['vɪlən] *n* villano(a) *m,f*; *Cin & Th* malo(a) *m,f*

vinaigrette [vɪneɪ'gret] *n* vinagreta *f*

vindicate ['vɪndɪkeɪt] *vt* justificar, vindicar

vindictive [vɪn'dɪktɪv] *adj* vengativo(a)

vine [vaɪn] *n* vid *f*; *(climbing)* parra *f*

vinegar ['vɪnɪgə(r)] *n* vinagre *m*

vineyard ['vɪnjəd] *n* viña *f*, viñedo *m*

vintage ['vɪntɪdʒ] **1** *n* **(a)** *(crop, year)* cosecha *f* **(b)** *(season)* vendimia *f* **(c)** *(era)* era *f*

2 *adj* **(a)** *(wine)* añejo(a) **(b)** *(classic)* clásico(a); **v. car** coche *m* de época

vinyl ['vaɪnɪl] *n* vinilo *m*

viola [vɪ'əʊlə] *n* viola *f*

violate ['vaɪəleɪt] *vt* violar

violence ['vaɪələns] *n* violencia *f*

violent ['vaɪələnt] *adj* **(a)** violento(a) **(b)** *(intense)* intenso(a)

violet ['vaɪəlɪt] **1** *n* **(a)** *Bot* violeta *f* **(b)** *(colour)* violeta *m*

2 *adj* violeta

violin [vaɪə'lɪn] *n* violín *m*

violinist [vaɪə'lɪnɪst] *n* violinista *mf*

VIP [vi:aɪ'pi:] *n Fam (abbr* **very important person**) personaje *m* muy importante

viper ['vaɪpə(r)] *n* víbora *f*

virgin ['vɜ:dʒɪn] **1** *n* virgen *f*; **the V. Mary** la Virgen María; **to be a v.** ser virgen

2 *adj* virgen

virginity [və'dʒɪnɪtɪ] *n* virginidad *f*

Virgo ['vɜ:gəʊ] *n* Virgo *m*

virile ['vɪraɪl] *adj* viril

virtual ['vɜ:tjʊəl] *adj* virtual; *Comput* **v. reality** realidad *f* virtual

virtually ['vɜ:tjʊəlɪ] *adv (almost)* prácticamente

virtue ['vɜ:tju:] *n* virtud *f*; **by v. of** en virtud de

virtuous ['vɜ:tjʊəs] *adj* virtuoso(a)

virulent ['vɪrʊlənt] *adj* virulento(a)

virus ['vaɪrəs] *n* virus *m inv*; *Comput* **v. check** detección *m* de virus

visa ['vi:zə] *n* visado *m*, *Am* visa *f*

vis-à-vis [vi:zɑ:'vi:] *prep* **(a)** *(regarding)* respecto a **(b)** *(opposite)* frente a

viscose ['vɪskəʊs] *n* viscosa *f*

viscount ['vaɪkaʊnt] *n* vizconde *m*

vise [vaɪs] *n US (tool)* torno *m* de banco

visibility [vɪzɪ'bɪlɪtɪ] *n* visibilidad *f*

visible ['vɪzɪbəl] *adj* visible

vision ['vɪʒən] *n* **(a)** visión *f* **(b)** *(eyesight)* vista *f*

visit ['vɪzɪt] **1** *vt* **(a)** *(person)* visitar, hacer una visita a **(b)** *(place)* visitar, ir a

2 *n* visita *f*; **to pay sb a v.** hacerle una visita a algn

visiting ['vɪzɪtɪŋ] *adj* **v. card** tarjeta *f* de visita; *Med* **v. hours** horas *fpl* de visita; *Sport* **v. team** equipo *m* visitante

visitor ['vɪzɪtə(r)] *n* **(a)** *(guest)* invitado(a) *m,f*; **we've got visitors** tenemos visita **(b)** *(in hotel)* cliente(a) *m,f* **(c)** *(tourist)* turista *m*

visor ['vaɪzə(r)] *n* visera *f*

> 🖉 Note that the Spanish word **visor** is a false friend and is never a translation for the English word **visor**. In Spanish, **visor** means ;viewfinder".

vista ['vɪstə] *n* vista *f*, panorama *m*

visual ['vɪʒʊəl] *adj* visual; **v. aids** medios *mpl* visuales

visualize ['vɪʒʊəlaɪz] *vt* **(a)** *(imagine)* imaginar(se) **(b)** *(foresee)* prever

vital ['vaɪtəl] *adj* **(a)** *(lively)* enérgico(a) **(b)** *(essential)* fundamental **(c)** *(decisive)* decisivo(a); *Fam* **v. statistics** medidas *fpl* del cuerpo de la mujer **(d)** *Med (function, sign)* vital

vitality [vaɪ'tælɪtɪ] *n* vitalidad *f*

vitally ['vaɪtəlɪ] *adv* **it's v. important** es de vital importancia

vitamin ['vɪtəmɪn, *US* 'vaɪtəmɪn] *n* vitamina *f*

viva ['vaɪvə] *n Br* examen *m* oral

vivacious [vɪ'veɪʃəs] *adj* vivaz

vivacity [vɪ'væsɪtɪ] *n* viveza *f*, vivacidad *f*

vivid ['vɪvɪd] adj (a) (bright, lively) vivo(a), intenso(a) (b) (graphic) gráfico(a)

vixen ['vɪksən] n zorra f

V-neck(ed) ['viːnek(t)] adj con el cuello en pico

vocabulary [vəˈkæbjʊləri] n vocabulario m

vocal ['vəʊkəl] adj vocal; **v. cords** cuerdas fpl vocales

vocalist ['vəʊkəlɪst] n cantante mf

vocation [vəʊˈkeɪʃən] n vocación f

vocational [vəʊˈkeɪʃənəl] adj profesional; **v. training** formación f profesional

vociferous [vəʊˈsɪfərəs] adj (a) (protest) enérgico(a) (b) (noisy) clamoroso(a)

vodka ['vɒdkə] n vodka m

vogue [vəʊg] n boga f, moda f; **in v.** de moda

voice [vɔɪs] **1** n voz f; **to lose one's v.** quedarse afónico; Fig **at the top of one's v.** a voz en grito; Comput **v. mail** buzon m de voz

2 vt (a) (express) manifestar (b) Ling sonorizar

void [vɔɪd] **1** adj (a) **v. of** sin (b) Jur nulo(a), inválido(a)

2 n vacío m

volatile ['vɒlətaɪl] adj volátil

volcanic [vɒlˈkænɪk] adj volcánico(a)

volcano [vɒlˈkeɪnəʊ] n (pl **volcanoes**) volcán m

volition [vəˈlɪʃən] n Fml **of one's own v.** por voluntad propia

volley ['vɒlɪ] **1** n (a) (of shots) descarga f (b) Fig (of stones, insults) lluvia f (c) (in tennis, football) volea f

2 vt (in tennis, football) volear

volleyball ['vɒlɪbɔːl] n voleibol m

volt [vəʊlt] n voltio m

voltage ['vəʊltɪdʒ] n voltaje m

voluble ['vɒljʊbəl] adj locuaz

⚠ Note that the Spanish word **voluble** is a false friend and is never a translation for the English word **voluble**. In Spanish, **voluble** means "fickle, changeable".

---

volume ['vɒljuːm] n (a) volumen m (b) (book) volumen m, tomo m; Fig **to speak volumes** decirlo todo

voluntary ['vɒləntəri] adj voluntario(a); **v. organization** organización benéfica

volunteer [vɒlənˈtɪə(r)] **1** n voluntario(a) m,f

2 vt (help etc) ofrecer

3 vi (a) ofrecerse (**for** para) (b) Mil alistarse como voluntario

voluptuous [vəˈlʌptjʊəs] adj voluptuoso(a)

vomit ['vɒmɪt] **1** vt & vi vomitar

2 n vómito m

voracious [vəˈreɪʃəs] adj voraz

vortex ['vɔːteks] n (pl **vortices** ['vɔːtɪsiːz]) vórtice m; Fig vorágine f

vote [vəʊt] **1** n voto m; (voting) votación f; **v. of confidence** voto de confianza; **to take a v. on sth** someter algo a votacíon; **to have the v.** tener derecho al voto

2 vt (a) votar (b) (elect) elegir (c) Fam proponer

3 vi votar; **to v. for sb** votar a algn

voter ['vəʊtə(r)] n votante mf

voting ['vəʊtɪŋ] n votación f

vouch [vaʊtʃ] vi **to v. for sth/sb** responder de algo/por algn

voucher ['vaʊtʃə(r)] n Br vale m

vow [vaʊ] **1** n voto m

2 vt jurar

vowel ['vaʊəl] n vocal f

voyage ['vɔɪɪdʒ] n viaje m; (crossing) travesía f; **to go on a v.** hacer un viaje (en barco)

vulgar ['vʌlgə(r)] adj (coarse) vulgar, ordinario(a); (in poor taste) de mal gusto

vulgarity [vʌlˈgærɪtɪ] n (coarseness) vulgaridad f, ordinariez f; (poor taste) mal gusto m

vulnerable ['vʌlnərəbəl] adj vulnerable

vulture ['vʌltʃə(r)] n buitre m

vulva ['vʌlvə] n vulva f

W, w [ˈdʌbəljuː] *n (the letter)* W, w *f*

W (a) *(abbr* **West)** O **(b)** *(abbr* **Watt(s))** W

wad [wɒd] *n (of paper)* taco *m; (of cotton wool)* bolita *f; (of banknotes)* fajo *m*

waddle [ˈwɒdəl] *vi* andar como los patos

wade [weɪd] *vi* caminar por el agua; **to w. across a river** vadear un río

▸ **wade through** *vt insep* hacer con dificultad; **I'm wading through the book** me cuesta mucho terminar el libro

wading pool [ˈweɪdɪŋpuːl] *n US* piscina *f* para niños

wafer [ˈweɪfə(r)] *n* barquillo *m; Rel* hostia *f*

waffle¹ [ˈwɒfəl] *n Culin* = tipo de barquillo

waffle² [ˈwɒfəl] *Br Fam* **1** *vi* meter mucha paja; **to w. on** parlotear
2 *n* paja *f*

waft [wɑːft, wɒft] **1** *vt* llevar por el aire
2 *vi* flotar (por *or* en el aire)

wag [wæg] **1** *vt* menear
2 *vi (tail)* menearse

wage [weɪdʒ] **1** *n (also* **wages)** salario *m*, sueldo *m;* **w. earner** asalariado(a) *m,f;* **w. freeze** congelación *f* salarial
2 *vt (campaign)* realizar **(against** contra); **to w. war (on)** hacer la guerra (a)

wage-packet [ˈweɪdʒpækɪt] *n* sueldo *m*

wager [ˈweɪdʒə(r)] **1** *n* apuesta *f*
2 *vt* apostar

waggle [ˈwægəl] **1** *vt* menear
2 *vi* menearse

wa(g)gon [ˈwægən] *n (horse-drawn)* carro *m; Br Rail* vagón *m*

wail [weɪl] **1** *n* lamento *m*, gemido *m*
2 *vi (person)* lamentar, gemir

waist [weɪst] *n Anat* cintura *f; Sewing* talle *m*

waistcoat [ˈweɪstkəʊt] *n Br* chaleco *m*

waistline [ˈweɪstlaɪn] *n Anat* cintura *f; Sewing* talle *m*

wait [weɪt] **1** *n* espera *f; (delay)* demora *f;* **to lie in w.** estar al acecho
2 *vi* **(a)** esperar, aguardar; **I can't w. to see her** me muero de ganas de verla; **while you w.** en el acto; **to keep sb waiting** hacer esperar a algn **(b) to w. at table** servir la mesa

▸ **wait about, wait around** *vi* esperar

▸ **wait on** *vt insep* servir

waiter [ˈweɪtə(r)] *n* camarero *m, CAm, Col, Méx* mesero *m, Chile, Ven* mesonero *m, Perú, RP* mozo *m*

waiting [ˈweɪtɪŋ] *n* no **w.** *(sign)* prohibido aparcar; **w. list** lista *f* de espera; **w. room** sala *f* de espera

waitress [ˈweɪtrɪs] *n* camarera *f, CAm, Col, Méx* mesera *f, Chile, Ven* mesonera *f, Perú, RP* moza *f*

waive [weɪv] *vt Fml (rule)* no aplicar

wake¹ [weɪk] **1** *vt (pt* **woke;** *pp* **woken) to w. sb (up)** despertar a algn
2 *vi* **to w. (up)** despertar(se)
3 *n (for dead)* velatorio *m*

wake² [weɪk] *n (in water)* estela *f; Fig* **in the w. of** tras

waken [ˈweɪkən] *vt Literary* despertar

Wales [weɪlz] *n* (el país de) Gales

walk [wɔːk] **1** *n* **(a)** *(long)* caminata *m; (short)* paseo *m;* **it's an hour's w.** está a una hora de camino; **to go for a w.** dar un paseo; **to take the dog for a w.** sacar a pasear al perro **(b)** *(gait)* modo *m* de andar **(c)** *(social status)* **people from all walks of life** gente *f* de toda condición
2 *vt* **(a)** **we walked her home** la acompañamos a casa **(b)** *(dog)* pasear
3 *vi* **(a)** andar **(b)** *(go on foot)* ir andando

▸ **walk away** *vi* alejarse; *Fig* **to w. away with a prize** llevarse un premio

▸ **walk into** *vt insep* **(a)** *(place)* entrar en; *Fig (trap)* caer en **(b)** *(bump into)* chocarse contra

▸ **walk out** *vi* salir; *Ind* declararse en huelga; **to w. out on sb** abandonar a algn

▸ **walk up** *vi* **to w. up to sb** abordar a algn

walkabout [ˈwɔːkəbaʊt] *n (by Queen etc)* = paseo informal entre la gente

walker [ˈwɔːkə(r)] *n* paseante *mf; Sport* marchador(a) *m,f*

walkie-talkie [wɔːkɪˈtɔːkɪ] *n* walkie-talkie *m*

walking [ˈwɔːkɪŋ] **1** *n* andar *m; (hiking)* excursionismo *m*
2 *adj* **at w. pace** a paso de marcha; **w. shoes** zapatos *mpl* de andar; **w. stick** bastón *m*

Walkman® ['wɔːkmən] n (pl **Walkmans**) walkman® m

walkout ['wɔːkaʊt] n Ind huelga f

walkover ['wɔːkəʊvə(r)] n **it was a w.** fue pan comido

walkway ['wɔːkweɪ] n paso m de peatones

wall [wɔːl] n (a) (freestanding, exterior) muro m; Fig **to have one's back to the w.** estar entre la espada y la pared; **city w.** muralla f; **garden w.** tapia f (b) (interior) pared f; **w. map** mapa m mural (c) Ftb barrera f
▸ **wall up** vt sep (door, fireplace) tabicar

walled [wɔːld] adj (city) amurallado(a); (garden) cercado(a) con tapia

wallet ['wɒlɪt] n cartera f

wallflower ['wɔːlflaʊə(r)] n (a) Bot alhelí m (b) Fam **to be a w.** ser un convidado de piedra

wallop ['wɒləp] Fam **1** n golpazo m
2 vt (a) (hit) pegar fuerte (b) (defeat) dar una paliza a

wallow ['wɒləʊ] vi revolcarse (en in); Fig **to w. in self-pity** sumirse en la autocompasión

wallpaper ['wɔːlpeɪpə(r)] **1** n papel pintado
2 vt empapelar

wally ['wɒlɪ] n Fam idiota mf

walnut ['wɔːlnʌt] n nuez f; (tree, wood) nogal m

walrus ['wɔːlrəs] n morsa f

waltz [wɔːls] **1** n vals m
2 vi bailar un vals

wan [wɒn] adj (**wanner, wannest**) pálido(a); (look, smile) apagado(a)

wand [wɒnd] n (**magic**) **w.** varita f (mágica)

wander ['wɒndə(r)] **1** vt **to w. the streets** vagar por las calles
2 vi (a) (aimlessly) vagar, errar; **to w. about** deambular; **to w. in/out** entrar/salir sin prisas (b) (stray) desviarse; (mind) divagar; **his glance wandered round the room** recorrió el cuarto con la mirada

wandering ['wɒndərɪŋ] adj errante; (tribe) nómada; (speech) divagador(a)

wane [weɪn] vi menguar; (interest) decaer

wangle ['wæŋgəl] vt Fam agenciarse

wank [wæŋk] Br Vulg **1** n paja f
2 vi hacerse una paja

wanker ['wæŋkə(r)] n Br Vulg mamón(ona) m,f

want [wɒnt] **1** n (a) (lack) falta f; **for w. of** por falta de (b) (poverty) miseria f

2 vt (a) (desire) querer, desear; **to w. to do sth** querer hacer algo (b) Fam (need) necesitar; **the grass wants cutting** hace falta cortar el césped (c) (seek) buscar; **you're wanted on the phone** te llaman al teléfono
▸ **want for** vt insep carecer de; **to w. for nothing** tenerlo todo

wanting ['wɒntɪŋ] adj (a) **she is w. in tact** le falta tacto (b) **he was found w.** no daba la talla

wanton ['wɒntən] adj (a) (motiveless) sin motivo; **w. cruelty** crueldad gratuita (b) (unrestrained) desenfrenado(a); (licentious) lascivo(a)

war [wɔː(r)] n guerra f; **to be at w. (with)** estar en guerra (con); Fig **to declare/wage w. on** declarar/hacer la guerra a; **w. crime** crimen m de guerra

warble ['wɔːbəl] vi gorjear

ward [wɔːd] n (a) (of hospital) sala f (b) Jur pupilo(a) m,f; (minor) pupilo(a) bajo tutela judicial (c) Br Pol distrito m electoral
▸ **ward off** vt sep (blow) parar, desviar; (attack) rechazar; (danger) evitar; (illness) prevenir

warden ['wɔːdən] n (of residence) guardián(ana) m,f; **game w.** guardia m de coto

warder ['wɔːdə(r)] n Br carcelero(a) m,f

wardrobe ['wɔːdrəʊb] n (a) armario m, ropero m (b) (clothes) guardarropa m (c) Th vestuario m

warehouse ['weəhaʊs] n almacén m

wares [weəz] npl mercancías fpl

warfare ['wɔːfeə(r)] n guerra f

warhead ['wɔːhed] n (nuclear) **w.** ojiva f nuclear

warm [wɔːm] **1** adj (a) (water) tibio(a); (hands) caliente; (climate) cálido(a); **a w. day** un día de calor; **I am w.** tengo calor; **it is (very) w. today** hoy hace (mucho) calor; **w. clothing** ropa f de abrigo (b) (welcome, applause) cálido(a)
2 vt calentar; Fig alegrar
3 vi calentarse; **to w. to sb** cogerle simpatía a algn
▸ **warm up 1** vt sep (a) calentar; (soup) (re)calentar (b) (audience) animar
2 vi (a) calentarse; (food) (re)calentarse; (person) entrar en calor (b) (athlete) hacer ejercicios de calentamiento (c) Fig (audience, party) animarse

warm-blooded [wɔːm'blʌdɪd] adj de sangre caliente

warm-hearted [wɔːm'hɑːtɪd] adj afectuoso(a)

warmly ['wɔːmlɪ] *adv Fig* calurosamente; *(thank)* con efusión

warmth [wɔːmθ] *n (heat)* calor *m*; *Fig* cordialidad *f*

warn [wɔːn] *vt* avisar (**of** de), advertir (**about/against** sobre/contra); **he warned me not to go** me advirtió que no fuera; **to w. sb that** advertir a algn que

warning ['wɔːnɪŋ] **1** *adj* **w. light** piloto *m*; **w. sign** señal *f* de aviso
2 *n* (**a**) *(of danger)* advertencia *f*, aviso *m* (**b**) *(replacing punishment)* amonestación *f* (**c**) *(notice)* aviso *m*; **without w.** sin previo aviso

warp [wɔːp] **1** *vt* (**a**) *(wood)* alabear, combar (**b**) *Fig (mind)* pervertir
2 *vi* alabearse, combarse

warrant ['wɒrənt] **1** *n* (**a**) *Jur* orden *f* judicial; **death w.** sentencia *f* de muerte (**b**) *(authorization note)* cédula *f*; *Com* bono *m*
2 *vt* (**a**) *(justify)* justificar (**b**) *(guarantee)* garantizar

warranty ['wɒrəntɪ] *n Com* garantía *f*

warren ['wɒrən] *n* conejera *f*; *Fig* laberinto *m*

warrior ['wɒrɪə(r)] *n* guerrero(a) *m,f*

Warsaw ['wɔːsɔː] *n* Varsovia

warship ['wɔːʃɪp] *n* buque *m* or barco *m* de guerra

wart [wɔːt] *n* verruga *f*

wartime ['wɔːtaɪm] *n* tiempos *mpl* de guerra

wary ['weərɪ] *adj* (**warier, wariest**) cauteloso(a); **to be w. of doing sth** dudar en hacer algo; **to be w. of sb/sth** recelar de algn/algo

was [wɒz] *pt of* **be**

wash [wɒʃ] **1** *n* (**a**) *lavado m*; **to have a w.** lavarse (**b**) *(of ship)* estela *f*; *(sound)* chapoteo *m*
2 *vt* (**a**) *lavar*; *(dishes)* fregar; **to w. one's hair** lavarse el pelo (**b**) *(of sea, river)* arrastrar
3 *vi* (**a**) *(person)* lavarse; *(do the laundry)* hacer la colada (**b**) *(lap)* batir
▸ **wash away** *vt sep (of sea)* llevarse; *(traces)* borrar
▸ **wash off** *vi* quitarse lavando
▸ **wash out 1** *vt sep* (**a**) *(stain)* quitar lavando (**b**) *(bottle)* enjuagar
2 *vi* quitarse lavando
▸ **wash up 1** *vt sep Br (dishes)* fregar
2 *vi* (**a**) *Br* fregar los platos (**b**) *US* lavarse rápidamente

washable ['wɒʃəbəl] *adj* lavable

washbasin ['wɒʃbeɪsən], *US* **washbowl** ['wɒʃbəʊl] *n* palangana *f*

washcloth ['wɒʃklɒθ] *n US* manopla *f*

washer ['wɒʃə(r)] *n (on tap)* junta *f*

washing ['wɒʃɪŋ] *n (action)* lavado *m*; *(of clothes)* colada *f*; **(dirty) w.** ropa sucia; **to do the w.** hacer la colada; **w. line** tendedero *m*; **w. machine** lavadora *f*; **w. powder** detergente *m*

washing-up [wɒʃɪŋ'ʌp] *n Br* (**a**) *(action)* fregado *m*; **w. bowl** barreño *m*; **w. liquid** (detergente *m*) lavavajillas (**b**) *(dishes)* platos *mpl* (para fregar)

washout ['wɒʃaʊt] *n Fam* fracaso *m*

washroom ['wɒʃruːm] *n US* servicios *mpl*

wasp [wɒsp] *n* avispa *f*

wastage ['weɪstɪdʒ] *n* pérdidas *fpl*

waste [weɪst] **1** *adj* (**a**) *(unwanted)* desechado(a); **w. food** restos *mpl* de comida; **w. products** productos *mpl* de desecho (**b**) *(ground)* baldío(a)
2 *n* (**a**) *(unnecessary use)* desperdicio *m*; *(of resources, effort, money)* derroche *m*; *(of time)* pérdida *f*; **to go to w.** echarse a perder (**b**) *(leftovers)* desperdicios *mpl*; *(rubbish)* basura *f*; **radioactive w.** desechos radioactivos; **w. disposal unit** trituradora *f* (de desperdicios); **w. pipe** tubo *m* de desagüe
3 *vt (squander)* desperdiciar, malgastar; *(resources)* derrochar; *(money)* despilfarrar; *(time)* perder
▸ **waste away** *vi* consumirse

wasteful ['weɪstfʊl] *adj* derrochador(a)

wasteland ['weɪstlænd] *n* baldío *m*

wastepaper [weɪst'peɪpə(r)] *n* papeles usados; **w. basket** papelera *f*

watch [wɒtʃ] **1** *n* (**a**) *(look-out)* vigilancia *f*; **to keep a close w. on sth/sb** vigilar algo/a algn muy atentamente (**b**) *Mil (body)* guardia *f*; *(individual)* centinela *m*; **to be on w.** estar de guardia (**c**) *(timepiece)* reloj *m*
2 *vt* (**a**) *(observe)* mirar, observar (**b**) *(keep an eye on)* vigilar; *(with suspicion)* acechar (**c**) *(be careful of)* tener cuidado con; *Fig* **to w. one's step** ir con pies de plomo
3 *vi* *(look)* mirar, observar; **w. out!** ¡cuidado!
▸ **watch out for** *vt insep (be careful of)* tener cuidado con

watchband ['wɒtʃbænd] *n US* = **watchstrap**

watchdog ['wɒtʃdɒg] *n* perro *m* guardián; *Fig* guardián(ana) *m,f*

watchful ['wɒtʃfʊl] *adj* vigilante

watchmaker ['wɒtʃmeɪkə(r)] *n* relojero(a) *m,f*

watchman ['wɒtʃmən] n vigilante m;
night w. (of site) vigilante nocturno
watchstrap ['wɒtʃstræp] n correa f (de
reloj)
watchtower ['wɒtʃtaʊə(r)] n atalaya f
water ['wɔːtə(r)] 1 n (a) agua f; **w. bottle**
cantimplora f; **w. lily** nenúfar m; **w. main**
conducción f de aguas; **w. polo** water
polo m; **w. sports** deportes acuáticos;
w. tank depósito m de agua; **territorial
waters** aguas jurisdiccionales; Fig **it's all
w. under the bridge** ha llovido mucho
desde entonces (b) **to pass w.** orinar
  2 vt (plants) regar
  3 vi **my eyes are watering** me lloran los
ojos; **my mouth watered** se me hizo la
boca agua
  ► **water down** vt sep (drink) aguar
watercolour, US **watercolor** ['wɔːtə-
kʌlə(r)] n acuarela f
watercress ['wɔːtəkres] n berro m
waterfall ['wɔːtəfɔːl] n cascada f, (very
big) catarata f
waterfront ['wɔːtəfrʌnt] n (shore) orilla f
del agua; (harbour) puerto m
watering ['wɔːtərɪŋ] n (of plants) riego m;
w. can regadera f; **w. place** abrevadero m
waterline ['wɔːtəlaɪn] n línea f de flota-
ción
waterlogged ['wɔːtəlɒɡd] adj anega-
do(a)
watermark ['wɔːtəmɑːk] n filigrana f
watermelon ['wɔːtəmelən] n sandía f
waterproof ['wɔːtəpruːf] 1 adj (material)
impermeable; (watch) sumergible
  2 n (coat) impermeable m
watershed ['wɔːtəʃed] n Geog línea divisoria de aguas; Fig punto decisivo
water-skiing ['wɔːtəskiːɪŋ] n esquí
acuático
watertight ['wɔːtətaɪt] adj hermético(a)
waterway ['wɔːtəweɪ] n vía f fluvial
waterworks ['wɔːtəwɜːks] npl central f
de abastecimiento de agua; Fig **to turn
on the w.** empezar a llorar
watery ['wɔːtərɪ] adj (a) (soup) agua-
do(a); (coffee) flojo(a) (b) (eyes) lacrimo-
so(a) (c) (pale) pálido(a)
watt [wɒt] n vatio m
wave [weɪv] 1 n (a) (at sea) ola f (b) (in
hair) & Rad onda f (c) Fig of anger, strikes
etc) oleada f (d) (gesture) saludo m con la
mano
  2 vt (a) agitar; (brandish) blandir (b)
(hair) ondular
  3 vi (a) agitar el brazo; **she waved (to
me)** (greeting) me saludó con la mano;
(goodbye) se despidió (de mí) con la

mano; (signal) me hizo señas con la
mano (b) (flag) ondear; (corn) ondular
wavelength ['weɪvleŋθ] n longitud f de
onda
waver ['weɪvə(r)] vi (hesitate) vacilar
(between entre); (voice) temblar; (courage) flaquear
wavy ['weɪvɪ] adj (wavier, waviest) on-
dulado(a)
wax¹ [wæks] 1 n cera f
  2 vt encerar
wax² [wæks] vi (a) (moon) crecer (b) **to
w. lyrical** exaltarse
waxworks ['wækswɜːks] n sing museo m
de cera
way [weɪ] 1 n (a) (route) camino m; (road)
vía f, camino; **a letter is on the w.** una
carta está en camino; **on the w.** en el
camino; **on the w. here** de camino para
aquí; **out of the w.** apartado(a); **to ask
the w.** preguntar el camino; **to go the
wrong w.** ir por el camino equivocado; **to
lose one's w.** perderse; **to make one's w.
through the crowd** abrirse camino por
la multitud; **which is the w. to the station?** ¿por dónde se va a la estación?; Fig
she went out of her w. to help se des-
vivió por ayudar; **w. in** entrada f; **w. out**
salida f; Fig **the easy w. out** la solución
fácil; **I can't find my w. out** no encuentro
la salida; **on the w. back** en el viaje de
regreso; **on the w. up/down** en la subida/
bajada; **there's no w. through** el paso
está cerrado; **you're in the w.** estás es-
torbando; **(get) out of the w.!** ¡quítate de
en medio!; Fig **to get sb/sth out of the w.**
desembarazarse de algn/algo; **I kept out
of the w.** me mantuve a distancia; Aut
right of w. prioridad f; **there's a wall in
the w.** hay un muro en medio; **to give w.**
ceder; Aut ceder el paso
  (b) (direction) dirección f; **come this w.**
venga por aquí; **which w. did he go?** ¿por
dónde se fue?; **that w.** por allá; **the other
w. round** al revés
  (c) (distance) distancia f; **a long w. off**
lejos; Fig **he'll go a long w.** llegará lejos;
Fig **we've come a long w.** hemos hecho
grandes progresos
  (d) **to get under w.** (travellers, work)
ponerse en marcha; (meeting, match)
empezar
  (e) (means, method) método m, manera
f; **do it any w. you like** hazlo como
quieras; **I'll do it my w.** lo haré a mi
manera
  (f) (manner) modo m, manera f; **in a
friendly w.** de modo amistoso; **one w. or**

another de un modo o de otro; **the French w. of life** el estilo de vida francés; **the w. things are going** tal como van las cosas; **to my w. of thinking** a mi modo de ver; *Fam* **no w.!** ¡ni hablar!; **she has a w. with children** tiene un don para los niños; **by w. of** a modo de; **either w.** en cualquier caso; **in a w.** en cierto sentido; **in many ways** desde muchos puntos de vista; **in some ways** en algunos aspectos; **in no w.** de ninguna manera

(**g**) *(custom)* hábito *m*, costumbre *f*; **to be set in one's ways** tener costumbres arraigadas

(**h**) *(state)* estado *m*; **leave it the w. it is** déjalo tal como está; **he is in a bad w.** está bastante mal

(**i**) **by the w.** a propósito; **in the w. of business** en el curso de los negocios

2 *adv Fam* mucho, muy; **it was w. off target** cayó muy desviado del blanco; **w. back in 1940** allá en 1940

waylay ['weɪ'leɪ] *vt (pt & pp* **waylaid** [weɪ'leɪd]) (**a**) *(attack)* atacar por sorpresa (**b**) *(intercept)* abordar, detener

wayside ['weɪsaɪd] *n Fig* **to fall by the w.** quedarse en el camino

wayward ['weɪwəd] *adj* rebelde; *(capricious)* caprichoso(a)

WC [dʌblju:'si:] *n (abbr* **water closet)** wáter *m*, WC *m*

we [wi:] *pers pron* nosotros(as) *(usually omitted in Spanish, except for contrast)*

weak [wi:k] *adj* débil; *(argument, excuse)* pobre; *(team, piece of work, tea)* flojo(a)

weaken ['wi:kən] **1** *vt* debilitar; *(argument)* quitar fuerza a

2 *vi* (**a**) debilitarse (**b**) *(concede ground)* ceder

weakling ['wi:klɪŋ] *n* enclenque *mf*

weakness ['wi:knɪs] *n* debilidad *f*; *(character flaw)* punto flaco

wealth [welθ] *n* riqueza *f*; *Fig* abundancia *f*

wealthy ['welθɪ] *adj* (**wealthier, wealthiest**) rico(a)

wean [wi:n] *vt (child)* destetar; *Fig* **to w. sb from a habit** desacostumbrar (gradualmente) a algn de un hábito

weapon ['wepən] *n* arma *f*

wear [weə(r)] **1** *vt (pt* **wore**; *pp* **worn**) (**a**) *(clothes)* llevar puesto, vestir; *(shoes)* llevar puestos, calzar; **he wears glasses** lleva gafas; **to w. black** vestirse de negro (**b**) *(erode)* desgastar

2 *vi* **to w. (thin/smooth)** desgastarse (con el roce); *Fig* **my patience is wearing thin** se me está acabando la paciencia

3 *n* (**a**) ropa *f*; **leisure w.** ropa de sport (**b**) *(use) (clothes)* uso *m* (**c**) *(deterioration)* desgaste *m*; **normal w. and tear** desgaste natural

▶ **wear away 1** *vt sep* erosionar

2 *vi (stone etc)* erosionarse; *(inscription)* borrarse

▶ **wear down 1** *vt sep (heels)* desgastar; *Fig* **to w. sb down** vencer la resistencia de algn

2 *vi* desgastarse

▶ **wear off** *vi (effect, pain)* pasar, desaparecer

▶ **wear out 1** *vt sep* gastar; *Fig* agotar

2 *vi* gastarse

wearily ['wɪərɪlɪ] *adv* con cansancio

wearisome ['wɪərɪsəm] *adj* fatigoso(a)

weary ['wɪərɪ] **1** *adj* (**wearier, weariest**) (**a**) *(tired)* cansado(a) (**b**) *(fed up)* harto(a)

2 *vt* cansar

3 *vi* cansarse (**of** de)

weasel ['wi:zəl] *n* comadreja *f*

weather ['weðə(r)] **1** *n* tiempo *m*; **the w. is fine** hace buen tiempo; *Fig* **to feel under the w.** no encontrarse muy bien; **w. chart** mapa meteorológico; **w. forecast** parte meteorológico; **w. vane** veleta *f*

2 *vt Fig (crisis)* aguantar; *Fig* **to w. the storm** capear el temporal

weather-beaten ['weðəbi:tən] *adj* curtido(a)

weathercock ['weðəkɒk] *n* veleta *f*

weatherman ['weðəmæn] *n* hombre *m* del tiempo

weave [wi:v] **1** *n* tejido *m*

2 *vt (pt* **wove**; *pp* **woven**) (**a**) *Tex* tejer (**b**) *(intertwine)* entretejer (**c**) *(intrigues)* tramar

3 *vi (person, road)* zigzaguear

weaver ['wi:və(r)] *n* tejedor(a) *m,f*

web [web] *n* (**a**) *(of spider)* telaraña *f* (**b**) *(of lies)* sarta *f* (**c**) *Comput* **the W.** la Web; **w. page** página *f* web; **w. site** sitio *m* web

webbed [webd] *adj Orn* palmeado(a)

wed [wed] *vt Literary (pt & pp* **wed** or **wedded**) casarse con

wedding ['wedɪŋ] *n* boda *f*, casamiento *m*; **w. cake** tarta *f* nupcial; **w. day** día *m* de la boda; **w. dress** traje *m* de novia; **w. present** regalo *m* de boda; **w. ring** alianza *f*

wedge [wedʒ] **1** *n* (**a**) cuña *f*; *(for table leg)* calce *m* (**b**) *(of cake, cheese)* trozo *m* grande

2 *vt* calzar; **to be wedged tight** *(object)* estar completamente atrancado(a)

Wednesday ['wenzdɪ] *n* miércoles *m*

wee¹ ['wiː] *adj esp Scot* pequeñito(a)

wee² ['wiː] *Fam* **1** *n* pipí *m*

2 *vi* hacer pipí

weed [wiːd] **1** *n Bot* mala hierba

2 *vt* (a) *(garden)* escardar (b) *Fig* **to w. out** eliminar

3 *vi* escardar

weedkiller ['wiːdkɪlə(r)] *n* herbicida *m*

weedy ['wiːdɪ] *adj* (**weedier, weediest**) *Pej* debilucho(a)

week [wiːk] *n* semana *f*; **a w. (ago) today/yesterday** hoy hace/ayer hizo una semana; **a w. today** justo dentro de una semana; **last/next w.** la semana pasada/que viene; **once a w.** una vez por semana; **w. in, w. out** semana tras semana

weekday ['wiːkdeɪ] *n* día *m* laborable

weekend [wiːk'end] *n* fin *m* de semana

weekly ['wiːklɪ] **1** *adj* semanal

2 *adv* semanalmente; **twice w.** dos veces por semana

3 *n Press* semanario *m*

weep [wiːp] **1** *vi* (*pt & pp* **wept**) llorar; **to w. for sb** llorar la muerte de algn

2 *vt* (*tears*) derramar

weeping ['wiːpɪŋ] *adj* **w. willow** sauce *m* llorón

weigh [weɪ] **1** *vt* (a) pesar (b) *Fig* (*consider*) ponderar (c) **to w. anchor** levar anclas

2 *vi* (a) pesar (b) *Fig* (*influence*) influir

▸ **weigh down** *vt sep* sobrecargar

▸ **weigh in** *vi* (a) *Sport* pesarse (b) *Fam* (*join in*) intervenir

▸ **weigh up** *vt sep* (*matter*) evaluar; (*person*) formar una opinión sobre; **to w. up the pros and cons** sopesar los pros y los contras

weight [weɪt] *n* (a) peso *m*; **to lose w.** adelgazar; **to put on w.** subir de peso; *Fam Fig* **to pull one's w.** poner de su parte (b) (*of clock, scales*) pesa *f* (c) *Fig* **that's a w. off my mind** eso me quita un peso de encima

weighting ['weɪtɪŋ] *n Br* (*on salary*) suplemento *m* de salario

weightlifter ['weɪtlɪftə(r)] *n* halterófilo(a) *m,f*

weighty ['weɪtɪ] *adj* (**weightier, weightiest**) pesado(a); *Fig* (*problem, matter*) importante, grave; (*argument*) de peso

weir [wɪə(r)] *n* presa *f*

weird [wɪəd] *adj* raro(a), extraño(a)

welcome ['welkəm] **1** *adj* (*person*) bienvenido(a); (*news*) grato(a); (*change*) oportuno(a); **to make sb w.** acoger a algn calurosamente; **you're w.!** ¡no hay de qué!

2 *n* (*greeting*) bienvenida *f*

3 *vt* acoger; (*more formally*) darle la bienvenida a; (*news*) acoger con agrado; (*decision*) aplaudir

welcoming ['welkəmɪŋ] *adj* (*person*) acogedor(a); (*smile*) de bienvenida

weld [weld] *vt* soldar

welfare ['welfeə(r)] *n* (a) (*well-being*) bienestar *m*; **animal/child w.** protección *f* de animales/de menores; **w. work** asistencia *f* social; **w. worker** asistente *mf* social (b) *US* (*social security*) seguridad *f* social

well¹ [wel] *n* (a) pozo *m* (b) (*of staircase, lift*) hueco *m* (c) (*of court, hall*) hemiciclo *m*

▸ **well up** *vi* brotar

well² [wel] **1** *adj* (a) (*healthy*) bien; **are you keeping w.?** ¿estás bien de salud?; **to get w.** reponerse (b) (*satisfactory*) bien; **all is w.** todo va bien; **it's just as w.** menos mal (c) **it is as w. to remember that** conviene recordar que

2 *adv* (**better, best**) (a) (*properly*) bien; **he has done w. (for himself)** ha prosperado; **the business is doing w.** el negocio marcha bien; **she did w. in the exam** el examen le fue bien; **w. done!** ¡muy bien!; **he took it w.** lo tomó a bien (*thoroughly*) bien; **I know it only too w.** lo sé de sobra; *Culin* **w. done** muy hecho(a) (c) **he's w. over thirty** tiene treinta años bien cumplidos; **w. after six o'clock** mucho después de las seis (d) (*easily, with good reason*) **he couldn't very w. say no**; **I may w. do that** puede que haga eso (e) (*as well*) **as w.** también; **as w. as** así como; **children as w. as adults** tanto niños como adultos

3 *interj* (a) (*surprise*) ¡bueno!, ¡vaya!; **w. I never!** ¡no me digas! (b) (*agreement, interrogation, resignation*) bueno; **very w.** bueno; **w.?** ¿y bien? (c) (*doubt*) pues; **w., I don't know** pues no sé (d) (*resumption*) **w., as I was saying** pues (bien), como iba diciendo

well-behaved ['welbɪheɪvd] *adj* (*child*) formal, educado(a)

well-being ['welbiːɪŋ] *n* bienestar *m*

well-built ['welbɪlt] *adj* (*building etc*) de construcción sólida; (*person*) fornido(a)

well-earned ['welɜːnd] *adj* merecido(a)

well-educated [wel'edʊkeɪtɪd] *adj* culto(a)

well-heeled ['welhiːld] *adj Fam* adinerado(a)

well-informed ['welɪnfɔːmd] *adj* bien informado(a)

wellingtons ['welɪŋtənz] *npl* botas *fpl* de goma

well-known ['welnəʊn] *adj* (bien) conocido(a)

well-mannered ['welmænəd] *adj* educado(a)

well-meaning [wel'miːnɪŋ] *adj* bien intencionado(a)

well-off [wel'ɒf] *adj* (*rich*) acomodado(a)

well-read [wel'red] *adj* culto(a)

well-spoken [wel'spəʊkən] *adj* con acento culto

well-to-do [weltə'duː] *adj* acomodado(a)

well-wisher ['welwɪʃə(r)] *n* admirador(a) *m,f*

Welsh [welʃ] **1** *adj* galés(esa); **W. rarebit** = tostada con queso fundido
2 *n* (a) (*language*) galés *m* (b) **the W.** los galeses

Welshman ['welʃmən] *n* galés *m*

Welshwoman ['welʃwʊmən] *n* galesa *f*

welterweight ['welterweɪt] *n* (peso *m*) wélter *m*

wench [wentʃ] *n Old-fashioned* moza *f*

went [went] *pt of* **go**

wept [wept] *pt & pp of* **weep**

were [wɜː(r), *unstressed* wə(r)] *pt of* **be**

west [west] **1** *n* oeste *m*, occidente *m*; **in/to the w.** al oeste; *Pol* **the W.** los países occidentales
2 *adj* del oeste, occidental; **the W. Indies** las Antillas; **W. Indian** antillano(a)
3 *adv* al oeste, hacia el oeste

westerly ['westəlɪ] *adj* (*wind*) del oeste

western ['westən] **1** *adj* del oeste, occidental; **W. Europe** Europa Occidental
2 *n Cin* western *m*, película *f* del oeste

westward ['westwəd] *adj* in a w. direction hacia el oeste

westwards ['westwədz] *adv* hacia el oeste

wet [wet] **1** *adj* (**wetter, wettest**) (a) mojado(a); (*slightly*) húmedo(a); **w. paint** (*sign*) recién pintado; **w. through** (*person*) calado(a) hasta los huesos; (*thing*) empapado(a); **w. suit** traje isotérmico (b) (*rainy*) lluvioso(a) (c) *Fam* (*person*) soso(a); **w. blanket** aguafiestas *mf inv*
2 *n Fam* apocado(a) *m,f*
3 *vt* (*pt & pp* **wet**) mojar; **to w. oneself** orinarse

whack [wæk] **1** *vt* (*hit hard*) golpear fuertemente
2 *n* (a) (*blow*) porrazo *m* (b) *Fam* (*share*) parte *f*, porción *f*

whale [weɪl] *n* ballena *f*

wharf [wɔːf] *n* (*pl* **wharves** [wɔːvz]) muelle *m*

what [wɒt, *unstressed* wət] **1** *adj* (a) (*direct question*) qué; **w. (sort of) bird is that?** ¿qué tipo de ave es ésa?; **w. good is that?** ¿para qué sirve eso?
(b) (*indirect question*) qué; **ask her w. colour she likes** pregúntale qué color le gusta
2 *pron* (a) (*direct question*) qué; **w. are you talking about?** ¿de qué estás hablando?; **w. about your father?** ¿y tu padre (qué)?; **w. about going tomorrow?** ¿qué te parece si vamos mañana?; **w. can I do for you?** ¿en qué puedo servirle?; **w. did it cost?** ¿cuánto costó?; **w. did you do that for?** ¿por qué hiciste eso?; **w. (did you say)?** ¿cómo?; **w. does it sound like?** ¿cómo suena?; **w. is happening?** ¿qué pasa?; **w. is it?** (*definition*) ¿qué es?; (*what's the matter*) ¿qué pasa?; **w.'s it called?** ¿cómo se llama?; **w.'s this for?** ¿para qué sirve esto?
(b) (*indirect question*) qué, lo que; **he asked me w. I thought** me preguntó lo que pensaba; **I didn't know w. to say** no sabía qué decir
(c) (*and*) **w.'s more** y además; **come w. may** pase lo que pase; **guess w.!** ¿sabes qué?; **it's just w. I need** es exactamente lo que necesito
(d) (*in exclamations*) **w. a goal!** ¡qué *or* vaya golazo!; **w. a lovely picture!** ¡qué cuadro más bonito!
3 *interj* (*surprise, indignation*) ¡cómo!; **w., no dessert!** ¿cómo, no hay postre?

whatever [wɒt'evə(r), *unstressed* wət'evə(r)] **1** *adj* (a) (*any*) cualquiera que; **at w. time you like** a la hora que quieras; **of w. colour** no importa de qué color (b) (*with negative*) nothing w. nada en absoluto; **with no interest w.** sin interés alguno
2 *pron* (a) (*what*) **w. happened?** ¿qué pasó? (b) (*anything, all that*) (todo) lo que; **do w. you like** haz lo que quieras (c) (*no matter what*) **don't tell him, w. you do** no se te ocurra decírselo; **w. (else) you find** cualquier (otra) cosa que encuentres; **he goes out w. the weather** sale haga el tiempo que haga

whatsoever [wɒtsəʊ'evə(r)] *adj* anything w. cualquier cosa; **nothing w.** nada en absoluto

wheat [wiːt] *n* trigo *m*; **w. germ** germen *m* de trigo

wheedle ['wiːdəl] *vt* **to w. sb into doing sth** engatusar a algn para que haga algo;

to w. sth out of sb sonsacar algo a algn halagándole

wheel [wi:l] **1** n rueda f

2 vt (bicycle) empujar

3 vi (**a**) (bird) revolotear (**b**) **to w. round** girar sobre los talones

wheelbarrow ['wi:lbærəʊ] n carretilla f

wheelchair ['wi:ltʃeə(r)] n silla f de ruedas

wheeze [wi:z] vi respirar con dificultad, resollar

when [wen] **1** adv (**a**) (direct question) cuándo; **since w.?** ¿desde cuándo?; **w. did he arrive?** ¿cuándo llegó? (**b**) (indirect question) cuándo; **tell me w. to go** dime cuándo debo irme (**c**) (on which) cuando, en que; **the days w. I work** los días en que trabajo

2 conj (**a**) cuando; **I'll tell you w. she comes** se lo diré cuando llegue; **w. he was a boy …** de niño … (**b**) (whenever) cuando (**c**) (given that, if) si (**d**) (although) aunque

whence [wens] adv Fml Literary (from where) de dónde

whenever [wen'evə(r)] **1** conj (when) cuando; (every time) siempre que

2 adv **w. that might be** sea cuando sea

where [weə(r)] adv (**a**) (direct question) dónde; (direction) adónde; **w. are you going?** ¿adónde vas?; **w. did we go wrong?** ¿en qué nos equivocamos?; **w. do you come from?** ¿de dónde es usted? (**b**) (indirect question) dónde; (direction) adónde; **tell me w. you went** dime adónde fuiste (**c**) (at, in which) donde; (direction) adonde, a donde (**d**) (when) cuando

whereabouts **1** adv [weərə'baʊts] **w. do you live?** ¿por dónde vives?

2 n ['weərəbaʊts] paradero m

whereas [weər'æz] conj (**a**) (but, while) mientras que (**b**) Jur considerando que

whereby [weə'baɪ] adv por el/la/lo que

whereupon [weərə'pɒn] conj Fml después de lo cual

wherever [weər'evə(r)] **1** conj dondequiera que; **I'll find him w. he is** le encontraré dondequiera que esté; **sit w. you like** siéntate donde quieras

2 adv (direct question) adónde

wherewithal ['weəwɪðɔːl] n Fam pelas fpl

whet [wet] vt **to w. sb's appetite** abrir el apetito a algn

whether ['weðə(r)] conj (**a**) (if) si; **I don't know w. it is true** no sé si es verdad; **I doubt w. he'll win** dudo que gane (**b**) **w.**

he comes or not venga o no

which [wɪtʃ] **1** adj (**a**) (direct question) qué; **w. colour do you prefer?** ¿qué color prefieres?; **w. one?** ¿cuál?; **w. way?** ¿por dónde?

(**b**) (indirect question) qué; **tell me w. dress you like** dime qué vestido te gusta

(**c**) **by w. time** y para entonces; **in w. case** en cuyo caso

2 pron (**a**) (direct question) cuál/cuáles; **w. of you did it?** ¿quién de vosotros lo hizo?

(**b**) (indirect question) cuál/cuáles; **I don't know w. I'd rather have** no sé cuál prefiero

(**c**) (defining relative) que; (after preposition) que, el/la cual, los/las cuales, el/la que, los/las que; **here are the books (w.) I have read** aquí están los libros que he leído; **the accident (w.) I told you about** el accidente del que te hablé; **the car in w. he was travelling** el coche en (el) que viajaba; **this is the one (w.) I like** éste es el que me gusta

(**d**) (non-defining relative) el/la cual, los/las cuales; **I played three sets, all of w. I lost** jugué tres sets, todos los cuales perdí

(**e**) (referring to a clause) lo cual, lo que; **he won, w. made me very happy** ganó, lo cual or lo que me alegró mucho

whichever [wɪtʃ'evə(r)] **1** adj el/la que, cualquiera que; **I'll take w. books you don't want** tomaré los libros que no quieras; **w. system you choose** cualquiera que sea el sistema que elijas

2 pron el/la que

whiff [wɪf] n (**a**) (quick smell) ráfaga f; (of air, smoke) bocanada f (**b**) Fam (bad smell) tufo m

while [waɪl] **1** n (**a**) (length of time) rato m, tiempo m; **in a little w.** dentro de poco; **once in a w.** de vez en cuando (**b**) **it's not worth your w. staying** no merece la pena que te quedes

2 conj (**a**) (time) mientras; **he fell asleep w. driving** se durmió mientras conducía (**b**) (although) aunque (**c**) (whereas) mientras que

► **while away** vt sep **to w. away the time** pasar el rato

whilst [waɪlst] conj = while

whim [wɪm] n capricho m, antojo m

whimper ['wɪmpə(r)] **1** n quejido m

2 vi lloriquear

whine [waɪn] vi (**a**) (child) lloriquear; (with pain) dar quejidos (**b**) (complain) quejarse (**c**) (engine) chirriar

whip [wɪp] **1** *n* (**a**) *(for punishment)* látigo *m*; *(for riding)* fusta *f* (**b**) *Br Pol* = oficial encargado(a) de la disciplina de un partido

2 *vt* (**a**) *(as punishment)* azotar; *(horse)* fustigar (**b**) *Culin* batir; **whipped cream** nata montada (**c**) *Fam (steal)* mangar

▸ **whip away** *vt sep* arrebatar

▸ **whip up** *vt sep (passions, enthusiasm)* avivar; *(support)* incrementar

whipping ['wɪpɪŋ] *n Fig* **w. boy** cabeza *f* de turco

whip-round ['wɪpraʊnd] *n Fam* colecta *f*

whir [wɜ:(r)] *vi* = **whirr**

whirl [wɜ:l] **1** *n* giro *m*; *Fig* torbellino *m*

2 *vt* **to w. sth round** dar vueltas a *o* hacer girar algo

3 *vi* **to w. round** girar con rapidez; *(leaves etc)* arremolinarse; **my head's whirling** me está dando vueltas la cabeza

whirlpool ['wɜ:lpu:l] *n* remolino *m*

whirlwind ['wɜ:lwɪnd] *n* torbellino *m*

whirr [wɜ:(r)] *vi* zumbar, runrunear

whisk [wɪsk] **1** *n Culin* batidor *m*; *(electric)* batidora *f*

2 *vt Culin* batir

▸ **whisk away**, **whisk off** *vt sep* quitar bruscamente, llevarse de repente

whisker ['wɪskə(r)] *n* **whiskers** *(of person)* patillas *fpl*; *(of cat)* bigotes *mpl*

whisky, *US* **whiskey** ['wɪskɪ] *n* whisky *m*

whisper ['wɪspə(r)] **1** *n* (**a**) *(sound)* susurro *m* (**b**) *(rumour)* rumor *m*

2 *vt* decir en voz baja

3 *vi* susurrar

whistle ['wɪsəl] **1** *n* (**a**) *(instrument)* pito *m* (**b**) *(sound)* silbido *m*, pitido *m*

2 *vt (tune)* silbar

3 *vi (person, kettle, wind)* silbar; *(train)* pitar

white [waɪt] **1** *adj* blanco(a); **to go w.** *(face)* palidecer; *(hair)* encanecer; **w. coffee** café *m* con leche; **w. hair** pelo cano; **a w. Christmas** una Navidad con nieve; *Fig* **a w. lie** una mentira piadosa; *US* **the W. House** la Casa Blanca; *Pol* **w. paper** libro blanco; **w. sauce** bechamel *f*

2 *n* (**a**) *(colour, person, of eye)* blanco *m* (**b**) *(of egg)* clara *f* (**c**) **whites** ropa *f* blanca

white-collar ['waɪtkɒlə(r)] *adj* **w. worker** empleado *m* de oficina

whiteness ['waɪtnɪs] *n* blancura *f*

whitewash ['waɪtwɒʃ] **1** *n* (**a**) cal *f* (**b**) *Fig (cover-up)* encubrimiento *m* (**c**) *Fig (defeat)* paliza *f*

2 *vt* (**a**) *(wall)* enjalbegar, blanquear (**b**) *Fig* encubrir

whiting ['waɪtɪŋ] *n* *(pl* **whiting**) *(fish)* pescadilla *f*

Whitsun(tide) ['wɪtsən(taɪd)] *n* pentecostés *m*

whittle ['wɪtəl] *vt* cortar en pedazos; **to w. away at** roer; *Fig* **to w. down** reducir poco a poco

whiz(z) [wɪz] *vi* (**a**) *(sound)* silbar (**b**) **to w. past** pasar volando; *Fam* **w. kid** joven *mf* dinámico(a) y emprendedor(a)

who [hu:] *pron* (**a**) *(direct question)* quién/quiénes; **w. are they?** ¿quiénes son?; **w. is it?** ¿quién es? (**b**) *(indirect question)* quién; **I don't know w. did it** no sé quién lo hizo (**c**) *rel (defining)* que; **those w. don't know** los que no saben (**d**) *rel (nondefining)* quien/quienes, el/la cual, los/las cuales; **Elena's mother, w. is very rich ...** la madre de Elena, la cual es muy rica ...

whodun(n)it [hu:'dʌnɪt] *n Fam* novela *f*/obra *f* de teatro/película *f* de suspense

whoever [hu:'evə(r)] *pron* (**a**) quienquiera que; **give it to w. you like** dáselo a quien quieras; **w. said that is a fool** el que dijo eso es un tonto; **w. you are** quienquiera que seas (**b**) *(direct question)* **w. told you that?** ¿quién te dijo eso?

whole [həʊl] **1** *adj* (**a**) *(entire)* entero(a), íntegro(a); **a w. week** una semana entera; **he took the w. lot** se los llevó todos (**b**) *(in one piece)* intacto(a)

2 *n* (**a**) *(single unit)* todo *m*, conjunto *m*; **as a w.** en su totalidad (**b**) *(all)* totalidad *f*; **the w. of London** todo Londres (**c**) **on the w.** en general

wholefood ['həʊlfu:d] *n* alimentos *mpl* integrales

wholehearted [həʊl'hɑ:tɪd] *adj (enthusiastic)* entusiasta; *(sincere)* sincero(a); *(unreserved)* incondicional

wholemeal ['həʊlmi:l] *adj Br* integral

wholesale ['həʊlseɪl] *Com* **1** *n* venta *f* al por mayor

2 *adj* al por mayor; *Fig* total

3 *adv* al por mayor; *Fig* en su totalidad

wholesaler ['həʊlseɪlə(r)] *n* mayorista *mf*

wholesome ['həʊlsəm] *adj* sano(a)

wholly ['həʊllɪ] *adv* enteramente, completamente

whom [hu:m] *pron Fml* (**a**) *(direct question) (accusative)* a quién; **w. did you talk to?** ¿con quién hablaste?; *(after preposition)* **of/from w.?** ¿de quién?; **to w. are you referring?** ¿a quién te refieres? (**b**) *rel (accusative)* que, a quien/a quienes; **those w. I have seen** aquéllos a quien he

visto (**c**) *rel (after preposition)* quien/
quienes, el/la cual, los/las cuales; **my
brothers, both of w. are miners** mis hermanos, que son mineros los dos

En la actualidad, sólo aparece en contextos
formales. **Whom** se puede sustituir por
who en todos los casos salvo cuando va
después de preposición.

whooping cough ['huːpɪŋkɒf] *n* tos ferina

whopping ['wɒpɪŋ] *adj Fam* enorme

whore [hɔː(r)] *n very Fam Pej* puta *f*

whose [huːz] **1** *pron* (**a**) *(direct question)*
de quién/de quiénes; **w. are these gloves?**
¿de quién son estos guantes?; **w. is this?**
¿de quién es esto? (**b**) *(indirect question)*
de quién/de quiénes; **I don't know w.
these coats are** no sé de quién son estos
abrigos (**c**) *rel* cuyo(s)/cuya(s); **the man
w. children we saw** el hombre a cuyos
hijos vimos

2 *adj* **w. car/house is this?** ¿de quién es
este coche/esta casa?

why [waɪ] **1** *adv* por qué; *(for what purpose)* para qué; **w. did you do that?** ¿por
qué hiciste eso?; **w. not go to bed?** ¿por
qué no te acuestas?; **I don't know w. he
did it** no sé por qué lo hizo; **that is w. I
didn't come** por eso no vine; **there's no
reason w. you shouldn't go** no hay motivo para que no vayas

2 *interj* (**a**) *(fancy that!)* ¡toma!, ¡vaya!,
w., it's David! ¡sí es David! (**b**) *(protest,
assertion)* sí, vamos

wick [wɪk] *n* mecha *f*

wicked ['wɪkɪd] *adj* (**a**) malvado(a) (**b**)
Fam malísimo(a); *(temper)* de perros

wicker ['wɪkə(r)] **1** *n* mimbre *m*

2 *adj* de mimbre

wickerwork ['wɪkəwɜːk] *n (material)*
mimbre *m*; *(articles)* artículos *mpl* de
mimbre

wicket ['wɪkɪt] *n (in cricket) (stumps)*
palos *mpl*

wide [waɪd] **1** *adj* (**a**) *(road, trousers)*
ancho(a); *(gap, interval)* grande; **it is 10
m w.** tiene 10 m de ancho (**b**) *(area,
knowledge, support, range)* amplio(a); **w.
interests** intereses muy diversos (**c**) *(off
target)* desviado(a)

2 *adv* **from far and w.** de todas partes; **to
open one's eyes w.** abrir los ojos de par en
par; **w. apart** muy separados(as); **w.
awake** completamente despierto(a); **w.
open** abierto(a) de par en par; **with
mouth w. open** boquiabierto(a)

wide-angle ['waɪdæŋɡəl] *adj Phot* **w.**

lens objetivo *m* gran angular

widely ['waɪdlɪ] *adv (travel etc)* extensamente; *(believed)* generalmente; **he is w.
known** es muy conocido

widen ['waɪdən] **1** *vt* ensanchar; *(interests)* ampliar

2 *vi* ensancharse

wide-ranging ['waɪd'reɪndʒɪŋ] *adj (interests)* muy diversos(as); *(discussion)*
amplio(a); *(study)* de gran alcance

widespread ['waɪdspred] *adj (unrest, belief)* general; *(damage)* extenso(a); **to
become w.** generalizarse

widow ['wɪdəʊ] *n* viuda *f*

widowed ['wɪdəʊd] *adj* enviudado(a)

widower ['wɪdəʊə(r)] *n* viudo *m*

width [wɪdθ] *n* (**a**) anchura *f* (**b**) *(of
material, swimming pool)* ancho *m*

wield [wiːld] *vt (weapon)* blandir; *Fig
(power)* ejercer

wife [waɪf] *n (pl wives)* mujer *f*, esposa *f*

wig [wɪg] *n* peluca *f*

wiggle ['wɪgəl] **1** *vt (finger etc)* menear;
to w. one's hips contonearse

2 *vi* menearse

Wight [waɪt] *n* Isle of W. Isla *f* de Wight

wild [waɪld] **1** *adj* (**a**) *(animal, tribe)* salvaje; **w. beast** fiera *f*; *Fig* **w. goose chase**
búsqueda *f* inútil

(**b**) *(plant)* silvestre

(**c**) *(landscape)* agreste; **the W. West** el
Salvaje Oeste

(**d**) *(temperament, behaviour)* aloca-
do(a); *(appearance)* desordenado(a);
(passions etc) desenfrenado(a); *(laughter, thoughts)* loco(a); *(applause)* fervoro-
so(a); **to make a w. guess** adivinar al
azar; *Fam Fig* **she is w. about him/about
tennis** está loca por él/por el tenis

(**e**) *Br Fam Fig (angry)* furioso(a)

2 *adv Fig* **to run w.** *(children)* desmandarse

3 *n* **in the w.** en el estado salvaje; *Fig* **to
live out in the wilds** vivir en el quinto pino

wildcat ['waɪldkæt] *n* **w. strike** huelga *f*
salvaje

wilderness ['wɪldənɪs] *n* desierto *m*

wildfire ['waɪldfaɪə(r)] *n* **to spread like
w.** correr como la pólvora

wildlife ['waɪldlaɪf] *n* fauna *f*; **w. park**
parque *m* natural

wildly ['waɪldlɪ] *adv* (**a**) *(rush round etc)*
como un(a) loco(a); *(shoot)* sin apuntar;
(hit out) a tontas y a locas (**b**) **w. enthusiastic** loco(a) de entusiasmo; **w. inaccurate** totalmente erróneo(a)

wilful, *US* **wilfull** ['wɪlfʊl] *adj* (**a**) *(stubborn)* terco(a) (**b**) *Jur* premeditado(a)

will¹ [wɪl] **1** n (a) voluntad f; **good/ill w.** buena/mala voluntad; **of my own free w.** por mi propia voluntad (b) Jur (testament) testamento m; **to make one's w.** hacer testamento

2 vt **fate willed that ...** el destino quiso que ...

will² [wɪl] v aux (pt **would**)

> En el inglés hablado, y en el escrito en estilo coloquial, el verbo **will** se contrae de manera que **I/you/he** etc **will** se transforman en **I'll**, **you'll**, **he'll** etc y el verbo **would** se contrae de manera que **I/you/he** etc **would** se transforman en **I'd**, **you'd**, **he'd** etc. Las formas negativas **will not** y **would not** se transforman en **won't** y **wouldn't**.

(a) (future) (esp 2nd & 3rd person) **they'll come** vendrán; **w. he be there? – yes, he w.** ¿estará allí? – sí(, estará); **you'll tell him, won't you?** se lo dirás, ¿verdad?; **don't forget, w. you!** ¡que no se te olvide, vale!; **she won't do it** no lo hará

(b) (command) **you w. be here at eleven!** ¡debes estar aquí a las once!

(c) (future perfect) **they'll have finished by tomorrow** habrán terminado para mañana

(d) (willingness) **be quiet, w. you! – no, I won't!** ¿quiere callarse? – no quiero; **I won't have it!** ¡no lo permito!; **w. you have a drink? – yes, I w.** ¿quiere tomar algo? – sí, por favor; **won't you sit down?** ¿quiere sentarse?

(e) (custom) **accidents w. happen** siempre habrá accidentes

(f) (persistence) **if you w. go out without a coat ...** si te empeñas en salir sin abrigo ...

(g) (probability) **he'll be on holiday now** ahora estará de vacaciones

(h) (ability) **the lift w. hold ten people** en el ascensor caben diez personas

willing [ˈwɪlɪŋ] adj (obliging) complaciente; **I'm quite w. to do it** lo haré con mucho gusto; **to be w. to do sth** estar dispuesto(a) a hacer algo

willingly [ˈwɪlɪŋlɪ] adv de buena gana

willingness [ˈwɪlɪŋnɪs] n buena voluntad

willow [ˈwɪləʊ] n **w. (tree)** sauce m

willpower [ˈwɪlpaʊə(r)] n (fuerza f de) voluntad f

willy-nilly [ˈwɪlɪˈnɪlɪ] adv por gusto o por fuerza

wilt [wɪlt] vi marchitarse

wily [ˈwaɪlɪ] adj (**wilier, wiliest**) astuto(a)

wimp [wɪmp] n Fam (physically) debilucho(a) m,f; (lacking character) blandengue mf

win [wɪn] **1** n victoria f

2 vt (pt & pp **won**) (a) ganar; (prize) llevarse; (victory) conseguir (b) Fig (sympathy, friendship) ganarse; (praise) cosechar; **to w. sb's love** conquistar a algn

3 vi ganar

▶ **win back** vt sep recuperar

▶ **win over** vt sep (to cause, idea) atraer (**to** a); (voters, support) ganarse

▶ **win through** vi conseguir triunfar

wince [wɪns] vi tener un rictus de dolor

winch [wɪntʃ] n cigüeña f, torno m

wind¹ [wɪnd] **1** n (a) viento m; Fig **to get w. of sth** olerse algo; **w. farm** parque eólico; **w. tunnel** túnel aerodinámico (b) (breath) aliento m; **to get one's second w.** recobrar el aliento (c) Med flato m, gases mpl (d) **w. instrument** instrumento m de viento

2 vt **to be winded** quedarse sin aliento

wind² [waɪnd] **1** vt (pt & pp **wound**) (a) (on to a reel) enrollar; **to w. a bandage round one's finger** vendarse el dedo (b) **to w. on/back** (film, tape) avanzar/rebobinar (c) (clock) dar cuerda a

2 vi (road, river) serpentear

▶ **wind down 1** vt sep (window) bajar

2 vi Fam (person) relajarse

▶ **wind up 1** vt sep (a) (roll up) enrollar (b) (business etc) cerrar; (debate) clausurar (c) (clock) dar cuerda a

2 vi (meeting) terminar

windfall [ˈwɪndfɔːl] n Fig ganancia inesperada

winding [ˈwaɪndɪŋ] adj (road, river) sinuoso(a); (staircase) de caracol

windmill [ˈwɪndmɪl] n molino m (de viento)

window [ˈwɪndəʊ] n ventana f, (of vehicle, ticket office etc) ventanilla f; (shop) **w.** escaparate m; **to clean the windows** limpiar los cristales; **w. box** jardinera f; **w. cleaner** limpiacristales mf inv

windowpane [ˈwɪndəʊpeɪn] n cristal m

window-shopping [ˈwɪndəʊʃɒpɪŋ] n **to go w.** ir a mirar escaparates

windowsill [ˈwɪndəʊsɪl] n alféizar m

windpipe [ˈwɪndpaɪp] n tráquea f

windscreen [ˈwɪndskriːn], US **windshield** [ˈwɪndʃiːld] n parabrisas m inv; **w. washer** lavaparabrisas m inv; **w. wiper** limpiaparabrisas m inv

windswept [ˈwɪndswept] adj (landscape) expuesto(a) a los vientos; (person, hair) despeinado(a) (por el viento)

windy ['wɪndɪ] *adj* (**windier, windiest**) *(weather)* ventoso(a); *(place)* desprotegido(a) del viento; **it is very w. today** hoy hace mucho viento

wine [waɪn] *n* vino *m*; **w. cellar** bodega *f*; **w. list** lista *f* de vinos; **w. merchant** vinatero(a) *m,f*; **w. tasting** cata *f* de vinos; **w. vinegar** vinagre *m* de vino

wineglass ['waɪnglɑːs] *n* copa *f* (para vino)

wing [wɪŋ] *n* (**a**) *Orn & Av* ala *f* (**b**) *(of building)* ala *f* (**c**) *Aut* aleta *f*; **w. mirror** retrovisor *m* externo (**d**) *Th* (**in the**) **wings** (entre) bastidores *mpl* (**e**) *Ftb* banda *f* (**f**) *Pol* ala *f*; **the left w.** la izquierda

winger ['wɪŋə(r)] *n Ftb* extremo *m*

wink [wɪŋk] **1** *n* guiño *m*; *Fam Fig* **I didn't get a w. (of sleep)** no pegué ojo
2 *vi* (**a**) *(person)* guiñar (el ojo) (**b**) *(light)* parpadear

winner ['wɪnə(r)] *n* ganador(a) *m,f*

winning ['wɪnɪŋ] *adj (person, team)* ganador(a); *(number)* premiado(a); *(goal)* decisivo(a); **w. post** meta *f*

winnings ['wɪnɪŋz] *npl* ganancias *fpl*

winter ['wɪntə(r)] **1** *n* invierno *m*
2 *adj* de invierno; **w. sports** deportes *mpl* de invierno
3 *vi* invernar

wintry ['wɪntrɪ] *adj* (**wintrier, wintriest**) invernal

wipe [waɪp] *vt* limpiar; **to w. one's brow** enjugarse la frente; **to w. one's feet/nose** limpiarse los pies/las narices
▸ **wipe away** *vt sep (tear)* enjugar
▸ **wipe off** *vt sep* quitar frotando; **to w. sth off the blackboard/the tape** borrar algo de la pizarra/de la cinta
▸ **wipe out** *vt sep* (**a**) *(erase)* borrar (**b**) *(army)* aniquilar; *(species etc)* exterminar
▸ **wipe up** *vt sep* limpiar

wire [waɪə(r)] **1** *n* (**a**) alambre *m*; *Elec* cable *m*; *Tel* hilo; **w. cutters** cizalla *f* (**b**) *(telegram)* telegrama *m*
2 *vt* (**a**) **to w. (up) a house** poner la instalación eléctrica de una casa; **to w. (up) an appliance to the mains** conectar un aparato a la toma eléctrica (**b**) *(information)* enviar por telegrama

wireless ['waɪəlɪs] *n* radio *f*

wiring ['waɪərɪŋ] *n (network)* cableado *m*; *(action)* instalación *f* del cableado

wiry ['waɪərɪ] *adj (wirier, wiriest) (hair)* estropajoso(a); *(person)* nervudo(a)

wisdom ['wɪzdəm] *n* (**a**) *(learning)* sabiduría *f*, saber *m* (**b**) *(good sense)* cordura *f*; *(of action)* sensatez *f* (**c**) **w. tooth** muela *f* del juicio

wise [waɪz] *adj* (**a**) sabio(a); **a w. man** un sabio; **the Three W. Men** los Reyes Magos (**b**) *(remark)* juicioso(a); *(decision)* acertado(a); **it would be w. to keep quiet** sería prudente callarse

wisecrack ['waɪzkræk] *n Fam* salida *f*, ocurrencia *f*

wisely ['waɪzlɪ] *adv (with prudence)* prudentemente

wish [wɪʃ] **1** *n* (**a**) *(desire)* deseo *m* (**for** de); **to make a w.** pedir un deseo
(**b**) **best wishes** felicitaciones *fpl*; **give your mother my best wishes** salude a su madre de mi parte; **with best wishes, Peter** *(at end of letter)* saludos cordiales, Peter
2 *vt* (**a**) *(want)* querer, desear; **I w. I could stay longer** me gustaría poder quedarme más tiempo; **I w. you had told me!** ¡ojalá me lo hubieras dicho!; **to w. to do sth** querer hacer algo
(**b**) **to w. sb goodnight** darle las buenas noches a algn; **to w. sb well** desearle a algn mucha suerte
3 *vi (want)* desear; **as you w.** como quieras; **do as you w.** haga lo que quiera; **to w. for sth** desear algo

wishful ['wɪʃfʊl] *adj* **it's w. thinking** es hacerse ilusiones

wishy-washy ['wɪʃɪ'wɒʃɪ] *adj Fam (person)* soso(a); *(ideas)* poco definido(a)

wisp [wɪsp] *n (of wool, hair)* mechón *m*; *(of smoke)* voluta *f*

wistful ['wɪstfʊl] *adj* melancólico(a)

wit [wɪt] *n* (**a**) *(intelligence) (often pl)* inteligencia *f*, *Fig* **to be at one's wits' end** estar para volverse loco(a); *Fam Fig* **to have one's wits about one** ser despabilado(a) (**b**) *(humour)* ingenio *m* (**c**) *(person)* ingenioso(a) *m,f*

witch [wɪtʃ] *n* bruja *f*; *Fig* **w. hunt** caza *f* de brujas

witchcraft ['wɪtʃkrɑːft] *n* brujería *f*

with [wɪð, wɪθ] *prep* con; **a room w. a bath** un cuarto con baño; **do you have any money w. you?** ¿traes dinero?; **the man w. the glasses** el hombre de las gafas; **he went w. me/you** fue conmigo/contigo; *Fam* **w. (sugar) or without (sugar)?** ¿con o sin azúcar?; **I have six w. this one** con éste tengo seis; **w. all his faults, I admire him** lo admiro con todos sus defectos; **w. your permission** con su permiso; **we're all w. you** *(support)* todos estamos contigo; **you're not w. me, are you?** *(understand)* no me entiendes, ¿verdad?; **he's w. Lloyds** trabaja para Lloyds; **she is popular w. her colleagues**

todos sus colegas la estiman mucho; **to fill a vase w. water** llenar un jarrón de agua; **it is made w. butter** está hecho con mantequilla; **she put on weight w. so much eating** engordó de tanto comer; **to be paralysed w. fear** estar paralizado(a) de miedo; **w. experience** con la experiencia

withdraw [wɪð'drɔ:] **1** *vt* (*pt* **withdrew**; *pp* **withdrawn**) (**a**) retirar, sacar; **to w. money from the bank** sacar dinero del banco (**b**) (*go back on*) retirar; (*statement*) retractarse de; (*plan, claim*) renunciar a

2 *vi* (**a**) retirarse (**b**) (*drop out*) renunciar

withdrawal [wɪð'drɔ:əl] *n* retirada *f*; (*of statement*) retractación *f*; (*of complaint, plan*) renuncia *f*; **w. symptoms** síndrome *m* de abstinencia

withdrawn [wɪð'drɔ:n] **1** *adj* (*person*) introvertido(a)

2 *pp of* **withdraw**

withdrew [wɪð'dru:] *pt of* **withdraw**

wither ['wɪðə(r)] *vi* marchitarse

withering ['wɪðərɪŋ] *adj* (*look*) fulminante; (*criticism*) mordaz

withhold [wɪð'həʊld] *vt* (*pt & pp* **withheld** [wɪð'held]) (*money*) retener; (*decision*) aplazar; (*consent*) negar; (*information*) ocultar

within [wɪ'ðɪn] **1** *prep* (**a**) (*inside*) dentro de (**b**) (*range*) **the house is w. walking distance** se puede ir andando a la casa; **situated w. 5 km of the town** situado(a) a menos de 5 km de la ciudad; **w. sight of the sea** con vistas al mar; *Fig* **w. an inch of death** a dos dedos de la muerte (**c**) (*time*) **they arrived w. a few days of each other** llegaron con pocos días de diferencia; **w. the hour** dentro de una hora; **w. the next five years** durante los cinco próximos años

2 *adv* dentro; **from w.** desde dentro

with-it ['wɪðɪt] *adj Fam* **she is very w.** tiene ideas muy modernas; **to get w.** ponerse de moda

without [wɪ'ðaʊt] *prep* sin; **he did it w. my knowing** lo hizo sin que lo supiera yo; *Fig* **to do** *or* **go w. sth** (*voluntarily*) prescindir de algo; (*forcibly*) pasar(se) sin algo

withstand [wɪð'stænd] *vt* (*pt & pp* **withstood** [wɪð'stʊd]) resistir a; (*pain*) aguantar

witness ['wɪtnɪs] **1** *n* (**a**) (*person*) testigo *mf*; **w. box**, *US* **w. stand** barra *f* de los testigos (**b**) (*evidence*) **to bear w. to sth** dar fe de algo

2 *vt* (**a**) (*see*) presenciar, ser testigo de (**b**) *Fig* (*notice*) notar (**c**) *Jur* **to w. a document** firmar un documento como testigo

witticism ['wɪtɪsɪzəm] *n* ocurrencia *f*, salida *f*

witty ['wɪtɪ] *adj* (**wittier, wittiest**) ingenioso(a), agudo(a)

wives [waɪvz] *pl of* **wife**

wizard ['wɪzəd] *n* hechicero *m*, mago *m*

wizened ['wɪzənd] *adj* (*face*) arrugado(a)

wobble ['wɒbəl] *vi* (*table, ladder etc*) tambalearse; (*jelly*) temblar

woe [wəʊ] *n Literary* infortunio *m*; **w. betide you if I catch you!** ¡ay de ti si te cojo!

woeful ['wəʊfʊl] *adj* (**a**) (*person*) afligido(a) (**b**) (*sight*) penoso(a); **w. ignorance** una ignorancia lamentable

woke [wəʊk] *pt of* **wake**

woken ['wəʊkən] *pp of* **wake**

wolf [wʊlf] *n* (*pl* **wolves** [wʊlvz]) lobo *m*; *Fig* **a w. in sheep's clothing** un lobo con piel de cordero

woman ['wʊmən] *n* (*pl* **women**) mujer *f*; **old w.** vieja *f*; *Fam* **women's libber** feminista *mf*; *Fam* **women's lib** movimiento *m* feminista; **women's rights** derechos *mpl* de la mujer

womanhood ['wʊmənhʊd] *n* (*adult*) edad adulta de la mujer

womanizer ['wʊmənaɪzə(r)] *n* mujeriego *m*

womanly ['wʊmənlɪ] *adj* femenino(a)

womb [wu:m] *n* matriz *f*, útero *m*

women ['wɪmɪn] *pl of* **woman**

won [wʌn] *pt & pp of* **win**

wonder ['wʌndə(r)] **1** *n* (**a**) (*miracle*) milagro *m*; **no w. he hasn't come** no es de extrañar que no haya venido (**b**) (*amazement*) admiración *f*, asombro *m*

2 *vt* (**a**) (*be surprised*) sorprenderse (**b**) (*ask oneself*) preguntarse; **I w. why** ¿por qué será?

3 *vi* (**a**) (*marvel*) maravillarse; **to w. at sth** admirarse de algo (**b**) **it makes you w.** (*reflect*) te da qué pensar

wonderful ['wʌndəfʊl] *adj* maravilloso(a)

wonderfully ['wʌndəfʊlɪ] *adv* maravillosamente

wont [wəʊnt] *Fml* **1** *adj* **to be w. to** soler

2 *n* costumbre *f*; **it is his w. to ...** tiene la costumbre de ...

woo [wu:] *vt Literary* (*court*) cortejar; *Fig* intentar congraciarse con

wood [wʊd] *n* (**a**) (*forest*) bosque *m* (**b**)

(material) madera *f*; *(for fire)* leña *f*; *Fam Fig* **touch w.!** ¡toca madera! **(c)** *(in golf)* palo *m* de madera **(d)** *(bowling)* bola *f*

woodcarving ['wʊdkɑːvɪŋ] *n* **(a)** *(craft)* tallado *m* en madera **(b)** *(object)* talla *f* en madera

woodcutter ['wʊdkʌtə(r)] *n* leñador(a) *m,f*

wooded ['wʊdɪd] *adj* arbolado(a)

wooden ['wʊdən] *adj* **(a)** de madera; **w. spoon/leg** cuchara *f*/pata *f* de palo **(b)** *Fig* rígido(a); *(acting)* sin expresión

woodlouse ['wʊdlaʊs] *n* cochinilla *f*

woodpecker ['wʊdpekə(r)] *n* pájaro carpintero

woodwind ['wʊdwɪnd] *n* **w. (instruments)** instrumentos *mpl* de viento de madera

woodwork ['wʊdwɜːk] *n* **(a)** *(craft)* carpintería *f* **(b)** *(of building)* maderaje *m*

woodworm ['wʊdwɜːm] *n* carcoma *f*

wool [wʊl] **1** *n* lana *f*; *Fig* **to pull the w. over sb's eyes** dar gato por liebre a algn **2** *adj* de lana

woollen, *US* **woolen** ['wʊlən] **1** *adj* **(a)** de lana **(b)** *(industry)* lanero(a)
2 *npl* **woollens** géneros *mpl* de lana or de punto

woolly, *US* **wooly** ['wʊlɪ] *adj* **(woollier, woolliest,** *US* **woolier, wooliest) (a)** *(made of wool)* de lana **(b)** *Fig (unclear)* confuso(a)

word [wɜːd] **1** *n* **(a)** *(spoken, written)* palabra *f*; **in other words ...** es decir ..., o sea ...; **words failed me** me quedé sin habla; *Fig* **a w. of advice** un consejo; *Fig* **I'd like a w. with you** quiero hablar contigo un momento; *Fig* **she didn't say it in so many words** no lo dijo de modo tan explícito; **in the words of the poet ...** como dice el poeta ...; *Fig* **w. for w.** palabra por palabra; **w. processing** tratamiento *m* de textos; **w. processor** procesador *m* de textos

(b) *Fig (message)* mensaje *m*; **by w. of mouth** de palabra; **is there any w. from him?** ¿hay noticias de él?; **to send w.** mandar recado

(c) *Fig (rumour)* voz *f*, rumor *m*

(d) *Fig (promise)* palabra *f*; **he's a man of his w.** es hombre de palabra

2 *vt (express)* formular; **a badly worded letter** una carta mal redactada

wording ['wɜːdɪŋ] *n* expresión *f*; **I changed the w. slightly** cambié algunas palabras

word-perfect [wɜːd'pɜːfekt] *adj* **to be w.** saberse el papel perfectamente

wore [wɔː(r)] *pt of* **wear**

work [wɜːk] **1** *n* **(a)** *(labour)* trabajo *m*; **his w. in the field of physics** su labor en el campo de la física; **it's hard w.** cuesta trabajo

(b) *(employment)* trabajo *m*, empleo *m*; **out of w.** parado(a)

(c) *(action)* obra *f*, acción *f*; **keep up the good w.!** ¡que siga así!

(d) a piece of w. un trabajo; **a w. of art** una obra de arte

(e) works obras *fpl*; **public works** obras (públicas)

(f) works *(machinery)* mecanismo *m*

(g) *Br* **works** *(factory)* fábrica *f*

2 *vt* **(a)** *(drive)* hacer trabajar; **to w. one's way up/down** subir/bajar a duras penas; *Fig* **to w. one's way up in a firm** trabajarse el ascenso en una empresa

(b) *(machine)* manejar; *(mechanism)* accionar

(c) *(miracles, changes)* operar, hacer

(d) *(land)* cultivar; *(mine)* explotar

(e) *(wood, metal etc)* trabajar

3 *vi* **(a)** trabajar **(on** *or* **at** en); **to w. as a gardener** trabajar de jardinero

(b) *(machine)* funcionar; **it works on gas** funciona con gas

(c) *(drug)* surtir efecto; *(system)* funcionar bien; *(plan, trick)* salir bien

(d) *(operate)* obrar; **to w. loose** soltarse; **we have no data to w. on** no tenemos datos en que basarnos

▶ **work off** *vt sep (fat)* eliminar trabajando; *(anger)* desahogar

▶ **work out 1** *vt sep* **(a)** *(plan)* idear; *(itinerary)* planear; *(details)* desarrollar **(b)** *(problem)* solucionar; *(solution)* encontrar; *(amount)* calcular; **I can't w. out how he did it** no me explico cómo lo hizo

2 *vi* **(a) things didn't w. out for her** las cosas no le salieron bien **(b) it works out at five each** sale a cinco cada uno **(c)** *Sport* hacer ejercicio

▶ **work through** *vi* penetrar (**to** hasta)

▶ **work up** *vt sep (excite)* acalorar; **to get worked up** excitarse; **to w. up enthusiasm (for)** entusiasmarse (con)

workable ['wɜːkəbəl] *adj* factible

workaholic [wɜːkə'hɒlɪk] *n* *Fam* trabajoadicto(a) *m,f*

workbench ['wɜːkbentʃ] *n* obrador *m*

worker ['wɜːkə(r)] *n* trabajador(a) *m,f*; *(manual)* obrero(a) *m,f*

workforce ['wɜːkfɔːs] *n* mano *f* de obra

working ['wɜːkɪŋ] **1** *adj* **(a)** *(population, capital)* activo(a); **w. class** clase obrera; **w. man** obrero *m* **(b)** *(clothes, conditions, hours)* de trabajo; **w. day** día *m* laborable;

(number of hours) jornada *f* laboral (**c**) **it is in w. order** funciona (**d**) *(majority)* suficiente; **w. knowledge** conocimientos básicos

  2 *n* **workings** *(mechanics)* funcionamiento *m*; *Min* explotación *f*

workman ['wɜːkmən] *n (manual)* obrero *m*

workmanship ['wɜːkmənʃɪp] *n (appearance)* acabado *m*; *(skill)* habilidad *f*, arte *m*; **a fine piece of w.** un trabajo excelente

workmate ['wɜːkmeɪt] *n* compañero(a) *m,f* de trabajo

work-out ['wɜːkaʊt] *n* entrenamiento *m*

worksheet ['wɜːkʃiːt] *n* plan *m* de trabajo

workshop ['wɜːkʃɒp] *n* taller *m*

worktop ['wɜːktɒp] *n* encimera *f*

work-to-rule ['wɜːktəˈruːl] *n* huelga *f* de celo

world [wɜːld] *n* mundo *m*; **all over the w.** en todo el mundo; **the best in the w.** el mejor del mundo; *Fig* **there is a w. of difference between A and B** hay un mundo de diferencia entre A y B; *Fig* **to feel on top of the w.** sentirse fenomenal; *Fig* **to think the w. of sb** adorar a algn; *Fam Fig* **it is out of this w.** es una maravilla; **the W. Bank** el Banco Mundial; *Ftb* **the W. Cup** los Mundiales; **w. record** récord *m* mundial; **w. war** guerra *f* mundial

world-class ['wɜːldˈklɑːs] *adj* de categoría mundial

world-famous ['wɜːldˈfeɪməs] *adj* de fama mundial

worldly ['wɜːldlɪ] *adj* mundano(a)

worldwide ['wɜːldwaɪd] *adj* mundial

worm [wɜːm] **1** *n* (**a**) gusano *m*; **(earth) w.** lombriz *f* (**b**) *Med* **worms** lombrices *fpl*

  2 *vt* **to w. a secret out of sb** sonsacarle un secreto a algn

worn [wɔːn] **1** *adj* gastado(a), usado(a)

  2 *pp of* **wear**

worn-out ['wɔːnaʊt] *adj (thing)* gastado(a); *(person)* rendido(a), agotado(a)

worried ['wʌrɪd] *adj* inquieto(a), preocupado(a)

worry ['wʌrɪ] **1** *vt* (**a**) preocupar, inquietar; **it doesn't w. me** me trae sin cuidado (**b**) *(pester)* molestar

  2 *vi* preocuparse (**about** por); **don't w.** no te preocupes

  3 *n (state)* inquietud *f*, *(cause)* preocupación *f*

worrying ['wʌrɪɪŋ] *adj* inquietante, preocupante

worse [wɜːs] **1** *adj (comp of* **bad**) peor; **he**

gets **w. and w.** va de mal en peor; **to get w.** empeorar; *Fam* **w. luck!** ¡mala suerte!

  2 *n* **a change for the w.** un empeoramiento; *Fig* **to take a turn for the w.** empeorar

  3 *adv (comp of badly)* peor; **w. than ever** peor que nunca

worship ['wɜːʃɪp] **1** *vt* adorar

  2 *n* (**a**) adoración *f* (**b**) *(ceremony)* culto *m* (**c**) *Br* **his W. the Mayor** el señor alcalde; *Jur* **your W.** señoría

worshipper ['wɜːʃɪpə(r)] *n* devoto(a) *m,f*

worst [wɜːst] **1** *adj (superl of* **bad**) peor; **the w. part about it is that …** lo peor es que …

  2 *n* (**a**) *(person)* el/la peor, los/las peores (**b**) **the w. of the storm is over** ya ha pasado lo peor de la tormenta

  3 *adv (superl of badly)* peor; *Fig* **to come off w.** salir perdiendo

worth [wɜːθ] **1** *adj* (**a**) **to be w. £3** valer 3 libras; **a house w. £50,000** una casa que vale 50.000 libras (**b**) *(deserving of)* merecedor(a) de; **a book w. reading** un libro que merece la pena leer; **for what it's w.** por si sirve de algo; **it's w. your while, it's w. it** vale *or* merece la pena; **it's w. mentioning** es digno de mención

  2 *n* (**a**) *(in money)* valor *m*; **£5 w. of petrol** gasolina por valor de 5 libras (**b**) *(of person)* valía *f*

worthless ['wɜːθlɪs] *adj* sin valor; *(person)* despreciable

worthwhile [wɜːθˈwaɪl] *adj* valioso(a), que vale la pena

worthy ['wɜːðɪ] *adj* (**worthier, worthiest**) (**a**) *(deserving)* digno(a) (**of** de); *(winner, cause)* justo(a) (**b**) *(citizen)* respetable; *(effort, motives, action)* loable

would [wʊd, *unstressed* wəd] *v aux* (**a**) *(conditional)* **I w. go if I had time** iría si tuviera tiempo; **he w. have won but for that** habría ganado su no hubiera sido por eso; **we w. if we could** lo haríamos si pudieramos; **you w. have to choose me!** ¡tenías que elegirme precisamente a mí!

  (**b**) *(reported speech)* **he said that he w. come** dijo que vendría

  (**c**) *(willingness)* **the car wouldn't start** el coche no arrancaba; **they asked him to come but he wouldn't** le invitaron a venir pero no quiso; **w. you do me a favour?** ¿quiere hacerme un favor?

  (**d**) *(wishing)* **he w. like to know why** quisiera saber por qué; **I'd rather go home** preferiría ir a casa; **w. you like a cigarette?** ¿quiere un cigarrillo?

(e) *(custom)* we w. go for walks solíamos dar un paseo

(f) try as I w. por mucho que lo intentara

(g) *(conjecture)* it w. have been about three weeks ago debe haber sido hace unas tres semanas; w. this be your cousin? ¿será éste tu primo?

(h) *(expectation)* so it w. appear según parece

would-be ['wʊdbiː] *adj* en potencia; a w. politician un aspirante a político; *Pej* a w. poet un supuesto poeta

wound¹ [waʊnd] *pt & pp of* **wind²**

wound² [wuːnd] **1** *n* herida *f*

2 *vt* herir

wove [wəʊv] *pt of* **weave**

woven ['wəʊvən] *pp of* **weave**

wow [waʊ] *Fam* **1** *vt* encandilar

2 *interj* ¡caramba!

WP *n* (a) *(abbr* word processor*)* procesador *m* de textos (b) *(abbr* word processing*)* tratamiento *m* de textos

wrangle ['ræŋɡəl] **1** *n* disputa *f*

2 *vi* disputar (over por)

wrap [ræp] **1** *vt* to w. (up) envolver; he wrapped his arms around her la estrechó entre sus brazos; *Fam* we wrapped up the deal concluimos el negocio

2 *vi Fam* **w. up well** abrígate

3 *n (shawl)* chal *m*; *(cape)* capa *f*

wrapper ['ræpə(r)] *n (of sweet)* envoltorio *m*; *(of book)* sobrecubierta *f*

wrapping ['ræpɪŋ] *n* w. paper papel *m* de envolver

wreath [riːθ] *n (pl* wreaths [riːðz, riːθs]*)* *(of flowers)* corona *f*; laurel w. corona de laurel

wreck [rek] **1** *n* (a) *Naut* naufragio *m*; *(ship)* barco naufragado (b) *(of car, plane)* restos *mpl*; *(of building)* ruinas *fpl* (c) *Fig (person)* ruina *f*

2 *vt* to w. (ship) hacer naufragar (b) *(car, machine)* destrozar (c) *Fig (health, life)* arruinar; *(plans, hopes)* desbaratar; *(chances)* echar a perder

wreckage ['rekɪdʒ] *n (of ship, car, plane)* restos *mpl*; *(of building)* ruinas *fpl*

wren [ren] *n* chochín *m*

wrench [rentʃ] **1** *n* (a) *(pull)* tirón *m* (b) *Med* torcedura *f* (c) *(tool) Br* llave inglesa; *US* llave

2 *vt* to w. oneself free soltarse de un tirón; to w. sth off sb arrebatarle algo a algn; to w. sth off/open quitar/abrir algo de un tirón

wrestle ['resəl] *vi* luchar

wrestler ['reslə(r)] *n* luchador(a) *m,f*

wrestling ['reslɪŋ] *n* lucha *f*

wretch [retʃ] *n (poor)* w. desgraciado(a) *m,f*

wretched ['retʃɪd] *adj* (a) desdichado(a); *(conditions)* deplorable; *Fam (bad, poor)* horrible (b) I feel w. *(ill)* me siento fatal (c) *(contemptible)* despreciable (d) *Fam (damned)* maldito(a), condenado(a)

wriggle ['rɪɡəl] **1** *vt* menear

2 *vi* to w. (about) *(worm)* serpentear; *(restless child)* moverse nerviosamente; to w. free escapar deslizándose

wring [rɪŋ] *vt (pt & pp* wrung*)* (a) *(clothes)* escurrir; *(hands)* retorcer (b) *Fig (extract)* arrancar, sacar

wringing ['rɪŋɪŋ] *adj* to be w. wet estar empapado(a)

wrinkle ['rɪŋkəl] **1** *n* arruga *f*

2 *vt* arrugar

3 *vi* arrugarse

wrist [rɪst] *n* muñeca *f*

wristwatch ['rɪstwɒtʃ] *n* reloj *m* de pulsera

writ [rɪt] *n* orden *f* judicial

write [raɪt] **1** *vt (pt* wrote; *pp* written*)* escribir; *(article)* redactar; *(cheque)* extender

2 *vi* escribir (about sobre); to w. for a paper colaborar en un periódico

▸ **write back** *vi* contestar

▸ **write down** *vt sep* poner por escrito; *(note)* apuntar

▸ **write in** *vi* escribir

▸ **write off 1** *vt sep (debt)* condonar; *(car)* destrozar

2 *vi* to w. off for sth pedir algo por escrito

▸ **write out** *vt sep (cheque, recipe)* extender

▸ **write up** *vt sep (notes)* redactar; *(diary, journal)* poner al día

write-off ['raɪtɒf] *n* the car's a w. el coche está hecho una ruina

writer ['raɪtə(r)] *n (by profession)* escritor(a) *m,f*; *(of book, letter)* autor(a) *m,f*

writhe [raɪð] *vi* retorcerse

writing ['raɪtɪŋ] *n* (a) *(script)* escritura *f*; *(handwriting)* letra *f*; in w. por escrito (b) writings escritos *mpl* (c) *(action)* escritura *f*, w. desk escritorio *m*

written ['rɪtən] *pp of* **write**

wrong [rɒŋ] **1** *adj* (a) *(person)* equivocado(a); I was w. about that boy me equivoqué con ese chico; to be w. no tener razón; you're w. in thinking that ... te equivocas si piensas que ...

(b) *(answer, way)* incorrecto(a), equivocado(a); my watch is w. mi reloj anda mal; **to drive on the w. side of the road** conducir por el lado contrario de la carretera; **to go the w. way** equivocarse de camino; *Tel* **I've got the w. number** me he confundido de número

(**c**) *(unsuitable)* impropio(a), inadecuado(a); *(time)* inoportuno(a); **to say the w. thing** decir algo inoportuno

(**d**) *(immoral etc)* malo(a); **there's nothing w. in that** no hay nada malo en ello; **what's w. with smoking?** ¿qué tiene de malo fumar?

(**e**) **is anything w.?** ¿pasa algo?; **something's w.** hay algo que no está bien; **what's w.?** ¿qué pasa?; **what's w. with you?** ¿qué te pasa?

2 *adv* mal, incorrectamente; **to get it w.** equivocarse; *Fam* **to go w.** *(plan)* fallar, salir mal

3 *n* (**a**) *(evil, bad action)* mal *m*; **you did w. to hit him** hiciste mal en pegarle

(**b**) *(injustice)* injusticia *f*; *(offence)* agravio *m*; **the rights and wrongs of a matter** lo justo y lo injusto de un asunto

(**c**) **to be in the w.** *(be to blame)* tener la culpa

4 *vt (treat unfairly)* ser injusto(a) con; *(offend)* agraviar

wrongdoing ['rɒŋduːɪŋ] *n* maldad *f*

wrongful ['rɒŋfʊl] *adj* injusto(a)

wrongly ['rɒŋlɪ] *adv* (**a**) *(incorrectly)* incorrectamente (**b**) *(mistakenly)* equivocadamente (**c**) *(unjustly)* injustamente

wrote [rəʊt] *pt of* **write**

wrung [rʌŋ] *pt & pp of* **wring**

wry [raɪ] *adj* (**wrier, wriest** *or* **wryer, wryest**) sardónico(a)

XYZ

xenophobia [zenə'fəʊbɪə] *n* xenofobia *f*

Xerox® ['zɪərɒks] **1** *n* fotocopia *f*, xerocopia *f*

2 *vt* fotocopiar

Xmas ['krɪsməs, 'eksməs] *n* (*abbr* **Christmas**) Navidad *f*

X-ray ['eksreɪ] **1** *n* (*radiation*) rayo *m* X; (*picture*) radiografía *f*; **to have an X.** hacerse una radiografía

2 *vt* radiografiar

Y, y [waɪ] *n* (*the letter*) Y, y *f*

yacht [jɒt] *n* yate *m*; **y. club** club náutico

yachting ['jɒtɪŋ] *n Sport* navegación *f* a vela; (*competition*) regatas *fpl*

yachtsman ['jɒtsmən] *n* balandrista *m*

yachtswoman ['jɒtswʊmən] *n* balandrista *f*

yam [jæm] *n* (**a**) ñame *m* (**b**) *US* (*sweet potato*) boniato *m*, batata *f*, *Andes, CAm, Carib, Méx* camote *m*

Yank [jæŋk] *n Br Pej* yanqui *mf*

yank [jæŋk] *vt Fam* tirar; (*tooth*) arrancar

Yankee ['jæŋkɪ] *adj & n Pej* yanqui (*mf*)

yap [jæp] *vi* (*dog*) aullar; *Fam* (*person*) darle al pico

yard¹ [jɑːd] *n* (*measure*) yarda *f* (*aprox* 0,914 m)

yard² [jɑːd] *n* patio *m*; *US* jardín *m*

yardstick ['jɑːdstɪk] *n Fig* criterio *m*, norma *f*

yarn [jɑːn] *n* (**a**) *Sewing* hilo *m* (**b**) (*story*) historia *f*, cuento *m*; **to spin a y.** (*lie*) inventarse una historia

yawn [jɔːn] **1** *vi* bostezar

2 *n* bostezo *m*

yawning ['jɔːnɪŋ] *adj* (*gap*) profundo(a)

yd (*pl* **yds**) (*abbr* **yard**) yarda *f*

yeah [jeə] *adv Fam* sí

year [jɪə(r)] *n* (**a**) año *m*; **all y. round** durante todo el año; **last y.** el año pasado; **next y.** el año que viene; **y. in, y. out** año tras año; **I'm ten years old** tengo diez años (**b**) *Educ* curso *m*; **first-y. student** estudiante *mf* de primero

yearly ['jɪəlɪ] **1** *adj* anual

2 *adv* anualmente, cada año

yearn [jɜːn] *vi* **to y. for sth** anhelar algo

yearning ['jɜːnɪŋ] *n* anhelo *m* (**for** de)

yeast [jiːst] *n* levadura *f*

yell [jel] **1** *vi* gritar

2 *n* grito *m*, alarido *m*

yellow ['jeləʊ] **1** *adj* amarillo(a); *Fam Fig* (*cowardly*) cobarde; *Tel* **Y. Pages®** páginas amarillas

2 *n* amarillo *m*

yelp [jelp] **1** *vi* aullar

2 *n* aullido *m*

yen [jen] *n* (**a**) (*currency*) yen *m* (**b**) **to have a y. for sth** tener ganas de algo

yeoman ['jəʊmən] *n Br* **Y. of the Guard** = alabardero de la Casa Real británica

yes [jes] **1** *adv* sí; **you said y.** dijiste que sí

2 *n* sí *m*

yesterday ['jestədeɪ] *adv & n* ayer *m*; **the day before y.** anteayer; **y. morning** ayer por la mañana

yet [jet] **1** *adv* (**a**) **not y.** aún no, todavía no; **as y.** hasta ahora; **I haven't eaten y.** no he comido todavía (**b**) (*in questions*) ya; **has he arrived y.?** ¿ha venido ya? (**c**) (*even*) más; **y. again** otra vez; **y. more** todavía más (**d**) (*eventually*) todavía, aún; **he'll win y.** todavía puede ganar

2 *conj* sin embargo

yew [juː] *n* tejo *m*

yield [jiːld] **1** *n* (**a**) rendimiento *m* (**b**) *Agr* cosecha *f* (**c**) *Fin* beneficio *m*

2 *vt* producir; *Agr* dar; (*money*) producir

3 *vi* (**a**) (*surrender, break*) ceder (**b**) *US Aut* ceder el paso

YMCA [waɪemsiː'eɪ] *n* (*abbr* **Young Men's Christian Association**) ACJ *f*, Asociación *f* Cristiana de Jóvenes (*que regenta hostales económicos*)

yob(bo) ['jɒb(əʊ)] *n Fam* gamberro(a) *m,f*

yoga ['jəʊgə] *n* yoga *m*

yog(h)urt ['jɒgət] *n* yogur *m*

yoke [jəʊk] **1** *n* yugo *m*

2 *vt* (*oxen*) uncir; *Fig* unir

yokel ['jəʊkəl] *n Pej* paleto(a) *m,f*

yolk [jəʊk] *n* yema *f*

yonder ['jɒndə(r)] *adv* más allá

you [juː, *unstressed* jə] *pers pron* (**a**) (*subject*) (*usually omitted in Spanish, except for contrast*) (*familiar use*) (*singular*) tú; (*pl*) vosotros(as); **how are y.?** ¿cómo estás?, ¿cómo estáis?

(**b**) *(subject) (polite use) (singular)* usted; *(pl)* ustedes; **how are y.?** ¿cómo está?, ¿cómo están?

(**c**) *(subject) (impers use)* **y. never know** nunca se sabe

(**d**) *(object) (familiar use) (singular) (before verb)* te; *(after preposition)* ti; *(pl) (before verb)* os; *(after preposition)* vosotros(as); **I saw y.** te vi/os vi; **it's for y.** es para ti/es para vosotros(as); **with y.** contigo/con vosotros(as)

(**e**) *(object) (polite use) (singular) (before verb)* le; *(after preposition)* usted; *(pl) (before verb)* les; *(after preposition)* ustedes; **I saw y.** le vi/les vi; **it's for y.** es para usted/es para ustedes; **with y.** con usted/con ustedes

(**f**) *(object) (impers use)* **alcohol makes y. drunk** el alcohol emborracha

> In Spanish, the formal form **usted** takes a third person singular verb, and **ustedes** takes a third person plural verb. In many Latin American countries, **ustedes** is the standard form of the second person plural (**vosotros**) and is not considered formal. Note also that in some of those countries **usted** is used in the second person singular (**tú**), and is likewise not considered formal.

young [jʌŋ] **1** *adj (age)* joven; *(brother etc)* pequeño(a); **y. lady** señorita *f*; **y. man** joven *m*

2 *npl* (**a**) *(people)* **the y.** los jóvenes, la juventud (**b**) *(animals)* crías *fpl*

youngster [ˈjʌŋstə(r)] *n* muchacho(a) *m,f*

your [jɔː(r), *unstressed* jə(r)] *poss adj* (**a**) *(familiar use) (singular)* tu/tus; *(pl)* vuestro(a)/vuestros(as) (**b**) *(polite use)* su/sus (**c**) *(impers use)* **the house is on y. right** la casa queda a la derecha; **they clean y. shoes for you** te limpian los zapatos (**d**) *(formal address)* Su; **Y. Majesty** Su Majestad

yours [jɔːz] *poss pron* (**a**) *(familiar use) (singular)* el tuyo/la tuya/los tuyos/las tuyas; *(pl)* el vuestro/la vuestra/los vuestros/las vuestras; **the house is y.** la casa es tuya (**b**) *(polite use) (singular)* el suyo/la suya; *(pl)* los suyos/las suyas; **the house is y.** la casa es suya (**c**) *(in letters)* **y. faithfully** le(s) saluda atentamente; **y. sincerely** reciba un cordial saludo de

> In Spanish, the forms **tuyo(a)**, **suyo(a)** and **vuestro(a)** require a definite article in the singular and in the plural when they are the subject of the phrase.

yourself [jɔːˈself, *unstressed* jəˈself] *(pl* **yourselves** [jɔːˈselvz]) **1** *pers pron* (**a**) *(familiar use) (singular)* tú mismo(a); *(pl)* vosotros(as) mismos(as); **by y.** *(tú)* solo; **by yourselves** vosotros(as) solos(as) (**b**) *(polite use) (singular)* usted mismo(a); *(pl)* ustedes mismos(as); **by y.** *(usted)* solo(a); **by yourselves** *(ustedes)* solos(as)

2 *reflexive pron* (**a**) *(familiar use) (singular)* te; *(pl) (familiar use)* os; **enjoy y.!** ¡diviértete!; **enjoy yourselves!** ¡divertíos! (**b**) *(polite use)* se; **enjoy y.!** ¡diviértase!; **enjoy yourselves!** ¡diviértanse!

> In many Latin American countries, **se/ustedes** is the standard form of the second person plural and is not considered formal.

youth [juːθ] *n* (**a**) juventud *f* (**b**) *(young man)* joven *m*; **y. club** club *m* juvenil; **y. hostel** albergue *m* juvenil

youthful [ˈjuːθfʊl] *adj* juvenil, joven

Yugoslav [ˈjuːɡəʊslɑːv] *adj & n* yugoslavo(a) *(m,f)*

Yugoslavia [juːɡəʊˈslɑːvɪə] *n* Yugoslavia

Yugoslavian [juːɡəʊˈslɑːvɪən] *adj & n* yugoslavo(a) *(m,f)*

YWCA [ˈwaɪdʌbəljuːsiːˈeɪ] *n (abbr* **Young Women's Christian Association**) ACJ *f*, Asociación *f* Cristiana de Jóvenes *(que regenta hostales económicos)*

Z, z [zed, *US* ziː] *n (the letter)* Z, z *f*

zany [ˈzeɪnɪ] *adj* (**zanier, zaniest**) *Fam* (**a**) *(mad)* chiflado(a) (**b**) *(eccentric)* estrafalario(a)

zap [zæp] **1** *interj* ¡zas!

2 *vt Fam* (**a**) *(hit)* pegar (**b**) *(kill)* cargarse a

3 *vi TV* hacer zapping

zeal [ziːl] *n (enthusiasm)* entusiasmo *m*

zealous [ˈzeləs] *adj (enthusiastic)* entusiasta

zebra [ˈziːbrə, ˈzebrə] *n* cebra *f*; *Br* **z. crossing** paso *m* de cebra

zenith [ˈzenɪθ] *n Astron* cenit *m*; *Fig* apogeo *m*

zero [ˈzɪərəʊ] *n* cero *m*; **z. hour** hora *f* cero

zest [zest] *n (eagerness)* entusiasmo *m*

zigzag [ˈzɪɡzæɡ] **1** *n* zigzag *m*

2 *vi* zigzaguear

Zimbabwe [zɪmˈbɑːbweɪ] *n* Zimbabue

zinc [zɪŋk] *n* cinc *m*, zinc *m*

zip [zɪp] **1** *n* (**a**) *Br z.(fastener)* cremallera *f* (**b**) *Fam* brío *m*; *US* **z. code** código *m* postal

2 *vi* cerrarse con cremallera

▶ **zip by** *vi* pasar como un rayo

▸ **zip up** *vt sep* cerrar con cremallera; **to z. sb up** cerrar la cremallera a algn

zipper ['zɪpə(r)] *n US* cremallera *f*

zodiac ['zəʊdɪæk] *n* zodiaco *m*, zodíaco *m*

zombie ['zɒmbɪ] *n* zombie *mf*

zone [zəʊn] **1** *n* zona *f*
2 *vt* dividir en zonas

zoo [zuː] *n* zoo *m*

zoological [zuːə'lɒdʒɪkəl] *adj* zoológico(a)

zoologist [zuː'ɒlədʒɪst] *n* zoólogo(a) *m,f*

zoology [zuː'ɒlədʒɪ] *n* zoología *f*

zoom [zuːm] **1** *n* (**a**) *(buzz)* zumbido *m*
(**b**) **z. lens** zoom *m*, teleobjetivo *m*
2 *vi* (**a**) *(buzz)* zumbar (**b**) **to z. past** pasar volando

▸ **zoom in** *vi (camera)* acercarse rápidamente

zucchini [zuː'kiːnɪ] *n US* calabacín *m*, *CSur* zapallito *m*

Zulu ['zuːluː] *adj & n* zulú *(mf)*